WYCLIFFE
Bible Encyclopedia

The New Church of the Annunciation, Nazareth. See Luke 1:25–38. HFV

WYCLiFFe
Bible Encyclopedia

Volume 1
A-J

Editors:

CHARLES F. PFEIFFER, B.D., Th.M., Ph.D.
HOWARD F. VOS, Th.M., M.A., Th.D., Ph.D.
JOHN REA, B.D., Th.M., M.A., Th.D.

MOODY PRESS

CHICAGO

ISBN: 0−8024−9697−0

Library of Congress Catalog Card Number: 74−15360

Library of Congress Cataloging in Publication Data

The Wycliffe Bible encyclopedia.

    Includes bibliographies.
    1. Bible−Dictionaries. I. Pfeiffer, Charles F.,
ed. II. Rea, John, 1925-   ed. III. Vos, Howard
Frederic, 1925-   ed.
BS440.W92   220.3   74-15360
ISBN 0-8024-9697-0

PREFACE

The two volumes of the *Wycliffe Bible Encyclopedia* are the product of the combined efforts of more than two hundred scholars in the several fields of biblical studies. While most of them are Americans, a number are citizens of other countries.

The project was begun in 1959 when the staff of Moody Press recognized the need to replace older Bible dictionaries and encyclopedias with a work that would be abreast of recent trends in theology and the newest discoveries in archaeology and linguistic research.

The committee established several basic guidelines for the WBE. First of all, its doctrinal articles must adhere to Christian orthodoxy, the fundamentals of the faith generally accepted by believers of conservative, evangelical persuasion. No article should contradict the belief that all Scripture is inspired of God and was verbally inerrant in its original manuscripts. In matters of eschatology the return of Christ is considered as occurring before His millennial reign on earth.

Second, the encyclopedia should be complete in the sense that every place and personal name in the Bible be listed and discussed, as well as all important doctrines and theological terms. Various articles on nonbiblical subjects have been included to provide historical and cultural background for the setting of the events in the Bible. This has been done because frequent references are made to such subjects as the Amarna letters, the Nuzu tablets, Hammurabi, Sumer, and the Moabite Stone. There terms are meaningless to the average reader of the Bible unless explained. Because the encyclopedia is limited to a discussion of subjects contributing directly to one's understanding of the Bible and Bible times, little attention has been given to matters of church history.

Third, the articles should be comprehensive enough to satisfy the informed layman, yet clear enough for the understanding of the average reader. For this reason Hebrew, Greek, and other foreign words have been transliterated.

Since the King James Version is still the most widely read Bible in evangelical churches, it has been followed for the spelling of proper names in the titles of the individual articles. Within the articles, however, the more accurate translations or transliterations found in the recent revisions are frequently used. Certain names and important words or terms which occur in newer versions but not in the KJV are discussed for the convenience of the reader. Names as spelled in newer versions are also listed, and are followed by a cross reference to the name as spelled in the KJV. For example, by the entry on Quirinius the notation is found: *See* Cyrenius. The latter is the spelling as given in the KJV. In referring to the personal name of God in the OT the editors have chosen the spelling *Yahweh* rather than *Jehovah*. The former spelling is now generally accepted by most OT scholars as more nearly approximating the correct pronunciation in ancient Israel.

The authors of all articles of 150 words or more in length are identified by their initials. Their position in the academic community is given in the List of Contributors. The reader is assured of having at his disposal an accurate, reliable, and up-to-date source of information for his study of God's Word. Differing viewpoints (within the boundaries of an evangelical position) are expressed, so that a rigid uniformity has not been imposed on the various articles.

Bibliographies attached to the longer articles are by no means exhaustive, but are added as a help to the reader by referring him to books and periodicals usually obtainable in the libraries of most Christian colleges in America. A special effort was made to refer to the more important articles in G. F. Bromiley's excellent translation of Kittel's famous work, the *Theological Dictionary of the New Testament*.

The usefulness of the encyclopedia has been greatly extended at the same time that duplication has been largely avoided by a system of cross references within and at the end of most articles. Another subject may be referred to either by the abbreviation *q.v.* (Latin *quod vide*, "which see") in parentheses following the mention of that word, or by the actual instruction "*See* . . ." naming that article.

In a number of areas it was deemed best to discuss the related individual items or units under a general topic instead of in separate articles. For example, all the animals, birds, fish, insects, and reptiles are discussed under Animals. Other examples are the long articles on Bible Manuscripts; Dress; Festivals; Food; Gods, False; Jewels; Minerals and Metals; Occupations; Plants; Versions, Ancient and Medieval; and Weights, Measures, and Coins. This arrangement enables the reader more easily to gain a comprehensive knowledge of a particular subject, if he so desires.

The original staff of editors was headed by Charles F. Pfeiffer. Associated with him were E. Leslie Carlson in Old Testament, Walter M. Dunnett in New Testament, R. Allan Killen in theology, and Howard F.

Vos for illustrations and archaeology. John Rea was later asked to fill the vacancy created by the death of Dr. Carlson. Subsequently, Dr. Rea was brought in as manuscript editor to expedite the editorial task through to completion. He was especially assisted by Dr. Vos, who as textbook editor of Moody Press, and later textbook consultant, read and evaluated the entire contents of the encyclopedia; and by James Mathisen, for several years assistant editor of Moody Press. Others who have rendered invaluable editorial assistance include Dwight P. Baker, Kenneth A. Domroese, Fred Dickason, Stanley N. Gundry, and Alan F. Johnson.

Special thanks are due to Miss Nettie Cox, who after her retirement from Moody Bible Institute as editor of promotional materials has served so ably and tirelessly as chief copy editor. Without her ability to organize the accumulating mass of manuscripts, her memory of details and sharp eye for errors, this project would have foundered. She was assisted by Mrs. Dorothy Martin during the many months of proofreading. Nor would the project have been completed without the constant supervision and practical involvement of Howard Fischer, production manager at Moody Press.

The authors and the editors acknowledge their indebtedness to the many fine Bible dictionaries and encyclopedias published in this century. Especially useful have been *Unger's Bible Dictionary* and *The New Bible Dictionary,* in all aspects; the *Pictorial Biblical Encyclopedia* (by G. Cornfeld), the *Seventh-Day Adventist Bible Dictionary* (by Siegfried H. Horn), *The Interpreter's Dictionary of the Bible* , and *The Biblical World* (by Charles F. Pfeiffer) in matters of archaeology, ancient history, and biblical customs; and *Baker's Dictionary of Theology* in doctrinal matters. *The Interpreter's Dictionary of the Bible* has served as the standard for the spelling and pronunciation of most of the names of persons, places, and events in the ancient history of the Near East. The table of abbreviations for periodicals, reference works, dictionaries, and versions reveals in fuller measure the wide scope of materials consulted by the contributors of the articles and by the editors. Color maps are inserted by special arrangement with C. S. Hammond and Company.

Numerous individuals and agencies have supplied illustrations for this work. A credit line appears with each picture but special recognition goes to those listed below who have all furnished a sufficiently large number of pictures to commend the use of abbreviations to designate them. Such abbreviations appear in parentheses in the following listing: British Museum, London (BM); Israel Information Service, New York (IIS); Lehnert and Landrock, Cairo (LL); Louvre Museum, Paris (LM); Moody Institute of Science (MIS); Metropolitan Museum of Art, New York (MM); Matson Photo Service, Los Angeles (MPS); Oriental Institute of the University of Chicago (ORINST); Dr. John Rea (JR); and Dr. Howard F. Vos (HFV).

LIST OF CONTRIBUTORS

Entries are made in order of authors' last names

W.A.A. ALCORN, Wallace A., Ph.D., Associate Professor of New Testament, Northwest Baptist Seminary, Tacoma, Wash.

G.A.A. ANDERSON, George A., Th.M., Professor of Bible, King College, Bristol, Tenn.

G.L.A. ARCHER, Gleason L., Jr., Professor of Old Testament, Trinity Evangelical Divinity School, Deerfield, Ill.

D.P.B. BAKER, Dwight P.

N.B.B. BAKER, Nelson B., Ph.D., Professor of English Bible Emeritus, Eastern Baptist Theological Seminary, Philadelphia, Penn.

D.B. BALY, Denis, Kenyon College, Gambier, Ohio.

D.C.B. BARAMKI, D.C., Ph.D., Curator of Museums, American University of Beirut, Lebanon.

L.B. BARBIERI, Louis, Th.D., Member of Faculty, Moody Bible Institute, Chicago, Ill.

G.W.Ba. BARKER, Glenn W., Th.D., Dean & Professor of Christian Origins, Fuller Theological Seminary, Pasadena, Calif.

K.L.B. BARKER, Kenneth L., Ph.D., Associate Professor of Semitics and Old Testament, Dallas Theological Seminary, Dallas, Tex.

D.M.B. BEEGLE, Dewey M., Ph.D., Professor of Old Testament, Wesley Theological Seminary, Washington, D.C.

R.H.B. BELTON, Robert H., Th.M. Member of Faculty Emeritus, Moody Bible Institute, Chicago, Ill.

T.H.B. BENDER, Thorwald W., Th.D., Professor of Philosophy of Religion and Theology, Eastern Baptist Theological Seminary, Philadelphia, Penn

T.M.B. BENNETT, T. Miles, Th.D., Professor of Old Testament, Southwestern Baptist Theological Seminary, Fort Worth, Tex.

S.H.B. BESS, S. Herbert, Ph.D., Professor of Old Testament and Hebrew, Grace Theological Seminary, Winona Lake, Ind.

E.M.B. BOHNETT, Earl M., M. Div., M.A., Dean of Education, Baptist Bible College, Denver, Col.

A.B. BOWLING, Andrew, Ph.D., Associate Professor, Biblical Studies and Philosophy, John Brown University, Siloam Springs, Ark.

J.L.B. BOYER, James L., Th.D., Professor of New Testament and Greek, Grace Theological Seminary, Winona Lake, Ind.

G.W. Br. BROMILEY, Geoffrey W., Ph.D., Professor of Church History and Historical Theology, Fuller Theological Seminary, Pasadena, Calif.

W.B. BROOMALL, Wick, M.A., Th.M., Atlanta School of Biblical Studies, Atlanta, Ga.

W.G.B. BROWN, W. Gordon, D.D., Dean Emeritus, Central Baptist Seminary, Toronto, Ontario, Canada.

S.G.B. BROWNE, S.G., Leprosy Research Unit, Uzuakoli, Eastern Nigeria

F.F.B. BRUCE, F.F., M.A., D.D., Rylands Professor of Biblical Criticism and Exegesis, University of Manchester, England.

S.F.B. BRYAN, Sigurd F., Th.D., Professor of Religion, Samford University, Birmingham, Ala.

D.W.B. BURDICK, Donald W., Th.D., Professor of New Testament, Con-

ix

servative Baptist Theological Seminary, Denver, Col.

J.O.B.   BUSWELL, J. Oliver, Jr., Ph.D., Dean Emeritus, Covenant Theological Seminary, St. Louis, Mo.

D.K.C.   CAMPBELL, Donald K., Th.D., Dean, Dallas Theological Seminary, Dallas, Tex.

E.L.C.   CARLSON, E. Leslie, Th.D., Professor Emeritus, Southwestern Baptist Theological Seminary, Fort Worth, Tex.

F.G.C.   CARVER, Frank G., Jr., Ph.D., Professor of Biblical Theology and Greek, Pasadena College, Pasadena, Calif.

G.H.C.   CLARK, Gordon H., Ph.D., Professor of Philosophy, Butler University, Indianapolis, Ind.

E.W.C.   CLEVENGER, Eugene W., Th.D., Professor of Bible, Abilene Christian College, Abilene, Tex.

J.W.C.   COBB, John W., Th.D., Professor Emeritus of Religion, University of Corpus Christi, Corpus Christi, Tex.

W.B.C.   COBLE, William B., Th.D., Professor of New Testament Interpretation and Greek, Midwestern Baptist Theological Seminary, Kansas City, Mo.

S.M.C.   CODER, S. Maxwell, Th.D., Dean of Education Emeritus, Moody Bible Institute, Chicago, Ill.

S.C.   COHEN, Simon, D.D., formerly Hebrew Union College, Cincinnati, Ohio.

ꞏR.O.C.   COLEMAN, Robert O., Th.D., Associate Professor of Biblical Backgrounds and Archaeology, Southwestern Baptist Theological Seminary, Fort Worth, Tex.

C.W.C.   CROWN, C.W., M.D., Physician, Chicago, Ill.

T.B.C.   CRUM, Terrelle B., M.A., Professor of Biblical Studies, Barrington College, Barrington, Rhode Island.

W.C.   CULBERTSON, William, D.D., President Emeritus and Chancellor, Moody Bible Institute, Chicago, Ill.

R.D.C.   CULVER, Robert D., Th.D., Professor of Systematic Theology, Trinity Evangelical Divinity School, Deerfield, Ill.

J.J.D.   DAVIS, John J., Ph.D., Professor of Old Testament and Hebrew, Grace Theological Seminary, Winona Lake, Ind.

V.G.D.   DAVISON, Vernon G., Ph.D., Professor of Religion and Greek, Samford University, Birmingham, Ala.

W.T.D.   DAYTON, Wilber T., Th.D., President, Houghton College, Houghton, N.Y.

D.W.D.   DEERE, D.W., Th.D., Professor Emeritus of Old Testament, Golden Gate Theological Seminary, Mill Valley, Calif.

R.B.D.   DEMPSEY. Robert B.

C.E.D.   DE VRIES, Carl E., Ph.D., Research Associate (Associate Professor), Oriental Institute, University of Chicago, Chicago, Ill.

C.F.D.   DICKASON, C. Fred, Th.D., Member of Faculty, Moody Bible Institute, Chicago, Ill.

R.L.D.   DOBSON, Robert L., Th.D., Professor of Bible, Howard Payne College, Brownwood, Tex.

H.L.D.   DRUMWRIGHT, Huber L., Jr., Th.D., Dean and Professor of New Testament, Southwestern Baptist Theological Seminary, Fort Worth, Tex.

W.M.D.   DUNNETT, Walter M., Ph.D., Member of Faculty, Moody Bible Institute, Chicago, Ill.

D.G.E.   EADIE, Douglas G., Th.D., Ph.D., Professor of Religion, University of Redlands, Redlands, Calif.

R.E.   EARLE, Ralph, Th.D., Professor of New Testament, Nazarene Theological Seminary, Kansas City, Mo.

L.R.E.   ELLIOTT, L.R.

C.L.F.   FEINBERG, Charles L., Ph.D., Dean, Talbot Theological Seminary, La Mirada, Calif.

P.F.   FEINBERG, Paul, Ph.D., Assistant Professor of Philosophy of Religion, Trinity Evangelical Divinity School, Deerfield, Ill.

E.F.   FERGUSON, Everett, Ph.D., Professor of Bible, Abilene Christian College, Abilene, Tex.

P.W.F.   FERRIS, Paul W., Jr., M.Div., Graduate Student, Dropsie College, Philadelphia, Penn.

H.E.Fi.   FINLEY, Harvey E., Ph.D., Professor of Old Testament, Nazarene Theological Seminary, Kansas City, Mo.

F.L.F.   FISHER, Fred L., Th.D., Professor of New Testament Interpretation, Golden Gate Baptist Theological Seminary, Mill Valley, Calif.

H.D.F.   FOOS, Harold D., Th.D., Member of Faculty, Moody Bible Institute, Chicago, Ill.

C.T.F.   FRANCISCO, Clyde T., Th.D., Professor of Old Testament Interpretation, Southern Baptist Theological Seminary, Louisville, Ky.

H.E.Fr.   FREEMAN, Hobart E., Th.D., Lecturer and Author, Graceland, Ind.

L. Ga.   GALLMAN, Lee, Th.D., Profes-

J.F.G.   GATES, John F., S.T.D., Professor of Bible and Philosophy, St. Paul Bible College, Bible College, Minn.

N.L.G.   GEISLER, Norman L., Ph.D., Professor of Philosophy of Religion, Trinity Evangelical Divinity School, Deerfield, Ill.

J.M.G.   GERSTNER, John M., Ph.D., Professor of Church History, Pittsburgh Theological Seminary, Pittsburgh, Penn.

G.A.G.   GETZ, Gene A., Ph.D., Associate Professor of Christian Education, Dallas Theological Seminary, Dallas, Tex.

R.G.   GODDARD, Robert, Th.D., Member of Faculty, Moody Bible Institute, Chicago, Ill.

L.Go.   GOLDBERG, Louis, Th.D., Member of Faculty, Moody Bible Institute, Chicago, Ill.

J.H.G.   GREENLEE, J. Harold, Th.D., Missionary, OMS International

J.K.G.   GRIDER, J. Kenneth, Ph.D., Professor of Theology, Nazarene Theological Seminary, Kansas City, Mo.

V.C.G.   GROUNDS, Vernon C., Ph.D., President, Conservative Baptist Theological Seminary, Denver, Col.

S.G.   GUNDRY, Stanley, S.T.D., Member of Faculty, Moody Bible Institute, Chicago, Ill.

G.H.G.   HADDOCK, Gerald H., Ph.D., Associate Professor of Geology, Wheaton College, Wheaton, Ill.

E.F.Hai.   HAIGHT, Elmer F., Th.D., Professor Emeritus of Religion, Louisiana College, Pineville, La.

P.S.H.   HAIK, Paul S., Th.D., Member of Faculty, Moody Bible Institute, Chicago, Ill.

F.E.H.   HAMILTON, Floyd E.

H.A.Han.   HANKE, H.A., Th.D., Professor of Religion, Asbury College, Wilmore, Ky.

G.L.H.   HARDING, G. Lankester, Daroun-Harissa, Lebanon.

L.O.H.   HARRIS, Lindell O., Th.D., Chairman, Division of Religion, Hardin-Simmons University, Abilene, Tex.

R.L.H.   HARRIS, R. Laird, Ph.D., Professor of Old Testament, Covenant Theological Seminary, St. Louis, Mo.

E.F.Har.   HARRISON, Everett F., Ph.D., Senior Professor of New Testament, Fuller Theological Seminary, Pasadena, Calif.

G.W.H.   HARRISON, G.W., Th.D., Professor of Religion, Samford University, Birmingham, Ala.

fessor of Old Testament and Hebrew, New Orleans Baptist Theological Seminary, New Orleans, La.

C.K.H.   HARROP, Clayton K., Th.D., Professor of New Testament Interpretation, Golden Gate Baptist Theological Seminary, Mill Valley, Calif.

R.E.H.   HAYDEN, Roy E., Ph.D., Professor of Biblical Literature, Oral Roberts University, Tulsa, Okla.

A.K.H.   HELMBOLD, Andrew K., Ph.D., Professor of Humanities, Tidewater Community College, Portsmouth, Va.

E.W.H.   HELSEL, E. Walter, Th.M., Professor of Religion, Seattle Pacific College, Seattle, Wash.

C.F.H.H.   HENRY, Carl F.H., Ph.D., Professor at Large, Eastern Baptist Theological Seminary, Philadelphia, Penn.

D.E.H.   HIEBERT, D. Edmond, Th.D., Professor of New Testament, Mennonite Brethren Biblical Seminary, Fresno, Calif.

H.W.H.   HOEHNER, Harold W., Ph.D., Associate Professor of Bible Exposition, Dallas Theological Seminary, Dallas, Tex.

H.A.Hof.   HOFFNER, Harry A., Jr., Ph.D., Associate Professor of Hittiology and Assyriology, Yale University, New Haven, Conn.

S.H.H.   HORN, Siegfried H., Ph.D., Professor of Archaeology and History of Antiquity, Andrews University, Berrien Springs, Mich.

C.M.Ho.   HORNE, Charles M., Th.D., Associate Professor of Theology, Graduate School of Theology, Wheaton College, Wheaton, Ill.

S.M.H.   HORTON, Stanley M., Th.D., Professor of Bible, Hebrew, and Theology, Central Bible College, Springfield, Mo. /

H.E.H.   HOSCH, Harold E.

F.D.H.   HOWARD, Fred D., Th.D., Professor of Religion, Wayland Baptist College, Plainview, Tex.

G.E.H.   HOWARD, George E., M.A., Th.M., Ph.D., Associate Professor, Philosophy of Religion, University of Georgia, Athens, Ga.

F.R.H.   HOWE, Frederic R., Th.D., Professor of Theology, Dallas Theological Seminary, Dallas, Tex.

H.A.Hoy.   HOYT, Herman A., Th.D., President, Grace Theological Seminary, Winona Lake, Ind.

F.B.H.   HUEY, F.B., Jr., Th.D., Associate Professor of Old Testament, Southwestern Baptist Theological Seminary, Fort Worth, Tex.

K.H.   HUJER, Karel, D.Sc., Professor of

xi

Astronomy and Physics, University of Tennessee at Chattanooga, Tenn.

C.J.H.   HURST, Clyde J., Th.D., Professor of Bible and Philosophy, Hardin-Simmons University, Abilene, Tex.

C.M.Hy.   HYATT, Cecil M., Th.D., Professor of Bible and Religion, California Baptist College, Riverside, Calif.

E.C.J.   JAMES, Edgar C., Th.D., Member of Faculty, Moody Bible Institute, Chicago, Ill.

J.E.J.   JENNINGS, James E., M.A., Assistant Professor of Archaeology, Wheaton College, Wheaton, Ill.

P.K.J.   JEWETT, Paul K., Ph.D., Professor of Systematic Theology, Fuller Theological Seminary, Pasadena, Calif.

A.F.J.   JOHNSON, Alan F., Th.D., Associate Professor of Bible and Apologetics, Wheaton College, Wheaton, Ill.

P.C.J.   JOHNSON, Philip C. Th.D.,

R.L.J.   JOHNSON, Robert L., M.A., Associate Professor of Bible, Abilene Christian College, Abilene, Tex.

E.S.K.   KALLAND, Earl S., Th.D., Dean, Conservative Baptist Theological Seminary, Denver, Col.

J.L.K.   KELSO, James L., Th.D., Professor Emeritus of Old Testament History and Biblical Archaeology, Pittsburgh Theological Seminary, Pittsburgh, Penn.

H.A.K.   KENT, Homer A., Jr., Th.D., Vice President and Dean, Grace Theological Seminary, Winona Lake, Ind.

R.A.K.   KILLEN, R. Allan, Th.D., Professor of Contemporary Theology, Reformed. Theological Seminary, Jackson, Miss.

W.H.K.   KIMZEY, Willis H., Jr., Th.D., Professor of Religion, Union University, Jackson, Tenn.

M.A.K.   KING, Marchant A., D.D., Professor Emeritus, Los Angeles Baptist College, Newhall, Calif.

M.E.K.   KLINE, Meredith E., Ph.D., Professor of Old Testament, Gordon-Conwell Theological Seminary, Wenham, Mass.

F.H.K.   KLOOSTER, Fred H., Th.D., Professor of Systematic Theology, Calvin Theological Seminary, Grand Rapids, Mich.

J.W.K.   KLOTZ, John W., Ph.D., Professor of Natural Science, Concordia Senior College, Fort Wayne, Ind.

G.W.K.   KNIGHT, George W., III, Th.D., Associate Professor of New Testament, Covenant Theological Seminary, St. Louis, Mo.

C.H.K.   KRAELING, Carl H., Ph.D., Director Emeritus of Institute of Oriental Studies, University of Chicago, Chicago, Ill.

F.C.K.   KUEHNER, Fred C., Th.D., Dean, Professor of Biblical Languages, The Theological Seminary of the Reformed Episcopal Church, Philadelphia, Penn.

W.L.L.   LANE, William L., Th.D., Professor of New Testament and Judaic Studies, Gordon-Conwell Theological Seminary, Wenham, Mass.

H.C.L.   LEUPOLD, H.C., D.D., Professor of Old Testament Theology, Evangelical Lutheran Seminary, Columbus, Ohio.

J.P.L.   LEWIS, Jack P., Ph.D., Professor of Bible, Harding Graduate School of Religion, Memphis, Tenn.

N.R.L.   LIGHTFOOT, Neil R., Ph.D., Professor of Bible, Abilene Christian College, Abilene, Tex.

R.P.L.   LIGHTNER, Robert P., Th.D., Assistant Professor of Systematic Theology, Dallas Theological Seminary, Dallas, Tex.

F.D.L.   LINDSEY, F. Duane, Th.D., Assistant Professor of Systematic Theology, Dallas Theological Seminary, Ft. Worth, Tex.

G.H.L.   LIVINGSTON, G. Herbert, Ph.D., Professor of Old Testament, Asbury Theological Seminary, Wilmore, Ky.

G.C.L.   LUCK, G. Coleman, Th.D., Member of Faculty, Moody Bible Institute, Chicago, Ill.

E.L.L.   LUEKER, Erwin L.

L.A.L.   LUFBURROW, Lawrence A.

J.C.M.   MACAULAY, J.C., D.D., Dean, New York School of the Bible, New York City.

W.R.L.Mc.   MC LATCHIE, Wm. R.L.

W.H.M.   MARE, W. Harold, Ph.D., Professor of New Testament Language and Literature, Covenant Theological Seminary, St. Louis, Mo.

J.Ma.   MATHISEN, James, M.A., Assistant Professor of Sociology, Aurora College, Aurora, Ill.

A.M.   MERCER, Arthur, Th.D., Private Business, Dallas, Tex.

C.S.M.   MEYER, Carl S., Ph.D., Graduate Professor of Historical Theology, Concordia Seminary, St. Louis, Mo.

J.R.M.   MICHAELS, J. Ramsey, Th.D., Professor of New Testament and Early Christian Literature, Gordon-Conwell Theological Seminary, Wenham, Mass.

R.A.M.   MITCHELL, Richard A., Institute for Mediterranean Studies, Berkeley, Calif.

H.M.M.   MORRIS, Henry M., Ph.D., Institute for Creation Research, San Diego, Calif.

L.M. MORRIS, Leon, Ph.D., Principal, Ridley College, Melbourne, Australia.

R.M. MOUNCE, Robert, Ph.D., Professor of Religious Studies, Western Kentucky University, 'Bowling Green, Ky.

W.M. MUELLER, Walter, Th.M.

J.K.M. MUNRO, John Ker, Th.M., Director of Admissions, Columbia Bible College, Columbia, S.C.

J.M. MURRAY, John, Th.M., Professor of Systematic Theology Emeritus, Westminster Theological Seminary, Philadelphia, Penn.

W.E.N. NIX, William E., Ph.D., Director of Education, Beverly Hills Hospital, Dallas, Tex.

H.W.N. NORTON, H. Wilbert, Th.D., Dean of Graduate School of Theology, Wheaton College, Wheaton, Ill.

R.P. PACHE, Rene, J.D., President of Emmaus Bible School, Lausanne, Switzerland.

F.P. PACK, Frank, Professor of Bible, Abilene Christian College, Abilene, Tex.

J.B.P. PAYNE, J. Barton, Th.D., Professor of Old Testament Language and Literature, Covenant Theological Seminary, St. Louis, Mo.

A.T.P. PEARSON, A.T.

J.D.P. PENTECOST, J. Dwight, Th.D., Professor of Bible Exposition, Dallas Theological Seminary, Dallas, Tex.

G.W.P. PETERS, George W., Ph.D., Professor of World Missions, Dallas Theological Seminary, Dallas, Tex.

I.G.P. PETERSON, Irving G.

C.F.P. PFEIFFER, Charles F., Ph.D., Professor of Ancient Languages, Central Michigan University, Mt. Pleasant, Mich.

C.H.P. PINNOCK, Clark H., Ph.D., Professor of Systematic Theology, Regent College, Vancouver, British Columbia.

R.E. Po. POWELL, Ralph E., Th.D., Professor of Theology and Philosophy of Religion, North American Baptist Seminary, Sioux Falls, S.D.

R.E. Pr. PRICE, Ross E., Ph.D., D.D., District Superintendent, Rocky Mountain District, Church of the Nazarene, Billings, Mont.

W.T.P. PURKISER, W.T., Ph.D., Associate Professor of English Bible, Nazarene Theological Seminary, Kansas City, Mo.

A.F.R. RAINEY, Anson F., Institute for Holy Land Studies, Jerusalem, Israel.

R.G.R. RAYBURN, Robert G., Th.D., President, Covenant Theological Seminary, St. Louis, Mo.

J.R. REA, John, Th.D., Theological Lecturer and Editor

A.M.R. RENWICK, Alexander M., D.D., Professor Free Church College, Edinburgh, Scotland.

R.L.R. REYMOND, Robert L., Ph.D., Associate Professor of Systematic Theology, Covenant Theological Seminary, St. Louis, Mo.

J.A.R. REYNOLDS, J.A., Th.D., Professor of Religion, Mary Hardin-Baylor College, Belton, Tex.

R.C.R. RIDALL, R. Clyde, Th.D., Associate Professor of Theology and Biblical Literature, Olivet Nazarene College, Kankakee, Ill.

R.V.R. RITTER, R. Vernon, Th.D., Professor of Religious Studies, Westmont College, Santa Barbara, Calif.

D.M.R. ROARK, Dallas M., Ph.D., Professor of Philosophy, Kansas State College of Emporia, Emporia, Kan.

J.W.R. ROBERTS, J.W., Ph.D., Professor of Bible, Abilene Christian College, Abilene, Tex.

I.R. ROBERTSON, Irvine, Th.M., Member of Faculty, Moody Bible Institute, Chicago, Ill.

E.B.R. ROBINSON, Earl B.

D.R.R. ROSE, Delbert R., Ph.D., Professor of Biblical Theology, Asbury Theological Seminary, Wilmore, Ky.

C.C.R. RYRIE, Charles C., Ph.D., Dean of Doctoral Studies, Dallas Theological Seminary, Dallas, Tex.

A.C.S. SCHULTZ, Arnold C., Th.D., Lecturer in History, Roosevelt University, Chicago, Ill.

S.J.S. SCHULTZ, Samuel J., Ph.D., Professor of Bible and Theology, Wheaton College, Wheaton, Ill.

D.R.S. SIME, Donald R., Ph.D., Vice President, University Affairs, Pepperdine University, Malibu, Calif.

J.H.S. SKILTON, John H., Ph.D., Professor of New Testament, Westminster Theological Seminary, Philadelphia, Penn.

E.B.S. SMICK, Elmer B., Ph.D., Professor of Old Testament, Gordon-Conwell Theological Seminary, Wenham, Mass.

R.L.S SMITH, Ralph L., Th.D., Professor of Old Testament, Southwestern Baptist Theological Seminary, Fort Worth, Tex.

W.M.S. SMITH, Wilbur M., D.D., Professor Emeritus of English Bible, Trinity Evangelical Divinity School, Deerfield, Ill.

J.A.S. SPRINGER, J. Arthur, D.D., Member of Faculty Emeritus,

B.C.S. STARK, Bruce C., Th.D., Professor of Philosophy, Ashland College, Ashland, Ohio

Moody Bible Institute, Chicago, Ill.

F.R.S. STEELE, Francis R., Home Director, North Africa Mission

D.S. STEPHENS, Douglas, Th.D., Member of Faculty, Moody Bible Institute, Chicago, Ill.

H.G.S. STIGERS, Harold G.

N.J.S. STONE, Nathan J., Th.M., Member of Faculty Emeritus, Moody Bible Institute, Chicago, Ill.

R.S. STRICKLAND, Rowena, Th.D., Professor of Bible, Oklahoma Baptist University, Shawnee, Okla.

G.G.S. SWAIM, Gerald G.

M.C.T. TENNEY, Merrill C., Ph.D., Professor of Bible and Theology, Graduate School of Theology, Wheaton College, Wheaton, Ill.

J.D.T. THOMAS, J.D., Ph.D., Professor of Bible, Abilene Christian College, Abilene, Tex.

J.A.T. THOMPSON, John A., Cairo, U.A.R.

D.D.T. TIDWELL, D.D., Th.D., Professor in Christianity, Houston Baptist College, Houston, Tex.

G.H.T. TODD, G. Hall

W.B.T. TOLAR, William B., Th.D., Professor of Biblical Backgrounds, Southwestern Baptist Theological Seminary, Fort Worth, Tex.

S.D.T. TOUSSAINT, Stanley D., Th.D., Assistant Professor of Bible Exposition, Dallas Theological Seminary, Dallas, Tex.

A.E.T. TRAVIS, Arthur E., Th.D., Professor in Christianity, Houston Baptist College, Houston, Tex.

J.L.T. TRAVIS, James L., Th.D., Faculty (Bible), Blue Mountain College, Blue Mountain, Miss.

J.W.T. TRESCH, John W., Jr., Belmont College, Nashville, Tenn.

G.A.T. TURNER, George A., Ph.D., Professor of Biblical Literature, Asbury Theological Seminary, Wilmore, Ky.

R.V.U. UNMACK, Robert V., Th.D., Professor of New Testament, Central Baptist Theological Seminary, Kansas City, Kan.

C.V. VAN TIL, Cornelius, Ph.D., Professor of Apologetics Emeritus, Westminster Theological Seminary, Philadelphia, Penn.

E.J.V. VARDAMAN, E. Jerry, Th.D., Associate Professor of Biblical Archaeology, Southern Baptist Theological Seminary, Louisville, Ky.

H.F.V. VOS, Howard F., Th.D., Ph.D., Professor of History, The King's College, Briarcliff Manor, N.Y.

L.L.W. WALKER, Larry L., Ph.D., Associate Professor of Old Testament, Southwestern Baptist Theological Seminary, Fort Worth, Tex.

W.B.W. WALLIS, Wilber B., Ph.D., Professor of New Testament, Covenant Theological Seminary, St. Louis, Mo.

J.F.W. WALVOORD, John F., Th.D., President, Dallas Theological Seminary, Dallas, Tex.

B.M.W. WARREN, Bern M., Th.D., Professor of Biblical Studies, Western Evangelical Seminary, Portland, Ore.

J.W.W. WATTS, J. Wash, Th.D., Professor Emeritus of Old Testament and Hebrew, New Orleans Baptist Theological Seminary, New Orleans, La.

J.D.W.W. WATTS, John D.W., Th.D., Professor of Old Testament, Serampore College, India.

C.J.W. WENZEL, Charles J., B.D., Member of Faculty, Columbia Bible College, Columbia, S.C.

W.W.W. WESSEL, Walter W., Ph.D., Professor of New Testament, Bethel College, St. Paul, Minn.

J.C.W. WHITCOMB, John C., Th.D., Director of Postgraduate Studies, Grace Theological Seminary, Winona Lake, Ind.

J.T.W. WILLIS, John T., Ph.D., Associate Professor of Bible, Abilene Christian College, Abilene, Tex.

D.L.W. WISE, Donald L., M.A., Member of Faculty, Moody Bible Institute, Chicago, Ill.

D.J.W. WISEMAN, Donald J., O.B.E., M.A., Professor of Assyriology, University of London, London, England

A.W.W. WONDER, Alice W., Th.D., Professor of Religion, Texas Wesleyan College, Fort Worth, Tex.

G.E.W. WORRELL, George E., Director of Youth Evangelism, Texas Baptist Convention

E.M.Y. YAMAUCHI, Edwin M., Ph.D., Associate Professor of History, Miami University, Oxford, Ohio

K.M.Y. YATES, Kyle M., Jr., Th.D., Associate Professor of Old Testament and Archaeology, Golden Gate Baptist Theological Seminary, Mill Valley, Calif.

J.D.Y. YODER, James D., Th.D., Professor of English Bible and Biblical Languages, Evangelical Congregational School of Theology, Myerstown, Pa.

E.J.Y. YOUNG, Edward J., Ph.D., Professor of Old Testament, Westminster Theological Seminary, Philadelphia, Pa.

F.E.Y.   YOUNG, Fred E., Ph.D., Dean, Professor of Old Testament, Central Baptist Theological Seminary, Kansas City, Kan.

R.F.Y.   YOUNGBLOOD, Ronald F., Ph.D., Professor of Old Testament, Bethel Theological Seminary, St. Paul, Minn.

ABBREVIATIONS

Books of the Bible

Old Testament

Gen	II Chr	Dan
Ex	Ezr	Hos
Lev	Neh	Joel
Num	Est	Amos
Deut	Job	Ob
Josh	Ps	Jon
Jud	Prov	Mic
Ruth	Eccl	Nah
I Sam	Song	Hab
II Sam	Isa	Zeph
I Kgs	Jer	Hag
II Kgs	Lam	Zech
I Chr	Ezk	Mal

New Testament

Mt	Eph	Heb
Mk	Phil	Jas
Lk	Col	I Pet
Jn	I Thess	II Pet
Acts	II Thess	I Jn
Rom	I Tim	II Jn
I Cor	II Tim	III Jn
II Cor	Tit	Jude
Gal	Phm	Rev

Apocrypha and Pseudepigrapha

Bar (Baruch)
Bel (Bel and the Dragon)
Ecclus (Ecclesiasticus) or Sir (Wisdom of Jesus
 Son of Sirach)
I Esd (Esdras)
II Esd
I Macc (Maccabees)
II Macc
Tob (Tobit)
Wisd (Wisdom of Solomon)

Bible Translations, Reference Works, Periodicals, etc.

AASOR — *Annual of the American Schools of Oriental Research*
AB — Amplified Bible
AJA — *American Journal of Archaeology*
AJSL — *American Journal of Semitic Languages and Literatures*
ALUOS — *Annual of Leeds University Oriental Society*

ANEP — *The Ancient Near East in Pictures*, J. B. Pritchard
ANET — *Ancient Near Eastern Texts*, J. B. Pritchard
ANT — *Apocryphal New Testament*, M. R. James
AOTS — *Archaeology and Old Testament Study*, D. Winton Thomas
ARE — *Ancient Records of Egypt*, J. H. Breasted
Arndt — Arndt-Gingrich, *Greek-English Lexicon*
A-S — Abbott-Smith, *Manual Greek Lexicon of the New Testament*
ASAE — *Annales du service des antiquités de l'Egypte*
ASOR — American Schools of Oriental Research
ASV — American Standard Version (1901)

BA — *Biblical Archaeologist*
BASOR — *Bulletin of American Schools of Oriental Research*
BC — *The Beginnings of Christianity*, Foakes-Jackson and Lake
BDB — Brown, Driver, and Briggs, *Hebrew-English Lexicon of the Old Testament*
BDT — *Baker's Dictionary of Theology*
BETS — *Bulletin of the Evangelical Theological Society*
BJRL — *Bulletin of the John Rylands Library*
BS — *Bibliotheca Sacra*
BW — *Biblical World*, Charles F. Pfeiffer

CAH — *Cambridge Ancient History* (12 vols.)
CBQ — *Catholic Biblical Quarterly*
CHT — *Christianity Today*
CornPBE — G. Cornfeld, *Pictorial Biblical Encyclopedia*

D — Deuteronomist source
DeissBS — Deissmann, *Bible Studies*
DeissLAE — Deissmann, *Light from the Ancient East*
DOTT — *Documents from Old Testament Times*
DSS — Dead Sea Scrolls

E	Elohist source	JBL	*Journal of Biblical Literature*
EA	El-Amarna letters or tablets	JBR	*Journal of Bible and Religion*
EBC	*Everyman's Bible Commentary*	JCS	*Journal of Cuneiform Studies*
EBi	*Encyclopaedia Biblica*	JEA	*Journal of Egyptian*
EDNTW	*Expository Dictionary of New*		*Archaeology*
	Testament Works, W. E. Vine	JerusB	Jerusalem Bible
EGT	*The Expositor's Greek Testa-*	JETS	*Journal of the Evangelical*
	ment, W. R. Nicoll		*Theological Society*
EQ	*Evangelical Quarterly*	JewEnc	*Jewish Encyclopaedia*
ERV	English Revised Version	JFB	Jamieson, Fausset and Brown,
	(1881–85)		*A Commentary on the*
Euseb. Hist.	Eusebius, *History of the*		*Old and New Testaments*
	Christian Church	JNES	*Journal of Near Eastern Studies*
EV	English Versions	Jos *Ant.*	Josephus, *Antiquities of the*
ExpB	*The Expositor's Bible*		*Jews*
ExpGT	*The Expositor's Greek*	Jos *Wars*	Josephus, *The Jewish Wars* .
	Testament	JPS	Jewish Publication Society,
ExpT	*The Expository Times*		*Version of the Old Testament*
		JQR	Jewish Quarterly Review
FLAP	Jack Finegan, Light from the	JSS	*Journal of Semitic Studies*
	Ancient Past	JTS	*Journal of Theological Studies*
		KB	Koehler and Baumgartner, *Lexi-*
GTT	*Geographical and*		*con in Veteris Testamenti Libros*
	Topographical Texts of the Old	KD	C. F. Keil and Franz Delitzsch,
	Testament, J. Simons		*Commentary on the Old*
			Testament
HBD	*Harper's Bible Dictionary*	Kittel	Rudolf Kittel, *Biblica Hebraica*
HDAC	*Hastings' Dictionary of the*	KJV	King James Version (1611)
	Apostolic Church		
HDB	*Hastings' Dictionary of the*	LAE	see DeissLAE
	Bible	LB	Living Bible
HDCG	*Hastings' Dictionary of Christ*	LSJ	Liddell, Scott, Jones,
	and the Gospels		*Greek-English Lexicon*
HE	*The Ecclesiastical History of*	LXX	Septuagint – Greek translation
	Eusebius		of the Old Testament
HERE	*Hastings' Encyclopaedia of*		
	Religion and Ethics	MM	Moulton and Milligan,
HGHL	*Historical Geography of the*		*The Vocabulary of the*
	Holy Land, G. A. Smith		*Greek Testament*
HNTC	*Harper's New Testament*	MNT	*Moffatt's New Testament*
	Commentaries		*Commentary*
HR	Hatch and Redpath,	MSt	McClintock and Strong, *Cyclo-*
	Concordance to the Septuagint		*paedia of Biblical, Theological*
HTR	*Harvard Theological Review*		*and Ecclesiastical Literature*
HUCA	*Hebrew Union College Annual*	MT	Masoretic Text
IB	*Interpreter's Bible*	NASB	New American Standard Bible
ICC	*International Critical*	NBC	*New Bible Commentary*,
	Commentary		F. Davidson
IDB	*Interpreter's Dictionary of the*	NBD	*New Bible Dictionary*,
	Bible		J. D. Douglas
IEJ	*Israel Exploration Journal*		
ILN	*Illustrated London News*	NEB	New English Bible
Interp	*Interpretation*	Nestle	Nestle (ed.), *Novum*
IOT	*Introduction to the Old*		*Testamentum Graece*
	Testament, R. K. Harrison	NIC(NT)	*New International Commentary*
IQM	War Scroll from Qumran Cave 1		*(on the New Testament)*
ISBE	*International Standard Bible*	NJPS, NJV	New Jewish Version of the
	Encyclopaedia		Jewish Publication Society
		NPOT	*New Perspectives on the*
J	Jehovah (Yahwist) source		*Old Testament*
JAOS	*Journal of the American*	NT	New Testament
	Oriental Society	NTS	*New Testament Studies*
JASA	*Journal of the American*		
	Scientific Affiliation	Onom.	*Onomasticon*, Eusebius

OT	Old Testament	ZPBD	*Zondervan Pictorial Bible Dictionary*
P	Priestly source	ZPBE	*Zondervan Pictorial Bible Encyclopedia*
PEQ	*Palestine Exploration Quarterly*		
Phillips	J. B. Phillips, New Testament in Modern English		

OT		Old Testament
P		Priestly source
PEQ		*Palestine Exploration Quarterly*
Phillips		J. B. Phillips, New Testament in Modern English
Ptol.		Ptolemy of Alexandria (Claudius Ptolemaeus)
PTR		*Princeton Theological Review*
RA		*Revue d'assyriologie et d'archéologie orientale*
RB		*Révue Biblique*
RSV		Revised Standard Version
RV		Revised Version
SBK		Strack and Billerbeck, *Kommentar zum Neuen Testament aus Talmud und Midrasch*
SCM		Student Christian Movement
SDABD		*Seventh-day Adventist Bible Dictionary*
SHERK		*New Schaff-Herzog Encyclopedia of Religious Knowledge*
SOTI		*A Survey of Old Testament Introduction*, Gleason L. Archer
SP		Samaritan Pentateuch
SPCK		Society for the Promoting of Christian Knowledge
Tac. Ann.		Tacitus *Annals*
TAOTS		D. Winton Thomas, *Archaeology and Old Testament Study*
Targ.		Targum
TBC		*Tyndale Bible Commentaries*
TDNT		*Theological Dictionary of the New Testament*, Kittel
TNTC		*Tyndale New Testament Commentaries*
TR		Textus Receptus (Received Text)
TWNT		*Theologisches Wörterbuch zum Neuen Testament*, Kittel
UBD		*Unger's Bible Dictionary*
VBW		*Views of the Biblical World*, Benj. Mazar
VT		*Vetus Testamentum*, Martin Noth
Vulg.		Vulgate Version
WBC		*Wycliffe Bible Commentary*, Pfeiffer and Harrison
WC		*Westminster Commentaries*
WH		Westcott-Hort, *Text of the Greek New Testament*
WHG		*Wycliffe Historical Geography of Bible Lands*, Pfeiffer and Vos
W Int D		*Webster's International Dictionary*
WTJ		*Westminster Theological Journal*
ZAW		*Zeitschrift für die alttestamentliche Wissenschaft*

General

A.D.	*anno domini* (in the year of our Lord)
Akkad.	Akkadian
Arab.	Arabic
Aram.	Aramaic
art.	article
B.C.	before Christ
c.	*circa* (about)
CA	critical apparatus
cen.	century
cf.	*confer* (compare)
chap(s).	chapter(s)
col.	column
com.	commentary
d.	died, or date of death
E	east
ed.	edited, edition, editor
e.g.	*exempli gratia* (for example)
Egyp.	Egyptian
Eng.	English
et al.	and others
f., ff.	following (verse or verses, page, pages, etc.)
fem.	feminine
fig.	figuratively
ft.	foot, feet
gal.	gallon(s)
Gr.	Greek
Heb.	Hebrew
ibid.	*ibidem* (in the same place)
id.	*idem* (the same)
i.e.	*id est* (that is)
illus.	illustration
intro.	introduction
L., Lat.	Latin
l.	line
lit.	literal, literally
loc. cit.	*loco citato* (in the place cited)
marg.	margin, marginal reading
mil.	millennium
MS(S)	manuscript(s)
N	north
n.d.	no date
NE	northeast
No.	number
NW	northwest
op. cit.	*opere citato* (in the work cited)
orig.	original
p., pp.	page, pages
par.	paragraph
pl.	plural
publ.	publication, published
q.	source
q.v.	*quod vide* (which see)
re	pertaining to, connected with, concerning
rev.	revised, revision
Rom.	Roman

S	south		trans.	translation
SE	southeast		viz.	*videlicet* (namely)
sec.	section		vol.	volume
sing.	singular		v., vv.	verse, verses
s.v.	*sub verbo* (under the word)		W	west
SW	southwest			

GUIDE TO PRONUNCIATION

ā as in late
ă̄ as in vacation
â as in care
ă as in add
a as in infant
ä as in father
a as in ask
á as in testament
ē as in eve
ē̮ as in depend
ĕ as in pet
ĕ as in silent
ė as in porter
ī as in like

ĭ as in till
i as in glory
î as in marine
ō as in oat
ō̮ as in obey
ô as in Lord
ŏ as in hot
ŏ as in connect
ōō as in moon
ŏŏ as in book, put
ū as in fuse
ŭ as in unite
û as in turn
ŭ as in rub
ŭ as in consensus

WYCLIFFE
Bible Encyclopedia

Mount Nebo from the Springs of Moses © MPS

A

AARON (âr'ŭn). Aaron is known best as the head of the Heb. priesthood. He was a descendant of Levi, the son of Amram and his wife Jochebed (Ex 6:20). A younger brother of Miriam, he was three years old when his brother Moses was born (Ex 7:7). He had four sons by his wife Elisheba: Nadab, Abihu, Eleazar, and Ithamar. The first two died before the altar (Lev 10:1-2) and the succession went to Eleazar upon the death of his father (Num 20:26).

Aaron first appears in the biblical narrative as Moses' assistant and spokesman. In response to God's command, Aaron, who had remained in Egypt during the 40 years of Moses' absence, went forth to meet Moses at "the mount of God" and reintroduced him to the Heb. community in Egypt (Ex 4:27-31). Moses was to receive God's message directly and it was Aaron's task to relay this message to the people (Ex 4:16). Aaron also accompanied Moses when they appeared in Pharaoh's presence with the request that Israel be permitted to hold a feast in the wilderness (Ex 5:1). It was Aaron who did miracles in Pharaoh's presence as evidence that their authority came from God Almighty (Ex 7:10). Later, during the battle with the Amalekites, Aaron, assisted by Hur, held up the hands of Moses until Israel was victorious (Ex 17:8-12).

Aaron appeared at Mount Sinai as an elder who, as representative of his people, was allowed, with Moses, Aaron's two sons, and 70 elders, to approach the very presence of the Lord (Ex 24:1-11). After this, while Moses was to be alone with God in the mountain, Aaron was appointed by Moses to be the interim leader of the people (Ex 24:12-18). It was during this period of Aaron's greatest responsibility that he failed his trust most tragically. Less than 40 days after he had been face to face with the God of Israel, Aaron yielded to popular pressure and sanctioned the people's lapse into idolatry. When confronted by Moses, he attempted to evade responsibility for his role in the apostasy (Ex 32:21-24). Strangely, no mention is made of any punishment for Aaron.

Later, his weakness showed up in petty jealousy which led him to join with his sister Miriam in a complaint against Moses because of the latter's claim to be God's spokesman and because of his marriage to a Cushite woman (Num 12). Miriam was punished, but again Aaron was not disciplined, perhaps because of his priestly office. Aaron and Moses together later faced a rebellion which subsided when Aaron with his censor made intercession for the people (Num 16:47). The consequent budding of Aaron's rod served to vindicate Aaron and

his priesthood before the entire nation (Num 17). He died in Mount Hor at the age of 123 (Num 20:28).

Aaron's chief significance was his establishment of the priesthood. His was the responsibility of appearing in God's presence, as representative of the nation, to intercede for them and to present their sacrifices. The priesthood, thus established, lasted until A.D. 70. Although not listed among the heroes of the faith (Heb 11), Aaron is named as the God-appointed high priest who helped prepare the people for the greater high priesthood of Christ (Heb 5:4).

G. A. T.

AARONITE (âr'ŭn-īt). A term descriptive of one whose descent was from Aaron, the founder of the priesthood and brother of Moses. In I Chr 12:27 the 3,700 fighting men under Jehoiada who joined David at Hebron are so designated (translated in RSV as "of the house of Aaron"). The same Heb. phrase is translated "for Aaron" (RSV) in connection with Zadok (I Chr 27:17), distinguishing descendants of Aaron from the other Levites (Josh 21:4, 10, 13).

AB (ăb). The Babylonian name of the fifth Heb. religious month (July-August) and the eleventh civil month. See Calendar.

ABADDON (a-băd'ŏn). This word occurs six times in the OT (RSV) as the name of a place (Job 26:6; Prov 15:11; 27:20; Job 28:22; Ps 88:11; Job 31:12). In the first three it is a synonym for Sheol, in the next for death, in the next for grave, and in the last it is possibly to be taken in a general sense for ruin. In the NT the word occurs once (Rev 9:11) as the name of the angel who reigns over the world of the dead (Gr. *Apollyon*), especially of punishment. See Apollyon; Dead, The.

ABAGTHA (a-băg'tha). Name of one of the seven eunuchs of Ahasuerus (Xerxes I) mentioned in Est 1:10 (one of several Persian characteristics of the book). Abagtha was sent by the king to accompany Queen Vashti to the royal feast, since he was a guard for the king's harem. See Eunuch.

ABANA (ăb'a-na). The first of the two rivers of Damascus which Naaman (*q.v.*) preferred to Jordan (II Kgs 5:12); modern Nahr Barada. Both Abana and Barada may have been used at one time, the former partially preserved in the name of one of Barada's branches, Nahr Banias (HDB). The latter is taken from the mountain

The Abana River (modern Barada) as it flows through downtown Damascus. HFV

which is its source, Amana (Song 4:8), Amana of Assyrian writers (Montgomery, *Kings*, ICC, p. 377), modern Zebedani.

Rising in the Anti-Lebanon range 23 miles NW, it is doubled in volume by the torrential 'Ain Fijeh as it cascades down the mountain. Crossing the plain of Damascus it fans out into several branches, at last to be lost in a marshy lake to the E. The beauty and fertility of Damascus are primarily because of its clear, cool waters creating what Arabic writers have fondly called "the garden of Allah." If appearance were all, Naaman's partiality could hardly be avoided.

ABARIM (ăb'á-rĭm). The promontories at the western edge of the plateau of Moab, overlooking the Jordan Valley and the Dead Sea. Viewed from the W in the valley below, they appear to be a mountain range rising to a height up to 4,000 feet above the Dead Sea. Here the Israelites camped briefly (Num 33:47–48). From Mount Nebo (Pisgah, *q.v.*) Moses saw Canaan (Num 27:12; Deut 32:49). Jeremiah (22:20, RSV) links Abarim with Lebanon and Bashan because of the hilly nature of its terrain.

ABBA (ăb'á; Aramaic "father"). Especially a name by which God was addressed in prayer. In the NT it occurs three times, being accompanied by the Gr. equivalent (Mk 14:36; Rom 8:15; Gal 4:6). But this Aramaic term may lie behind numerous references to God as Father where only the Gr. is given in the NT.
See Adoption; God.

ABDA (ăb'dá)
1. The father of Adoniram, an officer in charge of forced labor under Solomon (I Kgs 4:6).
2. The son of Shammua, a Levite of the family of Jeduthun, who resided in Jerusalem after the Exile (Neh 11:17). In I Chr 9:16 (RSV) he is called "Obadiah, the son of Shemaiah."

ABDEEL (ăb'dĕ-ĕl). Father of Shelemiah (Jer 36:26), who served Jehoiakim. Shelemiah was ordered by the king to help arrest the prophet Jeremiah and his scribe Baruch.

ABDI (ăb'dĭ)
1. A Levite, father of Kishi and grandfather of David's singer Ethan (I Chr 6:44).
2. A Levite, father of Kish who served at the beginning of Hezekiah's reign, considered by some to be the same as 1 above (II Chr 29:12).
3. One of the sons of Elam in Ezra's time who put away his foreign wife (Ezr 10:26).

ABDIEL (ăb'dĭ-ĕl). A son of Guni, father of Ahi, who was a Gadite living in Gilead or Bashan (I Chr 5:15–17).

ABDON (ăb'dŏn)
1. A Levitical city in Asher, assigned to the Gershonites (Josh 21:30; I Chr 6:74). It is probably modern Khirbet 'Abdeh, in the hills 12 miles NE of Acre. Possibly "Abdon" should also be read where RSV has "Ebron" and KJV "Hebron" in Josh 19:28 (Kittel, BH; BDB, p. 715).
2. A judge of Israel for eight years (Jud 12:13–15). He was son of Hillel of Pirathon, an Ephraimite hill-country town seven miles SW of Shechem; modern Far'atah. A special point is made of the family status symbols—70 ass colts ridden by his 70 sons and grandsons.
3. A courtier of Josiah, king of Judah, sent to inquire the meaning of the book of the law found in the temple (II Chr 34:20). He is also called Achbor (II Kgs 22:12, 14; probably also in Jer 26:22; 36:12).
4. A Benjamite of Gibeon, firstborn of Jehiel and Maacah, and brother of Saul's grandfather, Ner (I Chr 8:30; 9:35–36).
5. One of several Benjamites dwelling in Jerusalem (I Chr 8:23, 28).

ABEDNEGO (á-bĕd'nĕ-gō). The Babylonian name given to Azariah, a companion of Daniel in exile (Dan 1:1–7). The name, meaning "servant of Nebo," was given him by his captors. Since Nebo was a chief god of Babylon, it is believed that scribes changed it to "nego" to avoid honoring a heathen deity.

Abednego was among the Heb. captives taken to Babylonia by Nebuchadnezzar in 605 B.C. (Dan 1:1). With his compatriots he refused to eat the "unclean" food while learning Chaldean culture in the king's court. After this he became one of the king's counselors or wise men (Dan 1:20) and was later promoted to an administrative position (Dan 2:49). His fame comes from his refusal to deny his God even under threat of death (Dan 3:12–18). After miraculously surviving the fiery furnace he was given a further promotion by the chastened tyrant. He is named in I Macc 2:59 and referred to in Heb 11:33–34.

ABEL (ā'bĕl)

1. The second son of Adam, who was a shepherd. His offering to God was from the "firstlings of his flock," an offering more acceptable than Cain's offering of grain and vegetables. Whether Abel's was preferred because it involved the shedding of life and hence was symbolic of life, or whether it was offered in a more sincere spirit, is not made explicit. In jealous rage Cain killed Abel and tried to evade responsibility. Abel became a type of the martyrs who suffer for their faith (Mt 23:35). He was honored by Jesus and appears in the catalog of heroes of the faith (Heb 11:4). While his offering was superior to that of Cain, it was inferior to that of Jesus Christ (Heb 12:24). Of Abel it may be said that he was the first shepherd, the first to offer animal sacrifices, the first righteous man (Mt 23:35; I Jn 3:12), and the first martyr. He was victim of the same kind of insane jealousy which took the life of Jesus.

2. Abel ("meadow") is a term compounded with several other place names; e.g., Abel-maim.

3. Apparently identical with Abel-beth-maachah (q.v.) in II Sam 20:18.

G. A. T.

ABEL-BETH-MAACHAH (ā'bĕl-bĕth-mā'á-kà).
Alternately Abel (II Sam 20:18); Abel-maim (II Chr 16:4); Beth-maachah (II Sam 20:14–15, RSV). See each.

A fortified city in the tribe of Naphtali, located W of Dan, about 12 miles N of Lake Huleh in the N of Israel. It overlooked the intersection of the important trade route running from the Mediterranean to Damascus with the one coming N from Hazor. It is the place where Sheba, son of Bichri, took refuge when his revolt against David failed (II Sam 20:13–18). It was among the Israelite towns captured by Ben-hadad of Damascus (I Kgs 15:20) and later by Tiglath-pileser (II Kgs 15:29). It corresponds to modern Tell Abil in Israel.

ABEL-MAIM (ā'bĕl-mā'ĭm). An alternate form of Abel-beth-maachah (q.v.) in II Chr 16:4.

Tell Abil, the site of Abel-Beth-Maachah. JR

ABEL-MEHOLAH (ā'bĕl-mĕ-hō'là). Probably a place E of Jordan, though the site is not exactly located, to which the Midianites fled when pursued by Gideon (Jud 7:22). It is best known as the home of the prophet Elisha (I Kgs 19:16, 19–21). In Solomon's administration it was a part of the district which lay on both sides of Jordan, centered in Bethshean (I Kgs 4:12).

ABEL-MIZRAIM (ā'bĕl-mĭz'rā-ĭm). Alternate place name of Atad, which lay E of the Jordan and N of the Dead Sea, at which the funeral procession of Jacob paused to mourn the patriarch before entering Canaan to bury him (Gen 50:11). Previously called the "threshing floor of Atad," it now became known as the "mourning of Egypt" because of the mighty men of Egypt who took part in the ceremony (Gen 50:7). There is a possible play on the words 'ābel, "meadow," and 'ēbel, "mourning." Apparently new inhabitants of the Negeb made the direct route to Hebron too dangerous.

ABEL-SHITTIM (ā'bĕl-shĭt'ĭm). A place earlier called Shittim (q.v.) on the plains of Moab at which Israel camped before crossing the Jordan to attack Jericho. During this encampment (Num 33:49), the Balaam episode (Num 22–24), the invasion of the camp by Midian idolatry (Num 25), and the war with Midian (Num 31) took place.

ABEZ (ā'bĕz). A name used for the town Ebez (see Josh 19:20, RSV), located in the territory of Issachar.

ABI (ā'bī). In II Kgs 18:2 Abi is cited as the name of the mother of Hezekiah, king of Judah. She is alternately called Abijah (q.v.) as in II Chr 29:1.

ABIA (à-bī'á)

1. Grandson of Solomon through Rehoboam, father of Asa (I Chr 3:10; Mt 1:7).

2. Descendant of Aaron, who was head of the eighth division of David's priestly order (I Chr 24:10, "Abijah"). Zacharias, father of John the Baptist, belonged to this division (Lk 1:5).
See Abijah.

ABIAH (à-bī'á). Variant form of Abijah (q.v.).

1. The second son of Samuel who was appointed judge of Beer-sheba, whose conduct hastened Israel's demand for a king like other nations (I Sam 8:2–5; I Chr 6:28).

2. The wife of Hezron (I Chr 2:24).

3. One of the sons of Becher and grandson of Benjamin (I Chr 7:6, 8).

ABI-ALBON (ā'bī-al'bŏn). One of the 30 mighty men (II Sam 23:31) surrounding David, serving him as a bodyguard. Abi-albon is called Abiel (q.v.) in the parallel passage in I Chr 11:32.

ABIASAPH (à-bī'á-sāf). Probably same as Ebiasaph. A Levite who is the last mentioned de-

scendant of Levi through Korah (Ex 6:24). There exists a difference of opinion as to his identity with Ebiasaph, an ancestor of the great musician Heman of David's time (I Chr 6:23, 37; 9:19).

ABIATHAR (a-bī'a-thár). A priest of the old line of Eli. Apparently his father's name was Ahimelech (I Sam 22:20) and one of his sons had the same name (II Sam 8:17). (*See* Ahimelech.) When Saul slew the priests of the Lord at Nob, Abiathar escaped and fled to David, before whom he served and bore the ark of the Lord when occasion demanded. Frequently (at least eight times) Zadok and Abiathar are mentioned together (Zadok always first) as the high priests of David's time. In Absalom's rebellion, Abiathar remained true to David's cause. However, afterward in Adonijah's attempt to secure the throne, Abiathar cast in his lot with Adonijah and was therefore ultimately deposed by Solomon, and commanded to dwell in his home town Anathoth. Solomon spared him for having faithfully shared in David's afflictions. In the deposition of Abiathar, the doom foretold upon the house of Eli was fulfilled, as noted in I Kgs 2:27. If in II Sam 8:17 Zadok and Ahimelech are unexpectedly mentioned together, it may be that Abiathar had Ahimelech as his assistant because of his own old age.

When Jesus says in Mk 2:26 that David came to request the showbread when "Abiathar was priest," whereas I Sam 22:11 ff. says that Ahimelech filled that office, apparently the son Abiathar is named as the one who stood out more prominently.

H. C. L.

ABIB (a'bĭb)
1. Young ears of barley (Heb. of Ex 9:31; Lev 2:14), ripe but still soft, eaten either rubbed or roasted (KB).
2. This Canaanite name was applied to the month (March-April) in which the barley ripened. As "the beginning of months" (Ex 12:2) and "the first month" (Lev 23:5) of Israel's national life, Abib was a witness year by year to the Lord's part in the crisis experience of the Exodus events, ritually remembered in the Feast of Unleavened Bread (Ex 13:4; 23:15; 34:18) and the Passover (Deut 16:1) during this month.

Abib is equivalent to the Babylonian Nisan, by which name the month was called after the Captivity (Neh 2:1; Est 3:7). It is not clear whether Josephus' distinction between the ritual and civil years, beginning, respectively, in the spring (Nisan) and fall (Tishri), is of early or late origin (Jos *Ant.* i.3.3). *See* Calendar.

ABIDA, ABIDAH (a-bī'dá). A son of Midian and a grandson of Abraham and Keturah (I Chr 1:33). The name is spelled Abidah in Gen 25:4 (KJV).

ABIDAN (a-bī'dán). The son of Gideoni (Num 1:11). As a prince of the tribe of Benjamin he represented that tribe at the census in the wilderness (Num 2:22), and was also present at the dedication of the tabernacle (Num 7:60, 65).

ABIEL (a'bĭ-ĕl)
1. A Benjamite, probably the father of Ner, who was Saul's and Abner's grandfather (I Sam 9:1; 14:51).
2. An Arbathite, one of David's mighty men (I Chr 11:32), called in II Sam 23:31 Abi-albon. The name occurs also in Akkadian and in ancient S Arabic, meaning "El is my father."

ABIEZER (ăb'ĭ-ē'zĕr), **ABIEZERITES** (ăb'ĭ-ē'zĕ-rīts)
1. Founder of a family to which the judge Gideon belonged, called Jeezer or Iezer in Num 26:30 (see KJV and RSV). The term Abiezerites identifies the descendants of Abiezer (Jud 6:11, 24; 8:32).
2. A family descended from Manasseh to which land in Canaan was given (Josh 17:2; I Chr 7:18).
3. A member of David's 30 mighty men, a Benjamite (II Sam 23:27; I Chr 27:12).

ABIGAIL (ăb'ĭ-gāl)
1. The wife of Nabal of Maon, near Carmel, in the territory of the tribe of Judah. She was a woman "of good understanding and beautiful." When Nabal treated David churlishly and so irritated him that he would have taken vengeance on Nabal, Abigail, hearing of her husband's folly, prepared a substantial gift of food and took it to David and his men. With discreet words of reconciliation she checked David's anger and saved her husband's life. But about ten days later Nabal died, apparently of a stroke. David admitted that the woman had prevented him from committing grievous folly by seeking to take his own vengeance on his enemy (I Sam 25).

David felt free to woo the woman after this, having been deeply impressed by her practical discretion and levelheadedness. When David was constrained to flee to Gath, he took Abigail with him (I Sam 27:3). Abigail was but one of the six wives David had in those early days. In Hebron she bore him a son by the name of Chileab, his second son (II Sam 3:3). However in I Chr 3:1 this son is called Daniel.
2. The name of a sister of David, who became the mother of Amasa (I Chr 2:16 f.).

H. C. L.

ABIHAIL (ăb'ĭ-hāl)
1. A Levite, the father of Zuriel, who was chief of the family of Merari in Moses' day (Num 3:35).
2. The wife of Abishur, a Jerahmeelite of the tribe of Judah (I Chr 2:29).
3. The son of Huri of the tribe of Gad, head of a family in Bashan in the time of Jotham, king of Judah (I Chr 5:14).
4. One of the wives of Rehoboam, a descendant of Eliab, David's older brother. She was

not strictly a daughter of Eliab as the text states or she would have been far too old for Rehoboam (II Chr 11:18).

5. The father of Esther and uncle of Mordecai (Est 2:15; 9:29).

ABIHU (*a*-bī′hū). The second son of Aaron (Ex 6:23), who was consecrated to the priesthood with his three brothers, Nadab, Eleazar, and Ithamar (Ex 28:1; Num 3:2; I Chr 24:1). With his older brother Nadab, Abihu went with the elders of Israel and with Moses and Aaron up the mountain of God (Ex 24:1, 9). When he and his brother Nadab offered "strange fire" on the altar, they were instantly killed (Lev 10:1-2). The prohibition against the use of intoxicants which follows this account (v.9) has led some commentators to assume that the brothers were drunk when they died. They were childless (Num 3:4; I Chr 24:2).

ABIHUD (*a*-bī′hŭd). A Benjamite, the third son of Bela (I Chr 8:3).

ABIJAH (*a*-bī′ja)

1. A son of Jeroboam I, king of Israel. When the boy was gravely ill, Jeroboam sent his wife in disguise to appeal to the prophet Ahijah. The prophet, warned by God, told her that for the sin and apostasy of Jeroboam God's judgment would sweep his descendants away, and as for Abijah, "when thy feet enter into the city the child shall die" (I Kgs 14:12). The child died as prophesied, saved from the wrath to come, "because in him there is found some good thing toward Jehovah" (I Kgs 14:13, ASV).

2. The son of Rehoboam and his successor on the throne of Judah (II Chr 12:16). He is also called Abia in I Chr 3:10 and Abijam in I Kgs 14:31; 15:1-8. His mother was Maachah (I Kgs 15:2) or Michaiah (II Chr 13:2), the granddaughter of Absalom. The chief episode of his brief reign of three years was the battle in which he decisively defeated Jeroboam of Israel. The remarkable thing about the battle was a speech by Abijah to the opposing army in which he proclaimed God's presence with Judah and rebuked the Israelites for their apostasy (II Chr 13). Nevertheless he walked in the sins of his fathers, imitating their debasing polygamy with 14 wives (I Kgs 15:3; II Chr 13:21).

3. A descendant of Aaron and a priest in the time of David. He was made head of the eighth of the 24 courses into which David divided the whole priesthood for service (I Chr 24:10).

4. The daughter of Zechariah and wife of King Ahaz (II Chr 29:1). Her name is given as Abi in II Kgs 18:2. She was the mother of King Hezekiah.

5. A priest, the father of Zichri (Neh 12:1-4, 17), who returned with Zerubbabel to rebuild the temple after the Exile. If it is the same one, at a great age he also sealed the covenant of Nehemiah, binding the people in rededication to God (Neh 10:7).

P. C. J.

ABIJAM (*a*-bī′jam). A king of Judah, successor to his father Rehoboam (I Kgs 14:31 – 15:8). Abijam may be an alternate spelling since he is also referred to as Abijah (*q.v.* 2).

ABILENE (ăb-ī-lē′nē). A territory on the eastern slopes of the Anti-Lebanon Mountains, named after its capital, Abila, which was about 18 miles NW of Damascus on the SW bank of Wadi Barada, the ancient Abana River (II Kgs 5:12). It was the tetrarchy of Lysanias (Lk 3:1, only Bible reference). *See* Lysanias. A contemporary inscription at Abila confirms this. In A.D. 37 it was given by the emperor to Herod Agrippa I. From A.D. 44 to 53 the territory was administered by procurators. In the latter year it was confirmed by Emperor Claudius to Herod Agrippa II. Toward the end of the century it was once more made a part of the province of Syria. It is identified with the village called es-Suk, or Suq Wadi Barada, in a wild and scenic region of limestone cliffs and gorges.

ABIMAEL (*a*-bĭm′a-ĕl). One of the sons of Joktan, a descendant of Shem, supposed founder of a tribe among the Arabians (Gen 10:28; I Chr 1:22). Such names with a medial *m* are found both in S Arabic (*Abmi-'athtar*) and Akkadian (*Ili-ma-abi*).

ABIMELECH (*a*-bĭm′e-lĕk)

1. The earliest OT man to bear this name was the king of Gerar, an early Philistine inhabitant of Palestine, who should be distinguished from the later warlike Philistines who at the end of the 2nd mil. migrated from their homeland in Caphtor (probably Crete, *q.v.*) and settled along the southern coast. It is highly probable that these "sea people" arrived in Palestine in waves of migration throughout the 2nd mil., Abimelech's clan being among the early settlers. Gerar is believed to be located some few miles SE of Gaza.

Abraham told Abimelech the half-truth that Sarah was his sister (Gen 20:2-18). Abimelech, whose wife was barren, assumed Sarah was unmarried and espoused her to be his wife. He became cognizant of the whole truth through a dream by which he learned also that Abraham was a prophet of the Lord who could pray for him. After some chiding of Abraham, the good Philistine Abimelech not only returned Sarah untouched but also gave Abraham gifts of cattle, servants, and silver. Abraham's prayer for Abimelech was answered with fruitfulness of womb for his entire household. Later there was a slight rift between the two wealthy households over possession of a well (Gen 21:22-32). The swearing of a covenant brought peace and gave the Hebrews their name for the oasis at Beer-sheba ("the well of swearing"). *See also* Philistines.

2. Another king of Gerar in the time of Isaac was called Abimelech (Gen 26:1, 6-17). Isaac's experience was very similar to that of his father Abraham. He too went to Gerar be-

Probable ruins of the Temple of Baal Berith (Judg 9:46–49) at Shechem. HFV

cause of famine. Fearful of his life because of his wife's beauty, Isaac said that she was his sister. Abimelech learned the whole truth and rebuked Isaac. Isaac's success through agriculture and reopening the wells dug by his father made the people envious, so that Abimelech asked him to leave. Later, a covenant was made between Isaac and Abimelech, as had been done between Abraham and the first Abimelech (Gen 26:26–31).

3. In the title of Ps 34 Achish, the Philistine king of Gath in the time of David (I Sam 21:10), is called Abimelech. It is possible that Achish (q.v.) was his native name and that he was known among the Canaanites as Abimelech (cf. the Assyrian king Tiglath-pileser III who was also called Pul in parts of his realm). Or Abimelech may have been a popular title for kings among the Hebrews. It is a well-known fact that Egyptian titulary consisted of five names for each king.

4. The son of Gideon (Jud 8:30 – 9:54) bears the title Abimelech. Related through his mother to the people of Shechem who worshiped the god Baal-berith, Abimelech received money from the treasury of Baal-berith and with it procured wicked men to help him slay his 70 brothers. The people at Shechem quickly proclaimed him king. Jotham, the youngest, however, escaped and lived to speak a parable against his presumptuous brother. In this parable he likened Abimelech to a bramble bush lording it over all the trees, and prophesied that the men of Shechem and Abimelech would destroy each other. In three years the prophecy began to be fulfilled when the people of Shechem turned against Abimelech.

Another complication is introduced into the narrative with the appearance of Gaal, the son of Ebed, who gained the confidence of most of the men of Shechem. However Zabul, a ruler of Shechem, informed Abimelech of this situation, and Abimelech by means of an ambush drove Gaal and his people away.

But Abimelech still had to win the city of Shechem, which took some ingenious military tactics (Jud 9:43–45). Finally the city was taken and sown with salt, a measure designed to spoil the soil for years to come. As was usually the case, many of the lords of Shechem took refuge in their citadel in the temple of the god Berith. The bloody Abimelech set fire to the temple tower and burned them alive. In the process of taking Thebez, a nearby city, the people likewise took refuge in their strong tower, but Abimelech's purpose to burn it was frustrated by a woman who dropped a piece of millstone on his head breaking his skull, and thus ending his wicked career.

E. B. S.

ABINADAB (á-bĭn′á-dăb)

1. An older brother of David (I Sam 16:8; 17:13).

2. A son of Saul who died with him in the battle of Gilboa (I Sam 31:2; I Chr 8:33; 9:39; 10:2). He is also called Ishui in I Sam 14:49.

3. The best known personage who bore this name was the man of Kirjath-jearim in whose house the ark of God rested for 20 years and from whose house David, not without trouble, brought the ark up to Jerusalem (I Sam 7:1; II Sam 6:3–4; I Chr 13:7).

4. The "son of Abinadab" (I Kgs 4:11, KJV) is rendered "Ben-Abinadab" in ASV, RSV.

ABINOAM (á-bĭn′ō-ăm). A native of Kadesh in Naphtali, father of Barak (Jud 4:6, 12; 5:1, 12). The name is found also in ancient S Arabic inscriptions.

ABIRAM (á-bī′răm)

1. A Reubenite, son of Eliab, who with his brother Dathan joined On and Korah (a Levite) in organizing a jealous conspiracy against Moses and Aaron in the wilderness (Num 16:1,12,24–27; 26:9; Deut 11:6; Ps 106:17). He perished miserably (with Korah and Dathan) when the earth miraculously cleft asunder and "swallowed them up" (c. 1430 B.C.).

2. The firstborn son of Hiel the Bethelite (I Kgs 16:34), who died when his father foolishly relaid the foundation of Jericho (c. 870 B.C.). His tragic death fulfilled Joshua's remarkable prophecy (Josh 6:26). (Perhaps Hiel revived an ancient Canaanite custom and offered his firstborn son as a foundation sacrifice.)

ABISHAG (ăb′ĭ-shăg). According to I Kgs 1:4. this was an exceedingly beautiful unmarried young woman (Heb. na′arâ bᵉtulâ) who cared for King David in his old age. Though one of her duties, in the words of the king's servants, was to be "in thy bosom, that my lord the king may get heat" (I Kgs 1:2), there can be no inference that she became his wife (v. 4, RSV). Her purpose was only to make the aged man comfortable. "They covered him with clothes, but he gat no heat." After David's death Adonijah, an older half-brother of Solomon who was a rival contender for kingship, asked Solomon for Abishag's hand in marriage. Solomon interpreted this as a possible claim on the throne in the eyes of the people and forthwith had Adonijah put to death.

ABISHAI (á-bǐsh′á-ī). A grandson of Jesse and cousin of David, being the son of David's sister Zeruiah who bore three sons, Abishai, Joab, and Asahel (I Chr 2:15–16). Abishai appears to have been a capable though impetuous soldier completely devoted to David as the Lord's anointed In I Sam 26:6–9 Abishai went with David by night into the camp of the sleeping Saul and was restrained from killing Saul with the latter's own spear. He joined his brother Joab in pursuing the hapless Abner, who was forced to kill their brother Asahel during a skirmish resulting from a belt-wrestling joust (II Sam 2:18–24).

There are numerous examples of Abishai's devotion to David and his character as a military hero. Facing Ammonites and Syrians before and behind, Joab divided his army giving his brother Abishai the less heroic warriors to fight Ammon while Joab fought the Syrians; both experienced victory (II Sam 10). It took an army and the forceful General Abishai to slay 18,000 Edomites in the valley of salt and put up garrisons in Edom (I Chr 18:12–13). He was wholly the soldier in his thinking; treason deserved death. When the Benjamite Shimei cursed the exiled David, Abishai wanted to slay him immediately. "Why should this dead dog curse my lord my king? let me go over, I pray thee, and take off his head." But David looked on this misfortune as of the Lord (II Sam 16:7–14). Later, in II Sam 19:21 when David forgave Shimei, once again it was Abishai who called for execution.

Abishai commanded one of the three regiments of David's army-in-exile which brought the Absalom rebellion to a swift conclusion. In the Sheba rebellion, Joab and Abishai took command from their ill-chosen cousin Amasa and pursued after the rebel to the frontier settlement Abel-beth-maachah, whence Sheba's head was thrown over the wall to him (II Sam 20). In David's later years Abishai delivered the king out of the hand of a Philistine giant, after which David no longer went out to battle (II Sam 21).

According to II Sam 23:15–18, Abishai seems to have been the leader of the three mighty men who risked their lives to bring David a drink from the well in Bethlehem. Here also we are told he slew 300 with his spear.

E. B. S.

ABISHALOM (á-bǐsh′á-lôm). This is the fuller form found in I Kgs 15:2; II Chr 11:20 of the more common name Absalom (q.v.).

ABISHUA (á-bǐsh′ū-á)
1. A Benjamite, a son of Bela (I Chr 8:4).
2. A descendant of Aaron, he was the son of

Phinehas, the priest, and ancestor of Ezra (I Chr 6:4, 50; Ezr 7:5).

ABISHUR (á-bī′shûr). A man of Judah, the second son of Shammai, listed in the genealogy of Jerahmeel. He was the husband of Abihail (I Chr 2:28–29).

ABITAL (á-bī′tál). One of David's wives (fifth), the mother of Shephatiah, who was born in Hebron (II Sam 3:2, 4).

ABITUB (á-bī′tŭb). A Benjamite born in Moab, a son of Shaharaim (I Chr 8:8–11).

ABIUD (á-bī′ŭd). The Gr. form of Abihud (q.v.), who was a descendant of Zerubbabel and the father of Eliakim, being mentioned in the NT as an ancestor of Jesus (Mt 1:13).

ABJECT. A plural noun in Ps 35:15 from Heb. *nēkeh* probably meaning "slanderers" or "railers." RSV has "cripples."

ABLUTION. This is an act of washing the body. In Scripture there are only a few doubtful references to washing for sanitary purposes. These references, the bathing of Pharaoh's daughter (Ex 2:5), of Bathsheba (II Sam 11:2), and of the harlots of Samaria (I Kgs 22:38, RSV), are each also capable of explanation as religious ablutions. Religious ritual washings were universal in the ancient Near East. "In the minds of the ancients there was a close connection between the notion of purity or cleanness and the notion of being consecrated to God" (R. deVaux, *Ancient Israel, Its Life and Institutions,* p. 460).

The evolutionary religious concept explains the entire OT system of clean and unclean and of ritual washings as arising, like the idea of holiness, from taboo, and makes of it all a base element in Heb. religion ("Unclean," HDB; cf. de Vaux, *op. cit.,* pp. 463, 464, where taboos

Ruins of a highly decorated ablution tank adjacent to the temple of Jupiter at Baalbek. It measures about sixty-five by twenty-five feet.
HFV

are said to be "remains of old superstitious rites"). Whatever forms and ideas may have been carried over from pre-Mosaic times, it is certain that ablutions were designed by God, "having as their object the cultivation of holiness and of the spiritual life. . . . The great obstacle to holiness is sin; while that death again, which is the consequence of sin, puts an end to man's life . . . permeates the entire man; nor does it merely desecrate the soul . . . but it also defiles the body . . . turns it into the very dust of death" (C. F. Keil, *Biblical Archaeology,* I, 378).

Keil's view is further that water as a principal cleansing medium of ordinary life was used to symbolize spiritual forgiveness of sin. This connection between defilement and death explains how the Levitical purifications ranked side by side with sacrifices and together formed the main features of worship in the Mosaic system. Thus the law was able all the better to fulfill the purpose for which it was designed, of awakening and keeping alive in man the consciousness of sin and guilt and of the need for cleansing of the inner nature (see Keil, *ibid.,* pp. 378–384).

The Levitical ablutions were of four kinds: (1) washing of the hands (Lev 15:11); (2) washing of hands and feet (Ex 30:19; 40:31); (3) bathing of the whole body (Num 19:19; Lev 22:4–6); (4) sprinkling with a special water ("water of separation," Num 19:9).

Baptism is a form of ritual ablution which arose among the Jews apparently in connection with initiation of proselytes. Authorities state that a stranger who desired to become a proselyte of the covenant of righteousness, i.e., in the fullest sense an Israelite, had to be circumcised and baptized, and then offer sacrifice. Baptism was by self-immersion in a pool (see HDB, I, 239; Edersheim, *Life and Times of Jesus the Messiah,* II, xii; Schürer, *History of the Jewish People,* II, ii, par. 31, p. 319). Baptism and other ablutions were prominent among the Essenes (Jos *War* ii. 8.5) as witnessed by the findings at Qumran (F. M. Cross, Jr., *The Ancient Library of Qumran,* pp. 49, 50, 70). John's and Jesus' use of baptism is well-known.

Except for the rites of baptism and feet washing (Jn 13), ritual ablution is as foreign to NT Christianity as the sacrifices of the Mosaic law. For the Christian, ceremonial defilement does not exist (Mk 7:6–23; Mt 15:3–20), hence no need for ritual washing. Jesus fulfilled this aspect of the law as well as the others. Baptism by whatever mode and feet washing whether viewed as a rite or only as a Gospel incident have no connection with ritual uncleanness, hence no connection with OT ritual or interpretation.

See Baptism; Bathe, Bathing; Foot Washing; Hands, Washing of; Unclean.

Bibliography. A. Oepke, "*Louō,* etc.," TDNT, IV, 295–307.

R. D. C.

ABNER (ăb'nẽr). A cousin of Saul and commander of Israel's army (I Sam 14:50–51; 17:55). He occupied the place of honor at feasts and was Saul's bodyguard during the desert campaign against David (I Sam 20:25; 26:5–15). After the death of Saul and Jonathan, Abner became leader of Israel and made Ishbosheth king, succeeding his father Saul (II Sam 2:8–10). When offended by Ishbosheth, Abner decided to support David as king over all Israel (II Sam 3:8–10). Incensed by David's acceptance of this allegiance, and embittered because Abner had killed his brother Asahel (in self-defense), Joab murdered Abner at the gate of Hebron (II Sam 3:27). His death was mourned by David and all Israel (II Sam 3:31–34; I Kgs 2:32).

ABOMINATION. There are a total of 12 Heb. and Gr. words translated "abomination" or "abominable." The biblical languages, like our own, have a variety of expressions, some close synonyms, others not, to express degrees and varieties of abhorrence.

The chief idea represented in the four Heb. nouns is revulsion at great wrong in religious matters. Since there is only one true living God, an invisible spiritual being without bodily parts, all forms of idolatry and all ceremonies and objects connected with idolatry are abhorrent to God. This attitude is shared by His people and His prophets. Heb. *tôʿ ẽbâ* is the chief word in the OT used in this connection. The same abhorrence pertains to moral evil. Hence *tôʿẽbâ* is used of that as well (Jer 7:7–10). The verb *tāʿab* from which *tôʿ ẽbâ* is derived is less specialized in meaning, though translated similarly. It expresses displeasure of all sorts, from dislike of certain foods (Ps 107:18) to loathing for idols (Deut 7:26).

Heb. *sheqes* seems to be a technical word for revulsion at the use of flesh of unclean animals for food or sacrifice (Lev 7:21; 11:10–13, 20, 23, 41, 42). The related *shiqūs* is chiefly a term of contempt for idols and idolatry, especially in the prophets (Isa 66:3; Jer 4:1; 32:34; Ezk 7:20). The verb *shāqas,* translated "abomination" (Lev 11:11, 13), from which these two words are derived, likewise expresses the revulsion a Heb. was expected to have toward things morally or religiously wrong.

Disgust at petty dishonesty is expressed once as abomination (Mic 6:10, "abominable"), though the Heb. word used here ordinarily means to be angry.

The NT words rendered "abomination," "abominable," etc. (Mt 24:15; Lk 16:15; Tit 1:16; I Pet 4:3; Rev 21:8), are simply the OT Heb. ideas discussed above in Gr. garb.

See Sacrilege.

R. D. C.

ABOMINATION OF DESOLATION. This expression appears in Mt 24:15 and Mk 13:14. Matthew states that it is that "spoken of by Daniel the prophet." The Gr. phrase is quoted almost exactly from the LXX of Dan 9:27 (as well as Theodotion's Gr. translation which replaced the LXX in early Christian centuries). Similar expressions are found in Dan 8:13 ("transgression of desolation"), Dan 9:27 ("for the overspreading of abominations he shall make it desolate"), Dan 11:31 ("the abomination that maketh desolate"), of which, as stated, the LXX of Dan 9:27 is cited in the NT.

An act whereby a pagan idol is introduced. into the precincts of the holy temple at Jerusalem is obviously intended by Jesus. Liberal interpreters of Daniel hold that the three passages in Daniel all refer to an act of Antiochus Epiphanes, pagan king of Syria, who desecrated the temple in 165 B.C. Thus Jesus was mistaken or else never really said what is attributed to Him in Mt 24:15 and Mk 13:14. Certain conservatives feel the prophecy was fulfilled in events of the 1st cen. A.D. associated with the destruction of Jerusalem. Others assert that Paul's expansion of the prophecy in II Thess 2 (as most agree it is) requires that there is some reference here to a final Antichrist who shall make his appearance at the end of the present age (G. R. Beasley-Murray, *Jesus and the Future* and *A Commentary on Mark 13*). *See* Abomination; Antichrist; Beast (Symbolic).

R. D. C.

ABRAHAM (ā′brȧ-hăm)

Authenticity and Date of His Background

Though archaeology has provided no direct contact with Abraham, abundant evidence has accumulated which, far from contradicting the biblical story, has led many critical scholars to accept the account as a genuine reflection of the period it claims to represent. This evidence is in the form of documentary sources which establish the cultural traditions reflected in the biblical account.

The Nuzu texts which present the common law of the Hurrians (biblical Horites, *q.v.*), who dominated parts of Mesopotamia *c.* 1500 B.C., have cast light on such traditions as Abraham's adoption of his servant Eliezer as heir (Gen 15:2–4). In Nuzu such slave adoptions were common practice by childless couples. For the eventual inheritance, the adopted male adult traded his caring for the adopting parents in their old age and his providing them proper burial ceremonies. But Nuzu provided that a natural son like Isaac, even if born after such adoption, always received primary inheritance rights.

Again, both Nuzu and Hammurabi's law-code tell how a childless wife was obliged to provide her husband a handmaid with hopes a son might be born. Abraham's reluctance to send Hagar off (Gen 21:11) reflects the protection by Hurrian law of the handmaid under those circumstances.

Another cultural tradition, which does not fit later (Mosaic) Heb. law and therefore must come from an earlier time, is Abraham's purchase of the field of Machpelah (Gen 23). Cap-

The Plains of Mamre. HFV

padocian texts reflect Hittite feudal laws which apparently made it necessary for Abraham to pay full price (23:9, NASB) to obtain legal title and to purchase the entire field from Ephron the Hittite, because with full ownership went the feudal obligation or services due the ruler of the land, according to Hittite law (BASOR, # 129, pp. 15–18). Abraham was accustomed to such business transactions and was able to weigh out to Ephron the 400 shekels of silver as "current money with the merchant." It was not coinage, but as the Heb. says, "silver which passes to the merchant," meaning unalloyed bars or rings of silver.

Although Abraham himself is not known from extrabiblical sources, the name is attested in its Babylonian form, Abamram (BASOR, # 83, p. 34), as are the names Nahor (cf. city of Nahor, Gen 24:10), Terah and Serug (Gen 11:22, 24) as towns mentioned in the Mari texts and other Assyrian documents (cf. John Bright, *A History of Israel*, p. 70).

One of the most interesting chapters in the story of Abraham is Gen 14 which deals with the battle of the four kings of the E against the local monarchs. Archaeologists consider this chapter to be most detailed in its authenticity. (*See* Amraphel; Arioch; Chedorlaomer; Tidal.) The geographical accuracy of Gen 14 is undisputed. Moreover, the rare technical term (*hanîkim*) used for Abraham's retainers (Gen 14:14) appears in the Egyptian Execration texts and in a letter from Taanach dated to the first half of the 2nd mil. B.C. The occurrence of this rare, early word lends tremendous authenticity to the text.

Abraham's travels from Mesopotamia and his wanderings in Palestine accord well with the general picture that archaeology has obtained for the early 2nd mil. This was a time when Palestine was receiving new nomadic groups and the central hill country where Abraham chose to live was sparsely populated, while the Jordan Valley, coastal regions, and other agricultural domains were dominated by the Canaanites and others. Abraham was probably part of this great movement of people usually identified as Amorites (Gen 15:16), which would explain Abraham's alliances with the Amorites Aner, Eshcol, and Mamre (Gen 14:13, 24), and the justification for Ezekiel accusing the erring nation of having an Amorite father (Ezk 16:3–5). Abraham spent some time in the Negeb and along the trade route from Kadesh-barnea to Shur (eastern border of Egypt). Not for centuries before or after the Middle Bronze I period (2100–1850 B.C.) were there known settlements in the Negeb. Ruins of way stations, dated to that time by pottery, dot the inland caravan route through the northern Sinai desert.

An exact date for Abraham cannot be pinpointed by means of archaeology, though most authorities settle on the early 2nd mil. By using the biblical figures and assuming no gaps, a date of *c*. 2000 B.C. for the birth of Abraham may be obtained. This fits well with archaeological data.

Objection has been raised regarding the occurrence of the term Philistine *(q.v.)* in Gen 21:32, 34. The warlike Philistines of David's day did not arrive in the coasts of Palestine until *c*. 1200 B.C. It has been pointed out by C. H. Gordon, however, that the Indo-European Sea people, such as the Minoans from Crete, had been migrating into Canaan all through the 2nd mil. The Canaanized Abimelech of Gerar was probably part of an earlier wave of peace-loving "Philistines," although the name Philistine itself may be anachronistic, coming from the hostile peoples of Saul's and David's time. *See* Chronology, OT; Patriarchal Age.

History and Significance of His Life

Abram began his life in Ur of the Chaldees in Mesopotamia. From there Terah, his father, moved the family to Haran. Both Ur and Haran were centers of moon worship. His father's name, Terah, possibly means "Ter is (the divine) brother." Ter is believed to be a dialectic variant for the moon-god and was especially popular in the district of Haran as is borne out by Assyrian records (J. Lewy, HUCA, 19, p. 425). But Abram was called away from this pagan background by the voice of God to go to a land divinely promised to his seed.

After arriving in Palestine Abram spent his days mainly near three centers in the S, Bethel, Hebron (Mamre), and Beer-sheba. He had apparently entered Canaan from the E, as Jacob did on his return from Padan-aram, crossing the Jordan near Succoth and stopping first to worship God outside Shechem (Gen 12:5–7). Near Bethel, however, Abram built his second altar (Gen 12:8; 13:3) and called on the name of the Lord Yahweh. After a brief sojourn in Egypt because of famine, Abram returned to the place of the altar near Bethel and effected a separation with his nephew Lot, who chose to dwell in the verdant plain of the Jordan where the Canaanite cities of Sodom and Gomorrah were situated. Then Abram journeyed S to the highland plain called Mamre (Hebron) at the southern end of the central mountain range. Here he built another altar to the Lord.

Following the recovery of Lot and his household from the hands of their Mesopotamian captors, Abram paid tithes to Melchizedek, king of Salem. Whether or not Salem was Jerusalem cannot be proved, but the text is clear that Melchizedek was a priest-king representing El Elyon—another appellation for Abraham's God. Gen 20–22 tells of Abraham's sojourn in the Negeb, especially around Beer-sheba. The biblical account states that Abraham both dug the well and named the place Beer-sheba ("the well of swearing") because of the covenant he made with Abimelech, the Philistine chieftain in that area.

God renewed His promise to Abram on several occasions (cf. Gen 13:14–18; 15; 17; 22:15–19). Emphasis is laid on Abram's faith in the promise of God concerning both a land and a seed despite his wife's continued barrenness and age. Abram's name, meaning "exalted father" or "my father is exalted," was changed to "Abraham" meaning "father of a multitude." God's covenant with him was sealed by the sign of circumcision, and eventually Isaac, a son of promise (Gal 4:28), was given to this one who ever after was to be known as "the father of all them that believe" (Rom 4:11). Indeed, Abraham believed God's promise of a son in his old age and "it was reckoned to him for righteousness" (Gen 15:4–6; Rom 4:1–4; Jas 2:22–23; Gal 3:6; 5:6). Before Isaac was given through Sarah's dead womb (Heb 11:11), her Egyptian handmaid Hagar bore Ishmael, through whom the Arabs of this day trace their origin to Abraham.

Isaac's name comes from the Heb. root *ṣā-ḥaq*, meaning "to laugh." Abraham's laughter (Gen 17:17) seems to have been an expression of joy or even amazement, while Sarah's laugh-

The Mosque of Hebron which covers a cave thought to be the Cave of Machpelah, burial site of Abraham and other members of the Patriarchal family. HFV

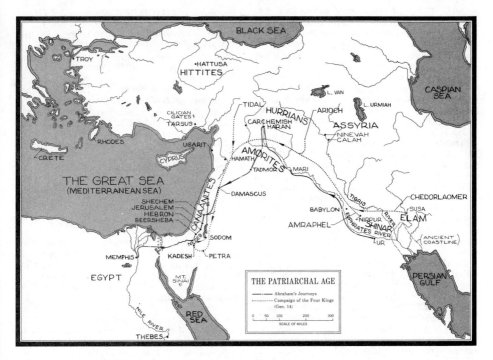

The Journeys of Abraham

ter (Gen 18:11–15) was an expression of disbelief which she shamefacedly disavowed. In due time Isaac became the focal point of all Abraham's hopes; this explains the importance of the episode of the offering of Isaac in Gen 22. The dilemma Abraham experienced was that God's promise could not be fulfilled if Isaac died and yet God was asking Abraham for Isaac. Heb 11:17–19 gives the divine commentary on this event, showing how Abraham's faith in God's faithfulness triumphed, "accounting that God was able to raise him [Isaac] up, even from the dead" (v. 19) if necessary, to fulfill His promise. See Abrahamic Promise.

Other episodes in the life of Abraham picture him not as a generic figure about whom legend has become encrusted (as certain critics have claimed) but in warm human tones. Most of the biblical account deals with him from his seventy-fifth year on (Gen 12:4). That Abraham was 100 and Sarah was 90 when Isaac was born, far from being late Midrash, is a key part of the original story, i.e., that Abraham worshiped the God who performs the impossible. It is true that the biblical account touches on a relatively small segment of his life, yet these comparatively few chapters (Gen 12–25) present a surprisingly well rounded picture of the patriarch. He was seminomadic but very different from the average bedouin of today, for Abraham was well-to-do in cattle, silver, and

servants. He was a man of peace, but could use his retainers (Gen 14:14) for an occasional skirmish.

Abraham had face-to-face encounters' with the Almighty, entertained angels (Gen 18:1–8), and received the word of God in dreams (Gen 15:12–17). Most importantly, he is called a prophet by God in Gen 20:7, where Abimelech, the king of Gerar, is warned that Abraham had the gift of intercession. He used this gift successfully in Abimelech's behalf (Gen 20:17–18) but was unsuccessful in his intercession for Sodom (Gen 18:23–30), undoubtedly because his estimate of that city was wrong. See Sodom; Bab edh-Dhra.

Twice Abraham seems to have been protecting his own skin by using the half-truth that Sarah was his sister while hiding the fact that she was also his wife (Gen 12:11–13; 20:5). Isaac did the same thing (Gen 26:6–11). See Abimelech. These episodes, however, when properly understood, show that Abraham and Isaac, although afraid, were not deliberately walking the borderline of moral turpitude. The patriarchs came from Haran, an area controlled by the Hurrians. Hence they were evidently both practicing a cherished Hurrian custom, which E. A. Speiser (The Anchor Bible, Genesis, pp. 91–94) calls the wife-sister relationship. Both Sarah and Rebekah were eligible for this privileged status according to Hurrian legal practice. The patriarchs hoped to use as a diplomatic device this special status of their wives, who enjoyed superior standing in their society. Neither the pharaoh of Egypt nor the ruler of Gerar, however, was familiar with this Hurrian custom, and had to be convinced it was a legitimate exercise of prerogative and protection enjoyed by sister-wives of upper-class Hurrian society. Yet God intervened for Abraham in both cases, teaching him that the walk of trust and obedience was the new course he should follow (Gen 12:17; 20:3, 17f.).

Abraham had another wife, Keturah (Gen 25:1-4), through whom he became the father of the Midianites and others, but as the Scripture says, "He gave all that he had to Isaac" (Gen 25:6). Abraham died "in a good old age" and was buried in the cave he had bought from the Hittites. His taking such a step for burial of his family and himself in the land promised to him instead of back in his ancestral homeland was strong demonstration of his faith in the covenant.

In II Chr 20:7 and Jas 2:23 Abraham is called the friend of God. The universality of this title for the father of the Heb. nation is reflected in the name of the mosque in honor of Abraham at Hebron, Al-Khalil ("The Friend"). No one can be sure that this mosque stands over Abraham's burial cave in the field of Machpelah, but Gen 23:19 states that it was indeed in the area of Hebron.

E. B. S.

Abraham in the NT

The name of Abraham occurs 74 times in the NT, more than that of any other OT saint except Moses (79 times). God is the "God of Abraham" (Mt 22:32; Acts 7:32), and Abraham lives on in conscious fellowship with Him (Lk 16:22; see Abraham's Bosom). Abraham was the ancestor of Messiah (Mt 1:1) and the father of the Israelites according to the flesh (Mt 3:9; Jn 8:33; Acts 13:26). But he becomes the spiritual father of all who share in his faith by the Spirit (Rom 4:11-16; 9:7; Gal 3:16, 29; 4:22, 31). Abraham's faith led to his justification and thus typifies the kind of faith we must exercise (Rom 4:3-11). The demonstrations of his faith in his obeying God's call to leave Mesopotamia and in his offering of Isaac are mentioned as outstanding examples of faith in action (Heb 11:8-19; Jas 2:21).

J. R.

Bibliography. William F. Albright, *Archaeology, Historical Analogy, and Early Biblical Tradition,* Baton Rouge: Louisiana State Univ. Press, 1966, pp. 22-41. Jack Finegan, *In the Beginning,* New York: Harper, 1962, pp. 85-121. Nelson Glueck, *Rivers in the Desert,* New York: Farrar, Strauss & Cudahy, 1959, pp. 60-110. Angel Gonzalez, *Abraham, Father of Believers,* trans. by R. J. Olsen, New York: Herder & Herder, 1967. James L. Kelso, *Archaeology and Our OT Contemporaries,* Grand Rapids: Zondervan, 1966, pp. 13-27. K. A. Kitchen, *Ancient Orient and OT,* Chicago: Inter-Varsity, 1966, pp. 41-56, 153-156. W. S. LaSor, *Great Personalities of the OT,* Westwood, N.J.: Revell, 1959, pp. 13-30. F. B. Meyer, *Abraham: or the Obedience of Faith,* London: Morgan & Scott, n.d. D. J. Wiseman, *The Word of God for Abraham and Today,* G. Campbell Morgan Memorial Lecture #11, London: Westminster Chapel, 1959. C. Leonard Woolley, *Abraham: Recent Discoveries and Hebrew Origins,* London: Faber & Faber, 1936. Geerhardus Vos, *Biblical Theology,* Grand Rapids: Eerdmans, 1954, pp. 79-105.

ABRAHAMIC PROMISE. The promises given to Abraham embodied in the Abrahamic covenant first appear in Gen 12:1-3, followed by three important confirmations and applications (Gen 13:14-17; 15:1-7; 17:1-19). The Abrahamic promise, first, concerned Abraham himself *(q.v.).* He was promised great personal blessing, his name would be great, and he himself would be a channel of blessing to others.

Second, the Abrahamic promise related to Abraham's descendants. He was to be the father of a great nation (Gen 12:2) with innumerable posterity, compared to the dust of the earth and the stars of heaven (Gen 13:16; 15:5). His descendants were to be famous, including kings and more than one great nation (Gen 17:6). It is significant that all these promises have already been literally fulfilled.

Third, the promise of title to the land to which God had directed Abraham was made sure to Abraham's posterity as an "everlasting" possession (Gen 17:7-8). The extensive boundaries of their possession are given in great detail (Gen 15:18-21) and confirmed by a solemn covenant sealed with blood (Gen 15:8-17). The implication that the nation would continue forever in keeping with its title to the land was later confirmed in Jer 31:35-37. To these broad promises detailed predictions are added, such as the sojourn in Egypt (Gen 15:13-14) and emphasis on the fact that only a portion of Abraham's seed would inherit the full promise.

Fourth, through Abraham "all the families of the earth" would be blessed. This promise went beyond Abraham's physical lineage and concerned all nations. It was fulfilled in the coming of Jesus Christ and His provision for the sins of the whole world. Through Abraham's posterity, also, the Scriptures have been written through which God speaks to the entire world. The antagonism between Gentiles and Israel is anticipated in Gen 12:3 in the statement that God would bless those who bless Abraham's seed and curse those who curse it.

Scholars have differed as to whether the promises to Abraham should be considered literally or nonliterally. The nonliteral interpretation regards Abraham's seed as the divine community or body of believers throughout all ages and the promise of the land is spiritualized to represent the promise of heaven.

Abraham, however, understood the promise concerning his seed to be literal, and this was confirmed by God's refusal to recognize Abraham's servant or Ishmael (Gen 15:2-4; 17:15-22). The specific promise to Abraham's seed was first narrowed to Isaac, later to Jacob, and through Jacob channeled to the 12 patriarchs, the sons of Jacob. The promise of the land was also interpreted literally throughout the OT. Not only was the promise of the land confirmed to Isaac (Gen 26:1-5) and then to Jacob (Gen 28:13-15), but it was given to Moses (Deut 30:1-5) and Joshua (Josh 1:3-4). Israel was assured that, though scattered, ultimately they would be restored to their land never to be dispersed again (Amos 9:14-15).

The NT seems to justify the concept that there is a sense in which all believers are children of Abraham. Gal 3:6-9 states that "they which are of faith, the same are the children of Abraham." However, the particular aspect of the Abrahamic promise cited relates this, according to Gal 3:8, not to Israel but to that aspect of the covenant which originally belonged to the Gentiles, namely, "in thee shall all nations be blessed." The fact that the NT uses the expression "children of Abraham" to include those who are not physical descendants of Abraham but who, like Abraham, believed in God (Gal 3:9) does not cancel the promises to Israel as a nation or the promise of the land to them.

The Abrahamic promise will involve the restoration of Israel to the land, as promised Abraham in Gen 15:18-21 and numerous other OT prophecies (Isa 11:11-12; 12:1-3; 27:12-13; 43:1-7; 48:8-17; 66:20-22; Jer 16:14-16; 23:3-8; 30:10-11; 31:8, 31-37; Ezk 11:17-21; 20:33-38; 34:11-16; 39:25-29; Hos 1:10-11; Amos 9:11-15; Mic 4:4-7; Zeph 3:14-20; Zech 8:4-8). The Abrahamic promises are, therefore, foundational declarations of the purposes of God beginning with Abraham's day and finding their fulfillment throughout human history.

See Covenants.

J. F. W.

ABRAHAM'S BOSOM. This figurative phrase depicts the blessedness of the believer in paradise following death. Although used in rabbinic Judaism, the only scriptural occurrence of this expression is in Christ's parable of the rich man and Lazarus (Lk 16:19 ff.). At his death Lazarus the beggar is carried by angels to Abraham's bosom, while the rich man after his burial is tormented in Hades.

According to the OT, at death one goes to be with his fathers (Gen 15:15; 47:30; Deut 31:16; Jud 2:10). Since Abraham was the father of the Jews (Lk 3:8; Jn 8:39 f.), a concrete form of this expression was to go to father Abraham (IV Macc 13:17). A simple variation of this was to speak of the life hereafter in terms of Abraham's bosom.

In rabbinic Judaism the phrase had two distinguishable meanings, and interpreters are divided as to the precise meaning of the phrase in this parable. To lie or sit in Abraham's bosom may express figuratively the loving fellowship which exists between Abraham and his believing descendants in heaven in analogy to the paternal tenderness of a father for his son (Jn 1:18). Others think the figure focuses primarily on the heavenly banquet where, according to the Roman manner of feasting employed also by the Jews, Lazarus reclined at table with his head in the bosom of Abraham, his host (Jn 13:23; 21:20).

Perhaps both elements are applicable to the parable. Since Scripture generally depicts the joy of heaven in terms of a banquet feast (Mt 8:11; Lk 13:28-29; 14:16 ff.), it is natural to see this implied in the picture of the poor beggar who was fed by the crumbs from the rich man's table now enjoying the abundance of the heavenly banquet. But intimacy and fellowship are not excluded from the picture. The lonely outcast beggar is now enjoying the blessedness of heaven in the intimate company of the father of believers. And since Lazarus is in Abraham's bosom, it also appears that he has received the place of honor at the banquet.

Interpreters also differ as to whether Abraham's bosom depicts a place which is a division or compartment of Hades. In Jewish writings Sheol-Hades is often the place of the dead in general, including both righteous and unrighteous. In the pseudepigraphal Enoch chap. 22, there are even four divisions to Hades where the dead await the day of judgment. But here Abraham's bosom and Hades are distinct places. Jesus speaks of the rich man only in Hades, and there he sees Abraham "afar off" and is told that "a great gulf" is fixed between them so that transfer is impossible. Abraham and Lazarus are in bliss, while the rich man in Hades suffers torment and requests water to cool his tongue. These dreadful conditions appear as the inherent consequences of being in Hades.

The eschatological implications are clear, for the faith of Lazarus leads to the joy of everlasting life (Abraham's bosom), while the riches of the unbelieving rich man cannot protect him from the torment of hell (Hades).

The context offers no support for the view of some Roman Catholics that Abraham's bosom refers to the *limbus patrum,* a place where the OT believers enjoy peace while awaiting Christ's perfect redemption. In Egypt other motifs led to an interpretation of Abraham's bosom in which the element of cool water and refrigeration were emphasized.

For further bibliographical references see SBK, II (1924), 226-227; SBK, IV (1928), 1018-1019; TWNT, III (1938), 825-826.

See Abraham; Death; Paradise; Sheol.

F. H. K.

ABRAM (ā'brăm). The original name used for Abraham *(q.v.)* in Gen 11:27 – 17:5. The name occurs in Old Babylonian, Egyptian texts of the 19th cen. B.C., ancient S Arabic, and on a Ugaritic inscription. To these heathen the name probably meant "my (divine) father is exalted."

ABSALOM (ăb'sá-lŏm). David's third son, born to Maacah the daughter of Talmai, king of Geshur, at Hebron (II Sam 3:2–3; I Chr 3:1–2). The author of the book in which the Absalom narratives occur (II Sam 13 – 19) is primarily concerned with the Lord's righteous acts in the formative years of the Davidic dynasty. For the author, Solomon (and not the firstborn Amnon nor the third son Absalom nor the fourth Adonijah, etc.) was God's choice as David's successor. An appreciation of this emphasis helps to explain the selection of two events in Absalom's life (Amnon's murder, II Sam 13:1–38; and Absalom's conspiracy and rebellion, II Sam 13:39 – 19:8) in preference to others. The writer intends to show how the Lord punished David for adultery and murder, and yet kept His promise to perpetuate David's dynasty (announced by Nathan in II Sam 12:10–14; 7:12–16).

Nathan announced three ways in which God would punish David. (1) Bathsheba's child (a son, II Sam 11:27, and thus possible heir to the throne) would die (II Sam 12:14). Who would succeed David? Could it be Amnon? Prodded by Jonadab (his "friend," II Sam 13:3–7, a "court confidant"; cf. Hushai, David's "friend," II Sam 15:37; 16:16; I Chr 27:33),

Traditional tomb of Absalom in the Kidron Valley, Jerusalem. HFV

Amnon raped his half sister (Absalom's full sister) Tamar; and (David having failed to avenge this act) two years later Absalom had Amnon killed and then fled to his maternal grandfather. Could, then, David's successor be Absalom? Five years passed before David fully reinstated him. But now Absalom moved swiftly to gain the throne. Adopting pagan customs (which Talmai taught him?), he appeared publicly in a chariot escorted by a cortege of runners. He secured the sympathy of the ten northern tribes by posing as their advocate. Within four years (LXX; not 40 years – apparently due to mishearing, a Heb. copyist wrote *'arbā 'îm shānāh* for *'arbā' shānîm* in II Sam 15:7), under pretense of fulfilling a vow, Absalom went to Hebron and claimed the title "king" (II Sam 15:10); then seized Jerusalem for his capital. But his success ended when Joab had him murdered (defying David's explicit command) in the forest of Ephraim. Finally, could the successor to David be Adonijah? He attempted to seize the throne in David's old age, only to be denounced by the aged king's own appointment of Solomon (Bathsheba's son!) as his successor.

(2) The sword would not depart from David's house (II Sam 12:10). Absalom had Amnon murdered for raping his sister; Joab had Absalom slain for conspiracy and rebellion; and Benaiah killed Adonijah for asking to marry Abishag (I Kgs 2:13–25).

(3) One of David's own house would conspire against him and go in publicly to his concubines (II Sam 12:11–12). Absalom stole the hearts of the men of Israel (II Sam 15:6), proclaimed himself king at Hebron, and seized Jerusalem without a battle. Following Ahithophel's advice, he went in to David's ten concubines publicly, thereby strengthening his claim to the throne and asserting his complete domination of David's empire (II Sam 16:20–23).

But despite the magnitude of David's sins and the period of uncertainty concerning the identity of his successor, God remained faithful to His promise that David's dynasty would be established forever in Israel. Solomon became king in his father's stead (I Kgs 1).

Bibliography. E. R. Dalglish, "Absalom," IDB, I, 22–23. H. W. Hertzberg, *I and II Samuel: A Commentary,* Old Testament Library, Philadelphia: Westminster, 1964. Eugene H. Maly, *The World of David and Solomon (Backgrounds to the Bible Series),* Englewood Cliffs, N.J.: Prentice-Hall, 1966. J. Weingreen, "The Rebellion of Absalom," VT, XIX (1969), 263–266.

J. T. W.

ABSTINENCE. This is a general term applicable to any object or action from which one refrains for a certain time and for some particular purpose, especially for the cultivation of the spiritual life. It is usually a voluntary self-discipline and may consist in an entire renunciation or a very slight partaking of some pleasure or necessity, as eating, drinking, etc. Sometimes it pertains to the total abstinence from something positively harmful or forbidden, as fornication, prohibited food, intoxicating alcoholic beverages, or debilitating drugs. Extreme abstinence may take the form of asceticism. It may be distinguished from temperance, which is a moderate use of food or drink, etc. Fasting is a specific form of abstinence, namely, from food. *See* Fasting.

In the OT the eating of blood was forbidden (Gen 9:4). Other instances of mandatory abstinence are recorded (Gen 32:32; Ex 22:31; Lev 3:17; 10:9; 11:4 ff.; Num 6:3; Deut 14:21), related to the dietary regulations of the Israelites in general and the priests and Nazarites in particular. These dietary restrictions were largely set aside in the NT (Acts 15:19-20, 28-29). Paul leaves the matter of abstinence from food up to the individual's conscience and the Spirit's guidance, and urges loving consideration for one another (Rom 14; I Cor 8). In matters involving morals, apostolic commands to abstain from evil are obligatory (I Thess 4:3; 5:22; I Pet 2:11).

While His life was the supreme example of self-denial, our Lord neither taught nor practiced asceticism, although His public ministry was preceded by 40 days of fasting in the wilderness. He condemned artificial piety and ostentation (Mt 6:16-18).

Abstinence, according to the Bible, is never good and valuable in itself, but is so only when it fosters a holy and useful life. It is a means, not an end in itself.

R. E. P.

ABYSS (lit., "no bottom"). This word appears only nine times in the NT. It is translated seven times as "the bottomless pit" (Rev 9:1, 2, 11; 11:7; 17:8; 20:1, 3). In two other occurrences the rendering is "the deep" (Lk 8:31; Rom 10:7).

The NT usage apparently grew out of its frequent usage in the Septuagint. Here it usually is the translation of *te hôm*, beginning at Gen 1:2. Primary reference in each case is simply to the depths of the ocean (e.g., Ps 77:16). Those interpreters who suppose the Hebrews adopted the pagan cosmology of the ancient Near East imagine all sorts of references to mythology in the word (see BDB, pp. 1062-1063). This much only needs to be conceded: that the language and outlook of the OT being phenomenal, i.e., employing the common language of appearance, the depths of the sea are cited poetically as the opposite of the vault of heaven above. Paul employs similar language, using the word abyss in Rom 10:6-7.

Taken, then, as the remote opposite of heaven, the abode of God, the word is employed as a name for the present abode of wicked spirits. This is the better understanding of Rom 10:7 (Jesus did not send demons to dwell in a lake, Lk 8:31), and of every other NT use save Rom

10:6-7 where the word simply designates the farthest possible position downward.

Study of the word in the LXX, classics and NT supplies no information for a geography of the nether world. *See* Bottomless Pit; Dead, The; Hell.

R. D. C.

ACACIA. *See* Plants.

ACCAD (ăk'ăd). Spelled Accad in English Bibles (KJV, ASV, RSV), it is in Heb. *'akkad* (Gen 10:10). The city of this name (in modern historical literature commonly spelled Akkad) was located in lower Mesopotamia not far S of present day Bagdad and a bit N of ancient Babylon. In certain early tablets the spelling is Agade. The exact site of Agade is not known.

Lower Mesopotamia (i.e., S and E of the neck formed by the near approach of the Tigris and Euphrates) in later OT times was called Babylonia, but as early as the Third Dynasty of Ur (Abram's city), located in the far S of the territory, the area was known as Sumer and Akkad (ANET, p. 159 *et al.;* FLAP, p. 10), indicating the early prominence of Akkad. During the Old Akkadian period (c. 2360-2180 B.C.) a certain Sargon founded a dynasty of Semitic-speaking kings at Akkad (Agade) who ruled all of lower Mesopotamia. Under Sargon I and Naram-Sin, his grandson, the realm was extended till the king of Agade could be styled "the mighty, god of Agade, king of the Four Quarters." His empire extended from Elam to Syria.

The strong impression left by this kingdom of Agade upon later generations is seen in the fact that more than a millennium and a half later Nabopolassar, Nebuchadnezzar and Nabonidus, kings of the Neo-Babylonian Empire, were sometimes called "the king of Akkad" (FLAP, pp. 220, 222, 227; Donald J. Wiseman, *Chronicles of the Chaldean Kings,* pp. 67-69). Furthermore, the chief Semitic language of the region and the cuneiform writing came to be known as Akkadian (of which Assyrian and Babylonian are dialects), referred to respectfully by Ashurbanipal, king of Assyria (668-633 B.C., the Asnapper of Ezr 4:10), as "the obscure Akkadian writing which is hard to master" (FLAP, p. 216).

R. D. C.

ACCEPT, ACCEPTABLE. These English words translate a variety of Heb. and Gr. words. In the OT "to accept" (from *rāṣâ*) means "to receive with pleasure and kindness" (Deut 33:11; Ps 119:108), becoming part of the sacrificial terminology that indicated the acceptability (*rāṣôn*) of an offering to God (Lev 22:20; 23:11; Isa 60:7).

Contrary to pagan belief, the biblical teaching is that one's sacrifices and prayers are acceptable to God only when the man's person is first of all acceptable to Him (Hos 8:13; Jer 6:20; Mal 1:9 f.; note the order in II Sam

Crusaders' Wall, Accho. IIS

24:23–25). Only moral uprightness (Prov 21:3; Job 42:7–9) and the sacrifices of a repentant, sincere heart (Ps 19:14; 40:6–8; 51:15–17) are recognized as truly acceptable with God. The Lord's acceptance of Abel's offering (Gen 4:4f.) was a witness that Abel's person had already been accepted. Through his offerings presented in faith "he received approval as righteous, God bearing witness by accepting his gifts" (Heb 11:4, RSV), whereas Cain was admonished that his offering would be accepted if he would do well (Gen 4:7).

An "acceptable time" (Ps 69:13; Isa 49:8; II Cor 6:2) or "acceptable year" (Isa 61:2) is a time of favor or grace (*rāṣôn*), hence the favorable season or opportune moment when God is still offering His salvation.

The basic Gr. word for "accepted," "acceptable" (*dektos*) means "welcomed," "appreciated," as in Lk 4:24. In the NT the grounds of divine acceptance are never ceremonial, but always spiritual (Rom 12:1; Phil 4:18; I Tim 2:3; I Pet 2:5). Our Lord does not accept the person (shows no partiality, lit., does not receive the face) of anyone (Lk 20:21; Gal 2:6); rather, the one who fears God and practices righteousness is acceptable to Him (Acts 10:35), demonstrating genuine repentance by appropriate works (Acts 26:20). None, however, can achieve perfect acceptability by his own works, for all have fallen short of the glory of God (Rom 3:9–23). Jesus Christ alone is

fully accepted by the Father. ("This is my beloved Son, in whom I am well pleased," Mt 3:17.) In Him as the Beloved and through Him as the Mediator, men secure their standing and fundamental acceptance with God (Eph 1:6).

J. R.

ACCESS TO GOD. "1. The act of bringing to. 2. Access, approach ... that friendly relation with God whereby we are acceptable to Him and have assurance that He is favorably disposed toward us" (Thayer).

The OT believer approached God through a priest, after offering sacrifices for his sins; the NT believer approaches Him directly because of and through Jesus Christ. The concept of access can be properly understood only by the OT revelation that God is King, and therefore to be approached through a worthy and qualified representative (Ps 47:7).

Christ reconciled both Jew and Gentile to God by the cross, broke down the middle wall of partition between Israel and the Gentiles, and removed the hostility between God and man (Eph 2:16), thus making possible access to God for both (Eph 2:18).

Access to the grace of God through saving faith—the ability to believe in Christ as our Saviour—also is dependent upon His having first made peace with God through the blood of His cross (Rom 5:2; Col 1:20).

Because of what Christ did and because He is ever at the throne of God as our Advocate, even when we have sinned (I Jn 2:1), we are encouraged to come to God with boldness (Eph 3:12; Heb 4:16).

R. A. K.

ACCHO (ăk'ō). A town on a promontory across the bay to the N from Haifa and Mount Carmel. Furnishing the best anchorage in the area, it long commanded the approach to the rich plains of Esdraelon and the coast road to the N. Though within the territory of Asher, it was not conquered by the Hebrews (Jud 1:31). During the Greek and Roman sway it was called Ptolemais after the first Egyptian king of that name. Paul visited it (Acts 21:7). The Crusaders, considering it the key to the Holy Land, won it at great cost. Now Haifa and Beirut have overshadowed it as centers of trade.

ACCOUNTABILITY. Not a biblical term but it expresses the biblical concept of man's responsibility to God. Man knows by what he learns through consciousness that he is answerable for his actions, and this is confirmed by his conscience and by the revelation of Scripture.

Christ says man is accountable for what he says, even for idle words (Mt 12:36), and for what he does, particularly for the way he uses the money, gifts, and talents which the Lord has bestowed (Mt 25:14–30; Lk 19:11–27). Paul speaks of the deeds done by the Christian while alive "in the body" (II Cor 5:10); of his responsibility to consider a weaker brother in his actions (Rom 14:10) even though all things are lawful for him (I Cor 6:12; 10:23); of his own responsibility to keep his body under and control his passions lest he become disapproved in the ministry—a castaway (I Cor 9:27). In Romans Paul also speaks of responsibility for obedience to civil rulers, and hence to laws of the state (Rom 13:1-7).

The Christian will not be judged with the unbeliever, since he is judged regarding possible rewards; there is no condemnation possible for him (Rom 8:1), only the exposure of what is proved to be dross (I Cor 3:12-15). His judgment occurs before the Millennium, as proved by the fact Christ promises rulership over cities to the good servants in the parable of the pounds (Lk 19:17, 19). It is clear this judgment of the believer's works must be complete before he reigns with Christ on the earth (Rev 5:10; 20:4-6). See Rewards.

R. A. K.

ACCURSED

1. Heb. $q^e l\bar{a}l\hat{a}$, a form of curse used throughout the ancient Near East as a malediction expressing a wish that evil may overtake someone. In the ancient usage, curses frequently had the effect of protecting the terms of treaty contracts by being directed toward future violators of the agreement. As translated in Deut 21:23, "he that is hanged is accursed of God," it refers to the abject criminal who after he has been put to death is impaled on a tree or stake. Only the worst of cases was so punished and hence the person was considered accursed of God (cf. Josh 8:29; 10:26-27; II Sam 4:12; Gal 3:16). In Isa 65:20 a form of this word occurs denoting the longevity of life even on the accursed sinner in the future millennial age. RSV translates this word "accursed" in Ps 119:21.

2. Heb. ḥerem, a word meaning "devoted thing," used especially in the book of Joshua (cf. 6:17, 18; 7:1 ff.; 22:20) in connection with Canaanite cities and all their inhabitants. A thing which is accursed or banned is irrevocably withdrawn from common use. Consequently it was either set apart for the use of the Lord in the priestly service or utterly exterminated. It was common in ancient warfare to "devote," or put under the ban, the enemy and everything which belonged to him. So Mesha, king of Moab (c. 830 B.C.), relates how he "devoted to destruction" for the god of Ashtar-Chemosh the entire Israelite city of Nebo, "slaying all, seven thousand men, boys, women and girls and maid-servants" (ANET, p. 320). It was also practiced by the Assyrians (II Kgs 19:11). Whoever took the "devoted" thing for himself, as Achan did (Josh 7), became himself "banned" and was mercilessly destroyed with all persons and property attached to him. In later rabbinical use the practice became equivalent to excommunication.

3. RSV translates Heb. zā'am as "accursed" in Mic 6:10 (KJV "abominable").

4. NT use. Each of the four occurrences of this word in the KJV are renderings of Gr. anathēma (cf. Rom 9:3; I Cor 12:3; Gal 1:8-9) which is the LXX word for section 2 above. In pagan usage it referred to a "votive offering." Paul desired that it might be possible for him to be "banned" from Christ in order, as it is commonly inferred, that his Jewish brethren might find Christ as their Lord (Rom 9:3).

On another occasion Paul remarks that no man speaking by the Spirit of God can say Jesus is "accursed" (I Cor. 12:3). Apparently some in the church (gnostics?) made certain esoteric statements that in fact degraded the high position of Jesus to that of one who deserved the death He died (Godet). Hence Paul states that all true manifestations of the Holy Spirit exalt Jesus as Lord.

Again, Paul relegates to "utter destruction" all those who do not love the Lord Jesus Christ (I Cor 16:22). He also states that the gospel he proclaimed was the only way of salvation, and those who pervert it are accursed or irremediably assigned to judgment because of the serious consequences of invalidating the grace of God in the preaching of Jesus Christ (Gal 1:8-9).

See Achan; Anathema; Curse; Devote; Oath.

A. F. J.

ACCUSED. Three important examples in the Bible of persons being accused are Daniel, Christ and Paul.

Daniel was accused of praying to his God when all were ordered to make supplications to Darius only (Dan 6:4-24). Daniel's three Heb. companions had previously been accused of disloyalty because they would not bow to the image of King Nebuchadnezzar (Dan 3:8-12).

Christ was accused of many things but of six in particular:

1. Desecrating the Jewish sabbath, because (a) His disciples gathered and ate some grain on the sabbath (Mt 12:1-8). He replied by citing two examples from the OT and giving three reasons for permitting His disciples to do this. David entered the house of God and took the sacred showbread for his famished soldiers (I Sam 21:6); and the priests on the sabbath day profaned the sabbath and were blameless (Num 28:9-10, 24). The reasons given are that Christ is greater than the temple, i.e., He has authority over it and what is holy (Mt 12:6); God is seeking mercy and compassion from His own above ritual sacrifice (v. 7); Christ, the Son of Man, is the one who has authority over the sabbath itself (v. 8). (b) Christ also healed on the sabbath. Jesus defended His action by pointing out that His accusers did good and saved life on the sabbath (Mt 12:11; Lk 6:9), and that man is worth much more than the sheep they would rescue (Mt 12:12). The sab-

bath was made for man anyway, and not man for the sabbath (Mk 2:27).

2. Fellowshiping with publicans and sinners, that is, with the common people and the unsaved (Mt 9:11; Lk 7:34). His defense was that He came not for the righteous but to bring sinners to repentance (Mt 9:13).

3. Forbidding men to pay tribute to Caesar (Lk 23:2). This accusation was untrue because He had paid tribute Himself (Mt 17:24–27), and declared that appropriate tribute should be given both to God and to Caesar (Mt 22:17–21; Mk 12:14–17).

4. Claiming to be God by forgiving sin, which of course He did (Lk 5:20–24).

5. Planning to destroy the temple and to rebuild it in three days, though He really spoke of His own body (Mt 26:61; Jn 2:19–21).

6. Claiming to be Christ the very Son of God (Mt 26:63), and to this He gave His assent (Mt 26:64).

Paul was falsely accused of the Jews as the instigator of sedition against the Roman government, and as being a profaner of the temple and a member of the Nazarenes (Acts 24:5–6).

The Christian realizes that he is being accused by Satan daily before the throne of God (Job 1:6–12; 2:1–8; Rev 12:9–10), but rejoices that Christ stands there also as his Advocate to plead His shed blood and to defend him (I Jn 2:1–2). Christians shall also suffer from false accusations by those around them, but are not to allow themselves to be found in a position to which they are rightfully accused of wrongdoing (I Pet 3:17; 4:12–19). Believers in Christ can overcome Satan, the accuser of the brethren, on the basis of the blood of the Lamb and the word of their testimony (Rev 12:11). *See* Accuser.

R. A. K.

ACCUSER

1. A human accuser, plaintiff in any lawsuit (Gr. *katēgoros,* Jn 8:10; Acts 23:30, 35; 24:8; 25:18); an opponent in court or in general (Gr. *antidikos,* Mt 5:25, RSV; Lk 12:58; 18:3); "false accuser" (Gr. *diabolos,* II Tim 3:3; Tit 2:3).

2. Satan (the adversary, I Pet 5:8) is an accuser of the believers (Rev 12:10). He comes before the throne of God and points out all their weaknesses and faults and sins (Job 1:6 f.; 2:1–8). But the day will come, just before the time of the Great Tribulation, when he and his angels will be cast out of heaven into the earth (Rev 12:7–10). Meanwhile, in the face of Satanic accusations, Christ intercedes on behalf of believers at the right hand of God the Father. He pleads for them on the basis of His sacrificial death (Rom 8:34), so that no other being has any right to condemn the Christian. *See* Adversary; Devil.

ACELDAMA (*à-kĕl'dà-mà*). This term for "field of blood" is found only in Acts 1:19. The piece of land, which was formerly known as the potter's field (cf. Jer 18:2; 19:1, 2; Mt 27:7), was purchased by the priests with the betrayal money which Judas returned (Mt 27:3–10). Their intention was to use the ground as a cemetery for strangers. Tradition locates the site S of Jerusalem, on the S side of the valley of Hinnom near its junction with the Kidron Valley. The name apparently has reference to the blood money used in its purchase (Mt 27:6–7) and to the gruesome death of Judas (Acts 1:18–19).

ACHAIA (*ā-kā'yà*). In the NT Achaia refers to the southern portion of Greece, Macedonia being the northern portion (Acts 19:21; Rom 15:26; II Cor 1:1; I Thess 1:7, 8). By Claudius' direction, in A.D. 44 it was governed by a proconsul (e.g., Gallio in Acts 18:12, ASV), appointed by the Roman senate; the emperor governed his provinces through procurators. Its chief cities were Athens *(q.v.)* and Corinth *(q.v.)* the capital with its seaport Cenchrea, although Sparta to the S and Megara, Thebes, and Delphi to the N were famous from antiquity.

ACHAICUS (*à-kā'ĭ-kŭs*). A companion of Stephanas and Fortunatus, who visited Paul at Ephesus and perhaps brought a letter from the church at Corinth (I Cor 7:1; 16:17).

ACHAN (*ā'kăn*). Variant of Achar in I Chr 2:7; also in certain LXX and Syriac MSS.

A man of Judah who secretly appropriated for himself some of the spoils of war at the fall of Jericho (Josh 7:1–26; 22:20). The Lord revealed to Joshua that Israel's defeat at Ai was caused by the presence of sin in the camp. When the sacred lot specified Achan as the offender, he confessed to coveting, stealing, and concealing in his tent fine clothing, silver, and gold, all of which was under the sacrificial ban,

South bank of the Hinnom Valley showing Potter's Field with burial caves. HFV

"devoted to the Lord for destruction" or "for the treasury" (Josh 6:17-19, RSV; cf. S. R. Driver on I Sam 15:33). Achan and his family were stoned to death, and their bodies and possessions were burned in the valley of Achor ("troubling") S of Jericho.

Theft would have carried only the penalty of restitution with double indemnity (Ex 22:4, 7) even in a peacetime situation. Achan violated the special sanctity of "devoted things" which were forever removed from common use. He had dared to put them among his "own stuff" (Josh 7:11).

The ancient concept of community solidarity everywhere underlies the story: (1) the covenant unity of Israel as a "devoted" (i.e., "sanctified") people (cf. Ex 13:11-15; 4:23) assured them of the Lord's protection; (2) Achan's offense associated him with the Canaanites who were "devoted to the Lord for destruction" (i.e., "accursed") and separated him from the protection of the covenant (Josh 6:17-18; 7:15); (3) Achan's offense became Israel's offense until they separated themselves from the "devoted things" whose end had to be destruction (Josh 6:18; 7:11-12); (4) all Achan's family and possessions had suffered the taint of the "devoted things" and shared his responsibility and destruction (Josh 7:24-25).

R. V. R.

ACHAR (ā'kär). This is a variant form of Achan (q.v.) found in I Chr 2:7.

ACHAZ (ā'kăz). In Mt 1:9 the KJV makes use of this name for Ahaz (q.v.)

ACHBOR (ăk'bôr)
1. The father of Baal-hanan, a king of Edom (Gen 36:38-39; I Chr 1:49).
2. An officer in the government of Josiah who was deputized to examine the book of the law (II Kgs 22:12, 14; Jer 26:22; 36:12). He is called Abdon in II Chr 34:20.

ACHIM (ā'kĭm). According to Mt 1:14, Achim was the fifth of the ancestors of Joseph the husband of Mary.

ACHISH (ā'kĭsh). King of Gath (home of Goliath and member of the Philistine pentarchy) to whom David twice resorted when a fugitive from Saul. Achish still ruled early in Solomon's reign (I Kgs 2:39, here, "son of Maachah"; cf. "son of Maoch," I Sam 27:2; consonantal similarity suggests identity).

David first fled to Achish alone (I Sam 21:10-15) offering himself for service in the palace (21:15). Recognized as the slayer of Goliath (cf. v. 11 with 18:7), in fear David feigned madness and escaped (22:1).

On his second flight to Achish, now accompanied by his 600 seasoned guerrillas, David was made welcome (I Sam 27:1-12). The Philistine king granted him and his men the border town of Ziklag. This association was hardly an

The mound of Gath, where Achish was king and where Goliath lived. HFV

unmixed blessing for either, since it contained for David self-contradictory elements: a sense of responsibility to Achish, whose feudatory vassal he had become (I Sam 28:1-2); a built-in loyalty to his own nation resulting in raiding Philistine allies instead of the Judean Negeb as claimed (I Sam 27:8-12); a deep sense of divine mission and personal restraint. David was spared fighting Israel in the battle on Gilboa by Philistine skepticism of David's loyalty (I Sam 29:1-11).

Achish has left his imprint on the sacred record: (1) he appears as Abimelech (q.v.) in the superscription of Ps 34; (2) David, appointed to the bodyguard of Achish (I Sam 28:2), maintained a Pelethite (Philistine) bodyguard when king (II Sam 8:18, et al.).

R. V. R.

ACHMETHA (ăk'mĕ-thả). A city reaching at least back to the days of Cyrus (about 550 B.C.). Here the decrees of Cyrus were found that authorized the Jews to rebuild the temple at Jerusalem (Ezr 6:2). The city is on high elevation (about 6,000 ft.) and thereby provided a good summer resort. Darius I may have used it for a part-time capital of Persia.

Achmetha is referred to many times in the Apocrypha but under the name of Ecbatana. Known today as Hamadan, this city of Iran has a population of about 50,000 and is located on the road from Baghdad to Teheran.

ACHOR (ā'kôr). A valley lying W of Jericho where Achan (Achar, I Chr 2:7) and his family were stoned to death (Josh 7:24, 26). It is also on the N boundary of Judah (Josh 15:7). A future millennial change is found in Isa 65:10; Hos 2:15.

ACHSA, ACHSAH (ăk'sả). The name of Caleb's daughter (I Chr 2:49). Caleb had been assigned the unconquered Kirjath-sepher. He promised his daughter to anyone who would capture it for him. Caleb's kinsman Othniel won the right to marry Achsah (Josh 15:16 ff.; Jud 1:12 ff.).

ACHSHAPH (ăk'shăf). A city in the land given originally to the tribe of Asher (Josh 19:25). It was a city-state under one of the kings allied against Joshua (Josh 11:1; 12:20). Though its exact location is disputed by authorities, all agree it was near the Mount Carmel ridge.

ACHZIB (ăk'zĭb)

1. A town in the Shephelah of Judah near Keilah and Mareshah (Josh 15:44; Mic 1:14). Micah makes a pun on its name, which means "deceitful" or "treacherous." Achzib seems to be mentioned in Lachish letter #8. Perhaps it is the same as Chezib (*q.v.;* Gen 38:5).

2. A Canaanite town assigned to Asher (Josh 19:29) on the Mediterranean coast eight miles N of Acre. It is doubtful whether the tribe of Asher ever occupied this city (Jud 1:31). Sennacherib claims to have overwhelmed the fortress city Akzibi (ANET, p. 287). In 1941–42 two large cemeteries with over 70 rock-cut tombs were excavated, from which were recovered quantities of Phoenician pottery, figurines, scarabs and jewelry. Recent excavations at the site have revealed a Hyksos-type fortification, plus six more levels of occupation dating from the 9th to the 4th cen. B.C. Many pieces of imported Gr. and Cypriot pottery testify to Achzib's commercial connections in the Israelite, Persian and Hellenistic periods.

J. R.

ACRE

1. An area, lit., "yoke" (I Sam 14:14, RSV; Isa 5:10), which likely means the amount of ground a yoke of oxen could plow in a day.

2. A Western name since the Crusades for the city of Accho *(q.v.),* which was given to Asher but never conquered (Jud 1:31). This city lies at the N end of a fine plain about eight miles long, with modern Haifa on the S end. It was called Ptolemais during the period of Hellenistic influence, and is the port where Paul landed on his way to Caesarea (Acts 21:7).

ACROPOLIS (á-crŏp'ŏ-lĭs). The higher part of a city; especially a fortified eminence overlooking an ancient Gr. town. Among cities with an acropolis were Philippi, Athens, and Corinth, which Paul visited on his second missionary journey.

By far the most famous acropolis was that of Athens. On the plateau at its summit, magnificent structures were erected in classical times. Celebrated for their architectural excellence were the Parthenon, preeminent shrine of Athe-

The Acropolis at Corinth (which towers to a height of almost 1900 feet) with the temple of Apollo in the foreground. HFV

Entrance to the Acropolis at Athens today.
HFV

na; the Erechtheum, another temple dedicated to Athena and Poseidon; the Propylaea; and the temple of Athena Nike. In the Parthenon was a statue of Athena, more than 40 feet in height, made by Phidias of gold and ivory. Between the Parthenon and the Erechtheum was the bronze statue of Athena Promachos, 30 feet high, also made by Phidias. The shining helmet and spear were visible far off at sea. On the summit of the acropolis and on its sides were additional temples, statues, and other structures. Here human artistic effort achieved some of its most notable triumphs, but the dedication to false religion pointed up the inability of the natural man to find the truth of God. The spiritual need of a city filled with idols deeply moved the apostle Paul (Acts 17:16–34).

J. H. S.

ACROSTIC. A literary device found in some of the poetry of the OT either to aid memory or to provide strophic divisions. The kind employed in the OT is alphabetic in character. The best example is Ps 119 in which the first word in each of the first eight verses begins with the first letter of the Heb. alphabet; the next eight verses begin with the second letter of the alphabet. In succession, eight verses are assigned to the rest of the 22 Heb. consonants, making a total of 176 verses. However, Ps 34 has only 22 verses, since the first word of each verse begins with a Heb. letter in alphabetic order. Ps 25, 37, 111, 112, and 145 are similar but are not quite so regular; some have one or more letters missing or transposed. Parts of Ps 9 and 10, which are one psalm in the LXX, are alphabetic.

In Prov 31, each verse of 10–21 begins with a Heb. letter in alphabetic order. Several alphabetic acrostics occur in Lamentations. Chaps. 1, 2 and 4 each contain an acrostic of 22 verses, with one verse to each Heb. letter, but not always in precise order. Chap. 3 has three verses for each letter of the alphabet. Nah 1:2–10 is thought by some to be partially alphabetic, but this is not clear in the Heb. text. Some have held that acrostic poems are late in date, but the position is not founded on fact.

G. H. L.

ACTS, THE BOOK OF. The Acts of the Apostles, the fifth book of the NT, is the second volume of the earliest history of Christianity, of which the first volume is the Gospel according to Luke. The essential unity of the two volumes is marked by the common address to Theophilus (Lk 1:1–4; Acts 1:1); by the allusion in Acts to a "former treatise . . . concerning all that Jesus began both to do and to teach" (ASV), which fits the content of the Gospel; by a common emphasis on the person and work of the Holy Spirit; by the

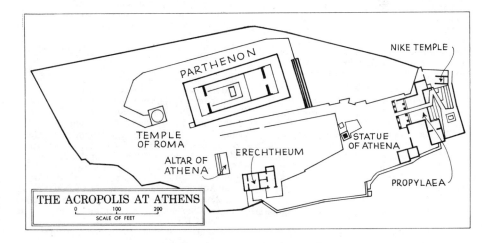

THE ACROPOLIS AT ATHENS

0   100   200
SCALE OF FEET

PARTHENON

NIKE TEMPLE

TEMPLE OF ROMA

ALTAR OF ATHENA

ERECHTHEUM

STATUE OF ATHENA

PROPYLAEA

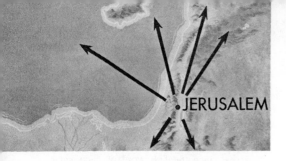

JERUSALEM

The Book of Acts tells how believers preached the Gospel in Jerusalem, Judea, Samaria, Syria and in much of the Eastern Mediterranean World (cf. Acts 1:8). MIS

close resemblance of the language of the two documents; and by the confirmation of tradition which uniformly ascribes the authorship to Luke, the friend and companion of Paul. The title was probably given to it when the Gospel was combined with Matthew, Mark, and John into a distinct group of narratives of the life of Jesus, leaving Acts to become the chronicle of a later period. The division took place at an early date, since the oldest extant list of canonical books treats it as a separate writing.

Content

Although it is called the Acts of the Apostles, or even Acts in some MSS, it does not narrate the deeds of all the earliest followers of Jesus. The record is selective, and is apparently motivated by a desire to trace the growth of the Gentile church from the day of Pentecost through the expansion to Antioch, and then through the Pauline mission to Rome. The organization is largely biographical, focusing on such personalities as Peter, Stephen, Philip, Barnabas, and Paul.

Acts is organized in three stages, based on the words of Jesus quoted in Acts 1:8: "But ye shall receive power, when the Holy Spirit is come upon you: and ye shall be my witnesses both in Jerusalem, and in all Judea and Samaria, and unto the uttermost part of the earth" (ASV). The first stage marks the Jewish foundation beginning in Jerusalem; the second stage of transition involves the development of new ideas and movements in the direction of the Gentile world; and the third stage covers the Gentile mission of Paul which carried him from Antioch across Asia Minor to Rome.

Outline

The Beginnings of the Christian Church

I. The Period of Inception: Jerusalem, 1:1–8:3
  A. The Commission of Christ, 1:1–8
  B. The Preparation for Pentecost, 1:9–26
  C. The Founding of the Church at Jerusalem, 2:1–6:7
  D. The Ministry of Stephen, 6:8–8:3
II. The Period of Transition: Antioch, 8:4–11:18
  A. The Ministry of Philip (Samaria), 8:4–40
  B. The Conversion of Paul, 9:1–31
  C. The Ministry of Peter (Caesarea), 10:1–11:18

III. The Period of Expansion: Rome, 11:19–28:31
  A. The Transfer to Antioch, 11:19–12:25
  B. The First Missionary Tour, 13:1–14:28
  C. The Council at Jerusalem, 15:1–35
  D. The Second Missionary Tour, 15:36–18:22
  E. The Third Missionary Tour, 18:23–21:14
  F. The Arrest and Defense of Paul, 21:15–28:31

The first section of Acts introduces the theme by reference to the last words of Jesus before His ascension, in which He commanded the disciples to remain in Jerusalem for the coming of the Holy Spirit. At His descent on the day of Pentecost they were empowered to preach that Jesus had risen and that He was the true Messiah. Peter's sermon called for repentance and baptism on the part of believers. Three thousand converts were added to the band of disciples. Through a series of persecutions the church grew until it numbered at least 5,000, including converts from the Jewish priesthood.

The ministry of Stephen extended the church into foreign-speaking synagogues. His arrest and trial before the Sanhedrin marked a turning point in the life of the church. His statement that "the Most High dwelleth not in houses made with hands" (Acts 7:48) implied an outlook broader than that of Judaism, and the persecution accompanying his death compelled the Christians to scatter into other fields.

The period of transition marked advance into new territory and the commencement of a ministry among other peoples. Philip's preaching to the Samaritans and to the Ethiopian eunuch (8:5–40), Peter's entrance into the household of the Roman centurion Cornelius (10:1–11:18), and the startling conversion of the chief persecutor, Saul of Tarsus (9:1–30), broke down the barriers of prejudice and fear. Some of the refugees began a work among the Gentiles at Antioch, which became the basis for an empire-wide missionary movement.

The missionary campaign comprised three successive tours. The first, conducted by Paul and Barnabas, covered Cyprus and the southern part of the province of Galatia (Acts 13:1–14:28). The second by Paul, Silas, Timothy, and Luke, revisited the churches of S. Galatia, and penetrated the provinces of Macedonia and Achaia (15:36–18:22). The third included a three-year ministry in the province of Asia, centering in Ephesus, followed by a thorough inspection of the churches in Macedonia and Achaia (18:23–21:14). The council at Jerusalem settled the important question whether the Gentiles needed to keep the law in order to become Christians (15:1–35).

The arrest of Paul in Jerusalem, his imprisonment and hearings before Jewish and Roman officials, and his voyage to Rome conclude the narrative with his preaching in the imperial city (21:15 – 28:31). The story ends abruptly, perhaps because the author had finished the account as he knew it and had no more to say. He had, however, achieved his objective of tracing the progress of the gospel message from Jerusalem, the center of Judaism, to Rome, the metropolis of the Gentile world.

Authorship

Acts has been traditionally ascribed to Luke, a Gr. physician, who was a companion of Paul on his second and third journeys. His presence is indicated by the use of the pronoun "we," which occurs first in Acts 16:10–17, reappears in 20:5 – 21:17, and again in 27:1 – 28:16. The author joined Paul at Troas, went with him to Philippi, where he apparently remained until Paul returned on the third tour, and then accompanied him all the way to Rome. He did not share Paul's imprisonment in Jerusalem and Rome, but remained near him. Paul alluded to "Luke, the beloved physician" in his correspondence from prison (Col 4:14; Phm 24), and at a later date spoke of him again (II Tim 4:11).

Irenaeus, one of the early Church Fathers (c. A.D. 180), quotes Acts as the product of Luke, "the disciple and follower of the apostles" (*Against Heresies* I. xxiii.1). It is possible that Luke was the brother of Titus, another of Paul's companions, who is never mentioned in Acts, and that he is characterized by Paul in II Corinthians as "the brother whose praise in the gospel is spread through all the churches" (II Cor 8:18, ASV). The letter was written while Luke presumably was still in Philippi and when Titus was in Macedonia.

Internal evidence shows that the author was a highly literate Greek who had traveled widely and who was a keen observer. Hobart *(The Medical Language of St. Luke)* argued that Luke's language proved that he was a physician because of the medical terms he used. It may be that Hobart exaggerated the technical significance of Luke's vocabulary, but Luke seems to have had a greater interest in disease and in healing than other Christian writers. All indications that can be drawn from Acts support the traditional authorship.

Date

The *terminus a quo* of Acts is the close of Paul's first imprisonment, c. A.D. 61/62, for the book could not have been written earlier than the events which it describes. The Tübingen School of the 19th cen. assigned it to the middle of the 2nd cen., believing it to be an apologetic work written to gloss over differences in the church that occurred in the preceding era. Others have dated it late in the 1st cen. on the assumption that Luke used as a source the works of Josephus, which were not written before A.D. 90. Luke, however, may have had independent access to the same information that Josephus used. The general accuracy of his allusions to places, persons, and events, insofar

as they can be corroborated by archaeology and history, indicates that Luke was a contemporary of what he described. Despite the author's keen interest in Paul, the absence of any reference to his epistles is scarcely explicable if Acts were written after their collection and publication. For these reasons a date before A.D. 65 seems most acceptable.

The Value of Acts

Acts is a document of primary historical value both for the history of the church and of the ancient world. Apart from Acts the gap between the Gospels and the epistles would be almost unbridgeable, for no explanation would be available for the transition from the ministry of Jesus to the doctrine and evangelism of the church. Almost all authentic extant knowledge concerning the apostolic leaders and the geographical extent of their mission is derived from this book. Acts does not afford a complete account, but it provides leading facts and general principles that aid historical interpretation.

The allusions to contemporary occurrences enable scholars to relate Christianity to the world of its day. The death of Herod Agrippa I (Acts 12:21–23); the proconsulship of Gallio (18:12–17); the administrations of Felix (23:24) and Festus (24:27), procurators of Judea; the technical names of officials in the districts of the Roman Empire, such as praetors and lictors at Philippi (16:35, ASV marg.); "rulers of the city" at Thessalonica (Gr. *politarchs*, 17:6), and Asiarchs at Ephesus (19:31, ASV); the linguistic differences that obtained in different sections of the empire (14:11; 21:37, 40); and the accurate geographical detail of the final voyage to Rome (Acts 27–28)) provide reliable information for modern historians, and show that the author was accurately informed.

The doctrinal and spiritual value of Acts is great. The primitive teaching of the church is outlined in the speeches which Acts preserves; and the emphasis upon the work of the Holy Spirit and upon the basis of the missionary enterprise constitutes a pattern for the experience and practice of succeeding generations.

Bibliography. E. M. Blaiklock, *The Acts of the Apostles (Tyndale Commentaries),* Grand Rapids: Eerdmans, 1959. F. F. Bruce, *Commentary on the Book of Acts (The New International Commentary),* Grand Rapids: Eerdmans, 1954. F. J. Foakes-Jackson and Kirsopp Lake, *The Beginnings of Christianity,* Part I: *The Acts of the Apostles,* 5 vols., London: Macmillan, 1920–35. Richard B. Rackham, *The Acts of the Apostles,* WC. A. T. Robertson, *Luke the Historian in the Light of Research,* New York: Scribner's, 1923.

M. C. T.

ADADAH (ăd'ădà). A town in the southern part of Judah, associated with Kinah and Dimonah (Josh 15:22).

ADAH (ā'dá)

1. One of the two wives of Lamech (Gen 4:19–23), the mother of two famous sons, Jabal and Jubal.

2. Esau had a Hittite wife by the name of Adah who was the mother of his son Eliphaz (Gen 36:2–16).

ADAIAH (á-dā'yá)

1. A native of Boscath in Judah. He was the father of Jedidah, wife of Amon and mother of Josiah king of Judah (II Kgs 22:1).

2. A Levite of the family of Gershom, an ancestor of Asaph, a celebrated musician in the time of David (I Chr 6:41). Probably the same as Iddo (v. 21).

3. A son of Shimei or Shema of Benjamin, an important resident of Jerusalem before the Exile (I Chr 8:13, 21).

4. A priest and important family head who served in the temple after the return from Exile (I Chr 9:10–12; Neh 11:12).

5. The father of Maaseiah, one of the captains used by Jehoiada to guard the child Joash when he was proclaimed king (II Chr 23:1).

6. A son of Bani after the Exile who was condemned as one who had taken a foreign wife (Ezr 10:29).

7. The son of another Israelite named Bani, also listed with those who had put away their foreign wives (Ezr 10:39).

8. A man of Judah, father of Hazaiah, whose descendants were prominent men in Jerusalem after the return from Exile (Neh 11:5).

P. C. J.

ADALIA (á-dā'lĭ-á). One of the ten sons of Haman who was slain by the Jews at the order of Mordecai (Est 9:8).

ADAM (ăd'ám). The first man, from whom the entire human race descended. The NT presents Adam as the representative of humanity and relates the whole problem of sin to his original transgression.

As to the meaning of this name, etymology cannot offer any positive help. Three possibilities rival one another. The word may come from the similar word 'ádāmâ, which means "the red soil"; or from the root dāmâ, which means "be like" (reference to d^{e}mût, i.e., "likeness," Gen 1:26; 5:1); or from the Akkad. root adāmu, which means "to make or produce." Perhaps the last deserves the preference.

The Bible states that God created Adam (Gen 2:7), placed him in the garden of Eden (2:8–15), gave him the command regarding the tree of the knowledge of good and evil (2:16–17), and lastly put woman at his side as his mate in a separate act of creation (2:18–25). God blessed them, conferring prosperity on them by the power of His spoken word, and ordered them to multiply and to be masters of all living creatures on earth (1:28). When subjected to a temptation by the serpent, Adam succumbed, as his wife had before him. This marks the event commonly known as the Fall. Immediately after the Fall, the altered lot of our first parents became known through their actions and through the doom that God assigned to them. They were not cursed. In His great mercy, the Lord suffered them to continue to live for a while and provided them with their first garments. But He did expel them from the garden in which they had dwelt. They had children, in fact a number of them (cf. Gen 5:4). Adam himself died at the age of 930 years (Gen 5:5).

Adam was a historic personage, not merely a poetic figure or a mythical person. In the OT the word 'ādām is used more than 500 times in the sense of mankind as well as in the sense of a proper name. Both uses appear in the Genesis record, but only from Gen 4:25 onward can it definitely be claimed that the specific person Adam is exclusively under consideration. Before that, he usually is thought of as the representative man, although the term Adam in Gen 3:17, 21 seems to occur without the definite article, suggesting that in these verses the name is meant and the specific person is in view. See also Gen 5:1, 3–5.

There are two accounts of Adam's creation: Gen 1:26–28 and 2:4–7, 20–23. The usual explanation of this fact by modern higher critics is that these two accounts trace back to two separate sources that the author used, and to reinforce this point, the near incompatibility of the two accounts is often stressed. But quite apart from sources, about which we must always speak with great caution, it appears that the account of Gen 1 is quite summary in fashion and agrees with the pattern of the work of the six creation days; whereas the record of Gen 2 is supplementary — in no sense contradictory to chap. 1 — supplying certain details that are very essential to the understanding of what follows. This latter viewpoint is generally held by conservative biblical scholars.

In this dual record two factors are found in man: God made him of the dust of the earth (2:7) and breathed into his nostrils the breath of life. There was a lower and a higher strain in his being. Secondly, he was made in "the image of God" (1:26–27), a meaningful claim which is not defined by the writer in any way. The supplementary account (Gen 2) also gives the exact manner in which Eve was created; it tells of the location of the garden, and also of the two unusually significant trees. So also man's duties in this early state of existence were outlined: he was to till and keep the garden (2:15).

Divine grace manifested itself in that only one commandment was laid upon the man, that he was not to eat of the tree of the knowledge of good and evil. This command was violated with tragic consequences.

The almost startling fact about this narrative of Adam and the Fall is that there are very sparing references to it in the OT. A comparison of the original Heb. would show that there could be a reference to Adam in Deut 32:8; Job 31:33; Hos 6:7, ASV. It may be safe to assume that the basic character of the event of man's creation and Fall was generally accepted without further ado. The full theological evaluation of the Fall came later, in the writings of the apostles.

Almost equally strange is the fact that in the apocryphal books, the references to Adam and his basic importance are numerous.

The passages of the NT that refer to Adam are Mt 19:4–6; Rom 5:12–21; I Cor 15:22, 45; I Tim 2:13–14; Jude 14. In each of these, it can hardly be doubted that Adam is regarded as a historical figure. Rom 5 is particularly strong: two persons are contrasted — Adam and Christ — and the wide sweep of the consequences of their deeds. Of these two, the one is as much a historical figure as the other.

See Anthropology; Creation.

Bibliography. James O. Buswell, III, "Adam and Neolithic Man," *Eternity,* XVIII (1967), 29 ff., for various views of the date of Adam. J. Barton Payne, *The Theology of the Older Testament,* Grand Rapids: Zondervan, 1962, pp. 213–231, helpful both for content and further bibliography. Geerhardus Vos, *Biblical Theology,* Grand Rapids: Eerdmans, 1954, pp. 37–55.

H. C. L.

ADAMAH (ăd′á-má). A fortified city assigned to Naphtali (Josh 19:36).

ADAMANT. *See* Minerals.

ADAMI (ăd′á-mī). The lone mention of this border town in Naphtali (Josh 19:33) has brought various suggestions from scholars. The translators of the KJV decided it was a separate town from Adami-Nekeb, while the ASV translators made the two one town. (*See* Nekeb.) Its identification is not certainly known. Perhaps it may be associated with the pass in the hills going to the Jordan River S of modern Tiberias, possibly with Khirbet Damiyeh, a large Bronze Age site five miles SW of Tiberias.

ADAR (ā′där)
1. Used in KJV as the name of a city in Judah (Josh 15:3), but perhaps it should have been spelled Addar (*q.v.*).
2. Most likely this word came from Babylonia and was first used by the Jews there to indicate the twelfth month of their sacred calendar; therefore, it appears in Ezr 6:15; Est 3:7, 13; 8:12; 9:1, 15, 17, 19, 21. It was timed from the new moon in our February until the new moon in March. *See* Calendar.

ADBEEL (ăd′bĭ-ĕl). The third son of Ishmael and therefore the name of an Arabian tribe (Gen 25:13; I Chr 1:29). It was located in NW Arabia close to Kedar and Nebaioth.

ADDAN (ăd′án), **ADDON** (ăd′ŏn). Some of the people who returned to Jerusalem from Babylon with Zerubbabel were from Addan in Babylonia (Ezr 2:59). They were unable to establish their identity with Israel (Neh 7:61).

ADDAR (ăd′är)
1. A city on the border of Judah W of Kadesh-barnea (Josh 15:3, RSV), called by the double name Hazar-addar in Num 34:4.
2. The son of Bela and grandson of Benjamin (I Chr 8:3). Elsewhere called Ard (Gen 46:21).

ADDER. *See* Animals: Cobra IV.8.

ADDI (ăd′ī). The father of Melchi and the son of Cosam (Lk 3:28) in the Lucan genealogy of Jesus.

ADDON (ăd′ŏn). *See* Addan.

ADER (ā′dĕr). A distinguished man of Benjamin, son of Beriah, who lived at Aijalon (I Chr 8:15).

ADIEL (ā′dĭ-ĕl)
1. One of the noted warriors of the tribe of Simeon who helped to take certain cities from the original inhabitants (I Chr 4:36).
2. A priest, the son of Jahzerah, who was among the people returning from the Exile (I Chr 9:12).
3. The father of the treasurer Azmaveth in the days of King David (I Chr 27:25).

ADIN (ā′dĭn). The representative of a family in Exile some of whom returned to Jerusalem under Zerubbabel (Ezr 2:15), and some later perhaps under Ezra (Neh 7:20; 10:16).

ADINA (ăd′ĭ-ná). One of the mighty men under David, captain of 30 men, a member of the tribe of Reuben (I Chr 11:42).

ADINO (ăd′ĭ-nō). The reference in II Sam 23:8 may not be the name of a person, and perhaps should be related to I Chr 11:11. One of the shades of meaning of the word Adino in Heb. is "slender," which may suggest the spear used by these mighty warriors of David.

ADITHAIM (ăd-ĭ-thā′ĭm). A city in the Shephelah section of Judah (Josh 15:36).

ADJURE. To make or cause one to swear by some higher being or object, which put one under obligation to speak the truth. Two Heb. and two Gr. words carry the same general thought. The Heb. words 'alâ and shāba' are used in connection with oaths (I Sam 14:24; Josh 6:26; I Kgs 22:16; II Chr 18:15). The Gr. words are *exorkizō* and *horkizō,* used where Jesus was put under oath (Mt 26:63), and where demons spoke to Him (Mk 5:7; see also Acts 19:13). *See* Oath.

ADLAI (ăd'lā). The father of Shaphat, a shepherd of David's royal flocks in the valleys (I Chr 27:29).

ADMAH (ăd'må). One of the towns in the Dead Sea basin with Sodom and Gomorrah, conquered with them by the kings from the E, and then destroyed with them in divine judgment (Gen 10:19; 14:2, 8; Deut 29:23). The fate of Admah is presented as a warning against all Israel (Hos 11:8).

ADMATHA (ăd-mā'thå). The third in rank of the princes of Persia who sat with King Xerxes (Ahasuerus); these were counselors to the king (Est 1:14; cf. Ezr 7:14).

ADNA (ăd'nå)
1. One of the men from Pahath-moab who was condemned by Ezra because of his marriage to a foreigner (Ezr 10:30).
2. A priest who served during the high priesthood of Joiakim in the days of Nehemiah (Neh 12:15).

ADNAH (ăd'nå)
1. When it was learned that the Philistines refused to allow David and his force to join them against Saul, some of Saul's own men deserted him and joined David at Ziklag. One of these was a captain named Adnah (I Chr 12:20).
2. One of the captains under Jehoshaphat (II Chr 17:14).

ADONI-BEZEK (a-dō'nĭ-bē'zĕk). A petty king of the Canaanite town of Bezek, he had unmercifully amputated the thumbs and great toes of 70 other "kings." (This incapacitated them for ancient warfare; they could neither handle weapons nor pursue an enemy.) When Bezek fell before the fierce warriors of Judah and Simeon, Adoni-bezek fled. However, he was captured alive and received the same cruel treatment which he had inflicted upon his royal captives. Incredible as it may seem, he recognized his punishment as an act of retributive justice (Jud 1:5-7). He died at Jerusalem.

ADONIJAH (ăd'ō-nī'jå)
1. The fourth son of David by Haggith (II Sam 3:4; I Chr 3:2). When David was at the brink of death, Adonijah desired to succeed David to the throne, for at that time he was the oldest living son. Gathering chariots, horsemen, and 50 men, Adonijah enlisted the aid of Joab, commander of the army, and Abiathar, the high priest. However, other generals, priests, Nathan the prophet, and David's bodyguard refused to follow him. They favored Solomon as the new king. While Adonijah called for a meeting of his supporters at En-rogel in the valley below Jerusalem, Bathsheba, Solomon's mother, and Nathan the prophet made an urgent plea to David that Solomon be crowned immediately. David quickly granted their petition and gave instructions for the coronation of Solomon at the spring of Gihon close by Jerusalem. Zadok the priest anointed Solomon king, and he was proclaimed king of Israel amid the wild acclaim of the people (I Kgs 1). In a few days, Adonijah rashly requested that Abishag, David's last attendant, be given him for a wife. In anger, Solomon sent Benaiah to kill Adonijah. The command was promptly carried out (I Kgs 2:13-25).
2. In Jehoshaphat's reform, another Adonijah, a Levite, assisted a group of princes and priests in teaching the people the law of God (II Chr 17:7-9).
3. Among those returning to Jerusalem from Exile was an Adonijah (also called Adonikam) who set his seal to the covenant made during Ezra's reform (Ezr 2:13; Neh 7:18; 10:16).

G. H. L.

ADONIKAM (ăd-ō-nī'kăm)
1. The representative of a family that returned with Zerubbabel from Exile and that numbered 666 (Ezr 2:13), or including the representative, the family numbered 667 (Neh 7:18).
2. Part of the above family waited to come with Ezra. This group was composed of 60 males (Ezr 8:13).

ADONIRAM (ăd'ō-nī'răm). A public official in charge of forced labor during the reigns of David, Solomon, and Rehoboam (I Kgs 4:6; 5:14; 12:18). After the ten northern tribes revolted, Rehoboam foolishly sent Adoniram (perhaps to collect their taxes), but the insulted Israelites stoned him to death at Shechem (c. 922 B.C.). He is also known as Adoram (II Sam 20:24; I Kgs 12:18) and Hadoram (q.v.; II Chr 10:18). When the latter spelling occurs one should carefully distinguish this unpopular taskmaster from (a) Hadoram, a son of Joktan in the genealogy of Shem (Gen 10:27; I Chr 1:21), and (b) Hadoram, a son of Tou, king of Hamath (I Chr 18:10).

ADONI-ZEDEK (a-dō'nĭ-zĕ'dĕk). An Amorite king of Jerusalem at the time of the Conquest (Josh 10). Impressed by the initial successes of Israel and by the military potential of their newly formed alliance with Gibeon (Josh 9), he took the initiative in forming a five city military alliance against Israel. By attacking the city of Gibeon he hoped to greatly weaken the Israelite position as well as punish the Gibeonites for their defection. Joshua made an overnight march, arriving in time to assist his ally. The miraculous intervention of God and the resultant decisive Israelite victory were celebrated in song in the Book of Jashar, a portion of which is quoted in Josh 10:12-13.

Adoni-zedek and his royal allies hid in a cave at Makkedah. After the destructio᾽ of all their armies they were taken out, humbl᷍ed and slain, and, after sundown, entombed in the same cave.

ADOPTION. The word itself is used in the Bible only in a theological sense. In a civil or legal sense the practice of adoption was exemplified outside the cultural milieu of Israel in the adoption of Moses (Ex 2:10; Acts 7:21, RSV) and of Esther (Est 2:7, 15).

In patriarchal times the ancient Near East practiced something akin to adoption. The discovery of the Nuzu tablets has disclosed the custom whereby a childless couple adopted an adult son who would serve them in life and bury them at death. In return this adopted son would receive the inheritance, unless a son were later born to the couple, in which case the natural born son would then become chief heir (see ANET, pp. 219 f.). While no laws of adoption are found formulated in the OT, such a custom may well be reflected in the relationship of Abraham and Eliezer (Gen 15:2-4). Something close to legal adoption may also be seen in respect to Jacob's grandsons Manasseh and Ephraim (Gen 48:5), with a recognized adoption formula, "let my name be named on them," appearing in v. 16 (cf. Code of Hammurabi #185, ANET, p. 174). Possibly Laban placed Jacob in the status of an adopted son wherein Jacob had to perform service (Gen 29:15) and which gave Laban legal rights to Jacob's children (Gen 31:28, 43, 55). Other cases of adoption may be alluded to in I Kgs 11:20 and I Chr 2:34-35.

The details of these OT practices do not appear to have a direct bearing on the NT usage of the term. Paul is the only one to employ the Gr. word *huiothesia* and then he does so only five times (Rom 8:15, 23; 9:4; Gal 4:5; Eph 1:5). In Rom 9:4 he refers to the privileged position of the Jews as God's elected people, alluding to Ex 4:22 where the Lord calls Israel His son, His firstborn (cf. Deut 7:6-8; Isa 43:6; Jer 3:19; Hos 11:1).

In the other passages, however, the apostle's usage reflects not the Hebraic but the Hellenistic world, emphasizing the freedom of a son in the household contrasted to the bondage of a slave.

Adoption was a very common part of the Graeco-Roman way of life. If there were no children in a family, the husband would adopt a son to whom he could give the inheritance. The person being adopted might have living parents but this would not prevent the adoption proceedings, because families were often willing to give up their children if they would thereby have a better chance in life. Once a child was adopted, the natural father had absolutely no more authority over him, and the adoptive father had complete control over his new son. A notable example of this practice in Roman history comes from the administration of the emperor Augustus. Realizing he had no responsible heir to his throne, he adopted an heir. When he outlived one heir, he adopted another, and finally settled on Tiberius, who succeeded him in A.D. 14.

Reflecting this understanding of adoption in the Hellenistic world, Paul employed the term to denote that legal act of God's grace by which believers become sons of God. Their relationship to God *as children* results from the new birth ("He gave the right to become children of God," Jn 1:12, NASB); whereas their adoption signifies that they as children have been placed in the position of *adult sons* (Gal 4:1-7). This is in contrast with the unique ("only begotten") sonship of Jesus Christ, who is Son of God by nature (Jn 1:14).

As in civil adoption, so in a spiritual sense, the following features may be noted: (1) Adoption is taking one for a son who was not so by nature and birth. (2) It is being adopted to an inheritance—in the spiritual sense, an inheritance which is incorruptible and undefiled (Rom 8:15-17; Gal 4:5-7). (3) It is the voluntary act of the adopter—spiritually the heavenly Father exercises His sovereign will in the matter (Eph 1:5)—mediated by Christ through the instrumentality of the Holy Spirit (Gal 4:4-6). (4) It means that the adopted bears the name of the adopter and can call him "Father" (Isa 56:5; 62:2; 65:15; Rev 2:17; Rom 8:15; I Jn 3:1). (5) It means that the adopted becomes the recipient of the compassion and care of his heavenly Father (Eph 1:3-6; cf. Lk 11:11-13), and is accepted into full family rights and privileges, received back as a son and not a servant in the case of the prodigal (Lk 15:19-24). (6) In the eschatological aspect the entire creation will benefit from the adopted one receiving the deliverance of his body from decay and death (Rom 8:23).

See Family; Inheritance.

Bibliography. Sherman E. Johnson, "Adoption," HDB rev., p. 11. C. F. D. Moule, "Adoption," IDB, I, 48 f. CornPBE, p. 319.

C. M. H.

ADORAIM (ăd'ō-rā'ĭm). A city in southern Judah rebuilt and fortified by Rehoboam (II Chr 11:9). It has been identified with Dura, five miles SW of Hebron.

ADORAM (á-dō'răm). Alternate form of Adoniram *(q.v.)*.

ADORATION. This term does not occur in KJV, ASV, or RSV, although the idea is expressed in the OT *shāhâ*, "worship," "bow oneself before"; and in the NT *proskuneō*, "worship," "kiss the hand," "do reverence to," "adore," and less frequently by *sebomai*, "revere," "adore," "be devout," and *latreuō*, "worship publicly," "minister," "serve," "render religious homage." *See* Worship.

ADORN. A word meaning "to polish" or "to arrange," it came to be used for dress, especially women's dress (I Tim 2:9; I Pet 3:3, 5; Rev 21:2). Figuratively, we are to adorn the doctrine of God (Tit 2:10).

ADRAMMELECH (*á*-drăm'*ĕ*-lĕk)

1. One of the Syrian or Mesopotamian gods brought to Samaria when the kingdom of Israel fell (II Kgs 17:31), likely the deity Adad-milki ("Adad is king"). *See* Gods, False.

2. A son of Sennacherib. He and a brother assassinated their father and fled to Armenia (II Kgs 19:37; Isa 37:38).

ADRAMYTTIUM (ăd-rá-mĭt'ĭ-ŭm). Mentioned only once in the Scriptures (Acts 27:2) when Paul was placed on a ship from this seaport in Mysia of the Roman province of Asia.

ADRIA (ā'drĭ-á). Paul and the party with him being taken to Rome drifted in Adria for 14 days (Acts 27:27). The northern part of the body of water between Italy and Dalmatia was from Etruscan times called the Adriatic Sea, but according to Livy, Strabo, Ptolemy and Josephus, the sea as far S as the island of Crete was designated as Adriatic. Thus when Luke wrote in the 1st cen. A.D. about the voyage, he used the current designation and called the waters "Adria" in which they were drifting.

ADRIEL (ā'drĭ-ĕl). King Saul had promised his daughter Merab to David, but instead he gave her in marriage to Adriel (I Sam 18:17–19). Later Saul gave his daughter Michal to David in marriage. Perhaps some scribal corruption accounts for Michal being recorded as the mother of five boys that David allowed the Gibeonites to hang in payment for Saul's offense to them. Their mother was Merab the wife of Adriel (II Sam 21:8). The RSV has corrected this on the authority of two Heb. MSS and the LXX.

ADULLAM (*á*-dŭl'*á*m), **ADULLAMITES** (*á*-mīts). A city in the Shephelah of Judah, usually listed with some other cities that can more easily be identified (Josh 12:15; 15:35; II Chr 11:7; Neh 11:30; Mic 1:15). Near the city were several caves in which David and his men stayed for a while (I Sam 22:1; II Sam 23:13; I Chr 11:15). The Adullamites were citizens of Adullam.

ADULTERY. Sexual intercourse of a married person with other than the marriage partner. Adultery was generally condoned in pagan cultures, particularly on the part of the male, who though married was not charged with adultery unless he cohabited with another man's wife or a betrothed maiden.

Adultery is strictly forbidden in both the OT (the seventh commandment, Ex 20:14; Deut 5:18; punishable under the law with death by stoning, Lev 20:10; Deut 22:22 ff.) and the NT (Rom 13:9; Gal 5:19; Jas 2:11). Jesus extended guilt for adultery, as He did in the case of other commandments, to the purpose or will to commit it as well as to the act itself (Mt 5:28).

Adultery is technically distinguished from fornication, which is intercourse between unmarried persons. However, the Gr. *porneia*, uniformly translated "fornication" in the KJV, properly includes all lewdness and sexual irregularity (cf. MM; and Vine, EDNTW). For this reason, many churches regard Mt 5:32 and 19:9 as allowing divorce with remarriage in cases where the prior marriage was broken by reason of adultery. Others refuse to acknowledge any valid basis for remarriage after divorce, and view all such as resulting in adultery in the sight of God. However, it must not be concluded because this exception is absent from the Synoptic parallels and from Paul's analogy in Rom 7:2–3 or his treatment in I Cor 7:10–11 that it therefore is not authentic. Exactly the reverse may be the case. It may have been so universally recognized as not to require restatement each time divorce and remarriage were mentioned.

The attitude of Jesus toward the woman taken in adultery as recorded in Jn 8:1–11 has been questioned on the grounds that this passage is lacking in the best ancient MSS, and where it does occur, the readings vary widely. However, "it is unquestionable that it forms part of the authentic tradition of the church" (A. J. MacLeod, "John," NBC). Christ did not condone sin in the woman, nor did He condemn her to death by stoning as her accusers suggested. "The truth in Him rebuked the lie in the scribes and Pharisees. The purity in Him condemned the lust in her" (C. J. Wright, *Mission and Message of Jesus*, p. 795), and He bade her go and sin no more.

A consistent biblical use of the term adultery (Heb. *nā'aph;* Gr. *moicheia*) is metaphorical, to represent the idolatry or backsliding of the nation and people espoused to God. Examples of this are Jer 3:8–9; Ezk 23:27, 43; Hos 2:2–13; Mt 12:39; Jas 4:4. Such use is based on the analogy of the relationship between God and His people as resembling the relationship of husband and wife, a common feature of both OT (Jer 2:2; 3:14; 13:27; Hos 8:9) and NT (Jn 3:29; Rev 19:8–9; 21:2, 9). Marriage as involving both a legal covenant and a bond of love is a fitting symbol of the relationship between Christ and His Church (Eph 5:25–27).

Polygamy as a legalized relationship between the male and subordinate wives and concubines was permitted in OT times, but forbidden in the NT (e.g., I Tim 3:2, 12). It did not involve the sin of adultery.

In spite of strict biblical injunctions, adultery became widespread at different times, being particularly offensive as part of the Canaanite worship of the Baals, involving "sacred" prostitution. Indications of common moral laxity are found in such references as Job 24:15; 31:9; Prov 2:16–19; 7:5–22; Jer 23:10–14. The case of David was particularly notorious, giving occasion for the enemies of God to blaspheme (II Sam 11:2–5; 12:14). That general laxity prevailed in NT times is clearly seen in Mk 8:38; Lk 18:11; I Cor 6:9; Gal 5:19; Heb 13:4, and in more than 50 references in the NT to the concept of fornication *(porneia, porneuō, pornē, pornos)*. *See* Fornication.

Bibliography. F. Hauck, "*Moicheuō*, etc.," TDNT, IV, 729-735.

W. T. P.

ADUMMIM (*à*-dŭm'ĭm). The pass through red marl hills with the modern Arabic name of Tal'at ed-Damm ("ascent of blood") is thought to be the ancient Adummim. The Scriptures indicate it is on the general line between Jericho and Jerusalem (Josh 15:7; 18:17). It may be the setting for Jesus' story of the good Samaritan (Lk 10:30).

ADVENT, SECOND. *See* Christ, Coming of.

ADVERSARY. In 32 of its 57 KJV occurrences, "adversary" is the translation of *ṣar* (or related forms) meaning "foe." It refers primarily to enemies of Israel (Ex 23:22; Jer 50:7; cf. Est 7:6; Ps 69:19), but also to a rival wife (I Sam 1:6) or sinful Judeans (Isa 1:24). Adversaries execute God's wrath (Ps 89:42; Amos 3:11; cf. Lam 2:4), but will be overcome (Ps 81:13-14; Jer 30:16; cf. Isa 59:18; Nah 1:2). Heb. *śāṭān* (*see* Satan) may describe a human adversary (I Sam 29:4; II Sam 19:22), or even the angel of the Lord (Num 22:22).

Of NT words rendered "adversary," *antikeimenos* means simply "opposer" (Lk 13:17; 21:15; I Cor 16:9; Phil 1:28; I Tim 5:14; cf. Arndt); but *antidikos* signifies opponents in a lawsuit (Mt 5:25; Lk 12:58; cf. Job 31:35; Isa 50:8), as well as more generally the devil (Lk 18:3; I Pet 5:8).

See also Devil.

ADVOCATE. Arndt defines the Gr. word *paraklētos* for "advocate" as "one who appears in another's behalf; mediator, intercessor, helper" (p. 623). *See* Paraclete.

John says that one only deceives himself when he says he has no sin (I Jn 1:8), while he makes God a liar when he says he has never sinned (v. 10). At the same time, if anyone commits sin he does have an "advocate with the Father, Jesus Christ the righteous" (I Jn 2:1). To understand what John means, one must realize he also has an adversary who constantly stands to accuse him before God, even Satan (cf. Zech 3:1-7; Job 1:6-12; 2:1-7; Rev 12:10). In Christ's work as Advocate He pleads His own substitutionary atonement for the believer's sins and defends him against the attacks of Satan before God.

AENEAS (ĕ-nē'ás). The name of a paralytic "sick of the palsy" and bedridden for eight years whom Peter healed, saying, "Jesus Christ maketh thee whole" (Acts 9:32-35). The healing resulted in a great spiritual awakening at both Lydda and Sharon. It illustrates very well the purpose of NT miracles as an attestation by God to the ministry of the early church, and identifies the disciples' work with that of Christ. *See* Healing, Divine; Miracles.

AENON (ē'nŏn). John baptized here because there was much water. In Jn 3:23 it is said to be near Salim. Though the exact site is unknown, it is located by Eusebius (*Onomasticon* 40:1-4) W of the Jordan, eight miles S of Scythopolis or Beth-shan.

AEON. This represents a Gr. word which is used in the NT of an age (cf. the present age, this age, the coming age, that age, Mt 12:32; Mk 10:30; Lk 18:30; 20:35; Gal 1:4, RSV). It is also used of worlds and universe (Heb 1:2). It is employed especially in certain phrases to express the ideas of forever and forever and ever (Jn 6:51, 58; Gal 1:5). For an introduction to recent discussion of its force as applied to eternity, see James Barr, *Biblical Words for Time.* Barr contends that Cullmann's vocabulary study has failed to prove that there is lexical foundation for his view that no qualitative distinction can be drawn between the NT conceptions of time and eternity, and claims that eternity is merely time in its entirety or time without end or limit. *See* Eternity; Time.

J. H. S.

A lively controversy exists over the use of the word in such a passage as Mt 24:3 (cf. Mt 13:39-40; Lk 18:30; I Cor 10:11; Heb 9:26) where the disciples said to our Lord, "Tell us, when shall these things be? and what shall be the sign of thy coming, and of the end of the world [age or aeon]?" Young, in his concordance, sees it as being used here in the sense of age, and classifies it along with many other NT uses which, though translated "world" in the KJV, express time and can be, therefore, better translated "age" or "dispensation."

Actually the decision as to which translation is correct is dictated in such places not so much by exegetical details as by the fact one is either amillennial or premillennial. The premillennialist has no difficulties with the literal translation "age," but the amillennialist feels he must eliminate such a meaning for such verses as this and Mt 13:39, "the harvest is the end of the aeon" (cf. II Cor 4:4; Gal 1:4), lest it support the literal idea of the thousand year reign of Christ on the earth. The primary meaning "age" should be given preference over the secondary one "world" except where it does not fit (e.g., Heb 11:3; cf. I Cor 2:6; II Cor 4:4), or the context demands the meaning "world" (Heb 1:2).

At the same time it should be realized that the Heb. concept of time and of dispensations in time was applied in a much wider sense than our term age; everything was related to particular periods or points of time. *See* Dispensation.

Bibliography. James Barr, *Biblical Words for Time,* Naperville: Allenson, 1962. Oscar Cullmann, *Christ and Time,* London: S. C. M. Press, 1951.

R. A. K.

AFFLICTION. The unsaved suffers afflictions because of his sins (Ps 107:10, 39); the Christian, because of the curse of sin and death upon the world, because of Satan (Job 1:6–12; 2:1–7), and because the fallen world hates righteousness and the light (Jn 15:18; 3:20). Moses chose to "suffer evil [literal] together with the children of God, rather than to enjoy the pleasures of sin for a season" (Heb 11:25).

Yet this does not explain fully the afflictions which come upon the believer. Seen in a deeper dimension, they are all part of Rom 8:28 – "all things work good to them that love God" – in the sense God sends afflictions for the Christian's good. Paul, who knew the greatest of trials, calls the believer's afflictions "light" compared with the glory which follows when he goes to be with the Lord (II Cor 4:17).

According to our Lord, the time of greatest affliction, the Great Tribulation, will occur just prior to His second coming (Mt 24:21, 29–30; cf. Rev 7:14; Rev 6–19), and He says except those days be shortened, no one will be left on the earth (Mt 24:22).

The term "the afflictions of Christ," used by Paul in Col 1:24, does not refer to any lack in the sufferings of Christ which is completed by believers. The Roman Catholics teach that it is possible to help fill out these sufferings and add to the work of Christ, just as it is possible to do works of merit which are added to His works. Paul is here referring to the sufferings borne by Christ's Body, the Church, and speaks in this way because of the close spiritual union between the Lord and His own. The Lord refers to this union in Jn 17:21 as He prays, "That they all may be one; as thou, Father, art in me, and I in thee, that they also may be one in us."

See Agony; Suffering.

R. A. K.

AGABUS (ăg'à-bŭs). A prophet from Jerusalem (Acts 11:27–30) who predicted a widespread famine in the inhabited world (the Roman Empire). This occurred in the days of Claudius (A.D. 41–54), relief being sent probably between the years 45–46 by the Antioch church in Syria to the Jerusalem Christians. Presumably, the same Agabus is intended in Acts 21:10, 11, where his prediction made in A.D. 59 to the church at Caesarea was dramatically presented by his binding himself with Paul's girdle, warning Paul of impending imprisonment if he insisted on going up to Jerusalem.

That Agabus may have been a native of Antioch rests on the very slender evidence of a few MSS which read "one of us" instead of "one of them" in Acts 11:28.

AGAG (ā'găg). The king of the Amalekites, who was captured and his life spared by Saul, although the prophet Samuel had commanded that all Amalekites be put to death. When Samuel went out to meet Saul after the king had returned from the victory, the bleating of the sheep belied his claim of perfect obedience. He tried to blame the people for sparing Agag and the cattle, but Samuel would not accept the excuse. Saul then confessed his sin, but it was too late, for Samuel predicted the loss of his kingdom. Samuel demonstrated the need of full obedience by personally slaying Agag in the presence of the people (I Sam 15:8–33). Earlier, an Agag had been mentioned in the prophecy of Balaam, who declared that Israel's king would be higher than Agag (Num 24:7).

AGAGITE (ā'gà-gīt). Haman (*q.v.*), who was the first officer in command under Ahasuerus (Xerxes I), was an Agagite (Est 3:1, 10; 8:3, 5; 9:24). Josephus (*Ant.* xi.6.5) associated this name with Amalek. It was Agag the king of the Amalekites whom Saul brought back to Israel and thus aroused the anger of Samuel (I Sam 15:8, 33). If this association is correct, one can understand Mordecai's disrespect for Haman.

An Akkadian inscription of Sargon II mentions Agag as a district in Media.

AGAPE (ä-gä'pā). The agape (Gr. for "love") was the common meal or love feast of the early church. Besides satisfying hunger and distributing to the poor, it was a means for expressing unity and brotherly love. *See* Love Feast.

Though mentioned specifically only in Jude 12 and II Pet 2:13 (in some MSS), the custom was known in the NT (Acts 2:42, 46; 20:11; I Cor 10:16; 11:24) and in post-canonical literature (Didache, Ignatius, Tertullian, Chrysostom, Augustine, *et al.*). Jewish feasts and Gentile guilds furnished precedent for such an expression of fellowship.

At first, after the pattern of the Lord's Supper, the meal seems to have been associated with the Eucharist. Later, the sacerdotal emphasis tended to separate the two and to associate the latter with fasting. Never having been entirely universal or essential to Christian practice, faced with abuses from within, and coming under suspicion of the heathen who imagined an evil motive, the meal fell more and more into disuse by the 4th cen. However, it is still preserved by some religious bodies (Mennonites, Dunkards, and some German Baptists).

W. T. D.

AGAR (ā'gär). The Gr. version of the Heb. Hagar *(q.v.).* It is used allegorically by Paul in Gal 4:24–25.

AGATE. A precious stone. *See* Jewels; Minerals.

AGE. *See* Eternity; Time.

AGEE (ā'gē). The father of Shammah, one of

David's mighty men. He is called a Hararite (II Sam 23:11).

AGONY. This word (Gr. *agōnia*) is found but once in the NT (Lk 22:44). It describes the climax of the mysterious conflict and unspeakable suffering of our Lord in the garden. Coming from *agōn*, "contest," and *agō*, "to drive or lead," as in a chariot race, it has the root idea of the struggle and pain of the most severe athletic contest or conflict. From Demosthenes on, it has been used of severe mental struggles and emotions.

The agony of soul wrought pain upon the body of Jesus until "his sweat became as it were great drops of blood falling down upon the ground" (Lk 22:44, ASV). Blood mixing with the ordinary watery perspiration is medically termed diapedesis. It results from agitation of the nervous system, turning the blood out of its natural course and forcing the red particles into the skin excretories (Fausset, *Bible Encyclopedia*). Other cases are on record, such as Charles IX of France on his death bed and a Florentine youth unjustly condemned to death by Sixtus V.

The anguish of Christ seems to have reached an unbearable level even before the bloody sweat, for an angel came and strengthened Him (Lk 22:43). It was then that He was able to pray the more earnestly and to sweat blood.

The meaning of the agony is in the thrice repeated cry, "If it be possible, let this cup pass from me" (Mt 26:36–46; Mk 14:32–42; Lk 22:39–46). It was not the pains of physical death from which Jesus shrank. It was the prospect of becoming the bearer of sin. There was an instinctive, agonizing shrinking of His whole being from the horror of bearing the sin of the whole world and the withdrawal of the light of God's face. None but the perfect Christ could compass the weight of all man's guilt, anguish, sorrow, and pain as He consented to be bruised and crushed by our iniquities. The NT reserves the word agony for this one supreme redemptive contest. *See* Affliction; Suffering.

W. T. D.

AGORA (ăg'ŏ-rȧ). The gathering place was the public open space in town, city, or country where the people congregated. From its use for display and exchange of goods, it was called the marketplace or bazaar. It was often at or near the gate of the city, as the bazaar of Old Jerusa-

The Church of All Nations at the foot of the Mount of Olives covers the traditional rock of agony. To the left of the church is the Garden of Gethsemane. HFV

The Agora at Athens with the reconstructed Stoa of Affalos in the background. HFV

lem just inside the Damascus Gate. But business fanned out into adjoining areas, which came to be known as the street of the bakers or of the coppersmiths.

Marketing was only one of the activities. Children assembled for song, dance, and play (Mt 11:16, 17; Lk 7:32); the idle awaited employment or sought the latest gossip (Mt 20:1-16); those who wanted to attract attention came where people assembled (Mt 23:3-7; Mk 12:38; Lk 11:43; 20:46); the sick sought treatment (Mk 6:56); preliminary hearings for trials were held here where rulers could be found (Acts 16:19); and the public gathering served as a sounding board of free speech for religious, philosophical, and political discussion (Acts 17:17). The agora of Athens was the scene of peripatetic (sauntering) schools of philosophy.

W. T. D.

AGRAPHA (ăg'rȧ-fȧ). Commonly used to refer to alleged sayings of Christ not written in the Gospels (or in the NT; as, e.g., a few of His sayings which appear in Acts and the epistles).

A number of alleged sayings of Jesus are found in non-canonical sources. First, a few are preserved in later MSS of the NT; e.g., the one in Codex Beza after Lk 6:4 (in the footnotes of Nestle). Also some of the early Church Fathers added a number of sayings of Jesus, like that of Justin: "In whatsoever things I shall take you, in these I shall judge you" (Dial. with Trypho 47). These are, however, very few, unimportant, and are probably only fanciful citations.

In 1897 and 1903 Grenfell and Hunt found three papyri in Egypt that occasioned much interest. These included about 14 "sayings" of Jesus, half of which equal sayings in the Gospels. The non-canonical sayings are out of character; therefore surely not genuine. One of the more famous ends, for example, in pantheism: "Raise the stone and thou shalt find me; cleave the wood and there I am." The source of these sayings is unknown, but it has been argued that they came from a 2nd cen. collection of sayings of Jesus (ISBE art. *Logia*). This conclusion is now largely confirmed, though some reconstruction of damaged portions has been shown to be fallacious.

In 1946 there was discovered in Egypt at Chenoboskion (q.v.) an amazing cache of documents. Some of these are in Coptic and include Gnostic works and apocryphal materials composed in Gr. in the 2nd cen. Related finds are the Bodmer papyri, including important early copies of books of the Gr. NT. The Gnostic works include a Gospel of Thomas (not the previously known Gospel of the Infancy allegedly by Thomas), which is a collection of 114 sayings of Jesus. These include the sayings discovered earlier by Grenfell and Hunt. Some of the others parallel our Gospels; some do not. Again, the non-canonical sayings are usually widely out of character and have little chance of being genuine. A work entitled The Gospel of Truth is a discussion of Gnostic views but gives no sayings of Christ. Another work is entitled The Gospel of Philip. All three are dated by F. L. Filson (BA, XXIV, 1961, pp. 8–18) and others as in the 2nd cen. They are Gnostic and help greatly in studying that movement. But there is no clear indication that any of these sayings are genuine. They add nothing clear, sure, or of value to our Gospels.

See Gnosticism.

R. L. H.

AGRICULTURE. The production of crops from the soil and the raising of livestock. The word "agriculture" is not used in the Bible, but the idea is conveyed by the term "husbandry" (Heb. *'ădāmâ*, II Chr 26:10; Gr. *geōrgion*, I Cor 3:9). The term "husbandman" is frequently used; e.g., Gen 9:20; Jer 31:24; 51:23; Mt 21:33–41; Jn 15:1; Jas 5:7.

Agriculture in the Bible. The importance of agriculture in the Bible is indicated by numerous references to the farmer and the shepherd. The many agrarian laws in the OT reflect the fact that throughout the whole period of Israel's national history the principal occupation was agriculture.

It is mentioned in connection with the earliest activities of the human race. Cain is said to have cultivated the ground (Gen 4:2). God was regarded as the founder of husbandry (Isa 28:26). No other area of Israelite life has supplied so many figures of speech to enrich the thought and language of the Bible as agriculture. The blessings of the messianic future are described in terms of fertile fields, fruit trees, and vineyards (Amos 9:14; Zech 8:12), while the disappointment of a crop failure was symbolical of sorrow or judgment (Isa 16:10). The language of Jesus illustrates the importance of figures related to the agricultural life of Palestine (Lk 6:43–44). Good examples are seen in the parable of the fig tree (Mt 24:32), the parable of the laborers in the vineyard (Mt 20:1–16), the parable of the sower (Mk 4:1–20).

The calendar and methods of the husbandman. The land was thought of as being the property of the Lord (Lev 25:23), and the husbandman enjoyed the privilege of its use. *See* Land and Property. The crops depended on the seasons, which in turn were determined by God. In many ways the religious calendar of the Israelites reflected the agricultural life of the people. The so-called Gezer Calendar (*see* Calendar), in seven lines of doggerel, provides a summary of the agricultural activities in the period of the beginning of the divided monarchy. The months are mnemonically arranged according to the main agricultural activities of the year. The three major festivals (Feast of Unleavened Bread, Feast of Weeks or Pentecost, and Feast of Tabernacles, Ex 23:14–17; Deut 16:16), which the Israelite was under obligation to attend in Jerusalem, were basically agricultural in character. They were related to the seasons and the products of the soil, and were observed at the beginning and at the end of the grain harvest, and the final ingathering of all the crops of the year.

The agricultural year began with the advent of the early rains, which had the effect of softening the ground baked hard by the heat of the summer sun. The early or former rains began during the latter half of October. Delay of these rains, or scanty rains in the spring or the "latter rain," would endanger the crop.

The major supply of water for agriculture was from the rains and dew (Gen 27:28, 39; I Kgs 17:1; Hag 1:10), but underground water sources were sometimes utilized. Some irrigation was developed by the use of Jordan River water, and by channels from cisterns hewn out of rock (Ps 1; Deut 8:7; Ezk 17:8). Israel's greater dependence on the rains is contrasted with Egypt's total dependence on irrigation (*q.v.*) in Deut 11:10–12. The dependence of Israel upon the Lord for His gift of rain is indicated in many references (Deut 11:14; Jer 3:3; 5:24; Joel 2:23; Zech 10:1). The farmer's major enemy was drought; but locusts, plant mildew, hot sirocco winds and pillaging in war also might take a heavy toll.

The principle of crop rotation is suggested in the regulation that a field (*q.v.*) should lie fallow for one year in every seven (Ex 23:10). Plowing was done usually with a simple plow drawn by oxen or cows, and reaping with a sickle of

A terracotta model of a plowing scene, third millennium B.C. Cyprus Museum

Israelis harvesting olives. IIS

dicate the variety of foods which could be grown in ancient times. Three products dominated the market in Palestine—wheat, wine, and olive oil (Ps 104:15; Joel 2:19); these were also the chief exports. Thus the four most important branches of agriculture were the growing of grain, vineyards, olives and the raising of flocks. *See* Vine; Wine; Plants; Shepherd; Animals.

Of the grains, wheat was the most valuable product (I Kgs 5:11). It was sown in late October or early November when the rains had started, and was harvested during the end of May or the beginning of June. Barley was more common and was used for bread (Jud 7:13; II Kgs 4:42). It was also used for fodder (I Kgs 4:28), which perhaps indicates that it was considered an inferior grade of food. Barley was sown the same time as wheat but could be grown on poorer soil and was harvested about a month earlier (Ruth 2:23). Spelt was also cultivated (Ex 9:32). The Heb. word is translated "rie" in the KJV. Spelt was sown around the edges of the barley and wheat fields (Isa 28:25). It apparently was an inferior species of wheat. Flax was another important crop (Josh 2:6; Isa 19:9; Hos 2:5, 9). Rope and linen cloth were made from flax.

The fig was a significant delicacy. It was, together with the date, an important source of sugar. The sycamore fig, which was an inferior type, was treated in a special way to improve its quality. In Amos 7:14, the prophet says that he was "a dresser [or pincher] of sycomore trees." The fig was used for medicinal purposes as appears from Isa 38:21. The date palm tree was widely used and was grown especially in the Jordan Valley (Deut 34:3; Jud 1:16). Dates were made into cakes, as were figs, and there was also date honey and date syrup.

Legume-producing plants were lentils and beans, which were sometimes used for the making of bread (II Sam 17:28; Ezk 4:9). Melons and cucumbers constituted part of the diet and were particularly refreshing in such a hot cli-

wood and flint, or of iron (Deut 16:9; 23:25; Jud 14:18; I Kgs 19:19; Job 1:14; Amos 6:12). Threshing *(q.v.)* and winnowing were done on a hard threshing floor. Oxen trod out the grain and sometimes a threshing sledge was used (Isa 28:27*a*; 41:15). Flails or sticks were sufficient to beat out the smaller harvests (Isa 28:27*b*; Jud 6:11, RSV). In winnowing the threshed grain, the workers tossed it by means of a pitchfork, shovel, or "fan" *(q.v.)* into the air to permit the breeze to blow away the fine chaff (Mt 3:12; Ps 1:4). The heavier kernels fell at their feet. To remove bits of straw the grain was sifted (cf. Lk 22:31). The cut straw and stubble could be used as fuel, or was left in the field and burned (Lk 3:17; Isa 47:14; Mal 4:1).

The ass and the mule also served as draft animals. The farmer used his goad also to break the clods. The ground was leveled with an implement resembling a stone boat, or with a roller (Job 39:10; Isa 28:24–25; Hos 10:11). The seed was sown by hand. Spelt, barley, and wheat were frequently placed in the furrow, and in the time of the Mishna the seed was plowed in.

The products of agriculture. The general diet of Israel is reflected in such references as I Sam 25:18 and Num 11:5, and together they in-

A threshing scene near Jerash, Jordan. HFV

mate. As is the case today, the poor might live for months on bread and melons or cucumbers alone. Leeks, garlic, and onions were used for seasoning. Cummin and coriander are mentioned (Isa 28:25; Ex 16:31). The NT adds anise, mint, rue, and mustard (Mt 13:31; 23:23; Lk 11:42). *See* Food; Harvest.

Bibliography. ANEP, figs. #84–102. Denis Baly, *The Geography of the Bible*, New York: Harper, 1957, especially pp. 97–108. A. C. Bouquet, *Everyday Life in NT Times*, New York: Scribner's, 1954, pp. 74–94. CornPBE, pp. 17–30, 238–243. E. W. Heaton, *Everyday Life in OT Times*, New York: Scribner's, 1956, pp. 97–112. Madeleine S. and J. Lane Miller, *Encyclopedia of Bible Life*, New York: Harper, 1944, pp. 1–24. William M. Thomson, *The Land and the Book*, Grand Rapids: Baker, 1954. Lucian Turkowski, "Peasant Agriculture in the Judean Hills," PEQ, CI (1969), 21–33, 101–112. G. Ernest Wright, *Biblical Archaeology*, rev. ed., Philadelphia: Westminster, 1962, pp. 183–187.

A. C. S.

AGRIPPA I, HEROD (hĕr'ŏd á-grĭp'á). He is called Herod the King in Acts 12:1. He was a son of Aristobulus and Bernice, and grandson of Herod the Great and Mariamne. The royal Asmonean line, though nearly extinguished by the murderous jealousy of Herod the Great, was preserved in Agrippa. In him the kingdom of Herod came again to glory.

Agrippa was born about 10 B.C. and moved to Rome at the age of six. He was brought up with Drusus, son of Tiberius; with Antonia, wife of Drusus; and with Claudius. Though but a private citizen, he was far-seeing and cultivated every opportunity of advancement. His brilliant prospects made available a supply of money for luxury and extravagance. But after Drusus died suddenly in A.D. 23, the emperor declined to receive the high-spirited young man. His companions forsook him. Deeply in debt, he fled from Rome to a fortress in Malatha in Idumea.

His wife, Cypros, through his sister Herodias, wife of Herod Antipas, obtained a position for him as a market overseer at Tiberias with aedile rank and a small annuity (Jos *Ant.* xviii.6.2). Having quarreled with his brother-in-law, who made him feel his dependent position, he fled to Flaccus, proconsul of Syria. Convicted of a bribe, he fled again, and, as he was about to sail for Italy, was arrested for a sum of money owed to the Roman treasury. He escaped to Alexandria, where his wife procured a loan for him. Thence he sailed to Puteoli and was favorably received by the aged Tiberius. Back in Rome, he made fast friends with Caius Caligula, heir presumptive to the Roman throne. One day he expressed the wish that Caius might soon succeed to the throne. Reported to the emperor, he was cast in prison.

When Caligula succeeded Tiberius (A.D. 37),

A plowing scene from a tomb of a noble at Thebes, Egypt. Gaddis, Luxor

he freed Agrippa, gave him the tetrarchy of Philip and the territory of Lysanias II with the title of king, exchanged the iron chain with which he had been bound for a gold one of the same weight, and induced the Senate to invest him with the rank of praetor. Herod Antipas and his wife, being jealous of the distinctions conferred, sailed to Rome to supplant him in the emperor's favor. Agrippa anticipated the action by countercharges against Antipas of treasonous correspondence with the Parthians. When the charges were not answered, Antipas was exiled, and the tetrarchies of Galilee and Perea were added to Agrippa in A.D. 39. Then when Caligula was assassinated and the imperial crown was offered to the weak and indifferent Claudius, it was Agrippa who led him to accept the honor. In A.D. 40 Claudius added Judea and Samaria to Agrippa and confirmed the grant of the tetrarchy of Lysanias. He then possessed the entire kingdom of Herod the Great. In addition, he begged from Claudius the kingdom of Chalcis for his brother (who was then called Herod of Chalcis) and obtained consular rank for himself.

His reign over the total domain was for only three years, but it was considered a happy one for the Jews. He was the most affable and popular ruler of the Herodian family. He showed such tact and respect for the feelings of his countrymen that the Talmud and other Jewish literature praise him as a pious and beloved devotee of their religion.

The first act by which Agrippa celebrated his return to Palestine was one of piety. The golden chain which Caligula had bestowed on him, he hung up within the limits of the temple, over the treasury, as a memorial. At the same time, he presented a thankoffering, "because he would not neglect any precept of the law," and bore the expenses of a large number of Nazarites that they might discharge the obligation of their vows (*Ant.* 19.6.1).

Agrippa won the gratitude and good wishes of the Jews by persuading Caligula to desist from his attempt to have his own statue placed in the temple in Jerusalem. This was done with real hazard to his own security and fortunes. Two other attempted favors to the Jews were less successful. In order to strengthen the fortifications of Jerusalem, the capital, he began to build on the N of the city a powerful new wall which, according to Josephus, would have made the city impregnable. But at the instigation of Marsus, governor of Syria, Claudius issued an injunction against its continuance. Of still more importance was Agrippa's conference of princes at Tiberias. Five Roman vassal kings answered the invitation. Again the governor of Syria was suspicious of their designs. He appeared at Tiberias and ordered the other guests to return home without delay.

Agrippa I liked to live in Jerusalem and was strictly careful of the laws of the Jews while there, letting no day pass without its appointed sacrifice. The Talmud relates how as a simple Israelite, he with his own hand presented the firstfruits in the temple (Mishna, *Bikkurim,* iii. 4). When he betrothed his daughter Drusilla to King Antiochus of Commagene, he made him promise first to be circumcised. By such displays of piety he gave abundant satisfaction to the people and befriended the Pharisees. At the Feast of Tabernacles in A.D. 41, he read Deut 17:15, according to the old custom, and burst forth in tears at the words, "Thou mayest not set a stranger over thee, which is not thy brother." The people cried out, "Be not grieved, Agrippa! Thou art our brother!" His strong desire to please the Jews seems to be the reason for his persecution of the Christians (Acts 12:1–3), whom the Jews hated.

It is too much to believe that Agrippa was a Pharisee by conviction. His piety was only in the Holy Land. Elsewhere, he was a liberal patron of Gr. culture. In Berytus he cultivated pagan magnificence, building a beautiful theater, an amphitheater, baths, and piazzas. Games and sports of all kinds were celebrated, including gladiatorial combats in which, on one occasion, 1,400 men were killed. While coins stamped in Jerusalem had no offensive images, those minted outside bore likenesses of Agrippa or the emperor. He was more affable and sly than Herod the Great, but was moved more by a desire for peace than by piety.

In A.D. 44 he celebrated games at Caesarea to honor the emperor and to make vows for his safety. A number of principal persons in the province attended. The second day he appeared in the theater in a garment interwoven with silver. At the close of his address to the people they saluted him as a god. He did not rebuke them. A sharp pain seized him and he died five days later, in his fifty-fourth year. The NT calls it an act of God (Acts 12:23). With him the Herodian power had virtually run its course. He left three daughters (Bernice, Mariamne, and Drusilla) and a son of 17 (Agrippa), to whom the Romans were not yet ready to entrust the government.

See Herod. For bibliography *see* Herod.

W. T. D.

AGRIPPA II, HEROD. The only son of Agrippa I and Cypros, he was the last of the royal Herodian line. Marcus Julius Agrippa, as he was named, received a royal education at Rome in the palace of the emperor. Being only 17 when his father died in A.D. 44, he was considered too young to rule over the difficult kingdom of the Jews. Claudius sent Cuspius Fadus as procurator and thus restored the land of the Jews to a Roman province. In the meantime, the youth was useful to his countrymen at Rome through his influence at the court.

When his uncle, Herod of Chalcis, died (A.D. 48), Claudius conferred on Agrippa the little province of Chalcis with the oversight of the temple and the right to appoint the high priest. This latter right he exercised from time to time down to A.D. 66, but his impulsive appointments offended the Jews. Agrippa continued to reside in Rome, for the most part at least, until A.D. 53, when Claudius, in exchange for Chalcis, bestowed on him the larger tetrarchies which had formerly been held by Lysanias and Herod Philip. Later, Nero added important parts of Galilee and Perea, including Tiberias, Tarichea, and the lands belonging to them. The title of king was permitted.

Agrippa's private life was blighted by scandal. His sister Bernice, widow of Herod of Chalcis, moved to his house in A.D. 48 and soon had the weak man in her control. Their incestuous relationship was commonly discussed in Rome as well as among the Jews. To stop the report, Bernice married Polemon of Cilicia, but soon returned to her brother and apparently resumed the old relations.

The public policy of his reign reflected complete dependence upon Rome. He provided auxiliary troops in the Parthian campaign of A.D. 54. When the new procurator Festus arrived in Palestine, he and Bernice hastened with great pomp to offer him a welcome (Acts 25:13, 23). His coins, almost without exception, bore the names and images of the reigning emperor (Nero, Vespasian, Titus, and Domitian). He seems to have been more of a visitor at Jerusalem than a resident. His gestures toward Jewish law were less extravagant than his father's and proved less convincing to the people.

However, Agrippa did seek to keep on good terms with Judaism. His brothers-in-law, Azizus of Emesa and Polemon of Cilicia, were required to be circumcised. Questions of law were put by the king directly or indirectly to Rabbi Elieser. Even Bernice took a vow in Jerusalem, shaving her head and going barefoot. But the general, undisguised mood was one of indifference. Rather than please the Jews by quick condemnation of Paul, as his father would likely have done, he indulged his curiosity with a hearing (Acts 26:1). Then admitting the force of Paul's argument, he straightway dismissed it (Acts 26:28). His interest was in external matters. He imported wood from Lebanon to support the temple when its foundations began to sink, allowed the psalm-singing Levites to wear the linen garments of the priests, and paved Jerusalem with marble. But he had no reputation for personal piety.

When in A.D. 66 the revolution broke out, Agrippa earnestly warned the nation against revolt. When the peace party was defeated, Agrippa stood unflinchingly loyal to Rome, even though much of his territory joined the rebellion. He entertained the Roman general Vespasian magnificently in Caesarea Philippi, fought on the Roman side, was wounded at the siege of Gamala, became a companion of Titus (to whom the war had been entrusted), and almost certainly joined in the festive celebration at Caesarea Philippi to rejoice over the destruction of the Jews in the war. His loyalty to Rome was rewarded by additions to his territory. But he and Bernice resided in Rome, where he died in the reign of Trajan in A.D. 100 without heir. His kingdom was undoubtedly incorporated in the province of Syria.

See Herod.

W. T. D.

AGUR (ā'gûr).The writer of Prov 30.

AH. An emotional term usually expressing hesitance or complaint (Jer 1:6; 4:10; 14:13; 32:17; Ezk 4:14; 9:8; 11:13; 20:49).

AHAB (ā'hăb)

1. A false prophet, son of Kolaiah. He was deported to Babylon and denounced by Jeremiah (Jer 29:21).

2. The seventh king of Israel, son and successor of Omri. In the book of Kings he appears as both a politically strong and a spiritually weak king. On the secular side, he was able to win the respect of both friend and foe. On the religious side, his syncretistic practices spelled the doom of the house of Omri. His reign is listed as 22 years (I Kgs 16:29), which Thiele gives as 874 to 853 B.C. (*The Mysterious Numbers of the Hebrew Kings*, p. 61).

His political marriage with Jezebel resulted in mixed blessing and curse. The attendant alliance with Ethbaal, king of the Tyrians and father of Jezebel, brought increased trade, wealth, and a growing merchant class to Israel. However, Jezebel brought with her a form of Baalism which clashed head on with the worship of the Lord. With fanatical zeal, she pushed forward the cult associated with Baal-Melcarth and Asherah, gradually engulfing Ahab by her ruthless vigor. Later Ahab introduced this form of Baalism into Judah by giving his daughter Athaliah in marriage to Jehoram, son of Jehoshaphat.

Ruins of Ahab's palace, Samaria. HFV

Neither Ahab nor Jezebel was able to stand unopposed. Elijah, the Tishbite, appeared repeatedly as an accusing conscience. He was the champion of the common man as he confronted Ahab in the vineyard of Naboth. He was the champion of the worship of God in the victory on Mount Carmel.

While the Elijah stories present Ahab as weak and dominated by Jezebel, other aspects of his reign demonstrate his stronger points. His building operations were extensive and outstanding. At Samaria, he continued the construction begun by his father Omri. Excavations at Samaria have illustrated how strong were the walls which later were to withstand three years of siege. Carved ivories from Samaria are illustrative of the furnishings which went into his "house of ivory" at Jezreel. It was during his reign and possibly on his orders that Jericho was rebuilt by Hiel of Bethel. Other cities were rebuilt and fortified during this period.

Ahab's reign was a time of constant international conflict. He is shown fighting against the Syrian kingdom of Damascus (I Kgs 20), fighting with them against the Assyrians in the battle of Qarqar (records of Shalmanezer III), and finally aligned with Judah against Ben-hadad of Syria at Ramoth-gilead (I Kgs 22). In this battle to win back Ramoth-gilead from the Syrians, Ahab was struck down by an arrow shot at random. The king died, and his kingdom declined rapidly after his death, Moab and other subject areas rebelling and winning independence from Israel (II Kgs 1:1).

K. M. Y.

AHARAH (à-hâr'à). A son of Benjamin (I Chr 8:1). The list of the sons of Benjamin given in Gen 46:21 does not include Aharah, but Ehi may be the same. In Num 26:38 the third son of Benjamin is called Ahiram.

Ahasuerus (Xerxes) here stands behind his enthroned father (Darius); from the treasury at Persepolis, the Persian capital. ORINST

AHARHEL (*a*-här′hĕl). Perhaps a descendant of Caleb. It is certain he was of the tribe of Judah and son of Harum (I Chr 4:8).

AHASAI (*a*-hā′sī). A priest among those who returned from Exile (Neh 11:13). This name is spelled Ahzai in RSV. He is also called Jahzerah (I Chr 9:12).

AHASBAI (*a*-hăs′bī). A Maachathite, the father of Eliphelet, one of the mighty men of David known as the "thirty" (II Sam 23:34). In the parallel passage (I Chr 11:35*b*–36*a*), his name seems to be Ur.

AHASUERUS (*a*-hăzh′ŏo-ĕr′ŭs). Better known by his Gr. name Xerxes (486–465 B.C.), he was the son of Darius I and father of Artaxerxes I. Scripture indicates that he ruled a vast empire from India to Ethiopia (Est 1:1; cf. Herodotus 7:9), deposed Vashti as queen in 483 B.C., and chose Esther in 478 B.C. Four years later he gave permission to Haman to destroy the Jewish nation; but the plot was thwarted by the providence of God (473 B.C.). This great deliverance is celebrated at the Feast of Purim (Est 9:28). *See* Esther; Esther, Book of.

Ahasuerus (Xerxes) is depicted in the book of Esther as a fickle and vain monarch, and this seems to be confirmed by other historical sources. Because of a rebellion in Babylon, he had the city partially destroyed (482 B.C.). Two years later his great fleet was defeated at Salamis and Samos, and his army was routed at Plataea when he tried to conquer the Greeks.

The taking of a new wife in his seventh year (Est 2:16) fits Herodotus' description of the new interest he manifested in his harem after the disastrous Gr. campaign (9:108). Various court intrigues plus work on the new palace at Persepolis occupied his remaining years until he was assassinated in his bedchamber, August, 465 B.C.

Ezr 4:6 was formerly applied to Cambyses (530–522 B.C.), but it is definitely a reference to Xerxes, constituting part of a parenthetical summary of opposition to the rebuilding of Jerusalem and its walls (Ezr 4:6–23). Although he is not named, Xerxes was probably the fourth Persian king after Cyrus mentioned in Dan 11:2 (following Cambyses, Pseudo-Smerdis, and Darius I): "the fourth shall be far richer than they all: and when he is waxed strong through his riches, he shall stir up all against the realm of Greece" (ASV).

The Ahasuerus of Dan 9:1, father of Darius the Mede, is not otherwise known to history.

J. C. W.

AHAVA (*a*-hā′vȧ). A Babylonian town along a small river or canal of the same name on whose banks Ezra assembled the Jews who were to return to Jerusalem with him (Ezr 8:15, 21, 31).

AHAZ (ā′hăz). The twelfth ruler of Judah, son of Jotham. He was 20 years of age when he ascended the throne, and he reigned for 16 years (732–716 B.C.; see II Kgs 16:2; II Chr 28:1). Ahaz was given to idolatry, following the practices of the northern kingdom. He even went so far as to sacrifice a son to pagan gods.

Politically, Ahaz was at odds with Pekah, king of Israel, and with Rezin, king of Syria. They decided to attack Jerusalem and set a puppet, "the son of Tabeel" (Isa 7:6), on the throne of Judah, but they were unsuccessful. However, the Edomites took advantage of Judah's plight by capturing Elath on the Gulf of Aqaba (II Kgs 16:5–6).

The prophet Isaiah lived in Jerusalem at the time and sought to encourage Ahaz by giving him the virgin birth prophecy as a sign of God's delivering power (Isa 7:3-17), but Ahaz refused to accept the challenge to believe God. Instead, he sent messengers, with some of the temple treasure, to enlist the aid of Assyria's Tiglath-pileser III, who promptly destroyed Damascus (c. 732 B.C.). Ahaz went to Damascus where Tiglath-pileser gave him specifications for a new altar for the temple court (II Kgs 16:7-10).

The Chronicles give a more vivid account of Ahaz's wickedness and the devastation of Judah by Syria and Israel. Pekah is said to have slain 120,000 soldiers and taken captive 200,000 of the inhabitants of Judah. However, the prophet Obed warned Pekah to be merciful or else suffer divine punishment. In response to this message, the Israelites properly clothed the captives and returned them to Judah (II Chr 28:5-15). The Chronicler notes that the Philistines also had taken several cities from Ahaz at this time, and that after the Assyrians had helped Ahaz by destroying Syria and Israel, they turned on him, exacting tribute. Ahaz spent his last days as a helpless puppet of Assyria (II Chr 28:16-27).

G. H. L.

AHAZIAH (ā'hȧ-zī'ȧ)

1. Ahaziah followed Ahab, his father, to the throne of Israel in 853 B.C. and reigned two years. He joined Jehoshaphat, king of Judah, in building a merchant fleet, but it displeased God and the fleet was destroyed (I Kgs 22:40, 48-53; II Chr 20:35-37). Ahaziah accidently fell out a second story window and was severely hurt. He sent messengers to Ekron to inquire of Baalzebub whether he would recover, but Elijah, at God's bidding, stopped the messengers and sent them back with word that Ahaziah would die. In anger, Ahaziah sent 50 soldiers twice to bring Elijah to him, but fire from heaven struck each company dead. The captain of a third company of 50 soldiers begged Elijah for mercy; so at God's command Elijah went to Ahaziah and warned him personally of his coming death. Within a short time, Ahaziah died (II Kgs 1). His brother Jehoram became the next king.

2. There was also a king of Judah by the name of Ahaziah who reigned but a short time in 841 B.C. He was a nephew of Ahaziah of the northern kingdom of Israel and a grandson of Ahab, for his mother was Athaliah, Ahab's daughter. His father was Jehoram, son of Jehoshaphat. Ahaziah was 22 years old when he ascended the throne and soon joined with Joram, king of Israel, in an expedition against Syria. The battle was lost, Joram was wounded, and Jehu, one of his generals, rose in revolt. He killed Joram and Jezebel and wounded Ahaziah, who later died at Megiddo but was buried in Jerusalem (II Kgs 8:28-9:37). The account in II Chr 22:7-9 emphasizes the guilt of Aha-

ziah and condemns his alliance with Joram (Jehoram) by stating that it was because of their close friendship that Jehu killed him. Ahaziah was also called Jehoahaz (q.v.; II Chr 21:17; 25:23).

G. H. L.

AHBAN (ä'băn). One of the sons of Abishur by Abihail in the genealogy of Jerahmeel, a man of Judah (I Chr 2:29).

AHER (ā'hĕr). A Benjamite (I Chr 7:12). Identified in the ASV marg. as the Ahiram of Num 26:38.

AHI (ā'hī)

1. Chief of the Gadites in Gilead in Bashan (I Chr 5:15).

2. A son of Shamer (I Chr 7:34).

AHIAH (ȧ-hī'ȧ). Three OT characters are so identified in KJV, though elsewhere (and throughout ASV) this same name appears as Ahijah (q.v.).

1. A warrior (I Chr 8:7; possibly the same as the earlier Ahoah, 8:4), who, with Naaman, was led by Gera to take captive two sons of Ehud.

2. A great-grandson of Eli, through Phinehas and Ahitub (brother of Ichabod), and high priest during Saul's early reign (I Sam 14:3). He brought the ark to Gibeah at the battle of Michmash (14:18) and later encouraged Saul to seek God (14:36). Ahiah was succeeded by his younger brother Ahimelech (I Sam 22:9), unless these two are to be equated (KD, *Samuel*, pp. 136-7).

3. A son of Shisha (I Kgs 4:3) who, with his brother Elihoreph, served Solomon as "scribe" (secretary of state, or finance, II Kgs 22:3-9; Isa 22:15; 36:3; *see* Scribe), as his father (q.v.) had under David (II Sam 8:17; 20:25; I Chr 18:16).

J. B. P.

AHIAM (ȧ-hī'ȧm). One of David's mighty men of the company of "thirty," a son of Sacar (I Chr 11:35) or Sharar (II Sam 23:33).

AHIAN (ȧ-hī'ȧn). Of the family of Shemidah, of Manasseh's tribe (I Chr 7:19).

AHIEZER (ā'hī-ē'zēr)

1. A representative of the Danites who assisted Moses in the census. The son of Ammishaddai (Num 1:12; 2:25), he was also captain of the rear guard for the march (Num 10:25).

2. From Gibeath, he came to David's aid at Ziklag. He was a leader of the Benjamite bowmen (I Chr 12:3).

AHIHUD (ȧ-hī'hŭd)

1. An Asherite leader, son of Shelomi (Num 34:27). He was appointed to divide the W Jordan territory among the ten tribes in that area.

2. A head of the house of Benjamin (I Chr 8:7), a son of either Heglam (RSV) or Gera

(KJV). The Heb. phrase "he removed them" (KJV), may be rendered as the name "Heglam," thus changing the father from Gera to Heglam.

AHIJAH (á-hī'já). In KJV this name sometimes appears as Ahiah (q.v.).

1. An Ephraimite from Shiloh, a prophet of God, who, meeting Jeroboam returning from exile in Egypt, tore his own new garment into twelve pieces and gave ten pieces to Jeroboam, indicating God's intention to make him king over the ten tribes of the northern kingdom (I Kgs 11:29–39). Much later, when he had become king, at the serious illness of his son, Jeroboam sent his disguised wife to now blind Ahijah to inquire whether the child would recover. By revelation, Ahijah knew the disguised queen and predicted the child's death (I Kgs 14:1–18). He wrote of Solomon's "acts" (II Chr 9:29).

2. The father of Baasha, king of Israel (I Kgs 15:27, 33).

3. A son of Jerahmeel, and descendant of Judah through Pharez and Hezron (I Chr 2:25).

4. A Pelonite, one of David's mighty men (I Chr 11:36). *See also* Paltite.

5. A Levite set over the treasures of the house of God in David's reign (I Chr 26:20). LXX translates the Heb. as "the Levites, their brethren."

6. A chief of the people in Nehemiah's day, among those who sealed a covenant to walk uprightly before God (Neh 10:26; cf. 10:14). The name is translated Ahiah in RSV.

H. G. S.

AHIKAM (á-hī'kăm). The son of Shaphan the scribe, he was a companion of Shaphan and Hilkiah the priest when Shaphan read to King Josiah a copy of the law found in the course of repairing the temple. He was sent with Hilkiah, Achbor, Shaphan and Asahiah to inquire of Huldah the prophetess concerning the future of Judah relative to the curses read out of the law (II Kgs 22:8–14). Through the protection of Ahikam, Jeremiah was saved from death at the hands of false prophets (Jer 26:24). Ahikam was the father of Gedaliah, governor of Judah under the Babylonians (II Kgs 25:22).

AHILUD (á-hī'lŭd). Father of the recorder Jehoshaphat under rule of David (II Sam 8:16; I Kgs 4:3; I Chr 18:15) and, probably, the father of Solomon's district officer Baana (I Kgs 4:12).

AHIMAAZ (á-hǐm'á-ăz)

1. The father of Ahinoam, wife of Saul first king of Israel (I Sam 14:50).

2. One of two sons of Zadok who was high priest in David's time when Absalom raised rebellion against David (II Sam 15:27; I Chr 6:8, 53). With Jonathan, son of Abiathar a priest, Ahimaaz was to carry information to David concerning Absalom's plans and move-

ments from Zadok and Abiathar in Jerusalem (II Sam 15:35–36). News of Absalom's plan to trap David in some corner was transmitted to them in En-rogel by a woman. They were seen by one who informed Absalom, but after concealment by a woman in Bahurim safely took the news to David (II Sam 17:15–21). At the death of Absalom in the Wood of Ephraim (q.v.), when Ahimaaz requested permission to bear the news to David, Joab refused it, but Ahimaaz persisted and finally was given permission. He gave David incomplete news, however; but Cushi soon made known the fact of Absalom's death (II Sam 18:19–32).

3. An officer of Solomon in the tribe of Naphtali responsible for provisions for Solomon's table for the seventh month. His wife was Solomon's daughter Basmath (I Kgs 4:7, 15).

H. G. S.

AHIMAN (á-hī'măn)

1. A son of Anak, and probably founder of a family of Anakim (Num 13:22), he was one of the giants (*see* Anak) driven from Hebron by Caleb (Josh 15:14; Jud 1:10).

2. A Levite who served as porter for the house of God (I Chr 9:17).

AHIMELECH (á-hǐm'é-lěk)

1. A son of Ahitub, a priest at Nob (I Sam 22:9), from whom David, pretending to be on King Saul's business, received showbread for food and the sword of Goliath when he fled from Saul (I Sam 21:1–9). (Mk 2:26 places this event in the time of Abiathar [q.v.], son of Ahimelech.) Ahimelech's aid to David was reported to Saul by Doeg the Edomite, who had observed them. Saul interpreted it as treachery on the part of all the priests. On the basis of this unsubstantiated report Saul ordered Doeg to slay Ahimelech and 84 other priests. Doeg also put the sword to the town of Nob, from which Abiathar alone escaped to bear the news to David (I Sam 22:6–20).

2. Son of Abiathar and grandson of Ahimelech. He was a priest with Zadok, son of Ahitub, in David's reign (II Sam 8:17; I Chr 24:3, 6, 31).

3. A Hittite and follower in David's band when Saul pursued him (I Sam 26:6).

H. G. S.

AHIMOTH (á-hī'mŏth). A Levite, son of Elkanah and brother of Amasai (I Chr 6:25).

AHINADAB (á-hǐn'á-dăb). A purveyor in Mahanaim for Solomon, he was the son of Iddo (I Kgs 4:14).

AHINOAM (á-hǐn'ō-ăm)

1. The daughter of Ahimaaz and wife of Saul (I Sam 14:50).

2. One of David's wives, a woman of Jezreel (I Sam 25:43). Captured by the Amalekites, she was rescued by David (I Sam 30:5), and lived

with him in Hebron while he was king of Judah (II Sam 2:2). She was mother of David's eldest son, Amnon (II Sam 3:2).

AHIO (*a*-hī'ō)
1. The son of Abinadab, who with his brother Uzzah was entrusted with the ark when David made his first attempt to take it to Jerusalem (II Sam 6:3–4).
2. Considered the proper name of a Benjamite, son of Elpaal (I Chr 8:14–16).
3. Son of Jehiel, brother of Kish; a Benjamite (I Chr 8:30–31; 9:35–37).

AHIRA (*a*-hī'ra). A prince of the tribe of Naphtali and son of Enan. He helped Moses with the census during the wilderness wanderings (Num 1:15; 2:29; 7:78; 10:27).

AHIRAM (*a*-hī'ram). The third son of Benjamin; the head of the family called Ahiramites (Num 26:38). Also referred to as Aharah (I Chr 8:1).

AHISAMACH (*a*-hĭs'*a*-măk). From the tribe of Dan, father of Aholiab, he was one of the craftsmen of the tabernacle and its equipment (Ex 31:6; 35:34; 38:23).

AHISHAHAR (*a*-hĭsh'*a*-här). A descendant of Benjamin through Bilhan and Jediael (I Chr 7:10).

AHISHAR (*a*-hī'shär). The household overseer for Solomon (I Kgs 4:6).

AHITHOPHEL (*a*-hĭth'ō-fĕl). A resident of Giloh, a town in SW Judah (II Sam 15:12; Josh 15:51). One of David's counselors (II Sam 15:12), he was the father of Eliam, one of David's mighty men (II Sam 23:34). Though a discerning and skillful counselor (II Sam 16:23), he was morally unstable, ready to betray David by giving counsel as to how to destroy him (II Sam 17:1–4). When Absalom accepted instead the adverse counsel of delay of Hushai, who was there purposely to defeat Ahithophel's counsel (II Sam 15:34), Ahithophel understood the result to mean the end of the rebellion, and anticipating his punishment when David would return, he went home and hanged himself (II Sam 15:31–34; 16:15; 17:23).

AHITUB (*a*-hī'tŭb)
1. A priest in the line of Ithamar, son of Aaron. He was grandson of Eli the priest at Shiloh, son of Phinehas, and father of Ahimelech the priest (I Sam 14:3).
2. A priest in the line of Eleazar, son of Aaron (I Chr 6:3–7), son of Amariah the priest, and father of Zadok, priest in David's time (I Chr 6:8). He was an ancestor of Ezra (Ezr 7:1–2).
3. A priest, also in the line of Eleazar, son of Aaron, son of a second Amariah and father of a second Zadok (I Chr 6:3–11).

AHLAB (ä'lăb). A town in the territory of Asher from which the Canaanites were not driven out (Jud 1:31). Probably a textual corruption of Mahalab (Josh 19:29, RSV), a town on the coast between Tyre and Achzib, mentioned by Sennacherib as Mahalliba.

AHLAI (ä'lī)
1. The daughter of Sheshan (I Chr 2:31, 34).
2. The father of Zabad (I Chr 11:41).

AHOAH (*a*-hō'*a*). Son of Bela of the family of Benjamin (I Chr 8:4).

AHOHITE (*a*-hō'hīt). A descendant of Ahoah (II Sam 23:9, RSV; I Chr 11:12,29). Apparently used to designate a hero of David's time.

AHOLAH (*a*-hō'lä). A symbolic name (hinting at Israel's schismatic tent-shrine) used in Ezk 23 for the kingdom of Samaria. The unfaithfulness of Israel and Judah was symbolically portrayed in the persons of Aholah and Aholibah (Oholah and Oholibah in RSV), who became harlots while married to the Lord. Aholah's activities were painted in lurid detail in order to show the heinousness of Israel's sin against a background of the unchangeable character of God (Ezk 23:49). Israel's unfaithfulness, begun in Egypt, included political involvement with Assyria and syncretistic worship (Ezk 23:5–10). In poetic justice these very paramours became ministers of divine judgment (Ezk 23:9–10). Samaria was defeated and carried captive by Assyria in 722 B.C.

AHOLIAB (*a*-hō'lĭ-ăb). A craftsman of the tribe of Dan, son of Ahisamach, appointed by Moses to assist Bezaleel in the construction of the tabernacle and its furnishings (Ex 31:6). He was filled with the Spirit of God for his construction task and teaching ministry (Ex 35:34–35). *See* Bezaleel.

AHOLIBAH. *See* Aholah.

AHOLIBAMAH (*a*-hōl-ĭ-bā'ma)
1. The wife of Esau, granddaughter of Zibeon the Horite (Gen 36:20, 25; cf. v. 2). In Gen 36:2 Zibeon is called a Hivite, evidently a textual corruption, since in v. 20 he is clearly a Horite (Kittel), i.e., the name applied to the early occupants of Seir (Gen 14:6), whose personal names were Semitic in contradistinction from the Horites of central Palestine who were non-Semitic Hurrians, called Hivites in Heb. (Gen 34:2) (E. A. Speiser, AASOR, XIII [1931–32], 26–31). Aholibamah's name is not found in the other lists of Esau's wives (Gen 26:34; 28:8–9).
2. Chief of an Edomite clan (Gen 36:41; I Chr 1:52).

AHUMAI (*a*-hū'mī). Head of a family of Judah, the son of Jahath (I Chr 4:2).

AHUZAM (a-hŭz'ăm). In the genealogy of Judah, he is mentioned as a son of Ashur (I Chr 4:5–6).

AHUZZATH (a-hŭz'ăth).The adviser and friend of Abimelech, king of Gerar. He went with Abimelech to Beer-sheba to make a covenant with Isaac (Gen 26:26–31).

AI (ā'ī). A city of the Canaanites situated E of Bethel. Its name means "ruin." After Joshua had conquered Jericho, he sent men to spy out Ai. On the advice of the spies, Joshua sent 3,000 soldiers against Ai, but they suffered defeat. In distress, Joshua prayed for guidance. God answered that someone had sinned by stealing some of the devoted spoil of Jericho. Achan of Judah was singled out as the culprit and, with his family, was promptly stoned to death. Joshua then sent out 30,000 soldiers and by clever strategy captured and destroyed Ai (Josh 7–8).

Evidently a new town was built nearby, for Isaiah speaks of an Aiath through which the Assyrians marched on their way S to Jerusalem (Isa 10:28). Among those who returned from Exile were 223 from Bethel and Ai (Ezr 2:28; see Neh 7:32 where the number is 123). Nehemiah also speaks of an Aija near Bethel (Neh 11:31). Jeremiah mentions an Ai, but it was E of the Jordan in Ammonite territory (Jer 49:3).

The identification of Ai with any known site near Bethel has been a difficult problem for archaeologists. In 1933–35 Judith Marquet-Krause partially excavated a mound known as et-Tell two miles SE of Bethel, but found that though the site had been founded about 3000 B.C., it had been destroyed no later than 2000 B.C. It was occupied again after 1200 B.C., for about a century. This would mean that no city existed on this mound at Joshua's time.

Some scholars then suggested that the story of the destruction of Ai was actually that of the fall of Bethel (q.v.), since excavations at the village of Beitin (Bethel?) have revealed that that city was reduced to ruins by the invading Israelites (see reference to Bethel in Jud 1:22–26). On the other hand, legitimately it could be argued that ancient Ai was located elsewhere near Bethel, or that the remains of the city destroyed by Joshua had been washed or blown away, or that its ruins lay under the present village of Deir Dibwan immediately SE of et-Tell (R. K. Harrison, *Introduction to the Old Testament,* Eerdmans, 1969, pp. 121f., 177, 327ff.; John Rea, WBC, pp. 213f. at Josh 7).

G. H. L.

Attempting to solve the problem of Ai, Joseph A. Callaway began in 1964 a new series of excavations at et-Tell. Four seasons of digging confirmed that the site was not occupied between 2500 and 1200 B.C. Furthermore, his investigations within Deir Dibwan and at several nearby ruins, including Khirbet Haiyan that might possibly have been Ai, revealed nothing earlier than the Herodian period. Callaway believes the large (25 acre) Early Bronze Age city commanded the trade route into the hill country from Jericho from *c.* 2900 to 2500 B.C. and may have become a center of Egyptian influence before it was burned and left a stark ruin. The Iron I Age Israelite village on et-Tell covered less than three acres and was unfortified (BA, XXVIII [1965], 26–30; JBL, LXXXVII [1968], 312–320). David Livingston has suggested a new possibility for the location of Bethel (q.v.) at Bireh, and that Ai may then identify with the small unnamed ruins a mile and a half SE of Bireh ("Location of Biblical Bethel and Ai Reconsidered," WTJ, XXXIII [Nov., 1970], 43).

J. R.

AIAH (ā'yà)
1. Son of Zibeon, brother of Anah, a Horite (Gen 36:24 [Ajah]; I Chr 1:40).
2. The father of Saul's concubine Rizpah (II Sam 3:7; 21:8, 10, 11).

AIATH. *See* Ai.

AIJA. *See* Ai.

AIJALON. *See* Ajalon.

AIJELETH SHAHAR (ā'jĕ-lĕth shā'här), **AIJELETH HASH-SHAHAR** (ā'jĕ-lĕth hăsh-shā'här). Perhaps the name of a tune used by the chief musician for Ps 22. The tune name probably means "hind of the dawn." *See* Music.

AIN (ä'ĕn)
1. The name of the sixteenth letter of the Heb. alphabet. *See* Alphabet.
2. In OT times, several towns bore this name, meaning "well," which was also compounded with place names in NT times. In an account of the boundaries of Israel's inheritance (Num 34:1–12; cf. Ezk 47:15–23), Ain is said to lie within the eastern boundary near Riblah and N of the Sea of Galilee.

Et-Tell, supposed site of Ai. JR

Another Ain is designated as a city in the Negeb within Judah's portion (Josh 15:32) but also belonging to the tribe of Simeon, whose heritage was within Judah (Josh 19:7; I Chr 4:32). A parallel account in I Chr 6:59 calls this place Ashan. This city was occupied by Aaronic priests and was located near Hebron (Josh 21:16).

In the post-Exilic period, Ain appears to be identified with En-rimmon (Neh 11:29), although these places are distinctly separated in the references above. Tradition has held that Ain Karem, a village four miles W of Jerusalem, was the birthplace of John the Baptist. A spring, Ain Feshkha, on the W shore of the Dead Sea, was important in the life of the Qumran community.

G. H. L.

AIN FESHKHA (ä'ēn fĕsh'kȧ). A slightly mineral spring on the NW shores of the Dead Sea, emerging at the foot of the Judean hills which here are close to the sea. It lies about two miles S of Khirbet Qumran, at the southern extremity of the narrow plain which represents the end of the Jordan Valley. Immediately S of the spring the cliff descends steeply into the sea and blocks further progress except on foot.

A group of buildings at the spring belonging to the Essene settlement of Qumran was discovered in 1956 and excavated in 1958. These are contemporary with the main settlement, *c.* early 1st cen. B.C. to A.D. 69. The connection is clearly attested by identical pottery and coins found at the two sites. The installations can be divided into three groups of which the central, a rectangular building with inner courtyard surrounded by rooms, would seem to be partly living quarters, while the southern part was connected with agricultural affairs, and the northern, as suggested by the excavator Père de Vaux, was concerned with the tanning of hides and skins. The practice of a modest form of agriculture would certainly have been possible, for there are several smaller, slightly mineral springs there and the remains of long walls which appear to be ancient field boundaries. The soil is, however, rather salty, setting a limit to the type of vegetation which could be grown.

The suggestion that the northern group of buildings was concerned with tanning is based on the peculiar layout of cisterns, channels and shallow basins which constitute this group, and is difficult to explain in terms of ordinary everyday usage. Analyses of deposits from basins and channels do not contradict the suggestion, and experts in the trade consider the installation perfectly suitable for such a purpose; but nothing can be proved definitely. The community, however, was a self-contained one, and it is probable that they produced somewhere on the premises the skins necessary for writing material, etc., and this is certainly the most likely place for such work.

See Archaeology; Dead Sea Scrolls.

G. L. H.

The Valley of Ajalon where the sun stood still.
HFV

AIR. Used in the language of the supernatural as the lowest of the three divisions: the atmosphere or air, the sky, and the highest or third heaven (II Cor 12:2, 4). The air is the dwelling place of Satan, "the prince of the power of the air" (Eph 2:2), and of his demonic hosts (cf. Eph 6:12).

AJAH. *See* Aiah.

AJALON (ăj'a-lŏn). Variant of Aijalon.

1. A valley town on the Philistine border in the Shephelah (Josh 10:12; II Chr 28:18). It is mentioned in the Amarna letters and the list of Shishak's conquests in Palestine. Ajalon is identified with modern Yalo, 13 miles NW of Jerusalem, guarding the lower end of the pass of Beth-horon. It was a Levitical city of Dan for the Kohathites (Josh 21:20, 24; I Chr 6:69). Later it was included in Benjamin (I Chr 8:13). Fortified by Rehoboam (II Chr 11:10), it was then captured by the Philistines (II Chr 28:18).

2. A village in the tribe of Zebulun, site unknown, where Elon was buried (Jud 12:12).

AKAN (ā'kăn). A Horite (Gen 36:27). *See* Jaakan.

AKELDAMA. *See* Aceldama.

AKHENATON (ä'kĕ-nä'tŏn). Succeeded his father, Amenhotep III, as ruler of Egypt *c.* 1370 B.C. He inspired the Amarna revolution (*see* Amarna, Tell el-), which displaced the older gods by the Aton, or sun disk. He deified the light of the sun, devising a new symbol for the new god: the sun disk with diverging rays radiating downward, each ending in a human hand. Some of these hands held the *ankh*, "life" symbol. There is evidence that this "solar monotheism" had its roots in the time of

Akhenaton, Nefertiti, and a daughter worship
the sun disk with rays ending in human hands.
LL

A statue of Akhenaton in the Cairo Museum.
LL

Amenhotep III, and perhaps as far back as
Thothmes IV.

Since Akhenaton sought to exterminate the
old gods, he chiseled from the inscriptions the
plural "gods" and every occurrence of the word
"Amon." However, attempts to eliminate the
old cults never penetrated to the masses. The
priests of Amon in Thebes, the capital, stirred
up trouble. As a result, Akhenaton was compelled to choose a new location for the capital
near the site of modern Tell el-Amarna. Here,
300 miles N of Thebes, he built Akhetaton,
"Horizon of the Aton," and occupied it in the
sixth year of his reign. Aton worship was made
the official state religion. The king changed his
own name from Amenhotep IV, "he in whom
Amon is content," to Akhenaton (variously
spelled Ikhnaton), "he who is beneficial to
Aton."

He married his sister, Nefertiti, a zealous
devotee of Aton worship. Due to his preoccupation with the religious, literary, and artistic reforms, the great empire erected by
Thothmes III crumbled. The Hittites absorbed
the vassal states in Syria. Nomads overran Pal-

estine. (Some see in this the early period of the
judges following Joshua's conquest. Others believe that certain archaeological evidence would
favor a later date for that event.) The Egyptian
fortifications and center at Gaza were destroyed. The priests and army began to conspire against Akhenaton. He married his daughter Merit-Aton to his brother Smenkhare, and
made him co-regent. Shortly after Akhenaton
died, c. 1357–1353, he was succeeded by
Tut-ankh-Amon, Nefertiti's half brother, and
Enekhes-en-Amon, who returned the capital to
Thebes.

A. K. H.

AKKUB (ăk'ŭb)
1. The son of Elioenai, descendant of David
(I Chr 3:24).
2. A Levite who was head of a family of
gatekeepers in the post-Exilic temple (Ezr 2:42;
Neh 7:45; 11:19; 12:25; I Esd 5:28).
3. The name of a Nethinim family of temple
servants (Ezr 2:45; I Esd 5:30).
4. An expounder of the law; a Levite (Neh
8:7; I Esd 9:48).

44

AKRABBIM

ALEXANDRIA

AKRABBIM (ă-krăb'ĭm). The name (meaning "scorpions") of the ascent of a mountain pass on the southern border of Canaan on the route up from the Arabah through the Negeb highlands to Beer-sheba (Num 34:4; Josh 15:3, RSV; Jud 1:36). *See* Hazazon-tamar.

ALABASTER. *See* Minerals.

ALAMETH (ăl'ă-mĕth). A Benjamite, the son of Becher and the grandson of Benjamin (I Chr 7:8). In RSV the name is spelled Alemeth (*q.v.*).

ALAMMELECH (ă-lăm'ĕ-lĕk). A town located in Asher. The exact site is unknown but probably it was on the border of Zebulun in the southern region of the plain of Acco (Josh 19:26).

ALAMOTH (ăl'ă-mŏth). A term in music, likely referring to the falsetto or maiden soprano voice, or to a musical instrument used for accompaniment (I Chr 15:20). *See* Music.

ALARM. A sound of battle, usually used in relation to blowing the trumpet for announcing war or victory (Num 10:5–6; Jer 4:19; 49:2; Zeph 1:16).

ALEMETH (ăl'ē-mĕth)
1. A descendant of King Saul. His father was either Jarah (I Chr 9:42) or Jehoaddah (I Chr 8:36).
2. Known also as Almon, a city of Benjamin (I Chr 6:60; Josh 21:18).

ALEPH (ä'lĕf). The first letter of both the Phoenician and Heb. alphabets. It is a consonant having no counterpart in the English alphabet. From aleph the Gr. *alpha*, a vowel, is derived. It is used to begin the first word of each verse in the first section of Ps 119, called the acrostic psalm. *See* Alphabet.

ALEXANDER (ăl'ĭg-zăn'dĕr). A fairly common NT name.
1. Alexander, son of Simon of Cyrene who was compelled to carry the cross for Jesus (Mk 15:21). Because of this allusion to Alexander as one known to the Christian community, it has been assumed that he and his brother became Christians.
2. An Alexander in the Sanhedrin (Acts 4:6) before whom Peter and John were brought for trial. Nothing further is known of him.
3. A leader of the Jews in Ephesus at the time of the riot against the Christians (Acts 19:33). Prompted by his fellow Jews because of his prominence, he attempted to quiet the uproar, fearing, perhaps, that the heathen would not distinguish between Jew and Christian in their fanaticism.
4. Alexander the coppersmith (II Tim 4:14), an enemy and antagonist of Paul who "did me much harm." If this warning to Timothy implies

that he lived in Ephesus, this Alexander may be the same as 3, thus a fellow craftsman of the silversmiths. However, the reference may mean an opposing witness to Paul at his Roman trial. In this case, further identification would be very difficult.
5. Another Alexander in Ephesus (I Tim 1:20) is mentioned as one who had made shipwreck of his faith and had been sternly disciplined by Paul. Since the name was so common, it would be precarious to identify this fallen Christian with either 3 or 4.

P. C. J.

ALEXANDRIA (ăl'ĭg-zăn'drĭ-ă). An important Gr. city founded by Alexander the Great in 332 B.C. and built around a small Egyptian town called Rakote, dating back to 1300 B.C. It is located near the point where the western branch of the Nile empties into the Mediterranean. With two spacious harbors, it became a famous commercial center, exporting Egyptian grain to Rome and serving as a focal point for trade with India, Arabia, and parts of Africa.

Alexander never saw the completed city, but his body was brought there from Perdiccas for interment. His Egyptian territories were taken over by his general Ptolemy, who left Memphis and made Alexandria his capital and founded the dynasty which continued until the death of Cleopatra (30 B.C.). Alexandria reached its height under the first three Ptolemies: Ptolemy I (Soter), 323–285 B.C.; Ptolemy II (Philadelphus), 285–247 B.C.; and Euergetes, 247–222 B.C.

A "museum" was established and became a center of learning and culture. Like a modern university, the museum had research professors and included lecture halls, laboratories, observatories, parks, zoos, and a library approaching 700,000 volumes. Jewish legend says the Septuagint translation of the OT was made especially for the museum.

Other famous structures included the Pharos lighthouse, towering nearly 450 feet high over the harbor; the Temple of Serapis, which was

Alexandrian waterfront and skyline. Egyptian State Tourist Administration

45

designed for the worship of the god which combined the Osiris cult with the Apis (bull) cult; the royal tombs, and the palace in the Rakote sector. Here the apocryphal book of Wisdom was written, and the famous Philo tried to reconcile Gr. philosophy and Heb. religion in the 1st Christian cen. *See* Philo.

Famous men of Alexandria included the mathematicians Euclid, Eratosthenes and Hipparchus, and the astronomers Aristarchus and Claudius Ptolemy, who respectively viewed the universe as heliocentric and geocentric.

By the 1st Christian cen. Alexandria was the second city of the Roman Empire, with a population of at least 600,000. It was the home of Apollos (Acts 18:24), and from its port sailed two of the grain ships used by the centurion to transport Paul to Rome (Acts 27:6; 28:11). It had a large Jewish community because Alexander had treated the Jews kindly, and some Jews from Alexandria returning to Jerusalem had formed a synagogue (Acts 6:9). There was a tradition, according to Eusebius, that John Mark founded the church at Alexandria, but this lacks support.

Following in the footsteps of Philo's allegorical method of interpreting the Scriptures, early converts to Christianity from Judaism turned to Gnostic (*see* Gnosticism) forms of thinking and formed a school at Alexandria under the direction of Basilides. Clement of Alexandria (*c.* A.D. 150–*c.* 220) and his foremost pupil Origen (*c.* 185–*c.* 254) directed a Christian catechetical school that was more orthodox and more closely attached to the church at large, although it, too, preferred allegorical or "spiritual" interpretation. The Epistle to the Hebrews *(q.v.)*, because of its use of terminology beloved at Alexandria and its frequent reference to the OT, has been associated with an Alexandrian background, perhaps even with Apollos.

A. K. H.

ALEXANDRIAN (ăl′ĭg-zăn′drĭ-ăn). A native of the Egyptian city of Alexandria (*q.v.*), which numbered more than 600,000 inhabitants in the first Christian century. The Alexandrians were quite cosmopolitan, as their location and previous history would prescribe. Most of the inhabitants of the city were either Egyptians (in the sector of Rakote), Greeks (in Brucheum), Romans, or Jews (in the eastern sector). The latter, comprising about one-fourth of the population, had equal rights with Greeks until Caligula took them away. The great museum, with its eminent scholars, had given the city two centuries of cultural and literary pre-eminence. As a result of the siege of Alexandria by Julius Caesar, when much of the library in the museum was burned, this importance had about disappeared by the end of Cleopatra's reign, only to be replaced 200 years later by another period of greatness when Alexandria led the world in philosophy and theology.

A. K. H.

ALGUM, ALMUG. *See* Plants.

ALIAH (*à*-lī′ă). A duke of Edom, descended from Esau (I Chr 1:51). The name is also spelled Alvah (*q.v.*).

ALIAN (*à*-lī′ăn). A son of Shobal in Edom (I Chr 1:40). The name is also spelled Alvan (*q.v.*).

ALIEN. A foreigner (*q.v.*), one who is denied the privileges of a specific group to which he is not considered to be a member; sometimes the sense of the word stranger (KJV).

ALLEGORY. A "prolonged metaphor" (longer and more detailed) in which objects or events are understood as symbolic or typical of meanings in another realm of discourse. An allegory is distinguished from a parable in that an allegory makes each detail representative of truth or meaning, whereas a parable stresses one central truth. A hard and fast line is difficult to draw, since many parables lend themselves to allegorizing. The allegory differs from the fable in that it is more true to life and fact than is the fable, in which animals or objects may speak or act in human ways (cf. Jotham's fable of the trees choosing a king, Jud 9:7–15).

The word occurs but once in the KJV (Gal 4:24, *allēgoroumena*, "being allegorized") in connection with the application of the history of Sarah and Hagar to the covenant of grace in contrast with the covenant of law. The Gr. word is derived from *allos,* "other," and *agoreuō,* "to speak in a place of assembly"; and came to mean speaking not in the primary sense of the words but in such a way that the stated facts illustrate principles.

Other biblical allegories occur in Ps 80:8–19; Isa 5:1–7, and in the allegory of the sower and the seed, Lk 8:4–15. The door of the fold and the Good Shepherd of Jn 10:1–16, 26–29 are properly regarded as allegories. It must be noted, however, that the meaning of *parabolē,* "parable, a placing beside" (derived from *paraballō,* "to throw or lay beside, to compare") may in fact include what is meant by allegory. RSV translates Heb. *māshāl* (KJV, "parable") with "allegory" in Ezk 17:2; 24:3. Outside the Bible, Bunyan's *Pilgrim's Progress* is the best-known example of a religious allegory.

The allegorical interpretation of the OT became prominent in Alexandria with Philo, and was taken over by such Christian Fathers as Justin, Clement, and Origen. Origen distinguished three levels of truth in Scripture: the literal or "fleshly," the moral, and the spiritual. These were said to correspond to man's body, soul, and spirit. Jerome introduced the use of allegory into Roman Christianity, but it was largely rejected by the reformers. Unrestrained allegorizing is subject to the obvious abuses of excessive subjectivity and imagination.

It must be recognized, however, that the NT

itself views parts of OT history allegorically; e.g., the Church is the new Israel, delivered from bondage to sin in a new Passover, receiving a new covenant in Christ's blood, subject to a new law given from a new mount, and led into a second rest by a new Joshua. Paul so speaks in I Cor 10:1–12 (cf. also Heb 3–4). *See* Parable; Type.

W. T. P.

ALLELUIA. This word occurs only in Rev 19:1, 3, 4, 6, KJV (ASV and RSV spell the expression hallelujah). It is a transliteration of the Gr. *allēlouia,* which in turn is a transliteration of the Heb. *halelûyāh,* a liturgical expression which means "praise the Lord." In the LXX, the Gr. word occurs as the title of Ps 104–106, 110–118, 134–135, 145–150. It is found within the LXX text only in Ps 150:6. The word has come directly into the English language without change as a religious expression. Within the psalms to which it is attached there is an emphasis on the power and wisdom of God as these are witnessed to in His deeds.

ALLIANCE. Although this word does not occur in the KJV or ASV, it does appear four times in the RSV. Its basic idea is conveyed by the Heb. noun *berît,* meaning "league," "confederacy," "covenant"; the verbs *ḥātan,* meaning "affinity," "join in marriage"; and *nûaḥ,* meaning "to be at rest," "to be confederate"; and the noun *qesher,* which usually has the negative meaning "conspiracy," "treason."

The earliest alliance described in Scripture was between Abraham and the Amorites Mamre, Eshcol, and Aner. They joined forces long enough to rescue Lot from his captors (Gen 14:13–24). Abraham entered a more lasting alliance with Abimelech at Beer-sheba (Gen 21:22–32), as did Isaac later (Gen 26:26–31).

No prohibition or stigma was placed against these early alliances; but the Mosaic law later repeatedly placed a ban against foreign alliances, particularly with Canaanites. The prohibition against joining the Canaanites was based chiefly upon religious grounds. The newly formed nation was as yet too weak to withstand the enticements of Canaan's sex worship, so God through Moses sought to isolate Israel. The pagan altars, temples, and images were torn down lest the young people become ensnared by Baalism (Ex 23:32–33; 34:12–13). To protect the Israelites further from this corruption, intermarriage was prohibited, lest in the intimacy of marriage the pagan idolator corrupt the Israelite (Deut 7:2–4). After the Conquest, when Israel became entangled with waywardness, the reason for God's judgment upon them was traced back to Israel's violation of this ban (Jud 2:2).

Besides the alliance which the Gibeonites by trickery concluded with Joshua, there were no official ties with other nations until the time of Solomon. David had friendly relationships, based on personal covenants, with the kings of Moab, Ammon, Gath, and Hamath; but it seems that Solomon was the first to establish an international league with a foreign nation. This was done with Hiram of Tyre in connection with building the temple and operating fleets in the Red Sea and in the Indian Ocean (I Kgs 5:1–18; 9:26–28). The full implications of this league did not come to light until the marriage of Ahab with Jezebel, a daughter of a king of Tyre. Baalism immediately took over the religious life of Israel but was vigorously opposed by Elijah, Elisha, and Jehu. Judah felt some evil results of this marriage when Jezebel's daughter, Athaliah, became queen of Judah.

In the triangular quarrels of Judah, Israel, and Syria, several leagues were forged. At one time, Asa of Judah purchased the aid of Ben-hadad of Syria against Baasha of Israel (I Kgs 15:18–19; II Chr 16:3). Later, Ahab of Israel gained the help of Jehoshaphat of Judah against Syria (I Kgs 22; II Chr 18:1). After Ahab's death, Ahaziah of Israel sought to join Jehoshaphat in building a merchant fleet, but God was displeased and the fleet was destroyed (II Chr 20:35–37). In Isaiah's time, Rezin of Syria and Pekah of Israel joined against Judah, but Ahaz of Judah purchased the help of Assyria, which quickly destroyed Syria, reduced Israel to the status of a satellite, and finally made Ahaz its puppet (II Kgs 16:5–8). The last tragic alliance was between Zedekiah and Egypt, which act brought Babylon against Judah and utterly destroyed Jerusalem (Jer 37:1–8; Ezk 17:15–17). *See* Covenant.

G. H. L.

ALLON (ăl'ŏn)

1. A Simeonite prince, a descendant of Shemaiah (I Chr 4:37).

2. In Josh 19:33 it is better translated (see ASV, RSV) as a common noun meaning "oak." The word "plain" in Jud 4:11 should also be rendered "oak" as in ASV and RSV.

ALLON-BACHUTH (ăl'ŏn-băk'ŭth). Rebekah's nurse Deborah was buried under this tree (its name meaning "oak of weeping"), near Bethel (Gen 35:8). It also may have been the site of the palm tree of the prophetess Deborah located between Ramah and Bethel (Jud 4:5).

ALLOTMENT. The terms "allotment," "inheritance" (*q.v.*) and "portion" (*q.v.*) are used of land and, by extension, of one's position in life.

Josh 13–19 describes the allotment assigned to each of the Israelite tribes in Canaan following the conquest. Reuben, Gad, and half the tribe of Manasseh had settled E of the Jordan, but the remaining nine and a half tribes were assigned land in the area W of the Jordan and the Dead Sea (cf. Num 32; 33:54; 34:13). Since the Promised Land belonged to the Lord, He had the right to assign it as He chose. Eleazar, the priest at Shiloh, and Joshua, Moses' successor, in cooperation with the tribal leaders (Josh

14:1-2; 19:51), determined the will of God and revealed to the people their tribal inheritance. The means of determining the allotment is not specified. It may have been by the use of Urim and Thummim, two stones in the breastplate or pouch on the ephod of the high priest (Ex 28:28-30).

The land of Canaan is described as the "lot of the righteous" (Ps 125:3). The tribe of Levi had no territorial allotment, but Levitical cities were established among the tribes (Josh 21).

C. F. P.

ALMIGHTY. Used 48 times in the OT, of which 31 are in the book of Job, to translate Heb. *shaddai. See* God, Names and Titles of; El.

ALMODAD (ăl-mō'dăd). A people who lived in southern Arabia descended from the first son of Joktan (Gen 10:26; I Chr 1:20).

ALMON (ăl'mŏn). A Benjamite city in which the priests lived (Josh 21:18). It is also called Alemeth (I Chr 6:60).

ALMON-DIBLATHAIM (ăl'mŏn-dĭb'lá-thā'ĭm). A stopping place in the journeyings of Israel after Dibon-gad and before the mountains of Abarim (Num 33:46-47). Probably the same as Beth-diblathaim (*q.v.*; Jer 48:22).

ALMOND. *See* Plants.

ALMS, ALMSDEEDS. These words occur in the NT only, as the translation of the Gr. *eleēmosynē*, derived from *eleos*, "mercy"; *eleeō*, "to show mercy"; and *eleēmōn*, "merciful." The Gr. word means "pity, mercy, kindness," as well as the kind act or benefaction itself, in which the effect is taken for the cause. Essentially, alms is relief to the poor in the modern sense of charity. ("Charity" in the KJV is a translation of *agapē*, "love," and is a much broader term, as e.g., I Cor 13:3.) "Alms" and "almsdeeds" are now archaic as English words.

The OT uses *sedeq* or *ṣᵉdāqâ*, "righteousness," "justice," in a number of instances to mean the duty of caring for the poor (e.g., Deut 24:13; Ps 24:5; Prov 10:2; 11:4; Mic 6:5), and this term is translated *eleēmosunē* in the LXX of Deut 25:15 and Dan 4:27. The propriety of this usage is seen in view of the constant OT concern for widows, the fatherless, strangers, and the poor—a complete contrast with ancient Gr. and Rom. attitudes. To do what the law so clearly required was *ṣᵉdāqâ*, "righteousness."

The law of Moses was very definite on the care of the poor. In the Book of the Covenant (Ex 20-23), the poor were protected against usury and the taking of garments in pledge for loans (Ex 22:25-27; cf. Lev 25:35-36), and were provided for in the sabbatical year (Ex 23:11). In the Holiness Code (Lev 17-22) provision was made that gleanings be left in the

field for the poor (Lev 19:9-10; cf. Ruth 2) and that wages be paid promptly (Lev 19:13). Later provisions in Leviticus protected the property of the poor from permanent alienation (25:25-30). Deuteronomy is replete with directions for a second tithe for the poor (14:28-29); generosity in providing for their needs (15:7, 11); provision for them at the stated festivals (16:11-14); and permission to satisfy hunger in vineyard and field (23:24-25). See also Deut 24:13, 19-22; 26:12-13.

Job in his "oath of purgation" cites his generosity to the poor (Job 29:12-16). Special blessing was promised those who assisted the oppressed (Neh 8:10; Prov 19:17). The prophets declare the care of the poor to be God's will (Isa 58:4-7; Ezk 18:7; Dan 4:27; Amos 2:6-7).

In the NT the same concern is seen. Jesus gives directions for almsgiving as characteristic of the religious spirit (Mt 6:1-4). Luke particularly stresses the Lord's sympathy for the poor and outcast (Lk 3:11; 6:30; 12:33). The early church viewed almsgiving as an evidence of Christian love (Acts 9:36; 10:2, 4; Rom 12:13; Eph 4:28; I Tim 6:18; Heb 13:16; I Jn 3:17-19). The NT gives particular attention to the motive in giving in relation to ability (Mk 12:42-44; II Cor 8:12; Acts 11:29).

W. T. P.

ALMUG TREE. *See* Plants: Algum.

ALOES. *See* Plants.

ALOTH (ā'lŏth). Used only in I Kgs 4:16. *See* Bealoth.

ALPHA AND OMEGA (ăl'fà, ō-mĕg'à). The first and last letters of the Gr. alphabet, used in Rev 1:8; 21:6 as a title of God, and in Rev 22:13 of Christ. In the latter reference the added phrases give the meaning of the expression: "the beginning and the end, the first and the last." Additional parallel phrases indicating the same basic concept appear subjoined to the expression, such as, "the Lord, which is, and which was, and which is to come, the Almighty" (Rev 1:8). Thus is signified the sovereignty of Christ, as of God in Isa 44:6; 48:12.

As the Alpha, He alone is in possession of the knowledge of the origin of the earth and man; and having absolute authority over them, He alone has the power to make all things new (Rev 21:5-6). As the Omega, the last, He is in possession of the future and alone can "tell us what is yet to be" (Isa 44:7, RSV). He can banish death and Hades (Rev 20:14), punish the wicked eternally (Rev 21:8), and determine the final reward for all men (Rev 22:12; Jn 5:22).

The importance of this term being applied to Christ (Rev 22:13) cannot be overlooked. In other terms the NT concurs with John's designation by asserting the primacy of Christ in and over all creation (Col 1:15-18; Heb 1:1-3; Mt

28:18), His absolute power over life and resurrection (Jn 5:21, 25–26, 28–29), and His sovereignty in the final judgment (Jn 5:22, 27). Rev 1:17–18 asserts that the firstness and lastness of Christ are supremely validated by His resurrection from the dead.

W. M. D. and A. F. J.

ALPHABET. An alphabet is a series of letters which represent significant phonetic values arranged in a socially accepted order. The word alphabet is a combination of the names of the first two letters of the Gr. alphabet, *alpha* and *beta*.

Alphabetic writing was preceded by other methods of written communication. Pictures etched in ancient caves conveyed meaning, although the words they were intended to represent cannot be read. By 3000 B.C. two systems of writing, both based on pictorial characters, developed in the Near East. The Egyptian system of picture writing, or hieroglyphs, so called because of their association with the priesthood, contained both syllabic and alphabetic elements. Pictures could represent sounds, corresponding in some instances to individual letters of later alphabets. The Egyptians, however, never dropped the nonalphabetic elements from their writing system, so that they cannot be credited with actually producing an alphabet.

The Sumerians, who were dominant in the Tigris-Euphrates valley during the last half of the 4th and the 3rd mil. before Christ, used a system of wedge-shaped characters impressed in clay or cut into stone. Originally a system of picture writing, the cuneiform characters, as the wedges are now called, developed into a system of syllables and word signs in which the earlier pictorial element lost its significance. The cuneiform system of writing was adopted by the successors to the Sumerians — Assyrians, Babylonians, Hittites, and other peoples of the Fertile Crescent. *See* Writing.

Discoveries at Serabit el-Khadem in the Sinai Peninsula show that slaves of the Egyptians who worked the turquoise mines used alphabetic writing in the early 15th cen. B.C. A dagger with an alphabetic inscription dating to the 16th cen. B.C. has been discovered at Tell ed-Duweir (biblical Lachish), and comparable material has been excavated at Gezer, Shechem, Megiddo, and Beth-shemesh.

In 1929 documents in an alphabetic cuneiform script were discovered at Ras Shamra (*q.v.*), ancient Ugarit, in northern Syria. The Canaanite cuneiform alphabet seems to have been invented by someone who knew both the alphabetic principle and the cuneiform system of writing. By combining both ideas he invented an alphabet which would be suitable for writing on clay tablets. Hundreds of texts were found at Ras Shamra, dating from the 15th and the 14th cen. B.C. Other texts using the same alphabet were subsequently discovered at Beth-shemesh and in the vicinity of Mount Tabor. In 1949, Professor C. F. A. Schaeffer found at

The Ahiram Sarcophagus, from Gebal, with an alphabetic inscription from the eleventh century B.C. National Museum, Beirut

Ras Shamra a tablet of the 14th cen. B.C. listing the 30 letters of the Canaanite cuneiform alphabet in their alphabetic order. The arrangement of the letters is similar to that used for the Phoenician or NW Semitic alphabet, with which the Sinai script is related.

The Old Hebrew (palaeo-Hebrew) script is the form of Heb. writing which is similar to that used by the Phoenicians. A royal inscription of King Shaphat-baal of Gebal (Byblos) in this alphabet dates back to 1600 B.C. The sarcophagus of a Phoenician king named Ahiram contains an inscription which tells how the son of Ahiram made the coffin for his father "as an abode forever." Ahiram, whose name is similar to the biblical Hiram of Tyre, probably reigned in the late 11th cen. B.C.

The oldest extant Heb. writing, the Gezer Calendar, dated around the 10th cen. B.C., is written in this Old Hebrew–Phoenician type script, as is the Moabite Stone (*c.* 840 B.C.), which gives the Moabite version of the revolt mentioned in II Kgs 1:1; 3:4–5.

A variant of the Old Hebrew–Phoenician method of writing was used by the Arameans, whose alphabet used "square letters" in contrast to the more angular shape of the NW Semitic alphabet. About 200 B.C. the Hebrews, influenced by the Aramaic language which was commonly spoken by post-Exilic Jews, adopted the square form of the letters. With few exceptions, this is the form of the alphabet used in the Dead Sea Scrolls, dated from the 2nd cen. B.C. to the 1st cen. after Christ. The square letters are used in printed Heb. Bibles and in other printed literature in Heb.

According to Gr. tradition, the alphabet was brought to Boeotia in central Greece by a Phoenician prince of Tyre named Cadmus. Since *kedem* is the Semitic word for east, the tradition with the name Cadmus derived from the root *K-d-m* seems to reflect the fact that Greece received her alphabet from the east, i.e., Phoenicia. The Semitic origin of the Gr. alphabet is further illustrated by the names of

DEVELOPMENT OF THE ALPHABET

	Sinai 1500 BC	Phoenician 1000 BC	Early Hebrew (Siloam) 700 BC	Old Greek 8th cen. BC	Formal Greek 5th cen. BC	Formal Hebrew 2nd cen. AD	Roman		Sinai 1500 BC	Phoenician 1000 BC	Early Hebrew (Siloam) 700 BC	Old Greek 8th cen. BC	Formal Greek 5th cen. BC	Formal Hebrew 2nd cen. AD	Roman
oxhead	K				A alpha	X aleph	A	staff, oxgoad					lambda	lāmedh	L
house	9	9	6	B	beta	bēth	B	water					mu	mēm	M
throwstick			1	Γ	gamma	gimel	G	snake					nu	nūn	N
door	q	△		△	delta	dāleth	D	fish					xi	samek	X
man praising				E	epsilon	hē	E	eye	O		O	O	omicron	'ayin	O
neck prop	Y			Y	digamma	waw	F,Y	mouth					pi	pē'	P
?	I	I	I	Z	zeta	zayin	Z	?						ṣadē	
twisted hank					H ēta	ḥēth	H	monkey?						qōph	Q
?					thēta	ṭēth		head					rho	rēsh	R
?				I	iota	yōdn	I	tooth?					sigma	shīn	S
palm of hand				K	kappa	kāph	K	mark of a cross	X	X		T	tau	taw	T

Chart showing development of alphabet. JR

the letters. Gr. *alpha, beta, gamma* are clearly parallel to Semitic *aleph, beth, gimmel*. The words mean nothing in Gr. except the letters they name, whereas in Heb. they reflect early picture writing when they represented, respectively, an ox, a house, and a camel. It is thought that the Greeks learned of the alphabet through trade with the Phoenicians. After it proved useful for commercial purposes, it was adopted for literary use. By 700 B.C. even painters of pottery jars had learned the art of writing.

While cuneiform writing continued in use to the 1st cen. B.C., the simplicity of alphabetic writing caused it ultimately to displace other systems. Cuneiform and hieroglyphic writing were used by learned and priestly classes, but all normal persons could readily learn to communicate through alphabetic writing. All the biblical writers seem to have used alphabetic writing—Hebrew, Aramaic, or Greek. By the time of the judges, a young man whom Gideon met by chance could write down the names of the chief men of his city (Jud 8:14, RSV). *See* Languages; Writing.

Bibliography. W. F. Albright, "The Early Alphabetic Inscriptions from Sinai and Their Decipherment," BASOR #110 (1948), pp. 6–22; *The Proto-Sinaitic Inscriptions and Their Decipherment*, Harvard Theological Studies #22, Cambridge, Mass.: Harvard Univ.

Press, 1968. Frank M. Cross, Jr., "The Evolution of the Proto-Canaanite Alphabet," BASOR #134 (1954), pp. 15–24. David Diringer, *The Alphabet*, New York: Philosophical Library, 1948. Ignace J. Gelb, *A Study of Writing*, Chicago: Univ. of Chicago Press, 1952.
C. F. P.

ALPHAEUS (ăl-fē'ŭs). One of many Gr. names in common use by Jews in 1st cen. Palestine.

1. The father of Levi the tax collector (Mk 2:14).

2. The father of James, one of the disciples of Jesus (Mk 3:18). The identification with either Cleophas (Jn 19:25) or Cleopas (Lk 24:18) seems unlikely. On these problems *see further* under Cleophas, Cleopas, James, Levi, Matthew.

ALTAR. In the Heb. OT, the usual word for altar is *mizbēaḥ*, "place of sacrifice," which is derived from the verb *zābaḥ*, "to slaughter," "to sacrifice." In Ezr 7:17 there occurs the Aramaic *madbaḥ*, formed from the same word. Such Aramaic words may be expected after the return from the Captivity. Two other terms for altar seem to be derived from the Akkad. language. In Ezk 43:15–16 the expressions *har'ēl*, "mountain of God"(?) and *'ărī'ēl* (of uncertain meaning) are translated "altar" in KJV, and "altar hearth" in ASV.

Patriarchal Altars

As far as is recorded, Noah is the first person in the OT to have built an altar. Upon it he offered as a burnt offering one animal from each kind of clean animal and bird which had been preserved in the ark. Abraham built an altar at Shechem, one near Bethel (Gen 12:6-8), and one at "Mamre, which is in Hebron" (Gen 13:18). Later, he built one on Mount Moriah where God provided a substitute sacrifice for Isaac (Gen 22:9-13). According to the record, Isaac built only one altar, that at Beer-sheba (Gen 26:23-25), whereas Jacob erected one at Shechem (Gen 33:18, 20) and one at Bethel (Gen 35:1-7). No description is given of the size, shape, or construction of any of these altars.

Mosaic Altars

Apart from the altars of the tabernacle, Moses is said to have reared an altar after the battle with the Amalekites (Ex 17:15), and also after the revelation of the covenant law on Sinai (Ex 24:4-5). Beside this altar 12 pillars, one for each tribe, were erected, and upon the altar burnt offerings were placed. The Pentateuch also mentions two other occasions when altars were built apart from the tabernacle. Balaam, a non-Israelite, built seven altars at each of three different places, and upon each altar sacrificed a bullock and a ram (Num 23:1, 14, 29). Moses instructed the elders of Israel to erect an altar of unhewn stones on Mount Ebal. Upon this altar they were to sacrifice peace offerings, and on large plastered stones near the altar they were to inscribe the words of the law (Deut 27:4-8). Joshua carried out this injunction faithfully several years later (Josh 8:30-32).

Though only the construction of the altar on Mount Ebal is described in these passages, the Pentateuch contains several sets of instructions concerning the building of altars. After Moses came down from Mount Sinai, he told the people that altars could be constructed either of earth or of unhewn stones. Steps could not be used with either type, lest the nakedness of the priest be exposed (Ex 20:24-26). The altar on Mount Ebal was of this kind and, presumably, also those built by the tribes of Reuben, Gad and the half tribe of Manasseh (Josh 22:10, 34), by Gideon (Jud 6:26-27), Samuel (I Sam 7:17), Saul (I Sam 14:35), David (II Sam 24:18, 25), and Elijah (I Kgs 18:30).

Tabernacle and Temple Altars

Moses received word from the Lord that the tabernacle should have two altars: the brazen altar of burnt offering, which was located in the courtyard, and the altar of incense in the holy place.

The brazen altar, built by Bezaleel (Ex 27:1-8; 31:2-5; 38:1-7), was made of acacia wood and was covered with bronze. It was seven and one-half feet square, four and one-half feet high, and had horns on its upper four corners. Within, it was equipped with a

Canaanite altar at Megiddo, dating to about 2700 B.C. HFV

grating of bronze which had four bronze rings, one at each corner. The altar could be transported by means of two wooden poles overlaid with bronze, which were slipped through rings on the sides of the altar.

The brazen altar was placed just inside the main entrance of the courtyard and was in direct line with the door of the tabernacle. Upon it were sacrificed the animal and cereal offerings of Israel (Ex 40:6, 29). When the altar was consecrated, a sin offering was made for its atonement each day for seven days. It was also anointed with oil. After its consecration, the altar was holy, and whatever touched it was regarded as holy (Ex 29:36-37, 44; 30:28; 40:10; Lev 8:11; Num 7:10-88).

The brazen altar of burnt offering was also a place for refuge for the innocent man accused of murder (Ex 21:12-14; I Kgs 1:50; 2:28). He could plead for mercy by holding on to the horns of the altar.

The brazen altar which Solomon designed for the temple was larger than that in the tabernacle. It measured 20 cubits (30 feet) square and 10 cubits (15 feet) high (II Chr 4:1). It was repaired by Asa (II Chr 15:8), but was replaced by Ahaz, who constructed a new altar after an Assyrian model (II Kgs 16:14-17). Hezekiah ordered the altar to be restored and cleansed for service (II Chr 29:18-24). Manasseh at first ignored the brazen altar, but in later life restored it to its proper function (II Chr 33:16).

Evidently the brazen altar was destroyed by the Babylonians after the fall of Jerusalem (II Kgs 25:14). Before the second temple was built, the returned exiles rebuilt the altar in the courtyard and reestablished its proper service (Ezr 3:1-6).

While in captivity, Ezekiel envisioned a great altar in a future temple, and recorded its size and shape in some detail. There were to be three stages. The base would be 24 feet square, the second stage 21 feet square, and the final stage 18 feet square. The total height would be about 16 feet. Steps would ascend to the altar on its E side (Ezk 43:13–27). Some speculate that rather than a vision of a future temple this is a description of the altar built by Ahaz which was still standing in the temple court at the time Ezekiel was taken away as a captive.

Limestone altar of incense, Megiddo. Palestine Archaeological Museum, Jerusalem

The golden altar, or altar of incense, was much smaller than the brazen altar. It was covered with gold, and was placed in the holy place of the tabernacle before the curtain of the holy of holies. The frame of the altar of incense was made of acacia wood measuring one and one-half feet square by three feet high. Its upper four corners had horns or projections and its sides had rings. Through the rings were slipped wooden poles covered with gold for carrying the altar. On it the high priest offered incense morning and evening. Once a year the high priest made atonement by placing blood upon its horns (Ex 30:1–10; 40:5, 26–27). After the sons of Korah had rebelliously offered incense contrary to the law and were punished by death, their bronze censers were fashioned into a cover for the golden altar as a memorial (Num 16:36–40).

Solomon made an altar of cedar, overlaid it with gold, and placed it in the holy place of the temple (I Kgs 6:20, 22; 7:48). However, David is said to have given his son the specifications for the temple and its furniture, including the altar of incense (I Chr 28:18). This altar is not mentioned again in the OT. Presumably, it also was destroyed when Jerusalem was captured by the Babylonians. Although the OT has left no record to this effect, it is likely the second temple was equipped with an altar of incense, since the NT speaks of such an altar in Herod's temple that followed it.

Nonbiblical Jewish Literature

References to the altars of the temple appear in Jewish literature of the intertestamental period. In the Letter of Aristeas (100 B.C.), the author makes the observation that water was piped to the base of the brazen altar from underground cisterns in order that the blood of the animal sacrifices might be washed away (*The Apocrypha and Pseudepigrapha of the Old Testament,* ed. by R. H. Charles, Oxford: Clarendon Press, II, 83–122). Antiochus, the Gr. ruler of Syria and Palestine (175–163 B.C.), carried away the golden altar and other valuables from the temple, and erected a sacrilege, an image of Jupiter, by the altar of burnt offering (I Macc 1:21, 54). After defeating the Greeks, Judas the Maccabee tore apart the altar of burnt offering and built a new one of unhewn stones (I Macc 4:44–49; *ibid.,* I, 59–124).

Both altars of the tabernacle are described by Josephus (*Ant.* iii. 6.8). His description of the altar of incense differs from the scriptural record only in one detail. Josephus noted that at the top of the golden altar there was a golden grate edged with a golden crown to which the rings were attached. In another place, Josephus (*Wars* v. 5.5–6) observed that in the temple of his day (1st cen. A.D.) 13 kinds of incense were offered on the golden altar in order to honor God as the possessor of all things. Also, he noted that the altar of burnt sacrifice was 75 feet square at the base and 23 feet high. A gradual incline approached it from the E. In the Mishnah (treatise "Middoth" III, trans. by H. Danby, pp. 593–595) mention is made that the measurements in Ezk 43:13–27 are from the center to the outer edge, so each figure should be doubled, i.e., the base should be 48 feet square instead of 24, etc. Further, the men who returned from the Exile added a six foot extension to the S and to the W sides of the base. The inclined ramp is located on the S side of the altar and is said to be 24 feet wide and 48 feet long.

Altars Found by Archaeologists

In Palestine, archaeologists have identified many objects as altars. The use of altars of burnt offering and of incense was widespread among the pagan non-Israelite people in ancient Palestine and in neighboring countries. From a small Early Bronze Age shrine built against the inner side of the city wall at Ai, archaeologists have brought to light an altar of plastered stones.

At Megiddo the remains of three temples from c. 1900 B.C. were unearthed. Against the back wall of each was a raised mud-brick platform serving as an altar table not only for offerings but also for images of the gods. In the temple courtyard in obvious relation to these buildings was found a round mound of stones and rubble which was used for burnt offerings. It is six and a half feet high and 29 feet in diameter, with six steps on one side. The period of 1475–1225 B.C. at Lachish yielded three successive temples, each with benches and mud-brick altars. The latest of these was approached by means of three steps at one side and measured about 29 inches square and three feet high. An irregular mound with steps was found in a Late Bronze temple courtyard at Bethshan. At Hazor about 1300 B.C., an altar was hewn from a huge block of limestone, about 40 inches square and 90 inches long and weighing around five tons. It had a place for burnt offerings and a basin for either blood or liquids. Clay stands from many locations have been thought to have been incense burners.

From the 10th cen. B.C. have come relatively small cut stone altars, some with horns on their upper corners. Most are from Megiddo, Tell Beit Mirsim, and Shechem. These have been regarded as altars of incense. In II Chr 34:4, 7; Ezk 6:4, 6 and other passages the Heb. word ḥammanîm, translated "images," is found. This is now known to refer to small stone incense altars with four feet, of the 6th to the 5th cen. One such altar inscribed in Aramaic, beginning with the word "incense offering," came to light at Lachish.

Significance and Abuse of Hebrew Altars

The altars built for the tabernacle and for the temple, then, were not completely different from those of Israel's neighbors, but their function in worship was brought in line with the covenant concept of the relationship between God and Israel. The altar of burnt offering was the place where sacrifices for atonement and communion were to be offered. The golden altar was where God's majesty was honored by means of burning incense.

Actually, the sanctuary altars were not always employed in the worship of Israel's true God. Frequently, idolatry polluted the spiritual life of the Israelites, and the sacrifices offered on the altars became a snare to them (Amos 3:14; 5:21–22; Isa 1:11–13; 27:9). When Jeroboam formed the rebellious ten tribes into a nation, he built altars and sacrificed to the calves which he had made (I Kgs 12:32). This act was condemned by a prophet of God (I Kgs 13:3–5). Ahab set up an altar to Baal in Samaria, an act which angered God (I Kgs 16:32; cf. Hos 8:11; Jer 17:2). Josiah was commended because he destroyed pagan religious tools

A small altar in the theater at Salamis, Cyprus. Sacrifices were commonly made before dramas were performed. HFV

which were used at the temple altars, and also destroyed unlawful altars which were located outside Jerusalem (II Kgs 23:4–20).

In the New Testament

The Gr. word for altar most frequently appearing in the NT is thysiastērion. Referring to the altar of burnt offering in the temple, it occurs in Mt 5:23–24; 23:18–20, 35; Lk 11:51; Rom 11:3; I Cor 9:13; 10:18; Heb 7:13; Rev 11:1. But in a few places altar has a spiritual sense (Heb 13:10; Rev 6:9). In reference to the golden altar of incense, this Gr. term appears in Lk 1:11 and a very similar word in Heb 9:4 to designate the altar in the earthly temple built by Herod. But elsewhere the golden altar is symbolic of intercessory prayer (Rev 8:3–5) or of judgment (Rev 9:13; cf. Rev 14:18; 16:7). In order to explain the seeming contradiction in Heb 9:4, which states that the golden altar of incense stood in the holy of holies, it has been suggested that on the Day of Atonement the high priest brought this altar inside the veil for that part of the ceremony involving the burning of incense before the ark (Lev 16:13).

Another Gr. word for altar, bōmos, is used in Acts 17:23 for a pagan altar in Athens. An altar of this type has been unearthed in Ephesus.

Bibliography. W. F. Albright, *Archaeology and the Religion of Israel,* Baltimore: Johns Hopkins Press, 1946. G. Cornfeld, *Adam to Daniel,* New York: Macmillan, 1961. W. Harold Mare, "The Greek Altar in the NT and Intertestamental Periods," *Grace Journal,* X(1969), 26–35. Roland de Vaux, *Ancient Israel,* New York: McGraw-Hill, 1961. G. E. Wright, *Biblical Archaeology,* Philadelphia: Westminster, 1957.

G. H. L.

AL TASCHITH (ăl-tăs′kĭth; Heb. "do not destroy"). More correctly Al-tashheth (RSV). A title annotation found in Ps 57, 58, 59, 75. Its significance is uncertain, but it may have been the name of a Heb. tune to which these psalms were sung. Or, as in the case of other musical terms in the psalm titles, it may be a subscript belonging to the previous psalm. Psalms 56, 57, 58, and especially 74, seem to voice the pleas of David and Asaph for God not to destroy them nor allow the righteous to be destroyed by their enemies.

ALUSH (ā'lŭsh), One of the encampments of the Hebrews as they fled Egypt under the leadership of Moses, between Dophkah and Rephidim. Mentioned only in Num 33:13–14.

ALVAH (ăl'vá). A chief of Edom descended from Esau, referred to in Gen 36:40 and again in I Chr 1:51, where the same name is spelled Aliah.

ALVAN (ăl'ván). The eldest son of Shobal, a clan chief in the land of Edom (Gen 36:23). The name is spelled Alian in I Chr 1:40. It is probably a Hurrian (Horite) name.

AMAD (ā'măd). A city of Canaan assigned to the tribe of Asher in the division of the land after the Conquest (Josh 19:26).

AMAL (ā'măl). A son of Helem listed among the descendants of Asher in I Chr 7:35.

AMALEK (ăm'á-lĕk), **AMALEKITES** (á-măl'ĕ-kīts)
1. A grandson of Esau and son of Eliphas by Timna, his concubine. Amalek became a chieftain in Edom and gave his name to a semi-nomadic group roaming the wilderness S of Canaan (Gen 36:12, 16).
2. A people called Amalek or Amalekites against whom the Israelites often fought from the days of Moses to the reign of David. The mention in Gen 14:7 of "all the country of the Amalekites" through which Chedorlaomer campaigned does not prove that Amalekites already existed in Abraham's time, but simply designates the territory as it was known to the author of Genesis and his readers.

The main territory of the Amalekites seems to have been the Negeb desert (Num 13:29) between Beer-sheba and Sinai. The extent of their wanderings is summed up in I Sam 15:7 as "from Havilah as far as Shur, which is east of Egypt" (RSV) – from NW Arabia to the eastern border of Egypt along the line of the modern Suez Canal.

Migrating in search of suitable oases in what may have been a drought year, the Amalekites attacked Israel at Rephidim near Mount Sinai (Ex 17:8), for which ultimate destruction was decreed for them (v. 14; Deut 25: 17–19). They were declared the objects of perpetual warfare (Ex 17:16), and continued to be numbered among the enemies of Israel (Ps 83:7). After rebelling against the Lord, the Israelites sought to enter Canaan from the S, but were disastrously defeated by the Amalekites and Canaanites in the hills of the Negeb N of Kadesh-barnea (Num 14:43, 45). Balaam de-

scribed Amalek as "the first of the nations" (Num 24:20), either because of their antiquity in that region (I Sam 27:8) or because they were the first to attack the fledgling nation of Israel (Ex 17:8).

The Amalekites joined with neighbors twice in oppressing Israel during the period of the judges. They helped Eglon, king of Moab, to capture Jericho (Jud 3:13; for "the city of palm trees" – Jericho see Deut 34:3). As camel-riding bedouin they accompanied the Midianites in their harvesttime raids throughout Israel in the time of Gideon (Jud 6:3), but Gideon defeated them in the valley of Jezreel (6:33; 7:12–22). At one time there had been a settlement of Amalekites on a hill in the land of Ephraim (Jud 12:15; cf. 5:14).

King Saul carried out a systematic military campaign against the Amalekites (I Sam 14:48; 15:1–8). He selfishly refused to slaughter their healthy cattle and to execute their king Agag (15:9–33). Evidently he also failed to exterminate all of them, for they continued to raid the settled communities in S Judah during the later reign of Saul (I Sam 30:1–2). David made a reprisal raid to recover the wives and children taken from Ziklag (30:3–20). It was he who effectively crushed Amalek (I Sam 27:8–9; II Sam 8:11–12), so that they are heard of no more until the last remnant was wiped out by 500 Simeonites in Mount Seir in the reign of Hezekiah (I Chr 4:43).

H. G. S.

AMAM (ā'măm). One of the villages near Beer-sheba assigned to the tribe of Judah in the division of the land. Mentioned only in Josh 15:26.

AMANA (á-mā'ná), A peak in the Anti-Lebanon range (Song 4:8), probably S of the Amana (Abana) River valley. It is called Umânum and Ammana in Akkad. inscriptions. Sargon II obtained alabaster there.

AMARIAH (ăm-á-rī'á)
1. A descendant of Aaron through Phinehas, the son of Meraioth, and father of Ahitub (q.v.; I Chr 6:3,4,7,52); an ancestor of Ezra (Ezr 7:3).
2. A second priest, son of Azariah who was high priest in the time of Solomon (I Chr 6:9–11).
3. A descendant of Levi through Kohath, the father of Hebron, of whom he was the second son (I Chr 6:1,2; 23:19; 24:23).
4. A third priest, declared high priest by Jehoshaphat in Jerusalem in his reforms in Judah after the death of Ahab (II Chr 19:1, 8–11). He was probably the Amariah who was the son of Azariah (I Chr 6:11).
5. A Levite under Kore, the son of Imnah the Levite, appointed by Hezekiah to distribute among the Levites the freewill offerings of the people, as well as the oblations and the most

holy things (II Chr 31:14–15). He officiated in one of the cities of the priests.

6. A descendant of Bani (called Binnui in Neh 7:15) whose descendants returned with Zerubbabel from Babylon. In the time of Ezra he had taken a "strange" (non-Israelite) wife (Ezr 10:42; Neh 12:2, 13), from whom Ezra took an oath that he would put away his foreign wife (Ezr 10:19).

7. A priest in the time of Nehemiah who sealed a covenant with him and others (Neh 10:1–8) to serve the Lord (9:38). He was probably the same one who married a strange wife (cf. Neh 12:1–7 with 10:1–8).

8. A descendant of Judah through Perez (Neh 11:4), some of whose descendants dwelt in Jerusalem after the Exile.

9. A descendant of Hezekiah, king of Judah, and ancestor of Zephaniah the prophet who prophesied in the days of Josiah, king of Judah (Zeph 1:1).

H. G. S.

AMARNA LETTERS (à-mär'nà). The group of official letters found in 1887, with subsequent discoveries, at Tell el-Amarna in Egypt (*see* Amarna, Tell el-) now comprises about 375 clay tablets. They were written mostly in Babylonian cuneiform to the pharaohs Amenhotep III and Akhenaton (*q.v.*). This correspondence, covering the period roughly from 1400 to 1360 B.C., came from (1) rulers of the four nations comparatively equal in strength to Egypt: Assyria, the Hittites, Mitanni, and Kassite kings in Babylon; (2) vassal princes in Canaan and Syria under Egyptian control; and (3) various Egyptian officials in those lands. It is evident that Akkadian was the diplomatic language of the entire Near East at this time, even between the Egyptian overlord and his Asiatic vassals. This great influence of Babylonian culture on Canaan is confirmed by the discovery in 1946 at Megiddo of a fragment (*c.* 1400 B.C.) of the Gilgamesh Epic (Babylonian flood account). The Amarna letters, therefore, possess extraordinary importance for reconstructing the culture and history of the Near East in the early 14th cen. B.C. More than 200 of the Amarna tablets are in the Berlin Museum, over 80 are in the British Museum, and the rest are in museums in Cairo, Oxford, Paris, and Brussels.

Among the vassal princes heard from are those of Byblos or Gebal, Sidon, Tyre, Hazor, Akko, Megiddo, Gezer, Ashkelon, Lachish, Shechem, and Jerusalem. But never mentioned in these letters are the towns of Jericho, Ai, Bethel, Gibeon, and Hebron, taken or destroyed by Joshua. The vassals in Canaan complain to the pharaoh of hostility between their own city and neighboring towns, and call for help to meet the raids of small bands of Habiru or 'Apiru (*see* Hebrew People). These cannot be exclusively identified, however, with the invading Israelite army under Joshua, for Habiru are mentioned in various documents all during the 2nd mil. B.C. and throughout the Near East

as mercenary troops or vagrants. Nevertheless it is possible to see a picture of conditions in Palestine that prevailed early in the period of the judges when the Israelites were no longer operating as a united force.

In the Amarna period there were only four main city-states left in southern Palestine, whereas in Josh 10 nine cities having a king are mentioned. The Israelites had initially conquered and even recaptured some of these cities (e.g., Hebron and Debir), but in other cases, such as Jerusalem, they were unable to take the stronghold, or the Canaanites reoccu-

Amarna letters from King Labaia and Arzawa to Akhenaton in the Cairo Museum. LL

55

pied and held the city (e.g., Lachish) after the Israelite army returned to Gilgal. Disunity prevailed in the Amarna age, quite unlike the league of Amorite kings (Josh 10) or the Canaanite confederacy (Josh 11) that unitedly opposed Joshua. In certain specific instances the term Habiru in the Amarna letters may refer to Israelites. If so, the fact that according to tablets from 'Abdu-Heba of Jerusalem (ANET, pp. 487 ff.) Lab'ayu the prince of Shechem was in league with the Habiru may explain why Joshua did not find it necessary to attack and capture that city when the Israelites held the covenant ceremony at nearby Mount Ebal (Josh 8:30–35).

Bibliography. W. F. Albright, "The Amarna Letters," ANET, pp. 483–89. Gleason L. Archer, Jr., SOTI, pp. 164, 253–59, 265. F. F. Bruce, "Tell el-Amarna," TAOTS, pp. 3–20. Edward F. Campbell, Jr., "The Amarna Letters and the Amarna Period," BA, XXIII (1960), 2–22; *The Chronology of the Amarna Letters,* Baltimore: Johns Hopkins Univ. Press, 1964. CornPBE, pp. 40 ff. J. A. Knudtzon, *Die El-Amarna Tafeln,* Leipzig, 1907–15. George E. Mendenhall, "The Hebrew Conquest of Palestine," BA, XXV(1962), 66–87. Samuel A. B. Mercer, *The Tell el-Amarna Tablets,* New York: Macmillan, 1939. Charles F. Pfeiffer, *Tell el-Amarna and the Bible,* Grand Rapids: Baker, 1963.

J. R.

AMARNA, TELL EL- (tĕl-ĕl-*a*-mär'n*a*). The modern name of ruins and tombs on the E bank of the Nile, *c.* 190 miles S of Cairo. Tell el-Amarna is the site of ancient Akhetaton, "Horizon of Aton," built *c.* 1370 B.C. by Pharaoh Amenhotep IV, who changed his name to Akhenaton (*q.v.*) and instituted the so-called Amarna revolt. This revolution, possibly stemming from the cosmopolitanism of the empire of Thutmose III, involved religious, artistic, and literary changes. In religion, there was a new universalism, tending toward monotheism. Aton, the sun disk, was worshiped by the pharaoh and his family as the

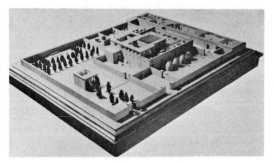

A model of a house and estate at Amarna, *c.* 1375–1330 B.C. ORINST

creator of all men, the benevolent father caring for all his creatures. Those in the court worshiped Akhenaton, the reputed son of this solar deity. Initiating this new worship brought so much opposition in Thebes, the royal residence and center of the worship of Amon-Re, that the young pharaoh moved the capital down stream to this new site. After his death the weakling pharaoh Tutankhamon was forced to return the capital to Thebes.

Excavations of the unimposing ruins of Tell el-Amarna, which stretches about five miles along the Nile but is only about 1,100 yards in width, indicate that the city was built in haste. The site had lain unnoticed and unidentified until 1887. In that year a local woman, while digging in the ruins for waste to use as fertilizer in her garden, happened on the royal archives of Akhetaton. These are known as the Amarna letters (*q.v.*) or tablets. Beginning in 1891 W. M. Flinders Petrie uncovered much of the palace. Later expeditions traced the plan of the city and explored about 25 tombs cut into the side of the hills to the E where Akhenaton's nobles were buried.

A hymn to Aton (ANET, pp. 369 ff.), with many parallels to Ps 104, was discovered at Amarna in the tomb of Eye, a courtier of Akhenaton. Direct dependence of Ps 104 on this hymn is doubtful, however, since contemporary Egyptian literature abounds in similar expressions, and the monotheism of the psalm goes far beyond the monolatry of the Aton worship.

Along with the Aton worship, Akhenaton fostered *ma'at,* "truth," in art and social life. Animals were depicted as if caught in action by a high-speed camera. Scenes of the royal family are presented in an informal, natural manner which differs from the earlier stylized art forms. The natural and familiar scenes, however, were so overdone that Akhenaton's own sickly figure, with pot belly, became the norm for all Egyptian portraits in that period.

A. K. H.

AMASA (*a*-mā's*a*)

1. Nephew of David, son of his sister Abigail and Jether an Ishmeelite (I Chr 2:13–17); cousin of Joab, son of Zeruiah, Abigail's sister (II Sam 17:25). After Absalom's revolt failed, David forgave Amasa and made him captain of his forces in place of Joab (II Sam 19:13). On the fall of Absalom, Sheba sought to keep the revolt alive (II Sam 20:1–2). David instructed Amasa to assemble the army to pursue Sheba, but he delayed too long (II Sam 20:4–5). David then sent Abishai, cousin of Amasa and brother of Joab (II Sam 20:6; I Chr 2:16), who was among the troops. At Gibeon the forces of Amasa and Abishai met (II Sam 20:7–8). Feigning to kiss him, Joab seized Amasa by his beard and slew him with his sword (II Sam 20:9–10).

2. An Ephraimite who helped deliver the Judeans taken captive by Pekah (II Chr 28:12).

AMASAI (*à*-mā'sĭ)

1. A Levite of the family of Kohath. He was the father of Mahath, the ancestor of Samuel (I Chr 6:25, 35).

2. One of the chief captains of David. With a group of men from Judah and Benjamin he deserted Saul and joined David at Ziklag. By some he is supposed to be the same as David's nephew Amasa *(q.v.)*, the son of Abigail (I Chr 12:18).

3. A priest in the time of David who blew a trumpet before the ark as it was brought up from the house of Obed-edom to Jerusalem (I Chr 15:24).

4. A priest in the days of Hezekiah. His son Mahath took an active part in the great revival and cleansing of the temple under Hezekiah (II Chr 29:12, 15).

AMASHAI (*à*-măsh'ī). Son of Azareel among the priests chosen by lot to live in Jerusalem at the time of Nehemiah (Neh 11:13).

AMASIAH (ăm'*à*-sī'*à*), Son of Zichri; a commander from Judah in Jehoshaphat's army who had volunteered for the Lord's service (II Chr 17:16).

AMAW (ā'mô). The name of the homeland of the prophet Balaam (Num 22:5, RSV), translating Heb. *'ammô*, "his people" (KJV). W. F. Albright (BASOR #118 [1950], 14–20) recognized this term to be the name of the country called *'Amau* on the inscribed statue of Idrimi excavated by Leonard Woolley at Alalakh, which may be dated variously *c.* 1450 B.C. (Albright) or 1375 (Woolley, Sidney Smith). Amaw, which lay between Aleppo and the Euphrates River, was ruled at that time by the king of Alalakh (near Antioch-on-the-Orontes). Amaw was also mentioned by an Egyptian officer of Amenhotep II. These references to Amaw from *c.* 1400 B.C. tend to confirm an early date for Moses, the Exodus, and Balaam. After *c.* 1370 B.C. that area was under Hittite control and was known to biblical writers as "the land of the Hittites" (cf. Josh 1:4; Jud 1:26). *See* Pethor; Balaam.

AMAZIAH (ăm'*à*-zī'*à*)

1. The ninth ruler of Judah, a son of Joash and Jehoaddan (Jehoaddin in II Kgs 14:2, RSV). Twenty-five years of age when he ascended the throne, he reigned for 29 years. There is disagreement on the dates of his reign. E. R. Thiele has placed the beginning of Amaziah's reign at 796 B.C. with a co-regency with his son Uzziah from 790 to 767 B.C. (*The Mysterious Numbers of the Hebrew Kings*, pp. 71–72). But W. F. Albright has proposed the dates 800–786 B.C. without a co-regency (*From the Stone Age to Christianity*, pp. 404 ff.). Because his father had been assassinated by servants in the royal household, Amaziah first had to ferret out and kill these murderers before his

throne was secure (II Kgs 12:19–21; 14:6; II Chr 24:25–27; 25:3–4).

Though accounted as a good king, Amaziah was warlike in temperament. He soon organized a large army of 300,000, plus 100,000 hired from Israel. However, on the advice of a man of God, he discharged the soldiers from Israel, making them so angry that they killed 3,000 Judahites. Amaziah attacked and subdued the Edomites, but preserved their idols for his personal use, for which a prophet condemned him (II Chr 25:5–16). Amaziah challenged Jehoash, king of Israel, to battle. The battle was fought at Beth-shemesh, and Amaziah was defeated and captured. Jehoash broke down the N wall of Jerusalem and robbed the temple of its treasure (II Kgs 14:8–14; II Chr 25:17–24). Judah apparently became a vassal of Israel throughout the remainder of Amaziah's reign. Amaziah was assassinated at Lachish by rebels who pursued him from Jerusalem. He was buried in Jerusalem (II Kgs 14:19, 20; II Chr 25:27, 28).

2. A Simeonite, father of the prince Joshah (I Chr 4:34, 38).

3. A Levite, an ancestor of Ethan, a singer in the services of David's tabernacle (I Chr 6:45).

4. A priest during the reign of Jeroboam II, known because he commanded Amos to cease prophesying at Bethel (Amos 7:10–17).

G. H. L.

AMBASSADOR. In the KJV the following three Heb. words are translated "ambassador"; *mal'āk*, meaning "messenger" (II Chr 35:21; Isa 30:4; 33:7; Ezk 17:15); *melîṣ*, meaning "intercessor" or "interpreter" (II Chr 32:31); and *ṣîr*, meaning "ambassador" (Josh 9:4; Prov 13:17; Isa 18:2; Jer 49:14; Ob 1). The general OT use of the term was to designate a temporary messenger sent on a special mission representing a king or a government (*see* Herald).

In the NT the Gr. word *presbeia*, "embassage," is used in Lk 14:32 of a group of ambassadors sent with a request for a peaceful settlement of difficulties (cf. Lk 19:14 where *presbeia* is translated "message"). Paul employed the verb *presbeuō* (II Cor 5:20; Eph 6:20) in a figurative sense describing his ministry as a representative of Christ. The Gr. papyri show that both these words were commonly used in the Hellenistic world in the official relationships of cities and rulers (MM). Deiss LAE, p. 374, indicates that *presbeuō* and *presbeutēs* were the terms used to designate the emperor's legate. Thus, Paul claimed for himself the lofty dignity of representing heaven's King, Jesus Christ, and as Christ's ambassador he brought the message of reconciliation to a world at enmity with God. In Eph 6:20 the apostle appears as an ambassador in prison because of the message which he proclaimed.

D. W. B.

AMBER. *See* Minerals.

AMBUSH. A military tactic involving the placing of armed men in a hidden or unexpected location for a surprise attack. Used effectively by Joshua against Ai (Josh 8), by the men of Shechem and Abimelech (Jud 9:25, 35), in the battle against Gibeah (Jud 20), and by King Jeroboam (II Chr 13:13). Paul's life also was threatened by an ambush (Acts 23:16, 21; 25:3). Because of the deceit involved, ambush is sometimes used in a derogatory sense (Jer 9:8; Ps 17:12; Ps 64:4; Prov 1:11, 18, RSV).

AMEN (ā'měn'). This was the customary Jewish assent to commands (I Kgs 1:36) and prayers (Neh 5:13; 8:6), and is rendered in LXX by the optative of wish (*genoitō*), "So be it." Jesus used it before statements to certify what followed (Mt 5:18, "verily"). Christians employed it after prayers to signify the listener's approval (I Cor 14:16). The noun is used as a title for Jesus (Rev 3:14); cf. "God of (the) Amen" (Isa 65:16, Heb.). The Heb. *'āmēn*, "firmness," is derived from the verb root *'āman*, "to believe." In Gen 15:6 Abram believed in the Lord and said "Amen" to God's promise (see Meredith G. Kline, "Abram's Amen," WTJ, XXXI [1968], 1–11).

AMETHYST. See Jewel.

AMI (ā'mī). The head of a family included among the descendants of Solomon's servants who returned from Exile to Judah under the leadership of Zerubbabel (Ezr 2:57). He is also called Amon (Neh 7:59).

AMIABLE. An older English word meaning "lovely," and used to describe God's dwelling place in Ps 84:1 (KJV).

AMINADAB (à-mĭn'à-dăb). This name appears in the genealogies of Jesus (Mt 1:4 and Lk 3:33) in KJV only. It has been changed to Amminadab in RSV. See Amminadab.

AMITTAI (à-mĭt'ī). The father of the prophet Jonah (II Kgs 14:25; Jon 1:1).

AMMAH (ăm'à). A hill facing Giah on the way to the wilderness of (i.e., E of) Gibeon, which marked the end of Joab's pursuit of Abner (II Sam 2:24). The hill probably was at the crest of the wilderness descent into the Jordan Valley.

AMMI (ăm'ī). Heb. word meaning "my people," given by Hosea as the new name of the third child of his adulterous wife Gomer (Hos 2:1). The original name, Lo-ammi ("not my people," Hos 1:9), symbolized the sad rejection of God's covenant by His wayward people Israel. Ammi conveyed the hope of restoration (Hos 2:21–23) and is applied to the new Israel by NT writers (Rom 9:25; I Pet 2:10).

AMMIEL (ăm'ĭ-ĕl)
1. A man of the tribe of Dan. One of the 12 spies sent out by Moses to look over Canaan. He was with the majority who brought an unfavorable report and died under God's judgment (Num 13:12).
2. A Manassite of Lodebar in Gilead. He was the father of Machir who protected Mephibosheth, the lame son of Jonathan, and also received David fleeing from Absalom (II Sam 9:4–5; 17:27).
3. The father of David's wife Bathsheba (I Chr 3:5). In II Sam 11:3, by transposition of the second and third consonants, he is called Eliam.
4. A Levite, doorkeeper in the temple. One of the sons of Obed-edom (I Chr 26:5).

AMMIHUD (à-mĭ'hŭd)
1. The father of Elishama, who was chief of the tribe of Ephraim in the days of Moses (Num 1:10).
2. The father of Shemuel who was appointed from the tribe of Simeon as a divider of the Promised Land (Num 34:20).
3. The father of Pedahel, prince of the tribe of Naphtali, a divider of the land (Num 34:28).
4. The father of Talmai, king of Geshur and father-in-law of David. Absalom fled to his grandfather's court after slaying his brother Amnon (II Sam 13:37).
5. A descendant of Perez of the tribe of Judah. His son Uthai was among the first to return to Jerusalem after the Exile (I Chr 9:4).

AMMINADAB (à-mĭn'à-dăb)
1. The father of Nahshon, prince of the tribe of Judah in the days of Moses (Num 1:7; 2:3; 7:12, 17; 10:14). He was the father also of Elisheba, the wife of Aaron (Ex 6:23). Amminadab was the ancestor of Boaz and David and is listed in the genealogy of Jesus Christ (Ruth 4:19–20; I Chr 2:10; Mt 1:4; Lk 3:33; spelled Aminadab in NT).
2. Named in I Chr 6:22 as the son of Kohath and father of Korah. In I Chr 6:2, 18 and in Ex 6:18, 29 he is called Izhar (*q.v.*).
3. One of the chief Levites of the family of Kohath in the time of David. He was one of those privileged to carry the ark of the Lord from the house of Obed-edom to Jerusalem (I Chr 15:10).
4. The name occurs on two ancient Ammonite seals and in an inscription of Ashurbanipal, where it is the name of the king of Ammon (ANET, p. 294).

AMMINADIB (à-mĭn'à-dĭb). Occurs only in Song 6:12, KJV where it is taken to be the name of a charioteer otherwise unknown. RSV regards it not as a proper name but emends it to read "in a chariot beside my prince." The text of this verse is generally regarded as having been corrupted in transmission, as it does not clearly make sense as it stands in the existing Heb. texts.

AMMISHADDAI (ăm'ĭ-shăd'ī). The father of Ahiezer of the tribe of Dan at the time of the Exodus (Num 1:12). This Heb. name was borne by an Egyptian official in the late 14th cen. B.C.

AMMIZABAD (à-mĭz'à-băd). The son of David's military leader Benaiah (I Chr 27:6).

AMMON (ăm'ŏn).The son of Lot by his younger daughter (Gen 19:38). His descendants are called Ammonites (q.v.), and sometimes Ammon (Ps 83:7). Ammon is also used as a place name in Neh 13:23.

AMMONITES (ăm'ŏ-nīts). A people descended from a son of Lot by his younger daughter, who gave birth to Benammi in a cave near Zoar, now called Zi'ara. They dispossessed the Zamzummims and dwelt in their place (Deut 2:20–21). Their country lay between the Arnon and Jabbok Rivers to the NE of Moab, protected by a strong border on its N side (Num 22:24). Rabbah (q.v.) or Rabbath (modern 'Ammān) was its chief city (Deut 3:11). In 1961 a fragment of a royal Ammonite monument from the 9th cen. B.C. was discovered in the ruins of the ancient citadel at Amman, written in Aramaic script (BASOR #193 [Feb., 1969], pp. 2–19).

No Ammonite could enter the nation of Israel even to the tenth generation (Deut 23:3). The Israelites were not to meddle with nor distress them on the way to Canaan (Deut 2:19).

The Ammonites joined with the Amalekites and Eglon the king of Moab to smite Israel in the time of the judges and to occupy Jericho, "the city of palm trees" (Jud 3:13). Israel later worshiped the Ammonite gods, was subjugated by these enemies for 18 years, and was finally delivered by Jephthah (Jud 10:6—11:33). Nahash, king of the Ammonites, threatened Jabesh-gilead, but was routed by Saul (I Sam 11:1–11; 12:12). David was a friend of Nahash or of his son with the same name (II Sam 10:2), but Nahash's son insulted David's messengers of peace and David thereupon sent Joab and Abishai to punish the people (II Sam 10:1—11:1). When David fled from Absalom, Shobi, son of Nahash and brother of Hanun, brought supplies to David at Mahanaim (II Sam 17:27–28). Zelek, one of David's mighty men, was an Ammonite (II Sam 23:37). Solomon loved Ammonite women among other foreign women, and worshiped Milcom, the god of the Ammonites, building a high place for his worship (I Kgs 11:1, 5, 7, 33). This god was the chief deity of their religion. Naamah, the mother of Rehoboam, was an Ammonite (I Kgs 14:21, 31).

When the Ammonites joined with the Moabites and Edomites to attack Jehoshaphat, God sent confusion among them so that they destroyed each other (II Chr 20:1–23). Zabad, son of the Ammonitess Shimeath, with Jehoza-

A street scene in Amman, Jordan, site of Rabbath-Ammon, capital of the Ammonites. Richard E. Ward

bad, son of the Moabitess Shimrith, conspired against Joash, king of Judah, and slew him (II Chr 24:26; II Kgs 12:21). Uzziah received tribute from the Ammonites among others whom he subjected (II Chr 26:8). Jotham, son of Uzziah, again subjected them to tribute (II Chr 27:5). In his reforms Josiah defiled the high place which Solomon had built in Jerusalem for Milcom, the god of the Ammonites (II Kgs 23:13). The Lord sent the Ammonites against Jehoiakim and Judah because of the sins of Manasseh (II Kgs 24:1–4).

The practices of the Ammonites still infected Israel in the days of Ezra (Ezr 9:1). Tobiah, an Ammonite, obstructed the rebuilding of both the temple and city of Jerusalem (Neh 2:10, 19; 4:3, 7). The Ammonites were threatened with destruction (Amos 1:13–15; Zeph 2:8–11), punished (Jer 9:26), and were to become obedient to God's people (Isa 11:14).

Archaeological evidence indicates that the Ammonite civilization flourished from 1200 to 600 B.C. The W approaches to the capital at Rabbah were protected by a strong line of border fortresses. The fortress towers could be circular, square or rectangular. Ammonite tombs in the vicinity of Amman reveal a prosperous material culture during the Iron II period (900–600 B.C.), made possible by controlling the lucrative caravan trade across the desert from Arabia. Yet the Ammonites seem to have retained an essentially nomadic type of social structure as late as the 7th cen. B.C. (George M. Landes, "The Material Civilization of the Ammonites," BA, XXIV [1961], 65–86).

H. G. S.

AMNON (ăm'nŏn)

1. Oldest son of David, born at Hebron (II Sam 3:2; I Chr 3:1). He raped his half sister Tamar, and in retaliation was murdered by order of Absalom, her full brother (II Sam 13).

2. One of the sons of Shimon of the tribe of Judah (I Chr 4:20).

AMOK (ā'mŏk). One of the leading priests who returned to Judah with Zerubbabel after the Exile (Neh 12:7, 20).

AMON (ăm'ŏn)

1. Governor of the city of Samaria under Ahab, keeper of the prophet Micaiah, while Ahab with Jehoshaphat fought Syria (I Kgs 22:2, 10, 26; II Chr 18:25).

2. King of Judah, son of Manasseh, who succeeded his father at age 22 and reigned two years (II Kgs 21:19-21). He was distinguished by his evil deeds. Worshiping idols (v. 21), he thus forsook God (v. 22). Unlike his father Manasseh, Amon did not repent of his wickedness, exceeding his father in his evil deeds (II Chr 33:23). He was murdered in his palace by his servants (II Kgs 21:23), and the people made his son Josiah king in his stead (v. 24). Amon is numbered among the ancestors of Christ (Mt 1:10).

3. A descendant from among the servants of Solomon (Neh 7:57, 59).

4. The name of an Egyptian divinity in the name of the Egyptian city No-Amon (called "No," Jer 46:25); also called Thebes, the capital of upper Egypt. Amon replaced the sun-god Ra as head of the Egyptian pantheon. Under his ensign, the Hyksos were expelled from Egypt. *See* Gods, False.

H. G. S.

AMORITES (ăm'ŏ-rīts). The Amorites of the OT derived their name from a Semitic word (Akkad. *Amurru*) which means "westerner." The Amorites in Palestine were a part of a movement of western Semitic nomads *c.* 2100- 1900 B.C. who appeared in all parts of the Fertile Crescent. They are included in the Genesis table of nations as a people of Canaan (Gen 10:16), reflecting the mid-2nd mil. B.C. viewpoint of that passage. The Beni-Hasan tomb paintings of Egypt (*c.* 1900 B.C.) depict 37 bearded Amorites bringing their wares into Egypt on donkeys. Kathleen Kenyon believes the single burials of the Early Bronze-Middle Bronze period (2100- 1900 B.C.) at Jericho may be those of invading Amorite seminomads. Oldenburg contends that the Amorites introduced the worship of Baal-Hadad in the region of Canaan, which eventually displaced the worship of the god El.

In southern Babylonia the Larsa Dynasty (*c.* 1950 B.C.) was founded by Amorites. In the following century the Amorites took over such important centers as Babylon and Eshnunna. Mari on the mid-Euphrates had an Amorite king during the days of Hammurabi (*c.* 1750 B.C.) whose own dynasty had been founded by an Amorite. The Amorites formed the basis of the Assyrian stock who settled on the Tigris between the Zab tributaries. It has been conjectured that Abraham's family was among the

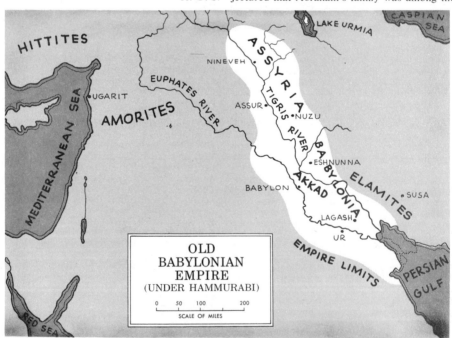

In the days of Hammurabi (*c.* 1700 B.C.) and the Old Babylonian Empire, the Amorites were one of the most powerful peoples of the Near East. Hammurabi's dynasty was Amorite, and Amorites controlled much of Palestine and Syria at the same time.

Amorite invaders of Canaan. Ezk 16:3 tends to support this by saying of Judah, "Thy father was an Amorite, and thy mother a Hittite."

The Amorites, who spoke a NW Semitic dialect, settled in various regions of Palestine, notably N of the Arnon but especially N of the Jabbok River. It was here that the Israelites under Moses encountered them and their king Sihon, who, like the Moabites and Edomites, refused to let Israel pass. The Hebrews celebrated their victory over the Amorites in the ballad song of Num 21:27-30. Moses also conquered the land of Og, king of Bashan, who is designated an Amorite in Deut 4:47.

According to Gen 14:13 some of the Amorites who settled in the Hebron area were allies of Abraham. Some of these Amorites dwelt on the W bank of the Dead Sea at En-gedi (Hazezon-tamar, Gen 14:7). They were subdued by the four kings from Mesopotamia (Gen 14). Shechem who fell in love with Dinah (Gen 34) was an Amorite. Jacob alludes to this episode in Gen 48:22 (Heb. text) when he bequeathed the town of Shechem to Joseph. Joseph's bones were eventually buried near this old Amorite-Hebrew stronghold (Josh 24:32).

After Joshua's invasion of Canaan, a league of five Amorite kings headed by Adonizedek of Jerusalem opposed the Israelite army near Gibeon (Josh 10). During the time of the judges the descendants of the Amorites in the S of Judah were still in the land. Their pressure forced the Danites to move N, while another pocket of Amorites who lived near the valley of Aijalon was put to forced labor by the Ephraimites (Jud 1:34-36). Solomon eventually put to slave labor all the remnants of non-Israelites left in the land, including the Amorites (I Kgs 9:20-21) who had tricked Joshua into an alliance (Josh 9).

Sometimes the OT seems to use the term Amorite as representative of all the Canaanite tribes in Palestine (cf. Gen 15:16). Perhaps this reflects the fact that their dialect was practically undistinguishable from their 3rd mil. predecessors in Palestine commonly called Canaanites. The Amarna letters use the term Amurru of the entire region of Syria-Palestine, revealing how numerous the Amorites became in Canaan. On the other hand, there are passages which make a distinction between the Amorite and the Canaanite and other groups, especially when the people whom the Lord would drive out were listed (cf. Ex 34:11). Also the Amorite had a common preference for the hill country along with the Hittite and the Jebusite (Hurrian), while the Canaanite dwelt by the sea (Num 13:29).

Later in history the autonomous Canaanite seafarers were called Phoenicians by the Greeks, while the Amorites were assimilated and disappeared as a distinct people in Palestine. Because of their degraded religious practices, this assimilation was stoutly resisted by the spiritual leaders of Israel from Joshua (Josh 24:15) down to Ezra (Ezr 9:1-3).

Bibliography. Giorgio Buccellati, *The Amorites of the Ur III Period,* Naples: Institute Orientals di Napoli, 1966. Kathleen M. Kenyon, *Amorites and Canaanites,* London: Oxford Univ. Press, 1966. Ulf Oldenburg, *The Conflict Between El and Baal in Canaanite Religion,* Leiden: E. J. Brill, 1969, pp. 151-163.

E. B. S.

AMOS (ā′mŏs). An 8th cen. prophet, Amos (Heb. '*āmôs,* "burden bearer") was unique in his bold ministry to the kingdom of Israel in that he was a native of Judah. He did not have his training in the religious schools or prophetic guilds of his day. To the contrary, he denied any previous connection with the formal religious community (Amos 7:14-15). He placed himself in the midst of the world in which he lived, a shepherd (1:1) and a dresser of sycomore fig trees (7:14). His familiarity with rural life is reflected in his selection of language: lion, bear, and serpent (5:19); locusts and grass of the land (7:1); and basket of summer fruit (8:1). He made his living in the wilderness or dry pastureland near Tekoa (cf. II Chr 11:6; Jer 6:1), a village situated about ten miles S of Jerusalem and 12 miles W of the Dead Sea.

Three statements in Amos 1:1 indicate the time Amos lived: (1) Uzziah was king of Judah; (2) Jeroboam was king of Israel; (3) it was two years before the earthquake. Critical study seems to place the convergence of these three near 760 B.C.

Amos was a prophet, a speaker for God, but not of his own choosing (cf. Paul, Jeremiah and Isaiah); it was rather at the command of God (7:15). His comprehension of the spiritual scene of his day has led many to classify him as the beginning of a new order of prophets. His ministry led him to Bethel, the center of religious apostasy in the northern kingdom (I Kgs 12:26-33). The last years before the fall of Israel were characterized by great material prosperity. Still enjoying the luxury of military victory during the reign of Jeroboam II, Israel allowed temporal security to replace her trust in the living God.

Amos' denunciation of Israel (Amos 2:6-16) can serve as an outline for a study of the social, moral, and religious condition of the people. Socially, two distinct classes had developed, the poor and the rich. The rich were seeking greater riches by any means (2:6-7). Moral evils were rampant. Drunkenness and sexual license were at an abominable level (2:7-8). Religious perversion was at a gross high. For the most part idolatry was common (2:8). The faithful were scorned, chastised and mocked (2:12). The depth to which the people had fallen is characterized in their seeming indifference to their position as a delivered and cared-for nation (2:9-11). Repentance and obedience were imperatives, the only escape from imminent judgment.

Amos or the compiler (cf. superscription and third person portions of the narrative) arranged this material into three major divisions. Likely the book contains only a portion of Amos' words spoken at Bethel. If the book had an editor other than Amos himself, possibly he was also from Judah and was a companion of the prophet on his trek northward, for the nature of the text indicates early recording of the prophet's message.

Chaps. 1 and 2 are viewed as one division, including a preface (1:1-2) in which Amos' theme is announced that the wrath of the Lord is imminent, and a setting forth of judgments against Israel and her neighbors. A second division is comprised by chaps. 3-6. These are in turn subdivided, each section introduced by "Hear this word" (3:1; 4:1; 5:1). The final division, chaps. 7-9, contains a series of five visions (7:1-3; 7:4-6; 7:7-9; 8:1-14; 9:1-10) interrupted by an historical account of his visit to Bethel (7:10-17). Perhaps at that time he proclaimed the warning messages of chaps. 1-6. His preaching seems to have been inspired by the words accompanying the fourth vision found in 7:4-6 (cf. 2:6-7). An epilogue (9:11-15) foretelling the restoration of the Davidic kingdom closes the work.

The key verses of the book may be 3:2—that judgment is determined according to privileges, so that God's chosen covenant people above all others will not escape—and 4:12, a summons to covenant renewal.

The book may be outlined in this way:

I.   Judgments Against Near Eastern Nations, Chaps. 1-2
     1. Prophecies against heathen neighbors, 1:3-2:3
     2. Wrath upon the two covenant nations, 2:4-16
II. Proclamations Against Israel, Chaps. 3-6
     1. The fact of Israel's guilt, 3:1-15
     2. The depravity of Israel, 4:1-13
     3. Coming punishment for Israel's sin, 5:1-17
     4. The inescapable captivity, 5:18-27
     5. The peril of complacency, 6:1-14
III. Five Visions Concerning Israel, 7:1-9:10
     1. Devouring locusts, 7:1-3
     2. Flaming fire, 7:4-6
     3. Plumbline; opposition of the priest of Bethel, 7:7-17
     4. Basket of ripe fruit, 8:1-14
     5. Judgment of the Lord on Bethel's apostate altar, 9:1-10
IV. Promise of Restoration, 9:11-15

Amos' theological motifs can be summarized briefly as the holy character of the sovereign God, the requirement by God of social justice, the moral and religious infidelity of the covenant people shown in utter disregard for the law of Moses, the reality of judgment, salvation through repentance, and the ultimate restoration and realization of God's purposes.

See Israel, Kingdom of; Prophet.

Bibliography. W. Brueggemann, "Amos IV: 4-13 and Israel's Covenant Worship," VT, XV (1965), 1-15. B. B. Copass, *Amos,* Nashville: Broadman, 1939. Richard S. Cripps, *A Critical and Exegetical Commentary on the Book of Amos,* London: SPCK, 1929. William R. Harper, *Amos and Hosea,* ICC, 1905. R. L. Honeycutt, *Amos and His Message,* Nashville: Broadman, 1963. A. S. Kapelrud, *Central Ideas in Amos,* Oslo: Aschehoug, 1956. H. G. R. Mitchell, *Amos, an Essay in Exegesis,* New York: Houghton Mifflin, 1900. Norman H. Snaith, *Amos, Parts I and II,* London: Epworth Press, 1945-6; *Amos, Hosea and Micah,* London: Epworth, 1956. John D. W. Watts. *Vision and Prophecy in Amos,* Grand Rapids: Eerdmans, 1958.

R. O. C.

AMOZ (ā'mŏz). The father of the prophet Isaiah (Isa 1:1; II Kgs 19:2, *et al.*). A Palestinian seal bearing the inscription "Amoz the Scribe" may have belonged to Isaiah's father since Amoz is a rare name. This may indicate Isaiah was from a family prominent in government.

AMPHIPOLIS (ăm-fĭp'ō-lĭs). Mentioned once in the NT (Acts 17:1). This city was visited by Paul on his second missionary journey. It was called Amphipolis ("surrounded city") because the site on which it was located was enclosed on three sides by the Strymon River which curved around it, the E side being open. According to Thucydides (*Peloponnesian War,* iv. 103 ff.), a wall protected this E side, and it was

The Lion of Amphipolis stands guard at the ancient site as it did in Paul's day. HFV

strengthened and enlarged at various times. Thucydides was intimately familiar with Amphipolis, since he tried unsuccessfully to relieve it in time of seige (*c.* 422 B.C.). His failure resulted in his 20-year exile from his country. He mentions that the town was valuable for "the timber that it afforded for ship building."

Jackson and Lake (*Beginnings of Christianity, Acts,* IV, 202) point out that Paul's journey between Philippi and Thessalonica along the Egnatian Way was 100 Roman miles and seems to have been divided into these three stages: Philippi to Amphipolis (33 Roman miles); Amphipolis to Apollonia (30 Roman miles); Apollonia to Thessalonica (37 Roman miles). This suggests to them that Paul used horses to make this part of his journey.

The coins of Amphipolis during Paul's time frequently depict Artemis Tauropolis riding on a bull, indicating the close contact the area had with Asia, being located only three miles from the Mediterranean. No archaeological work has been carried on as yet at Amphipolis (which reaches back to the 1st cen. A.D.), though a Byzantine-period Christian complex has been discovered.

E. J. V.

AMPLIAS (ăm'plĭ-ăs). A common name, frequently given to slaves. It is a shortened form of Ampliatus. Paul greets Amplias in Rome by calling him "my beloved in the Lord" (Rom 16:8). An early Christian tomb in the cemetery of Domitilla in Rome bears the inscription "Ampliat."

AMRAM (ăm'răm)

1. Grandson of Levi, son of Kohath, and the father of Moses and Aaron (Ex 6:18, 20; Num 26:59).

2. A son of Bani, who had married a foreign wife and was required by Ezra to put her away (Ezr 10:34).

AMRAMITES (ăm'ră-mīts). The descendants of Amram who formed a branch of the priestly family of Kohathites (Num 3:27; I Chr 26:23).

AMRAPHEL (ăm'ră-fĕl). The king of Shinar, who joined with other kings in a battle in the valley of Siddim during the days of Abram (Gen 14). *See* Abraham. Because of some similarity of the names in Heb., attempts formerly were made to identify him with Hammurabi, the famous king of Babylon. The first and last Heb. letters of Amraphel, however, cannot be equated with the Akkad. *ḫ* and lack of an *l*, respectively, in the name Hammurabi. It more likely would be the Amorite name *Amur-pi-el* or *Amuru-âpil(i)*.

W. F. Albright believes the name "Amraphel" may be associated with Emudbal, the name of an important Amorite tribe which gave its name to a region between Elam and Babylonia at least by 1800 B.C., according to the Mari tablets (BASOR # 163, pp. 49 f.; *Yahweh*

and the Gods of Canaan, Garden City: Doubleday, 1968, pp. 68 f.
See Chedorlaomer.

AMULET. Amulets are decorative or magical objects worn on the person or installed in the home. They are usually made of semiprecious stone, such as carnelian or soft stone covered with glaze. As objects of magic they are intended to protect against evil spirits and assure the welfare of the wearer and his family. Amulets are usually pierced and worn around the neck.

Styles of amulets discovered in Palestine were often borrowed from Egypt where scarabs were common. The scarab was shaped like a beetle, usually made of stone, with a religious design or name on its under flat surface. Horus eyes served as symbols of the magic activity of the goddess Isis in restoring life to her husband Osiris.

Images of gods or teraphim (*q.v.*) were also common amulets (Gen 35:4). Palestinian excavations have yielded many Astarte figurines—images of the fertility goddess with exaggerated sexual features designed to insure fertility. Isaiah denounced the women of Israel for their pride and their ostentatious display of a variety of jewelry including crescent-shaped ornaments and amulets, which may have been more for decorative than magical use (Isa 3:18–21, NASB; cf. Jud 8:21, 26). *See* Magic.

C. F. P.

AMZI (ăm'zī)

1. Son of Bani of the tribe of Levi (I Chr 6:46).

2. A priest, the son of Zechariah (Neh 11:12).

ANAB (ā'năb). A town in the hill country of Judah conquered by Joshua (Josh 11:21) and allotted to the tribe of Judah (Josh 15:50). The site is now called Khirbet 'Anab, 13 miles SW of Hebron. The city was repeatedly mentioned in Egyptian texts of the Nineteenth Dynasty as Qrt-'nb, corresponding to the Heb. Kiriath-anab ("city of Anab").

ANAH (ā'na). Son of Zibeon and father of Aholibamah, the wife of Esau (Gen 36:2, 24). In I Chr 1:38–41 Anah is identified as a brother of Zibeon. This may be a different person, or the name may be loosely used to refer to a family group.

ANAHARATH (*a*-nā'*a*-răth). A town allotted to the tribe of Issachar in the conquest of Canaan (Josh 19:19), now en-Na'urah, five miles NE of Jezreel. Also mentioned in the list of towns captured by Thutmose III about 1479 B.C.

ANAIAH (*a*-nā'y*a*). One of the post-Exilic leaders who stood at Ezra's right hand when he read the book of the law (Neh 8:4), and who assisted Nehemiah in sealing the covenant (Neh 10:22).

ANAKIMS (ANAKIM, ANAK) (ăn'á-kĭm). A tribe inhabiting the land of Palestine especially in the S near Hebron in pre-Israelite times. The term probably developed from the ascriptive title "people of the neck" or "necklace" (from Heb. 'ānāq, "necklace," cf. Prov 1:9; Song 4:9) to a proper name for the tribe. Apparently all these tribal groups were destroyed by Joshua except the coastal settlements at Gaza, Gath, and Ashdod (Josh 11:21–22).

Twice the Bible refers to "the city of Arba the father of Anak" (Josh 15:13; 21:11), which could indicate either that a prominent man or ancestor of the Anakim was called Arba, or that we should understand the expression as a proper name of the city, i.e., "Kiriath-arba" or Hebron (cf. Gen 23:2), in which case the city was the ancestral home of the Anakim.

In the Execration texts of Egypt now in the Berlin Museum, dated c. 1900 B.C., there is an incantation directed toward certain enemy cities and territories among which are Palestinian areas and which names specific rulers of an area called "Iy-'aneq," who could well be the Anakim of biblical materials (ANET, p. 328). These pottery fragments represent the ritual cursing of Pharaoh's enemies by breaking jars upon which the names were inscribed.

The biblical materials indicate that very large stature (perhaps exaggerated by their neighbors) was attributed to the Anakim which tended to produce fear among their enemies (cf. Num 13:22, 28, 33; Deut 2:10–11, 21; 9:2). *See* Dolmens; Giant. In Num 13:33, RSV, they are mentioned as descendants of the "Nephilim," who are elsewhere described as being the pre-Flood sons of the union between the sons of God and the daughters of men (Gen 6:4). The Anakim were also known as Rephaim (*q.v.;* Deut 2:11, RSV).

E. C. B. Maclaurin believes that the term Anak may have been a Philistine title of rank, and that the Anakim were hereditary rulers of the Philistines who early came to Palestine from the Mycenaean world ("Anak/'Anax," VT, XV [1965], 468–474). A cuneiform tablet from Asshur mentions Anaku as a place in the Aegean area. R. de Vaux suggests the Anakim made up a corps of mercenary troops for one of the Canaanite principalities (*Ancient Israel,* p. 219).

A. F. J.

ANALOGY. The relation of similarity or likeness between two objects of thought, used as a basis for inferring other resemblances less obvious. The word is derived from the Gr. *ana,* "according to"; and *logos,* in this use, "proportion" or "ratio." The Gr. word occurs twice in the NT: Rom 12:6, translated "proportion," from which comes the phrase "analogy of faith"; and Heb 12:3 in the verb form, translated "consider," pointing out the resemblance

between the sufferings of Christ and those of His followers.

Analogies are widely used in the Bible in the effort to convey truth about God and spiritual things to minds limited by the human and material. Thus, God is our heavenly Father (Deut 32:6; Ps 68:5; Isa 63:16; Mt 6:9; 23:9; Rom 8:15–16), we are joint heirs with Christ (Rom 8:17; Gal 4:7), and many more too numerous to list. All parables involve an element of analogy.

The anthropomorphisms of the Bible (i.e., attributing to God human form, feelings, and actions) must be considered as analogies; e.g., God is spoken of as having hands (Ex 7:17), eyes (II Chr 16:9), ears (Isa 5:9), mouth (Isa 1:20); and being able to walk (Gen 3:8), sleep (Ps 44:23), see (Gen 6:12), hear (Ex 16:12), write (Ex 31:18), breathe (Job 4:9), smell (Gen 8:21), and many others. *See* Anthropomorphism.

The strength and value of analogical reasoning depends on the degree to which the objects compared are essentially similar. Incidental resemblances are never safe bases for analogy. Analogy in theology is inescapable, but must be used with caution.

W. T. P.

ANAMIM (ăn'á-mĭm). An Egyptian group (Anamin in RSV) referred to only in Gen 10:13 and I Chr 1:11.

ANAMMELECH. *See* Gods, False.

ANAN (ā'năn). One of the post-Exilic leaders who assisted Nehemiah in sealing the covenant with God (Neh 10:26).

ANANI (á-nā'nī). The seventh son of Elioenai of the tribe of Judah (I Chr 3:24).

ANANIAH (ăn'á-nī'á)
1. The father of Maaseiah and grandfather of Azariah (Neh 3:23), the grandson assisting in the rebuilding of a section of the wall of Jerusalem.
2. A town in the territory of Benjamin (Neh 11:32) which was inhabited by Jews after the Exile. It is possibly to be identified with Bethany ("house of Ananiah"), which is two miles E of Jerusalem, probably taking its name from the members of the family of Ananiah who settled there.

ANANIAS (ăn'á-nī'ás)
1. Ananias and Sapphira (*q.v.*), husband and wife, of Acts 5:1–11. In sharp contrast to the unselfishness of other church members, they pretended to give to the Jerusalem church the total sale price of their property while they actually retained part for themselves. Peter rebuked Ananias, who was immediately struck down in death by divine judgment. A few hours later Sapphira was likewise judged for the same effort to deceive. It is important to notice that Peter predicted rather than decreed these judgments which were God's act. The severity of

God's judgment is a warning to all, and not repeated in later cases because of His forbearance and desire for our repentance. These two may not have been sent into eternal punishment, as often assumed, but rather taken from this life in order that they might not be condemned with unbelievers (see I Cor 11:29-32).

2. Ananias in Acts 9:10-19 was a disciple of Damascus (c. A.D. 31-35) whom God instructed in a vision to go to Saul of Tarsus, to restore his sight, baptize him, and introduce him to the Christian believers. Later, when giving his testimony (Acts 22:12-16), Paul describes Ananias as a "devout man according to the law, having a good report of all the Jews" in Damascus.

3. In Acts 22:5; 23:2; 24:1 ff., the high priest before whom Paul was on trial (c. 58) in Jerusalem is named Ananias. From Josephus we learn he was a son of Hedebaeus and served in the office of high priest c. 47-59. He had come down to Caesarea in person to accuse Paul before Felix, the Roman procurator. Because of his unpriestly behavior, Paul rebuked him but promptly apologized. Paul's behavior has been explained as due either to his supposed nearsightedness or to momentary forgetfulness.

T. B. C.

ANATH (ā'năth)

1. Name of a Canaanite goddess. *See* Gods, False: Anath.

2. The town of Anata (Anathoth, the home of Jeremiah), three miles NNE of Jerusalem, bears the name of the goddess Anath, as do other place names, such as Beth-anoth (temple of Anath) in Judah (Josh 15:59) and Beth-anath in Naphtali (Josh 19:38; Jud 1:33).

3. The form of the word Anath standing alone appears only as the name of the parent of Shamgar the judge (Jud 3:31). Since the term could hardly be the name of a male, some modern scholars have suggested this is a case of ascribing to a hero divine parentage (the goddess, Anath) as is sometimes the case in Near Eastern mythology. But such a view is contrary to OT usage. Jud 5:6 contains a clue to the right view. It is sufficient to say that Anath was the mother of Shamgar and that this man's mother rather than father is mentioned because the text is stressing the role of women deliverers. So Deborah singles out Shamgar in her song, because he was the son of Anath (cf. Zeruiah, the mother of the hero Joab, II Sam 17:25), and Jael because she was the woman who killed Sisera (Jud 5:6).

E. B. S.

ANATHEMA. The Heb. term *ḥerem*, translated in LXX by Gr. *anathema*, came to have a double meaning: (1) something devoted or consecrated to a god, and thus withdrawn irrevocably from man's use; or (2) something or someone dedicated to destruction, and lying under a divine curse. For this use in the OT, see examples in Lev 27:28 f.; Josh 6:17 f. For the former usage in the NT see Lk 21:5 (KJV, "gifts"; NASB, "votive gifts").

The second meaning is the usual one, however. By a solemn oath *(anathema)* the conspirators against Paul pledged to kill him or to die themselves (Acts 23:14). Paul used the term *anathema* with reference to someone who is the object of a curse calling for destruction or death and implying moral worthlessness (Rom 9:3; I Cor 12:3; 16:22; Gal 1:8-9). A. Deissmann has shown that the word was used in pagan religions. In Judaism and the early church it came to have the sense of excommunicate.

See Accursed; Curse; Devote.

W. M. D.

ANATHOTH (ăn'a-thŏth). A small village three miles NE of Jerusalem. It was the home of Abiathar the priest and of Jeremiah, his descendant (I Kgs 2:26; Jer 1:1; 11:21 ff.). Located in the land of Benjamin (Josh 21:18), it was assigned to the sons of Aaron. Two of David's men of valor, Abiezer and Jehu, came from Anathoth (II Sam 23:27; I Chr 12:3). Here, by revelation, Jeremiah purchased a field which had belonged to his ancestors (Jer 32:7 ff.). Upon their return from Exile, the Benjamites again occupied it (Neh 11:32).

To the N of Anathoth was Michmash and to the SW was Jerusalem (Isa 10:28-32). It has been identified with the modern 'Anātā, though the ancient site seems to have been about 850 yards SW of it on the summit *Rās el Kharrūbeh,* which is about 150 feet higher than the present village. Archaeologists have found here the remains of a settlement that endured from the time of ancient Israel to the 7th cen. A.D. From here, the eye surveys the Dead Sea to the SE, the highlands of Transjordan to the E, and the northern uplands. It is exposed to the withering siroccos which blow from the deserts of Transjordan.

R. E. Pr.

The Village of Anathoth. @ MPS

ANCHOR. Larger ships of NT times carried several anchors. In form, they had evolved from heavy stones (ANEP, fig. 42) to large wooden shanks with upturned flukes and wooden stocks or crossbars filled with lead, weighing hundreds of pounds (*Archaeology*, XXI [1968], 63).

Luke's masterful account of Paul's voyage and shipwreck contains the only reference to literal anchors in the biblical narrative (Acts 27:29–40). The violence of the storm made the issue doubtful even with four anchors. Anchoring from the stern was unusual (William Ramsay, *St. Paul, the Traveller*, p. 335), but best if planning to run ashore soon. It was the usual practice of anchoring from the bow that gave plausibility to the pretense of the sailors, who used it as an excuse for lowering the boat in which they hoped to abandon ship and passengers. This ruse was detected and exposed by Paul.

In Hebrews "anchor" expresses symbolically the stabilizing influence of a hope grounded (anchored!) in the inner sanctuary of heaven in the Forerunner Himself (Heb 6:19–20), who in turn is fulfillment of the unchangeable divine purpose based on two immutable facts: God's person and oath (Heb 6:13–18).

R. V. R.

ANCIENT OF DAYS. This expression appears only three times, all in Aramaic, in Dan 7:9, 13, 22. Though the second and third appearances are properly translated with the article as "*the* Ancient of Days," this is only by way of identifying the person so designated with that of v. 9 where there should be no article, since the Aramaic word is anarthrous. This indicates that "ancient of days" is not a name and that the capitalization is a mistake, at least in v. 9, even though the adjectival expression does refer to God. It simply means that the prophet saw one of advanced age. Liberal commentators, in support of a late date of the book of Daniel, are fond of supposing a contrast in this designation of the God of Israel with other new gods of Gr. origin. Devout students have been correct in finding here a symbolical representation of the eternity of the Godhead (see Isa 9:7; Ex 3:6, 14).

It is good Aramaic for "an old man," corresponding to the Heb. of Gen 24:1 (lit., "gone in days"). Authorities cite other cases in ancient nonbiblical Aramaic.

R. D. C.

ANCIENTS. Refers to the wise sages of Israel who were the source and transmitters of traditional wisdom sayings. Used in RSV only in I Sam 24:13, but other verses may refer to them in veiled fashion, e.g., Job 12:12 and Isa 3:2. The "elders of Israel" probably also refers to these venerable teachers.

ANDREW (ăn'drōō). This Gr. name means "manly." It is found in Josephus, Dio Cassius, and other early Gr. writings. However, in the Gospels only one person bearing this name is mentioned, the brother of Simon Peter, son of Jonas (i.e., Jonah, because the Gr. alphabet had no final "h").

Andrew was a native of Bethsaida on the northern shore of Galilee (Jn 1:44), but lived in nearby Capernaum (Mk 1:21, 29) and worked with his married brother Simon as a fisherman. He became a disciple of John the Baptist (Jn 1:35, 40), who was preaching and baptizing near Jerusalem (Jn 1:28) and pointed out Jesus as the Lamb of God (Jn 1:29, 36). Andrew became convinced Jesus was the Messiah (Jn 1:41); then brought his brother Simon to Jesus (Jn 1:42).

Probably it was about a year later when Jesus called Andrew and Simon to leave their fishing business and become His disciples (Mk 1:16–18; Mt 4:18–20). On the first sabbath of Jesus' ministry they witnessed His teaching and healing power (Mk 1:21–39), a striking introduction to the great Galilean ministry.

Some months afterward Jesus appointed Andrew to be one of the twelve apostles (Mk 3:18; Mt 10:2; Lk 6:14; Acts 1:13). Although always mentioned among the first four, he seems to have been noticeably absent at Jesus' raising of Jairus' daughter (Mk 5:37; Lk 8:51), the transfiguration (Mk 9:2; Lk 9:28), and Jesus' prayer of agony in Gethsemane (Mk 14:33). Why is this? Was he much younger than Peter and the Zebedee brothers? Was he the deputized leader of the remaining nine apostles?

At the feeding of the 5,000, both Philip (also a native of Bethsaida) and Andrew voiced the doubts of the disciples as to how so many people could be fed with their meager supply of money and one little lad's lunch of bread and fish (Jn 6:6–9). In Jerusalem at the last Passover when certain Greeks would see Jesus, Philip and Andrew together escorted them (Jn 12:20–22). At the close of Jesus' final day of teaching in the temple, Andrew, with Peter, James, and John, asked Jesus privately for a fuller explanation of His prediction that the temple would be destroyed (Mk 13:3).

Acts 1:13 suggests Andrew was active in the early churches, being included whenever the Twelve are mentioned. Traditions of questionable value describe Andrew's preaching in Scythia, and his martyrdom in Achaia on an X-shaped cross, today known as St. Andrew's cross.

T. B. C.

ANDRONICUS (ăn-drŏn'ĭ-kŭs). A Christian leader and kinsman of Paul. The recipients of the Roman letter were asked by Paul to greet him (Rom 16:7). He had been in jail with Paul at sometime in the past and was prominent among the apostles. He is mentioned along with Junia as having come to Christ before Paul.

ANEM (ā'nĕm). A town with its pasture land in the area of the tribe of Issachar given to the Gershomites (I Chr 6:73).

ANEMONE. *See* Plants.

ANER (ā'nĕr)
1. One of three Amorite brothers who were allies of Abram in the story of Gen 14.
2. A city of refuge located in the half tribe of Manasseh (I Chr 6:70).

ANETHOTHITE (ăn'ĕ-thŏth-īt'), **ANETOTH-ITE** (ăn'ĕ-tŏth-īt). A form of Anathothite, an inhabitant of the village of Anathoth *(q.v.)* in Benjamin (II Sam 23:27 and I Chr 27:12, KJV only).

ANGEL (Heb. *mal'āk* and Gr. *aggelos,* "agent," "messenger")

The Nature and Rank of Angels

Angels are a supernatural order of heavenly beings separately created by God before the creation of the world (cf. Job 38:6-7) and called spirits (Heb 1:4, 14). Though without bodily organism, they have been permitted often to appear in the form of man (Gen 19:1, 5, 15; Acts 1:11). Scripture describes them as personal beings, higher than mankind (Ps 8:4-5) and not mere personifications. Nor are they glorified human beings (I Cor 6:3; Heb 1:14). They possess more than human knowledge but still are not omniscient (II Sam 14:20; 19:27; Mt 24:36; I Pet 1:12). They are stronger than men but are not omnipotent (Ps 103:20; II Pet 2:11; II Thess 1:7). Nor are they omnipresent (Dan 10:12-14). At times they are enabled to perform miracles (Gen 19:10-11). The NT reveals that there are great multitudes of angels in heaven (Mt 26:53; Heb 12:22; Rev 5:11).

Individual angels have different endowments and ranks (*see* Cherubim; Seraphim), and are highly organized (Rom 8:38; Eph 1:21; 3:10; Col 1:16). Two of the more important angels are Gabriel (Dan 8:16; 9:21; Lk 1:19, 26) and Michael the archangel (Dan 10:13, 21; 12:1; Jude 9; Rev 12:7). Satan was one of the cherubim and was called "the anointed cherub that covereth" (Ezk 28:14). Thus he was one of the highest as well as most gifted of the heavenly host (Ezk 28:13-15) until he fell. *See* Satan.

The Ministry of Angels

The work of angels is varied. Their chief role in the NT is that of divine messengers or spokesmen. An angel spoke to Zacharias (Lk 1:11-20), to Mary (Lk 1:26-38), to Joseph (Mt 1:20-24; 2:13, 19), to the shepherds (Lk 2:9-15), to Cornelius (Acts 10:3, 7, 22), to Paul (Acts 27:23), to John in Revelation. Angels proclaim divine judgments throughout Revelation.

The holy angels stand in God's presence and worship Him (Mt 18:10; Heb 1:6; Rev 5:11-12). They minister to the saints (Heb 1:14) through giving assistance, protection and deliverance (Gen 19:11; Ps 91:11; Dan 3:28;

6:22; Acts 5:19); guide them (Acts 8:26; 12:7-10); at times give encouragement (Dan 9:21; Acts 27:23-24); interpret God's will (Dan 7:16; 10:5, 11; Zech 1:9ff.), and carry it out with regard to both individuals and nations (Gen 19:12-16; II Sam 24:16). In this capacity the angels of God are often called "guardian angels," one being assigned to watch over each believer and to represent him in heaven (Acts 12:15; Ps 34:7; Mt 18:10). *See* Watchers. The six men of Ezk 9:1-7 were apparently *divine* executioners. Angels carried the beggar Lazarus to Abraham's bosom (Lk 16:22). They are used of God to punish His enemies (II Kgs 19:35; Acts 12:23) and punish even His own (II Sam 24:16). One of their great privileges is to show the features of heaven to the redeemed (Rev 21:9 – 22:6), over whose conversion they have rejoiced (Lk 15:10).

Angels had a large part in the life of Christ, appearing both before and at His birth (Mt 1:20; Lk 1:30; 2:9, 13), and to strengthen Him after His temptation (Mt 4:11) and in the garden of Gethsemane (Lk 22:43). One rolled away the stone at His resurrection (Mt 28:2-7), and two appeared and confirmed His return at the ascension (Acts 1:11). He could have called upon His Father for 12 legions of angels to deliver Him from His enemies (Mt 26:52).

Fallen Angels

The evil angels, of whom Satan is the prince (Jn 12:31; 14:30; Eph 2:2; cf. 6:12), oppose the good (Dan 10:13), hinder man's welfare at times by acquiring control from God over the forces of nature (Job 1:12-19) and disease (Job 2:4-7; cf. Lk 13:16; Acts 10:38). They tempt man to sin (Gen 3:1-7; Mt 4:3; Jn 13:27; I Pet 5:8) and spread false doctrine (I Kgs 22:21-23; II Cor 11:13-14; II Thess 2:2; I Tim 4:1). However, their freedom to tempt and test man is subject to the permissive will of God (Job 1:12; 2:6).

While they still have their abode in heaven, and have access at times to the very throne of God (Job 1:6), they will be cast out by Michael and his angels into the earth just prior to the Great Tribulation (Rev 12:7-9), and finally be consigned to the lake of fire and brimstone "prepared for the devil and his angels" (Mt 25:41).

Angels as separately created beings do not marry nor give in marriage (Mt 22:30; Lk 20:36). In contrast, men are all part of the human race and descended from the first pair, Adam and Eve. God, therefore, cannot deal with the angels through a representative, and thus fallen angels cannot be redeemed through a federal head like man (e.g., "in Adam" and "in Christ," Rom 5:12ff.; I Cor 15:22).

Upon what basis did God, then, separate the holy angels (Mt 25:31; Mk 8:38) from those that sinned (II Pet 2:4; cf. Jude 6)? Upon that of their obedience, love and loyalty to Him. Those who followed Lucifer in his rebellion against God (Isa 14:12-17; Ezk 28:12-19) thereby sinned and fell. Some of these were put in everlasting chains (Jude 6), but the others are still free and active and called demons. Those angels that continued steadfast in love, loyalty and obedience were confirmed in a character of righteousness. Thus angels could either sin or remain sinless till they were fully tested and confirmed in righteousness.

Since God is unchangeable, we learn from this that Adam and Eve likewise could have either loved God, remained loyal to Him, and obeyed Him and been confirmed in righteousness; or rebelled and sinned, as they did, and be lost. The great difference between the fallen angels and man is that while man can be saved through a representative substitute, namely, Christ, by taking Him as Saviour and coming under His federal headship, the fallen angels cannot. Christ would have to die once for each separate lost angel to save any of them.

See Angel of the Lord; Archangel; Demonology; Devil.

Bibliography. W. Grundmann, G. von Rad, and G. Kittel, *"Aggelos,* etc.," TDNT, I, 74–87. Donald G. Barnhouse, *The Invisible War,* Grand Rapids: Zondervan, 1965, pp. 127–132. CornPBE, pp. 107–110. T. H. Gaster, "Angel," IDB, I, 128–134. J. Barton Payne, *The Theology of the Older Testament,* Grand Rapids: Zondervan, 1962, pp. 167–170, 205–207, 284–291.

R. A. K.

ANGEL OF THE LORD. It is disputed whether the angel of the Lord (Gen 16:7–14; 22:11, 14, 15; Ex 3:2; Jud 2:1, 4; 5:23; 6:11–24; 13:3) or angel of God (Gen 21:17–19; 31:11–13) is one of the angels or an appearance of God Himself. The fact that the angel speaks not merely in the name of God but as God in the first person singular leaves no doubt that the angel of the Lord is a theophany—a self-manifestation of God (Gen 17:7 ff.; 22:11 ff.; 31:13). The angel identifies himself with God and claims to exercise the prerogatives of God. Sometimes he is distinguished from God (II Sam 24:16; Zech 1:12 f.). Yet when distinguished, the identity as Deity remains (cf. Zech 3:1 f.; 12:8). Therefore, any distinction between the angel and the Lord is only a distinction between the Lord invisible and the Lord manifest. Since the angel of the Lord ceases to appear after the incarnation of Christ, it is often inferred that the angel is in the OT a preincarnate appearance of the Second Person of the Trinity.

C. C. R.

ANGELIC HYMN. A liturgical or poetic refrain described as being sung by superhuman messengers or servants of God. Examples include the Trisagion of the seraphim (Isa 6:3), the Gloria in Excelsis (Lk 2:14), and several in the book of Revelation (e.g., Rev 5:9–10).

ANGELS OF THE SEVEN CHURCHES. Rev 2–3 contains a series of letters addressed to the "angels" of the churches at Ephesus, Smyrna, Pergamos, Thyatira, Sardis, Philadelphia, and Laodicea—all in Asia Minor. The letters contain words of praise, censure, and exhortation, with attendant warning in the event of continuing unfaithfulness. From the context it is clear that each letter was primarily meant for the church to which it was addressed.

The Gr. *angelos* may refer either to an angelic being or to a human messenger. Among suggestions as to the meaning of the term "angel" in Rev 2–3 we find: (1) the heavenly representative or guardian angel of the church (cf. Dan 10:13; 12:1; Mt 18:10; Acts 12:15; *see* Angel); (2) the personification of the church itself, in which the life of the church finds embodiment; (3) the spiritual core of mature persons within the church; (4) the representative sent by the church in Asia Minor to John on Patmos; (5) the bishop (overseer) or presbyter (elder) of the church as God's messenger to that church.

The name of the prophet Malachi in Heb. means "My messenger" or "My angel," perhaps analagous to the use of the term in Rev 2–3. Malachi as a prophet was the messenger of the Lord to Israel.

C. F. P.

ANGER. The Bible predicates anger as a strong feeling of displeasure both of God and of man. In the case of man, anger is often mixed with hostility and hatred. The most common OT terms are *'aph,* derived from a primitive root, "to breathe hard," translated "anger" 171 times and "wrath" 42 times in the KJV; and *kā'as,* "to trouble, provoke, be angry, grieved." Five other Heb. terms are translated "anger" in KJV. The NT term is *orgē,* translated "anger" three times, "wrath" 31 times; also "indignation, vengeance."

In general, usage in the English Bible distinguishes anger from wrath (*q.v.*), the latter being the more explosive, active manifestation of displeasure. Anger and wrath are not incompatible with love. The carnal anger of man is anger in which hatred is a large element. God's anger is essentially expressed against that which and those who would destroy the objects of His love; described by Luther as His "strange work" (cf. Isa 28:21). *See* Fury.

W. T. P.

ANGLE
1. Heb. *pinnâ.* A portion of the wall of Jerusalem fortified by King Uzziah (II Chr 26:9, RSV) and repaired under Nehemiah (Neh 3:19–25, RSV).
2. Heb. *ḥakkâ.* In KJV (Isa 19:8; Hab 1:15) this is the translation of the word for "hook," i.e., a fishhook, and is so rendered in Job 41:1.

ANIAM (*á-nī'ám*). One of the sons of Shemida in the genealogy of Manasseh (I Chr 7:19).

ANIM

ANIM (ā′nĭm). A town allotted to the tribe of Judah after the conquest under Joshua (Josh 15:50). Identified with Khirbet Ghuwein et-Taḥta, 11 miles S of Hebron.

ANIMALS OF THE BIBLE. The biblical approach to animal classification is quite different from that used by the scientific community today. Thus, in Gen 1:20–30; 2:19–20 organisms are classified as great sea monsters, aquatic creatures, winged birds (1:21), cattle (domesticated animals), creeping things, and beasts of the earth, i.e., wild beasts (1:24). A similar scheme of the classification of fauna is found in Lev 11. Essentially the approach of the Bible to classification is an ecological one, i.e., the Bible classifies organisms on the basis of the habitat which they occupy, and lumps together, for example, all aquatic organisms regardless of their anatomical structure.

The modern system of classification is based on structure—anatomy and morphology—and consequently biologists place into one category the whale, the lion, and the bat because of anatomical similarities even though they occupy three different habitats. The Bible, on the other hand, would classify together the shark, the fish, and the mollusk even though their internal and external structures are different.

Any system of classification is arbitrary. There is no right way, nor can any series of categories that show some system be regarded as wrong. Most scientists today find a system of classification based on anatomy and morphology to be the most useful one; however, there are some men today who believe it would be profitable to pay more attention to ecology and other branches of biology in classifying organisms.

Classification by Anatomy and Morphology

I. Porifera
Sponge

II. Coelenterates
Red Coral

III. Annelida
1. Leech
2. Worm

IV. Arthropoda
A. Arachnids
1. Scorpion
2. Spider

B. Insects
1. Ant
2. Bee
3. Beetle
4. Crimson Scale
5. Flea
6. Fly
7. Gnat
8. Locust
9. Louse

10. Moth
11. Wasp

V. Mollusca
1. Mollusk, Purple
2. Oyster, Pearl

VI. Chordates
A. Fish
B. Amphibians
Frog
C. Reptiles
1. Cobra
2. Crocodile
3. Gecko
4. Leviathan
5. Lizard
6. Lizard, Dabb
7. Serpent
8. Viper

D. Birds
1. Buzzard
2. Cormorant
3. Crane
4. Cuckoo
5. Dove, Turtledove
6. Eagle
7. Fowl, Domestic
8. Goatsucker
9. Goose
10. Hawk, Sparrow
11. Heron
12. Hoopoe
13. Ibis
14. Kestrel
15. Kite
16. Lammergeier
17. Ostrich
18. Owl, Barn
19. Owl, Little
20. Owl, Long-eared or Great
21. Owl, Scops
22. Partridge
23. Peacock
24. Pelican
25. Pigeon, Rock
26. Quail
27. Raven
28. Sea Gull
29. Sparrow
30. Stork
31. Swallow
32. Swan
33. Swift
34. Vulture, Black
35. Vulture, Egyptian
36. Vulture, Griffon

E. Mammals
1. Antelope
2. Ape
3. Ass
4. Bat
5. Bear
6. Boar, Wild

7. Camel
8. Cattle
9. Coney
10. Deer
11. Dog
12. Dugong
13. Elephant
14. Fox
15. Gazelle
16. Goat
17. Hare
18. Hedgehog
19. Hippopotamus
20. Horse
21. Hyena
22. Ibex
23. Jackal
24. Leopard
25. Lion
26. Mole Rat
27. Monkey
28. Mouse
29. Mule
30. Onager
31. Ox, Wild
32. Pig
33. Porcupine
34. Sheep
35. Sheep, Mountain
36. Vole
37. Weasel
38. Whale
39. Wolf

Classification by Biblical System

I. Cattle
1. Ass or Donkey
2. Beeves; see Cattle, I.6
3. Bull, Bullock; see Cattle, I.6
4. Calf; see Cattle, I.6
5. Camel
6. Cattle
7. Dog
8. Dromedary; see Camel, I.5
9. Goat
10. Greyhound; see Fowl, Domestic, III.14
11. Horse
12. Mule
13. Ox; see Cattle, I.6
14. Pig
15. Sheep
16. Swine; see Pig, I.14

II. Beasts of the Field
1. Antelope
2. Ape
3. Ass, Wild; see Onager, II.29
4. Badger; see Dugong, V.3
5. Bear
6. Behemoth; see Hippopotamus, II.20
7. Boar
8. Chamois; see Sheep, Mountain, II.36
9. Coney or Rock Badger

10. Deer, Hart or Stag, Hind or Doe, Roe, Roebuck
11. Dragon
12. Elephant
13. Ferret; see Gecko, IV. 16
14. Fox
15. Gazelle
16. Hare
17. Hart; see Deer, II.10
18. Hedgehog
19. Hind; see Deer, II.10
20. Hippopotamus
21. Hyena
22. Ibex or Wild Goat
23. Jackal
24. Leopard
25. Lion
26. Mole; see Mole Rat, IV.25
27. Monkey; see Peacock, III.40
28. Mouse; see IV.27
29. Onager or Half Ass
30. Ox, Wild, or Unicorn
31. Porcupine
32. Pygarg; see Antelope, II.1
33. Roe; see Gazelle, II.15
34. Roebuck; see Deer, II.10
35. Satyr
36. Sheep, Mountain
37. Unicorn; see Ox, Wild, II.30
38. Weasel; see IV.36
39. Wild Ass; see Onager, II.29
40. Wild Ox; see II.30
41. Wolf

III. Flying Creatures
1. Bat
2. Bee
3. Bittern; see Hedgehog, II.18; Heron, III.21
4. Buzzard
5. Cock; see Fowl, Domestic, III.14
6. Cormorant
7. Crane
8. Cuckoo or Cuckow
9. Dove or Turtledove
10. Eagle; see Vulture, Griffon, III.54
11. Eagle, Gier; see Vulture, Egyptian, III.53
12. Falcon; see Kestrel, III.25
13. Fly
14. Fowl, Domestic
15. Glede; see Kite, III.26
16. Gnat
17. Goatsucker or Nighthawk
18. Goose
19. Hawk, Sparrow
20. Hen; see Fowl, III.14
21. Heron or Bittern
22. Hoopoe
23. Hornet; see Wasp, III.55
24. Ibis
25. Kestrel or Falcon
26. Kite or Glede
27. Lammergeier
28. Lapwing; see Hoopoe, III.22
29. Locust

30. Moth; see IV.26
31. Nighthawk; see Goatsucker, III.17
32. Osprey; see Vulture, Black, III.52
33. Ossifrage; see Lammergeier, III.27
34. Ostrich
35. Owl, Barn or White
36. Owl, Little
37. Owl, Long-eared or Great
38. Owl, Scops
39. Partridge
40. Peacock
41. Pelican
42. Pigeon or Dove
43. Quail
44. Raven
45. Seamew or Sea Gull; see Cuckoo, III.8
46. Sparrow
47. Sparrow Hawk; see Hawk, Sparrow, III.19
48. Stork
49. Swallow
50. Swan
51. Swift
52. Vulture, Black, or Osprey
53. Vulture, Egyptian
54. Vulture, Griffon, or Eagle
55. Wasp or Hornet

IV. Creeping, Swarming Things
1. Adder; see Cobra, IV.8; Serpent, IV.30; Viper, IV.34
2. Ant, Harvester
3. Asp; see Cobra, IV.8
4. Beetle
5. Cankerworm; see Locust, III.29
6. Caterpillar; see Locust, III.29
7. Chameleon; see Lizard, IV.21
8. Cobra
9. Cockatrice; see Serpent, IV.30
10. Cricket; see Beetle, IV.4
11. Crimson Scale Insect
12. Dragon; see II.11
13. Flea
14. Fly; see III.13
15. Frog
16. Gecko
17. Gnat; see III.16
18. Grasshopper; see Locust, III.29
19. Hornet; see III.55
20. Horseleach; see Leech, V.6
21. Lizard
22. Lizard, Dabb
23. Locust; see III.29
24. Louse
25. Mole Rat
26. Moth
27. Mouse
28. Palmerworm; see Locust, III.29
29. Scorpion
30. Serpent, Snake
31. Spider
32. Tortoise; see Lizard, Dabb, IV.22
33. Turtle; see Dove, III.9
34. Viper
35. Vole

36. Weasel
37. Worm

V. Aquatic Organisms
1. Coral
2. Crocodile
3. Dugong or Sea Cow
4. Fish
5. Frog; see IV.15
6. Leech
7. Leviathan, Sea Monster
8. Mollusk, Purple
9. Onycha
10. Oyster, Pearl
11. Sea Monster (Lam 4:3); see Jackal, II.23
12. Sponge
13. Whale

Following the biblical system of classification we find mention of:

I. Cattle

Cattle are domesticated animals which include:

1. **Ass** or **Donkey,** *Equus asinus.* The ass is of purely African origin. Three wild races are known: a NW African race which is extinct; a NE African race which, if not extinct, is close to extinction; and a Somalian race which survives to the present but did not play an important part in domestication. The second of these, the Nubian ass, was believed to have been domesticated in the Nile Valley in early historic times. (For Old Kingdom tomb reliefs see VBW, I, 109; II, 184.) Bones of this form have been found in Palestine at Tell ed-Duweir and date from between 3000 and 2500 B.C.

The first mention of the ass in the Bible includes male and female asses among the animals which Abram acquired in Egypt (Gen

A Palestinian Ass. HFV

Oxen and an ass hitched together for threshing near Jerash, Jordan. HFV

12:16). The ass was primarily a beast of burden (Gen 42:26; I Sam 16:20; 25:18); it was driven but never bridled. W. F. Albright has emphasized the widespread use of asses for trade by the 20th cen. B.C. In caravans of 300 up to 1,000, each carrying loads of 150–200 pounds, the donkey needed fodder and water en route. Hence way stations with cisterns filled from dammed-up wadis were built in the Negeb and along the Sinai road to Egypt in Abraham's time (*Archaeology, Historical Analogy, and Early Biblical Tradition,* Baton Rouge: Louisiana State Univ. Press, 1966, pp. 28–40).

From the time of the Middle Kingdom on, the ass was used for riding in Egypt, but only the Jews and Nubians rode asses regularly. The ass was also used for threshing grain and for pulling the plow. In Arab countries today peasants plow with an ass and a cow or a camel hitched together (VBW, I, 279). The law, however, forbade plowing with an ass and an ox hitched together (Deut 22:10).

The ass was rather highly regarded by the Jews. It was considered an economic asset. An individual had to have an ass for minimum existence (Job 24:3), and the individual's wealth was counted by the number of asses which he possessed (Gen 12:16; 24:35; Job 1:3). The ass was an acceptable gift (Gen 32:13–15). The ass shared the rest of the sabbath (Deut 5:14). Numbers records the report of Balaam's ass which spoke (Num 22:22–35). People of influence rode asses (Jud 10:4; 12:14; I Sam 25:20); and the ass became a symbol of the Messiah's peaceable coming (Zech 9:9; Mt 21:1–7).

Elsewhere the ass was almost universally despised. Apparently its stolid temperament annoyed man. It has been considered inferior to the horse and the mule, and it has been generally regarded as the beast of the poor. Its patience has been likened to that of a slave. Yet the milk of asses was supposed to have medicinal properties and was highly regarded. The ass was often used to turn the large millstone of

Roman times (cf. Mt 18:6, NASB marg.). Its dietary requirements are very simple: it can live on stubble, thistles, straw and a very small amount of grain.

See also Onager, II.29.

2. **Beeves.** *See* Cattle, I.6.

3. **Bull, Bullock.** *See* Cattle, I.6.

4. **Calf.** *See* Cattle, I.6.

5. **Camel,** *Camelus dromedarius* L. The camel is unintelligent, ill-natured and quarrelsome; it is a slow breeder. Yet it is a blessing to tribes living on the border of deserts because it is especially adapted to this habitat. Its feet padded with a thick elastic mass of fibrous tissue are adapted to walking on desert soils. It can go without water for a long period of time, and it can subsist on vegetation which grows on saline soils (photo, VBW, II, 85).

The camel is used primarily for transportation of merchandise, household equipment, and persons. It can carry a load weighing 600 pounds or more. A camel can be hitched to a plow where lands are temporarily arable. Because they are smelly and cannot be kept penned, camels are not used in cities.

There are two varieties within the one-humped species, the slow burden-bearing camel (Gen 37:25) and the fast dromedary (I Sam 30:17). Because Babylon is seen being attacked by Elam and Media, Isa 21:7 may refer to the Bactrian camel, *C. bactrianus.* This camel has two humps and longer hair but is not as fast as the swift dromedary.

Abraham had camels in Egypt (Gen 12:16), and Job at first had 3,000 camels (Job 1:3) and then 6,000 (42:12). While large scale camel nomadism does not seem to have begun until toward the end of the 2nd mil. B.C. (Jud 6:5), Sumerian texts from the Old Babylonian period list camels and indicate their domestication. Also camel bones and figurines have been found at various Near Eastern sites well before 1200 B.C. (K. A. Kitchen, *Ancient Orient and OT,* 1966, pp. 79 f.).

A camel at market day in Beer-sheba. HFV

Camels were used for swift travel (Gen 24:31). A riding camel can cover from 60 to 75 miles in a day as opposed to a normal day's journey of 20 miles. They were also used as mounts in time of war (Jud 6:5). Camels were used as burden bearers, especially of spices (Gen 37:25). Their wool was important (Mt 3:4); a rough cloak of camel's hair is still worn by Bedouin today. A camel's hair garment was also a sign of the prophetic office (Zech 13:4). Camels were eaten by the Arabs, who also drank their milk (Gen 32:15). However, the camel was forbidden to the Jews as food (Lev 11:4; Deut 14:7).

6. **Cattle,** *Bos primigenius.* The term "cattle" (Heb. *b^ehēmâ* or *miqneh*) is frequently used to refer to all domestic animals or livestock (Gen 1:24; 2:20; 7:23; 47:6, 16, 17; Ex 9:3–7; Num 3:41, 45). Occasionally it is used to refer to all large domestic animals (Num 31:9; 32:26), though sometimes the English word in KJV refers only to sheep and goats (Gen 30:32, 39–43; 31:8, 10; Isa 7:25; 43:23); in such cases it renders either Heb. *śeh* or *ṣō'n.* *See* Herd.

Usually, however, the English word refers to what we commonly speak of today as domestic cattle of the bovine species. Domestication is believed to have begun before 4000 B.C. (For reliefs, paintings, and models of cattle from Egyptian tombs see VBW, I, 59, 104, 117.) Cattle require considerable attention from the community and a reasonably high degree of community organization.

Some authors believe that milk rather than meat was the foremost consideration in the domestication of cattle and that in early civilization meat supplies came chiefly from wild game. Cattle also supplied strong hides that supplanted wood in the manufacture of shields. Their dung was a source of fuel when wood was scarce (Ezk 4:15). They were also used as beasts of burden and for traction, though oxen were more commonly used in this way. Still it is believed that the development of wheel transportation was associated more closely with cattle than with any other animal.

Bulls are referred to in Gen 32:15, so that cattle breeding was widely practiced by patriarchal times. Successful breeding by a bull is referred to in Job 21:10. Inlaid friezes found at Tell el-Obeid near Ur, dating to the middle of the 3rd mil. B.C. show bulls and a dairy scene with the milking of cows (ANEP, #98, 99). Strict laws in Mesopotamia and Israel penalized the owner of a bull that gored a man or other cattle (Ex 21:28–36). Bulls are sometimes employed figuratively as pictures of strength or violence (Deut 33:17; Ps 22:12; 68:30; Isa 10:13).

Bulls were widely used for sacrifices (for Egyptian tomb painting see VBW, I, 181). For this purpose they had to be at least eight days old (Lev 22:27). They might be used as a general sacrifice (Lev 22:23; Num 23:1) or for special sacrifices (Jud 6:25; I Sam 1:24). They were also used in particular sacrifices such as the consecration of priests (Ex 29:1), the dedication of the altar (Num 7), purification of Levites (Num 8), sin offerings (Lev 16), the day of the new moon (Num 28:11), the Passover (Num 28:19), the Feast of Weeks (Num 28:27), the Feast of Trumpets or of the new year (Num 29:1–2), the Day of Atonement (Num 29:7–8), and the Feast of Booths (Num 29:12–38). The latter feast exacted the largest number of bulls for burnt offerings of all the annual feasts, with a total of 71 being slaughtered during the course of eight days.

Calves are referred to as "sons of the herd" in Gen 18:8–9; I Sam 6:7; 14:32. The calf or heifer (*'ēgel*) was a symbol of peacefulness (Isa 11:6). It also was used figuratively to refer to Gentile peoples (Ps 68:30). A calf's head decorated the back of Solomon's throne (I Kgs 10:19, RSV). Calves were sometimes fattened in the stall (Amos 6:4; Mal 4:2; Lk 15:23) or kept around the house (I Sam 28:24). They supplied veal (Gen 18:7), which was considered a delicacy for the wealthy (Amos 6:4); yet calves also supplied meat for all Saul's army at the great slaughter of the Philistines (I Sam 14:32).

Cattle were subject to the law of firstlings (Ex 13:12). Cattle were a mark of wealth (Gen 13:2) and were considered proper booty of war (Josh 8:2).

Aaron made the golden calf as a rival for the

Farmers leading well-fattened cattle. Wall relief from the tomb of Ptah-hotep. Saqqara. Egypt. LL

Sacrificing a bull (lower register), Tomb of Menna, Thebes. Gaddis, Luxor

7. Dog, *Canis familiaris.* The dog is believed to have been the earliest of all domesticated animals. It is thought to have been valuable as a scavenger and to have been associated with man in hunting. The modern dog is thought to have come from the Indian wolf, *C. lupus pallipes.*

The dog is generally looked down on in the Bible (Prov 26:11; II Pet 2:22), and biblical writers seem to show no familiarity with the warm personal human-dog relationship which we know. The dog is pictured as a scavenger haunting streets and dumps (Ex 22:31; I Kgs 22:38; Mt 15:26; Lk 16:21). Isa 66:3 seems to point to a non-Yahvistic cult which sacrificed dogs.

Dogs were often used in hunting, according to paintings in Egyptian tombs, and there is reference to dogs herding sheep in Job 30:1. In general, however, "dog" was a term of contempt (I Sam 17:43) or of excessive humility (II Sam 9:8; 16:9; II Kgs 8:13). The "price of a dog" (Deut 23:18) meant the earnings of a male cultic prostitute. Dogs are also used to refer to lascivious and wicked persons (Isa 56:10-11; Mt 7:6; Phil 3:2; Rev 22:15).

8. Dromedary. *See* Camel, I.5.

9. Goat, *Capra hircus mambrica.* The goat is probably the earliest ruminant to be domesticated. Its wild ancestor seems to have been the bezoar goat, *C. aegagrus* Erxleben. The Mesolithic Natufians are believed to have tamed wild goats in Palestine by *c.* 9000 B.C. The goat of Bible times was probably the Syrian or Mamber variety (photo, VBW, I, 183).

Sheep are more important where cattle can be kept for milk, but where pasture is scarce and thorny scrub dominates over grass, and where cattle are difficult to keep because of lack of good food and water, goats become important. Not only are they able to live under conditions that do not suit sheep, but they also produce large quantities of milk. The goat does not supply fat as does the sheep, and since its hair is coarse the wool is rather scarce.

ark of the covenant (Ex 32; Deut 9:16, 21). Even if the image was intended only to be the pedestal for the invisible Yahweh (cf. Egyptian and Syrian deities standing on a lion or a bull, ANEP, #470-474, 486, 500, 501, 522, 531, 534, 537), it was especially offensive because the calf was a symbol of fertility related to Egyptian and Canaanite cultic practices. Two calves were made by Jeroboam I for his shrines at Bethel and Dan (I Kgs 12:28-33); denunciations of calf worship were directed at these (Hos 8:5-6; 13:2).

The ox is the adult castrated male of *Bos primigenius.* Oxen were used as draught animals (Num 7:3; Deut 22:10; 25:4). They usually fed on grass (Num 22:4; Ps 106:20), but they also ate straw (Isa 11:7) and salted fodder (Isa 30:24, NASB). They could be kept in a stable (Lk 13:15). Oxen could not be offered as sacrifices because they had been castrated (Lev 22:24). In passages (e.g., Ex 20:24; I Sam 6:13) which seem to say that oxen were sacrificed to God, it must be noted that the Heb. words *bāqār* and *shôr* can also mean "cattle" and "bull," respectively. Oxen could be used as food but they were not a common article of diet. Possession of an ox and an ass was regarded as the bare minimum for existence in an agricultural economy (Job 24:3; cf. Ex 20:17). *See also* Ox, Wild, II.30.

A herd of goats, Jerash, Jordan. HFV

Goats have voracious appetites and they were responsible for much of the damage done to the land in Palestine, breaking down terraces, destroying forests, and bringing about soil erosion by eating off all cover.

In Palestine the goat has hollow backward curving horns and is of lighter build than the sheep. It is commonly black and was the principle source of milk (Prov 27:27). Its flesh served as meat (Lev 7:23; Deut 14:4), and its hair was the raw material used for weaving tent cloth and for various domestic purposes (Ex 26:7; 36:14; I Sam 19:13, 16). The skin was tanned as leather, and a whole hide was turned into a skin bottle by sewing shut the leg and neck apertures (Gen 21:14; Josh 9:4).

The goat was a recognized form of wealth. It was subject to the law of firstlings (Num 18:15), and had to be eight days old before it could be offered as a sacrifice. A year-old male goat was one of the animals offered at the Passover (Num 28:22), and two goats were offered on the Day of Atonement (Lev 16:7 ff.; see Azazel). It was also used for many other specific sacrifices.

The goat is used in a figurative and symbolical sense in Song 4:1 and 6:5 for the bride's black hair; in Mt 25:30-46 for the wicked; and in Isa 14:9; Ezk 34:17; Dan 8:5-8; Zech 10:3 for various human leaders. See also Satyr, II.35.

10. **Greyhound.** See Fowl, Domestic, III.14.

11. **Horse,** *Equus caballus orientalis.* Two races of wild horses have survived into modern times: Przewalski's horse, which roamed about Mongolia until modern firearms put an end to most of them after World War I and the Russian Revolution; and the tarpan, a horse of southern Russia which became extinct in the Ukraine in 1851. The domesticated horse seems to be derived from the tarpan. The original site of domestication is believed to be Turkestan (see Hilzheimer, "The Evolution of the Domestic Horse," *Antiquity,* IX [1935], 133-139).

The horse apparently was domesticated, according to skeletal remains, at Sialk on the Iranian plateau by the 5th mil. B.C. and perhaps at Beer-sheba in the next millennium. It was known in Sumer during the Ur III Dynasty, mentioned in the Cappadocian (19th cen. B.C.) and Mari (18th cen.) tablets, and shown on 19th-18th cen. B.C. Anatolian seals with four horses drawing a solid-wheeled chariot (BASOR #77, p. 31; #163, p. 43). A horse skeleton was found at the Middle Kingdom Egyptian fortress of Buhen in the Sudan. The Hyksos conquerors achieved success largely by horse and chariot warfare.

The horse was introduced only very gradually into Israel, however. Joshua was commanded to hough or hamstring the horses of the Canaanites (Josh 11:6, 9), and David hamstrung most of the horses captured from Zobah, though he kept enough for a hundred chariots (II Sam 8:4). Solomon greatly increased the number of horses in the Jewish kingdom and maintained large stables at various cities (I Kgs 10:26) such as Megiddo, Hazor, and Gezer (I Kgs 9:15), major regional defense centers. Ahab's horses are mentioned in I Kgs 18:5, and records of Shalmaneser III state that Ahab furnished 2,000 chariots in the coalition against Assyria. Ruins of stables excavated at Megiddo date to his reign and reveal stalls and mangers for 450 horses.

In early Israel the horse was opposed as a symbol of pagan luxury and dependence on physical power for defense (Deut 17:16; I Sam 8:11; Ps 20:7; Isa 31:1). In addition, horses may have been used in heathen religious processions (II Kgs 23:11). Horse trading is mentioned already in Gen 47:17, and was carried on by Solomon between Egypt and Syro-Hittite principalities (I Kgs 10:28-29, RSV).

Most biblical references to horses refer to their use in war, but horses were also used in transportation. Riding seems to have been much less popular than the use of chariots, and cavalry units were not introduced until the 12th cen. B.C., by the Medes and Cimmerians. Joseph rode in Pharaoh's second horse-drawn chariot (Gen 41:43) and Absalom made a display by riding a horse-drawn chariot (II Sam 15:1). Naaman traveled by horse and chariot (II Kgs 5:9). Later, horses were so common in Jerusalem that the royal palace had a special horse gate (II Chr 23:15), and a gate of the city itself was known as the horse gate (Neh 3:28; Jer 31:40). See Jerusalem: Gates. Mordecai rode the royal horse as a sign of honor (Est 6:8-11). See Horseman.

Horses were also used by the wealthy for hunting (ANEP, #183, 184, 190); the only biblical reference to such hunting (Job 39:18) connects them with pursuing the ostrich. Horses were forbidden as food though they may have been eaten in Samaria during the siege (II Kgs 7:13). There seems to have been little use of horses in connection with agriculture or in the bearing or pulling of burdens. Isa 28:28 may refer to the use of horses in threshing grain, though this is uncertain. Horses are often spoken of figuratively (Ps 32:9; Song 1:9; Jer 5:8;

Horses were used by the wealthy for hunting. Here King Ashurbanipal of Assyria hunts lions. From his palace at Nineveh. BM

12:5; etc.) and in contexts of judgment (Hab 3:8; Zech 1:8; 6:1-8; Rev 6:2-8; 9:17; 19:11 ff.).

12. **Mule.** This is a hybrid, ordinarily sterile, the offspring of a male ass and a mare. Gen 36:24 reports that mule breeding was developed by the Edomites and Horites, though this may be a mistranslation; RSV uses the words "hot springs" rather than "mules." Because cross breeding was forbidden in the law (Lev 19:19), the Israelites procured mules from the Gentiles. They may have been obtained from the Phoenicians, since Tyre imported horses and mules (Ezk 27:14). They did not appear in Israel until David's reign (II Sam 13:29), possibly because of the rarity of horses among the Hebrews. Mules were used chiefly by members of the royal palace and by nobles. King David rode on a mule, and Solomon rode to his anointing upon King David's mule (I Kgs 1:33). Absalom met his death riding on a mule (II Sam 18:9). Mules were less common than horses, camels, and asses in the post-Exilic community (Ezr 2:66).

13. **Ox.** See Cattle, I.6.

14. **Pig,** *Sus scropha.* The pig is the most prolific and abundant supplier of meat and fat for the kitchen. Pigs cannot be driven; they are of value only to a settled farmer.

Wild pigs were found in Palestine, as well as in many other countries today. Ps 80:13 refers to the destructiveness of the wild boar which attacks growing crops. See Boar, II.7.

The pig symbolizes filth and ugliness. It eats fecal material, vermin, rodents, carrion, and the like (II Pet 2:22). Prov 11:22 refers to the incongruity of a golden ring in the nose of an animal showing these characteristics. There is a similar reference in our Saviour's statement in Mt 7:6 about casting pearls before swine. The prodigal's degeneration is shown by his being forced to feed pigs and eat their food in his poverty (Lk 15:15-16). The Gadarene demons took refuge in the herd of swine feeding on the bluff, overlooking the Sea of Galilee (Mt 8:28-32).

According to Lev 11:7 and Deut 14:8 the eating of the flesh of pigs was forbidden to the Jews. Pre-Semitic inhabitants of Palestine killed and ate pigs freely. In intertestamental times Antiochus used the pig as a test of loyalty to the Jewish faith by requiring its consumption (II Macc 6:18). Pig blood was also sprinkled on the temple altar to desecrate it (I Macc 1:47).

Pigs were frequently used in worship among heathen people (Isa 65:4; 66:3, 17), and this may account for their being forbidden to the Jews as food. Evidence in Palestine shows that

A shepherd anointing his sheep (cf. Ps 23:5). @ MPS

swine were sacrificed long before Hellenistic times. Pig bones were found in the grotto below the rock-cut place of sacrifice at Gezer. A similar underground chamber with vessels containing piglet bones at Tirzah dates to the Middle Bronze Age; and at Ai were unearthed alabaster fragments of a statuette of a pig ready to be sacrificed. Among the Greeks the agrarian rites of the swine god Adonis were popular. Swine were sacrificed to Aphrodite, and in Greece and Asia Minor to Venus. In addition, pigs were sacrificed in connection with oaths and treaties; in the *Iliad* Agamemnon sacrificed a boar to Zeus and Helius.

It is possible that the eating of pork was forbidden because the pig carries many worm parasites such as the trichina; yet this is true of other meat animals. Some people are allergic to pork in hot weather, and this has also been suggested as the reason for the Jewish taboo. The same taboo exists among the Moslems and existed in certain social strata in Egypt.

15. **Sheep,** *Ovis orientalis.* Next to the goat the sheep is believed to be the earliest ruminant tamed by man. It may have been domesticated as early as the 6th mil. B.C. with the aid of the dog, before agriculture itself was fully developed. However, the Bible reports that Abel kept sheep (Gen 4:2). The first sheep to be domesticated was probably the argali *(Ovis ammon),* a variety of the urial *(Ovis vignei)* which is a mountainous species still existing in Turkestan and Mongolia. Five breeds had reached Mesopotamia by 2000 B.C.; these were all of urial stock. *See also* Sheep, Mountain, II.36.

There are more than 500 references to sheep in Scripture, including mention of rams and lambs. Sheep represented the chief wealth and total livelihood of pastoral peoples, providing food to eat, milk to drink, wool for making of cloth and covering for tents. Its skin and bones were also used. In addition, the sheep was a medium of exchange and a source of sacrifices. The number of sheep raised in ancient times was prodigious. Mesha, king of Moab, paid a tribute (annually?) of 100,000 lambs and the wool of 100,000 rams (II Kgs 3:4). Reuben, etc., took 250,000 sheep from the Hagrites (I Chr 5:21). Thutmose III carried off 20,500 sheep from Megiddo (ANET, p. 237).

Good grades of wool suitable for garments developed on the sheep in climates with relatively cold winters; flax was grown to make linen in milder climates. Wool has finer quality as a fabric than does flax.

Sheepshearing (VBW, II, 150) was often a time for festival (II Sam 13:23). The sheep known in Israel (photo in VBW, I, 182; II, 81) was the broadtailed sheep *(O. orientalis vignei* or *O. laticaudata)* of which the tail weighs from 10 to 15 pounds and has always been considered a delicacy. Thus the Lord asked for this choice part as a sacrifice (Ex 29:22–25, RSV).

The ram represented great strength and fittingly symbolized Medo-Persia in Daniel's vision (Dan 8:3). For Persian ram's head made of gold, see VBW, IV, 207.

Because of the very nature of the sheep—gentle and submissive (Isa 53:7; Jer 11:19, RSV), defenseless (Mic 5:8; Mt 10:16), and in constant need of guidance and care (Num 27:17; Mt 9:36)— the Bible often draws an analogy between sheep and the believer. *See* Shepherd; Flock.

16. **Swine.** *See* Pig, I.14.

II. Beasts of the Field

A number of general references to wild animals may be found in the OT (Lev 26:22; II Kgs 14:9; Job 39:15; Ps 50:11; 80:13; Hos 13:8).

1. **Antelope,** *Oryx leucoryx.* These animals are very graceful and carry their heads considerably above the level of the back. They live in arid plains and deserts but are also found on rocky hillsides and in thick bush forests. Both sexes have long, permanent, hollow horns (not antlers) which go straight back. They are alert, wary, and keen sighted and form herds of from two to a dozen. When injured or brought to bay, the antelope attacks with his head lowered so that the sharp horns can point forward; in this way he can defend himself even against a lion.

Antelope feed on grasses and shrubs; they go to streams and waterholes to drink. When water is scarce they will eat melons and succulent bulbs.

The antelope was ceremonially clean. While exact identification of the Heb. terms is difficult, probably the *te'ô* is the antelope (Deut 14:5; Isa 51:20, both RSV). The *dîshōn* (Deut 14:5) is translated "pygarg" in KJV following the LXX. It is a white-rumped antelope, perhaps the *Addax nasomaculatus* of N Africa and Arabia; RSV has "ibex."

A female antelope in the Biblical Zoo in Jerusalem. HFV

2. **Ape.** This term as it is used in Scripture (Heb. *qôph*) may well refer to monkeys and baboons rather than to true apes. Baboons were well known in Egypt where the god Thoth was often represented by a baboon. The common baboon is *Papio hamadryas.*

The term *qôph* is probably not a Heb. word. It may be derived from the Sanskrit *kapi* and from the Gr. word *kepos* which means long-tailed monkey. The LXX renders it "the tailless ape." If Ophir is India as some believe, or Somaliland on the African coast as others believe, or some place on the Persian Gulf as still others believe, the animals which Solomon received were in all probability a mixed lot (I Kgs 10:22; II Chr 9:21). Quite likely they were tailed primates, not true apes, like those the Egyptians brought back from Punt (tomb painting, VBW, II, 224).

3. **Ass, Wild.** *See* Onager, II.29.

4. **Badger.** *See* Dugong, V.3; *also* Coney or Rock Badger, II.9.

5. **Bear,** *Ursus arctos syriacus.* The bear is a large, heavy, big-headed mammal with short powerful limbs and a short tail. The eyes and ears are small. Bears have a plantigrade walk: they walk on both sole and heel as a man does.

Bears are usually peaceful and inoffensive, but if they think they must defend themselves (Lam 3:10), their young (II Sam 17:8; Prov 17:12; Hos 13:8), their food supply (Prov 28:15), or their own territory (II Kgs 2:24; Amos 5:19), they are formidable and dangerous adversaries (see Egyptian relief, VBW, II, 255). David was the champion bear killer of the Bible (I Sam 17:34–37).

The senses of sight and hearing of the bear are not too good, but their sense of smell is excellent. Bears are omnivorous: they subsist largely on a diet of vegetables, fruits, insects, and fish. The Palestinian bear is a Syrian version of the brown bear. In biblical times it seems to have roamed over all parts of Israel.

6. **Behemoth.** *See* Hippopotamus, II.20.

7. **Boar,** *Sus scropha.* Wild boars do not attack unless molested, but they are dangerous when aroused. They travel in bands of from six to 50 and are most active in the evening and early morning hours. The body is covered with

Catching deer in a net, palace of Ashurbanipal, Nineveh. BM

stiff bristles and usually some finer fur, but the body covering is often quite scant. They have four continually growing tusks, two in each jaw. Boar hunts were common in Mesopotamia.

Wild pigs are mainly vegetarian, feeding on roots, nuts, grains, and plant stems. They may damage gardens and farms (Ps 80:13). *See also* Pig, I.14.

8. **Chamois.** *See* Sheep, Mountain, II.36.

9. **Coney** or **Rock Badger,** *Procavia capensis.* The coney is a small ungulate, the only species of the group found outside Africa. It looks like a rabbit, but its ears are quite inconspicuous. It does not burrow as rabbits do, but lives in rocky regions (Ps 104:18; Prov 30:26). It has black whiskers that may be as long as seven inches.

The coney is not a ruminant, but the constant motion of its jaws may suggest that it chews its cud. While for this reason it was probably included with other cud-chewing animals, it did not have cloven hoofs; thus God forbade it as food to the Jews (Lev 11:5; Deut 14:7).

The coney lives in small colonies of from six to 50 animals. It is mainly diurnal, but also comes out on warm moonlit nights. The animal is exclusively a vegetarian. Its flesh is eaten by some natives.

10. **Deer, Hart** or **Stag, Hind** or **Doe, Roe, Roebuck.** Deer are ruminants and were considered clean animals (Deut 12:15, 22; 14:5). Only the males have antlers. Deer antlers grow annually and are solid; this distinguishes the deer from the antelope and gazelle.

Three species of deer are known from Palestine: the red deer, *Cervus elaphus;* the Persian fallow deer, *Dama mesopotamica;* and the roe deer, *Capreolus capreolus.* The red deer (probably the Heb. *'ayyāl,* "hart" or "stag"; fem. *'ayyālâ,* "hind") stands about four feet high at the shoulder. It is gregarious, each group remaining in a definite territory. They graze and browse (Lam 1:6) during the morning and late afternoon. The sexes remain in separate herds. It was celebrated for its leaping (Isa 35:6) and sure footedness in the mountains (Ps 18:33; Song 2:8–9, 17; 8:14; Hab 3:19). Its thirst is evident when pursued (Ps 42:1). (For Assyrian relief of stag attacked by lion see ANEP, #355.)

The Persian fallow deer (I Kgs 4:23, KJV) may now be extinct. The antlers were flattened and palmated (VBW, II, 96). This deer traveled in small groups, feeding mainly on grass in the morning and evening.

The roe deer (Heb. *yaḥmûr,* Deut 14:5; I Kgs 4:23, RSV) is a small graceful animal, dark reddish brown in summer and yellowish gray in winter. Its antlers are about one foot long and have three points. This deer prefers sparsely wooded valleys and the lower slopes of mountains, grazing in open grasslands. These usually associate in family groups of the doe and her offspring. They are shy, yet very curious. The roe deer barks like a dog when disturbed. They are excellent swimmers with all senses well developed.

The hind or doe usually has a single offspring (Job 39:1; Ps 29:9; Jer 14:5), though twins occur with some degree of regularity. (For photo of fawn, see VBW, IV, 143.) The fawn is able to stand on its legs within a few hours of its birth. The hind illustrated grace and charm (Gen 49:21; Prov 5:19).

11. **Dragon.** The KJV translates the plural Heb. word *tannîm* as "dragons" when it clearly refers to desert animals (e.g., Ps 44:19; Isa 13:22; Jer 9:11; Mic 1:8; Mal 1:3), most likely meaning the jackal (*see* II.23). The similar word *tannîn* is singular with a plural form *tannînîm*, also rendered "dragon" or "dragons" in KJV and often in RSV. It refers to serpents in Ex 7:9, 10, 12; Deut 32:33, and perhaps in Ps 91:13; to the crocodile in Ezk 29:3; 32:2; to primordial sea monsters and possibly dinosaurs in Gen 1:21; Job 7:12; Ps 148:7; Jer 51:34; and perhaps in Ps 74:13; Isa 27:1; 51:9 to creatures familiar to the ancient reader from his general knowledge of Canaanite and Babylonian mythology. *See* Leviathan and Whale, V.7, 13.

The mythology of Babylonia describes such monsters or dragons in primordial conflict with Marduk (ANEP, #523); they represented the principle of evil (Tiamat and her troupe of dragons and demons, ANET, pp. 62–67). In Babylon, dragons constructed in relief with glazed bricks decorated the Ishtar Gate (ANEP, #761). Horned serpents appear frequently in Mesopotamian art (ANEP, #454, 511, 519, 520, 537).

In the book of Revelation the dragon is primarily a symbol of Satan, the archenemy of God and His people (12:3–17; 13:2, 4, 11; 16:13; 20:2).

12. **Elephant,** *Elephas africanus* and *E. indicus.* While there are no references in Scripture to the elephant itself, there are a number of references to ivory (I Kgs 10:18, 22; 22:39; Ps 45:8; Song 5:14; 7:4; Ezk 27:6, 15; Amos 3:15; 6:4). The elephant's tusk is the source of ivory, which is carved into ornaments and jewelry and used in making various pieces of furniture. *See* Ivory. At least four Assyrian kings reported hunting elephants and capturing them.

There are two species of elephants: the African and the Indian. The Indian elephant once roamed wild in N Syria and was hunted near Carchemish by Pharaoh Thutmose III (ANET, p. 240). Tiglath-pileser III as late as 735 B.C. received elephant hides and ivory as tribute (ANET, p. 283; cf. ANEP, #353). Elephant tusks have been found in the Jordan Valley.

The Indian elephant lends itself readily to domestication. In addition to its use as a beast of burden, it was used in battle in the ancient world. The Seleucid leader Lysias employed 32 elephants against the Jews in the Maccabean war (I Macc 6:30).

The African elephant is larger than the Indian elephant and untameable. The elephant is

A fox in the Biblical Zoo, Jerusalem.IIS

the largest land mammal, weighing about three tons. The tusks may weigh up to 200 pounds.

13. **Ferret.** *See* Gecko, IV.16.

14. **Fox,** *Vulpes vulpes palaestinae.* The fox is a small dog-like carnivore with a bushy tail half its body length. It is smaller than a wolf and is normally a nocturnal solitary animal. The fox is omnivorous: it eats small animals, insects and fruit (Song 2:15). The fox is intelligent and has considerable endurance. It can run at speeds up to 30 mph. It has a keen sense of sight, smell, and hearing, and at times seems almost to have a sense of humor.

Usually the fox excavates its own burrow. It is known for its slyness, but the Hebrews also thought of the fox as insignificant (Neh 4:3; Lk 13:32). Some OT references, such as Ps 63:10 and Lam 5:18, are to jackals, for only the latter hunt in packs and tend to act as scavengers. Tristram found two varieties of fox in Palestine in the 19th cen. Feliks reports three varieties of fox in Israel today. How many of these existed in biblical times is not known.

15. **Gazelle,** *Gazella dorcas* and *G. arabica.* The gazelle (Heb. *ṣebî*, KJV "roe," "roebuck"; Gr. *dorkas*) is a small, dainty, graceful antelope with recurved horns. Two varieties exist in Palestine, the dorcas gazelle, which is pale fawn in color and 21 or 22 inches tall; and the Arabian gazelle, which is dark smoky fawn color and 24 or 25 inches tall. Both sexes have hollow horns.

Gazelles formed an important part of the diet of the early inhabitants of Jericho. The dorcas gazelle may have been domesticated and kept in the same way as goats. Apparently gazelles were kept as domestic animals in the Old Kingdom of Egypt. It could not be used for Jewish sacrifice, but could be eaten as food (Deut 12:15, 22; 14:5; 15:22, RSV).

In biblical times the gazelle was probably the game animal most hunted by the Jews (Prov 6:5; Isa 13:14). Pharaoh Tutankhamon hunted gazelles and ostriches with bow and dogs (ANEP, #190). The gazelle is said to have graced Solomon's table (I Kgs 4:23, RSV). It was not easy to catch because of its great speed (II Sam 2:18; I Chr 12:8; Prov 6:5, all RSV). It is also referred to in Song 2:7; 4:5; 7:3 (all RSV).

Herds are still found in the Negeb. Herds usually consist of from five to ten animals, but larger herds assemble in the varieties that migrate in the fall to lower elevations and new feeding grounds. The Bedouin hunt gazelles with falcons and dogs. The falcon annoys the gazelle and injures it so that dogs can overtake it.

16. **Hare,** *Lepus europaeus judaeus, L. capensis,* and *L. arabicus.* The hare is found in both open country, preferably near or on cultivated land, and in woods, usually deciduous. It is an herbivorous rodent and is different from the rabbit; no rabbits are found in Palestine.

A man sacrificing a gazelle, palace of Sargon II, Khorsabad, Assyria. LM

While not a true ruminant according to modern classification in that it does not have a four-chambered stomach, the hare does rechew its food. There is a process of partial regurgitation of material that is too hard for little cells in the stomach to absorb initially; thus the hare actually chews food previously swallowed (E. P. Schulze, "The Ruminating Hare," *Bible-Science Newsletter,* VIII [Jan. 15, 1970], 6).

Hares have very long ears and large hind feet; their feet are well furred (Egyptian relief, VBW, I, 186). Hares do not dig or occupy burrows; in this way they differ from true rabbits which do. Hares are mainly nocturnal and spend their inactive hours hiding in vegetation. They eat grasses and herbaceous matter, also twigs and the young bark of woody plants.

The hare was ceremonially unclean (Lev 11:6; Deut 14:7) apparently because while it appeared to chew its cud it did not have cloven hoofs. The consumption of hares is forbidden also among the Arabs, Chinese and Lapps.

The hare was widely hunted by other peoples in ancient and modern times (Assyrian relief, ANEP, #185). Yet its great speed, its prolific breeding, its timidity and its caution save it from extermination by its many enemies.

17. **Hart.** *See* Deer, II.10.

18. **Hedgehog,** *Erinaceus* sp. L. The hedgehog is an insectivore; the porcupine (*q.v.,* II.31), often confused with the hedgehog, is larger and is a rodent. This animal is characterized by a slow rolling walk, but it can run rapidly. It is a good swimmer and is generally active at night. Its spines are used to cushion itself as well as for protection.

The hedgehog roots in the fallen leaves of hedges and thickets, feeding on seeds and grubs, beetles, snails, snakes, lizards, young birds, mice, and carrion. It rolls into a ball for defense, covering its vulnerable belly.

Bodenheimer reports three species in Palestine. The Egyptian regarded the hedgehog as a bad omen. It is used in Scripture as a symbol of an inhabited area that has become desolate (Isa 14:23; 34:11; Zeph 2:14, all NASB; KJV, "bittern").

19. **Hind.** *See* Deer, II.10.

20. **Hippopotamus,** *Hippopotamus amphibius.* The hippopotamus is a large, thick-skinned amphibious ungulate with a large head, a bulky hairless body, and short legs. At the present time it is found only in the rivers of Africa, but there is considerable fossil evidence of hippopotami in Palestine, and they may have existed in the swamps of northern Galilee and the Jordan Valley. They are frequently found in the art and literature of pharaonic Egypt (VBW, IV, 132). Many have thought that this may be the animal principally in mind in Job 40:15-24 called behemoth. The Egyptian *pehemu* means "ox of the water."

21. **Hyena,** *Hyaena hyaena.* The hyena is a stockily built carnivore with coarse hair and an erect mane of long hairs along the neck and

back. Hyenas live in holes in banks or among rocks. They are mainly nocturnal but are not ordinarily noisy or aggressive. Their cry, however, is a disagreeable, unearthly sound. Usually they feed on carrion; they have jaws so powerful that they can crush bones. When the carrion supply is inadequate, they will kill sheep, goats, and small animals. If threatened, they growl and erect their mane, but they rarely fight.

Hyenas are known as scavengers; in Africa they eat the domestic refuse in the villages. The striped hyena is said to be the second most common predator in Palestine; here it prefers rocky districts and even rock tombs. It may exhume human bodies.

The hyena is not mentioned in KJV but appears as Zibeon in Gen 36:2, 14, 20, etc., as a personal name and in Gen 14:2, 8; Deut 29:23; I Sam 13:18 as a place name, Zeboim, which seems to indicate hyenas were common in the area. RSV translates *ī* as "hyena" in Isa 13:22; 34:14; Jer 50:39. The hyena is mentioned in Sir 13:18.

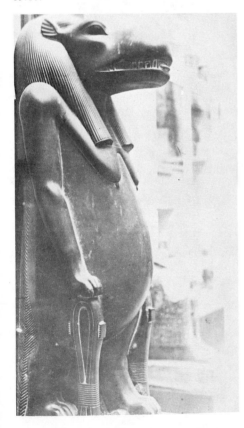

A statue in green schist of Thueris, Egyptian hippopotamus goddess in the Cairo Museum.
LL

22. **Ibex** or **Wild Goat,** *Capra ibex nubiana.* The ibex (Heb. *yā'ēl,* "wild goat," KJV) is a species of wild goat which still lives in small numbers in the cliffs close to the Dead Sea (I Sam 24:2). Its slender legs and sharp cloven hoofs enable it to cling to narrow rock ledges, to jump between them, and to climb steep cliffs. Usually the ibex is found in rugged mountain country, rocky crags and meadows, just below the snow line (Ps 104:18). In Job 39:1 they are called *ya'ălê-sāla',* "goats of the crag or rock"; in RSV, "mountain goats."

These animals frequently gather in herds of from five to 20. They graze and browse, being active in the afternoon and sometimes feeding throughout the night.

The large horn of the ibex was at one period made into the shofar, which was blown in the second temple to announce the new year and the jubilee year.

23. **Jackal,** *Canis aureus.* The jackal (Heb. *tan,* often "dragon" in KJV) is smaller than the true wolf, and its tail is shorter (for photo see VBW, III, 258). It is similar to the fox (*q.v., II.*14) but with shorter ears and longer legs. Its tail is drooping or erect compared with the long and horizontal tail of the fox. These animals usually prowl at night, singly, in pairs, or in packs through open savannah country. They eat small mammals, poultry, fruit, vegetables, and carrion. They spend their days in thickets and in clumps of vegetation. Often they obtain scraps from the kill of the larger carnivores. They are fast runners; their running speed is about 33 mph.

The cry of the jackal is an unnerving wailing howl (Mic 1:8, RSV; cf. Job 30:28–29). Scripture references in the RSV and NASB are chiefly to jackals prowling around ruined cities and wilderness areas. References include Neh 2:13; Ps 44:19; Isa 13:22; 34:13; 35:7; Jer 9:11; 14:6; 49:33; 51:37; Lam 4:3; 5:18; Mal 1:3.

24. **Leopard,** *Panthera pardus tulliana.* The leopard has the widest range across the earth of any of the large cats. In rocky areas it lives in caves, but in forested regions it lives in thick vegetation. Many lived in the vicinity of Mount Hermon in OT times (Song 4:8). It is a wary and cunning animal, formidable and ferocious (Jer 5:6; Hos 13:7; cf. Isa 11:6). It has survived in Palestine into the 20th cen. A.D.

The leopard is swift on the ground (Hab 1:8) and agile in trees. When it cannot consume all its prey, it caches the remainder in a tree. Its color is yellowish bespeckled with black spots (Jer 13:23; photo and tomb painting, VBW, III, 109). Daniel and John saw leopards in their visions as symbols of world powers (Dan 7:6; Rev 13:2).

25. **Lion,** *Panthera leo persica.* The lion is a large tawny colored carnivore which preys chiefly on hoofed mammals and charges by a series of leaps and bounds. Within the historic period, the lion ranged in Europe and Palestine. The Palestinian animal was the Asiatic or Per-

King Ashurnasirpal of Assyria hunting lions
from his chariot. BM

sian lion. The males are heavily maned. The
mane stops at the shoulders but covers much of
the belly. It cannot climb and is mainly nocturnal, returning to its lair or thicket by day (Jer
4:7; 25:38; Nah 2:11–12).

Lions were common in biblical times in all
parts of Palestine. The Heb. language has at
least seven words for lion and young lion, and
the beast is referred to over 130 times in the
Bible. It gradually declined and became extinct
shortly after A.D. 1300. The lion was present in
Mesopotamia until the end of the 19th cen.
Lion hunting was the sport of kings in Assyria
(ANEP, #184) and Egypt (ANET, p. 243).

The roaring of the lion comes only on a full
stomach, i.e., after it has consumed its prey (Ps
22:13; Ezk 22:25; Amos 3:4). The lion is a
bold (II Sam 17:10; Prov 28:1), destructive
animal (Ps 7:2; Jer 2:30; Hos 5:14; Mic 5:8),
the enemy of the flock (Amos 3:12), whose
roaring inspires fear in domestic animals (Amos
3:8; see VBW, III, 174–235; I Pet 5:8). Like
all great cats, lions sometimes become man-
eaters (I Kgs 13:24–28; 20:36; II Kgs
17:25–26; Ps 57:4; Dan 6:7–27). They prefer
open country, savannas, and plains.

Lions played an important part in the political (I Kgs 10:19–20) and religious symbolism
of the Near East (see many references in
ANEP). In Assyria and Babylonia the lion was
regarded as a royal beast (Dan 7:4). A large
basalt stela from the mid-2nd mil. B.C. was
found at Beth-shan depicting a dog and a lion
fighting (ANEP, #228). The lion was the
mightiest of beasts to the Jew and illustrated a
king's regal bearing (Prov 30:29–31). Thus it
symbolized rulership (Gen 49:9; Num 24:9)
and even became a title of Christ (Rev 5:5).
The lion remains a favorite zoo animal among
oriental-style rulers; the emperor of Ethiopia
still exhibits the royal lions.

26. **Mole.** See Mole Rat, IV.25.
27. **Monkey.** See Peacock, III.40.
28. **Mouse.** See Mouse, IV.27.

Diorite statue of the Egyptian lion goddess
Sekhmet. MM

29. **Onager** or **Half Ass**, *Equus hemionus hemihippus.* The onager or Syrian wild ass (Heb. *pere'*) is intermediate between the true horse and the true ass. Its ears are longer than those of a horse but shorter than those of the ass. It is also known as the kulan, the kiang, and the djiggetai. For Assyrian bas reliefs see VBW, III, 98; IV, 128; ANEP, #186. The front hoofs are narrow, there are chestnuts on the forelegs only, and the tail is short haired for a long distance from its root so that it appears to be tufted.

The Sumerians were able to domesticate the onager, but the horse superseded it. In Ur it was used to draw chariots, for a number were buried with their vehicles in a royal grave *c.* 2500 B.C. Later it was a favorite quarry of the Babylonian and Assyrian kings.

The onager seems to have been very common in the steppe lands near Israel where it is described as a freedom-loving desert animal (Job 24:5; 39:5–8; Ps 104:11; Isa 32:14; Jer 2:24; Hos 8:9). Ishmael was to be a wild ass of a man (Gen 16:12, RSV), one who could not adjust to communal life. Drought seems to have been responsible for the decimation of the onager in biblical times (Jer 14:6). Nebuchadnezzar dwelt among the wild beasts including the onager (Aram. *'ărād,* Dan 5:21).

30. **Ox, Wild** or **Unicorn**, *Bos primigenius.* This animal (Heb. *re'ēm,* Akkad. *rīmu,* described in Job 39:9–12; for Assyrian relief see VBW, IV, 129) is clearly the wild ox, a large, fierce, fleet, intractable animal. It has a long lean rump with a straight back and a long narrow head. The two horns (Deut 33:17, RSV; "unicorns" should be singular in KJV) are straight and as long as the head. These were its outstanding characteristics (Num 23:22; 24:8; Ps 22:21).

It is also known in Europe as the aurochs. In Germany it is known as *Auer;* in Latin it was *urus.* It existed in the wild state until the 17th cen. A.D. when it became extinct, though Bodenheimer reports rumors of individual specimens surviving in the mountain valleys of Kurdistan. Hunting of this animal was the preferred sport of the Assyrian kings. Tiglath-pileser I hunted it in the Lebanon Mountains *c.* 1100 B.C. (cf. Ps 29:6).

At one time *re'ēm* was thought to be the oryx or antelope; the Arabs call the oryx *ri'm.* The translators of the LXX called *re'ēm* "monokeros" (unicorn) on the basis of relief representations of the aurochs in strict profile which they found on Babylonian mosaics and Egyptian drawings. Because it was in strict profile, only one horn was seen, hence "unicorn." The Vulgate translated *re'ēm* "unicornus" and Luther followed with the phrase "Einhorn." There is no question today that the *re'ēm* is the wild ox and that the author of Job was referring to this and not to a mythological animal (see also ANEP, #183; VBW, I, 228).

Kings often symbolized their dominion by wearing a helmet with two wild ox horns (VBW, IV, 57; cf. Ps 92:10 with 132:17–18).

31. **Porcupine,** *Hystrix* sp. The porcupine is a true rodent as opposed to the insectivore hedgehog, and lives in forested areas, rocky hills, ravines and valleys. It has long quills, which when raised give the appearance of a crest. This animal is almost entirely nocturnal. It burrows by day into a natural cavity or crevice. The old world porcupine rarely climbs trees as the new world porcupine does. Porcupines eat fruit, bark, roots and other succulent vegetation. They may also eat carrion. While its flesh is edible, it was not classed among the clean animals for the Israelite. A porcupine may weigh as much as 60 pounds.

Heb. *qippôd* in Isa 34:11 is translated "porcupine" in ASV and RSV, but "bittern" in KJV; KJV also has "bittern" for this word in Isa 14:23; Zeph 2:14, where RSV has "hedgehog."

32. **Pygarg.** *See* Antelope, II.1.

33. **Roe.** *See* Gazelle, II.15.

34. **Roebuck.** *See* Deer, II.10.

35. **Satyr.** The satyrs (Heb. *śā'îr*) of Isa 13:21; 34:14 (KJV, RSV, JerusB) were evidently hairy creatures (from Heb. *śē'ār,* "hair") and almost certainly wild goats, since Heb. *śā'îr* is also the word for "he-goat." RSV also translates this Heb. word as "satyrs" in Lev 17:7 and II Chr 11:15, where KJV has "devils." At the latter reference WBC (p. 400) suggests that instead of mythological satyrs or hairy demons, "as claimed by 'liberal' criticism," the *śe'îrîm* were simply goat idols, used in conjunction with the golden calves which Jeroboam I of Israel had set up.

36. **Sheep, Mountain,** *Ovis orientalis.* The European chamois *(Rupicapra)* is not found in Bible lands. Thus in Deut 14:5, for Heb. *zemer* the KJV "chamois" may refer to one of several varieties of wild sheep known in the Mediterranean area. The above species occurs wild in Armenia and Persia. For *zemer* Tristram suggested the *Ovis tragelaphus,* a sheep about three feet high with long curved horns, familiar to the Bedouin.

37. **Unicorn.** *See* Ox, Wild, II.30.

38. **Weasel.** *See* IV.36.

39. **Wild Ass.** *See* Onager, II.29.

40. **Wild Ox.** *See* II.30.

41. **Wolf,** *Canis lupus.* The wolf travels in bands of up to 30 animals that arise from a family group (for photo see VBW, III, 280). They hunt singly or in relays, usually at night (Jer 5:6). Wolves have acute hearing and sight, but rely chiefly on scent and usually catch their prey in a swift and open chase. The wolf is known for its boldness, fierceness, and voracity (Gen 49:27; Hab 1:8). It commonly kills more than it can eat or take away. Its usual food is small mammals, such as mice, fish, crabs, and carrion. In Egypt, Rome, and Greece the wolf was considered sacred.

Wolves are intelligent, social creatures, faithful to their own kind; they mate for life. Wolves were well known in Palestine. Except for Isa 11:6; 65:25; Jn 10:12, the scriptural references to wolves are all figurative, usually the symbol of enemies and wicked men (e.g., Ezk 22:27; Zeph 3:3; Acts 20:29).

III. Flying Creatures

1. **Bat.** Bats are flying mammals; they have hair and provide milk for their young. They orient themselves by echo location and take shelter in caves, crevices, tree cavities, buildings, and also in exposed places on trees. In colder areas they hibernate or migrate. The normal resting position for a bat is hanging head downward. Because they fly with their legs as well as with their wings, they may properly be said to swim through the air.

Most bats are insectivorous. These bats are relatively small in size and obtain insects in flight. Many insectivorous bats also eat some fruit. In addition, there are fruit-eating bats which feed exclusively on fruit and some green vegetation. These usually live and feed in groups. They are tropical because they can live only where fruit is constantly ripening, although some have been observed in Palestine. Fruit-eating bats may be large with a wing spread of almost five feet. A third group are flower-feeding bats which eat pollen and nectar. They are small with long pointed heads and long tongues. They are found only in the tropics and semitropical regions.

Vampire bats are known only from the New World. There are only three species; these eat blood by making a small incision and lapping it up. Carnivorous bats are of all sizes; these prey on birds, lizards, and frogs. Fish-eating bats catch fish at or near the water surface.

Tristram reports eight varieties of bats in Palestine in the 19th cen. One of these, the little brown bat, *Myotis* sp., is worldwide in its distribution. It is insectivorous and probably actually has the widest natural distribution of any terrestrial mammal except man. Little brown bats are mostly cave dwellers. The females form maternity colonies which may number in the tens of thousands.

Two species of mouse-tailed bats, *Rhinopoma* sp., are found in Palestine. The tail is nearly as long as the head and body combined. These are often colonial. They roost in caves, rock clefts, wells, pyramids, palaces, houses, and they are insectivorous.

The slit-faced or hollow-faced bats also are found in Palestine. These, too, are insectivorous and roost in groups of from six to 20.

The bat is unclean (Lev 11:19; Deut 14:18), and is a symbol of desolation (Isa 2:20–21).

2. **Bee,** *Apis mellifica.* There are many references to bees in the Bible. The land of Israel was described as a land flowing with milk and honey. Honey and dates were the only major sources of sugar available to ancient man. It is believed that the honeybee was not domesticated until the Hellenistic period in Palestine so that earlier references are to wild honeybees. Passages such as Jud 14:8 refer to honey; other passages such as Deut 1:44; Ps 118:12; and Isa 7:18 allude to the irritable, vindictive nature of the bee and the painful stings which it inflicts.

In getting honey every attempt was made by the ancients to protect the colony in order to preserve this source of sugar. In Egypt the bee was considered sacred. The Philistines and the Hittites practiced beekeeping in their cities. A bee swarm was as valuable as a sheep, though the price of honey itself was low. Honey was sometimes eaten with the honeycomb (Song 5:1).

3. **Bittern.** *See* Hedgehog, II.18; Heron, III.21.

4. **Buzzard,** *Buteo buteo.* This bird was ritually unclean (Heb. *'ayyâ*, Lev 11:14; Deut 14:13, both JerusB), as were all predatory and carrion-feeding birds. It resembles the kite (KJV in above verses), though its tail is straight and not cleft. It is said to have wonderfully sharp eyesight (Job 28:7*b*) and will trail its prey for hours.

5. **Cock.** *See* Fowl, Domestic, III.14.

6. **Cormorant,** *Phalacrocorax carbo carbo.* The Heb. word *shālāk* implies a bird that hurls itself or dives upon its prey (Lev 11:17; Deut 14:17). The common cormorant is a large black goose-like bird which feeds on fish. It is known from the Mediterranean coast, from the Jordan River, and from the Sea of Galilee. The cormorant is repeatedly depicted in Egypt and in Palestine.

7. **Crane,** *Grus grus.* Cranes are tall wading birds resembling the stork and the heron but with shorter talons. Its plumage has a silvery gloss, and the feathers of the tail are wavy. It feeds on plants, insects, and worms. Large flocks of cranes flying in a wedge-shaped formation pass over Palestine annually on their way to Africa from the northern countries of Europe and again on their return flight. Jer 8:7 refers to the crane's migratory habits. Their general call is best described as a bellowing, but during flight they are said to emit a chattering sound; this latter seems to be what is referred to in Isa 38:14.

8. **Cuckoo** or **Cuckow,** *Cuculus canorus canorus.* The term used in Lev 11:16 and Deut 14:15 (KJV) may refer either to the common cuckoo or to the great spotted cuckoo, *Clamator glandarius.* The cuckoo is a small, drab brown bird. It is best known because of its parasitic habits. It acts as a brood parasite, laying its eggs in the nest of another species after pushing out one of the eggs of the host species. The young cuckoo hatches before the host species and evicts the young host species. The foster parents raise it as their own.

The cuckoo is an insect eater, yet in Scripture it is considered unclean, implying that either it is a predator or a carrion eater. For that reason some believe that the term actually refers to the sea gull (RSV, JerusB) or sea-mew (ASV) and not to the cuckoo. Gulls, terns, and petrels are all common on the seashore and lakes of Palestine.

9. **Dove** or **Turtledove,** *Streptopelia turtur.* The plumage of the dove or turtledove (Heb. *tôr;* Akkad. *tūrtu;* Gr. *trugōn*) is of many hues — red, blue, and violet. It migrates to Israel in the spring (Jer 8:7) and awakens the groves with its call (Song 2:12, RSV). It is smaller than the pigeon but is more beautiful. It cares for its young much as does the pigeon by regurgitating food. The psalmist employed the word metaphorically as a term of affection, "the soul of thy dove" (Ps 74:19). It was a clean bird that could be used for sacrifice (Gen 15:9; Lev 1:14; 5:7; 12:6; Num 6:10; Lk 2:24). *See also* Pigeon, III.42. (See Heinrich Greeven, *"Peristera,"* TDNT, VI, 63–72.)

10. **Eagle.** *See* Vulture, Griffon, III.54.

11. **Eagle, Gier.** *See* Vulture, Egyptian, III.53.

12. **Falcon.** *See* Kestrel, III.25.

13. **Fly,** *Musca* sp. Flies (Heb. *zᵉbûb)* are important causes of epidemics and food spoilage. The reference in Eccl 10:1 seems to be *Musca domestica* which ruins the ointment. The fly symbolizing Egypt in Isa 7:18 seems to refer to *Tabanus arenivagus* which attacks both man and animal. The swarms of insects in the fourth plague (Ex 8:21–31) may refer to the house fly, to the bluebottle fly *(Calliphora erythrocephala),* the dog fly, the Barghas midge, or the Tabanid fly *(Stomoxys calcitrans).*

The maggots of Job 25:6 and Isa 14:11, and the worms of Ex 16:24; Job 7:5; 17:14 are probably fly larvae. *See* Worm, IV.37. The domestic fly is very common in all parts of Israel, chiefly in dung heaps and garbage. The female lays her eggs out of which a white maggot emerges which feeds on refuse. After a few days the maggot develops into a cocoon out of which the adult insect emerges. In the summer this whole cycle lasts just about twelve days so that a fly can breed about twenty generations a year. Philistine inhabitants of the city of Ekron worshiped a god named Baal-zebul, "Baal the Prince," who was dubbed Baal-zebub, "Lord of flies," by God-fearing Israelites in a mocking pun (II Kgs 1:2).

14. **Fowl, Domestic,** *Gallus gallus domesticus.* Domesticated poultry are probably derived from the red jungle fowl of India. They seem to have been known already in OT times (Prov 30:31, RSV; not the "greyhound," KJV). A seal of Jaazaniah (cf. II Kgs 25:23) dating *c.* 600 B.C. bears the figure of a fighting cock; it was found at Tell en-Nasbeh, the site of ancient Mizpah.

Poultry were considered a symbol of fertility. The Jews carried a cock and a hen in front of bridal couples. The cock is still used as a timekeeper and an alarm clock in eastern countries (cf. Mt 26:34). *See* Cockcrowing. The motherly concern of the hen was familiar to Jesus' hearers (Mt 23:37). The reference in Neh 5:18 to fowls or poultry for Nehemiah's table is probably to wild game.

15. **Glede.** *See* Kite, III.26.

16. **Gnat,** *Culex, Anopheles,* etc. The references in Ex 8:20–28; Ps 78:45; 105:31 to "swarms of flies" (KJV, RSV) may be to the mosquito, to the harvester gnat, to the Barghas of the Arabs, or to the sandfly. These references seem to fit a swarm of these insects that plagued the inhabitants and pestered them in their daily life not unlike the lice which occurred in the preceding plague. Gnats frequently had to be strained out of wine to which they were drawn while it fermented (Mt 23:24).

17. **Goatsucker** or **Nighthawk,** *Caprimulgus* sp. There are several species of these birds found in Palestine, similar to the American whippoorwill (Lev 11:16b; Deut 14:15b). The goatsuckers were thought by the ancients to milk goats. They resemble owls with a flat head, large eyes and soft plumage which results in a noiseless flight. They are insectivorous, catching their prey on the wing. They migrate from Africa to Europe each year.

18. **Goose,** *Anser anser.* Geese are longnecked, web-footed water birds. They are easily domesticated. They were known to the Greeks, and domestic geese are mentioned in the Odyssey. They may have been domesticated already in Egypt in the Old Kingdom and certainly were domesticated by New Kingdom times. They were used for food and for sacrifice.

Geese were similarly used for food and sacrifice in ancient Mesopotamia. The breeding of geese was widespread in Canaan in biblical times; ivory carvings of the 13th or 12th cen. B.C. showing geese found at Megiddo attest to this fact (VBW, II, 210). Geese graced the table of King Solomon, according to I Kgs 4:23, where they are referred to as "fatted fowl."

Snaring ducks and geese. Wall relief in tomb of Ka-Gemni, Saqqara, Egypt. LL

The Egyptian god Horus represented as a hawk. LL

19. Hawk, Sparrow, *Accipiter nisus.* The Heb. *nēṣ* was ceremonially unclean (Lev 11:16; Deut 14:15) and probably is the sparrow hawk. It is not a permanent resident in Palestine, but stops off as it migrates from N to S. This southward migration is mentioned in the book of Job (39:26).

The sparrow hawk (photo, VBW, I, 188) is slightly larger than the kestrel with short feathers and a long tail. The tail acts as a rudder and helps the bird change its course very swiftly in flight, so that it can maneuver in the air when it chases small warblers and other birds. It does not seize its prey on the ground as does the kestrel, but hunts small birds in flight and attacks them. The Egyptians embalmed sparrow hawks as well as kestrels; all hawks were highly regarded by them. The god Horus was depicted with the head of a hawk or falcon. The sparrow hawk's back is grayish brown and its belly white with black and brown bars.

20. Hen. *See* Fowl, Domestic, III.14.

21. Heron or **Bittern,** *Ardea* sp. The heron is a wading bird with a long thin neck and long legs (photo, VBW, I, 188). There are at least seven varieties reported by Tristram in Palestine. According to Deut 14:18 and Lev 11:19, the heron was ceremonially unclean. Driver believes these references are to the cormorant, but most scholars believe they refer to one of the herons.

The characteristic mark of these birds is a comb-like growth on the inner side of the third toe. The white heron attains a length of over three feet, while the dwarf heron is only about 22 inches long. All herons feed on fish, small reptiles, and insects. They are a nuisance in artificial fish ponds.

22. Hoopoe, *Upupa epops.* The hoopoe (Lev 11:19; Deut 14:18, both RSV; "lapwing," KJV) is one of the most beautiful birds of Israel with colored plumage, a lovely crown-shaped crest on its head, and a long slender curved bill. In the fall it migrates to the S. It is listed as unclean, possibly because it searches for grubs and small insects in repulsive places such as dunghills.

23. Hornet. *See* Wasp, III.55.

24. Ibis, *Threskiornis aethiopica aethiopica.* The ibis (Lev 11:17, RSV following the LXX; "great owl," KJV) is a wading bird unknown in Palestine in the 19th and 20th cen. A.D., but possibly known there in biblical times. It was well known in ancient Egypt where it was sacred to Thoth. The ibis was classed as unclean; it eats mollusks and crustaceans. At one time it was very common in Egypt, but it has largely vanished today with the disappearance of the swamps along the Nile. The RSV does not consistently translate *yanshûp* as "ibis"; in Deut 14:16 and Isa 34:11, RSV follows the other versions by rendering it "great owl" or "owl."

On right, herons; on left ducks, geese, and pigeons. Wall relief from tomb of Ptah-hotep, Saqqara, Egypt. LL

25. **Kestrel** or **Falcon,** *Falco tinnunculus.* The kestrel or falcon (Heb. *'ayyâ*) is ceremonially unclean (Lev 11:14; Deut 14:13, "kite," KJV). This bird is abundant in Palestine both in town and country, nesting in roof tops and among the rocks. It is a small hawk about a foot long with brown, black, and yellow-colored feathers on the breast (for photo, see VBW, I, 188). Like most hawks it floats on the air and swoops down on its prey (mice, small reptiles, and insects) seizing them with its sharp, hook-like talons. The kestrel, like most hawks, is a useful bird, destroying rodents and venomous snakes.

Embalmed kestrels are found in ancient tombs in Egypt, where the bird was highly regarded. The Egyptians also embalmed the hunting kestrel, *F. cherug,* which can be tamed and trained to hunt deer and rabbit. Falconry, or hunting with hawks of various sorts, was well known among the ancients and is still practiced today. The Assyrians were familiar with it as seen in the records of Ashurbanipal.

26. **Kite** or **Glede,** *Milvus milvus.* The red kite or glede (KJV, Deut 14:13) is a medium-sized unclean bird of prey, called *rā'â* in Heb. because of its sharp sight (from *rā'â,* "to see"). It has a small head, and the edges of the upper part of the bill overlap with the lower ones, forming a sharp scissors. Its tail is forked or cleft like that of a fish. Its cry is loud, often with sharp, whistling notes.

The black-winged kite, *Elanus caeruleus,* is also known in Palestine. Both these birds eat refuse, carrion, small birds, and mammals. They have the habit of expelling undigestible material from their stomachs. They are impudent scavengers in Oriental towns, flying almost into the hands of man.

27. **Lammergeier,** *Gypaetus barbatus.* The lammergeier is a larger vulture and less common than other vultures. It is partial to marrow bone — the Latin *ossifragus,* "crusher of bone," refers to this — and to tortoises. Aeschylus is supposed to have lost his life when a lammergeier mistook his bald head for a rock and dropped a tortoise on it. It may attack deer and goats, carrying them aloft and dropping them on rocks.

The lammergeier is greyish brown with white streaks. It has a black tuft which gives it the name "bearded vulture." It is called "ossifrage" in KJV and "vulture" in RSV in Lev 11:13; Deut 14:12.

28. **Lapwing.** *See* Hoopoe, III.22.

29. **Locust,** *Schistocerca gregaria.* The locust has a number of names — at least 12 in the Bible. These refer to the different stages of its development from larva to adult, or to the type of damage which it causes. Sometimes two different species are referred to. Locusts were considered clean as food (Lev 11:22), though later the Talmud applied this only to varieties in which the wings covered the whole body.

Locusts are characterized by swarming and mass migration; in modern times they have

Behind the head of an Egyptian Pharaoh, a falcon, emblem of the god Horus, spreads his wings to protect the king. LL

caused frightful vegetative destruction. Grasshoppers do not swarm or migrate en masse; this differentiates them from locusts.

The OT mentions several different species of locust. Lev 11:22 seems to refer to the slant-faced locust and also to the katydid or long-horned grasshopper. The reference in Deut 28:42 may be to the mole cricket. In Joel 1:4; 2:25; Nah 3:16–17 the successive stages of the insect's development are described. See VBW, III, 224 f. for excellent illustrations and discussion.

A locust plague was one of the most severe evils to come to the ancient world (Deut 28:38; Joel 2:1, 11). Special days of prayer, fasting, and trumpet blowing were prescribed to remove the plague (I Kgs 8:37; II Chr 6:28; Joel 2:12–17). Locusts are still a serious problem, particularly in E Africa. At present there is a locust control program supervised by the Desert Locust Control Organization of East Africa. In 1958 aircraft measured a 400 square mile swarm of locusts in Ethiopia. At that time crop losses were estimated at $30 million, and four million people lost two years' supply of food. A 1969 locust invasion was successfully halted by the Desert Locust Control Organization.

Bedouin still eat locusts today, raw, roasted or cooked. They are preserved by drying and threading. They may also be crushed and ground and the grist put into dishes or eaten

A ceremonial fan from the tomb of Tut-ankhamen, originally fitted with ostrich feath-ers fixed in holes around the edge. Its is cov-ered with gold and shows the king hunting ostriches in the desert near Heliopolis. LL

with bread sometimes mixed with honey and dates. The Greeks ground locusts in stone mor-tars and made a flour of them.

Locusts symbolized the powerful and large enemy armies which completely destroyed the earnings of man's toil (Jud 6:5; Isa 33:4; Jer 46:23; 51:27; Nah 3:15).

Only three of the hundreds of Acridids found in Bible lands are capable of multiplying into great swarms, and only the *Schistocerca gre-garia* can be considered widespread in all Bible lands. This is the desert locust whose native home is the Sudan. It shows two phases, a solitary phase and a gregarious phase, with a possible third phase known as "transiens." There are differences in the immature and adult forms of these phases in color and physiology.

The quantity and distribution of rains is an important factor in determining whether there will be a plague; moist soil is needed for depos-iting the eggs and permitting them to develop. Each female deposits from one to six egg pods which contain anywhere from 28 to 146 eggs each. The larvae emerge in 15 to 43 days.

In the gregarious phase from the second in-star or stage of metamorphosis and afterward, the locust is overwhelmed by a strong wander-ing instinct, and masses of them form a random procession of overflowing bodies which ignore any obstruction. They swarm over everything (Joel 2:4–9). The only regulator to their acti-vities is temperature; temperatures that are too high or too low will immobilize them. They take to the wing and fly and may move 1,200 miles from their native home. This movement seems to be controlled by hormones. The direction is also influenced by the wind. They consume al-most every plant, but spare the carob, syca-more, castor tree, and oleander bush. Modern anti-locust campaigns have reduced the damage but have not solved the problem which has existed from biblical times.

The ancients considered the two large hind legs or jumping legs of the locust as a separate limb and had a special name for them. Hence locusts are described as having four legs; this is a reference to the four smaller walking legs. Aristotle refers to this in his "Parts of Ani-mals," IV, 6. "Going on all fours" refers to creeping or walking as opposed to jumping, and does not mean these unclean insects had only four legs in all.

30. **Moth.** *See* IV.26.

31. **Nighthawk.** *See* Goatsucker, III.17.

32. **Osprey.** *See* Vulture, Black, III.52.

33. **Ossifrage.** *See* Lammergeier, III.27.

34. **Ostrich,** *Struthio camelus.* The ostrich is a two-toed, swift-running flightless bird. It lives in deserts or in areas covered with stunted bushes. Heb. *bath hayya'ănâ,* "daughter of the desert" (Lev 11:16; Deut 14:15; Job 30:29; Isa 13:21; 34:13; 43:20; Jer 50:39, all RSV), prob-ably refers to the ostrich, though Driver con-tends these passages refer to the owl, as in KJV. According to the first two references, it was unclean.

The ostrich is the largest of all birds, attain-ing a height of about ten feet and a weight of 175 pounds. For Egyptian tomb painting see VBW, IV, 130. In biblical times ostriches were found over the entire wasteland of the Negeb, but they have since become extinct there.

The ostrich is omnivorous; it eats grass, fruits, small mammals, birds, snakes, and liz-ards, as well as large pebbles to assist the breakdown of food in the gizzard. The night cry of the ostrich, "like the hoarse lowing of an ox in pain," is referred to in Mic 1:8. Lam 4:3 refers to its apparent indifference to its brood: the male may transfer the young of one female into the nest of another. The ostrich is hunted (Assyrian cylinder seal scene, VBW, III, 38 f.), but its eggs are even more important than the bird itself. They are traded throughout the en-tire Mediterranean area. They may be used as utensils or they may be broken up and the shell converted into beads.

Occasionally the ostrich is used for riding and even for pulling small carts. Ostrich feath-ers are in great demand. Ostrich plumes graced ancient royal courts as fans. An ivory-handled fan of Pharaoh Tutankhamen with its lovely plumes may be seen in the National Museum at Cairo. Attempts at domestication have not been very successful, though there are ostrich farms in South Africa.

Job 39:13–18 refers to some familiar features and habits of hen-ostriches (*rᵉnānîm,* v. 13, KJV "peacock"). The many eggs of the ostrich are laid in a shallow nest in the sand, and some are left uncovered; thus they appear to be ne-glected by day, but this is only apparent, for they are incubated at night. The cock does most of the incubating. Unhatched eggs placed into the vicinity of the incubated eggs are intended to serve as food for the young.

The stupidity of the ostrich appears when it is hunted and cornered because it fails to take the evasive action which might save it. In open country, however, it is very wary and runs at great speed to escape. In contrast to the partridge, it will run away from its eggs and chicks when pursued. Its speed is proverbial: Tristram reports the maximum stride from 22 to 28 feet and a speed of 26 mph. To bag an ostrich was considered the feat of a hero (ANEP, #190, 706).

35. Owl, Barn or **White,** *Tyto alba.* Tristram reported that in 19th cen. A.D. Palestine there were eight varieties of owls, of which five were quite plentiful. It is difficult, however, to identify a particular variety with a certain Heb. word in the OT. Thus the following four owls can be only approximate identifications.

The barn owl (Heb. *tinshemeth*) is ritually unclean (Lev 11:18a; Deut 14:16c). It may get its Heb. name from the snoring sound that it makes when breathing. It has a frightening voice and somewhat sinister features so that at times it has been considered to be demonic; yet it is a useful bird that devours rodents that ravage the fields and damage houses. It sleeps during the day and is active at night. Its sense of hearing and sight are well developed. Its color is light brownish-yellow with a white mask around the eyes and cheeks. The whole leg is covered with feathers that protect it against the bites of its struggling victims. It has a large head and wide pop eyes; for this reason it is sometimes called the monkey-faced owl.

The KJV follows the Vulgate in translating *tinshemeth* as "swan," while the RSV renders it "water hen" after the LXX.

An ostrich in the Biblical Zoo. Jerusalem. HFV

36. Owl, Little, *Athene noctua lilith.* Like all other owls, this is ritually unclean (Heb. *kôs,* Lev 11:17a; Deut 14:16a). It is the smallest of all nocturnal birds of prey (photo, VBW, I, 188). Chiefly insectivorous, at times it feeds also on tiny birds. It is the most common owl in Palestine, dwelling among ruins (Ps 102:6b, RSV), tombstones, rocks, and in thickets. Its voice sounds like that of a dying person. On occasion it may be observed perching on a rock with its large eyes gazing off into the distance. It was this pose that the ancient Greeks considered a sign of wisdom. They considered it sacred to the goddess Athena.

The famous "owl" of Athens, standard currency of the Eastern Mediterranean during the Athenian Empire period (fifth cen. B.C.). G. L. Archer & W. S. LaSor

37. Owl, Long-eared or **Great,** *Asio otus.* This bird is mentioned in the Bible among the birds of desolation that will inhabit the devastated Edom (Isa 34:11). It gets its Heb. name *yanshûph* ("hisser," from *nāshap,* "to blow, hiss") because of the snoring or panting sound which it makes when breathing. For this reason G. R. Driver thinks it is the screech owl. It feeds on rodents, rats, and mice, devouring them skin and all and expelling the undigested waste through its mouth. It hibernates in Israel among ruins and in groves.

The great owl stands nearly two feet tall. The color is mouse gray with gray-brown spots and black stripes. As its name indicates, it has tufted "ears." Like other predatory birds, it was considered ritually unclean (Lev 11:17; Deut 14:16). For another possible translation of *yanshûph* see "Ibis."

38. Owl, Scops, *Otus scops.* The scops owl has two horn-shaped crests of hair-like feathers on its head, perches in an inclined posture, and hops and dances like a goat. During the hatching period the male's hooting sounds like a moan. It feeds chiefly on insects and mice. During an invasion by mice or locusts these owls appear in large flocks and help destroy the pest.

Biblical references may be either Isa 13:21 (NASB, Heb. *'ōaḥ,* KJV "doleful creatures") or Isa 34:15 (Heb. *qippôz,* KJV "great owl"). Others think the *qippôz* is a variety of snake (NASB, JerusB).

39. **Partridge,** *Alectoris graeca werae, A. graeca cypriotes,* and *Ammoperdix heyi heyi.* The partridge referred to in I Sam 26:20 is probably the sand partridge *(Ammoperdix)* found near the Dead Sea; in Jer 17:11, the chukar *(Alectoris).* They are the most common game birds in Palestine. The main hunting season seems to have been in July. It is caught by continuously chasing it (cf. I Sam 26:20), by snares, or by a hunter hiding in a deer blind. The bird finds refuge among the bushes with which its brownish-green feathers blend. It is a prolific breeder, otherwise it probably would have become extinct. The young are able to run about seeking food and shelter almost immediately after hatching. The explanation of the partridge's gathering a brood which she did not hatch (Jer 17:11, RSV) seems to lie in the fact that the hen partridge lays two batches of eggs, one for herself and one for the cock to incubate.

40. **Peacock,** *Pavo cristatus.* The peacock is a native of India where it is a shy, fast runner. Occasionally the peacocks fly in small flocks. Because it is not native to Palestine, the Heb. word *tukkîyîm* in I Kgs 10:22 and II Chr 9:21 is thought by some to be a reference to old world monkeys brought from E Africa, or to guinea hens from the Upper Nile. Since *tukî* is mentioned along with ivory, most likely from the African elephant, the *qōph* (*see* Ape, II.2), the monkey is the most probable identification

A pelican in the Biblical Zoo, Jerusalem. HFV

(see IDB, II, 252a). The Heb. term is similar to an Egyptian word for monkey in inscriptions regarding expeditions to Punt (Somaliland). Large and small monkeys were among the tribute received by the Assyrian king Ashurnasirpal II (ANET, p. 276).

41. **Pelican,** *Pelecanus onocrotalus.* Pelicans were known to the ancient Egyptians and Assyrians. Many scholars doubt that the Heb. *qā'at,* an unclean bird (Lev 11:18; Deut 14:17) that inhabited the wilderness (Ps 102:6) and ruins (Isa 34:11; Zeph 2:14, KJV "cormorant"), refers to the pelican and believe the *qā'at* is one of the owls or vultures. But the roseate pelican, with white plumage and large yellow pouch under its· lower bill, does frequent rivers, lakes, and marshes of Palestine. After flying out to sea as far as 20 miles to swoop down upon fish near the surface, the pelican often retires inland to a deserted spot to digest its enormous meal. Thus the pelican may well be the lonely bird of the psalmist (102:6).

42. **Pigeon** or **Dove,** *Columba livia.* The dove (Heb. *yônâ;* Gr. *peristera*) or young pigeon (Heb. *ben yônâ*) mentioned in the Bible seems to be the wild rock pigeon from which our domestic pigeon is descended; the term is a loose one applying to any small species of pigeon. Some were colored silvery gray with greenish-gold irridescent plumage on the wings (Ps 68:13; for photos, see VBW, I, 184; III, 88).

The pigeon or dove was apparently one of the first birds to be domesticated, since Noah released a dove toward the end of the Flood (Gen 8:8–12). One variety still lives in a semiwild state on the roofs of Jerusalem. It roves over the fields, feeds on weeds, and returns at dusk to its home (Isa 60:8). The dove was offered as a sacrifice by the poor and the Nazarite (Lev 5:7; Num 6:10). It was widely used for food. Its throaty moaning is referred to in Isa 38:14; 59:11; Ezk 7:16; Nah 2:7. Its powers of flight were well known (Ps 55:6). Solomon comments on the beauty of its eyes (Song 1:15; 4:1; 5:12). He also calls attention to its gentleness and loyalty to its mate (Song 2:14; 5:2; 6:9). The dove often built its nest in the rocks and cliffs (Song 2:14; Jer 48:28). Usually the dove was regarded as a symbol of innocence (Mt 10:16); yet in Hos 7:11 the dove is said to be senseless and foolish. In II Kgs 6:25 there is a reference to the sale of dove dung *(q.v.),* presumably used for food because of famine conditions during the siege of Samaria. *See also* Dove, III.9.

43. **Quail,** *Coturnix coturnix.* These are short-winged, sandy-colored gallinaceous (poultry-like) birds, the smallest of the subfamily *Phasianinae* which includes pheasants and partridges. Quail of the Mediterranean region winter in the Sudan and migrate northward in vast flocks in the spring. Their flight at night with the wind is exhausting, so that when they alight they are easily caught with nets and even with bare hands (for painting, see VBW, I, 149).

Tristram says that quail are considered the most delicate eating of all game.

Enormous flocks of quail twice served as food for the Israelites in the wilderness of Sinai when they were driven down in the desert miraculously by the winds (Ex 16:13; Num 11:31; Ps 105:40). In the second case they must have been flying along the Gulf of Aqaba and were blown off course by an east wind (Ps 78:26–28). They are preserved by drying in the sun (Num 11:32).

44. **Raven,** *Corvus corax.* The raven is a large (three pound, 26 inch long) passerine (sparrow-like) bird related to the rooks, jackdaws, magpies, and jays. Its most conspicuous feature is its glossy-black, irridescent plumage (Song 5:11; for photo, SEE VBW, I, 189). Other members of the *Corvidae* are less soberly colored. It is found almost everywhere in the world except in the South Pacific.

Noah sent out a raven first from the ark (Gen 8:7); it must have fed on floating victims of the Flood. The raven is essentially a scavenger and thus was ceremonially unclean (Lev 11:15; Deut 14:14); but it will attack defenseless young animals (Prov 30:17). Aristophanes in his *Birds* similarly reports that crows peck out the eyes of their prey. It will even attack lambs, small mammals, birds, and reptiles. Ravens find food for themselves and their young quite readily, without help from man (Job 38:41; Ps 147:9; Lk 12:24). They pair for life. They prefer desolate uninhabited areas as their home territory (I Kgs 17:4, 6; Isa 34:11). Apparently the Heb. *'ōrēb,* "raven," refers to the entire family of *Corvidae.* Tristram reports eight species of the family in Palestine: three ravens, two jackdaws, one crow, one rook, and one chough.

45. **Seamew** or **Sea Gull.** *See* Cuckoo, III.8.

46. **Sparrow,** *Passer domesticus.* The sparrow referred to in Ps 84:3; 102:7 (KJV); Prov 26:2 (RSV); Mt 10:29, 31; Lk 12:6–7 is a passerine bird of the finch family and is generally considered to be of little worth. The Heb. word *ṣippôr* is the general term for "bird" and especially would refer to small birds, such as sparrows, finches, thrushes, blackbirds, and starlings. The common or house sparrow was known in ancient Greece and Egypt. There it had the reputation of invading fields in big swarms and picking seeds from them.

47. **Sparrow Hawk.** *See* Hawk, Sparrow, III.19.

48. **Stork,** *Ciconia alba.* The stork is a long-legged, wading white bird with glossy black wings, which eats aquatic organisms, garbage, small mammals, birds, and reptiles. It is related to the heron and is ceremonially unclean (Lev 11:19; Deut 14:18). Flocks of storks pass through Israel during the September migration on their way to central and southern Africa, and likewise in the spring on their return flight to their home in northern Palestine, Syria, and the whole of Europe. Their faithful tending of the young is proverbial, as is also their habit of returning annually to the same nesting place.

Jeremiah mentions the uncanny instinctive knowledge the stork has of the time of his migration (Jer 8:7; for photo, see VBW, III, 103). Ps 104:17 refers to its nesting in a treetop when a suitable building is not at hand. Tristram reported the black stork, *C. nigra,* as well as the white stork in 19th cen. Palestine. The black stork is common around the Dead Sea valley and nests in trees; hence it may be the species referred to in Ps 104:17.

The stork has large powerful wings, the flapping of which produces a strong rushing sound referred to in Zech 5:9. It has very long legs and connecting membranes between the toes to prevent it from sinking in the mud. The red bill is sharp and long, serving to seize and lift the prey out of water. In Europe the stork nests on rooftops and lives in the same place year after year.

49. **Swallow,** *Hirundo rustica.* The swallow is a small, nearly black, fork-tailed passerine bird with long, tapered wings, noted for its graceful flight. It resembles the swift in shape and life habits, but it has a shorter tail. The Heb. *dĕrôr* (Ps 84:3; Prov 26:2) is quite certainly the sparrow; but in Isa 38:14; Jer 8:7 the *sîs* should rather be translated as the swift (*q.v.*).

50. **Swan,** *Cygnus* sp. Two species of swans are found in the Middle East as passing migrants, *C. olor, C. musicus.* Swans are the best musicians known among the birds and were considered sacred to Apollo. They sound like flutes and harps. Swans will fight only if attacked. They are often attacked by eagles. The scriptural references in Lev 11:18a and Deut 14:16c (both KJV) may not be to the true swan, but the Heb. term *tinshemet* may be the water hen (RSV) or the barn owl (*q.v.,* III.35).

51. **Swift,** *Apus* sp. Swifts (Heb. *sîs*) arrive in Palestine in late winter (Jer 8:7), and immense flocks fill the cities with their cries. They usually arrive sometime between February 20 and 25. The swift, like the swallow, has long, bent wings and a cleft tail which enables it to attain great speed as it skims the ground and sweeps through the air. It is a useful bird devouring a great many harmful insects which it catches in its mouth in flight. The swift makes its nest in the rooftops, in nooks and crannies of the walls in Palestinian cities. To build its nest it uses straw and feathers which are cemented together with saliva from its mouth. Other swifts live in caves and clefts of rocks. The plaintive cry of the swift is referred to in Isa 38:14.

52. **Vulture, Black,** or **Osprey,** *Aegypius monachus.* The black vulture is ceremonially unclean ("osprey," Lev 11:13; Deut 14:12, KJV, RSV). Its Heb. name (*'oznîyâ*) may be derived from a root meaning "powerful." Its body length is a little over a yard with a wing spread of over three yards. The feathers are black, and the head and the upper part of the neck are bald like those of other carrion eaters. It nests in

the Jordan Valley and seems to have been rather abundant in biblical times, but today it is quite rare. It has a cere, a small waxlike membrane at the base of the beak, of livid flesh color. It feeds on carcasses and on carrion (e.g., II Sam 21:10; see VBW, II, 195). Some observers report that it drives goats and sheep over precipices and then it devours them.

53. **Vulture, Egyptian,** *Neophron percnopterus.* This vulture, too, is ceremonially unclean (*rāḥām*, "gier eagle," KJV; "carrion vulture," RSV; in Lev 11:18; Deut 14:17). It is also known as Pharaoh's hen and has a plumage that is basically white with a naked head and a yellow neck. Its feet are pink. The Egyptian vulture breaks bones left by other vultures. Its flight is slow and easy and its voice a croak. It is the smallest of all the carrion-eating birds found in Palestine.

An eagle or vulture in the Biblical Zoo, Jerusalem. HFV

54. **Vulture, Griffon,** or **Eagle,** *Gyps fulvus.* Until a generation ago the griffon vulture, the "eagle" of the OT (Heb. *nesher,* Lev 11:13; Deut 14:12; VBW, I, 188) was one of the most common birds in Palestine, but today it is on the verge of extinction. Many have been killed by eating poisonous bait meant for foxes and jackals. In addition, its reproduction is limited; the female lays only one or two eggs a year. It nests in crags and on clifftops (Job 39:27–28; Jer 49:16; Obad 4), and gives special care to the fledglings for seven weeks (Deut 32:11; VBW, I, 292). It often basks on rocks at midday and can fly swiftly (Deut 28:49; Job 9:26)

or can hover with easy movements. It can soar until it almost disappears in the sky (Prov 23:5; 30:19; Isa 40:31). Its call is a growling note.

The vulture was considered a symbol of sovereignty and domination in the ancient Near East. Thus Ezekiel compared the kings of Egypt and Babylon to mighty vultures (Ezk 17:3, 7). The Egyptian goddesses Nekhbet and Mut were represented as vultures (VBW, III, 171).

Like other carrion eaters (Prov 30:17), its neck is bald or very thinly covered with white down (Mic 1:16). This baldness seems to prevent the clumping of the feathers through the clotting of the blood as it plunges its head into the viscera of the carrion. The griffon vulture is the largest bird of Palestine, about four feet in length and measuring ten feet between its wing tips. Its beak is extremely strong but its toes are short, fitted with blunt talons. The middle toe is equal in length to the others, unlike that of other birds of prey which use it to seize their victims. Keen-sighted, it hovers at great height watching for dying or dead animals. It plummets swiftly upon the corpse (Job 39:29–30; Hab 1:8).

In some passages the true eagle must be meant. Ezekiel saw in vision four living creatures, each with four faces, one of which was like an eagle's (Ezk 1:10), and John saw similar beings, one like a flying eagle (Rev 4:7). Palestine has two varieties, the more common imperial eagle, *Aquila heliaca heliaca,* and the golden eagle, *Aquila chrysaëtos.* The latter can fly three or four miles in ten minutes, and may have evoked the comparison in II Sam 1:23; Jer 4:3; Lam 4:19.

Other biblical references include Ex 19:4; Ps 103:5; Jer 49:22; Hos 8:11; Mt 24:28; Rev 12:14.

55. **Wasp** or **Hornet,** *Vespa orientalis.* The hornet, a large stinging wasp, is mentioned three times in the Bible (Ex 23:28; Deut 7:20; Josh 24:12). The common species in Palestine, a yellow and red-brown insect, is larger and more dangerous than an ordinary wasp. Its sting paralyzes its victim before it sucks out the vital fluids. The hornet is an important enemy of the honey bee; it lies in ambush for honeybee workers and then invades and destroys the hive.

The hornet is a social insect with the division of labor among queen, workers, and drones. It builds a comb with characteristic hexagonal cells of a paper-like substance. In addition to feeding on honey it feeds on fruit and gnaws at the bark of trees using this in building its comb.

The biblical references may be figurative for the panic and terror that the invading Israelites would instill in Canaanite hearts (cf. Deut 11:25); or the hornet may symbolize actual military power. John Garstang (*Joshua-Judges,* New York: Richard R. Smith, 1931, p. 259) believed the hornet represented the armies of Egypt because the wasp was one of the emblems of the pharaohs (VBW, I, 158).

IV. Creeping, Swarming Things (Chiefly insects, amphibians, and reptiles)

1. **Adder.** *See* Cobra, IV.8; Serpent, IV.30; Viper, IV.34.

2. **Ant, Harvester,** *Messor* sp. Ants are exceedingly abundant all over Palestine; 31 kinds are now known in that land. Ants only rarely enter houses made of stone or mud brick; thus a long, ancient omen listed the dire consequences to a house or its owner if one of many varieties of ants would be seen in it (Bodenheimer, *Animal and Man in Bible Lands,* pp. 97 f.).

Ant nests are ordinarily underground in Palestine to protect the ants against excessive heat. They frequently have special chambers which serve as nurseries, granaries, or fungus gardens.

Particularly interesting are the references in Prov 6:6–8 and 30:25 to ants which store up grain in the summer. At one time critics doubted the activity of these harvester ants. It was even suggested that these references resulted from faulty observation: that Solomon had seen the white larval cases and had mistaken these for grains of wheat. We now know that several species of this genus build granaries, flat chambers connected by galleries and irregularly scattered over an area averaging two yards in diameter and about a foot deep in the soil. They collect seeds from the ground or pluck them from plants, remove the envelopes, and discard the chaff and the empty capsules on kitchen middens outside the nest. During the winter an average-sized nest may contain a half pint of seeds. The ants first bite off the head or radicle, the softest part of the kernel, which prevents germination in the seeds, or they may spread them out in the sun to dry; some seeds germinate in spite of this. The individual granaries may be five inches in diameter and a half inch high. Some nests may be 25 to 40 feet in diameter and six to seven feet deep with several entrances.

3. **Asp.** *See* Cobra, IV.8.

4. **Beetle,** *Coleoptera.* Beetles are insects with chewing mouth parts and two pairs of wings, the fore pair of wings being hard and sheath-like and the hind pair being membranous and folded under the fore pair. Some beetles are carnivorous, others chiefly herbivorous. Some are aquatic, some produce a secretion which blisters the skin, some damage fabrics, some damage crops, and some feed on other insects which are harmful to man.

The beetle is referred to in Lev 11:22 (Heb. *ḥargōl*), where it is mentioned as edible. The reference here may well be to the cricket (RSV), one of the orthoptera (related to grasshoppers and locusts), rather than to the beetle. In ancient Egypt the beetle or sacred scarabaeus, the *kheper*, was a symbol of the sun-god Ra, and the scarab seal and amulet became extremely popular.

5. **Cankerworm.** *See* Locust, III.29.

6. **Caterpillar.** *See* Locust, III.29.

7. **Chameleon.** *See* Lizard, IV.21.

8. **Cobra, Egyptian,** *Naja haje.* References to the adder or asp (Heb. *pethen,* Job 20:14–16; Deut 32:33; Ps 58:4–6; 91:13; Isa 11:8) seem to be to the Egyptian cobra. It is one of the most poisonous snakes, attaining a length of about 80 inches. It is common in Egypt, but at the present time it has become extinct in Palestine. Cobras extend a hood when disturbed by expanding ribs on the sides of the neck and head. Their fangs are permanently erect, not movable as in the vipers. The poison attacks the nervous system of the victim causing muscular paralysis; that of the viper attacks chiefly the circulatory system. The Egyptian cobra is related to the Indian cobra which is frequently charmed. Ps 58:6 may be a reference to the practice of snake charmers in extracting the fangs of cobras. The "fiery serpents" (Num 21:6; Deut 8:15) perhaps were cobras, "fiery" (Heb. *sārāph*) referring to the burning fever caused by their venom. The winged or flying serpents (*sārāph*) of Isa 14:29; 30:6 may refer to the extended hood or to the lightning-like strike.

9. **Cockatrice.** *See* Serpent, IV.30.

10. **Cricket.** *See* Beetle, IV.4.

11. **Crimson Scale Insect,** *Kermes* sp. The scriptural references to "scarlet" (KJV) or crimson (Heb. *tôla'at shānî,* lit., "scarlet worm"; e.g., Ex 25:4; 26:1; 39:1 ff.; Lev 14:4–6; 14:51 f.; Num 19:6; Prov 31:21; Song 4:3; Isa 1:18; Jer 4:30) refer to a dye derived from the larvae or the eggs on the bodies of female kermes or cochineal scale insects. The Arabs called the insect *qirmiz,* from which our word "crimson" is derived. The LXX translated the color as *kokkinos,* normally rendered "scarlet" in English, from the Gr. *kokkos,* so named because the female insect looks like a berry. The females actually secrete and remain under waxy scales on plant tissue. These attach themselves to the kermes oak, Q. *coccifera,* a native of the Near East and the Mediterranean area (illus., VBW, I, 190).

The dye industry and trade in the paste made from these insects undoubtedly flourished among the Phoenicians, although "scarlet" thread was used in patriarchal times (Gen 38:28, 30), and the merchant Ili-ittiya of Nuzu promised to deliver by caravan to the palace "rouge extracted from worms," along with other products. It takes 70,000 insects to make a pound of dye which today sells for about three dollars a pound and is used in cosmetics, rouge, food coloring, beverages, and medicine. Today the insects live on the prickly pear and other cacti. The rich red color is actually extracted from the eggs of the female. By applying pressure on the part of the body containing the eggs the red substance oozes out. *See* Color: Crimson.

12. **Dragon.** *See* II.11.

13. **Flea,** *Pulex irritans.* There are many species of fleas in Palestine besides the common flea. They are wingless parasites that have

sharp jaws and suck out blood from the bodies of humans and animals. The body is wedge shaped, enabling the flea to burrow into the folds of the skin and hide there. The female lays her eggs in dust heaps which accumulate in the corners of rooms, and the eggs hatch into small white larva which pupate in a cocoon. Soon adult fleas appear which immediately attach themselves to the body of their host. The female requires blood for the development of her eggs.

The most dangerous fleas are those of the rat which transmit the organism responsible for bubonic plague.

The references in I Sam 24:14 and 26:20 seem to be to a very small and despicable creature.

14. **Fly.** *See* III.13.

15. **Frog,** *Rana* sp. The frog is mentioned as the second of the ten plagues inflicted on the Egyptians (Ex 8:2–14; Ps 78:45; 105:30). Frogs are amphibians, living part of their lives in the water and part on land. The female lays her eggs in the water; after about a week the eggs hatch into tadpoles. Gradually through metamorphosis the tail is lost and limbs are acquired. Frogs must maintain a moist skin since they must take in oxygen through the skin as well as through their lungs; thus they must always remain close to water. They feed on insects and worms. Frogs are found throughout Israel. They inhabit chiefly lowlands where their croaking is heard in the spring and on summer evenings.

The frog would be expected to fall in the category of the creeping or swarming creatures which in general were termed ceremonially unclean (Lev 11:29–31). However, since the frog was not specifically listed, the rabbis did not consider it one of the animals that defiled through contact. Maimonides said, "Only those animals mentioned in the law are defiling, but not the serpent, the frog, and the tortoise." Instead, the Jews classified the toad as unclean, believing it to be the *ṣāb*, the last creature of

Lev 11:29 (*see* Lizard, Dabb, IV.22).

In Rev 16:13 certain foul spirits are said to look like frogs. The ancient Egyptians made the frog a symbol of life and origin, and an emblem of Heqet, the patron-goddess of birth. She is depicted with a frog's head, giving life to the newborn. Thus the deity was discredited when the power of Yahweh afflicted Egypt with the very animal that was her symbol (cf. Ex 12:12).

16. **Gecko,** *Hemidactylus turcicus.* The gecko is a reptile listed in Lev 11:30, RSV (KJV, "ferret"), as a ritually unclean creeping creature similar to the lizard. The reference in Prov 30:28 is to the insectivorous Turkish gecko which climbs walls and enters through the windows with the help of hand-shaped limbs. There are seven species of geckos in the Holy Land; all of them are insectivorous.

17. **Gnat.** *See* III.16.

18. **Grasshopper.** *See* Locust, III.29.

19. **Hornet.** *See* III.55.

20. **Horseleach.** *See* Leech, V.6.

21. **Lizard,** *Lacerta* sp. Lizards are listed as ceremonially unclean (Lev 11:29–31); in addition, their carcasses defile through contact (11:32–36). There are ten types of lizards, including the land crocodile and the chameleon, in Palestine which vary in color and size (see photos of chameleon and green lizard, VBW, I, 189). Lizards are reptiles: their skin is covered with scales. The lizard is a useful creature because it captures harmful insects and worms. Like other reptiles it lays eggs with shells softer than those of the birds and with no clear division between the yolk and the white. Both extreme heat and cold inactivate them, since they are variable-temperature organisms.

22. **Lizard, Dabb,** *Uromastix aegyptius.* In Lev 11:29 (RSV) the Heb. *ṣāb* is described as ceremonially unclean. KJV translates this "tortoise" but the reference seems to be to a lizard. It attains a length of about 24 inches and is found chiefly in the Negeb. The Dabb lizard is herbivorous, an unusual trait since most lizards are insectivorous. It has a hard rough skin. The

A lizard in the Biblical Zoo, Jerusalem. IIS

body is green with brown spots. It has a short, rounded head and a powerful tail encircled with a row of strong spines which it uses as a weapon of defense.

23. **Locust.** *See* III.29.

24. **Louse,** *Anoplura*. Lice (Heb. *kēn, kinnām*) were one of the ten plagues inflicted upon the Egyptians (Ex 8:16–19; Ps 105:31). The identification of these with lice is in dispute, though Feliks believes they were lice. Others suggest that the term refers to the gnat, the mosquito, or some other insect. The reference, they suggest, may be to the harvester gnat, the Barghas of the Arabs, a small midge which enters the eyes, ears, and nose of field workers during harvest (RSV above and Isa 51:6); to the Anopheles mosquito which transmits malaria (JerusB), or to the sandfly which carries dengue fever. Some identify the flies of the next plague with gnats (*see* Gnat, III.16) which seems likely, so that these may well have been true lice.

Lice were such a pest in biblical times that Egyptian priests and others shaved their heads. The Talmud distinguishes between the head louse and the body louse. Lice suck blood and are nuisances in this way. In addition they carry a number of diseases.

25. **Mole Rat,** *Spalax ehrenbergi ehrenbergi Nhrg*. The mole rat is neither a mole nor a rat, but rather a rodent from six to nine inches long which burrows in any area where the soil is suitable for digging. It is heavy-bodied, short-legged, and powerful, with projecting incisors and small claws. It has no tail and is mole-like in appearance, but neither true moles nor shrews have ever been found in Palestine. The mole rat builds breeding mounds in the wet winter season, which resemble those of pocket gophers, and less complex resting mounds in the summer. Both have rather complex tunnel systems. The mole rat feeds on roots, bulbs, tubers, and various other subterranean plant parts and does extensive damage to agriculture. Its body is adapted to underground life; it has no ears and only rudimentary eyes. The Libyans believe that touching a mole rat will result in blindness. Scriptural references are Isa 2:20 (Heb. *ḥăparpārâ*, from *ḥāpar*, "to dig") and probably Lev 11:29 (JerusB; "weasel," KJV and RSV; Heb. *ḥōled*).

26. **Moth,** *Tineola* sp. The clothes moth lays its eggs on wools or furs and the larvae feed on these. The destructive qualities of this insect are referred to in Job 13:28; Ps 39:11; Isa 50:9; Hos 5:12; Sir 42:13; Mt 6:19–20; Lk 12:33; and Jas 5:2. Isa 51:8, "worm," refers specifically to the larvae of the clothes moth. In all cases it is the larvae which does the damage; the adult is quite harmless and feeds mainly on the nectar of flowers. It is easily crushed (Job 4:19, JerusB). The moth is used as a symbol of disintegration, decay, and weakening. There are hundreds of species of moths other than the clothes moth in the Holy Land; they are harmful to leaves, flowers, fruits, trees, and seeds.

As with the clothes moth, it is the larva which damages.

27. **Mouse,** *Mus musculus praetextus*. The mouse (Heb. *'akbār*) was pronounced unclean because being short-legged it was considered to be one of the creeping creatures (Lev 11:29). Both commensals, which inhabit dwellings, and wild forms of mice are known. The commensal forms tend to have longer tails and to be darker in color. The wild forms are active chiefly at night. Mice are good climbers and even good swimmers. Wild mice eat many kinds of vegetables, such as seeds, fleshy roots, leaves, and stems. At times they store food.

The word *'akbār* (Lev 11:29; I Sam 6:4–5; Isa 66:17) is probably a general term for various rats and mice. Tristram reports 23 varieties of mouselike rodents in 19th cen. Palestine. Mice and rats cause food spoilage, damage to household articles, and transport the host fleas of typhus, spotted fever, and bubonic plague bacteria. The latter may have caused the tumors or swellings among the Philistines (I Sam 6:5); but *see* Vole, IV.35. Isa 66:17 refers to a pre-Exilic Canaanite cultic practice in which mice were eaten; in this case the rodent may have been the hamster. For image of mouse found in Middle Bronze Age obelisk temple at Byblos, see VBW, II, 119.

28. **Palmerworm.** *See* Locust, III.29.

29. **Scorpion,** *Buthus quinquestriatus*. There are a dozen species of scorpions found in Palestine, but 90 percent are yellow scorpions. These are arthropods, three to five inches long (for photo, see VBW, III, 160), belonging to the same group (arachnids) as the spiders, slow nocturnal invertebrates which rest beneath stones by day and prey on insects and other arachnids. It carries at the end of its tail a poisonous sting which is fatal to its prey and extremely painful to man (Rev 9:3, 5, 10; cf. I Kgs 12:11, 14) and often dangerous (Lk 11:12). Scorpions symbolized Ezekiel's evil countrymen (Ezk 2:6) and the demonic forces of Satan (Lk 10:19). The scorpion is mentioned as frequenting the Sinai desert (Deut 8:15).

30. **Serpent, Snake,** Suborder *Ophidia*. Nine Heb. words and four Gr. words are found in Scripture referring to snakes or to various species of them. Heb. *naḥash* (31 times) and Gr. *ophis* (14 times) are the generic terms, always translated "serpent." The Heb. word is an onomatopoeic imitation of its hissing as it scrapes its scales along the ground (cf. Jer 46:22). Many types of snakes lay eggs (Isa 59:5), although some retain the eggs in the body until ready to hatch.

The asp is probably the cobra (*q.v.*, IV.8), while the adder belongs to the viper class (*q.v.*, IV.34). The cockatrice of the KJV (Isa 11:8; 14:29; 59:5; Jer 8:17) was a fabulous serpent in English literature, supposedly hatched from a cock's egg, and thus has been replaced by "adder" in RSV.

Serpents were associated with worship in the Canaanite religion, and symbolized evil deities among many other peoples. Stelas have been unearthed at several sites in Palestine and Syria which depict a god or worshiper with a snake winding around the legs or body (W. F. Albright, *Archaeology of Palestine*, Penguin Books, 1960, p. 97, fig. 20; see also references to "serpent" in ANEP). Because the Israelites were burning incense in pagan worship of the bronze serpent of Moses (cf. Num 21:8–9), King Hezekiah destroyed it in his religious reform (II Kgs 18:4). *See* Brazen Serpent.

See also Cobra, IV.8; Viper, IV.34.

31. **Spider.** There are between 600 and 700 different species of spiders in Palestine. These are different from insects in that they, like scorpions, have four pairs of legs instead of the three pairs which characterize insects. All are equipped with poison glands, the effectiveness of which varies. A few can kill insects only, but others can kill even birds and mice. Most spiders are web builders. In Job 8:14 and Isa 59:5, 6 the web is referred to as a symbol of frailty and insecurity. Prov 30:28 seems to refer not to the spider but to the gecko (*q.v.,* IV.16).

32. **Tortoise.** *See* Lizard, Dabb, IV.22.

33. **Turtle.** *See* Dove, III.9.

34. **Viper,** *Cerastes* sp., *Echis colorata* and *Vipera palaestina.* For photos of the second and third species, see VBW, III, 87. There are several species of true vipers (*Viperidae*) in SW Asia, all poisonous with curved fangs that spring down when ready to strike; they are difficult to identify exactly. Pit vipers *(Crotalidae),* with facial or sensory pits such as the rattlesnake and copperhead, inhabit only the Americas. Heb. *'eph'eh* is the word translated "viper" in most English versions (Job 20:16; Isa 30:6; 59:5), but its exact identity is uncertain. The extremely venomous horned viper *Cerastes Hasselquistii* which is found in Palestine may attack horses (Heb. *sh*ep*îpōn,* Gen 49:17). It is 12 to 18 inches long and lies in ambush, sometimes burrowing in the sands so that only the two eyes and the hornlike protrusions on its head are visible. These two "horns" may be employed as bait for small birds which frequent caravan routes looking for refuse. The "adder" (KJV) or "viper" (RSV) of Ps 140:3 (Heb. *'akshûb*) may be a very similar species of horned viper *(Cerastes cornutus).*

The reference in Acts 28:3 (Gr. *echidna;* also Mt 3:7; 12:34; 23:33) is probably to *Vipera aspis,* which is smaller than the common viper and is found in southern Europe. It is pugnacious and lies flat glaring at its opponent. Each time it inhales and exhales it hisses. This viper strikes very rapidly.

35. **Vole,** *Microtus guentheri.* The reference in I Sam 6:5 (Heb. *'akbār*) is probably to a vole, very likely the Levant vole, *Microtus guentheri.* They have short tails; this distinguishes them from the mice. Voles prefer moderately moist meadow lands and swampy areas, where they have clearly defined surface runways. Some dig short round burrows and live among the rock crannies. The vole is strictly vegetarian, having substantial food requirements; within 24 hours most voles consume nearly their own weight in seeds, roots, bark, and leaves. The Levant vole not only ravishes agriculture but may also spread disease.

The vole is cyclic; e.g., in the western U.S. at peak periods, they may number up to 12,000 per acre. Others believe the *'akbār* is a mouse (*q.v.,* IV.27) or rat which carries the bacteria of bubonic plague and of a type of typhoid fever transmitted to human beings by fleas. Some believe the emerods or tumors of I Sam 5:9–12 refer to bubonic plague attacking the abdominal parts of the body.

36. **Weasel,** *Mustela* sp. Weasels are small carnivorous mammals mentioned in Lev 11:29 (KJV, RSV, based on the LXX and Vulgate); they are listed among the creeping things that swarm and that were ceremonially unclean. They are characterized by long slender bodies and short legs. They have well-developed anal scent glands. Weasels are solitary animals and tend to be nocturnal. They hunt by scent.

It is possible that the animal (Heb. *hōled*) referred to in Leviticus is not the weasel but the mole rat (*q.v.,* IV.25).

37. **Worm.** In most cases references to worms are to maggots (Heb. *rimmā;* feeding on spoiled manna, Ex 16:24; on corpses, Job 21:26; 24:20; Isa 14:11; on open wounds, Job 7:5) or to the larvae of insects (Heb. *sās,* Isa 51:8). In Deut 28:39; Jon 4:7 the vine weevil *(Cochylis ambiguella)* is probably referred to; it destroys vines by boring into their stems.

In some cases men are humiliated by being likened to worms (Job 25:6; Ps 22:6; Mic 7:17) which may be *Lumbricus terrestris,* a segmented worm which lives in burrows consuming soil and leaf mold.

The Gr. *skōlēx* (Mk 9:48) refers to the worm or maggot that eats dead flesh. In Acts 12:23 the related adjective *skōlēko-brōtos,* "eaten by worms," describes the fatal abdominal worm disease of King Herod Agrippa.

V. Aquatic Organisms

1. **Coral,** *Corallium rubrum.* Corals represent the calcareous skeletons of marine organisms of a low order. The famous red coral of the Mediterranean and Red Sea is widely used for jewelry. While alive it is green in color and shrublike in appearance, looking very much like a plant growing in the water, since the animals are sessile or immobile. As soon as the coral is removed from the water it grows hard and red in color. The red coral is fished with nets or cut off with sharp iron tools. It is also used both externally and internally as a medicine. Two words in Heb. may refer to coral, *rā'mōt* (Job 28:18; Ezk 27:16) and *p*en*înîm* (Job 28:18; Prov 8:11; 20:15; 31:10; Lam 4:7); but the latter almost certainly are pearls (*q.v.,* V. 10).

Sobek the Egyptian crocodile god in bronze.
LM

2. **Crocodile,** *Crocodilus vulgaris.* The crocodile is the largest of all existing reptiles, attaining a length of 25 feet (photo, VBW, IV, 133). Until the beginning of the 20th cen. it was found in marshes and small coastal rivers of western Palestine. It was considered sacred by the Egyptians (for Sixth Dynasty relief see VBW, III, 187). The description of the leviathan (Heb. *lôtan*) in Job 41 is almost certainly based on that of the crocodile, although in other passages leviathan was a mythical creature used symbolically of the forces of evil (*see* Leviathan, V. 7). The pharaoh is probably symbolized by a crocodile, the "dragon" of Ezk 29:3, and Nebuchadnezzar likewise (Jer 51:34).

3. **Dugong** or **Sea Cow,** *Dugong dugong.* The dugong (Heb. *tahash*) is an herbivorous aquatic mammal, similar to the manatee of Atlantic tropical coastal waters, about 11 feet long and weighing up to 650 pounds. It occasionally swims along the shores of the Red Sea to sleep or feed its young in one of the caves. It has a large, thick skin which the Bedouin made into footwear (cf. Ezk 16:10). This may be the animal referred to as badgers (KJV) or goats (RSV) in Ex 25:5; 26:14; 35:7, 23, the skin of which was used for the covering of the tent of testimony. The dugong was also caught for its blubber and oil and now is almost extinct. In view of the human-like breasts of the female, dugongs are probably the sirens and mermaids of mythology.

4. **Fish,** *Pisces.* Fish are frequently mentioned in the Bible without ever giving specific names which enable us to identify a particular species. Since time immemorial fish have constituted one of the staple foods of mankind, and they still serve as the chief source of protein throughout the world. For photos of catfish and edible fish from the Sea of Galilee, see VBW, I, 187.

The trade in fish was highly developed in biblical times. One of the gates of Jerusalem was called the Fish Gate (Neh 3:3; Zeph 1:10). In Egypt fish were speared and netted; hook-and-line fishing was also practiced. Lev 11:10–12 permitted the Jews to eat the bony fish or pisces which have fins and scales, but forbade the eating of cartilaginous fish such as the shark, the eel and the catfish which have no scales. *See* Occupations: Fishing; Fins.

5. **Frog.** *See* IV.15.

6. **Leech,** *Haemopis* or *Aulostoma gulo.* These are wormlike blood-sucking animals which are referred to in Prov 30:15. It is likely that the reference here is to the horseleech, though it may be to the ordinary medicinal leech, *Hirudo medicinalis.* This latter is abundant in springs and ponds from the Negeb to Galilee. It adheres to the body of human beings and animals which submerge themselves in water, injects an anticoagulant, and sucks their blood.

At one time leeches were widely employed in medicine to draw blood when it was thought that disease was caused by bad blood.

7. **Leviathan, Sea Monster.** This term (Heb. *liwyāthān*), which occurs in Job 3:8; 40:38 (MT); Ps 74:14; 104:26; Isa 27:1, may refer to larger marine animals, such as the large jellyfish, whales (*see* V. 13), sharks, or to large reptiles, such as the crocodile (*see* V. 2). In addition, this may well include some forms now extinct, such as the ichthyosaurs and the plesiosaurs, extinct marine reptiles similar to the dinosaurs. The scriptural term may also recollect some of the dinosaurs which spent part of their lives half-submerged in shallow streams, lakes, and oceans. *See also* Dragon, II.11.

8. **Mollusk, Purple,** *Murex trunculus* and *M. brandaris.* In the ancient world purple dyes of all shades ranging from red to purple were highly valued. These were obtained from a mollusk or sea snail which inhabited the waters off Crete and Phoenicia (photo, VBW, V, 177). The secretion is produced by the hypobranchial

gland of the mollusk, and the shade is regulated by using different species, altering the ratio, adding ingredients such as kermes (*see* Scarlet Scale Insect, IV.11), or varying air and light exposure time in the process of producing the dye. Tyrian purple was obtained by a double dyeing. Deposits of *Murex brandaris* and *M. trunculus* shells have been found in dyeing beds along the Mediterranean.

The Hebrews had to import purple goods (Ezk 27:16). Purple was a sign of distinction, royalty, and wealth. Lydia was a "seller of purple" or of cloth so dyed (Acts 16:14). Other Scripture references include Ex 25:4; 28:5–6, 15; Num 15:38; II Chr 2:7; Est 8:15; Prov 31:22; Song 3:10; Ezk 27:7; Dan 5:7. *See also* Purple.

9. **Onycha.** An ingredient of the sacred perfume (Ex 30:34), probably an aromatic oil obtained by roasting the closing valve muscle of certain marine mollusks or the Red Sea snail.

10. **Oyster, Pearl,** *Pinctada margaritifera.* While the word "pearl" does not occur in the OT of the KJV, it is found in the RSV, JerusB, and others, for Heb. $p^e n \hat{n} \hat{m}$ (Job 28:18; Prov 8:11; 20:15; 31:10; Lam 4:7; KJV "rubies"). The pearl is a highly valued gemlike deposit, chiefly calcium carbonate, formed around a grain of sand in the shells of oysters or certain other mollusks. Pearls of fine quality are obtained from oysters in the Persian Gulf, off Ceylon, and in the Red Sea. In the latter area the pinna oyster occasionally yields translucent pink pearls, which may explain the comparison with ruddy bodies in Lam 4:7 (see *Unger's Bible Dict.,* 1957, p. 742).

In the NT the Gr. *margaritēs* unquestionably means "pearl." Pearls were in great demand for jewelry then as now (Mt 13:45–46; I Tim 2:9; Rev 17:4; 18:12, 16). Likening spiritual wisdom and other blessings to pearls, Jesus warned against casting them before swine (Mt 7:6). Each of the gates of the New Jerusalem is described as consisting of a single pearl (Rev 21:21).

11. **Sea Monster** (Lam 4:3, KJV). *See* Jackal, II.23.

12. **Sponge,** *Euspongia* sp. The sponge is the skeleton of a simple marine animal, *Euspongia officianalis.* It is a porous body composed of tubules and cells, lined with amoeboid substance. The vital action of these protozoa keeps up a steady action of water through the channels. Sponge fishing was well known in the Mediterranean area in ancient times. It was practiced particularly along the Anatolian and Syrian coasts. The references in Mt 27:48 and Mk 15:36 are to the use of sponges in absorbing liquids. Sponges were harvested by divers; their work was considered "hard and woeful."

13. **Whale,** *Balaenoptera physalus, Physeter catodon.* This is the largest of all living creatures, including those that have become extinct. Whales are air-breathing mammals. Their young are born alive and nourished with milk. They are generally devoid of hair except for a few stray whiskers. When they spout they are actually breathing; moisture from their exhaled breath condenses, giving the appearance of a spout.

Two varieties of whales visit the shores of Palestine at times. The fin whale weighs about 200 tons and lives mainly in the arctic region but sometimes passes through the Straits of Gibraltar to reach the eastern Mediterranean. It feeds on small marine organisms which it strains through its whale bone; it does not have teeth. The esophagus is narrow.

The sperm whale, about 60 feet long, has a curiously shaped head which looks like a battering ram and has teeth. It feeds on big fish, even on sharks. It has a large throat opening.

The "great fish" of Jon 2:1 need not have been a whale but could have been a large shark such as the Rhineodon, the whale-shark, which grows 70 feet and lacks the terrible teeth of other sharks. In any event, Jonah's deliverance was miraculous.

The KJV translates Heb. *tannîn* as "whale" in Gen 1:21; Job 7:12; Ezk 32:2. The latter reference probably is to a crocodile. The Heb. word, elsewhere in the KJV translated "dragon" (*q.v.,* II.11), is a general term for any sea or river monster. In Mt 12:40 the Gr. for "whale" is *kētos,* evidently following the LXX in Jon 2:1, *kētei megalō,* "great fish." The Gr. word also is a general term for sea monster or huge fish.

Bibliography. Emmanuel Anati, *Palestine Before the Hebrews,* New York: Knopf, 1963. Michael Avi-Yonah and Abraham Malamat, eds., *Views of the Biblical World,* 5 vols., Jerusalem: International Publishing Co., 1960. Raoul Blanchard and M. DuBuit, *The Promised Land,* New York: Hawthorn, 1966. F. S. Bodenheimer, *Animal and Man in Bible Lands,* Leiden: Brill, 1960; "Fauna," IDB, II, 246–256. George S. Cansdale, *All the Animals of the Bible Lands,* Grand Rapids: Zondervan, 1970. Robert A. M. Conley, "Locusts: Teeth of the Wind," *National Geographic,* CXXXVI (1969), 202–226. George R. Driver, "Birds in the Old Testament," PEQ, LXXXVI (1955), 5–20; LXXXVII (1955), 129–140. Jehuda Feliks, *The Animal World of the Bible,* Tel-Aviv: Sinai, 1962. Joseph P. Free, "Abraham's Camels," JNES, III (1944), 187–193. Frederick R. and George F. Howe, "Moses and the Eagle: An Analysis of Deut. 32:11," JASA, XX (1968), 22–24. George F. Howe, "The Raven Speaks," JASA, XXI (1969), 22–25; "Job and the Ostrich," JASA, XX (1968), 107–110. Willy Ley, *The Lungfish, the Dodo, and the Unicorn,* New York: Viking, 1948. Alice Parmelee, *All the Birds of the Bible,* New York: Harper, 1959. James B. Pritchard, ed., *The Ancient Near East in Pictures,* Princeton Univ. Press, 1954. William M. Thomson, *The Land and the Book,* Hartford: Scranton, 1910. H. B. Tristram, *The Survey of Western Palestine: The Fauna and Flora of Palestine,*

London: Palestine Exploration Fund, 1884. Ernest P. Walker, et al., *Mammals of the World*, Baltimore: Johns Hopkins, 1964. Robert S. Wallace, "Birds of the Bible," Atlanta, Georgia, 1939, unpublished sermon quoted in George J. Wallace, *An Introduction to Ornithology*, New York: Macmillan, 1955. Lulu Rumsey Wiley, *Bible Animals*, New York: Vantage, 1957. Frederick E. Zeuner, *A History of Domesticated Animals*, New York: Harper and Row, 1963.

J. W. K.

ANIMATION. Animation means "making animate" or "alive," "quickening." Two main examples are found in Scripture. (1) The creation of man. "The Lord God formed man of the dust of the ground, and breathed into his nostrils the breath of life; and man became a living soul" (Gen 2:7). (2) The vision of the valley of dry bones, when, as the prophet prophesied to the wind, these came together and lived, signifying the regeneration of the nation Israel at the second coming of Christ (Ezk 37; cf. Rom 11:26-29; Zech 12-14).

Animation is to be distinguished from resurrection, which has to do with the body, in that it signifies the giving of life itself to the lifeless. In the first example, Adam was made a living soul; and in the second example, new life, which comes with the soul's regeneration, will be given to the Jews who are alive at the second coming of our Lord.

The term is sometimes used theologically to denote that quality of Holy Scripture which through the Holy Spirit produces spiritual life in receptive lives. Thus, "The word of God is living and active . . ." (Heb 4:12, ASV); and "being born again . . . by the word of God, which liveth and abideth for ever" (I Pet 1:23). This quality is one of many features which distinguishes the canonical Scripture from other mere human writings.

R. A. K. and A. F. J.

ANIMISM (ăn'ĭ-mĭz'm). This is the view that such things as trees, rocks, mountains, etc., are possessed of separate spirits which can either help and bless, or hinder and curse man. Such spirits are to be placated by certain acts and offerings. Animism differs from pantheism, which sees one spirit or god as present and identified with all things, in that it attributes separate spirits to each object. It agrees, however, in seeing the divine as present in the material.

Many evolutionary anthropologists place animism as the fourth of seven upward evolutionary steps in the progressive development of religion: dynamism, manaism, fetishism, animism, totemism, polytheism, and monotheism. The whole theory of such an evolutionary development is to be rejected for three reasons. (1) It is impossible to prove such a development ever occurred. (2) Even the lower forms of primitive religion have myths concerning a "high god" or a "sky god" who is a perfect, holy being and never does anyone any harm. Such a study of the mythology and folklore of any pagan tribe reveals the fact that a primal revelation of God is to be found in their mythology, even though it has disappeared from their direct historical knowledge. (3) The Bible teaches that at the very beginning God created man in His own image and after His own likeness, and that He talked with man and taught him about Himself. This particular primal revelation is, of course, found only in the Bible, but it fits and explains, as no other view can, the presence of the myths of the "high god" and the "sky god" in paganism.

R. A. K.

ANISE. *See* Plants.

ANKLET. An ornament worn around the ankle like a bracelet on the wrist. As found in tombs and numerous excavations, usually anklets were made of bronze. When used in pairs or with ankle chains, they would make a tinkling sound as one walked. Denounced by Isaiah as frivolous (Isa 3:18, RSV). *See* Dress.

ANNA (ăn'ä). This is the Gr. form of Hannah, meaning "grace." *See* Hannah.

Anna the aged prophetess who was present at the dedication of the infant Jesus was the daughter of Phanuel, a descendant of Asher (Lk 2:36-38). Her age has been variously reckoned from 84 to 105 years. She had been married for seven years, following which she had been a widow, either for 84 years or until her eighty-fourth year. That she actually had living quarters in the temple is unthinkable, for no one lived there permanently. Luke's account suggests that Anna was one of the godly remnant looking expectantly for Israel's Messiah.

ANNAS (ăn'äs). The Jewish high priest appointed about A.D. 6 by Quirinius, governor of Syria. While Annas was deposed in A.D. 15, his prestige and control of the temple still continued in that five of his sons and his son-in-law Caiaphas became high priests after him. Luke was indicating the real state of affairs when he deliberately wrote, "Annas and Caiaphas being high priest" (singular, Lk 3:2, Gr.). Thus Annas took a leading part at the time of the crucifixion of Jesus (Jn 18:13, 24) and at the trial of Peter and John (Acts 4:6).

ANOINT. In the Scriptures, the practice of anointing with oil, either with or without perfume, had both a secular and a religious significance. In the Heb., two words were used: *sûk* (which occurs only nine times) and the more common word *māshaḥ*, from which comes the noun *māshîaḥ*, known in English as Messiah, "the Anointed One." The Gr. words are: *aleiphō*, which is comparable to *sûk;* and *chriō*, from which comes the title Christ, the counterpart of Messiah.

The Heb. *sûk* designated an everyday practice of rubbing the body with olive oil after bathing, or pouring oil on the head of a guest (Deut 28:40; Ruth 3:3; Est 2:12). However, it was prohibited during mourning (II Sam 12:20; 14:2; Isa 61:3; Dan 10:3). In Ex 30:31–32, where the term is translated "pour," it is specifically stated that the sacred oil was not to be used for common purposes.

In only one place in referring to persons does the term *māshaḥ* seem to indicate a nonreligious act of anointing the body (Amos 6:6). The basic meaning of *māshaḥ* is "to smear." It appears in Jer 22:14 in the sense of painting a royal chamber. Mention is made in II Sam 1:21 (RSV) and Isa 21:5 of anointing shields, which may mean no more than applying oil as a preservative.

In classical and in NT Gr. *aleiphō* is the preferred term for the secular practice of anointing the body after bathing or to show honor to a guest (Lk 7:38, 46; Jn 11:2; 12:3). It can, however, designate the act of anointing the sick (Mk 6:13; Jas 5:14) and the dead (Mk 16:1). In Jn 9:6 *epichriō*, "to rub on," is used of the mud with which Jesus anointed the eyes of the man born blind, and Rev 3:18 employs *egchriō*, "to rub in," for anointing the eyes with salve. The spiritual application was derived from the use of olive oil in physical healing. The Gr. *myrizō*, "to anoint with aromatics," is found in Jesus' statement that Mary had anointed His body beforehand for burying (Mk 14:8).

For a religiously oriented act of anointing, the Heb. OT prefers verbal and nominal forms of *māshaḥ*. The first such instance was Jacob's deed of anointing the stone at Bethel after his vision (Gen 31:13). Priests and high priests were anointed (Ex 28:41; 29:7, 36). Kings were anointed (I Sam 9:16; 16:3, 12–13; II Sam 2:4). Prophets were sometimes anointed (I Kgs 19:16). The tabernacle, its furniture, and its vessels were anointed (Ex 30:26–28). The anointing separated the thing or person unto God for special service, thus becoming sacred and untouchable (I Sam 24:6; 26:9). Frequently, the anointing was regarded as an act of God, because He commanded it to be done (cf. I Sam 9:16 with 10:1), and was associated with the outpouring of the Spirit of the Lord (I Sam 10:9; 16:13; Isa 61:1).

In the OT, the concept of anointing is associated with the future Messiah (Ps 45:7; 89:20; Isa 61:1; Dan 9:24). The Gr. word *chriō* carries these concepts into the NT, where God is always involved. In references to OT priests, kings, and prophets, it has the same function as *māshaḥ*. In Lk 4:18, Jesus applied the anointing mentioned in Isa 61:1 to Himself. Peter related the anointing of Jesus with the Holy Spirit (Acts 10:38), and Paul connects the anointing with the seal of the Spirit and proof of the Christian's relationship to Christ (II Cor 1:21–22). Thus the NT writers understood anointing metaphorically, that it is an enduement of spiritual power and understanding (I Jn

2:20, 27). In the OT it is associated with the kingly office (I Sam 10:1–9; 16:13), but in the NT it is associated with Christ and with Christian witnesses within a context of proclaiming the gospel.

G. H. L.

ANSWER. *Noun.* Chiefly from Heb. *dābār*, "word," and *mā'ănâ*, "answer," in OT; and *apokrisis*, "answer," and *apologia*, "defense," in Gr. NT. In the OT, the idea is that expressed by the English "answer" (II Sam 24:13; Job 32:3; Prov 15:1)–"a soft answer turneth away wrath." In the NT, *apokrisis* appears four times in the sense of giving an answer to a question; *apologia* appears eight times conveying the idea of making a defense–although II Cor 7:11 is best translated "clear yourselves" (ASV), and I Pet 3:15 "answer" in the sense of explaining or defending one's faith.

Verb. In the OT chiefly from Heb. *'ānâ*, "to answer," and *'āmar*, "to say"; in the NT from Gr. *apokrinomai*, "to answer," which occurs almost 200 times. The principal uses are: (1) reply to a question (I Sam 4:20; Mt 11:4; Lk 3:11); (2) reply to a request or command (Mt 4:4; 12:39); (3) response to a situation that demands a reply, although no question has been asked (Mt 17:4; Jn 2:18; I Sam 9:17); (4) rebuttal (Job 9:14; Mt 3:15; 27:12); (5) continuation of a discourse (Mt 11:25; Mk 10:24).

J. McR.

ANT. *See* Animals, IV.2.

ANTEDILUVIANS. In contrast to evolutionary concepts of human origins, the Scriptures clearly assert that the very earliest men were possessed of all the necessary talents for high cultural achievement. Cain, the son of Adam, built a city, and his immediate descendants lived in tents, domesticated cattle, invented musical instruments ("the harp and pipe"), and forged "every cutting instrument of brass and iron" (Gen 4:17–22, ASV). Noah had sufficient tools and skills for building a gigantic ark according to divine specifications (Gen 6:14–16). Great length of life and a unity of language doubtless contributed to a rapid development of the arts and sciences.

Parallel to the growth of civilization was the ripening of spiritual depravity. Cain, the first man born of woman, set the pattern for the age by murdering his own brother and complaining that God's punishment was unfair (Gen 4:1–15; I Jn 3:12). To be sure, some outstanding men of God lived during this period, such as Abel, Enoch, Lamech, and Noah; but the race as a whole sank to abysmal depths of sin (Gen 6:5–12; Mt 24:38; Jude 14–15). It is possible to interpret Gen 6:1–4 in terms of a race of wicked men of giant stature (Heb. *nᵉphīlîm*; cf. Num 13:33) born of men who had permitted themselves to be totally possessed by demons ("sons of God," Job 1:6). Because of such widespread acts of depravity, God's long-suffering came to an end (Gen 6:3; I Pet 3:20). With the exception of Noah's family, "the world that then was, being overflowed with water, perished" (II Pet 3:6), and another chapter of human history began.

See Anthropology; Ark, Noah's; Creation; Flood.

J. C. W.

ANTELOPE. *See* Animals, II.1.

ANTHROPOLOGY. The science or the knowledge of man, where he came from, what he is, and what are his future potentialities and destiny. The term anthropology can be used to define the entirely secular scientific study of these details when such theories as (1) organic evolution and theistic evolution, entirely apart from or versus fiat (i.e., by order) creation, are considered as explanations of man's origin; (2) pure behaviorism and operationalism, either apart from or versus the biblical view of the image of God in man and its effacement by sin, are examined to explain man's present condition; and (3) pure naturalism, with its extinction of individual personal existence at death, is adopted either apart from or versus the biblical supernaturalistic view of the immortal soul, which teaches that the soul is destined to an endless future existence after death.

Generally, as taught in colleges or universities, anthropology is presented according to theories which entirely disregard revealed biblical anthropology. When biblical anthropology is considered, secular theories can throw some light on the principles revealed in Scripture. This is more by contrast, however, than by common agreement, as is seen in the following study of the Bible's revelation concerning man.

The origin of man. God created man (male and female) by an act of fiat creation (Gen 1:27). The Bible allows no room for any theory of either organic or theistic evolution so far as the creation of man is concerned. Adam was created first, and immediately started to name the animals God had already created as God brought them before him. He looked for the fellowship of an I-thou relationship, similar to that which he already enjoyed with God from the beginning, but could not find it among the lower form of creation (Gen 2:20). Then, and only then, did God create Eve as his helpmeet (2:21-22).

Modern anthropologists usually ignore the biblical explanation altogether. To keep abreast of biological research the Christian may wish to allow much more room for development of phyla (those groups, larger than species, now considered the basic separate classes of beings created by God, from which species and kinds developed). However, he cannot accept the biblical record and go further in any theory of man's origin than to see him as a separate phylum, created from the beginning as a fully developed, self-conscious moral being. There are the clear statements of Genesis (chaps. 1-3)

and the NT teaching that sin entered the world by one man, Adam, and passed upon all mankind through him as the federal head of the human race (Rom 5:12 ff.), as well as Christ's statement that God made man male and female at the beginning (Mt 19:4; Mk 10:6). These are evidences for man's creation as man, apart from any evolutionary development from protoplasm up to rational being.

A straightforward, literal acceptance of man's direct creation as a fully developed individual (rather than as the result of a long evolutionary process, even though that process is theistic evolution) is required by the following considerations: (1) The Genesis account clearly states such to be the case. (2) Jesus Christ declares the same to be true (Mt 19:3 ff.). (3) Paul in Rom 5:12-21 (as he holds that Adam is the first man) and in I Cor 15:45-47 expresses the same view. (4) The doctrine of the federal headship of Christ rests upon the federal headship of Adam, so that we read, "As in Adam all die, even so in Christ shall all be made alive" (I Cor 15:22). If Adam was not a real person, how can the Scripture compare him with Christ? The comparison is faulty and fails except they both are true representatives. (5) The reason that no fallen angel can be redeemed, while fallen men can be redeemed, is that angels are not members of a race, and therefore Christ could not die as their representative and be their Saviour. Never is Satan called the representative of even the fallen angels. Each one who rebelled did so as individually as each one who went on to eternal righteousness, both by individual decision.

The Shorter Catechism states that God created man "for His own glory," and declares that man's chief end is to enjoy God and glorify Him forever. God did not need man! Already in the Trinity He enjoyed an I-Thou relationship and the blessings of personal communion, as well as a social relationship in that any two persons of the Trinity could join to minister to the third. Why then did He create? To show forth His person with all its glories and bring glory and honor to His own name. This was to be demonstrated not only by those who worship Him with the homage due the Creator by the creature, but also by those who love Him for His sovereign grace and love manifested to them in their redemption through Christ. The angels could never be an illustration of the latter. *See* Creation.

The antiquity of man. Few if any scholars now feel that Ussher's chronology gives a satisfactory answer (creation in 4004 B.C.). It is quite commonly accepted by evangelicals that many of the names mentioned in OT genealogical tables stand for leading genealogical names, and that the lists cover much longer periods of time (and often cover hundreds of years) than at first thought. By the carbon 14 method (*see* Carbon 14 Dating) and the potassium-argon method anthropologists have tried to push the age of man back many millennia and even over a million years. Some conservative scholars are now speaking of a possible 100,000 years. Further knowledge with regard to radioactive factors and changes in cosmic radiation above the earth, however, may well cause the figures to be revised back much closer to a possible 25,000 to 10,000 years, or even less. For ethnic divisions of mankind *see* Nations.

The nature of man. Man is the highest of God's creatures, aside from the angels (Ps 8:5-8; Heb 2:6-9). He was the consummation of God's creation and given dominion over the earth and a charge to subdue it (Gen 1:26-27). For men's salvation alone did God send His only begotten Son to redeem them by the cross.

Man is bipartite in nature. He is composed of both body and soul or spirit. The angels are simply unipartite and pure spirit. The trichotomist position that man is tripartite — spirit, soul, and body — is based primarily on I Thess 5:23, "I pray God your whole spirit and soul and body be preserved blameless . . . ," and on Heb 4:12, "piercing even to the dividing asunder of soul and spirit." In the light of other Scripture, these seeming distinctions between soul and spirit can best be explained as differences of function or different aspects of the personality of the immaterial part of man. *See* Inner Man.

Certain important consequences follow: (1) Men are all members of a race, the human race. (2) Men as bipartite creatures will never be entirely complete without some physical "tabernacle" to house the soul. Hence, resurrection becomes a very important fact for man (cf. II Cor 5:1 ff.). (3) Being a combination of body and soul, man is subject to problems which arise from sin. The soul is subject to what are called psychosomatic problems (where difficulties in the mind cause sickness in the body), and somatic-psychic problems (where a sickness of the body becomes such an obsession of the mind that it becomes the cause of mental illness). (4) Since man was ordained to have a body, he must, except in the case of the creation of Adam and Eve, come into existence by physical generation and be a member of the human race.

So far as his spirit or soul is concerned, man was made by God according to His own image, after His own likeness (Gen 1:26-28). In what does this image consist? (1) Man, like God, is a person; both he and God have the characteristics of personality: intellect, will, emotion, self-conciousness, and a moral nature. Animals, in contrast, while they may show something of the first three, lack self-consciousness and a moral nature. (2) Man enjoys in a finite degree the communicable attributes of God: wisdom, power, holiness, goodness, love, justice, and truth. Yet he is entirely distinguishable from God in that he does not possess God's infinity, eternity, and unchangeableness, nor His omniscience, omnipotence, and omnipresence.

The fall affected God's image in man. Roman Catholics maintain that image and likeness are distinct qualities and that man lost only the latter. The "likeness" (Lat. *similitude*) of God was a *donum superadditum,* an additional supernatural gift extended to man at creation, by means of which he was to be able to control the degenerating effects of the physical body. This man lost when he fell but regains in salvation.

Protestants claim that the image of God was not entirely lost by man when he fell, but was only defaced. (Barth is an exception at this point, first, in that he sees the image in the fact God made man male and female and, second, that he insists the creation-image was entirely lost by his fall, yet retained by Christ and restored to man in redemption, and that these two facts exist simultaneously for every man whether he accepts them or not.) Man is still man but has become totally depraved by sin. Beginning with regeneration, the image, which is of course perfect in Christ, is gradually restored as the believer is renewed in knowledge (Col 3:10), righteousness, and true holiness (Eph 4:24). *See* Image of God.

God's original goal for man. This can only be understood properly when compared with that of the angels. It coincided with their goal to the extent that both angels and mankind started out in a state of innocency, and that both were given the opportunity to attain to a state of confirmation in righteousness. It differed in the manner in which this was to be accomplished. The holy angels so kept God's law and obeyed His will that they were individually confirmed; those that sinned defied His law and were eternally lost. Adam and Eve, on the other hand, were warned of the consequences (negative results) if they would not love God but disobey through eating of the forbidden fruit, and thereby sin and fall. Thus, God made an agreement, which, for the sake of simplicity and because of its particular character, has been called by the Reformed theologians the covenant of works. If man had kept this agreement, or covenant, he would have been confirmed in righteousness and would have gone on to eternal blessedness, just as the holy angels did (positive results).

But how do we come to this conclusion since it is not stated in the Bible? God, who is unchangeable, must deal with all His moral creatures in the same manner, whether they are angels or men. Does He not say, "I am the Lord, I change not" (Mal 3:6)? The development and confirmation of a holy, righteous character became a fact in the existence of the holy angels; the same, therefore, must have been a possibility for God's other personal creatures, men.

The redemption of man. But all mankind fell in Adam. The guilt and taint of Adam's sin were inherited and the lack of original righteousness was accompanied by the corruption of each man's entire nature. Therefore if man was to be saved from eternal separation from God and hell, an adequate plan of salvation was demanded. This provision of salvation is called in the NT the gospel or good news. Though regarded by worldly philosophers as foolishness (I Cor 1:18), and proving to be a stumbling block to the self-righteous who would save themselves by their own good works (v. 23), this gospel is God's almighty power to salvation and contains God's highest wisdom (v. 24). It corresponds completely to the needs of sinful, rebellious, fallen man.

By a study of the life of Christ, plus the revelation found in Ps 40:6-8, we are able to understand to some extent the plan of redemption developed in eternity past: (1) Christ was to lay aside His glory and become a man, taking upon Himself a physical body and a complete human nature (Ps 40:6-8; Heb 10:5-9; Phil 2:5-8). (2) He was to keep God's law as a man, the God-man, perfectly (Gal 4:4; cf. Mt 3:15; Heb 2:10). That He did so is proved by the fact that He led a sinless life (Jn 8:46; Heb 5:8-9; 9:14; I Pet 2:22). (3) He was to offer Himself as a substitutionary sacrifice in our place (Isa 53:10-11; Heb 10:5-9; I Pet 2:24) and die under the penalty of our sins. (4) The result or reward would be the salvation (Jn 1:29; 3:16) of all who repented of their sins and believed, and this salvation would cover believers of all ages (Rom 3:25-26).

In that Christ was made of a woman and made under the law, and kept that law perfectly in His life, He fulfilled in our stead the covenant of works which had been given to Adam. In that He died under the condemnation pronounced for breaking that covenant, He bore its penalty.

The present results for us of Christ's active and passive obedience, outlined above, are: (1) justification of believers before God, who sees us in Christ as having judicially fulfilled the law and borne its penalties; (2) deliverance from the penalty and power of sin; (3) the presence of the Holy Spirit in the believer. He can now dwell in us fully, since sin in us, our fallen nature, is a judged and condemned thing (Rom 8:3); and He can keep the law of God through us (8:4).

The future results of Christ's obedience are: (1) the complete removal of the fallen nature at the believer's physical death or at the second coming of Christ, whichever occurs first; (2) the reception of a resurrection body like that of Christ's (Rom 8:23; Phil 3:21; see Resurrection of the Body); (3) enjoyment of all the bliss and glory of eternal life in the presence of God.

Man's eternal future. In matters of eschatology and the prophecies concerning the future, wide variances of opinion appear. While the facts of a visible return of Christ and the future resurrection are accepted by all evangelicals, there is not agreement about the events which will occur afterward. Three main views are held: (1) Amillennialism—There will be no literal, physical rule of Christ on the earth. The OT prophecies predicting a glorious kingdom encompassing the earth (see Kingdom of God)

and Rev 20:4 ff. are to be taken spiritually rather than literally. The OT references speak of the effect of the gospel in the Church Age; Rev 20, of the condition of those who have died in Christ. After Christ's second coming will occur the one final resurrection and great judgment. (2) Postmillennialism—The church, by its preaching prior to Christ's second coming, will usher in the Millennium on earth, a period of peace of approximately 1,000 years. (Some say we are in the Millennium now.) (3) Premillennialism—After Christ's second coming, He will establish a thousand years of peace in which the gospel will continue to be preached on earth. Satan will be bound for all this period, but will be loosed again at its close. Then those who have refused the gospel in spite of Christ's presence on the earth will rise against the Church. At that time Christ will destroy His enemies, and the final judgment of the wicked will take place. *See* Eschatology.

This last view does particular honor to the unfathomable grace of God in that it teaches that God's patience and mercy extend far beyond anything the other views can admit. (Acceptance of the premillennial position is based on many additional arguments from Scripture, however.) At the same time, it stresses even more clearly the total sinfulness of sin. There might be some seeming rational excuse for rejecting Christ and the gospel today, but what excuse can there be during the visible, personal reign of Christ on the earth when men have demonstrated before their very eyes the wonderful blessings of salvation in the lives of the resurrected saints who shall reign with their Saviour? Those in the first resurrection, namely, the righteous dead, and those believers who are alive on the earth at the rapture, will all have resurrection bodies like Christ's resurrection body and be freed of their fallen nature.

All who are saved now receive the earnest or down payment of their complete salvation in the form of the Holy Spirit (Eph 1:14; II Cor 1:22; 5:5). Other future installments of salvation for all believers are the removal of the fallen nature at death or when Christ comes, depending on which comes first, and then a resurrection body at Christ's second coming.

Bibliography. Herman Bavinck, *Our Reasonable Faith,* Grand Rapids: Eerdmans, 1956, pp. 184-220. Wayne Frair and P. William Davis, *The Case for Creation,* Chicago: Moody Press, 1967. R. Laird Harris, *Man: God's Eternal Creation,* Chicago: Moody Press, 1971. Charles Hodge, *Systematic Theology,* Grand Rapids: Eerdmans, 1952, II, 1-306. John W. Klotz, *Genes, Genesis and Evolution,* St. Louis: Concordia, 1955. J. Gresham Machen, *The Christian View of Man,* Grand Rapids: Eerdmans, 1937. Russell L. Mixter, *Evolution and Christian Thought Today,* Grand Rapids: Eerdmans, 1959. James M. Murk, "Anthropology," *Christianity and the World of*

Thought, ed. by Hudson T. Armerding, Chicago: Moody, 1968, pp. 185-211. Erich Sauer, *The King of the Earth* (The Nobility of Man According to the Bible and Science), Grand Rapids: Eerdmans, 1962. A. E. Wilder-Smith, *Man's Origin, Man's Destiny,* Wheaton: Shaw, 1968. P. A. Zimmerman, ed., *Darwin, Evolution and Creation,* St. Louis: Concordia, 1959.

R. A. K.

ANTHROPOMORPHISM AND ANTHROPOPATHISM. By anthropomorphism is generally meant the ascription of human form to God, and by anthropopathism, the ascription of human feelings, passions, emotions and suffering to God. Theologians in general agree that both anthropomorphic and anthropopathic terms in the Bible are ascribed to God in a metaphorical sense. Only the sect of the Audians (in the 4th and 5th cen.) held to a strictly literal interpretation of such words. Christians differ greatly as to the real nature of this phenomenon.

In ascribing various attributes to God the Bible represents Him as:

Having human organs — eyes and eyelids (Ps 11:4; 34:15; Hab 1:13), fingers (Ps 8:3), feet (Ex 24:9-11; Isa 66:1), nose (Ex 15:8; II Sam 22:9), ears (Ps 17:6; 31:2), hands (Ps 95:4; 139:5), and even hair (Dan 7:9).

Having human emotions. Scripture speaks of God as having joy (Isa 65:19; Zeph 3:17), grief (Jud 10:16; Heb 3:10, 17), anger (Deut 1:37; Jer 7:18-20), hatred (Ps 5:5-6; Prov 6:16), wrath (Ex 32:10; Ps 2:5, 12; Rev 15:7), love (Jer 31:3; Jn 3:16; I Jn 4:16).

Executing human actions. The Scripture describes God as knowing (Ex 3:7; Lk 16:15), thinking (Ex 32:14; Ps 40:17), remembering (Gen 9:16; Jer 31:34), speaking (Gen 2:16; Ex 7:8), hearing (Ps 6:8-9; Acts 7:34), repenting (regretting, feeling sorry, Gen 6:6; Ex 32:14), and resting (Gen 2:2; Ex 20:11).

Having human relations. The Lord is called a shepherd (Ps 23:1; cf. Jn 10:11), a judge (Gen 18:25; Isa 33:22), a farmer (Jn 15:1), a bridegroom (Mk 2:19-20), a husband (Isa 54:5; Jer 31:32), a builder (Ps 127:1; Heb 11:10), a doctor (Ex 15:26; Ps 103:3; 147:3). Further He is likened to a lion (Rev 5:5), a lamb (Rev 5:6, 12), an eagle (Deut 32:11-12), a hen (Mt 23:37), the sun (Mal 4:2), a star (Rev 22:16), a rock (Ps 18:2), a tower (Ps 61:3; Prov 18:10), and a shield (Ps 28:7; 84:11).

Though the Bible speaks of God in such terms, they are only figures of speech which convey deeper truths. God is spirit and therefore beyond any human description. For example, since He is omniscient, all expressions of His knowing, thinking, and remembering really show that He is intensely and constantly interested in the world and man; since He is omnipotent, the expression of His forming the heavens with His fingers reveals that He was infinitely precise and personal in creation and forming all things, including man.

Two approaches are helpful in considering the anthropomorphic descriptions given in the Bible. The first is based upon a study of the particular nature of our knowledge of God. What is the nature of these descriptions? It can be any one of three: (1) Univocal. The anthropomorphic expression means literally exactly what it says. This theologians in general reject. (2) Equivocal. A statement does not mean what is says and therefore can communicate no certain meaning or knowledge. Some Reformed theologians have come very close to taking this viewpoint when they have overstressed the inability of human words to communicate truth from God and any revelation concerning Him in particular. (3) Analogical. A statement is to be taken as a comparison based either upon comparatives that are absolutely different (Aquinas) or comparisons which do have a univocal element in them. It is the univocal element in an analogy which enables it to communicate knowledge. For example, "Like as a father pitieth his children, so the Lord pitieth them that fear him" (Ps 103:13). The univocal element in this is the concept of a father and his mercy toward his own child. We know what fathers are and how they pity their errant children, and to this extent we can understand God's compassion for those who reverence Him. Further, since man is made in the image and likeness of God, man's organs, actions, feelings, emotions and relations can all become legitimate means for the description of God.

Specific data given in the Scripture can offer a sound approach to the question of anthropomorphism. For example, such a categorical statement as that given by Christ to the woman at the well, "God is a Spirit: and they that worship him must worship him in spirit and in truth" (Jn 4:24). Again, there are some descriptions of God given both in the OT and the NT. The closest to a visual one may be that given in Ex 24:9-11: "There was under his feet as it were a paved work of a sapphire stone, and as it were the body of heaven in his clearness." The two "as it weres" clearly indicate that the description is figurative. Though Moses saw God in Ex 33:18-23 he saw only His "after parts," or as R. Laird Harris translates this along with J. O. Buswell, His "after effects," namely, evidences of His glory and power (*A Systematic Theology,* J. O. Buswell, p. 31). Warnings against making images and likenesses of God point to the supernatural non-corporeal nature of God. Moses wrote, "Ye heard the voice [sound] of the words, but saw no similitude; only ye heard a voice" (Deut 4:12), and warned against all images and likenesses (Deut 5:6-9, 22-28).

How are the anthropomorphic terms used of God to be understood? Though they are clearly figurative in nature, they communicate such real knowledge of God as that He is active, attentive even to the smallest details of man's life, sympathetic with all his weaknesses, patient, kind, and loving. *See* Analogy.

104

Certain problems arise with anthropopathisms. How can God who is immutable (Ps 102:26–27; Mal 3:6; Heb 13:8; Jas 1:17) be said to change His mind and to repent (Jon 3:10; Ex 32:14; I Sam 15:35), particularly when Scripture says He cannot repent (Num 23:19; I Sam 15:29)? Looked at from man's standpoint, God appears to change His mind—remember He does have feelings and emotions—but looked at from the fact of His omniscience, He knows what is to come to pass and has already ordained that it be so.

Divergent views are held about anthropomorphisms and anthropopathisms. Karl Barth, for example, sees them as a part of the *welthaftigkeit*, the "worldliness" that adheres to Scripture because man cannot express the "absolute otherness" of God. Only in the ineffable event of a personal experience of revelation does man come to know God. The difficulty with this view is that it actually makes any real knowledge of God impossible, that is, any knowledge that can be communicated from man to man. If Barth is right, then the anthropomorphisms in the Bible are really the perversions of revelation caused by man's forcing timeless eternal truth into time-space categories.

In paganism man himself has built up concepts of God made in the image and likeness of fallen man (Rom 1:23). Feuerbach rejected the Bible's explanation at this point and said that in Christianity man had simply projected an image of himself and turned and worshiped this image, and that this is the explanation of the origin of Christianity (*The Essence of Christianity*). But in Rom 1:18 ff. Paul by revelation explains how man once knew God, yet did not want to retain Him in his knowledge and therefore made images of himself, of fourfooted beasts and creeping things, and turned and worshiped these instead of God.

Anthropomorphism plays a very necessary part in revelation. It shows that God is really a person with intellect, will and emotions, a moral nature and self-consciousness, giving proofs of all these marks of personality. In recent years the "God is Dead" theologians have claimed that the transcendent God of the Scripture is either dead or died at Calvary (T. J. J. Altizer, cf. Wm. Hamilton); or that the concept given in the Bible of God is outdated, is no longer tenable and needs to be changed (Paul Tillich. Bishop Robinson); or that the term God is empty and meaningless and illogical (Paul Van Buren), and in at least one if not all of these senses dead. The anthropomorphisms and anthropopathisms of the Bible offer a needed answer to such views, in that they prove the image of God and the image of man are sufficiently alike that man can have a knowledge of God and know Him personally.

Bibliography. Herman Bavinck, *The Doctrine of God,* Grand Rapids: Eerdmans, 1951, pp. 83–98. J. O. Buswell, *A Systematic Theology,* Grand Rapids: Zondervan, 1962, 1, 29–36.

Charles Hodge, *Systematic Theology,* Grand Rapids: Eerdmans, 1952, 1, 335–345. A. H. Strong, *Systematic Theology,* Philadelphia: Judson Press, 1953, pp. 250 f.

R. A. K.

ANTICHRIST. *Names and references.* The term "Antichrist" appears only in I Jn 2:18, 22; 4:3; II Jn 7. If one holds that the Scriptures present a growing unity on this doctrine, and that an eschatological person, the final Antichrist to be indwelt by Satan (Rev 13), is yet to be manifest, he must relate a large number of biblical names and references to him. These begin with the "seed" of the serpent (Gen 3:15) and end with "the beast" (Rev 20:10). Most important are the "little horn" on the fourth beast of Dan 7:7 ff.; "the prince that shall come" (Dan 9:26); "one who makes desolate" (Dan 9:27, RSV); the willful king of Dan 11:36–39; "man of sin" and "son of perdition" as well as "the lawless one" (II Thess 2:3, 8, ASV); and "the beast" (Rev 11:7; 13:2 ff.). Jesus referred to Antichrist as one setting up an idol in God's temple in the days just before His second advent (Mt 24:15; *see* Abomination of Desloation).

Meaning. Antichrist means one who is against Christ or who is a substitute for Him. John saw his "spirit" or doctrine (Docetism?) in the world in the 1st cen. (I Jn 4:3). The OT doctrine of Belial (the Heb. *bᵉlîya'al* occurs 27 times in OT; once in NT, II Cor 6:15; cf. Beelzebub, Lk 11:15–19) probably refers to the same concept. *See* Belial.

Interpretations. Emphasizing one aspect or another of Scripture teaching, several types of interpretation have appeared in Christian circles.

1. "Principle of evil" view. Advocates propose that Antichrist is a personification of some evil principle, power(s), or idea(s) of the world, always until the end of time in opposition to the kingdom of God. I and II John seem to portray Antichrist in this way, and surely this must be part of the truth. At various times this principle has been identified with current movements (e.g., Communism, Fascism).

2. "Institution of evil" view. This is an appropriate name for the idea that the Roman Empire or the Papacy or the Muslim religion, etc., is the Antichrist. This approach is common among preterist and historicist interpreters of Revelation.

3. "Person of evil" view [not personification] is still another. Some contemporary man who seems particularly dangerous to Christianity in the opinion of the interpreter has frequently been held to be the man of sin of II Thess 2 or the Beast of Revelation and Daniel. In the early Middle Ages Muhammad was the favorite candidate. Later the popes would find various offending emperors or heretics likely holders for the label while conversely these men or their followers put the label on the current pope. In Reformation times, depending on whose side the interpreter was, the pope or

Martin Luther would be charged with the unwelcome name. Napoleon, Kaiser Wilhelm II, Mussolini, etc., have been proposed.

4. "Popular fallacy" view. Liberal (modernist) writers usually hold that Antichrist in the NT only reflects ancient pagan myths still believed by the early Christians, or Jewish notions carried over into Christianity by the first Christians. Such interpreters read II Thessalonians and Revelation not as God's Word but only as a source of early Christian opinion.

5. Among evangelicals, far more common is what may be called the "organic" view. This is the opinion that good and evil have parallel development and reach ultimate consummation in a personal Christ and in a personal Antichrist, and that these meet in final conflict at the second advent of Chirst. Postmillennialists (e.g., A. H. Strong, *Systematic Theology*, p. 1008), amillennialists (e.g., C. F. Keil, *Commentary on Daniel* at 9:26 – 27), and premillennialists (e.g., Alva J. McClain, *The Greatness of the Kingdom*, pp. 452 – 453) agree in this.

The doctrine. Though Daniel and Revelation have more material on this subject, the most detailed systematic treatment is in II Thess 2. Examination yields information that a con-summately evil person called "the man of sin," "son of perdition," and "lawless one" (ASV) shall some day "be revealed." This revelation is to take place before (presumably shortly before) "the day of the Lord." With revelation of the man of sin will come a general apostasy from true religion, or "falling away." He will oppose God, exalt himself, demand divine honors, and in a general way be consummate godlessness and Antichrist. His coming will be the fruition of evil forces ("the mystery of lawlessness") now operating (II Thess 2:7). His success shall come, temporarily, by Satanic power and divine permissive providence (vv. 9 – 12), but ultimately he shall be slain by Christ's own manifestation at His coming (v. 8). (See also Rev 13:1 ff.; Dan 7:8 ff.; 11:36 ff.) Jesus speaks of him as one who comes in his "own name" (Jn 5:43).

See Beast (symbolic); Man of Sin; Devil.

Bibliography. W. Bousset, *The Antichrist Legend*, 1896. James Oliver Buswell, *A Systematic Theology of the Christian Religion*, Grand Rapids: Zondervan, 1962, II, 371 – 383, 390 – 396, 465 – 481.

R. D. C.

Excavations at Antioch of Syria. Princeton University

ANTIOCH (ăn′tĭ-ŏk). Sixteen Antiochs were established by Seleucus Nicator, founder of the Seleucid Empire in 312 (or 306) B.C. in honor of his father, Antiochus. Only two of these are mentioned in the NT: one in Syria, the other in Pisidia.

1. Antioch in Syria, the capital, was one of five Antiochs in Syria alone. Founded in 301 B.C., it became the greatest of all the Antiochs. In the 1st cen. it was the third largest city of the Roman Empire, with a population frequently estimated to have been 500,000. It was called "the Beautiful and the Golden," the "Queen of the East" from its location and magnificent buildings.

Located some 15 miles from the Mediterranean harbor of Seleucia, it lay on the N bank of the Orontes River in a broad and fertile valley at the foot of the snow-crested peaks of Mount Silpius. Crowding caravans from N, S, and E converged upon its marketplaces, while boats from the Mediterranean waited in port to unload their burdens and be refilled again. Retired government officials spent their fortunes there, surfeiting themselves with its exotic delicacies, gambling their gold coins on the chariot races, and relaxing daily in its great public baths. From its founding it was cosmopolitan. Jews enjoyed the same privileges given to Greek traders.

The city was divided into four quarters from 175 B.C. onward, separated by one long colonnade and a second shorter one intersecting it obliquely. Temples, theaters, baths, and Roman streets, when destroyed by earthquakes (as in A.D. 37) or by wars (several revolts in 1st cen.) were promptly rebuilt by the vigorous citizens. Today its population numbers barely 42,000.

Syrian Antioch is very important in the early history of the Christian church. Nicholas, one of the original deacons, was a proselyte of Antioch (Acts 6:5). During the persecutions following Stephen's stoning, many Jerusalem Christians fled to Antioch where they preached to Greek-speaking Jews (Hellenists) and to Greeks (Hellenes). (Gr. MSS are divided and we can argue for either word as original in Acts 11:20, but the context clearly implies both Hellenists and Hellenes were found in the congregation.)

Barnabas greatly strengthened the ties of fellowship between the Antiochian congregation and the mother church at Jerusalem (Acts 11:22–30), secured Paul's services for them as a teacher (Acts 11:25–26), and in company with Paul carried their relief money to Jerusalem (Acts 11:27–30). The disciples were given the name "Christians" first in Antioch (Acts 11:26). Paul was sent out from the Antioch church on his three great missions to Cyprus, Asia Minor, and Greece (Acts 13:1 ff.; 15:36 ff.; 18:23 ff.). The first great church council at Jerusalem was occasioned by the question whether it was necessary to circumcise Gentile converts, and it is fair to say the broader view of Antioch prevailed over the narrower view of Judea (Acts 15; cf. Gal 2:4–14).

In the ancient church, Antioch was famous for Ignatius, the bishop and martyr (c.A.D. 110) whose letters we still read; and for its school and great teachers, Chrysostom (c. 390) and Theodore of Mopsuestia (c. 390) who urged a literal and historical interpretation of the Bible over against the allegorizing tendencies of Clement and Origen of Alexandria in Egypt. *See* Archaeology.

The chalice of Antioch (found near Syrian Antioch in 1916), sometimes claimed to be the Holy Grail used by Jesus and His apostles at the first communion, is a plain silver cup set in a filigree holder bearing figures thought to represent Jesus and several apostles. It is now believed to date from the 4th or 5th cen. A.D.

See Archaeology.

Bibliography. Glanville Downey, *Antioch in the Age of Theodosius the Great,* Norman: Univ. of Oklahoma Press, 1962; *A History of Antioch in Syria,* Princeton: Univ. Press, 1961. Bruce M. Metzger, "Antioch-on-the-Orontes," BA, XI (1948), 69–88. Richard Stilwell (ed.), *Antioch-on-the-Orontes,* Princeton: Univ. Press, 1938.

2. Antioch near Pisidia, a city of Phrygia in southern Asia Minor. It was called Pisidian Antioch to distinguish it from the many other cities of the same name founded by Seleucus Nicator in honor of his father, probably soon after 301 B.C. It was a garrison point commanding the great Roman road connecting Ephesus with the Cilician Gates, a mountain pass just above Tarsus. After 25 B.C. Rome made it a city of Galatia, then elevated it to colony status shortly before 6 B.C. Roman roads henceforward connected it with the other colonies (e.g., Lystra) founded in the district.

On his first mission Paul planted a church in Pisidian Antioch (Acts 13:13–52) and its witness was heard throughout the "region" (Acts 13:49); only in Ephesus and Thessalonica were there comparable results. Jews were present in great numbers from 200 B.C. onward and no doubt their proselyting efforts had prepared many Gentile hearts for the gospel. By reaching "the Jew first" (Rom 1:16), Paul could furnish leadership to the infant church which knew the OT Scriptures and the synagogue service upon which Christian worship was based. (Note in Acts 13:43 ff. emphasis on Jews and proselytes.) Noble women among the Gentiles were drawn in great numbers from paganism to Judaism, according to Juvenal VI:543 and Jos *Wars* II.20.2, and likewise they readily embraced the Christian faith (Acts 13:50). Paul's sermon is given at length in Acts 13.

The "South Galatian" theory (*see* Galatia) claims Pisidian Antioch belonged to the region of Phrygia (a geographical term used by Greeks) and Galatia (a political term used by

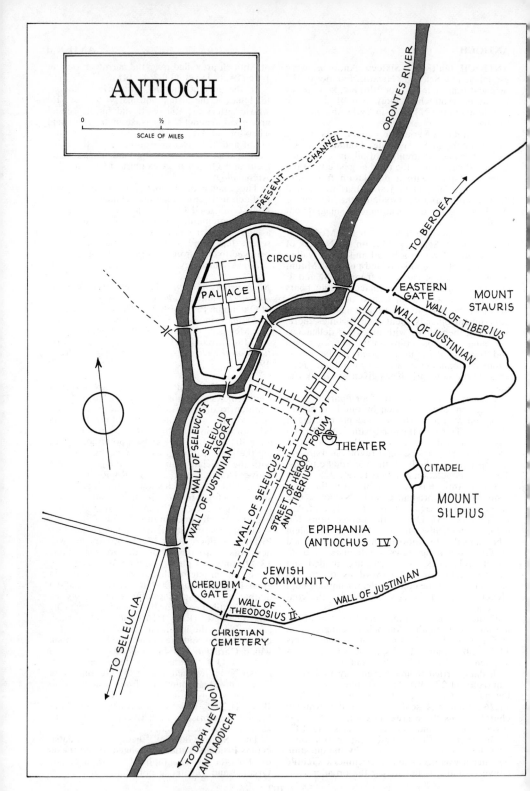

A Map of Antioch of Syria in New Testament Times.

108

the Roman government) according to Acts 16:6 and 18:23. Along with Iconium, Lystra, and Derbe, Antioch is one of the "Galatian" churches to which Paul wrote his letter.

On the less probable "North Galatian" theory, Pisidian Antioch lay too far S in Phrygia to be one of the churches to which Paul wrote; they were rather at Tavium. Ancyra and Pessinus, cities not mentioned in Acts or the NT except as Acts 16:6 and 18:23 refer to Phrygian (geographical) and Galatian (geographical northern part of the political province) territory.

Bibliography. David Magie, *Roman Rule in Asia Minor*, Princeton: Univ. Press, 1950, I, 457–463. David M. Robinson, "A Preliminary Report on the Excavations at Pisidian Antioch and at Sizma," AJA, XXVIII (Oct., 1924), 435–444.

T. B. C.

ANTIPAS (ăn'tĭ-păs). A contraction of Antipater.

1. While this was the name of the father of Herod the Great (Jos *Ant.* xiv. 1.3–4), it was best known as the name of one of the several sons of Herod the Great. He was the son of Herod and Malthace, and the brother of Archelaus (Mt 2:22) and Philip, known as Herod the tetrarch (Lk 3:1, 19) and notorious for his marriage to Herodias, Philip's wife.

After John the Baptist had appeared before him and had been beheaded for accusing Herod of adultery (Mk 6:17–29), Jesus was sent to him by Pilate to be examined (Lk 23:7–11). He was known for his evil deeds (Lk 3:19) and was called "that fox" by Jesus (Lk 13:31–32), an expression probably referring to his slyness. *See also* Aretas; Herod.

2. An early Christian martyr mentioned in Rev 2:13 as "my faithful martyr" resident at Pergamum (*q.v.*).

W. M. D.

ANTIPATRIS (ăn-tĭp'ă-trĭs). This city is mentioned only once in the NT (Acts 23:31). Paul and the 470 Roman soldiers guarding him stopped there when he was being transferred by night from Jerusalem to Caesarea. The site overlooks the plain of Sharon, *c.* 30 miles NW of Jerusalem and 28 miles S of Caesarea. The town was elaborately beautiful in the time of Herod (*c.* 9 B.C.) and renamed after Herod's father, Antipater; it was originally known as Kaphar Saba (see Jos *Ant.* xiii, 15.1; xvi.5.2).

Unquestionably a town stood there many centuries before the time of Jesus. Antipatris most likely was located at Ras el-'Ain ("head of the spring"), which spring is the most copious in all of Palestine and forms the main constant source for the Aujeh River (i.e., the Yarkon). Today most of this water is drained off by pipeline to the Negev.

Pre-Christian pottery (Hellenistic, Iron and Bronze Ages) was found here in 1946, corroborating the view that this site was OT Aphek

(*see* Aphek 3). Josephus said it was located near the tower of Aphek (*Wars* ii.19.1), and in the Hellenistic period it was probably called *Pēgai* ("springs"; it is referred to in a document from the time of Ptolemy Philadelphus, cf. *Pap, d. Soc. Ital.* IV, 406). There are impressive remains (a large fortress and caravansary, etc.) from the Arabic-Crusader period there today. It invites excavation, which has not been carried on to any real degree as yet. In the Talmudic period it was on the border between northern Judea and Galilee (cf. *Gittin* VII.7; *Yoma* 69a). From the 4th cen. on it was one of the main stations for pilgrims.

Bibliography. Conder and Kitchener, *Survey of Western Palestine, Memoirs* II, 134, 258 ff. Emil Schürer, *History of the Jewish People in the Time of Jesus Christ*, New York: Scribner's, 1891, II, 1, 130–131.

E. J. V.

ANTITYPE. "Something that corresponds to or is foreshadowed in a type or symbol" (Webster). Christ is the messianic reality which fulfills many particular pre-messianic figures in the OT. For example, as the Lamb of God He is the antitype and fulfillment of the Passover lamb (I Cor 5:7). Christian baptism symbolizes the salvation which is in Christ and is the antitype (Gr. *antitypon*) of the salvation which was offered in Noah's ark (I Pet 3:21, NASB). In Heb 9:24 the term is used in a slightly different manner as the sections of the OT tabernacle are called the antitypes of God's heavenly tabernacle in the sense that the Mosaic tabernacle was the fulfillment or subsequent earthly reality of the eternal heavenly tabernacle, its pattern (cf. Heb 8:2, 5). *See* Types.

Reconstruction of the Castle of Antonia. Sisters of Zion, Jerusalem

ANTONIA (ăn-tō'nĭ-ǎ). A fortress rebuilt by Herod the Great NW of the temple, not named in the Bible but referred to in connection with Paul's arrest in Jerusalem. In the time of Nehemiah it was a citadel related to the temple (Neh

2:8; 7:2, RSV). Later this site was occupied by a castle of the Asmonean high priest-kings (Jos *Ant.* xv.11.4; xviii.4.3; *Wars* i.21.1). When Herod ordered the temple to be rebuilt (*c.* 22 or 19 B.C.), this structure at the NW corner of the temple area was also remodeled as a palatial guard tower and royal residence, and renamed in honor of Mark Antony, the friend and patron of Herod. It stood on a cliff of the Tyropeon Valley nearly 75 feet high, and had four massive towers, each 75 – 100 feet tall, at its four corners. Its courtyard was paved with great stone slabs three feet square and a foot thick.

For the NT student the primary importance of Antonia rests in the fact that Paul was imprisoned in the barracks (Gr. *parembolē*, "castle," KJV) until he was transferred to Caesarea (Acts 21:37; 22:24; 23:10, 16, 32). The high priest's garments were also stored here and released by the Romans only during the time of the Jewish festivals.

H. P. Vincent has argued that Antonia is to be identified with the pretorium with its pavement (Jn 18:28; 19:13) and that Jesus was tried here before Pilate. Strong reasons weigh against Vincent's view. The pretorium more likely referred to Herod's palace in Jerusalem. *See* Pretorium.

Bibliography. Soeur Marie Aline de Sion, *La forteresse Antonia à Jérusalem et la question du Prétoire,* Paris: Galbalda, 1956. P. Benoit, "Pretorie, Lithostrotos," *Revue Biblique,* LIX (1952), 531 – 550. Millar Burrows, "The Fortress Antonia and the Praetorium," BA, I (1938), 17 – 19. Superior Godeleine, *Le Lithostrotos d'apres des Fouilles Recentes,* Jerusalem: "Notre-Dame de Sion," 1932. Soeur Marie Ita of Sion, "The Antonia Fortress," PEQ, C (1968), 139 – 143. E. Schürer, *A History of the Jewish People in the Time of Jesus Christ,* 5 vols., 1896, see references to Josephus, Tacitus, etc. H. P. Vincent, "Le Lithostrotos Evangelique," *Revue Biblique,* LIX (1952), 513 – 530.

E. J. V.

ANTOTHIJAH (ăn'tō-thī-jȧ). A descendant of Benjamin. In RSV the spelling is Anthothijah (I Chr 8:24).

ANTOTHITE (ăn'tō-thīt). A short form of Anethothite (*q.v.*), a dweller in Anathoth.

ANUB (ā'nŭb). The son of Coz of the tribe of Judah (I Chr 4:8).

ANVIL. A heavy piece of metal used by smiths to receive hammer taps or blows when shaping metal implements or objects. Referred to only in Isa 41:7.

APE. *See* Animals, II.2.

APELLES (ȧ-pĕl'ēz). A Christian in Rome whom Paul greeted and designated as one "approved in Christ" (Rom 16:10). It was a frequently used name among Greeks and Jews according to inscriptional evidence.

APHARSACHITES (ȧ-fär'sȧ-kīts), **APHARSATHCHITES** (ȧ-fär'săth-kīts). A name used to transliterate an Aramaic or Persian term, understood in KJV as referring to the name of a people resettled in Samaria by Asnapper (Ashurbanipal), the Assyrian king. Found in Ezr 4:9; 5:6; 6:6, KJV. RSV translates the word as "governors" following the example of I Esd 6:7.

APHARSITES (ȧ-fär'sīts). Found only in Ezr 4:9, KJV, referring to a tribe resettled in Samaria by the Assyrian king Asnapper (Ashurbanipal). RSV translates the word as "Persians." Herzfeld believes it refers to neo-Babylonian officials (IB, III, 601).

APHEK (ā'fĕk)

1. A city by this name (Aphik in Jud 1:31), perhaps to be identified with Tell el-Kurdaneh six miles SE of Acco, was within Asher's territory (Josh 19:30) but was not conquered at first by the Israelites.

2. The Syrians fled to a city named Aphek in Bashan (E of the Sea of Galilee) after being defeated by Ahab (I Kgs 20:26 – 30).

3. An ancient Canaanite city which lay within the territory of Ephraim in the plain of Sharon. It was located at Ras el-'Ain, a copious spring that forms the headwaters of the Yarkon River. The presence here of Middle Bronze, Late Bronze, and Iron I Age potsherds agrees with the mention of Aphek in the Egyptian Execration texts and as the first town captured by Amenhotep II on his second Asiatic campaign (*c.* 1440 B.C.). Aphek appears again in an Aramaic letter of a Palestinian prince, Adon, to Pharaoh Hophra *c.* 600 B.C. (BASOR, # 111 [Oct., 1948], 24 – 27). Its king was slain by Joshua (Josh 12:18), but later the Philistines defeated the sons of Eli near the place and captured the ark (I Sam 4:1 – 11). The Philistines used Aphek as a staging area for their forces before attacking Saul in Jezreel. At the time, David and his men were a part of the Philistine forces, but were dismissed before the battle began because some Philistine generals did not trust David (I Sam 29).

In Roman times, the city of Antipatris (*q.v.*) was built near the ancient ruins of Aphek by Herod the Great and named after his father. After his arrest in Jerusalem, Paul was brought by night to this place while on his way to Caesarea (Acts 23:31).

G. H. L.

APHEKAH (ȧ-fē'kȧ). A town in the southern hill country of Judah allotted to that tribe after Joshua's conquest (Josh 15:53).

APHIAH (ȧ-fī'ȧ). A Benjamite ancestor of King Saul (I Sam 9:1).

APHIK (ā'fĭk). *See* Aphek.

APHRAH (ăf'rá). *See* Beth-le-aphrah.

APHSES (ăf'sēz). A descendant of Aaron appointed by lot to priestly duties under King David (I Chr 24:15, KJV). Appears as Happizzez in RSV.

APOCALYPSE. From the Gr. word *apokalypsis*, an uncovering or unveiling, a disclosure of truth, a manifestation or return to view, the English word has come to mean a certain type of prophetic literature featuring end-time judgments of this world and visions of the next world. In addition to the canonical apocalypses in the books of Ezekiel, Daniel, and Zechariah in the OT and of John in the NT (*see* Revelation, Book of), there were numerous fanciful Jewish and early Christian apocalypses included among the Apocrypha (*q.v.*).

APOCRYPHA (á-pŏk'rĭ-fá). Commonly used to designate a collection of edifying books not included in the canon of Scripture.

Terminology

Apocrypha as a Gr. adjective, neuter plural, meaning "hidden things," is to be found in Dan 2:22 (Theodotian); Sir 14:21; 39:3, 7; 42:19; 43:32; 48:25; and in the NT in three passages (Mk 4:22; Lk 8:17; Col 2:3). In early usage it was about equivalent to *esoterikos* — writings intended for the inner circle and capable of being understood by no others — "kept for the wise among people" (cf. IV Ezr 14). But with Augustine (*De civ. dei* xv.23), a second idea of obscurity of origin or authorship is suggested. Since the time of Jerome it has designated noncanonical books, and since the time of the Reformation a definite collection of such books. Carlstadt defined "Apocrypha" as writings excluded from the canon whether or not the true authors of the books were known.

Attitudes Toward OT Apocrypha

The OT Apocrypha is comprised of 14 or 15 books which are usually found in MSS of the LXX or the Vulgate, but which are not included in the Heb. canon. The Prayer of Manasseh and II Esdras are exceptions. The latter appears in no Gr. MSS and the Prayer of Manasseh is not in all of them. In contrast, the books of the Pseudepigrapha with few exceptions are never found in biblical MSS.

No exact record has survived giving the process and basis by which the apocryphal books were excluded from the canon. The exclusion for Pharisaic Jews had already taken place by the time of Josephus (cf. *Apion i.* 8), who states that the canonical books are 22 in number and that they date between the time of Moses and Artaxerxes. The apocryphal books, commonly dated from the 2nd cen. B.C. to the 1st cen. A.D., were too late to qualify. Some of the books have historical mistakes and represent questionable ethics and theology.

The earliest list of OT canon (Melito of Sardis; cf. Eusebius H. E. iv. 26.14) does not include the Apocrypha. No book of the Apocrypha is directly quoted in the NT; but the books are frequently cited by early Christian writers. In the Eastern and Western churches the books came to form an integral part of the canon and were scattered throughout the OT, generally placed near the books with which they have affinity.

OT Apocrypha deals in the main with persons, events, and themes closely related to OT and post-OT figures. Though composed by Jewish writers, likely in Hebrew and Aramaic, and though communities like the Dead Sea group possessed an undefined number of outside books, the Apocrypha has largely been preserved by Christians. However, despite Akiba's threat that he who reads the outside books has no part in the world to come, there were medieval Jewish translations of some of the books.

The Apocrypha has exercised considerable influence upon art and upon English literature through the centuries. Common proverbs and familiar names have been derived from these books. Most early English Bibles (Wycliffe, Coverdale, and Geneva) contained these books as an appendix, but as early as 1629 they were omitted from some editions of the KJV. The major translating committees have translated the Apocrypha as a separate volume; but since 1827 Bibles published by the British and American Bible Societies have omitted these books.

Four attitudes have crystallized toward the Apocrypha since the time of the Reformation. The Council of Trent (1546) affirmed the canonicity of these books as found in the Vulgate edition and anathematized him who denied their place. This declaration was further confirmed by the Vatican Council of 1870. In Catholic writers the books are often called "Deutero-canonical" with no distinction of authority to be implied from the term. Catholics tend to use the term Apocrypha to designate the group of books the Protestants call Pseudepigrapha.

A second attitude is to be found in Protestant writers. When Luther issued his German Bible, he put six books in an appendix at the end of the OT with an introduction: "Aprocrypha: these books are not held equal to the sacred Scriptures and yet are useful and good for reading." The sixth article of the Church of England states: "And the other books the church doth read for example of life and instruction of manners, but yet doth it not apply them to establish any doctrines." On special holy days sections of Tobit, Wisdom, and Sirach are read by the Episcopal Church in America.

The third attitude is seen developing with the rise of the Puritans who rejected the books as of no religious value: "Not to be otherwise approved or made use of than any other human writing." The term Apocrypha came to have a derogatory sense meaning unauthentic.

A fourth attitude, widely held today, shifts

the point of emphasis from that of the canonical status of the books to that of their historical value for supplying information on the times between the OT and NT period. They are invaluable for supplying information on the historical and religious conditions out of which they arose. The messianic idea, the doctrines of wisdom, law, sin, good works, demonology, angels, and eschatology are all dealt with.

Contents of OT Apocrypha

I Esdras is a narrative survey of events, parallel to the narrative of Ezra and Nehemiah, surrounding Zerubbabel and the return of Ezra and his work. The most charming part is the story of the three guardsmen who debate over the strongest thing in the world and conclude that it is Truth.

II Esdras is an apocalypse in which the writer has Ezra raise questions seeking to justify the ways of God in permitting calamities to befall Zion.

Tobit is a novel purporting to depict the life of the Jew in captivity. Its purpose is to teach moral lessons. Prayer and almsgiving are praised. The duty of burying the dead and of marrying within Judaism is set forth.

Judith is a patriotic short story extolling the deeds of a Jewish widow who delivered her people even as Esther brought deliverance.

The Additions to Esther are six supplementary passages added to complete the canonical story. They must be read in their proper place in the story as they stand in the LXX, rather than as a collection at its end as in the RSV, in order to be intelligible. They add a religious note to an otherwise secular book.

The Wisdom of Solomon consists of Wisdom-type literature in which idolatry is mocked and wisdom is praised. The fates of the righteous and the wicked are contrasted.

Ecclesiasticus is a miscellaneous collection of wise sayings dealing with all areas of life. Proverbs is the nearest canonical parallel. The book culminates in the "Praise of the Fathers" which surveys the merits of the OT worthies.

Baruch is a lament over the fall of Jerusalem which confesses the guilt of Israel and promises a restoration in prophetic fashion.

The Letter of Jeremiah is a satire on the follies of idolatry.

The Prayer of Azariah is an addition to Daniel which purports to express sentiments of the three Hebrews when in the fiery furnace.

Susanna is a detective story designed to extol the wisdom of Daniel, who demonstrates the innocence of the falsely accused woman.

Bel and the Dragon also extols the wisdom of Daniel and satirizes idolatry.

The Prayer of Manasseh purports to express the penitence of the OT's most wicked king. The theme is suggested by II Chr 33:12.

I Maccabees is a narrative of events leading up to and covering the Maccabean revolt. The book is a historical source of considerable merit.

II Maccabees covers the same material as the first part of I Maccabees, but adds religious sentiments and attempts to demonstrate that the miraculous played a significant part in the victory. See Maccabees.

NT Apocrypha

The Aprocryphal NT is a body of literature of undefined limits. It differs from the OT Apocrypha in that it is seldom found in biblical MSS. In general, infancy and passion Gospels, acts, epistles, and apocalypses are the categories treated. It is unlikely that they preserve any authentic deeds or sayings of their heroes. Rather, they are amplifications of themes suggested by the canonical books. The writers attempted to supply information on periods where biblical material is wanting, such as the hidden years of Jesus' life or details about what the man might have seen who was caught up into the third heaven (II Cor 12:2). The miraculous element is usually heightened.

The books tend to make propaganda for views which the writer thought were significant. Early heretics used these means to spread their views. In 1947 the known material of this sort was considerably enlarged by the discovery of a Gnostic library in Egypt containing portions of 13 codices in Coptic. Back of these are thought to lie Gr. materials that may be dated in the 2nd cen. A.D. See Chenoboskion; Gnosticism.

Considerable misimpression has been fostered about the Apocrypha by such titles as "The Lost Books of the Bible," for it has by no means been established that these books were ever a part of the Bible. Some NT apocryphal writings were already known to early Church Fathers. On the other hand, composition of this type of material has continued on down to modern times. The materials of the earlier period are most satisfactorily presented in the edition of M.R. James, while modern examples are evaluated by E. J. Goodspeed.

Bibliography. L. H. Brockington, *A Critical Introduction to the Apocrypha*, London: Duckworth, 1961. E. J. Goodspeed, *Modern Apocrypha*, Boston: Beacon Press, 1956. Robert M. Grant, *Gnosticism*, New York: Harper, 1961. M. R. James, *The Apocryphal New Testament*, Oxford: Clarendon, 1924. Bruce M. Metzger, *An Introduction to the Apocrypha*, New York: Oxford, 1957. B. F. Westcott, *The Bible in the Church*, London: Macmillan, 1905.

J. P. L.

APOLLONIA (ăp′ŏl-lō′nĭ-à). Apollonia of Mygonia in Macedonia was one of the dozen or so towns of this name in the ancient world. (For list of other places named Apollonia, see A. H. M. Jones, *Cities of the Eastern Roman Provinces*, p. 560; see also B. V. Head, *Historia Numorum*, pp. 895 ff.). There were three Macedonian towns of this name. The one referred to in Acts 17:1 was situated S of Lake Bolbe.

According to Strabo, Cassander took the people from Apollonia, as well as other surrounding cities, and settled them in Thessalonica when he built that town for his wife (daughter of Philip of Macedonia) and named it after her (Strabo, *Geography,* Fragments of Book VII, Loeb ed. III, 343).

The apostle Paul passed through Apollonia on his second missionary journey as he traveled the Egnatian Way from Philippi to Thessalonica, a distance of *c.* 85 miles. It was *c.* 34 miles from Philippi to Amphipolis, 21 from Amphipolis to Apollonia, and 30 from Apollonia to Thessalonica. The whole district of Macedonia was much more fertile and prosperous than the region around Athens. The economic importance of this area is not generally recognized, but is quite obvious to the modern traveler. Adequate rainfall accounts for the lush aspect of this region. Apollonia (modern Pollina) is still settled by a small handful of people. See also W. M. Leake, *Travels in Northern Greece,* iii.458.

E. J. V.

APOLLOS (*á*-pŏl'*ŏs*). The name is a shortened form of Apollonius. He is described in Acts 18:24 – 28 as an Alexandrian Jew, an eloquent man, and one "mighty in the scriptures." He had been "instructed" (lit., "catechized," cf. Lk 1:4) in "the way of the Lord"; that is, he knew of the teachings of the followers of Jesus (cf. Acts 9:2, "the Way"). His teaching, done with fervency, concerned "the baptism of John" (cf. Lk 7:29).

His preaching in Ephesus, listened to by Priscilla and Aquila, was not incorrect; rather, it was incomplete. They explained to him "the way of God" more accurately; that is, the rest of the message was made known to him, particularly concerning the ascension of Christ and the advent of the Holy Spirit. That these elements seemed to be lacking in his initial preaching is implied by Acts 19:1 – 3.

Other NT passages giving information about Apollos are I Cor 1:12; 3:4 – 6, 22; 4:6; 16:12 and Tit 3:13. We learn there that he had been associated with Paul, and that he had become one of four "party favorites" in the church at Corinth (along with Cephas, Paul, and Christ). Paul referred to him as a "fellow worker" and as "our brother," although making it clear that he himself had "laid the foundation."

Apparently Apollos' eloquence had made an impression on the Corinthians, and Paul took pains to emphasize that he (Paul) "did not come with superiority of speech or of wisdom" (I Cor 2:1, NASB), and that their faith "should not rest on the wisdom of men, but on the power of God" (v. 5).

Apollos seems to have become aware of the problem of tensions in the Corinthian church, and although Paul encouraged him to revisit them, he declined to go at that time (I Cor 16:12). Tit 3:13 appears to indicate that he was with Titus in Crete at a later date.

W. M. D.

APOLLYON (*á*-pŏl'y*ŭn*). A Gr. word meaning "destroyer," translating the Heb. *'ăbaddôn* (the lower or nether world, "perdition"), used of the angel of the bottomless pit (Rev 9:11). In Prov 15:11 (RSV) Sheol and Abaddon are linked together as the location and the state of the dead. Bunyan, in his *Pilgrim's Progress,* equated Apollyon with Satan.

APOLOGETICS. The term is derived from the Gr. verb *apologeomai,* meaning "to give an answer back," "reply," "defend one's position," and the Gr. noun *apologia.* In its narrowest sense it means the defense of the faith of the individual Christian. In a broader sense it is the answer of the Christian to attacks upon himself, his doctrine and faith, and all the revelation given in the Scriptures. In its fullest sense apologetics is the defense and justification of the Christian faith and of the revelation given in the Holy Scriptures against the attack of doubters and unbelievers, plus the development of a positive evangelical presentation of the facts given in the Bible, the reasonableness of God's revelation to man in Scripture, and its ample sufficiency alone to meet the complete spiritual needs of man. Apologetics is then not only a negative and defensive but also a positive and offensive exercise. It is not only to be used in defense of the gospel but also in its propagation.

The study of apologetics. This can be divided into three periods as found in three eras of church history.

1. *New Testament apologetics.* The Gr. verb *apologeomai* is used to express the idea of self-justification or self-excuse (Rom 2:15; II Cor 12:19) and also the noun *apologia* (II Cor 7:11); but particularly in the sense of replying to attacks on one's faith and convictions, and offering a defense. Acts 7 is often called Stephen's apology as he replied before the Jewish Sanhedrin to the accusations of false witnesses (Acts 6:11 – 15).

Paul speaks of being set for "the defense of the gospel" (Phil 1:7, 17). He made two "apologies" for his position: the first before Festus (Acts 24:10; 25:8; cf. v. 16), and the second before Agrippa (Acts 26:2). When he appealed for the privilege to do the same before Caesar (Acts 25:8 – 16), his request was finally granted. Each of these apologies contains both a negative defensive and a positive evangelistic element. For example, Paul used his defense as an introduction to the gospel in such an effective manner that Felix trembled (Acts 24:25), while Agrippa cried, "Almost thou persuadest me to be a Christian" (Acts 26:28). Even if the other interpretation of the latter verse, "Would you so easily persuade me to be a Christian?" is adopted, the positive evangel in Paul's apology still clearly appears by the effect produced in Agrippa.

2. *Apologetics in the early and medieval church.* Justin Martyr wrote his *Dialogue with*

Trypho (c. A.D. 150). Origen answered many antichristian arguments in his *Kata Kelsou* (*Contra Celsus*) (c. 235), and Athanasius published his *Contra Gentes* (c. 315). But the most important apology of all was Augustine's *City of God* (A.D. 426).

Until the church became recognized by Constantine the Great, it found itself accused of cannibalism and sexual promiscuity because of having to meet in secrecy in such places as the catacombs. In contrast, after it was imperially recognized, it had to face charges of worldliness. It was to explain the latter that Augustine wrote and took as his thesis the City of God in contrast to the city of the world.

In the Middle Ages apologetics struggled with the questions of faith — with regard to facts such as the Trinity and the incarnation, knowable only by faith — versus reason, and the facts of science and of the material world which are amenable to reason. Aquinas made a partial synthesis which has become the official position of Romanism: by reason man can argue to the existence of God and even know God, and yet the Trinity and the incarnation are inaccessible to reason, given by revelation, and received by faith alone.

3. *Modern apologetics.* For the purpose of study and helpful analysis it proves valuable to consider both Roman Catholic and Protestant apologetics.

(a) Roman Catholic apologetics is characterized by the fact it attributes both the origin and (infallible) interpretation of the Scriptures to the church; and by the fact that it teaches that rational theology is possible and exists as well as revealed theology: by the use of the human reason man can come to a knowledge of the person and existence of God and even to salvation. The reason why man fails to come to the truth by rational theology is not his fallen condition, but rather the indolence of those mentally equipped to achieve by this means and the rational inability of the rest. Because of this laziness on the part of some and inability of the rest, God has chosen in His grace to give revelation.

The Roman Catholic church has developed a very thorough apologetic of its own. Starting in 1908, the pope appointed continuous commissions to investigate thoroughly and issue reports on the Deutero-Isaiah problem, the J.E.D.P. theory, form-Geschichte, etc. Able church writers have produced such effective books on apologetics as *The Faith of Our Fathers* by Cardinal James Gibbons, a defense of the Roman Catholic church; and *Katholieke Geloofsverdediging* by Cardinal Brocardus Meijer, a very thorough, able work on apologetics in general, in Dutch. As a result of Rome's scholarly commissions and of such a complete work in apologetics as that by Meijer, the Roman Catholics are presenting a convincing defense of their faith which is winning many from the modernist fold where no such defense is given for a Christian faith.

(b) Protestant apologetics. There is a strong element of apologetics present in Calvin's *Institutes* where it is presented in combination with theology. The most famous and effective works in apologetics proper, however, before our times, are Joseph Butler's *Analogy of Religion* (1736) and A. B. Bruce's *Apologetics or Christianity Defensively Stated* (1892). The latter has been the standard orthodox work in English for many years. Its place has been taken lately largely by the writings of Edward John Carnell: *An Introduction to Christian Apologetics* and *A Philosophy of the Christian Religion,* and of Bernard Ramm: *Protestant Christian Evidences, Types of Apologetic Systems,* and *The Christian View of Science and Scripture.*

While Carnell and Ramm have led the evangelical cause in apologetics with admirable work in many areas of the field, both have had difficulties in places, particularly with regard to the absolute infallibility of the Bible in the original writing, and others have had to come to their rescue at this point.

The value and place of apologetics. Considering its length, the OT contains relatively little use of apologetics. In Job 32 – 37, however, is a corrective by Elihu to the false or inadequate views of Job and his three friends regarding God and theodicy. The Lord Himself replies to Job to convince of His sovereignty and Job's inability (Job 38 – 41). A number of the psalms appeal to God's activity, in providential care (e.g., Ps 104, 107) and history (Ps 105, 106), to evoke praise and trust and to show the folly of idolatry (Ps 115). Especially Isaiah among the prophets proclaimed God's apology against the pagan deities, challenging the idol-worshiping Gentiles to prove the reality and power of their gods by the test of prophecy and fulfillment (Isa 41:21 – 29; 43:8 – 13; 44:6 – 20; 45:18 – 25; 46:1 – 11; 48:1 – 6).

The NT gives apologetics a much more important place. The early Church Fathers were constantly called upon to defend their faith against heathen philosophers, agnostics, and heretics.

In apologetics we are called upon to show the reasonableness and rationality of the Christian faith and of its revelation as given in the Bible. This is accomplished by such means as a comparison of science with Scripture, a consideration of archaeology and biblical facts and history, an appeal to the fulfillment of predictive prophecies, a study of the proofs of inspiration and infallibility of the Bible, and an application of reason to the question of the existence and nature of God.

The Protestant apologists do not teach that a complete natural theology is possible merely by the application of man's reason in the formulation of five or more theistic proofs (proofs of the necessary and actual existence of God). Rather, as far as the human reason can go — and that includes the formulation of the theistic arguments, namely, the cosmological (existence of world), ontological (existence of an idea of God), the teleological (existence and manifestation of design and purpose in the world and man) and the moral arguments (existence of a moral nature in man) — it is only reasonable to conclude that a rational, purposeful, moral Person exists and is the cause of both the universe and man. The Bible states by revelation that such is the case, and in Rom 1:18 ff. we learn that God holds man responsible to come to the conclusion that God exists.

Therefore the Protestant apologist neither fully rests his case upon reason — as the Roman Catholic with his natural theology, nor does he completely reject the place of reason — as some of the extreme orthodox Protestants (e.g., Abraham Kuyper in his *Principles of Sacred Theology* and Cornelius Van Til in his *The Defense of the Faith,* who emphasize the helplessness of the human mind in sin and the necessity of the renewing power of the Holy Spirit). Instead, recognizing the frailty of human reason since the Fall of man, he gives it a corroboratory function subsidiary to revelation. In other words, the laws of logic, the facts of life and of the cosmos, and the propositional revelations found in the Bible are all to be given their proper place in the attainment of final truth and the formulation of our apologetic system.

Apologetic methods. It becomes most important to develop a thorough and satisfactory apologetic method. This is all the more necessary since the Christian must defend himself against not only the passing theories of science but also the errors of worldly philosophy. No successful defense is possible until one is able not only to see the error or errors against which he contends, but also to understand their philosophical foundations.

Therefore our cause is greatly strengthened when we insist upon the fact that we have a Christian philosophy of existence, namely, an explanation for *(a)* the origin of reality, consisting of the world and men; *(b)* reality itself, as consisting of objects *(res extensa),* and ideas or thoughts *(res cogitata)* — the two of which we clearly define and distinguish; *(c)* the destiny of the world and man. All philosophers are called upon to give their own explanation of these three things.

A workable and thorough defense of the Christian viewpoint on any opinion sought, therefore, includes the following: (1) a fair and thorough description of an opponent's view; (2) a presentation of the value of that view to one who holds it; (3) a consideration of its philosophical basis and a clear presentation of its fallacies, both on logical and philosophical grounds; (4) an examination of the view in light of the confessions and creeds of the church; (5) an examination to see what theological advantages it may offer and what theological problems it may raise; (6) a presentation of the scriptural view of the matter in discussion and proof of its reasonableness, and a clear description of how the biblical view escapes the philosophical and the theological problems raised by an erroneous view.

Besides the main works in apologetics already mentioned, there have been many very valuable books on specific aspects of the faith, such as the virgin birth, the resurrection, miracles, the infallibility of the Scriptures, etc. These can be found readily in the extensive bibliographies attached to books by Carnell and Ramm mentioned above.

The aim of apologetics. This includes: (1) making contact with those who hold an erroneous or dangerous view, or who attack the Christian revelation and faith; (2) finding an area in which the problem can be discussed impartially, and proving the weakness of the view in question first in some neutral area common to all, such as philosophy or logic; (3) showing the theological problems raised; (4) expounding the church's convictions in its confessions and creeds and exegeting what the Scripture teaches, while showing the reasonableness thereof. The common ground sought for conversation with the adversary does not have to entail any compromise, such as attempted by some recent apologetics, nor does it force Scripture upon the doubter or the agnostic. By considering every aspect of a problem before taking up the Scripture itself, it opens the mind of an opponent to consider God's own position and answer.

Bibliography. A. B. Bruce, *Apologetics,* Edinburgh: T. & T. Clark, 1892. E. J. Carnell, *An Introduction to Christian Apologetics,* Grand Rapids: Eerdmans, 1952; *A Philosophy of the Christian Religion,* Grand Rapids: Eerdmans, 1952. Robert Flint, *Agnosticism,* New York: Scribner's, 1903; *Anti-Theistic Theories,* Edinburgh: Blackwood, 1879. Brocardus Meijer, *Katholieke Geloofsverdediging,* Roermond: Romen & Zonen, 1946. Bernard Ramm, *Protestant Christian Evidences,* Chicago: Moody Press, 1953; *Types of Apologetic Systems,* Wheaton, Ill.: Van Kampen Press, 1953; *The Christian View of Science and Scripture,* Grand Rapids: Eerdmans, 1954.

R. A. K.

APOSTASY (Gr. *apostasia,* "a falling away or defection from the faith").

While the Gr. word is used only twice in the NT (Acts 21:21; II Thess 2:3), it is found in the LXX several times, as in Josh 22:22, to express rebellion of the people from God, and in II Chr 29:19 of the casting away of the holy temple vessels.

Apostasy is possible only for nominal Christians. In the case of real believers, the Scripture declares that God either brings them back through suffering and chastisement (I Cor 11:29 – 30; I Cor 5:5) or removes them through death (I Cor 11:30). In the case of apostates, though He may allow them to remain, He withdraws from them all possibility of repentance and salvation (Heb 6:1 – 6; 10:26 – 31).

Apostasy is to be distinguished from ignorance or a lack of knowledge, as well as from heresy, which is mistaken knowledge (II Tim 2:25 – 26). Men can be saved from ignorance but not from apostasy. It is characterized by a deliberate rejection of Christ's deity (I Jn 2:22 – 23; Jude 4) and His atoning death (Phil 3:18; II Pet 2:1; Heb 10:29). *See* Backsliding.

R. A. K.

APOSTLE. The Gr. *apostolos* comes from the verb *apostellein,* "to send away," "send forth." Noun and verb are used by the LXX to translate Heb. *shālah* and its derivatives. These Heb. and Gr. words are occasionally used for messengers with emphasis on the sender, so that the agent becomes an extension of the personality and influence of the master (Gen 45:4 – 8; I Kgs 14:6). K. H. Rengstorf, T. W. Manson, and others have attempted to trace the NT word to the Jewish *shālîah* (used of a representative whose functions cannot be transferred; representative of religious authority, either of an individual or group; God's agent). *Apostolos,* used for "messenger" or "agent," is also found in classical Gr. (Herodotus i.21; v. 38; cf. Euripides, *Iphigeneia in Aulis,* 688).

In the NT the word "apostle" is used with both a broad and a narrow meaning. All apostleship focuses on Jesus, who is *the Apostle* (Heb 3:1 – 6) sent by God to be the Saviour of the world (I Jn 4:14). Although John does not use the noun, he frequently uses the verb and describes functions of Jesus as the Apostle of God. He was sent by God (Jn 7:28 – 29; 8:42) to speak the words of God (3:34), to do God's works (5:36; 6:29) and will (6:38), to reveal God (5:37 – 47), to give eternal life (17:2 –3). All subsequent apostleship centers in God through Jesus Christ (Jn 17:18 – 26; 20:21 – 23) and mediates Christ in word and person (Mt 10:40; Lk 10:16).

Matthew and Mark use "apostle" only once for the Twelve who were sent on a missionary journey (Mt 10:2; Mk 6:30). Here the word designates a function rather than status. During Jesus' ministry, the Twelve were not primarily messengers but select men who were initiated into the coming kingdom and therefore regarded it their duty to call Israel to repentance and ultimately judge it (Mt 19:28 – 30).

Luke frequently and almost exclusively calls the Twelve "apostles" (Lk 6:13; 9:10; 17:5; 22:14; 24:10; Acts 1:26; 2:43; 4:35, 37; 5:2, 12, 18; 8:1. Exceptions: Lk 11:49; Acts 14:4, 14). The apostles were eyewitnesses of the earthly activity of Jesus and hence testified that Jesus was the risen Lord (Lk 24:45 – 48; I Jn 1:1 – 3). The prerequisites for apostolic replacement in this unique function are given in Acts 1:21 – 22. Luke's list of the apostles (Lk 6:14 – 16; Acts 1:13) corresponds to the list of the Twelve given in Mt 10:2-4 and Mk 3:16 – 19. Matthew lists the disciples in pairs, supposedly as sent out by Jesus. Thaddaeus (Matthew and Mark) was identical with Judas the son of James (Luke). Peter, James, and John formed an inner circle within the Twelve and were present at the transfiguration (Mt 17:1 –9; Mk 9:2 – 10; Lk 9:28 – 36) and in Gethsemane (Mt 26:36 – 46; Mk 14:32 – 42; Lk 22:39 – 46). The Twelve were selected to be the companions of Jesus and proclaim the gospel (Mk 3:14). During Jesus' ministry, the Twelve served as His representatives, a function shared by others (Lk 10:1).

Apparently the position of the apostles was not permanently fixed before the resurrection (Mt 19:28 – 30; Lk 22:28 – 34; cf. Jn 21:15 – 18). The risen Christ made this select group of witnesses of His ministry and resurrection permanent apostles and witnesses that Jesus is the Lord, commissioned them as missionaries, instructed them to teach and baptize (Mt 28:18 – 20; Mk 16:15 – 18; Lk 24:46 – 48), and completed the process with the sending of the Holy Spirit on Pentecost (Lk 24:49; Acts 1:1 – 8; 2:1 – 13). In the earliest period, the 12 apostles were the only teachers and leaders of the church, and other offices were derived from them (Acts 6:1 – 6; 15:4). Apostleship did not imply permanent leadership. Though Peter initiated missions to Jews (Acts 2) and Gentiles (Acts 10:1 – 11:18), James replaced him as leader among Jews, and Paul among Gentiles.

Paul uses "apostle" in a broad sense for a messenger or agent (II Cor 8:23; Phil 2:25; possibly Rom 16:7). This broader usage made it possible to speak of false apostles (Rev 2:2). Usually, however, Paul uses the word for a group of witnesses who had seen the risen Lord and had received a specific call to an apostleship. This group was larger than the Twelve (Acts 15:5 – 6). Included in it were James the Lord's brother (Acts 15:13; Gal 1:19), Paul (Rom 1:1; I Cor 1:1; 9:1 – 2; 15:8 – 10; Gal 2:7 – 8), probably Barnabas (I Cor 9:1 – 6; Gal 2:9; cf. Acts 14:4, 14), and possibly others (Rom 16:7). The risen Lord, however, whom Paul witnessed is identical with the historical Jesus witnessed by the Twelve. Hence Paul's

The Sea of Galilee near the place where some of the apostles must have been called to be "fishers of men." CCR

proclamation must be identical with that of the Twelve (I Cor 15:11; Gal 1:18; 2:7 – 10; cf. Acts 15).

John emphasizes the work of the Spirit who witnesses through the words of the apostles (Jn 15:26 – 27). Through the preaching of the gospel, Jesus the risen Lord is contemporary to the hearers, and places them on the same footing with the eyewitnesses (cf. I Cor 3:21 – 23).

The members of the church are priests, kings, servants of God, and saints who use their gifts for the edification of the whole church (I Cor 12:1-11; I Pet 2:9; Rev 1:6; 5:8, 10; 7:3) and, like the apostles, mediate Christ (Mt 25:40, 45; Mk 9:37; Lk 9:48) and will reign with Him (Rev 3:21).

The apostles, however, through the witness of their word, will always be the norm and foundation on which Christ builds His church (Eph 2:20; Rev 18:20; 21:14). Apostles are the first of Christ's gifts to the church (Eph 4:11) and of God's appointed ministers in the church (I Cor 12:28-29).

For details on the Twelve, see under name of each, including Matthias.

Bibliography. Oscar Cullmann, "The Tradition," *The Early Church,* ed. by A. J. B. Higgins, Philadelphia: Westminster, 1956. J. N. Geldenhuys, *Supreme Authority,* Grand Rapids: Eerdmans, 1953. E. J. Goodspeed, *The Twelve,* Philadelphia: Winston, 1957. Arnold Ehrhardt, *The Apostolic Succession,* London: Lutterworth, 1953. J. B. Lightfoot, *Saint Paul's Epistle to the Galatians,* rev. ed., London: Macmillan, 1890, and subsequent reprints, pp. 92 – 101. T. W. Manson, *The Church's Ministry,* Philadelphia: Westminster, 1948. K. H. Rengstorf, *"Apostellō-apostolos,"* TDNT, I, 398 – 447.

E. L. L.

APOSTOLIC, APOSTOLICAL. Pertaining to or descending from the apostles. The term is used to designate men who were companions of the apostles and those Church Fathers who were contemporary with the apostles. A supposed apostolic source was claimed by use of the titles Apostolic Constitutions and Apostolic Canons for writings of the 4th cen.

In an ecclesiastical sense, apostolic succession refers to the assumed uninterrupted line of Christian ministry descendant from the apostles. The assembled bishops of the Councils of Orleans (A.D. 511) and Macon (A.D. 581) were described as apostolic. In time the popes restricted the term to themselves as spiritual descendants of Peter, and the Council of Rheims (A.D. 1049) declared the pope to be the sole apostolic primate. The Roman Catholic church has since employed the term in various connections; e.g., apostolical decree.

APOSTOLIC AGE. The time from Pentecost (c. A.D. 30) to the death of the apostle John (c. A.D. 100) during which the apostles were exerting influence among the churches. The era readily divides itself into the pre-Pauline (c. A.D. 30 – 40), Pauline (c. A.D. 40 – 67), and post-Pauline (c. A.D. 67 – 100) periods. During the first period Christianity was largely confined to Jerusalem and the Jewish people. There was no attempt to make a definite break with Judaism as yet. Church life was marked by simplicity, purity, and power. In the Pauline period a transition occurred from a Jewish to a Gentile-Jewish church with a corresponding empire-wide expansion. Numerous problems began to take shape, such as the Judaistic perversion in Galatia, irregularities in Corinth, and the Colossian heresy. The chief figure of the post-Pauline period was the apostle John, whose death brought the Apostolic Age to its close. By that time Christianity had been firmly planted in all the lands from Jerusalem to Rome.

D. W. B.

APOSTOLIC COUNCIL. The designation sometimes used of the Jerusalem assemblage of apostles and elders (c. A.D. 49 – 50) recorded in Acts 15. As a result of the reception into the churches of uncircumcised Gentiles (Acts 11:19-21, RSV; 13:46-48; 14:27), the ultra-Judaistic party began to press strenuously for the adoption of the Jewish law in addition to faith in Christ as a condition of Gentile salvation. The ensuing controversy led to a council in Jerusalem (Acts 15:1 – 2), which apparently developed along the following lines: an open meeting of the church (15:4 – 5), a session of the church leaders (15:6 – 11), and a resumption of the general church meeting (15:12 – 29). After testimony from Paul, Barnabas, and Peter concerning the evident fact that God had saved uncircumcised Gentiles, the council agreed on a twofold decision: (1) Gentiles were not to be required to submit to the law of Moses (15:19), and (2) Gentiles were to be asked to abstain from practices which would hinder social relations between Jewish and Gentile believers (15:20, 28 – 29). Historically and theologically, this was an epoch-making decision. As a result, Christianity was to be not merely a Jewish phenomenon but a universal faith. Furthermore, it became the accepted view of the church that salvation is by faith alone.

D. W. B.

APOTHECARY. See Occupations.

APPAIM (ăp′ī-ăm). A descendant of Hezron of the tribe of Judah (I Chr 2:30–31).

APPAREL. See Dress.

APPEAL. A judicial term referring to the request of an inferior to his superior for either mercy or justice. The Shunammite woman appealed to the king of Israel for her land (II Kgs 8:3). Job appealed to God for mercy (Job 9:15). Paul appealed to Caesar for justice (Acts

25:11). Used also in RSV in an informal sense in NT epistles as a request for godly Christian behavior (e.g., Rom 12:1; I Cor 1:10; Heb 13:22). *See* Exhortation.

APPEARANCES OF CHRIST. The Gospels record five appearances of Jesus on the day of His resurrection. The first was to Mary Magdalene (Jn 20:11 – 18). The second was to "Mary Magdalene and the other Mary" as they were returning from the empty tomb (Mt 28:1 – 10). It is obvious that these might be taken as the same incident. But Mark adds a third person to the group (Mk 16:1) and seems to suggest that the first appearance was to Mary Magdalene alone (Mk 16:9, if genuine). The third appearance was to the two disciples on the way to Emmaus (Lk 24:13 – 32). The fourth was to Simon Peter (Lk 24:34; I Cor 15:5). The fifth was to the disciples, with Thomas absent (Lk 24:36 – 43; Jn 20:19 – 25).

In the following 40 days Jesus appeared: (1) to the eleven disciples (Jn 20:26 – 31); (2) to the seven disciples beside the Lake of Galilee (Jn 21:1 – 14); (3) to "above five hundred brethren" (Mt 28:16 – 20; I Cor 15:6); (4) to James (I Cor 15:7); (5) at the ascension (Lk 24:44 – 51; Acts 1:3 – 11).

The purpose of these appearances was to convince the disciples of the bodily resurrection of Jesus, and therefore the validity of His saving work in His life and on the cross as the true Messiah. They also fulfilled Scripture and taught the disciples things they could not grasp beforehand.

For OT appearances of the pre-incarnate Son of God *see* Theophany.

R. E. and E. B. R.

APPEARING. *See* Christ, Coming of; Millennium.

APPHIA (ăf'ĭ-à). A Christian woman in Colossae, one of the addressees of the book of

The Appian Way. HFV

Philemon, probably the wife of Philemon (*q.v.*). Apphia was a common female name in western Asia Minor, as inscriptions show.

APPII FORUM. Used in Acts 28:15; Forum of Appius in RSV. It is still called Foro Appio. This commercial station is one of the two places ("Three Taverns," nine to ten miles N, is the other) mentioned in Paul's itinerary between Puteoli and Rome. Inscriptions have been found here. One of Emperor Nerva states explicitly: ". . . at the Forum of Appius." In the same vicinity a milestone was discovered which indicated that Appii Forum was located 43 Roman miles (*c.* 40 English miles) from Rome.

The place itself was named after the censor, Appius Claudius Caecus, who also initiated (*c.* 312 B.C.) the famous Appian Way as well as the aqueduct named in his honor. Pliny (III.v.9) mentions Appii Forum among the towns of Latium. Strabo (v.233) says that a mule-operated canal cut through the Pontine marshes and ran parallel to the road, which was especially used by travelers at night: ". . . embarking in the evening, and landing in the morning to travel the rest of their journey by road." Horace (*Satires* I.v.3 – 6) interestingly describes the activity of its boatmen and travelers. The marshes nearby (largely drained in the time of Mussolini) then added to the tedium of its life since mosquitoes and other insects were spawned there in great numbers. Horace complains that the waters about the town were bad, its rooms were crowded and expensive, and travelers could not sleep because of the noise of frogs and the sting of mosquitoes. It is easy to understand how much Paul needed encouragement when Christian brethren from Rome met him here!

E. J. V.

APPLE. *See* Plants.

APPROVE. The Gr. verb *dokimazō* and its derivatives are used particularly of testing and purifying metals, and hence metaphorically of the testing of the Christian in such passages as I Pet 1:7: "That the proof [*dokimon*] of your faith, being more precious than gold which is perishable, even though tested [*dokimazomenou*] by fire . . ." (NASB). Four main uses of "approval" are:

1. Self-examination of the Christian to prove himself as to his faith (II Cor 13:5), his own works (Gal 6:4), and particularly before attending communion (I Cor 11:28).

2. Examination of others, such as when Israel tested God (Heb 3:9); deacons are tested for office in the church (I Tim 3:10); and the spirit in others is tested to see if they are orthodox and have the Holy Spirit or the spirit of Antichrist (I Jn 4:1).

3. Self-preparation for God's approval. Paul urges young Timothy in II Tim 2:15, "Study [*spoudason*, lit., "hasten"] to show thyself approved [*dokimon*] unto God, a workman that

needeth not to be ashamed, rightly dividing the word of truth." The idea of preparation through study is so apparent in this verse that the translators chose to bring out this aspect rather than Paul's stress upon the need of speed in the preparation of oneself for the Lord's service.

4. God's testing of His servants through trials and tribulations before He is ready to open new and greater doors of service. James speaks of this in his epistle, urging one to "count it all joy when ye fall into divers temptations . . . for when he is tried, he shall receive the crown of life . . . " (Jas 1:2, 12). Just as examinations precede entry to high school, university, etc., so trials precede promotions in the life of the believer in God's economy.

At the same time, the Christian is constantly in danger of losing God's approval and blessing upon his ministry because of allowing his fallen nature to have its own sinful way. Therefore even Paul as a mature missionary writes: "I keep under my body, and bring it into subjection: lest by any means, when I have preached to others, I myself should be a castaway" (*adokimos*, "become disapproved," I Cor 9:27).

R. A. K.

APRICOT. *See* Plants.

APRON. *See* Dress.

AQABAH, GULF OF (ä′kȧ-bä). An arm of the Red Sea reaching N, located E of the Sinai peninsula and W of Midian in Arabia. Geologically it is part of the Arabah and Jordan rift which continues the fault northward. Elath (*q.v.*), a seaport, is located at its northern end. *See also* Ezion-geber.

AQUILA (ăk′wĭ-lȧ). A Jew from Pontus in N Asia Minor, resident in Rome, where he and his wife Priscilla (*q.v.*) became Christians. The edict of the emperor Claudius (*c.* A.D. 49) expelling Jews from Rome, forced this couple to migrate to Corinth, where they set up a branch of their tentmaking or leather-working business, and met Paul, who joined them because that was his trade too (Acts 18:1–3). When Paul left Corinth in A.D. 52, they accompanied him as far as Ephesus, where they settled for some years. Early in their residence there, they gave hospitality to the Alexandrian Jew Apollos (*q.v.*) and repaired deficiencies in his knowledge of Christianity (Acts 18:18–26). By A.D. 57 they were probably back in Rome, according to Rom 16:3. Claudius' expulsion edict doubtless lapsed for practical purposes with his death in A.D. 54. According to II Tim 4:19, they seem to have located in Ephesus again. The picture of such tradespeople moving from place to place, probably leaving branches of their business here and there in charge of a manager, is quite true to conditions of life under the Roman Empire. Wherever they lived, Aquila and Priscilla provided the local church with accommodation in their home (Rom 16:5; I Cor

16:19). On one occasion, possibly in Ephesus, they risked their lives for Paul (Rom 16:4).

F. F. B.

AR (är). A Moabite city located near the Arnon gorge E of the Salt Sea (Num 21:15, 28). When Isa 15:1 was written it had been destroyed. Its exact site has not yet been determined.

ARA (âr′ȧ). A descendant of Asher (I Chr 7:38).

ARAB (âr′ăb)

1. A city, identified with Khirbet er-Rabiyeh, seven miles SW of Hebron, allotted to the tribe of Judah after the conquest by Joshua (Josh 15:52).

2. A bedouin inhabitant of the Arabian peninsula, neighbors of the Hebrews to the S and E of Palestine. The word originally meant "waste" or "desloation." That they were tent-dwellers in the wilderness is indicated in Isa 13:20 and Jer 3:2.

The Arabah from Petra. JR

ARABAH (ăr′ȧ-bȧ). A Heb. word (′ărābâ) usually translated "plain" or "wilderness" in KJV. Literally the word means "arid"; hence it implies desert or wasteland (Job 39:6*a*; Isa 35:1, 6). With the article, this word is often transliterated in the RSV and in Josh 18:18 (KJV) as the name of the great Rift Valley extending S from the Sea of Galilee through the Dead Sea and continuing to the Gulf of Aqabah. Sometimes this name is connected with the northern part of this valley, called el-Ghôr by the Arabs (Deut 1:7; 3:17; Josh 11:2, 16) and sometimes with the portion S of the Dead Sea, which the Arabs call Wadi el-'Arabah (Deut 1:1; 2:8). This depression reaches the lowest point on the earth's surface at the Dead Sea (l,275 feet below sea level at the surface of the sea; in addition, the Dead Sea is 1,300 feet deep at its lowest point). It divides eastern from western Palestine, geographically and historically.

Archaeological remains confirm indications in the patriarchal narratives that this valley was more thickly populated in the Bronze Age than later. In ancient times, especially during Solomon's reign, copper and iron were mined and smelted in the southern Arabah, notably at Punon (modern Feinan), Mene'iyeh, Khirbet en-Nahas, and Mrashrash. Such deposits were known or foretold in Moses' day (Deut 8:9).

The plains ('arābôth) of Moab (Num 22:1; 26:3; etc.) are the Moabite portions of the Arabah. Likewise the plains of Jericho (Josh 4:13; 5:10; II Kgs 25:5; Jer 39:5) refer to the Arabah near that city.

The Sea of the Arabah (Deut 3:17; 4:49; Josh 3:16; 12:3; II Kgs 14:25, RSV) is the Dead Sea. The Brook of the Arabah (Amos 6:14, RSV) is a stream flowing into the Arabah and marking the southern boundary of Jeroboam II's kingdom, perhaps the valley of Zered (Wadi el-Hesa. Num 21:12; Deut 2:13). *See* Dead Sea; Jordan; Palestine II.B.3. f.

J. A. T.

ARABIA (*ȧ-rā'bǐ-ȧ*). A peninsula in SW Asia, bounded on the W by the Red Sea, on the S by the Indian Ocean, on the E by the Persian Gulf, and on the N by modern Jordan, Syria, and Iraq. Its area is almost one million square miles, about one-third the size of continental U.S.A. Classical geographers divided it into three parts: Arabia Petrea, including Sinai, Edom, Moab, and eastern Transjordan, named after the area's greatest city, Petra; Arabia Deserta, the Syrian and central deserts; and Arabia Felix, the "happy," fertile southern area.

In S Arabia kingdoms arose which owed their prosperity largely to trade and spices: the Sabean kingdom, or Seba (Ps 72:10; Isa 43:3; 45:14), organized at least as early as the 10th cen. B.C.; the Minaean kingdom of Ma'în *c.* 400 B.C.; the kingdom of Qataban in the 4th cen. B.C.; and the two Himyarite kingdoms from the 1st cen. B.C. to the 6th cen. A.D. Much of Arabia is desert, except for some fertile areas in the mountainous section of the S coast, which precipitates rainfall. Oases, including biblical Dedan, Tema, and Dumah, line the caravan routes along which perfumes of S Arabia and products of Africa and India were carried to Palestine and thence to Mediterranean countries.

Biblical references to Arabia sometimes include both the N and S portions (II Chr 9:14), but sometimes indicate only the NW portion, Arabia Petrea (Gal 1:17; 4:25). The many places in Arabia mentioned in the Bible show

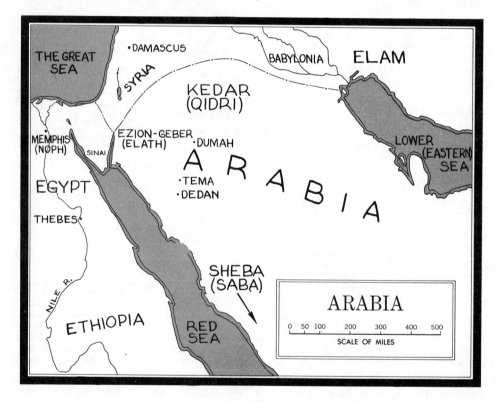

120

an early and detailed knowledge of this country and include Buz, Dedan, Dumah, Ephah, Havilah, Hazarmaveth, Hazor (Jer 49:28), Massa, Mesha, Midian, Parvaim, Raamah, Sabtah, Seba, Sephar, Sheba (called "the south" in Mt 12:42), "the hill country of the east" (Gen 10:30, RSV). Some important biblical events took place in the NW portion of Arabia, notably the giving of the law at Sinai and the wandering in the wilderness.

Products of Arabia mentioned in the Bible include frankincense and perfumes (I Kgs 10:2, 10), gold (I Kgs 10:2, 10, 15), precious stones (Ezk 27:22), onycha (Ex 30:34), coral and pearls (Job 28:18, RSV), camels (Gen 37:25), sheep and goats (Ezk 27:21), asses (Num 31:28), horses (Job 39:19–25), dates (Ex 15:27). Since A.D. 1932 oil has been marketed from the world's largest known petroleum deposits.

Wild animals connected with Arabia in the Bible are lion (Job 38:39–40, no longer found in Arabia), mountain goat (Job 39:1–4), wild ass (Job 39:5–8), wild ox or unicorn (Job 39:9–12, now extinct), jackal and hyena (Isa 34:13–14, RSV), gazelle (Isa 13:14, RSV), poisonous serpents (Num 21:6), and flying, i.e., springing, serpents (Isa 14:29). The following birds are associated with Arabia: raven (Job 38:41), ostrich (Job 39:13–18, last seen in Arabia in A.D. 1941), hawk (Job 39:26), eagle (Job 39:27–30), quail (Num 11:31), owl and kite (Isa 34:15, RSV).

See Arabians.

J. A. T.

ARABIANS (á-rā'bĭ-áns). The Heb. *'ărab* literally denotes "arid," the dry steppe land. The Arabah (*'arabâ*), the dry Dead Sea valley, comes from the same word root. Hence the *'ar^ebîm* were the wanderers in the desert wilderness, or nomads (II Chr 17:11; 21:16; 22:1; 26:7). In Assyrian cuneiform records they are called *Arubu* and *Aribi*, a term used for the nomads of Media as well as for those of Arabia. Even the Koran uses *a'rab* (plural of *'arab*) for the Bedouin, as contrasted with the settled people.

As for the inhabitants of Arabia, some of the sons of Joktan (Gen 10:25–30), of Cush (Gen 10:7), of Keturah (Gen 25:1–4), and of Ishmael (Gen 25:13–16) can be identified with places and tribes in Arabia. Other Arab tribes mentioned in the OT include the Amalekites, Hagarites, Kedarites, Kenites, Meunim (identified by LXX with Minaeans), and perhaps (though some of these may be Canaanites) the Gezrites, Kadmonites, and Kenizzites. Another name for Arabians is "children of the east" (*b^enê qedem*, Jud 6:3). *See* Arabia.

Historical events involving Arabians in the OT include the Midianite raids on Palestine in the time of Gideon (Jud 6–8), the first recorded large-scale use of camels; and the Queen of Sheba's visit to Solomon (I Kgs 10:1–10), reflecting the wealth and commerce of S

Arabia. Arabians paid tribute to Jehoshaphat (II Chr 17:11), raided Jerusalem in the reign of Jehoram (II Chr 21:16–17; 22:1), and were defeated by Uzziah (II Chr 26:7). The conquest of N Arabian tribes by the Assyrians is referred to in Isa 21:13–17 and by the Babylonians in Jer 25:23–24; 49:28–30. By the 5th cen. B.C. Arabs pushed the Edomites out of Mount Seir (Ob 7). Nehemiah was opposed by Geshem the Arabian (Neh 2:19), who is known from inscriptions as king of Kedar, a tribe who then dominated the N Arabians.

In the Apocrypha, "Arab" (e.g., I Macc 11:16–17) usually refers to the Nabataeans (I Macc 5:25), who made Petra their capital and controlled the trade routes around Palestine. They were sometimes allied with the Maccabees (I Macc 9:35) and sometimes with the Syrians (I Macc 5:39; 12:31). *See* Nabataeans.

Arabians were among the Jews and proselytes who heard the gospel in Jerusalem at Pentecost (Acts 2:11). They may have come from the Nabataean kingdom in Transjordan, or perhaps from farther S. The governor of Damascus, representing the Nabataean king Aretas IV (9 B.C.–A.D. 40), set guards to catch Paul, who nevertheless escaped (II Cor 11:32–33).

In culture, Arabians are Semites (Gen 10:25–30), as indicated by their languages. N Arabians lived in the wilderness (Jer 3:2) in tents (Isa 13:20) made of black goats' hair (Song 1:5). They were camel riders (Gen 37:25). Arabian caravans brought spices, gold, and precious stones from S Arabia, and sheep and goats of N Arabia to Palestine and Syria (I Kgs 10:2; Ezk 27:20–22), and Arab merchants also transferred products of Africa and India (I Kgs 10:22). Jer 9:26; 25:23; 49:32 (RSV) mention the Arab custom of cropping the hair, which is referred to by Herodotus (iii.8) and is depicted in Assyrian bas reliefs of Arabs fighting from their camels.

Arabia was known for its wise men (I Kgs 4:30), among whom were Agur (Prov 30:1) and Lemuel (Prov 31:1), two kings of Massa, a tribe of Ishmael (Gen 25:14). The wisdom book of Job reflects its background in NW Arabia. The advanced culture of the ancient S Arabians is illustrated by the great temple of Ilumquh, the moon-god at Ma'rib, the Sabaean capital; large dams and canals for irrigation; sculpture in stone; casting in bronze; goldsmith's work; and by many religious and historical inscriptions.

The general Arabian term for god was *il* (cf. Heb. *'el*) or *ilah* (cf. Heb. *'elôah*), but the ancient Arabians revered many gods, including a moon-god; a sun-goddess, Shamash; and their son, the morning star, 'Athtar. The Koran mentions several pagan gods: al-Lat, al-'Uzza, and al-Manat (Qur'an 53:19, 20), Wadd, Suwa', Yaghuth Ya'uq, and Nasr (71:23). Arabians feared demons called jinn (Qur'an, 72).

Like the Israelites, the Arabians practiced circumcision, pilgrimage, and sacrifice, including a sin offering. Among their religious functionaries were priest-diviners and seers.

Bibliography. R. L. Bowen and F. P. Albright, *Archaeological Discoveries in South Arabia,* Vol. II, Baltimore: Johns Hopkins Univ. Press, 1958. CornPBE, pp. 116 – 120. Butrus Abd al-Malik and John A. Thompson, "Arabia," BW, pp. 45 – 50. P. K. Hitti, *History of the Arabs,* 6th ed., London: Macmillan, 1956. J. A. Montgomery, *Arabia and the Bible,* Philadelphia: Univ. of Pennsylvania Press, 1934. G. Ryckmans, *Les religions arabes préislamiques,* 2nd ed., Louvain: Publications Universitaires, 1951. J. Starcky, "The Nabataeans: A Historical Sketch," BA, XVIII (1955), 84 – 106. G. W. Van Beek, "Recovering the Ancient Civilization of Arabia," BA, XV (1952), 2 – 18; "Frankincense and Myrrh," BA, XXIII (1960), 70-95. Brian Doe, *Southern Arabia,* New York: McGraw-Hill, 1971.

            J. A. T.

ARAD (âr′ăd)

1. A son of Beriah, a Benjamite (I Chr 8:15).
2. ·A Canaanite city in the Negeb whose king fought against the Israelites when they were on their way to Mount Hor (Num 21:1, 33:40, RSV). In the KJV of these verses "king Arad" should read "king of Arad." Joshua later vanquished its king (Josh 12:14). Arad is mentioned again in Jud 1:16 as a city on the border of the wilderness of Judah where the Kenites settled.

The site has generally been identified with Tell ′Arâd, about 17 miles S of Hebron, but the excavations carried out there under the direction of Y. Aharoni and R. Amiran since 1962 have shown that Tell ′Arâd was inhabited only during two periods: from *c.* 3200 to *c.* 2900 B.C. and from the 10th cen. B.C. to the Byzantine period. Hence this site was uninhabited during the period of the wilderness wandering of Israel and at the time of Joshua's conquest, and the Arad of Moses' and Joshua's time must have been somewhere else. The excavators have therefore come to the conclusion that Tell ′Arâd represents another Arad which, although not mentioned in the Bible, appears in the victory inscription of Pharaoh Shishak, while the Canaanite Arad of the Bible existed at Tell Malḥata, *c.* eight miles SW of Tell ′Arâd, where Middle and Late Bronze Age Canaanite remains have been found (IEJ, XII [1962], 144 – 145; Yohanan Aharoni and Ruth Amiran, "Arad: a Biblical City in Southern Palestine," *Archaeology,* XVII [1964], 43 – 53). B. Mazar argues on the basis of Jud 1:16 – 17 that the entire region of the eastern Negeb was called Negeb Arad, so that there was no *town* of Arad during the 2nd mil. B.C. ("The Sanctuary of Arad and the Family of Hobab the Kenite," JNES, XXIV [1965], 297 – 303).

            S. H. H.

During Solomon's reign a strong square fortress with casemate walls *c.* 165 feet on a side and a typical Solomonic city gate was erected on Tell′Arâd to guard the kingdom's SE border

with Edom. After this fortress was destroyed, probably by Pharaoh Shishak, another with a solid wall 13 feet thick and a second smaller wall on the lower slope was built in the 9th cen. A water tunnel below the latter wall enabled water carriers using donkeys to fill large plastered cisterns beneath the citadel buildings. Over 200 ostraca were found during five seasons of excavations, over half of them written in Heb. from the time of the monarchy. Seventeen are addressed to Eliashib, evidently the commander of the fortress in the time of Nebuchadnezzar. One of these mentions the "house of Yahweh" and was apparently sent from Jerusalem. Another orders men to be sent from Arad to Ramath-negeb against a threatening Edomite attack (Y. Aharoni, "Three Hebrew Ostraca from Arad," BASOR #197 [1970], pp. 16–42).

The most surprising discovery at Tell ′Arâd was an Israelite temple within the citadel rebuilt several times and in use from the 10th to the 7th cen. B.C. It evidently functioned as a royal border sanctuary until King Josiah's reform (II Kgs 23:5, 8) along with other such probable temples at Gilgal, Beer-sheba, and Geba (Amos 5:5; 8:14; II Kgs 23:8), just as the northern kingdom had border temples at Dan and Bethel. Its E-W axis was the same as that of the tabernacle and Solomon's temple, and in a courtyard until the time of Hezekiah's reign (cf. his reform, II Kgs 18:4) there was an altar for burnt offerings built of many stones exactly five cubits square and three cubits high, as in the tabernacle (Ex 27:1). Heb. ostraca found in these levels contain names of priestly families known from the OT (Y. Aharoni, "Arad: Its Inscriptions and Temple," BA, XXXI [1968], 1 – 32).

            J. R.

ARAH (âr′ä). A man of the tribe of Asher (I Chr 7:39). His numerous descendants returned from the Exile with Zerubbabel (Ezr 2:5; Neh 6:18; 7:10).

ARAM (âr′ăm), **ARAMEANS** (ăr′ä-mē′ănz). Aram was the name of at least three men in the Bible:

1. The fifth son of Shem (Gen 10:22 – 23). From this lineage came several Semitic groups.
2. Son of Kemuel, nephew of Abraham (Gen 22:20 – 21). This kin group settled about Haran, whereas Abraham moved to Canaan. Hence Aram came to designate a land area and a language called Aramaic.
3. The third son of Shamer of the tribe of Asher (I Chr 7:34).

As the name of a people called the Arameans, the term occurs about 65 times in the books of Samuel, Kings, and Chronicles. Following the LXX (*Syria*), the KJV calls these people Syrians (Amos 1:5; 9:7; Isa 7:2, 4, 5, 8; 9:12; 17:3; Jer 35:11; Ezk 16:57; 27:16).

As a reference to the land of the Arameans, the translation "Syria" appears in KJV in

II Sam 15:8; Hos 12:12, but in Num 23:7 KJV has Aram. Of the people and the land together, or of the gods of that country, "Syria" occurs in Jud 10:6; Isa 7:8 and more than 40 times in Kings and Chronicles.

Aram is most likely a non-Semitic appellation. In geographical terms Aram seemed to refer to that land area which was bounded by the Tigris River, the Arabian Desert, the Taurus Mountains, and the land of Phoenicia. Assyrian inscriptions usually limit Aram to the plains E of the Euphrates River.

Sometimes Aram is connected with other names, which seem to designate limited land areas. Aram of Damascus (II Sam 8:6, RSV) would refer to territory immediately about Damascus. Aram-maacah (I Chr 19:6, RSV), Beth-rehob and Zobah populated by Syrians or Arameans (II Sam 10:6) all designate small provinces E of the Jordan and NE of Galilee. The KJV uses Syria instead of Aram in each of the above instances.

Late in the 3rd mil. B.C., nomadic Arameans pushed westward out of the NE section of the Arabian Desert and were deflected to the NW by the Amorite settlements on the Euphrates River. They settled around Haran, sometimes called Aram-Naharaim (KJV has Mesopotamia in Gen 24:10; Deut 23:4; Jud 3:8). See also Padan-aram (q.v.) in Gen 25:20; 28:2, 6, 7; 31:18; 33:18, and Padan in Gen 48:7. From Aram came Rebekah (Gen 24) and to it Jacob fled (Gen 28).

The Arameans are first mentioned in Akkad. texts, perhaps c. 2250 B.C., but certainly in some around 2000 B.C. From the Amorite city of Mari have come texts which refer to the Arameans as early as the 18th cen. B.C. Tablets from Ugarit (14th – 13th cen. B.C.) also mention Aram, as well as the Amarna letters.

By the 12th cen. B.C., Aram was strong enough to make itself felt in international affairs. By the 9th cen. B.C. it had become an effective buffer state between Assyria and Palestine. Damascus, a fruitful oasis on the plain E of the Anti-Lebanon range, was made the capital of Aram (Syria).

David conquered Syria and controlled it during his reign (II Sam 8:5 – 6; I Chr 18:5 – 6). After the breakup of the kingdom during the reign of Rehoboam, the Syrians became independent, with the dynasty of Hezion in power-er.

During the kingdom period, Israel, Judah, and Syria were a quarrelsome triad. At one time Judah and Syria teamed up against Israel (I Kgs 15:18 – 20). At another time Israel and Syria joined forces against Judah (II Kgs 16:5); and according to Assyrian inscriptions, Israel under Jehu united with Ben-hadad (q.v.) of Syria and others to stop the westward march of the Assyrian Shalmanezer III at Qarqar in 853 B.C. Finally, Ahaz of Judah joined with Assyria against Israel and Syria (II Kgs 16:7 – 18). As a result, Tiglath-pileser III destroyed Damascus in 732 B.C., and the power of Aram (Syria) was

broken forever. Many of its people were carried into captivity by the Assyrians. *See* Aramaic; Syria; Damascus.

Bibliography. R. A. Bowman, "Arameans, Aramaic, and the Bible," JNES, VII (1948), 65 – 90. CornPBE, pp. 121 – 126. A. Malamat, "The Kingdom of David and Solomon in Its Contact with Aram Naharaim," BA, XXI (1958), 96 – 102. Benjamin Mazar, "The Aramean Empire and Its Relations with Israel," BA, XXV (1962), 98 – 120. Roger T. O'Callaghan, *Aram Naharaim,* Rome: Pontifical Biblical Institute, 1948. Merrill F. Unger, *Israel and the Arameans of Damascus,* London: James Clarke, 1957.

G. H. L.

ARAMAIC (ăr′á-mā′ĭk). A general term for some Semitic dialects related to Hebrew. Besides isolated words in the OT, Aramaic is found in Ezr 4:8 – 6:18; 7:12 – 26; Dan 2:4b – 7:28; Jer 10:11. Some Aramaic expressions occur in the NT. The originals of some of the apocryphal and pseudepigraphal books were written in Aramaic. The translations of the OT into Aramaic are called Targums. Inscriptions in an Aramaic alphabet on stone from Syria are dated as early as the 10th and 9th cen. B.C.

In their rise to power, the Assyrians developed Aramaic into the common language of their empire, for rulers and merchants. Inscriptions of this official Aramaic occur on weights, seals, pottery, and on cuneiform tablets as summaries of their content. At Sinjirli, a statue of Bar Rekub shows a scribe as though writing Aramaic letters. There is reference to Aramaic as a diplomatic medium in II Kgs 18:13 – 37. A bronze bowl with Aramaic letters has been found in Greece, and inscriptions have been found in Egypt dating from the Assyrian period.

Both the neo-Babylonian (605 – 538 B.C.) and Persian (538 – 330 B.C.) empires utilized Aramaic in their correspondence, of which abundant samples have been found. The Borchardt collection has 13 letters in Aramaic written on leather. These came from Egypt and were official Persian correspondence. Aramaic written on papyri has been found in Egypt, the most famous coming from Elephantine and dating from the 5th cen. B.C. *See* Elephantine Papyri.

During the Exile the Jews adopted Aramaic as their tongue and borrowed the Aramaic script for their Scriptures. In Jesus' day Galilean Aramaic was common. Among the Christians who went to the upper Euphrates Valley the language soon became known as Syriac, written with a different script.

G. H. L.

ARARAT (ăr′á-răt). A high plateau on the far E border of modern Turkey, N of biblical Haran and SE of the Black Sea. The Tigris and Euphrates Rivers are formed by the confluence of streams which spring up in this region. Gen 8:4 records that Noah's ark rested "upon the mountains of Ararat" after the Flood. This does not necessarily mean that the ark stood upon one of the two peaks which rise from the plateau. These peaks, Great Ararat, which rises some 17,000 feet above sea level, and Little Ararat, which is nearly 13,000 feet high, have been given the name of the region of which they are a part, just as Sinai may be either the mountain on which the commandments were given or the desert or peninsula surrounding this summit. In II Kgs 19:37 and Isa 37:38, the "land of Ararat" is translated "land of Armenia" in the KJV. In Jer 51:27, the "kingdom of Ararat" (Urartu of Akkad. inscriptions, e.g., ANET, pp. 305, 316) is one of the kingdoms summoned to destroy Babylon. *See* Armenia.

Since World War II several expeditions have explored in this region looking for Noah's ark. Their efforts have frequently been hampered by Soviet suspicion that continued activity near the Russian border involved spying. A large wooden structure has been found encased in ice on Mount Ararat. Wood samples taken from the site have been tested by the carbon 14 method of dating, but interpretations of the results conflict. In any case, these materials do not seem to date early enough to have anything to do with Noah. Much further investigation of the area will evidently be required.

G. A. A.

ARAUNAH (*ȧ-rô′nȧ*). A Jebusite, an inhabitant of Jebus ("which is Jerusalem," Jud 19:10; I Chr 11:4). The non-Semitic form of his name may stem either from the Hittite title *arawanis*

meaning "noble," or from the Hurrian title *iwirne* meaning "chief, ruler, lord." In II Sam 24:16 his name is preceded by the definite article in Heb. and explained in v. 23 as *hammelek*, "the king." In either case it would tend to confirm the foreign ancestry of some of Jerusalem's aboriginal inhabitants (Ezk 16:3).

Araunah (also called Ornan, I Chr 21:15) owned a threshing floor on Mount Moriah which he sold to King David as a place for an alter to Yahweh. God had smitten Israel three days with a plague and 70,000 died because of King David's sin in numbering the people (II Sam 24:10 – 15; I Chr 21:1, 8 – 14). According to God's instructions, the prophet Gad told the king to build an altar on the threshing floor. Araunah would have given the land and oxen for sacrifice, but David felt he must pay fully (50 silver shekels in II Sam 24; 600 gold shekels in I Chr 21, the higher figure probably for the whole area). Heaven answered by sending fire to consume David's offerings (I Chr 21:26) and Yahweh stopped the plague. David determined this as the place for the temple, and it was here that Solomon later built the temple (II Chr 3:1).

W. G. B.

ARBA (är′bȧ). A leader of the Anakim and founder of the city of Hebron (Josh 14:15), whose original name, Kiriath-arba, means the "city of Arba" (also Josh 15:13; 21:11).

ARBATHITE (är′bȧ-thīt). Abialbon, one of David's mighty men, was so designated (II Sam 23:31; cf. I Chr 11:32). The word indicates an inhabitant of Beth-arabah.

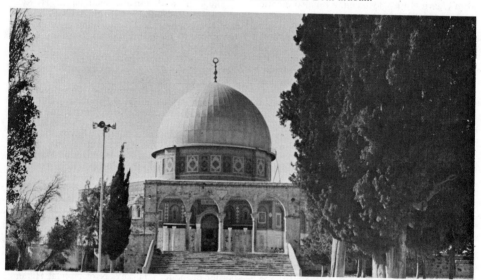

The Dome of the Rock on the site of the threshing floor of Araunah. HFV

ARBITE (är'bĭt). A dweller in the town of Arab (Josh 15:52). Paarai, one of David's warriors, is so designated (II Sam 23:35).

ARCH. The English word "arch" occurs 15 times in the KJV and only in the plural (Ezk 40:16 – 36). It is the translation of two similar forms of the Heb. word *'êlām,* which is related to Heb. *'ûlām,* "porch," "vestibule." The words thus mean generally "porch," differing slightly in emphasis. They designate an entry room or pillared hall or covering of some sort in front of a building or gate. The three main gates to the outer court of Ezekiel's temple are described as each having a vestibule at its inner end (Ezk 40:7 – 26), while each of the three gates leading to the inner courtyard have a vestibule at its outer end (Ezk 40:27 – 37).

The earliest known true arch in Palestine occurs at Lachish in a 5th cen. B.C. Persian residence. The arch and vault became common in the great buildings of Herod the Great's reign. The arch as a weight-carrying device was developed in Mesopotamia and then borrowed by other countries. This architectural feature was highly perfected and widely utilized by Roman engineers of the empire period. Greeks and Egyptians generally employed the post-and-lintel type of construction, though the corbeled arch was used by the early Aegean builders (e.g., in the Mycenaean "beehive" tombs).

See Architecture; Porch.

H. G. S.

ARCHAEOLOGY

Nature and Purpose of Biblical Archaeology

The word "archaeology" comes from two Gr. words, *archaios* and *logos,* which mean literally "a study of ancient things." But the term has been much more refined than that and usually applies to a study of excavated materials belonging to a former era. Bible archaeology may be defined as an examination of ancient things which have been lost and found again, as those recovered objects relate to the study of Scripture and the portrayal of life in Bible times.

While archaeology is defined variously in the popular mind, it is basically a science. Knowledge in the field is acquired by systematic observation or study, and facts discovered are evaluated and classified into an organized body of information. Moreover, archaeology is a composite science because it seeks assistance from many other sciences, such as chemistry, anthropology, and zoology.

Of course, some subjects of archaeological investigation (such as obelisks and temples of Egypt and the Parthenon at Athens) have never been "lost" at all, but perhaps a knowledge of their original form and purpose and the meaning of inscriptions on them have been lost.

Corbeled arch at Mycenae. HFV

Functions of Biblical Archaeology

Archaeology performs the very useful service of helping us to understand the Bible. It reveals what life was like in biblical times, what obscure passages of Scripture really mean, and how the historical narratives and context of the Bible are to be understood.

Archaeological study also helps to confirm the accuracy of the biblical text and its contents. It has shown the falsity of some higher critical theories of biblical interpretation. It has helped to establish the accuracy of the Gr. and Heb. originals and to show that the biblical text has been transmitted with a remarkable degree of accuracy. And it has confirmed the accuracy of many passages of Scripture, e.g., statements concerning numerous kings and the whole patriarchal narrative.

One should not be dogmatic in his statements concerning confirmation, however. Archaeology has also created numerous problems for the Bible student. For instance, recovered Babylonian and Sumerian accounts of the creation and the Flood having striking parallels to the OT and questions of origin plague the Bible scholar. One is also troubled by the problem of interpreting the relationship between the Ras Shamra texts and the Mosaic code. But one can confidently believe that answers to the problems will be forthcoming. To date there has not been an instance of archaeology conclusively demonstrating the Bible to be in error

Why Ancient Cities and Civilizations Disappeared

It may be argued that ancient civilizations and cities disappeared because of the judgment of God. Scripture is full of such indications. But there are simple naturalistic explanations that can also be briefly noted. Cities were usually built on easily defensible sites possessing a good water supply and located near important trade routes.

Such sites were at a premium in the ancient Near East. So if some catastrophe brought about the destruction of a town, the tendency was to rebuild on the same location. A town might be largely destroyed by earthquake or invasion. Famine or pestilence might depopulate a city or territory. In the latter instance, the inhabitants might conclude that the gods had leveled a curse on them and they might fear to return. Uninhabited sites would quickly fall into ruins. And when former inhabitants returned or when new settlers came into the area, they usually simply smoothed out the rubble and built a new city. Thus mounds or tells rose up with many superimposed layers of habitation. Sometimes the water supply dried up, rivers changed their courses, trade arteries were rerouted or political fortunes changed—resulting in the permanent abandonment of a site.

Excavating a Mound

The biblical archaeologist may undertake excavation of a mound for many reasons. If the mound he attacks is known to cover a biblical site, he probably seeks to uncover the layer or layers of occupation having relevance for the biblical narrative. He may be looking for a city which is known to have existed but has not yet been identified. Perhaps he seeks to resolve doubts concerning proposed identification of a site. Possibly he is searching for information concerning Bible characters or events that will help to illuminate the Scripture narrative.

Once the excavator has chosen a site to dig and has made proper arrangements to do so (including permits, finances, equipment and staff), he is ready to begin operations. A careful surface exploration is usually carried out first to learn all that can be ascertained from pottery or other artifacts on the surface, to discover whether a configuration of ground houses the remains of a building, or to figure out something of the history of the mound. Then a contour map of the mound is drawn and a sector or sectors chosen where digging is to be carried on during a season of excavation. These sectors are then usually subdivided into one meter squares to facilitate labeling of finds.

The usual method of excavation today is stratigraphic. That is, each successive layer or stratum of occupation is carefully uncovered until bedrock is reached. All objects are photographed where found, and then carefully lifted from location and labeled and recorded. The pieces of a broken jar are put in a basket and later glued together. Since stratigraphic excavation is so expensive, time-consuming, and destructive, the tendency is to clear only part of

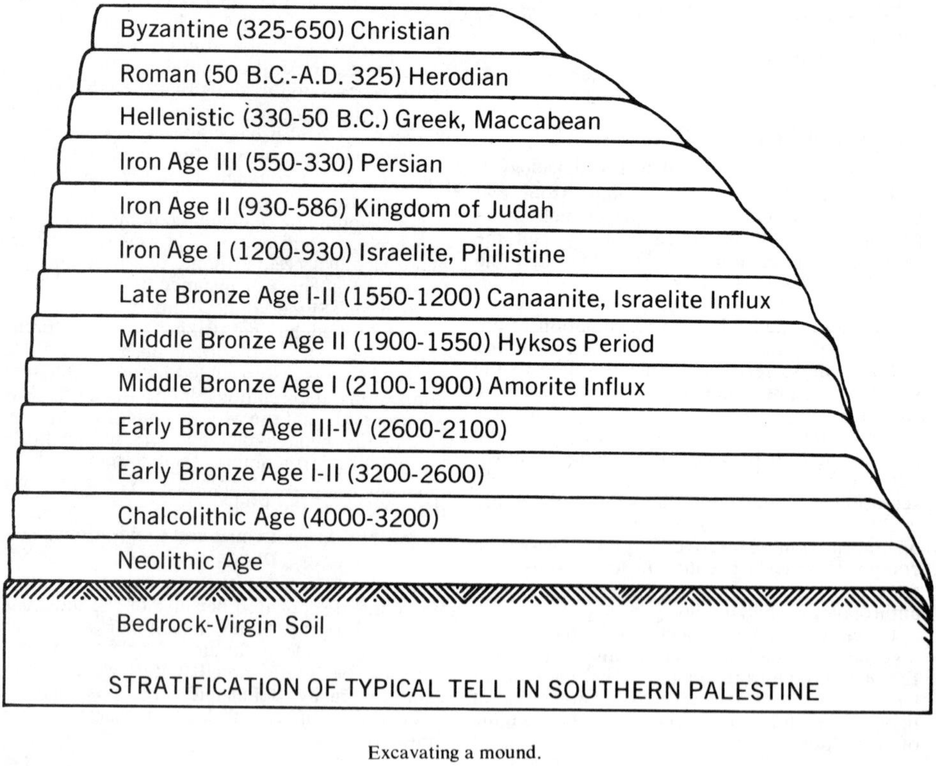

Byzantine (325-650) Christian

Roman (50 B.C.-A.D. 325) Herodian

Hellenistic (330-50 B.C.) Greek, Maccabean

Iron Age III (550-330) Persian

Iron Age II (930-586) Kingdom of Judah

Iron Age I (1200-930) Israelite, Philistine

Late Bronze Age I-II (1550-1200) Canaanite, Israelite Influx

Middle Bronze Age II (1900-1550) Hyksos Period

Middle Bronze Age I (2100-1900) Amorite Influx

Early Bronze Age III-IV (2600-2100)

Early Bronze Age I-II (3200-2600)

Chalcolithic Age (4000-3200)

Neolithic Age

Bedrock-Virgin Soil

STRATIFICATION OF TYPICAL TELL IN SOUTHERN PALESTINE

Excavating a mound.

a layer. In that way a fairly clear picture of the history of the mound may be drawn and there will be something left for future excavators to evaluate if they desire to do so.

Archaeology and the Text of the Bible

While most people think of huge monuments and museum pieces and exploits of kings when biblical archaeology is referred to, they have become increasingly aware that inscriptions and manuscripts also have an important contribution to make to biblical study. Although most archaeological work used to center on biblical history, today it is increasingly concerned with the text of the Bible.

Intensive study of the more than 3,000 NT Gr. MSS dating from the 2nd cen. A.D. and following has shown that the NT text has been remarkably preserved in transmission from the 3rd cen. to the present. Not one doctrine has been perverted, and Westcott and Hort concluded that only about one word in a thousand of the Gr. original has serious question upon it.

It is one thing to demonstrate that the NT text has been remarkably preserved from the 2nd cen. to the present; it is quite another to show that the Gospels, for instance, did not gradually evolve into their present form during the early centuries of the Christian era or that Christ was not gradually deified by Christian legend. At the turn of the 20th cen. a new science was born that would help to show that neither the Gospels nor the Christian view of Christ evolved into their present form. B. P. Grenfell and A. S. Hunt excavated in the Fayum district of Egypt (1896–1906), finding large quantities of papyri and launching the science of papyrology.

The papyri, written on a kind of paper made from the papyrus reed of Egypt (*see* Papyrus), include a wide variety of topics presented in several languages. The number of fragmentary papyrus MSS containing portions of the NT now stands at 77. These fragments help to confirm the general text found in the longer vellum MSS dating to the 4th and following centuries, and to bridge more of the gap between the later MSS and the originals.

Phenomenal has been the impact of papyrology upon biblical study. Many of the papyri date to the first three centuries after Christ. Thus it is possible to establish the development in the grammar of that period, and on the basis of the argument from historical grammar, to date the composition of NT books to the 1st cen. A.D. In fact, one fragment of the Gospel of John found in Egypt can be dated on the basis of paleography *c.* A.D. 125. Allowing time for the book to get into circulation, a date toward the end of the 1st cen. must be assigned to the fourth Gospel—and that is what Christian tradition has always assigned to it. No one doubts that the other three Gospels date to a period somewhat earlier than John. If the NT books were written during the 1st cen., they were written close to the events they record and

there was no time for an evolutionary development to occur.

But the contributions of the mass of papyri of all types do not stop here. They have shown that NT Gr. is not some form of language invented by NT writers, as formerly thought. Instead it was generally the language of the people of the first centuries of the Christian era. Fewer than 50 words in the NT were coined by the apostles. Moreover, the papyri have shown that NT grammar was good grammar, judged by 1st cen. standards rather than those of the classical period. Furthermore, the non-biblical Gr. papyri have helped to clear up the meaning of uncertainly understood NT words and to throw new light on others fairly well understood.

The story of OT textual criticism can hardly be told here. Suffice it to say that OT MSS are not as close to their originals in time as those of the NT, but they were copied with greater care and have fewer variations.

Until recently, the oldest-known Heb. MS of any length did not date earlier than the first part of the 10th cen. after Christ, and the oldest complete Heb. Bible dates about a century later. Then, in the spring of 1948, the religious and academic worlds were rocked with the announcement that an ancient Isaiah manuscript had been found in a cave near the NW corner of the Dead Sea. Since that time a total of 11 caves in that area have disgorged their treasures of scrolls or fragments. Tens of thousands of leather fragments and some of papyrus have been recovered. While most of the materials are non-biblical, fragments representing over a hundred MSS bear Scripture portions. So far, all OT books except Esther are represented in the finds. As might be expected, fragments of OT books quoted most in the NT (Deuteronomy, Isaiah, Psalms) are most numerous there also. The longest and most nearly intact biblical scrolls include two of Isaiah, one of Psalms and one of Leviticus.

The significance of the Dead Sea Scrolls is tremendous. They have pushed the history of the OT text back 1,000 years (after much controversy the date has been assigned to the first centuries B.C. and A.D.). They have provided an abundance of critical material for research on the OT comparable to what has been available to NT scholars for many years. Third, the Dead Sea Scrolls have provided a more adequate context for the NT, demonstrating, for instance, the essential Jewish background of the Gospel of John — rather than a Gr. background as scholars have frequently asserted. Fourth, they help to establish the accuracy of the OT text. The Septuagint (Gr. OT) has been shown by studies in the scrolls to be more nearly accurate than often thought. And it has been demonstrated that there were other families of texts besides the Masoretic (traditional), which has served as the text of Heb. Bibles for so long. Yet, when all of the evidence is in, perhaps it will be demonstrated that the true text of the

OT is 95 percent or more what has been in the Masoretic Text all along. In this connection, it is interesting to note that one of the Isaiah MSS tallies almost exactly with the Masoretic Text. Fifth, the scrolls provide new material to help establish the meaning of Heb. words. *See* Dead Sea Scrolls.

The Dead Sea Scrolls are not the only important textual discovery of this century bearing on OT textual study. The Ras Shamra texts of the 15th and 14th cen. B.C. (see below under excavations) unearthed in 1929 ff. have done much to put Heb. religious practices into their proper context and to shed light on the meaning of certain Heb. words. The Mari and Nuzu texts (see below) have also played their part in illuminating the OT text. *See* Bible Manuscripts.

The Temple of Zeus at Athens. HFV

Excavations of Biblical Sites

No two writers will agree on a selection of excavated biblical sites for comment in a short survey such as this. Since hundreds of cities have now received archaeological attention, the choice becomes increasingly difficult. Some have been chosen because of their importance in ancient times, some because they figure prominently in the Bible narratve, and others because they illuminate the biblical narrative.

1. *Antioch of Syria.* Excavations were carried on at this early headquarters of Christianity (1932 – 39) by Princeton University, with the cooperation of the Baltimore Museum of Art, the Worcester Art Museum, and the National Museum of France, under the general direction of Richard Stillwell. The main features of the city were recovered, and the near equivalent was accomplished for the suburb of Daphne and the port of Seleucia. The acropolis of the city was discovered on Mount Stauris; the location of the two principal intersecting

colonnaded streets was plotted; and the circus, probably erected originally in the 1st cen. A.D., was found and excavated. Villas, aqueducts, and baths in abundance were found at Antioch and her suburbs. Several churches were uncovered, but none date to the 1st cen. Probably most amazing of all the finds at Antioch were the well executed mosaics, dating from the 1st to the 6th cen. after Christ. *See* Antioch.

2. *Athens.* Archaeological work at Athens began after the Greek Archaeological Society was founded in 1837. Since then French, German, American, British, Austrian, Italian, and Swedish schools have been established there, in that order. Excavations of structures or areas familiar to Paul during his ministry at Athens include the Gr. and Rom. marketplaces, the acropolis and the structures of the S slope of the acropolis, and the great temple of Zeus. The most prodigious single undertaking involved clearance of 16 acres of the Gr. agora by the American School of Classical Studies since 1931, largely financed by John D. Rockefeller, Jr. Gr. archaeologists excavated the acropolis down to bedrock 1884 – 1891, and the 367- by-315-foot Roman market between 1890 and 1931. The Greek Archaeological Society (1886 – 1901) and the German School (1922 – 23) worked on the temple of Zeus which measured 286 by 62 feet. *See* Athens.

3. *Babylon.* Knowledge of ancient Babylon comes from the excavations of Robert Koldewey, who excavated there for the German Oriental Society, 1899–1914. Since he found the earliest strata of occupation to be under seepage water, nearly everything uncovered dated to the time of Nebuchadnezzar, except for one

Reconstruction of Babylon (after Unger). ORINST

spot where a few houses of the Hammurabi period were reached. Despite the general destruction of the city, the excavators were able to gain an accurate picture of the layout of the city, to outline its major buildings, procession street, and the famous Ishtar Gate. One of the major structures was the great brick ziggurat or staged tower some 295 feet high and composed of seven successively smaller stages or stories, on the topmost level of which stood a temple. *See* Babylon.

Remains of the Roman Period at Caesarea. IIS

The Temple of Apollo at Corinth. HFV

4. *Caesarea.* Built by Herod the Great and dedicated about 10 B.C., Caesarea (*c.* 25 miles S of Haifa) was the Rom. capital of Palestine in subsequent decades. Here Paul was imprisoned for two years and here Origen and Eusebius lived and ministered. The Crusaders occupied the site for almost two centuries, and it has lain in ruins ever since the Muslims destroyed it in the 13th cen. The massive crusader walls and some adjacent areas were excavated by the Israelis in 1960. In the same year the Link Expedition conducted extensive underwater exploration around the harbor of this first good artificial port the Hebrews built on the Mediterranean. The circular breakwater which enclosed the harbor was charted and numerous pieces of pottery and other artifacts were found, the most important of which was a coin interpreted as picturing the ancient harbor and waterfront. In 1961 Italian archaeologists discovered a stone inscription in the theater bearing the name of Pontius Pilate. *See* Caesarea.

5. *Corinth.* Corinth was the great commercial center of Greece where Paul ministered for 18 months. In 1896 the American School of Classical Studies began excavation here under the general direction of R. B. Richardson and has continued intermittently ever since, working on the city proper, the acropolis, and the nearby sanctuary of Poseidon where the Isthmian games were held. Of special interest to the Bible student is the excavation of the great agora, or commercial and political center of the city, measuring 600 feet E and W, and 300 N and S. In the center of the agora still stands the bema or judgment seat at which Paul appeared before Gallio. *See* Corinth.

6. *Ephesus.* John T. Wood launched archaeological work at Ephesus in 1863 when he began his search for the great temple of Diana. This he finally located in 1869, and then spent five more years excavating the structure. At the same time he cleared the immense theater (Acts 19:31) on the W slope of Mount Pion. In 1897 Austrian excavators began to work on the city proper and have, with interruptions, continued there to the present. They have uncovered the street that led to the harbor and a great street that ran through the city, as well as numerous structures along both sides of the thoroughfare. The great 360-foot square Hellenistic agora is very largely excavated, and shops of silversmiths have been found there. *See* Ephesus.

Shops adjoining the Hellenistic Agora at Ephesus. HFV

Entrance to the water supply system, Hazor.
HFV

7. *Ezion-geber.* Ezion-geber (Tell el-Kheleifeh) is known in the OT as the headquarters of Solomon's fleet (1 Kgs 9:26) and was built by him at the N end of the Gulf of Aqabah. Nelson Glueck's excavation of the site in 1938 revealed that it was also an important copper smelting center where partially roasted ore from the Arabah to the N was prepared for shipment. Glueck also found that there were five main periods of occupation beginning with Solomon. What were thought to be blast furnaces or foundries of the Solomonic town were considered to be the finest yet discovered in the ancient world.

This feature of the excavations, however, has recently been challenged by Beno Rothenberg who has shown the improbability of the structures being used as smelting furnaces, and suggests that they were rather warehouses for goods being shipped along the trade routes which intersected at Ezion-geber (PEQ, 94 [1962], pp. 5–61). *See* Ezion-geber.

8. *Hazor.* Prominent in the leadership of opposition to Joshua in northern Palestine (Josh 11), Hazor was one of the largest cities of Canaan. It was located nine miles N of the Sea of Galilee and consisted of a high bottle-shaped mound some 2,000 feet long and 25 acres in extent and a lower rectangular plateau about 2,300 feet wide and 3,300 feet long. John Garstang excavated here briefly in 1928, but a more detailed excavation was made by a Hebrew University expedition under the direction of Yigael Yadin, 1955–58 and 1968–69. The last city in the rectangular enclosure had an estimated population of 40,000 and presumably was destroyed by Joshua or by Barak. Solomon and Ahab were probably responsible for building towns on the upper mound during the 10th and 9th cen. B.C. *See* Hazor.

9. *Jerash.* Jerash (perhaps the NT Gerasa) was one of the Decapolis, a chain of ten Hellenistic cities located in the Palestinian region. Many followed Jesus from the Decapolis (Mt 4:25; Mk 5:20; 7:31). Serious excavation began

A view across the ancient site of Jerash from one of the theaters. MIS

there in 1920 under the supervision of the Palestine Department of Antiquities, and since 1948 the government of Jordan has continued the work. The magnificent city which has been laid bare provides a good example of the Graeco-Roman influence of Decapolis in the midst of Jewish religious exclusivism. While many of the remains date to the 2nd cen. A.D., a theater and temples to Zeus, Artemis, and Tiberius are among the structures dating to Jesus' day. *See* Gerasa.

10. *Jericho.* Excavations at OT Jericho were first carried on by Ernst Sellin and Carl Watzinger for the German Oriental Society, 1907 – 9. The archaeologists demonstrated that the town had covered only some six to eight acres, small enough for the Israelites to have marched around in 15 minutes. The British archaeologist John Garstang worked at the site 1929 – 36 and identified the double walls of City D as belonging to the city of Joshua's day. He claimed that they fell outward around 1400 B.C. Kathleen Kenyon, reopening the Jericho excavations 1952 – 58 for the British School of Archaeology in Jerusalem, concluded that the walls Garstang dated to Joshua's time actually dated to the period 3000 – 2000 B.C. She believed Joshua captured Jericho 1350 – 25 B.C. Excavations at nearby NT Jericho were conducted by James Kelso in 1950 and James Pritchard in 1951. They found remains of the Herodian palace and other structures of this winter capital of the Herods. *See* Jericho.

11. *Jerusalem.* The beginnings of archaeological work in Jerusalem date to the establishment of the Palestine Exploration Fund in 1865 and the work of Charles Warren in 1867 ff. From 1894 to 1897 F. J. Bliss and his architect A. C. Dickie did important archaeological and architectural work in the old Heb. capital. Captain Parker in 1909 – 11 cleared the entire system of tunnels related to the Gihon spring. E. L. Sukenik undertook excavation of the line of the N wall between 1925 and 1940.

In addition to these few examples, many other archaeological efforts have been undertaken in Jerusalem, but it will of course be impossible to carry on any large scale expeditions there because the ancient city is largely covered by modern habitation. Since nearly all these expeditions were conducted before proper stratigraphical records were understood, the British School of Archaeology in Jerusalem and the Ecole Biblique undertook in 1961 to survey the old city. In 1962 and succeeding years they were joined by the Royal Ontario Museum. Père R. de Vaux, A. D. Tushingham, and Kathleen M. Kenyon were codirectors. A significant step has been made in clearing up problems related to the E wall and the area of the old Jebusite city. New evidence was also found to suggest that the site of the Church of the Holy Sepulcher was outside the wall of Jerusalem at the time of the crucifixion. Israeli soundings in 1969 found that the Herodian bridge across the Tyropeon Valley to the W side

Excavations adjacent to the Western Wall of the Temple in Jerusalem. HFV

of the temple area was as wide as a four-lane highway. *See* Jerusalem.

12. *Megiddo.* Among the fortress cities constructed by Solomon (I Kgs 9:15), Megiddo (Tell el-Mutesellim, located S of the plain of Esdraelon) was excavated by the Oriental Institute of the University of Chicago (1925 – 39) under the leadership of Clarence Fisher, P. L. O. Guy, and Gordon Loud. Stratum IV has been identified as the Solomonic level. There two stable compounds were found, capable of holding about 450 horses and a large number of chariots. Although Yigael Yadin of the Hebrew University in more recent excavations at the site feels that these stables date to Ahab's day, it seems probable that Solomon built them and that they were remodeled by Ahab. *See* Megiddo.

13. *Nineveh.* Excavations at Nineveh were begun by A. H. Layard in 1847 and continued during the last century by Hormuzd Rassam and George Smith for the British Museum and Victor Place for the French. Later, British Museum expeditions there were led by L. W. King and R. C. Thompson in 1903 – 5, and M. E. L. Mallowan in 1931 – 32. Ancient Nineveh is represented by 7½ miles of ramparts surrounding two great mounds — Kouyunjik and Nebi Yunus. Most of the archaeological work has centered on the former, where Layard uncovered the palace of Sennacherib, and he and others worked on the palace of Ashurbanipal with its great library. The palace of Esarhaddon was discovered in the mound of Nebi Yunus. Nineveh is as yet only partially excavated. *See* Nineveh.

14. *Pergamum* (Pergamos). Since 1868, when Carl Humann began to excavate at Pergamum, German archaeologists have been working at the site, which consists of an older hill city and a lower city of Roman imperial times. The hill city has now been largely excavated. There the great altar of Zeus was uncovered, identified by some as Satan's throne

The Altar of Zeus, Pergamum. HFV

(Rev 2:13), as well as two agoras, the gymnasium, several temples, the world-famous library, and palaces and a theater. The lower city, which was just being built in the apostle John's day, is largely covered by the modern city; but archaeological work was attempted there just prior to World War II. Near the lower town was the world-famous health center dedicated to Asklepius, god of healing, which is still receiving archaeological attention. *See* Pergamum.

15. *Philippi*. The first city in Europe to hear the Christian gospel was Philippi, and the church there was dear to the heart of the apostle Paul. While some excavation has been conducted at Philippi since World War II, the main work was done at the site by the French School at Athens, 1914–38. The 300-by-150-foot rectangular forum has been completely uncovered. Though rebuilt in the 2nd cen., it had essentially the same plan in Paul's day. The French also worked on the acropolis and uncovered the theater and Byzantine churches. *See* Philippi.

16. *Rome*. While archaeological work in Rome has been extensive, only a fraction of it has any relation to Scripture. Excavations on the Palatine Hill began about 1725 and have continued intermittently to the present. Part of the palace of Tiberius (reigning emperor when Christ was crucified) has been uncovered, but most of the construction on the hill was built by Domitian (who exiled John to the Isle of Patmos). Since 1907 work has been in progress on the recovery of Nero's Golden House on the Oppian Hill. First archaeological work at the Forum (political, social and economic center of the city and probable place where Paul appeared before Caesar) was done in 1788, and it has been carried on periodically to the present. A considerable amount of attention has also been devoted to the Circus Maximus, a great entertainment center in Paul's day, located between the slopes of the Aventine and Palatine.

Excavation under the Vatican began in 1940 and has continued since World War II. Opinions of archaeologists vary on whether Peter's tomb was located there and whether it has been found. *See* Rome.

17. *Samaria*. Excavations at Samaria, capital of the northern kingdom, began with a Harvard expedition under the leadership of George A. Reisner, 1908–10. J. W. Crowfoot led a second expedition, 1931–33, in which Harvard cooperated with four other institutions. The British School of Archaeology in Jerusalem and others excavated at the site in 1935. Excavations at Samaria uncovered the palace begun by Omri and Ahab and added to by later kings, the city walls, cisterns for water storage during long sieges, large amounts of ivory, and ostraca. The latter, about 70 in number, were inscribed pieces of pottery dating to the early 8th cen. B.C., and tell something of the handwriting, religious and economic conditions of the time. Remains of construction by Herod the Great also came to light. *See* Samaria.

18. *Shechem*. Shechem (Tell Balatah) figures often in the OT narrative. It was, e.g., the town near which Abraham built his first altar, and served as the first capital of the kingdom of Israel under Jeroboam. I. E. Sellin and others connected with the German Oriental Society excavated at Shechem between 1913 and 1934. G. Ernest Wright, now at Harvard, began a new series of excavations at the site in 1956 under the auspices of Drew University, McCormick Theological Seminary, and the American Schools of Oriental Research. Various institutions have cooperated in the almost annual expeditions of recent years. Shechem probably reached its height between 2000 and 1500 B.C. A discovery of particular interest to the Bible student is an extensive Late Bronze Age temple which may have been the house of Baal-berith of Jud 9:4. *See* Shechem.

19. *Susa* (Shushan). Winter capital of the Persian Empire, Susa appears in the OT under the name Shushan (Neh 1:1; Est 1:2; Dan 8:2). The royal palace there was begun by Darius I

A griffon in bas relief from the palace at Susa, fifth to fourth century B.C. LM

ARCHAEOLOGY

(522 – 486 B.C.) and enlarged and beautified by later kings. Darius tells of bringing materials for it from Egypt, Lebanon, and India. French excavators have conducted the work at Susa. M. A. Dieulafoy pioneered there in 1884 – 86 and Jacques de Morgan and others directed excavations at the site 1897 – 1912. The three fragments of the Code of Hammurabi were discovered at Susa in 1901 – 2. Especial attention was devoted to the palace, which included three courts of varying size surrounded by large halls and apartments. The walls of sun-dried brick were covered with whitewash on the inside but were decorated with panels of beautifully colored glazed bricks probably during the reign of Artaxerxes II (404 – 359), well after the days of Esther and Nehemiah. Motifs of these panels included winged bulls, winged griffins, and spearmen of the guard. *See* Shushan.

20. *Ur.* In 1854 J. E. Taylor identified Tell Mukayyan in S Iraq as Ur and excavated there briefly. R. Campbell Thompson and H. R. Hall led two expeditions there in 1918 under the auspices of the British Museum. But the main work at the site was done by a joint expedition of the University Museum of Philadelphia and the British Museum in a protracted excavation headed by Sir Leonard Woolley (1922 – 34). Woolley found that Sumerian civilization flourished at Ur at a very high level as early as 2500 B.C. But the city was at its height 2070 – 1960 B.C., during which time Abraham may have left it, depending on how one figures the OT chronology. At that time its population numbered in the tens of thousands, and its people engaged in extensive commercial and industrial activity, enjoyed substantial educational opportunities, and built such great public structures as the brick ziggurat or stage-tower of Nanna (200 feet long by 150 feet wide and 70 feet high). *See* Ur.

Excavations of Sites Important for Biblical Study

1. *Ain Feshkha* and *Qumran.* The spring Ain Feshkha is located some 10 miles S of Jericho, and it is in this region just W of the Dead Sea that the caves are located which contained the Dead Sea Scrolls. To date at least 11 caves in the region have yielded scrolls and scroll fragments since the original discovery in 1947. Immediately N of Ain Feshkha was Khirbet Qumran, excavated in 1953 – 56 and discovered to have been the center of an ascetic sect akin to the Essenes and a place where many of the DSS were produced. The scrolls include portions of all OT books except Esther. A complete Isaiah MS, a second fairly complete Isaiah scroll, an almost complete scroll of Leviticus, and an almost complete copy of about 40 psalms are the longest and most important biblical MSS among the discoveries. The DSS provide important new information on the historical background of Scripture and important new materials for textual criticism. *See* Ain Feshkha; Dead Sea Scrolls.

The ziggurat at Ur. BM

2. *Boghazköy.* Mentioned many times in more than a dozen books of the OT, the Hittites were an important people of Asia Minor hardly known until Hugo Winckler led a German Oriental Society excavation at Boghazköy (the Hittite capital 90 miles E of Ankara) in 1906 ff. A find of special importance was the royal archives, consisting of about 10,000 cuneiform tablets. Temples, walls, and other construction have come to light in subsequent seasons of excavation. German excavators have again been working at this great 300-acre site regularly since World War II. *See* Hittites.

3. *Mari.* Mari (Tell Hariri) is located on the Euphrates almost due E of Byblos. André Parrot of the Louvre led annual excavations at the site 1933 – 38 and 1951 – 56. Most dramatic of the finds were the royal palace and the royal archives of the early 2nd mil. B.C. The palace boasted more than 250 rooms, courts, and corridors and covered more than six acres. More important to biblical study, however, were the royal archives, containing upward of 20,000 clay tablets. These consist of royal correspondence from many kingdoms of western Asia and a large number of business documents. These tablets have helped to modify our knowledge of the chronology of the 2nd mil. B.C. and have told much about the Amorites and thus about the patriarchal period. The names Peleg, Serug, and Nahor (Gen 11:16, 22, 24, 27) appear as names of towns in the Mari tablets. *See* Mari.

4. *Nippur.* Nippur, some 50 miles SE of Babylon, was an important Sumerian site. The first excavations there were conducted by the University Museum of Philadelphia, 1889 – 1900, under the leadership of J. P. Peters and others. Since Nippur was a religious and commercial center dedicated to the great earth-god Enlil, the city's principal building was the temple of Enlil. Near the temple was found the temple library comprising some 20,000 tablets of the 3rd and early 2nd mil. B.C. Among the religious texts important for biblical study were the Sumerian flood account and Sumerian King List, which mentions long-lived

patriarchs. Among the business houses of the mound thousands of tablets were found, dating from the 3rd mil. to the 5th cen. B.C. Since World War II many seasons of excavation have been conducted at the site by the Oriental Institute of the University of Chicago and the University Museum of Philadelphia with notable success. Several large temples have been investigated, foundation deposits discovered and additional tablets excavated. *See* Nippur.

5. *Nuzu.* Excavations at this NE Iraq site were conducted 1925–31 by the American Schools of Oriental Research under the direction of Edward Chiera. Harvard, the University Museum of Philadelphia, and other institutions cooperated in the operation. Of particular significance was the discovery of about 1,500 clay tablets in Nuzian private homes, dating to about 1500 B.C. and revealing striking parallels to the patriarchal narrative. Moreover, it should be pointed out that the Nuzians were Hurrians, related to the long-lost Horites of the OT. *See* Nuzu; Horites.

6. *Persepolis.* Persepolis was one of the great capitals of Persia and became the main capital under Darius I. Xerxes (probable husband of Esther) and Artaxerxes I (to whom Nehemiah ministered) continued construction there. The Oriental Institute of the University of Chicago excavated at Persepolis 1931–39 under the direction of Ernst Herzfeld and Erich Schmidt. The chief buildings were erected on a large rectangular terrace and included the palace of Darius, a building which probably served as his reception hall, and an audience hall begun by Darius I and completed by Xerxes (195 feet square). It was covered by a wooden roof supported by 72 stone columns. Also on the terrace stood a third large reception hall with 100 columns started by Xerxes and finished by Artaxerxes I, the harem of Darius, and the royal treasury. *See* Persia.

7. *Ras Shamra.* Ras Shamra (ancient Ugarit) was located on the Syrian coast opposite Cyprus. Excavated from 1929 until World War II and since 1950 by C. F. A. Schaeffer, the site has provided hundreds of texts dating from the 15th and 14th cen. B.C. These Canaanite documents are very significant for understanding the Heb. language, and reveal as well the nature of Canaanite religious practices in the time of the Heb. Conquest. *See* Ras Shamra.

Bibliography. William F. Albright, *The Archaeology of Palestine,* rev. ed., Harmondsworth, Middlesex: Penguin, 1960. George A. Barton, *Archaeology and the Bible,* 7th ed., Philadelphia: American Sunday School Union, 1937. George E. Bean, *Aegean Turkey,* London: Ernest Benn, 1966. Millar Burrows, *What Mean These Stones?* New Haven: American Schools of Oriental Research, 1941. Jack Finegan, FLAP. Joseph P. Free, *Archaeology and Bible History,* 2nd ed., Wheaton: Scripture Press, 1956. David N. Freedman and Jonas C. Greenfield (eds.), *New Directions in Biblical Archaeology,* Garden City: Doubleday, 1969. Nelson Glueck, *Rivers in the Desert,* Philadelphia: Jewish Publication Society, 1959. Kathleen Kenyon, *Archaeology in the Holy Land,* 2nd ed., New York: Praeger, 1965. William S. LaSor, *Amazing Dead Sea Scrolls,* 2nd ed., Chicago: Moody, 1959. Paul MacKendrick, *The Greek Stones Speak,* New York: St. Martin's Press, 1962. Charles F. Pfeiffer, ed., BW. Ira M. Price, O. R. Sellers, and E. L. Carlson, *The Monuments and the Old Testament,* Philadelphia: Judson, 1958. James B. Pritchard, ed., ANET, ANEP. D. Winton Thomas, ed., AOTS. John Arthur Thompson, *The Bible and Archaeology,* Grand Rapids: Eerdmans, 1962. Merrill F. Unger, *Archaeology and the Old Testament,* Grand Rapids: Zondervan, 1954. Donald J. Wiseman, *Illustrations from Biblical Archaeology,* Grand Rapids: Eerdmans, 1958. G. Ernest Wright, *Biblical Archaeology,* rev. ed., Philadelphia: Westminster, 1962.

H. F. V.

ARCHANGEL. That there are ranks among both the good and evil angels is clear in Eph 3:10 and 6:12. The evil angels are led by Satan and the elect angels by the archangel Michael (Rev 12:7).

The word "archangel" occurs only twice in the Bible (I Thess 4:16; Jude 9) and there is only one angel so designated—Michael ("who is like God"). In the OT he appears as the guardian angel of Israel (Dan 10:21; 12:1) and he has great authority (Dan 10:13). His power and authority will be used in behalf of the Israelites particularly during the time of Jacob's trouble.

Rabbinical traditions concerning Michael are many. He is called "great high priest in heaven" and "great prince and conqueror." In the Book of Enoch he is called one of the archangels (implying others).

A relief from the palace area at Persepolis.
ORINST

In the NT the voice of the archangel will be heard at the return of the Lord for His people (I Thess 4:16). Michael is seen in the apocalyptic vision of John as leading the angelic armies of heaven against Satan and his host of evil angels (Rev 12:7). As a result of this conflict Satan is cast out of heaven. The reference in Jude 9 poses problems for some in connection with its being quoted from the Assumption of Moses. However, if one believes that its inclusion in the inspired text guarantees the accuracy of the facts reported (but only those facts which are included and not the entire account in the Assumption), then we learn that the archangel (1) had something to do with the burial of Moses; (2) had no prerogative in himself to pronounce judgment on Satan; and (3) is dependent on the greater power of God.

See also Angel; Michael.

C. C. R.

ARCHELAUS (är′kē-lā′ŭs). Son of Herod the Great by the Samaritan woman Malthace; governor over Idumea, Judea, and Samaria (4 B.C.—A.D. 6). On the death of his father, Archelaus at first appeared to be conciliatory to the Jews, but in a short time his true nature was revealed by the slaying of 3,000 persons during an uprising at the Passover season. As a result, when he went to Rome to obtain Caesar's confirmation of his rulership, the Jews also sent a delegation to protest his appointment (Jos *Ant.* xvii.11.1 f.). Some are of the opinion that Christ referred to this event in Lk 19:12–27. His brother Antipas also appeared before Augustus to contest their father's will, desiring to obtain the kingdom for himself. Finally, however, Archelaus was appointed ethnarch of Idumea, Judea, and Samaria, with the promise that he was to become king if he proved to be worthy (Jos *Ant.* xvii.11.4).

His rule, like his father's, was marked by numerous building projects. By many unwise and cruel acts he brought the hatred of the people upon himself. His domestic relationships were particularly offensive to the Jews. After being married to Mariamne for some time, he fell so deeply in love with Glaphyra, the widow of his half-brother Alexander, that he divorced his first wife and married Glaphyra (Jos *Wars* ii.7.4). He was also guilty of replacing the high priests at will. His treatment of his subjects is described by Josephus as barbarous and tyrannical (*Ant.* xvii.13.2; *Wars* ii.7.3). The only mention of him in the NT occurs in Mt 2:22, where Joseph is said to have settled in Galilee because he feared Archelaus. After ruling for more than nine years, Archelaus was recalled to Rome following accusations made by both Jews and Samaritans. On his arrival, he was deposed and banished to Vienna in Gaul (Jos *Ant.* xvii.13.2).

D. W. B.

ARCHERS. Men armed with bows and arrows. For many centuries archers, on foot, riding in

Archers from the guard of king Ashurbanipal at Nineveh, seventh century B.C. LM

chariots, or mounted, formed the backbone of the armies of the ancient Near East. In the OT the archer stands for military activity, and bows and arrows for military equipment generally (Gen 49:23–24; Ps 127:4–5; Hos 1:5; R. de Vaux, *Ancient Israel,* pp. 243–244). When Job wished to say God was making war against him, he said he had been made a target for God's archers (Job 16:12–13). Saul, Uriah, and Josiah were shot by archers (I Sam 31:3; II Sam 11:24; II Chr 35:23).

Bows were usually of wood. To string a bow with its ox gut string, one end was secured with the foot while being bent, hence the archer was one who "treads a bow" (I Chr 8:40; Jer 51:3). Arrows were tipped with bone, stone, bronze, or iron and were called "sons of his quiver" (Lam 3:13, ASV marg.) or "son of the bow" (Job 41:28, ASV marg.).

See Bow and Arrow.

ARCHEVITES (är′kē-vīts). A group of people deported to Samaria by the Assyrian king Asnappar or Ashurbanipal (Ezr 4:9). They are identified with the Babylonian city of Erech of Gen 10:10 (IB, III, 601) and translated in RSV as "the men of Erech." *See* Erech.

ARCHI (är′kī).*See* Archite.

ARCHIPPUS (är-kĭp′ŭs).Mentioned twice in the NT (Col 4:17; Phm 2). In Colossians, Archippus is urged to take heed to his ministry. Paul is here perhaps commending Archippus for past service and encouraging him for future tasks, with no thought of a rebuke. In Philemon, Paul greets Archippus after Philemon and Apphia in a manner suggesting he may have been their son, and calls him a "fellow soldier," likely because Archippus had shared with Paul in some experience of service or suffering for the sake of Christ (cf. Phil 2:25).

Lightfoot has argued that Paul in Colossians is reproving Archippus for being remiss in the service of Christ. Believing that Archippus served the church at Laodicea, Lightfoot thinks of Archippus as being lukewarm like the whole church at Laodicea later became (cf. Rev 3:14 ff.). John Knox, however, has argued that Archippus was the main addressee of the so-called Epistle to Philemon and thus likely the pastor of the church at Colosse, not Laodicea; and that the service *(diakonia)* which Archippus was urged to perform was, as the owner of Onesimus, to release him so that he might do the work of an evangelist. This is not an obvious interpretation, however, of "the ministry which thou hast received in the Lord" (Col 4:17). *See* Philemon, Epistle to.

Bibliography. Henry Cowan, "Archippus," HDAC, 1, 89. John Knox, *Philemon Among the Letters of Paul,* rev. ed., New York: Abingdon, 1959. J. B. Lightfoot, *Colossians,* 3rd ed., London: Macmillan, 1879, pp. 72 ff. For the occurrence of this name in Egyptian papyri and inscriptions from Asia Minor, see Arndt.

E. J. V.

ARCHITE (är′kīt). An inhabitant of a town or clan along the border of Ephraim and Benjamin between Luz and Ataroth (Josh 16:2, RSV). Hushai, David's loyal counselor, was an Archite (II Sam 15:32; 16:16; 17:5, 14).

ARCHITECTURE. The art of building, herein limited to Palestine from 2000 B.C. to A.D. 100.

In the Old Testament

The usual city of several thousand people was perched atop a hill or city mound five to ten acres in extent, and was protected by a strong wall with one or two gates. With no proper street planning before the Hellenistic age, the city contained only an unimpressive assortment of houses crammed together,

A diagram of the northern gate at Megiddo.
HFV

reached by winding unpaved alleys. Many people, mainly the peasants engaged in agriculture, lived in surrounding unwalled villages (Deut 3:5) or in huts and tents outside the fortified city, seeking refuge within it only in time of attack. Most essential to the location was an adequate fresh water supply. Thus many towns (e.g., Jerusalem, Gibeon, Megiddo, Lachish, Gezer, Zarethan) had elaborate stepped tunnels to reach the spring or well when besieged. Around 1300 B.C. plastered cisterns and catchbasins came into use to collect rainwater, supplementing the town well. On the whole, building styles were simple and practical, for Israel was always the cultural borrower and never the innovator.

Fortifications. For centuries after the Hyksos period the Canaanites and even the Israelites made use of any remaining features of the Middle Bronze Age defenses. These consisted of stone or brick walls perhaps 25 to 30 feet high at the top of an artificial slope (or glacis) of battered earth with a ditch at the bottom to protect the walls from enemy battering rams. Egyptian sculptured reliefs depict bearded Canaanite defenders standing on crenellated battlements. Early in the Israelite monarchy casemate walls were constructed, consisting of two parallel walls connected by a series of cross walls. The "rooms" thus formed could be filled with earth in times of siege to strengthen the wall against battering machines (cf. Ezk 26:9). Later in the monarchy, single walls 20 feet or more thick were built with alternating recesses and salients to expose attackers.

The gate was the key to the city's defense since it was the most vulnerable point. While Jerusalem had a number of gates, most Israelite cities had only two, one for chariots and, on the opposite side of town, a smaller one for donkeys and pedestrians only. The road leading up to the main gate was planned so that attackers carrying shields with their left hands would have the wall and its defenders on their right flank. The gate was part of a strong tower or had bastions on each side (II Chr 26:9). Usually in the gateway the road ran between two sets of massive stone piers (pilasters) or projecting jambs—sometimes three as at Shechem—with guard chambers between (II Sam 18:24). Stairs gave access to the tower roof where a sentinel stood watch (II Kgs 9:17). The double doors of the gate (Isa 45:1; Neh 6:1) consisted ordinarily of two wooden sections, sometimes overlaid with bronze plating (Isa 45:2) and held shut with one or more horizontal bars of wood, bronze (I Kgs 4:13), or iron (Ps 107:16), passing into openings in the gateposts (Jud 16:3). At Megiddo, as in the present Damascus Gate of Jerusalem, the axis of the gate turned 90 degrees between the two sets of portals to prevent a straight shot through the gate by enemy archers. Solomon's architect planned identical gates with four pairs of pilasters for Hazor, Megiddo, and Gezer (cf. I Kgs 9:15).

Public buildings. In Canaanite cities the local king of the city-state and a few of his nobles built two-story houses with ceilings supported by stone pillars. Solomon rebuilt certain cities as centers for his administrative districts (I Kgs 4:7–19). As at Megiddo, these probably contained near the gate a "palace" with many rooms to house the city garrison as well as the provincial governor and his retinue, and stables for the horses of the royal chariotry (I Kgs 9:19). Storehouses held the jars of grain, wine, and olive oil collected as taxes, as at Dothan, Shechem, and Gezer. A large stone-lined silo pit was constructed at Megiddo during the reign of Jeroboam II to store the grain harvested from the fertile plain of Esdraelon. The fortified building at Ezion-geber, formerly dubbed a copper smelter, is now interpreted as having been a storehouse granary.

Except at these store-cities and the royal citadels at Samaria, Jerusalem, and Ramat Rahel, Israelite Palestine gives little evidence of monumental architecture of the styles current in Egypt and Phoenicia. But King Solomon did hire carpenters and masons from Tyre and Gebal to prepare the cedar timber and stones for his temple (I Kgs 5:6, 18). Quite clearly Phoenician masons were also employed at Megiddo, and by King Omri and King Ahab at Samaria later on. At these sites parts of walls remain consisting of closely jointed and smoothed limestone blocks laid in a pattern of alternating headers and stretchers. The oldest known masonry of this type was uncovered at Ugarit.

Solomon's courtyard was built with a foundation of three rows of hewn stones topped by a row of cedar beams (I Kgs 6:36; 7:12), a common architectural feature in the ancient Near East to withstand earthquake shocks. Probably above the timber joists bonding the stones together were laid further courses of stones or of bricks, as at Ezion-geber and Samaria. The citadel enclosed by two walls on the summit of Samaria was approached from the E through a gate with a monumental forecourt ornamented by pilasters with "proto-Ionic" capitals. These have been found also at Megiddo and Ramat Rahel near Jerusalem, at the latter site decorating the facade of a palace in the royal citadel built probably by King Jehoiakim (cf. Jer 22:13 ff.). An Egyptian-style monolithic tomb of the period of the Jewish monarchy can be seen at Silwan across the Kidron Valley from old Jerusalem. Perhaps the sepulcher of the pro-Egyptian steward Shebna (Isa 22:16) or even of King Hezekiah (II Chr 32:33) followed this architectural style.

See Temple for special features of these buildings.

Private houses. The house of the better-class Israelite consisted of several rooms facing a courtyard, which was used for all household tasks (II Sam 17:18), the largest room for the family, another for the cattle, and a third for a general storeroom ("closet," Mt 6:6). These

A casemate wall of ancient Hebrew construction at Ramat Rahel, near Jerusalem. HFV

rooms were small, 12 to 15 feet square or less. As at Gezer, house walls generally consisted of common field stones with wide, irregular joints filled with mud and stone chips. Each family built its own house, expert masons being employed only on royal residences, temples, or city walls. The average man plastered the inside walls with mud; the wealthy could afford to panel their walls with cypress or cedar wood ("cieled," Hag 1:4, KJV). In all periods the floors were made of hard-packed clay or plaster polished with rubbing stones.

Roofs were flat, supported by wooden beams laid from wall to wall. Smaller rafters (Song 1:17) crossed these, then brushwood or reeds, above which was a layer of earth several inches thick coated with heavy plaster, rolled after a rain to keep the roof watertight. The roof was reached by an outside staircase from the courtyard and was made safe by a parapet required by the Mosaic law (Deut 22:8). Such a roof, sometimes shaded by awnings, had many uses (Josh 2:6; I Sam 9:25; Isa 15:3; Acts 10:9). Some built roof chambers (I Kgs 17:19; II Kgs 4:10, RSV), in effect making theirs a two-story house. Only a palace, however, would have an ornamental or latticed window balustrade such as the one from which Jezebel looked out (II Kgs 9:30–33), in accordance with a favorite artistic theme of the ancient Near East showing a lady standing at the state window. Stone-lined sewers have been discovered in many Canaanite and Israelite towns.

Paneled effect of Herodian masonry on the Western Wall of the Temple. HFV

In the New Testament

One lasting result of the Hellenization of the Mediterranean world was the founding or rebuilding of some 350 Hellenistic cities, more than 30 of them in Palestine. These 30, among them the cities of the Decapolis (q.v.), were concentrated mainly in Transjordan and along the coast. They stood out architecturally because of their systematized town planning with principal streets and rectangular blocks, monumental arches, theaters, public baths, gymnasiums, temples, and above all the typically Gr. agora (forum or marketplace). Gerasa in Gilead with its spectacular ruins is the chief example of one of these cities. The Nabateans incorporated many of these architectural features in their rock-cut city of Petra. Predominantly Jewish towns, however, had refused to Hellenize, even though prominent Jewish families took on western ways, as seen in the mausoleum of the Tobiads in Transjordan and the Maccabean-age tombs in the Kidron Valley. The average Jewish houses remained small and crowded together, with flat roofs and the rooms opening on a courtyard separated from the street by a wall with its gate-door (Acts 12:13), all purely utilitarian in architectural style.

It was the great building program of Herod the Great (30–4 B.C.) that most deeply affected the architecture of Judea. He erected a remarkable chain of castles with aqueducts, great cisterns, and dungeons. Remains of these can still be seen at Masada and Herodium near Bethlehem. His supreme achievements were the complete renovation of the second temple in Jerusalem, and the transformation of Caesarea and Samaria (which he renamed Sebaste) into major cities. His masonry is recognizable everywhere by squared blocks of faultless jointing with drafted borders producing a paneled effect. He introduced cut-stone vaulting, making possible the harbor at Caesarea, the vast substructures of the Jerusalem temple area, and great viaducts that spanned the Tyropean valley (Wilson's and Robinson's Arches). His attempts, however, to ingratiate himself with the Jewish populace by this program only earned him their undying hatred. By and large, they bitterly opposed his temples built in other cities as tributes to the Greek and Roman gods, and they refused to appreciate the blending of prevailing Hellenistic forms in structure and ornament with their native Oriental motifs. See Arch.

See articles on the various cities mentioned herein.

Bibliography. "Ancient Cities"; "Cities, Canaanite, Israelite, Hellenistic," Pictorial Biblical Encyclopedia, ed. by Gaalyahu Cornfeld, New York: Macmillan, 1964. J. W. Crowfoot, Kathleen M. Kenyon, E. L. Sukenik, The Buildings at Samaria, London: Palestine Exploration Fund, 1942. R. W. Hamilton, "Architecture," IDB. G. Ernest Wright, Biblical Archaeology, rev. ed., Philadelphia: Westminster, 1962.

J. R.

ARCTURUS (ärk-tūr′ŭs). A large bright star or constellation referred to in Job 9:9; 38:32, KJV. RSV translates the Heb. word as the "Bear." The precise modern equivalent is not known, although either the constellation of Ursa Major, the Great Bear, or of Aldebaran is a possible reference. See Astronomy.

ARD (ärd), **ARDITE** (är′dīt). One of the descendants of Benjamin who founded a clan in Egypt (Gen 46:21; Num 26:40).

Ard is alternately Addar (q.v.; I Chr 8:3).

ARDON (är′dŏn). One of the sons of Caleb of the tribe of Judah (I Chr 2:18).

ARELI (á-rē′lī), **ARELITES** (á-rē′līts). A son of Gad who went to Egypt with the house of Jacob (Gen 46:16). The Arelites were descendants of Areli (Num 26:17).

AREOPAGITE (ăr′ē-ŏp′á-gīt). A member of the Areopagus council. One such member is named in Scripture, Dionysius (q.v.; Acts 17:34). See also Areopagus.

AREOPAGUS (ăr′ē-ŏp′á-gŭs). Philosophers of Athens brought Paul to the Areopagus to hear an explanation of his teachings. Areopagus (Acts 17:19) is the equivalent of Mars Hill (Acts 17:22), for Mars was the Roman name for the god of war and Ares the Gr. name. Actually Areopagus could signify a 377-foot hill in Athens NW of the acropolis, or the name of the venerable council which traditionally had met on the hill. By Paul's day the council did sometimes meet in the agora, but the Gr. of Acts 17:19 probably should be translated "up to" and seems to signify that this meeting took place on the hill. Acts 17:19 probably refers to the hill and Acts 17:22 to the council ("in the midst of Mars hill" is an impossible rendering of the Gr.).

While the Areopagus had once held a place of supreme importance in the political and religious affairs of the state, during the 5th cen. B.C. it lost its political power and became largely a criminal court. In Roman times it was charged mainly with religious and educational affairs. Sir William Ramsay believed that the Areopagus had power to appoint or invite lecturers at Athens and that for that reason Paul was brought before the council. *See* Athens; Dionysius the Areopagite.

H. F. V.

The Areopagus. HFV

ARETAS (ăr′ĕ-tăs). Mentioned only in II Cor 11:32 in the NT. The name was used by the kings of Nabatean Arabia whose capital was Petra. This was Aretas IV (9 B.C.–A.D. 40), whose daughter was married to Herod Antipas (*q.v.*) until the latter divorced her to marry Herodias. As a result of Herod's act, along with border disputes between the two (cf. Jos. *Ant.* xviii.5.1), Aretas declared war in A.D. 36, a war which resulted in the destruction of Herod's army.

Probably about this same time the incident recorded in II Cor 11:32 took place. Exactly what Aretas' jurisdiction in Damascus was is not clear, for the province of Syria was officially under Roman jurisdiction. Some scholars think that the governor or ethnarch at Damascus under Aretas was ruler only of the Nabatean citizens resident in the vicinity of the city. Others suppose that the Roman emperor Caligula (A.D. 37–41) may have handed over the control of Damascus to Aretas as a friendly gesture.

See Damascus; Ethnarch.

W. M. D.

ARGOB (ăr′gŏb)

1. The southern part of Bashan in northern Transjordan, extending on the S to the Yarmuk River and on the W to Geshur and Maachah (Deut 3:4–5, 13–14). It included the 60 fortified cities which comprised the northern por-

tion of the kingdom of Og. It should be distinguished from northern Gilead, S of the Yarmuk where the "unwalled towns" of Deut 3:5*b* (i.e., the *ḥavvôth* Jair, Deut 3:14*b*; Jud 10:4) were located (I Kgs 4:13). This distinction, however, is not clear in Josh 13:30. Rabbinic Targums identified Argob with Trachonitis (modern el-Leja), but this is generally rejected in favor of the more fertile area to the W (Driver, *Deuteronomy*, pp. 48–50). Moses assigned this area to the half tribe of Manasseh (Deut 3:13–14). In Solomon's fiscal administrative organization Argob was the northern half of the district assigned to the son of Geber, one of Solomon's 12 administrative officials responsible for the supply of food for the court (I Kgs 4:13).

2. An Israelite noble associated with Pekah (II Kgs 15:25). However, Argob and Arieh possibly should be omitted from v. 25 and added to v. 29 as place names, as in RSV (cf. also KB; BDB; Kittel marg.; Smith, *An American Translation;* James A. Montgomery, ICC, *The Books of Kings*).

R. V. R.

ARIDAI (âr′ĭ-dī). One of the ten sons of Haman slain by the Jews in the story of Queen Esther (Est 9:9).

ARIDATHA (ăr′ĭ-dā′thá). A son of Haman killed in Susa by Jewish loyalists (Est 9:8). This was probably a Persian name of uncertain meaning.

ARIEH (âr′ĭ-á). Along with Argob, Arieh was involved in the conspiracy of Pekah and the murder of King Pekahiah (II Kgs 15:25, KJV and RSV marg.).

ARIEL (âr′ĭ-ĕl)

1. The hearth of the altar of burnt offering in Ezekiel's temple (Ezk 43:15–16). *See* Hearth.

2. A leader whom Ezra sent to Casiphia, presumably a Babylonian Levitical settlement, to seek ministers for the temple (Ezr 8:16–17).

3. A symbolic name for Jerusalem (Isa 29:1–2, 7). Its usage favors the root meaning "hearth of God" rather than the similar root for "lion." Jerusalem under divine judgment, despite its holy associations, will be as a great bloody altar with the slain everywhere around it.

4. Its occurrence in the Heb. text of II Sam 23:20 (ASV) and I Chr 11:22 (ASV) is enigmatic, but may suggest the strength of the two slain (KJV). Preferably, by introducing "sons of," the Septuagint makes it the name of a Moabite whose two sons were slain by Benaiah (RSV).

ARIMATHAEA (ăr′ĭ-má-thē′á). A town mentioned only in the Gospels as the home of Joseph who requested the body of Jesus from Pilate and buried it in his own new tomb (Mt 27:57; Mk 15:43; Lk 23:51; Jn 19:38). Luke's reference, which states it was a city of the

Jews, would identify it with the territory of Haramantha (Rathamin) mentioned in I Macc 11:34 as being added to the northern border of Judea by the Syrian king Demetrius II Nicator (145 B.C.) from possessions then belonging to Samaria. Eusebius' *Onomasticon* apparently calls it "Remphthis" (Rantis) and locates it as part of the city territory of Diospolis. While sometimes also called Ramah, it should not be confused with Ramah (Ramleh or er-Ram) in Benjamin, six miles N of Jerusalem. However, Arimathaea is identified by some as Rama-thaim-zophim ("the two Ramahs" or "twin heights") in the land of Ephraim where Samuel was born (I Sam 1:1, 19). The exact location still remains uncertain although many place it about 20 miles E of Tel-Aviv and Joppa. *See* Ramah.

A. F. J.

ARIOCH (ăr'ĭ-ŏk)

1. King of Ellasar, one of the Mesopotamian coalition, who campaigned successfully against the rebellious cities of the Arabah (Gen 14:1, 9), capturing Lot who was in turn rescued by Abram. He is not clearly identifiable from extrabiblical sources. Most recent attempts, through the Mari tablets, to equate with Arriwuk, son of Zimrilim of Mari, would demand a 17th cen. B.C. date, seemingly too late for Abraham (cf. Gerhard von Rad, *Genesis,* p. 171; Martin Noth, VT, I, 136–140; W. F. Albright, "Archaeology of Palestine," *Old Testament and Modern Study,* p. 7; H. H. Rowley, *From Joseph to Joshua,* pp. 63–66). The similarity to Arriwuk does show that Arioch was an authentic Hurrian name during the 2nd mil. B.C. in N Mesopotamia.

See Abraham; Ellasar.

2. Nebuchadnezzar's captain of the guard, commissioned to slay the wise men for their inability to tell Nebuchadnezzar his dream (Dan 2:14–15, 24–25). His commission was never executed. He informed Daniel, who through divine revelation succeeded where the other wise men had failed.

R. V. R.

ARISAI (âr'ĭ-sĭ). A son of Haman slain in the revenge of the Jews under Queen Esther (Est 9:9).

ARISTARCHUS (ăr'ĭs-tär'kŭs). A Macedonian from Thessalonica (Acts 19:29; 27:2), probably of Jewish ancestry (Col 4:10–11), who accompanied Paul on his third missionary journey. At Ephesus he was dragged into the theater in the silversmiths' riot (Acts 19:29). From there he journeyed with Paul through Macedonia to Greece (Acts 20:2), and with others sailed directly to Troas where they awaited arrival of Paul who followed by way of Philippi (Acts 20:3–6). Aristarchus sailed with Paul to Rome for trial (Acts 27:2), and evidently shared his imprisonment (Col 4:10). Paul's alternating references to him and Epaphras as "fellow prison-er" and "fellow worker" in the closing greetings may suggest that this was a voluntary sharing in which these faithful friends took turns (cf. Phm 23–24). According to tradition he was martyred under Nero.

ARISTOBULUS (ăr'ĭs-tŏb'ū-lŭs). Paul sent greetings to "them which are of Aristobulus' household" (Rom 16:10). Lightfoot's well-known view is that this man was a brother of Herod Agrippa I and that these people were his slaves, now the property of the emperor. Bruce suggests that the next verse, "Salute Herodion my kinsman" (Rom 16:11), is thus very fitting. Possibly Herodion was a member of the household of Aristobulus.

ARK, NOAH'S. Noah's ark was a colossal barge which God commanded Noah to build for the purpose of keeping alive members of his family and two of every kind of land animal through a universal flood (*see* Flood) which would come upon the earth in 120 years (Gen 6:3, 14–21). The ark (Heb. *tēbâ,* from the Egyptian *db*ᵗ*t,* meaning "chest," "box," or "coffin," and found elsewhere only in Ex 2:3, 5) was not a ship with sloping sides, rudder, and mast, but rather a bargelike repository intended only to float and to withstand the impact of waves. Shaped thus, its carrying capacity was one-third greater than a ship of similar length and width, and it would have been almost impossible to capsize.

The ark was constructed of gopher wood (cypress?) and was protected by an inner and outer coating of pitch or bitumen (Heb. *kōper*). The three decks were divided into rooms (Heb. *qinnîm,* "nests"). Around the entire vessel just below the roof was an opening for light; and on one side was a door (Gen 6:14–16). See Alexander Heidel, *The Gilgamesh Epic and Old Testament Parallels,* pp. 233–35; and Bernard Ramm, *The Christian View of Science and Scripture,* pp. 229–31.

The ark was 300 cubits long, 50 wide, and 30 high (Gen 6:15). Assuming that the basic Heb. cubit was 17.5 inches (cf. R. B. Y. Scott, "Weights and Measures of the Bible," BA, May, 1959, pp. 22–27), the ark was 437.5 feet long, 72.92 feet wide, and 43.75 feet high. Since it had three decks, its total deck area was about 95,000 square feet. The total volume of the ark would have been 1,396,000 cubic feet, giving it a gross tonnage of about 13,960 tons, which is well within the category of large metal ocean-going vessels today. As early as 1609–21, Peter Janson of Holland built a large model of the ark and demonstrated the efficiency of its design and proportions. Not until the last half of the 19th cen. was a ship built with dimensions exceeding that of the ark.

Noah and his sons probably hired many men to assist them in the construction of the ark. By the very nature of the case, the project must have gained worldwide attention, and the universal rejection of Noah's faithful warnings during this final testing period of 120 years was the basis upon which Noah "condemned the world" (Heb 11:7). Noah's ark-building faith stood out in startling contrast to the unbelief of the human race "when the long-suffering of God waited in the days of Noah, while the ark was a preparing, wherein few, that is, eight souls, were saved through water" (I Pet 3:20, ASV).

For well over a century, scholars have debated whether the ark was sufficiently large to carry two of every kind of air-breathing animal in the world, plus an additional five of each "clean" kind. It must be recognized, in the first place, that two or more similar "species" of modern taxonomy may be included within one Genesis "kind." But more important, the vast majority of the nearly one million species of today are marine creatures which could have survived outside the ark. A leading systematic taxinomist, Ernst Mayr, lists 17,600 species of mammals, birds, reptiles, and amphibians. So we may assume that there were probably not more than 35,000 individual vertebrate animals in the ark, the average size being that of a sheep. Since a standard two-decked railroad stock car (with an effective capacity of 2,670 cubic feet) can carry about 240 sheep, only 146 stock cars would be needed to carry 35,000 animals of this average size. But the ark had a carrying capacity equivalent to that of 522 stock cars; so it is obvious that it was entirely adequate for its God-intended purpose (see John C. Whitcomb, Jr., and Henry M. Morris, *The Genesis Flood*, pp. 65–70).

When fully laden with its cargo (Gen 6:21), the ark sank into the water 15 cubits, or one-half its height. This seems to be the implication of Gen 7:20 ("fifteen cubits upward did the waters prevail"), for if the Flood had not covered the mountains by at least 15 cubits, the ark could not have floated over them. On the same day that the waters began to assuage (exactly 150 days after the Flood began), the ark rested on the highest peak of the mountains of Ararat (Gen 8:4); but an additional 221 days elapsed before Noah was permitted to disembark (8:14–16).

Concerning the subsequent history of the ark, Scripture is silent. In spite of rumors to the contrary, it is doubtful that its remains will ever be discovered. Sufficient for the Christian is the testimony of God's Word that such a structure once existed and that for more than a year it served as the only refuge for the human race and air-breathing animals in the judgment of a universal deluge. *See* Ararat.

Bibliography. Alexander Heidel, *The Gilgamesh Epic and Old Testament Parallels*, 2nd ed., Chicago: Univ. of Chicago Press, 1949. John C. Whitcomb, Jr., and Henry M. Morris, *The Genesis Flood: The Biblical Record and Its Scientific Implications*, Philadelphia: Presbyterian and Reformed, 1961.

J. C. W.

The traditional spot where Moses was rescued from the Nile. HFV

ARK OF BULRUSHES. When the mother of Moses could no longer hide the baby Moses, she placed him in an ark made of rushes or papyrus reeds caulked with pitch (Ex 2:3), to avoid killing the child in accord with Pharaoh's cruel decree (Ex 1:22). Bulrushes (*q.v.*) of this type were plentiful on the shores of the Nile River. There is no support that Moses' mother used papyrus reeds for the small basket because she was following an ancient belief that such rushes were effective in warding off crocodile attacks.

ARK OF THE COVENANT. This was a chest made of acacia wood, about four feet long, two and a half feet wide, and two and a half feet high. It was overlaid with gold inside and out (Ex 25:11) and had a ring of gold at each corner or foot through which poles were passed to carry it. The lid of the ark, the *kapporeth* or "mercy seat" (Ex 25:17), was made of pure gold. At each end of the mercy seat was a cherubim made of hammered gold.

The ark (*'aron*) is referred to some 200 times in the OT under 22 different designations. It is called the ark (Ex 25:14), the ark of Jehovah (I Sam 4:6, ASV), the ark of God (Elohim, I Sam 4:18), the ark of the covenant (Josh 3:6), the ark of the testimony (Ex 25:22). This various terminology for the ark may reflect a difference in date and authorship of the various sources, but this is not necessarily so.

The ark seems to have served various functions during its history. It was built by Moses (Deut 10:5), or actually by Bezaleel (Ex 31:2, 6–7; 37:1–9), at Sinai. According to Num 10:33–36 it served as a guide to Israel in the wilderness, and Num 14:44 adds that when the rebels at Kadesh-barnea went out to possess the Promised Land, neither Moses nor the ark went with them. In these passages the ark serves as a symbol of the presence of God. The ark is spoken of as the throne of God (I Sam 4:4; II Sam 6:2; cf. Jer 3:16).

The idea of the ark as a war palladium is a

very common one in the OT. The ark was very prominent in the story of the capture of Jericho (Josh 6-7), and in the struggle with the Philistines when the ark was captured (I Sam 4:11), at which time it is said that "the glory is departed from Israel" (I Sam 4:21). Even in defeat God did not abandon His throne on the ark but wrought havoc among the Philistine captors. The power of the ark can be seen in the curses it brought upon the Philistines (I Sam 5) and upon Uzzah (II Sam 6:7). G. Henton Davies has argued that the ark may be mentioned a number of times in the Psalms under the term *'ōz,* "strength" (cf. "The Ark in the Psalms," *Promise and Fulfillment,* F. F. Bruce, ed.; also cf. Ps 132:8; 78:59-61; 105:4).

One other function of the ark was to serve as the container of the tablets of the law or covenant. This concept is reflected in the name "the ark of the testimony" (Ex 25:16; Num 4:5; Josh 4:16).

When the ark was returned from the Philistines, it came to Beth-shemesh (*q.v.*) and then was removed to the house of Abinadab in Kirjath-jearim where it stayed for approximately 20 years (I Sam 7:2). Although the ark was now in Israel, it was probably, in effect, still under the control of the Philistines. This fact would explain why Saul had nothing to do with the ark and why "all the house of Israel lamented after the Lord" (I Sam 7:2).

When David came to the throne he set out to make Jerusalem the political and religious capital of all Israel. In doing so he brought the ark to Jerusalem and made it the center of worship (II Sam 6; Ps 132). Solomon built his temple to house the ark (I Kgs 6:19; 8:1-9). From this time on the historical books seldom mention the ark (cf. II Chr 35:3). It is very probable, however, that it was used in some of the great religious festivals in Jerusalem during the monarchy. At least four psalms (24, 68, 118, 132) reflect a cultic procession around Jerusalem probably during one of the major festivals,

at which time the ark may have been carried in front by the priests (cf. Ps 68:24-25; 118:26-27; 24:7-10; 132:8-9).

The final fate of the ark is a mystery. A reference to it in Jer 3:16 seems to suggest that it would be destroyed or captured (by the Babylonians in 586 B.C.). The prophet was saying that in the latter days the ark (as the throne of God) would not be missed, or come to mind, or be made again, because Jerusalem shall be called the throne of God. There is an apocryphal tradition found in II Esd 10:22; II Macc 2:4-5 which claims that Jeremiah hid the ark along with the tent and the altar of incense in a cave on Mount Nebo before Jerusalem was destroyed. George Adam Smith says, "This was a most unlikely thing for him to do" (*Jerusalem,* Vol. 2, footnote 4, p. 256).

The ark was the visible symbol of the presence of God. It had served a real need in the early days of Israel's history. But when the danger arose that it might become a fetish in Israel, God allowed it to be captured and destroyed.

See Tabernacle.

Bibliography. Frank M. Cross, Jr., "The Priestly Tabernacle," *The Biblical Archaeologist Reader,* ed. by G. Ernest Wright and David Noel Freedman, Anchor Books, Vol. I, Garden City: Doubleday, 1961. G. Henton Davies, "The Ark of the Covenant," IDB, I, 222-226. Roland de Vaux, *Ancient Israel,* trans. by John McHugh, New York: McGraw-Hill, 1961, pp. 297-301. Walther Eichrodt, *Theology of the Old Testament,* trans. by J. A. Baker, Philadelphia: Westminster, I (1961), 107-112. Gerhard von Rad, "The Tent and the Ark," *The Problem of the Hexateuch and Other Essays,* trans. by E. W. Trueman Dicken, Edinburgh: Oliver & Boyd, 1966, pp. 103-130. Marten H. Woudstra, *The Ark of the Covenant,* Philadelphia: Presbyterian and Reformed, 1965.

R. L. S.

ARKITES (är'kīts). A tribe descended from Canaan (Gen 10:17; I Chr 1:15). The present site, Tell 'Arqah, is located in Syria along the coast N of Tripoli. The city is mentioned in several Egyptian records from the 19th to the 14th cen. B.C., as well as by Tiglath-pileser III of Assyria (ANET, p. 283).

ARM. As a noun it is used mostly in a poetic sense in the Bible to symbolize strength or power. The "outstretched arm of God" refers to His providential care (Ex 6:6; Deut 4:34; 9:29; Ps 89:10; Isa 51:9; *et al.*). The breaking of an arm means the loss of power or health (Job 31:22; Ps 10:15; Jer 48:25; *et al.*). Although frequent in the OT, it appears but three times in the NT and in each case in imitation of OT usage of the arm of the Lord (Lk 1:51; Jn 12:38; Acts 13:17).

The Plain of Armageddon or Jezreel. IIS

ARMAGEDDON (är-mȧ-gĕd'ŭn). A Heb. name used only in Rev 16:16 for the gathering place for the "battle of that great day of God Almighty" associated with Christ's second coming (Rev 16:14-15). It is usually interpreted as Mount (Heb. *har*) Megiddo. The pass of Megiddo leads through the Carmel range and has been the scene of many famous battles.

It is possible that the Revelation uses Megiddo as a type of bloody conflict as it uses Sodom as a type of sinful Jerusalem (Rev 11:8). Since the eschatological battle (Zech 14:2 and elsewhere) is at Jerusalem, some have identified Armageddon with Jerusalem. But the verse may merely mean that Megiddo (*q.v.*) will be the bivouac area for the great conflict. It is important to note that Rev 16:13-16 only announces the battle. The actual conquest of the three evil powers by Christ in His coming is given in the succeeding section, Rev 19:11-20:3, which describes in detail the battle of the great day of God Almighty.

R. L. H.

ARMENIA (är-mē'nĭ-ȧ). The KJV translation of Ararat (*q.v.*), following the LXX in II Kgs 19:37; Isa 37:38. A later name for Ararat, it first occurs as Armina in the inscriptions of Darius I at Behistun. The Assyrians had used Urartu.

Armenia centered about Lake Van and the Araxes Valley. Traditionally, Mount Ararat has been located in the mountains of Armenia. The Araxes Valley linked the Iranian plateau with the plateau of Asia Minor, and served as the sanctuary for oppressed people from the S.

The Urartian kingdom flourished in the 9th and 8th cen. B.C. It was very rich in mineral resources, with fertile plains along its deep river valleys. After Assyria regained her might under Tiglath-pileser III, the Assyrian kings frequently pillaged Urartu and took thousands of captives. See T. Özgüç, "Urartu and Altintepe," *Archaeology*, XXII (1969), 256-263.

The Medes conquered Urartu early in the 6th cen. B.C. A people with an Indo-European language moved into the plateau and blended with the natives. These newcomers seem to have belonged to the Thraco-Phrygians of Asia Minor.

The Seleucids took over from Persia, but Armenia revolted in 190 B.C. Artaxias founded Armenia, which was strongest under Tigranes I (96-55 B.C.). He was defeated, however, by the Romans in 69 B.C. and surrendered to Pompey (66 B.C.), giving up Syria which he had ruled for over 14 years. In A.D. 303 Tiridates III was converted to Christianity, which became the state religion.

G. H. L.

ARMINIANISM. Arminianism is that form of Protestant theology which bears at least some resemblance to the teachings of James Arminius (1560-1609). In its authentic form it refers especially to the doctrine that predestination is conditioned upon man's free response to grace—as taught by Arminius, the Remonstrants, John Wesley, and conservative evangelicals of this century, such as the late H. Orton Wiley (see his three-volume *Christian Theology*, 1940-46). In its unauthentic form, it has come to be associated with Socinian, Unitarian, Universalist, Latitudinarian, and other liberal theologies, which carried to extremes certain germinal persuasions of Arminius, especially his tolerance and his emphasis upon human freedom. Lambertus Jacobus van Holl, referring to these unauthentic developments, speaks of "the increasing involvement of Arminianism in liberal theology" ("From Arminius to Arminianism in Dutch Theology," *Man's Faith and Freedom*, p. 27).

Antecedents of Arminianism

Arminius did not originate what is called Arminianism, but was simply its ablest exponent. Just before he became associated with such teachings as conditional predestination, a whole array of scholars were either tending in that direction or teaching that doctrine.

Well known is the fact that the erudite Erasmus taught human freedom, as opposed to Luther's Augustinian view, although Erasmus was humanistic and therefore quite unlike the later Arminius.

Melanchthon seems to have gravitated in the direction of conditional predestination (see Caspar Brandt, *The Life of James Arminius*, pp. 32-34).

Anabaptists, later better known as Mennonites, taught that the provision for salvation is universal and that men cast the deciding vote on whether they will be damned or redeemed.

While Zwingli and Calvin taught unconditional predestination, their view was by no means held universally even in their own Switzerland. At Zurich, the distinguished Bullinger questioned for a time Calvin's teaching; and Jerome Bolsec of Geneva opposed the view, as did Charles Perrot of Geneva.

In Holland, a few decades before the Synod of Dort (1618-19), most ministers tended to conditional predestination. Theodore Beza, Calvin's son-in-law and successor at the Geneva Academy where so many ministers were trained for the Reformed churches, came to expect that many of the students from the Low Countries would be conditionalists—although he himself was a supralapsarian, i.e., one who believed that the decree to elect some individuals and to damn others was made prior to Adam's creation and fall.

At the newly founded university at Leyden in Holland, most of the teachers were "Arminian" during the six years Arminius studied there (1775-1781). Nor had the Belgic Confession and the Heidelberg Catechism, the two main creeds for the Reformed churches prior to the Canons of Dort, taught unconditional predestination—unless it was by implication. Arminius was quite sure that they had not clearly taught that doctrine.

In England, in 1595, William Barrett was denied the B.D. degree at Cambridge because he rejected the Calvinistic views of Cambridge's William Perkins. At about this time, theologian Peter Baro was deposed from his position at Cambridge for the same reason (see Carl Bangs, "Arminius and the Reformation," *Church History*, June, 1961, p. 7).

But of all these, Arminius was distinctly the ablest. "Of all the actors in that movement [the recoil from Calvinism], so fertile of mighty actors, no one played a more conspicuous, important, and trying part than Arminius" (John Guthrie, "Translator's Preface," *The Life of James Arminius*, by Caspar Brandt, p. XIV).

Arminius' Teachings

Arminius' "Declaration of Sentiments" (see *The Writings of James Arminius*, I, 193), delivered by him before the governmental authorities at The Hague in 1608, spells out his own views and gives 20 arguments against the supralapsarianism of Leyden University's Francis Gomarus. Arminius' arguments condensed say that the doctrine is unsound because it makes God the author of sin.

It is in this treatise, too, that Arminius presents his distinctive doctrine of the divine decrees. Whereas the supralapsarians taught that the decree to save and to damn certain individuals preceded the decree to create them, Arminius taught that the first decree was to send Christ to redeem sinful men; the second was to receive into favor those who repent and believe; the third was to help all men to do this repenting and believing (prevenient grace); and the fourth was to save and damn individuals according to God's foreknowledge of the way in which they would freely respond to His offer of grace.

Important to an understanding of Arminius' teachings, too, is his view of human freedom. He was not a Pelagian in this regard, although he was so accused even in his own lifetime. Unlike the ancient Pelagius, he believed in a racial fall caused by Adam's sin; and while he believed that "the power of willing" was retained in men after the Fall, he believed that it is not possible for fallen men, unaided by prevenient grace, to exercise that capacity of freedom toward any good thing. Of fallen, natural man, Arminius wrote: "In this state, the free will of man toward the true good is not only wounded, maimed, infirm, bent, and weakened; but it is also imprisoned, destroyed, and lost. And its powers are not only debilitated and useless unless they are assisted by grace, but it has no powers whatever except such as are excited by divine grace. For Christ has said, 'Without me ye can do nothing' " (*The Writings of Arminius*, ed. by Nichols, I, 526).

He also wrote: "The mind, in this state, is dark, destitute of the saving knowledge of God, and, according to the apostle, incapable of those things which belong to the Spirit of God. For 'the animal man has no perception of the things of the Spirit of God' (I Cor 2:14)" (*ibid.*). Hear him also say: "Exactly correspondent to this darkness of the mind, and perverseness of the heart, is the utter weakness of all the powers to perform that which is truly good, and to omit the perpetration of that which is evil" (*ibid.*, p. 527). In support, he quotes Christ: "A corrupt tree cannot bring forth good fruit" (Mt 7:18), and "how can ye, being evil, speak good things?" (Mt 12:34). Among other supports, he also mentions Jn 6:44: "No man can come to me, except the Father draw him." After quoting Jn 8:36, that only those are free "whom the Son hath made free," he says: "It follows, that our will is not free from the first fall; that is, it is not free to good, unless it be made free by the Son through his Spirit" (*ibid.*, p. 528).

It has often been supposed that Arminius held the doctrine of entire sanctification, or Christian perfection (see this error in *Man's Faith and Freedom*, pp. 66–79). But Arminius did not teach this doctrine. It is true that at times he seemed to suggest the Wesleyan teaching. Of sanctification he says that it is for believers only, that it is an act, that it is received by faith (*Works*, II, 120). He even says that it is "the purification from sin" (*ibid.*, p. 121). Yet he withdrew such suggestions of a Wesleyan understanding right within such passages, saying, e.g., "This sanctification is not completed in a single moment; but sin . . . is weakened more and more . . ." (*ibid.*). He also wrote, "Who can deny, when the Scriptures affirm, that there are in us the remains of sin and of the old man as long as we survive in this mortal life" (II, p. 263).

Arminius tried to make theology really biblical. He felt that Stoic philosophy instead of the Bible was the basis of Augustine's doctrine of unconditional predestination; for the Stoics taught that there is a law of necessity written into the very nature of existence, to which law both God and men are subject. Arminius felt also that the creeds often become more authoritative than Scripture, and he believed that both the Belgic Confession and the Heidelberg Catechism should be interpreted, and perhaps corrected, by the Bible.

Arminius was also irenic. He was a peace-loving man who called not for rigid uniformity of belief but for tolerance. It is ironic that during his last years and just after his death the people of Holland took sides so heatedly on the matter of predestination that some wondered if the issue might give rise to a civil war.

Arminius followed practical interests instead of the merely speculative. He wrote, "For the theology which belongs to this world is practical . . . . Theoretical theology belongs to the other world . . . . For this reason, we must clothe the object of our theology in such a manner as may enable it to incline us to worship God, and fully to persuade and win us over to that practice" (*Writings*, I, 60).

For centuries it was generally thought that Arminius had earlier been a supralapsarian Calvinist, and that he had switched to the espousal of conditional predestination. Supposedly this change took place after he had been asked to support supralapsarianism against the type of conditional predestination which the Dutch humanist Richard Coornhert was advocating, and against the sublapsarianism of certain ministers of the town of Delft — sublapsarianism being the view that God's decree to save or damn certain individuals was made after the free sin and fall of Adam. Peter Bertius had stated that Arminius changed from supralapsarianism to conditional predestination. Bertius made this claim in a funeral oration at the time of Arminius' death, and the statement seems to have influenced those who have written about Arminius ever since.

While the matter has not been resolved, Carl Bangs, the principal authority on Arminius of the present time, has made an interesting case for the theory that Arminius was a conditionalist right through the years, and did not earlier espouse supralapsarianism (see Carl O. Bangs, *Arminius and Reformed Theology*, Univ. of Chicago Library, 1958). Bangs mentions the fact that the only primary evidence contrariwise is the statement of Bertius, but that Bertius had not been so close to Arminius as some have supposed. Bangs also says that Beza expected his Dutch students to be conditionalists, and thus did not clash with Arminius, but instead recommended him highly on the completion of his studies. As to why Arminius was asked to support supralapsarianism, Bangs points out that, (1) another person, Martin Lydius, had first been asked, who in turn asked Arminius; and that (2) perhaps the request for Arminius to do this was designed to drive him out into the open with his conditionalism. One factor which this does not explain, however, is why Arminius should have accepted such an assignment, if indeed he was already an opponent of supralapsarianism.

Arminianism in Holland

In 1610, the year after Arminius' death, 42 ministers and two educators met at The Hague and drew up and signed a statement which in general concurred with what Arminius had taught. Written by John Uytenbogaert, Arminius' close friend from student days at Geneva onward, it came to be called the *Remonstrance*, and its signers, the Remonstrants. This document, addressed to the government of Holland, enumerated five doctrines held by Uytenbogaert and his associates, and was designed to gain official permission for the promulgation of those doctrines in Holland's Reformed churches.

The *Remonstrance* discusses certain problems and also outlines five doctrinal differences between Calvinism and what was soon called

Arminianism. In the first part of the document, the Remonstrants treated the place of confessions in the church, and stated that they are helpful, but that they may be changed at any time, and that only the Holy Scriptures are authoritative.

An interesting statement in the first part of the document, also, is its view that secular authorities have the right to enter into theological disputes in order to preserve peace and prevent schisms. The Remonstrants probably figured that secular authorities would be more tolerant and more objective as arbiters of theological disputes than ecclesiastical authorities would be. Aside from the matter of whether this would give the state the right to dominate the church, it was a stance on the part of the Remonstrants which, if followed in the upcoming years in Holland, might well have guaranteed for Arminianism an official status. As it turned out, an ecclesiastical "court" was later called (1618-19) which outlawed Arminianism.

The second part of the *Remonstrance* rejects the five articles of Calvinism and sets forth the five opposing positions of the Remonstrants. The first of the five, summarized, is what might be called conditional predestination: that God purposes to save those who repent and believe, and to damn those who do not.

The second main point of the Remonstrant position is that Christ died "for all men and for every man," and not simply for a segment of the race who had been previously destined for salvation (see Philip Schaff, *The Creeds of Christendom*, III, 545 ff.).

The third point has to do with what can be called prevenient grace — God's purpose to help sinful men to turn to God.

The fourth point is that this grace may be resisted, and is not, as the Calvinists were saying, irresistibly received.

The fifth and last point is that, having become "incorporated into Christ by true faith," Christ "keeps them from falling" only if they continue to believe. But while the Remonstrants are cautious on the matter, they imply that if a saved person does not continue to cooperate with Christ he will become "devoid of (saving) grace."

When the *Remonstrance* was published, the Calvinist party issued a Counter-Remonstrance in which they answered it.

Arminianism Outlawed in Holland

Holland was now divided. In 1610 and 1612 conferences were held to help heal the dispute, but were not successful. In 1614 the government forbade pulpit discussion of the disputed doctrines. Then in 1617 Prince Maurice, who wanted the dispute decided in favor of Calvinism, called for a national synod to meet at Dort the following year. According to the Memoirs of Simon Episcopius, this prince was enlisted by the Calvinists on their side of the controversy against the great statesman van Olden Barnevelt. Maurice was jealous and afraid of him, and saw in the religious dispute an opportunity to unite the provinces under his control.

It was decided to make the meeting at Dort a national synod for the United Netherlands, composed of six delegates from each of the seven provinces. These delegates were to be chosen by provincial synods; and because of certain maneuverings, even from the provinces of Holland and Utrecht, where the Arminians were in the majority, almost all the delegates were Calvinists. Indeed, in all there were only three Arminians among the 42 official delegates; and in addition to the official ones, 33 foreign delegates were invited as guests, all of them Calvinists. Besides all this, the three Arminian members were prevented by the rules from defending Arminianism, and they quit the sessions before taking the "Calvinistic" oath as delegates. While Arminian spokesmen were permitted on a few occasions to answer the charges made against them, there was no open debate on the merits of the two theologies.

This synod condemned Arminianism as heresy, and forbade its propagation in the Low Countries — in the seven states, that is, of the 17 states which comprised the entire Low Countries, the seven being officially called the United Netherlands, or the Dutch Republic. The synod's sessions concluded in May, 1619, having begun in November, 1618. In July, 1619, the synod's *Sentence* was approved by the government, and the Arminian leaders were ordered banished or imprisoned. It was illegal to hold Remonstrant meetings, or to support or harbor any of their ministers. Spies were hired to report the leaders if any of them returned to their families for visits. Some 18,000 became martyrs, slaughtered by hired mercenaries of the contra-Remonstrant party.

In spite of all these deterrents to their faith, the Remonstrants often met together; and survived, even if they did not flourish. In 1619 they set up an organization called the Remonstrant Reformed Brotherhood, led by John Uytenbogaert, Simon Episcopius (a pupil of Arminius), and one Grevinchovius. When Prince Maurice died in 1623, the ban against the Remonstrants was lifted. They organized the Remonstrant Reformed Church Community, which still exists as the Remonstrant Brotherhood. In 1634 they started a theological college at Amsterdam with Episcopius as its head and as its first professor of theology. The college still exists as a part of the University of Leyden (see G. O. McCulloh, ed., *Man's Faith and Freedom*, 1962, pp. 5-7).

Outside of Holland

Arminius and Arminians in general have made frequent mention of the fact that both the Greek and the Latin Fathers prior to Augustine (354-430) had been conditionalists. Already it has been mentioned that the Mennonites, who flourished in Germany, were Arminians.

The Moravians, who moved to Count Zinzendorf's large estates at Herrnhut in Germany and who went forth from there as missionaries to many world areas, were Arminian. Their belief that anyone may be saved, thrust them into extensive and committed missionary work at a time when not many Christians were similarly motivated. It was through their work in America and England that their Peter Böhler met John Wesley in London and helped him to experience the strangely warmed heart.

In England, there were some conditional predestinationists prior to Arminius' espousal of that doctrine with disputations and publications. Peter Baro, at Cambridge, has already been mentioned. His successor (1608), John Playfere, lectured and published on free will and redemption as possible for all men. So did Archbishop Laud early in the 17th cen., although he went to Pelagian extremes, denying original sin (see John Fletcher, *Works*, II, 276, 277).

The Quakers, mystical and not doctrinal in their interests, and therefore "Arminians without Arminius," nonetheless taught basically what Arminius did — that anyone may be saved.

John Goodwin taught Arminianism in England in the middle of the 17th cen., and directly influenced Wesley in that direction (see William Strickland's Ph.D. dissertation on Goodwin, Vanderbilt University, 1967). Jeremy Taylor and William Law also taught Arminianism and likewise helped to mold the founder of Methodism.

Many English divines prior to the time of John Wesley (1703-1791) taught an aberrant Arminianism. Pelagian, Socinian, Arian, Universalist, and Latitudinarian impurities were introduced into the Arminian opposition to Calvinism. This is why John Wesley wrote, "To say, 'This man is an Arminian,' has the same effect on many hearers as to say, 'This is a mad dog.' It puts them into a fright at once..." ("The Question, 'What Is an Arminian?' Answered," *The Works of John Wesley*, X, 358). Yet when Wesley started a periodical in 1778, he was brave enough to call it *The Arminian Magazine*.

Actually, in England, and in Wales as well, there were and are two wings of the Arminian movement. Geoffrey Nuttall, in a paper presented in 1960 in Holland at the four hundredth anniversary of Arminius' birth, says: "Self-confessed Arminianism in England is to be found, in the main, in one or the other of two contrasting movements. One of these two movements leads into Arianism, Socinianism, and Unitarianism, and eventually decreases in numbers and influence. The other remains Trinitarian and evangelical, and increases" ("The Influence of Arminianism in England," *Man's Faith and Freedom*, ed. by G. O. McCulloh, 1962, p. 50). Nuttall actually traces the "unauthentic" wing in the records of local congregations in Wales and England, and supports by first-hand historical study his statement that the unauthentic wing tends to decrease in numbers.

It would not take such a study to prove that the other wing, Wesleyan Arminianism, "Arminianism on fire," has tended to increase in numbers and influence. So effective, in fact, is the influence of Wesleyan Arminianism that university students in England, a few years ago, found themselves writing an examination on the topic "Since Wesley We Are All Arminians."

Methodism is the movement through which Arminianism was most widely disseminated in America. With the word that anyone may be saved, Methodist circuit riders, lay and ordained, spread the doctrine of conditional predestination as America's frontier moved westward. Thus Methodism became the largest Protestant denomination in the United States, being overtaken by the Southern Baptists only in the 1950's.

Besides being promulgated in America by Methodism, authentic Arminianism has been taught in this country by the United Brethren, the Salvation Army, many Wesleyan denominations including the Church of the Nazarene, and by numerous other groups.

The Present Situation

Arminianism and Calvinism are not now so far apart as they were, say, during the first half of the 20th cen.

On the Arminian side, even within its Wesleyan strain, i.e., "Arminianism on fire," Pelagian tendencies had developed. John Miley, who taught at Methodism's Drew Theological Seminary during the latter years of the 19th cen., opposed the representative theory of original sin's "transmission," which theory both Arminius and Wesley had espoused, and taught a so-called genetic mode view: that original sin is received from one's parents (see his *Systematic Theology,* II, 506). In addition, Miley taught that no racial guilt resulted from Adam's sin, whereas Arminius and Wesley had taught that guilt as well as depravity accrued to the race, but that the guilt was removed by Christ's atonement as a "free gift" (Rom 5:16-17) for the entire race (cf. Robert E. Chiles, *Theological Transition in American Methodism 1790-1935,* 1965).

Besides Miley, who was studied widely by Wesleyans, Olin Alfred Curtis, his successor at Drew, also tended in a Pelagian direction, away from an emphasis upon grace and toward an overemphasis upon free will. His major work, *The Christian Faith* (1905; reprinted by Kregel in 1956), was probably the most widely used theology textbook in Wesleyan-Arminian circles prior to the publication of H. Orton Wiley's three-volume *Christian Theology* (1940-46). Curtis is Kantian in that volume when he says, "Deeds are moral . . . only when they express a man's own conception of duty . . ." (p. 61). So Kantian is Curtis that he cannot let God's grace come through unconditionally to infants who die. He has them accepting Christ for themselves in the intermediate state. Says he, "In the intermediate

state all these children come to full personal experience just as surely as our children do in this life" (p. 404). For Curtis, man is so free that "any motive in the conscious range can be selected . . ." (p. 44).

Also Pelagian in tendency were Boston University's E. S. Brightman and A. C. Knudson. Brightman's *A Philosophy of Religion* (1940) shows this, as well as others of his works. Knudson defined freedom as the power of "contrary choice" (*The Principles of Christian Ethics,* p. 82). He could say that, apart from grace, men can choose contrariwise, because, for him, the Fall is "legendary" (p. 94).

Such men as Miley and Curtis, Brightman and Knudson were mentors to many Wesleyan-Arminians and influenced them in a Pelagian direction.

What Arminius taught on freedom has been shown. John Wesley was in basic agreement with Arminius on freedom. Like Arminius, he taught that man casts the deciding vote whether he will be saved or damned. But for Wesley, as for the earlier "freedomist," man does not, cannot, of himself, cast an assenting vote. Speaking of John Fletcher and himself, Wesley says that they "absolutely deny natural free will" (see Burtner and Chiles' *Compend of Wesley's Theology,* pp. 132-133). Wesley continues, "We both steadily assert that the will of fallen man is by nature free only to evil" (*ibid.*).

Believing that to deny original sin is to be a heathen, Wesley held a view of the racial fall which is a bit extreme. He taught that all men are " 'conceived in sin,' that hence there is in every man a 'carnal mind,' which is enmity against God; which is not, cannot be, 'subject to' His 'law'; and which so infects the whole soul that 'there dwelleth in' him, 'in his flesh,' in his natural state, 'no good thing'; but 'every imagination of the thoughts of his heart is evil,' only evil, and that 'continually' " (*Standard Sermons,* II, 223). Wesley even figures that every descendant of Adam is ". . . dead to God, wholly dead in sin; entirely void of life of God; void of the image of God" (*Works,* ed. by Emory, 401).

If man is not "void" of the image of God, the image is at least utterly defaced. This is why Arminian-Wesleyans agree with Wesley that "salvation begins with what is termed (and very properly) preventing grace; including the first wish to please God, the first dawn of light concerning his will, the first slight transient conviction of having sinned against him" (*ibid.,* VI, 509).

Within the past decade or two, within "Arminianism on fire," Pelagian tendencies have waned and authentic Wesleyan-Arminianism has exerted itself. This is in part because of the widespread use of the late H. Orton Wiley's *Christian Theology,* which is admittedly more idealistic in places than Arminius and Wesley were (e.g., I, 255-319), but which nonetheless is basically Arminian in the authentic sense. It is in part because of a revival of first-hand study of Arminius and Wesley. The waning of purely philosophical interests and the resurgence of biblical engagement have figured most importantly in this return to the persuasions of Arminius and Wesley. For proof of such a return, see *The Word and the Doctrine*, a composite volume issued in 1965 by the National Holiness Association, containing 37 papers given at a 1964 national conference on Wesleyan-Arminian theological distinctives.

At the same time, Calvinism is tending to become less Calvinistic. Not many prominent Calvinists at present espouse the supralapsarianism of Theodore Beza and Francis Gomarus of Arminius' time, nor even the sublapsarianism of the Synod of Dort. Nor do such scholars, by and large, teach the unconditional predestination contained in the Westminster Confession. Those of the Christian Reformed Church (Calvin Seminary) still do, along with distinguished scholars at Westminster Theological Seminary. But several Calvinist scholars connected in recent years with Fuller Theological Seminary, for example, write quite as evangelical Arminians might. *Christianity Today*, by far the most widely disseminated and influential evangelical magazine for ministers in our time, is not at all rigidly Calvinistic. Many such persons now teach that anyone may be saved; but in general they do still teach the unconditional security of believers—eternal security. Yet it is an interesting fact that Robert Shank, in his *Life in the Son*, 1960, a Baptist, has tended to undermine even the doctrine of eternal security.

It may be that in the future there will be still more of a convergence of the Arminian and Calvinistic theologies, as the vain philosophies of men wane in their influence and as evangelicals are taught more and more by Holy Scripture.

Bibliography. James Arminius, *The Writings of James Arminius*, trans. by James Nichols and W. R. Bagnall, Grand Rapids: Baker, I–III, 1956. Carl Bangs, *Arminius and Reformed Theology*, Ph.D. dissertation, Dept. of Photoduplication, Univ. of Chicago Library, 1958; "James Arminius and the Remonstrants," unpublished B.D. thesis, Nazarene Theological Seminary, 1949. E. S. Brightman, *A Philosophy of Religion*, New York: Prentice-Hall, 1940. Edward John Carnell, *The Kingdom of Love and the Pride of Life*, Grand Rapids: Eerdmans, 1961. Robert E. Chiles, *Theological Transition in American Methodism 1790–1935*, New York: Abingdon, 1965. George L. Curtiss, *Arminianism in History*, New York: Hunt and Eaton, 1894. Simon Episcopius, *Memoirs of Simon Episcopius*, ed. by Calder Frederick, London: Simpkin and Marshall, 1835. J. Kenneth Geiger, ed., *The Word and the Doctrine*, Kansas City: Beacon Hill Press, 1965. John Guthrie, *The Life of James Arminius*, Nashville: Stevenson and F. A. Owen, 1857. A. C. Knudson, *The Principles of Christian Ethics*, New York: Abingdon-Cokesbury, 1943. Gerald O. McCulloh, ed., *Man's Faith and Freedom*, New York: Abingdon, 1962. O. Glenn McKinley, *Where Two Creeds Meet*, Kansas City: Beacon Hill Press, 1959. John Miley, *Systematic Theology*, New York: Eaton and Mains, 1894. Robert Shank, *Life in the Son: A Study in the Doctrine of Perseverance*, Springfield, Mo.: Westcott Publishers, 1960. Wm. Fairfield Warren, *In the Footsteps of Arminius*, New York: Phillips and Hunt, 1888. H. Orton Wiley, *Christian Theology*, Kansas City: Beacon Hill Press, 1940–46. Mildred Bangs Wynkoop, *Foundations of Wesleyan-Arminian Theology*, Kansas City: Beacon Hill Press, 1967.

J. K. G.

Armlets and bracelets adorn this mythical figure at the Assyrian palace of Nimrud. LM

ARMLET. A ring or band usually of metal worn on the upper arm, as distinguished from a bracelet, worn on the wrist. It was an ornament or status symbol and could be worn by either men or women (Ex 35:22). Armlets were counted as spoils of war (Num 31:50). King Saul wore one (II Sam 1:10), but later Isaiah condemned them as frivolous (Isa 3:19).

ARMONI (är-mō'nī). A son of King Saul and his concubine Rizpah. David delivered him along with others of Saul's family to the Gibeonites to be hanged, to avenge Saul's slaughter of the Gibeonites (II Sam 21:8–9).

ARMOR, ARMS. Various kinds of weapons are mentioned frequently in the Bible, both literally and figuratively (as illustrative of spiritual warfare). Yet little detailed description is given of the many different weapons. However, it is known that the weapons of the nations of the Near East were essentially the same, with certain modifications and variations. Representations in sculpture of the weapons of the Assyrians, Chaldeans, Egyptians and Hittites on their ancient monuments greatly assist us in knowing more definitely what the battle pieces of the Hebrews were like.

Offensive Weapons

The rod or staff was the simplest implement, which might have been weighted on one end with a stone or copper mace-head like a club. It could be quite a threatening weapon, whether used in self-defense or in attack of an enemy (Prov 25:18, "maul," KJV; "war club," RSV). It was either carried in the hand or attached to the wrist by a loop. *See* Rod; Staff.

The sling was another simple instrument among the most ancient devices of warfare (Job 41:28), used commonly by shepherds to drive off animals attempting to attack or molest their flocks or to turn straying sheep. *See* Sling. The sling was usually made from a strip of leather, although sometimes it was woven into a belt from rushes, hair, or animal sinews, which widened to about two inches in the middle and formed a hollow in which a smooth object was placed. After being swung several times around the head with great force, one of the strings of the sling was released to discharge the missile. Both smooth stones and pellets of lead were used, carried in a bag or piled at the feet of the soldier. They could be hurled as far as six hundred feet!

Slingers formed a part of the regular army and at times certain nations employed large numbers of slingers in their armies as part of the light infantry, together with the archers. It will be remembered that this was the weapon used by David to kill the giant Goliath (I Sam 17:40–50). The chosen 700 left-handed Benjamites were noted for their skill and accuracy with the sling (Jud 20:16).

The bow and arrow constituted a very important weapon of war, as well as for hunting, and is thought to have been the principal weapon of offense. Evidence indicates its early use among the Hebrews (Gen 21:20; 27:3; 48:22). Use was not limited to common soldiers, but captains high in rank and even kings' sons employed the bow and arrow and were skilled in its use (II Kgs 9:24; I Sam 18:4). The tribe of Benjamin seems to have been particularly ex-

pert in archery (I Chr 8:40; 12:2; II Chr 14:8; 17:17). *See* Bow and Arrow; Archer.

Bows were made of flexible seasoned wood, copper, or bronze, and ranged greatly in size and style. The string was made from bindweed, natural cord, hide, or the intestines of animals. The bow was strung by hand, usually bending it with the foot since it required much strength. Arrows, constructed from reed or light wood, were tipped with sharp stone, bronze, and iron, and were often poisoned and provided with barbs. They were about 30 inches long and winged with three rows of feathers. In times of siege they were dipped in pitch, wound with flax or hemp, and ignited to start fires. The quiver in which arrows were kept was carried on the soldier's back, at his side, or fastened to a chariot. Archers on foot and mounted comprised a formidable element of the fighting forces.

A Persian panel showing spearmen of the guard from the palace at Susa. LM

The spear, javelin, or lance had a wooden shaft of varying lengths and weight with a metal point or head made from brass or iron, usually with a double edge. Infantry spears were shorter (about the height of a man) than those of the cavalry. Javelins were generally lighter and shorter than spears. When not in use these weapons were carried across the soldiers' backs (I Sam 17:6, RSV). They were employed by the heavy-armed troops and were used both for thrusting and throwing. Stuck in the ground in front of a tent, a spear indicated the quarters of a king (cf. I Sam 26:7). It was the heavier spear, *ḥănît*, Saul's favorite weapon, that he hurled at David (I Sam 18:11; 19:10) and later at Jonathan (I Sam 20:33), and not a javelin as KJV translates. There also existed a lighter missile called a dart, but little is known about it.

The sword or dagger (Heb. *ḥereb*) is the most frequently mentioned weapon in the Bible, being used both for offense and defense. The blade was constructed of iron or bronze and varied greatly in length, weight, and style, usually being two-edged. It normally hung on the left side from a girdle, housed in a sheath. Often the hilt was highly ornamented, especially those

An Assyrian archer draws his bow. From the palace of Ashurbanipal, seventh century B.C. LM

150

Two Assyrian servants armed with swords, from the palace at Khorsabad, eighth century B.C. LM

of kings. Swords were used to hit, cut, and thrust. Short swords or daggers sometimes had three sides and were carried under the belt or the clothing (Jud 3:16, 21). In the hands of a skilled soldier the sword was a deadly and much-feared weapon.

Battle-axes and maces were among the most primitive weapons. They were used for cleaving, as clubs, and as throwing missiles. Wooden maces were bound with bronze, had metal hand guards, and were probably studded with iron spikes. Used by the heavy infantry in hand-to-hand fighting, they were also issued to charioteers. Battle-axes were two or more feet long with variously shaped metal blades (often curved or circular), wielded by infantrymen to batter down enemy gates and towers (Ezk 26:9). See Axe.

Chariots were not used by the Israelites until the time of Solomon, who built 4,000 stalls for his horses and chariots (I Kgs 4:26). They were boxlike vehicles closed in front and open in the rear, likely made of wood and overlaid with iron or bronze, resting on an axle which connected the two wheels. Usually three persons stood in the chariot, the driver, the warrior, and the shield bearer. See Chariot.

Siege weapons, such as the battering ram, engine *(q.v.),* and catapult, were used for breaching walls and throwing stones, arrows, darts *(q.v.),* and other objects (up to 300 pounds weight; some missiles could be hurled more than a quarter of a mile). Some rams required as many as 200 men to move; others were hung in movable towers and were threat-

ening instruments of war. The Hyksos built sloping ramparts to defend their cities against battering rams as early as 1600 B.C.

Defensive Armor

The shield or buckler was the oldest and most common weapon of defense. The Israelites had chiefly two varieties. A large shield *(ṣinnâ)* used by the heavy-armed infantry, covered the whole body, and was either oval or rectangular in shape (Ps 5:12; II Chr 11:12; 25:5). Sometimes a special shield bearer was employed. A small light shield *(māgēn),* used by archers and for hand-to-hand fighting, was round (II Chr 17:17). Shields were made of wood or wicker overlaid with leather, although sometimes bronze and copper were used. They were rubbed with oil to preserve them and to make them shine in the sun (II Sam 1:21; Isa 21:5). Ornamental shields were plated or made with gold. When not being used in actual combat, the shield was strapped over the shoulder and kept in a cover (Isa 22:6).

Helmets were made of differing materials and in various shapes by the ancient nations. Originally they were more like skullcaps and worn only by prominent persons, but later it became common for ordinary soldiers to wear them for protection. Materials from which they were made included wood, linen, felt, rushes, leather, and brass. Sometimes helmets were furnished with flaps and covered with metal scales to protect the ears, neck, and shoulders. See Helmet.

The coat of mail, habergeon, cuirass, or breastplate was also used at first only by prominent men. At a later period when the soldiers were provided with such body armor, theirs were made of leather, linen or felt, whereas the leaders' were made of bronze. Often it protected the back as well as the breast; sometimes it had leather flaps which hung from the waist-

King Ashurnasirpal II of Assyria in his chariot. BM

line. Certain styles had small iron plates fitting closely over each other and sewn on a leather jacket. The "nails" used in its construction were likely the pins which were used to fasten the metal scales. Smaller plates or scales and narrower rows were used where greater flexibility was needed, as at the throat and neck. Some coats of mail covered the thigh nearly to the knee, being bound with a girdle at the waist to prevent its pressing too heavily on the shoulders. More often a second piece was employed to cover the body below the waist, like a short skirt detached from the girdle. Wire netting was also used to cover the top part of the body. Kings and principal chariot warriors wore long coats of mail reaching to the ankles or to the knees. *See* Cuirass; Corselet; Habergeon.

The girdle, from which the sword usually hung, was of leather studded with nails or metal plates. With light armor it was sometimes broad and placed around the hips. It was known also to have been worn from the shoulder like a scarf.

Greaves, armor to protect the leg between the knee and the ankle, were widely used among the ancients, but apparently not commonly among the Israelites. Made of brass or leather, they were tied with thongs around the leg and above the ankle. Military boots are mentioned in Isa 9:5 (RSV), likely a leather half-boot studded with heavy nails.

Greek armor of the fifth century B.C. BM

Spiritual Armor

In the well-known passage in Eph 6:10–17 the Christian is exhorted to put on the whole armor of God (*panoplia tou theou;* 6:11, 13). The word *panoplia,* "full armor" (NASB), is a fusion of two Gr. words, *pan* ("all") and *hopla* ("weapons"), and refers to the full combat equipment of a soldier: It is used figuratively to indicate the complete provision of spiritual virtues with which God endows His child for the war against evil (see also Rom 13:12; II Cor 6:7; 10:4–6). Every believer is inextricably engaged in the warfare that rages in the spirit realm between Christ with His angels and Satan with his demonic forces of wickedness.

The apostle Paul symbolizes vital elements of Christian character for one's defense against the accusations of the devil (cf. Rev 12:10) by various pieces of the Graeco-Roman armor of his day. Truth in the sense of personal honesty, sincerity, and dependability must be girded on the loins, the biblical seat of one's emotions (cf. Isa 11:5). The breastplate of practical uprightness in daily life protects the heart, the biblical seat of one's personality, conscience, and will (cf. Isa 59:17). The sandals are equated to preparedness in, or a skillful working knowledge of how to apply, the promises of the gospel of peace, so that one need not be anxious but have firm footing on the slippery ground of external circumstances. The large (four-by-two-feet) rectangular shield (*thyreos*), which could interlock with those of the soldiers on either side to form a solid wall, suggests one's faith acting together with that of fellow believers to present a united front against insidious, devilish attacks. The helmet of salvation perhaps symbolizes assurance of salvation, so necessary to protect one's mind from doubts and fears. The only offensive weapon listed by Paul is the sword of the Spirit, here described as the Word (*rhēma*) of God, i.e., every spoken command or prophetic utterance coming from God through one of His servants (Lk 1:37 [ASV], 38; 5:5; Mt 4:4; Heb 1:3; cf. Hos 6:5; Mt 10:19 f.; I Cor 12:8–10).

Bibliography. CornPBE, pp. 126–136. A. Oepke and K. G. Kuhn, "*Hoplon,* etc.," TDNT, V, 292–315. Yigael Yadin, *The Art of Warfare in Biblical Lands,* 2 vols., New York: McGraw-Hill, 1963.

R. E. Po.

ARMOR BEARER. A companion to an important warrior in the period of the Conquest and monarchy who was responsible for carrying a shield and perhaps weapons to assist in battle. Stories of Abimelech, Jonathan, and Saul all involve their armor bearers (Jud 9:54; I Sam 14 and I Sam 31). Joab, David's general, had ten armor bearers (II Sam 18:15).

ARMORY. Refers to military equipment kept in a storehouse (II Kgs 20:13) or to the place where such collections were kept (Neh 3:19).

Used poetically of God's power against the Chaldeans (Jer 50:25). In Song 4:4 the Heb. word *talpîyôth* ("armoury," KJV) perhaps refers to the courses of stone in the tower of David, likened to the rows or layers of the beloved's necklace.

ARMY. The Israelites were not intended by God to be a warlike people with a large standing army. Because of their strategic location at the crossroads of three continents, however, they found it necessary to make adequate preparations for their defense against hostile attacks. In the OT two Heb. words often signify "army": *hayil*, literally meaning "strength, force" (cf. armed forces), and *sābā'*, "host, army." God is frequently called Yahweh of hosts, and the name is transliterated as Lord of Sabaoth in Rom 9:29 and Jas 5:4.

The first recorded use of armed forces in the history of the Jews is that of Abraham's conflict with the king of Elam and his confederates (Gen 14), in which Abraham displayed heroic military leadership with a band of 318 retainers.

Military organization of the Jews began with the Exodus from Egypt. It was not so much, especially at first, that they were armed for warfare as that they were arranged by tribes and divisions as a body of troops for the march through the wilderness. After Sinai they were divided into divisions or army corps; certain gradations of military rank existed. Except for the Levites, men of 20 years of age and older who were fit to go to war were assigned a post in the army (Num 1:3, 47-50; 31:14). Certain individuals were exempt from military service: those who were newly married, those who had built a new house or planted a vineyard, the fearful and fainthearted (Deut 20:5-8). As footmen in the desert their weapons were the simple arms for attack and defense. It is evident that their journeyings in the wilderness prepared them for the discipline and tactics of a military company.

Under the brilliant leadership of Joshua and following the conquest of Canaan, there was further development of military organization, strategy, and equipment. United action of the armed forces was jeopardized, however, by tribal jealousies and rivalries which threatened the national solidarity. Individual tribes generally defended their own territory and people; only great emergencies united the armies of the various tribes in common action. There was no regular, permanent army at this time. When emergencies arose, God raised up a leader who summoned the men of Israel to war against their enemies, and when the exigency passed the forces were disbanded. Armies thus drafted were divided into companies of thousands, hundreds, fifties, and still further into families under appointed officers. Provisions for the army were the responsibility of each tribe (Jud 20:10), were supplied by rich landowners (I Sam 25), or from the natural resources of the

Wooden models of a contingent of Egyptian soldiers found in a tomb dating to about 2000 B.C. LL

land. The soldiers' pay generally consisted only of supplies, plus a portion of the spoil.

It was not until the monarchy that Israel had a professional or standing army. (Comparatively little progress had been made in military affairs from the time the Jews had entered Palestine.) Saul and David had bands of select warriors, the nuclei of which served as the kings' bodyguards. David developed a national militia of 12 regiments, each of which was called up for duty for one month in the year under their appointed officers. Over the entire army there was a commander-in-chief or "captain of the host" (I Sam 14:50; II Sam 24:2), a role only rarely assumed by the king himself after Saul's reign.

Samuel had warned the leaders of Israel that a professional soldiery would be needed under a monarchy (I Sam 8:10-12). But the severe oppression of the mighty Philistines necessitated systematic military preparations on the part of King Saul to withstand invasions and to free the people from their heavy yoke of bondage, as well as to achieve a national unity in Israel. General Joab of David's army, though rough and unscrupulous, was well known for his military genius. His tactical brilliance revolutionized Israel's warfare, particularly his skill in the art of siege warfare which he taught David's soldiers.

Although peace generally prevailed during Solomon's reign, there was no diminution of the armed forces. Many cities resembled fortresses and required strong garrisons for their defense. Disregarding the divine prohibition of horses (Deut 17:16; I Kgs 10:26-29), Solomon added vast numbers of horses and chariots to the army's equipment, and later lancers and mounted archers were also added. Palestine's hilly interior was not suited for the use of chariots, but as the foreign relations of Israel extended in the direction of Syria and Egypt in later times, it was thought advantageous and militarily necessary to employ chariots against enemy forces, especially in the flat plains regions. But this proved to be an expensive and often impractical addition to Israel's army. The oppressive cost and the forced military service and labor created intense dissatisfaction, eventually contributing to the disruption of the kingdom. Foreign troops, such as the Cherethites and Pelethites, mainly of Philistine origin, were sometimes hired as mercenaries.

Extraordinarily large numbers are sometimes given for the military statistics (e.g., I Sam 11:8; II Chr 26:12–13). It is thought that some of these are not necessarily to be understood in a strictly literal numerical sense, but may have been figurative or territorial terms. Or the numbers may not have been transmitted correctly in the recopying of MSS. Another possibility is that the Heb. *'eleph* translated "thousand" can also mean in various contexts "clan" or "clan leader, chieftain." In some passages such men are further designated as mighty men of valor (e.g., II Chr 14:8; 17:13–18). *See* Number.

Little is known about the order of battle and the exact arrangement of troops in the field, but it seems that the heavy-armed troops (spearmen) came first, followed by slingers and archers, supported by horses and chariots. Division into three bodies is frequently mentioned, the heavy-armed troops and two divisions of light-armed soldiers. Various purposes were served by this arrangement: the provision of a center and two wings for combat; various strategic combinations of the divisions according to special needs; relays for the night watches. Maneuvers varied according to the strategy of the enemy forces or the lay of the land.

Fighting was generally limited to the dry season. Operations were suspended when the rainy autumn weather came and resumed again in the spring. Sentries were appointed to keep a vigilant guard of the camp at night. When the army went forth into battle a detachment remained to protect the camp and to serve, if necessary, as a reserve or to provide an escape for the chief.

In the NT, the Roman army is most frequently mentioned, especially the Roman legions (varying from 3,000 to 6,000 soldiers), which were commanded by chief captains or tribunes. Legions were divided into bands or cohorts, which were subdivided into maniples, which in turn were divided into centuries (originally comprised of 100 men) under the command of centurions. Special groups, independent cohorts of volunteers, are mentioned in Scripture, such as the Augustan and the Italian bands (Acts 10:1; 27:1); also there was the praetorian guard (Phil 1:13, RSV).

See Armor; Host; Legion; War.

Bibliography. Yigael Yadin, *The Art of Warfare in Biblical Lands,* 2 vols., New York: McGraw-Hill, 1963.

R. E. Po.

ARNAN (är'năn). A remote descendant in the royal family of David through Zerubbabel (I Chr 3:21).

The Arnon River. JR

ARNON (är'nŏn). A perennial stream of Transjordan flowing 30 miles through a deep gorge into the Dead Sea slightly N of its mid-point; modern Wadi el-Mojib. At the time of the Conquest it separated Moab from the Amorite kingdoms to the N. It was from this vicinity that Israel issued its challenge to Sihon, king of Heshbon (Num 21:13–14, 21–24, 28), and moved northward to conquer the whole of Gilead and Bashan (Deut 2:24, 36; 4:48; Josh 12:1–2). Upon assignment of tribal allotments, the Arnon became the southern boundary of the territory of Reuben (Deut 3:12, 16; Josh 13:15–16). Balak, king of Moab, met Balaam here to solicit his favor and to seek his curse on Israel (Num 22:36).

The territory N of Arnon had previously been controlled by Moab so that the portion opposite Jericho was still called the "plains [fields] of Moab" (Num 22:1; 26:3; 36:13; *et al.*), but Sihon had driven the Moabites over Arnon (Num 21:26, 28). The Moabites under Eglon attempted its recovery in the period of the judges (Jud 3:12–30), as also in the late 9th cen. when Mesha claimed victory over Israel in his votive stela (Moabite Stone), building a highway and numerous forts along the N of the Arnon (line 26; cf. Nelson Glueck, *The Other Side of the Jordan,* pp. 138–139). An elegy over the ultimate fall of Moab witnesses indirectly to the temporary successes Moab had enjoyed (Isa 15:4; Jer 48:20).

R. V. R.

AROD (âr'ŏd), **ARODI** (ăr'ō-dī). A son of Gad (Gen 46:16) and founder of the clan. The Arodites were descendants of Arod (Num 26:17).

AROER (à-rō'ẽr)

1. A city strategically located on the N bank of the Arnon gorge; modern Arair, three miles SE of Dhiban. It was the southernmost city of the Amorite king Sihon (Deut 2:36; 4:48; Josh 12:2), hence also Reuben's southernmost city (Josh 13:16). This was David's starting point in

Transjordan for his census (II Sam 24:5). Aroer appears also in the Heb. of Jer 48:6, but the text is uncertain (RSV: "like a wild ass"). Aroer was lost to Hazael (II Kgs 10:33). Mesha records rebuilding it (Moabite Stone, line 26). Jeremiah represents Aroer as Moabite at that time (Jer 48:18-19). Hotham, the "Aroerite" in a Reubenite context, suggests this Aroer (I Chr 11:44; cf. v. 42).

2. A town in the territory of Gad "opposite" (RSV: "east of") Rabbah (modern Amman), capital of the Ammonites (Num 32:34; Josh 13:25); exact location uncertain. LXX of Isa 17:2 is to be preferred to the Heb., reading "her cities" (RSV) instead of "Aroer."

3. A town of southern Judah to whom David gave a part of the spoil retrieved from the Amalekite raiders of Ziklag (I Sam 30:28); modern Ararah, 12 miles SE of Beersheba. "Adadah" of Josh 15:22 should probably also be so read.

R. V. R.

ARPAD (är'păd). Twice spelled Arphad (Isa 36:19; 37:13). A N Syrian city-state, spelled *'Arpad* in Heb., *'rpd* in an Aram. inscription, and *Arpadda* in Akkad. records. The site of Arpad, now *Erfâd*, lies 30 miles N of Aleppo. The Assyrians under Adad-nirari III despoiled the city first in 806 B.C., and again under Ashurdan III in 754 B.C. Tiglath-pileser III after another conquest of the city in 740 B.C. made its territory into an Assyrian province. Twenty years later Arpad rebelled and received its punishment by Sargon II. In the OT it is most often mentioned in connection with its destruction by the Assyrians (II Kgs 18:34; 19:13; Isa 10:9; 36:19; 37:13; Jer 49:23).

ARPHAD (är'făd). *See* Arpad.

ARPHAXAD (är-făk'săd). Listed in Gen 10:22, 24 as a son of Shem, born two years after the Flood (Gen 11:10) and living to the age of 438 years (Gen 11:13). The name may refer not only to an individual but to a tribe of people descended from Shem. The name Arrapachitis (Ptol. vi. 1-2), a region between lakes Van and Urmiah in Armenia, perhaps stems from his name.

ARROW. *See* Armor; Bow and Arrow.

ARTAXERXES (är'tă-zûrk'sēz). The fifth monarch after Cyrus the Great to rule over the Persian Empire. To distinguish him from two later kings of the same name, he was known as Artaxerxes I (Longimanus). He reigned from 464 to 423 B.C., twice as long as his father Xerxes (Est 1:1). *See* Ahasuerus.

Not a dynamic ruler, Artaxerxes had suffered humiliations at the hands of the Greeks and by revolts in Egypt and Syria. Enjoying life in his palace cities, he entrusted military campaigns to his generals and the rule of the provinces to relatives and friends. Thus he was only too glad to stabilize matters in Palestine by heeding the requests of first one faction and then another.

In 458 B.C., he gave Ezra permission to return to Jerusalem to revive and strengthen the temple services (Ezr 7). A few years later the Jews must have begun to repair the city walls too, for about 446 B.C. Artaxerxes allowed Rehum and Shimshai to halt the project (Ezr 4:7-23). Not only did they stop this work, but also broke down the walls and burned the gates (Neh 1:3). This led the cupbearer of Artaxerxes, a Jew named Nehemiah, to ask permission to rebuild the city walls, which favor was graciously granted in 445 B.C. (Neh 2:1-8). In 443 B.C., Nehemiah obtained permission from Artaxerxes to return again to Jerusalem to carry out reforms (Neh 13:6).

J. C. W.

ARTEMAS (är'tē-mĭs). A companion of Paul whose name is linked with Tychicus in a proposed mission to Crete to relieve Titus (Tit 3:12). The name is generally considered to be Gr. (*contra.* Jerome), possibly a shortened form of Artemidorus, a familiar name in Asia Minor, or the masculine form of Artemis. According to tradition, he was one of the 70 disciples of Lk 10:1.

ARTEMIS. *See* Gods, False.

ARTILLERY. The KJV translation of the word rendered "weapons" in I Sam 20:40, RSV. From the context ("Jonathan gave his weapons to the lad") and from the modern meaning of the word "artillery," it is clear that the RSV is a more accurate translation. *See* Armor.

ARTS. *See* Occupations.

ARUBOTH (a-rōō'bŏth). The town of Ben-hesed, one of Solomon's officers (I Kgs 4:10). It may be identified with the modern Arab town of 'Arrabeh, two miles SW of Dothan in Manasseh.

ARUMAH (a-rōō'ma). A town near Shechem where Abimelech resided (Jud 9:31, 41).

ARVAD (är'văd), **ARVADITE** (är'va-dīt). A port city of northern Phoenicia, located on the island of Ruad, which lies c. two miles off the mainland and c. 30 miles N of Tripolis. The city is mentioned first in the Amarna letters (14th cen. B.C.) as Arwada, in Assyrian records as Armada, Aruda, Aruadi, etc., in classical writings as Aradus, and in Hebrew as *'Arwād*.

The Arvadites are listed in Gen 10:18 and I Chr 1:16 as descendants of Canaan, while Ezekiel mentions the mariners and soldiers of Arvad as having served the city of Tyre in its defense (Ezk 27:8, 11). The city repeatedly fought against the Assyrians, and at other periods was tributary to Assyria. Nebuchadnezzar II mentions its king as one of his vassals.

ARZA (är′zà). The steward of King Elah of Israel at whose house in Tirzah the king was drunk when he was assassinated by Zimri (I Kgs 16:9).

ASA (ā′sà). The third king of Judah, son and successor of Abijah. His 41-year reign began with a ten-year period of peace, during which a program of religious reform was started. His aim was to rid the land of heathen idols and worship. His zeal for God was shown by the dethroning of Maachah, his grandmother, the acting queen mother, for erecting an image of Asherah, the Canaanite goddess of fertility (I Kgs 15:12–13; II Chr 15:16). (For the problem of Asa's mother and grandmother having the same name, see Maachah.) Also during this period Asa built fortified cities and fielded an army (II Chr 14:1–8).

It was probably in the 11th year of his reign that a great army invaded Judah from the S, led by Zerah, the Ethiopian. Asa put his trust in the Lord and attacked the invaders. God gave the victory (II Chr 14:9–15). See Zerah.

Following this victory, Asa heeded the advice of Azariah, the prophet, and completed the reformation begun earlier. The people were called together and induced to renew their covenant with God (II Chr 15:1–15).

During the 16th year of his reign (the 36th year of the divided kingdom), the border war with Israel was continued. Baasha, king of Israel, invaded the territory of Benjamin and fortified the city of Ramah. His purposes were (1) to recover the territory lost to Abijah, Asa's father, and (2) to control the area N of Jerusalem. Asa took what was left of the temple treasures and sent them to Ben-hadad, king of Syria, asking him to break his pact with Baasha and attack Israel. Ben-hadad complied, forcing Baasha to withdraw from Ramah. Asa conscripted labor and used the materials gathered at Ramah to fortify the cities of Geba and Mizpah (I Kgs 15:16–22; II Chr 16:1–6).

Hanani, the seer, condemned Asa for his alliance with Syria instead of reliance upon the Lord. Asa became enraged, casting Hanani into prison (II Chr 16:7–10).

During his 39th year as king, Asa became diseased in his feet and failed once more to seek help from God, calling on the physicians instead (I Kgs 15:23; II Chr 16:12). Asa died in the 41st year of his reign and was buried with royal honors in the city of David (I Kgs 15:24; II Chr 16:13–14).

R. O. C.

ASAHEL (ăs′à-hĕl)
1. A brother of Joab (David's army commander) and one of the three sons of Zeruiah (David's sister). Asahel was an officer in David's army (II Sam 23:24; I Chr 11:26). He was known for his fleetness ("as swift of foot as a wild gazelle") in his pursuit of Abner following the battle of Gibeon. This event ended in his own death by impalement upon Abner's spear (II Sam 2:18–23). The whole incident issued in the treacherous murder of Abner at Hebron and David's lament for Abner's politically untimely death (II Sam 3:26–39).
2. A Levite named Asahel was commissioned by King Jehoshaphat as an itinerant instructor of the law and sent through "all the cities of Judah" teaching (II Chr 17:8).
3. Another Levite bearing this name was placed under Cononiah by Hezekiah with the group charged with overseeing "the contributions, the tithes and the dedicated things" (II Chr 31:12–13).
4. The father of the Jonathan who, in the time of Ezra, opposed the appointment of a commission to study Jewish intermarriage of the period (Ezr 10:15, ASV).

R. O. C.

ASAHIAH. See Asaiah.

ASAIAH (à-zā′yà)
1. "King's servant" to Josiah, member of a delegation he sent to Huldah the prophetess to inquire the meaning of the words of the book of the law found in the renovation of the temple (II Chr 34:20). Incorrectly written "Asahiah" in II Kgs 22:12, 14, KJV.
2. Princely descendant of Simeon who in the time of Hezekiah dispossessed the Mennim near Gedor (Gerar?) (I Chr 4:34–41).
3. A Levite, chief of the 250 descendants of Merari assembled by David to assist in bringing up the ark from the house of Obed-edom to Jerusalem (I Chr 15:6, 11). Probably the same as in I Chr 6:30.
4. A "Shilonite" (i.e., descendant of Shelah, son of Judah, Num 26:20) dwelling in Jerusalem after his return from captivity (I Chr 9:5, RSV). Possibly the same as Maaseiah in Neh 11:5 (RSV) since the list is otherwise similar.

ASAPH (ā′săf)
1. Asaph the son of Berachiah, a Levite, is the most prominent of this name in the Bible. An outstanding musician in the days of David, he was appointed along with another Levite, Heman, as minister of music in the center of worship in Jerusalem (I Chr 6:39; 15:17, 19; 16:5, 7, 37; 25:1–2, 6–9). Eleven of the psalms (73–83) are attributed to Asaph by the traditional editorial notes. The descendants of Asaph for hundreds of years retained this office of musicians before the Lord, and the term "sons of Asaph" became almost equivalent to chorister or musician (Ezr 2:41; 3:10; Neh 7:44; 11:17, 22; 12:35–36). See Psalms, Book of.
2. The father of Joah, the court chronicler or recorder in the days of Hezekiah (II Kgs 18:18, 37; II Chr 29:13; Isa 36:3, 22).
3. The ancestor of some of the Levites who returned from the Exile (I Chr 9:15). This may be the same as 1.
4. A Levite of the family of Korah whose descendants were appointed gatekeepers of the

Lord's house by David (I Chr 26:1; called Ebiasaph in 9:19).

5. An officer of the king of Persia who may have been a Jew; he was "keeper of the king's forest" (Neh 2:8).

A Heb. seal bearing the name Asaph was found at Megiddo.

P. C. J.

ASAREEL (á-sâr′ĭ-ĕl). One of the four sons of Jehaleleel of the tribe of Judah (I Chr 4:16).

ASARELAH (ăs′á-rē′lá). A son of Asaph who was selected by David for the service of prophesying (I Chr 25:2). Also called Jesharelah (v. 14).

ASCENSION OF CHRIST. The bodily transfer of our Lord from the earthly to the heavenly sphere of existence. The primary account of this event appears in Acts 1:9-11; the secondary references in Mk 16:19 and Lk 24:51 are rendered questionable by inferior textual evidence. However, the ascension is assumed as the foundation for numerous statements in the NT (e.g., Col 3:1; Rom 8:34; Heb 8:1). In fact, there is hardly a NT writer who does not give testimony, direct or indirect, to the truth of the ascension.

According to Luke, the event took place 40 days after the resurrection (Acts 1:3) near Bethany (Lk 24:50) on the Mount of Olives (Acts 1:12). The text explains that He was taken up into a cloud (Acts 1:9). Whether the cloud was that of the Shekinah glory or a natural cloud of vapor, the record does not make clear. The ascension was anticipated in the OT in Ps 68:18; 110:1, and Christ spoke of it prophetically in Jn 6:62; 20:17.

Objection has been raised concerning the ascension by those who approach the record from a purely naturalistic viewpoint. They assert that such violation of the law of gravity is unthinkable. However, for those who accept the possibility of supernatural intervention in the world, the ascension is no problem. Given an omnipotent God, both resurrection and ascension are easily conceivable.

Others view the ascension as being merely a symbolical representation of Christ's entrance into divine glory. This is an attempt to retain the spiritual value of the ascension account without sacrificing the concept of the natural world as a closed system not susceptible to supernatural intrusion.

The significance of the ascension is manifold. (1) For Christ Himself it meant exaltation to a position of glory as victorious Lord, the Head of the Church (Eph 1:20-23; Phil 2:9). (2) It also made possible the coming of the Holy Spirit to indwell the believer as Divine Helper (Jn 16:7; Acts 2:33) and to convict the world of sin, righteousness, and judgment (Jn 16:8-11). (3) The ascension signifies the identification of the Christian with Christ; he is seated with Him positionally in the heavenlies (Eph 2:6; Col

Chapel of the Ascension atop the Mount of Olives. HFV

3:1-3). (4) The ascension initiated Christ's high priestly advocacy before the Father in the believer's behalf, a truth which is given major treatment in the Epistle to the Hebrews (4:14-16; 6:20; 7:25; 8:1; 9:24). (5) For the future, the fact that Christ ascended means that He will return to the earth in the same manner in which He left (Acts 1:11).

D. W. B.

ASENATH (ăs′ē-năth). Daughter of Potipherah, Egyptian priest of On, who was given to Joseph for his wife by Pharaoh. She was the mother of Ephraim and Manasseh (Gen 41:45, 50). In Heb. her name is a transliteration of the Egyptian name ′Iws-Nĭt ("she belongs to [the goddess] Neith").

ASER (ā′sér). The Gr. form of the Heb. Asher found only in the NT (KJV) in Lk 2:36 and Rev 7:6. Asher (q.v.) was a son of Jacob by Zilpah, and the tribe descended from him.

ASH A tree. *See* Plants.

ASHAN (ā′shăn). A village allotted to Judah after the Conquest (Josh 15:42), reassigned to Simeon (Josh 19:7; I Chr 4:32), and finally given to the sons of Aaron (I Chr 6:59). It has been identified with Khirbet ′Asan, four miles NW of Beer-sheba. The Chor-ashan (Bor-ashan, ASV, "cistern of Ashan") of I Sam 30:30 is the same town.

ASHBEA (ăsh′bē-á). The town in the tribe of Judah noted for its linen workers (I Chr 4:21). RSV renders it Beth-ashbea.

ASHBEL (ăsh′bĕl), **ASHBELITES** (ăsh′bĕ-līts). One of the sons of Benjamin (Gen 46:21) and ancestor of the Ashbelites (Num 26:38; I Chr 8:1). Apparently Ashbel was also called Jediael (I Chr 7:6).

ASHCHENAZ (ăsh′kĕ-năz). Another form of Ashkenaz (q.v.). Ashchenaz is used in I Chr 1:6 and Jer 51:27.

ASHDOD (ăsh′dŏd). Probably the capital of the five Philistine cities. Located three miles inland and 18 miles NE of Gaza, it controlled a junction on the coastal trade route. Tablets discovered at Ugarit indicate that Ashdod was one of three Palestinian cities that traded with the northern Canaanite capital in Syria during the 14th and 13th cen. B.C.; the other two were Acco and Ashkelon. Ashdod was allotted to the tribe of Judah (Josh 15:46 f.), but its Anakim inhabitants enabled the city to resist Joshua's army (Josh 11:22; 13:1-3).

When the Philistines captured the ark of the covenant, they placed it in the temple of Dagon there. On each of two nights the image fell, and finally broke. A plague of tumors also descended upon the city. In panic, the Ashdodites gave the ark to Gath and then to Ekron, which returned it to the Israelites (I Sam 5-6). Ashdod was not captured by Judah until the reign of Uzziah (II Chr 26:6).

The Assyrians took the city in the 8th cen., calling it Asdudu. A revolt occurred while Ahimiti was governor, and the city was destroyed by Sargon II in 711 B.C. (ANET, pp. 284-287; cf. Amos 1:8; Isa 20:1). During the next century Ashdod was weak (see Jer 25:20; Zeph 2:4; Zech 9:6).

In Nehemiah's day the city joined with others to oppose the rebuilding of Jerusalem's walls. Nehemiah protested that half the children of Jews who had wives from Ashdod did not speak Hebrew (Neh 4:7-8; 13:23-24). Idolatry in Ashdod, by Hellenistic times called Azotus, provoked the Maccabees to attack it (I Macc 5:68; 10:84). In the NT, the city is referred to in Acts 8:40. It had been restored by Herod and Gabinius and was presented to Salome, Herod's sister, by Augustus Caesar.

Ashdod is now known as Esdud. The ruins consist of an acropolis of 17 acres and a lower city spreading over at least 90 acres. Excavations beginning in 1962 have revealed 20 levels of human settlement, from Early Bronze Age II to the end of the Byzantine period. Throughout the Late Bronze Age (1550-1200 B.C.), Ashdod was a large walled city. A cylinder seal of the Middle Babylonian style belongs to the period, and many pottery imports show commercial relations with Cyprus and the Mycenaean cultural area of Greece. The last Late Bronze Age city was totally destroyed, leaving

a thick level of ash after 1250 B.C., but the conqueror is still unknown.

Five strata belong to the era of the Philistines (q.v.). The ruins reveal that they reached the peak of their power in the first half of the 11th cen., i.e., before Saul became king. The city wall, built of sun-dried bricks, was 20 feet wide. The earliest Philistine stratum yielded pottery resembling in decoration a style found in Cyprus from the period after 1230 B.C. This suggests Ashdod was settled by an early wave of Sea-Peoples coming via Cyprus. Three seals have been found engraved with signs resembling the Cypro-Minoan script in use in the E Mediterranean sphere c. 1300-1150 B.C. A potters' quarter was unearthed in the lower city area dating to the 8th cen. B.C. Its destruction may be attributed to Uzziah. Fragments of a basalt stela bearing cuneiform characters of a type found in Sargon's capital attest to the Assyrian domination by that king.

Bibliography. Moshe Dothan, "Ashdod: a City of the Philistine Pentapolis," *Archaeological Discoveries in the Holy Land,* New York: Thomas Crowell Co., 1967, pp. 129-137; "Ashdod of the Philistines," *New Directions in Biblical Archaeology,* ed. by D. N. Freedman and J. C. Greenfield, Garden City: Doubleday, 1969, pp. 15-24; "Tel Ashdod, 1969," IEJ, XIX (1969), 243 ff.

G. H. L.

ASHDOTHITES (ăsh′dŏth-īts). Found in Josh 13:3, it is a less acceptable form of Ashdodites, resulting from anglicizing the name. See Ashdod.

ASHER (ăsh′ẽr). *Personal history.* Asher was the eighth son of Jacob and the second by Zilpah, Leah's maid (Gen 30:12-13; 35:26). Jacob's blessing on Asher is found in Gen 49:20. He had four sons and a daughter (Gen 46:17; I Chr 7:30).

The tribe. Descendants from Asher at the time of the Exodus numbered 41,500 adult males (Num 1:41). At the second census the number was 53,400 (Num 26:47). On the march this tribe was placed with Dan on the N of the tabernacle along with Naphtali. It was allotted territory in the N, which formed the northern boundary of Palestine. This extended southward to S of Carmel, about 60 miles in extent. On the E were the territories of Zebulun and Naphtali; on the W was the Mediterranean (Josh 19:24-31).

This territory brought the tribe into contact with the Phoenicians, who were famous for their extensive commerce. But Asher failed to drive the Canaanites out of their cities (Jud 1:31-32). The method of taking possession of their allotted land seems to have been by peaceful penetration rather than by outright conquest. They gave their energies to the cultivation of the olive; thus the mention in Deut 33:24 that they would dip their feet in oil.

Egyptian records from the reigns of Seti I (1319- 1304 B.C.) and Rameses II (1304- 1234 B.C.) speak of the hinterland of Phoenicia as *'I-ś-r* or *Asaru,* which seems to indicate that the tribe of Asher had already settled in this area. Here is clear evidence for the earlier date of the Exodus and Conquest. *See* Exodus, The.

The tribe did not distinguish itself during all of Israel's history. It was not adventurous or enterprising (Jud 5:17). In David's time it was not even mentioned in the list of chief rulers (I Chr 27:16 ff.). In Hezekiah's godly reign it responded to his call for observance of the Passover (II Chr 30:11). Anna, the prophetess, was a member of this tribe (Lk 2:36).

C. L. F.

ASHERAH.*See* Gods, False.

ASHES

1. A special word, *deshen,* really "fatness," denotes the burnt wood of the altar soaked with fat (I Kgs 13:3, 5), which was in pots (Ex 27:3), or on the E side of the tabernacle altar (Lev 1:16), or deposited outside the camp (Lev 4:12; cf. Jer 31:40).

2. Another word, *pîaḥ,* used twice, is really "soot." Moses tossed skyward before Pharaoh two handfuls from a kiln to bring sores on man and beast (Ex 9:8, 10).

3. The common word *'ēper* is the same as "dust," loose and crumbled. These ashes may be useless remains of complete destruction, as when God turned Tyre "to ashes upon the earth" (Ezk 28:18; cf. Mal 4:3; II Pet 2:6; Lam 3:16). To express dire distress, whether of mourning or repentance, the impassioned Oriental often used ashes. They might be on the head, as of dishonored Tamar crying aloud (II Sam 13:19); in the garment of sackcloth, as of Mordecai bewailing the decree to annihilate the Jews (Est 4:1; cf. v. 3); sat on to show deepest repentance, as the king of Nineveh (Jon 3:6; cf. Isa 58:5; Mt 11:21 parallel to Lk 10:13); mixed with dust (Job 42:6); or used more fervently to seek the Lord (Dan 9:3).

Ashes, then, symbolized deepest humility, as when Abraham pled for Sodom (Gen 18:27); or even humiliation, as when Job had "become like dust and ashes" (Job 30:19). They might symbolize futility, as of idolatry (Isa 44:20) or paltry proverbs (Job 13:12). Ceremonially, the ashes of the red heifer were used in "the water for impurity" (Num 19:9; Heb 9:13).

What a wonderful promise of the evangelical prophet that the Lord would grant mourners a diadem instead of ashes (*pe'ēr* instead of *'ēper,* Isa 61:3)! *See* Beauty.

W. G. B.

ASHIMA.*See* Gods, False.

ASHKELON (ăsh'kĕ-lŏn). This city on the Mediterranean coast, about 30 miles S of Tel-Aviv, was among five principal cities of the

The Goddess of Victory standing on the globe supported by Atlas in the antiquities park, Ashkelon. HFV

Philistines (Gaza, Ashdod, Gath and Ekron being the other four, Josh 13:3). Each city was controlled by a "lord." Together, the cities posed the most serious threat to the independence of Israel during the period of the judges.

From Ashkelon, the Philistines sent back with the ark one of the golden tumors (I Sam 6:17). With Gaza, Ashdod, and Ekron, the city was bitterly denounced by Amos (Amos 1:7 f.). It is mentioned also by David (II Sam 1:20) and the prophets (Jer 25:20; Zeph 2:4, 7; Zech 9:5). Worship of Dagon by the inhabitants of Ashkelon is indicated in the Tell el-Amarna tablets c. 1380- 1350 B.C.

Ashkelon was captured by Jonathan, brother of Judas the Maccabee (I Macc 10:86; 11:60). Though the Herodian family was connected with Idumaea, there is evidence that Herod the Great was born at Ashkelon (Eusebius, *Eccles. Hist.* 1.7.11 and Justin *Dialogue, c.* 52). Herod built baths and costly fountains there (Jos *Wars* i.21.11). Ruins from the time of his reign were uncovered in excavations in the 1920's, in addition to evidence of occupation from the Philistine period and as early as 1800 B.C.

R. L. J.

ASHKENAZ (ăsh'kĕ-năz). The eldest son of Gomer and great-grandson of Noah through Japheth (Gen 10:3; I Chr 1:6, ASV). Also the name of a tribe mentioned in Jer 51:27 (ASV), coming from eastern Armenia, associated with Ararat and Minni, who as barbarians were instruments of God's wrath against Babylon. The identification with Assyrian *Aš-gu-za-a*, the Scythians of the 7th cen. B.C., is reasonably certain, because cuneiform documents of Esarhaddon mention them as allies of the Mannai (Minni) in their revolt against Assyria. Medieval Jews wrongly connected the term with Germany, so that German Jews are called Ashkenazim.

ASHNAH (ăsh'nà). Two villages in the Shephelah or foothills of Judah are given this name (Josh 15:33, 43). Their exact location has not been determined. The first is thought to be 'Aslin, located on the edge of the coastal plain W of Jerusalem. The second has been identified by some with Idhna between Hebron and Lachish, about 30 miles SW of Jerusalem.

ASHPENAZ (ăsh'pē-năz). Master of the eunuchs in the court of Nebuchadnezzar, king of Babylon (Dan 1:3). The meaning of the name is unknown. It is perhaps of Persian origin, and has been found on an incantation text at Nippur.

Ashpenaz held a position which was common in Oriental courts. One in this position could attain great influence with the ruler and was sometimes treated by him as a confidential servant. His office placed him in control of the other eunuchs employed in the palace, and consequently put the royal harem in his charge. He was also entrusted with the training of youths for the service of the king. This latter responsibility does not necessarily imply, however, that Daniel and his three friends were made eunuchs. Yet see Isaiah's prediction in Isaiah 39:7.

ASHRIEL (ăsh'rĭ-ĕl). Found only in I Chr 7:14. The name is more properly spelled Asriel *(q.v.)*.

ASHTAROTH (ăsh'tà-rŏth)

1. The plural form of Ashtoreth, a Canaanite goddess (Jud 2:13; 10:6; I Sam 7:3–4; 12:10; 31:10). *See* Gods, False.

2. One of two chief cities, along with Edrei *(q.v.)*, of Og, king of Bashan (Deut 1:4; Josh 9:10; 12:4; 13:12, 31; I Chr 6:71; cf. Gen 14:5), located at Tell Ashtarah about 20 miles E of the Sea of Galilee. This area is traditionally in the region of Uz, homeland of Job (HDB, rev. ed., p. 63). The name may be an abbreviated form of the place name Ashteroth-karnaim *(q.v.)*, either the name of the Canaanite goddess Ashtoreth compounded with Karnaim ("two horns") meaning "Ashtoreth of the two horns," or it may designate one of the twin cities along the King's Highway which alternated as the capital of Bashan. It is known as *Aštarti* in the Amarna tablets.

ASHTEROTH-KARNAIM (ăsh'tĕ-rŏth-kär-nā'ĭm). A city in Bashan occupied by the

Rephaim, prehistoric inhabitants of Canaan (Gen 14:5), and apparently dedicated to the worship of the primary female deity of the Canaanites, the goddess of fertility. By Hellenistic times Atargatis, the Syrian goddess, may have been worshiped there (II Macc 12:26) rather than Ashteroth. Ashteroth was often represented in art wearing a two-horned headdress like the Egyptian cow-goddess Hathor.

A more probable meaning of the name according to Eusebius' *Onomasticon*, however, is "Ashteroth near Karnaim," in which case it may be identified with the town Ashtaroth *(q.v.)*, capital of King Og (Deut 1:4), at modern Tell Ashtarah, 21 miles E of the Sea of Galilee. Under Aramaean and Assyrian rule a town called Karnaim (Carnaim) by the Jews (Amos 6:13, RSV; I Macc 5:26, 43 f.) eclipsed Ashtaroth in size and became the regional capital. It may be identified with the site of *Sheikh Sa'ad*, three miles NE of Tell Ashtarah.

H. L. D.

ASHTORETH. *See* Gods, False.

ASHUR (ăsh'ŭr). A great-grandson of Judah, born posthumously to Hezron by his wife Abiah (I Chr 2:24). The name is more correctly spelled Ashhur in RSV (Heb. *'ashḥûr*). He became the founder of Tekoa through the seven children that were borne by his two wives, Helah and Naarah (I Chr 4:5). The LXX makes him a son of Caleb by Ephrathah.

ASHURBANIPAL (ăsh'ŭr-băn'ĭ-păl). The last of the great kings of Assyria (668–626 B.C.). The Assyrian Empire was supreme by this time, but this supremacy had to be maintained by the constant strong arm of the military to keep down revolts. Though not without military ability, Ashurbanipal appears to have had more

A fragment of the Babylonian creation epic from Ashurbanipal's palace. BM

interest in cultural pursuits than conquest. Under his father, Esarhaddon, Assyrian suzerainty spread into Egypt, and Ashurbanipal inherited an uprising by Tirhakah the Nubian (Ethiopian, cf. II Kgs 19:9). The revolt was crushed and Memphis taken, but Ashurbanipal restored the Delta princes to their positions. The man who was to become Pharaoh-necho (II Kgs 23:29) was carried to Assyria, later released and was set up as ruler in Sais. A final attempt to restore Nubian power by Tirhakah's nephew, Tanutamon (Tandamane), in 663 B.C., brought the Assyrian army all the way S to Thebes. The sacking of this famous city by Ashurbanipal left a lasting impression, as can be seen from Nahum's reference to it (Nah 3:8, RSV). Ashurbanipal himself considered this triumph a noble accomplishment.

Almost immediately a native Egyptian ruler, Psamtik I (663–609 B.C.), started another rebellion and this time with the aid of Lydian mercenaries he overcame rival princes and succeeded in driving Assyrian forces out of Egypt. Ashurbanipal's apparent indifference to this loss may have been for two reasons. First, Assyria was overextended in Egypt; and secondly, Ashurbanipal preferred peaceful enterprises. A less aggressive policy is evidenced also by the swift conclusion of the inherited seige of Tyre, accomplished probably by offering Ba'alu, its king, easier terms of surrender. On the other hand, the presence of the Cimmerians, hordes of wild nomads in the N, may have made many a prince happy to wear the protective mantle of Assyrian might. Gyges of Lydia (in western Asia Minor) felt it wise to flatter Ashurbanipal by acknowledging the latter's supremacy, though he was beyond the Assyrian sphere of power. But at almost the same time Gyges encouraged Psamtik's liberating of Egypt with Lydian mercenaries. Left alone to face an overwhelming enemy, Gyges' capital city Sardis fell into the hands of the Cimmerians in 652 B.C.

In 652 Ashurbanipal also became absorbed with the rebellion of his own brother Shamash-shum-ukin, who ruled over the Babylonian province. It was perhaps the preoccupation of Ashurbanipal together with the Egyptian success which encouraged this general movement toward rebellion. Elam had been reduced to a dependent state and new princes appointed in 663 B.C., the very year of Psamtik's success. The southern Chaldeans had a long history of opposing Assyrian domination of Babylonia. An unwise administration of Babylonia, in which Shamash-shum-ukin was king but all local governors were responsible to Ashurbanipal, and constant pressures from anti-Assyrian elements like the Chaldeans, finally led Shamash-shum-ukin secretly to ally himself with Elam, the Chaldeans, the Arameans, the Aribi, Egypt and others. The result was the most difficult struggle the Assyrian army had faced for decades. It was the first time the Assyrians were met by warriors trained in their

Ashurbanipal in his war chariot. LM

own school. The struggle continued from 651 to 648 B.C. Internal strife weakened the Elamites, which gave Ashurbanipal opportunity to cut off the city of Babylon and to starve it into submission. Shamash-shum-ukin died in the flames of his own palace. Ashurbanipal did not sack the city but devoted himself to a year of personal rule and restoration, after which another puppet king, Kandalanu, was set up.

Ashurbanipal was not as generous with the Elamites who stubbornly championed the rebellious activities of the Chaldean leader Nabu-bel-shumati. This action provoked Ashurbanipal's last campaign against Elam when he virtually exterminated the Elamite nation, leaving the capital Susa uninhabitable. Elamite history thus came to an end and a void existed in this region until the coming of the Persians.

From 669 to 639 B.C., when the sources for his reign came to an abrupt end, Ashurbanipal was a successful ruler, as Assyrian rulers go. In the last years of his reign, however, ill-health and internal dissensions plagued the king. He died in 626 B.C. and Ashur-etil-ilani, his chosen son, had to fight a usurper to take the throne. This marked the beginning of the end of the Assyrian Empire.

Ashurbanipal was a scholar and archaeologist, or at least an antiquarian. As a trained scribe he took avid interest in literary and cultural matters. He had scribes collecting and copying into late cuneiform writing thousands of documents which became the basis for his famous library in Nineveh. The discovery of this library by Layard and Rassam in the mid-19th cen. gave birth to the serious study of all the languages written on clay and stone in cuneiform.

Like many of his predecessors, Ashurbanipal was a great builder. He embellished his architecture with the usual reliefs. The quality of this art was unequalled in Assyria and, in the depiction of animals, ranks with the best relief work in the world. Assyrian culture had reached its apex but was destined to be short-lived.

It appears that the Asnapper of Ezr 4:10 is Ashurbanipal, for among the people this Asnapper brought to Samaria were Susanchites and Elamites (Ezr 4:9), which agrees well with the final destruction of Elam described above.

Ashurbanipal ruled approximately during the period paralleled by the reigns of Manasseh, Amon, and Josiah, kings of Judah. The Israelites had already fallen to the Assyrian Sargon II (721 B.C.). The prophetic ministries of Isaiah, Micah, Nahum, and possibly Zephaniah were also contemporary with his reign.

E. B. S.

Ashurnasirpal II at a banquet. BM

ASHURITES (ăsh′ŭ-rīts). A tribe in northern Israel, located between Gilead and Jezreel, part of the realm of Ishbosheth (II Sam 2:9). Many follow the Targum emendation, reading this name as the men of Asher (cf. Jud 1:32). It could hardly be the Asshurim of Gen 25:3, for these were a tribe in northern Arabia.

ASHURNASIRPAL II (ăsh′ĕr-năs′ĭr-păl). After nearly two centuries of decline, the Assyrian army began again the work of conquest in the reign of Tukulti-Ninurta, the father of Ashurnasirpal II (884–859 B.C.). To the latter fell the task of completing the conquest and organizing the realm. Though with typical Assyrian cruelty, this work was done efficiently and with considerable forethought. His greatest expansion was to the W where he marched to the Mediterranean coast, assimilating many new provinces and placing numerous Aramean princes under heavy tribute. In his annals he frequently boasts of the ferocity with which he put down many a revolt, crucifying thousands and flaying alive captured rulers. His, however, was a time of comparative peace for Assyria, and he sometimes avoided battle, especially in strong and distant places such as Damascus.

Ashurnasirpal was interested in building and art. He moved the capital from Nineveh to Calah (Gen 10:11) and rebuilt this city with the help of captured Aramean artisans. He invited 69,574 persons to a great feast when he dedicated the new capital in 879 B.C. (cf. the 120,000 persons of Nineveh in Jonah's times, Jon 4:11). But the Assyrians themselves were artists of no little talent as is evidenced by the great inscribed reliefs of Ashurnasirpal and the man-headed lion colossus discovered in his palace at Nimrud (Calah). The lone example of Assyrian sculpture in the round is itself a statue of this notable Assyrian monarch (ANEP, #439). *See* Assyria; Calah.

E. B. S.

ASHVATH (ăsh′văth). A great-grandson of Asher, the last of the three sons of Japhlet of the family of Heber (I Chr 7:33).

ASIA (ā′shá). In the NT, Asia generally refers to the Roman province created *c.* 129 B.C. after Attalus III had earlier (133 B.C.) willed his kingdom of Pergamos to Rome. Asia included the countries of Mysia, Lydia, Caria, and most of Phrygia, plus several islands and coastal cities. At first Pergamos was the capital, but the seat of government was later moved to Ephesus. Asia was governed by a procurator or a proconsul appointed by the Senate. The annual assembly of representatives from all districts was presided over by the Asiarch (*q.v.*). The city of Smyrna also vied with Ephesus for chief honors.

Jews from Asia were present in Jerusalem on the day of Pentecost (Acts 2:9). On his second journey, Paul was prevented from preaching in Asia (Acts 16:6); but on the third journey his ministry was extensive, and all Asia "heard the word" (Acts 19:10). Rev 1:11 lists the "seven churches of Asia" as Ephesus, Smyrna, Pergamum, Thyatira, Sardis, Philadelphia, and Laodicea.

R. L. J.

ASIA, CHURCHES OF. *See* under their respective names. *See* Asia.

ASIARCHS (ā′shĭ-ärk). These were officials and possibly "high priests of the temples of Asia" (Ramsay and Lightfoot), though some authorities challenge this designation. There were chief men of equal rank in other provinces (cf. Syriarch, Pamphyliarch, etc.). They must have been men of means, as they incurred considerable expense while presiding over the public games held in celebration of religious rites in honor of the gods and the emperor. It is believed that they formed a type of council which managed the business of the *Commune Asiae*. They offered friendly advice to Paul at Ephesus (Acts 19:31, ASV). The office was one of power and prestige in view of the control exercised over the priesthood and of religion in general.

ASIEL (ăs′ĭ-ĕl). Great-grandfather of Jehu, a Simeonite "prince" mentioned in I Chr 4:35.

ASKELON. *See* Ashkelon.

An inscription from Izmir bearing the title Asiarch in the fourth line. HFV

The province of Asia occupied the western third of Asia Minor.

ASNAH (ăs'nȧ).The head of a family of Nethinim who returned from the Exile with Zerubbabel (Ezr 2:50).

ASNAPPER (ăs-năp'ĕr).This spelling is used in Ezr 4:10. RSV uses Osnappar. *See* Ashurbanipal.

ASP. *See* Animals: Cobra, IV.8.

ASPATHA (ăs-pā'thȧ).The third son of Haman, put to death by the Jews (Est 9:7).

ASPHALT. *See* Minerals: Bitumen.

ASRIEL (ăs'rĭ-ĕl), **ASRIELITE** (ăs'rĭ-ĕ-līt). A Gileadite family descended from Manasseh through Machir (Josh 17:2; Num 26:31). The spelling of the name as Ashriel in I Chr 7:14 is probably a scribal error.

ASS. *See* Animals, I.1. For Wild Ass, *see* Animals: Onager, II.29.

ASSEMBLY. From several Heb. words, especially *qāhāl* (tribal gathering-council, Gen 49:6), which came to signify the community of Israel in whole or in part. From Gr. *ekklēsia*, originally it meant any public assembly of citizens summoned by a herald. In a Gr. city, the *ekklēsia* was the whole assembly of free-born citizens. Though sometimes translated "assembly" (Acts 19:32), *ekklēsia* in the NT chiefly means church (*q.v.*). The original word is from *ek-kaleō* ("call out"), but various meanings are associated; e.g., "the meeting" (convened) assembly, community or society of Christ's disciples, association, *et al.*; also *synagōgē*, a "coming together." as in Jas 2:2. *See* Synagogue; Congregation; Church.

ASSHUR (ăsh'ŭr), **ASSUR** (ăs'ŭr)
1. A son of Shem (Gen 10:22; I Chr 1:17), from whom the Assyrians were descended. The name appears in Gen 10:11 (KJV) as if it were the name of a person, but the verse should be rendered as in the RSV: "From that land he [Nimrod, vv. 8-10] went into Assyria, and built Nineveh."
2. The land of Assyria (Ezr 4:2; Ezk 27:23; 32:22; Hos 14:3). The Assyrian city named Asshur is not mentioned in the Bible. *See* Assyria. The chief god of the Assyrian pantheon bears this name.
3. An Arabian tribe (Num 24:22, 24; Ps 83:8), also known as the Asshurim (*q.v.;* Gen 25:3) and perhaps the Ashurites of II Sam 2:8-9.

ASSHURIM (ăsh'ŭr-ĭm). Found only in Gen 25:3. A son of Dedan, or his descendants, traced back to Abraham and Keturah.

ASSIR (ăs'ĕr)
1. A son of Korah of the Kohathite branch of the tribe of Levi (Ex 6:24; I Chr 6:22)

2. A son of Ebiasaph, descendant of 1 above (I Chr 6:23, 37).
3. A son of Jeconiah (Jehoiachin) (I Chr 3:17), the king of Judah who was carried captive to Babylon by Nebuchadnezzar in 597 B.C. (II Kgs 24:8-15). The fact that a son of that name is mentioned nowhere else, and that the line of descent was carried through Salathiel (Mt 1:12; Lk 3:27, RSV, Shealtiel) has led to the conjecture that the supposed name should be translated as a common noun, "the captive" (I Chr 3:17, RSV). If this translation is correct, the article in the Heb. text must have been dropped in textual transmission.

ASSOS (ăs'ŏs). Referred to once in the NT (Acts 20:13-14) in connection with the final stages of Paul's third missionary journey. On leaving Troas, the companions of Paul traveled by ship around Cape Lectum, sailed between the island of Lesbos and the mainland, and took Paul on board at Assos (a distance of 35 miles by sea). Paul took the shorter land route between Troas and Assos (21 miles in a straight line, but somewhat farther as the road ran). There must have been some practical reason for this plan, but the author of Acts does not make it clear. Perhaps contrary winds indicated that Paul would have much more time at Assos if he journeyed by land rather than by sea.

Assos was on the site of the present village of Behramkoi. It was founded by Aeolians of Lesbos (Mytilene) *c.* 900 B.C. The acropolis, which was located on a steep volcanic cone *c.* 770 feet above sea level, overlooked the Gulf of Adramyttium, half a mile away. A temple of Athena crowned the top. Assos has excellent architectural remains and city walls which date from the Hellenistic and Roman periods. Its 4th cen. B.C. fortifications are some of the best preserved of their kind. Strabo (XIII.1.58) indicated they were two miles around and 65 feet high.

Assos was famous as the home of Cleanthes, who succeeded Zeno as leader of the Stoic school (3rd cen. B.C.). Aristotle also lived there three years. It was noted for various products in the ancient world. It seems to have been a center for animal breeding, for we hear incidentally that Eumenes II bought some famous white boars there (see Rostovtzeff, *Social and Economic History of the Hellenistic World*, Oxford: Clarendon Press, 1941, I, p. 563). Assos also was a center for the finest white limestone *(lapis Assius)*, used for the manufacture of sarcophagi (see Pliny, *Natural History*, II.95; Augustine, *City of God*, XVIII.5). In the Hellenistic period Assos was renamed temporarily Apollonia (Pliny, *Natural History*, V.123). It was well known for the fine wheat which grew in the area and was exported to Rome in Paul's day (cf. Acts 27:2).

A bronze plaque from Assos dating from the time of Caligula (A.D. 37) has been discovered which mentions that the people of Assos welcomed the reign of this emperor (who had visited Assos with his father Germanicus, in A.D. 18) and pledged their loyalty to him (see for convenience a photo of this bronze tablet in *The Good News: The New Testament with Over 500 Illustrations and Maps*, New York: American Bible Society, n.d., p. G18). For drawing and translation of original text of this plaque to Caligula, see Clarke, Bacon, Koldewey in bibliography below, p. 66). Interestingly, in this tablet the people take an oath to be faithful by swearing to ". . . Zeus Soter and the Deity Caesar Augustus [i.e., Octavian], and the pure Virgin [i.e., Athena Polias], whom our fathers worshipped . . . ."

Bibliography. J. T. Clarke, *Report on the Excavations at Assos*, 1881, Boston: A. Williams and Co., 1882. The inscriptions of Assos were published separately by J. R. S. Sterrett, *Papers of the American School of Classical Study at Athens*, Vol. I, Boston: Damrell and Upham, 1885, pp. 1–90. J. T. Clarke, *Report on the Investigations at Assos*, 1882, 1883, Part 1, New York: Macmillan, 1898. See especially the combined volume, J. T. Clarke, Francis H. Bacon, Robert Koldewey, *Investigations at Assos*, 1881–1882–1883, Cambridge, Mass.: Archaeological Institute of America, 1902 (yet as the Epilogue by Bacon on p. 315 notes, this book was not finally released until 1921 due to high printing costs).

E. J. V.

ASSUR. *See* Asshur.

ASSURANCE. The realization by redeemed people that they are truly saved. Eternal security is the work of God which guarantees salvation forever, while assurance is the realization of this fact by the individual. The Gr. word usually translated "assurance" is *plērophoria* (Rom 4:21; Col 2:2; I Thess 1:5; Heb 6:11; 10:22).

The ground for assurance is threefold. First, there is the objective revelation from God that those who believe in Jesus are truly redeemed (Rom 3:25; I Jn 5:13). Second, there is the certainty of the committal of faith which results in God's keeping His promise to save (Rev 3:20). Third, there are the subjective experiences of the realities of the Christian faith. The experiences of being led by the Spirit, answers to prayer, love for the brethren are such that nurture assurance in the believer's life (Rom 8:14; I Jn 3:21–22; 2:10).

ASSYRIA (á-sĭr´ĭ-á). Assyria is a triangular-shaped section of land E of the middle Tigris between 35° and 37° N latitude, bounded in antiquity on the N by the mountains of Armenia and Kurdistan, on the E by the Median range, on the S by the Upper Zab River, and on the W by the Tigris River. The later Assyrian Empire at its height was bounded on the W by the Mediterranean and the Libyan Desert, on the E by the Persian Gulf and what later became Persia, on the N by the old Hittite Empire in Asia Minor and the Caucasus, and on the S by the Arabian Desert.

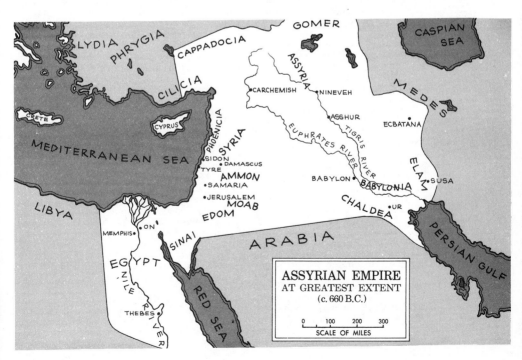

Assyrian relief showing fight between gods and a monster. ORINST

Since Assyria proper was a highland limestone plateau, it had a more invigorating climate than that of Babylonia. It was cold and wet in the winter, but rather warm during the summer months. The major river in the country was the Tigris (biblical Hiddekel, cf. Gen. 2:14), which originated in the mountains of Armenia about 25 miles from the source of the Euphrates. It flowed swiftly (Hiddekel means "the arrow-swift river") through the hills of Assyria and joined the Euphrates before emptying into the Persian Gulf. Other important rivers were the two Zab Rivers and the Khoser River, on which was situated Assyria's best known city, Nineveh. For the most part, the land was hilly, with well-watered plains along the Tigris River. The hills were covered with oak, plane and pine trees, while the main products of the country were fruits, dates, olives, wine, wheat and barley. Larger wild beasts included bears, panthers, wolves, lynxes, foxes, marmots, deer, lions, and wild boar. Domesticated animals included goats, camels, sheep, oxen, horses, and dogs.

Assyria was undoubtedly founded by Babylonian colonists. "From that land he [Nimrod and his descendants] went into Assyria, and built Nineveh, Rehoboth-Ir, Calah, and Resen between Nineveh and Calah; that is the great city" (Gen 10:11–12, RSV). Some Sumerians apparently lived in Asshur, the early capital, for a temple dedicated to Ishtar was found there with Sumerian architectural designs. The Assyrian people were Semitic with strains of Hurrian, Sumerian, and Hittite.

An early literary reference to Assyria was found in a tablet from Nuzu written during the Old Akkad. period (c. 2350 B.C.). Nuzu (Yorgan Tepe) lay E of Asshur, the capital, near Kirkuk in modern Iraq. It was here that much evidence was also found that related to the social and religious customs of the patriarchs (see Nuzu).

The Assyrians of historic times were a fierce, war-loving (cf. Isa 33:19) people, much more aggressive than their neighboring Semitic cohorts of Babylonia. This spirit of competitiveness may have derived from the more temperate climate or the circumstances that

faced Assyria. The most important cities of Assyria were Calah (q.v.), Nineveh (q.v.), Asshur (q.v.), Arbela and Khorsabad (see Sargon).

The language of the Assyrians differed only dialectally from that of the Babylonians. Under the influence of the Babylonians, the Assyrians wrote in cuneiform script on clay tablets. These tablets were usually pillow-shaped, about two by one and a quarter inches, or large flat pieces 16 by 10 inches. Sometimes a barrel-type clay prism was used to record important materials. The contents of the tablets varied from royal and private letters, lists of taxes, bills of sale and receipts, to mythological, astrological and incantation texts. In the Assyrian vocabulary, there were a number of Sumerian loan words. This necessitated grammars and vocabulary lists.

In the cultural program of Ashurbanipal (q.v.), agents were employed to ransack the libraries of Babylonia and to send their contents to Nineveh, where royal scribes copied and edited the ancient texts. Later there came commentaries on these texts, and there were prepared even some interlinear translations of the texts to help students understand the ancient language of the Sumerians. Many thousands of these tablets were discovered by excavators in the royal library of Nineveh. So much literature and of such a varied nature has been found that a separate department on Assyriology has been created in leading institutions in both America and Europe.

Often a tyrant at home, the king was general of the army in the field and rarely missed an annual expedition to exact tribute or to plunder some country. The whole organization of the state in Assyria was built around the king and was military in nature. The king was supreme. The palace dominated, and the temple was merely a royal chapel attached to the palace. This accounts for the preponderant size of the king's palace in comparison to the temples of Assyria. In Babylonia, a theocratic state, the temples were larger than the palace.

The culture and religion of Assyria were essentially Babylonian except for the predominance of the national god, Asshur. Asshur was the incarnation of war, represented in art by the sun disc, topped by an archer shooting a shaft. He was always honored as the divine founder of the nation. Babylonian deities were also worshiped in Assyria. Two important triads worshiped there were Anu, Bel, and Ea, and Shamash (sun deity), Sin, and Ramman (storm-god). Sometimes Ishtar replaced Ramman in the second triad.

Since there was an abundance of stone in Assyria, the natives did not build with brick as in Babylonia. Instead of painted or tiled walls, as in Babylonia, they faced the palaces with sculptured slabs. However, the quality of sculpture lagged behind that of relief, and thus the statuary was quite inferior to that of Babylonia. Soft alabaster was used to decorate the halls with sculptures in low relief, while fine marbles, hard limestone, and basalt were worked into stone vessels, pillars, altars, etc. The winged lion and the human-headed bulls at the entrance to buildings were famous forms of Assyria (cf. Dan 7:4). The British Museum and the Louvre afford excellent opportunities to see the Assyrian wall reliefs. There are war scenes, triumphal processions, pictures of private life, etc., depicted on the walls that were removed from Assyria by British and French excavators during the 19th cen.

The early history of Assyria was permeated with Babylonian influence. Although there is evidence of Assyrian merchant colonies in Asia Minor shortly after the fall of the Ur III Dynasty (*c*. 2000 B.C.) in the thousands of clay business documents (Cappadocian tablets) found at Kanesh (Kultepe), the early authority in Assyria was Babylonian and Amorite. Even when Assyria asserted her independence under Shamshi-Adad I (1813–1781 B.C.), there continued from 1800 to 1380 B.C. to be exerted strong pressures by the Hittites from Asia Minor, by the Hurrians from the N, and in particular by the Egyptians under the influence of Thutmose III, the Napoleon of Egypt.

Knowledge of Assyrian history has come largely through the efforts of excavators. To launch archaeological investigations, Layard dug at Calah and Nineveh 1845–51 and Botta at Khorsabad 1843–45. Rawlinson and others continued activities during the 19th cen. The British School of Archaeology in Iraq has done thorough excavation from 1949 to 1963 at Nimrod (Calah, *q.v.*). From these excavations has come a mine of inscriptions. As these inscriptions were translated and interpreted, the history of Assyria began to unfold. Because of the widespread influence of Assyria, evidences important for Assyrian history have been located in non-Assyrian sites. A stele of Sargon was found in Cyprus; a stele of Esarhaddon at Zinjirli on the borders of Cilicia; a letter from Ashur-uballit, king of Assyria, to Amenhotep IV, king of Egypt, at Tell el-Amarna in Egypt; and statues of Assyrian kings at Dog River near Beirut. The biblical record is very helpful for the later period, but the classical histories of Greece and Rome add little to the accurate knowledge of ancient Assyria.

While the Babylonians dated their years with names, the Assyrians devised a modification of the year name by a system known as the eponym canon. They named each year after a particular official who was selected by lot to govern that year. Lists of these officials, in their order of succession, are fairly complete from 911 to 668 B.C. In these lists, the ruling official sometimes added a chronological statement, and thus a sketchy history of the past could be ascertained.

One of the early rulers, Tiglath-pileser I (1114–1076 B.C.), left a rather full account of a lengthy reign and a series of conquests. He claimed to have conquered 42 countries with their princes. He was distinguished by his res-

toration of cities and the acclimatizing of all sorts of useful trees and plants.

Shalmaneser III (858–824 B.C.) also had a long and effective rule. His record relates 33 campaigns. He strengthened his conquests by placing governors over the conquered districts. During his reign, Assyria began to loom large on the horizon of Israel. The Kurkh stele tells of contact between Shalmaneser and Israel at the battle of Qarqar (853 B.C.). Here Shalmaneser met the combined forces of Damascus, Hamath, Bedouin Arab nomadic forces, and King Ahab of Israel. According to the Assyrian record, Ahab provided 2,000 (or 200) chariots and 10,000 foot soldiers. The battle was not decisive, as Shalmaneser had to fight the same foes in 849 B.C., and again in 846 B.C. In 842 B.C., he defeated Hazael of Damascus, and according to his famous Black Obelisk (now in the British Museum) he claimed tribute from Tyre, Sidon, and Jehu, king of Israel. Jehu's tribute is interesting: it included silver, golden cups and buckets, a golden bowl, a golden vase with pointed bottom, tin, a scepter, and *puruḥati*-fruits (ANET, p. 281; DOTT, pp. 48 f.).

Tiglath-pileser III (745–726 B.C.) was one of Assyria's most celebrated warriors. He took the title of the 12th cen. Assyrian hero, causing many scholars to see in the careful destruction of his predecessor's records and his scanty remarks about his origin, the rise of a commoner to kingship. He was tremendously successful in his concerted drive to revive the Assyrian Empire. He secured the boundaries to the N, E, and S, and then moved W to claim for Assyria a port on the Mediterranean. His drive was not

Bas relief showing Ashurnasirpal II of Assyria being anointed by a magical figure. BM

ASSYRIE

A human-headed winged bull from the palace of Sargon II of Assyria, weighing thirty to forty tons.
LM

just to annex land, but to gain control of the caravan routes that plied the coastal regions and thus to pour the wealth of the world into the coffers of Assyria. Tiglath-pileser III is the Pul of II Kgs 15:19–20, according to I Chr 5:26 (Anchor Bible). After defeating the Chaldean king who had made himself king of Babylon, Tiglath-pileser III was crowned king of Babylon in 728 B.C. He took there the name of Pulu. Previously, in 732, he had defeated Syria and annexed it along with the northern part of Israel to the Assyrian Empire (II Kgs 15:29).

Sargon II (722–705 B.C.) seems to have been a son of Tiglath-pileser III. He tried to reproduce the reign of the great Sargon of Akkad. In 722 B.C. he was present at the fall of Samaria and deported more than 27,000 Israelites to cities in Assyria and Media (cf. II Kgs 18:9–11). He replaced the deportees with natives from Syria and Babylonia. These intermarried with the Israelites left in Samaria and were called by the Hebrews the Samaritans.

Sennacherib ("Sin [the moon-god] has increased the brothers"), 705–681 B.C., followed Sargon II. He claimed ancestry from Gilgamesh, the semidivine Babylonian hero. He conducted many campaigns, one of which was at Kish against Merodach-baladan, the Chaldean, who sent an embassy to visit King Hezekiah of Judah (Isa 39:1–2). Sennacherib took from him the city of Babylon in 703 B.C. and spoiled it, deporting over 208,000 people as captives. In 701 B.C., Sennacherib appeared on the Mediterranean coast, accepted tribute from Phoenicia, isolated Tyre and took, according to his records, 46 cities of Judah, deported 200,150 people, and shut up Hezekiah "like a bird in a cage" in Jerusalem (ANET, p. 288). Where he deported all these people is not known. Apparently he took much of his spoil to the capital city of Nineveh. Some say his records really meant that he claimed an oath of allegiance from that number. Others conjecture that he displaced them to Babylon from where he had taken approximately the same number. This is an interesting conjecture; but according to Assyrian records, he destroyed the city of Babylon for its insurrection.

One of the great puzzles concerning Sennacherib is the account of his great loss of soldiery in an attack on Jerusalem. One suggestion has been made that there were really two campaigns, and that the loss of 185,000 soldiers occurred in the second investiture. Esarhaddon's annals suggest that there was a second campaign. The biblical narrative says that Tirhakah, king of Ethiopia, was on the scene of battle. This would make this battle c. 691 B.C. (see Sennacherib). The Assyrian king died c. 681 B.C. and was succeeded by his son, Esarhaddon, whom he had apparently appointed regent of Babylonia. Even before Sennacherib's death, Esarhaddon began to restore the city of Babylon.

Ashurbanipal (q.v.) succeeded Esarhaddon

and ruled 668–633 B.C. He was noted for his cultural interests and for the famous Nineveh library whose cuneiform treasures have unlocked the door to many secrets of Assyriology.

About 612–609 B.C., the Assyrian Empire gave way to the Neo-Babylonian Empire led by Nabopolassar and his son Nebuchadnezzar II. After the fall of Nineveh in 612 B.C. to the Babylonians and Medes, Haran and Carchemish soon surrendered, and the lion of Assyria gave way to the eagle of Babylon.

Bibliography. Georges Contenau, *Everyday Life in Babylon and Assyria,* New York: St. Martin's Press, 1954. CornPBE, pp. 136–146. C. J. Gadd, *The Fall of Nineveh,* London: Oxford Univ. Press, 1923; *The Stones of Assyria,* London: Chatts and Windus, 1936. M. E. L. Mallowan, *Twenty-five Years of Mesopotamian Discovery,* London: British School of Archaeology in Iraq, 1956. A. T. Olmstead, *History of Assyria,* 1923, Chicago: Univ. of Chicago Press, 1960 (reprint). A. Leo Oppenheim, "Assyria and Babylonia," IDB, I, 262–304; *Ancient Mesopotamia: Portrait of a Dead Civilization,* Chicago: Univ. of Chicago Press, 1964. Andre Parrot, *Nineveh and the Old Testament,* London: SCM Press, 1955. H. W. F. Saggs, *The Greatness That Was Babylon,* New York: Hawthorn Books, 1962.

F. E. Y.

ASTAROTH (ǎs′tȧ-rŏth). The KJV spelling of the town Ashtaroth (*q.v.*) in Deut 1:4. *See also* Gods, False: Ashtoreth.

ASTARTE. *See* Gods, False: Ashtoreth.

ASTONISHMENT. The translation of five Heb. words and one Gr. word. Most important in the OT is *shammâ* ("astonishment" or "desolation," as in Jer 8:21), along with *shāmēm, shimmāmôn, timmāhôn* ("astonishment" or "consternation," as in Deut 28:28) and *tar'ēlâ* ("astonishment," "reeling," or "staggering," as in Ps 60:3). The lone word in the NT is *ekstasis* ("astonishment," "amazement" or "trance," as in Mk 5:42). There are in addition a number of related verbal forms, particularly in the NT, where *ekplēssomai* (Mk 1:22), *existēmi* (Lk 2:47), *thambeomai* (Mk 10:24) and *periechō* (Lk 5:9) occur.

In the OT, *shammâ* is used 14 times, ten being in Jeremiah, and is closely associated with such words as "desolation," "hissing," and "curse." Most of the references apply to a disobedient Israel and dismay over the fate that would consequently befall the nation. Moses prophesied that if Israel would not hearken to the voice of the Lord her God, she would be scattered among the nations of earth, and she would become "an astonishment, a proverb, and a byword" among these nations (Deut 28:37).

Jeremiah, living at the time of the Babylonian destruction of the nation, described its impending fate. Eight of his references (8:21; 25:9, 11, 18; 29:18; 42:18; 44:12, 22) apply to the state of the Jews under judgment. The same word is then applied to their captor Babylon. She, in turn, would become "an astonishment" among the nations of the earth (Jer 51:37, 41) at the hand of the Lord.

Thus the word was usually related to the dread of judgment, and often included the idea of the unexpected or the awesome. Sinful man stood in the presence of a holy and righteous God.

The NT word *ekstasis* (in this sense) occurs only in Mk 5:42 where it is combined with *existēmi:* "And they were astonished with a great astonishment." Here the context includes the response to one of Jesus' miracles (raising the daughter of Jairus from the dead), where those present were "beside themselves" (NEB).

People were astonished *(ekplēssomai)* at Jesus' teaching (Mt 7:28), for it was full of fresh vigor and came with great authority. Even as a lad in the temple, He caused astonishment (*existēmi*) at His insight (Lk 2:47). His parents, too, were amazed (*ekplēssō,* Lk 2:48). The reports of His resurrection also caused the disciples to be astonished (Lk 24:22). In fact, the chief human reaction to the manifestations of deity in Jesus Christ, as emphasized throughout the Gospel of Mark, is that of fear, amazement, astonishment, and the like. The short ending of that Gospel closes with the note of awe in the hearts of the women disciples who had seen the empty tomb (Mk 16:8).

In Acts the same kind of response to divine intervention is described. For instance, the Jews were astonished when God imparted the Holy Spirit to Gentiles (Acts 10:45). The disciples were astonished that Peter had been released (miraculously) from prison (12:16). Sergius Paulus, the Roman proconsul of Cyprus, was astonished when he saw and heard the power of God through Paul (13:12), and he became a believer.

There is only one occurrence of any of the Gr. terms cited above later than Acts. In II Cor 5:13 *existēmi* is translated "beside ourselves," in the sense of being ecstatic and considered insane. Evidently the word "astonishment" (and its related terms) is primarily tied to a description of the wonderful, supernatural works of God through our Lord (in the Gospels) and His designated apostles (in Acts).

See Fear; Holiness.

Bibliography. Georg Bertram, *"Thambos,* etc.," TDNT, III, 4–7; *"Thaume,* etc.," TDNT, III, 27–42.

W. M. D.

ASTROLOGY. *See* Astronomy; Magic.

ASTRONOMY. The science of the stars, the most ancient of all human intellectual pre-

occupations. Its beginnings are lost in the dawn of prehistory of man's civilization. Since the age of mythology, astronomy has occupied a leading role among all the sciences and arts. By the very nature of the object of its study — heavenly appearances — it was closely associated with man's religious life and observances.

Its original name was astrology, generally described as the mother of astronomy. By the 18th cen. A.D. this designation was abandoned because of the exclusive astrological drift into horoscopic prognostication of man's future based on the 12 zodiacal signs. This practice, a remnant of the age of mythology, became unacceptable to the scientific and rational discipline of the science of astronomy. Yet even rational astronomy continued to be the source of religious inspiration, with Newton himself and later Eddington as outstanding examples.

With the rise of the French school of materialistic philosophy at the turn of the 19th cen. and the formation of Laplacian determinism in the evolution of the physical world, astronomy also became the source of agnostic and atheistic tendencies. This concurred with the emergence of a new astronomy in which the universe was thought to consist only of matter and energy. The new science became cosmical physics or astrophysics. But simple faith continued to be sustained by the overwhelming wonders of the universe. "The heavens declare the glory of God." However, triumphant victories in such intellectual fields as spectrum analysis, which in the nature of light of radiant stars established the universality of matter, kept undermining the ancient faith. Consequently, there then emerged that school of philosophy which advocates the primacy of matter in the universe, a universe with nothing supernatural in its character. The result of this trend is dialectic materialism.

If classical, descriptive astronomy was concerned in the position of celestial objects, in the orbits of planets, comets and multiple stars, astrophysics today investigates the nature, origin, and behavior of matter and energy that constitutes all the stars in the universe. Astrophysics, therefore, becomes closely related to atomic or nuclear physics. For this very reason, astrophysics encourages the student of creation to consider such speculations on the origin of matter and of the universe that continue to follow the trend of mechanistic determinism and the picture of a universe without God. Some authoritative doctrinaires holding this school of thought go even so far as to advocate that all wisdom is now attainable. They boast of the triumphs of experimental science, which maintains that the universe consists only of matter without any supernatural character, and that all the laws of the universe and the higher forms of life, including consciousness, are mere results of more complex and arbitrary oscillations of some ultimate particles of the universe, such as electrons, protons, or neutrons.

They further maintain that the entire universe is knowable, which means that it is only a question of time when man will learn everything so far unknown.

However, the contemporary revolution in physics, known as quantum physics, reveals entirely new and unpredictable regions of an unknown universe which indicates an inevitable end of the transient Laplacian illusion. New phases of quantum physics, combined with unforeseen aspects of the Einsteinian universe, reveal that the objective character of physical phenomena is undescribable in imaginative terms. On the borderline of the perceptible, comprehensible, and conceivable, the explorer once again encounters a certain transphenomenal realm. This realm is irrevocably forever inaccessible both to man's perception and his imagination; it can neither be perceived nor imagined. In other words, after the most ingenious language of modern mathematical astrophysics and the seemingly genial cosmogony of most advanced intellects, man once again returns to the simple biblical statement: "In the beginning, God created the universe."

In biblical times the science of astronomy was in its infancy. The Egyptians observed that the heliacal rising of the Dog Star Sirius—which they identified with their god Soth—at times coincided with the annual rising of the water of the Nile. Such readings were made for practical agrarian purposes, not for theoretical studies. Around 700 B.C. systematic reports of the movements of heavenly bodies were given to the Assyrian kings, especially data pertaining to eclipses. But such information largely aided the court diviners, and no mathematical computations were made.

Much earlier texts from the time of Hammurabi record observations of the planet Venus. Various German scholars, such as O. Neugebauer, T. G. Pinches, A. J. Sachs, and J. N. Strassmaier, have studied the mathematical and astronomical texts of ancient Mesopotamia and have concluded that early Babylonian astronomy was very crude. Yet as early as the time of Job, or of the writing of his book, the major constellations were noted and designated by specific names (Job 9:9; 38:31 ff.; cf. Isa 13:10; Amos 5:8).

It was not until the Hellenistic era that texts reveal any consistent mathematical theory of lunar and planetary motion. In this period the concept of the 12 signs of the zodiac and the accompanying horoscopes seem to have been developed. The terms "height" and "depth" (Rom 8:39) were used by astrologers for the celestial spaces above and below the horizon, to speak of the rising and setting of the stars which supposedly control the fate of men (Merrill C. Tenney, *New Testament Times*, p. 123).

In Greece it was during the Classical Age that astronomy first began to develop as a true science. Thales (d. 546 B.C.) declared the theory of the earth's roundness and predicted the

year of a solar eclipse. The mathematician Anaximander (611–547 B.C.) taught that the earth revolves about its own axis and that the light of the moon is reflected sunlight. Pythagoras and his school (530–400 B.C.) held that the sun is the center of the planetary system, and also believed that the earth rotates on its axis.

The Israelites do not appear to have devoted much attention to astronomy, perhaps because astrology (*see* Magic) and worship of the heavenly bodies were forbidden by the law (Deut 4:19; 18:10–11; see also II Kgs 17:16; Jer 19:13; Ezk 8:16). Such worship was practically universal among the neighboring nations (Isa 47:13; Jer 27:9; Dan 2; Amos 5:26).

In I Cor 15:41 the apostle Paul refers to the differing degrees of brightness or glory between sun, moon, and stars in order to illustrate the possibility of variations among those who will receive glorified resurrection bodies. These will be celestial *(epourania)* bodies (I Cor 15:40, 48–49), of another or different *(hetera)* kind from the terrestrial *(epigeia,* I Cor 15:40; II Cor 5:1) or natural human bodies we now have (I Cor 15:44–46). Angels at present are considered as celestial or heavenly beings *(epouranion,* Phil 2:10; cf. Lk 9:26).

See Star; Magi; Magic; Arcturus; Orion; Pleiades; Moon; Sun; Calendar.

Bibliography. CornPBE, pp. 146–150. M. J. Dresden, "Science," IDB, IV, 236–244. O. Neugebauer, *The Exact Sciences in Antiquity,* 2nd ed., Providence, R.I.: Brown Univ. Press, 1957. Merrill C. Tenney, *New Testament Times,* Grand Rapids: Eerdmans, 1965.

K. H. and J. R.

ASUPPIM (á-sŭp′ĭm). The KJV in I Chr 26:15, 17 transliterates this as a proper noun. Literally, it means "gatherings," "stores." The RSV translates here as the temple "storehouse," and in Neh 12:25 as "the storehouses of the gates."

ASYLUM. The custom of flight to sacred places to secure at least the temporary protection of a deity was known to ancient man in all areas of the earth. The ancient Greeks and Romans found asylum at the altars, temples, and holy shrines. Even the statues of Roman emperors afforded such, and the Roman legions in their campaigns used the standard with the eagle to provide asylum.

The two chief places among the Hebrews were their altars and the cities of refuge. Ex 21:14 provided that a person be taken from the altar to be executed. I Kgs 1:50; 2:28 indicate that the altar of the house of God was so used. Laws preventing abuse of such a place of refuge for criminals deserving of death appear in Lev 4:2 ff.; 5:15–18; Num 15:27–31. The cities of refuge *(q.v.,* Num 35:6; Josh 20:7–9) served as asylums complementary to the law of the avenger of blood *(see* Blood, Avenger of). Here one could flee and be shielded from the avenger until his trial. Here also the inadvertent slayer found refuge. (Cf. also II Sam 14:4–11.)

Among Christians, the church altar (later the building and grounds) served as such. But many abuses necessitated definite reforms. Modern law affords asylum to the accused until he is convicted.

R. E. Pr.

ASYNCRITUS (à-sĭng'krĭ-tŭs). A believer greeted by Paul in Rom 16:14. The name, meaning "incomparable," appears among the freedmen of Augustus.

ATAD (ă'tăd). A threshing floor in Transjordan (Gen 50:10). *See* Abel-Mizraim.

ATARAH (ăt'à-rà). The second wife of Jerahmeel and mother of Onam (I Chr 2:26).

ATAROTH (ăt'à-rŏth)

1. A town E of the Jordan given to the tribe of Reuben but evidently fortified by Gad; modern Khirbet 'Attârûs, about eight miles NW of Dibon (modern Dhiban) (Num 32:3, 34). On the Moabite Stone *(q.v.)* Mesha said the Gadites had "always" dwelt there (ANET, p. 320).

2. A town on the S border of Ephraim toward the W (Josh 16:2), perhaps the same as Ataroth-addar (Josh 16:5), probably Khirbet 'Attâra near Tell en-Nasbeh.

3. A border town of Ephraim (Josh 16:7), perhaps the prominent mound of Tell el-Mazar, according to Nelson Glueck, which guards the route up the Wadi Fari'a from the Jordan valley toward Shechem and overlooks the ford across the Jordan at Adamah leading to the Jabbok valley.

4. A town in Judah near Bethlehem; referred to as "Ataroth, the house of Joab" (I Chr 2:54).

ATER (ā'tẽr)

1. The ancestral head of one of the large families of returning exiles (Ezr 2:16; Neh 7:45).

2. The chief of a family of returning exiles who with Nehemiah sealed the covenant (Neh 10:17).

ATHACH (ā'thăk). A city in S Judah, probably near Ziklag, to which David sent gifts from the booty taken from the defeated Amalekites (I Sam 30:30).

ATHAIAH (à-thā'yà). A man of Judah, son of Uzziah. He was a post-Exilic inhabitant of Jerusalem (Neh 11:4).

ATHALIAH (ăth'à-lī'à). Her father, Ahab, was seventh king of the northern kingdom of Israel; her mother, Jezebel, Ahab's Phoenician wife. Her husband was Jehoram, fifth king of Judah, who, evidently under his wife's influence, murdered his six brothers and restored Baal worship which his father Jehoshaphat had sup-

pressed. The marriage seems to have been prompted by a political desire to bring Judah under the control of Israel. Apparently even the nonaccession year system of Israel was adopted by Judah at this time. After Jehoram's death in 841 B.C., the Arabs killed all his sons except Ahaziah, who became king under Athaliah's guidance. Athaliah saw to it that her son promoted Baalism and fully cooperated with Joram, king of Israel. But Ahaziah was killed along with Joram that same year by Jehu, one of Joram's generals, when a joint expedition against the Syrians failed.

Taking advantage of the fact that none of Ahaziah's sons were old enough to ascend to the throne, Athaliah seized power and proceeded to exterminate the royal household of Judah. However, the infant Joash was saved by Ahaziah's sister Jehosheba. Unknown to Athaliah, Joash was hidden in the temple for six years by Jehosheba and her husband Jehoida, the priest (II Kgs 11:1–3; II Chr 22:10–12). Athaliah promoted a reign of terror against all her opponents and installed Baalism as the religion of Judah. She made the high priest Mattan her personal priest in Baal worship.

At an opportune time, Jehoida publicly proclaimed Joash the new king of Judah in the temple court with the support of the temple guard. When Athaliah heard the celebration which followed the coronation ceremony, she ran into the temple area crying, "Treason! Treason!" but no one rose to aid her. So she was seized and slain near the horse gate of the palace (II Kgs 11:12–20; II Chr 23:11–15). Her reign was 841–835 B.C.

G. H. L.

ATHEISM. The biblical adjective *atheos* occurs only once in the NT (Eph 2:12). It is translated "without God," and signifies an idolatrous religious state, not a state of atheism as the word is now commonly understood. There is no biblical noun for "atheism" or "atheist," but the idea is described in such passages as "The fool hath said in his heart, There is no God" (Ps 14:1; 53:1).

The American Association for the Advancement of Atheism was incorporated in New York state in 1925; and in 1929 the League of Militant Atheists was organized "to carry out the communist aim of destroying the religious foundations of the old society." (Very brief bibliographical references to these two atheistic movements are found in the *Twentieth Century Encyclopedia of Religious Knowledge,* I, 91 f.). One can find no information about these dogmatic atheistic movements in current editions of such general reference works as the *Encyclopaedia Britannica* nor even the compendious *World Almanac.*

The history of atheism, ancient (Lucretius) and postmedieval, is well set forth in Robert Flint's *Anti-Theistic Theories.* Albert Camus gives a history of European atheism in his book, *The Rebel.*

Dogmatic atheism today is far from being dead, but it generally prefers to wear other names, such as naturalism. In *Naturalism and the Human Spirit,* H. T. Costello gives as a thesis of the naturalists, "There is no supernatural." He continues, "The naturalist now looks up to the great white throne, where once sat great Jove himself, and exclaims, 'Thank God, that illusion is gone'" (pp. 295 f.).

Ludwig A. Feuerbach (1804–1872) is correctly classed as a materialistic atheist. He taught that *"Mann ist was er isst"* ("Man is what he eats") (see Wilhelm Windelband's *History of Philosophy,* p. 641). Yet a current article on "Atheism" (*Encyclopaedia Britannica, II,* 600) suggests that one is not an atheist if, as Feuerbach claims (*Essence of Christianity,* Eliot tr., p. 21), though denying the existence of God, he accepts the value of the attributes "love, wisdom, justice."

The atheism about which Christians are chiefly concerned is not so much the dogmatic denial that in some form "God is," as the denial that in Christ He is the "rewarder of them that diligently seek him" (Heb 11:6).

J. O. B., Jr.

ATHENIAN (*a-thē'nē-an*). A dweller of the ancient city of Athens (Acts 17:21).

ATHENS (ăth'ĕnz)

Geography. Athens was the political, cultural, and economic center of Attica in eastern Greece. The Athenian city-state was coextensive with the roughly triangular 1000-square mile peninsula of Attica (about equal to Rhode Island). Located about four miles from the Aegean, Athens was served during her most important period by her seaport at the Piraeus. The driest region of Greece with

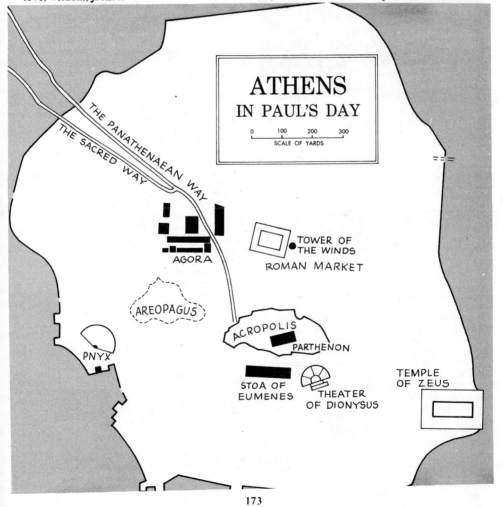

173

The Tower of the Winds. HFV

an annual rainfall of only 16 inches, Attica had a soil only about one-quarter arable. Resources in ancient times included excellent clay beds for pottery manufacture, the famous marble of Pentelicus, and the lead and silver mines of Laurium in the S of the peninsula (exhausted by the Christian era).

History. Although Athens was an important center in Greece during the Mycenaean era (*c.* 1400–1150/1100 B.C.), the city lost much of her early power and prestige during the subsequent Dorian invasion and Dark Ages. For centuries it remained a backward little country town with little interest in trade. During the 7th cen. the power of the monarchy was broken and an aristocracy established in its place.

Discontent resulting from agrarian problems opened the way for Solon to make sweeping economic, political, and social changes early in the 6th cen. He wiped out slavery for debt, strengthened the power of the assembly, and encouraged foreign artisans to settle at Athens. Development of the Athenian olive oil and pottery-making industries date to this time. The Pisistratid family ruled as tyrants or dictators during the latter half of the 6th cen., bringing about land reforms and encouraging the industrial and commercial development of the state and urbanizing Athens.

In the struggle that followed the expulsion of the tyranny from Athens, Cleisthenes rose to power and in 508 was given authority to reform the government. He became the real founder of the Athenian democracy and was responsible for creation of the famous Council of 500.

Athens was heavily involved in the Graeco-Persian wars. She supported the revolt of Miletus against Persia in 499 and defeated the Persians at Marathon in 490. In 480 Persians occupied Athens but the population was evacuated. The next year Athens led in the great naval victory over Persia at Salamis. In 478 Athens organized the Delian League as a defense against Persia but later turned it into an Athenian Empire.

Income from the empire made possible the golden age of Athens in the days when Pericles held the reins of government (461–431). The full democracy was developed in those days and extensive beautification of the Acropolis *(q.v.)* engaged in to make Athens a fit center of the empire and a fit home for her patron goddess Athena.

Rivalry with Sparta led to the Peloponnesian War (431–404), which resulted in destruction of Athens' empire, fortifications, and fleet. During the 4th cen. Athens built a small empire, but she was defeated by Alexander the Great and contributed to his invasion of Persia. Macedonia continued to control Athens during much of the 3rd cen., and during the 2nd cen. Athens fell under control of Rome.

Athens suffered terribly during the occupation by Mithridates of Pontus in 88–87 B.C. and the subsequent revenge of the Roman Sulla. During the 1st cen. A.D. Athens was primarily known for her cultural prowess and her university. The empire and the silver mines were gone and great rival centers of the E Mediterranean competed effectively for her trade. Despoiling of the city's art treasures came with Nero's rebuilding of Rome after the fire of A.D. 64. But Roman emperors of the 1st and 2nd cen. contributed heavily to building and other needs of Athens.

Biblical connections. Paul stopped briefly in Athens on his second missionary journey to wait out the storm of opposition raised against him at Thessalonica. Apparently he did not have a plan for evangelization of the city. He ministered in the Athenian synagogue and

Acropolis at Athens in classical times. After D'ooge

agora (Acts 17:17). At the latter he would have seen such important structures as the council chamber, the mint, the stoa of Attalus, and the temple of Hephaestus on an adjoining hill.

Epicurean *(q.v.)* and Stoic *(q.v.)* philosophers brought him before the Areopagus *(q.v.)*, which probably met on the 377-foot hill S of the agora *(q.v.)*. There he delivered his famous speech, in which he referred to "temples made with hands" (Acts 17:24), no doubt alluding to the famous temples of the Acropolis to the E of Areopagus. There the Parthenon, Erechtheum and temple of Athena Nike still stood intact. Farther E stood the great temple of Zeus. His reference to an inscription "TO THE UNKNOWN GOD" is supported by the 2nd cen. Gr. writer Pausanias, who saw altars at Athens to "gods called unknown." The American School of Classical Studies has excavated the agora and worked in other areas of Athens. *See* Archaeology.

H. F. V.

ATHLAI (ăth'lī). An Israelite who in the days of Ezra was one of those compelled to put away his foreign wife (Ezr 10:28).

ATONEMENT. The word "atonement" is an Anglo-Saxon term which has the force of "at-one-ment," a "making at one." It speaks of a process of bringing those who are enemies into harmony and unity, and thus it means reconciliation.

In the NT, the Gr. *katallagē,* "reconciliation," is once translated "atonement" in KJV (Rom 5:11); it describes the work or action of God in Jesus Christ by which the sinner is reconciled to God. This reconciliation, however, is not merely any reconciliation. It takes place in a definite setting of OT teaching and practice, so that the English Bible not unjustly uses the term "to make atonement" for the Heb. verb *kippēr,* which signifies appeasement or propitiation *(q.v.).*

Under the Mosaic law atonement for sin was achieved by the death of a sacrificial victim. The shedding of its blood was the evidence of its death. "For the life of the body is in the blood; and I have appointed it for you to make atonement upon the altar in behalf of your lives; for it is the blood that makes atonement by reason of the life [of the victim]" (Lev 17:11, orig. trans.).

Biblical atonement has a definite form, this specific reconciliation being effected by the death of Jesus Christ in His incarnation, life, death, resurrection and ascension. Thus this particular atonement is to be understood in terms of its specific background and reality, rather than in terms of the general concept. *See* Reconciliation.

The biblical concept. In both the OT and the NT the need of reconciliation is posed by the gracious, wise, and omnipotent resolve of God to satisfy His holiness and justice and yet fulfill His purpose even for sinful, guilty, alienated, and impotent man. Man in his sin is obviously unfit for fellowship and an eternal destiny with God. Yet man is neither able to absolve his guilt nor to free himself from transgression. The OT sacrifices were certainly not designed as a means of human self-atonement. They pointed to the atonement offered by Christ. For the fulfillment of the divine purpose in man, there is need of a substitutionary sacrifice as the basis of forgiveness, liberation, and restitution.

On a human reckoning, this might not seem to present any problem. God might simply abandon man on the one side, or declare and make him righteous on the other, in an arbitrary acceptance in spite of sin. As self-revealed in Holy Scripture, however, God is holy and loving as well as righteous, and therefore He was not willing that man should perish. But being righteous, He neither would nor could condone man's guilt or receive him in his sin. Reconciliation as accomplished by God is thus His self-consistent action for the divine restoration of fellowship between Himself, an absolutely holy God, and fallen, sinful man.

The problem of reconciliation was that of saving man in an act of perfect righteousness and judging him in an act of love. It should be emphasized, however, that this was no problem with God. He was not as it were brought to a stand and forced to seek a solution. He was not confronted by an inner tension in His own being which demanded integration. It may seem to us that the love and the righteousness of God pulled different ways, so that the first reconciliation had to take place within God Himself; but this is a false conception. We perceive the problem only as we see it in the light of the answer, and it was a problem only in terms of human understanding.

How could there be an action in which justice was done both to the righteousness of God on the one side and His love on the other, when it was a matter of saving guilty and impotent men? In His eternal wisdom and power, in the inner consistency of His own being, God had in Himself from the very first the answer to this question. Worked out historically in the action recorded in Scripture, this answer lay in the person and work of Jesus Christ, the incarnate Son, in whom all the demands of righteousness were met, both actively in His life as He kept the law perfectly in our stead, and passively in His death as He died under the penalty of the broken law. Thus the purpose of absolute justice and love was accomplished, man being freed from the guilt and power of sin and restored to eternal fellowship with God.

Four aspects of Jesus Christ and His work are here considered.

1. He was both God and man, so that He could act for both parties and yet also in one cause. While the incarnation was not itself the atonement, it was its indispensable basis. God now dealt with mankind only in the one Man who is Himself both God and man, so that

already there was in this new work an indissoluble relationship.

2. He fulfilled the law of God and attained righteousness, overcoming temptation and manifesting consistent obedience even to the death of the cross. He thus merited to the full the divine good pleasure, but in such a manner that there was in Him no rift between the divine love and the divine righteousness.

3. In fulfillment of His obedience, He bore the righteous judgment of sin as the one for the many. Thus sin was not condoned, yet it was judged in an act which was itself the crown of obedience and therefore acceptable to the Father. Judged in the innocent Saviour, sinful man can be accepted in Him even in judgment. The act of judgment was thus both an act of grace and salvation.

4. He was raised the third day from the dead, so that the sinner judged in Him is also victoriously renewed through Him. In virtue of the new life in Christ, the sinner is thus freed from the power as well as the guilt and penalty of sin, and can live the new life of fellowship to which he is restored.

Scriptural formulations. To describe the tremendous and inexhaustible reality of this great work of reconciliation, the Bible uses many forms of expression. It was an act of redemption in which the price paid by another, and finally by God Himself, was the precious blood of Christ (cf. Mk 10:45; Gal 3:13; Eph 1:7; I Pet 1:18–19). It was an act of conquest, in which the powers of evil, i.e., sin, death, the devil and hell, were overthrown (cf. Rom 8:37; Col 2:15). It was an act of sacrificial propitiation, in which the pleasing self-offering of the Innocent was accepted representatively for the guilty (cf. Rom 3:25; 5:12–21; Heb 2:17). It was an act of penal judgment, in which the divine wrath was suffered by the Just for the unjust (Isa 53:10–11); and therefore in one act God was just and yet also the justifier of those who trust in Jesus Christ (Rom 3:26 ff.).

In all these statements there is an element of metaphor. They are drawn from familiar social, military, cultic and forensic situations. Yet this does not mean that the metaphors do not represent facts. They are not to be evaluated simply as the efforts of the writers to express God's work in familiar concepts and categories. They cannot be dismissed as relative expressions which may be replaced by new and better ones as insight into the work of God increases. As the divine order lies behind human life in general, so there is a reality of divine and eternal content behind these descriptions of the divine work of reconciliation, even though some of the details in the divine wisdom may remain a mystery. Man is in fact enslaved, and God liberated him at a price. There is in fact a conflict, and Jesus Christ on the cross triumphed in and by the defeat of Satan and the powers of evil. Separation between the holy God and sinful man is a reality, but it was bridged by the offering of Christ which was well-pleasing to

God. There is a holy, wise, just, good law and God is righteous. Transgression and guilt exist and therefore bring judgment. But judgment was executed as the penalty fell on the righteous One in place of the guilty. These are solid and enduring realities which cannot be ignored in any attempted restatement.

The history of the doctrine. In the patristic age the discussion of the doctrine of atonement was largely dominated by the concepts of redemption and victory, though other motifs were also present. Irenaeus stressed the full identification of Christ with man as the second Adam, and His freeing of man from the devil by the ransom of death. Later writers, like Athanasius and Gregory of Nyssa, brought out the great importance of the incarnation in this regard, either in the principle of God's identification with man, or by the stratagem whereby the devil was lured by the bait of humanity and caught on the hook of divinity (cf. also Augustine and John of Damascus). The latter idea introduced a certain incongruity, as does also the discussion whether the ransom was paid to God or to the devil (Origen). Perhaps an even greater danger lurked in the approximation to a cosmic or metaphysical reconciliation by the simple equation of God and man irrespective of the cross. Nevertheless, the period shows a fine grasp of reconciliation not only as victory but also as intellectual and physical as well as spiritual liberation, and for the most part, the crucifixion was seen to be the critical point in the whole downward and upward movement of Christ the Reconciler.

The medieval period gave fresh prominence to the legal aspect which Augustine appreciated. A particularly fine statement is made in the famous *Cur Deus homo?* of Anselm, where the greatness of sin, the significance of divine holiness, the demand for satisfaction, and therefore the absolute necessity of the incarnation and crucifixion, are all convincingly declared. If Anselm also added less satisfactory elements, e.g., the idea of an equivalent payment and the transfer of a merited but superfluous reward, he certainly held the essentials of a true biblical concept. Bernard of Clairvaux preferred the more common patristic understanding, and Thomas Aquinas attempted a large-scale synthesis in his usual mode. Abelard sounded a new but defective note with his suggestion that the death of Christ was a demonstration of love which brought reconciliation by changing the sinner; and Scotus and Occam introduced the element of arbitrariness with their argument that it was only because of the inscrutable divine will that the death of Christ was an acceptable basis of forgiveness.

The Reformation fathers followed for the most part the Anselmic line, though with significant modifications. True, Luther loved to speak in terms of victory and liberation, but he also spoke plainly of Christ bearing the actual punishment of sin (as distinct from offering an equivalent satisfaction). Melanchthon developed this thought of penal suffering in his *Loci communhes,* and Calvin gave it forceful formulation in the definition: "Christ took upon Himself and suffered the punishment which by the righteous judgment of God impended over all sinners, and by this expiation the Father has been satisfied and His wrath appeased" (*Institutes,* II, 16, 2). For all the legal emphasis, Calvin's understanding was perhaps that one which stresses the primary scriptural aspect. Christ is the High Priest who reconciled us by His self-oblation and who still ministers on our behalf in His heavenly intercession.

In the post-Reformation age, Grotius tried to see in Christ an example given on a governmental basis to deter man from sin and yet satisfy the principles of good government. Moberly attempted to preserve the thought of a vicarious offering, but primarily in terms of penitence rather than punishment. Many recent writers, e.g., Rashdall, Storrs, Hanson, and to some degree Dodd, show great hostility to the full biblical Reformation understanding. Yet few are prepared to make it entirely subjective, that is, to make it rest on the response of the sinner aside from the satisfaction of God's holiness. In the most diverse circles there may be seen an insistence on the objectivity and even the penal nature of the work of Christ. B. B. Warfield, James Denney, J. K. Mozley, E. A. Knox, and Leon Morris may be quoted in this regard. But so, too, may L. Hodgson and Vincent Taylor to some degree, though in more guarded terms. The exegetes are almost unanimous that this is the witness of Scripture itself, as admitted by candid opponents like Rashdall and Storrs, who explained their position by claiming a better insight than the apostles. Emil Brunner and especially Karl Barth, with his thoroughgoing outworking of substitution, have added some scriptural and historic facets again, but have fallen into Schliermacher's error of a realistic view of true atonement which logically negates the need of personal faith in Christ.

Three points may be briefly made in conclusion. First, the reality of reconciliation is so vast that no single simple statement of one aspect can claim to be adequate. The Bible itself presents different aspects in order the better to encompass the whole. From this it follows, secondly, that we are not confronted by sharp alternatives in which the choice of one necessarily excludes all others. The various presentations all bring out elements of the truth of reconciliation comprehensively. Thirdly, however, this does not mean that we are in a sphere of relativity where each view of the Church Fathers is as good as another, and therefore we may pick and choose either arbitrarily or at random. There is an absolute reality of atonement which can be expressed fully only by accepting all of the biblical aspects or formulations. Proper weight must thus be attached to each of these if there is to be comprehension of what God Himself has really done for the redemption of His elect.

See also Christ, Passion of; Forgiveness; Salvation; Reconciliation.

Bibliography. Karl Barth, *Church Dogmatics,* IV, 1, 2, 3, trans. by G. T. Thomson, Edinburgh: T. & T. Clark, 1936. John Calvin, *Institutes of the Christian Religion,* 8th Am. ed., Grand Rapids: Eerdmans, 1949, I, 506–512, 551–585. Thomas J. Crawford, *The Doctrine of the Holy Scripture Respecting the Atonement,* 4th ed., Grand Rapids: Baker, 1954. Robert H. Culpepper, *Interpreting the Atonement,* Grand Rapids: Eerdmans, 1966. James Denney, *The Christian Doctrine of Reconciliation,* New York: Doran, 1918; *The Atonement and the Modern Mind,* London: Hodder & Stoughton, 1903. Vernon C. Grounds, "Atonement," BDT, pp. 71–78. J. Hermann and F. Büchsel, *"Hilaskomai, etc.,"* TDNT, III, 300–323. David Hill, *Greek Words and Hebrew Meanings,* Cambridge: Univ. Press, 1967, chap. on *hilaskesthai.* Thomas H. Hughes, *The Atonement, Modern Theories of the Doctrine,* London: Allen & Unwin, 1949. R. B. Kuiper, *For Whom Did Christ Die?* Grand Rapids: Eerdmans, 1959. Leon Morris, *The Apostolic Preaching of the Cross,* Grand Rapids: Eerdmans, 1956, pp. 114–117, 142–156, 161–223, 277–280. John K. Mozley, *The Doctrine of the Atonement,* London: Duckworth, 1947. J. Barton Payne, *The Theology of the Older Testament,* Grand Rapids: Zondervan, 1962, pp. 246–257, 378 ff.

G. W. Br.

ATONEMENT, DAY OF. *See* Festivals.

ATROTH (ăt'rŏth). The KJV translation of a town of Gad listed in Num 32:35, near Jogbehah. The name should be combined with Shophan, giving the compound name Atroth-shophan, as in RSV. The town was probably near the larger Ataroth (Num 32:3, 34), from which its name was derived, and acting as its outpost. A site, Rujm 'Atarus, on a lofty hill a mile and a half NE of Ataroth (Khirbet 'Attarus), may be its location.

ATTAI (ăt'ī)

1. A half Egyptian, father of Nathan; mentioned in genealogy of Jerahmeel of the tribe of Judah (I Chr 2:35–36).

2. A Gadite, one of David's mighty men who joined him at Ziklag (I Chr 12:11).

3. Son of Rehoboam and younger brother of Abijah, king of Judah (II Chr 11:20).

ATTALIA (ăt'á-lī'á). A city on the coast of Pamphylia, visited by Paul on his first missionary journey (Acts 14:25). It was founded *c.* 165–150 B.C. (see A. H. M. Jones, *Cities of the Eastern Roman Provinces,* p. 130) by Attalus II Philadelphus (159–138 B.C.) of Pergamum to be an outlet to Egypt and Syria (Strabo XIV. 667). Strabo placed Attalia to the W of the Catarrhactes River; Ptolemy on the other hand

Augustus Caesar. HFV

4, 1169, n. 20, 1365, 1615 f. W. M. Ramsay, *Historical Geography of Asia Minor,* London: John Murray, 1890, p. 420. An inscription published in the *Bulletin de correspondence hellenique* (1883, p. 260) proves that in the late 3rd cen. Attalia became a Roman colony. It reads: ". . . the glorious colo[ny] Attalia . . ." For other inscriptions from Attalia see Robert, *Revue des Etudes Greques,* LXI (1948), 198 f.

E. J. V.

ATTIRE. *See* Dress.

ATTITUDES. *See* Mind and Attitudes.

AUGUSTUS (*ȧ-gŭs'tŭs*). The first of the Roman emperors (27 B.C.–A.D. 14) and the successor of the noted Julius Caesar. His reign was especially marked by two things: a time of peace (the *Pax Augusta*) and his great building programs ("I found Rome built of sun-dried bricks; I leave her clothed in marble"). He gave impetus to the restoration of religion.

In the NT, his name is indelibly inscribed together with the story of the birth of Jesus (Lk 2:1-20). It seems not accidental, either, that the angel's words on that occasion included "peace among men."

His full name was Gaius Julius Caesar Octavianus, and the title Augustus was bestowed upon him by the Senate in 27 B.C., making him the commander-in-chief of the armies. The title implied divinity, but he did not claim such for himself.

Although he was Julius Caesar's adopted heir, Augustus had to fight to inherit Caesar's legacy. First he and Mark Antony had to defeat forces responsible for Caesar's assassination led by Brutus and Cassius. The battle took place near Philippi in 42 B.C. Later he was forced to war against Antony and Cleopatra, defeating them at Actium in western Greece in 31 B.C. Augustus brought an end to the Roman Republic and introduced the empire period. By careful organization of the provinces, he consolidated the empire, leaving a conquered area

placed it to the E (v. 5.2). Perhaps the river changed its course. It was punished by the Roman consul P. Servilius Isauricus (*c.* 77 B.C.) for aiding Zenicetes in his piracy (see Jones, p. 105) by being added to the Roman province thereafter.

Coins were struck from the time of the founding of the city and its name is spelled thereon as *Attaleōn* ("belonging to Attalia"). When Paul was there, the main type of coin showed Claudius on the obverse, and on the reverse Athena dressed in a crested Corinthian helmet (cf. G. F. Hill, *B. M. C., Catalogue of Greek Coins; Lycia, Pamphylia, Pisidia* [London: 1897], Plate XXIII, 8). It should be remembered that the people of Attalia claimed kinship with the Athenians. Attalia struck coins as late as Cornelius Valerianus (d. A.D. 255).

The situation of this port city, rising as it does by tiers from its harbor, is still picturesque and is partly responsible for its continued existence and commercial activity. Ruins there are traceable to the Roman and Hellenistic periods. It is called Antalya today.

Bibliography. A. H. M. Jones, *Cities of the Eastern Roman Provinces,* Oxford: Clarendon, 1937, pp. 105, 130-131, 133-134, 145, 557. Karl Lanckoroński-Brzezie, *Städte Pamphyliens und Pisidiens,* Wien: F. Tempsky, 1890, pp. 7-32, 153-163. David Magie, *Roman Rule in Asia Minor,* Princeton: Univ. Press, 1950, I, 28, 261 f., 285, 288, 291, 620, 691; II, 1133, n.

Tomb of Augustus, Rome. HFV

of more than three million square miles at his death. He was succeeded by his adopted heir Tiberius.

See also Caesar.

Bibliography. William James Durant, *Caesar and Christ, The Story of Civilization,* New York: Simon and Schuster, III (1935), Chap. XI. Herbert Jennings Rose, *Ancient Roman Religion,* London: Hutchinson's Univ. Library (1948), Chap. IV. Suetonius, *The Twelve Caesars,* trans. by Robert Graves, Harmondsworth: Penguin, 1957.

W. M. D.

AUL. A thin, sharp instrument mentioned in the Bible only in connection with the piercing of the ear of a Heb. slave who out of love willingly took a vow of perpetual slavery (Ex 21:6; Deut 15:17). Many specimens of auls made of bone, wood, flint, or metal have been unearthed in the Near East from earliest periods onward.

AUTHORITY

Terms. The Gr. *exousia* is the chief word translated as "authority" in the NT. Originally it signified the power and freedom of choice (e.g., I Cor 7:37, NEB). Ancient wills expressed the "right" of the testator to dispose of his property as he wished. In the NT *exousia* is used in the sense of one's rights. Paul spoke of his rights as an apostle (I Cor 9:1-14). Those who wash their robes have the right to the tree of life (Rev 22:14), even as Christ gives the right to become children of God to those who receive Him (Jn 1:12).

Then *exousia* came to mean the rightful power to act or possess or control, as in the case of the sale proceeds of the property of Ananias and Sapphira (Acts 5:4). Whereas *dynamis* primarily denotes physical power or ability, *exousia* usually signifies the warrant or power that is in some sense lawful (e.g., Acts 9:14; 26:10, 12). The uniform teaching of the Bible is that the only rightful power in the created universe is that of the Creator. Absolute authority belongs to God alone, all other authority being subordinate and derivative.

While the English word is not used of God in the OT, the concept of His authority appears in passages speaking of His sovereign and everlasting rule (Ps 66:7; 89:9; 103:19; Isa 40:10; Dan 4:17, 34-35) and His universal kingship (Ps 47; 93; 95:3-5; etc.). He is recognized as the Judge of all the earth (Gen 18:25) who has the last word in all the affairs of men. In OT times God exercised authority over and governed His people through the agency of the elders and also the priests, judges, and kings whom He raised up or appointed (Jud 2:16; II Sam 7:8). They were enabled to govern by God-given wisdom (Prov 8:15-16). See "Government, Authority and Kingship," CornPBE, pp. 354-369. Especially the prophets were His servants to proclaim His messages (Jer 1:7-10) and write down His authoritative instruction

(tôrâ). They were bound to no earthly superior and so spoke with His divine authority to people, priest, and king alike.

The ultimate authority of God. The Bible plainly states that the true source and seat of authority is in God. Paul writes that there is no authority except from God (Rom 13:1), and Jesus argues that God alone need be feared, because He alone has authority to cast into hell (Lk 12:5). God's authority over mankind consists in His unchallengeable right and power to deal with men as He pleases, just as the potter has *exousia* over the lump of clay (Rom 9:21). Man is not to attempt to unravel the mystery of future times and epochs which God the Father has fixed by His own authority (Acts 1:7).

Jesus Christ's authority is both original and derived. As the Son of God, His authority is original because He is Himself God, the Co-creator and sharer in all the Father's works (Jn 5:19-21). He had within Himself the power or authority to lay down His life and to take it up again, although the charge or directive to do so He had received from His Father (Jn 10:18). He did not have to pray to God for help or hesitate to assume complete authority in the presence of storms or disease or demon-possession. He took it upon Himself to forgive sins, the prerogative of God alone (Mk 2:5-10). He dared to go beyond the precepts of the law of Moses, which was accepted as of divine origin (Mt 5:22, 28, 34); thus He taught as one having authority in Himself (Mt 7:29).

Because the Word of God is fully inspired by the Spirit of God, it has supreme authority for men (*see* Inspiration). The prophets spoke the word of the Lord — "thus saith the Lord"; and the apostles were Christ's commissioned witnesses and representatives (Mt 10:40; Jn 14:26; 15:26-27; 20:21; Acts 1:8; 26:16-18). They were given His authority to build up the Church (Mt 16:18-19; II Cor 10:8; 13:10). God bore witness with them by signs and miracles and gifts of the Holy Spirit (Heb 2:3-4). Their message was received "not as the word of men, but for what it really is, the word of God, which also performs its work in you who believe" (I Thess 2:13, NASB). *See* Apostle.

Even Jesus Christ as man accepted and submitted to the authority of the OT. During His temptation He quoted Scripture to Himself in the presence of Satan as the reason why He should not follow the devil (Mt 4:1-10). In His controversies He appealed over and over again to the Scriptures as the final authority to answer His critics (e.g., Jn 10:33-36; Mt 22:23-46). He clearly demonstrated that the proper school of authority is not the individual's reason or conscience (rationalism) or religious tradition (Mk 7:1-13) but the Word of God, the Bible.

The documents of the NT were early recognized as Scripture (cf. I Tim 5:18 with Lk 10:7; II Pet 3:15-16) and considered profitable and thus authoritative (II Tim 3:16). It is through the Bible, then, that God the Son now speaks and exercises divine authority.

The authority delegated to men. As man and Messiah, Christ's authority is not only original but also delegated to Him by His Father (Jn 17:2). He implies as much when He counters the question of the Jewish leaders who asked, "By what authority are You doing these things, and who gave You this authority?" (Mt 21:23-27, NASB). He praises the centurion for recognizing that He too is under authority (Mt 8:8-10). He plainly states that the Father gave Him authority to pass judgment, gave it to Him because He is Son of man—the *human* Messiah (Jn 5:27). This is clearly reminiscent of the vision of Daniel in which one like a Son of Man stood before the Ancient of Days and received everlasting sovereignty and glory and kingship (Dan 7:13-14; *see* Son of Man). His great commission to His disciples has finality because all authority has been given to Him in heaven and on earth (Mt 28:18).

Men have authority only as God commits it to them (Jn 19:11). This is true both within the church and in the realm of civil government where secular (Roman) officials are called "authorities," ministers of God to punish evildoers (Rom 13:1-7). Christians are to honor and submit themselves to these kings and governors (I Pet 2:13-17; Tit 3:1; cf. Mt 22:21), unless it requires a direct disobedience to God (Acts 4:19; 5:29).

Within the God-ordained family unit the man is "head," has authority over the woman (Eph 5:23) and over his children (I Tim 3:4, 12). Thus the wife should not teach or exercise authority over her husband (I Tim 2:12) but be subject to him (Eph 5:22; I Pet 3:1-6). The husband should exercise leadership of the home as his duty in all humility, gentleness and love, recognizing that Christ as his Head has granted authority to him (I Cor 11:3). In turn, he should fully respect his wife's sphere of responsibility and show appreciation for her competence in handling the details of housekeeping. Children are to obey their parents in harmony with the fifth commandment (Eph 6:1-3; Col 3:20).

Christ delegated His authority not only to the apostles who had, properly speaking, no successors in the matter of producing inspired Scriptures, but also to every disciple. He gave power and authority over all demons and to heal diseases both to the twelve (Lk 9:1) and to the seventy (Lk 10:1, 9, 17, 19). Miraculous signs, the credentials of the ambassador of Christ, accompanied those who believed in the apostles (Mk 16:16-20).

Such power is granted to the believer because by God's grace he is seated or enthroned with Christ in the heavenly places, in the spirit realm or sphere of all spiritual activity (Eph 1:19-20; 2:6). Every Christian, therefore, occupies potentially the throne of Christ. In the spiritual warfare with Satanic forces the believer should exercise his delegated authority and in faith compel the powers of evil to obey in the name of Jesus (Eph 6:12; Acts 3:16; 4:30; 16:18). He is to bring every thought captive to the obedience of Christ (II Cor 10:4-5). He can reckon on the power of the Holy Spirit (Rom 15:13, 19) and the protection of the blood of Christ (Rev 12:11), symbolic of Christ's victory at Calvary over the Satanic principalities and powers (Col 2:14-15).

The authority usurped by Satan. The exercise of power by the devil and his demonic spirits and their domain are often termed *exousia* (Lk 4:6; 22:53; Acts 26:18; Eph 2:2; Col 1:13). While Satan has usurped his power from God, it nevertheless has been handed over to him (Lk 4:6). Thus he holds it only by God's permission and as God's unwilling agent (Rev 2:10).

Angelic beings are sometimes called "powers" or "authorities" (*exousiai,* Eph 3:10; Col 1:16), and these include the evil spirits (Eph 6:12; Col 2:15). But in every case their authority is only secondary, for Christ has been raised "far above all rule and authority and power and dominion, and every name that is named, not only in this age, but also in the one to come" (Eph 1:21, NASB). The great claim of the NT is that the whole world of supernatural beings and their authority are entirely subordinate to God.

Bibliography. Werner Foerster, *"Exousia,* etc.," TDNT, II, 562-575. J. Norval Geldenhuys, *Supreme Authority,* Grand Rapids: Eerdmans, 1953; "Authority and the Bible," *Revelation and the Bible,* ed. by Carl F. H. Henry, Grand Rapids: Baker, 1958, pp. 371-386. J. I. Packer, "Authority," NBD, pp. 111-113. Bernard Ramm, *The Pattern of Religious Authority,* Grand Rapids: Eerdmans, 1957. T. Rees, "Authority," ISBE, I, 333-340. Benjamin B. Warfield, *The Inspiration and Authority of the Bible,* Philadelphia: Presbyterian and Reformed, 1948.

J. R.

AUTHORIZED VERSION. The King James Version (KJV) of A.D. 1611. *See* Bible, English Versions.

AVA (ăv′à). A city from which colonists were sent to Samaria to replace the Israelites removed by the conquest of the Assyrians in 722 B.C. (II Kgs 17:24). The Avites made idols which were called Nibhaz and Tartak (II Kgs 17:31), perhaps deliberate Jewish corruptions of the names of Syrian deities. Ava may be identified with Ivah (II Kgs 18:34), probably modern Tell Kefr 'Aya on the Orontes River. *See* Ivah.

AVEN (ā′vĕn)
1. Aven is the name applied by Ezekiel (Ezk 30:17) to the famous Egyptian worship center of On (Gen 41:45), also called Heliopolis. As he prophesied of the desolation to be visited by God upon Egypt, this world renowned city for the worship of Ra the sun-god

is described by the prophet as Aven— "nothingness."

2. The same scorn of idolatrous places of worship is found in Hos 10:8 where the sites of Israel's apostasy are described as the "high places of Aven, the sin of Israel."

3. Amos 1:5 speaks of the "plain [or valley] of Aven" in connection with God's judgment of Syria. If this reference is to Baalbek, the center of Baal worship in Syria, the false gods are again scorned as "vanity."

AVENGER OF BLOOD. *See* Blood, Avenger of.

AVIM (ăv'ĭm), **AVITES** (ăv'īts)
1. An aboriginal Canaanite people who lived in the area around Gaza. At the time of the Philistine invasions, all except a small remnant were destroyed (Deut 2:23; Josh 13:3). *See also* Hazerim.
2. A city S of Bethel in Benjamin (Josh 18:23).
3. Inhabitants of Ava (*q.v.;* II Kgs 17:24) in Syria, mentioned in II Kgs 17:31 as an idolatrous people transported to Samaria.

AVITH (ā'vĭth).The city or home of Hadad, son of Bedad, fourth king of Edom, who ruled before there were any kings in Israel (Gen 36:35; I Chr 1:46).

AWL. *See* Aul.

AXE. Axes were among the commonest tools of Palestine (Isa 10:15). With other such tools they required hard toil (II Sam 12:31; I Chr 20:3, both RSV).

As to material, earliest cutting tools were of bone, flint, or stone, later bronze, and beginning about 1200 B.C., iron. (The "axe head" in II Kgs 6:5 is really "iron," as in v.6.) The Philistines tried to prevent Israel from using this superior metal when they overflowed the lowlands of Palestine at the beginning of the Iron Age; at least I Sam 13:19-22 is so interpreted (G. Ernest Wright, *Biblical Archaeology,* rev. ed., Philadelphia: Westminster Press, 1962, pp. 91-94).

The butt of the axe head might be perforated to receive a thong by which to fasten it to the wooden helve or handle. The accidental murder anticipated in Deut 19:5 and the loss of the borrowed axe in II Kgs 6:5-6 suggest that the head often worked loose.

The shape of the axe varied, so that the seven different Heb. words which the KJV renders "axe" could be translated axe, pick-axe or adze (with cutting edge at right angle to the handle), billhook, chisel, pick—all of them cutting tools, mostly for wood, sometimes for stone (in Palestine especially limestone).

Abimelech and his men cut brush with axes to set fire to the tower of Shechem (Jud 9:47-49). Attackers of cities cut down trees (Jer 46:22) for siegeworks, for which no fruit trees might be taken (Deut 20:19-20). An axe might be used as a blade for shaping the wood-

en core of an idol, to be overlaid with precious metals (Jer 10:3-4). The enemies of Israel hacked down the wooden decorations of the temple with axes (Ps 74:4-7). Pick-axes or adzes were employed to cut stones for altars (but Israel's altars were to be of natural stones only, Ex 20:25), or for the temple of Solomon, whose stones, some of tremendous size, were all prefabricated (I Kgs 6:7; 7:9-11).

The axe occurs in the NT only in the words of John the Baptist (Mt 3:10; Lk 3:9), who illustrated threatened judgment by an axe laid at the roots of a fruit tree, ready to cut it down if the tree were useless.

W. G. B.

AX HEAD. *See* Axe; Armor.

AZAL (ā'zăl). Found only in Zech 14:5 (KJV). It is conjectured that this is the name of a site near Jerusalem. Two places are suggested: Beth-ezel (Mic 1:11), or the name of a place that ceased to exist and is suggested in the name of Wady Yasul, a tributary of the Kidron. The Heb. meaning is "side or slope."

AZALIAH (ăz-ȧ-lī'ȧ). A son of Meshullam and father of Shaphan, the scribe under Josiah (II Kgs 22:3; II Chr 34:8).

AZANIAH (ăz-ȧ-nī'ȧ). A Levite, son of Jeshua, who signed the covenant after the Exile (Neh 10:9).

AZARAEL (ăz'ȧ-rā'ĕl), **AZAREEL** (ăz'ȧ-rēl)
1. One of the family of Korah who defected from Saul to David at Ziklag (I Chr 12:6). He is listed with the warriors of Benjamin, especially skilled in using the sling with either right or left hand.
2. A Levite, son of Heman, who was appointed by David to minister in music in the sanctuary (I Chr 25:18). He is called Uzziel in I Chr 25:4.
3. A prince of the tribe of Dan who was appointed by David to be chief captain over his tribe at the time of the numbering of the people (I Chr 27:22).
4. An Israelite of the family of Bani after the return from Exile. He had taken a foreign wife and thus came under the judgment of Ezra (Ezr 10:41).
5. A priest in the days of Nehemiah (Neh 11:13; 12:36). He was the father of Amashsai, a "mighty man of valor," residing in Jerusalem. He is probably the man mentioned as a member of the band of trumpeters at the dedication of the wall.

P. C. J.

AZARIAH (ăz-ȧ-rī'ȧ).This was a common name in Heb., especially among the families of the priestly line of Eleazar, whose name means "whom Yahweh has helped." It is closely related to the name Ezra, which means simply "help." The Scriptures mention the following persons as having borne this name:

1. The son of Ahimaaz (I Chr 6:9) who, according to I Kgs 4:2, seems to have succeeded his grandfather Zadok in the high priesthood under Solomon. Since his father died before Zadok, the notation in I Chr 6:10 undoubtedly applies to him rather than his own grandson.

2. A son of Nathan who served as captain of Solomon's tax collectors (I Kgs 4:5).

3. The tenth king of Judah whom Isaiah refers to as Uzziah (*q.v.;* II Kgs 14:21; 15:1, 6, 7, 8, 17, 23, 27; I Chr 3:12. See also II Kgs 15:13; II Chr 26:1; Isa 1:1; 6:1).

4. A son of Ethan of the tribe of Judah (I Chr 2:8).

5. The son of Jehu with Egyptian descent through the daughter of Sheshan (I Chr 2:38–39).

6. The son of Johanan, who served as high priest during the reigns of Abijah and Asa (I Chr 6:10).

7. The son of Hilkiah and the father of Seraiah (I Chr 6:13–14).

8. The son of Zephaniah the Kohathite, ancestor of the prophet Samuel (I Chr 6:36; see also I Chr 6:24).

9. A prophet during the reign of Asa whose father's name was Oded (II Chr 15:1–8).

10. and 11. Two of the sons of Jehoshaphat, king of Judah (II Chr 21:2).

12. King of Judah (II Chr 22:6; also called Ahaziah in v. 1).

13. A son of Jehoram, and a captain in Judah. He helped overthrow Athaliah and enthrone Joash (II Chr 23:1).

14. The high priest who withstood King Uzziah when he took to himself priestly prerogatives (II Chr 26:17–20). A contemporary of Isaiah.

15. The son of Johanan and a captain of Ephraim during the reign of Ahaz (II Chr 28:12). He returned the captives and the spoil that were taken in the invasion of Judah by Pekah.

16. A Kohathite who was father of Joel in the reign of King Hezekiah (II Chr 29:12).

17. A Merarite who was the son of Jehalelel in the time of Hezekiah (II Chr 29:12).

18. A chief priest during the reign of Hezekiah who cooperated with the king in the cleansing of the temple (II Chr 31:10, 13).

19. A bitter enemy of Jeremiah (Jer 43:2 ff.).

20. The companion of Daniel whose name was changed to Abed-nego, a royal captive in Babylon (Dan 1:6, 7, 11, 19).

21. The son of Maaseiah, who helped repair the walls of Jerusalem (Neh 3:23–24).

22. A Levite who assisted Ezra in expounding the law (Neh 8:7). Possibly the same as 21.

23. One of the priests who sealed the covenant with Nehemiah, and who probably is to be identified with the one who assisted with the dedication of the city wall (Neh 10:2; 12:33). Possibly the same as 21.

R. E. Pr.

AZAZ (āʹzăz). A Reubenite, the son of Shema and father of Bela (I Chr 5:8).

AZAZEL (*á-zāʹzĕl*). This word means "scapegoat," "removal," or "far removed" (Lev 16:8, 10, 22, 26). A footnote in the Berkeley Version says: "The name Azazel is derived from Azalzeh ('dismissed one') thus properly thought of as the scapegoat." Gesenius in his Heb. lexicon declares: "I have no doubt that it should be rendered *averter.*" He suggests a more correct form to be *ʻazalzêl* meaning "to remove," "to separate." It may be considered as an intensified form of the Semitic root *ʻazal,* found in Arabic. Thus the term seems to stand (in its untranslated form in recent versions) as a symbol of the transfer of guilt and the complete removal of sin.

The Gr. term used by the LXX translators signifies "a sending away, or a getting rid of." Jerome seems to have considered the term to be a compound of *ʻēz* and *ʼāzal,* "goat" and "to depart," for his Latin term is *Caper emissarius* in the Vulgate Version. Brown, Driver, and Briggs (*Hebrew Lexicon,* p. 736) remind us that "in the ritual of the Day of Atonement" it indicates "entire removal of sin and guilt from sacred places into the desert on the back of a goat; symbolic of entire forgiveness." Oehler, in his *Theology of the Old Testament,* thinks it has reference to "an evil spiritual power" (p. 350) or to "a wicked demon" (p. 159).

The name appears in the pseudepigraphical book of Enoch where Azazel designates the angel of cutlery, weapons, and metallurgy (8:1); a teacher of unrighteousness (9:6); who is bound and cast into darkness in the desert pit or abyss (10:4); to whom there is no peace, but severe sentence of bonds (13:1); and is later named among the fallen angels (69:2).

Among the Arabs, the name refers to an evil demon. Those who regard it as a demon of the wilderness appeal to such passages as Ps 106:37; Deut 32:17; Lev 17:7; II Chr 11:15; Isa 13:21; 34:14; Mt 12:43 ff.; Lk 11:24 ff.; Rev 18:2.

The Epistle of Barnabas (7:6–11; mid. 2nd cen. A.D.) definitely considers this scapegoat to be a type of Christ our Sinbearer (cf. Isa 53:4–6). And so it has been treated frequently in later Christian thought.

Others suggest that the term has special reference to the place of banishment, or that it may specify a curse offering to the author of demoniacal sin (cf. Gal 3:13).

Radical liberals view it as simply a relic of some ancient magical pagan rite which was incorporated into Judaism. The Caffers of South Africa have a ceremony in which a goat is taken into the presence of a sick man, where the sins of the kraal are confessed over it and a few drops of blood from the sick are allowed to fall on the head of the goat, which is then turned out into an uninhabited part of the veldt. Thus the animal becomes a vehicle for the expulsion of evil, which evil, being transferred to the animal, is lost in the desert.

Evangelical Christians see here a type of the removal of sin and guilt achieved in the person of our Saviour, and for that reason, they are loath to think of the "scapegoat" as an offering for the placating of a demon.

See Festivals: Day of Atonement.

R. E. Pr.

AZAZIAH (ăz-à-zī'à)

1. A Levitical musician appointed to play the harp when the ark was brought to Jerusalem from Obed-edom (I Chr 15:21).

2. The father of Joshea, prince of Ephraim, in the reign of David (I Chr 27:20).

3. A Levite overseer of the tithes under Hezekiah (II Chr 31:13).

AZBUK (ăz'bŭk). The father of a certain Nehemiah (not the governor of the same name) who took part in rebuilding the wall of Jerusalem after the Exile (Neh 3:16).

AZEKAH (à-zē'kà). A city located on a high hill NE of Lachish and SW of Jerusalem. Her king joined the enemies of Israel in Joshua's day and suffered defeat at the hands of the Hebrews (Josh 10:10–11). Near this city the Philistines encamped when David killed Goliath (I Sam 17:1). During the divided monarchy Rehoboam fortified Azekah (II Chr 11:9) and it remained an important fort when Nebuchadnezzar attacked Jerusalem in 588 B.C. On that occasion it was one of the last remaining strongholds of Judah (Jer 34:7). One of the Lachish letters (No. IV), written at that time by an officer in charge of an outpost near Azekah, mentions that he could not see fire signals from Azekah (ANET, p. 322). It is not certain whether this implies Azekah had already fallen to the Babylonians. The city again figured in Heb. history after the return from Babylonian captivity (Neh 11:30).

It is identified with Tell Zakariyeh in the Shephelah or foothills region of Judah (Josh 15:35), guarding the lower end of the valley of

Mound of Azekah. HFV

Elah (Wadi es-Sant), *c.* 16 miles W of Bethlehem. F. J. Bliss and R. A. S. Macalister in 1898–99 uncovered an inner citadel fortified with eight large towers, perhaps built during Rehoboam's reign.

H. F. V.

AZEL (ā'zĕl). A Benjamite, a descendant of Jonathan (I Chr 8:37).

AZEM (ā'zĕm). A town in the Negeb district of Judah later assigned to Simeon (Josh 15:29; 19·3). It is spelled Ezem in I Chr 4:29. Since it is mentioned near Arad in the list of towns pillaged by Pharaoh Shishak, it may be identified with Umm el-'Azam, 12 miles SE of Beer-sheba.

AZGAD (ăz'găd). The head of a family, of whom 1,222 male members returned to Palestine with Zerubbabel (Ezr 2:12; Neh 7:17 [2,322]), and again 110 male members returned with Ezra (Ezr 8:12). Azgad set his seal to Ezra's covenant (Neh 10:1, 15). The name occurs in the Aramaic papyri from the ruins of the Jewish colony at Elephantine in Egypt.

AZIEL (ā'zĭ-ĕl). A shortened form of Jaaziel *(q.v.;* I Chr 15:18). A Levitical singer who played the psaltery (I Chr 15:20).

AZIZA (à-zī'zà). One of the sons of Zattu who obeyed Ezra and put away his foreign wife (Ezr 10:27).

AZMAVETH (ăz-mà'vĕth)

1. A member of David's elite corps of 30 valiant men (II Sam 23:31; I Chr 11:33). He was a native of the town of Bahurim in Benjamin, just E of Jerusalem. He was probably the father of the two young Benjamites who deserted Saul to join David at Ziklag (I Chr 12:3).

2. The son of Jehoaddah, a descendant of Jonathan through Mephibosheth (Meribbaal) (I Chr 8:36; 9:42).

3. The son of Adiel and an important officer over the king's treasury in the time of David (I Chr 27:25).

4. A village, also called Beth-Azmaveth *(q.v.),* on the border of Judah and Benjamin, five miles NE of Jeruslaem; modern Hizmeh. The village might well preserve the name of the mighty man of David's day (i.e., see 1 above). From this town came 42 exiles who returned in the days of Zerubbabel (Ezr 2:24; Neh 7:28; 12:29).

AZMON (ăz'mŏn). A place on the southern border of Judah; location uncertain (Num 34:4–5; Josh 15:4).

AZNOTH-TABOR (ăz'nŏth-tā'bŏr). A place at the SW corner of the border of Naphtali, evidently on the lower slopes of Mount Tabor (Josh 19:34). *See* Tabor, Mount.

AZOR (ā'zŏr). One of the post-Exilic ancestors of Jesus (Mt 1:13–14).

AZOTUS (a-zō'tŭs). The LXX and NT form (Acts 8:40) of Ashdod (q.v.).

AZRIEL (ăz'rĭ-ĕl)
1. One of the heads of the half tribe of Manasseh E of the Jordan (I Chr 5:24).
2. The father of Jerimoth who was a chief of Naphtali (I Chr 27:19).
3. The father of Seraiah who was commanded by King Jehoiakim to arrest Baruch and Jeremiah (Jer 36:26).

AZRIKAM (ăz'rĭ-kăm)
1. One of the sons of Neariah, a descendant of Zerubbabel in the family of David, in the period after the return from Exile (I Chr 3:23).
2. One of the six sons of Azel, a Benjamite descendant of Saul and Jonathan, probably after the Exile (I Chr 8:38; 9:44).
3. A Levite of the family of Merari, one of whose descendants is listed as a dweller in Jerusalem in Nehemiah's time (I Chr 9:14; Neh 11:15).
4. The most prominent Azrikam was "commander of the palace" under Ahaz (II Chr 28:7, RSV). He was slain by Zichri of Ephraim during the attack of Pekah and Rezin on Judah.

AZUBAH (a-zū'ba)
1. A wife of Caleb and mother of three sons (I Chr 2:18–19).
2. A daughter of Shilhi and the mother of King Jehoshaphat (I Kgs 22:42; II Chr 20:31).

AZUR (ā'zŭr)
1. The father of Hananiah, the false prophet from Gibeon (Jer 28:1).
2. The father of Jaazaniah, one of those who gave wicked counsel to the city of Jerusalem (Ezk 11:1).
3. One of the chief Israelites who signed the covenant in the days of Nehemiah (Neh 10:17, Azzur).

AZZAH (ăz'a). The KJV translation of Heb. 'azzâ in Deut 2:23; I Kgs 4:24; Jer 25:20. The Gr. form, Gaza, is more commonly used. See Gaza.

AZZAN (ăz'an). The father of Paltiel, a prince of the tribe of Issachar who was one of the commissioners selected to divide the land among the tribes (Num 34:26).

AZZUR (ăz'ŭr). Found only in Neh 10:17. See Azur.

B

BAAL, BAALIM. See Gods, False.

BAALAH (bā'a-lă)
1. A border city of northern Judah, better known as Kirjath-jearim or Kirjath-baal (q.v.), five miles W of Jerusalem on the road descending to the coast (Josh 15:9–10, 60), where the ark remained after its return from Philistia (I Chr 13:6).
2. A ridge, probably the hill of Mughar, some 20 miles farther W, arising out of the Philistine plain between Ekron and Jabneel (Josh 15:11).
3. A city of Simeon in southern Judah (Josh 15:29), modern Tulul el-Medhbah, identifiable with Balah (Josh 19:3) and Bilhah (I Chr 4:29), which see.

BAALATH (bā'a-lăth). A town fortified by Solomon (I Kgs 9:18; II Chr 8:6). It was in the original territory of Dan (Josh 19:44), probably near Gezer.

BAALATH-BEER (bā'a-lăth bē'ẽr). A border city of the tribe of Simeon, apparently also known as Ramah (q.v.) of the Negeb (Josh 19:8; I Sam 30:27). The shrine of a Canaanite goddess was located here and was simply referred to as Baal (I Chr 4:33). An early 6th cen. B.C. Heb. ostracon from Arad mentions Ramath-negeb and illuminates the area of the S boundary of the kingdom of Judah (BASOR # 197 [1970], pp. 16–28).

BAALBEK (bāl'bĕk). A site of magnificent ruins, about 40 miles NW of Damascus in the Beqa', the wide plain between the Lebanon and Anti-Lebanon. Some scholars have identified it with the Aven of Amos 1:5 (RSV). It seems to have been a center for the worship of Baal or Hadad before it became known as Heliopolis, "City of the Sun," in the Seleucid period. Under Augustus the city became a Roman colony and its cult was much favored. The first three centuries of the Christian era witnessed its greatest prosperity. Magnificent temples were erected to the god Bacchus and to the triad Jupiter (identified with Baal, at that time recognized as the sun-god), Mercury, and Venus. The great Jupiter temple was commenced by

Antoninus Pius (A.D. 138 – 161) and completed under Caracalla (211 – 217), whose mother was a Syrian lady.

When the Arabs conquered Baalbek in 634 the great temple was converted into a citadel. Two severe destructions were carried out by the Mongols, first by Hulagu in 1260 and later by Tamerlane in 1401. It again suffered greatly from an earthquake in 1759. Since 1900 excavations and restoration work of the ruins have intermittently been carried out, first by a German expedition and recently by the Lebanese government.

S. H. H.

The temple of Bacchus at Baalbek. HFV

BAAL-BERITH. *See* Gods, False.

BAALE OF JUDAH (bā'ȧ-lē of Jū'dȧ). A town of Judah (II Sam 6:2), the same city as Baalah or Kirjath-jearim (*q.v.*; I Chr 13:6).

BAAL-GAD (bāl-găd'). Located in the valley of Lebanon, near Mount Hermon, marking the northern boundary of Joshua's conquests (Josh 11:17; 12:7; 13:5). May have been where Gad, the god of fortune, was worshiped. Site unknown.

BAAL-HAMON (bāl-hā'mŏn). Solomon had an extremely successful vineyard here (Song 8:11). Site is unknown.

BAAL-HANAN (bāl-hā'năn)
1. A king in Edom, son of Achbor (Gen 36:38; I Chr 1:49).
2. A man appointed by David as caretaker of the olive and sycamore trees in the Shephelah (I Chr 27:28).

BAAL-HAZOR (bāl-hā'zôr). A height NE of Bethel where Absalom apparently had a farm and invited the other sons of David to a festival. Ammon was slain by the servants according to Absalom's plans (II Sam 13:23– 29).

BAAL-HERMON (bāl-hûr'mŏn). A height near Mount Hermon on the N border of Manasseh, E of the Jordan. It was not captured by the Israelite conquest (Jud 3:3; I Chr 5:23).

Reconstruction of the temple complex at Baalbek in the National Museum, Beirut. Entrance through the massive propylea leads up to the temple of Jupiter. The temple of Bacchus stands on the left. HFV

BAALI (bā'ȧ-lī). The Heb. word *ba'al* means "owner," "husband," "master" (KB), and the suffix *ī* adds the personal possessive "my." The term "Baal" had come to be applied to a Semitic deity (particularly the storm-god Hadad) and to local fertility deities, "owners," of the cities. There was also another word for husband (*'îsh*) which, in contrast, had its cultural association in the primitive marriage relationship (Gen 2:22– 24). In Hos 2:16 there is a play on these two words (cf. KJV and RSV) with respect to the Lord. The prophet pointed to a time of regeneration and covenant renewal when the Lord's steadfast love would have triumphed over Israel's unfaithfulness, and she would call Him "my Husband" (*'îshî*). The names of the Baals no longer in her heart, they will no longer be on her lips (Hos 2:17– 23).

BAALIM. *See* Gods, False: Baal.

BAALIS (bā'ȧ-lĭs). An Ammonite king who sent Ishmael to murder Gedaliah shortly after Nebuchadnezzar's capture of Jerusalem (Jer 40:14).

BAAL-MEON (bāl-mē'ŏn). An Amorite city of N Moab, assigned to the Reubenites and rebuilt by them. Also known as Beth-baal-meon (*q.v.*; Josh 13:17; Ezk 25:9). It is mentioned on the Moabite Stone (line 9) as held by Mesha, king of Moab, *c.* 830 B.C., and later taken by the Israelites (Ostracon 27 from Samaria); but by Ezekiel's time it was back in the hands of Moab (Ezk 25:9).

BAAL-PEOR. *See* Gods, False.

BAAL-PERAZIM (bāl-pē-rā'zĭm). A place near the valley of Rephaim where David won a victory over the Philistines shortly after he became king of Israel (II Sam 5:18– 20; I Chr 14:9– 11; Isa 28:21). *See* Perazim, Mount of.

BAAL-SHALISHA (bāl-shăl'ĭ-shà). A fertile valley where early crops were raised. It was from here that a man brought 20 loaves of barley and fresh ears of grain to Elisha and the school of the prophets at Gilgal (II Kgs 4:42). Some scholars identify the site with Shalisha mentioned in I Sam 9:4, SW of Shechem.

BAAL-TAMER (bāl-tā'mär). A place near Gibeah in Benjamin where the Israelite army took its last stand and successfully attacked the city (Jud 20:33). The site has not been positively identified.

BAAL-ZEBUB. *See* Gods, False.

BAAL-ZEPHON (bāl-zē'fŏn). One of the three sites mentioned near the Red Sea in connection with the Israelites' crossing (Ex 14:2, 9). The exact location is unknown, but the divinity for whom the place was named is mentioned in Ugaritic, Egyptian and Phoenician literature as a sea- and storm-god. *See* Exodus, The.

BAANA (bā'à-nà)

1. The son of Ahilud, an overseer for Solomon in the S district of the plain of Jezreel from Megiddo to the Jordan (I Kgs 4:12).

2. The father of Zadok, who helped in rebuilding the walls of Jerusalem in the time of Nehemiah (Neh 3:4).

See also Baanah 3.

BAANAH (bā'à-nà)

1. Son of Rimmon, of the tribe of Benjamin. He and his brother Rechab were captains in Ishbosheth's army. They traitorously slew Ishbosheth while he was sleeping at noon in his house. Taking his head, they fled to Hebron and presented it to David. Enraged by their act, David ordered them slain. With hands and feet cut off, their bodies were hung by the pool in Hebron (II Sam 4:2-12).

2. The father of Heleb, one of David's 30 heroes (II Sam 23:29; I Chr 11:30).

3. A son of Hushai, overseer of one of the 12 districts of Solomon in Asher and Bealoth (I Kgs 4:16). His name should be translated Baana, as in RSV.

4. One who returned from Babylon with Zerubbabel, and signed Ezra's covenant (Ezr 2:2; 7:7; 10:27).

BAARA (bā'à-rà). A wife of Shaharaim (I Chr 8:8).

BAASEIAH (bā'à-sē'yà). An ancestor of Asaph, the musician, and a Levite of the family of Kohathites (I Chr 6:33, 40). Perhaps the name should be Maaseiah (*q.v.*).

BAASHA (bā'à-shà). A son of Ahijah of the tribe of Issachar. He became third king of Israel by destroying Nadab, son of Jeroboam I, at Gibbethon (I Kgs 15:27). He thoroughly exterminated all members of Jeroboam's family, thus fulfilling prophecy (I Kgs 14:6-16). After establishing his capital at Tirzah, he made war against Asa, king of Judah. Baasha entered the territory of Benjamin and began to build a fortress at Ramah, about five miles N of Jerusalem. Since the E-W trade route crossed the highlands just N of Ramah, this move threatened to set up an economic blockade against Jerusalem. He withdrew because Asa persuaded Ben-hadad of Syria to attack Baasha from the N. The prophet Jehu predicted judgment because of Baasha's wicked ways. Baasha reigned for 24 years and was buried at Tirzah. The destruction of Baasha's dynasty by Zimri (I Kgs 16:9-12) became a symbol of divine judgment (I Kgs 21:22; II Kgs 9:9). His story is found in I Kgs 15:16-22, 27-34; 16:1-7; II Chr 16:1-6.

G. H. L.

BABBLER. The English word refers to one who talks incoherently or foolishly. The term is supposed to have been formed from the childish ba ba (cf. Eccl 10:11). The Gr. word *spermologos* was applied contemptuously to Paul by some Athenian philosophers (Acts 17:18). The word means literally a seed picker, and was applied to a bird, or a man "lounging about the market place and picking up a subsistence by whatever may chance to fall from the loads of merchandise . . . getting a living by flattery . . . an empty talker" (Thayer, p. 584).

BAB EDH-DHRA (băb'ĕd-drä). A site about five miles E of the Dead Sea, just E of the tongue of land (el-Lisan) that juts out into the Dead Sea. It was discovered and explored in 1924 by W. F. Albright, who thought it to be a place of pilgrimage and annual religious feasts where people of the adjacent valley came several days a year.

Several excavation campaigns have been conducted at the site since 1965, directed by Paul W. Lapp. Before 3000 B.C. people began to camp at the site and buried their dead there in underground chambers radiating outward from the tomb shafts they dug. About 2800 B.C. massive mudbrick and stone defense walls were constructed, some up to 40 feet thick. Apparently this was a fortified town, occupied down to the 23rd cen. B.C. Its inhabitants continued the use of shaft tombs but mainly constructed single-room mudbrick charnel houses which were found filled with human bones and pots as well as some copper weapons. The destroyers of this Early Bronze Age town, and their descendants, camped in the vicinity until *c.* 2000 B.C. and continued to use the site as their cemetery also, employing cairn burials consisting of a shallow pit in which was placed a single skeleton together with some jars. All in all, an estimated 20,000 tombs with some three million pots made up the cemetery of Bab edh-Dhra.

If this was the burial ground and religious center or "high place" for Sodom (*q.v.*) and the other cities of the nearby plain, as Albright suggested, it would be expected that a sudden destruction of those cities would cause discontinuance of the use of their cemetery, as did in fact occur about 2000 B.C. Two similar walled hilltop sites for pagan worship have been found in the Negeb, all dating around 2000 B.C.

J. R.

The ziggurat at Babylon, cast in the Oriental Institute Museum. ORINST

BABEL, TOWER OF (bā'bĕl). This expression does not occur in the OT, but is used to describe the tower built by the early inhabitants in the plain of Shinar. The word "tower" is *migdol* (Canaanite, "watch tower"). Basically, the people built the tower to fortify their city against God in their refusal to spread out and repopulate the earth after the Flood (Gen 11:4).

The Mesopotamian temple towers, called in Assyro-Babylonian *zigguratu* ("pinnacle, mountain top"), are often thought to help in understanding the form of the Tower of Babel. The oldest extant ziggurat, however, at ancient Uruk (biblical Erech, Gen 10:10, modern Warka), dates back only a little before 3000 B.C. These temple towers were rectangular, built in stages, accessible by stairs from the court to the top of the second story, and from there to the top by outside staircases.

The foundation consisted of stamped down clay, buttressed with layers of brick and bitumen. In Babylonia there was no stone locally available in the alluvial plain near the rivers, but an abundance of clay. Thus many elaborate buildings were constructed entirely of sun-dried or kiln-baked clay bricks. Bitumen (slime, pitch, tar) was also available and was used for mortar. Normally in a ziggurat there were three stages, but some reached seven stages. The chapel atop the tower held the image of the deity in whose honor the ziggurat was built. The temple tower at Borsippa had seven different colors, one for each stage.

There are two suggestions for the location of the biblical Tower of Babel. (1) Most writers follow the tradition handed down by Jews and Arabs identifying it with the temple of Nabu in Borsippa (Birs Nimrud), *c.* ten miles S of Baby-

lon. Birs Nimrud is explained as a corruption of Birj Nimroud—Tower of Nimrod (cf. Gen 10:9). (2) Others locate it in Babylon. There was in Babylon an ancient ziggurat which was begun in the second millennium B.C. Called Etemenanki ("the house of the foundation of heaven and earth"), it stood a short distance to the N of Esagila, the temple of Marduk. It was like a step pyramid, 300 feet square at the base and about 300 feet high above the foundation. Nebuchadnezzar called it the Tower of Babylon.

The writer of Genesis sees this tower as the symbol of human pride and ambition, and says that it was destined to fall even before it was finished. No one knows where it was or is. One Jewish tradition claimed that fire fell from heaven and split it to its foundation. Another tradition maintained that the wind blew it down. The biblical writer used the story to account for the origin of various languages in the human race. Man's pride and disobedience led to confusion and dispersion, as did Adam and Eve's sin. *See* Tongues, Confusion of.

Bibliography. Hugo Gressmann, *The Tower of Babel,* New York: Univ. Publishers, 1960. Alfred Jeremias, *The Old Testament in the Light of the Ancient East,* New York: Putnam's, 1911. André Parrot, *The Tower of Babel,* trans. by E. Hudson, New York: Philosophical Library, 1955. Merrill F. Unger, "Semites and Babel Builders," *Archaeology and the Old Testament,* Grand Rapids: Zondervan, 1954

F. E. Y.

BABYLON (băb'ĭ-lŏn). An ancient city-state situated on both banks of the river Euphrates in the land of Shinar (later called Chaldea), *c.* 40–50 miles S of modern Baghdad and 300 miles N of the Persian Gulf. Its name was derived from the Akkad. *babilu*—"gate of god." It eventually became the capital city of the Babylonian Empire, and the name was used in the OT to designate both the city and the country.

The beginnings of the city are obscure, except for the biblical passage that ascribes founding of Babylon to the descendants of Cush and the followers of Nimrod (Gen 10:8–10). According to Gr. tradition, Belus (Babylonian Bel or Merodach) was the founder. Archaeological excavations have revealed the presence of a Sumerian culture in and around Babylon that antedates the Akkadian-Semitic civilization.

Description. Many ancient writers have given accounts of the size, splendor, and significance of Babylon. Although there is some disagreement among them concerning the actual size of the city, all are agreed on its magnitude and its influence. Since stone was scarce in the area, and the quality of wood (mainly palm trees) was inferior, the city was constructed largely of brick made from the clay deposits

Reconstruction of Babylon, showing the Procession Street, the Ishtar Gate, and in the right background the Hanging Gardens and the ziggurat. ORINST

nearby (cf. Gen 11:3, ASV marg. – "brick for stone, and bitumen for mortar"). Herodotus, the Gr. historian who visited Babylon after the conquest of Cyrus while it still preserved much of its original splendor, related that the city was a great square 56 miles in circuit. He also referred to the huge moat that surrounded the double walls of the city. These walls were very high and quite wide (cf. Jer 51:58). Atop the walls were chambers facing each other, with space between the rows for a four-horse chariot to turn around. One hundred gates, 25 on each side, all with bronze-plated doors, pierced the city walls (cf. Isa 45:2). The streets of the city were laid out in an orderly fashion as symmetrical as a modern American housing development. Houses three and four stories high lined the well-planned streets. The two halves of the city were joined by a bridge consisting of stone piers covered with movable platforms of wood. Royal palaces, heavily guarded, were at either end of the bridge, and a tunnel beneath the river connected the palaces.

Another famous structure in the city was the temple of Belus, described by Herodotus as occupying one of the squares into which the city was divided. This temple was greatly enlarged and beautified by Nebuchadnezzar. Berossus, the Babylonian historian in the days of Alexander, wrote his history of Babylonia from the inscriptions taken from the temple walls. The temple tower or ziggurat was devoted to astronomical purposes, for which the Babylonians were famous. The first recorded eclipse of the sun was observed with accuracy in Babylon in 721 B.C.

The palace of Nebuchadnezzar also adorned the city of Babylon, as did the Hanging Gardens, said to have been built by Nebuchadnezzar to gratify his wife Amytis, who retained strong sentiment for the hills and groves in her native Media. These gardens were called one of the seven wonders of the ancient world.

The famed Processional Avenue led from the Ishtar Gate to the Ishtar (comparable to Ashtoreth in the OT) temple and to the Esagila temple. Both sides of the street were lined with life-size lions and dragons in relief on enameled brick.

Rulers. The first famous ruler of Babylon was the Amorite Hammurabi (*c.* 1728–1686 B.C.), sixth king of the strong First Dynasty of Babylon. Especially known for the law code which bears his name, he also extended the boundaries of his empire to Mari in the N. A Hittite raid ended this dynasty shortly after 1600 B.C. Kassites from the NE overran the country for several centuries, ruling from Dur Kurigalzu (modern 'Aqarquf), a few miles W of Baghdad. From the time Tukulti-Ninurta I (1235–1198 B.C.) captured Babylon, it was periodically under the sway of the Assyrians, until the death of Ashurbanipal late in the 7th cen. B.C. In 626 B.C. Nabopolassar declared himself king of the city, and under his son Nebuchadnezzar II (605–562 B.C.) Babylon reached her

most glorious heights. Merodach or Marduk, patron deity of the city, became, with the gradual rise of Babylon to supremacy in the area, the head deity of the Babylonian pantheon, and is called in the OT Bel. He is pictured symbolically on monuments as a fiery dragon.

Babylon and the Bible. Mentioned along with Babylonia more than 200 times in the Bible, Babylon played a significant role in the life of the Hebrews. Abraham brought with him in his pilgrimage from this area, the language, culture, and faith that left certain influences upon the stream of Heb. life. Babylonia, along with Assyria, constantly affected the development of the Heb. nation, and Babylonia served as a second Egypt in influencing Heb. life and thought through the enforced Babylonian Exile that followed the fall of Jerusalem and the collapse of the Judean state. Merodach-baladan, ruler of Babylon in the 8th cen. B.C., carried on correspondence with Hezekiah, king of Judah (II Kgs 20:12–19; Isa 39:1–8); and Daniel and his three Heb. companions were the captives of the Babylonians in the capital city (Dan 1–5).

Isa 13–14; 21:1–10; and Jer 50–51 spoke of the coming fall of Babylon. They pictured it as an earth-shaking event in the magnitude of its impact upon civilized nations. It would become a desolated, ruinous heap. According to ancient Mesopotamian records, Sennacherib first invested the city and flooded it by means of canals to wreak vengeance on the city for its insurrection. Cyrus the Great, Darius Hystaspes, Xerxes (who punished rebellions in the city by destroying palaces, temples, and walls *c.* 480 B.C.), and finally Alexander the Great made conquest of the city. Alexander planned to restore the city and make it the capital of his empire, but failed because of his untimely death. Then in 312 B.C., Seleucus Nicator founded and fortified Seleucia on the Tigris, some distance from Babylon, and transferred the seat of the empire to that city. From that time, Babylon rapidly declined and never regained the status of a city. At the beginning of the Christian era only a small group of astronomers and mathematicians were living in Babylon. Many of the cities in the vicinity, such as Hilla, used the sun-dried and kiln-baked bricks of the once great city to build new walls, houses, and dams, even as prophesied (Isa 13:19–22; Jer 50:23–26; 51:24–26). Babylon thus lives only in the building of new cities.

In the NT, therefore, the references in Rev 14:8; 16:19; 17:18 to Babylon probably refer to the city of Rome. Tertullian, Jerome, and Augustine so viewed these references. A less likely theory is that the reference to Babylon in I Pet 5:13 referred to a place in Egypt now located in Old Cairo.

Excavations. The major archaeological undertaking at Babylon was led by Robert Koldewey, who excavated there for the German Oriental Society, 1899–1914. Since the earliest strata of occupation at the site now lie under water, nearly everything found is dated to the

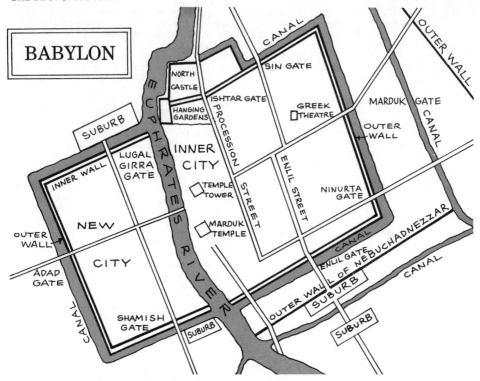

time of Nebuchadnezzar. Although the whole city had been badly ruined, it was possible for the expedition to recapture an accurate picture of the layout of the city and to outline its major buildings. *See* Archaeology.

Bibliography. Albert Champdor, *Babylon,* trans. by Elsa Coult, New York: Putnam, 1959. Edward König, *The Bible and Babylon,* trans. by W. T. Pilter, London: The Religious Tract Society, 1905. Gerald A. Larue, *Babylon and the Bible,* Grand Rapids: Baker, 1969. G. F. Owen, *Archaeology and the Bible,* Westwood, N.J.: Revell, 1961. André Parrot, *Babylon and the Old Testament,* London: SCM, 1958. H. W. F. Saggs, *The Greatness That Was Babylon,* New York: Hawthorne, 1962; "Babylon," TAOTS, pp. 39 – 56.

F. E. Y.

BABYLON, MYSTERY. A term used in Scripture (Rev 17:5, 7; cf. 18:2, 10) to typify paganism in an all-inclusive sense, as it is seen by God. In certain passages of the OT the concept of Babylon emerges into an archetypal figure for the proud, God-defying forces of this world (Isa 13 – 14; 21:1 – 10; 47; Jer 50 – 51). In the NT it is even more clearly a type of pan-deism formed from a synthesis of Christianity and paganism; this is indicated symbolically in the description of the woman riding on the Beast (Rev 17:1 ff.). The designation "mystery" does not mean that it refers to something unrevealed, but rather something revealed from heaven to all who will listen and read, though it can be understood only by the believer in Christ and with the aid of the Holy Spirit.

The Jerusalem Bible translates the term "mystery" (Rev 17:5) as, "On her forehead was written a name, a cryptic name," indicating that "Babylon" is meant symbolically. In John's day Rome (city, empire, civilization, emperor worship) was the contemporary embodiment of Babylon. Rome was built on seven hills (Rev 17:9), and "blasphemous names" (Rev 17:3) or divine titles were given to Roman emperors. Roman harlots customarily displayed their names on their brows (Rev 17:5).

But Babylon is more than the Rome of history. It prefigures the apostate ecclesiastical system of the end time (Rev 17; 19:2) as well as the political power of the Antichrist (Rev 14:8; 16:19; 18:10–24). It is a demonic kingdom, the habitation of demons and the haunt of every unclean spirit (Rev 18:2). This Babylon is clearly considered to be the successor of the pagan kingdom denounced in the OT prophetic books, for echoes from the taunt songs of the prophets concerning Babylon are heard in Rev 17 – 18 (Rev 17:1, 15 with Jer 51:13; Rev 17:2, 4; 18:3, 9 with Jer 51:7; Rev 18:2 with Isa

21:9; 13:21–22; Rev 18:5 with Jer 51:9; Rev 18:7 with Isa 47:7–8; Rev 18:8 with Isa 47:9; Rev 18:21 with Jer 51:63–64).

R. A. K. and J. R.

BABYLONIA (băb-ĭ-lō'nĭ-à)

The Land and Its People

Babylonia is located in the alluvial plain between the Euphrates and Tigris Rivers at the eastern end of the Fertile Crescent in western Asia. Scarcely 40 miles wide, it comprises about 8,000 square miles and is approximately the size of New Jersey. The city of Babylon (*q.v.*) was its capital, and the land of Babylonia was called "land of Shinar" (Gen 10:10; 11:2; Isa 11:11) and the "land of the Chaldeans" (Jer 24:5; 25:12; Ezk 12:13). It is bounded on the N by Assyria, on the E by the plains at the foot of the Zagros Mountains, on the S by the Persian Gulf, and on the W by the Arabian Desert from which it is separated only by a narrow strip. The deposits of silt, carried by the Tigris and Euphrates Rivers in their course toward the Persian Gulf, extend the land area approximately 72 feet a year, or one and one-half miles each century. Some scholars believe that the rate of deposit was much greater in antiquity.

The climate is extremely warm in summer. The rainy season continues from November through February, but total rainfall during those months is less than ten inches. The fertility of the soil was fantastic. Two harvests each year and 50- to 100-fold reaping of grain sown was not unknown in antiquity. Irrigation canals, well arranged and properly attended, added to the productivity of the soil, which was enriched annually by the new topsoil silt brought into the valleys by the yearly inundations of the Euphrates and the Tigris. Ancient authors called Babylonia the bread basket of the world and the cradle of civilization – the site of the Garden of Eden. However, long neglect of cultivation has rendered much of Babylonia an arid waste. Only the visible embankments and trenches attest the presence and courses of those ancient irrigation canals so vital to the teeming masses that once filled the Babylonian plain. Recent estimate of the population of this area is given as 7 million, but with a potential of 50 million should the full use of the waters of the Euphrates and the Tigris be utilized.

Wheat was the main harvest, while sesame was also grown. Date palms were introduced from Arabia, providing for the inhabitants wine, vinegar, honey, sugar, flour for baking, matting for wicker work, wood for construction, and even food for fattening oxen and sheep. Man could live almost exclusively from the fruit of the date palm. Reeds that grew along the river canals were used in construction of boats and for fencing around the fields.

The canal systems virtually joined the Euphrates to the Tigris and became in themselves means of transportation as well as the sources for irrigation. One was called the royal canal and joined the two rivers, with water sufficiently deep and wide to convey large boats. Tradition makes it the canal built by the biblical Nimrod, while critical scholarship accredits it to a Babylonian king. Ps 137:1–2 speaks of the rivers (canals) of Babylon. Lions, panthers, jackals, foxes, wild boar and wild oxen roamed the marshlands, while cattle, sheep, goats, donkeys, and dogs served the needs of man in domesticated service. The elephant, the wild ass, and the camel were also known.

Since stone was extremely scarce in the alluvial plain, and the date palm was of inferior quality for construction purposes, most of the cities in Babylonia were constructed on mounds with the use of sun-dried or kiln-baked bricks made from the abundant clay found everywhere. The bricks varied considerably in size, and many of them were stamped with the name of the king for whose use they were made, which lends considerable assistance in deciding the chronology and history of the many structures. The kiln-baked bricks were used to finish the outer layers of public buildings and in important foundation structures, for their resistance to weather made them more durable than that of the sun-dried bricks. Stones were imported when necessary for special monuments or other building needs.

In the early period, the country was divided between the Akkadians in the N and the Sumerians in the S. Babylon, Borsippa, Kish, Kutha, Sippar, and Agade (founded by Sargon I) were Akkadian cities; Ur (the home of the patriarch Abraham), Eridu, Nippur, Lagash, Umma, Larsa, and Erech were Sumerian cities. Some of these cities go back to 4000 B.C. or even earlier.

The Sumerians spoke an agglutinative language (like Turkish) which belongs to an unclassified group of languages called for convenience, Turanian. They developed a cuneiform script from an earlier pictographic writing form. The language spoken by the Babylonians belongs to the N group of Semitic languages and is related to Phoenician, Aramaic, and Heb. It was called cuneiform from the Latin *cuneus* – "wedge," which was the form the signs took from the stylus used to form the symbols. The script ran from right to left with no spaces between the words. Writing was usually done on clay tablets, virtually indestructible when baked. Thus extensive records of Mesopotamia have been preserved and large collections have been uncovered by excavators. The Akkadians, upon defeating the Sumerians, borrowed their form of writing, modified it, and made it the basis of all cuneiform writing which continued in existence until a century before the Christian era.

The origin of the Sumerian peoples is uncertain. Some scholars have seen in the root *smr* the basic root *sm* (shem) with a phonetic complement "r" and maintain that they are the descendants of Shem and are really a Semitic people. From the monuments they have left, it appears that their facial features resemble Asiatics, and from the trees and animals portrayed on their cylinder seals, it has been conjectured that they came from the mountains to the N and E. Their work with metals and inlaid jewelry has never been excelled. *See* Sumer.

Historical Developments

At first, the cities of Babylonia were independent kingdoms — city-states. But finally dynastic centers began to arise to protect the area from invaders and to organize the indispensable irrigation systems. About 2500 B.C. Ur established a hegemony over most of Sumer. Sargon I of Agade, *c.* 2350 B.C., created in the true sense a Semitic empire when he defeated all the Sumerian cities and founded the city of Agade (Accad) as the first capital of the Semitic Empire. Their dynasty continued until about 2200 B.C.

Among the early conquerors of Babylonia were the Gutians and the Amorites. Hammurabi (18th cen. B.C.), an Amorite, led Babylon in a victorious campaign against neighboring cities and made of it the capital of a political empire. His administration was excellent, great public works were instituted, law and order prevailed, and his fame became immortal in his codifying of the laws known as the code of Hammurabi. It was a law code that protected the interests of the noble and furthered the interests of the upper classes. Many comparative studies of the Heb. and Hammurabi codes have been made. While there do appear to be many similarities, the differences are greater. Heb. law was unique in its elevated monotheism, its rejection of administration of justice according to one's social class, and its concept of moral law. *See* Hammurabi.

After the Hammurabi dynasty came to an end in the 16th cen., Babylonia did not figure significantly in world history until the Chaldean Empire of Nebuchadnezzar (6th cen. B.C.) became the terror of western Asia. *See* Babylon; Chaldea; Chaldeans; Nebuchadnezzar.

Babylonian Religion

With the rise to supremacy of the city of Babylon, Marduk, the patron deity of the city, became the head deity of the Babylonian pantheon. A new year festival called the "akitu" festival was held annually in his honor, wherein a mock battle between the king and the dragon of the deep was reenacted to commemorate Marduk's primeval victory over chaos. The purpose of the festival was to usher in the new year with a ritual form so as to ensure peace, prosperity, and happiness throughout the entire year.

Other deities worshiped by the Babylonians were Anu, god of heaven; Enlil, god of wind and earth; Ea, god of the underworld — who together formed a triad of deities. Another important triad was Sin, the moon-god of Ur and Haran, the early haunts of the family of Abra-

OLD
BABYLONIAN
EMPIRE
(UNDER HAMMURABI)

0   50   100   200

SCALE OF MILES

ham; Shamash, the sun deity; and Ishtar, goddess of love and war, the counterpart to Astarte of the Phoenicians, Ashtoreth of the Bible, and Aphrodite of the Greeks. Other significant deities were Nabu, the god of writing, and Nergal (brother of Marduk), the god of war and famine. *See* Gods, False.

The gods of Babylonia were, in their origin, personifications of the various forces of nature. Babylonian religion was thus a worship of nature in all its parts, paying homage to both friendly and hostile superhuman beings, often depicted in the human, animal, or human-animal form. No deity was all-powerful — not even the heads of the various triads of deities. Each deity had a province wherein he or she ruled. In fact, each large city had its own deity to whom the inhabitants of that city gave homage. The deities were created out of the existing materials of the world and were subject to the natural order. Some deities died as did man. The rising gods were the Babylonian expressions of man's longing for transcending the pattern of the natural order. Beneath the deities was the world of demons, endowed with various qualities and characteristics, but of limited influence.

The deities were worshiped in various temples, many times on temple towers. The temple towers (ziggurats) consisted of lofty structures rising in huge stages one above the other, composed for the most part of solid brick and ascended by a staircase on the outside. Several of these temple towers were three or four stories high with extremely wide bases. At the top of the structure was a shrine in which stood an image of the deity to whom the tower temple was dedicated. Some of the ziggurats were constructed so that the angles were oriented toward the points of the compass. These temple towers dominated the surrounding houses and were more imposing than the royal palaces.

To each temple was attached a trained and highly organized priesthood devoted to the worship of its god and to the preserving of the ritual and body of traditions. The priests were remunerated with the regular offerings and the revenue from endowed temple lands. The role of priesthood in Babylonia was higher than that exercised in Assyria. Babylonia was a theocratic society, governed by the priestly order, which sanctioned a kingship that was subordinate to the religious order, but powerful enough to carry out the law that regulated Babylonian society.

Several great pieces of literature have come from Babylonia. Besides the law code of Hammurabi are the Creation and Flood stories found at Nippur and elsewhere and the Descent of Ishtar into Hades.

Babylonian influence in Heb. affairs was at its highest peak during the period of the Exile. Several Heb. families of the Captivity were involved in business transactions in the area of Nippur as stated in tablets found there, and the

Marduk, chief god of Babylon, became the head of the Babylonian pantheon as the city extended its power over the whole area of Babylonia.

coinage of Babylon influenced the monetary system of the Hebrews. It is quite likely that the synagogue movement developed among the Hebrews in the Babylonian Exile, and the spirit of Judaism, born in this period, was carried by Ezra the scribe from Babylonia to Jerusalem.

During the early Christian centuries, the Babylonian Talmud was created in the Heb. schools in and about Nehardea, Pumbeditha, and Sura. These schools eventually died out, and the center of Judaism shifted to Palestine and Europe.

Bibliography. Georges Contenau, *Everyday Life in Babylonia and Assyria,* trans. by K. R. and A. R. Maxwell-Hyslop, London: E. Arnold, 1954. G. S. Goodspeed, *A History of the Babylonians and Assyrians,* New York: Scribner's, 1906. Samuel N. Kramer, *History Begins at Sumer,* New York: Doubleday, 1959. A. Leo Oppenheim, *Ancient Mesopotamia,* Chicago: Univ. of Chicago Press, 1964. H. W. F. Saggs, *The Greatness That Was Babylon,* New York: Hawthorne, 1962.

F. E. Y.

BABYLONISH GARMENT. (Heb. "mantle of Shinar") Shinar was the name by which the Israelites knew Babylonia. The garment stolen by Achan (Josh 7) cannot be described exactly but probably was very fine embroidered cloth, woven entirely of gold thread.

BACA (bā'ka). If the valley of Baca (Ps 84:6) was ever an identifiable place, its location is now unknown but may have taken its name from the presence of balsam trees (cf. II Sam 5:23 – 24, RSV). The word, however, is from a root meaning "to weep" (BDB and KB *s.v.*). It is probably preferable here to consider it a common noun rather than a place name and translate as "valley of tears" (Arthur Weiser, *The Psalms*, pp. 565, 567; *et al.*). Men who find their strength in the God to whose sanctuary they make pilgrimage, men "in whose heart are the highways to Zion" (Ps 84:5, RSV), discover hidden springs and enjoy refreshing rains even in the place of desolation (cf. Ps 23:4; Hos 2:15). The eyes which can see the springs through the tears can also see Zion's God (Ps 84:7).

BACKBITE. The Heb. word so translated means "to wander about as a slanderer" (Ps 15:3). Another Heb. word is used in similar manner to describe evil speaking (Prov 25:23).

BACKSLIDING. A term used in the OT by God of Israel, particularly in Jeremiah, where the nation is spoken of as backsliding children (Jer 3:22), a backsliding daughter (Jer 31:22), and in Hosea where He calls Israel a backsliding heifer (Hos 4:16). Children who get into evil and a daughter who chooses a life of sin are familiar examples to people of all ages, and a backsliding heifer is a particularly expressive term to any farmer to portray stubbornness.

In the OT, backsliding speaks of a return or turn back to the old life of sin and the worship of false gods; in this day, a return to a former life of sin and spiritual idolatry, that is, to materialism and the worship of things rather than God. As used today in modern religious parlance, the term refers to the spiritual state of individual Christians.

The view that the backslider who though once saved has become lost again, fails to see that the Christian's *standing* must be distinguished from his *state*. Positionally, that is. as far as his standing is concerned, he is in Christ and eternally justified. He is safe against anything or anyone taking away his eternal life, since both Christ and the Father hold him in their hands (Jn 10:28 – 29). And yet the Christian's *state* is subject to change, since he is still imperfect and able either to progress or regress. The Christian's *standing* is spoken of in Col 2:10 – 13 as a perfection equal to Christ's; his *state* (I Cor 3:1 – 4; Rom 7), as one in danger of a constant degeneration into carnality. Backsliding invokes chastening from God (Heb 12:6; I Cor 11:32), and results in the loss of rewards (II Cor 5:10; I Cor 3:15), loss of fellowship (I Jn 1:7), removal from a place of usefulness (I Cor 5:5; 11:30), and sometimes even calls for removal from this life by death (I Cor 11:30). *See* Apostasy.

R.A.K.

BADGER. *See* Animals: Dugong, V. 3.

BAGS. Bags in OT times were of bark, cloth, and skin, and of varied size. They were often purses (Isa 46:6; Prov 1:14; 7:20) and, since money was uncoined metal, might be of considerable size (II Kgs 5:23; Gen 42:35). The figurative use in I Sam 25:29 (translated "bundle"), suggests sealing (cf. Hos 13:12, "bound up"; Job 14:17); but in Hag 1:6 such a sealed money bag was worthless if it had holes, and figuratively illustrated a man's life when God was neglected. A bag was often used for weights of stone (Prov 16:11); the deceitful man had two kinds in his bag (Deut 25:13; Mic 6:11). The shepherd's bag appears in both the OT and NT (I Sam 17:40, 49; Mt 10:10; Lk 10:4, RSV).

In the NT the bag functioned as a purse for coins (Lk 12:33; 22:35). Judas' "bag" (KJV), however, was actually a small case or "money box" (Jn 12:6; 13:29, RSV) (Arndt, *s.v. glōssokomon*).

BAHARUMITE (ba-hä'rū-mīt). An inhabitant (I Chr 11:33) of Bahurim (*q.v.*); also called a Barhumite (II Sam 23:31).

BAHURIM (ba-hū'rĭm). Modern Ras et-Temim, a highway village E of Olivet, where Phaltiel and Michal parted as she was being returned to David (II Sam 3:15 – 16). Here Shimei cursed David (II Sam 16:5; 19:16; I Kgs 2:8), and Jonathan and Ahimaaz hid in the well of a man in Bahurim (II Sam 17:18).

BAIL. *See* Surety.

BAJITH (bā'jĭth). A Moabite place name found only in Isa 15:2. Some suggest that the Heb. *bayit* may be an altered reading for *bat* ("daughter"), which would then be rendered: "The daughter of Dibon has gone up to the high places to weep" (RSV). Such a rendering is grammatically weak because the verb is masculine in Heb. RSV marg. reads: "The house and Dibon are gone up to the high places to weep," which may be the proper rendering. *See* NASB.

BAKBAKKAR (băk-băk'ēr). A Levite of the sons of Asaph and resident of Jersulaem (I Chr 9:15).

BAKBUK (băk'bŭk). Family head of post-Exilic temple servants, one of the Nethinim (Ezr 2:51; Neh 7:53).

BAKBUKIAH (băk'ba-kī'a)
1. A high official of the Levites in Jerusalem immediately after the Exile (Neh 11:17).
2. A gatekeeper of the temple in Nehemiah's time (Neh 12:25) related to or the same as 1.

BAKE. *See* Food: Cook, Cooking.

BAKEMEATS. *See* Food.

BAKER. *See* Occupations.

BALAAM (bā'lăm). A prophet whose sin and failure made him an example to warn later ages (Num 22 – 24). Having defeated the Amorite kings Sihon and Og, and thus acquiring all the land from the Arnon to Mount Hermon, the Israelites settled in the plains of Moab to prepare for the invasion of Canaan. Though they had already passed by Moab in peace, the sight of this victorious host on his borders alarmed Balak, king of Moab. After consulting with his Midianite allies, he sent an embassy to Pethor in Amaw, part of Mesopotamia, to call the renowned prophet Balaam to their aid. If the identification of Pethor (*q.v.*) with Tell Ahmar near Carchemish should prove correct, it would locate the home of Balaam near Haran, once the home of Abraham. This suggests the possible source of Balaam's knowledge of God. *See* Amaw.

The embassy from Balak offered rewards of wealth, honor, and power if Balaam would come to curse Israel, but God's will was very clear. "Thou shalt not go with them; thou shalt not curse the people: for they are blessed" (Num 22:12). Refusing the first delegation, the covetous prophet succumbed to the tempting offer of a second embassy and obtained permission from God to depart for Moab. On the journey, an angel of the Lord, unseen by Balaam but manifest to the ass he rode, barred the way. The poor beast three times sought to avoid the apparition and brought the angry prophet to the point of beating him, when Balaam's eyes were opened and he was made aware of the Lord's opposition. In fear, he offered to return home, but he was ordered to continue on to Moab where he would speak "only the word that I shall speak unto thee" (Num 22:35).

Balak received the prophet with great expectation and led him to a Baal sanctuary high above the plain where he could look upon Israel. After the appropriate sacrifices, Balaam opened his mouth to speak, but the words that came forth were the words of the Lord; not in cursing but in blessing. A second and third high place only brought forth more blessings, until the frustrated and enraged king commanded the unhappy prophet to begone.

Before he departed, Balaam proclaimed one more word from the Lord. This famous prophecy told of a star, the symbol of a great king, who would arise in Israel in the far off future days. The sign of a star in connection with the promised King-Messiah is found only here in the OT. It is significant that the wise men who followed that star to Bethlehem came from the east, possibly the same area from which Balaam himself came.

The defeated and humiliated prophet departed for home, but not to stay. Determined still to gain the promised reward, Balaam conceived a plan whereby God Himself would destroy Israel. Let Balak send the young people of Moab to mingle with the Israelites and draw them away from God to the degrading worship of Baal. The plan was highly successful (Num 25), but the results were not as Balaam had planned. God's judgment came quickly upon His people, and the sinners were thoroughly cleansed from the congregation. Then the Lord commanded Moses to smite Moab for their wily attack (Num 25:16 – 18). In the ensuing battle, the prophet Balaam was slain, falling in defeat with those who had sought his aid (Num 31:8).

The NT warns against the "error" (Jude 11) and the "way" of Balaam (II Pet 2:15). Balaam is a type of all those who, knowing God, yet turn their backs upon Him to grasp at the temporal goods of an evil world. Rev 2:14 speaks of the wicked "doctrine of Balaam," the teaching that would lead God's people to indulge in the sins of the flesh as though God were indifferent. *See* Divination; Prophecy.

P.C.J.

BALAC (bā'lăk). The same as Balak (*q.v.*). Balac is found only in Rev 2:14.

BALADAN (băl'a-dăn). The father of Merodach-baladan, king of Babylon (II Kgs 20:12, RSV; Isa 39:1).

BALAH (bā'lä). A town of Simeon in the Negeb, perhaps SE of Beer-sheba (Josh 19:3). It may be the same as Bilhab (*q.v.*) in I Chr 4:29 and Baalah (*q.v.*) in Josh 15:29.

BALAK (bā'lăk). A king of Moab who was frightened by Israel's conquest of the kingdoms of Sihon and Og and in desperation hired Balaam (*q.v.*), from Pethor on the Euphrates, to curse Israel. The Lord would not permit Balaam to curse but rather bless. However, Balak succeeded in a roundabout way by following Balaam's advice and seducing the men of Israel to idolatry, thus bringing God's judgment upon themselves (Num 22 – 25; 31:8, 16; Josh 24:9; Jud 11:25; Mic 6:5; Rev 2:14).

BALANCES. Three words are used to picture balances: *qāneh*, "cane, beam of the scales" (Isa 46:6 only); *peles*, "indicator, level beam of the scales" (Isa 40:12; Prov 16:11 only); and *mō'zᵉnayim*, "a pair of pans, balances" (16 times). The only NT reference is *zugos*, "yoke or beam of the balance" (Rev 6:5). Down to the Persian period, money consisted of lumps or rings of gold or silver and was weighed (e.g., Gen 23:16; Jer 32:10).

"Balance" is used mostly in connection with the divine demand for business honesty (Lev 19:36; Ezk 45:10). A just balance is God's work (Prov 16:11)! But "balances of deception are the Lord's abomination" (Prov 11:1), for that is oppression (Hos 12:7). Here "diverse weights" (Heb. "a stone and a stone," Prov 20:10, 23), "a bag of stones of deception," and

Weighing of the heart of the scribe Ani in the afterlife by the gods Anubis and Thoth. Egyptian scales are clearly shown. BM

"balances of wickedness" (Mic 6:11) to falsify (Amos 8:5), imply a heavier weight to buy with and a lighter one to sell with. *See also* Weights, Measures, and Coins.

The balance might also represent heavy calamity (Job 6:2 – 3), or simply moral integrity (Job 31:6) or the lack of it (Dan 5:27; Ps 62:9).

W. G. B.

BALDNESS. Mentioned infrequently in the OT and not at all in the NT, natural baldness was probably uncommon in biblical times. Semites or Asiatics are usually depicted in ancient Near Eastern art with long hair and beards. Baldness was considered a defect which detracted from one's beauty (Isa 3:24), for gray and white hair were looked upon as a crown of glory (Prov 16:31; 20:29). *See* Hair. It was the duty of the priest to distinguish between natural baldness and that caused by leprosy (Lev 13:40–44).

The address to Elisha, "Go up, thou bald head" (II Kgs 2:23), may be an allusion to a tonsure worn by prophets and thus a mockery of his office, for Elisha was not yet an old man.

Baldness artificially produced was a mark of mourning in the ancient Near East in later times (Isa 15:2; 22:12; Jer 16:6; Ezk 7:18; Amos 8:10; Mic 1:16), although it had been forbidden to the Israelites on the ground of their being a holy people (Deut 14:1–2). It is thought that the pagan Canaanites shaved off hair to provide their dead with that life-giving stuff (cf. Samson's hair) which would enable the dead to live on in the realm of death. Arabs today often lay hair on the grave of the dead. A female prisoner-of-war whom her captor desired to marry was first to be allowed to mourn her parents with the sign of shaving her head

(Deut 21:10 – 13). The priests especially were not to follow heathen mourning rites and customs such as shaving the head and cutting off the corners of their beards; thus wearing tonsures was forbidden to them at any time (Lev 21:1–5, RSV; Ezk 44:20). Yet for the Nazarite, who was to let his hair grow long, shaving the head marked the conclusion of his vow (Num 6:9, 18).

J. R.

BALM. *See* Plants.

BAMAH (bā′mȧ). The word is retained in its Heb. form only in Ezk 20:29. Doubtless the prophet's question is a contemptuous play on words regarding the people's worship at a heathen high place: "What [*mȧ*] is the high place [*bāmȧ̂*] whereunto ye go [a form of the verb *bȧ*]?" *See* Bamoth.

BAMOTH (bā′mŏth). This name appears in KJV in Num 21:19 – 20 as a camping ground on the journey of Israel N of the Arnon canyon. The site may have been identical with Bamoth-baal (*q.v.*; Num 22:41, RSV; KJV, ASV, "the high places of Baal") where Balak took the prophet Balaam to observe Israel, a locality mentioned in Josh 13:17.

The name is plural form of *bāmȧ̂*, "elevation," "a height," and appears in Heb. in this sense in Deut 32:13; II Sam 1:19, 25; Ps 18:33; Mic 3:12; Ezk 36:2; Hab 3:19. In a specialized sense the Heb. word means a sacred hill shrine with an altar or chapel (e.g., I Kgs 11:7; 12:32; 13:32; 14:23; Jer 7:31; etc.). *See* High Place.

BAMOTH-BAAL (bā'mŏth-bāl'). A place N of the Arnon River in Moab where Balak took Balaam that he might see Israel. There he sacrificed and sought to curse Israel (Num 22:41, RSV; 23:1–12). Later it was assigned to the tribe of Reuben (Josh 13:17). Apparently the same city is called Beth-bamoth in the Moabite inscription (ANET, p. 210).

BAND. A term used in describing army units, such as a cohort. *See* Army.

BANI (bā'nī)
1. A Gadite warrior, one of David's 30 mighty men (II Sam 23:36).
2. A chorister of the Levitical family of Merari in David's time (I Chr 6:31, 46).
3. The progenitor of a family of the tribe of Judah whose descendants are listed among those returning from the Exile (I Chr 9:4; Ezr 2:10; 10:29, 34).
4. A member of the family of Bani with the same name. He is listed among those condemned by Ezra for having a foreign wife (Ezr 10:38).
5. A Levite prominent in the reforms of Nehemiah (Neh 8:7; 9:4–5; 10:13–14). One of his sons, Rehum, was active in the building of the wall (Neh 3:17). He is one of the men who assisted Ezra at the great reading of the law, by causing the people to understand the meaning of that which was read, probably by "targumming," that is, translating into Aramaic. He took part also in the prayer of dedication of the wall and sealed the covenant. Another of Bani's sons was appointed overseer of the Levites (Neh 11:22). *See also* Binnui.

P. C. J.

BANISH. The Hebrews had no legal banishment prescribed by the Mosaic law as a punishment, as did the Greeks and Romans. But individuals cast out of the land by war (Isa 16:3–4), or self-exiled because of crime (II Sam 13:37–38; 14:13–14) or some other reason (e.g., David), were all "banished."

The Heb. formula for serious crimes not worthy of death was "to cut off" (Lev 17:4; Ex 12:15; Num 19:20). This has been taken to mean death, but more probably it was a form of excommunication (Ezr 7:26). The individual was barred from all communion, social and religious, within the fellowship of Israel. In later times, this took the form of exclusion from the temple or synagogue (Jn 9:21, 34–35).

BANK. The ancient world did not have banks in the modern sense of the institution. The word translated "bank" in the NT is the common word "table." It is used to refer to the ordinary dining table, and also for the tables of the money changers (Lk 19:23). These exchangers would take deposits of money on which they paid interest and use it either for trade or for lending at a higher rate of interest. That is Jesus' reference in Mt 25:27. Another aspect of the business was to exchange coins of one denomination for another, or foreign money for current coins, which was a highly lucrative business. From the Phoenicians, who seem to have invented the practice, the business of money changing had spread throughout the Roman Empire by NT times. *See* Occupations: Money Changers. In Moses' day, the simple pastoral economy of Israel did not call for such complicated financial transactions. Loans were made between friends in case of need, and taking interest was forbidden (Ex 22:25; Lev 25:37). For commercial loans in Solomon's time see note on Prov 6:1 in *Wycliffe Bible Commentary*. *See* Borrow; Occupations: Banker.

P. C. J.

BANNER. Two words are used in Heb. in the sense of a banner: *degel*, "something conspicuous," and *nēs*, "lifted up, exalted." The banners of Bible times were poles or standards with some identifying marking or figure, rather than the flags and pennants of our day. They were used as rallying points either in peace or war (Num 21:8–9), and served as identification for the various tribes and nations (Num 1:52; 10:14, 25; Ps 20:5). The ancient standard of Ur (from 2500 B.C.), a wooden panel inlaid with a mosaic of shell and lapis lazuli, shows the antiquity of standards. A 13th cen. B.C. silver-plated bronze cult standard, showing a goddess head with snakes, was found at Hazor. The banners of Rome with their eagles and other insignia are familiar ensigns (*q.v.*).

BANQUET. *See* Food.

BAPTISM (Gr. nouns *baptismos* and *baptisma*; Gr. verbs *baptizō* and *baptō*).
Three different views are held concerning the real meaning of baptism. The Baptists and others who baptize by immersion maintain that it signifies the believer's identification with the death, burial, and resurrection of Christ, and therefore insist it must be done by a complete immersion in the waters of baptism. Those who practice pouring maintain it signifies the outpouring of the Holy Spirit upon the believer and his infilling with the Spirit. The Reformed, Methodists, and Anglicans, who sprinkle, maintain baptism signifies the cleansing away of the believer's sins by the blood of Christ. They, and those who pour, baptize infants, while immersionists baptize only those who have reached sufficient maturity to themselves believe in Christ.

The reasons for these wide divergences stem, first, from the use of *baptō* and *baptizō* in classical Gr. For example, Charles Hodge, the great Presbyterian theologian, says the following: "*Baptō* means (1) to dip, (2) to dye by dipping, (3) to dye without regard to mode.... (4) It also means to gild ... (5) to wet, moisten or wash, (6) to temper ... (7) to imbue.... As to the classical use of *baptizō*, it means (1) to

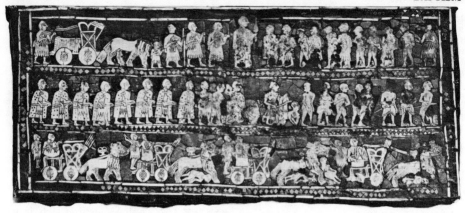

Apparently the Standard of Ur, pictured here, served as a kind of flag or banner. BM

immerse or submerge . . . (2) to overflow or cover with water . . . (3) to wet thoroughly or moisten, (4) to pour upon or drench, (5) in any way to be overwhelmed or overpowered" (*Systematic Theology*, III, 527). However, this only introduces the arguments which ensue and which are summarized below. The actual question is, how are the words used in the OT and particularly in the NT? Second, the fact that several different things are spoken of as baptism, such as the outpouring of the Holy Spirit (Mt 3:11; Acts 1:5); identification with Christ's death, burial, and resurrection (Rom 6:3–5; cf. Mk 10:38; Lk 12:50; Col 2:12); and OT cleansings by sprinkling (Heb 9:10, 13, 19, 21).

The Case for Immersion

This rests upon the following arguments:

1. The general use of *baptō* and *baptizō* in secular and classical Gr. Both those who teach immersion and those who teach sprinkling accept the fact that it is largely used there to express to dip and to immerse. Thus the meaning to sprinkle appears to have been a secondary meaning in Gr.

2. A simple acceptance of the translation of *baptizō* in several places in the KJV and other English versions of the NT gives the impression immersion was the mode (Mt 3:6; Mk 1:5, 8 – 10; Acts 8:38).

3. A stress upon certain passages in the OT in which both of the Gr. words are used of immersion. For example, Naaman was told to dip (*baptizō*) seven times in the Jordan (II Kgs 5:10, 14); Nebuchadnezzar was wet (*baptō*) with the dew of heaven (Dan 4:33); and the priest was told to dip the tip of his finger in the blood (Lev 4:17; cf. Josh 3:15; I Sam 14:27; Ps 68:23).

4. The baptism of proselytes in the intertestamental period. The Dead Sea Scrolls throw some light upon this custom, though it is a question whether they prove very much. First, they reflect customs of such an extremely ascetic group as the Essenes and these cannot be regarded as being identical with the customs of orthodox Jews; and, second, the mode of cleansing they required of proselytes is not too clear.

5. Since the exhortations to be baptized by John the Baptist were directed to adults who repented of their sins, and by Christ and the disciples to those old enough to believe, it is argued that baptism is a sacrament or ordinance to be dispensed only to those who have first believed. Certain pertinent rational arguments are added to support the view, such as the futility of baptizing a baby who cannot know what is being done either to him or for him, in contrast to the meaningfulness of baptism when it is given to those who have already believed in Christ.

6. The difference between the OT and NT and between law and grace. In the OT the stress is upon "this do and thou shalt live," and in the NT, upon God's grace and man's faith. The emphasis upon obedience in the old dispensation stands in contrast to that of belief in the new. Circumcision and the covenant which accompanied it have been discontinued, and baptism and personal confession of faith have been introduced.

7. The NT teaching that believers are baptized into Christ's death, burial, and resurrection. This is taken to express the true significance of baptism. Only immersion can properly and fully express what burial with Christ in His death means (Rom 6:3–5).

8. Christ's particular teaching. He said of His coming death on the cross, "I have a baptism to be baptized with: and how am I straitened till it be accomplished!" (Lk 12:50); and he asked His disciples, "Can ye

drink of the cup that I drink of? and be baptized with the baptism that I am baptized with?" (Mk 10:38).

Highpoints in the immersionist view. (1) The atoning death of Christ and His bodily resurrection are witnessed to, and thus the gospel is given in a most dramatic form. (2) Saving faith is stressed. (3) This method enables the participant to confess his faith publicly and even add a personal testimony, which enhances the sealing aspect of baptism as the sign or token of the new covenant on the one hand, and witnesses to salvation on the other. (4) A most important phase of the gospel is expressed. (5) This particular meaning for baptism has strong support from Christ and the Scripture.

The Case for Pouring

This rests upon the NT teaching concerning baptism and the Holy Spirit. When clean water is poured upon the participant, it signifies the outpouring of the Holy Spirit upon the believer. Certain arguments are presented to support this mode, such as:

1. John the Baptist's teaching. John, when baptizing those who had repented of their sins, said that he baptized only with water, but Christ would baptize with the Holy Ghost and fire (Mt 3:11).

2. Christ's teaching. Though Christ left all baptisms to His disciples (Jn 4:2), still they soon were baptizing more than John (Jn 4:1). After His resurrection and just before the ascension, Christ told the disciples to wait for the promise of the Father, and, taking up the teaching of John, He said, "For John truly baptized with water; but ye shall be baptized with the Holy Ghost not many days hence" (Acts 1:5). This appears, in contrast to Rom 6:3-5, to

identify baptism with the infilling of the Holy Spirit. Some Reformed writers place much of their stress upon this passage (cf. Robert G. Rayburn). Of course Peter explained the actual outpouring of the Spirit at Pentecost as a fulfillment of Joel's prophecy (Acts 2:16-21; Joel 2:28-32) and preached that those who repented and were baptized should receive the Holy Spirit (Acts 2:38-39).

Highpoints of the pouring view. (1) It stresses the person and work of the Holy Spirit and the importance of the Spirit-filled life. (2) It emphasizes a particular truth in baptism stressed by both John the Baptist and Paul. (3) It has the support of Christ's own words and interpretation in Acts 1:5.

The Case for Sprinkling

This rests upon the following considerations:

1. Certain OT commands to sprinkle. Consideration is given to OT passages where sprinkling is enjoined for cleansing (Ex 24:6-8; Lev 14:7; Num 19:9, 17), and their classification in Heb 9:10 as divers baptisms (*diaphorois baptismois*). In the ensuing passage in Hebrews the sprinkling of the ashes of the red heifer on the unclean (Num 19:9, 17), the sprinkling of both the Book of the Covenant and of the people by Moses (Ex 24:6-8) after the giving of the law, and cleansing of certain other sins are all given as examples of baptism.

2. The continuity between circumcision and baptism. This is taught in Col 2:11-12 where the two are used of circumcision and baptism in Christ, either interchangeably or as two parts of the same thing. Peter concluded his plea at the end of his sermon at Pentecost, when calling upon those present to repent and to be baptized that they might receive the Holy Ghost, with the declaration, "For the promise is unto you,

A baptism in the Jabbok River, Jordan. Courtesy Richard E. Ward

and to your children [*teknois*]" (Acts 2:38 – 39), making clear that the blessings of baptism extend to the whole family and to their descendants. Had he not included their children, the Jews who heard him would have objected that the gospel in the NT offered them less than the law in the OT.

3. Continuation of the covenant. At circumcision the children of OT believers came under a covenant relationship with God – they became children of the covenant. Unless baptism extends to children, this aspect of covenantal relationship for infants ceased with the coming of Christ. Since this was a very precious doctrine to the OT saint, and entitled him to special blessings from God, it would be amazing that it could have disappeared without mention or controversy in the NT, and adult baptism have taken its place to the exclusion of the believer's children, particularly since the dropping of circumcision itself brought such a strong reaction (cf. Acts 15:1 ff.; Gal 2:1 ff.). The conviction that the covenantal relationship for children continued, with the baptism of children taking the place of circumcision, is strengthened by the fact that there is not even a suggestion of any objection being raised that with the introduction of baptism a covenantal relation had been removed.

Baptismal pool in the sixth century church of St. John at Ephesus. HFV

4. The unity of the plan of salvation. If God commanded His OT saints to circumcise their children and to enter into a covenant with Him to rear them in the fear and nurture of the Lord, promising to be their God and the God of their children, and if He is unchangeable, why should He change His way of dealing with children in the NT age? A covenant sealed by circumcision was God's way of bringing salvation to the OT family, and unless otherwise revealed, a covenant sealed by baptism should be His way in this present age. God's unchangeability and the unity of the plan of salvation, by faith through sovereign grace, call for a continuation of His same plan for the salvation of children in the NT age.

5. John the Baptist's office and training. John was an OT Levite and a priest in his own right. His father was a priest who served in the course of Abia (Lk 1:5). John, as the forerunner of Christ and the liaison between OT and NT believers, had to follow exactly the instructions given to Moses in the Pentateuch for sacrifices and cleansings. However, the OT cleansings were by sprinkling, except in cases where the body of an individual had actually become infected with sores or contaminated by disease and in certain cases of bodily discharges (cf. Lev 15:1 ff.; 22:1-9; Num 5:2; cf. Lev 14:2 f.). That John's mode of baptism was a sign of cleansing is also clear from the fact that he connected it with repentance from sin on the participant's part, and purging or cleansing on God's part: "He shall baptize you with the Holy Ghost, and with fire . . . and . . . thoroughly purge his floor" (Mt 3:11- 12), and that the only dispute over his baptism was regarding purification (Jn 3:25) or cleansing.

Yet the question as to whether John the Baptist might have practiced the mode of baptism administered to proselytes, namely, immersion (G. F. Moore, *Judaism,* I, 334 f.), is admittedly impossible to answer dogmatically. First of all, the Jewish evidence from the Mishnah and the Talmud comes too late to be entirely conclusive (from A.D. 200 to 400). Then the earliest Christian evidence for the use of immersion comes from about A.D. 100. Even if the Jewish evidence proves that immersion was practiced for proselytes entering Judaism by John's time, this does not necessarily mean John adopted this practice. It is to be remembered that no Jew would readily submit to what was reserved as a proselyte baptism without real objections. Would John have used a mode which would appear certain to raise protests? Or did he simply follow the OT modes of ceremonial priestly cleansing? The latter conclusion appears certain to the Reformed people, particularly since no controversy arose concerning his mode. The only question discussed regarding John's baptism so far as the NT records go, was the broad doctrine of purification or cleansing itself (Jn 3:25).

If John by revelation introduced a new kind of cleansing, namely, by immersion rather than by sprinkling, then of course that should be adopted. However, at no point did he suggest he was bringing in some new method of cleansing. Nor did he ever have to explain or defend the mode he used.

6. Lack of any NT passages that conclusively prove immersion. The Reformed group maintains there is no passage on baptism in the NT which cannot be explained more naturally by sprinkling than by immersion, whether it be the baptism of John, that of the 3,000 at Pentecost, of the Philippian jailer at midnight, or the Ethiopian eunuch in the desert. Further, in no place does the Gr. require translation of a particular instance of baptism as by immersion. For example, as certain writers point out (E. B. Fairfield, *Letters on Baptism*, pp. 73-76; John Scott Johnson, *Baptism*, p. 30), to express "from" the Gr. is merely *ek* or *apo*, and to express "to" is *eis;* but to express "out of" it is unquestionably *ek*, once with the verb and once with the noun (Mk 5:8; 7:31; Lk 4:22), and to express "into" *eis* is unquestionably used, once with the verb and once with the noun (Jn 20:3-6). At His baptism Jesus was baptized by John *eis* the Jordan (Mk 1:10) and went up *apo* the water (Mt 3:16), but in neither case is the preposition repeated so as to prove absolutely that Christ either went fully under the water or came up from immersion in the water.

At the same time the Reformed group sees particular cases in the NT in which they feel immersion would seem to be impossible. How could Jews immerse couches before they took their meals, and how could Pharisees accuse Christ of not taking a bath by immersion before He ate when water was very scarce and kept in home cisterns (Mk 7:3-4)? How could 3,000 be baptized by immersion right in the city of Jerusalem, or a jailer at midnight (Acts 16:30-34)?

7. The stress upon the gospel in sprinkling. In sprinkling, the Reformed people signify that the blood of Jesus Christ alone can cleanse from sin. They maintain that they thus express the gospel in its most fundamental form. Someone may never understand the doctrine of identification with Christ in His death, burial, and resurrection, biblical and wonderful as that truth is, and yet he may go to heaven. But no one can go to heaven except he accept and believe that the blood of Jesus Christ cleanses from sin.

8. Family salvation retained. In the OT God ordered the parents to make a covenant to rear their children in His fear and nurture, and commanded circumcision as a seal of their faith. God is intensely interested in the salvation of children and does not entrust them to believers of either Testament without requiring a pledge, or covenant, binding the parents to teach and instruct the children and bring them up for God.

The Reformed feel that few understand what the baptism of a child really means. It is first of all a confession of the faith of the parents that only the blood of Jesus Christ can cleanse away their own sin, and that that same precious blood alone can take away the sin of their child. Second, it is an agreement and pledge to care for and train the child whom God has given, for God; to teach him the Scriptures and how to pray, and to endeavor to lead him to a saving faith in Jesus Christ. When parents do this, God promises to be the God of their children. Thus it becomes a covenant between the parents and God, and the child is the child of the covenant. But the covenant does not save. Salvation is possible only by God's sovereign grace; thus the salvation of the child is actually and finally of grace. When he comes to the age of accountability, he must himself accept and confess Christ as his own personal Saviour.

Highpoints of the sprinkling view. (1) This particular mode signifies and stresses the fact that only by the shedding of Christ's blood can one's sins be washed away. Therefore, like immersion, it gives the gospel in baptism, though in an even simpler and more fundamental form. (2) It maintains what is called the unity of the covenant of grace, or the continuity of the one plan of salvation in the OT and NT. (3) It supports the doctrine of the unchangeability of God. (4) Family salvation becomes a reality for believing parents of both Testaments. The importance of children, and of their nurture in the faith and their being won to Christ, is emphasized. (5) The acceptance of John the Baptist's mode of baptism by the Jews is explained.

Why Are There Three Modes of Baptism?

Is one mode in particular, and its peculiar significance, to be maintained so completely over the others as to deny that blessing can be found in the others too? This would be hard to sustain, since the Baptists and other immersionists appear to have won more to Christ than those who practice either of the other modes. The answer is to be found in the facts that: (1) Each mode of baptism teaches a separate, vital biblical truth. Immersion teaches identity with Christ's death, burial, and resurrection; pouring teaches the baptism or infilling of the believer with the Holy Spirit; and sprinkling teaches the washing away of sins by the blood of Christ. Therefore each, when properly understood and taught, brings great blessing. (2) They all are only phases or parts of what baptism in its entirety covers. Each mode is based upon what is called in the NT a baptism—and yet the Scripture categorically states there is only one baptism. Paul writes in Eph 4:4-6 that there is one Holy Spirit, one God and Father of us all, "one Lord, one faith, one baptism." This leads to the realization that all three modes or "baptisms" are only parts of a greater whole. But what is this whole?

In the Lord's Supper Christ's substitutionary death is commemorated until He comes again. It would be strange if baptism only repeated the same truth. The problem of the two sacraments or ordinances signifying the same thing is solved when we see that, while the Lord's Supper signifies Christ's death, baptism covers the application of the benefits of Christ's death to the believer by the Holy Spirit.

The first thing the Holy Spirit does is to apply the blood of Christ to cleanse away sin — signified by sprinkling; the next is to identify the believer with the death, burial, and resurrection of Christ — signified by immersion; and the last is to come and indwell God's purchased vessel — signified by pouring. Thus we are led to see that baptism signifies more than many scholars at first thought; that each of the three views is true as far as it stresses a phase of the total meaning of the sacrament or ordinance, and therefore is accompanied by blessings when properly understood and taught and used; that immersion has brought blessing to countless thousands, and still, sprinkling is blessed as it stresses an equally fundamental truth of the gospel. All inclination to ridicule and make light of each other's viewpoint vanishes when once the particular biblical truth others are trying to demonstrate and teach is understood. Baptists learn a new respect for Presbyterians and Presbyterians for Baptists, and those who omit the ordinances both of baptism and the Lord's Supper (Salvation Army and the Quakers) receive a new understanding of the different views and modes practiced by others.

Bibliography. Herbert S. Bird, "Professor Jewett on Baptism," WTJ, XXXI (1969), 145–161. J. Oliver Buswell, Jr., Systematic Theology, Grand Rapids: Eerdmans, Vol. II. Edmund B. Fairfield, Letters on Baptism, Philadelphia: Gordon Holdcrott, n.d. Charles Hodge, Systematic Theology, Grand Rapids: Eerdmans, III (1952), 526–611. Paul Jewett, "Baptism (Baptist View)," Encyclopedia of Christianity, ed. by E. H. Palmer, 1964, I, 517–526. Albrecht Oepke, "Baptō, etc.," TDNT, I, 529–546. A. H. Strong, Systematic Theology, Philadelphia: Judson, 1953, pp. 930–959.

R. A. K.

BAPTISM FOR THE DEAD. Paul speaks of this practice when presenting his arguments for the bodily resurrection in I Cor 15. He argues: (1) "If there be no resurrection of the dead, then is Christ not risen . . . then is our preaching vain . . . . But now is Christ risen" (vv. 12–20). (2) If the dead do not rise, why are some baptized for (or above, hyper) the dead (v. 29)? (3) If He be not risen, why do we risk our lives hourly to preach a risen Lord (v. 30)?

Many explanations have been given of the expression "baptism for the dead." These may be divided into two classifications.

Early views: (1) Early Christian writers suggested a vicarious baptism undergone by believers for other believers who died unbaptized. Tertullian offers this explanation (de Resurr.

48; Adv. Marc. 5:10). Epiphanius speaks of such a custom among the Cerinthians but not among Christians (Haer. 28:6). H. A. W. Meyer (Critical and Exegetical Handbook to the Epistles to the Corinthians, pp. 364–368) accepts such a view. (2) Chrysostom considers that it means the believer is baptized for his dead body, in order to show he believes it will live as a resurrection body.

Modern views: (1) That some were being baptized on behalf of those who died unbaptized, whether believers or not. This view is held and practiced by Mormons today. (2) That some were encouraged to be baptized by the example of early Christian martyrs, this being a testimony to their faith in the resurrection of the body. (3) That all who are baptized are baptized "for the good of the dead," in the sense the resurrection cannot occur till a certain number are saved (Olshausen). (4) That erstwhile Gentile pagans who became Christians through the testimony of loved ones now departed were baptized for the sake of their dead, i.e., in order to be reunited with them at the resurrection (J. K. Howard, "Baptism for the dead: a Study of I Corinthians 15:29," E.Q., XXXVII [July, 1965], 137–141). (5) That many are baptized over the graves of departed (G. J. Vossius; F. W. Grossheide, Korte Verklaring, I Corinthians, pp. 196–7).

Though the explanation offered by Vossius and Grossheide may not appear so convincing to Western minds, it has several points in its favor. It offers a view that may fit the person and the writings of Paul. He would not use an unscriptural vicarious baptism as an argument to true believers for the resurrection, and if he did, certainly not without any explanation. In Europe and Asia burial beneath the floor of a church is a common practice. Those being baptized in such churches would testify by their baptism that they believed their bodies, and those of the dead beneath them, would rise at the resurrection. In the 1st cen. A.D., however, Christians were not yet building their own churches, but baptized their converts in convenient pools or rivers.

R. A. K.

BAPTISM OF FIRE. In announcing the baptism of the Spirit, John the Baptist twice declared that Christ would also baptize with fire. Having said that, he immediately mentioned the judgment by which the Saviour ". . . will burn up the chaff with unquenchable fire" (Mt 3:11–12; Lk 3:16–17). The "baptism of fire" is therefore the terrible punishment by which sinners will be judged in the last day (cf. Mt 13:30, 41–51; 25:41, 46; see also in Mal 3:2–3 the appearance of Him who will be like "the refiner's fire"; see Occupations: Refiner).

In a similar passage, Christ declares that "every one shall be salted with fire" (Mk 9:49). This appears to be applied to believers as well as unbelievers, but with this tremendous difference: the believer recognizes that he is guilty and liable to judgment, but he believes that Jesus has been smitten in his place and judged by the fire of divine justice. If now such a man "shall not come into condemnation" (Jn 5:24), it is because in Christ the fire has already passed on him. Henceforth he is willing that the Spirit of holiness judge and burn in him all impurity, "for our God is a consuming fire" (Heb 12:28-29). On the other hand, *the unbeliever* will know all the severity of the "unquenchable fire," the "everlasting fire," and the "lake of fire and brimstone" (Mt 3:12; 25:41; Rev 20:10, 15). *See* Brimstone; Punishment.

R. P.

BAPTISM OF THE SPIRIT. After the repeated announcements of John the Baptist concerning the baptism of the Holy Spirit (Mt 3:11; Mk 1:8; Lk 3:16; Jn 1:33), Christ solemnly stressed the promise of the Spirit's coming (Acts 1:4-5). The two historical fulfillments mentioned in the NT occurred at Pentecost (Acts 2:1-4) and in the house of Cornelius (Acts 11:15-16). These two groups of believers were added to the church at the very moment they received the baptism of the Spirit. Paul confirms this by giving in I Cor 12:13 the clearest definition in the NT.

Effected by the divine Spirit, this baptism has as its result the placing of every believer "in Christ," making him a member of Christ's Body, and at the same time uniting him to all the other children of God. The tense of the verb "we were all baptized . . ." (RSV) indicates that here it is a matter of the initial experience coinciding with the new birth. The man already regenerated need not therefore look again for the baptism of the Spirit, nor for a "new baptism" (that which does not exist), but rather for the fullness of the Spirit constantly renewed.

Baptism shows death and resurrection, the burial of the crucified sinner with Christ, and the birth of the regenerated man, born from above by the Holy Spirit (Jn 3:3). It marks the break with the past and the entrance by faith into the new sphere of life in Christ: "Buried with him in baptism, wherein also ye are risen with him through the faith of the operation of God. . . [you] hath he quickened together with him" (Col 2:12-13). We "were baptized into his death . . . buried with him by baptism into death: that like as Christ was raised up from the dead . . . even so we also should walk in newness of life" (Rom 6:3-4). "For as many of you as have been baptized into Christ have put on Christ" (Gal 3:27). These texts speak first of all of the baptism of the Spirit, which alone is capable of producing such a work in us: death and resurrection with Christ, new birth and the receiving of a superior nature which is the basis of a transformed life.

Water baptism shows by an external and visible means that which the baptism of the Spirit has produced in the spiritual realm. Since the believer dies and is resurrected with Christ, it is understandable that the church often practiced water baptism by the immersion of the convert (*see* Baptism). The old man, crucified with Christ, disappears under the water, and it is a new man which comes out of it, dead to sin and regenerated unto a new life (Rom 6:3-4; Col 2:12). Water baptism is, therefore, the affirmation and sign of that which the baptism of the Spirit has effected in the depth of the heart. The two are so bound together that Paul could state in reality that there is only *one baptism* (Eph 4:5). It is the baptism of the Spirit (death and resurrection with Christ) that saves a believer, and in water baptism he gives the answer of a good conscience toward God (I Pet 3:21).

Participation in this gracious operation of God is assured to all who become members of the Body of Christ by faith (Col 2:12; I Cor 12:13).

See Holy Spirit, Filling of; Unction.

R. P.

BAR

1. A piece of wood or metal (Heb. *berîah*) used as a support, fastening or barrier (e.g., Ex 26:26-29; Neh 3:3; Jon 2:6).

2. A bolt or bar (Heb. *min'āl*, "to fasten"). The word is used only in Deut 33:25, RSV ("shoes" in KJV).

BAR-. A prefix, this is the Aramaic for the Heb. *ben* ("son"), e.g., Bar-jonah, "son of Jonah" (Mt 16:17). *Bar* is the original word translated "son" in Ps 2:12 and Prov 31:2.

BARABBAS (băr-ăb'ás). All four Gospels (Mt 27:16; Mk 15:15; Lk 23:18; Jn 18:40) mention this man who was released by Pilate in preference to Jesus. A notorious prisoner arrested for robbery, sedition, and murder, he has become the source of many imaginative narratives describing what may have happened to him when the full realization broke upon his conscience that a "good man," God's Son, had been crucified in his place. The custom of releasing a prisoner at Passover is not mentioned outside the NT.

The reading of his name as Jesus Barabbas (Mt 27:16 f.) was known to Origen (c. A.D. 200), is found in the early Syriac version (c. A.D. 200), and a few cursive MSS (dating after A.D. 900), but it is not found in the oldest and best texts. Probably it originated as a scribal error due to the proximity of Jesus' name in Mt 27:17.

See Crime and Punishment; Pilate; Zealot.

T. B. C.

BARACHEL (băr'á-kĕl). A descendant of Buz (Gen 22:21), Barachel was the father of Elihu, one of Job's friends (Job 32:2, 6).

BARACHIAH. *See* Berechiah.

BARACHIAS (băr′á-kī′ás). In Mt 23:35 he is called the father of Zacharias, who seems to have been the Zechariah referred to in II Chr 24:20–22, the son of Jehoiada the priest (*see* Zacharias for discussion of the problem of parentage).

Barachias is also spelled Berechiah (*q.v.*) in the OT.

BARAH. *See* Beth-barah.

BARAK (bâr′ák). A military leader from the tribe of Naphtali who, under the direction and encouragement of the prophetess Deborah (*q.v.*), delivered the northern tribes of Israel from bondage imposed by Jabin, king of Hazor. Jabin (*q.v.*) had a seemingly invincible army with 900 chariots of iron, led by a mercenary Sisera, possibly an Egyptian or a Hittite. Deborah, a judge in Ephraim, called upon Barak as the chosen of the Lord to gather an army from Zebulun and Naphtali. The Israelites met on Mount Tabor, while Sisera, alarmed by the revolt, assembled his army on the plain of Esdraelon by the river Kishon. A violent thunderstorm caused the Kishon to overflow its banks, rendering the iron chariots useless in the swampy ground. Attacked by the Israelites, the Canaanites fled in panic. Sisera himself died at the hands of a woman, Jael, in whose tent he had sought refuge (Jud 4–5).

Barak is named among the great heroes of faith in Heb 11.

P. C. J.

BARBARIAN. This word is not found in the OT, though the LXX uses it; e.g., Ps 114:1. It is used five times in the NT. "Barbarian" may be a repeated syllable imitative of a foreigner, "bar bar." Similarly Egyptians called non-Egyptians *berber.* So it means speaking an unintelligible tongue in I Cor 14:11.

Plato divided his world into barbarians and Hellenes. The word may therefore mean non-Greek of both language and culture. Luke does not in any derogatory way call the Semitic Maltese barbarians, that is, non-Greeks, natives (RSV), in Acts 28:2, 4.

After the Persian War (493–479 B.C.) the Greeks came to use "barbarian" with the sense of rough and crude. So Rom 1:14 may mean that Paul is "debtor to those who speak Greek and to those who do not, and (so) to the cultured and to the uncultured." In Col 3:11 he defines "Greek and Jew" as "circumcision and uncircumcision," and puts Scythian right after barbarian, for Scythians were barbarians par excellence. *See* Foreigner.

W. G. B.

BARBER. *See* Hair; Occupations.

BAREFOOT. Two words are used in the Heb.: *yāḥēp,* "unshod" (II Sam 15:30; Isa 20:2–4); and perhaps *shôlāl* in Mic 1:8, "stripped," and in Job 12:17, 19, "spoiled."

BARHUMITE (bär-hū′mīt). A probable variant of Baharumite (cf. II Sam 23:31 with I Chr 11:33), denoting an inhabitant of Bahurim (*q.v.*).

BARIAH (bā-rī′á). A descendant of David in the Zerubbabel line, son of Shemaiah (I Chr 3:22).

BAR-JESUS (bär-jē′sŭs). Alternative name for the magician Elymas, who opposed Barnabas and Saul in Cyprus (Acts 13:6). *See* Elymas.

BAR-JONA (bär-jō′ná). A surname of Simon Peter (Mt 16:17). *See* Bar-.

BARKOS (bär′kŏs). Ancestor of certain Nethinim (*q.v.*) who returned with Zerubbabel and were temple servants (Ezr 2:53; Neh 7:55).

BARLEY. *See* Plants.

BARNABAS (bär′ná-bás). A Levite of Cyprus and member of the primitive church of Jerusalem. His personal name was Joseph; the patronymic Barnabas was given him by the apostles to indicate his character ("son of encouragement," Acts 4:36, RSV). He is first mentioned for his generosity in selling some land and handing over the price to the apostles for the relief of the poorer members of the church (Acts 4:36 f.). He next appears in Acts 9:27 as lending his good offices to Saul of Tarsus when Saul returned to Jerusalem in the third year after his conversion, and commending him to the apostles as a genuine believer. This suggests that he was previously acquainted with Saul.

When, some years later, news came to the apostles in Jerusalem of the large-scale Gentile evangelization being undertaken in Syrian Antioch by Christian Hellenists, refugees from the persecution which started in Judea after Stephen's death, they sent Barnabas to Antioch as their commissioner to investigate the situation and take such action as he judged appropriate. They could not have sent a more suitable man.

The nearer harbor area pictured here is where Barnabas and Paul landed at Salamis on Cyprus on the first missionary journey. HFV

Far from being shocked at the innovations that he found, Barnabas was delighted to see how the grace of God was at work in the conversion of pagans at Antioch, and he encouraged the evangelists and the young converts with all his might. After some time, he felt the need of a colleague in the supervision of this growing work, and brought Saul/Paul from Tarsus to help him.

After a year's collaboration in Antioch, Barnabas and Paul were released by the church there to undertake a more extensive ministry. They traversed Cyprus from E to W, and then crossed to Asia Minor, where they preached the gospel and planted churches in the cities of S Galatia. Barnabas' young cousin, John Mark of Jerusalem, accompanied them on this journey as far as the coast of Asia Minor, and then returned home.

The incident of Gal 2:11 ff. may be dated shortly after Barnabas and Paul returned to Antioch. Even Barnabas was disposed to follow the example of Peter and others and withdraw temporarily from table-fellowship with Gentile Christians to avoid offending visitors from Jerusalem.

On two occasions Barnabas and Paul visited Jerusalem as delegates from the church of Antioch. The first was when they brought a gift for the relief of the Jerusalem church in time of famine (Acts 11:30). It was probably during this visit that they had the interview with the Jerusalem leaders at which their apostleship to the Gentiles was recognized (Gal 2:1-10). The second was when they attended the Jerusalem council (Acts 15) to discuss and decide with the Jerusalem leaders the terms on which Gentile converts should be admitted to church fellowship.

Shortly after this, Barnabas and Paul parted company because they disagreed about taking Mark with them again. Barnabas took Mark and continued to evangelize Cyprus. But Paul always refers to him with affectionate esteem as a fellow missionary among the Gentiles (I Cor 9:6). From the fact that Paul requested John Mark to be sent to help him years later, "for he is profitable to me for the ministry" (II Tim 4:11), we can conclude that Barnabas did as much for Mark as he had earlier for Paul.

F. F. B.

BARREL. The word used in KJV refers to a large earthenware jar used for carrying water, storing grain, etc. (I Kgs 17:12, 14, 16; 18:33). The Heb. word *kad* is more properly translated "pitcher" (KJV) or "jar" (RSV) in Gen 24:14-20; Eccl 12:6; Jud 7:16-20. *See* Pottery.

BARREN. To the Hebrews, children were a blessing from the Lord (Ps 127:3-5), and childlessness was an affliction, a judgment of God (Ex 23:26; Deut 7:14; Lev 20:21). For a woman to be barren was the ultimate in sorrow and shame. She felt that she had failed in the prime

reason for her existence, and she was looked upon as one whom God had smitten. Regardless of her position or other blessings, she was in sorrow until a child should be born (I Sam 1). It was a legal practice in Abraham's day to claim the child of one's husband by a handmaid as one's own to avoid the disgrace of sterility (Gen 16:1-2; 30:3-4). *See* Family; Marriage.

BARSABAS (bär′sȧ-bȧs)

1. Joseph, surnamed Justus, nominated with Matthias to succeed Judas Iscariot (Acts 1:23).

2. Judas, a prophet in the Jerusalem church, who with Silas accompanied Paul and Barnabas to deliver the decision of the Jerusalem council to Antioch. He later returned to Jerusalem and nothing more is known of him (Acts 15:22-33).

BARTHOLOMEW (bär-thŏl′ō-mū). The English and Gr. forms simply transliterate the Aramaic name meaning "son of Tolmai" or "Talmar," a name found in the Gr. OT in several forms and in Josephus. Bartholomew is named in all four lists of the 12 apostles (Mt 10:3; Mk 3:18; Lk 6:14; Acts 1:13) and always immediately after Philip. Study of the lists indicates pairing and grouping into four. This suggests Bartholomew and Philip were companions in the second group headed by Philip.

It is also conjectured that Nathanael (meaning "God's gift") is a surname of Bartholomew since the Synoptic Gospels pair Philip and Bartholomew, whereas John pairs Philip and Nathanael. In addition, the Synoptics never mention Nathanael, and John never mentions Bartholomew. Attempts to identify him with Matthew or Matthias, or John the son of Zebedee have proved vain. On the other hand, some scholars give up the attempt to identify Nathanael with one of the Twelve. If his identification with Nathanael is correct, however, then Philip brought Bartholomew (Nathanael), a native of Cana of Galilee (Jn 21:2), to acknowledge Jesus as the Messiah (Jn 1:45-46). The beautiful description of his encounter with Jesus is found in Jn 1:47-51. An Israelite indeed, without guile, Jesus disclosed Himself to him as God's Son, Israel's King, and then promised more and fuller divine insights through the days of discipleship to come.

Nothing further is known of Bartholomew from the NT. Traditions concerning him are very untrustworthy. They begin with Eusebius (A.D. 325), state several fields of preaching, and several forms of martyrdom. He is often made one of the 70 disciples (Lk 10:1).

See Nathanael.

T. B. C.

BARTIMAEUS (bär-tĭ-mē′ŭs). The name of a blind beggar whose eyes Jesus opened as He went on His last journey from Jericho to Jerusalem. Bartimaeus' healing as recorded in Mk 10:46-52 presents a remarkable profession of faith in the person of Christ—"thou son of David"—and His power—"Lord, that I might receive my sight" (vv. 47, 51).

A problem, however, has arisen since Lk 18:35-43 speaks of a blind man receiving his sight as Jesus "was come nigh unto" Jericho, while Mark says as He left Jericho. Further, Mt 20:29-34 speaks of two blind men, while Mark and Luke mention only one. These may well be three separate incidents. Yet they can be reconciled as one if the expression "was come nigh" (Lk 18:35) merely means Jesus was near, and the two writers Mark and Luke picked out the blind beggar who did the speaking and ignored a second with him.

R. A. K.

BARUCH (bâr'ŭk)

1. The son of Neriah and brother of Seraiah (King Zedekiah's chamberlain, Jer 51:59), said by Josephus (*Ant.* x.9.1) to have come from a very illustrious family (cf. Jer 51:59; Bar 1:1). He was Jeremiah's friend and private secretary (Jer 32:12; 36:4). *See* Jeremiah.

Upon being forbidden to prophesy in the temple area, Jeremiah dictated his oracles to Baruch, who then read them to the people. Baruch was arrested by King Jehoiakim, and the scroll (*q.v.*) containing Jeremiah's prophecies was cut to pieces with a knife and burned in the fire. Baruch and Jeremiah then were obliged to rewrite the oracles.

Along with Jeremiah, Baruch witnessed the destruction of Jerusalem by the Babylonians in 586 B.C. and thereafter went to live at Mizpah. But after the untimely death (murder) of Gedaliah, the newly appointed Babylonian governor of Judea, at the hands of the anti-Babylonian faction, Baruch was accused of unduly influencing Jeremiah (cf. Jos *Ant.* x.9.6) to dissuade the people from leaving Judea (Jer 43:3). Along with Jeremiah, he was forced to accompany those who fled into Egypt for fear of Babylonian reprisals (Jos *Ant.* x.9.6).

Tradition says he survived Jeremiah and went eventually to Babylon, where he lived for 12 years after the fall of Jerusalem, his death occurring in 574 B.C. But another tradition holds that he and Jeremiah died at the same time in Egypt.

A large number of spurious writings have been attributed to him, the most important of which are the apocryphal book of Baruch and the pseudepigraphical Apocalypse of Baruch.

2. The son of Zabbai (Zacchai, ASV marg.), who aided Nehemiah as he repaired the wall of Jerusalem (Neh 3:20).

3. One of the priests who sealed the covenant in Nehemiah's time (Neh 10:6); possibly the same as 2.

4. The son of Col-hozeh, descendant of Perez the son of Judah (Neh 11:5).

R. E. P.

BARZILLAI (bär-zĭl'ā-ī)

1. A wealthy octogenarian of Gilead, E and N of Jordan, who met David at Mahanaim

(Gen 32:2) near the Jabbok River during the king's flight from Absalom, and gave provisions to David's men (II Sam 17:27-29). As he and David parted at the Jordan on the king's return, he refused the royal invitation to move to the palace and its delights, and asked rather to die at home, though at Barzillai's suggestion his son Chimham (*q.v.*) took his place (II Sam 19:31-40). David, dying, charged King Solomon to show loyalty to Barzillai's sons (I Kgs 2:7).

2. Barzillai's name continues as that of returning priests of Ezra's time, descended from one of "the daughters of Barzillai the Gileadite" (Ezr 2:61 parallel to Neh 7:63).

3. Another Barzillai, of Meholah, possibly also in Gilead, was paternal grandfather of five of the seven sons of Saul, whom the Gibeonites hanged (II Sam 21:8 f.).

W. G. B.

BASHAN (bā'shăn). Bashan, meaning "fertile plain," was the name of the area E of the Sea of Galilee and the Jordan River. It was bounded on the N by Mount Hermon and on the E by Jebel Druse, extending on the W to the slopes of the Sea of Galilee and the upper Jordan. Bashan extended S about six miles beyond the Yarmuk River. It was a tableland 1600-2300 feet high with excellent wheat fields, pastures for cattle (Mic 7:14; Jer 50:19), and the groves of oak trees which have now disappeared. Bashan includes 350 square miles of petrified lava fields from which the Gr. name Trachonitis (Lk 3:1) was given to the region.

Bashan was the kingdom of Og at the time of the Exodus. It boasted 60 cities (Num 21:33; Deut 29:7) including Karnaim his capital, Ashtaroth (Deut 1:4), Salcah, Kenath and Edrei where he was defeated. Later, Gr. cities of Hippos, Dion and Abila were in the region, which included the districts of Argob and Golan (Deut 3:4; 4:43). Bashan was assigned to the E half of the tribe of Manasseh.

Archaeologists claim that the area was continuously occupied from about the 32nd cen. B.C. Its fields of dolmens (*q.v.*) may date to that early period. Taken from the Amorite king Og at the time of the Conquest (Deut 3:1-3), Bashan subsequently became a battleground between Israel and the Arameans (II Kgs 10:32-33). The area may have been mentioned as *Ziri-bashani* in the Amarna letters. In later times it was identified with Hauran and Hellenistic-Roman Batanaea.

In the Bible, the prosperity of Bashan is frequently used as a symbol of arrogant pride. The cruel enemies that beset the righteous are "strong bulls of Bashan" (Ps 22:12). The pleasure-seeking women of Samaria are addressed as "cows of Bashan" (Amos 4:1). God's judgments will be on the haughty and proud who are like "the cedars of Lebanon" and "the oaks of Bashan" (Isa 2:13). The rich city of Tyre, soon to meet God's judgment, had oars for its ships made from the oaks of Bashan (Ezk 27:6).

In Moses' blessing on the tribes we read, "Dan is a lion's whelp: he shall leap from Bashan" (Deut 33:22). Lions lurked among the trees of Bashan, affording the imagery of Dan as a tribe that could be ferocious like a lion. *See* Palestine II.B.4.*a*.

C. F. P.

BASHEMATH (băsh'ĕ-măth)

1. Esau's wife, the daughter of Elon the Hittite (Gen 26:34), probably to be identified with, or considered a sister of, Adah who is listed as the wife of Esau (Gen 36:2).

2. Another wife of Esau, the daughter of Ishmael and sister of Nebajoth (Gen 36:3, 4, 10, 13, 17). She is also called Mahalath (Gen 28:9). As a daughter of Ishmael she would also be a descendant of Abraham. Esau married her because his parents were displeased with his other wives (Gen 28:8; 26:34-35).

3. A daughter of Solomon, the wife of Ahimaaz, a quartermaster in the service of King Solomon for the province of Naphtali (I Kgs 4:15). The name is here spelled Basmath.

BASIN, BASON. Several words are translated "basin" (or "bason") in KJV. Basins were usually metal.

1. The Heb. word 'aggān, a large banqueting bowl or crater; used also for catching and sprinkling blood in sacrifice (Ex 24:6). A smaller size may also have existed ("cups," Isa 22:24).

2. Heb. kepôr ("bowl," RSV), somewhat smaller, used in the temple service; of gold and silver (I Chr 28:17; Ezr 1:10; 8:27).

3. Heb. mizrāq, a large banqueting bowl (Amos 6:6), similar to 1 above. When used in a sacrificial ritual, it was of bronze (Ex 27:3; Num 4:14; I Kgs 7:40, 45), silver (Num 7:13; II Kgs 12:13), or gold (I Kgs 7:50; II Kgs 25:15).

4. Heb. sap, a bowl of indeterminate size with both sacrificial (Ex 12:22; Jer 52:19) and secular uses (II Sam 17:28).

5. Heb. niptēr, a washbasin (Jn 13:5). Such a foot basin is also mentioned in Ps 60:8; 108:9 (sîr raḥaṣ, "washpot," KJV; "washbasin," RSV). Examples have been excavated at Samaria and Mizpah (Tell en-Nasbeh).

See Pottery.

R. V. R.

BASKET. Woven or plaited of reeds or straw, baskets had many uses; exact size and shape is not always clear. One type, often carried on the head, was used for both secular and sacrificial purposes (Gen 40:16-18; Ex 29:3, 23, 32; Lev 8:2, 26, 31; Num 6:15, 17, 19; Jud 6:19). A rough wicker basket was used for transporting the heads of the sons of Ahab (II Kgs 10:7), figs (Jer 24:1-2), and the burdens of the slave laborer (Ps 81:6, "pots"). A type used as a fruit basket in Amos 8:1-2 doubled as a cage for birds (Jer 5:27, *see* Cage). Another was used for produce (Deut 26:2-4; 28:5, 17).

The ark of bulrushes in which the baby Moses was placed by his mother (Ex 2:3, 5) was probably a small basketlike chest with a cover made of bulrushes or papyrus (*see* Ark of Bulrushes; Bulrush; Reeds).

By the use of different Gr. words Mark (8:19-20) differentiates the types of baskets used for collection of the fragments after the feeding of the 5,000 (Mt 14:20 and parallels) and the feeding of the 4,000 (Mt 15:37 and parallels). The latter kind was used to lower Paul over the wall (Acts 9:25, but cf. II Cor 11:33 where the word used is one for a large rope basket).

R. V. R.

BASMATH (băs'măth).*See* Bashemath 3.

BASTARD. An illegitimate child or, particularly in the OT, a child sprung from an incestuous union (BDB, *s.v.*), or from a marriage within the prohibited degrees of affinity (Lev 18:6-20; 20:10-21). In the Deuteronomic law, such offspring were to the tenth generation (Deut 23:2) excluded from the covenanted community, "a people holy to the Lord your God" (Deut 14:2; Ex 19:5-6). The Moabites and Ammonites as a result of their incestuous origin (Gen 19:30-38) suffered the same blemish and the same exclusion (Deut 23:3; cf. Driver, *Deuteronomy*, ICC, pp. 260 f.). That this applied only to the males of these peoples was generally recognized by rabbinic interpreters. Witness also the acceptability of Boaz's marriage to Ruth the Moabitess. David the king was a third generation descendant of this union (Ruth 4:17).

The same Heb. word translated "bastard" in Zech 9:6 is better rendered "mongrel people" (RSV), that is, the proud Philistine city of Ashdod would as a result of divine judgment suffer the humiliation of being inhabited by a mixed population.

The illegitimate child's second-rate position in the family (e.g., Jud 11:1-3) resulted in lack of parental attention, including the discipline that would normally be exercised toward those in whose future the parent was most concerned. This fact lies behind Heb 12:7-8 where God's discipline of His spiritual children is the mark of their having the full standing of sonship (cf. Prov 3:11-12; Arndt, *s.v.*; MM, *s.v.*).

R. V. R.

BAT. *See* Animals, III.1.

BATH. *See* Weights, Measures, and Coins.

BATHE, BATHING. There is no distinction in terminology between bathing and washing only part of the body. References to the former, apart from ritual ablutions, are very limited: Pharaoh's daughter (Ex 2:5); Bathsheba (II Sam 11:2, RSV); possibly Ruth (3:3). The bathing of Naaman (II Kgs 5:14) and the impotent man at Bethesda (Jn 5:2–7) had therapeutic aspects. The hot climate and dusty roads of Palestine made washing of hands, face, and feet a frequent necessity (Gen 19:2; 24:32; 43:31; II Sam 11:8). Guests were provided water to wash their feet (Gen 18:4; Jud 19:21; Lk 7:44). To do so for them was the responsibility of a servant (I Sam 25:41), hence the significance of Jesus' example in humility (Jn 13:1–10; cf. I Tim 5:10).

Most of the biblical references are related to ritual washings: of offerings (Ex 29:17; Lev 1:9, 13; 8:21; 9:14; *et al.*); of priests (Ex 30:20; Lev 8:6; Num 8:21); of clothing and/or bodies of those ceremonially unclean (Lev 14:9; 15:5–27 *passim;* Num 19:10; *et al.*).

To wash the hands on the occasion of possible or presumed guilt was an assertion of innocence (Deut 21:6–7; Mt 27:24).

It was only after contact with Hellenistic civilization that gymnasia and public baths found a place in Palestine (Jos *Ant.* xix.7.5; I Macc 1:14). The hot springs at Tiberias and Gadara were renowned for their therapeutic powers (Jos *Ant.* xvii.6.5; xviii.2.3).

See Ablution; Unclean.

R. V. R.

BATHSHEBA (băth-shē′bá). The daughter of Eliam (II Sam 11:3) and granddaughter of Ahithophel the Gilonite (II Sam 23:34), the trusted friend and counselor of David who later betrayed him. She was married to Uriah the Hittite, one of the many foreign mercenaries attracted to the court of David. In the absence of Uriah in the Ammonite war, David took Bathsheba as his paramour. The illicit love affair ended with the murder of Uriah and the death of the child born of the adulterous union (II Sam 11 – 12).

David and Bathsheba were then married legally and she became the mother of four sons: Solomon, Shimea, Shobab, and Nathan (I Chr 3:5; Bath-shua is an alternate spelling of Bathsheba). As Solomon's mother, Bathsheba is included in the genealogy of Christ (Mt 1:6).

It was at the insistence of Bathsheba, supported by the prophet Nathan and the priest Zadok, that Solomon was crowned king, preventing the plot of his brother Adonijah to seize the succession to the throne. Bathsheba last appears as the unwitting tool of Adonijah who, in asking for the hand of David's wife Abishag in marriage, laid a claim to the kingdom (I Kgs 1 – 2).

P. C. J.

BATH-SHUA (băth-shū′á). An alternate form of Bathsheba (*q.v.*), mother of Solomon (cf. I Chr 3:5; II Sam 12:24).

BATTERING RAM. *See* Armor.

BATTLE. *See* Warfare.

BATTLE AXE. Used only in Jer 51:20. *See* Armor; Axe; Maul.

BATTLE BOW. *See* Armor.

BATTLEMENT. A row or course of stones with openings on top of walls or fortifications. From these openings stones, arrows, lances were hurled on attacking soldiers (Zeph 1:16; 3:6, RSV).

In Deut 22:8 a battlement or parapet was to enclose the open flat roof of a house, mainly to keep people from falling from it. The flat roof was used for recreation and entertaining guests, since there one could be cooled by the evening breeze.

BAVAI (băv′ī). Son of Henadad who aided in the rebuilding of the wall of Jerusalem (Neh 3:18); perhaps called Binnui in Neh 3:24.

BAY (COLOR). *See* Colors.

BAY (COVE)
1. The bay or cove at the NW corner of the Dead Sea (Josh 15:5; 18:19), formed by the delta of silt at the mouth of the Jordan River.
2. The shallow bay at the S end of the Dead Sea (Josh 15:2), S of el-Lisan, the "tongue" or delta-peninsula extending from the E shore of the sea. The waters of this bay may now cover the ruins of Sodom and Gomorrah.

BAY TREE. *See* Plants.

BAZLITH (băz′lĭth). The ancestor of a family group included among the Nethinim (*q.v.*), members of which returned from Babylonian Exile. The spelling is sometimes Bazluth and Bazloth; the correct rendering is difficult to determine (Ezr 2:52; Neh 7:54).

BAZLUTH (băz′lŭth). Another form of Bazlith (*q.v.*).

BDELLIUM. *See* Minerals: Bdellium; Plants: Bdellium.

BEALIAH (bē-á-lī′á). One of the Benjamites who joined David's outlaw band at Ziklag. He was one of the mighty men who could shoot arrows and sling stones with either the right or the left hand (I Chr 12:2, 5).

BEALOTH (bē′á-lŏth)
1. A town in southern Judah (Josh 15:24), perhaps the same as Baalath-beer (Josh 19:8).
2. A town or locality in Solomon's ninth administrative district (Aloth, KJV) located in the old territory of Asher in the N (I Kgs 4:16, RSV).

BEAM. A word used to translate several Heb. and Gr. terms referring to large timbers in constructing floors and ceilings or roofs of buildings (I Kgs 6:9; 7:2–3; II Kgs 6:2, 5). The word also refers to the large bar on which the warp was wound in the loom, called "the weaver's beam" (Jud 16:14; I Sam 17:7; I Chr 11:23). In I Kgs 6:36; 7:12 reference is made to an architectural feature common in the Near East during the 2nd mil. B.C., the use of a framework of wooden beams to strengthen a wall on a stone foundation against the shock of earthquakes. The term was used by Jesus in a figurative sense in contrast to a mote (*q.v.*) or speck (Mt 7:3).

BEANS. *See* Plants.

BEAR. *See* Animals, II.5.

BEAR (CONSTELLATION). Translated "Arcturus" in Job 9:9; 38:32, but "Bear" in RSV. *See* Astronomy.

BEARD. *See* Hair.

BEAST. *See* Animals.

BEAST (SYMBOLIC). This expression is frequently used in Scripture in a figurative or symbolic sense. It may symbolize especially tyrannical monarchies. The four beasts in Dan 7:3, 17, 23 represent four kingdoms (Babylon, Medo-Persia, Greece, Rome). The fourth beast (Dan 7:7-8, 19-26) is said to have ten horns. Among these ten (symbolic of ten contemporary kings immediately before the coming of the Most High) arises an eleventh ("little horn") who destroys three and dominates the rest.

Christian interpreters generally unite in identifying this "little horn" with the beast "out of the sea" of Rev 13:1 ff. and 17:3 ff. who has "seven heads and ten horns." This is the same as the man of sin or son of perdition of II Thess 2:3-10 (*see* Man of Sin; Antichrist). Identification is based on similarity and doctrinal unity rather than specific scriptural statement.

Most of the features of the fourth beast of Dan 7 are incorporated into John's vision of "the beast," a final personal Antichrist. This beast forms an unholy trinity with a second beast "out of the earth" (Rev 13:11) and the "dragon" (Satan, Rev 13:2) in imitation of and opposition to the Holy Trinity. The first beast apparently even fakes a resurrection (13:3) and performs other false miracles (13:13 ff.). He persecutes the saints (13:7) and gains world power, but is destroyed by Christ at His coming (19:20). *See* Abomination of Desolation; Deceiver.

For a preterist view see H. B. Swete, *The Apocalypse of John. The Apocalypse* by Joseph Seiss provides an elaborate premillennial futurist interpretation. An excellent homiletical treatment is found in *The Apocalypse Today* by Thomas F. Torrance.

"Beast" in Rev 4 translates a Gr. word which should be rendered "living creature" (*q.v.*).

R. D. C.

BEATING. This was a common form of punishment throughout the East. Beating administered with a rod should be distinguished from scourging inflicted with a whip of several lashes, often reenforced with sharp pieces of metal or bone (II Macc 6:30; 7:1; Mt 10:17; Acts 22:25).

Israel's foremen were beaten by Egyptian taskmasters for failure to meet brick production quotas (Ex 5:14, 16). (Cf. Egyptian Eighteenth Dynasty tomb painting where taskmaster says to brickmakers, "The rod is in my hand; be not idle," Alleman and Flack, *Old Testament Commentary*, p. 214.) Such beatings as legal punishment in OT law were administered to the prisoner in a prone position and proportioned to the offense with a 40 stroke maximum. Jewish practice reduced it to "forty stripes save one" to avoid breaking the Deuteronomic law by miscalculation (II Cor 11:24). Beating of a child was essential as a disciplinary measure to save him from worse evil (Prov 23:13-14). An owner might beat his slave, short of immediate death, without penalty (Ex 21:20-21).

Paul and Silas were beaten before being thrown in prison at Philippi (Acts 16:22-23). On the ground that this was an infraction of his rights as a Roman citizen, Paul demanded and received a public apology (Acts 16:37-39); yet

The dungeon at the traditional site of the Palace of Caiaphas showing the place where prisoners were beaten. The prisoner's hands were tied at the two holes over the archway at the left. Courtesy St. Pierre en Gallincante

he was beaten on two other occasions (II Cor 11:25).
See Crime and Punishment; Punishment; Scourge.

R. V. R.

BEATITUDES. *See* Sermon on the Mount.

BEAUTY. The biblical concept of beauty blends two areas: the aesthetic that touches man's experiences of beauty and art, as well as the recognition of the moral, ethical and spiritual aspect of what is divinely and eternally good and righteous. The Bible does not purport to supply answers for a critique into the meaning and value of human experiences in beauty and art; the Gr. thinkers speculated philosophically concerning the aesthetic. As the divinely inspired writers speak of their encounters with the majesty, honor and glory of the one holy God in His being as well as in His work, one cannot help seeing something of the "beauty of holiness" of God and the work of His creation (though marred now) pronounced as "good." Out of this, in a practical way, the Bible recognizes beauty in every area of the human experience.

A number of terms express in a variety of meanings the many facets of beauty. In the OT there is *pā'ar*, "to beautify," "glorify." The nouns *tip'ārâ* and *tip'eret* are "beauty," "finery," "glory" (Isa 44:13; 52:11). The Heb. verb *yāpâ* means "be fair," "be beautiful" (Ezk 16:13), while the noun and adjective *yāpeh* carries the same meaning. The Heb. root *tā'ar* ("mark out," "delineate") emphasizes as a noun *tô'ar*, "fair of form," "handsome form" or "shapely figure" (Est 2:7). *Hādar* (root idea of "to swell") and its derived forms denote "beauty," "majesty," "honor," "splendor" (Ps 8:5; 29:4). *Nā'â* (or, *nāwâ*) emphasizes "to be comely," "beautiful" (Song 1:10). *Ṣābâ*, "to swell" (or, Arabic "to shine"), carries in its derivative *ṣeḏî* the ideas of "beauty," "glory," "ornament" (Ezk 7:20). The same word is the Heb. for the beautiful, graceful gazelle (Song 8:14). The noun *hôd* indicates "glory," "majesty," "honor," "comeliness," "beauty" (Ps 45:3). *Ḥāmad*, "to desire," "to delight" in a good sense ("covet" in an evil sense), expresses the same idea in its derivatives (Ezk 23:6, 23; Hag 2:7). *Nā'ēm*, "to be delightful," indicates through its derivatives "pleasant," "agreeable," "lovely" (II Sam 1:23; Ps 16:11). Other words are, e.g., *tôb*, "handsome," "fair," "goodly," "pleasant," "pleasure"; and *hēn*, "grace" or "beauty" in several instances (Prov 1:9; 3:22; 17:8).

In the NT, there are *asteios*, "elegant," "fair," "comely"; *euprepeia*, "well-looking," "grace," "beauty"; *kalos*, "beautiful"; *timē*, "honor"; and *hōraios*, "prime" or "blooming," thus, "attractive."

Usages of the various terms from concordances indicate wide ranges of descriptions. *Women* are described as beautiful: Rachel was "fair of form" and "beautiful to behold" (Gen 29:17). Certain *men* are described as handsome: David had "beauty of eyes and good appearance" (I Sam 16:12); the ruler of Tyre was "perfect in beauty" which made him proud (Ezk 28:12, 17). Specific *body parts* are mentioned: Ezekiel had "a pleasant voice" (Ezk 33:32); the feet of the messenger of God's news are comely (Isa 52:7; Rom 10:15); the "fair" woman in the Song had beautiful eyes, hair, teeth, lips, etc., described with appropriate similes (Song 4:1 f.). *Garments* are considered as beautiful and attractive: the high priest's garments were for "honor and beauty" (Ex 28:2); Joseph was arrayed in fine linen of an important office (Gen 41:42); and the glorified saints are ornamented in white garments (Rev 3:4–5).

Countries, cities, Jerusalem, temple, etc., are all described as beautiful under various terms and figures; e.g., Zion (Ps 48:2 f.), the temple (Acts 3:2), the crown of Ephraim (Samaria, Isa 28:1–4), Tyre (Ezk 27:3), nature (Mt 6:29), etc. *Art work* of all kinds was the product of the wise-hearted (Ex 35–39), and the aesthetic in architectural designs was recognized and appreciated (I Kgs 6–7; Eccl 2:4–10). In *eschatological* expressions, the Jerusalem of the future is described as a city of brightness and beauty (Isa 62:1–4).

Moving into the *moral, ethical,* and *spiritual* aspects, a strong emphasis is noted: the face of an old man is to be honored (Lev 19:32); the woman who anointed Jesus before His passion did a beautiful work to be remembered as a memorial (Mt 26:10, 13); the sons who are wise in God's wisdom wear a crown of beauty (Prov 4:9); the right kind of speech is likened to art work in apples of gold (Prov 25:11); the commandments of God (or, the Word of God) are to be regarded greater than the best art work (Ps 119:127); the Lord is to be worshiped in the "beauty of holiness" (Ps 96:9), etc. The *Messiah* in the days of His flesh had no comeliness (Isa 53:2), but "in that day" He will be "for beauty and honor" (Isa 4:2).

Therefore, the Bible has distinctive terms describing the God of majesty, who is arrayed in glory and beauty, and deals "in grace and loving-kindness." His activities are a delight to the heart and eye. Thus, within a theocentric context, in a unique presentation, there is seen the proper union of moral and spiritual beauty and the aesthetic. The lines of contact between the human and divine in the appreciation of beauty are, in the end, an emphasis upon the uniqueness of the God of the whole cosmos.

In Zech 11:7, 14 God as the divine shepherd of Israel is depicted as taking two staffs which He calls "Beauty" (*nō'am*) and "Bands" (*ḥōbelîm*), the first representing the Lord's gracious, pleasant covenant relationship with His people, and the second, the brotherly union (RSV) of Judah and Israel. The breaking in half of the staffs represented the annulment of the covenant and the dissolution of the bonds uniting the descendants of Jacob.

L. Go.

BEBAI (bē'bī). A chief of returning exiles from the Captivity (Ezr 2:11; 8:11; 10:28; Neh 7:16; 10:15).

BECHER (bē'kẽr)
1. Second son of Benjamin (Gen 46:21; I Chr 7:6, 8). The other available lists of the sons of Benjamin do not mention Becher (Num 26:38–41; I Chr 8:1–40). There may have been considerable confusion in textual transmission. On the other hand, the Benjamin genealogy in I Chr 8 probably contains lists of Benjamite families and their dwelling places at a particular period (Jacob M. Meyers, *I Chronicles*, Anchor Bible, XII, 59 f.), perhaps in the time of Ezra. Becher is thought to have been omitted in Num 26 because of the small number of his descendants in the early history of the tribe. By David's time the Becher clan could send 20,200 men to war (I Chr 7:2, 9). But after the Exile the clan had once again become insignificant.
2. A son of Ephraim, progenitor of the Bachrites (Num 26:35; Becherites, RSV). This son and clan are not included in the LXX. In I Chr 7:20 there is a "Bered" but no "Becher." BDB considers the former the correct form in Num 26:35 (cf. Gray, *Numbers*, ICC, p. 393). Evidence is inconclusive.

R. V. R.

BECHORATH (bĭ-kôr'ăth). One of Saul's ancestors of the tribe of Benjamin, the father of Zeror (I Sam 9:1).

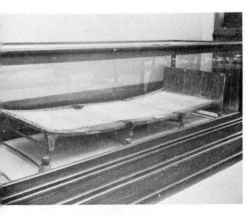

Wooden bedstead covered with thick gold and mesh of linen cord, from the tomb of Tutankhamon. LL

BED. A number of terms are used, often interchangeably, which are rendered "bed" or the equivalents: "pallet," "couch," or "litter." The form depended on the economic status of the individual. The simplest was a place on the dirt floor where a person might recline with his only covering his outer garment (Ex 22:27; Deut 24:13), or a rug or blanket (Jud 4:18; Isa

28:20). Most common was a reed mat or pallet rolled out along the wall at floor level or on an elevated ledge that would serve as a seat during the day. Such a bed could be carried with ease (II Sam 17:28; Lk 5:25; Jn 5:5–8), and could also serve as a litter for transporting the sick (Mk 6:55). Larger homes had separate bedrooms (II Kgs 11:2) often on a second level (I Kgs 17:19); the balustraded rooftop was a common sleeping place.

That beds on legs were rather common would appear from Jesus' use of them as illustrations in teaching the masses (Mk 4:21; Lk 8:16). Among the wealthy they were very elaborate and highly ornamented. Amos charged the luxury-loving Israelites with sleeping on "beds of ivory" (i.e., ivory inlay, Amos 6:4). The harlot of Proverbs enticed to a couch "decked with coverings, colored spreads of Egyptian linen," and "perfumed with myrrh, aloes and cinnamon" (Prov 7:16–17, RSV). Ptolemy of Egypt sent ten beds with silver feet as a gift to Eleazar, high priest at Jerusalem (Jos *Ant.* xii.2). Sennacherib of Assyria listed beds with ivory inlay as a part of Hezekiah's tribute (ANET, p. 288). Xerxes' palace could boast beds of gold and silver (Est 1:6).

R. V. R.

BEDAD (bē'dăd). The father of Hadad, king of Edom (Gen 36:35; I Chr 1:46).

BEDAN (bē'dăn)
1. A judge mentioned only in I Sam 12:11. Bedan is probably a corruption of either Abdon or Barak, as found in LXX. In Jud 12:13–15 Abdon is recorded as one of the regular judges of Israel, while Barak and Deborah's exploits are told in Jud 4 and 5.
2. From the tribe of Manasseh, a son of Ulam (I Chr 7:17).

BEDCHAMBER. Two Heb. expressions are so translated.
1. The Heb. words *ḥădar mishkāb*, enclosure or room for lying down (Ex 8:3; II Sam 4:7; II Kgs 6:12; Eccl 10:20).
2. The Heb. words *ḥădar hammiṭṭôth*, rooms for (storing) beds (II Kgs 11:2; II Chr 22:11). *See* Chamber.

BEDEIAH (bē-dē'yà). A son of Bani who was compelled to give up his foreign wife in the time of Ezra (Ezr 10:35).

BEDSTEAD. *See* Bed.

BEE. *See* Animals, III.2.

BEELIADA (bē-ė-lī'à-dà). A name meaning "Baal knows," given to a son of David born in Jerusalem (I Chr 14:7). According to II Sam 5:16 and I Chr 3:8 perhaps the name was altered to Eliada, "God knows."

BEELZEBUB (bē-ĕl'zē-bŭb). This name designates Satan as the "chief of the devils" (Lk

11:18). The perverted Pharisees accused Jesus of exorcising demons (Lk 11:15, 19), of having (Mk 3:22), or even being, this fallen prince (Mt 10:25; 12:24). Beelzebub (from II Kgs 1:2) is the Syriac and Latin Vulgate (hence KJV) rendering of the Gr. NT's *Beelzeboul* (cf. ASV marg.), probably meaning "lord of the height" (IDB, SBK, TWNT; cf. Eph 2:2, "prince . . . of the air"). Ugaritic myths thus speak of *z-b-l B-'-l,* "exalted Baal." No definite connection can be made between Baalzebub (II Kgs 1:2, "lord of flies") and the NT *Beelzeboul.* Alternative doubtful derivations include *Ba'al zebûl,* "lord of the dwelling" (cf. Mt 10:25; "they have called the *master of the house* Beelzebul"), or "lord of dung" (II Kgs 1:2; the Philistine deity Baalzebul [?] mocked as Baalzebub, "lord of flies"). *See* Baal-zebub under Gods, False; Devil.

J.B.P.

BEER (bē'ĕr)

1. A stopping place on the NE border of Moab as Israel approached Canaan (Num 21:16–18). Here the Lord provided water in a well dug by their princes and remembered in song. This may be the Beer-elim ("well of heroes") mentioned in a Moabite context in Isa 15:8, possibly in Wadi eth-Themed NE of Dibon.

2. The city to which Jotham fled after reciting the parable in which he denounced his brother Abimelech to the men of Shechem (Jud 9:21). Location is uncertain, possibly modern el-Bireh about eight miles N of Beth-shan (Beisan). This is not to be confused with the el-Bireh N of Jerusalem.

BEERA (bē'ê-ra). A descendant of the tribe of Asher, the eleventh son of Zophah (I Chr 7:37).

BEERAH (bē-ê'ra). A prince of the tribe of Reuben who was deported by Tiglath-pileser III in the 8th cen. B.C. (I Chr 5:6).

BEER-ELIM (bĭr-ē'lĭm). A village name meaning "well of Elim" in Moab (Isa 15:8); possibly the same as Beer (*q.v.*; Num 21:16) where the Israelites stopped during their wilderness journey.

BEERI (bē-ē'rī)

1. Name of a Hittite whose daughter Judith was one of Esau's wives (Gen 26:34).

2. Father of the prophet Hosea (Hos 1:1).

BEER-LAHAI-ROI (bĭr'la-hī'roi). The Heb. *be'ēr laḥay ro'î* means "well of the Living One who sees me." This was a fountain of water in the wilderness, between Kadesh and Bered on the road to Shur (the eastern line of Egypt's border fortresses), where the Lord's watch care was revealed to Hagar. Also a place where Isaac dwelt for some time (Gen 25:11, RSV). The site is unknown, possibly about 50 miles SW of Beer-sheba.

Excavations of an underground Chalcolithic settlement at Beer-sheba. HFV

BEEROTH (bē-ē'rŏth). One of the cities of the Gibeonite alliance with whom Joshua made a treaty of peace (Josh 9:16–18). It was assigned to Benjamin (Josh 18:25) and was evidently near the Ephraimite border (II Sam 4:2–3, 5–9). It was the home of Ishbosheth's assassins. One of David's "mighty men," Naharai, armor bearer of Joab, was from Beeroth (II Sam 23:37; I Chr 11:39). Men of Beeroth are listed among the post-Exilic community (Ezr 2:25; Neh 7:29).

Exact location is disputed, several sites having strong advocates: (1) el-Bireh, one mile E of Ramallah; (2) Tell en-Nasbeh, one mile S of el-Bireh (Albright), but more likely to be Mizpah; (3) Nebi Samwil, about two miles SW of Tell en-Nasbeh.

BEEROTHITE (bē-ē'rō-thīt). A native or inhabitant of Beeroth (*q.v.*). These inhabitants succeeded in deceiving Israel and in making a covenant with them (Josh 9:3 ff.). *See also* Berothite.

BEER-SHEBA (bĕr-shē'ba). A city in the territory of Simeon (Josh 19:1–2) and reckoned among "the uttermost cities of the tribe of the children of Judah" (Josh 15:21, 28). It marked the southern extent of the land (cf. Jud 20:1; I Sam 3:20; II Sam 3:10; 17:11). Its name may mean "well of seven" (Gen 21:30 f.), or "well of (the) oath" (Gen 26:31–33).

In this area Hagar wandered with Ishmael (Gen 21:14). Abimelech of Philistia and Abraham entered into a covenant here (Gen 21:27–32). Abraham planted a tamarisk tree at Beer-sheba (Gen 21:33), and returned to the town after the offering of Isaac on Moriah (Gen 22:19). Isaac returned here from his sojourn in the valley of Gerar (Gen 26:17, 23). Jacob fled from Beer-sheba to escape the wrath of Esau (Gen 27:41; 28:10). On his way to Egypt, Jacob offered sacrifices at Beer-sheba (Gen 46:1).

Joel and Abiah, sons of Samuel, judged in Beer-sheba (I Sam 8:2). Elijah stopped at

Beer-sheba on his way to the Mount of God (I Kgs 19:3). The mother of Joash, king of Judah, was from Beer-sheba (II Kgs 12:1; II Chr 24:1). During the divided monarchy the town had a sanctuary that was visited by pilgrims from the northern kingdom (Amos 5:5; 8:14; cf. II Kgs 23:8). The family of Shimei of the tribe of Simeon lived here (I Chr 4:28). Some of the children of Judah lived here after the Captivity (Neh 11:27, 30).

Beer-sheba's importance spiritually is attested by God's appearance here to Hagar (Gen 21:17), to Isaac (Gen 26:23–24), and to Jacob (Gen 46:1–2).

Twenty-eight miles SW of Hebron the 25-acre Tell es-Seba' lies c. two miles to the E of the modern city. Here Israeli archaeologists noticed ruins of a fortress of the kingdom of Judah, measuring approximately 465-by-265 feet, headquarters for controlling the Negeb trade routes (IEJ, XVII [1967], 9, 15). Four seasons of excavation, begun in 1969 and directed by Yohanan Aharoni, revealed Roman, Hellenistic and Israelite structures. The oldest city wall, over 13 feet thick, was built in the late 10th cen. B.C. The well-preserved 8th cen. wall from the reign of Uzziah or Hezekiah was of brick casemate construction atop a steep glacis reminiscent of Hyksos fortifications, testifying to the great pains taken in protecting the city. Inside the walls were two royal store houses, each c. 55 feet long, with a row of pillars for supporting the roof. Astarte figurines, a small incense burner, and a miniature horned altar suggest the spiritual condition of the inhabitants. The city reached its greatest extent in the 7th cen. B.C. It was similar in nature to the fortress at Arad (q.v.). Excavations at a site S of the present city by Jean Perrot uncovered dwellings of the Chalcolithic Age (4000–3100 B.C.), with stone and copper maceheads and fertility cult images.

Beer-sheba is a rapidly growing Israeli city (c. 70,000–75,000 in 1968) which serves as an administrative and distribution center for the Negev. The environs, particularly to the N and the W, are being developed agriculturally, thanks to irrigation largely from the Yarkon River project.

W. C.

BEESHTERAH (bē-ĕsh'tē-rȧ). A Levitical city given to Manasseh; also called Ashtaroth (q.v.; cf. Josh 21:27; I Chr 6:71). Beeshterah is an abbreviation or contraction for Beth-Ashtaroth, "the temple of Ashtoreth."

BEETLE. See Animals, IV.4.

BEEVES. See Animals: Cattle, I.6.

BEGGAR. The Gr. word ptōchos has reference to "crouching" or "cringing," hence to one who was "a beggar." According to MM, Lexicon, it always had a bad sense before biblical usage (in the Gospels).

In the NT, a "beggar" might wait for food scraps (Lk 16:21) or money (Acts 3:2 f.). The word was also associated with Jesus' disciples, who were not allowed to carry a "beggars' bag" but were dependent on people for their food (Mt 10:10, NASB marg.), and with the virtue of "poverty" (e.g., "Blessed are the poor in spirit," Mt 5:3).

BEGINNING. The word "beginning" appears in Gen 1:1 and Jn 1:1 in a specialized, absolute sense. In Gen 1:1 the beginning is not the first of the creative acts, but rather the act by which the whole of creation is initiated. The beginning is thus apart from that which begins, transcending time (cf. "the beginning of his way," Prov 8:22; cf. also Heb 1:10, quoting Ps 102:25). It is the immediate act of God, prior to time and transcending time. Creation is seen as dependent on the God who was in the beginning—before time.

Jn 1:1 states that the logos, "the Word" by which the eternal, invisible God is revealed to man, was with God (the Father) and was in essence Deity "in the beginning." The Father and the Son are thus presented as co-equal and co-eternal. Before time, before the beginning of the creative process by which the universe and mankind came into being, God was—without beginning or end—and the "Word" was present sharing in the divine essence and glory. John contrasts the position of the Word as "in the beginning" with God, yet in historical time entering the world and dwelling among us (Jn 1:1; 1:14).

The Lord Jesus Christ is called the Beginning (archē) by both Paul (Col 1:18) and John (Rev 3:14; 21:6; 22:13; cf. the Alpha and the Omega, Rev 1:8). The Gr. philosophers expressed the First Cause of all things by the same term, archē.

See Creation; Logos; Time.

Bibliography. Gerhard Delling, "Archē, etc.," TDNT, I, 479–484.

C. F. P.

BEGOTTEN. See Only Begotten.

BEGUILE. See Guile.

BEHEMOTH. See Animals: Hippopotamus, II.20.

BEKAH. See Weights, Measures, and Coins.

BEL. See Gods, False.

BELA, BELAH (bē'lȧ)
1. Another name for Zoar (q.v.), one of the five cities of the plain with Sodom and Gomorrah (Gen 14:2, 8).
2. A descendant of Esau who is listed as the first king of Edom (Gen 36:32–33; I Chr 1:43–44). From the name of his father, Beor, the same name as the father of Balaam, some

have thought he may have been a Chaldean rather than an Edomite.

3. The eldest son of Benjamin (Gen 46:21). From him were descended the Belaites, one of the main family groups of Benjamin in the time of Moses (Num 26:38, 40; I Chr 7:6–7; 8:1, 3).

4. The son of Azaz of the tribe of Reuben who dwelt in Gilead (I Chr 5:8).

BELAITE (bē′lā-īt). A descendant of Bela (Num 26:38).

BELIAL (bē′lĭ-ĕl). The literal meaning of the OT Heb. word *belĭya'al* is "useless," "without worth." It is usually employed as a term descriptive of a person; e.g., "a son of Belial" or "a man of Belial." An approximate meaning is our colloquial expression "a good-for-nothing." But the contexts of most passages suggest definite forms of evil, not just the absence of good. The evil men of Gibeah who abused the Levite's concubine in Jud 19:22 f. are called "sons of Belial." When Hannah prayed for a son in the temple, moving her lips but making no sound, Eli the priest, concluding she was drunk, thought her to be "a daughter of Belial" (I Sam 1:16). In Prov 6:12 the term is equated with the Heb. *'āwen* which often means "iniquity." In Ps 41:8, "a thing of Belial" (Heb.) is an evil disease, while in II Sam 22:5 and Ps 18:4 "the floods of Belial" are equated with "the waves of death."

E. B. S.

BELIEVE. The verb form is related to faith, meaning "to have confidence in," "to trust," "to accept as true and reliable." In the NT it often has the force of "obey"; e.g., "believe the gospel" (Mk 1:15; I Thess 2:13) and "obey the gospel" (Rom 10:16; II Thess 1:8; I Pet 4:17; cf. Rom 1:5).

"Believe" is used to translate the Heb. *'āman,* "to build up or support," "to render firm or faithful," "to trust," "to stand still"; and the Gr. *pisteuō,* "to have faith or trust," "put trust in," "commit"; or more rarely *peithomai,* passive, "to assent, rely," "have confidence in," "be persuaded."

When used with God or Christ as its object, to believe means three things: (1) to assent to the truth of what He says or makes known; (2) to receive and trust Him personally; and (3) to commit oneself to Him in obedience. "Believe" is often used with the preposition "in" or "on"; e.g., "Believe on the Lord Jesus Christ, and thou shalt be saved" (Acts 16:31), to stress elements of trust and commitment. Believing must not be intellectualized and considered only in terms of assent to truth. Truth about God is necessary ("He that cometh to God must believe that he is, and that he is a rewarder of them that diligently seek him," Heb 11:6), but it is not sufficient ("Thou believest that there is one God; thou doest well: the devils also believe, and tremble," Jas 2:19, and are still demons!).

In the religious sense, believing depends upon divine revelation, and is always related to that revelation in the personal and written Word. Believing is thus the human response to the initiative God has taken in His redemptive acts, which are made known to men through the written and preached Word: "For whosoever shall call upon the name of the Lord shall be saved. How then shall they call on him in whom they have not believed? and how shall they believe in him of whom they have not heard? and how shall they hear without a preacher? and how shall they preach, except they be sent? . . . So then faith cometh by hearing, and hearing by the word of God" (Rom 10:13–15, 17). In the high priestly prayer Jesus said, "Neither pray I for these alone, but for them also which shall believe on me *through their word*" (Jn 17:20).

Since faith is response to grace, it involves no element of merit. We are not, strictly speaking, saved *by* faith; rather it is *through* faith: "By grace are ye saved through faith; and that not of yourselves: it is the gift of God: not of works, lest any man should boast" (Eph 2:8–9).

See also Faith.

W. T. P.

BELIEVERS. A term (from Gr. *pisteuō,* "to trust," "to rely upon") applied to Christian converts (Acts 5:14; I Tim 4:12). It is thought by B. B. Warfield that "believer" was the first name given to Christians ("The Biblical Doctrine of Faith," *Biblical Doctrines*). Certainly the great stress in the teachings of Christ is that men are to believe in Him (Jn 3:16, 38; 5:24; 10:26–30; cf. Rom 10:9–10; I Jn 5:1; Heb 11:6). The Philippian jailer asked what he must do to be saved and was told, "Believe on the Lord Jesus Christ, and thou shalt be saved, and thy house" (Acts 16:31). In Romans and Galatians Paul stresses that Abraham was justified by faith, that is, by believing God, and that this is the only way in which man can be saved (Rom 3:28; Gal 2:16, 21).

Believers are those who have exercised saving faith by taking Christ as their own personal Saviour on the authority of the Word of God, the Bible, and thus have obtained a position of sonship to God. They are spoken of as "in Christ" (Eph 1:3; I Cor 1:2; Rom 8:1). Their position in Christ is sealed in the Holy Spirit, in whom they are baptized unto the death, burial and resurrection of Christ (Eph 1:13; I Cor 12:13; Rom 6:3; Gal 3:27). This position is the basis of all the Christian's spiritual possessions. Because of his sonship, he is obligated to live in accordance with his position and with the character of his heavenly Father (Eph 4:1; Mt 5:48; Rom 6:11).

R. A. K.

BELL. Two different Heb. words are translated "bell."

1. Heb. *pa'ămôn,* lit., "striker." A bell of

gold which, alternating with pomegranates of blue, purple, and scarlet fabric, encircled the bottom of the high priest's blue linen robe (Ex 28:33 f.; 39:25 f.). Ben Sirach stated the purpose thus: "to send forth a sound as he went, to make a sound that might be heard in the temple, for a memorial to the children of his people" (Sir 45:9). That is, the sound of the bells reminded the worshiper of the effective mediatorial ministry of the priest in his behalf before God. Ex 28:35 (RSV) states: "Its sound shall be heard when he goes into the holy place before the Lord, and when he comes out, lest he die." The sound of the bells indicated to the worshiper that his mediatorial representative was properly robed to minister acceptably in his behalf in the Divine Presence. That these bells were a relic of a primitive fear of evil spirits that might otherwise assemble about the doors of the sanctuary can hardly be proved (cf. Driver, *Exodus, Cambridge Bible*, p. 308). Bells were not used as a call to worship before the Christian era.

2. Heb. *mᵉṣillâ*, lit., "a tinkler." A bell was used as an ornament on the harness of horses (Zech 14:20). When inscribed "Holy to the Lord," they became symbols of the total integration of life within the all-pervasive divine holiness in the Messianic Age. Since a cognate of this Heb. word meant "cymbals" (I Chr 13:8; Ezr 3:10, *et al.*), some have supposed these bells to be more like bangles which made a tinkling sound from striking together when the horses moved. However, Assyrian excavations have illustrated the use of clapper type bells as ornaments on the harness of war horses.

R. V. R.

BELLOWS. Although the word *mappuaḥ*, "bellows," occurs only in Jer 6:29, there are allusions to the use of bellows in Isa 54:16 and Ezk 22:21. Since wood and charcoal burn easily and may be simply fanned, bellows were used in forges and furnaces for smelting and refining purposes. Pictures of bellows may be seen in the tomb of Senusert II (*c.* 1892 B.C.). They were made of two leather bags secured and fitted on a frame, from each of which a large reed pipe extended to carry the air to the fire. They were worked by the operator's foot pressing alternately upon the two skins till they were deflated, and then pulling up the skins by means of a string in each hand. Two pairs of bellows were used for one forge, one on either side.

BELLY. The words translated in Scripture as "belly" are from various roots signifying "soft," "hollow," "round," that describe the physical features of the abdominal region. The term is used quite generally to refer to the outer belly (Song 5:14), womb (Ps 22:10), stomach (Ps 17:14), and the lower abdomen in general.

The term is also widely used in a figurative sense. Because of its connection with food, it sometimes stands for carnal, worldly satisfactions (Phil 3:19). Because it designates the in-

ner anatomy, it is used in Heb. thought as a figure of the inner self, of the intellectual and emotional life (Jn 7:38; Job 20:20).

BELOMANCY. A method of divination by arrows, a number of which were marked in certain ways, then mixed and drawn at random. References in the OT are in Hos 4:12 and Ezk 21:21. This practice was condemned by the prophet Hosea. *See* Magic.

BELOVED DISCIPLE.*See* John the Apostle.

BELSHAZZAR (bĕl-shăz'ár).The ruler in Babylon who was killed when the city was captured in October, 539 B.C. His name (Babylonian *Bel-shar-uṣur*) means "May Bel protect the king." The LXX and Theodotion in his Gr. version called him Baltasar. Although he is mentioned in Dan 5:2, 11, 13, 18 as having Nebuchadnezzar as his father, he was really the son of a later king called Nabonidus (Akkad. *Nabu-na'id*). Yet there is a likelihood that Belshazzar's mother was the daughter of Nebuchadnezzar (*q.v.*), making him the grandson of the great Chaldean king. At any rate, the use of "father" here can signify simply a predecessor, just as in ancient usage the term "son" often referred to a successor in the same office whether or not there was a blood relationship (e.g., "son" in the nomenclature "Jehu, son of Omri" in the Assyrian inscriptions, which must mean successor).

Critical scholarship had long questioned the statements in Dan 5 regarding the kingship of Belshazzar, for it is certain that Nabonidus remained alive until after the fall of Babylon in 539 B.C. Various clay tablets from Babylonia, however, have revealed that Belshazzar shared the throne as coregent or king with his father. From the site of Ur came a tablet with the text of two dreams for which the man involved studies the stars in regard to a favorable interpretation "for my lord Nabonidus, king of Babylon, as well as to a favorable interpretation for my lord Belshazzar, the crown prince" (ANET, p. 309, n. 5). Also there exist two legal documents dated to the twelfth and thirteenth years of Nabonidus that include oaths sworn by the life of Nabonidus, the king, and of Belshazzar, the crown prince, a unique type of oath in cuneiform literature.

A tablet in the series known as the Babylonian Chronicle states that Nabonidus (556/555-539 B.C.) stayed in Tema from the seventh through the eleventh years of his reign, while the crown prince, his officials, and his army were in Akkad (i.e., Babylonia), and that during those years the festival of the new year was omitted (ANET, p. 306). The so-called "Verse Account of Nabonidus" complains that the king, when his third year was about to begin, "entrusted the 'Camp' to his oldest son, the firstborn, the troops everywhere in the country he ordered under his command. He let everything go, entrusted the kingship to him and, himself, he started out for a long journey," invading Arabia, capturing Tema (*q.v.*), rebuilding the town, and making his residence there (ANET, p. 313). A Harran inscription gives ten years for the exile of Nabonidus. Just why he chose to live in Tema for so long a time is not known, but it may be conjectured that he needed to be near this important outpost to keep down the Arab tribes that threatened his commercially lucrative caravan route that passed through Tema, or that in favoring Sin, the chief god of Ur and of Harran, his home town, he found himself at odds with the hierarchy and formalized worship of Marduk, the city-god of Babylon.

Therefore Daniel is not unhistorical in portraying Belshazzar as the reigning king in Babylon. Nabonidus did eventually return to Babylonia, and was present in the land when Cyrus' army attacked. He had brought idol-gods from other cities to Babylon, perhaps for safekeeping, but was in Opis at the time. Nearby Sippar was seized without battle, and Nabonidus fled. After Cyrus took Babylon, Nabonidus returned there and was arrested, all according to the Nabonidus section of the Babylonian Chronicle (ANET, p. 306).

Other Babylonian inscriptions give details of Belshazzar's administration and of his gifts to sanctuaries in Babylon and to the temples in Erech and Sippar, up to the fourteenth year of his father's reign. The scriptural record, however, emphasizes his blasphemous feast during which he used the sacred vessels brought by Nebuchadnezzar to Babylon from the conquest of Jerusalem.

Bibliography. Raymond P. Dougherty, *Nabonidus and Belshazzar,* Yale Oriental Series, XV, New Haven: Yale Univ. Press, 1929. FLAP. ANET. H. H. Rowley, *Darius the Mede and the Four World Empires in the Book of Daniel,* Cardiff: Univ. of Wales Press, 1959. E. J. Young, *The Prophecy of Daniel,* Grand Rapids: Eerdmans, 1949.

F. E. Y. and J. R.

BELTESHAZZAR (běl-tě-shăz'ĕr). The name given by the prince of the Babylonian eunuchs to Daniel (Dan 1:7). *See* Daniel.

BEN

1. Ben is the Heb. word for son. Usually it referred to the male child. However, it was used also as a term of kindliness or endearment even when no blood relationship existed. In I Sam 3:6, 16, Eli calls Samuel his son. It was frequently used as a prefix in proper names; e.g., Ben-oni, "son of my sorrow" (Gen 35:18); Benjamin, "son of the right hand" (Gen 35:18); Ben-ammi, "son of my people" (Gen 19:38).

On occasion it was used descriptively when followed by a word indicating a characteristic. "Strong man" in I Sam 14:52 is literally, "son of strength." "Sons of Belial" (Jud 19:22) were worthless, base fellows or scoundrels.

The term may also designate membership in a guild or class, as one who had learned the trade from his father or by apprenticeship. The "sons of Mahol" (I Kgs 4:31) were members of a musical guild.

2. A Levite (I Chr 15:18), in KJV included in the second rank of Levites, but probably in error. The name is omitted in LXX, and does not occur in the similar list of v. 20.

R. B. D.

BENAIAH (bē-nā'yả)

1. A Levite, the son of Jehoiada of Kabzeel (II Sam 23:20) from southern Judah (Josh 15:21). Jehoiada was probably the leader of the priests who joined with the army at Hebron to place David on the throne of all Israel (I Chr 12:23, 27). Benaiah began his career as the commander of a division of 24,000 soldiers in the third month on a monthly basis during David's reign (I Chr 27:5). He was listed in the second rank among the heroes of David's great men (II Sam 23:20–23; I Chr 11:22–25). His feats of prowess included the killing of a lion that strayed into the Judean hills, the slaying of two lionlike (mighty) men of Moab, and the disarming and slaying of an Egyptian giant. He served as commander of David's chosen troops, the Cherethites and the Pelethites (II Sam 8:18). In the rebellion of Absalom (II Sam 15:18; 20:23), and in the attempt of Adonijah to seize the throne (I Kgs 1:8), Benaiah remained loyal to David. Along with Nathan and Zadok, Benaiah espoused the cause of Solomon and assisted in Solomon's coronation at Gihon, just outside Jerusalem (I Kgs 1:38–40). As chief of the bodyguard of the king, he executed Adonijah (I Kgs 2:25), Joab (I Kgs 2:34), and Shimei (I Kgs 2:46) on the orders of Solomon. During Solomon's reign, Benaiah replaced Joab as commander-in-chief of the army.

2. A Pirathonite, one of David's heroes of the second rank (II Sam 23:30; I Chr 11:31) who commanded the army in the eleventh month (I Chr 27:14).

3. A prince of the families of Simeon who was among those who took Gedor from the Amalekites for pastureland (I Chr 4:36, 39–41).

4. A Levite who played a musical instrument before the ark when David brought it to Jerusalem (I Chr 15:18, 20; 16:5).

5. One of the priests appointed to blow the trumpets before the ark when David brought it to Jerusalem (I Chr 15:24; 16:6).

6. A Levite, descendant of Asaph, the son of Jeiel and grandfather of Jahaziel (II Chr 20:14).

7. A Levite in the time of Hezekiah appointed to be one of the overseers of the temple offerings (II Chr 31:13).

8–11. Four men who put away their foreign wives in the days of Ezra and Nehemiah (Ezr 10:25, 30, 35, 43).

12. The father of Pelatiah, a prince in Israel (Ezk 11:1).

F. E. Y.

BEN-AMMI (bĕn-ăm'ī), Son of Lot's younger daughter, from whom sprang the Ammonite tribe (Gen 19:38). This son was born soon after the destruction of Sodom. The account of his birth, as well as that of Moab, was commonly regarded as an expression of Israel's intense hatred and contempt toward these two nations.

BENCH. In the prophet's lamentations over Tyre in Ezk 27:6, he says: "They have made thy benches of ivory inlaid in boxwood, from the isles of Kittim" (ASV). The word benches here evidently stands for the benches of the boat whose mast (v. 5) and oars (v. 6) have just been described in the vivid figures of speech in which the city itself is pictured as a merchant ship. Since the Heb. word *qeresh* in the plural denotes boards in the tabernacle (Ex 26:15–29) but here is used in the singular, the more recent versions and lexicons have suggested "deck" or "prow" as the meaning.

BENE-BERAK (bĕn'ē-bĕr'ăk). A city in the territory of Dan (Josh 19:45), represented by the modern village of Ibn Ibrak, about four miles SE of Jaffa.

BENEDICTION. The invocation of blessing, and the expression in prayer for happiness and well-being. Technically, benediction is the act of a minister in pronouncing blessing upon others in the name and in the stead of the divine Lord. Thus benediction may be distinguished from prayer for blessing in which a minister voices the desire of his own heart and of the people for God's blessing. In the narrower sense, the Aaronic benediction in the OT (Num 6:24–26) and the apostolic benediction in the NT (II Cor 13:14) are true benedictions. Eph 3:20–21; Heb 13:20–21; and Jude 24–25 are often used as benedictions in a broader sense of the term, but are more properly prayers for the blessing of the Lord upon the people.

Benediction is implied in the "blessing" of patriarchal times; e.g., Melchizedek (Gen 14:19–20; Heb 7:6), Isaac, and Jacob (Heb 11:20–21). The Aaronic benediction was pronounced by the priest with uplifted hands after the morning and evening sacrifices, the people responding with "amen" (cf. Lev 9:22; Lk 1:10, 21–22). Levites (II Chr 30:27) and kings (II Sam 6:18; I Kgs 8:55) in OT times also pronounced benedictions. Benediction is expressed as Jesus blessed the children (Mk 10:16), and His disciples (Lk 24:50).

Protestants reject the Roman Catholic view that the value of the benediction increases with the hierarchical rank of the functionary pronouncing it. Catholic dogma claims objective worth for the benediction by authorized officials. Protestants recognize the subjective and spiritual value of the benediction as received in faith by its subjects.

W. T. P.

BENE-JAAKAN (bĕn-ē-jā'á-kăn). Described as "Beeroth of the children of Jaakan" (Deut 10:6), the place is called Bene-jaakan in the list of stations (Num 33:31–32). From Gen 36:27 (ASV marg.) and I Chr 1:42 the Bene-jaakan seem to be descendants of Seir, the Horite. The western border of Seir or Edom near Mount Hor is the probable situation of the wells of this clan.

BENE-KEDEM (bĕn-ē-kē'dĕm; "children of the East"). From references such as Gen 29:1; Job 1:3; Jud 6:3, 33, it seems that the term Bene-kedem refers to the peoples of the Arabian deserts, and primarily to the tribes of Ishmael and Keturah. Some of these seem to have spoken a dialect which was understood by the Israelites (Jud 7:11–15).

BENEVOLENCE, DUE. The KJV of I Cor 7:3 reads, "Let the husband render unto the wife due benevolence," but ASV and most other versions read simply "her due" (Gr. *opheilēn*), what she has the right to expect (Jerusalem Bible), what he owes her. It is a direction dealing with "the duty of cohabitation" (Alford).

BEN-HADAD (bĕn-hā'dăd). Contemporary with the rise of the state of Israel under David and Solomon, a dynasty of forceful kings built up the powerful rival kingdom of Syria N and E of Israel, with its capital at Damascus. Until both nations were finally swept away by Assyria, there was continual warfare between them.

1. Ben-hadad I, the son of Tabrimmon (I Kgs 15:18), was one of the strongest and most aggressive of the Syrian kings. About 890 B.C., opportunity was given him to advance greatly his kingdom and authority. Attacked by Baasha of Israel, who fortified Ramah just five miles N of Jerusalem, Asa, king of Judah, sent a great treasure to Ben-hadad, begging him to attack Israel in the N. Asa was saved, but Syria was placed in a position of great advantage, threatening both Heb. kingdoms (I Kgs 15).

In the days of Ahab of Israel, Ben-hadad invaded the country with a great host and besieged Samaria. Whether this was the same Ben-hadad has been questioned, but the inscribed stela of Ben-hadad found in northern Syria in 1940 seems to settle the fact that it was (W. F. Albright, "A Votive Stele Erected by Ben-hadad I of Damascus to the God Melcarth," BASOR #87 [1942], 23–29). The siege was broken and the Syrians driven out. A year later on the plains of Aphek Ahab again defeated the Syrian king (I Kgs 20). Instead of exercising the rights of victor, Ahab entered into an alliance with his defeated enemy. The strange action, unexplained in Scripture, is made clear from Assyrian records. The rising great empire of Assyria threatened both kingdoms, and the alliance was for mutual protection. The Monolith inscription of Shalmaneser III describes the decisive battle of Karkar in 853 B.C. when Assyria was halted, at least for a time, by a coalition, prominent among whom were Ahab and Ben-hadad.

Ben-hadad I seems to have been the Syrian king who was warring against Israel in II Kgs 6:8 – 7:16 (see 6:24), and not the ineffective Ben-hadad II, who did not begin to reign until c. 800 B.C. at the very end of Elisha's life. The king of Israel in Samaria at the time (6:9, 23, 26; 7:12) was probably the wicked Jehoram (q.v.). After a long reign Ben-hadad was assassinated in 841 B.C. by the hands of a trusted general, Hazael (II Kgs 8:7 – 15).

2. Ben-hadad II, a weak king, son of Hazael, is mentioned in the Aramaic inscription of Zakir, king of Hamath, under the name of Bar-hadad. He was defeated by Jehoash of Israel, as prophesied by both Amos (Amos 1:4) and Elisha (II Kgs 13), losing all the territory gained by his father.

P. C. J.

BEN-HAIL (bĕn-hāl'). One of the princes of Judah who was sent by Jehoshaphat to teach in the cities of Judah (II Chr 17:7).

BEN-HANAN (bĕn-hā'năn). A son of Shimon, registered with the tribe of Judah (I Chr 4:20).

BENINU (bē-nī'nū). A Levite who with Nehemiah and others sealed a covenant with the Lord (Neh 10:13).

BENJAMIN (bĕn'jȧ-mĭn)

1. A son of Bilhan, the head of a family of warriors (I Chr 7:10).

2. An Israelite, the son of Harim, who divorced his foreign wife after the Exile (Ezr 10:32). He assisted in the rebuilding of the walls of Jerusalem (Neh 3:23) and the Benjamin gate in the temple area (Neh 12:34), the scene of one of Jeremiah's imprisonments (Jer 20:2).

3. The youngest of the children of Jacob and the only one of the 13 born in Palestine. He was born somewhere between Bethel and Ephrath (Bethlehem), his mother Rachel dying in the act of giving birth. She called him Ben-oni ("son of my sorrow"). Jacob, fearing the consequences of such a name, renamed him Benjamin ("son of the right hand," or "son of the South," i.e., southerner, Gen 35:16–18). The Samaritan Codex gives his name as Benjamin, "son of days," i.e., "son of old age" (cf. Gen 44:20). Philo, the Testament of the Twelve Patriarchs, and Ibn Ezra preferred this reading.

After Joseph was sold to the Ishmaelites, Benjamin became the favorite of his father Jacob, as well as of his brothers. Since he is called a lad in Gen 44:20, 22, his sons and grandsons were most likely born after Jacob brought the entire clan to Egypt during the famine (Gen 46:21; see Leupold, *Genesis*, p. 1115). There is little besides the events in Gen

24 – 44 concerning Benjamin himself; later references concern the tribe of Benjamin.

Tribe of Benjamin. In the census list in Num 1:36–37, Benjamin is next to the smallest tribe with 35,400 members; and in the census list in Num 26:41, the tribe is in sixth position with 45,600 members. In the wilderness journeyings, Benjamin was on the W side of the tabernacle along with Ephraim and Manasseh (Num 2:18–24).

In the allotting of the land by Joshua and the elders, Benjamin drew the hill country S of Ephraim and N of Judah. It was in the form of a parallelogram, 26 miles long by 12 miles wide. The eastern boundary was the Jordan; the western one was Kirjath-jearim (the later western boundary included Ono and Lod). The northern boundary was Bethel, and the southern, the Valley of Hinnom. The boundary between Benjamin and Judah ran next to the city of the Jebusites (Jerusalem). Therefore the temple was built adjacent to the old tribal border. This may have played some part in Benjamin's choice to stand with Judah when the northern tribes seceded.

The territory of Benjamin was, for the most part, hilly. The names of Geba, Gibeah, Gibeon all suggest hills, and Ramah, Ramathaim and Mizpeh indicate heights. The other significant cities in Benjamin were Bethel, the site sacred to Jacob's theophany, and Kirjath-jearim, the place where the ark rested for 20 years. The land was open to attack from the Moabites on the E and from the Philistines on the W. The fortress cities in the land of Benjamin made life hard for the courageous Benjamites. They are characterized by the epithet "fierceness." They were the only tribe to have pursued archery to any purpose, and their skill with the bow (I Sam 20:20, 36; II Sam 1:22) and the sling (Jud 20:16) was celebrated.

The second deliverer in the period of the judges was the Benjamite Ehud (Jud 3:15). This tribe joined with Deborah and Barak in the struggle against Jabin and Sisera (Jud 5:14). It gave to Israel her first king, Saul, the gentleman farmer from Gibeah (I Sam 9:1–2). The tribe was nearly exterminated when it protected miscreants who attacked the concubine of the Levite sojourner at Gibeah (Jud 19–20). The tribe of Benjamin stayed with Judah in the drive to restore Israel to the dynasty of Solomon (I Kgs 12:21; II Chr 11:1). Rehoboam strengthened Judah by fortifying and garrisoning several cities in Benjamin and dispersing members of his own family throughout the tribe in order to secure his position.

The history of Benjamin finally merges with that of Judah. Men of Benjamin returned with the Judeans under Zerubbabel (Ezr 2; Neh 7) and took back their old towns (Neh 11:31–35).

Extrabiblical references. In 1933 the city of Mari on the middle Euphrates yielded a store of clay tablets that dated back to the 18th cen. B.C. Among these tablets were some that told of the Banu Yamina (sons of the South). The French excavator of Mari, A. Parrot, attempted to tie these references to those of Benjamin in the OT and concluded that the tribe of Benjamin was of Mesopotamian origin. However, in the same tablets were references to the "sons of the North." These designations may have been to distinguish two tribes in Mesopotamia rather than to refer to the Benjamites of the OT.

F. E. Y.

BENJAMIN GATE. See Jerusalem.

BENJAMITE (běn'jȧ-mīt). One belonging to the tribe of Benjamin (e.g., Jud 3:15; I Sam 9:1–2; II Sam 20:1; Phil 3:5). See Benjamin.

BENO (bē'nō). A descendant of Merari through Jaaziah (I Chr 24:26–27), if Beno is a proper name, as it seems in v. 27.

BEN-ONI (běn-ō'nī). The name, which means "son of my sorrow," that was given by the dying Rachel to her new-born son. But the name was changed by his father Jacob to Benjamin (Gen 35:18). See Benjamin.

BEN-ZOHETH (běn-zō'hěth). A son of Ishi of the house of Judah (I Chr 4:20).

BEON (bē'ŏn). An old Amorite city on the frontiers of Moab, known fully as Beth-baal-meon (q.v.; Josh 13:17); more briefly Baal-meon (q.v.; Num 32:38) or Beth-meon (Jer 48:23), as well as Beon (Num 32:3). It was assigned to the Reubenites and rebuilt by them (Num 32:2–5). The city was held by Mesha, king of Moab, and was in the possession of the same people in the 6th cen. B.C. (Ezk 25:9; Jer 48:23). In Jerome's day it was still a considerable town, about nine and three-quarter miles from Heshbon. The ruins, now called Main, lie in the N Moabite territory, four miles SW of Medeba.

BEOR (bē'ôr)

1. The father of Bela, king of Edom (Gen 36:32).

2. The father of the seer Balaam (Num 22:5). He is called Bosor in II Pet 2:15.

BERA (bêr'ȧ) King of Sodom (Gen 14:2), who in the battle of Siddim was subdued by Chedorlaomer.

BERACHAH (bĕr'ȧ-kä)

1. A Benjamite who joined David at Ziklag (I Chr 12:3).

2. A valley where an army invading Judah in the days of Jehoshaphat was destroyed (II Chr 20:26). The name still lingers as Bereikut, a ruin about four miles NW of Tekoa, six miles SW of Bethlehem, and a little E of the road from Bethlehem to Hebron.

BERACHIAH. See Berechiah.

A street scene in Berea. Courtesy E. W. Saunders

BERAIAH (bē-rā'yȧ). One of the sons of Shimhi, listed as a member of the tribe of Benjamin (I Chr 8:21).

BEREA (bē-rē'ȧ). A city of southern Macedonia in the district of Emathia (Ptolemy's *Geography*, iii.12). Strabo says distinctly that the "city Berea lies in the foothills of Mount Bermium" (Strabo *Fragments*, VII.26; see the Loeb edition, Vol. 3, 351). The region about Berea was watered by the river Haliacmon. A few miles to the SE this river left the Olympian range and flowed into the Thermaic Gulf. Berea was c. 50 miles SW of Thessalonica, the chief metropolis of Macedonia at this time; 30 miles S of Pella, the birthplace of Alexander the Great; and c. 20 miles W of the Thermaic Gulf. Leake (*Travels in Northern Greece*, III, 290 ff.) describes the town as beautifully situated and states that its modern name is Verria. In NT times it was evidently a prosperous city with a Jewish colony.

Paul and Silas found their way to Berea when pressure forced them out of Thessalonica (Acts 17:10). They had hoped to return to Thessalonica, but since this was not permitted (I Thess 2:18), they made their way to Athens, where Timothy later met them. Apparently Paul and Silas had a rather brief stay in Berea, but it cannot be exactly determined how many days they were there. Ramsay, however, conjectures that Paul and Silas stayed in Berea some months (*St. Paul the Traveller and the Roman Citizen*, p. 234). The Jews in Berea were more openminded than those in Thessalonica, listening eagerly to Paul's message and studying the Scriptures to see if what he said was really true (Acts 17:11).

Finally, Paul and Silas were forced to leave Berea due to rabble-rousers who stirred up the people against these apostles (Acts 17:13–14). Acts 20:4 mentions that Sopater, one of Paul's close friends and fellow travelers, was from Berea. According to the Apostolic Constitutions, VII, 46, Onesimus was the first bishop of the church of Berea.

E. J. V.

BERECHIAH (bĕr'ē-kī'à)

1. A descendant of Jehoiakim and Jehoiachin born in captivity. He was a brother or son of the leader of the return from Exile, Zerubbabel (I Chr 3:20).

2. A Levite of the family of Gershom, the father of the celebrated musician of Israel, Asaph. Berechiah was appointed as one of two "doorkeepers of the ark" when it was brought up from Obed-edom to Jerusalem (I Chr 6:39, RSV; 15:17, 23).

3. A Levite, son of Asa, who returned from the Exile to settle near Jerusalem (I Chr 9:16).

4. A prince of Ephraim in the time of Pekah. When Oded the prophet warned the Israelites against taking into bondage the host of captives they had secured in their war against Judah, Berechiah and three others led the way in persuading their brethren to restore the captives (II Chr 28:12).

5. The father of Meshullam, a family head who assisted in building the wall of Jerusalem in Nehemiah's day (Neh 3:4, 30; 6:18).

6. The son of Iddo and father of Zechariah the prophet (Zech 1:1, 7).

P. C. J.

BERED (bĕr'ĕd)

1. A place in the wilderness of Shur, to the W of Kadesh, and not far from Beer-lahai-roi (Gen 16:7, 14).

2. The son of Shuthelah of the house of Ephraim (I Chr 7:20), supposed by some to be the same as Becher (Num 26:35). *See* Becher 2.

BERI (bĕr'ī). An Asherite, son of Zophah, of the family of Heber (I Chr 7:36).

BERIAH (bē-rī'à)

1. The son of Asher and ancestor of the family of Beriites (*q.v.*; Gen 46:17; Num 26:44–45; I Chr 7:30–31).

2. One of the sons of Ephraim. He was born after some of his brothers had been slain by the Gathites, and was called Beriah "because it went evil with his house" (I Chr 7:23).

3. A Benjamite, the son of Elpaal, who with his brothers settled in the area of Aijalon (I Chr 8:13, 16).

4. A Levite of the family of Gershom in the time of David. Because they had few sons, he and his brother Jeush were counted as one house in the ordering of the Levitical courses (I Chr 23:10–11).

BERIITES (bē-rī'īts). The descendants of Beriah, a son of Asher, and father of Heber and Malchiel, and head of the family of the Beriites (Num 26:44).

BERITES (bĕr'īts). The descendants of Beri, a warrior of Asher (I Chr 7:36). They are mentioned only once in Scripture (II Sam 20:14) as followers of Sheba, whose abortive rebellion against David followed closely the defeat of

Absalom (II Sam 20). They followed him to the city of Abel of Beth-maachah where he was killed. After the death of their leader, the Berites were permitted to depart in peace.

The RSV translates the word "Bichrites" (*see* Bichri) following the lead of both the LXX and Vulgate. Sheba was the son of Bichri of the tribe of Benjamin, and the RSV editors have conjectured that it was his own kinsmen who followed him, not the obscure northern Berites.

BERITH. *See* Gods, False: Baal-berith.

BERNICE (bĕr-nēs'). The name occurs three times in the NT designating the oldest daughter of Herod Agrippa I (Jos *Ant.* xviii.5.4). She was born in A.D. 28 and was early married to Marcus, the son of Alexander (Jos *Ant.* xix.5.1). After his death, Bernice was given by Agrippa to his brother Herod, king of Chalcis. To this union two sons were born (Jos *Ant.* xviii.5.4). When Herod of Chalcis died in A.D. 48, she "lived a widow a long while" and was assumed to have been involved in incestuous relations with her brother Agrippa II (Jos *Ant.* xx.7.3) with whom she appears in the book of Acts (25:13, 23; 26:30). "She persuaded Polemo, who was king of Cilicia, to be circumcised and to marry her" (Jos *Ant.* xx.7.3), but soon left him and returned to her brother. Eventually she came into contact with the Roman rulers Vespasian and Titus, to both of whom she became a mistress (Tacitus, *Hist.* ii.81; Suetonius, *Titus,* 7). *See* Herod; Agrippa I; Agrippa II.

J. McR.

BERODACH-BALADAN. *See* Merodach-Baladan.

BEROTHAH (bē-rō'thà), **BEROTHAI** (bē-rō'thī). A town situated between Hamath and Damascus (Ezk 47:16). It is probably identical with Berothai, a city which was once subject to Hadadezer, king of Zobah, but was captured by David and yielded him large booty in brass (II Sam 8:8; in I Chr 18:8 called Chun, *q.v.*). Identified with Ain Berdai or Bereitan, S of Baalbek.

BEROTHITE (bē-rō'thīt). Probably a man of Beeroth (*q.v.*). The name is associated with Naharai, Joab's armor bearer (I Chr 11:39).

BERYL. *See* Jewels.

BESAI (bē'zī). One of the Nethinim (*q.v.*) and founder of a family who returned with Zerubbabel to Jerusalem (Ezr 2:49; Neh 7:52).

BESODEIAH (bĕz'ō-dē'yà). Father of Meshullam, who helped to repair the gate of Jerusalem (Neh 3:6).

BESOM (bē'zŏm). This word occurs only once in Scripture: "I will sweep it with the besom of destruction" (Isa 14:23). This refers to what was in store for Babylon. The Heb. word *maṭʾăṭēʾ*, rendered "besom," is close of kin to the verb *ṭēʾṭēʾtî*, rendered "I will sweep." In early English "besom" was synonymous with "broom," and is still so used in some parts of England.

BESOR (bē'zôr). A torrent bed or brook S of Ziklag mentioned in the account of David's pursuit of the Amalekites (I Sam 30:9– 10, 21). Perhaps it is the present Wadi Ghazzeh, which rises near Beer-sheba and empties into the Mediterranean SW of Gaza.

BETAH (bē'tá). A city of Aram-zobah taken by David from the king of Zobah, called Tibhath in I Chr 18:8.

BETEN (bē'tĕn). A village of Asher (Josh 19:25) mentioned between Hali and Achshaph. Eusebius identified it with the village of Beth-beten, about seven and a half miles E of Acre.

BETH (bĕth; "house"). The second letter of the Heb. alphabet. *See* Alphabet. Originally it was a rude representation of a dwelling, whence it derives its name. In compound place names Beth means "place of," "abode of," "temple of," "house of." It came also to be used for the number "two." It became Gr. *beta* and Latin and English *b*.

BETHABARA (bĕth-ăb'á-rá). A place beyond the Jordan at which John baptized (Jn 1:28). The name survives at the ford called Abarah, 12 miles S of the Sea of Galilee and NE of Bethshean. This is the only place where this name occurs in Palestine. The site is as near to Cana as any point on the Jordan, and within a day's journey. The principal Gr. MSS here read "Bethany" (*q.v.*). Others connect Bethabara with the Beth-barah (*q.v.*) of Jud 7:24.

BETH-ANATH (bĕth-ā'năth). An ancient fenced town in Naphtali (Josh 19:38) from which the Canaanites were not expelled (Jud 1:33). Today it is the modern village of Ainatha in the mountains of upper Galilee about 12 miles NW of Safed.

BETH-ANOTH (bĕth-ā'nŏth). A town in the mountains of Judah near Gedor (Josh 15:59). It is the present Beit 'Ainun, a mile and a half SE of Halhul.

BETHANY (bĕth'á-nĭ)
1. The village of Bethany, the home of Lazarus, Mary, and Martha (Jn 11:1), was situated on the E side of the Mount of Olives about two miles E of Jerusalem (Jn 11:18). Jesus visited Bethany on occasion (Mt 21:17; 26:6; Mk 11:1, 11, 12; Jn 11:1; 12:1) and chose a spot near it to be the site of His ascension (Lk 24:50).

Bethany. HFV

2. "Bethany beyond the Jordan" was on the E side of the Jordan River where John baptized (Jn 1:28). There is some evidence that the site might have been called Bethabara ("house of the ford") as well as Bethany (FLAP, p. 301).

BETH-ARABAH (bĕth-ăr'á-bà). One of the six cities in the wilderness of Judah on the NE boundary between Judah and Benjamin (Josh 15:6, 61; 18:22), called simply Arabah in Josh 18:18. It is situated near 'Ain-el-Gharba in the Wadi el-Kelt.

BETH-ARAM (bĕth-ā'răm). In Num 32:36 called Beth-haran (*q.v.*). A town in the E Jordan Valley in the territory of Gad and rebuilt by the Gadites (Josh 13:27). It is identified with Tell Iktanû on the S side of the Wadi er-Rameh (Wadi Hesban), about seven miles NE of the mouth of the Jordan. It is also known as Beth-aramphtha, where Herod had a palace. The place was called Livias by Herod Antipas in honor of the wife of Augustus. Here Herod possibly celebrated his birthday (Mt 14:6– 12).

BETH-ARBEL (bĕth-ăr'bĕl). A place mentioned as having been plundered by Shalman (Hos 10:14). Some have identified Beth-arbel with Arbela of Galilee (Jos *Ant.* xii.11.1; xiv.15.4), modern Irbid in the hills W of the Sea of Galilee. However, it is more likely that Eusebius was correct in identifying it with Irbid in Gilead, which was called Arbel in his time (*Onomasticon* 14:18). This site was occupied from the Bronze Age until the Persian period. The city was probably conquered by Shalmaneser III during one of his campaigns in Syria and Bashan (841 and 838 B.C.).

BETH-AVEN (bĕth ā'vĕn). A town in the territory of Benjamin, near Ai, E of Beth-el (Josh 7:2), W of Michmash (I Sam 13:5; cf. 14:23), and on the border of a wilderness (Josh 18:12). This name, meaning "house of wickedness," was given in contempt to Beth-el by Hosea after it had become a seat of idolatry and corrupt worship (Hos 4:15; 5:8; 10:5).

BETH-AZMAVETH (bĕth-ăz′má-vĕth). A village in the vicinity of Jerusalem, also called Azmaveth (*q.v.*), where 42 of its inhabitants returned from the Babylonian Captivity (Neh 7:28; Ezr 2:24). Some of the singers at the dedication of the restored walls resided on its field (Neh 12:29). Its site is perhaps Hizmeh, midway between Geba and Anathoth.

BETH-BAAL-MEON (bĕth′bāl-mē′ŏn). The town's full name (Josh 13:17), but also written Baal-meon (Num 32:38; I Chr 5:8; Ezk 25:9), Beth-meon (Jer 48:23), and Beon (*q.v.*; Num 32:3). The town was built by the children of Reuben along with Nebo, "their names being changed" (Num 32:38). As Beth-baal-meon it was given by Moses to the tribe of Reuben (Josh 13:15–17). King Mesha named it on the Moabite Stone as a city he fortified. It appears in Jer 48:23 as one of the cities of Moab. Eusebius' *Onomasticon* speaks of it as a large village near the hot springs, i.e., Callirrhoe, in Wadi Zerka Ma'in, nine miles from Heshbon.

BETH-BARAH (bĕth-bâr′à). A place on the Jordan S of the valley of Jezreel. Some suppose it to be the same as Bethabarah (*q.v.*). Owing to its waters, it was a locality difficult for the Midianites to cross (Jud 7:24). This is probably S of Beth-shean in the region N of the mouth of the Wadi Farah.

BETH-BIREI (bĕth-bĭr′ī). A town belonging to Simeon in the Negeb (I Chr 4:31), called Beth-lebaoth (*q.v.*) in Josh 19:6 and Lebaoth (*q.v.*) in Josh 15:32. The site is not identified.

BETH-CAR (beth-kär′). A place, probably a height, to which the Philistines were pursued by the Israelites after the second and decisive battle of Ebenezer (I Sam 7:11). Ain Karim, four and a half miles W of Jerusalem, is a possible site.

BETH-DAGON (bĕth-dā′gŏn)
1. A city in the territory of Judah in the lowlands of the Shephelah (Josh 15:41). It is provisionally identified with Khirbet-Dajun.
2. A town on the border of Asher (Josh 19:27), apparently to the E of Carmel, and is probably Jelamet el-Atiqa, at the foot of Carmel.
Both places were doubtless once seats of Dagon worship.

BETH-DIBLATHAIM (bĕth-dĭb-lá-thā′ĭm). A town on the tableland of Moab once in possession of Israel and mentioned with Dibon and Nebo (Jer 48:22). It is probably the same as Almon-diblathaim (*q.v.*; Num 33:46 f.). Mesha claims to have fortified it along with Medeba and Baal-meon. It has been identified with the double ruin Deleilât esh-Sherqîyeh two and one-half miles NE of Khirbet Libb.

James Kelso excavating a Canaanite worship center at Bethel. HFV

BETHEL (bĕth′ĕl; "house of God")
1. A town in the southern part of Israel, evidently in the vicinity of Ziklag. Probably Bethel, Bethul and Bethuel (*q.v.*) are names by which it was known (Josh 19:4; I Sam 30:27; I Chr 4:30). Its site is not currently identified.
2. A town on the border between Benjamin and Ephraim, about ten miles N of Jerusalem and S of Shiloh (Jud 21:19), near Ai (Gen 12:8).
Originally called Luz (*q.v.*; Gen 28:19; Josh 18:13), it was visited by Abram early in his sojourn in the Promised Land (Gen 12:8). Later he stopped here on his return from Egypt and the Negeb (Gen 13:3). Jacob had his dream here while on his way to Padan-aram (Gen 28:19). Upon Jacob's return from Padan-aram, he built an altar here and called the place El-bethel (*q.v.*; Gen 35:6–7). Deborah, Rebekah's nurse, was buried here (Gen 35:8). The town was assigned by the drawing of lots to Benjamin (Josh 18:22). Afterward, the Ephraimites possessed it (I Chr 7:28). It was a place of worship (Jud 20:18; I Sam 10:3). Samuel judged Israel here as one of the places in his circuit (I Sam 7:16).

Jeroboam I made Bethel one of the two seats of worship for Israel, erecting here one of the golden calves (I Kgs 12:28–29; cf. Jer 48:13). A man of Judah came to Bethel to announce the birth of Josiah (I Kgs 13:2). An old prophet, who proved the undoing of this man of God, lived here (I Kgs 13:11). The contemporary prophets Hosea and Amos both spoke against Bethel (Hos 10:15; also known as Bethaven [*q.v.*], 5:8–9; 10:5, 8; Amos 3:14; 5:5). The king of Assyria established a priest in Bethel (II Kgs 17:27–28). Josiah (cf. I Kgs 13:2) destroyed the altar and high place of Bethel (II Kgs 23:15–16). People of Bethel returned here after the Captivity (Ezr 2:28; Neh 7:32).

Archaeological research was carried on at the supposed site of ancient Bethel (modern Beitîn) by W. F. Albright in 1934 and by James L. Kelso in 1954, in 1956–57, and in 1960. The modern town is built on a large section of the southern part of ancient Bethel, preventing excavation here. It has been ascertained that a street N of Beitîn is built over the N wall of the old city. Pottery from a house adjoining the N wall of the ancient town would indicate that this level was occupied by the Hyksos, *c.* 1700 B.C. No recognized ruins of the holy place erected by Jeroboam I have been discovered. His shrine may have been outside the city walls on the site of Abraham's or Jacob's altar.

In 1957 Kelso discovered an inscribed S Arabian clay stamp seal at Beitîn, almost identical to one found *c.* 1900 by T. Bent at Meshed in the Hadhramaut region of Arabia. The stamp was used to seal the bags or sacks used as containers in the incense trade between Israel and S Arabia *c.* the 9th cen. B.C. (BASOR #151, pp. 9–16; #163, pp. 15–18; #199, pp. 59–65).

There is no evidence of a break in occupation between the early 8th cen. and the 6th cen. (BASOR #56, p. 14). Bethel was destroyed late in the 6th cen. B.C. There are references to the town in Josephus (*Ant.* xiii.1.3; *Wars,* iv.9.9).

More recently David Livingston has argued that Bethel should be located at el-Bireh just E of modern Ramallah and two miles SW of Beitîn. It is dominated by the height Ras et-Tahuneh, where Jeroboam may have built his temple, and lies on the natural crossroads for the whole area ("Location of Biblical Bethel and Ai Reconsidered," WTJ, XXXIII [Nov., 1970], 20–44).

W. C.

BETHELITE (bĕth'ĕl-īt). The term was applied to a man named Hiel (*q.v.*) who was a native of Bethel and in the days of Ahab rebuilt the city of Jericho (I Kgs 16:34).

BETH-EMEK (bĕth-ē'mĕk). A town within the territory of Asher (Josh 19:27). It is probably modern Tell Mimas, about six and a half miles NE of Acre.

Stone cups for watering sheep at the Pool of Bethesda, illustrative of Psalm 23:5. HFV

BETHER (bē'thĕr). Found only in Song 2:17, translated in RSV by the adjective "rugged"; ASV, "craggy." Probably it refers either to a type of difficult terrain over which, however, a mountain deer could move swiftly and safely, or to the city of Bether which is presently identified with Khirbet el-Yehud, just above modern Bittir, about seven miles SW of Jerusalem.

BETHESDA (bē-thĕz'dà). The name of a pool with five porticoes mentioned only in Jn 5:2 where the afflicted came for healing when the waters were troubled. Here Jesus healed the man who had been unable to walk for 38 years. In 1888, N of the temple area in Jerusalem, K. Schick uncovered the outlines of a large double pool, i.e., twin rectangular pools lying N and S, with a rock partition 20 feet thick on which the fifth portico was constructed. The area of the pools measured *c.* 150-by-300 feet.

One of the best ancient MSS of the NT (Codex Sinaiticus), one other later Gr. MS and Eusebius have *Bēthzatha* (the name of the northern extension of Jerusalem according to Josephus—Arndt, p. 139) rather than *Bēthesda.* This name has been included in recent editions of Gr. texts (e.g., Nestle; Aland-Black). The copper scroll from Cave III near Qumran, however, lists 64 different hiding places for the temple treasures, with locations 57–60 in and around "Beth-Eshdatain." Since this Heb. form of the name has a dual ending, it fits in precisely with the archaeological discovery that Bethesda was, in fact, a double pool (Jerry Vardaman, "Bethesda, Pool of," BW, pp. 140 ff.; VBW, V, 142).

J. Mc R.

BETH-EZEL (bĕth-ē'zĕl). Probably a town in the Philistine plain (Mic 1:11). The reference may suggest that no help will be found in a neighbor town, for it has its own "mourning." It is probably Deir el-'Aṣal, two miles E of Tell Beir Mirsim.

BETH-GADER (bĕth-gā'der). An unidentified town in Judah, listed with Bethlehem and Kirjath-jearim. It is associated with Hareph, son of Hur and grandson of Caleb (I Chr 2:51). Hareph was "father" or founder of the city. *See* Geder; Gedor.

BETH-GAMUL (bĕth-gā'mŭl). Town of Moab in the tableland near the Arnon River, marked for divine judgment (Jer 48:23).

BETH-GILGAL (bĕth-gĭl'găl). Probably a town eight miles NE of Jerusalem mentioned by Nehemiah (Neh 12:29) as residence of a group of Levites belonging to the clans of singers.

BETH-HACCEREM (bĕth-hăk-kē'rĕm). A town in Judah, modern Khirbet Salih, near Ramat Rahel, two miles N of Bethlehem. Its name means "settlement of the vineyard." The list of hidden treasure on the Dead Sea Copper Scroll locates Beth-haccerem just before the tomb of Absalom which was in the Valley of the King (II Sam 18:18). A similar identification is made in the *Genesis Apocryphon,* another of the Qumran scrolls (BW, p. 142).

Because of its height, Jeremiah mentions Beth-haccerem as a signal point in a time of invasion (Jer 6:1). Predicting a terrible imminent invasion from the N, *c.* 625 B.C. (Jer 1:13 ff.; 4:6; 6:22; 10:22), Jeremiah calls on Tekoa ("blast"), 11 miles S of Jerusalem, to give a trumpet blast, and on "Vineyard Settlement," a third of the way there, to raise a fire signal on its hill.

Such signals are known in the Euphrates Valley from the Mari letters 11 centuries earlier. In the last days of Judah's kingdom, before Nebuchadnezzar destroyed it, signal telegraph was used by the Jewish army, according to correspondence of 589 B.C. found at Lachish, where the word for "signal" is the same as

Bethlehem. HFV

Jeremiah used (*maś'ēt,* "sign of fire," KJV, properly a "lifting up"; in Jud 20:38, 40 "flame," KJV, or "smoke signal," JerusB).

In post-Exilic times when the walls of Jerusalem were being rebuilt, men from the district of "Vineyard Settlement" repaired the Gate of Ash Heaps (Neh 3:14), just as other groups from N, E and S of the capital labored on other gates.

Bibliography. Yohanan Aharoni, *"Beth-haccherem,"* TAOTS, pp. 171–184.

W. G. B.

BETH-HAGGAN (bĕth-hăg'ăn). Translated "the garden house" in II Kgs 9:27, but probably the name of a town seven miles S of Jezreel toward which Ahaziah fled. This is modern Jenin, also called En-gannim (*q.v.*).

BETH-HARAN (bĕth-hâr'ăn). A fortified town of Gad with folds for sheep (Num 32:36), identical with Beth-aram (*q.v.*).

BETH-HOGLA (bĕth-hŏg'lá). A town near the mouth of the Jordan River mentioned as marking the N border of Judah (Josh 15:6) and the S border of Benjamin (Josh 18:19), about five miles SE of Jericho ('Ain Hajlah).

BETH-HORON (bĕth-hôr'ŏn). The name of twin towns near the old shrine of the Canaanite god Horon, on the road from Jerusalem to the Mediterranean.

Joshua, after a surprise attack to defend the new ally Gibeon against the confederacy formed in alarm by five kings under Adonizedek of Jerusalem, chased the fleeing enemy through the pass of the two Beth-horons some four miles W (Josh 10). More destruction during the rout was done by "great stones from heaven" than by Israel's swords. Joshua even commanded the sun to "be silent," that is, "be motionless," or, as the story continues, it "stood in the middle of the sky." As Joshua stood on the height of the pass, the sun was on Gibeon to the E and the moon on the "Valley of Stags" to the W, which increased the slaughter. This crucial victory assured the conquest of southern Judah. *See* Sun.

Among the tribes the Beth-horons lay near the boundary between Ephraim (Josh 16:3, 5) and Benjamin (18:13–14). These two towns and surroundings were a possession for the Kohathite Levites (Josh 21:22). In the time of Saul parties of Philistine raiders spread from their central camp at Michmash toward Beth-horon (I Sam 13:18).

Solomon's fortifications through his kingdom included the two Beth-horons, upper and lower (I Kgs 9:17; II Chr 8:5). After overrunning the territory of Rehoboam, Egyptian Shishak listed Beth-horon among the 156 places taken, on the sculpture celebrating the victory. The captives appear to be Amorites with fair skin, light hair, blue eyes, and long heads. King Amaziah of

Judah spent 100 talents hiring mercenaries of Israel against Seir. But when he did not use them, they fell upon cities of Judah, including Beth-horon, for slaughter and booty (II Chr 25:13).

Here Judas Maccabaeus won his second victory over Syria (I Macc 3:16, 24). Here, too, in the Roman war against them the rebellious Jews cut in pieces a considerable army under Cestius Gallus in A.D. 66 (Jos *Wars*, ii.19.8–9).

W. G. B.

BETH-JESHIMOTH (bĕth-jĕsh'ĭ-mŏth), **BETH-JESIMOTH** (bĕth-jĕs'ĭ-mŏth). A town three miles E of the mouth of the Jordan River. Mentioned (Num 33:49) as the point from which the camp of Israel stretched five miles N to Abel-shittim; as S end of Jordan Valley (Josh 12:3); and in the allotment of Reuben (Josh 13:20). In an oracle against Moab, Ezekiel (25:9) mentions it as a frontier town of Moab. It is probably Tell el-'Azeimeh.

BETH-LE-APHRAH (bĕth-lē-ȧf'rȧ; "house of dust"). An unknown place name (Mic 1:10, RSV), probably same as Ophrah of Benjamin or of the Philistine plain. There is here a play on words, for Micah declares, "Roll thyself in the dust" as an act of mourning.

BETH-LEBAOTH (bĕth-lē-bā'ŏth). A town in the S of Judah, assigned to the Simeonites (Josh 19:6). It is the same as Lebaoth (*q.v.*) in Josh 15:32 and as Beth-birei (*q.v.*) in I Chr 4:31.

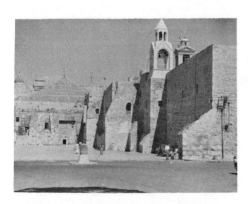

Church of the Nativity, Bethlehem. HFV

BETHLEHEM (bĕth'lĕ-hĕm; "house of bread"). A name used 40 times in the OT and eight times in the NT.

1. A place in Zebulun's territory seven miles NW of Nazareth (Josh 19:15). It is suggested by some that Ibzan, one of the judges, came from this Bethlehem in the N (Jud 12:8).

2. A village on a Judean hill about five miles

Interior of Church of the Nativity, Bethlehem.
Courtesy Semerdjian, Jerusalem

S of Jerusalem, center of a fruitful area also called Ephrath or Ephratah ("cornland"; cf. Ruth 4:11; I Chr 2:5; 4:4). In this territory, though not right at Bethlehem (Zelzah, I Sam 10:2, near Ramah, Jer 31:15), Rachel died and Jacob buried her (Gen 35:16 – 20; 48:7).

In one of the Amarna letters (# 290), dating a little after 1400 B.C., the prince of Jerusalem tells that *Bit-Lahmi*, a town in his domain, has gone over to the side of the 'Apiru (ANET, p. 489). In the time of the judges Bethlehem was the home of a self-seeking Levite (Jud 17:7–9) and a run-away concubine (19:1–2, 18). From this city Ruth's in-laws fled to Moab in a time of famine (Ruth 1:1–2). In Bethlehem her great-grandson David was born (I Sam 17:12) and there Samuel anointed David king (I Sam 16:13). Three of his mighty men broke through the Philistine garrison to draw David a drink from the well near Bethlehem's gate (II Sam 23:13–17; I Chr 11:15–19). His relative Asahek was buried here (II Sam 2:32). Rehoboam fortified the town (II Chr 11:6). After the Exile some "sons of Bethlehem" returned (Ezr 2:21; Neh 7:26).

Prediction had been made that "great David's greater Son" would be born here (Mic 5:2), as the scribes of Herod's day knew (Mt 2:4–6), and their people had heard from the Scripture (Jn 7:42). Indeed, here Joseph and Mary came to be enrolled in the empire's census (Lk 2:4–5), and to the shepherds the angel said that the Saviour, Christ the Lord, was born "in the city of David" (Lk 2:11). Emperor Constantine's Christian mother Helena built the original church in A.D. 325 on the site of the traditional cave of the virgin and her Son.

See City of David.

W. G. B.

BETHLEHEMITE (bĕth'lĕ-hĕm-īt). An inhabitant or native of Bethlehem (*q.v.*), a town of Judah five miles S of Jerusalem. It identifies Jesse, father of David (I Sam 16:1, 18; 17:58), and Elhanan (II Sam 21:19) who slew a brother of the giant Goliath.

BETH-MAACHAH (bĕth-mā'ȧ-kȧ). A city far to the N near source of the Jordan River. So named in II Sam 20:14 – 15, but also named Abel-beth-maacah (*q.v.*) in I Kgs 15:20 and II Kgs 15:29, as well as Abel (*q.v.*) in II Sam 20:14, 18. In II Samuel it is the city in which Joab besieged rebelling Sheba. In I Kings it is included among cities smitten by Ben-hadad of Damascus. In II Kings it is mentioned as a city in Naphtali captured by Tiglath-pileser, king of Assyria, about 732 B.C.

BETH-MARCABOTH (bĕth-mär'kȧ-bŏth). A city of Simeon in extreme S of Judah (Josh 19:5; I Chr 4:31). It is conjectured that this might be one of the stations Solomon built for his chariots and horsemen (I Kgs 9:19; 10:26).

BETH-MEON (bĕth-mē'ŏn). A city of Moab included by Jeremiah with others in the coming destruction of the nation (Jer 48:23). Same as Beth-baal-meon, Baal-meon and Beon (*q.v.*).

BETH-NIMRAH (bĕth-nĭm'rȧ). A city in Transjordan opposite Jericho originally assigned to Gad (Num 32:36; Josh 13:27), a fenced city with folds for sheep. It was also named Nimrah (*q.v.*; Num 32:3) and Nimrim (*q.v.*; Isa 15:6), and was included by the prophet among the cities of Moab whose ample springs would dry up and whose territory would produce no grass. The site has been identified with Tell el-Bleibil, six miles E of the Jordan in the Wadi Sha'îb.

BETH-PALET (bĕth-pā'lĕt). Listed by Joshua (15:27) among "the uttermost cities of . . . Judah" (v. 21), near the border of Edom S of Beer-sheba. In Neh 11:26 (here called Beth-phelet) it is mentioned as a village of Judah. The site is uncertain; Aharoni suggests Tell es-Saqati (*The Land of the Bible*, Westminster, 1967, p. 356). Tell el-Far'ah, 18 miles S of Gaza, with which Flinders Petrie identified the town, is now identified with Sharuhen. Beth-pelet (RSV spelling) must have been a settlement of the Pelethites (*q.v.*).

BETH-PAZZEZ (bĕth-păz'ĕz). A town in the land allotted to Issachar (Josh 19:21) in the N.

BETH-PEOR (bĕth-pē'ôr). A town *c.* ten miles E of Jordan at its mouth. When Moses delivered the messages of Deuteronomy, the Israelites were encamped in the valley "over against Beth-peor" (Deut 3:29; 4:46). Moses was buried in this valley by the Lord (Deut 34:6) but the exact spot was unknown to man. Beth-peor is included in the allotment of land made by Moses to the tribe of Reuben (Josh 13:20). It perhaps can be identified with Baal-peor (*q.v.*)

and with Khirbet esh-Sheik Jāyil, six miles W of Heshbon at the edge of the Moabite plateau. *See also* Peor.

BETHPHAGE (bĕth'fȧ-jē). A town on the E slope or ridge of the Mount of Olives on or near the Jericho-Jerusalem road. Mentioned by Synoptic Gospels (Mt 21:1; Mk 11:1; Lk 19:29) in connection with Jesus' journey with His disciples from Bethany to Jerusalem on the day of the triumphal entry. Tentatively it has been located at the present Kefr et-Tur, NW of Bethany, on the summit of the Mount of Olives (Emil G. Kraeling, *Bible Atlas*, Chicago: Rand McNally, 1956, pp. 396 – 398). Here Jesus' disciples secured the young donkey for Him to ride.

BETH-PHELET. *See* Beth-palet.

BETH-RAPHA (bĕth-rā'fȧ). A name occurring in the genealogy of Judah (I Chr 4:12), possibly referring to a clan which dwelt in a place by the same name.

BETH-REHOB (bĕth-rē'hŏb). A town, probably identical with Rehob (*q.v.*; Num 13:21), in the N of Canaan, near which the Danites built Laish-Dan (Jud 18:28). It is probably the same as the Rehob (No. 87) in Pharaoh Thutmose III's list of captured towns. In II Sam 10:6, 8 Rehob designates a city-state and district occupied by the Aramaeans, who supplied soldiers to assist the Ammonites against David. The site, though uncertain, possibly lay in Coele-Syria between the Lebanon ranges N of Dan. (See M. F. Unger, *Israel and the Aramaeans of Damascus*, p. 42).

BETHSAIDA (bĕth-sā'ĭ-dȧ). This name is Aramaic for "house of hunting," in Bible instances, "of fishing"; so in English it could be called "fishtown." Two cities by this name are mentioned seven or eight times in all four Gospels.

1. Bethsaida-Julias, on the E bank of the upper Jordan about a mile N of the Lake of Galilee, was named by Herod Philip, tetrarch of Ituraea and Trachonitis (Lk 3:1), after the daughter of Caesar Augustus – Julia's Bethsaida (Jos *Ant.* xviii.2.1). It is probably to be identified with modern et-Tell. Near here, in "a desert place," i.e., a sparsely inhabited region, our Lord in a tremendous nature miracle fed the 5,000 on "an extensive plain" (Lk 9:10 ff.). In another retirement from Galilee E across the lake, on His way to the region of the same Philip's Caesarea near Mount Hermon, Jesus stopped at this Bethsaida to restore the sight of a blind man in two unique stages (Mk 8:22 ff.).

2. The home of Philip, Andrew and Peter (Jn 1:44) was NW of the lake in the fertile plain of Gennesaret (Mk 6:45, 53) near Capernaum (Jn 6:17) in the province of Galilee (Jn 12:21). Its name could refer to the fishing quarter of that important town on the lake, except that Jesus twice denounced Bethsaida separately from Capernaum for its blind unbelief (Mt

Mound of Bethshan, Roman theater in foreground. IIS

11:21, 23; Lk 10:13, 15). If there was another city of the same name on the W shore of the lake, probably all the biblical references refer to it rather than some to Bethsaida-Julias.

Some further confusion arises in connection with the reference to the pool of Bethesda in Jn 5:2. In certain ancient Gr. MSS (B, W, P[66]), "Bethsaida" is read instead in this passage. It is probably a corruption for either Bethesda (KJV) or Bethzatha (RSV).

W. G. B.

BETH-SHAN (bĕth'shăn), **BETH-SHEAN** (bĕth-shē'ăn). The first spelling occurs in I and II Samuel; the latter in Joshua, Judges, I Kings and I Chronicles.

Beth-shan was the most important fortress guarding any Jordan River crossing. It was located at the E end of the vale of Jezreel (modern Tell el-Husn), whose road carried the heavy traffic from Egypt and the Mediterranean coast to Damascus. Identification is confirmed by two Egyptian texts which mention the name. Although the site of Beth-shan was occupied as early as 4000 B.C., the city's major historical period occurred during Egyptian suzerainty when, for approximately three centuries during the Late Bronze Age, it served as a key fortress

in that nation's Asian empire. The last Pharaoh to occupy it was Rameses III during whose reign the Philistines entered Palestine in force.

Joshua was unable to capture Beth-shan, for his troops were infantry only and unable to cope with the iron chariots of its defenders (Josh 17:16). In hopes that the larger tribe might later take the city, Joshua allotted Beth-shan to Manasseh in the distribution of the land, although geographically it was in the territory of Issachar (Josh 17:11); but Manasseh also failed (Jud 1:27). During the Amarna period men of Gath-carmel acted as a garrison for the Egyptians. Pharaoh Seti I c. 1310 B.C. placed two stelae in Beth-shan, one of which mentions that the Habiru were attacking a nearby town (ANET, pp. 253 ff.). An Egyptian father and son dedicated a stele to the Sumerian god Mekal in a temple found in Level IX (14th cen. B.C.). Many cult objects were found in this and the next four levels that show Beth-shan was a center of snake worship.

The Philistines later occupied the city, evidenced by anthropoid clay coffins showing the Philistine style headdress. Saul's last battle was fought at nearby Mount Gilboa. His armor was placed as a votive offering to Ashtaroth, the greatest of the Canaanite goddesses. Her temple (I Sam 31:10) is probably the north-

227

ernmost of the two sanctuaries found by the excavators in Level V. Saul's body and those of his sons were displayed on the walls of Beth-shan, from which they were rescued at night by the valiant men of Jabesh-gilead as a token of respect for his earlier rescue of that city (I Sam 31:12). David added Beth-shan to his empire, and Solomon incorporated it into the new fiscal district whose capital was Megiddo. Shortly after Solomon's death, Pharaoh Shishak plundered Beth-shan, according to his inscription at Karnak.

The next historical reference to the city is in intertestamental times when the city is also called Scythopolis. In Maccabaean times, John Hyrcanus captured the city but spared its population of mixed Jews and Gentiles. Pompey made it a free city, and it remained such throughout Roman times.

As one of the Decapolis (q.v.), Beth-shan gained considerable prosperity. This fact is attested to by remains of the magnificent theater and other structures of the period. Major excavations at the site were conducted by the University of Pennsylvania 1921–23, 1925–28, 1930–33, revealing 24 strata of settlement back as far as the 4th mil. B.C.

Bibliography. G. M. Fitzgerald, "Beth-shean," TAOTS, pp. 185–196. Henry O. Thompson, "Tell el-Husn—Biblical Beth-shan," BA, XXX (1967), 109–135. J. A. Thompson, "Beth-shan," BW, pp. 143 ff.

J. L. K

BETH-SHEMESH (bĕth-shĕm'ĭsh). The name Beth-shemesh means "house of the sun (god)," reflecting the fact that the pre-Israelite Canaanites had shrines to many deities in the land of Canaan. Many of these names continued into Israelite times. At least four places named Beth-shemesh are mentioned in the OT:

1. A town in the valley of Sorek on the N border of Judah (Josh 15:10) 15 miles W of Jerusalem and 15 miles NE of Tell ed-Duweir (Lachish). Located in the Shephelah on the site of Tell er-Rumeileh, Beth-shemesh was a frontier post near the border between Judah and the Philistines. It was doubtless also called Ir-shemesh (q.v.; Josh 19:41), which was jointly allotted to the tribe of Dan. At the division of the land of Canaan, Beth-shemesh was assigned to the Levites (Josh 21:16) as one of 48 Levitical cities (Josh 21:41–42).

After the Philistine victory at Aphek (I Sam 4) the ark was taken to Ashdod, and then to Ekron, Philistine cities where God's judgment brought a plague on Israel's enemies (I Sam 5). The Philistines then sent the ark to Beth-shemesh (I Sam 6:10—7:2), where it remained until it was taken to Kirjath-jearim, in the hills W of Jerusalem. Beth-shemesh was in Solomon's second administrative district (I Kgs 4:9).

It was the scene of a battle between Jehoash

of Israel and Amaziah of Judah in which Amaziah was defeated and taken prisoner (II Kgs 14:11–14; II Chr 25:20). As a border city it was frequently threatened by the Philistines (cf. II Chr 28:18).

Beth-shemesh was excavated by Duncan Mackenzie from 1911 to 1913 for the Palestine Exploration Fund, and by C. S. Fisher and Elihu Grant under the sponsorship of Haverford (Pa.) College from 1928 to 1931. Archaeological evidence indicates that the first settlement (Stratum VI) was during the Early Bronze Age, from the 23rd to the 21st cen. B.C. It apparently was taken and settled by the Hyksos (Stratum V) and later destroyed, perhaps by Amenhotep I of Egypt or his successor Thutmose I, c. 1525 B.C. Beth-shemesh flourished during the 15th to the 13th cen. B.C. as is evidenced by its houses, lime-plastered cisterns, granaries, and heavy fortifications (Stratum IV). A smelting furnace of this period used imported copper ore. Two interesting inscriptions were found in this level: an ostracon with proto-Sinaitic characters, and a 14th cen. tablet in the alphabetic cuneiform used at Ugarit. From the period of the judges (Stratum III) bronze work was discovered, with some iron weapons and jewelry of probable Philistine origin. Much of the pottery was also of Philistine design. Stratum III was destroyed by fire, probably in the wars between Israel and the Philistines in the time of Saul or David.

To the period of David (c. 1000 B.C., Stratum IIa) belong granaries and a palace or citadel on an earth-filled platform, or Millo, such as was built in Jerusalem. Protection (presumably from the Philistines) was afforded by a casemate wall. Evidence of oil and wine production comes from grape and olive presses.

Occupation ended during the 10th cen., perhaps at the time of Shishak's invasion (925 B.C.). Rehoboam did not rebuild Beth-shemesh, but instead he strengthened Zorah on the hill above. Beth-shemesh was reoccupied during the 9th cen., but it was a poorer city (Stratum IIb). During the time of Ahaz, the Philistines took the city (II Chr 28:18) but it was retaken, probably by Josiah. A jar handle seal bears the inscription, "Belonging to Eliakim, steward of Yaukin" (i.e., Jehoiachin, king of Judah, 597 B.C.). The armies of Nebuchadnezzar destroyed Beth-shemesh (Stratum IIc) along with other cities of Judah (588–587 B.C.).

Following the return from captivity the Jews did not regain Beth-shemesh, which was possibly in Philistine territory (cf. the mention of Ashdodites in Neh 4:7). The site was not reoccupied until the Hellenistic period (Stratum I). The last archaeological remains are of a 4th or 5th cen. A.D. monastery.

Bibliography. J. A. Emerton, "Beth-shemesh," TAOTS, pp. 197–206. Elihu Grant, *Beth Shemesh,* Progress of the Haverford Archaeological Expedition, 1929; *Ain Shems Excavations,* I-III, Haverford, 1931–34. Elihu

Grant and G. E. Wright, *Ain Shems Excavations,* IV–V, Haverford, 1939.

2. A city in Issachar near the Jordan River (Josh 19:22). It may be el-'Abeidiyeh guarding a ford over the Jordan *c.* two miles S of the Sea of Galilee.

3. A Canaanite city in Naphtali (Josh 19:38) which Naphtali was not able to occupy (Jud 1:33). Possibly the same as 2, or the village of Haris, SSE of Tyre.

4. The Heb. rendering of On in Egypt. The temple of the sun-god Re was at On, which the Greeks called Heliopolis. The city of On is five miles NE of modern Cairo. Jeremiah prophesied that the Lord would break the images of Beth-shemesh and burn with fire the houses of the gods of Egypt (Jer 43:13).

C. F. P.

BETH-SHEMITE (bĕth-shēm'īt). An inhabitant of Beth-shemesh (*q.v.*) on the western edge of Judah, specifically, Joshua the Beth-shemite (I Sam 6:14, 18), in whose field the cart bearing the ark of the covenant came to rest.

BETH-SHITTAH (bĕth-shĭt'à). A town between the valley of Jezreel and the Jordan on the route followed by the Midianites in flight before Gideon (Jud 7:22).

BETH-TAPPUAH (bĕth-tăp'ū-à). A town in the mountains of Judah (Josh 15:53), probably the modern village of Taffuh, about three and a half miles NW of Hebron. Another town was known simply as Tappuah (*q.v.*).

BETHUEL (bē-thū'ĕl)
1. The youngest child of Nahor, Abraham's brother, and Milcah (Gen 22:20, 22). He became father-in-law to Isaac (Gen 22:23; 24:50). This close relationship stemmed from Abraham's desire that his only son by Sarah should not marry a Canaanite but an Aramaean (Gen 25:20) from "home" (Gen 24:3–4). Isaac's desire, in turn, for his son Jacob was like Abraham's for him, a wife from the same family (Gen 28:2).
2. The name Bethuel is attached to a town in the territory of Simeon (I Chr 4:30), spelled Bethul in Josh 19:4. *See* Bethel 1.

BETHUL (bĕth'ŭl). A city in Simeon (Josh 19:4), the same as Bethuel (*q.v.*).

BETH-ZUR (bĕth-zûr'). A fortified town in the hill country of Judah (Josh 15:58). It is identified with Khirbet et-Tubeiqah, four and a half miles N of Hebron, settled by Calebites (I Chr 2:45) and fortified by Rehoboam (II Chr 11:7).

Resettled after the Babylonian Exile in the time of Nehemiah (Neh 3:16), Beth-zur was the most important strong point on the border facing Idumea. Near here Judas Maccabaeus defeated a Syrian army in 165 B.C., and then fortified the city (I Macc 4:29, 61). Beth-zur was later starved into surrender by the Syrians (I Macc 6:31, 49–51). It was finally recovered *c.* 143 B.C. by Judas' brother Simon (I Macc 11:65 f.).

Excavations on the site by Albright and Sellers in 1931 and by Sellers in 1957 revealed huge defense walls of the Hyksos period and occupation during the 12th–11th cen., the 8th and 7th cen., and the Hellenistic age. They showed that *c.* 110 B.C. the town was abandoned, suggesting that after John Hyrcanus conquered Idumea, the Jewish garrison at Beth-zur was no longer needed there and was withdrawn.

S. C.

BETONIM (bĕt'ō-nĭm). A town in the territory of Gad, E of the Jordan, given by Moses (Josh 13:26). It is identified with Khirbet Batneh near es-Salt.

BETRAY. The underlying Gr. words mean "to deliver over." This is precisely what Judas did in betraying Christ (Mt 26:14–16, 47–50; Mk 14:10–11, 43–46; Lk 22:3–6, 47–48; Jn 18:3–5), which accounts for most occurrences of the word in the KJV. The hideousness of betrayal is made more poignant by the Lord's quotation from Ps 41:9: He "which did eat of my bread hath lifted up his heel against me." The circumstances of Judas' treachery and the awful results for himself have forever stamped him as a "devil" (Jn 6:70) and the "son of perdition" (Jn 17:12).

Judas' motivation for his act of treachery has been traced to ambition, covetousness, and jealousy. Baffled ambition turned him to treachery when he did not find in Christ the worldly advantages he desired. Covetousness and jealousy were manifest in his reaction to Jesus' anointing and the subsequent rebuke he received from the Lord when he hypocritically lamented the "waste" (Jn 12:1–8). Frank Morison in *Who Moved the Stone?* (pp. 30–39) shows how Judas was in a most favorable position for carrying out his resolve to betray Christ. *See* Judas.

W. B. W.

BETROTHAL. *See* Marriage.

BEULAH (bū'là). A name prophetically applied to the land of Palestine after it should be repeopled by an Israel restored to God's favor after the Captivity (Isa 62:4). As Israel's name is changed from "forsaken," to "my delight is in her" (Hephzibah), so the once desolate land shall be called "married" (Beulah), for it will again be populated.

BEWITCH. This word, found in Acts 8:9, properly means "astonish" or "amaze," and is so translated in the ASV and RSV. The Gr. word *baskainō* in Gal 3:1 means "bewitch" or "deceive." Judaizers had charmed the Galatian Christians to a point where they had ceased to reason.

BEYOND JORDAN, BEYOND THE RIVER.
The deep rift of the Jordan River divides Palestine E and W. The Heb. term "beyond the Jordan" is used numerous times of the land E (Deut 1:1; 3:8, RSV) and also a number of times of the land W of the Jordan (Deut 3:20, 25; 11:30). The phrase thus acquires a technical meaning something like "Jordania." In the KJV the same Heb. phrase is sometimes rendered "this side Jordan" (Deut 1:1; 3:8, etc.). While some have maintained that the term indicates the geographical proximity of the author, it is a reasonable supposition that the phrase had become a standard designation for the territory E of Jordan regardless of where the writer happened to be (SOTI, p. 244). In the instances where the term refers to the W area, it should be understood literally rather than as the technical term.

In the NT the Gr. term "beyond the Jordan" is translated numerous times as the territory E of the Jordan known as Perea (e.g., Mt 4:25) and only once as the region W of the Jordan (Mt 19:1)

The term "beyond the river" is the Persian designation for the land W of the Euphrates, and in the reign of Darius I included Palestine-Syria within its bounds (cf. Ezr 4:10–20; 5:3; Neh 2:7, 9; 3:7). This is the same Heb. expression for the KJV "on this side the river."

W. G. B. and A. F. J.

BEZAI (bē′zī)

1. One whose descendants, numbering 323, returned from Exile with Zerubbabel (Ezr 2:17; Neh 7:23).

2. The name of a chief or clan that, with Nehemiah, sealed the covenant with God (Neh 10:18).

BEZALEEL (bĕ-zăl′ē-ĕl)

1. The son of Uri, son of Hur, of the tribe of Judah. This gifted artist, endowed by the Spirit of God with knowledge and ability in all sorts of craftsmanship, was called by God to be the chief artisan in the construction of the tabernacle in the wilderness. With him was associated another gifted man, Aholiab (q.v.) of the tribe of Dan (Ex 31:1–6). These two not only had the responsibility of designing the various parts of the tabernacle, according to the divinely revealed plan, but of teaching other Israelites the skills necessary for the actual building (Ex 35:30–35). Bezaleel himself was not only chief artist but chief artisan, and as the ultimate authority he is said to have made all the various parts of the tabernacle (cf. Ex 37:1 ff.). Skills necessary for fabricating structures similar to the tabernacle, for working the precious metals and for cutting and mounting the jewels were practiced and highly valued during the 2nd mil. B.C. in Syria, Palestine and Egypt (R. K. Harrison, IOT, pp. 403 ff.). See Jewel; Occupations: Metalworker, Woodworker.

2. A priest of the family of Pahath-moab in the days of Ezra. One who had married a foreign wife (Ezr 10:30).

P. C. J.

BEZEK (bē′zĕk)

1. The residence of Adoni-bezek ("lord of Bezek") in Judah, near Gezer, inhabited by Canaanites and Perizzites, taken by Judah and Simeon (Jud 1:4–5). See Adoni-bezek.

2. The place where Saul marshaled his army before going to the relief of Jabesh-gilead, probably Khirbet Ibziq, in Ephraim, about 13 miles NNE of Shechem (I Sam 11:8).

BEZER (bē′zĕr)

1. A city of refuge designated by Moses and also Joshua in the territory of Reuben E of the mouth of Jordan in the tableland (Deut 4:43; Josh 20:8). It was assigned by lot as also a place of residence for the family of Merari of the tribe of Levi (Josh 21:36; I Chr 6:63, 78).

2. A son of Zophah of the family of Asher (I Chr 7:37).

BIBLE. That collection of books of the OT made by the Jews, and of the Gospels, Acts, epistles, and book of Revelation made by the early Christian church, which the church recognizes as the divinely inspired record of God's revelation of Himself and of His will for mankind.

Names. The Gr. *biblion*, sing.; *biblia*, pl., are diminutive of *biblos*, which means any kind of written document, though originally one written on papyrus (*biblos*). The English word "Bible" comes from the Latin *biblia*, a fem. sing., meaning "book." The singular in Latin witnesses that the 66 books—39 in the OT and 27 in the NT—reveal such a unity of thought and purpose that together they form one book.

The first usage in the early church of the term *ta biblia*, "the books," for the Bible in the above sense is reported to be found in II Clement XIV:2 (c. A.D. 150), "The books and the apostles declare that the church existed from the beginning." Daniel, however, had already spoken of the Scriptures, particularly the prophecies existent in his time, as "the books" (Heb. *sepārîm*, Dan 9:2). Several synonymous expressions referring to the OT are found in the NT, such as "the writings" or "the scriptures" (*hai graphai; ta grammata*). The briefest is simply "the scriptures" (Mt 21:42—called "this scripture" in Mk 12:10, the parallel passage; Mt 22:29; Lk 24:32; Jn 5:39); "the scripture" (Acts 8:32; Gal 3:22); "the holy scriptures" (Rom 1:2; II Tim 3:15, "the sacred writings," RSV); "the other scriptures" (II Pet 3:16).

Several other terms descriptive of the OT canon are found in the NT, such as "the law" (Mt 5:18; Lk 16:17; Jn 12:34); "Moses and the prophets" (Lk 16:29; 24:27); "the law and the prophets" (Mt 22:40; Lk 16:16); or possibly even more fully, "the law of Moses... the prophets... and... the psalms" (Lk 24:44).

Languages. The OT was written in Heb., except for a few passages in Aramaic found in Ezr 4:8–6:18; 7:12-26; Jer 10:11; Dan 2:4–7:28. The original Heb. text contained no vowels. These were added by the Jewish Masoretic scholars in the 6th cen. A.D. and later, following ancient traditional pronunciation.

The Heb. text was translated into Gr. between 250 and 150 B.C. This earliest version of the OT is called the Septuagint or the LXX (the "seventy," since it was purported to be the work of 70 translators). Using the Dead Sea Scrolls as a basis, R. Laird Harris dates the LXX at about 200 B.C. (*Inspiration and Canonicity of the Bible,* p. 99). In numerous cases the NT quotes from the LXX rather than from the Heb. text.

The discovery of Gr. papyrus fragments in the Egyptian desert written in Koine, that is, in the common or vernacular Gr. of NT times, has explained the main differences between the NT and classical Gr. The NT was written in the common (Koine) vernacular language of the 1st cen., even as Martin Luther used the common German of the times in his translation of the Bible. *See* Bible Versions.

Scope and dimensions. The Bible used by Protestants contains 66 books, 39 in the OT and 27 in the NT. The books accepted in the OT are the same as the books accepted by the Jews as canonical. They speak of 24 books in the OT because of the fact that they consider I and II Samuel, I and II Kings, I and II Chronicles, Ezra-Nehemiah, and the 12 Minor Prophets as each one book. Josephus (*Against Apion* i. 8) refers to the fact that there are only 22 books in the OT to correspond to the 22 letters in the Heb. alphabet, but he probably combines Ruth with Judges and Lamentations with Jeremiah in order to arrive at 22.

The Roman Catholic church includes in the OT as canonical most of the Apocrypha: Tobit, Judith, Wisdom, Ecclesiasticus (also called Sirach or Ben Sirach), Baruch, I and II Maccabees, and some additions to Esther and to Daniel. The Greek Orthodox church does likewise. The Church of England, in accord with the Lutheran church, follows Jerome in holding that the apocryphal books may be read "for example of life and instruction on manners; but yet doth not apply them to establish any doctrine" (Article VI). The Ethiopic Bible includes I Enoch and the Book of Jubilees. *See* Apocrypha.

The Jews divided the OT into three sections: (1) the Law, the five books of the Pentateuch written by Moses; (2) the Prophets, which was subdivided into the Former Prophets, and included Joshua, Judges, Samuel and Kings, and the Latter Prophets, which included Isaiah, Jeremiah, Ezekiel, and the book of the Twelve Prophets; (3) the Writings, which contained the rest of the OT: the Psalms, Proverbs, and Job; then the five Scrolls: Canticles, Ruth, Lamentations, Ecclesiastes, and Esther; and finally Daniel, Ezra–Nehemiah, and Chronicles.

The Jews used the above order in their text, but the LXX revised this to form a more chronological and logical order. The LXX order has been retained by the Christian church.

The books of the OT are divided by the Christian church into four sections: (1) Law, namely, the Pentateuch. (2) History, comprising Joshua, Judges, Ruth, I and II Samuel, I and II Kings, I and II Chronicles, Ezra, Nehemiah, and Esther. (3) Wisdom and poetry, namely, Job, Psalms, Proverbs, Ecclesiastes, Song of Solomon. (4) Prophecy, namely, Isaiah, Jeremiah, Lamentations, Ezekiel, Daniel, Hosea, Joel, Amos, Obadiah, Jonah, Micah, Nahum, Habakkuk, Zephaniah, Haggai, Zechariah, and Malachi. Isaiah, Jeremiah, Ezekiel, and Daniel are called the Major Prophets, the other 12, the Minor Prophets.

The NT is composed of 27 books which are usually divided into four parts also: (1) Gospels, namely, Matthew, Mark, Luke, and John. (2) History of the early church, namely, Acts. (3) Epistles. These are sometimes divided into (a) Church Epistles: Romans, I and II Corinthians, Galatians, Ephesians, Philippians, Colossians, I and II Thessalonians; (b) Pastoral Epistles: I and II Timothy, Titus, and a personal epistle to Philemon; (c) Catholic (or General) Epistles: Hebrews, James, I and II Peter, I, II, and III John, and Jude. (4) Prophecy: book of Revelation.

Text of Scripture. The Bible was written over a period of approximately 1,500 years. The five books of Moses can be dated *c.* 1400 B.C. and the last book of the NT, Revelation, *c.* A.D. 90. In spite of the fact that the original manuscripts are not now extant, and that only handwritten copies existed down to the invention of printing, still the condition of the text has been remarkably preserved. The Heb. OT has been substantially verified by the LXX, and by the Heb. biblical manuscripts of the Dead Sea Scrolls which date in places back to the same period as the LXX. The existence of around 4,500 manuscripts of the NT in Gr., dating from *c.* A.D. 125 up to the invention of printing, provide a wealth of attestation to the NT. Added to this evidence are the versions, such as the Old Latin and Syriac, going back to A.D. 150, and the Latin Vulgate translation made by Jerome (382–405).

Chapter and verse divisions. The books of the Bible originally had neither chapters nor verses. Jews of pre-Talmudic times divided the OT into sections of convenient length for reading in the synagogues. Verse division marks of the OT appeared somewhat later, but our modern system was devised by Rabbi Nathan in the 15th cen. and came into Christian usage through Paginius' Latin Bible of 1528. Probably it was Stephen Langton (d. 1228), archbishop of Canterbury and supporter of the Magna Charta, who worked out the present chapter divisions. The verse divisions of the NT appeared first in a Gr. NT published in 1551 by Robert Stephens, a Paris printer. In 1555 he

Thus far all Old Testament books except Esther have been represented in the Dead Sea Scrolls. Here scholars scrutinize scroll fragments. Palestine Archaeological Museum, Jerusalem

published an edition of the Latin Vulgate, which was the first Bible to have the present chapters and verses. The first English Bible with such divisions was the Geneva edition of 1560.

Message. The Bible, though written over a long period of time, and by writers who often did not know each other, reveals a marvelous unity of thought. The writers all agree in their views of a divine revelation concerning: (1) Man's condition and needs. They depict man's sinful, fallen condition; his inability to save himself; God's revealed will to save man through a substitutionary sacrifice, and the salvation of man through saving faith alone. (2) God's covenant with Israel. He covenanted with Israel through Abraham to give them both a Saviour and a kingdom. This covenant was expanded and developed in all the ensuing covenants, namely, the Sinaitic with Moses and Israel, and the Davidic. It was both expanded and replaced by the new covenant in the NT (Mt 26:28; Heb 8:6–13). The term OT actually refers to the old covenant, the Latin word "testament" having been adopted to translate the Heb. *berîth* and the Gr. *diathēkē* (Mt 26:28). (3) Types and antitypes. All the types given in feasts, ceremonies, and sacrifices in the OT are fulfilled in Christ and the Church in the NT. For example, the Feast of Passover typified Christ as our passover and sacrificial lamb (Jn 1:29; Mt 26:19; I Cor 5:7). *See* Antitype. (4) Prophecies. Many specific prophecies con-

cerning the coming of Christ the Messiah and of His sacrificial death were fulfilled in His life and death. Others concerning His coming to rule in His kingdom are still future.

The Bible and criticism. Two forms of criticism have been applied to the Bible, lower and higher. Lower criticism concerns the establishment of the exact wording of the text of Scripture, and great progress and much reason for confidence have attended its scholarly application. The Dead Sea Scrolls have done much to confirm the reliability of the words of the OT in particular, and to clear up quotations by the NT writers from the Septuagint at the points in which it differs from the Masoretic Text.

Higher criticism, which can be used constructively to study the origin of the facts in the Bible and the authenticity of the authorship of the different books, has all too often been used in a destructive manner. Rejecting supernaturalism as a general principle, the critics have endeavored to prove that Moses did not write the Pentateuch; that Isaiah did not write all the book designated by his name; that the fourth Gospel was not written by John the apostle; and that the Synoptic Gospels are not the product of the three evangelists, Matthew, Luke, and a man called Mark who was guided by Peter, but are accounts based upon sources or documents which have been drastically edited and collated. Detailed studies by evangelical scholars have answered in a careful manner the attacks on the OT. Some of these are James

Orr, Oswald T. Allis, Edward J. Young and Gleason L. Archer. In refuting the attacks of the higher critics on the NT, the following men among others have given worthwhile and scholarly answers: R. Laird Harris, Donald Guthrie and Ned B. Stonehouse. See bibliography below.

See Bible, English Versions; Bible Interpretation; Bible Manuscripts; Canon of Scripture, the OT and the NT; Versions, Ancient and Medieval.

Bibliography. Oswald T. Allis, *The Five Books of Moses,* 1943; *God Spake by Moses,* 1951; *The Unity of Isaiah,* 1950, Philadelphia: Presbyterian and Reformed Pub. Co. Gleason L. Archer, *A Survey of Old Testament Introduction,* Chicago: Moody Press, 1964. William Henry Green, "The Canon," *General Introduction to the Old Testament,* New York: Scribner's, 1898. Donald Guthrie, *New Testament Introduction,* London: Tyndale Press, 3 vols., 1965. R. Laird Harris, *Inspiration and Canonicity of the Bible,* Grand Rapids: Zondervan, 1957. James Orr, *Problem of the Old Testament,* New York: Scribner's, 1906. Ned B. Stonehouse, *Origins of the Synoptic Gospels,* Grand Rapids: Eerdmans, 1963. Edward J. Young, *Introduction to the Old Testament,* Grand Rapids: Eerdmans, 1949.

R. A. K.

BIBLE DICTIONARIES. In the last 300 years there have been nearly 300 Bible dictionaries published in the English language — some small and some extending to many volumes, some carrying the names of many of the greatest biblical scholars of their respective generations, while some appear anonymously.

Augustine, as early as A.D. 367, expressed a wish that someone would produce a work on the names found in Scripture, "such as Eusebius has done in regard to the history of the past." But the church had to wait 12 centuries before any such volume appeared.

Early Dictionaries

The earliest work of this kind probably was done by John Marbeck (1550), followed by a Latin dictionary of the Bible by a German Lutheran, M. I. Flacius (1567). The beginnings of a dictionary of the Bible in English was a work by William Patten. This appeared in London in 1575 (200 pages), the title of which indicates its scope — *The Calendar of Scripture, wherein the Hebru, Chaldean, Arabian, Phenician, Syrian, Persian, Greek and Latin names of — Men, Weemen, Idols, Cities, etc., in the Holly Byble — is set and Turned into Our English Toung.*

The first really important Bible dictionary appearing in English was the one compiled by Thomas Wilson, *Complete Christian Dictionary,* first published in 1612, and appearing in four other editions within 35 years. The text

extends to 948 unnumbered pages, concluding with a unique dictionary for the book of Revelation of 131 pages, and a dictionary of the Song of Solomon of 49 pages.

The greatest Bible dictionary appearing in Europe before the middle of the 19th cen. was by one of Europe's great Catholic scholars, Augustin Calmet (1672–1757), published in Paris in 1722. It was translated into English and published in London in 1732 in six folio volumes with the title *An Historical, Critical, Geographical, Chronological, and Etymological Dictionary of the Holy Bible.* This was the ideal of biblical encyclopedias from the time of its first appearance. It was published in revised form in four volumes, then in five volumes, and again in abbreviated editions, even being published in Boston in 1832 and in London in 1847, thus still being issued 125 years after its first appearance. The last volume contains an enormous bibliography of biblical literature extending to 600 columns. This was probably the only great Bible dictionary in English that was translated from a European language.

John Brown of Haddington (1722–1787) published *A Dictionary of the Holy Bible Containing Definitions of All Religious and Ecclesiastical Terms . . . and a Biographical Sketch of Writers in Theological Science,* in the middle of the 18th cen. A fifth edition of Brown's work appeared in 1839 embracing about 95,000 words. Early in the 19th cen. Charles Buck (1771–1815) published his *Theological Dictionary,* London, 1802, in two volumes. It has often been reprinted and revised, down to as late as 1850. It is a work of great erudition.

The earliest important Bible dictionary by an American was *The Dictionary of the Bible* by Howard Malcolm (1799–1879), London, 1828; third edition, Boston, 1830; and an enlarged edition, Boston, 1853. It sold 130,000 copies within 20 years.

A New Era for Bible Dictionaries

One might say that a new era for Bible dictionaries began with the appearance in 1845 of the *Cyclopedia of Biblical Literature* by John Kitto (1804–1854). His enlarged edition of 1862–67 extended to about 3,340,000 words. Here for the first time an edition of a Bible dictionary made use of a great number of contemporary biblical scholars, more than 40 of them, from Great Britain, Germany, and America. Some biblical subjects are treated with greater fullness than any other similar work; e.g., ten double-column pages are devoted to the subject of Adam, 45 pages are devoted to "Burial in Tombs," and there is a superb survey of biblical concordances, etc. An abridgment of the third edition appeared as late as 1894.

In this same decade (1849) there appeared an excellent one-volume work, *The Biblical Cyclopedia,* by John Eadie (1810–1876), which called for 17 editions within 40 years.

233

In 1860, the first volume of the *Dictionary of the Bible,* edited by Sir William Smith (1813–1893), was published. This proved to be the most influential Bible dictionary of the 19th cen. The complete three-volume work contains more than 3,100 pages. This dictionary saw innumerable editions, the most important of which was the American revision edited by Professor H. B. Hackett, to which an additional staff of 27 scholars contributed. With this work began the strong emphasis on articles relating to historical and geographical subjects, incorporating the constantly multiplying results of archaeological discovery. Smith's dictionary has appeared in many forms, revised, abbreviated, etc., and parts of it stolen for other later dictionaries.

In the same decade, Patrick Fairbairn (1805–1874) issued his *Imperial Bible Dictionary* (1865), which in the later edition of 1885 appeared in six quarto volumes. It is still a treasure house of biblical lore.

The well-known biblical commentator A. R. Fausset (1821–1910) published his *Englishman's Critical and Expository Bible Encyclopedia,* London, in 1878, a work of some 950,000 words, with excellent articles on prophetic subjects, and with unusually full treatment of such subjects as David, Christ, etc. This was republished by an American firm in 1949.

William Blackwood, an American clergyman, in 1873 published his *Potter's Complete Bible Encyclopedia* in two quarto volumes of 2,000 pages, certainly the most beautiful Bible dictionary that had been published up to that time, with more than 3,000 illustrations.

The most important one-volume Bible dictionary edited by an American was the *Dictionary of the Bible* by John D. Davis (1854–1926), first appearing in 1898; the fourth edition in 1924, which was reprinted in 1954. A revision by H. S. Gehman appearing in 1944 with the title *The Westminster Dictionary of the Bible* was more liberal than the original work by Davis.

In 1899 there began to appear in four large volumes the most liberal of all Bible dictionaries up to that time, *The Encyclopedia Biblica,* edited by T. K. Cheyne and J. S. Black, London, 1899–1903. A large number of articles in this encyclopedia were written by the German rationalist P. W. Schmiedel, who repudiated all biblical miracles including the resurrection. A noted review commented, "It is not a dictionary of the Bible: it is a dictionary of the historical criticism of the Bible."

Twentieth Century Dictionaries

In the first decade of the 20th cen. began to appear the remarkable series of dictionaries edited by James Hastings (1852–1922). A *Dictionary of the Bible* in five volumes was published in 1898–1904, followed by a single volume in 1909, really an improvement over the

preceding work. A thoroughly revised edition edited by F. C. Grant and H. H. Rowley appeared in 1963, with 150 contributing editors. The latter is a beautiful piece of typography, with excellent colored maps, but lacking bibliographies.

In 1908 appeared the two-volume work *A Dictionary of Christ and the Gospels;* and in the next decade, 1916–1918, *The Dictionary of the Apostolic Church,* also in two volumes. These last two works are far more important for the Bible student today than the earlier five-volume work. Some of the best scholars in the Western world contributed to these volumes on NT subjects. The volumes relating to the Gospels include articles by B. B. Warfield; "Fact and Theory" by C. W. Hodge; an article on the Holy Spirit by James Denny; and an extended article on "The Character of Christ" by T. B. Kilpatrick.

A one-volume work, *A Standard Bible Dictionary,* edited by Nourse and Zenos, appeared in 1909, revised by M. W. Jacobus as *A New Standard Bible Dictionary,* New York, 1936, with 55 contributors, extending to nearly a million words.

The most helpful conservative Bible dictionary of this century, up to the time of its publication, was the *International Standard Bible Encyclopedia* (ISBE), edited by James Orr, Chicago, 1915, in five volumes of more than four million words. It includes articles by 200 contributors, with discussions of such subjects as Chronology, Astronomy, Jesus Christ, Inspiration, etc. It has proved a boon to students of the Scriptures for the last half century, and a revision is now being carefully prepared. One of the invaluable features of this work is the five exhaustive indexes extending to over 840 columns.

Necessarily passing by numerous Bible dictionaries, certainly the most important one-volume work published in the last half century is *The New Bible Dictionary* under the editorship of the staff of the Inter-Varsity Fellowship of London, a work of over 1,400 pages, appearing in 1962, produced by 140 contributors, with many illustrations and the most modern maps. Of great value are the rich articles on OT historical subjects by K. A. Kitchen and Donald J. Wiseman, together with the latter's carefully prepared tables setting forth the most important archaeological discoveries since early in the 19th cen., with full bibliographic references.

The largest Bible dictionary attempted since ISBE is *The Interpreter's Dictionary of the Bible* (1962), in four volumes, in modern format, the work of 253 biblical scholars and authorities on various related subjects. There are something over 1,000 illustrations, together with a series in color of the Westminster maps. Historical and archaeological subjects are considered with fullness and general satisfaction. In many places, however, the work is extremely liberal, with the denial of the Mosaic authorship of the Pentateuch, insisting that Daniel was a product of the 2nd cen. B.C., etc. The NT articles are far more conservative and satisfying than the OT.

Other important one-volume Bible dictionaries that have appeared since World War II include *Harper's Bible Dictionary* (1952) by Madeleine S. and J. Lane Miller; *Unger's Bible Dictionary* (1957) by Merrill F. Unger, a thorough revision of the *Bible Encyclopedia* (1900) by Charles R. Barnes; the *Seventh-Day Adventist Bible Dictionary* (1960) by Siegfried H. Horn; *The Zondervan Pictorial Bible Dictionary* (1963) edited by Merrill C. Tenney with more than 65 contributors; and the *Pictorial Biblical Encyclopedia* (1964) edited by Gaalyahu Cornfeld and assisted by over two dozen Israeli Bible scholars and archaeologists.

Word Studies

Mention should be made of some volumes that are devoted exclusively to the study of specific words found in the Scriptures. Among these, one of the most widely used was *The Bible Word Book, a Glossary of Archaic Words and Phrases in the Authorized Version of the Bible,* compiled by William Aldis Wright, first published in London in 1866, with a second revised edition in 1884. There is also *The Theological Word Book of the Bible* edited by Alan Richardson, London, 1950. Some of the articles here are quite extensive, as the one on the Spirit of 26 columns, with a good bibliography. Another very helpful work is by W. E. Vine, *An Expository Dictionary of New Testament Words,* published in London in 1940, in four volumes.

Some of the more important dictionaries of theology include one of extended significance, *The Dictionary of Doctrinal and Historical Theology* by J. H. Blunt, second edition 1872, a work of 800 double-column pages. Though very few probably consult it now, there are still great treasures in *The Cyclopedia of Biblical, Theological, and Ecclesiastical Literature* edited by John M'Clintock (1814–1870) and James Strong (1822–1894), New York, 1867–1881, two volumes, with two supplementary volumes. There is also the still valuable work *The New Schaff-Herzog Encyclopedia of Religious Knowledge,* published in 12 volumes, appearing in 1908. A work that contains a great mass of invaluable information but today almost wholly forgotten is *The Concise Dictionary of Religious Knowledge* edited by Samuel Macauley Jackson (1851–1912), first appearing in two volumes, 1889 and 1890, with a third edition in 1898.

Geoffrey W. Bromiley is performing a tremendous service to English readers by translating the voluminous German work *Theologisches Wörterbuch zum Neuen Testament* edited by Gerhard Kittel (1888–1948) and Gerhard Friedrich (1908–). The original work was begun in 1932.

An excellent recent volume is *Baker's Dictionary of Theology* edited by Everett F. Harrison, 1960. This is an invaluable work from a conservative standpoint, with articles by 140 contributors. The bibliographies are most commendable.

From time to time a number of denominations have issued separate ecclesiastical encyclopedias. The still very important work, *The Catholic Encyclopedia,* was published in New York from 1907 to 1914 in 16 volumes. *The Jewish Encyclopedia,* 12 volumes, appeared earlier, 1901–1906.

W. M. S.

BIBLE—ENGLISH VERSIONS. The Bible came to the British Isles in a Latin version. In the 1st cen. there were two versions of the OT, Heb. and Gr. But the early Christians found a Latin version necessary, both for the OT and the growing NT, especially because of their missionary work in N Africa where Latin was the dominant language. Before the end of the 2nd cen. some of the books of the Bible had been translated into Latin, for writers of the 3rd cen. show wide acquaintance with Latin versions.

These versions became so multiplied and varied that Pope Damasus assigned to Jerome the task of producing a standard Latin text, which was completed in A.D. 405. This came to be called the Vulgate, which was the standard text most widely used for more than a thousand years, and is still the official text of the Roman Catholic church. It could be that some of the Roman soldiers sent to Britain had copies of portions of the Bible in Latin, though of this we have no evidence.

For nearly 200 years following the departure of the last Roman troops from Britain, A.D. 410, almost nothing is known of the experiences of Christians in England. But monasteries were springing up throughout Ireland so that by A.D. 600 the study of sound literature held the uppermost place and was pursued with a thoroughness and intensity unknown elsewhere in Europe at that time. During this period the Book of Armagh was written, partly in Irish, partly in Latin, containing a non-Vulgate text of the NT. There is no trace of a vernacular Bible in the Celtic church.

Following the coming of Christianity to England in 597 through the mission of Augustine, the first archbishop of Canterbury, Bibles were sent to the early church at Canterbury by Pope Gregory (540–604), some of the volumes adorned with silver and jewels, all in the Latin tongue.

Early English Translations

The earliest translation of any part of the Bible into Anglo-Saxon was expressed in songs, initiated by the beautiful songs of Caedmon (d.680), of whom Bede says, he "sang first of the creation of the world and the beginning of mankind and of the story of Genesis . . . and of Christ's incarnation, and of His passion, and of His ascent into heaven; of the coming of the Holy Ghost and the teachings of the apostles." Many of these songs were carefully preserved and can be read today. About this time the famous Christian epic known as *The Christ* was composed, and also that exquisite gem of literary composition *The Dream of the Rood*.

The greatest scholar in Britain in the 8th cen., the Venerable Bede, confessed, "I gave all my attention to the study of the Scriptures." While Bede's writings were in Latin, he did undertake the translation of the Gospels into Anglo-Saxon, and on the day of his death (735) was dictating the concluding lines of the Gospel of John. None of these translations have come down to us.

The earliest written translation of the Gospels into Anglo-Saxon now existing dates from about the 10th cen. The elegantly written Lindisfarne Gospels were originally in Latin (*c.* 700), but *c.* 950 an interlinear translation in Anglo-Saxon was inserted. Alfric, the abbot of Eynsham, writing *c.* 990, acknowledged that the English at that time "had not the evangelical doctrines among their writings . . . those books excepted which King Alfred wisely turned from Latin into English." About 1000 there was a Wessex version of the Gospels.

For two centuries following the Norman invasion (1066) there was an almost total check upon the producing of vernacular literature in Britain, for the Normans introduced and constantly used the French language. By the 14th cen., however, the general use of the French language in England had practically ceased, and there began the production of genuine native literature accompanied by a revival of vernacular Bibles and portions of the Bible. Two English versions of the Psalter were produced at this time. The work by Richard Rolle (d. 1349), which attained great popularity, contained the Latin text of the Psalter, following verse by verse with an English translation and commentary.

Great Bible Translators

The first of the great Bible translators of Britain was *John Wycliffe* (1320 – 1384). Wycliffe's one great desire was to make the Scriptures available in the language of the people, even though a large part of the population of Britain at that time could not read. He also hoped that the availability of the Scriptures in the vernacular would bring about a reformation in the church, and for this reason he has since been called "the morning star of the Reformation." His NT translation was completed in 1380 and the OT in 1382, making this the first complete Bible in the English language. The Apocrypha (*q.v.*) was included, interspersed among the OT canonical books, but with a note in the preface to the OT that these

were "without the authority of belief." At least 170 manuscript copies of this Bible, in one edition or another, have survived, and for 150 years it was the only complete English Bible in use. Its greatest shortcoming was that it was a translation from the Latin Vulgate and not from the original Heb. and Gr. Scriptures.

The next distinguished translator of the Bible was *William Tyndale* (1492 – 1536). Educated at Oxford, Tyndale was thoroughly acquainted with Heb. and Gr., and thus for the first time an English NT was produced translated directly from the Gr. Tyndale was in frequent fellowship with the great Gr. scholar Erasmus, and may have met Luther.

It was Tyndale who said to an opponent, "I defy the Pope and all his laws; if God spare my life, ere many years I will cause a boy that driveth the plow shall know more of the Scriptures than thou dost." Since the Wycliffe Bible had appeared, Gutenberg had invented printing with movable type, and had produced the great Mazarin Bible, the Latin Vulgate text, in 1456. Soon manuscript Bibles ceased to be written. Tyndale's NT, and later the OT, appeared in printed form, and thus with copies available for the common man, they were eagerly purchased by people throughout Britain.

The printing of Tyndale's Bible had to be carried on outside Britain, at Hamburg, Worms, and Cologne. Not for the first time but now with greatest intensity, the authorities vigorously attempted to suppress all these efforts of Tyndale and his group. King Henry VIII issued a proclamation in 1530 that read in part as follows: "His highnes hath therfore semblably

A page from the Wycliffe Bible. BM

there vpon consulted with the sayd primates and vertuous, discrete, and well lerned personages in diuinite forsayde, and by them all it is thought, that it is not necessary, the sayde scripture to be in the englisshe tonge, and in the handes of the commen people: but that the distribution of the sayd scripture . . . dependeth onely vpon the discretion of the superiours, as they shall thynke it conuenyent. And that hauing respecte to the malignite of this present tyme, with the inclination of people to erronious opinions, the translation of the newe testament and the olde in to the vulgare tonge of englysshe, shulde rather be the occasion of contynuance or increace of errours amonge the sayd people, than any benefyte or commodite towarde the weale of their soules. And that it shall nowe be more conuenient that the same people haue the holy scripture expouned to them, by preachers in their sermons, accordynge as it hath ben of olde tyme accustomed before this tyme . . . that the same bokes and all other bokes of heresy, as well in the frenche tonge as in the duche tonge, be clerely extermynated and exiled out of this realme of Englande for euer."

Betrayed by a friend, Tyndale was martyred in Brussels in 1536. He himself never saw a completed English Bible as a result of his own labors. However, a complete translation by *Miles Coverdale* (1488–1569), later the bishop of Exeter, did appear based upon Tyndale's work. In contrast with the persecution of Tyndale and the attempt to suppress his version, Coverdale did his work under the patronage of Thomas Cromwell.

Miles Coverdale's English translation of the Bible was based on Latin versions, Tyndale's work, and Luther's and Zwingli's German translations. Appearing in 1535, this was the first Bible to be published (i.e., printed) in English, although not all of it based on the original Gr. and Heb. Here for the first time in English Bibles, the books of the OT were arranged in the order in which they are found in Bibles today. Interestingly, from Coverdale's Bible onward the Apocrypha (*q.v.*) has not been printed along with the canonical books of the OT but is placed in a separate appendix at the close of the OT.

A folio edition of the Scriptures appeared in 1537 affirming the translation to be by one *Thomas Matthew*, now recognized as John Rogers, an associate of Tyndale. This translation was "set forth with the King's most gracious license."

A later edition revised by Coverdale (1539) contained a preface by Archbishop Cranmer, and so became known as the *Cranmer Bible* (also called the *Great Bible* because of its size). This was the first authorized Bible and copies were placed in every church. Various editions underwent careful revision. In 1541 King Edward issued a proclamation for the English Bible to be set up in churches, and a part of this proclamation may be read again with profit:

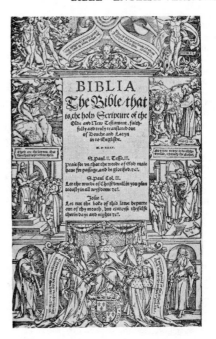

Title page of the Coverdale translation, the first printed English Bible. BM

"It was ordenyed and commaunded . . . that in al and synguler paryshe churches, there shuld be prouyded by a certen day nowe expyred, at the costes of the curates and paryshioners, Bybles conteynynge the olde and newe Testament, in the Englyshe tounge, to be fyxed and set vp openlye in euery of the sayd paryshe churches. The whiche Godlye commaundement and iniunction was to the onlye intent that euery of the kynges maiesties louynge subiectes, myndynge to reade therin, myght by occasyon thereof, not only consyder and perceyue the great and ineffable omnipotent power, promyse, iustice, mercy and goodnes of Almyghtie God, but also to learne thereby to obserue Gods commaundementes, and to obeye theyr soueraygne Lorde and hyghe powers, and to exercyse Godlye charite, and to vse themselues, accordynge to theyr vocations: in a pure and syncere christen lyfe without murmure or grudgynges. . . . and not that any of them shulde reade the sayde Bybles, wyth lowde and hyghe voyces, in tyme of the celebracion of the holy Masse and other dyuyne seruyces vsed in the churche, nor that any hys lay subiectes redynge the same, shulde presume to take vpon them, any common dysputacyon, argumente or exposicyon of the mysteries therein conteyned, but that euery suche laye man shulde humbly, mekely and reuerentlye reade the same, for his owne instruction, edificacion and amendment of hys lyfe, accordynge to goddes holy worde therin mencioned."

237

Title page of the Bishops' Bible.

Other Early Bibles

During the reign of Queen Mary (1553–1558), no Bible was printed in England, and its use in the churches was forbidden. However, a group of scholars in Geneva, in 1560, produced an unauthorized English version called the *Geneva Bible*. This was the most accurate version up to that time. The NT was edited by William Whittingham, who was married to Calvin's sister. Calvin wrote an introductory epistle.

For the first time, marginal notations called attention to variations in the Gr. MSS. This was the first English version to use numbered verses as separate paragraphs. The verse divisions of Robert Estienne (or, Stephanus), originally employed in his Gr. NT in 1551, were also used. It was the first Bible to be printed in Roman type instead of the old block letters, the so-called Old English type.

This was the Bible used by Shakespeare, John Bunyan, Oliver Cromwell, so fervently studied by the Puritans and brought over on the *Mayflower*. Designated as "the People's Book," it held a preeminent place among English versions for 75 years.

From 1560 to 1644, 140 editions of the Geneva Bible or NT appeared. Certain Geneva Bibles printed in 1599 omitted the apocryphal books for the first time. The first Bible to be printed in Scotland was a Scottish edition of the Geneva Bible, in 1579.

The popularity of the Geneva Bible persuaded the Anglican authorities, after the accession of Queen Elizabeth to the throne in 1558, that they should produce a Bible which could bear the authority of the Church of England. Proposed by Archbishop Parker, he appointed a committee for such a work. Since the scholarship of these bishops was not equal to that of the group that had produced the Geneva Bible, they used the Great Bible as their basis, checking with the Gr. and Heb. text. The finished work was called the *Bishops' Bible*. Nineteen editions were printed from 1568 to 1606. It was endorsed by convocation in 1571. In the 1572 edition Parker published in parallel columns the Psalter of the Great Bible and the Psalter of the Bishops' Bible.

Until the rather free translation (NT, 1944; OT, 1949) by the late Msgr. Ronald A. Knox, the *Douay Bible* had been the only English Bible approved by the Roman Catholic church. The NT, translated from the Latin, was published under the leadership of Gregory Martin in 1582 by the English Catholic University, then located in exile at Rheims in northeastern France and it was thus known as the *Rheims New Testament*. The OT, for the most part a translation of the Latin Vulgate by Martin, was published in 1609–10 when the English University had returned to Douay in northwestern France and hence the name the Douay Bible.

The poorest part of this version is acknowledged to be the Psalter, which has been rightly characterized as "a translation of a translation of a translation." There is heavy emphasis in this version on ecclesiastical terms. "Repentance" is here translated "penance." Here are such unfamiliar words as "exinanited," "donanes," and "commersation." Instead of "shewbread," this version reads "proposition of loaves." "Deacon" is translated "minister" and "elder" is translated "priest." Eph 3:9 is made to read, "the dispensation of the sacrament." The Douay NT was extensively used by the King James revisers, but the OT was published too late for any such influence. An authority on this subject does not exaggerate in saying that today "the Douay Old Testament is a forgotten book." The apocryphal books appear interspersed throughout the OT in this version.

Translation of the King James Version

With all these various translations available, and with a growing knowledge in Britain of Heb. and Gr., the time was ripe for the greatest single undertaking in the area of translation in the history of English literature, the production of what came to be known as the Authorized Version, or the King James Version (KJV).

In the summer of 1603, King James I, on his way to London to receive the English crown, was presented with a petition of grievances by the clergy of Puritan convictions, which led him to call for a conference at Hampton Court, January 14-16, 1604. During this conference, Dr. John Reynolds, president of Corpus Christi College, Oxford, moved that a new translation of the Bible be undertaken. Though opposed by the majority, this motion was accepted by the king, and the undertaking was begun at once with 54 of the outstanding biblical scholars in Great Britain engaged in this task. They were divided into six groups, three to work on a translation of the OT, two on the NT, and one on the Apocrypha.

Dr. H. Wheeler Robinson has well summarized the qualifications of this group: "The Oxford group was headed by Dr. John Hardinge, regius professor of Hebrew, and included Dr. John Reynolds, the originator of the project, 'his memory and reading were near to a miracle'; Dr. Miles Smith, who 'had Hebrew at his fingers' ends'; Dr. Richard Brett, 'skilled and versed to a criticism in the Latin, Greek, Chaldee, Arabic and Ethiopic tongues'; Sir Henry Saville, editor of the works of Chrysostom; and Dr. John Harmer, professor of Greek, 'a most noted Latinist, Grecian and divine.'

"The Cambridge committee was at first presided over by Edward Lively, regius professor of Hebrew, who died in 1605 before the work was really begun, and included Dr. Lawrence Chaderton, 'familiar with the Greek and Hebrew tongues, and the numerous writings of the rabbis'; Thomas Harrison, 'noted for his exquisite skill in Hebrew and Greek idioms'; Dr. Robert Spalding, successor to Lively as professor of Hebrew; Andrew Downes, 'one composed of Greek and industry'; and John Bois, 'a precocious Greek and Hebrew scholar.'

"The Westminster group was headed by Lancelot Andrewes, dean of Westminster, afterward bishop of Chichester, of Ely, and finally of Winchester, 'who might have been interpreter general at Babel . . . the world wanted learning to know how learned he was'; and included the Hebraist Hadrian Saravia, and William Bedwell, the greatest living Arabic scholar."

In method, the separate panels were to consider the work of each other panel, and differences were to be resolved first by correspondence, and that failing, by the general meeting at the end, which was composed of two representatives from each of the three main centers of translation (Oxford, Cambridge, Westminster). The final session, which brought together and edited the whole work, lasted nine months. Though begun in 1607 the translation was not completed until 1610 and published in 1611.

In the famous preface to this version is a superb statement regarding the work and value of translation: "Translation it is that openeth the window, to let in the light; that breaketh the shell, that we may eat the kernel; that putteth aside the curtaine, that we may looke into the most Holy place; that remooueth the couer of the well, that we may come by the water, euen as *Iacob* rolled away the stone from the mouth of the well, by which meanes the flockes of *Laban* were watered. Indeede without translation into the vulgar tongue, the vnlearned are but like the children at *Iacobs* well (which is deepe) without a bucket or some thing to draw with: or as that person mentioned by *Esay,* to whom when a sealed booke was deliuered, with this motion, *Read this, I pray thee,* hee was faine to make this answere, *I cannot, for it is sealed."*

It was not long before the KJV crowded out all preceding translations as far as the public reading of the Scriptures was concerned. At last England was reading the same Bible at home which they also heard read from the pulpits of their churches. The distinguished English scholar of a generation ago, Dr. Albert S. Cook well said: "It thus became bound up with the life of the nation. Since it stilled all controversy over the best rendering, it gradually came to be accepted as so far absolute that in the minds of myriads there was no distinction between this version and the original texts, and they may almost be said to have believed in the literal inspiration of the very words which composed it."

The translators of the Revised Version nearly three centuries later declared: "We have had to study this great version carefully and minutely, line by line; and the longer we have been engaged upon it the more we have learned to admire its simplicity, its dignity, its power, its happy turns of expression, its general accuracy, and, we must not fail to add, the music of its cadences, and the felicities of its rhythm."

Even such a non-Christian as Thomas Huxley gladly acknowledged that the KJV "is written in the noblest and purest English, and abounds in exquisite beauties of pure literary form; and, finally, that it forbids the veriest hind who never left his village to be ignorant of the existence of other countries and other civilizations, and of a great past stretching back to the furthest limits of the oldest civilizations of the world."

English and American Standard Versions

While a number of versions appeared during the 17th and 18th cen., and particularly some important new translations from the Gr. NT, more than 250 years went by before there was any united effort to produce a new standard version. Much had happened in the world of biblical scholarship since 1611, e.g., the discovery of the great Sinaitic manuscript by Tischendorf (*see* Bible Manuscripts). On February 10, 1870, Bishop Wilberforce submitted the following resolution to the Upper House of Convocation of the Province of Canterbury: "That a committee of both Houses be appointed, with power to confer with any committee that may be appointed by the Convocation of the Northern Province, to report upon the desirableness of a revision of the Authorized Version of the New Testament, whether by marginal notes or otherwise, in all those passages where plain and clear errors, whether in the Hebrew or Greek text originally adopted by the translators, or in the translation made from the same, shall, on due investigation, be found to exist."

In May of the same year, a committee made some suggestions. Among them were: "1. That it is desirable that a revision of the Authorized Version of the Holy Scriptures be undertaken. 2. That the revision be so conducted as to comprise both marginal renderings and such emendations as it may be found necessary to insert in the text of the Authorized Version. 3. That in the above resolutions we do not contemplate any new translation of the Bible, or any alteration of the language, except when in the judgment of the most competent scholars such change is necessary."

Fifty-four of the best biblical scholars in Britain pledged themselves to cooperate in this undertaking. Two groups of 27 members each commenced work in June of that same year, the NT company meeting on 407 days within 11 years, and the OT company on 792 days in 15 years. The NT appeared on May 17, 1881, and the OT in 1885.

Among other virtues, the poetical passages throughout the Bible were printed as such. Many words that had become outdated and antique were modernized, and innumerable passages were more accurately translated. A great number of varied renderings were inserted in the margin, and the entire system of cross-references was completely revised. While verse numbers were retained, apart from the poetical passages the text was printed in paragraphs, and these paragraph divisions were most carefully determined.

The text of the English revision of the NT was sent ahead to New York and published in America May 20, 1881. Two Chicago daily newspapers received the text of Matthew through Romans in history's longest telegram (c. 118,000 words). Type for the remainder was set from copies arriving by fast train in the evening of May 21, so that they published the entire NT for their public May 22. Three million copies of this were sold in the United States and Great Britain in the first twelve months.

The verdict of Prof. F. F. Bruce exactly states what is the general opinion by the best authorities, that this version "is still the most useful edition of the Bible for the careful student who knows no language but English." But concerning the NT Charles H. Spurgeon once remarked, "It is strong in Greek, weak in English." This evaluation still stands and the fact observed has hindered this version and its American counterpart from being a "people's" version.

The English committee invited American biblical scholars to participate with them in this undertaking, an invitation that was gladly accepted. But differences arose about certain methods of procedure and the American committee decided to publish its own revised version, though exchanging notes with the British revisers, and promising not to publish its complete work for 14 years after the English revision had appeared. It has been generally agreed that the American Standard Version (ASV), which was published in 1901, was in many ways superior to the English one. It is estimated that in the NT of these revised versions there are about 30,000 alterations from the KJV text or, as someone has estimated, about four and one-half alterations for each verse.

Revised Standard Version

In 1937 the International Council of Religious Education initiated work for a complete new revision, undertaken by 32 American biblical scholars. The Revised Standard Version (RSV) NT was published in 1946 and the entire Bible in 1952. While many passages in this text aroused fierce criticism, in some places there was actually a return to the earlier KJV. For example, II Tim 3:16, which had been badly mutilated in the ASV, was now made to read, "All scripture is inspired by God and profitable, etc."

The chairman of this work, Dean Luther Weigle of Yale, wrote of this new version at the time of its publication: "It was in effect a new translation, and for three reasons. The first is that no adequate revision can be made except upon the basis of a thorough study of the Greek text, and as careful procedure in putting its meaning into English, as would be required in the case of a new translation. The second is that the committee has used the new evidence concerning the Greek text and the new resources for understanding the vocabulary and grammar of the Greek New Testament which have been afforded by the remarkable discoveries of the past sixty years since the revisions of 1881 and 1901 were made. The third is that the present committee was not obliged, as the former committees were, to maintain the peculiar forms of Elizabethan English in which the King James Version is cast." In this text the use of the name "Jehovah" was dropped and the title "Lord" was substituted. While archaic forms of pronouns were discarded, quotation marks were not introduced.

W. M. S.

Translations into Modern Speech by Committees or Groups of Scholars

New English Bible (NEB). In 1946 the General Assembly of the Church of Scotland approached the Protestant churches of Great Britain suggesting a completely new translation of the Bible into contemporary English. The proposal met with approval, and a translation called the New English Bible was produced.

This version stems from an interdenominational joint committee of English Protestants under the direction of C. H. Dodd, commissioned to make a "completely new translation" of the Bible "rather than a revision of any earlier version." It was to be both a "faithful rendering of the best available Greek text into the current speech of our time and a rendering which should harvest the gains of recent biblical scholarship."

The NT appeared in March, 1961, and has been widely adopted by many British and American groups. Since a new Gr. text has been constructed for this project, it marks an innovation in committee translations where formerly standard critical editions of the Gr. text were used. However, in a number of cases, in our judgment, this new text follows questionable and slender manuscript evidence in the readings it adopts (e.g., Jn 13:10; 19:21; Mk 8:26; Phil 2:16). The OT was published in March, 1970.

Many attractive features and qualities, ranging from a pleasing format and style to clarity and forcefulness, have contributed to the NEB's present popularity. However, a number of general weaknesses can be cited. It falls prey to excessive interpretive paraphrases and free translations in many instances (e.g., Jn 16:8-11; Rom 5:15). For this reason, it is difficult to classify the NEB as either a literal translation with some paraphrase, or as a true paraphrase. Furthermore, there are no italics to indicate where words and phrases are added in English in order to complete the sense. Parentheses are used ambiguously for both the added words and parenthetical thought.

New American Standard Bible (NASB). A well-qualified group of evangelical American biblical scholars issued the NT of the New American Standard Bible in 1963, and the whole Bible in 1971. They stated as their purpose "to adhere to the original languages of the Holy Scriptures as closely as possible and at the same time to obtain a fluent and readable style according to current English usage." The basis for their work was the ASV of 1901.

In this revision helpful marginal notes and cross-references are found on the outer edge of the page; paragraphs are designated; quotation and punctuation marks follow modern practice. "Thou," "thy" and "thee" are changed to "you" except in the language of prayer when speaking to Deity. The number of the word "you" is designated "you^s" or "you^{pl}" when it cannot be determined from the context. Italics indicate words not present in the Gr. text but justified in the translation.

The translators indicate that, while giving attention to the latest available Gr. MSS, the attempt is made "to render the grammar and terminology of the ASV in contemporary English." Where the literalness of the ASV is not possible, a more current English expression is used, but the literal rendering is indicated in the margin.

This version is an accurate translation free from archaic expressions and suitable for careful Bible study and for Scripture memorization, which is not always the case with paraphrases or amplified versions.

Confraternity Version. The NT was first published in 1941 by the Episcopal Confraternity of Christian Doctrine. It is a revision of the Rheims-Challoner NT translated from the Latin Vulgate. The latest evidence for the Vulgate text is followed, but it is indicated that ". . . if the Latin disagrees from the Greek to such an extent to affect the meaning, attention is given in the footnotes" and the Greek is followed. The text is divided in paragraph style but with the verses numbered within the paragraphs.

There is a colloquialism in this translation that lends itself to a good understanding of the Scripture. Some of the footnotes, however, contain Roman Catholic dogma, as in I Tim 2:5 where this is said to mean "mediatorship as a man," or in Mt 1:25 which is said to mean that "Mary's perpetual virginity" is not impaired in the least.

In 1948 a new translation of Genesis appeared and therefore a start was made on a translation of the OT based on the Heb. rather than the Latin. The entire Bible was published in 1970 under the title New American Bible.

The translation has an easy reading style and follows the text quite closely, though in the introductions there are evidences of higher critical scholarship.

Revised Standard Version Roman Catholic Edition. The Catholic Bible Association of Great Britain has been responsible for this Roman Catholic edition. The statement in the foreword has been that the different religious branches – Protestant, Catholic and otherwise – can use just about the same Bible. However, this edition, while not changing the bulk of the NT RSV, does incorporate some 67 changes that reflect Roman Catholic dogma.

But in the OT, "it was not thought necessary to make any changes at all." The usual amount of footnotes is carried. Of course the apocryphal books are included along with the OT text. Thus the objections already indicated concerning the regular RSV apply to the Roman Catholic edition as well.

Berkeley Version in Modern English (1958). The NT portion is a private version by Gerrit Verkuyl, whose desire was to produce a translation less interpretive than Moffatt's, more American than Weymouth's and less tied to the KJV than the RSV. Working from the best Gr. MSS, Verkuyl did produce a version with clear idiomatic English. The archaic expressions with obscurities of speech are minimized. Yet there are a number of stiff expressions.

Much the same is true of the OT. Many scholars, each responsible for his own work, did the translation on portions assigned to them, but the whole Berkeley Version is essentially a series of private ventures with no formal committee revision procedure. Messianic prophecies with regard to Christ are carefully preserved.

The version carries chronological notations in the headings of many of the chapters, while the footnotes have moral and ethical suggestions along with the other explanatory remarks.

The Torah, the Five Books of Moses. Published in 1963, this is the first phase of a Jewish translation of the entire OT, of which the other books are still in process of translation. There is an English translation by Jewish scholars of the Heb. OT dating from 1917, largely modeled on the idiom of the ASV, but the present version is a new translation into modern English. The text reads smoothly and is free from expressions difficult to understand. In instances where the context demands extra words that are not in the Heb. text, paraphrase is used, but the additional words are bracketed. Where the text is controversial, there are variant readings in the footnotes, thus allowing some choice for the reader. It is noted that in Ex 3:14, the holy name for God is left untranslated. The reading is, "Thus shall you say to the Israelites, '*Ehyeh* sent me.'" Some questionable translations may be seen in Gen 2:17; 3:15; Num 24:17; Deut 6:4.

The translation is basically the work of one man, Harry M. Orlinsky, noted Jewish scholar, although two other scholars (H. L. Ginsberg and E. A. Speiser) and three rabbis acted as a reviewing committee. The three rabbis represented the three branches of American Judaism.

The Anchor Bible. It is known as an ecumenical venture and is under the editorial supervision of William F. Albright and David N. Freedman. The first volumes were published in 1964, Genesis and the Epistles of James, Peter and Jude. For each book of the Bible there is an accurate English translation conveying the meaning of the Heb. and Gr. texts and yet adapting the translation to modern American English. However, in many instances the translation follows the biblical text quite literally (e.g., Ps 1; Jn 1). There are some curious paraphrases (e.g., in Jn 3:1 where Nicodemus is "a member of the Jewish Sanhedrin").

With the translation there are explanatory notes and a commentary considering historical and critical matters. There is no ecclesiastical organization behind the project, which is international and interfaith since Catholic, Protestant, and Jewish scholars from many parts of the world contribute the individual volumes. Each Bible book is the work of one scholar who is an expert in that area of Bible study. It should be noted that most scholars hold the theologically liberal view.

Amplified Bible. This appeared in several stages, the NT in 1958 and culminating in the whole Bible in 1965. The complete edition has been extensively revised, especially in the OT.

The translation is new and generally accurate in the revised edition. As its chief feature it amplifies different shades of meaning in the original Heb. and Gr. by multiplying English words. For example, whereas in Isa 7:14 the KJV reads, "Behold, a virgin shall conceive," the AB has, "Behold, the young woman *who* is unmarried *and* a virgin, shall conceive." Footnotes bring together a multitude of conservative comments on the text of every page.

While in some instances it is no doubt helpful to have more than one English word to translate the original, yet out of the several shades of meaning represented by the various word amplifications, only one – not all – of the meanings fit a given context. In other words, though a single English word seldom says all an author intended, a multiplication of words usually says more than he actually meant to convey. However, many find enrichment in the understanding of Scripture through the approach of the AB.

The Jerusalem Bible (1966). This Roman Catholic version produced in England is the English equivalent of the French *La Bible de Jerusalem* (1956) prepared by the Dominican Biblical School in Jerusalem under the general editorship of Père Roland de Vaux. The introductions and copious footnotes are a direct translation from the French, while the text was usually translated directly from the original languages and simultaneously compared with the French when questions of variant reading or interpretation arose. The desire of the English general editor Alexander Jones and his collaborators was to translate the Bible into "contemporary" English.

The divine name Yahweh is used throughout the OT. As one would expect, the books of the Apocrypha are distributed among the Historical Books, the Wisdom Books, and the Prophets instead of keeping them in a separate section. The poetic passages are printed as verse and the lines with fewer stresses in the Heb. are indented. The text is divided by bold-type section and paragraph headings to enable the reader to see at a glance what is the subject matter before him.

The introductions and the interpretive notes follow the trend among Roman Catholic scholars to accept a modified documentary theory of the Pentateuch, believing there are three streams of tradition in Genesis to Numbers; to hold to composite authorship for the book of Isaiah; and to date the writing of Daniel to *c.* 165 B.C. On the other hand, messianic prophecies are clearly noted and often explained in the footnotes (e.g., the passages in Isaiah regarding the "servant of Yahweh," at 42:1). The explanatory footnotes in the NT are in general theologically sound; with the book of Romans, e.g., they are nearly as long as the text of that book and provide excellent evangelical comments. Helpful supplements include an extensive chronological table for general and biblical history, and an index of the biblical themes in the footnotes.

The New World Translation. Published by the Watchtower Bible and Tract Society in 1953, this version indicates how a distinctive cult (Jehovah's Witnesses) can translate the Bible to suit its own purposes, often without the substantiation of any kind of good biblical exegesis. Of course where no theological bias is involved, the translation can be in fairly good idiom. Yet this cult denies the deity of Christ and the equality of the Son with the Father, and thus Jn 1:1 is translated ". . . and the word was *a god.*"

Also, the word "Jehovah" is often substituted in the NT for the word "Lord," although "Jehovah" is not used when referring to the Lord Jesus Christ personally. Thus there is an inconsistency to support a particular bias.

Some Private Translations into Modern Speech

The New Testament in Modern Speech. This is perhaps the first modern speech version translated by an individual (1902). R. F. Weymouth first ascertained the sense of the Gr. text and then proceeded to express that sense in 20th cen. English. In other words, Weymouth was interested in how an inspired writer would have written had he lived in this age. The values of Gr. verbs, shades of meaning of words used and a keen appreciation of Gr. cases are all reflected in this translation. Note how I Jn 1:6 is translated: ". . . while we are living in darkness," or note the expression in Lk 15:1: "Now the tax-gatherers and the notorious sinners were everywhere in the habit of coming close to Him to listen to Him."

In general the earlier editions were doctrinally sound. Later editions, revised by Weymouth's successors, were somewhat influenced by liberal doctrine.

Twentieth Century New Testament. This British translation began in 1890 when a mother and pastor's wife, Mrs. Mary Higgs, together with Ernest Malan, an engineer, decided to produce a translation of the NT in everyday speech that young people could understand. They were joined gradually by more housewives, businessmen, and ministers until the committee had grown to 35 persons, including three recognized scholars. Their work was done with meticulous care and a thoroughly sound procedure; it was released in 1904 (Moody Press reprint, 1961). TCNT contains a minimum of paraphrase and interpretation and shows both accuracy and clarity.

The Bible by James Moffatt. The translation of the whole Bible by Moffatt was completed and published in 1926. He attempted to provide an entirely new version that would produce the same effect as the original text on those who read and heard it. Moffatt was a careful scholar, especially in the NT (1913). The version is free and quite vigorous. It does not sound like the familiar KJV (e.g., Gen 1:1,

"This is the story of how the universe was formed"). Finer shades of meaning in the Gr. tenses are graphically brought out in the NT (cf. Lk 7:45; 8:23; Rom 8:13; I Jn 1:6).

In spite of these qualities, Moffatt's version has serious weaknesses. He affirmed that he found "freedom from the theory of verbal inspiration," and this view is reflected in his rendering of some of the great doctrinal passages of both OT and NT. In the Pentateuch, in accord with the documentary theory, he attempted to indicate the multiple authors by alternating Roman and italic type. He also rearranged the text as he thought best in some places (cf. Jn 13 – 16), and since he held to a diminished view of the deity of Christ, he reduced to a minimum the thrust of the great passages on that doctrine (e.g., Jn 1:1 – 5; Phil 2:5 – 8; Col 1:15 – 18; Heb 1:3). The virgin birth of Christ is placed in question by using a decidedly inferior text reading that refers to Joseph as "the father of Jesus" (Mt 1:16).

The New Testament in the Language of the People. This was translated and first published in 1937 by C. B. Williams, then professor of Greek at Union University, Jackson, Tenn., and reprinted by Moody Press in several editions. It is noted primarily for its accuracy in rendering the tenses, word pictures, and fine shades of grammatical meaning in the Gr. which are often passed over in other translations. While it lacks something in literary quality and smoothness, it rewards the careful reader of the NT by additional help from the Gr. in a modern-speech rendering.

This translation is not to be confused with the *New Testament in Plain English* by Charles Kingsley Williams, published in 1949 and reprinted by Eerdmans in 1963. The latter volume is an excellent basic English version with about a 2,000 word vocabulary suitable for children or foreigners learning English.

The New Testament in Modern English by J. B. Phillips (1958). This version is highly colloquial, a deliberate presentation of vivid and idiomatic language, using paraphrase very freely to bring out the meaning of difficult passages. It has become one of the most widely used translations of the NT in recent years.

With his *Four Prophets* (1963), Phillips began the translation of the OT using Amos, Hosea, Micah and Isa 1-35. These four prophetic passages were chosen because of their relevance today. Phillips admits that the OT cannot be translated so quickly and readily as the NT.

On the whole, the OT is a good and intelligible translation, although some objectionable features might be cited. In Isa 6:5 the prophet describes himself as a "foul-mouthed man," which can have an altogether different doctrinal meaning than the KJV of "a man of unclean lips." Hos 2:2 reads, "Tell her to wash the paint from her face," instead of "Let her put away her harlotries from before her presence," thus giving the passage a different connotation from what was intended. In general, however, many a difficult passage has been clarified, while paragraph headings are an aid to understanding.

The New Testament in the Language of Today by William F. Beck (1963). Prompted by the desire to put the NT in "the living language of today and tomorrow," Beck, aided by the most recent manuscripts and papyri discoveries, prepared a completely new translation, which was published by Concordia Publishing House. It has also been included in the *Four Translation New Testament* published in 1966 by Moody Press.

While lacking in forcefulness, NTLT is generally accurate, clear, and free from interpretation and paraphrases. It does a good job of following the Gr. text and at the same time attempts to render the words in their nearest single-word English equivalent. For example, "behold" in the KJV becomes "look" in the NTLT; "serpent" in KJV is simply "snake" in Beck's rendering; "blessed" in the beatitudes (Mt 5:3–12) of the KJV becomes "happy" in the NTLT.

The Letters of Paul by F. F. Bruce (1965). This is an avowed extended paraphrase by one of England's greatest evangelical NT scholars.

Bruce points out that in a paraphrase "the paraphrast includes much more of his own interpretation and exposition than a translator would deem proper." Therefore, the accuracy of such a rendering hinges largely on the scholarly ability of the translator. To guard against false conclusion from his paraphrase, Bruce has included on each facing page the ERV, which he deems the most accurate literal rendering.

Living Bible. Starting in 1962 with *Living Letters*, a paraphrase of the NT epistles, Kenneth N. Taylor published the *Living New Testament* (1967) and has now completed the series covering the entire Bible. His work immediately gained popularity so that by 1967 three million copies of Living Letters and Living Gospels had been printed. Also available is a parallel edition of the Living New Testament with the KJV. The earlier translations were carefully revised for the 1967 edition of the complete NT, and a general revision by a paraphrase revision committee is planned for every five years.

There is an undeniable freshness and clarity in Taylor's style that awakens interest. This results from the paraphrast's skill in using colloquial speech and free rendering of passages. Another reason for the clarity is interpretive selection. In practically every instance where the Heb. or Gr. texts are ambiguous, allowing alternatives, Taylor has adopted one view and rendered it clearly.

For example, the problem of what kind of faith James is talking about is decided by the additional interpretive word "real" faith (Jas 2:20); the problem of the sense of "she shall be *saved* in childbearing" (KJV) is interpreted in Living Letters as "He will save their souls"

(I Tim 2:15); the meaning of "Can two walk together, except they be agreed?" is fixed by the interpretive paraphrase, "For how can we walk together with your sins between us?" (Amos 3:3). This leads to clarity, but it also fixes interpretation when equally sound alternate views are possible.

Much of Taylor's very free paraphrase is plainly commentary and should be so recognized. True paraphrase involves the modernized English equivalent of what is in the text itself, while the commentary introduces something which is not there in order to elucidate the meaning of what is there. In Jn 1:11, e.g., Taylor adds the whole sentence, "Only a few would welcome and receive Him." Besides being historically inaccurate, this statement is not in the Gr. text, but the reader is not informed of this.

The New Testament, An Expanded Translation by Kenneth S. Wuest, late professor of Greek at Moody Bible Institute (1961). Using "as many English words as are necessary to bring out the richness, force and clarity of the Gr. text," the translation is intended as "a companion to, or commentary on, the standard translations."

Wuest wished to stay clear of paraphrase and interpretation. The translation is commendable for attempting to reproduce the feeling of the Gr. text as a Gr. student would read it. For example, the KJV of Lk 15:20 reads, "... and fell on his neck and kissed him," while Wuest translates, "... he fell on his neck and tenderly kissed him again and again." Sometimes the expansion gets out of hand, as in Acts 17:18 where the one Gr. word *spermologos* (KJV, "babbler") is rendered, "This ignorant plagiarist, picking up scraps of information here and there, unrelated in his own thinking and passing them off as the result of his own mature thought."

Despite certain weaknesses of paraphrase and some questionable Gr. exegesis, this version is helpful as a commentary-type translation and a supplement in understanding certain idioms and shades of thought in the Gr. text.

Good News for Modern Man, the New Testament in Today's English Version (TEV). Published by American Bible Society, this translation has had an unexpected sales boom since its publication in 1966. Its author, Robert G. Bratcher, steers a healthy course between the inaccuracies of excessive paraphrase that have spoiled many recent translations and the obscurity of meaning in the more literal versions. This has the combined strengths of general accuracy with everyday language, conservative handling of the text, and general theological faithfulness to the intent of Scripture. Interesting line drawings on almost every page, outlines and cross-references of the general material, and a glossary of Bible terms at the back offer several added and helpful features.

The TEV, however, contains some weaknesses of various types. While interpretive paraphrase is at a minimum, the author unnecessarily biased the translation in a few places toward a particular interpretation of the text. In I Jn 5:6, ". . . he came with the water of his baptism and the blood of his death," Bratcher interpreted the words "water" as Christ's "baptism," and "blood" as His "death." The different "tongues" of I Cor 12 and 14, which may well be languages, are rendered as "strange sounds," which is not justified by the Gr. text and biases the interpretation toward ecstatic utterances.

Some criticism has been offered in the way the version translates certain passages referring to the "blood" of Christ by the "death" of Christ (cf. Eph 1:7; Col 1:20; Rom 3:25; 5:9; Acts 20:28; 1 Pet 1:19; Rev 1:6). While it would be easy to accuse the translator of theological motives in these cases, the fact that in numerous other places the word "blood" is retained (cf. Lk 22:20; Jn 6:53–56; I Cor 10:16; 11:27; Heb 9:22) seems to indicate he is not opposed to this concept but has been motivated out of concern for modern readers understanding that the "blood" was often used as a synonym for "death" in ancient days (cf. Mt 27:4, 25).

A. F. J. and L. Go.

Bibliography. Ward Allen, trans. and ed., *Translating for King James* (the notes of John Bois), Nashville: Vanderbilt Univ. Press, 1969. Dewey Beegle, *God's Word into English,* New York: Harper, 1960. F. F. Bruce, *The English Bible,* London: Oxford Univ. Press, 1961. Charles C. Butterworth, *The Literary Lineage of the King James Bible,* Philadelphia: Univ. of Pennsylvania Press, 1941. Herbert Dennett, *A Guide to Modern Versions of the New Testament,* Chicago: Moody, 1966. Stanley L. Greenslade, ed., *The Cambridge History of the Bible,* Cambridge: Cambridge Univ. Press, 1963 (a monumental work). Geddes MacGregor, *A Literary History of the Bible,* Nashville: Abingdon, 1968. Gustavus S. Paine, *The Learned Men,* New York: Crowell, 1959 (about those who produced the KJV). Alfred W. Pollard, *Records of the English Bible,* New York: Oxford, 1911. Hugh Pope, *English Versions of the Bible,* rev. and amplified by S. Bullough, St. Louis: Herder, 1952 (by a Roman Catholic scholar, with a full bibliography and extended lists of versions and translations). Ira Price, *The Ancestry of Our English Bible,* New York: Harper & Bros., 3rd rev. ed., 1956. H. Wheeler Robinson, ed., *The Bible in Its Ancient and English Versions,* London: Oxford Univ. Press, 1940, rev. ed., 1954. Philip Schaff, *A Companion to the Greek Testament and English Version,* 4th ed., New York: Harper & Bros., 1894. Luther A. Weigle, *The English New Testament from Tyndale to the Revised Standard Version,* New York: Abingdon-Cokesbury Press, 1949. B. F. Westcott, *A General View of the History of the English Bible,* 1868; 3rd ed. rev. by W. A. Wright, New York: Macmillan, 1927.

BIBLE INTERPRETATION. All communication must be properly interpreted by the bearer or reader. Witness Philip's question to the Ethiopian treasurer, "Do you understand what you are reading?" (Acts 8:30), indicating the need for interpretation.

The basic word hermeneutics (Gr. *hermēneia,* verb *hermēneuō*) means "to interpret," "to expound," "to explain," and further includes to translate from a foreign language into a familiar language (Jn 1:38, 42; 9:7). In the OT the English term occurs, e.g., in Prov 1:6 regarding the interpretation of a proverb.

Joseph was enabled to interpret (Heb. *pātar*) dreams in Egypt (Gen 40:12; 41:8–15), and Daniel was given the interpretation (Aram. *peshar*) of several dreams (Dan 2; 4; 7:16) and the mysterious handwriting (Dan 5). The term *pesher* was used by the Qumran community for their interpretations of OT prophetical passages (*see* Dead Sea Scrolls).

In the NT the compound Gr. word *diërmēneuō* is used of Jesus expounding the OT prophecies regarding His suffering and glory (Lk 24:27) and of interpreting a message in an unknown tongue (I Cor 12:30; 14:5, 13, 27).

A distinction ought to be maintained between inspiration (*q.v.*) and interpretation. Inspiration relates to the nature of the Bible, its trustworthiness, because it is the word of God written (II Tim 3:16); interpretation relates to the meaning of the Bible. It is, therefore, quite possible for persons to agree on the former while having great difference of opinion regarding the latter. For example, two persons might agree that Gen 1 is a trustworthy record, yet disagree about the meaning of the word "day" in the passage.

During the early centuries of church history two basic schools of interpretation arose, one in Alexandria, Egypt, the other in Antioch, Syria. Only a summary of their principles can be included here, described by way of contrast. First, the Alexandrian school emphasized the allegorical approach (one thing stands for or teaches something else), while the Antiocheans insisted upon a more literal meaning, or the original sense of any passage.

Second, the Antiocheans laid more stress upon a study of any passage within its immediate and wider context, a practice not always followed by the Alexandrians.

Third, greater reliance upon the traditions of the church in interpreting Scriptures was found in Alexandria than in Antioch. For the latter, Scripture was its own interpreter.

Fourth, with regard to the inspiration of the Bible, the Alexandrian stressed the abnormal, or trancelike, state of the writer, while the Antiocheans emphasized his consciousness and the heightening of his perceptions by the work of the Holy Spirit. Thus the latter provided for a greater degree of individuality being preserved in the writing of Scripture.

The interpreter of the Bible is similar to a

workman with a task before him. He is an intelligent being, and he sees what needs to be done. What else is required? Two things: *spiritual insight* and *good tools*. The former is supplied by the ministry of the Holy Spirit in the life of the believer (Jn 14:26; I Cor 2:10–13; I Jn 2:27; cf. Eph 1:17); the latter we now discuss. Admittedly, some of these tools, or principles, will be more available to some than others.

1. Determine the meaning of the original language of any passage for the original readers. Ideally, this calls for a knowledge of Hebrew, Aramaic, and Greek. Practically, it means the interpreter needs to use the best translations of the Bible available to him. In this connection, he ought to learn something of the purpose for which the author wrote and the historical circumstances out of which the writing arose. The Scriptures are part of a larger historical and cultural context. In the OT, Israel was related, in one way or another, to the Egyptians, the Assyrians, the Babylonians, the Persians (to name a few); in the NT, the church emerged from a Jewish background and arose in the Greco-Roman world. The languages of the Bible reflect these various cultures; thus the interpreter must be knowledgeable of and sensitive to the use of words in their various settings.

For example, the word "save" (Gr. *sōzō*) was a common term of the 1st cen. world. The secular usage included saving from death, rescuing from physical danger, saving from disease or demon-possession, and preserving one's physical well-being (e.g., Mt 8:25; 14:30; Mk 3:4; 15:30–31; Jas 5:15). In addition to these, in the NT the word is used of saving from spiritual or eternal death (e.g., Lk 9:24; 19:10; Jn 3:17; 5:34; 10:9; Rom 5:9–10).

2. Interpret the words of any given verse or paragraph within its immediate context. The context is the ultimate determinant of word meanings. While the dictionary will provide various possibilities, the context will aid in narrowing the choice. For example, why translate the Gr. word *paraklētos* as "Comforter" in Jn 14:16 and as "Advocate" in I Jn 2:1? Or what is the difference between the word "law" in Rom 7:9 and in Rom 8:2? Furthermore, the context of the Bible as a whole must be included. The principle of "the analogy of Scripture" is a corrective to isolated interpretations and a guard against the danger of pet theories based upon limited data.

3. Discover the literary nature of the passage under study. Is it to be taken in the natural, normal sense of the language? Or is it figurative? Is it a narrative of events? Or is it discourse or didactic material, meant to teach a specific idea? This calls for some knowledge of customs within the culture involved, and of the idioms by which ideas are made clear.

Often there is no problem in deciding matters of this kind. For example, the parables of Jesus are regarded as illustrations of ideas, figurative

language to clarify concepts. Idea: the kingdom of heaven. Illustration: a man who sowed good seed in his field (Mt 13:24–30). Not so simple is the meaning of the words "a great mountain burning with fire was cast into the sea" (Rev 8:8). Is it a description of a meteorite-like object falling into water? Or is it depicting the fall of some great ruler, rejected by God and cast down among men? Possibly more difficult yet is the interpretation of the phrase "a thousand years" (Rev 20:2–7). Does it mean an actual thousand years? Or a round number of years? Or a long period of time (regardless of specific length)? Or is it a symbol of completeness? The history of biblical interpretation shows that these questions are not always easily decided.

4. Interpret the Bible in terms of the principle of progressive revelation. Put simply, this means that God revealed things gradually, not all at one time. Partly, this was because of the stages in which the divine program was being fulfilled (cf. Heb 1:1–2); partly, because of man's state of unreadiness to receive and understand the message (cf. Jn 16:12).

On occasion, this principle involved adding to what had been given earlier. Jesus told His disciples, "I have yet many things to say unto you, but ye cannot bear them now" (Jn 16:12); the Holy Spirit would teach them when He came. In other instances, there was a fuller interpretation of previous teachings, e.g., "Ye have heard that it was said. . . but I say unto you" (Mt 5:21–22). Here our Lord explained the essential character of the commandments.

5. Interpret the language of the Bible regarding the natural world as that of appearance and popular rather than technical or scientific. Yet, at the same time, *popular* terminology is not synonymous with *errant* or *invalid*. The Bible does not theorize about nature; it simply states facts in a non-technical manner.

Illustrations of this form of language are found in expressions describing the sun rising (Eccl 1:5; Mt 5:45), or the earth having four corners (Isa 11:12), a form of speaking preserved in our speech until this day. Notice, too, the manner in which the various elements in the creation are described: a "firmament" (Gen 1:6–8); "grass," "herb," "fruit tree" (Gen 1:11); "living creature" and "fowl" (Gen 1:20). None of these are technical names. They are all common, popular terms, intelligible to the ordinary reader. Simply put, too, are observations of the water cycle of nature: the rivers flow from their sources into the sea; then by evaporation and condensation the waters return again to their sources (Eccl 1:7).

Another illustration of this same principle is found in the book of Ecclesiastes as a whole. The writer makes observations on various human experiences and natural conditions, then draws certain deductions therefrom. The book is essentially a commentary on life by nature, a continual round of activity, unsatisfying to the one caught in it. A final solution to the human dilemma occurs at the end of the book (12:13-14).

To return to the question of the identification and interpretation of various literary types, a knowledge of these is indispensable to the interpreter. A concise discussion has been written by J. Stafford Wright from which the following are adapted, with some added illustrations:

Literal fact. A statement of events as they occurred, to be interpreted in its simple sense (e.g., Jn 1:35-42).

Substantial or compressed fact. A statement compressing irrelevant details in the interest of a main impression (cf. Lk 24:44-53 with Acts 1:1-11, the latter indicating that there were 40 days between the resurrection and the ascension, a fact not given in the former passage).

Metaphor. A word or group of words indicating a resemblance between two ordinarily different things (e.g., Gen 2:7 which describes God's creative activity under the figure of a potter; cf. Rom 9:20-21).

Parable. A story based on an ordinary life situation, used to convey the meaning of an idea or concept. Commonly used in the teaching of Jesus, this literary device could drive home a point effectively. See the examples in Lk 10:30-35 (where one point is basic, answering the question, "Who is my neighbor?") and Mt 13:24-30, 36-43 (where Jesus explains both the one point and the many details).

The recent key works on this figure are by C. H. Dodd, *The Parables of the Kingdom* New York: Scribner's, 1936; J. Jeremias, *The Parables of Jesus* (trans. by S. H. Hooke), London: SCM Press, 1954; A. M. Hunter, *Interpreting the Parables,* Philadelphia: Westminster, 1960; and in a number of his other books on the Gospels. Among the older, standard books mention should be made of R. C. Trench, *Notes on the Parables of Our Lord,* 14th ed. rev., London: Macmillan, 1882; A. B. Bruce, *The Parabolic Teaching of Christ,* New York: A. C. Armstrong & Son, 1894; and G. Campbell Morgan, *The Parables and Metaphors of Our Lord,* New York: Revell, 1943. The last three tend to be more conservative in their attitude toward the Bible, while the first three have indicated many new insights into the problems related to interpreting the parables. *See* Parable; Parables of Jesus.

Symbol. An object or person which has no importance in itself but rather in what it portrays. Many of these are found in the visionary apocalyptic writings (e.g., Dan 7:2-3,17; Rev 1:12, 16, 20), as well as in the prophets' teaching techniques (e.g., Ezk 37:15-28). *See* Symbol(ism).

Type. An object or person having significance of its own, yet is used to represent something or someone else. While often abused by interpreters, the type holds a large place in Scripture. The original plan of the tabernacle (Acts 7:44; Heb 8:5), the first Adam (Rom 5:14), and the experiences of the Israelites in the wilderness (I Cor 10:6, 11) are all called types (Gr. *typos*) of something greater. Probably the NT use of certain OT figures is the proper starting point for interpretation of others. *See* Type.

Allegory. The use of a story, which may or not be factual, to depict a certain truth. Jotham's tale (sometimes called a "fable") in Jud 9:7-15 is one clear example; the story in the Song of Solomon may be another; while Paul's use of Hagar and Sarah (Gal 4:21-31) seems to be a third. *See* Allegory.

Myth. While the use of this word is always in an unfavorable sense in the NT (I Tim 1:4; 4:7; II Tim 4:4; Tit 1:14; II Pet 1:16), probably resulting from the apostles' response to Gnostic excesses, the term basically means an account, whether or not true in itself, used to teach a truth about human experience.

For the OT, much formerly regarded by liberal critics as mythical (e.g., the patriarchal narratives in Genesis) has been shown by archaeological investigation to be a part of early Semitic culture (the Nuzu tablets and the Mari documents are important evidence here). A valuable monograph on the historical and theological backgrounds is G. E. Wright's *The Old Testament Against Its Environment*; see also W. F. Albright, *The Biblical Period*; and W. Keller, *The Bible as History.*

For the NT, the arguments of Rudolf Bultmann for the mythical nature of much of the Gospel narratives has been countered by recent arguments for the historicity of early Christianity (e.g., F. V. Filson, J. W. Montgomery, W. Pannenberg, N. Stonehouse, M. C. Tenney). Within the NT itself, see I Cor 15:1-4; I Jn 1:1-4; II Pet 1:15-18. Luke wrote of the factual nature of the events of the life of Christ, even His ascension into heaven (Acts 1:1-11). *See* Myth(ology).

Saga. A psychological and interpretative reaction of some person involved in an important event. Examples of this figure would be the song of Deborah (Jud 5) or the song of Moses and the Israelites after crossing the Red Sea (Ex 15). Saga fills a relatively minor role in biblical literature. In modern critical theories it is often suggested as the source of various other OT and NT types of literature, thus casting doubt on their authenticity.

The interpreter of the Bible, therefore, needs genuine spiritual insight into that which he reads, and honest diligence in his pursuit of understanding. And what he understands ought to end in glory to God and to richness of life in Christ.

A final summary of the approach to study is as follows: (1) Read the text prayerfully, asking God for wisdom; (2) study the immediate and surrounding contexts; (3) give attention to other major related biblical passages; (4) investigate available theological, historical, archaeological, and psychological/sociological evidences which bear upon the problem involved; (5) choose the resulting interpretation which seems most in harmony with clear evidence (including the whole of Scripture); (6) be willing to await further light rather than make a bad choice at the moment.

Bibliography. E. C. Blackman, *Biblical Interpretation,* Philadelphia: Westminster, 1959. F. J. Denbeaux, *Understanding the Bible,* Philadelphia: Westminster, 1958. A. M. Derham, *A Christian's Guide to Bible Study,* New York: Revell, 1963. F. C. Grant, *How to Read the Bible,* New York: Collier, 1961. A. M. Hunter, "The Interpreter and the Parables," *New Testament Issues,* R. Batey, ed., London: SCM, 1970. A. B. Michelsen, *Interpreting the Bible,* Grand Rapids: Eerdmans, 1963. B. Ramm, *Protestant Biblical Interpretation,* Boston: Wilde, 1956. Milton S. Terry, *Biblical Hermeneutics,* Grand Rapids: Zondervan, n.d. J. D. Wood, *The Interpretation of the Bible,* London: Duckworth, 1958. J. Stafford Wright, *Interpreting the Bible,* London: Inter-Varsity, 1955.

W. M. D.

BIBLE MANUSCRIPTS

The Old Testament

The original MSS of the OT (*autographa*) are not available, but the Heb. text is amply represented by both pre- and post-Christian MSS.

I. The Number of Hebrew Old Testament Manuscripts

The first collection of Heb. MSS made by Benjamin Kennicott (A.D. 1776-80), published by Oxford, listed 615 MSS of the OT. Later Giovanni de Rossi (1784-88) published a list of 731 MSS. The main MS discoveries in modern times are those of the Cairo Geniza (*c.* 1890f.) and the Dead Sea Scrolls (DSS) (1947f.). In the Cairo synagogue attic storeroom alone were discovered some 200,000 MSS and fragments (Paul E. Kahle, *Cairo Geniza,* p. 13; Ernst Würthwein, *The Text of the Old Testament,* p. 25); some 10,000 of these are biblical (Moshe Goshen Gottstein, "Biblical Manuscripts in the United States," *Textus* [1962], p. 35). According to J. T. Milik, fragments of about 600 MSS are known from the DSS, not all biblical. Gottstein estimates that the total number of OT Heb. MS fragments throughout the world runs into the tens of thousands (Gottstein, *op. cit.,* p. 31).

II. Major Collections of Old Testament Manuscripts

Of the 200,000 Cairo Geniza MS fragments, some 100,000 are housed at Cambridge. The largest organized collection of Heb. OT MSS in the world is the Second Firkowitch Collection in Leningrad. It contains 1,582 items of the Bible and Masora (see V. Nature of OT MSS, 3) on parchment, 725 on paper, plus 1,200 additional Heb. MS fragments (the Antonin Collection, Würthwein, *op. cit.,* p. 23). The British Museum catalog lists 161 Heb. OT MSS. The

Bodleian Library catalog lists 146 OT MSS, each one containing a large number of fragments (Kahle, *op. cit.,* p. 5). Gottstein (*op. cit.,* p. 30) estimates that in the United States alone there are tens of thousands of Semitic MS fragments, about 5 percent of which are biblical (500 plus MSS).

III. Description of Major Old Testament Hebrew Manuscripts

The most significant Heb. OT MSS date from between the 3rd cen. B.C. and the 14th cen. A.D. (For terms and names pertaining to the Masoretes see V. Nature of OT MSS, 3.)

1. Dead Sea Scrolls. The most remarkable MSS are those of the DSS (*q.v.*) which date from the 3rd cen. B.C. to the 1st cen. A.D. They include one complete OT book (Isaiah) and thousands of fragments which together represent every OT book except Esther.

2. Nash Papyrus. Besides these unusual finds, which are about a thousand years older than most of the earliest OT Heb. MSS, there is extant one damaged copy of the Shema (from Ex 20:2 f.; Deut 5:6 f. and 6:4 f.). It is dated between the 2nd cen. B.C. (William F. Albright, "A Biblical Fragment from the Maccabean Age: The Nash Papyrus," JBL, LVI [1937], 145-176), and the 1st cen. A.D. (Kahle).

3. Oriental 4445 (Or 4445). This British Museum MS is dated by Ginsburg between A.D. 820 and 850 (*Introduction,* pp. 249 f., 269 f.), the Masora notes being added a century later. But Kahle (*op. cit.,* p. 118) argues that both consonantal Heb. texts and pointing (the added vowel points or marks) are from the time of Moses ben Asher (10th cen.). Since the Heb. alphabet normally consists only of consonants, Heb. writing normally shows only these letters, with a few of the letters being used in varying degrees to represent some of the vocalic sounds. This MS contains Gen 39:20 – Deut 1:33.

4. Codex Cairensis. A codex is a manuscript in book form with pages. According to a colophon or inscription at the end of the book, this Cairo Codex was written and vowel-pointed in A.D. 895 by Moses ben Asher in Tiberias in Palestine (Würthwein, *op. cit.,* p. 25). It contains the Former Prophets (Joshua, Judges, I and II Samuel, I and II Kings) and the Latter Prophets (Isaiah, Jeremiah, Ezekiel, and the Twelve). It is symbolized *C* in Kittel's *Biblia Hebraica* (BH).

5. Aleppo Codex of the whole OT. It was written by Shelomo ben Baya'a (Kenyon, *Our Bible and the Ancient Manuscripts,* p. 84), but according to a colophon it was pointed (i.e., the vowel marks were added) by Moses ben Asher *c.* A.D. 930. It is a model codex, and although it was not permitted to be copied for a long time and was even reported to have been destroyed (Würthwein, *op. cit.,* p. 25), it was smuggled from Syria to Israel. It has now been photographed and will be the basis of the new Heb. Bible to be published by the Hebrew University (Gottstein, *op. cit.,* p. 13). It is a sound authority for the Ben Asher text.

6. Codex Leningradensis (B 19 A). According to a colophon or note at the end, it was copied in Old Cairo by Samuel ben Jacob in A.D. 1008 from a MS (now lost) written by Aaron ben Moses ben Asher c. A.D. 1000 (Kahle, op. cit., p. 110), whereas Ginsburg held it was copied from the Aleppo Codex (pp. 243 f.). It represents the oldest dated MS of the complete Heb. Bible that is known (Kahle, op. cit., p. 132). Kittel adopted it as the basis for his BH from the 3rd ed. on, where it is rep. e-sented under the symbol L.

7. Babylonian Codex of the Latter Prophets (MS Heb. B 3). This is sometimes called the Leningrad Codex of the Prophets (Kenyon, op. cit., p. 85) or the [St.] Petersburg Codex (Würthwein, op. cit., p. 26). It contains Isaiah, Jeremiah, Ezekiel, and the Twelve. It is dated A.D. 916, but its chief significance lies in the fact that through it, punctuation added by the Babylonian school of Masoretes was rediscovered. It is symbolized as V (ar)P in BH.

8. Reuchlin Codex of the Prophets, dated A.D. 1105, now at Karlsruhe. Like the British Museum MS Ad. 21161 (c. A.D. 1150), it contains a recension of Ben Naphtali, a Tiberian Masorete. These have been of great value in establishing the fidelity of the Ben Asher text (Kenyon, op. cit., p. 36).

9. Cairo Geniza MSS. Of the about 10,000 biblical MSS and fragments from the Geniza (storehouse for old MSS) of the Cairo synagogue now scattered throughout the world, Kahle identified over 120 examples copied by the Babylonian group of Masoretes. In the Firkowitch Collection are found 14 Heb. OT MSS dating between A.D. 929 and 1121. He contends also that the 1,200 MSS and fragments of the Antonin Collection come from the Cairo Geniza (Kahle, op. cit., p. 7). Kahle provided a list of 70 of these MSS in the prolegomena to BH, 7th ed.

There are other Geniza MSS scattered over the world. Some of the better ones in the United States are in the Enelow Memorial Collection housed at the Jewish Theological Seminary, New York (cf. Gottstein, op. cit., p. 44 f.).

10. Erfurt Codices (E 1, 2, 3) are listed in the University Library in Tübingen as MS Orient. 1210/11, 1212, 1213. Their peculiarity is that they represent more or less (more in E 3) the text and Masora of the Ben Naphtali tradition. E 1 is a 14th cen. MS containing the Heb. OT. E 2 is also of the Heb. OT, probably from the 13th cen. E 3 is the oldest, being dated by Kahle and others before A.D. 1100 (cf. Würthwein, op. cit., p. 26).

11. Some lost codices. There are a number of significant but now lost codices whose peculiar readings are preserved and referred to in BH. Codex Severi (Sev.) is a medieval list of 32 variants of the Pentateuch (cf. CA to Gen 18:21; 24:7; Num 4:3), supposedly based on a MS brought to Rome in A.D. 70 which Emperor Severus (A.D. 222–235) later gave to a synagogue he had built. Codex Hillel (Hill.) was

Samaritan high priest and Samaritan Pentateuch. HFV

supposedly written c. A.D. 600 by Rabbi Hillel ben Moses ben Hillel. It is said to have been accurate and was used to revise other MSS. Readings from this MS are cited by medieval Masoretes and are used in the critical apparatus (CA) of BH in Gen 6:3; 19:6; Ex 25:19; Lev 26:9 (cf. Würthwein, op. cit., p. 27). A critical apparatus lists the variant readings to the text which the editor considers are significant for translators or necessary for establishing the text.

12. Samaritan Pentateuch. The separation of the Samaritans from the Jews was an important event in the history of the post-Exilic period of the OT. It probably occurred during the 5th or 4th cen. B.C., and was the culmination of a long process. At the time of this schism one would suspect that the Samaritans took with them the Scriptures as they then existed, with the result that there came into being a second Heb. recension or revised text of the Pentateuch. This Samaritan Pentateuch (SP) is not a version in the strict sense of the word, but rather a MS portion of the Heb. text itself. It contains the five books of Moses, and is written in a Paleo-Heb. script quite similar to that found on the Moabite Stone, Siloam inscription, Lachish

letters, and in particular some of the older biblical MSS from Qumran. Because the Samaritan script is a derivative of the Paleo-Heb. script which was revived in the Maccabean era of nationalistic archaizing, and because of the full orthography of the SP, Frank M. Cross, Jr., believes that the SP branched off from the pre- or proto-Masoretic text in the 2nd cen. B.C. (*The Ancient Library of Qumran*, Garden City: Doubleday, 1958, pp. 127 f.).

The Samaritans were the descendants of those members of the ten northern tribes who were not deported by the Assyrian kings in their conquest of the kingdom of Israel. After the capital city of Samaria fell to Sargon II in 722 B.C., this ruler claims to have led away 27,290 of its inhabitants (ANET, pp. 284 f.). He brought in Gentile colonists from other parts of his empire, who eventually intermarried with the remaining Israelites. The Samaritan Sanballat (*q.v.*) opposed the relief measures of Nehemiah because Zerubbabel earlier had refused to let the Samaritans help rebuild the temple in Jerusalem. The rift between the Jews and the Samaritans widened, so apparent in the Gospels describing the time of Christ. Alexander the Great gave them permission to build their own temple on Mount Gerizim (later destroyed by John Hyrcanus in 128 B.C.), and they made their own recension of the Heb. books of Moses with modifications to provide scriptural authority for worshiping on that mountain. *See* Samaritans.

A form of the SP text seems to have been known to such early Church Fathers as Eusebius of Caesarea and Jerome. It did not become available to scholars in the West, however, until 1616 when Pietro della Valle discovered a MS of the SP in Damascus. A great wave of excitement arose among biblical scholars. The text was published in an early portion of the Paris Polyglot (1632) and later in the text of the London Polyglot (1657). It was quickly regarded as being superior to the MT; but it became relegated to relative obscurity after Wilhelm Gesenius in 1815 adjudged it to be practically worthless for textual criticism. In more recent times the value of the SP has been reasserted by A. Geiger, Paul E. Kahle, Frederic Kenyon, *et al.*

So far as is known, no MS of the SP is older than the 11th cen. A.D. Although the Samaritan community esteems one roll, which it claims was written by Abisha, the great-grandson of Moses, in the thirteenth year after the conquest of Canaan, their authority is so spurious that the claim may safely be dismissed. The oldest codex of the SP bears a note about its sale in A.D. 1149 – 50, but the MS itself is much older. One MS was copied in 1204, while another dated 1211 – 12 is now in the John Rylands Library at Manchester, and still another, dated *c.* 1232, is in the New York Public Library.

The standard printed edition of the SP is in five volumes by A. von Gall, *Der hebräische Pentateuch der Samaritaner* (1914–18). It provides an eclectic text based on 80 late medieval MSS and fragments. Although Gall's text is in Heb. characters, the Samaritans wrote in an alphabet quite different from the square Heb. Nevertheless, their script, like the Heb., descended from old Paleo-Heb. characters.

In all there are about 6,000 deviations of the SP from the MT, many of them being merely orthographic and trivial. In about 1,900 instances the Samaritan text agrees with the LXX against the MT. It must be argued, however, that some of the deviations from the MT are alterations introduced by the Samaritans in the interests of preserving their own cultus as well as the N Israelitic dialectal peculiarities, while the MT perpetuates any Judean dialectal features.

In the early Christian era the SP was translated into the Aram. dialect of the Samaritans, known as the Samaritan Targum. It was also translated into Gr., called the *Samaritikon*, from which about 50 citations are preserved in the notes on Origen's *Hexapla*. After the 11th cen. several translations of the SP were made into Arabic (cf. Paul E. Kahle, *The Cairo Geniza*, 2nd ed., pp. 51–57). [This section on the SP is by W.E.N. – Ed.]

IV. *Printed Hebrew Bibles*
(See Kenyon, *op. cit.*, pp. 86–88; Gottstein, *op. cit.*, pp. 8–10; Würthwein, *op. cit.*, pp. 27–30.)

1. Bologna ed. of the Psalms (A.D. 1477).

2. Soncino ed. of the complete OT with vowel pointing (A.D. 1488). There were also editions in Naples (1491–93) and Brescia (1494).

3. Complutensian Polyglot Bible by Cardinal Ximenes at Alcala, Spain (1514–17) in Heb., Gr., Aram. Targum, and Latin. A polyglot is a multiple-columned edition containing the original language and various other translations for means of comparison.

4. Antwerp Polyglot (1569–72).

5. Paris Polyglot (1629–45) ten vols.

6. London Polyglot (1654–57) six folio vols.

7. First Rabbinic Bible (1516–17). Produced by Felix Pratensis and published by Daniel Bomberg. It was a considerable critical achievement (in four vols.) and served as the basis of the Second Rabbinic Bible.

8. Second Rabbinic Bible (1524–25) by Jacob ben Chayyim and published by Daniel Bomberg in four vols. It was based on late MSS which provide the basis of the *textus receptus* (TR), a text presumed to be identical to that of the original MSS. Until 1929 it was found in Kittel's 1st and 2nd eds. of BH (where it is called Bombergiana or B).

9. J. H. Michaelis ed. (M¹) (A.D. 1720). A Protestant pietist of Halle who followed in the main the text of Jablonski's 1699 ed. Its critical apparatus (CA) contains the most important readings of the Erfurt MSS.

10. Kennicott ed. (1776–1780) used 615 MSS (mostly late) and 52 printed eds. The text follows the ed. of van der Hooght (1705).

11. Meir Halevi Letteris (1852) two vol. Heb. Bible based to a marked extent on MS Erfurt 3, readings of which are found in Michaelis (1720). He may have used MS or folio 121 of Marburg (Gottstein, *op. cit.*, p. 8).

12. De Rossi (1784–88) produced not an ed. but a collection of variants from 1,475 MSS and eds. The collection is greater than Kennicott's but most variants are not substantial.

13. S. Baer (B) (1869–95) with the collaboration of Franz Delitzsch endeavored to produce a correct form of the Masoretic text using old MSS and eds., but their methods of "correcting" the text are questionable, according to Kahle and Würthwein. They followed the text of Wolf Heidenheim (1757–1832).

14. Ginsburg ed. (1894) used earlier and better MSS.

15. C. D. Ginsburg (G) produced for the British Foreign Bible Society (1926) a new ed. of Ginsburg's earlier work (1894) with variants of 70 MSS and 19 printed eds. (mostly 13th cen.) including Or 4445 which Ginsburg dated A.D. 820–50.

16. *Biblia Hebraica* (1929) 1st and 2nd eds. based on Bomberg (1524–25), containing variants from 10th and 11th cen. *Codicis Jemensis* (*V*[ar]J) edited by R. Hoerning (1889).

17. *Biblia Hebraica* (1939) 3rd ed. based on codex Leningradensis (L) or B19A (from A.D. 1008) with the small Masora of Ben Asher in the margin.

18. *Biblia Hebraica* (1951) 7th ed. includes DSS Isaiah and Habakkuk variants for the first time.

V. *Nature of Old Testament Manuscripts*

Although the official text of the OT was transmitted with great care, it was inevitable that certain copyist errors would creep into the texts over the hundreds of years of transmission into thousands of MSS.

1. Types of MS errors. There are several kinds of copyist errors which produce textual variants (cf. Archer, SOTI, pp. 48–50): (*a*) Haplography is the writing of a word, letter, or syllable only once when it should have been written more than once. (*b*) Dittography is writing twice what should have been written only once. (*c*) Metathesis is reversing the proper position of letters or words. (*d*) Fusion is the combining of two separate words into one. (*e*) Fission is the dividing of a single word into two words. (*f*) Homophony is the substitution of one word for another which is pronounced like it (e.g., "two" for "to"). (*g*) Misreading of similarly shaped letters. (*h*) Homoeoteleuton is the omission of an intervening passage because the scribe's eye skipped from one line to a similar ending on another line further down the page. (*i*) Accidental omissions where no repetition is involved (as "Saul was . . . year(s) old," I Sam 13:1, RSV). (*j*) Misreading vowel letters for consonants.

2. Rules for textual criticism. Scholars have developed certain criteria for determining which reading is the correct or original one. Seven may be suggested (cf. Archer, *op. cit.*, pp. 51–53): (*a*) The older reading is to be preferred since it is closer to the original. (*b*) The more difficult reading is to be preferred because scribes were more apt to smooth out difficult readings. (*c*) The shorter reading is to be preferred because copyists were more apt to insert new material than omit part of the sacred text. (*d*) The reading which best explains the other variants is to be preferred. (*e*) The reading with the widest geographical support is to be preferred since such MSS or versions are less likely to have influenced each other. (*f*) The reading which is most like the author's usual style is to be preferred. (*g*) The reading which does not reflect a doctrinal bias is to be preferred. (Cf. Würthwein, *op. cit.*, pp. 80–81, for further textual principles.)

3. History of the OT text. The Sopherim (from Heb. meaning "scribes") were the Jewish scholars and custodians of the OT text between the 5th and the 3rd cen. B.C. whose responsibility it was to standardize and preserve the OT text. They were followed by the Zugoth ("pairs" of textual scholars) in the 2nd and 1st cen. B.C. The third group were Tannaim ("repeaters" or "teachers") who extended to A.D. 200. Their work can be found in the *Midrash* ("textual interpretation"), *Tosefta* ("addition"), and *Talmud* ("instruction") which latter is divided into *Mishnah* ("repetitions") and *Gemara* ("the matter to be learned"). The Talmud gradually was written between A.D. 100 and 500.

Between A.D. 500 and 950 the Masoretes added the vowel pointings and pronunciation marks to the consonantal Heb. text received from the Sopherim, on the basis of the *māsôrâ* ("tradition") which had been handed down to them. The Masoretes were scribes who codified and wrote down the oral criticisms and remarks on the Heb. text. There were two major schools or centers of Masoretic activity, each largely independent of the other, the Babylonian and the Palestinian. The most famous Masoretes were the Jewish scholars living in Tiberias in Galilee, Moses ben Asher (with his son Aaron) and Ben Naphtali, in the late 9th and 10th cen. A.D. The Ben Asher text is the standard text for the Heb. Bible today as best represented by Codex Leningradensis (B 19A) and the Aleppo Codex.

4. Families of OT texts. Despite the minor variations within the Masoretic Heb. text (MT), it represents one broad textual family, even if all the MSS cannot be traced to a single archetype (as Kahle has argued that they cannot be).

The other two basic families of similar variants are the LXX and the Samaritan Pentateuch (SP). Thanks to the discovery of the DSS there are now Heb. MS representatives of all three text types: (*a*) The Proto–Masoretic text type is represented by findings of MSS of Isaiah, Ezekiel, the Twelve, and most MSS of

One of the most important of the Dead Sea Scrolls is the complete manuscript of Isaiah (1QIs^a), dating prior to 100 B.C. Courtesy *Biblical Archaeologist*

the law from Cave IV of Qumran. (*b*) The Proto-Septuagint text type, which often varies in its use of numbers from the MT, is represented by MSS of Samuel (4Q Sam^{a,b}), Exodus (4Q Ex^a), and Jeremiah (4Q Jer^a) which is one-eighth shorter in the LXX. (*c*) The Proto-Samaritan text type is also represented by the DSS Paleo-Heb. MS of Exodus (4Q Ex^b) (cf. Patrick W. Skehan, "Exodus in the Samaritan Recension from Qumran," JBL, LXXIV [1955], 182–187), and one of Numbers (4Q Num^b in "square" script).

5. Quality of the OT text. What does a comparison of the OT textual variants among the three textual families reveal about the state of the OT text? The SP contains *c*. 6,000 variants from the MT, but most of these are a matter of orthography (spelling, etc.). Some 1,900 of the variants agree with the LXX (e.g., in the ages given for the patriarchs in Gen 5, 10). Some of the SP variants are sectarian, such as the command to build the temple on Mount Gerizim, not at Jerusalem (e.g., after Ex 20:17). It should be noted, however, that most MSS of SP are late (13th–14th cen.) (see von Gall, *Der hebräische Pentateuch der Samaritaner*, 1914–18) and none is before the 10th cen. (Kenyon, *op. cit.*, p. 93). Many of the LXX variants from the MT are a matter of numbers, as "75 souls" (LXX) rather than "70 souls" (MT) in Ex 1:5. The LXX is now supported by fragments from the DSS (cf. Millar Burrows, *The Dead Sea Scrolls*, New York: Viking Press, 1955, and *More Light on the Dead Sea Scrolls*, New York: Viking Press, 1958, chaps. 13–14).

With the discovery of the DSS, scholars have Heb. MSS one thousand years earlier than the great MT MSS which enable them to check on the fidelity of the Heb. text. The result of comparative studies reveals that there is a word-for-word identity in more than 95 percent of the cases and the 5 percent variation consists mostly of slips of the pen and spelling (Archer, *op. cit.*, p. 19). To be specific, the Isaiah scroll (1Q Isa) from Qumran led the RSV translators to make only 13 changes over the MT, eight of which were known from ancient versions and

few of which are significant (cf. Burrows, *The DSS*, p. 320). More specifically, of the 166 Heb. words in Isa 53 only 17 Heb. letters in 1Q Is^b differ from the MT. Ten letters are a matter of spelling, four are stylistic changes, and the other three comprise the word for "light" (add in v.11) which does not affect the meaning greatly (Laird Harris, "How Reliable Is the Old Testament Text?" *Can I Trust My Bible?* Chicago: Moody, 1963, p. 124). Furthermore this word is also found in that verse in the LXX and 1Q Is^a.

We may conclude then with Kenyon that "the Christian can take the whole Bible [see NT below] in his hand and say without fear or hesitation that he holds in it the true word of God, handed down without essential loss from generation to generation throughout the centuries" (*op. cit.*, p. 55).

The New Testament

The original MSS of the NT are not available but, like the OT, they are represented by an abundance of MS copies.

I. *The Number of Greek New Testament Manuscripts*

In 1964 there were known to be 4,969 Gr. MSS of the NT: 76 papyri, 250 uncials, 2,646 minuscules, and 1,997 lectionary MSS (Metzger, *The Text of the New Testament*, pp. 31–33). But it must be remembered that this total increases yearly as new MSS come to light. About 95 percent of these date from the 8th through the 13th cen. (Greenlee, *Introduction to New Testament Textual Criticism*, p. 62). This would mean that there are *c*. 250 MSS from the 2nd through the 7th cen.

Compared to other books from the ancient world, the total ages and numbers of NT MSS are remarkable. Some ancient works survive on a single MS, e.g., Velleius Paterculus' compendious history of Rome, which was lost in the 17th cen. Even the first six books of the *Annals* of Tacitus are known through one MS dating from the 9th cen. Homer's *Iliad* survives by 647 MSS. Compared with almost 5,000 NT MSS the evidence for most other ancient works is meager. Of course most of these MSS are only portions of the NT; about 50 of them are of the complete NT. The least well attested book of the NT, Revelation, is preserved by about 300 Gr. MSS, only ten of which are uncials (Metzger, *op. cit.*, p. 34).

II. *Nature and Date of New Testament Greek Manuscripts*

Textual critics today classify the Gr. text of all NT MSS, according to the similarity of the slight variations in wording, into four main types or families—Alexandrian, Caesarean, Western, and Byzantine (Greenlee, *op. cit.*, pp. 117 f.). This classification relates to the characteristics of the Gr. text contained in the MSS. But when considered in terms of appearance and date, the NT MSS are divided into three major groups, all in codex form with pages—papyri, uncials, minuscules:

A. Papyrus MSS. MSS from the 2nd and 3rd cen., so named because written on material made from the pith of the papyrus reed. Of the 76 papyrus MSS of the NT, the following are the earliest and most significant.

1. P 52 John Ryland Fragment (A.D. 117-138). It contains Jn 18:31-33, 37-38 and is the oldest known fragment of the NT. Because of its early date and where it was found (Egypt) it tends to confirm that the Gospel of John was a 1st cen. composition.

2. P 66, 72, 75 Bodmer Papyri (c. A.D. 200). P 66 contains most of John (mixed Alex. and West. text types). P 72 is the earliest known copy of Jude, I Peter and II Peter (similar to Alex. type). P 75 contains the earliest copies of Luke and John (Alex. type like B).

3. P 45, 46, 47 Chester Beatty Papyri (c. A.D. 250) together contain most of the NT. P 45 consists of 30 leaves from the Gospels and Acts (mostly Alex. and West. text type). P 46 has 86 leaves of Paul's epistles (mostly Alex. text type). P 47 contains ten leaves of the book of Revelation (Alex. text type).

B. Uncial (Majuscule) MSS. MSS from the 4th to the 9th cen., so named because the Gr. letters were formed or printed as large, separate letters called "uncials."

1. B, Codex Vaticanus (A.D.325-350). This is the oldest extant uncial MS, on vellum. It contains both OT (LXX) and NT, except Gen-

The Bodmer Papyrus showing John 1:1-14.
Bodmer Library

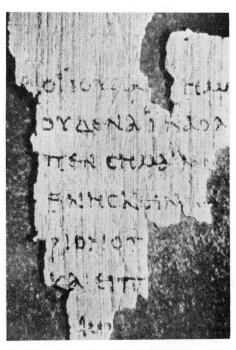

The John Rylands Fragment of John 18:
31-33. John Rylands Library

esis (1-46), some of Kings (10-13), Psalms (106 – 138), and Heb 9 through Revelation. Mk 16:9 – 20 and Jn 7:53 – 8:11 are intentionally omitted from the text. It is a good example of the Alex. text type.

2. Aleph (χ), Codex Sinaiticus (A.D. 340). Because of its antiquity, accuracy, and completeness (all of the NT and half of the OT), it is one of the most important of all Gr. biblical MSS. It too leaves out Mk 16:9-20 and Jn 7:53 – 8:11. It is generally Alex. text type with strains of West. readings.

3. C, Codex Ephraemi Rescriptus (c. 345). Most of the OT is missing and II Thessalonians and II John of NT plus parts of other books. It is a palimpsest ("rubbed out") rescriptus ("rewritten"), i.e., the codex in which the Gr. text of Scripture was originally copied was much later erased by Ephraem, who wrote his sermons on the pages. By chemical reactivation Tischendorf was able to decipher the almost invisible original writing. The text type is a compound of all major types, but it agrees frequently with the Byzantine.

4. A, Codex Alexandrinus (c. A.D. 425). Originally this vellum MS contained the entire Gr. Bible plus I and II Clement and the Psalms of Solomon. The NT now lacks Mt 1:1 – 25:6; Jn 6:50 – 8:52; and I Cor 4:13 – 12:6. The text

is written in two columns to the page. It is, as its name might suggest, of the Alex. text type.

5. D, Codex Bezae (*c.* A.D. 450 or 550). This is the oldest known bilingual (Gr. and Latin) MS of the NT. It contains the Gospels, Acts, and III Jn 11 – 15 with many small omissions (Latin only). It is representative of the West. text type but has a remarkable variation from the usual NT text type.

6. D², Codex Claromontanus (*c.* A.D. 550). It is also bilingual and contains much of the NT missing in D, with distinctly West. readings.

7. E, Codex Basiliensis (8th cen.) is a MS of the four Gospels with a Byzantine text type.

8. E², Codex Laudianus (6th or 7th cen.) is the earliest MS with Acts 8:37. The text is mixed but mostly Byzantine.

9. H³ (or H^P), Codex Coislinianus (6th cen.) is an important codex of Paul's epistles with an Alex. text type.

10. I, Codex Washingtonianus II (5th or 6th cen.) has portions of all Paul's epistles and Hebrews except Romans, with a good Alex. text resembling Aleph and A.

11. L, Codex Regius (8th cen.) is a badly written copy of a good text type, often like B. It contains two endings for Mark, a shorter one (see RSV footnote of Mk 16:8) and the longer one (vv. 9– 20 of KJV).

12. P², Codex Porphyrianus (9th cen.) has

Codex Sinaiticus opened to John 21:1–25. BM

all the NT but the Gospels (with some omissions). One of the few uncials containing the book of Revelation. The text type is mixed.

13. W, Codex Washingtonianus I (4th or 5th cen.). It contains the Gospels, portions of all Paul's epistles except Romans (with some omissions). Mark has a different insertion following the long ending (see Metzger, *op. cit.,* p. 54). The text is a mixture of types.

14. Theta (*θ*), Codex Koridethi (9th cen.) is a MS of the Gospels, mostly Byzantine except that Mark resembles the 3rd or 4th cen. text used by Origen and Eusebius, a Caesarean text type.

It should be noted that of the many uncial MSS of the NT the most important ones (Aleph, B, A, and C) were not available to the KJV translators prior to 1611. The only uncial available for the KJV was D and it was used only slightly.

C. Minuscule MSS. These NT MSS from the 9th to the 15th cen. are so named because the style of handwriting used was modified cursive (small letters which were sometimes connected and capable of being written rapidly) called "minuscule." Although the minuscule MSS are late, some of them have value as copies of good and earlier texts. Of these the following families may be mentioned.

1. The Alex. family represented by MS 33, "the Queen of the cursives," which contains

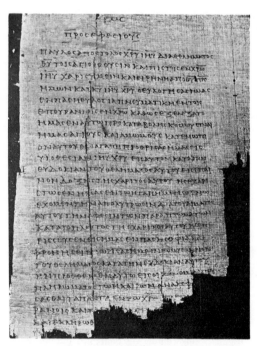

The first page of Ephesians from a Beatty-Michigan papyrus. University of Michigan Library

the whole NT except Revelation. It is mostly Alex. with traces of Byzantine text.

2. The Caesarean text type is represented by family 1 which includes MSS 1, 118, 131, and 209 (from 12th–14th cen.). Mark is similar to Theta (θ), a Caesarean text type.

3. An Italian subfamily of the Caesarean (11th–15th cen.) is represented by family 13 including MSS 13, 69, 124, 230, 346, 543, 788, 826, 828, 983, 1689, and 1709 (the first four MSS were formerly thought to be Syrian text type). An interesting characteristic of family 13 MSS is that they contain the passage on the woman taken in adultery (Jn 7:53–8:11, KJV) after Lk 21:38.

Some other noteworthy MSS. MS 28 (11th cen.) is of the Gospels, having many noteworthy Caesarean readings in Mark. MS 61 (15th or 16th cen.) is of the whole NT and the first one containing 1 Jn 5:7, the single basis on which Erasmus reluctantly inserted this doubtful passage in his Gr. NT (A.D. 1516) and which eventually came into the KJV. MS 81 (A.D. 1044) of Acts is one of the most important minuscules, frequently agreeing with Alex. text type. MS 565 is very beautiful with gold letters on purple vellum. It has all four Gospels, closely akin to Theta (θ) in support of Caesarean text. MS 579 (13th cen.) of the Gospels is a good Alex. text of all but Matthew, often agreeing with Aleph, B, and L. MS 700 (11th or 12th cen.) has some 2,724 deviations from the received text, 270 of which are found in no other MSS (cf. Metzger, op. cit., p. 64). MS 1739 (10th cen.) is an important copy of 4th cen. Alex. type with marginal notes from Origen, Eusebius, et al.

Space does not permit a listing and description of lectionaries, church service books containing selected Scripture readings usually from the Gospels and sometimes from Acts or the epistles. About 2,000 Gr. lectionaries are known, most of them dating from the 7th to the 12th cen.

III. *History and Editions of the Greek New Testament*

A. Period of composition (1st cen.). Most if not all the NT books were composed between A.D. 50–100. Some authors hold that Galatians and James were composed before this (see Merrill C. Tenney, *NT Survey,* Eerdmans, 1962, pp. 262–268).

B. Period of reduplication (2nd and 3rd cen.). During this period the books of the NT were usually copied rather carefully by professional scribes, but sometimes hastily and imperfectly, often because of persecution. For this reason there arose a multiplicity of early variants in the text. And even though the Christian scholars at Alexandria attempted an early criticism and editing of the Gr. text, the unnoticed textual errors which they inherited, plus the unintentional errors which they created by editing and revision, were transmitted in the MSS which they ordered to be written. Thus there came

into being the basis of textual problems later scholars would have to face.

C. Period of standardization (4th–15th cen.). Beginning with Eusebius there was a new era of more careful and faithful copying of the NT text. But critical comparison and revision of the text were rare. Rather than criticism there was a process of standardization so that by the 8th cen. the older text types (Alex., Caesarean, West.) were standardized and replaced by the Byzantine. As a result, the mass of NT MSS produced between 8th and 15th cen. (95 percent of all NT MSS) are largely Byzantine in type.

D. Period of crystallization (16th and 17th cen.). With the invention of printing came some editorial revisions of the Gr. text, but basically it was a matter of crystallizing in printed form what was already abundant in MS forms (viz., the late Byzantine text). What previously had been standardized now became established.

1. The Complutensian Polyglot (A.D. 1514) of Cardinal Ximenes was the first to be printed, but it was not approved by the pope for publication until 1520. The MS basis has never been determined, though he claimed they were ancient MSS lent to him by the pope (cf. Metzger, op. cit., p. 98).

2. The Erasmus Gr. NT (A.D. 1516) was the first to be published. In order to beat Cardinal Ximenes, Erasmus made a hurried ed. based on about a half dozen Gr. MSS (10th–12th cen.) only one of which was non–Byzantine (MS 1) but which he used least. In his 3rd ed. he included I Jn 5:7 (KJV) on the basis of MS 61. In his 4th and 5th eds. he omitted this verse and used better MSS, but the cheaper more popular 3rd ed. became the basis for the later "received text" or *textus receptus* (TR), the Gr. text presumed to underlie the KJV of 1611.

3. Robert Estienne (Latinized as Stephanus of Paris) issued four eds. of the Gr. NT (1546, 1549, 1550, 1551). The 3rd ed. was the first Gr. NT to have a critical apparatus (CA), using 14 codices including D and the Complutensian Polyglot. His 3rd ed. followed Erasmus' 4th and 5th eds. almost exactly. The text of Stephanus' 4th ed. (1551) is the same as in his 3rd ed., but for the first time the text was divided into numbered verses. It was the work of Stephanus that was considered the TR in Great Britain and America (Greenlee, op. cit., pp. 70-71). The first English NT (Geneva, 1557) to incorporate both the modern chapter and verse divisions was based on his 4th ed.

4. Theodore Beza published four eds. of the Gr. NT (1565, 1582, 1588–89, 1598) plus five reprints. Despite the fact that Beza annotated his work with several Gr. MSS which he had collected, including D and D² as well as MSS collated by Henry Stephanus (son of Robert S.), the text he printed differed little from that of Stephanus (1551). Beza's NT succeeded in popularizing the TR, and the KJV translators made large use of his last two eds.

5. The Elzevir brothers (Bonaventure and

Abraham) published seven eds. of the Gr. NT between A.D. 1624 and 1678 (Greenlee, *op. cit.,* p. 71). Their purposes were more commercial than critical, and their 2nd ed. (1633) was so widely sold that it became the accepted Gr. text in continental Europe.

E. Period of criticism (18th to 20th cen.). With the Gr. NT widely available, scholarly interest in the best possible text increased and new MSS came to light. The goal has been to produce an edited critical text of the Gr. NT which, by critical comparison and evaluation of all the MS evidence, most closely would approximate what was in the autographs or original MSS.

1. Dr. John Fell issued a Gr. NT (1675) drawn from the Elzevir NT (1633) which claimed to use variants from 100 MSS and ancient versions including the Gothic and Bohairic versions for the first time.

2. John Mill published a Gr. NT in 1707 using the Stephanus text of 1550, but including a prolegomena and index using nearly 100 MSS and 32 printed eds. of the NT. Mill refers to 3,041 of the almost 8,000 verses of the NT, collecting some 30,000 variants.

3. Richard Bentley did not publish a NT but a prospectus (1720) for a work he never completed; this contained a specimen of Rev 22 which forsakes the TR more than 40 times.

4. Daniel Mace anonymously published *The New Testament in Greek and English* (1729), choosing from Mill's CA the variants that common sense told him were better than the TR; thus he often anticipated the readings of much later scholars.

5. Johann Albert Bengel published a Gr. NT (1734) which printed the text of the TR with preferred variants in the margin chosen on the textual principle that "the difficult is to be preferred to the easy reading." Bengel was also the first to classify MSS into two great groups: Asiatic and African.

6. Johann Jacob Wettstein published the TR (1751-52) with the preferred readings in the CA, arguing that "manuscripts must be evaluated by their weight not by their number." He was the first to designate uncials by capital Roman letters and minuscules by Arabic numbers—a system used to the present.

7. Johann Salomo Semler (1725 -91) did not publish a Gr. NT, but he further developed Bengel's classification of MS families into three recensions: Alex., West., and Eastern.

8. William Bowyer, Jr., produced a critical ed. of the Gr. NT (1763) largely following Wettstein's judgment, bracketing familiar passages which lacked good textual support (as Mt 6:13; Jn 7:53 – 8:11; Acts 8:37; I Jn 5:7).

9. Johann Jacob Griesbach published three eds. of the Gr. NT (1774-1806), collated a large number of MSS, categorized the families as Alex., West., and Byzantine, and developed 15 canons of criticism of which the following is a sample: "The shorter reading . . . is to be preferred to the more verbose" (cf. Metzger,

op. cit., p. 120). Because of his influence, scholars began to abandon the TR.

10. Karl Lachmann published the first Gr. NT (1831) whose text rested wholly on critical principles. A second ed. followed (1842-50) in which he explained his principles and silenced some criticism.

11. Constantin von Tischendorf published eight eds. of the Gr. NT (1841-1872) plus 22 vols. of texts of NT MSS, the most important of which was Aleph, which he had discovered in the St. Catherine monastery at Mount Sinai. His 8th ed. of the Gr. NT (1869-72), based primarily on Aleph, differs in 3,572 places from his 7th ed. and it contains a comprehensive CA with all the variants known to his time.

12. Samuel P. Tregelles published his critical Gr. NT (1857 -72) based on sound textual principles; he is responsible for leading England away from the TR.

13. In 1881-82 B. F. Westcott and F. J. A. Hort published *The New Testament in the Original Greek,* but it was used in advance by the translators of the ERV (1881). The work of Westcott and Hort (WH) was so extensive and prevailing that with it the TR was vanquished. On the basis of their study they formulated four families or similar groupings of MSS: Syrian (A and late minuscules), West. (D, D²), Alex. (C, L), and Neutral (Aleph, B).

14. John W. Burgon (1813-88) and F. H. A. Scrivener led a futile battle against the WH text in favor of the TR.

15. Bernhard Weiss edited a Gr. NT (1894- 1900), using intrinsic probability as a guide, concluding that B is the best and resulting in a text like WH.

16. Alexander Souter's Gr. NT (1910) reproduced that of Archdeacon Edwin Palmer, which lies behind the ERV (1881), but added a CA. In the 1947 ed. evidence of the Chester Beatty Papyri was added.

17. Von Soden's Gr. NT (1913) is based on principles different from WH and results in a text closer to the TR than any other modern critical text but generally confirms the WH text. He classes all MSS into K (Koine or Syrian), H (Hesychian of Egypt), and I (Jerusalem or Palestinian), all three recensions based on a lost archetype used by Origen and corrupted before him by Marcion and Tatian. Other scholars feel he gave too much value to K and that I is too heterogeneous (Metzger, *op. cit.,* pp. 142- 143).

18. Present state of the NT text. Recently Canon Streeter has rejected WH "Neutral" and discovered a new family, the Caesarean, thus leading to a reclassifying of the families in order of preference: Alexandrian (including WH "Neutral"), Caesarean, Western, Byzantine (formerly "Syrian").

From 1898 until recently Erberhard Nestle's *Novum Testamentum Graece* has been the most widely used critical Gr. NT. It is based on a combination of WH, Tischendorf, and Weiss texts. It was slightly revised for the British and

Foreign Bible Society by G. D. Kilpatrick (1958). The United Bible Societies have published *The Greek New Testament* (1966), edited by Kurt Aland, Matthew Black, Bruce Metzger, and Allen Wikgren, which for the first time includes readings from 52 important lectionary MSS (9th–14th cen.).

IV. *Nature of New Testament Manuscripts*
1. John Mill had collected some 30,000 variants in NT MSS by A.D. 1707.
2. F. H. A. Scrivener counted nearly 150,000 variants by A.D. 1864. It is estimated that there are some 200,000 to date (Neil R. Lightfoot, *How We Got the Bible,* Grand Rapids: Baker, 1963, p. 53). On the surface this seems like an enormous number; but it is a very misleading figure, for the variants occur in only 10,000 different places in the NT (e.g., if one word is misspelled in 2,000 MSS it is counted as 2,000 variants). Furthermore, the vast number of variants do not affect the meaning of a passage (see Geisler and Nix, *General Introduction to the Bible,* pp. 360–367).
3. WH estimated that only one–eighth of all variants had any weight and only about one–sixteenth rise above "trivialities" and can be called "substantial variations." This would leave the text over 98 percent pure.
4. Ezra Abbot estimated that nineteen-twentieths (95 percent) of the variants were "various" rather than "rival" readings and nineteen-twentieths (95 percent) of the "rival" readings make little difference in the sense of the passage.
5. Philip Schaff calculated that of the 150,000 variants known in his day only 400 affected the sense, only 50 were of real significance, and not one of these affected any article of faith.
6. A. T. Robertson said that the real concern is about one–one thousandth of the text (i.e., the text is 99.9 percent pure of significant variants). When this is compared with Homer's *Iliad* where 5 percent of the text is in doubt, or the Mahabharata which has 10 percent corruption, it may be safely concluded that the Bible is the most accurately transmitted major work from the ancient world (cf. Metzger, *Chapters in the History of New Testament Textual Criticism,* pp. 144 f.).

Bibliography. Norman L. Geisler and William E. Nix, *A General Introduction to the Bible,* Chicago: Moody Press, 1968. Harold J. Greenlee, *Introduction to New Testament Textual Criticism,* Grand Rapids: Eerdmans, 1964. Paul E. Kahle, *Cairo Geniza,* 2nd ed., Oxford: Blackwell, 1959. Frederic Kenyon, *Our Bible and the Ancient Manuscripts,* 5th ed., rev. by A. W. Adams, New York: Harper, 1958. Bruce M. Metzger, *The Text of the New Testament,* New York: Oxford Univ. Press, 1964. Bleddyn J. Roberts, *The Old Testament Text and Versions,* Cardiff: Univ. of Wales Press, 1951. Bruce K. Waltke, "The Samaritan Pentateuch and the Text of the Old Testament," NPOT, pp. 212–239. Ernst Würthwein,

The Text of the Old Testament, trans. by Peter R. Ackroyd, Oxford: Blackwell, 1957.

                     N. L. G.

BIBLIOMANCY. A form of divination by which the Bible is opened at random and the reader is guided by the first verse that meets the eye. The practice goes back to ancient times, when the Greeks and Romans in the same way consulted the works of Homer and Virgil. In the Middle Ages such things as the demands of duty and the discerning of the future were divined from the Bible. It is not to be doubted that instruction and comfort can come from chance readings of Scripture, but it is to be denied that God's Word should be so studied.

BICHRI (bĭk′rī). The father of Sheba, a Benjamite, who rebelled against David. Sheba is identified as the son of Bichri eight times in II Sam 20.

BIDKAR (bĭd′kär). A captain in the service of Jehu when he killed King Jehoram and earlier a fellow officer serving King Ahab (II Kgs 9:25).

BIER (bēr). Found only twice in KJV. King David followed the bier bearing the body of Abner (II Sam 3:31). Christ touched the bier of the only son of a widow in Nain (Lk 7:14). The word means "coffin" and refers to a simple open litter or flat wooden frame on which the dead body was borne from the house to the grave. *See* Burial.

BIGTHA (bĭg′thà). One of the seven eunuchs or chamberlains in charge of the harem of the Persian king Xerxes (Ahasuerus). He was commanded to bring Vashti to the king's banquet (Est 1:10–11).

BIGTHAN (bĭg′thăn), **BIGTHANA** (bĭg-thā′nà). One or two eunuchs or chamberlains of Xerxes (Ahasuerus) whose conspiracy against the king was known to Mordecai. Upon Mordecai's testimony through Queen Esther, the men were hanged (Est 2:21; 6:2). Bigthan was possibly identical with Bigtha (*q.v.*).

BIGVAI (bĭg′vī)
1. The head of a great family that returned in 536 B.C. with Zerubbabel to rebuild the temple (Ezr 2:2). The importance of the family can be judged by the fact that the "sons," probably including all retainers, are numbered 2,056 (Ezr 2:14). Two sons of Bigvai, Uthai and Zaccur, returned with Ezra in 458 B.C. in a company of 72 men (Ezr 8:14, RSV).
2. In Neh 10:16 there is a Bigvai listed with the princes of Israel who set their seal to the covenant made in 444 B.C. under Nehemiah. Unless he was very old this is unlikely to be the same as 1.

BILDAD (bĭl′dăd). Bildad, the Shuhite, was the second of Job's three friends (Job 2:11; 8:1;

18:1; 25:1; 42:9). The patronymic Shuhite has been taken to refer to Shuah, one of the sons of Abraham and Keturah (Gen 25:2). The Assyrian land of *Shûḫu* was S of Haran, near the middle Euphrates and may have been the land of Bildad.

Bildad attributes the sufferings of Job to his sins, as do the other friends. Bildad's argument is based upon the traditions of the wise and ancient words that had come down from past ages. His appeal to tradition is irrelevant to the situation and fails to convince Job. Although Bildad is solemn and gracious in manner, his second speech is a horrible description of the unrighteous man, as he assumes Job to be (Job 18).

BILEAM (bĭl'ē-ăm). A town of Manasseh W of Jordan assigned to the Levite family of Kohath (I Chr 6:70). *See* Ibleam.

BILGAH (bil'gȧ)
1. A descendant of Aaron, and in the time of David head of the 15th of the 24 divisions of the priests who officiated in the temple (I Chr 24:14).
2. A priest or priestly family who accompanied Zerubbabel on the return from Captivity (Neh 12:5, 18).

BILGAI (bĭl'gī). Found only in Neh 10:8. It is probably the same as Bilgah (*q.v.*), but named among those who sealed the covenant (Neh 10:1).

BILHAH (bĭl'hȧ)
1. A slave girl whom Laban gave to his daughter Rachel when she married Jacob (Gen 29:29), and whom Rachel gave to Jacob as a concubine (Gen 30:3-4). She became the mother of Dan and Naphtali by Jacob (Gen 30:5-8). After the death of Rachel she committed incest with Reuben (Gen 35:22).
2. Town in the territory of Simeon, S of Judah (I Chr 4:29), probably the same as Balah and Baalah (*q.v.*).

BILHAN (bĭl'hăn)
1. A Horite chief, son of Ezer, descendant of Seir (Gen 36:20, 27; I Chr 1:42).
2. A descendant of Benjamin, son of Jediael, father of seven sons who were heads of houses (I Chr 7:10).

BILL
1. Heb. *sēpher kerîtût*, "scroll," "document of cutting off"; LXX *biblion apostasion*, "a bill of divorcement" (cf. Deut 24:1, 3; Isa 50:1; Jer 3:8). According to the law of Moses, divorce transactions were to be formally certified by written documents. Archaeological discoveries have furnished modern students of the Bible with extensive evidence of these materials so that it is possible to study actual copies of such divorce contracts. Document 19 published in

Les Grottes de Murabba'at (*Discoveries in the Judean Desert*, II, Oxford: Clarendon Press, 1961) tells of a certain "Mary and Joseph" who divorced each other. The document is prepared in duplicate, witnesses attested it, the woman was free to marry any other Jew. Each document was written twice, so that if the divorcing partner lost a copy of the bill, another original copy could be supplied! (See also V. A. Tcherikover and A. Fuks, *Corpus Papyrorum Judaicarum*, II, Cambridge, Mass.: Harvard Univ. Press, 1960, p. 10, No. 144 and the references there.) In the Hellenistic period, Jewish divorce contracts written outside Palestine used the legal forms customary in the same pagan contracts of time and place.

2. In the NT Gr. *biblion apostasion*, "a document of divorce" (Mk 10:4) follows the LXX expression. Jesus showed familiarity with the Mosaic provisions of divorce, but went beyond Moses as interpreted by certain rabbis of His day, in taking a position against the laxity with which divorce was granted.

Gr. *gramma*, "writing," "bond," "letter" (Lk 16:6). The papyri supply students with thousands of examples of receipts, I.O.U.'s, business contracts, accounts, etc. A. Deissmann raises the possibility that perhaps the "bill" of Lk 16:6 is to be explained by the practice of drawing up such a document in two copies, one "inner" (closed) and the other "outer" (open). He describes a receipt in which the outer text reads *30* drachmae, while the inner text reads *40* (Deiss LAE, p. 33, n. 3).

E. J. V.

BILSHAN (bĭl'shăn). One of 10 or 11 chief men or princes who returned to Jerusalem from Babylon with Zerubbabel (Ezr 2:2; Neh 7:7).

BIMHAL (bĭm'hăl). A son of Japhlet of the line of Asher, who was a son of Jacob (I Chr 7:33).

BINDING AND LOOSING. These words were common in rabbinical circles in both a legislative and a judicial sense. They were employed to mean: (1) to forbid or permit, (2) to condemn or acquit, and (3) to retain sins or to forgive.

Christ's conferral on Peter of the power to bind and loose (Mt 16:19) has been variously interpreted through the Christian centuries as referring to binding decisions concerning right and wrong, to the power to excommunicate or restore church members, and to the retention or forgiveness of sins. The Roman Catholic church insists that this power is legislative, judicial, and administrative, and that it was committed to Peter and his successors, the popes.

It should, however, be noted that the power was not only promised to Peter (Mt 16:19) but also to the other disciples (Mt 18:1, 18). Another significant factor is the tense of the verbs employed. The assertion that the earthly binding and loosing are accompanied by similar actions in heaven is expressed by the Gr. future perfect periphrastic construction, meaning that whatever is bound or loosed by the apostles shall have (already) been bound or loosed by God Himself. The apostles, therefore, are merely repeating or declaring what God has already done.

In view of the preceding context in Mt 16:19, it would appear that the power to bind and loose is related to that of the keys, which, in turn, were to be employed to open the doors for entrance into God's kingdom, misused by Jewish scribes (cf. Mt 23:13; Lk 11:52). Some, however, explain the passage eschatologically, as applying to the reign of the saints over the earth in the Millennium (A. J. McClain, *The Greatness of the Kingdom*, pp. 329 f.).

Parallelism with Jn 20:23 suggests that binding and loosing refer to forgiving or retaining sins, the factors which determine entrance into the kingdom. An instance of the exercise of such authority is afforded in Acts 10:43. Peter announced that acceptance of Christ and the gospel brings loosing from sin's penalty, and rejection leaves one bound for judgment. These terms may also include the power to excommunicate or reinstate (Mt 18:15–18), as well as the authority to prohibit or permit various actions such as those described in Acts 15:23–29 and I Cor 5. It should be clearly understood, however, that this latter power was given to the apostles, and there is no scriptural indication or example that it was to be transmitted to papal successors.

According to Mt 18:18 disciple-believers may bind the power of Satan and his demonic hosts or loose persons from his grip by declaring what Christ has already accomplished in destroying the works of the devil (cf. Heb 2:14–15; I Jn 3:8; Rev 12:11).

D. W. B.

BINEA (bĭn'ĭ-å). A son of Moza, a descendant of King Saul through Jonathan (I Chr 8:37; 9:43).

BINNUI (bĭn'ū-ī). A name common at the time of Israel's return from Exile.

1. The father of a Levite named Noadiah (Ezr 8:33). The latter assisted in weighing the silver, gold, and vessels which Ezra brought from Babylon.

2. The son of Pahath-moab (Ezr 10:30). During the revival under Ezra, this lay Israelite agreed to put away his foreign wife (or wives).

3. The son of Bani who did the same (Ezr 10:38).

4. A Levite, the son of Henadad, who accompanied Zerubbabel to Jerusalem (Neh 12:1, 8). He helped repair the wall (Neh 3:24), and signed a covenant of loyalty to the Lord (Neh 10:9). He may also be the same as Bani (*q.v.*) who assisted in the great assemblies under the ministry of Ezra (Neh 8:7; 9:4–5).

5. The head of a large family who came to Jerusalem with Zerubbabel (Neh 7:15). He is to be identified with the Bani of Ezr 2:10, and

probably with the Bani of Neh 10:14 or Bunni (Neh 10:15).

D. W. B.

BIRD. *See* Animals, III.

BIRSHA (bûr'shå). King of Gomorrah who joined in a league in an unsuccessful war against Chedorlaomer. The latter made Lot and his family captive (Gen 14:1–12).

BIRTHDAY. There are two biblical references to birthdays: (1) On Pharaoh's birthday he made a feast for his servants and granted amnesty to his chief butler whom he had previously imprisoned (Gen 40:20). (2) The birthday of Herod Antipas was celebrated with a banquet for his "courtiers and officers and the leading men of Galilee." Entertainment included the dancing of Salome, daughter of Herodias, who was rewarded with the head of John the Baptist on a platter (Mt 14:6; Mk 6:21–28, RSV).

The Gr. *genesia* originally was a celebration on the birthday of a deceased person (Arndt, *s.v.*), but came to have broader application, and in the papyri it was always a birthday feast (MM, *s.v.*). That it might also be a feast on the anniversary of the accession date of a ruler has never been demonstrated (cf. Edersheim, I. 672).

The birth of a son was an occasion for rejoicing (Ruth 4:14; Jn 16:21; Jos *Ant.* xii. 4.7), but Jeremiah, in great despondency, came to curse the day of his birth (Jer 20:14–15; cf. Job 3:3). According to Herodotus, the ancient Persians also celebrated a birthday with a feast (i.133). In Egypt such celebrations can be documented back to the 13th cen. B.C. apart from the biblical reference above.

R. V. R.

BIRTHRIGHT. *See* Firstborn.

BIRZAVITH (bûr-zā'vĭth)

1. Son of Malchiel, great-grandson of Asher (I Chr 7:31).

2. A town "fathered" or settled by Malchiel, a descendant of Asher. Because several Asherite clans seem to have settled in the hill country of Ephraim, it is possibly the present Khirbet Bir Zeit, four miles NW of Bethel (Beitin), where Judas Maccabeus pitched his last camp (Jos *Ant.* xii.11.1) (Aharoni, *The Land of the Bible*, p. 223).

BISHLAM (bĭsh'lăm). A Persian official, possibly satrap, who complained to Artaxerxes against the Jews under Zerubbabel who were rebuilding the city (Ezr 4:7).

BISHOP. The word *episkopos* occurs five times in the NT: once of Christ (I Pet 2:25), and in four places of "bishops" or "overseers" in local churches (Acts 20:28; Phil 1:1; I Tim 3:2; Tit 1:7). The verb *episkopeō* occurs in Heb 12:15 ("watching") and (in some NT MSS) I Pet 5:2 ("exercising the oversight," ASV), while the noun *episkopē* in the sense of an "office of an overseer" appears in Acts 1:20 ("bishopric") and I Tim 3:1.

It is generally agreed that the term "bishop" in the NT is equivalent to "elder" (*presbyteros*), the latter occurring often in Acts as well as in I Tim 5:17, 19; Tit 1:5; Jas 5:14; I Pet 5:1, 5. *See* Elders. (The sense in II Jn 1 and III Jn 1 is not wholly clear, as is the case of the "four and twenty elders" in Revelation.)

Lightfoot (*Philippians*, pp. 96 f.) summarizes the NT evidences for the identity of the terms as follows: (1) In Phil 1:1, Paul salutes the "bishops and deacons," and it seems incredible that he would omit the second order (viz., elders) if it was distinct, as elders formed the staple of the ministry of a NT church; (2) in Acts 20:17, Paul summoned the "elders" of Ephesus to Miletus, yet addressed them as "bishops" (Acts 20:28, ASV); (3) Peter appealed to the "elders" to fulfill the office of bishops (I Pet 5:1-2); (4) Paul described the qualifications for the office of a "bishop" (I Tim 3:1-7) followed by a "deacon" (I Tim 3:8-13), yet in I Tim 5:17-19 he calls these ministers "elders"; (5) yet more plainly in Tit 1:5 the apostle speaks of "elders," then of a "bishop" (Tit 1:7).

Both the Gr. and Jewish backgrounds of "bishop" are illuminating, though not as conclusive NT usage. In its etymology, the word means an "overseer" or "one who watches." On the other hand, in usage it was varied. The one who "watched" or "protected" assumed an attitude of graciousness toward the one under his care. Further, the word came to denote an office of one kind or another, whether financial, administrative, or social, either secular or religious.

The Greeks thus described their gods: a being who gave particular attention to the one who worshiped him. And the god had a particular sphere of responsibility, protection, and judgment. When used of men, the idea of protective care is still essential to the activity of the individual. In Gr. life the word also designated an office. The *episkopos* could be an official of the state, an officer of a local society (as those who supervised the relief of the poor in a city), or those who supervised building projects and possibly controlled the money designated for the work.

Jewish usage was similar. In the LXX at Job 20:29, the Heb. word for "God" (*'ēl*) is rendered *episkopos* (*para tou episkopou*). Thus, the "Episkopos" is the One who judges the wicked, rendering to him his heritage. Men are so designated also, whether as officers (Num 31:14), overseers (or supervisors, II Chr 34:12,17) responsible for money for workmen, or, in a religious sense, as officers (or watchmen) in the temple (II Kgs 11:18). The Syrian king Antiochus IV appointed "inspectors" (or governors) over Israel (I Macc 1:51), men who were to enforce his policies.

Both the name and the office of "elder" are

essentially Jewish (Lightfoot, *op. cit.,* p. 96; cf. Beyer, TDNT, II, 618). Particularly, the name is linked with the governing council of every Jewish synagogue, whether in Palestine or the Diaspora. Both in the OT (cf. Josh 20:4; Ruth 4:2; Ezr 10:14) and the NT (cf. Lk 7:3) the case is the same. And in the Jerusalem Sanhedrin "elders" formed a part of the group (cf. Mk 8:31; Lk 20:1; Acts 4:5). *See* Elder.

It seems hardly surprising, therefore, that these terms *episkopos* and *presbyteros* were employed for leaders in the NT church. They were terms at hand, and already connected with organizations current in Gr. and Jewish life. While certain changes were, of course, necessary in view of the nature of the Christian church and the prevailing circumstances, the familiar names were kept and used.

The NT usage of *episkopos* and *presbyteros* is important. That they both referred to the same individual in the NT has already been considered, but what was the function fulfilled by each? From an examination of Acts 20:17, 28 it would seem that the term "elder" designated the status of the men, i.e., they were the recognized leaders of the Ephesian church. On the other hand, "bishop" or "overseer" is used with particular reference to their ministry: to feed the church of God. In I Pet 2:25 the terms "shepherd" and "bishop" are linked together of Christ. Selwyn (*I Peter,* p. 182) regards the latter term as an interpretation of the former, rather than the introduction of a new idea, appealing to Acts 20:28 for support. Ezk 34:11-13 combines the same two terms, as does also I Pet 5:2.

In Phil 1:1, the term *episkopos* is joined with *diakonos* ("deacon"), the latter appearing here for the first time, but the function of neither is specified. It is only in the Pastoral Epistles that the description of this ministry is made clear (I Tim 3:1-7; 5:17 ff.; Tit 1:5-9). The following seems to characterize the teaching given there:

1. In I Tim 3:1, the word *episkopē* has reference to an office which a man may seek. Both in Acts 14:23 and Tit 1:5, the "elders" were appointed. The word used in Acts (*cheirotonēsantes*) occurs again in the NT only in II Cor 8:19 where one was "appointed by the churches" to travel with Paul. In Athenian life it referred to voting "by stretching out the hand." The term in Titus (*katastēsēs*) occurs also in Acts 6:3, where the apostles told the congregation to "look out" (*episkepsasthe*) from among them seven men whom they would "appoint" (*katastēsomen*), over the serving of tables.

2. The "bishop" in I Tim 3:1-7 must be a man possessed of high moral qualities (vv. 2-3), an apt teacher (v. 2), one in control of his own family (vv. 4-5), spiritually mature (v. 6), and held in high regard by unbelievers (v. 7). The necessary qualifications for "elders" in Tit 1:5-9 are similar. God's work calls for godly and gifted men.

3. In the NT, the number of these persons in

any particular place was plural. The use of the singular in I Tim 3:2 and Tit 1:7 refers to "the bishop as a type" rather than number. "There is no reference to monarchical episcopate" (Beyer, TDNT, II, 617).

In I Tim 5:17 ff., there may be indicated a bridge between the NT "presbyter" and the later development into the elevation of one above the others. Those elders who "rule well" were to be counted "worthy of double honor." That some would labor particularly "in the word and in teaching" seems to indicate already a division of responsibility. Does this possibly stand in contrast to the apostles' word in a much earlier day: "It is not fit that we should forsake the word of God, and serve tables" (Acts 6:2, ASV)?

The historical progression of the meaning of *episkopos* into "the episcopate" may be traced in the writings of the Church Fathers. It was not thus advanced in Clement of Rome (First Epistle to the Corinthians), but begins to appear in the *Didache*, in Ignatius (Epistles), where it is "your godly bishop and your presbyters"; then is well developed in Irenaeus (*Against Heresies*), and Cyprian (Epistles). Yet it is notable that even in the 2nd cen. and on into the Middle Ages, the 1st cen. equivalence of the terms was maintained (e.g., by Chrysostom, Jerome, Augustine, and others).

Bibliography. Hermann W. Beyer, "*Episkopos,* etc.," TDNT, II, 599–622. T. M. Lindsay, *The Church and the Ministry in the Early Centuries,* London: Hodder and Stoughton, 1910.

W. M. D.

BISHOPRIC (Gr. *episkopē*). The English word is found only in Acts 1:20 (KJV; "office" in RSV) and quoted by the apostle Peter from Ps 109:8. The reference is to Judas' position as an apostle. In I Tim 3:1 the same Gr. word is used of the office of bishop; in I Pet 2:12 the word is translated "visitation."

Bishopric in later times was the office of overseer or the district over which the bishop or elder was in charge. *See* Bishop; Elder.

BIT. A part of the bridle or halter inserted in the animal's mouth to which the reins were fastened to control the animal's movement (Ps 32:9; Jas 3:3). *See* Bridle.

BITHIAH (bĭ-thī'à). An Egyptian princess, a daughter of Pharaoh and wife of Mered of the tribe of Judah. The meaning of her name ("daughter of Yah[weh]") suggests that she became a believer in the Lord (I Chr 4:18).

BITHRON (bĭth'rŏn). Found only in II Sam 2:29. Bithron apparently is not a proper place name but designates the ravine or shortcut by which Abner and his men came up from the Jordan Valley to his capital at Mahanaim, S of the brook Jabbok. RSV translates the phrase, "the whole forenoon."

BITHYNIA (bĭ-thĭn'ĭ-à). A Roman province (after 74 B.C.) of NW Asia Minor situated near the Bosphorus and the Propontis (modern Sea of Marmara). It is mentioned only twice in the NT (Acts 16:7; I Pet 1:1). On his second missionary journey (c. A.D. 49–50) Paul was restrained from entering Bithynia by the "Spirit of Jesus" (RSV), and thus he proceeded on to Europe via Troas.

It is obvious that Christian work was started in Bithynia before A.D. 63 since I Peter is addressed to believers in this area by that time. It is possible that Christianity was planted in Bithynia long before Paul attempted to go there. Since Pontus was at that time connected with Bithynia (after 65–63 B.C.), Christianity could have been introduced there shortly after Pentecost (cf. Acts 2:9). At an early period Paul determined not to labor where other missionaries had already laid a foundation of believing Christians before him (Rom 15:20). In the NT period Bithynia was a senatorial province (after 27 B.C.) and its capital was at Nicomedeia. The propraetor Pliny the Younger was sent by Trajan to Bithynia as governor (c. A.D. 111–122). He reported (see Letter 96) that Christianity (which he calls a "superstition") was so strongly rooted in Bithynia at that time that it ". . . has spread not only in the cities, but in the villages and rural districts as well. . . ." The strength of the Christian movement then is also shown by the fact that prominent Roman citizens were included in the fellowship of Christians, and it is significant that many of the pagan temples in Bithynia were "almost deserted" according to Pliny.

Bibliography. J. Weiss, *Realencyclopädie für protest. Theol. und Kirche,* X, 553 ff. For a convenient source on Pliny and Trajan's reply, cf. Henry Bettenson, *Documents of the Christian Church,* London: Oxford Univ. Press, reprinted 1959, pp. 3–6. For convenient maps of Bithynia and Pontus in relation to other provinces see William M. Ramsay, *Historical Commentary on the Galatians,* London: Hodder and Stoughton, 1899, map facing p. 1. For coins see *B.M.C. Catalogue of Greek Coins: Pontus, Paphlagonia, Bithynia, Bosporus,* London: 1889.

E. J. V.

BITTER. In one form or another, the word is used 65 times, mostly in the OT. It may be of things concrete, as herbs (Ex 12:8; Num 9:11); or water, as at Marah, "bitter," i.e., brackish (Ex 15:23); or in the water trial for a woman's adultery (Num 5:16–28); of the stomach (Rev 10:9–10); and even of people (Hab 1:6).

The word may describe actions, whether with words (Ps 64:3), or weeping (e.g., Peter's, Mt 26:75 parallel to Lk 22:62), of cursing (Rom 3:14 from Ps 10:7), or crying out (Gen 27:34).

Again it may describe feeling of soul (Job 3:20), whether in resentment (Col 3:19; Heb 12:15) or total wickedness (Acts 8:23), or even evil destiny (Prov 5:4; Eccl 7:26).

BITTER HERBS. *See* Plants.

BITTERN. *See* Animals, III.3.

BITUMEN. *See* Minerals.

BIZJOTHJAH (bĭz-jŏth'jà). A town in the S of Judah near Beer-sheba (Josh 15:28).

BIZTHA (bĭz'thà). One of seven eunuchs or chamberlains serving King Ahasuerus or Xerxes (Est 1:10).

BLACK. *See* Colors.

BLASPHEMY. The concept involved an intentional and defiant dishonoring of the nature, name, or work of God by word or action (II Kgs 19:3, 6, 22; cf. 18:22) Sometimes it was directed toward men or objects closely associated with God; e.g., Israel (Isa 52:5), the mountains of Israel (Ezk 35:12), the temple (I Macc 7:38). The idea was also expressed euphemistically by use of the root *bārak*, the usual term for "bless," the actual intent being obvious from the context (I Kgs 21:10, 13; Ps 10:3; Job 1:5, 11; 2:5, 9; cf. A. Murtonen, VT, IX [1959], 171).

Blasphemy is often stated as being against the name of the Lord (Lev 24:11, 16; Ps 74:10, 18; Isa 52:5). This terminology led the Jews to a superstitious regard for the name itself. Some of the Qumran MSS, e.g., although written in the later "square" script, have the divine name written in the older script, to avoid profaning it with the newer, common characters. Likewise, the Jews dared not pronounce it, so in reading they substituted "Adonai" for "Yahweh." As a reminder to the reader, they wrote the vowel signs of Adonai with the consonants of Yahweh, and in the LXX wrote *kurios*, the Gr. of Adonai, "Lord."

Blasphemy was a capital offense, execution among the Jews being traditionally by stoning (Lev 24:11-16; cf. Naboth's fate, notwithstanding the falsity of the charge, I Kgs 21:10, 13). In the case of Jesus, the charge of blasphemy was based on His having claimed divine prerogatives (Mt 9:3; 26:64-65; Mk 2:7; Jn 10:33, 36; 19:7), but since the capital punishment entailed was administered under Roman jurisdiction, execution was by crucifixion. Stephen was stoned for blasphemy (Acts 6:11; 7:56-58).

In the NT, following classical Gr. usage, *blasphēmeō* and its substantives are often related to men and an injury of reputation; i.e., "slander" (Rom 3:8; I Cor 4:13; 10:30; Tit 3:2; cf. Arndt, *s.v.*).

For blasphemy against the Holy Spirit, *see* Sin; Holy Spirit, Sin Against.

Bibliography. Hermann W. Beyer, *"Blasphēmeō, etc.,"* TDNT, I, 621-625.

R. V. R.

BLASTING. This word refers to the effect upon grain or other plants caused by the hot E wind which blows upon Palestine from the Arabian Desert. The winds usually continue for two to three days at a time, and in the ripening time will cause severe damage. This blight is included among the divine curses upon a disobedient Israel (Deut 28:22-24; Amos 4:9; Hag 2:17). In Solomon's prayer (I Kgs 8:37; II Chr 6:28), blasting is included among the curses removed by a merciful God in response to the cry of His people. Occasionally the wind brought with it a cloud of locusts (II Chr 6:28).

BLASTUS (blăs'tŭs). Described in Acts 12:20 as "the king's chamberlain," he was appealed to by the populace of Tyre and Sidon in the face of the wrath of Herod Agrippa I. These cities were dependent upon the king for their food, even as they had been dependent upon Solomon in the days of Hiram (I Kgs 5:9-11; 9:11-13).

BLEMISH. The English word occurs often in KJV, mostly in Leviticus, Numbers and Ezekiel, representing three Heb. and two Gr. words. Of the Heb. words, *tāmîm* means "entire" or "complete," hence "without blemish." Heb. *me'ûm, mûm* means "something stained," or "spot" or "blot." The third, *teballul* (used only in Lev 21:20) denotes a white spot in the eye causing obscure vision, probably a cataract (*see* Diseases). Blemish occurs only three times in the NT. Each time the Gr. word *mōmos* means "blot" or "flaw" (or, negatively, "without flaw").

To summarize: the sacrifices of the OT were to be "without blemish"; Christ was a sacrifice "without blemish" (I Pet 1:19); and the Church is to be one day "without blemish" (Eph 5:27).

BLESS, BLESSING. The act of one person blessing another can be considered under several headings.

1. God blessing man (Gen 1:28; 12:2; 22:17; 32:29; Ex 20:24; 23:25; Deut 1:11; 15:10; II Sam 6:11; Ps 28:9; 45:2; 107:38; Eph 1:3; Heb 6:14). God's blessing, since it is that of an omniscient, omnipotent, omnipresent God, is always fully effective, both in supplying man's needs in this life and eternal life in the world to come (Mt 6:33; Jn 10:27-30; Mt 25:34; Rev 22:14).

2. Man blessing God (Ps 63:4; 103:1-2; 104:1; 145:1-3) in which man recognizes and praises those great qualities which adhere to God's person, and expresses thanks and gratitude to Him and His name.

3. Men blessing each other in particular prayers, such as a father blessing his sons just before his expected death, which prayers were accompanied by a prophecy, as when Isaac blessed Jacob and Esau (Gen 27:26-40), when Jacob blessed his sons (Gen 49:1-27), when Moses blessed the children of Israel (Deut

262

33:1-29), and when Simeon blessed the holy family (Lk 2:34).

4. Priests in the OT blessing the Lord's people (Lev 9:22-23; Num 6:24-26; I Sam 2:20), and Christian leaders doing so in the NT (Col 1:9-14; Heb 13:20-21) in prayers and benedictions.

5. The blessing of food before it is eaten, as for example the cup at Jewish feasts, which was done by Christ as He instituted the new covenant in His blood (Mt 26:26-28). The church continued this custom in the Lord's Supper as indicated in I Cor 10:16: "The cup of blessing which we bless, is it not the communion of the blood of Christ?"

The description of the state of blessedness or happiness is often introduced by the distinctive words Heb. *'asherê* (Ps 1:1; 2:12; 32:1-2; etc.) and Gr. *makarios* (Mt 5:3-11; 11:6; etc.), both of which denote one who is truly happy before the Lord.

Bibliography. Hermann W. Beyer, *"Eulogeō, etc.,"* TDNT, II, 754-765.

R. A. K.

BLESSING, CUP OF. The apostle Paul in I Cor 10:16 states that participation in drinking the cup at the Lord's Supper brings a blessing, for in so doing we commemorate the Lord's death on the cross. *See* Lord's Supper.

BLESSINGS AND CURSINGS. *See* Covenant: Mosaic or Sinai Covenant.

BLIGHT. *See* Blasting (I Kgs 8:37; II Chr 6:28; Amos 4:9; Hag 2:17, RSV).

BLINDNESS. One of the many common physical ailments of biblical times. It was often inflicted upon prisoners of war by barbaric nations (Jud 16:21; II Kgs 25:7). On occasion it was a punishment of God for sin (Gen 19:11; Acts 13:11). The physically blind are frequently listed with the dumb (Mt 15:30) and the lame (Lk 14:21) who received healing from Jesus. It is not strange that the reign of the Messiah should be described by Isaiah as a time when "the eyes of the blind shall be opened" (Isa 35:5). *See* Diseases.

In a figurative sense the word is used of spiritual ignorance caused by unbelief (II Cor 4:4; Mt 15:14; 23:17), and of spiritual immaturity (II Pet 1:9). *See* Judicial Blindness.

BLOOD (Gr. *haima*). The red fluid circulating in the bodies of animals and men which signifies the "life" principle in the OT (Gen 9:4; Lev 17:11; Deut 12:23). Because "the life is in the blood" the OT forbade eating blood or bloody meat (Lev 3:17; Deut 12:16). Though all foods were made clean by Christ (Mk 7:18-19; Acts 10:13-15), this prohibition was applied to Gentile Christians in the apostolic decree of Acts 15 out of consideration for the consciences of their Jewish brethren (Acts 15:19-20).

Blood denotes the physical origin of human life (Jn 1:13; Acts 17:26). The expression "flesh and blood" speaks of man in his weakness, brief life, and limited knowledge (Mt 16:17; Gal 1:16; I Cor 15:44-50; Eph 6:12). It stands for human nature in Heb 2:14 where Christ shares fully our humanity, even to the giving of His life.

Shedding blood is violently taking the life of another, or murder (Acts 22:20; Rom 3:15). God condemns the shedding of the blood of the righteous and the innocent (Gen 9:6; Prov 6:17; Mt 23:35; 27:4; Rev 6:10). The term "blood" is sometimes used for the bloody death itself (Mt 23:30; 27:24; Lk 11:51). To have another man's blood on one's hands was to bear the guilt for the death of another (II Sam 1:16; I Kgs 2:37; Prov 28:17). Symbolically Pilate washed his hands to be free from the innocent blood of Jesus, while the mob shouted, "His blood be on us, and on our children" (Mt 27:24-25). Judas' betrayal of Jesus brought "a reward for a bloody deed" (Arndt, p. 22) and with this reward "the field of blood" was bought with blood money (Mt 27:6, 8).

Blood also played a significant role in the religious practices of the OT. It is worthwhile noting that blood was not a basic element of sacrifice and had no special function or meaning in the rituals of any of the other ancient Near Eastern or Mediterranean peoples (McCarthy, "The Symbolism of Blood and Sacrifice"). The sacrificial system of the law, based on the earlier animal sacrifices of the patriarchal period, called for the slaying of the victim on behalf of the sinner, and the sprinkling of its warm blood by the priest as proof of its death for atonement for sins (Lev 17:11-12). In the sacrifices death was required of the victim so that its life might be offered to God as the substitute for the repentant sinner. Sin was thus cleansed ("covered with blood") and guilt taken away (Heb 9:22).

This background forms the basis for the place of the blood of Christ in the NT. The shedding of His blood on the cross ended His earthly life, which He voluntarily gave to die in our place as the Lamb of God slain to redeem us (I Pet 1:18-20; Rev 5:6, 9, 12); and the sprinkling of that blood made atonement for the sins of all men (Rom 3:25). Following the pattern of the Jewish Day of Atonement (Lev 16), Christ is our atoning sacrifice (Heb 9:11-14; I Jn 2:2; Rev 1:5), and also our sin offering (I Pet 1:18-19; Rev 5:9). As Moses sealed the covenant between God and ancient Israel at Sinai with sprinkled blood (Ex 24:8; cf. Heb 9:19-21), so the new covenant of Jer 31:31-34 was sealed by Christ's blood (Heb 9:14-15; 10:14-19, 29; 13:20). In instituting the Lord's Supper, Jesus spoke of the cup as "the new covenant in my blood" (I Cor 11:25; Lk 22:20; cf. Mk 14:24).

Christ is also referred to as the great peace offering, reconciling Jew and Gentile (Eph 2:14-17) as well as all things through His blood (Rom 5:9-10; Col 1:20). The sinner is delivered from slavery to sin through the release (redemption) which Christ's blood has purchased (Eph 1:7; Col 1:14). Thus the Church is described as "purchased with his own blood" (Acts 20:28). By the blood of Christ Christians have been justified (Rom 5:9), loosed from sins (Rev 1:5), sanctified (Heb 13:12), and will be redeemed eternally (Rev 7:14 - 15). To "eat the flesh and drink the blood" of Christ is to receive all the gracious benefits which His death and life-giving blood can bring to the believer (Jn 6:53 - 56).

See Atonement; Sacrificial Offerings; Sacrifices.

Bibliography. Johannes Behm, *"Aima,* etc.," TDNT, I, 172- 177. Dennis J. McCarthy, *"The Symbolism of Blood and Sacrifice,"* JBL, LXXXVIII (1969), 166- 176. Leon Morris, *The Apostolic Preaching of the Cross,* Grand Rapids: Eerdmans, 1956, pp. 108- 124 (Chap. III, "The Blood"); "Blood," BDT, pp. 99 f. A. M. Stibbs, *The Meaning of the Word 'Blood' in Scripture,* Monograph Series, London: Tyndale Press, 1947.

F. P.

BLOOD AND WATER. *See* Cross; Diseases: Sufferings and Death of Christ.

BLOOD, AVENGER OF. In the OT, if a man killed another, the man closest of kin to the dead was expected to kill the slayer and was called "the avenger of blood" (Heb. *gôʾēl haddām*).

This practice may perhaps be traced to Gen 9:5 f., where God lays down the rule for mankind after the Flood that he who sheds man's blood shall in turn have his blood shed by man. Antiquity finds this rule in force among many nations and tribes. In the course of time it is not surprising that this law of blood revenge came to include the accidental slayer along with the guilty murderer, and so the practice came to be the source of unwholesome feuding between individuals and tribes.

The need of curtailment of this practice was so strongly felt in Mosaic days that in the covenant law (Ex 20:22 – 23:33) a clear distinction was made between intentional murder and accidental slaying, and provisions were made for the safeguarding of the innocent (Ex 21:12- 14).

This led to the establishment of cities of refuge (*q.v.*; Num 35:9- 34; Josh 20:1- 9), where the man who had accidentally slain another might take refuge from the avenger of blood and be safe until a fair trial had established either guilt or innocence. In the former case he would be handed over to the proper authorities, but in the second instance he could claim asylum in the city of refuge until the death of the incumbent high priest. Then the whole case was declared closed, evidently a legal custom comparable to the expiration of our statutory period of limitations.

Nothing directly messianic is involved in the term "avenger of blood."

Bibliography. Moshe Greenberg, "Avenger of Blood," IDB, I, 321.

H. C. L.

BLOOD, ISSUE OF. *See* Diseases.

BLOODY SWEAT. The expression comes from the statement in Lk 22:44, "his sweat was as it were great drops of blood." Only Luke, a physician (Col 4:14), tells of this unusual phenomenon in the agony of Christ in Gethsemane. Many insist that his statement was written in medical terminology (e.g., W. K. Hobart, *Medical Language of Luke,* p. 82) and that he was describing a physiological rarity – the emitting of blood through the transpiratory glands. Cases are on record of such phenomena caused by extreme grief or terror (cf. Henry Alford, *Greek Testament,* 7th ed., I, 648). It is further urged that the word "blood" would not have been used at all for mere comparison, for why should drops of sweat resemble blood any more than anything else? Luke could simply have said, "His sweat became great drops."

Others feel equally strongly that "Luke by the use of Gr. *hōsei* says plainly enough that he is using a simile, and is speaking neither of a change of the sweat into drops of blood nor of a mixture of sweat with blood" (Norval Geldenhuys, *Commentary on the Gospel of Luke,* p. 577). *See* Diseases: Sufferings and Death of Christ.

The exact nature of the visible signs of Jesus' agony may be irrelevant, because textual evidence suggests verses 43 and 44 may not have been in Luke's original manuscript.

J. McR.

BLOT. Two Heb. words and one Gr. word are used for "blot," "blotted," "blotteth," and "blotting." One Heb. word means basically "to rub" or "blot out." The other means a spot or blemish (*q.v.*). The Gr. word means to "erase" or "obliterate." Usually, the word is followed by "out."

Two things in particular are referred to in connection with being blotted out: names and sins. God threatens to blot out the name of Israel (Deut 9:14), and the name of the Israelite who breaks His covenant (Deut 29:20); but says He will not blot out of the book of life the name of the overcomer (Rev 3:5).

David prays for his own sins to be blotted out (Ps 51:1, 9); Jeremiah and Nehemiah for the sins of certain enemies not to be blotted out (Jer 18:23; Neh 4:5). Ps 109:14 is similar. The blotting out of sins has a very definite theological meaning, in the sense of forgiveness. God is the One who blots out Israel's sins for His own sake (Isa 43:25; 44:22), and Peter says sins will be blotted out upon repentance and conversion (Acts 3:19).

J. A. S.

BLUE. *See* Colors.

BOANERGES (bō'á-nûr'jēz; "sons of thunder"). A surname Jesus gave James and John, sons of Zebedee, when He ordained them apostles (Mk 3:17), referring to their fiery zeal (see Mk 9:38; Lk 9:54).

BOAR. See Animals, II.7.

BOAST. See Glory.

BOATS. The people of ancient Israel were not a seafaring people, a fact that is strikingly illustrated by the very scattered mention of ships or boats in Scripture. The Jordan River was not safely navigable and the Dead Sea had no value for fishermen or other voyagers. For ventures on the great seas the Israelites depended upon the Phoenicians and other nations to bring their goods from afar or transport them. Except for a "ferry" described in II Sam 19:18 to cross the Jordan, and the small lifeboat mentioned by Paul in Acts 27, the boats of Scripture, as distinguished from large ships (*q.v.*), almost entirely refer to the small fishing vessels that in Jesus' day swarmed on the Sea of Galilee.

These little boats were the tools of a great industry that in later times almost completely disappeared. William M. Thomson, in *The Land and the Book* (p. 401), which described 19th cen. A.D. Palestine, could find hardly a boat on Galilee where once they had been so numerous, because of the Arab's dislike for open water.

The fishing boats were small, scarcely larger than a good sized row boat. They carried one sail, but for the most part were propelled by rowing. They were large enough to carry Jesus and His disciples and even provided a place where Jesus might rest on the steerman's "cushion" (Mt 8:23 f.; Mk 4:38"; Lk 8:22 f.; KJV misleadingly translates "ships"). Although these boats were very small, at times pirates used them on the Sea of Galilee to raid towns along the shore. Miniature naval battles were fought as the authorities sought to clear the waters of these pirates.

For the Christian these little boats will always have a special appeal. It was from them that Jesus preached, in them that He passed across the sea to His ministry. To such a boat He walked on the waves and from it He stilled the storm.

See Ships.

P. C. J.

BOAZ (bō'ăz)

1. A Bethlehemite of the tribe of Judah, great-grandfather of David (Ruth 2:4; I Chr 2:12). He was an honorable and wealthy landowner from Bethlehem (Ruth 2:1-3), a kinsman of Elimelech, Naomi's husband (1:1; 2:1). Ruth went to glean in the fields (cf. Deut 24:19) and happened to select the fields of Boaz (Ruth 2:3). Acting under Deut 25:5, the law of levirate marriage, Naomi instructed Ruth what to do in order to have Boaz perform the part of redeemer-kinsman (Ruth 3:1-11). However, a kinsman of nearer relation had first rights and obligations (3:12-13). When he had to decline the duty of near kinsman, Boaz announced he would do so and married Ruth (4:1-11). Their union was blessed by a son who was named Obed.

2. The left pillar of the two at the front of Solomon's temple (I Kgs 7:15-22). *See* Jachin.

BOCHERU (bō'kĕ-roō). A son of Azel, a descendant of King Saul through Jonathan (I Chr 8:38).

BOCHIM (bō'kĭm). A place W of Jordan near Gilgal, probably so named (lit., "the weepers") because Israel wept there at the remonstrance of the angel of the Lord (Jud 2:1, 5).

BODY. In the KJV no less than 14 Heb. words are translated "body" in the OT. But most of these indicate a part of the body. Five of them literally mean "back." A common one, *beten*, means "belly" or "womb." Another refers to the "thigh." Still another describes the body as a "sheath." Another word means "bone" or "skeleton." Heb. *geshem* is most commonly translated "rain." But five times the identically appearing Aramaic word is rendered "body" in Dan 3-7. Another word means "carcass." Heb. *nephesh* is translated "body" four times, but its most common renderings are "soul" (428 times) and "life" (119 times). It means a living organism. The Hebrews did not have the concept of a physical body as we have it now. Nor did they seem to differentiate sharply between the body and the spirit, as we do. Perhaps *bā-śār*, "flesh," comes the nearest to making this distinction.

A Roman merchantman of the first century. Department of Classics, New York University

265

In the NT the common Gr. word for "body" is *sōma* (145 times). Here the difference between body and spirit is more evident. But *sōma* is used mostly in a figurative sense in the NT—for the whole man, for the body of sin, and for the Church.

Bibliography. E. Schweizer and F. Baumgärtel, "*Sōma,* etc.," TDNT, VII, 1024 - 1094.

R. E.

BODY OF CHRIST

1. A human body was prepared for the eternal Son of God that He might dwell among men (Heb 10:5). This He assumed in the incarnation (*q.v.*), when the Word became flesh (Jn 1:14; I Jn 4:2). To achieve our salvation it was essential that He take a real human body (Heb 2:14 - 16; 10:20); thus He is a perfect High Priest (Heb 2:17 – 3:1; 4:14 – 5:10) and a perfect substitute (Heb 9:12 - 14, 26 - 28; I Pet 2:24). The transformation of His own body in His resurrection is a prototype and guarantee of a similar resurrection body for each believer (Phil 3:21; I Cor 15).

2. The bread which was broken and appointed to be eaten at the Lord's Supper (*q.v.*), over which Christ spoke the words, "This is my body" (Mt 26:26; etc.). The broken bread represented His body which was to be wounded and scourged for our healing (Isa 53:4 - 5; Mt 8:17; I Pet 2:24).

3. The beautiful figure of the human body with its component parts is used by Paul in I Cor 12 (cf. Rom 12:4 - 8; I Cor 10:17; Eph 1:22 - 23; 2:16; 4:15 - 16; 5:23; Col 1:18, 24; 2:19; 3:14 - 15; Heb 13:3) to describe the relationship and unity of all believers in the Church of Jesus Christ (cf. Gal 3:27). The Church is *metaphorically* the body of Christ in relation to His headship (Eph 1:22 f.). But the NT nowhere indicates that the Church is the continuation of the incarnation or is to be identified with Christ's incarnate body or is Christ Himself. All believers are indwelt by and baptized in the one Holy Spirit unto or with reference to this one body (I Cor 12:13). Each believer is given particular spiritual gifts with which to minister in the body (v. 11); each fulfills some very necessary function in regard to the other members of the body (vv. 14 - 31), which function is chosen by God according to His own wish and plan (vv. 11, 18). The full spiritual understanding of this figure to express the life and internal ministrations and order of the Church is the secret to a successful, efficiently operating church. *See* Church; Head of the Church; Spiritual Gifts.

Bibliography. Alan Cole, *The Body of Christ: A New Testament Image of the Church,* Philadelphia: Westminster, 1964.

R. A. K. and J. R.

BOHAN (bō'hăn). A descendant of Reuben after whom a stone was named which marked the NE boundary of Judah where it bordered on Benjamin (Josh 15:6; 18:17).

BOILS. *See* Diseases: Skin.

BOLDNESS. The concept of boldness is seldom expressed verbally in the OT. Prov 28:1 does state: "The righteous are bold as a lion," where the verb *batah* connotes their confidence based upon active trust in the Lord. In like manner courage in the OT is not thought of as an independent virtue but as an inner strength and determination inspired by God (Deut 31:7; Ps 27:14; 31:24).

In the NT, however, there are three different word roots that carry the idea of boldness. The verb *tolmaō* contains the element of daring, of action that rises above fear (Mk 12:34; 15:43; Acts 7:32; Rom 5:7; II Cor 11:21; Phil 1:14). The second, *tharrheō,* denotes confidence and hope in God (II Cor 5:6, 8; Heb 13:6), confidence in men (II Cor 7:16), and boldness in human relations (II Cor 10:1 - 2). It is the third word, *parrhēsia,* however, which strikingly characterizes the early Christians. It denotes speaking freely and boldly, and carries the old Athenian tradition of unhindered, democratic speech. The disciples followed the example of their Teacher, who spoke out openly (Jn 7:26) and plainly (Mk 8:32; Jn 11:14). The apostles on numerous occasions exercised great boldness of speech in the face of their opponents (Acts 4:13, 29; 9:27; 13:46; 14:3; 28:31). Such boldness is attributed to the filling of the Holy Spirit (Acts 4:31). Paul testifies of his own boldness to preach and teach the gospel to his converts (I Thess 2:2; II Cor 3:12; Phm 8). At times, however, he felt the need of prayer that he might continue to speak boldly for the Lord (Eph 6:19 f.).

This new outspoken courage marked Christian believers in every phase of their lives (Phil 1:20). Absolutely devoid of self-confidence, they were fully assured of the finished work of Christ in their behalf, of His continual power and presence with them, and of all the mighty promises of God. Thus the Christian knows he can approach God directly with full confidence of an immediate audience (Heb 4:16; 10:19, 22). This provides strong assurance in prayer (I Jn 3:21 f.; 5:14 f.). Nor need the believer shrink from Christ at His second coming but he may have bold confidence before Him on the day of judgment if His love is perfected in him (I Jn 2:28; 4:17). It is by holding fast to his confidence in Christ (*parrhēsia,* Heb 3:6; Eph 3:12)—not throwing it away (Heb 10:35)—that the believer may enter the rest which God has provided for him by Jesus Christ, who has accomplished the necessary work of conquering the Christian's enemies (Heb 3:14; 4:3, 11).

Bibliography. Heinrich Schlier, "*Parrhēsia,* etc.," TDNT, V, 871 - 886.

J. R.

BOLSTER. In KJV the word is found only in I Sam 19:13, 16, where it designates the head of the bed where a "pillow of goat's hair" had been placed, and in I Sam 26:7, 11, 12, 16, where it indicates the place Saul's spear had been stuck in the ground at the side of his head.

BOLT. *See* Lock.

BOND. In the KJV, bond represents four Gr. and four Heb. words meaning "chain," "fetter," "slave," or, in a figurative sense, a moral or legal obligation.

In Acts 8:23, the "bond of iniquity" seems to mean the fetter that consists of unrighteousness. In Eph 4:3, "bond of peace" means the bond that consists of peace; that is, peace itself is the bond. In Col. 3:14, love is the bond which unites all the virtues in perfect unity. This word *syndesmos* also means "ligament" in an anatomical sense (Col 2:19, RSV).

In Col 2:14 (ASV and RSV) "bond" appears as the translation of *cheirographon* (KJV, "handwriting"). Here the figure refers to a written document. What was this bond? The just condemnation of the law against sin. Christ blots out, takes out of the way and nails to the cross, the cancelled bond. The reference to ordinances refers to the specific requirements of the law, or the specifications, in legal usage, of the general charge against us. When the law condemns, God and conscience bring to bear specifications of our transgressions. Paul became aware of the law when an awakened conscience specified transgression of the command, "Thou shalt not covet" (Rom 7).

W. B. W.

BONDAGE. *See* Service.

BONDMAID, BONDMAN, BONDSERVANT. *See* Service.

BONE. Four words are used for "bone" in the Bible.

1. The Heb. word *gerem* is used metaphorically of character or personality in Prov 17:22; 25:15.

2. Heb. *'eṣem* refers to bone or substance (Gen 2:23; Ex 13:19; II Sam 21:12); to the body or physical frame (Lam 4:8); to the substance of the sky, i.e., to "very" heaven (Ex 24:10, ASV); to the center of one's being or the seat of sensation (Job 20:11; Jer 20:9).

3. Heb. *qāneh* is used in Job 31:22 and translated "socket" in the RSV.

4. The Gr. word *osteon* is translated "bone" in Mt 23:27; Lk 24:39; Jn 19:36; and in some MSS of Eph 5:30 and Heb 11:22.

BONNET. *See* Dress: Dress of Priests.

BOOK. *Old Testament.* The Heb. word for "book" is usually *sēper*, which is probably a loan word from the Akkadian. It is suggested that in Akkad., the root signified a "task," then the document outlining the task, then the verb meaning "to send" a document. At all events, *sēper* means "book" or "letter." The derived verb signifies "count" or "relate." The participle *sōper* designates either a scribe or the officer who mustered troops.

The form of the book in OT times varied. The "letters" of II Kgs 20:12 were likely clay tablets as had been used in Mesopotamia since the invention of writing before 3200 B.C. In Palestine, the Hebrews usually used Egyptian papyrus, or possibly skins, for writing material. The Heb. alphabet was not adapted to writing on clay. The Heb. book, such as the Book of the Covenant (Ex 24:7), was doubtless a scroll such as is seen in Egyptian pictures. Such scrolls (*q.v.*) were well adapted for long literary pieces. Five scrolls would easily hold the five books of Moses. The later word for such a scroll is *megillā* (Jer 36:28). The Dead Sea Scrolls (*q.v.*) now give us many examples of such rolls written on leather as early as 225 B.C. The whole book of Isaiah coming from 150 B.C. is in a fine state of preservation.

Shorter writings were sometimes folded up and tied or sealed. Examples of this format are found in the papyri of *c.* 500–400 B.C. from the Jewish colony of Elephantine in Egypt. *See* Elephantine Papyri.

Many books are mentioned in the OT, some known and some unknown. The book of the law of Moses is repeatedly mentioned. Joshua also wrote a section in the book of the law of God (Josh 24:26). Several of the prophets refer to their books. Daniel evidently had a collec-

A Hebrew scroll book—the Habakkuk Commentary from the Dead Sea Scrolls. Y. Yadin and The Shrine of the Book.

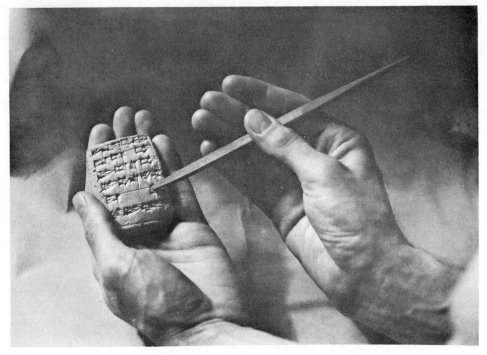

A Babylonian "book" written on a clay tablet. ORINST

tion of sacred books among which was Jeremiah (Dan 9:2; cf. BDB, p. 707).

Ancient kings kept court records in books (Est 6:1; Ezr 4:15). There were such chronicles of the kings of Israel and Judah (I Kgs 14:19, 29). Chronicles refers to the books of successive prophets as its sources (II Chr 9:29; 20:34; 32:32; etc.). Since we know its sources were Samuel-Kings, we may argue that these books were the very works of those prophets. An enigmatic reference is to the book Jasher (Josh 10:13; II Sam 1:18). Jasher means "the upright," and Israel was named Jeshurun (Deut 32:15; 33:26). Jasher just may have been an early chronicle of the history of the nation.

New Testament. The Gr. for "book" is *biblion* or *biblos* from which we get Bible, *the* Book. The Gr. word in turn seems to be derived from the name of the town Byblos, the Syrian port through which the Egyptian papyrus was imported into Palestine and Syria and transshiped to Greece.

The word "book" in the NT several times refers to OT writings, which were clearly scrolls (Lk 4:17). The shorter compositions of Paul and Peter are called "epistles." They would perhaps have been folded instead of rolled into scrolls. Revelation and John's Gospel are called "books" (Rev 22:18; Jn 20:30). Matthew's Gospel begins, "The book of the generation of Jesus Christ" which reminds us at

once of Gen 5:1. Paul asks for his books in II Tim 4:13.

It is regularly supposed that the apostles wrote on scrolls except for the shorter letters. But the Rylands papyrus fragment of John's Gospel dating from *c.* A.D. 125 was written on pages like our books in the form called a codex. It is possible that some of the NT writings were originally in codex form. This would explain the very early collection of the Gospels into one unit of material and the Pauline epistles into another unit. The modern codex form of book probably helped in the spread of the NT as a unit, and, conversely, the wide use of the NT helped in the widespread adoption of the codex form of books. *See* Scroll; Writing.

R. L. H.

BOOK OF LIFE.*See* Life, Book of.

BOOK OF THE COVENANT. Moses read from "the book of the covenant" when reporting to the people the laws given to him by God on Mount Sinai (Ex 24:7). The expression probably refers to the collection of laws found in Ex 20:22 − 23:33.

BOOT. The word does not occur in KJV, but in the RSV the word is found in Isa 9:5, which is translated "battle" in KJV. The Heb. word involved, $s^{e'}\bar{o}n$, probably is derived from an Assyrian word meaning "shoe" or "sandal." *See* Sandal; Dress.

BOOTH. A hut made of wattled twigs or branches, common as temporary buildings for a person (Jon 4:5), for soldiers (II Sam 11:11; I Kgs 20:12), for harvesters (Lev 23:33 ff.). Job (27:18) used a watchman's booth as a symbol of impermanence. *See* Festivals: Feast of Tabernacles.

BOOTY. *See* Spoil.

BOOZ (bō'ŏz). The Gr. form of Boaz (Mt 1:5; Lk 3:32). *See* Boaz.

BORDER. In the OT the Heb. word is $g^e b\hat{u}l$, meaning "border," "boundary line," "edge," "margin" (Num 34:6; Deut 3:16; Jud 11:18; Ezk 43:13). It can mean a bounded country or district included within borders (Gen 10:19). In the NT the Gr. word is *horion*, meaning "limit" or "border" and always in the plural (Mt 4:13; cf. 2:16; 8:34).

BORN AGAIN. To be born again is to experience the creative, life-giving work of the Holy Spirit. He regenerates (Jn 3:5) those who are dead in trespasses and sins, so that they are quickened or made alive spiritually (Eph 2:1, 5), and are changed from being the children of the devil (Jn 8:44; Eph 2:2–3) to becoming the children of God (Jn 1:12), His sons and daughters (Rom 8:16–17). When a person is born again he becomes a partaker of the divine nature of Christ (Gal 2:20; Eph 2:10; Col 1:27; I Pet 1:23; II Pet 1:4).

Interpretations of the expression "born of water and of the Spirit" (Jn 3:5) have been various. (For details see commentaries.) Both in John's Gospel (see 1:33; 7:37–39) and in the OT (see Ezk 36:25–27; Isa 44:3) the two elements are joined. In Nicodemus' own day, the ministry of John the Baptist, which emphasized both cleansing through repentance and the coming of the Spirit, would have been illustrative. The water was the sign; the work of cleansing by the Spirit was the thing signified. Both are important, and joined together they complement the ideas of repentance and fai·h (Acts 20:21) which bring salvation.

Need for the new birth. God warned Adam and Eve that the day they rebelled against Him by disobeying His command they would die (Gen 2:17). They died spiritually when they ate of the forbidden fruit (Rom 5:12), with the result that no matter how moral, upright, and law-abiding any of their descendants may be, each man in his heart is totally depraved and sinful. He has a fallen nature, being blind to sin and unable to save himself (Jn 3:6; Ps 51:5; I Cor 2:14; Rom 8:7–8), and needs cleansing from his sins and personal salvation (Ps 51:7; Mt 26:28; Jn 13:8; Tit 3:5; Heb 1:3; 10:14).

Christ explained to Nicodemus, who was a member of the Jewish Sanhedrin and a leading theologian of his day, that he must be born again (or "from above," as some translate *anōthen* in Jn 3:3, 7). For "that which is born of the flesh is flesh"—by our parents we experience a physical birth and enter into the world as human beings, and "that which is born of the Spirit is spirit"—by the Holy Spirit we receive spiritual birth and become children of God.

The tests of the new birth. One reason men have sometimes ignored the doctrine of the new birth is that they have overlooked the fact it is set forth not only in John 3 but also in I John. In John's epistle he goes into the matter of the new birth more fully, giving the marks or proofs whereby a man may know whether he has been born again. (1) Such a one does not practice sin (I Jn 3:9; 5:18). (2) He has true Christian love toward others (4:7, 20; cf. 3:14–15), particularly toward other Christians (5:1). (3) He loves God and keeps His commandments (5:2–3). (4) He overcomes the world, that is, lives a victorious Christian life (5:4–5). When these proofs are missing, either the person is only a nominal Christian and not really saved, or he is a Christian who is living a defeated, disobedient life. *See* New Birth; Regeneration.

Bibliography. F. Büchsel and K. H. Rengstorf, "*Gennaō*, etc.," TDNT, I, 665–675. Herman A. Hoyt, *The New Birth*, Findlay, Ohio: Dunham Pub. Co., 1961.

R. A. K. and W. M. D.

BORROW, BORROWING. In its usual sense in Scripture, borrowing means just what it does in our own times. The root meanings of the Heb. words "to be joined (to another)" (Deut 28:12; Ps 37:21; Neh 5:4) and "interweave" (Deut 15:6) suggest the close relationship that obtains between borrower and lender. We lend not only our goods but ourselves, and we not only borrow another's possessions but become a part of his life. For borrowing as a commercial transaction, *see* Bank; Loan.

Chief interest in the term comes as a result of the unfortunate KJV translation in Ex 3:22; 11:2; 12:35, where the word "ask" was translated "borrow." Modern versions have translated correctly according to the context. The word so translated in these verses is the usual Heb. word "to ask." In some cases, as here, it bears the implication "to demand."

The use of the word "borrow" has given rise to a serious ethical question. It is assumed that the Lord was commanding the Israelites to deceive their neighbors into thinking that they intended only to borrow their valuables for a few days, but then they departed forever from the land with these goods thus fraudulently obtained. Actually the Israelites were told to demand from their masters that which would represent the wages of the many years of slavery when they labored without pay. God said, "Ye shall not go out empty" (Ex 3:21). They were to "despoil" the Egyptians (Ex 3:22; 12:36) as surely as though they had been a great army, conquering and despoiling its foe. Thus God's victory over Egypt would be clearly marked. It is obvious, then, that in these passages there is no moral problem of a God who counsels fraud and deceit. Any attempts to justify Israel's "borrowing" have been unnecessary. In two other passages (Ex 22:14; II Kgs 4:3) the verb "ask" seems to be translated properly by "borrow."

P. C. J.

BOSCATH. *See* Bozkath.

BOSOM
1. Bosom refers to the human breast both literally and figuratively in Scripture. One holds a child or clasps a loved one to one's bosom (Num 11:12; Ruth 4:16; I Kgs 3:20). The bosom is also the place of affection and love, the inner self (Deut 13:6; Ps 89:50; Prov 6:27). It describes the place of special intimacy (Jn 1:18). The term "Abraham's bosom" *(q.v.)* refers to heaven, where the "Father of the faithful" receives His children to final peace and rest (Lk 16:22).
2. A use of the term "bosom" peculiar to the East is also found. The long flowing garments, bound at the waist by a girdle, provide a convenient carrying place, like a bag, in the fold of material over the breast. Thus the word often refers to this pocket where bread, grain, even lambs were carried (Ex 4:6-7; Prov 17:23; Isa 40:11).

BOSOR (bō′sôr). Gr. form of Beor, father of Balaam (II Pet 2:15). *See* Beor.

BOTCH. *See* Diseases: Skin.

BOTTLES. The most widely used bottles in the East, even today, are made of leather. Usually the skin of a kid or goat, though even a cow, camel, or buffalo, was used. The animal's head

A goatskin "bottle." JR

and feet were cut off, and it was then skinned. The hide was usually tanned and smoked, the openings were sewn up and sometimes sealed with pitch, and the "bottle" was ready for use. It was a highly portable vessel. Carried on the back, filled with water or milk, it was one of the most essential articles of any household. It was even used as a churn; when filled with milk it was shaken until it formed an oily butter.

By use the skins became stretched and dry and in time would split. This is the point of Jesus' parable of new wine in old wine skins (Mt 9:17). The new wine would ferment and expand; the old skin, having no stretch left, would split and lose the wine.

Earthenware bottles and jars were also used, but these were fragile and easily broken. For costly perfumes there were tiny flasks of glass, gold, or silver. *See* Cruse.

P. C. J.

BOTTOMLESS PIT. The expression occurs only in Rev 9:1-2, where at the sound of the fifth angel the pit was opened by one possessing the key and beings came forth resembling locusts but having faces like men (Rev 9:7). Their physical make-up equipped them for their mission, "to hurt men five months" (Rev 9:10).

The word abyss *(abyssos),* however, stands alone frequently, and in both Scripture and early religious literature indicates the opposite extreme of heaven (cf. Testament of Levi 3:9 where the plural is used of a third category or realm of things, along with the heavens and the earth, that are shaken by the presence of God. In I Clement 28:3 the plural is used in the same categorization in a quotation from Ps 139:7-8). Paul makes a similar categorization in Phil 2:10 and speaks of "things under the earth" *(katachthonios).* This third realm called the abyss was also called Hades (Gr. in LXX of Ps 139:8) and considered to be the abode of the dead (Rom 10:7; Acts 2:31) and of demons (Lk 8:31). The devil himself is kept in the abyss according to John's revelation (Rev 20:3). Some feel that the word thus means "the depths of hell" (Arndt, p. 55), but this cannot be clearly established. *See* Abyss; Hades; Hell.

J. Mc.R.

BOW, BOWING. An act of obeisance. Many Heb. and Gr. words signify the act of bending one's knees and bowing down in humility before a superior. The custom symbolized (1) servitude (Gen 27:29); (2) homage, respect, or reverence, e.g., when Abraham bowed before the three angels (Gen 18:2), Lot before the two angels (Gen 19:1), Ruth before Boaz (Ruth 2:10), Bathsheba before David (I Kgs 1:16); (3) worship (Ex 20:5; Ps 72:9; Mic 6:6; Ps 99:9, "worship," lit., "bow down"); (4) mourning and sorrow (Ps 38:6; 44:25).

In many cases the suppliant bowed so completely that hands and face were on the ground, i.e., he prostrated himself (Gen 48:12; Num

22:31; I Kgs 1:31; Lk 24:5). The custom of bowing seven times, as Jacob did before Esau (Gen 33:3), is verified by the frequently used statement in the Amarna letters that the writers "fall seven times and seven times" at the feet of Pharaoh (ANET, pp. 483–490). The Roman soldiers showed their contempt for Christ by mockingly bowing before Him as the king of the Jews (Mt 27:29; Mk 15:19).

See Worship.

A. F. J.

BOW AND ARROW. Used as an instrument in hunting and warfare from very earliest days in biblical lands. In the Bible references, the bow (Heb. *qeshet*) dates back to the patriarchal period where it appears to have been used both as a weapon by the nomad (cf. Gen 21:20) and for hunting (Gen 27:3). Later references indicate it became part of the warriors' equipment (Isa 13:18). The Philistines seemed to excel in the art of archery which led David to require special training to be given to the Israelites (II Sam 1:18). Seen in the hand of the symbolical white-horseman of the apocalypse (Rev 6:2), it may indicate warfare and conquest or, as others interpret, a bloodless victory (no arrows).

The earliest bows were constructed of wood often plaited with leather or bark for added strength (Job 20:24; Ps 18:34, RSV). The Hyksos introduced the compound bow, which contained laminations of bone, horn or ivory to increase its elasticity and shooting power. Some bows were even laminated with bronze strips for the same purpose. Such bows were expensive and were carried usually by princes and leaders. For example, in the campaign of the Egyptian pharaoh Thutmose III at Megiddo (*c.* 1480 B.C.), only 502 bows were taken while over 900 chariots and 2,000 horses were captured (ANET, p. 237). Larger battle bows (Zech 9:10; 10:4) were strung by placing the foot on one end of the bow and bending down the upper end to notch the string. Apparently from this procedure archers were known as "bow treaders." Strings were made of ox gut.

Arrows were made of reed or light wood notched at one end for the string and tipped at the other with flint, bone, or bronze. Tips were often barbed or dipped in poison (Job 6:4).

Arrows are once associated in the Bible with the occult divination (Ezk 21:21) practiced by the Babylonians, and were used in magical or symbolic rites (II Kgs 13:15–19). The bow and/or arrow sometimes symbolizes divine judgment (Ps 7:13; 38:2; 64:7), violence (Ps 11:2; 57:4), or military might (Gen 49:24; I Sam 2:4; Hos 1:5). *See* Archers; Armor; Arms; Hunt; War, Warfare.

A. F. J.

BOW IN THE CLOUDS. The regular Heb. word *qeshet* for "bow" is used in Gen 9:13, 14, 16 for the rainbow, which symbolized God's covenant with mankind that He would never again

An Assyrian warrior, palace of Sargon II of Assyria at Khorsabad. LM

flood the earth with water as in the days of Noah. Whether this phenomenon appeared for the first time in nature at this point, as C. F. Keil concludes in commenting on Gen 9:8–17 (KD, *Pentateuch*, I, 154), or gained a new significance as a "sign" to the inhabitants of the earth, is not clear.

Both Ezekiel (1:28) and John (Rev 4:3; 10:1) see the rainbow associated with the throne of God's judgment, probably signifying the grace and mercy of God in the midst of judgment.

BOWELS. The KJV rendering of several Heb. words and the consistent rendering of the Gr. *splagchna*. In addition to its literal meaning (II Sam 20:10; Acts 1:18), the word is also used to refer to the reproductive capacity of man (II Sam 7:12; Isa 48:19), and the center of his emotions (Song 5:4), equivalent to the heart in Western literature. The ASV renders the Gr. *splagchna* in various ways to indicate emotion: (1) tender mercy (Lk 1:78; Phil 1:8; 2:1); (2) affections (II Cor 6:12; 7:15); (3) heart of compassion (Col 3:12); (4) heart (Phm 7, 12, 20); and (5) compassion (I Jn 3:17).

The bowels were probably felt to be the center of emotion because of the reaction of the stomach to excitement. Though "heart" is a more poetic word than "bowels," it is no more accurately used, because emotion originates in the mind.

BOWL. A shallow, hollow-shaped vessel, such as a basin or cup. *See* Dish. The word bowl is used to translate a variety of Heb. words. Bowls were made of earthenware, metal, or wood. *See* Pottery.

Gideon wrung water from fleece into a bowl (Jud 6:38). Bowls like cups in the shape of almonds decorated the lampstand in the tabernacle (Ex 37:17-20). Larger gold and silver bowls were used for the ritual service in the temple (I Chr 28:17). Dissolute revelers in Israel would drink wine from costly bowls (Amos 6:6). "Bowl" is used instead of "vial" in the revised versions of Revelation (e.g., Rev 16:1 ff.).

BOWMAN. *See* Armor; Bow and Arrow.

BOWSHOT. A way of indicating the distance (only in Gen 21:16) between an archer and his target, about 50 yards.

BOX. A small case, cruet, or flask with cover for keeping oil or ointment, such as Elisha used in anointing Jehu (II Kgs 9:1, 3); alabaster jar *(alabastron)* of the NT (Mt 26:7; Mk 14:3; Lk 7:37).

BOX TREE. *See* Plants.

BOY. Two Heb. words are used: *yeled,* "one born" (Joel 3:3; Zech 8:5), and *na'ar,* "youth" (Gen 25:27), used of young Esau and Jacob. The latter word covers the age range from an infant (I Sam 4:21) to a warrior such as Absalom (II Sam 18:5, 12), with a stress on youthfulness.

BOZEZ (bō'zĕz). Name of the northern of two cliffs which stand on each side of the valley of Michmash (I Sam 14:4). *See* Geba; Michmash.

BOZKATH (bŏz'kăth). A town in the lowlands of Judah between Lachish and Eglon (Josh 15:39), the birthplace of the mother of King Josiah (II Kgs 22:1).

BOZRAH (bŏz'rà)
1. A very ancient city, a capital of Edom, about 18 miles SE of the Dead Sea (Gen 36:33; I Chr 1:44; Isa 34:6; 63:1; Jer 49:13, 22; Amos 1:12), identified with the village of Buseirah on a virtually impregnable spur of a ridge, guarded on three sides by deep wadis.
2. Mentioned in Jer 48:24 as a city of Moab, possibly the Reubenite city of refuge known as Bezer *(q.v.).*

BRACELET. Used to translate five Heb. words which describe an ornament worn by both men and women. King Saul wore a bracelet on his arm (II Sam 1:10) and the Israelites gave bracelets as an offering to the Lord (Ex 35:22). Bracelets were used as a sign of wealth (Gen 24:22). Isaiah prophesied the removal of such finery as a future punishment by the Lord for the proudness of women (Isa 3:19).

Bracelets were made of bronze, iron, glass, ivory, silver, and gold and are found in many shapes and designs, some inlaid with many precious stones. They are found in abundance throughout the lands of biblical times.

See Dress; Jewels, Jewelry.

BRAMBLE. *See* Plants.

BRANCH. This term translates 18 Heb. and four Gr. words. These include six distinct connotations:
1. The natural meaning is evident when it is said, "the fowls of the heaven . . . sing among the branches" (Ps 104:12), or that the fig tree's budding branches are a sign of approaching summer (Mt 24:32). *See* Plants.
2. The three arms on each side of the central shaft of the golden candlestick or lampstand are termed branches (Ex 25:31-36; 37:17-22).
3. The making of booths of tree branches under which to dwell during the Feast of Tabernacles gives a ceremonial connotation (Lev 23:40 ff.; Neh 8:14 f.).
4. Branches may be part of a figure representing some important person, as Job (Job 29:19); the chief butler (Gen 40:9 f.); Joseph (Gen 49:22); Nebuchadnezzar (Dan 4:12, RSV).
5. "Branch" depicts God's blessings on faithful Israel, as well as His chastisement for their disobedience. Israel under chastisement: "The Lord will cut off from Israel . . . branch and rush in one day" (Isa 9:14); Israel the "green olive tree . . . the branches of it are broken" (Jer 11:16); and many others. Like judgment is visited on heathen nations and rulers because of their sins: Moab (Isa 16:6-8); Egypt (Ezk 31:2-14); Nebuchadnezzar (Dan 4:13-14). Paul also uses the metaphor of natural branches broken off the olive tree to describe the result of Israel rejecting Jesus (Rom 11:19-21). Jesus employs a similar figure to warn fruitless disciples (Jn 15:6). Israel under blessing: "But you, O mountains of Israel, shall shoot forth your branches, and yield your fruit to my people Israel; for they will soon come home" (Ezk 36:8, RSV; also Ezk 19:10 f.; Ps 80:8-11).
6. The culmination of all OT branch symbolism is found in those foregleams of the coming Messiah (Heb. *ṣemaḥ,* "sprout," Isa 4:2; Jer 23:5; 33:15; Zech 3:8; 6:12; Heb. *neṣer,* "green shoot," Isa 11:1 f.). Isa 4:2 ("In that day shall the branch of the Lord be beautiful and glorious") does not give the branch definite personality as does Isa 11:1 f., but the results of His presence (4:3-6) are so similar as to leave little doubt that both passages refer to the

coming Branch. The remaining passages are clearly personal and messianic.

After His resurrection Jesus became the Vine and His disciples the branches (Jn 15:1–8).

L. R. E.

BRAND. Three Heb. words are used in connection with this expression: (1) *'ûd,* "a bent stick," used to stir the fire (Amos 4:11; Zech 3:2); also "firebrand" (Isa 7:4; *see* Firebrand); (2) *lappîd,* a waving torch similar to a lightning flash (Jud 15:4–5); (3) *ziqqîm,* "sparks, embers, or firebrands" (Prov 26:18; Isa 50:11).

BRASS. *See* Minerals and Metals: Bronze.

BRAY. Two Heb. words are translated "bray."

1. In Job 6:5 *nāhaq* is used to refer to the harsh cry of the ass; and in Job 30:7, figuratively, to the senseless talk of mockers.

2. In Prov 27:22 *kātash* is used to refer to the severe but futile chastisement of a fool, which is likened to being crushed or pounded small in a mortar.

BRAZEN. Used of articles made of brass. *See* Metals.

BRAZEN SEA. *See* Tabernacle: Laver.

BRAZEN SERPENT. During the period of the wilderness wanderings, Israel murmured against the Lord. As a disciplinary measure, God sent "fiery serpents" among them (Num 21:5–9). Probably these were cobras, whose bite produced a burning fever. When the stricken people imploringly turned to Moses, he at the command of God made a brass (copper) serpent, no doubt a replica of the viper with the stinging, deadly bite which had already bitten them. One should not consider this as sympathetic magic, for it probably served as a symbolic reminder of the divine displeasure. Centuries later it became a rallying point for idolatrous worship in Israel which caused the godly Hezekiah to destroy it (II Kgs 18:4). Christ refers to it figuratively as a type of His own approaching death on the cross (Jn 3:14), as being "made sin for us" (II Cor 5:21) and as bearing our judgment.

See Animals, IV.8, 30.

J. F. G.

BRAZIER. A pan, usually metal, for holding live coals, placed for heating on the floor in the middle of the room. In Jer 36:22–23 (KJV, "hearth") it refers to the heating device in King Jehoiakim's winter palace on which he burned Jeremiah's scroll as he cut it to pieces with a knife. *See* Hearth.

BREAD. *See* Food.

BREAD OF FACES, BREAD OF PRESENCE. The Heb. term referring to the showbread in the tabernacle or temple. Twelve loaves were kept on the table in the holy place at all times, being exchanged for fresh loaves every week (Ex 25:30). *See* Showbread.

The significance of the "bread of faces" is seen perhaps best in its literal meaning, "bread of the presence" (Num 4:7, RSV). Not only was the never-ceasing presence of God thus symbolized, but also the fact that God's presence was to be considered as more vital than bread.

BREAKER, THE. A messianic title found only in Mic 2:13. The KJV translation of Heb. *happōrēṣ* (RSV, "He who opens the breach"), it is used of the Lord as the deliverer of regathered Israel pictured as a flock in an enclosure and besieged by its enemies. In an earlier time God had broken through *(pāraṣ)* David's enemies the Philistines like a bursting *(pereṣ)* flood, so that King David had named that place Baal-perazim—"the Lord of breaking through" (II Sam 5:20, RSV marg.). A literal rendering of Mic 2:13 follows: "The Breach-maker will go up before them; they will break through and pass through the gate and will go out by it; yes, their King will pass on before them, even Yahweh at their head." Christ is also the Breaker figuratively for the individual believer as "He breaks the power of cancelled sin and sets the prisoner free." (Cf. Lev 26:13; Isa 61:1; Ezk 34:27.)

J. R.

BREAKFAST. *See* Food: Meals.

BREAST. The common Heb. word, translated variously in the KJV as "breast" (Gen 49:25), "teats" (Isa 32:12), and once by the Old English "paps" (Ezk 23:21), always refers to the female breast. In the NT, the Gr. word *stēthos* translated "breast" refers always to the male chest (e.g., Lk 18:13; Jn 13:25; Rev 15:6). The Gr. *mastos* is apparently synonymous, but is rendered "pap" in the NT (Lk 11:27; 23:29) and refers to the female breast, except in Rev 1:13 where it is used of Christ. *See also* Bosom.

BREASTPLATE. *See* Armor; Dress (of High Priest); Priest, High.

BREECHES. *See* Dress: Dress of Priests.

BRETHREN. *See* Brother.

BRIBE, BRIBERY. The Heb. word *shōḥad* means a gift; but in a corrupt sense, a bribe. Heb. law condemned the giving or receiving of gifts or bribes in order to pervert justice (Ex 23:8). References are made to its use to corrupt judges and rulers (Job 15:34; I Sam 8:3; Ps 26:10; Isa 33:15; Ezk 22:12). In this sense *kōper* is used in I Sam 12:3 and Amos 5:12. This Heb. word is used of the atonement money or ransom, and in the latter passage implies a payment for a man that was murdered so that the rich murderer might go free.

BRICK. The earliest bricks of which there is written record were in the city and tower of Babel (Gen 11:3). The ruins of Mesopotamian houses reveal the use of beaten clay and bricks in their foundations as early as approximately 4000 B.C. (Joseph Free, *Archaeology and Bible History*, pp. 37–38). Ancient Babylonia, Egypt, Assyria, and even Palestine found them a cheap and convenient building material, especially where stone was scarce or hard to use. The exact extent of their use is hard to trace because unburned bricks, after the houses and walls fall, gradually form a heap of earth not distinguishable from the surrounding soil.

In Egypt the bricks were invariably crude or unburned. When kiln-burned bricks are found, they are known to be of Roman time. Crude bricks were made of a black loamy earth or mud which was thoroughly "slipped" or mixed and formed in a bottomless box, which came off to let the brick bake in the sun. It often became so hard that a blow of a hammer would be required to break it. To render it more cohesive, chopped straw or stubble was added (Ex 5:7–18). (See *ibid.*, pp. 91–92, for confirmation of the cohesive action of straw and even of water in which straw has soaked.) When feed was in short supply, the straw was consumed by the beasts. This greatly added to the difficulty of the brickmakers, who had to collect stubble, or labor under severe handicap. Mod-

ern excavations at Pithom (Ex 1:11) show that most of the bricks of the store city were made of mud and straw baked in the sun (probably the work of the Heb. slaves). In some of the upper courses rushes had been substituted for straw, and still other bricks had no fibrous material.

Egyptian bricks were generally about 16 x 8 x 6 inches. For walls they were laid flat. For arches they were laid edgeways. They were frequently stamped on one side with hieroglyphics of the name of the pharaoh or of some edifice belonging to the pharaoh. The bricks that have survived from early Egypt appear to have been made under government monopoly. The rulers gave the distasteful and unhealthful task to captive Asiatic foreigners, among whom were the Israelites. In the tomb of the grand vizier Rekh-mi-Re at Thebes is a much-publicized picture of some light colored bondsmen (possibly Hebrews) employed in bringing water, digging clay, kneading it, pressing it into molds, carrying the bricks and piling them up for use. The picture is complete with whips and goads and the superintending officer.

In Palestine and Syria the same methods were often used. Where building stone was scarce, houses were made of sun-baked brick. When the bricks were laid, the house was plastered inside and out with the same material and whitewashed or painted with gray or yellow earth. The outer coating had to be renewed from year to year. Isa 9:10 refers to the superiority of hewn stone over brick.

Brick-making along the Nile. Wet clay is poured into a wooden frame, which is then lifted and used to repeat the process. HFV

Ancient Babylon used kiln-baked bricks which were frequently held together by hot bitumen (Gen 11:3). These bricks were generally about 12 x 12 x 3½ inches. They were often stamped with cuneiform characters. Many thousands bore the name of Nebuchadnezzar. Vitrified bricks of different colors were common. Assyrians used sun-baked bricks more freely for buildings, though they also used kiln bricks for flooring or paving of courts or palaces. Painted, glazed, and even gilded bricks have also been found at Nineveh and other Assyrian cities.

See Architecture; Building.

W. T. D.

The clay brick wall of the hall of justice at Ur.
Carl DeVries

BRICKMAKER. *See* Occupations.

BRIDAL GIFT. *See* Marriage.

BRIDE, BRIDEGROOM. The bride is a translation of Heb. *kallâh* and Gr. *nymphē*, referring to a betrothed or recently wedded woman (Isa 61:10; 62:5; Jer 7:34; Jn 3:29). The same Heb. word is translated "spouse" in Song 4:8 – 5:1. The most important usage is with reference to the Church as the Bride of Christ (Rev 21:2, 9; 22:17; also II Cor 11:2; Eph 5:25 ff.). The Gr. word *gynē*, "wife," is also closely related, as in Mt 1:20.

The bridegroom is the counterpart of the bride. The Gr. *nymphios* is the "bridegroom" (Jn 3:29; Rev 18:23). The Heb. word *hātān* means "bridegroom," "husband," or "son-in-law" according to the context. Christ used the term of Himself in the parable of the ten virgins (Mt 25:6). The "friend of the bridegroom" was one who arranged the details of the marriage and had a prominent place in the wedding festivities (Jn 3:29).

See Bride of Christ; Marriage.

Bibliography. J. Jeremias, "*Nymphē,* etc.," TDNT, IV, 1099–1106. T. C. Mitchell, "The Meaning of the Noun *HTN* in the OT," VT, XIX (1969), 92–112.

W. M. D.

BRIDE OF CHRIST. One of the seven figures used to set forth the relationship of the Church to Christ: the branches and the Vine (Jn 15:1–11), the sheep and the Shepherd (Jn 10:1–30), the stones and the Chief Cornerstone (I Pet 2:4–8), the priests and the High Priest (Heb 2:17; 4:14; 7:26; I Pet 2:9), the new creation and the Last Adam (I Cor 15:45–50), the members and the Head of the Body (I Cor 12; Eph 4:4–16), the bride and the Bridegroom (Rev 19:7–9; cf. Eph 5:21–32). *See* Bride, Bridegroom.

The Church, composed of those who have been saved by grace through faith, forms the Bride of Christ. Those already with the Lord, together with those still alive at the rapture, will at that event receive resurrection bodies (I Thess 4:14–17; I Cor 15:51 f.). As members of the Church they will celebrate the marriage supper of the Lamb with Christ (Rev 19:7–9) close to the time of His return to put down His enemies (Rev 19:11–21). Our Lord Himself foretold the occurrence of this marriage in the parable of the ten virgins in which He stressed the fact that the day and the hour of His coming for His own is unknown (Mt 24:36; 25:1–13), and the consequent need to be ready at all times with oil in our lamps—perhaps a figure of salvation in the sense that the Christian is the temple of the Holy Spirit (I Cor 6:19). *See* Marriage of the Lamb; Head of the Church.

At present, then, the marriage of the Church to Christ has not been consummated. She is to be living as a virgin betrothed to her future husband (II Cor 11:2), belonging to Christ under marriage contract (i.e., the covenant of redemption). He has sought His bride in love and is even now sanctifying her that she might be without spot or blemish when He will present the Church to Himself in splendor (Eph 5:23–27, RSV). This present time of purification of the Church is reminiscent of the twelve months of beautifying through which Esther and the other maidens went, before being brought in to the king (Est 2:12). The Bride of Christ joins in the last prayer of the Bible as she waits for Him to return for her: "And the Spirit and the bride say [to Jesus], Come! . . . Amen. Even so, come, Lord Jesus" (Rev 22:17, 20).

In connection with the theme of the bride and the Bridegroom, NT teaching speaks of wedding guests (Mt 22:1–14), "sons of the bridechamber" (Mk 2:19 f., ASV), and even a best man or friend of the Bridegroom, viz., John the Baptist (Jn 3:27–30). OT imagery includes bridal attendants along with the king's daughter or bride in the beautiful poetic prophecy of the coming messianic wedding (Ps 45:13–15). The interpretation as to the identity of these guests and attendants is not theologically certain.

Ultimately the Bride will reign with her Husband over the new earth, as the joint metaphor of the holy city, the new Jerusalem, "coming down from God out of heaven, prepared as a bride adorned for her husband" (Rev 21:2, 9–10), seems to indicate.

R. A. K. and J. R.

BRIDECHAMBER. *See* Marriage.

BRIDLE. The several words in Heb. and Gr. for "bridle" are used rather loosely in the Bible to refer to either bit *(q.v.),* bridle, rein *(q.v.),* or halter, whatever may have been used to guide or check an animal. Usually it was no more than a leather strap with a loop over the upper lip. Sometimes a ring was placed in the nose or lip and the animal was led about. A basket of rope network was also in use as a sort of muzzle.

The references in Scripture are largely figurative. The nations, and particularly Israel, are spoken of as though they were refractory animals who must be trained and curbed, or punished (II Kgs 19:28; Isa 30:28; 37:29; Ezk 29:4). That these expressions are not entirely figurative is seen by some of the Assyrian monuments in which captives of war are actually led on a strap with a ring through the lip.

God's law is also referred to as that which controls and guides (Ps 32:8–9). The point of Ps 39:1 is somewhat dimmed by the KJV translation "bridle." The psalmist actually says, "I will muzzle my mouth."

P. C. J.

BRIER. *See* Plants.

BRIMSTONE. *See* Minerals.

BRONZE. *See* Minerals and Metals.

BROOCH. Used in plural by RSV (KJV, "bracelets") for a class of gold jewelry brought as offerings by men and women of Israel (Ex 35:22). Keil and Delitzsch suggest "clasp or ring." It could be "buckle or brooch." *See* Bracelet.

BROOK. In the OT "brook" derives its meaning from the following Heb. words: (1) *nahal,* which describes a valley with a stream or a river in it (Num 21:12), or the stream alone (Deut 9:21); (2) *'āphîq,* which refers to the actual bed of the stream (Joel 1:20, RSV); (3) *yeʾōr,* which almost always refers to a large river such as the Nile, the canal-arms of the Nile, or the Tigris; but in Isa 19:6–8 it is translated "brook" in referring to the channels of the Nile in the delta; (4) *mîkāl,* which is found only in II Sam 17:20 and is of uncertain meaning.

In the NT the Gr. word for the brook Kidron in Jn 18:1, *cheimarrhos,* describes a stream which flows in the winter.

BROOM. *See* Plants.

BROTHER. This term is used extensively in Scripture to express a wide variety of relationships. The natural use has reference to a blood relationship, whether immediate or remote: (1) sons of the same parents or parent (Gen 43:29; Gal 1:19); (2) near relatives (Gen 29:15); (3) fellow tribesmen (Num 16:10); (4) kindred

tribes (Jud 20:23); (5) fellow countrymen (Ex 2:11); (6) cognate nations (Ob 10); (7) fellow human beings (Gen 9:5).

The figurative use expresses a relationship of affinity or similarity which is not necessarily based on a physical connection: (1) likeness (Job 30:29; Prov 18:9); (2) similarity in rank or office (Ezr 3:2); (3) friendship (II Sam 1:26); (4) relationship of allies (Amos 1:9).

The most distinctive NT usage of the term "brother" is that which expresses a spiritual relationship. It is a common designation for a Christian (Acts 9:17; I Cor 5:11; Phm 16), and is suggestive of the family nature of the Christian community (Gal 6:10) in which God is Father (Phil 1:2; I Jn 5:1) and all believers are brothers. This relationship is not merely figurative but is based on a spiritual birth which makes its recipients fellow possessors of a new life (II Pet 1:4). The Christian community is called a brotherhood (I Pet 2:17) and as such is to be marked by love (I Jn 5:1). Its members are to cultivate brotherly love (Gr. *philadelphia*) toward each other (II Pet 1:7). The fact that they are brothers should significantly affect their conduct. They are to share with the needy brother (I Jn 3:17–18); they are to show hospitality to one another (III Jn 5–6); they are not to take each other to court (I Cor 6:1–8); they are not to place a stumbling block before a weaker brother (I Cor 8:9–13); they are to admonish those who sin (II Thess 3:15).

Background for this distinctive NT use of the term is obviously to be found in its OT employment to refer to a fellow Israelite. However, it may well be that the custom of the Pharisees of calling themselves *ḥăbērîm,* "companions" or "brethren," has a bearing upon the Christian usage. It may also be significant that the members of the Qumran community referred to one another as brothers.

D. W. B.

BROTHERLY KINDNESS. Translated thus twice in II Pet 1:7 from the Gr. *philadelphia;* more literally, "love of the brethren" (I Pet 1:22, ASV marg.), or as the same noun is elsewhere rendered, "brotherly love" (Rom 12:10; I Thess 4:9; Heb 13:1). The biblical connotation of *philadelphia* is not that of love simply for one's blood brothers, as in all previous pagan writings, but for the broader brotherhood of true believers (cf. Arndt). Those who have been adopted into divine sonship through faith in Christ (Jn 1:12) become necessarily brothers in their relation to each other (Mt 23:8; Rom 8:17; Eph 4:15–16; cf. "neighbor" in OT, Lev 19:17). Brotherly kindness thus forms an indispensable (I Jn 4:20) element in the Christian's growth in sanctification (II Pet 1:7) and exhibits itself in harmoniousness (Acts 2:46; Rom 12:16), sincerity (I Pet 1:22), affection and esteem for fellow disciples (Rom 12:10; cf. Gal 6:10; Lev 19:34 for others also), zealously maintained (Heb 13:1; I Pet 1:22). Pagans witnessing this unique selflessness could only exclaim, "Behold how they love one another!" (Tertullian, *Apologeticus,* cf. Jn 13:35). *See* Love; Charity; Brother.

J. B. P.

BROTHERLY LOVE. *See* Brotherly Kindness.

BROTHERS OF OUR LORD. The NT contains a number of references to the brothers of Christ (Mt 12:46 ff. and parallels; Jn 2:12; 7:3, 5, 10; Acts 1:14; I Cor 9:5; Gal 1:19). Their names, as listed in Mt 13:55, were James, Joses, Simon, and Judas.

Since the days of the early church, the relationship of these individuals to Jesus has been under discussion. Some have held that they were stepbrothers, sons of Joseph by a former marriage. This theory, which was advanced by such men as Origen, Eusebius, and Epiphanius, is based on the conjecture that Joseph was considerably older than Mary. A similar view postulates that the brothers were sons of Joseph by a levirate marriage with the widow of Cleophas, his brother. Neither of these theories has sufficient basis to warrant serious consideration.

Of much wider acceptance is the view, which is officially held by the Roman Catholic church, that the brothers were in reality cousins of Jesus. James, the Lord's brother, is identified with James the son of Alphaeus (Lk 6:15) and with James the less (Mk 15:40), and is thus considered to be one of the 12 apostles (Gal 1:19). Judas and Simon (Mt 13:55) are also taken to be apostles (Lk 6:15-16). Mary, the wife of Cleophas, is said to be a sister of the mother of Jesus (Jn 19:25), and Cleophas is identified with Alphaeus (cf. also Mk 6:3; 15:40). It is asserted, therefore, that these brothers were sons of Mary, the sister of Christ's mother, and thus cousins of Christ.

This view, however, is open to several serious objections: (1) It is not possible to identify Christ's unbelieving brethren (Jn 7:5) with the apostles. (2) Scripture clearly distinguishes the brothers of the Lord from the apostles (Jn 2:12; Acts 1:13-14). (3) It is unthinkable that sisters would have the same name. Jn 19:25 probably refers to four women rather than three. (4) There is no sound basis for identifying Alphaeus with Cleophas. (5) This view is in reality based on the Roman Catholic dogma of the perpetual virginity of Mary.

The most natural interpretation of the passage involved considers the brothers to be half brothers of Jesus, born of Mary subsequent to the birth of Christ. It is significant that they are repeatedly associated with Jesus' mother (Mt 13:55-56; Jn 2:12; Acts 1:14). Furthermore, Luke, writing a number of years later, calls Jesus Mary's firstborn son (Lk 2:7), which indicates that other sons followed. In addition, Matthew's statement that Joseph "knew her not till she had brought forth her firstborn son" (Mt 1:25) argues against perpetual virginity. The NT contains nothing which demands anything other than the natural interpretation of the term brother. In fact, history indicates that it was the development of the Roman Catholic Marian doctrine which made necessary the deviations from the natural view.

D. W. B.

BROTHER'S WIFE. A brother's wife is to be respected and her person not violated (Lev 18:16; 20:21). *See* Levirate Marriage.

BROWN. *See* Colours.

BRUISED. This word appears a number of times in the Bible as a translation for several different words. It is used principally of grain that has been crushed (Lev 2:14, 16; II Sam 17:19) and of reeds that have been broken (II Kgs 18:21). But the latter use always has a deep religious significance. (1) Egypt is the reed that is to be crushed (II Kgs 18:21); (2) weak disciples are bruised reeds for whom God cares (Isa 42:3; Mt 12:20); (3) Satan would bruise the heel of Christ, i.e., cause suffering and death; but Christ would bruise the head of Satan, i.e., destroy his power (Gen 3:15); (4) through the bruising of Christ (i.e., crucifixion) salvation from sin has been made possible (Isa 53:5, 10; Lk 4:18); (5) God will bruise Satan ultimately (i.e., triumph) (Rom 16:20).

BRUISES. *See* Diseases.

BRUTISH. One who is irrational and unreasonable. RSV usually translates the word "stupid" (Ps 49:10; 73:22; 92:6; Jer 10:8, 14, 21; 51:17), and therefore unteachable. Such are also crude, uncultivated, thoughtlessly ignorant. Brutish counsel (Isa 19:11) is foolish and unreasonable. In self-criticism Agur regarded himself as brutish (Prov 30:2), indicating his lack of knowledge.

BUCK. *See* Animals, II.10.

BUCKET. Found only in Isa 40:15 and Num 24:7. The bucket was a skin with two wooden crosspieces at the top attached to a rope, for drawing water.

Leather bucket used at a well. JR

BUCKLE. *See* Brooch.

BUCKLER. *See* Armor.

BUFFET. The Gr. word *kolaphizō*, "to strike with the fist," "to beat," signifies rude maltreatment, whether in derision (Mt 26:67; Mk 14:65), affliction (I Cor 4:11), opposition (II Cor 12:7), or punishment (I Pet 2:20).

BUILDERS. *See* Occupations.

BUILDING. Buildings included homes, temples, city walls and other fortifications. *See* Architecture. Mud bricks dried in the sun (*see* Bricks) were used for the ordinary home, or stone if available. Roof timbers would be covered with clay or thatch.

Solomon's and Herod's temples were made with costly materials by trained artisans of their times. The disciples shared the great pride of the Jews in their magnificent temple (Mk 13:1).

Foundations were often laid on the leveled ruins of previous towns and villages destroyed by invaders or fire.

"Building" is used figuratively also. It may refer to a family line, as in God's promise to build David a house (II Sam 7:27); or to the building which is God's church (I Cor 3:9); or to the building of Christian character (Jude 20).

See Occupations.

BUKKI (bŭk′ī)
1. Son of Jogli and representative Danite chief who assisted in the division of the land (Num 34:22).
2. Fourth in descent from Aaron through Eleazar (I Chr 6:5, 51), and ancestor of Ezra (Ezr 7:4).

BUKKIAH (bŭ-kī′á). A Levite, a son of Heman, leader of the sixth company of 12 musicians who served in the temple worship (I Chr 25:4, 13).

BUL (bōōl). Name of the eighth month of the pre-Exilic Jewish year (I Kgs 6:38), corresponding to October-November. The name appropriately means rain or shower, for this is the beginning of the rainy season. *See* Calendar.

BULL. *See* Animals, I.3.

BULLOCK. *See* Animals, I.3.

BULRUSH. *See* Plants.

BULWARK. Translation of five Heb. words: (1) *ḥēl* (Isa 26:1) and (2) *ḥêlâ* (Ps 48:13), meaning "strong objects," ramparts or citadel; (3) *māṣôd* (Eccl 9:14) and (4) *māṣôr* (Deut 20:20), meaning a fortress or siegeworks used against a city; (5) *pinnâ* (II Chr 26:15), corner tower(s) of a fortification. *See* Fort; Citadel.

Mummy-shaped coffin of wood of King Tutankhamon of Egypt. LL

BUNAH (bū′ná). The son of Jerahmeel of the line of Judah (I Chr 2:25).

BUNCH. Only one word is properly translated "bunch," *'ăguddâ*, "a bunch of hyssop" (Ex 12:22). "Bunch" in II Sam 16:1 and I Chr 12:40 (Heb. *ṣimmûq*) means a cluster or bunch of raisins. In Isa 30:6 *dabbeshet* means a "camel's hump," as in RSV.

BUNDLE. A pouch which could be closed and used especially for items of value (e.g., money, Gen 42:35; Prov 7:20) and designed to be kept near the person for safekeeping. The essential concepts are those of safety and value. In Hag 1:6, since the bag has holes, it is the life without God, soon empty of all value, even material. The supreme and intimate preciousness of the lover (Song 1:13) is expressed by the bundle of costly perfume pressed close to the breasts. Abigail tells David he is "bound in the bundle of the living" (I Sam 25:29, RSV), literally, "with the Lord thy God." God had seen value in David and had become his intimate associate and guarantor of his safety (cf. the variant concepts of being enrolled in the "book of the living," Ps 69:28, RSV; Ex 32:32–33; Dan 12:1).

BUNNI (bŭn'ī), Apparently the name of three Levites:

1. A Levite who helped Ezra teach the people (Neh 9:4).

2. An ancestor of Shemaiah (Neh 11:15).

3. A leader or family that, with Nehemiah, sealed the covenant (Neh 10:15).

BURDEN

1. The Heb. word *maśśā'* literally comes from the root *nāśā',* which means "to lift up" any load carried by beast (Ex 23:5) or man (Num 4:15). Figuratively, as a responsibility of a leader, people may be a burden (Num 11:11); a man may be a burden to himself (Job 7:20); the psalmist speaks (38:4) of iniquities as a burden. Possibly taxes are referred to as a burden in Hos 8:10.

The word *maśśā'* is frequently used of the message and utterance of a prophet (Isa 13:1; 15:1; etc.) against the nations, and translated "oracle" in RSV. It is used also of the words of Agur and Lemuel in Prov 30:1; 31:1, translated "oracle." The term *mas'ēt,* of the same derivation, is used of foolish oracles (Lam 2:14) by false prophets.

2. Other words, e.g., *sēbel* (Neh 4:17) and *sōbel* (Isa 9:4) are derived from *sābal,* "to bear a load," translated "burden." In Exodus (1:11; 2:11; 5:4–5; 6:6–7), *sᵉbālâ* is used and refers to the total hardship placed upon the Hebrews by the Egyptians.

E. F. Hai.

BURIAL. The manner of disposing of dead bodies in biblical times varied from country to country. In Egypt the outstanding burial practice for nobles and royalty was the unique method of embalming (*see* Embalm). The internal organs were removed from the body cavity and replaced by linen cloth and a resinous gum. The body was then wrapped in yards of linen bandages from the toes to the head. If the deceased was a king or high official, the body was enclosed in a case of plaster-like substance which was painted with the face of the dead person and otherwise engraved with various markings. The mummy was then encased in several coffins. Such was, no doubt, the method used in embalming Joseph (Gen 50:26), though Jacob's preservation would probably have been less elaborate (Gen 50:2–3). In the case of pagan Egyptians, the body was buried with helpful items for the future life and often with portions from the Book of the Dead. Kings were buried in elaborately prepared tombs, some of which were housed in pyramids as late as the Twelfth Dynasty in the time of the patriarchs.

Excavated Babylonian tombs also indicate that great care was taken to prepare the body for burial and for the future life. Personal items to be used in the next life were placed with the body, as in the royal tombs of Ur (*q.v.*). The greater the dignity of the deceased, the larger the tomb and the more extensive were the provisions for the hereafter. Poorer people were buried in simpler graves accompanied by food and personal effects. For Canaanite tombs at Jericho with well-preserved furniture and dried food, *see* Tomb.

Heb. burials, like those in other countries with warm climate, usually took place on the day of death (Deut 21:23; Acts 5:5–10). The seeming haste, a sanitary measure occasioned by the heat, was also necessitated by the ceremonial laws of the clean and unclean which warned against the touching of a dead body (Num 19:11–14). If the family was prosperous enough to own property, a cave was used (Gen 49:29–31), or a tomb was hewn out of rock in which were carved a number of shelves or niches for the various members of the family (II Kgs 21:18, 26; 23:30). In NT times such a tomb would often be closed with a circular rolling stone set in an inclined groove (Mk 16:3-4). The rocky hills around Jerusalem, as well as those in other places, contained many

Sarcophagus of Ramses III of Egypt. LM

Phoenician sarcophagus from Byblos, late second millennium B.C. HFV rock-hewn tombs (Lk 23:53; Jn 19:41; Mk 5:3).

Poorer people buried their dead in graves dug in the earth and covered them with stones. Such a cemetery was found near the monastery at Qumran by the Dead Sea with 1,200 graves placed in rows. The Early Bronze Age cemetery at Bab edh-Dhra contained thousands of graves. Only leading men were allowed to be buried within the city walls (I Kgs 2:10). A graveyard for paupers was located outside the S wall of Jerusalem (Mt 27:7-8; Acts 1:19).

The Hebrews neither embalmed nor cremated their dead except in rare instances (Gen 50:2-3, 26; I Sam 31:11-13). It was customary to wash the body (Acts 9:37), apply spices and ointment (Lk 23:56; Jn 19:39-40), and wrap it in strips of linen cloth (Jn 19:40). The face was tied separately with a napkin and the hands with linen cloths (Jn 11:44). The body was carried to the burial place on a bier or litter (Lk 7:12, 14). The use of professional mourners was quite common where finances permitted (Mk 5:38).

The denial of proper burial to a man or to toss his body into a common pit of corpses indicated the greatest disgrace heaped upon the reputation of the deceased (Isa 14:18-20; Jer 22:18-19). Burning the body was a punishment fit for a criminal (Lev 20:14; 21:9; Josh 7:25). The Mishna forbade cremation as idolatry ('Abodah Zarah I.3).

Christian burial in NT times was viewed in the light of the resurrection hope. Death was referred to as sleep (I Thess 4:13) and the grave as a place of rest (Gr. koimētērion from koimaō, "I sleep," the source of the English word "cemetery"). The body, as the temple of the Holy Spirit (I Cor 6:19) and as the subject of resurrection (I Cor 6:13-14), was viewed with respect. Pagan excessiveness in mourning was discouraged (I Thess 4:13). Burial was also used symbolically to depict the believer's posi-

A graveyard for paupers located just east of the Kidron Valley (center) in Jerusalem. Pictured are some of the caves in which burials took place. HFV

tional identification with Christ in death to sin (Rom 6:4-5). Many also view this passage as referring to burial in the waters of baptism.

A Chalcolithic practice of placing the bones of a decomposed corpse in an ossuary (a terra-cotta or stone box two to three feet long) was revived about the 3rd cen. B.C. In a tomb dating c. A.D. 50, between Jerusalem and Bethlehem, E. L. Sukenik in 1945 found eleven ossuaries on which charcoal inscriptions had been made. These included the sign of the cross, possible laments to Jesus, and the name Simeon Barsaba. The latter name is not known elsewhere except in Acts 1:23; 15:22. Here may be "the earliest evidence for the presence in Jerusalem of the first Christian community" (André Parrot, Golgotha and the Church of the Holy Sepulchre, p. 119). In another cemetery on the Mount of Olives were discovered in 1954 a number of ossuaries with NT names, such as Jairus, Salome, Martha, Mary, Simon son of Jonas, one with a carefully drawn cross, and another with the three letters I, X, B standing undoubtedly for Iēsous, Xristos, Basileus (i.e., Jesus Christ King). The Christian catacombs in Rome contain many inscriptions expressing the faith of the early church (see FLAP, pp. 451-491).

See Bier; Cross; Dead, The; Embalm; Funeral; Grave; Mourning; Tomb.

Bibliography. Eric M. Meyers, "Secondary Burials in Palestine," BA, XXXIII (1970), 1-29. Roland de Vaux, Ancient Israel, New York: McGraw-Hill, 1961, pp. 56-61.
D. W. B. and J. R.

BURNING. Burning, the act of consuming combustible material by fire, is used in Scripture in both a literal and a figurative sense. Sacrifices were burned on the altar of burnt offering, signifying total consecration to God (Lev 6:9). Lamps burned continually, with pure olive oil as the fuel (Lev 24:2; Rev 4:5). Incense was continually burning on an altar in the holy place

Sarcophagus of the Greek period at Tyre. HFV

of the tabernacle and, later, the temple (I Kgs 9:25). The burning of spices near the body of King Asa was performed as a royal funeral rite (II Chr 16:14; cf. 21:19; Jer 34:5). The bush from which God called Moses (Ex 3:2; *see* Burning Bush) and the mountain from which the law was given, are both described as burning (Deut 5:23). A burning coal from the altar was applied to the lips of Isaiah (Isa 6:6-7, NASB).

Punishment by fire was practiced in Babylonia (Jer 29:22). Shadrach, Meshach and Abed-nego were cast alive into a burning, fiery furnace (Dan 3:6, 11, 15-26). In ancient Israel, however, burning as a punishment was used only in cases of aggrieved prostitution and incest (Gen 38:24; Lev 20:14; 21:9). Some scholars suggest that stoning preceded burning in these instances. It is known that the corpses of criminals executed by stoning were sometimes burned with fire, as in the case of Achan and his family (Josh 7:25). Divine punishment by fire sometimes fell directly from God (Lev 10:2, 6).

Figuratively the word "burning" is used to describe the anger of the Lord (Josh 7:26; Ps 69:24, RSV); everlasting punishment (Isa 33:12, 14; Rev 19:20; 21:8); physical pain (Job 30:30); idolatrous or sexual lust (Isa 57:5, RSV; I Cor 7:9); and fervent, flattering lips (Prov 26:23). In the context of worship, burning indicates purification (Isa 6:6-7; I Pet 1:7) and total devotion to God (Lk 24:32; Jn 5:35). In human relationships, a burn or burning speaks of the sense of pain and suffering, either physical (Lev 13:24-25) or emotional (II Cor 11:29).

See Fire.

C. F. P.

BURNING BUSH. The flaming bush by which God attracted Moses' attention and revealed Himself at the time of Moses' call to become Israel's deliverer (Ex 3:2-4). The Heb. word for "bush," *seneh*, is found only in this passage and Deut 33:16. It was probably an unidentified thorn bush of the acacia family. *See* Plants: Bush.

The blazing flame which did not consume the bush and with no human agent to kindle it illustrated to Moses the self-sufficiency and unapproachable holiness of God; it was not a symbol of the afflictions of Israel in Egypt, as many commentators have suggested. The JerusB brings out the proper sense of Ex 3:2: "There the angel of Yahweh appeared to him in the shape of a flame of fire, coming from the middle of a bush." Thus the flame as a symbol of deity (cf. Gen 3:24; 15:17; Ex 13:21; 19:18) and the audible voice of God declaring the holi-

ness of the place enabled Moses to recognize that God was dwelling in the bush, as he later recalled (Deut 33:16). That he used the term "the angel of the Lord" (KJV) in v. 2 in narrating this incident is no contradiction, because this expression often signifies a special manifestation of Yahweh, a theophany or appearance of the pre-incarnate Son of God. *See* Moses.

J. R.

BURNT OFFERING. *See* Sacrificial Offerings.

BUSH. *See* Plants.

BUSHEL. *See* Weights, Measures and Coins.

BUSYBODY. Three different Gr. words are used, all meaning the same thing: (1) *periergos*, meaning "to be overly officious," "to be a busybody" (I Tim 5:13); (2) *periergazomai*, meaning "to make oneself always too busy," "to be a busybody" (II Thess 3:11); (3) *allotriepiskopos*, meaning "a meddler in other men's matters" (KJV, ASV), "mischief maker" (RSV). The use of *episkopos* suggests that Peter was referring to an "overseer" or "bishop" (I Pet 4:15).

BUTCHER. *See* Occupations.

BUTLER. *See* Occupations.

BUTTER. *See* Food.

BUZ (bŭz)
1. The name of a region (Jer 25:23) probably somewhere in N Arabia, possibly the Bazu of the Assyrian inscriptions. *See* Buzite.
2. The second son of Nahor and Milcah, and nephew of Abraham (Gen 22:21).
3. A descendant of the tribe of Gad (I Chr 5:14).

BUZI (bū'zī). The father of the prophet Ezekiel (Ezk 1:3), and consequently a member of the priestly house of Zadok.

BUZITE (bū'zīt). One belonging to the Arabian tribe of Buz. Elihu, one of the friends of Job (Job 32:2), is called a Buzite, and may have belonged to a tribe of that name, against which judgments were denounced by Jeremiah (Jer 25:23).

BUZZARD. *See* Animals, III.4.

BYBLOS. *See* Gebal.

BYWAYS. Used in Jud 5:6 to mean a back road or path that a traveler sometimes took.

C

CAB. *See* Weights, Measures and Coins.

CABBON (kăb'ŏn). An unidentified place in the Shephelah or foothills of Judah near Eglon (Josh 15:40). It is possibly the same as Machbenah (I Chr 2:49).

CABUL (kā'bŭl)
1. A village in the borderland between Asher and Zebulun, about ten miles NE of Mount Carmel, in the Galilean hills (Josh 19:27).
2. A region embracing 20 villages given to Hiram of Tyre by King Solomon (I Kgs 9:10 – 13). Hiram was displeased with the gift, calling it "Cabul," by some taken to mean worthless or good-for-nothing, but by others taken to mean a borderland region, perhaps unproductive, and as an inland area of small value to a sea power. According to II Chr 8:2, Solomon fortified this region and colonized it with Israelites, suggesting that he regained possession of it.

CAESAR (sē'zẽr). The term was the surname of the Julian family, as in the name Caius Julius Caesar. In the NT it is applied to four Roman emperors: (1) Caesar Augustus (Lk 2:1); (2) Tiberius Caesar (Lk 3:1); (3) Claudius Caesar (Acts 11:28; 17:7, where he is called only Caesar; Acts 18:2, where he is called Claudius); Nero (Acts 25:10–12; 26:32; Phil 4:22). *See* each name.

The expression "the things that are Caesar's" (Lk 20:25) came to be used in opposition to "the things that are God's," that is, the earthly realm versus the heavenly realm. Thus a principle was introduced to guide the disciple of our Lord in the extent of his responsibilities to the world and to God (cf. Acts 4:19 f.; 5:29).

Crusader Walls and Moat at Caesarea. HFV

CAESAREA (sĕs'á-rē'á). Two cities in the NT are so named.
1. Caesarea was the capital of Judea under the Roman procurators (e.g., Pilate). It had been rebuilt and renamed from Strato's Tower to Caesarea Sebaste (in honor of Augustus) by Herod the Great. Located on the coast about 30 miles N of Jaffa (old Joppa) and about 65 miles NW of Jerusalem, it was a magnificent city containing many palaces and lavish public buildings, and a seaport, in this latter respect being adulated by Josephus. It was here that King Herod Agrippa I, in Luke's account, "was eaten of worms, and gave up the ghost" (Acts 12:19b–23).

A city of mixed population, leading to frequent Jewish-Gentile friction, it is connected in Acts with various evangelistic efforts. Here lived Philip the evangelist (one of the seven deacons, Acts 6:5), together with his four daughters who prophesied (Acts 21:8–9). Peter, while residing at Joppa, was called to preach to "a certain man in Caesarea," the Roman centurion Cornelius, a God-fearer (Acts 10:1–2, 24; 11:11–12). Paul saluted the church at Caesarea on his return from his missionary journey (Acts 18:22); then later he was held prisoner here for two years under Felix and Festus (Acts 23:23 – 26:32). He "reasoned" with Felix and often the procurator "communed with him" (Acts 24:25–26). And before Festus and Herod Agrippa II Paul expressed his fervent desire for their conversion (Acts 26:29).

An Italian expedition excavating the site in 1959–61 discovered a stone inscription from the city theater bearing the word "Tiberieum" (dedicated to the emperor Tiberius), and on the next two lines, "[Pon]tius Pilatus . . . Military Procurator." This is the first reference to Pilate (cf. Lk 3:1) on an inscription (BW, p. 156). In 1962 excavators found in a synagogue at Caesarea part of a list of the 24 priestly courses and the cities in which the priests lived, including a reference to the 18th course as coming from the city of Nazareth (BW). *See also* Archaeology.
2. Caesarea Philippi was N of the Sea of Galilee on the SW slope of Mount Hermon. It was renamed by Herod Philip (the tetrarch), son of Herod the Great and Cleopatra of Jerusalem, in honor of Tiberius Caesar (Jos *Ant.* xviii.2.1). This Gr. city (earlier called Paneas after the god Pan) is notable in the NT as the scene of Peter's great confession (Mt 16:13 ff.; Mk 8:27), and probably the transfiguration of Christ (Mt 17:1–8). The name "Philippi" distinguished it from the Caesarea on the sea. In NT times the city was an important center for

Remains of the Temple of Augustus at Caesarea. HFV

Greco-Roman civilization and culture. Josephus indicates that its population was largely
pagan (*Life*, xiii). Some suggest the city was the
OT Baal-gad (Josh 11:17; 12:7; 13:5). *See*
Baal-gad.

Ewing (HDB), in a descriptive passage, says
that "no spot in Palestine can compare with this
in romantic beauty." Its abundant vegetation,
the beauty of Mount Hermon to the NE, its
crag towering up to 8,000 feet above the valley,
and the waters which comprise the fountainhead of the Jordan River, all combine to a magnificent scenery. The modern village of Banyas
stands among the ruins of the once splendid
city.

W. M. D. and A. F. J.

CAGE. In Jer 5:27 the Heb. word means the
wicker basket in which the fowler placed the
captured birds. Such baskets, filled to capacity
with living birds, were probably a familiar scene
in the markets of ancient cities. *See* Basket.

CAIAPHAS (kā'á-făs). Joseph Caiaphas was
high priest *c.* A.D. 18–36. He was son-in-law
and successor of Annas. Appointed by the Roman procurator Valerius Gratus (Pilate's immediate predecessor), he was deposed by Vi-
tellius, "president of Syria" (Jos *Ant.* xviii.2.2;
4.3).

The earliest mention of him is in Lk 3:2:
"Annas and Caiaphas being the high priests."
This odd expression evidently reflects the fact
that whereas the latter legally held the position
of high priest, Annas continued to wield the
power of that office. *See* Annas.

The next notice is in Jn 11:49–53, where
Caiaphas advised that Jesus' life should be sacrificed to save the nation. He feared that the
Prophet from Nazareth would precipitate a political revolution, which might result in the
whole nation being destroyed by Rome. The
evangelist comments (Jn 11:51) that Caiaphas
spoke better than he knew. As high priest he
uttered a prophecy that Jesus would die on
behalf of the Jews and all mankind. Reference
is made to this again in Jn 18:13–14.

Steps leading to St. Peter's in Gallicantu, presumably the site of Caiaphas' palace. Jesus
may have walked on these Roman steps. HFV

The Jewish leaders followed the advice of
Caiaphas and from that very day "took counsel
together" to put Jesus to death (Jn 11:53). Matthew (26:3–5) describes a meeting of the Sanhedrin—"the chief priests, and the scribes, and
the elders of the people"—at the palace of "the
high priest, who was called Caiaphas," two
days before the Passover of the Passion. Here
the leaders of the nation conspired to take Jesus
"by subtilty" and kill Him. They did not wish
to arrest Him during the feast, for fear of an
uprising of the people. But Judas Iscariot's offer
to betray Him secretly caused them to change
their minds.

After a preliminary hearing before Annas,
Christ was sent to Caiaphas (Jn 18:24)—perhaps just from one apartment to another in the
same palace. Here the Sanhedrin had gathered
(Mt 26:57). The true character of the high
priest is shown in this Jewish trial of Jesus. The
Sanhedrin "sought false witness against Jesus,
to put him to death" (Mt 26:59). When Christ
refused to reply to these false accusations,
Caiaphas put Him under oath to tell whether
He was the Messiah. When He answered in the
affirmative and applied to Himself the language
of Dan 7:13, the high priest "rent his clothes"
and declared that Jesus had uttered blasphemy
(Mt 26:65). The Sanhedrin gave judgment that
He was guilty of death, and delivered Him to
the Roman governor for execution. The last
mention of Caiaphas is in Acts 4:6.

R. E.

CAIN (kăn)

1. The older brother of Abel, Cain is pictured in Genesis as the first child to be born of the first parents, Adam and Eve. The name is explained as meaning "gotten" (from Heb. *qānâ*, Gen 4:1), but the exact form *qayin* can also mean "spear" or "smith." He was a "tiller of the ground" (v.2).

Cain brought an offering to the Lord "of the fruit of the ground," while Abel offered "of the firstlings of his flock" (vv. 3-4). God accepted Abel's offering, but not Cain's. Three reasons for God's rejection of Cain's offering have been suggested. The first is that Abel offered the best he had, while Cain did not. But there is no clear indication of that in the account. The second is that Cain brought a bloodless offering, and thus offended Deity by posing as righteous and not in need of any sacrifice for sin. This theory has strong theological appeal. It assumes previous divine instruction as to what type of offering must be brought for making atonement for sin. There is indication that such a revelation had been given by the use of the verb form in Gen 4:3 that can mean customary action.

Without ruling out the possible validity of these two theories, we must note that a third one seems to have also a firm scriptural support. This holds that Cain's attitude was wrong. Heb 11:4 says it was "by faith" that Abel offered a "more excellent sacrifice" than did Cain.

Cain was reproved by the Lord for his jealous anger. Instead of repenting, he killed his brother, and was cursed away from home for his sin (Gen 4:6-12). He moved to Nod, where he built a city and raised a family. He must have married a daughter or granddaughter of Adam and Eve.

In the NT Cain is mentioned in Heb 11:4; I Jn 3:12; Jude 11.

2. A town in the southern part of Judah (Josh 15:57).

R. E.

CAINAN (kā'năn)

1. Son of Enos and great-grandson of Adam, mentioned in Gen 5:9-14 and Lk 3:37.

2. Son of Arphaxad, mentioned in Lk 3:36, which seems to follow Gen 10:24; 11:12-13 of the LXX (and also I Chr 1:18 of the Alexandrine text of the LXX).

CAKE. *See* Food.

CALAH (kă'lȧ). This Assyrian city, now called Nimrud after its founder Nimrod (Gen 10:11-12), was already ancient when the Assyrian king Ashur-nasir-pal II (884-859 B.C.) chose it for his capital. It lay at the confluence of the Great Zab and Tigris Rivers *c.* 20 miles S of Nineveh.

Here the pioneer archaeologist Sir Austen Henry Layard began his excavations in Assyria, digging this site 1845-51. Rassam and Loftus followed him, 1852-55. The British School of Archaeology in Iraq resumed work at Calah, with a series of campaigns directed by

Ivory panels from Calah showing Egyptian influence. BM

walled city from the acropolis Shalmanezer III erected *c.* 840 B.C. a tremendous fortified palace and arsenal, 18 acres in extent. The greater walled city with its armories and gates covered nearly 900 acres, and had a population of perhaps 60,000.

From Calah Tiglath-pileser III (744–727 B.C.) and Sargon II (721–705 B.C.) marched via Nineveh across the N Syrian plains to attack Palestine. After the latter conquered Samaria, he stored much booty in Calah, and a list of Jewish names written in Aramaic seems to suggest that captives from the northern kingdom were removed to Calah. Late in his reign Sargon built a new royal city at Khorsabad, and Sennacherib removed the capital to Nineveh; but Calah remained the military headquarters of the empire until it was burned in 612 B.C. by the Medes and Babylonians.

Other notable finds from Calah are the famous Black Obelisk showing the Israelite king Jehu (or his ambassador) paying tribute to Shalmanezer III; the rare statue in the round of Ashur-nasir-pal II; glazed tile and many objects of ivory and bronze showing Egyptian motifs and Phoenician craftsmanship; the great treaty

A royal servant from the palace at Calah, ninth century B.C. LM

The Black Obelisk of Shalmaneser III; in the second panel Jehu of Israel pays tribute to the Assyrian king. ORINST

M. E. L. Mallowan and David Oates 1949–61.

The main citadel was built by Shalmaneser I *c.* 1250 B.C. In the first years of his reign Ashur-nasir-pal II constructed in Calah (Heb. *Kālaḥ*, Akkad. *Kalḫu*) a new canal partly underground from the Upper Zab River to the city wall. He added a palace of brick faced with stone, decorated with characteristic Assyrian reliefs of religious ceremonies, hunting and battle scenes. Its doors were guarded by two colossal winged man-headed lions. This monarch was also responsible for the temple of Ninurta, in which were found an unusually excellent lion in high relief and two poorly preserved statues of Nabu with inscriptions by the city governor Bel-tarṣi-ilsuna. These mention Adad-nirari III (811–782 B.C.) and his queen mother Sammu-ramat (Semiramis of Gr. legend).

This latter king was so proud of his control of Babylonia that he built in Calah a replica of the temple of Ezida at Borsippa. Across the

tablet of Esarhaddon of 672 B.C. made with various Iranian princes; and the Banquet Stele, discovered in 1951, which describes the feast of dedication in 879 B.C. for the newly rebuilt capital to which Ashur-nasir-pal II invited 69,574 guests. They came from all parts of the kingdom and spent ten days consuming 2,200 oxen, 16,000 sheep, 10,000 skins of wine, and 10,000 barrels of beer. Cf. the number of sacrificial animals offered at the dedication of Solomon's temple — 22,000 oxen and 120,000 sheep, for seven days (I Kgs 8:62–66).

See Assyria.

Bibliography. M. E. L. Mallowan, *Nimrud and Its Remains,* 2 vols., London: Collins, 1966.

E. B. S.

CALAMUS. *See* Plants.

CALCOL (kăl'kŏl). Variant of Chalcol (I Kgs 4:31).

A Judahite (I Chr 2:6), one of several brothers, "sons of Mahol," each of whom was celebrated for wisdom. In I Kgs 4:31 they are compared in wisdom with Solomon. Since the word *māḥôl* is elsewhere found as a musical term (Ps 149:3; 150:4), "sons of Mahol" may mean members of an orchestral guild, with exceptional wisdom or skill in the composition of hymns. The name Kalkol appears in a 13th cen. B.C. Egyptian inscription found at Megiddo, as the name of a great Canaanite musician at Ashkelon.

CALDRON. An earthenware vessel for cooking, of undefined size and characteristics. In I Sam 2:14 the vessel was for use in the sanctuary; in Mic 3:3 the vessel was for domestic use. The Heb. word *sîr* is translated caldron in Jer 1:13 (ASV); 52:18 (KJV); Ezk 11:3, 7, 11. It was distinctly a large pot, employed both for domestic use and in the sanctuary.

CALEB (kā'lĕb)
1. Caleb, the son of Jephunneh of the tribe of Judah, was one of the 12 spies sent in from Kadesh-barnea to explore the land of Palestine (Num 13:6). While ten of the spies brought back an adverse report, discouraging the people from attempting the conquest of the Promised Land because of the great cities and the fearsome inhabitants, "the sons of Anak" (Num 13:33), Caleb and Joshua pleaded with Israel to go forward, trusting in the Lord (Num 13:30; 14:6–9). Although Israel failed to enter the land at that time because of unbelief, the Lord promised Caleb and Joshua that they would have a part in the occupation of the country because of their faith and loyalty (Num 14:24, 30). Caleb stands as a great monument of faith because he "wholly followed the Lord" (Num 32:12; Deut 1:36).

At the end of the 40 years of wandering under God's judgment, Caleb with Joshua entered the Promised Land and was a part of the great conquest. After the decisive victories of Joshua had subjugated the land as a whole, it became the responsibility of each tribe to occupy the territory that had been assigned to it by lot. Although he was now an aged man, Caleb set an example to the nation by the faith and vigor with which he claimed his possessions. Caleb asked for the city of Kiriath-arba in the hill country to the S. This was the city of Arba, "the greatest man among the Anakim," those giants who had so frightened the spies many years earlier (Josh 14:6–15, RSV). It is as though Caleb wished to show the people of Israel that their fathers could have entered the land 40 years before had they only believed.

As an inducement to the young men of his tribe, Caleb offered his daughter Achsah in marriage to the young man who would take the city of Kirjath-sepher (Josh 15:16; Jud 1:12). It was his own nephew Othniel, inspired by the reward and his own faith, who led the assault that took the city, and with it won the hand of Achsah (Josh 15:17 ff.; Jud 1:13 ff.). Othniel became the first of the judges of Israel in the years that followed (Jud 3:9).

There is no discrepancy between this account of the conquest of Caleb and the statement that Joshua "wiped out the Anakim" (RSV) and "took the whole land" (Josh 11:21, 23). It is clear in the book of Joshua that organized resistance to Israel was broken by the two great victories at Gibeon and Hazor (Josh 10–11). After that it was only a question of the individual tribes moving into the assigned territories and taking over the cities one by one. As in modern warfare, the commander-in-chief is accredited with the whole operation. In great measure the tribes failed fully to possess the land because of their lack of faith and courage in wholly following the Lord (Jud 1:27 ff.). Here, as at Kadesh-barnea, the valiant Caleb set an example of what it means to follow God.

There is some question as to the exact ancestry of Caleb. The genealogy in I Chr 2:18 mentions Caleb as the son of Hezron. On the other hand, Jephunneh the Kenezite is called Caleb's father in Num 32:12. The Kenezites, descendants of Kenaz, seem to be one of the Edomite tribes roaming the deserts of Sinai (Gen 36:15). It was into one of these tribes, the Kenites, that Moses had married (Jud 1:16; 4:11). The migration of Israel northward attracted some of these people, and they joined themselves in faith to the Lord and to His people. Caleb's family was attached to the tribe of Judah, and Caleb quickly gained a place of leadership. Although the chief of the tribe was Nahshon, son of Amminadab (Num 2:3), it was Caleb who represented the tribe as a spy and later as one of those who divided the land into tribal areas (Josh 21:12). It is said that Caleb was given his portion "among the children of Judah" (Josh 15:13), implying that he was not actually a member of that tribe. Centuries later, in the days of Saul and David, the Calebites were still a distinct family in Judah and their part of the country seems to have been a separate enclave in the tribe (I Sam 25:3; 30:14).

2. The son of Hezron (I Chr 2:18-19) and grandson of Judah (I Chr 2:3-5). He was the great-grandfather of Bezaleel (Ex 31:2; I Chr 2:20), chief artisan of the tabernacle. He is called Chelubai in I Chr 2:9. Possibly he is the same as 1.

3. The son of Hur (I Chr 2:50) and grandson of 2 according to the Heb. The LXX and Vulgate connect this Caleb with the preceding verses (cf. I Chr 2:42-50 with I Chr 2:18-19), which would make him the same as 1.

P. C. J.

CALEB-EPHRATAH (kā′lĕb-ĕf′rȧ-thȧ). On the basis of I Chr 2:24, this is thought to be a place in the vicinity of Bethlehem where Caleb, the son of Hezron, an ancestor of David, died. This place is not mentioned elsewhere in the Bible, and the LXX of the passage reads: "And after the death of Hezron, Caleb went in to Ephratha, the wife of Hezron his father; and she bore him Ashur the father of Tekoa." It is possible that Ephratah was a second wife of Caleb's father Hezron whom Caleb took to establish his claim to the inheritance (cf. II Sam 16:22).

The Gezer Calendar. ORINST

CALENDAR. Palestine was a land without political unity until the time of the Heb. united monarchy. Among peoples who lived under city-state unity centered around an important temple, the tendency was to develop separate menologies or ecclesiastical calendars. In the ancient Near East the best documented calendars of this type were those of the Sumerians. One determines the provenience of a Sumerian business document by the month name appearing in the date formula. Not until the strong central government of Hammurabi did the Babylonian month names begin to take the place of local menologies.

The evidence from Palestine bears witness to a similar system of local rather than national menologies.

First, there is a noticeable silence of any official month names used continuously by the Jews before they took the Babylonian names during the Babylonian Exile.

Secondly, it is important to note that three of the month names which were used in pre-Exilic Israel are Phoenician names. These are Ziv (*ziw*), Ethanim (*'ētānîm*) and Bul (*bûl*), which are mentioned only in I Kgs 6 and 8 in connection with building and dedicating the temple. The month Abib (*'ābîb*, Ex 13:4; 23:15; 34:18; Deut 16:1) usually associated with the above names is not attested in Phoenician sources.

Thirdly, *yeraḥ* is primitive Semitic and in Heb. is the older poetic word for "month." In Phoenician, Ugaritic and the Gezer Calendar, *yeraḥ* is regularly employed. The more common prosaic Heb. idiom in the Bible is *ḥōdesh*. The contrast between these two words is striking in I Kgs 6:38, "in the month (*yeraḥ*) Bul, which is the eighth month" (*ḥōdesh*).

In this light it is significant that in every usage of *'ābîb* the term *ḥōdesh* is employed. This, along with the fact that *'ābîb* is not attested in Phoenician sources, gives reason for assuming it belonged to another calendar.

The fourth piece of evidence comes from the meaning of *'ābîb*. In Ex 9:31 Pharaoh's barley was ruined by the hail because *haśśᵉ'ōrā 'ābîb*, "the barley was freshly ripened." In Ex 13:4 the phrase *bᵉḥōdesh hā'ābîb* clearly means "in the month of the freshly ripened barley." Therefore *'ābîb* is an agricultural common noun incorporated in the month name of an early agricultural menology in use among the Hebrews.

The evidence for a fifth menology is the Gezer Calendar written by a schoolboy on a limestone tablet dating from the late 10th cen. B.C. It is still another completely distinct local calendar based on agricultural seasons.

Both *yeraḥ* and *ḥōdesh* are words associated with lunation, the time elapsing between two successive new moons, averaging 29 days, 12 hours, 44 minutes and 2.8 seconds. Although *ḥōdesh* (from *ḥādāsh*, "new") originated from observation of the moon's renewal, the word was by no means limited to this exact connotation. This is seen in Gen 29:14, where Jacob dwelt with Laban *ḥōdesh yāmîm*, "a month of days."

Egypt developed a solar calendar having 30-day months irrespective of the renewing of the moon, but here again the 30-day period must have originated from lunation since 30 days is an approximate lunation and could refer

HEBREW MONTHS, FESTIVALS, AND SEASONS

Lunar Month	Preexilic Hebrew Name	Postexilic Babylonian Name	Modern Equivalent	Festivals	Agricultural Season
1	Abib (Ex 13:4; 23:15; 34:18; Deut 16:1)	Nisan (Neh 2:1; Est 3:7)	Mar.-Apr.	1st: New Moon 10th: Passover lamb selected (Ex 12:3) 14th: Passover lamb killed (Ex 12:6-7; Lev 23:5) 15th-21st: Unleavened Bread (Lev 23:6-8) 16th: Wave sheaf offered (Lev 23:10-14)	Latter (spring) rains Green figs and leaf buds Barley harvest begins Flax harvest
2	Ziv (1 Kgs 6:1,37)	Iyyar	Apr.-May	1st: New Moon 14th: Later Passover for those unclean in 1st month (Num 9:10-11)	Dry season begins
3		Sivan (Est 8:9)	May-June	1st: New Moon 6th: Feast of Weeks (Feast of Wheat Harvest, Pentecost; loaves of wheat flour offered on 50th day from 16th of Nisan (Ex 23:16; Lev 23:19-21)	Wheat harvest Early or first-ripe figs
4		Tammuz	June-July	1st: New Moon	Vine-tending
5		Ab	July-Aug.	1st: New Moon	First-ripe grapes Olives in lowlands
6		Elul (Neh 6:15)	Aug.-Sept.	1st: New Moon	Olive and grape harvest Dates and summer figs
7	Ethanim (1 Kgs 8:2)	Tishri	Sept.-Oct.	1st: Blowing of Trumpets (Rosh Hashanah, New Year, Lev 23:24). Beginning of civil year 10th: Day of Atonement (Yom Kippur; Lev 16; 23:27-32) 15th-21st: Feast of Ingathering (Ex 23:16) or Tabernacles (Succoth, Booths, Lev 23: 34-43) 22nd: Holy convocation (Lev 23:36; Num 29:35)	Olive harvest completed Vintage Early (autumn) rains begin Plowing begins
8	Bul (1 Kgs 6:38)	Marcheshvan	Oct.-Nov.	1st: New Moon	Barley and wheat sown
9		Kislev (Neh 1:1; Zech 7:1)	Nov.-Dec.	1st: New Moon 25th: Dedication (1 Macc 4:52-59; Jn 10:22)	Planting continued
10		Tebeth (Est 2:16)	Dec.-Jan.	1st: New Moon	Winter rains, occasional snow in hill country
11		Shebat (Zech 1:7)	Jan.-Feb.	1st: New Moon	Almonds blossom
12		Adar (Ezr 6:15; Est 3:7)	Feb.-Mar.	1st: New Moon 14th-15th: Purim (Est 9:17-28)	Citrus fruit harvest; hoeing flax
(13)		Adar Sheni	c. 7 times in 19 years		

to nothing else, and the hieroglyph for "month" is the crescent.

There is no evidence in the Bible of any such uniform solar month; indeed, the new moon festivals are quite important and called for special sacrifices, the blowing of trumpets, and feasts (Num 28:11-15; Ezr 3:5; Neh 10:33; II Chr 2:4; 8:13; I Sam 20:18-34).

Since lunation and agricultural seasons are two phenomena early employed by the Hebrews for time reckoning, when they are used together as is clear from these calendars, one concludes that intercalation was necessary. Otherwise the agricultural festivals, which were based on annual solar seasons though expressed in terms of lunar months, could not have kept on representing the proper agricultural event. The Sumerian lunar calendars were also tied to the seasons, hence they also intercalated according to need. For example, a second month of *še-kin-kud* is frequently attested in order to keep the season of harvest approximately in place in the calendar.

The Hebrews in rustic simplicity achieved a solar year by making the months agree with agricultural seasons and intercalating when necessary. The Egyptians, though pioneers in the sophisticated non-lunar months which we have inherited through the Romans, made a small error; small, though big enough to send the "seasons" on a 1,460 year cycle around the true solar year, commonly called the Sothic Cycle because the year was measured by the first appearance of the star Sothos on the horizon at exact sunrise. They neglected the one-quarter of a day which we make up with our leap year.

The Hebrews outgrew their simple agricultural calendars as they too became more sophisticated. When Solomon built the temple, he employed Phoenician technicians. Just as Phoenicians supplied materials and served as craftsmen, it is reasonable to believe that Phoenicians also kept the records of building progress. The Phoenician month names Ziv, Ethanim, and Bul were used by Phoenician scribes, and are found in the OT only in connection with the building and dedicating of Solomon's temple. That these months are defined by the Heb. numbered months suggests that sometime during the monarchy, for administrative reasons, this system of numbered months was employed. It was quite likely instituted all at once by the central authority of the crown.

The numbered system was evoked by the administrative needs of the monarchy when, for example, tax collection and conscription brought about the need for a uniform calendar throughout the realm. Tax administration might become an acute problem if each community had its own menology. The Egyptians had for a long time numbered the months from one to four within each of the three seasons. The Heb. monarchy merely improved on this by straight 1 to 12 numbering. Such may not have originally affected the common people who would con-

tinue their provincial ways, but crown officials would be forced to go by the national reckoning. In the book of Jeremiah only the numbered system is used.

After the Exile the Jews, like other subject peoples in the world empires of Assyria, Babylonia, and Persia, were gradually forced into using the Babylonian names. This change was effected by a strong central government that cut across national lines. Although a Persian government official, Nehemiah seems to have preferred the Babylonian names. Ezra, the scribe and priest, in all but one instance uses the Judean numbered designation. The book of Esther uses both, giving dual references. Likewise the Elephantine papyri use dual references giving both the Babylonian and Egyptian month names; for in Egypt of Persian times the old numbered system was given up in favor of festival names. Gradually later Judaism adopted the Babylonian names to the exclusion of other systems.

The Jews at various times in the OT employed at least five different calendars:

1. The *'ābîb* calendar, a local agricultural menology, this being the only month name we have from it. The new year began in the spring, the system followed for the festivals outlined in the Levitical law.

2. The Gezer Calendar, which is the only extant example of another local menology. It began with the two months of olive harvest, our early autumn. This inscription is on a small tablet of soft limestone discovered during Macalister's excavation of Gezer in 1908. W. F. Albright believes it was written *c.* 925 B.C. in verse in good biblical Hebrew:

> *His two months are (olive) harvest,*
> *His two months are planting (grain),*
> *His two months are late planting;*
> *His month is hoeing up of flax,*
> *His month is harvest of barley,*
> *His month is harvest and feasting;*
> *His two months are vine-tending,*
> *His month is summer fruit*

(ANET, p. 320; see also DOTT, pp. 201 ff.).

3. A Phoenician calendar with months named *Ziv*, *'Ētānîm*, and *Bûl*, all attested in Phoenician sources and used in the Bible only where Phoenician personnel were concerned.

4. The numbered system which came about through practical demands under the monarchy. We know that Gezer was incorporated into Solomon's realm upon the capture of Gezer by Solomon's Pharaonic father-in-law. The multiplicity of such local calendars doubtless precipitated the numbered system. Solomon's civil year apparently began in the autumn with the Feast of Trumpets (Lev 23:24 f.). The dedication of his temple (I Kgs 8:2) was postponed for eleven months (cf.6:38), apparently in order to make it a part of the autumnal new year festival (Rosh Hashana).

5. The Babylonian month names, which were forced on the entire Near East as a con-

sequence of the ancient world empires. Their new year was in the spring.

During the intertestamental period pious Jews developed a perfectly regular calendar in order to insure the proper observance of their holy days. As learned from the Book of Jubilee (written between 135 and 105 B.C.) the year consisted of 364 days divided into four series of three months each, the first and second months always having 30 days and the third 31 days. The first day of the first month was always Wednesday, so that the eve of the Passover was on Tuesday every year. This was the calendar observed by the Qumran community for dating their religious festivals (see Finegan, *Light from the Ancient Past,* pp. 580–587). Some scholars have suggested Jesus and His disciples were following this system in eating the Passover meal in advance of the date officially observed in Jerusalem (Finegan, pp. 596 f.).

See Era; Festivals; Time.

Bibliography. F. F. Bruce, "Calendar," NBD, pp. 176–179. CornPBE, pp. 176 ff. S. J. DeVries, "Calendar," IDB, I, 483–488. Jack Finegan, *Light from the Ancient Past,* 2nd ed., Princeton: Princeton Univ. Press, 1959, pp. 552–598. J. van Goudoever, *Biblical Calendars,* 2nd ed. rev., Leiden: E. J. Brill, 1961.

E. B. S.

An Apis bull. LM

CALF. *See* Animals, I.6.

CALF, GOLDEN

1. While Moses was absent in Mount Sinai, Aaron made an image of a bull calf which he announced as the god who brought Israel out of Egypt (Ex 32:1–20). The worship and play conducted before this image so angered Moses upon his return that he broke the tablets of stone containing the law of God and made the people ingest the image, reduced to fine powder, with their drinking water. This idolatry may have been patterned after Egyptian and Semite bull-cults in the Egyptian Delta with their symbolism of strength and fertility.

2. In order to hold the loyalty of the people after their revolt from Rehoboam by cutting them off from the temple at Jerusalem, Jeroboam set up rival centers of worship in Bethel and Dan and installed a golden (bull) calf in both places (I Kgs 12:28–32). Whether Jeroboam intended to displace the worship of God or merely to give some visible aid to His worship, these calves did become objects of worship (Hos 10:5–6; 13:2).

It should be noted that some peoples of this part of the world thought of their gods as invisibly seated or standing on the back of an animal that would be reproduced in wood or metal at a cultic center. Possibly Jeroboam had this in mind when setting up the calves in Israel.

J. K. M.

CALKER. *See* Occupations.

CALL, CALLED, CALLING. Although "call" has many ordinary usages in the Scriptures, its chief importance is as a specifically theological term. The verb form *(kaleō),* when used technically, refers to God's (rarely Christ's) call to men to participate in the blessings of redemption. The benefits may be described as God's call unto His glory (I Pet 5:10; II Pet 1:3); to eternal life (I Tim 6:12); unto fellowship with His Son (I Cor 1:9); and from darkness unto His marvelous light (I Pet 2:9).

The call is dependent upon God's divine purpose (Rom 8:30; 9:11), established through the free grace of God (Gal 1:6, 15), and reaches men through the proclamation of the gospel (II Thess 2:14), so becoming man's one hope (Eph 4:4). The calling is directed not only to man's salvation but to his behavior. Thus Christians are called not to uncleanness but to sanctification (I Thess 4:7); to patience in suffering (I Pet 2:21); to freedom (Gal 5:13); and to life in peace (I Cor 7:15).

The noun form "calling" *(klēsis)* appears in the NT in a technical sense exclusively. The invitation to enter the kingdom of God, to receive it as a gift and possession. Included in the invitation is a decided emphasis on the sovereign initiative of God. "For the gracious gifts of God and his calling are irrevocable" (Rom 11:29, NEB). "Think what sort of people you are, whom God has called ... God has chosen what the world counts folly . . . so there is no place for human pride" (I Cor 1:26-28, NEB; cf. Eph 4:4). But this divine call requires a human response as well. "All the more then, my friends, exert yourselves to clinch God's choice and calling of you" (II Pet 1:10, NEB; cf. also II Thess 1:11).

The call may be spoken of as a call from heaven (Heb 3:1) and as a call to the heavenly life (Phil 3:14). It is also a holy calling (II Tim 1:9), which is not open to human understanding but requires spiritual discernment (Eph 1:18).

The verbal adjective "called" (klētos) is used in two ways. In the majority of cases it has in view the call to salvation (so Rom 1:6-7; I Cor 1:24; Jude 1; Rev 17:14); but a new dimension appears in Rom 1:1 and I Cor 1:1 where calling becomes effectual in terms of an office — "called to be an apostle."

It is Matthew's parable about the wedding feast ("many are called [klētos], but few are chosen" [eklektoi], Mt 22:14) that provides the text with the greatest difficulty. Contrary to the practice in other instances (see especially Rev 17:14; but also Rom 8:28 f.), the elect here are distinguished from those who are called. In spite of K. L. Schmidt's warning that we do not know the Aramaic wording behind the text (TWNT, III, 496), the context clearly supports the distinction. The dialectic tension of which the verse speaks cannot be located in the fact that in some instances many are called and in other instances only few are called, as Schmidt maintains. It is rather that many are invited but few are accepted. What the text asserts is that God as the inviter has the sole prerogative to qualify those who may attend. The purpose of the utterance is not to give comfort to the chosen few. In the parable the call to the many has been extended and refused. Those who are gathered are men originally passed by. But even they are not exempt from judgment. Each must have his wedding garment to be accepted (chosen).

The parable is a warning. It reiterates what is taught elsewhere in Matthew (cf. Mt 5:20) and particularly in the immediate context. In the parable of the vineyard just preceding, the conclusion is that he "will rent out the vineyard to other vinegrowers, who will pay him the proceeds at the proper seasons . . . . Therefore I say to you, the kingdom of God will be taken away from you, and be given to a nation producing the fruit of it" (Mt 21:41, 43, NASB).

In Mt 23:3 the theme is continued in Jesus' condemnation of the Pharisees who preached but did not practice righteousness. Merit consists not in being one of the few, but in possessing a righteousness acceptable to God. See Chosen; Election; Vocation.

Bibliography. Alan Richardson, *A Theological Word Book of the Bible,* New York: Macmillan, 1960, pp. 39 f. J. L. Schmidt, "*Kaleō,* etc.," TDNT, III, 487-501. K. Stendahl, "The Called and the Chosen," *The Root of the Vine,*

New York: Philosophical Library, 1953, pp. 63-80.

G. W. Ba.

CALNEH (kăl'nĕ), **CALNO** (kăl'nō). The name of a city or village in NW Syria referred to in Amos 6:2 and Isa 10:9. Although today Calneh is often equated with Assyrian *Kunalū'a (Kinalū'a),* the present site of which is believed by some to be a large tell one mile E of Ḥarîm, the best identification still remains that of I. J. Gelb (cf. *American Journal of Semitic Languages and Literatures* 51 [1935], pp. 189-191) who equates Assyrian *Kullāni* (Calneh) with modern Kullan Köy, about ten miles SE of Arpad. Canneh (q.v.), though located in the same general area (cf. Ezk 27:23), was perhaps a different site.

Heb. *kalnēh* in Gen 10:10 should doubtless be revocalized to read *kullānû,* "all of them" (cf. RSV), as in Gen 42:36 (cf. also Prov 31:29), since no Calneh is known in Babylonia (cf. W. F. Albright in JNES, III [1944], 254 f., R. Youngblood in *Bethel Seminary Quarterly,* XI [1962], 8 f.). LXX *pántes,* "all," translating the Heb. consonants k-l-n-h in Amos 6:2, further demonstrates such a revocalization to be not without foundation.

R. Y.

CALNO (kăl'nō). A city which had fallen to the Assyrians, cited as an example to Israel of the futility of offering resistance to them (Isa 10:9). This is probably the Kulnia associated with Arpad and Hadadezer in the Assyrian "tribute list." It is also called Calneh (q.v.) and mentioned with Hamath in Amos 6:2. It may be modern Kullan Köy, 20 miles NW of Aleppo.

CALVARY (kăl'vá-rĭ). The word occurs in only one place in the Bible (Lk 23:33). It comes from the Vulgate, which in all four Gospels (Mt 27:33; Mk 15:22; Lk 23:33; Jn 19:17) translates the Gr. word *kranion* ("a skull") by *calvaria,* the Latin word for skull. Strangely, the KJV translators gave the correct English equivalent, "a skull," in three of the Gospels. For some unknown reason they varied this in the

Gordon's Calvary. Garden Tomb Assn.

The Church of the Holy Sepulchre covers the traditional site of Calvary. G. Semerdjian

case of Luke, adopting a Latinism. Thus by literary accident the term appeared in what became the most widely used English version. Though based on this one odd occurrence, the term "Calvary" has taken on such rich devotional and theological associations that its value guarantees it a permanent place in the Christian vocabulary.

The location of Calvary is uncertain. The traditional site, fixed in the 4th cen. by Helena, the mother of Emperor Constantine, is in the Church of the Holy Sepulchre. But this is inside the present N wall of Jerusalem (where the N wall was in Jesus' day is not yet established by archaeologists) and it is implied that Christ died outside the wall (Heb 13:12). For this reason some have preferred "Gordon's Calvary," a skull-shaped rock some 250 yards NE of the Damascus Gate.

See Cross; Golgotha.

R. E.

CALVINISM.This is the name of that system of theological thought which was brought to its most complete expression by the great Swiss reformer John Calvin (1509-64). It is also called Reformed doctrine. Its emphases include predestination and the sovereignty of God. It must not be forgotten that Calvinism holds, besides its distinctives, to those doctrines common to all historic Christianity, such as the full truthfulness of Scripture, the Trinity, the deity of Christ, His supernatural miracles, bodily resurrection, etc. Without these basic and fundamental doctrines a theology cannot properly be called Calvinistic or Reformed.

Although Calvin gave the Reformed doctrine its most thorough formulation, the theology had long been held. Calvin would have been the first to have denied its novelty. He found it in the Church Fathers and, of course, in the Bible. This theology and its main opposing view, now called Arminianism *(q.v.)*, were much discussed through the Middle Ages in the Latin church. Augustine was a prominent protagonist of the position later held by Calvin. Indeed, Calvinism is often called Augustinianism. In the Council of Trent in 1545, the Roman Catholic church, partly in reaction to the reformers, officially espoused the Arminian view.

Martin Luther's view on the sovereignty of God was very similar to Calvin's. His tract on *The Bondage of the Will* speaks strongly of total depravity. Later, Lutheran thought on these matters inclined more toward Melancthon's Arminian views. In post-Reformation days a reaction set in and in Holland Jacob Arminius (1560-1609) advocated a greater emphasis on free will. His five theses were condemned by the Synod of Dort (1618) which formulated the famous five points of Calvinism remembered by the acronym TULIP: total depravity, unconditional election, limited atonement (now often called definite atonement), irresistible grace, and perseverance of the saints

(or as now sometimes put, the perseverance of God in the saints).

Prominent Calvinistic creeds are the Westminster Confession, the Heidelberg Catechism, the Belgic Confession, and the Scotch Confession of 1560. The Arminian position has been adopted especially in Methodism; the Calvinistic, in Presbyterian, Reformed, the older Episcopal, and many of the older Baptist churches.

It must be remembered that Calvinism does not deny free will. It declares that God's sovereignty extends to all things and persons, but that His sovereign control in some inscrutable way does not deny man's free moral agency and responsibility. Note also that the problem of sovereignty and freedom was not originated by Calvinism or even by Christianity. Plato struggled with the problem and concluded with belief in a creator limited by his refractory materials. Muslim theologians also face the problem and adopt the position of fatalism. Calvinism does not claim to solve the problem, but only to put it in the Scripture focus and leave it there, not going beyond what is written.

R. L. H.

CAMEL. *See* Animals, I.5.

CAMEL'S HAIR. In Mt 3:4 and Mk 1:6 the outer garment of John the Baptist is said to have been of camel's hair. It is rather long and woolly in texture, and when woven makes a coarse, durable textile which both ancient and modern Bedouins have found suitable for clothing or tent coverings. Toward the spring when the camel is shedding, the hair of the neck, back and hump is either clipped or pulled in handfuls or licks. It is then woven on hand looms and made into camel's hair cloth. Elijah's mantle of "haircloth" (II Kgs 1:8, RSV) and the "hairy mantle" mentioned in Zechariah (13:4, RSV) may be OT references to this textile.

CAMON (kā'mŏn). Camon is found in KJV, but in other versions is spelled Kamon. It was where Jair, the Gileadite judge, was buried (Jud 10:5), probably in Gilead.

CAMP

1. The most common Heb. word for camp is *maḥăneh*, which probably comes from a root meaning "to bend or curve." Hence it is thought that the Heb. camp in the seminomadic period was usually in a circle with the tents surrounding the cattle and sheep, and wagons surrounding the women and children in times of travel, for protection from attack. The same Heb. word is used of a caravan of travelers (Gen 32:7-8, "company"); of a band of angels (Gen 32:2); of all the tribes of Israel encamped around the tabernacle (Num 2:17); of the camp of the armies of Israel (Josh 6:11; I Sam 4:3, 5); of the funeral "company" of Jacob (Gen

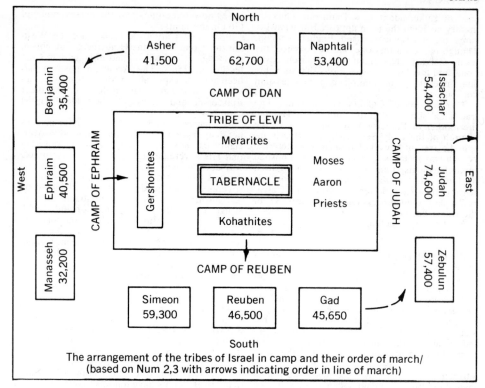

North

| Asher 41,500 | Dan 62,700 | Naphtali 53,400 |

Benjamin 35,400

Issachar 54,400

CAMP OF DAN

TRIBE OF LEVI

CAMP OF EPHRAIM

West

Ephraim 40,500

Gershonites

Merarites

TABERNACLE

Kohathites

Moses

Aaron

Priests

CAMP OF JUDAH

Judah 74,600

East

Manasseh 32,200

Zebulun 57,400

CAMP OF REUBEN

| Simeon 59,300 | Reuben 46,500 | Gad 45,650 |

South

The arrangement of the tribes of Israel in camp and their order of march/
(based on Num 2,3 with arrows indicating order in line of march)

50:9). The temple is even called "the camp of the Levites" in I Chr 9:18 (RSV).

2. Once (II Kgs 6:8) the Heb. *taḥănōt,* "camp," "encampment," occurs. The form of the word is related to 1 above.

3. The Gr. word for camp, *parembolē,* refers to the barracks of the Roman army in Acts 21:34 (RSV). In Heb 13:11, 13 the sin offering is mentioned as being burnt outside the camp of Israel. A figurative reference to the militant saints is made in Rev 20:9.

R. L. S.

CAMPHIRE. *See* Plants.

CANA (kā′nȧ). A Galilean village mentioned only in the fourth Gospel as the site of Jesus' first miracle (Jn 2:1, 11), as the place where He spoke the word to heal a nobleman's son lying sick in Capernaum (Jn 4:46), and as the home of Nathanael (Jn 21:2).

The location of Cana in Galilee (so called to distinguish it from a Cana in Coelesyria) has long been an open question in Gospel geography. Various identifications are:

1. Khirbet Kana, overlooking the Battof Valley (also called Plain of Zebulun or Plain of Netophah) nine miles N of Nazareth. This site was reidentified by Robinson (*Biblical Researches . . . ,* III, 204–207). Dalman also ar-

gues for this site (*Sacred Sites . . . ,* pp. 101–106). Etymologically, historically, archaeologically, and geographically, a strong case can be made for this locale as the true site of Cana. Archaeologists in 1963 discovered pottery of the Iron II, Hellenistic, Herodian, Late Roman, Arabic, and Crusader periods. This is important since Tiglath-pileser III mentions his capture of a town in Galilee named Qana (see ANET, p. 283). The Iron II sherds of Khirbet Kana strengthen its case as being the true Cana. Surface coins of the 1st cen. A.D. have been found here according to reports (cf. Kraeling, *Bible Atlas,* pp. 372–373), and the name ("reeds") is naturally accounted for by the fact that reeds once grew bountifully in the marshy Battof Valley (called the Asochis Valley in the NT period; cf. Jos *Life,* 41). This Cana was inhabited as late as the time of Quaresimus (17th cen.).

2. Others (De Saulcy, Vilnay?, Pilter, Farrar) favor Kefr Kenna. There is little tangible evidence to support this view, which was never popular before the Franciscans settled there in the 16th cen. "Tradition" located the site at Kenna to make it more convenient for travelers, since it was on the main road between Nazareth and Tiberias. But Eusebius says that Cana was in the area of the tribe of Asher, near Sidon (cf. *Onomasticon,* ed. Klostermann, pp.

116–117). Besides, other pilgrims speak of Sepphoris as being located between Nazareth and Cana, which would be out of the question for Kenna.

3. Ain Kana, S of er-Rene, has also been so identified, but this location has never been widely accepted.

Cana must have remained a strictly Jewish community throughout the Roman period, since the priestly family of Eliashib was settled here after the destruction of the temple in A.D. 70. The stone jars, used by the Jews for purifying (cf. Jn 2:6), are explained by several examples of such jars which still are to be found at 3rd cen. synagogues in Galilee (see photos), or certain pedestal urns, made of soft limestone, which date from the Herodian period and have been found at various places in Palestine (cf. *Gallery Book, Palestine Archaeological Museum; Persian, Hellenistic, Roman, Byzantine Periods*, p. 35, freestanding 1092; and for a photograph [of one found at Ain Feskha], cf. Roland deVaux, *L'Archelogie et Les Manuscrits de la Mer Morte*, London: 1961, p. xxxiv). The Talmud speaks of lustral vases which contained the water and the ashes of a red heifer located at the entrance of the court of Israel in the temple enclosure (cf. Parah, iii.3).

Bibliography. See books referred to above. M. Avi-Yonah, *Views of the Biblical World*, Jerusalem: International Publishing Co., 1961, V, 138. Ch. Clermont-Ganneau, "La mosique de Kefr Kenna," *Recueil d'Arch. Or.*, Paris: Leroux, 1901, pp. 345–360, 372–373. W. H. Dixon, "Itineraries of Our Lord," PEQ (1878), pp. 67–73. Samuel Klein, *Beitrage zur Geographie und Geschichte Galiläas*, Leipzig: Rudolf Haupt, 1909, pp. 56 ff. Clemen Kopp, *Das Kana des Evangeliums*, 1940. E. W. G. Masterman, "Cana of Galilee," PEQ (1914), pp. 179 ff. W. T. Pilter, "Where is Cana of Galilee?" PEQ (1883), pp. 143–148. W. M. Thomson, *The Land and the Book*, Hartford: Scranton, II, 303–306. Zeller, "Kefr Kenna," PEQ I (1869–70), 71–73.

E. J. V.

CANAAN (kā′nȧn), **CANAANITE** (kā′nȧ-nīt). A personal name applied to the youngest son of Ham (Gen 9:18); a tribal name for peoples supposedly descended from him; and a geographical name describing the territory occupied by those descendants.

As a tribal name, Gen 10:15–19 lists eleven subdivisions, Ex 13:5 lists five, Ex 23:23 lists six, Deut 7:1 lists seven, and Gen 15:19–21 lists ten. Omission in the other lists of the last five names of the Gen 10 list may result from their unimportance. The additions to the Gen 15 list may be primarily of tribes in the Negeb and the Sinai peninsula.

As a geographical term, Canaan at one time was the name of the land along the Mediterranean from modern Syria to S of Gaza. However, throughout most of OT times it referred

Remains of the Canaanite city of Hazor destroyed by Joshua. Yigael Yadin

to all the territory W of the Jordan. Taking its name from the chief tribal group inhabiting it, the land was called *Kena'an*, according to both Gen 10 and native Canaanite-Phoenician tradition as transmitted by Sanchuniathon and preserved by Philo of Byblos.

The Canaanites can be traced back before 3000 B.C. to the founding or rebuilding with strong walls of such cities as Jericho, Beth Shean, Beth Yerah and Megiddo. About 2200/2100 B.C. a wave of Amorite (q.v.) invasions into Syria and Canaan greatly influenced Canaanite civilization. The Early Bronze Age cities of the Canaanites fell before the nomadic chieftains, who often camped on the ruined sites and buried their dead in tombs nearby, as at Jericho. As these Amorites amalgamated with the Canaanites, towns again began to multiply in Palestine *c.* 1900 B.C., revealing a change from nomadic to urban civilization. This is documented by comparing the 20th cen. Egyptian Execration texts now in Berlin with the similar 19th cen. texts in Brussels. The earlier series lists several headmen with Amorite names for several localities, suggesting seminomadic conditions. In the latter set of texts the following are some of the Canaanite towns listed, naming only one ruler for each: Jerusalem, Shechem, Accho, Achshaph, Tyre, Hazor, Aphek, Ashtaroth, Pella, Shutu (Sheth, Num 24:17), and Byblos (BASOR #83, pp. 33 f.).

Beginning *c.* 1750 B.C. the Canaanites broke with Egyptian and other cultural influences and began to develop their own culture and art. Known at this time as the Hyksos, they established many commercial contacts with the Aegean world. From 1800 until 1500 B.C. there was a great movement of Hurrians (biblical Horites) and some Indo-Iranians (including Hittites) into Syria and Palestine, so that the Canaanites of the Late Bronze Age became a very mixed race.

Linguistic evidence shows the presence or influence of Canaanites in the Sinai peninsula about 1500 B.C. Their culture reached its peak

Roman columns frame the Crusader castle, below which stand the Canaanite walls of Gebal (Byblos).

at Ras Shamra (Ugarit) about 1500 B.C. After 1400 B.C. the Canaanites in Canaan were being disrupted by the Israelite and Aramaean invasions as documented by the Amarna tablets. *See* Joshua, Book of. In the 12th cen. the Sea Peoples (including the Philistines) from the Aegean Sea region took possession of the Canaanite seacoast from Gaza to S of Joppa and destroyed Ugarit and Tyre. Shortly afterward Aramaeans took over most of the northern territory of the Canaanites, establishing the kingdom of Damascus (Syria), which became so troublesome to later Israelite and Judean kings. As a result of these invasions, the Canaanite territory shrank to one-tenth of its original extent. This led to a new Canaanite capital being established at Tyre as the center of a colonizing empire. Byblos and Sidon became leading cities in this era.

From these outposts, traders and colonizers set forth in the 9th cen. to found colonies on Sardinia, with settlements on Cyprus antedating them, and those at Carthage not much later. These traders even colonized Spain (ancient Tartessus or Tarshish, *q.v.*). However, historians make a division in Canaanite history and culture at *c.* 1100–1000 B.C., calling the period subsequent to that date "Phoenician" *(q.v.)*. This term probably is derived from Gr. *phoinos,* "purple" *(q.v.),* referring to a famous and expensive dye made by the Phoenicians from the murex shellfish. With the defeat of Tyre by Nebuchadnezzar in 572 B.C. the Canaanites/Phoenicians ceased to be of importance in biblical history.

Linguistically, the Canaanites spoke and wrote a language very closely related to, if not the antecedent of, classical biblical Heb. The earliest evidence for a Canaanite dialect is found in the inscriptions of the Sinai turquoise mines at Serabit el-Khadem, dating to *c.* 1500 B.C. The decipherers say these inscriptions are adaptations of Egyptian hieroglyphics by the acrophonic principle to a Canaanite dialect. These adapted figures were later stylized into the Canaanite script of *c.* 1000 B.C., the almost identical Phoenician script of the 8th cen. (as known at Karatepe). Probably most of the OT was written in a similar script. Although they were in contact with four other styles of writing—Egyptian hieroglyphs, Byblian syllabic writing, Akkadian syllabic cuneiform, and Ugaritic alphabetic cuneiform—the Canaanites rejected them in developing their own alphabetic script. From the Phoenicians, *c.* 800 B.C., the Greeks borrowed the alphabet which is used by most modern Western languages. *See* Writing.

The literary character of the Canaanite civilization is attested by a whole library of religious literature found in the house of the chief priest between two temples at the site of ancient Ugarit. Beginning in 1929, an extensive literature in a dialect closely related to early Heb. was recovered in the Ras Shamra Ugaritic tablets. The mythological texts, Ba'al and Anath, Dan'el and Aqhat, and Keret (cf.

ANET, pp. 129 ff. for H. L. Ginsburg's translations; also translated in T. H. Gaster's *Thespis*), not only show the religious myths and ideas of Canaanite culture, but also are verbally and stylistically quite similar to early Heb. poetry, especially the song of Miriam (Ex 15), the song of Deborah (Jud 5), the blessing of Moses (Deut 33), and Ps 29 and 68. The Heb. poets borrowed much of their style and vocabulary from the Canaanites without, however, taking over their religious ideas. Through the Bible, the Canaanites have passed on some of their literary forms to the world.

Canaanite religion left its impress upon the OT in two ways: (1) certain mythological themes (e.g., Leviathan) were borrowed by the Hebrews for illustrative purposes and some practices and cult objects (e.g., incense altars) adapted to the worship of God; (2) the reaction of the Heb. prophets against the false theology and impure, idolatrous worship. The former category includes some architectural features of the Solomonic temple and some of its furnishings. The latter classification includes the Heb. rebellion against Canaanite polytheism, its sensuality, worship of idols, and practices such as human sacrifice, sacred prostitution, eunuch priests, and serpent worship.

The pantheon of the Canaanites, according to the Ugaritic literature, was headed by El, the creator god, whose wife was Asherah. Their son (or grandson), Ba'al, was the god of fertility, the "activator" of all life, and the real power to be worshiped. His wife was Anath, the goddess of love and war. Other gods were Dagon, the grain god; Resheph, god of plagues; Shulman, god of healing; Koshar, the inventor god; and Mot, the god of death *(see* Gods, False). The OT presents a slightly different picture of the pantheon, with Ashtoreth (Ishtar) being the wife of Ba'al. Such variations from region to region are common in the ancient Near East. *See* Ras Shamra.

Canaanite cultic practices centered around elaborate rites of sacrifice of cattle, rams, ewes, lambs, wild animals, birds, doves. There is some evidence that they offered up the front shoulder as did the Hebrews. Altars were erected at high places; in connection there were sacred groves, trees, or carved wooden images of Asherah *(see* Gods, False; Heb. *'ăshērâ,* cf. Jud 6:25, RSV). Canaanite temples had a "holy of holies" with an idol enshrined, an altar of incense before its entrance, libation bowls and small lamps. Divination, snake worship and sacred prostitution were practiced. The latter was supposed to make the lands, domesticated animals, and human beings fertile and productive.

Evidence of the widespread influence of Canaanite religion can be seen in the mention of Ba'al-zephon in Egypt (Ex 14:2). This probably refers to a site where Ba'al of Saphon, "the lord of the North," was worshiped.

In material culture, from the middle to the end of the 2nd mil. B.C. the Canaanites were quite advanced as evidenced by their walled cities, buildings, pottery, ivory inlays and other artifacts.

Bibliography. William F. Albright, *The Archaeology of Palestine,* 2nd ed., Harmondsworth: Penguin Books, 1960; *Archaeology and the Religion of Israel,* 2nd ed., Baltimore: Johns Hopkins Univ. Press, 1956; *From the Stone Age to Christianity,* 2nd ed., Baltimore: Johns Hopkins Univ. Press, 1957; "The Role of the Canaanites in the History of Civilization," appendix to *The Bible and the Ancient Near East,* G. Ernest Wright, ed., New York: Doubleday, 1961; *Yahweh and the Gods of Canaan,* Garden City: Doubleday, 1968. CornPBE, pp. 179–196, 210–211. J. Gray, *The Legacy of Canaan* (supplement to VT, V), Leiden: Brill, 1957. Kathleen Kenyon, *Archaeology in the Holy Land,* London: Ernest Benn, 1960. George Ernest Wright, *Biblical Archaeology,* Philadelphia: Westminster 1957.

A. K. H.

CANAANITE, SIMON THE.*See* Simon; Zealot.

CANAL. The word "canals" occurs in several places in the ASV marg. (Ex 7:19; 8:5; Isa 19:6; Nah 3:8). In the account of the plagues (Ex 7:19), names are used descriptively to designate the different waters of Egypt: *nehā-rôt,* "flowing streams," for the main branches or channels of the river Nile in the Delta, and *ye'ōrîm* for other streams, which by contrast must mean, as it should according to its use by the Egyptians, "the sluggish streams," i.e., "canals." It is so rendered by the revisers. It refers to the network of connecting waterways and irrigation canals from the Nile.

CANDACE (kăn'dá-sē). Queen of ancient Ethiopia or Cush, who is mentioned in Acts 8:27. Her kingdom, which is not to be confused with modern Ethiopia or Abyssinia, was the area known as Meroë in S Nubia or the modern Sudan (*see* Cush 3 and Ethiopia).

The writings of Strabo, Dio Cassius, and Pliny, and the inscriptions of pyramid tombs indicate that Candace was a common title (not name) used by a number of reigning queen-mothers between *c.* 300 B.C. and A.D. 300. The occasion for the reference in Acts was the conversion, under Philip, of the treasurer of one of these queens, a eunuch who may well have been a proselyte to Judaism returning from a Jewish feast. *See* Ethiopian Eunuch. John A. Wilson believes the queen referred to was Amanitēre, whose title appears in a cartouche as *Kntky,* "Candace." She ruled from A.D. 25 to 41 (JNES, XVIII [1959], 287).

D. W. B.

CANDLE. This word is found nine times in the OT as the rendering of *nēr,* and in the NT for *luchnos.* In all these references in the ASV the more exact rendering "lamp" is used. The candle, in our sense of the term, was unknown in antiquity. *See* Lamp; Pottery.

CANDLESTICK, GOLDEN. *See* Tabernacle.

CANE. *See* Plants.

CANKER. *See* Diseases.

CANKERWORM. *See* Animals: Locust, III.29.

CANNEH (kăn'ĕ). Mentioned only in Ezk 27:23. Located in Syria, it was connected with Haran and Eden as one of the places with which Tyre had commercial relations. The site is unknown. It is possibly the same as Calneh (*q.v.*).

CANON OF SCRIPTURE – OLD TESTAMENT. By "canon" is meant that list of OT books which is regarded as inspired and which can be accepted as the rule of Christian faith and conduct. In English Protestant Bibles there are 39 books in the OT canon. How and when were these books accepted as canonical and why were these accepted and no others?

The study of the OT canon is made somewhat difficult by the fact that the process of canonization took place in a distant time and there are practically no extrabiblical materials from those days to provide details of the process. Some points and general principles can be learned from the books themselves, but for some matters meager information must suffice. Of great assistance has been the discovery of the Dead Sea Scrolls. These copies of biblical and non-biblical books push back available information to the first and second pre-Christian centuries. They have greatly helped to confirm many points previously held by orthodox students of this subject.

Christ and the Canon

Fortunately, we are not left entirely to speculation or to the evaluation of meager information concerning the OT canon. Specific instruction concerning the books and how they are to be received comes from the teaching of the Lord Jesus Christ Himself. For the Christian, this is the highest authority. And it must be remembered that the teaching of Christ and the apostles is not only authoritative, but also is the best witness for the situation among the Jews in the 1st cen.

The witness of Christ and the NT is clear and explicit. Christ accepted the present 39 OT books and no others as being the Word of God, entirely true and authoritative for His people. Inasmuch as this conclusion is widely accepted, it is only necessary to summarize the evidence.

In the Gospel of Matthew alone, Christ in His teaching specifically quotes from or refers to the OT some 31 times, referring to it as authoritative Scripture, the Word of God, etc. Many other instances occur in the remaining Gospels. In the whole NT, the OT is specifically quoted more than 250 times, according to lists of quotations in Nestle. There are many more allusions of equal significance. The OT is quoted for its ethical teaching, and for its spiritual revelations as well as for its historical facts. Jesus appeals to the OT account of the creation of Adam and Eve, to Noah's flood, to Jonah's experience in the fish. He refers to the necessity of Scripture being fulfilled (Mt 26:54; Lk 24:44). He says that it was written by the Holy Spirit (Mk 12:36) and that even a tittle of it shall never fail (Lk 16:17). Much more could be added, but these passages are sufficient to show that Christ and the apostles utterly believed in and trusted the OT. Even in Mt 5, where Jesus sets His own word against what had been "said by them of old time," He is not contradicting the OT, but the scribal traditions. Note Mt 5:43 where He expresses agreement with the OT part of the quotation, but contradicts the scribal addition to it. For further discussion, see R. Laird Harris' *Inspiration and Canonicity of the Bible*, pp. 48–56.

All parts of the OT are given equal reverence. The three most frequently quoted books are Deuteronomy in the Pentateuch, Isaiah among the prophetic books, and the poetical book of Psalms. All the books are quoted or alluded to except Ruth, Ezra, Esther, Ecclesiastes, Song of Solomon, Lamentations, Obadiah and Nahum. These eight are all short books and doubtless were not referred to for lack of occasion. Moreover, the Jews included Obadiah and Nahum in one book with the other Minor Prophets, and these the NT often appeals to. They likewise often united Ezra with Nehemiah, which is probably alluded to. Ruth also was united into one book with Judges, as 1st cen. evidence shows. Thus only four small books of the OT are without specific NT witness.

At the same time, no other books are quoted as authoritative. Not one of the seven apocryphal books accepted in Roman Catholic circles is quoted in the NT. Three times Paul quotes from Gr. authors (Acts 17:28; I Cor 15:33; Tit 1:12). The last reference speaks of the Cretan author as a prophet, but all three quotations are obviously given for illustrative purposes and their sources are not regarded as authoritative. Likewise, in Jude 14 there is a quotation from the book of Enoch, where Enoch is said to have prophesied condemnation of sinners. Here too it seems justified to say that Enoch is quoted for purposes of illustration and confirmation. The text of Enoch is uncertain, as it exists only in a translation of a translation, except for portions found in the Dead Sea caves. It was not accepted by the Jews as authoritative, nor does it ever appear in any Christian list or enumeration of canonical books. It can therefore be presumed that Jude quoted it for its inherent value and not as authoritative. It is thus clear from the quotations that Christ and the NT used the 39 books of the OT and no other as canonical.

This witness from quotations is fully supported by the references of Christ and the apostles to the OT as a whole. Once Christ spoke of the OT as the "law of Moses . . . the prophets and . . . the psalms" (Lk 24:44). In the context it is plain that this was a name for the "scriptures" or "all the scriptures" (Lk 24:45, 27). More often, Christ used the designation "the law and the prophets" or "Moses and the prophets" (Mt 5:17; 7:12; 11:13; 22:40; Lk 16:16, 29, 31; 24:27), which is used also by the apostles (Jn 1:45; Acts 13:15; 24:14; 26:22; 28:23; Rom 3:21).

There is no doubt as to what books were included by these designations. Josephus was a Jewish historian who was a contemporary of the apostles. In a well-known passage (*Against Apion* i.8) he states that the Jews held sacred only 22 books – 5 of the Law of Moses, 13 of Prophets, and 4 of "hymns to God and precepts for the conduct of human life." These 22 books are quite obviously the present 39. The difference arises because the 12 Minor Prophets were written on one scroll and called one book; I and II Samuel, I and II Kings, I and II Chronicles were each counted as one book; so also were Ezra and Nehemiah, Judges and Ruth, Jeremiah and Lamentations.

Various authors in the centuries after Josephus also counted the books as 22 (or 24 with Lamentations and Ruth counted separately). Thus Melito (A.D. 170) gives a list including exactly the present canon except for Esther. Origen (A.D. 250) counted 22 books, Tertullian (A.D. 200) counted 24. Jerome (A.D. 400) says that the Jews accepted 22 books, counted by some as 24. Augustine (c. 400) is the only ancient authority for including the extra apocryphal books, but even he declares the apocryphal books not fully authoritative (see evidence given in detail in William Henry Green, *General Introduction to the OT, the Canon*, pp. 160–175). It is therefore clear that "Moses and the prophets" on the lips of Jesus meant just the present 39 OT books and none other. On the authority of Christ one can be confident that the present canon of the OT is the correct one.

The Dead Sea Scrolls and the Canon

It is of some importance, however, to inquire further and learn how this canon arose. Obviously, Christ only approved a canon that was already recognized. Discovery of the Dead Sea Scrolls has opened up the whole picture of the intertestamentary times in a way not heretofore thought possible. Indeed, the contribution of the Dead Sea Scrolls to study of the OT canon may prove to be one of their major values. Evidence from the scrolls is of two kinds. First, they witness to the existence and widespread use of the OT books at an early date. Second, they show the attitude of Jews of those times toward the Scriptures.

As is well known, the scrolls contain copies of every book of the OT except Esther, which has not yet been identified. The dates range from the 3rd cen. B.C. to the 1st cen. after Christ, with the majority, apparently, falling in the 1st cen. B.C. Copies are in various states of preservation, from the first scroll of Isaiah, readable and practically complete through the entire book, to the fragments of Chronicles, which are only about six lines long and badly eaten by ancient bookworms. Some books, notably Deuteronomy, Psalms, Isaiah, and the Minor Prophets, are found in several copies. Important finds from the 3rd cen. include fragments of Exodus, Samuel and Jeremiah. Other portions of special value include a copy of Ecclesiastes from 150 B.C. and portions of Daniel from *c.* 110 B.C. For details, see J. T. Milik, *Ten Years of Discovery in the Wilderness of Judea,* pp. 20–43. *See also* Dead Sea Scrolls.

It can thus be said that all OT books (except possibly Esther) were known, loved, and used by the Essenes. But this alone does not prove that these books were regarded as canonical. For this, it is necessary to turn to the second type of evidence, quotations of these books in the non-biblical writings of the Essenes.

The chief non-biblical writings quoting Scripture extensively are the Manual of Discipline, the Thanksgiving Hymns, the Damascus Document (previously known but now authenticated by portions found in the caves), and the Rule for the Final War. Further information comes from commentaries on sacred texts and on testimonial booklets stringing together messianic passages.

The Manual of Discipline insists that the law of Moses is inviolate and a man shall be excommunicated if he "transgress a single word of the law of Moses" (viii, 22; translation by Theodor H. Gaster, *The Dead Sea Scriptures,* Doubleday Anchor Books, 1956, p. 57). Both Exodus and Isaiah are quoted as Scripture.

The attitude of the Damascus Document is similar, but its witness more extensive. It also speaks largely of the law of Moses and explicitly quotes every book of the Pentateuch as Scripture. It does the same for the prophets:

War of the Sons of Light and the Sons of Darkness (DSS) quotes from Deuteronomy, Numbers, and Isaiah as the Word of God.
Palestine Archaeological Museum

Isaiah, Ezekiel, Hosea, Amos, Micah, Nahum, Zechariah, and Malachi. Even the book of Proverbs is specifically quoted as Scripture. Many other biblical books are alluded to. Some non-canonical books might perhaps be used by the author, but there is only one clear allusion or reference to such a book. It says that certain matters "are spelled out with equal exactness in the Book of the Divisions of the Times into their Jubilees and Weeks" (xvi, 4; Gaster, *op. cit.,* p. 85). This is obviously the Book of Jubilees written, probably, early in the 2nd cen. B.C.

The Thanksgiving Hymns give a picture of the devotional life of the Dead Sea community. They have no formal citations of Scripture, but the comment of Gaster is: "It is true that they are, in the main, mosaics of biblical quotations" (*op. cit.,* p. 112). According to Gaster's notes, all OT books are utilized except Joshua, Ruth, Chronicles, Nehemiah, Esther, Song of Solomon, Joel, and Haggai. The authors were steeped in the present OT books, though in this type of devotional literature specific quotations are not to be expected. There is little if any dependence on non-canonical books.

The piece often called the War of the Sons of Light and the Sons of Darkness adds little to the above. It quotes from Deuteronomy, Numbers, and Isaiah as the Word of God.

In addition to this evidence, several commentaries exist on portions of Scripture. Non-canonical scriptures were not thus used, giving further witness on the limits of the Dead Sea canon. So far, commentaries have been identified on portions of Genesis, Isaiah, Habakkuk, Hosea, Micah, Nahum, and Psalms.

Also some documents have been found which string together Scripture passages, especially verses bearing on messianic prediction. Such documents use verses from Numbers, Deuteronomy, Joshua, Isaiah, Ezekiel, Amos, and Psalms. Daniel is reported to be thus used, although all the passages are not yet published. A non-canonical book, provisionally called Psalms of Joshua, seems to be quoted in one of the testimonia (not yet published in full), but the piece may be quoted because of the verses from the canonical Joshua cited therein (J. M. Allegro, "Further Messianic References in Qumran Literature," JBL, LXXV [1956], 185 f.).

To summarize, the extant Dead Sea sectarian writings quote or refer to as Scripture the five books of Moses and Joshua, I and II Samuel, Psalms, Proverbs, Isaiah, Ezekiel, Daniel, Hosea, Amos, Micah, Nahum, Habakkuk, Zechariah, and Malachi. This is a total of 20 books out of the present 39. It is to be noted that books of all sections of the OT are treated as equally inspired. Furthermore, many of the remaining books are utilized in the Thanksgiving Hymns as explained above. For instance, Job does not appear among the books just listed, but it was repeatedly used in the Thanksgiving Psalms, as is also the case with Jeremiah. If the usage in the Thanksgiving Hymns is added to the positive evidence of canonicity, all 39 OT books are covered except Ruth, Chronicles, Nehemiah, Esther, Song of Solomon, Joel, and Haggai. But the last two were united with the other Minor Prophets in the term "the twelve prophets" (Sir 49:10, before 180 B.C.), and Ruth was by the Jews attached to Judges, and Nehemiah to Ezra. Thus actually all but Chronicles, Esther, and Song of Solomon are covered. The evidence for canonical acceptance may not be watertight and conclusive for all, but it is positive for most of the books, and satisfactory for all but these three.

Divisions of the Canon

The earliest witness to the Jewish classification of the OT is the prologue to the apocryphal book of Ecclesiasticus (Wisdom of Jesus the Son of Sirach), which speaks three times of "the law and the prophets and the other books of our fathers" in slightly varying phraseology. It has been argued in slightly that the third division was not yet definite, because it is referred to three times in different words.

The next time this threefold division is used is in Lk 24:44 where Jesus speaks of the "law of Moses and . . . the prophets . . . and the psalms." The next instance is Josephus (*Against Apion* i.8), referred to above, where for the first time the contents of the three divisions are given as 5 books of Law, 13 books of Prophets, and 4 books of "hymns to God and precepts for the conduct of human life." Philo of Alexandria, a contemporary of Christ, also says of the sect of the Therepeutae that they had "laws, and oracles uttered by prophets, and hymns and the others by which knowledge and piety are increased and perfected" (*de vita contemplativa*, § 3). This sounds much like Josephus' division and seems to be usually passed over by those who suppose the Egyptian canon was different from that in Palestine. This threefold division does not occur in the Mishna of *c.* A.D. 200. It apparently does not appear again until about A.D. 400 in the Talmud (Baba Bathra, 14*b*–15*a*) and the writings of Jerome. The Talmud names 5 books in the Law, 8 in the Prophets, and 11 in the Writings—24 in all.

Many conclusions have been drawn from the threefold division of the canon as found in the present Heb. Bible and the Talmud and these four ancient witnesses. But there are two things to observe about it. First, it is by no means sure that the threefold division of today—substantially that of the Talmud—goes back much before A.D. 400. The only previous witness as to the details of the grouping of the books is Josephus who groups them as 5 of Law, 13 of Prophets, and 4 of hymns and precepts. For some strange reason, authors have paid little attention to this witness of Josephus, but his testimony is clear and weighty. Indeed, Philo's terminology seems to support it.

The second observation concerning this threefold division is that parallel to it there was

another, the twofold division. This is clearly seen in the NT witness as outlined earlier. Fourteen times the NT speaks of Moses and the Prophets or uses similar terms. It is out of the question to say that the NT authors did not yet recognize the third division books as canonical. All the major books of the third division of the Talmud are quoted in the NT and quoted as authoritative. It is clear, rather, that there was a twofold classification of the whole OT parallel with the threefold. Later Christian authors use this terminology also (Ignatius, *Epistle to Smyrnaeans*, chap. 5; *Epistle to Diognetus* [*c*. A.D. 130], chap. 10; Irenaeus, *Against Heresies*, i.3.6).

But the new evidence of the Dead Sea Scrolls is that this terminology is pre-Christian and Palestinian. It existed at an early date side by side with references to a threefold classification.

Such a reference has long been known in II Macc 15:9 where Judas comforted his army out of "the law and the prophets." The assumption has sometimes been made that this only referred to the first two divisions of the Heb. Bible (5 books of Law and 8 of Prophets), the third division not yet having been canonized. This was pure assumption. To begin with, the first two divisions of Josephus' day would have 5 books of Law and 13 of Prophets. Besides, who can now think that the Psalms were not canonized by the days of II Maccabees?

The Dead Sea Scrolls clarify the matter, for side by side with clear acceptance of practically all the books of the OT canon they evidence usage of the twofold division, so common in the NT.

Thus the Manual of Discipline exacts a pledge of all initiates to do what is good "in accordance with what He has commanded through Moses and through His servants the prophets" (i.2–3; Gaster, *op. cit.*, p. 39). This clearly refers to the entire sacred corpus and is as early as the reference in the prologue of Ecclesiasticus. Another probable reference speaks of the "study of the law which God commanded through Moses to the end that, as occasion arises, all things may be done in accordance with what is revealed therein and with what the prophets also have revealed through God's Holy Spirit" (Manual of Discipline, viii.15–16; Gaster, *op. cit.*, p. 56). The Prophets, notice, are not a lesser revelation than is the Law and they are quoted repeatedly in the Dead Sea literature as the word spoken by God.

In the Damascus or Zadokite Document twice again such terminology is used. In interpreting Amos 5:26–27 the writer(s) used a slightly variant text; Gaster translates the portion as follows: "I will exile *Sikkuth* your king and *Kiyyun* your image, the star of your God . . . beyond Damascus." The comment is made that "the expression 'Sikkuth your king' refers to the books of the law" and that "the expression 'Kiyyun your image' refers to the books of the prophets" (*Zadokite Document*, vii.15-18; Gaster, *op. cit.*, p. 70). Another instance is translated by Gaster as follows: "The commandments of God which he had given through Moses and through his holy anointed priest Aaron" (v.21-vi.1; Gaster, *op. cit.*, p. 67). But the words "priest Aaron" are not in the original. It is better to translate more strictly: "The commandments . . . through Moses and through his holy anointed ones." This is suggested by Chaim Rabin (*The Zadokite Documents*, 1954, p. 20). He remarks (p. 8n.) that "anointed ones" is equivalent to "prophets."

Thus the Dead Sea Scrolls show that substantially the present OT was held by the community as of divine authority and these books were subsumed under the names "the law and the prophets," or "Moses and the prophets."

Although it has been argued that the original designation of the OT was twofold, and that later a threefold classification was used (R. L. Harris, *Inspiration and Canonicity of the Bible*, p. 147 f.). further reflection suggests that the varying usage may be due to sectarian differences. It is not impossible that the Jerusalem Jews of official Pharisaic and Sadducean opinion divided the canon into three parts and that the Essene sect divided it into only two parts. In that case it would explain the NT terminology which here as often would tend to reflect Essenic usage.

The Critical View

There is no justification whatever for the view held by destructive critics in general, which makes the threefold division a basis for a theory of three stages in the development of the canon. This view alleges that the Pentateuch was canonized first about 400 B.C. After that, the Prophets (Joshua, Judges, Samuel, Kings, Isaiah, Jeremiah, Ezekiel, and the 12 Minor Prophets) were accepted about 200 B.C. Last of all, the 11 other books called the Writings (Heb. *Kethuvim;* Gr. *Hagiographa*) were canonized at the Council of Jamnia about A.D.90.

Evidences for this view are not impressive. There is no proof of any canonizing of the Pentateuch at 400 B.C. There are no contemporary non-biblical documents bearing on the question. As far as evidence goes, the Pentateuch could have been canonized much earlier. But critical thought will not allow this because, it is held, the Pentateuch was not completed until about 400. There are biblical verses to the contrary, as is noted subsequently, but these are explained away.

The Prophets were canonized somewhat later, the theory holds. If the Prophets had been accepted at 400, they would have been included in the Law. But they were not, so they must have been canonized at a later time. It is known that the 12 Minor Prophets were canonized by about 180 B.C. when Ecclesiasticus mentions

them as a unit (49:10). So likely this canon was closed shortly before that date. The clinching argument is that Daniel is not among the Prophets. Clearly Daniel belongs among the Prophets. Chronicles also belongs among the Prophets as truly as does Kings. But Chronicles was written around 200 B.C. and Daniel about 168 B.C. (they say) – just too late to get into the canon of the Prophets. This suggests that 200 B.C. was the closing date. The Psalms also were not fully collected until after 168 B.C. as there are some Maccabean psalms allegedly after that time.

The Writings are therefore a miscellaneous collection which were accepted at various times from 200 B.C. to A.D. 90. At this date there supposedly was a council held in Jamnia in Palestine at which the Jews, now dispersed and seeking guidelines for faith, discussed the canonicity of several books, notably Ruth, Esther, Proverbs, Ecclesiastes, Song of Solomon, and Ezekiel. Objections were at last overcome and the canon forever closed.

This is a neat theory almost universally held by destructive criticism. Orthodox students following William Henry Green (*op. cit.*, p. 81) have usually countered by alleging that the three divisions answer to three types of authorship, rather than to three periods of time. The Law was by Moses, the next eight books were by prophets, the Writings were by men who had the gift of prophecy but not the prophetical office. One may ask, however, how we know that Judges was written by a prophet and Daniel was not! And can we say that David the king had not the office of a prophet (cf. Acts 2:29 f.), whereas Joshua the captain did?

Other questions must embarrass the views of criticism. Dead Sea discoveries have moved F. M. Cross now to claim that Chronicles was written c. 400 B.C. (F. M. Cross, *The Ancient Library of Qumran*, p. 141). Fragments of Ecclesiastes dated at 150 B.C. have convinced most that it was written by 250 B.C. at least. Why then were these not included in the canon of the Prophets? As mentioned above, the book of Proverbs was quoted as Scripture in the Zadokite Documents which were written close to 200 B.C. When we add the considerable regard shown for Proverbs by Ecclesiasticus at 180 B.C., we wonder why Proverbs did not make it into the canon of the Prophets, which was supposedly closed only very shortly before. Now with the Dead Sea copies available, practically no one speaks of Maccabean psalms any more!

Also, the so-called Council of Jamnia is a very shadowy thing. There is no contemporary information on it. Moreover, the books there questioned were questioned not for admittance into the canon, but as to their continued acceptance. This is clear, because Ezekiel was also questioned and it was admittedly among the Prophets since 200 B.C.! The questioning of Proverbs means nothing, because, as already seen, the Dead Sea Scrolls accepted it as Scripture long before. So did the NT. Any discussion of rabbis at Jamnia proves absolutely nothing about the close of the canon. It only shows that questions of canonicity keep popping up!

But the main fact opposed to the critical view (and also the view of Green *et al.*) is that the threefold canon of the Talmud is simply not the exclusive and original division. Why explain the absence of Daniel from the Prophets when the oldest definite witness, Josephus, makes it quite explicit that this book was among the Prophets! Why explain the presence of Daniel among the Writings when the Dead Sea Scrolls and the NT show that many Jews in that time used no such classification at all!

Some branches of Jewry indeed had a threefold division. But the contents of those three divisions were subject to change without notice. Josephus (and probably Philo) had only four books among the Writings. The Talmud had 11. Origen counted 22 books and thus did not have Ruth and Lamentations among the Writings. Tertullian, counting 24, would have placed them there if, indeed, he used the threefold scheme.

It has been suggested that this shifting of books from one division to another was for liturgical reasons. The Law and Prophets were divided at an unknown date into weekly synagogue lessons. Some of the other small books were read entire at annual feasts. Such practices may have caused these differences in the Jewish divisions of their Scriptures, but this is only theorizing. The facts, however, are sure. The threefold division cannot be made the basis of a three-stage canonization.

The Old Testament Witness to Its Canon

It may yet be asked if the OT itself gives an indication as to when and why these 39 books were accepted. For the period before the Dead Sea Scrolls there is no non-biblical information, but the OT books themselves speak with considerable clarity, though not in detail.

That the OT in general accepted the law of Moses as canonical is clear. Moses commanded that it be read at the Feast of Tabernacles every seventh year (Deut 31:9-11). Nehemiah records that he did this (Neh 8:1-18), and further says that the people lived in booths fulfilling the law of Moses. This law is given in Lev 23:40 ff.

Joshua recognized the law of Moses as the law of God (Josh 1:7, 8; 23:6). But Joshua added a writing to the law of God (Josh 24:26) and 600 years later the book of Joshua is quoted as the word of the Lord (I Kgs 16:34).

Deut 18:15-22 predicts a succession of prophets culminating in the great Prophet and demands credence for the Lord's prophets. Certain tests are given that the people may know a true prophet—fulfilled prophecy, miracle, agreement with God's previous word.

It should be noted that the OT historical books follow in connected sequence. The death

of Joshua is recorded in Jud 2:7-9 and these verses form the conclusion of Joshua. Judges and Ruth go together, and Ruth ends with a genealogy going up to the time of David. Samuel-Kings carry the story to the Captivity. The parallel history in Chronicles ends with two verses which are repeated in Ezr 1:1-2.

As is well known, Chronicles used the books of Samuel-Kings as its sources. What is not so well known is that Chronicles in a series of verses declares that its sources (Samuel-Kings) were written by a succession of prophets from Samuel to Jeremiah (see I Chr 29:29; II Chr 9:29; 12:15; 13:22; 20:34; 26:22; 32:32; 33:19; 35:25). Many of these prophets are known to us. They rebuked kings, preached reform, comforted God's people, and some have left books in their own names. The people were taught to heed their spoken words. Their writings were equally authoritative. Note the reception Jeremiah's writings had with the faithless king and the faithful remnant (Jer 36:4-32). Jeremiah's writings were to be accepted at once as the word of the Lord. Jer 36:4-6 says they were to be accepted because of prophetic authorship.

Likewise, II Kgs 14:6 refers to King Amaziah who about 825 B.C. heeded Deuteronomy as the word of the Lord by Moses. Jer 26:18-19 quotes a verse from the prophet Micah as the pronouncement of the Lord. Dan 9:2 says that Daniel had read in "the books" (Heb. "the article") a prophecy of the word of the Lord to Jeremiah.

The fact is that the OT is permeated with the idea of canonicity. Many prophets claimed to speak the word of the Lord, and their books repeat the claim. False prophets were exposed, but tests revealed the true prophet. In not a few places the prophets quote each other as canonical. In many more places the books refer to each other, as Hos 10:9 refers to Jud 20; Hos 11:8 to Deut 29:23; Prov 9:10 to Job 28:28.

Evidence is obviously not complete for all the OT books. But evidence is clear for the principles of their acceptance. Those written by prophets were accepted, and kings and priests were also sometimes prophets. Any man to whom God revealed His word was a prophet. Thus David and Solomon were prophets as truly as Joshua and Daniel. There are, of course, some books whose authorship is now not known. These were, however, classified by the Jews and by Christ as among the Prophets, and in the absence of the slightest evidence to the contrary, they may be thus accepted. God gave the Jews no test of an inspired book or list of canonical books. But He did give them very obvious and practical tests of a prophet, and it is clear that they accepted the writings of these prophets equally with their spoken words.

Some have held other tests of canonicity than prophetic authorship. The authority of the OT congregation has been suggested, but that certainly would not have helped in Jeremiah's day! Nonetheless, acceptance by the believing congregation or church universal is a significant point. Providential leading has been mentioned, and this doubtless operated insofar as God used providential means in preserving the writings of these prophets. But there is no hint in the OT that the messages oral or written of other than prophets should be revered. Likewise, there is no hint in the OT of Green's distinction between the gift of prophecy and the office of a prophet. Only one prophet in the whole OT was ever ordained to his office as far as is known – Elisha, and he wrote no book.

More common today is the idea that canonicity is determined by the inner testimony of the Holy Spirit. There is truth in this concept, but it is not always accurately expressed. The reformers emphasized this testimony, but not for questions of canonicity of particular books. The Spirit testifies rather to our being saved through being led to repentance and faith by the sacred doctrine, and thus testifies to the writings which contain that teaching. As Abraham Kuyper well puts it, the Spirit testifies to the *centrum* (*Principles of Sacred Theology*, pp. 560 ff.). From these central truths we can work out to other truths. From the fact of our salvation through Christ, we can conclude to His authority and the inspiration of the Scriptures that He recommends. But we cannot merely by reading a short passage such as the 25 verses of Jude know beyond a doubt that this is Scripture. At least Luther could not so identify James! And the question of the verses in Mk 16:9-20, which is a section almost as long as Obadiah, cannot be decided by an inner voice.

By and large the testimony of the Holy Spirit confirms the canonization of the 39 OT books. The apocryphal books have many good points and have been accepted as Scripture by many Christian people. But they will not stand *all* the tests or indeed any one of them – prophetic authorship, approval of Christ, acceptance by the church universal, or the testimony of the Holy Spirit. The 39 canonical books will pass them all.

See Hagiographa.

Bibliography. Archibald Alexander, *Evidences of the Authenticity, Inspiration, and Canonical Authority of the Holy Scriptures*, Philadelphia: Presbyterian Board of Publication, 1836. F. F. Bruce, *Second Thoughts on the Dead Sea Scrolls*, 2nd ed., Grand Rapids: Eerdmans, 1961. F. Buhl, *Canon and Text of the OT*, Edinburgh: T. & T. Clark, 1892. F. M. Cross, *The Ancient Library of Qumran*, Garden City, N.Y.: Doubleday, 1958. T. H. Gaster, *The Dead Sea Scriptures*, New York: Doubleday Anchor, 1956. Samuel R. L. Gaussen, *Theopneustia: The Inspiration of the Holy Scriptures*, reprint, Chicago: Moody, 1949. W. H. Green, *General Introduction to the OT, the Canon*, New York: Scribner's, 1899, xvii. R. Laird Harris, *Inspiration and Canonicity of the Bible*, Grand Rapids: Zondervan, 1957; "Was

the Law and the Prophets Two-thirds of the OT Canon?" BETS, IX (1966), 163-171. Meredith G. Kline, "Canon and Covenant," WTJ, XXXII (1969), 49-67. W. S. LaSor, *Amazing Dead Sea Scrolls*, Chicago: Moody, 1956. J. T. Milik, *Ten Years of Discovery in the Wilderness of Judea*, London: SCM, 1959. E. J. Young, *Introduction to the OT*, Grand Rapids: Eerdmans, 1949.

R. L. H.

CANON OF SCRIPTURE – NEW TESTAMENT.
What books belong in the NT? This is a question not often asked because there is such a complete agreement on the subject. All branches of Christendom explicitly state that they receive the 27 books of our NT as properly belonging to the sacred collection – the canon. There is considerable material to support this universal judgment of the church. It is true that because of the ravages of time, some of the evidence is lacking which was available in the early centuries of this era. On the other hand, some new material has been recently discovered. The evidence must therefore be scrutinized with care. This evidence comes largely from the writings of the early Church Fathers and from the works also of heretics of those days. Some evidence can be gleaned from the pages of the NT itself.

For this article the general conclusions of conservative NT scholarship with regard to the origin of the individual books are assumed. If one held the old liberal view that John's Gospel is a late 2nd cen. production, then of course its apostolic authorship would be ruled out. Happily, that view has been adequately disproved and our study may be based upon the conclusion that John, and the other Gospels, too, are from the 1st cen., even from the middle decades for the Synoptics. The point is that general introduction, which considers the canon, must base itself in part on special introduction, which considers in detail the date and authorship of the individual books. For these details, reference may be made to articles on the books themselves.

There is considerable evidence available for study of the early use and acceptance of the NT books. The first witness comes from the days when John, the last surviving apostle, was still alive. Clement of Rome wrote an extensive epistle at about A.D. 95. The epistles of Ignatius and of Polycarp come from only a few years later. These men had probably all talked with one or more of the apostles. They knew some of the NT authors firsthand. They had surely seen some of the original writings.

The next stage of the investigation concerns the second generation of Christians – those who wrote at about A.D. 140. These had talked with those who had known the apostles. More extensive writings have survived from this period. The names of Justin Martyr and Papias stand out. By this time also, there were some who had departed from the faith. We must reckon with Marcion and also with the heresy of Gnosticism. New information is available on Gnosticism. Former students sometimes felt that Christianity was heavily influenced by this heresy. It appears now that the Gnostic philosophy — which claimed a secret and esoteric knowledge — was a later and somewhat weird attempt to unite Christian doctrine with Gr. philosophy. Of especial interest now is the recently discovered work called "The Gospel of Truth" written, evidently, by the Gnostic Valentinus at about this time.

A third stage of study is at about A.D. 170 when evidence becomes abundant for almost all parts of the NT. From this period there are the extensive writings of Irenaeus and the nearly complete listing of NT books called the Muratorian Canon. Of course, there is also much other minor material bearing on the subject. Even this age — 70 years after the death of the last apostle — is not so far removed from the earliest times. Irenaeus was a pupil of Polycarp who in turn had been a disciple of the apostle John. So the extensive information given by Irenaeus is of great value even though not from the earliest time.

There is no great need to trace the subject through the giants of the later ages — Tertullian and Clement of Alexandria, and Cyprian of about A.D. 200; then Eusebius, the church historian, and Athanasius, the defender of orthodoxy, in A.D. 325. These men in some cases round out the picture, but their witness is hardly necessary. The NT canon was fixed to all intents and purposes before their time. This can be said in spite of the fact that the first listing of NT books exactly agreeing with our Bibles was in Athanasius' Festal Letter of A.D. 367. The point is, that although no list before this exactly agrees with our own (there actually are very few earlier lists in any case), there still is a great deal of evidence from which the canon of the earlier periods may be constructed.

Furthermore, absolute unanimity on the canon at an earlier time does not preclude someone's reopening the discussion at a later date. It is well known that Luther questioned somewhat the canonicity of James. Yet James had been accepted by the whole church for well over a thousand years. Likewise, in an earlier day there was a group of heretics called the *Alogi* (those who were opposed to the Logos doctrine of Jn 1:1). These people in the 3rd cen. denied the canonicity of all the Johannine writings. Yet before this all the Johannine writings had been fully accepted as canonical. The lesson is that every witness is not to be accepted at face value. There are offshoots and backslidings which need not seriously trouble us. As van Unnik reminds us, "The way that led to the formation of the canon was, however, a zig-zag road" (H. C. Puech, G. Quispel and W. C. van Unnik, *The Jung Codex*, p. 125). Van Unnik holds that the canon was substantially settled earlier, despite these controversies of the 3rd cen. regarding certain books.

For these reasons it is possible to omit detailed study of the later centuries and concentrate on the history of the acceptance of the NT books in three stages. First may be chosen the period of A.D. 170 when data becomes really abundant. Working backward to about A.D. 140, we find there is a broad witness in several authors. Finally we shall study the period from A.D. 95 to 120 in the writings of those who were themselves contemporary with and companions of the apostles. We shall finish this survey of history by an investigation of the claims and witness of the NT itself.

The Period of A.D. 170

The writings of Irenaeus which remain fill 263 large pages in *The Ante-Nicene Fathers* (A. Roberts and J. Donaldson, ed., Vol. 1). Irenaeus was an important figure in France in the early days. He was born in Asia Minor about A.D. 130 and was a friend of Polycarp in his youth. He became a bishop of the church in Lyons, Gaul, and was in close touch with the church at Rome, opposing it more than once. He wrote his great work *Against Heresies* after the intense persecution of A.D. 177, and finally gave his life with many of his flock in the awful times of Severus (A.D. 202). His witness is of great value because of its extent and also because he was in a position to know the facts of the origin and acceptance of the NT books.

In Irenaeus we perceive a kindred spirit. His trust in Christ was deep, and his regard for the NT is clear. In one passage he presents an early form of the Apostles' Creed (*ibid.*, p. 330). In another place he likens the inspiration of God by the Holy Spirit to a man playing music on a lyre (*ibid.*, p. 276). He says, "I am entirely convinced that no Scripture contradicts another" (*ibid.*, p. 230), thus evidencing belief in its inerrancy. He evidently regarded the NT as a unit, for he calls it "the evangelists and apostles," paralleling it with the term "the law and the prophets" for the OT (*ibid.*, p. 320).

The extent of the canon for Irenaeus is rather plain. He quotes extensively from the NT, summarizes the teaching of all the Gospels, tells how they were written, and then goes on to summarize from the apostolic epistles arguments against the Gnostic heresies of his day. Irenaeus refers by name (i.e., citing the author) to 18 NT books, and seven more are quoted. Only the tiny books of Philemon and Jude pass unnoticed, and this is surely because he lacked occasion to use them.

Irenaeus' references are interesting. He declares that there are necessarily four Gospels as there are four winds of heaven, four faces on the cherubim, etc. (*ibid.*, p. 230). He insists that Paul was truly an apostle (*ibid.*, p. 439) and quotes by name most of his epistles in Book V of his work. In the second Pfaffian fragment preserved from a lost work, he quotes Hebrews as Pauline (*ibid.*, p. 574). He cites Revelation as written by John the apostle "no very long time since, but almost in our day, towards the end of Domitian's reign" (i.e., about A.D. 95, *ibid.*, p. 559 f.). In fact, Irenaeus quotes practically the whole NT, referring to it as Scripture, apostolic, verbally inspired, and absolutely true. No other book written in the Christian era is quoted as Scripture. Indeed, the spurious Gospel of Thomas and the Gnostic Gospel of Truth are indignantly rejected (*ibid.*, pp. 345 and 429), as "agreeing in nothing with the Gospels of the apostles." Irenaeus bases everything on "the scriptural proof furnished by those apostles who did also write the Gospel," and adds, "The apostles, likewise, being disciples of the truth are above all falsehood" (*ibid.*, p. 417).

Supplementing the testimony of Irenaeus is the Muratorian Canon. This interesting list of NT books is known from a Medieval fragment and was composed about A.D. 170. The history of the fragment is not known, and it is tantalizingly brief. The first lines are missing, but it begins by mentioning "the third Gospel," Luke, and therefore it witnesses to Matthew and Mark as well. All the other NT books are listed with brief comments, except Hebrews, James, I and II Peter. Inasmuch as Hebrews, James and I Peter are well attested before this and II Peter also is used by Irenaeus, Westcott concludes that the fragment was copied from a MS with a break in it (B. F. Westcott, *A General Survey of the History of the Canon of the New Testament*, 6th ed., p. 219). The fragment mentions two epistles of John, which are taken by Westcott to be II and III John. It also quotes from I John. Thus the fragment agrees with Irenaeus and complements his witness. The two together give our NT exactly.

The Muratorian Canon (printed in *Ante-Nicene Fathers*, V, 603 f.) rejects the Shepherd of Hermas as not from the apostles. It mentions the Apocalypse of Peter as received by some but not by others, and names some spurious epistles of Paul. It is a discerning witness both in what it accepts and what it rejects. Other witnesses from this period tell the same story with individual variations.

Two translations of the NT were made around this time. The Eastern Church made the Syriac version called the Peshitta. Little is known of its origin, and early MSS do not remain. It apparently lacked II and III John, II Peter, Jude, and Revelation. There were no extra books. The Old Latin Version, used largely in Carthage, was made before A.D. 200. It apparently lacked II Peter, James, and Hebrews, though the evidence on Hebrews is unsure. Again, there were no added books. Putting these two versions together, we may say that the church agreed on our NT books and none other, except that some doubts were expressed on the shorter epistles and Revelation. Actually, we have abundant evidence for Revelation at an early time. The Eastern Church was clearly in error in excessively narrowing its list.

The Days of Justin Martyr – A.D. 140

Justin is the earliest Christian author whose writings have been preserved in considerable extent. His two *Apologies* and the *Dialogue With Trypho* cover 110 large pages of material. His date is not certain, but he seems to have been born in Neapolis (modern Nablus near ancient Shechem) and to have been martyred in A.D. 148 (Westcott, *op. cit.*, p. 99 n); others say 165 (*Ante-Nicene Fathers*, Vol. 1, 159 f.). He was a philosopher in his early days and carried over his philosophic bent into his writings. They show a boldness and a Christian humility which are still impressive. We also have fragments and shorter pieces from several of his contemporaries which add to the evidence for his age.

Justin refers to a number of the NT books by name and clearly uses others. According to Westcott, he uses all the Gospels, Romans, I and II Corinthians, Colossians, II Thessalonians, Hebrews and Revelation (Westcott, *op. cit.*, pp. 114 f., 167 ff.). His treatment of the Gospels is interesting. Writing as he did for non-Christians, he used the unique phrase "Memoirs of the Apostles," adding that they "are called Gospels" (*Ante-Nicene Fathers*, p. 185). He describes a Christian Sunday worship service as consisting of reading of the "Memoirs of the apostles, or the writings of the prophets," with a sermon, prayer, communion service, and collection (*ibid.*, p. 186)!

Justin's doctrine of Scripture is clearly that of full belief: "I am entirely convinced that no Scripture contradicts another." He adds that if a contradiction be imagined, "I shall admit rather that I do not understand what is recorded" (*ibid.*, p. 230). It is true that in this passage he was discussing the OT, but his reverence for the Memoirs is so clear that the statement can fairly be applied to the rest of the NT that he used.

Justin gives valuable information on the authorship of the Gospels. He says, "The apostles, in the Memoirs composed by them, which are called Gospels" have delivered to us the Lord's Supper. But he also quotes an item found only in Luke and says it is recorded "in the Memoirs which I say were drawn up by His apostles and those who followed them" (*ibid.*, p. 251).

Also he refers to an incident recorded only in Mark saying, "When it is said that He changed the name of one of the apostles to Peter; and when it is written in the Memoirs of him that this so happened, as well as that He changed the names of other two brothers . . . this was an announcement of the fact that it was He by whom Jacob was called Israel" (*ibid.*, p. 252). Westcott has noted that "him" in this quotation can only refer to Peter, and thus the Gospel of Mark is designated as the Memoirs of Peter (*op. cit.*, p. 114). Justin was doubtless aware that Mark wrote the second Gospel, but he was also aware of the witness of Papias and others that Mark wrote it down as Peter gave it. This could put Mark in a position similar to Tertius who wrote down Romans for Paul (Rom 16:22) or Silas whom Peter used on another occasion (I Pet 5:12). In this sense the Gospels are referred to by Justin indiscriminately as the work of "apostles" or as the work of "apostles and those who followed them." Note also the expression of Justin quoted above: "It is written in the Memoirs of him [Peter]." This formula of citation is one regularly used for the quotation of Scripture. It is clear that Justin had our Gospels, called them Gospels, and used them as Scripture. As already mentioned, he also uses seven other NT books. He refers to these more or less informally, but on one occasion quotes Revelation by name, ascribing it to the apostle John (*Ante-Nicene Fathers*, Vol. 1, 240).

Several other shorter witnesses for Justin's day have long been known. Basilides, the Gnostic heretic, and the Epistle of Barnabas add very little to Justin's testimony, but it is interesting that Basilides quotes I Corinthians and Romans as Scripture. The Epistle to Diognetus, probably somewhat earlier than Justin, includes allusions to Acts, Galatians, Ephesians, Philippians, I Timothy, Titus, and I Peter in addition to some of those quoted by Justin. Diognetus has one of the early references to the Bible as a unit: "The fear of the law is chanted, and the grace of the prophets is known, and the faith of the Gospels is established, and the tradition of the apostles is preserved, and the grace of the church exulted" (*ibid.*, p. 29). It is clear that the central books of the NT were received on a par with the OT at this time.

Papias is another witness, somewhat earlier than Justin. His works included a five-volume exposition of the oracles of the Lord, but unfortunately all have perished except a few quotations in other books. He is noted for his statement that Mark wrote down Peter's preaching and Matthew wrote his Gospel originally in Aramaic. Papias also mentions I John and "the Epistle of Peter" by name (*ibid.*, p. 155).

Until quite recently, only these half dozen witnesses remained from the mid-2nd cen. Now, however, the sands of Egypt have yielded new treasures. At Chenoboskion (*q.v.*), a little N of Thebes, peasants in 1945 found a cache of Gnostic writings (known as the Nag Hammadi Gnostic Texts, see BW, pp. 402–410). There were 13 books containing about 49 works. One of these books, the Jung Codex, was eventually spirited out of Egypt and is being published.

One of the interesting writings of the Jung Codex is the Gospel of Truth, written by the heretic Valentinus about A.D. 140. Irenaeus had attacked this work in his book *Against Heresies* (III.11.9), but no copies of it had survived. Now it is available (Kenneth Grobel, *The Gospel of Truth*). It is not an attempted fifth Gospel, but an exposition of what Valentinus thought to be the true gospel, i.e., Gnosticism.

But in his writing Valentinus quotes from or alludes to many NT books. Tertullian at A.D. 200 had written that Valentinus, though a heretic, had used all the NT. This one writing of Valentinus supports Tertullian's estimate.

In the study, *The Gospel of Truth and the New Testament,* van Unnik parallels the wording of Valentinus with many passages of the Gr. NT and concludes, "It is clear that the writer of the Gospel of Truth was acquainted with the Gospels, the Pauline epistles, Hebrews and Revelation, while there are traces of Acts, I John and I Peter" (*The Jung Codex,* by H. C. Puech, G. Quispel, and W. C. van Unnik, 1955, p. 122). This covers all the NT except small books totaling 11 chapters! He adds, "Round about 140–50 a collection of writings was known at Rome and accepted as authoritative which was virtually identical with our New Testament" (*ibid.,* p. 124). It will be remembered that Diognetus already put this collection on a par with the OT Scripture. The testimony of Valentinus is a welcome voice confirming the previously known witnesses and adding important details.

The Earliest Age – A.D. 95-120

Now take a further step backward to A.D. 95-120. This period overlapped the times of the apostle John. It includes three well-known witnesses, Clement of Rome, Ignatius, and Polycarp, all three of whom had known the apostles and two of whom sealed their faith in blood.

Clement wrote to the Corinthians at about A.D. 95. He quotes from I Corinthians by name and clearly uses Matthew, John, Romans, Ephesians, Hebrews, James, and possibly I Timothy and Titus (cf. Westcott, *op. cit.,* pp. 25 f., 48). Some of the quotations from Matthew have parallels in Mark and Luke, so it is not impossible that these Gospels are included in Clement's testimony.

Ignatius was a bishop in Antioch around the end of the 1st cen. The *Martyrdom of Ignatius (Ante-Nicene Fathers,* Vol. 1, 129) places his arrest in the reign of Trajan, but there is some uncertainty whether he was martyred in 107 or 116. In any case, his witness is valuable and significant. He wrote epistles to seven different churches as he was being carried to Rome for martyrdom. In these letters he quotes Ephesians by name. In his letter to the Philadelphians he seems to refer to NT writings as a corpus: "I flee to the Gospel as the flesh of Jesus and to the apostles as to the presbytery of the church. And let us also love the prophets" (*ibid.,* p. 82). We may compare the similar wording of Justin given above.

Again, he refers to some whom "neither have the prophets persuaded nor the law of Moses, nor the Gospel even to this day" (*ibid.,* p. 88). Another such reference is that we should "give heed to the prophets, and above all, to the Gospel" (*ibid.,* p. 89). He quotes verbatim from

Matthew, I and II Corinthians, and Ephesians, and clearly uses the phraseology of Luke, John, Romans, Galatians, Philippians, I Thessalonians, and I Timothy. Gregory remarks, "The Gospels of Matthew and John appear to have been either his favorites or the ones better known to him. He knew the epistles of Paul well" (C. R. Gregory, *Canon and Text of the New Testament*, p. 71). Ignatius and Clement together witness to the bulk of the present NT.

Shortly after Ignatius' martyrdom, Polycarp wrote a letter to the Philippians which has fortunately been preserved. Polycarp was instructed by the apostles, according to Irenaeus, and was in turn Irenaeus' teacher. He therefore directly links Irenaeus to the Apostolic Age. Polycarp was martyred in his old age about A.D. 155. But the best date for this epistle is shortly after Ignatius' death, therefore either 108 or 118 (cf. Westcott, *op. cit.*, p. 38). It is an early and precious monument of Christian antiquity.

Polycarp quoted the NT copiously. In the *Ante-Nicene Fathers* quotation marks are used to set off excerpts from Matthew, Luke, Acts, Romans, I Corinthians, Galatians, Ephesians, I and II Thessalonians, I and II Timothy, I Peter, and I John. Other books are clearly alluded to. Westcott claims the use of II Corinthians, Philippians, and possibly Ephesians and II Peter in addition (*ibid.*, p. 49). In Chap. XII Polycarp quotes Eph 4:26 as Scripture and in his previous chapter, he quotes I Corinthians and Philippians by name.

Putting together these three great men who began their Christian life in apostolic times, we see that they used the bulk of the NT. They refer by name to I Corinthians, Ephesians, and Philippians, and speak of the NT books as a united whole and as Scripture. The only NT books not witnessed to in these very early writings are Mark, Colossians, Philemon, II and III John, Jude, and Revelation.

Even these omissions are not unexplainable. Matthew and Mark are so very parallel that it is likely that quotations from Mark are concealed under the material from Matthew. Colossians was fully recognized in the next age, and was probably omitted in these early writings for lack of an occasion to quote it. The absence of Philemon, II and III John, and Jude from the list is not surprising either, as they are each but a chapter long and would have less chance of being quoted. With regard to Revelation, we should remember that it was probably written only about 20 years before the last of these men wrote. But Polycarp's pupil Irenaeus gives very explicit testimony concerning the date and authorship of Revelation. Indeed, Irenaeus uses all these books except Philemon and III John. We need not question them because of the silence of the very earliest witnesses.

The New Testament Testimony to Itself

Having traced the reception of the NT books back to the very edge of the apostolic times, we have found that there is evidence that practically all of them were accepted by the men who had learned from the apostles themselves. What was the beginning of this practice? What principle did the early church follow in selecting these books?

Two points should be emphasized to begin with. First, the apostles did not unthinkingly write miscellaneous letters and histories which were piously gathered only in a later age. Rather, the apostles wrote their works consciously and commanded the faithful to receive them.

Secondly, the early church did not pick and choose 27 books out of a mass of good literature, even apostolic literature. No early author refers to a lost writing of the apostles or clearly quotes from such, as far as we can tell. There may have been lost letters of Paul, but none were consciously rejected by the early church. Actually, it may be questioned if any were ever lost. Col 4:16 may well refer to the epistle to the Ephesians which may have been a general letter ("Ephesians" is not in some texts of Eph 1:1), and I Cor 5:9 may be an epistolary aorist referring to the letter Paul was then writing. Contrary to some statements, the spurious books of Barnabas, Apocalypse of Peter, Shepherd of Hermas, etc., may have fooled a few people, but they were never accepted in any serious fashion.

As to Paul's conscious intention in writing there is clear witness in his next to earliest epistle, "If any man obey not our word by this epistle . . . have no company with him" (II Thess 3:14). In his first epistle he claims that his preaching is not the "word of men," but "the word of God" (I Thess 2:13). In his great epistle of I Corinthians he speaks similarly (I Cor 2:13), and further he insists that "the things that I write unto you are the commandments of the Lord" (14:37). This is not contradicted, as some think, by his statements in I Cor 7:10, 12, etc., where he distinguishes his word from the Lord's. There he is only concerned to quote the words of Jesus on earth. It should be noted that Paul — and Luke — often refers thus to Jesus as "the Lord" before His crucifixion (cf. Mt 26:75 with Lk 22:61). Paul quotes the spoken words of Jesus where possible, but adds his own where the direct command of Jesus was lacking.

There is a reason why Paul could make these claims. He was an apostle. He makes much of this office (I Cor 15:8-9; 9:1; II Cor 11:5; 12:11-12). So do the early authors Clement, Ignatius, etc. They never confuse themselves with the apostolic circle. Similarly, John makes the claim of inspiration in Rev 1:1-3 and 22:18-19.

Christ had chosen the apostles for a purpose. He had promised them the Spirit in a special way. Jn 14:26 promises that He will quicken their memory concerning the words of Jesus. Jn 16:13 promises them that the Spirit will show them future things. The apostles are counted equal to the OT prophets by all the early authors. It is no wonder that their works were promptly equated to the OT Scripture.

This was already done in the NT itself. Three times one author calls the work of another inspired. The best known is II Pet 3:15–16 which refers to the epistles of Paul as Scripture. I Tim 5:18 quotes Lk 10:7 as Scripture. And Jude 17–18 quotes II Pet 3:3 as part of the words spoken by the apostles. These witnesses are not inconsequential. But they are directly in line with the witness of the post-apostolic fathers.

The above study of the early Church Fathers, plus other passages on the subject that could be cited, shows that the early church received as authoritative all the books written by apostles. This is stated categorically by Stonehouse: "It is clear that apostolicity was the organizing principle of the NT of the Old Catholic Church," i.e., the church of about 170 (Ned B. Stonehouse, *The Apocalypse in the Ancient Church*, pp. 4–5).

Warfield in his valuable studies on this subject admits that "apostolic authorship was, indeed, early confounded with canonicity" (B. B. Warfield, *Revelation and Inspiration*, p. 455). Warfield's own view is that those books were canonized which the apostles either wrote or declared that the church should accept. This view is quite safe, for the early witnesses show that the NT books were all by apostles except possibly Mark, Luke, Acts, Hebrews, James, and Jude. These books were used as early as the others, however (though the witness for Jude is not clear in the earliest time), and it is surely clear that they were accepted in the age of the apostles.

But there is more. The same witnesses who tell that Mark wrote his Gospel also tell that he wrote down Peter's preaching. The Gospels of Mark and Luke are called works of apostles by Justin Martyr. Tertullian later presents the same view (*Ante-Nicene Fathers*, Vol. 3, 252). Apparently these books were written under the superintendence of the apostles and thus were certified by them.

Much has been made of Hebrews as if it were not written by Paul. But we should note that no voice before A.D. 200 said it was non-Pauline. It was used by Clement at A.D. 95. The newly found Gospel of Truth by Valentinus makes definite use of it. In Egypt the claim of its Pauline authorship can be traced back through Clement of Alexandria to Pantaenus of about 140. And in Rome, Irenaeus not only uses Hebrews extensively, but in the second Pfaffian fragment refers to it as Pauline (see details in R. L. Harris, *Inspiration and Canonicity of the Bible*, p. 264). There has always been the problem that the language of Hebrews seems somewhat different from that of Paul's other epistles, but the thought and argument is quite Pauline. The truth may be that the book is by Paul, but was written for him by another helper (but not by Luke).

As to James and Jude, these were written by brothers (Jude 1) and we apparently have a twofold choice. There was a pair of brothers, James and Jude, in the apostolic company (Lk 6:16). There seems to have been another pair who were half brothers of Jesus – though this has been denied (Mt 13:55). The problems are complicated, but it would seem possible for men in this station to whom Christ had especially appeared after His resurrection (I Cor 15:7) to be counted as apostles extraordinary, if indeed these passages do not refer, after all, to the one pair of brothers, the sons of Alphaeus, the apostles.

In conclusion, it should be reemphasized that the early church did not falter in establishing its rule of faith, nor was there a welter of conflicting opinion with many different books now accepted, now rejected. In the later times of the 3rd cen. when the living witnesses had passed away, there was actually more debate and uncertainty than in the age immediately following the apostles. At first all the Gospels were fully accepted, and were not questioned in the 2nd cen. except by the heretic Marcion who denied the authority of all the apostles except Paul. Moreover, most of the Pauline epistles, including Hebrews, were used and several were quoted by name by the early writers who had known the apostles. We may lack as full evidence as we would wish for some of the smaller epistles, because the works of Papias and others have perished; but we should always remember that though we lack full evidence, Irenaeus, Justin, and such men had abundant evidence in their possession. As Tertullian challenged, if one questions these things, he may go to the churches where the original writings of the apostles were preserved (*Ante-Nicene Fathers*, Vol. 3, 260). These early men had the facts. We have most of them too. But as to some of the lesser supported epistles where our evidence is meager, we can safely rest in the testimony of such valiants for truth of the early days.

See Epistles, General; Inspiration.

Bibliography. A. H. Charteris, *The New Testament Scriptures,* New York: Carter, 1882. C. R. Gregory, *The Canon and Text of the New Testament,* New York: Scribner's, 1907. R. Laird Harris, *Inspiration and Canonicity of the Bible,* Grand Rapids: Zondervan, 1957. Everett F. Harrison, *Introduction to the New Testament,* Grand Rapids: Eerdmans, 1964. H. Puech, G. Quispel and W. C. van Unnik, *The Jung Codex,* ed. by F. L. Cross, New York: Morehouse-Gorham, 1955. Herman Ridderbos, "The Canon of the New Testament," *Revelation and the Bible,* ed. by C. F. H. Henry, Philadelphia: Presbyterian and Reformed, 1958. A. Roberts and J. Donaldson, ed., *The Ante-Nicene Fathers,* 9 vols., Buffalo: Christian Literature Publishing Co., 1886. H. C. Thiessen, *Introduction to the New Testament,* Grand Rapids: Eerdmans, 1954. Theodor

Zahn, *Introduction to the New Testament,* Grand Rapids: Kregel, 1953.

R. L. H.

CANTICLES. *See* Solomon, Song of.

CAPER, CAPERBERRY. *See* Plants.

CAPERNAUM (kȧ-pûr′nȧ-ŭm). After His rejection at Nazareth, Jesus determined to make Capernaum, on the Sea of Galilee, His headquarters. Matthew called it "his own city" (9:1). Here occurred some of the most significant events of His ministry. Nearby, the Master called as disciples the fishermen Simon, Andrew, James, and John (Mk 1:16–21, 29), and the tax collector Levi (Mt 9:1–9; cf. Mk 2:13–14). In the town He healed the centurion's servant (Mt 8:5 f.; Lk 7:1 f.), Peter's mother-in-law (Mt 8:14–15; Mk 1:30; Lk 4:38–39), the paralytic (Mt 9:1 f.; Mk 2:1 f.; Lk 5:18), and a demon-possessed man. Here also occurred the dispute over greatness (Mk 9:33–37), the discourse of Jn 6 (see v. 59), and other events in the life of Christ.

The location of Capernaum has been problematical, but the town is now almost certainly identified with Tell Hum on the NW shore of the Sea of Galilee about two and a half miles SW of where the Jordan enters the sea. Capernaum is a Gr. corruption of the Heb. *Kefar-Nahum,* "village of Nahum," so-called because the prophet's tomb used to be shown there. Tell ("mound of ") (Na) Hum is linguistically equatable with Capernaum.

It is to be remembered that Jesus pronounced a curse on Capernaum for her unbelief (Mt 11:23). The town degenerated in the 6th cen., and became uninhabited. The Franciscans bought the site in 1894 and cleared the ruins of an ancient synagogue there. This limestone structure had an interior of about 70 by 50 feet. Oriented S toward Jerusalem, it was joined on the E by a colonnaded court. Along the E and W sides of the lower floor of the prayer hall were stone benches for worshipers. An upper floor was probably used by women. The synagogue was decorated with figures of palm trees, vines, eagles, lions, centaurs, and boys carrying garlands. Although the structure probably dates to the 3rd cen. A.D., it very likely stood on the site of an earlier synagogue—perhaps in the same place and following the same plan as the

The Capernaum Synagogue. IIS

310

one built by the Roman centurion (Lk 7:5) and the one in which Jesus taught. Excavations are presently being conducted in an area between the synagogue and the shore of the Sea of Galilee. Remains of an early Christian church have come to light there.

H. F. V.

CAPH. The eleventh letter of the Heb. alphabet. *See* Alphabet. This letter is used in the KJV as the heading of the eleventh section of Ps 119, where each verse begins with this letter.

CAPHTOR (kăf'tôr), **CAPHTORIM** (kăf'tô-rĭm). According to the Bible, Caphtor is the place of origin of the Philistines (Amos 9:7; Jer 47:4; cf. Gen 10:14; Deut 2:23). The name appears first as Kaptara in an Akkadian text which locates it "beyond the Upper Sea" (*c.* 2200 B.C.), available in a later MS copy. Other references are found in tablets from Mari and Ugarit. By the term *keftiu* Egyptian texts of *c.* 2200 to 1200 B.C. identify this with Crete (*q.v.*), an island kingdom with which Egypt had commercial relations. Some scholars think it more likely that the term was used by the 13th cen. to designate the Aegean islands. The Philistines are called Cherethites (*q.v.*) in Zeph 2:5 and Ezk 25:16, and the LXX translates this "Cretans." The theory that Caphtor is to be identified as Crete rests, therefore, upon the LXX and the Egyptian texts. *See* Philistines.

A recently published tablet from Mari, dated *c.* 1780–1760 B.C., mentions a Caphtorite merchant stationed at Ugarit to whom a shipment of tin was sent (IEJ, XXI [1971], 31–38).

G. A. T.

CAPPADOCIA (kăp'à-dō'shà). An inland province of Asia Minor, bounded on the E by the Euphrates River, on the N by Pontus, on the W by Lycaonia, and on the S by the Taurus Mountains. It was a wild, barren, mountainous country, with the highest peak (Arqâeus) reaching 13,100 feet. The earliest references to Cappadocia are from the time of Hammurabi, when it was part of the Babylonian Empire. It was occupied by Hittite civilization from 2000 B.C. In later years, it was a satrapy of Persia, and was made a Roman province in A.D. 17. Visitors from Cappadocia were in Jerusalem at Pentecost (Acts 2:9), and Peter addresses one of his epistles to scattered Christians in this province (I Pet 1:1). Caesarea in Cappadocia was an early center of Christianity, and Basil was its most famous son. It remained a part of the Eastern Empire until captured by the Seljuk Turks in the 11th cen.

C. K. H.

CAPTAIN. This term occurs some 214 times in the canonical Scriptures (KJV), of which 182 occurrences are in the OT. The word is the KJV translation of 14 different Heb. and four Gr. terms. It means an officer or leader either civilian or military.

1. By far the most frequent term in the OT is *śar* where it means "the captain of the guard"

Decorations of the Capernaum Synagogue. HFV

(Gen 37:36), the "captain of the host" (II Sam 10:16), or chariot officer (I Kgs 22:31). Among the men in the Bible thus designated were Joseph's master Potiphar, Abner (II Sam 2:8), Phicol (Gen 21:22), and captains of thousands, hundreds, fifties and tens in the army of Israel (Num 31:48; Deut 1:15).

2. Heb. *nāśî'* or "exalted one," was applied exclusively to the tribal leaders in the book of Numbers.

3. "Governor" is the meaning of *pehâ*, usually a reference to officers in foreign armies; e.g., Dan 6:7, "the princes, the counselors, and the captains" (see RSV).

4. Heb. *rab* (25 occurrences) designated the leader of the occupying troops of the Babylonians (Jer 39:9).

5. Heb. *shālîsh* is translated "captain" 13 times and refers to subordinate officers in Israel's army (II Kgs 10:25).

6–14. Heb. *rō'sh*, the word which is translated "captain" in ten instances, means "head." The other eight Heb. synonyms occur from one to six times each and are rendered in the RSV as "prince," a charismatic leader (I Sam 9:16), "sentry" (Jer 37:13), "marshal" (Jer 51:27), and "chief" (Josh 10:24). It is remarkable that such a variety of terms existed for which there seems to have been no technical precision in meaning.

15. The NT term normally used in the Roman army to designate the officer over the centurions was the *chiliarchos*, "chief captain," meaning the ruler of a thousand (Acts 21:31).

16. Gr. *stratēgos* in the term "captain of the temple" refers to the chief of police among the Jewish leaders. Such an officer was in charge of the men who went to arrest the apostles (Acts 4:1; 5:24, 26).

17. The *stratopedarchēs* occurs once (Acts 28:16) and means "chief of the camp."

18. Gr. *archēgos* means "pioneer" (RSV), "leader," or "founder," and is applied to Jesus in Heb 2:10.

G. A. T.

CAPTIVITY. The term "captivity" in the Bible can refer to the captivity of Israel or to that of other nations (Amos 1:5). From very ancient times victorious armies followed the practice of taking from their captives those they desired for slaves and wives (Deut 21:10 ff.). Such removal from their land nearly always meant the destruction of national existence and a feeling of severance from the care and protection of their local or national god; indeed, it implied the defeat of that deity (cf. Isa 52:2-5; Jer 50:29). Beginning with the Assyrians, a new technique for dealing with captive peoples was used, that of deportation. Great numbers of people were captured in war and deported and settled in another part of the empire. This practice was continued by the Babylonians, but was reversed by the Persians in 536 B.C.

There was hardly a time in Israel's history when all her people were at home in Palestine. In fact, Israel's history began in Egyptian bondage, and though that bondage is not referred to as a captivity, the people were slaves nonetheless and were not free to leave. There are three main oppressions of the people of Israel on foreign soil mentioned in the Bible: in Egypt, in Assyria, and in Babylon (cf. Isa 52:3-6).

Limited captivities for some Israelites probably began as early as the reigns of Rehoboam and Jeroboam I (c. 926 B.C.), when Shishak, pharaoh of Egypt, invaded Palestine (I Kgs 14:25-28). Tiglath-pileser III of Assyria (745-727 B.C.) captured the cities of Naphtali

(II Kgs 15:29) and carried the inhabitants of the tribes of Naphtali, Reuben, Gad and E Manasseh (I Chr 5:26) captive to Assyria (c. 733 B.C.). In 722/21 B.C. the city of Samaria fell to Sargon II of Assyria and the captives were taken to Halah (cf. Ob 20, RSV) on the Habor, the river of Gozan, and to the cities of the Medes (II Kgs 17:6; 18:11). Sargon's inscription indicates that 27,290 Israelites were deported. By following heathen deities they had brought upon themselves the covenant curse pronounced by Yahweh their God for such disobedience (Deut 28:25, 32, 36, 41; II Kgs 17:7-23).

With the fall of the northern kingdom to Assyria, the fate of the covenant people lay with Judah. Again certain individuals or small groups were carried away captive until Jerusalem herself was destroyed in 586 B.C and many of the people were deported to Babylon by Nebuchadnezzar. Three of Judah's last five kings were carried into captivity: Jehoahaz to Egypt, Jehoiachin and Zedekiah to Babylon. Daniel, Hananiah, Mishael, and Azariah were also carried away to Babylon. Jeremiah and Baruch were carried to Egypt against their wishes by some of their own countrymen. There were Jewish settlements already in Egypt when Jeremiah arrived. Such groups had come either as mercenaries or as refugees from Assyrian and Babylonian oppression.

Those taken as captives to Babylonia must have had times of bitterness. They were humili-

Prisoners of war represented on a relief in the palace of Ashurbanipal, Nineveh. LM

ated by the memory of the destruction of their beloved Jerusalem. If faithful to their God, they were subjected to the scorn and taunts of their captors (Ps 137). Yet life for the majority of the Israelites born in captivity does not seem to have been too hard. When the opportunity came for the Jews to return to Palestine in 536 B.C., only a small percentage came back. It has been estimated that at the time of Christ a million Jews were living in Egypt, a million more were living in Asia Minor and Syria, another million were living in Babylon, one hundred thousand were living in Italy and Sicily, and another hundred thousand were living in N Africa.

The Babylonian exile or captivity of Israel produced some remarkable prophetic personages, such as Ezekiel and Daniel. It was a period of great literary activity. It gave birth to the synagogue. It was at the very heart of the biblical understanding of divine judgment and revelation.

See Israel; Dispersion; Chronology, OT; Restoration and Persian Period.

R. L. S.

CARBON 14 DATING. This is a method of dating ancient objects made from organic substances, all of which contain carbon, by measuring the amount of radioactive carbon remaining after years of disintegration. The method was elaborated by Willard Libby of the University of Chicago and has been widely applied. It has proved useful and reliable in many instances, but problems and inconsistencies also have been observed. Its usefulness is admittedly limited to the last 50,000 years.

The method is based on the fact that there are two kinds (or isotopes) of carbon atoms—the normal kind called carbon 12 (atomic weight 12) and a heavy type with two extra neutrons in the nucleus called carbon 14. The latter kind is unstable and decomposes by radioactive decay into nitrogen. In the upper atmosphere cosmic rays strike atoms of nitrogen, which has seven neutrons and seven protons in its nucleus, and transform them into carbon 14, which has eight neutrons and six protons. This mingles with the normal carbon 12, which is in the atmosphere in the form of carbon dioxide and constitutes about one part in a trillion of the carbon in the air.

The carbon in the air is taken in by growing plants, and by photosynthesis is joined to water and becomes cellulose, starch, sugars, etc. These plants are then eaten by the animals, and thus all living things have the same proportion of carbon 14 and carbon 12 that the atmosphere does—about one part in a trillion. Even sea water has dissolved carbon dioxide, and the carbonates of seashells show approximately this same proportion.

However, when a living organism dies, it ceases to take in any more carbon from the atmosphere directly or indirectly. The radioactive carbon 14 in the dead organism slowly throws off energy and changes into nitrogen. The result is that after a sufficiently long time the object will have no carbon 14 left, but only the stable carbon 12. By measuring the amount of carbon 14 remaining in a sample, the age of the sample can thus be calculated. Experiments have determined that if a gram of pure carbon 14 is left for 5,570 years, one-half of it will have turned into nitrogen. If this is left another 5,570 years, another half will have changed and only one-fourth gram of carbon 14 will remain. After a third 5,570 year period, only one-eighth gram of carbon 14 will remain, and so on. This figure of 5,570 years is called the half-life.

In analyzing a sample of old organic material we must determine how much carbon 14 was there originally. This is done by assuming that the proportion of carbon 14 to carbon 12 in living things many years ago was the same as it has been recently, i.e., one to one trillion. Thus if we have a sample of old carbon weighing one trillion grams it would have had in it originally one gram of carbon 14 and all the rest carbon 12. If now we measure this sample and find only one-fourth gram of carbon 14, we conclude that the sample has lain dead for two half-lives, or 11,140 years. One gram of carbon taken from a living organism gives rise to approximately 15 disintegrations per minute from the carbon 14 it contains; a gram of carbon from a sample dead 5,570 years yields about 7.5 disintegrations per minute.

The method of analysis is relatively simple. A specimen of organic matter containing carbon is collected. It is carefully separated from any modern roots or mold, etc. Then it is burned and the carbon dioxide collected. This carbon dioxide is purified and the carbon from it is redeposited in a container. The container is placed in a space heavily shielded from stray radiation and the carbon 14 present is measured with a Geiger counter or similar device which counts the rate of breaking down of carbon 14. From these data the amount of carbon 14 can be calculated, and from the amount of carbon 12 present the original amount of carbon 14 can be calculated. The difference is a measure of the time taken for the carbon 14 decomposition.

There are certain assumptions and limitations in the method of which we should be aware. First, it is held that the rate of carbon 14 decay never changes. Experiments with pressure and temperature variation do not vary it. However, it is not so clear that stray radiation might not have some effect—probably slight in most cases.

A second assumption is that the proportion of carbon 14 to carbon 12 in the air has always been constant. This involves two other assumptions. First, that cosmic rays have always been the same. Actually we can observe minor variations in them but do not directly know the past situation. Their intensity in space may have been invariable, but their intensity in the stratosphere may indeed have changed. Secondly, it is assumed the amount of carbon 12 in the air has always been the same. But this is a questionable assumption. Coal-burning factories in recent years have increased the carbon 12 in the air. Volcanic activity could have changed it, as could other unknown circumstances. The extent of such variation would presumably not have been great, unless there were a revolution of climate or of the earth's circumstances. It could be theorized that if there were a great change of climate at the time of Noah's flood, dates determined from objects prior to the deluge would possibly be inexact.

One obvious limitation of the method is that it must be used on carbon. It therefore cannot date dry fossil bones, as these are largely calcium phosphate. If fresh bones were burned over a camp fire and the fat and marrow turned to charcoal, the charcoal could be dated, however. Wooden beams in Egyptian tombs have been dated satisfactorily. Charcoal from camp sites is another good subject.

A last limitation that comes to mind is that this method cannot date very old material. After about 50,000 years the carbon 14 remaining becomes so scarce that measurement is not practical. Therefore this method cannot date directly the bones of fossil men nor can it substantiate the claims of ages of 100,000 years, 300,000 years, etc., for them. These ages are still reckoned by the older geological methods, usually by comparison with glacial deposits.

The dates have proved acceptable with some exceptions back to 3000 B.C. when history begins in Egypt. The lowest levels of Jericho have been dated to 7000 B.C. by a series of self-consistent readings. The most glaring inconsistencies have been the datings of Jarmo in Iraq, which was clearly inhabited only a short time but whose datings vary from about 3300 B.C. to 9275 B.C. Something here is badly wrong. With this in mind, there is a tendency not to trust too implicitly an individual age determination, but to get a series of consistent dates, if possible.

On the positive side, carbon 14 of spruce logs in Wisconsin and of some glacial remains in Europe has, in the minds of most, brought down the age of the last glacier from 25,000 years ago to about 11,000 years. Since the interval after the last glacier is used to calculate the ages of the other glaciers, their dates should be correspondingly reduced, though this is usually not yet done. A notable exception is Albright (*Archaeology of Palestine*, pp. 51–61), who formulates a much lower chronology based on radiocarbon dating.

Another striking use of the method is to date the entombment of the Siberian mammoths at about 11,000 years ago. Albright suggested a correlation of the last glacier and what he speaks of as "traditions of the Great Flood" at about 9000 B.C. (*From the Stone Age to Christianity*, 2nd ed., p. 9). Much work remains to be done, but certainly something of major proportions happened at a time given as about 9000 B.C. by carbon 14 dating.

Bibliography. L. J. Briggs and K. F. Weaver, "How Old Is It?" *National Geographic Magazine,* CXIII (1958), 234–255. W. F. Libby, *Radiocarbon Dating,* 2nd ed., Chicago: Univ. of Chicago, 1955. E. A. Olson, "Radiocarbon Dating," JASA, XI (1959), 2–11.

R. L. H.

CARBUNCLE. *See* Jewels.

CARCAS (kär'kăs). One of seven chamberlains ordered to summon Queen Vashti before King Ahasuerus (Est 1:10).

CARCASE. The spelling is now carcass. It refers to the dead body of a beast (Jud 14:8), or sometimes in a contemptuous way to the dead body of a human being (Josh 8:29). The use of the word as applied to a living body is not found in either the OT or NT.

A Syro-Hittite bas relief from Carchemish. Hittite Museum, Ankara

CARCHEMISH (kär'kĕ-mĭsh). Also spelled Charchemish in II Chr 35:20 (cf. Jer 46:2).

A city on the upper Euphrates mentioned in ancient records from the beginning of the 2nd mil. B.C. as *Karkamis* in Babylonian documents, as *Kargamish* and *Gargamish* in Assyrian inscriptions, as *Krkmsh* in Egyptian records, and as *Karkᵉmish* in Hebrew. It was an important administrative center in the Hittite Empire;

several Syrian city-states (such as Ugarit) were, as vassals of the Hittite king, subject to Carchemish, according to royal Hittite archives found at Ras Shamra. After the end of the Hittite Empire (c. 1200 B.C.), Carchemish retained its Hittite culture and became an independent and important Hittite city-state. It paid tribute to Ashurnasirpal II of Assyria (884–859 B.C.) and to Shalmaneser III (859–824 B.C.), but was also often at war with Assyria. In 717 B.C. the city was destroyed and its population deported by Sargon II (722–705 B.C.). However, it rose again to importance, and after the fall of Nineveh in 612 B.C. was occupied by the Egyptians under Pharaoh Necho (see II Chr 35:20), who made it the center of his control over Syria for a few years. In 605 B.C. he was defeated there by Nebuchadnezzar II, according to the Babylonian Chronicle and Jer 46:2.

The site of ancient Carchemish, now called Jerablus, lies 63 miles NE of Aleppo, on the W bank of the Euphrates. It was excavated for the British Museum 1876–79 and 1912–14. In the first season of excavations in 1878 a large number of Syro-Hittite sculptures and Hittite hieroglyphic inscriptions came to light. Excavators of the second expedition discovered a fortified citadel at the summit of the mound, below which lay the city which was protected by a wall pierced with monumental gateways set between flanking towers. The lower part of the walls of these towers was covered with Hittite sculptures and inscriptions. Remains of a temple and a palace were also found, but they were not sufficiently investigated.

The main feature of the city was an irregular piazza or town square at the foot of the citadel approached from the S section of the city by a processional gateway. A monumental stairway led from this piazza up to the citadel on the N.

Bibliography. William Hallo, "Carchemish," BW, pp. 165–169. D. G. Hogarth, C. L. Woolley and T. E. Lawrence, *Carchemish,* London: British Museum, 1914, 1921, and 1952.

           S. H. H. and D. C. B.

CARE, CARES. A number of Heb. and Gr. words are translated by the English word "care." In the OT the following terms are each so rendered once: *de'āgâ,* meaning anxious care (Ezk 4:16); *hărādâ,* referring to a fearful anxiety (II Kgs 4:13); and *dābār,* meaning word or matter (in I Sam 10:2 a matter for concern). In Phil 4:10 the infinitive *phronein,* which is translated substantivally, refers to the act of thinking of someone. In II Cor 7:12; 8:16, *spoudē* is used in the sense of earnest concern. The NT term most commonly rendered by the noun "care" is *merimna* (Mt 13:22; Lk 21:34; II Cor 11:28; I Pet 5:7), which depicts anxiety as a destructive attitude or state of distraction.

CAREAH (kȧ-rē'ȧ). Father of the captains Johanan and Jonathan, who came to Gedaliah, the Babylonian governor of Judah (II Kgs 25:23). In other Scriptures the name is spelled Kareah (*q.v.*).

Mount Carmel with Haifa at its foot. IIS

CARMEL (kär'měl)

1. A mountain promontory 556 feet high situated between the plain of Esdraelon and the Mediterranean Sea (Jer 46:18). It was so called because of its thickly wooded aspect, which was even more striking in ancient times than it is today (Isa 33:9; Amos 1:2; 9:3; Mic 7:14). From a single peak, however, the name passed to the range of hills associated with it, thus designating the mountainous ridge more than 20 miles in length, from three to eight miles in breadth to the W and NW of Esdraelon, 1,742 feet above sea level at its summit.

Because of exposure to the sea winds, Carmel is well watered. Ancient sanctuaries to the weather deities were built on its heights; thus it was a fitting site for the contest between Elijah and the prophets of the Canaanite storm-god Baal (I Kgs 18). The Egyptians called Carmel a sacred cape, and in the Amarna letters from Canaanite princes it was known as Ginti-Kirmil. Carmel, meaning "garden" or "orchard," is famed in literary composition for its natural beauty (Song 7:5; Isa 35:2; Nah 1:4).

From 1929 to 1934 Garrod and McCown, under the auspices of the British School of Archaeology and the American School of Prehistoric Research, excavated caves on the lower western slopes of Mount Carmel known as Wadi el Mugharah, "valley of the caves." Specimens include evidence of a flint industry from early Paleolithic to Mesolithic times, as well as human bones of both Neanderthal man and Homo Sapiens. Animal bones in the caves have also thrown light on climatic changes in Palestine during the Stone Age (BW, p. 397).

2. A city of Judah, in the uplands near Hebron, named with Maon and Ziph (Josh 15:55). It was the scene of incidents in the lives of Saul and David. Saul set up a memorial stone there

Carmel Caves. HFV

(I Sam 15:12). It was the home of Nabal, the churlish and drunken flock-master, whose widow Abigail David married (I Sam 25); and also of Hezrai, one of David's mighty men (II Sam 23:35; I Chr 11:37). It is represented by the modern el-Kermel, about ten miles to the SE of Hebron. There are considerable ruins from Crusader days.

V. G. D.

CARMELITE (kär′mĕ-līt). A native of the Judean Carmel. Among those thus named were Nabal, the husband of Abigail (I Sam 30:5, etc.), and Hezrai, one of David's mighty men (II Sam 23:35).

CARMI (kär′mī), **CARMITES** (kär′mīts)
1. A son of Reuben, and founder of a tribal family (Gen 46:9; Ex 6:14; Num 26:6).
2. A Judahite (I Chr 2:7), son of Zabdi, according to Josh 7:1, and father of Achan, who is given the name of "Achar" in I Chr 2:7. The Carmi of I Chr 4:1 is probably a scribal variant of Caleb (q.v.).
The Carmites were a family of Judah whose head was Carmi.

CARNAL. This word occurs only in the NT, although "carnally" is found three times in the OT (KJV). "Carnal" appears in the NT 11 times, "carnally" once. "Carnal" means "pertaining to the flesh." The noun *sarx* basically means the flesh of an animal or person, or the meat of an animal. However, in the NT, "carnal" has sometimes to do with literal flesh, and sometimes with the old Adamic fallen human nature to be found in all men alike. For the literal use, see Rom 15:27; I Cor 9:11; II Cor 10:4; Heb 7:16; 9:10; for the metaphorical, Rom 7:14; 8:7; I Cor 3:1, 3, 4 where reference is to the old nature, or "old man."
Paul admits to being carnal, that is, still having a fallen nature. He says the carnal mind is enmity against God, and brands the Corinthian Christians as carnal, which he defines as behaving like natural, unregenerate men. When he says "to be carnally minded is death" (Rom

8:6), he is talking of those who have only a fallen nature and have not the new nature, those who are unsaved.
See Anthropology; Flesh.

J. A. S.

CARNELIAN. *See* Jewels.

CAROB. *See* Plants.

CARPENTER. *See* Occupations: Carpenter, Craftsman.

CARPUS (kär′pŭs). Mentioned only in II Tim 4:13 as a man of Troas with whom Paul left his cloak. Such a reference seems to indicate a degree of friendship, or possibly that Paul had stayed in his home. The word *phelonēs* (alternate spelling of *phainolēs*) was used of a coarse outer garment worn to protect one against the elements while traveling. Had Paul just "forgotten" his cloak? Or possibly, due to warm weather, had he temporarily left it behind?

CARSHENA (kär-shē′nà). The first named among the "seven princes of Persia and Media" under King Ahasuerus (Est 1:14).

CART. The Heb. term *'ăgālâ* is translated both "cart" and "wagon" (q.v.). In I Sam 6:7–14 the Philistines made a new cart to transport the ark of God back to Israel. Such Philistine carts with two solid wheels are depicted in a relief of Rameses III at Medinet Habu, c. 1170 B.C. In II Sam 6:3 and I Chr 13:7 a cart was used by Uzzah and Ahio to bring the ark to Jerusalem from the house of Abinadab. Isa 28:27–28 refers to a cart wheel used as a threshing instrument, and Amos 2:13 may refer to the same thing in the words "a cart . . . full of sheaves."
In Ps 46:9 the Heb. term *'ăgālâ* is translated "chariot" in the KJV, and probably refers to supply wagons used for military purposes.

CARVING. *See* Occupations.

CASEMENT. *See* Lattice.

CASIPHIA (kà-sĭf′ĭ-à). An unidentified place in N Babylonia near the river Ahava, on the route from Babylonia to Jerusalem, to which Ezra sent for "ministers for the house of our God" (Ezr 8:17).

CASLUHIM (kăs′lŭ-hĭm). The name of an unidentified people mentioned in Gen 10:14 and I Chr 1:12 as descended from Mizraim (Egypt).

CASSIA. *See* Plants.

CASTANET. *See* Music.

CASTAWAY (Gr. *adokimos*, "not approved, rejected, disqualified").
While this Gr. term occurs a number of times in the NT, the only passage where the KJV

translates it "castaway" is I Cor 9:27. Etymologically it is related to the verb *dokimazein*, which means to test or to approve as a result of testing. *Adokimos*, then, describes a person or an object which has been tested and disapproved. These words were used of such things as metals, coins, and horses.

In I Cor 9:27, however, the context demands an athletic setting, perhaps drawn from the Isthmian games held near Corinth. The picture is that of a contending athlete who is disqualified because of an infraction of the rules. In saying that he had preached (Gr. *kēryssein*) to others, Paul seems to be drawing upon the imagery of the herald (Gr. *kēryx*) who announced the rules of the game. The apostle was engaged in the contest of Christian life and service. In fact, he had proclaimed to others the standards for that life. It would have been most tragic if the very one who had announced the rules should, through submission to his carnal nature, violate those rules and be disqualified from further participation and thus from the reward. In so speaking, Paul is not referring to the loss of salvation, but to the forfeiture of reward for service. The crown (Gr. *stephanos*) of I Cor 9:25 was the wreath of pine or olive leaves placed on the head of the victorious athlete, a figure commonly used in the NT to picture the believer's reward. *See* Crowns.

D. W. B.

CASTING. *See* Occupations: Metal, Workers in.

CASTLE. Ordinarily a fortified place, building, or citadel (*q.v.*). Several words are translated "castle" in the KJV; only two in the RSV. It is used in the sense of encampment in Gen 25:16; Num 31:10; I Chr 6:54 (KJV). "Castle" (RSV is better than "palace" in Neh 7:2. The castle referred to in Acts 21:34 was the Roman fortress of Antonia attached to the temple area. The RSV and NASB "barracks" does not sufficiently indicate its strength as a fortress.

CASTOR AND POLLUX. *See* Gods, False.

CASTRATION. The act of emasculating by removing the testicles. Castrated animals were not acceptable as sacrificial offerings (Lev 22:24, RSV). This operation performed on a human resulted in his being known as a eunuch (*q.v.*). The Mosaic law excluded such a man from the congregation (*q.v.*) of the Lord (Deut 23:1, RSV), but God promised through Isaiah to relax this prohibition (56:3–7), which was fulfilled under the new covenant (see Acts 8:27, 38).

CATAPULT. An ancient military machine used for discharging darts, stones, or other objects. The motive power was obtained by a strong lever working on an axis, which was tightly strained with twisted ropes and suddenly released. Although this machine is not mentioned specifically in the Bible, it was in common us-

age by the Assyrians and other peoples during the 1st mil. B.C. It may be referred to under the term "engines" in II Chr 26:15, invented to shoot arrows and great stones. *See* Engines; Armor.

CATERPILLAR. *See* Animals: Locust, III.29.

CATHOLIC EPISTLES. A traditional designation for the last seven epistles in the NT. *See* Epistles, General.

The term "catholic" is derived from Gr. *katholikos*, "general," "worldwide," "universal." With the exception of II and III John, each of which is written to an individual person or church, these epistles were addressed to a wider audience than one local church or individual. Later, the word "catholic" was applied to epistles which were universally accepted by the church and were orthodox in doctrine; thus the term became synonymous with "genuine" or "canonical."

CATTLE. *See* Animals, I.6.

CAUL

1. A word applying to a membrane fastened to the liver and mentioned along with fat and kidneys which Aaron's sons were to burn on the altar (Lev 3:4–5). One explanation is that it refers to the fatty mass which covers the liver (*q.v.*). Another is that it denotes the "liver-net, or stomach-net, which commences at the division between the right and left lobes of the liver" (KD on Lev 3:4).

2. In Hos 13:8 "the caul of their heart" may be understood to mean "the enclosure of the heart, i.e., their ribs or their breast" (IB).

3. In Isa 3:18 the word "cauls" refers to a kind of headdress.

CAUSEWAY. This word occurs in I Chr 26:16, 18, and refers to a series or flight of steps leading up into the temple.

CAVALRY. *See* Army; War.

CAVE. The soft limestone hills of Palestine are marked by innumerable artificial and natural caves. During prehistoric times many of the caves were used for human shelter, as shown by the artifacts discovered in them. Later, Lot and his daughters occupied a cave (Gen 19:30), as did David (I Sam 22:1), and Elijah (I Kgs 19:9). Human occupation of caves continued all through the biblical period. Jewish sectarians apparently lived in some caves and stored precious manuscripts in others near Qumran by the Dead Sea. The inn at Bethlehem at the time of the birth of Jesus was built over a cave which was used as a stable. Even today many caves in Judea are used as places of shelter for man and beast.

Caves were used in conducting heathen ritualistic practices (Isa 65:4, Berkeley), as at Gezer. There are many references in the Bible to

Numerous caves dot the cliffs at Qumran.
HFV

caves used as places of refuge (Josh 10:16; Jud 6:2; I Sam 13:6; 22:1; II Sam 23:13; Heb 11:38). Caves were natural burial places and were used as tombs in every period of human history. Abraham purchased the cave of Machpelah for use as a tomb for Sarah (Gen 23:19). This cave became the sepulcher of Abraham, Isaac, Rebekah, Leah, and Jacob (Gen 25:9; 49:30-31; 50:13). In the NT the tomb of Lazarus was a cave (Jn 11:38). Caves were also used as prisons (Jer 37:16-17; 38:6), and as cisterns. *See also* Den; Pit.

A. C. S.

CEDAR. *See* Plants.

CEDRON. *See* Kidron.

CELESTIAL BODIES. *See* Astronomy.

CELIBACY. Remaining in an unmarried state for conscientious, religious, or moral reasons. The term is often confined to men, but applies equally to women, such as the vestal virgins of heathenism and the nuns of Roman Catholicism.

As a phenomenon, celibacy is not confined to Roman Catholicism. The Buddhist priests and many of their laity practice the strictest and most exacting rules of celibacy, as do many heathen witch doctors.

The practice is justified among Roman Catholics, first, upon the basis of Christ's words in Mt 19:4-12: "There be eunuchs, which have made themselves eunuchs for the kingdom of heaven's sake" (v. 12); and, second, upon Paul's insistence that the unmarried state is preferable (I Cor 7:8, 40). Christ's statement certainly does not command celibacy—only some can bear it. Rather, He commended marriage as ordained of God from the beginning (Mt 19:3 ff.). Paul saw celibacy as expedient for him and certain others in his day. He thought the Lord's coming was too near, the time too short to become involved in marriage (I Cor 7:29). Celibacy leaves men free of the cares of marriage. Yet it can be dangerous, and must

then not be attempted (v. 36 f.). Paul spoke of himself as being as free to have a wife of his own as Peter and the brothers of Christ (I Cor 9:5). Paul's position was that celibacy, in his opinion, was the best for him (I Cor 7:6, 40).

The Roman Catholic view of physical nature actually lies behind this practice of celibacy. Having adopted the heathen view that the material, the body in particular, is inherently evil, as it is expressed in neo-Plotinian philosophy, this church seeks holiness for its priests and nuns through a life of absolute poverty, chastity, and obedience led in monasteries and nunneries. The pagan practices of a similar nature also have contributed to a certain syncretistic adoption of heathen customs in the matter. Celibacy often leads to great evil and gross sin, since it places impossible burdens upon both men and women, as has often been proved by the testimony of those who have left Romanism.

Paul thoroughly condemns those who forbid to marry (I Tim 4:3; cf. Col 2:16-23) when he says this will be a mark of apostates in the latter days. The mention of the 144,000 as virgins in the Great Tribulation of Rev 14:1, 4 may bear out Paul's conviction that in times of great persecution it can be expedient that the Lord's servants be unmarried.

R. A. K.

CELLAR. In I Chr 27:27-28 the word means merely storehouses or rooms where wine and oil were stored. In Lk 11:33 (ASV) the Gr. word means literally "a hidden place," i.e., anything similar to a vault, crypt, or cellar.

CENCHREA (sĕn′krē-à). This seaport of Corinth was about nine miles from the metropolis, on the E side of the isthmus. Paul embarked from Cenchrea at the close of his first visit to Corinth (Acts 18:18). It was the site of a church by the time of the writing of Romans, where mention is made of Phoebe, a servant (deaconess) of that church (Rom 16:1).

Area of the old port of Cenchrea. JR

CENSER. The Heb. *maḥtâ,* commonly translated "censer," is a general word meaning any sort of firepan. It is used not only for true censers, i.e., vessels in which coals of fire were placed to burn incense (Lev 10:1; 16:12; Num 16:6 ff.), but of ordinary firepans used to carry away the ashes of the altar (Ex 27:3) and of snuffdishes, the trays used to catch the debris of the lamps when they were trimmed (Ex 25:38; 37:23).

Another Heb. word, *miqtereth,* means literally "a vessel to burn incense" (II Chr 26:19; Ezk 8:11). This specialized utensil may have been a decorated rod ending in a small hand-shaped bowl as found in Egypt. In the NT the KJV translation "golden censer" of Gr. *thumiatērion* in Heb 9:4 probably refers to the golden altar of incense in the holy place of the tabernacle rather than a censer (cf. RSV). *See* Altar; Incense.

The censers were ordinarily made of copper or bronze, but in some cases they were of gold (I Kgs 7:50; II Chr 4:22; Rev 8:3, 5). Since they were a part of the tabernacle or temple, they were treated as sacred objects (Num 4:14), and even in the hands of rebels they were holy, having been dedicated to God (Num 16:36 - 40).

Scripture contains no description of size or shape of the censers. They were probably either shallow pans or bowls when used as true censers, or flat, shovel-like utensils when used as ash pans. The censers of Korah and his company could be flattened out and used to plate the altar of burnt offering (Num 16:39). According to Jewish tradition they were of various sizes and had long or short handles (Mishnah Yoma iv.4). *See* Firepan.

A similar utensil was the small ladle or spoon *(kaph),* literally a "hand" or "palm" (Ex 25:29; 37:16; Num 4:7; I Kgs 7:50; II Kgs 25:14). Stone or marble incense spoons have been found at Tell Beit Mirsim (ANEP, #592), at Megiddo (BA, IV [1941], 30), and at Hazor (BA, XX [1957], 40 and fig. 7). On some of these a hand is carved with the fingers grasping the "cup" of the ladle. A hollow tube opens into the cup, perhaps to enable one to blow on the incense to speed its burning. The Twelfth Dynasty tomb of Amenemhet depicts a priest carrying a long white (ivory?) handle ending in a cupped "hand" supporting a bowl in which incense is burning (*Illustrated Family Encyclopedia of the Living Bible,* II, 75).

P. C. J.

CENSUS. The biblical concept of enrollment, numbering, or census is found in the Heb. *pāqad,* "to visit," "examine," "review," "muster," "number"; also *sāpar* and *mānâ;* the Septuagint *arithmos,* "number," "amount," "sum," "unit of troops"; the NT *apographē,* "list," "inventory," "taxing" (KJV), "census," "registration" (cf. *kēnsos,* "tribute money," "poll tax," Latin *census*); and the Latin *descriptio,* "a marking out," "transcript," "copy."

An instance of numbering is found in Ex 38:26, soon after the Exodus, while Israel first encamped at Sinai. It was to raise necessary funds to build the tabernacle. Another census occurred one year later (Num 1:2-3; cf. Jos *Ant.* iii.12.4), to ascertain the people's military strength. A later census revealed the number of males 20 years and upward (Num 26:1 -2). *See* Number. In the reign of David a census revealed his military potential (I Chr 21:1-6; cf. differing totals in II Sam 24:1, 9; Jos *Ant.* vii.13.1). Solomon completed David's census and included the foreigners and aliens (I Chr 22:2; II Chr 2:17-18). During the centuries that followed, numerous instances of the recorded military strength of both Israel and Judah appear (see I Kgs 12:21; II Chr 13:3, 17; 14:8-9; 17:14-19; 25:5-6; 26:11-15, etc.). Such information was essential for taxation.

Each country had its system of taxation and census taking. Fluctuating property values caused differing evaluations. In Athens, for example, an assessment was held every year, or every third or fifth year (Aristotle, *Polit.* v.7.6). Before and after the days of the Republic, it was customary for the Romans to have "enrollments by households," where persons and property would be taxed by families. The censors would query each family head regarding the name, age, financial and legal status of each member of his household (cf. Cic. *Laws* iii.3; Livy xliii.14).

In NT times, rather complete records were kept by Emperor Augustus because of his thorough reorganization of the Roman Empire. Papyri finds from Egypt reveal that at this time a census was taken every 14 years (cf. P. Oxy. 255 in Milligan, *Greek Papyri,* pp. 44-47), and such general procedures would affect Palestine. Mention is made of three enrollments taken during the rule of Augustus (Sue. *Aug.* xxvii; cf. Tac. *Ann.* i.11). The second of these is generally understood to have been around 8-4 B.C. Most biblical scholars identify the taxing of Lk 2:1-2 with this particular census and thus show reason for the journey of Joseph and Mary to Bethlehem. Josephus (*Ant.* xviii.1.1), however, mentions a taxing while Quirinius ruled Syria, which the latter administered after Archaelaus, the son of Herod the Great, was deposed from office in A.D. 6. How long or often Quirinius remained in office is a matter of dispute. This census mentioned by Josephus is associated with the one which caused Judas the Galilean to revolt (Acts 5:37). For a complete discussion of this intricate problem, *see* Chronology of the NT; Cyrenius; Taxing.

Bibliography. F. F. Bruce, "Census," NBD, p. 203. CornPBE, pp. 196-199. G. E. Mendenhall, "The Census Lists of Numbers 1 and 26," JBL, LXXVII (1958). George Milligan, *Selections from the Greek Papyri,* Cambridge: Univ. Press, 1927. Alfred Plummer, "Quirinius," HDB, IV. William M. Ramsay, *The Bearing of Recent Discovery on the Trust-*

worthiness of the New Testament, London: Hodder and Stoughton, 1915. Ramsay, *Was Christ Born at Bethlehem?* London: Hodder and Stoughton, 1898. J. A. Sanders, "Census," IDB, I, 547.

R. V. U.

CENTURION. An officer in the Roman army (Acts 21:32; 22:26; 23:23) in command of a century (100 foot soldiers, more or less). The number of centurions in a legion was 60 and in a cohort (KJV, "band") was ten.

In the NT, four centurions are mentioned, all in a favorable light: Cornelius, stationed at Caesarea, through whom it was made evident that Gentile believers also received the Holy Spirit (Acts 10); Julius, who treated Paul kindly on his trip to Rome (Acts 27:1, 3, 43); the centurion of Capernaum who sought aid for his servant (Mt 8:5–13); and the centurion who announced his faith at the cross (Mt 27:54).

CEPHAS (sē'făs; Gr. *kēphas,* from Aram. *kēpa',* "rock or stone").

A name given by Jesus to the apostle Simon (Jn 1:42; I Cor 1:12; 3:22; 9:5; 15:5; Gal 2:9). Peter is the Gr. equivalent of Cephas. *See* Peter; Simon; Simeon.

CHAFF. *See* Plants.

CHAIN. The term "chain" is used in two different senses. Chains were used, as were ropes, for binding prisoners (Jer 39:7; 52:11; Nah 3:10; Acts 12:6; 21:33; 28:20). More frequently we read of ornamental chains and necklaces strung with precious stones, particularly pearls (Jud 8:26; Ezk 16:11). Such chains were made of precious metals and often served as a sign of rank. Both Joseph and Daniel were given such chains or necklaces (Gen 41:42; Dan 5:29). Ornamental necklaces are also mentioned in Prov 1:9 and Song 1:10; 4:9. Ornamental chains formed part of the decoration of the Jerusalem temple (I Kgs 6:21; 7:17; II Chr 3:5–16). *See* Jewels, Jewelry; Fetters.

CHALCEDONY. *See* Jewels.

CHALCOL. The same as Calcol (*q.v.*).

CHALDEA (kăl-dē'à). From at least the 10th cen. B.C. southern Babylonia bordering the Persian Gulf was called by the Assyrians *Kaldu*-land (Babylonian *kashdu;* Heb. *kaśdîm*). In 626 B.C. a dynasty from this area ruled in Babylon and subsequently the name was used by foreigners (Jer 50:10; Dan 3:8; Ezk 11:24) as a synonym for the whole of Babylonia. *See* Babylonia; Chaldeans.

CHALDEANS (kăl-dē'ăns). The Gr. name *Chaldaioi* (Heb. *kaśdîm*) designated a group of Semitic tribes living in the "sea-lands" of southern Babylonia. It is first found in texts of *c.* 1000 B.C. but is probably a much older name. It

is likely that seminomads of the Kaldu occupied the deserts of N Arabia (Job 1:17) and settled in the Persian Gulf area late in the 3rd mil. B.C. Thus the city of Ur in their territory continued to be called "of the Chaldees" (Gen 11:28; Acts 7:4), perhaps to distinguish it from a city (Ura') of the same name in northern Mesopotamia.

During the 2nd mil. Babylon was ruled by chiefs from these "sea-lands" for brief periods. From the reign of Adad-nirari III (*c.* 810 B.C.) the Chaldean tribes paid homage to the Assyrian conquerors of N Babylonia. Then in 734 Ukin-zēr, head of the Chaldean tribe of Bit-Amukkani, seized the throne of Babylon for a few months before he was defeated at Sapia. Two other tribal leaders, Balasu of Bit-Dakkuri and Marduk-apla-iddina (the biblical Merodach-baladan) of Bit-Yakin, paid their dues, and their lands were spared.

The latter took the initiative at a time of Assyrian weakness to regain the throne for the Chaldeans in 721–710 B.C. His embassy to Hezekiah of Judah seeking support for his opposition to Assyria, despite Isaiah's warning of the dangers of such action to Judah (Isa 23:13) and his prophecy of the coming defeat of the Chaldeans (Isa 43:14), could be dated to the time of Merodach-baladan's defeat by Sargon II in 710 B.C. or by Sennacherib after the Chaldeans had once more seized the throne in Babylon in 703/2 B.C. Isaiah referred to Babylon itself by the poetic phrase "daughter of the Chaldeans" (Isa 47:1) and correctly used Chaldean as a synonym for Babylonia at this time (Isa 13:19; 47:1; 48:14).

In 626 B.C. Nabopolassar, another native Chaldean, was enthroned in Babylon by popular acclaim. He soon won the whole country as far N as the Middle Euphrates and, with the Medes, sacked Nineveh in 612. He was succeeded by his son Nebuchadrezzar II (605–581 B.C.), who defeated the Egyptians at Carchemish in 605 and made all the kings of Palestine, including Jehoiakim of Judah, his vassals. Jeremiah makes frequent reference to the Chaldeans at this time since the Babylonian army marched annually to Palestine in the first 12 years of Nebuchadrezzar's reign (Jer 21:4, *et al.*).

In 601 B.C. the Babylonian army was defeated by the Egyptians, and Jehoiakim, who had been a vassal for three years, now broke with Babylon. Retribution followed in late 598 and early 597 when, according to the Chaldean (or Babylonian) Chronicle (626–594 B.C.), which is an objective and accurate source for the history of this period, "Nebuchadrezzar marched to the city of Judah, capturing it and its king. He put a king of his own choice on the throne. He took much spoil and sent it back to Babylon." This capture of Jerusalem and Jehoiachin on March 16, 597 B.C., at the beginning of the great Exile, as at the sack of Jerusalem ten years later, was the work of Chaldean army units (II Kgs 24).

The Chaldean or Neo-Babylonian Empire at its height.

Later rulers of the Chaldean dynasty included Evil-Merodach (Awel-Marduk), Nabonidus, and his co-regent Belshazzar, whom Daniel calls "king of the Chaldeans" (Dan 5:30). Darius the Mede ruled "the kingdom of the Chaldeans" after the fall of Babylon to Cyrus in October, 539 B.C. (Dan 9:1). *See* Babylon. Daniel used "Chaldean" to describe the whole of Babylonia and its inhabitants (Dan 3:8). Ezekiel extended the use to those neighboring countries under its jurisdiction (Ezk 23:23).

The language of the Chaldeans (Dan 1:4) was only a dialect of Aramaic; thus "Chaldee" as at one time applied to the non-Hebrew sections of Daniel and Ezra is .technically incorrect.

While others used Chaldean to describe all the people, the Babylonians themselves later reserved the name for priests who specialized in astronomy and mathematics (the science of which originated in Babylonia) or used these sciences for astrology, horoscopes, or other omen practices. This special use of Chaldean to denote a "wise man" (attested by Herodotus) appears to have been developed in the 6th cen. B.C. (Dan 2:10; 5:11).

Bibliography. A. Leo Oppenheim, *Ancient Mesopotamia: Portrait of a Dead Civilization,* Chicago: Univ. of Chicago Press, 1964. D. J. Wiseman, *Chronicles of Chaldean Kings* (626–556 B.C.), London: British Museum, 1956.

D. J. W.

CHALDEE. *See* Aramaic; Chaldeans.

CHALK. *See* Minerals and Metals.

CHAMBER. Equivalent to a room, especially a private one (Gen 43:30; Jud 16:9). The word "room" is preferred in present-day English. Chamber is used of the rooms in the temple, whether in Solomon's temple (I Chr 9:26, 33) or the post-Exilic temple (Ezr 8:29), or especially in the temple of Ezekiel's vision (Ezk 40:17, *et al.*).

Sometimes the chamber was a room on the upper level of a house, either the second story or on the roof (II Sam 18:33). The Lord cautioned the disciples against any rumor that He would be in a secret chamber at the time of His final return (Mt 24:26).

CHAMBERING. A sexual sin mentioned as one of the works of darkness in Rom 13:12–13 (Gr. pl. *koitais,* "debauchery," "illicit intercourse"). The sing. form *koitē* occurs in Lk 11:7 as "bed," and in Heb 13:4 as the marriage "bed." In Rom 9:10, Rebekah "conceived" (*koitēn*) by Isaac. Thus the original passage condemns the prostitution of a natural (and divinely ordained) relationship.

CHAMBERLAIN. *See* Occupations: Chamberlain.

CHAMELEON. *See* Animals: Lizard, IV.21.

CHAMOIS. *See* Animals: Sheep, Mountain, II.36.

CHAMPION. In I Sam 17:51 *gibbōr*, rendered "champion," means "hero," "mighty man." In I Sam 17:4, 23, "champion" is a good translation of the Heb. word meaning "man of the middle places," i.e., the man who stands between two armies to decide the case of one against the other.

CHANAAN. *See* Canaan.

CHANCE. To the Hebrews Yahweh was a God of law and order, and therefore there is very little room for "chance" in their theology. In most instances where the idea is used it is the thinking of someone other than a Hebrew. In the Gr. translation of the OT (LXX), the word *tychē* is found twice, once in Gen 30:11 where Leah said, "With *fortune*" (ASV marg.; KJV, "a troop cometh"); and in Isa 65:11 (lit.), "preparing for the demon a table, and filling up for *chance* a mixed drink." In view here is the heathen god of chance, called Fortuna by the Romans. The idea of chance is found in the statement of the Philistines, that if their effort to determine the cause of their calamities turned out a certain way, they would call them a chance, that is, bad luck (I Sam 6:9). There are other instances where the same word is used: "chanceth him by night" (Deut 23:10); "her chance was to light on the portion of the field" (Ruth 2:3); "something hath befallen him" (I Sam 20:26); "one event happeneth to them all" (Eccl 2:14–15).

There is also the Heb. word *qārā'*: "If a bird's nest chance to be before thee in the way" (Deut 22:6); again, "and there happened to be there a base fellow" (II Sam 20:1, ASV). *Pegaʻ* is the Heb. word used in Eccl 9:11: "Time and chance happeneth to them all," and I Kgs 5:4, "neither adversary nor *evil occurrent* [misfortune, RSV]."

V. G. D.

CHANCELLOR. The title of Rehum (Ezr 4:8, 9, 17) meaning literally "lord of judgment." The term designates a Babylonian office, viz., that of the "master or lord of official intelligence," or "postmaster" (Sayce).

CHANGE OF RAIMENT. This expression occurs in three different passages in the OT (Gen 45:22; Jud 14:12, 13, 19; II Kgs 5:5, 22–23). The peoples of the ancient Near East were fond of brightly colored and ornamented garments and changed into such at weddings and other festive occasions. Kings and men of rank kept a large wardrobe of these (cf. II Kgs 10:22), partly for their own use (Prov 31:21; Job 27:16; Lk

15:22), partly to give away as presents (Est 6:6–11; and see above). Included in long lists of gifts exchanged between the pharaoh in the Amarna age and various kings in Babylonia, Syria and Palestine are many types of clothing, with up to 41 garments of a certain kind (e.g., EA #14, 22, 25, 29, 31a, 34). Another Heb. word, *mahălāṣôt* (KJV, "changeable suits of apparel," Isa 3:22; "change of raiment," Zech 3:4) is better translated "festal robes" as in NASB. *See* Dress.

J. R.

CHANNEL. In the KJV two words are translated "channel."

1. Heb. *'apîq* refers to the streambed or riverbed (Isa 8:7; cf. Joel 3:18, RSV), or to deep ravines in the ocean floor (II Sam 22:16; Ps 18:15; cf. Ezk 35:8; 36:4, 6, RSV).

2. Heb. *shibboleth* refers to the flowing stream of the Euphrates River (Isa 27:12). The Heb. term appears as a test of dialect in Jud 12:6, where it refers to the channel or stream of the Jordan.

See Canal.

CHAOS. The Gr. term from which this word is transliterated *(chaos)* does not occur in the Bible. In ancient mythologies it carried the idea of confusion and is commonly used to describe the condition of the earth at the time the Spirit of God moved upon the face of the waters (Gen 1:2–4). In this passage the concept of chaos would then be a synonym for the word "void" (Heb. *bōhû*, Gen 1:2) in the expression "waste and void."

The idea of Gen 1:2, however, is not best understood by the English "confusion." Rather, the original Gr. meaning of *chaos* as void or desolate should be understood. The Heb. word (*bōhû*) never occurs in the OT except with the corresponding word, as in Gen 1:2, "waste" (Heb. *tōhû*), which is used in Isa 45:18 to mean "uninhabited" and both terms appear in Jer 4:23 referring to Jerusalem after the Babylonian invasion in the 6th cen. B.C. Jeremiah says, by way of further explanation, "I beheld, and, lo, there was no man" (Jer 4:25).

J. McR.

CHAPEL. An expression in Amos 7:13 (KJV), elsewhere translated "sanctuary." Here it is indicative of the dependence of this national shrine at Bethel on the court of King Jeroboam II of Israel.

CHAPTER. Chapter is the rendering of three Heb. words used in Kings, Chronicles, and Exodus to designate the topmost part of a pillar.

The capitals of the two pillars of Solomon's temple were called *kōteret*, "crown" (I Kgs 7:16 ff.). *See* Jachin and Boaz. They had bowls (pommels, II Chr 4:12–13), apparently to hold oil for a continuing flame. The exact style of the pillars is unknown. The Heb. *ṣepet*, "capital," in II Chr 3:15 is a synonym. *See* Architecture.

The tops (rô'sh, "head or top") of the pillars of the door of the tabernacle tent were gold leafed (Ex 36:38). The tops of the pillars of the fence (rô'sh) were silver plated (Ex 38:17, 19, 28). This treatment caused the parts to glisten in the sunlight.

CHARASHIM (kär'ȧ-shǐm, "craftsmen"). The expression "valley of Charashim" is found in I Chr 4:14 (KJV). In ASV and RSV Ge-harashim is used. This valley in Judah was where a certain Joab founded a community of metal craftsmen, inhabited after the Exile by the tribe of Benjamin (Neh 11:35, see also ASV marg.). It may be identified with Sarafand el-Kharab, about five miles SW by W of Lydda (Lod) in a dale that slopes into the valley of the Nahr Rubin, or with the broad valley between Lod and Ono on the main road between Joppa and Jerusalem.

CHARCHEMISH. See Carchemish.

CHARCOAL. See Coals; Minerals and Metals.

CHARGER. Two Heb. words and one Gr. word denote this utensil.

1. The Heb. word qeʿārâ, originally meaning "hollowness" but later signifying "plate" or "dish," indicates one of the gifts the tribal chiefs presented at the tabernacle dedication (Num 7:13, et al.).

2. The Aramaic word ʾăgarṭāl (etymologically uncertain) is used of the "vessels" or "basins" given to the returning Jewish exiles by Cyrus (Ezr 1:9).

3. The Gr. word pinax, "board" or "plank," came to denote anything flat as "tablet, disc, dish, platter." Such a flat, narrow-rimmed charger, usually one to three feet in diameter (HDCG), was used to bring John the Baptist's head to Salome when her dancing pleased Herod Antipas (Mt 14:8, 11; Mk 6:25, 28). "Charger," an English word, is better translated "platter."

CHARIOT. The common Heb. words for chariot, rekeb and merkāb, probably come from a root meaning "to mount and ride." Heavy-wheeled vehicles drawn by asses are attested in Mesopotamia as early as the end of the 4th mil. and throughout the 3rd mil., as seen at Ur, Kish, and Tell Aqrab. The lighter spoke-wheeled, horse-drawn war chariot is depicted on Cappadocian cylinder seals in the time of Hammurabi (c. 1750 B.C.). It was the use of the speedy horse-drawn chariot that enabled the Hyksos to overrun Syria and Palestine and to conquer and control Egypt from about 1730 to 1580 B.C.

The first reference in the OT is to Joseph's chariot (Gen 41:43), probably patterned after the solid-wheeled chariots drawn by four horses shown on 19th–18th cen. B.C. seals from Anatolia. Other references to Egyptian chariots are in Gen 46:29; 50:9; Ex 14–15; Josh 24:6; II Kgs 18:24.

State chariot of King Tutankhamon of Egypt.
LL

When the Israelites came into Canaan, they found inhabitants in the plains whom they could not drive out because of their chariots of iron (Josh 11:4–9; Jud 1:19; 4:13). Joshua burned the chariots and hamstrung the horses that he captured in the battle against Jabin, possibly because they would have been of little use to people living in the hill country (see also the commandment of the Lord in Deut 17:16). See Armor.

Although David hamstrung some horses he captured, in one battle he saved enough horses for 100 chariots (II Sam 8:4). It was Solomon who built the chariot cities of Hazor and Megiddo to protect the northern frontier, Beth-horon, Gezer, and Baalath overlooking the Philistine plains, and Tamar in the Arabah to guard against the Edomites (I Kgs 9:15–19). Solomon had 1,400 chariots and 12,000 horsemen (I Kgs 10:26). He was also a middleman in the trade of horses from Cilicia (Kue) and chariots from Egypt (I Kgs 10:28–29, RSV).

The stele of Shalmaneser III mentions Ahab's 2,000 chariots which he furnished for the battle of Qarqar. The stables for 450 horses excavated at Megiddo are now dated to his reign.

Chariots continued to be used on a much smaller scale in Israel until NT times. The most familiar reference to a chariot in the NT is that which the Ethiopian eunuch was riding when Philip preached the good news of Jesus to him (Acts 8:27–28).

R. L. S.

CHARITY. Used 27 times in the KJV, including eight times in I Cor 13 for agapē, to signify human love for another person, often in the sense of benevolence. It is not used for the Gr. charis, which indicates grace, favor, goodwill. The Gr. agapē goes far deeper than the modern concept of charity, welfare, and generosity.

The use of "charity" in I Cor 13 (KJV) does not refer to almsgiving, since v. 3 uses it in the broad sense of love to all. The KJV translates the Gr. agapē as "charity" 27 times and as "love" 82 times, both mostly in Paul's writings. The difference must be determined by the context.

Charity shows man's love to man predicated on God's love to man. The word comes from the Latin *caritas*, which influenced Wycliffe and the Roman Catholic translators. Tyndale and most modern translators prefer to translate the Gr. *agapē* as "love," which avoids the narrower modern implication of generosity to needy people or worthy causes, and conveys the idea of man's loving attitude and action to his fellowman as a result of divine grace (Mt 22:37–40; Rom 13:8; I Cor 13). *See* Brotherly Kindness; Love.

E. B. R.

CHARM, CHARMER, CHARMING. *See* Magic.

CHARRAN. *See* Haran.

CHASE. *See* Hunting.

CHASTE, CHASTITY. Used to indicate inward, personal purity which shrinks from contamination or pollution, consequently free from defilement generally (I Pet 3:2), and from carnality and sexual sins (II Cor 11:2, "pure," RSV; Tit 2:5). *See* Purity.

CHASTEN. *See* Chastisement.

CHASTISEMENT. This is the KJV translation for the Heb. word *mûsār* and the Gr. word *paideia*. RSV prefers to use "discipline," which more closely represents the basic meaning of the original words. The primary significance is that of education, correction, guidance. The idea of punishment may be involved in the word, but unless the context indicates otherwise, punishment is to be viewed as corrective, as a part of the training process.

The basic idea involved in the biblical use is that God deals with His people as a father deals with His children. He disciplines and trains His people (primarily the nation Israel in the OT and the individual believer in the NT) to produce in them the qualities that conform to His own desire for them. The basic passage in the NT is Heb 12:6–8 where the writer states that chastisement (discipline) is a sign of sonship; the absence of it is a sign of illegitimacy.

Chastisement from God is to be viewed as an act of love and mercy. The believer, rather than rebelling against God's discipline, should recognize it as an act of fatherly love on God's part and correct his ways. Christian fathers are admonished by Paul to emulate God in bringing up their children in the discipline *(paideia)* and admonition of the Lord (Eph 6:4).

See Punishment.

F. L. F.

CHEBAR (kē'bär). A river in the land of the Chaldeans, on the banks of which some of the Jewish exiles, including the prophet Ezekiel, were settled. It was there that Ezekiel (*q.v.*) saw some of his visions (Ezk 1:1, 3; 3:15, 23; 10:15, 20). It has been identified as a navigable canal called *naru Kabari,* "great river," in Akkadian cuneiform tablets, just E of the ancient site of Nippur adjoining one of the great ship canals of Babylonia.

CHECKER WORK. Network or latticework used as ornamentation on the top of the pillars of Jachin and Boaz before the porch of the temple (I Kgs 7:17, 21). *See* Jachin and Boaz.

In Ex 28:4, 39 a different Heb. word is translated by RSV as a "coat of checker work" or "broidered coat," referring to the checked design used in making the high priest's tunic.

Checker work also refers to a net (Job 18:8) and a lattice (II Kgs 1:2). *See* Lattice.

CHEDORLAOMER (kĕd'ŏr-lā-ō'mēr). A king of Elam who led a coalition of Mesopotamian and northern Syrian kings to put down a rebellion of five vassal kings in the Vale of Siddim, the Salt Sea (Dead Sea) area (Gen 14:1–5). The latter may have stopped tribute payment of bitumen, copper or salt, natural resources highly prized in Mesopotamia. After the defeat of Sodom and Gomorrah and capture of Lot by Chedorlaomer and his allies, Abram pursued them to Hobah, N of Damascus (Gen 14:15), and rescued Lot (Gen 14:17). *See* Abraham; Ellasar.

Although the places and peoples named and linguistic archaisms establish the antiquity of Gen 14, it is not possible to suggest an historical identification of Chedorlaomer free of problems. The proposal by W. F. Albright (BASOR #88 [1942], p. 34) that he may be Kutir-nahhunti I of Elam (*c.* 1625 B.C.) has chronological difficulties (see now BASOR # 163, pp. 49 f.). The name Chedorlaomer is a genuine Elamite construction, *Kutir* (or *Kudur*)-*lagamar,* and means "servant of the (goddess) Lagamar"; however, it cannot be equated with any known Elamite ruler.

Since Abraham lived *c.* 2000 B.C., the most likely time in Mesopotamian history when such a campaign could have taken place would be after the collapse of Sumerian rule during the Ur III Dynasty (2113–1991) and before the powerful control of Babylonia under Hammurabi (1792–1750 B.C.). Elamites, Amorites (*see* Amraphel) and Hurrians (*see* Arioch) are known to have been active in Mesopotamia during the Isin and Larsa dynasties (1991–1786 B.C.).

H. E. Fi.

CHEEK. The freshness and roundness of the cheek was a sign of youthful beauty (Song 1:10; 5:13). To be smitten on the cheek was regarded as a deadly insult (Job 16:10; Mic 5:1; Mt 5:39). Even a slave preferred a blow to a buffet on the cheek. "Thou dost smite all my enemies on the cheek" (Ps 3:7, RSV) is symbolic of their utter destruction.

CHEESE. *See* Food.

CHELAL (kē'lăl). One of the eight sons of Pahath-moab who were forced by Ezra to give up their foreign wives after their return from Captivity (Ezr 10:30).

CHELLUH (kĕl'ä). One of the sons of Bani, mentioned in a group having foreign wives who were forced by Ezra to give them up after their return from Captivity (Ezr 10:35).

CHELUB (kē'lŭb). May be a variant of Caleb.
1. A descendant of Judah, a brother of Shuah and father of Mehir (I Chr 4:11).
2. Father of Ezri, one of David's officers and evidently his chief gardener (I Chr 27:26).

CHELUBAI (kĕ-lū'bī). A form of Caleb (I Chr 2:9, 18). He is mentioned here as the brother of Jerahmeel and Ram, and son of Hezron. Caleb (or Chelubai) is listed also as the son of Jephunneh the Kenezite (Num 32:12) and as the brother of Kenaz, Othniel's father (Josh 15:17). He was one of the men sent by Moses to spy out the land of Canaan (Num 13:6, 30), and was the conqueror of Hebron (Josh 14:13). *See also* Caleb.

CHEMARIM (kĕm'ä-rĭm). A word of Aramaic origin meaning "priest." The RSV translates this plural form as "idolatrous priests." The KJV transliterates the term "chemarims" in Zeph 1:4, but as "idolatrous priests" in II Kgs 23:5 and "priests" in Hos 10:5. All three passages show these priests involved in false worship. The Peshitto, however, uses the term favorably in connection with the Levitical priests and Jesus (Isa 61:6; Heb 2:17; 3:1; 4:14–15). The root idea is still uncertain. The word occurs in ancient Phoenician, Palmyrene, and Nabataean texts, and in the Amarna letters as *kamiru*. Jews at the fortress of Elephantine near Aswan used the word when speaking of the Egyptian priest of the god Khnum.

CHEMOSH. *See* Gods, False.

CHENAANAH (kĕ-nā'ä-nä)
1. The father of Zedekiah, the false prophet who incited Ahab against Micah (I Kgs 22:11, 24; II Chr 18:10, 23).
2. One of the seven sons of Bilhan, son of Jediael of the tribe of Benjamin, a mighty warrior at the time of David (I Chr 7:10).

CHENANI (kĕ-nā'nī). One of eight Levites mentioned as singing some religious song at Ezra's public reading of the law (Neh 9:4). The names represent either Levitical houses or individuals chosen to lead the worship of the people.

CHENANIAH (kĕn-ä-nī'ä)
1. A leader of the Levites over "the songs," or the "lifting up" of the ark of the covenant as it was brought by David's command from the house of Obed-edom to Jerusalem (I Chr 15:22, 27).
2. An Izharite, who with his sons was appointed "to outside duties for Israel, as officers and judges" (I Chr 26:29, RSV). This probably refers to duties outside the temple.

CHENOBOSKION (chĕn-ō-bŏs'kĕ-ŏn). The ancient Gr. name of a village (Coptic *Shénésit*) in upper Egypt where a large collection of Gnostic books was discovered. Now called Qasr es-Sayyad, Chenoboskion lies near the town of Nag Hammadi, some 30 miles NW of Luxor. Here, sometime in 1945, natives accidentally discovered 13 well-preserved Coptic codices on papyrus with leather covers. One of them found its way to the Jung Institute at Zürich, Switzerland, while the other 12 codices came eventually to the Coptic Museum in Cairo. These volumes contain 49 treatises, of which some are duplications, but 44 of them are different. The majority of these works had been lost for many centuries and were known only by name or through quotations given in the writings of Church Fathers who refuted them. Most of these works are written in the Sahidic dialect of Coptic, but several appear in the Subakhmimic dialect. These manuscripts were written in the 3rd and 4th cen. A.D., but they are all translations of Gr. works of greater antiquity, which originally were composed in the 2d cen. A.D.

The Chenoboskion papyri contain Gnostic works of a great variety: discussions and treatises, dialogues, prayers, gospels, epistles, and apocalypses. From early church writings it is known that some of these works were attributed to the Gnostic Valentinus (middle of the 2nd cen. A.D.), and others to the Gnostic sects of the Sethians, Archontics and Barbelognostics. Up to the present time only a few of the Chenoboskion have been published in full, but even these few provide some idea of the literature of these sects. Among the most important of the published works belong the following three so-called gospels: (1) the Gospel of Thomas, a collection of 114 sayings of Jesus, of which some were already known from Gr. papyrus fragments found at Oxyrhynchus in Egypt; (2) the Gospel of Philip, also a collection of sayings, which is characterized by a strong dualism and which stresses the four elements of water, earth, wind, and air that correspond to faith, hope, love, and knowledge; and (3) the Gospel of Truth, which is a conglomeration of different phases of Gnostic philosophy, but has no semblance of what ordinarily is considered a gospel.

See Agrapha; Canon of Scripture — NT; Gnosticism.

Bibliography. J. Doresse, *The Secret Books of the Egyptian Gnostics*, New York: Viking Press, 1960. F. V. Filson, BA, XXIV (1961), 7–18. V. R. Gold, BA, XV (1952), 70–88. Andrew K. Helmbold, *The Nag Hammadi*

Gnostic Texts and the Bible, Grand Rapids: Baker, 1967. W. C. van Unnik, *Newly Discovered Gnostic Writings,* Naperville, Ill.: Allenson, 1960.

S. H. H.

CHEPHAR-HAAMMONAI (kē'fár-hā-ăm'ō-nī). A settlement meaning "village of the Ammonite" in the territory of Benjamin (Josh 18:24), so called perhaps because Ammonites lived there. Some identify it with Kefr'ana, a site of ruins about two miles NE of Bethel.

CHEPHIRAH (kĕ-fī'rạ). A Hivite city in Benjamin's territory (Josh 18:26) which followed Gibeon's lead in making peace with Israel (Josh 9:17). It was resettled after the return from Babylonian exile (Ezr 2:25; Neh 7:29). The present-day site is Khirbet Kefireh SW of el-Jib (Gibeon).

CHERAN (kĕr'án). The fourth son of Dishon, a Hurrian clan chief, listed in the genealogical tables of Seir. Evidently the founder of a Hurrian subclan in Edom (Gen 36:26; I Chr 1:41).

CHERETHITES (kĕr'ĕ-thīts)
1. A body of people in the Negeb or southern Palestine (I Sam 30:14), neighbors to the SE of the Philistines (cf. Ezk 25:16; Zeph 2:5). Ezekiel predicts judgment on them because of the Philistine revenge against Judah, indicating the close association of the two. The name (Heb. *keréṯî*) probably echoes the word Crete *(q.v.),* ancient Caphtor *(q.v.).* They would thus be Cretans, relatives of the Philistines. The Carites were probably the same peoples (II Sam 20:23, variant reading in the *Kethibh;* II Kgs 11:4, 19, RSV, not "captains" as in KJV).
2. Mercenaries along with the Pelethites forming David's bodyguard, led by Benaiah son of Jehoiada (II Sam 8:18; 20:23; I Chr 18:17), probably recruited from the Cherethites during the time he fled from Saul. They stood by David when Absalom rebelled (II Sam 15:18), and proved their loyalty once again by being present at Solomon's coronation (I Kgs 1:38, 44). Foreign mercenaries have no family or local loyalties and tend to be well disciplined, as Cyrus H. Gordon points out, who equates these Cherethites with Cretans (*The World of the Old Testament,* pp. 171 f.). *See* Philistines.

H. G. S.

CHERITH (kĕr'ĭth). A brook where Elijah was told to hide from Ahab and was miraculously fed by ravens (I Kgs 17:2–7). The expression "facing" or "before" Jordan seems to favor a site in Gilead E of Jordan rather than the Wadi Qelt, the traditional site W of Jordan near Jericho.

CHERUB
1. Cherub (kĕr'ŭb) was an Israelite who returned from Captivity but was of a group who "could not prove their fathers' houses or their descent, whether they belonged to Israel" (Ezr 2:59; Neh 7:61, RSV). It could possibly be an unknown Babylonian place name instead of a person.
2. Cherub (chĕr'ŭb; pl., cherubim) is a celestial being of the angelic order belonging to the spiritual realm. The Semitic peoples pictured the cherubim as winged lions and bulls, having human faces, guarding temples and palaces. The biblical representations stress the human likeness but also indicate the animal characteristics. They guarded the way to the tree of life (Gen 3:24); a representation was fastened to the mercy seat of the ark (Ex 25:18 ff.) in the holy of holies (II Chr 3:7–14). They evidently have to do with the holiness of God violated by sin. Ezekiel identified them as the "living creatures" *(q.v.)* which he saw by the river Chebar (Ezk 1:5 f.; 10:20). Many identify the living creatures of the book of Revelation (4:6 f., RSV) with the cherubim. The number of wings varies. *See* Angel.

L. O. H.

CHESALON (kĕs'á-lŏn). A city on the northern boundary of Judah, bordering Dan (Josh 15:10). Usually identified with modern Kesla, about nine miles W of Jerusalem on a mountain ridge to the S of Wadi el-Humar.

CHESED (kē'sĕd). The fourth son of Nahor (Abraham's brother) and Milcah (Gen 22:22). Probably the ancestor of an Aramean tribe referred to as the Casdim or Chaldeans.

The Monastery of Elijah by the traditional Brook Cherith. G. Semerdjian

CHESIL (kē'sĭl). A town in the extreme S of Judah named with Eltolad and Hormah (Josh 15:30). The name is not mentioned again. Chesil evidently corresponds with Bethul (Josh 19:4), Bethuel (I Chr 4:30), and Bethel (I Sam 30:27). *See* Bethel.

CHEST. Two Heb. words mean "chest," referring to an object rectangular in shape and usually made of wood.

1. Heb. *'arôn* is uniformly used for the ark of the covenant except in two instances: (1) The bones of Joseph were placed in a "coffin" which was carried to Palestine (Gen 50:26). (2) King Joash and Jehoiada the priest had a chest placed in the temple beside the altar to receive free-will offerings for the repair of the temple (II Kgs 12:9; II Chr 24:8–11).

2. Heb. *genāzîm* is used in its plural form in connection with things collected or hidden, as treasures (Est 3:9), and chests for keeping valuables, treasure chests (Ezk 27:24).

CHESTNUT. *See* Plants.

CHESULLOTH (kĕ-sŭl'ŏth). A town in Issachar on the border of Zebulun (Josh 19:18). It seems to be the same as Chisloth-tabor (*q.v.;* Josh 19:12). It is identified with the modern Iksal on the northern edge of Esdraelon, about three miles SE of Nazareth.

CHETH. The eighth letter of the Heb. alphabet. *See* Alphabet. This letter is used in KJV as the heading of the eighth section of Ps 119, where each verse begins with this letter.

CHEZIB (kĕ'zĭb). The place where Judah's third son, Shelah, was born (Gen 38:5). It is probably to be identified with Achzib (*q.v.*), a town in western Judah, mentioned along with Mareshah and Keilah as belonging to Judah (Josh 15:44). From its grouping it seems to be the same also as Chozeba (I Chr 4:22).

CHICKEN. *See* Animals: Fowl, Domestic, III.14.

CHIDON (kī'dŏn). The name of the threshing floor where Uzzah was struck dead for touching the ark when the oxen stumbled (I Chr 13:9–10). However, the parallel passage in II Sam 6:6 has the threshing floor of Nachon (*q.v.*). The reference may indicate the owner of the threshing floor. There is no certain knowledge concerning either name.

CHIEF. The translation of a large group of Heb. words in the OT, usually designating the leader of a family, clan, or tribe, or in connection with certain official terms and titles. The ASV and RSV use "chief" where the KJV uses "duke" in referring to clan and tribal leadership (Gen 36:15; Ex 15:15; I Chr 1:51). Certain official terms are used, such as "chief butler" (Gen 40:9), "chief of the captains" (I Chr 11:11),

"chief of the fathers of Israel" (II Chr 19:8), "chief of the nations" (Amos 6:1), and "chief priest" (II Chr 19:11). The NT uses such terms as "chief of the demons" (Lk 11:15), "chief Pharisee" (Lk 14:1), "chief of the Jews" (Acts 28:17), "chief city" (Acts 16:12), and "chief captain" (Gr. *chiliarchos*, RSV, "tribune," NASB, "commander," Acts 21:31, etc.). *See* Captain; Tribune.

CHIEF OF THE THREE. The official title of Adino the Ezrite, or Eznite (II Sam 23:8). The ASV reads: "These are the names of the mighty men whom David had: Josheb-basshebeth a Tahchemonite, chief of the captains; the same was Adino the Eznite, against eight hundred slain at one time." The obscure Heb. of this verse has led the RSV to omit the phrase "the same was Adino the Eznite," substituting the phrase "he wielded his spear." The phrase "chief among the captains" (KJV) is then translated as "chief of the three" in RSV.

CHIEF PRIEST. *See* Priests.

CHIEFS OF ASIA. *See* Asiarchs.

CHILD SACRIFICE. *See* Sacrifice, Human.

CHILDBEARING. One evidence that creation lies under God's curse is the travail which ordinarily accompanies the birth of a child (Gen 3:16). Often, indeed, the Bible alludes to the pangs of parturition as pain at its most painful (Ps 48:6; Isa 13:8; 21:3; 26:17; Jer 4:31; 6:24; 13:21; 22:23; 50:43). Yet from a biblical perspective childbearing is not just a burden; it is, paradoxically, a woman's highest privilege and greatest joy (Ps 113:9; Isa 54:1; Jn 16:21). Sterility, on the contrary, is a supreme affliction (Gen 11:30; I Sam 1:1–2:5; II Sam 6:23; Lk 1:7).

Under the Mosaic law childbearing rendered a woman ceremonially unclean; 50 days for a daughter, 40 days for a son. At the end of that time a sacrifice for purification was presented (Lev 12; Lk 2:22–24). The older practice of the "churching" of women, a public thanksgiving for the safe deliverance of child and mother, no doubt developed from this OT purification ordinance. This observance, in Protestant churches at any rate, has been largely abandoned.

Paul's statement concerning childbirth in I Tim 2:15 has called forth a number of diversified views, ranging from ordinary childbirth to an allusion to the incarnation (cf. Dean Henry Alford, *The Greek New Testament*).

V. C. G.

CHILDHOOD OF CHRIST. Knowledge of the childhood of Christ depends upon three sources: historical, cultural, and indirect evidence.

1. *Recorded facts.* These are the recorded incidents surrounding the birth and early babyhood of Christ, followed by complete silence

until His twelfth year when He went with Joseph and Mary to the temple to attend the Feast of the Passover at Jerusalem. The main events at His birth include the time and place (Mt 2:1 ff.; Lk 2:1 ff.), and the annunciation to the shepherds and their visit to the manger to worship the Christ Child (Lk 2:8-20). On the eighth day He was circumcised, and at that time He received His name (Lk 2:21). At His presentation in the temple on the fortieth day, Mary offered a pair of turtledoves or two young pigeons, as was appropriate for the poor (Lev 12:8; Lk 2:22-24).

This last ceremony was marked by Simeon's prophecy that Jesus was God's means of salvation for both Jew and Gentile, though His coming would be rejected by many in Israel (Lk 2:25-35). This prophecy was corroborated by Anna, an aged woman serving God day and night in the temple with fasting and prayer, who foretold that Jesus was the one sent for the redemption of Jerusalem (Lk 2:36-38).

It was probably after the circumcision and dedication that the wise men inquired in Jerusalem and then visited Mary and Joseph and the Babe in Bethlehem, since the flight to Egypt followed that visit so shortly (Mt 2:1-14). After the death of Herod, Joseph and Mary and the Child returned to Palestine and lived quietly in Nazareth (Mt 2:19-23). We may well surmise that Joseph and Mary told Jesus the amazing events and the prophecies attending His birth, and that these details greatly enriched His childhood.

In Lk 2:42-50, the boy Jesus, at 12 years of age, showed great insight into His peculiar relationship to God. His question addressed to Joseph and Mary, "Did you not know that I had to be in My Father's house?" ("in the things of My Father?" NASB and marg.) shows a consciousness that God, not Joseph, was His true Father. These first quoted words of Jesus, referring to His sonship, were the mark of His awareness of His mission on earth.

2. *Culture and customs.* A study of Jewish customs and culture, particularly as they are recorded in the OT and were revealed to Israel as the will of God, adds much to our knowledge of the childhood of Christ. The feasts and religious observances filled much of the life of the Israelite (*see* Worship). The Feast of the Passover was celebrated in every family, followed by the Feasts of Unleavened Bread, First Fruits, Pentecost, Trumpets, Day of Atonement, and Feast of Tabernacles. Some of these feasts lasted a week. Although the main celebrations occurred at Jerusalem, nevertheless observances of a lesser nature must have been held in the local synagogues.

The Jewish home had Scripture on its doorposts, the constant daily teaching and discussion of the Bible (Deut 7:6-9; 11:18-20), and memorization of the Heb. Scriptures, in addition to the weekly sabbath services in the synagogue. We know that Christ learned to read (Lk 4:17) and write (Jn 8:6-8). Like every

Jewish boy. He was taught a trade, and by carpentry probably supported Himself, His mother Mary, and the family after Joseph's death, until He was baptized and led by the Holy Spirit into His public ministry (Mt 3:13-17; Lk 4:1, 14). Justin Martyr speaks of His making "plows and yokes" (*Dial.* 88).

3. *Inferences from Christ's own references to childhood.* Jesus must have been intensely interested in nature because of His references to foxes, birds (Mt 6:26; 8:20; 13:32; Lk 9:58; 12:6), hen and chickens (Mt 23:37), flowers (Mt 6:28-30), and the weather (Mt 16:2-3; Lk 12:56). He must have entered into and played the games which other children played (Mt 11:16-17).

In all, Jesus enjoyed a very normal and healthy childhood. His parents were humble, honest, hard working, and devout. His mother in particular was an example of patience and love (Lk 2:19, 51); Joseph a man of integrity, yet compassionate (Mt 1:19-25) and of real faith. Christ's childhood experiences undoubtedly were those of a boy who spent much time in the out-of-doors, coupled with a thorough training in a trade. Through it all He developed both mentally and physically. His teaching proved the former and His physical endurance the latter. Besides this, He matured spiritually in His fellowship with God, and socially in His relationships with His fellowmen (Lk 2:40, 52).

The so-called infancy gospels, the Protevangelium of James and the Gospel of Thomas, are apocryphal writings of the 2nd cen. A.D. They contain purely legendary incidents such as miracles wrought by Jesus as a small boy. In later centuries other writings copied and enlarged on these imaginative stories.

R. A. K.

CHILDREN. Parenthood, as the Bible sees it, is an incontestable proof of God's favor. The pious Israelite, therefore, responded to the birth of his child with gratitude and joy (Ps 127; 128:3), and his wife shared these emotions (Ps 113:9). Indeed, the larger their family, the greater was the thankfulness of a heaven-blessed couple. In the context of a rather simple agricultural economy, this reaction was entirely understandable. Hence the problem of planned parenthood never appeared on the horizon in ancient Palestine. Hence, too, voluntary childlessness was viewed as reprehensible.

The birth of a boy, however, was far more welcome than that of a girl. To the Jews the pagan practice of destroying female infants was anathema, yet only mild enthusiasm greeted a daughter's arrival.

Hebrew mothers, one may assume, prided themselves on delivering their own children with ease (Ex 1:19), although on occasion they had the help of midwives (Gen 35:17; 38:28; Ex 1:15-19). Immediately after parturition infants were bathed; then they were rubbed with salt to harden their skin; after that they were wrapped in swaddling bands (Ezk 16:4; Lk

2:7). Suckling was the rule rather than the exception (I Sam 1:21–23; Isa 49:15; cf. Ex 2:7; II Kgs 11:2). The weaning of a child at two or three years of age was the occasion for both feast and sacrifice (Gen 21:8).

When only eight days old, males were circumcised, a rite which Yahweh explicitly commanded in Gen 17:10. Circumcision was not primarily an act of purification; essentially it was an act of incorporation, the sign that a boy had become a member of the covenant community (Lev 12:3). A parallel ceremony for girls evolved to mark their official entrance into God's people.

Names were customarily bestowed at the same time (Lk 2:21). Since in Semitic culture a spiritual significance, a kind of numinous influence, was attached to names, the father had the privilege of choosing what his child would be called; no doubt in practice the choice was a matter of mutual agreement between husband and wife (Lk 1:57–63).

The firstborn male in a family occupied a unique position; his status as future head of the family was indicated by a special designation, $b^e k \hat{o} r$, the Heb. term Mary must have applied to her own Son (Lk 2:7). In remembrance of the Exodus judgment upon Egypt, the firstborn belonged to the Lord. Within a month after his birth, however, following official presentation in the temple, he was ransomed by an offering (Ex 13:12–16; Num 8:17; Lk 2:22–23).

For the first few years of life both boys and girls were in the care of their mothers. The girls, of course, remained under maternal supervision, helping in the home, carrying water, learning to spin, or perhaps tending sheep, and gleaning in the fields. Boys, as they grew, were supervised by their fathers, serving as apprentices in the paternal occupation.

Education, too, was the father's responsibility. This was chiefly religious and moral in nature (Ex 13:8; Deut 4:9–10; 6:4–7; 7:9; Josh 4:4–8), a thorough indoctrination in history, Torah, and ritualism. Something of the tenderness of a child's upbringing in Israel may be glimpsed in passages such as Isa 66:12; Hos 11:3; cf. Mk 9:36–37. Something of the severity which likewise prevailed, a severity which sprang from the absolute authority of the parents, may be seen in passages like Ex 21:15–17 and Deut 21:18–21. And something of the play in which children engaged may be gathered from passages like Zech 8:5 and Mt 11:16–17.

Formal schools seem to have appeared about a century before our Lord was born. Extensions of the synagogue, they enrolled a child at five and subjected him to a program of rote memorization which centered in the Torah. By 13 this training ended, as a boy legally came of age, entered into the court of men, and assumed the duties of reciting the Shema, fasting regularly, and making pilgrimages. Some rabbis argued that girls should not be educated, but they seem to have acquired a rather thorough knowledge of Scripture; e.g., Mary's repeated allusions to the OT in her Magnificat (Lk 1:46–55).

The duties of parents (q.v.) with respect to their children are set forth in, e.g., Prov 22:6; Eph 6:4; Col 3:21; I Tim 5:8; Tit 2:4. The duties of children, on the other hand, are stated in, e.g., Ex 20:12; Eph 6:1–3; and Col 3:20.

In the Bible, references to childhood are sometimes used psychologically to denote a stage of ignorance and immaturity (Lk 7:32; I Cor 13:11; Eph 4:14; Heb 5:13); sometimes they are used ethically to denote a state of innocence, simplicity and trust (Mt 7:9–11; 18:1–5; 19:13–15; I Cor 14:20); and sometimes they are used spiritually to denote a faith-established relationship to God (Mt 5:9; Jn 1:12; Rom 8:14–17).

See Family; Education.

Bibliography. Henri Daniel-Rops, *Daily Life in the Time of Jesus,* New York: Hawthorn, 1962, pp. 118–133. Edith Deen, *Family Living in the Bible,* New York: Harper, 1963, pp. 86–93. Albrecht Oepke, *"Pais,* etc.," TDNT, V, 636–654.

V. C. G.

CHILDREN OF GOD. With a few exceptions, this phrase is equivalent to sons of God. In the OT it denotes chiefly a relationship to God by covenant, not by physical descent as is found in other Semitic or pagan religions. Man was *created* in the image of God, not begotten, and Israel's sonship was dependent upon grace not nature. Moreover, not all men are addressed as children of God. Israel collectively can be spoken of as God's son (Ex 4:22), or the nation generally may be called the children of God (Deut 14:1); but only the actual or messianic King can be called the Son of God (Ps 2:7).

In the NT, sonship is indissolubly linked with the sonship of Christ (Rom 8:17; Jn 1:12). Because He is Son (Mt 2:15; 3:17), He also leads many other sons to glory (Heb 2:10).

In Pauline parlance men become children of God by adoption (Rom 8:15, 23; Gal 4:5; Eph 1:5). This is made possible by coming to God the Father through Christ (Gal 3:26). Sonship is attested to by the Spirit (Rom 8:14, 16). Although on earth it is imperfect and incomplete, in the resurrection at the return of Christ it will be made perfect (Rom 8:21, 23, 29; I Jn 3:1).

In the language of John and Peter, sonship is described in terms of rebirth (Jn 1:12–13; I Jn 3:9; 4:7; 5:1, 4; I Pet 1:23). Some have held that in the NT the children of God *(tekna)* and the sons of God *(huioi)* should be differentiated, the former term being more appropriate for the birth metaphor and the latter to adoption. Such a distinction should be advanced with great caution. It is true that John uses *tekna* for Christians and reserves *huios* for Christ. Paul, however, seems to use *huios* and *tekna* interchangeably when referring to Christians.

G. W. Ba.

CHILDREN OF ISRAEL. *See* Israel.

CHILEAB (kĭl'ĭ-ăb). The second son of David, born to him at Hebron by Abigail, the widow of Nabal the Carmelite (II Sam 3:3). He is called Daniel in a corresponding account (I Chr 3:1).

CHILION (kĭl'ĭ-ŭn). One of the two sons of Elimelech and Naomi, who migrated from Bethlehem to Moab. Chilion married the Moabitess Orpah, and died childless in Moab (Ruth 1:2, 5; 4:9).

CHILMAD (kĭl'măd). A city or district mentioned along with Asshur, Haran, Canneh, and Eden as having supplied merchandise to Tyre (Ezk 27:23). Chilmad may possibly be identified with Charmon (Charmande), a town in Babylonia near the Euphrates.

CHIMHAM (kĭm'hăm). One of the sons of Barzillai the Gileadite (Jos *Ant.* vii.11.4), who remained loyal to David while the latter was in exile at Mahanaim (II Sam 19:37–40). David urged Barzillai *(q.v.)* to return to Jerusalem with him and receive royal favors, but he declined because of his age and asked that David confer the favors upon Chimham (II Sam 19:31–40). Chimham seems to have received a pension and some land near Bethlehem, known four centuries later as the "habitation of Chimham" (I Kgs 2:7; Jer 41:17).

CHIMNEY. The word more properly means "lattice" or "window." The word "chimney" is found only in Hos 13:3. RSV translates the passage: ". . . like smoke from a window." The houses had no chimneys.

CHINNERETH (kĭn'ĕ-rĕth), **CHINNEROTH** (kĭn'ĕ-rŏth)
1. An early name, probably Canaanite, for the Sea of Galilee (Num 34:11; Deut 3:17; Josh 11:2; 12:3; 13:27), perhaps because the lake is lyre or harp shaped (from Heb. *kinnôr*, "lyre"). *See* Galilee, Sea of.
2. A fortified city of Naphtali (Josh 19:35). It was included as *knnrt* in a list of towns conquered by Thutmose III of Egypt (c. 1475 B.C.). Its site is Tell el-'Oreimeh, on the lake shore two and a half miles SW of Capernaum.
3. The area around the city of Chinneroth (Josh 11:2), usually identified with the plain of Gennesaret (Mt 14:34), and thus a district of Naphtali W of the Sea of Galilee, conquered by Ben-hadad of Syria (I Kgs 15:20), spelled Cinneroth in KJV. The Gr. name *Gennēsaret* was more correctly *Gennēsar*, according to I Macc 11:67, Josephus, the Talmud, Gr. MS D, and several ancient versions of Mt and Mk. The derivation of the Gr. name is not certain.

L. O. H.

CHIOS (kī'ŏs). A rocky and mountainous island in the E central region of the Aegean Sea, about five miles from the mainland of Asia Minor, W of Smyrna. It was famous for its wines, figs, and aromatic resins. Paul's ship anchored for the night off Chios as he returned to Jerusalem at the end of his third missionary journey (Acts 20:15). Along with other places, it claimed to be the birth place of Homer. Its chief city and port, also called Chios, was a free city belonging to the Roman province of Asia in Paul's time. Today Chios (Khios) is a town of 22,000.

CHISEL. A carpenter's tool used in the making of a wooden idol (Isa 44:13, JerusB). The Heb. term *maqṣu'ôth* is probably better translated "chisels" instead of "planes" (KJV, RSV, etc.). In Isaiah's time the more primitive chisel and adz still were used in place of the plane.

CHISLEU (kĭs'lū). The third civil or ninth ecclesiastical month of the Jewish year corresponding to November-December (Neh 1:1; Zech 7:1). The derivation seems to be from the Akkad. word *kislīmu. See* Calendar.

CHISLON (kĭs'lŏn). The father of Elidad, who as one of the leaders of Benjamin was selected to help divide the portion of Canaan W of the Jordan among the nine and one-half tribes (Num 34:21).

CHISLOTH-TABOR (kĭs'lŏth-tā'bŏr). A town in Galilee bordering the territories of Issachar and Zebulun. It seems to be the same as Chesulloth *(q.v.;* Josh 19:18). It is identified with the modern Iksal, a village about four miles W of Mount Tabor near Nazareth.

CHITTIM (kĭt'ĭm). The Heb. word is used in both a broad and narrow sense. In its narrower sense it meant the island of Cyprus (Isa 23:1, 12; Jer 2:10; Ezk 27:6). Josephus refers to Cyprus as follows: "Cethimus possessed the island Cethima; it is now called Cyprus: and from that it is that all islands, and the greatest part of the sea-coasts, are named Cethim [equals Kittim] by the Hebrews" *(Ant.* i.6.1). The city of Citius, or Cition, on Cyprus seems to have given its name to the island. In Num 24:24; Dan 11:30 Chittim evidently refers to Rome. The earliest reference (Gen 10:4) makes this term apply to the descendants of Javan, indicating the Greek-Latin races of the Mediterranean area including Cyprus.

CHIUN. *See* Gods, False: Kaiwan.

CHLOE (klō'ē). A woman, evidently a Christian, whose household servants or slaves informed Paul, who was working in Ephesus at the time, of partisan divisions and moral disorders in the church at Corinth (I Cor 1:11). It is not known whether she lived in Corinth or Ephesus. However, she was well-known to Paul and the Corinthian church.

CHOENIX. *See* Weights, Measures, and Coins.

CHORASHAN (kôr-ā'shăn). Found only in I Sam 30:30 (KJV). RSV refers to the city as Borashan. It is probably the same as Ashan. Located in the Shephelah, it was originally assigned to Simeon, but in David's administration it became a Levitical city of Judah (Josh 15:42; 19:7; I Chr 4:32; 6:59). See Ashan.

CHORAZIN (kō-rā'zĭn). A small town in the hills, about two miles N of Tell Hum (Capernaum) and thus as far inland from the Sea of Galilee. Identified with Kerazeh, the town exhibits extensive ruins from the 3rd to 4th cen. A.D., including a synagogue of black basalt stones richly decorated with sculptures of animals and representations of grape gathering and grape pressing. Jesus performed many great works there without winning disciples, and upbraided the townsfolk for their unbelief (Mt 11:20-22; Lk 10:13).

CHOSEN. The Heb. and Gr. words translated "chosen," based on the verbs *bāḥar* and *eklegomai,* involve a comparison of two or more objects or persons. The choice suggests a certain privilege, position, or purpose. Human choices on the basis of character or skill are evident in Scripture, such as choosing wives (Gen 6:2), captains and soldiers (Ex 15:4; 17:9; Jud 20:15-16), and Yahweh as one's God (Josh 24:15, 22). The church in Jerusalem chose seven deacons on the basis of their spirituality and wisdom (Acts 6:3, 5); and the church chose men who had already risked their lives for Christ to accompany Paul and Barnabas to Antioch with the decision of the Jerusalem council (Acts 15:22, 26).

God also chooses, but His choice depends upon grace rather than merit. Israel was not chosen to be His special people because of its numbers (Deut 7:6-7; 10:15; Neh 9:7-8; Isa 43:20; 44:1-2; Acts 13:17); nor is the Christian believer selected because of his natural talents (I Cor 1:26-31) but for God's glory and to manifest His love. He chose David to be king over Israel not on the basis of his outward appearance (I Sam 16:7, 12). The Servant of Yahweh (Isa 42:1) would have no stately form or majesty but would be despised and rejected by men (Isa 53:2-3). As individual believers we were "chosen before the foundation of the world" (Eph 1:4; cf. Rom 8:29).

Can any of the chosen of God fail? What about Israel, for example? In Rom 11 Paul discusses at length their being rejected for a time and their final redemption, concluding his revelation with the words, "So all Israel shall be saved . . . for the gifts and calling of God are without repentance" (Rom 11:26, 29). Similarly, those whom God has foreknown as His own He will carry safely through every step of salvation to their final glorification (Rom 8:29-30). See Election.

Certain difficult questions arise concerning God's election or choice. How can man be called free if only those who are chosen are

The Chorazin Synagogue. HFV

saved? In other words, where do God's sovereignty and grace and man's freedom meet in salvation? Briefly, man's freedom since the Fall is essentially a freedom to do evil. Without God's grace he may desire but cannot actually choose the good. At the same time God does not ignore the freedom of man but includes it in His sovereign grace when He does save a man.

Again, how can God be righteous and choose some while rejecting others? The answer to this is that God does not have to save any; and therefore those who are saved are actually the subjects of His unmerited favor, while those He passes by are victims of their own rebellion and sin.

See Call; Election.

R. A. K.

CHOSEN PEOPLE. In the OT the term *bāḥar* expresses "choose," and first occurs in connection with Israel in Deut 7:6, where they are commanded to destroy all pagan cult objects in Canaan because "thou art a holy people unto Jehovah thy God: Jehovah thy God hath chosen thee" (ASV). This was no matter of nationalistic pride, for God's choice was based upon His gracious love and His promise to Abraham, rather than upon the numbers or merit of the nation (v. 7). Hence, they were a people saved only by grace and unconditionally committed to God's will and cause (Ps 105:6; 135:4). God's choice was later reaffirmed by His delivering Israel from Babylonian captivity (Isa 14:1) to fulfill a missionary role to the world as His servant (Isa 41:8; 44:1-2), especially in the person of the coming Christ, God's Chosen One *par excellence* (Isa 42:1). Other occurrences of the chosen people concept are in I Kgs 3:8 and Ezk 20:5. Important references in the NT are I Cor 1:26-28; Eph 1:4; Jas 2:5; and especially I Pet 2:9-10. See Election.

G. L. A.

CHOZEBA (kō-zē'bȧ). A city in Judah whose men were descendants of Shelah (I Chr 4:22). It is to be identified with Chezib (Gen 38:5) and Achzib (Josh 15:44). See Chezib; Achzib.

CHRIST. *See* Jesus Christ.

CHRIST, APPEARANCES OF. *See* Appearances of Christ.

CHRIST, ASCENSION OF. *See* Ascension of Christ.

CHRIST, COMING OF. The first and second comings of Christ as the Messiah are foretold in many OT prophecies. He was to come the first time as the suffering Messiah and to die as an atoning sacrifice (Isa 7:14; 52:13 – 53:12; Ps 16; cf. Acts 2:22- 31; Ps 22:1- 21; 31; 40:5- 8; 41:9; 69:8- 9, 21). He is to come the second time as the reigning, ruling Messiah, whose kingdom is to be a literal reign on the earth (Isa 9:6- 7; 11:1 ff.; 66:15 ff.; Zech 12:10; 13:6; 14:1 ff.). The book of Revelation says the reign will be for one thousand years (Rev 20:4- 6).

On the details of His first coming all Christians agree. On those of His second coming there is a wide divergence of opinion. The post-millennialist says the church will inaugurate a period of perfect peace, a millennium, and then Christ will come. The amillennialist says there is no literal earthly millennium; for them the passages which speak of a physical rule of the Messiah on the earth are not to be taken literally. The premillennialist says since the prophecies of His first coming were fulfilled literally, even though the Jewish leaders rejected their literal interpretation and would not receive Christ, the prophecies of His second coming are to be accepted as literal.

Four Gr. words are used for Christ's second coming: (1) *erchomai,* "to come" (Mt 24:3; 25:27; Lk 12:45; 18:5; 19:23); (2) *epiphaneia,* "appearing," "presence," which occurs six times, one in II Thess 2:8 and five times in the pastoral epistles (I Tim 6:14; II Tim 1:10; 4:1, 8; Tit 2:13); (3) *apokalypsis (apokalyptō),* "revelation" (apocalypse) or "unveiling" (Lk 17:30; I Pet 1:13); (4) *parousia,* which means "presence" and is used more frequently. It expresses the arrival and subsequent visit of a king or emperor (Mt 24:3, 27; I Cor 15:23; I Thess 2:19; 3:13; 4:15; II Thess 2:1, 8- 9; Jas 5:7- 8; II Pet 1:16; 3:4, 12; I Jn 2:28). See Albrecht Oepke, "*Parousia,* etc.," TDNT, V, 858- 871.

Christ's second coming includes two phases: His coming in the air for His own at the rapture (Jn 14:3; I Cor 15:51- 53; I Thess 4:13- 18; Rev 16:15), and His coming to rule over the nations of the world (Zech 14:1 ff.; Rev 20:4- 6).

The time of the rapture is a question to which three answers are given. It may be immediately preceding the Great Tribulation – the pre-Tribulation rapture view; in the middle of the Tribulation – the mid-Tribulation rapture view; or after the main part of the Great Tribulation but before the seven vials of wrath – the post-Tribulation rapture view.

The important thing, and that on which all premillennialists agree, is that the Scriptures of

the OT and NT both teach Christ will rule in His millennial kingdom upon the earth. They base their conclusion upon a grammatical-historical interpretation of both fulfilled and unfulfilled prophecy in OT and NT. *See* Eschatology; Rapture.

R. A. K.

CHRIST, CRUCIFIXION OF. *See* Cross.

CHRIST, DEATH OF. *See* Atonement; Christ, Passion of; Cross.

CHRIST, DEITY OF. Jesus Christ is the Son of God and very God of very God. He is of the same substance with the Father and the Holy Spirit, and equal in power and glory (*see* Godhead). Everything, therefore, that can be said of the Father and of the Holy Spirit can be said of the Son. He is the Creator (Jn 1:1- 3; Col 1:16; Heb 1:2), even as the Father (Gen 1:1; Rev 4:11) and the Holy Spirit (Gen 1:2) created. He is the Upholder and Sustainer of all things (Col 1:17; Heb 1:3), even as are the Father (Gen 8:21- 22) and the Holy Spirit (Job 27:3; 33:4). He is the Redeemer (Rev 5:9; Rom 3:24; Titus 2:14), even as the Father (Isa 63:16).

Biblical proofs of the deity of Christ. The deity of Christ is proved by certain express statements in Scripture (Immanuel, or "God with us," in Isa 7:14 and Mt 1:23; Jn 1:1; Jn 1:18, RSV marg.; Rom 9:5; Tit 2:13, RSV; Heb 1:8). He claimed to be able to forgive sins (Mk 2:5, 10- 11; Lk 7:48), which is the prerogative of God alone and was so recognized (Mk 2:7; Lk 5:21). He healed the sick (Mt 4:23 – 24; 8:14 – 17; 9:18 – 35; Lk 5:17 – 26; 7:18- 23), and raised the dead (Lk 7:11- 15; 8:41- 42, 49- 55; Jn 11:38- 44; cf. 5:25- 29). He controlled nature by stilling the waves (Mt 8:23- 27). He acted creatively in multiplying the loaves and fishes (Mt 14:19- 21; 15:32- 38). He claimed to be God (Jn 10:33) and to be pre-existent with God (Jn 8:58; 17:5). He is equal with the Father (Jn 14:9; Phil 2:5- 8) and one in essence with the Father (Jn 10:30). He alone of all men is worthy to be worshiped, an act prohibited toward mere created beings and reserved for God only (Jn 9:38; Phil 2:9- 11; Rev 5:11- 14; 19:10; 22:8 f.; Acts 10:25 f.).

Philosophical and theological proofs. If we are to have a God who is infinite in His person and in His relationships, this God must be triune in nature. *See* Trinity; Theism. Any view – such as the Muslim faith, Judaism, Jehovah's Witnesses – which states that there is only one person in the Godhead proves inadequate. Such a view presents a God who for the first time would have known a true subject-object relationship (the I-It relationship), would have had a real person relationship (the I-Thou relationship), or would have experienced an actual social relationship (the We-You), only after He had created both the world and man. This is the fatal defect in all Unitarian views. In that man knows and enjoys all these relationships, he would be greater in these respects than a non-triune God would have been before He created the world and man. Thus the eternal sonship and deity of Christ is philosophically tenable and necessary.

The deity of Jesus Christ is of the greatest importance for our salvation. Only an infinite person could offer an infinite sacrifice sufficient to satisfy God's divine justice and to atone for the sins of all who would believe. While sin started with a single act of disobedience, such as a forest fire starts with a single spark, it spread to all mankind; and its atonement — after sin had enveloped all of nature and of mankind — required not merely the act of a man but of the Almighty in His own omnipotent Son. *See* Incarnation.

R. A. K.

Nicene creed. In the 2nd and 3rd cen. A.D. widely divergent views of the relation of Jesus to God were expressed in the writings of various Christian leaders. Justin Martyr held that the Logos incarnated in Jesus Christ was a second God. Irenaeus emphasized the unity of God, or monotheism, while Paul of Samosata stressed the humanity of Jesus, saying He was a sinless man from birth. Sabellius believed the Father was born as Jesus Christ and suffered as the Son, the Father, Son, and Holy Spirit being three modes or aspects of God. Tertullian declared that God is one substance but three persons or parties in the divine administrative activity, and that Jesus was both God and man, one person but two substances or natures. Origen was basically orthodox but taught that while the Son was coeternal with the Father, yet Christ as the image of God is dependent upon the Father and subordinate to Him.

Early in the 4th cen. Arius, a presbyter in the Alexandrian church, maintained that the Son had a beginning and is not a part of God. The Father had created the Son in order that He might create the world. Such a controversy developed in the eastern part of the Roman Empire that Emperor Constantine summoned a council of the entire church that met at Nicaea in Asia Minor in A.D. 325. It was the first ecumenical council, with more than 300 bishops in attendance. The young Athanasius, a deacon of Alexandria, championed the orthodox position. The creed adopted by this council states that the Son is of the same substance (*homoousios*) with the Father. It reads as follows:

"We believe in one God, the Father Almighty, maker of all things visible and invisible, and in one Lord, Jesus Christ, the Son of God, the only-begotten of the Father, that is, of the substance (*ousias*) of the Father, God from God, light from light, true God from true God, begotten, not made, of one substance (*homoousion*) with the Father, through whom all things were made, those things that are in heaven and those things that are on earth, who for us men

and for our salvation came down and was made flesh, suffered, rose again on the third day, ascended into the heavens, and will come to judge the living and the dead" (K. S. Latourette, *A History of Christianity,* New York: Harper, 1953, p. 155).

While Arius was banished and his position anathematized, in the decades that followed his disciples tried to override the council's decision. Athanasius for a time was given so little support by others that historians speak of *Athanasius contra mundum,* "Athanasius against the world." He died in 373. Three outstanding bishops from Cappadocia, Gregory of Nazianzus, Basil of Caesarea, and Gregory of Nyssa, took up the contest and argued that there is only one *ousia* (substance, essence) in which Father, Son, and Holy Spirit share, but that there are three *hypostases* (translatable into Latin by *personae,* persons). A second ecumenical council met at Constantinople in 381 to make a final end of the Arian controversy. The orthodox doctrine established at Nicaea was reaffirmed and the Nicene creed modified and enlarged to its present form.

J. R.

Bibliography. G. C. Berkouwer, *The Person of Christ,* Grand Rapids: Eerdmans, 1954, pp. 155–192. Loraine Boettner, *Studies in Theology,* Eerdmans, 1947, pp. 140–182. H. P. Liddon, *The Divinity of Our Lord and Saviour Jesus Christ* (Bampton Lectures, 1866), 15th ed., London: Longmans, Green & Co., 1891. Wilbur M. Smith, *The Supernaturalness of Christ,* Boston: Wilde, 1940.

CHRIST, HUMANITY OF. The Scripture bears witness in numerous ways to the humanity of Jesus Christ. He was "the son of Abraham" (Mt 1:1), "made of the seed of David according

During His earthly life, Christ spent many hours by the Sea of Galilee. IIS

to the flesh" (Rom 1:3), conceived of Mary the virgin (Lk 1:31), "made of a woman" (Gal 4:4), born of Mary (Mt 1:25; 2:11; Lk 2:7), "made flesh" (Jn 1:14; cf. Rom 1:3; I Tim 3:16). He was an infant (Mt 2:11, 14, 20, 21; Lk 2:7, 16), He "increased in wisdom and stature" (Lk 2:52), wrought as a carpenter (Mk 6:3), hungered (Mt 4:2; Mk 11:12), thirsted (Jn 4:7; 19:28), experienced the emotions of joy and sorrow (Lk 10:21; Jn 12:27), was crucified, and rose again from the dead. He is expressly called man (Jn 1:30; Acts 17:31; Rom 5:15; I Cor 15:21, 47; I Tim 2:5; Heb 2:6–9). Four characterizations sum up the doctrine of Christ's humanity.

1. The *reality* must be emphasized in opposition to any view which either asserts or implies mere appearance or semblance. It was this heresy John was called upon to combat, and he says it was of Antichrist (I Jn 4:1–3). There are more subtle ways, however, in which the reality of Christ's humanity may be compromised. Human nature is finite and there are, therefore, the limitations inseparable from Jesus' manhood. The meaning of many of His words and actions in the days of His flesh are missed if one does not take account of His speaking and acting in terms of His human nature, and thus with the limitations incident to it. Conspicuous in this respect is Mt 24:36 which, so far from being a difficulty, is a clear index to the limited knowledge belonging to His human consciousness and His dependence upon revelation for all that came within its compass.

2. The *integrity* of Christ's humanity means that all the attributes essential to manhood were His. He was body and spirit. He had human understanding, feeling, and will, and these must not be submerged in the attributes of Deity which were also His. The jealousy with which the church must maintain this integrity appears in what was central in His mission. In human nature He suffered and died. It would impinge upon the reality of the atonement to impair to any extent the completeness with which He acted in terms of human nature.

3. The *sinlessness* of Jesus distinguishes His human nature from that of all others. Limitations are not to be equated with sinful infirmities nor with fallibility. From conception He was the holy thing begotten (Lk 1:35); born of a virgin. He was holy, harmless, undefiled, and separate from sinners (Heb 7:26), and no one could convict Him of sin (Jn 8:46). Though tempted in all points like as we are, yet it was the qualification "without sin" that imparted to His ability to sympathize its matchless grace and virtue (Heb 4:15).

4. The *continuance* of His humanity is indispensable to the discharge of His heavenly ministry. In death, body and spirit were separated, the body laid in the tomb and the spirit dismissed to the Father. But body and spirit were reunited in the resurrection. In the integrity of human nature physically and psychically constituted He ascended to heaven,

and continues His mediatorial ministry until at His advent He will return in this same human nature to judge the world and consummate the kingdom of God.

See Incarnation.

J. M.

CHRIST, HUMILIATION OF. The title "Christ" means "anointed"; it refers to that office which was undertaken in pursuance of God's saving and redeeming purpose. It is more proper, therefore, to speak first of all in terms of the humiliation of the Son of God. The latter title bespeaks His eternal and divine identity, and only against the background of such dignity may His humiliation be understood.

It would have been humiliation for the eternal Son of God to have come into this world and become man under the most ideal earthly conditions, a humiliation merely because of the disparity between God and man. It was not, however, into an ideal world that the Son of God came, but into this world of sin, and misery, and death. All the circumstances of His coming were conditioned by these facts. Not only so, He came to deal with sin, misery, and death; He took these upon Himself as the Sin-bearer to make an end of sin and abolish death for His people. The cross of Christ was self-humiliation to the lowest depths conceivable. Because of the dignity of His person as the one "in the form of God" and "on an equality with God" (Phil 2:6), and the damnation He took upon Himself as Sin-bearer, there is no parallel to this humiliation; it is inimitable and unrepeatable.

The humiliation began with the begetting in the womb by the Holy Spirit and conception by the virgin. The entrance into and development in the womb of one who was herself sinful, as all other members of the race, are indicative of the condescension. Jesus did not partake of Mary's sin but He did of her substance. The conditions under which Jesus was born at Bethlehem are expressive of the humiliation through which this Person must fulfill the design of His coming. The humble station in life at Nazareth, baptism of John at Jordan, temptation in the wilderness, weariness with toil, hunger and thirst, sufferings and persecutions, mockeries and insults in arraignment before the high priest and Pilate, the agony of Gethsemane—all exemplify the humiliation that converged upon and reached its climax in Calvary.

The humiliation did not end with the cross. His spirit went to paradise but His body was laid in the tomb. The Son of God was in the grave as respects His body and He remained under the power of death for a season. Only with the resurrection was humiliation ended. The resurrection was the first phase of that exaltation whereby is bestowed upon Him the highest exaltation conceivable (Phil 2:9).

See Kenosis.

J. M.

CHRIST, OBEDIENCE OF. *See* Obedience of Christ.

CHRIST, PASSION OF. The expression "passion of Christ" has its origin in the translation of the aorist infinitive of the verb *pascho* in Acts 1:3, where Luke speaks of the fact that Christ "showed himself alive after his passion by many infallible proofs." The verb here translated as a noun means "to suffer," and is used frequently to refer to the sufferings and death of Christ (Mt 16:21; 17:12), and specifically to the death of Christ in Lk 22:15; 24:26. The expression should not be confused with the "passions of men" referring to human emotion (Acts 14:15; Jas 5:17). Used of Christ, it embodies the thought of His sufferings and death on the cross.

The Garden Tomb, where many believe Christ was buried. HFV

The Prophetic Fulfillment

The sacrificial death of Christ was anticipated in the OT in the sacrificial system, and it was also the frequent subject of OT prediction (Ps 22; 69; Isa 53; Zech 12:10; 13:7; cf. Rev 1:7). Christ predicted His own sufferings and death constantly throughout His life ministry and especially toward its end (Mt 16:21; 17:22-23; 20:17-19; 26:12, 28, 31; Mk 9:31; 14:8, 24, 27; Lk 9:22, 44-45; 18:31-34; 22:20; Jn 2:19-21; 10:17-18; 12:7). It was anticipated in the announcement of John the Baptist (Jn 1:29) when Christ was introduced as "the Lamb of God, which taketh away the sin of the world," and especially in the Gospel of John in a number of classic passages (3:14-16; 6:51; 10:11; 11:49-52; 12:24; 15:13).

The crucifixion, a torturous death prescribed by Roman law for those who were not Roman citizens, together with the burial of Christ, is described in all four Gospels (Mt 27:31-56; Mk 15:20-41; Lk 23:26-49; Jn 19:16-37). The order of events in the Gospels includes the attempt of Jesus to carry the cross to the place of crucifixion. When He was unable to do this, Simon of Cyrene was compelled to carry the cross (Mt 27:32; Mk 15:21; Lk 23:26). John alone does not mention Simon. The place of crucifixion, described as Golgotha, is in-terpreted as "the place of a skull" (Mt 27:33; Mk 15:22; Jn 19:17). Luke alone calls it Calvary (Lk 23:33).

The order of events which followed the act of crucifixion is: (1) Christ's refusal of the drugged vinegar (Mt 27:34; Mk 15:23); (2) Christ's crucifixion along with two thieves (Mt 27:35-38; Mk 15:24-28; Lk 23:33-38; Jn 19:18-24); (3) His first statement on the cross, "Father, forgive them" (Lk 23:34); (4) the soldiers casting lots for His garment, in fulfillment of prophecy (Ps 22:18; Mt 27:35; Mk 15:24; Lk 23:34; Jn 19:23-24); (5) the mocking of the Jews (Mt 27:39-44; Mk 15:29-32; Lk 23:35-37); (6) the mocking of the two thieves, though later one believed (Mt 27:44; Mk 15:32; Lk 23:39-43); (7) the second statement of Christ, "Today shalt thou be with me in paradise" (Lk 23:43); (8) the third statement of Christ, "Woman, behold thy son" (Jn 19:26-27); (9) the three hours of darkness (Mt 27:45; Mk 15:33; Lk 23:44); (10) the fourth statement of Christ, "My God, my God, why hast thou forsaken me?" (Mt 27:46-47; Mk 15:34-35); (11) the fifth statement of Christ, "I thirst" (Jn 19:28); (12) the sixth statement of Christ, "It is finished" (Jn 19:30); (13) the seventh and final statement of Christ, "Father, into thy hands i commend my spirit" (Lk 23:46); (14) Christ dismissed His spirit (Mt 27:50: Mk 15:37; Lk 23:46; Jn 19:30). *See* Cross.

Immediately after His death, the veil of the temple was rent from top to bottom and graves were opened. Later, soldiers broke the legs of the two thieves, but finding Christ dead they pierced His side in fulfillment of Scripture (Jn 19:31-37; cf. Zech 12:10; Rev 1:7). The body of Christ was claimed by Joseph of Arimathea, who with Nicodemus prepared His body for burial and laid it in a new sepulcher in a garden. Christ's burial was followed by His resurrection on the first day of the week.

The Theological Significance of the Death of Christ

The central significance of the death of Christ is contained in three great words—redemption, propitiation, and reconciliation. According to Rom 3:24, believers in Christ are "justified freely by his grace through the redemption that is in Christ Jesus." The thought of redemption is that of deliverance by the payment of a price. The imagery involves both the redemption by purchase and the setting free of the object of redemption. Christ in His death also constituted a propitiation or satisfaction of the righteousness of God (Isa 53:11), as explained by the apostle Paul in Rom 3:25-26. Likewise, in His sacrifice "God was in Christ, reconciling the world unto himself, not imputing their trespasses unto them" (II Cor 5:19). Through the death of Christ, the sinner is transformed both in position and in nature, given eternal life, and thereby reconciled to God and His holy standards. *See* Propitiation; Reconciliation; Redemption.

The crypt in the Garden Tomb where Christ is believed to have been buried. Photo Leon, Jerusalem

Different Theories of the Atonement

In the history of the church, various theories of the atonement have been advanced. Historic orthodoxy has supported the concept of a *substitutional atonement*, also described as vicarious or penal. This regards the death of Christ as primarily directed toward God and the satisfaction of His holy character and righteous demands in relation to sinners (cf. Jn 1:29; II Cor 5:21; Gal 3:13; Heb 9:20; I Pet 2:24). Substitutionary atonement is indicated by the use of prepositions *peri, hyper,* and *anti,* used in relating the sacrifice of Christ to the sinner. The view of A. H. Strong, called "ethical atonement," and that of Louis Berkhof are variations of this point of view.

A number of alternative viewpoints have been advanced. Early Church Fathers, such as Origen, Augustine, and others, held to the *ransom theory,* that the death of Christ was a penalty paid to Satan in the form of a ransom, a view largely abandoned today. The *recapitulation theory,* supported by Irenaeus, viewed the death of Christ as a phase of Christ's reenactment of all phases of human life, including being made sin, without excluding the idea of the satisfaction of divine justice.

The *commercial theory,* advanced by Anselm in the 11th cen., regards the atonement as essentially commercial or one of the satisfactions of God in the sense that it satisfies the honor of God. While not necessarily contradicting the substitutionary view, it falls short of being penal. The *moral influence theory,* introduced by Abelard in opposition to Anselm, is based on the premise that God did not require the death of Christ as an expiation of sin but only to demonstrate His love and fellowship in suffering. This view is followed by modern neoorthodox and liberal scholars in its modern form as the *example theory,* that Christ died as merely an example.

Various combinations of these theories have been offered, such as that of Thomas Aquinas, usually considered the norm for Roman Catholic theology, which accepts substitutionary atonement with some qualification. Aquinas held that God was under no necessity to offer atonement. Another view, that of Duns Scotus, denies the necessity of the atonement as far as the nature of God is concerned, and makes it an arbitrary choice on the part of God that He accepts the sacrifice of Christ as sufficient apart from whether it is or not.

Schleiermacher and Ritschl offered a *mystical experience theory,* a variation of the moral influence theory, that the death of Christ in a mystical way influences the sinner for good. The *governmental theory* of Grotius is another compromise between the example theory and orthodox substitutionary atonement, in which the death of Christ proceeds from the government of God rather than the character of God. The *vicarious confession theory* is based on the idea that God could forgive if man could adequately repent and confess his sins. Because he could not, Christ did it in his place.

The Scriptures support the substitutionary concept that Christ actually died in the sinner's place and that this provided a righteous ground for God to forgive and to save (Isa 53:11; Rom 3:25–26; I Pet 2:24). The death of Christ is therefore essential not only to human faith and salvation but to the divine program of redemption, and constitutes a fundamental of Christian doctrine.

See Kenosis; Atonement.

Bibliography. Lewis Sperry Chafer, *Systematic Theology,* Dallas: Dallas Seminary Press, 1948, III, 35–164. James Denney, *The Death of Christ,* ed. by R. V. C. Tasker, London: Inter-Varsity, 1952. Leon Lamb Morris, *The Apostolic Preaching of the Cross,* Grand Rapids: Eerdmans, 1955. Andrew Murray, *The Power of the Blood of Jesus and The Blood of the Cross,* London: Marshall, Morgan & Scott, 1951.

J. F. W.

CHRIST, RESURRECTION OF. *See* Appearances of Christ; Resurrection of Christ.

CHRIST, SECOND COMING OF. *See* Christ, Coming of.

CHRIST, SINLESSNESS OF. This expression refers to Christ's perfect freedom from sin not only in its outward aspect of acts of sin but also in its inward aspect of an inclination to sin.

Scriptural statements. The perfect sinlessness of Christ is foretold in the OT under the figure of the holiness and righteousness of the coming Messiah (Ps 45:7; 89:19; Isa 11:5; 32:1; 49:7; 53:9; 59:17; Jer 23:5; Zech 9:9). In the NT it is declared in many passages (Mk 1:24; Lk 1:35; 4:34; 23:40–41; Jn 1:29; 8:46; 10:36; 16:10; Acts 3:14; 4:27, 30; 13:28; Rom 8:3; II Cor 5:21; Heb 4:15; 7:26–27; 9:14; I Jn

3:5; I Pet 1:19, 23; 3:18; I Jn 2:29; 3:5; Jas 5:6; Rev 3:7).

Christ's sinlessness is typified in the OT by the perfection required of the sacrifices (Ex 12:5; Deut 15:21; cf. Jn 1:29; I Pet 1:19). It was declared in the NT by the testimony of the demons (Mk 1:24; Lk 4:34); by Pilate's wife as she pleaded, "Have thou nothing to do with that just man" (Mt 27:19); by Pilate as he said, "I . . . have found no fault in this man" (Lk 23:14); by Judas as he cried, "I have betrayed the innocent blood" (Mt 27:4); by the centurion as he said, "Truly this was the Son of God" (Mt 27:54; cf. Lk 23:47). It is evidenced by the fact that while others admitted they were sinners, Christ maintained Himself to be sinless (Jn 8:46); while others had sins to confess, Christ confessed no sins; while others must be born again. He never spoke of the need for Himself. He was not, as we, dead in trespasses and sins (Eph 2:1), but rather He was the resurrection and the life (Jn 11:25).

Theological aspects of Christ's sinlessness. Man finds himself guilty of three kinds of sin: (1) original sin, that is, the sin of Adam which is imputed to every man (Rom 5:12 ff.); (2) a sinful fallen nature which leads man to want to sin (Rom 7:17 ff.); (3) individual acts of sin. It is because man under the federal headship of Adam is fallen in Adam, that the NT says, "By one man sin entered into the world . . . for that all have sinned" (aorist, Rom 5:12), and "in Adam all die" (I Cor 15:22).

But Christ did not enter the world under the federal headship of Adam. He introduced a new headship, His own (I Cor 15:20-22, 45-49). In order to do this it was necessary that He not follow in Adam's line, but be born of a virgin. This the angel made clear to Mary as he said, "The Holy Ghost shall come upon thee . . . therefore also that holy thing which shall be born of thee shall be called the Son of God" (Lk 1:35). A better translation, supported by the margin in Nestle and by Westcott and Hort, is, "therefore also that which is born shall be holy, the Son of God." This reading answers Mary's question, "How can this be, seeing I know not a man?" (The Son of God can be born of Mary and be holy because this will occur by the power of the Holy Spirit.) This is the attestation of the angel Gabriel to Christ's incarnation in innate holiness.

Some problems. Certain passages have raised problems. Why did Christ say to the rich young ruler in Mark, "Why callest thou me good? There is none good but one, that is, God" (Mk 10:18; cf. Lk 18:19)? And why did He ask a different question in Matthew, "Why do you ask me about what is good? One there is who is good" (Mt 19:17, RSV)? The answer is possibly the fact that Christ asked two separate questions. He was leading the young man on, stepwise, from the question, "Why do you ask Me about what is right?" (Matthew), to, "Why callest thou Me good?" (Mark and Luke), in an endeavor to evoke saving faith and the answer,

"Because You are God!" Thus seen, there is no hint given here by Christ that He is not God, but rather a pair of persuasive questions are so presented as to lead the young ruler toward making the conclusion that Jesus is God.

Concerning Christ's baptism, was not John's baptism one of repentance for the remission of sins? Yes, but Christ identified Himself with those He came to save. "He was made of a woman, made under the law," and, therefore, He must keep the law in its entirety. He was circumcised the eighth day (Lk 2:21), presented in the temple after the days of purification were over (Lk 2:22-24), and baptized in order "to fulfill all righteousness" (Mt 3:13-17; Lk 3:21-22).

Does the statement in Heb 5:7-8 regarding Christ learning obedience imply a stage in which Christ was not obedient? Christ learned obedience in connection with His suffering. He had come to do God's will (Heb 10:7-9), but this entailed terrible suffering and the agony of the sinless Son of God becoming sin, a sin bearer, for sinful man (II Cor 5:21). In this is seen the contrast between Adam's disobedience and Christ's obedience (Rom 5:19). *See* Temptation of Christ for the nature of Christ's sinlessness.

R. A. K.

CHRIST, TRANSFIGURATION OF. *See* Transfiguration of Christ.

CHRISTIAN. One who belongs or is devoted to Christ. This is one of several NT terms applied to followers of Christ. It is formed from Christ (Messiah) and the *-ianos* ending, which is from the Latin and is used only with proper names (cf. Herodians in Mk 3:6). The word occurs only three times in the NT: Acts 11:26; 26:28; I Pet 4:16. It was used first in Antioch, *c.* A.D. 43, and seems to have been given to the disciples by outsiders. (For a contrary opinion see Elias J. Bickerman, "The Name of Christians," *Harvard Theological Review,* XLII [1949], pp. 109-124.) The name most likely was used by Gentiles, since the Jews were still looking for the Messiah. The occasion was probably the large number of Gentiles who for the first time had become followers of Christ.

Several scholars feel that the name was given by enemies of the Christians. In favor of this view it is argued that the NT uses of the term have a note of hostility, and that the term *chrēstianos* was often applied to Christians. The word *chrēstianos* means "kindly" and was most likely used in derision. While it is true that in the NT "Christian" is used in relation to the outside world, it does not necessarily carry the implication of hostility in any of its three occurrences. Also, the word *chrēstianos* may have been a confusion of the word *christianos* and not the origin of it. If so, the term *christianos* most likely was used in a general way by outsiders to designate the followers of Christ, and not just by their enemies. Several considerations show the appropriateness of the term to designate the followers of Christ: the prophecy of a new name (Isa 65:15); references by Jesus (Mk 9:41; Lk 6:22); the apostles spoke in the name of Jesus (Acts 5:40); and believers were baptized in the name of Jesus (Acts 2:38).

D. R. S.

CHRISTIANITY. The religion founded by Jesus Christ. Following His ascension, the apostles in the power of the Holy Spirit preached in His name. They taught that He was God's Son, the Messiah; they gathered a community of believers; and they exhorted all to a holy life.

There is both a continuity and a discontinuity of Christianity with the religion of the OT. The life and teachings of Jesus, upon which Christianity is founded, are the culmination and fulfillment of the OT; and at the same time they represent the incarnation of the Spirit of God in a way radically different from anything which preceded. Although believing in the deity of Christ and the reality of the Holy Spirit in human affairs, Christianity has a strong monotheistic emphasis.

There has been great latitude in the historical development of Christianity. It is possible, however, to say that in the main the followers of Christ have stressed the historic and factual nature of the biblical revelation, and have attempted to follow it as the guide to faith and practice. Counting all adherents to Christianity there are at the present time about one billion Christians, the largest of all the world religions.

D. R. S.

CHRISTMAS. Tourists taking the Christmas pilgrimage to Jerusalem and Bethlehem are apt to be surprised at finding it celebrated there on three different days. Roman Catholics and most Protestants observe December 25. The Eastern Orthodox church holds to January 6, while the Armenian church observes January 19.

There is no evidence for the observance of December 25 before *c.* A.D. 300. Hippolytus, in his commentary on Daniel, is supposed to have been the first to compute the date. He believed that from the conception to the crucifixion of Jesus was exactly thirty-three years, and that both these events took place on March 25. That would make the birth, nine months later, fall on December 25. The weakness of these premises is obvious. In the 3rd cen. some favored April 18 or 19 for the birth of Christ, others March 28. A. H. Newman says: "The earliest record of the recognition of December 25 as a church festival is in the Philocalian Calendar (copied 354, but representing Roman practice in 336)" (SHERK, III, 47).

One objection often raised against observing Christmas is the claim that it is simply the old heathen festival of the sun Christianized. But it may have been intended to link this with the birth of the Sun of Righteousness (HDCG, I, 261).

R. E.

CHRISTS, FALSE. Those who claim to be the Messiah but are not. Jesus warned His disciples during the Passion week against such, saying that many would come in His name claiming to be the Messiah, and would deceive many. These pretenders were not to be believed (Mt 24:4, 11, 23–25; Mk 13:21–23; Lk 21:8). *See* Antichrist.

CHRONICLES, BOOKS OF. In the Heb. Bible Chronicles is called *dibrê hay-yāmîm,* "the words (affairs) of the days," meaning "the annals" (cf. I Chr 27:24). Other annals (now lost) are referred to in Kings (e.g., I Kgs 14:19, 29); but they cannot be our present I and II Chronicles, which were written a full century after I and II Kings. Jerome (A.D. 400) first entitled these books "Chronicles." Written as one book, they were divided into I and II Chronicles in the LXX (*c.* 180 B.C.). In the Heb. Bible, Chronicles closes the OT canon. Christ (Lk 11:51) therefore spoke of all the martyrs from Abel in the first book (Gen 4) to Zechariah in the last (II Chr 24).

Authorship

Chronicles does not explicitly state when or by whom it was written. The last recorded event is the decree of Cyrus in 538 B.C., releasing the Jews from their Babylonian captivity (II Chr 36:22). The book's genealogies extend to Pelatiah and Jesaiah (*c.* 500 B.C., I Chr 3:21), two grandsons of Zerubbabel, the leader of the returning exiles. The style and subject matter of Chronicles closely parallel Ezra, which carries on the history of the Jews from Cyrus down to 457 B.C. Both emphasize lists and genealogies, priestly activities, and reverence for the law of Moses. The last verses of II Chronicles (36:22–23), moreover, reappear as the opening verses of Ezra (1:1–3). Scholars, such as Albright (JBL, 40 [1921], 104–124), therefore, confirm the ancient Heb. tradition that Ezra may have written both Chronicles and Ezra. His total history would then have been finished *c.* 450 B.C.

Authorship by the "scribe" (Ezr 7:6) may explain Chronicles' repeated acknowledgment of written sources. These include prophetic records by Samuel (I Chr 29:29), Isaiah (II Chr 32:32), and a number of others (II Chr 9:29; 12:15; 20:34; 33:19), but especially "the book of the kings of Judah and Israel" (II Chr 16:11; 25:26; etc.). This last source cannot be our book of Kings, for verses such as I Chr 9:1 and II Chr 27:7 refer to it for further details on matters about which I and II Kings are silent. It must have been an extensive court record from which both Kings and Chronicles drew before it perished.

Contents

Chronicles seems to have been written as a part of Ezra's crusade to revitalize post-Exilic Judah in devotion to the law of Moses (Ezr 7:10). Starting in 458 B.C., Ezra campaigned to restore temple worship (Ezr 7:19-23, 27; 8:33-34), to save the Jews from mixed marriages with pagan neighbors (Ezr 9-10), and to rebuild Jerusalem and its walls (Ezr 4:8-16; 9:9). Chronicles, accordingly, consists of these four parts:

I.   Genealogies, Adam to 500 B.C., I Chr 1-9
     To establish family descent (cf. Ezr 2:59)

II. The Kingdom of David, I Chr 10-29
     The ideal theocratic state

III. The Glory of Solomon, II Chr 1-9
     Stressing the temple and its worship

IV. The History of the Southern Kingdom, II Chr 10-36
     Especially, religious reforms and military victories of Judah's more pious kings

While paralleling the events of Samuel and Kings, the priestly annals of Chronicles lend greater emphasis to the building of the temple (I Chr 22, etc.), the holy ark, the Mosaic sacrifices, Levites, and the singers (I Chr 13; 15-16). At the same time they omit certain moralistic, personal acts of the kings (II Sam 9; I Kgs 3:16-28) and biographies of the prophets (I Kgs 17:1-22:40; II Kgs 1:1-8:15). This agrees with the placement of Chronicles in the third (non-prophetic) part of the Heb. canon; contrast the location of the prophetically authored and more homiletically minded books of Samuel and Kings in the second (prophetic) division. Finally, the Chronicler seems deliberately to pass over the deteriorating reign of Saul (I Sam 8-30, except his death, 31), David's disputed accession and later shame (II Sam 1-4, 11-21), Solomon's failures (I Kgs 11), and the whole deviant history of the northern kingdom of Israel. The disenchanted, struggling Jews of 450 B.C. were painfully aware of the results of sin; what they needed was the encouragement and inspiration of their former, God-given victories (such as II Chr 13-14, 20, 25).

Authenticity

These very emphases, however, have caused the majority of modern critics to reject Chronicles as mere Levitical propaganda, dreams of "what ought to have happened" (IB, III, 341), with numerous conflicting revisions as late as 250 B.C. (e.g., Robert H. Pfeiffer, Adam C. Welch, and W. A. L. Elmslie). The book's high numbers (e.g., one million invading Ethiopians, II Chr 14:9) have been particularly ridiculed, despite the clarifications of believing scholars (see Edward J. Young, *An Introduction to the Old Testament*, pp. 420-421). But once a liberal writer denies the Mosaic origin of the Pentateuch and of OT religion, as all do, then an open-minded evaluation of Chronicles becomes impossible. Chronicles' repeated validations of the laws of the Pentateuch leave him no alternative but to reject its historicity. Yet excavations at Ras Shamra, the Canaanitish city of Ugarit of Moses' own day, have confirmed the authenticity of just such religious practices (J. W. Jack, *The Ras Shamra Tablets: Their Bearing on the Old Testament*, pp. 29 ff.). Albright further observes that archaeological discoveries have established the historicity of many of the statements that were formerly found in Chronicles alone (BASOR # 100 [1945], 18). Though Chronicles does indeed emphasize the brighter side of Israel's history, it is not unmindful of the defeats (cf. I Chr 29:22 on the undisputed second anointing of Solomon, and II Chr 17:3 on the more creditable first ways of David). Both the prophetic woes of Kings and the priestly hopes of Chronicles are true, and both are necessary. While the moralizing sermons of Kings are indispensable, it is the sacrificial redemption of Chronicles that constitutes the distinctiveness of NT Christianity.

Bibliography. William F. Albright, "The Date and Personality of the Chronicler," JBL, XL (1921), 104-124. Willis J. Beecher, "Chronicles," ISBE, I, 629-635. Edward L. Curtis and A. A. Madsen, ICC. H. L. Ellison, "I and II Chronicles," *The New Bible Commentary*, ed. by Francis Davidson, Grand Rapids: Eerdmans, 1953, pp. 339-364. W. A. L. Elmslie, *The Books of Chronicles (Cambridge Bible for Schools and Colleges)*, Cambridge: Univ. Press, 1916; "The First and Second Books of Chronicles," IB, III, 339-548. J. K. F. Keil and F. J. Delitzsch, KD. J. Barton Payne, "Chronicles," *Wycliffe Bible Commentary*, Chicago: Moody, 1962. A. M. Renwick, "I and II Chronicles," *The Biblical Expositor*, ed. by Carl F. H. Henry, Philadelphia: Holman, I (1960), 351-377. Israel W. Slotki, *Chronicles (Soncino Books of the Bible)*, Bournemouth, England: Soncino, 1952.

J. B. P.

CHRONOLOGY OF THE OLD TESTAMENT.

Biblical chronology in general and OT chronology specifically present many intricate and in some cases insoluble problems. For some periods of biblical history no detailed chronological sources are available, and even where such information is provided, the data often seems to be contradictory or incomprehensible. It is for these reasons that many differing chronological schemes have been worked out by scholars, and that absolute unanimity has still not been reached in the field, though an intensive study of the biblical and extrabiblical data has led to a great measure of agreement for the later periods of OT history.

Many editions of the KJV contain in the

margins OT dates which are the result of computations made by Archbishop James Ussher, first published in his *Annales* (1650–58). According to his scheme of reckoning, the creation of the world took place in 4004 B.C., exactly 4,000 years before Christ's birth. Since Ussher's dates were computed at a time when chronological data of the nations surrounding Israel was not yet available or only incorrectly understood, it is not surprising to find that his dates can no longer be considered a valid system of chronology. Three centuries of increasing knowledge in the field of ancient history have thoroughly outmoded them.

From the Creation to the Deluge

The only biblical data for this period is contained in the genealogical list of Gen 5 to which Gen 7:11 must be added. This list contains the age of one representative patriarch of each of ten successive generations. By adding up the ages which each patriarch had reached at the time his first son was born, a total figure of 1,656 years is obtained, according to the figures of the Masoretic Hebrew Text. These 1,656 years represent the time from the creation of Adam to the Flood in the six hundredth year of Noah's life.

However, the Samaritan Pentateuch, the LXX, and the statements of the Jewish historian Josephus vary greatly with regard to these figures, as Table I shows. In the LXX six of the ten patriarchs are given ages at the time of the birth of their sons that are 100 years higher than in the Masoretic Text. This lengthening of ages has the result that the period between the creation and the Flood according to the LXX is

2,242 years long. On the other hand, the figures of the Samaritan version are shorter in several instances, with the result that the period from the creation to the Flood is only 1,307 years long. According to Josephus, who follows closely but not completely the figures of the LXX, this period has a length of 2,256 years. These great divergences between the ancient sources make it understandably difficult to establish a convincing case for acceptance of one set of figures and rejection of the others.

Furthermore, it should be pointed out that commentators differ in their understanding of these genealogical lists. Some take them to indicate a direct succession of one generation after the other, from father to son, while others assume that a number of links have dropped out and that only some representative patriarchs are listed. A third group of interpreters considers the names given as dynasties of peoples. The two last-mentioned groups of interpreters therefore deny that the figures given in Gen 5 provide a basis for an estimate of the length of the period which lay between the creation and the Deluge.

In this connection it must be stated that the ancient methods of composing biblical genealogical lists are unknown to us. A comparison of such lists shows that hardly two parallel lists ever completely agree with each other. That the knowledge of the methods employed was already forgotten in the time of the apostles, with the result that the study of genealogies presented great difficulties and caused differences of opinion, can be concluded from the admonition of the apostle Paul to avoid disputations concerning "endless genealogies" (I Tim 1:4).

TABLE I

GENEALOGY OF THE PATRIARCHS FROM CREATION TO THE FLOOD

	Hebrew		*Samaritan*		*LXX*		*Josephus*	
	Age at Son's Birth	Age at Death	Age at Son's Birth	Age at Death	Age at Son's Birth	Age at Death	Age at Son's Birth	Age at Death
Adam	130	930	130	930	230	930	230	930
Seth	105	912	105	912	205	912	205	912
Enos	90	905	90	905	190	905	190	905
Cainan	70	910	70	910	170	910	170	910
Mahalaleel	65	895	65	895	165	895	165	895
Jared	162	962	62	847	162	962	162	962
Enoch	65	365	65	365	165	365	165	365
Methuselah	187	969	67	720	167*	969	187	969
Lamech	182	777	53	653	188	753	182	777
Noah	500	950	500	950	500	950	500	950
Noah's age at Flood	600		600		600		600	

*Later editions of the LXX give Methuselah's age at the birth of Lamech as 187 years, in an attempt to avoid the obvious difficulty of having Methuselah live 14 years after the Flood.

Secular records are entirely lacking for this period, and those given in the later Sumerian King Lists are legendary data. According to some lists ten kings, according to others eight kings, reigned over the country before the Deluge, to whom are given reigns averaging more than 20,000 years each.

It must therefore be concluded that neither the biblical records nor secular documents can give a final and definite answer to the question how long man has been on earth.

From the Deluge to Abraham

The biblical sources for the chronology of this period and problems connected with them are similar to those of the preceding era. Again nothing is available but genealogical lists (Gen 11:10-26), and they differ widely among the Masoretic Text, the LXX, the Samaritan Pentateuch, and Josephus, as Table II shows.

An additional uncertainty lies in the fact that the age of Terah at the time of Abraham is not clearly given. Gen 11:26 seems to imply that Terah was 70 years old when Abraham was born, but a comparison of Gen 11:32; 12:4; Acts 7:4 indicates that Abraham was probably born when his father had reached the age of 130 years. Taking this latter figure, the data of the Masoretic Text lead to a total of 352 years from the Flood to the birth of Abraham, the data of the Samaritan Pentateuch to 942 years, and of the LXX to 1,232 years. Both the Samaritan and the Gr. texts give to several patriarchs a higher age at the birth of their firstborn son than the Masoretic Text does. Furthermore, the LXX adds Cainan, with 130 years, to

the list by putting him between Arphaxad and Salah. This additional name is also found in Lk 3:35-36, where the same genealogical list is preserved. This fact provides powerful support to the views of those who see in the genealogical lists of Gen 5 and 11 no absolutely complete records, but only selections or excerpts of longer lists of generations.

Exact chronologies of early Egypt and Mesopotamia, two countries from which early historical records are available, have not yet been established, but all available evidence indicates that history based on written records began in both countries about 3000 B.C. Hence, the Deluge, which preceded the establishment of historical Egypt and of Sumer, must have occurred at an earlier time.

From Abraham to the Exodus

For this period not only genealogical information is available but also some chronological data, although they also pose problems. A key statement for this period claims that the total length of Israel's sojourn at the time of the Exodus was 430 years (Ex 12:40). However, the Samaritan Pentateuch and the LXX include in this number not only the years spent in Egypt but also the years of the patriarchs' sojourning in Canaan, and the apostle Paul accepts this reasoning, as is seen from Gal 3:16-17. Paul here clearly shows that he considered the 430 years as beginning at the time when the promises were made to Abraham (Gen 12:1-4) and terminating with the giving of the law at Sinai.

If this interpretation is correct, the actual

TABLE II

GENEALOGY OF THE PATRIARCHS FROM THE FLOOD TO ABRAHAM

	Hebrew		Samaritan		LXX		Josephus
	Age at Son's Birth	Remaining Years	Age at Son's Birth	Remaining Years	Age at Son's Birth	Remaining Years	Age at Son's Birth
Shem (age 2 years after the Flood)	100	500	100	500	100	500	(omits)
Arphaxad	35	403	135	303	135	430*	135
Cainan					130	330	
Salah	30	403	130	303	130	330	130
Eber	34	430	134	270	134	370*	134
Peleg	30	209	130	109	130	209	130
Reu	32	207	132	107	132	207	130
Serug	30	200	130	100	130	200	132
Nahor	29	119	79	69	179*	129*	120
Terah	70	135	70	75	70	135	
Terah (at Abram's birth)	130	75	70	75	130	75	70

*Ancient texts of the LXX disagree on these figures. The figures here given are from the oldest LXX texts known.

time spent by the Israelites in Egypt from the time Jacob entered Egypt until the Exodus could have been only 215 years, because the migration of Jacob's family to Egypt took place 215 years after Abraham came to Canaan, as can be seen from the following data. Abraham was 75 years old at the time he entered Canaan and received God's promises (Gen 12:4). Abraham was 100 years old when Isaac was born (Gen 21:5), hence 25 years after Abraham's entry into Canaan. Isaac was 60 at the time of Jacob's birth (Gen 25:26), and Jacob was 130 at the time of his migration to Egypt (Gen 47:9, 28). Adding up the 25, 60, and 130 years makes 215 years from the beginning of the sojourn in Canaan to the beginning of the sojourn in Egypt, and if the 215 years are part of the total period of 430 years, the time spent by the Israelites in Egypt was another 215 years.

No other chronological statements are preserved for this period, and the genealogical data covering Israel's stay in Egypt are of doubtful value. Some of the people who lived at the time of the Exodus, such as Moses, Aaron, and Miriam, seem to be removed from Jacob by only four generations (Num 3:17–19; 26:57–59; etc.), while others, such as Joshua, are said to be removed from Jacob by 11 generations (I Chr 7:20–27). Hence, the genealogical lists cannot decide the question whether the Israelites spent the long period of 430 years or the shorter period of 215 years in Egypt. [Actually the LXX and Samaritan reading of Ex 12:40 merely state that "the children of Israel"—not including Abraham and Isaac—sojourned in Canaan and in Egypt 430 years. A few more than 30 years passed from Jacob's return from Padan-aram until he and his sons migrated to Egypt.—Ed.]

The date of the Exodus is disputed. Many scholars place the Exodus in the 13th cen. B.C. during the reign of the Nineteenth Dynasty kings, while others favor an Exodus date in the 15th cen. during the reign of the powerful kings of the Eighteenth Dynasty. The crucial text to determine the date of the Exodus is I Kgs 6:1, according to which Solomon began to build the temple in the fourth year of his reign, which coincided with the 480th year after the Exodus. The dates of Solomon's reign are fairly well established (see sections under United and Divided Kingdoms), and his fourth regnal year was the year 967/6 B.C. The month Zif, in which the work began, was a spring month, hence the building activity began in the spring of 966 B.C. Since this was the 480th year after the Exodus, that event must have taken place in 1445 B.C. *See* Exodus, The.

The invasion of Canaan took place 40 years after the Exodus (Num 33:38; Deut 1:3; Josh 5:6), hence after 1405 B.C. when the Hebrews began to make their inroads into Canaan in the Amarna period. The final destruction of the reused Hyksos-built city wall of Jericho possibly may be attributed to this invasion, as well as the fact that Jericho's cemetery shows that

no burials took place after *c.* 1375 B.C. Also the destruction of a gateway in Area K at Hazor and of Debir's city C_1 may be attributed to the Israelite campaigns under Joshua (Josh 6:20–21; 10:39; 11:13). The destruction of Hazor and Debir in the 13th cen. B.C., of which the ruins also contain clear evidence, must therefore have occurred in the period of the judges. Recent discoveries at various sites in Transjordania have revealed that in some spots a sedentary population occupied eastern Palestine, contrary to earlier claims that it had been unoccupied from the 18th to the 13th cen. B.C. These evidences and others not mentioned here make it therefore plausible to believe that the Exodus took place in the 15th cen. B.C.

Using the year 1445 B.C. as the end of the period which begins with Abraham and terminates with the Exodus, the migration of Abraham to Canaan took place in 1875 B.C., his birth in 1950 B.C., and the migration of Jacob's family to Egypt in 1660 B.C.—during the Hyksos period. Joseph's position as vizier of Egypt can better be visualized under the foreign Hyksos rulers than in any other period of Egypt's history. The fact that horses and chariots are also first mentioned in the Bible in connection with the Joseph stories (Gen 41:43; 47:17) agrees with the historical fact that the Hyksos introduced horses and chariots into Egypt for the first time.

The Period of the Judges

A definite chronology for the period of the judges cannot be established for the following reasons: (1) no information is available with regard to the length of time that elapsed from the beginning of the conquest under Joshua (40 years after the Exodus) until the oppression of Chushan-rishathaim started, some time after Joshua's death; (2) the length of Samuel's judgeship is unknown; and (3) the total of all figures given in the book of Judges for the periods of oppression and of rest under the rule of judges considerably exceeds the total number of years available for this period. Therefore it must be concluded that some of the periods of oppression and rest overlapped.

Archaeological evidence has shown that Shechem and its great temple of Baal were destroyed *c.* 1150 B.C., which helps to date the approximate reign of Abimelech, since he was the king responsible for Shechem's destruction (Jud 9:46–49). Furthermore, the excavations of Shiloh revealed that that city was destroyed *c.* 1100 B.C., thus providing an approximate date for Eli's death, which occurred after the battle of Aphek and the capture of the ark (I Sam 4:11, 18), for it must be assumed that Shiloh was at that time destroyed by the victorious Philistines (Jer 7:12, 14; 26:6, 9).

The period of the judges began with the oppression of Chushan-rishathaim, the result of an apostasy of the Israelites. This apostasy had set in some time after the death of Joshua and the elders, during whose time Israel had served the

TABLE III

TENTATIVE CHRONOLOGY OF PERIOD OF THE JUDGES

	B.C.
Invasion of Canaan	c.1405
Israel under Joshua and the elders (Jud 2:7)	c.1405 – c.1364
Othniel's liberation from Chushan-rishathaim's eight-year oppression (Jud 3:8)	c.1356
Rest of 40 years (Jud 3:11)	c.1356– c.1316
Ehud's liberation from 18-year Moabite oppression (Jud 3:14– 15)	c.1298
80 years' rest of southern and eastern tribes (Jud 3:30)	c.1298–c.1218
Deborah and Barak's liberation after Jabin's 20 years of oppression in the N (Jud 4:3)	c.1258
Rest of 40 years in the N (Jud 5:31)	c.1258–c.1218
Gideon's liberation from seven-year Midianite oppression (Jud 6:1 ff.)	c.1211
Gideon's rule of 40 years (Jud 8:28)	c.1211–c.1171
Abimelech's kingship over Shechem (Jud 9:22)	c.1171–c.1168
Tola, Jair (Jud 10:1– 3)	c.1168–c.1123
Jephthah's liberation from 18-year Ammonite oppression (Jud 10:8 – 11:33)	c.1105
Jephthah, Ibzan, Elon and Abdon (Jud 12:7–9, 11, 13– 14)	c.1105–c.1074
Philistine oppression of 40 years (Jud 13:1)	c.1119–c.1079
Samson's exploits (Jud 14:1 – 15:20; 16:31)	c.1101–c.1081
Ark taken, Eli's death (I Sam 4:18)	c.1099
Battle of Ebenezer, Philistines defeated (I Sam 7:2– 12)	c.1079
Samuel as judge (I Sam 7:15– 17)	c.1079–c.1050

Lord (Jud 2:7– 11; 3:7– 8)—perhaps some 30 to 40 years after the conquest (c. 1370 B.C.). It ended c. 1050 B.C. when Saul was elected king (see next section). Hence, the whole period of the judges, from Othniel to Samuel, lasted approximately 320 years. Table III gives dates for the various periods of oppression, of political rest, and of the years of reign of the several judges. All dates are only approximate and are based on 1445 B.C. as the year of the Exodus, as well as on the statement of the judge Jephthah that in his time the conquest lay 300 years in the past (Jud 11:26). If the Exodus took place 200 years later, i.e., in the 13th cen. B.C., as many scholars believe, the period of the judges would have been only c. 120 years in length and all dates presented in Table III would have to be revised accordingly.

The United Kingdom

The OT provides no information with regard to the length of Saul's reign, but Paul in one of his sermons gives the length as "40 years" (Acts 13:21). Since he makes no point of exact chronology, it is entirely possible that the term "40 years," like that of the "450 years" in the preceding verse, was meant as a round number.

David's 40-year reign, however, may be regarded as established, since the number 40 is the sum of seven years of reign in Hebron and of 33 years in Jerusalem (II Sam 5:4– 5; I Kgs 2:11; I Chr 29:27). One event is dated in his fortieth year (I Chr 26:31).

Solomon also reigned 40 years (I Kgs 11:42), which again may be a round number. His reign began before his father's death (I Kgs 1:32– 48), but no information is given concerning the length of this coregency. However, the context of the story and the expressions used in I Chr 23:1 give the impression that Solomon's coronation took place shortly before David's death. Hence, we should not count on a great overlap of the reigns of the two kings. Solomon's death, which marked the division of the kingdom, occurred in 931 B.C. (see next section). This date can be considered to be fairly accurate, while the other dates given here for the reign of Saul, David, and Solomon are only approximate, since they depend on the accuracy of the number 40 for the length of reign of each of the three kings involved, and the assumption that Solomon came to the throne in the year of David's death.

Saul	c. 1050 – c. 1011 B.C.
David	c. 1011 – c. 971 B.C.
Solomon	c. 971 – c. 931 B.C.

In the section on Abraham to the Exodus reference was made to the beginning of the building of the temple by Solomon in the spring of 966 B.C., which according to I Kgs 6:1 marked 480 years after the Exodus. The correctness of this date hinges on the accuracy of the length of Solomon's reign. While the year of his death (931 B.C.) is fairly well established, the beginning of his reign in 971 B.C. is based on I Kgs 11:42, which mentions 40 years as the length of Solomon's reign. If Solomon came to the throne in 971 B.C., his first year began with the following New Year's Day in the autumn of 970 B.C., and his fourth year was 967/66 B.C. (autumn to autumn). Since the month Zif, during which the actual building activity started, was a spring month, we have to conclude that the beginning of the building of the temple must be dated in the spring of 966 B.C.

The Divided Kingdoms — Israel and Judah

For this period precise chronological data are available, giving for each king the length of reign, and also many synchronisms by dating the beginning of a king's reign in the regnal year of the monarch who at that time reigned in the rival kingdom. The mention of Assyrian kings in the records dealing with the history of the divided kingdoms also provides chronological evidence, as does the mention of kings of Israel or of Judah in Assyrian records. Furthermore, several synchronisms between kings of Judah and of Babylon are given in the OT, which serve as helps to establish an accurate chronology for the last period of the kingdom of Judah.

A study of all available evidence leads to certain conclusions with regard to the chronological methods employed by ancient scribes who produced the source material which forms

TABLE IV

CHRONOLOGY OF THE KINGS OF ISRAEL AND JUDAH			
Israel		*Judah*	
	B.C.		B.C.
Jeroboam I	931–910	Rehoboam	931–913
		Abijam	913–911
Nadab	910–909	Asa	911–869
Baasha	909–886		
Elah	886–885		
Zimri	885		
Omri	885–874		
(Tibni	885–880)		
Ahab	874–853	Jehoshaphat	872–848*
Ahaziah	853–852	Jehoram	854–841*
Joram	852–841	Ahaziah	841
Jehu	841–814	Athaliah	841–835
Jehoahaz	814–798	Joash	835–796
Jehoash	798–782	Amaziah	796–767
Jeroboam II	793–753*	Azariah (Uzziah)	791–739*
Zachariah	753–752		
Shallum	752		
Menahem	752–742	Jotham	750–731*
Pekahiah	742–740		
Pekah	752–732*	Ahaz	735–715*
Hoshea	732–722	Hezekiah	729–686*
		Manasseh	696–641*
		Amon	641–639
		Josiah	639–608
		Jehoahaz	608
		Jehoiakim	608–598
		Jehoiachin	598–597
		Zedekiah	597–586

The dates follow Edwin R. Thiele, except with regard to King Hezekiah.

*The Hebrew reigns thus marked (*) are reckoned as overlapping; that is, the earlier years of one reign coincide with the closing years of the preceding reign, representing coregencies. The one exception is Pekah, whose years seem to have been reckoned from 752 B.C., ten years before he took over actual control of the kingdom by murdering Menahem's son Pekahiah.

the basis for a reconstruction of the history of the Heb. kings. The regnal years of all kings always coincided with the existing calendar years, and were not anniversary years as are the regnal years of modern rulers. However, the official years of kings in the ancient Near East were reckoned according to at least two different methods, and both methods were employed in the OT with regard to the kings of Israel and Judah. One method of reckoning was to count the year in which a king came to the throne as his "accession year" and then begin his "year one" with the following New Year's Day. According to the other method, a king began to count the year of his accession as "year one," and began "year two" at the following New Year's Day. In the latter case the calendar year in which a king came to the throne was officially counted twice, i.e., as the last year of the dead king, and as the first year of the incoming king. A study of all available evidence shows that the kings of Israel applied the non-accession-year system from Jeroboam I to Jehoahaz, but the accession-year system from Jehoash to the end of the kingdom, while the kings of Judah employed the accession-year system throughout their history, except for a short period from Jehoram to Joash, when, under the influence of the northern kingdom, the non-accession-year system was followed.

The chronology of this period is further complicated by two facts: (1) The kingdom of Israel used a calendar year that began in the spring with the month later called Nisan as its initial month, while the kingdom of Judah employed a calendar year that began in the autumn, with the month later called Tishri as its first month. (2) The scribes of both countries recorded synchronisms and other data of their own kings as well as that of the rival country according to the system employed in their own land.

Several kings associated their sons with them on the throne and thus created coregencies. Only one such coregency is expressly mentioned in the biblical record, that between Azariah (Uzziah) and Jotham (II Kgs 15:5), while other coregencies can be recognized either by double synchronisms such as those given for Jehoram (II Kgs 1:17; 3:1) and Hoshea of Israel (II Kgs 15:30; 17:1), or by a careful study of all available data. In Israel, King Pekah evidently counted a large portion of his regnal years simultaneously with those of his two rivals, Menahem and Pekahiah.

Because of the contact between the Heb. kings and the rulers of the Assyrian and Babylonian empires, whose chronologies from the 10th cen. B.C. are well established, a fairly accurate chronology in terms of B.C. dating can be obtained. The first of these contacts is the battle of Qarqar in the sixth year of Shalmaneser III, in which, according to the Assyrian records, King Ahab of Israel took part. The second contact is King Jehu's payment of tribute to the same Assyrian king in his eighteenth year. The Assyrian chronology of this period is firmly established by means of the Assyrian eponym lists through their mentioning of a solar eclipse that took place on June 15, 763 B.C. *See* Eclipse. Combined with the biblical synchronisms and regnal years of the Israelite kings involved, the information given by Shalmaneser III thus enables us to date with reasonable certainty Ahab's death in 853/52 B.C. and the accession of Jehu in 841/40 B.C. A further result of this information is the fixation of the chronology of the kings of Israel and Judah before the reign of Ahab and after that of Jehu. The computations based on this evidence lead to 931 B.C. as the year of the accession of Jeroboam I of Israel and of Rehoboam of Judah in the year of Solomon's death. This date has been used in the sections from Abraham to the close of the judges as the basis for the computation of chronological dates of the earlier biblical periods.

Also, the reign of some of the last kings of Judah can be dated fairly accurately through synchronisms with Nebuchadnezzar II of Babylon, such as those given in Jer 25:1–3 and in II Kgs 24:12, 17; 25:1–2, 8–9, since Nebuchadnezzar's regnal years are well established by an astronomical tablet of his thirty-seventh year, by many dated economic records, and by the Babylonian Chronicle.

Table IV presents the results of the most recent studies of all data as applied to the chronology of the kings of Israel and Judah. The dates presented follow for the most part the studies of E. R. Thiele (see bibliography), and deviate from them only with regard to the period of King Hezekiah. (The writer believes he has a more satisfactory solution of the chronological problems than has Thiele.)

Exile and Post-Exilic Period

The OT contains records of three successive captures of Jerusalem by Nebuchadnezzar II, each accompanied by the carrying away of captives. The first capture took place in the third year of King Jehoiakim (Dan 1:1–3), in 605 B.C. The second capture occurred March 16, 597 B.C., when young Jehoiachin surrendered to Nebuchadnezzar (according to the Babylonian Chronicle and II Kgs 24:12), while the third and final fall of Jerusalem took place in the eleventh year of King Zedekiah (II Kgs 25:2), in 586 B.C.

Babylon fell to Cyrus of Persia on October 12, 539 B.C. The same king allowed the Jews to return to their homeland, issuing a decree to this effect in his first year (II Chr 36:22; Ezr 1:1). Cyrus' first regnal year, according to Persian reckoning, lasted from the spring of 538 B.C. to the spring of 537 B.C., but according to Jewish reckoning from the autumn of 538 B.C. to the autumn of 537 B.C. Neh 1:1 and 2:1 provide evidence that the Jews in post-Exilic times reckoned the years of Persian kings according to their own calendar year, which began in Tishri, and not according to the Persian calendar year, which began in Nisan. The Aramaic papyri from Elephantine have furnished evidence that the same custom was employed by the Egyptian Jews in the 5th cen. B.C. (see bibliography under Horn and Wood). Hence, it can be concluded that Cyrus' decree was issued in 537 B.C., and that the return of the Jews took place during the following year, which was the seventieth year after the first captivity had begun, thus fulfilling the prophecy of Jeremiah concerning the length of the Exile (Jer 25:12; 29:10).

After the return of the Jews under Cyrus, the work of rebuilding the temple was commenced at once, but due to various difficulties it soon came to a halt. However, in the second year of Darius I (520/19 B.C.) the building activity was resumed, chiefly as the result of appeals made by the prophets Haggai and Zechariah (Ezr 4:24; 5:1–2; Hag 1:1–15; 2:1–9). The building was completed on Adar 3 of the sixth year of Darius (Ezr 6:15), which was March 12, 515 B.C.

The last events recorded in the OT took place under Artaxerxes I (465–423 B.C.). Ezra was sent to Jerusalem as plenipotentiary in Artaxerxes' seventh year (Ezr 7:7–9). If the reckoning of Ezr 7 follows that of Nehemiah, as there is every reason to believe it does since Ezra and Nehemiah were originally one book, Artaxerxes' seventh year was reckoned from the autumn of 458 B.C. to the autumn of 457 B.C. Accordingly, Ezra began his journey in the spring of 457 B.C. and arrived in Jerusalem in the summer of the same year.

After Nehemiah, a Jewish royal courtier, heard of the sad state of affairs at Jerusalem in the month Chislev of the twentieth year of Artaxerxes (Neh 1:1), he obtained an appointment as governor of Judah in Nisan of the same twentieth year (Neh 2:1–8). That was in April, 444 B.C. The last date mentioned in the OT is the thirty-second year of Artaxerxes (433/32 B.C.), when Nehemiah's first term as governor of Judah came to an end (Neh 13:6).

Bibliography. W. F. Albright, "The Chronology of the Divided Monarchy of Israel," BASOR #100 (Dec., 1945), 16–22. Joachim Begrich, *Die Chronologie der Könige von Israel und Juda,* Tübingen: J. C. B. Mohr, 1929. S. H. Horn and L. H. Wood, "The Fifth Century Jewish Calendar at Elephantine," JNES, XIII (1954), 1–20; "The Chronology of King Hezekiah's Reign," *Andrews University Seminary Studies,* II (1964). P. van der Meer, *The Ancient Chronology of Western Asia and Egypt,* 2nd ed., Leiden: E. J. Brill, 1955. R. A. Parker and W. H. Dubberstein, *Babylonian Chronology 626 B.C.-A.D. 75,* Providence: Brown Univ. Press, 1956. L. Pirot and V. Coucke, "Chronologie biblique," *Supplément au Dictionnaire de la Bible,* ed. by L. Pirot, A. Robert and H. Cazelles, Paris: Letouzey et Ane, I (1928), cols. 1244– 1279. Edwin R. Thiele, *The*

Mysterious Numbers of the Hebrew Kings, 2nd ed., Chicago: Univ. of Chicago, 1955; "The Question of Coregencies Among the Hebrew Kings," *A Stubborn Faith,* ed. by Ed. C. Hobbs, Dallas: Southern Methodist Univ. Press, 1956, pp. 39–52; "Synchronisms of the Hebrew Kings," *Andrews University Seminary Studies,* I (1963), 121–138; II (1964). D. J. Wiseman, *Chronicles of the Chaldean Kings (626–556 B.C.) in the British Museum,* London: British Museum, 1956.

S. H. H.

CHRONOLOGY OF THE NEW TESTAMENT. The NT contains chronology in the sense that it records its story accurately and in orderly sequence. But it does not give a carefully dated chronicle. Hence attempt is made to take its historical data, compare it with information from other available sources, and to arrive if possible at specific dates for its major events.

Dates in the Life of Christ

His birth. The scriptural facts which are involved in the date of the birth of Christ are these:

1. Herod was king of Judea (Mt 2:1). The birth of Christ took place while Herod was still living, not long before his death (Mt 2:20, 22), yet possibly as much as two years before (Mt 2:7, 16). The Jewish historian Josephus identifies the year of this Herod's death as 4 B.C. He even tells the time of year, just before Passover, and records an eclipse of the moon which preceded his last illness. This eclipse has been dated astronomically as March 12, 4 B.C. So the spring of 4 B.C. was the date of Herod's death and the latest possible date for Jesus' birth. In light of Herod's concern for the precise time of the appearance of the star and his order to kill all the children of Bethlehem "from two years old and under, according to the time which he had diligently inquired of the wise men" (Mt 2:16), it seems probable that the birth took place at least one, perhaps two years earlier, therefore 6 or 5 B.C. It is clear, then, that the monk Dionysius Exiguus, who *c.* A.D. 525 introduced the present method of dating forward and backward "from the year of the incarnation of our Lord Jesus Christ," made an error in his calculations. On the basis of the data at his command, he fixed the birth of Christ as the year 754 of the Roman era instead of 750 or earlier.

2. The enrollment under Quirinius (Lk 2:2, RSV). What is known of this Roman official from outside the Bible is in harmony with what the Scripture here says of him, but it does not fix the date of this enrollment. *See* Census; Cyrenius.

3. Jesus' age at His baptism (Lk 3:23). "And Jesus himself began to be about thirty years of age" at the time of His baptism. Assuming that this means His age was close to 30, it ought to be possible to reckon back to the birth date of Jesus. The date of the beginning of John's min-

istry is carefully given by Luke (see below) and, as is shown later, was probably in A.D. 26. If the baptism of Jesus took place shortly after, which is the impression gained from reading the account, then subtracting "about thirty years" brings us to "about" 5 B.C. as the date of His birth. Obviously this is a very inexact reckoning, but it coincides with the date figured from the death of Herod.

4. The star of Bethlehem. Attempt has been made to fix the date of the nativity by identifying the star seen by the wise men as a natural phenomenon. Astronomers have pointed out that unusual conjunctions of planets did occur in 7 or 6 B.C. In China there is recorded a comet or nova which occurred in March, 5 B.C., and in April, 4 B.C. However, several arguments weigh against such an identification. The conjunction of planets was never close enough to be called "a star," and the date is too early, unless it is assumed that the wise men saw it long before they arrived in Jerusalem. Most important, however, is Matthew's statement that the star "stood over where the young child was." This would be impossible for any natural star; it demands a supernatural phenomenon, and renders the natural explanation unwarranted. Perhaps the unusual natural occurrence might have served to awaken interest on the part of the wise men, but it cannot help to date the birth of Christ.

5. What about December 25? Here it must be admitted freely that the date is only traditional, and relatively late tradition at that (4th cen. A.D.). Even the late tradition is divided between Dec. 25 and Jan. 6 (still observed by the Eastern church as celebrating both the birth and baptism of Christ). Both dates were previously observed as pagan celebrations, and were probably taken over in an attempt to replace the pagan ceremonies with Christian ones. The Scripture itself gives no clue. The winter season does not fit well with the gospel story. It is unlikely that shepherds would be in the fields with their flocks in midwinter.

The beginning of His public ministry.
1. The fifteenth year of Tiberius (Lk 3:1-2). Luke here gives a detailed date-reference for the beginning of the preaching of John. The baptism of Jesus followed soon after. This fifteenth year of Tiberius may be figured variously, depending on whether his years are counted from the time he succeeded Augustus, Aug. 19 or Sept. 17, A.D. 14, or from the time he was named joint ruler of the eastern provinces as coregent with Augustus, A.D. 12. Luke, as a provincial, may have chosen the latter method. To complicate the reckoning further, it is uncertain whether his regnal years were figured according to the accession year system or the non-accession year system. Thus the possible dates for "the fifteenth year of the reign of Tiberius Caesar" (Lk 3:1) are four: A.D. 26, 27, 28, or 29. Of these, the first is most probable.

2. The forty-sixth year of the temple (Jn 2:20). This reference to the temple cannot mean that in the past it had taken 46 years to complete it, for the building was still going on and was not completed until almost 40 years later. The statement is usually taken to mean that the temple had been begun just 46 years before that time: "It has taken forty-six years to build this temple" (RSV). Josephus says it was begun in the eighteenth year of Herod, or 19 B.C. The forty-sixth year, then, at Passover, would be the spring of A.D. 27. If Jesus' baptism occurred the preceding fall, A.D. 26, this coincides with and confirms the date arrived at above for the fifteenth year of Tiberius.

The length of His public ministry.
1. In the Synoptic Gospels. These Gospels give no information on which the length of the Lord's public ministry can be determined. It is often claimed that they reflect a ministry of only one year. But this certainly is overstating the case, for even in these Gospels there are indications of at least two other spring seasons besides the Passover at which He was crucified (Mt 12:1; Mk 2:23, "ripe grain"; Mt 14:19; Mk 6:39, "green grass").

2. The Passovers named in John's Gospel. John carefully lists a number of the annual Jewish festivals and relates them to the Lord's public ministry. This list includes at least three Passovers (Jn 2:13; 6:4; 12:1), necessitating a public ministry of more than two years. Taking the unnamed feast of Jn 5:1 to mean another Passover—and there are many arguments for so understanding it—this would add another year. Since the baptism and the beginning of Christ's ministry in Galilee preceded that first Passover by perhaps six months, the total period of the public ministry would be about three and one-half years.

The date of the crucifixion.
1. From previous findings. If, as indicated above, Christ's public ministry began in A.D. 26 and lasted through four Passovers, then the death of Christ occurred at the Passover season in the year A.D. 30. This is the most satisfying and fruitful method of figuring. All other methods presented here only confirm the results thus obtained, or are of such a nature that they may be made to fit whatever result has been previously obtained by this method.

2. Pontius Pilate. The governorship of Pilate, according to Josephus, was from A.D. 26 to 36. At the trial of Jesus it appears that Pilate already had had trouble with the Jews, the Galileans, and Herod; therefore it must not have been at the very beginning of his term in office. A Passover earlier than A.D. 28 would hardly fit.

3. Annas the high priest. The high priesthood of Annas offers another point of contact. Josephus states he was deposed about the time of Herod Philip's death, or about A.D. 34. This then becomes the latest possible date of the crucifixion.

4. Astronomical calculations. Elaborate attempts have been made to fix the year by calcu-

lating in what year the Passover fell on Friday. Assuming that the crucifixion was on Friday, and that the last supper was the Passover meal, it should be possible to arrive at an exact date. But this method of reckoning is beset by many difficulties. (a) While the almost universal tradition has placed the crucifixion on Friday, there have been and still are some scholars who dispute that interpretation, putting it instead on Thursday, or Wednesday. (b) Again, there is disagreement on the nature of that last supper, whether it was an ordinary meal or the Paschal meal. (c) There is disagreement whether the first day of the feast was Nisan 14 or 15. Of course anyone may choose his own from these alternatives and proceed to figure an exact date. Actually the many who have attempted to do so have come up with widely divergent results. However, the chief and fatal objection to this method is (d) the uncertainty as to how the Jews determined their calendar. If they calculated the first day of the month astronomically, the method ought to work. If they did it by actual observance of the appearance of the new moon, which is much more likely, then certainty is impossible. The unknown factors involved, therefore, would seem to make this method all but useless in ascertaining the date of the crucifixion.

Dates in Early Church History

Points of contact. Several references in the historical narratives of the book of Acts mention contact with persons or events in extrabiblical history. Only a listing of these and a brief summary of the information contributed by them are here given. For fuller treatment consult the bibliography.

1. Aretas, king of the Nabataeans (Acts 9:23–25; II Cor 11:32). There is no extrabiblical evidence that Damascus was under a Nabataean governor appointed by Aretas, but if it was, it must have been after A.D. 34, for there is clear evidence that the Romans governed the city before that date. But if this reference is to an ethnarch over only the Nabataean segment of the Damascus population, this could be true even when the Romans governed the city, and therefore nothing can be fixed as to date.

2. Death of Herod Agrippa I (Acts 12:21–23). Josephus and almost all other sources agree that Herod's death came in A.D. 44. An attempt to fix the time of year by identifying the occasion of Herod's display and oration seems unconvincing. From Acts 12:1–4, 19 it would appear that it followed Passover.

3. The famine under Claudius (Acts 11:28–30). Secular history confirms that widespread famine, or dearth, marked the reign of Claudius, but does not single out any date. Josephus tells of "the great famine in Judea" and the generous help of Queen Adiabene, but unfortunately his dating is not clear; either in the governorship of Fadus (A.D. 44–46) or of Alexander (A.D. 46–48), probably not earlier than 46.

4. Sergius Paulus, proconsul in Cyprus (Acts 13:7–12). Inscriptions have attested both the name and the title of this Roman official in Cyprus, but have not fixed the date.

5. The edict of Claudius (Acts 18:2). Again, extrabiblical sources mention Claudius' edict of expulsion of the Jews from Rome. The fifth century historian Orosius gives the date as the ninth year of Claudius, or about A.D. 49.

6. The proconsulship of Gallio in Achaia (Acts 18:12). Here there is strong possibility that the precise date may be fixed by extrabiblical sources. An inscription from Delphi mentions Gallio with the official title used in Acts, and is dated in the first half of the year A.D. 52. Since Roman proconsuls usually arrived at their posts and entered office in the early summer, this date may represent either the end or the beginning of his term. The incident in Acts seems to have taken place shortly after the arrival of Gallio; therefore Paul's 18 months in Corinth coincide fully or in part with the year between the summers of A.D. 51 and 52.

7. The procuratorship of Felix (Acts 23–24). Felix became procurator of Judea in A.D. 52. There is some evidence that he had held a subordinate position under his predecessor, so that Paul's statement that he had been "many years a judge" (Acts 24:10) does not demand a date later than A.D. 55 or 56. Also, Drusilla (Acts 24:24) could not have been his wife before A.D. 54 (she had been given in marriage to another in A.D. 53). So Paul's first appearance before Felix might have been as early as A.D. 55 or 56, but not before A.D. 54.

8. Festus succeeds Felix (Acts 24:27). This very crucial time-reference, unfortunately, cannot be dated with certainty. There is abundance of information from Josephus and other sources, but it has been understood in widely different ways. For full discussion, see the works listed in the bibliography and E. M. B. Green, "Festus," NBD, p. 421. The most that can be concluded is that Festus (q.v.) replaced Felix between A.D. 57 and 60, perhaps earlier than later.

9. The days of unleavened bread (Acts 20:6–7). Attempt has been made to reason backward from Monday when Paul left Troas to Thursday as the day of the week when the Passover occurred that year; then to identify the year by astronomical calculation; result, A.D. 57. For reasons indicated above (see date of the crucifixion) this line of reasoning is unconvincing.

10. The single prefect (Acts 28:16). According to Conybeare and Howson, after the death of Burrus (A.D. 62), Rufus and Trogellinus were made joint prefects. Since at Paul's arrival in Rome a single prefect is mentioned, it could not have been after A.D. 61.

An illustration. In spite of these many contacts with extrabiblical history and many more references to periods of time within the Acts and the epistles, there is still only a relative chronology. The precise date for even a single event is not fixed, yet the order of events and their relative position have been carefully checked and confirmed. An illustration may help. The various events described in the book of Acts may be likened to the links of a chain. Certain of these links, which represent the points of contact described, are fastened so that they can come and go only within certain definite limits. It is readily seen that such a chain would be quite flexible, and could be stretched or compressed into many different patterns according as one might pull one link to its latest extremity or push another to its earliest limit. But with all its flexibility, the links would still remain in the same order and the same relative position with respect to one another and to the outside facts to which they were linked. To carry the illustration one step further, if the size of the various links is narrowed down by reasonable deductions from the events themselves, the chain will become more and more fixed. To this we turn next.

Additional data from the NT. Besides these direct points of contact with secular history, there are many indications within the book of Acts and the epistles which help to date with some confidence the intervening events.

1. The council at Jerusalem (Acts 15). Two lines of approach are open. It is possible to reason forward from the famine in Claudius' time, which, as seen above, must be not earlier than A.D. 46. Acts 13:1 suggests that Paul and Barnabas must have spent some time in Antioch before they started out on the first missionary journey, and Acts 14:28 indicates a considerable period after their return before the calling of the council at Jerusalem. The first journey itself must have taken at least a year and a half (Turner's estimate; Ramsay makes it two years and three or four months). If the whole interval then be estimated at a minimum of three years, A.D. 49 would be the earliest probable date for the council. Or reasoning back from the year 52 (or 51) for Paul's trial before Gallio (the interval includes the entire second journey and the 18 months in Corinth), any date later than 49 for the council seems improbable.

2. Paul's visits to Jerusalem. The book of Acts lists five visits of Paul to Jerusalem, while in his epistle to the Galatians Paul mentions two and gives some important chronological data in relation to them. There seems little doubt that the first visit of Gal 1:17-18 refers to the first visit of Acts 9:26. This is dated three years after his conversion. But there is sharp difference of opinion regarding the visit mentioned in Gal 2:1. The older traditional view identified it with Acts 15 and the council at Jerusalem. Others argue that it should rather be identified with the famine relief visit of Acts 11:27-30; 12:25. Paul says this visit came "fourteen years after" (Gal 2:1). If Paul made this trip to attend the Jerusalem council A.D. 49,

then beginning with that date and taking the inclusive way of figuring, the conversion of Paul would be in A.D. 35. Taking the 14 years as being in addition to the three, his conversion would be in A.D. 32. If this visit is identified instead with the famine relief visit in A.D. 46, the conversion of Paul would be in A.D. 32. Of course the 14+3 manner of reckoning would be impossible in this case.

3. The date of Paul's martyrdom. It may be inferred from several factors that Paul was not martyred at the end of his two years imprisonment of Acts 28. The way Acts mentions the "two whole years" (v. 30) gives the impression that the period had come to an end. Paul's letter to the Philippians, usually thought to have been written during that Roman imprisonment, reflects Paul's own expectation that he would be released. The Pastoral Epistles seem best explained on the theory that Paul was released and carried on a continuing ministry for some time, and then again was imprisoned in Rome. This reconstruction of the last years of Paul's life is strongly confirmed by early Christian tradition.

The only evidence for the date of Paul's death is found in this early tradition, and it is quite clear and definite. It associates the martyrdom of both Peter and Paul with the persecution of Nero which followed the great fire of A.D. 64.

One of the arguments which has been strongly urged for a later date than A.D. 64 is the supposed difficulty in fitting a release from the first imprisonment, a more or less extended further missionary career, a rearrest and second imprisonment, into the period between Paul's first imprisonment in Rome, and the year 64. This difficulty was especially prominent in the older traditional system of dating which accepted a late date for the procuratorship of Festus. If Paul appeared before Festus as late as A.D. 60, he would have arrived in Rome in 61, and the two years of this imprisonment would be 61-63. No time is left for these later travels before 64. But if Paul's meeting before Festus were in 57 or 58, as seen above is possible and probable, then his first Roman imprisonment would have ended in 60 or 61 and plenty of time is left before A.D. 64.

A Resultant Table of Approximate Dates

Birth of Christ	6 or 5 B.C.
Death of Herod	March, 4 B.C.
Beginning of John's ministry	A.D. 26
Baptism of Jesus	A.D. 26
Duration of Christ's public ministry	3½ years
Crucifixion and resurrection	Passover, A.D. 30
Conversion of Paul	32
Martyrdom of James, death of Herod Agrippa I	44
Famine relief visit of Paul and Barnabas to Jerusalem	46

Bibliography. James L. Boyer, *New Testament Chronological Chart*, studygraph chart, Chicago: Moody Press. Jack Finegan, *Handbook of Biblical Chronology*, Princeton: Univ. Press, 1964. F. R. M. Hitchcock, "Dates," HDCG I, 408–417. W. M. Ramsay, *St. Paul the Traveller and the Roman Citizen*, Grand Rapids: Baker, 1951. Merrill C. Tenney, *New Testament Times*, Grand Rapids: Eerdmans, 1965, pp. 134–138, 158 f., 164–178, 203, 206 ff., 216, 242–246, 275 ff., 294 ff. C. H. Turner, "Chronology of New Testament," HDB I (1903), 403–425.

J. L. B.

CHRYSOLYTE. *See* Jewels.

CHRYSOPRASUS. *See* Jewels.

CHUB (kŭb). A place or nation in alliance with Egypt and mentioned along with Ethiopia, Libya and Lydia (Ezk 30:5). The ASV transliterates a corrected Heb. reading by "Cub," while the RSV translates the corrected reading as "Libya" (*q.v.*).

CHUN (kŭn). One of the cities of Hadarezer, king of Syria, plundered by David for its brass and copper for use in building the temple (I Chr 18:8). The city is called "Cun" in ASV and RSV. The parallel passage in II Sam 8:8 has "Berothai" (*q.v.*).

CHURCH

Origin of the Term

The English word "church" is derived from the Gr. adjective *kyrikon (kyriakon)* which means "belonging to the Lord." The substantival form can be rendered simply as "the Lord's house" and is used to designate a Christian place of worship.

In the NT, however, "church" translates the Gr. *ekklēsia* which never refers to a place of worship but has in view an assembly of people. In the overwhelming majority of cases, *ekklēsia* indicates a local company of believers.

The circumstances under which *ekklēsia* became the accepted term for Christian congregations remain uncertain. The word does appear in the NT in the utterance of Jesus recorded in Mt 16:18 and 18:17. However, unless Jesus spoke Gr. on these two occasions, a possibility which remains much in doubt, *ekklēsia* in this text more likely reflects the terminology of Matthew and the early church. Moreover, there is no way to determine what Heb. or Aram. word Jesus may have used, for *ekklēsia* could be used to translate at least three different Semitic words.

Neither is it probable that *ekklēsia* owes its origin to the first believers in Jerusalem. In Acts there is a variety of what appear to be self-designations of the members of this community, such as "the brethren," "the disciples," "followers of the way," or "saints"; but there is no evidence that they called themselves "the church."

More than likely it was among the Gr. speaking Jewish Christians and their Gentile adherents that the name was first introduced and that in the context of their own cultural tradition. In the Gr. world *ekklēsia* commonly referred to an assembly. It was also used technically to refer to the regularly scheduled assemblies of the citizens of a Gr. city. Acts 19:39 provides an example of this usage when the town clerk of Ephesus remonstrates with the people that they should refer any action against Paul's companions to the lawfully constituted *ekklēsia*.

It is also possible that Jewish Christians in the Hellenistic world introduced the term *ekklēsia* because it was one of the two primary expressions used in the LXX to designate the people of God. Nearly 100 times *ekklēsia* renders the Heb. word *qahal*, meaning "assembly." The other main word used to translate *qahal* was *synagōgē*, but this term had already been appropriated by the Gr.-speaking Jewish community to designate their gathering places. *See* Assembly.

By whatever means the word *ekklēsia* drew the attention of Christians, its swift rise to general usage and its predominance over other competing terms cannot be accepted as accidental. Two factors appear responsible. First in importance is the awareness on the part of Christians of the parallel development which they sustained to the people of God in the OT. The OT "assembly" was established when God summoned Israel at Mount Sinai (Deut 5:22; 9:10; 10:4; 18:16) and by His own word and act the covenant community was created. From this time forth the Israelites became the *qahal (ekklēsia)* of God, "actively engaged in God's purposes of revelation and salvation, caught up in the mighty events whereby God intervenes redemptively in history and involved in the forward thrust of the covenant toward final and universal fulfillment" (T. F. Torrance, "The Israel of God," *Interpretation*, X, 306).

Correspondingly, the NT *qahal* or *ekklēsia* was duly summoned of God by His own divine Word, the Eternal Logos. It too had been ordered into existence as a "covenant" community, and receiving the new covenant in Jesus' blood was "caught up" in God's great redemptive program. Thus believers, by the use of this name, bore witness that they stood in direct succession to Israel as inheritors of the hope of Israel. The use by Christians of other expressions that had traditionally referred to Israel would support this contention. Early Christians are spoken of in the NT as "the elect," "Abraham's seed," "the twelve tribes," "strangers of the dispersion," and the "Israel of God."

The coming into existence of the church was recognized by Christians as a fulfillment in part of the covenant made with Abraham and Moses. With the Israelites God had covenanted that He would establish a people for His own possession who should receive His promises. They would be His "own possession," "a kingdom of priests," "a holy nation," the bearer of His light to the nations (Ex 19:5-6).

In I Peter it is precisely in these terms that the community of the NT is addressed. They are "elect according to the foreknowledge of God the Father, through sanctification of the Spirit, unto obedience and sprinkling of the blood of Jesus Christ ... begotten ... again unto a lively hope by the resurrection of Jesus Christ from the dead, to an inheritance incorruptible, and undefiled, and that fadeth not away" (1:2-4). They are "precious, ... living stones ... built up a spiritual house, an holy priesthood, to offer up spiritual sacrifices" (2:4-5). They have become "an elect race, a royal priesthood, a holy nation, a people for God's own possession, that [they] may show forth the excellence of him who called [them] out of darkness into his marvelous light" (2:9, ASV).

The second factor in the eventual choice of the term *ekklēsia* by the Christian community is related to the Jewish rejection of Messiah. A new people of God had been established. Appropriate to this people was the selection of a term from the LXX which historically referred to the people of God, a name familiar by its usage and associations, sacred because of its appearance in the divine Book, and unappropriated by the Jewish opponents.

G. W. Ba.

What could be more natural than the selection of *ekklēsia,* a term neutral enough that it could be adapted to the many fresh understandings which belonged to the new hope?

Origin of the Church

Much difference of opinion exists concerning the date of the origin of the church. Did it begin at Pentecost, or was it merely constituted in its NT form at that time?

Those who believe it started at Pentecost point out that Christ's statement in Mt 16:18, "I will build my church," is in the future tense and alludes to a time at least subsequent to this utterance. Further, they argue that one be-

St. Peter's Church at Antioch of Syria. A Crusader facing encloses a cave believed to have been used by Christians for worship purposes in the early days of the Church. HFV

comes a member of the church by the baptism in the Holy Spirit, which act joins him to or identifies him with the mystical body of Christ (I Cor 12:13 ff.). The baptism in the Holy Spirit was future in the Gospels (Mt 3:11; Mk 1:8; Lk 3:16; Jn 1:33) and in Acts 1:5. It is past in Acts 11:15-16. Where else could one logically begin the baptism than at Pentecost? If the beginning of the baptism in the Holy Spirit, by which one becomes a member of the church, occurs at Pentecost, then the church must begin there.

Moreover, they refer to Paul's teaching in Eph 3:2-11 and stress that he speaks of "the mystery ... which in other ages was not made known unto the sons of men, as it is now revealed unto his holy apostles and prophets by the Spirit" (vv. 3-5).

Others reply that this passage clearly does not deny the prior existence of the church but only says that its extension was not made known to them as it was to the apostles. In other words, while the OT certainly gave indications that the Gentiles would receive the gospel when the Messiah came (Isa 9:2; 11:10; 42:6; 49:6; 60:3; 66:12; Amos 9:12), it did not make clear the abolishment of the division or middle wall of partition between Jew and Gentile (Eph 2:14; 3:9).

To this they add that the unity of the covenant of grace—that salvation has at all times and under all dispensations been offered on the basis of God's grace through believing faith—and the teaching of Rom 4 concerning justification by faith, before the law in Abraham's case, under it in David's case, and in the NT times, call for the existence of the church in the OT and its continuity into the NT.

R. A. K.

Nature of the Church

The true church is one, as indicated by the singular use of the term in Ephesians and several other passages when referring to all believers (I Cor 15:9; Gal 1:13; Col 1:18, 24; I Tim

3:15). Yet there were many local groups known as "the church" in that locality. W. C. Robinson explains the paradox: "Wherever the church meets she exists as a whole, she is the church in that place. The particular congregation represents the universal church, and through participation in the redemption of Christ mystically comprehends the whole, of which it is the local manifestation" (BDT, p. 124).

The significant feature of each local church and the universal church is its relationship to God and to Jesus Christ: "the churches of God in Christ Jesus" (I Thess 2:14, NASB). The church is God's because He has established it by the supernatural acts of coming to earth in the person of the Son via the virgin birth, purchasing a people by the substitutionary sacrifice of His Son, raising Him from the dead to provide eternal life, and sending forth the Holy Spirit to fill and equip His saints.

At least eight NT figures represent the relation of Christ to His church: (1) the Shepherd and the sheep (Jn 10:1-30; Acts 20:28; Heb 13:20); (2) the Vine and the branches (Jn 15:1-17); (3) the Cornerstone or Foundation and the stones of a holy temple (Eph 2:20-22; I Cor 3:9-17; I Pet 2:4-8); (4) the High Priest and the kingdom of priests (Heb 5:1-10; 6:13-8:6; I Pet 2:5, 9; Rev 1:6); (5) the Head and the many membered body (Eph 1:22-23; 4:4, 12, 15; 5:23, 30; I Cor 12:12-27; Col 1:18; 2:19); (6) the Bridegroom and the bride (Jn 3:29; II Cor 11:2; Eph 5:25-33; Rev 19:7-8); (7) the Firstborn or Firstfruits among many brethren (Rom 8:29; I Cor 15:20, 23; Rev 1:5); (8) Master and slaves (Eph 6:5-9; Col 3:22-4:1; I Cor 7:22-23; Rom 6:18, 22; Phil 1:1). These and other descriptions reveal that the life of the church, her holiness, and her unity are in Christ (Col 3:3-4; I Cor 1:30; Gal 3:28; Jn 17:21-23).

Ministry and Mission of the Church

As a body, a living organism, the church was to grow to mature manhood, "to the measure of the stature which belongs to the fulness of Christ" (Eph 4:13, NASB; cf. vv. 14-16). To aid in this development Christ gave gifts to His church in the form of men to fulfill various tasks. Some were apostles, and others were prophets, evangelists, and pastor-teachers, to equip the saints for the work of ministering (Eph 4:11-12). Since every member of the church was baptized in the Spirit, every member had one or more spiritual gifts to edify the others in the community of believers (I Cor 12:4-13; Rom 12:3-8; see Gifts, Spiritual). Each was to serve according to his calling and ability (I Pet 4:10-11).

The church was also to grow in the sense of expansion. Every believer was to be a witness of Christ through the empowering of the Holy Spirit (Acts 1:8), taking the gospel to every creature and making disciples of all the nations (Mk 16:15; Mt 28:19; see Commission, Great).

While every believer enjoyed an equal position under Christ the Head, the church was organized in order to insure its practical, orderly functioning here on earth. In one sense the apostles and prophets were its foundation (Eph 2:20), the authorized representatives of Jesus Christ to complete the revelation of His Word to His people. In this primary sense of apostleship there could be no succession of apostles subsequent to those who had witnessed the ministry and resurrection of Jesus (Acts 1:21-22; see Apostle). In order to preside over and give direction in the local churches, the apostles instituted the offices of deacon (Acts 6:1-6) and elder (Acts 14:23; 20:17-38; Phil 1:1; I Tim 3:1-7; Tit 1:5-9; I Pet 5:1-4; Jas 5:14).

In whatever capacity each believer served, it is significant to note that he was chosen and then guided and energized by the Spirit. In a manner not specified, the Holy Spirit revealed that Barnabas and Paul were to be sent out as missionaries (Acts 13:1-3). Similarly the elders at Ephesus were made leaders of the community by the Spirit (Acts 20:28). Prophetic utterance accompanied the charismatic gift bestowed on Timothy at his ordination (I Tim 4:14). Paul and Silas were directed by the Spirit to Troas (Acts 16:6-8).

Thus the chief ministry of the church was to minister to her Lord (Acts 13:2a), to worship Him as priests by the indwelling Spirit (Phil 3:3) and to carry out His will on earth by performing His works through the power of His Spirit (Jn 14:12, 16-17). The aura of the supernatural characterized the church at every turn.

J. R.

Bibliography. James Barr, *The Semantics of Biblical Language,* London: Oxford Univ. Press, 1961, p. 119. J. Oliver Buswell, Jr., *Systematic Theology,* Grand Rapids: Zondervan, 1963, I, 418-429; II, 216-280. J. Y. Campbell, "The Origin and Meaning of the Christian Use of the Word *Ecclesia*," JTS, XLIX (1948), 130. Edmund P. Clowney, "Toward a Biblical Doctrine of the Church," WTJ, XXXI (Nov., 1968), 22-81. Charles Hodge, *Systematic Theology,* Grand Rapids: Eerdmans, 1952, III, 546 ff. P. H. Menoud, "Church, Life and Organization of," IDB, I, 617-626. Paul S. Minear, "Church, Idea of," IDB, I, 607-617. Leon Morris, "Church Government," BDT, pp. 126 f. William Childs Robinson, "Church," BDT, pp. 123-126; "The Nature of the Church," *Christian Faith and Modern Theology,* ed. Carl F. H. Henry, New York: Channel Press, 1964, pp. 389-399. K. L. Schmidt, "*Ekklēsia*," TDNT, III, 501-536. T. F. Torrance, "The Israel of God," *Interpretation,* X (1956), 305.

CHURL. The word occurs only in Isa 32:5, 7. It probably means "avaricious" or "fraudulent." The RSV translates the term as "knave." The term "miserly" also fits the context very well.

CHURLISH. The term means "severe," "hard," or "rough." Nabal, whose widow Abigail later married David, was described as "churlish and ill-behaved" (RSV), "evil in his doings" (I Sam 25:3).

CHUSHAN-RISHATHAIM (kū'shăn-rĭsh-à-thā'ĭm). A king of Mesopotamia (Aram-Naharaim) who oppressed Israel for eight years not long after the time of Joshua. He was defeated by Othniel, the first of the judges (Jud 3:7–11). The identity of the king is a mystery. Even his name is actually an epithet, "doubly wicked Chushan," probably applied by his Israelite subjects. The most likely identification is with an obscure Hittite conqueror from Qusana-Ruma, a district in northern Syria. He had overcome the Mitanni (Mesopotamia; *see* Horites) in Aram and then turned S against Israel (cf. Unger, *Israel and the Aramaeans of Damascus,* pp. 40 f.).

Because Cushan is used as a parallel to Midian in Hab 3:7, some have conjectured that the king was from this country and overcame only Judah, from whence the deliverer Othniel came.

CHUZA (kū'zà). Steward of Herod Antipas, probably managing his property. He was the husband of Joanna, a Galilean woman who, having been cured of a disease or possession of an evil spirit, followed and supported Jesus (Lk 8:2–3; 24:10).

CIEL, CIELD, CIELING. *See* Architecture: Private Houses.

CILICIA (sĭ-lĭsh'à). Geographically Cilicia referred to the area of SE Asia Minor between Pamphylia on the W, the Amanus Mountains on the E, Lycaonia and Cappadocia on the N, and the Mediterranean on the S. It had a coastline of about 430 miles, extending from the E boundary of Pamphylia to the S end of the Gulf of Issus. It was roughly co-extensive with the modern Turkish Vilayet of Adana. Politically (in Paul's day at least) Cilicia designated the Roman province first organized in 102 B.C. to deal with the pirate menace. It encompassed the E part of the geographical area. When Luke spoke of the "sea of Cilicia" (Acts 27:5), he probably had in mind the Mediterranean opposite the entire geographical region. Since Paul used Roman political terminology, he must have applied Cilicia to the Roman province only (Acts 21:39; 22:3; 23:34).

Cilicia was commonly divided into two territories almost as dissimilar in their physical characteristics as they could be. The W part, Cilicia Tracheia ("Rugged Cilicia"), was a tangled mass of mountains of the Taurus range descending abruptly to the sea, with a narrow tract of land along the coast and little or no plain country. The mountains of Tracheia were valuable only for their timber (chiefly cedar),

The Cilician Gates, strategic pass through the Taurus Mountains about thirty miles north of Tarsus. Robert McKay

and this rugged terrain succeeded effectively in cutting off the inhabitants from much peaceful contact with the rest of the world. In 67 B.C. Pompey wiped out the pirates who had their hideouts in the impassable hills.

The E part of Cilicia was known as Cilicia Pedias ("Lowland Cilicia"). This region had much in its favor from a geographical standpoint. Its land was fertile and grew cereals of all kinds, and its flax made possible a thriving linen industry. Timber from the nearby mountains moved through Cilician ports. Goats living on the slopes of the Taurus, where snow lies until May, grew magnificent coats used in the famous tentmaking industry of the area. It will be remembered that Paul followed this trade (Acts 18:3). Pedias was located on one of the great trade arteries of the ancient world. Trade routes from the Euphrates and Syria met about 50 miles E of Tarsus (*q.v.*), chief city of the province and Paul's birthplace, and entered the city as a single road. It then proceeded through the Cilician gates, a pass through the Taurus Mountains 30 miles to the N, and led across south central Asia Minor to Ephesus. Paul, accompanied by Silas, undoubtedly took this route to Derbe on his second missionary journey (Acts 15:41; 16:1).

Around 38 B.C. Cilicia Pedias was transferred to the province of Syria. It seems to have been administered by the Roman governor of Syria until A.D. 72, when Vespasian recombined both regions of Cilicia into a single province. Therefore Paul and Luke, both writing before A.D. 72, are strictly correct in speaking of Syria and Cilicia together (Gal 1:21; Acts 15:23, 41).

Jews had settled in Tarsus and other Cilician cities after the conquests of Alexander the Great. A certain synagogue in Jerusalem was frequented by Jews who returned from Cilicia and other lands of the Dispersion (Acts 6:9); one of them may have been Saul of Tarsus.

In OT times the region of Cilicia Pedias was known to the Hittites as Kizzuwatna. Its Mycenean Greek settlers apparently called it Khilakku, mentioned in late Assyrian records (ANET, pp. 284, 297). The Syrians named the area Qu'e, according to annals of Shalmaneser III and Tiglath-pileser III (ANET, pp. 277, 282 f.) and the Old Aramaic inscription of Zakir, king of Hamath and Lu'ash, from the early 8th cen. B.C. (DOTT, pp. 242–246). The name Kue appears in modern versions of the Bible as a land from which Solomon imported horses (I Kgs 10:28; II Chr 1:16, RSV, NASB). Cilicia was famous for raising great numbers of horses.

Bibliography. W. F. Albright, "Cilicia and Babylonia under the Chaldean Kings," BASOR, #120 (1950), pp. 22–25. J. D. Bing, "Tarsus: A Forgotten Colony of Lindos," JNES, XXX (1971), 99–109. M. J. Mellink, "Cilicia," IDB, I, 626–628. H. F. Vos, "Asia Minor," WHG, pp. 336–344.

H. F. V.

CINNAMON. *See* Plants.

CINNEROTH. *See* Chinnereth 3.

CIRCLE. The word has reference to the vault of the heavens (Isa 40:22). The same word is also translated "circuit" (*q.v.;* Job 22:14). Yahweh is represented by Isaiah as sitting upon the circle of the earth and by Job as walking upon the vault of heaven as it arched over the earth.

CIRCUIT. Used to represent several Heb. words in various meanings.

1. Heb. *sābab,* "to revolve"; a regular tour of inspection (I Sam 7:16). Eccl 1:6 mentions the circuit of the winds.

2. Heb. *teqûpâ,* "revolution"; the sun's orbit (Ps 19:6); the completion of a year (Ex 34:22).

3. Heb. *ḥûg,* "circle"; the vault of the heavens (Job 22:14).

CIRCUMCISION (Heb. *mûlâ,* Gr. *peritomē*). Circumcision is literally the surgical removal of the prepuce or foreskin of the male sexual or-

gan. Similar operations on women are known but are infrequent and religiously meaningless. Circumcision is practiced by many peoples, especially in tropical and subtropical regions. Their number is variously estimated to include one-seventh to one-fifth of the earth's population.

In Egypt (Jer 9:25–26; Josh 5:4–9) and among Semitic peoples generally, circumcision seems to have been practiced in antiquity. A relief in the Sixth Dynasty tomb of Ti (*c.* 2300 B.C.) at Saqqarah in Egypt depicts the operation of circumcision on 13-year-old youths. Exceptions in the Near East were the Babylonians, Assyrians, and Philistines. Apparently among many the practice was given up in later times, or only employed loosely. Under the Roman Caesars in Egypt, only sons of priests were circumcised. Josephus (*Ant.* xiii.9.1) reports that John Hyrcanus had to force the Edomites to be circumcised.

The original significance of this practice is uncertain. Various possibilities include hygiene in preventing infection; facilitating intercourse; initiation into manhood; sacrifice similar to that for the firstborn; or as a protective measure against demons. All of these may have had significance somewhere, and all are in some sense reflected in the OT.

Apparently circumcision was first given religious significance in the OT where it is prescribed as the required external sign or seal (Gen 17:11; Acts 7:8; Rom 4:11) that one belonged to the covenant people of the Lord. Of course, this applied only to the male members of the people. Circumcision was a fitting sign for the chosen people of God because spiritual purity and holiness were to characterize their walk. Since the corruption of sin often manifests itself with peculiar force in the sexual life, God required His people to symbolize the sanctifying of their lives by the purifying of the organ by which life is reproduced.

Curiously, this prescription occurs chiefly in narrative passages of Scripture (Gen 17:10–14; 34:15–17; Josh 5:2–7). In the actual legal sections it is required only in Lev 12:3. It appears again in the narrative related to Passover (Ex 12:44, 48). Nowhere are there instructions as to how it is to be carried out. Apparently stone (flint) knives were used by the child's father (Ex 4:24–26; Josh 5:3). Gen 17:12; 21:4; Lev 12:3 set the time as the eighth day after birth. It was vitally important that Moses, God's newly appointed leader of His covenant people, carry out the rite of circumcision on his own son(s), lest God slay Moses for disobedience (Ex 4:24–26; cf. Gen 17:14). Some think Moses himself may not yet have been circumcised (Jerusalem Bible, p. 83, note *e.* See also H. Kosmala, "The 'Bloody Husband,'" VT, XII [1962], 14–28).

Circumcision gained in importance during the Exile as a sign to distinguish Jews from Babylonians, but its earlier significance is stressed in the repeated scorn poured on the

Philistines as "uncircumcised" (Jud 14:3; 15:18; I Sam 14:6; 17:26, 36; 18:25; 31:4; II Sam 1:20; 3:14; etc.).

The OT also uses the term in an applied or symbolic sense. In Deut 30:6 the Lord promises to "circumcise thine heart" (cf. also Deut 10:16; Lev 26:41; Jer 4:4; 6:10; Ezk 44:7, 9). Circumcision of the heart or ear evidently was understood to mean overcoming spiritual hindrances to obedience. (Cf. reference to Moses as of "uncircumcised lips," Ex 6:30.)

Post-biblical Judaism under the influence of Pharisaic emphasis on individual piety through keeping the law laid great stress on circumcision. This only made the position of the Jews more difficult in the Graeco-Roman world and provided occasion for taunts and even persecution under Hadrian. The pressure led some to attempt a second operation to disguise or remove the sign of circumcision. Orthodox Jews reacted by placing even greater value on it as Israel's highest honor and badge (Midrash Rabbah on Numbers, 12:10; Midrash Tehilloth, 40; etc.). They even ascribed circumcision to Adam, Seth, Noah, and Melchizedek. It is therefore strange that neither the Mishna nor any other official document of the times has a section on circumcision. It is possible to follow the exact prescription for the rite in Talmudic times. The Babylonian Talmud states that the Jews accepted the ceremony with joyfulness (*Shabbath* 130*a*).

Islam took over circumcision from the Jews. It is not demanded by nor even mentioned in the Koran, but is practiced by tradition which traces Arab ancestry to Abraham through Ishmael (Gen 17:20). The normal age for circumcision is 13, since Ishmael was circumcised at that age (Gen 17:25). In Islam circumcision is clearly a puberty rite in which the boy is led to the scene in girl's clothes. They also occasionally have parallel rites for girls. But circumcision in Islam never has had the importance that it does for Jews.

In the NT circumcision was first recognized as a proper prescription of the law (cf. the accounts of Jesus, Lk 2:21; John the Baptist, Lk 1:59-60; Paul, Phil 3:4-5. See also Jn 7:22). But in Antioch the Christians first denied its necessity for church membership (Acts 15). This decision was later supported in the so-called Jerusalem council (Acts 15:6ff.). Evidently the argument continued, however, as seen in the writings of Paul (especially Romans and Gal 5:2, 6; 6:15; Col 3:11). It was linked with the larger question of the necessity for the Christian to fulfill the whole law.

The positive meaning of circumcision in the NT lay not in fulfilling the law but as the sign of God's chosen people in the previous history of revelation (Acts 10:45; 11:2; Rom 3:1-2; 4:12; 15:8; Gal 2:7-9, 12; Eph 2:11; Col 4:11; Tit 1:10). Circumcision is a part of God's order which contained the promise of the Messiah. True circumcision was a seal of faith (Rom 4:9-11). Faith was essential. True circumcision

"not done with human hands" consists in laying aside the "body of flesh" in the Christ-circumcision, i.e., being buried with Him in baptism and raised with Him (Col 2:11-12). Whoever serves God in spirit and boasts only of Christ is truly circumcised (Rom 2:28-29; Phil 3:3).

The OT stresses spiritual as well as fleshly circumcision. The NT values only the former while giving it deeper meaning in relating it to Christ's crucifixion and resurrection.

See Concision.

Bibliography. L. H. Gray, L. Spence, G. Foucart, D.S. Margoliouth, G.A. Barton, "Circumcision," *Encyclopaedia of Religion and Ethics*, III (1910), 659-680. Rudolf Meyer, *"Peritemnō,* etc.," TDNT, VI, 72-84.

J.D.W.W.

CIS (sĭs).The Gr. form of Kish (*q.v.*), the father of King Saul (Acts 13:21).

Cistern and altar at the high place, Petra.

CISTERN. The Heb. word *bôr* means "pit, dungeon, sepulchre."

Usually cisterns were tanks hewn from the porous limestone rock, or pits artificially constructed, of varying dimensions with sides and bottom sealed by lime plaster, invented about 1200 B.C. Most of the cisterns were roughly bottle shaped with one or more openings at the top through which water was drawn in containers. In a land where rainfall is small, it is exceedingly important that the water supply, collected during the rainy season (November-April), be carefully preserved. Water was essential for domestic use, irrigation, and ceremonial cleansings. Excavations reveal that it was not uncommon for cisterns to have steps leading to the bottom, chiefly to assist in the cleaning operations or in ceremonial cleansing.

In ancient times, cistern users would often close the opening with flat stones or boards, over which sand was spread, to prevent its use by unlawful hands. A cracked rock, a split wall, or an insufficiently sealed tank, resulting in a broken cistern was looked upon as a great calamity (Jer 2:13). The reference to a wheel broken at the cistern (Eccl 12:6) not only symbolizes the ending of life but suggests the way water was pulled up for use.

Cisterns have been used as dungeons. Examples of this are seen in the experiences of Joseph (Gen 37:22–24) and Jeremiah (Jer 38:6–13). It also was customary to make men responsible for their cisterns, for if a man's animal should fall into a neighbor's unclosed cistern, the cistern owner was required to pay for the loss (Ex 21:33–34; cf. Jos *Ant.* iv.8.37). By persuasive speech, the Rabshakeh, the crafty Assyrian commander, tried to lure the people of Judah to surrender Jerusalem by offering every man "his own fig tree and his own cistern" (II Kgs 18:31). The remains of ancient cisterns are still to be seen.

R. V. U.

The citadel of Aleppo, Syria. JR

CITADEL. This term means a stronghold or fortress. Several Heb. terms are used to describe the various aspects and elements of fortification. The Heb. word *'armôn* suggests a stronghold of a city, a palace, castle, or citadel (I Kgs 16:18; II Kgs 15:25). The most famous stronghold in the OT was the citadel of Jerusalem which David conquered, and thus conquered the city (II Sam 5:7–9; I Chr 11:5, 7). The term usually comprehends many buildings. This word and other Heb. words are translated variously, such as tower (Ps 122:7, RSV), fenced city or fortress (Isa 17:3), siegeworks (II Kgs 25:1, RSV), high fortifications (Isa 25:12, RSV), stronghold (Jud 6:26, RSV), palace (Isa 32:14), and fortress of the temple (Neh 2:8, RSV). *See* Fort; Bulwark.

CITIES OF REFUGE. Among the 48 cities given to the Levites throughout Israel, six were by the command of God to be appointed as cities of refuge, or asylum, "for the manslayer" (Num 35:6–7). Moses himself selected three of these on the E side of the Jordan River: Bezer in Reuben, Ramoth-gilead in Gad, and Golan in Manasseh (Deut 4:41–43). Later under Joshua the other three were named, being in the main part of the land W of Jordan: Kedesh in Naphtali, Shechem in Ephraim, and Hebron in Judah (Josh 20:7). These were conveniently located in northern, central, and southern areas of the land. Roads were to be built and kept open to these important cities (Deut 19:3).

An ancient practice, said to exist even now in the Near East, was for the closest relative of a slain man to act as "avenger of blood" (Num 35:12, 19; Deut 19:12). This custom was permitted to continue under the Mosaic law, but with certain restrictions. If one had killed another unintentionally ("unawares," Num 35:15), he could flee immediately to one of these cities of refuge and there find sanctuary. The deliberate murderer who had killed intentionally was not allowed to claim this privilege (Num 35:16 ff.). The one to whom it properly belonged, however, was safe from the avenger as long as he stayed inside his city of refuge. When the high priest died, he was free to leave the city and dwell safely at home again (Num 35:25–28). *See* Blood, Avenger of.

That the cities of refuge were a type of Christ is hinted in Heb 6:18. "The apostle alludes to this when speaking of those who fled for refuge to lay hold upon the hope set before them" (Fairbairn, *Imperial Standard Bible Encyclopaedia,* IV, 161). To Christ we flee for refuge, and in Him we are safe from the divine Avenger of blood (Rom 5:9; 8:1, 31, 34). The greatest sin of this age – the murder of Jesus Christ – is classified by God as a sin of ignorance (Acts 3:17; I Cor 2:7–8). Unsaved men little realize the "exceeding sinfulness of sin." Sanctuary is open to all who will flee for refuge to Christ (Jn 6:37). The saved ones will never again leave this "city of refuge" because their High Priest will never die (Heb 7:25).

G. C. L.

CITIES OF THE PLAIN. The Heb. word *kikkār,* for "plain," refers to the "basin" of the Jordan. These cities included Sodom, Gomorrah, Admah, Zeboiim, and Bela (Zoar), located in the Valley of Siddim or Salt Sea (Gen 14:8). By far the most famous (or infamous) of these cities were Sodom and Gomorrah (*q.v.*), which according to Gen 19 were completely destroyed by fire. The wickedness of these cities, along with the resulting judgment, is often referred to in the Scriptures (Deut 29:23; Isa 1:9; 3:9; Jer 50:40; Ezk 16:46; Mt 10:15; Rom 9:29) as a precedent to be avoided.

Opinion differs among scholars as to whether these cities were located at the northern or southern end of the Dead Sea. According to tradition and the judgment of most scholars, the probable site was at the southern end of the Salt Sea. The abundance of salt and bitumen in this area lends credence to this theory. Reports that the remains of the cities have been seen from the air have not been substantiated. It is not improbable that the cities are underneath the shallow water at the southern quarter of the sea.

The cities are first glimpsed in biblical history in Gen 13:10 where the apparent proximity to the "well watered" Jordan Valley might seem to argue for a location to the N. Because of the fertility of the valley compared to that of the hill country of Canaan, Lot chose it as his residence.

The cities were really city-states, each with its own "king" (Gen 14:2). After a war with Mesopotamian kings, these cities became vassal states of Chedorlaomer, king of Elam, for a period of 12 years. In the thirteenth year they rebelled and found themselves at war again with Chedorlaomer and his three allies (Gen 14:9). They were defeated and Lot's family and others were captured and taken away. Abraham attacked the victorious allies, defeated them, and recovered both the captives and the goods (Gen 14:13–16).

The destruction of two of these cities, Sodom and Gomorrah, is detailed in Gen 18–19. The destruction, as a result of a fire from heaven, consumed four of the cities, the inhabitants of the valley, and "what grew on the ground" (Gen 19:25). The small town of Zoar apparently was located at some distance from Sodom and Gomorrah. Lot and his daughters lodged here temporarily after leaving Sodom and before they fled to the hills behind the city (Gen 19:20–30). In Wisd 10:6 these cities are called the Pentapolis (Five Cities).

G. A. T.

CITIZENSHIP. *Hebrew citizenship.* Among the Jews in OT times the stress was on the membership of the Israelite in a religious organization, rather than on his relationship to the city or the state (Eph 2:12, "commonwealth of Israel"). Non-Israelites had the protection of the same law as the Israelites, but were not allowed to insult the Israelites in any way concerning their religious beliefs. The good citizen was the good member of the Jewish theocracy. The advantage of the Jew over the Gentile was spiritual and not judicial.

Roman citizenship. This made persons equal in judicial rights to the inhabitants of Rome. It was granted by emperors to provinces and cities, or to individuals because of special services rendered to the emperor or the state, and was even obtainable by purchase at times (Acts 22:28). It entitled the holder to exemption from such shameful punishments as scourging or crucifixion, and also gave the right of appeal to Caesar in certain cases.

Paul's citizenship. Either Paul's father or an ancestor had obtained Roman citizenship and Paul had it by birth. He sometimes used his Roman privileges (Acts 16:37–39; 22:25–29; 23:27; 25:10–12; 26:32).

Christian citizenship. All believers are citizens of a heavenly commonwealth and ought therefore to live in accordance with such a position (Phil 1:27; 3:20; cf. Acts 23:1). As citizens of the kingdom of God (Heb 11:16; 12:22 f.; 13:14; I Pet 2:9–11), they shall reign with Christ in His millennial kingdom and then enter the new heavens and the new earth (Rev 5:10; 20:4–6; 21–22). *See* New Heavens and New Earth; Millennium; Eternal State and Death.

R. A. K.

CITRON. *See* Plants.

CITY. As in modern times so also in the ancient world, the line of demarcation between "city" and "town/village" was nebulous. There seems to have been no distinction in the several Heb. words for city: *'îr, qiryâ* and *qāret.* Heb. *sha'ar* ("gate") frequently stands by *synecdoche* for "city," especially in Deuteronomy. A rule-of-thumb classification characterized the city as walled, the village or town as unwalled (Lev 25:29–31; Deut 3:5). All such distinctions, however, were more convenient than scientific, since Bethsaida, e.g., is called a city in Mt 11:20–21; Lk 9:10; Jn 1:44, but a town in Mk 8:22–23. In ancient Israel, it was typical for a city (the "mother," cf. II Sam 20:19, RSV) to be surrounded by a cluster of villages (the "daughters," cf. Num 21:25, Heb.), the former exercising a certain hegemony over the latter in a characteristic city-state relationship (cf., e.g., Josh 15:32).

Such city-states (cf. Latin *cīvitās*) with all the refinements of civilization sprang up originally in Mesopotamia during the Proto-Literate period (*c.* 3500 B.C.), in turn stimulating a similar development in Egypt and the Indus Valley slightly later. Hazor (Josh 11:1–5, 10) was the largest city in Palestine in the second millennium B.C. with a population of perhaps 50,000. During the Amarna period (*c.* 1375 B.C.), there were four main city-states (Gezer, Jerusalem, Lachish, and probably Hebron) in southern Palestine, whereas in the time of Joshua's conquest the number was nine (including in addition Debir, Eglon, Jarmuth, Libnah, and Makkedah; cf. Josh 10).

The earliest cities in the hill country of Palestine usually occupied a limestone knoll near a spring. Successive periods of habitation and destruction would result in the formation of mounds or "tells" (cf. Josh 11:13, Heb.), many of which modern excavators have laid bare. The more important of such cities would be enclosed by massive, buttressed walls (Num 13:28; Deut 1:28; 9:1) with towers at the corners and flanking the gates (II Chr 26:9), fortified as a last means of defense by a citadel (*q.v.*) or a "strong tower within the city" (Jud 9:51), and interlaced by a network of streets

A reconstruction of Megiddo in the days of Solomon and Ahab. ORINST

which were often narrow, crooked, and dirty (Isa 10:6). Occasionally certain cities were set aside for specialized functions and became, e.g., chariot cities (II Chr 1:14), store cities (I Kgs 9:19), or merchant cities (Ezk 17:4).

During the Hellenistic period, many of the old cities were rebuilt, but new ones were also established by Gr. conquerors and colonists. These newer cities (Gr. *polis*) were plotted according to the city plan devised by Hippodamus of Miletus, consisting of streets intersecting at right angles with a centrally located marketplace. The same pattern was followed by city builders during the early Roman period (cf. Mt 6:5). Somewhat later the Roman city came to be characterized by an avenue of columns leading from a triple gate through the center of the city and crossed by one or more secondary streets. *See* Acropolis.

Spiritually speaking, the Bible recognizes that while the city is the repository of cultural life (Gen 4:17, 21-22), it also tends to become the receptacle of evil propensities (Gen 4:19, 23-24; 19:1-38) which concentrate themselves in the capital city (Mic 1:5). Eventually all earthly cities will thus have to be destroyed (Mic 5:11, 14) in anticipation of the final establishment of the heavenly and "holy city, new Jerusalem" (Rev 21:2). *See* Babylon; Jerusalem, New.

Bibliography. "Ancient Cities (of Palestine)," CornPBE, pp. 44-107, 210-221.

R. Y.

CITY, FENCED. The Heb. expressions *'îr bᵉṣûrâ, 'îr (ham)mibṣār,* and *'îr mᵉṣûrî* are all translated "fenced city" in KJV and refer to cities surrounded by walls or fortifications as opposed to unwalled villages. Such a rendering is found in I Sam 6:18; II Sam 20:6; Jer 5:17; Ezk 36:35; Dan 11:15; Hos 8:14; Zeph 1:16, and more than once each in Numbers, Deuteronomy, Joshua, II Kings, and II Chronicles. Heb. *'îr māṣôr* is similarly so rendered in II Chr 8:5. "Defenced city" renders *'îr bᵉṣûrâ* three times in Isaiah and *'îr (ham)mibṣār* four times in Jeremiah, while *qiryâ bᵉṣûrâ* is so translated in Isa 25:2.

In all the above references, ASV and RSV translate "fenced" and "defenced" uniformly as "fortified."

See further Fence; Fort; Gate; Tower; Wall.

CITY, HOLY

CITY, HOLY. For Christians and Jews, there is but one "holy city"—Jerusalem (Neh 11:1, 18; Isa 48:2; 52:1; Mt 4:5; 27:53; Rev 11:2; 21:2). For Muslims, Jerusalem is the third holiest city next to Mecca and Medina, and Palestinian Arabs call it El Kuds, "the holy (place, city)." Most major religions of the world have their "holy cities," including Eleusis in Greece, Thebes in Egypt, Benares in India, and Kyoto in Japan. In the Bible, rivals for this distinction included Shechem (Gen 12:6-7, RSV; cf. Josh 8:30-35), Gilgal (Josh 4:20; I Sam 11:14 – 12:25), Mizpah (I Sam 10:17-25), and Bethel (I Kgs 12:26-33). For Christians, not even Nazareth or Bethlehem rank with Jerusalem in emotional appeal. *See* Jerusalem; Jerusalem, New.

CITY, LEVITICAL. *See* Levitical Cities.

CITY OF DAVID

1. This name is applied to the most ancient section of Jerusalem, the SE hill of Jerusalem also called Mount Zion. The Jebusite fortress which stood here was conquered by David, who then moved his capital from Hebron and built a new palace and citadel (II Sam 5:7, 9; I Chr 11:5, 7). He made his new royal city the center of Israel's religious life by bringing to it the ark of the covenant from the house of Obed-edom (II Sam 6:10- 16). King Solomon brought up the ark out of the city of David to the temple on Mount Moriah to the N (I Kgs 8:1; II Chr 3:1; 5:2).

Hezekiah, in constructing the Siloam tunnel, brought the waters of Gihon down to the W side of the city of David (II Chr 32:30). Manasseh rebuilt and considerably heightened the outer wall of the citadel of David; his repairs encircled the Ophel (*q.v.*) as far as the Fish Gate in the Tyropean valley (II Chr 33:14, JerusB). David, Solomon, and many other kings of Judah were buried within David's original city. *See* Jerusalem.

2. The town of Bethlehem in Judea, the home of David, is called the city of David (Lk 2:11). *See* Bethlehem 2.

L. O. H.

CITY OF DESTRUCTION. *See* Irhaheres.

CITY OF GOD

1. A term used to describe Jerusalem (Ps 46:4; 48:1, 8). It was the city which God chose to be His habitation among the tribes of Israel (Deut 12:5). *See* Jerusalem.

2. This term is used also to describe heaven, or the New Jerusalem (Heb 11:10; 12:22; Rev 3:12; 21; 22). *See* Jerusalem, New.

CITY OF PALM TREES. *See* Jericho.

CITY OF SALT. *See* Salt, City of.

The Jerusalem David conquered is now barren (foreground) and lies south of the later Temple area. HFV

CITY, TREASURE. The Israelites built two such cities, Pithom and Raamses, for Pharaoh (Ex 1:11). The produce of the land was stored in the cities. Certain cities were set aside by Solomon for stores of food, chariots, and horsemen (I Kgs 9:19). Benhadad conquered the store cities of Naphtali (II Chr 16:4). Jehoshaphat built store cities in Judah (II Chr 17:2). *See* Pithom; Raamses.

CLASPS. This word means "a bend," especially a hook made to fit in an eye for fastening. The KJV translates the term as "taches" (an English word of French origin) or as "hooks," while the ASV and RSV translate the term as "clasps" (Ex 26:11; 35:11; 36:13; 39:33). The clasps were fastenings of gold (Ex 26:6; 36:13) or bronze (Ex 26:11; 36:18) by which the linen curtains and the goat skin hangings of the tabernacle were held together.

CLAUDA (klô'dã). A small island about 23 miles from the SW shore of Crete. Spelled Cauda in ASV and RSV, it is now called Gaudos or Gozzo. On Paul's journey to Rome his ship sailed under the lee of Clauda after a storm prevented its reaching a safe harbor at Crete (Acts 27:16).

CLAUDIA (klô'dĭ-á). A Christian woman at Rome who sent her greetings to Timothy (II Tim 4:21). This is all that Scripture tells of her. Legend has made her the mother of Linus, mentioned in the same verse (*Apostolical Constitutions* vii, 21), and identified by Irenaeus and Eusebius as a bishop of Rome.

So great a modern scholar as Alford (*Greek Testament*, III, 104– 105) has given considerable attention to the hypothesis that Claudia may have been a British maiden, converted to Christianity and later married to Pudens (mentioned before Linus in II Tim 4:21). This conjecture, based on an inscription found in England, is admittedly rather fanciful and very doubtful.

CLAUDIUS (klô'dĭ-ŭs). The fourth Roman emperor, who reigned A.D. 41-54. He was a nephew of Tiberius Caesar (A.D. 14-37), under whose rule Jesus' ministry was carried on. Between these two emperors came the short rule of Caligula, who greatly antagonized the Jews by his cruel policies toward them. Claudius revived the more generous attitude of Augustus and Tiberius, the first two Roman emperors, who had been conciliatory toward the Jews.

The Emperor Claudius. BM

At the beginning of his reign Claudius issued an edict in favor of the Jews of Alexandria, who had been undergoing persecution. Josephus reports part of it as reading thus: "I will, therefore, that the nation of the Jews be not deprived of their rights and privileges on account of the madness of Caius; but that these rights and privileges, which they formerly enjoyed, be preserved to them, and that they may continue in their own customs" (*Ant.* xix. 5.2). Josephus further relates that Claudius sent an edict throughout the world in which he wrote: "Upon the petition of king Agrippa and king Herod, who are persons very dear to me, that I would grant the same rights and privileges should be preserved to the Jews which are in all the Roman empire, which I have granted to those of Alexandria, I very willingly comply therewith" (*Ant.* xix. 5.3). "Agrippa" was Herod Agrippa I, grandson of Herod the Great. Claudius gave him the territory ruled by his grandfather, with the title of king.

Claudius is mentioned by name only twice in the NT. In Acts 11:28 a famine is recorded as

occurring in his reign. Historical records indicate that famines were frequent and severe in this period (Suetonius, *Claudius* 18). In fact, the emperor's life is said to have been threatened on this account (Tacitus, *Annals* xii. 43). The situation was partly due to the carelessness of his predecessor.

Aquila and Priscilla are said to have been compelled to leave Rome when Claudius made a decree expelling all Jews from that city (Acts 18:2). The correctness of this reference is confirmed by Suetonius (*Claudius* 25).

The unfortunate emperor was murdered by his wife Agrippina in A.D. 54.

R. E.

CLAW (lit., "hoof"). The mark of a "clean" animal was: "Every animal that parts the hoof and has the hoof cloven in two, and chews the cud, among the animals, you may eat" (Deut 14:6, RSV). The KJV describes the worthless shepherd as tearing off even the "claws" of the sheep, while the RSV uses the term "hoofs" (Zech 11:16).

CLAY. *See* Minerals.

CLEAN, CLEANNESS. The translation of several Heb. and Gr. words having the idea of physical cleanness, and then of moral purity. The term is used in the physical, ceremonial, ethical, figurative, and spiritual senses, with the uses frequently overlapping. The chief usage is the ceremonial, applied to persons, places, or things (Lk 5:14; Heb 9:13, 22; II Chr 23:19; Isa 52:11). The idea of cleanness is also applied to animals and birds (Gen 7:2; Deut 14:11). *See* Food; Meat.

The importance of "cleanness" for Israel is that the nation should reflect in her national life the qualities which she ascribes to Yahweh. The spiritual ideal of cleanness is reflected in the OT mainly in Job, Psalms, and the Prophets. "Cleanness" is necessary to fellowship with Yahweh (cf. Ps 15). The greater emphasis concerning spiritual cleanness is found in the NT (Jn 13:11; Acts 18:6; I Jn 1:7, 9). *See* Chaste; Purity; Sanctification.

Bibliography. R. Meyer and F. Hauck, "*Katharos, etc.*," TDNT, III, 413-431.

CLEFT

1. A space or opening, usually narrow, made by cleavage, as the "clefts of the rocks" (Ex 33:22; Isa 2:21; Amos 6:11; Mic 1:4).

2. The split in the hoof of an animal (Deut 14:6; cf. Lev 11:3).

CLEMENT (klĕm'ĕnt). A fellow worker with Paul at Philippi and saluted by Paul in his letter to the Philippian church as one whose name was in the book of life (Phil 4:3). Attempts to identify him with Clement of Rome fail largely because Clement of Rome lived at the end of the 1st cen., and Paul's friend was evidently a mature person at the time of Paul's letter, c. A.D. 63.

CLEOPAS (klē'ō-pás). One of the two disciples to whom Jesus revealed Himself in the breaking of bread at Emmaus on the afternoon of His resurrection (Lk 24:18). Some would identify this Cleopas with Cleophas (KJV) or Clopas (RSV) in Jn 19:25, the husband of one of the Marys who stood at the cross. Others would go further and identify both of these with Alphaeus (Mt 10:3; Mk 3:18; Lk 6:15; Acts 1:13), the father of James the apostle (the second by that name). While Clopas and Alphaeus may well come from the same Heb. root (Alford, *Greek Testament*, I, 101), it does not appear that these men should be identified with Cleopas.

CLEOPHAS (klē'ō-fás). A close relative of a woman named Mary who stood by the cross (Jn 19:25). The Gr. text does not indicate whether his relationship was that of husband, son, or father, although it would be most probable that he was her husband. The following attempts at further identification have been made:

1. Cleophas (Gr. *klōpas;* RSV, Clopas) has been identified with Cleopas (Gr. *kleopas,* Lk 24:18), which is doubtful since the latter is a thoroughly Gr. name while the former seems to be of Semitic origin.

2. Cleophas has also been identified with Alphaeus (Mt 10:3), on the assumption that both names are transliterations of the Aramaic *ḥalpay*. That this view is based on a number of arbitrary assumptions weakens its possibility.

3. Cleophas has been thought to be the brother of Joseph, as Hegesippus suggested, but there is no biblical indication of such a relationship.

In view of the lack of evidence, it would seem best to view Cleophas, Cleopas, and Alphaeus as different individuals.

D. W. B.

CLERK. *See* Town Clerk.

CLOAK, CLOKE. The outer garment. *See* Dress.

CLOSET. In Heb. *ḥŭppâ*, KJV, "closet," means a canopy, as in Isa 4:5, RSV; the verb form means "to cover." Originally it evidently referred to the tent set apart for the bride. Later it signified the bride's chamber (Joel 2:16). In the NT the Gr. term *tameion* (Mt 6:6; Lk 12:3, 24) refers to a store chamber or inner chamber. The NT stresses the ideas of privacy, even secrecy, and storage, as suggested in the terms store chamber, upper chamber, secret chamber, inner room, and private room.

CLOTH, CLOTHES, CLOTHING. *See* Dress.

CLOTHES, RENDING OF. *See* Rend.

CLOUD. The word is used many times. Basically, it refers to the literal clouds in the sky, as in Gen 9:13, 14, 16; Lk 12:54. However, it is frequently used figuratively as in Ezk 8:11; Heb 12:1. The word is also used in another sense to indicate the presence of God to guide His people (Ex 13:21, 22; 40:34-38), or to protect them (Ex 14:19).

Literal. Unlike Lower Egypt, Palestine enjoys considerable rainfall, but it is limited almost entirely to the winter—from October 15 to May 1. During the summer—May 1 to October 15—there is practically no rain and few clouds. Hence, "the winter is past, the rain is over and gone" (Song 2:11).

Figurative. The dissipation of a thick cloud is used to represent the blotting out of Israel's sins (Isa 44:22). A cloud veiled the glory of the Lord from Moses' sight, and the people's, when the law was given (Ex 19:9; 24:15-18), and at other times also (Ex 16:10; 34:5). The Lord promised to appear in a cloud upon the mercy seat in the most holy place on the Day of Atonement (Lev 16:2). A cloud representing the glory of God appeared when the tabernacle was originally set up (Ex 40:34-35), and when the ark was brought into the first temple (I Kgs 8:10-11). Clouds are often spoken of in connection with the unapproachableness of God, as in Job 22:14; Ps 18:11, 12; 97:2.

At the transfiguration, a cloud overshadowed the three disciples and the voice of God spoke from it acknowledging Jesus as His beloved Son (Mt 17:5; Mk 9:7; Lk 9:34-35). Jesus said He would come again "in a cloud with power and great glory" (Lk 21:27; see also Mt 24:30; Mk 13:26; Rev 1:7). Paul speaks of believers being caught up in the clouds (or, in clouds) when Christ comes for His own (I Thess 4:17). Thus clouds, being in the sky, seem to be used repeatedly in Scripture to remind us of God: His glory and His guidance, His distance and His presence.

J. A. S.

CLOUD, PILLAR OF. *See* Pillar of Cloud and Fire.

CLOUT. A patch or piece of cloth, a rag, a portion of cloth applied to mend a tear. The Gibeonites in deceiving Joshua came with "old shoes and clouted" (Josh 9:5). Rags and torn bits of cloth were used to prevent the ropes from cutting Jeremiah's flesh when he was being pulled up from the dungeon (Jer 38:11-12).

CLUB. An offensive weapon, probably the most primitive of all weapons. Several words may be translated "club."

1. Heb. *tôtāḥ*, "bludgeon" or "club" (Job 41:29). The LXX translated it as "hammer," "mallet"; the KJV has "dart."

2. Heb. *mappēṣ*, "war club" (Prov 25:18; Jer 51:20). The KJV has "maul" and "battle axe"; the RSV has "war club" and "hammer."

3. Gr. *xulon,* something made of wood such as a "cudgel," "stick," "staff" (Mt 26:47, 55; Mk 14:43, 48; Lk 22:52). The KJV has "staves," while the RSV has "clubs." These were carried by the crowd in arresting Jesus in Gethsemane.

CNIDUS (nī'dŭs). A Gr. city of Caria on the coast of SW Asia Minor. It was located at the tip of a long narrow peninsula jutting out into the sea for 90 miles. Its location placed it between the islands of Rhodes and Coos (Cos). Paul sailed by Cnidus on his journey to Rome (Acts 27:7). The ruins of Cnidus are the only objects of interest on the peninsula today.

COALS. This translates five different Heb. words in the OT and two different Gr. words in the NT. Although no mineral coal has been found in Palestine, wood was used to make a fire of coals such as is described in Jn 18:18; 21:9. The coal was actually charcoal made by subjecting wood to a smothering process, and was used then as in recent times for heat (Isa 47:14) as well as cooking (Isa 44:19; Jn 21:9), and by the blacksmith (Isa 44:12). The Gr. *anthrax* (Rom 12:20) refers to charcoal when Paul says (quoting Prov 25:22) that one may heap coals of fire upon someone's head by returning good for evil. *See* Minerals and Metals.

COAST. This word is translated variously as "border," "boundary," "coast," "territory," or "region" in the RSV (Num 34:11; Josh 1:4; Jud 1:18; Acts 27:2). Where the KJV has "coast," the RSV usually has "border" or "boundary." The seacoast itself is seldom mentioned (Acts 27:2; Lk 6:17). *See* Border.

COAT. *See* Dress.

COAT OF MAIL. *See* Armor.

COBRA. *See* Animals, IV.8.

COCK. *See* Animals, III.14.

COCKATRICE. *See* Animals: Serpent, IV.30.

COCKCROWING. All four Gospels give Jesus' prophecy that Peter would deny Him three times: Mark, "before the cock crows twice" (14:30); the others merely, before the cock crows (Mt 26:34; Lk 22:34; Jn 13:38). Mark therefore refers to a "second" cockcrowing (14:68, 72), the others do not (Mt 26:74-75; Lk 22:60-61; Jn 18:27). Numerous explanations for this difference are offered. Possibly Mark's two cockcrowings give the more precise and detailed account—consistent either with the priority of Mark or with Peter himself as Mark's source of information—while the other evangelists generalize into the one cockcrowing which was later and more commonly heard.

COCKLE. *See* Plants.

COFFER. A small chest or box which the Philistines placed upon the cart with the ark (I Sam 6:8, 11, 15). In this they placed the golden mice and emerods when they returned the ark to the Hebrews.

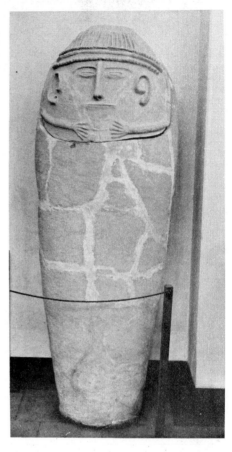

A pottery coffin from Bethshean. Palestine Archaeological Museum

COFFIN. Coffins were seldom used by the Hebrews, who buried their dead wrapped in cloths or sheets. The only exception in the Bible is the case of Joseph, who died as a nobleman in Egypt (Gen 50:26). His embalmed body was likely placed in a wooden Egyptian coffin or mummy case. For this unusual instance the Heb. word *'ārôn* was employed; it is rendered "chest" in II Kgs 12:9-10 and very frequently "ark." Numerous coffins from the Middle Kingdom period of Egypt (*c.* 2050-1750 B.C.) are displayed in our museums. These are often shaped in human form and elaborately decorated inside and out. Joseph's remains were carried, presumably in his coffin, by the Israelites into Canaan for final burial (Josh 24:32). *See* Burial; Tomb.

COHORT. The tenth part of a legion, usually about 600 men. The KJV has "band," while ASV marg. has "cohort" (Mt 27:27; Mk 15:16; Acts 10:1; 21:31; 27:1). It may also be used of a small detail (Jn 18:3, 12, ASV marg.). A cohort was stationed in Jerusalem in the tower of Antonia adjacent to the temple (Jos *Wars* v.5.8). *See* Army; Legion.

COIN. *See* Weights, Measures, and Coins.

COL-HOZEH (kŏl-hō′zĕ). A man of Judah whose father was Hazaiah (Neh 11:5). His son Shallum rebuilt the Fountain Gate in the time of Nehemiah (Neh 3:15).

COLLAR
1. The opening of a robe or shirt through which the head is inserted (Job 30:18; cf. Ex 28:32; Ps 133:2, RSV). *See* Dress.
2. A decorative ornament hung around the necks of Midianite camels (Jud 8:26).
3. A pendant or necklace (Prov 1:9; Song 4:9).
4. A pillory or instrument of torture into which a person's head was placed (Jer 29:26, RSV; Ps 105:18, RSV).

COLLECTION. The word collection is found in two passages in the KJV (II Chr 24:6, 9; I Cor 16:1). However, in the OT the original is more properly rendered "tax." In the NT the word *logeia* is used (found only here) which refers to a voluntary gathering of money for charitable purposes. The use of this word in the sense of "collection" is abundantly confirmed by the papyri. It is closely related to the usage of *koinōnia* ("contribution") in Rom 15:26. The collection made among the Gentile churches for the poor saints at Jerusalem by Paul and delivered at the peril of his life (Acts 21:17-36; 24:17) was a visible sign of the inward and essential unity of apostolic Christianity. *See* Alms.

COLLEGE. The residence of the prophetess Huldah (II Kgs 22:14; II Chr 34:22). The Heb. term evidently means a district or suburb of the city. The KJV has "college" while the RSV has "second quarter." The same term is translated as "second" in Zeph 1:10 where the reference is to a quarter of the city.

COLLOPS. The only reference to this term is in Job 15:27. The KJV reads "maketh collops of fat on his flanks," while the RSV reads "gathered fat upon his loins."

COLONY. A group of self-governing Roman citizens settled in foreign communities. Roman colonies were established primarily for three purposes: (1) to serve as strategic outposts; (2) to resettle poor citizens and thus take them off the relief rolls; (3) to provide land for veterans. In addition, sometimes a community would be

granted colonial status by Rome to honor its inhabitants and to strengthen its ties with the imperial government.

The word "colony" occurs only once in the NT (Acts 16:12). Philippi was a Roman colony originally settled by the veterans of the battle fought between the forces of Antony and Octavian (later Emperor Augustus) and Brutus and Cassius in 42 B.C. Subsequently Octavian settled other colonists there.

COLOR, COLORS. *See* Colours.

COLOSSE (kŏ-lŏs′ĕ). A city located on both sides of the Lycus River in Phrygia, about 12 miles from Laodicea in SW Asia Minor. The histories of Colosse, Laodicea, and Hierapolis were closely associated. The great trade route from Ephesus to Tarsus and Syria went through Colosse and made it a prosperous city by the time of Xerxes (Herodotus vii.30). The city had owed its wealth chiefly to its red or violet woolens, called *colossinus*. But it was already declining in importance by Paul's day because of competition especially from Laodicea (*q.v.*), and no letter was sent there by John when he wrote the churches in Asia (Rev 1-3).

The Christian church in Colosse may have been founded by Epaphras (Col 1:2; 4:12). Paul had not visited Colosse previous to his epistle to them (Col 2:1). The church seems to have met in the home of Philemon, a prominent layman (Phm 2).

COLOSSIANS, BOOK OF. The Epistle to the Colossians is almost universally regarded as a genuine writing of the apostle Paul. Three times the writer calls himself Paul (Col 1:1; 1:23; 4:18). The great concepts of the person and work of Christ, death and resurrection with Christ, harmonious domestic relationships, and the new man in Christ are unmistakably Pauline. Repeatedly the genuineness of Ephesians is argued because of its similarity to Colossians, assumed without question to be Pauline. Furthermore, "the external attestation to Colossians is all that can be desired" (H. C. Thiessen, *Introduction to the New Testament*, p. 229).

One of four writings usually called the Prison Epistles, Colossians is a companion epistle to Philemon, both of which were apparently written about the same time (perhaps A.D. 60-61) and carried to their destination by Paul's co-worker Tychicus (Col 4:7-9), who was to take the slave Onesimus back to Philemon. Because of these associations, it is argued that Philemon lived at Colosse and was a leading member of that church, which may have met in his house (Phm 2). As far as we know, Paul never personally ministered in Colosse; however, the assumption that his co-laborers evangelized there while he was at Ephesus (Acts 19:1-10) is valid. At least, he felt a personal responsibility for this church.

Purpose for Writing

The immediate occasion of writing to the Colossians was the projected mission of Tychicus, coupled with a report brought to Paul from Colosse by Epaphras (1:7-9; 4:12). Apparently this report informed Paul of insidious errors, both doctrinal and practical, that had crept into the church. Often called the Colossian heresy, these errors combined Judaistic elements with ascetic and Gnostic teachings akin to those features which later developed into a full-blown Gnostic system. Designating it as an example of man-made religion, R. H. Lightfoot summarizes the features of this heresy as: rationalism, heresy of intellect (Col 2:8); ceremonialism, heresy of religious instinct (Col 2:16, 20-22); mysticism, heresy of spiritual consciousness (Col 2:18); and asceticism, heresy of the moral will (Col 2:23) (*St. Paul's Epistles to the Colossians and to Philemon*, pp. 71-111).

The basic purpose of Colossians is to combat these heresies, which Paul meets "not by indignant controversy, for as yet they were only undeveloped; not by personal authority, for these Christians were not his converts; but by the noblest of all forms of controversy, which is the pure presentation of counter truths" (F. W. Farrar, *Messages of the Books*, p. 312). Hence, a key idea for the entire epistle is in 2:9-10 and 1:19-20. The complete Christ, giver of a complete salvation, when personally experienced, is the complete answer to error, both theological and practical.

Plan of the Epistle

The emphasis in Col 1:12-20 is on Christ in whom dwells all the fullness of the Godhead bodily. As to His person, He is the image—the likeness, representation, manifestation—of the invisible God. In reference to creation, He is its Sovereign, Creator, Sustainer, and to it He gives essential meaning. First to be resurrected from the dead, He is the beginning, the Head of the Body, the Church. The work of Christ is here described as reconciliation, both cosmic and personal, made possible by the peace He secured by His death.

In Col 2:11-3:4, Paul then shows how that "in Him ye are made full." This vital experience in Christ is described negatively as being buried with Christ and is symbolized by spiritual circumcision and baptism. Positively, being in Christ is to be made alive with Him. The means of realizing this experience is faith in the workings of God. God raised Christ from the dead after our Lord had defeated all spiritual enemies and cancelled the indictment of sin by assuming in full the demands of its penalty (2:11-15). This work, then, constitutes the basis of personal salvation. Practical consequences follow. Negatively, they are a rescue from the error and a repudiation of the error with all its features. This is involved in dying to the old way and manner of living (2:16-23).

Positively, vital experience in Christ will mean a new kind of living—seek heaven, think heaven—and a new hope (3:1-4).

What follows in Col 3:5-4:6 are detailed practical expressions of new life in Christ. New character must come—put to death the old nature, seeing that the new nature has been put on (3:5-14); new life principles must be adopted—peace ruling in the heart, the Word dwelling there, and grace inspiring the heart's song (3:15-17); new conduct must show in domestic relationships, in evangelism among the worldly (3:18-4:6).

Outline

The Christian in Christ—
Antidote to Error

I. The Gospel at Work Among the Colossians, 1:1-14

II. The Person and Work of Christ, 1:15-23
   A. Christ as seen in all His relationships is pre-eminent, vv. 15-20
   B. Christ's work is described as reconciliation, vv. 21-23

III. Paul's Ministry of the Mystery of Christ, 1:24-2:5: His spirit, authority, message, method, strength, goal

IV. The Personal Experience of Christ, 2:6-3:4
   A. Man-made religion—the enemy of faith
   B. The complete Christ and complete experience in Him is the answer to all error
   C. Vital Christian experience
      1. Described negatively: buried with Christ
      2. Described positively: raised with Christ
      3. Means of realization: faith in the working of God
      4. Grounds or basis: the working of God
   D. The practical consequences of experience in Christ, negative and positive

V. Life in Christ Expressed in Personal Character and Relationships, 3:5-4:6

VI. Paul's Personal Interests and Salutations, 4:7-18

Bibliography. John Eadie, *Commentary on the Epistle of Paul to the Colossians*, Grand Rapids: Zondervan, reprint. R. C. H. Lenski, *The Interpretation of St. Paul's Epistle to the Colossians*, Columbus: Lutheran Book Concern, 1937. J. B. Lightfoot, *St. Paul's Epistle to the Colossians*, Grand Rapids: Zondervan, reprint. Alexander Maclaren, "The Epistle of Paul to the Colossians," ExpB. H. C. G. Moule, *The Epistle of Paul the Apostle to the Colossians*, Cambridge: Univ. Press, 1894. W. R. Nicholson, *Oneness with Christ*, Grand Rapids: Kregel, 1951. A. T. Robertson, *Paul and the In-*

tellectuals, rev. by Archie Robinson, Nashville: Broadman, 1959. James S. Stewart, *A Man in Christ,* New York: Harper, 1935.

E. W. H.

COLOURS

1. "Under colour" in Acts 27:30 (KJV) means simply "on the pretense of" (NASB).

2. The abstract word for color does not actually occur in the OT or NT. In each case where the translators have so employed our English word, the word in the original has a different basic meaning.

In most OT occurrences the Heb. word means simply "appearance" (cf. Lev 13:55; Num 11:7; Ezk 1:4, 7, etc.; Dan 10:6). The coats of many colors of Joseph (Gen 37:3) and Tamar (II Sam 13:18-19) were most probably ankle-length coats with long sleeves which, as the Tamar reference illustrates, were worn by the upper classes. The ordinary coat reached only to the knees and had no armholes. Several Heb. words with meanings like "variegated," "many colored" also occur (cf. Ezk 16:16; 17:3; I Chr 29:2; Prov 7:16, RSV).

All NT references are not separate Gr. words but extensions of the basic color mentioned.

3. Color as a specific light phenomenon in both OT and NT. When one seeks to identify the various names of colored objects in the Bible he is perplexed at the paucity of words used and the difficulty of matching the terms with standard colored objects which we know. This does not necessarily mean that the Oriental lacked a sense of appreciation for color, but rather that he failed to analyze and define color effects. The biblical indefiniteness should be understood as part of the general cultural heritage of the ancient Near East and not a particular defect of the Hebrews.

In the ancient use of colors on pottery, glazed bricks, glassware, tomb walls, sarcophagi, wood, and fabrics there does not seem to be the elaborate blending of colors which characterizes modern coloring, but rather the striking effects produced by highlighting the basic colors. It may be noted in this connection that often the main distinction in reference to the color of an object is not in its specific hue, but rather its classification as somber or brilliant, lightish or darkish. This concern for color value or brilliance is apparently a phenomenon noticed in other ancient literature such as Homer and Old English poetry (R. W. Corney, "Colors," IDB, I, 657).

The following is an attempt to identify the main specific colors mentioned in the OT and NT:

Bay, or red. Probably better understood as a reference to the strength or vigor of the horses referred to in Zech 6:3, 7 and not to the color (so RSV, "steeds," v. 7; cf. JerusB).

Black. The English word translates at least eight different Heb. words indicating shades of darkness from dark brown to gray to blackish.

Black is used to describe the color of hair (Lev 13:31, 37; Song 5:11), skin (Job 30:30; Song 1:5-6, where the reference is not necessarily racial but "sunburned" or dark brown), human face (Lam 4:8), horses (Zech 6:2, 6), flocks (Gen 30:32 ff., RSV), heavens (I Kgs 18:45, as a sign of rain), brooks because of ice (Job 6:16). The Gr. word for black in the NT is used of hair (Mt 5:36), one of the four horses of the Apocalypse (Rev 6:5), and the darkened sun (Rev 6:12). In Heb 12:18 a different Gr. word signifies blackness or darkness of Mount Sinai when the law was given, and the same word literally describes the "blackness of darkness" (II Pet 2:17; Jude 13, NASB marg.; RSV has "nether gloom of darkness").

Blue. Probably a purple-blue obtained from Mediterranean mollusks or shellfish and, although considered inferior to the royal purple dye, was a very popular color used in the tabernacle fringes, veil and priestly vestments (Ex 25:4; 26:1; Num 4:6-7, 9; 15:38) and in Solomon's temple (II Chr 2:7, 14; 3:14). This color appears also in Ahasuerus' palace and his royal robes (Est 1:6; 8:15). Qumran (Essene) priests wore an embroidered purple and blue girdle at the occasion of battle (1QM 7:10; cf. Ex 39:28-29). The word blue does not occur in the KJV or RSV of the NT.

Brown. The KJV form of the same word for black (*q.v.*) in the sense of "sunburnt" or "swarthy" in Gen 30:32-33, 35, 40.

Crimson. A red color of varying shades derived from the eggs of female kermes or cochineal insects. After the eggs were removed from under the outer shell of the female insect, they were carefully rolled into a large ball from which the dye was then extracted. This color is applied to materials used in Solomon's temple (II Chr 2:7, 14; 3:14); metaphorically to the blood redness of Israel's sins of shedding innocent blood (Isa 1:18), and apparently to the face paint of a harlot (Jer 4:30). *See* Scarlet; Animals: Crimson Scale Insect, IV.11.

Gray. Applied to the color of the hair of the aging (Gen 42:38; 44:29, 31; Deut 32:25; I Sam 12:2; Job 15:10; Ps 71:18; Prov 20:29; Isa 46:4; Hos 7:9). The same word is rendered "hoar" or "hoary" in other passages (cf. I Kgs 2:6, 9; Isa 46:4; etc.).

Green. Several Heb. words are so translated. In each case the usual reference is to the color of vegetation, and along with red and white forms one of the definite color words in the OT (cf. Gen 1:30; 9:3; Ex 10:15; Job 39:8; Ps 37:2). Sometimes the color is a yellow-green such as "green gold" (Ps 68:13, RSV) or the greenish color of leprous spots (Lev 13:49; 14:37). In the NT the references are all to green grass or trees (Mk 6:39; Rev 8:7; 9:4). A metaphorical usage occurs in Lk 23:31 where Jesus apparently likens the future distress to come upon the rebelling Jewish people to the rapid burning of a "dry" tree, contrasting it to the undeserved distress He was encountering in

His scourging and crucifixion which He alluded to as the burning of a "green" tree.

Grisled ("dappled" in RSV). The term denotes literally, "spotted with hail" and is used of the "mottled," "spotted" or perhaps "dappled gray" color of certain apocalyptic horses (Zech 6:3, 6) and goats (Gen 31:10, 12).

Purple. Probably this color was considered the most valued of the ancient dyes. Its various red-purple hues were derived from Mediterranean mollusks or shellfish of the Gastropoda class. Phoenicians (from Gr. *phoinos,* "red-purple") have been cited in ancient documents as the discoverers of this dye color (cf. Ezk 27:7). The name Canaan ("land of the purple") was apparently derived from the dye. According to Pliny, the most valuable shade was that of congealed blood. Garments dyed in the color were used in the tabernacle (Ex 26:1, 31) and in the priestly attire (Ex 28:4 – 6; 39:1, 28 – 29; cf. 1QM 7.11, where along with blue, white, and scarlet clothing the Qumran priests attired themselves for battle). Royal garments customarily contained the purple dyed fabrics (cf. Midianite kings, Jud 8:26; Solomonic chariot seat, Song 3:10; Babylonian and Persian kings' apparel, Dan 5:7, RSV; Est 1:6), as well as those of wealth (Prov 31:22; Jer 10:9; Ezk 27:7, 16). Apparently the earlier Roman kings did not wear purple (cf. I Macc 8:14).

In the NT Lydia of Thyatira (Acts 16:14) was a dealer in the costly purple dye. The rich man was clothed in purple in the story Jesus told about the beggar Lazarus (Lk 16:19). The symbolical significance of purple denoting royalty figures in the robes of mockery in Jesus' trial (Mk 15:17, 20; Jn 19:2, 5), and the whore mentioned in Revelation (cf. 17:4; 18:12, 16). *See* Purple; Animals: Purple Mollusk, V.8.

Red. While this color may be a dye artificially obtained from insects, vegetables, and minerals (Ex 25:5; 26:14; etc.), the most frequent use in the Bible is to designate the natural color of certain objects. For example, red is used of the color of skin (Esau's, Gen 25:25; David's, "ruddy," I Sam 16:12; 17:42); the color of the eyes after wine has been drunk (Gen 49:12; Prov 23:29); of pottage (Gen 25:30); of the sacrificial purification heifer (Num 19:2, 5 – 6, 8 – 10); of spots of suspected leprosy (Lev 13:19); of war shields (Nah 2:3). In Isa 63:1–2, a word-play exists between the word Edom ("red," v. 1) and red in "red [Heb. *'ādōm*] like him that treadeth in the winefat" (v. 2). The latter statement refers to the Messiah's blood-spattered clothing resulting from His work of judgment (v. 3). A different Heb. word *(hāmar)* occurs in Ps 75:8 translated "red" but the meaning is probably "foaming" (RSV) or "fermented."

In the NT the Gr. word *pyrros* and cognates are used of the color of the sky as "fiery red" (Mt 16:2–3); one of the four horses in the Apocalypse (Rev 6:4); and the color of the satanic dragon (Rev 12:3).

Scarlet. A dye color indistinguishable in the Bible from crimson (*q.v.*) and derived in the same manner from the bodies of certain female insects and used for fabrics and yarn (Gen 38:28, 30; Josh 2:18, 21; II Sam 1:24; Nah 2:3; Prov 31:21); lips (Song 4:3); figuratively for sins (Isa 1:18). Scarlet was also part of the Qumran priests' attire (1QM 7.11). In the NT scarlet is used to designate the color of wool (Heb 9:19); the robe put upon Jesus by the Roman soldiers in mockery (Mt 27:28); and together with purple comprises the clothing worn by the symbolic woman in Revelation (17:4) which may signify her magnificence. The businessmen of the world mourn over the loss of their market for scarlet when the woman is destroyed (Rev 18:12). *See* Animals: Crimson Scale Insect, IV.11.

Sorrel. Found in Zech 1:8, RSV, as one of the colors of the apocalyptic horses. The Heb. word is related to the Assyrian and Arabic word for "red blood" or "redness." It may refer to having a ruddy tinge over white (BDB).

Vermilion. A bright red pigment made in modern times from mercuric oxide, but probably from an iron oxide in ancient times that was known as red ocher. It was a brilliant color and apparently connected with costly painting of rooms and pottery. Jeremiah accused King Jehoiakim of building himself a house painted with vermilion while he neglected justice and practiced oppression (Jer 22:14). It is connected with the figures of Babylonian men painted on the walls by which the adulterous Judah was seduced to intercourse (Ezk 23:14). These figures were war scenes, depicting the triumphal processions of the Babylonian rulers with which the Assyrian palaces were adorned (cf. Keil, *Ezekiel,* KD). Heathen idols are described as being painted with this red ocher in the apocryphal book of the Wisdom of Solomon (13:14) and the Greeks used the color for painting pottery (Pliny, *Nat. Hist.,* XXXV.152).

Violet. Found in the RSV of Jer 10:9 (KJV, blue). The Heb. word is everywhere else rendered "blue."

White. While there are several Heb. words which are rendered white, the most common is *lābān,* which can be detected in the word "Lebanon" that probably was so named because of Mount Lebanon's snow-tipped peaks. It is generally the natural color of various objects, such as teeth (Gen 49:12), snow (Isa 1:18), hair (Mt 5:36), horses (Zech 1:8; 6:3), tree branches (Joel 1:7), bleached garments (Eccl 9:8; Dan 7:9). In the NT "whitewashed" (Mt 23:27; Acts 23:3; KJV, "whited") is used metaphorically much like our use of a deliberate attempt to portray outwardly something as good but which in reality is bad. White garments clothed the transfigured Christ (Mt 17:2), angels (Mt 28:3; Jn 20:12; Acts 1:10), and various clothed personages in the book of Revelation (3:4; 4:4; 7:9; 19:8, 14).

Yellow. A word describing the color of gold

in Ps 68:13, but elsewhere a greenish-yellow, and hence translated greenish in Lev 13:49; 14:37. In Lev 13:30, 32, 36 a different Heb. word describes the color of the hair in a person afflicted with leprosy in the region of the head or beard.

Color symbolism. It is very difficult to assign specific symbolic significance to the colors found in the Bible because of the general lack of emphasis on distinctive hues in the majority of cases, and because only a few colors in a few places are given any definite meaning in the text. Furthermore, there is no principle that demands that once a color is mentioned in a certain symbolic sense it always retains that same sense uniformly through the biblical periods. The contemporary cultural significance of colors appears to have influenced the biblical writers more than a uniform scriptural fixity. The following colors seem to be identified in some contexts with the stated associations.

Black: mourning (cf. Jer 4:28; 8:21; 14:2; Isa 50:3; Job 30:30), treachery (Job 6:15-16), perhaps hopelessness (Mic 3:6, RSV; Jude 13).

Blue: bonds of wisdom compared to a cord of blue in the apocalyptic book of Ecclesiasticus (6:30); associated with kings, therefore figurative of royalty.

Crimson: sin is so described (Isa 1:18).

Green: occasionally used to refer to places of idolatrous practices (cf. Deut 12:2; I Kgs 14:23) which were luxuriant with trees. Since the color is usually associated with luxuriance and abundance of vegetation, it easily suggests that which is flourishing and healthy (cf. Job 15:32; Ps 23:2; 37:35; Jer 11:16).

Purple: usually associated with kings and the wealthy, hence the color of royalty, honor, status.

Scarlet: associated with sins (Isa 1:18); some suggest it as the color of sacrifice or blood-shedding.

White: symbolic of purity, holiness, righteousness (Dan 11:35; 12:10; Isa 1:18).

Most of the other symbolic designations that are made can offer no more than educated guesses. Even regarding the rich tabernacle colorings, some suggest that they all imply nothing more than that the presence of the King of kings is there, as opposed to others who find a symbolic significance in each of the colors used.

A. F. J.

COLT. See Animals, I.1.

COMB. The honeycomb (e.g., I Sam 14:27; Prov 24:13; Lk 24:42). See Animals: Bee, III.2; Food: Honey.

COMFORT. The OT terms *nāḥam,* "to sigh with," and *sāʿad,* "to support and refresh," imply an expression of sympathy, giving of encouragement. The NT terms express the idea of strengthening, encouragement, speaking with consolation. The most common, *parakaleō,* means "to call to one's side" particularly to

help. Men comfort one another (Gen 37:35; Job 6:10; Phil 2:19), and God is the divine source of comfort (Ps 119:76; Isa 49:13; II Cor 1:4). The actual experience of comfort in the fellowship of the church is the work of the Holy Spirit, appropriately termed "the Comforter" (Jn 14:16, 26; 15:26; 16:7). See Paraclete. Comfort is one of the three main results of prophesying (I Cor 14:3). KJV often translates the original terms with "consolation" (*q.v.*). See Exhortation.

Bibliography. Gustav Stählin, *"Paramytheomai,* etc.," TDNT, V, 816-823.

COMFORTER, THE. See Holy Spirit.

COMING OF CHRIST. See Christ, Coming of.

COMMANDMENTS, TEN. See Ten Commandments.

COMMERCE. While this word is not used in KJV, it includes in its scope the terms "merchant," "merchandise," "trade" and "traffic." *See* Occupations: Merchant.

Palestine was situated on or near the chief commercial highways of the ancient world, being traversed by roads connecting Babylonia and Egypt and the Far East with the Mediterranean area. See Travel and Communication. International trade early benefited those who lived in Canaan. Abraham, for example, was rich in cattle, silver and gold (Gen 13:2). W. F. Albright suggests that Abraham may have been involved in the profitable caravan trade, leading donkey caravans back and forth across the Negeb and the Sinai desert between Palestine and Egypt (*Yahweh and the Gods of Canaan,* 1968, pp. 58-73).

The patriarch had come from one of the great commercial centers of the ancient world, Ur, the capital of Sumer. The Sumerian cities traded far and wide. Tablets from the Ur III dynasty (2070-1960 B.C.) deal with the exchange of slaves and houses, the borrowing of commodities, and the loaning of grain, dates and silver at interest. Even before that, Gudea, king of Lagash, tells of obtaining gold from Anatolia and Egypt, silver from the Taurus Mountains, cedar from Lebanon, copper from the Zagros ranges, diorite from Ethiopia, and timber from Dilmun, which may refer to Bahrain or the Indus Valley civilization (S. N. Kramer, "Sumer," IDB, IV, 457). From *c.* 1950 to 1750 B.C. the Assyrians traded extensively with Asia Minor where they established as many as nine merchant colonies. Over 3,000 tablets from Kanesh (Kültepe) reveal that Assyrian traders lived under the protection of native princes while they bartered their goods in exchange for the gold and silver which was so plentiful in E Anatolia.

The earliest biblical account of bargaining and selling is Abraham's transaction with Ephron the Hittite (Gen 23:3-20). The use of the word "merchant" (v. 16) implies that the standard of the silver weighed out was fixed by usage among the merchants of that period. Reparations or compensation could be made for intangible damages by means of such money (Gen 20:16). Gold and silver in the form of bars or rings, as well as manufactured vessels and jewelry, were in use among the settled inhabitants of the area, although the metals were probably imported. Eliezer gave jewels of silver and earrings and bracelets of gold to Rebekah (Gen 24:22, 53). The *qesitah* was a specific form of money in the early 2nd mil. B.C., probably an ingot of precious metal (Heb., Gen 33:19; Job 42:11). The book of Job mentions iron, bronze, lead, crystal, jewels, the art of weaving, merchants, gold from Ophir, sapphire (lapis lazuli) whose only ancient source was Afghanistan, topaz from Ethiopia, all indicating an advanced state of commerce during the patriarchal period. The inhabitants of Arabia, living between India and Egypt, seem to have had a monopoly of trade between these countries, as well as with spices grown in S Arabia.

Egypt was prominent among the trading nations, along with the Ishmaelites or Midianites. It was a caravan of the latter, carrying spices, balm and myrrh, that took Joseph to Egypt (Gen 37:25; 39:1). Slaves were obviously also a part of their merchandise. Grain was exported from Egypt and paid for by silver (Gen 41:57; 42:3, 25, 35). The colored cloth used in the tabernacle was probably made and dyed in Egypt (Ex 25:4, 5). Evidences of widespread trade with Babylonia and Syria, known from the Amarna tablets, are seen in Num 31:50; Josh 7:21; Jud 5:30; 8:24.

After their settlement in Canaan, the Israelites became involved in commerce. At first, they had a natural self-sufficient economy. Each household grew its food and made all the tools and clothing needed. Other necessary articles or metals were supplied by wandering blacksmiths such as the Kenites (*q.v.;* Jud 1:16; 4:11)—the name means "smith"—and merchants. The latter were mostly Canaanites or Phoenicians. The word "Canaanite" became a synonym for "merchant," "trader" or "trafficker" (Job 41:6; Prov 31:24; Isa 23:8; Hos 12:7; Zech 14:21, RSV).

Previous to the Exile, Israel was not usually noted for commerce; trade was not the occupation of many of its people. The law made little regulation of such. Rather, just and righteous dealings were emphasized in general (Lev 19:35-36; Deut 25:13-16; 28:12). This absence of any manufacturing code is in itself a witness to the early date of the laws of the Pentateuch. The tribes near the sea and near Phoenician territory may have had some maritime trade (Gen 49:13; Deut 33:18; Jud 5:17).

During the reign of Solomon, however, Israel developed extensive external trade. A number of the wise sayings in Proverbs pertain to business matters, such as warnings regarding surety (Prov 6:1; 11:15; 17:18; 20:16; 22:26). The

virtuous wife is commended for her small-scale commercial endeavors (Prov 31:13-18, 24). Solomon levied tariffs on merchantmen (I Kgs 10:15). He apparently exploited the copper deposits in the Arabah and was also a large exporter of wheat and oil, which was paid to Hiram of Tyre for timber and the use of skilled workmen (I Kgs 5:6 ff.). Sidon and Tyre with the nearby mountains furnished the best and most durable timber for shipbuilding. Their craftsmen built ships and made other products for export. The Phoenicians led by Tyre were esteemed as the great commercial nation and famed for knowledge of navigation (Ezk 27).

Solomon also acted as middleman in the profitable trading of horses and chariots between Kue (Cilicia) and Egypt, and his royal merchants as agents sold many to the Hittite and Aramean principalities (I Kgs 10:28-29, RSV). Every three years from Ezion-geber (*q.v.*) he sent ships to Ophir for gold, silver, ivory, apes and peacocks. He had built for him a fleet of cargo ships designed like those the Phoenicians were sailing to their mining colonies at Tarshish in Spain (I Kgs 10:22). He also fostered the spice trade with Arabia (I Kgs 10:15). His example apparently could not be followed on any large scale by his successors, although Jehoshaphat vainly tried to revive trade to Ophir (I Kgs 22:48). Jonah had to embark on a ship with Gentile sailors for Tarshish, showing that his countrymen were not active in maritime affairs at that time.

After the division of the kingdom, Israel traded with Phoenicia and Syria, while Judah dealt with Egypt, its southern neighbor, olive oil being its chief export (Hos 12:1). Ahab of Israel gained the right to establish trading markets or bazaars (KJV, "streets") in Damascus of Syria (I Kgs 20:34). The treasuries of the kings must have been accumulated partly at least by trade. Isaiah (3:18-24) speaks of the luxuries of feminine apparel not native to Israel. Tribute was often paid in kind, as sheep

Model of a ship used by Queen Hatshepsut of Egypt in trading expeditions about 1500 B.C.
Art Gallery and Museum, Glasgow

and wool from Moab (II Kgs 3:4). Hezekiah paid Sennacherib with silver and gold stripped from the house of the Lord (II Kgs 18:15 – 16).

During this period certain towns seem to have specialized in certain trades, such as the dyeing industry evidenced by the many stone vats in the excavations of Tell Beit Mirsim. Gibeon enjoyed a prosperous business in making and selling wine. See Occupations.

It is probable that the commercial genius of the Jews began to appear during the Exile. They acquired both wealth and positions of importance in Babylonia (Neh 1:11; 5:17). Many of those who stayed there became clients or agents of big commercial firms, such as the business house of the Murashu sons in Nippur, according to tablets written in the reign of Artaxerxes I (ANET, pp. 221 f.). After the return from the Exile, the Jewish community in Judah was poor and there was little business except at Jerusalem. Ezra (3:7) mentions oil exported to Tyre and cedar imports. Tyre sent fish to Palestine (Neh 13:16). Nehemiah's exhortation to the people to stop profaning the sabbath indicates that buying and selling were carried on.

Domestic trade in Israel included the shipping of salt from the Dead Sea, cattle and wool from the pastures E of the Jordan, and grain from the plain of Esdraelon. These were sent to various markets. Zephaniah implies one at Jerusalem (1:11).

The town markets were chiefly open spaces near the gates to which the producer brought his goods for direct sale to the consumer (II Kgs 7:1; Neh 13:15-16; Zeph 1:10). Later, traders intruded into the temple where the outer courts were utilized (Zech 14:21; Mt 21:12; Jn 2:14).

During the Hellenistic period, Jews did business with colonies in Alexandria, Antioch of Syria, Asia Minor, Greece, and even in Rome. Greek mercenary troops, craftsmen and merchants had been active along the E Mediterranean coast for centuries (Edwin Yamauchi, *Greece and Babylon*, pp. 26–93). Herod built the port of Caesarea, as Simon Maccabeus had built Joppa, to care for the maritime trade.

In Maccabean times it had become customary for villagers to carry products to town once a month. Later, market days were traditionally twice a week, on Monday and Thursday. Special services were held in synagogues on these days.

While its position was extremely unfavorable for trade, Jerusalem was the commercial center of the entire country in the time of Christ. Woolen garments were produced there and sold in the markets of the city. Tanners obtained skins from the temple sacrifices. Olives were processed in and around Jerusalem in such presses as Gethsemane, and the oil was probably the only export of the city. Spices were made into ointments and sold in its markets (Mk 16:1; Lk 23:56; Jn 19:39). The craftsmen were organized in guilds and grouped their small shops, open to the street or bazaar, in separate sections or quarters. The building trade flourished in Jesus' day, and stone was easily quarried in the vicinity. As Joachim Jeremias concludes, it was the religious significance of the Holy City which made its trades flourish and the enormous revenues of the temple which enabled Jerusalem to import its necessary food (*Jerusalem in the Time of Jesus*, p. 28; see his chapters on industries and commerce, pp. 3 – 57).

Bibliography. G. A. Barrois, "Trade and Commerce," IDB, IV, 677–683. "Trade," CornPBE, pp. 687–691. Walter Duckat, *Beggar to King*, Garden City: Doubleday, 1968, Appendix 1: "Commerce and Trade," pp. 287–298. Donald Harden, *The Phoenicians*, London: Thames & Hudson, 1962, pp. 157–179. Joachim Jeremias, *Jerusalem in the Time of Jesus*, Philadelphia: Fortress Press, 1969. J. L. Kelso and E. M. Blaiklock, "Trade and Commerce," NBD, pp. 1287–1290. W. F. Leemans, "Old Babylonian Letters and Economic History," *Journal of the Economic and Social History of the Orient*, XI (1968), 171–226. Nimet Özgüc, "Assyrian Trade Colonies in Anatolia," *Archaeology*, XXII (1969), 250–255. H. W. F. Saggs, *The Greatness That Was Babylon*, New York: New American Library, a Mentor Book, 1962, pp. 262–287. Edwin Yamauchi, *Greece and Babylon*, Grand Rapids: Baker, 1967.

I. R.

COMMISSION, GREAT. The post-resurrection command of Jesus Christ to His disciples as recorded in Mt 28:19-20; Mk 16:15-18; Lk 24:46-49; Jn 20:21-23; and Acts 1:4-5, 8.

Its integrity. The authenticity and genuineness of the Great Commission passages, especially as found in Matthew and Mark, have been assailed by representatives of rationalism and higher criticism, the former on theological grounds and the latter on manuscript evidence. Evangelical scholarship, however, has defended both the genuineness as well as the authenticity of the passages and held its line well on the basis of internal and external evidences.

Its interpretation. The interpretation of the Great Commission passages has differed greatly through the centuries and has caused considerable discussion. Debate has revolved around numerous questions: Were these words spoken to the disciples as apostles of Jesus Christ? Did they constitute a part of the unique assignment to the apostolic office? Or were they addressed to the apostles as representatives of the church of Jesus Christ and thus are a part of the church's commission unto the end of the age? Again, what is the interrelationship between baptizing and teaching? Is the latter a coordinate with or a subordinate to the former since the conjunctive "and" is missing between vv. 19 and 20 of Mt 28? Or is teaching associated with baptizing and not merely subsequent to it? And how are baptizing and teaching related to making disciples? What is the real meaning of baptizing "into" the name? Why is the word "name" used in the singular when it is followed by an enumeration of the three persons of the Godhead?

Evangelical scholarship has sought to answer these questions very much in keeping with the presentation which follows, believing that the commission is addressed to the church and must be obeyed to the end of the age, and that it must be interpreted in the light of total revelation.

Few commentators deal exhaustively with the Great Commission passages. Recently two exegetical studies of note have appeared. The first is by Karl Barth, the second by Robert D. Culver. Neither man attempts to investigate the full scope of the Great Commission; both limit their studies to the Gospel of Matthew passage. Thus these are only partial considerations of the Great Commission.

Its relationship to Christianity. The Great Commission is not an isolated command arbitrarily imposed upon Christianity. It is a logical summation and natural outflow of the character of God as He is revealed in the Scriptures (Ezk 33:11; I Tim 2:4; II Pet 3:9); of the missionary purpose and thrust of God as unfolded in the OT (e.g., Isa 49:6; 56:3-8; Jon 3:10; 4:2, 11), and historically incarnated in the calling of Israel (Gen 12:1-3; Ex 19:5-6; Isa 42:6-7, 19); of the life, theology and saving work of Christ as disclosed in the Gospels (Mt 9:35 — 11:1; Lk 19:10; Jn 10:16); of the nature and work of the Holy Spirit as predicted by our Lord and manifested on and after Pentecost (Acts 2:17; 13:2, 4; 16:6- 10); and of the nature and design of the church of Jesus Christ as made known in Acts (2:9- 11, 21, 39; 13:46- 49; 15:7- 18) and the epistles (Rom 10:18; Eph 2:11- 22; 3:8- 11; Col 1:6, 23). Christ prophetically declared that His gospel will be preached throughout the whole world as a testimony to all nations before the end comes (Mt 24:14). The fulfillment of this is previewed in the heavenly scene described in Rev 7:9- 10. The commission is thus firmly anchored in the total body of revelation, both OT and NT. It forms an organic unit and an integral part within that revelation, and receives its true meaning and force only if seen in this larger relationship.

The Great Commission does not make Christianity a missionary religion. The latter is such because of its source, nature, and total design. The apostles became missionaries not because of a commission but because Christianity is what it is and because of the indwelling Holy Spirit who is a Spirit of missions. Christ Himself speaks of the mission of the Holy Spirit as a witnessing mission (Jn 15:26; 16:8- 15). Thus, if the particular words of the Great Commission had never been spoken, or if having been spoken they had not been recorded or preserved, the missionary thrust and responsibility of the church would not be in the least affected. The thrust of missions prospers wherever Christianity is truly known, thoroughly believed and genuinely experienced.

Its value. Nevertheless, it is of immense value that the Great Commission was spoken by our Lord and recorded by the Holy Spirit through the Gospel writers. While it does not create new duties for Christianity, this final order of Jesus Christ sharply focuses the missionary thrust and responsibility beyond reasonable doubting and disputing. Again, its singularity as the principal command of the Lord in His resurrection ministry marks it off as unique among His words and makes it more than just one commission among many commands to the disciples. Its restatement by every one of the Gospel writers witnesses to its living tradition in the early church, and the book of Acts demonstrates its dynamic in the original movement of Christianity.

Its composite nature. The Great Commission is a composite command. Its record in all four Gospels and in Acts is unique among the words of Christ and points up its significance in the mind of each writer, its richness and fullness of content, and the unity and design of each of the Gospels. They all culminate in the Great Commission and point in a common direction. Christianity is centrifugal in nature and thrust.

The fact that each of the four evangelists gives the Great Commission in one form or another needs to be noted. No one gives it in its completeness. While each of the evangelists presents it from his own point of view and with his own emphasis, together they supplement each other, making a complete whole as the following outline shows:

Matthew – the authority, the all-inclusive goal and the time-extension of the work

Mark – the method and geographical scope of the work

Luke – the message and the universality of the work

John – the spiritual equipment and the spiritual nature of the work

Only as we see the whole outline as presented in the four Gospels do we see the total Great Commission.

Its scope and pattern. An analysis of the Great Commission reveals two imperatives in the original Gr. that give direction to the commission. These are found in Matthew and Mark in the words "make disciples" and "preach the gospel." Thus the Great Commission is like an ellipse with its twofold foci. While in former years of the modern missionary movement beginning with William Carey the emphasis was upon the Markan focus — "preach the gospel" — and evangelism was the all-out thrust of missions, the emphasis today is upon Matthew's focus — "make disciples" — and church planting has come to the foreground. The Bible would emphasize both and keep them in proper balance. The two imperatives are supplemented by the participles "going" (Mk 16:15; Mt

28:19), "baptizing" (Mt 28:19; cf. Mk 16:16), "teaching" (Mt 28:20).

There are no imperative verbs relative to witnessing or preaching in Luke, John or Acts. However, there is a scriptural ("thus it is written," Lk 24:46) and a spiritual ("receive ye the Holy Spirit," Jn 20:22) force back of these words so that a command to witness is not necessary; indeed, it would seem out of place. The dynamic of the Word and the Spirit take the place of the imperative.

A study, then, of the composite Great Commission as recorded in the four Gospels produces the following facts. The all-inclusive *goal* is to *"make disciples"* of all nations. In order to accomplish this purpose:

1. Christians must engage in an intensive and extensive heralding of the gospel among the nations of the world, communicating meaningfully the gospel of God as recorded in the Scriptures.

2. Christians must lead people into an experience of the grace of God made available through the death and resurrection of Jesus Christ and offering forgiveness of sin in His name to all who will believe the gospel.

3. Christians must separate people from their old sinful relationships (without deculturizing them) and build them into the new congregation of God through the practice of baptism.

4. Christians must indoctrinate them in the precepts of the Master and thus by the renewing of their minds mold them into true Christian discipleship.

Such is the pattern of our ministry according to the Great Commission. None of the essentials may be omitted or neglected. Neither does time exhaust the dynamics nor the validity of the commission. Christ's commands bind every Christian to the task until the end of the age. *See* Evangelists; Witness.

Bibliography. Karl Barth, *The Theology of the Christian Mission*, ed. by Gerald Andersen, New York: McGraw-Hill. Robert D. Culver, "What Is the Church's Commission? Some Exegetical Issues in Matthew 28:16-20," *Bulletin of Evangelical Theological Society*, X (1967), 115-126. Joachim Jeremias, *Jesus' Promise to the Nations*, trans. S. H. Hooke, Naperville, Ill.: Allenson, 1958, includes an excellent bibliography. George E. Mendenhall, "Missions," IDB, III, 404 ff. John R. W. Stott, "The Great Commission," ChT, XII (1968), 723-725, 778-782, 826-829. John M. L. Young, "Theology of Missions, Covenant-centered," CT, XIII (1968), 162-165.

G. W. P.

COMMUNION. *See* Lord's Supper.

COMMUNION OF SAINTS. Gr. *koinōnia*, translatable as "communion" or "fellowship," designates a common sharing or participation in

something. It (and its cognate forms) describes the fellowship of true believers with their Lord and with one another. The essential teachings regarding this truth may be set forth thus:

Communion arises out of the new birth (Jn 3:1-12), and is therefore restricted to those who are "in Christ" (II Cor 5:17). Their common spiritual paternity makes them one common brotherhood (Heb 2:11-13).

Thus communion represents the spiritual unity that binds believers to Jesus Christ and to each other (Jn 15:1-10; 17:21, 23; Eph 4:3-16). This unity transcends natural bounds (Gal 3:28; Col 3:11), although it does not thereby abolish providential differences between believers (I Cor 7:20-24; Eph 6:5-9).

This communion finds its visible outlet in the mutual sharing of material blessings (Rom 12:13; 15:26-27; II Cor 8:4; 9:9-14; Gal 6:6; Phil 4:14-16). In the apostolic community at Pentecost this sharing took the form of a community of goods, although it is not evident that this innovation became a precedent for subsequent times (but cf. I Tim 6:18; Heb 13:16).

On a higher level, communion provides for the free use of spiritual gifts, even though these gifts are not equally bestowed upon all believers (Mt 25:15; I Cor 12:1-31). Within the Christian community places of leadership are just as important as places of submission (Phil 2:29; I Thess 5:12-13; II Thess 3:14; Heb 13:7, 17).

Restricted to the regenerate, the communion of saints necessarily excludes all other relationships incompatible with it. The child of God can no longer participate on the spiritual level in the plans and programs of unregenerate humanity (Ps 1:1-2; 26:4-5; I Cor 5:9-11; II Cor 6:14-18; Eph 5:7, 11; I Tim 5:22).

This communion may be interrupted or hindered either by sin (I Cor 5:1-7; I Jn 1:6-10), or by error in conduct (II Thess 3:6-15), or in doctrine (I Jn 2:19; II Jn 9-11). It is therefore very necessary for the believer to safeguard his life scrupulously (I Cor 6:1-20).

In the present life the communion of saints finds its highest realization in the fellowship with the Triune God (I Cor 1:9; II Cor 13:14; Phil 2:1; I Jn 1:3). In Christ's sufferings (Phil 3:10; I Pet 4:13) the believer finds a fellowship that is visibly portrayed in the Lord's Supper (I Cor 10:16, 20-21; 11:20-34).

This blessed communion reaches its consummation in the eternal fellowship of believers with the Triune God and with one another (Ps 73:23-26; Mt 8:11; Heb 12:22-24). This communion constitutes a paramount blessing of the glory of heaven (Rev 5:9-14; 7:9-17). *See* Fellowship.

W. B.

COMMUNITY OF GOODS. With a large segment of the world's population under the political and economic control of communism and with an increasingly widespread discussion of communist theory everywhere in the world, the question often arises whether the Bible recommends or even enjoins communal ownership of goods.

It is true that Jesus commanded a rich young ruler to sell his goods and give to the poor (Lk 18:18–30), but the reason for the command was to test the extent of his faith, not to enforce a social or economic leveling. It should be remembered that on another occasion when the disciples argued that Mary's anointing of the Master was a waste and that the money might better be given to the poor, Jesus remarked, "Ye have the poor always with you; but me ye have not always" (Mt 26:11).

As far as the early church and Scripture regarding it are concerned, there is only one locale where communal ownership of goods was practiced and only two passages referring to it. In Jerusalem, after the descent of the Holy Spirit on Pentecost, the brethren of the new fellowship of Christians enjoyed a remarkable unity, extending to holding all things in common. Those who had wealth pooled it, and all drew from the common treasury as they had need (Acts 2:44–45).

After an outbreak of persecution, the Holy Spirit again moved upon the believers in Jerusalem. Again it is said that they held all things in common; no one was in need. Barnabas was singled out as a well-to-do person who sold property and contributed to the common treasury. In this context appears the account of the death of Ananias and Sapphira. They sold property too, but were more concerned with a reputation for philanthropy than for honesty. They kept back part of the proceeds though they said they gave all as they presented their gift to the common treasury. God would not condone sin in the nascent Christian church any more than in the early days of Heb. national occupation of Canaan (when He judged Achan, Josh 7), and He struck down both Ananias and Sapphira. Power was linked to purity in the launching of the Christian church (Acts 4:32–5:11).

What conclusions may be drawn, then, concerning the biblical approach to communism? In the first place, the Bible certainly does not support Marxist Communism with its anti-God philosophy and its concept of class warfare. Numerous passages (e.g., Eph 6:5–9; Col 3:22–4:1) admonish good relations between workers and employers. Second, communal ownership of property among believers seems to have been restricted to Jerusalem. Whether in Antioch of Syria, Philippi or Thessalonica, believers practiced private ownership of property, and there is no indication they were encouraged to pool their resources. They were, however, urged to give to various collections for the poor saints in Jerusalem. Moreover, there is no proof that communal ownership of property continued indefinitely in Jerusalem. Furthermore, apparently communal ownership of property was optional in Jerusalem. In his judgment, Peter focused on Ananias' dishonesty. He made it clear that Ananias did not have to sell his property, and once he did, he did not have to give the proceeds to the common treasury. His sin was in claiming to have given all, when he held back a part (Acts 5:3–4).

There seems to have been a special, temporary need for a communal ownership of property in Jerusalem. Many Jews of the Dispersion, in Jerusalem for the Jewish feast of Pentecost, were converted and lingered on, enjoying spiritual blessing. There was little means of support for them. Probably many of them would have been cut off by their families socially and economically if they had returned home. Likewise, many Palestinian Jews were cut off from their society after conversion and no longer had a means of livelihood. Moreover, at best Jerusalem Jews in NT times had a difficult economic position. The economic pinch on believers there was great indeed. A communal treasury seemed necessary for the time being, as did numerous collections by Paul for the "poor saints in Jerusalem."

If believers today wish to live in an arrangement where Christians have communal ownership of goods, they should feel free to do so; but the Scripture does not oblige them to live in this fashion. And they should not sit in judgment on other believers who prefer to enjoy the private ownership of property. All should remember that they are merely stewards of all God has given them and that they are enjoined to exercise a faithful stewardship of possessions entrusted to them. *See* Fellowship; Steward.

H. F. V.

COMPASS. Various Heb. words are used. The noun forms suggest a circle or sphere (Prov 8:27; Job 26:10); a compass, circuit, or margin (Ex 27:5; 38:4); compass or instrument for describing a circle (Isa 44:13); what is round about (I Kgs 7:35). The verb forms frequently mean to surround, go round about (Gen 2:11; Deut 2:1; Jer 31:22; Ps 18:4; Isa 50:11); to be or go round about (Josh 15:10; 18:14; 19:14); to encircle (I Sam 23:26; Lk 21:20); to set around (II Kgs 6:14); and other variations.

COMPASSION. *See* Mercy.

COMPEL. The English word carries the ideas both of force and persuasion. Several words convey various aspects of these ideas. (1) It may mean "to urge or constrain" (I Sam 28:23); (2) "to force" (II Chr 21:11), "to press" (Est 1:8), "impress" for service (Mt 5:41; 27:32), "to constrain" by force or entreaty (Lk 14:23).

CONANIAH (kŏn-á-nī′á). A chief of the Levites in the reign of King Josiah (II Chr 35:9).

CONCISION (Gr. *katatomē*, "to cut down or cut off," "mutilate").

Used by Paul once in Phil 3:2 where he

contemptuously speaks of physical circumcision, considered by the Judaizers to be necessary for salvation, as a type of mutilation in comparison with the true spiritual circumcision of those who worship God in the Spirit. He suggests that those who were unsettling the Galatians should mutilate (Gr. *peritomē*) themselves (Gal 5:12). This passage may refer to emasculation, such as found in the Cybele-Attis cult. In Col 2:10–11 Paul speaks of a circumcision "made without hands" in Christ, and equates it with baptism into Christ's death (cf. Rom 6:3–5). True circumcision then is that phase of baptism in which the Holy Spirit identifies the believer with all Christ has done for his justification. *See* Baptism; Circumcision.

CONCUBINE. Though lawfully united to a man in marriage, the concubine was a secondary type of wife and inferior to a full wife. Concubinage was a natural part of a polygamous society. The custom was recognized and regulated in the code of Hammurabi (13th cen. B.C.), and also in the laws of Moses (Ex 21:7–11; Deut 21:10–14). Concubines were usually taken from among Heb. or foreign slaves or from foreign captives. They enjoyed no particular rights in family affairs and could be sent away with a mere present and their children excluded from an inheritance (e.g., the sons of Hagar and Keturah, Gen 25:1–6). Though their children were regarded as legitimate, they were treated as secondary when it came to inheritances.

In patriarchal times following Mesopotamian customs concubines particularly served to continue the line of a family when the real wife was barren (Gen 16:3). Levirate marriage, on the other hand, supplied this need when the husband died without descendants. Then his brother was to take the widow to wife (Deut 25:5–10; cf. Mt 22:23 ff.).

Some men who had concubines in the OT were Nahor (Gen 22:24), Abraham (Gen 25:6), Jacob (Gen 35:22), Eliphaz (Gen 36:12), Gideon (Jud 8:31), Saul (II Sam 3:7), David (II Sam 5:13; 15:16; 16:21), and Solomon (I Kgs 11:3). The problems and dangers of the practice are shown in the OT, particularly in Solomon's case where his many wives and concubines caused him to permit pagan worship and thus to sin (I Kgs 11:1–8).

The later prophets encouraged monogamy (Mal 2:14 ff.). Prov 31 urges this as the ideal. In His teaching on marriage (Mt 19:3–9) Christ implied that polygamy was among the things permitted by Moses only because of the hardness of men's hearts (Mt 19:8), thus showing that it is excluded for all Christians. The teaching of the epistles is clear that any leader of a church must be the husband of only one woman (I Tim 3:2, 12; Tit 1:6), and that every believer should love his wife (singular) as himself (Eph 5:33). *See* Family; Marriage.

R. A. K.

CONCUPISCENCE (kŏn-kū′pĭ-sĕns). A term used theologically to express the evil desires and lusts which beset fallen man (Rom 7:8; Col 3:5; I Thess 4:5).

There exists a great difference of opinion among Roman Catholics over the true nature of this word, and between Catholics in general and Protestants. Augustine confined it to sexual lusts; others extended it to all inordinate desires, hence the lack of agreement. Aquinas saw it as sin, but in general Roman Catholics do not regard concupiscence itself as sin. The Council of Trent spoke in negative terms and straddled the issue. It was thought of as something that gives cause to sin. Man was created with it, and the *donum superadditum*, the added gift of original righteousness, held it in control until man fell. It is counteracted in baptism and by *gratia infusa*, infused grace, at regeneration. It is clear that it is something for which man cannot be held responsible when looked upon in this way.

The biblical Reformed view sees concupiscence as the lust which leads to sin, developed when man rebelled against God and fell. It is sinful in itself, and reveals the corruption of man's whole nature and sin in him. Not only acts of the will are sinful, but willful thoughts (Gen 6:5; Mt 5:28). Paul speaks of it in Rom 7 as that which caused him to sin. It can be conquered only through recognizing that the fallen nature in us is judged (Rom 8:3); then walking by the Spirit and letting Him keep the law of God in us (Rom 8:4), which is the Spirit-filled life. *See* Covetousness; Lust.

R. A. K.

CONDEMNATION (CONDEMN). An unfavorable decision or sentence rendered by either human or divine agency. In the OT, the verb "condemn" in almost every instance translates the Heb. word *rāsha'*, meaning "condemn as guilty," and is used in civil relations (Deut 25:1; Ps 94:21; Job 34:17) and in ethical and religious relations (Job 9:20; 10:2; Ps 37:33; Prov 12:2; Isa 50:9; 54:17).

In the NT, occasionally the English words "condemn" and "condemnation" are used to translate the shorter Gr. words for "judge" and "judgment" (*q.v.*). The context makes it clear whether it is simply a decision rendered or an unfavorable sentence imposed by God or man (cf. Jn 3:17, 19; 5:24; Lk 23:40; Jas 5:12).

The more frequent Gr. word is *katakrinō* and is to be distinguished from the previously mentioned words in that it refers either to the sentence or to the punishment following the sentence (MM, p. 328) rather than to the simple act of deciding in judgment. Only the context can determine the precise nature of the sentence. For example, in Mk 10:33 and Mt 20:18 the condemnation or sentence is to physical death; in II Cor 7:3 Paul refers to a condemnation or reprimand of behavior before others. In some places the reference is to God's condemnation and seems to refer to God's sentence of permanent judgment upon the sinner and all that that implies (Mt 12:41-42; I Cor 11:32; II Cor 3:9; II Pet 2:6).

In Rom 5:16, 18 Paul refers to the divine condemnation of the whole human race in Adam. While some make a distinction here between the sentence and its legal punishment or execution (e.g., Deissmann, *Bible Studies,* pp. 264 ff.), others perhaps rightly point out that in divine condemnation in distinction to human, the sentence and its execution—the beginning at least—can never be separated (TWNT, p. 951). For those who are "in Christ Jesus" there is no longer either the divine sentence or the legal punishment for sin resting upon them (Rom 8:1). The difficult expression of Paul that "God condemned sin in the flesh" (Rom 8:3) seems to assert that God both judged and executed punishment for man's sin upon Jesus who became flesh (incarnate).

A further word *(katadikazō)* is used in basically the same sense as *katakrinō* for the rich landlords punishing the poor innocent laborers (Jas 5:6); for the words untruthfully spoken and held as evidence to sentence those who reject Christ (Mt 12:37); for the act of holding persons personally guilty rather than acquitting them (Lk 6:37); and for the Pharisees' pronouncement upon the disciples of their guilt for threshing and eating grain on the sabbath day (Mt 12:7).

A somewhat different word *(kataginōskō)* is used in I Jn 3:20-21 concerning our heart condemning us. The word means to "scorn" and is used of self-judgment, perhaps in the idea of "guilt feeling," and admits either to the sense that God is behind the guilt feeling showing us that something is wrong, or that God's knowledge is greater than our own feeling of guilt and we should persuade our hearts to His point of view (cf. Rom 14:22; Gal 2:11).

A. F. J.

CONDUIT. Expressed in Heb. by *teʻālâ,* "channel," "trench"; in Gr. by *hydragōgos,*

Roman aqueduct at Caesarea. HFV

"water carrier," "irrigation channel"; and in Latin by *aquaeductus,* "conduit," "aqueduct."

Usually a conduit was an open trench running along the surface of the ground; but there were also underground piped channels. Remains of numerous conduits may be seen in the Near East; for example, at Caesarea, Qumran, and Jerusalem. Clay pipes fitted into stone blocks can be seen at Laodicea. Such a conduit brought water from the neighboring hills. Biblical references are to the water works of Jerusalem in Isaiah's time (II Kgs 18:17; 20:20; Isa 7:3; 36:2; cf. Sir 24:30; 48:17; FLAP, pp. 190 f.).

CONEY. *See* Animals, II.9.

CONFECTION. A perfume made by the temple apothecary (Ex 30:35). The KJV translates the same term as "ointment" while the ASV has "confection," referring to a mixture of medicines or perfumes made by the sons of the priests (I Chr 9:30).

CONFECTIONARY. This term is found only once in the KJV of the OT. I Sam 8:13 reads: "He will take your daughters to be confectionaries" ("perfumers," ASV). They seemed to have formed part of a perfumers' guild (Neh 3:8; II Chr 16:14).

CONFECTIONER. *See* Occupations: Perfumer.

CONFESSION. The word means to make an open avowal, usually with undertones of a change of position. Nearly all the biblical passages can be classified under two heads: a confession of sin, or a confession of faith. Confession of sin is made to God (Ps 32:3-6; I Jn 1:9), to the one who has been wronged (Lk 17:4), to a spiritual adviser (II Sam 12:13), to the congregation of believers (I Cor 5:3 ff.; cf. II Cor 2:6 f.). Confession of faith is to be made openly before men (Mt 10:32; Rom 10:9; I Tim 6:12-13; Heb 3:1; 4:14; 10:23). In the end, all men will be forced to confess the lordship of Christ (Phil 2:11). *See* Forgiveness.

Bibliography. Otto Michel, "*Homologeō,* etc.," TDNT, V, 199-220. John R. W. Stott, *Confess Your Sins: The Way of Reconciliation,* Philadelphia: Westminster Press, 1964.

CONFIDENCE. *See* Boldness.

CONFUSION OF TONGUES. *See* Babel; Tongues, Confusion of.

CONGREGATION. The Heb. words *qāhāl* ("assembly") and *ʻēdâ* ("congregation") are the most frequently used terms to designate a gathering of Israel for religious or political purposes (BDB). It has been supposed, on the basis of Ex 12:6 and Num 14:5, that the "assembly" constituted only a part of the "congregation";

Water channel atop the Roman aqueduct at Caesarea. HFV

but this distinction, in the light of Lev 4:13 and Num 16:3 (ASV and RSV), cannot be pressed too far. Prov 5:14 uses the two terms as synonyms.

The only valid distinction between these terms seems to be in the fact that *qāhāl* represents Israel as the ideal people of God, whereas *'ēdâ* designates the nation as a political entity here upon earth. This latent meaning of *qāhāl* in certain messianic passages in the Psalms (22:22, 25; 35:18; 40:9-10; 89:5; 107:32; 149:1) puts this term in the forefront as the spiritual prototype of the Christian *ekklēsia* ("church"). Justification for this word parallelism may be seen in the quotation of Ps 22:22 in Heb 2:12, where *qāhāl* is translated by *ekklēsia*. However, *'ēdâ* also has its spiritual implications (Ps 1:5; 74:2).

It should be noted that ASV translates *qāhāl* as "assembly" in all places except in Genesis (28:3; 35:11; 48:4), Jeremiah (31:8; 44:15; 50:9), and Ezekiel (16:40; 17:17; 23:24, 46-47; 26:7; 27:27, 34; 32:3, 22-23; 38:4, 7, 13, 15). "Assembly" is, however, used in Jer 26:17; and strangely, "congregation" is found in II Chr 31:18. "Company" is used in the passages noted as exceptions. On the other hand, ASV translates *'ēdâ* as "congregation" in all places except where, designedly, it uses "swarm" (Jud 14:8), "multitude" (Ps 68:30) and "company" (Num 16:5 f., 11, 16, 40; 27:3; Job 15:34; 16:7; Ps 22:16; 86:14; 106:17-18).

Membership in the congregation of Israel was on the basis of circumcision (Gen 17:1-14). However, "strangers" could become members by submitting to this same rite (Ex 12:48 f.). They thus assumed the same rights and responsibilities as native-born Israelites (Ex 12:19; Num 9:14; 15:15 f., 29). Membership could be lost ("cut off") by rebellion against God's laws (Gen 17:14; Ex 12:15, 19; 31:14; Lev 17:10, 14; Num 9:13; Ezr 10:8). Some were automatically excluded because of physical deformity or ancestral sins (Deut 23:1-8; Neh 13:1-3; Lam 1:10).

The congregation was called together by trumpets (Num 10:2-8). Such purposes as the following justified the calling of the congregation: to receive new legislation (Lev 8:1-4); to perform religious ceremonies (Ex 12:47; II Chr 30:1-13); to hear important messages (Josh 23:2; 24:1; Ezr 8:15 f.); to act on moral issues (Jud 20:1; Ezr 10:1-19); to ratify a covenant (II Chr 15:9-15); to crown a king (I Sam 10:17-25; II Sam 5:1-3; I Kgs 12:20). Often, however, the nation was represented by elders and/or chiefs (Ex 3:16; 4:29 f.; 12:21; 17:5; 24:1, 9-11; 34:31 f.; Num 31:13). Their decisions were accepted as final (Josh 9:15, 18; 22:30-34; Ezr 10:14, 16).

The congregation of Israel during and after the conquest of Canaan met at such places as Shiloh (Josh 18:1; 22:12), Shechem (Josh 24:1, 25), and Mizpeh (Jud 10:17; 11:11; 20:1; I Sam 10:17). The congregation met at Hebron to crown David king (II Sam 5:1-3), but afterward Jerusalem became the focal point of national gatherings (I Chr 13:2; 15:29; II Chr 23:2 f.; 30:1-13, 25-26). The Jews continued to make Jerusalem their national center after returning from exile in Babylon (Ezr 10:1, 9).

In two passages in the NT (Heb 10:25; Jas 2:2), the Christian gathering is called a synagogue *(synagogē)*. Once Israel is called an *ekklēsia* (Acts 7:38). But *ekklēsia*, "a called out group," eventually became the specific term for the Christian church as the divide between the church and Judaism grew wider and wider. Although some features of the church, e.g., rule by elders (Acts 15:2, 23), undoubtedly came from the Heb. "congregation," the church was a new society, a separate community. It was made up of men of various nations and classes who by salvation were transformed into "one body in Christ"; they were no longer Jews or Gentiles, slaves or freemen (Gal 3:28-29; Col 3:11, 15). Their new citizenship was in heaven (Phil 3:20, NASB).

The members of this new congregation were commanded to keep themselves "unstained by the world" (Jas 1:27, NASB), because friendship with the world (Jas 4:4) crowds out love for God (I Jn 2:15-17). They could expect persecution from the world. While they did not belong to the world, their Leader had not chosen to remove them from the world (Jn 17:14-15) and had given them a responsibility to win as many from the world as possible (*see*

375

Commission, Great). Thus the Christian church as a whole has not isolated itself from the rest of human society. See Assembly; Church; Synagogue.

Bibliography. John W. Flight, "Man and Society," IDB, III, 250 ff. Marvin H. Pope, "Congregation, Assembly," IDB, I, 669 f. J. A. Selbie, "Congregation," HDB, I, 466–467.

W. B.

CONGREGATION, MOUNT OF THE. This phrase is found in Isa 14:13, which places the mountain in the sides or recesses of the N. It does not refer to Zion, for Zion was neither in the northern part of the earth nor was it located to the N of Jerusalem. In his predictive taunt song Isaiah depicts the kings of the nations speaking to the king of Babylon (cf. v. 4) in terms of the thinking of his people, who did not have the throne of their god in the midst of them as did the Israelites. The Babylonians placed the abode of their god on the summit of the northern mountains which were lost in the clouds. The high boast of the Babylonian king of self-deification, inspired by Satan (Lucifer), doomed him to be cast down to the lowest depths. Various terms in Isa 14:12–14, RSV, such as "Day Star," "son of Dawn," "the Most High," and "the mount of assembly" of the gods, are common also in Canaanite mythology as known from the Ras Shamra (q.v.) texts. The Canaanites located this mountain at Jebel 'Aqra, N of Ugarit. See Lucifer.

W. B.

CONGREGATION, TABERNACLE OF. See Tabernacle.

CONIAH (kō-nī'á). This king of Judah is called Coniah in Jer 22:24, 28; 37:1, but he was known also as Jeconiah and Jehoiachin (q.v.).

CONONIAH (kŏn-ō-nī'á). A Levite, appointed with his brother Shimei by Hezekiah the king and Azariah the ruler of the house of God, to oversee the oblations, tithes and dedicated things (II Chr 31:12–13).

CONQUEST. See Exodus, The; Joshua; Joshua, Book of.

CONSCIENCE. Conscience is that faculty of a person that tells him he ought to do that which he believes to be right and that he ought not to do that which he believes to be wrong. It is not that by which one distinguishes right and wrong, since that is learned from teaching or environment, but that which prods one to do right and to refrain from wrong. The apostle Paul once did wrong, yet in a "good conscience" (Acts 23:1), which means that he was misinformed as to right conduct, but he still did that which he at that time believed right.

Conscience is an innate characteristic, found universally in men, that becomes active when one reaches the age of accountability. It is the "sense of moral awareness" or of *oughtness* in man, called the "categorical imperative" by Kant. The word is from the same root meaning as the words for consciousness and conscientiousness, but in its common NT usage means moral awareness. The conscience serves: (1) to accuse or excuse us (Rom 2:14–15), (2) to punish us when violated, and (3) to give us a sense of divine approval as well as self-approval when we do right. This is true since the very existence of the conscience calls for the existence of a Moral Governor of the universe, to whom we must all some day give account. See Law.

Bibliography. Christian Maurer, "*Synoida, Syneidēsis,*" TDNT, VII, 898–919. Roy B. Zuck, "The Doctrine of the Conscience," BS, CXXVI (1969), 329–340.

J. D. T.

CONSECRATION. This is primarily an OT word in the KJV and is used to translate a number of Heb. verbs and their derivative nouns (*ḥāram,* "to devote"; *qādash,* "to set apart"; *mālē',* "to fill the hand"; and *nāzar,* "to separate"). The common idea of these Heb. words brought out in KJV seems to be that of setting something or someone apart to the peculiar service of the Lord: priests (Ex 28:1–3; 30:30), things (Josh 6:19), feast days (Ezr 3:5), sacrifices (Lev 7:37), gain (Mic 4:13). The word is also used to describe the procedure by which one who has been defiled may regain admittance to the Lord (Num 6:7–12).

In the NT, the KJV uses the word to translate two Gr. words. Heb 10:20 declares that Jesus has consecrated (*enkainizō,* "renewed") a new and living way to God. Heb 7:28 shows that Jesus is eternally consecrated (*teleioō,* "perfected") as our great High Priest.

RSV prefers to use this word to translate *hagiazō,* usually translated in KJV by "sanctify" or "sanctification." The root idea is still that of separating from secular (worldly) use to divine service. There are a few instances of things being separated to God (cf. Mt 23:17, 19), but primarily the idea is that of separating people to God. The emphasis shifts from the exceptional individual to the whole body of Christians. The act of consecration takes place primarily at the time of conversion. The actor is always God; the object is man (cf. Heb 2:11). However, the idea of separation to and equipment for service is found in the case of Jesus (Jn 17:19) who is said to have consecrated Himself, and of the apostles (Jn 17:17) whom God so consecrated. A few passages seem to involve the growth or development of the Christian in holy living (cf. I Thess 5:23).

Of particular interest is the fact that the adjective for this verb *(hagios)* is one of the most common designations for the believer, usually translated "saint." The idea in the word is that every believer is a saint, a consecrated one, one who is separated from the world and belongs to God. Being a saint is our vocation, and becoming saintly is our goal in life. The modern practice of applying the word only to great Christians, especially of a previous age, is completely unbiblical. The biblical usage justifies us in saying that every true believer is a saint; he has been consecrated by God to Himself through Jesus Christ. *See* Saint; Dedicate.

F. L. F.

CONSOLATION. *See* Comfort; Holy Spirit.

CONSTELLATIONS. *See* Astronomy; Star.

CONSUMPTION
1. Heb. *shaḥepheth,* "wasting away." A punishment which would follow disobedience to God and His laws (Lev 26:16; Deut 28:22). Other diseases and punishments are also listed.
2. Heb. *kālâ,* "destruction," "completion," or "full end." The KJV uses the term "consumption," but the ASV and RSV use the terms "destruction" (Isa 10:23; 28:22), "full end" and "decreed end" (Dan 9:27).
3. In Isa 10:22, "consumption" ("full end," RSV) is the rendering of a different Heb. term from the above references.

CONTENTION. Several Heb. and Gr. words are used to suggest contention, strife, and wrangling. The contention may be physical, oral, or spiritual. It may describe a man's nature (Jer 15:10; Hab 1:3). Pride may bring contention (Prov 13:10). Christians are admonished to avoid contentious wrangling (I Cor 1:11; Tit 3:9). The sharp dispute between Barnabas and Paul (Acts 15:39) may refer more to a state of irritation and inner incitement than to an outward expression of contention.

CONTENTMENT. "The acceptance of 'things as they are' as the wise and loving providence of a God who knows what is good for us, who so loves us as always to seek our good" (IDB).
Moses was content to dwell with Jethro (Ex 2:21). The brothers of Joseph were pleased to listen to Judah in selling Joseph (Gen 37:27). Jesus urges contentment (Mt 6:19–34) with regard to desires for material things. John the Baptist urged the Roman soldiers to be content with their wages (Lk 3:14). Paul reminds Timothy that godliness with contentment is great gain (I Tim 6:6–8). The secret of contentment lies in the Christian's fellowship and union with God (Phil 4:11–13; 3:8–9).

CONTRACT. *See* Covenant.

CONTRITION. Found only in the OT in KJV (cf. Ps 34:18; Isa 57:15; Ps 51:17; Isa 66:2). The literal meaning of the word is to be bruised or broken. Biblical usage is limited to a description of the worshiper who approaches God with a "crushed" spirit over his sins. The implication is always that God will receive and forgive one who comes to Him in such a spirit. A NT parallel is found in II Cor 7:10 where "godly sorrow" for sin is looked upon as a precondition of true repentance. Possibly parallel in thought is the beatitude, "Blessed are they that mourn: for they shall be comforted" (Mt 5:4).

CONVERSATION. The KJV translation of Heb. *derek,* "way (of life)" in Ps 37:14; 50:23, and of Gr. *anastrophē, politeuma,* and *tropos* (once, Heb 13:5). This 17th cen. meaning of conversation always connoted ethical and moral conduct, behavior, or life-style in contrast with the modern meaning of the term as social intercourse and friendly talk.
The Gr. words translated "conversation" in Phil 1:27 (*politeuō*) and 3:20 (*politeuma*) refer to discharging one's obligations as a citizen in his civil life and to "citizenship," respectively.
The KJV uniformly rendered the 13 occurrences of the noun *anastrophē* by "conversation," whereas the modern English versions have employed a variety of terms to render the word; e.g., "manner of life," "behavior," "conduct." In Paul's epistles KJV has "ye have heard of my conversation" (Gal 1:13); "put off concerning the former conversation" (Eph 4:22); and "be thou an example . . . in conversation" (I Tim 4:12). Paul used the verb *anastrephō* in II Cor 1:12, "we have had our conversation in the world"; in Eph 2:3, "we all had our conversation in times past"; and in I Tim 3:15, where KJV does have "how thou oughtest to behave thyself in the house of God."
Peter employed the noun frequently in exhorting his readers to demonstrate holy, honorable, chaste conduct in keeping with a holy life (I Pet 1:15; 2:12; 3:2, 16; II Pet 3:11). By her godly behavior the Christian wife may without nagging win her husband who is disobedient to the word of God (I Pet 3:1). James used the noun in 3:13 to teach that individual deeds of the man with godly wisdom must stem from consistent good behavior. Heb 13:7 speaks of the model behavior of Christian leaders, "whose faith follow, considering the end of their conversation."
Placed in a contemporary setting, the dynamic Christian life is relevant. By his words and deeds the Christian communicates meaningfully the truth of God which he has believed and received into his own life. Honesty and love are the normal experiences of Christian living (Heb 13:18), in contrast with the deceitful, vain and filthy life-style of the non-Christian (I Pet 1:18; II Pet 2:7, 18). *See* Example; Liberty.

H. W. N.

CONVERSION. This means literally to turn, and is used to translate the Heb. word *shûb,* and the Gr. word *strephō* and its derivatives, especially *epistrephō.* The words are sometimes used in the Bible in a literal sense of turning physically to or from something (cf. Mt 9:22; Acts 9:40). The meaning which is primary and spiritual denotes a spiritual revolution. It is used in the bad sense of being converted from the right to the wrong in two passages (Gal 4:9; II Pet 2:21). However, the good meaning of turning from the undesirable to the desirable is the usual one. In this sense, it is used both of unbelievers and Christians.

When used of unbelievers, it denotes the change of heart or mind (related to repentance and faith) which enables one to receive the grace of God in salvation (cf. Acts 3:19). Though conversion is thought of as an act of man in contrast to justification and regeneration which are solely acts of God, the implication is always present that thoroughgoing conversion can only be accomplished by the help of the Holy Spirit. Conversion implies a complete repudiation of sin and a trustful surrender to Christ as Lord. See Repentance.

When used of believers, it denotes a return to a proper relationship with God which may have been broken by moral failure (cf. Peter, Lk 22:32) or by departure from true doctrine (cf. Jas 5:19-20).

The spiritual use of this word is illustrative of the fact that the Christian vocabulary, at first, was primarily figurative. The necessity of expressing spiritual concepts without an established vocabulary drove the apostles to adopt many common words and convert them to their own uses.

Bibliography. Georg Bertram, "*Strephō,* etc.," TDNT, VII, 714-729.

F. L. F.

CONVICTION. Used only in the NT and primarily with the meaning of bringing one to a realization of his own guilt or attempting to do so. The Gr. word *elegchō* is variously translated in the KJV by "convict," "convince," "reprove," "rebuke," and "tell one's fault." The various means by which conviction is brought about are: the reproof of a wronged brother (Mt 18:15); the message of the preacher (cf. Lk 3:19; I Tim 5:20; II Tim 4:2; Tit 1:9, 13; 2:15); the Holy Spirit dwelling in the congregation (Jn 16:8); coming to the light (Jn 3:20; Eph 5:13); the law (Jas 2:9); the Lord (Heb 12:5; Rev 3:19); the church (Eph 5:11; I Cor 14:24); and the coming of the Lord (Jude 14-15).

Faith is said to be the means by which men come to a conviction of the truth of creation (Heb 11:3). The Jews were challenged to convict Jesus of any sin (Jn 8:46); perhaps the judicial idea of convicting by evidence in court is approximated in this passage. In general, conviction is thought of in the NT as a necessary precondition to repentance and conversion.

F. L. F.

CONVOCATION. A religious gathering on a sabbath or certain sacred days. Usually "holy" precedes the word (Lev 23:2-4, 7-8, 21, 24, 27, 35-37; Num 28:18). It is a technical phrase in priestly regulations. The same Heb. words appear elsewhere (Ex 12:16; Isa 1:13; 4:5) meaning a "solemn assembly." A summoned assembly held under particularly holy circumstances for the observance of sacred rites and occasions, such a convocation was part of the great festivals in Israel. They were called sabbaths and were regarded as rest days. Such assemblies belonged to the picture of eschatalogical hope (Isa 4:5). The same Heb. word (without the qualifying "holy") is once used in the sense of "reading aloud" from the Torah (Neh 8:8). Jews came to use the term as a synonym for Scripture.

COOK, COOKING. *See* Food; Occupations: Cooks.

COOS (kō'ŏs). An island off the coast of Asia Minor near the province of Caria, 111 square miles in area. It was at the entrance to the Thermaic Gulf. The island is famous as a fertile place and as an emporium for various products and for banking. Coos (or Cos) lay on the main shipping route between Greece and the E. Josephus states that Herod the Great provided for perpetual annual revenues for the people of Coos to maintain the office of Gymnasiarch (see *Wars* i.21.11). An important inscription has been found on the island which mentions Herod Antipas, tetrarch of Galilee. This inscription can be translated: "To Herod [the] Tetrarch, son of Herod the Great, Philo, son of Aglaos [by adoption?], but by physical nature son of Nikon, his host [lit., 'guest friend'] and friend of Herod the Tetrarch [has erected this monument]."

Just when Herod Antipas made a journey to Coos is not certain, but it was probably in connection with a stop he also made on the island of Delos some time during A.D. 6-10. Around the year A.D. 6, Archelaus, his brother, who had been ethnarch of Judea, was removed and likely Herod Antipas made a trip to Rome at that time to protect his own interest, which might have been threatened, since he gave a donation about this time to the temple of Apollo on the island of Delos. It is highly probable that at this same time he also gave new benefits which his father Herod the Great had earlier provided (see above reference in Josephus). The inscription, therefore, is likely to be dated at that time.

Coos is mentioned in the NT in Acts 21:1 in connection with Paul's final journey to Jerusalem. It was natural that the famous island of Coos should be mentioned in connection with Paul's journey. It was a well-known and historic isle (it is mentioned as early as Homer) and as such was a well-known landmark. Coos was the site of the first school of scientific medicine.

Here the great Hippocrates, father of medicine, practiced early in the 4th cen. B.C.

One of the best short descriptions of Coos is by W. M. Ramsay in HDB. The island is referred to in Strabo, *Geography,* p. 657 ff.

E. J. V.

COPING. An obscure architectural term used in connection with the building of the temple by Solomon (I Kgs 7:9). It reads: "All these were made of costly stones, hewn according to measure . . . from the foundation to the coping" (RSV). It evidently refers to the highest or covering course in the wall. *See* Architecture.

COPPER. *See* Minerals and Metals.

COPPERSMITH. *See* Occupations.

COPY. *See* Type.

COR. *See* Weights, Measures, and Coins.

CORAL. *See* Animals, V.1; Jewels.

CORBAN (kôr'băn). A sacred gift, money or service dedicated to God to be used for a religious purpose (Lev 1:2; 2:1; 3:1; Num 7:12-17; Mk 7:11). The Pharisees, who were zealots for the temple, held that when a person said to his father or mother concerning his possessions, "That wherewith thou mightest have been profited by me is Corban" (Mk 7:11, ASV), the possessions were consecrated to God and he was released from using any of them to benefit his parent. Jesus condemned this practice as a casuistic use of religion to avoid the obligation of the commandment to honor father and mother by aiding them in their needs. Josephus (*Wars* ii.9.4) shows that Corban money could not be diverted for secular use even if for public welfare. *See* Vows.

Bibliography. K. H. Rengstorf, *"Korban,"* TDNT, III, 860-866.

CORD. Used to translate the Heb. words *hebel, hût, yeter, mêtār, 'ăbōt,* and the Gr. *schoinion,* the most frequent being *hebel.* The meaning includes not only cord or rope but also string, thread, twine, measuring line, bowstring, etc. The materials used depended on what was available for the strength required. They included flax, goat's hair, camel's hair, date tree fibers, reeds, rushes. Strong cords were made of camel's hide, still used by the Bedouin for drawing water.

The following are some of the uses of this word in the OT: (1) To lower men over walls and Jeremiah into a dungeon (Josh 2:15; Jer 38:6, 11-13). (2) To drag stones so as to destroy a city, or to draw a cart (II Sam 17:13; Isa 5:18). (3) As the tacklings of ships (Isa 33:23). (4) To bind expensive clothing or hangings of a palace (Ezk 27:24; Est 1:6). (5) As a

The harbor at Coos. E.W. Saunders

measuring line (Amos 7:17; Mic 2:5). (6) As an easily broken thread (Jud 16:12). (7) As a scarlet thread, or literally, "the cord of this thread of scarlet" (Josh 2:18). (8) As a threefold cord (Eccl 4:12). (9) As a bowstring (Job 30:11). (10) To hold up a tent, or as the cords of the tabernacle (Ex 35:18; 39:40; Num 3:26, 37; 4:26, 32; Isa 54:2; Jer 10:20). (11) As a twisted cord used as a fetter (Jud 15:13-14; Ps 118:27). (12) As twisted cords or golden chains on the high priest's breastplate (Ex 28:14, 22; 39:15).

Cord in the NT is made of rushes and used only once, where Jesus made a whip (Jn 2:15). However, the same Gr. word is used for the ropes that hold a ship's boat in place (Acts 27:32).

Figurative uses of cord include the following: (1) Of one who is bound with his sins (Prov 5:22). (2) The cords of wickedness (Isa 5:18) or affliction (Job 36:8). (3) The cord of life (Eccl 12:6). (4) The cords of a father training his child to walk, which is figurative for a guiding principle (Hos 11:4). (5) A figure of authority or restraint (Ps 2:3; 129:4).

E. C. J.

CORE (kō'rĕ). A Gr. or variant form in Jude 11 of Korah (*q.v.*). Korah was a cousin of Moses and Aaron (Ex 6:21), who led in a rebellion against their leadership (Num 16:1-49).

CORIANDER. *See* Plants.

CORINTH (kŏr'ĭnth). A very ancient city; the earliest settlers came in the 5th or 6th mil. B.C. But Corinth of the classical period was really established with the Dorian invasion. About 1000 B.C. these Gr. people settled at the foot of the acropolis of Corinth. Occupying a place of safety, they also controlled the main overland trade route between the Peloponnesus and central Greece, as well as the Isthmian route. Coming early to a height of prosperity, the city colonized Syracuse on Sicily and the island of Corcyra and achieved a peak of prosperity

379

through commercial and industrial development. Corinthian pottery and bronzes were exported widely over the Mediterranean. About the middle of the 5th cen. the city's fortunes declined as a result of the effective competition of Athenian industrial production. During the classical period Corinth controlled about 248 square miles of territory, approximately one-fourth the size of Rhode Island.

It is not possible to tell the history of Corinth in detail. Suffice it to say that she clashed with Rome during the 2nd cen. B.C., was finally destroyed by the Romans in 146 B.C., and lay virtually uninhabited until Julius Caesar refounded it in 44 B.C. The growth of Corinth was rapid, and by the time of Paul or soon thereafter it became the largest and most flourishing center in S Greece. It served as capital of the Roman province of Achaia, with a population estimated variously from 100,000 to several hundred thousand.

The later history of Corinth has no special value to the NT student. The city suffered various catastrophes until in 1858 when obliterated by an earthquake it moved to a new site on the Corinthian gulf; hence excavators of the American School of Classical Studies were able to discover what the place was like in NT times.

In Paul's day the city lay about one and a half miles S of the Corinthian gulf on the N side of its acropolis at an altitude of *c*. 400 feet. The Acrocorinthus or acropolis hill towered *c*. 1,500 feet over the city to an altitude of 1,886 feet. The city and its acropolis were enclosed by a wall over six miles in circumference. Outside the walls in the surrounding plain stretched grain fields, olive groves, vineyards, and other agricultural holdings of the city.

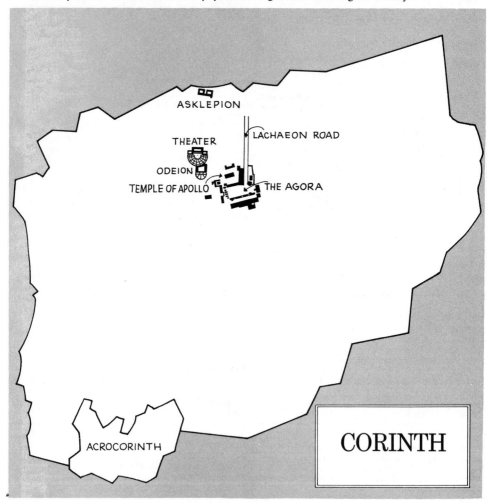

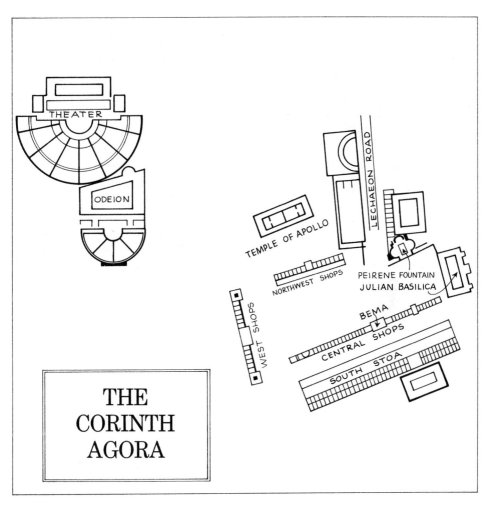

THEATER

ODEION

LECHAEON ROAD

TEMPLE OF APOLLO

NORTHWEST SHOPS

PEIRENE FOUNTAIN
JULIAN BASILICA

WEST SHOPS

BEMA

CENTRAL SHOPS

SOUTH STOA

THE
CORINTH
AGORA

In the N central part of town stood the Agora, nerve center of the metropolis. The Agora was almost 700 feet E and W and about 300 feet N and S. Following the natural configuration of the land, the S section was about 13 feet higher than the N part. At the dividing line of the two levels was a row of low buildings flanking a rostrum or bema, which served as a speaker's stand for public addresses and a judgment seat (*q.v.*) for magistrates. Here Paul appeared before Gallio (*q.v.*), governor of Achaia, as a result of Jewish accusations to the effect that he had broken the law (Acts 18:12–13). Along the S side of the Agora stood a stoa or colonnaded shopping center about 500 feet long. Here and on the NW side near the temple of Apollo were shops for meat and wine merchants, probably the "shambles" or market which Paul referred to in I Cor 10:25 (KJV).

An inscription was found near the theater stating that Erastus (*q.v.*; probably mentioned in Rom 16:23) the aedile (city treasurer) had laid the pavement at his own expense.

As to nonphysical aspects of Corinth, it should be noted that much of the population was mobile (sailors, businessmen, government officials, *et al.*) and was therefore cut off from the inhibitions of a settled society. To make matters worse, religious prostitution was commonly practiced in connection with the temples of the city. For instance, according to Strabo, 1,000 priestesses or slave girls of the Temple of Aphrodite on the acropolis were employed in religious prostitution. An inscription reveals they had their own seats in the theater NW of the Agora. From the social mobility and the evils of religious practices there arose a general corruption of society. "Corinthian morals" be-

The Bema at Corinth where Paul stood before Gallio. HFV

came a byword even in the pagan Roman world. It is no wonder Paul had so much to say about the sacredness of the body in his first Corinthian letter.

Near Corinth the Isthmian games were held every two years in honor of Poseidon, god of the sea. Athletic events included footraces, two-horse chariot racing, the pentathlon (running, jumping, discus and javelin throwing, wrestling) and the pankration (a combination of boxing and wrestling). The victor's crown seems to have been withered wild celery during the 1st cen. A.D., a corruptible crown indeed (I Cor 9:25).

Bibliography. Oscar Broneer, "Corinth, Center of St. Paul's Missionary Work in Greece," BA, XIV (1951), 78–96. Rhys Carpenter, *Ancient Corinth,* rev. by Robert L. Scranton and others, 6th ed., Athens: American School of Classical Studies at Athens, 1960. William A. McDonald, "Archaeology and St. Paul's Journeys in Greek Lands, Part III: Corinth," BA, V (1942), 36–48.

H. F. V.

CORINTHIANS, I AND II. These letters belong to the second group of Paul's writings, usually designated as soteriological because of their concern for the message of salvation. The others in the same group are Galatians and Romans.

In the course of his European mission Paul came to Corinth from Athens and began his labors in the synagogue. Doubtless Priscilla and Aquila assisted. Later, Silas and Timothy helped in the work (II Cor 1:19). After Paul's departure at the end of a ministry of 18 months, Apollos came and carried on for a time (Acts 18:24, 27–28; I Cor 3:5). The church seems to have been composed mainly of Gentiles, for the testimony in the synagogue was soon terminated by the opposition of the Jews (Acts 18:6–7). This conclusion is supported in several respects by the first epistle (e.g., I Cor 12:2).

According to his custom, Paul made contact with the church after his departure. Knowledge of conditions among his converts reached him through the household of Chloe (I Cor 1:11), a letter sent to him by the congregation (I Cor 7:1), and the coming of three men (I Cor 16:17). In addition Apollos, who had returned to Ephesus before Paul wrote I Corinthians, could furnish information (I Cor 16:12). Paul had written a letter, probably brief and limited in its scope, which has not been preserved (I Cor 5:9). Everything considered, the church at Corinth gave the apostle more trouble than any other that he founded, as his letters to this congregation abundantly demonstrate. Despite the necessity for correction and warning, Paul does not fail to mingle with these his assurances of love and concern.

Outline of I Corinthians

Introduction, 1:1–9
 I. Problems in the Congregation, 1:10–6:20
  A. Spirit of faction, 1:10–4:21
  B. Disorders, 5:1–6:20
 II. Questions Practical and Doctrinal, 7:1–15:58
  A. Concerning marriage, 7:1-40
  B. Concerning things sacrificed to idols, 8:1–11:1
  C. Concerning conduct of women in the assembly and the Lord's Supper, 11:2–34
  D. Concerning spiritual gifts, 12:1–14:40
  E. Concerning the resurrection, 15:1-58
Conclusion, 16:1–24

Following the introduction (1:1-9), the apostle turns immediately to deal with a pressing problem, the spirit of faction which was threatening to rend the church (1:10–4:21). Some had a fierce loyalty to Paul as the founder of the assembly, others were attached to Apollos, and still others to Cephas (Peter), even though, as far as is known, he had not visited the place. A fourth segment, disgusted with their fellows, turned against all human leadership (1:12). Paul shows that only Christ merits their devotion. He died for them. They were baptized in His name. The ministry has a place, but only in the sense of workers who labor together under God (3:9). All the ministry belongs to the church as a whole, not to a section of it (3:21-22). Christianity is not a philosophy with various schools of thought led by teachers who have their own coteries of disciples.

The next problem to be faced was a grievous case of immorality (5:1-13). In being lax about discipline and even being puffed up over this situation, the church must share in the guilt. Blame attaches to the believers also for taking their grievances against one another to pagan magistrates for settlement (6:1–8). Reverting to the problem of morality along broader lines than in chap. 5, the apostle teaches the sanctity of the body (6:9–20).

Marriage and related matters claim attention (7:1–40); then the question of eating food which has been offered to idols (8:1–11:1). It was hard for these young Christians to break the hold of their former environment. They needed help, too, regarding the conduct of women in the assembly and the proper observance of the Lord's Supper (11:2–34).

The Corinthians, being Greeks, loved self-expression, so they treasured the gift of tongues. Paul treats the whole question of spiritual gifts, not forbidding tongues but calling for greater interest in the gift of prophecy, and for supreme concern for love, which is greater than all the gifts (12:1–14:40).

The letter comes to a climax with its teaching on resurrection (15:1–58). Gr. philosophy was not hospitable to a doctrine of bodily resurrection. But if Christ was so raised (and the Corinthians had accepted this, 15:3–11), the resurrection of believers is guaranteed thereby.

The closing chapter deals with plans and personalities (16:1–24).

This letter was written about A.D. 55 or 56. The identity of the bearer is not certainly known.

Outline of II Corinthians

I. Gratitude for God's Consolation, 1:1–2:13; 7:5–16
II. The Glory and Suffering of the Christian Ministry, 2:14–7:4
III. Christian Giving, 8:1–9:15
IV. Paul's Ministry Contrasted with That of False Apostles, 10:1–13:14

Opposition to Paul, which had been fostered to some extent by the factions (I Cor 4:18–21) and which centered in his apostleship and authority (I Cor 9:1–3), was fanned by the arrival in Corinth of men who claimed to belong to the Christian fellowship and to be of apostolic rank (II Cor 11:13). One of the believers, apparently taken in by their propaganda, turned against Paul and encouraged others to do so (II Cor 2:5 ff.; 7:12). It seems that the apostle felt it necessary to leave his work at Ephesus temporarily to make a hurried trip to Corinth to settle the unrest (II Cor 2:1; 12:14; 13:1–2). Even this face-to-face encounter was not successful. On his return to Ephesus Paul penned a letter filled with anguish and tears (II Cor 2:4; 7:8), sending it by the hands of Titus. Anxiety over the outcome compounded his troubled situation at Ephesus, where he faced the danger of death (II Cor 1:8 ff.). Leaving the city, he passed through Troas (II Cor 2:12–13) and finally met Titus in Macedonia and learned with relief of the improvement of conditions at Corinth (7:5 ff.).

This news led to the writing of II Corin-

thians, wherein the apostle defends and expounds his ministry (2:14–7:4). He had some unfinished business with the church, including the raising of a fund for the poor saints at Jerusalem (cf. I Cor 16:1–4). To this he now gives attention (chaps. 8–9).

The unwholesome influence of his opponents, the false "apostles," still lingered to some extent, so Paul levels an attack on them (chaps. 10–13). He challenges them to match his record of service tinged with suffering for Christ's sake (11:22–29). Nothing in Paul's writings is so critical as these chapters. He complains that his friends have allowed themselves to be browbeaten by these interlopers (11:19–20), and by failing to stand up for him themselves have forced him to make his own defense against these attacks (12:11).

Some students have seen in these final chapters of the book the letter to which Paul makes reference as written following his trip from Ephesus. The great difficulty in accepting this judgment is that the character of the two portions is quite different. There is nothing to suggest tears of anguish and sorrow in this broadside with which the second letter closes, yet such was the nature of the communication which Paul wrote in that crisis.

It appears that II Corinthians, written only a few months after the first epistle, was sent by the hand of Titus (8:6).

Bibliography. James Denney, *The Second Epistle to the Corinthians,* ExpB, New York: Armstrong, 1900. Frederic Godet, *Commentary on St. Paul's First Epistle to the Corinthians,* 2 vols., Edinburgh: T. & T. Clark, 1889. F. W. Grosheide, *Commentary on the First Epistle to the Corinthians,* NICNT, Grand Rapids: Eerdmans, 1953. Charles Hodge, *An Exposition of the First Epistle to the Corinthians,* 1857, Grand Rapids: Eerdmans, 1950 (reprint); *An Exposition of the Second Epistle ...,* 1859, Eerdmans, 1950 (reprint). P. E. Hughes, *Paul's Second Epistle to the Corinthians,* NICNT, Grand Rapids: Eerdmans, 1962. G. Campbell Morgan, *The Corinthian Letters of Paul,* New York: Revell, n.d. Leon Morris, *The First Epistle of Paul to the Corinthians,* TNTC, Grand Rapids: Eerdmans, 1958. Alfred Plummer, *A Critical and Exegetical Commentary on the Second Epistle of St. Paul to the Corinthians,* ICC, New York: Scribner's, 1915. Archibald Robertson and Alfred Plummer, *A Critical ... Commentary on the First Epistle ... Corinthians,* ICC, 2nd ed., Scribner's, 1911. A. T. Robertson, *The Glory of the Ministry,* New York: Revell, 1911. R. V. G. Tasker, *The Second Epistle of Paul to the Corinthians,* TNTC, Grand Rapids: Eerdmans, 1958. A. F. Walls, "Corinthians, Epistles to the," NBD, pp. 252–257.

E. F. Har.

CORMORANT. *See* Animals, III.6.

CORN. A term found in Bibles published in England (KJV, NEB, etc.). It is the translation of several Heb. and Gr. words for cereal grains such as wheat and barley (e.g., Gen 27:28; 41:35; 42:1; Deut 16:9; Mt 12:1). Modern American versions usually have "grain" where KJV has "corn." The term must not be mistaken for Indian maize, a cereal native only to the Western Hemisphere.
See also Food.

CORNELIUS (kôr-nēl'yŭs). This man is of particular significance in two ways: he is the first recorded Gentile convert to Christianity; and the story of his conversion is told twice. Apart from the threefold repetition of Saul's epochal conversion, this is unique in Acts. The conversion of Cornelius is related in Acts 10. Peter, when reproached at Jerusalem for eating with uncircumcised Gentiles, retold the incident as his best defense (Acts 11:1-18). At the famous council of Jerusalem (A.D. 48) he alluded to this significant event as proof that God designed to save the Gentiles by grace apart from the Mosaic law (Acts 15:7-11).
Cornelius is identified as a centurion (*q.v.*) of the Italian cohort stationed in Caesarea (Acts 10:1). Since Publius Cornelius Sulla in 82 B.C. had freed 10,000 slaves and given them the family name Cornelius, this was a common name in the Roman Empire at this time, and also an honorable one.
The centurion is described as "a devout man, and one that feared God with all his house, who gave much alms to the people, and prayed to God always" (Acts 10:2, ASV). There has been considerable dispute as to exactly what this means. Was he a full proselyte to Judaism? Most scholars are agreed that he was not. He has commonly been labeled a "proselyte of the gate." But Kirsopp Lake maintains that there was no such category. Gentile worshipers in Jewish synagogues were proselytes only if they were circumcised and observed all the regulations of the Mosaic law ("Proselytes and God-Fearers," *Beginnings of Christianity,* V, 74-96). Cornelius was not a proselyte but a God-fearer. The Gr. word for "devout" means "pious, godly." It seems clear that Cornelius had accepted monotheism, and worshiped the true God in the synagogue. It appears equally clear that he had not heard the definite Christian gospel preached before this. In a vision he was instructed to send for Peter who would tell him how to be saved (Acts 11:12-14). Peter preached salvation through the name of Jesus (Acts 10:43). Cornelius and his company accepted the message of Christ and the Holy Spirit was poured out on them (Acts 10:44).

R. E.

CORNER GATE. A gate at the NW corner of Jerusalem. Located 400 cubits from the Ephraim Gate (II Kgs 14:13; II Chr 25:23), its defenses were torn down by Jehoash, king of Israel. Uzziah later built a tower there (II Chr 26:9). Jeremiah prophesied that Jerusalem would be rebuilt "from the tower of Hananel to the Corner Gate" (Jer 31:38, RSV).
See Jerusalem.

CORNERSTONE. Either a stone tying two walls of a building together (Isa 28:16), or the keystone capping and completing the building (Ps 118:22). Figuratively, Christ's passion and resurrection are the "cornerstone" or fulfillment of the OT (Mk 12:10 f.; Acts 4:11; I Pet 2:4-7; Rom 9:33; 10:11). The Church is represented as a building erected on the foundation of the prophets and apostles, Christ Jesus being the cornerstone (Eph 2:20). Daughters are referred to as cornerstones, to be regarded as of great worth (Ps 144:12).
The significance of the keystone in an arch is often ascribed to a cornerstone. In modern architecture its value is slight, frequently only as the stone giving the date of the building. For churches and sacred edifices a special dedicatory service is generally held for the laying of the cornerstone. Sometimes documents are deposited in it, symbolizing that the past is the foundation for the future. *See* Headstone.

CORNET. *See* Music.

CORRECTION. This word is used for reform, amendment, restoration, discipline. Correction is a function of a father with his children (Prov 23:13; 29:17; Jer 2:30; Heb 12:9) and of God with His people (Job 5:17; Prov 3:12; Heb 12:7, 9). Both Heb. and Gr. terms imply a twofold meaning: to instruct, guide, reason with; and to punish, chastise, reprove. The whole process of child rearing is in view in correction, as suggested by the most common Gr. term *paideuō*, "to train up a child," involving both positive guidance and negative discipline in the case of wrongdoing. That the Word of God is profitable for correction (II Tim 3:16) refers to its value for improvement of life and character in the believer. The Gr. term here means "restoration to an upright state." *See* Chastisement.

CORRUPTION. This word translates various nouns from the Heb. root *shāḥat* (OT) and Gr. root *phtheirō* (NT), "to ruin," "destroy." Corruption may be physical: blemished animals (Lev 22:25); disfigured faces (Dan 10:8); desecrated shrine, whose high place is therefore called "mount of corruption" (*q.v.*; II Kgs 23:13); perishable bodies (I Cor 15:42, 50; Acts 13:36; cf. Isa 38:17, pit of *belî*, "nothingness," bodily annihilation); or creation under the curse (Rom 8:21). The very important passage in Ps 16:10 predicts Christ's resurrection (Acts 2:27, 31; 13:34-35, 37) from decomposition (Job 17:14, worm-eaten; cf. Ps 49:9; Jon 2:6). The RSV renders Ps 16:10 as if the reference is to David's deliverance from approaching the "pit" of death (from another Heb. root, *shûâh,* "sink down," hence "pit trap," Ezk 19:4, 8; cf. *The Biblical Expositor,* II, 58–60). Corruption also denotes moral depravity (II Pet 1:4; 2:19) and final spiritual judgment (Gal 6:8; II Pet 2:12*b,* Arndt, p. 865). *See* Death; Immortality; Pit; Sheol.

CORRUPTION, MOUNT OF. A hill E of and near to Jerusalem where Solomon had built places for the worship of Ashtoreth, Chemosh, and Milcom (I Kgs 11:7, RSV). Josiah destroyed them (II Kgs 23:13). The site evidently referred to the southern height of the Mount of Olives. Later, Christian tradition referred to it as the "Mount of Offense." It was also called the "Mount of the Ointment," a term used for the Mount of Olives (*q.v.*).

CORSELET. Defensive armor for the body. It evidently refers to the protective covering for the chest, abdomen, and back. It is referred to as "breastplate," "habergeon," and "coat of mail." Armor of this nature was worn by Nehemiah's workers (Neh 4:16), by the soldiers of King Uzziah (II Chr 26:14), by Goliath (I Sam 17:5), and by Ahab (I Kgs 22:34, "harness," KJV). Paul uses this term figuratively (Eph 6:14). *See* Armor.

COSAM (kō'săm). An ancestor of Jesus, the son of Elmodam and the father of Addi, in the fifth generation before Zerubbabel (Lk 3:28).

COSMETICS. Materials used for beautification. Ointments, perfumes, eye paint, and possibly henna were widely used by Egyptian and Hebrew women in biblical times (Prov 27:9; Rev 18:13). Jezebel painted her eyes (II Kgs 9:30, RSV), and beauty applications were valued by many (Jer 4:30). Ivory combs, hairpins, alabaster flasks and palettes for ointment, bronze mirrors, and rouge pots have been found in many excavations. The hot, dry climate made the use of lotions for the skin essential, and perfumes counteracted body odors. The offering of ointments for guests was a part of the hospitality pattern of NT times (Lk 7:37 f.).

COSMOS. *See* World.

COTTAGE. This word appears in the KJV in Isa 1:8 (Heb. *sukkâ,* "hut"); Isa 24:20 (Heb. *mᵉlûnâ;* "hut" in RSV); Zeph 2:6 (Heb. *kãrôth,* "hewn out place"; translated "Crete" in LXX, and "meadows" in RSV).

The word "cottage" has changed considerably in meaning from its original significance. It is related to the word "cote," a stall for animals (cf. Milton, *Comus,* 344). "Might we but hear the folded flocks, penned in their wattled cotes." Chaucer used the term to signify a humble dwelling: "A poore widow somedeal stoopen in age, was whilom dwelling in a narrow cottage" (*Canterbury Tales:* "Nun's Priest's Tale," 1:2).

A bronze mirror of the Egyptian Empire period. LM

The term as found in the OT always preserves this connotation of a lowly kind of structure, and not the neutral significance of the word as employed in contemporary usage. In Isa 1:8 it refers to a temporary frame which would be covered with foliage to protect a worker from the sun while he guarded the vineyard during the time the grapes ripened. The other Heb. words translated "hut" or "cottage" also suggest a flimsy type of construction.

E. J. V.

COTTON. *See* Plants.

COUCH. *See* Bed.

COULTER. Plowshare, a sharp metal point attached to plowbeam (from Heb. "to cut in or dig"). The Philistines sharpened these tools for the Israelites before iron became plentiful in Palestine (I Sam 13:20–21). *See* Plow.

COUNCIL. This is the KJV translation for three biblical words: (1) Heb. *rigmâ,* "crowd," "assembly" (Ps 68:27); (2) Gr. *symboulion,* "a joint council" (Mt 12:14; Acts 25:12); (3) Gr. *synedrion,* often transliterated "sanhedrin." Except for Mt 10:17 and Mk 13:9, where it refers to lesser courts, the latter form always represents the high Jewish tribunal located in Jerusalem (Mt 26:59). This body was composed of 70 members drawn from the elders, scribes, and priests, plus the current high priest who presided. While it exercised religious authority over all Jews, its civil power was restricted to Palestine and concerned only those matters not preempted by the Roman authorities. *See* Sanhedrin; Apostolic Council.

COUNCIL OF JERUSALEM. *See* Apostolic Council.

COUNSELOR. *See* Occupations: Counselor.

COUPLING. Used to indicate joining together, as the curtains of the tabernacle (Ex 26:4–5; 36:11–12, 17). A similar Heb. word refers to timbers used to bind walls together (II Chr 34:11) or to clamps of iron (I Chr 22:3, RSV). *See* Joining.

COURSE. A word used in reference to one's way of life (Jer 8:6; 23:10), suggesting a fast, loose style of living or running around.
For the priestly courses *see* Course of Priests and Levites.

COURSE OF PRIESTS AND LEVITES. Twenty-four divisions or classes of priests and Levites performed the daily duties in the temple at Jerusalem, each for one week at a time. Arranged by David (I Chr 24), each division, named after a prominent member of the family, was subject to its president. Zacharias, John the Baptist's father, belonged to the eighth division, that of Abia (Lk 1:5).
In 1962 while excavating a synagogue at Caesarea archaeologists discovered fragments of a marble inscription that originally named the 24 priestly courses and the city where each moved after the destruction of the temple in A.D. 70. Nazareth is listed as the city of the 18th course, the town's earliest mention outside the NT (IEJ, XII, 137 ff.).

COURT. An area without a roof enclosed by buildings or walls. The tabernacle had an outer court enclosed by curtains (Ex 27:9 ff.). Solomon's temple had an inner court for the priests marked off by stone walls (I Kgs 6:36), and another outer court. *See* Tabernacle; Temple.
Ancient houses were often protected from direct entrance from the street by a forecourt enclosed by a wall; in other houses the living quarters would be built around a central court. The RSV has "court of the high priest" instead of "palace" (KJV, Jn 18:15). Rev 11:2 speaks of a huge court outside the temple proper in John's vision. *See* House; Architecture.

COURTS, JUDICIAL. *See* Law, Administration of.

COUSIN. There is no word for cousin in the OT, but "kinsman" or "relative" was used to denote that relationship. Marriage between cousins was common (Gen 24:15; 28:2; 29:10, 19; 36:3).

COVENANT. In Heb. "covenant" is designated *berît*, and *berît kārat* signifies "to make (lit., 'cut') a covenant." In Gr. the term is *diathēkē* (which can mean both "pact" and "last will and testament"), and the verb *diatithēmi* (cf. Acts 3:25; Heb 8:10; 9:16; 10:16).
A covenant is an agreement between two or more persons in which the following four factors or elements are present: parties, conditions, results, security.
The biblical covenants are important as the key to two great facets of truth: *Soteriology*—God's plan through Jesus Christ to redeem His elect is unfolded in an ever-widening and deepening manner in the successive covenants. *Prophecy*—the Abrahamic, Palestinian, Davidic, and new covenants open up the whole panorama concerning Christ's first and second advents, and His thousand year millennial reign on the earth. Most of the great covenants reveal facts concerning both the suffering, sacrificial Messiah, and the ruling, reigning Messiah. The manner in which these two lines of prophecy are to be interpreted finally determines one's eschatology, whether it is to be amillennial, postmillennial, or premillennial. The question must be faced as to whether the method to be applied to both lines of prophecy is the same or different. Upon this must depend the decision on the millennial question and the interpretation of much contained in each of the covenants. *See* Millennium.
Parties. These may be: (1) Individual men, such as Abraham and Abimelech (Gen 21:27) or Jacob and Laban (Gen 31:44–46), when each man subjected himself to certain conditions and offered a proof to secure the covenant made. (2) Nations, as when Nahash the Ammonite tried to force a covenant upon Jabesh-gilead in I Sam 11:1 ff., or the Israelites were foolishly led to make a covenant with the Gibeonites (Josh 9:6–16). (3) God and man were the parties of the great kingdom-messianic covenants, such as the Abrahamic covenant (Gen 12:1–7; 15; 17:1–14; 22:15–18), the Palestinian covenant (Deut 29–30), and the Davidic covenant (II Sam 7:4–16; Ps 89:3–4, 26–37; 132:11–18). (4) God the Father and Jesus Christ were the chief originating parties of the covenant of redemption (Ps 40:6–8; Heb 10:5–14), Christ being the Mediator of this covenant, while God and individual men (Heb 7:9 ff.) and God and Israel (Jer 31:37) were its efficacious partners. The Father and the Son were the chief parties of the covenant of grace. God the Father covenanted with Christ to save by grace those who believe in the Son and His substitutionary death. This covenant became the foundation of Rom 4 and Heb 11, the two

loci classici or main passages concerning justification by faith in the NT. Individuals in the OT entered into this covenant through their saving faith in and acceptance of the type of Christ in the OT, and in the NT by the same faith with acceptance of the antitype, even Jesus Christ Himself.

Conditions. In every covenant certain conditions are stated. This applies both to those covenants which are unilateral, namely, announced by God to man and promulgated as certain to come to pass, and to this extent unconditional; and also to those covenants which are bilateral, namely, to those covenants which are entirely conditional upon the acceptance and fulfillment thereof by both parties. All human covenants are bilateral and conditional. Covenants between God and man can be mainly unilateral, e.g., the Abrahamic covenant, Davidic covenant, new covenant; or bilateral, e.g., the Mosaic covenant. Still there is confusion if we do not see that even the essentially unilateral covenants have a bilateral aspect insofar as their application has regard to individual men. This can be seen in the fact that, as Paul writes in Rom 9, though the covenants belong to Israel, "they are not all Israel, which are of Israel . . . the children of the promise are counted for the seed" (Rom 9:6, 8). They apply to the elect.

Further, we see that the seal or sign or token of one's having accepted the covenant relationship by an act of individual faith is a step of obedience, even in the Abrahamic covenant, the sign of which was circumcision (cf. Gen 17:10-11 where the sign was stated as a part of the individual application of the covenant, "This is my covenant . . . every man child among you shall be circumcised"). Any attempt to separate the unilateral element of the Abrahamic covenant from its individual application becomes artificial, and the acknowledgment therefore of both factors—unilateral and bilateral—in such a covenant becomes necessary. In like manner water baptism is the sign or seal of one's membership in the new covenant community. Examination shows that the unilateral elements in a covenant are prophetic, and thereby immutable; and the bilateral elements are soteriological, and therefore conditional to the extent they are dependent upon personal acceptance by faith, with motivation coming through God's sovereign grace.

Results. These can either be promises of blessing when the covenant is kept, or warnings of punishment when the covenant is broken, or both. For example, in the Abrahamic covenant there was promise of a seed (who according to Gal 3:16 was Christ; cf. Gen 12:1-3; 13:16; 22:18), of a land, of fame, and of a great posterity. These facts were prophetic and certain. At the same time there was a conditional aspect, for each believing participant had to be circumcised as a seal of his faith, even as in the case of Abraham (Gen 17:9-17; Rom 4:11). Those who refused to be circumcised broke the covenant (Gen 17:14). This rite pointed to

Christ "in whom we [Christians] are circumcised . . . by the circumcision of Christ" (Col 2:11). All this is conditional to the extent it is based upon saving faith.

Security. The security given to guarantee the fulfillment of a covenant was usually an oath. For men, it was an oath of such solemn character that it partook of the nature of a will or testament. The idea is that just as a testator cannot change his will when dead, so neither can a covenanter change his covenant. One way in which this was signified was by the slaying of an animal, dividing it into two parts, and then the passing of both parties between the halves (Gen 15:9 ff.). Christ sealed the new covenant with His death (Heb 9:15-17), having instituted the Lord's Supper to commemorate that death (Mt 26:28; Mk 14:25; I Cor 11:25-26). Again, sometimes a gift was made (Gen 21:30), or a sign set up, such as a cairn or heap of stones (Gen 31:52).

Since God can swear by nothing greater than Himself, He confirmed His covenants either by swearing by Himself (Deut 29:12; Heb 6:13-14), as when confirming His covenant with Abraham, or by swearing by His providential control of the world, as when He announced the new covenant in Jer 31:35; 33:20.

Kinds of Covenants

Two main kinds of covenants in the Bible need to be considered, those specifically designated as covenants, and those implied but not so designated. For the sake of distinction they can perhaps best be called biblical and theological covenants.

Specific Biblical Covenants

1. *Noahic covenant.* This is the first clearly mentioned covenant in the Scriptures. It was promised to Noah in Gen 6:18 and is recorded in Gen 8:20—9:17. This covenant was chiefly unilateral in that God was the initiator and maker, not requiring a promise of acceptance and compliance on the part of Noah as the Israelites vowed at the foot of Mount Sinai (see Ex 19:8).

The *parties* to this covenant were God and the earth (Gen 9:13) or Noah and all his descendants (Gen 9:9, 16, 17). Hence it was universal in its scope. Nevertheless it had *conditions*, namely, that mankind would be fruitful, multiply, and fill the earth (9:1, 7), and that they must not eat flesh with the life, i.e., the blood, still in it (9:4). In this sense the covenant was conditional, for God brought judgment upon mankind at the Tower of Babel in the form of confusion of language in order to force them to scatter and populate the earth when they were deliberately defying the purpose and command of God (Gen 11:4-9). The *results* were the promise of God never again to destroy the earth by deluge (Gen 8:21; 9:11, 15), with the concomitant promise of the regularity of seasons (Gen 8:22). The *security* that God would keep this covenant as long as earth shall last is found in its sign or token, the rainbow (9:12–17).

2. *Abrahamic covenant.* This is generally considered to be a unilateral covenant in the sense that it was announced by God in the first place without any attached conditions. A bilateral element does appear, however, in Gen 17:1: "I am the Almighty God; walk before me, and be thou perfect," and in the last repetition and confirmation of the covenant to Abraham in Gen 22:16 ff., when God says, "By myself have I sworn . . . because thou hast done this thing, and hast not withheld thy son, thine only son: that in blessing I will bless thee . . . because thou hast obeyed my voice."

The *parties* to this covenant were God and Abraham. The *condition,* as revealed above by God to Abraham after he had shown his willingness to obey God's command to offer up Isaac, was faithful obedience (cf. Heb 11:17–19). The *results* were the promises of God to make Abraham's posterity into a great nation (Gen 12:2); to increase his seed as the sands of the sea (Gen 22:17); to bless those who should bless the Jewish people and curse those that should curse them (Gen 12:3); and to give to Abraham's seed, that is, to Israel, Palestine and the territory from the River of Egypt to the Euphrates. Finally, and most important of all, the whole world was to be blessed through his seed, which was Christ (Gal 3:16), and Christ in turn was to have rulership over all His enemies (Gen 22:17–18). The *security* for this great covenant was God's oath by Himself and His great name (Gen 22:16; Heb 6:13–18), as well as the shedding of the blood of sacrifices (Gen 15:9, 10, 17).

3. *Mosaic or Sinai covenant.* In this covenant there is the appearance of a new factor, that of a particular form. The Abrahamic covenant was very simple and direct. The Mosaic, while still direct, was much more complex. It employed the contemporary form of suzerain-vassal covenants then in vogue in the ancient Near East in which the great lord or suzerain dictated an agreement to his vassals or servants. A recent study of Hittite treaties or covenants of the mid-2nd mil. B.C. has revealed that a parallel form existed between these and God's covenant with Israel. Each had six elements.

(1) A preamble: "I am the Lord thy God" (Ex 20:2*a*). This identified the author of the covenant and corresponded to such an introduction as, "These are the words of the son of Mursilis, the great king, and king of the Hatti land, the valiant, the favorite son of the storm-god, etc. . . ." (ANET, p. 203).

(2) A historical prologue: "which have brought thee out of the land of Egypt, out of the house of bondage" (Ex 20:2). In Deuteronomy, which is the second giving of the covenant and of the law, the historical prologue is greatly expanded in order to cover how God led Israel through the wilderness right to the threshold of the Promised Land (Deut 1:6–4:49). Moses is

repeating and expanding the covenant given at Sinai to bring it up to date and to prepare Israel for entry into the Promised Land. In the Hittite covenants the suzerain reminded the vassal ruler of the benefits he had enjoyed hitherto as a vassal of his kingdom, as a basis for the vassal's gratitude and future obedience.

(3) The exclusive stipulations or obligations of the covenant: "Thou shalt have no other gods before me. Thou shalt not make unto thee any graven image . . . thou shalt not bow down . . " (Ex 20:3–5). One typical Hittite covenant reads: "But you Duppi-Tessub remain loyal to the king of the Hatti land. . . . Do not turn your eyes to anyone else" (ANET, p. 204). In its first form in Ex 20 the covenant opens with the Ten Commandments and continues on through Ex 31. In Deuteronomy it opens with the law in chap. 5 and continues on through chap. 26.

(4) Sanctions, namely, blessings and curses which accompanied the keeping or breaking of the covenant. In its first promulgation in Exodus, the Mosaic covenant contains those specifically attached to the Ten Commandments, e.g., "visiting the iniquity . . . and showing mercy" (Ex 20:5–6); and, "Honor thy father and thy mother; that thy days may be long . . ." (Ex 20:12). In addition, further sanctions and warnings are given with the promise of guidance and protection by the Lord's presence (Ex 23:20–33; for other blessings and curses see Lev 26). But in Deuteronomy there are two chapters of blessings and curses to be read publicly and expounded at the covenant renewal ceremony (27–28), followed by the so-called Palestinian covenant (29–30). Blessings and curses were also written into the ancient treaties of western Asia.

The biblical confirmation or surety for keeping a covenant was either an oath or the death of the one who made the covenant. "The terms oath and covenant often are used as synonyms in the OT, as are the terms oath and treaty in extrabiblical texts"—so Gene M. Tucker concludes ("Covenant Forms and Contract Forms," VT, XV [1965], p. 497). In essence, an OT covenant was an oath, a sworn agreement. God confirmed the Mosaic covenant by an oath, called in Deut 29:12 ff. "his oath, which the Lord thy God maketh with thee" (cf. Deut 32:40; Ezk 16:8; Neh 10:29). The parties making a covenant were to become as if dead so that they could no more change their minds and revoke it than can the dead (Gen 15:8–18; Heb 9:16–17). Thus the blood of sacrificed animal substitutes was sprinkled at the covenant ratification ceremony to represent the "death" of the parties to the covenant (Ex 24:3–8). In the current Hittite treaties of Moses' time an oath on the part of the suzerain was not a feature; rather they stressed the oath of loyalty on the part of the vassal.

(5) Witnesses. The Hittite treaties called a long list of deities to witness the document. In the Sinai and other biblical covenants pagan

gods were obviously excluded. Instead, memorial stones could be a witness (Ex 24:4; cf. Josh 24:27); heaven and earth were called upon as witnesses (Deut 30:19; 31:28; 32:1; cf. 4:26); the scroll of the law was deposited by the side of the ark to be a witness (Deut 31:26); and Moses' song itself would remind the people of their covenant vows (Deut 31:30–32:47). In the covenant renewal service at the end of Joshua's life the people themselves acted as the witnesses (Josh 24:22).

(6) The perpetuation of the covenant. This was seen in the care for the safekeeping of the treaty documents by depositing them before or under the idol of a heathen god of the nation which was party to the treaty, in contrast to the tablets of the Mosaic covenant being placed within the ark of the covenant in Israel (Ex 25:16, 21; 40:20; Deut 10:2); and in the periodic reading in public and instruction to children both of the Hittite covenants and the Mosaic covenant. The law was recorded on plastered stones and read aloud at the ceremony when the blessings and the curses were pronounced by half of Israel on Mount Ebal and half on Mount Gerizim after they entered the land (Deut 27:9 ff.; Josh 8:30–35). The whole law was reread publicly every seven years at the Feast of Tabernacles (Deut 31:9–13).

Several important conclusions have been reached as a result of the comparison of the Mosaic covenant with ancient suzerainty treaties of that day: (a) God spoke to Israel in a form which was suitable for His purpose but which also was familiar to the people of that day. Some of the finer details of the form even prove that the Mosaic covenant must be placed before 1200 B.C., because Aramaic and Assyrian treaties of the 1st mil. B.C. lack several of the distinctive elements common to the Hittite and the Sinai covenants (see Meredith G. Kline, *The Treaty of the Great King*, p. 42 f.). (b) The particular Hittite covenantal form of Deuteronomy leads us to see that the stress is more upon its covenantal meaning than its legal meaning. (c) Study shows the two tablets of the law were not two stones with four commandments on the first and six on the second, but two stone copies of the same treaty or covenant, one for God—kept in the ark—and one for Israel. The same was true of all Hittite and Assyrian treaties: two copies were made, one for the suzerain king and one for the vassal king.

Certain important differences must not, however, be overlooked. The Mosaic covenant as made by God was based upon love and grace rather than mere power. Further, it had as its goal the salvation of God's elect rather than their mere submission and obedience.

Returning to the spiritual significance of this covenant, we might conclude that the conditional element outshadows the unconditional. Does it teach "this do, and thou shalt live" (cf. Lk 10:28) in the sense that eternal life for the OT believer depended on keeping God's law?

If so, works were of meritorious value up until the cross! Or does God mean that we are to live in the light of this law? Christ in the Sermon on the Mount taught the latter view when He exegeted several commandments and said, "Be ye therefore perfect, even as your Father which is in heaven is perfect" (Mt 5:48). He applied the law for the purpose of the continuing sanctification of the believer and not for his justification. In Lev 18:5 the same application of the law is made: "Keep my statutes . . . which if a man do, he shall live in them" (that is, in their sphere). When we see that this covenant opens with grace: "I am the Lord thy God, which brought thee out of the land of Egypt; out of the house of bondage" (Ex 20:2), and we add to this a consideration of the facts given above, we are led to see it as full of grace. The Mosaic covenant then becomes both a schoolmaster to bring us to Christ, with all its types which point to Him, and a standard to guide the deportment of both the OT believer and the Christian.

4. *Palestinian covenant* (Deut 29-30). Though a part of the renewal of the Mosaic covenant, this covenant is considered separately by some. The *parties* are God and Israel. The *conditions* are that God will bless Israel if she remains faithful to Him, and He will curse her if she turns from Him, as expressed in the blessings and the curses promulgated from Mount Gerizim and Mount Ebal (Deut 27:9 ff.). The *results,* after all the blessings and the curses have been experienced by Israel in the course of her history, are that, if and when she repents, God will regather her from the utmost parts of the earth, reestablish her in Israel and bless her. The *security* for the covenant is found in the ordinances of heaven and of earth (Deut 30:19).

This covenant has a unilateral aspect—promises and rewards for keeping the covenant, and curses as the consequence of breaking it. The assurance was given that national repentance of Israel will most surely occur (Deut 30:1–10). Yet there is also a bilateral aspect—Israel must repent. This repentance will come to pass because of God's sovereign grace in the lives of individual Jews when Christ returns (Zech 12:10-14; 13:6; cf. Isa 66:19–20). God's ordinances take into consideration both what man will do in his freedom, and what God plans to do in His sovereign grace. Both these elements appear in the Palestinian covenant.

5. *Davidic covenant* (II Sam 7:4-16; Ps 89:3-4, 26-37; 132:11-18; cf. Isa 42:1, 6; 49:8; 55:3-4). This was basically a unilateral covenant in which God promised David first a secure reign for his son and successor Solomon, and then a kingship that should continue forever in the Messiah. Isaiah speaks of the Messiah Himself as both this covenant and its fulfillment (Isa 42:1, 6; 49:8). Yet it had a bilateral element, in that for the individual king it contained conditional elements (II Sam 7:14–15).

6. *New covenant.* Like the Sinaitic covenant, with Moses as the mediator between God and His chosen people (Acts 7:38; Gal 3:19), so the new covenant was also established between God and a redeemed people, with Christ the Son of God acting as mediator (I Tim 2:5; Heb 8:6; 9:15; 12:24). In contrast, however, the new covenant is far superior to the old or Mosaic covenant, for it is based on better promises and a better sacrifice (Heb 8:6; 9:23). It speaks of a time when God will write His will within the minds and hearts of His people in such a manner that men will no more need to teach one another His will, and when He will forgive the sin of His people Israel (Jer 31:31-37). The writer of Hebrews uses the OT revelation of this covenant to prove that Christ is both the Redeemer and the Mediator for man's sins (Heb 9:7-9; 10:5-16). Christ referred to this covenant as He announced at the institution of the Lord's Supper, "This is my blood of the new testament [covenant]" (Mk 14:24).

Is there any conditional element in this covenant? Yes, to the extent the believer takes Christ as his Saviour and testifies to his faith that Christ's blood was shed for the remission of his sins, and thus individually becomes partaker of the new covenant. Yet there is an unconditional, unilateral, prophetic aspect to this covenant in that it also speaks of a time when all Israel, all the Jews, will know its blessings. Certainly this Gosepl Age cannot yet claim that no man needs to teach his neighbor or brother God's law. This part of the covenant can be applied only to the Millennial Age. *See* Covenant, New.

Theological Covenants

These covenants are thus named because they are discovered by applying the definition of covenant to an agreement recorded in Scripture. Where such facts as contracting parties, conditions, results, and security are present, there is a covenant. Such covenants, which some theologians consider to be woven into the warp and woof of the Scriptures, are the covenant of works, the covenant of grace, and the covenant of redemption. These are usually discussed in the writings of Reformed theologians who follow the covenant theology of Johannes Cocceius (1603-1669).

To those who object to the classification of God's agreement between Himself and Adam before the Fall as a covenant of works, and His agreement with men for their salvation after the Fall as a covenant of grace, the following may be said: (1) God's agreement with David in II Sam 7 is not designated a covenant there, but it is named a covenant in Ps 89:3, 28. (2) It is only possible to develop a true systematic theology by the application of inductively developed definitions. This is what is done in establishing the theological covenants. (3) We are faced with the necessity of laboriously repeating the agreement God announced to Adam when He created him, and its conditions and results, or classifying the same. When we call it a covenant we are simply using a definitive term rather than unnecessarily repeating data.

1. *Covenant of works.* The *parties* were God and Adam before the Fall. The *conditions,* positive: love God and obey Him and love others; negative: do not disobey God or rebel against Him; do not eat of the tree of the knowledge of good and evil. How can we determine the positive result when it is not stated? Quite simply. God is holy and unchangeable; therefore the way in which He dealt with the earliest order of rational beings, the angels, is the way in which He must deal with all the rest of His creatures. Those angels who loved and obeyed Him became the holy angels—they were confirmed in righteousness; those who rebelled became the fallen angels. The tree of the knowledge of good and evil in Eden was the test for man. Not to eat of it represented obedience and love; to eat, disobedience and distrust. The *results* revealed in this covenant were life for obedience and love, as for the holy angels; and death for disobedience and rebellion, as for the fallen angels. God's word, because He is the truth, was the *security.*

2. *Covenant of grace.* The *parties* are God and man through the Lord Jesus Christ, or, perhaps better, God and Jesus Christ and men as they become united with Christ by faith in Him. This concept of a covenant of grace between the Father and the Son in which salvation is offered to sinners may be found in Eph 1:3-6, where it is written that God chose us in Christ before the foundation of the world. See also II Tim 1:9; Tit 1:2; Jn 3:17; 17:4-10, 21-24. The *condition* again is saving faith, expressed in the OT by such acts of faith as that of Abel (Heb 11:4), Abraham and David (Rom 4:3, 6-8), and by acceptance of Jesus Christ as revealed in the NT. The *results* are eternal life for the believer and eternal condemnation for the unbeliever.

3. *Covenant of redemption.* Whether there is an additional covenant of redemption to the covenant of grace is debated by the covenant theologians. Charles Hodge was the leader of those in the United States who make a distinction and see two separate covenants. J. O. Buswell, Jr., argues strongly that they are one and the same (*Systematic Theology,* II, 122 ff.).

The covenant of redemption may be defined as a unilateral agreement between the Father and the Son, which contains a second covenant between God and His people. This covenant appears clearly in two places: in Ps 40:6-8, where the Son is talking to the Father and speaks of the sacrifice God desires from Him; and in a passage which quotes these verses, Heb 10:5-16, where we are told God takes away the first covenant, namely, the Mosaic, to establish the second: "By the which will we are sanctified through the offering of the body of Jesus Christ once for all" (v. 10). We are then told (Heb 10:15-17) that the Holy Spirit endorsed this truth when He foretold the new covenant in Jer 31:33–34. The insight of Archibald McCaig is particularly helpful at this point: "The 'New Covenant' here spoken of is practically equivalent to the Covenant of Grace established between God and His redeemed people, that again resting upon the eternal Covenant of Redemption made between the Father and the Son, which, though not so expressly designated, is not obscurely indicated by many passages of Scripture" ("Covenant, The New," ISBE, II, 731).

It is of value to distinguish the covenant of redemption from the new covenant, since the covenant of redemption becomes a most important test in the detection of a Unitarian view, such as found in the teachings of Karl Barth. If there is no ontological Trinity of three Persons in the Godhead, there can be no covenant of redemption between the Father and the Son. Since Barth teaches merely three modes of revelation of one single Person, he must reject this covenant. His Unitarianism excludes a covenant or direct communication in word or prayer between the Persons of the Godhead.

Interrelationship of the Covenants

This connection between the various covenants can be likened to a series of stair-steps—each is added to and based on the ones preceding it. The interrelationship may be illustrated by the fact that the Davidic and the new covenants are both contained in and are extensions of the Abrahamic covenant. Abraham was promised a kingdom and a land, and these were given in further detail in the Davidic covenant. He was also given the gospel, for "the scripture . . . preached the gospel beforehand to Abraham" (Gal 3:8, RSV), and this was delineated much further and in greater detail in the new covenant.

Again, the covenant of works, though broken by Adam and though its consequences came upon all mankind, was taken up by Christ, as He was "made of a woman, made under the law, to redeem them that were under the law" (Gal 4:4–5), and kept perfectly by Him for us and in our stead. Further, on the cross He bore the penalty of the broken law for us. We in turn are saved by the covenant of grace, which depends upon Christ having ended for us the covenant of works; first by fulfilling its demands, and second by bearing its penalties against sin (Rom 10:4).

Bibliography. Karl Barth, *Church Dogmatics,* Edinburgh: T. & T. Clark, 1936. Louis Berkhof, *Systematic Theology,* Grand Rapids: Eerdmans, 1949. J. Oliver Buswell, Jr., *A Systematic Theology of the Christian Faith,* Grand Rapids: Eerdmans, 1962. K. A. Kitchen, *Ancient Orient and Old Testament,* Chicago: Inter-Varsity, 1966, pp. 90–102. Meredith G. Kline, *The Treaty of the Great King,* Grand Rapids: Eerdmans, 1963; *By Oath Consigned,* Grand Rapids: Eerdmans, 1968; "Canon and Covenant," WTJ, XXXII (1969), 49–67; "The Correlation of the Concepts of Canon and Covenant," NPOT, pp. 265–279. George E. Mendenhall, *Law and Covenant in Israel and the Ancient Near East,* Pittsburgh: Biblical Colloquium, 1955. John J. Mitchell, "Abram's Understanding of the Lord's Covenant," WTJ, XXXII (1969), 24–48. J. Barton Payne, *The Theology of the Older Testament,* Grand Rapids: Zondervan, 1962; "The B'rith of Yahweh," NPOT, pp. 240–264. Gottfried Quell and Johannes Behm, "*Diathēkē,*" TDNT, II, 106–134. Gene M. Tucker, "Covenant Forms and Contract Forms," VT, XV (1965), 487–503. Donald J. Wiseman, "The Vassal-Treaties of Esarhaddon," *Iraq,* XX (1958), 1–28. John M. L. Young, "Theology of Missions, Covenant Centered," ChT, XIII (Nov. 22, 1968), 162–165. *See also* Covenant, New.

R. A. K. and J. R.

COVENANT, ARK OF. *See* Ark of the Covenant.

COVENANT, BOOK OF THE. *See* Book of the Covenant.

COVENANT, NEW. This is God's arrangement by which He established a new relationship of responsibility between Himself and His people (Jer 31:31–34). The phrase the new covenant also is a synonym for the NT, and thus refers to the 27 books of the NT or the New Covenant. But in this article the phrase is considered only in connection with that covenantal relationship between God and His people which is designated as a new covenant.

The designation of the covenant. When first mentioned, this covenant was called "new" (Jer 31:31), for it was set in contrast with Israel's primary or older covenant, namely, the covenant of the Mosaic law. This same contrast is also made in Heb 8:6–13.

The provisions of the covenant.

1. The new covenant provides an unconditional, grace relationship between God and "the house of Israel and the house of Judah." The frequency of the use of the phrase "I will" in Jer 31:31–34 is striking.

2. It provides regeneration in the impartation of a renewed mind and heart (Ezk 36:26).

3. It provides for restoration to the favor and blessing of God (Hos 2:19–20).

4. It includes forgiveness of sin (Jer 31:34b).

5. The indwelling ministry of the Holy Spirit is one of its provisions (Jer 31:33; cf. Ezk 36:27). This also includes the teaching ministry of the Spirit.

6. It provides for the exaltation of Israel as head of the nations (Jer 31:38–40; cf. Deut 28:13).

The foundation of the covenant. The foundation of all the covenant blessings is the blood of Christ. In the upper room the night before His death, the Lord stated that the cup symbolized "the blood of the new covenant" (Mt 26:28), and that this blood shed would be the foundation for all the blessings of that covenant. The disciples would have thought of no other covenant than the one prophesied by Jeremiah.

The people of the covenant. There is no question that the OT revelation of the new covenant links it with the nation Israel. This is specifically stated in the words of establishment (Jer 31:31). This fact is reaffirmed in Isa 59:20-21; 61:8-9; Jer 32:37-40; 50:4-5; Ezk 16:60-63; 34:25-26; 37:21-28. It is also a logical deduction from the fact that the contrasting Mosaic covenant was made with Israel, and from the fact that in its establishment, the perpetuity of the nation Israel and her restoration to the land is vitally linked with it (Jer 31:35-40). The NT adds the truth that believers in Christ have a better covenant (Heb 8:6) and that they are ministers of the new covenant (II Cor 3:6).

Amillennialists understand the NT teaching to indicate that only the Church is now fulfilling the promises of the new covenant and that there will be no other fulfillment. Premillennialists disallow an exclusive fulfillment by the Church and teach either that the covenant is still only for Israel, and will be fulfilled by her in the millennium; or that the Church has some relationship to the covenant but that this does not replace the future millennial fulfillment by Israel.

The amillennial interpretation is based on its consistent insistence that the Church during this age is fulfilling all of Israel's promises, which would quite naturally include the promises of the new covenant. The premillennial interpretation is built on the sharp distinction made in the system between Israel and the Church. (Cf. O.T. Allis, *Prophecy and the Church,* pp. 154 ff., and C. C. Ryrie, *The Basis of the Premillennial Faith,* pp. 105-125.)

The fulfillment of the covenant. Whatever relationship the Church may have to the new covenant, it seems clear from the NT that it will be fulfilled in its original provisions to Israel at the second coming of Christ (Rom 11:26-27). There is no question that the covenant to be fulfilled at that time is the new covenant, for the reference to taking away sin is a promise contained in the new covenant. The question is only, who is "Israel," who will be saved then, and who will enjoy the benefits of the new covenant? Premillennialists and even some amillennialists (Charles Hodge, *Epistle to the Romans,* pp. 584-5) say that this is a reference to the Jewish people, but other amillennialists insist that it is the Church and that fulfillment is now, not at the second coming of Christ (Allis, *op. cit.,* p. 156). This appears inconsistent with the principle of plain interpretation, since the nation of Israel is so clearly mentioned.

Premillennialists are faced with the question of the relation, if any, of the believer today to the new covenant. Some have said that there is no relationship (J.N. Darby, *Synopsis of the Books of the Bible,* V, 286). Others follow the view of the notes of the Scofield Reference Bible (p. 1297), which applies the one new covenant to both Israel in the future and the Church in the present. A few others see two new covenants—one for Israel and one for the Church (L. S. Chafer, *Systematic Theology,* IV, 325). Note that all agree on a future fulfillment by Israel in the millennium.

Concerning the Church's relation to the covenant, it seems best understood in the light of the progress of revelation. OT revelation of the new covenant concerned Israel alone. The believer today is saved by the blood of the new covenant shed on the cross. All spiritual blessings are his because of this, and many of his blessings are the same as those promised to Israel under the OT revelation of the new covenant. However, the Christian believer is not promised blessings connected with the restoration to the Promised Land, and he is not made a member of the commonwealth of Israel. He is a minister of the new covenant, for there is no other basis than the blood of that covenant for the salvation of any today. Nevertheless, in addition to revealing these facts about the Church and the new covenant, the NT also reveals that the blessings promised to Israel will be experienced by her at the second coming of Christ (Rom 11:26-27).

See Church; Covenant; Kingdom.

Bibliography. O. T. Allis, *Prophecy and the Church,* Philadelphia: Presbyterian and Reformed, 1945. Alva J. McClain, *The Greatness of the Kingdom,* Grand Rapids: Zondervan, 1959, pp. 157-160. Leon Morris, "Covenant," *The Apostolic Preaching of the Cross,* Grand Rapids: Eerdmans, 1955, pp. 60-107. Charles C. Ryrie, *The Basis of the Premillennial Faith,* New York: Loizeaux Bros., 1953; "Covenant Theology," *Dispensationalism Today,* Chicago: Moody Press, 1965, pp. 177-191. Wilber B. Wallis, "Irony in Jeremiah's Prophecy of a New Covenant," JETS, XII (1969), 107-110. *See also* under Covenant.

C. C. R.

COVENANT OF SALT. Agreements or compacts between individuals were usually ratified by eating together (Gen 31:44, 54; Ex 24:7-11). Seasoning the food to be eaten with salt signified the permanence and inviolability of the treaty or covenant being made or remembered (II Chr 13:5; Ezr 4:14, RSV). When the covenant was made with God, the food was first sacrificed to Him (Lev 2:13; Num 18:19; Ezk 43:24). Nomads of the Middle East still eat "bread and salt" together as the sign and seal of a brotherhood covenant.

COVERING THE HEAD. In I Cor 11:2-16 Paul commanded women to have their heads covered while at public worship. In the plan of God, man has headship over the woman. It was unseemly, then, in a gathering where both men and women were present in the house of God, that women should be without a token of this subjection. Women should not therefore object to wearing a veil, for this simply answered to the long hair covering which they already had. Women who refused to wear a veil manifested a spirit of independence, which was unbecoming and which would find its logical expression in cutting the hair so as to look like a man (vv. 5-6). This condition was considered by Paul contrary to nature (vv. 14-15). In no church at that time was it the custom to permit the women to be without a veil (v. 16). Actually, in the final analysis, the covering of the head represented the subjection of the woman to the man.

F. C. K.

COVERLET. Found in II Kgs 8:15, RSV. A mat or coarse cloth used to smother Ben-hadad.

COVERT FOR THE SABBATH. See Sabbath, Covert for the.

COVETOUSNESS. The tenth commandment forbids covetousness of all sorts when it speaks of a neighbor's house, wife, servant, cattle, draft animal, and of any of his possessions (Ex 20:17). The NT declares covetousness to be a form of idolatry (Col 3:5) or worship of goods and possessions, and condemns it along with other cardinal sins (Mk 7:22; Lk 12:15; Rom 1:29; Eph 5:3; Col 3:5; I Thess 2:5; II Pet 2:3).

It was covetousness which Christ saw in the rich young ruler when the Lord quoted him five of the six commandments of the second table of the law, and then challenged him with the tenth by enjoining him to sell all he had and give the proceeds to the poor (Lk 18:20-22). Barnabas, in contrast, probably fearing covetousness and knowing of the rich young ruler, sold all he had and gave it to the church (Acts 4:36-37). Paul cites covetousness as a key illustration of sinfulness, saying that "sin, finding occasion, wrought in me all manner of coveting" (Rom 7:8, ASV). In I Tim 6:10 we read, "The love of money is the root of all evil." The Gr. says "a root." This love stems from covetousness and can become the source of all kinds of evil (e.g., Ananias and Sapphira, Acts 5:1-11; cf. Ahab and Naboth's vineyard, I Kgs 21:1-19).

Some forms of covetousness are even more subtle, such as gambling, lotteries, bingo, etc., in which the player or participant often fails to analyze his own motive and detect covetousness. It is essentially covetousness which causes one to want to keep up with others when he knows that doing so extends him beyond his means and causes him to purchase what he really does not need.

Bibliography. Gerhard Delling, *"Pleonektēs,* etc.," TDNT, VI, 266-274.

R. A. K.

COW. See Animals, I.6.

COZ (kŏz). The father of Anub and Zobebah. Coz is found only in I Chr 4:8. It is also spelled Koz (*q.v.*).

COZBI (kŏs'bĭ). A Midianite princess slain by Phinehas, thus averting a plague (Num 25:6-15). In Akkadian *kuzbu* means "voluptuousness."

CRACKLING. The noise of burning thorns or stubble sometimes used as firewood, which flashes up and burns out quickly, leaving nothing but ashes (Eccl 7:6).

CRACKNELS. Used only in I Kgs 14:3. See Food.

CRAFT, CRAFTSMAN. See Occupations.

CRAFTINESS, CRAFTY. These terms are used for cunning or guile. Crafty refers to one who is sly and tricky in getting his own way (Job 5:12-13; 15:5; I Cor 3:19), or who is even unscrupulous or deceitful (Lk 20:23; II Cor 4:2; Eph 4:14). Paul caustically quotes the Corinthians' opinion of him in II Cor 12:16 in order to refute their insinuation.

CRANE. See Animals, III.7.

CREATION. The work of God in bringing all things into existence. The definitive passage is Gen 1:1, upon which must rest all biblical theology. God the Creator is a personal trinity, omnipotent, omnipresent, and omniscient. God alone is eternal, and is both immanent and transcendent with respect to His creation.

True creation must be *ex nihilo* (from nothing). The idea that the present universe has been developed out of prior materials, though commonly held in other religions and philosophies, has no basis in either Scripture or physical science. The translation of Gen 1:1 which treats it as a dependent clause (i.e., "When God began to create the heavens and the earth, the earth was without form and void") is inadmissible. This opening verse is rather an absolute statement asserting the initial creation of the heavens and the earth out of nothing. Neither is it a mere title nor summary of that which follows; rather, it is the first statement in the narrative of the order of the events of creation.

Since Gen 1:1 is the only verse in the chapter which mentions the creation of the heavens, it must be comprehended within the scope of the summary statement of Gen 2:1, which asserts the completion of the creation of both the heavens and the earth.

CREATION

CREATION

Complete creation. It is of paramount importance to recognize that Scripture teaches a *finished* creation. This fact is emphasized by the repeated statements to this effect in Gen 2:1–3, and by the institution of the sabbath as a memorial of God's finished work (see also Ex 20:11; 31:17; Ps 33:6, 9; Neh 9:6; Heb 4:4, 10; II Pet 3:5). Thus creation is no longer taking place, except in occasional acts of a miraculous nature. The normal, uniform processes of nature by which God now is providentially upholding all things (Heb 1:3; II Pet 3:7) are thus not processes of creation at all. Scientific study of present processes can therefore lead to no understanding whatever of the events of the creation period, since these events were brought about by divine creative processes which we are not now able to investigate.

A fragment of the Babylonian Creation epic from the palace of King Ashurbanipal of Assyria. BM

This teaching of Scripture is supported scientifically by the law of conservation of mass and energy, the first law of thermodynamics, which is the most basic and best-proved law of all science. Neither energy nor mass (except in mass-energy interchanges) is now being either created or destroyed. The universal reservoir of energy (which really includes everything in the physical universe) must therefore date from a primeval period of creation, just as the Bible declares.

Apparent age. If creation was not brought about by means of present processes, then the *only* way by which we can know anything of the events, manner, order, or date of creation is for God to reveal these things. This is exactly what He has done in the creation record in Gen 1 and 2, as well as in many other passages of Scripture. There is therefore no valid reason to

doubt in any way the exact accuracy of the events recorded in these passages. These great events occupied a six-day period. Each act was complete and each was adjudged by God to be "good." The total creation He called "very good" (Gen 1:31). Necessarily, these created entities must, at the instant of their creation, have had an "appearance of age." This is most obvious in the case of Adam and Eve, who were created as mature individuals, but it must also have been true in the case of all other objects, both animate and inanimate. The entire universe was established as a functioning whole from the instant of creation. In fact, it is philosophically as well as scripturally impossible even to conceive of a substance truly created without some appearance of age. This does not in any wise involve God in deception, as some claim, since He has clearly revealed this to be the case in His Word.

Evolution. It may therefore be categorically asserted that processes of evolution, whether theistic or atheistic, cannot account for the constitution of the universe and its inhabitants. Evolution by definition involves a general increase in order and organization, from simple to complex and from lower to higher. In its usually presented scientific framework, it involves great ages of slow changes, guided upward by the process of natural selection. This is purportedly explained by the principle of uniformity of operation of present processes—a principle explicitly contradicted by the creation account.

Furthermore, the Scriptures indicate that because of the entrance of sin there now exists a universal curse on the earth (Gen 3:17–19; Rom 8.19–22), manifested in a universal tendency toward decay and death. Thus, although change is everywhere evident in the world, this change is not evolutionary but rather deteriorative. This teaching of Scripture is verified scientifically by the second law of thermodynamics, which states that there is in every system—whether physical or biological—an innate tendency toward decrease of order and complexity. At the most, therefore, evolution can only be a local and temporary phenomenon, and cannot possibly have the status of a universal law such as the laws of conservation and deterioration. Thus it is impossible to attribute the creation to any form of evolution.

Summary. Creation, according to Scripture, was accomplished as a series of divine acts, bringing material entities into existence out of nothing. These were highly organized and completely functioning from the beginning, and thus were formed with an appearance of age. The creation was completed and finished during a special period in the past, following which God "rested" and is no longer creating, except in isolated instances of supernatural intervention. Present physical and biological processes are providential rather than creative, and so can give no information whatever concerning the creation period. This information can come only by divine revelation, which is given in the Bible.

Thus there remains no reason why we cannot or should not accept the creation record of Genesis as a historical, literal, factual account of the specific events which took place during that period. *See* Adam; Genesis.

Bibliography. J. O. Buswell, Jr., *A Systematic Theology of the Christian Religion,* Grand Rapids: Zondervan, 1962, pp. 135–137. J. O. Buswell, III, "Adam and Neolithic Man," *Eternity,* XVIII (1967), 29–30, 39, 48–50. Alexander Heidel, *The Babylonian Genesis,* Chicago: Univ. of Chicago Press, 1951, pp. 89–92. W. G. Lambert and A. R. Millard, *Atra-Hasis: the Babylonian Story of the Flood,* New York: Oxford Univ. Press, 1969. James M. Murk, "Evidence for a Late Pleistocene Creation of Man," JASA, XVII (1965), 37–49. Robert C. Neville, *God, the Creator,* Chicago: Univ. of Chicago Press, 1968 (a philosophical defense of the theory of divine creation). J. Barton Payne, *The Theology of the Old Testament,* Grand Rapids: Zondervan, 1962, p. 133. A. E. Wilder Smith, *Man's Origin, Man's Destiny,* Wheaton: Shaw, 1968. John C. Whitcomb and Henry M. Morris, *The Genesis Flood,* Nutley, N.J.: Presbyterian and Reformed Pub. Co., 1961, pp. 223–227, 232–234, 344–346. Edward J. Young, "The Relation of the First Verse of Genesis 1 to Verses 2 and 3," WTJ, May, 1959, pp. 134–145. R. Laird Harris, *Man—God's Eternal Creation,* Chicago: Moody, 1971, pp. 25–71.

H. M. M.

CREATURE(S). In Heb. a creature, *nepesh,* is any living being (Gen 1:21, 24; 2:19), even as God breathed "the breath of life" into man and he became a living "soul" (*nepesh,* Gen 2:7). The English word is also used to refer to all created animate beings both human and animal in the total creation (Gen 2:19; Rom 8:19–22), but elsewhere is applied specifically to animals or water creatures (Gen 1:20–21, 24; 9:10, 12, 15–16; Lev 11:46).

In the NT the word so translated (Gr. *ktisis*) means either (1) an individual thing or being created, "created thing" or "creature" (Rom 8:39; Heb 4:13); (2) the sum total of everything created, "creation" (Mk 13:19; II Pet 3:4).

Paul describes a redeemed man as a "new creature" (II Cor 5:17; Gal 6:15). Since the word is Gr. *ktisis,* Paul means that a redeemed man is a "new creation."

See Living Creatures.

CREATURES, LIVING. *See* Living Creatures; Cherubim.

CREDITOR. *See* Debt; Loan.

CREEK. Found only in Acts 27:39 ("bay" in RSV) as a translation of the Gr. *kolpos* meaning "bay," "gulf" of the sea (Arndt, p. 443).

Paul was shipwrecked on the shore of the bay of the island of Melita (*q.v.*) or Malta. The traditional gulf is located on the NE tip of the island and is known today as St. Paul's Bay.

CREEPING THING. *See* Animals, IV.

CRESCENS (krĕs'ĕnz). Crescens was the assistant of Paul mentioned in II Tim 4:10. He went to Galatia, but there is no indication of the reason. No trustworthy tradition exists concerning him, though tradition has suggested that he was one of the 70 sent out by Jesus, and that he founded the church in Vienna.

CRESCENTS. Used in Jud 28:21, 26, RSV. It is translated ornaments in KJV. *See* Amulets.

CRETANS. *See* Crete.

CRETE (krēt). The fourth largest island in the Mediterranean (Sicily, Sardinia, and Cyprus being larger). Located 60 miles S of Cape Malea in the Peloponnesus and 110 miles W of Cape Krio in Asia Minor, Crete became a seed bed and distributing center for the cultures of the Near East from the 4th to the 1st mil. B.C.

Comprising an area of 3,200 square miles, Crete is of elongated form—160 miles from E to W and 6 to 35 miles from N to S. In the center of the southern coast is Cape Lithinos, the southernmost point of the island. Immediately to the E of that is the small bay of Kali Limenes or Fair Havens, where the ship carrying Paul took refuge (Acts 27:8). A little less than 25 miles SW of Cape Lithinos lay the rocky, treeless isle of Clauda (Cauda, RSV; modern Gavdo), which Paul's ship passed as it began to fight the storm which eventually blew it to Malta (Acts 27:16).

During the 2nd mil. B.C. Crete was the center of the famous Minoan civilization (CornPBE, pp. 13–17). Caphtor (*q.v.*), home of the Philis-

A reconstructed entrance to the palace at Knossos, Crete. Mimosa

A large storage jar (*c.* 4–5 feet high) from the palace at Knossos (1500–1400 B.C.) in the British Museum. BM

tines (Jer 47:4; Amos 9:7), is commonly identified with Crete. *See also* Cherethites. Rome conquered the island 68/67 B.C. and made it a separate province. Paul may have evangelized it on a fourth missionary journey. At any rate, he sent Titus to organize the church there (Tit 1:5). He quoted one of the Cretan philosophers, Epimenides (*c.* 600 B.C.) who said of his countrymen, "Cretans are always liars, evil beasts, lazy gluttons" (Tit 1:12, NASB), a line in the same poem which Paul also quoted in Acts 17:28.

H. F. V.

CRIB. A feeding trough for animals (Prov 14:4; Isa 1:3; Job 39:9). Government stables at Megiddo during the era of the kings had mangers hollowed out of stone blocks. *See* Manger.

CRICKET. *See* Animals: Beetle, IV.4.

CRIME AND PUNISHMENT. A crime is an act or omission that violates the law forbidding such an act. Punishment (*q.v.*) imposes a penalty to the one responsible for the crime. Crime in the secular sense is regarded as an offense against society, and punishment ensues in the name of society. However, in biblical administration of justice, punishment ranges widely in

extent and refinement, from prosecution by injured individuals as in the time of the patriarchs (Gen 38:24), to a well defined prosecution by society through a recognized body of judges and courts as in the NT. In all this development, there is a religious basis.

The body of the law in the OT provides the fundamental biblical base for the definition of crime and punishment. Extrabiblical Jewish traditional materials in the intertestamental period give amplification and modification of these bases which are reflected in the NT. The presence of Roman penal law is also seen in the NT. The body of law in the OT should also be seen against the wider background of ancient Middle Eastern law, in agreement with it in many facets but also divergent from it because of a distinctive theocratic tie with Israel's special revelation.

An OT Theology of Crime and Punishment

The OT view of crime. Since Israel was a theocracy, criminal law in the OT differs from the Middle Eastern legal procedures of other ancient peoples. Crimes are regarded as an offense against Yahweh, and thus, crime is sin. The theocracy had a body of divinely given law and was held responsible for its practice. If there was any laxity in disciplining individual offenders, God held the whole community responsible and He would bring judgment on the community (Lev 26:3–45; Deut 28). These passages indicate that idolatry, immorality and murder were crimes involving the whole community in its common share of guilt and therefore punishment involved itself in public action.

Thus, laws existed in the theocratic relationship between the nation and Yahweh pertaining to the community's responsibility as well as to the individual's moral choices. There was also overlap in the two considerations that posed some real problems in legal procedure of determining guilt and punishment; e.g., in the slaying by the "avenger of blood" of one involved in an accidental homicide when the latter left the city of refuge before the appointed time. While the action would be wrong, the avenger would not be charged, since "blood-guilt" consideration was a serious community responsibility.

The most often used words describing crimes come from the root verbs *ḥāṭā'* ("miss the mark," usually rendered "sin"), *pāsha'* ("revolt," or "refuse subjection to rightful authority," usually rendered "transgress"), and *'āwâ* ("bent," or "crooked," usually rendered "do iniquity"). The words are rendered differently in various situations; thus the contexts need to be examined to see if the criminal acted against God or man.

A number of terms are used to describe those committing offenses and crimes. There is the "wicked" or "guilty" one (Deut 25:2) and the "offender" (I Kgs 1:21). An offender guilty of a capital crime was "guilty of death" (Num 35:31) and the offense could be described as "worthy of death" (Deut 19:6). Another penalty was to be "cut off" (Lev 7:20), and seems to imply the death penalty (cf. Lev 18:8, 29; 20:11). Later development of the law in *Mishnah Makkoth* 3:1, 2 implies that "cut off" standing by itself suggested another penalty, e.g., scourging, etc. Other terms for crimes speak of "breach of faith against the Lord" (Lev 6:2, RSV), wrongdoing as "punishment" (I Sam 28:10), and to commit "folly" (Josh 7:15). A more complete list of crimes and their punishments is given later.

The OT view of punishment. "The judgment is God's" (Deut 1:17) and the punishment of evildoers is an expression of divine justice. A person who was punished for a misdeed was reckoned to have appeared in judgment before the Lord (Deut 19:17). The penal laws were meant to be obeyed, with dire consequences of punishment for disobedience, because observing the law was doing "that which is right in the eyes of the Lord thy God" (Deut 13:18). Other expressions in the administration of justice need to be recognized; e.g., "If the thief is not found, the owner of the house shall come near to God . . ." (Ex 22:8, RSV; KJV has "judges" for "God"). "God" is understood here as the judge himself called Elohim and who was the representative of God.

Source Materials

The Pentateuch. In the establishment of the theocracy, one sees a stricture of exercise in function by taking from the head of a family the power of life and death exercised in the time of the patriarchs (Gen 38:24; Ex 21:20). Blood revenge was still retained but restricted under theocratic controls. At Sinai and Abel-shittim God gave the theocratic nation a revelation of detailed legislation, codified in the Mosaic writings.

The historical development of criminal law seems to involve four major codes: (1) the Decalogue (Ex 20:2–17); (2) elaboration in the judicial and ritualistic specifications of "the book of the testament" (Ex 20:22–23:33) which united the nation in its religious and political life; (3) the priestly codes (comprising primarily Leviticus and Num 5; 6; 9:1–14; 10:1–10; 15; 18; 19); (4) the Deuteronomy codes.

However, Moses received all this material during the period of the wilderness experience, beginning with the Decalogue on Mount Sinai in 1447 B.C. and ending with the Deuteronomy materials given on the plains of Moab in 1407 B.C., just before Israel entered Canaan. One can discern development in the details of a law, e.g., the law of accidental homicide, from the book of the testament to Deuteronomy as additional material was added (Ex 21:13; Num 35:9–15, 22–28; Deut 19:1–10). Also, depending on particular needs, a given judicial aspect was emphasized in one area more than in another, or it was mentioned in one code and not discussed in

another. For example, the Exodus materials treat in detail concerning injuries to person and property, but deal with only one aspect of immorality concerning seduction; Deuteronomy treats the matter of crimes upon women, wedded or single, but does not mention seduction. This does not mean, however, that offenses involving chastity were not known during the Sinai encampment.

In general, the body of the Mosaic law emphasizes that God is the Lawgiver and the One who validates the law; that accidental death and murder must be treated differently; that there is no death penalty in a crime pertaining to a property right; that punishment in cases of the principle of *lex talionis* excludes the practice of one human dying for another; and that no class distinction is observed in ascertaining punishment. The body of the law is also distinct in its comprehension and application from that of other law codes of Middle Eastern peoples in the 2nd mil. B.C. (see below).

Upper part of the Code of Hammurabi, showing Hammurabi receiving his laws from the sun god. LM

Middle Eastern law. A knowledge of other law codes of Middle Eastern countries contemporary with the patriarchs and Moses is necessary in order to provide proper background and contrast. Pertinent to this period are the laws of Eshnunna of the 19th cen. B.C., the Hammurabi code of the 18th cen. B.C., the Middle Assyrian laws of the 15th–13th cen. B.C., and the Hittite laws ranging from the 19th–13th cen. B.C.

In treating the well-known Hammurabi's *lex talionis,* appearing earlier than the book of the testament, some scholars have questioned the divine origin of Moses' laws. It is granted that there were legal patterns present as a part of a common Middle Eastern culture and heritage familiar to all peoples of the region. However, there were important points of contrast between the Pentateuchal codes and the Hammurabi code and other codes of the ancient Middle East. Thus, it was God who sanctioned the Mosaic materials throughout, while Hammurabi's code existed in no such form (except for one initial reference to its supposed receipt from the sun-god). Moses' law had one standard of justice for all, while Hammurabi's material presented an elaborate class distinction. The Pentateuchal insisted on sexual purity, with divorce permitted only for one specific cause (Deut 24:1), but Hammurabi's code recognized temple prostitutes as one social class and divorce was common. Moses' laws had a unique regard for social consciousness that reached even to an enemy (Deut 23:7); it forbade replacement of the slain by another person and sacrificing life to protect property.

What has been indicated for the Hammurabi code applies to a greater or lesser extent to the other codes. The primary thrust of the penal law was economic, and a secular legal system represented the state and the king as the ones who gave and validated the codes, in contrast to the Mosaic law.

Further development in the OT. Extrabiblical material from Palestine covering the period from the judges to the end of the OT monarchy is almost lacking as contrasted with a wealth of material in criminal cases, court documents, etc., in Mesopotamia. In 1960 an ostracon from the time of Josiah was found in Israel near Yavneh-Yam. It is the plea of a conscripted agricultural worker to the local governor that his overseer had wrongly impounded his garment for not delivering a full quota of grain (S. Talmon, "The New Hebrew Letter from the Seventh Century B.C. in Historical Perspective," BASOR #176 [Dec., 1964 , pp. 29–38). The few biblical references in the non-legal literature to criminal situations in the period just indicated are brief and treat only some unusual circumstances.

When there are references to points of law in the Prophets and Writings, there is sometimes an agreement with the criminal code and sometimes a deviation from it. In most instances deviations resulted from the people's syncretization of Canaanite practices, which had a thoroughly adverse effect upon public morals and led to an increase in criminal actions. The prophets denounced this synthesis and championed greater adherence to the revealed materials. But the greatest amount of biblical mate-

rial dealing with ethics, which in turn would aid in the control of criminal situations, was in the Proverbs of Solomon. This book should be regarded as second to the Pentateuchal codes in explaining and amplifying the precepts in the laws. Prevention of crime is stressed in Proverbs concerning the sanctity of life, regard for private property, and the use of sex as God had prescribed.

Non-legal biblical literature gives some application of the law concerning crimes involving the state and the king. Saul abused the criminal code in slaughtering the priests of Nob contrary to the concept of vicarious punishment (I Sam 22:19), while in another place he condemned the trafficking in spiritism (I Sam 28:9). David was involved in criminal action in the Bathsheba affair. Also he indicated a knowledge of the penal codes in Nathan's story of the confiscation of the poor man's lamb (II Sam 12:1–6). One full account of a legal procedure, although an abuse, is the case of Naboth and the false charge of cursing God and the king (I Kgs 21:10, 13). During his reign, Jehoshaphat saw that Judah had need for the application of a good judicial system (II Chr 19:4–11). A trial for treason appears in Jer 26; prosecution and defense argued alternately for Jeremiah, who was charged with "worthy of death." Jeremiah was cleared, but Uriah, another prophet, suffered a miscarriage of justice. The period of the monarchy closed with a wide gap between an actual legal practice and the demands of the Mosaic law.

Jewish traditional materials. The post-Exilic period began to see, under Ezra, a restoration of the ordinances of the law in the life experiences of a resettled people. There was no official monarchy, but Ezra and those who succeeded him fenced the legal system with further restrictions to guard against the deviations from the commandments.

The end of the intertestamental period and the 1st cen. A.D. saw the production and further development of a body of literature and materials concerning views on the biblical law. The *ḥiṣōnîm* literature (that outside the canon)—the Apocrypha (e.g., Tobit and Judith) and the Pseudepigrapha (e.g., Jubilees)—is a valuable witness. Main line Judaism had its legal sources in appropriate materials of the Tannaim (lawyer rabbis of the 1st cen. B.C. to c. A.D. 200). This material appeared in written form by A.D. 200 in the Mishnah (first part of the Talmud). Included with the Mishnah are the Tannaitic commentaries on the legal materials in the Pentateuchal books, e.g., the *Mekilta* on Exodus, the *Sifra* on Leviticus, and the *Sifre* on Numbers and Deuteronomy. This literature is still used as source materials for judicial rendering on points of Jewish law in connection with biblical materials. The writings of Philo (*On the Special Laws*) and Josephus (*Ant.* iv.8) are also pertinent.

Crime and Punishment in the OT

Crimes concerning society as a whole. These were crimes that affected the whole nation. One of these was to *defy the law.* It was a gross crime to act with impudence and defiance toward the priest and the judge as these officials sought to minister. The penalty in this case was death in order to put away evil from Israel (Deut 17:12). This was to serve as a warning to the rest of the people that they should not act in defiance of the law either.

Another crime of this nature involved *perverting and obstructing justice.* False reports were not to be received, and one was not to join with the wicked to be an unrighteous witness. One was not to join in a false cause to twist judgment, especially when the poor were involved inasmuch as the latter could not defend themselves (Ex 23:1-2, 6-7). There was to be impartiality; equal justice was to prevail for both poor and wealthy (Lev 19:15). Here was a unique contrast with other Middle Eastern codes that had respect for all kinds of classes and many times favored the wealthy over the poor.

Bribery as a crime against society was forbidden; bribes were regarded as blinding the ones receiving them (Ex 23:8).

Closely associated with bribery was *perjury,* which was strictly forbidden (Deut 5:20). The penalty for perjury consisted in punishing the false witness to the extent that he had thought to do to his victim (Deut 19:16-20).

Crimes against individuals. Within the biblical context, individual life has dignity and grace associated with it and any harm to that life is of a serious nature. Accordingly, a number of areas whereby harm could come to the individual life was spelled out.

At the head of the list of crimes which could result in bodily harm was *murder.* The Decalogue indicated that one was not to murder (Ex 20:13). Murder was regarded as marring the image of God (Gen 9:6). The unrequited blood of the murdered one was considered as polluting the land (Num 35:33). Some of the cases of premeditated murder were spelled out: coming presumptuously in guile upon a neighbor to kill him (Ex 21:14); smiting a person with various instruments in enmity or with hatred so that death ensues (Num 35:16-21). Striking a father or mother was considered murder (Ex 21:15, RSV). It was regarded as murder when death was caused from an induced miscarriage (Ex 21:22-23). It was considered murder to sacrifice a child to a foreign god (Lev 20:2-3). The penalty in all these instances was death. In cases of murder, the offender was not allowed to ransom his life (Num 35:31-33). There is no parallel in this matter between the biblical codes and other Middle Eastern codes, e.g., Assyrian, Hittite and the Hammurabi codes. The biblical text emphasizes the sanctity of human life.

Different degrees of guilt were recognized when human life was taken. When the killing was without premeditation, the offense was called manslaughter. When there was accidental death, the offending party was to flee to a city of refuge (Ex 21:13; Num 35:15). An appropriate penalty would then be established by the judges (Num 35:22-28). Death as a result of self-defense seems to have been recognized and the one who killed was blameless (Ex 22:2).

The cursing of one's parents was considered heinous and was regarded as having his blood upon him (Lev 20:9), a form of murder. The case of a rebellious son who would not listen to his parents, and who had established a pattern of perversity in spite of continued correction and chastening, was considered the same as a murderer; this action carried the death penalty (Deut 21:18-21).

Also considered crimes against individuals were *rape* and *seduction* (see next section dealing with crimes of a sexual nature).

Assaults of various categories were also treated in the code. In the case of a fight between two individuals, and one was harmed but did not die, the offending party had to pay for any damages as well as lost wages (Ex 21:18-19). When a master struck his servant so that he died, then the servant would be avenged; but if the servant continued to live, the master would not be punished (Ex 21:20-21). One sees here an unparalleled law in the Middle East for its interest in the slave as a human being rather than as chattel. However, if the master struck the servant so that he lost either an eye or a tooth, the servant was to be freed (Ex 21:26-27). When a man caused a pregnant woman to miscarry but the woman did not die as a result, then the offender had to pay damages as assessed by the wronged husband and the judges (Ex 21:22). In the case of an assault by an animal, the animal was to be put to death (Ex 21:28-32; see section below under penalties for murder).

A householder could slay a burglar breaking into his house at night, but was forbidden to do this in the daytime (Ex 22:2-3). The assumption was that the burglar at night would not hesitate to kill, and thus the case of law at this point. The Hammurabi code did not make this distinction since theft alone was sufficient to justify killing the offender. Other Middle Eastern laws did make the distinction of night and daytime robbery as the biblical law does.

Crimes of an ethical nature were also considered an affront against individuals. There was to be no *lying* one to another (Lev 19:11*b*). In the same category, *slander* and *talebearing* were expressly forbidden (Ex 23:1; Lev 19:16).

Honest weights and measures were to be used in dealing with each other and any *falsifying* was also considered an injustice against God. The penalty inferred here was that dwelling in the land could be jeopardized (Deut 25:13-16).

Stealing and selling a man was an extreme ethical violation and a disgrace to human dignity. This practice carried the death penalty (Ex 21:16; Deut 24:7).

Specific crimes of a sexual nature. Strict regulatory procedures were spelled out in the area of morality with measures of penalty which might sound harsh from the modern point of view. However, moral deviations were regarded as serious, especially since the basic structure of society was involved, the family unit. While similar in a number of ways, distinction in one aspect from other Middle Eastern codes is that biblical law regarded the marriage bond as divinely sanctioned.

In the case of *rape,* the penalty for the man who committed this crime was death (Deut 22:25 – 26). Concerning *seduction,* when a man enticed a maid who was not engaged into sexual intercourse, then the maiden was to be married to this individual. However, if the maiden's father refused this action, then the offender had to pay money for the dowry of the misused maiden (Ex 22:16 – 17).

Adultery was considered a crime and was forbidden (Ex 20:14). A number of instances of adultery were spelled out in the law. When there was coition between a married woman and a man not her husband, and they were caught, then both suffered the penalty of death (Deut 22:22). The same would apply if an engaged woman in a populated area had illicit relations with a man not her fiancé: both suffered the penalty of death (Deut 22:23–24). However, if an engaged woman in a sparsely settled area entered into illicit relations, only the man was put to death inasmuch as the woman could always claim she had protested but no one heard her cries (Deut 22:25–27).

In still another case, if a virgin not engaged had been forced by a man into sexual intercourse, then the man had to pay 50 shekels of silver and she had to be his wife; the man had no right to put her away as long as he lived (Deut 22:28–29). In a further curious situation, if a man was suspicious of his wife's actions, he could appeal to the "law of jealousies," the instruction for cases of jealousy (Num 5:29–30). In an oath before the priest, the suspected woman would drink water mixed with the dust from the tabernacle floor and rest her case before the Lord. If she was guilty, she would become ill, and thus her guilt would be established (Num 5:12–31). A man and another man's bondmaid caught in immorality were to be scourged but not put to death, since the slave was not a freewoman. In this case the man could obtain forgiveness through the proper sacrifice (Lev 19:20–22).

Sexual relations with those near of kin were expressly forbidden. The list of persons considered close of kin included the immediate family, the immediate in-laws, step-mother or step-father, aunts, uncles, nieces, nephews, or double marriages involving a mother and daughter, or two sisters (Lev 18:6–18). The penalty in these cases of *incest* was death (Lev 20:11, 12, 14, 20, 21).

Sodomy (Lev 18:22) was punished by the death of both parties (Lev 20:13). In the case of bestiality (Lev 18:23), both the offending person and beast were put to death (Lev 20:15–16).

Indecent assault by a woman upon a man when defending himself resulted in a penalty in kind for the woman (Deut 25:11–12).

The case of *willful relations* with a woman during her menstrual period called for the death penalty (Lev 15:24; 18:19; 20:18).

Improper dress, where either sex wears the clothing that pertains to the opposite sex, is described as an abomination to the Lord; however, no penalty is prescribed by the law (Deut 22:5).

In the matter of *prostitution,* the law prohibited sacred or cult prostitutes of both sexes among the Israelites (Deut 23:17). While parents were forbidden to sell their daughters to be common harlots (Lev 19:29), it was recognized that such harlotry could not be strictly controlled (Deut 23:18).

Crimes of a religious nature. Because of the seriousness of these crimes, primarily against God, the penalties called for the death sentence.

Apostasy involved an individual's attempting to lead members of his family or close friends astray to worship gods other than Israel's true God (Deut 13:6–11). Or apostasy occurred in a case of proved subversion where whole communities were led astray to serve pagan deities (Deut 13:12–16). In addition there was the concept of *ḥerem,* pertaining to an object banned from common use or "devoted to destruction." This related to anything associated with paganism, the idols and their decorations (Deut 7:25), the people involved in sacrifices to them (Ex 22:20), or as indicated, subverted communities. One connected with *ḥerem* became *ḥerem,* and thus one who appropriated to himself objects regarded as *ḥerem* became *ḥerem,* accursed or under the ban (Josh 7:11–26).

Blasphemy of the name of the Lord, Israel's God, by either an apostate Israelite or a foreigner, was considered a heinous crime (Ex 20:7; Lev 24:16).

False prophets and *dreamers* prophesying in the name of foreign gods were not to have any audience. Even in cases where these individuals predicted short range prophecies that came to pass, they were not to receive attention for this demonstration. Their predictions were permitted by God to prove the Israelite in his loyalty to Him (Deut 13:1–5).

Sabbath desecration was another crime with serious consequences, for no labor was to be done on the day set aside particularly for worship (Num 15:32–36).

Men or women *possessing familiar spirits* (or

understood as being demon possessed) were not to be tolerated but must be executed (Lev 20:27). Neither was *sorcery* permitted (Ex 22:18).

Crimes concerning property. Personal property was held to be inviolate and each one was to respect the possessions of others. This high regard prompted a number of situations which were treated to demonstrate this respect. In all these cases specific restitution had to be made (see below, concerning punishment for crimes).

The eighth commandment definitely stated that no one was to steal, and therefore *theft* was condemned (Ex 20:15). Specific cases of theft are mentioned, e.g., stealing cattle or sheep (Ex 22:1, 7), and taking more of the neighbor's vineyard or grain fields than could be eaten at the moment (Deut 23:24–25).

Burglary as a specific case of theft was recognized, in which a thief would break into someone's property to steal for personal gain (Ex 22:1–4). *Arson* was a crime against property and considered loss where buildings containing stored grain as well as fields of grain were set on fire (Ex 22:6).

Killing someone else's beast of burden was forbidden (Lev 24:18, 21). If a hole or a pit was not covered and someone's beast fell into the pit or hole so that the animal was injured or killed, then the negligent party had caused a loss of property (Ex 21:33–34). Care was taken for property in the case of an animal injuring or killing a neighbor's animal. The live animal was to be sold and the money divided, or if a negligent owner did not properly guard an unruly animal, then payment was based on beast for beast (Ex 21:35–36).

Removing landmarks or changing boundary lines between neighbors was condemned (Deut 19:14).

It was regarded as *trespassing* when a man turned his beasts of burden loose in his neighbor's fields to cause loss or destruction (Ex 22:5).

Penalties for crimes. The criminal code recognized degrees of crimes and therefore recommended degrees of penalty. Some of these sentences seem inhumane from today's point of view, but it must be recognized that certain of these crimes, if allowed to go unchecked, had serious national consequences. Schooling a nation in its legal system would lead the people to recognize the holy position of their theocracy in which God Himself was regarded as the Ruler.

The rule of the *lex talionis* limited punishment to strict retaliation in order to prevent excessive revenge. In the case of murder, it was a life for a life, or capital punishment as we know it today (Gen 9:6). Note that this applied even before the Mosaic covenant. But the Mosaic law did also specify the eye for eye, the tooth for tooth, hand for hand as well as the life for life (Ex 21:24–25; Num 35:33). However, apart from murder, the emphasis too many times was on the negative outlook in the interpretation. The sacred Scripture emphasized positively the equity in the punishment. For example, if there was an eye injury, the life of the offending party could not be taken; or if there were an arson case, the offender was not to be maimed or killed. There was to be strict and equal justice, which seems to be the intent of the law.

In the case of murder, no ransom or fine was allowed. Neither was there any sacrifice specified in the sacrificial system for murder; e.g., David could only put himself at the mercy of God when confronted with his sins of adultery and murder (II Sam 12:13). The penalty for murder was the death of the murderer.

In only one instance was there an exception (Ex 21:28–32). This was the case where a negligent owner, after being warned of his rampaging ox, did nothing to restrain it and someone died as a result. In this case, both ox and owner were to be put to death. However, he could ransom himself with the consent and at a sum determined by the kin of the victim. Under the Hammurabi code, in cases of negligence where children died as a result of an unruly ox, etc., the child of the offender was put to death. Ex 21:31 and Deut 24:16 repudiate this practice in Mesopotamian law and emphasize a more humane outlook.

An extreme punishment of *burning* was reserved for those involved in unusual immorality cases; e.g., a man involved with both his wife and her mother, or in the case of a priest's daughter engaged in harlotry (Lev 20:14; 21:9). But even before the law was given, the penalty recognized by the patriarchs for a woman given over to the fertility cult rites of priestess-prostitute (*qedēshā*) was burning (Gen 38:24).

Mutilation was meted out to the woman attempting to help her husband engaged in a fight with another person. She was to lose her hand for indecent assault upon her husband's assailant (Deut 25:11–12). There are few other specific corporal penalties in biblical law. The Middle Eastern laws contain many mutilation specifications based on retaliation that involved ears, eyes, noses, lips, whole faces, etc. Unusual modes of execution, e.g., dismemberment as indicated in Hittite laws or being thrown to the beasts (Dan 6:12), were not a part of Israel's penal code.

Cutting off from the people was another general type of penalty, but the specific kind of punishment many times was not described. It could mean death, banishment, or loss of inheritance because there would be no children to carry on the family line. The context in a few cases indicates what is meant as to the kind of punishment.

Some examples deserving cutting off were: eating blood along with the flesh in violation of the sacredness of the blood (Lev 17:14), being engaged in the many moral deviations practiced by the pagans (Lev 18:29; 20:17–18), sacrificing children as burnt offerings to pagan deities (Lev 20:3), being engaged as accomplices to the ones offering their children (Lev

20:4), becoming involved with those having familiar spirits (Lev 20:6), disregarding the Passover (and thereby disregarding the whole religious system under the law, Num 9:13), continuing willful disregard of the Word of God (Num 15:30–31), and an obvious contemptuous disregard for the ceremonial purity under the law (Num 19:13, 20). *See* Cutting Off.

Hanging was used in certain instances where the crime was worthy of death; after death, the body was hanged or impaled on a stake and bore a special curse of God (Deut 21:22–23). The only specification was that the body was not allowed to remain on the tree overnight but was to be buried on the same day of the execution so that the land would not be defiled.

Stoning was the judgment for those proved to be apostates (Deut 17:5), for those who blasphemed the name of Israel's God (Lev 24:16), for those who sacrificed their children as burnt offerings to pagan idols (Lev 20:2), and for those who had familiar spirits or were wizards (Lev 20:27). In addition, stoning was the judgment for continually stubborn and rebellious sons (Deut 21:19–20), for a bride who could not disprove a charge of immorality (Deut 22:21), and for one who desecrated the sabbath day (Num 15:32–36). In the punishment of stoning, the witnesses to the crime had the privilege of throwing the first stones (Deut 17:7).

In cases where the judges meted out *scourging* and *beating* as a penalty for the wrongdoer in a controversy, any amount up to the limit of 40 stripes was the judgment. The limit of 40 was specific or else there would be no justice and the offender's dignity would be utterly degraded (Deut 25:2–6).

Banishment was a punishment meted out in the post-Exilic period for those who would disobey some of the laws of God or the land (Ezr 7:26). At that time *confiscations of property and excommunication* from the congregation were the penalty for those who refused to part with their non-Israelite marriage partners (Ezr 10:8).

Imprisonment mentioned in the Mosaic covenant lasted only a short time, until it could be ascertained from the Lord what penalty was to be applied to the offender; e.g., in the cases of sabbath desecration and blasphemy (Num 15:34; Lev 24:12). At a later point in Israel's history, imprisonment and the stocks were a part of the penal system of the government, since some of God's prophets were put in prison; e.g., Micaiah (II Chr 18:25–26), Jeremiah (Jer 20:2; 29:26).

Search warrants and sanctions were permitted in the case of a man who kept some of his neighbor's goods for a time and then couldn't return them when called for, indicating they had been stolen (Ex 22:8).

Restitution was an important part of the criminal code of the law. If a beast of burden harmed another, the repayment was animal for animal (Lev 24:18). Theft, denial of things found, burglary, things entrusted for safekeeping and falsely declared to be stolen, etc., were all the bases for restitution, and replacement was to be made plus 20 percent extra. Lev 6:1–7 and Num 5:5–8 deal with voluntary return of property. In all Middle Eastern law, in comparison, there were legal specifications of capital punishment for theft. In one exception in the Hammurabi code there were instructions for punishment in damages amounting to 10 and 30 times the amount stolen. However, this was almost tantamount to a death penalty, for if restitution could not be made, the thief suffered death. Continuing, restitution in kind was to be made for stolen or borrowed property; e.g., animals stolen which had been delivered for safekeeping, and animals or goods that were destroyed when the owner was not there to witness it (Ex 22:12, 14, 15).

In other cases of *compensation* and/or *damages,* an offending party in a fight had to pay lost wages and medical expenses for the injured party (Ex 19:21). A fine of 30 shekels of silver was assessed along with the loss of the ox, in case the ox gored a servant (Ex 19:32); the theft of an ox for food or profit required five oxen for payment, while four sheep were payment for the theft of one sheep (Ex 22:1). A burglar was to make full restitution for his theft, or if he had no money for payment, he was to be sold into servanthood (Ex 22:3). A burglar found with the stolen animal in hand was to repay double (Ex 22:4). A man who fed his animals in his neighbor's fields was to make repayment in kind out of the best of his own fields or vineyards (Ex 22:5), and an arsonist was to make full payment for crops or property destroyed (Ex 22:6).

Punishment was to be meted out for the offender's crimes only; no penalties were to be paid by the defendant's parents or children (Deut 24:16). Punishment was to be handled by the judges or elders and no one was to avenge himself when wronged (except in the case of the avenger of blood for premeditated murder, Lev 19:18; Deut 25:2).

Crime and Punishment in the NT

Jewish law. It should be recognized that the NT is not some kind of body of law. Many situations and instructions in the NT touch on points of the legal code; what is displayed is the Jewish and Roman practice of law (or lack of it) in that period. Legal situations are difficult to determine; the NT authors did not write comprehensive legal briefs and give majority and minority opinions. There are differences of opinion on points of law at crucial passages even in the trial of Jesus as well as in the lengthy trials of Paul in spite of the space devoted to the accounts. There are numerous sources in Jewish and Roman law, however, that give general background for NT materials concerning offenses and punishments.

Beginning with 37 B.C., Judea was governed

by Herod the Idumean in the name of Rome, and starting in the year A.D. 6, Roman procurators. In spite of the occupation, there was leeway in Jewish internal autonomy by the high priesthood and Sadducean hierarchy in matters involving Jewish law and custom. Religious jurisdiction also seems to have been granted by the Romans to Jewish communities in the Diaspora whereby Jewish religious matters could be handled by competent leadership under supervision by the Jerusalem high priesthood.

Jus gladii, or capital punishment, was largely under the jurisdiction of the Romans, taken from Jewish authority during Pilate's governorship (*Shabbath* 15a), although there were instances of capital trials and executions without known Roman interference. Tannaitic records indicate executions by burning in a strictly religious question (*Mishnah Sanh.* 7:1, 2). The NT records Peter's trial with the possibility of execution (Acts 5:27–33) and the power of the high priest to execute (Acts 26:10). Any foreigner, including Romans, could be slain if they trespassed into the well-defined temple area; the warning against entry on pain of death was plainly displayed in Greek (Jos *Ant.* xv. 11.5). Making the capital charge of blasphemy under the Mosaic code, the Sanhedrin voted for the death penalty when they felt that Jesus wrongfully testified He was the Messiah and equal with God (Mt 26:63–66). On this occasion, the Roman authority was involved as well in the death penalty since Pilate eventually concurred in the decision. However, *Mishnah Sanh.* 7:5 does not cover in the matter of blasphemy all that was involved in the trial of Jesus.

The Mishnah prescribes stripes as corporal punishment in the tractate *Makkoth.* Offenses against the codes carried certain penalties. When penalties were not specifically mentioned, 40 stripes were prescribed, although 39 stripes or less were applied also to show leniency or care for the culprit. The penalty of flogging served as a frequent deterrent to wrongdoing and was applied quite often (Mt 10:17; Acts 5:40). Religious authorities also used the penalty of excommunication from the synagogues as a means for enforcing conformity to the codes and traditions (Lk 6:22; Jn 9:22).

Roman law. It was within the jurisdiction of the Roman governors and procurators to handle all situations involving peace and order. Josephus gives illustrations of Roman pronouncements for sedition in the cases of Theudas and Judas the Galilean (Acts 5:36–37; *Ant.* xx.5.1). A similar illustration is provided concerning the execution of John the Baptist by Herod Antipas (*Ant.* xviii.5.2). Pilate's charge and basis for execution of Jesus seemed to be treason from the inscription, "King of the Jews." There were some who regarded the disciples of Jesus as rebels against Rome (Acts 5:34–39), while Paul was picked up by the authorities as a leader of sedition (Acts 21:38). Both Romans and Jews

could arrest and examine, but it was the prerogative of the Romans only to execute.

Roman execution of capital punishment was by crucifixion when slaves and other lower class people were involved, although beheading was also used on occasion (*Mishnah Sanh.* 7:3; Mt 14:10). Lifetime consignment to work in the mines, called *vincula* or "bonds" (word usage, Acts 23:29), was practically a punishment of living death. Scourging was used often, either as a punitive measure or to derive needed information for judicial proceedings (*Ant.* xv.8.4; Acts 22:24). Detention in jail was common, pending the court proceedings or execution (Acts 24:26–27), and sometimes the stocks were used to restrict further the prisoner's freedom (Acts 16:23–24).

A law enacted during the reign of Augustus prohibited scourging or imprisonment for a Roman citizen. Paul, having been born in the free city of Tarsus, was a Roman citizen, and appealed to this advantage on a number of occasions (Acts 16:37; 22:25–29). However, there were times when Paul was not able to prevent scourging (II Cor 11:25) or perhaps refused to claim this privilege (II Cor 11:24).

Roman citizens in the provinces, when tried for capital charges, had the right to a trial before a council comprised of the governor of the province and other leaders of the province (in the case of Paul, Acts 25:12, 23). However, the Roman citizen in this situation could also refuse this procedure and seek judicial audience with the emperor in Rome. As to Paul's case, a number of undesirable as well as technical factors induced him finally to appeal directly to the Roman emperor (Acts 25:11–12; 26:31–32).

Bibliography. H. J. Cadbury, "Roman Law and the Trial of Paul," *The Beginnings of Christianity,* V, New York: Macmillan, 1933. H. Danby, trans., *The Mishnah,* New York: Oxford Univ. Press, 1933. D. Daube, *Studies in Biblical Law,* n.p., 1937. G. R. Driver and J. C. Miles, *The Assyrian Laws,* New York: Oxford Univ. Press, 1935; *The Babylonian Laws,* I and II, Oxford: Clarendon Press, 1952 and 1955. E. W. Edersheim, *The Laws and Polity of the Jews,* London: Religious Tract Society, n.d. H. E. Goldin, *Hebrew Criminal Law and Procedure,* New York: Twayne, 1952. M. Greenberg, "The Biblical Conception of Asylum," *Journal of Biblical Literature,* LXXVIII, Philadelphia: Society of Biblical Literature, 1959. A. Gulak, "Law, Jewish," *Encyclopedia of the Social Sciences,* IX, New York: Macmillan, 1937. F. Josephus, *Antiquities of the Jews, Loeb Classical Library,* Cambridge: Putnam, 1930. J. Z. Lauterbach, trans., *Mekilta,* London: Routledge, 1949. P. L. Maier, *Pontius Pilate,* New York: Doubleday, 1968. G. F. Oehler, *Theology of the Old Testament,* Grand Rapids: Zondervan, n.d. J. B. Payne, *Theology of the Older Testament,* Grand Rapids: Zondervan, 1962. Philo, *On the Special Laws, Loeb Classical Library,* Cambridge: Harvard Univ.

Press, 1937-38. J. B. Pritchard, ed., ANET, Princeton: Univ. Press, 1955. H. W. Saggs, *The Greatness That Was Babylon,* New York: Hawthorne, 1962. A. N. Sherwin-White, *Roman Society and Roman Law in the New Testament,* Oxford: Clarendon Press, 1963. J. M. P. Smith, *The Origin and History of Hebrew Law,* Chicago: Univ. of Chicago, 1931.

L. Go.

CRIMSON. *See* Colours; Animals, IV.11.

CRISPING PINS. Once thought to refer to metal objects used for curling hair. RSV translates the Heb. *ḥărîṭîm* as "handbags" in Isa 3:22, here probably highly ornamented bags carried by women. The expression is defined in KB as a bag (originally made of bark) or purse. Naaman gave two talents of silver to Gehazi in two such bags (II Kgs 5:23). *See* Bags.

CRISPUS (kris'pŭs).The ruler of the synagogue *(archisynagōgos)* in Corinth who "believed on the Lord with all his house" (Acts 18:8). He was one whom Paul baptized, along with Gaius and the household of Stephanas (I Cor 1:14, 16). Tradition records that he became bishop of Aegina (Apostolic Constitutions, VII, 46).

See Synagogue.

CROCODILE. *See* Animals, V.2.

CROCUS. *See* Plants.

CROOKBACKED. *See* Diseases.

CROP. Craw or pouch which serves as a receptacle for food in the neck of birds or fowl, discarded before the sacrifice (Lev 1:16).

CROSS. An upright post with horizontal beam fastened across it near the top of which convicted persons were executed in the Roman world.

Forms. (1) *Crux simplex,* the simple cross, namely, a single post or upright stake; (2) *crux commissu* or *crux humilus,* St. Anthony's, in the shape of a *tau* or "T"; (3) *crux decussata,* St. Andrew's, in the form of an "X"; (4) *crux immissa,* the Latin cross; (5) St. George's, formed with two pieces of equal length; (6) triple cross, three crosses in a row, used by priests and church dignitaries from the 5th cen. on.

It is generally accepted that Christ was crucified on a *crux immissa,* or Latin cross, since the Scripture declares that the inscription, "This is Jesus the King of the Jews," was set over His head (Mt 27:37; cf. Mk 15:26; Lk 23:38; Jn 19:19). Neither the St. Andrew's cross nor the St. Anthony's would seem to have permitted this to be done. Early Christian tradition affirms that it was on a Latin cross that Jesus died (Irenaeus, *Against Heresies,* ii.24.4; Justin, *Trypho,* 91).

The *tau* cross consisted of the upright *stipes* or stake permanently planted in the execution field. Its top was tapered to a point. The *patibulum,* a wooden crossbar weighing some 125 pounds with a hollow cup whittled from its center, fitted over the tip of the *stipes.* Some authorities are convinced this was the cross preferred by Roman executioners and that the title plaque could be fastened to a stick and nailed to the *patibulum* above the criminal's head.

The sign of the cross may have been used by early Jewish Christians of Jerusalem before the city's destruction in A.D. 70. Ossuaries (rectangular stone chests for human bones) were found in 1945 in the suburb of Talpioth, one of which was marked on each of the four sides with a rough cross, like a plus sign. A similarly marked ossuary was included in an apparently Christian cemetery on the Mount of Olives (FLAP, pp. 331 ff.). At Herculaneum, destroyed in A.D. 79 by the eruption of Mount Vesuvius, a house was excavated which showed a Latin cross incised in the plastered wall above a small wooden cabinet taken to be a prayer stool or an altar (FLAP, pp. 363 f.).

Symbol or emblem. The cross is emblematic of a death died under the greatest guilt and the deepest curse. Thayer says of the cross that it was "the well-known instrument of most cruel and ignominious punishment, borrowed by the Greeks and Romans from the Phoenicians; to it were affixed among the Romans, down to the time of Constantine the Great, the guiltiest criminals, particularly the basest slaves, robbers, the authors and abettors of insurrections, and occasionally in the provinces, at the arbitrary pleasure of the governors, upright and peaceable men also, and even Roman citizens themselves" (J. H. Thayer, *A Greek-English Lexicon of the New Testament,* p. 586). For the Christian the cross therefore becomes the sign that Christ has borne the guilt and thus paid the penalty for his sins.

In the OT, death was by stoning (Deut 21:20-21), and then often the dead body was hung or impaled upon a tree or stake as a warning (Deut 21:22-23; Josh 10:26). This hanging of a body on a tree was regarded as a particular mark of accursedness (Deut 21:23), thus explaining Gal 3:13, "Christ hath redeemed us from the curse of the law, being made a curse for us: for it is written: Cursed is every one that hangeth on a tree." The cross *(stauros,* "stake") is often called the "tree" *(xylon)* in the NT (Acts 5:30; 10:39; I Pet 2:24), thus connecting it with the OT concept of the deepest humiliation and shame (Heb 12:2). Here may be seen the continuity of the one idea of shame and curse as it is expressed in two different cultures.

The one condemned to crucifixion was first scourged or flogged with a *flagrum,* a whip with several leather thongs the ends of which were tipped with lead balls or sheep bones. Then the near naked victim was forced to carry the heavy *patibulum,* or crossbar of his cross, to the place of his death. The intensity of Christ's sufferings even before His actual crucifixion is revealed by the fact that after a night of torture and scourgings He was too weak to carry His own cross. It was therefore placed upon Simon of Cyrene (Mt 27:32; Mk 15:21; Lk 23:26).

At Golgotha the soldiers would have flung Jesus to the ground and stretched His arms upon the crossbar for size. The executioner would take a square spike about a third of an inch thick at its head and drive it with a single blow between the carpal or wrist bones at the heel of the victim's hand (not through the palm). Usually it tore through the median nerve. Edward R. Bloomquist, M.D., explains that the tissue of the palm "cannot bear weight and the victim would drop to the ground within minutes after being elevated" (p. 48).

He further explains that the feet were nailed (through the second metatarsal space) in order to give the victim a cruel "step" to support himself so that he could breathe. Otherwise the sagging body hanging on its arms went into a tetanic spasm which prevented exhalation. The victim would then quickly suffocate from an inability to use his respiratory muscles. As the hours wore on the body became soaked with perspiration, thirst became intense, and pain and shock were tremendous. *See* Nail for 1968 discovery in a tomb near Jerusalem of an iron nail through the heel bones of a crucified victim.

Breaking the legs meant that the victim could no longer lift himself on the nail in order to breathe, and he soon died (Jn 19:32). Since Jesus was already dead, the soldiers merely administered their usual *coup de grace* by stabbing a lance along the right side of the sternum and into the heart ("A Doctor Looks at the Crucifixion," *Christian Herald* [March, 1964], 35, 46–48).

When one discovers what it meant to be hanged upon a tree in the OT dispensation, and to be crucified in Christ's day, he understands one of the reasons the cross was a stumbling block to the Jews (I Cor 1:23; Gal 5:11). Another reason was that it signified the utter impossibility of justification by works, even by keeping the perfect law of God (Rom 9:31–33). At the same time the preaching of the cross was foolishness—the thoughts of a moron—to the Greeks with their philosophies. Yet it frees the power of God to save men and reveals His infinite wisdom (I Cor 1:24). The more the believer understands of sin, its origin, nature and power, the fall of man and what devastation came thereby, the more he sees the wonder and sufficiency of Christ's substitutionary death upon the cross.

Figurative meanings of the cross.

1. Taking up one's cross. Christ says, "If any man will come after me, let him deny himself, and take up his cross [Luke adds, daily], and follow me" (Mt 16:24; Mk 8:34; Lk 9:23).

Here it becomes clear from the analogy of carrying the *patibulum,* mentioned above, that Christ calls upon believers to be ready to sacrifice their selfish interests and daily to bear reproach, misunderstanding and shame in their service for Him, even as He did in His life and death (Mt 10:38; 16:24–26; Mk 8:34–38; Lk 9:23–26).

2. The preaching of the substitutionary atonement. This is the meaning attached to the cross in many places in Paul's epistles (I Cor 1:18; Gal 6:14; Phil 3:18; Col 1:20). It expresses the whole concept of Christ bearing our sins as our representative (II Cor 5:21; I Pet 2:24). Through the cross, Christ reconciled the sinner to God and made peace between Him and the sinner (Col 1:20), so that God is now propitious or well-disposed toward the sinner, and Paul could therefore write, "We pray . . . in Christ's stead, be ye reconciled" (II Cor 5:20; cf. Rom 5:10). See Leon Morris, *The Apostolic Preaching of the Cross,* 1955.

3. A symbol of the believer's union with Christ and sharing in a new divine life. In Christ's death the believer died in Him to sin and to the world-system (Rom 6:4 ff.; Gal 6:14), and now is to live like Paul, who writes, "I have been crucified with Christ; and it is no longer I who live, but Christ lives in me; and the life which I now live in the flesh I live by faith in the Son of God, who loved me, and delivered Himself up for me" (Gal 2:20, NASB).

See Burial; Christ, Passion of; Golgotha.

Bibliography. Johannes Schneider, "*Stauros,* etc.," TDNT, VII, 572–584.

R. A. K. and J. R.

CROWN. An ornamental circlet or head covering symbolic of royalty or of special status or achievement.

Origin. Crowns in the ancient Near East are the development of two common headdresses, the turban and the cloth or leather headband. The headband early gave rise to the metal diadem, such as the ornate golden wreaths with beads and gold pendants or rosettes of Queen Shubad of Ur, dating back to the 25th cen. B.C. (ANEP # 72). A copper headband belonging to an Amorite chieftain from *c.* 2000 B.C. was found in a Jericho tomb, and Flinders Petrie discovered a diadem of strip gold patterned with dots at ancient Gaza (Tell el-'Ajjul). Such crowns were sometimes set with precious stones (Zech 9:16). Among the Greeks and Romans the headband became the garland of leaves or flowers given to victorious athletes or to prominent citizens. In imitation of the Hellenistic practice some Jews prior to the time of Christ were crowning themselves with roses and olive wreaths during times of revelry and rejoicing (Wisd 2:8; Jth 15:13).

Ancient monarchs in the biblical world wore a great variety of caplike crowns or turbans (q.v.). The conical headdress of Assyrian kings consisted of a cloth wrapped repeatedly around the head and adorned with bands of colored embroidery or precious stones. The turban and diadem were sometimes combined into a composite crown (Ezk 21:26, NASB). The elaborate double crown of Upper and Lower Egypt incorporated the red crown of Lower Egypt (a fez-like cap with spiraled wire at front and tall projection at rear) and the white crown of Upper Egypt (tall, conical cap with a bulbous top). Whatever crown the pharaoh wore, the royal insignia of the *uraeus* or cobra always adorned the front to symbolize power and terror to his enemies.

Old Testament. The official headpiece of the high priest of the Israelites, and later of their kings (II Sam 1:10; II Kgs 11:12), is denoted by the Heb. term *nēzer,* which means "consecration" (cf. Lev 21:12, KJV with NASB). It describes the diadem or plate of gold, inscribed

Queen Shubad of Ur (c. 2500 B.C.) shown wearing her crown. BM

with the words "Holy to the Lord," and attached to the priest's turban with a blue cord (Ex 29:6; 39:30; Lev 8:9; cf. Ex 28:36–38; *see* Diadem). The *nēzer* signified not only the rank and authority of the wearer but also the sacred nature of his office. In the cases of both priest (Ex 29:6–7) and king (II Kgs 11:12) the coronation involved anointing with the holy oil (IDB, I, 746). The crown of David was the emblem of God-given kingship in Israel (Ps 21:3; 132:18). When the crown was removed and profaned in the dust, the visible kingdom came to an end (Ps 89:39; cf. Prov 27:24; Lam 5:16; Ezk 21:26).

Heb. *ʾătārâ* is a more general word for crown, used for crowns and head ornaments of various sorts. It denotes the bejeweled gold crown taken by David from the king of Ammon at Rabbah (II Sam 12:30). It may be the queen's crown as well as that of the king (Jer 13:18), Mordecai's gold crown (Est 8:15), or King Solomon's on his wedding day (Song 3:11). The latter may refer to a garland of flowers worn by both bride and bridegroom (Ezk 16:12), a custom still observed in some parts of the Orient. Zechariah was commanded to make an ornate crown of silver and gold circlets for the head of Joshua the high priest, probably a double crown to symbolize the future uniting of the priestly and regal offices in the one person, Messiah (Zech 6:11–14, NASB).

This word for crown was also used metaphorically in the poetic and prophetic books of honor and glory (Job 19:9; Prov 4:9) conferred in the form of a bountiful harvest (Ps 65:11) and of riches to the wise (Prov 14:24), in the form of a virtuous wife (12:4) and of grandchildren (17:6), and appearing as gray hair on the head of the righteous (16:31). God has crowned man, represented now by Jesus the Son of man, with glory and majesty (Ps 8:5; Heb 2:7, 9). The Lord crowns the believer "with lovingkindness and tender mercies" (Ps 103:4), and will Himself be the beautiful crown of His people instead of the proud crowns worn by the drunken nobility of Ephraim (Isa 28:1, 3, 5). Millennial Jerusalem will be a glorious crown, a kingly diadem in the Lord's hand (Isa 62:3, NEB).

Persian royalty wore the tiara or crown (Heb. *keter*) made in the form of a skull cap encircled by a battlemented gold diadem decorated with rosettes and representations of jewels (ANEP # 462; Est 1:11; 2:17; 6:8). Originally the term diadem meant a blue band trimmed with white around the tiara and signifying royalty among the Persians (Arndt, p. 181). Figuratively, the prudent make knowledge their crown (Heb. *yaktirû,* Prov 14:18).

Other Heb. words rendered "crown" are *zēr,* a border or molding of gold around the edge of the ark, table of showbread, and altar of incense (Ex 25:11, 24; 30:3); and *qodqōd,* the crown or top of the head (Gen 49:26; Job 2:7; etc.).

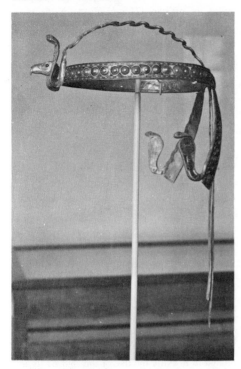

Crown of King Tutankhamon of Egypt. It is a gold band decorated with rosettes inlaid with carnelian. In front are the royal emblems of the vulture and cobra. LL

New Testament. Outside the book of Revelation the "crown" (*stephanos*) refers to a wreath, whether it be the literal crown of thorns mocking Jesus' claim to kingship (Jn 19:2, 5) or the garland of leaves symbolizing victory and reward. At the Isthmian games near Corinth winners were awarded a crown of celery leaves which would soon wither, suggesting the "corruptible crown" for which Paul says athletes in his day contended (I Cor 9:25; Oscar Broneer, "The Apostle Paul and the Isthmian Games," BA, XXV [1962], 16 f.). Instead, Christians seek the reward of an unfading crown of glory (I Pet 5:4), which has its basis in eternal life (Jas 1:12; Rev 2:10). Like the athlete, we must compete according to the rules (II Tim 2:5, NASB), for the crown may be taken from us (Rev 3:11). Paul states that it is the crown or reward for righteousness, awarded at the time of Christ's return to all those who have loved His appearing (II Tim 4:8). It is the hope of seeing Christ in His coming glory that causes believers to purify themselves (I Jn 2:28; 3:2–3). The apostle Paul also writes that his converts are his crown of rejoicing, his prize to be proud of (I Thess 2:19; Phil 4:1).

The golden *stephanos* in Revelation is worn by beings of high rank: the 24 elders (4:4, 10), the rider on the white horse (6:2), the demonic locust-like creatures (9:7), the woman Israel representing the people of God (12:1), and Christ waiting to come as judge (14:14). In 19:12, however, He wears the regal crown of many diadems (*diadēma*). Impersonating Christ and opposing God's sovereign rule, the devil and Antichrist will wear many diadems before their overthrow (Rev 12:3; 13:1).

See Diadem; Garland; Judgment; Rewards.

Bibliography. Walter Grundmann, "*Stephanos, etc.*," TDNT, VII, 615–636.

J. R.

CROWN OF THORNS. *See* Plants.

CRUCIBLE. The Heb. word means "to refine or melt." KJV uses the term "fining pot." It was a container, probably made of thick pottery, used for melting silver (Prov 17:3; 27:21, RSV). *See* Refine.

CRUCIFIXION. *See* Cross; Jesus Christ.

CRUSE. A small, elongated pottery decanter about four to six inches tall. Possibly a narrow-necked jar (Heb. "gurgler"), such as used by Jeroboam's wife to take a gift of honey to Ahijah the prophet (I Kgs 14:3; same word for "bottle" in Jeremiah's object lesson, Jer 19:1, 10); or a pan (open, shallow bowl) in which Elisha had put salt when he healed the water supply of Jericho (II Kgs 2:20); or a jug, flask, or canteen as a water bottle for Saul (I Sam 26:11, 12, 16) and Elijah (I Kgs 19:6), and an oil container for the widow of Zarephath (I Kgs 17:12, 14, 16). *See* Bottles; Pottery.

CRYSTAL. *See* Jewels.

CUBIT. *See* Weights, Measures, and Coins.

CUCKOO, CUCKOW. *See* Animals, III.8.

CUCUMBER. *See* Plants.

CUIRASS (kwē-răs'). A coat of mail made of interwoven heavy metal wire or links, or a breastplate (I Sam 17:5; Job 41:13, RSV; Neh 4:16, RSV; II Chr 26:14, RSV). *See* Armor; Breastplate; Coat of Mail.

CULTS. These are particular systems of religious worship with special reference to rites and ceremonies. The cult(us) is the focal point of a religion and eventually assumes forms and symbols which most clearly reveal the distinctive character of the religion. As the focus of religious life, the cult(us) becomes the point at which the sense of the sacred is most highly concentrated, and thus serves as an index to the innermost quality of religion. The term is also descriptive of minority religious groups holding beliefs regarded as unorthodox or spurious, and in this sense it was applied to early Christianity by the officials of the Roman state religion.

The religion of Israel was in constant conflict with, but eventually triumphed over, the base cults of her neighbors, such as the worship of Baal and Asherah with their many prophets and priests (I Kgs 18:19). The extremely degraded nature of these cults with temple prostitutes (*see* Harlot) and child sacrifices has been made startlingly clear by the Canaanite tablets found at Ras Shamra (*q.v.*) and Phoenician burials near Carthage.

The early Christian church doubtless inherited numerous forms and customs of worship from the Jewish synagogue; but it is very doubtful if pagan worship, such as that of the mystery religions, exercised an appreciable influence on early Christian worship. Research has rather conclusively shown that external and superficial resemblances do not necessarily prove dependence. In certain particular instances the most that seems probable is a similarity in terminology, a terminology to which Christianity gave a new content and meaning.

See Gods, False; Worship.

T. M. B.

CUMI (kū'mĭ). *See* Talitha Cumi.

CUMMIN. *See* Plants.

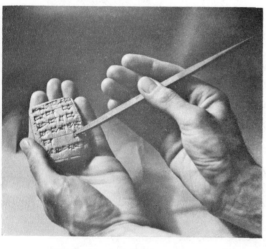

Babylonian clay tablet with stylus in correct position for writing Cuneiform. ORINST

CUNEIFORM. The name for the peculiar script developed in Mesopotamia around 3000 B.C. and used in modified form for many languages down to the 2nd cen. B.C. The name means, literally, "wedge-shaped" since the individual characters are composed of groups of wedge-shaped impressions made by a triangular

stylus in soft clay. Though used for the most part on clay, this script was also used on stone, metal, and terra cotta. (Other quite independent scripts using wedge-shaped characters were devised much later. See Ugaritic and Persian below.)

Apparently developed in its original pictographic form in order to signify personal ownership of goods, and especially offerings deposited in temples, the early incised pictures were scratched on lumps of soft clay used to seal jars. In time, as they changed into linear symbols, the underlying pictographs became entirely unrecognizable. Later, the symbols were constructed of complex groups of wedge-shaped impressions of varying size. Gradually the number and size of the wedges diminished until by the 6th cen. B.C. a sign once composed of 20 or more wedges required only five.

That the Sumerians invented the script is attested by the fact that the original reading of the signs was in the Sumerian language. For example, the picture of a fish was read *ha*, Sumerian for "fish," and the picture of a human head was read *sag*, Sumerian for "head." Soon pictures of objects were used for abstract ideas associated with the object. For example, the picture of a foot (Sumerian *DU*) was also read as *gub*, "to stand," and *gin*, "to go." A further development was the use of the individual signs for words that sounded like the word for the original pictured object though completely unrelated to it. Note the use of the sign *BI* (a jug) for the pronominal element "its" which is also pronounced *bi* in Sumerian. Next the signs were used in their syllabic value alone with no reference to the pictured object at all but simply as part of a spelled-out word. For example, the sign *RA*, originally the picture of a net, was used for *-ra*, a suffixal dative element in Sumerian.

Concomitant with this development in the use of the script for the Sumerian language there was adaptation so that it could also be used to write Semitic Akkadian. This development followed much the same lines. In addition, Akkadian translations were substituted for the various Sumerian readings of the signs, and at the same time, the syllabifying process was accelerated. The five basic types of signs in Akkadian documents were: word signs, syllabic signs, determinatives (symbols indicating that the following word was a personal name, a geographic term, a kind of stone, plant, animal, utensil, etc.), phonetic complements (a syllable written after a word sign to indicate its pronunciation), and numerals.

Perhaps the cuneiform syllabic system seems unwieldy to us, but it was sufficiently flexible to become the basic script for many languages beyond the tongue of its inventors. It was used by scribes to write Elamite, Hurrian, Hittite, and Urartean. On the other hand, Egyptian hieroglyphs remained local and were never used for any other language. In fact, syllabic cuneiform scripts continued in use long after alphabets were invented.

Its flexibility may be demonstrated in another way. The documents written in this fashion include just about every conceivable type of literature; e.g., business letters, contracts, receipts, lists, personal letters, myths, hymns, poems, proverbs, historic annals, monumental inscriptions, mathematical texts, grammatical texts and vocabularies. Literally hundreds of thousands of business documents have been recovered. Data from such documents together with government records have permitted a remarkably detailed reconstruction of daily life and political events more than 3000 years ago, in some cases to a greater degree than can be done for many parts of Europe of only a few centuries ago.

But first cuneiform inscriptions had to be deciphered. This was a difficult task performed with brilliance and diligence, chiefly by Grotefend, Rawlinson and Hincks, by the mid-19th cen. They began with Persian royal inscriptions of Darius and his successors in an entirely different script from that developed by the Sumerians. The script appears similar, however, in that it is composed of signs made up of groups of wedges. But the similarity ends there. The Persian script consists of 36 alphabet-like characters plus some special word signs, word dividers and determinatives.

These royal inscriptions were noticed by travelers to the Orient in the 17th cen., after having been unknown for centuries. Comparison of the Persian royal names found in these inscriptions with the same names in Sassanian and Gr. records provided vital clues. The larger number of signs in the parallel Neo-Babylonian inscriptions indicated a more complex script. It was assumed to be alphabetic in character with many helping signs. The multitudes of clay tablets uncovered by Botta at Khorsabad in 1843 and by Layard at Nineveh in 1845 helped considerably, especially by providing ancient lists of signs with their readings compiled by Assyrian scribes long ago. In fact, without the hundreds of similar tablets found later at Nippur, probably very little of the Sumerian language would yet be known.

Another cuneiform script of independent development consisting of 36 alphabetic signs arose in Syria in the 15th cen. B.C. It records a Semitic language called Ugaritic which is closely related to Hebrew. The tablets were discovered at Ras Shamra by Claude F. A. Schaeffer in 1929 and were deciphered by Hans Bauer, Edoward Dhorme, and Charles Virolleaud among others. The texts are chiefly poems of myths, epics and legends.

Eventually, Canaanite alphabetic scripts, with later modifications by the Greeks and Romans, completely replaced the cuneiform scripts and they passed into oblivion until archaeologists resurrected them and recovered the information they contained.

See Writing; Ras Shamra.

Bibliography. Edward Chiera, *They Wrote on Clay,* Chicago: Univ. of Chicago Press, 1938. Johannes Friedrich, *Extinct Languages,* New York: Philosophical Library, 1957. Samuel Noah Kramer, *From the Tablets of Sumer,* Indian Hills, Colo.: Falcon's Wing Press, 1956.

F. R. S.

The Chalice of Antioch is apparently a very early communion cup (some would date it to the first century) and may have representations of the apostles on it. MM

CUP. Besides its literal use as a drinking vessel, bowl, goblet or laver (*see* Pottery), the term is also used in a figurative sense in the Scriptures. By metonymy it may refer to what it contains (Prov 23:31). It is also used with the genitive of the person who bestows the drink (I Cor 10:21). Symbolically it is used of life itself, an expression of destiny in both the good and evil sense.

The inheritance of the saints is the portion of their cup (Ps 16:5); the state of the wicked is theirs (Ps 11:6). There is the cup of sorrow (Mt 26:39; Mk 14:36; Lk 22:42; Jn 18:11) and the cup of consolation (Jer 16:7). It symbolizes an abundant share of blessings, prosperity, joy, even salvation (Ps 23:5; 116:13); or a share of afflictions (Ps 75:8; Isa 51:17). It may be the cup of God's wrath, punishment, vengeance (Isa 51:17, 22; Lam 4:21; Ps 11:6; 75:8), the cup of judgment (Ps 11:6; 73:10; 75:8; Isa 51:17, 22; Jer 25:15–28; Ezk 23:31–34). The wine of harlotry, with which Babylon intoxicated the nations, becomes the wine of God's wrath for them, i.e., the wine cup of His passionate wrath (Rev 14:8, 10; 16:19; 18:3; 19:15).

Gold cup from Vaphio, Greece (c. 1500 B.C.).
Mimosa

For Christ Jesus it was the cup of violent death (Mt 20:22–23; Jn 18:11). The martyrdom of Christians is described as sharing in the cup of Christ (Martyrdom of Polycarp 14:2; cf. Mt 20:23; Mk 10:39). The cup which the Father gave His Son to drink makes the cup of the new covenant in His blood a cup of blessing (I Cor 10:16) for the forgiveness of sins.

The eucharistic cup is often made of precious metals, sometimes embellished with precious stones, although it is also made of less costly materials. The *calix ministerialis* was used in the Roman church until the high Middle Ages for communing the faithful *subutraque* (under both kinds, with bread and wine). The *calix offertorius* is used at the Roman Mass for the common participation by the officiant, but with bread alone. At baptism the *calix baptismalis,* which contained a mixture of milk and honey, was drunk.

In Bohemia the reform movement of the early 15th cen. demanded the giving of the cup to the laity, a concession granted by the Council of Constance, although this did not satisfy the calixists entirely. The European reformers of the 16th cen. denounced the withdrawal of the cup from the laity, for Christ commanded of this cup, "Drink ye all of it." In Protestant and Lutheran churches the sacrament is administered *subutraque,* under both kinds, as it is also in the Orthodox churches, both Eastern and Russian, and some of the Uniate churches. In many Protestant congregations individual communion cups are used; Anglican and many Lutheran churches use the "common cup" (one chalice from which all communicants drink in turn).

C. S. M.

CUPBEARER. *See* Occupations: Cupbearer.

CURE. *See* Diseases; Healing, Health.

CURIOUS ARTS. The translation "curious arts" ("magic arts," RSV) of a Gr. article (*ta*) and adjective (*perierga*) with this usage is found

only in Acts 19:19. The adjective originally means excessively busy; then meddlesome, relative to the concerns of others; and finally, as regards the future, inquisitive to the extent of using magical or occult arts as a means of information and discovery.

Such arts were a specialty in Ephesus (Acts 19). Magicians and astrologers were present in large numbers and carried on a brisk trade in charms, books of divination, and rules for interpreting dreams. The so-called "Ephesian spells," or "Ephesian writings," were small strips of parchment on which were written letters or monograms. These strips were kept in small silk bags which were worn on the arm as charms or amulets (*q.v.*).

In the OT such arts played a much less important role in Israel than in other countries of the ancient Near East. In fact, the Mosaic law forbade many such practices (Deut 18:9–13). That they were known among the Israelites, however, is seen from references to them in the prophets (Jer 27:9; Mic 5:12; Mal 3:5) and in certain incidents (e.g., the witch of Endor, I Sam 28), as well as the fact that amulets are often found in archaeological excavations in Palestine.

See also Magic; Divination.

T. M. B.

CURSE. The several Heb. and Gr. words for curse denote the expression of a wish or prayer that evil might befall another. This idea found a wide variety of uses in Israel's life and was universally known among her neighbors. The terms of a contract or treaty were protected by curses or imprecations directed at any future violator of the agreement (see ANET, pp. 205 f.). Similar security measures are found in royal inscriptions where curses were pronounced upon any one who might alter or destroy the inscription (ANET, pp. 267 f.). Curses were also directed against murderers (Gen 4:11–12), as well as against enemies who in the future might harm one (II Sam 18:32) or who were presently harming one (Jer 12:3). Indeed, wherever protective and punitive measures were lacking or inadequate, curses were employed.

Cursing, when applied to God, is an anthropomorphic term expressing divine displeasure or vindictive justice (e.g., Gen 3:14–19; 5:29; 12:3). The natural antithesis of all such curses is blessing.

The efficacy of a curse depended basically upon divine approval and execution. In the Heb. mind, the spoken curse was considered to be the active agent for harm, clothed with the power of the soul which sent it forth. But only the individual who was a faithful servant of Jehovah had a source of true power; hence it was the living God who ultimately wielded the power of the curse or spell. Therefore, a curse (or a blessing) once soberly uttered might not be recalled or revoked (Gen 27:27–40; cf. I Sam 14:24–30, 43–45).

The Mosaic law forbade the cursing of father or mother (Ex 21:17) on penalty of death, the prince of the people (Ex 22:28), and one that was deaf (Lev 19:14). Blasphemy, or cursing God, was a capital offense (Lev 24:10-16). But curses pronounced against individuals by godly men (e.g., Gen 9:25; 49:7; Deut 27:14-26; II Sam 3:29; 39; Josh 9:23) were not the expressions of passion, impatience, or revenge; they were prophetic predictions or statements of the divine decree, and therefore not such as God condemned.

Cursing or imprecatory psalms are those in which the psalmist pronounced a curse on the enemies of Israel (Ps 83:9-17) or on his personal opponents or oppressors (Ps 69:21-28). To understand these prayers which are so foreign to the NT, one must remember that the revelation of the OT was preparatory to that of the NT, and was therefore incomplete. Furthermore, the curse in the ancient Near East, including Israel, was considered a legitimate means of defense. Also, the language of the Oriental was more impassioned and for the Israelite more concrete than ours.

In the NT the cursing of enemies or persecutors is forbidden by the example and word of Jesus (Lk 23:34; Mt 5:44). Paul, however, cursed those who did not love Christ (I Cor 16:22) or who preached a gospel different from his (Gal 1:8 f.). He was willing to become accursed himself, if by so doing his own people would more readily accept his Christ (Rom 9:3). The "curse of the law" is the sentence of condemnation which is pronounced on the transgressor (Gal 3:10), and from which Christ redeemed us by having been made a curse for us (Gal 3:13). *See* Accursed; Anathema; Devote; Dedicate; Oath.

Bibliography. Herbert C. Brichto, *The Problem of "Curse" in the Hebrew Bible,* JBL Monograph Series, XIII, 1963. Chr. Senft, "Curse," *A Companion to the Bible,* J. J. von Allmen, ed., New York: Oxford Univ. Press, 1958. N. H. Smith, "A Study of the Words 'Curse' and 'Righteousness,'" *The Bible Translator,* III (1952), 111-114.

T. M. B.

CURTAINS. Ten curtains covered the tabernacle of Moses and became synonymous for the tabernacle itself (*q.v.*). Hangings were also used for the door and for the gate of the court about the tabernacle (Ex 26:1-14, 31-37; 27:9-18). A veil or curtain separated the holy of holies from the holy place.

The veil was torn at the death of Jesus Christ from the top to the bottom (Mt 27:51; Mk 15:38; Lk 23:45), and so access was opened to the inner sanctum (cf. Heb 6:19). This was symbolic of the direct access to God secured by Christ, since He opened the way through the veil, that is, through His flesh (Heb 10:20). *See* Veil.

CUSH (kūsh)
1. The son, possibly the eldest, of Ham and grandson of Noah (Gen 10:6-8). He was the father of several sons, or nations, including Nimrod.
2. A Benjamite enemy of David, according to the ancient title of Ps 7.
3. The people and land of Cush. The word is usually but not consistently translated Ethiopia in the KJV. The designation Ethiopia is misleading, for it did not refer to the modern state of Ethiopia or Abyssinia. The biblical Cush (Egyptian *Kôsh*) bordered Egypt on the S, the land of Nubia or modern Sudan. The dividing line seems to have been at the first cataract, at the city of Syene, modern Aswan (Ezk 29:10). Egyptian Dynasty XXIII was Cushite, and one of its kings is mentioned as the opponent of Sennacherib (II Kgs 19:9). *See* Ethiopia.
4. Another land, described as compassed by the river Gihon (Gen 2:13). Since this river flowed in the same area as the Tigris and the Euphrates (Gen 2:10-14), the land has been located in western Iran, home of the Kassites, a powerful people who ruled Babylonia in Moses' time.

P. C. J.

CUSHAN (kŏŏ'shăn). A name formed from Cush, whose meaning is in doubt. It is used as a parallel to Midian (Hab 3:7) and may be an older, poetical name for this land or its inhabitants who were descended from Cush. Some have suggested that the name stands for Chushan-rishathaim (*q.v.*), a Mesopotamian king who oppressed Israel some eight years before he was defeated by Othniel (Jud 3:8-10). This is highly improbable, even though Josephus refers to this king as Chusan (*Ant.* v. 3.2).

CUSHAN-RISHATHAIM. *See* Chushan-rishathaim.

CUSHI (kŏŏsh'ī)
1. Great-grandfather of Jehudi, a prince of Jeremiah's day (Jer 36:14).
2. The father of the prophet Zephaniah (Zeph 1:1).
3. In II Sam 18:21-32, the messenger sent by Joab to announce to David the success of the battle against Absalom as well as his death. Here the RSV renders the Heb. *the Cushi,* "the Cushite," i.e., the Ethiopian.

CUSHION. *See* Bed.

CUSTOM. The word refers in its widest legal sense to all rules of law not derived directly from specific acts of law-making bodies. In a more restricted sense it refers to a popular usage which under certain conditions may serve as a source of law.

In the OT it is one of a number of related words variously translated as "tax," "toll," "tribute," or "custom," depending on the version used (cf. Ezr 4:13, 20; 7:24). In the NT it is the rendering of the Gr. *telos,* usually meaning an indirect tax on goods, as opposed to a tax on property or person (Mt 17:25; Rom 13:7). *See* Taxes.

CUSTOM, RECEIPT OF. The place at which Matthew sat when Jesus called him (Mt 9:9; Mk 2:14; Lk 5:27). A revenue or tax office, which arose from the practice of the Roman government in selling to the highest bidder the privilege of collecting taxes within a certain province or city. The buyer paid a stipulated sum for the privilege and was free to collect more if he so desired.

Matthew's place of business was a toll booth or customs office (*telōnion*), perhaps near the wharves in Capernaum. He collected tariffs or duties levied on goods shipped across the Sea of Galilee from the territory of Philip to that of Herod Antipas, or on merchandise in transit on the road from Jerusalem to Tyre or Damascus. *See* Taxes.

CUTH (kūth), **CUTHAH** (kūth'â). An ancient city in Babylonia, *c.* 15 miles NE of Babylon. In 1880 Hormuzd Rassam identified Tel-Ibrahim, a mound about 3,000 feet in circumference and about 280 feet high, as the site.

The only mention of Cuth or Cuthah in the OT is found in II Kgs 17:24, 30, where it is listed as a source of the mixed population of Samaria. When Sargon II, king of Assyria, deported people from the northern kingdom of Israel, he transplanted inhabitants from other areas to take their place. Among these the Cuthians were sufficiently prominent that the rabbinical Jews applied their name to the Samaritans generally, and words peculiar to the Samaritans were called Cuthian. Contract tablets, the great temple Ê-meš-lam (dedicated to Nergal, god of the underworld), the ruins of the city itself, and the exterior remains extending for miles around, all indicate a flourishing city with foundations going back to Sumerian times. There are marks of greatly enhanced development after the destruction of Babylon.

Reference is made in II Kgs 17:30 to the introduction of the pagan cult of Nergal into Samaria. The racial amalgamation and the religious apostasies brought to Samaria go far to account for the animosities of Judah toward the Samaritans during the restoration.

W. T. D.

CUTTING OFF. In the OT a penalty or form of punishment used primarily, though not exclusively, for various offenses against the ceremonial laws (e.g., Lev 17:3-4). The agent of the "cutting off" was either God (Lev 17:10) or the community (Lev 18:29). Older interpreters held the view that this method of punishment always involved the death penalty. This is hardly correct in spite of the implication of such a passage as Ex 31:14. Although the death penalty was at times associated with "cutting off," its more probable meaning was that of expulsion from the religious or civil community.

CYPRUS

SCALE OF MILES

This type of punishment found in the early Israelitish community was doubtless the basis for the later "excommunication" among the Jews which resulted in exclusion from the synagogue, either temporarily or permanently depending on the nature of the offense committed. Evidence of a similar form of discipline has been found among the members of the Qumran community. Discipline in the early Christian communities was naturally patterned after that of the parent religion, and numerous similar practices are found in the NT (II Thess 3:14; I Cor 5:1–5, 13; I Tim 1:20).

See also Crime and Punishment; Excommunication.

T. M. B.

CUTTINGS IN THE FLESH. The biblical attitude gives no place in worship for cutting, gashing, or disfiguring the body in any way. (*See* Circumcision, an entirely different practice.) If not a belief in the sacredness of life, there was at least a profound respect for the body as God's creation, and therefore no place was given to mutilating or disfiguring it in the name of Yahweh. The common mourning practice of non-Israelites of scratching the arms, head, and face was prohibited by Moses (Lev 19:28; 21:5). In addition, the Mosaic law prohibited tattooing (Lev 19:28). Respect for a sound, whole body is emphasized in the bodily birth defects or injury sustained after birth which disqualified one of Aaron's family from the priesthood (Lev 21:18–24).

However, among the worshipers of Baal and Asherah it apparently was a common custom to cut and disfigure the body. This is illustrated by the frenzied action of the Baal priests during the contest between Elijah and Jezebel's priests on Mount Carmel (I Kgs 18:28). Adoni-bezek cut off the thumbs and great toes of his enemies (Jud 1:6–7); Philistines gouged out the eyes of Samson (Jud 16:21) and of the men of Jabesh-gilead (I Sam 11:2).

H. E. F.

CYMBAL. *See* Music.

CYPRESS. *See* Plants.

CYPRUS (sī'prŭs). The third largest island of the Mediterranean (after Sicily and Sardinia), it has an area of 3,572 square miles. Visible from both Asia Minor and Syria on a clear day, it is about 43 miles from the former and 60 miles from the latter. The surface is almost evenly divided between mountain and plain.

So extensive was Cyprus' export of copper in ancient times that the English word copper is derived from its Gr. name *kypros*, through the Latin *cuprum*. OT references to Kittim or Chittim (e.g., Gen 10:4; Num 24:24; Isa 23:1) are commonly identified with Cyprus (CornPBE, pp. 13–17). The Romans took the island in 58 B.C. and transferred the capital from Salamis (*q.v.*) on the E to Paphos on the W coast. Paul

and Barnabas landed at Salamis on their first missionary journey (Acts 13:5) and ministered throughout the island, embarking at Paphos for Asia Minor after some success in missionary efforts (Acts 13:6–13). Later, Barnabas and John Mark preached on Cyprus (Acts 15:39).

H. F. V.

Bronze statuette of a horned god, twelfth century B.C. Enkomi, Cyprus. Cyprus Museum

CYRENE (sī-rē'nĭ), **CYRENIAN** (sī-rē'nĭ-ăn). A city in N Africa midway between Carthage and Alexandria. Cyrene was founded as a Gr. colony in 630 B.C. In 331 B.C. it submitted to

Alexander, in 321 B.C. came under the Ptolemies, and passed to Rome in 96 B.C. Renowned as an intellectual center, at its zenith it had a population of 100,000. Ruins of beautiful buildings now mark the site. Cyrene and Cyrenians figure in Mt 27:32; Mk 15:21; Lk 23:26; Acts 2:10; 6:9; 11:20; 13:1.

CYRENIUS (sī-rē'nĕ-ŭs).The KJV form of Quirinius (ASV), taken from the Gr. *kyrēnios*. In Lk 2:2 he is called "governor of Syria," and was responsible for carrying out the census of Caesar Augustus.

Publius Sulpicius Quirinius was a Roman senator, later elected consul, and "of great dignity" (Jos *Ant.* xviii.1.1). He was sent to Syria by Augustus to carry out a taxation edict of the emperor. (To this point both Josephus and Luke [Acts 5:37] agree, for they both refer to an event *c.* A.D. 6, in the days of the rise of "Judas the Galilean.") At his death in A.D. 21, Tiberius requested the Senate that the occasion "be celebrated with a public funeral" (Tacitus, *Annals* iii.48).

The chronological problem arises in connection with the "first census" mentioned in Lk 2:2. Of this there is no other mention, and some have rejected Luke's history. Several factors, however, ought to be considered. First, it seems that Quirinius had been appointed by Augustus to serve as legatus of the emperor during the period 10-6 B.C. in the E, and may have held a governorship in Syria. Second, we know by the discovery of receipts and decrees among the papyri of Egypt that regular Roman enrollments were instituted on the basis of a 14-year cycle. Other inscriptions indicate Augustus first ordered the imperial census. The earliest known census papyrus document certainly dated is from A.D. 34; other similar papyri are regarded by some as belonging to A.D. 20 or even A.D. 6. Fourteen years earlier would thus fall in the period of about 8 B.C. Third, the example of an edict in Egypt in A.D. 104, issued by one Vibius Maximus, ordered all persons "to return to their domestic hearths" to be enrolled (Deiss LAE, p. 271). The similarity to Luke's language is clear. Finally, the fact that Luke calls this incident "the first census" taken by Quirinius in Syria may imply that Quirinius also supervised a second census, namely, the one of A.D. 6, mentioned in Acts 5:37. *See also* Census.

Bibliography. F. J. Foakes-Jackson and Kirsopp Lake, *The Beginnings of Christianity,* London: Macmillan, IV, 61 f. J. N. Geldenhuys, "Commentary on the Gospel of Luke," *New International Commentary on the New Testament,* Grand Rapids: Eerdmans, 1956, pp. 99-106. W. M. Ramsay, *Was Christ Born at Bethlehem?* New York: Putnam's Sons, 1898, pp. 227-248. Merrill C. Tenney, *New Testament Times,* Grand Rapids: Eerdmans, 1965, pp. 134-138.

W. M. D.

Tomb of Cyrus. ORINST

CYRUS (sī'rŭs). Son of the earlier Cambyses, of the royal race of the Achaemenians, and the founder of the Persian Empire. Isaiah prophesied of him as anointed of God to conquer kings and fortified places and to set the Jews free from captivity (Isa 44:28; 45:1-14). Under his liberal policies the Jews were permitted to return from the Exile (Ezr 1).

The history of Cyrus is complicated by early accretions of fable and romance. Even Herodotus, who lived within a century of the time of Cyrus, refers to these embellishments. Ctesias, a half century later, lived in the Persian court and drew from the Persian archives, but these were also affected. Xenophon's *Cyropaedeia* is thought to be more of a historical romance than accurate biography. The best sources are thought to be Herodotus, Persian and Babylonian chronicles, and inscriptions.

Cyrus was probably named for his grandfather, who had also been king of Anshan, capital city of Elam. The name Cyrus, being Elamite, is of doubtful meaning.

Herodotus (i.107 ff.) gives a stirring account of one version of Cyrus' origin. The wealthy Median king Astyages gave his daughter Mandane in marriage to Cambyses, a Persian ruler, to prevent any danger of her offspring being a rival to the Median throne. Persia was then a relatively poor and perhaps dependent land. It was also at a safe distance. Because of a dream, the Median king plotted to destroy the male offspring of this union. A shepherd, however, saved and reared Cyrus. As he became an extraordinary lad, he was discovered and returned to his parents and grandfather. Then he had access to the skills and resources of Median royalty and yet maintained the Persian hardy spirit. Friends and admirers in both countries paved the way for his sudden rise to power, as did the discontent of the people under the tyranny and injustice of the Median ruler.

Whether or not these events and relationships were all reported accurately, Cyrus first succeeded his father on the throne of the province of Anshan (559 B.C.), and then suddenly rose to the combined throne of Medo-Persia, aided by mass defection from the Median army. This was about 550 B.C., while Nabonidus reigned in Babylon. Cyrus took Ecbatana and carried its spoil to his own city.

Croesus, king of fabulous Lydia in Asia Minor, alarmed and covetous, made powerful Gr. alliances and crossed the Halys River to invade the dominions of the Medes and Persians. Cyrus overwhelmed him, conquered Lydia, and made Croesus a captive.

The great test was Babylon with its massive walls and its prestige of centuries of rule. It was particularly impregnable because of the vast area within the walls where food could be stored and even produced, because of its great wealth, and because of the Euphrates River which flowed through the city. Cyrus is said to have stationed a portion of his army at the place where the river entered the city and another where it left. The rest of the army deepened the canals in the Euphrates Valley and diverted the river temporarily. In October, 539 B.C., the army marched in by way of the riverbed under the leadership of Gobryas (Akkad. Ugbaru), who died a week later (ANET, p. 306).

The invasion seems to have been without battle. Dissatisfied with the reign of Nabonidus and Belshazzar, the people sued for peace and were granted it. They were governed by an official also named Gobryas (but Akkad. Gubaru; ANET, p. 306 does not clarify this distinction), whom Cyrus appointed vice-regent of the city. He is probably to be identified with Darius the Mede (Dan 5:31; 6; 9:1; see John C. Whitcomb, Jr., *Darius the Mede*).

With the throne of Babylon came the decision of the fate of the Heb. captives. In keeping with the generous policy of restoring people to their own lands and religion, Cyrus permitted the Jews to return from exile. Another reason may have been to create a buffer nation between Egypt and the Persian satraps.

The manner of Cyrus' death is uncertain. He crossed the Araxes to the N and attacked the Massagetae. His army was destroyed by the Scythians. It is thought that he lost his life in the battle. After a reign of 29 years, he was succeeded by his son Cambyses, in 530 B.C.

Cyrus is thought by most commentators to have been the subject of Daniel's vision of the ram with two horns, representing the Median and the Persian divisions of his empire (Dan 8:3-4, 20). *See* Babylon; Darius Hystaspes; Persia.

Bibliography. Ronald E. Manahan, "The Cyrus Notations of Deutero-Isaiah," *Grace Journal,* XI (Fall, 1970), 22-33. A. T. Olmstead, *The History of the Persian Empire,* Chicago: Univ. of Chicago Press, 1948, pp. 34-58.

W. T. D.

D

DABAREH (dăb'á-rĕ). A variant of Daberath (*q.v.*) found in Josh 21:28.

DABBASHETH (dăb'á-shĕth). A hill town (the name means "hump") of uncertain location on the border of Zebulun (Josh 19:11).

DABERATH (dăb'á-răth). Variant of Dabareh in Josh 21:28.

A Levitical town lying on the boundary line of Zebulun (Josh 19:12) and Issachar (Josh 21:28, RSV), probably modern Deburiyeh, at the foot of Mount Tabor. A strategic location, it may have been the site of the defeat of Sisera by Barak (Jud 4:14-22).

DAGGER. A short sword. Where the KJV translates the word "dagger," later versions translate it "sword" (Jud 3:16). Archaeologists arbitrarily distinguish swords from daggers by length, 40 centimeters (*c.* 16 inches) being the dividing point. Swords or daggers in biblical time were basically of two types: the straight and the bent (sickle). *See* Sword; Armor.

DAGON. *See* Gods, False.

DAILY. Pertaining to that which is done, occurs, or issues each day. Israelites counted their day from one sunset to the next (Ex 12:18; Lev 23:32). But the Israelites also understood by "day" the time during which the earth was lighted up in contrast to night (Gen 1:5; Dan 8:14).

For the expression "daily bread" in the Lord's Prayer, *see* Food: Bread.

DAILY OFFERING OR SACRIFICE. *See* Sacrifice.

DALAIAH (dá-lā'yà). Found only in I Chr 3:24 (KJV). This name is more correctly spelled Delaiah (*q.v.*).

DALE, THE KING'S. A valley in the immediate vicinity of Jerusalem, perhaps at the head of the Valley of Hinnom. It was the site where Abram after his victory over Chedorlaomer was met by the king of Sodom and by Melchizedek, king of

Damascus. HFV

Salem (Gen 14:17-18). It was the location of Absalom's memorial (II Sam 18:18). The latter reference calls it the King's Valley (RSV). According to Gen 14:17 it was in ancient times called the Valley of Shaveh.

DALETH (dä'lĭth).The fourth letter of the Heb. alphabet ("d" in English). *See* Alphabet. As such it is used in Ps 119 to designate the fourth part, each verse of which begins with this letter. The Heb. word *daleth* means "door," and this was the appearance of a daleth in its earliest pictographic form.

DALMANUTHA (dăl-ma-nū'thá). The place of landing by Jesus and His disciples after feeding the 4,000 (Mk 8:10). The location is unknown but thought to be on the W shore of the Sea of Galilee, somewhere S of the plain of Gennesaret. Probably the same as Magdala (Magadan, ASV) in Mt 15:39. Sometimes it is identified with the home of Mary Magdalene, but without evidence.

DALMATIA (dăl-mā'shĭ-à). A name originally applied to the land of Dalmatae, a warlike Illyrian tribe. Later, the southern portion of the province of Illyricum was called by this name. Finally it was applied to the entire province lying on the E shore of the Adriatic. Paul records in II Tim 4:10 the departure of Titus to this province. It is unknown whether churches had been established there before his visit.

DALPHON (dăl'fŏn).The second of the ten sons of Haman who were put to death by the Jews after the triumph of Queen Esther (Est 9:6-13).

DAM. The ordinary word for female parent. Heb. law prohibited the destruction of the dam on her nest and the young birds at the same time (Deut 22:6-7). An animal was not to be taken for slaughter before it had been seven days with its mother (Ex 22:30; Lev 22:27).

DAMAGES. The usual translation of a Heb. term expressing any affliction, or loss of value, or permanent injury to persons or things (Ezr 4:22).

DAMARIS (dăm'à-rĭs). A woman of Athens who, with Dionysius the Areopagite and certain others, was converted when Paul spoke on Mars Hill (Acts 17:34). The singling out of her name with that of Dionysius may indicate some personal or social distinction (cf. Acts 13:50; 17:12).

DAMASCENES (dăm'à-sēns'). The inhabitants of Damascus (*q.v.*) under Aretas, the Arabian or Nabataean ruler, were called Damascenes (II Cor 11:32).

DAMASCUS (dà-măs'kŭs). Damascus (Gr. *damaskos*, Heb. *dammaśeq*, Aram. *darmeśeq*, I Chr 18:5; II Chr 28:5), the chief city of ancient Aram (Isa 7:8), has had a long history reaching back to prehistoric times. The *'Aram Darmeseq* of I Chr 18:6 corresponds to modern Damascus. The city was known to the Egyptians as Apum according to the Saqqara Execration texts (19th cen. B.C.) and appears in both the records of Thutmose III (15th cen.) and the Amarna letters (14th cen.). The Assyrians knew it as *Dimashqi* and *Bît-Haza'-ili* (House of Hazael). It is well watered by the clear rivers called Abana and Pharpar (II Kgs 5:12).

It is first mentioned in the OT in Gen 14:15 as the scene of Abraham's rescue of Lot. His servant Eliezer may have come from there (Gen 15:2; see William F. Albright, *Yahweh and the Gods of Canaan*, Garden City: Doubleday, 1968, pp. 65 f., n. 30). By the time of David, Damascus was an influential city-state and the focal point of various coalitions. When the town sent troops to help Hadadezer of Zobah against David, David captured the city and placed a garrison there (II Sam 8:5-6; I Chr 18:5).

In Solomon's day Rezon of Zobah captured Damascus and made it the capital of the city-state of Aram (Syria, I Kgs 11:24). His successors Hezion and Tabrimmon strengthened the city. Asa of Judah made an alliance with Ben-hadad, son of Tabrimmon, when Baasha of Israel attacked him (I Kgs 15:18-19). Either the same king or Ben-hadad II (Akkad. Adad-idri) restored to Ahab cities which had been taken from Israel, and gave Ahab concessions in Damascus, perhaps to secure Ahab's help in an anti-Assyrian coalition (I Kgs 20:34). At the great battle of Qarqar in 853 B.C., Ahab of Israel fought beside Ben-hadad and ten other kings against Assyria. Some time later Ahab was killed fighting the "king of Aram" (I Kgs 22:29-36).

The prophet Elijah was sent by God to anoint a certain Hazael as the future king of Aram (I Kgs 19:15). Later, Elisha, who had healed the general Naaman (II Kgs 5), went to

Damascus and the sick Ben-hadad sent Hazael to inquire whether he would recover. Hazael slew the old king and ruled in his place (II Kgs 8:15). In the years that followed Hazael invaded Israelite lands. When Joram of Israel opposed him he was wounded in battle (II Kgs 8:29).

For some years prior to 800 B.C. Damascus suffered from repeated Assyrian attacks. In 843 B.C. Shalmaneser III besieged Hazael in Damascus. He withstood the siege but suffered badly. When the Assyrians withdrew, Hazael attacked Israel again and occupied all of Transjordan (II Kgs 10:32 f.). He even reached the coastlands of Judah in the days of Joash of Judah (II Kgs 12:17; 835–796 B.C.). In 805–803 B.C. the Assyrians under Adadnirari III attacked Hazael, and again in 797 B.C. King Shalmaneser IV attacked Damascus. These repeated assaults so weakened the city that J(eh)oash of Israel was able to recover the towns Israel had lost to Hazael (II Kgs 13:25).

During the years that followed, Aramaean states were at war with one another while Assyria was occupied elsewhere. Then in 739 B.C. both Menahem of Israel and Rezin of Damascus became vassals of Tiglath-pileser of Assyria. They broke free for a time and sought to

East Gate, Damascus. HFV

form an anti-Assyrian coalition. When Judah refused to join, Pekah of Israel and Rezin of Damascus marched on Judah (II Kgs 16:5; II Chr 28:5–8). Ahaz appealed to Tiglath-pileser for help and the latter launched a series of attacks in 734–732 B.C. which ended in the death of Rezin, the fall of Damascus in 732 B.C., and in the loss of areas of Israelite territory (II Kgs 15:29; 16:9 f.). This result had been foretold by Amos (1:4 f.) and Isaiah (8:4; 17:1).

At that time Ahaz of Judah was summoned to Damascus to pay homage and was required to place a copy of a pagan altar which was there in the temple in Jerusalem (II Kgs 16:10–12; II Chr 28:23). Thereafter, Damascus was a town in the Assyrian province of Hamath and lost all political significance, although it was a center of trade (Ezk 27:18). It was regarded as the ideal border of Israel (Ezk 47:16 ff.; 48:1; Zech 9:1 f.). See Aram, Aramaeans.

Under the Seleucid rulers Damascus was only the second city of Syria. In 111 B.C. Antiochus IX made it the capital of Coele-Syria. The Nabataeans took it in 85 B.C. but lost it to Tigranes the Armenian king. Finally it became a Roman town from 64 B.C. to A.D. 33. It was later governed by an ethnarch of Aretas IV (9

"Street Called Straight," Damascus. HFV

B.C.–A.D. 40), the Nabataean king (II Cor 11:32). Paul visited synagogues here after his conversion (Acts 9:8–25), but had to escape over the wall of the city when troubles arose (Acts 9:25; II Cor 11:33). He returned later after a period in Arabia (Gal 1:17).

The present East Gate of the old city probably dates from Roman times. It consisted of three archways, but two of the three arches are now walled up. The street which goes W from this gate becomes one of the bazaars of the city and is still called "Straight Street"; it probably preserves the line of "the street called Straight" of Acts 9:11.

In the early part of the Christian era Damascus was secondary to Antioch. It fell to the Arabs finally in A.D. 634.

Bibliography. A. Dupont-Sommer, *Les Araméens*, Paris: A. Maisonneuve, 1949. A. Jepsen, "Israel und Damaskus," *Archiv für Orientforschung*, XIV (1942), 153–172. Merrill F. Unger, *Israel and the Aramaeans of Damascus*, Grand Rapids: Zondervan, 1957. WHG, pp. 219, 234–239, 255–257.

J. A. T.

DAMMIM (dăm'ĭm). *See* Ephes-dammim; Pasdammim.

DAMNATION. The condition of being sentenced to eternal punishment is the idea underlying the KJV translation "damnation" of the three different Gr. words: *apōleia* in II Pet 2:1; *krima* in Mk 12:40; Rom 3:8, and elsewhere; and *krisis* in Mt 23:33; Jn 5:29. This meaning has come to be so fully identified with the word that damnation is almost universally associated with condemnation to future punishment. The root meaning of *krima* and *krisis* is simply "condemnation" or "judgment"; that of *apōleia* is "destruction." The idea of unending judgment is not in these words themselves, but is sometimes provided in the Scriptures by the modifying adjectives or prepositional phrases; e.g., Mt 23:33, RSV, "the judgment of hell [Gehenna]." In certain places, particularly I Cor 11:29, it is a mistake to imply eternal condemnation by translating *krima* as damnation, for the context indicates clearly that the apostle is speaking of penal judgment in this life which falls upon those who partake of communion in an unworthy or hypocritical manner. *See* Judgment.

R. G. R.

DAN (dăn), **DANITES** (dăn'īts). One of the sons of Jacob by Bilhah (Gen 30:5–6). He had an only son, Hushim (Gen 46:23) or Shuham (Num 26:42). His father Jacob's final prophetic benediction was figurative of Dan and his descendants. "Dan shall judge his people, as one of the tribes of Israel. Dan shall be a serpent in

the way, an adder in the path, that biteth the horse's heels, so that his rider falleth backward" (Gen 49:16–17, ASV). This is generally interpreted to mean that Dan would deal with the foes of Israel on a par with the other tribes. Moses referred to Dan as a lion's whelp that leapeth forth from Bashan (Deut 33:22).

The tribe of Dan was assigned an area in the central part of Canaan, facing the Mediterranean Sea. It had a common border on the N with Ephraim, on the E with Benjamin, and on the S with Judah. Its territory contained towns of Zorah, Aijalon, Ekron, Eltekeh, and the borders of Joppa (Josh 19:40–46; 21:5, 23–24; cf. Jud 5:17).

It is apparent that the Amorites restricted Dan's effort to possess the allotted area. Being pressed for extra living space the Danites sent spies to the extreme northern border of Palestine, near the southern slopes of Mount Hermon, to look for new territory. They found a desirable place in the vicinity of Laish and with an expedition of soldiers they seized the territory. Then they slew the inhabitants and rebuilt the city under the name of Dan (Josh 19:47; Jud 18).

The expression "from Dan to Beer-sheba" is sometimes used to denote the northern and southern boundaries of the inhabited area of the Promised Land (Jud 20:1; II Sam 3:10, etc.).

H. A. Han.

DAN, CAMP OF (Mahaneh-dan, ASV, RSV). A locality W of Kiriath-jearim in the SW part of Palestine. In the story of Samson (Jud 13:25), it is a stretch of territory where the tribe of Dan, the last of the Israelite groups to attempt to settle in Canaan, had temporary encampments, but were not able to establish any permanent settlements because of the Philistines. In the Micah story (Jud 18:11–12, RSV marg.), however, the name is given to the place where the warriors of Dan encamped on their march to the N. It is possible, therefore, that the same name was applied both to a place and a territorial area.

See Mahaneh-dan.

DAN, CITY OF. A town near the sources of the Jordan River, commonly identified with Tell el-Qadi because the Arabic name means "mound of the judge," which corresponds with Dan, "judge" (see AASOR, VI, 16). Proverbially, it was the northernmost point in Israel, as exemplified by the expression "from Dan to Beer-sheba" and its variations (Jud 20:1; I Chr 21:2, *et al.*).

The original name of the town was Laish or Leshem (Josh 19:47; Jud 18:7). Under this name (written *rws* in Egyp.) it appears before Hazor in Thutmose III's list of conquered towns (No. 31), and is found in the second group of Egyptian Execration texts from *c.* 1825 B.C. A Mari tablet, dated *c.* 1780–1760

418

The site of ancient Dan. JR

B.C., lists a tin shipment sent from the Euphrates city to the ruler of Laish with the Hurrian name of Wari-taldu (A. Malamat, "Syro-Palestinian Destinations in a Mari Tin Inventory," IEJ, XXI [1971], 35 f.). The Danites captured it and renamed it after their tribe (Josh 19:47; Jud 18).

In pursuit of the Mesopotamian invaders, Abraham had trekked as far as Dan (Gen 14:14). Some have suggested that this was another place, known from II Sam 24:6 as Dan-jaan. However, it seems more likely that Dan-jaan is a textual corruption which should be corrected on the basis of I Kgs 15:20 to read "Dan and Ijon."

The town had been known for its political and cultural association with Sidon (Jud 18:7, 28). After its conquest by the Danites, Jonathan, the son of Gershom, and his descendants served as priests until "the captivity of the land" (Jud 18:30). Jeroboam I established the cult of his golden calf there (I Kgs 12:28–30), which continued to thrive even after the reform of Jehu (II Kgs 10:29; Amos 8:14). Ben-hadad conquered it along with other towns in the region at the urging of Asa, king of Judah, who needed a diversionary action to help him escape the pressure of his rival Baasha, king of Israel (I Kgs 15:20; II Chr 16:4). A bowl with an Aramaic inscription "belonging to the butchers (or cooks)" was found at Dan and points to the Aramaean occupation of Ben-hadad I (PEQ, C [1968], 42 ff.).

In 1966 the Israeli Department of Antiquities began to probe the 65-foot-high mound. It was settled during the Early Bronze Age, and its chief fortifications were built in Hyksos times. All occupation in later periods was on the mound itself, except for an Iron Age II monumental building on the slope of the rampart and attached to the city wall. A thick layer of ash indicated destruction of the Late Bronze Age city, confirming the account in Jud 18:27 of the capture and burning of Laish by the Danites (IEJ, XVI, 144 f.).

In the following three seasons the city gateway on the E side of the mound was excavated, the largest ever discovered in Palestine. Probably built during the reign of Jeroboam I, the gate had a processional way of paved stones leading from the approaches of the mound and up into the city. Near the entrance were a 15-foot-long bench against the outer wall of one of the gate towers and a canopy-like structure with columns topped by decorated capitals at its four corners. Here the king may have sat in state (cf. I Kgs 22:10) during visits to Dan, or it may have served as the base for a statue with cultic significance. Near the NW corner of the mound the remains of the high place installation of Jeroboam possibly have been uncovered. Fine masonry using headers and stretchers enclosed the structure. It and the pottery, including five seven-spouted oil lamps, are typical of the period of the Israelite monarchy (IEJ, XIX [1969], 121 ff., 239 ff.).

A. F. R.

DANCE. The English word, in one form or another, occurs 25 or 30 times, mostly in the OT, and translates several Heb. and two Gr. words. One Heb. word means "to whirl, writhe"; another, "to spring, skip about"; and still another, "to revolve, whirl about." Of the two Gr. words, the more common suggests a "regular motion"; the other, "singing" (Lk 15:25), the word from which we get our English word "chorus."

There are various types of dancing in the Bible, usually by women: that representing joy, that representing worship, and that which might be classified as amusement. Examples of dancing for joy would include that referred to in Jud 11:34, where Jephthah's daughter met him, after his great victory over the children of Ammon, "with timbrels and with dances." Also included would be the rejoicing of the women at the victory of David over Goliath, when they sang and danced with tabrets (I Sam 18:6; 21:11; 29:5).

Examples of dancing in connection with worship are found in Ex 15:20; 32:19; Jud 21:19–23; II Sam 6:14–16. In the first of these references Miriam and other women are celebrating "with timbrels and with dances" the safe crossing of the Red Sea by Israel. In the second, the people are dancing, naked, before the molten calf of gold Aaron had fashioned for them to worship. In the third, the daughters of Shiloh, where the tabernacle and ark were located, go out into the fields to dance. Presumably this was a religious dance. In the last instance, King David, having brought the ark up to Jerusalem and being deeply stirred over this event, leaps and dances "before the Lord." The Psalms, too, refer occasionally to dancing (30:11; 149:3; 150:4).

The only example in the Bible of dancing as an amusement seems to be that of the daughter of Herodias (Mt 14:6; Mk 6:22). This was a prelude to the murder of John the Baptist. The dance as we know it today, performed by pairs of persons of opposite sex, seems to be entirely unknown in the Bible.

Acrobatic dancers pictured in the tomb of Mereruka, Sakkara, Egypt. LL

There are two other references to dancing in the NT which deserve notice. One is our Lord's comment in Mt 11:17 and Lk 7:32 concerning the people's rejection of John the Baptist and of Himself. He compares this to the refusal of children in the marketplace to respond either to gay music or to mournful. He says, "We have piped unto you, and ye have not danced; we have mourned unto you, and ye have not lamented." This and Job 21:11 f. indicate it was rather commonplace for children, at least, to dance for joy in biblical times. Probably this has always been true. The other instance is of similar import. In Lk 15:25, the elder son hears music and dancing in the house after his younger brother's return—again an example of dancing for joy.

Dancing in the Bible, therefore, except in the case of Herodias' daughter, seems to have little relationship to the sensual, but is rather associated ordinarily with joy, either because of circumstances or because of gratitude for the Lord's blessing.

See Games.

J. A. S.

DANIEL (dan'yăl). Daniel, an OT hero, is the main character of the book of Daniel. Of royal or noble birth (Dan 1:3), Daniel was taken captive to Babylonia by Nebuchadnezzar in 605 B.C., with other Jewish youths of like ability and attainments (1:1–7), where he spent the remainder of his life and gained distinction as statesman and prophet.

Daniel was instructed in the learning and language of the Chaldeans (1:4). He and his friends Hananiah, Mishael, and Azariah were offered the lavish menu of the heathen court. Since the royal fare was against the law of Moses and would render him less efficient, Daniel "purposed in his heart that he would not defile himself with the portion of the king's meat, nor with the wine" (1:8). At their request Daniel and his friends were allowed to eat vegetables and drink water for ten days and were then in better health than the other trainees. The supervisors discerned that these Jewish youths possessed great skill and wisdom. At the end of their training period they were recognized by the king as superior to all the other wise men at the royal court.

By divine revelation Daniel told the king his forgotten dream and its interpretation which included the doom of Nebuchadnezzar's kingdom (Dan 2). The king worshiped Daniel, honored his God, rewarded him with costly gifts (2:46–47), and "made him ruler over the whole province of Babylon, and . . . over all the wise men of Babylon" (2:48). Later, Daniel interpreted another of Nebuchadnezzar's dreams, telling the king that for a time he would lose his throne but would be restored to it after he had become thoroughly humbled (Dan 4).

God revealed through Daniel certain aspects of the messianic kingdom having to do with the course of history and the eternal age. *See* Daniel, Book of.

For more than 20 years (561–539 B.C.) nothing is recorded of Daniel, and he seems to have lost his position and fallen out of public favor. Then at the feast of Belshazzar (*q.v.*), coregent with his father Nabonidus, the queen (probably Belshazzar's mother, daughter of Nebuchadnezzar) remembered Daniel, who when sent for interpreted the strange handwriting on the wall (Dan 5:10–28). In accordance with his interpretation, Babylon fell that night (539 B.C.) to Darius the Mede. Though secular history at present does not know of a Darius the Mede, he is identified by competent scholars with Gobryas, governor of Babylon under Cyrus (John C. Whitcomb, *Darius the Mede*). Darius recognized Daniel's ability, made him chief of a board of three presidents, and "thought to set him over the whole realm" (Dan 6:3).

In religion Daniel still manifested the same uncompromising faithfulness. He defied Darius' decree and prayed to God rather than to the

Babylon as Daniel would have known it. The ziggurat stands in the foreground and Procession Street runs up the center of the picture. ORINST

king. He was cast into the den of lions, but was miraculously delivered (Dan 6). Daniel never compromised his convictions nor wavered in his loyalty to God. He lived until the third year of Cyrus (536 B.C.) being perhaps 90 years of age and still active.

Ezekiel referred to Daniel as a man of high wisdom and piety (Ezk 28:3) and placed Daniel alongside such worthies as Noah and Job (Ezk 14:14, 20), men renowned for their righteousness. Jesus referred to Daniel at least once (Mt 24:15).

C. J. H.

DANIEL, BOOK OF

General Characteristics

The book of Daniel occupies a unique place in the OT. It sets forth marvelous predictions of the coming of the Messiah and the kingdom of God. In the English Bible it is among the major prophets after Ezekiel; in the Heb. Bible it is among the Writings, the third division of the Jewish canon. In the Heb. Bible, Hebrew in Dan 1:1 — 2:4a and 8:1 — 12:13 points up Israel's significant role in international developments; Aramaic in Dan 2:4b — 7:28 indicates the order of succession, character, and destiny of heathen nations.

Outline

I. History of Daniel, chaps. 1 – 6
  A. Daniel's youth and education, chap. 1
  B. Nebuchadnezzar's image-dream, chap. 2
  C. Faithfulness of Daniel's companions, 'chap. 3
  D. Nebuchadnezzar's tree-dream, chap. 4
  E. Belshazzar's feast, chap. 5
  F. Daniel in the den of lions, chap. 6
II. Visions of Daniel, chaps. 7 – 12
  A. Vision of the four beasts, chap. 7
  B. Vision of the ram and the he-goat, chap. 8
  C. Daniel's prayer; vision of the 70 weeks, chap. 9
  D. Daniel's last vision, chaps. 10 – 12
    1. The angel appears to encourage Daniel and predict the future, chap. 10
    2. Persia and Greece; struggles between Ptolemies and Seleucids; oppression under Antiochus Epiphanes, chap. 11
    3. The Messianic Age and its consummation, chap. 12

Date and Authorship

From ancient times Jewish-Christian tradition has declared that Daniel wrote the book during the Exile in the 6th cen. B.C. That the men of the Great Synagogue wrote the book of Daniel during the time of Ezra and Nehemiah, according to the Talmud, means that they copied it. The book purports to be serious history and claims that Daniel gave forth the

prophecies contained therein. Jesus refers to "the abomination of desolation, spoken of by Daniel the prophet" in Mt 24:15.

The traditional view as to date and authorship has been seriously questioned. Porphyry, a Platonic philosopher of the 3rd cen. after Christ, held that the book was written in the 2nd cen. B.C. Many modern scholars hold that a pious scribe used the figure of Daniel, an ancient sage, to encourage loyalty to God and maintain enthusiasm for the national cause during the Maccabean revolt of 167– 164 B.C. against the Seleucid ruler Antiochus Epiphanes. In this view the book of Daniel consists of spurious stories of Daniel in the Babylonian courts during the Exilic period and of visions ascribed to Daniel which traversed Israel's history from this period to the writer's own time, concentrating on the years of persecution and their consummation in the inauguration of the kingdom of God.

Despite prevalent critical opinion against the 6th cen. dating of the book, a gradual trend is discernible toward earlier dating. The discovery of Belshazzar's (q.v.) name on Babylonian clay tablets, and the probable identification by Whitcomb of Darius the Mede (q.v.) with Gubaru (Gr. Gobryas) have gone far to vindicate the 6th cen. historical accuracy of the book. Alleged linguistic and exegetical problems have been more than adequately answered by conservative scholars (SOTI, pp. 368 ff.). Qumran fragments of the book of Daniel (150 B.C.) are also weighing heavily in pushing back the date of the authorship of the book toward the conservative date.

Interpretations

Three principal competing interpretations of the book of Daniel are noted.

1. The first view says the book was written to encourage the Jews to constancy under the persecutions of Antiochus Epiphanes. It deals with history no later than 164 B.C. The fourth kingdom of chaps. 2 and 7 is Greece with primary reference to Antiochus as the "little horn" of 7:8, parallel with 8:9. The anointed one cut off (9:26) probably refers to the murder of the high priest Onias III, c. 170 B.C. (II Macc 4:33– 38). The one who desolates in 9:27 is Antiochus, and the desolating abomination refers to his desecration of the altar in Jerusalem in 167 B.C. in the midst of Daniel's seventieth week (chap. 9). Sacrifices ceased, but were reinstituted in 164 B.C., the end of the seventieth week. The promise in chap. 12 is that God will vindicate the faithful and raise the martyrs from the dead to enjoy the blessings of the everlasting kingdom.

2. The second interpretation understands that the death of Christ occurred in the midst of the seventieth week, at which time Jewish sacrifices ceased and a covenant prevailed for many. Consequent upon the cutting off of the Messiah, a desolator appears over the temple which, now having become an abomination, is

destroyed. The fourth kingdom of chaps. 2 and 7 is Rome; the ten horns are ten early Roman emperors; the "little horn" is Titus Vespasianus who destroyed Jerusalem in A.D. 70. The emphasis in this interpretation is upon the messiah who, in being cut off, brought in eternal righteousness and made reconciliation for iniquity.

3. The third interpretation holds that Daniel's seventieth week is still future. The present Church Age was hidden from the OT prophets, but may be accounted for as a "parenthesis." The prophecy that "an anointed one shall be cut off" (9:26, RSV) looks to the death of Christ at the end of the sixty-ninth week. Israel will receive forgiveness for not having recognized their Messiah when "the times of the Gentiles" end and the Son of Man appears a second time. The second half of the seventieth week is identical with the Great Tribulation of Mt 24:15-28. The fourth kingdom of Dan 2 and 7 is Rome. The "little horn" is the Antichrist, the great leader of the revived Roman Empire who will appear at the end of the age in the midst of the seventieth week. At the end of the seventieth week the millennial reign begins.

See Nebuchadnezzar.

Bibliography. G. L. Archer, "The Aramaic of the 'Genesis Apocryphon' Compared with the Aramaic of Daniel," NPOT, pp. 160-169. R. D. Culver, *Daniel and the Latter Days,* New York: Revell, 1954. A. C. Gaebelein, *The Prophet Daniel,* New York: "Our Hope," 1911. E. W. Heaton, *The Book of Daniel,* London: SCM, 1956. G. R. King, *Daniel,* Grand Rapids: Eerdmans, 1966. H. Leupold, *Exposition of Daniel,* Columbus: Wartburg Press, 1949. D. J. Wiseman, *et al., Notes on Some Problems in the Book of Daniel,* London: Tyndale Press, 1965. E. M. Yamauchi, "The Greek Words in Daniel in the Light of Greek Influence in the Near East," NPOT, pp. 170-200. E. J. Young, *The Prophecy of Daniel,* Grand Rapids: Eerdmans, 1953.

C. J. H.

DAN-JAAN. *See* Dan, City of.

DANNAH (dăn'ȧ). A town in the mountain of Judah SW of Hebron, perhaps associated with modern Idnah (Josh 15:49).

DARA (där'ȧ). Found in I Chr 2:6. The preferred spelling is Darda (*q.v.*).

DARDA (där'dȧ). One of four men, sons of Mahol ("members of the orchestral guild," IDB), noted for wisdom, excelled only by Solomon (I Kgs 4:31). In I Chr 2:6 he is mentioned as a son of Zerah, son of Judah, and is called Dara (*q.v.*).

DARIC. A gold Persian coin worth about five dollars, known to the Jews after their return from Babylon (Ezr 8:27, RSV). The name is presumably derived from "Darius," the Persian king (522-486 B.C.), and is rendered "dram" in KJV. It is the first coin mentioned in the Bible. The writer in I Chr 29:7 may have been converting a monetary value of David's period to the equivalent amount in darics of his own day. The references in Ezr 2:69 and Neh 7:70-72 (RSV) to gold darics during the reign of King Cyrus (550-530 B.C.) prior to Darius' time may be similarly explained. *See* Weights, Measures, and Coins.

DARIUS (I) HYSTASPES (dȧ-ri'ŭs hĭs-tăs'pēz). The name in Old Persian was *Darayavaush;* in Babylonian, *Da-ri-ya-muš;* in Gr., *Dareios.* He is also known as Darius the Great.

Darius was a descendant through his father Hystaspes of Ariaramnes, a descendant of Hakhmanish (Achaemenae) the ancestor of Cyrus, but not of the royal succession. Darius was born in 550 B.C. and ruled from 522 to 486 B.C.

In his Behistun inscription Darius claims eight kings as his ancestors, but he came to the throne only by pressing energetically the claim of the elder side of Hakhmanish. At Cambyses'

Darius I enthroned with his son Xerxes standing behind him; from the treasury at Persepolis.
ORINST

Tomb of Darius, Naksh-i-Rustam. ORINST

death in 522 B.C., revolt flared up over the empire with contestants in Susiana, Babylon, Media, Sagartia and Margiana. By alliance with the heads of six leading families of Persia and starting with a surprise attack, Darius slew Gaumata, who pretended to be Bardiya (Gr. *Smerdis,* Cambyses' murdered brother), in 521 B.C., and by 519 B.C. had suppressed all rebellions.

Darius extended his empire to the Caucasus and by 513 B.C. marched beyond the Bosphorus and crossed the Danube. Complete Persian control over the area, however, was prevented by Scythian attacks. Though having added Macedonia to his realm, he failed to add Greece when his host was defeated at Marathon, 490 B.C. He recorded his exploits in a trilingual inscription high on the cliff near Behistun (Bisitun), along the main trade route between Ecbatana (Achmetha, Ezr 6:2) and Babylon.

Darius then proceeded to reorganize the empire, putting it under a bureaucracy centered in himself, removing many of the native officials installed by Cyrus. He fixed coinage and in-

troduced the daric. In the interests of E-W trade, he caused a canal to be dug from the Nile to the Red Sea and sent ships through it, according to hieroglyphic inscriptions.

He is the Darius mentioned by Haggai the prophet. In his second year, he affirmed Cyrus' benevolent policy respecting the Jews against the oppressions of Tatnai, governor of Samaria (Ezr 4:5; 6:6). On the request of the Jews, he ordered a search of the records, and the decree to restore the Jerusalem temple was found at Ecbatana (modern Hamadan) which he reaffirmed. To it he added the command that money and cattle be furnished to the project, forbidding at the same time further interference with it. The temple was completed in his sixth year, 515 B.C. (Ezr 6:1–15).

See Cyrus; Persia; Haggai.

H. G. S.

DARIUS THE MEDE. The ruler of "the realm of the Chaldeans" (Dan 9:1) under Cyrus (Dan 6:28), immediately following the death of Belshazzar (Dan 5:30–31). He is best remembered for his decree which resulted in the prophet Daniel's being cast into a den of lions (6:7–28). He is not to be confused with the later Persian monarch, Darius I Hystaspes (521–486 B.C.), for he was of Median extraction ("of the seed of the Medes," Dan 9:1), and his father's name was Ahasuerus (the Heb. equivalent of Xerxes; cf. the name of the son of Darius I; cf. Est 1:1). Darius the Mede was born in the year 601/600 B.C., for at the fall of Babylon (Oct., 539 B.C.), he was sixty-two (Dan 5:31).

One of the cardinal doctrines of negative criticism has been that the book of Daniel was authored by an unknown writer of the Maccabean age (*c.* 165 B.C.), who mistakenly thought that an independent Median kingdom ruled by Darius the Mede followed the fall of Babylon and preceded the rise of Persia under Cyrus. But Darius the Mede is not depicted in the book as a universal monarch. In fact, his subordinate position is clearly implied in the statement that he "was made king over the realm of the Chaldeans" (Dan 9:1). Also, the facts that Belshazzar's kingdom was "given to the Medes and *Persians*" (5:28); that Darius the Mede *received* the kingdom (5:31, ASV, RSV, NASB, JerusB); and that Darius found himself helpless to alter the "law of the Medes and *Persians*" (6:15) render the critical view untenable.

The publication during the early decades of this century of additional cuneiform texts from this period has enabled Bible students to gain a much clearer understanding of the fall of Babylon in 539 B.C. It seems quite probable that Darius the Mede was none other than Gubaru, the governor under Cyrus who appointed subgovernors in Babylon immediately after its conquest ("Nabonidus Chronicle," ANET, p. 306; cf. Dan 6:1). This same Gubaru (not to be confused with Ugbaru, governor of Gutium, the general under Cyrus who conquered Babylon and died three weeks later, according to the

Nabonidus Chronicle) is frequently mentioned in cuneiform documents during the following 14 years as governor of Babylon and the Region-Beyond-the-River (i.e., the entire Fertile Crescent). Gubaru thus ruled over the vast and populous territories of Babylonia, Syria, Phoenicia, and Palestine, and his name was a final warning to criminals throughout this area (cf. John C. Whitcomb, *Darius the Mede*, Presbyterian and Reformed Pub. Co., 1963, pp. 10–24). The fact that he is called "king" in Dan 6 is not an inaccuracy, even though he was a subordinate of Cyrus. Similarly, Belshazzar was called "king," even though he was the second ruler of the kingdom under Nabonidus (Dan 5:29).

The book of Daniel gives more information concerning the personal background of Darius the Mede than of Belshazzar or even of Nebuchadnezzar. He is the only monarch in the book whose age, parentage, and nationality are recorded. Although he was a subordinate ruler like Belshazzar, it is evident that he ruled Babylonia with far greater zeal and efficiency than did his profligate predecessor.

J. C. W.

DARIUS THE PERSIAN. Mentioned once in the OT in Neh 12:22. He was either Nothus, Darius II (423–404 B.C.) or Codomannus, Darius III (336–331 B.C.). Darius II authorized the keeping of the Passover by the Jews at Elephantine in Egypt (ANET, p. 491). Darius III was the king whose empire Alexander the Great conquered. The evidence for the identification rests on the fact that the priests Johanan and Jaddua are mentioned in the same verse. A Johanan appears as the high priest at Jerusalem in an Elephantine papyrus dated 407 B.C. (ANET, p. 492), which would favor an identification with Darius II. On the other hand, a Jaddua is mentioned as the high priest who greeted Alexander (Jos *Ant.* xi.7.2 and 8.4–5), which has inclined many scholars to favor an identification with Darius III.

The recent discovery of 4th cen. B.C. Samaritan papyri, which indicates that there was a sequence of governors called Sanballat, provides a new solution. It can be assumed that Darius the Persian was Darius II, and that the Jaddua mentioned in Nehemiah was not the same individual mentioned in Josephus but a grandfather of the latter. See Frank M. Cross, "The Discovery of the Samaria Papyri," BA, XXVI (1963), 121; "Aspects of Samaritan and Jewish History in Late Persian and Hellenistic Times," HTR, LIX (1966), 203 ff.

E. M. Y.

DARKNESS. This is expressed by 11 Heb. words, the most common of which is *ḥōshek* and several forms of *'ōpel;* and in Gr. by *skotia, skotos,* "darkness," and *zophos,* "gloom" or "blackness."

Physical darkness. This is particularly mentioned on four occasions in the Bible.

1. At the time of creation when "darkness was upon the face of the deep" (Gen 1:2). This was dispelled when God created light and commenced the generative process which is recounted in Gen 1:1–2:6, and ended in the creation of man (2:7–25).

2. The darkness of three days' duration which constituted the ninth judgment upon Egypt, "even darkness which may be felt" (Ex 10:21–23).

3. The darkness at the crucifixion (Mt 27:45), which continued for three hours, from the sixth to the ninth hour, as God hid from the wicked world the agonies of His Son upon the cross. This darkness was one of the series of miracles which happened at that time: earthquake (v. 51), darkness (v. 45), rending of temple veil from top to bottom (v. 51), resurrection of bodies of some of the saints (vv. 52–53).

4. Darkness at Christ's second advent. This darkness is prophesied by Isaiah, Joel, Christ and John (Isa 13:9–10; Joel 2:31; 3:15; Mt 24:29; Rev 6:12). It will be different from the second and third, though it too will accompany and signify judgment. While the others appear to have been local in nature, this darkness will cover the whole earth since the sun and the moon and stars are to be darkened.

Spiritual darkness. Darkness is also used in a figurative sense to designate spiritual ignorance and blindness (Eccl 2:14; 5:17; Isa 9:2; 29:18; 42:7; Jn 1:5; 8:12; I Jn 2:11) in contrast to light (Jn 1:5, 9; Isa 49:6).

The day of calamity and of sorrow is called a day of darkness (Isa 8:22; Joel 2:2; I Jn 2:8). The despair of the lost is as darkness (Mt 4:16; 6:23).

Since darkness offers a cover for committing evil, the expression "the works of darkness" is sometimes used (Rom 13:12; Eph 5:11).

Darkness is also used to express the condition of the dead apart from the light of the gospel (Job 10:21–22; 18:18; Col 1:13; I Pet 2:9); of the fallen angels kept in chains (II Pet 2:4; Jude 6); and of the final condition of the lost (Mt 22:13; 25:30; Jude 13).

R. A. K.

DARKON (där′kŏn). An ancestor of Solomon's servant Jaala. The "children of Darkon" returned from Exile with Zerubbabel (Ezr 2:56; Neh 7:58).

DARLING. A translation in KJV of the Heb. *yāḥîd,* "only" or "only one" (Gen 22:2, 12, 16). In Ps 22:20 and 35:17 later versions render it "life" or "dear life." It is poetically transferred to the psalmist's own life "as the one unique and priceless possession which can never be replaced" (*Oxford Hebrew Lexicon*).

DART. A sharp-pointed weapon as an arrow or light spear used for thrusting. Joab used three darts (pointed rods) to kill Absalom (II Sam 18:14). Darts or arrows were mechanically hurled in the Maccabean period (I Macc 6:51). At times these darts may have been wrapped in inflammable materials and ignited (Eph 6:16; cf. Ps 120:4). *See* Armor.

DATHAN (dā'thăn). A descendant of Reuben who, with his brother Abiram and others, followed Korah, the Levite, in rebellion against the authority of Moses and Aaron in the wilderness. Dathan and Abiram with their families and goods were swallowed up by the earth (Num 16; Deut 11:6; Ps 106:17).

DAUGHTER (Heb. *bath*, "daughter," "child," "descendant").One cannot determine the exact meaning of the Heb. word *bath* until he carefully considers the context, any more than he can for the word *ben*, "son," of which *bath* is the feminine counterpart.

The Heb. word *bath* appears about 150 times in the OT in contexts that would suggest the ordinary biological relationship. There is nothing unusual about this meaning of the word. Collectively, the term may refer to all the women of a community (Gen 34:1; Lk 23:28). It served also as a familiar form of address expressing respect and even compassion (Mk 5:34). *See* Family.

There are, however, figurative uses of the word which are of great significance. Seventy or more times in the Psalms and Prophets the word is so used, especially in the works of Jeremiah, where it appears 41 times. Sometimes the word "daughter" means a city (e.g., Isa 1:8; 10:32, referring to Jerusalem as the daughter of Zion). At other times the reference is to the inhabitants of a city or a kingdom (Isa 47:1 ff.; Jer 6:26; 46:24). Certain characteristics are heightened when used in conjunction with the term daughter (feminine beauty, Jer 6:2; the cry of anguish, Jer 8:19 ff.; the spirit of disobedience, Jer 31:22; or punishment decreed, Jer 51:33). The word is also applied to small villages attached to the mother city in a city-state community (Num 21:25; 32:42, marg., ASV).

J. W. C.

DAUGHTER-IN-LAW. This is the wife of one's son and is the translation of a term used also for "bride." The daughter-in-law joined her husband's family and came under the authority of her father-in-law (Gen 11:31). Incestuous relations with a man's daughter-in-law were forbidden, and death was the penalty for both, if this law was violated (Lev 18:15; 20:12).

DAUGHTER OF ZION. *See* Zion, Daughter of.

DAVID (dā'vĭd). The second king of Israel, founder of the united monarchy (1000–962 B.C.).

Sources

The main source for the life and times of David is the material found in the books of I

and II Samuel and I Kgs 1–2. These accounts, especially II Sam 9–20 (the court history of David), are a realistic presentation of David by a contemporary historian. I Chr 11–29 contains a parallel account to Samuel-Kings with some additions and omissions. It is fuller than the Samuel-Kings account in the details of the temple arrangement and of lists of royal officers, and presents David in a more idealistic way than does Samuel-Kings.

Numerous references to David are also found in other OT and NT books. Secondary sources to David are stories in the Talmud, Koran, and in the rabbinic and Christian traditions of David. These add to the luster if not to the light of Israel's most beloved figure after the patriarch Abraham.

Name and Family

The name David may mean "beloved" from the noun *dôd* (cf. Jedidiah, "the beloved of the Lord," II Sam 12:25, ASV marg.). Scholars thought a few decades ago that it might be a title such as "captain." The term *dawîdum*, "army officer," occurs a number of times in the Mari texts, and the word *dwdh* once on the Moabite Stone. This possible derivation of David's name, however, is now seriously doubted or discarded (K. A. Kitchen, *Ancient Orient and Old Testament*, pp. 84 f.).

David was born in Bethlehem of Judah, a city about six miles S of Jerusalem, mentioned in the Tel el Amarna letters. This was the home of Boaz and Ruth, and became best known as the birthplace of the son of David, the Messiah of Israel.

David was the youngest child of a family of ten children (I Sam 16:10–11; I Chr 2:13–16 lists only nine; perhaps one child died young). His brothers' names were Eliab (Elihu?), Abinadab, Shimma, Nethaneel, Raddai, and

David trying on Saul's armor, pictured on Byzantine silver dish, c. 625 A. D. MM

Ozem. His sisters' names were Abigail and Zeruiah. According to II Sam 17:25, these girls were daughters of Nahash. Apparently David's mother had the two daughters by a previous marriage. The name of David's mother is unknown. His father, Jesse, a well-to-do, respected elder in Bethlehem, claimed to be of the lineage of Boaz. David was a son of Jesse's old age (I Sam 17:12).

Early Life

The first mention of David occurs in the account of the visit of the prophet Samuel to Bethlehem to select a successor to King Saul. At the sacrifice to which Jesse was especially invited, Samuel began to interview his sons as possible candidates for the kingship. One by one Jesse presented his boys, but none seemed to meet the divine specifications which Samuel sought in the new leader-to-be. Finally, Samuel asked Jesse to present his youngest son; whereupon David was summoned from his chore of sheep tending and won the approval of the prophet as God's man for the nation.

Although David was anointed in the presence of his brethren (I Sam 16:13), the exact purpose of the anointing was not made known to all present. It is thought by many scholars that those at the feast interpreted the ritual act as Samuel's choice of David to succeed him in the prophetic office, as Elijah the prophet had anointed Elisha, the young man to succeed him.

I Sam 16:12 states that David was ruddy ('admônî, "red," also used of Esau, causing many to believe David to be redheaded), had beautiful eyes, and was handsome. Far more important to Samuel and to Israel was the assurance that "the Spirit of the Lord came mightily upon David from that day forward." He was the choice of the prophet and of God for the task which faced the nation. He was to become the people's choice at a later time.

David came to public attention in Israel through two important events, one related to music, the other to physical prowess. In the search for a skilled musician to soothe the melancholia of Saul, David was recommended by a member of the court for the position. I Sam 16:18 (RSV) lists among his qualifications "skilled in playing, a man of valor, a man of war, prudent in speech, and a man of good presence." In addition to good looks and excellent musical talent, he came from a good family background, could fight if called upon, knew how to ease difficult situations with the right word, and possessed the charm needed of one in public service. It seemed that David possessed all the requisites of a young man destined for greatness. Again it is noted that "the Lord is with him." David's versatility commanded the attention of Saul, and David quickly attained a dual role in the royal court, king's armor bearer and private musician to the king. Since Bethlehem was but a day's journey from Gibeah, the house of King Saul, it is believed that David returned often to his home to

The Valley of Elah, where the fight between David and Goliath took place. HFV

continue caring for his father's flocks (I Sam 17:15). His prestige grew in both Benjamin and Judah by leaps and bounds.

The other event in David's early life that commanded national attention was his victory over Goliath, the Philistine giant, in the battle that took place in the valley of Elah (I Sam 17). Chap. 17 may refer to events prior to Saul's hiring David to play in his court, parenthetically included by the author to explain David's qualifications (I Sam 16:18). David left his home in Bethlehem to carry food to his warrior brothers and to return word to Jesse on how the battle fared. When he arrived in the camp, he learned that Goliath had been challenging the Heb. army for 40 days to provide a Hebrew to engage him alone in a contest to determine the outcome of the war. It was customary in Gr. warfare for two warriors to fight a duel to determine the outcome of a battle, rather than for two armies to engage in locked combat. (Achilles and Hector finally settled the Trojan War by a duel.) Since the Philistines controlled the metal industry and were skilled warriors from their youth, the Heb. host was at a serious disadvantage. Their equipment and military tactics were inferior to the superbly trained Philistine giant. To volunteer to fight him was sheer suicide. Saul knew the odds of winning and offered high stakes to any one who would volunteer: freedom from taxation for his father's house, and the hand of Saul's daughter in marriage.

David offered to accept Goliath's challenge and Saul gave him the best military equipment the Heb. army could muster. David refused the armor as being unwieldy and chose his own weapons, the weapons of a shepherd, stone and sling. With this instrument he had protected the sheep of his father's flock; with it he would attempt to protect the people of his Father's flock. He accepted the offer of Goliath with an expression of his heroic faith in God to give

victory to His people. Goliath was defeated by
the shepherd boy, his head taken to the metropolis of Jerusalem as a trophy of war, and his
armor placed in David's tent (some would interpret "tent" to mean the tent at Nob).

The victory of David over Goliath brought
him more permanently into the court of Saul.
There he met Michal, the daughter of Saul, who
was to become his wife. Here he also met the
charming prince Jonathan. The story of their
friendship and loyalty to each other is a masterpiece in biblical literature. Their friendship was
of one soul in two bodies. The bond which
united Jonathan to David was neither mere admiration for his heroic courage and extraordinary skill in using the sling, nor mere sympathy with him in his fervent love of country and
common hatred of the uncircumcised Philistines, but was mainly their common faith in the
covenant love of God for Israel. This unity of
spirit won Jonathan to David, and he made with
him a covenant of friendship and exchanged
gifts in token of that friendship (I Sam 18:1–4).

Fugitive from King Saul

David performed his task so well that his
fame spread through all the land. He became
the favorite son of the common people and of
the court (I Sam 18:5). Hymns were composed
by the singing women lauding his exploits beyond those of the king himself. This caused a
breach to develop between Saul and David.
Saul attempted on several occasions to assassinate him (I Sam 18:11; 19:10), encouraged his
court to put him out of the way, sent him on
dangerous missions, and even proposed a
seemingly impossible feat with the pretext that
he should so distinguish himself in fulfilling it
that he could become the worthy son-in-law to
the king (I Sam 18:20–29). No plan of Saul nor
any member of his court was able to eliminate
David, for "the Lord was with him."

Saul's fears of David were legitimate, for he
saw quite clearly that David, rather than Jonathan, would succeed him in the kingship. Jonathan knew the reality of his father's fears, but
was of a gracious spirit and saw in David the
better man to succeed to the throne of Israel in
those troubled days. Jonathan tried several
times to heal the rift between Saul and David
but failed, and David finally had to flee for his
life. His wife Michal helped him to escape the
net of King Saul by a ruse. She placed a teraphim (household god) in David's bed, enlarged
the torso of the dummy with a goat hair quilt,
and covered it with a garment. Then she reported to the men whom Saul had sent to arrest
David that he was ill. Saul ordered his men to
bring David in his bed to the court, and the ruse
was revealed. Saul's inquiry of Michal was met
with carefully worded untruth (I Sam
19:11–17). Even Saul's family seemed to turn
from him in favor of youthful David.

David fled first to Samuel at Ramah (I Sam
19:18). Undoubtedly he sought the influence

and protection that the great religious leader
could provide. He also needed to be reassured
that God had a future for him in the scheme of
national affairs. Some have conjectured that
David offered to follow Samuel and to give up
the rocky road to the throne. Saul's repeated
attempts to capture David in Ramah met with
signal failure (I Sam 19:18–24). David's next
stop was at the sanctuary in Nob to secure
weapons and food for a flight to Philistine Gath
(I Sam 21). His method of securing aid has
been seriously questioned, for he lied to get
bread and a sword.

David made a wise choice in fleeing to the
land of the Philistines. He received his basic
boot training in warfare from the very people
whom he was to challenge later on for the right
to full control of Palestine. His newly acquired
military knowledge would better equip him to
fight Israel's most dreaded foe.

While in flight from King Saul, David collected a motley army. The dispossessed, those in
debt, and the discontents gathered around him,
and from this strange mixture David formed a
hard core of loyal adherents. Many were
non-Hebrews. With them he began a series of
movements in the Negeb area of Judah. His
flight from Saul offered him numerous opportunities to woo the clans of Judah to his cause.
Many were disillusioned in Saul's program and
in his tribal preferences, and were slowly but
surely becoming backers of the movement that
saw in David the champion of Israel's cause.
David made many fine gestures for the support
of Judah's clans by his gifts and protective policies. The marriages to Abigail and Ahinoam
(I Sam 25) strengthened the alliances with powerful clans in the hills of southern Judah.

David's patience with and respect for King
Saul are admirable. He did nothing that would
overthrow Saul's kingdom, but merely kept one
step ahead of the pursuing king. His healthy
and religious respect for the anointed of the
Lord and at the same time a steady building of
his own program so as to be prepared when
God should call him to assume leadership were
his paradoxical objectives. That time came in
the death of Saul and Jonathan in the battle on
Mount Gilboa. Most of Israel mourned the
death of the tragic King Saul. David wept with
the nation and composed an elegy in honor of
Saul and Jonathan (II Sam 1:17–27).

King of Israel

King at Hebron. David became king of the
tribe of Judah (II Sam 2:4) before he became
king of all Israel. His capital was in Hebron
about 30 miles S of Jerusalem. from where he
governed the affairs of Judah for seven and
one-half years. Among his most strategic moves
to enlarge his domain were the gestures of
friendship toward the men of Jabesh-gilead in
Transjordan (II Sam 2:4–7), recalling of Michal
his wife, and acts of courtesy toward key Benjamite leaders. Slowly but surely David was

able to woo the cohorts of the kingdom of Saul into the solid backing he had developed in Judah. All Israel finally crowned him king of Israel. He was the first king of united Israel and the founder of a dynasty which remained in power about 425 years. Few dynasties in the world have equaled the records of the family of David. The NT reveals the eternal nature of the kingdom of God in the true son of David, the King of kings, Jesus Christ.

King at Jerusalem. David had many wives and concubines who bore to him many sons and daughters. The most famous of his sons were Absalom, Adonijah, Amnon, and Solomon. Tamar was his most famous daughter. Tragedy struck hard and often in the family of David. Intrigue and rivalry always follow the careers of sons born to fathers who marry many wives. Absalom slew Amnon for the rape of Tamar; David's nephew Joab slew Absalom for treason; Solomon banished Adonijah for political reasons. The tragedy of David's life was his family problems. He could weld a nation of headstrong tribes into a solid unit, but his sons created chaos under his very eyes.

David's first act as king of all Israel was to choose a site for the capital that would be acceptable both to the northern and the southern tribes. Jerusalem was to become that place. David built his palace on Mount Zion, the SE hill captured from the Jebusites (II Sam 5:6-9), and he erected a number of government buildings to house his offices. His own experience and the period of the judges proved that a people's army was not dependable; he therefore created a professional army. It was composed of many Cherethites and Pelethites under the leadership of Benaiah of Kabzeel, and the 600 men under Ittai of Gath, an old friend from David's fugitive period. David waged war successfully against the Philistines, against Edom, Moab, Ammon, and Aram or Syria (II Sam 5; 8; 10; 12).

David's two most significant contributions to the life of Israel were (1) the unification of the 12 tribes into a monarchy whose capital was in Jerusalem; and (2) the plans for the centralization of worship in Jerusalem in a temple. He did this by establishing the worship of the people of Israel according to the Mosaic law as seen in the ritual of the ark. By placing the ark, the symbol of the invisible God, in the center of the state, David centralized the religious worship in Jerusalem and prepared the way for the temple. Subsequent history accredits to him not only the physical materials of the temple but much of the music that would constitute the worship of the temple (cf. I Chr 6:31; 16:7, 41-42; 25:1).

The Jews of later days looked back to David as the ideal king, and pictured as a second David the ruler of the happy day for which they hoped.

Evaluation

David was not without fault. The affair with

David ruled in Hebron for seven years before becoming king of all Israel. HFV

Bathsheba and the murder of Uriah indicate his human weaknesses. He often showed disrespect for the men who had been his staunchest supporters (e.g., Joab, and the army of Israel in the rebellion of Absalom). However, he was true to commitments, intensely loyal to friends, and more amenable to prophetic guidance than was Saul. He has been called the sweet singer of Israel; the founder of a dynasty of kings; a prophet; one beloved of God, for his heart was inclined toward God, and he knew how to repent and ask for God's grace.

Bibliography. William F. Albright, *The Biblical Period from Abraham to Ezra,* New York: Harper Torchbooks, 1963, pp. 50-53. John Bright, "The Age of King David," *Union Seminary Review,* Vol. 53 (1942), 87-109; *A History of Israel,* Philadelphia: Westminster, 1959, pp. 171-190. David Cooper, *David,* Los Angeles: Biblical Research Society, 1943. William J. Deane, *David: His Life and Times,* New York: Revell, n.d. James L. Kelso, *Archaeology and Our Old Testament Contemporaries,* Grand Rapids: Zondervan, 1966, chap. 5. Rudolf Kittel, *Great Men and Movements in Israel,* New York: KTAV Publishing House, 1968, chap. 6. F. B. Meyer, *David,* London: Morgan and Scott, 1910. Alan Redpath, *The Making of a Man of God: Studies in the Life of David,* Westwood, N.J.: Revell, 1962. Samuel J. Schultz, *The Old Testament Speaks,* New York: Harper, 1960, pp. 124-141.

F. E. Y.

DAVID, CITY OF. *See* City of David.

DAWN. *See* Dayspring; Time, Divisions of.

DAY. *See* Time; Time, Divisions of.

DAY OF ATONEMENT. *See* Festivals.

DAY OF CHRIST, THE. A NT expression occurring (with its equivalents) in I Cor 1:8; 5:5; II Cor 1:14; Phil 1:6, 10; 2:16. It looks more to a moment of time than to a period of time, the moment being when believers meet the Lord. It is that climactic time when the Church's pilgrimage is finished and she is joined to her Lord. It is related to believers only, and is associated with blessing, not judgment as is the day of the Lord (*q.v.*).

DAY OF GOD, THE. Found only in II Pet 3:12: "Looking for and hasting unto the coming of the day of God, wherein the heavens being on fire shall be dissolved, and the elements shall melt with fervent heat." It is identified by some with "the day of the Lord" (*q.v.*) spoken of in Isa 2:12-21; 13:9 f. (cf. Jer 46:10; Ezk 30:3; Joel 1:15; 2:1, 11; 3:14; Amos 5:18; Ob 15; Zeph 1:7, 14; Zech 14:1). It starts with the events which immediately precede the second coming of Jesus Christ and continues through the Millennium on till the creation of the new heavens and the new earth. That its duration is at least a thousand years is implied by the statement in II Pet 3:8 that "one day is with the Lord as a thousand years, and a thousand years as one day." The term is considered by others, especially those who are amillennial in viewpoint, as referring only to the renovation of the heavens and the earth by fire preparatory to the creation of the new heavens and the new earth. *See* Eschatology; Day of the Lord.

R. A. K.

DAY OF JUDGMENT. *See* Judgment.

DAY OF THE LORD, THE. This expression (and various equivalents, such as "that day") is the subject of both OT and NT revelation. An early occurrence (Amos 5:18-20) shows that the phrase was already a popularly used one. It is a time of judgment on Israel (Amos 5:18-20), of punishment on the nations (Isa 13:6, 9; Ob 15) and of the actual coming of the Lord and salvation for those who repent (Joel 2:28-32). Its coming will be as a thief in the night and will be preceded by signs (I Thess 5:1-2; II Thess 2:2). Thus the day of the Lord includes the period of the Tribulation and the millennial kingdom (II Pet 3:10). *See* Day of God.

DAY'S JOURNEY. *See* Weights, Measures, and Coins.

DAYSMAN. A judge, mediator, or arbitrator. Where the KJV translates the word "daysman," the RSV uses "umpire." "Daysman" is derived from "man's day" (I Cor 4:3, ASV marg.) in the sense of a day set for a man's trial. Job 9:33 says: "Neither is there any daysman betwixt us, that might lay his hand upon us both." The arbiter in the E lays his hand on both parties to show his authority and his desire to render an unbiased verdict. A good illustration of the daysman or mediator is found in Jesus Christ (cf. I Tim 2:5).

DAYSPRING. A poetic way of speaking of the dawn or of the sunrise (Job 38:12; Lk 1:78). In the latter passage the term refers to Messiah, with possible reference to Mal 4:2, "the Sun of righteousness shall arise."

DAY STAR (Gr. *phōsphoros*, "light giving"). Signifies the planet Venus (Lat. Lucifer), that star that precedes or accompanies the rising of the sun, the morning star. In II Pet 1:19 (cf. Lk 1:78; Rev 2:28; 22:16) the term is applied to Christ. Isaiah compares the king of Babylon to Lucifer (*q.v.*), son of the morning (Isa 14:12, RSV). The brightest of the planets is pictured as scheming to rise higher than the stars. In the desert the morning star is so brilliant that it appears as though the sun were about to rise. Even so Lucifer pretends to be the Sun rising with healing in his rays (cf. Mal 4:2). *See* Gods, False; Lucifer.

DEACON. The verb form (*diakonein*) means "to serve"; particularly, "to wait at table" (cf. Arndt, p. 183). It connotes a very personal service, closely related to a service of love. To the Greek, service was scarcely dignified; rather, one's goal should be self-development instead of self-abasement. While the LXX does not use the word *diakonein* ("to serve"), Judaism held a different view of service. It is exemplified in the second commandment: "Thou shalt love thy neighbour as thyself" (Lev 19:18; cf. Mk 12:31). Our Lord so taught when He washed His disciples' feet and then said, "For I have given you an example, that ye should do as I have done to you" (Jn 13:15).

The general uses of "deacon" in the NT have been classified by H. W. Beyer ("*Diakoneō*, etc.," TDNT, II, 81-93) and are given in the following adapted form: (1) "the waiter at a meal" (Jn 2:5, 9); (2) "the servant of a master" (Mt 22:13; Jn 12:26); (3) "the servant of a spiritual power," either good (Col 1:23; II Cor 3:6; Rom 15:8) or evil (II Cor 11:14 f.; Gal 2:17); (4) "the servant of God" (II Cor 6:3 ff.) or Christ (II Cor 11:23), as in Paul's case, or as applied to his fellow workers (I Thess 3:1-3; I Tim 4:6; Col 1:7; 4:7); (5) "the [heathen as] servants of God" (Rom 13:1-4); (6) "a servant of the church" (Col 1:24-25; I Cor 3:5).

In Gr. writings, the noun related closely to the verb in sense. It described a waiter at table, a servant, a messenger, a steward, and was even used with reference to specific occupations, as baker or cook. The term appears infrequently in the LXX, and then only in the secular sense. It describes the servants of the king in Est 1:10; 2:2; 6:3, 5. In Prov 10:4 (LXX only) the fool is to be "servant" of the wise. Josephus, historian of the Jewish nation, characterized Elisha as the "disciple and servant" of Elijah.

When did the diaconate first appear in the early church? Was it in Acts 6:1-6? In the passage dealing with the choosing and appointment of the seven, the word "deacon" does not appear. And while the terms *diakonia* ("ministry" or "service") and *diakonein* ("to wait at table") do appear (Acts 6:1, 2, 4), they are used, it would seem, in a nontechnical sense, i.e., they refer to workers and not to office bearers. This is indicated by the expressions "the ministry of waiting tables" and "the ministry of the word" where the same term applies to both types of service.

Lightfoot (*Philippians*, pp. 188f.) regards the seven as the first deacons, for (1) their duties were similar to what since that time has characterized the "diaconate," viz., the care of widows and orphans and deeds of charity; (2) it was a newly created office, neither patterned after the Levitical ministry nor the synagogue minister (the Chazan); and (3) the teaching ministry, e.g., of Stephen and Philip, was incidental to the office, being brought about by the necessity of the circumstances.

Rackham (*Acts,* pp. 82–86) concludes that the "office" in Acts 6 was "unique; i.e., unique in the same sense as was the apostolate." The seven correspond to the 12 disciples, and the full list of their names shows this relation. In these two groups, then, are the ancestors of presbyters and deacons.

In Rom 16:1, Paul made reference to Phoebe as a *diakonon* ("deaconess," *q.v.*) of the church in Cenchrea. Was she an officeholder or does the word simply describe her service in the Christian community? It is impossible to say, even as is the case in the reference to the "women" in I Tim 3:11 (RSV). Were these women the wives of deacons or were they "deaconesses"?

With reference to one who holds a specific office in the church, the word *diakonos* ("deacon") occurs in only two passages in the NT: Phil 1:1 and I Tim 3:8, 12. Phil 1:1 contains Paul's greetings to the "bishops and deacons." While no activities are specified here, they are two existent and related offices, regarded as distinct from the body of saints in general.

In I Tim 3:1–13, the same relation may be observed: "the bishop" (vv. 1–7) and "the deacons" (vv. 8–13). The "deacons" must be men of disciplined character and moral repute (vv. 8–9); they must qualify for the office by being "proved worthy" (v. 10); and they must be in control of their own households (v. 12). The fact that in their ministries of charity and aid they were in close contact with people and material possessions, called for special qualities of character. They were not to be "double-tongued," nor were they to be "greedy of filthy lucre" (v.8).

Paul does not specify how the deacons were to be chosen, yet they were to be first "proved," and Timothy was certainly expected to be able to approve them. The historical development of the office of deacon is linked with that of bishop. *See* Bishop for the question of selection.

Elsewhere in the NT Paul uses the term minister to denote his fellow workers in the gospel ministry — of Timothy (I Thess 3:2), Tychicus (Col 4:7), and Epaphras (Col 1:7). Paul's own ministry (I Cor 3:5; II Cor 3:6; 6:4; 11:15) and the ministry of Christ (Rom 15:8) are also so designated. These latter references indicate that the term is in no way applied to inferior service.

W. M. D. and A. F. J.

DEACONESS. The English translation of the Gr. *diakonos,* which is used of a helper or of a deacon as an official of the church. In Rom 16:1 Phoebe is mentioned as a *diakonos* in the church at Cenchrea. This would not necessarily imply that this was an official office. It could have been only an occasional or temporary act of service, or an office in the church. No clear recognition of the office of deaconess is found in the Pastoral Epistles. In the KJV and ASV Rom 16:1 is rendered "servant." In the ASV marg. it is translated "deaconess."

It is probable that there were in the different churches groups of women engaged in visiting those of their own sex in the same way as the deacons performed their duties. The rules given in I Tim 3:11 and Tit 2:3–5 as to the conduct of women have been referred to the office of the deaconess. I Tim 5:9 – 10 have also been suggested as requirements for the office. It is not certain that these passages refer to that office, although there existed such an order later in church history. Pliny the Younger, writing as governor of Bithynia to the emperor Trajan in A.D. 112, indicated that by that time there were deaconesses among the Christians whom he assigned to torture in that province.

D. L. W.

DEAD, THE. The word "dead" as an adjective is many times applied to individuals in the Bible from Sarah to Sapphira. The usual words referring to the dead are *môt* in the OT and *nekros* in the NT. The OT also uses the word *nepesh* (usually translated "soul") for a dead body, but this happens because the word often refers just to an individual and therefore to the body of the individual. Also the word *rᵉpāʾîm* is used, usually translated "shades" in the RSV. The etymological meaning "sunken," "powerless ones" is questionable. In the NT, forms of the verb *thnēskō*, "die" and similar words, are also used to designate the dead. None of these usages greatly elucidate the condition of those who have departed this life.

The OT Teaching

On this subject the OT is not very explicit. This is an interesting reticence in view of the wild speculations of the surrounding peoples. The OT verses bearing on the question come largely from Job, Psalms, Ecclesiastes, Isaiah, and Ezekiel, and are made more difficult by their poetic backgrounds. The subject is complicated also by the use of such words as Sheol (*q.v.*), which is of uncertain etymology and whose precise meaning is debatable. Critical studies on the subject, moreover, are often vitiated by a preconception which reverses the datings of some OT books and passages, and finds OT ideas of immortality and resurrection only in post–Exilic times under foreign influence.

But the Psalms are now accepted as largely pre–Exilic and Ps 16:8–11; 17:15; 49:14–15; 73:23–26 seem to speak clearly of resurrection and immortality. In Ps 16:8–11 David is said by Peter to be knowingly predicting Christ's resurrection (Acts 2:30–31). (See the writer's treatment of these verses in *The Biblical Expositor*, Vol.2, 59 f.) Ps 17:15 may also refer to future resurrection rather than to awaking after death in glory. It is significant that in the NT, resurrection is called an awaking (Jn 11:11), though this is somewhat figurative as is the reference to death as a sleep. Ps 49:14–15 and 73:19–26 may well refer to the present state of the dead. Ps 73:19, 24 and Isa 57:1–2 particularly seem to emphasize the distinction between the destiny of the righteous dead and of the wicked.

There are several specific verses in Job teaching immortality, but equally significant is the total argument of the book. Job sees the inequities of this life, yet holds fast to his trust in a righteous God. The only answer to this problem even today is in the concept of a future life of rewards and punishment. The classic passage is Job 19:25, "I know that my redeemer liveth." An extensive treatment of this passage and of the whole subject is found in a valuable but little known study on afterlife in the OT by A. Heidel, *The Gilgamesh Epic and OT Parallels* (2nd ed., Chicago: Univ. of Chicago Press, 1949, pp. 173–223). This verse in Job refers to resurrection rather than to the state of the dead today.

Isa 25:8 and 26:19 are clear and there is no necessity to place these passages later than the days of Isaiah himself. They speak of a resurrection of the dead as Israel's future hope. The former verse is quoted expressly with regard to the resurrection in I Cor 15:55. Dan 12:2 is also a landmark. It has been suggested that the verse may be read, "And the many that sleep in the dust of the earth shall awake," taking the *min* ("from") as explicative rather than as referring to a partial resurrection which does not seem to be in this context (cf. Heidel, *op. cit.*, p. 220f.). These passages do not reveal the present state of the dead, however, except that they forbid the doctrine of the extinction of the person inasmuch as there is a future hope. The instances of resurrection recorded in the OT reinforce this conclusion.

The translations of Enoch and Elijah and the bringing up of Samuel bear more on the state of the dead and emphasize also that Israel knew there was a life beyond for the people of God. Elijah was taken up body and soul to God in glory. The translation might well have suggested that the ascent of the soul of the godly was usual; the ascent of the body was obviously unique.

The raising of Samuel (I Sam 28:7–25) presents several problems, but in any case it argues that Samuel was in conscious existence after death. Some have argued that the appearance was that of an evil apparition and not the real Samuel (Heidel, *op. cit.*, p. 189 f.). Others hold that Samuel really appeared by a miracle of God — not by the conjurings of the necromancer, who apparently was quite surprised (cf. *Wycliffe Bible Commentary*, p. 292). That Samuel was brought *up* does not necessarily mean that his spirit was in the grave or in a subterranean netherworld. It may only be a figure of speech from the fact that Samuel had been let *down* into the grave (so Heidel).

This conclusion would doubtless be more widely accepted were it not that certain verses appear on the other side of the ledger. They are mainly: Ps 6:5; 30:9; 39:13; 88:11–12; 115:17; 143:3; Job 3:17; 10:21–22; Eccl 9:5,10; Isa 38:10–11. James Orr points out ("Eschatology of the OT," ISBE, II, 974) that these verses are not to be pressed too literally: "Part of it is the expression of a depressed or despairing . . . or temporarily skeptical . . . mood; all of it is relative." Thus, the skepticism of Eccl 3:19–4:3 is not the final answer of the book to the question of the chief end of man (Eccl 8:12–13; 12:13). It would seem that some at least of the descriptions in the above verses apply not to the state of the dead, but to the condition of the body in the grave. The grave is indeed a place of silence, of darkness, of the worm and corruption; a place where the body is soon forgotten and where the tongue ceases to give praise. "The death of the devout costs Yahweh dear" (Ps 116:15, Jerusalem Bible), because his service to the Lord of worship, sacrifice, and thanksgiving ceases on earth altogether. But these verses do not teach that this is the condition of the spirit after death. See R. L. Harris, "The Meaning of the Word Sheol," BETS, IV (1961), 129–135.

Other representations portray the dead kings of the earth rising from their thrones in Sheol to greet newly fallen potentates (Isa 14:9–20; Ezk 32:18–32). This also is highly figurative. Heidel argues (*op. cit.*, p. 198 f.) that the treatment in these verses is "almost exclusively of the grave and not of the spirit world." Sheol may be a poetic word for "grave" and this explains the statements about its being a place of darkness, silence, etc. But as to the abode of the spirit, the godly Israelite, trusting in the living God as he did, died in peace expecting to awake in God's likeness (Ps 17:15).

The NT Doctrine

The NT has more light on the state of the dead, but it only extends the OT teaching. It also clearly teaches a future resurrection. There are many such passages and the resurrection of Christ Himself is basic to the whole picture.

But there is also more light on the condition

of the dead today. Christians "sleep in Jesus" (I Thess 4:14). This seems clearly to be a euphemism arising from the appearance of the dead body, for the redeemed in glory are active (Rev 6:9 ff.) and are concerned with events on earth. The transfiguration scene shows Moses and Elijah speaking with Jesus of the coming crucifixion (Lk 9:30 – 31). The lost are also conscious, terribly so, and they too are concerned with the present world (Lk 16:19 – 31). Some have held that the record of Dives and Lazarus is a parable. It may be, though it differs essentially from other parables. But in any case, Jesus' parables were always true to life illustrations, and the conclusion is clear that the dead are either in bliss or in torment now.

This was the comfort that Christ gave to the dying thief (Lk 23:43; "paradise" is equated to heaven in II Cor 12:2, 4), and Paul declares that to depart and be with Christ is "far better" (Phil 1:23). To be absent from the body is, for the Christian, to be present with the Lord (II Cor 5:8). Stephen at death was given a glorious glimpse into this heavenly home (Acts 7:56) and so was the aged apostle on Patmos (Rev 4:1).

There is a view that before the cross there were two compartments in Sheol and that Christ entered Sheol and delivered the redeemed from there, taking them to heaven at His crucifixion. Aside from the strangeness of this view, it has poor exegetical foundation. Eph 4:9 is appealed to, but that verse may merely identify the ascended Christ with the Jesus who descended to the earth in His incarnation. Another passage often quoted is I Pet 3:19 – 20. This may only mean that Christ in the days before the Flood preached by the Holy Spirit to Noah's contemporaries who are now "in prison." Actually Christ told us, as has been noted, where He went at His death — to His Father and to paradise. The NT assures us that at our death we shall be there too with Christ until He comes again. See especially such expressions as are found in II Cor 5:8 and Phil 1:21 – 23. See Burial; Death; Embalm; Grave; Eschatology; Funeral; Hades; Heaven; Hell.

Bibliography. For treatment of the corpse and burial customs see Roland de Vaux, *Ancient Israel,* trans. by John McHugh, New York: McGraw-Hill, 1961, pp. 56 – 61. Aubrey R. Johnson, *The Vitality of the Individual in the Thought of Ancient Israel,* Cardiff: Univ. of Wales Press, 1949, pp. 11 – 14, 71 – 74, 89 – 94.

R. L. H.

DEAD, BAPTISM FOR THE. *See* Baptism for the Dead.

DEAD SEA. Called in the OT the Salt Sea (Gen 14:3; Num 34:12; etc.), the Sea of the Plain or Arabah (Deut 3:17; 4:49; etc.), the East Sea (Ezk 47:18; Joel 2:20; etc.). It lies in the great rift of the Jordan Valley resulting from a great

The Dead Sea

convulsion which shook the surface of the earth in prehistoric ages. At that time the mountain ranges of Lebanon and Anti-Lebanon rose above the great plain which embraced the entire area of Lebanon, Syria, Palestine, and Transjordan, and a deep cavity was formed between them, stretching from the foothills of the Amanus Mountains, through Coele-Syria, the Jordan Valley, the Dead Sea, and the Red Sea, and extending as far S as the Nyasa Lake in central Africa.

The surface of the Dead Sea averages about 1,290 feet below sea level. Its deepest point, near the NE corner, is some 1,300 feet lower. The sea today is about 50 miles long and up to 10 miles wide. It is fed principally by the river Jordan, but a number of springs and streams on both sides add their quota to its waters. It has no outlet, but the rate of evaporation is so great that the inflow of waters is able only to keep the surface level approximately constant. Thus the salt and potash deposits (25 percent of the water) have become more concentrated than in any other sea or lake in the world. The specific gravity of the water is greater than that of human beings and it is impossible for any person to sink in the Dead Sea.

The shallow area S of the peninsula El-Lisan, where Sodom and Gomorrah almost certainly lay, has at times been dry land, as submerged tree stumps testify. Ruins of an Edomite fort on the SW shore have been inundated at least twice since 1000 B.C. Between the days of Abraham (Gen 14:3) and the time of Moses the Dead Sea must have risen to cover the area of Sodom and the other cities of the plain.

There is a bed of asphalt at the bottom of the sea, from which fairly large pieces break loose from time to time and float on the surface (cf. Gen 14:10). The Greeks and Romans called it the Sea of Asphalt because of this feature. However, by the 2nd cen. after Christ it had acquired its more usual name from the fact that no fish or other marine animal can live in its waters. *See* Palestine, II.B.3.*e.*

The area around the Dead Sea has been inhabited by man since the Neolithic period, and the rugged country on both sides has afforded a refuge and a protection on numerous occasions to persecuted persons and groups. David, fleeing before Saul, took shelter at one time at the spring known as the waters of Engedi (I Sam 23:29 – 24:1). During the first Jewish revolt the Jews made their headquarters at the strategic position of Masada above the Dead Sea, whither they were followed by the Roman general Silva. Similarly, Herod the Great had refortified a Maccabean stronghold at Machaerus above its eastern shore. At his death it passed to Herod Antipas, and it was there that he slew John the Baptist. Below Machaerus, there is a hot water spring which was called Callirrhoë in ancient times because of its medicinal properties.

A short distance N of the Dead Sea, at a site called Ghassul, lie the ruins of a village which goes back to the Chalcolithic Age. The site has been excavated in recent years and has produced evidence to show that it was occupied between 4000 and 3200 B.C. at a time when Jericho appears to have been abandoned.

In recent years, the remains of a communal settlement which belonged to the Essenes have been discovered at Qumran, above the western shore of the Dead Sea. In the nearby caves, scrolls have been discovered, ranging in date from the 2nd cen. B.C. to the 1st cen. after Christ. See Dead Sea Scrolls.

D. C. B.

DEAD SEA SCROLLS

The Initial Discovery

The recovery of the Dead Sea Scrolls has been called "the greatest manuscript discovery of modern times." What enhances the value of the discovery is the paucity of written records from biblical times from Palestine.

In retrospect scholars were able to point to records of similar discoveries in the Dead Sea area. Origen used some texts found in A.D. 217 in jars near Jericho. A Nestorian patriarch, Timothy I (726–819), inquired about MSS found in a cave near Jericho, including "more than two hundred psalms of David." Al-Qirqisani of the 10th cen. A.D. referred to a sect called "Magharians" because their books were found in a cave. But in modern times no comparable MS discoveries had been made.

At the end of 1946 (or at the beginning of 1947) three members of the Ta'amireh Bedouin accidentally came upon a cave near Wadı Qumran NW of the Dead Sea. They discovered three sheepskin scrolls in a covered jar and removed them. In May or June, 1947, the Bedouin returned and removed four more scrolls from the cave. At the end of the year E. Sukenik of the Hebrew University purchased three of the scrolls (the incomplete Isaiah Scroll, the War Scroll, and the Thanksgiving Hymns).

It was not until April 11, 1948, that news of the discovery was released to the public. A month later Jewish–Arab hostilities erupted into a full–scale war, making further investigation by Israelis in the Qumran area impossible.

Early in 1949 Metropolitan Samuel of the Syrian Orthodox Church, who had secured the other scrolls (the complete Isaiah Scroll, the Manual of Discipline, the Habakkuk Commentary, and the Genesis Apocryphon), brought them to the U.S. In 1954 these were bought for Israel by Y. Yadin, the son of Sukenik, for $250,000, after they had been advertised in the Wall Street Journal.

Dating of the Manuscripts

Some scholars were skeptical of the antiquity of the documents. S. Zeitlin still vigorously argues that they are medieval MSS. The evidences for the date of the finds are as follows:

1. Paleography. J. Trever, who was at the American School of Oriental Research in Jerusalem in 1948, examined the scrolls in February and surmised their antiquity from a comparison of the script with that of the Nash Papyrus, a small fragment of the OT from Egypt and dated to the 2nd cen. B.C. His initial impression was confirmed by an authority on the subject, W. F. Albright.

2. Radio–carbon analysis. An analysis of cloth associated with the MSS yielded a date of A.D. 33 plus or minus 200 years (later revised to 20 B.C.).

3. Excavations at Khirbet Qumran. Excavations at Khirbet Qumran, the ruins of the monastery of Qumran, a mile S of the initial find, proved that the main levels of the settlement were in Hellenistic and Roman times.

4. Coins. Several hundred coins found in the excavations date the limits of the main period of occupation from 135 B.C. to A.D. 68.

Later Discoveries at Qumran

When the Ta'amireh Bedouin realized the monetary value of the MSS, they began to search the Judean desert for other finds. In 1952 they discovered Cave II close to Cave I. In the same year archaeologists led by R. de Vaux explored from 200 to 300 caves. In all, 11 caves have yielded MSS in the Qumran area.

In 1952, a mile N of the initial discovery, Cave III yielded the Copper Scroll. The most important discovery of all was that of a library in Cave IV in a terrace near Khirbet Qumran. This cave alone yielded some 40,000 fragments of 400 different MSS, one-fourth of which were biblical. Also in 1952 Caves V and VI were discovered near Cave IV.

In 1955 Caves VII–X were found in the area of Khirbet Qumran. These yielded relatively few MSS. In 1956 Cave XI was discovered to the N near Cave III. Next in importance to Caves I and IV, Cave XI gave up seven extensive MSS.

Some of the caves at Qumran. HFV

Other Discoveries Near the Dead Sea

1. *Murabba'at*. In 1951 the Bedouin discovered texts in caves in Wadi Murabba'at 11 miles S of Qumran. In 1952 archaeologists under L. Harding and R. de Vaux excavated four caves here. These caves yielded biblical documents, and also important letters and contracts from the period of Bar Kochba's revolt against the Romans in A.D. 132–135. One MS is the oldest Heb. papyrus ever found, dated to the 7th cen. B.C.

From the earliest level of occupation (4th mil. B.C.) came objects of wood, leather, basketry, and parts of a fish net—the first objects of such perishable material found in Palestine. The spectacular finds from Murabba'at have not received the notice they deserve, because they have been overshadowed by the even more spectacular Qumran materials.

In 1955 the Bedouin brought forward a MS which they said came from Murabba'at. It was a magnificent Heb. scroll, dated to the 2nd cen. A.D., of the Minor Prophets, extending from the middle of Joel to the beginning of Zechariah. It belongs to the proto-Masoretic Text type.

2. *Khirbet Mird*. Bedouin in 1952 discovered some Byzantine and early Arabic MSS at Khirbet Mird, six miles WSW of Qumran. This was the place where a famous monastery was established in A.D. 492 by Mar Saba. Explorations were conducted by R. de Langhe in 1953. MSS in Arabic, Gr. and Palestinian Aram. from the 5th to the 8th cen. A.D. were found. A Gr. fragment of *Andromache,* a play of Euripides, dates from the 6th cen. A.D. and is a thousand years older than the oldest MS of the play on parchment.

3. *Nahal Hever*. Here, three and a half miles S of En-gedi, the Israelis in 1960 made the first MS discoveries on their territory. They found 15 letters either to or from Bar Kochba: nine in Aram., four in Heb. and two in Gr. In 1961 in the same cave the Israelis found 65 more papyri and parchment documents, including important legal contracts. One of the letters from Bar Kochba was written on wooden tablets—the first such discovery in Israel. Bits of a MS were found by the Israeli team that proved to belong to a fragmentary copy of a Gr. version of the Minor Prophets purchased from the Bedouin in 1952. Its text is in agreement with that used by Justin Martyr c. A.D. 150. From Nahal Tse'elim, a few miles to the S of Hever, the first preserved arrow shafts of wood were found.

4. *Wadi Daliyeh*. In 1962 word reached Jerusalem that the Ta'amireh Bedouin had found still another cave, this time nine miles N of Jericho and seven miles W of the Jordan (therefore not strictly a "Dead Sea" site). The cave, called Mugharet Abu Shinjeb, was explored in 1963 under the direction of P. Lapp. Some 40 Aramaic papyrus documents were secured, pre-

cisely dated from 375 to 335 B.C. Hitherto very few texts from this century had been recovered. The MSS were entombed in the cave with perhaps 200 Samaritans attempting to flee from Alexander the Great in 331 B.C.

5. *Masada*. In 1963–65 Israelis under Y. Yadin excavated Masada, near the W shore of the Dead Sea opposite the Lisan peninsula. The last Jewish stronghold against the Romans in the first Jewish war, it fell in A.D. 73. In addition to a few biblical fragments and 26 fragments (some quite sizable) of the Heb. text of Ben Sirah, a scroll identical with the text of the Songs of the Sabbath Sacrifice from Qumran was found. This is the first time that a "Qumran" MS has been found outside a cave and in a stratified context.

OT Manuscripts from Qumran

Prior to the discovery of the Qumran MSS the oldest extant Heb. OT MSS came from the 9th and 10th cen. A.D., with the exception of a fragment known as the Nash Papyrus (2nd cen. B.C.), quotations in the Aramaic Magic Bowls (6th cen. A.D.), and fragments of over 120 6th–9th cen. A.D. biblical MSS from the geniza (storeroom) of a Cairo synagogue. The Jews made a practice of destroying worn-out MSS to save them from impious hands.

1. *Number and description*. The greatest importance of the Dead Sea Scrolls lies in the recovery of biblical MSS a full millennium earlier than the medieval copies. Of the some 500 MSS recovered from Qumran, 175, or one-third, are biblical. As of 1965 the following numbers of copies of OT books had been found in the 11 caves of Qumran: Genesis 15, Exodus 15, Leviticus 8, Numbers 6, Deuteronomy 25, Joshua 2, Judges 3, Ruth 4, Samuel 4, Kings 4, Chronicles 1, Ezra–Nehemiah 1, Job 4, Psalms 27, Proverbs 2, Ecclesiastes 2, Song of Solomon 4, Isaiah 18, Jeremiah 4, Lamentations 4, Ezekiel 6, Daniel 8, and the Minor Prophets 8. Of the Heb. canon only Esther is not represented. The most popular books were Genesis, Exodus, Deuteronomy, Isaiah, and Psalms.

The oldest text is an archaic Exodus fragment from Cave IV dated to 250 B.C. The text had to be read with the aid of infrared and ultraviolet photography.

Most of the texts were written in the so-called Aramaic script. But ten MSS including the books of the Pentateuch and Job were written in an archaizing script known as Paleo–Hebrew. The divine name was sometimes written in this script in other MSS.

2. *Textual traditions*

Masoretic Recension. The traditional Heb. text of the OT preserved in the medieval MSS is called the Masoretic Text (MT) after the editorial work of Jewish scribes known as Masoretes. They labored from the 5th to the

Professor H. Wright Baker of Manchester's College of Technology cutting the copper scroll from Cave Three. John M. Allegro

9th cen. A.D., introducing vowels into the consonantal text and adding notes in the margins.

Scholars were not sure how accurate the work of the Masoretes and their predecessors was. Some scholars dated the origin of the MT to the editorial activities of rabbis in the 2nd cen. A.D. Thanks to Qumran we now know that the MT goes back to an edition antedating the Christian era by several centuries, and that this recension was copied with amazing accuracy.

Most of the biblical MSS from Qumran belong to the proto–Masoretic tradition. This is especially true of the Pentateuch and the Latter Prophets. What effect the evidence of the complete Isaiah Scroll from Cave I (cited in the RSV as "one ancient MS") has made may be seen by comparing the RSV (1952) with the KJV in the following passages: Isa 3:24; 14:4, 30; 15:9; 21:8; 23:2; 33:8; 45:2, 8; 49:24; 51:19; 56:12; 60:19. Most of these 13 readings are not new, in that they have the support of some of the ancient versions. One may conclude therefore that in spite of the fact that the great Isaiah Scroll diverged considerably from the MT in spelling and grammar, it has not warranted any major changes in the substance of the text.

Septuagint Recension. The LXX, the Gr. translation of the OT begun *c.* 250 B.C., is next to the MT in importance for the reconstruction of the OT text. The majority of the 250 OT citations in the NT are from this version.

Where the LXX diverged from the MT, some scholars had assumed that the translators had taken liberties with their texts. Now it appears that many of these differences resulted from the fact that they were following a somewhat different Heb. text.

From Qumran have come Heb. texts that correspond to the LXX in the books of Exodus, Numbers, Deuteronomy, Job, Jeremiah and Samuel. The Jeremiah and Samuel MSS may help in obtaining a Heb. text superior to that of the MT.

Also found in Qumran were Gr. MSS of the LXX itself, of Exodus, Numbers and Leviticus. A text of Leviticus from Cave IV dated to 100 B.C. is now the oldest known LXX fragment. A Gr. MS of the Minor Prophets was recovered from the area of Wadi Khabra.

Other recensions. A Paleo-Heb. MS of Exodus from Cave IV is close to the Samaritan version. All known copies of the Samaritan version of the Pentateuch (SP) are written in a script derived from the Paleo–Heb. script used in some of the Qumran documents. The SP must now be dated to the 2nd cen. B.C. and not earlier as some had held. Since it exhibits expansive tendencies it is of little value in helping to obtain a better Heb. text.

There are also examples of Targums or Aramaic paraphrases of Leviticus and Job found at Qumran.

3. *Composition and canon.* The early dates of the biblical MSS from Qumran militate against extreme views of critics who place the

Qumran structures (airview). Palestine Archaeological Museum

composition of certain OT books in Maccabean times (2nd cen. B.C.).

Some critics dated the composition of Ecclesiastes to the 2nd or 1st cen. B.C. Yet Cave IV yielded a MS of Ecclesiastes dated to 175 – 150 B.C., which is certainly not the original text.

A 2nd cen. B.C. MS of the Psalms indicates that the collection of canonical Psalms was fixed before the Maccabean age. The 2nd to 1st cen. Hymns from Qumran are quite different from the canonical Psalms.

One MS of Daniel is dated to 120 B.C., bringing into question the alleged Maccabean date of its composition. A fragmentary Prayer of Nabonidus (*see* Nabonidus) shows that the Jews knew about the father of Belshazzar, though he is not mentioned by name in Daniel.

The biblical MSS from Qumran show affinities with a number of recensions. Those, however, from Murabba'at, including portions of the Pentateuch, Psalms, Isaiah and Minor Prophets, belong uniformly to the MT tradition. This lends credence to the Jewish tradition that the OT text was standardized at Jamnia in A.D. 95. Since all the texts from Masada (A.D. 73), including portions of Genesis, Leviticus, Deuteronomy, Psalms and Ezekiel, also belong to the MT tradition, standardization may have begun even earlier, at least in orthodox circles.

There is evidence that the sect at Qumran was more open than orthodox Jews in its concept of canonical books. They made use of a number of Apocryphal and Pseudepigraphical works, and probably considered the revelations embodied in their own sectarian writings as inspired. (Only commentaries that deal with canonical books have been found, it may be said.)

A Psalms Scroll from Cave XI, published in 1965, includes not only 36 canonical psalms but also eight other compositions. One of these is a prose piece ascribing to David the composition of 4,050 psalms. Another is a poem found in

Ben Sirah. One of the psalms is one known previously as Ps 151 of the LXX, Old Latin, and Syriac versions. Two others had been known from medievaı Syriac texts.

Apocrypha and Pseudepigrapha

1. *Apocrypha.* The Apocryphal and Pseudepigraphical works, rejected by the Jews from the canon, were known to us previously only in translations. Qumran has now furnished the Heb. and Aram. originals of some of these works. Cave IV has yielded four Aram. and one Heb. MSS of Tobit. The composition of Tobit dated by scholars to the 2nd–1st cen. B.C. may now be pushed back to the 5th–4th cen.

·A Heb. MS of Ben Sirah or Ecclesiasticus came from Cave II; a passage of chap. 51 was included in the Psalms Scroll from Cave XI. Fragments of the Heb. text of Sirah have also come from Masada. These are textually the same as the Heb. texts of Sirah recovered in the 1890's from the Cairo geniza, proving that the latter, though medieval MSS, were accurate copies of the text and not translations from Syriac as some had suggested.

A Gr. MS of the Letter of Jeremiah (Baruch 6 in the Vulg.) was found in Cave VII.

2. *Pseudepigrapha.* Fragments of ten MSS in Aram. of Enoch were found in Cave IV. Eleven MSS in Heb. of Jubilees were found in Caves I, II, and IV; fragments were also found at Masada. Three Aram. MSS of the Testament of Levi and one Heb. MS of the Testament of Judah were found. These MSS indicate that the date of composition for Jubilees and the Testaments must be pushed earlier than the end of the 2nd cen. B.C.

3. *The Genesis Apocryphon.* This scroll, called at first the Lamech Scroll, was one of the original seven documents from Cave I. It was not published until 1956, and then only in part. The MS is in Aram. and was copied at the beginning of the Christian era; its date of composition probably goes back to the early 1st cen. B.C. In style it resembles Jubilees or a Targum, commenting in a legendary vein on passages of Genesis. One passage, e.g., describes the beauty of Sarah in great detail.

Sectarian Documents

1. *The Damascus Document.* This composition, sometimes called the Zadokite Document, had been known from medieval MSS discovered in 1897 in the geniza (storehouse for old MSS) of a synagogue in Cairo. At least nine MSS of it have now been found at Qumran.

The Damascus Document gives important information about the history of the sect centered at Qumran. The reference to an exile to Damascus led some scholars to suggest an actual exodus to Syria after the earthquake of 31 B.C. struck Qumran. But since the oldest MS of the Damascus Document is dated back to 75–50 B.C., Damascus may be the prophetic name of Qumran itself.

2. *Manual of Discipline.* The manual was one of tł seven scrolls from Cave I. Eleven more fragmentary MSS have been found in Caves IV and X. This gives detailed instructions concerning the entrance requirements of the sect.

3. *The Thanksgiving Hymns.* Another of the seven MSS from Cave I contained hymns. It is called *Hodayot* in Heb. and is also represented by five fragments from Cave IV. In all they include some 30 hymns, probably composed by a single individual, perhaps the Teacher of Righteousness.

4. *Commentaries.* Commentaries, called *Pesharim* in Heb., have been found on Ps 37, Isaiah, Hosea, Micah, Nahum, Habakkuk, Zephaniah. The Habakkuk Commentary, one of the original MSS from Cave I, gives important details about the persecution of the Teacher of Righteousness by the Wicked Priest. The Nahum Commentary makes clear reference to historic persons: to Antiochus (probably the IV, 175–163 B.C.) and to Demetrius (probably the III, who ruled 95–88 B.C.). The mention of the "Lion of Wrath" who crucified men is probably a reference to Alexander Jannaeus (103–76 B.C.).

5. *The War Scroll.* Another of the original scrolls from Cave I, the War Scroll describes in detail the tactics, equipment, and prayers that the Sons of Light will use in defeating the Sons of Darkness. The eschatological war, which will also be waged by angels, will last 40 years: six years with Edom, Moab, Ammon, etc.; 29 years with the kings of the N and the Kittim; and five years off for the sabbatical years. Some scholars have identified the Kittim with the Seleucids and others with the Romans.

6. *Miscellaneous documents*

a. Descriptions of the New Jerusalem have been found.

b. Mishmarot, MSS describing the courses of the priests adjusted to the solar calendar of the sect, have been found.

c. Testimonia, collections of OT texts related to the Messiah, may be similar to those used by NT writers, including as they did composite quotations.

d. A liturgical calendar makes reference to Queen Alexandra, Hyrcanus (I or II), and Aemilius.

e. An angelic liturgy contains "Songs of the Sabbath Sacrifice." A MS of this work was also found at Masada, indicating that sectarians of the Qumran type fought with the Zealots there in the last stand against the Romans in A.D. 73. (Some, e.g., C. Roth and G. R. Driver, have argued indeed that the sectarians were Zealots!)

f. A messianic horoscope and a cryptic document indicate that the sectarians were not opposed to the astrology of their day.

g. A *Florilegium* or anthology of midrashic comments on II Sam 7 and Ps 1–2.

h. An allegory called "The Wiles of the Wicked Woman," describing a group hostile to the sect.

i. In 1967 after the June War, Yigael Yadin announced the acquisition of a remarkable Qumran document which he has called "the Temple Scroll." The scroll, over 28 feet long, is now the longest known from Qumran. The style of its Heb. script dates it to the Herodian period. The text, which is yet to be published, deals with four subjects: (1) religious rules concerning ritual cleanness; (2) sacrifices and offerings; (3) statutes of the king and the army; (4) a detailed description of the temple. The scroll gives detailed prescriptions as to the building of the temple, perhaps to supply the description which David was said to have given to' Solomon (I Chr 28:11). As the details of the projected temple do not accord with those of Herod's temple, this is further evidence that the sect had rejected the Jerusalem sanctuary. A unique feature of the new text is that the author seems to pass off the scroll as a divine decree from God. In quotations from the Pentateuch the third person singular of the text is regularly rendered as a first person singular.

The Copper Scroll

An unusual scroll of copper, eight feet long and 11 inches high, was found in Cave III in 1952. Because it had become very brittle it was not opened until 1955. The text, published in 1960 by J. Allegro, tells about the location in some 60 places of fabulous amounts of gold and silver. Allegro, who believes that it is a map of the temple treasures drawn up by Zealots fleeing from the Romans, made a survey of the identifiable sites in 1960 — unfortunately without any results. The text in Mishnaic Heb. is the earliest extensive document in that dialect. Cross dates the writing of the Copper Scroll to *c.* A.D. 75. He and Milik regard the text as folkloristic.

Excavations at Khirbet Qumran

Khirbet Qumran, i.e., the ruins of the monastery at Qumran, is located a mile S of Cave I. The ruins have been known for some time. In 1851 F. de Saulcy had mistakenly identified the site as Gomorrah. It was not until several years after the discovery of the MSS in the caves that excavations were conducted from 1951–56 under G. L. Harding and R. de Vaux.

1. *Levels of occupation.* The earliest occupation dates to the 8th–7th cen. B.C., perhaps a fortress built by King Uzziah (II Chr 26:10). A circular cistern dates back to this period. The major settlement, that which can be associated with the MSS from the caves, began in the time of Hyrcanus I (134–104 B.C.). The site was abandoned after the earthquake of 31 B.C. and reoccupied around the time of Herod's death in 4 B.C. The site was then taken by the Romans in A.D. 68 and occupied by a small Roman garrison until A.D. 86. It was finally occupied by the Jewish rebels under Bar Kochba in A.D. 132 – 135.

2. *Buildings and objects.* Although no MSS as such were found in the ruins, pottery similar to that in which MSS were stored in Cave I was found. One potsherd was found on which a budding scribe had practiced the writing of the alphabet. Several hundred coins were found which helped to establish the dates of the occupation levels.

The main settlement covered an area 80 meters square. The most striking feature of Qumran is the number of cisterns and pools, some of which were used for the ritual immersions of the sect. The cisterns were supplied with water by an open aqueduct from the mountain to the W.

Low plaster tables (or benches) 17 feet long and 20 inches high were found together with inkwells. These came from a second–story room which many have called the *scriptorium*, the room used for the copying of the MSS. The largest room, 22 meters long and four and a half wide, served as the refectory for the sect's communal meals.

Some two miles to the S farm buildings were found at the spring of Ain Feshkha.

It has been estimated that some 200–400 persons lived at Qumran at one time. Most lived in huts or tents outside the buildings. A few lived in nearby caves, where signs of occupation have been found in 30 of them.

3. *The cemetery.* Toward the Dead Sea, separated from the Khirbet by a wall, was a sizable cemetery. The main cemetery contains about 1,100 burials, with about 100 burials in secondary cemeteries. In the main cemetery 31 graves were dug, and 13 in the other sections. The main cemetery gave up but one female skeleton and three children's skeletons (from the ages of six to ten). On the other hand, the secondary cemeteries yielded five female skeletons and one of a child, a much higher proportion. Those who identify the sectarians with the normally celibate Essenes may argue that the burial of females in the secondary sections may be an indication that they were not full-fledged members of the community or that their bodies may have been brought to Qumran from the towns where married Essenes lived. More recently, however, further excavations have uncovered more female skeletons in the main cemetery itself.

The Life of the Sect

Although the Manual of Discipline seems to address itself to a celibate community, the Rule of the Congregation and the Damascus Document speak of women and children. Some explain the difference by ascribing it to different stages in the community's history. What is clear is that the sect excluded anyone who was lame, blind, deaf, dumb, or was so aged that he tottered.

Those who wished to enter the sect had to undergo a probationary testing of two years. In the third year one would be admitted to provisional membership. Upon becoming a member, one would give up his material wealth to a common treasury.

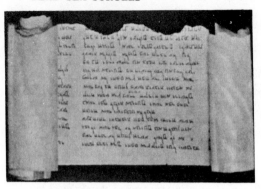

The Habakkuk Commentary. IIS

In addition to the manual work necessary to make the community self-sufficient, the members participated in the communal meals, ritual immersions, and above all in the study of Scriptures. In every group of ten, one man at least had to be studying or interpreting Scriptures at all times. The membership was divided into three shifts so that studies could be maintained throughout the night.

The sectarians were even stricter than the Pharisees in the maintenance of the sabbath. Discipline was severe. For falling asleep in the assembly one had to spend a month in isolation; likewise for foolish laughter; three months for indecent talk; six months for a deliberate lie; for slander against the community one was banished.

Beliefs of the Sect

1. *The angels and God.* Angels take a prominent role in the theology of Qumran. They fight along with the elect in the final war, and are more important than any messiah.

God is depicted as sovereign, predestinating men to either salvation or condemnation. The wicked, it seems, are not even allowed to repent.

2. *Sin and salvation.* Man is a frail creature, sunken in sin, "a spring of impurity, a furnace of iniquity." He can be saved only by the grace of God. The status of the elect is determined in part by his attitude to the Teacher of Righteousness. The sectarians explained Hab 2:4, which Paul cites as "The just shall live by faith," to mean faith in the Teacher. This does not, however, mean faith in an atoning Saviour but rather fidelity to the precepts of the Teacher. Salvation meant membership in the sect. One had a positive duty to hate outsiders.

3. *The Teacher of Righteousness.* This anonymous figure was not strictly speaking the founder of the sect, as he appeared some 20 years after the community had been groping "like the blind." He may possibly have been the author of the Thanksgiving Hymns, which give the greatest insight into the sect's views of sin and salvation. The Habakkuk Commentary, the Damascus Document, and the Commentary on Ps 37 provide but scanty information about the Teacher. He was a priest who was persecuted by the Wicked Priest, i.e., the corrupt high priest. Nowhere is it said that he was killed, let alone crucified as some have averred. Nor is there any justification in any of the scrolls for claiming the resurrection of the Teacher.

Scholars have tried to place the Teacher of Righteousness (TR) and the Wicked Priest (WP) in various historical contexts. (*a*) In the period 175–162 B.C. Rowley and Black would identify the TR with the Zadokite high priest Onias III and the WP with the Hellenizing Jason or his brother Menelaus. (*b*) In the period 162–152 B.C. Stauffer would identify the TR with the Hasidic Jose ben Joezer and the WP with Alcimus. (*c*) In the period 152–134 B.C. Milik, Cross, Sutcliffe, de Vaux, Vermes, Winter, J. Jeremias and Bruce would consider the TR some unknown person and the WP either Jonathan or his brother Simon. (*d*) In the period 134–76 B.C. Allegro and Brownlee would consider the TR some unknown person and the WP Alexander Jannaeus. The Hasmoneans from the time of Jannaeus' predecessor took over the high priesthood as well as the monarchy. (*e*) In the period 76–63 B.C. Dupont Sommer would consider Hyrcanus II as the WP. (*f*) At the time of the war with Rome in A.D. 66 Roth and Driver would identify the TR with the Zealot Menahem and the WP with Eleazar the son of Ananias the high priest. The most likely period seems to be 152–134 B.C. with Simon as WP.

4. *Messianic figures.* Many scholars see in the phrase "anointed ones of Aaron and Israel" a reference to two Messiahs, a priestly Messiah and a kingly Messiah, with the former having a role superior to the latter. This would correspond to the expectations reflected in the Testaments of the Twelve Patriarchs. Other scholars prefer to speak of one Messiah and a priestly companion. It is quite certain that the Teacher of Righteousness was not himself considered the Messiah. He may have fulfilled the role of the anticipated Prophet (Deut 18:18).

5. *Eschatology and afterlife.* The members of the sect believed that they were living in the last days before the coming of the Messiah(s) and the final battle with the wicked. The members believed in immortality for the elect. Certain passages in the Hymns may possibly reflect a belief in the resurrection of the dead. The wicked, however, were to be annihilated.

Identification of the Sect

The sect has been identified with many groups, ranging from the Hasidim, the Pharisees, the Zealots, on the one hand, to the Jewish-Christian Ebionites and medieval Karaites on the other hand. The most plausible identification is with the Essenes, a sect known from Josephus, Philo, and Pliny as an ascetic and generally celibate community living on the W shore of the Dead Sea.

Both the Qumran sectarians and the Essenes had a probationary period for initiates, ranked their members, held property in common, practiced immersion, partook of a common meal, refused the use of oil, held apart from the animal sacrifices of the temple, stressed God's predestination, and were intolerant of outsiders.

There are, to be sure, some discrepancies. The Essenes did not believe in the resurrection of the dead, whereas the sect may have held this belief. The Essenes rejected oaths, but the sect enjoined oaths on their initiates. These and other alleged differences are minor and can be explained. See Essenes.

Significance for NT Studies

1. *John the Baptist.* Since John was ascetic and celibate, lived in the Jordan Valley (thus near Qumran), and practiced baptism, some have suggested that he was reared at Qumran. But John's asceticism stemmed from the fact that he was a Nazarite. His baptism was a single rite and not the repeated washings of Qumran.

2. *Jesus.* Exaggerated comparisons between the Teacher of Righteousness and Jesus have been made, especially by A. Dupont-Sommer and J. Allegro. These views have been popularized by the journalist E. Wilson in a best seller. But in truth there are more contrasts than similarities.

Unlike the sect, Jesus did not withdraw from the world, did not reject the physically deformed, and did not hate outsiders. There is no evidence that the sect regarded the Teacher of Righteousness as pre-existent, as divine, as saving from sin by his death, as sinless, or as the Messiah of David who was also a priest after the order of Melchizedek.

3. *The Gospels.* Now that discovery has been made of actual documents in Heb. and Aram. from before the 2nd cen. A.D., the question of Heb. and Aram. originals of the Gospels may be reinvestigated.

The Gospel of John, considered to be very Hellenistic and dated by some scholars to the 2nd cen. A.D., is shown more clearly than ever to be a product of 1st cen. Palestine by virtue of its many parallels with the Qumran texts.

4. *Acts.* The communion of the church has been compared with the communal meals of the sect. The latter were not celebrated as sacraments, however; the elements did not represent anything. Both groups practiced a type of communism. This was voluntary in the book of Acts but required by the Qumran rules.

5. *Epistles.* Scholars sought to explain the use of the word "mystery" in Paul's epistles in terms of the Hellenistic mystery religions. This may now be explained more simply by the Sem-

itic background of Qumran. Scholars have argued that the office of bishop in the Pastoral Epistles indicates a late date. The functions of the *mebaqqer* or "overseer" at Qumran were the same as those of the bishops in the Pastorals. This fact therefore invalidates the argument.

Of major importance for understanding the Epistle to the Hebrews is a document from Cave XI which deals with the enigmatic figure of Melchizedek. This new text describes Melchizedek as a heavenly deliverer similar to the archangel Michael. He is also portrayed as the "heavenly one" who will proclaim God's salvation. This may help to explain why the author of Hebrews stresses not only Christ's superiority to the Aaronic priesthood but also to the angels. Heb 7:3, which speaks of Melchizedek without parentage, is usually explained on the basis that his ancestors are not mentioned in Gen 14, but may be now interpreted in the light that Melchizedek was regarded as a suprahuman being.

The Six Day War and the Scrolls

Fortunately neither scroll materials at the Palestine Archaeological Museum in Jerusalem nor those in the museum in Amman were harmed or pilfered during the Six Day War. The Israeli government has taken the position that all archaeologists approved for activity on the W bank by the Jordanian government will have permission to continue their projects. Of course this applies to work on the scrolls. Scholars working in E and W Jerusalem before the war had no contact with each other, even by telephone. Now that is changed and research on the scrolls may be expected to benefit by interchange between the international teams.

Bibliography

GENERAL WORKS. John Allegro, *The Dead Sea Scrolls**, Baltimore: Penguin, 1965. F. F. Bruce, *Second Thoughts on the Dead Sea Scrolls*, London: Paternoster Press, 1956. Millar Burrows, *The Dead Sea Scrolls,* New York: Viking Press, 1955. Frank M. Cross, *The Ancient Library of Qumran**, Garden City, N.Y.: Doubleday, 1961. David N. Freedman and Jonas Greenfield, eds., *New Directions in Biblical Archaeology,* Garden City, N.Y.: Doubleday, 1969, William S. LaSor, *Amazing Dead Sea Scrolls and the Christian Faith**, Chicago: Moody Press, 1956. M. Mansoor, *The Dead Sea Scrolls,* Grand Rapids: Eerdmans, 1964. K. Schubert, *The Dead Sea Community,* New York: Harper, 1959.

STORY OF DISCOVERY. Athanasius Samuel, *Treasure of Qumran**, Philadelphia: Westminster, 1966. John Trever, *The Untold Story of Qumran*, Westwood, N.J.: Revell, 1965. Yigael Yadin, *The Message of the Scrolls**, New York: Grosset and Dunlap, 1962.

ARCHAEOLOGY OF QUMRAN. John Allegro,

*Paperback edition is available.

The People of the Dead Sea Scrolls in Text and Pictures, Garden City, N.Y.: Doubleday, 1958. R. de Vaux, L'Archéologie et les Manuscrits de la Mer Morte, London: Oxford Univ. Press, 1961.

TRANSLATIONS. A. DuPont-Sommer, The Essene Writings from Qumran*, Cleveland: World Publ. Co., 1962. Theodor Gaster, The Dead Sea Scriptures*, Garden City, N.Y.: Doubleday, 1964. G. Vermes, The Dead Sea Scrolls in English*, Baltimore: Penguin, 1965.

DOCTRINES OF QUMRAN. F. F. Bruce, Biblical Exegesis in the Qumran Texts, Grand Rapids: Eerdmans, 1959. Helmer Ringgren, The Faith of Qumran*, Philadelphia: Fortress Press, 1963.

QUMRAN AND THE BIBLE. M. Black, The Scrolls and Christian Origins, New York: Scribner's Sons, 1961. W. H. Brownlee, The Meaning of the Qumran Scrolls for the Bible, New York: Oxford Univ., 1964. Jean Danielou, The Dead Sea Scrolls and Primitive Christianity*, New York: New American Library, 1962. R. Laird Harris, "The Dead Sea Scrolls and the Old Testament Text," NPOT, pp. 201-211. Lucetta Mowry, The Dead Sea Scrolls and the Early Church*, Notre Dame, Ind.: Univ. of Notre Dame, 1966. Roland Murphy, The Dead Sea Scrolls and the Bible*, Westminster, Md.: Newman Press, 1956. Jerome Murphy-O'Connor, ed., Paul and Qumran, Chicago: Priory Press, 1968. K. Stendahl, ed., The Scrolls and the New Testament, New York: Harper, 1957.

REFERENCE WORKS. Karl G. Kuhn, Konkordanz zu den Qumrantexten, Gottingen: Vandenhoeck and Ruprecht, 1960. A. M. Habermann, Megilloth Midbar Yehuda, Jerusalem: Machbaroth Lesifruth Publ. House, 1959. E. Lohse, Die Texte aus Qumran, Munich: Kösel-Verlag, 1964. [The last two works contain vocalized texts; Lohse also has a German translation facing the texts. For individual text editions with commentaries, see bibliographies below.]

BIBLIOGRAPHIES. C. Burchard, Bibliographie zu den Handschriften vom Toten Meer, Berlin: Töpelmann, 1957; 2nd vol., 1965. William S. LaSor, Bibliography of the Dead Sea Scrolls, Pasadena, Calif.: Fuller Theol. Seminary, 1958. Current bibliographies are being published in the journal Revue de Qumran. Cf. also James A. Sanders, "Palestine Manuscripts, 1947-1967," JBL, LXXXVI (1967), 431-440; J. Fitzmyer, "A Bibliographical Aid to the Study of the Qumran Cave IV Texts 158-186," CBQ, XXXI (1969), 59-71.

E. M. Y.

DEAF. Used in the Scriptures both in the physical sense and figuratively as expressing unwillingness to hear the divine message (Ps 58:4). It may also be used to signify incapacity to understand God's Word for want of spirituality (Ps 38:13).

*Paperback edition is available.

DEAL. See Weights, Measures, and Coins.

DEARTH. This word means scarcity or famine. The word originated from "dear"; that which is precious or dear is rare or scarce. The word is used in the KJV in Gen 41:54; II Kgs 4:38; II Chr 6:28; Neh 5:3; Jer 14:1; Acts 7:11; 11:28. In later translations "dearth" is replaced in most instances by such terms as "rare," "famine," "drought."

DEATH (Heb. māwet; Gr. thanatos). The cessation of natural or animal life; the state of having ceased to live; that separation, whether violent or otherwise, of the soul from the body whereby life as an organism is ended. So death has been variously defined as: "disunion of body and soul"—Tertullian; "departure of the mind from the body"—Cicero; "the suspension of personal union between the body and the soul, followed by the resolution of the body into its chemical elements, and the introduction of the soul into that separate state of existence which may be assigned to it by its Creator and Judge"—A. A. Hodge. Death may be thought of as that experience in which one's connection with the world of life is broken off or terminated. Theologically, it is the last event in the probationary history of the individual man.

Scientifically, death is a servant of the natural economy. Hence it is not a failure, but a sacrifice to secure a higher process of life, or at least to insure propagation of the species. Cf. Jesus' remark in Jn 12:24.

Scripturally, the idea of death is used or described: (1) In the sense of the process of dying (Gen 21:16). (2) Synonymously for poison (II Kgs 4:40). (3) To describe one in danger of perishing (Jud 5:18; cf. Paul's "in deaths oft," II Cor 11:23). (4) As a return to dust (Gen 3:19; Eccl 12:7). (5) As a removal of the breath of life (Ps 104:29). (6) As a departure or exodus from the body (Isa 38:12; II Cor 5:1; II Pet 1:13-15; cf. also II Cor 5:8-9). (7) As being unclothed of one's earthly garment (II Cor 5:3-4; II Pet 1:13-14). (8) As departure to a land of gloom and darkness (Job 10:21-22; 38:17). (9) As sleep (Ps 13:3; Jer 51:39; Jn 11:13 ff.; I Thess 4:15; Acts 7:60). (10) As loss of spiritual life (Rom 7:9-13; 8:6; Eph 2:1, 5; Col 2:13; Jude 12). (11) As an approaching ominous event that casts a deep, foreboding shadow (Heb. ṣalmāwet, "shadow of death," KJV; "deep darkness," RSV; Job 3:5; Ps 23:4; 44:19; 107:10, 14; Jer 2:6; Isa 9:2; Mt 4:16; Lk 1:79).

Death is personified (Job 28:22; I Cor 15:55; Rev 20:14) as a ruler, tyrant, or enemy (Job 18:13-14; Ps 55:15; I Cor 15:26; Rev 6:8); or as a hunter who lays snares for men (Ps 18:5; 116:3; Prov 13:14; 14:27).

Death appears constantly as the highest form of punishment that can be administered to transgressors (Gen 9:5-6; Ex 21:12; etc.). Capital punishment is therefore retributive and not merely reformatory. It served to purge out evil and to warn the nation (Deut 13:5-11). The final state of the unrepentant is called "the second death" (Rev 20:14; 21:8). But death in the scriptural sense never means annihilation of the person or extinction of being.

Death comes but once to each human organism (Heb 9:27), and while it is sure (Job 14:1-2), its advent is uncertain (Prov 27:1); but it is universal to mankind (Gen 3:19; Rom 5:12; I Cor 15:22). The grave is referred to as "the gates of death" (Job 38:17; Ps 9:13; 107:18), symbolizing the entrance to the abode of the dead and also the place from which death exercises its authority.

Man, in the case of his first parents, was placed only conditionally under the law of life. Eden yielded its rich fruitage to sustain his physical life. Deity walked and communicated with him to sustain his spiritual life, which was dependent upon communion with "the Father of his spirit."

Man's transgression of the will and commandment of God, involving as it did a breach of covenant, brought death as its penalty. Death is a consequence of sin (Rom 5:12; 6:23; Jas 1:15; Gen 2:17). Satan has instigated murders (Jn 8:44), and has used his power to inflict death as the means of gripping the human race in the bondage of fear (Heb 2:14). Therefore, Christ's redemptive work on behalf of mankind to deliver from both the penalty and the fear of death entailed His own death (I Cor 15:3; Rom 4:25; I Pet 3:18). By submitting to death He triumphed over it, abolished it, and brought to believers a blessed hope of life and immortality (II Tim 1:10). The sting of death has been removed (I Cor 15:55-56), and the grave has been robbed of its victory for those who are "in Christ" (I Cor 15:22).

Hence, because of Christ's victory over death, it may even be desirable to the righteous person (Lk 2:28-30), for he will gain rest from his labors (Rev 14:13) and death introduces him into felicity (II Cor 5:8).

See Abraham's Bosom; Dead, The; Eternal State and Death; Christ, Passion of.

Bibliography. R. Bultmann, "*Thanatos,* etc.," TDNT, III, 7-25. H. F. Lovell Cocks, "Death," *Handbook of Christian Theology,* New York: Meridian Books, 1958, pp. 70-73. Olin A. Curtis, *The Christian Faith,* New York: Eaton & Mains, 1905, Chap. XX. A. B. Davidson, *Theology of the Old Testament,* New York: Scribner's, 1906, pp. 495-532. Franz Delitzsch, *A System of Biblical Psychology,* Edinburgh: T. & T. Clark, 1899, pp. 467-476. John Laidlaw, *Bible Doctrine of Man,* Edinburgh: T. & T. Clark, 1897, pp. 171-176. Alex. Macalister and Herman Bavinck. "Death," ISBE, II, 811-813. McClintock and Strong, *Cyclopedia of Biblical, Theological and Ecclesiastical Literature,* II, 712-715. G. F. Oehler, *Theology of the Old Testament,* Grand Rapids: Zondervan, reprint, pp.

166-174. Alan Richardson, "Death, etc.," *Theological Word Book of the Bible,* New York: Macmillan, 1951, pp. 60-61. H. Orton Wiley, *Christian Theology,* Kansas City, Mo.: Kingshighway Press, 1943, III, 212-215.

R. E. Pr.

DEBATE. The English word comes from the Latin *de,* "down"; *batuere,* "beat," and now means to discuss in an open, friendly manner. In early English it was true to its Latin origin and meant to quarrel or wrangle or contend for something. In the KJV it is used only in this latter sense of strife (Prov 25:9; Isa 27:8; 58:4; Rom 1:29; II Cor 12:20).

DEBIR (dē'bĭr), A name given to a king and to three cities in Canaan. The word may mean "innermost room of a shrine," then, "sacred city," and ultimately may have been substituted for an older name, just as Zion ("citadel") became synonymous with Jerusalem.

1. A king of Eglon according to the Heb. MT (Josh 10:3). He was one of the five kings in the Amorite coalition that attempted to halt Joshua's invasion.

2. A Canaanite royal city (Josh 10:38 f.; 12:13), inhabited by the Anakim (Josh 11:21). It is listed as Kirjath-sannah (*q.v.*) in the hill country of Judah (Josh 15:49), and was also formerly known as Kirjath-sepher (Josh 15:15; Jud 1:11). The city of Debir was later assigned to the Levites (Josh 21:15). Debir was initially conquered by Joshua (Josh 10:38-39), but had to be recaptured by Othniel, the son-in-law of Caleb (Josh 15:15-19; Jud 1:11-15).

It has been tentatively identified with Tell Beit Mirsim, 12 miles SW of Hebron. Excavations of that site (1926-1932) have shown that it was founded *c.* 2200 B.C., became a fortified Hyksos city, and that it later underwent several destructions, including those probably by the Israelites, by Shishak of Egypt, and by Nebuchadnezzar. During the 9th and 8th cen. B.C. Tell Beit Mirsim was a center of the textile dyeing industry, according to numerous vats found by the excavators under the leadership of M. G. Kyle and Albright (W. F. Albright, "Debir," TAOTS, pp. 207-220).

Two other sites proposed for Debir, which have upper and lower springs (Josh 15:19) and are higher in the hill country (Josh 15:48-49), are Khirbet Terrameh, five and one-half miles SW of Hebron, and Khirbet Rabūd, nine miles SSW of Hebron (GTT, p. 282). Investigation of the latter site since 1967 has revealed Late Bronze Age occupation.

3. A city in Gad (Josh 13:26), also called Lo-debar (*q.v.*), located in the eastern part of Gilead. It is mentioned in the story of David's flight from Absalom (II Sam 17:27), and was a bone of contention between Aram and Israel in the wars of Jeroboam II (Amos 6:13).

4. A place on the N boundary of Judah (Josh 15:7), near the valley of Achor. It perhaps is

Thoghret ed-Debr, seven and one-half miles NE of Jerusalem, on the Jerusalem-Jericho road.

S. C. and J. R.

DEBORAH (dĕb'ŏ-rà)

1. Rebekah's nurse, who accompanied Rebekah to Canaan (Gen 24:59). Her death at Bethel is recorded in Gen 35:8.

2. A prophetess who "judged" Israel in the 13th or 12th cen. She was one of those rare individuals who had a special charismatic gift of the Spirit of God (cf. Jud 6:34; 11:29; 14:6); as such she was recognized as a prophetess (Jud 4:4). She had her headquarters under "the palm tree of Deborah" between Ramah and Bethel (Jud 4:5), where the people or leaders of the various tribes came to have their disputes arbitrated and settled. Although she probably gained her reputation as an ordinary, non-military judge, she was best remembered by later generations as the one able to rally the scattered tribes of Israel to loyalty to Jehovah, and hence as their savior or deliverer from the oppression of Jabin, king of the Canaanites (cf. Jud 5). Her own contemporaries respected her as a "mother in Israel" (Jud 5:7).

The song of Deborah (Jud 5:2-31) celebrates the victory of Deborah and Barak over Sisera and is one of the oldest pieces of literature in the OT. Recent studies by W. F. Albright, Frank M. Cross, Jr., and others have demonstrated the archaic style and form of this poem by comparison with the ancient Canaanite tablets from Ugarit (*see* Ras Shamra). Thus this poem is very important not only for a contemporary description of the historical situation and theological perspective of the period of the judges, but for the form and style of the poetry and language of the period as well.

R. L. S.

DEBT, DEBTOR. In OT times the debtor was to be pitied. In fact, it was a mark of divine favor to be in the class of the lender (Deut 15:6; 28:12, 44). The penalty of nonpayment often was slavery (Lev 25:47; Isa 50:1; Amos 2:6; 8:6). The harshness of this custom is graphically portrayed in the case of the widow's two sons (II Kgs 4:1-7). Debtors joined the distressed and discontented who followed David (I Sam 22:2).

Debts often involved pledges and usury and these were burdensome. The verb *ḥābal*, "to take in pledge" (Deut 24:6, 17; Job 24:3, 9), denotes something binding and painful as well. Interest or usury, Heb. *neshek*, literally means "something bitten off" (note Hab 2:7, ASV marg.). The deprivations caused by interest-seeking creditors are to be seen in the hardship cases of Neh 5:1-11.

On the other hand, the oppressive severity of life for the Israelite debtor was meant to be mitigated by regulations of the Mosaic law. The seventh year was the year of release from all pecuniary obligations (Deut 15:1-2). On the taking of pledges, a creditor was not to take a widow's garment (Deut 24:17), nor a millstone (Deut 24:6). Clothes taken as security from the poor were to be returned before sundown (Ex 22:26-27). Also, it was not the creditor's prerogative to determine the nature of the pledge (Deut 24:10-12).

Usury, especially from the poor, was condemned (Ex 22:25; Lev 25:35-37; etc.). Usury is linked with unjust gain in Prov 28:8. The righteous lend (Ps 37:26), and a rich kinsman might redeem his brother (Lev 25:47-49). Under the predominantly agricultural economy of the Israelite culture in the OT period, loans were not commercial in purpose but charitable, granted to tide a poor farmer over a time of hardship. Hence the Pentateuchal laws did not regulate mercantile pursuits but directed one's attitude to his unfortunate neighbor. *See* Loan; Mortgage; Surety; Usury.

According to the NT, we are to "owe no man anything" (Rom 13:8) and to show kindness and generosity (Mt 5:42; 6:12; Lk 6:35). Debts were forgiven (Mt 18:23-35; Lk 7:41-42). On the other hand, the parable of the unjust steward gives evidence of a commercial credit system in the Graeco-Roman civilization (Lk 16:1-7), and the parables on the talents and pounds condemn the unfaithful for not making gain by usury through the facilities of a bank (Mt 25:27; Lk 19:23).

This subject has rich theological overtones. The sinner and the debtor are most certainly related. Note the use of the word for debtor, *opheiletēs*, in Lk 13:4 (cf. v.2), and the usages in Lk 11:4 and Mt 6:12, 24. Sin makes us all debtors to God, and brings on an enslavement from which there is no release except through divine redemption and forgiveness, which in turn is to be expressed through us toward others.

I. G. P.

DECALOGUE. *See* Ten Commandments.

DECAPOLIS (dĕ-kăp'ŏ-lĭs; Gr. *deka*, "ten," and *polis*, "city," meaning "the league of ten cities"). Pliny called the territory "Decapolita regio" (*Natural History*, V, 16). It began on the W side of the Jordan where the plain of Esdraelon opens out into the river valley, being a part of Galilee at one time; it stretched across the Jordan to the E, embracing the territory given to the tribe of Manasseh at the time of the division of the land (Num 32:33-42).

As indicated by the name, there were originally ten cities in the league. Most of them were built by the followers of Alexander the Great, and to some extent were rebuilt by the Romans in 65 B.C., who conferred upon these cities the privileges of their own coinage, courts, and army. Other towns were added to the league until a total of 18 were included. The original cities were Scythopolis (Beth-shan), Hippos,

The circular forum and main street of Jerash, one of the cities of the Decapolis. G. Trimboli

Gadara (extensive remains are visible and are now called Um Qeis), Pella (modern Khirbet Fahil), Philadelphia (Rabbah and modern Amman), Gerasa, Dion, Canatha (OT Kenath), Raphana, and Damascus which alone has continuously remained a city to this day. Scythopolis (modern Beisan) was the only city W of the Jordan. (It was excavated by University of Pennsylvania, 1921-33; cf. BW, pp. 143-5.)

The Gospels indicate a repeated contact with this territory by Jesus during His itinerations. Multitudes coming from Decapolis followed Him in the beginning of His ministry (Mt 4:25). The Gadarene demoniac bore witness to his healing in the region of Decapolis (Mk 5:20), where Jesus on more than one occasion traveled (Mk 7:31). *See* Beth-shan; Gadara; Gerasa.

H. L. D.

DECEIT, DECEIVER. Many Heb. and Gr. words appear in English Bibles as forms of the word' "deceit." Basically it means a deliberate misrepresentation of the truth, especially in moral and spiritual matters, in order to mislead another person. The most frequently used Heb. root, *rāmâ*, and its derivatives, imply treachery and betrayal (e.g., I Sam 19:17; II Kgs 9:23). In the NT this concept is expressed chiefly by the Gr. *dolos*, "craftiness," "treachery" (Mk 7:22; Rom 1:29); by *apataō*, "to cheat," "seduce," "beguile" ("deceive you with vain words," Eph 5:6), and *apatē*, "seduction," "deceitfulness" (e.g., of riches, Mt 13:22; of evil, Heb 3:13); "deceitful lusts," Eph 4:22; and by *planaō*, "to go astray," "lead into error" (e.g., Mt 24:4-5,11,24).

While it is very possible to deceive oneself that he has no sin (I Jn 1:8; cf. I Cor 3:18), yet the source of all deceit and the arch-deceiver is the devil (*q.v.*), the one who deceives (Gr. *planōn*) the whole world (Rev 12:9; cf. 20:3,8,10). In the end time he will inspire a false prophet in league with the Beast (*q.v.*) to further his work of deception (Rev 13:14; 19:20; 20:10). The Antichrist himself, the man of lawlessness, will be energized by Satan to deceive many through signs and false wonders (II Thess 2:3-4, 8-10, NASB).

In the meantime many deceivers (*planoi*) have gone out into the world who refuse to acknowledge the truth about Jesus Christ (II Jn 7). John recognizes that these are antichrists, forerunners of the final Antichrist who is coming (II Jn 7; I Jn 2:18). Paul warns that there are false apostles, deceitful workers who masquerade as apostles of Christ (II Cor 11:13; cf. II Tim 3:13; Tit 1:10). He also states that in the latter times some will fall away from the faith because they pay attention to deceitful spirits and doctrines of demons (I Tim 4:1, NASB). While the Christian may be misunderstood and called a deceiver, even as were Paul (II Cor 6:8) and Jesus Himself (Mt 27:63), yet he will never resort to deceit or guile to extend the gospel (I Thess 2:3; II Cor 4:2).

See Guile.

Bibliography. Herbert Braun, "*Planaō*, etc.," TDNT, VI, 228-253.

J. R.

DECISION, VALLEY OF. The Heb. *'ēmeq heḥārûṣ* could be rendered "valley of judgment" or "valley of fate-decreed" (Joel 3:14). The

Heb. verb *ḥāraṣ* is used in Isa 10:22-23; 28:22 in the sense of destruction being decided or decreed for rebellious peoples. The valley of decision is identical with the valley of Jehoshaphat (*yᵉhôshāphāt*, "Yahweh hath judged," Joel 3:12). It is the place where someday God Himself shall judge all nations.

As early as the time of Eusebius of Caesarea (d. A.D. 340), this site was identified with the valley of the Kidron (E of Jerusalem). But this is pure conjecture. No valley of Palestine has ever borne this title. However, when our Lord returns for judgment, the Mount of Olives shall be cleft in twain and a new valley will extend from E to W (Zech 14:4). *Perhaps* this is the enigmatic valley of decision.

DECREE, ROYAL. Royal decrees are public proclamations, usually in writing, issued by rulers to their subjects. Isaiah (10:1) condemns rulers who proclaim unjust laws. Such proclamations seem to have been inscribed on stone by command of the king.

Hezekiah issued a decree concerning the observance of the Passover after it had been neglected for some time (II Chr 30:5). Nebuchadnezzar issued various decrees, such as the death penalty for his wise men who were unable to declare his dream (Dan 2:9, 13, 15) and his order for all people to worship the image that he set up on the plains of Dura (Dan 3:10). Darius the Mede was tricked into establishing an injunction against anyone who prayed to any god or man besides himself (Dan 6:7-15, NASB).

The Persian king Cyrus issued a decree permitting the Jews to rebuild their temple (Ezr 5:13), a decree which was subsequently confirmed by Darius (Ezr 6:1-12). When the Persian king Ahasuerus divorced Vashti, this fact was made known through the kingdom by a decree (Est 1:19-22). He also let a decree be issued in his name to destroy all the Jews in his domain (Est 3:8-15; 4:3, 8). This was forestalled by a subsequent decree which Mordecai sent out in the name of the king that the Jews might defend themselves (Est 8:8-9:1).

A decree for a census issued by Caesar Augustus brought Mary and Joseph to Bethlehem prior to the birth of Jesus (Lk 2:1). At Thessalonica the enemies of Christ accused the apostle Paul of acting contrary to the decrees of Caesar (Claudius) in asserting that there was another king, namely, Jesus (Acts 17:1-7). This anticipated the persecutions of Christians until the time of Constantine, for Christians were considered disloyal citizens since they rejected the gods of the state, including the emperor who was worshiped as a god.

Ps 2:7 speaks of a royal decree from God Himself declaring that His Anointed (the Messiah, the Christ) is His Son. The Most High God announced His decree of humiliation to Nebuchadnezzar through the vision which Daniel interpreted (Dan 4:17, 24).

C. F. P.

DEDAN (dē'dăn). The Dedanim (Isa 21:13) or Dedanites were an Arab people, descendants of Ham through Cush (Gen 10:7; I Chr 1:9), who intermarried with descendants of Abraham by Keturah (Gen 25:3; I Chr 1:32). That the name Dedan does not represent two separate peoples in these genealogies seems certain from the fact that in each case the brother of Dedan is named Sheba. They built the city of Dedan, 100 miles SW of Tema (*q.v.*), at a large oasis (el-'Ula, 175 miles NW of Medina, 350 miles SE of Petra) on the caravan route to S Arabia used by the Queen of Sheba. Thus they were known for their caravans and traders (Isa 21:13; Ezk 27:20; 38:13).

Dedan is mentioned in oracles against Edom (Jer 49:8; Ezk 25:13), indicating their close links with the Edomites and leading to the speculation that some Dedanites had settled in Edom. Dedan is mentioned in certain proto-Arabic Sabean and Minaean inscriptions, indicating its close contacts with these successive rulers of S Arabia (W. F. Albright, "Dedan," *Geshichte und Altes Testament*, Tübingen, 1953, pp. 1-12). See Arabia.

J. R.

DEDICATE, DEDICATION. To set apart or give to the deity or to a cause. Several Heb. terms are translated by this English concept, in verbal and substantive forms. The most frequent Heb. term, from the root word *qōdesh*, "apartness," "sacredness," "holiness," applies to men and to things set apart for divine service. Thus Ex 13:2, "Sanctify unto me all the firstborn." The things dedicated to God include treasure (Jud 17:3), spoils of war (I Chr 26:27), a field (Lev 27:18), and the temple (II Chr 7:5).

Of special usage is *ḥerem*, an antonym which denotes an object irrevocably devoted to one's God, or set apart for destruction. Any object or person that had been sacred to or associated with another deity must be "accursed," removed from any use by the layman (Deut 7:25-26; 20:17-18; Moabite Stone, line 17, ANET, p. 320). Usually this ban meant death or destruction, although certain objects captured in a holy war could be banned from common use and dedicated to sacred use in the sanctuary or by the priests (Num 18:14; Josh 6:19). See Curse. Achan disregarded the proscription imposed on Jericho and everything within it and was himself "devoted" (Josh 7:20-24; 8:26-27), while Rahab escaped a similar fate by aligning herself with God's covenant people (Josh 2:9-14).

See Consecration; Sanctification; Separation.

G. A. T.

DEDICATION, FEAST OF. *See* Festivals.

DEEP. The common Heb. root signifying "deep" or "low" is *'āmaq*. Another Heb. word, *tehôm*, refers to the ocean depths. While scholars have sought to derive this word from Akkad. *ti'amat,* the goddess of the salt water in the Babylonian creation epic (ANET, pp. 61–68), such borrowing cannot successfully be maintained, as Alexander Heidel has shown (*The Babylonian Genesis,* pp. 98–101).

The word *tehôm* is used: (1) of the primeval watery mass at creation (Gen 1:2; Ps 104:6; Prov 8:27); (2) of the sea (Ex 15:8; Isa 51:10; etc.); (3) of the subterranean reservoir of water (Gen 7:11; Deut 33:13); (4) in the figurative sense of profound: "Thy judgments are a great deep" (Ps 36:6; cf. 92:5); cf. " the deep things of God" (I Cor 2:10).

In the NT Gr. *abyssos,* "bottomless," refers literally to the depths of the Sea of Galilee (Lk 8:31, RSV) and figuratively to the underworld or abode of the dead (Rom 10:7, RSV) and of demons (Rev 9:1, 11; etc.). When used of water, *bathos* refers to the deep sea (Lk 5:4), and *buthos* is used only of ocean depths (II Cor 11:25). *See* Abyss; Hell.

R. L. D.

DEER. *See* Animals, II. 10.

DEFILE. In the OT this word is closely connected with the clean and the unclean (*see* Uncleanness) and the laws with regard thereto, as well as defilement of God's temple (Lev 15:31; 20:3; Num 19:13; Ps 79:1; Ezk 5:11), and the land (Jer 2:7; 3:9; 16:18). In the NT ceremonial defilement is shown to be only a type of moral defilement, and those who elevate the ceremonial above the moral are condemned by Christ (Mk 7:1–23). The extremes to which the Jews were going in cleansing cups, pots, tables and themselves were condemned by Christ. Not what enters the body defiles but what is said and done (v. 15). The keenness of the issue is revealed by the fact that the one known argument between John the Baptist and the Jews concerned purification (Jn 3:25). As a Levite and of the priestly order his baptism raised this question.

Peter had to learn by special revelation that nothing is actually unclean in itself (Acts 10:9–48). Paul advanced this teaching, though for expediency's sake he did once join in a Jewish purification ceremony. It is to be noticed, however, that this was the immediate cause of his Caesarean imprisonment (Acts 21:26 ff.).

R. A. K.

DEGREE. The Bible speaks of men of high degree (I Chr 17:17) and of low degree (Lk 1:52; Jas 1:9) with reference to their position in human society, whether they be exalted like David or of humble circumstances.

The deacons who serve well "purchase to themselves a good degree" (I Tim 3:13, KJV), i.e., they obtain for themselves a high standing or rank (Gr. *bathmos*) (NASB). Such a deacon gains a respected reputation in the church, and is also laying up treasures in heaven where he will have good standing at the judgment seat of Christ (H. A. Kent, Jr., *The Pastoral Epistles,* Chicago: Moody, 1958, p. 143).

For the "ten degrees" that the shadow of the sun turned backward for King Hezekiah (II Kgs 20:9–11; Isa 38:8) *see* Sun Dial. For a song of degrees (in titles of Ps 120–134) *see* Degrees, Song of.

DEGREES, SONG OF The KJV translation of the titles of Ps 120–134. The RSV and NASB call each "A Song of Ascents." The Heb. *ma'ălôt* literally means "goings up." The expression has been interpreted in different ways. Some see in it a reference to songs sung by pilgrims going up ("ascending") to Jerusalem (cf. Ps 122:4). Others suggest that it has specific reference to a supposed new year's festival with a ceremonial ascent to the temple, at which time these psalms were sung. The Mishnaic Tractate Middoth (ii.5) states that one of the 15 Psalms of Ascent was sung on each of the 15 steps leading from the women's court to the men's court of the second temple. The Levites sang these psalms, according to the Mishna, during the all-night ceremony of the first night of the Feast of Tabernacles.

Bibliography. J. Liebreich, "The Songs of Ascents and the Priestly Blessing," JBL, LXXIV (1955), 33–36.

C. F. P.

DEHAVITES (dē-hā'vīts). Mentioned among the groups for whom Rehum, the chancellor, wrote in Aramaic (Syrian) to Artaxerxes, the Persian king, filing a complaint against those who had recently returned from Babylonia to Jerusalem (Ezr 4:6–10). Along with the others they are identified as those who had been earlier transplanted by the great Asnapper (Ashurbanipal) from Babylonia and its neighboring regions to Samaria.

Formerly the Dehavites have been identified as a particular group like the Persians, Babylonians, etc. They were therefore thought to be the Daoi mentioned by Herodotus or the Dahae of Pliny and Virgil. This made them a tribe of the area to the E of the Caspian. The difficulty with this theory is that this region is far removed from Assyrian borders and, further, there is no mention of them in extant Assyrian documents. The more recent tendency is to follow a suggestion based on extrabiblical sources; that is, to read *dî-hû'* (or Targum *dîhû*) instead of *dehāwē',* meaning "that is" (cf. *hoi eisin* of Codex Vaticanus).

The resulting rendering is: "Susians, that is, the Elamites ..." (cf. Ezr 4:9, RSV, "the men of Susa, that is, the Elamites ...").

H. E. Fi.

DEKAR (dē'kar). The name of one of the 12 officers who provided food for King Solomon and his household (I Kgs 4:7, 9).

DELAIAH (dē-lā'yà)
1. A descendant of David through Zerubbabel; one of the seven sons of Elioenai (I Chr 3:24; KJV, Dalaiah).
2. A priest serving during David's reign who was leader of the 23rd course (I Chr 24:18–19).
3. A prince or officer, the son of Shemaiah, at the court of Jehoiakim. After hearing the words of prophecy from Jeremiah's scroll, he with Elnathan and Gemariah pleaded with the king not to burn the scroll (Jer 36:12, 25).
4. The ancestor of one of the post–Exilic families. Having lost the family genealogy, the sons "could not prove their fathers' houses or their descent" (Ezr 2:59–60, RSV; Neh 7:62).
5. The father of Shemaiah, a contemporary of Nehemiah. The builder rejected Shemaiah's counsel to flee and accused him of accepting hire from Tobiah and Sanballat (Neh 6:10–13).
R. O. C.

DELILAH (dĭ-lī'là). A Philistine woman living in the valley of Sorek c. 1100 B.C., to whom Samson revealed the secret of his strength (Jud 16:4–22). The Wadi Sorek is the main pass leading W down from Jerusalem, through the Shephelah or foothills to the Maritime plain.

Although there were at least three women in Samson's life, it is Delilah who receives the greatest attention in Scripture. She succeeded where all others had failed in defeating Israel's champion. Samson "loved" this woman (Jud 16:4) and saw her frequently. Noting this, the leaders of the Philistines sought by bribery to accomplish what they had been unable to do by force. The bribe by which they persuaded her to deceive Samson was so large that it may imply that her loyalties were with Israel. However, her attachment to Samson may have been so strong that a large sum was required to betray her lover, even if he were an enemy of her nation. Each of the five Philistine rulers promised to pay her 1,100 pieces of silver (Jud 16:5). If shekels are meant, the total amount was nearly fourteen times the price paid by Abraham for a place to bury his wife (Gen 23:15).

Samson suspected that Delilah was interested in something other than romance and three times he misled her as to the source of his strength. On the third attempt, Samson apparently slept on her lap while she wove his hair into fabric on a loom. This time he left with loom and all. On her fourth attempt, Delilah accused him of lack of love day after day until he relented and told her the truth. The secret of his strength lay in his Nazarite vow which separated him unto God for special service, the symbol of this vow being the uncut hair. Delilah perceived now that his secret was laid bare, and with confidence summoned the Philistines, who came bringing the money. She again got him to sleep in her lap and then called an assis-

tant to cut his hair. Delilah thus gained lasting infamy as the wily temptress who betrayed her lover for a large sum of money.
G. A. T.

DELIVERANCE. *See* Freedom; Liberation; Liberty.

DELUGE. *See* Flood.

DEMAS (dē'màs). Mentioned three times in the NT (Col 4:14; II Tim 4:10; Phm 24). This may be a shortened form of Demetrius (*q.v.*). He was a believer, and was evidently with Paul when he wrote Colossians and Philemon. Later, when writing II Timothy, Paul pens the dismal fact that Demas had forsaken him, "having loved this present world."

DEMETRIUS (dē-mē'trĭ-ŭs). At least five persons bore this name in biblical times.
1. Demetrius I, successor to Antiochus Epiphanes (162 B.C.), known for his intrigues, guile, and cruelty. In general he practiced repressive measures toward Jews in Palestine (I Macc 10:1–21).
2. Demetrius II, son of Demetrius I, who concluded a favorable treaty with Jonathan Maccabeus which he later violated. His generals were defeated at Hazor (I Macc 11:53 f.).
3. Demetrius III, ruler of Syria at the time of Alexander Jannaeus. During the latter's bitter quarrel with the Pharisees, he took their part, and thus extended his realm. Later, he was imprisoned and starved into submission by Philip Herod.
4. A Christian highly endorsed by John (III Jn 12).
5. The silversmith at Ephesus who accused Paul of endangering his trade and of imperiling the sanctity of the goddess Diana or Artemis (Acts 19:24 ff.). Because of this accusation, there ensued the riot in Ephesus which almost caused Paul and his companions to lose their lives. With the appearance of the town clerk, however, sanity was restored as he referred the rioters to their rights before the courts and their responsibilities as citizens (vv. 36–41).
J. F. G.

DEMONOLOGY. The study of the existence and activity of demons or evil spirits may be theologically classified under the doctrine of fallen angels. II Pet 2:4 and Jude 6–7 declare that some of the fallen angels are being kept in everlasting chains awaiting judgment. Some scholars consider this confinement merely a metaphor to express the fact that such beings are only specifically restrained by God as to their activities. Yet Christ's going in spirit during the time of His burial to proclaim His triumph to the imprisoned spirits that had been disobedient in Noah's day (I Pet 3:18–20,22b) points to an actual imprisonment of spirit-beings. By deduction one may infer that the demons which have been vexing mankind since the Flood are the remainder of the angels that followed Satan (Mt 25:41; Rev 12:7-9), for he is also called the prince of demons (Mt 12:24; cf. v. 26). Demons were considered to be evil angels in ancient Judaism.

Demons (devils, KJV) are unquestionably real, individual beings having personality and knowledge about God and humans (Jas 2:19; Acts 19:15). Their present domain is the spirit realm or supernatural sphere (Eph 6:12, Berkeley), but they desire to be embodied in living human or animal beings. Demons are able to invade or influence the minds of human teachers in order to suggest false doctrines (I Tim 4:1; I Jn 4:1-6; Jas 3:15). They actually commune with the souls of men in the case of mediums who yield to them. Demons will entice the rulers of the earth to assemble for the battle of Armageddon (Rev 16:14).

In the OT, evil or lying spirits possessed a certain freedom of action to tempt and thus test men, as revealed in the case of Job (Job 1-2). Yet they remained under God's ultimate control who uses or permits their activity to punish people for their sins (I Sam 16:14-16,23; 18:10; 19:9; I Kgs 22:21-23). Demons (shēdîm) were the reality behind the Canaanite gods or idols which many Israelites were tempted to worship (Deut 32:17; Ps 106:37; cf. I Cor 10:20-21; Rev 9:20). A specific form of such

Bronze figurine of the demon god Pazuzu, c. 800-600 B.C. ORINST

worship was the slaying of sacrifices for "devils" (KJV) or goat-idols (śe'îrîm, Lev 17:7; II Chr 11:15). In translating shēd by Gr. daimonion in the LXX, the Alexandrian Jews gave clear evidence that they considered the gods to be more than mere objects of wood, stone or metal. In the LXX daimonia is also found in Ps 96:(95:)5 for "idols" and in Ps 91:(90:)6 for "destruction" with an apparent allusion to the noonday demon of heat known in ancient Greece as Pan or Artemis-Hecate. The LXX translators used daimon instead of naming the Canaanite god Gad in Isa 65:11 (KJV, "troop"; RSV, "fortune").

In the NT, demons are frequently said to take possession of men, and Christ therefore cast them out (e.g., Mt 4:24; 8:16; 9:33; 15:22). At times more than one demon may possess one person, as in the cases of the maniac of Gadara (Mk 5:1-17; Lk 8:30-33, 36) and of Mary Magdalene (Lk 8:2). Such demons often produce uncleanness, whether ritual, moral or spiritual (Lk 4:33-36; 6:18; 8:27-29; 9:42; 11:24-26).

The disciples were empowered and commissioned to heal all manner of diseases and to cast out demons (Mt 10:8; Lk 9:1; 10:17-20). They had grave difficulty, however, with certain demons and were told by Christ that these could be cast out only after prayer and fasting (Mk 9:14-29). The apostles effected deliverance for victims of demonic oppression by use of the name of Jesus (Acts 16:16-18; 19:12-17). The writings of the Ante-Nicene Fathers indicate that the church continued to exorcise demons well after the Apostolic Age. Even if Christ's promise in Mk 16:17, "And these signs shall follow them that believe; in my name shall they cast out devils" (part of the questioned ending of Mk 16:9-20), were not canonical, it would then be descriptive of conditions early in the 2nd cen. A.D.

Pastors and foreign missionaries testify to demon possession among many peoples of the world today, from primitive heathen tribes with animistic beliefs to highly educated persons in Europe and America. In numerous cases those who commit mass murders or suicide seem to have been impelled by wicked demons. It is urgent that Christian workers take seriously this doctrine and learn to exercise the authority of Christ to set free those who are demon oppressed or possessed. See Angels; Devil; Divination; Exorcism; Familiar Spirit; Madness; Principalities.

Bibliography. Paul Bechtel, "Witches in the Air"; Ray B. Buker, Sr., "Are Demons Real Today?" Derek Prince, "Release from Depression," *Christian Life,* XXIX (March, 1968). William H. Chisholm, *Vivid Experiences in Korea,* Chicago: Moody Press, 1938, pp. 42-46. Werner Foerster, "*Daimōn,* etc.," TDNT, II, 1-20. Kurt E. Koch, *Christian Counseling and Occultism,* transl. by Andrew Petter, Grand Rapids: Kregel, 1965. Russell J. Meade, *Victory Over Demonism Today,* Wheaton: Christian Life Publications, 1962. John L. Nevius, *Demon Possession and Allied Themes*, 5th ed., Revell, n.d. Charles R. Smith, "The New Testament Doctrine of Demons," *Grace Journal*, X, 26-42. Merrill F. Unger, *Biblical Demonology*, Wheaton: Van Kampen Press, 1953.

R. A. K. and J. R.

DEN. A number of Heb. and Gr. terms are translated "den," "cave," "pit," "cleft," "covert," or "booth." In the limestone mountains of Palestine are many dens or caves large and small. Even on the plains there are numerous pits or "lime sinks" which were sometimes used by the Arabs to store straw or grain. Perhaps into such was Joseph cast by his brothers (Gen 37:20). Jackals, wolves and other wild animals inhabited these dens or caves. Even people frequently made their homes in such (Jud 6:2), and here also robbers would hide (Jer 7:11). *See also* Cave; Pit.

DEN OF LIONS. The account of Daniel in the den of lions (Dan 6:7,12,16-24) rings true with the Persian background of this chapter. The Persian rulers, being Zoroastrians, held fire to be sacred, so that for them it would have been improper to execute by fire (cf. Dan 3). Kings of the 1st mil. B.C. frequently kept lions in captivity. Ashurnasirpal II (883-859 B.C.) bred them and kept large numbers of them at Calah.

The construction of such lions' dens is not known, but on the basis of the text, Edward J. Young (*The Prophecy of Daniel*, Grand Rapids: Eerdmans, 1949, pp. 136 f.) suggests it was an underground pit with a small opening in the top like a cistern. Possibly there was also one at the side through which the beasts were admitted and normally fed. It was very likely such a side entrance that was closed by the stone and sealed (Dan 6:17). The hole at the top was evidently too high for a man to escape without assistance (6:23).

J.R.

DENARIUS. *See* Weights, Measures, and Coins.

DENIAL OF CHRIST. *See* Deny; Peter.

DENY. The verb "deny" appears in three forms in the Gr. NT and in the LXX where it translates three different Heb. words. The three Gr. terms have been illuminated by papyri discoveries of the 1st and 2nd cen. A.D.

Gr. *arneomai* was used in the early Christian centuries to mean "disown" (MM, p. 78) and bears this meaning in such NT passages as Acts 3:14; Mt 10:33; II Tim 2:12-13; I Jn 2:22; I Tim 5:8; Tit 2:12 (cf. Arndt, p. 107). It also means simply to deny in the sense of saying no as in Mt 26:70; Acts 4:16; Heb 11:24. To deny oneself (Mt 16:24; Mk 8:34; Lk 9:23) means to set aside or renounce all personal ambition and self-interest in favor of the new

claims of Christ upon one's life for unreserved commitment to Him and His gospel.

Gr. *aparneomai* was also used to mean "deny" in the sense of disown (MM, p. 53) as is seen especially in Peter's denials of Jesus in Mk 14:30-31, 72 and parallels, and in Mk 8:34 and parallels.

Gr. *antilegō* has been shown in the papyri to mean "contradict" in a passage where a man is told "not to agree now with his father, but to *oppose* him and make no contract" (MM, p. 48). This strong sense of "contradict" or "oppose" is found in Rom 10:21 (Isa 65:2), where God's judgment on Israel is that they were a disobedient and *opposing* people. Paul says the Jews opposed (*antilegō*, lit., "spoke against") his being set free at Caesarea (Acts 28:19). This word appears also in Tit 1:9; 2:9; Jn 19:12; Acts 13:45; and probably Lk 20:27. The church was everywhere "opposed" (Acts 28:22).

J. McR.

DEPRAVITY. *See* Fall of Man; Reprobate; Sin.

DEPUTY. The word occurs in the OT once (I Kgs 22:47) as the rendering of the verb *niṣṣāb*, to be appointed as a deputy or official; and twice (Est 8:9; 9:3, RSV) for *peḥâ*, a governor, subordinate to an official of higher rank. "Deputies" is also the RSV rendering of *segānim* (Jer 51:28, KJV, "rulers").

In the NT, "deputy" (KJV) appears for Gr. *anthypatos*, "in lieu of one higher," uniformly rendered "proconsul" by RSV. Under the Roman system proconsuls were appointed by the senate to preside over the senatorial provinces as distinct from the imperial provinces which were administered by direct appointees of the emperor. The proconsuls mentioned in the NT were Sergius Paulus of Cyprus (Acts 13:7-8, 12) and Gallio of Achaia (Acts 18:12). See Acts 19:38 for the only other NT mention of proconsuls.

See Governor.

DERBE (dûr′bĭ). A town in Asia Minor in the SE corner of Lycaonia on the main road from Lystra to Laranda. On Paul's first missionary journey he came to Derbe after having been stoned at Lystra and made many disciples there (Acts 14:6, 20). Paul passed through Derbe on his second journey from Cilicia to Lystra (Acts 16:1) and likely visited there on his third journey. Gaius, one of Paul's disciples and companions, was from Derbe (Acts 20:4).

Since Sir William Ramsay identified Derbe with Gudelisin in 1890, that view has been generally accepted. But two inscriptions found in recent years have demonstrated rather conclusively that Kerti Hüyük is the correct site of ancient Derbe. Gudelisin is about 30 miles W of the modern Turkish town of Karaman (66 miles by road SE of Konya), and Kerti Hüyük is some 15 miles NW of Karaman.

Bibliography. M. Ballance, *Anatolian Studies,* VII (1957), 147–151. B. Van Elderen, "Derbe," BW, pp. 195 f.

H. F. V.

DESERT. Various Heb. words are translated "desert" or "wilderness" in the KJV of the OT. *Midbār,* the most common, is found approximately 280 times. It is usually translated "wilderness" (*q.v.*) but 12 times is rendered "desert." The word derives from a root meaning "to drive," i.e., drive herds to the fields (cf. HGHL, p. 656; Selbie, HDB, IV, 917). It should be remembered that shepherds must lead their sheep from one spot to another to provide sufficient fodder if the flocks are to survive on the sparse vegetation of the desert (cf. Lk 15:3–7).

The term Jeshimon (Heb. *yᵉshîmôn*) is more expressive but is found less frequently (14 times). Apparently it derives from a root meaning "to be desolate" (*yāsham*). The mountain of Pisgah overlooked this area of Jeshimon (Num 21:20) as did the height of Peor (Num 23:28). The region around Ziph (near Hebron?) is similarly designated (I Sam 23:19, 24; 26:1, 3). It is thus a vivid term for the expanse of desert known to the sacred writers, particularly the rugged terrain that encircled the Dead Sea.

Arabah, Heb. *'ărābâ* (Isa 35:1, 6; 40:3; Jer 2:6; 17:6; etc.), is a broad term that refers frequently to depressed plains, such as the one in which the Jordan River is located, as well as the low desert region to the S of the Dead Sea. Today this large valley is called the Arabah. KJV translates the Heb. term 42 times as "plain."

Another term, *ḥorbâ,* is translated "desert" in KJV in Ps 102:6; Isa 48:21; Ezk 13:4, but generally means a ruined city or area.

The Gr. term used in the LXX and the NT for desert is regularly *erēmos,* a deserted, abandoned, lonely place. In later pilgrim texts in

In Egypt the desert begins at the edge of the rich soil deposited over the centuries by the Nile flood. HFV

Latin this term is transliterated as *heremus* or *eremus.*

The Judean desert has often exercised significant influences upon the changing tide of Palestinian history. Much evidence of the importance of this region has come to light recently in the form of ancient documents from biblical times. The recovery of the Dead Sea Scrolls, because of the bone-dry atmosphere of certain areas in this vicinity, is one of the more dramatic contributions of the Judean desert in our day. Written materials have been found especially in the area of the Dead Sea (at the Wadi ed-Daliyeh, N of Jericho; Qumran; Khirbet Mird; Nahal Tse'elim; Nahal Hever; Masada; etc.) and in certain centers of the Negev as well (Nessana, etc.). Thus, the practical monopoly which the Egyptian desert had held in years past on such ancient writing materials no longer exists. *See* Dead Sea Scrolls.

Glueck's researches in the Negev have brought to light many forgotten facts about the desert areas between Beer-sheba and the Gulf of Aqabah (where Solomon, Uzziah, and Jotham had a large warehouse and shipping center at Ezion-Geber). He has surveyed the centers where teeming populations once thrived (especially under the Nabataeans), carefully utilizing as they did their natural resources. Also he and his assistants have helped modern biblical research to discover anew the sites and the routes which Abraham and the Israelites followed in their desert sojourns.

The desert being close at hand (vegetation completely disappears six miles E of Jerusalem as one journeys toward the Dead Sea), it afforded criminals (cf. Lk 10:30), political exiles (I Sam 22–26, David fleeing from Saul), as well as false messiahs (Mt 24:26; Acts 21:38; Jos *Wars,* ii.13.5; vii.11.1) a suitable base for their operations.

The desert also reminded the sacred poets of the marvelous creative powers of God, blossoming as it does when drenched by the seasonal rains (Isa 35:1). For this reason a word which is sometimes used for the desert is *tohu,*

A typical scene in the Wilderness of Judea. HFV

a term descriptive of the primeval chaos ("without form," Gen 1:2) which abounded before God brought order to His created world (see "waste," Deut 32:10; "wilderness," Job 12:24; Ps 107:40).

Herod the Great, realizing the strategic importance of the defense posts, maintained various desert fortresses, such as Masada, Machaerus E of the Dead Sea, and Herodium near Bethlehem. John the Baptist, being reared in the desert, drew illustrations from its life (vipers fleeing before a brush fire, etc.; cf. Mt 3:7).

Bibliography. Frank M. Cross, Jr., "A Footnote to Biblical History," BA, XIX (Feb., 1956), 12–17. Gustav Dalman, *Sacred Sites and Ways,* New York: Macmillan, 1935, IV, 81–98. B. Z. Eshel, *The Dead Sea Region,* Jerusalem: Kirjath Sepher, 1958. Nelson Glueck, *The Other Side of the Jordan,* New Haven: ASOR, 1940; *Rivers in the Desert,* New York: Farrar, Straus and Cudahy, 1959. Edward Robinson, *Biblical Researches in Palestine, Mt. Sinai and Arabia Petraea* (various entries, see esp. II, 218–222). Beno Rothenberg, *God's Wilderness: Discoveries in Sinai,* London: Thames & Hudson, 1961. George Adam Smith, HGHL, 26th ed., pp. 263–265, 269–273, 312–317.

E. J. V.

DESIRE. For the occurrence of this word translating Heb. *'ăbîyônâ* in Eccl 12:5 (KJV, RSV) *see* Plants: Caperberry.

DESIRE OF ALL NATIONS. This phrase, found in Hag 2:7 (KJV), has traditionally been interpreted as a prophecy of Christ. In this, Christian expositors were following rabbinical interpretation which applied it to the Messiah. Another ancient interpretation, found as early as the LXX, has come into favor in recent times. While the noun "desire" is singular, yet because the verb "come" is plural, the phrase is translated "the desired things" or "the treasures of all nations shall come in" (RSV). The context of the passage is certainly messianic, since the splendor of the post-Exilic temple was found not in its beauty but in the coming of Christ. Both interpretations are acceptable. The passage speaks either of the coming of Christ or of the tribute which all nations will render to Him. I Sam 9:20 illustrates how the term "desire of Israel" may refer to a royal person, and Dan 11:37 infers that "the desire of women" is a divine being.

P. C. J.

DESOLATION, ABOMINATION OF. *See* Abomination of Desolation.

DESTROYER. This term refers to the angel of death employed in the destruction of the firstborn in Egypt not found under the blood (Ex 12:23; Heb 11:28); also in connection with the punishment for David's sin in numbering the people (II Sam 24:15–16); in smiting the camp of the Assyrians (II Kgs 19:35); and in smiting Herod in Acts 12:23. *See also* Destruction.

DESTRUCTION. Of 33 terms used in the OT, the most common are Heb. *'ăbăddôn,* "destruction," "perishing"; *'êd,* "calamity," "distress"; *mᵉḥittâ,* "dismay," "ruin"; *mᵉhûmâ,* "trouble," "destruction"; *sheber,* "breaking," "breach"; and of four in the NT, Gr. *apōleia,* "ruin," "loss"; *olethros,* "death," "destruction."

The word *'ăbăddôn* refers to a place of destruction, an abyss, and is very close in meaning to Sheol (Job 26:6; 28:22; 31:12; Ps 88:11; Prov 15:11). In the NT *apōleia* stresses the idea of utter loss (Mt 7:13; Rom 9:22; Phil 3:19; II Pet 2:1; 3:16) and can best be understood in the light of Christ's warning in Lk 9:25: "What is a man advantaged, if he gain the whole world, and lose [Gr. *apolesas*] himself, or be cast away?" Rev 9:11, ASV, speaks of "the angel of the abyss: his name in Hebrew is Abaddon, and in the Greek tongue he hath the name Apollyon" (i.e., the Destroyer). *See* Abaddon; Apollyon; Destroyer; Sheol.

DESTRUCTION, CITY OF. In Isa 19:18, by employing the phrase *'îr haheres,* "the City of Destruction" (NASB), the prophet seems to be making a deliberate punning allusion to *'îr haheres,* "the City of the Sun," a designation for the Egyptian city of On (*q.v.*), which the Greeks called Heliopolis. On the basis of certain MS evidence the RSV adopted the latter phrase, without however noting the emendation.

DEUEL (dū′ĕl). A Gadite, the father of Eliasaph, who was the leader of the tribe of Gad in the Exodus (Num 1:14; 7:42, 47; 10:20). The name probably comes from a Heb. term signifying "knowledge of God." In Num 2:14 the name is rendered Reuel, perhaps resulting from confusing the Heb. letters for "d" and "r." *See* Reuel.

DEUTERONOMY, BOOK OF. This is the last of the five books of the Pentateuch. Its name comes through the Latin Vulgate from the LXX title *deuteronomion,* "repetition of the law," based on a misunderstanding of the words "copy of this law" in Deut 17:18.

Ancient Jewish and Christian writers unanimously attribute this book to Moses. Jesus Christ and the various NT writers quote from it or allude to it nearly 100 times, often indicating that the citation came from Moses (e.g., Mk 12:19; Mt 19:8; Rom 10:19; I Cor 9:9). Modern critics deny that Moses wrote Deuteronomy, attributing the book in its present form to various writers and editors over a period of centuries.

The literary unity of this book of Moses is unmistakably evidenced by its remarkable structure. It exhibits in its total pattern and in numerous thematic emphases the legal form characteristic of ancient Hittite and Assyrian treaties; in particular, those of the vassal type. Moreover, in so far as there was an evolution in the documentary form of these treaties. Deuteronomy corresponds to the classic Near Eastern form attested in the time of Moses as over against that of the 1st mil. B.C. As sealed legal contracts these treaties were not subject to alteration.

The fact that Deuteronomy can be so identified confirms its own plain claims as to its Mosaic authorship and the occasion for which it was produced (see Deut 1:3; 31:9,22,24); and by the same token it belies the whole complex of modern higher critical theories concerning the origin of this book. Negative criticism since the days of Wellhausen regards Deuteronomy as the product of a prolonged process of expansion and alteration, completed, according to the majority opinion, in the 7th cen. B.C., though some date it in post-Exilic times and others trace it back to the pre-monarchic amphictyony.

The book may be outlined as follows:

I. Preamble: Covenant Mediator, 1:1–5
II. Historical Prologue: Covenant History, 1:6–4:49
III. Stipulations: Covenant Life, 5:1–26:19
IV. Sanctions: Covenant Ratification, 27:1–30:20
V. Succession Arrangements: Covenant Continuity, 31:1–34:12

Vassal treaties opened with the self-identification of the suzerain addressing himself to his servant. So the Deuteronomic preamble (1:1–5) identifies Moses as the speaker and mediator-representative of the heavenly King who was the true Lord of this covenant. The preamble also indicates the occasion to be the final assembly of Israel called by Moses just before his death. As was customary in the administration of covenants, the approaching death of the dynastic head (i.e., Moses) was the signal for a renewal of the covenant, requiring of the vassal (i.e., Israel) a recognition of the appointed dynastic successor (i.e., Joshua).

The purpose of the historical prologue was to cite benefits previously bestowed by the great King so that the vassal's allegiance might be motivated by a sense of gratitude. Beginning his rehearsal of the history of the Lord's relationship to Israel at the scene of the Sinaitic establishment of the covenant, Moses recalls God's faithful guardianship of Israel in spite of their fractiousness during the wilderness wanderings and the Transjordanian conquests, and he brings the account up to the present solemn ceremony with words of exhortation (1:6–4:49).

Stipulations dictated by the suzerain for the regulation of the vassal's life formed a third standard division in the treaties. Always the fundamental demand was for the vassal's per-

fect loyalty to the exclusion of allegiance to any other lord. Agreeably, the Deuteronomic laws open with the great commandment to love the Lord with all the heart, for He alone was Israel's God (5:1–11:32). The fact that suzerains, when renewing covenants, repeated their earlier demands with such modifications as might be necessary, explains the new version of the Decalogue (5:6 ff.). In the remainder of the legislation (chaps. 12–26), the primary principle was applied to specific areas of the Israelite theocracy in laws dealing with cultic-ceremonial consecration (12:1–16:17), judicial-governmental righteousness (16:18–21:23), the sanctity of the divine order (22:1–25:19), and the confession of God as Redeemer-King (26:1–19).

There follows the usual section presenting the treaty sanctions. It begins with directions for a concluding phase of the covenant renewal to be conducted by Joshua within Canaan (chap. 27). The curses and blessings of chaps. 28–30 provide a prophetic view of Israelite history, culminating in exile and restoration. They also constitute the divine threat and promise in terms of which Israel swore its oath of allegiance that day.

Gathered together in the final chapters (31–34) are elements relating to the continuation of the covenant; arrangements for Joshua's succession; the appointment of the covenant witnesses, namely, the treaty text deposited in the sanctuary, and the song of witness placed in Israel's mouth; Moses' testamentary blessings; and the record of Moses' death, the imminency of which was the occasion of the ceremony of which Deuteronomy is the documentary witness. *See* Covenant.

Bibliography. CornPBE, pp. 258–262, for recent theories of authorship. Kenneth A. Kitchen, "Ancient Orient, 'Deuteronism,' and the Old Testament," NPOT, pp. 1–24. Meredith G. Kline, *The Treaty of the Great King*, Grand Rapids: Eerdmans, 1963. Dennis J. McCarthy, *Treaty and Covenant*, Rome: Pontifical Biblical Inst., 1963. Gerhard von Rad, *Studies in Deuteronomy*, New York: Henry Regnery, 1953. Adam C. Welch, *The Code of Deuteronomy*, London: Oxford, 1924; *Deuteronomy: The Framework to the Code*, London: Oxford, 1932. Samuel J. Schultz, *Deuteronomy, The Gospel of Love*, Chicago: Moody Press, 1971.

M. G. K.

DEVIL (Gr. *diabolos*, "slanderer," "false accuser"). Identical with Satan, Adversary. He is once called *katēgor*, "accuser," in Rev 12:10, and is called Beelzebub (*q.v.*) in Mt 12:27.

The devil is a personal, superhuman, evil, created being, a fallen angel, without corporeal material form. He is represented in Scripture as the highest of all created archangels before his fall.

Though it is unpopular today to believe in

the personality of the devil, the Scripture teaches both his reality and his personality. The Bible credits Satan with the attributes, works, and names of a personal being. He is said "to deceive" the whole world (Rev 12:9), involving intellect; he goes forth with "great wrath" (Rev 12:12), exhibiting emotion; he "makes war" (Rev 12:17), thus doing the works of a person. Furthermore, he has various names which describe his character: "Satan," "Devil," "old serpent," "accuser" (Rev 12:9–10; 20:2).

Aside from Scripture the strongest argument for his being a real person is that denial of his personality would destroy our belief in the deity of Christ: ". . . if He [i.e., Christ] were not externally tempted to evil . . . if those evil suggestions to make stone into bread . . . did not come to Him from some living intelligence . . . external to Himself, then must they have come from *within;* and that being the case, He Himself needed a Saviour rather than *was one*" (F. C. Jennings, *Satan,* p. 5).

Satan is spoken of as "the adversary" in I Pet 5:8. He can and does transform himself into an angel of light (II Cor 11:14). At least some forms of sickness are caused by the devil, for Paul said his "thorn in the flesh" (II Cor 12:7) was "the messenger of Satan" (see also Lk 13:16; Job 2:7).

The devil assumed the form of a serpent to tempt Eve (Gen 3:1). He deceives and tempts men to sin (Eph 6:11; I Tim 3:7; Mt 4:1 ff.).

Satan was a created angel who apparently was included among the sons of God (Job 1:6). His original home was in heaven as the "anointed cherub that covereth" (Ezk 28:14, 16). The mention in Ezk 28:2 ff. of the prince of Tyre and the king of Tyre would seem to have reference to Satan, for he was said to have been in Eden (v. 13), and "thou wast perfect in thy ways from the day that thou wast created, till unrighteousness was found in thee" (v. 15, ASV). This would seem not to refer merely to the earthly prince of Tyre but to the devil who dwelt in him. Others do not see this as a reference to Satan.

The devil fell from his high estate by the sin of pride, and by seeking to usurp the throne of God. Jesus beheld Satan falling as lightning from heaven (Lk 10:18; cf. Isa 14:12–14). He is now called "the prince of the power of the air" (Eph 2:2), and "the prince of this world" (Jn 14:30). Some feel that before his power was broken by Christ's death and resurrection, Satan deceived the nations, but now, before the second coming of Christ, he is bound in respect to deceiving the nations, though not with respect to tempting people; and at the end of this age he will be loosed to deceive the nations once more (Rev 20:2, 7–8; cf. Mt 12:26–29). Others interpret Satan's binding to refer to the removal of his whole activity against God in the future Millennial Age and that today he is not only tempting people but also deceiving the nations by enticing them into complete independence of God (II Cor 4:4; 11:3).

Satan is the "father of lies," a "murderer," and the spiritual father, mentor, or master of evil men (Jn 8:44). But wicked as he is, he must still bow to the sovereignty of God (Job 1:10).

The devil is neither omniscient nor omnipresent, so apparently he depends on his followers, the wicked fallen angels (demons) who are subject to him, to be his agents in tempting men and indwelling those who are demon-possessed (Mk 1:23–27, 32–34; 3:11–12; etc.). He is called the "accuser of our brethren" (Rev 12:10; cf. Job 1).

He is already judged by God and awaits his doom at the final judgment (Rev 20:10; Mt 25:41). There is apparently no scriptural evidence for the common belief that the devil is now in hell presiding over the tortures of the damned. Peter declares in II Pet 2:4 that God cast down the sinning angels to Tartarus and committed them to pits of darkness to await the final judgment, but this is different from the lake of fire and brimstone (cf. II Pet 3:7).

See Accuser; Adversary; Antichrist; Belial; Deceiver; Demonology; Evil One; Lucifer; Satan.

Bibliography. Donald G. Barnhouse, *The Invisible War,* Grand Rapids: Zondervan, 1965. Lewis S. Chafer, *Satan,* Chicago: Moody, 1942. Werner Foerster and Gerhard von Rad, *"Diabolos,"* TDNT, II, 72–81. F. C. Jennings, *Satan: His Person, Work, Place and Destiny,* New York: A. C. Gaebelein, n.d. Merrill F. Unger, *Biblical Demonology,* 2nd ed., Wheaton, Ill.: Van Kampen Press, 1963, especially pp. 182–208.

F. E. H.

DEVILS. *See* Demonology.

DEVOTE, DEVOTED (Heb. *ḥērem*). This is a term connected with holiness, exclusion, separation, taboo, i.e., things placed under a ban and forbidden to common use. The *ḥarîm* was the area forbidden to all except the husband and eunuchs.

In the OT the "devoted thing" was that which was set apart to the Lord, and therefore belonged no longer to the owner, nor could it be used for sacrifice (Josh 6:18–19; 7:10–15; I Sam 15). Man was not to be offered in sacrifice, but certain persons and nations were doomed (devoted) by God, who alone has the prerogative of taking life as well as giving it. Sacrifice rests on a different ground, i.e., the voluntary offering of an innocent life of a creature without blemish, approved of God to represent the great Sacrifice. The pagan confounded the two ideas of the devoted thing under a ban (as criminals and captives), and the sacrifice of one's flock or herd as a voluntary offering in worship; but the Scripture writers keep them distinct. *See* Anathema; Curse.

R. L. D.

DEVOTED THING. *See* Anathema; Curse.

DEW. "Sprinkled moisture" is referred to indiscriminately as dew (i.e., condensation of water vapor on a cooled surface) and night mist (i.e., condensation of the air). Moisture and cold are necessary for the formation of dew. In moist areas, there is less dew because of the uniformity of the temperature night and day. Because of limited moisture in the atmosphere, there is little dew in the desert even though there is a marked change of temperature. Palestine, being located near the Mediterranean Sea, always had a large percentage of water vapor in the atmosphere. The clear skies contribute to rapid radiation of ground heat immediately following the sunset. This is turn cools the land, so that the moisture in the air condenses through contact with cool objects.

Since April through October is a dry season in Palestine, dew is imperative to revive vegetation. Dews are so heavy that the plants and trees are literally soaked with water. In Jud 6:38, the wetting of Gideon's fleece is indicative of the dew's heaviness. It is heaviest on the coast W of Beer-sheba, in the plain of Esdraelon, and at the sources of the Jordan beneath the slopes of Hermon (Ps 133:3). The dew descends mysteriously (Job 38:28); its origin is heavenly (Gen 27:28; Deut 33:28; Hag 1:10; Zech 8:12). It falls suddenly (II Sam 17:12), gently (Deut 32:2), and remains on the ground throughout the night (Job 29:19). Overexposure to dew is discomforting (Song 5:2; Dan 4:15, 23, 25, 33). It quickly evaporates in the morning (Job 7:9; Hos 6:4). Dew is normally expected during the hot summer harvest season (Isa 18:4; Hos 14:5; Mic 5:7). Its copiousness permits dry-farming.

Dew is a figure of speech for abundant fruitfulness (Gen 27:28; Deut 33:13); also it stands as a symbol of the "remnant of Jacob" blessing all people (Mic 5:7). Again dew serves as a figure of speech for an unaware thief (II Sam 17:12) and ephemeral religion (Hos 6:4; 13:3).

D. W. D.

DIADEM. Properly a diadem is not a crown but a band narrower than a crown; a circlet or ring for the head. The diadem originally was a strip of white cloth bound about the head, later of blue, and also ornamented with gold. The high priest's diadem (crown) was a gold plate tied to his turban by a blue cord and inscribed with the words "Holy to the Lord" (Ex 39:30, NASB). The Jerusalem Bible reads: "They also made the plate, the holy diadem, of pure gold, and engraved on it 'Consecrated to Yahweh,' as a man engraves a seal."

The bestowal of the diadem by God is a mark of His grace and favor, particularly the mark of Messiah (Isa 62:3). When Israel is to be restored to her millennial glory, God is said to be for her a diadem of beauty (Isa 28:5). Conversely, the withdrawal of the diadem indicates the debasing of the one wearing it, the removal of the favor of king or God (Ezk 21:26).

Job speaks of clothing himself with righteousness and justice as with a robe and a diadem (Job 29:14). In the NT the word diadem (Gr. *diadēma*) occurs only three times (Rev 12:3; 13:1; 19:12) as crown(s); it denotes a circlet. The last reference enumerates the crowns of the Son of God, denoting His sovereignty over all nations.
See Crown.

H. G. S.

DIAL, SUN. *See* Sun Dial.

DIAMOND. *See* Jewels.

DIANA (dī-ă'nà). This is the Latin name for the virgin goddess of hunting, also identified with the moon and Hecate, and patroness of childbirth. Her Gr. name was Artemis (meaning "prompt," "safe," or perhaps "pendant"). This twin sister of the sun-god Apollo, chaste goddess of nature and protectress of wild animals, especially of their young, was also regarded as the patroness of hunters. Armed with a bow and arrow and accompanied by a bounding stag, this goddess of the light by night (later of the moon) was a mighty huntress. To her the Spartans sacrificed a goat before each battle.

A statue of Diana excavated at Ephesus. HFV

455

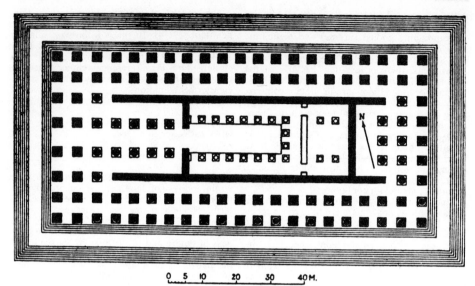

0   5   10   20   30   40 M.

Plan of the Temple of Diana, Ephesus. From I. H. Grinnell, *Greek Temples*,
Metropolitan Museum of Art

Young girls regarded her as the guardian of their maiden years. But in Asia Minor during Roman times she was identified with the Phrygian mother-goddess Cybele, a sensuous nature goddess, although images taken from the earlier yellow limestone temple at Ephesus picture her in less degrading light.

Diana of the Ephesians (Acts 19:24–37), as known from many statues of her image and as depicted on coins, had her thorax covered with three or four rows of pendant breasts, or possibly ostrich eggs, either of which were symbolic of fertility. The front of her garment was trimmed with sequences of lions, goats, and other sacrificial animals. Down the sides of her garment were alternate rows of nymphs, seashells, sphinxes, bees and roses. Her mural crown was decorated with signs of the Zodiac denoting the seasons, unlike the simple tiara symbolizing the crescent moon which was characteristic of the Gr. virgin huntress Artemis.

Originally the Artemis worshiped at Ephesus was not a Gr. divinity but was Asiatic. Ultimately the various goddesses of love in Syria and Asia Minor all owed their origin to the earlier Babylonian and Assyrian Ishtar through the link of the Phoenician Astarte. She impersonated the reproductive powers of man and animals and all other life. She assisted at childbirth. Associated thus with the various fertility cults she became the patroness of ceremonial prostitution, which was part of her worship at Ephesus.

The great temple of Diana at Ephesus, called the Artemision and considered as one of the seven wonders of the Hellenistic world, was the scene of an annual festival in her honor during the month of Artemisios (March–April). The religious ceremonies included athletic, dramatic and musical contests (*see* Games). Ephesus was proud of her position as "temple-keeper" of Diana (Acts 19:35), a boast which has been found on inscriptions excavated there. The temple treasury acted as a bank in which deposits were made by cities, kings and private persons (WHG, p. 362). Here the Ionians came with their wives and children, bringing costly offerings and presents to the priests. Her worship was characterized by sensuous orgies. Great throngs attended. Multitudes of female temple slaves or "priestesses" who came as virgins were here dedicated to service in the temple which may have included ritual or cultic prostitution.

· The silversmiths of Ephesus carried on a lucrative business by the forging and sale of images of this goddess (Acts 19:23 ff.). Hence it was inevitable that Paul's message of Christianity should arouse their indignation because it jeopardized their trade. *See* Demetrius; Ephesus; Gods, False: Artemis; Goddess.

Bibliography. E. J. Banks, "Diana, Artemis," ISBE, II, 842 f. C. Cobern, *New Archaeological Discoveries,* New York: Funk & Wagnall, 1921, pp. 461–482. W. K. C. Guthrie, *The Greeks and Their Gods,* Boston: Beacon Press, 1951, pp. 99–106. Jane E. Harrison, *Prolegomena to the Study of Greek Religions,* Cambridge: Cambridge Univ. Press, 1922. C. H. Moore, *The Religious Thought of the Greeks, from Homer to the Triumph of Christianity,*

Cambridge: Harvard Univ. Press, 1916. M. P. Nilsson, *A History of Greek Religion,* Oxford: Clarendon Press, 1925. Cf. also the articles by M. M. Parvis and F. V. Filson on Ephesus in BA, VIII (1945), 61–73, 73–80.

R. E. Pr.

DIBLAIM (dĭb'lĭ-ăm). Gomer, Hosea's wife, was a "daughter of Diblaim" (Hos 1:3). The name comes from a Heb. term signifying "lump or double cakes of figs and raisins." Some have thought the name to be figurative, i.e., "Gomer the daughter of raisin cakes," meaning that she was wholly given up to her harlotry, since raisin cakes were used in certain fertility cult rites.

DIBLATH (dĭb'lăth). This word in Ezk 6:14 occurs as "Diblah" in ASV and "Riblah" in RSV. In the Heb. the "r" and "d" could easily have been interchanged. The correct term is likely Riblah (*q.v.*).

DIBON (dī'bŏn), **DIBON-GAD** (dī'bŏn-găd')

1. Dibon was one of the principal cities of Moab, and under Mesha it became the capital of the kingdom. The city stood on the site of modern Dhiban, a low mound which lies on the plateau of Moab a short distance W of the main highway between Amman and Kerak and about 10 miles N of the Arnon gorge (Josh 13:9).

Prior to the Israelite conquest of Transjordan under Moses' leadership, Dibon and all Moab N of the Arnon was overrun by Sihon, king of the Amorites (Num 21:30). One of the stations of Israel on the journey toward Canaan (Num 33:45), Dibon was taken from Sihon with his other possessions and assigned by Moses to Reuben (Josh 13:17). The city, however, was rebuilt by the stronger tribe of Gad and given the name Dibon-gad (Num 32:34). It was later taken over by King Mesha of Moab, who rebelled against Israel after the death of Ahab *c.* 853 B.C. (II Kgs 1:1; 3:4–5). According to the biblical account (II Kgs 3), Israel was initially victorious over Mesha; but Mesha later (*c.* 830 B.C.) set up a stele at Dibon (the famous Moabite Stone [*q.v.*] found there in 1868), boasting of his defeating Israel. He seems to have given the name of Qarhoh to the citadel of Dibon. Isaiah (15:2) and Jeremiah (48:18, 22) pronounced judgment upon Dibon in their prophecies against Moab.

From 1950 to 1956 the site of Dhiban was sounded and parts excavated by the American School of Oriental Research. The earliest levels of occupation belong to the Early Bronze Age. The most important discovery was the section of a city wall and huge gate towers with corner guard rooms, built of large blocks of masonry, each measuring on the average about 32 inches in length, 24 inches in width and over 18 inches in depth, and going back to the 10th through the 8th cen. B.C. This wall was rebuilt in all probability by King Mesha after the reign of Ahab in Israel. On the summit of the site was uncovered the foundation of a Moabite official building with walls averaging five feet in thickness and paved stone floors. Since the central room contained a fine incense stand and two adjacent rooms had fertility figurines, the building may have been a temple or a palace with a royal chapel. Inside the city walls a Nabataean structure of the 1st cen. B.C. was discovered, as well as the remains of a Roman bath of about the 3rd cen. A.D., and the foundations of a church of the Byzantine period. The site was last occupied by the Arabs of the early Umayyad period and appears to have been abandoned sometime during the 9th cen. A.D. See William H. Morton, "Dibon," BW, pp. 200f.

2. A village in Judah reinhabited by some of the Jews who returned from the Babylonian captivity (Neh 11:25), perhaps the same as Dimonah (Josh 15:22) in the Negeb.

D. C. B. and R. L. D.

DIBRI (dĭb'rī). A Danite, father of Shelomith and grandfather of the blasphemer who was executed by stoning (Lev 24:11).

DICTIONARIES, BIBLE. See Bible Dictionaries.

DIDRACHMA. See Weights, Measures, and Coins.

DIDYMUS (dĭd'ĭ-mŭs). A transliteration of the Gr. *didymos,* an alternative appellation for the apostle Thomas (Jn 11:16; 20:24; 21:2), probably used by Gr. speaking Christians. It appears in the papri as a proper name as well as a common noun meaning "twin." This is also the meaning of Aram. *te'ôma'* (Gr. *thômas*). Instead of the name Didymus the RSV reads "the Twin." *See* Thomas.

DIET. The term applied to the daily allowance of food given by Evil-merodach, king of Babylon, to his royal captive Jehoiachin, king of Judah (Jer 52:34). The same Heb. word *'ărūhâ* is translated "allowance" in II Kgs 25:30.

DIGNITIES. Persons higher in honor or glory (Gr. pl. of *doxa,* "glory"); probably angels as spiritual beings of preeminent dignity (II Pet 2:10; Jude 8). RSV translated the expression "the glorious ones."

DIKLAH (dĭk'lâ). A descendant of Joktan (Gen 10:27; I Chr 1:21), and probably a tribe dwelling around an oasis (Diklah means "palm grove") in Arabia, perhaps at the S end of the Wadi Sirḥan *c.* 250 miles SE of the Dead Sea.

DILEAN (dĭl'ē-ăn). A town of Judah in the Shephelah or foothills near Lachish (Josh 15:38). Identification not certain.

DILL. *See* Plants.

DIMNAH (dĭm'nâ). A Levitical town in Zebulun

(Josh 21:35), probably a mistaken transcription for the name Rimmon, as given in I Chr 6:77. Rimmon (*q.v.*) may have been *c.* six miles NNE of Nazareth.

DIMON, WATERS OF (dī'mŏn). A stream E of the Dead Sea in the land of Moab (Isa 15:9), possibly the Arnon (Isa 16:2; Num 21:13, 26). The Vulg. and the famous Dead Sea Scroll (IQIsaa) read Dibon for Dimon. Jerome states that the two names were used interchangeably in his time. Some scholars think Isaiah purposely used the name Dimon to furnish a play on the sound of the Heb. word *dām*, "blood," in his line "the waters of Dimon shall be full of blood." RSV emends to Dibon.

DIMONAH (dī-mō'nả). A town in the Negeb of Judah, near Edom (Josh 15:22), not identified. It may be the same as the Dibon of Neh 11:25.

DINAH (dī'nả). The daughter of Jacob and his wife Leah (Gen 30:21). While going unescorted to visit with Canaanite girl friends she was raped by Shechem, son of Hamor the Hivite (Gen 34:2). Later the attacker wanted to take her in honorable marriage, and to this her brothers agreed, provided the Hivites would submit to circumcision. The stipulation was agreed upon and carried out; but despite the agreement, Dinah's two full brothers, Simeon and Levi, made a bloody attack upon the Hivite town and killed all the males, including Hamor and Shechem (Gen 34:1–29).

Jacob considered this treacherous act as unwarranted (Gen 34:30) and denounced it with horror just before he died (Gen 49:5–7). Because of this massacre the land fell to Jacob as the head of the tribe. At his death he bequeathed the land to Joseph (Gen 48:22).

DINAITES (dī'nả-īts). A name found in the KJV of Ezr 4:9, formerly understood as that of a people brought as colonists by Ashurbanipal (Asnapper) to Samaria. The word, however, is an official Aramaic title meaning "the judges" (so RSV, Jerusalem Bible, etc.), as the 5th cen. B.C. Elephantine papyri have shown.

DINE, DINNER. *See* Food: Banquet.

DINHABAH (dĭn'hả-bả). A city of Bela, king of Edom (Gen 36:32; I Chr 1:43). Location is uncertain.

DIONYSIUS THE AREOPAGITE (dī-ŏ-nĭsh'ŭs, ăr-ĕ-op'ả-gīt). An Athenian confessing Christ under Paul (Acts 17:34). As "the Areopagite" he was a prominent citizen, being one of the 12 judges forming the highest council. *See* Areopagus.

Tradition from another Dionysius, the bishop of Corinth in A.D. 171, through Eusebius and the Apostolic Constitutions, declares the Areopagite to be the first bishop of Athens, later suffering martyrdom under Domitian. Mis-

taken tradition also declares that he migrated to Rome, was sent to Paris, and is to be identified with the patron saint of France, Saint Denys (IDB). A considerable body of Neoplatonic literature bearing his name is forgery.

DIOTREPHES (dī-ŏt'rĕ-fēz). Mentioned only in III Jn 9–10, as one "who loves to be the first among them" (NASB), and who opposed the authority of the apostle John. Concerning those who did not agree with Diotrephes, it is said that he "cast them out of the church"—an early "excommunicator"!

DISCERNING OF SPIRITS. One of the gifts of the Spirit (I Cor 12:8–10; Eph 4:7–11). The discernment was as to whether or not one who prophesied, spoke in tongues, performed miracles, etc., was doing so by the Holy Spirit. The Gr. word *diakrisis* ("distinguishing," "discerning," "judging") is used only in two other places in the NT: in Heb 5:14, "to discern both good and evil," and Rom 14:1, "Now accept the one who is weak in faith, but not for the purpose of passing judgment on his opinion" (NASB). NT usage indicates that the meaning of I Cor 12:10 is an ability to judge as to whether one spoke or acted by the Holy Spirit or by a false spirit. *See* Gifts, Spiritual.

DISCIPLE. The Gr. word *mathētēs* for disciple used nearly 270 times in the Gospels and Acts denotes a pupil who submits to processes of learning under a teacher. The Gr. has entered the English language in the term mathematics, which means literally, "disposed to learn." In Attic prose, notably in Plato, it alludes to the students trained by a philosopher or rhetorician. The concept prevailed in the OT with "sons of the prophets," understudies of Samuel, Elijah, and Elisha, and later, Paul, "brought up at the feet of Gamaliel." In the NT, the term is used of the disciples of John the Baptist (Mt 9:14), the Pharisees (Mk 2:18), and Moses, indicating latter day adherents of his teachings (Jn 9:28).

In the epistles the term *mimētēs*, "follower," "imitator," occurs in exhortations to pattern one's life after God (Eph 5:1), the writer as an apostle (I Cor 4:16; 11:1; Phil 3:17; II Thess 3:7, 9), and other believers (Heb 6:12; 13:7). *See* Example.

In a broad sense, Jesus used "disciple" as descriptive of all His followers coming under the influence of His teaching, striving to conform to His principles. Luke refers to "the whole multitude of the disciples" (19:37). In Acts 6:2 he states that the Twelve summoned the multitude of the disciples. Jesus said, "If ye continue in my word, then are ye my disciples indeed" (Jn 8:31). Jesus' disciples then and ever are those who respond to His invitation, "Learn of me" (Mt 11:29).

In a restricted sense, disciple (also apostle) applies to the inner circle of the Twelve, called out of the greater company that they might be with Christ, hear Him expound the mysteries of the kingdom reserved for a select group, witness and later perform authenticating signs and wonders, and proclaim the gospel to the world.

The Twelve were as follows: Simon Peter, Andrew, James of Zebedee, John, Philip, Nathanael (also known as Bartholomew), Thomas, Matthew (called Levi), James of Alphaeus, Simon the Zealot or Canaanite, Judas the brother of James and sometimes called Thaddaeus, and Judas Iscariot.

Although lacking in higher education, as Hebrews they had a thorough grounding in the doctrines and history of their faith. Their obtuseness tried but never exhausted the patience of Jesus, who is no less forbearing with our limitations in His service. Their very dullness of comprehension constitutes an apologetic for the historical validity of what the Gospels relate concerning Jesus. Dr. A. B. Bruce said: "They were slow-minded persons, very honest but very unapt to take in new ideas. . . .We know that nothing but facts could make such men believe that which nowadays they get credit for inventing."

Bibliography. G. Kittel, *"Akolutheō,"* TDNT, I, 210–216. K. H. Rengstorf, *"Manthanō,* etc.," TDNT, IV, 390–461.

G. H. T.

DISEASES. It is difficult to discuss the diseases mentioned in the Bible with any degree of certainty. One reason for this is that diseases are named according to symptoms and not pathological processes. Thus palsy (paralysis) could be caused by polio, trauma, hysteria, or a number of other diseases. It is not at all certain that the consumption of Lev 26:16 and Deut 28:22 was tuberculosis. Secondly, references to sickness are almost always incidental in the narrative. They are recorded more for their historical than for their medical significance. Finally, we are not sure which diseases existed in OT times (though autopsies on Egyptian mummies have shown evidence of tuberculosis, arteriosclerosis, arthritis, cancer, gallstones, bladder stones, schistosomiasis and smallpox). For an informative survey of medical knowledge and practice in ancient Mesopotamia and Egypt, see A. Dudley Dennison, "Medicine," BW, pp. 368–373.

The Israelites obviously had a working knowledge of anatomy. This is seen in their descriptions of the organs of sacrificed animals. The blood was correctly held to be the vital principle: "The life of the flesh is in the blood" (Lev 17:11). Emotional functions were sometimes assigned to certain organs. The heart, for example, was considered to be the center of the mind and will (Ezk 18:31). The expression "bowels of mercies" (Col 3:12) emphasizes the relationship between *psyche* ("soul") and *soma* ("body"), which has been corroborated in our day by psychosomatic research.

The Heb. words for disease and sickness

come from the stems *ḥālâ* ("to be sick" or "weak") and *dawâ* ("to be ill"). These words are often modified by other descriptive phrases such as "sick and at the point of death." Heb. words for healing come from the stems *rāpā'* ("to heal," "stitch together," "repair"), and *ḥāyâ* ("revive," "restore to life"), and *'ārak* ("prolong").

The NT uses such Gr. expressions as *astheneia* ("weakness," "frailty"), *malakia* ("softness," "feebleness"), and *noseō* ("to be sick" or "ailing"). Gr. words for health and healing came from the stems *hygiainō* ("to be healthy" or "sound"), *therapeuō* ("to serve," "attend to," "heal," "cure," "restore to health"), and *iaomai* ("heal," "make whole").

Causes of Disease

Disease is but part of a broader concept—the suffering of man. In the Scriptures suffering is said to be one of the results of sin. God threatened to send disease on Israel if they disobeyed Him (Deut 28:15, 22, 27–28). Although disease was often considered as a direct punishment for disobedience (e.g., the sick man at the pool of Bethesda, Jn 5:14), it could also come from Satan, as it did in the case of Job (Job 2:7). Christ spoke of the crippled woman "whom Satan hath bound" (Lk 13:16). In addition, sickness could sometimes come for man's own good and for God's glory (e.g., Paul's "thorn in the flesh," *q.v.,* and II Cor 12:7–9).

The disciples, looking at disease only as punishment for sin, questioned Jesus about a man born blind. "Who sinned," they asked, "this man or his parents that he should be born blind?" (Jn 9:1–3). Jesus answered, "Neither hath this man sinned, nor his parents; but that the works of God should be made manifest in him."

It may not always be possible to distinguish whether an illness is the result of purely natural causes, an act of God, or the evil design of Satan. Perhaps all three may be active at the same time. Whatever the cause of a Christian's disease, however, he is promised that one day suffering will be removed, when God shall "wipe away every tear" and there will be pain no longer (Rev 21:4).

Physicians and Medicine

There are about a dozen references to physicians in the Bible. The Heb. root is *rāpā'* ("to heal"). Yahweh is referred to as "the Lord your healer" (Ex 15:26, RSV). The first reference to a physician is in Gen 50:2 (though it may be that these Egyptian physicians were only embalmers of the dead). Physicians in biblical times, also, were called upon to heal sickness and relieve suffering (Job 13:4; Jer 8:22; II Chr 16:12).

Physicians were held in high regard by the Jews. The son of Sirach wrote about 190 B.C.: "Honor a physician according to the need of him with the honors due unto him, for verily the Lord hath created him; for from the most High cometh healing; and from the king he shall receive a gift. The skill of the physician shall lift up his head; and in the sight of great men he shall be admired" (Sir 38:1–3).

Physicians in NT times were trained in one of two ways. Most commonly a man served an apprenticeship with an established physician. He could also go to a type of medical school, usually associated with a pagan temple. The two schools we know most about were the medical schools at Pergamos and Alexandria.

The medicines used in biblical times were rudimentary and in most cases not very effective. Among those mentioned in the Bible were locally applied ointments (Isa 1:6), poultices (Isa 38:21), and balms (Jer 8:22; Gen 37:25). The leaves of certain trees were apparently used for herbs (Ezk 47:12). The mandrake, a member of the potato family, was superstitiously thought to promote fertility (Gen 30:14–16). The citizens of Laodicea are known to have had a medical school and to have prepared a powder or salve for weak eyes (Rev 3:18).

Wine was suggested as a stimulant (Prov 31:6), and was also used as an antiseptic. The good Samaritan bound up his patient's wounds "pouring on them oil and wine" (Lk 10:34). Paul recommended a little wine to relieve Timothy's gastric discomfort (I Tim 5:23). Sour wine mingled with gall and myrrh would have some sedative properties. It was offered to Christ, probably to ease His suffering (Mk 15:23).

Surgical treatment was usually minimal. The only operations mentioned in the Bible are circumcision, castration and the closing of wounds. But the code of Hammurabi regulated the charge of physicians for major operations and eye surgery in Babylonia, as well as for setting a broken bone and healing a sprained tendon (ANET, pp. 175 f.). The Edwin Smith papyrus from Egypt describes 48 surgical cases including such contingencies as accidental injuries and battle wounds.

Was the writer of the third Gospel and the Acts a physician? Internal evidence suggests that he was. He uses a large number of medical words found in Hippocrates, Galen and other medical writings, yet not found in the rest of the NT. He also notes medical particulars, such as the intensity of a fever, whether a disease was congenital or acquired, and which side of the body was affected (Lk 4:38; Acts 3:2; Lk 6:6). In writing about the woman with the issue of blood (Lk 8:43), he honestly states that she could not be healed by the physicians; but he is more polite to his profession than Mark who adds that she had "suffered many things of many physicians, and had spent all that she had, and was nothing bettered, but rather grew worse" (Mk 5:26). These factors tend to corroborate the other evidence that Luke "the beloved physician" (Col 4:14) was the author of the third Gospel and Acts.

Mosaic Health Laws

The law given by God to Moses contained remarkable rules pertaining to public health. Although the primary purpose of these regulations was to render a man ceremonially clean, hygienic cleanliness nonetheless was involved. What are the primary concerns of a public health officer today? Water and food contamination, sewage disposal, infectious diseases, health education—these are all dealt with in the Mosaic health laws.

It has been said that some of the health laws were too strict and perhaps unnecessary for public health, but it must be remembered that ancient man did not have our understanding of disease. To be overly strict for the sake of simplicity is better than to err in the other direction. We with our medical ability to distinguish between the dangerous and the harmless would not need to observe some of these same precautions, but this would not be true in their day. Again, it must be remembered that the initial reason for these ordinances was ceremonial purity.

The Mosaic health laws (Lev 11–15) include rules of circumcision, meat consumption, parturition, skin infections, contamination by secretions and excretions, disposal of the dead, personal cleanliness, and sexual relations.

Miracles of Healing

A number of healing miracles are recorded in the Bible. Other miracles, while not of healing but of judgment, are medical in nature. These include the plagues on Egypt (Ex 9:13–15; 12:12–13), the slaying of the Philistines before the ark (I Sam 5:6), the decimation of Sennacherib's army (II Kgs 19:35), Jeroboam's withered hand (I Kgs 13:1–6), and Gehazi's leprosy (II Kgs 5:27). Though God may have used natural disease processes, the supernatural is involved in their timing.

Miracles in the OT seem to center around the time of the Exodus and the ministry of Elijah and Elisha. Those recorded are more frequently miracles of nature, with less than a dozen involving healing (e.g., Abimelech, Gen 20:17; Miriam, Num 12:10–15; the brazen serpent, Num 21:5–9; the widow's son, I Kgs 17:17–24; the Shunammite's son, II Kgs 4:18–37; Naaman, II Kgs 5:1–14; Hezekiah, II Kgs 20:1–7).

On the other hand, the NT records a greater proportion of healing miracles. These were either performed by Christ or in His name. Of the 35 miracles of Christ recorded in the NT, 26 involve healings. In six of these instances demons were expelled. Careful details are given about many of these cases, especially by Luke the physician. Some of the people are even identified by name (Bartimaeus, Jairus' daughter, Mary, Lazarus; also Aeneas, Eutychus, and Publius' father in the Acts).

Some have tried to explain the healing miracles of Christ on a psychological basis. According to this theory the diseases cured were only functional or psychosomatic. It is true that people may have their diseases relieved by "faith" in men or things. But this type of cure is far removed from Christ's cure of such organic diseases as congenital blindness (Jn 9:1), advanced arthritis of the spine (Lk 13:11), metorrhagia or prolonged hemorrhaging (Lk 8:43), leprosy (Lk 5:12; 17:12), and even death (Lk 7:12; 8:49-55; Jn 11:1-44). Only by denying the reliability of the NT documents can all the healings of Christ be made psychological.

In addition to their predominantly organic nature, the healings of Christ were complete and instantaneous (with the exception of the man whose sight returned in two stages, Mk 8:22-25). Furthermore, they consisted of a number of different diseases which are difficult to treat even by today's medical techniques. Few if any were likely to recover spontaneously. And there is no evidence of any relapses occurring after Christ's healings. *See* Healing, Health.

Demon Possession

Demon possession is a phenomenon which seems to have occurred with more frequency at the time of Christ. Of the 26 persons healed by Christ, six are mentioned as having been demon possessed. Many other persons with no apparent physical maladies were set free from demonic oppression (Mt 8:16; Mk 1:34, 39; Lk 6:18). Little if any mention is made of demon possession in the OT. Christ and the NT seem to distinguish between ordinary illnesses and those accompanied by demon possession (Mt 10:8; Mk 1:34; Acts 5:16). Demon possession could be accompanied by physical symptoms (e.g., blindness, deafness and dumbness, Mt 12:22; Mk 9:25), neurological manifestations (e.g., epilepsy, Lk 9:39, 42), or mental symptoms (Lk 4:33; 8:27; Mk 7:25).

The diagnosis of demon possession, however, raises some difficult problems. What distinguished it from natural illness? How could a person recognize it as such? If there are any distinguishing features which typify the condition, they are suicidal tendencies and the demon's use of the person as a mouthpiece.

On the other hand, physical illness is often attributed in the Scriptures to Satan. Christ spoke of the arthritic woman as "this woman whom Satan hath bound" (Lk 13:16). Was she demon possessed? Jesus did not address any demon when He healed her. A. Rendle Short suggests a solution: "It is not that the scribes and Pharisees and common people diagnosed demon possession too often, but that their ideas were too crude, and they failed to recognize that there may have been a very much wider work of the devil" (*The Bible and Modern Medicine*, p. 121).

If this is true, then it may not be possible always to find specific signs to diagnose and distinguish demon possession from other diseases. *See* Demonology.

Skin Diseases

A number of skin lesions are mentioned in the OT. Some of these were to be imposed as afflictions on Israel for disobedience to the Lord (Deut 28:27). The *itch* is probably scabies, still known by that descriptive name. It is caused by an insect, *Acarus scabei. Scurvy* (RSV) is not what we know today as scurvy (caused by vitamin C deficiency) but rather a "scab" (KJV). The word comes from a root meaning "to scratch" or "be rough." This possibly covers a range of skin diseases including eczema and psoriasis. The *botch* (KJV) or *boil* (RSV) comes from a root meaning "to be inflamed" or "hot." Boils are common today though better controlled, thanks to modern antibiotics. Hezekiah's boil may have been a carbuncle or possibly anthrax (II Kgs 20:1, 7). Anthrax is contracted from cattle or the dried hides and hair of infected animals. Without treatment it may be fatal.

Leprosy is frequently mentioned in the Bible. Miriam, Naaman, and King Uzziah all contracted this disease. Instructions for its diagnosis are given in Lev 13; it apparently included more than what we today call leprosy (caused by the *Lepra bacillus* of Hansen). Unfortunately, the term leprosy has changed its meaning in the English language. Even in the Middle Ages the word was used to describe a number of different skin disorders such as ringworm. Harold M. Spinka states, "It is my opinion, that leprosy as well as the diseases mentioned in the differential diagnosis, e.g., chronic psoriasis vulgaris, syphilis, pemphigus and dermatitis herpetiformis, smallpox, fungus infections as well as the pyodermas were included under the general label of leprosy" ("Leprosy in Ancient Hebraic Times," JASA, XI [March, 1959], 17-22). That the leprosy of the OT is not identical with the leprosy of today is also demonstrated in the fact that there was a leprosy of houses and garments (Lev 13:47; 14:37)—probably some type of mold or fungus. *See* Leprosy.

Job's affliction has been the subject of much speculation. It is unlikely that he had ordinary boils, as they would not extend from head to foot and would not itch so severely (Job 2:7-8). The description may fit smallpox, which is of sudden onset, extensive, and may itch at one stage. However, a person with smallpox would probably be too ill to talk as Job did. Pellagra, psoriasis, eczema, dermatitis herpetiformis, and exfoliative dermatitis have all been suggested as possibilities. Dermatitis herpetiformis, a rare skin disease, would itch intensely, and would not severely affect Job's general health. Exfoliative dermatitis is generalized, chronic, miserable, very itchy and associated with boils from scratching.

Eye and Ear Diseases

Both congenital and acquired blindness are mentioned in the Bible. Infection with *tra-*

CURRENT CLINICAL DATA OF DISEASES CONSIDERED AS BIBLICAL LEPROSY*		
Disease	*Degree of Contagion*	*Causative Agent*
Leprosy	++	Lepra bacillus of Hansen
Syphilis	++++	Treponema pallidum-bacteria
Smallpox	++++	Virus
Scabies	++++	Acarus scabei—a parasite
Favus	+++	Achorion Schoenleini-fungus
Tinea of scalp	++++	Microsporon audoini or lanosum fungus
Deep or systemic fungus infections	+++	e.g., Actinomysosis due to acti- nomyces bovis or Nocardia
Boils and furuncles	++	Staphlococcus and streptococcus- bacteria
Pemphigus	unknown	Unknown
Dermatitis herpeti- formis	unknown	Unknown
Cancer of skin	unknown	Virus?

*Harold M. Spinka, M.D., "Leprosy in Ancient Hebraic Times." Paper presented at the 13th annual convention of the American Scientific Affiliation at Iowa State College; August, 1958. Reprinted from *Journal of American Scientific Affiliation,* March, 1959.

choma is still a common cause of acquired blindness in many parts of the world. This virus causes unsightly discharge and may have been Leah's problem (Gen 29:17). Perhaps her eyes were crossed (*strabismus*). Trachoma could have been Paul's thorn in the flesh (II Cor 12:7-10); his own words suggest some sort of eye trouble (cf. Gal 6:11 with 4:14-15; Acts 23:2-5). Smallpox can also cause an unattractive ulceration and scarring of the cornea, with loss of vision.

Cataracts were probably the cause of Isaac's and Eli's blindness in their old age. This is a progressive opacification of the lens of the eye. In Lev 21:20 the Heb. word for "blemish" (*q.v.*) suggests a spot causing confused sight, probably a cataract.

Ophthalmia neonatorum causes a severe conjunctivitis and blindness in newborn infants. It is usually a result of a gonorrheal infection in the mother. This probably accounted for much of the blindness present from infancy. There are also many types of congenital anomalies of the eye, which could result in total blindness from birth. *See* Blindness.

Deafness was also common in biblical times though its cause is difficult to determine.

Orthopedic Deformities

Orthopedic deformities would have been pathetic in a day when little could be done to correct them. The lame beggar whom Peter healed is such a case (Acts 3:2-8). Since he was lame from birth he may have had a congenital club foot, *spina bifida,* or cerebral palsy. The woman healed by Christ of an 18-year infirmity had a severe form of arthritis which bowed her forward (Lk 13:11-13). This sounds like rheumatoid arthritis, which affects women more than men.

Jacob's limp, acquired by his wrestling with the angel of God, may have been caused by a dislocated hip (Gen 32:25, 31-32). One can walk with a limp on an anterior dislocation. The acute pain and lameness may also indicate a ruptured intervertebral disc producing sciatic pain.

Neurological Diseases

Paralysis was evident in the Jewish population of Jesus' day. It was, no doubt, frequently caused by accidents as well as tuberculosis of the spine and polio. Paralysis is seldom mentioned in the OT.

The paraplegic healed by Christ (Lk 5:18) possibly had an injury or bony lesion of the spine, causing compression of the spinal cord. This would result in paralysis of the lower part of the body. The man healed at the pool of Bethesda (Jn 5:5-8) was only partially paralyzed. A birth injury, polio, multiple sclerosis, or a stroke could have caused this. The man with the withered hand was also partially paralyzed (Lk 6:6-10). His muscle atrophy could have resulted from inability to use his hand. He may have been a victim of injury, polio, or possibly amyotrophic lateral sclerosis, which affects the small muscles of the hand. The medically significant fact is that Christ healed him instantly and completely.

The centurion's servant (Lk 7:2; Mt 8:5) was also paralyzed. However, his condition was acute; he was close to death, and in great pain. This would suggest tetanus or an acute spinal cord compression from tumor, abscess or hemorrhage.

The Shunammite woman's son had a sudden onset of headache (II Kgs 4:18-20). He died within six hours of what may have been sunstroke, meningitis, subarachnoid hemorrhage, or more likely cerebral malaria.

Obstetrics

Sterility or barrenness was a problem affecting couples in biblical times as well as today. Sarah, Rachel, Manoah's wife, Hannah, the Shunammite woman, and Elisabeth all had this malady.

Deliveries in ancient Israel were usually performed with the mother on a birth stool (Ex 1:16) or sitting on the lap of another (Gen 30:3). [In the latter passage the practice referred to may be that of placing the new-born infant on the knees of the one who could give it legitimacy or the right to inheritance. — Ed.] After the baby's birth, the navel was cut, the baby washed in water, salt applied, and the baby wrapped in swaddling cloth (Ezk 16:4). Tamar was skillfully delivered of twins with one of them in a transverse presentation (Gen 38:27-30).

Mental Illness

There are only a few references to mental illness in the OT. David convincingly feigned madness (I Sam 21:12-15); Saul had recurrent depressions and showed paranoid symptoms (I Sam 16:14, 23; 18:8-11, 28-29; 19:9-10). Nebuchadnezzar had psychotic symptoms, living like an animal for seven years. R. K. Harrison classifies his illness as lycanthropy or boanthropy, a specific form of paranoia (IOT, pp. 1114-1117).

The writer of Prov 17:22 relates the emotions to the body, and thus anticipated psychosomatic medicine when he wrote, "A cheerful heart is a good medicine, but a downcast spirit dries up the bones" (RSV).

The relationship between mental illness and demon possession is uncertain and controversial. The "wild" man of Gadara (Mk 5:2-5) resembles what we would today classify as psychotic, although the other "demoniacs" healed by Christ had organic symptoms of physical illnesses.

Internal Diseases

High fever is a symptom rather than a disease. It could refer to malaria, typhoid, paratyphoid, smallpox, sunstroke, typhus, or a number of other diseases (Lev 26:16; Deut 28:22; Lk 4:38).

The *pestilence* sent by God upon the Philistines (I Sam 5:6, 9-12; 6:5) was probably bubonic plague. This disease was described by Hippocrates 400 years before Christ. It swept across Europe in the Middle Ages and has the characteristics of heavy mortality, sudden incidence, transmission by dead rodents, and the presence of enlarged inguinal glands (in the groin). It is interesting to note that the Philistines placed five golden images of the tumors

and mice beside the ark. [Some have suggested that the "tumors" were hemorrhoids, following the KJV "emerods." — Ed.]

Another pestilence was used by God to destroy the army of Sennacherib (II Kgs 19:35). There are two diseases which could kill a large number of people within 24 hours — cholera and pneumonic plague. There would probably have been a few cases in the camp before the peak of the epidemic.

Giantism is caused by an endocrine disorder. Goliath is a familiar example and possibly had an anterior pituitary tumor. Og, king of Bashan, needed a bed about 13 feet long (Deut 3:11). A giant with 12 fingers and toes is described in II Sam 21:20.

Dropsy is caused by fluid in the tissues. It is symptomatic of certain diseases, the most common being heart failure. The man whom Christ healed with this condition may have been suffering with cancer, heart, liver or kidney disease (Lk 14:2).

Dysentery was the disease which caused the debilitating fever of Publius' father (Acts 28:8, NASB). In fulminating cases of bacillary dysentery there is evacuation of blood and mucous (hence the KJV "bloody flux"), and death may come quickly.

Medical science throws light on a number of *deaths* described in the Bible. King Asa died with a great disease of his feet (II Chr 16:12-14). His coffin was filled with perfumes. This suggests a gangrene of the feet which would have caused a foul odor. Gangrene (KJV "canker") was recognized as a decaying disease which eats away tissue in a part of the body, usually a limb (II Tim 2:17). It may be caused by injury or failure of the blood supply.

King Jehoram was stricken with an incurable disease which caused a prolapse of the rectum (II Chr 21:18-19). This may have been a severe amoebic dysentery or cancer of the rectum.

Nabal was probably a chronic alcoholic. Following an episode of acute alcoholism he apparently had a cerebrovascular incident (stroke). He was comatose for ten days and died without regaining consciousness (I Sam 25:36-38).

Ananias and Sapphira both died suddenly and without warning (Acts 5:1-10). They may have been struck with a coronary thrombosis.

Herod Agrippa was consumed by intestinal worms (Acts 12:23). He probably had an intestinal obstruction from parasitic round worms and may have died from a perforated bowel and its resulting peritonitis.

Sufferings and Death of Christ

Strong Christian tradition states that Jesus' sweat fell to the ground like great drops of blood as the result of His anguish in Gethsemane (Lk 22:44). This may have been the rare emitting of blood through the transpiratory glands. But verses 43 and 44 are doubted to have been written by Luke, according to the best MS evidence (*see* Bloody Sweat).

Over 100 years ago it was suggested by Stroud that Christ died of cardiac rupture (i.e., a broken heart). This has become a commonly held view, but it is quite unlikely. Cardiac rupture, apart from trauma, is rare and when it occurs affects those whose hearts are already seriously damaged. That Christ's heart was diseased is improbable in the light of His previous energetic activity and perfect physical condition to fulfill the sacrificial requirements (I Pet 1:19).

It has also been suggested that Christ died of asphyxia from impairment of respiration while on the cross. Prolonged upright positioning could also lead to venous pooling and to peripheral circulatory failure. The decrease in cardiac output and the resultant decrease in blood flow to the tissues would cause a lowered oxygen level in the brain.

Also compatible with both biblical history and medical probability is acute dilitation of the stomach. This is seen today as a rare and poorly understood post-operative complication. It may also follow a state of shock. The spear thrust would have released the accumulated watery fluid in the dilated stomach of our Lord. The blood probably came from the pierced heart and great vessels. Following this there would have been no question of death.

Whatever the immediate cause of His death, the importance of the crucifixion lies in the meaning of Christ's death. With Isaiah we can say, "He was wounded for our transgressions, he was bruised for our iniquities: the chastisement of our peace was upon him; and with his stripes we are healed" (Isa 53:5).

Bibliography. Charles J. Brim, M.D., "Job's Illness—Pellagra," *Archives of Dermatology and Syphilology,* XLV (Feb., 1942), 371–376. A. Dudley Dennison, "Medicine," BW, pp. 368–373. Roland K. Harrison, "Disease," IDB, I, 847–854; "Medicine," IDB, III, 331–334; *Introduction to the Old Testament,* Grand Rapids: Eerdmans, 1969, pp. 607–610 (on leprosy). Louis A. M. Krause, "Biblical Medical References," *Transactions of the New Jersey Obstetrical and Gynecological Society,* I (1956), 42–50. S. I. McMillen, *None of These Diseases,* Spire Book, Old Tappan, N.J.: Revell, 1967. "Medicine, Disease, Health," CornPBE, pp. 516–520. Albrecht Oepke. "*Iaomai,* etc.," TDNT, III, 194–215. A. Rendle Short, *The Bible and Modern Medicine,* Chicago: Moody Press, 1967. C. Raimer Smith, *A Physician Examines the Bible,* New York: Philosophical Library, 1950. Jacob Taub, M.D., F.C.A.P., "Endocrinology in the Bible," presented at the third World Assembly of the Israel Medical Assn., Jerusalem, August 16, 1955. J. V. Kinnier Wilson, "Gleanings from the Iraq Medical Journals," JNES, XXVII (1968), 243–247 (for a comparison of ancient and modern diseases). Nellie B. Woods, The

Healings of the Bible, New York: Hawthorne Books, 1958.

C. W. C.

DISH

1. The "lordly dish" (Jud 5:25, KJV) represents the Heb. *sēpel 'addîrîm,* lit., "a bowl of nobles." Possibly in the time of the judges this was a handsome Cypriote milk bowl with "wishbone" handle. Or Jael's dish, her one prized possession, may have been a large bronze bowl, since Heb. *sēpel* is cognate to Ugaritic *spl,* a huge metal vessel (C. H. Gordon, *Ugaritic Manual,* 1955, p. 301), and to Akkad, *saplu,* a golden bowl or basin given by Jehu as tribute to Shalmanezer III (ANEP, # 351 –355). Gideon obtained enough dew to fill a bowl (*sēpel*) when he wrung his fleece (Jud 6:38). Among the Arabs today the word *sifl* denotes a large earthenware washbasin (Millar Burrows, *What Mean These Stones?* ASOR, 1941, p. 255). For the view that Jael's "dish" was a bulging skin milk churn see J. Kaplan, "Skin Bottles and Pottery Imitations," PEQ, July – Dec., 1965, pp. 144 – 149.

2. Heb. *sallahat* (II Kgs 21:13) is likely the popular ring-burnished bowl of Iron II Age. Since it had no handles to hang it up, it was turned over to dry.

3. Heb. *qe'ārâ* (Ex 25:29; 37:16; Num 4:7) was a gold dish or platter holding the bread of the Presence on the table in the tabernacle. The word is translated "charger" or "plate" (RSV) 14 times in Num 7.

4. In connection with the Last Supper, Gr. *trublion* refers to a large, deep dish or bowl, either of metal or perhaps of Roman style *sigillata* pottery, from which all could take food together (Mt 26:23; Mk 14:20). *See* Bowl; Pottery.

J. R.

DISHAN (dī'shăn). A Horite, the seventh and last son of Seir, who possessed mountains S of the Dead Sea. Dishan became a "duke" or "chief" (Heb. *'allûp*), i.e., "thousand"-leader (Gen 36:21, 30; I Chr 1:38). The name probably also designates a Horite clan.

Heb. *dîshân* has been compared with the Hurrian name Tai-sheni. *See* Horite. God enabled the descendants of Esau, i.e., Edom, to dispossess the Horites (Deut 2:12, 22).

DISHON (dī'shŏn). The name of two descendants of Seir, the Horite. The Heb. *dishŏn* can mean "antelope," "mountain goat" (cf. Deut 14:5), but perhaps it is derived from the Hurrian name Tai-sheni.

1. Seir's fifth son, and head of one of the original Edomite tribes (Gen 36:21,30; I Chr 1:38).

2. Seir's grandson, the only son of Anah, and brother of Aholibamah, Esau's second wife (Gen 36:25; I Chr 1:41).

DISPENSATION. The Gr. word *oikonomia* means stewardship, management of a household, an economy or a dispensation. The greatest interest and importance centers around the last meaning.

While the term "dispensation" is used by all theologians to express God's method of dealing with men during different eras of biblical revelation before and since the Fall of man, great differences exist as to the correct meaning of the term. Dr. L. S. Chafer writes: "A dispensation is a specific, divine economy, a commitment from God to man of a responsibility to discharge that which God has appointed him" (*Systematic Theology,* VII, 122). The Scofield Bible states: "A dispensation is a period of time during which man is tested in respect to his obedience to some specific revelation of the will of God" (p. 5). Scofield also says, "Each of the dispensations may be regarded as a new test of the natural man and each ends in judgment" (*Rightly Dividing the Word of Truth,* p. 20).

Applying the above definitions, many dispensational theologians come to the conclusion that there are seven dispensations, namely: (1) Innocence—up to the Fall; (2) Conscience—from the Fall to Noah; (3) Human Government—from Noah to Abraham (Gen 8:20—9:27); (4) Promise—from Abraham to Moses (Gen 12:1—Ex 19:8); (5) Law—from Moses to Christ (Ex 20:1—31:18); (6) Grace—from the death of Christ until His second coming (Rom 3:24-26; cf. Eph 3:1-10); (7) Kingdom—the millennial reign of Christ on earth (Rev 20:4 ff.; cf. II Sam 7:8-17; Lk 1:31-33).

Reformed theologians in general reject both a dispensation of conscience and of human government, since conscience has been present always in man (Rom 2:15), and the command to subdue the earth was already given at creation (Gen 1:28). They teach from two to five dispensations: (1) two, namely, OT and NT (L. Berkhof); (2) three: OT, NT and kingdom (some premillennial Reformed theologians); (3) four: Adam to Abraham, Abraham to Moses, Moses to Christ, and the gospel dispensation (Charles Hodge); (4) five, namely, Hodge's four plus the millennial kingdom (some premillennial covenant theologians).

Reformed theologians in general are dissatisfied with Chafer and Scofield because they teach man has been under probation in each dispensation since the Fall, and that he could have met the specific test of any of the dispensational eras, and then the series would have ended. If so, the Reformed theologians reason, salvation was possible for man without the cross, and Christ therefore did not have to die. However, it must be realized that there are many who base their theology on a study of dispensations but reject the definition given by Scofield and Chafer. These groups may include the greater part of the evangelicals.

While the Reformed theologians differ in their opinions as to the number of the dispensations, they agree in asserting that only one plan of salvation has existed through all dispensations since the Fall of man. The divisions made—such as two by Berkhof and four by Hodge—are dependent on the detail into which each wants to carry his study of God's administration of salvation in the OT, rather than any disagreement in principle, and the question whether stress is placed upon dispensations or covenants or whether there is a balanced presentation of both.

It proves difficult to build a theology upon the biblical use of the Gr. word *oikonomia* since it is used in the sense of stewardship in nearly every case in the NT (Lk 16:2-4; I Cor 9:17; Eph 3:2; Col 1:25), except in Eph 1:10 where Paul speaks of God gathering all things into one "in the dispensation of the fullness of time." Nevertheless, great profit can come from a study of the increasing revelation of God's covenant of grace—namely, salvation by grace through faith—in the different eras or dispensations of OT and NT.

A study of the plan of salvation under each dispensation adds facets concerning soteriology which no fully developed system can afford to neglect.

See Covenant.

Bibliography. Louis Berkhof, *Systematic Theology,* Grand Rapids: Eerdmans, 1949, pp. 290-301. Lewis S. Chafer, *Systematic Theology,* Dallas: Dallas Sem. Press, 1948, IV, 16-21; VII, 121-123. Charles Hodge, *Systematic Theology,* Grand Rapids: Eerdmans, II (1952), 371-377. Charles C. Ryrie, *Dispensationalism Today,* Chicago: Moody Press, 1965.

R. A. K.

DISPERSION OF ISRAEL. From the time God gave Palestine to Abraham and his descendants as a permanent possession (Gen 13:14-17), the status of the nation Israel has been determined by its relation to that land. Those in the land were in the place of blessing. Those out of the land were "the captivity" (*gôlâ,* Ezr 1:11; 2:1), or the "dispersion" (*diaspora,* Jn 7:35). The former spoke of their relation to Palestine, and the latter of their relation to the peoples among whom they went. James (1:1, RSV) and Peter (I Pet 1:1, RSV) wrote to the converts among the Jews of the Dispersion.

The first absence of the nation from the land was predicted in Gen 15:13, where the Lord informed Abraham of the destiny of his descendants. A promise of restoration immediately followed (Gen 15:14). This prophecy was fulfilled in the Egyptian sojourn of the nation.

At the time of the return from the Egyptian bondage, God revealed to Moses, and through him to the nation, that dispersion would be His method of chastening them for disobedience and apostasy. This is clearly stated in Deut 28:15, 25; 30:1-4. Thus the nation was forewarned that unbelief and disobedience would be judged by expulsion from the land of promise. The prophets sent to both the northern and southern kingdoms warned of such an expulsion (Hos 9:3; Jer 8:3; Ezk 4:13) and stated clearly the cause for such a judgment (Jer 16:11-15), namely, that the nation had followed and served other gods and had forsaken the true God and refused to obey His law.

The northern kingdom (Israel) was carried into captivity by the king of Assyria, who relocated the deportees in Halah and in Habor by the river of Gozan and in the cities of the Medes (II Kgs 17:6). This deportation began in 722 B.C. when the Assyrians conquered Samaria. The indictment against Israel, listing the causes of the Exile, is given in II Kgs 17:7-20. In spite of the warnings by the prophets to the kingdom of Judah in the light of what happened to her N neighbor, the southern kingdom continued in unbelief and apostasy, and in 586 B.C. was carried captive to Babylon by Nebuchadnezzar (II Kgs 24:14; 25:6, 11). The reason for this dispersion is clearly stated to have been her rejection of the warning of the prophets and her continuance in idolatry (II Chr 36:13-16).

Other lesser deportations and relocations of Jews followed (*see* Elephantine papyri). Ptolemy I of Egypt (322-285 B.C.), at the time of his invasion of Palestine and capture of Jerusalem, transported many Jews to Alexandria, which subsequently became an important Jewish center. Antiochus of Syria (223-187 B.C.) transported about 2,000 families from Babylon, according to Josephus, and relocated them in Phrygia and Lydia (cf. the localities in I Pet 1:1). Pompey, after capturing Jerusalem in 63 B.C., carried many Jews to Rome to be sold as slaves. The latter, however, regained freedom and civil rights. After the destruction of Jerusalem in A.D. 70 by Titus, there was a further scattering.

In addition to these involuntary deportations, many Jews left Palestine voluntarily in pursuit of commercial interests. This took them to the important economic centers of the world, and most large cities had a Jewish settlement. Thus, it is not surprising to read in Acts 2:9-12 that Jews came to Jerusalem for the Feast of Pentecost from all over the known world. Although the deportees adjusted in language and culture to the society in which they settled, they maintained ties with Palestine and Judaism by pilgrimages to the three annual feasts, by the payment of the half-shekel temple tax as long as the temple stood, and by submission to the decrees of the Sanhedrin as long as it functioned.

During the 1st cen. of the Christian era it is estimated that a million Jews resided in Mesopotamia, another million in Antioch-on-the-Orontes and throughout present day Turkey, a million in Egypt centering around Alexandria, a hundred thousand each in

Italy and N Africa, and two and one-half million in Palestine. Philo Judaeus (20 B.C.-A.D. 40) listed dozens of countries where Jews were scattered (*Legatio Ad Caium* 36).

While in dispersion the Jews settled down, frequently in comfortable surroundings (Jer 29:4-7), and made themselves an invaluable part of the business community. Circumstances were so pleasant in Babylon that, when permission was granted the Jews to return to Jerusalem to rebuild the temple, only a small remnant desired to undertake the rigors of the work. From the time of the Babylonian Captivity the number of Jews outside Palestine greatly outnumbered those in the land.

Another feature of the dispersion must not be overlooked. While the scattering was a judgment on Israel and Judah for unbelief and apostasy, yet it was meant for the blessing of the Gentiles. According to Ex 19:6 the nation was set apart by God to be a kingdom of priests, that is, they were to mediate between God and the Gentiles. They were to disseminate the revelation of the true God entrusted to them. The blessing of God on Abraham's seed was to be for all men (Gen 12:3). Yet the nation did not fulfill the responsibility entrusted to it. The law, which hedged Israel in from the Gentiles, was used to hide the truth God had revealed to Israel for the Gentiles. However, through the dispersion, the knowledge of God was brought, involuntarily, to the nations. A worldwide expectation of a Messiah-Redeemer was aroused as the dispersion brought a knowledge of God's promises to the Gentiles. Writers such as Tacitus, Suetonius, and Virgil anticipated a Blesser who would appear in Judea. Without doubt the Magi came to Judea to seek the King of the Jews because of the star and also knowledge gained from the dispersed nation (Mt 2:1-12).

The dispersion of Israel also had its effects on the preaching of the gospel in the NT era. The apostle Paul, in spreading the gospel through the Roman world, always began a ministry in a new city in the synagogue of the Jews, for he felt obligated "to the Jew first," to announce the fact that Israel's Messiah had come. The dispersed Jews were the first in any community to hear the gospel. Only after their rejection of his message did Paul turn to the Gentiles (as in Acts 18:6).

In Mt 12:31-37 Christ warned the nation of the dire results of following the leaders in their rejection of Him as Messiah, and concluded with a warning of judgment (Mt 12:41-45). He prophesied further dispersion for the nation by predicting the coming desolation of Jerusalem (Mt 23:37-39), which was fulfilled in A.D. 70, and promising that the city would be occupied by Gentiles until the second advent (Lk 21:24). In the Olivet Discourse Christ graphically prophesied a yet future overthrow of Jerusalem (Mt 24:15-21). This is only a reaffirmation of the prophecy of Zech 13:8-14:2, where the prophet foretold of an invasion during the Tribulation period in which Jerusalem would be destroyed and many of the inhabitants killed or scattered.

This eschatological dispersion is God's final chastisement of the nation before the Millennium. At the beginning of the Tribulation the head of the Roman Empire will make a covenant with the nation Israel, guaranteeing safety in the land of Palestine (Dan 9:27). The nation will occupy the land, trusting this political alliance to defend it. It will go even further and acknowledge that this ruler is its Messiah and God, and will worship him (Rev 13:11-18). God will cause the Gentile nations to come against Jerusalem to destroy it and to scatter the inhabitants, as He punished Israel previously in chastisement for its apostasy.

The predictions of dispersion contain also a promise of restoration to the land. It was in keeping with the promise of Deut 30:3-5 that the nation returned from the Babylonian dispersion. It is in fulfillment of such a promise as Deut 30:1-10 and that found in Amos 9:14-15 that Israel will be restored at the second advent of Christ and resettled in its land. Ultimately the answer to Israel's dispersion is its complete conversion (Isa 66:6-9; Jer 31:31-34) and restoration to Palestine under its Messiah (Isa 54:1-17; 60:1-6; 62:1-12) at the second coming of Christ.

Bibliography. Karl L. Schmidt, *"Diaspora,"* TDNT, II, 98-104. Merrill C. Tenney, *New Testament Times,* Grand Rapids: Eerdmans, 1965, pp. 88-91, 182 f. A. F. Walls, "Dispersion," NBD, pp. 318 ff.

J. D. P.

DISPERSION OF MANKIND. By means of confusing the speech of the people at Babel, God scattered mankind over the entire earth (Gen 11:5-9). Thus the posterity of Noah was divided (from Heb. *pālag,* Gen 10:25; Heb. *pārad,* 10:32) after the Flood. This dispersal occurred in the days of Peleg, probably within two or three centuries following the Noahic deluge (cf. Gen 10:25 with 11:10-19). Historically, the event must have occurred prior to the migration of peoples to the W Hemisphere, and to the founding of neolithic villages in the Middle East and of such early cities as Jericho in Palestine, Jarmo in Mesopotamia, and Catal Hüyük in Anatolia (all dated archaeologically before 6000 B.C.), for these sites furnish no evidence of disturbance by flood waters.

It is conceivable that much cultural knowledge was lost to mankind as a result of the confusion of languages, since one man could no longer communicate the knowledge of his particular skill to another. Thus many arts and crafts — agriculture, metallurgy, music (cf. Gen 4:20-22), perhaps even writing — died out, only to be rediscovered by laborious process much later after perhaps millennia of dark ages and primitive existence.

Gen 10 and 11 present a list of the principal descendants of Noah who might likely be known to the Israelites, including an account of the event which precipitated the division into many nations. The main criteria for classifying the subdivisions of mankind in this so-called Table of Nations were geographical ("in their lands"), linguistic ("after his tongue"), and political ("in their nations," Gen 10:5, 20,31). The basis was essentially ethno-geographic, however, because language can change completely as a result of conquest or migration.

Assuming Mosaic authorship for these chapters, one can more readily understand that the list of 70-odd ethnic groups mentioned in Gen 10 was compiled from the knowledge available to one educated in the courts of Egypt in the middle of the 2nd mil. B.C. Egypt had widespread diplomatic and trade contacts at that time with Libya, Cyprus, Cilicia, Crete, up and down the Red Sea, and with the Hittites in Anatolia and the Kassites in Babylonia. As a result of the conquests of Thutmose III she controlled Nubia and large areas of Canaan and Syria. This may help to explain why the Philistines are grouped under Mizraim (Egypt, Gen 10:13-14) and Canaan comes under Ham, although all evidence proves the Canaanites spoke a Semitic language from 2000 B.C. onward. The table definitely reflects a time before 1200 B.C., for Gaza is said to belong to the Canaanites (Gen 10:19), not to the Philistines. The brown, yellow, and red races are not mentioned, probably because these had no contact with Egypt nor with the Israelites in those days. *See* Gentiles; Nations.

Bibliography. Gleason L. Archer, SOTI, pp. 201-203. T. C. Mitchell, "Nations, Table of," NBD, pp. 865-869. E. A. Speiser, "Man, Ethnic Divisions of," IDB, III, 235-242. Merrill F. Unger, *Archaeology and the OT,* Zondervan, 1954, pp. 73-104.

J. R.

DISTAFF. In the process of spinning, the spindle-and-whorl (Heb. *pelek;* cf. Akkad. *pilakku*) which winds up the twisted fibers (Prov 31:19b). It is manipulated by back-and-forth action of the palms. The Heb. word also occurs in II Sam 3:29 as "staff" (KJV; "one who holds a spindle," RSV), condemning the male descendants of Joab to the feminine task of spinning. In Prov 31:19a the term "spindle" (RSV, "distaff") refers to the stick, or to the spinning bowl noted in Egyptian tomb models, either of which was used to hold the loose fibers. *See* Spin; Spindle.

DIVERS. In the KJV an archaic English word generally meaning either "several," "many" (e.g., Heb 1:1) or "diverse," "different in kind" (e.g., Deut 22:9), the rendering of several Heb. and Gr. words.

The Israelites, probably to avoid idolatrous practices of the Canaanites, were forbidden to bring together different kinds of materials, ani-

467

mals, or products, such as: (1) weaving garments of two kinds of material, particularly of wool and linen; (2) sowing a field with mixed seed; (3) yoking an ox and an ass together; (4) breeding together animals of different species, e.g., an ass and a horse to procure mules (Lev 19:19; Deut 22:9–11).

DIVINATION. The attempt to discern future events by such means as trances, visions, etc., or physical objects. These were varied: (1) rhabdomancy, the throwing of sticks or arrows into the air (Ezk 21:21; cf. Hos 4:12); (2) hepatoscopy, examination of the liver or other organs of an animal (Ezk 21:21); (3) teraphim, images used for divination (I Sam 15:23; Ezk 21:21; Zech 10:2); (4) necromancy, communication with the dead (Deut 18:11; I Sam 28:8; II Kgs 21:6) which was condemned in the law (Lev 19:31; 20:6) and the prophets (Isa 8:19–20); (5) astrology, reading the stars and coming to conclusions on the basis of their positions and relations to each other, which was pronounced vain in Isa 47:13 and Jer 10:2; (6) hydromancy, divination with water, done either by noting the reflections, or inducing a trance by this means. In order to confuse his brethren, Joseph had his servants suggest the goblet found in their sacks was for that purpose (Gen 44:5, 15); no approval of such a practice is implied. God sternly condemns all means of seeking hidden knowledge and knowledge of the future apart from His divine revelation.

To be distinguished from divination are the use of the lot, dreams, and signs. In the OT God used the casting of the lot for certain purposes, such as the allocation of territory for the ten tribes (Josh 18:10), the choice of the goat to be sacrificed on the Day of Atonement (Lev 16), the choice of a guilty person (Josh 7:14; Jon 1:7), the assignment of temple service (I Chr 24:5), and once in the NT for the choice of a successor to Judas' lost apostleship (Acts 1:15–26). It is significant that the use of the lot ceased with Pentecost. *See also* Urim and Thummim.

Dreams were a means used of God also for revelation, though it is significant that we read of no one specifically asking for guidance in that manner (e.g., Joseph's dreams, Gen 37:5–11; Nebuchadnezzar's dream, Dan 2; the dreams of Joseph, Mary's husband, Mt 1:20; 2:19).

In several instances OT believers asked God for a sign to guide them, such as when Gideon put out his fleece (Jud 6:37–40) and Jonathan took the particular reply of the enemy as his guidance from God (I Sam 14:8–10). In the use of the lot, it was commanded of God only for decisions which required more than human wisdom. In the case of dreams, it was God's way of giving a divine revelation only for the most extreme emergencies.

See Demonology; Enchantment; Familiar Spirit; Hepatoscopy; Liver; Magic; Necromancer; Teraphim; Witchcraft.

Bibliography. Yehezkel Kaufmann, *The Religion of Israel,* trans. by Moshe Greenberg, Chicago: Univ. of Chicago Press, 1960, pp. 42–53, 87–93.

R. A. K.

DIVINE HEALING. *See* Healing, Health.

DIVORCE. *In the OT.* In Deut 24:1–4 Moses permitted divorce of a husband from his wife if the husband found *'erwat dābār,* "some uncleanness" in her (lit., "a case of nakedness," or "nakedness of a thing"). The nature of such an accusation was so general that it led to two interpretations at the time of Christ: a narrower one taught by the school of Shammai, which confined it to unfaithfulness; and a broader view, taught by the school of Hillel, which extended it to include anything that might displease the husband. The requirement that a man give his wife a bill of divorcement gave the act a legal and official status, since it needed the aid of at least a Levite to execute it properly. The further rule forbidding him to take his wife back after she had married another showed the gravity of the act (Deut 24:4).

There were several circumstances, however, in which divorce was forbidden. When a man had openly and wrongfully accused his young bride of premarital unfaithfulness, he must pay damages to her father and thereafter "he may not put her away all his days" (Deut 22:19). Again, if a man had premarital relations with a maiden, he must first pay an indemnity to the father and then marry the girl. Because he had humbled her, he also was not allowed ever to divorce her thereafter (Deut 22:28–29; Ex 22:16–17).

In the case of adultery with either another married person or between a married and an unmarried person, the OT penalty was death (Lev 20:10; Deut 22:22). The same penalty applied even to a wife who had practiced fornication before marriage (Deut 22:21; cf. v. 23). Thus the possibility of divorce was replaced by the penalty of death in such cases. *See* Fornication.

One more example of divorce remains. The Israelites were commanded to put away unbelieving heathen wives by Ezra (Ezr 9–10) and Nehemiah (Neh 13:23 f.; cf. Mal 2:10–16), since these wives were leading them astray. The command in II Cor 6:14, 17 not to be unequally yoked with unbelievers deals with the same problem, but in both cases would apply only when the strange wife or husband was leading the believer into unbelief or heathenism. (See William R. Eichhorst, "Ezra's Ethics on Intermarriage and Divorce," *Grace Journal,* X [1969], 16–28.)

In the NT. The Pharisees approached Christ concerning the views of Shammai and Hillel and asked, "Is it lawful for a man to put away his wife for every cause?" (Mt 19:3 ff.). His answer throws light on Deut 24:1–4. Moses did not "command" that a bill of divorcement be given, as they maintained (v. 7). He merely suffered or permitted it because of the hardness of their hearts (v. 8). From the beginning, that is, from the first revelation of the nature and meaning of marriage in Gen 2:23-24, man was to have only one wife—"they shall be one flesh" and to have her permanently (Mt 19:6)—"cleave unto his wife" (Gen 2:24). The one exception permitting divorce, which Christ mentioned at this point, was fornication (v. 9; Mt 5:32).

In I Cor 7:10 Paul gives the further teaching of Christ concerning marriage and divorce as he writes, "Unto the married I command, yet not I, but the Lord. . . ." Paul is saying that he is writing what Christ taught. The wife is not to leave her husband because he is an unbeliever, for the unbelieving husband is sanctified by the wife (vv. 10, 14). To express it in theological terms, the covenantal family relationship made by a believer with God for himself and his children cares for the marriage. If the believing party leaves, he is not to marry again (v. 11) unless the unbeliever breaks the marriage vow by adultery or remarriage (cf. Mt 5:32; 19:9). However, if the unbeliever deserts his believing wife, then the believer seems to be considered free to remarry: "A brother or a sister is not under bondage in such cases" (I Cor 7:15). Some feel that homosexuality is also a reason for divorce since it is listed as an even greater sin than adultery, being "against nature" (Rom 1:26-27).

Two difficulties have arisen over Christ's teaching in the Gospels.

1. In Mark 10:11-12 and Luke 16:18 Christ makes no room whatever for divorce on any grounds; only in Matthew (5:32; 19:9) does He mention that divorce is allowed in case of fornication. Here we have to apply the principle that all the details must be gathered and scripture must be compared with scripture before we come to final conclusions. A complete inductive synthesis requires that all Christ taught on divorce, as recorded both in the Gospels and in I Cor 7:10 ff., be assembled before a final decision is made on Christ's teachings. To this must be added all else found on the subject in the NT in order to be sure of the NT doctrine of divorce.

How is Christ's view of divorce to be reconciled with the OT? How could Moses have been instructed of God to give such general permission? The condition of mankind at that time needs to be considered. These instructions were given to Moses because of the demoralized attitudes of man since the Fall. The ideal conditions which existed when God gave the original ordinance of marriage no longer existed. Moses was told to promulgate a civil law which would regulate divorce rather than a divine law, such as later revealed by Christ, which they could never keep in their unregenerate state. Such being the case, this civil law can well be a guide to man as he deals with unsaved persons and for civil laws even today,

but it cannot be set up as the spiritual standard of the church. In the NT Christ removed the judgment of adultery and fornication from the realm of civil law, where they were punishable by physical death, and placed it fully under the judgment of the moral law and God Himself. Inasmuch as the moral law is a higher tribunal than the civil, He put it under an even severer judgment.

2. Christ did not mention adultery as a ground for divorce, but only fornication. Is it therefore not included? This can be explained first by the fact that the admission of the lesser sin of fornication implies the inclusion of the greater sin of adultery. Further, adultery was already considered in both Jewish and Roman law as a legitimate reason for divorce, and therefore would not require to be mentioned. To this must be added the fact that though fornication and adultery are separately mentioned in many cases (Mt 15:19; I Cor 6:9; Gal 5:19), fornication is often used alone to cover both (Acts 15:20; 21:25; Rom 1:29; Eph 5:3). The view generally held, therefore, is that by the use of the term fornication our Lord meant to cover the two. This is borne out further by the fact that the sinful conduct of Israel as Jehovah's wife is sometimes called adultery (Jer 3:8; Ezk 23:45) and sometimes fornication (Jer 3:2-3; Ezk 23:43). Again, in I Cor 7:2 fornication is used to cover either sin.

Summarizing the NT teaching, we find that divorce is permitted where there has been fornication or adultery, and in the case of willful desertion; but not because of some whim or even incompatibility. For such, only separation is permitted (cf. I Cor 7:10 ff.).

Some practical questions arise for the church. How is it to regard adultery and premarital relations? The latter is clearly the lesser sin. Paul was probably answering the question, "Is it good for a man to touch a woman?" in I Cor 7:1 ff., when he replied in the imperative mood, "Let every man have his own wife," or as Dr. J. O. Buswell, Jr., translates it, "Each man must have his own wife" (*Systematic Theology*, p. 386). The OT was very strict concerning fornication—the young people who had committed it must marry, yet it was lenient in comparison with adultery, when the offenders were to be stoned to death. The church should keep this in mind as it acts. *See* Incontinency.

What shall the church do about marrying divorced persons? Only the innocent party can be considered eligible for a church wedding. Some feel the same holds true for church membership. Others would urge a course of confession and discipline followed by restoration. Many churches refuse to give the divorced communicant membership, though with the open communion service not excluding him from the Lord's table. Churches with a closed communion tend to the former—discipline and restoration; those with an open one, to the latter.

See Bill; Family.

Bibliography. J. Oliver Buswell, Jr., *Systematic Theology,* Grand Rapids: Zondervan, 1963, I, 385–396. W. Fisher-Hunter, *The Divorce Problem,* Waynesboro: MacNeish Publishers, 1952. John Murray, *Divorce,* Committee on Christian Education, Orthodox Presbyterian Church, 1953; *Principles of Christian Conduct,* Grand Rapids: Eerdmans, 1957.

R. A. K.

DIZAHAB (dĭz'a-hăb). One of several places listed in Deut 1:1 as defining the route the Israelites took between Paran or Horeb (Mount Sinai) and Moab in Transjordan where Moses was speaking. Since the name means "having gold," at one time gold may have been found there. Location is uncertain.

DOCTOR, DOCTOR OF THE LAW. *See* Occupations: Doctor, Lawyer.

DODAI (dō'dī). An Ahohite (I Chr 27:4). *See* Dodo 2.

DODANIM (dō'da-nĭm). A family or race descended from Javan, the son of Japheth (Gen 10:4). If the Heb. spelling *dodānîm* is correct, this people may have been the ancient Danaoi (ANET, p. 262) or Dardani who were related to the Greeks and lived around Troy along the NW coast of Asia Minor. The LXX, however, reads *Rodioi,* and the MT of the parallel verse in I Chr 1:7 has Heb. *rôdānîm,* Rhodians or Greeks on the island of Rhodes (*q.v.*). The uncertainty is caused by the confusion of the very similar letters in Heb. of "r" and "d." Minoan, Mycenaean, and Dorian settlements have been identified on Rhodes from the OT period.

DODAVAH (dō'dä-vä). A man (RSV, Dodavahu) from Mareshah in Judah. His son Eliezer prophesied to King Jehoshaphat that for joining the wicked king Ahaziah of Israel in a maritime commercial venture, his fleet of ships would be wrecked (II Chr 20:37).

DODO (dō'dō). The name occurs in Akkad. as *Dudû.*
1. A descendant of Issachar, grandfather of the judge Tola (Jud 10:1).
2. An Ahohite, father of Eleazar, one of David's three mighty men or champions (II Sam 23:9; I Chr 11:12). He seems to be the same as the Dodai mentioned in I Chr 27:4 as commander of the division of David's royal troops for the second month.
3. A Bethlehemite, the father of Elhanan, one of David's 30 heroes (II Sam 23:24; I Chr 11:26).

DOE. *See* Animals, II.10.

DOEG (dō'ĕg). An Edomite who served King Saul. His name means "timid, anxious." He was "the chiefest of the herdmen that belonged to Saul" (I Sam 21:7). "As herds would form the main part of Saul's wealth, his chief herdsman would be a person of importance" (*Pulpit Commentary,* IV, 396).

When David, fleeing from Saul's insane wrath, received help from Ahimelech, the high priest at Nob, Doeg was present "detained before the Lord" (I Sam 21:7), perhaps in connection with some vow he had made. Later, he reported the incident to Saul (I Sam 22:9–10), who ordered the execution of all the priests. When Saul's bodyguard refused to obey this wicked command, the commission was transferred to Doeg, who fulfilled it with alacrity (v. 18), slaughtering 85 priests. (LXX increases this number to 305, while Josephus makes it 385.) It was a revolting crime and, though ordered by Saul, revealed also the bloodthirsty nature of Doeg. Evidently David, from previous experience with this Edomite, was not surprised when he received the sad report from Abiathar, son of Ahimelech, who alone escaped (I Sam 22:22). Allusion is made to Doeg and his part in this ugly affair in the title of Ps 52.

G. C. L.

DOG. *See* Animals, I.7.

DOLEFUL CREATURES. Animals or birds of uncertain identity (Isa 13:21). The Heb. *'ōhîm* means howling creatures (RSV).

DOLMENS. Ancient hut-like structures with walls built of large vertical slabs of stone, usually with a single massive horizontal roof stone, weighing several hundred pounds each. They are found in many parts of the E Hemisphere, from W Europe through N Africa and Malta to S Russia and SW Asia. In Palestine there are several thousand individual dolmens located in dozens of sites that overlook the Jordan Valley from both sides.

While dolmens are usually interpreted as tombs, there is no real proof as yet that the builders constructed them for this purpose. Because no artifacts have thus far been discovered in or beside the empty dolmens, it is impossible to know who built them or when, according to James L. Swauger in "Dolmen Studies in Palestine," BA, XXIX (1966), 106–114. David Gilead, however, believes from all available evidence that the dolmens in Palestine were used in the 4th mil. B.C. for primary burials, and that after complete decomposition the skeletons were removed and reburied in communal burial caves ("Burial Customs and the Dolmen Problem," PEQ,C [1968], 16–26, 84; see also D. Webley, "A Note on the Dolmen Field at Tell el-Adeimeh and Teleilat Ghassul," PEQ,CI [June, 1969], 42 f.). It has been suggested that the huge stones were erected by some of the aborigines who roamed Palestine in pre-Abrahamic times. Large giant-like peoples known as the Anakim, the Emim, the Rephaim, and the Zamzummim are mentioned in Deut 2:10, 11, 20, 21; 3:11 (RSV). *See* Anakim; Giant; Rephaim.

After the six-day war in 1967 Israeli archaeologists investigated a vast field of thousands of dolmens of different sizes on the Golan Heights. The site is called Rujum Hiri, *c.* 15 miles E of the N end of the Sea of Galilee. Like Stonehenge in England, the megalithic structure consists of large, crude basalt stones in a series of concentric rings whose outer circle is over 500 feet in diameter. The circles are *c.* six feet high, and at the center is a stone pile 31 feet high. The purpose served by the structure is not known, and its date is not certain, although it is assumed to belong to the 4th or 3rd mil. B.C.

J. R.

DOLPHIN. *See* Animals: Dugong, V. 3.

DONKEY. *See* Animals, I.1.

DOOR. Referred to many times in the Bible. In KJV it translates seven Heb. and one Gr. word. Two Heb. terms are used frequently: *delet*, referring to the door itself, and *petaḥ*, a doorway or entrance. "Door" is used both literally and figuratively.

Literal usage (e.g., Gen 19:6, 9; II Kgs 9:10). Doors ordinarily were of wood, but sometimes were made of thick slabs of stone, both for houses and for tombs. Locks of wood, brass, or iron were used (Jud 3:24–25). In tents, doors were openings covered with flaps (Gen 18:1–2). *See* Gate; Hinge.

Figurative usage. Probably the most frequent use of door in a figurative sense is as a symbol of opportunity, especially for Christian witness and service (e.g., I Cor 16:9; II Cor 2:12; Col 4:3; Rev 3:8). Door is also used to represent the way by which a person enters into something. Christ Himself is the door by which one enters into salvation (Jn 10:9; cf. Acts 14:27; Hos 2:15). That which is near is said to be "at the door" (Mt 24:33; Jas 5:9; Rev 3:20; Gen 4:7).

See Joachim Jeremias, *"Thura,"* TDNT, III, 173–180.

G. C. L.

DOORKEEPER. Mentioned a number of times in both OT and NT. It sometimes signifies a gatekeeper, since both Heb. and Gr. words can refer to either door or gate. In important buildings, such as the temple, the position was evidently one of dignity and honor. In Ps 84:10 the translation "doorkeeper" is inaccurate. The allusion is to one who "stands at the threshold" (ASV marg.), such as the beggar of Acts 3:2. In the temple, there were a considerable number of Levites who served as doorkeepers (or porters, the same word in original; see I Chr 9:22). A few priests were also given this designation (II Kgs 25:18). Possibly the former served under the latter. These doorkeepers not only guarded the gates but also performed other services (II Chr 31:14). At the trial of Christ, the

doorkeeper at the high priest's house was a girl (Jn 18:15–17). Sometimes private homes had doorkeepers (Mk 13:34).

See Porter.

G. C. L.

DOORPOST
1. Heb. *sap* (Ezk 41:16, KJV), better, "threshold" (*q.v.*).
2. Heb. *mashqôp* (Ex 12:7, KJV), "lintel" as in Ex 12:22, 23.
3. Heb. *mezûzâ* (Ex 12:7, 22, 23; 21:6; Jud 16:3; etc.), usually rendered "doorpost" in RSV and as "side post," "door post," or "post" in KJV. Just as the Passover blood was commanded to be smeared on the doorposts and lintel of the Israelite house (Ex 12:7), so the words of the Shema (Deut 6:4, 5) were to be inscribed on the doorposts (Deut 6:9). It may be argued from a similar command in Deut 11:20 that this instruction was meant to be understood figuratively. But the ancient Egyptians inscribed their doorways with favorable omens in the names of their pagan deities, so it may be that the Israelites were told to replace that custom with one honoring their God. In early times, at any rate, Jewish homes had portions of the law either carved or inscribed upon the doorposts and fixed on the right-hand door jamb of every room in the house. Moslems today often paint sentences from the Koran over their front doors.

J. R.

DOPHKAH (dŏf'kå). A campsite of the Israelites between the Wilderness of Sin on the shore of the Red Sea and the oasis valley of Rephidim (Num 33:12–13). Identification is not certain, but suggestions are (1) the area of Serabit el-Khadim, an Egyptian copper and turquoise mining center, or (2) more likely in the Wadi Magharah leading to Wadi Feiran and Mount Sinai. *See* Sin, Wilderness of.

DOR (dôr). A Canaanite city on the Mediterranean coast between Caesarea and Mount Carmel, at the site of el-Burj by the harbor town of et-Tanturah. Excavations led by John Garstang in 1923–24 proved occupation in the Late Bronze Age (1500–1200 B.C.). The king of Dor was a member of the confederacy of northern Canaanite kings headed by Jabin of Hazor, defeated by Joshua (Josh 11:2; 12:23). The city was assigned to Manasseh (Josh 17:11; I Chr 7:29), but was not taken over by Israelites (Jud 1:27) until the time of David and Solomon. Solomon made Dor the center of one of his administrative districts (I Kgs 4:11).

Meanwhile Dor had been occupied by the Tjekker who had invaded the coastal zone with the Philistines *c.* 1200 B.C. (ANET, p. 262), for the Egyptian emissary Wenamon found them living there *c.* 1100 B.C. (ANET, p. 26). The Assyrians claimed to have conquered Dor in the 8th cen. B.C. It fell into the hands of the Seleucids in the Maccabean struggle (I Macc 15:12–13,25). In 64 B.C. Dor was granted autonomy by Pompey. Josephus affirms that the Gentiles worshiped Apollo at Dor (Jos *Apion*, II. 10).

J. R.

DORCAS(dôr′kăs). A Christian woman of Joppa whom Peter raised from death (Acts 9:36–42). *See* Tabitha.

DOTHAN (dō′thạn). A picturesque site located a thousand yards E of the modern road from Samaria (Sebaste) to Jenin, said by Eusebius to be 12 miles N of Sebaste. The top of the tell is ten acres in area, dominating a broad fertile plain 1,000 feet above sea level. From the top an impressive view to the S and W is obtained of level fertile land under cultivation. A copious spring and large cisterns still supply water for the large flocks and herds in the area.

Dothan enters Bible history with the story of Joseph and his betrayal there, as he went to visit his brothers tending their flocks near the city (Gen 37). After the elder brothers had cast Joseph into a dry well or cistern, they decided to sell him to a caravan of spice merchants en route to Egypt. Then as now, the Dothan area has excellent pasturage, especially prized in dry seasons.

After this Dothan witnessed the invasion of Egyptians under Thutmose III (1504–1450 B.C.), who lists Dothan among the cities conquered (ANET, p. 242). Dothan is not mentioned in the Scriptures again until the Kingdom Period.

During the 9th cen. B.C., Elisha the prophet repeatedly warned the king of Israel of the movements of Syrian troops. The Syrian king suspected his own men of betraying his whereabouts, but was informed that Elisha knew the

The mound of Dothan. HFV

king's inner secrets and reported them to Israel's King Jehoram. Upon hearing this, Ben-hadad sent an army to capture the prophet. Dothan was surrounded during the night. The account says that in the morning, in answer to Elisha's prayer, the Syrian army was smitten by blindness, after which Elisha led them to Samaria where the king of Israel fed them and sent them home (II Kgs 6:8–23).

Dothan is mentioned several times in the fictional story of Judith (Jth 3:9; 4:6; 7:3, 18; 8:3). While the unknown author treats the geography of Palestine very loosely, he seems to place Dothan near the plain of Esdraelon and the range of hills known now as Mount Carmel and Mount Gilboa. His frequent mention of Dothan indicates it was a prominent town at the time of writing, c. 100 B.C.

Thus Dothan, located near the border between Manasseh and the plain of Megiddo, was near the caravan route and also near the scene of border conflicts. Even as late as 1967 its proximity to Jenin and the border between Jordan and Israel made Dothan a witness to armed conflict.

Dothan has been the scene of nine excavations, 1953–64, under the direction of Joseph P. Free with assistance of personnel from Wheaton College (Illinois). Approximately 20 levels of occupation have been identified. During the first season soundings 30 feet in depth at the crest of the S slope of the tell revealed 11 levels of occupation from the late Chalcolithic (3000 B.C.) to Iron I (1200–900 B.C.). An Early Bronze Age wall was exposed, 11 feet wide at the base, 9 feet wide at the top and 16 feet in height, vertical on the outside and sloping on the inside. A large stairway 13 feet wide with 18 steps was uncovered outside the city wall, presumably leading down to the springs and wells.

At the Middle Bronze level the skeleton of a two-year-old child was recovered, having been buried with a small jar and two juglets, all typical of the Middle Bronze Age. Since it had been placed in the foundation trench under the squared corner of a large wall, probably part of a rampart tower, this burial may well have been a child sacrifice incorporated in the wall during consecration (cf. Josh 6:26; I Kgs 16:34). The season produced nearly 400 artifacts, including flint blades, saddle querns, loom weights, bronze blades, a jar handle impressed by a Hyksos scarab, and a number of whole jars, pots, and bowls in stratification.

The second and third seasons concentrated on the top of the tell. Finds in the acropolis area included Hellenistic lamps and coins and Rhodian jar handles inscribed in Greek. Iron Age remains near the edge included a large Iron I crater or bowl with 14 handles, and an Assyrian "palace-ware" bowl from the Iron II level, mute evidence of 8th cen. B.C. Assyrian invasions.

The 1955 expedition revealed a section of "Wall Street" of the Iron II city, averaging four feet in width and extending, as the 1956 expedition revealed, more than 100 feet; the house walls on either side were still standing seven feet high in places. A small pyxis jar of Late Bronze II or Iron I was located containing 15 pieces of metal objects, most of which were silver rings, bracelets and jewelry.

The 1956 season disclosed evidence of a thriving Iron Age city during the Kingdom Period of Israel's history. Evidence of destruction by fire was abundant. A piece of charred wood in an Iron Age level was later tested by radio carbon process and dated by Columbia University scientists as 885–725 B.C., contemporary with the prophet Elisha. An Arabic palace with 25 rooms arranged around a central courtyard, dated A.D. 1200–1400, was uncovered at the summit of the mound. Five adjacent depressions representing other courtyards suggest this building may have had as many as 150 rooms.

The expedition of 1958 began to uncover a large two storied building with flagstone or plastered floors, doorways made of well-cut stones and a room filled with 96 broken storage jars of uniform type that could be stacked. Remains of dozens more were found in other rooms. Some of the jars contained grain and some olive pits. At least two drains led from the building. Subsequent seasons showed a kitchen area with stone water basin for servants or guards. Several storage bins up to 14 feet in diameter held the wheat collected in the storage jars. The accumulated evidence indicates this was an administrative building first constructed during Solomon's reign and rebuilt c. 800 B.C. Nearby houses showed a later rebuilding during the divided monarchy and one final time after the Assyrian conquest of the land in 725–722 B.C. Assyrian pottery and jar burials suggest the conquerors occupied Dothan.

At the end of the 1959 season below the Early Bronze city wall on the W slope, a shaft was discovered leading down to the doorway of a large cave-tomb of the period of the judges. Its ceiling had collapsed on more than 3,200 pottery vessels, including at least three seven-en-lipped lamps, plus over 50 bronze objects such as daggers, spearheads, rings, bowls, and a lamp. The tomb had four distinct levels of burial from 1400 to 1100 B.C. It is the richest tomb yet found in Palestine.

Bibliography. Joseph P. Free, BASOR, Nos. 131, 135, 139, 143, 147, 152, 156, 160.

G. A. T.

DOUBLE. From the Gr. *diplous* (I Tim 5:17; Rev 18:6; Mt 23:15) and several Heb. words from the verb root *kāpal* (Ex 26:9; 28:16; 39:9) and *mishneh* (Gen 43:12, 15; Ex 16:5,22). The latter Heb. word also means a "copy" (Deut 17:18; Josh 8:32) and even indicates "second" in rank (Gen 41:43; II Chr 35:24) as well as "second" in age (I Sam 8:2; 17:13).

In the church, elders who rule well are worthy to be paid as well as praised (I Tim 5:17, "double honor"; the Gr. *timē*, "honor," means also "compensation"). A double-minded (Gr. *dipsukos*, "double-souled") man (Jas 1:7–8; 4:8; cf. Ps 119) is one who is divided in his thinking. One who is double-tongued is perhaps "not truthful" rather than merely repetitious (I Tim 3:8).

DOUBT. Doubt is that undecided state of mind in which one hesitates between two opposite conclusions. The doubter may have some degree of belief while he wavers in his opinions. Such was Peter, called by the Lord Jesus a man of little faith after he began to sink beneath the waves (Mt 14:31); also some who saw the risen Christ and yet doubted (Mt 28:17). In these passages the Gr. *distazō*, "to stand divided," is used. In such cases doubt may be provisional, waiting for more light (e.g., Acts 10:17–20).

Unless the honest doubter presses on to full faith, his doubt becomes sin, "for whatever does not proceed from faith is sin" (Rom 14:23, RSV). One must "ask in faith, with no doubting" (Jas 1:6, RSV). Such was Abraham (Rom 4:20), of whom it is said that he did not stagger, hesitate, doubt (*diakrinō*) through unbelief or lack of faith (*apistia*). Assured faith, with no doubts in his heart, enables one to claim the promises of God (Mt 21:21; Mk 11:23).

Other Gr. words rendered as "doubt" or one of its verb forms in the KJV have different emphases. The Gr. root *poreomai* connotes uncertainty (Jn 13:22; Acts 25:20) or perplexity rather than reasoned doubt (see RSV at Acts 2:12; 5:24; 10:17; Gal 4:20). In Jn 10:24 the people ask Jesus how long He will keep them in suspense (RSV). Gr. *meteōrizō* (Lk 12:29) suggests those having anxious minds, wavering between hope and fear.

J. R.

DOUGH. *See* Food: Bread, Flour.

DOVE, TURTLEDOVE. *See* Animals, III.9.

DOVE'S DUNG. "The fourth part of a cab" (¼ cab equals *c.* ½ pint) of this substance was sold at an exorbitant price in Samaria during the siege (II Kgs 6:25). The Heb. words *hărê yōnîm* are plain as translated, an example of the actual extremity of the siege. Josephus records that in their dire circumstances people were reduced to eating cattle dung during Titus' siege of Jerusalem (*Wars,* v. 13.7). Some commentators (e.g., WBC, p. 347) suggest the possible comparison with an Arabic herb named "sparrow's dung," but a parallel Heb. plant has not been found. *See* Plants.

DOWRY. When arrangements for a marriage were being made, several types of exchange of property might take place.

1. The suitor could be expected to give a

certain "gift" (Heb. *mōhar*) to the bride's parents and/or brothers (Gen 34:12; Ex 22:16; I Sam 18:25). This could entail much negotiation (Gen 34:8-12). Some see this as a possible survival of an early custom to purchase wives (Gen 24:53; 31:15; Ex 22:16-17; I Sam 18:25; Ruth 4:10; Hos 3:2). It is better explained as a compensation given to the bride's family, for she herself was neither bought nor sold. The amount given (or paid) varied according to the status and wealth of the bride, as for example with Jacob's service to Laban (Gen 29:18, 27). It might be replaced by deeds of valor (Josh 15:16; I Sam 18:25; Jud 1:12).

2. Gifts (Heb. *mattān*) were made by the bridegroom to the bride herself, as in the case of Isaac to Rebekah (Gen 24:22, 53; cf. Gen 34:12; Hos 2:19-20). In Akkadian the bridegroom's gift is *zubullû;* the cognate Aramaic form is *zebed,* used by Leah when she said, "God has endowed me with a good dowry" (Gen 30:20, RSV), and then called her sixth son Zebulun with the name based on the Akkadian spelling (E. A. Speiser, *Genesis, Anchor Bible,* p. 231).

3. A dowry was often given by the father of the bride to his daughter who was to be married, such as land to Achsah (Jud 1:15) and to Pharaoh's daughter (I Kgs 9:16), or a maidservant to Rebekah (Gen 24:61) and to Leah (Gen 29:24).

R. A. K.

DOXOLOGIES (Gr. *doxologia,* from *doxa,* "glory," and *logia,* "word"). Used in ecclesiastical Gr. to describe formulas expressing praise and glory to the Trinity. While the word itself does not occur in the Bible, expressions of praise often are found. In Jewish worship such expressions as "To Thee be glory forever" accompanied Heb. prayers. Similar formulas are found in the NT and characterized the worship of the early church (cf. I Cor 14:16). While exhibiting considerable variety in expression, they show a basic structure.

Westcott (*Epistle to the Hebrews,* pp. 466-467) lists 16 doxologies in the NT (Rom 11:36; 16:27; Gal 1:5; Eph 3:21; Phil 4:20; I Tim 1:17; 6:16; II Tim 4:18; Heb 13:21; I Pet 4:11; 5:11; II Pet 3:18; Jude 25; Rev 1:6; 5:13; 7:12). These he classified into three major groups: those ascribing glory to God alone; those ascribed to God either directly or through Christ (Rom 16:27; Jude 25); and those ascribed to Christ alone (II Tim 4:18; II Pet 3:18; Rev 1:6). Only three doxologies are found at the close of epistles (Rom 16:27; II Pet 3:18; Jude 25). Every doxology with one exception (II Pet 3:18, according to the best MSS) ends with the characteristic Amen. Some scholars include among the doxologies those expressions that begin with "blessed."

In later church history, Lk 2:14 with additions was called the "greater doxology" while the Gloria Patri (completely extrabiblical) was the "lesser doxology."

F. P.

DRAG. A large fishing net or seine, equipped with weights on the lower edge and floats on the upper, so that the net may be dragged along the bottom of a river or lake. Then the two ends are drawn together, enclosing any fish caught within the net. The Babylonian armies are described as fishermen who sacrifice to their dragnet (Heb. *mikmereth*), deifying the very weapons of their military successes (Hab 1:15-16). In Ezk 32:3 the more general word for net, *ḥērem,* is used in the specific sense of a dragnet (so RSV), used figuratively as God's means of catching pharaoh, the monster of the Nile. *See* Fishing; Net.

DRAGON. *See* Animals, II.11; V.7.

DRAGON WELL. Identified by many as the fountain En-rogel (*q.v.*) SE of the Jebusite and Davidic city of Jerusalem (Neh 2:13). Yet a spring much further up the Valley of Hinnom, or a well now dry in the Tyropean Valley, would better conform to the assumed location of the gates which Nehemiah mentions on his nocturnal inspection tour. RSV translates the verse Jackal's Well.

DRAM. *See* Weights, Measures, and Coins.

DRAUGHT. The Gr. *aphedrōn* in Mt 15:17; Mk 7:19 signifies a latrine or toilet. *See* Dung.

DRAUGHT HOUSE. Jehu, in contempt of Baal, ordered the temple of that heathen god to be demolished and the place turned into a public latrine to make the spot altogether unclean (II Kgs 10:27). Excavated latrines of this type consist of a simple building with a row of holes in stone slabs covering a drain through which water could be flushed, similar to many toilet facilities in Middle Eastern lands today.

DRAWER OF WATER. One of the lowest classes of servant (Deut 29:11). Yet such servitude was preferred to death by the Gibeonites, who in fear had submitted to the invading Israelites (Josh 9:21,23,27). Women (Gen 24:11) and young men (Ruth 2:9) drew water from the well as part of daily chores, but as a full-time occupation it was despised. Until recently men have made it their trade in the Middle East to peddle water carried in goatskins slung on their backs.

DREAM. A dream is a series of images or thoughts occurring during sleep. When these are unpleasant the cause is sometimes a physical disorder. Dreams can also be caused by powerful stimuli or suggestions and emotions which may be pleasant or unpleasant. These need not be of recent occurrence but can lie buried in the subconscious for a long period and, even though apparently forgotten by the individual, can make themselves felt in disturbing dreams. The psychologist and psychiatrist are always interested in their patient's dream life to find, if possible, a clue to the personality problems.

Dreaming and the prophetic office in the Bible seem to have been closely associated, although the dream coming to pass was not always to be regarded as of God and proof that He had spoken (see Deut 13:1-3,5). God did communicate His will through dreams on some occasions. He spoke to Abimelech and forbade his taking Sarah to be his wife (Gen 20:1-7). He spoke to Jacob at Bethel and confirmed the covenant promise (Gen 28:12-15). At Haran He appeared to Jacob and told him to return to his own land (Gen 31:10-13). When Joseph was in Egypt he interpreted Pharaoh's dream of the fat and lean cattle (Gen 41:1-9). Gideon overheard a Midianite soldier tell another man his dream of a barley cake tumbling into the camp of Midian and upsetting a tent. When Gideon heard their interpretation he worshiped God and returned to the camp of Israel to lead his people to great victory (Jud 7:9-15). Daniel interpreted two of Nebuchadnezzar's dreams, that of the great statue (Dan 2) and of the tree (Dan 4:1-28). Daniel had a dream of four great beasts (Dan 7:1-14) and a vision of the ram and the he-goat (Dan 8:1-14).

There are six references in the NT to dreams. Four of them came to Joseph the husband of Mary. The angel of the Lord appeared to him prior to the birth of Jesus and told him to take Mary to be his wife (Mt 1:20-21). After the birth of Jesus, the wise men were warned of God to return to their country another way (Mt 2:12). Joseph likewise was warned to flee into Egypt to escape the wrath of Herod (Mt 2:13), and upon Herod's death he was told to return to Israel, while in another dream he was directed to go to Galilee (Mt 2:19-22). Pilate's wife was disturbed in a dream concerning the innocency of Jesus (Mt 27:19).

It is debatable whether God communicates directly or indirectly by dreams in this day, although it is not to be thought impossible. There is one citation in Peter's explanation of Pentecost in which he said, "Your young men shall see visions, and your old men shall dream dreams" (Acts 2:17). These could refer to "types of extraordinary spiritual influence, and not as the precise forms in which the promise was to be fulfilled." God has given His written revelation and His Spirit to instruct and guide into all truth, so there is not much need for dreams today. In the epistles there is an absence of reference to them.

See also Vision.

Bibliography. Albrecht Oepke, *"Onar,"* TDNT, V, 220-238. Richard L. Ruble, "The Doctrine of Dreams," BS, CXXV (1968), 360-364.

R. H. B.

DREGS

1. Dregs is the KJV translation of Heb. *shemārîm* in Ps 75:8; elsewhere "lees" of wine, as in Isa 25:6; Jer 48:11; Zeph 1:12. *See* Lees; Wine. As the wine was strained before drinking, so the psalmist uses the figure of the draught poured off from the top of God's cup of wrath to signify His restraint in judgment on the righteous, while the wicked shall drain the cup down to the dregs (cf. I Pet 4:17-18).

2. Heb. *qubba'at* means "goblet," "chalice" (Isa 51:17, 22). KJV renders, "Thou hast drunken the dregs of the cup of trembling, and wrung them out"; better, ". . . the chalice-cup of staggering and drained it" (51:17).

DRESS.

The types, styles, and customs of the dress of Bible times have been preserved to a large extent by indications in the biblical record and by the archaeological findings of sculptures and tomb paintings in Babylonia and Egypt which depict Palestinians and Syrians. Of special importance are the Beni Hasan tomb paintings for the patriarchal era, the Megiddo ivories for the time of the judges, and the Black Obelisk of Shalmanezer III and Sennacherib's bas reliefs portraying the siege of Lachish for the kingdom period. To a lesser extent the costumes and dress customs of the orthodox Jews and simple people of modern Palestine help explain the ancient garments.

Materials of dress. The materials of attire depended on the means of the wearer, the civilization and culture, and the geographical loca-

Hittite clothing of the post-empire period (after 1200 B.C.) as seen on a bas relief from Marash.
LM

Properly dressed members of the Roman Emperor Augustus' official family, as shown on his Altar of Peace in Rome. The Apostle Paul, a Roman citizen, probably would have worn the Roman toga, at least on occasion. HFV

tion. The first Scripture record of materials is in the statement that Adam and Eve "sewed fig leaves together, and made themselves aprons" (Gen 3:7). Animal skins were used early also (Gen 3:21), and sheepskins and goatskins were used widely (Heb 11:37). The sheepskin coat had sleeves and was worn over the tunic. Elijah's mantle may have been the skin of a sheep or other animal with the wool left on (I Kgs 19:19). Such rough garments were worn by prophets (Zech 13:4; Mt 7:15). Woven goats' hair was also known at an early period (Ex 26:7), and the sackcloth (*q.v.*) of mourners was of this material (cf. II Sam 3:31; Rev 6:12). The dress of John the Baptist was of camel's hair (Mt 3:4), which was a coarse woven cloth.

However, the favorite materials throughout Palestine were wool and linen (Lev 13:47–48, 52, 59). Sheepshearers were employed by Judah at an early time (Gen 38:12), and wool was a chief substance demanded as tribute (II Kgs 3:4). The prince of Megiddo wrote to the pharaoh that because of hostilities his men were not able to "pluck" the wool (EA #244, ANET, p. 485).

Linen (Heb. *bad;* Gr. *linon, sindōn*) was made from flax (I Chr 4:21; Prov 31:13; Mk 14:51; 15:46). It is interesting to note that angels appeared in linen (Dan 10:5; 12:6; Rev 15:6). The finest linen (Heb. *shēsh, būs;* Gr. *byssos*) was manufactured chiefly in Egypt (Gen 41:42; Ezk 27:7). Herodotus mentioned four qualities, one so fine that each thread con-

tained 360 fibers. The priestly vestments were made of this type of linen (Ex 28:6; etc.). *See* Linen.

The usual color of the Heb. dress was the natural white of the various materials or as bleached white by the fuller (*see* Occupations: Fuller). Such a color was appropriate not only for festive occasions but also as a symbol for purity (Eccl 9:8; Rev 3:4–5), since a spot or stain was readily detected (Isa 63:3; Rev 3:4). In Roman times the fuller also served as the cleaner of clothes.

Although it is not known when dyeing was introduced, scarlet thread was used at an early time (Gen 38:28), and purple was used as well (Acts 16:14; Rev 18:12). Purple was worn by Persian officers (Est 8:15), Midianite kings (Jud 8:26), and wealthy Tyrians (Ezk 27:7). Dyed robes were imported from other countries, particularly Phoenicia, and were worn only by the wealthy because of their expense.

Gold and silver thread were used for decoration. Figures too were added, much like the cherubim in the curtains of the tabernacle (Ex 36:8, 35). Such decorated robes were worn by royal personages (Ps 45:13; Acts 12:21) and the wealthy (Jud 5:30; Ps 45:14; Ezk 16:13). *See* Colors: Purple, Scarlet; Occupations: Dyer; Purple.

Articles of clothing. Because women's garments differed in detail not in kind, the usual articles of clothing were common to both men and women. The following articles were basic throughout Bible times. The most widely used term for clothing or garment in Heb. is *beged*, occurring some 200 times in the OT. In the NT Gr. *himation*, which has a specific meaning of robe or cloak, was also used in the general sense.

1. The loincloth or waistcloth (Heb. *'ēzôr*; KJV, "girdle") was a simple piece of cloth or leather worn by slaves and laborers about the hips like a kilt or apron and reaching from waist to above the knees (Isa 11:5; Jer 13:1–11). Elijah (II Kgs 1:8) and John the Baptist (Mt 3:4) wore leather waistcloths. Aprons were worn over the outer garment by workers in the Mediterranean world in Paul's day (Acts 19:12). A type of loincloth called an ephod was worn by those consecrated to God (I Sam 2:18; II Sam 6:14). *See* Girdle; Ephod 4.

2. The inner garment. The tunic or shirt (Heb. *ketōnet*; Gr. *chitōn*) was the principal ordinary garment worn by men and women. It was worn next to the skin and was actually a long, rather tight-fitting shirt (inappropriately translated "coat" in KJV). The material used was leather, haircloth, wool, linen, or in modern times, usually cotton. It was probably made in two pieces and sewn together at the sides. The simplest kind was sleeveless, reaching only to the knees. A girdle or sash worn around the waist permitted its wearer to tuck the lower part of the tunic under it for freer movement (Jer 1:17; I Pet 1:13).

Another type worn by favored persons reached to the wrists and ankles. This was the kind probably worn by Joseph (Gen 37:3, 23), Tamar (II Sam 13:18), and the priests (Ex 28:4, 39). The garment Jacob gave to Joseph (Gen 37:3), though rendered "coat of many colours" in KJV, may well have been a sleeved tunic. This would also have been a mark of aristocracy, as the working classes usually wore a sleeveless shirt tunic.

The inner garment was worn by women as well as men (Song 5:3, RSV), although there was no doubt a difference in style and pattern. The tunic (*chitōn*, wrongly translated "coat" in KJV) is the garment mentioned in Lk 3:11; 6:29; 9:3 (and parallel passages) and Acts 9:39. The lower classes often wore only the tunic in warm weather. However, the higher classes would put on an outer garment when receiving callers or going outside, although they might wear just the tunic while at home. A particularly fine grade of undergarment was the *sādîn*, a fine white linen sheet to wrap around the body (Jud 14:12–13; Prov 31:24; Isa 3:23).

The term "naked" was often used of men clad only with their tunic. Thus it is said of Saul (I Sam 19:24) when he had taken off his upper garments; of Isaiah (Isa 20:2) after he had put off his sackcloth; of a warrior (Amos 2:16) when he had taken off his military cloak; and of Peter (Jn 21:7) without his fisher's coat.

3. The outer tunic or robe (Heb. *meʿîl*). This was a looser and longer tunic, reaching to near the feet. It was open at the top so that it could be drawn over the head. It also had holes for the insertion of the arms. To cover a woman with one's "skirt" (*kānāp*) or corner of one's mantle or robe (I Sam 15:27; 24:4–5) symbolized protection and the right of marriage (Ruth 3:9). Uncovering the skirt of one's father meant lying carnally with one's mother or stepmother and was forbidden (Deut 22:30; 27:20).

Scripture indicates the use of tunic or robe by kings (I Sam 24:4), nobles (Job 1:20), prophets (I Sam 28:14), and sometimes youths (I Sam 2:19). However, these passages may refer to any robe worn over the inner garment. Nevertheless, when two tunics are mentioned as being worn at the same time (Lk 3:11), the second would be an outer tunic. Although travelers generally wore two tunics, disciples were forbidden to do so (Mt 10:10; Lk 9:3). The seamless tunic worn by our Lord (Jn 19:23, RSV) may have been of this outer type. Evidently this garment was optional, being worn by the higher classes or occasionally substituted for the outer garment.

4. The girdle. A loose tunic would hinder a person from walking freely, so a sash or belt was always worn when leaving home for any kind of journey (II Kgs 4:29; Acts 12:8). The "girdle" (Heb. *ḥăgôr*, *ḥăgôrâ*) normally was a long strip of cloth folded several times and wound around the waist over the tunic. The *ḥăgôr* could be simply a rope (Isa 3:24, RSV), but the waistband of a nobleman might be very elaborate, made of linen, embroidered with silk or gold and silver thread, and frequently studded with gold, precious stones, and pearls (e.g., "golden girdle," Rev 1:13; 15:6). It was generally a handbreadth in width. The girdles were fastened by a clasp or buckle of gold or silver. Fibula pins of bronze are regularly found

A wall painting from Tutankhamon's tomb showing Egyptian male and female dress about the time of Moses and the Exodus. LL

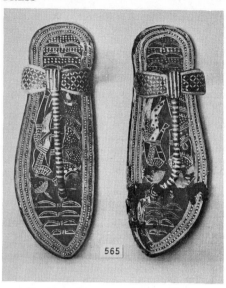
565

Sandals from the tomb of Pharaoh Tutankhamon. LL

in Palestinian excavations of Iron Age levels onward. The sash could also be tied in a knot so that the ends hung down in front.

The girdle was used to keep money (Mk 6:8, RSV). It also served as a belt to fasten a man's sword to his body (I Sam 25:13; II Sam 20:8). The girdle of women was generally looser than that of men and was worn about the hips, except when they were actively engaged (cf. Prov 31:17). See Girdle.

5. The outer garment or mantle (*simlâ* or *salmâ*). The ordinary outer garment was a large loose cloak which served the purpose of an overcoat. It was made of wool, goat's hair, cotton, or linen. It generally consisted of a large quadrangular piece of material, the size and texture varying with the demands of the wearer. It was worn over the shoulders in pleasant weather and wrapped like a heavy shawl around the body when necessary. When sleeping, the person would lie down on a rug or mattress and use his outer garment for a blanket. Thus the creditor was forbidden to keep the mantle of a borrower as a pledge overnight (Ex 22:26 f.; Deut 24:13). It was closely woven, warm, and in some cases waterproof.

This was the garment with which Elijah smote the waters of the Jordan, and it subsequently became Elisha's (II Kgs 2:8–13). Because of a violation of the sabbath, the Lord commanded the Israelites to make a fringe with a ribband or cord of blue on the borders of their mantles (Num 15:37–41). This was to remind them of the Lord and His commandments.

Because of its size, the outer garment could also be used to carry large burdens (Ex 12:34, RSV; II Kgs 4:39). Ruth even put six measures of barley into hers (Ruth 3:15, RSV). The *himation* of the NT ("cloak," "robe," Mt 5:40; 9:20; 24:18; Lk 6:29; 22:36; Jn 19:2; Acts 7:58; 22:20) was similar.

6. The headdress. Much of the time Israelites did not wear a head covering, except perhaps a headband of rope or cord (I Kgs 20:32). On occasions of war, a leather helmet was used. However, because of the direct rays of the sun, a turban (Heb. *ṣanîp*) was often worn by the better class of people. This was a piece of thick material wrapped several times around the head. It generally was made of linen or cotton and is mentioned by Job and Isaiah (Job 29:14, RSV; Isa 3:23, RSV). A single piece of cloth draped over the head and held in place with a cord or rope may have been used for protection by the Heb. peasant, just as the Bedouin wears the Arabic *kufiyeh* today.

7. The footgear. The shoes worn by the majority in Bible times were what we would call sandals (Heb. *na'al*; Gr. *sandalion*). The sole generally was made of leather, although felt, cloth, or wood were also used. It was bound to the foot by a leather thong (Gen 14:23; Mk 1:7). The sandals of women were sometimes made of animal skins. Women of rank had sandals elaborately embroidered with silk, silver, and gold. For some women, they were the richest articles of their attire. Sandals were universally worn throughout Palestine, even by the poor (Amos 2:6; 8:6). During mealtimes, the feet were uncovered (Lk 7:38; Jn 13:5–6); sandals were not worn indoors. They were used for military expeditions (Isa 5:27; Eph 6:15) and journeys (Ex 12:11; Josh 9:5, 13; Acts 12:8). The shoe could signify subjection or a transfer of property (Ps 60:8; 108:9; Ruth 4:7–8). See Sandal.

The dress of women. The dress of women was distinguished (Deut 22:5), not so much by kind, however, as by detail and quality of materials. They wore longer tunics and larger mantles than the men. The outer garment differed in elaboration, making it a distinctive robe. Isaiah mentions the "wimple" (KJV) or "cloak" (RSV), Heb. *miṭpaḥat* (3:22), a cape covering the head and neck. The skirt (*shûl*) means the lower flowing part of a garment. Figuratively, Jerusalem's "skirts" were lifted up to denote the shame of her illicit relationships (Jer 13:22, 26; Lam 1:9).

Women often wore veils, which were also distinctive. The veil (KJV, vail) was at first an article of ornamentation (Song 4:1, 3; 6:7, RSV), and both married and unmarried women appeared in public with their faces uncovered (Gen 12:14; 24:16; 29:10; I Sam 1:12). However, betrothed maidens did veil themselves in the presence of their future husbands, especially at the time of the wedding (Gen 24:65; 29:25). Tamar wore such a veil (*ṣā'îp*) to avoid recognition and to trick Judah by posing as a sacred prostitute (Gen 38:14, 19). The veil (*masweh*) which Moses would put on after being in the presence of God acted as a mask to conceal the departing of the radiance of his face (Ex 34:33 - 35; II Cor 3:13 - 16). Ruth's "vail" (*mitpaḥat*) in which she carried home six measures of barley was a large shawl or cloak (Ruth 3:15). The Koran is responsible for much of the strictness in the use of the veil, for it forbade women to appear unveiled except in the presence of their nearest relatives (Koran 33:55, 59).

Some of the veils of modern Syrian, Arabian and Egyptian women are embroidered with colored silks and gold, and extend almost to the ground. The extravagant costumes of the women living in luxury in Jerusalem in Isaiah's day included many articles of jewelry as well as purses and perfume boxes (Isa 3:16- 24, NASB). Since the woman's dress was distinct, the Mosaic law could forbid a man to wear woman's clothing and a woman to wear the garment of a man (Deut 22:5).

The dress of the priests. The priests and high priest were required to wear a distinctive dress when they were performing their priestly ministry. The *priests* were required to wear the following: (1) Drawers or short breeches (*miknesayim*, Ex 28:42), which reached from the loins to the thighs and were made of linen (Ex 39:28). (2) A long coat which had sleeves and was made of fine linen (Ex 39:27). (3) A girdle or sash (*'abnēt*) which was woven and variegated or embroidered with the same four colors used in the veil of the tabernacle and temple (Ex 39:29). (4) A cap or bonnet of linen. They were not allowed to have anything on their feet in the sanctuary (Ex 3:5; Josh 5:15).

The *high priest* was required to wear the following: (1) The breastplate, which was woven of blue, purple, scarlet, and fine linen yarn, embroidered with figures of gold. The 12 tribes of Israel were represented by 12 precious stones set in gold. It was securely fastened to the ephod and body by a series of cords and chains (Ex 28:13- 28; 39:8- 21). (2) The ephod was of the same material and fashion as the breastplate and was that upon which the breastplate was fastened (Ex 28:6- 12; 39:2- 7). *See* Ephod 2. (3) The robe of the ephod was blue, without seam, and worn under the ephod. The hem had blue, purple, and scarlet pomegranates alternating with bells of gold, which rang when the high priest went to minister (Ex 28:31- 35; 39:22- 26). (4) The girdle or sash was of the same material and fashion as the breastplate and ephod, and was used to hold the ephod firmly to the body (Ex 28:8). (5) The miter was a kind of turban which had a gold plate engraved, "Holy to Yahweh," and was fastened to the front of the miter with blue cord (Ex 28:36- 38; 39:30- 31).

The dress of the Pharisees. The Pharisees emphasized two articles of their religious garments which became distinctive to them. One of these, the phylactery (*q.v.*), was a small box of metal or a parchment band fastened by straps to the arm or forehead. It contained passages of Scripture referring to the Passover. The reason for wearing it is found in Ex 13:9, 16, where such objects, worn between the eyes, are called "frontlets" (*q.v.*). The other item was the blue fringes at the corners of the mantle (Num 15:37 - 38; Deut 22:12), which the Pharisees enlarged. Christ condemned them for their pride concerning these things without the appreciation of their true value, when He said that the Pharisees "make broad their phylacteries, and enlarge the borders of their garments" (Mt 23:5).

The dress of Jesus. In general, the clothes worn by Christ, as well as the disciples, were of

Bas relief of Shalmeneser III of Assyria showing King Jehu of Israel paying tribute to the Assyrian king and illustrating Hebrew and Assyrian dress of the ninth century B.C. ORINST

479

the simplest kind. It seems He wore a shirt or inner garment, since He removed His outer garments (pl., i.e., the tunic and mantle) before washing the feet of the disciples (Jn 13:4). His tunic was seamless (Jn 19:23, RSV) and therefore had short sleeves and fit closely at the neck. It would also indicate value and may have been given to Him by one of the women who ministered of their substance (Lk 8:3). Outside the tunic was a linen girdle or sash, wound several times around His waist. The mantle of woolen cloth was probably not white, for it became such during the transfiguration (Mk 9:3). It may have been blue or white with colored stripes and would have had the blue fringe or tassels at the corners. He wore leather sandals on His feet (Mt 3:11). He probably wore the customary white turban on His head, since no Jewish teacher of that day would appear with the head uncovered. This would have been wrapped around the head with the ends falling down over the neck. It probably fastened with a cord under the chin. Such a cloth, like a large handkerchief (KJV, "apron," *soudarion,* Lk 19:20, NASB; Acts 19:12), was used to cover the face of a corpse (Jn 11:44; 20:7). The disciples probably were dressed in similar fashion to Jesus.

The dress of foreign nations. The dress of foreign nations is occasionally referred to in Scripture. Included in the Babylonian garb worn by Daniel's three friends were the following articles (Dan 3:21, NASB): (1) the Aram. *sarbālîn* (KJV,"coats"), which were trousers or drawers and the distinctive feature of the Babylonian dress; (2) Aram. *peṭash* (KJV, "hosen"), which was a coat or inner tunic; (3) Aram. *karbelā'* (KJV, "hat"), the high pointed cap of the Cimmerians and Persians; and (4) Aram. *lebûsh* (KJV, "garment"), which was a general term for their other clothes.

Although the references to Gr. and Rom. dress are few, the traveling cloak referred to by Paul (II Tim 4:13) may have been a Rom. garment, the Lat. *paenula,* a circular cape used for protection against stormy weather.

The ornaments of dress. The Jewish men sometimes carried a staff or cane as an aid to travel through rough country or for purposes of protection. It was often ornamented at the top. Some men also wore a signet ring which served as the personal signature of its owner (Gen 38:18; Lk 15:22). This was generally worn on the right hand or suspended from the neck by a cord.

The women were more elaborate in their decoration and wore several types of ornaments. A favorite with them from the earliest times was the armlet or bracelet (Gen 24:22, 30, 47). Bracelets (*q.v.*) were sometimes worn even by men of rank (II Sam 1:10). These were made of ivory, precious metals, horn, cords, or chains. They could be worn on both arms, and some covered the forearm to the elbow.

The anklet (Isa 3:18) was generally so arranged that in walking a clanging or clapping sound was made which called attention to the wearer and enhanced her pride (v. 16). Sometimes small chains were fastened from one foot to the other in order to secure a more elegant step (Isa 3:20).

The necklace was another favorite ornament among the women. Men of rank and warriors of foreign nations also wore them. Persons of rank sometimes wore several. They were made of metal, stones, and pearls, and strung on a cord. Attached to them sometimes were other articles of finery, such as half-moons or crescents (Isa 3:18), smelling bottles (Isa 3:20, RSV), headbands with stellated studs (Isa 3:18), and serpent charms or amulets (Isa 3:20).

Earrings (*q.v.*) were universally worn by women (Ex 32:2; Ezk 16:12; Hos 2:13). They were made of bone, horn, or metal, and some that have been found have been rather large (as much as the width of four fingers in diameter). Some women would puncture the earlobe with as many openings as possible, and would then put a ring through each.

Nose rings were also a favorite and were used from the earliest times (Gen 24:22, 47, RSV). They were made of ivory or metal and often decorated with precious jewels. Isaiah lists these as well as other articles of ornamentation in rebuking the women of Jerusalem (Isa 3:18–26). *See* Jewelry.

Customs relating to dress. There are many significant customs associated with dress, and most arise from the particular type of wearing apparel. The outer garment or mantle had many secondary functions because of its size. It was used to carry a burden (Ruth 3:15) or as an impromptu saddle (Mt 21:7). It was used as a cover at night (Ex 22:27; Ruth 3:9). Because of its necessity, a creditor could not retain it after sunset (Ex 22:26; Deut 24:12–13).

Because the garments were loose and flowing, they were used in many symbolic ways. Rending them was a sign of grief (Gen 37:29, 34), fear (I Kgs 21:27), indignation (II Kgs 5:7; 11:14), and despair (Jud 11:35). Shaking the garments or shaking the dust off them was a token of renunciation (Acts 18:6). Spreading clothes before a person meant loyalty and joyous reception (II Kgs 9:13; Mt 21:8). If they were wrapped around the head, it was a sign of awe (I Kgs 19:13) or grief (II Sam 15:30). Casting them off meant excitement (Acts 22:23), and laying hold of them was a sign of supplication (I Sam 15:27; Isa 3:6).

Since the length of the outer garment made it inconvenient for active work, it was left in the house when working close by (Mt 24:18), thrown off when necessary (Jn 13:4; Acts 7:58), or girded up if traveling (I Kgs 18:46; II Kgs 4:29). Because the garments concealed the feet when sitting, a long, flowing robe was a sign of reverence (Isa 6:1). The greatest insult a Jew could receive was to shorten his garments (II Sam 10:4). Raising the skirt

A Syrian wears the typical pointed hat of his homeland as he presents tribute at the Persian palace at Persepolis. sixth century B.C.
ORINST

of a woman implied her unchastity and was a great insult (Isa 47:2).

In many cases, the presentation of a robe was a sign of installation into office (Gen 41:42; Est 8:15; Isa 22:21), and taking the robe away was dismissal from office (II Macc 4:38). Presenting a robe worn by the giver was a token of great affection (I Sam 18:4). Being given the best robe was a mark of special honor (Lk 15:22). The number of such robes or vestments stored for the purpose of presents might be very large and formed a great part of the wealth of the individual (II Kgs 10:22). Sometimes such a wardrobe was superintended by a servant (II Chr 34:22). *See* Change of Raiment.

Bibliography. ANEP, figs. 1–66. E. P. Barrows, *Sacred Geography and Antiquities,* New York: American Tract Society, 1875. CornPBE, pp. 221–227. George B. Eager, "Dress," ISBE, II, 875–879. H. F. Lutz, *Textiles and Costume Among People of the Ancient Near East,* New York: Stechert, 1923. John M'Clintock and James Strong, "Attire," *Biblical, Theological and Ecclesiastical Cyclopaedia,* I, 529–534; "Dress," II, 886–892. Madeleine S. and J. Lane Miller, "Apparel," *Encyclopedia of Bible Life,* New York: Harper, 1944, pp. 48–64. James B. Pritchard, ed. consultant, *Everyday Life in Bible Times,* Washington: National Geographic Society, 1967. E. A. Speiser, *et al., Everyday Life in Ancient Times,* Washington: National Geographic Society, 1951.

E. C. J.

DRINK. Both water and sour milk were drunk by the Jews, but a sour wine often called vinegar was also used extensively by the common people (Ruth 2:14). People of wealth drank wine of a better vintage often mixed with water and spices.

The word is also used figuratively: "drink iniquity like water" (Job 15:16); "drink of the wrath of the Almighty" (Job 21:20); "drink of the river of thy pleasures" (Ps 36:8); "drink the wine of astonishment" (Ps 60:3); "tears to drink" (Ps 80:5); "drink the wine of violence" (Prov 4:17); "let him come unto me, and drink" (Jn 7:37), referring to the manner of receiving the Holy Spirit. *See also* Drink, Strong; Banquet; Food; Wine.

DRINK OFFERING. *See* Sacrificial Offering.

DRINK, STRONG. Alcoholic beverages in Bible times were made from pomegranates, grapes, barley, dates, and raisins. The term "strong drink" referred most likely to a strong barley beer, known from archaeological discoveries to have been very popular among the Egyptians and the Philistines. Strong drink (Heb. *shēkār;* Akkad. *šikaru*) refers to an intoxicating drink. In Palestine wine was almost always fermented grape juice.

Scripture is emphatic in its denunciation of strong drink. Aaron and his sons were not to drink wine nor strong drink when ministering in the tabernacle (Lev 10:9). This injunction applied also to their descendants. God through Isaiah pronounced woe upon those who drank all day (Isa 5:11) and upon those in authority who drank, for this impaired their judgment (Isa 5:22–23). The priests and prophets had "erred through strong drink" (Isa 28:7). Strong drink is the cause of poverty (Prov 21:17–20) and much sorrow and dissoluteness (Prov 23:29–35). Compare also Lk 1:15: "shall drink neither wine nor strong drink" *(sikera).*

In days of increasing alcoholism the rebuke of Prov 20:1 needs to be sounded abroad: "Wine is a scorner, strong drink a brawler, and whosoever gets drunk is unwise" (Berkeley). *See* Drunk, Drunkard; Drunkenness; Wine.

R. H. B.

DROMEDARY. *See* Animals: Camel, I.5.

DROPSY. *See* Diseases.

DROSS. *See* Mineral and Metals: Silver.

DROUGHT. This expression is connected with famine, one of the Lord's judgments in the OT. Water is usually at a premium in Palestine. Since rain was the chief source of water for both crops and human consumption, a prolonged drought spelled disaster for Palestine (cf. I Kgs 17:1; Jas 5:17). In addition to the partial failure of winter rains, the OT mentions frequent summer droughts (cf. Ps 32:4) caused by the blighting E wind (cf. Hos 13:15).

Religion and nature were tied together in the OT. The Lord taught His people that He is the controller of nature. Thus throughout Israel's history He used droughts and other calamities of nature to urge them to repent (cf. I Kgs 17:1; 18:17–18; Hag 1:6, 9–11; 2:16–17). Obedience and prosperity (cf. Ps 1:1–3; Prov 3:7–10; Isa 1:19), disobedience and want (cf. Lev 26:14–16) were biblical siamese twins. One of the aspects of the Messianic Age will be abundance of rain and fertility of nature (Joel 2:23 f.).

D. W. D.

DROWN. The Egyptian charioteers pursuing the escaping Israelites were drowned in the Red Sea (Ex 15:4; Heb 11:29). Drowning was never a Jewish method of capital punishment, nor was it a common practice in Galilee in Jesus' day; but it was known among Gentiles in the Graeco-Roman world (Mt 18:6). The Gr. *buthizō* is used figuratively in I Tim 6:9 of foolish desires that drown or plunge men into ruin.

DRUM. *See* Music.

DRUNK, DRUNKARD. Drunkenness is expressed in the Gr. NT by *methē* and the verbs *methuō* and *methuskō*. In the LXX *methuō* translates most often the Heb. *shākar*, which is used both literally (Gen 9:21) and figuratively (Jer 25:27) of intoxication. The many injunctions against drunkenness in the OT show that such was prevalent among the people of Israel (Deut 21:20; Lev 10:9; Prov 20:1; 23:20–21, 30–35; Joel 1:5; Nah 1:10; *et al.*). The geography and climate of Palestine are especially suited for growing the grapes from which wine is made. The abundance of wine is seen in the fact that it was traded commercially for incense and spices from Arabia (cf. BA, II [1939], 40). Intoxicants were also made from grain, as well as apples, dates, honey, and pomegranates.

Although there is no absolute prohibition of the use of wine in the NT (I Tim 5:23; Jn 2:7–9; Mt 11:19; Lk 7:34), it is clear that those who would live godly, especially those who take positions of leadership, will not be guilty of using it excessively (I Pet 4:3; I Tim 3:3, 8; Tit 1:7; 2:3). Drunkenness is not only contrasted to spirituality (Eph 5:18; Rom 13:13), but drunkards are to be excluded from the kingdom of God (Gal 5:21; I Cor 6:10; 5:11). *See* Wine; Drink, Strong.

J. McR.

DRUNKENNESS. Holy Scripture contains many cases of individual drunkenness, such as Noah (Gen 9:20–24), Lot (Gen 19:30–35), Nabal (I Sam 25:36), Uriah (II Sam 11:12–13), Amnon (II Sam 13:28), King Elah of Israel (I Kgs 16:8–10), and Ben-hadad of Syria (I Kgs

20:16). Drunkenness is implied in the account of Belshazzar's feast (Dan 5:1–4, 23). It must have been common in the times of the judges, for Eli quickly suspected Hannah of being drunken (I Sam 1:13–14; see also Prov 23:29–35; Isa 5:11, 22; 28:1, 3, 7–8).

Jesus warned His disciples against drunkenness, lest they be caught unprepared to meet Him at His return (Lk 21:34). Paul severely reprimanded the Corinthian Christians for drinking to excess at the Lord's Supper (I Cor 11:20–21), and admonished believers in Rome concerning drunkenness (Rom 13:13). He forthrightly taught that continuance in alcoholism barred one from the kingdom of God (I Cor 6:9–11; Gal 5:21). His command is absolute: "Do not get drunk with wine, for that is debauchery" (Eph 5:18, RSV). *See* Drink, Strong; Drunk, Drunkard.

J. R.

DRUSILLA (drū-sĭl'å). The wife of Felix (*q.v.*), governor or procurator of Judea before whom Paul was brought at Caesarea (Acts 24:24). Born in A.D. 38, she was a Jewess, previously married to Azizus, king of Emesa, whom she left for Felix (Jos *Ant.* xx.7.1–2). As the youngest daughter of Herod Agrippa I, Drusilla belonged to the infamous family of the Herods. When Paul stood before Felix and Drusilla, the apostle spoke "concerning the faith in Christ Jesus," with the result that Felix was "terrified" as Paul "reasoned of righteousness, and self-control, and the judgment to come" (Acts 24:25, ASV). The effect on Drusilla is not recorded. *See* Herod.

DUGONG. *See* Animals, V.3.

DUKE. Around 1611 when the KJV was translated, "duke" was not a title but referred to a ruler or chieftain of a family or nation. Hence in Gen 36:15–43; Ex 15:15; I Chr 1:51–54 the KJV uses "duke" to translate Heb. *'allûph*, a tribal or clan leader of the Edomites or Horites. In Josh 13:21 (KJV) the Heb. plural of *nāsîk* is rendered "dukes," the ones anointed by Sihon, i.e., vassal princes to him.

DULCIMER. *See* Music.

DUMAH (dū'må)

1. A son of Ishmael and the presumed ancestor of a tribe in Arabia (Gen 25:14; I Chr 1:30), which gave its name to an oasis now called Dumat ej-Jendel, capital of the district known as the Jauf. Dumah lies about halfway between the Gulf of Aqabah and Kuwait on the Persian Gulf. It seems to be the same as the *Adumatu* conquered by Sennacherib (ANET, p. 691) and the *Adummu* overrun by Nabonidus of Babylonia on his campaign against Tema (ANET, p. 305). This may be the Dumah of Isa 21:11 (but see #2), if during the 8th cen. B.C. the Edomites had extended their control over

200 miles eastward to include the oasis of el-Jauf.

2. Perhaps a symbolic name for Edom (Isa 21:11); the Heb. word means "silence." LXX has *Idoumaias,* i.e., Edom. But see # 1.

3. A town in the mountain district of Judah (Josh 15:52), probably the present ed-Dômeh, ten miles SW of Hebron. The name Rumah in II Kgs 23:36 perhaps is a misspelling for Dumah in Judah.

J. R.

DUMB. Dumbness in Scripture is attributable to several causes: (1) inability to speak by reason of a physical defect (Mt 15:30-31; cf. Ex 4:11); (2) an oppression by an evil spirit binding one's center of speech (Mt 9:32-33; 12:22; Mk 9:17, 25); (3) a psychological fear (Dan 10:15-19) or a feeling of guilt (Ps 39:9-11) or of inferiority in not knowing how to express oneself (Prov 31:8; cf. Ex 4:10-16); (4) a temporary judgment from God (Lk 1:20; Ezk 3:26).

DUNG. In KJV "dung" is used to render nine Heb. and two Gr. words. While these possess different shades of meaning, all are used to refer to excrement—waste matter discharged from the body—either of human beings or of animals. Dung is alluded to in several ways:

In connection with sacrifices. In the sin offering and the sacrifice of the red heifer, dung with other portions was to be burned "without the camp" (Ex 29:14; Num 19:5). Mal 2:3 refers to such dung being smeared on the faces of hypocritical offerers, signifying that God would allow them to be shamefully treated.

As fertilizer. The barren fig tree was to be "dunged" (Lk 13:8). Several times it was threatened that the bodies of the Jews or their enemies would be "as dung for the earth" (Ps 83:10; Jer 8:2).

As fuel. Ezekiel was to use it thus in connection with a prophetic sign (Ezk 4:12, 15). Cattle dung is still used as fuel in Mesopotamia and other lands. (On this use, see instructive notes in KD, *The Book of Job,* I, 377; KD, *The Prophecies of Ezekiel,* I, 82; Doughty, *Travels in Arabia Deserts.)*

As food in a last resort during famine (II Kgs 6:25). Documents outside Scripture also record such actions in times of extremity.

As a figure of worthlessness. In connection with divine judgments it is several times said that the bodies of various ones will be cast like dung on the earth (I Kgs 14:10; Zeph 1:17). Comparison is made here with the use of dung for fertilizer. In Phil 3:8 the apostle Paul considers fleshly honors as "but dung" ("refuse") compared with the privilege of knowing Christ.

The Dung Gate (Neh 2:13; 3:13-14; 12:31) was the one through which refuse was taken from the city of Jerusalem. See Jerusalem: Dung Gate.

G. C. L.

DUNG GATE. *See* Jerusalem: Gates and Towers 10.

DUNGEON. *See* Prison.

DUNGHILL. In KJV "dunghill" is the rendering of several different words meaning (1) a manure pit (Isa 25:10) or heap (Ezr 6:11; Lk 14:35); (2) an ash heap or garbage dump where the poor and beggars often stayed (I Sam 2:8; Ps 113:7; Lam 4:5).

DURA (dŭr′à). The name of a plain in the province of Babylon where Nebuchadnezzar set up a golden image (Dan 3:1). Aram. *dûrā′* probably is derived from Akkad. *duru* meaning "wall," "circuit," perhaps referring to some of the outer fortifications of Babylon. The name survives in Nahr Dūra, a tributary which flows into the Euphrates *c.* five miles below Hilla. Nearby are some mounds or low hills called Tulūl Dūra.

DUST. Dust refers literally to small, powdery particles of earth, or is occasionally used as a synonym for the soil itself (Job 14:19; 38:38; Isa 25:12). From such humble material man's body was originally made by God (Gen 2:7), as well as the bodies of the other creatures (Eccl 3:20). To it the body eventually returns (Gen 3:19).

Dust is frequently used in the Bible as a figure of speech, and in a variety of ways. It sometimes speaks of a large number or great quantity (Gen 13:16; Ps 78:27; Zech 9:3). Conversely it is used to describe that which is very small (Deut 9:21; Ps 18:42; Isa 40:15). It speaks of a lowly position from which one is brought up (I Kgs 16:2) or a degraded position to which one is brought down (Ps 44:25).

To make something "like the dust" signifies complete destruction (II Kgs 13:7). Dust is frequently used as a synonym for the grave (Job 20:11; Dan 12:2). To speak of man as dust is to call attention to his frailty by an allusion to his humble origin (Gen 18:27; Ps 103:14). Dust is also a figurative expression for anything worthless (Zeph 1:17).

Most NT references have to do with Christ's command to His apostles to "shake off the dust of your feet" (Mt 10:14) when departing from a city which had rejected their divine message. "This symbolic act signifies that the feet of the heralds of the kingdom have actually been in the house or the town, and that they leave this their dust in witness to the fact that they were there but were forced to leave because they were unwelcome" (R. C. H. Lenski, *The Interpretation of St. Matthew's Gospel,* p. 396).

To throw dust at a person or in the air (II Sam 16:13; Acts 22:23) is said by some authorities to be a demand for justice (Conybeare and Howson, *The Life and Epistles of St. Paul,* p. 589). More likely, however, it was simply a gesture of contempt and hatred.

It was evidently quite common in Bible times to place dust on one's head as a sign of deep sorrow, grievous mourning, and complete humiliation (see e.g., Josh 7:6; Job 2:12; Lam 2:10; Rev 18:19). "The head, the noblest part of man, was thus placed beneath the dust of the ground from whence he was taken" (J. J. Lias in the *Pulpit Commentary*, Vol. 3, Part 2, p. 121).

G. C. L.

DUTY. Found six or eight times (excluding "due"). The duty of marriage is discussed in Ex 21:10; Deut 25:5, 7, in two different situations. Daily duty in connection with religious ritual is discussed in II Chr 8:14; Ezr 3:4. In Eccl 12:13, the word is supplied. The whole duty of man under the law was to fear God and keep His commandments. In Lk 17:10, Jesus says when we have done as commanded, we have merely done our duty. In Rom 15:27, Paul speaks of the duty of Gentiles to minister in material things to Jews who have ministered to them in spiritual things.

DWARF. The Heb. word *daq* is rendered "dwarf" in Lev 21:20, describing one who is physically disqualified from offering sacrifices. The term may indicate small size (perhaps caused by tuberculosis; *see* Diseases) or deformity resulting from withered limbs or some other malady. A dancing pigmy or dwarf was brought from central Africa as a gift to Pharaoh Pepy II of the Sixth Dynasty (*Everyday Life in Ancient Times*, National Geographic Soc., 1951, pp. 104 f.). The Egyptian god Bes was depicted as a grotesque dwarf figure (ANEP, # 663, 664).

DWELL. The translation of some 15 Heb. and Gr. words. Heb. *gûr* is often used of the stay of a foreigner, a transient, among the people (Lev 19:34).

Heb. *yāshab* conceives of one's dwelling as a sitting down, whether in a tent in the field or in a house in the town (Gen 13:12; Lev 18:3). Heb. *shākan* is used frequently of the Lord's dwelling among His people or in Jerusalem and means "to settle down and remain or dwell permanently." In the Gr. *katoikeō* (Acts 7:4) is similar to the Heb. *shākan*. Longer terms of stay are denoted by *menō*, "abide," "stay longer." *Oikeō* denotes "to have a house." *See* House; Tent.

The Gr. word for tent (tabernacle) is the root (*skēnē*) of a NT verb, *skēnoō*, describing the purpose of the life of Christ: like the tabernacle, He is the residence and manifestation of God's presence and glory among His people ("And the Word became flesh and tabernacled among us," Jn 1:14, NASB marg.). The Holy Spirit will abide (*menō*) in the Christian forever (Jn 14:17). The normal dwelling place or manner of life of the Christian is in the Father's love (I Jn 4:16).

H. G. S.

DWELLING. *See* Cave; Dwell; Habitation; House; Palace; Tabernacle; Tent.

DYERS. *See* Occupations.

DYSENTERY. *See* Diseases.

E

EAGLE. *See* Animals, III.53, 54.

EAR
1. The organ of hearing, our guarantee of God's ability to hear (Ps 94:9). Sometimes the external ear alone is meant, as in the piercing of a Heb. slave's earlobe for a sign of his choosing perpetual slavery (Ex 21:6; Deut 15:16 f.; Ps 40:6); also in the applying of blood on the right ear of the priest at his consecration (Ex 29:20), and of blood and oil at the leper's cleansing (Lev 14:14, 17). Figuratively, it speaks of an ability for spiritual understanding (Isa 50:4–5; contrast Isa 6:10; Jer 6:10).
2. Used of the fruiting spike of a cereal plant (Mk 4:28).
3. Archaic verb meaning to plow or till (I Sam 8:12; Isa 30:24).

Bibliography. Johannes Horst, "*Ous*, etc.," TDNT, V, 543–549. G. Kittel, "*Akouō*, etc.," TDNT, I, 216–225.

EARNEST (OF THE SPIRIT). "Earnest" is from the Gr. *arrabōn*, "surety," "pledge," a Semitic loan-word (cf. Heb. *'ērābôn*, Gen 38:17, 18, 20). It is a down payment given as a pledge or deposit that one will finally pay the full amount of the purchase price. The term "earnest money" is used today in the purchase of property.

The word is used three times in the NT (II Cor 1:22; 5:5; Eph 1:13–14). The last reference makes the biblical meaning clear: "In whom also after that ye believed, ye were sealed with that Holy Spirit of promise, which is the earnest of our inheritance until the redemption of the purchased possession unto the praise of his glory." The Holy Spirit was sent at Pentecost, just as money is given to guarantee a business transaction. His presence is a foretaste and pledge of what is finally to come. For the benefits to the believer in his completed salvation and total inheritance, *see* Salvation.

R. A. K.

EARRING. The Heb. word *nezem* signifies a ring and is used both of nose ring and earring. Its first use is in Gen 24:22 where the KJV has earring and the ASV has ring. From Gen 24:47 (ASV) it seems evident that nose ring is correct. Yet in Gen 35:4 earrings are definitely meant. Here the word is found in connection with Jacob's word to his household to discard the gods of the foreigner. They gave to him the foreign gods in their hand and the rings in their ears.

Gold earrings from the tomb of King Tutankhamon of Egypt. LL

From Ex 32:2-3 we learn that golden earrings were worn by Heb. women and both male and female children. Nothing is said of adult males wearing them. At this time they were fashioned into the golden calf. In Ex 35:22 either nose rings or earrings may be meant, but here the gold becomes an offering to the Lord for the construction of the tabernacle. Both men and women brought these rings, so if earrings were meant it shows that Heb. men did on occasion use them. However, Jud 8:24 indicates this was not the usual practice, for the men had earrings (or nose rings) because they were Ishmaelites.

The context of Prov 25:12 seems to favor earring instead of nose ring. Here it is used in a good sense of a thing of beauty. Thus the gold ring in itself was neither good nor bad, but could be used in idolatrous worship to make a golden calf, or given to the Lord, or worn as an object of beauty. In the NT the emphasis is that a Christian's adornment should not be outward but spiritual (I Tim 2:9-10; I Pet 3:3-4). *See* Dress.

A second word, *'āgîl*, translated earring in Num 31:50 and Ezk 16:12, emphasizes the idea of roundness.

The word *laḥash* means an amulet or charm. This word, translated in the KJV as "earring" in Isa 3:20, is "amulet" in ASV. The root means "to whisper" or "to conjure," and thus

refers to charms of metal or jewels which were thought to have protective powers. Sometimes they were inscribed with magical formulas or were shaped like god-emblems, as among the Egyptians. *See* Amulet; Jewels.

C. J. W.

EARTH. This word has several meanings in the English Bible.

1. The distinctive name for our planet (Job 1:7).

2. The solid matter of the globe in contrast to the water and air (Gen 1:10).

3. The soil; the ground as a farmer would speak of it (II Kgs 5:17).

4. The inhabitants of the globe (Gen 11:1).

5. The world as lying in the evil one; thus "the things upon the earth" are sinful and the opposite of that which is heavenly and spiritual (Col 3:2, 5; cf. Phil 3:19).

The main Heb. words translated earth are (a) *'ădāmâ*, which signifies the reddish soil or ground (cf. Heb. *'ādōm*, "red"), from which man's body was made, and so he was named *'ādām*, "man" or "Adam" (Gen 2:7; 3:19); and (b) *'ereṣ*, which is not only translated "earth" but "land," thus denoting a country (Gen 21:21). Since this word may mean either the whole earth or just part of it, some passages may read "earth" in one translation and "land" in another (cf. Isa 10:23, KJV and ASV). *See* Land.

In the NT the usual Gr. word is *gē*, translated either "earth" with its various meanings or "land," especially the land of Judea (Mt 27:45). See Lk 23:44 for the parallel account and note how "earth" is used in the KJV and "land" in the ASV. Another word, *oikoumenē*, denotes especially the whole inhabited earth (Lk 21:26), and particularly the Roman Empire in NT times (Lk 2:1, "world"). *See* World; Creation.

C. J. W.

EARTHEN VESSEL, EARTHENWARE. *See* Pot; Potter under Occupations; Pottery.

EARTHQUAKE. A vibration of the earth caused sometimes by a cracking and shifting of rock beneath the surface. There are two major types, volcanic and tectonic. The Bible mentions a few; e.g., when (1) the law was given on Sinai (Ex 19:18; Heb 12:26); (2) the earth "swallowed ... up" Korah, Dathan, and Abiram (Num 16:31-32); (3) Jonathan attacked the Philistine garrison at Gibeah (I Sam 14:15); (4) Elijah was on Horeb (I Kgs 19:11); (5) Uzziah was king of Judah (Amos 1:1; Zech 14:5); (6) Jesus died (Mt 27:51) and arose from the dead (Mt 28:2); (7) Paul and Silas were imprisoned at Philippi (Acts 16:26). Sometimes earthquakes are associated with divine judgment (Rev 6:12; 8:5; 11:13, 19). They will precede our Lord's second coming (Mt 24:7). The greatest earthquake of all time is yet future (Rev 16:18).

Natural theater on south side of Mount Ebal.
JR

EAST (Heb. *qedem*, lit., "front," or "before"; and *mizrāh̠*, "the place of dawning"; Gr. *anatolē*, "the rising" of the sun).

The Hebrews divided the world into four parts and described them as "corners of the earth" (Isa 11:12; Rev 7:1; 20:8), or as the "four winds" (Ezk 37:9). Like many Semitic peoples, the Hebrews looked to the East, "the place of dawning," as their basic direction. In describing the points of the compass, the "four corners," a person would face E, making that direction before, W to the rear, N to the left, and S to the right. *See* East, Children of the.

EAST, CHILDREN OF THE. The Heb. term *bᵉnê-qedem*, "sons of the east," was a general ancient designation of the peoples, mostly nomadic, living E of Palestine. They ranged as far N as Padan-aram where Laban (Gen 28:2; 29:1) and Balaam (Num 23:7) lived, and southward to Moab and Edom (Isa 11:14) and beyond (Ezk 25:4, 10) to Kedar among the Arab tribes (Jer 49:28). Many of these were descendants of Abraham by Keturah (Gen 25: 1–6). They invaded Israel along with the nomadic Midianites and Amalekites in the time of Gideon (Jud 6:3, 33; 7:12; 8:10–11).

The region of Qedem is mentioned in Ugaritic literature as well as in the Egyptian Tale of Sinuhe which reflects conditions in Palestine-Syria in the 20th cen. B.C. (ANET, p. 19). Job was "the greatest of all the men of the east" (Job 1:3). The men of the E had a special reputation for wisdom (I Kgs 4:30), which accords with the classification of the book of Job as Wisdom Literature.

J. R.

EAST GATE. *See* Jerusalem: Gates and Towers 14.

EAST SEA. The Dead Sea, on the eastern border of Canaan and Israel, is called the East Sea in Joel 2:20; Ezk 47:18; Zech 14:8 (RSV). *See* Dead Sea.

EAST WIND. *See* Wind.

EASTER. This word appears only once in the KJV (Acts 12:4). It is used there as a translation of the Gr. word *pascha*, which is translated correctly as "passover" in the 28 other places where it occurs in the NT. Revisions of the KJV consistently translate *pascha* as "passover" in all passages, including Acts 12:4 (cf. ASV, RSV, NEB). The English word "Easter" is thought to be derived from the name of a Teutonic goddess of spring, Eastre, and to have been adapted by Christians to its present usage about the 8th cen. after Christ.

EATING. *See* Food: Banquet.

EBAL (ē'băl)
1. An alternate form of Obal (*q.v.*; I Chr 1:22).
2. One of the sons of Shobal, son of Seir the Horite (Gen 36:20, 23; I Chr 1:40).
3. Mount Ebal, at the very center of Canaan, is the highest peak in the hill country of Samaria. Lying just N of Mount Gerizim and Shechem in the pass between, it rises to a height of 3,083 feet above sea level. Steep, barren, and rocky, Ebal was the site at which Joshua erected an altar of unhewn stones and wrote on plastered stones a copy of the law as Moses had commanded (Deut 11:29; 27:2 f.; Josh 8:30 ff.). The 12 tribes were divided upon Gerizim and Ebal for the blessings and curses, respectively, of the law.

EBED (ē'bĕd). Meaning "servant," Heb. *'ebed* is an element of many compound names. The following may be shortened from *'ebed-'ēl*, "servant of God," or *'ebed-yāh*, "servant of Yahweh":
1. The father of Gaal who headed the rebellion against Abimelech at Shechem (Jud 9:26–35).
2. The leader of the clan of Adin, who returned with Ezra from the Babylonian Captivity with 50 men (Ezr 8:6).

EBED-MELECH (ē'bĕd-mĕl'ĕk). This name meaning "servant of the king" may also have been a title equal to "king's minister." He was an Ethiopian (Cushite) eunuch at the court of King Zedekiah of Judah, perhaps in charge of the royal harem, an office which would give him private access to the king. He obtained Zedekiah's permission to rescue Jeremiah from the muddy bottom of an empty cistern (Jer 38:6–13). He was aided by three (one Heb. MS and LXX, v. 10) other men using ropes with old rags to pad the prophet's armpits. Later Jeremiah prophesied to Ebed-melech that for his kindness his life would be delivered in the approaching day of Jerusalem's destruction (Jer 39:15–18).

EBENEZER (ĕb'ĕ-nē'zĕr; "stone of help"). The name is mentioned three times in the Bible (I Sam 4:1; 5:1; 7:12). According to I Sam 7:12 it was the name given to a stone set up by

Samuel to commemorate the divine assistance given to Israel in battle, whereby they were victorious over the Philistines. Its position was carefully defined as a place between Mizpah and Shen, near Aphek. According to I Sam 4:1; 5:1, Israel 20 years previously had been soundly defeated there by the Philistines and the ark of God captured and taken to Ashdod. The writer used the name Ebenezer because the place was so known at the time of writing.

EBER (ē'bẽr)

1. Eber was a descendant of Shem (Gen 10:21, 24). He was the father of Peleg and Joktan, and the ancestor of various peoples called "all the children of Eber" (Gen 10:21; cf. Num 24:24), which phrase probably means the "Hebrews" in the broadest sense. Through Peleg, Eber became an ancestor of Abraham (Gen 11:16-26), and thus is in the messianic line (Lk 3:35). See Hebrew People.

2-5. Eber is also the name of a descendant of Gad (I Chr 5:13), two different descendants of Benjamin (I Chr 8:12, 22; cf. I Chr 8:17), and the name of a post-Exilic priest (Heb 12:20). See Heber.

EBIASAPH (ē-bī'a-săf). An ancestor of Heman, a musician in David's time (I Chr 6:23, 37; 9:19). Probably the same as Abiasaph (q.v.).

EBONY. See Plants.

EBRONAH. Translated Abronah in RSV. A campsite of the Israelites near Ezion-geber (Num 33:34-35). Possibly it was at 'Ain ed-Defiyeh, a shallow water hole in the Arabah c. seven and one-half miles N of Ezion-geber.

ECCLESIASTES, BOOK OF. A treatise on a proper philosophy of life, and an outstanding example of OT Wisdom Literature.

Title

The title comes to us by way of the Vulg. from the LXX, where it means a member of the ecclesia. The Heb. form qōheleth, which scholars often transliterate, is a feminine participle used idiomatically of the one who convenes and addresses a public assembly or school, i.e., the officer of a qahal, the common word for assembly.

Author

Did the writer assemble proverbs (cf. I Kgs 4:32)? Sections of the book are such (e.g., 7:1-13; 10). Or was he an orator or debater? But the book seems meditation rather than argument. Most translate the word as "preacher" (so five times in 1:1, 2; 12:8-10 according to KJV, ASV, RSV, Berkeley).

Qoheleth is declared to be "son of David, king in Jerusalem" (1:1). Is he Solomon, or is he merely quoting a saying of Solomon's in v. 2 as the theme of his study? Scholars are divided as to Solomon's being the author. Yet in 1:12 we read: "I the Preacher was king over Israel

in Jerusalem," i.e., up to the time of writing. The critical argument against Solomonic authorship is illogical, for the above statement is natural for one writing an autobiography. Beginning with chap. 3 Solomon uses proverbs which are based on his experience. He said, "I will be wise; but it was far from me" (7:23; contrast 1:16). It was a poor time compared to former days (7:10), for the government was corrupt near the end of his reign, and the subjects of the tyrannical king considered themselves oppressed (3:16; 4:1; 8:9; 10:5-7).

Was Qoheleth one or three? Some moderns say the preacher wrote in pessimism; he was augmented by a Wise Man with proverbs (e.g., 10:1 – 11:4), and he by a Pious One with more orthodox religious sentiments (e.g., 2:26). A final appendix (12:13 f.) commends the practice of the Jewish religion as man's whole duty. But could not one with keen mind both argue a case, adapt proverbs, and contend with doubts?

Qoheleth is never quoted in the NT, but Rom 8:20, speaking of creation subject to vanity, may have his theme as background; and our Lord's parable of the rich fool (Lk 12:16-21) is like the final sentence (Eccl 12:14).

While some scholars have suggested otherwise, the epilogue is by the preacher himself. He had wondered whether at death the spirit of man really does go upward to God (3:21), but now he is assured of a final judgment (12:14; cf. 11:9).

Time of Writing

The time of writing is held by some scholars to be the Persian period (which ended 333 B.C.) or even the succeeding Gr. period because of the occurrence of several words that seem to be Aramaic or Persian, but references to definite historical events seem quite indistinct. Solomon had more widely ranging international contacts than any after him (see Archer, SOTI, pp. 462-471).

Theme

The thought of these 12 chapters circles, rises and falls. At times it seems pessimistic, at times the cloud lifts. Though God is mentioned 20 times, 27 things vex the author with four main problems: life is unequal (2:12-26); the world is inscrutable (8:17); the future is uncertain (11:2, 6, 8 f.); death is dark (9:4-6, 10).

Yet there does appear to be a progression from an emphasis on vanity (Heb. hebel, "breath," "mist," anything transitory, frail, illusory, empty), mentioned 26 times in chaps. 1-6 and 12 times in chaps. 7-12, to an emphasis on wisdom, 11 times in chaps. 1-6 and 17 times in chaps. 7-12, and on being wise, 6 times in chaps. 1-6 and 15 times in chaps. 7-12.

The text, "How utterly futile, how utterly transitory, the whole thing is a puff of wind" (1:2; 12:8, orig. trans.), is true to realistic humanism. Life without God has no real meaning. Secularism can bring no lasting satisfaction. Faith, however, embraces the divine government. So in sum, "Banish moroseness from your heart; and remove evil from your flesh; for youth and the age of black hair are transient. Remember, then, your Creator in the days of your prime-of-life" (11:10 – 12:1, orig. trans.).

Outline

The Prologue, 1:1– 11

Life, while not in itself evil, is a meaningless cycle, vain when lived apart from God and not used for His glory.

I. The Vanity of All Things, 1:12–6:12
   A. The failure of all humanistic attempts to give meaning to existence, 1:12 – 2:23
   B. The contrast of a life lived in observance of God's ordained order, 2:24 – 3:22
   C. The disappointments of earthly life, 4:1– 16
   D. The futile efforts of the self-seeking life, 5:1– 20
   E. The inadequacy of attainments esteemed by the world, 6:1– 6
   F. Conclusion: Why argue with your Maker? 6:7– 12

II. Words of Wisdom for Dwelling Amidst Vanity, 7:1– 12:8
   A. General counsel about enduring values, 7:1– 29
   B. Exhortation to obey the earthly king and fear the heavenly King even in wicked, perplexing times, 8:1– 17
   C. How to cope with the fact of death, 9:1– 12
   D. Wisdom better than folly, 9:13 – 10:20
   E. Exhortation to benevolence and cheerful industry in spite of possible trouble, 11:1– 8
   F. Exhortation to youth to begin living for God while still young, before old age comes, 11:9 – 12:7
   G. Conclusion: Opening theme repeated that all is empty and transitory, 12:8

The Epilogue, 12:9– 14

Summary: Fear God, and keep His commandments.

See Wisdom.

Bibliography. Gleason L. Archer, *A Survey of Old Testament Introduction,* Chicago: Moody, 1964, pp. 459–472; "The Linguistic Evidence for the Date of Ecclesiastes," JETS, XII (1969), 167–182. H. L. Ginsberg, "The Structure and Contents of the Book of Koheleth," *Supplements to VT,* III (1955), 138–149. Robert Gordis, *Koheleth—The Man and His World,* New York: Block Publ. Co., 1955. G. S. Hendry, "Ecclesiastes," NBC. Ernst W. Hengstenberg, *Commentary on Ecclesiastes,* trans. by D. W. Simon, Edinburgh: T. & T. Clark, 1876. Herbert C. Leupold, *Exposition of Ecclesiastes,* Columbus: Wartburg Press, 1952. J. Stafford Wright, "The Interpretation of Ecclesiastes," EQ, XVIII (1946), 18–34.

W. G. B. and J. R.

ECCLESIOLOGY (Gr. *ekklēsia,* "that which is called out," "the church"). The doctrine of the Church based upon an inductive study of the Scriptures. *See* Church. The most basic question involved is that of the origin of the Church. Two main views are held by orthodox theologians.

1. According to some theologians, the Church began with the NT. It was foretold by Christ at the time of Peter's confession (Mt 16:18). Following Christ's resurrection, He was exalted as "head over all things to the church, which is his body" (Eph 1:22–23). Pentecost was the day when the Church actually began, for by sending the Holy Spirit, God "baptized into one body" (I Cor 12:13) all believers, whether Jews or Gentiles.

This view is supported by the argument that the Church was a mystery, "not known unto the sons of men" but established and revealed by Christ (Eph 3:5). In it there is "neither Jew nor Greek, there is neither bond nor free, there is neither male nor female: for ye are all one in Christ Jesus" (Gal 3:28), the middle wall of partition having been taken away by His death (Eph 2:14– 15). Those who were once separate, now through Christ "have access by one Spirit unto the Father" (Eph 2:18). This new relationship is based on our Lord's promise of the Spirit being "in" them (Jn 14:16– 17).

2. According to the other view, that held by the Reformed theologians, the Church is composed of all the elect of all ages. There was a Church in the wilderness (Acts 7:38). Believers in the NT come to the "general assembly and church of the firstborn, which are written in heaven" (Heb 12:22–23). The mystery "that the Gentiles should be fellowheirs, and of the same body" with Jews (Eph 3:5, 9) was known by revelation to the OT believers (Isa 42:1–4; 60:3; Lk 3:6; Acts 13:47; 15:17), but not as fully "as it is now revealed . . . by the Spirit" (Eph 3:5). Since the promises to Abraham are to be shared by believers of all ages (Rom 4:13– 16; Heb 11:39–40), the Reformed theologians see no possible distinction between the OT and the NT believers, either as to their basis of salvation in Christ and justification through faith (the unity of the covenant of grace), or their future destiny and rewards.

R. A. K.

ECLIPSE. The Bible contains no historical notice of an eclipse. The three-hour darkness beginning at noon during Christ's crucifixion cannot logically be attributed to an eclipse of the sun, because the moon is always full at the time of the Passover.

Eschatological descriptions of the "day of

the Lord," however, possibly foretell one or more eclipses in the future. Isaiah writes, "The sun will be dark at its rising and the moon will not shed its light" (13:10, RSV). Similarly, Joel says, "The sun and the moon shall be dark, and the stars shall withdraw their shining" (Joel 2:10; 3:15); "the sun shall be turned into darkness, and the moon into blood, before the great and the terrible day of the Lord come" (Joel 2:31; Acts 2:20). Amos even more clearly predicts a solar eclipse: "I will make the sun go down at noon, and darken the earth in broad daylight" (Amos 8:9, RSV). Other prophecies that may suggest such phenomena are Jer 4:23; Ezk 32:7-8; Zeph 1:15. Christ's Olivet discourse refers to these astronomical disturbances (Mt 24:29), and Rev 6:12 (RSV) repeats the thought, "And the sun became black as sackcloth, the full moon became like blood." At the sounding of the fourth trumpet there will be a partial restriction of solar, lunar, and stellar light (Rev 8:12).

James (1:17, RSV) may be implying the shadow of an eclipse by contrast when he writes, ". . . the Father of lights with whom there is no variation or shadow due to change" (i.e., in position of heavenly bodies, Arndt, pp. 97, 834). Job seems to have been aware of the phenomenon of the eclipse; in his cursing the day of his birth he exclaimed, "May murk and deep shadow claim it for their own, clouds hang over it, eclipse swoop down on it" (3:5, Jerus B).

The Bible is marked by the absence of belief in mythology, including astrology, such as the Babylonian myth of the eclipse of the moon, wherein the moon-god Sin is attacked by seven evil gods and must be rescued by the other great deities.

In ancient Assyria solar eclipses were observed and recorded, in one case as the chief event by which a year was distinguished in the lists of annual *limmu* officials. These records have been correlated with Assyrian king-lists giving the sequence and duration of reigns. In determining a chronological framework for a history of OT times the key is the note of that eclipse of the sun in the month *Simanu* in the *limmu*-ship of Bur-Sagale, the ninth year of King Ashur-dan III. By astronomical calculation this fell on June 15, 763 B.C., according to our calendrical system.

Other eclipses that would have been visible in Jerusalem occurred on Feb. 9, 784; June 5, 716; and Sept. 30, 610. Does Jeremiah allude to the latter in 15:9? Herodotus describes a battle that must have been fought about this date between Lydians and Medes when "day was suddenly turned into night" (*The Histories*, Penguin Classics, 1954, p. 42). In his canon or *Almagest* the Egyptian scholar Ptolemy (A.D. 70–161) recorded large amounts of astronomical data, including eight eclipses between 721 and 491 B.C. All his dates have been verified by modern astronomers. *See* Sun; Chronology, OT.

J. R.

ED (ĕd). A name appearing in Josh 22:34, transliterated from Heb. *'ēd,* "witness." The Heb. word has dropped out of the MT, but is obviously required by the context (see vv. 27, 28, 34b, where the word does appear). It is the name the two and one-half eastern tribes gave to an altar they built in the Jordan Valley, perhaps near the mouth of the Jabbok Valley. Their desire to have a monument to testify to the fact that they had a part in the Lord and in Israel was ill-founded, because God's method to preserve unity was to have *all* the tribes gather three times a year around the altar of sacrifice at *Shiloh* (Ex 23:17).

EDAR. *See* Eder 1.

EDEN (ē'dĕn; "plain" or "delight").

1. "And the Lord God planted a garden eastward in Eden" (Gen 2:8). Neither size nor boundaries of the garden are given. Adam, the first man, was put there to till and keep it. Eve was given to him as a helpmeet. Many fine trees were there: "The tree of life also in the midst of the garden, and the tree of knowledge of good and evil" (Gen 2:9). The man was told he could eat of the fruit of all the trees, "but of the tree of the knowledge of good and evil, thou shalt not eat of it: for in the day that thou eatest thereof thou shalt surely die" (Gen 2:17).

The term Eden gives the geographical location of the garden, an enclosed area. Eden (Heb. *'ēden*) is probably a common noun from the Sumerian *edin,* Akkad. *edinu* ("plain," "steppe land"), suitable for pasturage or cultivation, and characteristic of the Mesopotamian plain. "And a river went out of Eden to water the garden; and from thence it was parted, and became into four heads" (Gen 2:10). E. A. Speiser comments that the four separate heads, branches, or sources merged within Eden and went forth as one river *in* (locative use of Heb. *min*) Eden to water the garden (*Genesis,* The Anchor Bible, 1964, pp. 16–20). Two of these are well known: The Euphrates (*q.v.*), called in Scripture "the great river," and the Hiddekel, the old name for the river Tigris (*q.v.*). The other two, the Pison (*q.v.*) and Gihon (*q.v.*), which "compass" or meander through their respective lands, are not known. Some claim these are the four principal rivers of the ancient world, the latter two being the Indus and the Nile, respectively.

Many locations for Eden have been suggested, but the site cannot be determined because the surface of the earth after the Flood probably bears little resemblance to its antediluvian appearance. A likely site might be in the area of Babylon, where the Tigris and Euphrates come close together and the Diyala flows into the Tigris from the N and a large wadi drains into the plain from northern Arabia (Havilah?).

In the Sumerian texts the term *edin* was the pasturing ground of the Sumerian shepherds and seems to denote the grassy region between the plowed lands irrigated by canals from the

Tigris-Euphrates river system, specifically in the triangle between Nippur, Uruk (Erech), and Umma (Thorkild Jacobsen, "Mesopotamian Mound Survey," *Archaeology*, VII [1954], 54).

Sumerian literature contains the myth of the deities Enki and Ninhursag whose actions are centered around Dilmun, a fabled district near the head of the Persian or Arabian Gulf. The paradise-land of Dilmun is pure and clean and bright, with no death or sickness or old age, but lacking fresh water. Enki orders the sun-god to bring forth good water from the earth for Dilmun (cf. Gen 2:5–6). Later in the myth, a goddess is created for the healing of Enki's rib (*see* Eve). When Enki eats eight special plants, Ninhursag curses him, suggesting a parallel with the eating of the fruit of the tree of the knowledge of good and evil by Adam and Eve and the curse pronounced against them (see ANET, pp. 37–41; Samuel N. Kramer, *History Begins at Sumer*, pp. 144–149). While some scholars suggest that the Hebrews borrowed the concept of Eden from the Sumerians via the Babylonians or Canaanites, it is even more likely that both accounts refer to a real place and real events, the Sumerian version having become grossly distorted with mythological accretions over the centuries.

Paradise was apparently of short duration (cf. Gen 2:8 – 3:24). Following their sin, Adam and Eve were driven out of the garden, "lest he . . . take also of the tree of life . . . and live forever" (Gen 3:22). Their parting sight of that beautiful home was of a flaming sword guarding the way to the tree of life.

Strangely enough it was another sword, "the sword of the Spirit, which is the word of God" (Eph 6:17), that opened up to the sinner the fulfillment of the promise of a Redeemer first made in the Garden of Eden (cf. Gen 3:15). In the final chapter of the Bible the new paradise is seen. There the redeemed sinner can take of the tree of life and live forever (cf. Rev 22:14).

2. A locality in northern Mesopotamia (II Kgs 19:12; Isa 37:12; Ezk 27:23; Amos 1:5) mentioned as an embroidery market for Tyre; identified with Bit-adini in the Assyrian records, an Aramaean state between the Euphrates and the river Balikh. RSV has Beth-eden in Amos 1:5.

3. A son of Joah, a Gershonite Levite (II Chr 29:12; 31:15).

L. A. L. and J. R.

EDER (ē'dĕr), **EDAR** (ē'där), **ADER** (ā'dĕr)

1. A watchtower between Bethlehem and Hebron, where Jacob camped after Rachel's death and where Reuben had intercourse with Bilhah (Gen 35:21–22). KJV spells it Edar. Because of its proximity to Bethlehem where David was born, Micah (Mic 4:8) refers to it (*migdal 'ēder*, "O tower of the flock") and to Ophel ("the stronghold"), where David's citadel was built in Jerusalem, as symbols of the royal house of David.

2. A town in the Negeb of Judah (Josh 15:21), perhaps el-'Adar, five miles S of Gaza. The LXX, however, suggests that Arad (*q.v.*) is possibly the correct reading.

3. A Benjamite (I Chr 8:15, RSV), spelled Ader in KJV.

4. A Levite, descendant of Mushi, son of Merari (I Chr 23:23; 24:30).

EDIFICATION. The Gr. noun *oikodomē*, "edifice," "building up," "edifying," "edification," denotes the temple buildings in Mt 24:1; Mk 13:1–2, and appears metaphorically a dozen or more times in Paul's epistles. Believers as living stones (I Pet 2:5) are being built into the Church as a great "building" joined together and growing into a holy temple in union with the Lord Jesus Christ (Eph 2:21).

Each individual believer must be built up or edified for this ultimate purpose, strengthened and united with all other believers. The ascended Christ has given to His Church men with special ministries to equip the saints for this work of "building up" the body of Christ (Eph 4:12). This was the purpose of Paul's God-given authority, and his goal at all times (II Cor 10:8; 12:19; 13:10). Hence each Christian is to act unselfishly in order to edify his fellow believers in an attitude of love (Eph 4:15–16; Rom 14:19; 15:2; I Cor 8:1). His words should always be spoken to edify (Eph 4:29), especially in meetings of the local church (I Cor 14:26). Charismatic manifestations of the Spirit should always be controlled so that the hearers are edified. Prophesying best serves this purpose, although two or at the most three persons speaking in tongues, if followed by an interpretation in each case, may also edify the congregation (I Cor 14:3–13, 27–33).

Bibliography. Otto Michel, "*Oikodomeō*," TDNT, V, 136–144.

J. R.

EDOM (ē'dŏm). The term Edom means red. It has three possible origins: the red sandstone cliffs of the country (there is evidence that the country may have been called *'ĕdôm*, or "red," before Esau subjugated the Horites); Esau's red hair at birth; or the red pottage which Esau took in exchange for his inheritance (Gen 25:25–30).

Esau seems to have settled in a part of the Negeb S of Beer-sheba (Gen 28:9) which was called Seir at that time (Gen 32:3; 33:16; 36:8). This continued to be the homeland of the Edomites until after the time of Moses and Joshua, who came in contact with them just E of Kadesh-barnea (Num 20:14–21; 34:3; Deut 2:1–8) and S of Judah's tribal allotment (Josh 15:1, 21). *See* Esau.

The mountainous area which the Edomites (*q.v.*) invaded and made their headquarters from the 13th to the 6th cen. B.C. extends S from Moab, with the border at the river Zered, for about 70 miles to the Gulf of Aqabah. This territory consists of porphyry and colored sandstone mountains which contain the grandest rock scenery in the world. From these mountains of Transjordan the Edomites looked down upon a maze of cliffs, chasms, rocky shelves, and narrow valleys. This range E of the Arabah depression is actually the crested edge of a high, bleak plateau, covered by stones and spotted with patches of grain land and scattered woods. Its western cliff walls are steep and bare, black and red, rising from the pale yellow sands of the Arabah desert floor. So rugged is the terrain that the valley in which Petra is located can be reached by a deep gorge wide enough at times for only two horsemen to ride abreast. In addition to the wheat lands on the eastern plateau, the wider defiles provide some fertile fields and terraces for vineyards. Its 5,000 foot high promontories precipitate some of the moisture from the prevailing W winds that have passed over the Negeb, so that it is a comparatively well-watered land. Thus Mount Seir (q.v.) was a well-stocked fortress, with its copper and iron mines in the Arabah. Yet it was so high and lofty and locked in by precipice and jagged mountains that it was practically impregnable. It was this feature to which the prophet Obadiah referred in verses 3 and 4 when he wrote of Edom's dwelling in the clefts of the rock, setting his nest among the stars, and boasting, "Who shall bring me down to the ground?"

Living in this rich fortress-land, the Edomites enjoyed a civilization superior to that of the tribes of the surrounding deserts. Furthermore, they looked across to Palestine at their relatives the Israelites who were compelled because of their vulnerable borders to make alliances with surrounding nations in order to survive. The Edomites naturally absorbed something of the characteristics of their mountains. They were alone, aloof, unsympathetic and unmoved by the claims of pity and kinship. For this the Lord passed judgment on them: "For three transgressions of Edom, and for four, I will not revoke the punishment; because he pursued his brother with the sword, and cast off all pity, and his anger tore perpetually, and he kept his wrath for ever. So I will send a fire upon Teman, and it shall devour the strongholds of Bozrah" (Amos 1:11–12, RSV). This passage lists the two chief towns of Edom around 750 B.C., Bozrah (modern Buseireh), 20 miles SE of the Dead Sea, and Teman, identified by Nelson Glueck with a site strewn with Edomite potsherds known as Tawilan just E of the Petra valley.

Edom's self-sufficiency was enhanced by the position of the country located on several of the main trade routes of the ancient world. The masters of Mount Seir at times controlled the harbors of Aqabah, into which Solomon's ships had come with gold from Ophir. They swooped

Typical Edomite terrain. JR

down periodically upon the Arabian caravans and cut the roads to Gaza and Damascus. Mainly, however, the Edomites were traders, middlemen between Arabia and Phoenicia, thereby filling their caverns with both eastern and western wealth. This coveted position drew the envious fire of the Israelites — especially when the land of Edom was so cut off and so difficult to attack. Yet such kings of Judah as David, Amaziah, and Uzziah did invade Edom successfully and gained control of the oriental trade which flowed through the ports of Elath and Ezion-geber.

Bibliography. D. W. Deere, *The Twelve Speak,* New York: American Press, 1958, I, 45–50. Nelson Glueck, "Transjordan," TAOTS, pp. 433–445. G. A. Smith, *The Book of the Twelve Prophets,* New York: Harper, 1929, II, 177 ff.
D. W. D.

EDOMITES (ē′dŏ-mīts). The Edomites were a Semitic people descended from Esau (q.v.), who settled in the S of Palestine and Transjordan sometime during the 2nd mil. before Christ. Their kingdom was bounded on the N by the wilderness of Judea, the Dead Sea, and the river Zered (modern Wadi el-Hasa); on the E by the Syrian Desert; on the W by the Sinai Peninsula; and on the S by the Gulf of Aqabah. This territory, called Mount Seir (q.v.), was formerly occupied by the Horites (Gen 14:6), whom the Edomites dispossessed and settled in their place (Gen 36:8, 15–21). *See* Edom.

The Edomites are first mentioned outside the Bible in the Ugaritic tablets of Ras Shamra. In the Legend of King Keret, King Keret of Sidon is said to have advanced against the king of Edom, but the latter bought him off with some valuable presents and gave him his daughter Mesheb-Hory in marriage. Egyptian records from the late 13th cen. B.C. mention Bedouin tribesmen of Edom who were permitted to enter Egypt for food during a famine (ANET, p. 259).

The Edomites figure prominently in the Bible, often in the role of opponents to the Israelites. The first historical contact between the two took place when the Israelites were advancing on Palestine from the Sinai Peninsula. The Edomite territory lay along Moses' proposed route, so the Israelites sought permission to pass peacefully through their territory: "We will not pass through the fields, or through the vineyards, neither will we drink of the water of the wells; we will go by the king's highway, we will not turn to the right hand nor to the left, until we have passed the borders." The king of Edom refused this request even though an assurance was given to him by Moses that ". . . if I and my cattle drink of thy water, then I will pay for it" (Num 20:14–21).

The chief source of income of the Edomites came from trade and the fees collected for "protecting" the caravans carrying the incense from S Arabia to the Mediterranean coast. They also practiced agriculture, and cultivated wheat to a small extent; but rainfall is very scanty in that area. They grew vines and olives near those regions watered by natural springs. Another source of income came from copper mined in the Arabah. Their religion seems to have been polytheistic. Among the deities that can be traced from the names of their kings are Qos and Hadad.

The Edomites reached the height of their prosperity when the great empires of the past were weakened by the onset of the Aegean invasion and enjoyed an Indian summer between the 12th and the 10th cen. B.C. During

The Umm el Biyara or acropolis of Petra.

the 13th cen. the Edomites had expanded their territory to include the mountains and forests of Transjordan. To protect their eastern border from raids from the desert dwellers, they erected a series of fortresses close enough to one another to communicate by fire signals. Nelson Glueck roaming over the sites of their ruined cities has collected a large number of potsherds from this period.

With the rise of David, the Edomites became vassals of the kingdom of Israel. It was probably David who destroyed fortresses of the Edomites on their western frontier W of the Arabah, as in the case of two 11th cen. B.C. forts near Jebel Usdum, the "Mount of Sodom." They remained in that state during the reign of his son Solomon (I Kgs 11:14–17), who built the port of Ezion-geber (modern Tell el-Kheleifeh near the present port of Aqabah), in the heart of Edomite territory (I Kgs 9:26). Solomon also opened up a number of mines and constructed a large smelting industry which has been studied by Jewish archaeologists in recent years.

On the death of Solomon and the division of the kingdom of Israel, the Edomites regained their independence. However, with the rise of the Assyrian Empire in the 9th cen. the Edomites began paying tribute to Assyria, and became involved in the numerous revolts against Assyrian rule that were instigated by Egypt. The lot of the Edomites was, however, a harder one than that of their neighbors, as they often found themselves paying tribute to Assyria on the one hand, and to the kingdom of Judah on the other.

A revolt against Judah appears to have taken place sometime during the 9th cen. B.C., but this was put down by Amaziah with great severity (II Kgs 14:7); Amaziah slew many Edomites by throwing them down from the high rock bastion within Petra (II Chr 25:12), now known as Umm el-Biyara. This action greatly weakened the Edomites and they ceased to play a great role in the history of the Near East. Nevertheless, the Edomites stood by rejoicing when Jerusalem was captured by Nebuchadnezzar (Ps 137:7), and the prophets denounced them for ill-treatment of their brother nation Judah (Jer 49:7–22; Ezk 25:12–14). Because of similar callousness on the part of Edom when Jerusalem was plundered in his day, Obadiah had forewarned the house of Esau that judgment would befall them should they ever gloat over Judah again (Ob 10–14).

It must have been soon after this event that the Nabataeans began to dislodge the Edomites from their country and occupied it in their stead. Already in 646 B.C. Ashurbanipal of Assyria had met the Nabataeans (q.v.) on his campaign against the Arabs near the land of Edom (ANET, pp. 297–300). It appears that with the reduction of their number and the loss of the greater part of their territory, the Edomites withdrew to S Palestine which later came to be called Idumea (*q.v.*). There appears to have been no relationship between the Nabataeans and the Edomites or Idumeans. Antipater and his son Herod the Great were both Idumean, and looked upon the Nabataeans as an alien people.

D. C. B.

EDREI (ĕd'rē-ī)

1. A city in the land of Bashan, modern Deraʻa, about 30 miles E of the Jordan. Og, king of Bashan, came out of Edrei, which was built on a bluff overlooking the Yarmuk River and evidently on the S border of his kingdom, to intercept the invading Israelites. He lost the battle and his life, and all his territory was subjugated (Num 21:33–35; Deut 1:4; 3:1).

According to most biblical references, Og apparently used both Edrei and Ashtaroth (*q.v.*) as capitals (Josh 12:4; 13:12, 31). In one passage (Josh 9:10) it is simply stated that he lived in Ashtaroth. That this may be a textual problem is seen by examination of Deut 1:4 which, according to the Heb., could be rendered: "after he had defeated ... Og, king of Bashan, who lived in Ashtaroth, in Edrei." However, the Gr. text (followed by RSV) is in harmony with the passages listed above. It reads: "... who lived in Ashtaroth *and* in Edrei." Ashtaroth was no doubt the main city, and Edrei was a secondary capital.

After the Israelite occupation of Bashan, Edrei was apparently destroyed (Deut 3:1–6) and does not receive further mention in the Bible. However, it was known in Roman sources by the name Adra or Adraene. Eusebius (*Onomasticon* 8:84) mentions it as a well-known city of Arabia, 24 miles from Bosora and six miles from Ashtaroth. Though the ancient tell has only received surface investigation, pottery fragments testify to occupation as ancient as the Early Bronze Age, with a large portion of sherds from the Early Iron Age. Probably in Hellenistic or Roman times a subterranean city with streets, shops, and cisterns was constructed in underlying caves in the basaltic rock (HGHL, p. 576; UBD, p. 287).

2. A town in the tribal inheritance of Naphtali, listed among its fortified towns (Josh 19:37). Several variations are known among the Gr. texts: *Ias(s)eir, Assapei, Edrain, Edraei, et al.* In the list it appears between Kedesh and En-hazor. Its general location may also be inferred from its place in Thutmose III's list of conquered towns (No. 91) where the name is written *'itr'* (ANET, p. 242). There it appears among the towns of northern Galilee such as Abel (-beth-maacah). A possible location for the ancient site is Tell Khureiba, S of Kedesh. However, recent researches have pointed to the tentative suggestion that Edrei be located near the modern Aitaroun.

A. F. R.

EDUCATION

Mesopotamian

Mesopotamian education involved the arduous process of learning cuneiform script. Students generally came from the upper classes of society. On rare occasions girls must have been educated as there is evidence of a few female scribes.

The early schools were probably associated with temples, but the famous school at Mari was located in the palace. Here were found rows of benches together with a collection of writing materials.

This school was called the *e-dubba*, "the house of tablets." The *ummia*, "headmaster," had under him specialized assistants, such as the *dubshar nishid*, "the scribe of counting"; the *dubshar kengira*, "the scribe of Sumerian," etc. Much of the actual supervision lay in the hands of an older student, the *shesh-gal*, "older brother."

Pupils learned various cuneiform signs by copying tablets prepared by the teacher, writing with a stylus on a moist clay tablet. Later they would copy excerpts of literary texts and study mathematics and the division of land. After the 2nd mil. B.C. when Sumerian was no longer a living language, scribes would have to memorize bilingual lists of Sumerian words and their Akkadian equivalents.

Students woke up early in the morning, fearful of being late, and took with them two rolls of bread for lunch. Discipline was severe. One lad in an essay recalls how he received seven canings from seven different staff members for poor writing, for talking without permission, etc. More severe punishment involved being locked up for two months.

Egyptian

Egyptian education prepared a scribal class of civil servants. Students from humble beginnings were able to succeed to eminent positions by virtue of their education. Moreover it meant, as teachers often reminded their pupils, a life free from taxes, poverty, and physical labor.

Schools were located in temple precincts, such as the Ramesseum. They were supervised by high officials of the departments for which students were training. The child went to school from about four or five to about 16 years of age.

He learned to copy accurately the pictographic hieroglyphs. His first efforts were made on ruled limestone flakes or potsherds. Only later would he advance to writing on papyrus, and at first on palimpsests, i.e., papyrus that had already been used and erased.

He had to learn the specialized vocabulary of his intended profession, including, for example, 96 names of Egyptian cities, 48 different baked meats. If he planned to work with the army, he had to learn the geography of Palestine, the organization of a military campaign, and the distribution of provisions. In the New Kingdom period the scribe also had to learn Semitic, Cretan, and other foreign names.

The boys' lessons lasted for half the day. When noon was announced the children left school "shouting for joy." Lunch consisted of three rolls of bread and a jug of beer.

The Egyptian word for education *sb³jt* comes from the root *sb³*, "to chastise," "to punish." The teacher's motto was: "A youngster's ear is on his back; he only listens to the man who beats him." One student recalls how he was bound in the temple school for three months.

A painted limestone statue of a seated Egyptian scribe holding an open papyrus roll on his knees. LL

In spite of the rewards of a scribal career, there were delinquents. One teacher bemoaned a former pupil: "I am told, you are forsaking writing, and giving yourself up to pleasure. . . . You sit in the house and the girls encircle you. . . . A garland of flowers hangs about your neck, and you drum upon your belly."

Jewish

Jewish education was primarily religious, and until NT times was centered in the home. It was a father's duty to instruct his son about the religious traditions (Ex 12:26–27; Deut 4:9; 6:7).

It was essential that the child should learn to read the Scriptures. Happily the Heb. alphabet with its 22 letters was much easier than the hundreds of cuneiform or hieroglyphic characters of Israel's neighbors. In Isa 28:10, "precept upon precept" is literally, "*ṣ* after *ṣ*, and *q* after *q*," referring to the teaching of the alpha-

bet. In Isa 10:19 we read, "And the rest of the trees of his forest shall be few, that a child may write them." The young man of Jud 8:14 "wrote down" (not as in the KJV, "described") the names of the elders of the city.

Formal schooling away from the home is not attested until the intertestamental era. Ben Sirach (*c*. 180 B.C.) speaks of a "house of learning" (Gr. *oikos paideias* for Heb. *bêth-midrash*). Under Jason (175–171 B.C.), the Hellenizing high priest, a gymnasium was established in Jerusalem (I Macc 1:14; II Macc 4:9; Jos *Ant*. xii.5.1). The gymnasium was the chief educational institution of Hellenism.

Simon ben Shetaḥ (*c*. 75 B.C.) enacted a decree that children should go to school. The decisive development, however, came with the order of Joshua ben Gamala, high priest A.D. 63–65, that every town should have a school for children from the age of six.

According to a statement of Judah ben Tema (2nd cen. A.D.) in *Pirke Aboth* 5:21, the program of studies to be pursued was: (a) the Scriptures at the age of five; (b) the Mishnah — oral traditions — at ten; (c) the coming of age at 13; and (d) the Talmud — commentaries on the Mishnah — at 15. Young men were expected to marry at 18.

Girls were instructed at home, and were often betrothed at the age of 12 or 13. They did attend the synagogues, and some gained a good knowledge of the Scriptures (cf. the OT allusions in Mary's "Magnificat," Lk 1:46–55).

Most parents could not afford to allow their sons to have more than an elementary education. Some rabbis were contemptuous of those who had studied only the Scriptures, regarding them as ignorant *'am-hā'ārets*, "people of the earth" (cf. Jn 7:15; Acts 4:13). Those studying to become rabbis continued their education at the academy in Jerusalem, and were ordained at about 22.

Elementary classes met in the synagogues, with the *ḥazzan*, or attendant in charge of the scrolls, as the teacher. The teacher had to be a married man; no women were allowed to teach (cf. I Tim 2:12).

Children of various ages would sit on the floor before the teacher. The child would be taught to read the Scriptures aloud, beginning from Leviticus. He would proceed through most of the Scriptures, though some of the Hagiographa, e.g., the Song of Solomon, would not be taught to the immature student.

The stress was upon memory, and the method was repetition. One Mishnah teacher was said to have repeated the same lesson 400 times! Flogging was used with recalcitrant students. The Mishnah did not hold the teacher responsible if the student died from flogging. The Heb. word for education, *mûsār*, comes from the root *ysr*, "to chasten, to discipline."

The young boy's schooling began at daybreak and often continued until sundown. Some have questioned whether he took time

The "school" at Qumran.

out for a noon meal! School was shortened during the hot months of July and August to four hours. The day before the Sabbath was a half day, and there were holidays on religious festivals.

The academy at Jerusalem for prospective rabbis was distinguished by such teachers as Hillel and Shammai (1st cen. B.C.). Here Paul studied at the feet of Hillel's illustrious grandson, Gamaliel (Acts 22:3). Gamaliel was one of the few rabbis to permit students to study Gr. learning.

The rabbis, as a rule, did not receive recompense for their teaching, but supported themselves by working as millers, shoemakers, tailors, potters, etc. (cf. Acts 18:3). In fact, it was the duty of every father to teach his son a trade.

Greek

Gr. education or *paideia* (in the NT the word came to have the sense of "chastisement" in such passages as Heb 12:5, 7, 8, 11) was at first largely aristocratic and athletic. After about 450 B.C. the Sophists who taught rhetoric for pay revolutionized education. In the 4th cen. B.C. the great philosophic schools of Plato and Aristotle were established in two gymnasiums in the suburbs of Athens, the academy and the lyceum.

In the Hellenistic period the establishment of gymnasiums in every city founded by the Greeks in the Near East served as the primary means of preserving the Hellenic tradition and of assimilating non-Hellenes into Hellenic society.

Spartan education was a phenomenon by itself. Unlike the situation in other cities, education in Sparta was state sponsored. Girls received athletic training to make them robust mothers. At the age of seven boys were separated from their homes to live in barracks, to be subjected to a strict discipline intended to make them tough and obedient soldiers. Spartans were taught only the rudiments of reading and

writing, and were considered uneducated by Athenians.

In Athens girls were taught the domestic arts at home. Boys went to school at seven. It was a truism that richer children went to school earlier and left later than poorer children.

Most families would have a *paidagōgos*, usually an elderly slave, who carried the boy's equipment, accompanied him to school, and quizzed him on his lessons. He was a combination of "nurse, footman, chaperon, and tutor" (cf. I Cor 4:15; Gal 3:24-25).

Gr. education equally stressed *gymnasia* (I Tim 4:8) for the body and "music"—a term which included literature—for the soul. The former instruction would be conducted in private *palaistras*, or "wrestling arenas," under *paidotribes*, literally, "boy-rubbers" from the practice of rubbing the body with oil and dust before the exercises. Running and hurling the javelin would be practiced in the public gymnasiums. The latter also contained halls where teachers, such as Socrates, would lecture.

Every young boy would be taught to sing and to play the lyre. He would learn the *stoichea*, i.e., the ABC's or rudiments (cf. Heb 5:12). His main text would be Homer, and secondarily, the dramatists and lyric poets.

The pupil went to school at daybreak, accompanied by his pedagogue who carried a lamp on dark winter mornings. Schools held from 60 to 120 students. The pupils sat on benches with their waxed writing tablets on their knees. The teacher sat on a chair on a platform. Pedagogues usually sat in the class also. From illustrations on pottery we see that the children brought their pet cats, dogs, and even leopards!

From the Mime of Herondas (3rd cen. B.C.) we can learn what happened to truant boys. A mother complains that her son would rather play knucklebones than go to school. He is not able to spell from dictation, and can read only with hesitation. When he is scolded he runs away to his grandmother. She therefore has the teacher whip her son until his hide is as mottled as a water snake.

When the boy reached the age of 18 and became of age, he was at last freed from the restrictive care of his pedagogue. From 18 to 20, Athenian youths, called *ephebes* during this period, underwent a compulsory, state-sponsored course of military and athletic training. In Hellenistic times the graduates of the ephebic training formed the upper class of Hellenized citizens. In Roman times the institution of ephebes at Athens formed the basis for the university there.

Roman

Even before Greece became a Roman province in 146 B.C. her cultural influence was felt at Rome. Cato the Elder (234-149 B.C.), who opposed Gr. learning, is said to have learned Gr. at the end of his life.

The Gymnasium at Salamis, Cyprus. The Palestra or wrestling area was located in the rectangle surrounded by the columns. HFV

The Romans copied the Greeks in using pedagogues for their children, often employing Gr. slaves. The great Cicero (106–43 B.C.) was as well-versed in Gr. as in Latin, having been educated at Rhodes (as were also Caesar and Antony) and at Athens. Quintilian (A.D. 40–118), the great authority on Roman education, held that Roman children should be taught Gr. before Latin. The satirist Martial (A.D. 40–104) and his colleague Juvenal complained that the women even made love in Gr.!

The pragmatic Roman outlook introduced some striking differences. Mathematics, geometry, and music were taught only insofar as they had practical applications. Rhetoric, not philosophy, was the subject that ranked supreme in higher studies. The Romans had little liking for the nudity of Gr. athletics. More to their taste were the horse races of the hippodrome and the gladiatorial games of the colosseum.

Girls attended the elementary schools with boys. Beyond that, some women were able to get such a knowledge of literature on their own that Juvenal complained: "How I hate them. Women who always go back to the pages of Palaemon's grammar, keeping all of the rules, and are pedants enough to be quoting verses I never heard."

Schools were sometimes held in a *pergula*, or "shed," in front of a house separated from the public by a thin partition. Students would sit on benches, while the teacher sat on a chair. For writing they began with waxed tablets; later they would use papyrus or even the parchment of a worthless manuscript. For arithmetic the pupil would use an abacus with *calculi*, pebbles.

The children attended the elementary school, which was called *ludus*, or "play," from the age of seven to ten or eleven. The elementary teacher was known as the *ludi magister*. Parents demanded much from him but paid him little, and at times only at the order of the courts. It was his task to teach the three R's. For the teaching of reading, texts with Aesop's fables were popular.

School began early—too early for Martial, who complained that the scoldings of the teacher kept him from getting his sleep. Hurrying off to school without breakfast, the lad would buy a little cake as he passed a baker's shop. Upon arriving he would say, "Good-morning, everybody. Let me have my place. Squeeze up a bit." After his morning's lesson he went home for a lunch of white bread, olives, dry figs, and nuts. He then returned to school, where the master upon examining his copy said, "You deserve to be whipped! All right, I'll let you off this time. . . ."

Discipline was a synonym for education. The phrase *manum subducere ferulae*, "to withdraw the hand from the rod," meant to leave school. Quintilian protested against the universal practice of flogging. He felt that praise, the spirit of competition, and even of play were better incentives than fear.

The boys would have the summer off from July to October and extensive holidays in December and in March. Every eighth day, which was a market day, was also a holiday. This was not enough for some, who pretended illness, rubbing their eyes with olive oil or taking cumin to make themselves pale in order to play hooky.

From the age of 12 to 15 or 16 when the young Roman became of age and donned his white *toga virilis,* he would attend the secondary or grammar school. This was called the *ludus litterarius,* and the teacher was called the *litteratus* or *grammaticus.* The main subjects were technical grammar and literature, primarily Homer and other Gr. texts. It was not until 25 B.C. that Latin texts, such as Virgil and Cicero, were also introduced.

Beyond grammar school until the age of 18 or 20, the young men received training in rhetoric. As Rome was transformed from a republic to an empire with the consequent restriction of political liberties, training in rhetoric became more and more artificial. Students were asked to declaim on either *suasoria,* which proposed some action, such as "Should Agamemnon sacrifice his daughter?" or on *controversia,* which dealt with some far-fetched case involving a conflict of laws.

Various figures of speech were taught. Paul uses about 30 different rhetorical figures in his writing. F. W. Farrar suggests that he may therefore have received some rudimentary training in rhetoric at Tarsus. On the other hand, the paucity of his classical allusions (Acts 17:28; I Cor 15:33; Tit 1:12) and the quality of his Gr. show that he did not receive very advanced classical training at that famed center of learning. He was probably sent to Jerusalem before he came of age at 13. Some scholars have argued that the word *anatethrammenos,* "brought up," in Acts 22:3, places Paul in Jerusalem at an even earlier age.

Whatever his training may have been, Paul forswears (I Cor 2:1) the use of the elaborate and pompous rhetorical language so commonly used by orators of his day to gain applause (e.g., Tertullus, Acts 24:1-8). Even Roman writers were disgusted. Petronius, a contemporary of Paul's, wrote: "No one would mind this claptrap if only it put our students on the road to real eloquence.... Action or language, it's all the same: great sticky honeyballs of phrases, every sentence looking as though it had been plopped and rolled in poppyseed and sesame."

See Children; Family; School; Schools. Hebrew; Teach.

Bibliography—General. W. Barclay, *Educational Ideals in the Ancient World,* London: Collins, 1959. Georg Bertram, *"Paideuō,* etc.," TDNT, V, 596-625. E. B. Castle, *Ancient Education and Today,* Baltimore: Penguin, 1964. H. I. Marrou, *A History of Education in Antiquity,* New York: New American Library, 1964. Karl H. Rengstorf, *"Didaskō,* etc.," TDNT, II, 135-165. W. A. Smith, *Ancient Education,* New York: Philosophical Library, 1955.

Mesopotamian. Cyril J. Gadd, *Teachers and Students in the Oldest Schools,* London: Univ. of London, 1956. Samuel N. Kramer, "Schooldays," *Journal of the American Oriental Society,* LXIX (1949), 199-215; *The Sumerians,* Chicago: Univ. of Chicago, 1963, Chap. 5.

Egyptian. Adolf Erman, *Life in Ancient Egypt,* New York: Macmillan, 1894, Chap. 14; *The Ancient Egyptians,* New York: Harper & Row, 1966, pp. 54-85, 189-242. T. Säve-Söderbergh, *Pharaohs and Mortals,* Indianapolis: Bobbs-Merrill, 1958, pp. 195-205.

Jewish. Nathan Drazin, *History of Jewish Education,* Baltimore: Johns Hopkins, 1940. Eliezer Ebner, *Elementary Education in Ancient Israel During the Tannaitic Period,* New York: Bloch, 1956. Nathan Morris, *The Jewish School,* London: Eyre & Spottiswoode, 1937. Fletcher H. Swift, *Education in Ancient Israel,* Chicago: Open Court, 1919.

Greek. F. A. G. Beck, *Greek Education, 450-350 B.C.,* London: Methuen, 1964. W. W. Capes, *University Life in Ancient Athens,* New York: Stechert, 1922. C. A. Forbes, *Greek Physical Education,* New York: Century, 1929. Kenneth J. Freeman, *Schools of Hellas,* London: Macmillan, 1922. E. Norman Gardiner, *Athletics of the Ancient World,* Oxford: Clarendon, 1955, Chap. 6. Moses Hadas, *Hellenistic Culture,* New York: Columbia Univ., 1959, Chap. 6. W. Jaeger, *Paideia,* 3 vols., Oxford: Blackwell, 1936-45. H. Michell, *Sparta,* Cambridge: Cambridge Univ., 1964, Chap. 6. Paul Monroe, ed., *Source Book of the History of Education for the Greek and Roman Period,* New York: Macmillan, 1910. W. W. Tarn, *Hellenistic Civilization,* London: Edward Arnold, 1959, Chap. 8. John W. H. Walden, *The Universities of Ancient Greece,* New York: Scribner's, 1912.

Roman. Jerome Carcopino, *Daily Life in Ancient Rome,* New Haven: Yale Univ., 1960, Chap. 5. Donald L. Clark, *Rhetoric in Graeco-Roman Education,* New York: Columbia Univ., 1957. George Clarke, *The Education of Children at Rome,* New York: Macmillan, 1896. A Gwynn, *Roman Education from Cicero to Quintilian,* Oxford: Clarendon Press, 1926. Jack Lindsay, *Daily Life in Roman Egypt,* London: Frederick Müller, 1963, Chap. 5.

E. M. Y.

EFFECTUAL CALLING *See* Call.

EGGS. *See* Food.

EGLAH (ĕg'lă). A wife of David and mother of Ithream, David's son who was born in Hebron (II Sam 3:5; I Chr 3:3). Some Jewish tradition has identified her with Michal, daughter of Saul.

EGLAIM. *See* En-eglaim.

EGLON (ĕg'lŏn)

1. The king of Moab, who was noted for his obesity. In league with the Ammonites and Amalekites, he subdued Israel as a divine pun-

THE NILE
VALLEY

= CATARACTS

0   100   200   300

SCALE OF MILES

ALEXANDRIA   PORT-SAID

CAIRO

FAYUM

MINYA

ASYUT   QENA

LUXOR

ASWAN

WADI-HALFA

RED SEA

EGYPT

THE SUDAN

KHARTOUM

LAKE TANA

FASHODA (KODOK)

LAKE RUDOLF

LAKE ALBERT

VICTORIA LAKE

ishment for their sins (Jud 3:12–14), occupying the city of palms, Jericho. Subject to him for 18 years, the Israelites paid tribute. After Ehud, the second deliverer in the book of Judges, had assassinated Eglon (Jud 3:15–25), Ehud roused and led the people of Israel to victory against Moab (vv. 26–30). *See* Ehud.

2. A Canaanite royal city which became part of the inheritance of Judah after the conquest of Palestine under Joshua (Josh 15:39). After the defeat of Ai and the peaceful capitulation of Gibeon, Debir, the king of Eglon, entered into a league with kings of four other cities to make war against Gibeon. This Amorite coalition was routed at the battle W of Gibeon by the Israelites (Josh 10:5–10). The five kings were captured and executed (10:22–26). Joshua then marched on the cities of the league, capturing and destroying them, including Eglon (10:34–35).

Eglon may be identified most likely with Tell el-Hesi, seven miles SW of Lachish. Excavating in 1890–93, Petrie followed by Bliss first applied the stratigraphic method at this site. A clay tablet, scarab seals, and a stamped jar handle prove the city was inhabited in Joshua's time.

R. B. D.

EGYPT (ē'jĭpt).

Name

The name Egypt is derived from the Gr. *aigyptos,* generally believed to be a corruption of the Egyptian *Ḥt-k3-ptḥ,* "the house of Ptah," a name given to the ancient city of Memphis, which was the oldest capital of united Egypt. The Heb. name for Egypt was *Miṣrayim,* a term whose form and meaning are uncertain. Often it is taken as a dual form and as such a reflection of the Egyptian "the Two Lands," a common Egyptian name for the country, based on its origin in the union of Upper and Lower Egypt. The Egyptians had a number of names for their land. A geographical designation, for example, made Egypt *Kemet,* "the Black Land," which contrasted the dark alluvial soil of the valley and the reddish hues of the surrounding desert.

Geography

Though at times in its ancient history the Egyptian Empire extended as far S as the Sixth Cataract of the Nile or included Palestine and Syria to the NE as far as the Euphrates River, Egypt proper was limited to NE Africa. Its N boundary was the Mediterranean Sea; to the E was the Red Sea; the S border was regarded as Aswan and the island of Elephantine; to the W, Egyptian territory reached into the Libyan Desert and took in the oases prominent in that area.

In reality the land of Egypt was even more restricted. Egypt was essentially an agricultural country and the arable and habitable land was

Truly "Egypt is the Nile." Beyond the alluvium laid down by the annual Nile flood stretches desert as far as the eye can see.
HFV

limited to the Nile Valley, a narrow strip of extremely fertile soil, varying from one to 12 miles in width. Since the distance from Cairo to Aswan is nearly 600 miles, it is apparent that the primary dimension of Egypt was length and that the dominant feature of Egyptian geography was the Nile.

It is practically impossible to exaggerate the importance of the Nile River to Egypt, for without its waters the whole country would be barren desert waste. The ancients were vitally aware of the role of the river; and in later times Hecateus, echoed by Herodotus, declared that Egypt was "the gift of the Nile" (see Nile). The river scoured out the valley, freighted down the alluvium, and annually watered the land by its life-giving flood. The country is almost rainless. Several inches of rain fall each year along the Mediterranean coast and Cairo has an occasional winter shower, but in Upper Egypt rain is a phenomenon. The annual inundation of the river, by saturating the ground, adding new soil, and bringing some organic material as fertilizer, has been the basis for the agriculture which has typified Egypt. Irrigation and water control were important, and even today the economy of the land centers on the river.

Just N of Cairo the Delta spreads out in characteristic shape, about 125 miles long and 115 miles wide. It was in the E part of this area, along the Wadi Tumilat, that the land of Goshen was located.

These features, the long tube of the river and the Delta, were the primary geographic basis for the division of the country into Upper and Lower Egypt (these terms based on altitude), though the latter consisted of the Delta plus a short part of the valley to the S. This division antedated the historic period and was never forgotten, for the name "the Two Lands" remained a popular name for Egypt and in many

other traditional ways the bipartite origin of the country was remembered. For purposes of administration, the two areas were early divided into smaller parts, each with its distinctive name and emblem. In Gr. times these units were called nomes, with 20 of them in Lower Egypt and 22 in its S counterpart.

Geography contributed much to the course of the development of Egypt as a nation and as a center of culture. Though the dimensions of the land were a handicap to stable government and unified culture, the river was a good means of transportation and communication and served as a unifying and homogenizing factor. Over its long history Egypt lived in comparative security and stability, with opportunity to develop internally and to engage in the exchange of commodities and ideas with other lands.

By its unique setting the country was strikingly protected from periodic wholesale invasion. The valley was hemmed in by forbidding deserts of barren sand and jumbled rock cliffs. To the W lay the Libyan Desert and beyond that the vast Sahara; to the E was the Sinai Desert and farther S along the Red Sea the Nubian Desert. To the S the cataracts hindered foreign encroachment via the water route, and the addition of forts at strategic points made the S approach easily defended. The most vulnerable sections were the sides of the Delta, particularly near the sea. On the NW the Libyans sometimes posed a threat but generally were held in check by force of arms. The greatest danger lay in the NE, though Sinai formed a kind of buffer and the march along the desert coast was a tremendous feat for any army. In Middle Kingdom times this frontier was guarded by forts and checkpoints, for the kings were well aware of danger from this quarter. From this direction the infrequent invasions most characteristically came: Asiatics, Hyksos, Sea Peoples, Assyrians, Babylonians, Persians, Greeks.

Geography and climate were friendly to the Egyptians. Though the temperature range is quite great, it does not get down to freezing and the heat usually moderates at evening. Even the winds favored the land, for the prevailing N wind propelled sailboats on their upstream journey and provided refreshing coolness in houses oriented to receive the "sweet breezes of the north."

Its environment has made Egypt an outstanding area for the practice of archaeology. The presence of stone for building and art encouraged monumental architecture and statuary of both magnificent proportions and excellent finish. The absence of rain and frost preserved the monuments from these destructive elements, while the winds drifted in dry sand to cover them from sun and atmosphere, so that even fragile papyrus fragments and painted mud plaster are kept intact and fresh in appearance.

Religion

The study of Egyptian religion is exceedingly complex, for (1) the mass of source material is so great as to be unwieldy; (2) these materials vary greatly as to their nature, ranging from papyrus documents to the architecture and dec-

oration of vast temple complexes; (3) the sources cover a tremendous span of time; (4) many of the records are very heterogeneous, for the scribes uncritically combined writings from different places and times.

The history of religion in Egypt has been given considerable attention. Some scholars have thought that there is evidence of a primitive monotheism in Egypt, though there was a great multiplicity of local gods, whose fortunes often varied with political history. With the union of the two lands, the king was identified with Horus, the falcon-god of Upper Egypt. Other divinities of importance included Ptah, the god of Memphis; Re, the sun-god of Heliopolis, who gained prominence at the time of the Fifth Dynasty; Amon-Re, the Theban god of empire; Osiris and Isis, later adopted by the mystery religions of Greece and Rome; Set, the enemy of Osiris and Horus; Hathor, the cow-goddess; Khnum, the god of Elephantine; Thoth, the god of writing and wisdom. Often the gods were grouped into triads or enneads.

Much has been written of the religious innovations of Amenhotep IV (Akhenaton), who attempted to advance the sun disc, Aton, as the sole or leading divinity. Once widely heralded as a kind of monotheism, the religion of Akhenaton has in recent times been more critically evaluated. Certainly the movement had political

Egyptian gods in bronze encrusted with gold and silver; Osiris left and Ptah right. LM

overtones; much of its content was not original and its practice was very limited. With the death of Akhenaton, Atonism soon disappeared and the priests of Amon regained their supremacy.

Egyptian religion had high ethical concepts, but much of the literature is concerned only with life after death and it is evident from the innovations of various periods that no final answers were found.

The religious life of Egypt made no contribution to the religion of the Bible, but it did affect the religious history of Israel, for the gods of Egypt were a source of serious apostasy (Ezk 20:5-9; 23:3, 8, 19-21, 27). The golden calf made at Mount Sinai and the later calf worship of Jeroboam I are concrete examples of this idolatry.

The step pyramid and its temple. HFV

History

For some periods the chronology of Egypt is well established, but for others, such as the disturbed times called the "Intermediate Periods," considerably less is known. Egypt is fortunate, however, in the possession of fairly abundant materials for chronological study. From earlier historical times there is the Palermo Stone, which gives an abbreviated list of rulers and significant events down to the Fifth Dynasty. The Turin Papyrus extends the list of kings, but the document is incomplete and suffered irreparable damage during shipment to the Turin Museum. Other king lists are known from Sakkarah, Abydos, and Karnak. In addition, many historical references are dated in terms of the regnal year of the king. Records sometimes were cross-dated by the Sothic Cycle, a period of 1,460 years determined by the correspondence between the beginning of the yearly inundation and the heliacal rising of the Dog Star (Sothis, Sirius).

The cultures into which the predynastic period in Egypt is divided are named after "type-sites," at which a particular culture was first or most typically found by archaeologists. Consequently there are names such as Merimdian, Tasian, Badarian, Gerzean, etc. It is not possible to assign absolute dates to these cultures, though carbon 14 and similar tests may be used for approximate dating. Relative dates may be given on the basis of typology and for some of the periods the sequence is made certain by stratification, though excavated stratified sites are rare in Egypt. Sir Flinders Petrie, "the father of Egyptology," devised a system of sequence dating for Egyptian prehistory; this has been useful but now needs revision.

In the 3rd cen. B.C. an Egyptian priest-historian named Manetho divided the kings of Egypt into 30 dynasties, from the unification of the land until the conquest by Alexander the Great. Though little of his writing has come down to us, and that only as preserved by other writers, his system has been a convenience used by historians until the very present. The dynasties have been grouped into quite standard periods, which serve as useful labels in identification and discussion. Such an outline is presented here, with brief descriptions.

Protodynastic (Dynasties I-II; 3100-2700 B.C.). The traditional list of Manetho gives Menes as the first king of the Two Lands. Coming from Thinis in the S, he effected the union of Upper and Lower Egypt and set up his capital at "the White Wall," the city later known as Memphis. Some scholars believe that he is to be identified with Aha and/or Narmer. Large royal tombs of this period have been found at Sakkarah and Abydos.

Old Kingdom (OK, Dynasties III-VI; 2700-2200 B.C.). This period, the age of the great pyramid-builders, was one of the outstanding epochs of Egyptian history. Its architectural achievements are particularly famous; but equally noteworthy are its accomplishments in medicine, literature, and art. The proverbs of Ptahhotep, a vizier of Dynasty V, have been preserved and one of the best-known of the medical papyri, the Edwin Smith Surgical Papyrus, had its origins in the OK (*see* Diseases). The canons of Egyptian art were established, along with other cultural traditions which remained basically unchanged throughout Egyptian history.

The political dogma of this time pictured the king as an absolute ruler, aloof, austere, remote, unmoved by the vicissitudes of life and of time. The renowned statue of Khafre in the Cairo Museum conveys this impression of the king as a divinity incarnate but unapproachable, a most effective work of art.

Dynasty III saw the building of the step pyramid of Djoser at Sakkarah. Imhotep, the architect of this complex, was later regarded by the Greeks as identical with their god of medicine. Other pyramids were constructed during this period, but the largest of them still stand at Giza, the work of three kings of the Fourth Dynasty, Khufu, Khafre, and Menkaure, known to the Greek world as Cheops, Chephren, and Mycerinus.

Kings of the last two dynasties again had their pyramids at Sakkarah; from these tombs come the religious spells known as the Pyramid Texts. Fiscal difficulties, international problems, and related factors brought about the fall of the OK.

First Disintegration or First Intermediate Period (Dynasties VII–XI; 2200–2050 B.C.). This period was marked by political and social upheaval, confusion, and uncertainty. The breakdown of old values produced a pessimism reflected in the literature as men groped for meaning in life. Outstanding works include the Dialogue of a Man Weary of Life, the Song of Harper, and the writing of Ipuwer. Dynasties VII(?)–VIII had their capital at Memphis; IX–X, at Herakleopolis; XI, at Thebes.

Eventually the political situation stabilized when Mentuhotep II of Dynasty XI (*c.* 2060–2010 B.C.) crushed the rival king at Herakleopolis and another prosperous era eventuated with the *Middle Kingdom* (MK, Dynasty XI–XII; 2050–1786 B.C.). Many Egyptologists regard this as the greatest period of ancient Egypt. Art and architecture again flourished. This was the classical period of the Egyptian language and from the MK come the Story of the Eloquent Peasant, the adventures of the noble Sinuhe, and in religious literature the Coffin Texts. All the kings of Dynasty XII were named either Amenemhet or Senusert (Sesostris). The capital was located at It-towy near Lisht, not far from the Fayum.

This was an age of engineering projects, such as attempts to control the Nile waters and of imperialistic expansion. To the S, Nubia was occupied and protected by forts and to the NE there was increased activity in Sinai. During

Amenemhet III. LL

the dark times of disintegration the nobles had gained power, so that the early MK was a kind of feudal monarchy. About the middle of his reign Senusert III (1878–1843 B.C.) reduced the status of the provincial nobles and administered the entire country through the office of the vizier. How this was achieved is not revealed in the Egyptian records, but Joseph's purchase of the land for the pharaoh during the famine (Gen 47:20) supplies a possible explanation. The king was represented in statuary as a care-worn ruler, the concerned but efficient "shepherd" of the people. An increasing emphasis was placed on *ma'at*, "justice, right, the proper order of things."

The Second Intermediate Period (Dynasties XIII–XVII; 1786–1580 B.C.). Dynasties XIII–XIV were of minor importance; Dynasties XV–XVI were the Hyksos rulers, of whom later Egyptians spoke with contempt. The Hyksos, "rulers of foreign countries," became quite Egyptianized. Some scholars feel that they were able administrators and that Egyptian references to them were very biased. They introduced many elements into Egyptian culture including better weapons, which the native Egyptians adopted and used against them. Dynasty XVII, a local Theban house, initiated the fight to expel the Hyksos. The effort was successfully concluded by Ahmose, the first king of Dynasty XVIII. *See* Hyksos.

The great pyramid. Herbert Lockyer, Jr.

The New Kingdom or Empire (Dynasties XVIII-XX; 1580-1090 B.C.) was the high point of Egyptian territorial expansion, an age of conquest and material prosperity. The royal ideal now stressed the physical prowess of the divine king and made him the insuperable strong man and skilled athlete. Among the prominent rulers of this period the following may be singled out: (Dynasty XVIII) Hatshepsut, the woman-king, possibly the princess who found the infant Moses (Ex 2:5-10), is best known for her beautiful mortuary temple at Deir el-Bahri, with its fine reliefs showing her birth legend and a voyage to Punt. Thutmose III (1504-1450 B.C.) was the able military campaigner, whose 17 expeditions into Palestine-Syria really made the empire. According to the early date of the Exodus (*c.* 1445 B.C.), he would be the pharaoh of the oppression (Ex 2:15, 23; *see* Exodus, The); and his son Amenhotep II would then be the pharaoh of the Exodus (Ex 5 – 14). Amenhotep III, justly nicknamed "the Magnificent," noted for his luxurious living, and Amenhotep IV (Akhenaton), together were largely responsible for the temporary loss of the Asiatic empire through their rejection of pleas for help from that area (*see* Amarna Letters).

In Dynasty XIX, Seti I and Ramses II (1304-1234 B.C.) renewed Egyptian activity in the Asiatic provinces. According to the late date of the Exodus these two kings were the probable pharaohs of the oppression and the Exodus, respectively. The latter was famous also for his building achievements; his monuments and inscriptions mark him as a supreme egoist. His son Merenptah claimed to have destroyed Israel on a campaign to Palestine, the first extrabiblical mention of Israel.

Ramses III, the outstanding ruler of Dynasty XX, saved Egypt from an invasion of the Sea Peoples (including Philistines) and built his mortuary temple at Medinet Habu. The Empire Period was an age of cosmopolitanism, a characteristic which culminated in the collapse of the empire. Foreign influences sapped the strength of cultural features which were distinctively Egyptian; even the army became a mercenary force composed of foreigners.

The Post-Empire Period or Period of Decline (Dynasties XXI-XXX; 1090-331 B.C.) saw Egypt under foreign domination several times. In the Libyan Dynasty (XXII) Sheshonk (the biblical Shishak) successfully invaded Palestine (926 B.C.). Dynasty XXV was Kushite or Ethiopian, but these people were steeped in Egyptian tradition and were more Egyptian than the Egyptians of that time.

In spite of Assyrian invasions there was a resurgence of native energy in the *Saite Period* (Dynasty XXVI; 663-525 B.C.), but it was coupled with a backward look which generally hindered progress. Neco II (610-595 B.C.) tried unsuccessfully to dig a canal from the Nile to the Red Sea, but did send Phoenician ships which circumnavigated all of Africa.

A statue of Queen Hatshepsut from Deir el-Bahri. LL

In 525 B.C. Egypt came under Persian domination (Dynasties XXVII-XXX; 525-331 B.C.). In 331 Alexander the Great brought the native dynasties to an end; after his death (323 B.C.) Egypt was ruled by the Ptolemies until it became a province of Rome in 31 B.C.

Egypt and the Bible

Egypt appears in the Bible from Genesis to Revelation. The majority of the references are of an historic or prophetic nature and are found mostly in the OT. Egypt (Mizraim) is first mentioned in Gen 10:6, where the name appears in the Table of Nations as a son of Ham. It figures in the patriarchal narratives as a place of refuge for Abram at a time when famine swept through Palestine. Crop failure was rare in Egypt and its fertile soil produced both regularly and abundantly. It was natural for Egypt to play the role of breadbasket, and in Roman times large quantities of wheat were exported to Italy.

The presence of Asiatics in Egypt at about the time of Abram is illustrated by a frequently reproduced wall painting from the tomb of Khnumhotep II at Beni Hasan. Here some 37 Asiatics are shown bringing trade goods to Middle Egypt. Abraham's fears concerning his life and the seizure of Sarai for the king's harem were fulfilled in part. The varied literature from ancient Egypt provides no clear-cut parallels to this incident. Though the Tale of Two Brothers is sometimes cited in this respect, a reading of that story reveals that the circumstances were quite different. The wife of Bata wanted her husband killed so that she could be a member of Pharaoh's household.

The mention of camels in Egypt (Gen 12:16) early in the 2nd mil. B.C. is at present an unsolved problem, for there is no word for camel in hieroglyphic and the animal is not represented in the tomb scenes; further evidence is awaited. *See* Animals, I.5.

Since the Joseph narrative and the early part of Exodus are located in Egypt, the closest Egyptian-biblical relationships are found in these sections. Egyptian words and names, cultural practices, geographical features, and other aspects of Egyptian life appear in profusion. Some elements of Egyptian background include: Joseph's coat (Gen 37) of the style worn by Canaanite nobles bringing tribute to the pharaoh depicted in tomb paintings; the description of Potiphar as an Egyptian (Gen 39); the episode of the attempted seduction by Potiphar's wife, an account which has numerous parallels with the Tale of Two Brothers and its familiar sordid theme (Gen 39); the offices of royal butler and baker, the role of dreams in Egypt, the use of grapes (Gen 40); the raising of cattle, the relationship of cattle and the Nile, the production of grain (Gen 41); shaving (41:14); the destructive force of the east wind (41:27); the levying and collecting of taxes (41:34); the presentation of gold ornaments as an award for meritorious service (41:42); the use of chariots by royalty and nobility (41:42); the religious figure of the priest of On (Heliopolis) (41:45); divination (44:4–5); the location of the land of Goshen (Gen 45 ff.); embalming, mumification, and funerary ritual (Gen 50).

Ex 1 mentions the making of bricks, agricultural work, forced labor, and obstetrical methods. The description of the Nile in Ex 2 (babyhood of Moses) and Ex 7 (the first plague) is accurate and interesting. Moses' training in all the learning of the Egyptians (Acts 7:22) was not unusual, for children of W Semite nobles and officials were often sent to Egypt to be educated in court circles. The signs and the ten great plagues (*see* Plague) contain many evidences of a close acquaintance with Egypt, which testifies to the Mosaic authorship of the account. Familiarity with the excellence of Egyptian craftsmanship in gold and silver may be related to the Israelite demand for jewelry in Ex 11:2. The scene of the Egyptian chariotry pursuing the fleeing Israelites (14:9) reminds

one of the battle reliefs in many Egyptian temples. The despairing attitude of the Israelites reflects their experience of slavehood and their deep respect for the Egyptian military (14:10). The bitter irony of their reproach of Moses, "Is it because there are no graves in Egypt" (14:11, RSV), has considerable force when one realizes that the desert edges of both sides of the Nile virtually constitute one vast extended cemetery from the Delta to Nubia.

Thutmose III. LL

Though the Israelites were successfully delivered from the land of Egypt, they did not soon escape its influence. Even while God was conferring with Moses on Mount Sinai the people on the plain below were worshiping a calf of gold (Ex 32), a form of the cattle worship of Egypt which was a recurring temptation to Israel. The pleasures of Egypt were also recalled; while enduring monotonous rations in the desert, the Israelites recollected the good food they had enjoyed in Egypt—fish, cucumbers, melons, leeks, onions, and garlic (Num 11:5–6).

Having reached Palestine, the Israelites were relatively free from Egyptian interference for

EGYPT

some centuries. A few biblical scholars, however, have suggested a relationship between the oppressions and deliverances in the book of Judges and the periods of weakness and strength in Egypt. During this time the Egyptians were concerned mostly with the Great Road, the artery of commerce that lay in the maritime plain of Palestine (*see* Palestine II.B.1).

The decline of Egyptian power *c*. 1100 B.C. is evidenced in the account of the Egyptian representative Wen-Amon, who was treated with little respect on his venture to Phoenicia to obtain cedar wood (ANET, pp. 25-29). This weakness provided an opportunity for the rapid growth of the nation of Israel, particularly under David and Solomon. The first recorded contacts between Israelite and Egyptian rulers come in the time of Solomon, who married the daughter of the Egyptian king. The father-in-law captured and destroyed the city of Gezer and presented it to his daughter as a dowry (I Kgs 9:16). Solomon engaged in trade with Egypt (II Chr 1:16-17). His wisdom surpassed all the wisdom of Egypt (I Kgs 4:30).

Though Egypt had been a place of oppression for Israel, it was often considered a refuge. In Solomon's time it became a haven for political enemies of Solomon and a staging area from which they returned to plague him. Hadad, an Edomite who had fled to Egypt on the occasion of a foray by David into Edom, came back and became an active enemy of Solomon (I Kgs 11:14-20). Jeroboam the son of Nebat went to Egypt to escape Solomon's wrath. When he returned he became the first king of the northern tribes and "made Israel to sin" by his setting up of calf-idols at Bethel and Dan (I Kgs 12:26-33), another possible Egyptian influence on Israelite religion. With the division of the kingdom, Palestine was soon subjected to an Egyptian invasion. Sheshonk (biblical Shishak) sacked the temple of its treasures in the fifth year of Rehoboam (926 B.C.; I Kgs 14:25-26; II Chr 12:1-9).

Egypt continued to play a prominent part in Israelite political life and was overrated by those who saw in her a possible ally against the rising powers of Assyria and, later, Babylonia. Hoshea, the last king of Israel, in vain sent to So (the Delta city of Sais) to Pharaoh Tefnakhte (II Kgs 17:4). Isaiah and Jeremiah, as statesmen-prophets, saw the folly of this course and recognized Egypt under such a leader as Taharka (biblical Tirhakah, II Kgs 19:9) as only a "broken reed" (Isa 36:6; cf. II Kgs 18:21) on which one could not depend for support. Egypt was still much too strong for the military power of Judah, and when Neco II marched to aid the Assyrians in their last struggle against the Babylonians, Josiah, following his anti-Assyrian policy, made a foolhardy attempt against the Egyptians at Megiddo in 609 B.C. and lost his own life (II Kgs 23:29-30; II Chr 35:20-27). Ironically, the Babylonians won and later defeated Neco again at Carchem-

Statue of Ramses II at Luxor Temple. HFV

ish in 605 B.C. Apries (biblical Hophra) is mentioned in a prophecy of Jeremiah (Jer 44:30).

After the capture of Jerusalem by Nebuchadnezzar and the murder of Gedaliah, the Palestinian remnant fled to Egypt in spite of the strong speech of Jeremiah against such a course (Jer 44). In Egypt they scattered to many places. Later records, such as the Aramaic papyri from Elephantine, indicate that even at Egypt's S border there was a group of Jews who had a temple and service and who kept in touch with Palestine. Also in the inter-testamental period the translation of the OT into Greek (the LXX) was accomplished in Egypt (3rd cen. B.C.).

In the NT the references to Egypt are concerned mostly with the OT record of God's dealings with Israel. Egypt was part of the current scene, however, for God directed Joseph to take Jesus and Mary to Egypt to save the Baby's life from the vengeful fury of Herod (Mt 2:13-15; cf. Hos 11:1). Among the foreign Jews who heard the languages and message of Pentecost were those of Egypt (Acts 2:10). Egypt was important in the history of the early church; documents from Egypt bear on both this history and the transmission of the text of the Scriptures.

The final biblical allusion to Egypt is in Rev 11:8, where Jerusalem is called "Sodom and Egypt." This allegorical usage makes Egypt a symbol of evil and of the perishing world-order. Typologists have overworked this aspect of Egypt, forgetting God's use of Egypt to preserve Israel in the time of Joseph (Gen 45:5-9) and His direction of Jacob to go to Egypt (Gen 46:3-4). The prophets uttered many severe predictions against Egypt, but the Lord also gave to Isaiah an oracle concerning Egypt which included the promise that Egypt would finally turn to the Lord and the gracious words of the Lord of hosts, "Blessed be Egypt my people" (see Isa 19:18-25).

C. E. D.

Bibliography. Butrus Abd al-Malik, "Egypt," BW, pp. 207–218. I. E. S. Edwards, *The Pyramids of Egypt*, Baltimore: Penguin, 1961. Ahmed Fakhry, *The Pyramids*, Chicago: Univ. of Chicago Press, 1961. Henri Frankfort, *Ancient Egyptian Religion*, New York: Harper, 1961. Alan Gardiner, *Egypt of the Pharaohs*, Oxford: Clarendon Press, 1961. William C. Hayes, *The Scepter of Egypt*, 2 vols., Cambridge: Harvard Univ. Press, 1953, 1959; "The Middle Kingdom in Egypt," Fasc. 3 (Chap. XX) for rev. ed. of *The Cambridge Ancient History*, Vol. I, Cambridge: Univ. Press, 1964 (and many other similar fascicles on Egypt). Kenneth A. Kitchen, "Egypt," NBD, pp. 337–353, with excellent bibliography. Martin Noth, "Thebes," TAOTS, pp. 21–35. Charles F. Pfeiffer and Howard F. Vos, "Egypt," WHG, pp. 47–93. George Steindorff and K. C. Seele, *When Egypt Ruled the East*, 2nd ed., Chicago: Univ. of Chicago, 1957. John A. Wilson, *The Burden of Egypt*, Chicago: Univ. of Chicago, 1951; "Egypt," IDB, II, 39–66.

EGYPT, RIVER OF. *See* River of Egypt.

EHI (ē'hī). A son of Benjamin (Gen 46:21). This is probably a contraction of the name Ahiram (*q.v.*) or a distortion in the text.

EHUD (ē'hŭd)

1. The son of Gera of the tribe of Benjamin, who was noted for being "a man lefthanded" (Jud 3:15). Ehud was raised up by God as the second deliverer among the judges. Through Ehud's leadership the 18 years of Moabite rule over Israel was ended. This was accomplished by a clever ruse. For the sake of gaining familiarity with Eglon, the king of Moab, and his palace, Ehud joined those who bore to Eglon the usual tribute from Israel. On the homeward trip, Ehud returned alone to Jericho from the sculptured stones ("quarries," Jud 3:19) at Gilgal. Not even Israel knew of his secret mission to Eglon (*q.v.*). He was able to gain a private audience with Eglon by indicating that he had secret information for the king, and was able to slay the Moabite king in his rooftop chamber with his concealed and specially crafted two-edged sword. Due to the ineptness of Eglon's servants, Ehud escaped without detection. The judge then marshaled the Israelites together in the hills of Ephraim and led them in battle against Moab. Ehud's battle strategy was based on the control of the fords of Jordan. Without the leadership of their king, Moab was defeated. In Jud 3:28 Ehud acknowledged the hand of God in this victory. The land then had relative peace for 80 years.

2. The name of a son of Bilhan, and great-grandson of Benjamin (I Chr 7:10), who was renowned as a mighty warrior.

R. B. D.

EKER (ē'kĕr). A post-Exilic descendant of Judah through Hezron and Jerahmeel (I Chr 2:27).

EKRON (ĕk'rŏn). The northernmost of the five main cities of Philistia (Josh 13:3). It was first assigned to Judah (Josh 15:11, 45–46); then to Dan (Josh 19:43) before that tribe moved N, after which it was temporarily taken by Judah (Jud 1:18). It was prominent in all stages of Israel's history, from the time the ark was taken there (I Sam 5:10) until the time of the prophet Zechariah (cf. Zech 9:5, 7). Sennacherib captured Ekron from a group of rebels who had turned its king, Padi, over to Hezekiah, evidently the leader in the opposition to the Assyrians (ANET, pp. 287 f.).

The site is now disputed. Edward Robinson, in the 19th cen., suggested that Ekron be identified with 'Akir, ten miles NE of Ashdod. Others identify it with Khirbet el-Muqenna', six miles SE of 'Akir (BW, p. 219). The latter site was probably the largest Iron Age city in Palestine, a walled town that covered 40 acres (J. Naveh, "Khirbat al-Muqanna'-Ekron," IEJ, VIII [1958], 87–100, 165–170).

EL (ĕl). The generic name for Deity shared by Hebrews (*'el*) and Canaanites, appearing in the cognate form *ilu* in Akkadian, *allah* in Arabic. It is seldom found in the OT except in poetical passages. When it does occur in prose narratives, it is usually in titles, such as El Roi (Gen 16:13, ASV marg.), El Shaddai (Gen 17:1), El Elyon (Gen 14:18); or in descriptive phrases, such as "God, the God of Israel" (Gen 33:20, RSV marg.), or "Yahweh, God of gods" (Josh 22:22, Heb.).

The original meaning of the word is uncertain. Some trace it to the idea "in front" or "first," since the word for "leading ram of the flock" is similar. Others derive it from the same root as the preposition "toward," in the sense of describing the object of all worship. Still others see its meaning in the verb " to tie," thus denoting the one who holds all things together.

Most scholars prefer to identify the essential idea as the one in the idiom "in the power of my hand," literally, "in the *'el* of my hand" (Gen 31:29; also Deut 28:32; Mic 2:1; Prov 3:27; cf. Neh 5:5). God is the all-powerful One, the Almighty (*q.v.*). The only suffix found on this word is the first common singular "my." In the later history of Israel, Elohim (*q.v.*) was usually preferred to El, but this earlier title was retained as a time-honored term of endearment. *See* God, Names of.

In the Ugaritic tablets, El is a proper name, the "high god" of the Canaanites. His position as king of the Canaanite pantheon was evidently usurped by the Amorite deity Ba'al-Hadad in the religious revolution that followed the coming of the Amorites from the Syrian desert plateau *c.* 2000 B.C. *See* God; God, Names and Titles of.

Bibliography. William F. Albright, *Yahweh and the Gods of Canaan*, Garden City: Doubleday, 1968, pp. 119–121, 124–128. Ulf Oldenburg,

The Conflict Between El and Ba⁹al in Canaanite Religion, Leiden: Brill, 1969.

C. T. F.

ELADAH (ĕl'á-dá). A descendant of Ephraim (I Chr 7:20).

ELAH (ē'lá)

1. A prince of an Edomite clan (Gen 36:41; I Chr 1:52).

2. The father of Shimei, one of Solomon's administrative officers (I Kgs 4:18).

3. An Israelite king (*c.* 886–885 B.C.), son of Baasha (I Kgs 16:6, 8, 13–14). He was murdered by his successor Zimri.

4. Father of Hoshea, the last king of Israel (II Kgs 15:30; 17:1; 18:1, 9).

5. A family in the ancestry of Caleb (I Chr 4:15). Possibly this reference, as well as # 1 above, is to the place Elath (*q.v.*).

6. A family in the ancestry of Benjamin living in Jerusalem in post-Exilic times (I Chr 9:8).

ELAH, VALLEY OF (ē'lá). A valley which was the scene of the duel between David and Goliath (I Sam 17). Since the narrative indicates that the two armies confronted one another in strong positions on the heights, the valley is probably Wadi es-Sant, a steep-sided ravine W of Bethlehem, running from the heart of Judah to the Philistine plain.

ELAM (ē'lám) (PERSONS)

1. First son of Shem (Gen 10:22; I Chr 1:17); eponymous father of the Elamite people. *See* Elam (country), Elamites.

2. A chief man of the tribe of Benjamin who lived in Jerusalem (I Chr 8:24).

3. Son of Meshelemiah, a Korahite, one of the porters of the tabernacle in the time of David (I Chr 26:3).

4. The ancestral name of clans participating in the return from Exile (Ezr 2:7 and Neh 7:12; "the other Elam," Ezr 2:31 and Neh 7:34; Ezr 8:7; 10:2, 26).

5. A "chief of the people" (Neh 10:14). Possibly same as 4.

6. A priest and participant in the dedication of the wall of Jerusalem under Nehemiah (Neh 12:42).

ELAM (ē'lám) (COUNTRY). **ELAMITES** (ē'lá-mīts). Elam was located in SW Asia on a plain E of Babylonia and N of the Persian Gulf, watered by the Karun and Kerka Rivers. It corresponded approximately to Khuzistan in modern Iran.

Dating from the late 4th mil. B.C., the known history of the Elamites was one of constant strife and warfare with its more populous neighbors—Sumerians, Babylonians, Assyrians, and finally Persians, by whom the Elamites were ultimately absorbed. They seem, however, to have maintained rather consistently their independence in spite of repeated invasions attempting to gain control of the trade routes to the Iranian plateau.

The long history of this civilization is known through Mesopotamian documents and from inscriptions written by the Elamite kings in their own language. Most of the inscriptions were recovered at Susa, capital city of ancient Elam. In the early part of the 3rd mil. a proto-Elamite cuneiform existed alongside Sumerian cuneiform, but it died out as a result of the conquests of Sargon and the domination of his Akkadian Dynasty (*c.*2360–2180 B.C.). It was during this

Ruins at the ancient Elamite city of Susa as seen from the air. ORINST

period that the Elamite language produced the oldest known state treaty between Naram-Sin (Sargon's grandson) and the Avan Dynasty. Some proto-Elamite and Akkad. bilingual texts have come down to us from Puzur-Shushinak (2280 B.C.), a king of this Avan Dynasty. Later on, the Elamites used the Babylonian cuneiform signs for their language, as witnessed in that key to decipherment, the Behistun inscription written in Babylonian, Elamite, and Old Persian by the Persian king Darius I.

Many changes in Elamite culture took place during the Akkad. (Semitic) rule, for not only their peculiar form of writing but also their distinctive painted pottery disappeared, and the Sumero-Akkad. culture was adopted. Semites from Mesopotamia began to settle in this area in increasing numbers. Thus, while racially and linguistically the Elamites do not appear to have been of Semitic origin, it is probably on account of this Semitic influence that Elam is called a "son" of Shem in the Table of Nations (Gen 10:22; cf. I Chr 1:17).

Around 2000 B.C. the Elamites captured several cities in Babylonia, helping to bring to an end the supremacy of the Sumerian rulers of the Third Dynasty of Ur (2113–2006 B.C.) and sacking that city. It is in this period of Elamite strength that Chedorlaomer (q.v.; Gen 14:1–17) most likely rounded up confederates to march through Transjordan to collect tribute from the cities in the Dead Sea area. At the time of the Amorite First Dynasty of Babylon (c. 1894–1595 B.C.), whose sixth king was Hammurabi, several Elamite rulers are known, the first element of whose names was Kudur-. This fact tends to confirm that Chedorlaomer is an authentic Elamite royal name of that period.

Later, the Elamites periodically harassed Babylonia for several centuries (c. 1300–1120 B.C.). Shutruk-Nahhunte (c.1200 B.C.) returned from a successful raid against Babylon with the famous law code of Hammurabi as a trophy; it was rediscovered at Susa in 1901-2. Nebuchadnezzar I of Babylon reduced Elam once more, however, to the status of a Babylonian dependency, so that it is not heard of for some three centuries. After c. 740 B.C. the Elamites allied themselves with Babylonians as the almost constant enemy of the Assyrians, until Ashurbanipal nearly exterminated them (c. 645 B.C.). The void they left was filled in by Indo-European Persians, who made the ancient Elamite city of Susa into a Persian winter capital. It is called Shushan in the book of Esther; Neh 1:1; and Dan 8:2 (all KJV).

Isaiah had spoken of Elamite bowmen as captive mercenary troops in the Assyrian army that invaded Judah (Isa 22:6), and of Elamites in the army of Cyrus that would besiege Babylon (21:2). Jeremiah's prophecy against Elam (Jer 49:34–39) is puzzling unless it refers to the Persians who were overlords of the land formerly called Elam. Their return from captivity (v. 39) would then refer to the rise of the Persian Empire. Ezr 4:9 (RSV) names the "men of Susa, that is, the Elamites" as companions of Rehum and Shimshai, officials of the Persian government in Jerusalem, who opposed the rebuilding of post-Exilic Jerusalem. Elamites are also mentioned as present in Jerusalem on the day of Pentecost (Acts 2:9); these were Jews from the old region of Elam.

See Madai; Persia; Shushan.

T. M. B. and E. B. S.

ELASAH (ĕl-á/să)
1. Son of Shaphan and one of two messengers from Zedekiah to Nebuchadnezzar, who also delivered Jeremiah's message to the Judeans in Exile (Jer 29:3).
2. Son of Pashur and one of the post-Exilic priests who put away foreign wives (Ezr 10:22). Elsewhere the name is rendered Eleasah (q.v.).

ELATH (ē'lăth). Alternately Eloth. Elath was located in biblical times at the head of the Gulf of Aqabah (q.v.). The name is still used by the state of Israel for a similarly located town whose Jordanian counterpart nearby is called Aqabah. The area is delightful in the winter months, living up to the resortlike connotation suggested in the Heb. meaning of the term ('ēlat, "palm grove"). The port facilities became very important for modern Israel when the United Arab Republic closed the Suez Canal to Israeli ships. The natural deepwater harbor at Elath allows the largest freighters and oil tankers to discharge or load at the docks. Cargo and oil can then be transshipped by highway and pipeline through the Negev to Haifa on the Mediterranean.

The origins of Elath are unknown, but it was probably an old Edomite center, as is indicated in Deut 2:8, where Moses and the children of Israel passed through the Edomite plain (the Arabah) that began at Elath and went N to Moab.

With David's conquest of the Edomites the area became important to the Israelites. Solomon made it the main port of the nation, though he also used the Phoenician ports on the Mediterranean coast. In I Kgs 10:22 (RSV) mention is made of Solomon's "ships of Tarshish," that is, a deep-sea fleet like those used by the Phoenicians who helped provide him with sailors and nautical knowledge (II Chr 8:17–18). Later, Jehoshaphat attempted to rebuild this fleet, but the attempt met with disaster (I Kgs 22:48).

According to II Kgs 14:22 Azariah (Uzziah) restored Elath, while II Kgs 16:6 relates that King Rezin of Syria drove the Jews out of Elath in the days of King Ahaz. Some (RSV and JerusB) would take the Heb. text of the latter passage to say that Edomites, not Syrians ('dm for 'rm), actually occupied Elath, because of the northern attack on Judah by Resin and Pekah. According to II Chr 28:17, the Edomites were sharing in the spoils in those dark days, which was always the case when Judah was weak (II Kgs 8:20–22). See Ezion-geber.

E. B. S.

EL BERITH. *See* Gods, False: Baal Berith.

EL-BETHEL (ĕl-bĕth'ĕl; "God of Bethel"). The name given by Jacob to the scene of his vision of the ladder at Luz (cf. Gen 28:10- 15) as he returned to Canaan (Gen 35:7). *See* Bethel.

ELDAAH (ĕl-dā'à). The fifth son of Midian, the fourth son of Abraham by Keturah (Gen 25:2, 4; I Chr 1:32- 33).

ELDAD (ĕl'dăd). One of the 70 elders summoned by Moses to help assume the responsibility of government. For some reason Eldad did not formally present himself at the tabernacle for ordination, but notwithstanding this, he too received the Spirit of the Lord and prophesied. Joshua expressed concern for Moses' honor because Eldad had not been formally ordained. Moses expressed a charitable view by acknowledging that the Spirit of God had been conferred, and expressed a wish that the Lord might put His Spirit upon all the people (Num 11:24- 29).

ELDER. In the OT Heb. *zāqēn*, lit., "one who is bearded," designates a man of a certain official rank and position among his brethren. Among the Israelites there were two kinds of elders, the "elders of Israel" who were the heads of families or clans in the various tribes, and the "elders" of the towns built and settled after the Conquest.

Elders are mentioned in Mesopotamian texts from the 18th cen. B.C. onward as the representatives of the people, defending their rights but with no administrative functions. Many municipal duties were performed by the council of elders in the Hittite Empire. The elders of Gebal (Byblos) are mentioned in Ezk 27:9 and the assembly (of elders) of the prince of Byblos in the story of Wen-Amon (ANET, p. 29). The system of elders existed among other neighbors of Israel as well: Egypt (Gen 50:7; Ps 105:22, RSV), Moab and the Midianites (Num 22:4, 7), and the Gibeonites (Josh 9:11). The Heb. term is thus equivalent to the Homeric *gerontes*, the Spartan *presbys*, the Roman *senatus*, and the Arab *sheikh*.

The term *zāqēn* does not necessarily mean an old man, but does imply one of maturity and experience who has assumed leadership among his own kinsmen and in his town or tribe (cf. Num 11:16). Although the elders were not elected, during most of the periods from Moses to Ezra and on into the intertestamental era they were recognized as the highest authoritative body over the people. They acted as the religious representatives of the nation (Jer 19:1, RSV; Joel 1:14; 2:16) as well as handling many political matters and settling intertribal disputes (e.g., Phinehas and the ten tribal chiefs or elders, Josh 22:13- 33). The town elders were a sort of municipal council whose duties included acting as judges in apprehending murderers (Deut 19:12), conducting inquests (Deut 21:2), and settling matrimonial disputes (Deut 22:15; 25:7).

The "elders of Israel," first heard of in Ex 3:16- 18, were assembled by Moses to receive God's announcement of liberation from Egypt. The covenant was ratified at Mount Sinai in the presence of 70 of the elders of Israel (Ex 24:1, 9, 14; cf. 19:7), the "nobles" (KJV) or chief men of the nation (24:11). Later, 70 elders were specially anointed with the Spirit to aid Moses in governing the nation (Num 11:16- 25). In cases when the whole community sinned, the elders of the congregation or community were to represent it in making atonement (Lev 4:13- 15).

The authority of the elders was in principle greater than that of the king (cf. II Kgs 23:1). It was this group which demanded that Samuel appoint a king (I Sam 8:4- 6), and they were parties to the royal covenant which established David as king (II Sam 5:3). In Babylon the elders were the focal point of the Jewish community in exile (Jer 29:1; Ezk 8:1; 14:1; 20:1- 5), and after the return to Jerusalem they continued active (Ezr 5:5, 9; 6:7- 8, 14; 10:8, 14).

Out of the Council of Elders (*gerousia*) of the Hellenistic period in Judah developed the Great Assembly (*Knesset*) of the Jews which in 142 B.C. granted great power to Simon the Maccabean leader (I Macc 14:28). The Great Sanhedrin with its 71 members, the supreme legislative body prior to A.D. 70, was the ultimate form of the institution of the "elders of Israel." *See* Sanhedrin. (See also "Government, Authority and Kingship," CornPBE, pp. 354- 369.) For the office of elder in the NT churches *see* Bishop.

In his vision of heaven John saw 24 elders seated upon thrones surrounding the throne of God, clothed in white garments and wearing golden crowns (Rev 4:4). They fall down in worship and cast their crowns before God's throne (4:10; cf. 11:16; 19:4), and with their harps and bowls of incense, symbolizing the prayers of the saints, they sing a new song to the Lamb (5:8- 10). As elders they represent God's people; their thrones and crowns symbolize a kingly role, while their acts of worship and the bowls of incense suggest a priestly function. Thus they seem to be the chief representatives of the redeemed as a kingdom of priests (Rev 1:6; cf. 20:6; I Pet 2:5, 9; Ex 19:6). Whether the number 24 suggests the 24 courses of the Jewish priesthood, or a combination of the 12 tribes of Israel (indicative of the OT saints) and the 12 apostles (the leaders of the NT saints), is debatable. For a detailed discussion of the identity of these elders see G. H. Lang, *The Revelation of Jesus Christ,* London: Paternoster Press, 1945, pp. 124- 136.

Bibliography. W. Harold Mare, "Church Functionaries: the Witness in the Literature and Archaeology of the New Testament and Church Periods," JETS, XIII (1970), 229–239.

J. R.

ELEAD (ĕl'ĕ-ăd). A descendant of Ephraim, killed by the men of Gath while making a raid on their cattle (I Chr 7:21).

ELEALEH (ĕl-ē-ā'lĕ). A city of Transjordan in the area requested by the tribes of Reuben and Gad, rebuilt by Reuben (Num 32:3, 37); later a part of Moab (Isa 15:4; 16:9; Jer 48:34). Today it is identified as a mound called el-'Al.

ELEASAH (ĕl-ē-ā'să). This name has the same Heb. form as Elasah (q.v.).
1. A descendant of Judah through Hezron and Jerahmeel (I Chr 2:33, 39–40).
2. A descendant of Saul (I Chr 8:33, 37; 9:43).

ELEAZAR (ĕl'ē-ā'zàr). In addition to the following biblical references, the name appears also in a Jewish legal contract among the Dead Sea Scrolls.
1. The third son of Aaron and Elisheba (Ex 6:23; Num 3:2). He was consecrated to the priesthood with his father and brothers at Sinai (Ex 28:1, 4; Lev 8:2, 13). After God slew the older brothers when they presented unlawful fire (Lev 10:1–7), Eleazar and Ithamar continued to exercise priestly functions with Aaron (Num 3:1–4). Eleazar was placed over the Levites (Num 3:32) and assigned the care of the sanctuary and its vessels, etc. (Num 4:16; 16:37, 39; 19:3–4). He succeeded as high priest when his father Aaron died at Mount Hor (Num 20:25–28; Deut 10:6). Joshua was installed as Moses' successor before Eleazar the priest, who was to be Joshua's official counselor by making inquiry of the Lord (Num 27:18–22). He took part in the census at Shittim (Num 26:1, 63), and in the division of land to the eastern tribes (Num 32:2; 34:17) and later with Joshua to the western tribes (Josh 14:1; 17:4; 19:51; 21:1). He married a daughter of Putiel and she bore him Phinehas (Ex 6:25). Eleazar was buried near the home of his son, who succeeded him as high priest (Josh 24:33; Jud 20:28). Eleazar was the ancestor of the Zadokite priests, who in Solomon's time replaced Abiathar, a descendant of Ithamar, Eleazar's younger brother (I Chr 6:4–15; I Kgs 2:26–27, 35).
2. A Merarite Levite who died without sons. His daughters were married to kinsmen in order to keep the family inheritance within the tribe (I Chr 23:21–22; 24:28), in accordance with the regulation of Num 36:6–9.
3. The son of Abinadab, probably a Levite. He was consecrated to have charge of the ark while it was in his father's home in Kirjath-jearim after the Philistines had returned the ark (I Sam 7:1).

4. Son of Dodo; one of David's "three mighty men" (II Sam 23:9; I Chr 11:12).
5. A priest who assisted in the inventory of the temple treasure when it was brought back to Jerusalem by Ezra (Ezr 8:33).
6. A member of the clan of Parosh, listed among laymen in Israel who put away foreign wives during Ezra's reform (Ezr 10:25).
7. A priest who participated in the procession on the walls of Jerusalem during their dedication (Neh 12:42).
8. An ancestor of Joseph the husband of Mary (Mt 1:15).

J. R.

ELECT. "Chosen" or "selected." The main OT verb for this is *bāḥar*, a deliberated selecting of something or someone with attendant preference or pleasure. The NT verb *eklegomai* means to choose or select out of a larger group something or someone for oneself. The related adjectives *bāḥir* and *eklektos* are translated "elect" or "chosen" and are the result of an act of selection. The words are used of choices human (Gen 6:2; Deut 30:19; Lk 10:42; 14:7) and divine for salvation (Eph 1:4), and for service (Jn 15:16).

Various objects are termed "elect" or "chosen" by God: the nation Israel for special favor and purpose (Isa 44:1; 45:4); several individuals, such as Abraham (Neh 9:7), Aaron (Ps 105:26), David (I Sam 16:8 ff.); Jerusalem (II Chr 6:6); a remnant of Jews near the second coming of Christ (Mt 24:22; Isa 65:9); the Church, the body of Christ (I Pet 2:9; 5:13; Col 3:12; Tit 1:1); Christ Himself (Isa 42:1; I Pet 2:6); the "lady" (II Jn 1); and angels (I Tim 5:21). Elect men are chosen by God's grace (Rom 11:5) and love (Rom 8:33–39; 11:28; Eph 1:4–5) and according to His foreknowledge (I Pet 1:2); it is never on the basis of human merit (Rom 9:11; cf. II Tim 1:9). *See* Chosen; Election.

C. F. D.

ELECT LADY. A translation of the phrase *eklektē kyria* in II Jn 1. The meaning, long a puzzle to commentators, is probably to be found in one of two possible explanations: (1) a reference to an individual, named either "elect Kyria," Electa Kyria, or "the lady Electa"; or (2) a reference to a local Christian congregation under the symbol of a woman.

While the former meaning is possible, as the personal name Kyria was known in the ancient world, the contrast with III John makes it less likely. There John addressed his friend in the natural, normal way. On the other hand, the language of II John is indefinite and ambiguous.

More probably, then, John addressed a Christian congregation by use of the terms "the Lady chosen by God" (NEB). The idea of the election of the Church is common in the NT (see, e.g., Rom 8:33; Eph 1:4; Col 3:12; I Pet

1:1–2). Further, we find greetings being sent from "the church that is at Babylon, elected together with you" in I Pet 5:13. Furthermore, it was not uncommon to think of the community of God's people as a woman bearing children (Baruch 4:8 – 5:5; Gal 4:25; Rev 12).

Again, the alternating between the second person singular (II Jn 1–5) and the second person plural (vv. 6–12) and back again to the singular (v. 13) seems to favor the symbolic use of the phrase with reference to a church. Verse 13 could look in the same direction in the suggestion of sister churches greeting one another.

John's words in II Jn 5–6 are very similar to those in his first epistle (I Jn 2:3–10), a word given first by our Lord to His followers in Jn 13:34–35. Such words were given to the church generally, and seem less likely to have been written to one individual or family.

Bibliography. W. Foerster, TWNT (ExpT, Bromiley), III, 1095. B. F. Westcott, *The Epistles of St. John,* Grand Rapids: Eerdmans, 1950, pp. 223–224.

W. M. D.

ELECTION

Introduction

Election is the doctrine concerning God's divine choice of some individuals out of all mankind to become His own through regeneration and salvation. Election has to be related to but distinguished from God's decrees in general, predestination, foreordination and foreknowledge.

Election, the decrees of God, predestination and foreordination. The decrees of God encompass all that shall come to pass and include both foreordination and predestination. Predestination is confined in theological usage to God's decrees with regard to individual persons and their salvation, while foreordination covers all other events. They are the two parts of God's divine decrees in general.

Some Reformed scholars teach double predestination, that is, predestination to salvation for the elect and predestination to damnation for the lost (Augustine, Gottschalk, Calvin, Melanchthon and Luther, in their earlier period; L. Berkhof). Others teach the predestination of the elect and the passing by of the reprobate (C. Hodge, J. O. Buswell, H. C. Thiessen, L. S. Chafer). If God decrees to save one man and to damn another, then election and reprobation are two parts of the same. If predestination applies only to those whom God has chosen, then it describes that act in which God signs the projected life page or plan of the man whom He has chosen to save by divine grace. Foreordination, on the other hand, describes that act in which God signs the projected life page or plan of the man whom He has chosen to pass by and to leave to his own ways, which must inevitably lead to eternal loss.

Thus we see that for those who believe in double predestination, foreordination covers events but not individuals in any specific sense, while for those who believe in the predestination of the saved only, it applies to all God's decrees except those which have to do with the salvation of particular men.

Election and foreknowledge. Election is not simply foreknowledge, nor is it dependent upon foreknowledge. It includes God's foreknowledge as to what a man will do in his own freedom, but is dependent for its accomplishment upon God's sovereign grace. The Scriptures teach that God takes up what man will do in his freedom, and adds to this what He will do in His grace to save a man, to make effective His election of an individual.

Two controversies in particular have arisen within the church which have a bearing on election. First, that of Pelagianism versus Augustinianism. Pelagius argued for the ability of the natural man to accept Christ without sovereign grace, while Augustine maintained the doctrine of the total depravity of man and the need for sovereign grace. The Roman Catholic church chose a semi-Pelagian position, arguing that man has some ability but that this is insufficient without the help of seven kinds of steps of ascending grace. The Pelagian view leads to the conclusion that election, namely, God's choice of some, depends upon the foreknowledge of God; the Augustinian, that it depends on His good pleasure and grace. Arminius and the Arminians today argue like Pelagius, that election depends on God's foreknowledge.

Election and call. Two kinds of call are found in Scripture. A general call to all to repent and be saved (Isa 55:1; Mt 11:28), and an efficacious call (Jn 6:37, 44; Rom 8:29–30). The general call makes man cognizant of and responsible for what he ought to do; the efficacious call adds to this the sovereign enablement necessary to do it (Eph 2:8). It is the efficacious call which accompanies election. *See* Call.

We are now ready to consider the different phases of the biblical doctrine of election.

R. A. K.

The Vocabulary of Election

A wide variety of expressions is needed to describe the manifold aspects of election. Chiefly in the OT, *bāhar* indicates a selection of one among other possible choices. It may describe a natural choice (Gen 6:2; Deut 23:16), a moral choice (Deut 30:19; Josh 24:15, 22; Ps 119:30, 173), or a divine choice (Deut 7:6; I Sam 10:24; Isa 41:8–9). The Heb. *bāhar* and its cognate adjective *bāḥîr* are applied to such "chosen" objects as Abraham (Neh 9:7), Moses (Ps 106:23), Aaron (Ps 105:26), Israel (Ezk 20:5), David and Solomon (I Chr 28:4–6, 10), Jerusalem (II Chr 6:5 f.), the Messiah (Ps 89:3 f., 19; Isa 42:1), Zerubbabel (Hag 2:23), and the new Israel (Isa 43:20 f.; 65:9, 22). The verb *yāda'*, "to know," is often used as an evident synonym of election (Gen 18:19; Ex 33:12, 17; II Sam 7:20; Ps 1:6; Jer 1:5; Amos 3:2; Nah 1:7).

The NT Gr. verb *eklegomai*, "to choose out for oneself," designates a discriminate choice after careful scrutiny (Lk 6:13; 10:42; 14:7; Acts 6:5). Of the 21 occurrences of this verb in the NT, God is the subject in seven places (Acts 13:17; 15:7; I Cor 1:27 twice, 28; Eph 1:4; Jas 2:5) and Christ is the subject in eight places (Mk 13:20; Lk 6:13; Jn 6:70; 13:18; 15:16, 19; Acts 1:2, 24). The adjective *eklektos*, "elect," is applied to Christ (Lk 23:35; I Pet 2:4, 6), to angels (I Tim 5:21), and frequently to believers. The noun *ekloḡe*, "election," is applied to Paul (Acts 9:15), to God's purpose (Rom 9:11), to Israel's believing remnant (Rom 11:5, 7, 28), and to Christians (I Thess 1:4; II Pet 1:10).

The truth of election is also involved in such words as "purpose," *prothesis* (Rom 8:28; 9:11; Eph 1:11; II Tim 1:9), "give" (Mt 20:14, 23; Jn 1:12; 3:27; 6:37, 65; 10:28 f.; 17:11; Heb 2:13), "know" (Jn 6:64; 10:14, 27; II Tim 2:19), "appoint" (I Thess 5:9; I Tim 2:7; I Pet 2:8), "prepare" (Mt 20:23; 25:34, 41), "determine" (Lk 22:22), "call" (Rom 8:28, 30; 9:11, 24–26; I Cor 1:2, 9; 7:20–22; Eph 4:1, 4; I Thess 2:12; 4:7; II Tim 1:9; I Pet 1:15; 2:9; 5:10; II Pet 1:3; Rev 17:14), and "calling" (Rom 11:29; I Cor 1:26; Eph 1:18; 4:1, 4; Phil 3:14; II Tim 1:9; Heb 3:1; II Pet 1:10).

The elect are certainly designated by such terms as these: "sheep" (Ps 100:3; Ezk 34: 11–31; Mt 25:33; Jn 10:2–16, 26 f.), "flock" (Isa 40:11; Lk 12:32; I Pet 5:2), "one body" (I Cor 10:17; 12:12 f.; Eph 4:4), "the body of Christ" (I Cor 12:27; Eph 4:12), "seed" (Ps 22:23, 30; Isa 41:8; 45:25; 53:10; 61:9; 65:23; Rom 4:16; Gal 3:29; Heb 2:16), "people" (Hos 2:23; Acts 15:14; Rom 9:25 f.; 11:1 f.; II Cor 6:16; Tit 2:14; Heb 4:9; 8:10; I Pet 2:9 f.; Rev 21:3), "children," *teknia* (Jn 1:12, ASV; 11:52; Rom 8:16 f.; Gal 4:28), "sons," *hyioi* (Rom 8:14, 19; 9:26, ASV; II Cor 6:18; Gal 3:26, ASV; Heb 2:10; Rev 21:7), "brethren" (Mt 12:49; 25:40; Rom 8:29; Heb. 2:11 f., 17).

The Description of Election

Its selectivity. The doctrine of election excludes all theories of universal salvation. The following facts confirm this statement: (1) Selectivity is resident in the words designating election. For example, David "chose," *bāḥar*, five smooth stones for his sling (I Sam 17:40). It is perfectly evident, of course, that there were many more stones that David could have chosen. So likewise when God "chose" us in eternity (Eph 1:4), it is equally evident that He did not choose all. (2) Selectivity is confirmed by the "out of" passages dealing with this subject (Jn 15:19; 17:6; Acts 15:14; Gal 1:4; Col 1:13; I Pet 2:9; Rev 5:9; 7:9, 14; 14:3 f.). (3) Selectivity is manifested in the contrasting descriptions of the elect. They are the "sheep" (Jn 10:3–5, 11, 14–16); others are not (10:26). They are "written" in the Book of Life (Dan 12:1; Lk 10:20; Heb 12:23); others are excluded (Rev 13:8; 17:8). They respond to Christ (Jn 6:37, 39, 44, 65; 10:27 f.; Acts 13:48); others are unresponsive (Jn 8:43, 47; 10:26). (4) Selectivity is evidenced by the tragic descriptions of the lost. Such expressions as "not given" (Mt 13:11), "could not believe" (Jn 12:39), "perdition" (Jn 17:12; II Thess 2:3), "fitted unto destruction" (Rom 9:22), "were blinded" (Rom 11:7), "were appointed" (I Pet 2:8), "of old ordained" (Jude 4), "have not the seal of God" (Rev 9:4) point by way of contrast to the sovereign will of God in electing whom He chooses (Rom 9:14–24).

Its sovereignty. God's will is the sovereign cause of all His acts in eternity and in time. To His will are attributed His sovereignty (Eph 1:11), the creation (Rev 4:11), the course of history (Ps 115:3; 135:6; Dan 4:35; 6:27), the bestowal of blessings (Mt 11:25–27; 20:14–16), the Spirit's activity (Jn 3:8), regeneration (Jas 1:18), adoption (Eph 1:5), election (Rom 9:11, 18–24), and His good pleasure (Phil 2:13).

Thus, to be more specific, God's sovereignty in election is seen in His choosing (1) apart from the sinner's works (Rom 9:11; I Cor 1:26; Tit 3:4–7); (2) before the person's birth (Jer 1:5; Rom 9:11–13; Gal 1:15); (3) according to His sovereign purpose (Ex 33:19; Mt 11:25–27; Rom 11:33–36); (4) by sovereign discrimination (Rom 9:11–13, 19–23).

Its eternity. All of God's saving acts originate in eternity; therefore election must be eternal. (1) God's foreknowledge is eternal (Rom 8:29; I Pet 1:1–2); (2) God chose the elect in eternity (Eph 1:4; II Thess 2:13–14); (3) God promised the elect eternal life in eternity (Tit 1:1–2); (4) God inscribed the elect in His Book of Life in eternity (Rev 13:8; 17:8); (5) God chose the elect before their existence in this world (Jer 1:5; Gal 1:15; Eph 2:10; II Tim 1:9); (6) God gave the elect to Christ in eternity (Jn 17:2, 6, 24); (7) God prepared heaven, "eternal glory," for the elect (I Pet 5:10).

Its individuality. At this point we must recognize a distinction which is clearly indicated in the Scriptures. (1) The Bible speaks of a national election in the choice of Abraham and his posterity (Gen 12:1–2; Deut 4:37; 7:6–8; 10:15; Ps 105:6–15; Isa 41:8–9; Rom 9:4–5). But national election did not insure individual election (Mal 1:2–3; Rom 2:28–29; 9:27–33; 11:1–11; I Pet 2:8). (2) The Bible also speaks of an official election, that is, an election to some office or function. God sovereignly chose Moses (Ps 106:23), Aaron (Ps 105:26), the priests (Num 18:6 f.; Deut 18:5), Israel's kings (Deut 17:15; I Sam 10:24), the nations (Isa 45:1–7; Jer 27:5–7; Dan 2:37–40; 4:17, 25), the Messiah (Isa 42:1; I Pet 2:4, 6), and the apostles (Jn 15:16, 19) for their places in His plan. Sometimes, however, people were chosen to office, as illustrated in the lives of Saul (I Sam 13:14; 15:17-23) and of Judas (Jn 6:70; 13:2, 27; 17:12), who were not elected to salvation. (3) Apart from the limitations described above, the Bible never speaks of election as involving a race or group; election is always personal and individual. Those elected to salvation are described as individuals (Rom 16:13; Phil 4:2 f.); are referred to by personal pronouns (Rom 8:28-30; Eph 1:4); are distinguished from other individuals (Mt 24:22, 24, 31; Rom 9:21-29; I Cor 1:26-29); are declared to be from all groups of mankind (Rev 5:9 f.; 7:9).

Its certainty. God's plan of election is made definitely certain by the following factors: (1) God's purposes are definite and sure (Rom 11:29); no one can resist effectively His sovereign will (II Chr 20:6; Isa 45:9; Dan 4:35). God has eternally purposed the salvation of some (Rom 8:28-30). This purpose has been fulfilled (Rom 11:1-10) and is being fulfilled in the final completion of the entire number of the redeemed (Rom 11:11-36; Heb 11:39-40; 12:22-23). (2) The means ordained by God for the salvation of the elect are absolutely adequate. The Holy Spirit is sovereignly able to regenerate them (Jn 3:1-8). The gospel is God's power unto their salvation (Rom 1:16; I Cor 1:18, 24; 2:4; I Thess 2:13; Heb 4:12 f.; Jas 1:18; I Pet 1:3, 23). God convicts and brings them to salvation (Jn 16:8-11; Acts 16:14; Eph 2:1-10; Phil 2:13). Such persons come to Christ (Jn 6:37, 39; 17:2, 24) and are securely kept by God's power (Jn 10:27-29; I Pet 1:5; Jude 24). (3) The ultimate plan of God makes certain the salvation of those "ordained to eternal life" (Acts 13:48). God has prepared heaven for them (Jn 14:1-3); and He is now making equally certain that some will be there from all of earth's varied population (Rev 5:9; 7:9).

Its means. Those chosen to eternal life come to know Christ as their Saviour through the means ordained by God. They, like others, were in a state of spiritual deadness (Eph 2:1-3) before God worked faith in their hearts (Ps 110:3; Acts 11:18; 16:14; Eph 2:8) by the Spirit (I Cor 2:1-5; I Thess 1:4-5) and by His Word (I Thess 2:13; Heb 4:12; Jas 1:18). These God-given means are prerequisites of salvation (Rom 10:13-17). The gospel must be preached to all nations (Mt 24:14; 28:19; Acts 1:8); thus, by this means, the elect shall be gathered from all the earth (Mt 24:31; Rev 7:9). Through the ministry of God's elect others are brought into God's kingdom (Jn 17:20). Paul endured extreme suffering so that through his ministry the elect "may also obtain the salvation which is in Christ Jesus with eternal glory" (II Tim 2:10). The divine side stated in Acts 13:48 (those "ordained to eternal life believed") must not be divorced from the human side stated in Acts 14:21, ASV ("And when they had preached the gospel to that city, and had made many disciples," etc.). The mystery of election and human agency is the mystery of Deut 29:29.

Its assurance. It is absolutely certain, of course, that God knows those whom He has chosen (Num 16:5; Ps 37:18, 28; Nah 1:7). Christ likewise knows those chosen to eternal life (Mt 7:23; Jn 10:14, 27-30; 13:18; II Tim 2:19). God knows all things from eternity (Isa 41:26; 42:9; 45:21; Acts 15:18). The question arises, however, whether the elect can know their election and the election of others. The answer must be affirmative for these reasons: (1) God has revealed the election of certain ones. Ananias, for example, definitely knew that Paul was "an elect vessel" (Acts 9:15). Paul knew that Rufus was "chosen" (Rom 16:13; cf. II Jn 13). (2) Certain Christians evidently knew that they were among God's elect (I Thess 1:4; Jas 2:5; I Pet 1:1-2). They are even identified as such (Phil 4:3). (3) The elect are identical with the regenerate; therefore, since regeneration is knowable, election must also be knowable (Rom 8:15 f., 29-33; II Tim 1:12; I Jn 5:1-5, 13, 19-20). (4) God's Word declares the assurance of election to be one of the objectives of our Christian growth (Phil 2:12; II Pet 1:10). Christians can know that they belong to an elect people (I Pet 2:9-10).

Its results. Election is the positive side of predestination, and is thus the source of all good things planned for the redeemed. These good things are such as these: (1) Calling. Election always preceeds the historical call inviting the sinner to receive Christ (Rom 8:28-30; I Cor 1:26-29; II Thess 2:13 f.; II Tim 1:9; 2:10). This call becomes a living part of the Christian's experience of salvation (Rom 9:23 f.; I Cor 1:9, 24; I Thess 2:12; 5:24; II Thess 1:11; I Pet 1:15; 2:9; 3:9; 5:10). (2) **Faith.** Faith is God's gift (Eph 2:8) and the Spirit's fruit (Gal 5:22). The "vessels of mercy" are identical with those who believe (Rom 9:23-24, 33). Those "ordained to eternal life" believe (Acts 13:48). Those given to Christ by the Father believe in Christ (Jn 17:2, 6, 20). These "given ones" are "drawn" to Christ by a divine compulsion (Jn 6:37, 44, 47). (3) Justification. Faith is productive of the believer's justification (Rom 8:29-30, 33). Faith is described as the means of justification (Rom 3:22-30; 4:5, 20-24; 10:10; Gal 2:16; 3:11-14, 22); but the faith that justifies is "the faith of God's elect" (Tit 1:1). (4) Assurance. In addition to what is said above about assurance, it should be noted that a mutually reciprocal knowledge (*ginōskō*) exists between Christ and His sheep (Kn 10:14). Paul's "I know" is the human response to "the Lord knoweth them that are his" (II Tim 1:12; 2:19). (5) Perseverance. A necessary concomitant of election is perseverance. The elect are "kept by the power of God" (I Pet 1:1, 5). Those whom Christ knows as His sheep "shall never perish" (Jn 10:14, 27 f.). Those eternally called can never be separated "from the love of God" (Rom 8:30, 33, 35-39).

(6) Glorification. Here is the ultimate in the believer's election (Rom 8:30). God's elect will "obtain the salvation which is in Christ Jesus with eternal glory" (II Tim 2:10). This "eternal glory" follows earth's trials (I Pet 5:10). Those "redeemed from among men" are described as "without fault" (Rev 14:3–5; cf. Eph 5:27). Those who are "called, and chosen, and faithful" (Rev 17:14) are "clothed in fine linen, white and pure" (Rev 19:14, ASV).

Conclusions

It is quite evident that we should observe certain principles in teaching the doctrine of election. (1) We should go no further than God's Word takes us. There will always be mysteries about election that we can never fully explain or fathom. (2) Our duty is to preach the gospel in the power of the Holy Spirit to all (Mt 28:18–20; Acts 1:8; I Cor 2:1–5); God knows those who are His (II Tim 2:19). (3) Election should be a doctrine of hope and comfort to God's people—not a doctrine of horror and despair. Believers are encouraged to make their calling and election sure (II Pet 1:10).

These principles, held in proper balance, will enable us to avoid those extremes which are so often associated with this glorious truth.

See Chosen.

Bibliography. G. C. Berkouwer. *Divine Election,* Grand Rapids: Eerdmans, 1960. John Calvin. *Concerning the Eternal Predestination of God,* London: James Clarke, 1961. Hendley Dunelm. "Election." ISBE, III (1930), 925–927. John Gill. *The Cause of God and Truth,* London: W. H. Collingridge, 1855. G. E. Mendenhall. "Election." IDB, II, 76–82. G. Schrenk. "*Eklegomai,* etc.," TDNT, IV, 144–192. J. H. Thornwell. *Election and Reprobation,* Philadelphia: Presbyterian and Reformed, 1961. B. B. Warfield. "Predestination," HDB, IV (1902), 47–63. J. R. Willis, "Elect, Election," *Dictionary of Christ and the Gospels,* I (1906), 510–514.

W. B.

EL-ELOHE-ISRAEL (ĕl-ĕl′ō-hē-ĭz′rĭ-ĕl; "God is the God of Israel"). Jacob's altar at Shechem after he returned from Padan-aram (Gen 33:19–20). Here Abraham had erected an altar (Gen 12:7). The LXX renders Gen 33:20: "He built an altar and called upon the God of Israel."

ELEMENTS

1. The alphabet letters, thus symbolic of rudiments of a study or discipline, as in "the first principles [ASV, rudiments] of the oracles of God" (Heb 5:12).

2. Physical components of the world, which face destruction by fire (II Pet 3:10–12).

3. Spirits behind the physical components, which many Greeks personified as the ultimate principles of all existence and life and made

objects of worship. These Paul attacked in Colossians, particularly in 2:8, 20; possibly also in Gal 4:3, 9–although probably he referred here to Jewish legalism as rudimentary or infantile religious thought.

See Rudiments.

ELEPH (ĕ′lĕph). A place in the vicinity of Jerusalem allotted to the tribe of Benjamin. In RSV it is called Ha-eleph (Josh 18:28). Its exact location is uncertain.

ELEPHANT.*See* Animals, II.12.

ELEPHANTINE PAPYRI. A highly significant group of papyrus documents was discovered between 1893 and 1908 on the island of Elephantine, opposite the city of Aswan at the First Cataract of the Nile. These letters and records, dated in the 5th cen. B.C., were written in Aramaic, the *lingua franca* of that era, very similar in style to the Aram. section of the book of Ezra. Some of the official documents were dated in both Egyptian and Jewish months, making them of great value to the ancient historian. The papyri consist of three sets of about a dozen documents each, two being family records and the third a community archive. Together they provide the earliest known documentation for the life of a Jewish community in the Diaspora (*see* Dispersion of Israel).

On the island of Elephantine during the Persian Empire a colony of Jewish mercenary soldiers was established to man the border fortress. The ancestors of these Jews may have been refugees from the Assyrian conquest of the northern kingdom of Israel in 722 B.C. Again, they may have been sent as troops to Egypt in the middle of the 7th cen. B.C. by Manasseh when he allied himself with the pharaoh in an attempt to throw off the Assyrian yoke. Or they may have arrived as refugees from Judah following their defeat at the hands of Nebuchadnezzar in 586 B.C. (Jer 42–43).

One of the documents is a copy of a letter written in 407 B.C. to the Persian governor of Judah (ANET, p. 492). The Jewish priests complained that priests of the Egyptian god Khnum had destroyed the Jewish temple at Elephantine, dedicated to Yahu (i.e., Yahweh). This letter names men in Palestine who are also mentioned in the book of Nehemiah: Sanballat, the governor of Samaria (Neh 4:1, etc.), and Johanan, the high priest (Neh 12:22–23).

The Jewish worship at Elephantine did not adhere rigorously to the Mosaic law. Deut 12:5–28 forbade offering sacrifices in any place other than at the central sanctuary where God's name would dwell. Also, other Semitic deities were worshiped, such as Ishum-bethel, Anath-bethel, Herem-bethel, and Anath-yahu. The latter may indicate a syncretizing tendency, perhaps especially on the part of the Jewish women, identifying Yahweh with the queen of heaven (cf. Jer 7:18; 44:17).

Bibliography. BW, pp. 220 f. DOTT, pp. 256–269. Bezalel Porter, *Archives from Elephantine: the Life of an Ancient Jewish Military Colony,* Berkeley: Univ. of California Press, 1968.

J. R.

ELHANAN (ĕl-hā′năn)

1. In I Chr 20:5 it is said that Elhanan, the son of Jair, slew Lahmi, the brother of Goliath the Gittite, but II Sam 21:19 (RSV) states that Elhanan, the son of Jaare-oregim, the Bethlehemite, slew Goliath the Gittite. The "oregim" is perhaps a scribal error based on "weaver" in the following line, thus making Jair and Jaare the same person. These two verses coupled with I Sam 17 present the problem of who killed Goliath.

Some scholars have contended, without good reason, that Elhanan was David's original name. Others have maintained that the text of I Chr 20:5 is preferred to a corrupt text in II Sam 21:19. (The Masoretic Heb. text of I and II Samuel has a number of textual corruptions.) Still others have concluded that Goliath was slain by Elhanan and his name attributed to the anonymous giant slain by David in the Valley of Elah.

2. A son of Dodo of Bethlehem, one of the 30 heroes in David's guard (II Sam 23:24; I Chr 11:26).

F. E. Y.

ELI (ē′lī). The last judge of Israel's Dark Ages. Eli's dramatic life story is recorded in I Sam 1–4, the book named after his successor. He was the priest of the "house of the Lord" at ancient Shiloh (I Sam 1:3, 7, 9) *c.* 20 miles N of Jerusalem, to whom the boy Samuel was brought to fulfill Hannah's vow (I Sam 1:1 – 2:11). The "house of the Lord" evidently was the tabernacle of Israel (cf. Josh 18:1; Jud 18:31), and the ark resided there (I Sam 3:3), suggesting that this sanctuary was the central shrine of the Israelites.

The biblical record is silent concerning Eli's ancestry; hence two traditions have arisen about his family tree: one, that he came from the Aaronic house of Ithamar (cf. Jos *Ant.* v. 11.5; I Chr 24:3); another, Eli came from the rival house of Eleazar (cf. II Esd 1:2–3; Ex 6:23, 25). By comparing I Kgs 2:27 with I Chr 24:3, one concludes that Phinehas, his son, and Eli himself were probably descendants of Aaron's youngest son, Ithamar. Abiathar's son Ahimelech is of the "sons of Ithamar" (cf. I Chr 24:3 with II Sam 8:17). No doubt Eli's family was of the ancient priesthood which ministered at Shiloh. Eli's descendants through Phinehas and his son Ahitub may have perpetuated the priesthood at Nob for a time (I Sam 14:3; 22:9 ff.).

Associated with Eli in this priesthood were his two incorrigible sons, Hophni and Phinehas (I Sam 1:3). The two sons conducted themselves so outrageously that they excited deep disgust among the people and rendered the service of the tabernacle odious in the people's eyes (I Sam 2:12–17, 22). Of this conduct Eli was aware, but contented himself with mild and ineffectual remonstrances (I Sam 2:23–24) when his position demanded severe and vigorous actions (I Sam 3:13). Because of their scandalous conduct and the laxity of parental discipline, a man of God pronounced doom upon them and their posterity (I Sam 2:27–36). This prophecy was confirmed by a revelation to the child Samuel which predicted the irremediable punishment of Eli's household (I Sam 3:11–14).

This announcement of judgment was partially fulfilled in the death of Hophni and Phinehas in the battle with the Philistines at Aphek (I Sam 4:11) and the ruthless murder of the priests in Nob by King Saul (cf. I Sam 22:9–20). But Abiathar slipped through the net and shared with Zadok the priesthood under King David (II Sam 15:24–29; 19:11). However, his removal by King Solomon restored the line of Eleazar in the person of Zadok, and was the final fulfillment of the ancient prophetic oracle (cf. I Kgs 2:26 f.).

The sunset of Eli's life was one of defeat, disappointment, and disaster. His end followed the sad news of the loss of the ark to the Philistines in the battle near Ebenezer. He fell over backward, broke his neck, and died *c.* 1000 B.C.: "He fell from off the seat backward by the side of the gate, and his neck brake, and he died; for he was an old man [ninety-eight years, v. 15] and heavy" (I Sam 4:18).

His prematurely born grandson was named Ichabod, i.e., "the glory of the Lord has departed" (I Sam 4:19–21). Eli brought to a climax the long, disastrous age of the judges and paved the way for the new age of the kings. Eli judged Israel 40 years and combined in his own person the offices of high priest and judge (I Sam 4:18). However, his record was marred and blighted by the shameful practices of his sensual sons and his dismal failure to remove them from their priestly service.

D. W. D.

ELIAB (ĕ-lī′ăb). The name occurs in Akkad. texts as *Ili-abi.*

1. A representative or "prince" of the tribe of Zebulun who assisted Moses in the census, etc. (Num 1:9; 2:7; 7:24, 29; 10:16).

2. A Reubenite, father of the rebels Dathan and Abiram (Num 16:1, 12; 26:8, 9).

3. An ancestor of Samuel descended from the Levite Kohath (I Chr 6:27), possibly the Eliel of verse 34 and the Elihu of I Sam 1:1.

4. The eldest son of Jesse and brother of David, tall and of regal appearance (I Sam 16:6–7; I Chr 2:13). He was in Saul's army and became furious when he heard young David inquiring about the reward for killing Goliath (I Sam 17:13–28). His daughter Abihail mar-

ried David's son Jerimoth, and their daughter Mahalath married Rehoboam (II Chr 11:18).

5. A Gadite warrior who joined the outlaw David at his wilderness stronghold (I Chr 12:8-9).

6. A Levite singer and harpist appointed to accompany the procession which brought the ark up to Jerusalem (I Chr 15:18, 20).

ELIADA, ELIADAH (ĕ-lī'á-dá)

1. One of the sons born to David by a wife or concubine at Jerusalem (II Sam 5:16; I Chr 3:8). He is called Beeliada in I Chr 14:7.

2. Father of Rezon of Syria who was an implacable enemy of Israel during Solomon's reign (I Kgs 11:23; KJV, Eliadah).

3. A man of Benjamin, commander of 200,000 men in Jehoshaphat's army (II Chr 17:17).

ELIAH (ĕ-lī'á). A variant form of Elijah (q.v.).

1. One of the "heads of the fathers" of Benjamin (I Chr 8:27-28).

2. A son of Elam, a priest, and one who had taken a foreign wife (Ezr 10:26).

ELIAHBA (ĕ-lī'á-bá). A Shaalbonite, one of David's special guard of 30 mighty men (II Sam 23:32; I Chr 11:33).

ELIAKIM (ĕ-lī'á-kĭm). The name occurs on three scaraboid seals of the 6th cen. B.C. as "Belonging to Eliakim, attendant of Yaukin" (l'lyqm n'r ywkn). This Eliakim, not mentioned in the OT, was steward of Jehoiachin.

1. Son of Hilkiah; the royal chamberlain or official "over the household" of King Hezekiah, holding an office second only to the king. He represented Hezekiah during the interview with Sennacherib's officers (II Kgs 18:18, 26, 37). The king sent him on a delegation to Isaiah for advice (II Kgs 19:2-5). He must have been a highly capable and godly man, for Isaiah had prophesied that Eliakim would replace Shebna in office (Isa 22:20-24), and by the time of Sennacherib's invasion this had occurred.

2. A son of King Josiah. Pharaoh-nechoh placed him on the throne of Judah (II Kgs 23:34) and changed his name to Jehoiakim (q.v.).

3. A priest who took part in the dedication ceremony of the city wall (Neh 12:41).

4. The son of Abiud, descendant of David through Solomon and Zerubbabel (Mt 1:13).

5. The son of Melea, descendant of David through Nathan (Lk 3:30). These last two men occur in the genealogies of Jesus Christ.

J. R.

ELIAM (ĕ-lī'ám). The name has been found on an ancient Heb. seal.

1. The father of Bath-sheba (II Sam 11:3); called Ammiel (q.v.) in I Chr 3:5, the two basic elements of the names, 'ēl and 'am, being interchanged. The name would mean "my God is a kinsman."

2. Son of Ahithophel and one of David's "mighty men" (II Sam 23:8, 13, 34); possibly the same as #1.

ELIAS (ĕ-lī'ás).The NT form of Elijah (q.v.).

ELIASAPH (ĕ-lī'á-sáf)

1. A leader of the tribe of Gad, called the son of Deuel (Num 1:14; 10:20) or Reuel (Num 2:14). He presented Gad's offering at the tabernacle (Num 7:42-47).

2. Son of Lael, a chief of the Gershonites (Num 3:24).

ELIASHIB (ĕ-lī'á-shĭb)

1. A priest, head of the eleventh of the 24 courses into which David divided the priesthood (I Chr 24:1, 12).

2. A post-Exilic Levite singer who had married a foreign wife (Ezr 10:24).

3. A layman, son of Zattu (Ezr 10:27).

4. Another layman, son of Bani (Ezr 10:36), in the same list as 2.

5. The high priest who was contemporary with Nehemiah; the son of Joiakim and grandson of Jeshua the priest in Zerubbabel's day (Neh 12:10). He directed the priests in rebuilding the Sheep Gate under Nehemiah (Neh 3:1), but later was guilty of allying with the hostile Tobiah and assigning him a room in the temple area over which Eliashib had charge (Neh 13:4-7). He even had a grandson who married a daughter of Sanballat, another opponent of Nehemiah (Neh 13:28).

6. A descendant of Zerubbabel (I Chr 3:24).

ELIATHAH (ĕ-lī'á-thá). A son of Heman, whose family (sons and brothers) was appointed by lot to be the twentieth division of musicians to serve in the temple (I Chr 25:4, 27).

ELIDAD (ĕ-lī'dăd). Son of Chislon of Benjamin. He was the tribe's representative in the group who worked under Joshua and Eleazar in apportioning the land W of Jordan among the tribes (Num 34:21).

ELIEL (ĕ-lī'ĕl)

1. A Kohathite Levite (I Chr 6:34), probably the same as the Eliab of I Chr 6:27 and the Elihu of I Sam 1:1.

2 and 3. Two mighty men or heroes in David's army (I Chr 11:46-47).

4. The seventh of the Gadite warriors who joined David at his wilderness stronghold and became officers (I Chr 12:11).

5. A Levite mentioned in connection with the removal of the ark from the house of Obed-edom (I Chr 15:9, 11).

6 and 7. Two Benjamite family heads (I Chr 8:20, 22).

8. A family chief of the Transjordanian half-tribe of Manasseh (I Chr 5:24).

9. A Levite overseer appointed by Hezekiah to assist in collecting tithes and offerings (II Chr 31:13).

ELIENAI (ĕl'ĭ-ē'nī). A head of a family in the tribe of Benjamin (I Chr 8:20).

ELIEZER (ĕl-ĭ-ē'zẽr). A name not to be confused with Eleazar.

1. Eliezer of Damascus (Gen 15:2), a servant and heir of Abram's house. The custom of childless couples adopting a son who would serve them as long as they lived, then at their death would inherit their property, has long been known from the Nuzi texts (cf. John Bright, *A History of Israel*, p. 71; C. H. Gordon, "Biblical Customs and the Nuzi Tablets," BA, III [1940], 1–12).

2. The second son of Moses and Zipporah, so named because of God's help in delivering Moses from the sword of Pharaoh (Ex 18:4; I Chr 23:15, 17; 26:25).

3. The grandson of Benjamin (I Chr 7:8).

4. One of seven priests who blew the trumpet before the ark when David moved it from the house of Obed-edom to Jerusalem (I Chr 15:24).

5. A ruler of Reuben in the time of David (I Chr 27:16).

6. A prophet who rebuked Jehoshaphat for joining with Ahaziah, king of Israel, in an expedition to Tarshish (II Chr 20:37).

7. The first of a group of 11 leading men of insight sent by Ezra to Iddo to seek out Levites to return to Jerusalem (Ezr 8:16 ff.).

8–10. Three men, a priest, a Levite, and a son of Harim, who in the time of Ezra had married foreign women (Ezr 10:18, 23, 31).

11. A person in the genealogy of Jesus as recorded by Luke (3:29).

R. L. S.

ELIHOENAI (ĕl'ĭ-hō-ē'nī). Variant of Elioenai (*q.v.*).

Head of a family of 200 males who returned to Jerusalem with Ezra (Ezr 8:4).

ELIHOREPH (ĕl'ĭ-hôr'ĕf). Son of Shisha who, with his brother Ahijah, served as scribe in Solomon's court (I Kgs 4:3).

ELIHU (ĕ-lī'hū)

1. The grandfather of Elkanah, Samuel's father (I Sam 1:1); called Eliel in I Chr 6:34 and Eliab in I Chr 6:27.

2. A Manassite captain who deserted King Saul to join David and his guerrillas on their way back to Ziklag (I Chr 12:20).

3. A Korahite gatekeeper among the able descendants of Obed-edom (I Chr 26:7).

4. One of David's brothers (I Chr 27:18); called Eliab in LXX and in I Sam 16:6; 17:13, 28; I Chr 2:13.

5. Job's young friend (Job 32:2–6; 34:1; 35:1; 36:1), the son of Barachel of the clan of Ram, a Buzite (Job 32:2), and thus a distant relative of Abraham (Gen 22:21). Jer 25:23 indicates that Buz was in Arabia. Related to the Hebrews (which may imply a deeper knowl-

edge of their God), Elihu raises the discussion with Job to a higher theological level, showing that greater wisdom comes by inspiration than by human experience and tradition (Job 32:8–9), and urges Job to consider the wondrous works of God (37:14). *See* Job, Book of.

J. R.

Elijah and the widow's son. Stained glass, early sixteenth century Flemish. MM

ELIJAH (ē-lī'jà)

1. Elijah the prophet, whose name means "Yahweh is God," was active during the reigns of Ahab and Ahaziah in the northern kingdom (c. 875–850 B.C.). The account of his ministry begins in I Kgs 17 and concludes with the ascension of Elijah recorded in II Kgs 2. No genealogy, call to service, or background are given except the fact that he was identified as a Tishbite who resided in the land of Gilead E of the Jordan River.

Elijah was called to serve as a spokesman for God when the northern kingdom had expanded to its strongest position economically and politically since its secession from the Davidic rule in Jerusalem. Omri (885–874 B.C.), who introduced a policy of friendship with surrounding nations, sealed his alliance with Phoenicia by the marriage of his son Ahab to Jezebel, the daughter of Ethbaal, king of Tyre. Under the royal sponsorship of Ahab and Jezebel, the cult worship of the Tyrian Baal. Melqart, flourished in Israel. Ahab even erected a temple for Baal in the city of Samaria (I Kgs 16:32). Through his messages and miracles Elijah had the responsibility to remind the Israelites that they were God's people when the royal leadership was committed to Baal worship.

Elijah's first mission was to confront King Ahab with the announcement of an impending drought, reminding Israel's king that the Lord God of Israel, whom he had ignored, was in control of rain in the land where they lived (cf. Deut 11:10–12). Immediately Elijah secluded himself eastward toward the Jordan River. There he was sustained by water from the brook Cherith and by bread and meat miraculously supplied by the ravens. This "brook" (*nahal*) is possibly the deep valley of the Yarmuk River in northern Gilead. When the water supply terminated because of the drought, Elijah was divinely instructed to go to Zarephath in Phoenicia where he would be sustained by a widow whose supply of flour and oil was miraculously extended until rainfall was restored to the land. Elijah's identity as a prophet or man of God was confirmed by the divine manifestation when the widow's son was restored to life.

In the third year of this drought Elijah was divinely bidden to contact Ahab and announce that God was about to send rain. During this time Ahab had made an intensive search for water to sustain his livestock, while Jezebel had killed many of the Lord's prophets. Some of the Lord's prophets, however, were secretly hidden and sustained by one of Ahab's officers named Obadiah. When the latter met Elijah, Obadiah was gravely concerned since Ahab's search for Elijah had intensified. Assured by Elijah that he would not disappear, Obadiah arranged for a meeting between Ahab and Elijah.

Although Ahab charged Elijah with being responsible for Israel's drought problem, the prophet boldly confronted Israel's king with his guilt in breaking the first commandment in worshiping Baal instead of God. In quick order

Ahab complied with Elijah's instructions and arranged for a public meeting on Mount Carmel with the 450 prophets of Baal and 400 prophets of Asherah who were supported by Jezebel.

On Mount Carmel the issues were clearly drawn by Elijah. Ahab's prophets were completely helpless to initiate any power of Baal to ignite the sacrifice they had prepared. Elijah in the meantime repaired the altar of the Lord and prepared his sacrifice. After he prayed to the Lord God of Abraham, Isaac, and Israel, Elijah's sacrifice was miraculously ignited before the public assembly of Israelites. The people responded to this demonstration of God's mighty act and confessed that Yahweh is God. Immediately Elijah ordered the execution of the cultic prophets and instructed Ahab to hurry back to Jezreel before the impending rain, even though the sky was clear. After Elijah's prayer the rain came in abundance. Elijah through divine enablement outran Ahab to the entrance of Jezreel, 18 or 20 miles to the E.

Threatened by Jezebel, the prophet Elijah escaped southward a day's journey past Beer-sheba. He was discouraged to the point of requesting death, but was divinely supplied with nourishment and then continued on to Mount Horeb. There he received a threefold commission: (1) anoint Hazael king over Syria; (2) anoint Jehu king of Israel; (3) anoint Elisha as his successor. On his return Elijah called Elisha to become his associate. The communication of the divine message to Hazael and Jehu was subsequently implemented by Elisha.

The boldest personal confrontation with King Ahab occurred when Elijah met the king in Naboth's vineyard. Jezebel had plotted the execution of Naboth, ignoring the right of land inheritance in ancient Israel (cf. R. de Vaux, *Ancient Israel*, trans. by John McHugh, McGraw-Hill, 1961, pp. 53 ff., 166 f.). Divine judgment upon the royal family was the verdict as Elijah delivered God's message. Since Ahab repented, the judgment was temporarily postponed.

Elijah outlived Ahab, who was killed in an Israelite-Syrian battle in 853 B.C. Elijah's prediction concerning Ahab was fulfilled when the dogs licked the king's blood.

After Ahaziah succeeded his father Ahab on the Israelite throne, he had a crippling fall. When Ahaziah sent servants to inquire of Baal the god of Ekron (mockingly called Baal-zebub, "Baal of flies," a pun on the real name Baal-zebul, "Baal the prince"), to ask if he would recover, Elijah was divinely commissioned to intercept the messengers. They were bidden to return to the king rebuking him for ignoring the God of Israel and warning him of impending death. After several attempts to arrest Elijah failed, the prophet was bidden to go with the third captain dispatched by the king. This time Elijah went to the king to deliver his message directly. Ahaziah did not recover but died as Elijah had predicted.

Near the end of Elijah's ministry, Elisha and some of the prophets associated with them

Mount Carmel and modern Haifa. Palphot, Hertseliya, Israel

sensed that their master was about to leave them. Elisha, however, bound himself by an oath that he would remain with Elijah. After a miraculous parting of the Jordan so the prophets could cross the river on dry ground, Elisha requested a double or firstborn's share of his master's spirit, thus desiring to be Elijah's principal spiritual heir (cf. Deut 21:17). The granting of this request was assured as Elisha saw Elijah ascend into heaven in a whirlwind.

Although Elijah's ministry was primarily in the northern kingdom, he did send a written communication to King Jehoram of Judah who succeeded his father Jehoshaphat. Jehoram was rebuked for ignoring the godly ways of Asa and Jehoshaphat, and following the idolatrous pattern of the kings of Israel (II Chr 21:12-15).

The miraculous element is very prominent in the ministry of Elijah. By this means he was confirmed as a spokesman for God in a time when the kings in Israel were to set the example of wholehearted commitment to God, but were instead devoted to idolatry.

In the OT there is another reference to Elijah in Mal 4:5 where he is mentioned as the forerunner of "the great and terrible day of Jehovah." One of the two witnesses of Rev 11:3-12 is possibly Elijah reappearing in fulfillment of this prophecy. The Jews expected him to return, as indicated in Ecclus 48:10, the Qumran Manual of Discipline (IX.11), and the Mishnaic literature.

Other NT references for further study are: Mt 11:14; 16:14; 17:1-13; 27:47-49; Mk 6:15; 8:28; 9:2-13; 15:35-36; Lk 1:17; 4:25-26; 9:8, 19, 28-36, 54; Rom 11:2-4; Jas 5:17-18.

Bibliography. CornPBE, pp. 273-276. Joachim Jeremias, "*Helias*," TDNT, II, 928-941. James L. Kelso, "Elijah, the Abraham Lincoln of the Israelites," *Archaeology and Our Old Testament Contemporaries*, Grand Rapids: Zondervan, 1966, pp. 105-113. F. W. Krummacher, *Elijah the Tishbite*, trans. by John Cairns, London: T. Nelson & Sons, 1886. William S. LaSor, "Elijah: Rival Altars," *Great Personalities of the Old Testament*, Westwood, N.J.: Revell, 1959, pp. 126-135. F. B. Meyer, *Elijah, and the Secret of His Power*, London: Morgan & Scott, 1917. J. A. Montgomery and H. S. Gehman, *A Critical and Exegetical Commentary on the Books of Kings*, ICC, pp. 292-354. Leon J. Wood, *Elijah, Prophet of God*, Des Plaines, Ill.: Regular Baptist Press, 1968.

S. J. S.

2. A priest who had married a Gentile wife (Ezr 10:21).

3. A Benjamite chief (I Chr 8:27, RSV). *See* Eliah.

4. A layman who had married a foreign wife (Ezr 10:26, RSV). *See* Eliah.

ELIKA (ĕ-lī′kà). A Harodite, one of the 30 mighty men of David (II Sam 23:25). His name

Brook Cherith (at bottom of ravine) and St. George's Monastery, marking traditional spot where ravens fed Elijah.

is not included in the parallel list of I Chr 11:26-47.

ELIM (ē′lĭm). Israel's second encampment in the wilderness of Shur after crossing the Red Sea (Ex 15:22-27; Num 33:8-10). It offered refreshment from 12 springs ("wells," KJV) and 70 palms, in contrast to the bitter waters of Marah in the previous camp. It is traditionally identified as Wadi Gharandel, the usual camping place for travelers from Egypt to Mount Sinai.

ELIMELECH (ĕ-lĭm′ĕ-lĕk). A man of considerable importance and holdings in Bethlehem-judah in the time of the judges; husband of Naomi and father of Mahlon and Chilion (Ruth 1:1 f.). By moving to Moab the family escaped Judah's famine. The sons' marriage to Moabites and the death of the three men led to the return of Naomi and one daughter-in-law, Ruth, to Bethlehem; Ruth's marriage to Boaz; and the birth to them of Obed, grandfather of King David, as related in the book of Ruth.

ELIOENAI (ĕl′ĭ-ō-ē′nī). A contracted form of Elihoenai (*q.v.*).

1. One of the sons of Neariah, a descendant of Zerubbabel, and the father of seven sons (I Chr 3:23-24).

2. One of the Simeonite chiefs, head of a numerous family (I Chr 4:36).

3. Son of Becher of the tribe of Benjamin and head of a father's house (I Chr 7:8).

4. The seventh son of Meshelemiah, a Korahite, a gatekeeper in the house of the Lord (I Chr 26:3; RSV has Eliehoenai).

5. A priest, one of the sons of Pashur, who put away his Gentile wife in the reform of Ezra (Ezr 10:22).

6. An Israelite, of the sons of Zattu, who put away his Gentile wife (Ezr 10:27).

7. A musician priest who took part in Nehemiah's dedication of the wall. Perhaps the same as 5 (Neh 12:41).

ELIPHAL (ĕ-lī′făl). Son of Ur (I Chr 11:35) and

Oasis in Wadi Gharandel. JR

one of David's 30 mighty men. Some identify him with Eliphelet (*q.v.*), the son of Ahasbai (II Sam 23:34).

ELIPHALET (ĕ-lĭf'*á*-lĕt), **ELIPHELET** (ĕ-lĭf'*ĕ*-lĕt)
1. A son of David born in Jerusalem (I Chr 3:5–6; called Elpalet in I Chr 14:5).
2. The last of David's sons born in Jerusalem (II Sam 5:16, RSV; I Chr 3:8; 14:7, RSV).
3. A son of Ahasbai, one of David's mighty men (II Sam 23:34; cf. Eliphal [*q.v.*], I Chr 11:35):
4. A descendant of Jonathan (I Chr 8:33, 39).
5. A son of Adonikam who returned from Babylon with Ezra (Ezr 8:13).
6. A son of Hashum who divorced his Gentile wife after the Exile (Ezr 10:33).

ELIPHAZ (ĕl'ĭ-făz)
1. The eldest son of Esau who had a son named Teman (Gen 36:9–11), from whom the Edomite area took its name. Some have concluded that this was the Eliphaz (see 2) of Job's acquaintance.
2. The first and most prominent of the three friends of Job who came from great distances to comfort him when they heard of his affliction (Job 2:11). He is shown as a venerable sage of Teman in Edom, a place that was noted for its wisdom (Jer 49:7).
Doubtless the wisdom of Eliphaz was intended to be typical of the wisdom in the world of his time. This wisdom was a product of ages of thought, experience, and study. In his first speech (Job 4–5), he asserts that Job's condition is the natural effect of a cause, which cause he makes to include innate impurity and moral depravity. He promises restoration as a result of penitence. In his second speech (Job 15), Eliphaz is irritated by Job's words, which he feels hinder Job's devotion. He attributes them to iniquity and restates his depravity doctrine; he then goes into graphic detail concerning the

fate of the wicked man. In his third speech (Job 22), he actually attempts to accuse Job of crimes and frauds committed when God was too far away to observe him.
His speeches are well-composed and wise but lacking in true human understanding and divine insight so as to be cold and of no avail. Their error was in an unyielding presupposition of Job's wickedness, an unsympathetic clinging to this theory resulting in the suppression of human friendship.

R. O. C.

ELIPHELEH (ĕ-lĭf'ĕ-lĕ). One of 14 special porters "of the second order" (I Chr 15:18) who, among others under David's leadership, were chosen from and by the Levites as instrumental accompanists in the ceremony of bringing the ark of the covenant to Jerusalem from the house of Obed-edom.

ELISABETH (ĕ-lĭz'*á*-bĕth). The wife of the priest Zacharias (*q.v.*) and mother of John the Baptist (Lk 1:5–66). She was descended from Aaron and bore the name of his wife Elisheba (Heb. *'elīsheba'*, "my God has sworn," Ex 6:23). She and her husband, upright and blameless in their adherence to the law (Lk 1:6), could be included among those pious Jews who were eagerly awaiting the coming Messiah. The miraculous event (comparable to the births of Isaac and Samuel) of a son being born to this previously childless couple served both to confirm the announcement of the angel Gabriel to the virgin Mary (Lk 1:35–37), and to give the world a new prophet to prepare the way for the Messiah (1:76). When Mary her kinswoman (Gr. *sungenis,* 1:36) came to visit Elisabeth, the latter was filled with the Spirit and prophesied loudly, addressing Mary as the mother of her Lord (1:41–43). *See* John the Baptist; Mary.

J. R.

ELISEUS (ĕl'ĭ-sē'ŭs). The form of the name Elisha used in the NT (Lk 4:27) and throughout the Douay Version. *See* Elisha.

ELISHA (ĕ-lī'shà). The attendant of Elijah (*q.v.*) and his successor as prophet in Israel. His Heb. name *'ĕlishā'* means "God is salvation." Its Gr. form is *Elissaios,* as in Lk 4:27 (KJV, Eliseus).
Background. Elisha was the son of Shaphat from Abel-meholah (*q.v.*) in the Jordan Valley. The family must have had considerable means, for when Elijah came to extend him a call, Elisha was plowing with a yoke of oxen following eleven other teams. Although still quite young, Elisha responded eagerly and evidenced a godly upbringing by sacrificing his pair of oxen (I Kgs 19:16, 19–21).
Scope of ministry. His prophetic ministry covered the entire last half of the 9th cen. B.C. spanning the reigns of Jehoram, Jehu, Jehoahaz, and Jehoash of the northern kingdom. His influence extended from the widow in debt

(II Kgs 4:1) to the wealthy or prominent (4:8) and into the very palace of Israel itself (5:8; 6:9, 12, 21–22; 6:32–7:2; 8:4; 13:14–19). Furthermore, other kings (Jehoshaphat of Judah, II Kgs 3:11–19; Ben-hadad of Syria, 8:7–9) and high officials (Naaman of the Syrian army, 5:1, 9–19) sought his help. He changed the course of history by completing Elijah's commission (I Kgs 19:15–16) to anoint Hazael as king over Syria (cf. II Kgs 8:12–13) and Jehu as king over Israel (cf. II Kgs 9:1–10). Elisha's greatest contribution to the spiritual welfare of his country may well have been as principal of the schools of prophets at various centers, following in the tradition of Samuel (II Kgs 4:38–44; 6:1–7; cf. I Sam 19:20; *see* Sons of the Prophets).

Miracles. Elisha is best remembered, however, as a great miracle worker. No other person in sacred history is reported to have performed more signs and wonders, except Jesus Christ. A prophet like Moses (Deut 18:15), Elisha healed infected waters (II Kgs 2:19–22; cf. Ex 15:22–25) and produced water in the desert (II Kgs 3:9, 16–20; cf. Ex. 17:1–6). He paralleled the miracles of Elijah as he provided for the widow (II Kgs 4:1–7; cf. I Kgs 17:8–16) and restored the dead to life (II Kgs 4:18–37; cf. I Kgs 17:17–24). Anticipating the miracles of Christ, he healed the leper (II Kgs 5; cf. Mk 1:40–44; Lk 17:11–19) and multiplied the loaves (II Kgs 4:42–44; cf. Mt 14:16–21; 15:32–38). Again like our Lord, he was motivated by deep compassion as he responded to pleas for help by performing such feats as causing a borrowed axehead to float (II Kgs 6:5–7) and as he promised the Shunammite woman a son (4:11–17) and later advised her to flee the famine he predicted (8:1).

Character. In contrast to Elijah who tended to be an ascetic and to withdraw from the public eye, Elisha lived close to the people he served and enjoyed social life. He had a house in Samaria the capital city (II Kgs 6:32), but moved about the country constantly as Samuel had done. He frequently stopped to visit his

Traditional fountain of Elisha at Jericho. JR

friends at Shunem, even as Jesus stayed often with Mary and Martha. Elisha wept as he talked to Hazael, knowing full well the cruel suffering the latter would heap upon Israel (II Kgs 8:11–12). Yet he could pronounce judgment on the young fellows who ridiculed God's new prophet as a baldheaded leper (II Kgs 2:23–24; cf. Lev 13:40–46) and on the royal officer at Samaria for his mocking unbelief (II Kgs 7:1–2), just as severely as Elijah would have done and as Jesus called forth woe on the hypocritical Pharisees (Mt 23). Certainly Elijah's ministry was reproduced in John the Baptist (*q.v.;* Mt 17:10–13; *see also* Elijah); it is just as evident that the person and works of Elisha typify many aspects of our Lord's character and ministry.

Introduction to his ministry. Elisha's first public service, as a chaplain to the armies of Israel and Judah in the time of King Jehoshaphat (II Kgs 3:11–19), may well have preceded the translation of Elijah (2:1–18). Elijah lived to write a letter of judgment to King Jehoram, Jehoshaphat's son (II Chr 21:12–15). On that campaign, then, Elisha was still the attendant of Elijah, the one "who has poured water on the hands of Elijah" (II Kgs 3:11). He had not yet been endued with the full power and spirit of his master. Perhaps this explains why he resorted to the practice of the day of calling for a minstrel to play before he could prophesy (3:15; cf. I Sam 10:5–6; I Chr 25:1).

At the time of Elijah's departure Elisha's request for a double portion recalls the law of inheritance of Deut 21:17. He was asking for the portion and rights of the firstborn son, in this case for the privilege of being the mighty prophet's chief successor. According to the Heb. text, *berûḥăkā 'ēlāy,* he specified that the double portion might be in the form of (*bᵉ*) Elijah's spirit resting upon him (II Kgs 2:9). One should not infer, therefore, that Elisha was asking to be used twice as much or to be twice as powerful as his master.

Final ministry. When Elijah had gone up in the whirlwind, the younger prophet had acknowledged in his cry—"My father, my father, the chariotry of Israel and its horsemen!" (II Kgs 2:12)—that Elijah had been the real "army," the bulwark of spiritual defense for Israel in her time of apostasy. A half century later this same cry was directed by King Joash to Elisha (II Kgs 13:14). On his deathbed, the prophet was performing one last function, namely, to encourage the king to defend Israel against the Syrians (13:15–19). Such object lessons as having the king shoot an arrow and strike the ground repeatedly with his arrows, frequently accompanied prophetic oracles in the OT.

Even in his death the influence of Elisha continued. When a dead man was hastily buried in the same tomb during an enemy invasion, he was miraculously revived as his body touched the bones of Elisha (II Kgs 13:20–21).

J. R.

ELISHAH (ĕ-lī'shá)

1. Grandson of Japheth in the list of "heads of nations" in Gen 10:4 and I Chr 1:7. Josephus (*Ant.* i.6.1) identifies this name with the Aeolians.

2. A coastal region which sold blue and purple dye to Tyre (Ezk 27:7). Elishah is associated with Alashia, common to cuneiform records found in a number of places. Many call it a part of Cyprus other than Kittim (Ezk 27:6), possibly a non-Phoenician area. It has also been identified as Italy, northern Africa, Greece, and many other less prominent areas.

ELISHAMA (ĕ-lĭsh'á-má). The name occurs on ancient Heb. seals and in S Arabic inscriptions.

1. Son of Ammihud, leader of the tribe of Ephraim at the time of the Exodus (Num 1:10; 7:28). Joshua was his grandson (I Chr 7:26).

2. A son born to David in Jerusalem (II Sam 5:16; I Chr 3:8). The same name in I Chr 3:6 apparently stands for Elishua (*q.v.*; cf. II Sam 5:15–16; I Chr 14:5).

3. A prince and secretary to King Jehoiakim (Jer 36:12, 20–21), probably identical with the royal grandfather of Ishmael, who killed Gedaliah, the Babylonian-appointed governor of Judea (II Kgs 25:25; Jer 41:1).

4. A man of the line of Judah (I Chr 2:41).

5. A priest among a group of men appointed by King Jehoshaphat to teach the law in the cities of Judah (II Chr 17:7–9).

ELISHAPHAT (ĕ-lĭsh'á-făt). One of five "captains of hundreds" who joined with Jehoiada the priest to seize the throne from Athaliah and establish Joash as king (II Chr 23:1).

ELISHEBA (ĕ-lĭsh'ĕ-bá). Daughter of Amminadab, a leader of the tribe of Judah. She was the wife of Aaron and mother of Aaron's sons Nadab, Abihu, Eleazar, and Ithamar (Ex 6:23). Thus she was the mother of the entire line of Aaronic priests. *See* Elisabeth.

ELISHUA (ĕl'ĭ-shū'á). The sixth son born to David by a wife or concubine in Jerusalem (II Sam 5:15; I Chr 14:5). In I Chr 3:6 the name Elishama (*q.v.*) appears in his place in the list of David's sons.

ELIUD (ĕ-lī'ŭd). Listed in Matthew's genealogy of Jesus as the ancestor four generations before Joseph (Mt 1:15).

ELIZAPHAN (ĕl'ĭ-zā'făn), **ELZAPHAN** (ĕl-zā'făn)

1. A son of Uzziel who was a Kohathite Levite and a first cousin of Aaron (Ex 6:22; Lev 10:4; Num 3:30; in Exodus and Leviticus Elizaphan is contracted into Elzaphan). With his brother Mishael, he helped remove the bodies of Nadab and Abihu from the camp after they had offered "strange fire" on Yahweh's altar.

2. A son of Parnach who represented the tribe of Zebulun in the division of the land of Canaan under the supervision of Eleazar and Joshua (Num 34:25).

ELIZUR (ĕ-lī'zŭr). Chief of the tribe of Reuben who served as tribal military commander (Num 2:10; 10:18). He served under Moses and Aaron in the census of Israel taken in the second year of the Exodus travel (Num 1:5), and presented the tribe's offering at the tabernacle (Num 7:30–35).

ELKANAH (ĕl-kā'ná)

1. One of the sons of Korah who became the head of a clan (Ex 6:24; I Chr 6:23).

2. The father of Amasai and Ahimoth; son of Joel, descended from Korah through Ebiasaph (I Chr 6:25, 36).

3. The father of Zuph (Zophai) and Nahath, descended from No. 2 (I Chr 6:26, 35).

4. The son of Jeroham and father of Samuel (I Sam 1:1, 4, 8, 19, 21, 23; 2:11, 20; I Chr 6:27, 34). This man, descended from Elkanah Nos. 2 and 3, is described as an Ephraimite (Ephrathite) whose home was in Ramah in Ephraim (I Sam 2:11) and who, with his two wives, Hannah and Peninnah, made a religious pilgrimage to Shiloh each year to offer sacrifices (I Sam 1:3). Hannah was his favorite wife and this contributed, no doubt, to Peninnah's jealousy (I Sam 1:5–7).

5. One of the Levitical priests who dwelt in the hill country of Judea (I Chr 9:16).

6. A warrior from the tribe of Benjamin who deserted Saul's forces and joined David at Ziklag (I Chr 12:6).

7. A Levite in David's time charged with the responsibility for the custody of the ark (I Chr 15:23).

8. An official in the court of King Ahaz of Judah, who was said to have stood next to the king himself (II Chr 28:7).

The frequency of this name and the complexity of the genealogical lists have led some scholars to conclude that the term is used to denote the clan or family as well as individuals. Hence, in some cases one cannot be sure whether the individual or the clan is designated.

G. A. T.

ELKOSH (ĕl'kŏsh). The birthplace of the prophet Nahum (Nah 1:1). It is difficult to determine which city is meant; four suggestions have been made. (1) The 16th cen. Jewish writers identified Nahum as having been born of one of the ten northern tribes in exile in the town Al-Qush (Elkosh) N of Nineveh. (2) Capernaum in Galilee, the "village of Nahum." (3) Jerome's identification with Hilkesei (Elkoseh) in northern Galilee. (4) The more defendable position is the Elkosh in southern Judea near Beth-Gabre or the modern Beit-Jibrin between Jerusalem and Gaza.

ELKOSHITE. *See* Elkosh.

ELLASAR (ĕl'á-sär). The city or country ruled by Arioch (*q.v.*), an ally of Chedorlaomer (*q.v.*), who invaded Palestine in the time of Abraham (Gen 14:1, 9). Former identification of Ellasar with the S Babylonian city-state of Larsa must now be abandoned because the spellings of the two names cannot be equated. Also the cuneiform text bearing the name of the king of Larsa was formerly read as Eri-aku and thus seemingly was similar to Arioch; but now it is more correctly read as Warad-Sin. Recently scholars have suggested that Ellasar may be the town Ilanzura, between Carchemish and Harran in N Mesopotamia, mentioned in the Mari letters and in a Hittite text.

ELM. *See* Plants.

ELMODAM (ĕl-mō'dăm). Listed in Luke's genealogy (3:28) as Jesus' ancestor, the sixth generation before Zerubbabel and the twenty-fifth before Joseph.

ELNAAM (ĕl-nā'ăm). According to the Heb. text of I Chr 11:46, he was the father of Jeribai and Joshaviah, two of 16 men added by the Chronicler to the list of David's guard, the "thirty," as found in II Sam 23:24–39 (cf. I Chr 11:41 ff.). The LXX says, "Eliel the Mahavite and Jeribai and Joshaviah, his son, and Elnaam and Ithmah the Moabite," making Elnaam himself one of the soldiers.

ELNATHAN (ĕl-nā'thăn)
1. A Jerusalemite, maternal grandfather of Jehoiachin (II Kgs 24:8). He was possibly also the son of Achbor, Jehoiakim's court officer (Jer 26:22), who also pled with Jehoiakim not to destroy Jeremiah's scroll (Jer 36:12–25).
2. Two "chief" men (Heb. text of Ezr 8:16) and one "teacher" summoned by Ezra to his camp on the river to Ahava. I Esd 8:44 lists one "chief" man.

ELOHIM (ĕl'ō-hĭm). A plural form of the Heb. noun *'elōah* describing Deity. Some erroneously regard it as the plural of El (*q.v.*), but it is not from the same root. It is usually translated "God," although sometimes it is a true plural and must be understood as "gods" (Ex 12:12; Gen 35:2, 4; Deut 29:18; 32:17). It is sometimes applied to men as God's representatives (Ex 21:6, RSV; 22:8–9, 28, RSV). The term may refer to angels (Ps 8:5, cf. RSV; 82:1), although these passages are debated.

Usually Elohim takes a singular verb. However, it seems occasionally to govern a plural form of the verb (Gen 20:13; 35:7; II Sam 7:23; Ps 58:11, Heb.). What is the significance of this apparent inconsistency? Some would regard it as evidence of the polytheistic origin of the term. In fact, other people of the same era used divine titles in a similar way. The Akkad. plural *ilanu* (gods) was applied to a single deity. Pharaoh was addressed as *ilania* ("my gods") by his Canaanite vassals in the Amarna letters.

In the OT the plural Elohim is applied to Chemosh, the god of the Ammonites (Jud 11:24); Ashtoreth, the goddess of Sidon (I Kgs 11:5); and Baal-zebub of Ekron (II Kgs 1:2).

The significant fact, however, is not the origin of the word, for this cannot be definitely known. Rather, it is the way it is used of Israel's God in the OT. When used of Yahweh, it refers to the sole God of the world, who is addressed in the plural as the fullness of all Deity. We can be sure that no polytheistic elements are allowed to appear in Gen 1. Yet it is here that the plural is most obvious (Gen 1:26). Regardless of one's explanation of the reason for the plural emphasis here, he cannot ignore the plain meaning of the passage. In some sense God is plural; yet He is also singular (cf. the singular verbs in v. 27). Although the Christian doctrine of the Trinity is not taught in the chapter, it emerges from it.

See God; God, Names and Titles of.

C. T. F.

ELOI, ELOI, LAMA SABACHTHANI (ē-lō'ī, ē-lō'ī, lä'má sá-băk' thá́nî). The Heb. or Aram. words from Ps 22:1 spoken by Jesus in His fourth saying on the cross, quoted in Mk 15:34, and similarly in Mt 27:46, which has "Eli, Eli...." Under the agony of crucifixion our Lord recited the opening words of a Davidic psalm depicting sufferings far more intense than David ever endured personally.

Jesus seems to have voiced the words not in Heb., but in His native Galilean Aramaic, *'ĕlohî, 'ĕlohî, lemá shebaqtanî*, "My God, My God, why hast Thou abandoned Me?" The word "eloi" is thought to be the Gr. transliteration of Aram. *'ĕlāhî*, as in Dan 6:22 (v. 23, Aram.), the sound possibly changed to *'ĕlohî* by provincial pronunciation. The commonly accepted text in Matthew has *ēli*, which transliterates the Heb. *'ēlî;* but it is a form also widely used in Aram.

The best Gr. MSS have *lema* in both the Mark and Matthew passages, which better represents Aram. *lemá* than Heb. *lāmá* in either case meaning "why."

"Sabachthani" appears to transliterate an Aram. word, for the original word in Ps 22 is Heb. *'ăzabtānî*. The Aram. verb *shebaq*, "to leave, forsake, abandon," may be seen in Dan 4:23 and Ezr 6:7 ("let . . . alone"). The Targum of Ps 22 (the Targums were Aram. translations of the OT used in synagogues, still in oral form in the 1st cen. A.D.), has these words; thus it may have had a bearing on the form of Jesus' quotation.

Scholars, however, have reopened the debate whether Jesus would more naturally have used Heb. or Aram. The documents from Qumran and Wadi Murabba'at indicate that a form of Heb. influenced by Aram. may have been spoken quite generally in Palestine in the 1st cen. A.D., especially in religious contexts.

J. R.

ELON (ē'lŏn), **ELONITE** (ē'lŏ-nīt)

1. A Hittite, the father of Esau's wives Bashemath (Gen 26:34; 36:10) and Adah (Gen 36:2).

2. Second son of Zebulun, head of the family of Elonites (Gen 46:14; Num 26:26).

3. One of the judges, of the tribe of Zebulun, who served for ten years (Jud 12:11–12).

4. A town in the territory of Dan, the location of which is uncertain (Josh 19:43).

ELON-BETH-HANAN (ē'lŏn-bĕth-hā' nǎn). A Danite town which, with three others, provided one month's sustenance for Solomon's household (I Kgs 4:7–9). This may be the same as Elon 4 (*q.v.*).

ELOTH (ē'lŏth). An alternate form of Elath (*q.v.*).

ELPAAL (ĕl-pā'ǎl). The head of a family of the tribe of Benjamin (I Chr 8:11–12, 18).

ELPALET (ĕl-pā'lĕt). A son of David born in Jerusalem (I Chr 14:5). He is called Eliphelet (*q.v.*) in I Chr 3:6; but is not included in the list of David's sons in II Sam 5.

EL-PARAN (ĕl-pâr'ǎn). The southern extremity of the march of the kings with Chedorlaomer (Gen 14:6) before their swing northward through the city-states, which resulted in the capture of Lot and his rescue by Abraham. Many hold this to be another name for Elath (*q.v.*).

EL SHADDAI (ĕl-shǎd'ī). *See* God; God, Names and Titles of.

ELTEKEH (ĕl'tĕ-kĕ). A city in the area of Ekron, Gibbethon, and Timnah, assigned to the tribe of Dan (Josh 19:44); then to the Kohathite Levites (Josh 21:23); and later taken by Philistines. Probably the place called Altaku by Sennacherib (*Hexagon Prism*), where he defeated an army of Egypt and her allies during his invasion of that section in 701 B.C., though the site is uncertain.

ELTEKON (ĕl'tĕ-kŏn). A city in the hill country of Judah (Josh 15:59), probably N of Hebron and W of Bethlehem. The site is uncertain, but some identify it as Khirbet ed-Deir.

ELTOLAD (ĕl-tō'lǎd). A town of Judah near the border of Edom (Josh 15:30), given to the tribe of Simeon (Josh 19:4). It is probably the place called Tolad in I Chr 4:29. The site is unidentified.

ELUL (ē'lŭl). The sixth month in the Heb. sacred calendar and the last month of the civil calendar (Neh 6:15). It begins with the new moon of August and ends with the new moon of September. The Heb. name *'ĕlûl* seems to have been adopted during the Exile, as it does not appear in pre-Exilic writing. Early writings tended to refer to months by number. It was probably derived from the name of the Babylonian month of Elulu or Ululu. *See* Calendar.

ELUZAI (ĕ-lōō'zī). One of several warriors from the tribe of Benjamin, all noted for excellence with the bow and for ambidextrous use of the slingshot. They joined David's band at Ziklag (I Chr 12:5).

ELYMAS (ĕl'ĭ-mǎs). A Jewish magician at the proconsular court of Sergius Paulus in Cyprus who tried to dissuade Sergius from believing the message brought by Barnabas and Paul (Acts 13:6–11). For his opposition he was suddenly struck with temporary blindness. The name may be akin to Arabic *'alim*, "sage"; the Western text of Codex D reads *Hetoimas*.

See also Barjesus.

ELZABAD (ĕl-zā'bǎd)

1. One of several warriors from the tribe of Gad. Noted for use of the shield and spear, ferocity, and speed of foot, they joined David's band at Ziklag (I Chr 12:12).

2. One of six sons of Shemaiah, all Korahite gatekeepers (I Chr 26:7).

ELZAPHAN. *See* Elizaphan.

EMBALM. Processes of preparing the dead for burial varied considerably among Near Eastern countries during the biblical period. Embalming in antiquity differed somewhat in both tech-

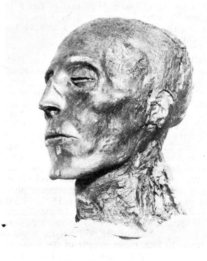

Mummified head of Seti I,
c. 1300 B.C. LL

nique and purpose from the practice of today. The word originally indicated the treating of the body with spices or perfumes, as a preservant and deodorant, and as a mark of respect or honor. Climate, geography and religion affected the preservation of the dead. In Egypt in predynastic times the dead were interred in shallow graves dug in the edge of the desert; in the dry sand the bodies desiccated rapidly and were remarkably well preserved. With the development of the tomb, some of these advantages were lost.

Since the theological concepts of the Egyptians emphasized the survival of the body, the process of mummification was originated in which various organs of the body were removed. Herodotus later described methods of mummification in various price ranges (II, 85–88). The only mentions of the word "embalm" in the Bible are in connection with the bodies of Jacob (Gen 50:2–3) and of Joseph (v. 26). The Heb. verb *ḥānaṭ*, "embalm," means to spice, make spicy. This work was performed by the *rōphe'îm*, "physicians," "repairers." Since spices such as natron, resins, and aromatics were used in mummification, the Egyptian context of Gen 50 indicates that the bodies of Jacob and Joseph were mummified. See Alfred Lucas, "Mummification," *Ancient Egyptian Materials and Industries*, 4th ed. rev. by J. H. Harris, London: St. Martin's Press, 1962, pp. 307–390.

The NT mentions the use of ointments in preparation for burial. The anointing of Jesus is described as burial preparation (Mt 26:12; Mk 14:8; Jn 12:7). In the burial of Jesus, Joseph of Arimathea and Nicodemus used "a mixture of myrrh and aloes, about an hundred pound weight" (Jn 19:39–40). The Galilean women also intended to anoint Jesus' body (Mk 16:1; Lk 23:55–24:1). The body was wrapped in linen cloth, with spices in the windings, according to Jewish custom (Jn 19:40; cf. Jn 11:44; Acts 5:6). Sometimes the corpse was merely washed and clothed to ready it for interment (Acts 9:37). Among the Jews no incisions were made in the corpse or organs removed, as in the mummification process.

See Burial; Dead, The; Funeral; Grave.

C. E. D.

EMBROIDERER. *See* Occupations.

EMEK-KEZIZ. *See* Keziz.

EMERALD. *See* Jewels.

EMERODS. *See* Diseases: Internal Diseases.

EMIM (ē'mĭm). These were giants inhabiting the land of Moab. They were once a tall and powerful people, comparable to the Anakim in stature (Deut 2:9–11). At the battle of the kings they were defeated by Chedorlaomer in the plain of Kiriathaim (Gen 14:5) during the time of Abraham. Apparently they belonged to the tribe of Rephaim although they are unknown outside the Bible. Their territory was later occupied by the Moabites. *See* Giant.

EMMANUEL (ĕ-măn'ū-ĕl). Gr. transliteration of the Heb. Immanuel, "God is with us." It is the form of the Heb. name in Mt 1:23 in which the evangelist quotes the words of Isaiah to King Ahaz (Isa 7:14), where the word is "Immanuel" in the prophetic announcement of the virgin birth of Christ.

See Edward E. Hindson, "Isaiah's Immanuel," *Grace Journal*, X (1969), 3–15.

EMMAUS (ĕ-mā'ŭs). A village mentioned only in Lk 24:13. One of the appearances of Jesus on resurrection Sunday was to two men walking from Jerusalem to Emmaus. The Lucan passage locates this village 60 stades from Jerusalem, or approximately six and three-quarter miles or 11 kilometers away. A variant reading, 160 stades, is found in a few uncial MSS. Si-

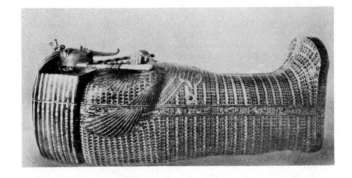

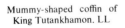
Mummy-shaped coffin of King Tutankhamon. LL

naiticus (4th cen.), N (6th cen.), K, Pi, and Theta (9th cen.), and a few minuscules and two versions; this distance is supported by Eusebius-Jerome, *Onomastikon.* The reading "60 stades" is found in P 75 (late 2nd or early 3rd cen.), B (4th cen.), A and C (5th cen.), and others. The evidence of P 75 (recently published Bodmer papyrus) and B (Codex Vaticanus) together establishes rather definitely the reading "60 stades."

Three identifications of Emmaus have been proposed: (1) The modern village of 'Amwâs (definitive publication: H. Vincent and F. M. Abel, *Emmaus: sa basilique et son histoire,* Paris: Librairie Ernest Lerous, 1932). However, this location would require the reading "160 stades," which is very doubtful in the light of the newer MS evidence. (2) A military colony of Vespasian, possibly present-day *Kaloniye,* called Ammaous by Josephus. The distance from Jerusalem is about 34 stades—rather difficult to correlate with the biblical record. (3) Present-day el-Kubêbe on the road to Joppa (definitive publication: P. B. Bagatti, *I Monumenti di Emmaus El-Qubeibeh e dei dintorni,* Jerusalem, Jordan: Franciscan Press, 1947). The remains here are definitely from the NT period, and the distance from Jerusalem agrees fairly well with the Lucan record, making this identification the preferred one.

B. Van E.

EMMOR (ĕm'ôr). The NT form of the Heb. name Hamor (*q.v.*) as transliterated into Gr. (Acts 7:16; cf. Josh 24:32).

EMPTIED. A word significant to the doctrine of Christ's incarnation (Phil 2:7, ASV, RSV, etc.). *See* Kenosis.

EN-. This prefix in Heb. stands for *'ayin* which primarily means "eye"; secondarily it means "fountain." Figuratively, it was anything which resembled the eye, a look or glance of the eye, an aspect or appearance of a thing. Thus, the usage for "spring" or "fountain" was derived. Many cities and places of Palestine and Syria were named from fountains in their vicinities, such as Engedi and En-gannim. Sometimes fountains themselves were so designated, as En-shemesh.

ENAM (ē'năm). A place in Judah adjacent to Adullam and Timnath in the Shephelah (Josh 15:34). It is conjectured that Enaim is another form of the same word (Gen 38:14, RSV). It was in the gate of Enaim or Enajim that Tamar sat before her interview with her father-in-law. The endings -im and -jim are interchangeable; thus the two names referred to the same place. In the KJV it is translated "an open place." The name means "double springs."

ENAN (ē'năn). A Naphtalite whose son Ahira was a prince at the time of the numbering of the children of Israel in the wilderness of Sinai (Num 1:15; 2:29; 7:83; 10:27). *See* Hazar-Enan.

ENCAMPMENT. *See* Camp.

ENCHANTER. *See* Magic.

ENCHANTMENT. In the KJV this is the translation of several Heb. words. It was used of the tricks of the Egyptian magicians (Ex 7:11, 22; 8:7), the auguries sought by Balaam (Num 24:1), the charming of a serpent (Eccl 10:11), and magical spells (Isa 47:9, 12).

Mosaic law forbad the practice of such enchantments (Deut 18:10; Lev 19:26; Isa 47:9). They constituted a peculiar temptation to Israel to apostatize.

See Magic; Divination.

END OF THE WORLD. *See* Eschatology.

ENDOR (ĕn'dôr). A town on the N side of the hill of Moreh, S of Mount Tabor which was assigned to the tribe of Manasseh, though it was located in the territory of Issachar (Josh 17:11). The ancient site was probably at Khirbet Safsafa about three-quarters of a mile NE of the former village of Indur which echoes the ancient name. Nearby are several ancient caves. Poetic tradition preserves the memory that Barak's victory took place in the vicinity of Endor (Ps 83:10). It was also the home of a witch consulted by King Saul (I Sam 28:7). *See* Familiar Spirit.

ENEAS. *See* Aeneas.

EN-EGLAIM (ĕn-ĕg'lĭ-ĭm). The name, found only in Ezk 47:10, refers to a site in conjunction with En-gedi between which places fishermen stand. Its exact location is in doubt; however, it is thought to have been on the W shore of the Dead Sea toward the mouth of the Jordan. Eglaim of Isa 15:8 is regarded as a different place since the initial letter is *alef* rather than *'ayin,* and the two letters are rarely if ever exchanged. The most probable location of En-eglaim is 'Ain Feshkha, one and a half miles S of Qumran.

ENEMY. One who hates another and seeks his hurt; a foe or adversary; also, a hostile nation or army.

A number of terms express in different ways the underlying idea of enemy. In the OT Heb. *'ōyēb* (possible original idea of breathing, blowing, puffing, an idea often applied to anger and hatred) is rendered "enemy" or "foe." Heb. *şar* (from *şarar,* "to press," "to compress" and thus to "oppress," or in this case, to treat one in a hostile manner) is translated as "adversary" and "foe" in addition to "enemy."

The noun *shōrēr* (specifically, a "defamer" or "slanderer," a Canaanism so used in the

Amarna letters according to M. Dahood, *Psalms II*, Anchor Bible, Garden City: Doubleday, 1968, pp. 25 f.) is also "enemy" in KJV and RSV.

Other words express the action of an enemy and are so indicated as such: *qûm*, "to rise up" against one; *śānē'*, "to hate" and in its participle, therefore, a "hater" or "enemy"; *shûr*, "to lie in wait" against one. In the NT, Gr. *echthros* is rendered "enemy" or "foe."

In most instances, "enemy" in the OT describes the national enemies of Israel (Jud 3:1-3; etc.), but there are also references to personal enemies (Ex 23:4; I Sam 18:29; I Kgs 21:20; Mic 7:6; etc.); note particularly the Psalms (7:5; etc.). In the NT "enemy" for the most part indicates personal enemies (Mt 5:44; II Thess 3:15; etc.), but it also depicts foreign powers (Lk 1:71; 19:43).

Man becomes the enemy of God when he disobeys the divine commandments. He can incur God's wrath and jealous zeal in his disobedience (Deut 5:8-10; 7:10). The imprecatory psalms (*see* Psalms) express the psalmist's feelings as he regards God's enemies as his own; he then implores God to vindicate His own honor and righteousness by judging and punishing those who flout His commandments. Sinners are named by Paul the enemies of God (Rom 5:8, 10). The friend of the world is the enemy of God (Jas 4:4). Satan (*see* Devil; Satan) is the greatest enemy of all (Mt 13:39; Acts 13:10; cf. Jn 8:44). Death is regarded as the last enemy (I Cor 15:26) to come under the dominion of Christ.

The OT describes God as an enemy. He was the enemy to the enemies of Israel (Deut 28:7; II Chr 20:29). The prophets express their hatred for Israel's enemies and despisers of the Lord. This is not necessarily a sub-biblical ethic, for the inspired men were not merely expressing some personal diatribe against Israel's national enemies; their words and writings were the thoughts and sentiments of a holy God expressed against *His* enemies (Isa 14:25-27; Ezk 35:7; Obadiah; Nahum; etc.). Thus God was for Israel so as to deliver them out of Egypt (Ex 3:8), to guide them through the desert, and ultimately to give them the land of Canaan. Not only is this seen in the books of Moses, but the prophets continue this emphasis (Hos 11:1; Amos 2:9-10).

God also abandoned Israel to their enemies as a means of judgment on His people (Isa 10:5-6; Ezk 14:13-21; Lk 19:41-44), and therefore the prophets called God Israel's enemy (Lam 2:5). The prophets, though, recognized the positive aspect of the judgment, because if God did not judge Israel, they would have disappeared into the sea of nations. As difficult as it was, there was the dominance of the love of God in preserving a remnant of His people (Isa 54:7-8; Jer 30:14, 18; Dan 9:16, 24). In a peculiar emphasis also on the personal level, Job calls God his enemy (Job 13:24; 19:11).

On the other hand, there are many OT examples where God did good to the national enemies of Israel (e.g., to Nineveh in the book of Jonah). Jeremiah, for the well-being of his kinsmen, instructed the Judean captives to pray for their Babylonian masters (Jer 29:7). In many ways and through a number of circumstances Israel was to be a blessing to foreign nations even though these countries were enemies at times (Gen 12:3).

The OT instructed the individual Israelite to love his neighbor (Lev 19:18). While the Israelite was not told to love his enemy, yet he was *never* told not to love him; indeed, he was told to do his enemy good. Thus, Moses instructed his kinsmen to return any enemy's lost ox or ass and even help his enemy with his beast of burden (Ex 23:4-5). Saul said David was more righteous than himself since David repaid good for his enemy's evil (I Sam 24:17-19). Job stated in defense of his righteousness that he would be denying God if he rejoiced at the defeat of his enemy (Job 31:28-29). The wisdom writer in Prov 25:21-22 stresses the righteous man's duty: "If thine enemy be hungry, give him bread to eat; and if he be thirsty, give him water to drink: for thou shalt heap coals of fire upon his head."

The NT filled in the gap in the OT when Jesus stated that one should love and pray for his enemies (Mt 5:43-44). This love is demonstrated when we realize that God gave His Son on behalf of a world of enemies (Jn 3:16), and thus reconciled those hostile to Him (Col 1:20-22). Christ (Lk 23:34) and Stephen (Acts 7:60) are examples for us as they prayed for their persecutors. Paul emphasized the love of Christians for their enemies when he made the OT imperative (Prov 25:21-22) the NT ethic (Rom 12:14-21).

See Adversary; Sin; War; Wrath.

L. Go.

EN-GANNIM (ĕn-găn'ĭm)

1. A town in the Shephelah of Judah in the proximity of Zanoah, Tappuah and Enam (Josh 15:34).

2. Josh 19:21 and 21:29 mention a second such city in the tribe of Issachar. The Gershonite Levites were assigned this city with its suburbs as one of their possessions. It probably corresponds to the Ginea of Josephus (*Ant.* xx. 6.1) and may certainly be identified with the modern Jenin, a prosperous village on the southern edge of the plain of Esdraelon, with beautiful gardens, fruitful orchards and plentiful supplies of water from the local springs. Its location is approximately seven miles SW of Mount Gilboa on the main road from Esdraelon through Samaria to Jerusalem. Beth-haggan (II Kgs 9:27, RSV) is probably an alternate name for En-gannim.

EN-GEDI (ĕn-gĕd'ī). In ancient times an agricultural settlement watered by a copious spring ("spring of the goat-kid" or "spring of abundant waters") on the W shore of the Dead Sea (Ezk 47:10), about midway between the N and S ends in the general direction or vicinity of Hazazon-tamar (II Chr 20:2). It was included in the territory of Judah (Josh 15:62). In Solomon's time it was a fertile oasis in the midst of the desert where spice plants and vineyards were cultivated (Song 1:14). En-gedi was also famed in Jewish and Roman literature for its fine date palms.

Saul pursued David to this region, whereupon David and his men hid in a cave (I Sam 23:29; 24:1) while Saul slept nearby.

In the Middle Ages the terraced gardens and buildings were abandoned and became a deserted waste. Today travelers approach the area after a long trek through the desert inferno along the shores of the Dead Sea. The plain of En-gedi stretches 1,500 yards between two wadis or canyons descending to the Dead Sea. It is located in Israel, only a few miles S of the 1948-1967 Israel-Jordan border. After one climbs upward for a few hundred yards inland from the Dead Sea, the beautiful falls of En-gedi come into view. A crystal clear spring in the cliff above, 670 feet above the sea, cascades into a beautiful pool below. Most of the water runs into the Dead Sea, but in recent years members of an Israeli kibbutz (a communal settlement, mainly for immigrants) have utilized some of the water for irrigation purposes. The plain between the canyons is very productive and grows an abundance of vegetables and fruits, especially bananas.

Five seasons of excavations by Israeli archaeologists (1961-1965) in the En-gedi area have discovered a late Chalcolithic Age (c. 3300 B.C.) enclosure above the spring, probably a sacred place for the nomads and villagers of the Judean desert and its oases; a fortified mound (Tell el-Jurn) with five levels of occupation; an Israelite square watchtower by the spring; and two ritual pools from before A.D. 70 and a Roman bath (A.D. 70-135). The mound was first occupied from the reign of Josiah to the time of Nebuchadnezzar's control (c. 625-580 B.C.). The unusual pottery vessels suggest that this was an industrial center for the preparation of perfume from the balm cultivated nearby. En-gedi likely became a royal estate under King Josiah, with the perfumers organized in a guild. Later levels of Tell el-Jurn indicate En-gedi prospered in the Persian period (c.525-475 B.C.), under the Hasmonean kings John Hyrcanus and Alexander Jannaeus (135-76 B.C.), in the 1st cen. until destroyed by the Roman legion (A.D. 1-68), and during the Roman-Byzantine era (3rd-5th cen. A.D.).

Bibliography. B. Mazar, "Excavations at the Oasis of Engedi," *Archaeology,* XVI (1963), 99-107; "En-gedi," TAOTS, pp. 223-230. Mazar and I. Dunayevski, "Third Season," IEJ, XIV (1964), 121-130; "Fourth and Fifth Seasons," IEJ, XVII (1967), 133-143. Mazar, T. Dothan, and Dunayevski, "En-Gedi," *Exca-*

vations in 1961-1962, Jerusalem: Dept. of Antiquities and Museums, 1966.

ENGINE. Translation of two words in Heb.: (1) *hishshebōnôt* (II Chr 26:15), devices of war for hurling stones and arrows, i.e., catapults (*q.v.*); (2) *mᵉḥî qᵉbōl* (Ezk 26:9), literally, "the smiting of an attacking engine," i.e., the blows of a battering ram (cf. RSV). *See* Armor.

ENGLISH VERSIONS, BIBLE. *See* Bible—English Versions.

EN-HADDAH (ĕn-hăd'á). A village in the tribal territory of Issachar, near Remeth (Josh 19:21). It is perhaps modern el-Hadetheh, six miles E of Mount Tabor and six miles SW of the southern tip of the Sea of Galilee.

EN-HAKKORE (ĕn-hăk'ŏ-rē). Jud 15:19 mentions the experience of Samson after his exploit with the jawbone of an ass. His thirst was great and he called upon the Lord for water. Water was provided at Lehi and the name thereof was En-hakkore, "the spring of him that called." Its location is unknown.

EN-HAZOR (ĕn-hā'zôr). Josh 19:37 locates this village in the tribe of Naphtali adjacent to Kadesh, Edrei and Iron. Its site is unknown; however, some speculation exists relative to its identification with Khirbet Hazireh or Hazzur on the slopes about nine miles W of Kedesh.

EN-MISHPAT (ĕn-mĭsh'păt). Gen 14:7 identifies this place as Kadesh, probably Kadesh-barnea (*q.v.*). It is thought that there was a sanctuary there at which in ancient times a pagan priest gave oracles and decided disputes. The names Kadesh and Kedesh are connected with Canaanite cities that had heathen sanctuaries.

ENMITY. The Heb. *'ēbâ* occurs five times in the OT (Gen 3:15; Num 35:21-22; Ezk 25:15; 35:5). The enmity in Gen 3:15 is between the serpent and Eve and between its seed and her seed, symbolic of the spiritual warfare between Satan and Christ and His followers. Individual hostility is in view in Num 35:21-22. The enmity in the Ezekiel passages is national.

The usage of the six occurrences of the Gr. *echthra* in the NT also reveals three kinds of enmity—hostility toward God (Rom 8:7; Jas 4:4), the enmity of individuals (Lk 23:12), and hostility between groups of people (Eph 2:14-16). The plural in Gal 5:20 (ASV) evidently refers to the various manifestations and forms of hostile feelings.

ENOCH (ē'nŭk)

1. The son of Cain (Gen 4:17) for whom a city was named.

2. The son of Jared (Gen 5:18) and the father of Methuselah (Gen 5:21; Lk 3:37). He is cited as a hero of faith (Heb 11:5).

It is said that "Enoch walked with God" (Gen 5:22), and as a reward for his holy walk he was translated to heaven without tasting death (Heb 11:5). Thus immortality or life after death was clearly taught in the early Genesis period. Jude 14–15 has excerpts from the Book of Enoch (1:9; 63:8; 93:3), which give a clear-cut sampling of the judgment which was preached by Enoch in this early period. While some may argue as to what source Jude actually used (written or oral tradition), it can be pointed out that inclusion of this quotation in a NT book canonizes his message and makes it Holy Writ. Some scholars believe that Jude was quoting from pseudepigraphical literature used by the false teachers in order to silence them with their own material.

The Book of Enoch was already in existence in the apostolic period. After being quoted in Jude and noticed by some of the Church Fathers, this book disappeared. No part of the Heb. original has come down to us, although there are fragments in Gr. and Ethiopic which scholars associate with this book. In caves near the Essene monastery by the Dead Sea were found parts of eight MSS. of I Enoch in Aramaic.

H. A. Han.

ENOS (ē'nŏs), **ENOSH** (ē'nŏsh). The son of Seth (Gen 4:26; 5:6) and the father of Cainan or Kenan (Gen 5:9–10; I Chr 1:1; Lk 3:37–38). The alternate spelling of Enos is Enosh. Little is known about him. His son Kenan was born when his father was 90 years of age and the length of Enos' life is recorded as 905 years. More significant is the statement that in his time men began to call on the name of Yahweh (Gen 4:26). The implication is that his birth is associated with the awakening of reverence and godly fear. The Genesis account presents Seth and Enos as successors of "righteous Abel." In contrast to Cain and his posterity, Seth and his descendants are portrayed as God-fearing and as custodians of the covenant relationship; this is the chief significance of Enos.

The Heb. term in the singular also occurs about 40 times as a common noun in the OT, chiefly in poetry, with the meaning parallel to that of 'ādām, "man, mankind, human being."

G. A. T.

EN-RIMMON (ĕn-rĭm'ŏn). Some suggest that the name Rimmon refers to the Canaanite weather god. Neh 11:29 names En-rimmon as one of the places which the men of Judah reinhabited after their return from the Captivity. From the names of the surrounding cities, it is possible that this site is the same as that named in Zech 14:10; Josh 15:32; 19:7; I Chr 4:32. In the last three references the two names are listed separately; however, they are in close proximity to one another. En-rimmon has been identified with Khirbet Umm er-Ramâmîn, eight and a half miles NE of Beer-sheba.

Present-day well at Bir-Ayyub, lower left to right above; Hinnom Valley, Southwest Hill, City Wall. JR

EN-ROGEL (ĕn-rō'gĕl). Josh 15:7; 18:16 locate this site on the border of Benjamin and Judah. II Sam 17:17 sets forth En-rogel as the location where Jonathan and Ahimaaz stayed while awaiting the messages to be taken to David during the revolt of Absalom. I Kgs 1:9 records the event of Adonijah's abortive ascension to the throne of Israel as having taken place in this area.

Some question exists relative to the location of the site. Some identify it with Gihon, or the Virgin's Fount, Ain Sitti Miriam, and 'Ain Umm ed-deraj. Their arguments are set forth as follows: (1) It is the only real spring close to Jerusalem. (2) It fits more concisely with the boundary of Benjamin than any other. (3) The tradition of the death of James relates that he was thrown from the temple wall and clubbed to death in the valley of Kidron. (4) This spring is opposite a cliff face called Zaḥweileh, said to be the equivalent of "the stone of Zoheleth, which is by En-rogel" (I Kgs 1:9).

On the other hand, En-rogel has been identified with Bir-Ayyub for the following reasons: (1) It is a well some 125 feet deep which is fed by a spring at the bottom. (2) According to the account in I Kgs 1:9, Adonijah was at En-rogel feasting when in I Kgs 1:38 Solomon was acclaimed king at Gihon. Thus two different sites seem to be set forth. (3) Since it was not on the immediate route from Jerusalem to Jordan, it seems apparent that there would have been a better hiding place among the caves that were in its proximity in which Jonathan and Ahimaaz could secrete themselves. Thus, En-rogel is set forth as being in the precincts of Jerusalem, and somewhere in the southern extremity of the valley of Hinnom. This is the site that is called by the natives the "Well of Job" or Bir-Ayyub, The Arabic version of Josh 15:7 sets forth En-rogel as the "Spring of Job" or Ain Ayyub.

A description of this well is revealing. The gradual filling of the valley necessitated walling up the top of the old well or spring with large square stones, the lowest stage perhaps dating to Roman times. The water is pure and sweet, but not very cold. At certain times of the year the well overflows, giving the sense of "spring." Although some question exists concerning this site of En-rogel, it seems apparent that the location is Bir Ayyub. Some commentators have identified the dragon or jackal well of Neh 2:13 with Bir Ayyub, but probably wrongly.

C. M. H.

ENROLLMENT. *See* Census.

ENSAMPLE. *See* Example.

EN-SHEMESH (ĕn-shĕm'ĭsh; "fountain or spring of the sun"). Josh 15:7 and 18:17 locate En-Shemesh on the border between Judah and Benjamin, En-rogel and Adummim. It was E of Jerusalem about a mile beyond Bethany toward Jericho. It is identified with 'Ain el-Hôd, also called "the Well of the Apostles," on account of a tradition dating back to the 15th cen. which stated that the apostles drank from this well. It is the last spring on the road to Jericho. The rays of the sun are on it the whole day. Thus it is appropriately called the "Fountain of the Sun."

ENSIGN, STANDARD. An emblem or flag; a signal or warning sign.

1. Heb. *'ôt*, the "sign" or token "of their father's house" and thus of a tribal subdivision (Num 2:2). Ps 74:4 refers to the idolatrous emblems (see ANEP #469–573) or military ensigns which foes of God set up in the holy place.

2. Heb. *degel*, the military standard or banner of a fighting unit (Num 1:52; 2:2, 3, 10, etc.; 10:14, 18, 22, 25; Song 6:10). The word came to mean a division of an army in post-biblical literature. It was used this way in the Elephantine papyri and the Qumran scrolls, and

the LXX translates *degel* by *tagma* or *taxis,* a body of soldiers (see Roland de Vaux, *Ancient Israel,* New York: McGraw-Hill, 1961, pp. 226 f.). The emblem was fastened to a wooden pole and was carried by a special standard-bearer as depicted in Sumerian and Egyptian art work (VBW, I, 202 f. on Num 2:2, 34).

Rabbinical tradition, continued in modern Jewish art, has perhaps partially preserved the figures portrayed on tribal standards of ancient Israel. The blessing of Jacob possibly provides a clue to the original emblems – Judah's, a lion (Gen 49:9); Zebulun's, a ship (Gen 49:13); etc. According to the Qumran apocalyptic scroll, "The War of the Sons of Light against the Sons of Darkness," inscriptions on the standards were to be changed with each new phase of the war. When the army of the righteous marched to battle their sign held high was to read: "The Community of God"; when fighting would begin it was to be changed to: "The War of God"; when their army returned to camp it was: "The Salvation of God."

The verb *dāgal* occurs in the victorious battle cry of trust in Ps 20:5, "In the name of our God we will set up our banners!" In Song 2:4 the beloved sings, "His banner over me was love." *See* Banner.

3. Heb. *nēs,* a standard or pole with an attached object. A bronze cult standard overlaid with silver found at Hazor bears the relief of a head of a goddess with two snakes on either side (VBW, I, 221 on Num 21:9). A bronze head covered over with gold, from a Late Bronze Age level at Beth-shan, probably adorned the top of a military standard (VBW, IV, 51 on Ps 115:4).

Moses placed a bronze serpent on a pole (*nēs*) as a signal for extending deliverance and healing (Num 21:8–9). In Num 26:10 the word translated "sign" indicates that Korah's death came as an act of judgment in order to convey a

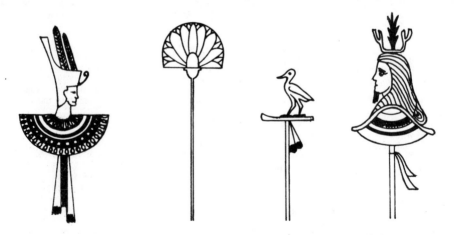

Egyptian Standards

warning. The simile of a signal standard alone on a bare hilltop depicts chastened Israel's lonely plight (Isa 30:17 – "ensign," KJV and ASV; "signal," RSV). Assyrian officers would desert their ensign or standard in panic (Isa 31:9, RSV).

As an object raised aloft accompanied by the sounding of a trumpet, in certain prophetic declarations the *nēs* represents God's signal to summon enemy nations for Judah's judgment (Isa 5:26; Jer 4:6, 21) and for Babylon's downfall (Jer 50:2; 51:12, 27). God signals for all the world to watch the defeat of Cush or Ethiopia (Isa 18:3).

The *nēs* is a part of the prophetic imagery in predictions concerning the future regathering of Israel: "The root of Jesse shall stand as an ensign to the peoples" (Isa 11:10, RSV; and 11:12). It symbolizes that mood, movement, or condition which God will establish among the nations in order to effect the return of His people to their land (Isa 49:22 – "standard," KJV; "ensign," ASV; "signal," RSV). It is the signal which will preface the heralding of the good news that salvation has come to the daughter of Zion (Isa 62:10).

Verbal forms of *nāsas*, considered to mean "lift up a standard," occur in Isa 10:18, "a standardbearer" (KJV); Isa 59:19, "the Spirit of the Lord shall lift up a standard against him" (KJV); Zech 9:16, "lifted up as an ensign upon his land" (KJV); and Ps 60:4, "Thou hast given a banner [*nēs*] to them that fear thee, that it *may be displayed* because of the truth."

H. E. Fi.

EN-TAPPUAH (ĕn-tăp'ŭ-à; "fountain of the apple or citron"). Located in Manasseh on the border of Ephraim (Josh 17:7). It is probably the same as or next to Tappuah (*q.v.*), located near the source of the river Kanah. Tappuah may be Sheikh Abu Zarad, nine miles SSW of Shechem, and the "spring of Tappuah" is probably to be identified with a spring about three miles N of Lebonah.

ENVY. Envy is an active principle of hostility aimed maliciously at the real or supposed superiority of another person. It originated in Satan's abortive attempt to usurp divine attributes (Isa 14:12–20). Eve imbibed this pernicious evil in yielding to Satan's insinuations (Gen 3:4–7). Envy prompted the first murder (Gen 4:5). Its ugly form appeared in Rachel (Gen 30:1), Joseph's brothers (Gen 37:11; cf. Acts 7:9), Saul (I Sam 18:8 f.), Israel (Ps 106:16). It even instigated the Jewish leaders to deliver Jesus to Pilate (Mt 27:18; Mk 15:10).

Gr. *phthonos*, which designates "envy" in all places except possibly Jas 4:5 (see ASV and NASB), characterizes human nature (Rom 1:29; Tit 3:3) and the "flesh" (Gal 5:19, 21). Its display among Christians is forbidden (Gal 5:26; I Tim 6:4; I Pet 2:1).

Gr. *zēlos* ("zeal"), while often righteously motivated (II Cor 7:7, 11; 9:2), can, when mis-

directed (Rom 10:2; Phil 3:6), easily become envy (Acts 13:45; 17:5; Rom 13:13; I Cor 3:3; II Cor 12:20; Jas 3:14, 16).

See Jealousy.

EPAENETUS (ē-pē'nē-tŭs). Paul's greeting to the Christians at Rome mentions Epaenetus as his beloved and as the first convert to Christ in Asia (Rom 16:5). The name was not uncommon; it is found in inscriptions both in Rome and Asia. In fact, one such inscription discovered in Rome makes reference to an Epaenetus as a native of Ephesus.

EPAPHRAS (ĕp'à-frăs). A "beloved fellow servant" and a "faithful minister of Christ," held in high esteem by Paul (Col 1:7–8; 4:12–13). In Phm 23 he is referred to as "my fellow prisoner in Christ Jesus." While the name is a contracted form of Epaphroditus, most do not connect him with the Philippian man of that name in Phil 2:25–30 (contra. Glover, *Paul of Tarsus*).

From Col 1:6–7 it appears that Colosse had received "the grace of God in truth" not from Paul himself but from Epaphras. On the basis of Col 4:13, he had been Paul's representative in evangelizing not only Colosse, but also Laodicea and Hierapolis. Later he shared Paul's imprisonment and sent greetings to Philemon.

EPAPHRODITUS (ē-păf'rō-dī'tŭs). One of two companions of Paul highly commended by him in Phil 2:25–30. The epithets are striking: "my brother and fellow worker and fellow soldier, and your messenger [*apostolon*] and minister to my need" (Phil 2:25, RSV). He had expended great energy both on behalf of the work of Christ and of Paul himself, even coming near death due to "hazarding his life" in aiding Paul (Phil 2:30), apparently in conveying to him the love-gift from Philippi (Phil 4:18).

EPHAH (ē'fà)

1. A branch of the Midianites (Gen 25:4; I Chr 1:33), living in NW Arabia, rich in camels and dromedaries (Isa 60:6). They are called Haiapâ in Assyrian inscriptions of Tiglath-pileser III.

2. A woman of the family of Caleb (I Chr 2:46).

3. A son of Jahdai, family of Caleb, of Judah (I Chr 2:47).

4. *See* Weights, Measures, and Coins.

EPHAI (ē'fī). Jer 40:8 mentions Ephai the Netophathite as the father of some of the captains of the forces who were left behind in Judah at the carrying away of the captives to Babylon. These captains were identified with Gedaliah, the governor of the scattered, poverty-stricken Jews at Mizpah. Concurrent with Gedaliah's assassination, they were also put to death by Ishmael, the son of Nethaniah (Jer 41:3).

EPHER (ē'fĕr)

1. The second son of Midian and a descendant of Abraham through his marriage to Keturah (Gen 25:4).

2. The third son of Ezrah of the tribe of Judah (I Chr 4:17, RSV).

3. One of the five heads of their fathers' houses in the half tribe of Manasseh who dwelt between Bashan and Mount Hermon (I Chr 5:24). He was regarded as a famous and mighty man of valor.

EPHES-DAMMIM (ē'fĕs-dăm'ĭm). The site of a Philistine encampment preparatory to the Philistine attack on the Israelites (I Sam 17:1). It is located between Shochoh and Azekah. Goliath went forth from the camp to challenge Israel to send out one warrior to represent them. It has been suggested that the name ("border of blood") was derived from the frequent sanguinary encounters between the Israelites and the Philistines. Another conflict between these two nations is recorded in I Chr 11:13, where the abbreviated form, Pas-dammim, is used. The land, when freshly plowed, has a deep red color and this may account for the name. *See* Pas-dammim.

EPHESIANS. *See* Ephesus.

The first page of Ephesians from Beatty-Michigan papyrus. University of Michigan Library.

EPHESIANS, EPISTLE TO THE. The tenth book of the NT, classified along with Philippians, Colossians and Philemon as one of the Prison Epistles of Paul.

EPHESIANS, EPISTLE TO THE

Authorship

Until the days of the 19th cen. higher criticism, Ephesians was universally held to be the work of Paul. Today, it is one of the four epistles which liberals in general deny as Pauline. (The others are I and II Timothy and Titus.) During the first three centuries it was ascribed to Paul by Marcion, Irenaeus, Clement of Alexandria, and Tertullian. Recent denial of Pauline authorship has, however, been based on internal evidence rather than external. Generally, four arguments are advanced in support of the critical position. (1) The vocabulary is said to contain 38 words not found elsewhere in the NT and 44 words not otherwise used by Paul. This argument fails to recognize the versatility of Paul and the influence of subject matter on vocabulary. (2) The style, it is noted, is smooth and deep-flowing, whereas Paul was a vigorous, rugged, controversial writer. Again, no room is left for Paul's versatility. Ephesians is, no doubt, an example of the apostle's style when he was not engaged in controversy, but, rather, in a more reflective type of writing. (3) Similarity to Colossians is taken to indicate that a later admirer of Paul used Colossians as his model in composing another letter in Paul's name. It is, however, much more natural to understand that Paul himself penned Ephesians shortly after Colossians, using with varying modification some of the terms and concepts employed in the letter to Colosse. (4) Doctrinal differences are interpreted as indicative of non-Pauline authorship. Careful analysis, however, reveals that the suggested differences are in no way inconsistent with Paul's teachings elsewhere. Allowance, again, must be made for the apostle's versatility. On the basis of the unanimous testimony of early church writers, and in light of the inconclusive nature of the critical arguments, it may be confidently asserted that Ephesians is the product of Paul's pen.

Recipients

Although the KJV contains the address, "to the saints which are at Ephesus," MS evidence and the general nature of the epistle have been taken to suggest that the letter was not confined to Ephesus alone. Two of the best MSS, the Vaticanus (c. A.D. 350) and the Sinaiticus (c. A.D. 375), as well as the Chester Beatty Papyrus P46 (c. A.D. 200), omit the words translated "at Ephesus." Furthermore, Basil the Great (A.D. 329–379) said that these words were not found in any ancient MSS. The impersonal nature of the epistle, and several passages which suggest that Paul was not personally acquainted with his readers (1:15; 3:2; 4:21), seem to call for a wider readership. There is, therefore, a reasonable possibility that Ephesians was originally a circular letter, perhaps sent to all the churches of the Roman province of Asia, of which the Ephesian church was the leading congregation. In time, because of the prominence of the latter church, the epistle may have come to be called by its name. The possibility that the letter was addressed to the church at Laodicea and is the so-called "lost" epistle to the Laodiceans ought to be carefully considered, particularly since there is considerable internal evidence to be found for its support.

An inscribed statue base along one of the main streets of Ephesus. HFV

Date and Place of Writing

The letter gives evidence of having been written during a prison experience (3:1; 4:1; 6:20). Although some, such as George S. Duncan in *St. Paul's Ephesian Ministry,* have argued for an Ephesian origin of the Prison Epistles, the traditional view of a Roman origin still commends itself to the majority of scholars. On this assumption, the epistle seems to have been written during Paul's first Roman imprisonment (cf. Acts 28:16–31), perhaps about A.D. 60–61. There is reason to believe that it was composed shortly after Colossians and sent along with that epistle and Philemon by the hand of Tychicus (Eph 6:21–22; Col 4:7–8).

Message of the Epistle

A key term in Ephesians is the word "mystery," the first occurrence of which is found in 1:9–10. Here Paul identifies the controlling theme of the epistle, namely, the design of God's overall plan. God purposes the ultimate union of all things in Christ, and the chief in-

strument which He is using during the present age to accomplish this goal is the Church. In this new community of redeemed people God has broken down the barrier between the Jew and the Gentile and united the two as one new man (2:14–15). This unification of two formerly opposing groups is but a token of the unity which is to be a reality among all who are members of the Body of Christ. In this new community of saints there are no legitimate barriers of nationality, race, color, or culture. The Church is one body in Jesus Christ, and as such it is, as Francis W. Beare asserts, the "harbinger of the ultimate unity of the whole creation" ("The Epistle to the Ephesians," IB, X, 606). From this first step in unification God will ultimately, according to His sovereign purpose, unite all things in Christ. This is the mystery of the grand design of God.

The unity of the Church is represented in Ephesians under three figures: the temple (2:19–22), the body (4:11–16), and the bride (5:21–33). Furthermore, in order that this unity may be more than theoretical, Paul insists that in its interpersonal relations the Church is to preserve "the unity of the Spirit in the bond of peace" (4:3).

Outline

I. Salutation, 1:1–2
II. Doxology, 1:3–14
    A. The choice of God the Father, 1:3–6
    B. The redemption wrought by Christ the Son, 1:7–12
    C. The sealing of God the Holy Spirit, 1:13–14
III. Thanksgiving and Prayer, 1:15–23
IV. Doctrinal Discussion, 2:1–3:21
    A. The redemption of Gentiles, 2:1–22
      1. Viewed personally, 2:1–10
      2. Viewed corporately, 2:11–22
    B. The ministry to Gentiles, 3:1–21
      1. Paul's commission, 3:1–13
      2. Paul's prayer, 3:14–21
V. Practical Discussion, 4:1–6:20
    A. Exhortation to unity, 4:1–16
    B. Exhortation to consistent living, 4:17–5:20
    C. Exhortations to various household groups, 5:21–6:9
      1. Wives and husbands, 5:21–33
      2. Children and parents, 6:1–4
      3. Slaves and masters, 6:5–9
    D. Exhortation to prepare for spiritual warfare, 6:10–20
VI. Conclusion, 6:21–24

Bibliography. F. F. Bruce, *The Epistle to the Ephesians,* Westwood, N.J.: Revell, 1961. Francis Foulkes, *The Epistle of Paul to the Ephesians,* TNTC. Charles Hodge, *A Commentary on the Epistle to the Ephesians,* Grand Rapids: Eerdmans, 1950. E. K. Simpson and F. F. Bruce, *Commentary on the Epistles to the Ephesians and the Colossians,* NICNT.

D. W. B

EPHOD

A view down one of the marble-paved streets of Ephesus, with the silted-in harbor visible in the distance between the first two columns on the right.
HFV

EPHESUS (ĕf'ē-sŭs). The capital of the Roman province of Asia, located at the mouth of the Cayster River on the W coast of Asia Minor. Because of its fine harbor facilities and the roads which converged at that point, this city of more than 300,000 people became the most important commercial center of Roman Asia. It boasted numerous warehouses lining the banks of the river. Remains of an amphitheater can still be seen, measuring about 495 feet in diameter and capable of seating 25,000 people.

The origin of the city is hidden in legendary antiquity. However, about 1044 B.C. Gr. colonists under the leadership of Androclus drove out the previous inhabitants and established a Gr. city on the site. In 133 B.C. Ephesus, after a rather varied history, became a part of the Roman province of Asia.

The city was most widely known for its temple of Artemis (Diana, KJV), one of the seven wonders of the world. When the first temple was constructed is not known. The structure standing in Paul's day was begun about 350 B.C. It measured 340 by 100 feet, and its 100 columns stood more than 55 feet high. The goddess Artemis was originally an Anatolian fertility deity who had become partially Hellenized. In addition to its religious significance, the temple served both as a bank for the deposit and lending of money and as an asylum for fugitives. *See* Gods, False; Diana.

On his third missionary journey, Paul spent almost three years in Ephesus (Acts 19), no doubt because of its strategic position as a radiating center for the dissemination of the gospel. Timothy was later stationed there as an apostolic representative, giving assistance to local church leaders (I and II Timothy). Irenaeus and Eusebius indicate that the apostle John spent his last years in Ephesus, from which he wrote the five NT books ascribed to him.

See Archaeology.

Bibliography. E. M. Blaiklock, *Cities of the New Testament*, Westwood, N.J.: Revell, 1965, pp. 62–67. Floyd V. Filson, "Ephesus and the New Testament," BA, VIII (1945), 73–80. Merrill M. Parvis, "Archaeology and St. Paul's Journeys in Greek Lands," Part IV – Ephesus, BA, VIII (1945), 61–73. Howard F. Vos, WHG, pp. 357–365. Alfons Wotschitzky, "Ephesus: Past, Present and Future of an Ancient Metropolis," *Archaeology*, XIV (1961), 205–212.

D. W. B.

EPHLAL (ĕf'lăl). A descendant of Judah through Pharez, Hezron, and Jerahmeel (I Chr 2:37).

EPHOD

1. Father of Hanniel, a Manassite leader who helped direct the distribution of W Jordanian Canaan among the occupying tribes (Num 34:23).

2. A sleeveless shoulder vestment worn by the high priest over other garments (Ex 28:28–29; 35:27; 39:2–21; Lev 8:7). *See* Dress. In color it was gold, blue, purple and scarlet and was part of the ceremonial dress to which the oracle pouch containing the Urim and Thummim was attached.

In 19th cen. B.C. Assyrian texts from Cappadocia, the Semitic word *epādum* appears, and *'epâdu* in Ugaritic materials (see G. R. Driver, *Canaanite Myths and Legends*, pp. 102 f.). W. F. Albright interprets the term as a wrap-around plaid robe, fastened at the shoulder and leaving one arm free. He believes the priestly ephod was similar to the Gr. *ependytēs*, a closely fitting outer garment which was often completely covered with gold, silver and other rich decoration (*Yahweh and the Gods of Canaan*, Garden City: Doubleday, 1968, pp. 200–203).

534

3. In I Sam 2:18 the boy Samuel and in II Sam 6:14 King David are described as being girded with a simple linen ephod, perhaps only a brief loincloth suitable for young children since Michal rebuked David for uncovering himself in public (II Sam 6:20). Thus it must have covered only the front of the body.

4. In several passages the meaning is obscure. The term ephod refers to an object used in obtaining oracles (I Sam 23:9–11; 30:7–8). In addition, in I Sam 14:18 the LXX reads: "Saul then said to Ahijah, 'Bring the ephod'; for it was he who carried the ephod in the presence of Israel" (JerusB), where "ephod" replaces the Heb. for "the ark of God" in the MT. I Sam 14:3 states that Ahijah was carrying (Heb. *nōśē'*, not "wearing") an ephod. In I Sam 2:28 Eli is reminded that the tribe of Levi was chosen, among other duties, "to carry the ephod" (JerusB; Heb. *lāśē'th*, from *nāśā'*). As Saul ordered Ahijah, so David on two occasions asked Abiathar to bring the ephod to him (I Sam 23:9; 30:7). Thus it was portable, yet large enough to hide Goliath's sword placed behind it (I Sam 21:9) in the sanctuary at Nob.

Gideon had made an ephod from the golden rings taken from the vanquished Midianites for his own city of Ophrah; it became the object of idolatrous worship for "all Israel" (Jud 8:26–27). Micah had such a cult object in his sanctuary (Jud 17:5; 18:14–20) along with teraphim and other images for the purpose of divination. Thus it may be concluded that this type of ephod was an oracular cultic instrument from which an answer could be obtained by means of inserting one's hand (I Sam 14:19). See Anthony Phillips, "David's Linen Ephod," VT, XIX (1969), 485–487.

R. O. C. and J. R.

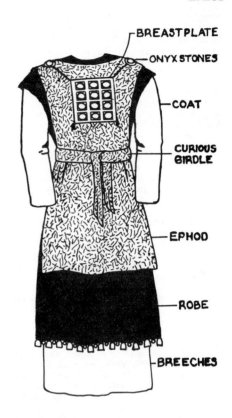

BREASTPLATE
ONYX STONES
COAT
CURIOUS GIRDLE
EPHOD
ROBE
BREECHES

Priest in Ephod

The great theater mentioned in Acts 19, capable of holding twenty-five thousand. HFV

535

EPHPHATHA (ĕf′á-thả). A transliteration of the Aramaic used by Jesus to the deaf-mute in Decapolis (Mk 7:34). It is the imperative form, "Be opened"; and at the sovereign word of Jesus the mouth and ears of the man were freed from their affliction.

EPHRAIM (ē′frȧ-ĭm). The name "Ephraim" is built upon a root meaning "to be fruitful" (Gen 41:52). Its dual form and prophecies added by Jacob (Gen 48:19) and Moses (Deut 33:17) indicate great fruitfulness.

1. *The son of Joseph.* The name was given by Joseph to his second son (Gen 46:20). Both sons were adopted by Jacob and ranked as his own sons (Gen 48:5). Though Ephraim was the second, Jacob insisted upon giving him the chief blessing (Gen 48:20).

2. *The territory.* Ephraim's name was also applied to the territory allotted to the tribe in the Promised Land (Josh 16; cf. I Chr 7:28-29). Boundaries have not been determined exactly. Roughly, however, they ran from Gilgal to Bethel and lower Beth-horon, W to Gezer, N to Lod, W toward the sea, N to tne Kanah River, E through Tappuah, Janobah, and Taanathshiloh to Ataroth, then S to Nasrath and Gilgal. This territory was hill country with fertile valleys and better rainfall than was enjoyed farther S.

3. *The tribe.* The tribe of Ephraim was prominent because of its numbers, its centers of influence, and the leaders that arose out of it.

Its numbers are revealed by the census lists in Num 1:33 (40,500) and in Num 26:37 (32,500). They fulfilled the predictions of Jacob and Moses.

Its centers at one time or another included: (1) Shechem, between Mount Ebal and Mount Gerizim, near the plot of ground willed by Jacob to Joseph and on which Joseph's bones were buried (Josh 24:32), near which the blessings and curses of the law were proclaimed from the lower slopes of the mountains (Josh

The Valley of Lebanon, north of Shiloh in the region of Mount Ephraim. JR

8:33-34); (2) Shiloh, where the ark was kept until the days of Eli (I Sam 1:3); (3) Bethel, the city on its southern border which became the more important of the two shrine centers established by Jeroboam I (I Kgs 12:26-33; Amos 7:10-13).

Its outstanding leaders included: (1) Joshua, the son of Nun, commander against the Amalekites at Rephidim (Ex 17:13), Moses' aid in the tent of meeting at Sinai (Ex 33:11), one of the 12 who spied out the Promised Land and one of the two who gave a good report (Num 14:6), successor of Moses as leader of all Israel, and who directed both the conquest and division of the land W of Jordan (Josh 14:1); (2) Samuel, the last of the judges, the seer to whom all Israel looked for the word of God, and the leader who prepared the way for the kingdom (I Sam 12:6-25); (3) Jeroboam, the son of Nebat, the first king over the ten tribes that rebelled against the house of David (I Kgs 12:19-20).

4. *The kingdom.* The name Ephraim was often used in the latter days for the northern kingdom (cf. II Chr 25:7; Hos 5:3; 6:10; 10:6; Isa 7:2; Jer 7:15). The calf worship set up by Jeroboam, the son of Nebat, led to moral corruption that ended in destruction and captivity, as prophesied by Amos, Hosea, Micah, and Isaiah. The prophets, however, predicted the restoration of a tiny remnant in the kingdom of the Messiah (Hos 14:8; Isa 11:13; Jer 31:7-9, 20; Ezk 37:16-23; 48:5; Zech 10:7).

J. W. W.

EPHRAIM, CITY OF. Jn 11:54 depicts Jesus leaving Judea and departing into the region near the wilderness to a town called Ephraim, because of the threat of violence by the priests after Lazarus' resurrection. The site may be modern et-Taiyibeh, situated on a conspicuous conical hill commanding a view over the valley of the Jordan and the Dead Sea. It is about five miles NE of Bethel and about 15 miles from Jerusalem. It has been identified with Ophrah (*q.v.*) of Josh 18:23 and I Sam 13:17, and also with Ephrain (Ephron, RSV), the city captured by Abijah from Jeroboam (II Chr 13:19). However, the Ephraim referred to in II Sam 13:23, to which Absalom invited all his family for the festivities relative to the sheepshearing, may be the same as the Mount Ephron of Josh 15:9; it is near Kirjath-jearim which is also called Baalah, corresponding to the Baal-hazor of II Sam 13:23.

C. M. H.

EPHRAIM GATE. *See* Jerusalem: Gates and Towers 6.

EPHRAIM, MOUNT OF. A comparison of Josh 17:15; 19:50; 20:7; 21:21; Jud 2:9; 3:27; I Sam 1:1 reveals the collective usage of the term; i.e., not any one single mount is set forth in every instance, but the reference is to the hill country or highlands which characterized the whole

The Shepherds' Fields with Bethlehem in the distance. HFV

territory of the tribe of Ephraim. This term applies to the greater part of the central ridge of Palestine on the W side of the Jordan, from N of Shechem S to Bethel.

EPHRAIM, WOOD OF. According to II Sam 18:6, the conflict between the forces of David and Absalom took place in this rugged tract which was overgrown with trees and shrubs. The context locates the area on the E of the Jordan River in the vicinity of Mahanaim. Since the territory of Ephraim lay W of the Jordan, the origin of the name of this thicket is unknown. Perhaps the name Wood of Ephraim resulted from the defeat of the Ephraimites at the hands of Jephthah and the Gileadites (Jud 12:1, 4–5); or the name may have been given at a later date, after the battle was over, as a reminder of Ephraim's folly. Another conjecture is that some Ephraimites were dissatisfied with their portion and made a colony in the area of Manasseh (Josh 17:14–18). The exact reason for this designation remains uncertain, however.

C. M. H.

EPHRAIMITE (ē'frà-mīt). In Josh 16:10; Jud 12:4, 5, 6, Ephraimite is used to denote anyone from the tribe of Ephraim (q.v.).

EPHRAIN (ē'frà-ĭn). One of the cities of Israel which Abijah took during his conflict with Jeroboam (II Chr 13:19; in RSV, Ephron, q.v.). It is conjectured that this is the same place referred to as Ephraim in the experience of Jesus recorded in Jn 11:54. See Ophrah; Ephraim, City of.

EPHRATAH (ĕf'rà-tà), or **EPHRATH** (ĕf'răth)
1. Ephrath is the ancient name of Bethlehem (Gen 35:16, 19; 48:7). Ruth 4:11 and Mic 5:2 seem to imply that Ephratah was a district in which Bethlehem was situated. Although the spelling differs they refer to the same area. Ps 132:6 mentions David's discovery of the ark after he heard of its being in Ephratah. The question is, what is meant by this use of the term? Does it mean the location in the area of Bethlehem, or can it mean some other? Some conjecture that it here means Kirjath-jearim, referred to as Ephratah. Since Kirjath-jearim was on the northern border of Judah, the term may also refer poetically to the tribal territories to the N of Judah. These are sometimes mentioned collectively by the name of their strongest tribe, Ephraim, whose nickname was Ephratah (meaning "fertility"; cf. Gen 49:22) as suggested by the usage of the term Ephrathite in I Sam 1:1; Jud 12:5 (Heb.); I Kgs 11:26.
2. The second wife of Caleb (I Chr 2:19, 50).

C. M. H.

EPHRATHITE (ĕf'rà-thīt). An inhabitant of Ephratah or Bethlehem (I Sam 17:12; Ruth 1:2). Elkanah, a Levite dwelling in the area of Ephraim, is called an Ephrathite (I Sam 1:1). Jeroboam is identified as an Ephrathite (I Kgs 11:26). The Ephraimites who sought to escape from Jephthah (Jud 12:5) were called Ephrathites (literal Heb.). See Ephratah.

EPHRON (ē'frŏn)
1. Son of Zohar, a headman among the sons of Heth who dwelt in an enclave at Mamre or

537

Hebron. He owned the cave of Machpelah (*q.v.*) which Abraham desired after Sarah's death for a family tomb (Gen 23:8-18). The elaborate purchase transaction between Abraham and Ephron, who required Abraham to buy also his land and its trees and thus pay all future dues on the property, parallels specific features and legal terms found in 2nd mil. B.C. Hittite laws and an Akkad. text from Ugarit (see K. A. Kitchen, *Ancient Orient and OT*, pp. 154 ff.). The price of 400 shekels of silver was exorbitant, for a hired laborer or craftsman earned only 1/30 shekel a day, or eight to 12 shekels a year (Code of Hammurabi, #273-277; ANET, p. 177). Yet in order to bury Sarah Abraham agreed to the price and terms without further argument. For the name Ephron cf. Apran in the Alalakh tablets. The "sons of Heth" may stem from proto-Hittites or Hattians migrating from Anatolia in the 3rd mil. B.C. *See* Hittites.

2. A mountain or hilly district between Nephtoah and Kirjath-jearim, on the border of Judah and Benjamin (Josh 15:9), probably in the forested region between Jerusalem and Beth-shemesh.

3. A town near Bethel which Abijah of Judah captured from Jeroboam I (II Chr 13:19, RSV, on the basis of the written MT, a Cairo Geniza fragment, LXX, and Vulg). The MT pointing or vocalization indicates *'eprayin,* KJV Ephrain (*q.v.*). It is probably the same as Ophrah (*q.v.*), a town of Benjamin (Josh 18:23), likely to be identified with the village of et-Taiyibeh, four and a half miles NE of Bethel.

J. R.

EPICUREANS (ĕp'ĭ-kū-rē'ánz). These were philosophers at Athens who confronted Paul along with the Stoics (*q.v.*; Acts 17:18). They followed the teachings of Epicurus (341-270 B.C.), an Athenian citizen though born on the island of Samos near Ephesus. Paul's familiarity with the philosophy is evident. Menander, writer and friend of Epicurus, is apparently quoted by Paul in I Cor 15:33 f. The Epicureans taught that the supreme good is pleasure or happiness (Gr. *hēdonē*); but it is the pleasure of the mind and the entire life, not the indulgence of momentary whims and instincts. Consequences of all actions should be considered before indulging in the activity. Epicurus was not a sensualist as is often charged. He denied providence, miracles, prophecy, and immortality, though modern writers claim he was not an atheist (cf. N. W. DeWitt, *Epicurus and His Philosophy*). Epicurus repudiated astrology and taught that religion was superstition; that to be happy one must be delivered from the fear of the gods. He developed an elaborate "atomic" theory. Lucretius (98-54 B.C.) was one of the best known interpreters of Epicureanism.

R. L. J.

EPILEPSY. *See* Diseases.

EPISTLE. In general usage the term epistle refers to written correspondence whether private or public. This broad use would include OT letters, although they are never specifically called epistles (II Sam 11:14-15; I Kgs 21:8-11; Ezr 4:11-22; Jer 29:1-29).

In the NT the Gr. *epistolē* occurs 24 times and is the designation of 21 of the NT writings. Of these, 13 are from the pen of Paul and seven or eight, depending on whether Hebrews is included or not, are traditionally classified as general or catholic epistles. The 13 letters of Paul are usually divided into four groups: eschatological (I and II Thessalonians), soteriological (Romans, I and II Corinthians, Galatians), prison (Ephesians, Philippians, Colossians, Philemon), and pastoral (I and II Timothy, Titus). The non-Pauline epistles have been called catholic because they were supposedly general in their destination. This, however, is not an accurate designation in the case of Hebrews and II and III John, which were sent to specific persons or groups.

In general, the NT epistles follow the standard form for an ancient letter as can be seen by study of the extensive papyrus correspondence which has been preserved. The usual epistolary order was: name of writer and recipients, greeting, prayer or wish for the readers' well-being, body of the letter, and closing greetings.

Some, following the lead of A. Deissmann, have made a distinction between letters and epistles. The former are said to be personal, non-literary pieces not intended for permanent use, whereas the latter are impersonal, literary pieces written for a more general readership and with the intention of permanency. Others have rightly insisted that this distinction is too sophisticated and oversimplified. Most of the NT epistles combine elements of both the letter and the epistle as distinguished by Deissmann. The NT correspondence was, for the most part, written in response to letters or personal word concerning problems or need which demanded authoritative treatment.

D. W. B.

EPISTLES, CATHOLIC. *See* Catholic Epistles; Epistles, General.

EPISTLES, GENERAL. Seven NT letters—James, I and II Peter, I, II, and III John, Jude—are so called because they do not contain specific addresses (notice the contrast with the Pauline epistles). The description "seven Catholic (*viz.,* indefinite and broadly addressed) epistles" was first given by the Church Father Eusebius (*Eccl. Hist.,* II, 23-25). However, even a cursory reading of the letters shows they are not all truly "general." I Peter was addressed to specific provinces in Asia Minor, III John was sent to one Gaius, and II John either to a local church or an individual.

Ready acceptance was not accorded these

letters in the early church. As late as the 4th cen. Eusebius stated that most of them were disputed, yet they were included in several important lists and manuscripts of the NT in the same century. Some of them, especially II Peter and James, have been contested in one way or another at various times until the present. (For details *see* Canon of Scripture, the NT.)

As far as major emphases are concerned, James and I Peter face the problem of suffering (see, e.g., Jas 1:2–4; 5:4–11; I Pet 1:6–7; 2:18–20; 3:14–17; 4:12–16). In fact, the words "suffer" or "suffering" appear at least 15 times in I Peter alone. The other letters reflect the rise of false teaching and how the early church opposed it (see II Pet 2:2–3; 3:1–7; I Jn 1:6–10; 2:22–23; 4:1–6; Jude 3–4).

See articles on the individual letters.

W. M. D.

EPISTLES, PASTORAL. *See* Pastoral Epistles.

EPISTLES, SPURIOUS. Among the apocryphal NT writings are a small number of epistles imitating those found in the NT canon but not ranking in importance with other types of apocryphal literature. The seven most important epistles are: the Epistle of the Apostles, Epistles of Christ and Abgarus, Epistle to the Laodiceans, Third Epistle to the Corinthians, Epistle of Lentulus, Epistles of Paul and Seneca, and the Apocryphal Epistle of Titus.

In the Epistle of the Apostles, 11 apostles (distinction is made between Peter and Cephas!) supposedly address "the churches of the east and west, of the north and south" and give a summary of the life and resurrection of Jesus. The work ends with an apocalypse from the risen Lord concerning the future.

The Epistles of Christ and Abgarus, found by Eusebius (*Ecclesiastical History*, I, 13), contains a letter addressed to Christ by Abgarus, king of Edessa, asking Him to come and heal the king and share his kingdom. Christ wrote and declined, but promised to send an apostle after His ascension. Thaddeus was sent, healed the king, and founded the Edessene church.

Both the Epistle to the Laodiceans and the Third Epistle to the Corinthians were suggested by references found in Paul's letters (Col 4:16; I Cor 5:9). Both had a rather wide circulation in the medieval period, though rejected by ancient scholars. The Laodicean epistle contains 20 verses copied from the genuine Pauline letters. This is not likely the same epistle mentioned in the Muratorian Fragment. The Apocryphal Epistle of Titus is a recent discovery.

The Epistle of Lentulus, written to the Roman Senate, gives a physical description of Jesus drawn from medieval paintings, although claiming to be from Lentulus, a Roman official in 1st cen. Judea.

The Epistles of Paul and Seneca are 14 short personal letters in which Paul and Seneca are represented as admiring each other, and Seneca extols Paul's inspiration.

F. P.

EPOCH. This is properly the starting point of an era or age, such as the first or second coming of Christ. However, the term is also used in a looser sense to signify an age or era which has been ushered in by a particular event and is characterized by that event. Thus we can speak of the epoch of the gospel, meaning the age of the dispensation of the gospel; and of the kingdom, signifying that of Christ's kingdom on the earth. *See* Time.

ER (ûr)

1. The firstborn son of Judah (Gen 38:7), whom the daughter of Shuah, a Canaanite, bore to him (vv. 3, 12; I Chr 2:3). Although Er was married to Tamar (Gen 38:6), he was childless, the Lord having slain him because of his wickedness (v. 7) in the land of Canaan (Gen 46:12; Num 26:19).

2. A descendant of Judah (I Chr 4:21), the namesake of his firstborn (cf. above).

3. The son of Jose and the father of Elmodam in the Lucan genealogy of Jesus (Lk 3:28–29).

ERA. An era is defined by Webster (2nd. ed. unabridged) as "a chronological order or system of notation computed from a given date as basis." There are no incontrovertible examples of such a concept in the OT, though some references border closely on it. The Exodus is used as the starting point for indicating the date of the building of Solomon's temple (I Kgs 6:1). The same very significant event is employed in connection with dating the death of Aaron (Num 33:38). It would seem natural for the Israelites to have continued to make the Exodus—which marked the beginning of the Heb. nation—the basis for their dating. Instead, they later followed the prevailing custom of the times in dating events by a certain year of a king's reign. This method was followed through the kingdom period, as both Kings and Chronicles testify.

Apparently the first era used by the Jews was the Seleucid era, which was widely observed in Syria. It dated from 312 B.C., when Seleucus Nicator took Babylon. The first distinctively Jewish era was that of the Maccabees, dating from Nov. 24, 166 B.C., the beginning of the Maccabean uprising against the Seleucids.

The Christian era supposedly dates from the birth of Christ. But that event took place at least as early as 4 B.C. Instead of B.C., Jewish writers use B.C.E.—before the common era (same as Christian era). The official Jewish era begins with the supposed date of creation, set at 3760 B.C. This has been used by the Jews since the 15th cen. A.D.

See Calendar.

R. E.

ERAN (ĭr'ăn). **ERANITES** (ĭr'á-nīts). The son of Ephraim's oldest son, Shuthelah (Num 26:36). He was the father or head of the family called the Eranites.

Inscription found at Corinth mentioning Erastus. JR

ERASTUS (ĭ-răs'tŭs). A name used three times in the NT of a friend or friends of Paul. The Erastus of Rom 16:23 was a chamberlain or treasurer of the city of Corinth who sent his greetings to the Christians at Rome. He appears to be the same as mentioned much later in II Tim 4:20 as remaining in Corinth. It is hard to say if the Erastus sent by Paul from Ephesus into Macedonia is the same man (Acts 19:22). He is mentioned as one who specifically ministered to Paul, and may have followed him from Corinth to Ephesus in order to help him there. A Latin inscription carved into a stone paving block near the theater at Corinth states that for receiving the position of *aedile* (treasurer) Erastus laid this pavement at his own expense. Scholars generally agree that he is Erastus of Rom 16:23.

ERECH (ē'rĕk; Akkad. Uruk; Arab. Warka). The city of Nimrod in the land of Shinar (Gen 10:10). Situated on the Euphrates a little less than halfway between Babylon and the Persian Gulf, it was considered to be the home of Gilgamesh, the hero of the Mesopotamian flood story. Excavations of its extensive ruins have shown that it was occupied continuously for nearly 4,000 years, and has yielded the oldest known examples of writing, from *c*. 3300 B.C. (cf. BW, pp. 605–6).

Ezr 4:9–10 (see RSV) states that Asnapper (*q.v.*), the Assyrian Ashurbanipal, deported citizens (Archevites, *q.v.*) from Erech to Samaria.

ERI (ĭr'ī). **ERITES** (ĭr'īts). The fifth of the seven sons of Gad (Gen 46:16). Eri was the father or head of the family called the Erites (Num 26:16).

ESAIAS (ē-zā'yǎs). NT (Gr.) form of Isaiah (*q.v.*).

ESARHADDON (ĕ'sár-hǎd'ŏn). An Assyrian king, son and successor of Sennacherib (II Kgs 19:37; Isa 37:38); he reigned 681–669 B.C. Esarhaddon had to fight for his throne when his father was murdered. After his accession he began to rebuild Babylon, which his father had cruelly destroyed, as well as other cities and temples of Babylonia, probably because his mother was a Babylonian princess. His chief military efforts were directed toward subduing Egypt, which was continually stirring up rebellion in Palestine and Syria. His first expedition to Egypt in 675 B.C. met defeat, but on the second expedition his general occupied the whole Delta, conquered Memphis, and drove Pharaoh Taharqa (the biblical Tirhakah) up the Nile Valley. On his way to quell a revolt in Egypt in 669, Esarhaddon fell sick and died.

He was an extremely able ruler, waging successful wars against Syrian kings, the Cimmerians, and the Medes. To prevent trouble for his successor such as he had faced, he made his younger son Ashurbanipal crown prince, who then assumed an important share of the administrative duties. In 672 B.C. the high officials of Assyria had to take an oath to assure the succession of Ashurbanipal, who became king without any difficulty upon his father's death. In his inscriptions Esarhaddon claimed that Manasseh, king of Judah, paid tribute to him (ANET, p. 291). Since he ruled in Babylon as well as Assyria, the statement in II Chr 33:11 that Manasseh was carried captive to Babylon is not historically out of place. The Bible also speaks of Esarhaddon as one of the Assyrian kings who settled foreign colonists in Samaria (Ezr 4:2).

J. R.

Portal of the palace of Esarhaddon on Nebi Yunus at Nineveh. JR

ESAU (ē'sô). The son of Isaac and Rebekah, the elder twin brother of Jacob (Gen 25:24–26; 27:1, 32, 42; I Chr 1:34), is the traditional ancestor of the Edomites (cf. Gen 36; Mal 1:2–3).

The theory of the derivation of the word

"Esau" is connected with the hairy covering on his body at birth: "The first came forth red, all his body like a hairy mantle; so they named him Esau" (Gen 25:25, RSV; cf. also Gen 27:11).

These twins struggled (lit., "crushed one another") in the womb before birth (Gen 25:22). This was a prenatal foreshadowing of the relationship of Esau and Jacob in life as well as in their descendants (cf. Gen 25:23). This motif of the prenatal struggle of twins is also found in the traditions of other ancient peoples (IB, I, 665). At birth Jacob seized Esau's heel, indicating further the locked struggle of the future between these brothers and their posterities, the Israelites (the sons of Jacob) and the Edomites (the sons of Esau, cf. Deut 2:4).

Jacob revealed an eagerness from the first to gain advantage of his brother (cf. Hos 12:3). Esau was the firstborn, but Jacob would be his master. This prophecy is reiterated by other Jacob-Esau passages (Jer 49:8; Ob 6; Rom 9:10-13).

Jacob was the introvert and meditative type; but Esau was an extrovert and a man of the field who became a skillful hunter. He was the favorite of his father Isaac, while Jacob became the favorite of his mother Rebekah. Esau provided his father with his favorite meats from his hunting expeditions, but Esau's love for the chase became his downfall. One day as Esau returned, tired and hungry, Jacob was waiting for him with a steaming hot vessel of red pottage. As the aroma of this food hit Esau's nostrils he exclaimed, "Give me some of that red stuff," literally, "Pray let me swallow some of that red stuff—that red stuff there—for I am famished" (Gen 25:30). Since his lack of self-control was a weakness from birth, Esau must have this food and at once to satisfy his appetite! He paid a dear price in hastily agreeing to the demands of Jacob to surrender his birthright (Gen 25:30-34). Esau's sale of his birthright to Jacob is paralleled in the Nuzu tablets where one brother sells to another an inherited grove of fruit trees for only three sheep (Cyrus Gordon, BA, III [1940], 5).

The term birthright denotes the advantages and rights normally enjoyed by the eldest son. These included natural vigor of body and character (Gen 49:3; Deut 21:17), a position of honor at the head of the family (Gen 27:29), and a double share of the inheritance (Deut 21:15-17). When applied to tribes or nations, it conveys the idea of political and material superiority. This impulsive act stripped Esau of the headship of the people through which the redemptive purpose of God would flow. Also he forfeited the secular advantage of the firstborn son's share in the father's temporal goods.

With his birthright gone, Esau was still eligible to receive from Isaac the blessing of the oldest son if cunning, shrewd Rebekah had not risen to the occasion (Gen 27:1-10). Jacob accepted his mother's scheme, being assured by her that this was the appropriate and opportune thing to do (Gen 27:13). So with the bowl of savory food (lit., "that which is hunted") and his hairy mantle of disguise, he went to blind Isaac and requested the final blessing. Isaac's suspicions were aroused by the quick return and by Jacob's voice; but he was lulled by the hairy touch. Strengthened by the meal, Isaac's soul poured out all of its dynamic force in this one last prophetic act. The word "soul" (nephesh) here means the totality of one's power. The OT frequently alludes to the peculiar efficacy of the utterance of a dying man of God (Gen 48:10-20; 49:1-28; 50:24; Deut 33; Josh 23; II Sam 23:1-7; I Kgs 2:1-4; II Kgs 13:14-19). As a prophecy it approximated the divine word which carried within itself the power of its own fulfillment (cf. Isa 55:11; Jer 23:29).

Oral blessings or deathbed wills were recognized as valid in Nuzu as well as in patriarchal society (Gordon, op. cit., p. 8). On the heel of the successful deception and the stolen covenant blessing, Esau returned from the field and served his father his favorite bowl of venison. As Isaac sadly related the theft, the loss suddenly dawned on Esau. He blamed Jacob altogether for his plight (Gen 27:34, 36), not recognizing that his earlier irreligious act of selling his birthright had become a fixed part of his character and he was unable to repent (Heb 12:16-17, RSV). So Esau received a blessing, but he was not to share in the fertile land of Palestine. "Behold, away from the fatness of the earth shall your dwelling be, and away from the dew of heaven on high" (Gen 27:39, RSV).

Esau at 40 years of age had married two Hittite wives which greatly distressed his parents. Isaac was gullible when Rebekah shrewdly used this parental heartbreak in her plan to send Jacob to Mesopotamia. Esau perceived that by marrying a non-Canaanite woman he would please his parents, so he married a relative of Ishmael (Gen 28:6, 9) in "the land of Seir." Since the land of Seir was a good environment for one who lived by the bow, Esau made it his permanent home.

Esau was living there when Jacob returned from Mesopotamia years later. As Jacob neared Palestine he dreaded to face his wronged brother and laid minute plans to allay Esau's anger. Also he earnestly petitioned God to soften Esau's attitude (Gen 32:3-21; 33:1-3). Esau, leading his 400 armed men, graciously embraced his guilty brother and received him without malice or recrimination (Gen 33:4-16). Although Esau cordially welcomed his brother, Jacob was dubious of Easu's complete forgiveness. With doubt in his mind, Jacob managed through deceit to travel a separate way toward Bethel, stopping long at Succoth and Shechem, while Esau returned to Seir (Gen 33:12-18).

In early life Esau lived shortsightedly as a youth of selfishness and impetuosity; but as a mature person he later exhibited generosity and forgiveness toward Jacob. Esau met his brother again about 20 years later at the death and burial of their father (Gen 35:29). Knowledge of Esau's latter years is nil.

If the old animosity was buried at the last meeting of the twin brothers, it was soon resurrected and handed down from generation to generation by their descendants. The history of their descendants is one of continuous fratricidal struggle. Israel's foes rose and fell like waves, but the Edomites were always their enemies. These two peoples scorned and hated each other with a relentlessness that finds no analogy between kindred and neighbor nations anywhere in history. From c. 1000 B.C. under King David to c. 120 B.C. under the Hasmoneans, Israel was at war with Edom. Between these two dates, prophet after prophet cried for vengeance upon Edom's heartless conduct. See Edom; Edomites; Idumaea.

Bibliography. Herbert Lockyer, *All the Men of the Bible*, Grand Rapids: Zondervan, 1958, pp. 113 f. A. Pieters, *Notes on Genesis*, London: Methuen & Co., 1913, pp. 245 ff., 255–263, 291–302, 312–321.

D. W. D.

ESCHATOLOGY. The term eschatology (Gr. *eschatos*, "last"; *logos*, "discourse"), meaning "the theology of last things," has been used since the 19th cen. to designate the division of systematic theology dealing with all that was prophetically future at the time it was written, i.e., prophecy now fulfilled, as well as unfulfilled prophecy. Important subjects of prophecy include predictions concerning Jesus Christ in both His first and second advents, Israel, the Gentiles, Satan, Christendom, the saints of all ages, the future Great Tribulation, the intermediate state, the resurrection of the dead, the millennial kingdom, the final judgments, and the eternal state. These themes may be classified as the divine revelation of the fourfold program of God for (1) Israel, (2) for the Gentiles, (3) for the Church, and (4) for Satan and the fallen angels.

Principles of interpretation. The concept of biblical prediction of future events depends upon the basic interpretive principles adopted. From the standpoint of historic orthodoxy, a detailed system of eschatology is impossible without assuming the authority and accuracy of the Scriptures. Radical liberalism has denied the possibility of the prediction of the future and has treated such Scripture as is seemingly prophetic as unauthoritative and merely expressing human hope or at best divine purpose already fulfilled. Moderate liberalism, represented by A. Schweitzer, recognizes that the NT taught the immediate end of the age, but holds that prophecy is not literally fulfilled and is only a vehicle to teach the general concept of future divine salvation and final judgment. Another deviation from historical orthodoxy is the view of C. H. Dodd who popularized "realized eschatology," the teaching that eschatology is

principally divine purpose as fulfilled in the life of Christ rather than a detailed prediction of events. Karl Barth, the representative neo-orthodox scholar, considered prophecy as anticipating a consummation but as being incapable of giving clear particulars. These varieties of interpretation depend on the premise that the Scriptures are fallible records of the past and incapable of accurate predictions of the future.

Within orthodoxy which accepts the inerrancy of prophecy, two principal schools of thought exist that are distinguished by the extent to which they interpret prophecy literally. The oldest view interprets prophecy with the same degree of literalness as other Scripture. A later view uses a dual form of interpretation. Though following the literal and grammatical interpretation of Scripture as a whole, it interprets prophecy in a nonliteral way. The application of these two principles has led to a threefold division of orthodox eschatology. The oldest and most literal form of eschatology is the chiliastic or premillennial interpretation, which holds that Christ will reign on earth for 1,000 years after His second coming. The nonliteral type of interpretation of prophecy made popular by Augustine has led to the amillennial form of eschatology, which first became prominent with Origen in the 3rd cen. This view interprets the kingdom of God as a reign of Christ in the hearts of believers between the first and second advents, and hence denies an earthly millennial reign following the second advent.

Postmillennialism is a later derivative of amillennialism, often credited to Daniel Whitby (1638–1726), an English Unitarian. This theory, now held by only a few, interprets the millennial reign of Christ more literally than amillennialism and regards it as the last 1,000 years of the period between the first and second comings of Christ. Though often confused with amillennialism, it may be distinguished as more optimistic and to some extent more literal in its interpretation. The view gets its name from the teaching that Christ will return at the end of the earthly Millennium or utopia to judge all mankind. The most important interpretative question in eschatology, apart from belief in the authority of Scripture, is the use of the principle of literal interpretation. The most determinative doctrine is whether there will be a literal reign of Christ on earth after the second advent.

Prophecies concerning Jesus Christ. Messianic prophecy is the most important subject of the OT, as the fulfillment of it is the most prominent theme of the NT. Christ was to be born in fulfillment of the promise of a Saviour (Gen 3:15), of the line of Abraham (Gen 12:1–3), Judah (Gen 49:10), and David (II Sam 7:12–13); to be born in Bethlehem (Mic 5:2; Lk 2:4–7) of a virgin (Isa 7:14; Mt 1:23). Christ was to be a prophet (Deut 18:15), the divine Son of God (Isa 9:6–7), a priest (Ps 110:4), and a king (Zech 9:9). He was to die a shameful death on the cross for the sin of the whole world (Ps 22; Isa 53), only to be raised from the dead (Ps 16:10) and glorified (Dan 7:14). In His historic birth, life, death, and resurrection, many prophecies were fulfilled, and the promise was left to His disciples that He would return to establish His kingdom on earth (Mt 24:3, 27-31; 25:31-46; Acts 1:6-7, 10-11; Rev 1:7; 19:11-16). *See* Christ, Coming of; Jesus Christ.

Prophecies concerning Israel. First announced to Abram (Gen 12:1-3), God's program for Israel, the descendants of Jacob, predicted their continuance as a nation forever (Gen 17:7; Jer 30:11; 31:35-37), and their ultimate and permanent possession of the Promised Land (Gen 12:7; 13:14-15; 17:8). Israel was warned of several dispersions from the land and promised final regathering (Gen 15:13-14; Deut 28:63-67; 30:1-3; Jer 23:2-8; Ezk 39:25-28; Amos 9:14-15). The broad outline of their prophetic program is given in Dan 9:24-27. Premillenarians expect literal fulfillment of these prophecies; amillenarians find a nonliteral fulfillment in the church today.

Prophecies concerning Gentiles. The OT abounds in prophecies relating to Gentiles, beginning with the predictions concerning Noah and his posterity (Gen 9:25-27). Many later prophecies concern the nations surrounding Israel. Of major importance, however, is the revelation given through Daniel (Dan 2, 7, 8, 11) concerning four empires: Babylon, Medo-Persia, Greece, and Rome, covering the period called by Christ "the times of the Gentiles" (Lk 21:24), i.e., the period during which Jerusalem will be under Gentile domination beginning 605 B.C. and ending at the second coming of Christ. Many premillenarians believe the latter part of the fourth empire refers to a time yet future, just preceding the second advent.

Prophecies concerning the Church. The divine program for the present age, announced by Christ (Mt 16:18), is the outcalling of a body of saints composed of both Jews and Gentiles (Eph 2:11-16; 3:6) to form the Church (*q.v.*). Related to Christ in various figures such as the vine and the branches (Jn 15), the body (Eph 1:22-23), and the bride (II Cor 11:2; Eph 5:23-32), the Church will be completed at the rapture or catching up of the Church to heaven (Jn 14:3; I Cor 15:51-52; I Thess 4:13-17).

Pretribulationists consider the rapture will take place approximately seven years before the second advent proper (Dan 9:27); posttribulationists regard it as a phase of the second advent. The living members of the Church will be translated, i.e., given heavenly bodies at the rapture, when the dead in Christ will be raised (I Cor 15:51-52; I Thess 4:14-17). Rewards will be given to the Church after the rapture (I Cor 3:11-15; II Cor 5:10-11), and the Church will be with the Lord forever (I Thess 4:17). Amillenarians regard the rapture and resurrection as occurring at the second advent

and as including all men, to be followed by the eternal state, in which the saved will be blessed and the unsaved will be punished. *See* Church; Rapture.

The intermediate state. Orthodox theologians hold that upon death all men go to the intermediate state, of torment for the unsaved and bliss for the saved, awaiting future resurrection and judgment (Lk 16:19-31; 23:39-43; II Cor 5:8; Phil 1:23; Rev 6:9-11; 7:9-17). *See* Dead, The; Death.

The millennial kingdom. According to the premillennial view, Christ will reign in person on earth for 1,000 years after His second advent. Satan will be bound and rendered inoperative (Rev 20:1-3). The period will be a golden age in which righteousness and peace will abound, war will be banned, and prosperity in the spiritual, economic, and political realms will be worldwide (Ps 72; Isa 2:2-4; 11:2-12; 65:17—66:24; Jer 23:2-8; 31:1-14, 31-34; 33:14-18; Amos 9:11-15). At the end of the Millennium, Satan will again be loosed, gain a large following, which will be destroyed by a judgment of fire from heaven (Rev 20:7-10). Amillenarians regard these prophecies as being fulfilled in the present age. *See* Kingdom of God; Millennium.

The final judgments. According to Scripture, all men will be judged (II Tim 4:1; Heb 9:27). Amillenarians regard this as a single event related to the second advent. Premillenarians view the final judgments as a series of events, beginning with the judgment of the righteous before the Millennium, and ending with the judgment of the wicked and Satan at the end of the Millennium (I Cor 3:11-16; II Cor 5:10; Rev 20:4-6, 9-15). The final destiny of the wicked is the lake of fire. *See* Gehenna; Hell.

The eternal state. Described in Rev 21-22, the locale of the eternal state is in a new heaven and a new earth in which is situated the New Jerusalem. The heavenly city is pictured as a place of great beauty, lavishly built of precious stones, the dwelling place of God as well as of the saints of all ages. *See* Eternal Life; Eternal State and Death; Heaven.

Taken as a whole, eschatology is the capstone of divine revelation, the grand culmination of the entire program of God for the ages and the principal reason for the creation of the material world. In it the eternal purposes of God for mankind will be realized with great blessing to all the saints.

Bibliography. Oswald T. Allis, *Prophecy and the Church*, Philadelphia: Presbyterian and Reformed, 1945 (amil.). Louis Berkhof, *The Kingdom of God*, Grand Rapids: Eerdmans, 1951 (amil.). Loraine Boettner, *The Millennium*, Philadelphia: Presbyterian and Reformed, 1958 (postmil.). John Bright, *The Kingdom of God*, Nashville: Abingdon, 1953 (neoorthodox). Herman A. Hoyt, *The End Times*, Chicago: Moody Press, 1969 (premil.). Alva J. McClain,

The fertile valley of Eshcol where the twelve spies picked grapes. HFV

The Greatness of the Kingdom, Chicago: Moody, 1959 (premil). René Pache. *The Future Life*, Chicago: Moody, 1962 (premil.); *The Return of Jesus Christ*, Chicago: Moody, 1955 (premil.). J. Barton Payne, *The Imminent Appearing of Christ*, Grand Rapids: Eerdmans, 1962 (posttrib.). Charles C. Ryrie, *The Basis of the Premillennial Faith*, New York: Loizeaux, 1953; *Dispensationalism Today*, Chicago: Moody, 1965. Wilbur M. Smith, *The Biblical Doctrine of Heaven*, Chicago: Moody, 1968. John F. Walvoord, *The Church in Prophecy*, Grand Rapids: Zondervan, 1964; *Israel in Prophecy*, Grand Rapids: Zondervan, 1962; *The Millennial Kingdom*, Findlay: Dunham, 1959; *The Nations in Prophecy*, Grand Rapids: Zondervan, 1967; *The Rapture Question*, Findlay: Dunham, 1957.

J. F. W.

ESDRAELON (ĕz-drā'lŏn). The Gr. name derived from Jezreel for the W portion of the valley of Jezreel (*q.v.*), including the valley of Megiddo (*q.v.*) or Armageddon (*q.v.*). *See* Palestine, II. B. 2. b.

ESEK (ē'sĕk). A flowing well dug under the direction of Isaac in the valley of Gerar near Rehoboth, over which the herdsmen of Gerar contended (Gen 26:20). Isaac gave it the name Esek because of the strife over it. The exact site is unknown.

ESHBAAL (ĕsh'bāl). The fourth son of Saul in the genealogical record of the tribe of Benjamin (I Chr 8:33; 9:39). In comparing this record with that found in II Sam 2:8, it appears that Eshbaal and Ishbosheth were the same person. Saul and three of his sons were killed in battle (I Sam 31:2). Only Eshbaal was left alive to assume the throne of his father. Because of later reluctance to pronounce the name "Baal," the uncomplimentary nickname Ishbosheth, "man of shame," was substituted. *See* Ishbosheth.

ESHBAN (ĕsh'băn). The second of four sons born to Dishon of the lineage of Seir the Horite, of the land of Edom (Gen 36:26; I Chr 1:41).

ESHCOL (ĕsh'kŏl)
1. A relative of Mamre and Aner, who formed an alliance with Abraham in Hebron, and joined his campaign in the rescue of Lot (cf. Gen 14:13-24).
2. A valley N of Hebron where the 12 spies sent out by Moses plucked huge clusters of grapes, symbolic of the fruitfulness of the land (cf. Num 13:23-24; 32:9; Deut 1:24). The vineyards in this wadi are still noted for their grapes.

ESHEAN (ĕsh'ĭ-ăn). A better spelling is Eshan (RSV). One of nine cities including Hebron in the hill country of Judah, grouped together in Joshua's division of the inheritance, according to Josh 15:52.

ESHEK (ē'shĕk). A Benjamite, brother of Azel, descended from Jonathan; he had three sons (I Chr 8:39).

ESHKALONITES (ĕsh'ká-lŏ-nīts). In Josh 13:3 (KJV), the inhabitants of the Philistine city of Ashkelon (*q.v.*).

ESHTAOL (ĕsh'tā-ŏl), **ESHTAOLITES** (ĕsh'tă-līts). One of the 14 cities occupying the foothills or Shephelah of Judah (Josh 15:33). Josh 19:41 names Eshtaol and Zorah as part of the inheritance of Dan. The fact that both Judah and Dan had claims at Eshtaol may have been one of the contributing factors in the Danites' feeling crowded and their seeking for more space (Jud 18:2). Between Eshtaol and Zorah at Mahaneh-Dan the Spirit of God first stirred Samson to move against the Philistines (Jud 13:25, RSV). On the death of Samson (Jud 16:31), his brethren and kinsmen took his body and buried it between Zorah and Eshtaol in the burying place of his father.

Probably two or three centuries prior to Samson's day the Danites decided to expand (Jud 18:2). They sent five men of valor from Zorah and Eshtaol to spy out land in northern Canaan. Returning to Zorah and Eshtaol (Jud 18:8) they reported that the people lived securely and the land was large and good. In the light of their report, the people of Zorah and Eshtaol sent 600 men of war (Jud 18:11) to secure the land. Ancient Eshtaol may have been on the site of modern Eshua, about 13 miles W of Jerusalem.

C. M. H.

ESHTEMOA (ĕsh-tĕ-mō'á), **ESHTEMOH** (ĕsh'tĕ-mō)
1. Son of Ishbah, Eshtemoa was a descendant of Caleb (I Chr 4:17).

2. A Maachathite, the son of Hodiah (I Chr 4:19).

3. The spelling Eshtemoh is found only in Josh 15:50. A city approximately eight miles S of Hebron, it is listed as one of a cluster of cities which occupied the hill country of Judah. Later, in distributing cities and their suburbs for occupation by the Levites (Josh 21:14), Eshtemoa was included. Thus, it became a Levitical city and a city of refuge in the territory of Judah. A family of Levites known as Kohathites became residents of Eshtemoa (I Chr 6:57). During his exile from Saul's court, David sent some of the spoil he had recaptured from the Amalekites to a number of towns in Judah including Eshtemoa (I Sam 30:28). The name of the present site is es-Semû'a.

C. M. H.

ESHTON (ĕsh'tŏn). A son of Mehir and the father of three sons, Beth-rapha, Paseah, and Tehinnah (I Chr 4:11–12), descendants of Judah.

ESLI (ĕs'lī). Esli is listed as the son of Nagge (Naggai, RSV) and the father of Naum (Nahum, RSV) in Jesus' genealogy, the eleventh generation before Jesus (Lk 3:25).

ESPOUSAL. Espousal, meaning "betrothal" or "engagement," was regarded almost as binding as marriage itself (Deut 20:7; 22:23, 25, 27–28; Hos 2:19–20; Lk 1:27; 2:5). This explains Joseph's concern over Mary and setting her aside (Mt 1:18–19). The betrothed man was sometimes called a husband (Deut 22:23; Mt 1:19) and the girl a wife (Gen 29:21; Deut 22:23–24; Mt 1:20). While the Bible does not legislate, except in Deut 22, about a broken betrothal, the code of Hammurabi did. It required that should the future husband break the engagement, the bride's father could keep the gift to the bride, and should the father of the bride renege, he would repay double the gift received. *See* Dowry. A man could declare his intentions and effect an engagement by spreading the skirt of his cloak over his beloved (Ruth 3:9; cf. Deut 22:30; 27:20; Ezk 16:8).

Figuratively, in the OT Israel is regarded as having been espoused or betrothed to Yahweh in the wilderness (Jer 2:2; cf. Ezk 16:8), but who through idolatry later became the adulterous wife of Yahweh (Hos 2:2, 16–23), now disowned but finally to be restored. In the NT the Church is called the espoused bride of Christ (II Cor 11:2; Eph 5:25–32; Rev 19:6–8).

R. A. K.

ESROM (ĕz'rŏm).This is the Gr. spelling of the OT name Hezron (*q.v.*). He is found in the genealogy of Jesus (Mt 1:3 and Lk 3:33).

ESSENCE, DIVINE. Our word "essential" comes from the word "essence." Both words are derived from the Latin *esse* which in English means "to be." The "essence" of a thing is that quality or characteristic which makes it to be what it is. For instance, the essence of a biped is that it has two feet, even as the essence of a quadruped requires an animal with four feet.

By divine essence is meant those characteristics God possesses which cause Him to be who He is. God is spirit, holiness, love, perfection. God possesses omniscience, omnipresence, and omnipotence. He does not depend for His existence on any other being; He is independent. He never changes in His character; He is immutable. He is not subject to the time process of the physical universe; He is eternal.

The revelation of the divine essence comes through God's actions. His revelation of Himself in Christ is the most authentic manifestation of His characteristics, attributes, and powers. "Divine essence" is but a generalized term for anything and everything that makes God to be uniquely Himself.

The word "essence" belongs to philosophy and theology rather than to the Scriptures. Theologians have argued as to whether man can really know the essence of God or only His attributes. Actually, to know God at all is to know Him through His actions. The actions of God reveal His character and powers. We can know God through what He has done and continues to do. God did not want us to know Him as an essence, a philosophical abstraction; but He revealed Himself, His divine essence, to us through Jesus Christ (Jn 14:9–11).

T. W. B.

ESSENES. For Judaism in the Roman period there were two alternatives to the issue of devout religious commitment: "party" life of the Pharisees and "sect" life of the Essenes. A party consists of people who join forces and efforts to make an impact upon society through reform. The purpose of the Pharisaic party was to restore sound life to Israel by being a good influence, and it accomplished its ends through careful organization, education and discipline. A sect, however, judges that society is beyond reform and sectarians withdraw in order to prepare for the judgment of God which must fall on a degenerate people. In the sectarian life of the Essenes, the cleavage between "the elect" and those outside the sect was emphasized by rites of initiation, acute discipline, and the claim that membership in the sect anticipates the messianic community.

Prior to the discovery and publication of the DSS material from Qumran, the Essenes had been known primarily through references made by Philo (*Quod omnis probus sit* xii–xiii (75–91), quoted by Eusebius (*Praeparatio Evangelium* viii. 12; *Hypothetica · apud* Eusebius, *Praep. Evang.* viii.11) and Josephus (*Wars* ii. 8.2–3; *Ant.* xiii.5.9; xv.10.5; xviii.1.5). These authors agree that the Essenes kept aloof from normal society, living in communities which had a single treasury; that they practiced community of property and lived a diligent and frugal life under strict discipline. Both writers speak of the deep piety of the Essenes. Josephus describes their daily worship; their communal meal which was initiated and terminated with grace spoken by a priest; and the several stages of a three year probationary period, climaxed by stringent oaths which preceded the right of a candidate to touch the food of the community (*Wars* ii.8.5, 7). Little more was definitely known, however, for both Philo and Josephus expressed themselves in Hellenistic categories which invited a variety of conflicting interpretations.

The discovery of the remains of a sectarian library in 1947 near the NW shore of the Dead Sea and of the wilderness center at Khirbet Qumran from which they came, altered this situation. The majority of scholars involved with the study of the DSS believe the Essenes best fit the clues for the identity of the Qumran monks. Piecing together the archaeological and literary evidence which has accumulated, the Essenes emerge as a Jewish priestly sect which expressed itself in thoroughly Semitic categories, familiar from biblical and apocalyptic materials, whose history and organization, communal life and hopes, are now quite clear. Thus when Philo states that the Essenes reject all logical and natural philosophy except that which treats of God and creation, and that they

are especially concerned with the ethical branch of philosophy, the Qumran texts clarify he is saying that the Essenes are interested only in biblical revelation and law.

The term "Essene" is probably a derivative from Aram. *'āsên, 'āsayyâ*, plural of *'āsê, 'āsyâ*, "healer"; or it may be the equivalent of Heb. *ḥasîdîm*, "pious ones." The *ḥasîdîm* are known from the Maccabean period and even before as those who were devoted to the law, and who chose death rather than violate their covenant with God (cf. I Macc 1:62 f.; 2:29–38, 42; 7:13–16; II Macc 14:6). From this group descended, apparently, both the Pharisees and the Essenes, each group developing along lines distinctive to itself, but claiming a common heritage. The name "Essene" was one given to the sect by outsiders, for it never occurs within the sectarian documents. The Qumran monks preferred to speak of themselves as "the Poor," "the Exiles," "the Sons of Light," or as "those who have entered into covenant," from which is derived the popular name for the group, "Covenanters."

The Essenes were a priestly movement. Although it is clear that both priests and laymen were to be found within the sect, priests dominated its councils and took precedence in its gatherings. The Manual of Discipline (1QS), by which the community was governed in the 1st cen. of this era, speaks often of "the priests and Levites" (e.g., 1QS i.18–24; ii.1–5, 11, 19–20),

Remains of the Qumran Community, Giovanni Trimboli

and more specifically of "the sons of Zadok the priests who keep the covenant" (1QS v.9; cf. ix.14; CD iii.21–iv.4). The Damascus Document (CD) speaks of "the sons of Zadok" as "the chosen of Israel, the men named with a name who shall stand at the end of the days" (CD iv.3–4). From this, and related evidence, it can be concluded that the Essenes were a priestly sect of the Zadokite line from which the high priests of Israel were to be anointed, but which was displaced by other lines in the priestly intrigues that preceded and accompanied the Maccabean revolt, c. 175–141 B.C.

The founder of the Essene movement is unknown by name, but is called in the documents "the Righteous Teacher," or perhaps "the Legitimate Teacher" (e.g., CD i.10–12). That he was a priest is now certain (4QpPs 37 ii.14–16; cf. 1QpHab ii.7–8), presumably of the legitimate but displaced Oniad-Zadokite line. Little is known of his life, but the texts indicate that he lived in a time of stress and was persecuted by a figure identified as "the Wicked Priest," who pursued him to his place of exile and violated the observance of the Day of Atonement among the Covenanters (1QpHab xi.4–16). The Righteous Teacher was primarily remembered by the Essenes as the man with revelatory insight, to whom God revealed the secrets of the prophets, and more specifically what would take place in the last generation (1QpHab viii.1–5; CD i.10–12).

The Damascus Document speaks of the Teacher having been "gathered in" (CD xx.1, 14), an expression used in the OT for natural death, but it remains uncertain how or when the Teacher died. The texts nowhere attach special significance to his death. The combined evidence of the texts and the coin sequence uncovered through excavation of the Essene center at Qumran suggests that it was toward the end of the troubled period, 175–141 B.C., that the Righteous Teacher led his faithful followers into exile where they could wait for God to vindicate them as His appointees to lead Israel in sacrifice and worship.

It was in 141 B.C. that the last of the Maccabean brothers, Simon of the priestly house of Hasmon, was confirmed as permanent ruling high priest by a nation grateful for the leadership the Hasmoneans had given to the successful revolt against Syria. The fact that the Hasmonean house was not of the legitimate Zadokite line was not considered a deterrent to this action. The decree confirming Simon in office expressly forbids any interference by laymen or priests, and prohibits the right of assembly without Simon's permission (I Macc 14: 44–45). To the Essenes there was no course of redress but to wait for divine intervention. It is this series of events which best explains the character of the sect and reason for its founding by the Legitimate Teacher, whose activity is presented in the sectarian documents against a backdrop of apostasy on the part of Israel.

The men of the community are described as those who show fidelity to the Teacher (1QpHab viii.2–3), i.e., who have confidence in his teaching. The Manual of Discipline states that they retreated into the wilderness "to separate themselves from the abode of perverse men" (1QS viii.12–13), in keeping with the Levitical prescription for purity imposed upon priests.

The character of Essene communal life may be reconstructed from the texts as illumined by the results of several seasons of excavation at Qumran. The complex of buildings, which was clearly the center of a monastic community, contained a number of pools and cisterns, presumably where lustrations were practiced. The group ate at a common table according to prescriptions set forth in the Manual of Discipline (col. vi). They carried on an active literary work, copying biblical manuscripts and both familiar and previously unknown apocryphal and pseudepigraphic works. The discovery of long plastered benches thought to be writing desks, and inkwells, as well as practice ostraca for young scribes, indicates that the hundreds of manuscripts and fragments found in eleven of the nearby caves were placed there by members of the sect. Pottery found in the vicinity of the communal kilns is of the same type found in some of the caves containing the remains of the Essene library.

Essene occupation of the center is marked off by two major destructions. While the exact date for the founding of the center on the site of an old Israelitish fortress is uncertain, it was probably built during the reign of John Hyrcanus I (135–104 B.C.), to judge from the coin sequence. The first period of communal occupation was interrupted in Herodian times by the earthquake of 31 B.C., the ravages of which are still visible in the faulted steps leading into one of the cisterns. The center was abandoned and not resettled, to judge again by coins, until the early years of the ethnarch Archelaus (A.D. 6–14).

The wilderness sect lived out its remaining existence without interruption until the turbulent days of the First Revolt, when Vespasian's Tenth Legion destroyed the center in the summer of 68. The walls of this period are mined through, and in the ruins sealed with a layer of ash are iron arrowheads used by Roman legionnaires. Prior to the destruction the Essenes hid their library in nearby caves, with the result that the knowledge of the sect was not extinguished with the sect itself. While it would be erroneous to conceive of the Essenes as a sect restricted to the community in the desert at Qumran, the fact remains that we know of their life and practices only from this one center.

The Essenes clearly regarded themselves as the true Israel, constituting a remnant within apostate Israel. The promises to Israel they understood as being fulfilled in their own experience as a righteous congregation assuming a holy posture before God. Their writings reflect a strong election consciousness, and they eagerly anticipated "the day of vengeance" when God would vindicate His own elect (1QS i.11; ii.9; iv.12; v.12; ix.23). Essene perspective can be seen especially in their biblical commentaries, interpretations of portions of Scripture which are understood as coming into meaningful focus in the experiences of the community.

The fullest text which has been preserved is the Commentary on Habakkuk (1QpHab) containing 13 columns of fragmentary text. The interpretation of the first two chapters of Habakkuk, verse by verse, is controlled by the conviction that the prophecy has received its fulfillment in the life-situation of the community and its founder, the Righteous Teacher. This understanding was the work of the Teacher himself "to whom God has made known all the mysteries of the words of his servants the prophets" (1QpHab viii.1–5). It was he who made clear that the general time to which Habakkuk's prophecy looked forward was the extended period into which the Qumran Covenanters had entered.

Theirs was the last generation, and they keenly anticipated, to a degree higher than is elsewhere attested in the literature of the intertestamental period, the consummation. These expectations were made concrete in terms of "the coming of a Prophet and the Anointed Ones of Aaron and Israel" (1QS ix. 10–11), from whom deliverance and restoration to office would come. Here, and elsewhere (e.g., CD vi. 10; vii.21; xii.23; xiii.20; xiv.19; 1QSa ii.12–17), there is reference to an Anointed High Priest and an Anointed King who appear to be messianic figures. It is distinctive of Essene thought that the Anointed Priest takes precedence over the royal figure, a direct projection of the priestly character of the sect.

Although the Essenes are not mentioned in the NT, it is possible that some aspects of Jesus' teaching show alertness to Essene concepts. In Mt 5:43–44 Jesus refers to those who teach "You shall love your neighbor and hate your enemy." The command to hate one's enemy is not found in the OT or in the more familiar intertestamental literature, but it is found in the sectarian documents (1QS i.10; ii.21 f.; cf. x.19 f.). It is clear that Jesus' attitude toward many questions was contrary to the doctrine of the Essenes, and especially concerning the sabbath. While Jesus, as an argument for helping a man, could appeal to the common custom of assisting a sheep which had fallen into a pit on the sabbath (Mt 12:11 f.), the Essenes taught that neither an animal nor a man could be helped on the sabbath (CD xi.13–17). To the Essenes, devotion to the law meant the exaltation of biblical prescription over human life itself. See Dead Sea Scrolls.

Bibliography. Frank M. Cross, *The Ancient Library of Qumran and Modern Biblical Studies,* Garden City: Doubleday, 1958. A. Dupont-Sommer, *The Essene Writings from Qumran,* New York: Meridian, 1962 (the texts in translation). W. R. Farmer, "Essenes," IDB, II, 143–149. John L. McKenzie, "Qumran Scrolls," *Dictionary of the Bible,* Milwaukee: Bruce, 1965, pp. 710–716. Krister Stendahl, ed., *The Scrolls and the New Testament,* New York: Harper, 1957.

W. L. L.

ESTHER (ĕs'tẽr). A Jewish exile who lived in Persia during the reign of Ahasuerus (Xerxes, 486–465 B.C.). The name Esther was from Persian *stara,* "star," or from Ishtar, a Babylonian goddess. Her Heb. name was Hadassah, "myrtle." Esther was an orphan and was raised by her cousin Mordecai. Her beauty was the reason for her being numbered among the virgins brought to Ahasuerus for the selection of a queen to reign instead of Vashti. Esther was chosen and made queen and lived in the palace at Shushan (*q.v.*).

Esther is also noted for her bravery and her loyalty to her people. Risking her own life by having to reveal for the first time that she was Jewish, she made supplication to the king to sign a new decree to undo Haman's decree against the Jews.

Some accuse her of being heartless and vengeful in asking that the Jews might defend themselves and slay their attackers. However, careful study does not sustain these accusations. She exposed the evil plot of Haman and sought to save her people, but the royal decree obtained by her intercession was limited to self-defense (8:11). Notice that the Jews abstained from plunder (9:10, 16), and that no reprisals against women and children are mentioned. The only request that would reflect on Esther is for a second day of bloodshed and the display of the corpses of Haman's sons on the gallows (9:13). This may have been done to extend the right of self-defense to the Jews if necessary, and to prevent more bloodshed by showing that the leaders of the campaign against the Jews were dead, thus indicating the folly of further attacks.

R. B. D.

ESTHER, BOOK OF. In the Heb. Bible this book comes last in a group of five books bearing the title Megilloth, following Ruth, Song of Solomon, Ecclesiastes, and Lamentations.

Textual Considerations

Textual problems in this book are few. Esther is generally accepted as a unit. Only 9:20–32 and 10:1–3 are questioned. Eissfeldt considers 9:20 ff. as an addition explaining a change of date for Purim; but the fact that this passage does not change the date denies Eissfeldt's view. The summary nature of 9:20–32 accounts for any stylistic differences.

Esther before Ahasuerus (Menescardi)). MM

Some dismiss 10:1-3 as annalistic and misplaced in an historical novel. However, its presence shows that the book of Esther is more than a novel. If 10:1-3 is obviously misplaced, no redactor would have included it in this fashion. Thus it may be concluded that the book of Esther in the Masoretic Text is in good textual condition and the work of one author.

Date

All evidence points to mid-5th cen. B.C. Est 10:2 indicates that it was written after the compilation of the annals of Ahasuerus (Xerxes, 486-465 B.C.). The author had an intimate acquaintance with the palace at Shushan (Susa), and this palace was burned within 30 years of the death of Ahasuerus (q.v.). Thus a date between 465 and the end of the reign of his successor, Artaxerxes I (464-424 B.C.), seems probable.

Author

The description of Mordecai in 10:3 precludes him as the author. The writer was probably an unknown Jew with personal knowledge of Shushan, the palace grounds and buildings, and Persian customs (see C. H. Gordon, *The World of the Old Testament*, Garden City: Doubleday, 1958, pp. 283 f., for the Iranian practice of *kitman* or dissimulation in Est 2:10; 8:17). He had access to Mordecai's writings, state annals, and royal decrees. Ezra or Nehemiah has been suggested as being the author, and the Heb. style compares closely with that of Ezra, Nehemiah, and Chronicles.

Outline of Contents

I. The Choice of a New Queen, Chaps. 1-2
 A. Vashti is deposed, 1:1-22
 B. Esther is made queen, 2:1-18
 C. Mordecai foils a plot against the king, 2:19-23
II. The Peril of the Jewish People, Chaps. 3-7
 A. Haman becomes furious at Mordecai, 3:1-5
 B. Haman plots to destroy the Jews, 3:6-15

 C. Mordecai persuades Esther to intervene, 4:1-17
 D. Esther invites the king and Haman to a banquet, 5:1-14
 E. The king makes Haman honor Mordecai publicly, 6:1-14
 F. Esther reveals Haman's plot to the king, 7:1-6
 G. Haman is hanged and Mordecai is promoted, 7:7-8:2
III. The Defense of the Jews, Chaps. 8-10
 A. A new edict is issued allowing the Jews to defend themselves, 8:3-17
 B. The Jews kill their enemies throughout the land, 9:1-16
 C. The Feast of Purim is inaugurated, 9:17-32
 D. Mordecai is advanced and is popular with his own race, 10:1-3

Historical Considerations

While Ahasuerus is commonly associated with Xerxes I (486-465 B.C.), in the LXX the name Ahasuerus was given throughout as Artaxerxes. The king in the book of Esther has therefore been identified by some scholars with Artaxerxes II (404-359 B.C.). The traditional identification seems correct for the following reasons:

Herodotus vii.8 relates that Xerxes called an assembly of princes in the third year of his reign to discuss a Grecian campaign. Est 1:3 refers to a princely gathering in that year. After the defeats of 480 and 479 B.C. Xerxes returned to Shushan several years later. Herodotus ix.108 states that he turned to private affairs. The book of Esther confirms this. Esther came to the harem in the sixth year (478 B.C.) and became queen (2:16) in the seventh (477 B.C.).

The book of Esther accurately describes the territory ruled by Ahasuerus (1:1, 3; 10:1). No other Persian ruler controlled the same domain.

Ahasuerus' character is correctly portrayed. He enjoyed the luxury and sensuality of court

A bull capital from one of the columns of the palace at Susa (biblical Shushan). LM

life and sometimes acted with brutality and cruelty. Thus Ahasuerus of the OT is characterized similarly to the Xerxes of Herodotus. Xerxes is known to have been capable of all attributed in the Bible to Ahasuerus. Although a law limited the Persian ruler to one wife, the palace ruins show that Darius and Xerxes had seraglios.

The author's accurate knowledge of the sections of the city and of details of the palace with its gorgeous furnishings (1:2, 5, 6; 2:11, 14; 3:15; 5:1; 6:4; 7:7–8) has been confirmed by French archaeologists. *See* Shushan.

A year's advance notice of the permission given to Haman by Xerxes to slaughter the Jews (Est 3:12–14) is historically understandable. It is in keeping with the value placed on lots among the Persians and with the psychological and military preparations necessary. If it be objected that so much notice would give the Jews opportunity to flee, it must be asked, where could they flee? There is no evidence of any mass migration of Jews during the 5th cen. B.C. to contradict Est 9:1–2 that they remained in their cities in the Persian Empire.

In recent years the historical accuracy of the story of Esther has been challenged on several counts. (1) Secular history knows nothing of a queen named Vashti or Esther in the reign of Xerxes, but rather his wife was Amestris, the daughter of a Persian general, according to Herodotus (vii.61). (2) Mordecai seems to be mentioned (Est 2:5–6) as having been carried away captive to Babylon (*c.* 597 B.C.) by Nebuchadnezzar. This would make him at least 122 years old when he was elevated to power in Xerxes' 12th year, while his young cousin Esther must have been at least 100 years younger. (3) The edict of Xerxes permitting the Jews to kill 75,000 of his subjects in one day (Est 9:16) seems improbable. These together with other problems of a more subjective nature form the main arguments against the historical accuracy.

In answer to these questions it may be noted that: (1) Herodotus omits many important people and events in his account. An outstanding example of this is his omission of Belshazzar (Dan 5), which recent archaeological discovery has verified. (2) The passage in Est 2:5–6 may be interpreted to mean that it was Mordecai's great-grandfather Kish who was taken captive by Nebuchadnezzar. A cuneiform inscription published by A. Ungnad in 1941 bears the name Marduk-ai-a (Mordecai), a Persian official and counselor in Susa during the reign of Xerxes. Late Babylonian inscriptions also reveal the frequent occurrence of the name Mordecai, indicating it was a common name of this period. *See* Mordecai. (3) The improbability of 75,000 Persians being slain in one day is not an impossibility. In the light of known Persian disregard for human life, especially when a member of the royal family was involved, and the thorough arming of the Jews throughout the province (Est 8:13; 9:5), "it is

by no means incredible that the Jews could have encountered and overcome such a large number of foes" (SOTI, p. 405).

The vengeful slaughter of 75,000 has been condemned by some as immoral. It must be remembered, however, that Medo-Persian laws could not be repealed (cf. Dan 6:8, 12, 15, 17 with Est 1:19; 8:8). All Xerxes could do was to provide for the Jews' own self-defense. While the city of Susa rejoiced at the promotion of Mordecai, his rise could not abate *all* anti-Semitic feeling throughout the land (8:15–17). In an empire of 100 million, for perhaps three million Jews to kill 75,000 was not an excessive number. Government officials even helped the Jews (9:3). The latter also undoubtedly suffered some casualties, but the general OT custom of mentioning only the dead of the vanquished seems to be followed (see Keil, *The Books of Ezra, Nehemiah and Esther*, KD, pp. 307–310).

Lack of Mention of God

Acrostics notwithstanding, God is not mentioned in this book. In an atmosphere of hatred and opposition, it was not always expedient for the Jews to display their religion publicly. The Gentile populace resented the Jewish attitude toward idols, religion, foods, and mixed marriages. Thus without flaunting his religion, the author of this book conveys a spiritual emphasis.

Mordecai is shown to stand in the tradition of Shadrach, Meshach, and Abednego in refusing obeisance to Haman (Est 3:2 ff.). His refusal is understandable only on the basis of his strict adherence to the Decalogue. Fasting is a further indication of Jewish religious practice (4:16; 9:31). Est 9:31 speaks of the Jews' cry for help. Help from whom? Mordecai expresses his faith in God by telling Esther that if she fails, help will come from another source.

The outstanding religious motif is divine providence. The Jews learned under God's affliction what they would not learn under His forbearance. The author weaves the pattern of providence. Before Haman quarreled with Mordecai, Vashti's dismissal provided the occasion for Esther, a Jewess, to gain a position which enabled her to save her people. Mordecai had indebted himself to the king. Xerxes had a sleepless night at the right time and read in the right portion of the state records. All fits together. No Jew could have penned this without the intention of presenting the providence of God in the sparing of His people.

Bibliography. R. K. Harrison, *Introduction to the Old Testament,* Grand Rapids: Eerdmans, 1969, pp. 1085–1102. A. Macdonald, "Esther," NBC, pp. 380–386. L. B. Paton, "The Book of Esther," ICC, 1916. John C. Whitcomb, "Esther," WBC, pp. 447–457. J. Stafford Wright, "Esther, Book of," NBD, pp. 392 ff.; "The toricity of the Book of Esther," NPOT, pp. 37–47.

R. B. D.

ESTHER, FAST OF. *See* Festivals; Purim.

ETAM (ē'tăm)

1. One of five cities belonging to Simeon (I Chr 4:32). Two adjacent cities were Ain and Rimmon. Etam was located in the extreme southern part of Simeon, among the Negeb hills near Beer-sheba. Its exact site is unknown.

2. In II Chr 11:6 mention is made of a second site named Etam adjacent to Bethlehem and Tekoa, built by Rehoboam for defense in Judah. It was probably founded by a descendant of Hur of the tribe of Judah ("father of Etam," I Chr 4:3). The LXX includes Etam in a list of 11 towns in the hill country district of Bethlehem, not found in the Heb. MT in Josh 15:59–60. Josephus, in talking about the activity and splendor of Solomon, related: "There was a certain place, about fifty furlongs distant from Jerusalem, which is called Etham, very pleasant; it is in fine gardens, and abounding in rivulets of water; thither did he use to go out in the morning, sitting on high" (*Ant.* viii.7.3).

In the writings of the Talmud, 'Ain Etan is mentioned as being the most elevated place in Palestine, and from it ran an aqueduct to the temple. The site of Etan (Etam) is on an isolated hill a little to the E of 'Ain 'Atan, two miles SW of Bethlehem. According to Josephus (*Ant.* xviii.3.2), Pontius Pilate used temple funds to construct a 23 mile long aqueduct to Jerusalem, evidently from the three Hellenistic-Roman reservoirs now called Solomon's pools at Etam.

Pools of Solomon near Etam. JR

3. The rock of Etam (Jud 15:8, 11), where Samson stayed in a cave after smiting the Philistines, was also in Judah but lower in altitude ("he went down," v.8) in the Shephelah foothills. A cavern known as 'Araq Isma'in, two and one half miles SE of Zorah, suits the requirements of the story and affords an excellent view from its mouth high up on the N cliffs of the Wadi Isma'in.

C. M. H.

ETERNAL LIFE. A phrase appearing 30 times in the NT (KJV), of which 15 usages occur in the Gospel and epistles of John; and 43 times in the RSV, with 25 occurrences in the Johannine writings.

The word eternal (*aiōnios*) is derived from the word meaning "age," an indefinite period of time, hence, agelong, and consequently unending. Eternal life refers invariably to the life of God, or to the future state of the righteous (Mt 25:46). The Johannine writings define it in terms of knowing, making it synonymous with the experience of God (Jn 17:3). It cannot be earned by men, but is bestowed upon them as a gift in response to faith (Jn 3:15–16; I Jn 5:11; Rom 6:23), and becomes a perpetual source of power and refreshment (Jn 4:14). Eternal life is the vitality which God imparts to the human soul at the moment of personal conversion to Christ.

Eternal life is mediated through Christ (I Jn 5:11) and represents the totality of Christian experience in its vitality, in its duration, in its quality, and in its associations and content. It enables the believer to enter directly into the presence of God at death and enjoy the eternal bliss of heaven. Its opposite is eternal death, or severance from God (II Thess 1:9).

See Immortality; Life.

M. C. T.

ETERNAL SECURITY. *See* Assurance.

ETERNAL STATE AND DEATH

Death

Death is spoken of in three senses in the Bible.

1. *Spiritual death.* This is what occurred to Adam and Eve, and passed from them to the whole human race by imputation when they sinned and fell, even as God had warned (Gen 2:17; Rom 5:12). The continuance of man in a state of spiritual death is spoken of throughout the Bible (Rom 3:10–18; 5:12; I Cor 2:14; Eph 2:1, 5). This condition is abolished only by regeneration or what is called the new birth (Jn 3:3, 5 ff.; I Jn 5:1; cf. Eph 2:1, 5). *See* Born Again.

2. *Physical death.* This is the appointed portion of every man since the fall of Adam (Heb 9:27), except for those Christians who will be still alive at the rapture, at the second coming of Jesus Christ (I Cor 15:51–52; I Thess 4:14–17).

Some have endeavored to explain the prophecies of the return of Christ for His own, especially in I Thess 4:14–17, as Christ receiving the believer at death. This does violence, however, to the clear teaching of Scripture concerning Christ's returning visibly for His own as He promised (Jn 14:3, 6; Acts 1:11). Also it conflicts with those prophecies which foretell the snatching away and rapture of the Christian (Mt 24:36–41; I Cor 15:51–52; I Thess 4:14–17; cf. Christ's coming "as a thief" in Rev

16:15 with Mt 24:43; I Thess 5:2), and with the promise that the believer will not suffer God's terrible wrath against sin at the second coming (I Thess 5:9; II Thess 1:7–10; cf. Rev 3:10; chap. 16 and the vials of wrath).

3. *The second death.* This is the final, irreversible separation of the wicked from God and the righteous as they are cast into hell after the judgment of the Great White Throne (Rev 20:6, 14; 21:8; cf. 2:11).

Rev 20:6 states: "Blessed and holy is he that hath part in the first resurrection: on such the second death hath no power." According to this verse and v. 14, the second death comes after the thousand year reign of Christ on the earth (cf. Rev 5:10). *See* Dead, The; Death.

The Eternal State

Just when the believer will enter the eternal state is not certain. Some say immediately after the second coming of Christ. These teach that there will be one general judgment of all men at that time. Others say that Christ first establishes His visible kingdom on earth at His second coming and that the eternal state begins only after the Millennium. *See* New Heavens and New Earth; Millennium; Rapture. The premillennialist maintains that on the basis of an inductive study of the Scriptures the latter view, as explained in the articles referred to, best fits the teaching of the whole Bible.

1. *The nature of the eternal state.* This can be best understood by contrasting, first, the difference between the state of the believer today and in the Millennium; and then, the difference between the state of the saints who enter and enjoy the Millennium and of the saints in their eternal reign in the new heavens and the new earth.

The rulership of Christ and His kingdom, i.e., the kingdom of God, began in its hidden "mystery" form during the ministry of Christ on the earth (Mt 12:28; Lk 11:20; cf. parables of the kingdom in Mt 13). It has continued throughout the so-called Gospel Age. The kingdom will enter its second phase as Christ comes with His resurrected saints to rule in person over the whole earth at His second coming (Isa 66:15 ff.; Zech 14:5; Jude 14; Rev 20:4). At that time the resurrected saints will minister with Christ in resurrected bodies fashioned after the resurrected body of Christ (Phil 3:20–21; I Thess 4:14–17; Rev 20:4). They will have been freed from their fallen natures and the earth will have been freed from the curse (Isa 11:6–9; 65:25; Rom 8:18–23). Yet sin and death will continue for the people surviving on the earth at the beginning of the Millennium and for those who will be born during that time (Isa 65:20; Rev 20:7 f.). Peace will prevail, but will be maintained only by the strict rule of Christ, because man will still be sinful (Isa 65:20; Rev 2:27; 19:15; 20:7–10).

The final, eternal state begins with the creation of the new heavens and new earth (*q.v.*)

"wherein dwelleth righteousness" (Rev 21:1; cf. II Pet 3:7–13). In it the wicked will be eternally separated from the righteous (Rev 21:27; 22:14–15), the former being finally consigned to the lake of fire and brimstone which is the second death (Rev 21:8).

The wicked will not be annihilated by the second death as judgment for their sins, any more than Christ was annihilated when He paid the penalty for our sins. The Beast and the False Prophet, cast into the lake of fire at Christ's return (Rev 19:20), do not suffer extinction of being, for they are still there in torment a thousand years later (Rev 20:10). The NT clearly teaches the endless duration of retribution (Mt 25:41, 46; II Thess 1:9; Jude 13; Rev 14:11; 19:3; 20:10). The nature of the punishment will include, in addition to whatever forms of physical suffering may continue, (1) exclusion from the immediate presence of God (II Thess 1:9) into outer darkness (Mt 25:30); (2) the gnawings of conscience and remorse (the undying worm, Mk 9:47–48; weeping and gnashing of teeth, Mt 25:30); and (3) probably the internal burning of the human spirit with no opportunity to express its sinful passions. *See* Gehenna; Hell.

2. *Blessings of the eternal state.* These include all the blessings enjoyed by the resurrected saints as they reign with Christ (see above), plus God's personal comfort as He wipes away all tears (Rev 21:4) and gives His own a specially prepared city, the New Jerusalem (Rev 21:9–22:5). In that city are the river of the water of life (Rev 22:1), the tree of life (Rev 22:2), and the very presence of God and His throne (Rev 22:3; cf. 21:22–23).

Certain questions arise concerning the final state of the believer. Will there not be sorrow over loved ones who died without Christ? Yes, but God will comfort us over such sorrows (Rev 21:4). Will there be time in heaven or will time cease? The meaning of the words "time shall be no more" in Rev 10:6 is not that time itself ceases but that the event being foretold is at hand. The idea that God is timeless or that eternity is static is not necessarily scriptural. Geerhardus Vos held that the eternal state will be progressive, opening up vista after vista, because hope, along with faith and love, will abide, and hope must have reference to a future even throughout eternity (Buswell, *Systematic Theology,* I, 46).

The philosopher Immanuel Kant saw God as timeless and spaceless, but only because he could not explain how the three infinites: God, time, and space, could all exist at one time. Kant therefore said that time and space are finite. However, this argument is fallacious since time and space are not created entities—as he supposed—but are merely relationships, for space between objects, and for time between events. It should be clear to all that more than one infinite can exist at one time. For example, God's infinite wisdom, power, holiness, etc., are not attributes of immensity and therefore do not conflict with infinite time and space. See Eternity; Time. Men are created beings, and thus are limited by time and space; but God is free from both time and space in the sense that His omnipresence overcomes the limiting effect of space, His omniscience that of time. See Eschatology; Eternity.

Bibliography. Rudolf Bultmann, *"Thanatos,* etc.," TDNT, III, 7–25. J. Oliver Buswell, Jr., *A Systematic Theology of the Christian Religion,* Grand Rapids: Zondervan, 1962, I, 29–54; II, 491–538. Harry Buis, *The Doctrine of Eternal Punishment,* Philadelphia: Presbyterian and Reformed, 1957. Herman A. Hoyt, *The End Times,* Chicago: Moody, 1969. C. S. Lewis, *The Great Divorce,* New York: Macmillan, 1946. S. D. F. Salmond, *The Christian Doctrine of Immortality,* 5th ed., Edinburgh: Clark, 1913. W. G. T. Shedd, *The Doctrine of Endless Punishment,* New York: Scribner, 1886. Henry B. Swete, *The Life of the World to Come,* New York: Macmillan, 1918.

R. A. K.

ETERNITY. In philosophic thought, both ancient and modern, eternity refers to something outside of or in contrast to time. In the biblical usage, however, the Heb. and Gr. terms for eternity always stand for time, either a specific era or a period of unknown and undivided quantity. The emphasis is on endlessness, indefinite duration.

The OT uses the Heb. word *'ôlām;* the NT employs the term *aiōn* (Herman Sasse, *"Aiōn,* etc.," TDNT, I, 197–209). These words may refer to exact periods as well as to undefined and incalculable duration. The eternity of God, for instance, means His continuous dominion over all time—past, present and future (Ps 10:16; 29:10; 90:1–2; 103:17–19; Isa 40:28; Jer 10:10–12). It must not be regarded as placing Him *outside* of time, as philosophy does. God effected our redemption at a specific moment in history. "When the fulness of the time came, God sent forth His Son" (Gal 4:4, NASB). Christ appeared to put away sins "at the climax of history" (Heb 9:26, NEB, lit., "at the consummation of the ages," His death viewed as the key event which completes or gives meaning to the ages), and He will appear a second time in history (Heb 9:28).

The Gr. NT frequently employs the plural *eis tous aiōnas,* "unto the ages," or *eis tous aiōnas tōn aiōnōn,* "unto the ages of the ages," to express the idea of eternity or forever (e.g., Rom 1:25; 9:5; 11:36; 16:27). The reference to God as the "King of ages" in I Tim 1:17 (RSV) really means the "eternal King."

See Aeon; Eternal State and Death; Time.

T. W. B.

ETHAM (ē'thám). This proper name is given to both a place in Egypt and the wilderness on the E of the Red Sea. Ex 13:20 locates Etham between Succoth and the wilderness. Thus it must have been near the eastern end of the Wadi Tumilat and probably N of Lake Timsah. It was quite likely a border fortress, since the Heb. name *'ētām* is cognate to Arabic *othom,* "citadel," "stone fortification." Also *'ētām* may represent the Egyptian word *ḥtm* meaning "fortress." Nineteenth Dynasty papyrus letters mention fortresses in this area (ANET, p. 259).

Num 33:6–8 tells of the progress of Israel from Etham to Pi-hahiroth, whence they were led through the Red Sea. On the E side of it they went into the Sinai desert, which was known as the wilderness of Etham.

ETHAN (ē'thán)
1. A son of Zerah, Judah's son by Tamar. He was the father of Azariah (I Chr 2:6, 8).
2. An Ezrahite of the tribe of Judah, known for his great wisdom (I Kgs 4:31) and mentioned in the title of Ps 89.
3. A Levite of the household of Merari (I Chr 6:44, 47; 15:17, 19) appointed as one of the temple singers by David. His name was apparently changed to Jeduthun after his appointment in the temple at Gibeon (I Chr 16:38–41).
4. A Levite of the household of Libni (I Chr 6:42–43; see also v. 20 and Num 26:58).

ETHANIM (ĕth'á-nĭm; "perennial"). In 1 Kgs 8:2 the seventh month of the Jewish year is named Ethanim, which corresponds to Tishri of the later calendar. It was regarded as the month when only perennial streams were still flowing. It is mentioned in Phoenician inscriptions. At the time of the Exile, the name was replaced by the Babylonian name of Tishri. It corresponds to our September–October and is regarded as the beginning of the civil year for the Jews. See Calendar.

ETHBALL (ĕth/baál). The king of the Sidonians and the father of Jezebel, wife of King Ahab of Israel (I Kgs 16:31). Josephus further identifies him as the king of the Tyrians and Sidonians (*Ant.* viii.13.1). Menander the Ephesian referred to Ithobalus, the priest of Astarte, who reigned for 32 years as the king of Tyre after assassinating Pheles, the former king (Jos *Apion,* 1.18).

ETHER (ē'thẽr)
1. In the first division of the land a town was assigned to Judah by the name of Ether, together with Libnah and Ashan, in the foothills or Shephelah (Josh 15:42). This town may be located at Khirbet el-'Ater, four miles N of Lachish.
2. In the lot that was cast for Simeon (Josh 19:7), an Ether was assigned along with Ashan. While some geographers consider it identical with the Ether assigned to Judah, others identify it with Khirbet 'Attir, 15 miles NE of Beer-sheba.

ETHICS. *See* Example.

ETHIOPIA (ē-thĭ-ō′pĭ-*à*), **ETHIOPIAN** (-*ăn*), Cush (Heb. *kùsh,* borrowed from Egyptian *k3sh*)in most of its OT occurrences refers to the land variously known as Ethiopia, Nubia or the Sudan. It is located S of Egypt (therefore its frequent bracketing with Egypt; cf. Gen 10:6–8; I Chr 1:8–10; Ps 68:31; Isa 11:11; 20:3–5; 43:3; 45:14; Ezk 30:4, 9; Dan 11:43; Nah 3:9) and at times a part of the W Arabian peninsula (II Chr 21:16 and certain Assyrian inscriptions). The Al Amran tribe of Arabia calls the region of Zebid in Yemen by the name Kūsh. Ezk 29:10; 30:6–9 (RSV) identifies its N border as Syene (modern 'Aswân, at the First Cataract of the Nile). Its S border was not clearly defined, but probably lay near Khartum at the junction of the Blue and the White Nile, a little upstream from the Sixth Cataract and a thousand miles S of Syene. Popular etymology defined the Gr. designation *Aithiopía* as the "Land of Scorched Faces" from *aíthein,* "to burn," and *ōps,* "countenance" (cf. Jer 13:23).

Nubia always attracted the attention of the Egyptian rulers because of its gold mines and the products of central Africa, such as ivory and ebony, which entered Egypt through Nubian traders (cf. Isa 45:14). The country was conquered by the strong kings of the Twelfth Egyptian Dynasty, lost during the Hyksos period, and reconquered by the Eighteenth Dynasty pharaohs. They penetrated as far S as the city of Napata at the Fourth Cataract and placed Kush under an Egyptian governor. The people of ancient Ethiopia – who were negroid, as appears from Egyptian art – adopted the Egyptian religion and culture so completely that the Egyptian way of life remained more conservative and lasted longer than in Egypt itself.

About 1000 B.C. Nubia regained its independence and established a kingdom with its capital at Napata. For an inscription telling of the nomination of an Ethiopian king of this period by the Egyptian god Amon-Re, see ANET, pp. 447 f. When Egypt became weak *c.* 750 B.C., the Nubians conquered Upper Egypt with its chief city of Thebes. About 725 Piankhi in a single campaign brought all the rest of Egypt under Nubian control except for a small portion in the Delta. Thus the Twenty-fifth Dynasty (715–663 B.C.) consisted of a series of Ethiopian rulers. The names of four of these have been preserved: Shabako, Shabataka. Taharka (the biblical Tirhakah, *q.v.*), and Tanutamun. These last two kings were driven back into Ethiopia by the Assyrian kings Esarhaddon and Ashurbanipal, who sacked Thebes in 663 B.C.

Nahum, who called Ethiopia the strength of Thebes (No-amon, 3:8–9), accurately reflects the Nubian control of that great city in Egypt. Toward the beginning of the Twenty-fifth Dynasty Isaiah delivered an oracle concerning the Cushites (chap. 18) and a prophecy (20:3–6) to warn Judah not to depend on Egypt and Ethiopia for help. Zephaniah (2:12) foretold Nubia's eventual doom, which was effected by the Persians (Est 1:1; ANET, p. 316). Meanwhile Ethiopian troops fought with Egypt in Jeremiah's day (46:9).

About 300 B.C. the royal residence of the Ethiopian rulers was transferred from Napata to Meroë at the Fifth Cataract. This kingdom, ruled by a succession of queens, each of whom carried the title Candace (*q.v.*; Acts 8:27), lasted until *c:* A.D. 355, and then gave way to the Abyssinian power of Aksum. During this period the population became predominantly Negro. The isolation of the Meroitic kingdom preserved its ancient Egyptian culture in stagnant form, as recent discoveries in the Nubian royal cemeteries at Meroë and Barkal indicate.

Other Ethiopians named in the OT are Zerah (*q.v.*, the leader of Egyptian mercenary forces, II Chr 14:9) and the slave Ebed-melech (Jer 38:7–12; 39:16). Joab sent a Cushite among his troops as one of his messengers to King David (II Sam 18:21–32, RSV). Ethiopian soldiers were frequently used as mercenaries in the Egyptian armies both before (II Chr 12:3) and after (Jer 46:9) their brief period of hegemony over Egypt. Persia later incorporated Ethiopia as the southwesternmost portion of its empire (Est 1:1; 8:9).

The hope expressed in Ps 68:31 that Ethiopia will stretch out her hands to God was realized in the conversion of the Ethiopian eunuch of Acts 8:26–39 who, according to tradition, became the first Christian evangelist to his people. *See* Ethiopian Eunuch.

Bibliography. Edward Ullendorff, *Ethiopia and the Bible,* New York: Oxford Univ. Press, 1968.

R. Y. and J. R.

ETHIOPIAN EUNUCH. Ethiopian tradition makes the man mentioned in Acts 8:26–40 the founder of Christianity in Ethiopia. Not identifiable from any reliable outside sources, he was possibly the state minister in charge of the treasury under Candace, queen of the Ethiopians. The designation "eunuch" is elsewhere translated "officer" or "chamberlain," and carries no special suggestion of mutilation. However, by usage the word had become synonymous with the Latin *castratus,* signifying one who had been emasculated. If physically a eunuch, the law of Deut 23:1 would have prohibited him from full communion in Judaism. He may have been a "proselyte of the gate." This is implied in his journey to Jerusalem to worship. *See* Candace; Ethiopia; Eunuch.

While traveling homeward, he was reading from the LXX, the Gr. translation of the OT. The place of his baptism, following his confession of faith in Christ, is believed to have been near Gaza.

I. R.

ETHIOPIAN WOMAN. The Cushite wife of Moses is so described in Num 12:1 (see RSV). Miriam and Aaron rebuked Moses for assuming authority beyond that which they possessed, and criticized his marriage to a person who was not of their national background, possibly lowering his prestige in the eyes of his contemporaries.

Two solutions are suggested for the problem of the Cushite woman. First, Zipporah, Moses' Midianitish wife (Ex 2:21), may have been called by this title. The name Cush has been applied to the territory stretching from Assyria on the E to Ethiopia on the W and S. The exploits of Nimrod, a descendant of Cush, in establishing Nineveh, are described in Gen 10:8-11. However, this term was never widely applied to this whole territory. Arabia may be recognized by the term Cush in I Chr 1:9, and by the related term Cushan in Hab 3:7. Thus, the term Ethiopian woman may reflect the fact that Zipporah came from a part of Arabia.

A second possible solution suggests that the term Ethiopian woman, as translated in KJV, applied to a second wife whom Moses married after the death of Zipporah. Neither event is stated in the Scriptures, however, and her background is not known. Josephus stated that Moses married a princess of Ethiopia after the battle of Saba (Meroë) and her delivering up of the city (*Ant.* ii.10.2). Another suggestion is that she may have been one of the mixed multitude who accompanied the children of Israel out of the land of Egypt (Num 11:4).

C. M. H.

ETHNAN (ĕth'năn). A son of Helah and member of the tribe of Judah (I Chr 4:7).

ETHNARCH (ĕth'närk). The Gr. term *ethnarchēs*, a governor of an ethnic group, occurs in II Cor 11:32, the "governor" of Damascus under the Nabataean king Aretas IV. "Ethnarch" was apparently a title of royalty granted to a dependent ruler, higher than "tetrarch" but lower than "king." Herod's son Archelaus was given the title of ethnarch of Judea (Jos *Ant.* xvii.11.4). After he was deposed in A.D. 6, "the government became an aristocracy, and the high priests were intrusted with a dominion over the nation" (*Ant.* xx.10). Thus Caiaphas had most of the powers of an ethnarch, and outranked the procurator Pilate in all matters not concerned with the safety of the state. That Caiaphas sent Jesus to Pilate for trial and sentencing suggests the nature of the crime attributed to our Lord. *See* Governor.

ETHNI (ĕth'nī). A Levite of the family of Gershom (I Chr 6:41). He was included in the genealogy of Asaph, one of the men set over the service of song in the house of the Lord after the ark had been restored by King David.

EUBULUS (ū-bū'lŭs). Paul listed Eubulus among the Christians who were active in the work at Rome by including a greeting to Timothy from him (II Tim 4:21). Since his was a Gr. name, it is assumed that he was a Gentile by birth. Nothing more is known about him.

EUCHARIST. *See* Lord's Supper.

EUNICE (ū-nīs). The name, meaning "victorious," occurs but once in the Bible (II Tim 1:5). Eunice was Timothy's mother, and this gives her a measure of importance. She and her mother Lois are both described as women of genuine faith in the Lord, and they had apparently encouraged a similar faith in young Timothy. Eunice was a godly Jewess, married to a Greek. It is unlikely that she was a Christian believer before Paul's first visit to Derbe and Lystra, where she lived, but evidently she had taught Timothy the OT Scriptures thoroughly (II Tim 3:15), although he was not circumcised until Paul's second visit.

EUNUCH (ū'nŭk). The Heb. word translated "eunuch" (*sārîs*) also means "officer." Usually it indicates an officer for the women's quarters in a king's court. There were married eunuchs (Gen 39:1), but usually they were castrated (*q.v.*). Such men could be high officials as in the case of Potiphar or the Pharaoh's chief butler and baker (Gen 37:36; 40:1). Eunuchs (*sārîs*) served in the court of Ahab and Jezebel (I Kgs 22:9, ASV marg.), and the Persian king had one over his harem (Est 2:3, 14). The Heb. law excluded them from worship in the temple (Deut 23:1), but they were used by David in his court (I Chr 28:1, ASV marg.). Captives were often made eunuchs, although not always. Probably those used in the courts of Judah were foreigners. Isaiah advocated that those eunuchs who sought to keep the covenant should have their worship privileges restored (Isa 56:4 f.). Two Ethiopian eunuchs are mentioned specifically: Ebed-melech, who asked that Jeremiah be released from the well (Jer 38:7-13); and the pious man, an officer of Queen Candace, who was baptized after Philip explained the Scripture to him on the Gaza road (Acts 8:27-40). *See* Ethiopian Eunuch. To be "a eunuch for Christ's sake" probably meant to voluntarily give up marriage and family life to work for the kingdom (Mt 19:12).

A. W. W.

EUODIAS (û-ō'dĭ-ăs). The KJV spelling, but it should properly be spelled Euodia (Phil 4:2, RSV). Euodia was a prominent woman in the church at Philippi who had a difference with another woman by the name of Syntyche. Paul exhorted them to settle their differences for the good of the church. What their difference was is not known. Some conjecture that it was a religious question rather than a personal quarrel. It is not known whether their positions in the church were official as deaconesses or if they were women in whose homes the church was accustomed to meet. However, the problem was so serious that it had been called to Paul's attention, and he sought even the intercession of a fellow worker in healing the breach of fellowship. An added incentive for this reconciliation was the memory of their former service with him in the work of the gospel.

C. M. H.

EUPHRATES (ū-frā'tēz). The largest river in western Asia. It has its source in central Armenia formed by the junction in Asia Minor of the Kara-su and Murad-su Rivers, from which it pursues a southeasterly course to the Persian Gulf. It is about 1,800 miles long. At Korna, about 100 miles from the gulf, it unites with the Tigris River. It is a very sluggish stream except in flood season and is not very deep until it combines with the Tigris, forming a delta which is composed of lakes and bays. The melting snow causes its rise about the middle of March, increasing gradually until June. The rise continues high for 30 to 40 days before it begins to fall. From the middle of September to the middle of October it is at its lowest.

The overflow of the Euphrates and the use of canals as in Egypt made possible bountiful crops that sustained a large population. Since the Mongolian and Mohammedan conquests, the land has been mostly unproductive, but now the Iraq government is restoring the canals and building dams.

Before its union with the Tigris it is navigable for only 1,200 miles by small boats. After its union, ocean-going vessels can go up as far as Basra. The Euphrates, with the Tigris, has carried silt to the Persian Gulf so that Ur, which some believe was just N of the gulf in Abraham's day, is now over 125 miles farther away.

Along or near its banks were such great cities in the historical past as Carchemish, Mari, Babylon, Ur, Erech, and Eridu. It is mentioned in the OT as "the river" (Deut 11:24), "the great river" (Gen 15:18; Deut 1:7; Josh 1:4), and twice in the NT (Rev 9:14; 16:12). It was the boundary of the Egyptian and Assyrian empires (II Kgs 24:7) and was prophesied to become the eastern boundary of the Heb. monarchy (Gen 15:18; cf. I Kgs 4:24).

E. L. C.

EUROCLYDON (û-rŏk'lĭ-dŏn). The term was commonly in use by sailors for an E or NE wind. It was a violent wind which frequently arose in the Cretan waters, swooping down from the mountains in strong gusts or squalls. The word is made up of two words, the Gr. *eyros,* meaning E wind, and a Latin word *aquilo,* meaning NE wind. Thus it seems to express a NE by E wind. It is still common that tempestuous winds from the E, S, and NE agitate the Mediterranean.

This was the tempestuous wind on the occasion of Paul's disastrous shipwreck (Acts 27:14). The ASV translates it Euraquilo.

An aerial view of the Euphrates. JR

EUTYCHUS (ū'tĭ-kŭs). The young disciple at Troas who sat in the open window of the third floor of a building where Paul was preaching. Falling asleep, Eutychus fell to the ground and was taken up dead. Paul extending himself upon the body restored him to life (Acts 20:5–12).

It has been disputed whether Eutychus was really dead or only in a swoon, and hence, whether a miracle was performed or not. Paul's words seem to indicate that the young man was not actually dead, but the words of Luke the physician are that he was "taken up dead." In Acts 14:19 Luke, referring to Paul's stoning, said the people, "supposing he had been dead," drew him out of the city. This is not the same phrase as in Acts 20:9 translated "taken up dead." The words in Acts 20:9 are too plain to justify modifying them to be read "taken up for dead," which the interpretation that he was not dead would require.

D. L. W.

EVANGELIST. One called to go about preaching the gospel, derived from the verb *euangelizō.* To evangelize is to bring good news to someone, specifically to announce information concerning Christian salvation (I Cor 15:1–4; *see* Gospel; Witness; Commission, Great).

The term is found three times in the NT. Evangelists are listed with apostles, prophets, pastors, and teachers as those called to share in building up the church (Eph 4:11 f.). Philip was called "the evangelist" (Acts 21:8). Although one of seven early chosen to relieve the apostles of the task of food distribution (Acts 6:5), he was especially noticed for his evangelistic activity. From Jerusalem he went to Samaria and preached with great success (Acts 8:4 ff.). From there he was sent to evangelize an officer of the Ethiopian court who was traveling home after visiting Jerusalem (Acts 8:26 ff.). He then preached the gospel from Azotus to Caesarea, where he had a home (Acts 8:40; 21:8).

Timothy, the young minister, was exhorted to do the work of an evangelist (II Tim 4:5) as an accompaniment of his pastoral oversight. It is clear that although apostles and others shared in the work of evangelizing, there were men whom God especially called for this task.

In later years the writers of the four Gospels were called evangelists because they recorded persuasively the foundations of the gospel of Christ.

N. B. B.

EVE (ēv; "life" or "life-giving"; exact meaning uncertain). Eve, the first woman, wife of Adam, and mother of Cain, Abel, Seth and other unnamed children, was made (lit., "built," Gen 2:22) by God from one of Adam's ribs. She was one with Adam yet subordinate to him and a helper for him (cf. I Tim 2:12; Gen 2:20).

The name Eve occurs only twice in the OT (Gen 3:20; 4:1), while the word "woman" is more commonly used. There is a biblical connection between the name Eve (from *ḥawwâ*, "to live") and her becoming the mother of the "living." Because Eve ate the forbidden fruit, she suffered certain judgments appropriate to her womanhood. (1) She and her seed were involved in the enmity between Satan and the redeemed. (2) Pain would accompany childbirth. (3) She would be subordinate to her husband.

In the Sumerian poem about the creation of deities at Dilmun (*see* Eden), the water-god Enki is dying from sickness in eight parts of his body. The goddess Ninhursag brings a cure for each member, including the rib, by giving birth to a special goddess. The one created for the healing of Enki's rib is called Nin-ti, "lady of the rib." But Sumerian *nin-ti* can also mean "the lady who makes live." Possibly this ancient literary play on words reflects in some way a common source with the Genesis account about Eve. (See Samuel N. Kramer, *History Begins at Sumer*, p. 146.) *See* Creation.

C. C. R.

EVEN, EVENING, EVENTIDE. *See* Time.

EVENING SACRIFICE. *See* Sacrifice.

EVERLASTING. *See* Eternity.

EVI (ē'vī). One of the five kings of Midian slain by the Israelites at the direction of Moses (Num 31:8). Josh 13:21 indicates that the land of Evi, along with that of the princes of Sihon and the other four chiefs of Midian, was given to the tribe of Reuben for an inheritance. It was on the E side of the Dead Sea.

EVIDENCE

1. The Heb. word *sēpher* means "writing," "letter," or "book." In Jer 32:10, 11, 12, 14, 16, 44 the prophet records the legal transaction involved in the purchase of a piece of property.

Repeatedly he refers to the title deed or bill of sale which was drawn up, witnessed, and sealed in confirmation of the purchase of the field in Anathoth belonging to his uncle. Then he placed the documents in an earthen vessel for preservation against the time when property would again be bought and sold in the land of Judah.

2. The Gr. word *elegchos* is translated "evidence" in Heb 11:1. In this instance, the idea is conviction (RSV), a proof or the result of putting to the test and proving a thing, a sure persuasion in the heart. The RSV paraphrases the word "mouth" as "evidence" in the expression, "by the mouth of witnesses" (Mt 18:16; II Cor 13:1; Num 35:30; Deut 17:6; 19:15) and introduces the word "evidence" in I Tim 5:19.

C. M. H.

EVIL. Evil is the opposite of good (Gen 2:9, 17). As not good, it always proves harmful and causes loss and suffering.

Several kinds of evil can be differentiated: religious, moral, social, and natural. Religious or spiritual evil is the opposite of righteousness; it is sin (Ezk 20:43; 33:11-13; Mk 7:21-23). Such evil may be in the heart of man even without any act of transgression on his part (Gen 6:5; Mt 5:28). In Scripture words, thoughts, desires, conscience and heart may all be evil. The only antidote to such evil is the cleansing work of Christ.

Moral evil may depend on the customs of a culture, the specific taboos or prohibitions of a society or community. It may be punishable as a crime by civil authorities (Mt 27:23; Acts 23:9; Rom 13:4). It may be something that seems morally unfair, contrary to what one judges to be right (Eccl 2:18-21; 5:13-17; 6:1-2; 10:5-7, RSV). It may or may not be sin according to the Bible, since it may only be a *human* judgment of another's conduct.

Social evil can be seen in such problems as alcoholism, cheating in business, corruption in politics, inadequate opportunities for education, unemployment, poverty, racial discrimination, and war (Zech 7:9-10; 8:16-17). There are also varying degrees of moral and spiritual responsibility involved in these problems, both collectively and individually.

Natural evil or calamity concerns the havoc, loss and suffering caused by earthquakes, famine, fire, floods, disease. It is evil in this sense that God says He has created (Isa 45:7; Amos 3:6).

Not all evil is willed by man or is in his control. Evil in its larger meaning cannot be equated with sin (Eccl 12:1).

See Evil One; Iniquity; Sin (for bibliography); Wickedness.

T. W. B.

EVILDOER. In the Heb. the word is the participial form of a verb meaning "to break or to break into pieces." Hence an evildoer is one who breaks into pieces, destroys, makes evil whatever he does, acts wickedly, and afflicts others. Thus in Ps 26:5; 37:1, 9; Isa 1:4, and other passages, the writers are describing those who were offenders against God's law as well as those who were personal offenders against their fellowmen. *See* Malefactor.

EVIL-FAVOREDNESS. This term is found in Deut 17:1. It states the ritual unfitness of any animal that possessed a blemish of any kind. This included the lack of symmetry or a lean-fleshed condition of the animal as set forth in Deut 15:21. God required perfect animals in the sacrificial offerings. These two unwanted features, ill-favored and lean-fleshed, are combined in a description of the seven cows seen by Pharaoh in his dream (Gen 41:3; etc.).

EVIL-MERODACH (ē'vĭl – mĕr'ŏ-dăk). Akkadian *Amel-Marduk,* king of Babylon (562–560 B.C.), the son and successor of Nebuchadnezzar. Confirmation of his existence turned up during excavations at Susa (biblical Shushan). The Bible tells of Evil-merodach's releasing Jehoiachin, king of Judah, from prison after nearly 37 years and treating him kindly by having him at the king's table and granting him a permanent living allowance for the rest of his life (II Kgs 25:27–30; Jer 52:31–34). Ration tablets which mention Jehoiachin by name have been found in Babylon and support the accuracy of the biblical statement. According to the Babylonian historian Berossus, Evil-merodach's reign was "arbitrary and licentious," and he was the victim of a murderous plot by his brother-in-law Neriglissar (Nergal-sharezer, *q.v.*), who succeeded him (Jos *Against Apion,* i.20, Loeb ed.). Nabonidus passes over Evil-merodach in silence when he mentions as his predecessors and models Nebuchadnezzar and Neriglissar.

J. R.

EVIL ONE. One of the names given to Satan. The parables of the kingdom of God in Mt 13 mention two of Satan's ways to thwart the gospel. In the parable of the sower, "the wicked one" (ASV, "evil one") snatches away the word sown in the hearts of those who do not understand the gospel (v. 19). In the parable of the tares among the wheat, Satan places his own children alongside the children of God, where they will remain until the harvest at the end of the age (vv. 36–42).

The "evil one" as a personality is undoubtedly referred to by Jesus in the Lord's Prayer ("deliver us from the evil one," Mt 6:13, ASV), and in His high priestly prayer (". . . but that thou shouldst keep them from the evil one," Jn 17:15, ASV).

See Devil; Evil; Satan.

EVIL SPIRIT. *See* Demonology.

EWE. *See* Animals, I.15.

EXACTOR. This term is from a Heb. word meaning "to drive." In Isa 60:17 ("taskmasters," RSV) the word refers to officials who had oppressed the people. The same word is used in Ex 3:7 where it is translated "taskmasters" in KJV.

EXAMPLE. The KJV translation of the Gr. words *typos, hypogrammos, hypodeigma,* and *deigma.* The English term is used in illustrating different aspects of Christian conduct. The proper life style and value systems are thus demonstrated individually and collectively in the lives of Christ (Jn 13:15; I Pet 2:21), the prophets (Jas 5:10), Paul (Phil 3:17; II Thess 3:9), and the churches and their leaders (I Thess 1:7; I Tim 4:12; Tit 2:7; I Pet 5:3).

The negative example (*deigma,* "a thing shown, a specimen," Jude 7; *hypodeigma,* "figure, copy, example," II Pet 2:6) testifies to the severity of the judgment of God upon gross sexual immorality. The examples of disobedience (Heb 4:11) and idolatry and grumbling (I Cor 10:6–11) in the wilderness journeys of the Israelites serve as warnings to Christian believers. The remaining occurrences of the word "example" are positive references to exemplary living. These demonstrate the relevance of the centrality of Christ to one's ethical motivation, and the positive effects of godly living in enabling other men to comprehend the meaning of the Christian life.

The primary example for the Christian to follow is Christ Himself. He came to fulfill the law and the prophets (Mt 5:17), and thus He is the end of the law for righteousness to everyone who believes (Rom 10:4). Only in Christ can the requirement of the law—the divine standard for morality—be fulfilled in us (Rom 8:4). He taught with authority (*q.v.*) and gave a new and deeper interpretation to the Ten Commandments, the heart of the law (Mt 5:17–48; *see* Law of Moses) and "the core of the biblical ethic" (Murray, *Principles of Conduct,* p. 7).

Jesus' new commandment to His disciples is to love one another "even as I have loved you" (Jn 13:34). We know what love is and how to demonstrate love because God first loved us in Christ (I Jn 4:19). Paul's classic description of love in I Cor 13:4–7 is very likely based on the life of Christ. Jesus had taught, "Greater love hath no man than this, that a man lay down his life for his friends" (Jn 15:13), and then performed this supreme sacrifice Himself.

Christ promised to send the same Spirit that empowered Him to enable us to do His works (Jn 14:12; 16:7) and to bear the fruit of love (Gal 5:22). Thus the Spirit of Christ is the source of Christian morality, for He enlightens the conscience, one's ability to make moral judgments.

The Lord Jesus Christ is also our pattern of humility (Phil 2:5–8), of not pleasing oneself

(Rom 15:2-3), of meekness and gentleness (II Cor 10:1), and of liberality (II Cor 8:9). We are to imitate God (Eph 5:1) and be perfect like our heavenly Father in the sphere of moral character such as love and mercy (Mt 5:44-48; Lk 6:36). Christ is the model missionary for the Church to follow in carrying out its commission (see Commission, Great), for He said, "As my Father hath sent me, even so send I you" (Jn 20:21).

Jesus expected His disciples to identify with Him in His purpose and destiny after He cleansed them by His symbolic washing of their feet (Jn 13:1-17). The event occurred during the last night He was with them before His crucifixion. The foot washing example (hypodeigma, "copy") of Jesus provided an audio-visual demonstration to draw His disciples into the heart of His life view and motivation (13:15). Jesus told Peter that without this cleansing experience "thou hast no part with me" (13:8).

Long afterward, with the insights of a lifetime of Christian experience, Peter referred to Jesus' pattern for our lives: "For even hereunto were ye called: because Christ also suffered for us, leaving us an example [hypogrammos], that ye should follow his steps" (I Pet 2:21). The Gr. word indicates that the very life of Christ is the "writing copy" for His disciples, drawing them to intimate involvement with Him in His life of suffering and crossbearing. Peter seems to have in mind Jesus' repeated instruction on discipleship that requires complete self-denial (Mt 10:38-39; 16:24-26; Lk 14:26-33; 17:33; Jn 12:24-26).

Jesus presented His own model life as the basis of the Christian ethic. To follow Christ would demand denying oneself and taking the cross as the principle of living and the goal of all life (Mt 16:24). The exemplary Christian life was emphasized by Jesus when He said, "I always do the things that are pleasing to Him," the Father (Jn 8:29), and, "I do not seek My own will, but the will of Him who sent Me" (5:30), and, "I have come down from heaven, not to do My own will, but the will of Him who sent Me" (6:38, all NASB). This is the heart of the Christian ethic – the life that demonstrates the principle of the cross in all of Christian conduct and behavior.

It must be recognized, however, that Christ did nothing simply for the sake of example. The ideal of His perfect life will only condemn the sinner. The cross has power to lead men to holiness only as it first reveals the atonement made for their sins.

James (5:10) stresses the "example" (hypodeigma) of the OT prophets, who mediated the revelation of God through their preaching and teaching. The example of their sufferings is a testimony to patience for all Christians.

Meanwhile Paul illustrates by his own life the meaning of "example" for the Christians of his time. He declared his identity with Christ in terms of the cross in writing to the Galatians:

"I have been crucified with Christ; and it is no longer I who live, but Christ lives in me" (2:20, NASB). Later he affirmed, "For to me, to live is Christ" (Phil 1:21).

Paul personalized the "example" by identifying himself with it in Phil 3:17, using the word typos, "mark of a blow, stamp, impress" (see Type). He urged the Philippians to observe those who walk according to the pattern they saw in him (3:17) and to practice these things themselves (4:9). His life-style and behavior stretched over a full generation of Christian witness and service. The Philippian Christians received his exhortation near the close of his confinement as a Roman prisoner. In one of his earliest epistles he had written to the believers in Thessalonica that he had worked to support himself "to offer ourselves as a model for you, that you might follow our example" (II Thess 3:9, NASB; cf. 3:7). Paul's conduct, therefore, demonstrated the validity of his message and the authority of the gospel in his life.

Such involvement in sacrificial living by faith in Christ enabled the two leading apostles to speak to both extremes of the generation gap of their times: Paul to Timothy, the NT representative of the youth generation, and Peter to the elders. Paul insisted that Timothy not allow any man to despise his youth; instead Timothy was commanded to be an example to the believers (I Tim 4:12). Peter, on the other hand, commanded the elders not to lord it over those allotted to their care, but to be "examples to the flock" (I Pet 5:3).

The Thessalonian Christians imitated the apostle Paul and the Lord, having received the word, the OT revelation as interpreted and fulfilled by Christ, "in much tribulation with the joy of the Holy Spirit." Consequently they became "an example to all the believers in Macedonia and in Achaia" (I Thess 1:6-7, NASB). The writer of Hebrews similarly describes the correlation of suffering and joy in the life of Christ, "who for the joy that was set before Him endured the cross" (Heb 12:2). The Thessalonians in their experience of suffering (I Thess 2:14; 3:3-4; II Thess 1:4-7) and joy seemed to fulfill Jesus' prayer for oneness with Christ in the Father and in the witness to God's love (Jn 17:21, 23).

Christian witness by example to other believers inevitably precedes the witness to non-believers on a broad scale. This was the case at Thessalonica (I Thess 1:7-8). Their witness to Christ was directly related to their behavior change. Their new conduct was clearly evident to the general population of Greece in that they had "turned to God from idols to serve the living and true God" (1:9).

The basis of such behavior change is established in the unique discipleship demonstrated by the same Thessalonian believers, who Paul said "became imitators of us and of the Lord" (I Thess 1:6, NASB). The key word to their discipleship is "imitators" (mimētai). Christian conduct, resulting in the change in behavior effected by conversion to faith in the living God, is based on imitating the Lord and His apostle Paul (cf. also I Cor 4:16; 11:1). The faith and patience of other believers and Christian leaders should also be imitated (Heb 6:12; 13:7).

In other words, Christian ethics has its foundations in the same principle of living as that of the Lord Jesus Christ. The commandments of God through His prophets and apostles and His Son, combined with the perfect example of Christ, provide the believer an absolute ethic rather than the ethical relativism of John A. T. Robinson's *Honest to God* (1963) and Joseph Fletcher's *Situation Ethics: The New Morality* (1966). The one all-inclusive principle of life is not intuitive love that relates to the need of another at the unique moment of personal encounter, but "whatever you do, do all to the glory of God" (I Cor 10:31), and to do it all in the name of the Lord Jesus (Col 3:17). The content of the Christian ethic is the will of God that must be done in love, "faith working through love" (Gal 5:6).

All of Christ's behavior was centered in His purpose to serve and to give His life a ransom (Mt 20:28). This was His pattern for His followers (20:25–27). Paul accepted it. So did the Thessalonian Christians. They had seen in Paul the example ("stamp") of Christ which gave meaning and understanding to them. They took this example for their own lives, including the affliction (*thlipsis*, "pressure, tribulation"). In such a context of Christian ethics, in the midst of suffering, imitating the life of Jesus and the conduct of Paul, those believers collectively and spontaneously shared a dynamically meaningful witness to Christ throughout Macedonia and Achaia.

The Christian example found first in Jesus and Paul issues in the kind of godly conduct that witnesses effectively through the combined body of the Church in any one area, strengthens the witness of Christian youth, and enables the behavior of the elders (pastors) to inspire a following in their flocks. The successful witness to Christ is centered on example.

See Conversation; Disciple; Grace; Justice; Law; Liberty; Love; Obedience.

Bibliography. Harvey Cox, ed., *The Situation Ethics Debate,* Philadelphia: Westminster, 1968. W. D. Davies, "Ethics in the New Testament," IDB, II, 167–176. J. Hempel, "Ethics in the OT," IDB, II, 153–161. John Murray, *Principles of Conduct,* Grand Rapids: Eerdmans, 1957. Sherwood E. Wirt, *The Social Conscience of the Evangelical,* New York: Harper & Row, 1968.

H. W. N.

EXCHANGER. *See* Occupations: Banker; Money Changer.

EXCOMMUNICATION. This is the judicial exclusion of unrepentant sinners from the rights and privileges of the communion of saints car-

ried out by a local congregation. After admonition by one has failed, then by two or three, then by the congregation, the offender according to Mt 18:16–17 is to be as a "heathen man and a publican," or according to I Cor 5:13 is to be "put away from among yourselves," or according to I Tim 1:20 "delivered unto Satan." The ultimate purpose is to bring the offender to a realization of the seriousness of his offense and to lead him to repentance. It also removes offense from the church. *See also* Cutting Off.

Excommunication was used already in the time of the apostles. The primitive church continued the practice. The question of restoring the lapsed raised serious problems. Various councils dealt with the question about who was to be excommunicated, among them the Council of Elvira (*c.* A.D. 305), the Council of Cirta in Numidia (March, 305), and the Council of Ancyra (*c.* 314–319).

During the Middle Ages the "greater" and the "lesser" excommunication were in use; the distinction was abrogated in 1884. The Roman church regards excommunication as the prerogative of the pope, bishops, a few other dignitaries, and councils. In some cases a definite sentence of excommunication must be pronounced (*ferendae sententiae*); in about 50 others it is automatic (*latae sententiae*). Kings and princes were excommunicated, even for political reasons. The bull *Clerices laicos* (1296) declared that those levying taxes on the church without the consent of the pope or paying such taxes "*ipso facto* incur excommunication."

In the Reformation era the Anabaptists and related groups placed great emphasis on excommunication or the ban, declaring that a congregation in which public expulsion or orderly process of excommunication does not take place is not a true Christian congregation. A controversy arose among them regarding the "shunning" of banned persons. Calvin and his followers held that the exercise of church discipline was one of the marks of the church. He urged moderation of discipline and emphasized the corrective aspect of excommunication (*Institutes,* IV, 12, 10.11). The Westminster Confession (Chap. XXX), the Thirty-nine Articles (Article XXXIII), and the Apology of the Augsburg Confession (Article XI) affirm the obligation of the churches to employ excommunication. In established or state churches it is generally not used; even in voluntary churches in recent years it has largely fallen into disuse.

C. S. M.

EXECUTION. *See* Crime and Punishment.

EXECUTIONER. In Israel no office of executioner was necessary, for executions were in general performed publicly by the people (cf. Deut 17:5; 22:21, 24; Josh 7:25). The term "executioner" appears rarely in the English versions of the Bible. In the KJV it occurs only in Mk 6:27, where the Gr. *spekoulator* (lit., "spy, scout," but also "courier" and "executioner") is used of the soldier who beheaded John the Baptist. In the RSV "executioner" is found only in Ezk 9:1, where men were commissioned to slay people in Jerusalem. Military leaders and particularly the bodyguard of rulers often served as executioners; Benaiah, for example, fulfilled this function for Solomon (see I Kgs 2:25, 46).

EXERCISE, BODILY. Paul frequently referred to the athletic contests of his day to illustrate spiritual truth (see I Cor 9:24–27; I Tim 6:12; II Tim 2:5; 4:7). He was not opposed to bodily exercise (Gr. *gymnasia,* I Tim 4:8), but to the ascetic mortification of the body as practiced by the Essenes and other fanatical groups of his day.

EXHORTATION. Exhortation refers to language which is intended to incite and encourage. Many ideas are associated with the Gr. word *paraklēsis* in the NT. It is one of the gifts of the Spirit (Rom 12:8), but seems to be one aspect or purpose of prophesying (I Cor 14:3). It is used as hortatory instruction and consolation (Lk 3:18; Acts 11:23; 13:15; I Tim 4:13; Heb 12:5; 13:22); as entreaty meaning earnest supplication (II Cor 8:4); as consolation or solace (Lk 2:25); as comfort and consolation (Acts 15:31; Rom 15:4–5; II Cor 1:3, 5–7); as inspiring suitable motives (Rom 12:8; I Tim 6:2; Heb 3:13); as comfort in the sense of a cheering and supporting influence (Acts 9:31); and comfort as giving joy, gladness and rejoicing (II Cor 7:13). *See* Comfort; Prophesy.

EXILE. *See* Captivity.

EXISTENTIALISM

What is Existentialism?

It is a philosophy which finds its starting point in man with his hopes and fears, his surging ambitions and his devastating anxiety, guilt and pessimism.

A full-fledged philosophy covers three areas: (1) origin – the origin of the world, the universe, and man; (2) reality – the nature of reality and ability to understand and know it; (3) destiny – a view of the goal or destiny of the universe and man.

Some philosophical systems lack one or more of these. Materialism and pragmatism give no explanation of origin or of destiny, confining themselves to the phenomenon of existence. Existentialism forms a distinct system of philosophy because it is characterized by a starting point in man, not just in the universe as in materialism. It starts, however, not just with man as a phenomenon – for the psychology of behaviorism and the philosophy of pragmatism do this – but with either his inborn hopes and fears, or his inner problems with knowledge.

Negatively defined, existentialism is the opposite of essentialism. The essentialist begins with Being, The Absolute, The All or God; the existentialist begins with man and his inner struggles. Positively defined, existentialism is that explanation of reality and the origin and destiny of man and the universe which chooses to make as the starting point man and his problems regarding the attainment of knowledge, along with his hopes and fears, his surging ambitions, and his anxieties and guilt.

Kinds of Existentialists

Because they all start with man, there can be theistic, atheistic and agnostic existentialists.

Theistic existentialists. These believe in a God but start with man, his estrangement, guilt and anxiety, on the one hand, and his problems in regard to the knowledge of eternal truth and God, on the other. They can be subdivided into: (*a*) Protestant theistic existentialists – examples of whom are Karl Barth and Emil Brunner; (*b*) Roman Catholic theistic existentialists – Jacques Maritain and Gabriel Marcel; and (*c*) pantheistic existentialists – Paul Tillich and John A. T. Robinson.

Atheistic existentialists. Jean-Paul Sartre is an example. Nietzsche may possibly also be classed with Sartre, for he starts with man and concludes, "God is dead."

Agnostic existentialists. Martin Heidegger is an example. His position has been essentially one of indecision as to the existence of anything beyond man and the universe.

The History of Existentialism

Existentialism as a real philosophy began with Sören Kierkegaard (1813–1855). Existential elements appeared in many earlier philosophers but they were combined with other philosophic tendencies. Neither man nor man's problem with knowledge was made the full starting point.

Immanuel Kant (1724–1804) had raised the problem of knowledge before the time of Kierkegaard, and it formed a large part of the predicament in which the first full existentialist found himself. Kant argued that through his physical senses man receives a stream of impressions which, as they enter the mind, are stamped upon by the outer form of the mind, namely, space or place, and by the inner form, time. But time and space, Kant reasoned, cannot belong to the really real, the noumenon, because God is infinite and time and space are only finite. Man, then, who knows all that he does by learning in finite categories of time and space, does not know anything as God knows it, nor can he know God or His eternal truths. These are all timeless and spaceless.

Even by pure thought, that is, by "pure reason," man cannot know things as they are in God and as God knows them, because all of man's thoughts include time – it is the inner form of the mind. The net result of Kant's reasoning is that God Himself cannot communicate directly with man because man has no containers, no timeless-spaceless categories in which to receive timeless-spaceless eternal or really real truth.

Kierkegaard was faced with Kant's arguments about knowledge, on the one hand, and man's problems with sin, on the other. His guilt complex which led him to break his engagement with his sweetheart Regina, left him full of anxiety, despair and pessimism. Trying to express his agony of soul, he spoke of "sickness unto death." Attacks on the Bible and on the historicity of Jesus Christ shook his faith in the Bible.

Kierkegaard solved his problems over the paradoxes and absurdities which arose for him in the Bible, and his own guilt complex and need of redemption, by a synthesis of Kant's view of the problem of knowledge of God and his own existential hopes and fears. He claimed that God cannot speak directly to man because man has no thought forms in which to receive eternal, timeless-spaceless truth. Only indirect communication is possible. Even as Kierkegaard was trying to speak indirectly to his estranged fiancée in his books, and tell her why he had to break his engagement because of his own unconfessed sin of fornication, so God was speaking indirectly to us. According to Kierkegaard, man forces the eternal truth he receives from God into time-space categories. This is to be seen in the myths found in the Bible. Satan, the Fall, etc., are not historical figures and events but myths which contain some eternal truth. Some later existentialists, such as Barth, have preferred to call them sagas, saying myths are stories of things that never happened, while sagas tell of what happens over and over and is truth.

In his lifetime, no theologian or philosopher took Kierkegaard really seriously. Man was living in an age of reason and unbounded hope, and Sören's despair and pessimism found no place in the optimism of the age. However, near the end of World War I, as Karl Barth listened to the guns booming just beyond the border of peaceful Switzerland and wrestled with the bankruptcy of the social gospel and liberalism, they did find a sympathetic listener.

Barth wrote his *Romans* using all Kierkegaard's terms and concepts of indirect communication, contemporaneity, disjunction, myth, saga, etc. Soon he was a professor at Basel and had a group of theologians around him, which included Thorneyson and Brunner. However, Barth received such a reaction to his existential theology, as presented in his *Doctrine of the Word of God* in 1927, that he rewrote the whole book and published it as 1:1 of his *Church Dogmatics*. The Kierkegaardian terms were eliminated and he claimed that all the existentialism had been removed along with them; but the Kierkegaardian views still remained thoroughly ingrained in this new presentation of the doctrine of revelation.

God was described as *totaliter aliter*, totally other, and only indirect communication was possible. He lives in a timeless-spaceless "eternal now," but man can enjoy contemporaneity and the "eternal now" in the subjective experience of revelation. Revelation and salvation become synonymous; they are the same thing. Revelation occurs in the form of myth and/or saga, in spite of and through contradictions, etc. Christ as the Word becomes the real revelation, as man reads or hears the Bible.

Emil Brunner stoutly defended the possibility of general revelation. But he did not make the same effort to eliminate Kierkegaardian terms and hide Kierkegaardian concepts.

In its first theological form existentialism remained thoroughly theistic. It was called Crisis Theology (stressing the idea of God's judgment on man and sin) and neoorthodoxy (claiming that it was a return to a new form of orthodoxy in contrast to the old biblicism and fundamentalism).

It remained for a liberal, Paul Tillich, to make a synthesis between liberalism and neoorthodoxy. Tillich, like his liberal forefather in theology Schleiermacher and his forerunner in philosophy Hegel, was actually a pantheist.

Others who were either agnostics (Martin Heidegger) or atheists (Sartre) and who therefore admitted no revelation in the first place, had no real epistemological problems over it. They picked up the existential predicament of hope and fear, and of freedom and destiny, and developed existential philosophies of their own.

The Characteristics of Existentialism

The predicament of man. Man finds himself in a threefold predicament:

1. Estrangement. He is estranged from the world, his neighbor and himself. The theists add that he is estranged from God.

2. Anxiety. Kierkegaard said man must progress from anxiety to despair before he can make the leap of faith to salvation. Sartre has the hero of *The Flies* cry, "Human life begins on the far side of despair."

3. Detachment and extreme individualization. There is a singular lack of interest in the social and political. Karl Barth urged opposition to Hitler and the Nazis because they denied God, but he did not urge any stand against the communists, because this would mean entering the political and social realms. Extreme individual detachment is manifest in many of the atheistic and agnostic existentialists. Paul Tillich, because of his pantheism, was an exception and stressed involvement in his tensional dialectic between individualization-participation.

The possibilities of man. These are four in number.

1. Freedom. This characteristic of Renaissance humanism is particularly stressed by the atheistic and agnostic existentialists. In the theistic existentialists, and the neoorthodox in particular, freedom fades away, excluded by

God's sovereign grace. On the other hand, since Kierkegaard left the initiative of the leap to man, he allowed him freedom.

2. Autonomy. Man makes his own laws and sets up his own ethical system. The Ten Commandments are not propositional truth and revelation for Barth, but the place we receive our commission or our orders.

3. Decision. Greater importance is placed on making decisions than on the nature of the decisions made. Kierkegaard spoke of the leap of faith, the decision to believe what is contradiction, paradox, the absurd. A decision is important to the degree it is made without or contrary to evidence. Decision is good, according to Tillich, if made with the motive of love, even if it is a wrong one.

4. Intuitive knowledge. Man finds knowledge within himself. Plato had spoken of knowledge as recollection, but the existentialist sees it as something intuitive. Tillich, as a pantheist, sees it welling up from the depth of reason present in man, to appear in art and culture. The neoorthodox, since they deny propositional revelation and yet claim to experience revelation, are manifestly replacing biblical revelation with some form of self-knowledge.

The problems of man. Man's greatest problems are time and truth, and the effect of these on his existence.

1. Two kinds of time. Timeless-time or the "eternal now" is vertical and contemporaneous, while earthly time is linear and continuous.

2. Two kinds of truth. According to theistic existentialists truth partakes of the same dualism as time: eternal truth is timeless and spaceless; earthly truth is cumbered with the categories of finitude, time and space. Earthly truth is useful and of temporary importance but of no eternal significance. Heavenly truth is of eternal significance and all-important, but impossible to express in human terms.

3. Two existences. Man can simply continue to live like the mass of mankind in unauthentic existence, or he can transcend himself and enjoy authentic existence. Barth added still another existence as he spoke of every man existing in Christ as "the rejected" and "the elected one." This is man's "proper" existence.

Personal consequences.

1. Subjectivism. Man's knowledge of anything beyond what he can know through the senses depends entirely on what wells up within himself. There is no direct revelation from God in words and statements for the theistic existentialist (Barth, Brunner, etc.). Even the commands and teachings of Christ were later surrendered by Him and do not hold for us, according to Tillich.

2. Pessimism. Existentialism is essentially a philosophy of pessimism, originating in the frustration and disillusionment caused by the First World War. The atheist has no hope for the future. The theistic existentialist, with his tendency to extreme detachment and individualism, has no answer for man's social or political needs. The future offered after death is contentless since impossible of meaningful description.

The destiny of man.

1. Revelation. Only the theistic existentialist can offer any theory of a divine heavenly revelation of truth. His theory of indirect communication, coupled with the identification of revelation and salvation, expresses his view of man's goal on earth.

2. Reconciliation. This too is possible only for theistic existentialism. It is accomplished by a realistic theory of man's identification with what Christ has done and leads therefore to the restoration of all things, and universal salvation (Barth).

3. Self-transcendence. This is the term used by atheistic and agnostic existentialists, and by Tillich as a pantheist. Man can transcend himself and the mass to become free and enjoy authentic existence. It is the counterpart of salvation for the theistic existentialists.

4. Either oblivion or static history. There is no future since death is the end of all for the atheistic existentialist. Man merges back into Being or the Power of Being in which subject-object relationships are merged and identified in Tillich's pantheism.

The neoorthodox can offer little more than oblivion with their concept of an eternal contemporaneous now. Man's future in a timeless-spaceless eternity is indescribable beyond saying that past, present and future will all be one grand present, just as the events of history are all present in an endless set of volumes of history.

See God; Liberalism; Neoorthodoxy; Theology; Time.

Bibliography. H. J. Blackham, *Six Existentialist Thinkers,* New York: Harper, Torchbooks, 1959. Marjorie Grene, *Introduction to Existentialism,* Chicago: Univ. of Chicago Press, Phoenix Books, 1960. F. H. Heinemann, *Existentialism and the Modern Predicament,* New York: Harper, Torchbooks, 1958. Milton D. Hunnex, *Existentialism and Christian Belief,* Chicago: Moody, Christian Forum Books, 1969. Carl Michalson, *Christianity and the Existentialists,* New York: Scribners, 1956. J. C. Mihalich, *Existentialism and Thomism,* New York: Philosophical Library, 1960. David E. Roberts, *Existentialism and Religious Belief,* New York: Oxford Univ. Press, Galaxy Books, 1959. J. M. Spier, *Christianity and Existentialism,* Philadelphia: Presbyterian and Reformed Pub. Co., 1953.

R. A. K.

EXODUS, BOOK OF

The Name

The second book of the Torah (the law) was named *shᵉmôth* by the Jews. They customarily entitled the books of their sacred Scriptures by one or more of the opening words, which for this book are *wᵉʾēlleh shᵉmôth*, "and these are the names. . . ." The English name is derived from its Latin name *Exodus*, in turn from the Gr. *exodos* of the LXX, meaning the "going out" or "departure" (occurring in the LXX at Ex 19:1; cf. Ps 104 [105]:38; 113 [114]:1; Heb. 11:22).

Theme and Contents

This is the great OT book setting forth redemption. Its purpose is to describe officially how Israel became the covenant nation of the Lord. While Heb. words translated "redeem" occur only in 6:6 and 15:13 (*gāʾal*) and in 13:13-15 and 34:20 (*pādâ*), the concept of liberation from death, enslavement, and idolatry is found throughout. Repeatedly God declares Himself to be Yahweh, His name as the sovereign Deity making covenant with Israel (*see* God, Names of; Lord). He delivers them and brings them out of the land of Egypt; He takes them to Himself to be His people and to be their God; and He will bring them into the land promised to Abraham, Isaac, and Jacob (e.g., 6:6-8).

The continuity of God's redemptive plan is carefully, if briefly, shown in the introductory chapter. Connected as it is with Genesis by the Heb. conjunction "and," it bridges the gap from the time of Joseph in the patriarchal period to the birth of Moses during enslavement in Egypt. The next few chapters describe the birth, training, and call of this man whom God chose to be the human deliverer and covenant mediator for His people. In a series of confrontations Moses was unable to persuade the pharaoh to let the Israelite slaves leave Egypt. Even nine unusually severe plagues did not change his attitude but only hardened him further. The Lord's warning of a tenth plague killing the firstborn male in every house and flock in Egypt set the stage for the Passover ceremony to protect the Israelite homes, and for the consequent gathering of His people and their march to the Sinai border. Trapped at the Red Sea, they experienced God's mighty deliverance through the parted waters and sang a hymn of triumph in honor of Yahweh (14:1-15:21).

Moses led the nation through the desert until they camped in front of Mount Sinai (19:1-2). Along the way they saw the Lord work supernaturally several times to supply their need of water, food, and victory in battle. When the people agreed to keep the stipulations of the covenant which God as their theocratic ruler was about to make with them (19:8), they purified themselves and assembled at the foot of the mountain on the third day to participate in the covenant ceremony (19:9-19). Moses went up the mountain (19:20) to receive orally God's statement of His covenant (vv. 20-23). Then Moses returned (19:25) and repeated to the people the moral, social, and religious obligations of the covenant, which they unanimously accepted (24:3). He then wrote

down all the words of the Lord and called it "the book of the covenant" (24:4a, 7), later receiving the moral code (the Ten Commandments) inscribed on two stone tablets by God Himself (24:12; 31:18). In the ceremony of covenant ratification the next day Yahweh's presence was represented by an altar and the 12 tribes by 12 pillars (24:4b-8). Then Moses as covenant mediator, the chief priests, and 70 elders representing the people ascended, saw the pavement of God's throne, and partook of the covenant meal (24:9-11).

Moses again climbed to the summit, this time for 40 days during which God revealed to him the plans for the tabernacle (*q.v.*), its furnishings and the priestly ministry in it, and the requirement to observe the sabbath as the sign of the covenant (chaps. 25-31). Meanwhile the people became impatient and demanded Aaron to make them an image of God (*see* Idolatry), thus breaking their covenant vow. Descending the mountain, Moses smashed the tablets of the law to symbolize this breach and had about 3,000 of the worst offenders executed (32:15-29). After Moses returned to the peak for another 40 days and interceded for the rest of the nation, God revealed Himself to His servant and promised to go Himself in the lead to Canaan (33:14) and drive out the heathen peoples (34:11). Fellowship was restored (34:31-33), and the people gladly responded with offerings to construct the tabernacle (35-39). When it was erected on the first day of the year, God sent His Shekinah glory to fill His earthly place of dwelling among His redeemed covenant people (40:34).

Outline

Preface: Link with Genesis, 1:1-7
I. God's Redemption of Enslaved Israel by Blood and Power from Egypt, 1:8-18:27
  A. Background of the Egyptian bondage, 1:8-22
  B. Preparation of the deliverer, 2:1-4:31
  C. Contest with the oppressor, 5:1-11:10
  D. Deliverance from Egypt, 12:1-15:21
    1. Redemption by sacrificial blood, 12:1-13:16
    2. Salvation by miraculous power, 13:17-14:31
    3. Song of triumph, 15:1-21
  E. Training in the wilderness, 15:22-18:27
    1. Testing the redeemed, 15:22-17:16
    2. Governing the redeemed, 18:1-27

II. God's Relationship with Redeemed Israel by Covenant at Mount Sinai, 19:1-40:38
  A. The covenant established with Israel, 19:1-24:18
    1. Preparations for receiving the covenant, 19:1-25

2. Statement of the covenant, 20:1 – 23:19
3. Sanctions of the covenant, 23: 20–33
4. Ratification of the covenant, 24: 1-'18

B. The worship of the covenant people, 25:1 – 40:38
   1. Divine plan for tabernacle and priesthood, 25:1 – 31:18
   2. Fellowship broken and restored, 32:1 – 34:35
   3. Offerings for the tabernacle, 35:1 – 36:7
   4. Its construction and erection, 36:8 – 40:38

Authorship and Date of Writing

The book of Exodus, as part of the Pentateuch, has been attributed by Jews to the hand of Moses ever since the time of Joshua (Josh 8:31-35; cf. "an altar of unhewn stones" with Ex 20:25). The Lord Jesus Christ quoted from the book of Exodus (3:6) and specifically called it "the book of Moses" (Mk 12:26; cf. Lk 20:37).

Internal evidences suggest that "the author must have been originally a resident of Egypt (not of Palestine), a contemporary eyewitness of the Exodus and wilderness wandering, and possessed of a very high degree of education, learning, and literary skill. No one else conforms to these qualifications as closely as Moses the son of Amram" (G. L. Archer, SOTI, p. 101).

The author of the Joseph narrative (Gen 37-50) and Exodus was well-acquainted with Egyptian names, titles, words, and customs. He correctly referred to the crop sequence for Lower Egypt (Ex 9:31-32). He spoke only of the shittim or acacia, the one known desert hardwood tree in the Sinai peninsula, as the source of lumber for the tabernacle (Ex 25:5, etc.); the acacia is not indigenous to Palestine except along the S shore of the Dead Sea. The "badger" skins used as the outer covering for the tabernacle (Ex 25:5; 26:14; etc.) were actually obtained from the dugong (Heb. *taḥash*), a sea mammal known in the Near East only in the waters of the Red Sea. He knew about the types of reeds in the marshes of the Nile delta (2:3) and that the desert sand begins abruptly at the edge of the cultivated fields (2:12). He seems to have been an eyewitness of the events and places mentioned in connection with the wilderness journey. For example, he listed for no apparent reason the exact number of springs (12) and of palm trees (70) at Elim (15:27). Moses was such an educated Israelite who had lived in Egypt (Acts 7:22) and who was thoroughly familiar with parts of the Sinai peninsula as well (see SOTI, pp. 101-109 for more details).

Furthermore, the book of Exodus states that Moses himself wrote down certain happenings.

and words soon after their occurrence. The "book" in which he recorded the battle with Amalek (17:14) was probably a leather scroll. It would be similar in function to the "annals" of Egypt and other ancient Near Eastern nations in which all the important events were recorded (cf. the daily records of the commanders of Thutmose III kept on "a roll of leather" in the temple of Amon, ANET, p. 237*a*). Moses personally transcribed all the words of the Lord contained in the Decalogue and the so-called covenant code (24:4). Later he was told by the Lord to write His additional directives when He renewed the covenant after the golden calf episode (34:27).

It is clearly stated that Moses put down in writing the complete words of the law when it

Thutmose III, Pharaoh of the Oppression according to the early date. LL

was renewed to Israel before his death, and that he delivered the record to the priests to place it beside the ark of the covenant (Deut 31:9, 24–26). He also wrote down the poem or song found in Deut 32 (Deut 31:19, 22). Thus there should be no question that Moses could write, that it was his habit to keep official records according to contemporary custom, and that he had his own source material which he could have used in writing the book of Exodus in its present form.

The date of writing, then, would be the date of Moses' life and the time of the Exodus (*see* Exodus, The: Date). Assuming he was the human author, he could have written the book during the 38 years of wandering in the desert around Kadesh-barnea after leaving Mount Sinai. Important confirmation of an early date for the book comes from a study of the ancient covenant or treaty forms used by sovereigns with their vassal nations in the middle of the 2nd mil. B.C. in the Near East. The pattern or format of God's covenant with Israel corresponds strikingly, e.g., with the suzerainty treaties of the Hittite emperors, suggesting that God employed the prevailing skeletal structure of covenant familiar to Moses from his education in the Egyptian court (*see* Covenant; G. L. Archer, "Old Testament History and Recent Archaeology from Moses to David," BS, CXXVII [1970], 103–106).

Another feature peculiarly reminiscent of the Egyptian New Kingdom (18th–19th Dynasties, 1570–1200 B.C.) is the structure of the tabernacle. Its linen curtains with figures of cherubim woven into the blue, purple, and scarlet tapestry work (Ex 26:1–6) were draped over a framework made of gilded shittim "boards" (KJV) or "frames" (RSV, 26:15–30). The closest known parallels in construction to this portable tent-sanctuary are the four rectangular gilded shrines, one within the other, over the sarcophagus of Pharaoh Tutankhamen (c. 1360–1352). These represented temples important in the life of the king. They were constructed of demountable wooden panels carefully joined together by means of mortice and tenon joints and sliding bolts, just as in the tabernacle, and assembled to fit neatly inside the royal burial chamber. A linen canopy or veil sprinkled with daisies of gilded bronze was over the second shrine (C. Desroches-Noblecourt, *Tutankhamen*, trans. by Claude, Garden City: Doubleday, 1965, pp. 49–54, 190–194). Since craftsmen trained or employed in Egypt, as Bezaleel may have been, could have known of this type of structure, it was not necessary at that period to spell out every detail in what to modern artisans is an enigmatic description (*see* Tabernacle; R. K. Harrison, IOT, pp. 403 ff.).

The members of the various schools of higher criticism have insisted that Exodus and the other books of the Pentateuch are composed of several independent documents and/or traditions compiled and edited many centuries after the time of Moses. The followers of the Graf-Wellhausen school divide Exodus into three main literary strata, the so-called J, E, and P sources. The post-Exilic Jerusalem priesthood supposedly interspersed background material and supplemented the older Jahwistic and Elohistic narratives with the account of the community's worship (Ex 25–31, 35–40). Wellhausen and other scholars held that the wilderness tabernacle was merely a late priestly idealization of the simple tent of meeting blended with the design and adornments of Solomon's temple. See a chart of the complicated division of the other chapters, verse by verse, into their documentary sources, reproduced in G. E. Wright, "Exodus, Book of," IDB, II, 193 f. Yet Wright recognizes that there are so many unknown factors in the transition of material that it is now considered difficult to be precise about such editorial work (*ibid*, p. 194).

Other scholars have propounded that there are additional documents that can be detected, a layman's source (Otto Eissfeldt) and a Kenite source giving Moses' history (Julius Morgenstern). Johannes Pedersen claims Ex 1–15 is the annual reliving of historical events, taking the form of a liturgical celebration of God's great victory, by the worshipers at the Passover festivals. Gerhard von Rad interprets the Sinai tradition (Ex 19–24) as a cultic legend. Martin Noth believes the book of Exodus is a combination of traditions: an oral Passover tradition of the deliverance from the plague and the miraculous rescue at the sea, with the story of Moses' birth, youth and call inserted into it; the recitation at certain central cultic festivals in Israel in which the making of the covenant was regularly re-enacted; narratives of the wanderings; and certain laws and creedal summaries inserted into the main Sinai narrative (*Exodus*, pp. 9–18). It is clear, therefore, that there is no consensus regarding authorship among the scholars who deny that Moses wrote the Pentateuch. *See* Canon of Scriptures, The OT; Genesis; Moses; Pentateuch.

The Hebrew Text

The Masoretic Text of Exodus is remarkably free from transcriptional errors (W. J. Martin, "Exodus, Book of," NBD, p. 405). A few affect the translation slightly. In 11:1 two Heb. words, k^eshall^{e}ḥô kālâ, "his sending away is final," may have been a scribe's marginal note that was later incorporated into the text (see JerusB and marg. note). In 23:3 an original *g* of the word gādôl, "a great man," may have been misread as *w*, forming w^{e}dāl, "and a poor man"; Lev 19:15 tends to corroborate this correction in that it has the same verbal construction, lō' tehdar, with gādôl. In Ex 34:19 apparently the Heb. definite article *h* became *t* in the uncertain form tizzākār; four ancient versions recognized this error and rendered the word "the male" (see RSV, NJV).

Many students of Exodus and Numbers have

questioned the magnitude of the numbers of the Israelites involved in the journeys. While it is probable that the transmission of numbers may have been more exposed to error than other words in the text, we cannot conclude that large figures are automatically suspect. There are problems in logistics of maintaining so many people and in tactics of getting a huge number of people to march quickly past a given point (e.g., the Red Sea) and through certain narrow valleys in the Sinai peninsula. Yet it is wiser to hold such difficulties in abeyance rather than to declare the text is corrupt. *See* Number; Numbers, Book of.

Bibliography. Gleason L. Archer, Jr., SOTI, pp. 209–226. Umberto Cassuto, *A Commentary on the Book of Exodus,* trans. by Israel Abrahams, Jerusalem: Magnes Press, 1967. G. A. Chadwick, "Exodus," ExpB. Samuel R. Driver, *Exodus (Cambridge Bible),* Cambridge: Univ. Press, 1911. Jack Finegan, *Let My People Go,* New York: Harper & Row, 1963. R. K. Harrison, IOT, pp. 566–588. Philip C. Johnson, "Exodus," WBC. H. R. Jones, "Exodus," NBC (rev. ed.). C. F. Keil and Franz Delitzsch, *Biblical Commentary on the OT, The Pentateuch,* Vols. I and II, Grand Rapids: Eerdmans (reprint), 1951. John Peter Lange, *Exodus,* trans. by Charles M. Mead, New York: Scribner, Armstrong, 1876. James Murphy, *Commentary on Exodus,* Edinburgh: T. & T. Clark, 1866. B. Davie Napier, *Exodus, The Layman's Bible Commentary,* Vol. 3, Richmond: John Knox Press, 1963. Martin Noth, *Exodus,* trans. by J. S. Bowden, London: SCM Press, 1962. J. Coert Rylaarsdam, "The Book of Exodus," IB, I, 831–1099.

J. R.

EXODUS, THE. The crucial event in Israel's history is the Exodus. It was the mighty deliverance performed by the Lord in bringing the entire people of Israel out from Egyptian slavery and into the Promised Land. This departure from Egypt and consequent migration toward Canaan under Moses' leadership was marked by many miracles. It resulted in the establishment of the Israelites as a nation in covenant agreement with God as their theocratic ruler. In its restricted sense the term covers the year of the ten plagues, the Passover, and the crossing of the Red Sea (Ex 7–15).

Historicity

No known Egyptian records refer to the Israelites in Egypt or to their departure. This complete lack of contemporary evidence has been used by some critics to argue against the Exodus as an historical event. But God's deliverance of Israel from bondage is referred to so often in the later books of the OT (see the numerous references to Egypt in a Bible concordance) that scholars now generally admit that a migration of some Israelites from Egypt

did take place. Scholarly opinion varies widely, however, as to the date and whether the whole nation was involved in the Exodus or only some of the tribes of Israel.

Large movements of peoples from one land to another were not uncommon in antiquity. God reminds His people of His sovereign actions in the past by asking, "Did not I, who brought Israel out of the land of Egypt, bring the Philistines from Caphtor, and the Aramaeans from Kir?" (Amos 9:7, JerusB). In the late 15th cen. B.C. Hurrians of some 14 districts apparently left their homes within the Hittite kingdom and fled to the land of Isuwa in Hurrian country. They were later forced to return, however, by the powerful Hittite king Suppiluliumas, and a treaty was signed with the Hurrian king Mattiwaza (K. A. Kitchen, "Exodus," NBD, p. 402; see ANET, pp. 205 f. for part of the treaty).

Thus the account of the Exodus is unique in all of ancient literature in describing an entire people who were successfully delivered from an oppressive regime by the supernatural acts of their Deity.

The Biblical Account

Jacob and his sons had gone down to Egypt at the direction of God (Gen 46:1–7) to seek relief from the widespread famine in the Near East. Joseph, who had been installed as vizier (41:41–43), had them placed in the pasture-land of Goshen near Egypt's E border (46:31–34). The Israelites came to Egypt some 400 years before the Exodus (Ex 12:40). If the Exodus occurred *c.* 1445 B.C. (*see* section under "The Date"), then Jacob entered Egypt *c.* 1875 B.C. (or 1845 B.C., if the reading "in Canaan and in Egypt" of SP and LXX is adopted) during the illustrious 12th Dynasty, a time of strength and peace and unity throughout the whole country (Gen 41:43–48).

Sometime after Joseph's death *c.* 1800 (or 1770) B.C. a new king arose over Egypt, who refused to recognize the value of Joseph's ministry (Ex 1:8). Since the Israelites were more numerous than the new king and his own people (1:9), it is very likely that Ex 1:8–12 refers to the time of the Semitic Hyksos kings in Lower Egypt (*c.* 1730–1570 B.C.), not to later Egyptian kings. Antipathy between the Hyksos and the enslaved Israelites would explain why the latter did not choose to leave Egypt, or were not expelled, along with the foreign rulers.

The powerful 18th Dynasty pharaohs continued the harsh oppression for several more generations. In spite of this the Heb. slaves kept multiplying (Ex 1:7, 12, 20). At the time of Moses' birth measures were being applied to hinder this increase by throwing the newborn sons into the Nile. The infant Moses, however, was rescued by an Egyptian princess who adopted him. Thus he was educated in royal court circles (Acts 7:22), where he could learn about the contemporary peoples and their cultures.

The Israelites needed to be redeemed not only from economic servitude but also from spiritual bondage. They had turned in large measure to heathen deities during their four centuries of residence in Egypt (Lev 17:7; Josh 24:14; Ezk 20:5-9; 23:3, 19, 27). Thus at Sinai specific commandments were given to guard against their worshiping other gods (Ex 20:5-9; 23:13). Yet the urge for an idol of Egyptian style quickly produced the golden calf (Ex 32; Acts 7:39 ff.).

God heard the cry of His oppressed people and called Moses from his self-appointed exile. Having killed an Egyptian taskmaster, he had fled from the pharaoh and remained in the Sinai desert until after that ruler had died (Ex 2:23). Soon after Moses returned, God began to unleash the plagues on Egypt to force the new pharaoh to let His people go. These disasters to the life and economy of Egypt were also judgments on the gods of Egypt (Ex 12:12; *see* Gods, False). Although the plagues were supernatural in the exact timing and severity, they consisted in phenomena that were also natural to Egypt. The account is replete with authentic local coloring. Wherever the capital of Egypt was at the time, the pharaoh obviously was staying near the land of Goshen (Ex 5:6, 15-20). He must have been living in a secondary residence such as a temple guest house in a city (9:33) by the Nile (7:20-23; 8:3, 24), if not in the main royal palace.

The Lord gave Moses and Aaron very detailed instructions regarding the selection and killing of the yearling male lamb and the application of its blood on the doorway. This sacrifice was exceptionally important both for Israel's immediate survival and for redemptive typology (Ex 12:1-27, 43-49; 13:1-16). It was to be a passover or protective offering to the Lord (12:11, NJV), an offering to insure their protection when the Lord would go through the land of Egypt and strike dead the firstborn in every house.

The Israelites must have marched several days and nights after eating the lambs before reaching the shore of the Red Sea (*see* section under "The Route"). The mighty miracle of deliverance through the divided waters could not have been on the same night as the Passover, although the shedding of blood marked the time their freedom began (Ex 12:42, 51; 13:3, 4). It is remarkable that nowhere is it claimed that the people made any fight at all (Hebert, p. 14).

It must be stressed that the OT uniformly represents all the tribes of Israel as having taken part in the Exodus. All 12 sons of Jacob were with him in Egypt, along with their families which became the 12 tribes (Gen 46:5-27; Ex 1:1-5). They all surrounded him on his deathbed when he prophesied over them (Gen 49). Ex 12:41 plainly states that "all the hosts

of the Lord went out from the land of Egypt." Moses erected 12 pillars at the foot of Mount Sinai to represent the tribes (Ex 24:4). All 12 names were to be engraved on the two shoulder stones of the ephod, and each of the 12 precious stones of the breastpiece was engraved with the name of a tribe (Ex 28:9-21; 39:6-14). Twelve loaves were to be placed on the table of showbread (Lev 24:5-6). The book of Numbers frequently mentions all 12 of the tribes of Israel. In Deuteronomy in referring to the spies Moses says, "I took twelve men of you, one man for every tribe" (1:23). All 12 tribes are named in connection with the command to pronounce the blessings and the curses between Mounts Ebal and Gerizim (Deut 27:12-13). The testimony of the book of Joshua is clear that all 12 tribes participated in the Jordan crossing (3:12; 4:2, 4, 9, 20-24).

Thus the OT teaches that the Exodus was a united movement from Egypt, all 12 tribes departing at once. And the entrance into Canaan was an invasion of the fighting men of all the tribes at the same time. Any evidence, therefore, concerning the history of one of the tribes during the latter half of the 2nd mil. B.C. is valid evidence for the history of the entire nation of Israel during that period.

This biblical data runs counter to the theories of many writers who follow the documentary hypothesis of the Pentateuch (*see* Exodus, Book of; Pentateuch). Most of them also subscribe to a late date for the Exodus. In order to handle certain extrabiblical evidence they have imagined either a twofold exodus and entry into Palestine in different centuries, or that some of the tribes of Israel never sojourned in Egypt at all. The interpretation of the Exodus event, then, is not merely a matter of chronology. It involves the origin of the religion of Israel, the historicity of the narratives, and the very inspiration of the Scriptures.

The Route

The exact route taken by the Israelites is difficult to determine. Nearly every place name mentioned in Ex 12-15 and the very meaning of the term "Red Sea" are in question. Therefore there are at least three main theories of the route of the Exodus. The higher critical attitude generally is that the account in Exodus appears to incorporate more than one geographical tradition, so that the present narrative is a reconstruction from several traditions without any certain knowledge of the places mentioned or of the actual route.

Those who believe the Heb. *yam sûph* refers to the Red Sea propose that the Israelites marched eventually S toward the head of the Gulf of Suez and crossed either the present gulf or the Bitter Lakes, connected at that time by a waterway with the Red Sea.

The proponents of a central crossing believe the Israelites proceeded E of Succoth to small Lake Timsah, the *yam sûph*, which should be

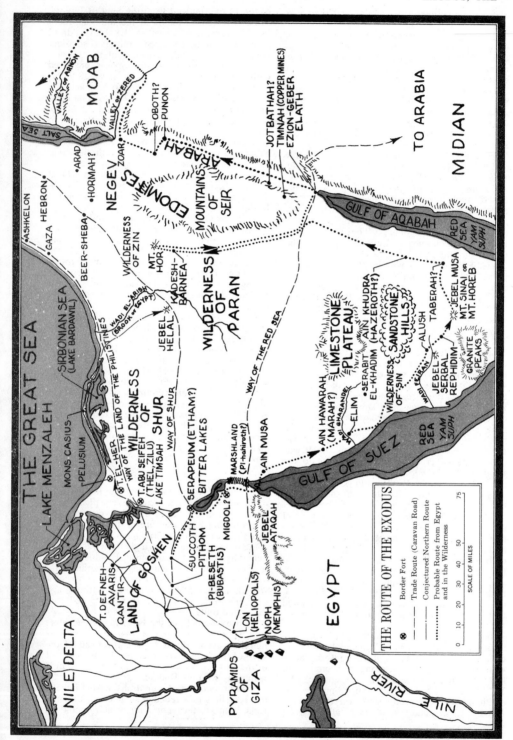

translated as the "Reed Sea." The Jews then left Egypt by "the way of the wilderness" (Ex 13:18), which they equate with "the way of Shur" (Gen 16:7) going to Beer-sheba.

The theory of an extreme northern route supposes that after leaving Succoth the Israelites could not safely pass the Egyptian border fortresses, and thus turned NE to the Mediterranean in order to flank the wall of Egypt. They avoided the way of the Philistines (Ex 13:17) by traversing the sandy spit which divides the Sirbonian Sea lagoon (the Reed Sea for this view), now called Lake Bardawil, from the Mediterranean. Baal-zephon (Ex 14:2, 9) is supposedly a temple site to be equated with Mons Casius where Zeus was later worshiped on this narrow strip of land. But this conjecture is improbable, because the proximity of this route to the military road or way of the Philistines would have endangered Israel (Cassuto, p. 156). Also, an Israeli archaeological survey in 1967 found no Late Bronze Age potsherds at Mount Casius (IEJ, XVII [1967], 279 f.).

A strange variant of the southern theory has the Israelites cross near Suez and continue E to Ezion-geber, then S through the land of Midian in Arabia to volcanic mountains. This view supposedly explains the fire and smoke on Mount Sinai (Ex 19 the peaks of the S Sinai peninsula are not volcanic), Horeb being in Midian (Ex 2:15; 3:1), and the references to Seir, Paran, and Teman in Deut 33:2; Jud 5:4–5; Hab 3:3. For all these routes see Emil G. Kraeling, *Rand-McNally Bible Atlas*, Chicago: Rand McNally, 1956, Map V.

W. F. Albright and G. E. Wright have championed a northern view that claims that Baal-zephon is Tell Defneh (Tahpanhes, *q.v.*) and the Reed Sea is Lake Menzaleh. After crossing it the Israelites turned S to go to the traditional Mount Sinai in the S end of the peninsula. But the association of the god Baal-zephon with the port of Tahpanhes is based on a late Phoenician papyrus letter of the 6th cen. B.C.

The geographical data are as follows. The Israelites dwelt in the land of Goshen, also called "the land of Rameses" (Gen 47:11). As slaves they had built for the pharaoh the military depot or "store" cities of Pithom and Raamses (Ex 1:11). The Heb. name *gōshen* is the Gr. Gesem (Gen 45:10; 46:34–LXX), probably the Egyptian "Kesem of the East." Goshen almost certainly refers to the region E of the Nile delta, including the fertile 30 mile long Wadi Tumilat stretching from Bubastis on the E branch of the Nile to Ismailia near Lake Timsah.

Archaeologists have examined two sites in Wadi Tumilat. Tell el-Maskhuta, nine and a half miles W of Lake Timsah, was excavated by Naville in 1883; and Tell er-Retabeh, eight and a half miles farther W, was explored by Petrie. Hieroglyphic inscriptions at the former site probably identify it as Tjeku or a town in the

Tjeku region, an area near the border of Egypt. Papyrus Anastasi VI mentions Tjeku as the place where famished Bedouin tribes of Edom were being sustained after being allowed to pass the fortress of Merneptah (ANET, p. 259). Another papyrus tells of the "enclosure-wall of Tjeku," evidently the line of fortresses guarding the desert border (*ibid.*). On philological grounds Tjeku may possibly be equated with Succoth (Ex 12:37; 13:20). This was the congregating point for the Israelites, their first encampment (Num 33:5) after leaving their slave dwellings. Heb. *sukkôth* literally means "booths," indicative of the temporary nature of their shelters on their journey.

Pithom (Pi-tum, Egyptian *Per-Atum,* "house of Atum") has been identified with Tell er-Retabeh by Sir Alan Gardiner. This is a small site, however, so that Uphill proposes Tell Hisn (Heliopolis, biblical On) in the NE suburbs of Cairo as Per-Atum (JNES, XXVII, 291–301). Thus the site of Pithom (Ex 1:11 only) remains uncertain.

Twenty-five miles NW of Tell el-Maskhuta and the area of Succoth lies Qantir. This is the probable site of Per-Rameses, the new capital city of Rameses II (see Uphill). Other scholars have equated Per-Rameses with Tanis (biblical Zoan, Ps 78:12, 43), the old Hyksos capital at San el-Hagar, 12–15 miles farther N. From the area of Rameses (Ex 12:37; Num 33:5) came many of the Israelites to begin the Exodus. The OT does not indicate, however, that this Rameses (or Raamses, Ex 1:11) was called Per-Rameses (which would be Pi-Rameses, after the pattern of Pi-tum=Per-Atum, Ex 1:11). The Heb. transcription omits the element *Pr* which always seems to precede the name of the city of Rameses in Egyptian inscriptions (Redford, VT, XIII, 409 f.). No 18th Dynasty inscriptions have been found at either Qantir or San el-Hagar, so that the biblical Rameses may have designated largely an agricultural area in Moses' time.

From Succoth the Israelites set out and encamped at Etham, at the edge of the wilderness (Ex 13:20). Because they were not led northward to take the shortest route to Canaan "lest ... they see war" (Ex 13:17), Etham (probably=Egyptian *ḫ t m*, "fort") cannot be one of the northern fortresses of the wall of Egypt. Rather a site to the E a day's journey (Num 33:6) would be expected. Ruins of such a fort are at Serapeum, half way between Lake Timsah and the Bitter Lakes, known later as "the fortress of Merneptah" (*see* above). It guarded the middle entrance route to Egypt known as "the way to Shur" (Gen 16:7).

Then the Lord ordered Israel "to turn back and encamp in front of Pi-ha-hiroth, between Migdol and the sea, in front of Baal-zephon ... by the sea" (Ex 14:2, RSV). The sea must refer to the Red Sea where the miraculous deliverance took place (15:4, 22; Deut 11:4; Josh 2:10; 4:23; 24:6; Neh 9:9; Ps 106:7, 9, 22;

136:13–15), for as Ex 13:17–19 summarizes the entire journey, God did not lead them by the nearest way, the way to the land of the Philistines, but "led the people by a roundabout way of the wilderness–by the Red Sea" (orig. trans. of 13:18*a*).

The Heb. term *yam sûph,* "Red Sea" in KJV and RSV, has become an enigma. Many modern scholars translate it as "the Sea of Reeds" because in Ex 2:3, 5 and Isa 19:6 *sûph* is the word for a plant growing in abundance on the banks of the Nile, and because *sûph* seems equivalent to Egyptian *twfi.* This etymological correspondence is not at all certain, however, and furthermore the Egyptian term *pr twfi* is used only for a territory and never for a sea or a river (Simons, GTT, pp. 77 f.). If it were to mean "Sea of Reeds," then it probably does not refer to the known Red Sea, because no reeds grow anywhere along its shores.

When *yam sûph* occurs in an OT passage not referring to the Exodus miracle, it may designate the E arm of the Red Sea, the Gulf of Aqabah (I Kgs 9:26; Ex 23:31; Jer 49:21). The way of the Red Sea (Num 14:25; 21:4; Deut 1:40; 2:1) is best explained as the trade route across the Sinai Desert from Egypt to Arabia, connecting the two tips of the Red Sea at Suez (Clysma) and Ezion-geber (Elat), respectively. The LXX (and Acts 7:36; Heb 11:29) constantly rendered *yam sûph* by *hē eruthra thalassa,* the Red Sea as we know it today, except in I Kgs 9:26, where the adjective *eschatēs,* "last, farthest, end," supposes the reading *sôph.* Heb. *sôph* means "end" (Eccl 3:11; 7:2; 12:13; II Chr 20:16). Thus the term may originally have been *yam sôph,* "the Border Sea," that sea at the end of Egyptian territory (M. Copisarow, "The Ancient Egyptian, Greek and Hebrew Concept of the Red Sea," VT, XII [1962], 1–13; N. H. Snaith, "*Yam-Sôph*: the Sea of Reeds: the Red Sea," VT, XV [1965], 395–398).

According to Ex 10:19, "a mighty strong west wind" blew all the locusts from the entire country of Egypt into the *yam sûph.* The "west wind" is in Heb. literally a "sea wind," which in Palestine would be a W wind; here in Egypt it would be more a NW wind. Only the presently known Red Sea (not a marshy lake) is properly placed and large enough to cause the death of a huge locust horde. If the S route and the traditional Mount Sinai are accepted, *yam sûph* in Num 33:10–11 is easily explainable as the Gulf of Suez shoreline beyond the mouth of Wadi Gharandel in which the oasis of Elim is found, at the plain of el-Marḥah.

The three place names in Ex 14:2 cannot be identified with certainty under any theory. But in keeping with the most likely S theory, the probable route can be traced. After turning back from the frontier at Etham, the Israelites detoured on a SW course around the NW shore of the larger Bitter Lake. Then passing Jebel Jenefeh on the W they moved SE between Jebel Abu Hasan and "the sea," camping at

Pi-hahiroth, which may mean "house of the marshes." Marshes exist around the S end of the Bitter Lakes, and on that height are ruins of a stone tower (Heb. *migdol,* Egyptian *mktl*), one of its three rooms being a shrine with hieroglyphic texts containing the names of Seti I and Rameses II.

While the possibility of identifying Baal-zephon with any of several sacred sites in the N is the crucial factor in the northern theories, the Canaanite deity Baal when introduced into Egypt was worshiped in many spots. C. Bourdon observed that an Egyptian papyrus giving an itinerary with the geographical names of the lakes lists four towers, one of which is the Tower of Baal-zephon (RB, LXI [1932], 370–392).

As early as the reign of Hatshepsut (1504–1483 B.C.), who sent ships via the Nile from Thebes to trade with Punt on the Somaliland coast, a channel must have connected the Bitter Lakes with the Gulf of Suez, and a canal in Wadi Tumilat joined the former with the E branch of the Nile near Bubastis. Therefore most scholars subscribing to the S route believe that the Bitter Lakes can rightfully be called part of the Red Sea, and propose that the Israelites crossed on a known ford at the narrow part of the lakes when the wind blew back all the water (a phenomenon observed by Napoleon, before the Suez Canal was dug).

On the other hand, the crossing path must have been very wide to enable all the Israelites to escape in one night. Also the waters returning to their normal state (Ex 14:27, NJV) were deep enough to cover all the chariot forces of Pharaoh. While the words of the song of Moses may be only figurative, they do speak of the depths of the sea, sinking to the bottom, the heart of the sea, and the mighty waters (Ex 15:5, 8, 10). Therefore a crossing through the present Red Sea S of the port of Suez or Clysma may best fit the data of the text. Here Israel would have been unable to escape by marching farther S along the W shore of the Red Sea, because the heights of Jebel Ataqah come right to the water. For the remainder of the route to Mount Sinai and Canaan, *see* Wilderness Wandering.

The Date

The key to the chronology of biblical events throughout the entire 2nd mil. B.C. is the date of the Exodus. There are two main views concerning this date: (1) the Israelites left Egypt during the 18th Dynasty *c.* 1450–1440 B.C., and (2) they did not depart until the 19th Dynasty during the 13th cen. The earlier date best accords with the 480 years between the Exodus and the beginning of Solomon's temple in the fourth year of his reign (*c.* 967 B.C.; I Kgs 6:1), the 300 years from the conquest of Transjordan to the time of Jephthah (Jud 11:26), and the length of the period of the judges. It claims Thutmose III (1504–1450 B.C.) to be the pharaoh of the oppression and Amenhotep II

(1450–1425) as the pharaoh of the Exodus. The chief arguments for the later date are the occurrence of the name of Rameses (or Raamses) in Ex 1:11 and 12:37, Glueck's surface explorations in Transjordan and the Negeb finding no important settlement ruins until after 1300 B.C., and destruction levels of a number of sites in W Palestine from 1250–1200 B.C.

Amenhotep II, Pharaoh of the Exodus according to the early date. HFV

The late date. The most reasonable explanation of this view is that the Exodus occurred early in the reign of Rameses II (1304–1237 B.C.), c. 1290 to 1280 B.C. Rameses' successor, Merneptah (1236–1223), claims on his victory stela about cities and peoples in Palestine to have laid Israel waste, along with his seed (ANET, p. 378). While "seed" may refer to offspring, more likely in keeping with Egyptian idiom the burning of growing crops is meant. Thus Israel seems already to have entered the Promised Land after the 40 years of nomadic wilderness wandering. But G. E. Wright and others insist that Israel must have been in Egypt at least during the early part of the reign of Rameses II in order to have worked on the construction of the city of Rameses (Wright, *Biblical Archaeology*, p. 60). They argue also that few if any building oper-

ations of Thutmose III are known to have taken place in the Nile delta, and that the 18th Dynasty capital was far upstream at Thebes.

The name Raamses in Ex 1:11 may not refer to the capital city Per-Rameses of Rameses II (*see* section under "The Route"). It may either be an anachronism, as it almost certainly is in Gen 47:11; or the name Rameses may go back to Hyksos times, even as the 19th Dynasty rulers traced their ancestry and tradition back to a Hyksos god or king named Seth, according to the "Stela of the Year 400" found at Tanis (ANET, pp. 252 f.).

The continuity of Ex 1 – 2 obviously implies that the beginning of the enslavement and the building of Pithom and Raamses took place before the birth of Moses. But Moses was 80 at the time of the Exodus (Ex 7:7). Thus, if the late date is correct, Moses would have been born c. 1370 in the 18th Dynasty (1570–1320). Therefore it is impossible both to hold that Rameses II was the pharaoh who ordered the Israelites to build the cities of Ex 1:11, and to believe Moses' age is correct.

The 18th Dynasty kings were very active in Lower Egypt. Thutmose III appointed two viziers over the country, one residing at Thebes and the other at Heliopolis near modern Cairo, where Thutmose erected two granite obelisks (now in New York and London). His son Amenhotep II is known to have left a monument to the god Amun-Re at Bubastis, at the W end of Wadi Tumilat. Here he also built a temple for the goddess Bastet. The armies of these two pharaohs must have used the facilities of this key city in the delta for their many Asiatic campaigns. A rock tablet at Tura shows that in Amenhotep's fourth year his overseer of works, Minmose, was still busy in the temples of the delta. Born at Memphis where he grew up (ANET, pp. 244 f.), Amenhotep took a keen interest in the affairs of Lower Egypt.

The late date proponents explain the 480 years of I Kgs 6:1 by suggesting this figure was an artificial date of secondary origin (Montgomery, *Kings*, ICC, p. 144). Supposedly it is based on a hypothetical 12 generations from Aaron to the priests of Solomon's day using the then accepted length of 40 years for a generation. But we know a generation is more closely 25 years long, giving a period of only 300 years from the Exodus to Solomon. While I Chr 6:3–8 and 50–53 list 11 priests from Aaron to Zadok (who anointed Solomon) inclusive, I Chr 6:33–37 has 18 generations from Heman in David's time to Korah in Moses' time. No accurate chronology, therefore, can be reckoned from the genealogies.

Nelson Glueck has charged that no Edomite or Moabite kings would have been encountered by Moses in the Negeb or Transjordan before they built their border fortresses in the 13th cen. B.C. (*The Other Side of the Jordan*, New Haven: ASOR, 1940, pp. 146 f.; *Rivers in the Desert*, New York: Farrar, Straus & Cudahy,

Huge fallen statue of Rameses II at Memphis, candidate for Pharaoh of Exodus according to the late date. HFV

1959, pp. 106, 109, 114 f.). He did not find one site or potsherd which could be ascribed to the Middle Bronze II or Late Bronze Ages (1900–1250 B.C.). His conclusions must now be modified, however.

A careful geographical study of the terms Edom (q.v.) and Mount Seir in Genesis to Judges reveals that Esau and his descendants lived in the Negeb W of the Arabah until after the time of Moses and Joshua. Not until the biblical records about Saul and David are the Edomites mentioned as residing in Transjordan (I Sam 14:47; II Sam 8:12–14, RSV; I Chr 18:11–13). Inscriptions from the reign of Thutmose III tell of his army warring in the Negeb (ANET, pp. 241, 243). Near ancient copper mines at Timnah (15 miles N of Elath, W side of Arabah) Beno Rothenberg excavated an Egyptian temple, dated by royal cartouches of Seti I (1318–1304 B.C.) and Rameses III (1198–1166). Much local pottery at the temple site and nearby smelting camps shows that tribes from Midian and the central Negeb hill country were employed in the Egyptian mining operations (PEQ, CI [1969], 57 ff.). The Canaanite king of Arad, who dwelt in the Negeb and fought against Israel (Num 21:1, RSV), evidently lived at Tell Malḥata (seven and a half miles SW of Tell Arad) which has a fine well and strong Canaanite fortifications including a solid brick glacis (IEJ, XIV [1964], 145 ff.).

Furthermore, the terms "king" of Edom (Num 20:14) and various "cities" of Edomite kings (Gen 36:32, 35, 39) need not prove that the Edomites were yet a sedentary people dwelling in fortified towns. The five kings of Midian (Num 31:8) in Moses' day and the two kings of Midian in Gideon's day (Jud 8:5, 12)

were only nomadic chieftains. Kadesh-barnea had no permanent buildings and fortifications during Israel's wanderings, yet it is called "a city in the uttermost of thy [i.e., Edom's] border" (Num 20:16). It was only a tent city, like the "camps" (maḥanîm) of Num 13:19. It was God who forbade Israel to cross the territories of the Edomites and Moabites, not the superior strength of these peoples who prevented it (Deut 2:4–9).

Since World War II a number of tombs in the Amman-Mount Nebo region have yielded hundreds of Middle Bronze II and Late Bronze I (1800–1400) pottery vessels and scarabs. A Late Bronze Age temple with a large quantity of imported Cypriote and Mycenean pottery was discovered in 1955 at the airport of Amman (PEQ, XC [1958], 10–12; XCVIII [1966], 155–162; BA, XXXII [1969], 104–116). Beginning excavations at Heshbon in 1968 unearthed some Late Bronze sherds. Thus it seems that there was some sedentary occupation in Transjordan around 1400 B.C.

The late 13th cen. B.C. destruction levels of Beitin (Bethel?), Lachish, Tell el-Hesi (Eglon?), Tell Beit Mirsim (Debir?), and Hazor are attributed to the Israelite conquest of Josh 10–11 by such writers as G. E. Wright (Biblical Archaeology, pp. 81–85). While the poorer style of houses above the levels of burning at these sites may or may not prove Israelite occupation, it cannot prove it was Joshua's army which destroyed the cities at that time. The tribes continued to subdue their territories long after Joshua's death. He burned only Jericho, Ai, and Hazor (Josh 6:24; 8:19; 11:13). Hebron and Debir had to be recaptured (15:13–17), for Joshua did not settle or leave garrisons in the cities he took but led his entire army back to Gilgal (10:43). He did not conduct siege warfare but rather a series of lightning-like raids against key Canaanite cities with the purpose of destroying the morale and fighting ability of the inhabitants.

The early date. Positive support for this view comes from a comparison of Moses' exile with the long reigns of certain pharaohs, from settlement conditions in Goshen, the Dream Stela of Thutmose IV, the time of Balaam, the fall of Jericho around 1400 B.C., the history of Hazor, Egyptian mentions of Asher, and correspondences between the Amarna letters and the early period of the judges.

The combination of Thutmose III and Amenhotep II best fits the requirements of the pharaoh of the oppression and the pharaoh of the Exodus, respectively. Thutmose would be the ruler whose death is recorded in Ex 2:23, the same one from whom Moses fled in 2:15 (cf. 4:19). He reigned alone for 34 years (1483–1450 B.C.). The only other pharaohs of the 18th and 19th Dynasties whose reigns were long enough to include even most of Moses' exile and sojourn with Jethro were Amenhotep III (1417–1379), Horemheb (1348–1320), and Rameses II (1304–1237). But each of these three is disqualified because the king who followed could not be the pharaoh of the Exodus. The effeminate Amenhotep IV (Akhenaten, 1379-1362) built a new capital at Amarna, 200 miles up the Nile from Goshen, and rather neglected the delta region as well as the Canaanite princes appealing to him for help. Horemheb was the last king of the 18th Dynasty, and his successor, Rameses I, first 19th Dynasty king, ruled only a year and four months. Merneptah, son of Rameses II, shows in his stela that Israel was already in Canaan.

The plagues of the flies and the hail fell on all the land of Egypt but not on Goshen (Ex 8:22; 9:25-26). This suggests that while Goshen was on the edge of the land of Egypt, it was removed to some extent from the territory where the native Egyptians were residing. This would have been true during the 18th Dynasty whose kings left no traces in the easternmost delta. But during the 19th Dynasty, when the capital was probably at Qantir (see "The Route"), many of the principal building projects of Rameses II were in the Wadi Tumilat or Goshen region itself.

Thutmose IV (1425-1417 B.C.), the son and successor of Amenhotep II, set up a remarkable stela between the legs of the Sphinx at Gizeh. In a dream he was told that he would be given the kingdom (ANET, p. 449). If he had been the eldest son of his father, there would have been no purpose in a divine promise that he should someday become king. One may reasonably infer that the oldest son of Amenhotep

must have predeceased his father, thus leaving the succession to his younger brother. This is in accord with the death of Pharaoh's firstborn son in the last plague (Ex 12:29).

In Num 22:5 we read that Balak "sent messengers to summon Balaam son of Beor, at Pethor on the River, in the land of the sons of Amaw" (JerusB). Pethor is the later Hittite city of Pitru, S of Carchemish on the Euphrates. The statue of Idri-mi from Alalakh, dated variously from 1450 to 1375 B.C., says he found sons of the land of 'Amau and sons of the land of Aleppo when he was in exile in Canaan (BASOR, # 118, p. 16). Only around 1400 B.C. was the land of 'Amau independent and not under the rule of either the Egyptians or the Hittites. From the time of Suppiluliumas (c. 1370 B.C.) Carchemish dominated the area, first within the Hittite imperial system and later as an independent city-state.

The first fortress city to fall before Joshua was Jericho. Miss Kathleen Kenyon has proved that Sir John Garstang misdated the parallel fortification walls that he attributed to Joshua's time. Nevertheless pottery evidence from the tell and from the tombs shows there was occupation of Tell es-Sultan in the Late Bronze I Age. Garstang's expeditions (1930-1936) discovered in 26 tombs containing pottery some 320 Late Bronze objects, including a series of royal Egyptian scarab seals ending with two of Amenhotep III (1417-1379 B.C.) but none of Akhenaten. Significantly, except in connection with the isolated Middle Building and two

The dream inscription of Thutmose IV shown on a stela between the paws of the Sphinx. LL

tombs which he attributes to the time of King Eglon (Jud 3:12-14), he found on the mound of Jericho next to no Mycenaen pottery. That began to enter Palestine c. 1400 B.C. Yet Pritchard at Tell es-Sa'idiyeh and Franken at Deir Allah 30 miles N in the Jordan Valley each found sizeable quantities of such ware. (See the penetrating analysis of the Jericho evidence in Wood, "Date of the Exodus," pp. 69-73).

On his northern campaign Joshua killed Jabin king of Hazor and set fire to the city (Josh 11:10-11). Later, Israelites under Deborah and Barak destroyed another king of Canaan that reigned in Hazor, also named Jabin (Jud 4:2, 23, 24). It is logical to associate the latest Canaanite level (1a) of the huge lower city with Jabin II. It was destroyed by fire in the second half of the 13th cen. B.C. and never reoccupied. In Area K of the lower city a gate (provisionally Late Bronze I of level 2) was destroyed in a violent conflagration. If it is correctly dated, this burning from around 1400 B.C. may have resulted from Joshua's action; there is no intervening evidence of destruction before the end of the Canaanite occupation.

The tribe of Asher settled in Galilee along the coast. An inscription of Seti I, dated c. 1310 B.C., lists a name in hieroglyphs 'i-s̆-r along with Megiddo and Kedesh (cf. Jud 4:6; J. Simons, Handbook for the Study of Egyptian Topographical Lists Relating to Western Asia, Leiden: E. J. Brill, 1937, p. 147, list XVII, 4). This may be the earliest extrabiblical reference to a specific Israelite tribe. It is mentioned again in Papyrus Anastasi I from the time of Rameses II (ANET, p. 477; Aharoni, The Land of the Bible, pp. 168, 171). Albright and K. A. Kitchen doubt that the Egyptian name is equivalent to Heb. 'āsher, but A. H. Gardiner believes that 'i-s̆-r may represent Asher (Ancient Egyptian Onomastica, I, 192 f.). In 1953 Aharoni found 19 small Iron Age settlements in upper Galilee which he believes were Israelite and began perhaps as early as 1300 B.C.

It is true that the small-scale forays of the Habiru and the inter-city fighting of the Amarna letters (q.v.) do not agree with the united invasion and disciplined campaigns of Joshua. The unrest in Canaan does harmonize with the early period of the judges, however, when the Israelites were turning to idols and "every man did that which was right in his own eyes" (Jud 17:6; 21:25). After Joshua died each tribe was responsible to conquer the Canaanites in its own possession, but in many cases the tribe was unsuccessful and co-existed with the heathen (Jud 1). The Habiru seem to have some connection with the Hebrews, however difficult that may be to define (see Hebrew People). It is significant that in Joshua's time there were nine city-states (cities with a king) in S Palestine, but Albright finds only four large ones c. 1375 B.C. according to a study of the Amarna tablets (BASOR, #87, pp. 37 f.). They are Gezer, Jerusalem, Lachish, and the city and land ruled

by Shuwardata; the first two were never captured by Joshua, and Lachish may well have been reoccupied by Canaanites as were Hebron and Debir. It is noteworthy that Jericho, Ai, Bethel, and Gibeon are not mentioned in those letters.

A mediating position between the early and late date views is that of Miss Kenyon. On the basis of her excavations at Jericho she dates the fall of that city to the Israelites 1350-1325 B.C. (Digging Up Jericho, London: Ernest Benn, 1957, pp. 260-263). This would tend to support the LXX translation of I Kgs 6:1, which says Solomon began to build the temple in the 440th year of the exodus of the sons of Israel out of Egypt. If the LXX were correct, the Exodus would have occurred c. 1407 B.C. and the conquest of Jericho 40 years later, c. 1367, quite close to Miss Kenyon's 1350 B.C. There is no textual support for the LXX instead of the Heb. MT in I Kgs 6:1, however, and Miss Kenyon did not find enough remains of the late Bronze period at Jericho to discount Garstang's earlier discoveries.

In summary, the factual evidence can better be explained by the early date view; and to those who believe strongly in the inspiration of all Scripture the statements in I Kgs 6:1 (MT) and Jud 11:26 and supporting passages are conclusive for a date of the Exodus c. 1445 B.C.

Bibliography. Gleason L. Archer, SOTI, pp. 164 f., 210-223, 253-259 (early date). U. Cassuto, Commentary on Exodus, Jerusalem: Magnes Press, 1967 (S route, late date). Jack Finegan, Let My People Go, New York: Harper & Row, 1963 (S route, late date). L. H. Grollenberg, Atlas of the Bible, trans. and ed. by J. M. H. Reid and H. H. Rowley, London, 1956 (S route, late date). Gabriel Hebert, When Israel Came Out of Egypt, London: SCM Press, 1961 (late date, liberal but helpful to show theological importance). Siegfried H. Horn, "Exodus," SDABD, pp. 330-333 (S route, early date). K. A. Kitchen, Ancient Orient and Old Testament, Chicago: Inter-Varsity, 1966, pp. 57-78 (conservative, late date). John Rea, "The Time of the Oppression and the Exodus," BETS, III (1960), 58-69; "New Light on the Wilderness Journey and the Conquest," Grace Journal, II (Spring, 1961), 5-13. Donald B. Redford, "Exodus I.11," VT, XIII (1963), 401-418. Irwin W. Reist, "The Theological Significance of the Exodus," JETS, XII (1969), 222-232. H. H. Rowley, From Joseph to Joshua, London: British Academy, 1950 (late date). J. Simons, GTT, pp. 233-266 (S route). E. P. Uphill, "Pithom and Raamses: Their Location and Significance," JNES, XXVII (1968), 291-316; XXVIII (1969), 15-39. C. De Wit, The Date and Route of the Exodus, London: Tyndale Press, 1960 (S route, late date). Leon Wood, "Date of the Exodus," New Perspectives on the Old Testament, ed. by J. Barton Payne, Waco: Word Books, 1970, pp.

66–87 (early date). G. Ernest Wright, *Biblical Archaeology*, rev. ed., Philadelphia: Westminster, 1962, pp. 53–85 (S route, late date).

J. R.

EXORCISM. One who extracts an oath, an exorcist; from *exorkizō, orkizō,* "to extract an oath, to adjure." The verbal form *exorkizō* is used once in Mt 26:63 where the high priest says to Jesus, "I adjure thee by the living God, that thou tell us whether thou be the Christ," while *orkizō* is used three times in the same sense (I Thess 5:27; Mk 5:7; Acts 19:13). The noun is used once in Acts 19:13 of the vagabond Jews — "exorcists."

The exercise of exorcism consisted in the use of magical words and ceremonies for the purpose of expelling demons or evil spirits. It should be very clearly distinguished from the ministry of Christ in casting out evil spirits since He did so by His own power and authority. When His disciples cast them out in His name, they were depending upon this same power and authority (cf. Acts 3:6). The difference between the casting out of evil spirits and exorcism is made clear by two passages which complement each other, namely, Mt 12:22–30 and Acts 19:13 ff. In Christ's defense against the accusation of the Jews in Mt 12, that He cast out devils by Beelzebub, we find the Jews held the view that Christ was working in cooperation with the devil (v. 27). Jesus said that if such were the case, Satan's kingdom was divided against itself and could not stand (v. 26). He claimed that He had the ability to restrain and bind Satan and cast out evil spirits by the power of God, and that this proved the kingdom of God was come (vv. 28–29). To stop their criticism, He asked whether their children were casting out devils by Satan's power (v. 27).

Apparently Christ was referring to what they taught their own children about exorcism. Something of what this was can be learned from Josephus, the Apocrypha, and rabbinical writings. Josephus writes of the wisdom of Solomon in exorcism, attributing to him what were clearly heathen practices (*Ant.* viii.5). The apocryphal book of Tobit speaks of burning the liver of a fish in the ashes of incense to drive away a demon. Rabbinical writers go into long and obnoxious details of methods for exorcism. Yet in spite of this conglomeration of strange ideas, the Jews certainly would not be ready to admit they were casting out demons by Satan, and teaching their children to do the same. This fact Christ uses in His own self-defense.

In Acts 19:11 ff. some of the reprobate Jews, thinking that Paul was practicing mere exorcism in casting out spirits by the name of Jesus, decided to copy him. The answer of the evil spirit, "Jesus I know, and Paul I know; but who are ye?" (v. 15), shows the difference between the magical use of a name in exorcism and casting out demons by the power of God.

The demon recognized the power of Jesus and the authority of Paul in Jesus' name, but not the magical exorcism in Jesus' name. Casting out evil spirits is different from exorcism.

See Demonology.

R. A. K.

EXPEDIENCY, EXPEDIENT. Expedient has two meanings: (1) the quality or principle of being adapted to ends which accomplish what is good; (2) the principle of doing what appears profitable or expedient under the particular circumstances apart from moral principles, often called pure expediency.

The wide scope of the word and its dual meaning causes much confusion. The second meaning is not found in the idea of expediency as used in Scripture. A distinction, therefore, needs to be made between the biblical use of the Gr. *sympherei,* the basic meaning of which is "what is profitable," and the idea of pure expediency. When Caiaphas says, "Consider that it is expedient for us, that one man should die for the people, and that the whole nation perish not" (Jn 11:50), and Christ, "It is expedient for you that I go away" (Jn 16:7), the idea of profit and the common good, rather than what suits the circumstances, is paramount. The Scriptures never teach us to make decisions apart from moral principles.

Again, when Paul says, "All things are lawful for me but all things are not expedient," while appearing at first glance to claim absolute Christian liberty, he still gives two reasons as the basis of decision: "I will not be brought under the power of anything"; "not all things edify" (I Cor 6:12; 10:23). Both are moral reasons and show that Paul's seeming amorality at this point is governed by good moral arguments, and his actions are determined by what will prove of permanent value, or real profit not only to himself but also to others.

Is pure expediency not present then in any sense in the NT? Yes, in the sense that eating things offered to idols or not eating them, and circumcision or uncircumcision are basically matters of Christian freedom. Still this is immediately tempered by the reaction of another man's conscience (Rom 14:13 ff.). In other words, while the Gr. word *sympherei* is not used to express pure expediency itself, there is an area of expediency revealed in Scripture. Since the ceremonial law has been done away with, there is nothing unclean in itself; since the antitype has come and fulfilled the law, circumcision has been fulfilled in Him (Col 2:11) and is revealed to be of the heart. Thus "expediency" in the NT is based upon what is profitable and morally good, first for others, whom we must not cause to stumble by doing what does not edify (I Cor 10:28); and second for ourselves, lest we become slaves to habit or "things," such as drink, etc. (I Cor 6:12).

See Flesh; Idols, Things Offered to.

R. A. K.

EXPERIENCE. Paul writes that "tribulation worketh patience; and patience, experience; and experience, hope" (Rom 5:3-4; cf. Jas 1:2-12), revealing a ladder of development which often occurs in the life of the Christian.

The proper relationship between revealed truth and experience must be carefully maintained, since revelation precedes Christian experience. We do not base our Christian ideas and decisions upon experience, but rather upon God's revelation, and experience corroborates the correctness of the decisions.

EXPIATE, EXPIATION. These terms are used in the RSV for Heb. *ḥaṭṭā't* (Num 8:7, "water of expiation") and *kāphar* (Num 35:33; Deut 32:43; I Sam 3:14; II Sam 21:3; Isa 27:9; 47:11), and for Gr. *hilastērion* (Rom 3:25), *hilaskomai* (Heb 2:17) and *hilasmos* (I Jn 2:2; 4:10).

The basic idea of expiation has to do with reparation for a wrong, the satisfaction of the demands of justice through paying a penalty. Propitiation carries in addition the idea of appeasing an offended person, of regaining the favor of a higher individual. Some feel that the idea of appeasing God, as one might appease an arbitrary tyrant, fails to do justice to the character of God as revealed in Christ. For this reason the term "expiation" is preferred as the translation for *hilastērion* by these recent scholars. But God is not seen as a temperamental, angry despot demanding his "pound of flesh." Rather we see Him in His holiness which cannot be undercut if He is to maintain His divine integrity. The demands of God's holiness are met in His love and mercy, His self-giving of Christ the only begotten Son as an expiation for our sins.

On the Day of Atonement in the history of Israel, the high priest entered the most holy place. First he sprinkled the blood of the sin offering upon the altar and then on the mercy seat "within the veil" where no one else dared enter (Lev 16:14). The writer of the Epistle to the Hebrews makes several references to Christ's ministry as our High Priest. After His death on Calvary, Christ entered the holy place of heaven once for all, not with the blood of bulls and goats, but with His own blood (Heb 9:11-14, 24-25; 10:10-14). Hebrews also tells us that the incarnation took place so that Jesus "might become a merciful and faithful high priest in the service of God, to make expiation for the sins of the people" (Heb 2:17, RSV).

Other NT writers also emphasize that through the sprinkling (shedding) of the blood of Christ reparation was made for our sins, a price was paid to remove the penalty from us (I Pet 1:18 f.). Forgiveness for sin could only be made by satisfying the holiness of God. God's reaction to sin cannot be anything else but judgment and condemnation, which Paul speaks of as the wrath of God (Rom 1:18 f.). The expiation made by Christ, His sin offering

on our behalf, provided the objective ground for God's forgiveness of our sins; we are then justified if we receive Christ's priestly ministry as the Lamb of God by faith (Rom 3:25, RSV).

We may say then that Christ propitiated the holiness of God through becoming an expiation for our sins. The atonement does not mean the appeasing of an arbitrary potentate; it is the love of God coming to us in the self-giving of Christ. In this expiating ministry Jesus is described as our "advocate with the Father" (I Jn 2:1-2). "In this is love, not that we loved God but that he loved us and sent his Son to be the expiation for our sins" (I Jn 4:10, RSV).

See Atonement; Propitiation.

T. W. B.

Ancient peoples of the Near East feared the evil eye. In this mosaic from Antioch of Syria of early Christian date, all sorts of attacks are made on the evil eye. HFV

EYE. Eye denotes the physical organ of sight of man and beast and is used in many figurative applications. The eyes are affected by age, emotions, sleep, and death. They show emotional qualities, such as generosity (Prov 22:9), greed (Ps 10:8), arrogance (Isa 2:11; 5:15; II Kgs 19:22), envy (I Sam 18:9; Prov 28:22; Mk 7:22), evil desire (Isa 3:16; II Pet 2:14; I Jn 2:16). They are used of God in an anthropomorphic sense, showing His omniscience.

Painting around the eye was common for women in ancient Egypt and Babylonia, but among the Hebrews it is mentioned chiefly in connection with women of ill repute. The eyelids above and below the eyes were blackened with black powder of antimony or stibium. However, the translators of the KJV sometimes translated the word "eyes" by "face." Thus Jezebel actually painted her eyes (II Kgs 9:30, ASV). Jeremiah says, "Though thou enlargest thine eyes with paint" (Jer 4:30, ASV; cf. Ezk 23:40). *See* Eyes, Painting the.

The word "eyes" is used in a variety of other ways: (1) a fountain (*q.v.*), as the Heb. word is sometimes translated, probably stemming from the eye as a fountain of tears (cf. Jer 9:1); (2) color or gleam, since the eye sparkles like metal or jewels (Ezk 1:4; 8:2; 10:9); (3) face (Num 14:14); (4) visible surface of the earth (Ex 10:5, 15; Num 22:5); (5) forehead, as in "between thine eyes" (Ex 13:9); (6) presence, as in "before the eyes" (Heb. Gen 23:11); (7) individual opinion, as "in your eyes" (Gen 19:8); (8) favor or anger, as in "to set thine eyes upon" (Heb. Jer 39:12; Amos 9:8). The phrase "to keep as the apple [or pupil] of the eye" (Deut 32:10; Ps 17:8) means to preserve something with particular care.

E. C. J.

EYE, BLINDING OF. *See* Punishments.

EYES, COVERING OF THE. A difficult phrase used in Gen 20:16 of different interpretations. If the words refer to Abraham, the idea may be that Abraham when he professes to be Sarah's husband would act as a veil to those who may desire her. If the words refer to the money received by Abraham, the money may be as a veil to protect her from the wanton desires of others. More likely it refers to the money as a compensation or an "atoning gift . . . so that he may forget a wrong done (cf. Gen 32:21, and Job 9:24, 'he covereth the faces of the judges,' i.e., he bribes them)" (KD, I, 241).

EYES, PAINTING THE. The practice of painting the eyes is very ancient, being well attested in Egypt from even predynastic times. The material used was ground on a stone palette and often was kept in small jars of alabaster, tubes of wood, or similar containers. The early preference was for a green color (chrysocalla or malachite), but later black (galena) became more popular. A black form is known in modern times as *kohl,* a term derived from Arabic. Kohl was applied to the edges of the eyelids by either the fingers or special rodlike applicators. The resulting dark rim was thought to add contrasting brilliance to the eye. Though used primarily as a cosmetic, eye paint also appears in prescriptions for eye ailments.

In the Bible the use of eye paint always has evil associations. The Heb. verb *kāhal,* "to paint (eyes)," occurs only in Ezk 23:40, in a description of the efforts of an adulteress to entice her victims. Eye paint (Heb. *pûk*) is mentioned twice in connection with makeup. Jezebel painted her eyes before she went to confront Jehu (II Kgs 9:30, RSV). Jer 4:30 (RSV) compares Judah and Jerusalem to a woman who enlarges her eyes with paint in an attempt to secure deliverance by seduction. Here the verb is *qāra',* basically "to tear," also "to make large or wide," graphically fitting the appearance of painted eyes. *See* Eye.

C. E. D.

EYESALVE. The medicine or powder referred to in Rev 3:18 was a compound of ingredients applied to the eyelids to strengthen the eyes. The medical school at Laodicea was famous for this preparation and its usage, according to Galen. The blindness of the Laodicean church was spiritual, however, and the intent of the command in Rev 3:18 was to urge those with inadequate spiritual discernment to seek a remedy for their condition.

EZAR (ē'zär). This spelling of the name is used in place of Ezer (*q.v.*) in I Chr 1:38 for a son of Seir, the Horite, in the land of Edom (cf. Gen 36:21).

EZBAI (ĕz'bī). The name of one of David's mighty men, the father of Naarai (I Chr 11:37).

EZBON (ĕz'bŏn)
1. A son of Gad (Gen 46:16), also called Ozni (cf. Num 26:15-16).
2. One of the sons of Bela, thus a grandson of Benjamin (I Chr 7:7).

EZEKIAS (ĕz-ē-kī'ăs). The Gr. form of Hezekiah (*q.v.*), a king of Judah (Mt 1:9-10).

EZEKIEL (ē-zē'ky'l). Ezekiel was one of the three writing prophets, along with Jeremiah and Daniel, at the time of the Babylonian Exile. While Jeremiah was ministering in Judah, and Daniel (deported in 605 B.C.) was serving at the court of Nebuchadnezzar (Dan 1:1-7), Ezekiel was preaching to the Jewish captives in Babylonia. He had been taken to Babylon with them and their king Jehoiachin (Ezk 1:2; 33:21) after the siege of Jerusalem in the eighth year of Nebuchadnezzar (597 B.C.; see II Kgs 24:10-16). The only other period of such fullness of prophetic testimony was the time of Isaiah, Hosea, Amos, and Micah in the latter half of the 8th cen. B.C. Ezekiel shows a closer relationship in concept and message to Jeremiah than to Daniel, who probably did not write down any of his prophecies until after the fall of Babylon in 539 B.C.

Ezekiel's name signifies "God strengthens." He was a priest (Ezk 1:3) of the family of Zadok. There is no evidence that Ezekiel had performed priestly functions in Jerusalem before he was exiled to Babylon, even though he seems to have been thoroughly familiar with the temple of Solomon and its cultus. Nothing is known of the personal history of Ezekiel beyond what is found in his book, and what is known of the times in which he lived. He is not mentioned in any other OT book, nor is he directly referred to in the NT, although much of the symbolism of the book of Revelation is clearly based on his visions.

Ezekiel is supposed to have been a young man at the time of the Exile, but it is claimed that his writings imply a more mature man. A number of his prophecies are carefully dated in the time of Jehoiachin's captivity. The date in Ezk 1:1 ("in the thirtieth year"), which has been the cause of much difference of opinion among the commentators, must refer to Ezekiel's own age of 30, the age when Levites entered their priestly duties (Num 4:23, 30, 39, 43). Thus he was born c. 627 B.C.

Ezekiel was married (Ezk 24:18) and lived probably in the village of Tel-abib near Nippur in Babylonia (3:15), in his own house (3:24; cf. Jer 29:1-7), to which the elders of Israel would come to consult with him (8:1; 14:1; 20:1). Most of the captives were settled along the river Chebar (1:3), now identified as a royal canal of Nebuchadnezzar, flowing from the vicinity of Babylon past Nippur to Erech (see Chebar). Fifth cen. B.C. clay tablets from Nippur tell of the Murashu Sons, merchants who did business with Jews during the Persian era, thus confirming the residence of Jews in this locale.

Ezekiel's wife died suddenly during his ministry, but the Lord expressly forbade him to mourn for her (24:16-18). The book is full of such personal experiences of the prophet (3:24-26; 4:4-8; 4:12; 5:1; 24:27). God intended the prophet to be a sign to Israel in the experiences of his life (24:24). He began his prophetic work in 592 B.C., in the fifth year of Jehoiachin's captivity when he was 30 years old (1:1-2). He prophesied for at least 22 years (29:17). Nothing is known concerning the end of his ministry.

At first Ezekiel's messages were not well received (14:1, 3; 18:19, 25), but with the passing of time his prophecies began to bear fruit, and finally the nation was cleansed of its idolatry. He began in a time of spiritual declension and uprooting. The prophet saw clearly that conditions among his people called for further judgment from the Lord, which did come in the third deportation from Judah in 586 B.C. When judgment had completed its work, then the need of the hour was consolation for the wounded nation.

Ezekiel has been spoken of as suffering from a mental disorder, even from a form of catalepsy, on the basis of such passages as 3:23-4:8 (H. Klostermann, *Theologische Studien und Kritiken*, 1877). Such a position arises from a failure to understand the nature of the visions and experiences of the prophet. His life and ministry were entirely under God's appointment.

He has been called "the father of Judaism" because of the influence he is said to have exercised on the later worship of Israel. A comparison may be drawn between the apostle John on the island of Patmos and Ezekiel at Chebar, both in a place of isolation and oppression by forces of the present evil world system.

C. L. F.

EZEKIEL, BOOK OF.

This major prophetic work is named for the prophet whose divinely inspired messages and visions are recorded in it. It is the 12th book (of 24) in the Heb. Bible, the 26th book in the English OT.

Authorship and Date

Not until the 1920's did any scholars ser-

iously challenge the genuineness and unity of the book of Ezekiel. J. Skinner wrote in 1898 (HDB, I, 817a): "Neither the unity nor the authenticity of Ezekiel has been questioned by more than a very small minority of scholars. Not only does it bear the stamp of a single mind in its phraseology, its imagery, and its mode of thought, but it is arranged on a plan so perspicuous and so comprehensive that the evidence of literary design in the composition becomes altogether irresistible." Nevertheless, critics have claimed several main difficulties in believing that the book is an authentic account of Ezekiel's ministry and that he wrote all the prophecies included in it.

First, Gustave Hölscher in 1924 claimed that all the pre-Exilic prophets of Israel and Judah proclaimed only doom and judgments against their respective nations, so that any passage promising a restoration and a golden age must necessarily have been added in the Persian period. Hölscher supported his criticism with a literary analysis based mainly on a contrast between the poetry and prose sections, and attributed to Ezekiel only 170 verses out of the total 1,273. But numerous writers, both ancient and modern, have composed beautiful poetry as well as prose. Furthermore, nearly all the OT prophets who warned of imminent divine punishment also predicted ultimate divine bestowal of grace upon a redeemed remnant of Israel.

Second, Robert H. Pfeiffer, following V. Herntrich, insisted that Ezekiel must actually have been living in Jerusalem when he delivered the prophetic messages of chaps. 4-24 (*Introduction to the OT*, Harper, 1948, pp. 535-543). His call to speak to a rebellious house (Ezk 2) and to be a watchman (Ezk 3) led him to return to Judah to address in person the Jews left in Jerusalem. He enacted symbolic prophecies for their benefit which they could not see if he were in Babylonia (e.g., 12:1-12); also he described conditions and events happening in his homeland, such as Pelatiah's sudden death (11:13) and Nebuchadnezzar's consulting omens at a crossroads as the Babylonian army approached Jerusalem (21:18-23).

Many modern scholars have adopted the view Pfeiffer has advocated because it would seem to be scientifically impossible for a man in Babylon to be ministering effectively to people hundreds of miles across the desert. But they discount the reality of visionary or spiritual transport (8:1-3; 11:24) and of direct revelation from God about immediate events in Jerusalem (e.g., 24:1-2). Furthermore, Ezekiel's words were relevant in Tel-abib, for in God's reckoning the 10,000 or more Jewish captives in Babylon (II Kgs 24:14) were as much His covenant people as those still in Judah. They were one in equally needing purification of heart and instruction concerning the reason for the destruction of their holy city. Moreover, as Jer 29 indicates, there was communication by ordinary travel between Palestine and Mesopotamia; thus the words and actions of Ezekiel could be reported to the Jerusalem community.

There are unconsciously designed bits of evidence that speak of a Babylonian locale for chaps. 1-24, such as a city map drawn on a clay tablet or brick (4:1-4)—a map of this kind has been found in the ruins of Nippur—and digging through a wall (12:1-7), possible of a mud-brick or adobe house common in Babylonia but not of the typical stone wall in the hill country of Judah. The many Babylonian words, idioms, and imagery also suggest that Ezekiel spoke and wrote in a proper Babylonian milieu (R. Tournay, "A propos des babylonismes d'Ezeckiel," RB, LXVIII [1961], 388-393). And as Carl G. Howie points out, Jews would have been very reluctant to admit that a genuine prophet was speaking outside the land, unless there were overwhelming evidence for such a conclusion (IDB, II, 206a; cf. Harry M. Orlinsky, "Where Did Ezekiel Receive the Call to Prophesy?" BASOR #122 [1951], 34-36). Therefore the interpretation of C. C. Torrey that the book was a pseudepigraph written in Palestine c. 230 B.C., a purely fictional account of events in the reign of Manasseh (*Pseudo-Ezekiel and the Original Prophecy,* 1930), may be dismissed.

Third, some scholars have argued that the presence of Aramaisms in the book must prove it was written in the post-Exilic period. But Aramaic had become the lingua franca of the Assyrian Empire from the latter half of the 8th cen. onward, and the Aramaic influence in Ezekiel is no more than one would expect for one writing in Mesopotamia in the 6th cen. B.C.

Others have rejected chaps. 38-39 and/or 40-48 as not belonging to Ezekiel because of their apocalyptic nature, this type of literature supposedly not having originated until the Hellenistic period. The same authors would date Daniel to the Maccabean period. Again one sees an antisupernatural bias at work, refusing to recognize the historical arguments in favor of the traditional 6th cen. B.C. date of these prophecies. The relative unimportance of Persia in Ezk 27:10 and 38:5 and its complete absence in chaps. 1-24 argue strongly for a time of writing before the rise of Cyrus c. 550 B.C. The gates of the future millennial temple (cf. 40:6-16) with three guardrooms on either side follow the pattern of excavated Solomonic gates at Megiddo, Gezer, and Hazor, whose plan was later discontinued, and was meaningful therefore only to one who had seen the temple of Solomon prior to its destruction in 586 B.C.

Purpose and Theme

The theme of Ezekiel is the glory and transcendence of the Lord. The Jews in exile must realize that their God has not been defeated by heathen powers but is justified in judging His own; that He is not limited to divine activity within the confines of Palestine but is present with them in far-off Babylon.

The vision of the throne-chariot of the Lord (Ezk 1) reveals the ability of God's governing power to go quickly anywhere on earth or above the earth—His omnipresence. He is enthroned above all creation—inanimate (represented by wind, cloud, and fire, 1:4) and animate (represented by the four cherubim; cf. Ezk 1:5-11 with 10:8; I Kgs 6:23-28)—symbolizing His omnipotence. Not only is He sovereign in His dealings with His chosen nation of Israel but also with the seven neighboring heathen nations that are exulting over her fall (Ezk 25-32). Them He will destroy for their pride and hatred of God's people (Babylon is not included, perhaps because that nation is the instrument of God's justice, cf. 29:17-20), but Israel He will purge and correct and restore as an act of His grace that will lead them to repentance (36:16-32). God's purpose is that both Israel and the nations "will know that I am the Lord"— a phrase that occurs some 30 times in 6:7-39:28.

The triumphant note of Ezekiel's prophecy is sounded in the last few words of the book: "the Lord is there." This will be the name, the very character, of the new, restored Jerusalem of the future millennial kingdom on earth. In a rebuilt literal temple, reminiscent of Solomon's, worship will be conducted with blood sacrifices, having sacramental but not propitiatory significance (Gleason Archer, SOTI, pp. 362 ff.). It will be a provisional economy pointing forward to the purely spiritual, eternal forms of worship without a temple promised in Rev 21:9-22:5.

Ezekiel was the first prophet to underscore the truth of individual responsibility (18:1-32; 33:1-20). Even though each may be a member of the covenant community, there is no such possession as inherited righteousness. Conversely, each may escape the judgment of his fathers by personally turning from his sins and observing God's ordinances.

Style and Literary Influence

Ezekiel uses more symbolism and allegory than any other OT prophet. His figures of speech are not dependent on heathen sources but have their foundation in the sanctuary of Israel and in the concepts of his predecessors, educated as he was under Levitical training. Nevertheless, he is unexcelled for the vividness of his poetic descriptions. Certainly he was a true mystic with an artistic imagination which the Spirit of God could employ to depict in human terms realities from the unseen spirit world (e.g., the king of Tyre evidently motivated by Satan, Ezk 28:11-19). None is so sensitive to the supernatural activity of the Spirit, and thus we turn to Ezekiel for much of the doctrine about the Holy Spirit in the OT.

Ezekiel shaped a type of prophecy known as the apocalyptic. It is characterized by the frequency of visions and emphasis on the future or eschatological period with its tremendous catastrophic movements and direct interventions from heaven. John was dependent on Ezekiel for many of the figures and concepts in the

Apocalypse (cf. Rev 1:15; 4:3, 6 with Ezk 1:22–28; Gog and Magog in Rev 20:8 with Ezk 38–39; the careful measuring and description of the city, etc., in Rev 11:1; 21:10–27 with Ezk 40–48; the river of life in Rev 22:1–2 with Ezk 47:1–12).

The significance of a good shepherd (Jn 10:1–30) is dependent on Ezk 34 as much as on Ps 23. The Lord Jesus seems to have turned to Ezekiel as well as to Dan 7:13–14 for the title He used most often of Himself, viz., the Son of Man. (For a thorough discussion of this term see Andrew W. Blackwood, Jr., *The Other Son of Man: Ezekiel/Jesus*, Baker, 1966, pp. 11–25.)

Contents

The book divides easily into two major parts separated by a collection of foreign oracles. The division is based on news of the siege and fall of Jerusalem (24:1–2; 33:21). Chaps. 1–24 in the main contain denunciations of the wickedness during the reign of Zedekiah, the last king of Judah, whereas chaps. 33–48 are occupied with promises to the future remnant of Israel.

A fourfold division of the book is also possible:

I.   God's Commissioning of Ezekiel, Chaps. 1–3

II.   Prophecies Concerning the Sins of Judah (dated 592–588 B.C., before the fall of Jerusalem), Chaps. 4–24

III. Prophecies Concerning the Punishment of Neighboring Nations (dated 587–585 B.C.; 29:17–21 dated 571 B.C.), Chaps. 25–32
    A. Against Ammon, Moab, Edom, Philistia, 25:1–17
    B. Against Tyre and Sidon, 26:1–28:26
    C. Against Egypt, 29:1–32:32

IV. Prophecies and Visions of Restored Israel in Their Land (dated 585–573 B.C., after the fall of Jerusalem), Chaps. 33–48
    A. Stages in the restoration and spiritual renewal of land and people, 33:1–39:29
    B. Visions of the future temple and worship in the glorious land, 40:1–48:35

Bibliography. G. A. Cooke, *The Book of Ezekiel*, ICC. H. L. Ellison, *Ezekiel: the Man and His Message*, Grand Rapids: Eerdmans, 1956. Carl G. Howie, *The Date and Composition of Ezekiel*, JBL Monograph Series, IV, 1950; "Ezekiel," IDB, II, 203–213. Anton T. Pearson, "Ezekiel," WBC, with bibliography of the older works. Samuel J. Schultz, *The OT Speaks*, New York: Harper, 1960, pp. 345–363. John B. Taylor, *Ezekiel: An Introduction and Commentary*, London: Tyndale Press, 1969. C. F. Whitley, *The Exilic Age*,

Philadelphia: Westminster, 1957. Walter Zimmerli, "The Message of the Prophet Ezekiel," *Interp.*, XXIII (1969), 131–157.

                                  J. R.

EZEL (ē'zĕl). There is wide difference of opinion as to the meaning of this word. Jonathan met David on their farewell parting (I Sam 20:19, 41 f.) by the stone Ezel (Heb. *hā'āzel*). The RSV, following the LXX, emends the passage to read, "beside yonder stone heap," and in v. 41 translates, "David rose from beside the stone heap." Regardless of the exact meaning, the field where David hid lay between Gibeah and Nob.

EZEM (ē'zĕm). *See* Azem.

EZER (ē'zĕr)
1. A son of Seir, the Horite, a native chief in Edom (Gen 36:21, 27, 30; I Chr 1:38, 42).
2. The father of Hushah, one of the descendants of Hur (I Chr 4:4).
3. A descendant of Ephraim who, with his brother Elead, was slain by the Gathites (I Chr 7:21).
4. The foremost of the Gadite warriors who joined David at Ziklag. They were famed for having boldly crossed the Jordan in the spring when it had overflowed its banks (I Chr 12:8–15).
5. A Levite, the son of Jeshua the ruler of Mizpah, who aided in building the wall of Jerusalem (Neh 3:19).
6. A priest who took part in the great dedication of the completed wall of Jerusalem in the days of Nehemiah (Neh 12:42).

EZION-GEBER (ē'zĭ-ŏn-gē'bĕr). In between the present-day cities of Elath and Aqabah in "no-man's land" lies the ancient site of the Solomonic fortified storehouse, which was built near the port anciently called Ezion-geber. It is identified with Elath (Eloth) in Deut 2:8; II Chr 8:17; I Kgs 9:26, and is also most probably to be identified with El-paran of Gen 14:6. *See* Elath. It is situated at the N end of the E arm of the Red Sea (*see* Aqabah, Gulf of). The Israelites encamped in this area when they left Sinai more than a year after departing from Egypt. From here they went on to Kadesh (Num 33:35–36).

Ezion-geber is not mentioned again in the OT until the time of Solomon. At this time (I Kgs 9:26–28; II Chr 8:17–18) Hiram (Huram), the king of Tyre, from whom Solomon had obtained both artisans and materials for building the temple, now sent him ships and sailors to ply the waters of the Red Sea from Ezion-geber. This commerce undoubtedly enriched both Solomon and Hiram and made good use of the products of copper mines located N of Ezion-geber along the Arabah, now known only from archaeological excavation. These "ships of Tarshish" (*q.v.*) took three years to make a round trip out of Ezion-geber to the foreign ports along the coasts of Africa, Arabia, and perhaps as far as India and Ceylon (I Kgs 10:22). Along with large quantities of gold (of Ophir) and silver, other articles of trade were ivory, spices, precious stones, wood (almug, I Kgs 10:11–12), apes, and peacocks. Solomon and his merchants became rich by shipping out of Ezion-geber copper, iron, olive oil, and possibly many products manufactured in Egypt, such as linen and chariots (I Kgs 10:28–29). Solomon had no great ports on the Mediterranean, but his alliance with the Phoenicians gave him access to their ports just as he gave Hiram of Tyre access to Ezion-geber. *See* Hiram; Navy.

Following Solomon, the activity of this port was a key to the prosperity of the land. Those kings of Judah who desired to show themselves powerful attempted to re-establish the fleet out of Ezion-geber. Jehoshaphat came nearest to success, but a storm or some other natural disaster destroyed the ships (I Kgs 22:48). A little known prophet, Eliezer of Mareshah, interpreted this disaster as punishment for Jehoshaphat's alliance with the wicked house of Ahab in the venture (II Chr 20:37). Throughout the rest of the history of the southern kingdom, whenever Judah was weak the Edomites took control of the Ezion-geber and Elath territory (cf. II Kgs 8:20–22; 14:22; 16:6; II Chr 28:17).

The port continued into Persian times as an important link between S Arabia, the coast of Africa, and the western world of the Mediterranean Sea. The excavations of Ezion-geber by Nelson Glueck prior to World War II (1938–40) amply prove this point. For example, Glueck discovered black Attic (Gr.) ware of the 5th cen. B.C., and two jars incised with S Arabian Minaean script in the 8th cen. B.C. level, which underline the prominence of Ezion-geber as a trade link (N. Glueck, BASOR #71 [1938], 15–16; #75 [1939], 19; #80 [1940], 3–10; #82 [1941], 3–16). Glueck's major find was Solomon's citadel with a large storehouse-granary for goods being shipped along the land and sea trade routes intersecting at Ezion-geber (BA, XXVIII [Sept., 1965], 70–87). A seal probably bearing the name of Jotham, the son of Uzziah, witnesses to the brief restoration of the port of Judah, according to II Kgs 14:22. *See* Archaeology; Commerce; Elath.

Bibliography. Y. Aharoni, "Forerunners of the Limes: Iron Age Fortresses in the Negev," IEJ, XVII (1967), 15–17. V. R. Gold, "Ezion-geber," BW, 233–237.

E. B. S.

EZNITE (ĕz'nīt). This word is used in a list of the mighty men of David, "Adino the Eznite" (II Sam 23:8). The meaning is uncertain. *See* Adino.

EZRA (ĕz'rá)

1. A priest who returned to Jerusalem with Zerubbabel (Neh 12:1, 13).

2. A priest in Nehemiah's time (Neh 12:33).

3. A priest-scribe, son of Seraiah (Ezr 7:1), who led a group of exiles back to Jerusalem. Best known from the book which bears his name, Ezra was designated in several ways: as priest (Ezr 10:10, 16; Neh 8:2), as scribe (Ezr 7:6; Neh 12:36), and as priest and scribe (Ezr 7:11–12, 21; Neh 8:9; 12:26). Although his work as scribe is well known, many fail to recognize the claim (Ezr 7:1–6) that his priestly lineage could be traced back through Zadok and Phinehas to Aaron. This placed him in the main stream of Jerusalem priesthood. His name is either a late form of *'ezrà*, "help," or an abbreviation of *'azaryahû*, "Yahweh helps."

Various sources of information are available for the reconstruction of Ezra's life and ministry. From the book of Ezra, the memoirs in the first person are of special importance (cf. most of Ezr 7:27–9:15). The Aramaic letters as well as the Heb. documents throughout the book give further background. The material in Neh 8–10 adds to the picture while also raising certain problems. There are also allusions to the work of Ezra in I and II Esdras of the Apocrypha.

His commission. In the seventh year of Artaxerxes (cf. below for problem of date), Ezra was commissioned by royal decree to go to Jerusalem for the purpose of evaluating the civil and religious conditions of the Judean community and instituting necessary corrective measures. He was given authority both in terms of money and goods for the temple and exemptions from taxation of the temple officials. Many have questioned the historicity of the sweeping authority given Ezra. Even though the powers are extensive, the king of Persia could well have needed the support of the provinces. He could gain gratitude without any risk to his empire by patronizing the needs of such neglected groups.

Ezra's commission also authorized him to gather a company of exiles who desired to return with him to Jerusalem. After mustering the group, fasting, and offering prayer, Ezra led them out on their journey. Reaching Jerusalem four months later, he presented his orders to the neighboring governors and turned over the temple vessels to the priestly officials. The community at Jerusalem was poor and backward compared with the culture of the Jewish group in Babylonia. It is difficult to estimate how much the arrival of Ezra meant to the struggling community at Jerusalem.

Date of his return. A superficial reading of the books of Ezra and Nehemiah leaves no doubt as to the chronological order of Ezra and Nehemiah. However, an unresolved controversy has raged since 1889 when Maurice Vernes made the suggestion that Nehemiah came first. (Cf. H. H. Rowley's essay, "Chronological Order of Ezra and Nehemiah," in *The Servant of the Lord and Other Essays on the Old Testament,* for a comprehensive listing of theories and scholars involved.) Rowley sums up the difficulty by saying: "It is therefore clear that bold claims, on the one side or the other, that the question is definitely settled are unjustified" (p. 135). Actually, no more than a balance of probability is justified at this point.

On the basis of the biblical text, Ezra appears to have arrived in 458 B.C., the seventh year of Artaxerxes I Longimanus (465-424 B.C.). According to many scholars, the king of Persia referred to should be Artaxerxes II Mnemon (404-358 B.C.). This would place Ezra's return in 398 B.C., long after Nehemiah's governorship. Three passages give the primary reasons for the later date: (1) Ezr 9:9 mentions the rebuilding of a wall, whereas the walls of Jerusalem were rebuilt by Nehemiah after his return in 444 B.C. (2) Ezr 10:1 suggests a greater population than Nehemiah found (cf. Neh 7:4). (3) Ezr 10:6 refers to Johanan (Jehohanan, RSV), as Ezra's contemporary, whereas Eliashib, the grandfather of a later high priest named Johanan, is the high priest in the time of Nehemiah (cf. Neh 3:1, 20; 12:22-23). It is known from the Elephantine papyri that a Johanan was high priest in 407 B.C. However, the arguments are not entirely conclusive, leaving the balance of probability in favor of the traditional order.

The long gap between the events in Ezra (458 B.C.) and the coming of Nehemiah (444 B.C.) also presents a problem. This has been explained as being occasioned by the alienation of the people toward Ezra over the compulsory divorces. However, Ezra may have returned to the Persian court and then have made a second visit to Jerusalem as a coadjutor to Nehemiah. Ezra's original commission may well have been a temporary appointment as in the case of Nehemiah. Surely the moral lapses which Nehemiah discovered would not have occurred if Ezra had been on the scene during the intervening years (458-444 B.C.). *See* Nehemiah.

His personality. Ezra was representative of those in Babylonia whose concern was for the nation's sacred heritage and writings. He was a diligent student of the law, a leading figure in the new order of scribes which had grown up during the Exile.

Much in Ezra reminds us of Nehemiah. They both demonstrated outstanding leadership qualities, unbounded energy, intense faith, and similar spiritual aims. However, Ezra's supreme work lay in his abilities as teacher, historian, critic, and linguist. While he was rigorous and narrow in matters of law, he was able to achieve lasting success. He gave determination and stubbornness to Judaism which made it able to resist the inroads of Hellenism. He was passionate and emotional but always exhibited strong faith in God. His asceticism was severe as he emphasized fasting and disciplined him-

self. Yet his interest in bringing back the temple vessels and treasures classifies him as a patron of sacred art.

His contribution. As a scribe, Ezra has always been remembered for his important editorial work on parts of the OT Scriptures. While much tradition has grown up around his name, he certainly was representative of those who helped in the collecting, arranging, and editing of the law.

As a religious leader, Ezra has a unique place in Jewish tradition, being often described as the true founder of Judaism, the second founder of the Jewish State, or the founder of the Great Synagogue. His work in renewing the spiritual power and vitality of Israel was indeed significant. Much of the work in adapting the pre-Exilic liturgical practices to post-Exilic Jewish worship can be credited to his spiritual leadership.

As a reformer, Ezra's name will always be linked with the enforced divorces with which he attempted to purify racial lines in order to preserve Israel's religious heritage. It is exceedingly difficult to justify the extreme measures employed as the homes of 17 priests, 6 Levites, 1 singer, 3 doorkeepers, and 86 laymen were torn asunder. However, it must be remembered that marriage in ancient times was viewed as a community matter.

Bibliography. John Bright, "The Date of Ezra's Mission to Jerusalem," *Yehezkel Kaufmann Jubilee Volume, Studies in Bible and Jewish Religion,* ed. by M. Haran, Jerusalem: Magnes Press, 1960, pp. 70-88. "Restoration and Persian Period; Ezra and Nehemiah," CornPBE, pp. 617-622. George Rawlinson, *Ezra and Nehemiah, Their Lives and Times,* London: Nisbet, 1891. H. H. Rowley, *The Servant of the Lord and Other Essays on the Old Testament,* London: Lutterworth, 1952. A. C. Welch, *Postexilic Judaism,* Edinburgh: Blackwood, 1935. J. S. Wright, *The Date of Ezra's Coming to Jerusalem,* London: Tyndale, 1947.

K. M. Y.

EZRA, BOOK OF. The book which bears Ezra's name was originally combined with Nehemiah as a single volume. This was true in Heb. MSS until separated in a MS dated in A.D. 1448. However, the books were known as separate works to Origen and Jerome in certain Gr. MSS.

Outline

I. The First Return, 1:1-2:70
   A. Permission to return, 1:1-11
   B. Register of returnees, 2:1-70
II. The Rebuilding of the Temple, 3:1-6:22
   A. Altar and foundations of temple set up, 3:1-13
   B. Hindrances to the work, 4:1-5, 24
   C. Later opposition, 4:6-23
   D. Completion of the temple, 5:1-6:22

III. The Activity of Ezra, 7:1 – 10:44
    A. Commission to Erza, 7:1–28
    B. Coming of Ezra, 8:1–36
    C. Problem of mixed marriages, 9:1– 10:44

Sources

The composite nature of the book is at once evident, especially so in the MT. The shift from first to third to first person pronouns and the alternating use of Heb. and Aram. are easily recognized. The book has combined the following:

1. Memoirs of Ezra (7:27 – 9:15). These were written in the first person. These may have been an abstract of the report which Ezra had to make to the Persian court.

2. Aramaic documents (4:7– 16; 4:18– 22; 5:7– 17; 6:3– 12; 7:12– 26). These include letters, official and semiofficial documents.

3. Hebrew documents (1:2-4; 2:1-70; 8:1– 14; 10:18– 44). These undoubtedly came mainly from state archives.

Authorship

According to the Talmud (*Baba Bathra* 15a) and other evidences of Heb. tradition, Ezra wrote both the book bearing his name and the book of Nehemiah. However, it is almost universally held today that Chronicles, Ezra, and Nehemiah originally formed one work. Since the closing verses of II Chronicles also stand at the beginning of Ezra, the order has probably been reversed. The term the Chronicler is usually assigned to the author of the entire work. Although many scholars recognize Ezra as the Chronicler, others place the work of compiling these books toward the end of the 4th cen. (c. 330 B.C.). The great linguistic similarities, however, with 5th cen. Aram. papyri from the Jewish community at Elephantine, Egypt, argue for a date in Ezra's period. *See* Elephantine Papyri.

K. M. Y.

EZRAHITE (ĕz′rá-hīt). A descendant of Zerah of the tribe of Judah, as Ethan the Ezrahite (I Kgs 4:31; I Chr 2:16; Ps 89, title), whose wisdom was exceeded only by that of Solomon. Heman, his brother, is called the Ezrahite in the title of Ps 88. Or I Kgs 4:31 could mean that Ethan was an *'ezrāḥî*, a native, i.e., Israelite trained, as opposed to Heman, Chalcol, and Darda, members of a Canaanite orchestral guild ("sons of Mahol").

EZRI (ĕz′rī). A servant of David, the son of Chelub, placed over the tilling of the ground (I Chr 27:26).

F

FABLE. In the KJV and ASV NT, fable (which does not occur in the OT) is used to translate *mythos*. This Gr. word has also been translated "fiction" (Goodspeed), "myth" (NEB), "fairy tale" (Phillips, Tit 1:14), etc. At one time the word was almost synonymous with the Gr. *logos* and *rhēma*, "word" (cf. Trench, p. 337). Before NT times it had come to mean that which was fictitious as opposed to *logos* – the true expression or utterance (Jn 1:1). In the NT it carries this sense in all its occurrences (I Tim 1:4; 4:7; II Tim 4:4; Tit 1:14; II Pet 1:16). In these letters the word probably refers to fictitious stories concocted by Jewish teachers (Tit 1:14), based on the OT and devised to turn Christians away from the truth.

There are fables in the OT, though the term is not used to so designate them. Compare Jotham's fable of the trees choosing their king (Jud 9:7–21), and Jehoash's fable of the cedar of Lebanon and the thistle (II Kgs 14:8– 10).

J. McR.

FACE. Used to denote the part of an object most exposed to view; hence, the face of the ground, water, sky, etc. In Scripture, it often denotes presence in the general sense; and when used of God, means His presence in a vivid sense. Adam and Eve hid from "the face of Jehovah," or from His presence. Because of the glory of God, Moses was told, "Thou canst not see my face: for there shall no man see me, and live" (Ex 33:20). Thus, no one in his present state of being can endure the full blaze of God's glory (I Cor 13:12; I Jn 3:2; Rev 22:4). However, when the brightness of His glory is veiled, man may behold such revelation (Gen 32:30; Jn 1:14). The "bread of the face" was the showbread, denoting God's presence. *See* Bread of Faces.

The word also implied favor, anger, justice, severity (Ps 44:3; 67:1; Dan 9:17; Gen 16:6, 8; Ex 2:15; Rev 6:16). "To hide the face" or "to fall on the face" expressed humility and reverence (Ex 3:6; Isa 6:2), and "the covering of the face" was a sign of mourning (II Sam 19:4). "To set one's face" denoted determination (Lk 9:51), and "to turn away one's face" expressed apathy or contempt (II Chr 29:6; Ezk 14:6).

Bibliography. Eduard Lohse, *"Prosōpon*, etc.," TDNT, VI, 768– 780.

E. C. J.

FAIR. Several shades of meaning are found in the use of this word.

1. Heb. *ṭāhôr* means "to shine," "be bright"; hence, "clean," "pure," thus "fair." It is used of physical, moral, or ritual fairness (Prov 22:11, KJV "pureness"). Used physically it is opposed to filthy (Zech 3:3– 5).

2. Heb. *ṭôb* means "to be bright," "cheer-

ful," "good," or "well." It also suggests beauty in the expression "fair young virgins" (Est 2:2).

3. Heb. *yāpeh* refers to "fairness as beautiful," such as a beautiful figure, beauty of aspect (Song 1:15-16; 4:1, 7; 6:10).

4. Heb. *leqaḥ*, "learning," is used of fair speech (KJV), captivating charms, learning or knowledge (Prov 7:21; cf. Rom 16:18).

5. Heb. *zāhāb* means "to shine or glitter" as gold, and suggests golden light as "fair weather" (Job 37:22, KJV); perhaps the aurora borealis is thus signified. In the NT "fair weather" translates the Gr. *eudia* (Mt 16:2).

FAIR HAVENS. A small bay on the S coast of Crete, about five miles E of Cape Lithinos. Paul's ship anchored there for a time while en route to Rome (Acts 27:8-12). The bay, which still retains its ancient name, is exposed on the E but protected on the SW by two small islands. Paul urged remaining there for the winter, but the ship's owner wanted to sail about 50 miles W of Phenice (Phoenix), a safer winter harbor. (Normally, ancient ships did not sail the Mediterranean during the stormy months of Nov. to Mar.) After leaving Fair Havens the vessel was driven from its course by a violent northeaster and ultimately was wrecked off Malta. *See* Melita.

FAIRS. Although "fairs" is one possible rendering of the Heb. word *'izzābôn*, it is translated in later versions by "wares," "merchandise." From Ezekiel's usage of the word it appears that it could mean either the place where trading was done or the objects involved in the trading (Ezk 27:12, 14, 16, 19, 27).

FAITH. Faith is a NT word. It occurs only twice in the OT of the KJV (Deut 32:20; Hab 2:4). The ASV translates the first reference (Heb. *'ēmùn*) "faithfulness." The ASV retains "faith" in the second text (giving "faithfulness" in the marg., Heb. *'ĕmûnâ*), possibly because of the frequent quotation of the text in the NT, in which the idea is clearly that of faith in the active sense (cf. Rom 1:17; Gal 3:11; Heb 10:38). The equivalent OT word is "trust." The word "trust" and its related forms occur more than 150 times in the OT, the translation of a number of different Heb. words. The NT word *pistis* (see Arndt) is used both in the sense of faithfulness (Rom 3:3; Gal 5:22; Tit 2:10) and of trust (Mk 11:22; Mt 8:10; Lk 5:20; Rom 3:22, 28; etc.). *See* Faithfulness; Fidelity; Amen.

Faith is the basic virtue in the NT (I Cor 13:13; Heb 11:6; II Pet 1:5-7). Even so, there is no formal definition of faith in the Bible. Concerning the passage sometimes so presented (Heb 11:1), Dean F. W. Farrar observed: "The famous words with which this chapter opens are not so much a definition as a description. They are not a definition, for they do not, as St. Thomas Aquinas says, indicate the essence of faith. They tell us what faith does, rather than what it is—its issues, rather than its nature. 'Faith,' the writer says, 'is the basis of things hoped for, the demonstration of objects not seen.' This is what faith is in its results. It furnishes us with a foundation on which our hopes can securely rest, and with a conviction that those things exist which are not earthly or temporal, and which, therefore, we cannot see."

A proper definition of faith must take into consideration its complexity, for while the exercise of it may be said to be simplicity itself, it involves the whole personality. Knowledge is necessary (Rom 10:13-17). However, while intellectual grasp of the truth to be believed is not faith, it is part of it. Assent to the truth to be believed is necessary (Mt 9:28; Jas 2:19); however, assent may be no more than admitting the veracity of the thing to be believed, without carrying any committal with it. The element without which we do not have biblical faith, is the consent of the volition, or "the consent of the will to the assent of the understanding" (cf. Jn 8:30-31, ASV).

Saving faith, therefore, involves active personal trust, a commitment of oneself to the Lord Jesus Christ. But it is not the amount of faith that saves, it is the object of faith that saves. Great faith in the wrong object does not alter man's lost estate one iota. Little faith (so long as it is faith) in the right object must result in salvation. As an article of religion puts it: "We may thus rely on Christ, either tremblingly or confidantly; but in either case it is saving faith. If, though tremblingly, we rely on Him in His obedience for us unto death, instantly we come into union with Him, and are justified. If, however, we confidantly rely on Him, then have we the comfort of our justification. Simply by faith in Christ are we justified and saved" (Reformed Episcopal usage). In general biblical usage, to believe is to have such full-fledged faith in Christ, to entrust oneself to Him. The first term which the Christians used to describe themselves was "the believers" (Acts 2:44; 4:32; 5:14; etc.). *See* Believe; Believers.

It should be observed that there are most blessed and real results when an individual truly trusts the Lord Jesus Christ. There is not only a changed position before God (justification), but there is the beginning of the redemptive and sanctifying work of God. While the transformation of life is not the ground of salvation, it is the evidence of salvation. And without some such evidence (in greater or lesser degree), a question must be raised as to the genuineness of the faith of the individual. Within bounds, we agree with the dictum of Dr. C. I. Scofield: "Faith which does not impel to action, which does not result in a changed relation to God and Christ, which does not work transformingly in life, is not biblical faith." Unbelief everywhere in the Bible is equated with disobedience (cf. Jn 3:36, KJV with ASV), and is considered the most serious of sins (Heb 3:12-18).

The good works of a Christian are the result of and the evidence for the genuineness of his faith. It is an understanding of this fact which will solve the problem of some as to an alleged discrepancy between Paul and James. Paul certainly relates good works to faith (Eph 2:8-10). James surely is clear that he is speaking of justification before men (Jas 2:18 – "show me," "show thee"; v. 22 – "thou seest"; v. 24 – "ye see"; v. 26), and that faith is proved by works (v. 22).

Faith is not only related to salvation from sin for the Christian, it is connected with God's providence and leading (Mk 11:22; Heb 11:6; Prov 3:5-6; Ps 37:3, ASV; Acts 27:25), with sanctification (Gal 3:1-3; Acts 26:18; II Cor 5:7; Gal 2:20, ASV; Col 2:6-7), with service (Rom 12:6; Gal 5:6; I Thess 1:3; II Thess 1:11; I Tim 6:12; Heb 11:33; Jas 2:22), and with prayer (Mt 21:22; Heb 11:6; Jas 1:5-8).

The relationship of repentance and faith is a frequently discussed theological question. In Paul's summation of his Ephesian ministry he spoke of "testifying both to the Jews, and also to the Greeks, repentance toward God, and faith toward our Lord Jesus Christ" (Acts 20:21; cf. 11:17-18; 26:18-20). It is probable that knowledge (*notitia*) and assent (*assensus*) precede repentance (a change of mind) as they precede trust (*fiducia*). Repentance, in this view, precedes trust. Thus faith is not genuine saving faith unless it involves repentance (*q.v.*).

Another theological question involving faith is that which is raised in any *ordo salutis* (order of salvation). One matter of concern is the relationship of regeneration and faith. The difference among evangelicals is represented by the Lutheran, the Arminian, and the Reformed conceptions. In the Lutheran view, calling, repentance, and regeneration are preparatory in the sinner's coming to Christ; since salvation is not imparted until the sinner exercises faith, it is necessary to maintain faith. The Reformed view regards regeneration, repentance, and faith as "blessings of the covenant of grace," not merely as preparatory or as conditions consummated by human initiative. In the Arminian concept, God grants grace to all men which enables them to believe and obey the gospel; a man is justified "on account of his faith."

Whatever view is held, it may be observed that there must be the response of faith for experiential salvation (Acts 8:37; 16:31; Eph 2:8). Indeed, such a concept is taught in the chapter on the new birth (Jn 3:14-16). Further, the Lord Himself spoke of the dead hearing His voice, and this reference must be to those spiritually dead (Jn 5:25-29; notice evident contrast in v. 29). However, there can be no question concerning either the sovereign choice of God (Acts 13:48; Rom 8:29, ASV; Eph 1:4-5), or the necessity of God's initiating the salvation of a man (Rom 3:10b-18; I Cor 2:14; Eph 2:8-9).

The expression "the faith" on occasion refers to "that which is believed, *body of faith* or *belief, doctrine*" (Arndt). The same lexicon says that "this objectivizing of the *pistis* concept is found as early as Paul." Even those scholars who acknowledge the usage of "the faith" in this sense, differ as to the references in which it appears. A suggested list follows: Lk 18:8; Acts 3:16; 6:7; 13:8; 14:22; 16:5; 24:24; I Cor 16:13; II Cor 13:5; Gal 1:23; 3:23-25; Eph 4:13; Phil 1:27; Col 1:23; 2:7; II Thess 3:2; I Tim 1:19; 3:9, 13; 4:1, 6; 5:8; 6:10, 21; II Tim 3:8; 4:7; Tit 1:13; Jas 2:1; Jude 3; Rev 14:12.

See Faith, The Christian; Faith, Rule of.

Bibliography. Rudolf Bultmann and Artur Weiser, "*Pisteuō*, etc.," TDNT, VI, 174-228. J. Oliver Buswell, Jr., *A Systematic Theology of the Christian Religion*, Grand Rapids: Zondervan, 1962, II, 175-186 (with good discussion of *pisteuō*, "to believe," in John's Gospel). Lewis Sperry Chafer, *Systematic Theology*, Dallas: Dallas Sem. Press, 1947-57, III, 372-378; VI, 293-294. Vernon C. Grounds, "The Nature of Faith," *Christian Faith and Modern Theology*, ed. by Carl F. H. Henry, New York: Channel Press, 1964, pp. 325-345 (including a discussion of Kierkegaard's understanding of faith and a full bibliography on the various aspects of faith). J. Gresham Machen, *What Is Faith?* Grand Rapids: Eerdmans, 1946 (the best volume on faith from an evangelical viewpoint). James I. Packer, "Faith," BDT, pp. 208-211. Benjamin B. Warfield, "Faith," HDB; *Biblical Doctrines*, New York: Oxford Univ. Press, 1929, Chap. 13; *Biblical and Theological Studies*, Philadelphia: Presbyterian and Reformed, 1952, pp. 375-444. See article on Theology for names and works of other recommended theologians.

W. C.

FAITH, THE CHRISTIAN. Christianity is that interpretation of existence which, as a thoroughgoing system of supernaturalism, stands in polar antithesis to atheistic naturalism. A radical monotheism, it is also the polar antithesis of polytheism. Teaching that God is self-subsisting, personal, living, ethical, dynamic, and sovereign, it is likewise the polar antithesis of pantheism and deism. Yet because it holds to the triunity of the Godhead, the Christian faith must be sharply differentiated from such species of monotheism as Judaism and Islam.

Structured upon the gracious activities of revelation and redemption, it postulates man's creation in the divine image; his apostasy, his guilt, his lostness; but his possibility of forgiveness through the miracles of incarnation, atonement, and resurrection – three history-splitting events which center in Jesus Christ. When the Mediator's person and work are appropriated by a sinner in trustful self-commitment, a new God-relationship is established. This experience is theologically formulated in the doctrines of regeneration, justification, and sanctification (*q.v.*). Christianity anticipates its Lord's second advent and His judgment of all mankind. Life, this faith holds, will continue eternally beyond death not in mere survival of disembodied souls but in a raising up of transformed bodies, with believers enjoying God's fellowship while unbelievers will endure unending punishment. And the dominant recurring theme of this cosmic drama is *sola gloria Deo* (to God be all the glory)!

V. C. G.

FAITH, RULE OF. Originally used to designate the summary of Christian doctrine taught to catechumens before baptism, the phrase, *regula fidei*, quickly became a technical term in theology; and as a synonym for the source and standard of belief, it likewise became the focus of significant controversy.

What is the norm of saving truth, the definitive criterion of dogma and practice, the canon of Christianity? Is it Scripture plus tradition, plus some ecclesiastical *magisterium* which functions as an authoritative interpreter? This has been the Roman Catholic and Greek Orthodox view, though Orthodoxy does not accept the papacy as the exclusive seat of interpretation, nor does it regard the pronouncements of any except the earlier church councils as binding. Is that criterion some mystical inner light? Disciples of Robert Barclay, the leading Quaker theologian, have so argued. Or is it a fusion of reason and conscience? With various modifications, liberalism has adopted that position. Or is it rather Scripture alone? This was the Reformation watchword, its *principium cognoscendi,* paralleling the material principle of justification by faith alone. Historic Protestantism contended—and still contends—that Scripture, Spirit interpreted, is the sole and sufficient norm of Christianity, rendering any extrabiblical supplement unnecessary.

Agreeing apologetically, Calvinists and Lutherans have divided on this issue polemically. Calvinists have taken rigorist ground, arguing that nothing is warranted unless Scripture expressly declares it. Lutherans have been less inflexible, accepting those practices which do not contradict Scripture. But all Reformed Christians concur with Chillingworth, "The Bible, the Bible alone, is the religion of Protestants."

Bibliography. Gabriel Moran, *Scripture and Tradition: A Survey of the Controversy,* New York: Herder & Herder, 1963. W. P. Patterson, *The Rule of Faith,* London: Hodder and Stoughton, 1912.

V. C. G.

FAITHFULNESS. God, as biblically revealed, is living and personal, hence the possessor of a certain character. Central to that character is faithfulness or utter dependability. Jas 1:17 brings out God's steadfastness, which is the antithesis of everything fickle and fluctuating. Very similar is II Tim 2:13 which declares that God's faithfulness is the corollary of His self-consistency. These NT passages highlight the same trait which is metaphorically expressed in those OT texts that call the Lord a Rock (Deut 32:4, 15, 18). In other words, God's character is the solid and unshakable foundation of reality. Hence His covenant is inviolable (Deut 7:9), His word more steadfast than the law-abiding framework of nature (Mt 7:24–27; 24:35; Lk 21:33). Because He is faithful, God's promises are infallibly reliable (Heb 10:23). God stands by His self-imposed commitments and carries through His self-initiated agreements. Forgiveness, therefore, is rooted in divine faithfulness (I Jn 1:9), as is His people's victory over life's hardest testings (I Cor 10:13; I Pet 4:19) and their perseverance as well (I Thess 5:24).

As the self-revelation of the divine character, Jesus Christ is fittingly designated the Faithful One (Rev 19:11), who with absolute fidelity discharges all the responsibilities of High Priest (Heb 2:17), Apostle (Heb 3:1–2), and Witness (Rev 1:5; 3:14).

This quality of the divine character finds its human reflection in men of faith (Hab 2:4). Like their divine Exemplar they manifest a steadfast trustworthiness in all their obligations (Mt 25:21; I Cor 4:2); they are tenaciously loyal even to the point of martyrdom (Rev 2:10). Responding to faith, the Holy Spirit produces in men this trait of faithfulness (Gal 5:22, RSV).

See Fidelity; God.

V. C. G.

FALCON. *See* Animals, III.25.

FALL OF MAN. *An historical event.* Scripture depicts the fall of Adam as a definite event taking place in human history. The account in Gen 3 is, therefore, not to be regarded as myth (so J. S. Whale: "Every man is his own Adam. Man's tragic apostasy from God is not something which happened once for all a long time ago. It is true in every moment of existence"). Nor is it to be taken as belonging to super-history (so Brunner: "The creation and the Fall both lie behind the historical visible reality"). Nor is it to be explained as an allegory, representing man's awakening to self-consciousness and personality (so Kant, Schiller, Hegel).

The NT takes the position that the fall of Adam is an historical event and an explanation of what happens today. Paul so closely links the respective headships of Adam and Christ that if Adam is looked upon as a myth, then Christ must be regarded as myth also (Rom 5:12 ff.; I Cor 15:21 ff.; see also I Tim 2:14). For Adam was the type of Him that was to come—"the last Adam" and "the second man" (I Cor 15:45, 47).

The details of the Fall are clear. Rather than confronting Adam, the tempter in the form of a serpent approached Eve. Not being the federal head of the race, and having received the command of God only indirectly, she would be less likely to assume a sense of responsibility. The course the tempter followed in Gen 3 lies behind every sin that is committed. First, there is the suggestion to doubt God's word ("Yea, hath God said. . . .?"). Second, there is the prompting to disbelieve God's word ("Ye shall not surely die"). Third, there is the appeal to pride and self-sufficiency ("Ye shall be as God," ASV). Fourth, there is the actual disobedience to God's word (they "did eat").

The consequences of the transgression struck immediately. First, Adam and his wife became overwhelmed with a sense of guilt ("they knew that they were naked"). Second, they were aware of an estrangement between them and God ("they hid themselves"). Third, they received a sentence of curse ("sorrow," "sweat," "unto dust shalt thou return"). Finally, they were banished from the presence of God ("he drove out the man").

A "Temptation Seal" from Mesopotamia, showing a man and woman, a tree, and a snake. BM

The effects of the Fall. Though the Fall was indeed an historical event, it was not an isolated event. The consequences it brought upon mankind's first parents did not cease with their death. In their transgression they implicated their posterity and all creation (cf. Rom 8:18–25).

For their posterity the Fall introduced the *universality of sin* throughout the human race (Ps 143:2; Rom 3:1–12, 19–20, 23; Gal 3:22; I Jn 1:8, 10). As the *New England Primer* put it, "In Adam's fall, we sinned all." It is in the Fall of the human race in Adam that we are given the explanation why children are born sinners, why some die in infancy, and why all who survive, regardless of race, culture, and ancestry, commit voluntary transgressions.

The sin thus transmitted to the human race is called *original sin.* It is so named because (1) it is derived from the original root of mankind; (2) it is present in each individual from the time of his birth; (3) it is the inward root of all actual sins that defile the life of man.

As the result of original sin man is both a guilty and a polluted creature. In Rom 5:12–19 Paul stresses the solidarity of the human race, the federal headship of Adam over it, the unique significance of his first sin for all his posterity, and the guilt with its consequences

under which all men now stand. The apostle reiterates the same truth in I Cor 15:22 ("In Adam all die"). If all die in Adam, it is because all sinned and are guilty in Adam. Every man is guilty, therefore, of having transgressed the expressed commandment of God and is, as a result, deserving of divine punishment.

Guilt, however, is but one result of original sin. The other is pollution. Man no longer possesses the original goodness with which he was created. In its place has come a perversity that controls his heart, mind, disposition, and will. This pollution of his entire nature is called *total depravity,* a term that needs to be guarded from misunderstanding. Total depravity does not suggest that every man is as bad as he can possibly become. Nor does it imply that he is incapable of thinking or doing any good whatsoever. Rather, we are to understand by the term that man is inherently corrupt in every part of his nature and is incapable of doing any spiritual good (that is, in relation to God). This total depravity is clearly taught in Scripture (Jn 5:42; Rom 7:18, 23; Eph 4:18; II Tim 3:2–4; Tit 1:15; Heb 3:12). *See* Depravity; Image of God.

But the effects of Adam's sin go beyond his descendants. Its consequences extend to the physical earth also. "Cursed is the ground for thy sake" (Gen 3:17; cf. Rom 8:20–22). As the image of God, the apex of creation, man was appointed God's vice-regent (Gen 1:26; Ps 8:4–8). When he, the crown of creation, fell, he brought catastrophe into everything over which he had dominion. This curse, which hangs like a pall over creation, will not be removed until Christ's second coming (Rom 8:18–23), at which time the effects of the Fall will finally be abolished, and a new heaven and a new earth, wherein righteousness dwells, will be established (II Pet 3:12–13). *See* Sin.

Development of the doctrine. Prior to the time of Augustine (5th cen.), not much can be found of formal exposition of the doctrine of the Fall of man in the writings of the Church Fathers. Augustine, in his controversy with Pelagius, stressed the fact that all men were seminally present in Adam and actually sinned in him. Pelagius, his opponent, denied such a connection between the sin of Adam and those of his posterity. Pelagianism taught that Adam's sin affected only himself, that every individual was born sinless, and was, therefore, inherently capable of living a sinless life. Only by way of setting a bad example did Adam's sin influence his descendants. The errors of Pelagianism have been perpetuated by the Socinians of the 16th and 17th cen. (forerunners of today's Unitarians), and by modern liberal theologians.

Roman Catholicism holds officially to a semi-Pelagian position, insisting that what man lost through the Fall was the gift of original righteousness. This gift was something extra added to man (*donum superadditum*) at the time of creation, and which, when lost, left man in his natural state. The Fall, therefore, constituted a negative evil (a loss of something added to man's nature) rather than a positive punishment. Thus, according to Roman Catholic theology, unregenerate man still possesses the ability to contribute works toward the attainment of his salvation.

Some of the reformers continued the Augustinian view that all men were seminally in Adam and thus shared in his transgression. Luther spoke of man's guilt because of the indwelling sin inherited from Adam. Calvin took the position that Adam was both the progenitor and the root of the human race; that therefore all his offspring are born with a corrupt nature; and that both the guilt of Adam's sin and their own inborn corruption are imputed to them as sin.

Later Reformed theologians laid greater emphasis on the federal or covenantal aspects of Adam's relationship to the race. According to them, Adam stood as the representative of the human race, and in his Fall mankind received both the guilt and the pollution of his sin. This view accords more with the parallel Paul sets up between Christ and those united to Him (Rom 5:12-19; I Cor 15:22, 45-49). In the case of Christ, it is representative headship that is indicated, a relationship that has its parallel in the one existing between Adam and his posterity.

In poetic terms Milton wrote one of the most profound statements concerning the nature of the Fall in the opening lines of his *Paradise Lost:*

"Of Man's first disobedience, and the fruit
Of that forbidden tree, whose mortal taste
Brought death into the world, and all our
*   woe,*
With loss of Eden. . . ."

Bibliography. H. Bavinck, "The Fall," ISBE, II, 1092 ff. L. Berkhof, *Reformed Dogmatics,* Grand Rapids: Eerdmans, 1941. Charles C. Hodge, *Systematic Theology,* Grand Rapids: Eerdmans, reprinted, 1952. J. Gresham Machen, *The Christian View of Man,* Grand Rapids: Eerdmans, 1937. J. Murray, *The Imputation of Adam's Sin,* Grand Rapids: Eerdmans, 1959. C. R. Smith, *The Bible Doctrine of Sin,* Naperville, Ill.: Alec R. Allenson, 1953.

F. C. K.

FALLOW DEER. *See* Animals, II.10.

FALLOW GROUND. The Heb. word *nîr* occurs twice in the OT (Jer 4:3; Hos 10:12), and is translated as "fallow ground" in the KJV. It signifies "tillable" or "untilled" ground.

The Heb. *nātash* has the thought of "fallow ground" in one instance (Ex 23:11). It means "to leave," "to let alone." The Israelites were required to allow the land to rest each seventh year.

FALLOW YEAR. *See* Sabbath.

FALSE CHRISTS. This term is found in Mt 24:24 and Mk 13:22. The idea is also expressed differently in Mt 24:5; Mk 13:6; Lk 21:8. Jesus said that many would come in His name claiming to be Christ. They would show signs and wonders, and thereby convince many that they were genuine. *See* Antichrist.

FALSE PROPHET, THE. The False Prophet (Rev 19:20; 20:10), also called the second Beast (Rev 13:11-18), is a religious leader who is associated with the first Beast, the political leader of the Tribulation period, as his subordinate. He appears in power in the middle of the Tribulation at which time the first Beast or Antichrist (*q.v.*) assumes worldwide political power (Rev 13:7) and he, religious power.

He is perhaps a Jew, since Rev 13:11 may indicate that he arises out of "the land," or Palestine. (In Gr. the word *gē* can mean either "earth" or "land.") He moves in the religious realm, for he appears as a lamb (Rev 13:11). He is energized by Satan, being given his power by the first Beast (Rev 13:12). He promotes the worship of the first Beast and forces the earth to worship him (Rev 13:12, RSV). His ministry and authority are authenticated by miracles and signs which he works by Satanic power (Rev 13:13-14). The unbelieving world is deceived by him and worships the first Beast as God (Rev 13:14-15). He holds the power of life and death to enforce the worship of the first Beast (Rev 13:15). His authority extends into the economic realm, and he uses this economic power to enforce his will (Rev 13:16-17). The believers of that day will be able to recognize him because of the sign given to identify him (Rev 13:18).

The False Prophet, together with Satan and the first Beast, form a triumvirate of evil, which is Satan's masterpiece of deception. The world will be dominated by them during the last half of the Tribulation period in the political, religious, and economic realms in imitation of God's worldwide rule over the earth in the Millennium by Jesus Christ, the Messiah.

J. D. P.

FAMILIAR SPIRIT. An expression occurring 16 times in the KJV, referring to a spirit of divination or to its medium or conjurer, translating Heb. *'ôb.* This term is related to similar words in Sumerian, Hittite, Akkadian, and Ugaritic, all probably coming from a common source. Originally it meant the ritual hole or pit dug in the ground to give underworld spirits access to the practitioner for a short time. Later the term was applied to the spirits which issued from the hole, and also to the necromancer himself/herself (Harry A. Hoffner, Jr., "Second Millennium Antecedents to the Hebrew *'ôb*," JBL, LXXXVI [1967], 385-401). The practice of necromancy in the ancient Near East is reflected in the Gilgamesh epic: "Forthwith he opened a hole in the earth. The spirit of Enkidu, like a wind-puff, issued forth from the nether world" (ANET, p. 98); and in Isa 29:4 (RSV): "Your voice shall come from the ground like the voice of a ghost ['*ōb*], and your speech shall whisper out of the dust."

The term "familiar" is used to describe the alleged spirit of a deceased person because it was regarded by the Genevan revisers (1557-1560) as a servant (*famulus*) easily summoned by the one possessing it, or as belonging to the family (*familiaris*) and thus on intimate terms with the deceased person (Merrill F. Unger, *Biblical Demonology*, p. 144).

A parallel term in Heb., always occurring with '*ōb*, is *yiddeʿōnî*, from Heb. *yādaʿ*, "to know," a "knowing" spirit, one with occult knowledge. The term is translated by "wizard" in KJV, RSV, etc., one who is made wise concerning the nether world by such a demon. The same medium might seek both types of demons: "one who consults a familiar spirit and a knowing-spirit" (Deut 18:11, lit.). Such a demon is well acquainted with the deceased human being and can imitate or impersonate him, deceiving the one desiring to communicate with the dead.

Other terms involved in necromancy are found in Deut 18:11, *dōrēsh el-hammēthîm* (lit., one who inquires of the dead; cf. Isa 8:19) and in Isa 19:3, *ha'ĕlîlîm* ("idols," or probably chthonic deities) and *ha'iṭṭîm* ("charmers"; better, "ghosts," from Akkad. *eṭimmu*), along with *hā'ōbōth* and *hayyiddeʿōnîm*.

The OT nowhere condemns necromancy on the ground that it is futile, but that it is rebellion against God on whom alone the Israelite believer was to depend (Lev 19:31; 20:6, 27; Deut 18:9-14), for the Lord had raised up prophetic spokesmen to reveal His will (Deut 18:15-22). Manasseh, as well as King Saul (I Chr 10:13), was guilty of trafficking with familiar and occult spirits (II Kgs 21:6; 23:4). In spite of these prohibitions many today find it fashionable to flock to spiritualist mediums for supposed messages from departed loved ones or for "proof" that there is no death or judgment to come.

The account of Saul when he sought counsel of the deceased Samuel through the medium of Endor (I Sam 28) exposes the fraudulency of spiritism. In the seance the witch, described as a *ba'ălath-'ōb*, "mistress of a familiar spirit," expected to bring up the "control" spirit which would impersonate Samuel, but instead shrieked in fear at what happened. In this sole instance God sovereignly permitted the actual spirit of Samuel to speak in order to deliver a solemn rebuke to the apostate king. Normally the alleged spirit would speak somewhat favorably; in this unique case the inquirer (Saul) was condemned to die on the morrow, a warning for all time to come. *See* Demonology; Divination; Magic; Necromancy.

Bibliography. Raphael Gasson, *The Challenging Counterfeit*, Logos International, 1966.

J. R.

FAMILY

Terminology. Several words expressing the idea of family appear in the Bible. In the OT, Heb. *bayith* (lit., "house") may signify the family living in the house (e.g., I Chr 13:14) and often is translated "household" (e.g., Gen 18:19; Ex 1:1; Josh 7:18, *re* Achan who lived in a tent). More frequently found is Heb. *mishpaḥa* with the meaning of "kindred" (e.g. Gen 24:38-41). "family" or "clan," usually with a broader connotation than our English word "family" (e.g., Gen 10:31-32). The NT uses Gr. *oikia* ("house," "home," "household," e.g., Lk 19:9; Acts 10:2; 16:31; 18:8; I Cor 1:16) and *oikiakos* ("members of one's family group," Mt 10:25, 36).

Extent. The Jewish family or household included not only immediate members closely related by ties of blood or marriage, but also embraced slaves, hired servants, concubines, and even foreigners. Abraham circumcised every male of his household, from his son Ishmael to the slaves born in his house and those purchased from foreigners (Gen 17:23, 27). Note how extensive Jacob's family was considered to be, numbering all his children and grandchildren as 66, not counting his sons' wives (Gen 46:5-7, 26). Children were greatly desired amd were extremely important in the family economy, especially sons (Ps 127:3-5; 128:3; Ruth 4:11).

Status and role. The father exercised practically absolute authority in the OT family; hence the need to caution him not to provoke his children to wrath in the NT (Eph 6:4; Col 3:21). He symbolized tradition, the family ancestry, and its hope for the future. His duty was to lead the family in worship. When he did, his uprightness and devotion to God became an example to his descendants (e.g., Job 1:5); when he failed, he was bitterly denounced (Ps 78:8; Amos 2:6-7). The mother also had great influence behind the scenes, as in the case of Rebekah's advising Jacob (Gen 27:11-17). She comforted her children (Isa 49:15; 66:13) and was loved and respected by them. The eldest or firstborn son normally was prepared and trained for the future role of head of the family. Perhaps because of the extra duties and responsibilities as clan leader he was granted a double portion of the inheritance.

Biblical basis and principles of family living. God's initial pattern for marriage is recorded in Gen 2:18-25. As originally planned, it involved one man and one woman, physical union (Gen 1:28), and a new social unit (Gen 2:24). Upon these foundational principles the family was built, and throughout the OT the family was considered basic in God's dealings with men. Children were considered to be a gift and blessing from God (Gen 4:1; 33:5; Ps 113:9; 127:3; 68:6). Parents were responsible to train them (Deut 6:6-9; Prov 22:6), and fathers particularly were responsible to provide a consistent example in godly living. Failure in this respect would bring devastating results (Ex 20:4-5; Num 14:18), well illustrated in the apostasy of Israel (II Kgs 17:14; II Chr 33:22-25; Acts 7:51-53).

NT writers built upon the principles and ideals for family living which were established in the OT. Referring to the Genesis account, Jesus clarified and confirmed the concept of earthly permanency in the marriage relationship (Mt 19:3-6). Though the term "shall cleave" (Gen 2:24) strongly implies that this union was to be lifelong, Jesus left no doubt when He said, "What therefore God hath joined together, let not man put asunder" (Mt 19:6).

Paul elevated marriage to its highest level when he likened the husband to Christ and the wife to the Church (Eph 5:22-23). The husband, says the apostle, should "love . . . even as Christ also loved," and the wife is to submit herself to her husband as the Church is to submit to Christ (Eph 5:25, 22-24). The man, as a loving husband reflecting the unselfish and sacrificial attitudes of Christ Himself, should be the "head of the wife," giving her security and protection.

Jesus also elevated children to a prominent place in His divine plan when He taught not to offend them (Mt 18:6), not to despise them (18:10), and not to forbid them to come to Him (19:14). Paul reiterates an OT principle when he places the primary responsibility for child training upon the father's shoulders (Eph 6:4).

Both the OT and the NT provide a variety of practical instructions for successful marital and family relationships. The book of Proverbs especially is replete with these teachings. The child's effect on family morale (10:1; 15:20; 17:25; 23:24-25); the value of strict discipline (13:24; 19:18; 22:15; 23:13-14; 29:15, 17; cf. Heb 12:5-11); warnings against disobedience to parents (19:26; 20:20); and the aggravation of a nagging wife (19:13; 27:15)—these are some of the wise sayings regarding family problems.

The prosperous home is warned not to forget the Lord (Deut 6:10-12). Marriage to unbelievers is forbidden for God's people to prevent turning away to other gods (Deut 7:3-4; II Cor 6:14). I Cor 7 gives practical instructions regarding the problem of selfishness in marriage (vv. 1-5), tells what to do when one's mate is unsaved (vv. 12-16), and warns against the problem of divided loyalties (vv. 32-35). Jesus deals with the issue of divorce (Mt 19:3-11). and Paul gives instructions regarding remarriage (I Cor 7:39-40; Rom 7:1-3). Practical advice for wives and mothers may be found in Tit 2:3-5 and I Pet 3:1-6.

In addition to specific instructions, the Scriptures also give many significant illustrations which in turn provide principles for Christ-like family living. For example, Eli's sons and David's children are a potent reminder as to what happens when parents fail (I Sam 3:13; II Sam

12:10). Joseph is no doubt the supreme example in demonstrating family forgiveness (Gen 50:15-21).

Jesus illustrated proper parental attitudes toward the straying child with His parable of the prodigal son (Lk 15:11-24), but He also lays bare parental motives that are selfish (Mt 20:20-28).

There is no doubt that the teachings of the Bible elevate the family and its function to a level duplicated in no other literature or society. Though this divinely instituted social unit has failed in many instances to function at a proper level within the Christian community, God's holy pattern for family living is in no way invalidated.

Figurative use of the concept of family. In the new creation there is a new family relationship, with one Father, who is in heaven (Mt 23:9). A man may have to renounce his old family ties (Lk 14:26, 33) or may discover that his foes are those of his own household (Mt 10:35-36). Jesus Himself experienced this cleavage (Mk 6:4; Jn 7:5) and declared that His true brother and sister and mother are they that do the will of God (Mk 3:31-35).

The church becomes the family or household of God (Eph 2:19; I Tim 3:15; Heb 3:6; I Pet 4:17). Paul counts Timothy, Titus, and Philemon as his "children," and he exhorts Timothy to treat the members of the church at Ephesus as his own relatives (I Tim 5:1-2). He compares elders to fathers of a family (I Tim 3:5), and himself "begets" churches like a father (I Cor 4:15; cf. II Cor 6:13) or gives birth to them like a mother (Gal 4:19). As God's people, as His sons and daughters, we are to be separate and touch nothing unclean (II Cor 6:14-18).

See Adoption; Children; Divorce; Education; Home; House; Household; Husband; Father; Mother; Son; Daughter; Marriage; Inheritance; Parent; Women.

Bibliography. O. J. Baab, "Family," IDB, II, 238-241. "The Family," CornPBE, pp. 310-320. Larry Christenson, *The Christian Family,* Minneapolis: Bethany Fellowship, 1970. John W. Drakeford, *The Home: Laboratory of Life,* Nashville: Broadman Press, 1965. Alta Mae Erb, *Christian Education in the Home,* Scottsdale, Pa.: Herald Press, 1963. Oscar E. Feucht, *Helping Families Through the Church,* St. Louis: Concordia, 1957. Gene A. Getz, "The Christian Home," BS, CXXVI (1969), 16-21, 109-114. Ralph Heynen, *The Secret of Christian Family Living,* Grand Rapids: Baker, 1965. E. A. Judge, *The Social Pattern of the Christian Groups in the First Century,* London: Tyndale Press, 1960. G. Quell and G. Schrenk, 'Patēr, etc.," TDNT, V, 945-1022.

G. A. G.

FAMINE. A general condition of extreme shortage of food. Bible history mentions numerous instances of famine during the days of Abraham (Gen 12:10), Isaac (Gen 26:1), Joseph (Gen 41:56-57), Elimelech and Naomi (Ruth 1:1), David (II Sam 21:1), Elijah (I Kgs 18:2; Lk 4:25), Elisha (II Kgs 6:25; 8:1), the final siege of Jerusalem (II Kgs 25:3).

During a famine in the "far country" the prodigal son was brought to his senses (Lk 15:14). One took place in the days of the Roman Emperor Claudius (Acts 11:28). In His Olivet discourse the Lord Jesus predicted famines during the tribulation period at the close of the age (Mt 24:7), and Revelation alludes to famine coming on Babylon the Great (Rev 18:8). One of the blessings promised to restored Israel is that there will be no more famines (Ezk 36:29-30).

There is reference to people paying high prices during famines for such unpalatable foods as asses' heads and doves' dung (II Kgs 6:25) and even turning to the most horrid kind of cannibalism (Deut 28:53-57; II Kgs 6:28-29).

Evidently in Bible days the natural causes most responsible for famine were drought (I Kgs 18:1, 2) and warfare in its various aspects (Ezk 6:11; II Kgs 25:2-3). However, it is many times pictured as a divine judgment on sin (II Sam 21:1; 24:13; I Kgs 8:37; II Kgs 8:1; Isa 51:19; Jer 14:12-18; Ezk 5:12). In this sense it is spoken of as one of God's "four sore judgments" (Ezk 14:21).

Yet promise is made that God will keep alive the godly in times of famine (Job 5:20, 22; Ps 33:19; 37:19), and best of all it is affirmed that famine, as well as other trials and tribulations, shall not separate us from the love of Christ (Rom 8:35-39). In a figurative sense "a famine . . . of hearing the words of the Lord" (Amos 8:11) is threatened to those who have despised and rejected the message of the Lord. This is the worst kind of famine of all.

G. C. L.

FAN. The noun forms are used twice in both the OT and NT (Isa 30:24; Jer 15:7; Mt 3:12; Lk 3:17). The meaning in all uses is simply "fan." Heb. *mizreh* is defined as a winnowing fan or fork, probably with six prongs, and Gr. *ptuon* is applied to the winnowing shovel used to toss grain into the wind. *See* Fork; Agriculture.

Forms of the verb *zārâ* are found four times translated as "fan" in the KJV (Isa 41:16; Jer 4:11; 15:7; 51:2), meaning "to winnow." The verb is used figuratively "to scatter" an enemy.

FANNERS. Used only once (Jer 51:2), and there the translation "fanners" is questionable. The ASV gives it the meaning of "strangers."

FARM, FARMERS. *See* Agriculture; Occupations: Farmer.

FARTHING. *See* Weights, Measures and Coins.

Ceremonial fan from the tomb of King Tutankhamon covered with gold. Around the edge of the head are holes into which ostrich feathers were fixed. LL

FAST, FASTING. Fasting in the Bible implies total abstinence (*q.v.*) from all food for a certain period. The length of time varied from daylight hours ("fasted that day until evening," Jud 20:26) up to 40 days, as in the cases of Moses, Elijah, and Jesus. People fasted either out of necessity during a food shortage (Acts 27:21, 33-36), because of loss of appetite resulting from deep emotions (as Hannah and Jonathan, I Sam 1:8, 18; 20:34), or for religious purposes.

The Heb. words are *ṣûm* (verb) and *ṣôm* (noun)—not found in the Pentateuch. The corresponding Gr. terms are *nēsteuō* and *nēsteia* from a root meaning "hunger." Other expressions used in the OT are "not eat bread" (I Sam 28:20; II Sam 12:17) and "to afflict one's soul." The latter is a phrase in the Mosaic law that may have included fasting (Lev 16:29, 31; 23:27, 32; *et al.*), and signifies to lower or humble oneself by self-denial as a proper expression of repentance.

The origin of the religious practice of fasting is lost in the dim past, but this discipline was widespread throughout ancient religions. In food-gathering (as opposed to food-growing) cultures fasting was often compulsory owing to the uncertainty of obtaining food. Possibly superstitious ignorance interpreted the scarcity of wild grains, fruits, and game as an expression of the divine will, and so men began to consider fasting as a religious duty. Thinking that the gods were jealous of the pleasures of mankind, men perhaps assumed that abstinence would propitiate their favor. On the other hand, the natural inclination to forego food during the grief of bereavement may have caused fasting to originate as a sign of mourning.

Fasting first appears in the OT as a voluntary act of individual piety. Moses twice fasted 40 days and nights in the presence of the Lord on Mount Sinai, taking neither food nor water (Deut 9:9, 18; Ex 34:28). While food may have been unavailable, abstention from water during these periods was probably voluntary, for there is a small well or spring in a cleft 100 feet below the summit of Jebel Musa. Yet Moses must have been supernaturally sustained, because the human body cannot endure lack of moisture for so long a time. Under ideal conditions a human has fasted from all food for 90 days and survived, according to Dr. Herbert M. Shelton who has supervised over 40,000 fasts (*Fasting Can Save Your Life,* Chicago: Natural Hygiene Press, 1964, p. 57). It is not specifically stated that Elijah (I Kgs 19:8) and Jesus (Mt 4:2) drank no water during their respective 40 day fasts. That they could continue to be active and not become weakened is the remarkable aspect in their cases (cf. Ps 109:24).

On long fasts hunger usually subsides by the end of the third day and does not return until the stored food reserves in the tissues of the body are used up ("and afterward he was hungry," Mt 4:2, RSV). This can take 40 days or longer; only then does starvation begin (Shelton, pp. 15, 23, 29–32). Before this stage fasting has many beneficial effects by permitting the body to secure physiological rest and be restored to health (*ibid.,* pp. 36–40, 48–52).

In most cases in the Bible fasting can be seen as a normal, voluntary result of the human state of mind. On his first prolonged stay on the mount Moses was too enraptured with the awesome presence of God, too absorbed with the divine revelations given him to want to eat. On his return he lay prostrate before God, heartbroken because of the rebellion of his people (Deut 9:18). The men of Jabesh-gilead and David mourned and fasted after bereavement (I Sam 31:11–13; II Sam 1:12; 3:35).

Fasting naturally seemed to reinforce the attitude of repentance and heartfelt confession, just as sackcloth and ashes did (I Sam 7:6; Ps 69:10–11; Jon 3:5, 8; Dan 9:3–5; Ezr 10:1, 6; Neh 9:1–2). After Elijah's rebuke, King Ahab thus repented of his crime toward Naboth (I Kgs 21:27–29). Perplexity, fear, and distress likewise evoked similar response (Jud 20:26; Est 4:3).

As an accompaniment of prayer, fasting often is something desirable to the godly man, not merely a matter of rigid self-discipline. During a fast one's mental and spiritual faculties seem more alert and sensitive to God's Spirit, and intercession seems easier, more effective. Thus David fasted while he prayed for his sick child (II Sam 12:16–23), and even for his sick enemies (Ps 35:13). Also Nehemiah fasted as he interceded for Israel (Neh 1:4–11).

The early Christians found fasting to be beneficial while seeking the will and direction of God (Acts 13:2–3; 14:23). During a three-week period of self-humbling and seeking

to understand the future, Daniel ate no "pleasant bread," i.e., delicacies, nor meat nor wine (Dan 10:2–3). Such a non-total fast can be an effective aid to spiritual concentration and prayer. It may be advisable for those who must remain active or are too weak to endure a total fast.

God never seems to command His people to fast regularly, unless the "affliction of the soul" on the Day of Atonement includes fasting (Lev 16:29). The OT stresses rather the positive enjoyment of God and His blessings with gladness of heart (Ps 4:7; Prov 15:13; 17:22; Eccl 3:13; 9:7–9). God is not impressed with the act of fasting, especially when it does not signify turning from strife and oppression (Isa 58:3–5). Instead, fasting is acceptable only if it eventuates in acts of social justice and true charity, only if the motive for self-denial is one of love and desire to help the poor (vv. 6–11).

Nevertheless, in times of national emergency kings and spiritual leaders proclaimed special fast days to seek help from the Lord. When invasion from E of the Dead Sea was imminent King Jehoshaphat summoned all Judah to fast (II Chr 20:3). After the disasters of locust plague and drought Joel was ordered to have the priests sanctify a fast (Joel 1:14; 2:12, 15), although he insisted that the primary need was inward repentance, to rend their hearts and not their garments (2:13). Jeremiah took advantage of a fasting day to have the words of the Lord read to the people (Jer 36:6, 9). Ezra proclaimed a fast to pray for a safe journey to Jerusalem (Ezr 8:21, 23). Queen Esther begged Mordecai and the Jews to fast with her three days and nights before she approached King Ahasuerus (Est 4:16). Later, a national fast in preparation for the observance of Purim followed this pattern (Est 9:31).

Four annual fasts had arisen during the Babylonian exile, but they were observed, apparently, without divine authorization. Through His earlier prophets God had already expressed His mind concerning mere ceremonial worship. The emphasis upon positive wholesomeness in fellowship with God is clearly heard in His declaration that the four exilic fasts would become "joy and gladness and cheerful feasts" (Zech 8:19; cf. 7:3–10; Jer 14:12).

The value of the discipline of fasting is pointed out frequently in the Jewish intertestamental literature, although no specific mention of the religious fast may be found in the Qumran MSS published thus far. The Manual of Discipline states only that serious offenses could be punished by fining a community member part of his food ration (1Q S vi. 25). In the temple itself the godly Anna served the Lord with fastings and prayers (Lk 2:37). The Pharisees made much of fasting and regarded it as a meritorious work. It became the custom of the pious to fast on Mondays and Thursdays (Lk 18:12). If a man began to fast, his fast took priority over making sacrificial offerings and was regarded as more efficacious than almsgiving. *See* Festivals: Extrabiblical Jewish sacred seasons.

Jesus never required His disciples to fast. The term "and fasting" is not found in the best Gr. MSS at Mk 9:29 (nor in Acts 10:30; I Cor 7:5); Mt 17:21 is omitted entirely in the best texts. Yet while He denounced the hypocrisy of the Pharisees, He emphasized that fasting done in secret out of true devotion to God will be rewarded (Mt 6:16-18). He took it for granted that after His ascension His followers would feel the need to fast, even as John the Baptist's disciples did (Mk 2:18-20). Whether Paul's fastings were voluntary or resulting from lack of food (II Cor 6:5; 11:27) cannot be settled. The absence of any problem of fasting in Paul's letters suggests that it was not a prominent matter in the Gentile churches. According to the Didache (8.1), Christians by A.D. 100 could be exhorted to fast twice a week—on Tuesdays and Fridays, however! In the 2nd and 3rd cen. the pre-Easter and pre-baptismal fasts came to be widely practiced.

Bibliography. Johannes Behm, "*Nētis*, etc.," TDNT, IV, 924-935. Arthur Wallis, *God's Chosen Fast*, Fort Washington, Pa.: Christian Literature Crusade, 1968.

J. R.

FAT. The subcutaneous layer around the kidneys and other viscera which, like the blood, was forbidden by the Mosaic law to be used for food but rather was burned as an offering to God (mentioned several times in Lev 3, 4, 7, 8, 9). The offering had to be made on the very day the animal was killed so as to remove the temptation to eat that portion. The ancients considered fat and blood as the source of vitality and strength. Fat was the richest portion of the sacrificial animal. For this reason the fat was offered to the Lord as representative of the best part of each sacrifice.

FATHER. This term in the OT has a wide spectrum of meanings. These may be divided into literal and figurative uses.

Basically it refers to the male parent (Gen 2:24; 22:7; 48:1; etc.). One of the most basic and foremost ethical precepts of the OT and NT relates to the honor and obedience due to fathers. This esteem of parents was a characteristic of godliness even before the Decalogue was given. The father's authority over his family in the OT was absolute. He could sell his children into slavery (Ex 21:7) or have them put to death (Gen 22:2-10; cf. 21:9-14). The blessing or malediction of a father was of special significance and conferred benefit or injury (Gen 9:25-27; 27:27-40; 48;15-20; 49:1-28). The father also functioned as priest of the family before the formation of a formal priesthood (Gen 8:20; 22:13; Job, 1:5). *See* Family.

The term is employed in a literal sense to describe a forefather. Here the relationship may be more immediate as a grandfather (Gen 28:13; 31:42; 32:9) or great-grandfather (I Kgs 15:3; cf. 15:11, 24), or it may be more remote (Gen 15:15; II Kgs 15:38; 16:2; Ps 45:16).

A third literal meaning is found in its usage to refer to the ancestral progenitor of a nation or a people, as Shem (Gen 10:21), Abraham (Gen 17:4-5), Moab (Gen 19:37), etc.

It is in the figurative meanings that the more colorful concepts are found. The term describes one who is the author, maker, originator, or creator of something. God is said to be the Father of Israel because He formed the nation (Deut 32:6; Isa 63:16; 64:8; Jer 31:9). By implication He is the Father of nature (Job 38:28). Man can also be called father in the sense of originator, as in Gen 4:20-21 where it looks at men who brought into being a new mode of life.

Father also is used in a nonliteral sense as a term of endearment. In II Sam 7:14; I Chr 17:13; 22:10; Ps 68:5; 89:26 it is applied to God in His relationship with men. It implies His love will move Him to nourish and sustain. The word is also employed of man's association with another (Job 29:16; Isa 22:21). While endearment still is in view, the concept of sustenance comes to the fore here.

The term may describe one who is a teacher (I Sam 10:12). Quite often it refers to an adviser who possesses some authoritative position (Gen 45:8; Jud 17:10; 18:19; II Kgs 2:12; 6:21; 13:14).

Figuratively it becomes a term of respect (I Sam 24:11; II Kgs 5:13; cf. 8:9).

Finally, it is used in the OT to refer to some unstated but intimate association (Job 17:14).

As a term in the NT father (*patēr*) is also employed with literal and metaphorical meanings. Its basic concept, that of referring to the male parent (*q.v.*), is seen in Mt 2:22; Mk 5:40; Jn 4:53; etc. In the plural the word may look at both parents, the mother and father (Heb 11:23; cf. Eph 6:4; Col 3:21). As in the OT it is used of genealogical forefathers (Mt 3:9; Lk 1:73; Jn 8:39; Rom 9:10). In II Pet 3:4 it seems to have a technical sense in referring to the whole group of OT patriarchs.

Although the figurative meanings of the word are not as broad as in the OT, there are some that are essential for a proper understanding of the NT. It is employed once of a spiritual father, that is, of one who by his witness brought others to faith in Christ (I Cor 4:15). It is employed as a term of respect and honor (Mt 23:9; Acts 7:2; 22:1). In I Jn 2:13-14 it evidently portrays Christians who have matured in the faith. Figuratively it looks at one who is a prototype or archetype, one who originates a company of people with kindred spirit (Jn 8:38, 44; Rom 4:11-12, 16; cf. I Pet 3:6).

The word is also used of God as Creator and Father. *See* Father, God the; God.

Bibliography. Gottlob Schrenk and Gottfried Quell, "*Patēr,* etc.," TDNT, V, 945-1022.

S. D. T.

FATHER, GOD THE. In four senses God is Father: as Creator, as Father of Israel, as Father of Christ, and as Father of believers.

God is Father of mankind by creation (Acts 17:28–29; Lk 3:38; cf. Gen 1:27; Jas 3:9). The fatherhood of God in this sense is not a frequent subject in the Bible. Angels are called "the sons of God" (Job 1:6; 2:1; 38:7; cf. Gen 6:2) because they were created by God and/or because of their spiritual ties with God.

In the OT God is especially the Father of the nation Israel (Isa 63:16; 64:8; Hos 11:1). He sustains this relationship because the nation was created by Him (Deut 32:6; Mal 2:10). Israel as God's firstborn possesses a privileged position (Ex 4:22; Jer 31:9) and as such owns great promises (Jer 3:19). As a son Israel is to honor and serve God (Ex 4:23; Mal 1:6). Just as a natural father rears his children, so God desires to sustain Israel and make it great (Jer 3:19; cf. Ps 103:13; Prov 3:12).

In a very special sense God is the Father of Jesus Christ. Several concepts are revealed in this relationship. Especially the deity of Christ is evidenced (Jn 5:18). In Mt 3:17 messiahship is in view (cf. 17:5; Mk 9:7; Lk 9:35). The equality of the Son with the Father is seen in the Trinitarian name (Mt 28:19). The Lord Jesus is careful to maintain a strict distinction between God as His Father and God as the Father of believers (cf. Jn 20:17). Christ as God's Son is the revelation of the Father and the way of access to God (Mt 11:27; Jn 10:30; 14:6–7).

In seed form God is portrayed as the Father of individual saints in the OT (II Sam 7:14; Ps 103:13; Mal 3:17), but this concept finds maturation in the NT with the coming of Christ (cf. Mt 6:4, 6, 8, 9, 32). By creation God is the Father of all; by His grace He is the spiritual Father of believers. Sonship in the NT is portrayed in three aspects—regeneration (Jn 1:12–13; 3:6), adoption (Rom 8:15, 23; Gal 4:5; Eph 1:5), and transferal into the Son's kingdom (Col 1:13).

The Christian's close relationship with God is particularly seen in the formula, "Abba, Father," literally meaning, "Father, Father" (Mk 14:36; Rom 8:15; Gal 4:6). The first is an Aram. word which became colloquial in Heb. expressing the more intimate association of child and father. It is never used of God in the OT, and rabbinic literature rarely refers to God by this name and then only in a specific formula. However, Christ boldly said, "Abba." The second word is the regular Gr. word for father. The persistence of the formula in the NT may be due to the deep impression made on the disciples by the Lord's use of it. He evidently employed both the Aram. and the Gr.

See God; God, Names and Titles of.
                                                    S. D. T.

FATHER-IN-LAW. The Heb. husband's father (Heb. *ḥām,* Gen 38:13, 25; I Sam 4:19, 21) had authority over his son's wife (Gen 38:24), but was forbidden to marry her (Lev 18:15). Jacob lived for an extended period (Gen 31:41) with his wives' father, as did Moses (Heb. *ḥōtēn,* Ex 2:21; 3:1; 4:18; 18:1–27; etc.). Caiaphas cooperated with his father-in-law (Gr. *pentheros*) Annas (Jn 18:13). *See* Marriage.

FATHER'S BROTHER. Abraham was Lot's uncle and guardian (Gen 12:5). An uncle (Heb. *dôd*) could act as redeemer of property (Lev 25:49). In inheritance, paternal uncles followed brothers of the deceased (Num 27:10). Mattaniah (Zedekiah), Jehoiachin's uncle, succeeded him as king (II Kgs 24:17).

FATHER'S HOUSE. This usage in the OT is always of earthly significance, referring to the dwelling place of the family (Gen 24:23), or to the family itself (Gen 12:1), or to the tribe (Gen 24:40), or to the entire nation (Neh 1:6). *See* Family.

In the NT Jesus added two further ideas. He referred to the temple as His Father's house (Jn 2:16). In Jn 14:2 He speaks of the Christian's future home as "in my Father's house." *See also* Father; Heaven; Mansion.

FATHOM. *See* Weights, Measures, and Coins.

FATLING. In all the uses of this word reference is to a young calf that has been fed and is fat and firm. A calf was sometimes used as an offering. It was considered valuable property (Isa 11:6; Ezk 39:18), and was looked on as a table delicacy (Mt 22:4).

FATTED FOWL. This term, referring to fatted birds, is used only once in the OT (I Kgs 4:23 [Heb., 5:3]). The term translated the Heb. words *barbūrîm 'ăbûsîm.* The first of the two words stems from the root *bārar,* meaning "be pure" and thus white. Since ivory carvings from Megiddo show a row of barefooted peasants bringing fattened geese into town (VBW, II, 210), the "fatted fowl" for Solomon's table were likely white geese. *See* Animals, III.18.

FEAR. A term used both in the OT and NT in several very significant ways. The Scriptures speak of the following kinds of fear:

1. A holy fear (Heb. *yir'à;* Gr. *phobos*) which amounts to awe or respect for the majesty and holiness of God, a godly reverence (Gen 20:11; Ps 34:11; Acts 9:31; Rom 3:18). David speaks of this fear as clean and pure (Ps 19:9); Job and the psalmist, as the basis or beginning of all true wisdom (Job 28:28; Prov 1:7; Ps 111:10). This fear is God-given and enables man to respect God's authority, obey His commands, turn from evil (I Sam 12:14, 20–25; Ps 2:11; Prov 8:13; 16:6), and to pursue holiness (II Cor 7:1; Phil 2:12). Gentile converts to Judaism who believed in God were called God-fearers (Acts 10:2, 22; 13:26). *See* Worship.

2. A filial fear (Lev 19:3) which is based

upon the proper reverence of the child of God for his heavenly Father (Ps 33:18; 34:6–11; Prov 14:26–27; II Cor 6:17–7:1).

3. A fear for unforgiven sin which is caused by the work of the law written in the heart (Rom 2:15) and the knowledge of God's Word; e.g., Adam's fear when he sinned (Gen 3:10; cf. Prov 28:1); Felix as he heard Paul preach (Acts 24:25); that of men who reject the preaching of the gospel (Heb 10:27–31).

4. A fear, dread or terror (Heb. *paḥad*) of God's holiness on the part of the wicked at the Lord's coming (Ps 14:5; Isa 2:10, 19; Rev 11:11; 18:10, 15). Along with this we may consider a fear of His people that God places in other men's hearts to protect His own (Deut 11:25; II Chr 20:29–30).

5. A fear of man is also mentioned in Scripture. This may either be a proper respect for those in authority (Rom 13:7; I Pet 2:18), or a senseless dread (Num 14:9; Isa 8:12).

6. A fear for others and the danger in which they stand (I Cor 2:3; II Cor 11:3; 12:20–21).

7. A terror of the unknown (Lk 21:26) or of the uncanny (Job 4:14–16).

8. Cowardice or timidity (Gr. *deilia*), as in "a spirit of fear" (II Tim 1:7), and "let not your heart . . . be afraid" (Jn 14:27; cf. Mt 8:26; Mk 4:40; Rev 21:8).

Fear is sometimes falsely assumed to be the origin of religion, but fear alone in the sense of dread is not the positive force that draws men to God with an attitude of reverence, worship, and respect.

The Kierkegaardian concept of *Angst zum tode*, that anxiety which pursues man right through life until his death, falls under the third classification above, since it expresses the nagging anxiety which besets the unsaved. This fear, and the dread of appearing before a holy God, is eliminated – or ought to be – in the lives of believers (I Jn 4:18; cf. Rom 8:1, 33–34), though the fear of reverence and of respect for authority remains.

R. A. K.

FEAST. *See* Food: Banquet. For the various OT Jewish feasts *see* Festivals.

FEAST OF CHARITY. *See* Agape; Love Feast.

FEEBLE KNEES. The idea expressed in these words is found three times in the Bible (Job 4:4; Isa 35:3; Heb 12:12). In Job the Heb. word is *kāra'* and speaks of the bending of the knee through weakness. There is no indication of the cause, whether through disease or weariness. Isaiah uses *kāshal*, which means to totter in the ankles, but no cause is indicated. In the letter to the Hebrews *paralelumena* is the word; it indicates a sort of paralysis resulting from a cutting off of vital strength. In all uses the idea seems to be more figurative than literal, suggesting weariness and discouragement.

See Feebleminded.

FEEBLEMINDED. In I Thess 5:14 believers are instructed to "comfort the feebleminded," i.e., encourage those who are fainthearted or discouraged (Gr. *oligopsychos*, often in LXX). In the LXX the term covers a wide range of attitudes from being fearful (Isa 35:4), humbled or dejected (Isa 57:15), grieved or depressed in spirit (Isa 54:6; Ex 6:9), wounded or broken in spirit (Prov 18:14), to being short-tempered (Prov 14:29). Thus the word suggests one who is laboring under such trouble that his heart sinks within him, or who is grieving because of the death of loved ones.

See Feeble Knees.

FEET. *See* Foot.

FELIX, ANTONIUS (ăn-tō'nĭ-ŭs fē'lĭks). Procurator of Judea under Claudius and Nero (A.D. 52–60), and one before whom Paul was brought to trial in Caesarea (Acts 23:24–24:27). The descriptions by Tacitus (*Annals* xii. 54 and *Histories* v. 9) are classic: "He thought he could do any evil act with impunity," and "(He) exercised the power of a king in the spirit of a slave."

Felix listened to Paul's defense, postponed any decision pending more information from Lysias, the Roman commander in Jerusalem who had originally arrested Paul (Acts 21:33), often listened to and conversed with the apostle, but left him in prison, hoping for a bribe and also as a move pleasing to the Jews.

He had married Drusilla, a Jewess and a sister of Agrippa II, when she was about 16 years of age, after having persuaded her to leave her husband for him. Paul's reasoning with them (Acts 24:25) may be analagous to John the Baptist's accusing Herod Antipas and Herodias of an illicit relationship (Mk 6:18).

In A.D. 60, Felix was recalled by Nero and was replaced in office by Festus. *See* Festus.

W. M. D.

FELLOES. The English word means the rims of wheels supported by spokes. In I Kgs 7:33 these are parts of the wheels of the stands for the bronze basins or lavers in the court of Solomon's temple. The KJV so translated *ḥishshuqîm*, which more accurately means the spokes, whereas the KJV word "naves" immediately preceding it should be "rims" or "felloes" (see RSV, JerusB).

FELLOW. A term denoting, as in Gen 38:12, a friend, companion, associate, i.e., a fellow companion; or less personally, a fellow citizen or neighbor (Lev 19:18). The feminine in Heb., *re'ûth*, means fellow (woman) or neighbor (Ex 11:2). The name Ruth, meaning "friendship," is from the same root. The term "fellow" sometimes denotes contempt when used derisively, as "vain fellows" (II Sam 6:20). Other OT terms are *ḥāber* (Ezk 37:16), and *'āmîth*, which is used prophetically of Christ in Zech 13:7. The NT synonyms are found in Mt 11:16;

20:13 (*hetairos*); Lk 5:7; Heb 1:9 (*metochos*). Cf. also fellow heir (Rom 8:17); fellow servant (Mt 18:28); fellow disciple (Jn 11:16).

FELLOWSHIP. Fellowship (Gr. *koinōnia*) means companionship or partnership and communion with others on the basis of something held in common. Christian fellowship can be considered under several headings.

Participants. The Christian's fellowship is first with God (I Jn 1:6), with Christ (I Cor 1:9), with the Holy Spirit (Phil 2:1; II Cor 13:14), with the Father and the Son (I Jn 1:3; Jn 14:6, 23, 26). It is second with fellow Christians (Jn 15:12; I Jn 1:3, 7).

Basis. The Christian's fellowship with men is, however, to be based, first, upon his clear confession that Christ is the promised Messiah and has truly assumed human flesh (I Jn 4:2-3; II Jn 7-11); and, second, upon his not living in open overt sins such as fornication, idolatry, covetousness, drunkenness (I Cor 5:11). Yet the Christian may company or mix with unsaved who have these sins, and will have to do so because he is a part of the world. That he is forbidden, however, to do so with Christians, shows the dangers of such overt sins not only to the Christian who lives in sin but also to others. Further, the Christian is forbidden to be unequally yoked together with unbelievers (II Cor 6:14-18). In the context Paul is speaking to those who have recently left heathenism. Still, the principle of separation from paganism is hard to distinguish from separation from those holding erroneous doctrines of Christ, particularly since the latter is forbidden by John (I Jn 4:2 f.; II Jn 7-11).

Means of fellowship. There are five specific kinds of fellowship or sharing enjoyed by the Christian.

1. Communion or fellowship together at the Lord's Supper (I Cor 10:16-21), in which the believer professes his faith in Christ's atoning blood and shows forth His death till He comes again (I Cor 11:23-26). Paul gives very careful instruction concerning this fellowship and warns us to examine ourselves before we take part in the Eucharist (I Cor 11:27-28).

2. Membership in the church. Our Lord established His NT Church, or body of called-out believers, on the public profession of Himself as Saviour (Mt 16:18). In Himself He established a vital unity, making of both Jew and Gentile one new "man" or "body" (Eph 2:14-16). He loved it as His own bride and gave Himself for it (Eph 5:25 f.). In the local churches or assemblies Christians are to be nurtured (Heb 10:24-25; cf. Mal 3:16) and to enjoy fellowship in the Word and prayer (Acts 2:42).

3. Giving, which is commanded (I Tim 6:18; Heb 13:16) and may consist in systematic giving on a regular basis (Rom 15:26; II Cor 8:4; 9:13), or it may occur in the gift of large sums or even all one owns at a particular time (Acts 4:36-37; 5:1-11). In cases where all is given, the gift is entirely at the discretion of the giver (Acts 5:4), though it may be necessary in certain cases because the particular individual is turning away from his besetting sin of covetousness (cf. the rich young ruler, Lk 18:18 f.).

4. Ministration to the saints, such as relief funds for other churches (Acts 11:29; Rom 15:25), help to Christians in need (Rom 12:13; II Cor 8:4) and perhaps other people as well (Heb 13:16), and sharing other people's burdens (Rom 15:1; Jas 5:16).

5. Fellowship in suffering. This refers to suffering as a member of Christ's body, partaking of "the fellowship of his sufferings" (Phil 3:10; cf. Col 1:24).

Is there not another fellowship, namely, that of the community of goods or Christian communism mentioned in Acts 4? The experiment of having all things in common was tried immediately after Pentecost. Since it is neither commended for future use nor condemned, and because it has never since been practiced by any except some of the smaller Christian groups, the general consensus is that it proved to be a failure, or was meant to be only a temporary expedient. *See* Community of Goods.

Limits of fellowship. The question as to how far the doctrine of Christian fellowship requires the church to go in the removal of denominational boundaries through merger and union has received increasing attention during the past 50 years. In 1923 all the Methodists, the Congregationalists and 55 percent of the Presbyterians united to form the United Church in Canada, and many other unions have occurred since in the U.S. Currently 25 million Protestants in the U.S. are working on a plan of church union. While undoubtedly many divisions within the body of Christ are unnecessary and harmful, the almost universal leveling of all distinctives in order to attain one great united church presents real questions and dangers.

Christ, it is true, prayed "that they may all be one . . . just as We are one" (Jn 17:21-22, NASB); nevertheless the basis upon which union is being fostered must be examined. Any unity founded upon the joining of those who truly believe Christ is the only begotten Son of God, who became incarnate, died on the cross to bear the sins of the believer, and rose in a resurrection body on the third day, with men or churches which do not believe these fundamentals of the faith, is unscriptural.

The move to bring about a reunion of Protestantism and Roman Catholicism also raises the problem of true biblical fellowship, though in another form. It is not the question as to who Christ is that separates Catholics and Protestants, but what Christ did. Did He offer the only sacrifice sufficient to save the sinner from his sin, or a sacrifice which was ineffectual without our good works? Is Christ the only mediator between God and man, or must we depend also on the intercessory work of Mary and the saints? Christ prayed for a unity of *fellowship,* not of *organization;* a unity in His new life and in the Spirit (II Cor 13:14) in which all the members of His one body are different (I Cor 12), not for a uniformity of structure. The eternal distinction and plurality of persons in the Trinity indicate that in making His comparison, Christ allows for diversity within the unity of His body (Jn 17:21–23). *See* Communion of Saints.

Bibliography. Friedrich Hanck, "*Koinos*, etc.," TDNT, III, 789–809.

R. A. K.

FEN. The Heb. word *biṣṣâ* is defined by BDB as a "swamp." The KJV translates the word in Job 8:11 as "mire" and in Job 40:21 as "fens." Thus a fen denotes a miry bog or marsh.

FENCE. Several Heb. words are used for fence.

1. The Heb. verb *gādar* designates "to surround with a wall," "to heap up stones for a wall" (Job 19:8; Lam 3:9). The nouns derived from the word mean either the wall itself or the area surrounded by it (Ps 62:3; "wall," Num 22:24; Prov 24:31; Isa 5:5).

2. Heb. *'āzaq* (Isa 5:2) really means "to dig and loosen with a mattock."

3. The verb *sākak* translated "fenced" in Job 10:11 (KJV) should be "knit together" as in RSV here and in Ps 139:13. *See* Hedge for passages containing the similar appearing root *sûk* or *śûk*, meaning "to hedge or fence up."

For fenced cities *see* City, Fenced.

FENCED CITY. *See* City, Fenced.

FERRET. KJV translation of *'ǎnāqa;* RSV has "gecko," a lizard. *See* Animals, IV.16, 21.

FESTIVALS. Observance of the sacred seasons and Jewish religious festivals constituted a significant aspect of the Heb. religion. These holy days and sacred seasons were decreed by God as His gifts to Israel. God purposed to preserve by them a remembrance of such sacred events as their divine election and deliverance (the Passover celebration), their sojourn in the wilderness (Feast of Tabernacles), their constant dependence upon Him for all temporal blessings and prosperity (Pentecost), their preservation in Persia (Feast of Purim), their need of cleansing and forgiveness (Day of Atonement). Many other spiritual lessons and blessings were also to be derived from the numerous festivals and holy days such as the sabbath, new moons, year of jubilee, and the like. Hence, the sacred seasons were based in large measure upon some significant historical event related to the national or religious life of Israel. Furthermore, like the temple and the Scriptures, the national religious festivals were important bonds of spiritual and national unity for the Heb. people.

Sabbatical Seasons

Weekly sabbath. In addition to the annual festivals, the celebration of the weekly sabbath

(*shabbāt*) and the sabbatical feast days are also called "holy convocations" (*miqrā'ê qōdesh*) in Lev 23:2 ff. During the wilderness wanderings a holy convocation appears to have been a religious convocation of all males at the tabernacle. After Heb. settlement in Palestine, however, the universal command to appear at the sanctuary had reference only in regard to the three festival pilgrimages in which all males were to attend the feasts of Passover, Pentecost, and Tabernacles at Jerusalem (Ex 23:14–17; Deut 16:16). The holy convocation commanded for the weekly sabbath was to be *in all your dwellings,* that is, the sabbath was to be observed where the people lived.

1. Origin. The creation narrative in Genesis is concluded with an account of the hallowing of the seventh day by God, who rested from all His creative activity on that day. Although the term "sabbath" does not occur in this account, its verbal root (*shābat*) meaning "he rested or ceased" does occur (Gen 2:3). The Decalogue in Ex 20:8–11 assigns as the reason for requiring Israel to observe the sabbath the fact that God rested on this day after six days of creative work. Although there is no distinct mention of the observance of the sabbath in Genesis, some scholars hold that Moses apparently treats it as an institution with which they were already familiar as indicated by the words, "Remember the sabbath day, to keep it holy" (Ex 20:8); furthermore, a seven-day period is referred to in Gen 1:1–2:3; 7:4–10; 8:10–12; 29:27–28.

The first definite mention of the sabbath as a religious institution is found in Ex 16:21–30 in connection with the giving of manna. God commanded Israel in the wilderness that she was to observe the seventh day as a sabbath of rest from all labor by gathering a double portion of manna on the sixth day. That the day was already known to them, some believe, is evidenced by the Lord's rebuke to those who disobeyed: "How long refuse ye to keep my commandments and my laws?" (Ex 16:28). A short time later the observance was enjoined as the fourth commandment at Sinai (Ex 20:8–11).

Modern criticism assigns the origin of the sabbath to two different sources, which allegedly give conflicting reasons for its institution. Ex 20:11, it is argued, makes the sabbath a memorial of God's rest upon the completion of creation, whereas Deut 5:15 states that the sabbath is a memorial of the deliverance of Israel from Egypt. However, this view ignores the context of Deuteronomy. The sabbath was to be a perpetual covenant between God and Israel as His gift of refreshing rest; as such it served as a memorial of His rest from creative activity and was not specifically a memorial of the Exodus. The reference to the Exodus event in Deuteronomy is for the express purpose of reminding Israel that out of gratitude for their freedom and rest after a long period of servile labor, they ought also to allow rest for their servants who now were in a similar situation to their former condition in Egypt as slaves (cf. Ex

CHART OF JEWISH FESTIVALS

MONTHS	FESTIVALS	MONTHS	FESTIVALS
A'BIB (Heb. 'ābîb, green ears), or NI'-SAN. Thirty days; first of sacred, seventh of civil, year. (March-April)	1. New moon (Num. 10:10; 28:11–15). 10. Selection of paschal lamb (Exod. 12:3). Fast for Miriam (Num. 20:1), and in memory of the scarcity of water (20:2). 14. Paschal lamb killed in evening (Exod. 12:6). Passover begins (Num. 28:16). 15. First day of unleavened bread (Num. 28:17). After sunset sheaf of barley brought to temple. 16. "First fruits," sheaf offered (Lev. 23:10, sq.). Beginning of harvest, fifty days to Pentecost (Lev. 23:15). 21. Close of Passover, end of unleavened bread (Lev. 23:6). 15 and 21. Holy convocations (23:7). 26. Fast for death of Joshua.	ETH'ANIM (Heb. 'ēthānîm, permanent), or TIS'RI. Thirty days; seventh of sacred, first of civil, year. (Sept.-October)	1. New moon; New Year; Rosh Hashanah Feast of Trumpets (Lev. 23:24; Num. 29:1, 2).· 3. Fast for murder of Gedaliah (II Kings 25:25; Jer. 41:2); high priest set apart for day of atonement. 10. Day of atonement (Yom Kippur), "the fast" (Acts 27:9), i. e., the only one enjoined by the law (Lev. 16; 23:27–32); the first day of jubilee years. 15–21. Feast of Tabernacles, or Ingathering (Ex. 23:16; Lev. 23:34–43). 22. Holy convocation, palms borne, prayer for rain. (Lev. 23:36; Num. 29:35). 23. Feast for law being finished; dedication of Solomon's temple.
ZIV (Heb. zîv, brightness), or IYYAR. Twenty-nine days; second sacred, eighth of civil year. (April-May)	1. New moon (Num. 1:18). 10. Fast for death of Eli and capture of ark (I Sam. 4:11, sq.). 14. "Second" or "little" Passover, for those unable to celebrate in Abib; in memory of entering wilderness (Exod. 16:11). 28. Feast for death of Samuel (I Sam. 25:1).	BUL (Heb. bûl), or MARCHESH'-VAN. Twenty-nine days; eighth of sacred, second of civil, year. (October-Nov.)	1. New moon. 17. Prayers for rain. 19. Fast for faults committed during Feast of Tabernacles. 26. Feast in memory of recovery after· the ·captivity of places occupied by the Cuthites.
SI'VAN (Heb. sîvän). Thirty days; third third of sacred, ninth of civil, year. (May-June)	1. New moon. 6. "Feast of Pentecost," or "Feast of Weeks," because it came seven weeks after Passover (Lev. 23:15–21). 22. Fast in memory of Jeroboam's forbidding subjects to carry first fruits to Jerusalem (I Kings 12:27). 27. Fast, Chanina being burned with books of law.	KISLEV (Heb. kisleu). Thirty days; ninth of sacred, third of civil, year. (Nov.-December)	1. New moon. 2. Fast (three days) if no rain falls. 6. Feast in memory of roll burned by Jehoiakim (Jer. 36:23). 14. Fast, absolute if no rain. 25. Feast of the dedication of the temple, or of Lights (eight days) in memory of restoration of temple by Judas Maccabaeus (cf. Jn. 10:22).
TAM'MUZ (Heb. tămmūz). Twenty-nine days; fourth of sacred, tenth of civil, year. (June-July)	1. New moon. 14. Feast for abolition of a book of Sadducees and Bethusians, intended to subvert oral law and traditions. 17. Fast in memory of tables of law broken by Moses (Exod. 32:19); and taking of Jerusalem by Titus.	TE'BETH (Heb. te'-bĕth). Twenty-nine days; tenth of sacred, fourth of civil, year. (December-Jan.)	1. New Moon. 8. Fast because the law was translated into Greek. 10. Fast on account of siege of Jerusalem by Nebuchadnezzar (II Kings 25:1).
AB (Heb. 'āb, fruitful). Thirty days; fifth of sacred, eleventh of civil, year. (July-August)	1. New moon; fast for death of Aaron, commemorated by children of Jethuel, who furnished wood to temple after the captivity. 9. Fast in memory of God's declaration against murmurers entering Canaan (Num. 14:29–31). 18. Fast, because in the time of Ahaz the evening lamp went out. 21. Feast when wood was stored in temple. 24. Feast in memory of law providing for sons and daughters alike inheriting estate of parents.	SHE'BAT (Heb. shᵉbät', or SE': BAT. Thirty days; eleventh of sacred, fifth of civil, year. (January-February)	1. New moon. 4 or 5. Fast in memory of death of elders. successors to Joshua. 15. Beginning of the year of Trees (q. v.). 23. Fast for war of the Ten Tribes against Benjamin (Judg. 20); also idol of Micah (18:11, sq.). 29. Memorial of death of Antiochus Epiphanes, enemy of Jews.
E'LUL (Heb. 'ĕlûl', good for nothing). Twenty-nine days; sixth of sacred, twelfth of civil, year. (August-Sept.)	1. New moon. 7. Feast for dedication of Jerusalem's walls by Nehemiah. 17. Fast, death of spies bringing ill report (Num. 14:26). 21. Feast, wood offering. (Throughout the month the cornet is sounded to warn of approaching new civil year.)	ADAR (Heb. 'ădär, fire). Twenty-nine days; twelfth of sacred, sixth of civil, year. (ADAR SHENI, c. 7 times in 19 years.) (February-March)	1. New moon. 7. Fast because of Moses' death (Deut.34:5). 8, 9. Trumpet sounded in thanksgiving for rain, and prayer for future rain. 13. Fast of Esther (Esth. 4:16). Feast in memory of Nicanor, enemy of the Jews (I Macc. 7:44). 14. The first Purim, or lesser Feast of Lots (Est.9:21). 15. The great Feast of Purim. 20. Feast for rain obtained in time of drought, in time of Alexander Jannaeus. 23. Feast for dedication of Zerubbabel's temple (Ezra 6:16). 28. Feast to commemorate the repeal of decree of Grecian kings forbidding Jews to circumcise their children.

A chart of the festivals.

5:14-15). Thus both passages connect the sabbath with rest.

Some scholars have drawn parallels between the Babylonian *shabbatu* and the Heb. sabbath, but no such relationship is indicated from available evidence. Furthermore, Ezk 20:12, 20, indicates that the sabbaths were signs God gave to Israel to distinguish her from other nations.

2. Character and observance. The sabbath was to be observed by abstaining from all physical labor, whether done by man or beast. But the sabbath was not intended for selfish use in idleness; it was a divinely given opportunity, in freedom from one's secular labors, to strengthen and refresh the whole man, physically and spiritually. The sabbath had a benevolent design and was intended as a blessing, not a burden, to man (cf. Deut 5:14-15; Isa 58:13-14; Mk 2:27). Sabbath legislation is found in several OT passages; e.g., Ex 16:23 ff.; 20:8-11; 31:12-17; Lev 19:3, 30; Num 15:32-36; Deut 5:12-15. *See* Sabbath.

Monthly new moon. The first day of each month was designated as *rō'sh ḥodesh,* "the first or head of the month," or simply as *ḥōdesh,* "new moon" (Num 10:10; I Sam 20:5). Unlike the new moon of the seventh month, which was the first day of the civil new year and celebrated with a great festival, the regular monthly new moons were subordinate feast days celebrated with additional burnt offerings (Num 28:11-15), the blowing of trumpets (Num 10:10; Ps 81:3), family feasts (I Sam 20:5), spiritual edification (II Kgs 4:23), and family sacrifices (I Sam 20:6). As on all sabbatical feast days, all servile work ceased, except the necessary preparation of food (cf. Ex 12:16). The new moon and sabbath are closely related in several passages (e.g., Isa 1:13; Ezk 46:1; Hos 2:11; Amos 8:5).

The moon occupied an important place in the life of the Hebrews, since it was the guide to their calendar based upon the lunar month or period of the moon's circuit. Because of this, and the importance of the uniform celebration of the various periodic religious festivals by Jews everywhere, it was extremely important to determine the exact time of the appearance of the new moon. Thus the appearance of the smallest crescent signified the beginning of a new month and was announced with the blowing of the shofar or ram's horn.

Sabbatical year. The *shenat shabbātôn,* "year of rest" or sabbatical year, like the weekly sabbath, was designed by God with a benevolent purpose in view. Every seventh year debts were to be cancelled and the land was to lie fallow, the uncultivated increase to be left to the poor Israelite.

1. Observance. According to II Chr 36:21, observance of the sabbatical year had been neglected for about 500 years, the 70 year Captivity allowing the land to enjoy its neglected sabbaths, "for as long as it lay desolate it kept sabbath, to fulfill three-score and ten years" (ASV). After the Captivity, the people under Nehemiah bound themselves to the faithful observance of the seventh year, covenanting that "we would forego the seventh year, and the exaction of every debt" (Neh 10:31, ASV). Its observance continued during the intertestamental period (I Macc 6:48-53) and afterward (Jos *Ant.* xiv. 10.6).

2. Purpose. (*a*) A rest for the land (Lev 25:1-7). After the land had been sown and harvested for six successive years it was "to rest" or to remain fallow on the seventh year. This included the vineyards and olive yards also (Ex 23:10). This provision insured greater productivity for the soil by the periodic interruption of the incessant sowing, plowing, and reaping. (*b*) To enable the poor to eat (Ex 23:10-11). During this year, that which grew of itself in the fields, vineyards, and olive yards was not to be harvested, but left so "that the poor of thy people may eat: and what they leave the beast of the field shall eat." Lev 25:6-7 also includes the owner, his servants, the sojourner, cattle and beasts, as well as the poor of Ex 23:11, as those who were eligible to consume the natural produce of the sabbatical year. (*c*) Debts were to be cancelled (Deut 15:1-6). Each creditor was to cancel the debts of a brother Israelite at the end of every seven years, for it was called also "the year of release" (Deut 15:9; 31:10). This did not apply to a foreigner, from whom the debt could be collected (Deut 15:3). The release was so that absolute poverty and permanent indebtedness would not exist among the Israelites. In addition, they were not to disregard the needs of their poorer brethren by refusing to lend merely because the year of release was near (Deut 15:7-11). (*d*) In the sabbatical year the law was to be read for the instruction of the people at the Feast of Tabernacles (Deut 31:10-13). (*e*) Not simply on the sabbatical year, but also at the close of any six year period, those Israelites who because of poverty had made themselves bondservants to their brethren were to be released (Deut 15:12-18). In this case the year of release would be ascertained from the first year of indenture. The legislation respecting the sabbatical year was confined to the Israelites in the Holy Land and went into effect upon their arrival there (Lev 25:2).

Year of jubilee. Seven sabbatic cycles of years (i.e., 49) terminated in the year of jubilee (*shenat hayyôbēl*), lit., "the year of the ram's horn," the fiftieth year being designated thus from the custom of sounding the ram's horn (*yôbēl*) announcing its arrival (Lev 25:8-17). The fiftieth year is called "the year of liberty" (*derôr*)in Ezk 46:17 (cf. Jer 34:8, 15, 17) on the basis of Lev 25:10: "And ye shall hallow the fiftieth year, and proclaim liberty throughout the land . . . it shall be a jubilee unto you."

1. Nature of celebration. According to Lev 25:9, the year of jubilee was announced by the sounding of rams' horns throughout the land on the tenth day of the seventh month, which was also the great Day of Atonement. The year of jubilee was not, as some have thought, the forty-ninth year, and thus simply a seventh sabba-

Samaritan priests celebrating the Passover.
Richard E. Ward

tical year, but, was, as Lev 25:10 states, the fiftieth year, thus providing two successive sabbatic years in which the land would have rest. Certain regulations were issued to take effect during the year of jubilee. (*a*) Rest for the land (Lev 25:11-12). As in the preceding sabbatical year, the land was to remain uncultivated and the people were to eat of the natural increase. To compensate for this, God promised: "I will command my blessing upon you in the sixth year, and it shall bring forth fruit for three years" (Lev 25:21). In addition, other sources of provision were available, such as hunting, fishing, flocks, herds, bees, and the like. (*b*) Hereditary lands and property were to be restored to the original family without compensation, in the year of jubilee (Lev 25:23-34). In this manner all land and its improvements would eventually be restored to the original holders to whom God had given it, for He said, "The land shall not be sold in perpetuity; for the land is mine" (Lev 25:23, ASV). This regulation did not apply to a house within a walled city, which stood in no relation to a family's land inheritance (vv.29-30). (*c*) Freedom of bondservants was to be effected in the year of jubilee. Every Israelite who had because of poverty subjected himself to bondage was to be set free (Lev 25:29 ff.).

2. Purpose. There were several divine purposes in these regulations and provisions for the year of jubilee. (*a*) It was to contribute toward the abolishment of poverty by enabling the unfortunate and victims of circumstances to begin anew. (*b*) It would discourage excessive, permanent accumulations of wealth and property, and the consequent deprivation of an Israelite of his inheritance in the land. "Woe unto them that join house to house, that lay field to field" (Isa 5:8; cf. Mic 2:2). (*c*) It preserved families and tribes inasmuch as it returned freed bondservants to their own blood relations and families, and thus slavery, in any permanent sense, would not exist in Israel.

Special festival sabbaths. In addition to the weekly sabbath and the monthly new moon,

there were seven annual feast days which were also classed as sabbaths. They were the first and last days of the Feast of Unleavened Bread (Lev 23:7-8), the Day of Pentecost (Lev 23:21), the Feast of Trumpets (Lev 23:24-25), the Day of Atonement (Lev 23:32), and the first and last days of the Feast of Tabernacles (Lev 23:34-36). There was one major distinction between these festival sabbaths and the weekly sabbath and Day of Atonement. On the latter, all work was strictly forbidden, whereas rest only from "servile" labor was required on the other sabbaths.

Pilgrimage Feasts

Feast of the Passover and Feast of Unleavened Bread. The Passover (*pesah*) was the first of three annual pilgrimage festivals and was celebrated on the 14th of Nisan (post-Exilic name; formerly Abib, Ex 13:4, approximately our April), thereafter continuing as the Feast of Unleavened Bread from the 15th to the 21st. Nisan marked the beginning of the religious or sacred new year (Ex 12:2). The Heb. term *pesah* is from a root meaning "to pass (or spring) over," and signifies the passing over (sparing) of the houses of Israel when the firstborn of Egypt were slain (Ex 12). The Passover itself refers only to the paschal supper on the evening of the 14th, whereas the following period, 15th to 21st, is called the Feast of Unleavened Bread (Ex 12; 13:1-10; Lev 23:5-8; Num 28:16-25; Deut 16:1-8).

1. Institution and celebration. The purpose for its institution was to commemorate the deliverance of Israel from Egyptian bondage and the sparing of Israel's firstborn when God smote the firstborn of Egypt. In observance of the first Passover, on the 10th of Nisan the head of each family set apart a lamb without blemish. On the evening of the 14th the lamb was slain and some of its blood sprinkled on the doorposts and lintel of the house in which they ate the Passover as a seal against the coming judgment upon Egypt. The lamb was then roasted whole and eaten with unleavened bread and bitter herbs. If the family was too small to consume a lamb, then a neighboring family could share it. Any portion remaining was to be burned the next morning. Each was to eat in haste with loins girded, shoes on the feet, and staff in hand.

2. Later observance. After the establishment of the priesthood and tabernacle, the celebration of the Passover differed in some particulars from the Egyptian Passover. These distinctions were: (*a*) the Passover lamb was to be slain at the sanctuary rather than at home (Deut 16:5-6); (*b*) the blood was sprinkled upon the altar instead of the doorposts; (*c*) besides the family sacrifice for the Passover meal, there were public and national sacrifices offered each of the seven days of the Feast of Unleavened Bread (Num 28:16-24); (*d*) the meaning of the Passover was recited at the feast each year (Ex 12:24-27); (*e*) the singing of the Hallel (Ps

113–118) during the meal was later instituted; (f) a second Passover on the 14th day of the second month was to be kept by those who were ceremonially unclean or away on a journey at the time of its regular celebration on the 14th of Nisan (Num 9:9–12).

The Passover was one of the three feasts in which all males were required to come to the sanctuary. They were not to appear empty-handed, but were to bring offerings as the Lord had prospered them (Ex 23:14–17; Deut 16:16–17). It was unlawful to eat leavened food after midday of the 14th, and all labor, with few exceptions, ceased. According to Josephus (*Wars* vi.9.3), each lamb was to serve ten to twenty persons, no ceremonially unclean men or women being admitted to the feast. After appropriate blessings a first cup of wine was served, followed by the eating of a portion of the bitter herbs. Before the lamb and unleavened bread were eaten, a second cup of wine was provided at which time the son, in compliance with Ex 12:26, asked the father the meaning and significance of the Passover feast. An account of the Egyptian bondage and deliverance was recited in reply. The first portion of the Hallel (Ps 113–114) was then sung and the paschal supper eaten, followed by third and fourth cups of wine and the second part of the Hallel (Ps 115–118).

3. Feast of Unleavened Bread. Both the Passover and the Feast of Unleavened Bread, which immediately followed, commemorated the Exodus, the former in remembrance of God's "passing over" the Israelites when He slew the firstborn of Egypt, and the latter, to keep alive the memory of their affliction and God's bringing them out in haste from Egypt ("bread of affliction," Deut 16:3). The first and last days of this feast were sabbaths in which no servile work could be done, except the necessary preparation of food. The Passover season marked the beginning of the grain harvest in Palestine. On the second day of Unleavened Bread (16th Nisan), a sheaf of the firstfruits of the barley harvest was presented as a wave offering (Lev 23:9–11). The ceremony came to be called "the omer ceremony" from the Heb. word for sheaf, *'ōmĕr*.

Feast of Pentecost. Pentecost, which is the Gr. word for "fiftieth," is called in Heb. *ḥag shābū'ōt*, i.e., "the feast of weeks" (Ex 34:22; Lev 23:15–22). It derived its name from the fact that it was celebrated seven weeks after the Passover on the fiftieth day (Lev 23:15–16; Deut 16:9–10). It is also called the "feast of harvest" (Ex 23:16) and the "day of firstfruits" (Num 28:26).

Pentecost was a one-day festival in which all males were to appear at the sanctuary, and a sabbath in which all servile labor was suspended. The central feature of the day was the offering of two loaves of bread for the people from the firstfruits of the wheat harvest (Lev 23:17). As the omer ceremony signified the harvest season had begun, the presentation of the two loaves indicated its close. It was a day of thanksgiving in which free-will offerings were made (Deut 16:10), rejoicing was expressed before the Lord, and special consideration shown the Levite, sojourner, orphan and widow (Deut 16:10–12). The festival day signified the dedication of the harvest to God as the provider of all blessings. *See* Firstfruits 3.

The OT does not specifically give any historical significance for the day, Pentecost being the only one of the three great agricultural feasts which does not commemorate some event in Jewish history. Later tradition, on the basis of Ex 19:1, taught that the giving of the law at Sinai was fifty days after the Exodus and Passover, and as a result *shābū'ōt* has also become known as the Torah festival. The book of Ruth, which describes the harvest season, is read at Pentecost. The significance of the day for the NT is set forth in Acts 2, when on the day of Pentecost the Church had its beginning. *See* Pentecost.

Feast of Tabernacles. The Feast of Tabernacles (*ḥag hassūkkôt*), the third of the pilgrimage feasts, was celebrated for seven days from the 15th to 21st day of Tishri, the seventh month (Oct). It was followed by an eighth day of holy convocation with appropriate sacrifices (Lev 23:33 ff.; Num 29:12–38; Deut 16:13–15). It was also called "the feast of ingathering" (Ex 23:16) for the autumn harvest of the fruits and olives, with the ingathering of the threshing floor and the wine press, which occurred at this time (Lev 23:39; Deut 16:13). It was the outstanding feast of rejoicing in the year, in which the Israelites, during the seven day period, lived in booths or huts made of boughs in commemoration of their wilderness wanderings when their fathers dwelt in temporary shelters. According to Neh 8:14–18, the booths were made of olive, myrtle, palm, and other branches, and were built upon roofs of houses, in courtyards, the court of the temple, and in the broad places of the city streets. Sacrifices were more numerous during this feast than at any other, consisting of the offering of 189 animals for the seven day period.

When the feast coincided with a sabbatical year, the law was read publicly to the entire congregation at the sanctuary (Deut 31:10–13). As Josephus and the Talmud indicate, new ceremonies were gradually added to the festival, chief of which was the *śimḥat bêt hashô'ēbâh*, "the festival of the drawing of water." In this ceremony a golden pitcher was filled from the pool of Siloam and returned to the priest at temple amid the joyful shouts of the celebrants, after which the water was poured into a basin at the altar (cf. Jn 7:37–38). At night the streets and temple court were illuminated by innumerable torches carried by the singing, dancing pilgrims. The booths were dismantled on the last day, and the eighth day which followed was observed as a sabbath of holy convocation. The feast is mentioned by Zechariah as a joyous celebration in the Millennium (Zech 14:16).

Festivals and Holy Days of the Seventh Month

Feast of Trumpets. The new moon of the seventh month (1st of Tishri) constituted the beginning of the civil new year and was designated as *ro'sh hashshanâ*, "the first of the year," or *yôm terû'â*, "day of sounding" (the trumpet). Lev 23:23-25 and Num 29:1-6 are the only OT references to Rosh Hashanah, the regulations, prayers, and customs of which today fill volumes. The blowing of the shofar or ram's horn occupied a significant place on several other occasions, such as the monthly new moon and year of jubilee, but especially so at the beginning of the new year, hence its name—Feast of Trumpets. The Heb. calendar (*q.v.*) actually began with Nisan in the spring as the beginning of months (Ex 12:2); but since the end of the seventh month, Tishri, usually marked the beginning of the rainy season in Palestine when the year's work of plowing and planting began, Tishri was constituted the beginning of the economic and civil year. Business transactions, sabbatical years and jubilee years were all determined from the first of the seventh month. Later, Judaism associated many important events with Rosh Hashanah: the creation of the world; creation of Adam; the births of Abraham, Isaac, Jacob, and Samuel; the day of Joseph's release from prison, etc. (Ben M. Edidin, *Jewish Holidays and Festivals*, pp. 53-54).

The day was observed as a sabbatical feast day with special sacrifices, and looked forward to the solemn Day of Atonement ten days later. Rosh Hashanah (New Year's) and Yom Kippur (Day of Atonement) constitute what are called "high holy days" in Judaism. Rosh Hashanah has come to be considered as a day of judgment for one's deeds of the previous year. It is a day for retrospection, prayer, and repentance. On this day God judges all men for their deeds and decides who shall live or die, prosper or suffer adversity.

The Day of Atonement. The annual Day of Atonement (*yôm hakkippūrîm*) is set forth in Lev 16; 23:27-32 as the supreme act of national atonement for sin. It took place on the 10th day of the seventh month, Tishri, and fasting was commanded from the evening of the 9th until the evening of the 10th, in keeping with the unusual sanctity of the day. On this day an atonement was effected for the people, the priesthood, and for the sanctuary because it "dwelleth with them in the midst of their uncleannesses" (Lev 16:16, ASV).

1. The ritual. This was divided into two acts, one performed on behalf of the priesthood, and one on behalf of the nation Israel. The high priest, who had moved a week previous to this day from his own dwelling to the sanctuary, arose on the Day of Atonement, and having bathed and laid aside his regular high priestly attire, dressed himself in holy white linen garments, and brought forward a young bullock for a sin offering for himself and for his house. The other priests who on other occasions served in the sanctuary on this day took their place with the sinful congregation for whom atonement was to be made (Lev 16:17). The high priest slew the sin offering for himself and entered the holy of holies with a censer of incense, so that a cloud of incense might fill the room and cover the ark in order that he not die. Then he returned with the blood of the sin offering and sprinkled it upon the mercy seat on the east, and seven times before the mercy seat for the symbolic cleansing of the holy of holies, defiled by its presence among the sinful people. Having made atonement for himself, he returned to the court of the sanctuary.

The high priest next presented the two goats, which had been secured as the sin offering for the people, to the Lord at the door of the tabernacle and cast lots over them, one lot marked for Jehovah, and the other for Azazel (ASV). The goat upon which the lot had fallen for the Lord was slain, and the high priest repeated the ritual of sprinkling the blood as before. In addition, he cleansed the holy place by a sevenfold sprinkling, and lastly, cleansed the altar of burnt offering.

2. The goat for Azazel. In the second stage of the ceremony the live goat, the goat for Azazel, which had been left standing at the altar, was brought forward. The high priest, laying hands upon it, confessed over it all the sins of the people, after which it was sent into an uninhabited wilderness bearing the iniquity of the nation of Israel.

The precise significance of this part of the ceremony is determined by the meaning which is attached to the expression "for Azazel" (KJV, "for a scapegoat"). Basically, there are four interpretations: (*a*) Azazel was a *place* to which the second goat was sent. But such a place would have been left behind in the constant movement of Israel from Egypt to Palestine. (*b*) Azazel was a *person*, either Satan or an evil spirit. But the name Azazel occurs nowhere else in Scripture, which is unlikely if he were so important a person to divide the sin offering with God, which suggestion in itself has an offensive connotation. Moreover, demon worship is condemned in the same law in Lev 17:7-9. (*c*) Azazel was an *abstract noun* meaning "dismissal" or "complete removal." (*d*) More likely Azazel designates the goat itself. This view was held by Josephus, Symmachus, Aquila, Theodotion, Luther, Bonar, LXX, Vulg., KJV ("scapegoat"), and others. Hence the goat was called in the Heb. Azazel, meaning "the removing goat": "And Aaron shall cast lots upon the two goats; one lot for Jehovah, and the other lot for Azazel" (ASV), *for the removing goat,* i.e., for the remover of sins (Lev 16:8). Both goats were called an atonement and both were presented to the Lord. Therefore, both goats were looked upon as *one offering.* Since it was physically impossible to depict two ideas with one goat, two were needed as a single sin offering. The first goat by its death symbolized atonement for sins; the other, by confessing over it the sins of Israel and sending it away, symbolized their complete removal. Compare the analogy in Lev 14:4–7. See Azazel.

Feast of Tabernacles. The third and final sacred observance in the seventh month commanded by Scripture was the Feast of Tabernacles. Inasmuch as it was also one of the three pilgrimage feasts in which all males were to appear at the sanctuary, it is discussed under that category (see above).

Post-Exilic Festivals

Feast of Purim. This feast was instituted by Mordecai to commemorate the preservation of the Jews of Persia from destruction through the plot of Haman, as recorded in the book of Esther. The term Purim (*pûrîm*), which means "lots," was given to the festival because Haman had cast lots to ascertain which day he would carry out the decree to massacre the Jews. The festival was to last for two days, the 14th and 15th of Adar, with "feasting and gladness, and of sending of portions one to another, and gifts to the poor" (Est 9:20–22, ASV). The feast has always been popular with the Jews as Josephus (*Ant.* xi.6.13) attests, its celebration continuing down to the present time. Later generations began to observe only one day (14th). The preceding day (13th) is known as the Fast of Esther in commemoration of Esther's fast before seeking audience with the king on behalf of the Jews (Est 4:15–16). Services at the synagogue on Purim include the reading of the book of Esther. See Purim.

Feast of Dedication. The Feast of Dedication (*ḥanukkâ*, "dedication"), also called the Feast of Lights, is a significant, although extrabiblical, feast originating during the Maccabean period in commemoration of the purification of the temple and restoration of the altar by Judas Maccabeus in 164 B.C. (I Macc 4:36–61). The dedication of the altar was observed eight days from the 25th of Kislev (Dec.) and ordained to be observed yearly thereafter. According to II Macc 10:6–7, the feast was likened to the Feast of Tabernacles and celebrated by the carrying of boughs, palms, and branches, with the singing of psalms. Josephus called the feast "Lights" for he writes: "We celebrate this festival, and call it Lights. I suppose the reason was, because this liberty [i.e., restored political and religious freedom] beyond our hopes appeared to us" (*Ant.* xii.7.7). The use of lights during Hanukkah celebrations has always played a significant part, especially in the homes, synagogues, and streets of Palestine. The feast is mentioned in connection with Jesus' ministry in Jn 10:22 ff.

Subordinate extrabiblical Jewish sacred seasons. The seventh day of Sukkot (Tabernacles), the 21st of Tishri, came to be known as *hôshă'nā' rabbā'*, "Great Hosanna" or "Great Help." The eighth day is now called *shĕmînî 'aseret*, "Eighth Day of Solemn Assembly," a holy convocation in which prayers for the

homeland are offered. The following day (23rd Tishri) is *śimḥat tôrâ*, "Feast of the Law," a day of rejoicing and celebration marking the close of the yearly cycle of reading the Torah in the synagogues. The "Fifteenth Day of Shebat," or *Ḥamishâ 'Asār Bishebāt*, marks the beginning of spring in Palestine and is celebrated by the planting of trees (cf. Lev 19:23; Deut 20:19). *Ḥag Bĕ'ōmĕr* is celebrated on the 33rd day of the "omer" season (18th of Iyar) to commemorate the attempt by the Jews to regain their independence under Simon bar Kokheba (A.D. 132–135).

Fasts include, besides the Fast of Esther (*Ta'ănît Esther*), *Asārâ Bĕṭĕbet*, "Tenth of Tebet," a fast in remembrance of the beginning of the siege of Jerusalem by Babylonia (II Kgs 25:1; Jer 39:1); *Shib'â 'Asār Betammûz*, "Seventeenth of Tammuz," in token of the day the city was entered by the invaders (Jer 39:2; 52:6–7); *Tishâ Bĕ'āb*, "Ninth of Ab," to lament the day of the destruction of the city and temple (II Kgs 25:8–9; Jer 52:12–13); and Fast of Gedaliah (third Tishri) to mourn the murder of Gedaliah in 586 B.C. See Fast.

Bibliography. Andrew A. Bonar, *A Commentary on the Book of Leviticus*, Grand Rapids: Zondervan, 1959. Ben M. Edidin, *Jewish Holidays and Festivals*, New York: Jordan Publ. Co., 1940. *Jewish Encyclopedia*, New York: Funk and Wagnalls, 1906. S. H. Kellogg, "The Book of Leviticus," ExpB. G. F. Oehler, "The Sacred Seasons,'" *Theology of the Old Testament*, Grand Rapids: Zondervan, n.d., pp. 323–352. J. Barton Payne, *The Theology of the Older Testament*, Grand Rapids: Zondervan, 1962, pp. 394–410, 524 f.

H. E. Fr.

FESTUS, PORCIUS (pôr'shŭs fĕs'tŭs). The successor to Antonius Felix as procurator of Judea under Nero. According to E. Schurer, he was unable to undo the damage done by his predecessor, although he himself was disposed to rule well. Josephus (*Ant.* xx.8.9–11) presents Festus as a wise and just official, an agreeable contrast to Felix and to Albinus his successor.

The generally accepted date for his accession is A.D. 60, but many chronological problems are involved, and consequently the beginning of Festus' office has been placed as early as A.D. 55 and as late as A.D. 60. See bibliography below for representative viewpoints.

According to Acts 24:27, Paul had been in prison two years when Festus arrived in Caesarea. When the procurator, anxious to gain favor with the Jews, asked Paul if he would consent to being tried in Jerusalem (Acts 25:9), the apostle objected to what (in his mind) would have been a risky situation, and then made his classic reply: "I appeal unto Caesar" (Acts 25:11). Because Festus had no charge to send to Nero with the prisoner (Acts 25:25–27), he appealed to Herod Agrippa II to hear the case. See Agrippa II.

As he listened to Paul's impassioned witness, Festus retorted, "Paul, you are out of your mind!" (Acts 26:24, NASB). Apparently the apostle either sounded absurd to the procurator, or he had come "too close to home" in the matter of conviction of sin.

Bibliography. For A.D. 56: F. J. Foakes-Jackson and Kirsopp Lake, *The Beginnings of Christianity,* London: Macmillan, 1933, V, 464–474. For A.D. 58: C. H. Turner, "Chronology of the New Testament," HDB, I, 418 f., 424 f. For A.D. 59: William M. Ramsay, *Pauline and Other Studies in the History of Religion,* London: Hodder & Stoughton, n.d., p. 348. H. J. Cadbury, *The Book of Acts in History,* New York: Harper, 1955, pp. 9–10. For A.D. 60: Theodor Zahn, *Introduction to the New Testament,* Grand Rapids: Kregel, 1953, III, 469–478.

W. M. D.

FETTERS. Instruments used in securing feet and hands of prisoners. Fetters were made in pairs, usually of iron or brass. The word is always used in the plural. "He sent a man before them, even Joseph, who was sold for a servant: whose feet they hurt with fetters" (Ps 105:17–18). The word is sometimes used figuratively, as in Job 36:8–9: "And if they be bound in fetters, and be holden in cords of affliction; then he showeth them their work. . . ."

FEVER. *See* Diseases: Fever.

FIDELITY (Gr. *pistis,* "faithfulness," "trustworthiness"). The adjective *pistos* is usually translated "faithful." The word *pistis* is translated "fidelity" only once in the NT (Tit 2:10), although it is possible that in Gal 5:22 it should be so translated. In Rom 3:3, "the faithfulness of God" (RSV) is clearly "the fidelity of God."

A stone watchtower in a field near Samaria.
HFV

There is a possibility that in Lk 18:8, "Shall he find faith on earth?" the meaning should be "fidelity." Two more passages, I Tim 6:11: "godliness, *faith,* love, patience," and II Tim 2:22: "follow righteousness, *faith,* charity," would make good sense if translated "fidelity." In all other NT uses of *pistis* the meaning would seem to be "faith" or "the faith" (*q.v.*).

When the word "fidelity" is used of God, as in Rom 3:3, the meaning is that God can be trusted not to change His character or disposition. He has the attribute of "fidelity." In Tit 2:10, "showing all good fidelity," slaves (servants) are enjoined to show the quality of faithfulness or fidelity. As Christians we are all to remain faithful to Christ, i.e., to have fidelity in our Christian life and faith, to manifest "the perseverance of the saints." In that way we will become "trustworthy." *See* Faith; Faithfulness.

F. E. H.

FIELD. The biblical term for "field" conveys the idea of an open area, while the term today may imply enclosure. The Heb. word *śādeh* (poetical form *śāday*) is the most common term for field in the OT. Frequently it is difficult to determine from the context the site and purpose of the territory (cf. Gen 2:5, 19; 4:8; Ex 1:14; 22:5; Deut 5:21, *et al.*). Sometimes the word is used to designate a large area ("country of Moab," RSV; or "field of Moab," KJV in Gen 36:35; parable of the tares in Mt 13:38, where "the field is the world"). The word is also used to designate a game resort (Gen 27:5), habitat of wild animals (Ps 80:13), a cultivated area (Ruth 2:2; Job 24:6; Ps 107:37), or a grazable pasture (Gen 34:5; Ex 9:21; Num 22:4). Jer 32:7 ff. records the details of the purchase of a field at Anathoth by Jeremiah during the siege of Jerusalem (588–586 B.C.).

Other Heb. words for a cultivated and non-cultivated field are: (1) *sh^edēmâ,* which is used only six times in the OT (cf. Deut 32:32; Isa 16:8); (2) *bar* (Aram.), used only in Dan 2:38; 4:12, 15, 21, 23, 25, 32; (3) *hûṣ,* sometimes translated "the outside" and frequently "abroad" (cf. Deut 23:13), but usually translated "field" as in Job 5:10; Prov 8:26, "in the open country"; (4) *ḥelqâ,* literally meaning "portion of ground," but usually translated "field" (II Sam 14:30); (5) *'ereṣ,* the common word for "earth" or "land"; (6) *y^egēbîm,* which occurs only once in the OT and is usually translated "fields" in the various English versions (Jer 39:10). The Gr. words *agros, chōra* and *chōrion,* translated "field," may refer either to areas limited in size or to the open country (Mt 6:30; Lk 15:25; Jn 4:35; Acts 1:18).

The biblical "field" was generally not enclosed, but was indicated by stone markers (or landmarks) at the corners. Such stones could be easily removed (Deut 19:14; 27:17). Because of the lack of enclosure and of the usually unsettled conditions, a watchman was ordinarily employed, especially when the crops were nearing maturity (*see* Agriculture). Besides the danger of human intruders, there was sometimes danger of straying cattle or even cattle rustling (Ex 22:5), and of fire if a Samson (Jud 15:5) or an angry Absalom (II Sam 14:30) were about.

Fields were occasionally named after remarkable events, as Helkath-hazzurim, "the field of strong men" (II Sam 2:16), or after their use, as "the fuller's field" (II Kgs 18:17) or "potter's field" (Mt 27:7). *See* Fuller's Field; Potter's Field; Aceldama.

D. W. D.

FIG, FIG TREE. *See* Plants.

FIG LEAVES. *See* Dress: Materials.

FIGHT. *See* Warfare.

FILLET (fĭl'ĕt). The Heb. word *ḥûṭ* in Jer 52:21 is translated "fillet" in KJV; ASV translates it "line." Gesenius gives the meaning "a thread, line, rope or cord."

The word *ḥishshaq* is given the meaning "filletted" by KJV in Ex 38:28; ASV and RSV give the meaning "made fillets." Gesenius gives the term "joinings," that is, the poles or rods used to join the top of the columns of the court of the tabernacle. In Ex 27:10–11, 17 these are prescribed to be made of silver.

FILTH, FILTHY. An alternate translation for Heb. *ṣô'â* which normally means "excrement" (Isa 4:4, a figure for sin), for Gr. *perikatharma* meaning "scrapings" or "refuse" (I Cor 4:13); or for *rhypos* (I Pet 3:21). Filthy can also be used in both literal (Isa 64:6; Ezk 36:25) and moral senses (Job 15:16; Ps 14:3; 53:3); or it may have the sense of "shameful" (Col 3:8).

FINE, FINES. *See* Crime and Punishment.

FINER. *See* Occupations: Refiner.

FINGER. This word is used literally of one of the five terminating members of the hand in relation to the OT priest and his ministry with the blood sacrifice (Lev 4:6; etc.); the rich man in Hades (Lk 16:24); Jesus' writing on the ground (Jn 8:6); doubting Thomas (Jn 20:25–27).

The term is also used figuratively or metaphorically to refer to the power or Spirit of God. Egyptian magicians said of the plagues, "This is the finger of God" (Ex 8:19). The tablets of stone were written by the finger of God (Ex 31:18; Deut 9:10). The heavens are the works of God's fingers (Ps 8:3). Jesus cast out demons with the "finger of God" (Lk 11:20).

FINING POT. A pot for refining metal, such as silver (Prov 17:3; 27:21). *See* Minerals and Metals; Silver; Occupations: Metal, Workers of.

FINISHER. This word (Gr. *teleiotes*) is used of Jesus in Heb 12:2. It is derived from *teleioō*

which means "to carry through completely," hence, "to make perfect." Perhaps the idea intended in Heb 12:2 is that it is Jesus who as author or pioneer-leader of the faith-life "fulfilled the ideal of faith Himself, and so, both as a vicarious offering and an example, He is the object of our faith.... In this He is distinguished from all those examples of faith in chap. 11" (JFB), who were not to be made perfect (*teleiōthōsis*) apart from us (Heb 11:40).

FINS. Among the water creatures that were clean and could be eaten by the Israelites (Lev 11:9–12) were those that had fins and scales. The word "fin" is only used in denoting what may be eaten in the sea. The Heb. word is of uncertain origin. Fins are the membraneous structures on the body of fish used to propel or guide them in swimming. *See* Animals: Fish, V.4.

FIR. *See* Plants.

FIRE. Words for fire are used about 450 times in Scripture with both literal and figurative meanings. The literal uses include its employment for domestic purposes in cooking (Isa 30:14), lighting and for warmth (Jer 36:22; Mk 14:54; Jn 18:18; Acts 28:2); for melting, casting, working, and refining of metals (Zech 13:9; Mal 3:2); for burning refuse and contaminated articles (Lev 13:52, 57); as a means of destroying idolatrous objects (Deut 7:5; I Chr 14:12); as a destructive force in the form of lightning (Ps 29:7) and the burning of cities in time of war (Isa 1:7; Jer 34:2); as a severe means of punishment for grievous offenses (Rev 16:8–9); as the common means of making sacrifices to God. (The pagan custom of burning children in fire as a sacrifice was condemned.) *See* Fire Worship.

Figurative or symbolic uses include the representation of the divine presence, holiness, glory, guidance, and protection (Ezk 1:4, 13, 27; 8:2); God's jealousy (Ezk 36:5), wrath against and punishment of sin (Isa 10:16–17; Mk 9:48; Rev 18:8; 19:20; *see* Gehenna); evil (Isa 9:18), lust (Prov 6:27), and greed; war, trouble, suffering, and affliction (Job 5:7; Isa 29:6); purification and testing (I Pet 1:7; 4:12); the power of the word and truth of God (Jer 5:14; 23:29); prophetic inspiration (Jer 20:9); the zeal of saints (Ps 39:3; 119:139) and of angels (Ps 104:4; Heb 1:7); the Holy Spirit (Acts 2:3) and the glorified Christ (Rev 1:14); and eschatological judgment (Rev 20:9–15; 21:8).

The most important aspect of fire in the Bible is its use in worship and sacrifices to consume the burnt offerings and incense. The first explicit reference is Noah's offering to God (Gen 8:20–21). Later it was a central part of the continual sacrifices and constant worship of both the tabernacle and the temple in which the fire upon the altar was never permitted to die out (Lev 6:12–13). Fire upon the altar was miraculously sent from God (Lev 9:24; II Chr 7:1-3). Any fire started by man or obtained elsewhere than from the altar ("strange fire," Lev 10:1-2) was ritually unacceptable and incurred the divine wrath. Nadab and Abihu were punished with death by fire from God for using strange fire upon the altar (Lev 10).

The perpetual altar fire was to be replenished with wood every morning (Lev 6:12). Acceptance of the sacrifices was indicated by the fire of God suddenly consuming the offering. Fire from God signified the acceptance of certain special sacrifices (Jud 6:21; I Kgs 18:24, 38; I Chr 21:26)—Yahweh is "the God who answers by fire." Animals slain for sin offerings were consumed by fire outside the camp (Lev 4:12, 21; 6:30). Upon completing his vow, a Nazarite shaved his head and put the hair into the altar fire in which the peace offerings were being sacrificed (Num 6:18).

The law forbade any fire to be kindled on the sabbath day, even for cooking (Ex 35:3). Because of the dryness of the land during the hot season, the law provided that a restitution must be made by anyone kindling a fire which caused damage and loss to a field of grain (Ex 22:6).

Bibliography. Friedrich Lang, "*Pyr,* etc.," TDNT, VI, 928-952.

R. E. Po.

FIRE BAPTISM. *See* Baptism of Fire; Gods, False: Molech.

FIREBRAND. A burning stick taken out of a fire. Specifically, "firebrand" can designate a stick for stirring a fire, a fire missile, or a torch made from a stick with flammable material fastened on the end. It is used symbolically of a nation almost consumed but mercifully rescued from destruction, "a firebrand plucked out of the burning" (Amos 4:11; Zech 3:2). The kings of Israel and Syria are spoken of contemptuously as "these two smoldering stumps of firebrands" (Isa 7:4, RSV). Firebrands (or, embers, cf. Isa 50:11) are among the objects hurled by a madman (Prov 26:18). In a fit of anger Samson tied firebrands or torches to foxes' tails and set them loose in the fields of the Philistines (Jud 15:3-6).

FIREPAN. A firepan was a tray attached to a long handle used to carry live coals of fire, and probably ashes also. It is listed as one of the vessels for the altar of burnt offering (Ex 27:3; 38:3). The Heb. word *maḥtâ* is also translated 15 times in KJV as "censer" (Lev 10:1; 16:12; Num 4:14; 16:6; etc.), because the firepan had this function when used to hold live charcoal for the burning of incense. The same shaped utensil was used to hold the tweezers and for removing the burnt portions of the lamp wicks of the golden lampstand. In this case it was translated "snuffdishes" in KJV, "trays" in RSV (Ex 25:38; 37:23). The firepans were made of copper as a rule, but those used with the golden lampstand were of pure gold (Ex 25:38). *See* Censer.

FIRES. In Isa 24:15 the KJV translates the Heb. *'urim* as "fires," but it is translated "east" in ASV and RSV. It is from the Heb. word translated "urim" in Urim and Thummim and denotes a glow as from fire—hence the idea of east as at sunrise. Where the KJV translates "burn with fire" (Ezk 39:9-10), the ASV and RSV use the words "make fires."

FIRE, STRANGE. *See* Fire.

FIRE WORSHIP. As a symbol of purity, or of the divine presence and power, or as one of the fundamental elements of nature, or as typifying the destructive forces of nature, fire has been worshiped by many peoples from the most ancient times. The idea of fire worship takes at least three directions in the Bible.

First, there is a definite relating of fire to God. This is evidenced by God's appearance to Abraham in ratifying His covenant (Gen 15:17), to Moses in the burning bush (Ex 3:2), and God's manifest presence in the pillar of fire over the camp of Israel (Ex 13:21). On Mount Sinai it is said that God descended in fire (Ex 19:18) and that the appearance of His glory was like devouring fire (Ex 24:17). Lev 9:24 states that fire came from the Lord and consumed the burnt offering. Lev 10:2 relates that fire from the Lord destroyed the two sons of Aaron. Because of the murmuring of the people against God, it is said that the fire of God burned among them (Num 11:1). These are only a few of the many instances where God is associated with fire in the OT.

In the NT John the Baptist promised that the Holy Spirit would baptize in fire (Mt 3:11, ASV). When the Holy Spirit came at Pentecost His presence is described as like cloven tongues of fire (Acts 2:3). Paul states that Christian service is to be tested by fire (I Cor 3:13). He says further that the Lord will return in flaming fire (II Thess 1:8). God specifically warns that His people must offer Him acceptable worship with reverence and awe, "for our God is a consuming fire" (Heb 12:29, quoting Deut 4:24).

Second, fire has to do with worship in a special way in the OT. The entire system of burnt offerings and, perhaps in a lesser way, the burnt incense, indicates that fire was instrumental in certain phases of worship. The offerings were consumed by fire and the aroma was wafted up to God symbolically. *See* Fire.

Third, the worship of fire as such did not enter into the Israelite concept and use of fire. However, there was a danger facing God's people because neighboring pagans perverted the use of fire in the worship of their deities. Outstanding were those who bowed to Molech, the god of the Ammonites. In Lev 18:21 and 20:1-5 Moses specifically forbids Molech worship, a part of which consisted in offering children by fire to him. The Israelites at times were enticed into this idolatry. Solomon went so far as to build a high place for Molech (I Kgs 11:7). Jeremiah reveals a practice of this worship (Jer 19:5; 32:35), and so does Ezekiel (20:31), although Josiah had seemingly purged the nation of this practice completely (II Kgs 23:10). See Gods, False: Molech. The article on fire worship in *Unger's Bible Dictionary* gives details of sacrifices to gods of fire in ancient Mexico and Peru.

A. E. T.

FIRKIN. See Weights, Measures, and Coins.

FIRMAMENT. The English term, derived from *firmamentum* in the Vulg., inadequately expresses the Heb. *rāqîa'*, which means "expanse" and describes the great vault or spread out expanse of sky surrounding the earth.

The firmament or atmosphere was created on the second day to separate the "waters from the waters" (Gen 1:6-7), i.e., the waters on the earth from the extensive water vapors (clouds) surrounding its surface. Into this expanse, which God called "heavens" (Gen 1:8), the sun, moon, and stars were set (Gen 1:14-18). The LXX renders the Heb. with *stereōma,* meaning a firm or fixed structure. In Col 2:5 this Gr. word, used metaphorically, is translated "stedfastness" (KJV) or "firmness" (RSV). However, it is the idea of expansiveness or extension rather than solidity that *rāqîa'* represents, a term derived from *rāqa',* "to beat, stamp, or spread out."

Heb. cosmogony, contends the critical school, represented pre-scientific concepts allegedly visualizing the firmament as a rigid, solid dome (Job 37:18; Prov 8:28) supported on pillars (II Sam 22:8; Job 26:11), and containing fixed stars. The rains descended from the waters above the firmament through windows (Gen 1:7; 7:11; Mal 3:10). Such interpretation is hermeneutically unsound, confusing poetical metaphor and phenomenal language with literal prose. The obvious poetic metaphor, expressing the expansiveness of the firmament, is seen in Isa 40:22: God "stretcheth out the heavens as a curtain, and spreadeth them out as a tent" (cf. Isa 45:12). The OT describes the firmament as bright and transparent like crystal, sapphire, or glass (Ex 24:10; Ezk 1:22; Dan 12:3; Rev 4:6), revealing the handiwork of God (Ps 19:1), and signifying the seat of His power (Ps 150:1).

H. E. Fr.

FIRST BEGOTTEN. See Firstborn.

FIRSTBORN

Old Testament

The Heb. word *behôr* makes no distinction between the firstborn of human beings and that of animals (Ex 11:5; 12:29; 13:2). The sacrifice of the firstborn, as of the firstlings of flocks and firstfruits of the produce of the earth, was com-

mon in early times (Ex 23:16). Reference is made in II Kgs 3:27 to the sacrifice of the heir to the throne by Mesha, king of Moab, in an effort to save his people in time of war. The influence of surrounding paganism had its effect upon Israel. Scripture gives instances of the sacrifice of the firstborn by various kings of Israel (II Kgs 16:3; 17:17; 21:6). Jeremiah the prophet denied that such offering was by instruction from the Lord (Jer 7:31; 19:5). Other prophets also denounced the practice (Ezk 16:20-21; 23:37; Mic 6:7). It was contrary to that which was known of the character of God.

At the time of the first Passover, when the firstborn of Egypt were slain, Moses gave command that Israel was to "set apart unto the Lord all that openeth the matrix" (Ex 13:12-13). The male firstborn was considered holy to the Lord (Num 3:13, 40; 8:15-18). By destroying the firstborn sons of Egypt and sparing those of Israel, God acquired a special ownership over the latter. Since it was not feasible to select the firstborn of the entire nation and thus disturb the family organization, the Levites were substituted for them (Num 3:12-13). Previously the firstborn had been priest of the whole family. Now the exercise of the priesthood was transferred by this command of the Lord from the tribe of Reuben to that of Levi. The service at the sanctuary had to be carried out by the Levites, but all the firstborn after the Exodus were the peculiar property of the Lord, and had to be redeemed (Num 8:18). When the Levites were set apart by Moses, they numbered 22,000 (Num 3:39), though the firstborn of the 12 tribes of a month old and upward totaled 22,273 (Num 3:46). Therefore 22,000 were redeemed by the Levites, and 273 were redeemed by payment of 1,365 shekels, which was given to Aaron and his sons as compensation (Num 3:50-51). The rate was five shekels per person.

Distinction is to be noted between the firstborn of inheritance, and the firstborn of redemption.

Firstborn of inheritance pertains to the firstborn of the father by any of his wives, if he practiced polygamy (Deut 21:16 ff.; Gen 49:3-4). The firstborn of the father had authority over the family in place of the father (Reuben in Gen 37:21-30; 42:37), a double share of the inheritance (Deut 21:17), and the right to the priesthood. When Elisha asked Elijah for a double portion of his spirit (II Kgs 2:9), he was in effect asking for the portion of the firstborn, that he might be Elijah's chief and worthy successor.

It appears that the promises of God to the patriarchs were considered as attached to the line of the firstborn. Note the story of Jacob and Esau in Gen 25:30-34; 27:36. As the cases of Ishmael, Esau and Reuben show, it was possible for the father to deprive the firstborn of this right. Such action is noted as having been practiced in various parts of the Middle East in patriarchal times, as confirmed by a tablet found at Alalakh in Syria. Deut 21:15-17 forbade the arbitrary transfer of the right from the actual firstborn to the son of a favored wife. *See* Birthright; Inheritance. In succession to the throne, primogeniture was always considered, but was not always decisive (I Kgs 1:1, 5-39; I Chr 26:10; II Chr 11:22).

Firstborn of redemption relates to the firstborn of the mother, and applies to both man and beast (Ex 13:2). All firstborn Israelite males had to be redeemed, since they belonged in a peculiar way to the Lord (Num 3:12-13, 45-51). According to Talmudic tradition, the firstborn acted as officiating priests in the wilderness, until the erection of the tabernacle, when the office was given to the tribe of Levi. In the matter of redemption, there were distinctions.

1. The firstborn of a clean animal had to be brought into the sanctuary on the eighth day after birth (Ex 22:30). If without blemish, it was to be sacrificed, its blood sprinkled, fat burned, flesh eaten (cf. Deut 15:19 with Num 18:17). If the animal had a blemish, it lost its holy character, and the priest to whom it was given might eat it outside Jerusalem, as any common food (Deut 15:21-23). It could also be eaten by other persons. Deut 15:19 suggests that no work could be done with the firstling of bullocks, nor wool shorn from that of sheep. They could not be sold. They became holy at birth, dedication being unnecessary. They had to be sacrificed during the first year.

2. The firstborn of an unclean animal had to be redeemed when a month old according to the estimation of the priest, with the addition of one-fifth (Lev 27:27; Num 18:15). The firstborn of an ass was either ransomed by a sheep or a lamb, or its neck had to be broken (Ex 13:13; 34:20). In later times, the unclean animals could be redeemed with money, or the neck was broken and the body burned.

3. The firstborn son of a mother (not of the father), at the age of one month, had to be redeemed with five shekels (Ex 13:13; 22:29; Num 18:15 ff.; Neh 10:37). This was given to the priest either in money or in valuables "according to . . . estimation" (Num 18:16). The husband of several wives would have to redeem the firstborn of each. If the father failed to redeem, Jewish law required that the son had to redeem himself when he grew up. Tradition added that priests, Levites and Israelites whose wives were daughters of priests or Levites needed not to redeem their firstborn. Because of deliverance from the tenth plague, the firstborn were required to fast on the day preceding the Passover. If too young, the father fasted for him. If the father was a firstborn, some say that both mother and father fasted, he for himself, and she for her son.

Figurative usages. In Job 18:13 "the firstborn of death" refers to the disease which would eventuate in death. In Ex 4:22 and Jer 31:9 God likens His relationship to Israel to that of a father and his firstborn son. In Ps 89:27 the reference is narrowed to King David and his dynastic line, culminating in Jesus the Messiah.

Bibliography. I. Mendelsohn, "On the Preferential Status of the Eldest Son," BASOR 156 (Dec., 1959), pp. 38-39.

I. R.

New Testament

Firstborn is used literally in Lk 2:7 and Heb 11:28. The word designates Christ as the unique and eternal Son of God in Rom 8:29 and Heb 1:6 (ASV), holding first rank and complete authority over angels and all His brethren on earth. Twice the words "firstborn from the dead" point to the fact that Christ was the first to arise from the dead in immortal form (Col 1:18; Rev 1:5, ASV).

Erasmus suggested that in Col 1:15 the word should be accented on the penult so as to mean "original One who brought forth." If this suggestion is not acceptable, then "firstborn" here designates the One who has the *rights* of primogeniture, who has authority over all creation. Certainly it does not indicate that He ever began to exist.

Heb 12:23 literally refers to "the church of firstborn ones who are written in heaven." Every child of God, enrolled in "the book of life from the foundation of the world," being "a joint heir with Christ," an heir of "all things" unlimited, has in a real sense the position of a "firstborn" in God's household, privileged above all other men.

Bibliography. Wilhelm Michaelis, *"Prōtotokos,"* TDNT, VI, 871-881.

J. O. B., Jr.

FIRSTBORN, DESTRUCTION OF. *See* Plagues of Egypt.

FIRST DAY OF THE WEEK. *See* Lord's Day.

FIRSTFRUITS

1. *Individual offering of firstfruits.* The Mosaic law required the Israelites to bring to the house of the Lord "the first of the firstfruits of thy land" (Ex 23:19; 34:26). This was to include grain, wine, and oil, and was to be used for the support of the priests (Num 18:12; Deut 18:4). Instructions were given as to the manner in which the firstfruits were to be brought to the house of God and turned over to the priests, along with the ritual to be used at that time (Deut 26). However, the actual amount is nowhere stated in Scripture. "The Talmud fixed on the sixtieth as the least to be given of the produce, a thirtieth or fortieth as a liberal offering" (A. R. Fausset, *Bible Encyclopaedia,* p. 232). Evidently, in actual practice the firstfruits were brought in abundantly by the people during times of revival and reform (II Chr 31:5). It is significant that on at least one occasion when the priests of Israel were

apostate, an individual brought barley loaves of firstfruits to the prophet Elisha instead (II Kgs 4:42). After the Captivity, the returnees to Jerusalem covenanted to give the firstfruits faithfully, Nehemiah seeing that these were cared for and distributed to the priests in a systematic way (Neh 10:35-37; 12:44; 13:31). The book of Proverbs promises prosperity to those who honor the Lord with the firstfruits (Prov 3:9).

2. *The Feast of Firstfruits* (Lev 23:9-14). This was to be observed at the beginning of barley harvest, the first grain to come in. The first sheaf of the new crop, together with a sacrifice, was presented as a wave offering before the Lord on the day after the Passover sabbath. By this, acknowledgment was made that all came from God and belonged to Him, and none was to be used for food until this ceremony had been performed. The firstfruits were also a sample or specimen of the bounteous harvest of golden grain which would eventually follow because of God's providence.

3. *The Feast of Pentecost.* This is called by various names in the OT. Since it took place on the fiftieth day after the Feast of Firstfruits, it came to be known as Pentecost ("fiftieth") by the Jews (Acts 2:1; 20:16). As it thus occurred at the completion of wheat harvest, the firstfruits of the wheat were to be brought to the Lord at this time (Ex 34:22; cf. Ex 23:16; Num 28:26). This wheat was to be baked into two wave loaves in which leaven was to be used (Lev 23:17, 20). This is significant, as the ordinary meal offering was to contain no leaven (Lev 2:11). However, part of the unleavened offering was wholly offered to the Lord by burning it (Lev 2:9), while the loaves at Pentecost were presented to the Lord simply by waving them before Him, with no portion burned.

4. *Figurative use of firstfruits.* Both OT and NT warrant us in believing that the ceremonial presentation of the firstfruits had, beyond its obvious implications, a typical and symbolical significance. The chosen nation Israel is spoken of as God's "firstfruits," dedicated wholly to Him (Jer 2:3). A curse is pronounced on those who consume and destroy Israel, because they have infringed on that which belongs to the Lord.

Christ in His resurrection is "the firstfruits of them that slept" (I Cor 15:20, 23). The Feast of Firstfruits took place on the first day after the Passover sabbath. On this very day Christ rose from the dead (Mk 16:1-6). At Pentecost, 50 days later, the Holy Spirit came to mold the believers into one body, the Church (Acts 2:1; I Cor 12:13). The two loaves waved before the Lord at this feast may possibly represent Jewish and Gentile believers made one in Christ (Eph 2:14). This would explain the usage of leaven (speaking of corruption) in these loaves, as the believer, though saved, still has sin *in* him.

In another sense believers are spoken of as a "kind of firstfruits" (Jas 1:18). The Lord Jesus in His resurrection is *the* firstfruits. In Him we see a wonderful specimen of what God will eventually do for all believers. In each Christian God is seeking to perfect a holy life and character so that he will be a specimen or example of what God desires to do for all. Thus believers are a *kind* of firstfruits. The Holy Spirit, given now to all who believe on Christ, is also spoken of as a firstfruits (Rom 8:23), a wonderful sample, so to speak, of the full and complete blessings that lie ahead.

The present saved remnant in Israel is spoken of as "firstfruits" (Rom 11:16) and the 144,000 of the Tribulation period are likewise so designated (Rev 14:4). They are foretokens of a prophesied turning to the Messiah by the nation Israel. In similar manner, the first converts in any particular area are spoken of as "firstfruits" (Rom 16:5; I Cor 16:15).

In Ezekiel's glorious vision of the millennial temple and kingdom, it is indicated that the priests will once again be given the firstfruits (Ezk 44:30). Their portion of the land is spoken of as a "firstfruits" which they are not to "alienate" or allow to pass to others (Ezk 48:14).

See Festivals; Pentecost; Sacrificial Offerings.

G. C. L.

FISH. *See* Animals, V.4.

FISHER, FISHING. *See* Occupation: Fishing.

FISH GATE. *See* Jerusalem: Gates and Towers 4.

FISHHOOK. In the KJV this term is found only in Amos 4:2, which employs the two Heb. words *sîr dûgâ|.* The word *sîr,* "hook," means literally "thorn," and likely came to be used of a hook because of its resemblance to a thorn. It was an Assyrian practice, known from their palace sculptures, to lead away captives by hooks or rings in their noses or lips (ANEP #440, 447; cf. Isa 37:29; Ezk 29:4; 38:4, where *hāh* is the word for "hook"). Job 41:1 asks if you can draw out leviathan with a hook (*hakkâ*). This word came to be used to denote a fishhook because the hook fastens to the roof of the mouth or palate (*hēk*). It also is translated as "hook" in Isa 19:8 and Hab 1:15 in the RSV. Jesus instructed Peter to cast a hook (Gr. *agkistron*) into the sea to catch a fish (Mt 17:27). Bone fishhooks have been found in prehistoric settlements in Palestine, and iron fishhooks were excavated at Ezion-geber from the time of Solomon. *See* Hook; Occupation: Fishing.

A. E. T.

FISHPOOL. The Heb. word *berēkâ* is translated "fishpool" in Song 7:4; but in II Sam 2:13; 4:12; Nah 2:8; Eccl 2:6 it is translated simply "pool." Versions other than KJV give the meaning in Song 7:4 as simply "pool." The word refers to an open pond of water.

FITCHES. *See* Plants.

FLAG

1. A standard. *See* Ensign.
2. A plant. *See* Plants.

FLAGON. In Isa 22:24 "flagons" (Heb. *neḇā-līm*) refers to a clay storage jar (Lam 4:2) or a bag, usually made of dried whole skins of a goat or other similar animal, and was used for water, wine, milk, or other liquids.

It is generally thought that the Heb. word *'ăshîshâ* translated "flagon" in other OT passages in the KJV (II Sam 6:19; I Chr 16:3; Song 2:5; Hos 3:1) designates a "cake of raisins," made of pressed grapes and carried on a journey. It was counted as a delicacy and was an important item of food.

FLAKE. In Job 41:23 the statement is made that the "flakes" of the flesh of leviathan (*q.v.*) are joined in such a way that they cannot be moved. A better rendering may be "horny epidermic scales" (ISBE). The same Heb. word is translated "refuse" in Amos 8:6.

FLAME. *See* Fire

FLANK. This word is used only in the plural, as in Job 15:27. It refers to the section of the animal carcass near the kidneys called the loins. It is used five times in Leviticus and is translated "loins" in the ASV (Lev 3:4, 10, 15; 4:9; 7:4).

FLASK. The ASV marginal translation of Gr. *alabastron* (KJV "alabaster box") in Mt 26:7; Mk 14:3; Lk 7:37. RSV renders it "flask" in Lk 7:37. *See* Minerals: Alabaster; Pottery: Cruse; Vial.

FLAX. *See* Plants.

FLEA. *See* Animals, IV.13.

FLEECE. The Heb. word *gēz* is translated "fleece" (Deut 18:4; Job 31:20) and also "mown" grass (Ps 72:6; Amos 7:1). It speaks of that which is shorn. The similar form *gizzâ* is also translated "fleece" in Jud 6:37-40 where Gideon's experiences with the fleece are related. It seems that the word refers primarily to wool after it was shorn.

FLEET. *See* Swift.

FLESH. The Gr. NT term is *sarx* which has specific meanings of its own but also translates the Heb. term *bāsār*. The word occurs 143 times in the Gr. NT. The main biblical meanings of flesh may be classified as follows:

1. The soft substance of the animal organism which may be stripped off from the bones and is made up of muscles, blood, tissue, etc. (Lk 24:39; Jn 6:51; I Cor 15:39; Jas 5:3; Rev 17:16; 19:18, 21; Gen 2:21; Ex 12:8; Isa 31:3; Ezk 23:20).

2. The body. The whole material part of a living being, i.e., that which makes up its somatic existence (Gen 40:19; I Kgs 21:27; II Kgs 4:34; Eccl 12:12; Heb 5:7), and used with "blood" the whole phrase "flesh and blood" (*q.v.*), signifies the body (Heb 2:14).

3. The basis or result of natural generation and kinship or kindred (Gen 2:24; 37:27; Jn 3:6; cf. Rom 4:1; 9:3, 5, 8; I Cor 10:18; Gal 4:23, 29; Eph 2:11; Rom 11:14).

4. Corporeally conditioned living things, usually man but also animals (Gen 6:13; Num 16:22; Jer 12:12; 25:31; Isa 40:5-6; Joel 2:28; Mt 16:17; 24:22; Mk 10:8; Lk 3:6; Jn 1:14; I Cor 1:29; Gal 1:16; 2:16; Eph 6:12; I Pet 1:24).

5. The weak creaturely side of man's constitution in contrast with heart and soul with which it often occurs to designate the whole man. Thus it is used to indicate the external and secular as distinguished from the spiritual and religious (Gen 6:3; Ps 16:9; Isa 31:3; Mt 26:41; Mk 14:38; Rom 6:19).

6. In the ethical sense it has reference to the carnal nature, or that disposition in man which is prone to sin and is opposed to God (Gen 6:12; Rom 7:18; 8:6-8; I Cor 3:3; Gal 5:17, 19; Col 2:18; II Pet 2:10, 18; I Jn 2:16). This is the most important use for the Christian. The flesh, or fallen nature, lusts and wars against the Spirit as He works through the new nature, resulting in spiritual paralysis and defeat (Gal 5:17-24; Rom 7:14-8:1). This condition is overcome in the following manner: (*a*) Learning to distinguish the works of the flesh from those of the Holy Spirit (Gal 5:19-23; cf. I Cor 6:9-11; Rom 8:4-13). (*b*) Realizing by faith that the fallen nature is already under condemnation, even though it is not yet removed (Rom 8:3), and therefore the Holy Spirit can and does indwell the believer (Rom 8:9). (*c*) Surrendering and submitting ourselves to the leading guidance of the Holy Spirit (Rom 8:4-13; Gal 5:24-25; Eph 5:18 ff.), which is spoken of as "walking by the Spirit." *See* Carnal.

7. There are other terms in Scripture which indicate flesh in the sense of "butcher's meat," or that which is used for food.

In no case does the biblical idea imply the inherent evil of matter, nor is the body looked upon as a thing of shame.

To summarize: flesh, *physically*, indicates the body as possessing a soul, which the Spirit of God enables to exist in individual form; *ethically*, that whole life of the soul which is of a unit with the body, after the body has fallen a prey to the power of the senses and the principle of sin, i.e., the whole personality wrongly directed.

Bibliography. Ernest DeWitt Burton, "Galatians," ICC, appended note on *Sarx*, pp. 492-5. W. P. Dickson, *St. Paul's Use of the Terms Flesh and Spirit*, Glasgow: James Maclehose & Sons, 1883. K. Grayston, "Flesh, Fleshly, Carnal," *Theological Word Book of the Bible*, Alan

Richardson, ed., New York: Macmillan, 1950, pp. 83–84. W. G. Künnel, *Man in the New Testament*, trans. by J. J. Vincent, Philadelphia: Westminster, 1963. John Laidlaw, *The Bible Doctrine of Man*, Edinburgh: T. & T. Clark, 1879, pp. 74–86. J. A. Motyer, "Flesh, Fleshly," BDT, pp. 222–224. G. B. Stevens, *The Pauline Theology*, New York: Scribner's Sons, 1911, Chap. VI. H. Wheeler Robinson, *The Christian Doctrine of Man*, Edinburgh: T. & T. Clarke, 1913, especially chaps. I and II.
R. E. Pr. and R. A. K.

FLESH AND BLOOD. A term used several times in the NT (Mt 16:17; I Cor 15:50; Gal 1:16; Eph 6:12; Heb 2:14; cf. Jn 1:13) to express the idea of man, human beings, men. It is neutral in connotation, and while it does not imply any moral condition, it portrays man as he is, with his own resources, in contrast to God. The term "flesh," on the other hand, while it may be used in a similar neutral sense (Jn 1:14; 6:63; Acts 2:17; etc.), generally implies fallen sinful man and man's fallen nature in particular (Rom 7:18 ff.; 8:1 ff.; I Cor 5:5; Gal 5:17–24; Eph 2:3; Phil 3:3). *See* Flesh.

FLESH HOOK. The directions given Moses for the altar of burnt offerings included the "flesh hooks" (Ex 27:3), which were to be made of bronze in the tabernacle and gold in the temple (I Chr 28:17). I Sam 2:13 describes the flesh hooks as having three teeth and being used by the priest to take up his portion of the meat from the pots as it was boiling.
See Hook.

FLESH OFFERED TO IDOLS. *See* Idols, Things Offered to.

FLESH POT. These were pots which the Israelite slaves had used in Egypt in cooking meats (Ex 16:3). No details are given of the material or size. One of the uses of the *sîr*, a rather general term for "pot," was for boiling meats and vegetables (e.g., II Kgs 4:38–41; Jer 1:13; Ezk 11:3, 7, 11 – "caldron"; 24:3–6; Mic 3:3). *See* Pottery.

FLINT. *See* Minerals.

FLOAT. A float was similar to a raft, formed of cedar logs tied together and floated to Joppa, as the word is used in I Kgs 5:9.

FLOCK (FIGURATIVE). This expression frequently was used of God's people. The prophets Isaiah, Jeremiah, Ezekiel, Micah and Zechariah all used flock in reference to Israel. For example, "He shall feed his flock like a shepherd" (Isa 40:11). Jeremiah accused false prophets of having scattered the flock of God (Jer 23:2). Ezekiel uses the word more than a dozen times in chap. 34 in a figurative sense of God's people. Jesus quoted Zech 13:7, using the term as applying to His disciples (Mt 26:31). He addressed His followers directly as "little flock" (Lk 12:32.) Paul admonished the Ephesian elders at Miletus to "take heed . . . to all the flock," and warned against the "wolves" who would ravage the flock (Acts 20:28–29). Jesus apparently used the expression "one flock" of the Church in Jn 10:16.
See Animals, I. 15; Shepherd.

FLOOD. The Noahic Flood, or Deluge, was the greatest single blow ever delivered by a holy God to this earth and its inhabitants. It was provoked by the universal apostasy and corruption of man, of whom it is written that "every imagination of the thoughts of his heart was only evil continually" (Gen 6:5). More space is devoted to a description of this universal aqueous catastrophe in the early chapters of Genesis than to the creation and the Fall. The technical term for "Flood" used in Gen 6–11 (and Ps 29:10) is *mabbûl*, which is translated by *kataklysmos* in the LXX, the same Gr. word being used in several of the NT references to the Flood (Mt 24:38–39; Lk 17:27; II Pet 2:5). The Flood is also referred to in Ps 104:6–9; Isa 54:9; Heb 11:7; I Pet 3:20; II Pet 3:3–7; and possibly Job 12:15.

The Chronological Order of Events

One hundred and twenty years before the Flood came, God began to warn men of their impending doom by instructing Noah to build a great ark (Gen 6:3, 14; I Pet 3:20). When the Flood began, only 40 days were required for the waters to reach their maximum depth, which was maintained for an additional 110 days (Gen 7.24). The ark settled on top of the highest peak in the mountains of Ararat and in 74 days the tops of the mountains were seen (Gen 8:5). Forty days later Noah sent out the raven, and then the dove three times at intervals of seven days. The covering of the ark was removed 29 days after this, and a final period of 57 days elapsed before the earth was sufficiently dry for disembarkation (Gen 8:14). Thus, the Flood lasted a total of 371 days (cf. E. F. Kevan, in *The New Bible Commentary*, p. 85).

The Geographical Extent of the Flood

A remarkable amount of biblical evidence is available for determining the geographical extent of the Flood. It is primarily to this evidence, rather than to the theories of modern scientists, that Christian students must pay heed in arriving at the correct answer to this highly controversial question. That the Bible clearly teaches a geographically universal flood in the days of Noah may be seen from the following considerations:

1. Gen 7:19–20 states that "all the high mountains that were under the whole heaven were covered" (ASV). Even if only one (instead of *all*) of the high mountains had been covered with water, the Flood would have covered the entire planet, for water must seek its own level.

2. Some of the most destructive floods in recorded history have come and gone within a matter of a few days, but the biblical deluge continued for over a year, seven months of this period being required for the waters to subside sufficiently for Noah to disembark from the ark in the mountains of Ararat.

3. Gen 7:11 states that "all the fountains of the great deep" (*tᵉhôm rabbâ*) were "broken up" at the commencement of the Flood, and Gen 8:2 (cf. 7:24) indicates that these geologic upheavals continued for five months. Since "the great deep" refers to the oceanic depths in this context (cf. Gen 1:2), the Flood could not have been a merely local catastrophe.

4. Assuming that the cubit was 17.5 inches long, the ark's three decks had an area of 95,700 square feet, a volume of 1,396,000 cubit feet, and a gross tonnage (figured at 100 cubic feet of usable storage space per ton) of 13,960 tons (*see* Ark, Noah's). It seems fantastic that God would have commanded Noah to build such a gigantic vessel merely for the purpose of escaping a local flood.

5. Even more compelling is the consideration that if the Flood was to be local in extent, there would have been no need for an ark at all! Noah and his family, to say nothing of the animals, could have moved to some other region to escape a local flood. But the fact that he was commanded to provide refuge for representatives of *all* land animals in the world constitutes final proof that the Flood was geographically universal, for no one would care to defend the view that all land animals could have been destroyed by a local flood.

6. The local flood concept cannot be harmonized with the divinely inspired statements of the apostle in II Pet 3:3-7, for the one single event which he sets forth as having brought about a transformation, not of the earth only but also of the very *heavens*, is the Flood. It was the Flood that provided the transition from "the heavens from of old" to "the heavens that now are." It was the Flood to which Peter appealed as his final and incontrovertible answer to those who chose to remain in willful ignorance of the fact that God had at one time in the past demonstrated His holy wrath and indignation against sin by subjecting "all things" to an overwhelming, cosmic (*kosmos,* II Pet 3:6) catastrophe that was on a par with the final day of judgment, in which He will consume the earth with fire and will cause the very elements to dissolve with fervent heat. It would not be easy to excuse the apostle of gross inaccuracy when he depicts the Flood in such cosmic terms and in such a universal context, if the Flood had been only a local inundation after all.

7. The Bible teaches emphatically that *all men* outside the ark were destroyed by the Flood (Mt 24:37-39; Lk 17:26-27; I Pet 3:20; II Pet 2:5; and frequently throughout Gen 6-7). But it is impossible to assume that the human race was confined to the Mesopotamian valley (where a local flood would presumably have occurred) during the sixteen or more centuries that elapsed between Adam and the Flood, for at least three reasons: (*a*) the longevity and fecundity of the antediluvians would provide for a very rapid increase in population; (*b*) the prevalence of strife and violence would encourage wide distribution rather than confinement to a single locality; (*c*) evidence of human fossils in widely scattered parts of the world makes it difficult to assume that men did not migrate beyond the Near East before the time of the Flood. Therefore, it would have required a geographically universal flood to destroy a widely scattered human race (cf. John C. Whitcomb, Jr., and Henry M. Morris, *The Genesis Flood,* pp. 1-35).

It is a significant commentary on the clarity of the biblical testimony to the universality of the Flood that no known commentator, Jewish or Christian, ever suggested the local-flood view before A.D. 1655, and that even then the view found scarcely any supporters until after the rise of modern geology in the middle of the 19th cen. (cf. Don Cameron Allen, *The Legend of Noah,* Urbana, Ill.: Univ. of Illinois Press, 1949, pp. 66-112).

The Sources of the Flood Waters

In Gen 7:11 we are informed that on the very day the Flood began, "all the fountains of the great deep [were] broken up, and the windows of heaven were opened." From this we may assume, first, that vast suboceanic upheavals caused the seas to encroach upon the continental coasts and lowlands. Second, the entire antediluvian, invisible vapor canopy, which had been suspended in the upper atmosphere since the second day of creation (Gen 1:6-8), fell upon the earth. It is now known that if all the water in our present atmosphere were suddenly precipitated, it would only suffice to cover the earth to an average depth of less than two inches. Therefore, a continuous rainfall of 40 days and nights (nearly 1,000 hours) over most of the earth would have required a completely different mechanism for its production than is available today.

The fact that antediluvian climatology was indeed different from that which we know today is supported by biblical references to a vast canopy of water vapor suspended high in the antediluvian atmosphere ("waters above the firmament," Gen 1:7), to the absence of rainfall as we know it today (Gen 2:5), and to the appearance of rainbows for the first time after the Flood ("I do set my bow in the cloud, and it shall be for a token of a covenant between me and the earth," Gen 9:13). Such a vast expanse of water vapor would, of necessity, have created a greenhouse effect in the entire world, providing warm climates even in the polar regions. (The presence of vast coal deposits and of the frozen remains of tropical animals in polar regions clearly points to a sudden climatic change on a nearly global scale.)

Recently, scientists have discovered a region in the upper atmosphere, called the mesosphere (from about 25 to 50 miles high), where temperatures rise to above 50 degrees Fahrenheit (cf. Arthur Beiser, *Life Nature Library: The Earth*, p. 58). A vapor blanket of stupendous magnitude could be supported in this region. Since water vapor weighs only 0.622 times as much as dry air for the same conditions, it would not be significantly affected by the presence or absence of air or other gases in the region, the temperatures would remain high both day and night, and condensation nuclei such as salt particles (apart from which water vapor cannot condense) would not rise to that level (cf. Whitcomb and Morris, *The Genesis Flood*, pp. 255–58). When the hour of judgment finally came, God caused this upper ocean to collapse upon the earth in the form of torrential rains that continued without interruption for six weeks.

Geology and the Flood

A universal Flood which attained a mountain-covering depth within six weeks, maintained that level for 16 weeks, and subsided into newly formed ocean basins in 31 additional weeks, must, of absolute necessity, have accomplished a vast amount of geologic work in the crust of the earth.

1. In the first place, erosion and resedimentation must have taken place on a gigantic scale. The rapid rise of water level within 40 days would have created great sediment-carrying currents. The Scriptures specifically state that the waters were "going and returning continually" (Heb., Gen 8:3) when they began to assuage. Previous crustal balances, of whatever sort they were, must have been entirely upset by the great complex of hydrostatic and hydrodynamic forces unleashed in the floodwaters, resulting very likely in great earth movements. Associated with the volcanic upheavals and the great rains must also have been tremendous tidal effects, windstorms, and a great complexity of currents, crosscurrents, whirlpools, and other hydraulic phenomena. For decades and even centuries after the Flood itself ended, much more geologic work must have been accomplished as the masses of water settled into new basins and the earth adjusted itself to new physiographic and hydrologic balances.

2. Since the Flood destroyed "every living thing that was upon the face of the ground" (Gen 7:23), and in view of the great masses of sediment being moved back and forth and finally deposited by the floodwaters ("I will destroy them *with the earth*," Gen 6:13), vast numbers of plants and animals must have been buried by the sediments, and under conditions eminently favorable to preservation and fossilization. This conclusion becomes inevitable when we realize that fossils are only rarely being formed in the earth today (cf. Wm. J. Miller, *An Introduction to Historical Geology*, 6th ed., New York: Van Nostrand, 1952, p.

12). Because the Flood was worldwide and comparatively recent (cf. below, "The Antiquity of the Flood"), most of the fossils that are now found in the earth's sedimentary rock beds must have been entombed there during the period of the Flood.

3. Finally, it may very fairly be inferred from the biblical record that it would now be impossible to discern geologically much of the earth's history prior to the Flood, at least on the assumption of continuity with present conditions. Whatever geologic deposits may have existed before the Flood, they must have been almost completely eroded, reworked, and redeposited during the Flood, perhaps several times. Such geologic time clocks as we may be able to use to date events subsequent to the Flood cannot therefore be legitimately used to extend chronologies before postdiluvian time. Even carbon-14 dating, which assumes basically unchanged atmospheric conditions indefinitely into the past, is valid only since the formation of a C-14 reservoir in the atmosphere following the collapse of the antediluvian vapor canopy. The basic premise of all such chronologies is uniformity; and, if the biblical record of the Flood be true, the premise of uniformity is, at that point at least, false. On the other hand, the relationship of the Flood to the earth's glaciers must be taken into consideration. Although many problems still remain, such as the exact chronology of the Pleistocene glacial period, the creation-catastrophe presupposition, based upon the inspired account of earth history in Genesis, has proved to be fruitful in approaching these problems.

The Antiquity of the Flood

Near Eastern cultures apparently have a rather continuous archaeological record (based on pottery chronology and occupation levels) back to at least the 5th or 6th mil. B.C.; and therefore it seems impossible to fit a universal flood into such an archaeological framework. Also the migration of man after the Flood to the Western Hemisphere, probably via the Bering Straits region, and the population expansion to the extremities of both North and South America, require a considerable amount of time. But there are several biblical evidences that point to rather long gaps in the genealogy of Gen 11, which would permit us to date the Flood long before Abraham.

(1) In the first place, the Scriptures give no total for the years between the Flood and Abraham, as they do for the time of Israel's sojourn in Egypt (Ex 12:40), even though totals are provided for the two numbers in the life of each antediluvian patriarch. (2) The genealogies of Gen 5 and 11 are symmetrical in form (ten patriarchs in each list, with the tenth in each case having three important sons named), suggesting the omission of other names, as in the parallel case of Mt 1. (3) If there were no gaps in the genealogy of Gen 11, *all* the postdiluvian patriarchs, including Noah, would still have

been living when Abram was 50 years old. *Three* of those who were born before "the earth was divided" at the judgment of Babel (Shem, Shelah, and Eber) would have actually outlived Abram. Eber, the father of Peleg, not only would have outlived Abram, but also would have lived two years after Jacob arrived in Mesopotamia to work for Laban. But Joshua said that Abram's fathers were idolaters, implying that Noah, Shem, and probably most of the others named in Gen 11 had long since died (Josh 24:2, 14, 15). (4) The biblical record implies that the judgment of Babel was a remote event in Abram's day, for he found ancient civilizations both in Canaan and Egypt. The strict chronology view, on the other hand, would date the Flood about 2460 B.C., several centuries after the building of the great pyramids of Egypt. (5) The term "begat" sometimes refers to ancestral relationships in the Bible. A careful comparison of Ex 6:20 with Num 3:17–19, 27–28 indicates that Amram was an ancestor of Moses and Aaron, separated from them by a span of 300 years. Similar wording in Gen 10:25, plus the fact that patriarchal life spans dropped suddenly between Eber and Peleg (Gen 11:16–19), suggests a large gap of generations between Eber and Peleg.

On the other hand, equally cogent arguments call for a date later than *c.* 7000 B.C. for the Flood: (1) The analogy of biblical chronology would be seriously strained if 5,000 years elapsed between the Flood and Abraham. Gaps of several centuries in OT genealogies are not unheard of, but gaps of thousands of years would be entirely out of proportion. (2) Because of the confinement of the human race to one region, it is highly improbable that Babel was judged more than a millennium after the Flood. But half of the postdiluvian patriarchs listed in Gen 11 lived in this pre-Babel period, leaving only Reu, Serug, and Nahor to link the judgment of Babel in the days of Peleg (cf. Gen 10:25) with the days of Terah. Thus, it is difficult to imagine how more than three or four thousand years could have elapsed between the judgment of Babel and the birth of Abram, or more than four or five thousand years from the Flood to Abram. (3) The remarkable similarities between the biblical and Babylonian Flood accounts preclude the possibility of a vast antiquity for the Flood, for the Babylonians could not have transmitted so many accurate details by oral tradition alone for more than a few thousand years (cf. Alexander Heidel, *The Gilgamesh Epic and Old Testament Parallels*). It may be concluded, then, that the judgment of the great Flood probably occurred from six to seven thousand years before Christ. *See* Chronology, Old Testament; Genesis.

Archaeological and Cuneiform Parallels

At the sites of several ancient Mesopotamian cities, notably Ur, Erech, Kish, Lagash, and Nineveh, levels of water-laid sediment of varying thickness have been discovered that can be dated to the 4th and 3rd mil. B.C. The archaeological contexts in each case indicate that the various destructions were local in character and do not all date from the same century. Hence these flood levels point to inundations of unusual severity caused by disastrous floodings of the Tigris and/or Euphrates Rivers, but not to a worldwide deluge of the proportions indicated in Genesis at the time of Noah.

Of more importance for a study of the biblical narrative are the various stories about the destruction of the world by a great flood which persist among many tribes on every continent and even on islands of the Pacific (Byron C. Nelson, *The Deluge Story in Stone*, pp. 165–190). The worldwide distribution of such flood stories cannot be accidental and should be considered as evidence for the historicity of the Genesis account.

Part of the Babylonian flood account from Ashurbanipal's palace. BM

Chief among extrabiblical narratives of a great flood is Tablet XI of the 12-tablet Gilgamesh epic written in Akkad. cuneiform. It was first discovered in 1872 by George Smith among the hoard of clay tablets brought back to the British Museum from the excavation of Ashurbanipal's palace at Nineveh. On his travels in search of immortal life, Gilgamesh met Utnapishtim, from whom he heard the story of the great catastrophe to mankind. The hero of the Deluge was called Ziusudra in the older Sumerian version written down by 2000 B.C. but circulating in Mesopotamia for many centuries before that. There are a number of close parallels between the experiences of Noah and Utnapishtim, as well as some obvious points of

FLOOR

The hero Gilgamesh in whose epic narrative the Babylonian flood account occurs. LM

divergence. Another Babylonian epic called the hero Atra-hasis.

In each case the hero was warned by deity of the impending flood; he built a boat in which he sheltered his family and animals; he sent out birds after the rain ceased; he sacrificed to deity after disembarking. But the polytheism of the Babylonian account stands in sharp contrast to the sober monotheism of Genesis 6-9. The gods of the Gilgamesh epic disagree with one another; they crouch like dogs and swarm like flies around Utnapishtim's sacrifice. The short duration of the flood—only seven days, and the proximity of Mount Nisir (in NW Persia, where Utnapishtim's craft came to rest) to Mesopotamia lead one to believe that details of a more recent local flood in the Tigris-Euphrates valley have been garbled with the oral tradition of the great Deluge of Noah's time. Certainly the many fanciful elements in the cuneiform accounts show that these are far less reliable than the Genesis narrative.

For a full translation of the Babylonian story see ANET, pp. 93-95, and for a translation of the Sumerian account, ANET, pp. 42-44.

Bibliography. Douglas A. Block, "Geology," *Christianity and the World of Thought,* Chicago: Moody Press, 1968, pp. 235-247. Alexander Heidel, *The Gilgamesh Epic and Old Testament Parallels,* Chicago: Univ. of Chicago, 1949. W. G. Lambert and A. R. Millard, *Atra-Ḥasīs: The Babylonian Story of the Flood,* New York: Oxford Univ. Press, 1969. Jack P. Lewis, *A Study of the Interpretation of Noah and the Flood in Jewish and Christian Literature,* Leiden: Brill, 1968. Byron C. Nelson, *The Deluge Story in Stone,* Minneapolis: Augsburg, 1931. André Parrot, *The Flood and Noah's Ark,* London: SCM, 1955. Donald W. Patten, *The Biblical Flood and the Ice Epoch,* Seattle: Pacific Meridian Publishing Co., 1966. A. M. Rehwinkel, *The Flood,* St. Louis: Concordia, 1951. Merrill F. Unger, *Archaeology and the Old Testament,* 3rd ed., Grand Rapids: Zondervan, 1956. J. R. van de Fliert, "Fundamentalism and the Fundamentals of Geology," JASA, XXI (1969), 69-81. John C. Whitcomb, Jr., and Henry M. Morris, *The Genesis Flood,* Philadelphia: Presbyterian and Reformed, 1961.

J. C. W.

FLOOR

1. The Heb. word *qarqa'* is used in referring to a floor of a building (Num 5:17). In the account of Solomon's building the temple, the word is used four times (I Kgs 6:15-16, 30). In I Kgs 6:5, 10 the noun *yāṣta'* ("chambers," KJV) probably means stories or floors.

2. Heb. *gōren* signifies a threshing floor. It was a level place swept clean and used for treading out the wheat, often just outside the city gate (I Kgs 22:10, "in a void place"; see ASV marg.). Isaiah uses it in a figurative sense (Isa 21:10) of God's people who are trodden down as grain on a threshing floor. *See* Threshing Floor.

3. Gr. *halōn* designates a threshing floor in Mt 3:12 and Lk 3:17.

The threshing floor at Samaria.

FLOTES. *See* Float.

FLOUR. *See* Food.

FLOWERS. The Heb. word *perah* is used figuratively in speaking of the blossom of the wicked going up like dust (Isa 5:24), of the blossom being ready for the pruning of judgment (Isa 18:5), and of the flower of Lebanon fading as a picture of judgment (Nah 1:4). Elsewhere this is the word for the blossoms on Aaron's rod that budded (Num 17:8), and it is used to speak of the flowerlike decorations on the branches of the golden lampstand (Ex 25:31-34; 37:17-20; Num 8:4; II Chr 4:21). The rim of the huge laver in Solomon's temple was shaped like the flower or calyx of a lily (I Kgs 7:26; II Chr 4:5, RSV, NEB).

Heb. *ṣîṣ* is used in comparing a man, his frailty, goodness, and works, to the fading flower (Ps 103:15). Heb. *ṣîṣâ* is used in a similar way of Ephraim's glorious beauty (Isa 28:4). The Gr. word *anthos* is found in the NT in a figurative sense in comparing man's life and glory to the frailty of a flower (Jas 1:10-11; I Pet 1:24).

Heb. *'ănāshìm* is translated in I Sam 2:33 (KJV, ASV) as the flower of age, denoting reaching the age of manhood (cf. our expression "in the bloom of life"). Similarly, Gr. *huperakmos* is used by Paul (I Cor 7:36) in speaking of a girl reaching womanhood, "the flower of her age."

The term *niddâ* is translated "flower" in KJV, but is given its more accurate meaning of "impurity" in ASV (Lev 15:24, 33).

See individual flowers under Plants.

            A. E. T.

FLUTE. *See* Music.

FLUX, BLOODY. *See* Diseases.

FLY, FLIES. *See* Animals, III.13.

FOAL. *See* Animals: Ass, I.1.

FOAM. Three words are thus translated. Heb. *qeṣep* refers to foam as on water (Hos 10:7). The marginal reference in ASV gives "twigs" as a possible rendering. The word comes from *qāṣap*, which means "to break off or out," or "to be angry." Thus it could mean twigs broken off, or foam as the result of angry waves.

Foaming as froth at the mouth is indicated by Gr. *aphrizō* in Mk 9:18, 20 (cf. Lk 9:39). Jude's use of Gr. *epaphrizō* pertains to the foaming of waves on the sea (v. 13).

FODDER. The Heb. word *beill* was used of a mixture of several kinds of grain as "wheat, barley, vetch and other seeds" (Gesenius), used in feeding livestock. The idea "mixed together" is indicated in the word. It is translated "fodder" in Job 6:5, "corn" in Job 24:6 and "provender" in Isa 30:24 in the KJV. *See* Provender.

FOLLOWER. *See* Disciples.

FOLLY. There is a variety of shades of meaning in the Heb. and Gr. words translated "folly." In general it expresses the unprofitable action or results of foolishness. Folly is the opposite of wisdom (*q.v.*).

1. Heb. *'iwwelet* is the word most often translated "folly," found frequently in Proverbs. It comes from the word meaning "to be a fool."

2. Heb. *kesel* is used twice (Ps 49:13; Eccl 7:25) and is related to the idea of confidence; hence, folly in the form of overconfidence. It is the folly that springs from inside a person.

3. Heb. *kislâ* is virtually the same word with a similar meaning as *kesel* (Ps 85:8).

4. Heb. *nebālâ* is folly signifying the weakness of decay from wickedness. This is the meaning of Nabal's name—emptiness or folly from inward wickedness (I Sam 25:25).

5. Heb. *sekel, siklût* suggest the folly that is due to thickheadedness (Eccl 2:3).

6. Heb. *tohŏlâ* denotes the folly that is sinful (Job 4:18).

7. Heb. *tiplâ* carries the idea of unsavory, without salt; hence, something silly because insipid. It is the folly of an idea or act when something is missing (Job 24:12; Jer 23:13).

8. Gr. *anoia* is the folly resulting from a lack of sense, without mind or understanding (II Tim 3:9), a madness expressing itself in rage (Lk 6:11).

9. Gr. *aphrosunē* (II Cor 11:1, 17, 21) is used by Paul to denote lightness or foolishness in speaking unwisely of himself in a way touching on self-glorying.

See Fool.

            A. E. T.

FOOD. Man as originally created was a vegetarian. God appointed the fruits, nuts and grains of the garden of Eden for his food (Gen 1:29; 2:16). Immediately after the Flood, which had destroyed earth's vegetation, God permitted man to eat the flesh of animals (9:3), although he was forbidden to consume the blood (9:4). The prohibition concerning blood (*q.v.*) was repeated to the Israelites in the law of Moses (Lev 3:17; 7:26; 17:10; etc.). God also designated that only certain ritually clean animals were proper for their food (Lev 11; Deut 14; *see* Animals).

The food of the Israelites varied somewhat according to the period of their history and the area in which they were living. When they wandered as nomads in the wilderness, their diet was more limited than after they settled down in Palestine. Their meals generally were simple and largely vegetarian (Ruth 2:14; I Sam 17:17-18), but they served a variety of foods when they entertained guests. Prominent and wealthy persons naturally enjoyed richer foods as well as a larger quantity (Lk 16:19). The table of King Solomon was provided daily with luxurious fare—"thirty measures of fine flour

FOOD

and sixty measures of meal, ten fattened oxen, twenty free-grazing oxen, one hundred sheep, besides deer and gazelles, roebucks and fattened cuckoos" (1 Kgs 4:22-23, JerusB).

Even after entering Palestine, food was often scarce because of droughts and the rocky soil and primitive methods of farming. *See* Famine. Food was therefore prized and used carefully, although the Jews did have their times of feasting. One of the factors which made Egypt and Babylonia prosperous was their abundant supply of food grown on well-irrigated and fertile soil.

The KJV often uses the terms "bread" and "meat" for food in general. There are, however, abundant references to specific foods which can be listed under various classes. Vegetables, fruits and grain comprised the chief foodstuffs of the Jews. An approximate idea of what these were may be obtained from a small limestone calendar found at Gezer from the 10th cen. B.C. *See* Calendar. It lists the chief crops and the months in which the farmer worked them.

The most important of the grains or cereals were wheat and barley. These were eaten raw, made into porridge, roasted or parched, or ground into flour or meal, and made into cakes or bread (leavened and unleavened). In times of famine bread was made from beans, lentils, millet and spelt. The pulse family included mainly lentils and coarse beans like our kidney bean. Other vegetables, most of which were eaten either raw or cooked, were squash, cucumbers, melons, leeks, onions, garlic, and various herbs (Num 11:5).

Fruit trees provided several varieties of food. Common were the olive, fig and vine, as suggested in Jotham's parable of the trees (Jud 9:8-15). Vines supplied grapes, a much prized food in the Orient, found in rich abundance in Palestine. Young grape leaves were used as a green vegetable; the older leaves were fed to sheep and goats. Grapes were eaten in their natural state, dried into raisins, and used to make wine. The date-palm tree is mentioned a number of times (Ex 15:27; Deut 34:3; Ps 92:12; Joel 1:12; Jn 12:13). Other fruits included pomegranates, various berries and nuts. The KJV "apple tree" was likely the apricot (Joel 1:12; Song 2:3; 8:5). Certain spices (cummin, dill, mint, mustard) and seasonings were grown or procured for cooking. Salt (*q.v.*) especially was considered to be a necessary ingredient.

**Use of meat was generally limited to special occasions, such as weddings, family festivals (Mt 22:2-4), entertainment of guests (Gen 18:2, 7), and sacrificial meals (Lev 7:11-27). Food from "unclean" animals was forbidden by Jewish law: swine, camels, rabbits, etc. (Lev 11; Deut 14). "Clean" animals most often prepared for the table included goats (also kids), sheep (especially lambs), and young bulls or steers. Gazelles, harts and fowl, animals of the chase, were valued for food. Domesticated birds, to-

Israeli olive harvest near Lydda. IIS

gether with their eggs (Lk 11:12), were a favorite by NT times.

Milk from animals was a principal item of food, from which sour milk, curds, and cheese were obtained (Gen 18:8; II Sam 17:29). Honey was much enjoyed and relished, especially by children (Ps 19:10; Song 5:1).

Fish are not often mentioned in the OT, but in the NT, especially in the Gospels, they are frequently referred to as a common food, both fresh and cured. Edible insects, generally of the locust family (Lev 11:22), were regarded as delicacies when dried, roasted, boiled in water, or ground into a paste.

In the course of time and especially during the period of the kingdom, there came advances in the art of cooking and a taste for the delicacies enjoyed by the kings and nobles of neighboring peoples. After the Exile the Israelites imported many new varieties of food.

Specific items of food, methods of cooking, and types of meals are discussed in the following subtopics. For other foods not mentioned, *see* Agriculture; Animals; Drink; Drink, Strong; Plants.

R. E. Po.

Bakemeats. Any kind of bread, cakes, pastries, or baked goods prepared by bakers for the pharaoh (Gen 40:17). Honey was used as the sweetening ingredient (Ex 16:31).

Banquet. Banqueting was a popular social and religious function of biblical times. Ordinarily an entire feast was involved, but at times the word was used only of the drinking (Est 5:5-6). Interestingly, the several Gr. and Heb. terms most often used of banqueting literally mean "to drink," and one function of the Jewish prophet and Christian apostle was to speak against the constant reduction of festive occasions to drunken revelry (Amos 6:7; Rom 13:13; Gal 5:19-21; I Pet 4:3), particularly when these were religious in nature. *See* Drink, Strong.

Sacrifices were generally accompanied by a banquet involving the eating of at least part of the sacrificed meat (I Sam 9:13; II Sam 6:18-19). It is felt that the "love feast" of NT

Ancient olive press at Capernaum. Phalpot

times (Jude 12) may have developed from the sacrificial banquet or as fulfillment of the predicted messianic banquet (Isa 25:6). Like the prophet of the OT, Paul rebuked those who failed to distinguish (Gr. *diakrinō*) the Lord's Supper from mere banqueting (I Cor 11:20-34), even though the supper itself had been instituted during a Jewish festival (Mt 26:20-29). *See* Festivals.

In addition to religious celebrations, banquets were held on such occasions as sheepshearing (II Sam 13:23), a marriage (Jud 14:10; Mt 22:2-4), the separation and reunion of friends (Gen 31:27; Lk 15:23-24), and the weaning of a son and heir (Gen 21:8). Banquets are mentioned at the birthdays of Pharaoh (Gen 40:20) and Herod (Mt 14:6), and there is evidence that mourners at a funeral took refreshments (Hos 9:4; II Sam 3:35).

Usually the banquet was held in the evening, and to begin too early was frowned upon as excessive (Isa 5:11). The cattle for the banquet were slaughtered in the early part of the day of the banquet (Mt 22:4). Some banquets lasted as much as seven days (Jud 14:12; Deut 16:13).

Invitations to the banquet were sent out by a servant (Mt 22:3), and in some cases, reminders were also later sent (Lk 14:17), but probably only in the case of larger banquets which required more extensive preparation. To spurn an invitation for insufficient reason was considered a great insult (Lk 14:18 ff.).

The normal posture at a feast before Amos' time was sitting (I Sam 16:11, Heb. "sit around"; I Sam 20:24 f.; I Kgs 10:5). During the monarchy the Syrian or Babylonian custom of reclining at meals was introduced among the nobility and wealthy (Amos 6:4; Ezk 23:41; Est 1:6). In the NT the phrase "to sit at meat" (*katakeimai*, lit., "to lie down," "recline") indicates that the banqueters lay on mats or couches around a central tray or low table (Mk 7:28). One supported himself on his left elbow, his right hand free for eating, his legs stretched out away from the table. Only this posture can explain how Mary could anoint Jesus' feet (Jn 12:3) or how the unnamed disciple could lean on Jesus' breast (Jn 13:23, 25).

In Graeco-Roman culture permanent benches were built U-shaped, called a triclinium, for nine to twelve or more persons. Each such setting had its place of honor (Lk 14:8-10, RSV). One assumes that in the case of large royal banquets where thousands were present (Dan 5:1) many tables with couches would have been used. Other terms also indicate that guests reclined during banquets (e.g., *anapiptō*, Lk 11:37; 17:7; Jn 13:12; *anaklinō*, Lk 7:36). Jesus spoke of the great joy and privilege of being in the kingdom of God in terms of "sitting down with Abraham, and Isaac, and Jacob" (Gr. *anaklinō*, Mt 8:11). This is taken by some to mean a great messianic banquet (Arndt, p. 55).

During the banquet, varying portions were given to guests by the host according to his desire (I Sam 1:5). Food at these banquets was also distributed to the poor (Neh 8:10) and to friends (Est 9:22). In addition to the meat and wine (often spiced, i.e., mixed, Prov 9:2, RSV), there were many kinds of food, the most choice of which was given to guests of special dignity (I Sam 9:24). *See* Drink; Drink, Strong; Wine.

Although at the three major feasts of the Jews it was the men who appeared before the Lord, women were not excluded from banquets (I Sam 1:9). The widow and the maid servant were to take part in the festivals (Deut 16:11). The practice of separating women at banquets was known among the Persians (Est 1:9).

Guests were received with a kiss as a matter of courtesy (Lk 7:45). The door was kept by a servant, and when the master was ready to

Dates almost ready for harvest. HFV

A banquet scene showing offering to Queen Makeri of Egypt. LM

begin the banquet, he shut the door himself to show that no more were to be permitted to enter (Lk 13:25). Thus the five foolish virgins were excluded from the marriage feast (Mt 25:10). Perfumes and scented oils were applied to the guests as anointing (Amos 6:6), and they also had their feet washed (Lk 7:36, 44). At weddings, garments were given to the guests for the occasion (Mt 22:11–12). It was considered an honor to be the recipient of a garment from a host (Rev 3:5).

In private banquets, the host presided over the festivities and cared for the details such as closing the door (Lk 13:25). When the banquets were larger and of mixed company, the custom was to choose a "ruler of the feast" (Gr. *architriklinos*) who would assume these duties (Jn 2:8). Guests were entertained by musical activities, dancing, and merrymaking in general (Jud 14:12; Isa 5:12; Amos 6:5; Mk 6:22; Lk 15:25). *See* Food: Meals.

J. McR.

Bread. The Heb. word *lehem* is used 297 times in the OT and the Gr. *artos* 99 times in the NT. Bread was the most common and important food of the peasant. It was made from grain, with or without yeast, in different shapes. Generally it was used for the table, though often also in sacrifices. The word is sometimes used figuratively of physical necessity or of spiritual sustenance, or even of eternal life.

Bread might be made of barley, as in the Midianite's dream (Jud 7:13) or the 20 loaves brought to Elisha (II Kgs 4:42). At the feeding of the 5,000, John indicates that the boy's five loaves were of barley (Jn 6:9, 13).

Greeks frequently referred to white bread as "pure," i.e., white. Most loaves for the tabernacle were made of wheat (e.g., Ex 29:2). Emmer and oats were also raised in Palestine, though they are not mentioned in Scripture.

Indian corn was unknown. ("Corn" in KJV is wheat or grain.) The dough was prepared simply by mixing the flour or meal with water and kneading the mixture. *See* Food: Dough; Flour.

"Little yeast ferments a big lump of dough" (a saying quoted in I Cor 5:6). The parable of the leaven had the woman baker "hide" a little yeast in three measures of flour (Mt 13:33). The rising took several hours. Kneading bowls are mentioned in Ex 8:3.

Unleavened bread was made at the time of the first Passover because Israel was hurried out of Egypt (Ex 12:39; cf. the witch of Endor hurrying to bake for Saul, I Sam 28:24, and Lot for his angelic visitors, Gen 19:3). In memory of Egypt the Jews ate this "bread of affliction" (Deut 16:3) for a week beginning with the Passover meal, but 51 weeks of the year they ate ordinary leavened bread. *See* Food: Leaven.

Fuel for baking was usually wood (Isa 44:14–15), but it might be dried grass inside a clay oven (Mt 6:30) with the loaves plastered on the outside and then turned (Hos 7:8). Fuel for baking might even be manure (Ezk 4:15). *See* Oven.

Professional bakers made bread in Jerusalem, for Jeremiah when in prison was given a loaf each day from "the bakers' street" (Jer 37:21). In the average home, however, bread was prepared by the wife (Gen 18:6) or a daughter (II Sam 13:8).

In size a loaf was one's thumb in thickness and as broad as a plate; thus loaves could be broken rather than cut. They usually were disk shaped, as indicated by the Heb. *kikkār* ("loaf," Jud 8:5; I Sam 10:3), but perhaps could be rings (Ex 29:23, Heb.), suspended around a pole to preserve them from mice, etc. So "breaking the staff or support of bread" meant famine (Lev 26:26; Ps 105:16; Isa 3:1; Ezk 4:16; 5:16; 14:13). *See* Food: Cake.

Bread kept too long became dry and crumbling (Josh 9:5, 12, JerusB). The Gilgamesh epic (XI, 225–229, ANET, p. 96) describes the various stages of bread mold.

Bread is a term used for food in general (II Sam 13:5–6, 10, RSV). To "eat bread" is to have a meal (e.g., Gen 3:19; 31:54; 37:25; 43:32; Prov 9:5; Eccl 9:7). Such food one should earn (II Thess 3:12). To "overflow with loaves" (Gr.) is to have plenty to eat (Lk 15:17). To go without a meal is not to eat bread (Mk 3:20). On a journey one usually took bread (Mk 6:8). Even animals and birds have their food or "bread" (Ps 147:9) and serpents their "meat" (leḥem; Isa 65:25).

A Jewish meal began with the father of the family taking a loaf, giving thanks, breaking and distributing it (cf. Christ in Mt 14:19; 26:26).

The uncommon Gr. adjective *epiousion,* translated "daily" in the only material petition of the Lord's prayer (Mt 6:11; Lk 11:3; *Didache* 8:2), may literally mean "for tomorrow"—the daily ration given out for the next day. The request may also be reminiscent of the provision of manna day by day to the Israelites.

Bread and clothing are essential for physical life (Deut 10:18), with water (Gen 21:14; I Kgs 18:4), or wine (Gen 14:18) and perhaps vegetables (Gen 25:34) or meat (I Kgs 17:6) or fruit (I Sam 30:12). It might be scant fare (I Kgs 22:27) or "bread of adversity and water of oppression" (Isa 30:20), or even "bread of pains," that is, bread earned by toil (Ps 127:2), the opposite of "bread of precious things," that is, delicacies (Dan 10:3; cf. Gen 49:20). But it is all important to remember that man does not live on bread or physical food alone, but in his total being on everything that proceeds from the mouth of the Lord (Deut 8:3; Mt 4:4).

Ceremonial use of bread was common. Much of it was unleavened (Ex 12:8, 18–20; 29:2; Lev 2:4), but leavened bread was used in a peace offering (Lev 7:13). The ceremonial loaf might be prepared from firstfruits and waved or swung in worship (Lev 23:17, 20).

What the KJV calls "shewbread"—continually (Num 4:7) supplied for a table in the tabernacle (Ex 25:23–30) and later in the temple (I Kgs 7:48), termed "holy bread" (I Sam 21:4), put there hot (I Sam 21:6), in rows (Ex 40:23; Neh 10:33, Heb.)—was by the Hebrews called "bread of (the) face," "presence bread," in the NT "loaves of the presentation" (Gr.; Mt 12:4; Heb 9:2). *See* Bread of Faces.

Manna was special "bread from heaven in abundance" (Ps 105:40; Neh 9:15), when God miraculously fed the multitudes of Israel 40 years in the wilderness (Ex 16:4, 15). It came with the dew (v. 14), six days a week (vv. 22, 25), and it could be cooked (v. 23). At times a complaining spirit loathed the light stuff (Num 21:5), though the apocryphal Book of Wisdom says this bread "provided every pleasure and suited every taste" (16:20)! *See* Food: Manna.

Metaphorical uses of bread in the OT are infrequent: the inhabitants of the land would be bread for Israel (Num 14:9), i.e., easily conquered. Bread and wine stand for the benefits of wisdom (Prov 9:5). But figurative uses play an important part in the NT. Leaven, ordinarily used in making bread, in the teaching of Jesus represented the teaching of the Pharisees and Sadducees (Mt 16:6, 11–12; parallel to Mk 8:15) and the hypocrisy or stage-play of the Pharisees (Lk 12:1). The parable of the leaven, like that of the mustard seed, illustrates the amazing growth of the kingdom, the mustard seed outward growth and the leaven inward. Leaven even here may represent evil, showing some kind of abnormal development. Paul in I Cor 5:6–8, employing rules for pre-Passover housecleaning, urged the corrupted church to "clean out the old leaven," which is "badness and wickedness." (Contrast Ignatius, d. A.D. 107, calling Christ the new leaven, Magnesians 10:2.)

Future bliss for the followers of Jesus was anticipated as eating bread at a banquet (Lk 14:15). In His discourse in Capernaum after the feeding of the 5,000, Jesus proclaimed Himself the bread of God that came from heaven (Jn 6:32–33 from Ex 16:4; Ps 78:24), and gives life to men (Jn 6:48, 51).

An ancient winepress in Jerusalem. HFV

In the supper which Jesus instituted, the broken bread represents His body smitten and broken for our healing (Mk 14:22 and the other Gospels; I Cor 10:16; 11:24; Isa 53:5; I Pet 2:24). For a believer to take of that bread is to show the most intimate communion with the Saviour. The one loaf also represents the many believers who form the mystical body of Christ (I Cor 10:17). *See* Lord's Supper.

Bibliography. T. Canaan, "Superstition and Folklore about Bread," BASOR #167 (Oct., 1962), 36–47.

W. G. B.

Butter. This is a milk product, translated "curds" in RSV, whether from camel, cow, goat, or sheep. With a cow and a couple of sheep one might live through hard times on butter and wild honey (Isa 7:15, 21, 22). Butter (Heb. *ḥem'â*) was made by pressing (sour) milk (Prov 30:33) so it would become curdled, like leben, yogurt, or cottage cheese. It was a staple article of diet, according to Abraham's menu (Gen 18:8), the lists of foodstuffs for Israel's land (Deut 32:13 f.), and the supplies taken to David in exile (II Sam 17:29). Sisera asked Jael for water and was given (sour) milk or curds, according to the use of synonyms in Heb. parallelism (Jud 5:25, RSV). Plenty of curds with olive oil made for a luxury diet (Job 20:17; 29:6). Parallel to oil, in Ps 55:21 it may be butter as we know it.

Cake. Several Heb. words translated "cake" in KJV describe the appearance of the loaf of bread (*q.v.*). Heb. *'ûgâ*, from a root meaning "to be round," signifies a round unsweetened cake or scone, a flat disk up to 18 inches in diameter. It was usually baked on hearthstones after raking away the coals (Gen 18:6; I Kgs 19:6). It needed to be turned to be properly done (Hos 7:8). Such cakes were never cut, always broken by hand. Manna could be crushed, boiled in a pot, and fashioned into round cakes (Num 11:8).

The *ṣelîl*, the barley cake which the dreaming Midianite saw rolling into his camp, must have been thicker. Heb. *ḥallâ*, from the root *ḥālal*, "to pierce, perforate," probably denotes ritual bread pierced with holes like the modern Passover cake (Ex 29:2, 23; Lev 2:4; *et al.*). The *rāqîq* was a thin, unleavened wafer (I Chr 23:29; Ex 29:2, 23; Lev 2:4; Num 6:15, 19) used in ceremonial offerings. Heb. *maṣṣôt*, translated "unleavened cakes" in Josh 5:11; Jud 6:19–21, is the usual term for unleavened bread (*see* Food: Leaven). The cakes (*kawwānîm*) of Jer 7:18; 44:19 (RSV) were marked with the features of the pagan goddess known as the Queen of Heaven, like a cookie pressed in a mold. Tamar made fancy cakes apparently in the shape of hearts, according to the Heb. *lebibôt*, from *lēb*, "heart" (II Sam 13:6, 8, 10).

J. R.

Cheese. The coagulated curd of milk pressed into a solid mass (I Sam 17:18; II Sam 17:29; Job 10:10). The making of cheese was an important industry for the people of antiquity. Cheese was prepared by salting the strained curds, shaping them into disks, and drying them in the open air.

The term *ḥem'â* (Prov 30:33, "butter") refers to curdled milk. The term *ḥālāb* is used for ordinary milk, but in I Sam 17:18 *ḥāriṣê heḥālāb*, lit., "cuttings of milk," refers to a cheese made from sweet milk. The proper designation for cheese is *gebînâ* (Job 10:10).

Cooking. While most meals were not elaborate and the food was cooked simply compared to our standards, preparation took much time (Prov 31:15) because of the primitive hearths, ovens, cooking vessels (*see* Pottery), and utensils and lack of any prepared or packaged foods. Cooking was universally the task of the women of the household (Sarah, Gen 18:6; Martha, Lk 10:40).

Meat was either stewed or roasted. In the former case it was cut up into pieces (Ezk 24:3–5; Mic 3:3) and, perhaps with crushed wheat and vegetables, allowed to stew in a "pan, or kettle, or caldron, or pot" (I Sam 2:13–14). The broth could be served separately (Jud 6:19–20). Roasting was the oldest method of cooking meat. At first it was merely laid upon hot stones after removing the coals. Jesus cooked a fish for the disciples by placing it on the charcoal itself (Jn 21:9). Later, the meat was spitted and held over the flame or baked in a preheated pit, as the Samaritans do at their annual Passover feast (cf. Ex 12:8–9).

Vegetables were generally boiled (*see* Food: Pottage) and then mixed with olive oil, similar to our flavoring with butter. Grain was often parched (*q.v.*). Coarse wheat or barley meal was sometimes prepared as a porridge. But most often the grain was ground into flour, mixed with olive oil, and baked as bread (*see* Food: Bread; Cake).

J. R.

Corn. The KJV uses this term to translate several Heb. and Gr. words referring to various grains. Later American translations use the term "grain" or the word for one of the various types of grain. In modern English "corn" refers mainly to the Indian maize of America which was unknown in Eurasia before the 16th cen. *See* Parched Corn. The most common types of grain in Palestine were wheat, barley, millet, and spelt (emmer). *See* Grain.

Cracknels. A kind of hard bread or cake (*niqqudîm*, I Kgs 14:3). In Josh 9:5, 12 the Heb. word is used of the dry and "mouldy" or crumbled bread carried by the delegation from Gibeon.

Dough. A mixture (Heb. *bāṣēq*) of wheat or barley flour (or meal) with water or olive oil, kneaded in a wooden bowl or trough (Ex 12:34, 39; II Sam 13:8; Jer 7:18; Hos 7:4). Into the dough being kneaded, a bit of dough set aside

A baker's shop of the New Testament period at Pompeii. In the center stand four flour mills; ovens are located to the left. HFV

from the previous mixing would be worked, in order to make leavened bread. Heb. *'ărîsâ* seems to designate dough in its first stage of mixing (Num 15:20–21; Neh 10:37; Ezk 44:30), an offering of firstfruits from the mixing bowl as well as from the threshing floor.

Gr. *phyrama* translates these Heb. words for "dough" in the LXX and appears figuratively as "lump" in the sense of the whole loaf in the NT. In Rom 11:16 "the firstfruit" and "the root" stand for Abraham, through whom all the nation of Israel, referred to by "the lump" and "the branches," has been consecrated. In I Cor 5:6–7 "the lump" represents the entire congregation of Christian believers, whether unleavened (pure) or leavened by malice and evil. *See* Food: Bread; Leaven.

J. R.

Egg. Eggs of domesticated chickens did not become common food until after the 4th cen. B.C. Eggs of small wild birds were gathered for food (Isa 10:14), but when found in Israel, the hen or mother bird could not be taken also (Deut 22:6). The ostrich's habit of leaving eggs to be hatched in warm sand is mentioned in Job 39:13–14. Hatching out adders' (KJV, "cockatrice") eggs symbolized scheming evil (Isa 59:5). Jesus' reference in Lk 11:12 was doubtless to a hen's egg.

Fish. *See* Animals, V.4.

Flour. Three ideas are conveyed in the three Heb. words translated "flour" in the KJV. The Heb. word *bāṣēq* speaks of dough made by mixing flour with water and a bit of the previous day's batch of leavened dough (II Sam 13:8). Heb. *sōlet* refers to fine crushed flour and is used more frequently than either of the other two (Lev 2:1). Heb. *qemaḥ* was used of a coarser flour or meal. It is translated "meal" in I Sam 1:24; II Sam 17:28; Jud 6:19, ASV. The

fine flour was made mainly from the inner kernels of wheat (Ex 29:2; Deut 32:14; Ps 81:16; 147:14), while barley, rye, and other grains were used for meal, the major difference being the texture since for the latter the entire kernel was used. Fine flour mingled with oil was used in unleavened bread (Ex 29:2) and in the meal offering (Ex 29:40). *See* Food: Bread.

After the grain was winnowed it was usually sifted (cf. Lk 22:31) and then ground into meal or flour between two millstones. Not until Hellenistic times did the rotary type of hand mill with two round stones become common. Throughout the OT the grinding was done by rubbing the upper, smaller stone back and forth over the grain placed on the larger stone. The sound of grinding early in the morning must have been common in the towns of Palestine before their destruction (Jer 25:10; Rev 18:22).

A. E. T.

Honey. Heb. *debash*, "honey," signified three sources of sweets: (1) grape or date honey, the Arabic *dibs*, a thick syrup made from dates or grape juice (Gen 43:11; I Kgs 14:3; II Kgs 18:32); (2) the honey of wild bees which was found dripping out of a honeycomb, perhaps in a hollow log, on the ground (I Sam 14:25 f.), in the skeleton of an animal (Jud 14:8–9), or in crevasses in the rocks (Deut 32:13; Ps 81:16; see also Mt 3:4; Mk 1:6); and (3) honey from domesticated bees (one of the products of "the field" collected as firstfruits during Hezekiah's revival, II Chr 31:5).

The term "honey" is used figuratively in the expression "a land flowing with milk and honey" (Ex 3:8, *et al.* 15 more times) to denote great fertility and abundance of food (PEQ, XCVIII [July–Dec. 1966], 166 f.). Canaan was indeed a source of much honey even before Moses' time. Thutmose III (1483–1450 B.C.)

brought back to Egypt hundreds of jars of honey from Syria-Palestine as tribute. Sinuhe sang the praises of that land *c.* 1950 B.C., exclaiming, "Plentiful was its honey, abundant its olives" (ANET, p. 19). At Ugarit the Canaanites lauded their country in the expression "The heavens rained oil; and the creeks ran with honey" (BA, XXVII [Dec., 1965], 121; cf. Job 20:17). Because of its sweetness honey is frequently employed in simile and metaphor in Heb. poetry (e.g., Ps 19:10; 119:103; Prov 16:24; Song 4:11; 5:1).

J. R.

Knead. Flour and water were placed in the kneading-trough in which a scrap of the previous baking had been left. The dough was worked by hand and allowed to stand until the scrap had leavened the lump (Gen 18:6; II Sam 13:8; Jer 7:18; Hos 7:4). The witch of Endor who hurriedly baked bread for King Saul did not have time for the fermenting, and thus baked unleavened bread (I Sam 28:24).

The kneading-trough was a shallow bowl usually made of wood or pottery. During the plague of frogs, even the kneading-troughs of the Egyptians were infested (Ex 8:3). The Israelites carried their kneading bowls as essential equipment when they left Egypt (Ex 12:34). The kneading-trough (KJV, "store") is among the objects of the Lord's blessing and cursing (Deut 28:5, 17).

Leaven. Bread was the staple commodity of food in biblical times, so much so that "our daily bread" was synonymous with one's whole diet. Except in times of unusual haste or unforseen circumstances (Ex 12:39), the bread was leavened. The leavening agent used to make the bread rise was a portion of a former mixture of leavened dough, preserved for the purpose, which was either dissolved in the water into which the flour was added in the kneading-trough, or "hid" in the flour itself which was kneaded into dough (Mt 13:33). *See* Food: Bread; Dough.

Unleavened bread (*maṣṣâ*) was used in the rituals of the Levitical law. There it seems to have had two special significances. 1. Unleavened bread was required in the Passover and the Feast of Unleavened Bread. It is also called "the bread of affliction" (Ex 12:34–39; 13:3; Deut 16:3–4). This kind of bread was required as a reminder that God had thrust the Israelites out of Egypt suddenly, without even sufficient time to allow their bread to rise. Hence they ate unleavened bread as they began their wilderness journey. Therefore, in both the Passover and the Feast of Unleavened Bread, designed as memorials of the deliverance from Egypt, unleavened bread was required. In these instances leaven does not seem to have an ethical significance. 2. Unleavened bread was required in the offerings made under the Levitical law (Lev 2:4; 6:16; 7:12). Leaven here does have an ethical connotation. It was excluded because the process of fermentation implied corruption. When used in an ethical sense, leaven speaks of evil or corruption.

Two exceptions to the general rule concerning the use of unleavened bread are to be noted. In the peace offering (Lev 7:13) and in the feast of the wave loaves (Pentecost) (Lev 23:17) leavened bread was to be offered. The explanation is to be found in the significance of these two events. The peace offering was a sweet-savor offering, revealing the Godward aspect of the death of Christ, in contrast to the nonsweet-savor offerings, which depicted the sinward aspect of Christ's sacrifice. In His death Christ reconciled the world to God (II Cor 5:19). He caused the warfare between man and God to cease, and established peace (Eph 2:14–18). Although "unleavened cakes mingled with oil" were offered (Lev 7:12) to show that Christ was separated from sin, leavened bread was also offered (Lev 7:13) as a symbol of the fact that Christ's reconciliation was for the sinful world.

In the feast of the wave loaves (Pentecost) it was also fitting to include leavened bread, for the two loaves symbolized the harvest that would be brought to God from among both Jew and Gentile by the work of Christ. That which was previously corrupt is after the cross offered to God as no longer corrupt but cleansed through the death of Christ.

In the figurative use of leaven in the NT, the ethical concept of the OT is retained. Christ used leaven as a figure of the false teaching of the Pharisees (Mt 16:6; Lk 12:1). This figure is explained in Mt 16:12, thus removing all doubt of its significance. Paul twice quoted a proverb using leaven in this ethical concept (I Cor 5:6; Gal 5:9), as the application of the proverb to the Corinthians shows (I Cor 5:7–8). This seems to be also the background of Peter's imagery in II Pet 1:4*b*. When Christ used leaven in the parable of the kingdom (Mt 13:33), while the ethical connotation may not be eliminated, the emphasis seems to be more on the effects of introducing leaven into meal: "all was leavened." In like manner, after the kingdom is introduced, it will ultimately encompass all. This is Christ's picture of the universality of His kingdom at His second advent.

J. D. P.

Manna. The word occurs first in KJV in Ex 16:15. Elsewhere in the OT all English versions uniformly render the Heb. word as "manna," which is merely an approximate transliteration; but in v. 15 ASV and RSV translate it as a question, "What is it?" Evidently, when the Israelites first saw it on the ground, they nicknamed it a "whatness," or colloquially a "whatdyacallit," which seems to be the literal meaning with reference to the mysterious quality of the divine bread.

Manna is said to have been small, round and white (Ex 16:14, 31). Left over night it ordinarily "bred worms, and became foul" (Ex 16:20, ASV). It melted in the hot sun. It was to be gathered daily, in the morning, an omer (about half a peck) per person. On the sixth day the people were to gather twice as much, to provide for the sabbath, when no manna was to be given. In this case it did not breed worms or become foul over the sabbath.

Manna tasted like "wafers made with honey" (Ex 16:31) or "butter cakes" (Num 11:8, NEB), and could be baked or boiled. Apparently it was like a seed in appearance and consistency, and like bdellium or gum resin in color. It was customarily ground before baking. After a time, many of the people came to dislike it violently (Num 21:5).

A pot of manna was gathered and kept as a memorial of this continuing miraculous provision by the Lord for the Israelites throughout the 40 years in the wilderness (Ex 16:32–35). Later, a golden pot of manna was placed in the ark in the tabernacle (Heb 9:4).

Manna is thought by many to be typical of Christ as the Bread of Life. The Lord's comments in Jn 6:31–35 seem to warrant this conclusion. "Hidden manna," which may refer to that in the ark, is promised in Rev 2:17 to the overcomer, implying the closest fellowship with the Lord in the coming kingdom.

See Food: Bread.

J. A. S.

Meal. This is the translation of two Heb. words, *sōlet* and *qemah*. The first refers to very fine flour or meal and is found in Gen 18:6; Ex 29:2; I Chr 9:29; Ezk 16:13, 19. The other word means flour or meal and is translated "meal" in the following passages: Gen 18:6; Num 5:15; I Kgs 4:22; 17:12, 14, 16; II Kgs 4:41; I Chr 12:40; Isa 47:2; Hos 8:7. The word "meal" occurs twice in the NT (Mt 13:33; Lk 13:21) where the Gr. word (*aleuron*) means fine flour or meal. The two most important grains among the Hebrews were wheat and barley (usually "corn" in KJV). When ground they were used for bread and for vegetable sacrifices ("meal offerings").

In Ruth 2:14 the Heb. word *'ōkel* ("meal") is used as a compound with the word for time (*'ēt*). The word denotes the portion of food eaten at any one time. In this passage the meaning is "mealtime" or "time of eating" (*see* Food: Meals).

Meals. Ordinary people in ancient Palestine ate only two regular meals a day — breakfast or lunch (our "brunch"), and supper or dinner (Ex 16:12; I Kgs 17:6). Heb. has no specific words to distinguish these meals, but in Gr. the former is *ariston* and the latter *deipnon* (see Lk 14:12, "luncheon or a dinner party," Phillips).

Aside from early snacks, the first proper meal came late in the morning, between 10:00 A.M. and noon (Ruth 2:14; cf. 2:7, 17). Peter became hungry about the sixth hour, i.e., noon (Acts 10:9–10). It was not a large meal. Boaz and his harvesters had only bread dipped in sour wine and parched grain (Ruth 2:14); Jesus provided bread and broiled fish (Jn 21:13). It was an hour for rest as much as for food.

The chief meal was eaten usually after sunset when it was too dark to work longer in the fields (Jud 19:16, 21). Unless a man had a slave (Lk 17:7–8), the women served the meal (Jn 12:2). If guests were invited, this meal became a feast or banquet (*see* Food: Banquet). Only men were seated at banquets (II Sam 13:23), although at ordinary meals women could eat with the men (Ruth 2:14). The communal practices of the Jerusalem church imply that after Pentecost male and female believers ate together daily (Acts 2:44, 46) as well as at the love feasts (I Cor 11:17–22, 33–34; Jude 12).

The Gospels reveal that "washing of hands" before meals was a religious requirement for Jews (Mk 7:1–5). At a banquet attendants brought bowls for washing the hands again after eating, since in biblical times no tableware was provided. Everyone ate out of the common bowl or platter with his fingers (Prov 26:15; Mk 14:20). Wine was usually not provided until the food had been served and eaten (Gen 27:25). At the Last Supper this order was followed as Jesus first broke the bread and then passed the cup.

Roman officials and wealthy persons often ate four meals a day, similar to our system with afternoon "tea" included. For a fuller description of Roman meals and cooking see A. C. Bouquet, *Everyday Life in New Testament Times*, Scribner's, 1954, pp. 70–73.

J. R.

Meat. This word was used in KJV for food in general, as it is in Scotland still. The "meat offering" (*minḥā*, "oblation") of Lev 2, *et al.* is more properly a meal or cereal offering. The term signifying meat in the modern sense is "flesh" in KJV, as in Ex 12:8, 46 speaking of the meat of the Passover lamb (cf. also Ex 16:8, 12; 29:14, 31–34; I Kgs 17:6; Ps 50:13; *et al.*).

The Levitical laws of purity regulated which animals were considered ritually clean and suitable for offerings to God (Lev 11:2–23; Deut 14:4–20). Later in Judaism ritually pure food was designated *kōsher* (from Heb. *kāshar*, "to be right, proper," cf. Est 8:5). The distinction between clean and unclean animals dates from the earliest times (Gen 7:2; 8:20). Any domesticated beast permissible as a sacrifice to Yahweh was also deemed fit to eat by His covenant people. The criteria were whether the animal chews the cud and has a cloven hoof (Lev 11:3).

An underlying reason for excluding other animals, such as the pig, may be found in the danger of contracting such diseases as trichinosis, carried by swine. The principal reason, however, was no doubt a religious taboo against animals which the Canaanites and other pagans offered to their gods. Horses, swine, dogs, and mice (or rats) were connected with the underworld rites often associated with the underworld (II Kgs 23:11; Isa 65:4; 66:3, 17). These and other beasts would be forbidden as food since animals were normally slaughtered only in connection with the offering of sacrifices. To eat their meat would make the Israelite "abominable" (Lev 11:43). For the prohibition con-

Peasant women bring offerings of a variety of food to Queen Ti as portrayed in her tomb at Sakkara, Egypt. LL

cerning stewing a kid in its mother's milk (Ex 23:19) *see* Food: Milk.

Many of the prohibited birds, insects, and reptiles (Lev 11:13–30) were worshiped in Egypt in the sense that as totems they represented Egyptian deities. No evidence exists that the game animals (Deut 14:5; 12:15; I Kgs 4:23) and birds not called unclean in the Mosaic code were ever totem gods in the ancient Near East. Egyptian Eighteenth Dynasty tomb paintings clearly show gazelle and quail as the object of the hunt (*see* Food: Venison). *See also* Clean.

The eating of any kind of blood, even of clean animals and birds, was absolutely forbidden on the grounds of the sacredness of life (Gen 9:4–6; Lev 17:10–14; Deut 12:16, 23–25; Acts 15:29). The life of the body was considered to flow in the blood, so that when the blood was shed, the very life itself was poured out. If not employed to make atonement (Lev 17:11), the drained blood was to be covered with dust.

Of the clean animals, a goat kid was the most frequently eaten, especially among the poor (hence the complaint of the prodigal's brother, Lk 15:29). But the favorite meal included a stall-fed calf (Prov 15:17) or choice sheep (Neh 5:18). Roast goose was a national dish in Egypt and may be the "fatted fowl" on Solomon's table (I Kgs 4:23). Chickens were known in Palestine by 600 B.C. (e.g., a seal showing a rooster found at Tell en-Nasbeh), but domestic poultry and eggs were uncommon before the Persian period.

J. R.

Mess. This nearly obsolete English word, now used only for meals in a military setting, occurs in KJV in Gen 43:34 and II Sam 11:8. Translating Heb. *maś'ēt*, the term means a portion of food or a gift "lifted" from the table of a ruler and given to an inferior as a largesse or token of friendship. The Heb. word occurs in this sense also in Est 2:18 ("gifts") and in Jer 40:5 ("reward," KJV; "present," RSV).

Milk. In biblical times people did not ordinarily drink fresh milk, probably because of lack of refrigeration. Milk was allowed to sour and then was made into curds (*see* Food: Butter) or cheese (*q.v.*). Goat's milk (Prov 27:27) was the most common, although sheep, cows, and even camels were also milked (Deut 32:14; I Cor 9:7). The importance of mother's milk for newborn infants is implied in Isaiah's figures (Isa 49:15; 66:11–12) and in Peter's simile regarding the necessity of spiritual nourishment from the Word of God (I Pet 2:2). For weaning from breast feeding (Isa 28:9), *see* Children.

The term "milk" was often used figuratively to denote abundance and fertility, both then (for the expression "milk and honey" *see* Food: Honey) and in the eschatological age (Isa 55:1; 60:16; Joel 3:18). In the NT "milk" represents the simplest form of the gospel, elementary Christian doctrine (I Cor 3:2; Heb 5:12–13). *See* Milk.

The prohibition of the Mosaic law against boiling or stewing a goat kid in its mother's milk (Ex 23:19; 34:26; Deut 14:21) evidently was given to combat a Canaanite sacrificial rite practiced to ensure the fertility of a field by sprinkling the resultant broth upon the earth.

Such a custom is mentioned in the Ugaritic poem, "Birth of the Gods" (G. R. Driver, *Canaanite Myths and Legends,* T. & T. Clark, 1956, p. 121).

J. R.

Parched Corn. This is roasted grain (Josh 5:11; Lev 23:14; Ruth 2:14; I Sam 17:17), probably wheat or barley (Ruth 2:14), not "corn" (*q.v.*). The threshed grain was roasted in a pan by keeping it in constant motion with a stirrer until the food was done. When prepared, such grain could be carried in quantity (I Sam 17:17) and used on a journey (Josh 5:11).

Pottage. Jacob made his famous pottage (Heb. *nāzîd*) by boiling red lentils (Gen 25:29–34). It was a common dish (Hag 2:12), a thick vegetable soup or stew, probably flavored with onions and occasionally bits of meat. Esau's sale of his birthright merely for a little pottage illustrates the cheap estimate he placed on his family rights. In Elisha's day one of the young prophets found a wild vine and cut up some of its gourds into the soup, inadvertently poisoning it (II Kgs 4:38–40).

Raisins. Raisins (Heb. *ṣimmûqîm*) were a favorite provision of persons on a journey (I Sam 25:18; 30:12; II Sam 16:1) because they were easily carried without spoilage (I Chr 12:40). Raisins were prepared by soaking bunches of grapes in oil and water, or in a solution of potash, and then spreading them in the sun to dry. Num 6:3 lists dried grapes as one of the prohibited foods for a Nazarite. The KJV "flagon," Heb. *'ăshîshâ,* more correctly is a raisin cake. *See* Flagon. These were considered delicacies suitable for feasts (II Sam 6:19; I Chr 16:3; Song 2:5). Cakes of raisins were used in pagan festivals (Hos 3:1) and no doubt as offerings to the fertility goddesses (cf. Jer 7:18; 44:19).

Savory Meat. Savory or tasty meat was requested by Isaac as he prepared to give his blessing to Esau (Gen 27:4, 7, 9, 14, 17, 31). The Heb. word means "delicacies" or "dainties" and was meat, particularly wild game, prepared in an appetizing way. Perhaps it was the deceiving of Isaac by Jacob that led the wise man to write the proverb that warns against desiring the "dainty meats" of the wicked (Prov 23:3, 6).

Venison. A KJV translation of two Heb. words (*ṣayid, ṣêdâ* from *ṣûd,* "to hunt") which technically referred to wild game of any kind (Gen 25:28; 27:3, 5, 7, 19 ff.). Venison came to mean usually deer, antelope, or gazelle meat. The Heb. term occurs also in Prov 12:27, in the KJV "hunting"; the Jerusalem Bible translates, "The idle man has no game to roast." BDB suggests, "The slothful man does not (even) flush his game." In Lev 17:13 Heb. *ṣayid* appears in the idiom "hunteth and catcheth," lit., "hunts a hunting of" or "hunts game whether animal or bird."

The same Heb. word was applied in a broad-er sense to any provisions of food (Job 38:41; Neh 13:15; Ps 132:15), especially to provisions for a trip (Gen 42:25; 45:21; Josh 1:11 ["victuals"[; 9:11, 14; etc.), perhaps because wild game was a frequent food of early nomads. *See* Food: Victuals.

Victuals. A common designation for food or provisions (cf. Gen 14:11; Lev 25:37; II Chr 11:11; Mt 14:15; *et al.*). This word is now seldom employed in the standard English language. KJV used it to translate such words as Heb. *'ōkel,* "food"; *leḥem,* "bread"; and *ṣêdâ,* "venison," "wild game," "provisions." *See* Food: Bread; Venison.

Bibliography. J. Behm, *"Esthiō,"* TDNT, II, 689–695. A. C. Bouquet, *Everyday Life in New Testament Times,* Scribner's, 1954, pp. 69–79. CornPBE, pp. 331–337. R. J. Forbes, *Studies in Ancient Technology,* III, Leiden: E. J. Brill, 1955, pp. 50–105; *op. cit.,* V, 1957, pp. 78–88, 97 f. E. W. Heaton, *Everyday Life in Old Testament Times,* Scribner's, 1956, pp. 81–115. K. A. Kitchen, "Food," NBD, pp. 429–433.

FOOL, FOOLISH. The term is used in Scripture with respect to moral and spiritual more than to mental or intellectual deficiencies. The "fool" is not one who does not think or reason, but who reasons selfishly and wrongly. In the OT the fool is the person who rejects the fear of the Lord, and thinks and acts independently as if he could ignore God's rule and blaspheme His name and mock at sin, all with impunity (Ps 14:1; 74:18, 22; Prov 14:8–9; etc.). In other passages the term has the more ordinary meaning, denoting one who is rash, loud-mouthed, or unreasonable.

The English word translates a number of Heb. and Gr. words. One word for "fool" in the Heb., *nābāl,* is also the name of an individual who personified folly, the man Nabal (I Sam 25:25). He was what he was not because of idiocy but because he was insensible to religious and ethical claims; even his own wife could not appeal to him (25:17). As such he might be termed spiritually senseless, as in Ps 14:1. Isa 32:6 gives a description of such a fool (see RSV): his mind plots iniquity, he practices ungodliness, utters error about the Lord, and neglects the hungry and thirsty. This type of person is actively irreligious and unkind. He is definitely a sinner (Gen 34:7; Josh 7:15; II Sam 13:12–13; Jud 19:23), practicing folly (*q.v.*).

Heb. *'ĕwîl* is found mostly in Proverbs and is described as one who despises advice and instruction (1:7; 10:8; 15:5), who lacks wisdom and good common sense (10:21; 11:29; 12:15; 24:7; Jer 4:22), and who is quick to talk back or act without thinking (10:14; 12:16; 14:17; 20:3, RSV; 29:9 RSV).

Heb. *kesîl* is used very frequently in both Proverbs and Ecclesiastes. This fool is characterized at length in Prov 26:1-12 and Eccl 7:4-9. The $k^e sîl$, one who is dull and obstinate, hates knowledge (Prov 1:22; 23:9) and has no capacity to get wisdom (Prov 17:16); he is complacent and self-confident (Prov 1:32, RSV; 14:16; 28:26); he enjoys doing wrong (Prov 10:23; 13:19) and displaying his folly (Prov 13:16; 18:2); he shrugs off a rebuke (Prov 17:10); his speech is perverse (Prov 19:1), and he is prone to make many rash promises (Eccl 5:1-6).

Heb. $sākāl$ occurs most often in Ecclesiastes; the term seems to stand for one who is willfully stubborn or thickheaded, who has eyes but does not see (Jer 4:22; 5:21; Eccl 10:3), as in the case of King Saul (I Sam 13:13; 26:21). Because this word is also applied to other kings in their transgression (David, II Sam 24:10; Asa, II Chr 16:9; Solomon [?], Eccl 2:12, 13, 19), perhaps $sākāl$ can connote foolishness at an official level with consequent greater guilt. Derek Kidner includes the simple ($p^e tî$) and the scorner ($lēṣ$) in the general category of fools (*The Proverbs*, Tyndale Press, 1964, pp. 39-42).

In the NT (using Gr. $ano\bar{e}tos$, "thoughtless") Christ rebukes the two on the Emmaus road and Paul rebukes the Galatians for lack of faith (Lk 24:25; Gal 3:1, 3). This term also describes the senselessness of the desires and lusts which drag men down into perdition (I Tim 6:9; Tit 3:3).

Gr. $asunetos$ denotes someone without understanding (Mt 15:16; Mk 7:18) and is used to depict the hearts or minds of the God-denying heathen (Rom 1:21, 31).

As the rich fool ($aphr\bar{o}n$) came to an untimely end because he failed to take into account the will of God, so Paul urges Christians not to be foolish but to understand what the will of the Lord is (Lk 12:20; Eph 5:15-17). This fool is heedless (Lk 11:40), without reason, ignorant (I Pet 2:15), and needs to be corrected (Rom 2:20). Paul uses this term of himself in sarcastically going along with the Corinthians' estimate of him (II Cor 11:16, 19; 12:6, 11).

In I Cor 1:18, 21, 25, 27; 2:14 $m\bar{o}ros$ and its derivatives seem to connote man's attitude toward something unusual that has no intellectual explanation or that does not fit in with one's preconceived ideas. In turn, those who try to get by in the spiritual realm on their human reasoning are called foolish in God's sight (I Cor 1:20; 3:19; Mt 23:17). Thus the five foolish virgins were dependent on their own natural understanding (Mt 25:2, 3, 8; see Georg Bertram, "*Moros*, etc.," TDNT, IV, 832-847).

In Mt 5:22 the expression "thou fool" ($m\bar{o}re$) may be the only pure Heb. (i.e., not Aramaic) word in the NT. Heb. $m\^oreh$ is an impious rebel against God, and is the expression which Moses used when he lost his temper at the chiding Israelites (Num 20:10). Its use would imply a murderous hatred.

I. G. P. and J. R.

FOOLISHNESS. *See* Folly; Fool.

FOOT. Great care was necessarily given the feet during Bible times because of the dusty roads, the absence of hose, and the open design of the sandals. Thus the host would wash the feet of a visitor, and this became synonymous with hospitality (I Tim 5:10). Such a menial task, done voluntarily, was a sign of complete humility, as exemplified by Christ (Jn 13:4-15).

The untying of the shoe latchets (*q.v.*) may refer to this same practice (Mk 1:7; Lk 3:16; Jn 1:27). Shoes were generally left outside one's house as well as the house of God. Moses was told to "put off thy shoes from off thy feet" (Ex 3:5; Acts 7:33), and Moslems still believe contact with the common ground brings defilement. The provision of shoes for Israel in the wilderness showed God's protection (Deut 8:4; 29:5). Nakedness of the feet in public was a sign of mourning (Ezk 24:17). Because of the delicacy of the Heb. language, the word was used for the private parts. Such phrases include "the hair of the feet," "the water of the feet," "to cover the feet," etc.

Other uses of the word are: (1) stability, "He set my feet upon a rock" (Ps 40:2); (2) the place of a learner, "to sit at the feet" (Deut 33:3; Lk 10:39; Acts 22:3); (3) affliction or calamity (Ps 35:15; 38:16; Jer 20:10); (4) take possession, to set one's feet (Deut 1:36; 11:24); (5) subordination, "to be under one's feet" (Ps 8:6; Heb 2:8; I Cor 15:27); (6) complete destruction, "treading under foot" (Isa 18:7; Lam 1:15). "To water with the foot" (Deut 11:10) may imply that channels of irrigation were turned with ease, as with the foot.

Bibliography. Konrad Weiss, "*Pous*, etc.," TDNT, VI, 624-631.

E. C. J.

FOOTMAN. Footman was used of a military infantryman (Num 11:21; I Sam 4:10; 15:4). An alternate Heb. word used stresses the activity of running and has the general idea of a runner or courier (I Sam 22:17). That the footman was often a runner is derived from the statement in Jer 12:5.

FOOTSTEPS. Two Heb. words are so translated.
1. Heb. '$āqēb$, literally, "the heel"; hence "heelprint," figuratively, "footstep" (Ps 77:19; 89:51; Song 1:8).
2. Heb. $pa'am$, "footfall," the tread of the foot on the ground; hence footstep (Ps 17:5). The idea is that of stepping or striding.

FOOTSTOOL. Heb. $kebesh$, translated "footstool," simply means that which is walked or stepped on, hence a stool, literally, "a stool of the foot" (Heb. $h\u{a}d\^om$ $regel$). In the description of Solomon's throne it is said that "there were six steps to the throne, with a footstool of gold" (II Chr 9:18).

Footstool is used figuratively especially as the place of God's feet, and refers to the temple which David planned to build for Him, and to the earth (I Chr 28:2; Ps 132:7; Isa 66:1). It is also applied to God's enemies as His footstool (Ps 110:1).

Gr. *hypopodion* means "what is under the foot." James uses it once (Jas 2:3) as a place to sit. Just as in the OT, it is also used in a metaphorical sense in Mt 5:35; 22:44, and parallel passages; Acts 2:35; 7:49; Heb 1:13; 10:13. Here it carries the idea of the subjection of those who are under God's feet.

A. E. T.

FOOT WASHING. Foot washing was a common custom in Eastern lands. The effect of dusty or muddy roads upon feet shod with open sandals made it customary for water and a basin to be available at the entry of homes. A slave or the visitor himself performed the washing (Gen 18:4), although the host might do so as a mark of special favor (I Sam 25:41). It was discourteous to neglect the practice (Lk 7:44).

The washing of the disciples' feet by Jesus (Jn 13:1–17) had a deeper significance. His remark to Peter that "what I do thou knowest not now" showed that Jesus' intention went beyond the well-known custom. Many hold that Jesus was giving a lesson in humility by His example. Humility was certainly displayed by the washer. Yet Jesus said that if He did not perform this act, it would be Peter and not He that would be at fault. Thus He must have been teaching something about Peter's need, not His own virtues.

That spiritual cleansing was basic to Christ's purpose is seen in Jn 13:10–11, where lack of cleansing is specified of Judas. All except Judas were said to have been bathed (*leloumenos*—complete bath), but they still needed to have their feet washed (*nipsasthai*—partial washing). The complete bath referred to salvation as symbolized in baptism. The washing of the feet depicted the need that even believers have for cleansing from defilement which comes from contact with a sinful world.

That Jesus intended this act to be perpetuated by the church may be inferred from Jn 13:14–15. The practice of the Pedilavium may be seen in the early church from I Tim 5:10, and from such patristic notices as Tertullian (*De Corona*, Chap. 8), Athanasius (*Canon 66*), and Augustine (*Letter to Januarius*). The Synod of Toledo (A.D. 694) specified that the rite should be observed on Maundy Thursday. It is still practiced by some Protestant groups, including Brethren, Mennonites, Waldensians, Winebrennarians, and a few Baptists.

For Jewish religious ritual washings *see* Ablution.

H. A. K.

FORBEARANCE. This noun translates the Gr. *anochē* in its two occurrences in the NT. The word literally means "holding back," "stopping" (especially hostilities), and thus was frequently used for an armistice or truce. In Rom 2:4 the delay in a just God's inflicting wrath or punishment on the sinner is explained by the truth of His goodness (or "kindness," RSV), forbearance, and long-suffering ("patience," RSV). This delay is to give opportunity for, and to lead the sinner to, repentance. In Rom 3:25 it is stated that God has passed over sins during the former dispensation(s) in His divine forbearance until the perfect substitutionary sacrifice should be offered by His Son Jesus Christ. This concept of God's forbearance is also found in Neh 9:30.

The related verb *anechomai* is translated by "forbear" in Eph 4:2; Col 3:13, where Christians are commanded to forbear one another in love, to make allowances for one another, because love "covers a multitude of sins" (I Pet 4:8).

Other Gr. and Heb. verbs translated as "forbear" have the sense "to stop," "to cease," "to refrain from." *See* Long-suffering.

J. R.

FORCES. A military term meaning an army or military force, resources, powers, or fortress. Examples of use meaning a military force are found in Jer 40:7, 13; 41:11, 13, 16; as resources, in Isa 60:5, 11 (ASV, RSV, "wealth"); and as fortifications, in Dan 11:38 (ASV, RSV, "fortresses").

FORD. Without bridges, fords in Bible times necessarily were places of easy passage across a river. In some instances, at least, fords were places not only for men and animals to wade across, but also for wagons or carts to be driven across. Two in Transjordan were the ford of the Jabbok—Wadi Zerqa (Gen 32:22), and the ford of the Arnon—Wadi Mojib (Isa 16:2). Other references to fords in nearly every instance are to crossing places of the Jordan. They are mentioned in connection with Joshua's spies (Josh 2:7), Ehud's victory over the Moabites (Jud 3:28), the Shibboleth incident (Jud 12:5–6), and David's flight (II Sam 15:28; 17:16—"fords of the wilderness," ASV, RSV). None of these crossings can be identified with certainty today, but they must be located somewhere in the lower stretch of the Jordan as it approaches and empties into the Dead Sea. II Sam 19:18 should probably be translated, "And they crossed the ford to bring over . . ." (RSV).

"Fords of Babylonia" (Jer 51:31–32, RSV) apparently refer to crossing places of the Euphrates and its canals.

H. E. Fi.

FOREFRONT. The front part of a building, a place, or a battle. The KJV and ASV translate several Heb. terms as "forefront"; *pānim*, "face" (II Kgs 16:14; Ezk 40:19; 47:1), but KJV renders Ezk 40:15 as "face" (ASV, "forefront"); *mûl pānîm*, "before or over against the face" (Ex 26:9; 28:37); *rō'sh*, "head" (II Chr

20:27); and *shēn,* "tooth" (I Sam 14:5; ASV, "front"). The RSV usually renders the first two expressions as "front," while it translates *rō'sh* literally and *shēn* as "crag."

FOREHEAD. This term is used frequently in its literal sense. Aaron and the high priests after him wore on their foreheads a gold plate (Ex 28:36, 38). The condition of the forehead aided the priest in determining leprosy (Lev 13:42–43; II Chr 26:20). David hit the forehead of Goliath with a stone (I Sam 17:49). Although cutting the body was forbidden (Lev 19:28), ownership markings were placed on the foreheads of slaves or devotees of a godhead. Such ownership by Yahweh is seen in Ezk 9:4, 6 where the word "mark" is the last letter of the Heb. alphabet (in early times made in the form of a cross). In the NT, the foreheads of the righteous (Rev 7:3; 9:4; 14:1; 22:4) and of the godless followers of Satan (Rev 13:16–17; 14:9; 17:5; 20:4) are marked. However, in Ezk 16:12, the jewel is a nose ring, not an ornament in the forehead as in the KJV.

Figuratively, forehead is used for obstinance (Ezk 3:7–9), and shame (Jer 3:3).

E. C. J.

FOREIGNER. Broadly, a Gentile or non-Israelite. The word included all aliens, wherever they resided. Foreigners could not partake of the Passover (Ex 12:43), enter the sanctuary (Ezk 44:9), be chosen king (Deut 17:15), or intermarry with Israelites (Ex 34:15–16). However, foreigners could be received into Judaism through circumcision (Gen 17:27).

A stranger (in ASV usually "sojourner") was one not having full citizenship but living in an Israelite home, in contrast with a foreigner staying in Israel temporarily. Although not an Israelite, the stranger had certain rights and duties. God admonished His people to be kind to him. "For ye know the heart of a stranger, seeing ye were strangers in the land of Egypt" (Ex 23:9). *See* Hospitality.

Many privileges and prohibitions were his, but not all the religious duties. He was free from circumcision, if he so chose. He could, on invitation, attend sacrificial feasts (Deut 16:11, 14). He was permitted to sacrifice to the Lord in the atonement for sins of the congregation unwittingly committed. He had the privilege of a sin offering, and the protection of a city of refuge. By circumcision, he was allowed to partake of the Passover (Ex 12:48). In early OT times, marriages with foreigners were frequently made, though not sanctioned. Later Ezra and Nehemiah vigorously tried to prohibit any foreign marriages (Ezr 10; Neh 13:23–31).

In the NT, among the Jewish people, foreigners and strangers were usually grouped together as Gentiles (*q.v.*). Strict Jews did not eat and drink with Gentiles (Acts 11:3). Due to conditions existing during and following the Exile, an attitude of hatred and scorn developed between Jew and Gentile, which continued through the

Christian era. Following the finished work of Christ on the cross, another group, the Church, is referred to in addition to the Jews and Gentiles. Full membership in the Church is open to all who will accept Christ's sacrifice on the cross for sin. "Now therefore ye are no more strangers and foreigners, but fellow citizens with the saints, and of the household of God" (Eph 2:19). *See* Proselyte.

Bibliography. K. L. and M. A. Schmidt and Rudolf Meyer, "*Paroikos,* etc.," TDNT, V, 841–853. Gustav Stählin, "*Xenos,* etc.," TDNT, V, 1–36.

L. A. L.

FOREKNOWLEDGE. *See* Election.

FOREORDINATION. *See* Election.

FORERUNNER. The English word "forerunner" is an exact translation of the Gr. *prodromos.* Forerunner is the term used of one sent ahead, either as a spy to reconnoiter for those who are to follow, or as a herald to prepare the way for a coming king.

Although John the Baptist was in truth the forerunner of Jesus (see Mal 3:1: "I will send my messenger, and he shall prepare the way before me"; cf. Mt 3:3 with Isa 40:3), the term "forerunner" is never used of him in Scripture. In its only use in the NT the word is applied to the Lord Himself. In Heb 6:20 He is described as our "forerunner" who has entered into the presence of God, preparing the way for us who by His grace are to follow (cf. Jn 14:2; Heb 10:19–20).

FORESHIP. The front part of a ship, the bow or prow. The KJV renders Acts 27:30 "as though they would have cast anchors out of the foreship," but in v. 41 the same Gr. word is translated "and the forepart stuck fast" (ASV, "foreship"). The RSV uses "bow" in both instances.

FORESKIN. The fold of skin (prepuce) removed from the male organ in circumcision (*q.v.*), as "a token of the covenant" between God and the Hebrews (Gen 17:11). David presented Saul with 200 Philistine foreskins as proof of their slaughter and of his prowess (I Sam 18:27). In Hab 2:16 it refers to indecent exposure, although the LXX and Syriac versions and the Qumran Habakkuk Commentary have a similar word meaning "stagger." It is used figuratively of the obstinacy of carnal man ("foreskin of the heart," Deut 10:16; Jer 4:4).

FORESKINS, HILL OF. A place near Gilgal where the rite of circumcision, neglected during the wilderness wanderings, was performed on the males of Israel (Josh 5:3).

FOREST. *See* Plants.

FORGIVENESS. The doctrine of forgiveness,

prominent in both the OT and NT, refers to the state or the act of pardon, remission of sin, or restoration of a friendly relationship. Central to the OT doctrine is the concept of covering of sin from the sight of God represented by the Heb. word *kāpar* (Ps 78:38; cf. Deut 21:8; Jer 18:23). This is indicated in the various translations of the word such as "appease," "be merciful," "make reconciliation," and the most prominent use in the expression "make atonement," occurring 70 times in the KJV. In Lev 4:20 it is coupled with another prominent OT word for forgiveness with the meaning "to send away or let go." Accordingly, in Lev 4:20 it is stated: "The priest shall make an atonement [from *kāpar*] for them, and it shall be forgiven [from *salaḥ*] them." A third Heb. verb, *nā'sā'*, occurs frequently with the idea of "lifting up" or "lifting away" sin (Gen 50:17; Ex 10:17).

From these passages it is clear that forgiveness depends upon just payment of the penalty for sin. The OT sacrifices provided this typically, and prophetically looked forward to the final sacrifice of Christ (cf. Acts 17:30; Rom 3:25). Forgiveness as a relationship between God and man depends upon the divine attributes of righteousness, love, and mercy, and is based upon the work of God in providing a suitable sacrifice. *See* Atonement.

The doctrine of forgiveness anticipated in the OT has its fullest revelation in the NT. Here three principal words are used in the original: (1) *aphiēmi* and *aphesis*, meaning "to send away," "remission" (Mt 6:12, 14–15; 9:2, 5–6; etc.); (2) *charizomai*, meaning "to be gracious" (Lk 7:43; Eph 4:32; Col 2:13; 3:13); and (3) *apoluō*, meaning "to loose away" (Lk 6:37). In the NT forgiveness is a part of the whole program of salvation provided for those who believe in Christ. In forgiveness the guilt of sin is pardoned and replaced by justification in which the sinner is declared righteous. Forgiveness is always included in the whole work of God for the sinner, is basically judicial, and provides pardon for the sinner. *See* Justification; Reconciliation.

Another major aspect of NT revelation concerns Christians who sin. Though judicially forgiven all sin, past, present, and future, when saved by faith (Jn 3:18; 5:24; Col 2:13; Rom 8:1), if sin enters the life of a Christian it affects his relationship to his heavenly Father. The forgiveness or restoration to fellowship which is necessary is accomplished by confession of sin (I Jn 1:9) and repentance (Lk 17:3–4; 24:47; Acts 5:31). The divine side is cared for by the efficacy of Christ's death and intercession (I Jn 2:1) in which Christ pleads for the sinner on the ground of His own sacrifice. *See* Confession; Repentance.

Two special cases related to forgiveness are cited in the NT: (1) the sin unto death, i.e., sin of such character that God takes His sinning child home to glory and cuts short any opportunity for further sin or testimony (I Jn 5:16; cf. I Cor 11:30–32); (2) the unpardonable sin,

defined as attributing the miraculous power of Christ to Satan rather than to the Holy Spirit (Mt 12:22–32; Mk 3:22–30). Technically, the unpardonable sin is impossible today as Christ is not performing miracles in the same way. However, all sin becomes unpardonable if an individual passes from this life without availing himself of divine grace.

Forgiveness is also an obligation in the relationship between men, and believers are exhorted to forgive one another (Eph 4:32; cf. Mt 6:12, 14).

Bibliography. J. O. Buswell, Jr., *A Systematic Theology of the Christian Religion,* Grand Rapids: Zondervan, 1962, II, 74–77, 128–131. Hugh R. Mackintosh, *The Christian Experience of Foregiveness,* London: Nisbet, 1947. W. C. Morro, "Forgiveness," ISBE, II, 1132–1135. Leon Morris, "Forgiveness," NBD, 435 f. John Owen, *The Forgiveness of Sin,* New York: American Tract Society, n.d. Vincent Taylor, *Forgiveness and Reconciliation,* London: Macmillan, 1958.

J. F. W.

FORK. Literally, a three-pronged fork, an agricultural tool on the order of a pitchfork, used once in KJV in an obscure passage (I Sam 13:21). ASV translates *mizreh* as "fork" (Isa 30:24; KJV, "fan"), while RSV renders *mazlēg* (I Sam 2:13–14) and *mizlāgâ* (Ex 27:3; 38:3; Num 4:14; I Chr 28:17; II Chr 4:16) as "fork," a utensil of the tabernacle and temple.

The "fan" of Mt 3:12 and Lk 3:17 (Gr. *ptuon*) was a "winnowing fork" (RSV). *See* Fan.

FORM *See* Image of God.

FORNICATION. Used of illicit sexual intercourse in general (Mt 5:32; 19:9; Acts 15:20, 29; 21:25; Rom 1:29; I Cor 5:1). In a technical sense it is to be distinguished from adultery or social promiscuity after marriage (Gr. *moicheia;* Mt 15:19; Mk 7:21; Jn 8:3; Gal 5:19), and from rape, which is a crime of violence without the agreement of the other party. *See* Adultery; Divorce; Harlot.

Fornication and adultery are used figuratively in the Bible to express the disloyalty of Israel to God when idolatry is in view (Jer 2:20–37; Ezk 16; Hos 1–3). The terms are all too fitting, however, because the idolatrous fertility cult worship of the Canaanites as well as of the Greeks (*see* Corinth) often involved fornication with sacred prostitutes or priestesses. In Rev 17 the idolatry of the final apostate church, formed by a merging of many religions, is likened to an adulterous woman because of the utter worldliness of the church and her synthesis with paganism through a form of pan-deism.

Bibliography. F. Hauck and S. Schultz, "*Pornē,* etc.," TDNT, VI, 579–595.

R. A. K.

FORT, FORTIFICATION, FORTRESS. The most ancient fortified site thus far discovered is the Palestinian city of Jericho, which *c.* 7000 B.C. was surrounded by a massive stone fortification strengthened in at least one place by a large stone tower. Other cities of Palestine are known to have been strongly fortified from the early Bronze Age, which began *c.* 3300 B.C. and encompassed the inception of the city-state system in Palestine, to the Roman period. The earliest builders tended to occupy easily defensible sites, fortifying their cities with walls. Fortifications generally followed the irregular outlines of the hills and spurs on which the cities were built.

During the Middle Bronze Age (*c.* 2100–1550 B.C.), fortifications became more elaborate and powerful than at any other time in Palestinian history. In connection with the Hyksos movements of this period, a new type of fortification appeared in Egypt and in Syro-Palestine. As enclosures for horse-drawn chariotry, great rectangular camps up to half a mile long were constructed. These were surrounded by enormous sloping ramparts of packed earth *(terre pisée).* The best example of such a camp in Palestine is at Hazor. Slightly later, similar ramparts, this time made of brick and stone and coated with hard-packed clay or with lime plaster, were used to strengthen city walls. They served to prevent erosion as well as to discourage invaders from attempting to scale the walls. In addition they probably served as an effective defense against the newly introduced battering ram. Other Middle Bronze Age innovations included new methods of constructing walls, gates, and towers in such a way as to force an enemy soldier, on entering the city, to expose his unshielded side. Such techniques greatly increased the difficulty of approaching and storming city gates.

Canaanite cities of the Late Bronze Age (*c.* 1500–1200 B.C.) were well fortified (cf. the description *'ārîm beṣûrôt,* "walled" or "fenced cities," used of them, e.g., in Num 13:28; Deut 1:28; 3:5; 9:1). At the beginning of Iron Age I (*c.* 1200–900 B.C.), however, the construction of fortifications in Palestine suddenly deteriorated. The feudal organization of the Canaanites had been able to make effective use of the corvée in building operations, while the loosely organized Israelite amphictyony was powerless to coerce its workmen. In addition, however, the introduction of bonded masonry made the previous massive construction techniques less necessary; and, indeed, Saul's castle at Gibeah (modern Tell el-Ful), though crudely built, demonstrates that Israelites were capable of erecting strong and relatively large buildings by the end of the period of the judges (last half of 11th cen.). It was a fortress built of massive polygonal masonry measuring *c.* 170 by 115 feet and surrounded by a double casemated wall (apparently with a tower at each of the four corners).

The casemate fortifications at Beth-shemesh

The King's Gate in the massive fortification walls at Boghazkoy, capital of the Hittite Empire. The gate is recessed in the wall and the walls are double, requiring a double gate. HFV

and Debir (modern Tell Beit Mirsim) can be confidently attributed to David. After capturing Jerusalem from the Jebusites, he proceeded to fortify it (David's Jerusalem is referred to as a "stronghold" in II Sam 5:9 [*meṣûdâ*] and I Chr 11:7 [*meṣād*]). Solomon, the great builder of united Israel, likewise shared in strengthening the fortified cities (cf. II Chr 8:5) of this period. Notable are the results of his labors still visible at Hazor, Gezer, and Megiddo. Defenses uncovered at Azekah (one of the "fortified cities" of Judah mentioned in Jer 34:7) and Mareshah have been attributed to Rehoboam (cf. the imposing list of "fortified cities" preserved in II Chr 11:5–10).

In the Transjordan region, many remains of Iron Age I fortifications have been discovered in recent years. Edomites and Moabites alike guarded their borders with fortresses (cf. the Moabite "strongholds" of Jer 48:18). The remains of the characteristic round tower forts of the Ammonites during the same period are often designated by the Arabic term *rujm el-malfûf* ("circular heap"). Transjordanian fortresses were commonly so situated that from each one those nearest on both sides were visible.

The best example of Iron Age II (*c.* 900–550 B.C.) fortifications in Palestine thus far excavated is the massive double wall of Tell en-Nasbeh (biblical Mizpah?) with its plastered revetment and well-preserved gate. The Judahite fortifications at this site witness to the ill will, not infrequently erupting into civil war, that obtained between Israel and Judah after Solomon's death. During this period Israel "built palaces" and Judah "multiplied fortified cities" (Hos 8:14, RSV).

Information regarding Iron Age III (*c.* 550–330 B.C.) fortifications is relatively scarce because of lack of physical remains, although Nehemiah restored the walls of Jerusalem during this period. Later strengthening of strategic Palestinian communities was stimulated by the Maccabean struggle for independence (cf., e.g., the remains of the Beth-zur fortress and those of the castle of Alexander Jannaeus on Qarn Sartabeh overlooking the Jordan Valley).

The arrival of the Romans in Palestine introduced changes in military architecture that sacrificed esthetic value for the sake of efficiency. The ruins of characteristically square Roman camps are observable throughout Palestine with many examples to be found in the Transjordan region. The most important of the massive fortifications of this period were constructed by Herod the Great, including particularly his fortress residence at Jerusalem and the Castle of Antonia (located at the NW corner of the temple area). He strengthened the defenses of Samaria (modern Sebaste) as well. His later namesake, Herod Agrippa I, is generally thought to be responsible for the so-called third wall of Jerusalem.

Since the nation of Israel was essentially and ideally a theocracy (cf. Ps 118:9, ASV), the OT emphasizes that true strength is found not in fortifications but in the Lord (Jer 5:17; Hos 8:14). Indeed, God is called a *mā'ôz* ("strength," "refuge") in II Sam 22:33; Prov 10:29; Isa 25:4; Jer 16:19; Joel 3:16; Nah 1:7; a *meṣûdâ* ("fortress," "stronghold") in II Sam 22:2; and a *miśgāb* ("high tower," "retreat") in 22:3. All three terms are also used of Him often in the Psalms. The character of Jeremiah resembled the unyielding nature of military defenses (Jer 1:18; 15:20), while Paul, in his well-known metaphor in II Cor 10:4, used the Gr. word *ochyrōma* ("stronghold") in reference to the vaunted arguments used by men to oppose the knowledge of God.

For descriptions of Assyrian, Babylonian, and Roman systems of fortifications *see* Babylon; Calah; Nineveh; Rome.

See also Bulwark; Citadel; City, Fenced; Gate; Tower; Wall.

Bibliography. Millar Burrows, *What Mean These Stones?* London: Thames and Hudson, 1957, pp. 97–104. Roland de Vaux, *Ancient Israel,* trans. by J. McHugh, New York: McGraw-Hill, 1961, pp. 229–236. Yigael Yadin, "Hyksos Fortifications and the Battering Ram," BASOR 137 (Feb., 1955), pp. 23–32; *The Art of Warfare in Biblical Lands,* 2 vols., New York: McGraw-Hill, 1963.

R. Y.

FORTUNATUS (fôr-tū-nā'tŭs). Mentioned but once (I Cor 16:17), Fortunatus is connected with two other men who, presumably, came from Corinth to Paul at Ephesus. The three are spoken of as having ministered to Paul in some way, and Paul uses this fact to administer a gentle rebuke to the Corinthian believers in general. He writes: "That which was lacking on your part they have supplied." Paul was evidently cheered by their coming.

FORUM. When mention is made of the forum, one usually thinks of the Imperial Forum at Rome. But every Roman city had a forum (roughly the equivalent of a Gr. agora), and some eastern cities (e.g., Athens) had a Roman agora or forum near the old Gr. agora. Moreover, near the Imperial Forum in Rome, Julius Caesar, Augustus, Nerva, Domitian, and Trajan built additional fora, as commercial and other needs demanded more space. The forum in every Roman city was the very hub of its life. *See* Agora; Market; Rome.

The Imperial Forum in Rome was bounded by the Palatine, Quirinal, Esquiline, and Capitoline hills. It was located where paths running down the valleys between the hills of Rome met. The Forum grew as Rome grew and was rebuilt from time to time. The area was drained by the Etruscans during the 6th cen. B.C. and became the political, religious, social, and economic center of Rome. As Rome grew, the more objectionable features of Roman business were removed from the Forum first. The

A reconstruction of the Castle of Antonia. Sisters of Zion, Jerusalem.

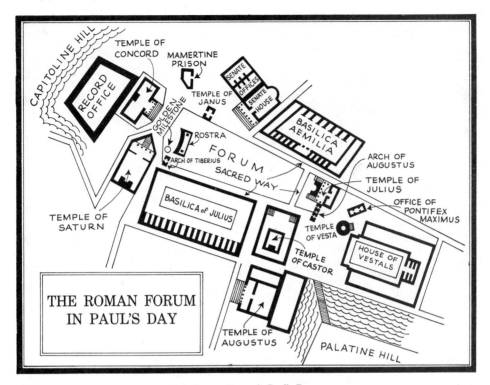

The Roman Forum in Paul's Day

smells of the fish market and the tumult of the vegetable market were removed about 300 B.C. In the early days there was no particular plan; the Forum was just a cluster of buildings. From about 200 B.C. to the time of Augustus a considerable amount of regularization took place. Augustus and Tiberius (about the time of Christ) gave the Forum its final ground plan but not its final buildings.

During these 200 years temples were rebuilt on a larger and more monumental scale and tended to take over the Gr. style. In addition, the Romans introduced the basilica, probably from Syria, with its large central hall and narrow side aisles. The Basilica Aemilia, the earliest in Rome, was built in the Forum c. 170 B.C. The Basilica Julia was started by Julius Caesar and finished by Augustus. The Romans used basilicas as law courts and business centers.

The Imperial Forum began to go out of regular use in the 5th and 6th cen. after Christ. During the medieval and early modern periods the area was used as a stone quarry. Stones found a use as building blocks as far away as Westminster Abbey in London.

As noted, the Forum was subjected to frequent reconstruction. Thus, effort is required to sort out the main buildings standing there when, for instance, the apostle Paul appeared before Nero. If he had entered the Forum on the Sacred Way from the E, he would have passed the large house of the vestal virgins, W of which was the Temple of Vesta. Vesta was the goddess of the hearth and was considered the patron of the fire that symbolized the perpetuity of the state. It was the responsibility of the priestesses to maintain this sacred fire and renew it annually on the first day of the year.

Just in front of the Temple of Vesta was the Regia or official residence of the head of the state religion. Next the apostle would have walked alongside the Temple of the Divine Julius (Caesar). When Paul came to the corner of the temple, the Sacred Way turned left, passed in front of the Temple of Julius and led straight to the steps of the Temple of Castor and Pollux. There the Sacred Way turned right again and passed the Basilica Julia, where Paul may have stood trial before Caesar (II Tim 4:16 f.).

As with municipal fora of Italy, so the Roman Forum was built up at one end. In Rome the W end dominated. Here on the Capitoline hill was a temple to Jupiter and at lower levels temples to Saturn and Concord. Before the lat-

The Roman Forum today. HFV

ter stood the Rostra where orators made public speeches. Under the northern slope of the Capitoline was the Mamertine Prison, where Paul was probably incarcerated (II Tim 1:16 f.; 2:9; 4:6). On the N side of the Forum stood the Senate chambers and the Basilica Aemilia.

H. F. V.

FORUM APPII. *See* Appii Forum.

FOUNDATION. Literally, the base or structure upon which a building or some object rests, as the foundation of the temple (II Chr 8:16), the base of the altar (Ex 29:12), the substratum of a mountain (Deut 32:22), a city (I Kgs 16:34) or its walls (Ezr 4:12). The Heb. *yāsad,* with its derivatives, and the Gr. *katabolē* are frequently used figuratively. Thus the term may refer to the security of the righteous described as "an everlasting foundation" (Prov 10:25), or to the frailty of man "whose foundation is in the dust" (Job 4:19). Temporally, it describes the beginning of the world; e.g., "the foundation of the world" (Mt 25:34; Eph 1:4); and poetically, the invisible foundational structure of the heavens (II Sam 22:8) and the earth (Ps 104:15).

Christ is designated in both Testaments as a "foundation" (Isa 28:16; I Cor 3:11). In the NT the term is used figuratively in reference to the first principles of the gospel (Heb 6:1–2); the teachings of the prophets and apostles (Eph 2:20); the eternal city (Heb 11:10; Rev 21:14); election (Eph 1:4; II Tim 2:19); the Christian life (I Cor 3); and is the subject of parables (Lk 6:48–49; 14:25 ff.).

Destruction of the foundation describes the overthrow of Egypt (Ezk 30:4), the wicked man by the figure of a house's foundation (Hab 3:13), and false prophets by the illustration of a wall (Ezk 13:14).

H. E. Fr.

FOUNDER. *See* Occupations: Goldsmith, Metal, Workers in, Refiner, Silversmith.

FOUNTAIN

1. A source of flowing water; a spring. This is to be distinguished from a well dug into the earth, or a cistern. One of the principal Heb. words translated "fountain" is *'ayin,* which also means "eye." In its compound form of *en (q.v.)* this word occurs in the names of many Palestinian cities, as En-rimmon (Neh 11:29); for Palestine, unlike Egypt, abounded in springs (Deut 8:7; 11:10). The Heb. *mabbúa'* has the idea of bubbling forth or gushing, as in Isa 35:7 where it is translated "springs."

2. A source of something other than literal water. The Heb. *māqôr* is often used this way. Thus is found the "fountain of life" (Ps 36:9), "of Israel" (Ps 68:26), "of her blood" (Lev 20:18). In Prov 16:22 and 18:4 it is translated "wellspring." The Gr. *pēgē* denotes both a spring of literal water (Jas 3:11–12) as well as the source of something else (Mk 5:29; Rev 21:6).

C. J. W.

FOUNTAIN GATE. *See* Jerusalem: Gates and Towers 11.

West end of the Roman Forum reconstructed.

FOWL. *See* Animals, III, 14.

FOWLER. In biblical times a fowler caught birds with snares. One kind of snare was a net *(reshet)* that pinned the bird to the ground (Hos 7:12). Another kind, called a gin, sprang up to cast a noose about a bird's neck *(môqēsh* in Amos 3:5*a*). Yet others, with doors or jaws which sprang shut when a bait was taken, have been found in Palestine and Egypt *(paḥ,* Ps 124:7; Amos 3:5*b*).

The action of a fowler in laying a snare has been used in the Bible in many different ways to illustrate the influence of evil persons and evil ways. In Jer 5:26 it is applied to wicked men that plot against others. In Jud 2:3 the worship of heathen gods is called a snare to Israel. In I Sam 18:21 Saul is said to have thought that the influence of his daughter Michal would be a snare for David. In II Sam 22:6 David spoke of the intention of his enemies as snares of death. In Prov 18:7 the lips of a fool are called "the snare of his soul." In I Tim 6:9 Paul said, "They that are minded to be rich fall into a temptation and a snare" (ASV).

See Snare.

J. W. W.

FOX *See* Animals, II.14.

FRANKINCENSE. *See* Incense; Plants: Frankincense.

FRAUD. *See* Crime and Punishment; Law.

FRAY. Literally, "to tremble, frighten, trouble," it is an archaic English word used in Deut 28:26; Jer 7:33; Zech 1:21. It is translated "frighten" in ASV and RSV in the first two references, and as "terrify" in the last.

FREEDOM. Freedom is exemption or release of one personality from domination by or obligation to another. The concept appears frequently in the Bible, especially in the passages dealing with the laws of slavery under the Mosaic regime, and also in the Pauline epistles, where the term is applied to individual spiritual life. When Abraham commissioned his servant to find a

The Peirene Fountain at Corinth. HFV

wife for Isaac, he required him to swear that he would not take Isaac back to the land from which Abraham had come, but that he would persuade the woman of his choice to come to Isaac. If the woman refused, the servant would be freed from his pledge (Gen 24:8, 41). To be free meant that the servant would not be expected to continue the search, but could consider his commission discharged.

Political freedom. Theory of government is not discussed at any length in the Bible. Autocratic rule prevailed in the time when it was written, but the germ of freedom can be found in the Christian revelation. In Paul's colloquy with the Roman colonel in charge of the garrison at Jerusalem, the latter said that he had bought his citizenship for a high price. Paul proudly affirmed that he was Roman born (Acts 22:28). Political freedom was usually inherited from one's ancestors, and was the privilege of the upper classes. It was an inalienable right unless some legal complications were involved.

Social freedom. Every member of the Jewish commonwealth was a free man except for captives of war who were made slaves, and for those who voluntarily sold themselves in order to pay a debt. Under the OT law a slave was usually freed upon completion of six years' service (Ex 21:2–6; Deut 15:12). When the slave had paid for his freedom by his labor, he was released to enter upon his own career.

Spiritual freedom. Freedom in the Bible is connected chiefly with the concept of liberation from sin. Jesus stated that every man who commits sin is the slave of sin, and that he can be freed only by the intervention of the Son of God who is able to break sin's yoke (Jn 8:32–36). The operation of the new life of the Spirit can deliver man from the depressing law of sin and death, and can engender the hope of ultimate liberation from the corruption that follows sin (Rom 8:2, 21). This freedom is not the product of legalism, but of faith (Gal 4:23–31).

Freedom, however, is not license, but is manifested in love (Gal 5:13). It is the voluntary operation of the will which motivates men to fulfill the purpose of God. To do right because it satisfies one's deepest desire is freedom.

The freedom of the human will is recognized by the Bible, though it is not discussed philosophically. It predicates the ability to choose one of two or more alternatives without external compulsion. God is also free; He may choose to do whatever He wishes (Dan 4:35). Because God is infinite personality and because man is finite, the freedom of man lies within the circle of the freedom of God. Man may at any moment decide to accept or to reject the alternative which that moment offers, but he cannot choose to avoid the consequences of his choice, nor can he refuse to respond to the alternative. To refuse to choose is in itself a choice. Furthermore, every choice modifies all subsequent choices. An act may be repudiated or counteracted, but it can never be recalled or

undone. Man's freedom, then, is circumscribed by his previous acts in time, since the past affects the present. Because the present affects the future, apart from the intervention of God, man lives in an ever-narrowing circle of cause and effect, which must finally bind him completely.

Man has sinned, and the horizon of his freedom is consequently limited. He may choose whether or not he will commit some particular sin, but he cannot choose whether or not he will be a sinner. He can only acknowledge the fact, and accept the deliverance which God can provide. He may have the freedom to refuse it, but not to avoid the consequences of his refusal.

God enjoys perfect freedom because He is never under the necessity of acting contrary to His own nature. No external compulsion can have any effect on Him, because He created the universe and is sovereign over it. As the Absolute Good, He is superior to all obligation or coercion.

Because God is completely righteous, He is not limited by the restraint of evil. He is free to exercise His creative and redemptive powers as He sees fit at any time, and whatever He does must ultimately eventuate in good for all concerned. There can be no real conflict between the moral responsibility of man and the sovereign will of God, since the constitution of the universe, which embraces the option of moral choice, is established by divine decree. God has created the world with the possibility of freedom because it is an essential part of His nature. Although man's freedom is circumscribed by finiteness, it is no less genuine than that of God, who is infinite. Within the sphere allotted to man, he is free.

This freedom, however, has been seriously curtailed by sin. The evils that have been produced by the wrong choices of the past handicap the full exercise of free will, not because God has arbitrarily so ruled, but because in an ordered universe liberty can survive only within law. Liberty is not synonymous with chaos. In order to restrain evil, and to keep it from enslaving the world permanently, God must intervene by redemption. He retains the prerogative of final decision.

Both the freedom of man and the sovereignty of God are presented in scriptural revelation, often in the same or contiguous passages. Freedom is contingent upon abiding in the work of Christ, which involves an act of the will (Jn 8:31–32), but freedom is a gift of God, who alone possesses it fully (Jn 8:36).

See Example; Liberation; Liberty.

Bibliography. Heinrich Schlier, "*Eleutheros,* etc.," TDNT, II, 487–502.

M. C. T.

FREEDOM, YEARS OF. *See* Festivals; Jubilee.

FREEMAN. The KJV does not use "freeman" in the OT. The RSV, however, so translates the

Heb. word *ḥôrîm* ("free born, nobles" in Eccl 10:17, ASV marg.). In the NT *apeleutheros* (I Cor 7:22) refers to a freed slave, and in this particular reference, to one who has received spiritual freedom, while *eleutheros* (Gal 4:22-23, 30; Rev 6:15) concerns a free man as contrasted with a slave. *See* Freedom.

FREEWILL OFFERING. *See* Sacrificial Offering.

FRIEND, FRIENDSHIP. Two OT words, Heb. *rēaʿ* (and its derivatives), "friend," "neighbor," "companion"; and *'ōhēb* (participle of *'āhab*, "to love"), "lover," "beloved friend"; and two NT words, Gr. *hetairos*, "comrade," "neighbor," "friend"; and *philos*, "beloved friend," refer to comrades and close friends. Thus both the OT and the NT have words for a mere friend and one for a deeply affectionate friend.

The Bible speaks of two kinds of friendship: (1) between man and God in the case of Abraham (II Chr 20:7; Isa 41:8; Jas 2:23) and Moses (Ex 33:11); (2) between man and man, such as that between David and Hushai (II Sam 15:37; 16:16), between Elijah and Elisha (II Kgs 2), and between David and Jonathan, which is the most famous case of friendship in Scripture, a love that was "wonderful, passing the love of women" (I Sam 18:1; II Sam 1:26). There is one outstanding example between women, namely, that of Ruth with her mother-in-law Naomi (Ruth 1:16-18).

Solomon spoke many words of wisdom about friendship, such as: "A friend loveth at all times" (Prov 17:17); "Faithful are the wounds of a friend" (Prov 27:6); "There is a friend that sticketh closer than a brother" (Prov 18:24); and "Make no friendship with an angry man" (Prov 22:24).

The relationship experienced between Christ and the Twelve developed from that of teacher to disciple, through that of Lord to servant (Jn 13:13), into that of friend to friend (Jn 15:13-15). Judas, called "mine own familiar friend" (Ps 41:9), is the terrible example of an unfaithful friend (Mt 26:14-16).

R. A. K.

FRINGE. One of three symbols (the others were phylacteries and cylinders containing a parchment scroll attached to the door posts) that continually confronted the Jew, reminding him of the Lord's commandments. Four blue (white was permitted later) fringes of woven cords with tassels were to be attached to the four corners of the Jew's outer garment (Num 15:38-39; Deut 22:12). Jesus condemned the Pharisees (Mt 23:5) who, to be seen by men, made their fringes long.

FROG. *See* Animals, VI.15.

FRONTLETS. Israel was told that the great redemption wrought for them by God in Egypt and the word of God revealed to them by Moses was to be laid up in their hearts and souls. It was never to be forgotten but was to be ever before them, like "frontlets," i.e., a band or ribbon about the head and before the eyes (Ex 13:16; Deut 6:8; 11:18; JerusB, "circlet"). In later days this symbolic representation was taken literally by the Jews. Strips of parchment or papyrus were inscribed with passages from Scripture, placed in a small leather box and bound with thongs to the forehead (Mt 23:5). *See* Phylactery. By this literal, outward observation, the great spiritual need and obligation was neglected and God's Word lost its proper place in Israel's heart.

See Dress.

FROST. Frost is common in the higher areas of Palestine during the winter and may damage early crops and fruits (Ps 78:47; Heb. *ḥănāmāl*). Hoarfrost (Heb. *kᵉpôr*) is referred to in Ex 16:14; Job 38:29; Ps 147:16; Sir 43:19. It is the term for small ice needles which form during a cold, still night. The Heb. word *qeraḥ* in Jer 36:30 is translated "ice" in Job 37:10 by ASV and RSV, and "cold" in Gen 31:40 by RSV.

FROWARD. The translation in the KJV of several Heb. words signifying "contrary," "perverse," "subversive," etc. Heb. *hăphakpak* ("devious," Prov 21:8, JerusB) and *tahpukôt* ("mutinous," Deut 32:20, NEB; "perverse," "perverted," Prov 2:12, 14; 6:14; 8:13; 10:31-32; 16:28; 23:33, RSV) are derived from *hāphak*, "to turn, overturn," and emphasize an obstinate persistence in turning away from or overthrowing what is right or good. Heb. *'iqqēsh* ("twisted," Prov 2:15, JeruB; "crooked," Ps 18:26; Prov 17:20, RSV) and *'iqqᵉshût* ("crooked speech," Prov 4:24; 6:12, RSV) describe an evil man or thing as something crooked or twisted out of shape, not aligned with God's ways. Other words rendered "froward" also bring out the devious nature and stubborn depravity of fallen mankind.

FRUIT. The product of many plants and trees. Those most frequently mentioned in Scripture are grapes, figs, and olives, all of which are still grown in Palestine today. *See* individual entries under Plants.

Figurative. The term "fruit" is often used symbolically. Children are referred to as fruit (Ex 21:22; Ps 21:10) in such phrases as "the fruit of the womb" (Ps 127:3; Deut 7:13; Lk 1:42) and "the fruit of the body" (Ps 132:11; Mic 6:7). Praise is poetically described as "the fruit of the lips" (Isa 57:19; cf. Heb 13:15), and a man's words are called "the fruit of the mouth" (Prov 12:14; 18:20).

The term "fruit" is applied to the consequences of our actions and motives. "They shall eat the fruit of their doings" (Prov 1:31; Isa 3:10). "The fruit of wickedness" is the judgment incurred from wrong action (Jer 6:19; 21:14); and "the fruit of righteousness" is the good works that spring from the heart of a godly man (Phil 1:11). "The fruit of the Spirit" are the gracious habits and principles which the Holy Spirit produces in a Christian (Gal 5:22–23; Eph 5:9). Thus in this sense "fruit" may be said to be the total result that issues from any specific action or attitude. The fruit may be evil (Mt 3:10; 7:15–20; 12:33; Lk 6:43–46; Rom 7:5), but more often it is good (Ps 104:13; Mt 3:8; 21:43; Rom 7:4; Jas 3:17).

The disciples were urged to "bear fruit" (Mk 4:20; Col 1:10; Jn 15:4–8), and were criticized for being spiritually unfruitful (Mk 4:19; Tit 3:14; II Pet 1:8; cf. I Cor 14:14).

J. R.

FRYING PAN. A vessel in which the meal offering was cooked (Lev 2:7; 7:9), more properly a deep-fat pan or kettle. The pan used by Tamar (II Sam 13:9) was probably a frying pan.

FUEL. In the KJV, "fuel" stands for two Heb. words both meaning "food"; in these cases, food for fire (Ezk 15:4, 6; 21:32; Isa 9:5, 19). Fuel in biblical times was wood, charcoal (KJV, "coals" in Prov 26:21; also in Isa 44:12; 54:16 for the fire of the metalworker), perhaps chaff (Mt 3:12), and dry hay (Mt 6:30). For cooking, thorns might be used (Ps 58:9; Eccl 7:6), and in cities suffering from shortages during seige, animal and even human excrement was used (II Kgs 6:25; Ezk 4:12, 15).

FUGITIVE. A translation of five Heb. words with varying shades of meaning. The Heb. *bārî-ah* means "one who flees or escapes" (Isa 15:5), as does *mibrāḥ* (Ezk 17:21); *nûa'* means "a roamer," "rover," "wanderer" (Gen 4:12, 14); *nōpēl,* "a deserter" (II Kgs 25:11), and likewise *pālit* (Jud 12:4). *See* Cities of Refuge.

FULFILL. *See* Prophecy, Fulfillment of.

FULLER. *See* Occupations.

FULLER'S FIELD. A well-known landmark of Hezekiah's day, just outside the city, near enough for the embassy of Sennacherib to be heard on the walls of Jerusalem. The uncertain site was near a conduit of the upper pool (II Kgs 18:17; Isa 36:2), probably near the Gihon spring in the Kidron Valley. Isaiah and his son met Ahaz here (Isa 7:3). The fuller's trade (*see* Occupation) required a water supply and ample area for drying the washed materials. *See* Field.

FULLER'S SOAP. *See* Occupations: Fuller.

FULNESS. The Gr. term *plērōma,* "fulness," that which has been filled, is used in Scripture in at least six ways.

1. *Time.* When the time had come and things were ready in God's plan: "When the fulness of the time was come, God sent forth his Son,

made of a woman, made under the law" (Gal 4:4).

2. *History of the Gentiles.* The "fulness of the Gentiles," namely, the completion of God's plan to give the gospel specially to the Gentiles in the Church Age (Rom 11:25; cf. Lk 21:24).

3. *The deliverance of the kingdom by the Son to the Father.* This is called the "dispensation of the fulness of times" in Eph 1:10, in the sense that it covers the complete work of Christ in subduing all things to Himself. It closes with Christ delivering up the consummated kingdom of God to the Father (I Cor 15:24–28).

4. *Fulness of Israel.* This occurs with the regrafting of Israel into the true olive tree and the marvelous salvation of all that nation, at the second coming of Christ (Rom 11:12, 26–29; cf. Isa 66:8–9; Zech 12:10 ff.).

5. *Fulness of Christ.* The presence of the whole divine nature and of all the attributes of God in Jesus Christ (Jn 1:16; Col 1:19). "For in him dwelleth all the fulness of the Godhead bodily" (Col 2:9). So "Christ is, in a unique and complete sense, the incarnation of God Himself. Thus it is (Eph 4:10) that He fills all things" (C. F. D. Moule, "Pleroma," IDB, III, 827). In Eph 4:13 the "fulness of Christ" must mean that completeness, that maturity already realized in Christ Himself.

6. *Christ's sufficiency for us.* The complete sufficiency of Christ in His ministry of redemption and salvation so that believers are seen as "complete [*peplērōmenoi*] in him" (Col 2:10). The perfect tense of the Gr. passive participle indicates that positionally true Christians have already been made complete, with the result that they always shall be filled or completed in Christ. For "from His fulness we have, all of us, received—yes, grace in return for grace" (Jn 1:16, JerusB), i.e., "a grace answering to the grace (that is in Christ)." By experiencing the love of Christ we become filled with all the fulness of God (Eph 3:19).

Bibliography. Gerhard Delling, "*Plērēs,* etc.," TDNT, VI, 283–311.

R. A. K. and J. R.

FUNERAL. A funeral is the performance of cial rites for the dead, especially in the presence of the body and preceding burial or cremation. In Palestine in biblical times few burials were accompanied by elaborate services. Burial (*q.v.*) was performed as soon as possible after death, because of ceremonial defilement of the living and for practical considerations. Where the temperature was often high and no embalming was practiced, decomposition of the body occurred rapidly (*see* Embalm). It was customary to bury the body within a few hours after death. Consequently there was a lack of ceremony in burial. (See CornPBE, pp. 338–346.)

Though a number of burials are mentioned in

the Bible, the word "funeral" does not appear in the English versions. The account of Ananias and Sapphira illustrates the simplicity of burial and the shortness of the interval between death and interment. When Ananias died, the young men wrapped him, probably using the garments he wore, and carried him out and buried him (Acts 5:6). His wife was not even informed of what had happened. Some three hours later she came in, and within minutes she too died and shortly was buried beside her husband (Acts 5:10).

Often a procession escorted the corpse to its resting place. The funeral procession of Jacob was impressive for size, because Jacob was the father of the vizier of Egypt (cf. Gen 50:4–14, esp. vv. 7–9). A much more simple procession is mentioned in Lk 7:12, where the only son of a widow of Nain was being carried to his grave, accompanied by his mother and a large crowd from the town (cf. II Sam 3:31). Ordinarily a coffin was not used; the body was borne on a bier and placed directly into the tomb or grave (*see* Grave; Tomb). The funeral of Asa, king of Judah, was exceptional; he was laid on a bier filled with spices and a great fire was made in his honor (II Chr 16:14).

Funeral services in other parts of the ancient Near East were often quite elaborate, those of Egypt particularly so, because of the importance of funerary beliefs in Egyptian religion (see Montet, *Everyday Life in Egypt,* pp. 300–301).

See Dead, The; Mourning.

C. E. D.

FURLONG. *See* Weights, Measures, and Coins.

FURNACE. The English word "furnace" translates several Heb. and one Gr. word. Some of these refer to firepots used to bake bread or provide heat in dwelling houses; others to smelting furnaces in which metal is refined, or to kilns where bricks, pottery, etc., are hardened.

In a few passages the term is used literally; e.g., Dan 3 where three Heb. youths were thrown into a furnace used by the Babylonians for capital punishment, and Ex 9:8, 10 in which Moses was commanded to sprinkle "handfuls of ashes of the furnace" in connection with the sixth judgment on Egypt.

More often, however, the word is used as a figure of speech: (1) as a symbol of God Himself in His glory, holiness, and wrath (Gen 15:17; Ex 19:18; Isa 31:9); (2) as a symbol of intense suffering viewed as a refining process (Deut 4:20; I Kgs 8:51; Isa 48:10; Jer 11:4; Ezk 22:18, 20, 22); (3) as a simile to describe a fierce conflagration (Gen 19:28); (4) as a simile to depict the absolute purity of the Word of God (Ps 12:6); (5) as a graphic picture of the awfulness of the place of future punishment of wicked men (Mt 13:42, 50).

G. C. L.

FURNACES, TOWER OF. *See* Jerusalem: Gates and Towers 8.

FURNITURE. Cooking equipment and bed mats constituted the furniture of the very poor, the furnishings increasing with the wealth of the owners. Elisha's guest chamber was one of the better equipped rooms (II Kgs 4:10). The palaces contained costly and luxurious furniture (Est 1:6).

Wooden bedstead covered with thick sheet gold with mesh of string from tomb of Tutankhamon. LL

The term "furniture" (Heb. *kelî*) in the OT, with only one exception, refers to the brazen altar, laver, table of showbread, altar of incense, lampstand, and ark of the covenant of the tabernacle (*q.v.;* Ex 31:7–9; 35:14; 39:33). In Nah 2:9 the reference is to furniture in the palace of Nineveh. In Gen 31:34 "furniture" *(kar)* refers to the saddle of Rachel's camel.

FURROW. A shallow incision made by a plow *(q.v.).* Three different Heb. words are translated "furrow": (1) *telem,* "ridge, furrow" (Job 31:38; 39:10; Hos 10:4; 12:11); (2) *gĕdûd,* "cut, gash" (Ps 65:10); (3) *ma'ănāh* (Ps 129:3), figurative use of "furrow." ASV and RSV translate I Sam 14:14, "half a furrow's length."

Two other Heb. words are rendered "furrow" in the KJV: *'ônāh* (Hos 10:10), which is probably better understood as "transgressions" (see ASV) and "iniquity" (RSV); and *'ărûgāh* (Ezk 17:7, 10), "bed" in ASV and RSV.

FURY. Used particularly to express the burning anger and rage of man (Gen 27:44; II Sam 11:20; Est 1:12; 2:1); of the he-goat in Daniel's vision (Dan 8:6); and of God (Lev 26:28; Isa 42:25; 51:17 ff.; Jer 4:4; 10:25; Ezk 5:13; Zech 8:2). *See* Anger.

FUTURE LIFE *See* Life; Immortality.

G

GAAL (gā'ăl). Son of Ebed, evidently a Canaanite, and leader of a roving band of his relatives similar to the bands of Habiru mentioned frequently in the Amarna letters (*q.v.*). He organized a revolt of the Shechemites against Abimelech's rule, but was defeated outside the city as he and his rebels sallied forth to fight Abimelech and his approaching army. Zebul, the lieutenant-governor of Shechem, barred the gate to Gaal and his fleeing brethren as they sought refuge within the city walls (Jud 9:26–41).

GAASH (gā'ăsh). A hill or mountain in the hill country of Ephraim, just S of Timnath-serah, where Joshua resided and was buried (Josh 24:30; Jud 2:9), and probably about 20 miles SW of Shechem. Hiddai (or Hurai) was a native of "the brooks of Gaash" (II Sam 23:30; I Chr 11:32), apparently a reference to the watercourses with sources in the vicinity of Mount Gaash.

GABA (gā'bà). A variant form of Geba in Josh 18:24; Ezr 2:26; Neh 7:30. *See* Geba.

GABBAI (găb'ī; "tax collector," "exactor of tribute"). A prominent Benjamite among a tenth of the people selected to reside in Jerusalem after the Babylonian Captivity (Neh 11:8).

GABBATHA (găb'à-thà). An Aramaic term for what in Gr. was called *lithostrōtos*. The Gr. word means "paved with stones" and is translated in KJV and ASV "the Pavement" (*q.v.*). The Heb. word does not exactly correspond with the Gr. It points to the raised character of the place rather than its tesselated or mosaic nature. Jn 19:13 indicates it was the place from which Pilate gave formal sentence against Jesus. It was located adjacent to the praetorium or governor's residence in Jerusalem. If the praetorium (*q.v.*) can be identified as Herod's Tower of Antonia (*see* Antonia; Castle), then the ancient pavement in the basement of the Convent of Our Lady of Zion is very likely Gabbatha. The central area of this paved court measures about 2,500 square yards, with paving stones a yard square and a foot thick.

D. L. W.

GABRIEL (gā'brĭ-ĕl). An angel sent to Daniel in Babylon to explain to the prophet the vision of the ram and he-goat and to announce the prophecy of the 70 weeks (Dan 8:16–27; 9:21–27). After an interval of several centuries, Gabriel was sent to Jerusalem as the herald to Zacharias of the birth of John the Baptist (Lk 1:11–22) and to Nazareth as the messenger to Mary of the birth of the Messiah (Lk 1:26–38). In identifying himself to Zacharias, Gabriel described himself as one standing in the presence of God (Lk 1:19). In the Book of Enoch (a late Jewish apocalyptic work), Gabriel appears with Michael, Raphael, and Phanuel (Uriel) as one of the four highest angels (chaps. 9, 10, 40), or as one of the seven highest (chap. 20). In Moslem literature (Koran) he is represented as the agent through whom Mohammed obtained his "prophetic lore."

F. C. K.

GAD (găd)

1. Gad, son of Jacob; Gadites. The seventh son of Jacob by Zilpah, Leah's maid (Gen 30:9–10). At his birth Leah said, "A troop cometh: and she called his name Gad" (Gen 30:11). The reference to "troop" was prophetic of the high spirit and valor which characterized the descendants of Gad. This seems to be affirmed in the words of blessing by Moses in which it is stated that Gad "dwelleth as a lioness, and teareth the arm, yea, the crown of the head" (Deut 33:20 ff., ASV).

Qualities of valor are ascribed to the Gadites in these words: "Of the Gadites there separated themselves unto David into the hold to the wilderness men of might, and men of war fit for the battle, and could handle the shield and buckler, whose faces were like the faces of lions, and were as swift as the roes upon the mountains" (I Chr 12:8).

Gad had seven sons (Gen 46:16), and with the exception of Ezbon, each founded a family tribe (Num 26:15–18). Even though much is said about the descendants of Gad, little is actually recorded about the patriarch himself. At the beginning of the Exodus from Egypt to Canaan, the tribe of Gad numbered 45,650 "from twenty years old and upward, all that were able to go forth to war" (Num 1:24).

The territory assigned to the tribe was E of the Jordan, but it was mutually agreed with the other tribes that their warriors would cross over and help subdue the rest of the land before they would settle down (Num 32:20–32). The land of the Gadites included the southern part of

The "Pavement" excavated beneath the Convent of Our Lady of Zion. Sisters of Zion

642

Mount Gilead from the Jabbok River to Heshbon and from Rabbath-Ammon on the E to the Jordan River.

H. A. Han.

2. Gad, the seer. A prophet who advised David, while a fugitive, to leave Moab (1 Sam 22:5). Later, he announced to David the Lord's choice of punishment for taking a census (II Sam 24:11-17; I Chr 21:9-17), and suggested the erection of an altar at "the threshing floor of Araunah" (II Sam 24:18-19; I Chr 21:18-19). He was one of the historians of David's reign (I Chr 29:29), and with Nathan encouraged David in forming the Levitical orchestra for "the house of the Lord" (II Chr 29:25). See Prophet.

3. Gad, a god of fortune. See Gods, False.

GADARA (găd'á-rá). Gadara (modern Umm Qeis) is located c. 1,200 feet above the Mediterranean Sea, yet c. 1,880 feet above the Sea of Tiberias, which it overlooks at a distance of six miles to the SE. It has a commanding view of the Jordan Valley and the Galilee area (on the hills behind, one can see all the way to Carmel), being situated on the W extremity of a mountain ridge between the valley of the Yarmuk to the N and the Wadi Arab to the S. Being surrounded on three sides by steep slopes, it was ideally situated to become a strong fortress. Its climate also is more bearable during the heat of summer than the Jordan Valley, or even the site of Amatha where famous warm springs were located three miles to the NE (the hottest spring being 115°).

A strategic road led from Tiberias to Damascus through Gadara, and another road branched off to go through Edrei all the way to the Persian Gulf. The aqueduct supplying the city with water came from Edrei, over 30 miles away. Important ruins similar to those at Gerasa (q.v.)—theaters, streets, buildings, inscriptions—are still visible, but practically no archaeological work has been attempted there.

Gadara served as an important Hellenistic fortress as early as c. 225 B.C., being taken by Antiochus the Great from Scopas, the general of Ptolemy Epiphanes. Later it was taken by Alexander Janneus (c. 100 B.C.), who forced its inhabitants to become Jewish proselytes. Pompey, being influenced by his freedman Demetrius, who was a Gadarene, rebuilt the city in 63 B.C. It was one of the original Decapolis (q.v.) cities and became the capital of Perea. Later (30 B.C.) Augustus gave the city to Herod the Great. After Herod's death (4 B.C.) it was transferred to the Roman province of Syria.

The character of the city was primarily Gr., but many Jews lived there and in the surrounding territory. At the beginning of the Jewish revolt its district was attacked by Jews, and as a means of revenge, Jewish citizens of the place were put to death or imprisoned. The citizens requested Vespasian to send a Roman garrison to defend the city against possible dangers,

which was finally done. Several famous teachers came from Gadara, such as Philodemus (whose works were found on charred papyrus rolls at Herculaneum), Meleager, Menippus, Theodorus the orator (tutor of the emperor Tiberius), Oemaus, and Apsines.

In the NT, the district of the Gadarenes is mentioned as the place where the demoniac was cured with the consequent destruction of the herd of swine. There is a difficult textual problem connected with this incident (the best MSS being for Mt 8:28—"Gadarenes"; for Mk 5:1—"Gerasenes"; for Lk 8:26, 37—"Gerasenes" or "Gergesenes").

W. M. Thomson discovered a village on the lake shore named Khersa (Gerasa?) which is supposed by some to have been in the larger district of Gadara, which also is surmised to have reached to the Lake of Galilee. As A. T. Robertson notes (*Harmony of the Gospels,* New York: Harper, 1950, p. 71, n.): ". . . then the locality could be described as either in the country of the Gadarenes, or in the country of the Gerasenes" (cf. also VBW, V, 36). While there are steep banks for the lake at this point, no tombs are to be found there at the present. Many scholars (Schürer, p. 104; G. A. Smith, p. 631; Wroth, p. lxxxvii, who allows it) have noticed the fact that certain coins of Gadara show depictions of ships or triremes, and interpret this as evidence that the territory of Gadara reached the Sea of Tiberias. But Dalman (*Sacred Sites and Ways,* p. 178) takes a contrary view; a coin he found at Gadara reads that naval battles were arranged "*on the river.*" See Gerasa.

Bibliography. G. Dalman, *Sacred Sites and Ways,* New York: Macmillan, 1935, pp. 176-180. E. Schürer, *History of the Jewish People,* II. 1, pp. 100-104 (still indispensable). G. A. Smith, *Historical Geography of the Holy Land,* New York: Harper, 1931, see index. W. M. Thomson, *The Land and the Book,* Grand Rapids: Baker, 1954, pp. 375-378. C. Warren, "Gadara, Gadarenes." HDB, II, 79 f. W. Wroth, BMC, *Greek Coins of Galatia, Cappadocia, and Syria,* London: 1899, pp. lxxxvi ff., 304 ff.

E. J. V.

GADDI (găd'ī). One of the 12 spies sent by Moses to spy out Canaan. The son of Susi, he was the representative of Manasseh (Num 13:11).

GADDIEL (găd'ĭ-ĕl). One of the 12 spies sent out by Moses to survey the land of Canaan. He was the son of Sodi and the representative of Zebulun (Num 13:10).

GADI (gā'dī). The father of Menahem, who became king of Israel after slaying Shallum (II Kgs 15:14, 17).

GAHAM (gā'hăm). One of the four sons of Nahor (q.v.) by his concubine Reumah (Gen 22:24).

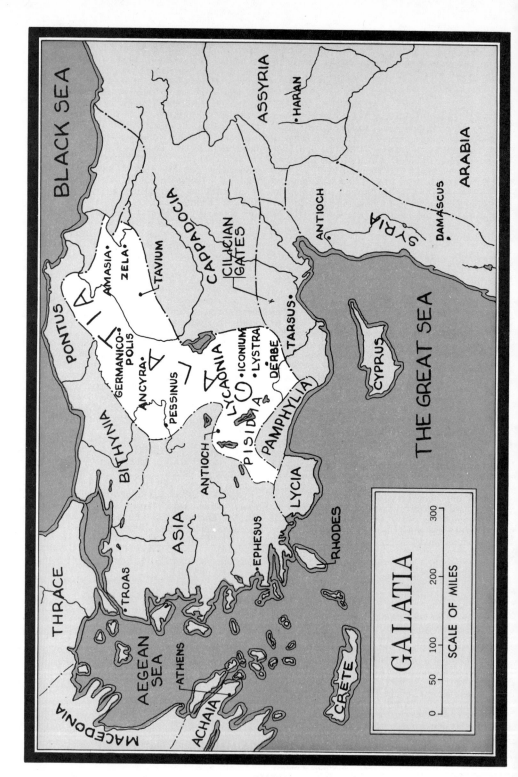

BLACK SEA

THRACE

MACEDONIA

AEGEAN SEA

ACHAIA

ATHENS

TROAS

ASIA

EPHESUS

ANTIOCH

BITHYNIA

PONTUS

AMASIA ZELA

TAVIUM

GERMANICO-POLIS

ANCYRA

PESSINUS

CAPPADOCIA

CILICIAN GATES

ASSYRIA

HARAN

ARABIA

DAMASCUS

SYRIA

ANTIOCH

TARSUS

ICONIUM

LYSTRA

DERBE

LYCAONIA

PISIDIA

PAMPHYLIA

LYCIA

RHODES

CYPRUS

THE GREAT SEA

CRETE

GALATIA

SCALE OF MILES

0   50   100   200   300

644

GAHAR (gā'här). One of the chief Nethinim whose descendants were among those returning from the Babylonian Captivity with Zerubbabel (Ezr 2:47; Neh 7:49). *See* Nethinim.

GAIUS (gā'yŭs). This common Roman name occurs five times in the NT. How many different persons are referred to is uncertain, but probably four.

1. A Macedonian Christian who accompanied Paul on some of his journeys and was one of two men seized at the riot in Ephesus (Acts 19:29).

2. A Christian of Derbe in Lycaonia who was with Paul on his return from Macedonia, probably on his way to Jerusalem (Acts 20:4).

3. Paul's host at Corinth in whose house the Christians were accustomed to assemble (Rom 16:23). He is doubtless the same man mentioned in I Cor 1:14 as one of the few converts Paul had baptized at Corinth.

4. A Christian leader to whom III Jn is addressed (III Jn 1). John was evidently sure of this man's spiritual health, for he hoped his physical health and prosperity might be as good. Since this epistle was written late (c. A.D. 90), it seems likely that this is a different Gaius from any of the others.

J. A. S.

GALAL (gā'lăl). The name of two Levites whose descendants were among the returning exiles from Babylon. One was a descendant of Asaph (I Chr 9:15), and the other a son of Jeduthun, whose descendants "dwelt in the villages of the Netophathites" (I Chr 9:16; Neh 11:17).

GALATIA (gà-lā'shà). In the time of the NT the term Galatia was used in two senses, ethnic and provincial. Thus there are now two theories about the location of the churches addressed in Paul's epistle to the Galatians.

1. Ethnic Galatia. This term refers to that northern region of the large inner plateau of what we term Asia Minor. It draws its name from the Gauls or Celts who first invaded Italy c. 390 B.C. and later crossed the Bosporus and overran Asia Minor c. 278–277 B.C. They were defeated by Attalus I, king of Pergamum, c. 239, and as a result were confined to NE Asia Minor. Their vigorous and aristocratic spirit contributed to their separation from and rule over the more numerous tribes of the Phrygians and Cappadocians. The geographer Strabo indicates that the Galatians were grouped in three tribes with four governing units or tetrarchies to a tribe. They enriched themselves at the expense of their neighbors by plunder and extortion, sometimes also serving as mercenaries in local conflicts. They eventually settled, with their chief cities as Tavium, Ancyra (modern Ankara), and Pessinus. Their territory was bounded on the N by Bithynia and Paphlagonia, on the E by Pontus, on the S by Cappadocia and Lycaonia, and on the W by Phrygia.

In 189 B.C. they were thoroughly defeated and plundered by the Roman army under Maulius Vulso, but were granted independence in 166 B.C. A Galatian leader, Deiotarus, sided with the Romans against Mithradates VI of Pontus (121–63 B.C.) in his continuing attempts to control all Asia Minor. After defeating Mithradates, Pompey confirmed Deiotarus in his ancestral kingdom and even added to his domains (63 B.C.):

2. The Roman province of Galatia. After the death of Amyntas, its last king, Augustus made Galatia a Roman province in 25 B.C., with Ancyra as capital. Its territory included, besides the old ethnic region, parts of Pontus, Phrygia, Lycaonia, Pisidia, Paphlagonia and Isauria. Included in provincial Galatia were the cities which the apostle Paul evangelized on his first missionary trip, i.e., Antioch, Iconium, Lystra, and Derbe (Acts 13–14). Lystra and Antioch were made Roman colonies, and all these cities attracted large numbers of Greeks, Romans, and Jews because of their geographical and economic importance. The Celtic tongue continued in private use in the N, but Latin became the official language, with Gr. permitted for business purposes.

3. The location of "the churches of Galatia." When Paul addressed his epistle to the Galatians, to what people did he refer? To those in the old northern and ethnic region, or to those in the southern region also included in the newer Roman province? The N Galatian theory holds that Paul addressed churches first contacted on his second missionary journey. After he had visited the southern territory he traveled through "the region of Phrygia and Galatia" (Acts 16:6). Advocates of this view say he entered old Galatia, visiting Pessinus and possibly Ancyra and Tavium before going on to Troas. They hold a second trip to the same territory is mentioned in Acts 18:23 where it says that he "went through the region of Galatia, and Phrygia, in order, establishing all the disciples" (ASV). This is the older of the two views, held by early Church Fathers and by more recent scholars such as Alford, Ellicott, Findlay, Godet, Lightfoot, and Moffatt.

The S Galatian theory holds that Paul wrote to the churches in the southern part of the Roman province which he contacted on his first missionary journey, i.e., Antioch, Iconium, Lystra, Derbe. These churches he revisited on his second journey (Acts 16:1–5) and possibly on the third (Acts 18:23). The main advocate of this view was Sir William Ramsay who did extensive archaeological research in Asia Minor. Most modern commentators, except for those in Germany, hold this view. Among them are Zahn, Burton, Duncan, Tenney, Bruce, and Hendricksen.

For an objective presentation of both N and S views see Everett F. Harrison, *Introduction to the New Testament*, pp. 257–59, and Donald Guthrie, *The Pauline Epistles, New Testament Introduction*, pp. 72–79.

While there is much to be said for either view and perhaps the issue cannot be settled with great certainty, the S Galatian view seems more probable for several reasons.

a. Paul's general habit of using official Roman terms, though not conclusive in itself, when coupled with the historical record in Acts and with the evidence of the epistle, strongly supports the view that Paul addressed the churches of the S as mentioned in Acts 13-14, and 16:1-5. Note I Cor 16:1 where Paul uses "Galatia" in context with other Roman provinces as Macedonia (16:5), Achaia (16:15), and Asia (16:19). Other references to Galatia are found in II Tim 4:10 and I Pet 1:1.

b. The lack of any definite evidence that Paul ever founded churches in N Galatia, in contrast to the easy connection to the southern cities whose extended historical background is supplied by Acts, is presumably in line with Luke's recognized purpose to supply background for Paul's epistles. Acts 16:6-8 and 18:23 are supports adduced for the N Galatian view. Acts 16:6-8 reads: "And they went through the region of Phrygia and Galatia, having been forbidden of the Holy Spirit to speak the word in Asia; and when they were come over against Mysia, they assayed to go into Bithynia; and the Spirit of Jesus suffered them not; and passing by Mysia they came down to Troas" (ASV). This passage indicates that after visiting the cities of S Galatia (16:1-5), Paul, being forbidden by the Spirit to go W into the province of Asia, headed N through a region ethnically Phrygian and Galatian (probably along the border of old Galatia). When he reached a point S of Bithynia and E of Mysia, he was directed by the Spirit to go W to Troas instead of N into Bithynia or E into old ethnic Galatia. There is no reference to extensive evangelism or founding of churches and no definite support here for the N Galatian theory.

In Acts 18:23 the order of the words is reversed and the reference is most likely to two adjacent regions. Paul departed from Syrian Antioch "and went through the region of Galatia, and Phrygia, in order, establishing all the disciples" (ASV). Burton prefers the explanation of the route that takes Paul to Tarsus and through the Cilician gates, through the extreme western part of old Galatia, and then through Phrygia, the eastern part of Asia. This would be consistent with Luke's ethnic use of the adjective "Galatian" in Acts 16:6 (NASB). Note there is no reference to cities or churches in any part of Galatia, either northern or southern. Luke gives no evidence of trying to furnish background to Paul's establishing churches at all. Thus there is no evidence in either passage cited of Paul's founding churches in the N.

c. A third reason for favoring the S Galatian view is that it better satisfies the exegetical considerations of the epistle. First, the southern portion of Galatia would more likely be familiar with the Jewish religion as Paul assumes. Sec-

ond, the Judaizing teachers opposing Paul would have easier, quicker, and more likely access to the S. Third, the form of Paul's reasoning is more understandable if we assume that the decrees of Acts 15 had been delivered to the southern churches, as in Acts 16:1-5, and that the error presented to the Galatians was not that of Acts 15 (Gal 2:1-10) concerning justification by faith, but was directed primarily to Christians living by Mosaic law (as in Gal 2:11-21). Of course the doctrine of justification was logically affected, but the peculiar form of argument in Gal 3-4 does not hit it directly as does Romans.

Bibliography. E. D. Burton, *A Critical and Exegetical Commentary on the Epistle to the Galatians,* ICC. D. Guthrie, *The Pauline Epistles, New Testament Introduction,* London: Tyndale Press, 1961. Everett F. Harrison, *Introduction to the New Testament,* Grand Rapids: Eerdmans, 1964. M. J. Mcllinck, "Galatia," IDB, II, 336 ff. W. M. Ramsay, *A Historical Commentary on St. Paul's Epistle to the Galatians,* New York: Putnam's, 1900; *St. Paul the Traveller and Roman Citizen,* London: Hodder and Stoughton, 1898. Howard F. Vos, WHG, pp. 332-337, 347-356, 383 ff.

C. F. D.

GALATIANS, EPISTLE TO THE

Significance

This short and fiery work of Paul is significant for several reasons. Interpretationally, there is a great contribution to the understanding of the gospel and ts practical implications. Historically, it saved Christianity from becoming a sect of Judaism in Paul's day, and later it fanned the fires of the Reformation. Doctrinally, it argues that since justification is by faith alone, so faith is the only proper sphere of Christian living. The new life is not legalism or license but liberty disciplined by grace and directed by the Spirit of God in love. It remains with exceeding relevance the protest against legalistic contamination of the gospel of grace and the proclamation of Christian liberty.

Authorship and Canonicity

Internal (within the book) and external (outside the book) evidence are both so decidedly in favor of the apostle Paul's authorship that it could not reasonably be doubted. Even destructive critics have recognized Galatians in the "normative group" of Paul (with Romans and I and II Corinthians). The writer calls himself Paul (1:1; 5:2). The book is so characteristic of Paul in vocabulary, style and content, so naturally developed in argument and personal allusions, so reflective of the heart and mind of the great apostle, that no one could have forged such a masterpiece. There is no suggestion of any worth from ancient times that anyone but Paul wrote it, or that it should not be in the canon of Scripture. It is found in the earliest lists of canonical books, in the earliest versions, and in references by Church Fathers and heretics. Galatians records God's words poured through the mold of Paul.

Date and Place of Writing

These cannot be fixed with certainty. Advocates of the N Galatian theory usually place it after Paul's second missionary journey, ranging from A.D. 52 in Ephesus to A.D. 57/58 from Macedonia or Achaia. S Galatian theorists vary from A.D. 48/49 at Syrian Antioch to the same later date and places as above. See Galatia. More exact dating depends on the interpretation of the Jerusalem visits mentioned in Gal 1-2. Exponents of the earliest date cannot allow that Gal 2:1-10 refers to the council of Acts 15 since these verses present a different emphasis and the decrees of the Jerusalem council are not cited as support by Paul; hence Galatians antedates the council (A.D. 48/49). The later dating by either theory identifies Gal 2:1-10 with Acts 15.

We may hold that Gal 2:1-10 refers to Acts 15 for several reasons. Lightfoot (St. Paul's Epistle to the Galatians, pp. 123-24) notes the determining similarities of geography, time, persons, subject of dispute, nature of the conference and result. Occurrence of two such similar incidents within a few years is so unlikely as to present great difficulty for any solution other than their identity. Those who hold this is not Acts 15 but Acts 11:30; 12:25 generally fail to see that Paul in Gal 1:13-24 does not intend to account for all his visits to Jerusalem, but only those which involved contact with the Twelve. There is no such contact in Acts 11; the Twelve may have fled from Herod (cf. Acts 12:1).

But if Paul wrote after Acts 15, why did he not appeal to the decision of the Jerusalem council to solve the Galatian problem? The answer is that he had done so in person (Acts 16:4); so later in his epistle he marveled at their deserting Christ (Gal 1:6). To refer to the Jerusalem decree would not now solve their problem, for it was a different one, like that of Peter (2:11-21); and both were logically the next step from the issue at the council. The issue had advanced to sanctification by faith and the relation of Christian living to Mosaic law. In Gal 2:1-10 Paul refers to a private aspect of the Jerusalem council; not primarily in support of his doctrine (independently received), but in support of his independence. Hence the different emphasis.

We may hold that Galatians was written on the third missionary journey from Ephesus, A.D. 52/53, or from Corinth or Macedonia, A.D. 54/55.

Recipients

Addressed to "the churches of Galatia," this is the only Pauline epistle written to a group of churches. They were all established by Paul (Gal 1:8, 11; 4:13-14, 19-20). If we hold the S theory and date the book after the Jerusalem council, Paul had delivered to them the council's decrees and they had prospered (Acts 16:4-5). The nucleus of the churches was Jewish, though they were composed mostly of Gentiles. To such a mixed group, a Judaizing compromise between Judaism and Christianity found many a point of contact. The question of Christian living according to Mosaic law and the breeding of two levels of righteousness (faith and faith plus law) might naturally arise and appeal to such a group. There appears no real evidence of the bold, assertive, proud character of northern Gauls; but the tone of Galatians and the type of problem that Paul dealt with in his letter would more naturally be expected of the subservient, susceptible S Galatians who were now seeking advancement under Rome. Such would well receive their new and inclusive title "Galatians."

Occasion and Purpose of Writing

Though some envision a dual problem of legalism and libertinism, the weight of the letter is directed against Judaistic and legalistic opponents. Jews outwardly espousing belief in Christ, to avoid persecution sought to promote the Mosaic law as a standard of Christian living. In doing this, they undercut the authority of Paul. They appealed to the Jerusalem apostles, to Abraham, and to the Mosaic law to picture Paul as a renegade apostle who, after he had received the gospel from the Twelve, stripped it of law to make it appeal to Gentiles; and by doing so, he offered a gospel with only half-standing before God. They insisted that a believer must also become a "son of Abraham" by being circumcised and keeping the law. Only this could he obtain full standing and inherit the fullest blessing of God in the Abrahamic covenant.

There is no evidence that the Judaizers outrightly denied justification by faith. They probably taught that faith in Christ was only the initial step into God's favor, and that the highest favor belonged to those who lived under the law. The Galatians had probably received the decrees of the Acts 15 council on justification by faith apart from law, and could not be confused by a frontal attack on that which Paul had delivered to them (Acts 16:1-5; Gal 1:9; 4:16). But this flank attack in the area of sanctification had "bewitched" the "unreflecting Galatians" (3:1), an address which immediately follows the story of Peter's similar error (2:11-21).

As a result, the Galatians were keeping Jewish seasons (4:9-10). They were hindered now in Christian living (5:7), in danger of becoming in bondage to law (4:21; 5:1) and losing fellowship with Christ (5:2, 4). There were seeds of division among them (5:15; 6:1). Of these things Paul was probably informed by a Galatian delegation.

Paul's purpose, then, is not to prove primarily that justification is by faith. His argument assumes this is true; and building upon the fact that justification has granted them perfect standing with God and full inheritance with Abraham, he seeks to establish that sanctification is in faith, apart from adherence to any part of Mosaic law (2:19; 5:18). This is the contention of the whole letter as seen in the key exhortation (5:1), the key question (3:3), and the significantly placed illustration of Peter's similar problem (2:11-21). Paul regards this error as a dangerous heresy, for the introduction of legalistic works anywhere into a grace system shatters grace and converts it into a system of works contrary to the gospel (1:6-9).

Paul must first reestablish his apostolic authority; then clarify that justification by faith has already granted them all the position they can gain; and finally exhort and instruct in regard to living by grace in faith.

Outline

Most analysts recognize three major divisions of thought with a salutation and a conclusion. Galatians may be outlined as follows:

I. Salutation and Denunciation, 1:1-10
   A. Salutation, 1:1-5
   B. Denunciation, 1:6-10
II. Personal: Authentication of the Apostle of Freedom, 1:11-2:21
   A. Proposition: Paul's message is independent of men and directly from God, 1:11-12
   B. Proof: History of Paul's independence from the 12 apostles, 1:13-2:21
      1. Independence verified: his authority separate from the apostles, 1:13-24
      2. Independence vindicated: his authority exercised with the apostles, 2:1-21
         a. Recognition at the council of Jerusalem, 2:1-10
         b. Refutation of Peter at Antioch, 2:11-21
III. Doctrinal: Justification of the Doctrine of Freedom, 3:1-4:31
   A. Principle argued: Righteousness and inheritance come by faith alone, not by law in any form, 3:1-4:7
      1. Personal experience, 3:1-5
      2. Progenitor Abraham, 3:6-9
      3. Pronouncement of law, 3:10-14
      4. Precedence of promise, 3:15-18
      5. Purpose of law, 3:19-22
      6. Position of superiority in faith, 3:23-4:7
   B. Personal appeal, 4:8-20
      1. Circumstance of appeal, 4:8-11
      2. Content of appeal, 4:12-16
      3. Cause of appeal, 4:17-20
   C. Pertinent allegory, 4:21-31
      1. Historical situation, 4:21-23
      2. Allegorical illustration, 4:24-27
      3. Personal application, 4:28-31

IV. Practical: Expression of the Life of Freedom, 5:1-6:10
   A. Life of liberty from the system of legalism, 5:1-12
      1. Command and injunction, 5:1
      2. Crucial issue, 5:2-12
   B. Life of love in the Spirit of God, 5:13-6:10
      1. Exclusion of the life of love: license and lust, 5:13-15
      2. Empowerment of the life of love: the Spirit's control, 5:16-24
      3. Expression of the life of love: the Spirit's direction, 5:25-6:10
V. Apostolic Conclusion, 6:11-18
   A. Final Warning, 6:11-16
   B. Final appeal, 6:17
   C. Final benediction, 6:18

Analysis of Contents

After a pointed salutation emphasizing his apostolic authority, Paul denounces the heresy and warns those who would follow it of its seriousness.

The first major division (1:11-2:21) is an extended defense of his genuine and independent apostleship, which is intrinsically a defense of his gospel. His ministry and message are completely independent of men and directly from the risen Christ.

Paul supports this proposition with two major lines of proof (see outline). The proof is essentially a history of Paul's independence from the 12 apostles and their headquarters in Jerusalem. His independence is verified (1:13-24) by a review of his limited contact with them. He was an apostle before he met the others. After God had commissioned him, he did not confer with anyone concerning the content of his gospel but exercised an independent ministry. His independence is vindicated (2:1-21) on two occasions when he did come in contact with other apostles. In the first, at Jerusalem, the apostles, whose gospel the Judaizers claimed to teach, recognized Paul's message and authority. In the second, Paul had to rebuke openly the leading apostle to the Jews. And Peter accepted the rebuke. In both cases the apostles submitted to Paul on the issue of grace versus law. We take it that Peter's problem was essentially the Galatians' problem—to live by faith or by law.

In 3:1-4:31 Paul enlarges upon the argument he used with Peter. He first establishes what justification by faith has done, that he might move on to sanctification by faith. The principle argued is that justification by faith has given the believer a perfect standing before God, superior to and unimprovable by anything supposedly gained by living under law. Paul supports this with six lines of evidence (see outline). The Galatians must recognize that their salvation and early Christian experience were based on faith and not law. How foolish they were to begin in faith and then to seek to complete their position and practice by strict law-keeping.

The first doctrinal argument declares that just as Abraham was declared righteous and made an inheritor of the promises of God by faith, so those who trust Christ are declared righteous and made heirs. Paul then shows that the law can only curse sinners and cannot make righteous. In fact, Christ redeemed us from law that we might inherit the promises. The promise to Abraham, by which we also are blessed in Christ, takes precedence over law in time and nature. The law was given to reveal sin as transgression and to restrict the sinner to faith. Since the cross, we are no longer under law as a rule of life, but are full-fledged sons of God and so "sons of Abraham" and "heirs of promise." There is now no distinction between persons racially, socially, or sexually. Note that these blessings come upon all nations through the universal aspect of the Abrahamic covenant (Gal 3:8) and do not fulfill or abrogate the personal and national aspects of the covenant (Gen 12:1–3) regarding the nation and land of Israel. Paul's main argument ends at 4:7.

A very warm personal appeal is followed by a story from the law that illustrates the principle that the law begets slavery and cannot provide inheritance; whereas the promise taken by faith begets freedom and secures inheritance.

The fourth section calls for the practice of a life of freedom for which Christ saved us. It is a life of liberty from legalism in any system or form, a life free from license and domination by the sin nature within, and a life in faith expressed through love which is produced by the indwelling Spirit. The Spirit replaces the law as the Christian's sphere and guide of life. He will not lead contrary to the abiding moral demands of the law, but will produce the spiritual life, reflective of Christ, which the law could never produce. The Spirit is the power and the director of the new life of freedom that honors Christ and serves men.

The last section contains a warning that contrasts the Judaizers' devotion to the flesh with Paul's devotion to the cross; a final appeal not to follow the errorists; and a benediction asking for grace that they might follow Christ.

Bibliography. G. W. Barker, W. L. Lane and J. R. Michaels, *The New Testament Speaks,* New York: Harper & Row, 1969, pp. 185–191. Conybeare and Howson, *The Life and Epistles of St. Paul,* London: Longmans, Green and Co., 1901. C. J. Ellicott, *Commentary on St. Paul's Epistle to the Galatians,* Andover: Warren F. Draper, 1896. Charles R. Erdman, *The Epistle of Paul to the Galatians,* Philadelphia: Westminster, 1930. G. G. Findlay, *The Epistle to the Galatians,* ExpB. Everett F. Harrison, "Galatians," WBC, pp. 1283–1299. William Hendricksen, *New Testament Commentary, Exposition of Galatians,* Grand Rapids: Baker,

1968. C. F. Hogg and W. E. Vine, *The Epistle of Paul the Apostle to the Galatians,* London: Pickering and Inglis, 1922. J. B. Lightfoot, *St. Paul's Epistle to the Galatians,* London: Macmillan and Co., 1896. H. N. Ridderbos, *The Epistle of Paul to the Churches of Galatia,* Grand Rapids: Eerdmans, 1953. J. H. Ropes, *The Singular Problem of the Epistle to the Galatians,* Cambridge: Harvard Univ. Press, 1929.

C. F. D.

GALBANUM. *See* Plants.

GALEED (găl'ē-ĕd). Jacob gave this Heb. name (which means "the heap of witness") to the heap of stones commemorating the covenant between him and Laban, his father-in-law. The latter called it Jegar-sahadutha, the Aramaic equivalent of the Heb. Galeed. The site was in Gilead where Laban overtook Jacob before he reached the Jabbok. The event was observed with sacrifices, a covenant meal, and a final parting in peace (Gen 31:47–48).

GALILEAN (găl-ĭ-lē'ăn). Either a native or inhabitant of Galilee (Mt 26:69; Mk 14:70; Lk 13:1; Acts 1:11). Jesus (Mt 26:69) and Peter (Mk 14:70) were called Galileans, and the 12 apostles were all Galileans except Judas Iscariot.

Galileans were rather common people who were generous, impulsive, pious, nationalistic, and often more Hellenistic than the Judeans were. Although Galilee and Judea were only 60 miles apart, the people differed from each other in many respects. One difference was speech in which the pronunciation and accent of Galilean Aramaic identified Peter to the maid (Mt 26:73; Mk 14:70).

Galileans had different customs and simpler religious practices than the Judeans, so that the term Galilean was a reproach used by the Pharisees. People outside Galilee had a poor opinion of Galileans and believed therefore that a prophet could not come from Galilee (cf. Jn 1:46; 7:41, 52). Thus the term Galilean signified both geographical location and cultural type.

E. B. R.

GALILEE (găl'ĭ-lē). The northernmost section of three in Palestine W of the Jordan River. Northern Galilee is mountainous (up to 4,000 feet above sea level) extending S from the Leontes River (Nahr el-Litani), which terminates the Lebanons, c. 30 miles to Wadi esh-Shaghur that flows toward Acco (Ptolemais). Southern or lower Galilee is more level and thus more suitable for living and farming, bounded as it is on the S by the fertile Plain of Esdraelon. Roads across Galilee from all directions brought commerce from Egypt, Arabia, and Syria. Fruit and olive orchards thrived on the hills, and grain and grass in the valleys.

The Canaanites continued to dominate Galilee for a long time after Joshua's invasion (Jud 1:30–33; cf. 4:2). In Solomon's time Galilee had a mixed population so that he felt he could give 20 of its cities to Hiram of Tyre without great loss to Israel (I Kgs 9:11). After the Assyrian conquests c. 732 B.C. (II Kgs 15:29), Galilee once again became predominantly Gentile. Thus Isaiah called it "Galilee of the nations" (Isa 9:1; cf. Mt 4:15).

After Herod joined it to his kingdom, Galilee attracted a great many Jews. Josephus claimed it had 240 cities and villages (*Life,* 45) and could field an army of 100,000 men to fight against the Romans (*Wars,* ii.20.6).

In Jesus' time Galilee was part of the tetrarchy of Herod Antipas (4 B.C.–A.D. 30). Its chief cities were Capernaum, Nazareth, and Tiberias the capital. Jesus' apostles were from here, and His ministry was mostly at the N and W end of the Sea of Galilee, using Capernaum as His center. Both Jews and Gentiles still made up the population, with the northern section more Gentile than the southern and having more contact with Gr. and Rom. culture.

E. B. R.

The western shore of the Sea of Galilee as seen from the air. IIS

GALILEE, SEA OF. Named Galilee in Mt 4:18, it was also called Sea of Chinnereth (Num 34:11), Lake of Gennesaret (Lk 5:1), and Sea of Tiberias (Jn 6:1).

Lying nearly 700 feet below sea level 60 miles N of Jerusalem in the province of Galilee, the Sea of Galilee is a fresh water lake fed by the Jordan River, bringing down the snows of Mount Hermon and the Lebanons with the rains of the hills to form a lake nearly 13 miles long, eight miles at its greatest width, and from 80 to an estimated 700 feet deep.

The mild climate of the Plain of Gennesaret on the NW shore produced a year-round supply of vegetables, fruit, and grain. Elsewhere steep cliffs and mountains enclose the lake rising on the E as high as 2,700 feet to the fertile Hauran plateau. Cool winds rush down these slopes and stir up frequent sudden and violent storms on the warm surface of the lake (Lk 8:22 ff.).

A fishing industry thrived there on the abundant supply of fish with 22 known species (Mk 1:20).

In spite of the steep shoreline, nine cities of 15,000 or more population bordered the lake. Most prominent were Bethsaida-Julias, Tiberias, and Capernaum.

Bethsaida-Julias (*q.v.*) on the NE shore was built by Tetrarch Philip, son of Herod the Great, and named Julias in honor of Emperor Augustus' daughter. The feeding of the 5,000 (Mt 14:13 ff.) occurred near here.

Tiberias (*q.v.*) on the W shore was built by Herod Antipas (c. A.D. 25) and named for Tiberius Caesar. Its warm mineral springs made it a health resort. Hellenistic manners and morals thrived there so that most Jews, including Jesus, avoided it.

Capernaum (*q.v.*), only six miles N of Tiberias, was the home of Peter and Andrew. Here Jesus had His headquarters, called it His own city (Mt 9:1), performed many miracles, and called Matthew from the tax collector's booth. But still the city did not repent and so faced ruin (Mt 11:23–24).

On and around the Sea of Galilee Jesus performed 18 of His 33 recorded miracles, gave many teachings, and called His disciples.

See Tiberias, Sea of.

E. B. R.

GALL
1. A plant with bitter or poisonous fruit (*see* Plants: Gall).
2. A bodily organ or its secretion. The Heb. word *mᵉrōrâ* denotes the gall bladder in Job 20:25 (cf. NEB) and the bile, a bitter yellowish liquid secreted by the liver and stored in the gall bladder, in Job 16:13; 20:14. It is used figuratively in Job 13:26, translated "bitter things."

GALLERY. An architectural term used in the KJV and ASV to translate *'attîq,* a Heb. word of uncertain meaning. It is used in describing Ezekiel's temple in Ezk 41:16, "the galleries round about on their three stories" (RSV, "all three had windows with recessed frames"), and in Ezk 42:3, 5. It is a loan word from Akkad. *etêqu,* "to pass," and may therefore have the sense of a balcony passage or walkway. A variant Heb. form of *'attîq* is found in Ezk 41:15 (RSV, "walls").

The obscure Heb. word *rahaṭ* rendered "galleries" in KJV is translated "tresses" by ASV and RSV (Song 7:5).

GALLEY. *See* Ship.

GALLIM (găl'ĭm). A town in Benjamin apparently near Laish ("Laishah," ASV, RSV) and Anathoth, and so N of Jerusalem (Isa 10:30). Perhaps it is Khirbet Ka'kûl, three-quarters of a mile W of Anathoth. It was the home of Phalti ("Palti," ASV, RSV), the second husband of Michal (I Sam 25:44).

GALLIO (găl'ĭ-ō). The Roman proconsul of Achaia in Greece when Paul labored in Corinth on his second missionary journey (Acts 18:12–17). He was the son of M. Annaeus Seneca and was born in Cordoba, Spain, *c.* 3 B.C. His two younger brothers were Seneca, the philosopher and tutor of Nero, and Marcus Annaeus Mela, the geographer and father of the poet Lucan. Nero forced all three brothers to commit suicide *c.* A.D. 66.

He assumed the name L. Junius Gallio Annaeus when he was adopted by his wealthy friend Lucius Junius Gallio and introduced to a political career. Besides holding the consulship once in Achaia, where the climate made him ill according to a letter of Seneca, Gallio became a senator of Rome.

An inscription found *c.* 1905 at Delphi (45 miles NW of Corinth) reveals that Gallio was proconsul of Achaia after the 26th acclamation of Claudius as *imperator.* Jack Finegan argues convincingly that Gallio's arrival in Corinth, therefore, must be dated *c.* July 1, A.D. 51, placing Paul's coming there early in the year 50 (FLAP, 2nd ed., pp. 362 f.).

Gallio proved himself an impartial judge and a worthy Roman official when Paul was brought before him, because he refused to become involved in matters of religion. He paid no attention to the ensuing anti-Jewish demonstration.

J. R.

GALLOWS. A pole with a projecting arm for the hanging up of a dead body (Est 5:14; 6:4; 7:9–10; 8:7; 9:13–14, 25; cf. Gen 40:19, 22; 41:13). In the book of Esther it may mean to impale a body on a stake. The victim was usually dead before the body was placed on the gibbet. *See* Crime and Punishment; Cross.

GAMALIEL (gȧ-ma'lĭ-ĕl)

1. Gamaliel I ("the elder") was the son of Simon and the grandson of the famous Rabbi Hillel. He occupied an important position in the Jewish council and was held in respect (Acts 5:34–40). He was the first to bear the title "rabban" (our master) instead of the more common "rabbi" (my master). On occasion he was counselor to the Herods in legal-religious matters (Pesahim 88*b*). His importance is seen in the statement: "When Rabban Gamaliel the Elder died, the glory of the Law ceased and purity and abstinence died" (*Sotah* 9.15).

Characteristic of the school of Hillel, Gamaliel was liberal in his outlook, showing moderate views toward the laws of the sabbath, marriage, and divorce (Rosh ha-Shanah 2:5; Yebamoth 16.7; Gittin 4.2, 3). In Acts 5:34–39 he is said to have counseled moderation in the treatment of the apostles. This can be interpreted as an example of his temperament. Another interpretation is that he spoke in irony against Sadducean skepticism toward the providence of God (James Moffatt, "Gamaliel," *Expositor,* 8th series, 5 [1913], p. 96). If this latter is true, the passage reflects the conflict between the

Ruins of ancient Corinth where Gallio was proconsul.

Pharisaic tradition of Hillel and the Sadducean tradition of Shammai.

Gamaliel's mention of Theudas in Acts 5:36 raises a problem in regard to chronology. Josephus mentions a rebel named Theudas who was killed *c.* A.D. 44 during the procuratorship of Fadus (*Ant.* 20.5.1 ff.). Gamaliel, speaking before this event, places Theudas prior to the enrollment which took place in A.D. 6. Swain has suggested that the speech should be placed in Acts 12 just before the death of Herod (Joseph W. Swain, "Gamaliel's Speech and Caligula's Statue," *Harvard Theological Review,* 37 [1944], p. 342). This solves little, however, since Theudas was put to death, according to Josephus, after the death of Herod. It is possible that Josephus refers to another Theudas. Also, the reliability of Josephus may be doubted, since his various accounts of the Jewish wars do not always correspond.

The statement in Acts 22:3 that Paul was brought up at the feet of Gamaliel raises another problem. If Paul was taught by the moderate Gamaliel, why did he show such radical hatred toward the church? Why did he not mention Gamaliel in his letters? And why was he so completely different in his attitude toward the law? Some suggest that *para tous podas gamaliel pepaideumenos* should be translated by the general phrase, "brought under the influence of Gamaliel" (G. Corrie Clanville, "Gamaliel," ExpT, 39 [1918], pp. 39 f.). Others say that Paul did not study in Jerusalem, and that it is Luke's theological bias that places him there (M. S. Enslin, "Paul and Gamaliel," *Journal of Religion,* 7 [1927], pp. 360–375). In some ways, however, Paul reflects the Pharisaic tradition of his teacher. For example, he calls Isaiah Torah (I Cor 14:21), an expression fitting for a student of Gamaliel, for the Pharisees considered all Scripture as Torah. Another piece of evidence that Paul studied under Gamaliel is the passages in the Talmud referring to a student of Gamaliel called "that pupil." This designation is possibly a reference to Paul (Joseph Klausner, *From Jesus to Paul,* pp.

310 f.). Why Paul did not mention his famous teacher in his letters is a moot question. His conversion experience and new orientation may have been important factors.

2. The prince of the tribe of Manasseh (Num 7:54, 59; 10:23). He was appointed assistant to Moses in numbering the people at Sinai (Num 1:10; 2:20).

G. E. H.

GAMES. The Hebrews seem not to have been interested in athletics as a sport. There are no references to any purely athletic contests in the OT such as abound in Greco-Roman literature. Even the reference in Ps 19:5, ". . . rejoiceth as a strong man to run a race," is not necessarily speaking of a contest. The Semitic peoples rather found recreation and expressed their humor and lighthearted attitude in song and dance (cf. Job 21:11–12). *See* Dance; Music.

Samson employed a guessing contest to entertain wedding guests (Jud 14:12). *See* Riddle. The grim contest with swords between picked soldiers from Abner's and Joab's troops cannot be classed as a game (II Sam 2:12–17). In the end time, the streets of Jerusalem will be full of boys and girls playing children's games (Zech 8:5) such as tug-of-war, known in Egypt (ANEP #216, 217).

Wrestling (*q.v.*) was a sport common in the ancient Near East as clay figurines and tomb paintings attest. Beautifully wrought game boards, some being inlaid with ivory, shell, gold, and blue paste, have been found at Ur, Meggido, and other towns in Palestine, and in Egyptian tombs (ANEP #212–215; R. F. Schnell, "Games, Old Testament," IDB, II, 352 f.). Clay dolls, toys, and models of furniture have survived the ravages of time to indicate that the life of a child was not overly dull.

Gaming board from Ur. *c.* 2500 B.C. BM

Games were of tremendous importance, however, in the Gr. and Rom. world. The Greeks are remembered for their public games, the names of them lingering even in a modern context: Olympian, Isthmian, Nemean, Pythian. The Olympian games were the chief national festival of the Greeks, being given in honor of Zeus at Olympia every four years, and were chiefly gymnastic, though equestrian and musical contests were added. The Isthmian games were held at Corinth in a grove sacred to Poseidon, in the second and fourth years of each Olympiad. The Nemean games were held in the valley of Nemea, given in honor of Zeus at the end of each first and third years of an Olympiad, and consisted of gymnastic, equestrian, and musical contests, as did each of the others. The Pythian were next to the Olympian in importance, taking place in the third year of each Olympiad below Delphi. The prize for the winners was only a wreath of leaves, such as olive or laurel, but great honor was shown them by their fellow citizens.

Starting lanes for runners in the Pythian Games at the stadium of Delphi, Greece. HFV

Among the Romans the number of the games increased until at the end of the Republic there were seven sets of games which occupied a total of 65 days. By the middle of the 2nd Christian cen., a total of 135 days out of the year was given over to these games, and by A.D. 354 the games claimed 175 days out of the year.

The major Roman games were the Ludi Romani, the oldest of the games, celebrated in honor of Jupiter; the Ludi Plebes which included dramatic entertainments; the Ludi Cereales, given in honor of the goddess Ceres; the Ludi Apollinares in honor of Apollo; the Ludi Megalenses in honor of the Great Mother; the Ludi Florales. The Ludi Circenses and the Ludi Augustales were celebrated during the period of the empire in memory of Augustus Caesar. These games were intimately connected with religious worship, being dedicated to the gods and goddesses. They were frequently under the direction of the priests, who superintended the games because they served the god in each instance.

For games that the government dedicated to the gods, the expense was met out of the public treasury. Eventually, the demands on the Roman public were so extravagant that the emperors found it necessary to underwrite a considerable part of the expense of public games out of the imperial purse. Not only Rome but other major cities and towns such as Ephesus found a considerable financial drain attached to the games that were celebrated locally, of which those at Rome would be more or less representative.

In addition to the public games that involved the entire population, many private games were given by individuals or organizations on occasions of special significance, such as births, marriages, and even funerals. Whereas admission to the public games was always free, private games many times charged admission and were frequently used by societies for fund raising. Sometimes these private games were donated by the wealthy to the public for the express purpose of gaining the good will of the populace. The cost of both the public and private games rose to staggering proportions by NT times.

Athletic games were especially favored by the Greeks but less favored by the Romans. The Romans favored those contests that involved danger and bloodshed. There were races, wrestling matches, throwing the discus and the javelin, and, of course, boxing. Among the Romans the chariot races in the circus were far more popular than the athletic races. The great race course in Rome, the Circus Maximus, could possibly accommodate 250,000 spectators. During the course of the race, the crowd went wild, and not infrequently there were riots. Large sums of money exchanged hands as the people bet on the outcome of the races; and the successful charioteer was able to amass a fortune.

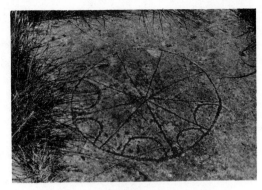

A Roman game cut into the pavement of the Agora at Philippi. HFV

The gladiatorial shows, which attained such popularity among the Romans, were the most objectionable of all the games to the Christians. Such combats came to be a part of every important public occasion. Julius Caesar at one festival presented more than 300 pairs of gladiators in combat, while Trajan, rejoicing over his victory in Dacia, matched together 10,000 gladiators. The majority of the gladiators were prisoners of war or slaves, although occasionally criminals were condemned to fight in the arena. In Spain, Africa, Gaul, and the East there was a craze similar to that in Rome for the gladiatorial combats. They were, however, never very popular in Greece, except at Corinth, which was a Roman colony in NT times.

The Roman games were usually held in a stadium or a large circus arena. Some were of a temporary nature; others were permanent, the remains of which can be seen in the ruins of ancient civilization to this very day. The circular arena, or amphitheater, was designed for the combats of gladiators and wild beasts, and was first used in Italy. Eventually, every large town had its amphitheater. The most famous in Rome itself, known as the Colosseum, was begun by Vespasian, consecrated by Titus (A.D. 80), and finished by Domitian. It was 158 feet high and accommodated some 50,000 spectators. In this arena large groups were engaged in mock battle, fights between wild animals were staged and, occasionally, the arena was flooded so that small ships were able to conduct naval battles before the very eyes of the crowd.

The ancients also had various social games that attained wide popularity. The Greeks and Romans both had ball games. There were also among these people games of chance that employed dice. There was a game very similar to chess that was played on a board divided into spaces, the movements on the board being made with stones. A widely popular game was called "Odd and Even" (in Gr. artiasmos and in Lat. ludere par impar) in which coins, stones, or nuts were held in the hand; the opponent

The second century B.C. stadium at Rhodes, rebuilt by Italians before World War II. HFV

was to guess whether the number was odd or even.

The leaders of the early Christian churches condemned the forms of amusement that associated themselves with pagan religion and which controverted the Christian ethic. In the Treatises attributed to Cyprian, the games and amusements of his day were denounced because it was felt that participation in them involved idolatry. Tatian, Tertullian, and Clément denounced the games and similar amusements because of idolatry, immodesty, and brutality. It was, in fact, the opposition of Christianity that brought them to an end.

The references in Paul's epistles which liken the Christian life to the course of the athlete are many. He speaks of the self-discipline that is necessary if one is to win, and the necessity of abiding by the rules (I Cor 9:24 ff.). He speaks of life and one's ministry as a course to run (Acts 13:25; 20:24; Phil 3:14; II Tim 2:5; 4:7), and of running in vain (Gal 2:2) or running well (Gal 5:7). The author of Hebrews even likens the Lord Jesus to a runner who has covered the course before us (Heb. 12:1 f.). Even today these references to the contests of strength and endurance arouse us to run "with patience the race that is set before us."

Bibliography. A. C. Bouquet, *Everyday Life in New Testament Times,* New York: Scribner's, 1953, pp. 180–190. Jerome Carcopino, *Daily Life in Ancient Rome,* New Haven: Yale Univ. Press, 1940. Henri Daniel-Rops, *Daily Life in the Time of Jesus,* New York: Hawthorne, 1962. E. Norman Gardiner, *Greek Athletic Sports and Festivals,* London: Macmillan, 1910. E. W. Heaton, *Everyday Life in Old Testament Times,* New York: Scribner's, 1956, pp. 75 f., 80, 91–94. Harold Mattingly, *Roman Imperial Civilization,* New York: Doubleday, 1959. Madeleine S. and J. Lane Miller, *Encyclopedia of Bible Life,* New York: Harper, 1944, pp. 391 f.

H. L. D. and P. C. J.

GAMMADIM (găm'á-dĭm). An obscure term found only in Ezk 27:11. It is translated "valorous men" by ASV, but the context seems to imply a proper name. Suggestions have been made to identify it with the city of Kumidi of the Tell el-Amarna letters, somewhere near Arvad in northern Phoenicia.

GAMUL (gā'mŭl). A chief of the Levites, who was chosen as head of the 22nd course of the priests when David organized them into 24 divisions (I Chr 24:17).

GANGRENE. *See* Diseases: Internal Diseases.

GAP. A break as through a wall, a tear, usually translated "breach," but as "gap" in Ezk 13:5; 22:30 (RSV, "breach").

GARDEN. *See* Plants: Garden.

GARDEN HOUSE. Mentioned in II Kgs 9:27, "when Ahaziah . . . fled by the way of the garden house." Since he fled in his chariot, pursued by Jehu, the "garden house" must have been some distance from the winter palace in Jezreel and may possibly be identified with En-gannim (*q.v.:* Josh 19:21), about "seven miles S of Jezreel at the foot of the ridge of Carmel" (IB, III, 235), modern Jenin.

GARDEN OF EDEN. *See* Eden.

GARDENER. *See* Occupations.

GAREB (gā'rĕb)

1. One of David's mighty men who was numbered among the 30 (II Sam 23:38; I Chr 11:40), an Ithrite (*q.v.*), a member of a Kirjath-jearim family (cf. I Chr 2:53).

2. The name of a hill of uncertain site near Jerusalem to which the city would expand, according to a prophecy of Jeremiah (Jer 31:39). It is literally, "Hill of the Leper."

GARLAND. Found only in KJV in Acts 14:13; where the priests of Jupiter (Gr. Zeus) "brought oxen and garlands" to worship Paul and Barnabas as deities. Whether the garlands (Gr. *stemma,* "wreath") were for the apostles or oxen is not clear.

The ASV and RSV translate the Heb. *pe'ēr* ("headdress," "turban," "chaplet") as "garland" in Isa 61:3 ("beauty," KJV) and also v. 10 ("ornaments," KJV).

GARLIC. *See* Plants.

GARMENT. *See* Dress.

GARMITE (gär'mīt). An appellation of uncertain meaning used of Keilah, a descendant of Caleb of the tribe of Judah (I Chr 4:19).

GARNER. An archaic English word for a granary, barn, or storehouse. It is used in Joel 1:17

(Heb. *'ôṣār*, "storehouses," RSV), but it is elsewhere rendered "store," "storehouse," "treasure," "treasury." The Heb. term *mezew* (*māzû* or *mᵉzāw*) is translated "garners" in Ps 144:13. The Gr. *apothēkē* is translated "garner" in KJV in Mt 3:12; Lk 3:17 (RSV, "granary") but elsewhere as "barn." *See* Storehouse.

GARNET. *See* Jewels.

GARRISON. A manned and provisioned military post or fortress. In the OT "garrison" is the translation of two Heb. words, both derived from the root *nṣb*. (1) Heb. *maṣṣāb* (I Sam 13:23; 14:1, 4, 6, 11, 15; II Sam 23:14) and a variant *maṣṣābâ* (I Sam 14:12). A similar form *maṣṣēbâ* is correctly rendered "pillars" by ASV and RSV in Ezk 26:11 where KJV has "garrisons." (2) Heb. *nᵉṣîb* (I Chr 11:16; and most likely II Sam 8:6, 14; I Chr 18:13; II Chr 17:2). This word must be translated "officer" (KJV, RSV), governor, deputy or the like in I Kgs 4:19; II Chr 8:10, but "pillar" in the account of the punishment of Lot's wife (Gen 19:26). How to render the word in I Sam 10:5; 13:3-4 is a question among translators. Did Jonathan smite a Philistine garrison (KJV, ASV, RSV), official (IB, II, 931 f., 946), or pillar (Jerusalem Bible)?

In II Cor 11:32 the KJV renders the Gr. *phrourein* by "keep with a garrison," where RSV and NASB have simply "guard."

D. D. T.

GASHMU (găsh'mū). A variant form of Geshem (*q.v.*) found only in Neh 6:6. This Arab was an associate of Sanballat and Tobiah in their opposition to Nehemiah.

GATAM (gā'tăm). An Edomite chief or duke, the son of Eliphaz and grandson of Esau (Gen 36:11, 16; I Chr 1:36).

GATE. The rendering of five Heb. and three Gr. words. It is used of cities (Deut 3:5, *deleth*, "door"; I Kgs 17:10, *pethaḥ*, "opening"; Gen 23:10, *sha'ar*, "gate"); of the tabernacle (I Chr 9:19, *saph*, "threshold"); of the king (Dan 2:49, *tᵉra'*, "gate"); of the temple (Acts 3:2, *thyra*, "door"); of hell (Mt 16:18; *pylē*, "gate") and cities (Lk 7:12; Acts 9:24); and of houses and cities (Lk 16:20; Acts 12:13-14; Rev 21:12-25, *pylōn*, "gate"). See J. Jeremias, "*Pylē, Pylōn*," TDNT, VI, 921-928.

City gates were made of wood (Neh 2:8; cf. 1:3; 2:13) and of bronze (KJV, brass; they were probably bound with heavy copper bands or sheathed in copper plates, as the gates of the Assyrian town of Balawat. ANEP #356-365). Some gates had towers as defensive elements (II Chr 26:9), and some were built of a series of gates hung on piers jutting out from a side wall, the outer gate sometimes protected by towers. *See* Tower. This was the Solomonic-type gateway with four pairs of evenly spaced piers found at Gezer, Hazor, and Megiddo (ANEP

#721; BA, XXI [1958], 29-30, 46; XXIII [1960], 62-68; XXX [1967], 39 f.; XIII [1950], 42 ff.). Bars secured the gates when closed (Deut 3:5), some being made of bronze (I Kgs 4:13). The doors were formed to pivot at the jambs in stone sockets which, in Babylonia and Assyria in the more important buildings, sometimes had dedicatory inscriptions giving the name of the king and the god to whom the building was dedicated.

Many of the houses unearthed in Tell Beit Mirsim of the period 900-600 B.C. did not have door sockets. In the period 2200-1600 B.C. the large stone sockets give evidence of heavy doors for the houses. The conclusion to be drawn is that in the earlier period, times were unsettled and strong doors were needed, there being no country-wide police force. In the later period, since doors were frequently missing, betokening only a hanging in the doorway, the conclusion is that times were much more settled and that David and his successors had set up a national police force to protect the people (cf. I Sam 25:7-9). Lot's door (Gen 19:1-10) was mob-proof, fitting the early period and not the later period. *See* Door.

Hadrian's Gate provided entrance to the east end of Athens in the second century A.D. HFV

The gateway in Palestinian and Babylonian cities became a place of public hearings, legal transactions, and business (I Kgs 22:10; Deut 21:19 ff.; 22:13-21; Gen 23:10, 18; Ruth 4:1 ff.; II Sam 15:2 ff.; 19:8; II Kgs 7:1). Gates in larger cities were named, sometimes in accordance with the type of market conducted

The Golden Gate
In the wall of Jerusalem as
seen from the Garden of
Gethsemane. It was
blocked up by the Turks in
1530 and is connected by
some with the prophecy of
Ezek. 44:1–3. Some
would identify it with the
Gate Beautiful. HFV

near it (e.g., Sheep Gate, Fish Gate, Old Gate, Neh 3:1, 3; 12:39). *See* Jerusalem: Gates. Gen 34:24 speaks of those going out at the city gate, and the context of the story would denote able-bodied males. The story of Ruth 4 would indicate them to be responsible men, and therefore Gen 34:24 and Ruth 4 would, by this phrase, denote the adult citizenry of the city. At Tell en-Nasbeh (biblical Mizpah) stone benches lining the walls forming the gate provided seats for the people conducting business there (ANEP #716, 717). Sometimes rooms for the gate garrison were provided above it (II Sam 18:24, 33).

In Heb 13:12 Jesus is said to have "suffered without the gate," i.e., outside the city. In this instance "gate" would signify the city of Jerusalem, fulfilling the OT type (Lev 4:12, 21; "camp" would be equal to "city"). Christ died to purify the "city" (household of faith) of God.

The term gate denotes the forces of hell in Mt 16:18; i.e., the devil and his armies of fallen

angels and demons. It is the same idiom as in Gen 34:24. These shall not prevent God's Church from fulfilling God's will, nor can they overthrow it (II Tim 2:19).

H. G. S.

GATE, BEAUTIFUL. The temple of Herod, which was the sanctuary in Jerusalem in the days of Jesus and the early church, was set in the midst of a huge courtyard, called the court of the Gentiles. Separating the outer court from the temple proper was a great wall, which in time of need made of the temple an actual fortress. This wall was pierced by nine gates by which Jews might enter to worship. According to the Mishnah, eight of the gates were 20 cubits high and 10 cubits wide. The great eastern gate, the principal entrance to the temple, was 50 cubits high and 40 cubits wide. This is undoubtedly that which the NT calls the Beautiful Gate (Acts 3:10). It was called the Gate of Nicanor in honor of its donor, and was also called the Corinthian Gate because its doors were made of Corinthian bronze. It was at this gate that the lame man sat who was healed by the power of the Lord through Peter (Acts 3:1–10). Against the background of this magnificent gate, Peter's words, "Silver and gold have I none" bear added significance.

P. C. J.

GATH (găth). A place name widely used in the Levant, meaning "wine press." Administrative documents from Ugarit list 29 different towns with a name of which the first element is *gt* (Gath) followed by a second element, e.g., *gt'ttrt*, "the wine press of Ashtaroth"; *gt gl'd*, "the wine press of Gilead." Therefore, it is not surprising to find several places with the name Gath in Palestine, since viticulture was a major industry in antiquity just as it is today.

Interior of the Golden Gate as seen from the
Temple area. HFV

There are numerous references to the Palestinian Gaths in both biblical and secular sources. Sometimes an additional element was added to the name to distinguish it from other Gaths, but in numerous instances the name Gath stands alone, and it is difficult for the interpreter to decide just which Gath is meant. The biblical Gaths which have such an additional designation are discussed under separate headings (*see* Gath-hepher; Gath of the Philistines; and Gath-rimmon). The locative ending *-ayim* may be added to produce the form Gittaim (*q.v.*). This town sometimes is referred to simply as Gath. The name Moresheth-gath contains this term as a second element, though it too may possibly be called simply Gath (II Chr 11:8; *see* Moresheth-gath).

At least four, or perhaps five, other Gaths in Palestine are known from sources outside the Bible. One of these is called *Gittipadalla* in the Amarna tablets (EA 250:12) and is written *ddptr* in Shishak's list (No. 34). From its position in the latter text, between Borim (No. 33; Khirbet Burin) and Yahem (No. 35; Khirbet Yamma) it is evident that this Gath-padilla should be identified with the village of Jatt on the northern coastal plain S of Mount Carmel. The same place is listed as *knt* in the list of Thutmose III (No. 70) in close association with other places known to be located in the northern Sharon, e.g., Soccho (No. 67; *swk*, Khirbet Shuweikat ar-Ras) and Yehem (No. 68).

The *Gintikirmil*, Gath-carmel, of the Amarna tablets (EA 288:26, 289:18) probably refers to the same town as Gath of the Philistines, now identified as Tell es-Safi (Y. Aharoni, "Rubute and Ginti-Kirmil," VT, XIX [1969], 137–145). Another Galilean Gath is indicated by No. 44 of Thutmose III's list, written *kniiśn*, listed after Ibleam (No. 43; Khirbet Bal'ama), which appears in an Amarna tablet (EA 319:5) as *Ginti-ashna.*

The fourth "Gath" in Thutmose's inscription, *kntit* (No. 93), probably represents the plural form *Gattoth*. Because of its position in the list alongside other towns in N Galilee, Aharoni has associated it with Gath Asher, written *qtisr* in two topographical lists of Ramses II. He suggests that this Gath be identified with Jatt, a village in the ancient tribal territory of Asher (Yohanan Aharoni, *The Settlement of the Israelite Tribes in Upper Galilee,* Jerusalem: Magnes Press, 1957, p. 65 [Heb.]).

A. F. R.

GATH-HEPHER (găth-hē'fĕr). A town on the boundary of Zebulun (Josh 19:13, RSV), listed after Daberath (Dabburiya) and Japhia (Yafa) and before Eth-kazin (location unknown). It is known as the birthplace of the prophet Jonah, the son of Amittai (II Kgs 14:25). Jerome, in his commentary on the book of Jonah, states that Gath-hepher was situated two miles from Sepphoris (Saffuriya) on the road to Tiberias, and that the local inhabitants in his day pointed out the tomb of the prophet to interested pass-

The Mound of Gath. HFV

ersby. This is evidently a reference to the village of Meshhed, which to this day displays a tomb of Nebi Yunas, an honor which it shares with several other places in Palestine, not to mention its famous rival at Nineveh. This village was only settled from the Roman period and later; but there was an Iron Age town on the nearby tell called Khirbet ez-Zurra', just SW of Meshhed.

A. F. R.

GATH OF THE PHILISTINES. Home of one of the five Philistine lords (Josh 13:3, RSV). It was known as the home of giants (Josh 11:22), Goliath in particular (I Sam 17:4; II Sam 21:19–20; I Chr 20:4–8). Achish (*q.v.*) ruled there as king with apparent hegemony over all of the Philistine region (I Sam 21:10–15; 27:1–12; 28:1–2; 29:1–11). Y. Aharoni (VT, XIX [1969], 141–144) believes that Gath-carmel of two Amarna letters from 'Abdu-Heba of Jerusalem (#288, 289: ANET, pp. 488 f.) is identical with the later Philistine Gath.

According to one passage (I Chr 18:1) David conquered Gath; but the parallel text has another reading (II Sam 8:1). A Philistine king still reigned there in Solomon's day (I Kgs 2:39). The town fortified by Rehoboam was probably Moresheth-gath (*q.v.*), which is on a more logical line with the other towns in that list (II Chr 11:8). Hazael captured Gath on a foray into Palestine (II Kgs 12:17); Uzziah neutralized its power when he expanded Judah's own influence (II Chr 26:6); and Sargon II's annals mention a Gimti in the land of Ashdod (*q.v.*). After this, the only reference to Gath is in a proverbial expression (Mic 1:10; cf. II Sam 1:20).

Excavations have shown that no Philistine settlement existed at either Tell Sheiʳk el-Areini (five miles NW of Lachish) or Tell en-Najila (eight miles SW of Lachish). For these two sites see BW, pp. 571-574. Scholars have recently returned (Aharoni, *op. cit.,* p. 144) to the older suggestion ("Gath," ISBE, II, 1177) that Gath was located at Tell es-Safi (21 miles due W of Bethlehem, ten miles N of Lachish) which would place Gath close to Ekron (Tell Muqanna) and which suits the LXX account of I Sam 17:52 (see RSV). Tell es-Safi is at the W end of the Valley of Elah in which David killed Goliath. The site on its narrow spur of the Shephelah foothills juts out like a bastion, with very steep slopes on the N and W.

In 1900 Bliss and Macalister made sound-ings at the site and discovered pottery that cor-roborates the biblical data regarding its occupa-tion. They noted a city wall of the Judean king-dom period and a Canaanite shrine enclosing an earlier high place with a series of standing stones (*Excavations in Palestine, 1898–1900,* pp. 28–43). But Moslem cemeteries on the mount have prevented large-scale excavations. *See* Gath; Philistines.

A. F. R.

GATH-RIMMON (găth-rĭm'ŭn). The name of one or two towns in ancient Israel.

1. It appears in the list of Danite cities (Josh 19:45) in association with Jehud, Bene-berak, and Me-jarkon, the "waters of Yarkon." How-ever, the city itself was to be a Levitical city (Josh 21:24; I Chr 6:69). It perhaps became an administrative center during the time of the united monarchy, since the area had remained unconquered by the Danites (Jud 1:34–35). Only during the expansion under David did Israel finally gain control over this region (cf. II Sam 8:1; I Chr 18:1).

The city called *knt* (No. 63), which is listed on Thutmose III's topographical list alongside Joppa (No. 62), Lod (No. 64), Ono (No. 65), and Aphek (No. 66), may be identical with Gath-rimmon because of the similarity of locale (for locations of the other towns mentioned above, cf. the respective articles). The city's apparent importance as a store city of the Le-vites under David's administration has led re-cent investigators to abandon the older identi-fication of Gath-rimmon with the small, though prominent, Tell Abu Zeitūn in favor of Tell Jerisheh ("Napoleon's Hill"), a large site near the junction of Wady Musrara with the Yarkon River. Excavations there revealed that the site was an important town during the Late Bronze Age and continued to exist until sometime near the end of the 10th cen. B.C.

2. A Gath-rimmon appears with Taanach as one of the cities of Manasseh in Cis-jordan which was assigned to the Kohathite families of the Levites (Josh 21:25). The validity of this reference is disputed because of a textual difficulty. The parallel passage in I Chr 6:70 gives two entirely different towns in place of Taanach and Gath-rimmon, viz., Aner and Bi-leam (*q.v.*). This reading is supported by the LXX of Josh 21:25 which has *Iebatha* (a pos-sible conflation of *Ieblaḏ[m]* and *Baithsa* or *Baithsan* which appear as variants in other LXX MSS in place of *Iebatha*). Whatever the solution to this knotty textual problem, the ex-istence of a Gath-rimmon close to Taanach re-ceives additional support from an Amarna tab-let, which refers to a Gimti-rimmunima (EA 250:46) in association with Shunem. The north-ern Gath-rimmon can perhaps be identified with Rummana (169–214) in the vicinity of Taa-nach.

Bibliography. Benjamin Mazar, "The Cities of the Territory of Dan," IEJ, X (1960), 65–77; "The Excavations at Tell Qasile," IEJ, I (1950), 63, n. 6. E. L. Sukenik, "Excavations in Palestine, 1933–1934: Tell el Jerishe," *Quar-terly of the Department of Antiquities, Pales-tine,* IV (1934), 208–209.

A. F. R.

GAULANITIS (gôl'a-nī'tĭs). The area E of Galilee and bounded by the Yarmuk on the S, Hermon on the N, the Jordan on the W, and the desert on the E. It is not mentioned by this name in the Bible, but is derived from Golan (*q.v.*), one of the six cities of refuge assigned to the Gershonites (Josh 21:27; I Chr 6:71).

GAY. Translated as "gay" with reference to clothing in Jas 2:3, but rendered "fine clothing" by ASV and RSV.

GAZA (gā'za). An important seaport town on the S coast of Palestine. The modern name Ghazzeh preserves the original first consonant (cf. Heb. *'azzâ,* Deut 2:23). During the Late Bronze Age it was the main Egyptian adminis-trative center in their province of Canaan, of which it marked the southernmost extremity (Gen 10:19; cf. Acts 8:26). The original in-habitants were Avim, later replaced by Caphto-rims (Deut 2:23; cf. Josh 13:3). Judah was supposed to inherit it (Josh 15:47) but failed to conquer it (Josh 13:2–3; Jud 3:3; Jud 1:18, LXX). Hence it became an important Philistine center (Jud 13:3; Jud 16; I Sam 6:17; *et al.*). The Assyrians conquered it several times in their struggle to control Palestine. King Heze-kiah subdued Gaza (II Kgs 18:8), but Sen-nacherib later gave some Judean towns to its king. Pharaoh Neco took over the city on his northward march in 609 B.C. (Jer 47:1).

The town maintained its importance in Per-sian. Hellenistic, and Roman times. Alexander spent five months besieging it. Jonathan, Simon, and Alexander Jannaeus all fought with it, and the latter finally devastated the town in 93 B.C., so that certain writers referred to it as *erēmos,* "desert(ed)." Pompey placed the region of Gaza under the jurisdiction of the Roman prov-ince of Syria (62 B.C.). The Roman general Ga-binius rebuilt Gaza in 57 B.C. on a new site by the sea, a little S of the old city. Thus in telling that Philip heeded the divine messenger to take the old road that descends from Jerusalem to Gaza, Luke correctly commented. "This city is deserted" (Acts 8:26, NASB marg.).

A. F. R.

GAZATHITES (gā'zȧ-thīts). The designation applied to the inhabitants of Gaza in Josh 13:3 ("those of Gaza," RSV) and rendered Gazites (*q.v.*) in Jud 16:2.

GAZELLE. *See* Animals, II.15.

GAZER (gā'zẽr). A variant form of Gezer (*q.v.*) in the KJV rendering of II Sam 5:25 and I Chr 14:16.

GAZEZ (gā'zĕz). A son and a grandson of Caleb bore this name (I Chr 2:46). The first Gazez was Caleb's son by his concubine Ephah, while the grandson was the son of Haran, another son of Caleb by Ephah.

GAZITES (găz'īts). The inhabitants of Gaza (*q.v.*), the southernmost of the five principal Philistine cities.

GAZZAM (găz'ăm). The founder of a family of the Nethinim (*q.v.*), whose descendants were among the first exiles returning from Babylon (Ezr 2:48; Neh 7:51).

GEBA (gē'bȧ). Spelled Gaba in Josh 18:24; Ezr 2:26; Neh 7:30, KJV.

A city in the inheritance of Benjamin (Josh 18:24), today Jebaʻ, an Arab village six miles NNE of Jerusalem between er-Ram (Ramah) and Mukhmas (Michmash). It occupies the hill (Heb. *gebaʻ* means "hill," "height") on the S side of the gorge of the Wadi Suweinit, opposite Michmash (*q.v.*) on the N rim (I Sam 14:5, RSV). Geba is one of the four Benjamite cities in which dwelt priestly families (Josh 21:17; I Chr 6:60). Some of the inhabitants traced their lineage back to Ehud (I Chr 8:6), apparently to be identified with the judge of that name (Jud 3:15 ff.). The "meadows of Gibeah" (Jud 20:33, KJV) is understood by the Peshitta, LXX, and Vulg. as "west of Geba."

Geba is doubtless the site featured in the account of Jonathan's daring attack on the Philistines, because in I Sam 13:16 and 14:5 the Heb. MT has *gebaʻ*, "Geba," not "Gibeah" (KJV). Most scholars believe that in I Sam 14:2, 16 *gibʻâ*, "Gibeah," is a scribal error for *gebaʻ*, because one cannot view Michmash from Gibeah (Tell el-Ful), but it can easily be watched from Geba across the deep valley. Earlier the Philistines had established a garrison at Geba (I Sam 13:3), also known as Gibeath-elohim ("the hill of God," I Sam 10:5, KJV) because of its high place.

During the Judean kingdom, King Asa dismantled the walls of Ramah to fortify Mizpah and Geba on the two main roads to Jerusalem from the N (I Kgs 15:22; II Chr 16:6). Geba is also mentioned as a station of the Assyrian advance against Jerusalem (Isa 10:29). With the first returnees from the Exile came 621 descendants of citizens of Geba and Ramah (Ezr 2:26; Neh 7:30). The town belonged to the post-Exilic province of Judah (Neh 11:31); in its territory dwelt many of the temple singers (Neh 12:28 f.).

Benjamin Mazar ("Geba," EBi, II, cols. 411–412 [Heb.]) argues that there must have been another Geba, a city on the northern border of Judah, probably Khirbet et-Tell overlooking Wadi Jib. King Josiah defiled all the high places from "Geba to Beer-sheba" (II Kgs 23:8). In the same chapter it is clear that Bethel was also within the bounds of Judah during Josiah's time (II Kgs 23:4, 16), and Bethel is N of the Jebaʻ discussed above. A similar expression is "from Geba to Rimmon south of Jerusalem" (Zech 14:10), which seems to support the view that this Geba is the northernmost point in the Judean kingdom. It is also significant to note that in Roman times the boundary between Judea and Samaria was along the line *Jeshanah*—Geba—Chanot—Barkai (cf. also II Chr 13:19).

Eusebius (Onomasticon 74:2) refers to a Geba which was five miles N of Gofna on the way from Jerusalem to Shechem. The identification with et-Tel is supported by the fact that remains from Israelite through the Byzantine periods have been found there.

However, as Y. Aharoni points out (*The Land of the Bible*, 1967, pp. 350 f.), there is no need to assume that this Geba was directly on the border. In the time of Josiah Geba, like Beer-sheba, was an administrative center near the border, where cultic sanctuaries had been located prior to Josiah's reform.

A. F. R.

Phoenician Fortifications, Gebal. HFV

GEBAL (gē'bȧl)

1. An ancient Phoenician seaport, 25 miles N of Beirut, known by the Greeks as Byblos; modern Jebeil. Gebal is one of the most ancient sites yet excavated in the Near East, yielding human bone remains enclosed in large earthen pots dating back to Neolithic times (4000–3000 B.C.). By about 3100 B.C. Byblos was a center

Ancient harbor of Gebal. ORINST

of Egyptian influence, and vessels, known as Byblos travelers, plied the Mediterranean between Phoenicia and Egypt (BW, p. 154).

One of the most important finds uncovered at Gebal is the Ahiram sarcophagus (c. 1000 B.C.), discovered in 1923, containing an inscription written in early Phoenician alphabetic characters. The Gebalites were skilled craftsmen (I Kgs 5:18, RSV) and furnished the caulkers for the ships of Tyre (Ezk 27:9). Because they saw there imported Egyptian papyrus reeds made into scrolls, the Greeks named the city Byblos, meaning "papyrus." Byblos also means "book," and our word Bible is derived from the same word. See N. Jidejian, *Byblos Through the Ages,* Leiden: Brill, 1968.

2. An area between the Dead Sea and Petra referred to in Ps 83:7 as allied with the enemies of Israel. It is modern Gibal.

For illustration of Ahiram Sarcophagus, *see* Alphabet.

D. D. T. and A. F. J.

GEBER (gē′bēr). The son of Uri and one of the 12 commissary officers of Solomon whose duty was to provide food and supplies for the king's household. He had charge of the 12th district consisting of Gilead (I Kgs 4:19).

Another of the commissary officers was Ben-Geber ("son of Geber," I Kgs 4:13), who was over the 6th district, consisting of 60 cities of Gilead and Bashan.

GEBIM (gē′bĭm). A city of unknown location in Benjamin between Anathoth and Nob, whose inhabitants are portrayed by Isaiah as fleeing before the approach of the Assyrian army (Isa 10:31).

GECKO. *See* Animals, IV. 16.

GEDALIAH (gĕd-á-lī′á)

1. Governor of Judah, appointed by Nebuchadnezzar after the destruction of Jerusalem c. 586 B.C. (II Kgs 25:22–26; Jer 40:6–41:18). Gedaliah was a member of a prominent and powerful family. His grandfather was Shaphan, probably the one who served as state secretary under King Josiah and reported the discovery of the book of the law to the king (II Kgs 22:10). Shaphan's son, Gedaliah's father, Ahi-

kam, became Jeremiah's protector after the famous temple sermon (Jer 26:24).

Gedaliah set up his government at Mizpah, which was five or six miles N of Jerusalem, either at the modern site of Tell en-Nashbeh or Nebi Samwil. The length of Gedaliah's governorship is not known. Suggestions have ranged from two months to five years. Ishmael, a leader of a fanatic nationalist band and a member of the exiled royal family, murdered Gedaliah while he was a guest in the official residence in Mizpah (Jer 41:2).

A seal impression on clay once attached to a papyrus scroll and bearing the words, "To Gedaliah who is over the house," was found at Lachish. This seal would suggest that Gedaliah was probably the last prime minister of Judah, or administrator of the palace, since such a seal was borne by the chief official of the land next to the king (cf. G. E. Wright, *Biblical Archaeology,* p. 178).

2. A son of Jeduthun, an instrumentalist leader of the temple choir (I Chr 25:3, 9).

3. Grandson of Hezekiah and grandfather of the prophet Zephaniah (Zeph 1:1).

4. Son of Pashur, one of the princes of Jerusalem who advocated putting Jeremiah to death (Jer 38:1–6).

5. One of the priests who put away his foreign wife (Ezr 10:18).

R. L. S.

GEDEON (gĕd′ĭ-ŏn). Gr. form of Gideon (*q.v.*).

GEDER (gē′dēr), **GEDERITE** (gē′dēr-īt). An unidentified city of southern Palestine, whose king was captured by Joshua (Josh 12:13). It is probably the same as Beth-gader (*q.v.*). Baal-hanan, who had charge of David's olives and sycamores "that were in the low plains" (Shephelah), was a Gederite, a native of Geder (I Chr 28:28).

GEDERAH (gĕ-dēr′á). A town in the Shephelah of Judah (Josh 15:36). I Chr 4:23 reads, "These were the potters and inhabitants of Netaim and Gederah; they dwelt there with the king for his work" (RSV). Gederah may possibly be identified with modern Jedireh, about 10 miles SE of Lud (Lod).

Some identify Gederah with a city of Benjamin from which came Jozabad, one of David's mighty men. It may be the same as a Jedirah near Gibeon or a Jedireh about three miles SW of Gezer.

GEDERATHITE (gĕd′ē-rá-thīt). An inhabitant of Gederah. This term is applied in I Chr 12:4 to Jozabad, one of David's mighty men, and in I Chr 4:23 in referring to the potters and inhabitants of Netaim and Gederah (ASV, RSV).

GEDEROTH (gĕ-dēr′ōth). A city in the Shephelah of Judah, named with Beth-dagon, Naamah, and Makkedah in Josh 15:41. It is mentioned along with Beth-shemesh and Aijalon as taken by the Philistines during the reign of Ahaz (II Chr 28:18). It has been identified with Kedron, a place fortified by Cendebeus who was defeated here by John, son of Simon Maccabeus (I Macc 15:39; 16:9).

GEDEROTHAIM (gĕ-dĕr'ō-thā'ĭm). A village in the Shephelah of Judah near Zorah-azekah (Josh 15:36). Joshua's account lists it as the fifteenth city in an enumeration which suggests "fourteen cities with their villages." Accordingly, some scholars feel that the term "and Gederothaim" should read "and her sheep folds," or "and her places of enclosure." Thus this statement would refer to the preceding cities and leave the total at 14 as the verse suggests.

GEDOR (gē'dŏr)
1. One of the sons of Jehiel, a Benjamite, the "father" or founder of Gibeon (I Chr 8:31; 9:37).
2. A city in the hill country of Judah, assigned by Joshua to Judah at the division of the land (Josh 15:58). Men from Gedor came to David at Ziklag (I Chr 12:7). I Chr 4:4 states that Penuel was a "father" of Gedor, and I Chr 4:18 that Jered was likewise a "father" of Gedor. Since in this section other men are obviously listed as "fathers" or Israelite rebuilders of former Canaanite towns—Socho and Zanoah (I Chr 4:18) are towns in Josh 15:35–35—we may conclude that Penuel and Jered were the founding fathers of Israelite Gedor.
3. A city or valley where some of the Simeonites settled (I Chr 4:39). The location is unknown. The LXX has "Gerar" for Gedor in this verse.

GEHAZI (gĕ-hā'zī). The servant or youth (Heb. na'ar) of Elisha. He is referred to by name on three occasions (II Kgs 4:12 ff.; 5:20; 8:4) and may be the unnamed servant in II Kgs 4:43 and 6:15.
It was Gehazi who suggested to Elisha that the Shunammite's hospitality should be rewarded with the promise of a son, and later carried Elisha's staff and laid it on the dead child's face in a vain effort to restore the child's life (II Kgs 4:8–37).
Gehazi's greed is seen in his deceitful request from Naaman of a talent of silver and two festal robes in the name of his master Elisha, who had previously declined to accept a reward from Naaman (II Kgs 5:20–23). As a consequence of this sin, Elisha pronounced a curse upon Gehazi and his descendants to the effect that the leprosy of Naaman would cleave to them forever (II Kgs 5:27). Leprosy is a general term in the OT used for many types of skin diseases. Evidently this type which Naaman and Gehazi had contracted did not require isolation (cf. II Kgs 8:1 ff.; Lev 13:12–13). *See* Diseases: Leprosy.
The last picture of Gehazi in the OT is that of his relating to King Jehoram "the great things that Elisha hath done," especially the raising of the Shunammite's son (II Kgs 8:4-6). *See* Elisha; Naaman.

R. L. S.

GEHENNA (gĕ-hĕn'ā). The Gr. form of the Heb. gē-hinnom, "valley of Hinnom" (Josh 15:8; 18:16); also called Topheth (II Kgs 23:10). The form *Gaienna* occurs in the LXX in Josh 18:16b. The word is used as the metaphorical name of the place of torment of the wicked after the final judgment. The valley was the place of the idolatrous worship of Molech, the fire god ("Ahaz . . . burnt incense in the valley of the son of Hinnom, and burnt his children in the fire," II Chr 28:3; cf. II Chr 33:6; Jer 7:31; 32:35; Lev 18:21). For this reason it was polluted by Josiah (II Kgs 23:10) to become a place of refuse and abomination.
The idea of a place of eternal spiritual punishment by fire is frequent in the OT (cf. Deut 32:22, "A fire is kindled in mine anger, and burneth unto the lowest Sheol," ASV. See also Lev 10:2; Isa 30:27, 30, 33; 33:14; 66:24; Dan 7:10; Ps 18:8; 50:3; 97:3). This concept combined with Jeremiah's prophecy of evil against the valley (Jer 19:2–10) developed a belief in a place of spiritual punishment to which the dread name Gehenna was given. Gaster (IDB) suggests that the application of the place name follows the analogy of using such Palestinian places as Armageddon (Rev 16:16; Zech 12:11), Jerusalem (Gal 4:26; Rev 21:2), or Sodom (Rev 11:8) for spiritual concepts.
It can be seen from Jewish literature that the idea was prevalent (Enoch 10:12–14: "[Sinners] will be led to the abyss of fire in torture and in prison they will be locked up for all eternity." Cf. also Enoch 18:11–16; 27:1–3; Judith 16:17; II Esd 7:36; Sir 7:17; Sibylline Oracles 1, 10:3; 1QM 2:8; Talmud, Aboth 1:6; Assumption of Moses 10:10). Some Jewish writers thought the chosen people would be exempt and that the duration would be limited. Philo, however, taught that wicked Jews would be punished also, and that eternally (De Praem. et Poen. 921). The spiritual nature of Gehenna is further indicated by the fact that it was placed in the third heaven (Ascension of Isaiah 4:14; II Enoch 40:12; 41:2).
But the doctrine is most explicitly affirmed in Jesus' teaching. Jesus spoke of Gehenna as a place of future punishment. He spoke of "being cast into Gehenna" (Gr.; see RSV marg. in Mt 5:29; 18:8–9; Mk 9:45, 47; Lk 12:5); "the Gehenna of fire" (Mt 5:22); "destroy both body and soul in Gehenna" (Mt 10:28); "the condemnation of Gehenna" (Mt 23:33); "make him a son of Gehenna," i.e., one worthy of its punishment (Mt 23:15). It is used elsewhere in the NT only in Jas 3:6, "the tongue is set on fire of Gehenna." The NT clearly teaches that the punishment of Gehenna is eternal (Mk 9:47–48; Mt 25:46; Rev 14:11).
The book of the Revelation gives to Ge-

henna the name "the lake of fire" (19:20; 20:10, 14, 15; 21:8). Furthermore, since the Revelation equates the lake of fire with the "second death" (20:14), this apparently is also a synonym for describing Gehenna. In further confirmation of the identity of these terms in the Revelation with Gehenna, it may be noted that unbelieving men are therein consigned (20:15; 21:8), as well as Satan himself (20:10). It is also the eternal place of condemnation (20:10*b*).

See Dead; Eschatology; Eternal State; Hades; Hell; Hinnom; Punishment; Sheol; Tophet.

Bibliography. Joachin Jeremias, *"Geenna,"* TDNT, I, 657 f.

J. W. R.

GELILOTH (gĕ-lī'lŏth). A technical Heb. term for administrative districts, as of the Philistines (Josh 13:2), translated "borders" or "regions." The Geliloth of Josh 18:17 lay on the boundary between Judah and Benjamin. It seems improbable to identify Geliloth with the Gilgal in the Jordan Valley, but it seems to be identical with the Gilgal of Josh 15:7. No positive identification is possible, but some point along the road from Jericho to Jerusalem. such as Tal'at ed-Damm, a hill near the so-called Good Samaritan Inn, may be intended. Josh 18:17, in speaking of the allotment to the tribe of Benjamin, reads: "Then it bends in a northerly direction going on to En-shemesh, and thence goes to Geliloth, which is opposite the ascent of Adummim" (RSV).

GEMALLI (gĕ-măl'ī). Father of the spy Ammiel from the tribe of Dan, sent out by Moses to spy out the land of Canaan (Num 13:12).

GEMARIAH (gĕm-*a*-rī'*a*)

1. The son of Shaphan and a scribe or priest who occupied a chamber in the New Gate of the temple during the reign of Jehoiakim (Jer 36:10). Gemariah was from an illustrious family. His father, Shaphan, was the secretary or a prominent minister in Josiah's time to whom Hilkiah first brought the book of the law when it was found in the temple (II Kgs 22:8). Gemariah's brother was Ahikam, who saved Jeremiah's life after his temple sermon (Jer 26:24). And Gemariah's nephew, Gedaliah, became governor of Judah after the fall of Jerusalem (Jer 39:14). Gemariah witnessed Jehoiakim's destruction of the first scroll of the book of Jeremiah. Together with Elnathan and Delaiah, he urged the king not to burn the scroll, but the king would not listen to them (Jer 36:25).

2. The son of Hilkiah, sent by King Zedekiah as an ambassador to Nebuchadnezzar, and the bearer of Jeremiah's letter to the Jewish captives in Babylon (Jer 29:3).

GENEALOGY

Definition

The Heb. word for genealogy, *yaḥaś*, occurs only once as a noun in the OT in the phrase "book of the genealogy" (Neh 7:5, ASV) where it is introducing a list of exiles returning to Jerusalem from Babylon. The verb *yāḥaś*, "to register," is always in the causative (*hithpael*) form and could be translated "to cause one's name to be recorded (enrolled) in genealogical tables" (I and II Chr, Ezr and Neh). In the NT the Gr. *genealogia*, "genealogy," occurs in I Tim 1:4 and Tit 3:9.

The idea is also conveyed in the OT by the Heb. word *tôledôth*, "generations" (*see* Generation), or the phrase "book of the generations" (Gen 5:1), and in the NT by Gr. *biblos geneseōs*, "book of the generation" (Mt 1:1). Thus the term "genealogy" can be defined as a list of names indicating ancestors or descendants of an individual or individuals, or it can mean the registration of the names of people for some reason.

Genealogical Lists

The principal lists are as follows:

1. Adam to Noah (Gen 5; I Chr 1:1-4). This gives the line of Seth, with ten names in each passage. In Genesis they are listed with a formula of A lived x years and begat B, and A lived after he begat B y years and begat sons and daughters, and all the days of A were z years, and he died. There are many variations for the x and y between the MT, SP, and the LXX, while the variations of the z in the various accounts are smaller.

2. The descendants of Cain (Gen 4:17-22). One notable feature of this earliest list in the Bible is that the occupation is mentioned for some of those listed.

3. The descendants of Noah (Gen 10; I Chr 1:4-23). This is the Table of Nations (*see* Nations).

4. The line from Shem to Abraham (Gen 11:10-26; I Chr 1:24-27). This list is similar to Gen 5 except the MT and the LXX do not give the total years that each man lived (conversely, the SP follows the formula of Gen 5 exactly).

5. The descendants of Ṭerah (Gen 11:27-31).

6. The descendants of Nahor, Abraham's brother (Gen 22:20-24).

7. The descendants of Lot, son of Haran, Abraham's other brother (Gen 19:36-38).

8. The descendants of Abraham (Gen 25:1-4; I Chr 1:28-33).

9. The descendants of Ishmael (Gen 25:12-17; I Chr 1:29-31).

10. The descendants of Isaac (I Chr 1:34).

11. The descendants of Esau (Gen 36; I Chr 1:35-54).

12. The descendants of Jacob/Israel (Gen 46:8-27; I Chr 2-8).

a. Descendants of Jacob by Leah (Gen 46:8- 15).

(1) Reuben (Gen 46:9; Ex 6:14; Num 26:5- 11; I Chr 5:1- 10).

(2) Simeon (Gen 46:10; Ex 6:15; Num 26:12- 14; I Chr 4:24- 38).

(3) Levi (Gen 46:11; Ex 6:16- 26). The genealogy of Levi is important and extensive in the post-Captivity books. The reason for this is to demonstrate the continuance of the Levitical priesthood, both before, during, and after the Exile. The Levitical priesthood can be traced from the post-Exilic books in the following way: (*a*) Pre-Exilic, before David (I Chr 6:16- 30); at the time of David (I Chr 6:31-48; 15:5- 24); Jehoshaphat (II Chr 17:8); Hezekiah (II Chr 29:12-14; 31:12- 17); Josiah (II Chr 34:8- 13; 35:8- 9). (*b*) Post-Exilic (Ezr 2:40-42; Neh 10:2- 13; 12:1- 24). (*c*) Aaronic high priesthood lineage (I Chr 6:1- 15; Neh 12:26; Ezr 5:2; Hag 1:1, 12, 14; 2:2, 4).

(4) Judah (Gen 46:12; Num 26:19- 22; I Chr 2:3 − 4:22). As with the Aaronic line, the line of Judah is important, for out of this line the Messiah was to come (Gen 49:9- 10) and more particularly, He was to come out of David's line (II Sam 7:12- 16; Ps 89:3- 4, 28- 30, 32- 37). For the Davidic line in particular see I Chr 3:10- 20; Ezr 3:2, 8; 5:2; Neh 12:1; Hag 1:1, 12, 14; 2:2, 23; Mt 1:6- 16; Lk 3:23- 31.

(5) Issachar (Gen 46:13; Num 26:23- 25; I Chr 7:1- 5).

(6) Zebulun (Gen 46:14; Num 26:26- 27).

b. Descendants of Jacob by Bilhah (Gen 46:23- 25).

(7) Dan (Gen 46:23; Num 26:42- 43).

(8) Naphtali (Gen 46:24; Num 26:48- 50).

c. Descendants of Jacob by Zilpah (Gen 46:16- 18).

(9) Gad (Gen 46:16; Num 26:15- 18; I Chr 5:11- 17).

(10) Asher (Gen 46:17; Num 26:44- 47; I Chr 7:30- 40).

d. Descendants of Jacob by Rachel (Gen 46:19- 22).

(11) Joseph (Gen 46:19- 20; Num 26:28- 37). However, two tribes came out of Joseph (cf. Gen 48:5, 8- 20), namely, Manasseh (Num 26:29- 34; I Chr 7:14- 19) and Ephraim (Num 26:35- 37; I Chr 7:20- 27).

(12) Benjamin (Gen 46:19, 21; Num 26:38- 41; I Chr 7:6- 12; 8:1- 40). King Saul was of Benjamin (I Chr 8:29- 38; 9:35- 44).

13. Genealogies of post-Exilic times. Those who returned with Zerubbabel (Ezr 2:2-61; Neh 7:7- 64), and with Ezra (Ezr 7:1- 7). Also there are several lists given in the post-Exilic books, two of which list both their names and their tribe (cf. I Chr 9:3- 9; Neh 11:4- 36). Post-Exilic genealogies are very important for establishing and preserving the homogeneity of the race. It was to show the continuance of the nation through a period of national disruption.

14. Genealogies of Christ (Mt 1:1-17; Lk 3:23- 38). Both of these genealogies fit within the purpose of each of the books. Matthew demonstrates that Jesus is Israel's Messiah and King; thus he traces Jesus' lineage back through Solomon and David to show His kingly right to the throne, and ultimately back to Abraham with whom God made an eternal covenant concerning Abraham and his seed. In showing that Jesus is the Son of Man, Luke traces Christ's line back to Adam, the father of mankind.

One can see that genealogical lists can be either of descending or ascending order. For example, one observes this in Aaron's genealogy which is given in the descending order (i.e., *A* begat *B*) in I Chr 6:3- 14, and in the ascending (i.e., *A*, the son of *B*) in Ezr 7:1- 5. The same phenomenon occurs in Christ's genealogy (cf. Mt 1:2- 16; Lk 3:23- 38 respectively).

Purposes of Genealogies

First, they show the history of Israel. The earlier genealogies show Israel's kinship with and distinction from her neighbors. Adam is father of all mankind, but later on nations develop. Israel was, of course, the main interest to the biblical writers since it was for the benefit of that nation that the Abrahamic and Mosaic covenants were made.

Second, they are given to show the ancestry and preservation of the different tribes in Israel.

Third, the genealogies are for the preservation and the purity of Israel's Aaronic priesthood and the Davidic line which ultimately led to Christ, the long-awaited Messiah as seen in the Gospels. These genealogies not only were for the preservation of the line but also they were used to demonstrate the legitimacy of an individual in his office.

Fourth, the post-Exilic genealogies serve to demonstrate the homogeneity of Israel as a nation after their captivities. Thus, in conclusion, it can be seen that these genealogies were essentially the skeleton on which the history of Israel rested.

Genealogies and Chronology

Right at the outset it is very evident that there are genealogical gaps, at least in some of the genealogies. For example, although in the lineage only three generations are listed between Jacob and Moses (Ex 6:16- 20; Num 3:17- 19; etc.), there are in the lineage of Joshua eleven generations listed between Jacob and Joshua (I Chr 2:2; 7:20- 29). Many more examples could be given (see Kitchen, pp. 54 f.).

The real crux of the relationship between genealogy and chronology comes in the genealogies of Gen 5 and 11. To say that other genealogies have gaps does not prove that these do, although Lk 2:36 includes the name Cainan as the son of Arphaxad, found in the LXX of Gen 11:12- 13 but not in the Heb. MT. These are the only genealogies which give the age of the father at the birth of the son who serves as the next link in the genealogy. It may be that there are genealogical gaps in Gen 5, but since the age is given of the father who gives birth to the child, it is quite another matter to say one can have chronological gaps. Thus there may be gaps in the genealogy but not in chronology.

To have genealogical gaps in Gen 11 is even more difficult, for it is unlikely that many would have been grandfathers or great-grandfathers in their late 20's or early 30's as would be the case for those listed in this chapter! To be sure, as Green has indicated, these genealogies may show the longevity of life early in the earth's history, but this does not preclude that they cannot be chronologically accurate. In conclusion, it must be stated that this is a rather complex problem which is further aggravated by the fact of great differences in the figures given in the SP and the LXX. *See* Chronology, OT.

Bibliography. R. A. Bowman, "Genealogy," IDB, II, 362-365. Philip W. Crannell, "Genealogy," ISBE, II, 1183-1196. E. L. Curtis, "Genealogy," HDB, II, 121-137. William Henry Green, "Primeval Chronology," BS, XLVII (April, 1890), 285-303, Marshall D. Johnson, *The Purpose of Biblical Genealogies,* Cambridge: Cambridge Univ. Press, 1969. K. A. Kitchen, *Ancient Orient and Old Testament,* Chicago: Inter-Varsity, 1966, pp. 53-56. Abraham Malamat, "King Lists of the Old Babylonian Period and Biblical Genealogies," JAOS, LXXXVIII (1968), 170. T. C. Mitchell, "Genealogy," NBD, 456 ff. John C. Whitcomb and Henry M. Morris, *The Genesis Flood,* Nutley, N.J.: Presbyterian and Reformed, 1961, Appendix II, 474-489.

H. W. H.

GENEALOGY OF JESUS CHRIST. *See* Chronology, New Testament; Jesus Christ; Genealogy.

GENERATION.

1. The Heb. word *dôr* occurs *c.* 130 times in the OT and has the idea of a circle or cycle to be completed. Hence, it means the cycle of a man's life. It could have the idea of a man's life span, as in Gen 15:16. Abraham's descendants were to return to Canaan "in the fourth generation" after being afflicted 400 years in a land that was not theirs (15:13). Here *dôr* seems to be equivalent to Akkad. *dāru,* a lifetime, as seen in an inscription of Shamshi-Adad I of Assyria (see Kitchen, p. 54, n. 99).

Generally, however, it has the idea of a cycle beginning with a man's birth and ending with the birth of his son. It may speak of the generations of the past (Isa 51:8-9), of the future (Ps 49:11; Ex 31:16), of the past and future (Ps 102:24), of the present (Gen 6:9), or of the men of that generation (Ex 1:6). Besides the normal meaning, it also is used of a class of men both in a good sense (Ps 14:5; 24:6) and in a bad sense (Deut 32:5, 20). The Aram. cognate is used only four times with the general meaning of "generation" (Dan 4:3, 34).

2. The term *tôl^{e}dôth* is used *c.* 40 times in

the OT. The word is always in the plural and hence it has the meaning "offsprings" or "generations," being formed from *yālad* which means "to beget," "to bear." This word is more concerned with the descendants of a man, and consequently it is the term that is used in the genealogical history of a man or family (cf. its repeated usage in Num 1:20-40). It occurs frequently in Genesis, and on this basis the book may be divided into 11 sections, each being styled with the words "the generations of..." (2:4; 5:1; 6:9; 10:1; 11:10; 11:27; 25:12; 25:19; 36:1; 36:9; 37:2). Whether the term *tôl^{e}dôth* introduces what is to follow (E. J. Young) or concludes what has preceded like a colophon on a cuneiform tablet (R. K. Harrison) is a technical point still being debated.

3. The Gr. word *genea* occurs around 40 times in the NT, and is the common term in the LXX as a translation of *dôr.* It has the concept of the sum total of those born at the same time—contemporaries (Mt 11:16; 12:41), a period of time (Acts 15:21, NASB; Eph 3:5, NASB; Col 1:26), or a kind of people (Lk 16:8).

4. The Gr. *genesis* occurs five times in the NT (Mt 1:1, 18; Lk 1:14; Jas 1:23; 3:6, see NASB marg.) and is used chiefly in the LXX as a translation of *tôl^{e}dôth.* It has the basic meaning of "origin," "birth," or "existence." Our name for the book of Genesis is from the Gr. title Genesis, which has the added meaning of "origin" or "generation." The whole book was thought of as the "Book of Generations" from this phrase as found in the LXX in 2:4*a* and 5:1.

5. Gr. *gennema* is used only four times in the NT (Mt 3:7; 12:34; 23:33; Lk 3:7). It has the basic meaning of "offspring" and in each case it is used in the phrase "generation of vipers," or "offspring of vipers."

6. Although *genos* occurs *c.* 20 times in the NT it is translated "generation" in the KJV only in I Pet 2:9. Basically the term connotes the meaning of "race," and it is so translated in the ASV, RSV and NASB.

In conclusion, the term "generation" has the basic meaning of a span of time, usually from a man's birth to the birth of his son. This span of time varies within the Scriptures, for according to Job 42:16 it was reckoned 30 to 40 years; in Deut 1:35; 2:14; etc., it was the 40 year period of the wilderness wanderings; and in Gen 15:13, 16 it was a period of approximately 100 years. The length of generations varies at different periods of history.

Bibliography. P. R. Ackroyd, "The Meaning of the Hebrew Dôr Considered," JSS, XIII (1968), 3-10. W. F. Albright, "Abram the Hebrew: A New Archaeological Interpretation," BASOR #163 (Oct., 1961), 50-51. R. K. Harrison, *Introduction to the Old Testament,* Grand Rapids: Eerdmans, 1969, pp. 543-551. K. A. Kitchen, *Ancient Orient and Old Testament,* Chicago: Inter-Varsity, 1966, pp. 53 f. F. J. Neuberg, "An Unrecognized Meaning of Hebrew Dôr," JNES, IX (1950), 215-217. E. J. Young, *An Introduction to the Old Testament,* Grand Rapids: Eerdmans, 1949, pp. 52-66.

H. W. H.

GENESIS (jĕn'ĕ-sĭs). The first book of the Bible and the first book of Moses is named from the Gr. title given to it in consequence of its subject matter. The name means "beginnings," or the name could refer to the genealogies which are so prominent in the early chapters (cf. Gen 2:4 and 5:1 with Mt 1:1). In Heb. the book was named after its first word, *berē'shît,* according to the usual Heb. practice. The word means "in the beginning."

Genesis is part of a larger work, the five books of Moses called the Pentateuch (*q.v.*). There is a uniform plan discernible in the Pentateuch. The early history goes down to the end of Genesis. Exodus carries on the history of Israel to the encampment at Sinai and the consecration of the tabernacle. Leviticus gives the laws, many of which were promulgated at Sinai. Numbers begins with the preparations for the first attempt to invade Canaan and carries the history to the end of the wilderness wanderings. Deuteronomy in large measure repeats the laws and histories of Sinai and the wilderness period in sermonic form, as the basis for the nation's renewal of its covenant vows. Genesis, then, seems to be part of the larger work, Scroll I of the Pentateuch. It is the only source for the pre-Exodus period; Deuteronomy does not rehearse this material. I Chronicles quotes extensively from the genealogies of Genesis, and other OT passages refer to it rather often. But Genesis is unique in its content.

Date and Authorship

The historic view. The time-honored view of the date and authorship of Genesis can be briefly stated. With one voice the Jews and the Christian church acknowledged the Mosaic authorship of the book until the rise of higher criticism in the 19th cen. It can hardly be doubted that this is the position witnessed in Neh 8-9. The book from which the Levites read is called the "book of the law of Moses" (Neh 8:1). But in Nehemiah's prayer (Neh 9) the history of Israel is summarized, beginning with creation and the call of Abram, continuing with the Exodus, Sinai, the rebellion at Kadesh-barnea, a quotation from Ex 34:6 (Neh 9:17), the wilderness experiences, the Transjordan conquest and, briefly, the later history of Israel. In short, the subject material of the whole Pentateuch beginning with Genesis is given. This witness gains somewhat from the tendency of recent scholars to agree with and ascribe the historic late 5th cen. dates to Ezra-Nehemiah and the books of Chronicles (F. L. Cross, *The Ancient Library of Qumran* [1961], p. 189; John Bright, *History of Israel* [1959], p. 383).

That Moses wrote the law is taught repeatedly in the OT (cf. Josh 1:7-9; 23:6; I Kgs

Abraham's well near Hebron as later incorporated into the temple of Hadrian. HFV

2:3; 8:53, 56; Ezr 7:6; etc.). In references to Israel's history, the events of Genesis are quoted in the same sequence with Exodus, Leviticus, Numbers, and Deuteronomy. In addition to the sequence in Neh 9, the historical Ps 105 is another case in point. Also the allusions in Hosea to the ancient history of the nation refer with equal facility to Genesis (Hos 12:3-4, 12), to Exodus (Hos 12:13; 13:4), to Leviticus (Hos 12:9), to Numbers (Hos 9:10), to Deuteronomy (ref. to Zeboim, Hos 11:8), and to later books. Genesis was clearly part of Israel's early sacred history.

In the NT Christ began at "Moses and all the prophets" expounding the messianic prophecies in "all the scriptures" (Lk 24:27). It is clear that Jesus considered the first book of the Bible Mosaic. Indeed, one of His names for the OT is "Moses and the prophets" (Lk 16:29, 31; cf. Jn 5:46-47; Mt 5:17; Lk 24:44). It is clear that the apostles used the terminology (Acts 26:22; 28:23). At the same time, Christ referred to many items in the Genesis record as part of the inspired Scriptures (Mt 19:4-6; 24:38; Lk 17:32; Jn 7:22). It is clear that Christ and the apostles held to the Mosaic authorship of Genesis. The Jewish historian Josephus expressly stated the same view in about A.D. 90 (*Against Apion* 1.8). No ancient authority of value brings this view into question.

As to the date of Genesis, the conservative position settles on the period of the wilderness wandering, about 1440-1400 B.C., because of the Mosaic authorship. The traditional date of the Exodus is calculated from the reference in I Kgs 6:1 as 480 years before Solomon began his temple. There is room for some slight elasticity here. The LXX text has 440 years. The date of Solomon's temple is about 960 B.C. With these figures the data in Jud 11:26 agree. An alternative dating of about 1250 B.C. is urged by some on the basis of certain archaeological data, but there seems to be no compelling reason to depart from the date most agreeable to the biblical text. *See* Exodus, Date of.

Critical views. With the rise of the rationalistic movement in Germany around A.D. 1800, the Mosaic authorship of all the Pentateuch was questioned. These views may be traced in any standard OT introduction (see Gleason L. Archer, *Survey of OT Introduction,* 1974, pp. 66–219).

The critical view has passed through several stages. First Genesis was divided into two documents on the basis of the different divine names Elohim and Jehovah (the Heb. consonants of which are YHWH). At first it was thought that these were two old documents woven together by Moses himself. Soon, however, the analysis was extended to the rest of the Pentateuch where the same phenomenon appears, and then the compiler was said to have lived long after Moses. The Mosaic authorship of the whole Pentateuch was thus denied.

It was noticed, however, that the general style of parts of the Elohim document differed from the Jehovah document, whereas other parts more or less resembled it. So the Elohim document was divided into an E_1 and E_2. The book of Deuteronomy was also isolated as containing much work of another source. There were thus four documents, E_1, E_2, J, and D. Some critics using similar criteria—that every alleged difference in style betokened a different author—divided up the Pentateuch into many fragments.

It remained for Wellhausen in about 1875 to set the patterns of thought for many years. He argued that these four documents, which he called J, E, D, P, could be dated by comparing their legal and historical references to the known history and legal picture of ancient Israel. If a document refers only to late legislation, the document is surely late.

One trouble with Wellhausen's theory was that in those days scholars were woefully ignorant of the history of the ancient Near East, let alone of the history of Israel, and Wellhausen all too often was left to reconstruct an artificial history. He did this quite confidently using the Hegelian philosophy of evolutionary progress, which was the last word in Wellhausen's day (1875). It is not remarkable, therefore, that when Wellhausen was done, he was able to show a beautiful progression in thought and culture from rude beginnings in Israel's history to its flowering expression in the 8th cen. prophets. It was a noble expression of Victorian ideology.

Two things have combined to overthrow Wellhausen's imposing edifice. First, the Hegelian philosophy of the evolutionary progress of history has largely given way to a more pessimistic existentialism since World War II. Secondly, the study of archaeology took great strides forward with the discovery of many additional clay tablets since the First World War and with the scientific unearthing of Palestinian cities. Whereas ancient history once began with Greece and Rome, and Herodotus was called the "father of history," now high school textbooks go back to 3000 B.C. for the start of written history, and there is much still earlier material in stratified sequence.

The notable thing, however, is that this wealth of ancient history fits beautifully with the biblical record. For example, the remains of people of Sumer who lived in lower Mesopotamia were discovered. The Bible called it the land of Shinar, which Heb. word is a good representation of "Sumer" (Gen 10:10; 11:2; 14:1). The Hurrian people were rediscovered with their customs and language. The Bible called them Horites. The ancient city of Uruk (biblical Erech) was uncovered and the oldest written tablets (from c. 3300 B.C.) were found there. The exploits of the great king Sargon of Accad of c. 2350 B.C. were discovered. Accad has not yet been identified, but Accad, Erech and Babel are all mentioned in Gen 10:10.

Ancient kings, ancient peoples, ancient cities, ancient cultures and ancient languages have been resurrected from centuries of oblivion. But the Bible all along preserved the kings,

The Patriarchs lived in tents and their "expanded families" must have created tent villages similar to those still to be seen in Palestine. HFV

cities and peoples in the right sequences and connections, and reflected the ancient cultures in the most natural ways. For a writing made up from a hodgepodge of sources by a later editor having very limited knowledge, this would be well·nigh a miracle. Archaeology has proved at least the substantial historicity of the biblical records. And nowhere has this work been more welcome than in the book of Genesis which, after all, concerns history of the distant past. Archaeological light is thrown on almost all parts of the book of Genesis. Further details are given. under the discussion of the book's content.

In the early portions of Genesis the Flood story was divided by Wellhausen into two documents J and P, the first source written *c.* 850 B.C., the second *c.* 450 B.C. Since then the Babylonian flood story has been discovered. It dates from long before the time of Moses. The relation between this story and the Bible is uncertain. Possibly both depended on ancient records and reports of the Flood itself. But at least both the J document and the later P document have interesting parallels with the early Babylonian flood story. A natural conclusion is that the documentary division is artificial and Wellhausen's datings are quite arbitrary.

Especially the patriarchal narratives of Genesis have been supported by tablets from the town of Nuzu and elsewhere which give the legal and family customs of Hurrian settlers in Semitic (Amorite and Aramaic) lands. These customs evidently were known by the patriarchs from their residence in Haran and Ur, and the close similarity of the patriarchal practices to the Nuzu laws is striking. Standard OT introductions give. details. One example will suffice. The birthright inheritance involving the double portion of a principal heir in Nuzu normally went to the oldest son. But it could be sold, and there is a case of the sale of a birthright for three sheep. Also it could be transferred by the father, and a case on record upholds the father's oral pronouncement in such a case (cf. Gen 48:17–20).

Notice that no such provisions or practices are found in Israel's later laws or history. The one passage in the Mosaic legislation dealing with birthrights forbids changing the natural order (Deut 21:15–17). Only in the patriarchal families are such customs witnessed. How would a late Israelite author like "J" at 850 B.C. or "P" at 450 B.C. know how to distinguish so accurately the ancient Mesopotamian background and customs of the patriarchs from the Mosaic legislation current in Israel?

Many such examples have driven recent OT scholars to accept the historicity even in detail of the patriarchal narratives. It is most difficult to combine this conclusion with Wellhausen's dictum of the late date of the alleged documents determined by comparing their background situations.

More recent critical study argues that the Pentateuch (and other historical books) were put together at a late date from early oral tradi-

The problem of water supply looms large in the patriarchal narrative. Here is the traditional well of Abraham at Beer-sheba. HFV

tions which were very faithfully preserved and transmitted. But opinions differ as to whether these oral traditions were all written down together after the Exile or were the background of J, E, D, and P, the usual Wellhausian documents which were combined after the Exile. In either case, the theory seems very unnatural. Writing was exceedingly common in all Mesopotamia and Egypt long before the patriarchal period. Why should it be thought that Israel alone of the nations had no written literature? This conclusion is especially odd when it is remembered that it was probably in Syria-Palestine that the alphabet was invented—the most convenient tool known for written expression!

It is true that ancient documents from Palestine have been almost completely lost except for the later Dead Sea Scrolls. But the explanation is not that they had no literature. It is simply that their literature has perished. If they had used cuneiform signs and had written on clay, the material would have lasted. But evidently they wrote on papyrus and skins. These items last well in the dry climate of Egypt, but in the rainy climate of Palestine they soon perish. It may indeed be true that the ancient Heb. people memorized much, and loved to recite their epics and religious literature. But that they did not also have the written word is pure theory. The archaeological support for the Genesis histories and laws is an impressive argument in favor of the witness of both the OT and the NT that Genesis and the rest of the Pentateuch is old, authoritative, and Mosaic.

Outline of Genesis

Content of the Book

Plan. It has often been pointed out that the author of Genesis wrote on a unified plan. In almost every case he tells the story of Israel proceeding from the general to the particular. He first tells of the entire world, or the entire race, or all the descendants of a man; then he concentrates on the specific, on a garden which he presents in detail, or the segment of the race important in the history, or the descendants of a man who carries on the line with which he is concerned.

Thus the first chapter deals with creation as a whole. Chaps. 2 and 3 give the picture of Adam, the fountainhead of the history. Chap. 4 gives the history and genealogy of Cain, who is not heard of again. Chap. 5, however, gives the genealogy of Seth which connects with Noah. After the Flood, the colonization of the whole Near East is given first in chap. 10; then comes the genealogy leading to Abraham. In the patriarchal histories, Ishmael is treated before Isaac; the descendants of Esau, before Jacob. Obviously Genesis as we have it is the work of one master mind, an author of competence using his materials skillfully and under the inspiration of the Spirit.

Creation narratives. Volumes have been written on the first chapter of Genesis. Two items are of special interest: first, the relation to Babylonian cosmogonies; and second, the relation to modern science.

As to the relation to Babylonian creation myths, the matter is discussed extensively in A. Heidel, *The Babylonian Genesis* (1951). The Babylonian story starts with warfare among the gods. The second generation of gods rebel against the first. Marduk is victorious. He vanquishes the goddess Tiamat and splits her dead body into halves making the heaven and earth. He creates man from the blood of her ally Kingu. There is no clear relation between the biblical account and the Babylonian stories.

As to scientific problems, the Genesis account gives few details. There is much truth in the statement that the Bible is not a book of science but of religion. Nevertheless, Genesis is clear that God made the worlds and is the Lord of nature as well as of spirits. Therefore where the Bible touches on science, it must be held to be correct when fairly and accurately interpreted. The Bible in Gen 1 and elsewhere declares that God created the worlds out of nothing. Matter is not eternal. With this view the current theories of science have no quarrel. One major claim is that all matter originated in a vast nuclear explosion some ten billion years ago. Science cannot say what caused the explosion. Genesis says, "In the beginning God. . . ."

The apparent great antiquity of the universe has been a problem. A theory of recent days has been that Gen 1:1 speaks of the distant creation of matter; v. 2 tells of a catastrophe which overtook creation at a fairly recent date; the following verses tell of quite recent events on the earth.

Another theory has been that the creative days of Genesis are not to be viewed as actual days in which events took place but as days on which God revealed certain items to Moses. They were "revelatory days." This view and variations of it do not seem to do justice to the meaning of the biblical text.

Another view, popularized by J. Whitcomb and H. Morris in *The Genesis Flood* (1961), suggests that the universe is not actually old. It appears to be old because God created it "fully grown" with the appearance of age. This view has some attractive features but has some philosophical problems too. Would God have created sedimentary rocks with fossils already in them? The view is usually associated with the idea that the Flood caused many fossils which are therefore of recent origin. It is a question if this view can be scientifically sustained.

A fourth view, held widely for many years, is that the days of Gen 1 were not 24 hour days but were periods of greater or longer extent. They began before the sun was established to mark the days, and the seventh day of God's rest from creation is still continuing, it would seem. This view is in general accord with scientific thought of today. Those who hold it argue that Gen 1:14 refers to the clearing away of dense clouds so that the sun and moon which were previously established became visible. The writer favors this view, but it should be remembered that scientific estimates of the age of the earth may well be wrong. Many present estimates depend upon astronomical and radiation theories which are of recent origin and which are not always self-consistent. There is room for reserve and further study of all these theories.

Gen 2:4-25 tells of the specific and separate creation of our first parents. The garden of

Eden was located in the Mesopotamian southland where the four rivers are located. (Ethiopia, Gen 2:13, is more properly Cush, the territory E of the Tigris.) Gen 2:5 probably refers not to the whole earth, but to paradise alone which was watered by irrigation from underground sources. (Heb. *'ēd,* "mist," from Akkad. *edû* seems to mean an underground flow.) Nothing in this section refers to anything in the earth outside of Eden. As to the alleged evolutionary origin of all species from one original germ and the evolutionary origin of man as well, cf. Carl F. H. Henry, "Theology and Evolution" in *Evolution and Christian Thought Today,* ed. R. Mixter (1959). *See* Creation.

The genealogical data. Four main genealogies are found in the early chapters: that of Cain (chap. 4), the antediluvians and postdiluvians (chaps. 5 and 11), and the Table of Nations (chap. 10). The contrast is plainest between chaps. 10 and 11. The so-called Table of Nations is not a genealogy at all. It is an outline of the result by Moses' time of the colonizing of the Near East after the Flood. In the movement of tribes and nations, some genealogical relations are involved; but in the peopling of Canaan, for instance (10:15-18), Canaan is said to "beget" peoples not individuals. Heth was apparently Indo-European, the Jebusite was probably Hurrian. The Amorite was of course Semitic but is found among the "sons" of Ham. One of the "sons" of Ham was Mizraim. This was the ancient name for Egypt and is a noun of dual formation referring to the union of upper and lower Egypt about 3000 B.C.

That there are omissions in the genealogies found in chaps 5 and 10 is a view widely held. Numerous other genealogies show such gaps. Thus four generations are reckoned from Levi to Moses (Ex 6:16-20), but the Levites in the generation of Moses and Aaron numbered 22,000 men (Num 3:39). Also, if the genealogy in Gen 11 is complete, Shem and his son. Arphaxad actually outlived Abraham! This is not the picture one gets from the Abrahamic narratives. Recognition of these and other points has convinced most that Ussher's dates for creation (4004 B.C.) and the Flood (2350 B.C.) must be pushed back by an undetermined number of years.

The Flood narrative. The Bible plainly says that there was a flood, worldwide in its extent, sent by God to eradicate sinful mankind. The Mesopotamian peoples had a flood tradition, as did many other cultures. The Babylonian story has been studied and compared with the Bible by A. Heidel in *The Gilgamesh Epic* (1949). It is reasonable to conclude that similarities are found because both accounts reflect the actual occurrence.

Scientific evidence for the Flood is lacking, but so is evidence against it. Calculation of the size of the ark has often been made, and it has been shown to have the requisite capacity for all the animals (A. M. Rehwinkel, *The Flood,* St. Louis: Concordia Pub. House [1951], pp. 68 ff.). It may be that the Flood was not so simple a phenomenon as has been imagined. It could possibly have been a heavy deluge of rain, plus movements in the earth's crust making the ocean levels rise, plus heavy and long-continued snow in the higher altitudes and northern latitudes. It seems clear that there was a great change of climate about 10,000 years ago. The widely publicized Siberian mammoths apparently lived in a climate with buttercups (found in their mouths) and abundant grass. They were instantaneously frozen, some still on their feet, and have stayed frozen ever since so that their meat is preserved! *See* Flood.

Abraham's life. Abraham was undoubtedly not the only God-fearing man of that time. God surely had spoken to many individuals, such as Enoch before the Flood and Melchizedek afterward. But with Abraham, God determined to do a new thing—to gather His people into one place and by intensive revelation of His word and grace to prepare a large cohesive group of people for the advent of Christ and the blessing of the nations. It may be noted that Palestine was a land bridge, and the caravans of three continents crossed its boundaries. The Jews in Palestine and by their Messiah were truly to be a light to the nations (Isa 42:6; 49:6; 51:4).

God chose Abraham, instructed him in sacrifice, and gave him the covenant sign of circumcision. Circumcision was practiced in Egypt and elsewhere at the age of puberty, but as far as is known the infant circumcision of the Jews was unique in antiquity. It was a sign of both race and grace (Gen 17:14; Deut 30:6; Rom 2:29). Later the Abrahamic clan became welded into a nation by Moses. But the bases of the faith of Israel were clear in Abraham. Indeed, the ritual of sacrifice was as old as Adam. Abraham, believing in one true, living God, had a spiritual and ethical monotheism. He recognized human sin, offered sacrifices for cleansing, hoped in the Redeemer to come and in eternal heavenly fellowship with God (Gen 22:8, 18; John 8:56; Heb 11:10). The cultural background of Abraham is now brilliantly illuminated from Ur, Mari, Nuzu, and other discoveries. *See* Abraham; Patriarchal Age.

Isaac and Jacob. Isaac's life is little known, as he was overshadowed by his more famous father and son. Isaac, however, was a peaceful man who turned the other cheek to Abimelech (Gen 26:17-31). He too received the messianic promise (26:4). *See* Isaac.

Jacob has perhaps been dealt with harshly. He (really his mother) schemed for the birthright. But it should be remembered that it had been promised by God to the younger twin (25:23), and Jacob apparently desired the birthright for spiritual rather than monetary reasons. Jacob at Bethel consecrated himself to the Lord (28:20-22). Jacob and his wives ascribed the birth of their children to God's answer to prayer (Gen 30). Even Jacob's increase of his sheep, though due in part to his industry, partly to his superstition about prenatal influence and in part perhaps to some observation of principles of heredity, is nonetheless ascribed in the last analysis to God's providence (31:9, 42). Jacob's prayer at Peniel was based on God's promises as well as obedience to God's commands (32:9–12). In the wrestling with the angel Jacob asked for God's blessing rather than for material advantage (32:25–30). In dealing with Esau he ascribed all his advancement to God (33:11). *See* Jacob.

Joseph in Egypt. The story of Joseph has been a perennial favorite. Its real message is not merely the story of rags to riches, but how God in fine details of providence accomplished His perfect will. Joseph's future was foretold by God. Apparently Joseph believed it, though the rest of the family were irritated at his dreams.

When young men leave home for trade or war they often either grow tall or fall badly. Joseph grew tall. When no one was watching but God, Joseph lived for God even though he suffered because of his integrity. But in prison he still believed and maintained his character, and at last God blessed him and used him like few other individuals.

Joseph apparently became the grand vizier of Egypt under one of the foreign Asiatic Hyksos kings. The Hyksos period was *c.* 1750–1570 B.C., though various dynasties reigned in this period. Some have held that Joseph's ascendancy happened before the Hyksos (Exodus at 1440 B.C., I Kgs 6:1; bondage of 430 years, Ex 12:40, making Joseph's date 1870 B.C.). This view is argued by Gleason Archer (*op. cit.*, pp. 205–208) following John Rea ("Time of the Oppression and the Exodus," BETS, III [1960], 58–59).

An alternative view supported by the LXX is that the period of 430 years includes both the patriarchal residence in Canaan (215 years) and the Egyptian bondage (1655–1440 B.C.). Thus Joseph's governorship began during the Hyksos dynasty. The Hyksos introduced chariots into Egypt (cf. Gen 41:43). They changed land tenure so that all land was owned by the crown except temple lands. Thereafter the crown exacted a 20 percent tax (cf. Gen 47:20–26). However, the details are obscure partly because little is known of the Hyksos. The date of the Exodus itself is under debate, although the biblical evidence as given above seems clear (cf. I Kgs 6:1; Jud 11:26).

Joseph's sterling character was finally shown not in adversity but in prosperity, where he wisely and carefully tested his brethren, then freely forgave *and forgot.* Thus by his magnanimity he laid the basis for the expansion of Israel into the nation that God had predicted. No other man was more aware of God's overruling providence. *See* Joseph.

Genesis closes with the great messianic prophecy of Jacob (Gen 49:10, treated by the writer in an appendix in J. O. Buswell's *Systematic Theology of the Christian Religion* [1963]. II, 544). The touching story is briefly told of Jacob's death and burial in the cave of Machpelah, and Joseph's directions for his own embalming and eventual burial in the land of Ca-

naan when God should have fulfilled His promises to Israel.

Bibliography. Gleason L. Archer, *A Survey of Old Testament Introduction,* Chicago: Moody Press, 1964. John Bright, *A History of Israel,* Philadelphia: Westminster Press, 1959. U. Cassuto, *Commentary on Genesis,* 2 vols., Jerusalem: Magnes Press, 1964. Jack Finegan, *Light from the Ancient Past,* 2nd ed., Princeton: Univ. Press, 1959. Cyrus H. Gordon, *The World of the Old Testament,* New York: Doubleday, 1958. Alexander Heidel, *The Babylonian Genesis,* 2nd ed., Chicago: Univ. of Chicago Press, 1951; *The Gilgamesh Epic and Old Testament Parallels,* 2nd ed., Chicago: Univ. of Chicago Press, 1949. Walter C. Kaiser, "The Literary Form of Genesis 1–11," NPOT, pp. 48–65. Ernest F. Kevan, "Genesis," NBC, 1953. Derek Kidner, *Genesis,* London: Tyndale Press, 1967. K. A. Kitchen, *Ancient Orient and the Old Testament,* Chicago: Inter-Varsity Press, 1966. H. C. Leupold, *Exposition of Genesis,* Columbus: Wartburg Press, 1942. E. A. Speiser, *Genesis* (Anchor Bible), Garden City, N.Y.: Doubleday, 1964. W. H. Griffith Thomas, *Genesis—A Devotional Commentary,* Grand Rapids: Eerdmans, 1946. J. A. Thompson, *The Bible and Archaeology,* Grand Rapids: Eerdmans, 1962. G. Van Groningen, "Interpretation of Genesis," JETS, XIII (1970), 199–218. John C. Whitcomb and Henry M. Morris, *The Genesis Flood,* Philadelphia: Presbyterian and Reformed Pub. Co., 1962. K. M. Yates, "Genesis," WBC, 1962; consult for further bibliography. Edward J. Young, *Genesis 3,* London: Banner of Truth Trust, 1966.

R. L. H.

GENNESARET (gĕ-nĕs′á-rĕt). The Gr. form of the Heb. name Chinnereth (*q.v.*) for the Sea of Galilee, found in the LXX and Mt 14:34; Mk 6:53; Lk 5:1. *See* Galilee, Sea of; Palestine, II. B. 3. *c.*

GENTILES. The plural of the word "nation" (Heb. *gôy;* Gr. *ethnos*) has sometimes been translated "nations," sometimes "Gentiles," sometimes "heathen." "Gentiles" has applied to all nations other than the Jewish without reflecting antipathy necessarily. "Heathen" has reflected a strong antipathy (II Kgs 16:3; Ezr 6:21; Ps 9:5, 15, 19).

In its early use, the word "Gentiles" or "nations" (*gôyim*) was applied without distinction to divisions among the descendants of Shem, Ham, and Japheth (Gen 10:5, 20, 31). The background for distinctions appeared in spiritual ideals for Israel held up by the Lord Himself. The promise concerning Abraham's seed (Gen 12:3) was interpreted by the first covenant at Sinai as making true believers in Israel an elect nation, chosen as a kingdom of priests to teach other nations about Yahweh (Ex 19:4–6). These ideals gave warrant for the description of

Israelites who "keep justice" and "do righteousness" as "thy nation," i.e., Yahweh's nation (Ps 106:5), while other nations are called "the nations," i.e., Gentiles (Isa 60:3; Acts 13:47). *See* Foreigners; Nations.

Perversion of the ideal relations led to emphasis upon the fact that "the nations" were identified with idolatry and basely corrupt (Lev 18:24). In turn Israelites often forgot to be priests of Yahweh. The forgetful Israelites considered Gentiles merely as "heathen" (Ps 9:5; 10:16).

The bitterness on both sides is marked for removal by missions. Hate is contrary to the heart of God (Jon 4:10-11). The Gentile nations are also to become the heritage of Messiah (Ps 2:8; Isa 42:1, 6; 49:6). Israelites and Gentiles are to be accepted as co-leaders in the messianic kingdom (Isa 66:12, 19-23). Followers of Jesus, Jews or Gentiles, are commanded to make disciples of all peoples (Mt 28:19-20). Paul described the redemption of Christ and faith in His work as resulting in the breaking down of "the middle wall of partition" between Jew and Gentile (Eph 2:14). This has reference to the partition wall which fenced out Gentiles from the inner courts of the Herodian temple. *See* Middle Wall of Partition; Commission, Great; Dispersion of Mankind; Nations.

J. W. W.

GENTILES, COURT OF THE. *See* Temple.

GENTLENESS. This term in English indicates moderation in action, refinement in mannerisms and disposition, and the absence of that which is precipitate and rough. The Heb. term is *ānâ*, with the basic meaning "to bend low," "to condescend." Cf. God's clemency toward mankind (Ps 18:35). Four terms are used for gentleness in the NT:

1. Gr. *chrēstotēs* (Tit 3:4; Rom 2:4; II Cor 6:6; Eph 2:7; Gal 5:22; Col 3:12), with the general meaning of "benignity," "sweetness," "potential goodness," "moral goodness and integrity." Josephus ascribes it to the nature of Isaac. Old mellow wine was referred to as *chrēstos*. The pagans seemed to confuse *chrēstos* with the name of Christ, *Christos*, which could not be considered a total mistake in the light of Christ's nature. He Himself speaks of His yoke (Mt 11:30) as being *chrēstos*, i.e., one which does not chafe or irk or gall, but is smooth and even. Hence, the term suggests that gracious nature which mellows that which otherwise would have been harsh and austere.

2. Gr. *prautēs*, "gentleness," "mildness," "meekness," "forbearance" (I Cor 4:21; II Cor 10:1; Gal 5:23). The term seems also to specify courtesy, considerateness, and a humble, unassuming spirit (II Tim 2:25).

3. Gr. *ēpios*, "affable," "kindness toward someone" (I Thess 2:7; II Tim 2:24).

4. Gr. *epieikeia*, which would indicate that which is equitable, fair, mild, gentle, seemly, or

a sweet reasonableness (Phil 4:5; I Tim 3:3; Tit 3:2). It is the opposite of contention and self-seeking, and is defined by Aristotle as "equity, or fairness of mind." Little wonder, then, that Paul specifies this as one of the qualities of a church official.

There is yet another similar term (*philanthrōpia*) which, while not translated "gentleness," carries the basic concept of "courtesy," "kindness," or "love to one's fellowman" (Acts 27:3; 28:2; Tit 3:4).

R. E. Pr.

GENUBATH (gḗ-nū'băth). Son of Hadad, the fugitive Edomite prince (I Kgs 11:19-20), who was brought up in Egypt with sons of Pharaoh. David's conquering of Edom necessitated the flight (I Kgs 11:15-20). Genubath's mother was a sister of Tahpenes, queen of the Pharaoh of Egypt.

GERA (gēr'á)

1. The son of Bela and grandson of Benjamin. In Genesis he is called the son of Benjamin and listed with those who went down to Egypt (Gen 46:21; I Chr 8:3, 5).

2. A Benjamite, the father of Ehud the judge (Jud 3:15).

3. A Benjamite of Bahurim, the father of Shimei who cursed David (II Sam 16:5; 19:16, 18; I Kgs 2:8).

4. The son of Ehud, a Benjamite, who was removed (KJV) or exiled (RSV) with his brothers to Manahath (I Chr 8:7).

GERAH. *See* Weights, Measures, and Coins.

GERAR (gēr'är). A city located in the southern extremity of Canaanite settlement. During the patriarchal period its inhabitants were known as Philistines (Gen 20:1 f.; 26:1, 6, 17, 20, 26). Some scholars suggest that Geder in Josh 12:13 may be a case of scribal confusion between *r* and *d* and should be read Gerar. This would associate the town with Hormah (*q.v.*) and Arad (*q.v.*). In I Chr 4:39-41 the LXX reads Gerara, while the MT has Gedor. The Simeonites occupied this area in Hezekiah's time. Asa defeated Zerah at Marisha and pursued his troops as far as Gerar (II Chr 14:13-14). Here the MT has Gerar, while the LXX has Gedor.

Eusebius (*Onomasticon*, 60. 7 ff.) described Gerar as being 25 miles from Eleutheropolis, which fits the location of Tell Abu Hureira (16 miles NW of Beer-sheba on the N side of the Wadi esh-Sheri'ah). Recent surveys have found ceramics on that site which show occupation during the Chalcolithic and in the Middle Bronze I and II plus the Iron Age periods. It is a huge tell of 40 acres with an upper citadel, possibly surrounded by a Hyksos glacis. Gerar is not mentioned in any existing Egyptian records or the Amarna letters.

A. F. R.

GERASA (gĕr'ă-să). One of a league of ten semi-independent cities (the Decapolis of Mt 4:25; Mk 5:20; 7:31). Gerasa (Jerash) is pleasantly situated in an open, fertile valley E of the Jordan, i.e., in the OT land of Gilead. Its spectacular archaeological remains are now readily accessible via the northward extension of the Dead Sea highway. The site was occupied in the Bronze Age and a city must have existed there under a Semitic name in the Iron Age, but it is not mentioned in the OT. The extant remains are those of the Gr. city, founded probably by Antiochus IV (175–163 B.C.) under the name Antioch on the Chrysorrhoas, a N tributary of the Jabbok. It was greatly expanded and monumentalized in the Roman and Byzantine periods. It had a territory and presumably a constitution of its own. Macedonian citizens are mentioned in inscriptions. Alexander Jannaeus (107–76 B.C.) incorporated it in the Jewish state, therefore its Jewish inhabitants. It was restored by Pompey (63 B.C.) to such independence as it and the other cities of the league enjoyed thereafter under the Roman governors of Syria and Arabia.

Mark (5:1), followed by Luke (8:26, 37), associates with the "land of the Gerasenes" Jesus' healing of a demoniac, the story implying that the city territory extended to the shore of the Lake of Galilee. This association seems to have been doubted by Matthew who, according to the preferred reading, substituted "land

Main street, Jerash. HFV

of the Gadarenes" (Mt 8:28). Scribes copying Gospel MSS adapted Matthew, Mark and Luke to each other. The Caesarean text, influenced by Origen, substituted "land of the Gergesenes," to complicate the attestation further. Borders of city territories are only rarely known and those of Gerasa are unknown. The fact that Gadara and its territory lie between Gerasa and the Lake of Galilee explains Matthew's reading, but Gadara too is S of the Yarmuk River. The only corresponding free city E of the lake is Hippos. The location of Origen's Gergesa is unknown. *See* Gadara.

Its colonnaded streets laid out in accordance with Roman city planning, Gerasa provides the best example of progressive urban development in Palestine in Roman times. Its monumental structures include a triumphal arch, hippodrome, temples of Zeus, of Artemis and of the Arabian god, a nymphaeum, two baths and two theaters. In Byzantine times the temple of the Arabian god was replaced by the Christian cathedral church, the fountain in its atrium being the site of the annual reenactment of the Cana miracle according to Epiphanius (*Panarion,* Her. 51:30, 1–2). It and ten other churches, one a rebuilt synagogue, have been excavated. Excavations (1927–1934) were conducted at the site by Yale University and the British and American Schools of Jerusalem. Further clearances by the Jordan Department of Antiquities are in process. See C. H. Kraeling, *Gerasa, City of the Decapolis,* ASOR, 1938. *See* Archaeology.

C. H. K.

GERASENE (gĕr'ă-sēn). A term derived from Gerasa, meaning an inhabitant of Gerasa (*q.v.*) or the nearby region. Two towns bear this name. The Roman Gerasa (Jerash) is too far distant from the Sea of Galilee. This term describes a district on the eastern shore of the Sea of Galilee where Jesus healed the demoniac (Mt 8:28; Mk 5:1; Lk 8:26, 37).

GERGESA. *See* Gadara.

GERGESENE (gûr'gĕ-sēn). To be identified with Gerasene. The terms "country of the Gerasenes" and "country of the Gadarenes" (Mk 5:1; Lk 8:26, 37, see KJV and RSV) are to be preferred to "country of the Gergesenes." *See* Gerasene.

GERIZIM (gĕr'ĭ-zĭm). A mountain 2,849 feet high in central Palestine S of the valley in which the city of Shechem was located. It is sometimes called the mount of blessing because Moses directed that the blessings were to be read from Gerizim while the curses were to be read from Mount Ebal on the opposite side of the valley (Deut 11:29; 27:12 f.; Josh 8:33).

A ledge part way up the mountain is popularly called Jotham's pulpit, from which he supposedly shouted his famous tree fable to the people below (Jud 9:7 ff.). The acoustic properties of the area make it possible for a voice to carry for great distances from certain spots on the mountain.

The Samaritans built a temple on top of Mount Gerizim, probably during the 4th cen. B.C. The Jewish Hasmonean king John Hyrcanus destroyed this temple in 128 B.C. However, the Samaritans still worshiped on Mount Gerizim in Jesus' day (Jn 4:20 f.), and continue to worship there now. The Samaritan synagogue is located in Nablus at the foot of Mount Gerizim.

Many traditions grew up around Gerizim. The Samaritans believe that there can still be seen the site of altars built by Adam, Seth, Noah, and Abraham. The last of these altars is said to have been erected for the sacrifice of Isaac.

Robert J. Bull of Drew University excavated at Tell er-Râs on the N slope of Mount Gerizim in 1964, unearthing the remains of a Roman temple in honor of Zeus erected by the emperor Hadrian (A.D. 117–138), and foundations of a Hellenistic structure which may have been the Samaritan temple destroyed by Hyrcanus (BASOR #180 [1965], pp. 37–41; AJA, LXXI [1967], 387–393).

In 1968 Robert Boling re-excavated a late Middle Bronze Age structure at Tananir, located on the lower N slope of Gerizim, c. 350 yards S of ancient Shechem. It was first discovered by G. Welter in 1931. The remains of four building phases (c. 1650–1540 B.C.) suggest a temple with rooms grouped around the central courtyard with a round stone pedestal for a sacred pillar. It is suggested Jotham may have stood on its ruins when he addressed the men of Shechem. A similar temple half the size was discovered at the Amman airport in 1955, also outside a city. One may assume these shrines served groups of tribes in covenant with one another (BA, XXXII [1969], 81–116).

R. L. S. and J. R.

GERSHOM (gûr'shŏm)

1. The firstborn son of Moses and Zipporah who was born in Midian (cf. Ex·2:22; 18:3; I Chr 23:13–16).

2. Same as Gershon, the eldest son of Levi (cf. Gen 46:11; Josh 21:6; I Chr 6:1, 16–17, 22, 43; 23:6–7). His descendants are termed Gershonites (q.v.) or the "sons of Gershom" (cf. I Chr 6:62, 71; 15:7).

3. A descendant of Phinehas, who was a priest and the grandson of Aaron. He was one of the "heads of houses" who returned with Ezra from Babylonia (cf. Ezr 8:2).

4. The father of Jonathan, who served as priest to the idolatrous worship practiced by the Danites in the times of the judges (Jud 18:30). An alternate textual tradition reads: "Gershom, son of Levi," thus equating him with the son of Moses (see 1). The substitution of "Manasseh" for "Moses" is explained in the Talmud by asserting that Jonathan did the work of Manasseh, and was therefore counted in his family.

Mount Gerizim. HFV

Descendants of Gershom were separated from the priestly line of Aaron in a post-Exilic genealogy (I Chr 23:13–16), and Shebuel is named as "chief officer in charge of the treasuries" (I Chr 23:16; 26:24, RSV).

D. W. D.

GERSHON (gûr'shŏn). See Gershom 2.

GERSHONITES (gûr'shŏ-nīts). The descendants of Gershon or Gershom (I Chr 6:17, 62, 71), one of the three sons of Levi; thus one of the three clans or main divisions of the Levites. Three apparent attitudes as to the order of importance of these three divisions may be noted in the OT.

1. Gershon, Kohath, and Merari are named in that order in Gen 46:11; Ex 6:16; Num 3:17; 26:57; I Chr 6:1, 16; 23:6, probably because Gershon was Levi's oldest son. Gershonites are mentioned first in a census notation (Num 26:57), in the genealogy of I Chr 6:16–30, and in the list of servants for the temple assembled by David (I Chr 23:7–11).

2. The Gershonites appear second after the Kohathites in Num 4:34–49 and Josh 21:6, 27–33, probably since the latter became dominant because the family of Aaron belonged to their clan. The Joshua passage shows that the cities assigned to the Gershonites were far removed from the city (Jerusalem) of the eventual temple.

3. They are mentioned third in the Chronicles account of David's bringing the ark to Jerusalem (I Chr 15:4–7) and third in II Chr 29:12. No Gershonites are mentioned in I Chr 24; II Chr 20:19 and 34:12.

J. R.

GESHAM (gĕsh'ăm). In I Chr 2:47 Gesham is listed as a descendant of Judah through Caleb. The KJV has "Gesham," but ASV has "Geshan."

GESHEM (gĕsh'ĕm). An Arabian who was one of the chief opponents of Nehemiah's plan to rebuild the wall of Jerusalem in 445 B.C. (cf. Neh 2:19; 6:1–2). He is almost certainly the Gashmu in Neh 6:6. In these verses he is simply referred to as "the Arabian," but the probability is that he was the ruler (king) of the whole province of Arabia.

Geshem is mentioned in at least two inscriptions. A Lihyanite inscription was found at al-ʿUla (biblical Dedan) in northwestern Arabia (cf. R. A. Bowman, IB, III, 681–682). An Aramaic inscription was on a silver bowl found at Tell el-Maskhutah (biblical Succoth) near the Suez Canal in Egypt. The inscription reads, "Qainu son of Geshem, king of Kedar." The bowl is now in the Brooklyn Museum. G. Ernest Wright says, "The evidence is accumulating that the territory ruled by his [Geshem's] dynasty was quite extensive, including southern Judah in which Lachish was a chief center, the ancient area of Edom, northern Arabia, Sinai, and some portion of the Nile Delta" (*Biblical Archaeology,* rev. ed., p. 207). He probably built the fine villa or palace and the so-called "solar temple" belonging to the Persian period found in the NE part of the ruined mound of Lachish.

R. L. S.

GESHUR (gĕsh'er). A small Aramean kingdom or city-state located in what is now Jaulan (NT period Gaulanitis), in the NW sector of Bashan.

It is mentioned several times in the story of Absalom (II Sam 3:3; 13:37; 14:23, 32; 15:8), as Maacah, the daughter of Talmai, its king, was the mother of Absalom, and Absalom fled to that country after killing Amnon. The kingdom was apparently later absorbed into the larger Aramean kingdom of Damascus.

GESHURI (gĕsh'ŭ-rī), **GESHURITES** (gĕsh'ŭ-rīts). The inhabitants of Geshur, an Aramean tribe on the W border of Bashan (Deut 3:14; Josh 12:5; 13:11). The Geshurites were not expelled by the half tribe of Manasseh to whom the land had been allotted (Josh 13:13). Talmai, a ruler of Geshur, gave his daughter Maacah to David in marriage (II Sam 3:3). The Geshurites and Aram seized the cities of Jair in the land of Gilead (I Chr 2:23). The land of the Geshurites is listed as land yet to be possessed (Josh 13:2). This may suggest another group of Geshurites in the Negeb.

GETHER (gē'thẽr). One of the sons of Aram (Gen 10:23), probably a grandson of Shem (I Chr 1:17). Evidently an Aramean town and kingdom. The clan of which Gether was the founder has not been identified.

GETHSEMANE (gĕth-sĕm'á-nẽ). From an Aramaic word probably meaning "oil press." It is mentioned in Mt 26:36 and Mk 14:32 as an "enclosed piece of ground" (ASV marg.) to which Jesus returned with His disciples. Lk

In the foreground is the Church of all Nations with the Roman Catholic Garden of Gethsemane to the left. Farther up the Mount of Olives is the Russian Orthodox Garden of Gethsemane. HFV

22:39-41 identifies it only as a "place" (*topos*) on the Mount of Olives. It is called "a garden" located E of the brook Kidron in Jn 18:1. It was a rather extensive area because the main body of disciples sat there while Peter, James, and John went farther up the hill with Jesus. Jesus went still farther in this large olive grove to be alone to pray, leaving the three between Him and the other eight.

There are four rival claimants for the authentic site: the Franciscan (Roman Catholic) garden nearest the highway with gnarled olive trees up to 900 years old and the Basilica of the Agony (the Church of All Nations) housing a traditional Rock of the Agony; the one near the Tomb of the Virgin to the N; the Greek Orthodox to the E; and the large Russian Orthodox orchard farther up the hill adjacent to the Church of Mary Magdalene, the latter being the most "restful."

G. A. T.

GEUEL (gū'ĕl). The son of Machi, a member of the tribe of Gad. He was sent out by Moses as one of the 12 spies to search out the land of Canaan (Num 13:15).

GEZER (gē'zĕr). A city at the border of the Philistine plain and the northern Shephelah (Judean foothills). It overlooked miles of fertile fields and controlled the juncture of the arterial highway from Egypt to Syria and the main road from the Mediterranean coast up the valley of Aijalon to the interior of the hill country and Jerusalem. The mound of its ancient ruins is now called Tell Jezer.

During the Middle and Late Bronze Ages Gezer must have been an important city-state, as the strength of its fortifications and various records would indicate. It appears on lists of cities conquered by the Eighteenth Dynasty pharaohs Thutmose III and Thutmose IV. The Amarna tablets reveal that the rulers of Gezer, Milkilu followed by two men who were possibly his sons, were intermittently rebellious and loyal to Egypt (J. F. Ross, "Gezer in the Tell el-Amarna Tablets," BA, XXX [1967], 62-70). In his famous stele Merneptah boasts that he has seized Gezer, apparently one of the keys in pacifying Canaan (ANET, p. 378).

At the time of the Israelite conquest of Canaan, the king of Gezer was named Horam. He rushed to the aid of Lachish but was defeated in the field by Joshua (Josh 10:33), and is therefore listed among the conquered rulers (Josh 12:12). The city, however, remained in Canaanite hands (Jud 1:29) until Israel became strong enough to put the inhabitants to forced labor (Josh 16:10). It was intended for a Levitical city in the inheritance of Ephraim (Josh 21:21; I Chr 6:67; cf. Josh 16:3; I Chr 7:28). During David's wars Gezer was a strategic point on the Philistine border (II Sam 5:25; I Chr 14:16; 20:4, although II Sam 21:18 reads "Gob"). KJV uses the alternate spelling "Gazer" in II Sam 5:25 and I Chr 14:16.

Gezer was one of Solomon's major fortified centers after Pharaoh (probably Siamun of the Twenty-first Dynasty) had conquered it and given it as dowry to his daughter, Solomon's wife (I Kgs 9:15-19). Recent discoveries have shown that a Solomonic gate and casemate fortification wall at Gezer were almost identical to those at Megiddo and Hazor, the other two major forts in this passage (Yigael Yadin, "Solomon's City Wall and Gate at Gezer," IEJ, VIII [1958], 80-86). From the period of Solomon comes the Gezer calendar, a small limestone tablet inscribed in Heb. that poetically describes the agricultural activities of the 12 months of the year (*see* Calendar). On a temple in Egypt Pharaoh Shishak lists Gezer as one of his conquests on his campaign to Palestine (I Kgs 14:25; II Chr 12:2-4).

The Assyrian Tiglath-pileser III conquered Philistia in 734 B.C. and depicted the siege of *Gazru* (Gezer) on a relief in his palace at Nimrud (Calah). Two 7th cen. B.C. tablets written in Akkad. and found by Macalister at Gezer confirm Assyrian occupation of the city. In 142 B.C. Simon the Maccabee captured Gezer from the Seleucids, and later installed his son John Hyrcanus as commander of the army with headquarters at Gezer (I Macc 9:52; 13:43-53). Persian and Hellenistic remains on the mound and in tombs attest occupation at this time. See H. Darrell Lance, "Gezer in the Land and in History," BA, XXX [1967], 34-47.

Major excavations have been conducted at Gezer by R. A. S. Macalister, 1902-09 (for resumé see Fred E. Young, "Gezer," BW, pp. 254-7); and more recently by the Hebrew Union College beginning in 1964 (Wm. G. Dever, "Excavations at Gezer," BA, XXX [1967], 47-62; "The Water Systems at Hazor and Gezer," BA, XXXII [1969], 71-78; "Further Excavations at Gezer, 1967-71," BA, XXXIV [1971], 93-132).

A. F. R. and J. R.

GEZRITE (gĕz'rīt). According to the LXX and the *qerē'* reading of the Heb. text, this is the correct name of a desert tribe which lived in the region S of Israel, in the same general area as the Amalekites and the Geshurites (I Sam 27:8). It was against these three tribes that David and his men made their raids during his stay at Ziklag. Some texts of the LXX do not contain this word at all; others have variants such as *gezraion* or *gesraion*. The written Heb. text was *girzî*, while the traditional reading was *gizrî*. For this reason some English versions will be found to have Girzites in this passage.

It has been suggested that the inhabitants of Gezer are meant in this reference, but David could not possibly have made raids so far N without his Philistine overlord knowing it.

GHOST. The word occurs about 20 times in the KJV in the archaic expression "gave up the ghost." As the translation of several different

Heb. and Gr. words, the thought is that one has breathed out his last breath and expired. The literal Heb. expression in Jer 15:9 is "she has breathed out her life (or soul)," similar to Job 11:20, "a breathing out of life." At His crucifixion, it is recorded that the Lord Jesus "yielded up [Gr. *aphēken*] His spirit" (Mt 27:50, NASB), "breathed His last" (*exepneusen*, Mk 15:37, 39, NASB), or "gave up [*paredōken*] His spirit" (Jn 19:30, NASB). The ASV and RSV render Gr. *phantasma* as "ghost" in the terrified cry of the disciples upon seeing Jesus walking on the water, "It is a ghost!" (Mt 14:26; Mk 6:49, NASB). *See* Holy Spirit.

GIAH (gī'a). An unidentified place on the route followed by Abner in his flight, pursued by Joab (II Sam 2:24). LXX renders the Heb. *gîah* as Gr. *gai*, corresponding to the Heb. *gay'*, meaning "valley."

GIANT. An abnormally tall and strong man of ancient times. "Giant" is a translation of several Heb. words.

1. Heb. *gibbôr* (Job 16:14) indicates simply a man great in deeds or in stature.

2. Heb. *rephā'îm* (*see* Rephaim), a race evidently including numerous giants who were among the original inhabitants of Canaan, Edom, Moab, and Ammon. Chedorlaomer in Abraham's time defeated them (Gen 14:5; cf. 15:20). Israel defeated Og (*q.v.*), king of Bashan, one of this race (Deut 3:11; Josh 12:4; 13:12). His bed (or sarcophagus) is said to have been nine cubits long and four cubits wide. Other names of these people are the Anakim (*q.v.*; Deut 2:21), Emim (Gen 14:5; Deut 2:11), and Zamzummin (Deut 2:20). When Israel occupied Canaan, the remnant of these giants took refuge with the Philistines (Josh 11:22). Goliath (*q.v.*) of Gath was a descendant of one of these bands of giants. Others are mentioned by name in II Sam 21:16-22; I Chr 20:4-8. The region near Jerusalem formerly occupied by these giants or Rephaim was for some time referred to as the Valley of the Giants (Josh 15:8; 18:16) or the Valley of Rephaim (II Sam 5:18, 22). In the Ugaritic tablets Dan'el was called the man of Rapha or the Rapha-man (ANET, pp. 149-155). The Rephaim were frequently mentioned in administration tablets of Ugarit as an ethnic group. Many believe they erected the dolmens (*q.v.*) in Palestine.

3. Heb. *nephilîm* is used in only two places (Gen 6:4; Num 13:33). The latter passage identifies the Nephilim (*q.v.*) with the sons of Anak, who in Deut 2:10-11 are connected with the Emim and in Deut 2:20 with the Zamzummim.

Identification of the Nephilim with the Rephaim, as in the foregoing references, does not fit so easily in Gen 6:4. One view of this passage holds that the "sons of God" were fallen angels which united physically with the "daughters of men" to produce a race of giants on earth. An opposing view holds that the relationship referred to here is simply the mingling of the godly line stemming from Seth with the ungodly line of Cain, the offspring of such unions being bold men, daring pioneers, individuals who flouted the laws of God and of society, as the latter part of the verse suggests: "these were the mighty men [*haggibbōrîm*] that were of old, the men of renown" (RSV).

The interpretation in Gen 6:4 hinges on the meaning given to Nephilim. Perhaps derived from *nāphal*, "to fall," the connotation may be "the fallen ones," referring to their fallen, wicked nature. Another meaning could be "the ones who fall" upon others, referring to their violent, tyrannical nature.

Extrabiblical evidence might lend support to the mixed angelic-human view, such as the Babylonian mythology with its Gilgamesh, a Sumerian demigod hero, and the whole Greek and Roman pantheon with its system of demigods and heroes, such as the rebellious Titans, born of the union between gods and mortals. Scriptures commonly cited in favor of this view include Job 1:6; 2:1; 38:7 (where "sons of God" are angelic beings), and Jude 6 with II Pet 2:4. But the latter passage implies that the fall and consignment to judgment of the angels was antediluvial, while Gen 6:4 states that however the "giants" were produced they reappeared after the Flood. Furthermore, Mt 22:30 states that angels are non-sexual.

Meredith J. Kline has suggested that the "sons of God" or "sons of the gods" of Gen 6:2 were antediluvian kings, following pagan terminology for divine kingship. They were noted for tyranny, city-building, and harems (cf. Gen 4:17, 19, 23). In taking as many wives as they wanted they were defying the pattern of monogamy which God had ordained (Gen 2:24), although as kings they acted as guardians of the general ordinances of God for human conduct (WTJ, XXIV [May, 1962], 187-204).

J. K. M. and J. R.

GIBBAR (gĭb'är). In Ezr 2:20 the "children of Gibbar" are mentioned among those who returned with Zerubbabel from Exile. However, the passage in Neh 7:25 has "children of Gibeon." It is possible that Gibbar is a corruption of "Gibeon."

GIBBET. *See* Gallows; Crime and Punishment.

GIBBETHON (gĭb'ě-thŏn). A town in west central Palestine in the territory of Dan listed with Eltekeh and Baalath (Josh 19:44). It was assigned to the Kohathite Levites (Josh 21:23). In early days of the northern kingdom Gibbethon belonged to the Philistines. Nadab was slain by Baasha while besieging it (I Kgs 15:27). Omri was besieging it when he was made king to succeed Zimri. It may possibly be identified with Kibbiah, which lies about 16 miles SE of Joppa.

GIBEA (gĭb'ē-à). A grandson of Caleb of the tribe of Judah (I Chr 2:49), whose father was

Sheva and whose mother was Maacah, Caleb's concubine (I Chr 2:48).

However, some think that the term is geographical rather than genealogical and refers more to a town in the hill country S of Hebron than to an individual (Josh 15:57). The term Gibea is probably a variation of the more common Gibeah (q.v.).

GIBEAH (gĭb′ē-à). This is a Heb. word meaning a "hill," especially one used for heathen worship. It is in contrast to the stronger word *har*, "mountain."

1. As a place name its primary reference is to Gibeah of Benjamin, best known as Saul's home town (I Sam 10:26) and later his capital for Israel (I Sam 11:4; 23:19). The earliest reference to the city is in the listing of the cities of Benjamin (Josh 18:28) where the spelling is Gibeath.

Although the shameful story of the Levite's concubine appears at the close of the book of Judges (chaps. 19–20), the episode itself (cf. Hos 9:9; 10:9) took place only shortly after Joshua's conquest when Phinehas, the son of Eleazar, was still high priest (Jud 20:28) and the ark was at Bethel (Jud 20:18). (After this episode the ark was moved to Shiloh.) Tragedy again struck the city when seven of Saul's descendants were hanged because of that king's killing of the Gibeonites (II Sam 21:1–14). Here too is the story of the faithful Rizpah.

Gibeah contributed one of the "thirty" champions of David's army—Ittai, son of Ribai (II Sam 23:29); and at Ziklag two other warriors of Gibeah came to David's aid (I Chr 12:1–3).

Isa 10:29 predicts the city as falling before the Assyrians. Hosea also hears the war trumpet here (Hos 5:8). Gibeah the city also gave its name to the county seat (I Sam 14:2; 22:6).

Tell el-Fûl, three miles N of the Damascus Gate of Jerusalem, covers the ruins of the biblical city. W. F. Albright conducted brief campaigns here in 1922–23 and 1933. Further excavations were made in 1964 to check his findings (BA, XXVIII, 2–10). The small village which Albright found built directly on bedrock was doubtless the one described in Jud 19–20. The site lay dormant for a century or two until the Philistines fortified the mound. Saul or Jonathan captured the town (I Sam 13–14), and Saul erected his palace-fortress, following the Philistine plan. It was a large building, at least 169 by 114 feet with four corner towers.

When David moved the capital to Jerusalem, Gibeah declined and it was not rebuilt until about the 8th cen. B.C. The new city was short-lived, apparently being destroyed by Pekah and Rezin in their attack on Jerusalem about 735 B.C. It was rebuilt in the 7th cen., only to be destroyed in Nebuchadnezzar's conquest of Jerusalem. Later, there was a Hellenistic occupation and also one after the Roman conquest of Palestine, 63 B.C. The city was finally destroyed by Titus the day before he laid

The Mound of Gibeah with an unfinished palace of King Hussein of Jordan on top. HFV

siege to Jerusalem in A.D. 70. King Hussein of Jordan began to construct a palace on top of the mound just before the Six Day War in 1967.

2. A minor town on the plateau SE of Hebron in the tribe of Judah (Josh 15:57).

Bibliography. W. F. Albright, "Excavations and Results of Tell el-Fûl (Gibeah of Saul)," AASOR, IV (1924), 1–89; "A New Campaign of Excavation at Gibeah of Saul," BASOR #52 (1933), pp. 6–12. Paul W. Lapp, "Tell el-Fûl," BA, XXVIII (1965), 2–10. Lawrence A. Sinclair, "An Archaeological Study of Gibeah (Tell el-Fûl)," BA, XXVII (1964), 52–64; AASOR, XXXIV–XXXV (1960), 1–52.

J. L. K.

GIBEATH (gĭb′ē-ăth). A town of Benjamin (Josh 18:28), usually identified with Gibeah, Saul's capital (*see* Gibeah 2). The name means "hill" and is sometimes the first element in compound place names. The hill of Phinehas (Heb. *Gibe 'ath-Phînehas*) was the burial place of Eleazar, the son of Aaron, in Mount Ephraim (Josh 24:33); its location is unknown. Other translations of Gibeath in English versions are the hill of Moreh (q.v.), Jud 7:1; the hill of Hachilah (q.v.), I Sam 23:19; the hill of Ammah (q.v.), II Sam 2:24; the hill of Gareb (q.v.), Jer 31:39.

RSV in I Sam 10:5 transliterates the name of a city where a Philistine garrison was stationed as Gibeath-elohim, in most other versions rendered "the hill of God." Since I Sam 13:3 states that the garrison was in Geba (q.v.), this town apparently was also known as Gibeath-elohim because of its high place and its group of prophets.

GIBEATHITE (gĭb′ē-à-thīt). An inhabitant of the city of Gibeah, a city of the tribe of Benjamin located between Jerusalem and Ramah (Jud 19:1l–15). Some of David's mighty men were "of Gibea" (II Sam 23:29; I Chr 11:31; 12:3).

The Mound of Gibeon. HFV

GIBEON, GIBEONITES (gĭbʹĭ-ŏn, gĭbʹĭ-ŏ-nīts; "hill, hill-dwellers"). A city and people in the territory of Benjamin, now identified with the village of el-Jib. In the Bible the name occurs 45 times, the city being alluded to on 15 different occasions in biblical history. Gibeon (el-Jib) is located on a hill about 2,600 feet above sea level, and near the intersection of three roads leading to Joppa via the valley of Ajalon. It lies about six miles NW of Jerusalem and four miles SSW of Ramallah, near the old Jerusalem airport.

The identification of Gibeon with el-Jib was first suggested by Franz von Troilo in A.D. 1666, followed by Richard Pococke in 1738. Edward Robinson in 1838 noted the correspondence between the biblical name and the modern Arabic name and substantiated these earlier suggestions. This identification was challenged by Albrecht Alt who believed that biblical Gibeon and Tell en-Nasbeh are identical. Excavations at Tell en-Nasbeh dispelled this hypothesis, and the excavations at el-Jib under James B. Pritchard (1956-62) confirmed the earlier identification. The identification was made certain by the discovery of 61 inscribed jar handles, on 31 of which the name. Gibeon had been incised in paleo-Hebrew. Few biblical sites have a more certain identification.

Gibeon's past, as reconstructed on the basis of excavations, can be traced to three millennia before Christ. Inhabitants of Gibeon in the Early Bronze Age (3100-2100 B.C.) built on bedrock as attested by the discovery of a room of this period containing 14 storage jars with distinctive Early Bronze handles. They were contemporary with similar jar finds in the Early Bronze remains at Tell en-Nasbeh, Jericho, and Ai. A burial cave which contained much pottery of this period was discovered in the hill on the E slope of the city.

During the Middle Bronze I period (2100-1900 B.C.) tent-dwelling seminomads dug shaft tombs, 55 of which have been cleared by the archaeologists halfway down the W slope of the hill. Each consisted of a cylindrical shaft c. four feet in diameter and from three to 13 feet in depth, which led down to a small opening into the burial chamber proper, measuring c. nine by six feet. In the chamber in 26 of these tombs were found four-spouted lamps, funerary jars, bronze javelins and daggers, or other artifacts characteristic of the Middle Bronze I period.

In the Middle Bronze II or Hyksos period the second actual city was built on the hill. A room belonging to this period, discovered on the NW edge of the site, contained 16 large MB II storage jars. The pottery of this period (1900-1550 B.C.) was far superior to that of Middle Bronze I in both design and texture. Artifacts in the 29 tombs of this period included bronze knives, toggle pins, scarabs, bone inlay and beads in addition to fine pottery. Multiple burials in one tomb was standard procedure of the period. This level of occupation came to an end at the close of the Hyksos period when the city evidently was destroyed by fire.

Evidence of the Late Bronze Age (1550-1200 B.C.) was found in seven tombs, revealing trade with Egypt and Cyprus. Among the finds were scarabs of Thutmose III (1504-1450 B.C.) and Amenhotep II (1450-1425). Cypriot imports included the distinctive long-necked jug (*bilbil*) of perfumed oil; pottery of domestic design and craftsmanship was inferior in technique to the imported wares. During this period the city entered into the mutual defense treaty with Joshua and the elders of Israel, thus avoiding the fate which befell their contemporaries among the Amorites (Josh 9).

Gibeon was the leading member of a group of four Hivite cities at the time of Joshua's conquest, the other three being Chephirah, Beeroth and Kirjath-jearim (Josh 9:17). These Hivite (or Horite) towns entered by deceit into a mutual assistance pact with Joshua and the elders of Israel, rather than remaining loyal to the Amorites of the area. As a result a coalition of five Amorite kings attacked Gibeon, but were defeated by Joshua's forces which had come from Gilgal in response to Gibeon's call for assistance as provided by the treaty (Josh 10:1-14). The episode indicates the binding obligations of an alliance made in the name of the Lord even when enacted without divine sanction (Josh 9:18). For comments concerning the sun and moon standing still, *see* Sun.

Gibeon was among the cities included in the territory of Benjamin (Josh 18:25) and was allotted to the descendants of Aaron (Josh 21:17). The Hivites inhabiting these cities were spared the fate of the other Canaanites but were made second-class citizens, assigned to be "hewers of wood and drawers of water" (Josh 9:27).

Iron Age I (1200-900 B.C.) was apparently the "golden age" of Gibeon. Archaeological discoveries which date from this period include two city walls. The older and outer wall was about five feet in thickness and more than a half mile· in circumference, enclosing the 16 acre site. An inner wall constructed in the 10th cen. B.C. was much stronger, averaging 13 feet in thickness.

The city now appears in the biblical record as the scene of a joust between soldiers representing Abner and those of David, with David's men victorious (II Sam 2:12–17). Gibeon marked the last time the Philistines were a menace to Israel. After they made a raid up the valley, David's men fell upon them and "smote the Philistine army from Gibeon to Gezer" (I Chr 14:16, RSV).

Later, in David's reign during the rebellion of Sheba, Joab murdered Amasa "at the great stone which is in Gibeon" (II Sam 20:8).

Gibeon seems to have been the religious center of Solomon's realm during the early days of his reign. Here was located the tabernacle, the altar of burnt offering, a priesthood, daily sacrifices, and the "great high place" (I Chr 16:37–40; 21:29). It was here that Solomon participated in the first public dedicatory service of his reign and received a vision from God (I Kgs 3:4–5; cf.9:2). The national religious center shifted from Gilgal (Josh 5:10) to the Shechem area (Josh 8:30–35) to Shiloh (I Sam 1:3) to Gibeon (I Chr 16:39) to Jerusalem.

Since no trace of Solomon's cultic installation has been discovered at el-Jib, Pritchard and others think it may have been located on Nebi Samwil, a conspicuous hill one mile S of el-Jib. Residents of Gibeon at this time included "Jehiel the father of Gibeon" (I Chr 8:29; 9:35). During the invasion by Pharaoh

Inside stairway to the pool of Gibeon.
James Pritchard

Shishak early in Rehoboam's reign (II Chr 12:2–9), Gibeon was among the many cities of Judah and Israel plundered according to Shishak's records in Egypt.

During the 6th cen. Gibeon again appears briefly in OT history as the hometown of the false prophet Hananiah, a contemporary of Jeremiah (Jer 28:1). During the Exile, in 582 B.C., Ishmael had murdered Gedaliah and his household at Mizpah and was returning with captives to the Ammonites. He was met by forces loyal to Johanan "at the great pool which is in Gibeon." A battle ensued in which the captives were released and their captor escaped by fleeing with eight companions to the sanctuary of the Ammonites in Transjordan (Jer 41:1–16).

In the memoirs of Nehemiah the Gibeonites are listed among those who helped build the walls of Jerusalem (Neh 3:7). The inhabitants of Gibeon had apparently been God-fearing people from the days of Joshua (cf. II Sam 21:4–6).

Josephus reports that in A.D. 66 the Roman governor Cestius camped at Gibeon as he traveled to and from Jerusalem via Beth Horon, to Joppa and the coast (Wars ii.19.1, 7).

Archaeologically speaking, Gibeon's most interesting era was during the kingdom period (Iron I and II, 1200–580 B.C.). The "great pool" of David's time may be the same as the enormous pit uncovered by Pritchard's expeditions of 1956 and 1957. This pit, dug perhaps in the early Iron Age, measures about 37 feet from rim to rim and has a depth of 35 feet, with a spiral stairway consisting of 40 steps and balustrade formed of the bedrock remaining when the pool was cut. Additional steps lead down through a rock tunnel to a large water chamber or cistern 82 feet below the surface. The largest of the eight springs near the city was reached by an enormous tunnel cut down through the rock with 93 steps leading from inside the city wall to the spring on the NE edge of the tell. In its walls were niches to hold lamps to provide light for the "drawers of water" (cf. Josh 9:27). Nearby were discovered more than 60 bell-shaped cellars cut out of the rock, capable of serving as cool storage places for wine kept in large jars and aged before being exported. Jar handles inscribed with the name GB'N (Gibeon) indicate a large distributing point in wine manufacture, and help to identify the site with certainty. The entire installation, including numerous winepresses and fermenting basins, the cellars, sherds of many jars, and more than 40 clay stoppers to fit into the mouths of the jars, could produce and store at least 30,000 gallons of wine. This winery was in use during the three centuries preceding the Exile, indicating that Gibeon was a thriving city engaged in industry and in trade with its neighbors.

Bibliography. James B. Pritchard, "The Water System at Gibeon," BA, XIX (1956), 66–75;

"Industry and Trade at Biblical Gibeon," BA, XXIII (1960), 23–29; "A Bronze Age Necropolis at Gibeon," BA, XXIV (1961), 19–24; "More Inscribed Jar Handles from El-Jib," BASOR #160 (1960), 2–6; *The Water System of Gibeon*, Philadelphia: Univ. of Penn. Museum, 1961; *Gibeon, Where the Sun Stood Still*, Princeton: Princeton Univ. Press, 1962; *The Bronze Age Cemetery at Gibeon*, Philadelphia: Univ. of Penn. Museum, 1963. W. L. Reed, "Gibeon," TAOTS, pp. 231–243.

G. A. T.

GIBLITES (gĭb'līts). Inhabitants of Gebal (*q.v.*).

GIDDALTI (gĭ-dăl'tī). A son of Heman (I Chr 25:4, 29), who was one of David's musicians, designated by David to prophesy with music in the sanctuary. The name is included in a list which seems to be a liturgical prayer in its origin.

GIDDEL (gĭd'ĕl)

1. The name of the head of a family of temple servants called Nethinim (Ezr 2:47; Neh 7:49).

2. Ancestor of one of the families of "Solomon's servants" among the returned exiles (Ezr 2:56; Neh 7:58; cf. I Kgs 9:21).

GIDEON (gĭd'ē-ŏn). A charismatic hero of Israel, son of Joash of the clan of Abiezer, of the tribe of Manasseh (Jud 6:11–8:35). He resided at Ophrah, E of the hill of Moreh between Beth-shean and Mount Tabor, a town in Issachar (cf. Josh 17:11). Like so many Israelites during the cycles of apostasy in the period of the judges, Gideon's father had turned to Baal worship. Few bothered to attend the feasts of the Lord at Shiloh, the one unifying factor that God had ordained to maintain a national sense of interdependency in Israel. Thus *c.* 1200 B.C. the Hebrews were easy prey for marauding Bedouin bands. Coming on camels from the deserts up Wadi Sirhan E of Amman, for seven consecutive years the Midianites invaded to steal livestock and plunder the ripening harvests. Likewise Amalekites, probably coming from the Negeb, raided as far as Gaza. Meanwhile the impoverished Jews, hiding in mountains and caves, began to cry to the Lord for deliverance.

During this oppression the angel of the Lord appeared to Gideon, probably then about 30 years old (cf. Jud 8:20). In order to keep his wheat hidden from the Midianites, he was beating it out in a winepress instead of treading it with animals on a threshingfloor, normally near the town gate. The divine messenger commissioned him to smite the Midianites, and manifested his true identity by having fire consume the food Gideon had prepared for him. That night the Lord tested Gideon's obedience by commanding him to destroy his father's altar of Baal and cut down the Asherah totem pole, and then to build a carefully constructed altar to Yahweh (Jud 6:11–27).

Gideon's other name, Jerubbaal (*q.v.*), is introduced in the account when his father shields him from the angry townspeople for his action by saying that Baal if a god should be able to contend for himself. Jerubbaal may have been the name given at birth to Gideon, "baal" meaning "lord" and signifying a title given to Yahweh, with the sense "May the Lord contend for me"; for it appears as his real name in Jud 7:1; 8:29, 35 and throughout chap. 9 as the father of Abimelech. ("Gideon," meaning "hewer," may have been a nickname or honorific title given him as a result of this incident.) Thus a new, popular explanation of his original name Jerubbaal arose: "Let Baal contend against him" (Jud 6:28–32). Later, when the name Baal was abhorred, this name was changed to Jerubbesheth ("Let the shameful one contend," II Sam 11:21).

The next time the Midianites and their allies swept into Israel, the Spirit of the Lord endued Gideon with power for a campaign of deliverance. He gathered an army from the tribes of Manasseh, Asher, Zebulun, and Naphtali. A novice in warfare himself, before going to battle he sought divine guidance and strengthening for his faith. God answered by signs of miraculous dew, first on the fleece, and the next night on the ground around it (Jud 6:35–40).

Because the highly mobile Midianites with their camels were encamped in the valley of Jezreel, Gideon and his men took position on Mount Gilboa above the spring of Harod ('Ain Jalud; cf. I Sam 29:1). At God's command in order to prevent pride, Gideon twice reduced his army, from an original 32,000 to 10,000 by sending home the cowards (cf. Deut 20:8), and then to a mere 300 by weeding out the careless. The faithful warriors, alert for ambushes, stood upright and kept one hand on their weapon while they dipped the other hand in the water and lapped from it, always ready for action (Jud 7:1–8).

God was revealing to Gideon step by step the only military tactics suitable for footsoldiers to defeat the vast camel-riding army of 135,000 (cf. 8:10). As A. Malamat shows, a small, closely knit, highly disciplined force—led by one thoroughly familiar with the terrain and knowing the morale of the enemy—could then stage a successful night assault ("The War of Gideon and Midian—A Military Approach," PEQ, LXXXV [1953], 61–65). Capitalizing on Bedouin fear of the dark, Gideon sprang the attack around midnight just after the Midianite watch was changed, the weakest moment in the sentry system. The element of surprise was augmented by every Israelite suddenly blowing a ram's-horn trumpet, breaking the jar which had concealed its smouldering torch (thus allowing it to burst into flame), and shouting the now-famous war cry, "A sword for the Lord and for Gideon" (7:20, RSV). Showing superb strategy, Gideon sent runners to have the Ephraimites cut off the enemy retreat at the fords of the Jordan (7:9–24). They captured two Midianite princes and brought the heads to

Gideon. He humbly and diplomatically allayed the bitterness of the men of Ephraim who reproached him for not summoning their help sooner (7:25 – 8:3).

Gideon continued the pursuit across the Jordan, capturing two more Midianite rulers. Because he had been refused assistance by the men of Succoth and Penuel, on his return he destroyed both places. He then executed Zebah and Zalmunna himself under the duty of blood revenge (cf. Num 35:19), because they had not spared his brothers living near Mount Tabor (Jud 8:4–21). The victory was so complete, so astounding, so wholly of God that "the day of Midian" seems to have become a proverbial expression for divine deliverance (Isa 9:4; cf. 10:26; Ps 83:11).

Gideon affords a splendid illustration of how God can use the least among men (Jud 6:15) when that one is fully yielded to His will and able to believe Him for miracles (6:13). Like Timothy, Gideon tended to be fearful (cf. 6:11, 22–23, 27; 7:10). But implicit reliance upon God and empowering by the Spirit made him a "mighty man of valour" (6:12), an outstanding example of one who "through faith subdued kingdoms" (Heb 11:32–33).

Gideon resisted the temptation of proffered hereditary kingship – his finest hour. But unwisely he made an ephod from the Midianite spoils given him (Jud 8:22–27). The ephod was probably a magnificent robe made of the gold and purple taken from his enemies. It proved a snare, however, to him and his house because he thus invaded the prerogative of the Aaronic priesthood, even though he perhaps meant only to use it in his office of civil magistrate (cf. I Chr 15:27). It also ensnared all Israel because they made it an object of worship. Like David, Gideon succumbed to the flesh in multiplying wives and concubines, with consequent tragedy among his offspring.

J. R.

GIDEONI (gĭd′ĭ-ō′nī). The father of Abidan, who was a leader of Benjamin in the wilderness (Num 1:11; 2:22; 7:60, 65; 10:24). Mentioned only in connection with his son.

GIDOM (gī′dŏm). The limit of the pursuit of Benjamin by the other tribes (Jud 20:45). It is a site in Benjamin near the rock Rimmon in the wilderness E of Gibeah. It may not be a proper name but may be used as an infinitive "till they cut them off." It is not mentioned elsewhere.

GIER EAGLE. See Animals, III.54.

GIFT. Several words with the basic meaning of "gratuity" come from the Heb. root *nāthan* meaning "to give." They were used of dowry (Gen 24:53; 34:12); a portion of inheritance (Gen 25:6; II Chr 21:3); a religious sacrificial offering (Num 18:11); an incentive to obtain favor from another (Prov 18:16; 21:14); and a bribe (Prov 15:27; Eccl 7:7).

Pecuniary assistance (Est 2:18) and a present given in token of respect (II Sam 19:42) are derived from the Heb. root *nāsā'* which means "to raise." It is translated "collection" in the KJV of II Chr 24:6, 9 and "tax" in the ASV. In II Sam 11:8 it is translated "mess" of food.

Heb. *minḥâ* is used of an oblation (II Sam 8:2, 6; I Chr 18:2, 6); *shōḥad* always means a bribe, a gift for the purpose of escaping punishment (Ex 23:8; Deut 10:17).

The Gr. words in the NT are related to the verb *didōmi: dosis* can be used with an active sense of "a giving" (Phil 4:15), or a passive sense of the "thing given" (Jas 1:17); *dōron* is used specifically of a "present" (Mt 2:11), yet not necessarily always gratuitous; *dōrea* denotes a gift which is also a gratuity (Rom 3:24, RSV).

God's supreme gift to mankind is His Son (II Cor 9:15; Jn 3:16). The Holy Spirit is the promised gift of the Father, sent by the Son, and to be received with active faith by Christian believers (Jn 14:16, 26; 15:26; 16:7; Acts 1:4–5; 2:33, 38–39; Gal 3:14). Through the Spirit are manifested spiritual gifts (I Cor 12:1–11). *See* Gifts, Spiritual.

Bibliography. Friedrich Büchsel, "*Didōmi,* etc.," TDNT, II, 166–173.

D. L. W.

GIFT OF TONGUES. *See* Tongues, Gift of.

GIFTS, SPIRITUAL. Three Gr. terms are involved in the apostle Paul's discussion of spiritual gifts in I Cor 12–14: *ta pneumatika* (I Cor 12:1; 14:1; see also Rom 1:11), "spiritual gifts, powers or manifestations"; *ta pneumata* (I Cor 14:12), "spirits" or manifestations of the Spirit; and *ta charismata* (I Cor 12:4, 9, 28, 30, 31; see also Rom 1:11; 12:6; I Cor 1:7; I Tim 4:14; II Tim 1:6; I Pet 4:10), "grace-gifts."

A spiritual or charismatic gift is a supernatural capacity or power bestowed upon a Christian believer by the Holy Spirit to enable him to exercise his function as a member of the Body of Christ (I Cor 12:4–27). These gifts are not to be considered natural abilities, but supernatural manifestations of the Spirit Himself (v. 7). They are not to be confused with spiritual graces or fruits of the Spirit – facets of Christ's character which every believer is to cultivate (Gal 5:22–23). They are not identical with spiritual offices – positions in the church whether for spiritual or temporal oversight of its affairs (elders, deacons, I Tim 3:1–13) or for public ministries (apostles, prophets, evangelists, pastor-teachers, Eph 4:11). Only certain believers are appointed to these spiritual offices (I Cor 12:28a, 29a) – Christ's gifts (*domata*) to His Church (Eph 4:8) – in view of specific charismatic endowments already evidenced in their lives.

In I Cor 12–14 Paul sets forth the unity, the diversity, the distribution, the order, the motivation, the permanence, the relative value, and the proper use of spiritual gifts. As to their unity, they are all given, administered and energized or inspired by the same Triune God

(12:4–6, 11). The one purpose of the Holy Spirit in so empowering Christians is always to glorify Christ (12:3), for the profit or common good of all (12:7).

As to their diversities or distinctions, they are called "gifts" (*charismata*) from the Spirit (12:4), "administrations," ministries or acts of service from the Lord (12:5), and "operations" or activities from God the Father (12:6). The apostle then names nine gifts: a word of wisdom, a word of knowledge, faith (not saving faith but exceptional faith to do the works of Christ, Jn 14:12), charismatic gifts of healings, workings of miracles or miraculous accomplishments, prophecy or prophetic utterances, discerning of spirits, speaking publicly in various kinds of tongues, and interpretation of tongues (12:8–10). Other charismatic gifts are mentioned in 12:28–30 (helps, administrations) and in Rom 12:6–8, so that no one list is exhaustive.

Various classifications of the gifts can be made, but perhaps that of I Pet 4:10–11 is the most satisfactory. Peter describes two main categories—gifts of utterance so that the possessor of the gift speaks forth as it were words spoken by God Himself, and gifts for practical service on a supernatural level. Paul makes a similar twofold classification when he states that the Corinthian believers were enriched with all utterance and all knowledge, not lacking in any charismatic gift (I Cor 1:5–7; cf. II Cor 8:7).

As to the distribution of the gifts, Paul says that they are given to "every man," i.e., to every believer (I Cor 12:7; see also I Pet 4:10). The Spirit is sovereign in granting these gifts, "distributing to each one individually just as He wills" (I Cor 12:11, NASB). It is possible for one individual to manifest more than one gift and to have more than one ministry. Paul, for example, was richly equipped, having the power to speak in tongues, to prophesy and to perform miracles, and was first a teacher (Acts 11:25–26; 13:1) and then an apostle (Acts 14:4, 14). Ordinarily, as in the church at Corinth, the gifts are widely distributed among the saints (I Cor 1:5–7; 12:29–30).

As to the order of the gifts, Paul teaches that some gifts are greater in their usefulness than others (I Cor 12:28, 31; 14:1–25). Yet none are to be ruled out or despised (I Cor 14:39; I Thess 5:20). The Corinthians were inclined to magnify the gift of tongues as most desirable, perhaps in keeping with the Gr. love of speech. But Paul puts it at the end of his lists (I Cor 12:8–10, 28–30).

As to the proper motive in desiring the gifts and the right motivation in using the gifts. Paul makes it very clear that love for others is the only true basis: "And moreover I am going to show you a way beyond comparison" (I Cor 12:31*b*, orig. trans.), a way *par excellence* (*kath' hyperbolēn*). Unless the gifts of tongues, prophesying, knowledge or helps are rooted in love, they are worthless (I Cor 13:1–3).

As to the permanence of the gifts, there is much difference of opinion. Obviously, the office of apostleship in the primary sense has been withdrawn. There is no proof in Scripture for apostolic succession from the Christ-appointed leaders of the church. In a secondary sense, however, many missionaries have done the work of apostles with extraordinary gifts and blessing from God. Again, the gift of prophecy in its primary sense of speaking forth and writing down the inspired, infallible Word of God has been sovereignly withdrawn; but believers may still speak forth a message impressed by God when they are under an anointing or prompting of the Spirit. Paul teaches that whereas love will never fail nor cease, the charismatic gifts will stop "when that which is perfect is come" (I Cor 13:10). Some have taught that by *to teleion,* "that which is perfect," Paul means the completed canon of holy Scripture; however, consideration of v. 12, which says that then we shall see face to face and know fully even as now we are fully known, seems to indicate that Paul is looking forward to the perfect state of things to be ushered in by the return of Christ from heaven (J. H. Thayer, *A Greek-English Lexicon of the New Testament,* p. 618).

A study of church history reveals that many of the charismatic gifts continued to be manifested long after the apostles were all dead (Adolf Harnack, *The Mission and Expansion of Christianity,* Harper Torchbooks, 1962, pp. 129–146, 199–205), and that on new mission fields and in times of spiritual revival the Lord still confirms His Word through the operation of supernatural gifts of the Spirit. Certainly the gifts of teaching, exhorting, sharing and ruling (Rom 12:6–8) or of helps and of governments (I Cor 12:28) are continuing functions, for the church will always need believers with such abilities.

As to the relative value of prophesying and speaking in tongues, Paul points out the limitations and the value of the latter gift to the individual for his own spiritual upbuilding and in his private praying and worshiping (I Cor 14:2, 4*a*, 14–18, 28*b*) as well as to the congregation for edifying when accompanied by the gift of interpretation (14:5, 13, 26–28). The one who prophesies, however, more directly and clearly helps the congregation by speaking a message of edification, exhortation or comfort, (14:3). A third function of the gift of tongues is to act as a sign. This is evident when a language unknown to the one speaking it is recognized by a "foreigner" or unbeliever in the meeting (14:22; Mk 16:17, 20), as on the Day of Pentecost (Acts 2:4–12).

As to the proper use of spiritual gifts, Paul carefully instructs the Corinthian church in the orderly display of the gifts of utterance in their fellowship meetings. Only one is to speak at a time, and he is to permit the others to test his message, in order to prevent confusion and that all might be edified (I Cor 14:26–40). To correct abuse he does not prohibit the practice of the gifts, but ends by saying, "Let all things be done decently and in order" (v. 40).

Bibliography. Arnold Bittlinger, *Gifts and Graces,* trans. by H. Klassen, London: Hodder & Stoughton, 1967, a commentary on I Cor 12–14. Donald Gee, *Spiritual Gifts in the Work of the Ministry Today,* Springfield, Mo.: Gospel Publ. House, 1963. James G. S. S. Thomson, "Spiritual Gifts," BDT, pp. 497–500.

F. C. K.

Entrance to Virgin's Fount. JR

GIHON (gī'hŏn)

1. Gihon (from *giah,* "to gush forth") was the name given to one of the four rivers emerging from Eden "which flows around the whole land of Cush" (Gen 2:13, RSV), apparently meaning the area E of Mesopotamia (or possibly the Nile, which would extend Eden as far as the entire Fertile Crescent).

2. The Nile in Jer 2:18 is translated in the LXX as *Gēōn* (Gihon), perhaps influenced by Gen 2:13.

3. A spring which is Jerusalem's only known natural source of water and lies in the Kidron valley, E of Ophel, directly S of the present temple area. This never-failing spring accounts for the fact that Jerusalem has been occupied continuously for some eight millennia. As its name implies, it gushes forth an extra amount of water from its natural cave once or twice a day as the dry season ends, four or five times daily after a rainy winter.

Solomon was crowned at Gihon after his brother Adonijah made a futile attempt to claim the kingship at En-rogel (Job's Well), a few hundred yards down the valley (I Kgs 1:33). As the Assyrian armies of Sennacherib approached, Hezekiah took measures to deny this water to the invaders (II Chr 32:3–4) and assure its availability to the defenders by cutting a tunnel through the hill so that it emerged on the W side inside the city wall in what is now called the Pool of Siloam (II Chr 32:30; cf. II Kgs 20:20). This winding tunnel, 1,777 feet in length, averaging six feet in height by three feet in width, is the most famous of several rock-cut tunnels designed to assure access to the water.

An older conduit on a slightly lower level, led down the W bank of the Kidron. It began as a tunnel leading S from Gihon's cave until it emerged and became a surface channel. Schick traced it in 1901 to the S end of the hill of Ophel, where it presumably led to a pool older than the Pool of Siloam (cf. the "old pool" of Isa 22:11). A vertical shaft, discovered by Warren, appears to have been used by the Jebusites in pre-historic times (*see* Gutter with reference to II Sam 5:8). A higher level aqueduct or rock-cut channel was discovered by Schick in 1866 and may have been used for irrigation of the king's gardens (cf. II Kgs 25:4), probably the "waters of Shiloah that go softly" mentioned in Isa 8:6. At present Gihon, now known as "the Virgin's Fountain," is in a cave 30 steps below the ground level and is still visited by the local women in quest of water. *See* Siloam; Jerusalem; Hezekiah.

G. A. T.

GILALAI (gĭ-lā'lī). A Levitical musician who took part in the dedication of the wall of Jerusalem rebuilt under the leadership of Nehemiah (Neh 12:36).

GILBOA (gĭl-bō'á). Usually identified with a range of hills today called Jebel Fuqû'ah with an average elevation of 1,600 feet at the SE end of the plain of Jezreel (Esdraelon). It forms a watershed between the river Kishon and the Jordan as its eight-mile length curves SE, then S to merge with the central uplands of Samaria. Between Gilboa and the hill of Moreh to the N is the valley leading from Jezreel down to Beth-shan. Near its northern cliffs is the well of Harod where Gideon encamped (Jud 7:1). Gilboa's chief fame comes from the death of Saul and his sons on its NW slopes (I Sam 28:4; 31:1–8; II Sam 1:21).

Mount Gilboa. JR

Another theory places Gilboa in the mountains of Samaria 15 miles or so E of Joppa near the Aphek of I Sam 29:1 (*see* Aphek 1), usually located at Ras el-'Ain (H. Bar-Deroma, " 'Ye Mountains of Gilboa,' " PEQ, CII [1970], 116–136).

GILEAD (gĭl'ē-ăd)

1. The founder of the tribal family by that name (Num 26:29–30; Josh 17:1).

2. The father of Jephthah (Jud 11:1).

3. A Gadite (I Chr 5:14).

4. A mountainous region E of the Jordan River with an average height of 3,000 feet above sea level. It is bounded on the N by Bashan, on the E by the Arabian Desert, and on the S by Moab and Ammon (Deut 3:12–17). It is also known as Mount Gilead (but it is difficult to identify it with any particular mountain), the "land of Gilead" (Josh 22:15, 32) and "Gilead" (Ps 60:7; Gen 37:25).

The Jabbok River divides this area into two parts (Josh 12:2). Because it receives a rainfall of from 28 to 32 inches a year, N Gilead has many perennial streams descending to the Jordan. Much of it is still thickly wooded as it was in Absalom's day (II Sam 18:6–9). Gad received the south-central part of Gilead and Manasseh the northern. Reuben occupied the extreme southern part extending into Moab. The last interview between Laban and Jacob took place in Mount Gilead (Gen 31:21). The region of S Gilead is well suited for cattle raising and was eagerly applied for by the Reubenites and the Gadites (Num 32:1–5). Moses rebuked them for their willingness to settle down on the E side of Jordan before Canaan was finally conquered for the rest of the tribes (Num 32:6–15), but he reluctantly agreed to let them settle here. For recent discussion and bibliography see Nelson Glueck, "Transjordan," TAOTS, pp. 428–453.

5. A city in the region of Gilead (Hos 6:8).

The King's Highway and the mountains of Gilead. HFV

6. A mountain on the edge of the Valley of Jezreel (Jud 7:3) where Gideon ordered a reduction in number of the men who were to fight the Midianites. Another interpretation of the command, "Let him return and depart early from mount Gilead," translates the Heb. preposition *min*, "from," in its occasional sense of "toward," as in Gen 2:8; 12:8; 13:11. Mount Gilead then would be the same region as 4.

H. A. Han.

GILEADITES (gĭl'ē-à-dīts). When the Heb. tribes arrived in the region E of the Jordan, Manasseh, Gad, and Reuben elected to take possession of that territory because they found it suitable for their flocks. Manasseh occupied the N, Gad the central, and Reuben the southern sector as far as the Arnon River. The exact borders between the three tribes cannot be defined with certainty because many of the cities named in the biblical record have not been identified.

One reference identifies the Gileadites with the descendants of Manasseh (Num 26:29). Jair and Jephthah are also identified as Gileadites (Jud 10:3; 11:1). Generally speaking, it is assumed that the Gileadites were the peoples occupying the greater Gilead region.

GILGAL (gĭl'găl)

1. Gilgal was Israel's first campsite after crossing the Jordan and main headquarters during the campaigns of conquest (Josh 4:19; 9:6; 10:6, 43; 14:6). Stones taken from the bed of the Jordan were set up in a memorial cairn. The name Gilgal, however, which means "circle," evidently belonged to the site already, for Moses seems to have known it (Deut 11:30). Perhaps to mark a burial site, as at Mycenae, the Canaanites had previously installed sculptured standing stones in a circle near Gilgal (Jud 3:19, RSV); the Israelites by establishing a memorial to Yahweh there, effectively counteracted the former idolatrous cult practices at the site. Nevertheless, Gilgal did not have an Israelite shrine until the 8th cen. B.C.; then, as at Bethel, unspiritual worship drew condemnation from Amos (4:4; 5:5) and Hosea (4:15; 9:15; 12:11). Both Gilgal and Bethel had been centers for the young prophets in training with Elijah and Elisha (II Kgs 2:1–2; 4:38), with an important road connecting the two towns.

Since Gilgal can be derived from the Heb. verb *gālal*, "to roll," the same was used by God through Joshua to serve as a reminder to Israel that He had rolled away the reproach or disgrace of all idolatrous Egyptian worship and lusting for Egyptian products still resident in their hearts by their submitting to circumcision there. Thus they were formally reinstated into covenant relationship with Yahweh and ceremonially fit to partake of the Passover festival (Josh 5:9–11). Later, Gilgal was the site of King Saul's coronation, his retreat and impetuous sacrifice, and his rejection as king (I Sam 11:15; 13:4, 7, 12; 15:12, 26, 33).

Gilgal is probably located just N of Khirbet el-Mefjir, about one and a quarter miles NE of OT Jericho (cf. Josh 4:19). James Muilenberg (BASOR #140 [1955] pp. 11-27) combines the testimony of the OT passages, Josephus' figure of ten stadia from Jericho, and his own small sounding in 1954 which unearthed pottery of the period 1200-600 B.C. to make this a convincing identification.

2. A place of the same name mentioned after Dor in a list of conquered kings (Josh 12:23), perhaps Jiljulieh bordering the plain of Sharon W of Shechem. In this verse, however, the LXX has Galilee instead of Gilgal.

3. A place on the border of Judah, "opposite the ascent of Adummim" (Josh 15:7, RSV); possibly the same as 1.

4. Many geographers seek to place the Gilgal of II Kgs 2:1 and 4:38, and perhaps of Deut 11:30, in the hill country of Ephraim, perhaps at Jiljulieh, eight miles NW of Bethel.

J. R.

GILOH (gī'lō). A city in the southern hills of Judah mentioned along with Jattir, Socoh, Debir, and Eshtemoh (Josh 15:48-51). It is called "Gilo" in II Sam 23:34 (RSV). Ahithophel came from here (II Sam 15:12). It is usually identified with Khirbet Jala, five miles NW of Hebron.

GILONITE (gī'lŏn-īt). An inhabitant of Giloh. Ahithophel is called a Gilonite (II Sam 23:34). The expression reads, "Eliam the son of Ahithophel of Gilo" (RSV).

GIMEL (gĭm'ĕl). The third letter of the Heb. alphabet, used in Ps 119 to designate the third section, each verse of which begins with this letter. *See* Alphabet.

GIMZO (gĭm'zō). A town in Judah bordering Philistia, captured by the Philistines in the days of Ahaz (II Chr 28:18). It is the modern Jimzu, a small village about three miles SE of Lydda.

GIN. Two words are translated "gin" in the KJV: *paḥ* in Job 18:9 and Isa 8:14; and *mô-qēsh* in Ps 140:5; 141:9; Amos 3:5. Both words are usually translated "snare." *Paḥ* is the snare and *môqēsh* is possibly the bait for the snare. It seems to have been a noose of hair or wire for snaring wild birds alive, horsehair for snaring small birds, and wire for snaring larger ones. *See* Snare; Trap.

GINATH (gī'năth). The father of Tibni, who was unsuccessful in his claim to the throne of Israel against Omri (I Kgs 16:21-22).

GINNETHO (gĭn'ĕ-thō). This term and Ginnethoi are evidently the same as Ginnethon (q.v.).

GINNETHON (gĭn'ē-thŏn). Variant of Ginnetho and Ginnethoi (Neh 12:4).

The head of a family of priests in the period of Joiakim (Neh 12:16). This name is also mentioned as being that of a priest who witnessed the covenant renewal under Ezra (Neh 10:6).

GIRDLE. There are several kinds of girdles, each used as an article of clothing. Heb. *'abnēt* was the special priestly linen sash (Ex 28:4, 39; 39:29; Lev 16:4; Isa 22:21); the *'ēzôr* was the common kilt or loincloth (II Kgs 1:8; Job 12:18; Isa 5:27; 11:5; Jer 13:1-11); the *ḥăgôr* or *ḥăgôrâ* was a soldier's belt (II Sam 20:8; I Kgs 2:5); and Gr. *zōnē* was a sash, belt, or loincloth. *See* Dress.

The word girdle is also used in a figurative sense. The girdle was a symbol of power, strength, and activity (Job 12:18, 21, ASV; 30:11; Isa 11:5; 22:21; 45:5; I Kgs 20:11), probably because it contained purses and weapons, or covered a man's vital and reproductive organs. Thus to gird (or girdle) up the loins denotes preparation for battle or any other activity (I Kgs 18:46; II Kgs 4:29; Lk 12:35; I Pet 1:13). *See* Armor.

To loose the girdle and give it to another was a token of great confidence and affection (I Sam 18:4). Girdles of sackcloth were worn in times of mourning to show humiliation and sorrow (Isa 3:24; 22:12). The "cleaving of the girdle to a man's loins" (Jer 13:11) illustrates the close adherence of the people of God to Him in loyalty. Righteousness and faithfulness are called the girdle or kilt of the Messiah (Isa 11:5). Because the *'ēzôr* was worn next to the skin, in figure it signifies that these are inseparable elements in His character.

E. C. J.

GIRGASHITES (gûr'gà-shīts). A Canaanite tribe (Gen 10:16; 15:21; Deut 7:1; Josh 3:10; 24:11; Neh 9:8; I Chr 1:14). In Heb. this term is always singular. These people were dispossessed by the Hebrews, with no sure indication of locality or to what branch of the Canaanites they belonged. The term is used in connection with the fifth son of Canaan (Gen 10:16).

The Girgashites evidently inhabited land to the W of Jordan (Josh 24:11). Some have identified the Girgashites with the Qirkishites of an Assyrian tablet. More likely the similarity is to the frequent personal names *Grgshy*, *Grgsh*, and *Grgshm* in the vowelless Punic texts from Carthage, and to the name *Grgsh* on a tablet from Ugarit. These occurrences would tend to confirm the Genesis record that the Girgashites were closely related to the Canaanites, later known as Phoenicians, who in turn founded Carthage.

GIRL. This term appears twice in the OT (Joel 3:3; Zech 8:5), in both instances in association with boys. The term may mean child, female, lass, or even damsel, as in Gen 34:4.

GISPA (gĭs'pà). An overseer of the Nethinim

(Neh 11:21). A comparison with Ezr 2:43 suggests that the term may be identified with Hasupha. This word may be a corruption of Hasupha, a family of temple servants among the returned exiles. *See* Hasupha.

GITTAH-HEPHER (gĭt′á-hē′fĕr). *See* Gath-Hepher.

GITTAIM (gĭt′á-ĭm). This is the name Gath with a common locative ending, -*ayim*, which is identical in form to the Heb. dual inflection. In II Sam 4:3 it is mentioned incidentally that the Beerothites (*q.v.*) had fled to Gittaim but that their town of origin, Beeroth, was reckoned to the tribe of Benjamin. In the post-Exilic period the Benjamites were also in possession of Gittaim (Neh 11:33). That the towns which follow Gittaim in this list, e.g., Hadid, Neballat, Lod, and Ono, are situated on the coastal plain inland from Joppa (for the location of each of these towns see their respective entries) is no coincidence. Eusebius (*Onomasticon* 72:2-3) located Gittaim between Antipatris and Yabneh. The town to which he referred is the Gitta of the Madebah map, which is placed between Beth Dagon and Lod (*q.v.*).

From the written texts it is clear that this town existed throughout the Israelite period, during the post-Exilic Age, and even into the Roman-Byzantine age. The Jewish community in Ramleh during the Middle Ages preserved the tradition that Gittaim was identical with their town. Ramleh was founded in the 8th cen. after Christ by Caliph Suleiman Ibn Abd el-Malik of the Umayyads. This combination of facts points to the identification of Gittaim with Ras Abu Hamid, a tell covering over 40 acres to the SE of the present town. Recent surface investigations of the site have shown that a large fortified town existed there from the Early Iron Age through the Early Arab period.

It is not impossible that some of the references to Gath (*q.v.*) are actually concerned with Gittaim. This was the suggestion of Mazar ("Gath and Gittaim," IEJ, IV [1954], 227-235; "The Cities of the Territory of Dan," IEJ, X [1960], 65-77), which was highly pertinent so long as Gath of the Philistines was thought to be in the southern part of the Philistine plain. However, with the tentative identification of that Gath with a more northerly locale (Tell es-Safi), the assumed confusion with Gittaim is no longer necessary. Nevertheless, it still deserves consideration, especially in regard to Hazael's campaign (II Kgs 12:17-18).

A. F. R.

GITTITE (gĭt′ĭt). An inhabitant of Gath. Gittites are mentioned along with the inhabitants of other Philistine cities (Josh 13:3). Some were found in Judah serving as a bodyguard to David with Ittai as their commander (II Sam 15:18 ff.; 18:2). Obed-edom, who cared for the ark for a time, was a Gittite (II Sam 6:10 f.; I Chr 13:13). Goliath and other giant Philistine warriors were Gittites.

GITTITH (gĭt′ĭth). A term found in the titles of Ps 8, 81, 84. It is a feminine adjective derived from Gath but with an uncertain meaning. It may denote a musical instrument manufactured at Gath. If this is right, the titles would mean "on the lyre which was brought from Gath." Some regard the term as denoting a melody or march popular in Gath, or "The March of the Gittite Guards." The LXX renders "concerning the vintage." It may indicate a vintage song, since the Heb. *gat* means "winepress."

GIZONITE (gī′zŏ-nīt). A designation which occurs in I Chr 11:34, "the sons of Hashem the Gizonite." Gizon is nowhere else mentioned in the OT.

GLAD TIDINGS. Good news; used in KJV in Lk 1:19; 8:1; Acts 13:32; Rom 10:15. *See* Gospel.

Hand mirrors might be made of bronze or silver. Here is a silver mirror with an obsidian handle from Egypt. LL

GLASS. Glass was manufactured as early as the Old Kingdom of Egypt (2850-2200 B.C.). Much of the sand of Egypt has a high content of calcium carbonate suitable for making glass. Because the technique of glassblowing was not developed until the 1st cen. B.C. by the Phoenicians, all glass objects in OT times were cast or made by welding sticks of glass around a core. By the time of Moses Egyptian craftsmen showed the greatest skill in beautiful colored beads, amulets and small vials for perfumes and unguents. Glass is mentioned only once in the OT (Job 28:17, RSV), Heb. *zᵉkûkît*, KJV "crystal," along with gold; this would indicate its rarity and high price in the ancient world.

By NT times the Romans were developing transparent glass. In his visions of heaven John saw a city of pure gold, like clear glass (Rev 21:18) and its street also of pure gold, "like transparent glass" (v. 21). He compared other surfaces to a "sea of glass" (Rev 4:6; 15:2). But the people still preferred bottles and other objects to be made of colored glass. The color was obtained by the addition of metal oxides. Even clear Roman glass objects have become iridescent because of the oxidation of mineral traces.

The "glass" in Ex 38:8; Isa 3:23; I Cor 13:12; Jas 1:23 refers to the highly polished bronze hand mirrors in vogue both in Egypt and in the Roman world. When Elihu said, "Hast thou with him spread out the sky, which is strong, and as a molten looking glass?" (Job 37:18), he had in mind the bronze mirror as a simile of the brazen summer sky.

See Minerals and Metals: Glass.

J. R.

GLASS WORKER. *See* Occupations.

GLEAN. To gather or to pick up what was left in the fields after reaping. It applied not only to grain but also to grapes and olives. Pentateuchal laws prohibited an owner from gleaning his own fields, so that the poor, the fatherless, the widow, and the stranger might have food (cf. Lev 19:9 ff.; 23:22; Deut 24:19–21; Ruth 2).

GLEDE. *See* Animals: Kite, III.26.

GLORIFY. With reference to the persons of the Godhead, glorify means to exalt, make glorious, and honor God in the human life of the believer by following those guides prescribed in the Bible. The Christian is to glorify God in his body (I Cor 6:20), that is, to set forth or manifest God's glory through a holy, godly, and completely yielded life. Primarily glorification came to Jesus Christ through His resurrection (Jn 12:16). The believer as sharing in this glorified resurrected life is to manifest Christlikeness and the fruit of the Holy Spirit (Mt 5:16; Gal 5:22). The Holy Spirit provides the source of power for this action (II Cor 3:17–18; Rom 8:13). *See* Glory.

GLORY. A major biblical concept, the word "glory" is the translation in KJV of a variety of Heb. and Gr. words, the most common being *kābôd* in the OT and *doxa* in the NT. Developing from the Heb. concept of "weight, heaviness, worthiness," the term "glory" in a doctrinal sense is used of God in Ps 19:1 and 63:2, speaking of the heaviness, awesomeness, or intrinsic worth of God's being.

Central to the OT usage of the term is the idea of the "glory of Yahweh" (Isa 6:3). In this sense, glory is linked to revelation, and consists

of the manifestation of God's nature. The specific issue in Isa 6 is the revelation of holiness, and the majestic holiness and glory of God are closely related. At times in the OT this manifestation approximates an overpowering physical appearance of glory, splendor, or brilliance (Lev 9:23; Ex 33:18 ff.). This is theologically represented by the terms "presence," or "Shekinah glory."

In the NT the glory of the Lord is seen in connection with Jesus Christ in a variety of ways. The birth narrative in the Lucan account shows that the first advent of Messiah was marked by the appearance of the glory of the Lord (Lk 2:9, 14, 32). This glory, the fullness or sum of all the perfections of the Godhead, was veiled during the earthly incarnate ministry of Christ, except for a brief glimpse at the transfiguration (Lk 9:28 ff.), and at crucial points in Christ's ministry (Jn 2:11; 11:40). Heb 1:3 delineates Jesus Christ as the effulgence or radiation of the glory of God.

By sovereign grace, the NT believer is seen as sharing to some extent in this glory now (Rom 8:30; II Cor 4:6). In the resurrected state the believer will be conformed to the glorified Saviour to a far greater extent than now realized, and will share in the eschatological glory of Christ (I Pet 5:4; Rev 21:23). He will be free of the fallen nature and have a resurrection body.

Bibliography. R. Bultmann, "*Kauchaomai,* etc.," TDNT, III, 645–654. Gerhard Kittel, "*Doxa,*" TDNT, II, 233–255. Bernard Ramm, *Them He Glorified,* Grand Rapids: Eerdmans, 1963.

F. R. H.

GLUTTON. Essentially a voluptuary or a debauchee. In both OT and NT it is connected with drunkenness (Deut 21:20; Prov 23:21). Because our Lord was friendly to and went to the homes of publicans and sinners, He was accused of being a glutton and winebibber (Mt 11:19; Lk 7:34).

GNASH. To bite with the teeth or to grind the teeth in such a fashion as to show anguish, rage, or remorse. The OT uses the term in Job 16:9; Ps 35:16; 37:12; 112:10; Lam 2:16. Jesus speaks of the "gnashing of teeth" in Mt 8:12; 22:13; 24:51; 25:30. See also Mk 9:18; Acts 7:54.

GNAT. *See* Animals, III.16.

GNOSTICISM (nŏs'tĭ-sĭz-ĕm). A name applied to (1) a broad religious movement, basically dualistic and syncretistic, which spread throughout the ancient Near East immediately before and after the time of Christ; and (2) the religious systems exemplified by the "Great Gnostics" which flourished from the 2nd to the 4th cen. A.D. Gnosticism is used here in this latter sense.

Origins. While many have attempted to trace

Gnosticism to Iranian, Greek or Egyptian sources, it is now commonly accepted that the movement arose in a Judeo-Christian milieu. This is not a denial of probable pre-Christian elements in Gnosticism. However, the peculiar synthesis of ideas that gave birth to the "Great Gnostics" seems to have occurred in the late 1st cen. or early 2nd cen. A.D. It is evident that the movement began in a Heb.-Christian environment, probably in Syro-Palestine, because of the large number of Semitic names, idioms, and ideas appearing in early Gnostic works, such as the Apocryphon of John, the Gospel of Thomas, the Gospel of Philip; and the presence of distinctly Christian ideas, such as the sacraments, Christ the Redeemer, and the appeal to NT Scriptures.

Beliefs and practices. The more prominent of the "Great Gnostic" sects taught a system of doctrines which included (in variant forms) the following basic ideas: (1) a transcendent, ineffable Deity who is pure spirit; (2) a basic dualism between spirit and matter which necessitated the Pleroma (the chain of emanated beings linking the Great God with matter) to account for the origin of the universe; (3) a split within the Pleroma which resulted in the creation of material things and man by a Demiurge, the God of the OT; (4) a spark of the divine implanted in man at his creation; (5) the redemption and release of this divine spark by means of illumination, resulting in self-awareness (sometimes called "awaking from sleep" or "arousing from drunkenness"); (6) a Christ who redeems by being the Revelator or Illuminator rather than the suffering Saviour; and (7) salvation by knowledge, essentially self-knowledge.

Little is known about the ritual or cultic practices of the Gnostics. The Gospel of Philip seems to indicate that its readers practiced five sacraments: baptism, sealing, eucharist, chrism (anointing with olive oil), and bridal chamber. All these, except the final one, are found in orthodox Christianity. The practices of the Gnostics ranged from extreme asceticism to extreme libertinism, both extremes based upon the belief that the body was essentially evil.

Sects. The main bodies of Gnostics were the Valentinians (founded by Valentinus at Rome, c. A.D. 140), the Sethites (worshipers of Seth), the Ophites or Naasenes (who worshiped the serpent), the Barbelo-Gnostics (who stressed the role of Barbelo—the lower Sophia in Valentinianism), and the Marcionites (followers of Marcion, c. A.D. 145). Lesser groups included the Simonians (presumably followers of Simon of Samaria, Acts 8), the Carpocratians, the Paulicians, the Phibionites, and the Peratae. The latter named groups are not well represented in the surviving Gnostic literature.

Other groups closely related to the Gnostics include the Cerinthians and the Encratites of the 2nd cen. A.D., the Hermetics, and the Docetists. Lineal descent from the Gnostic movement can probably be ascribed to the Man-

deans, a group still surviving in Iraq. Either through the Mandeans or directly, the Manicheans (who flourished 3rd to 5th cen. A.D.) borrowed certain Gnostic doctrines. The Manicheans left medieval manifestations in the Cathari (Albigenses) and the Bogomils.

Literature. Prior to 1955 the Gnostics were known mainly through (1) the descriptions of their beliefs and practices in the works of the Church Fathers, chiefly Irenaeus, Hippolytus and Epiphanius; and (2) the surviving Gnostic literature in Codex Brucianus (two Books of Jeu and an untitled work), and in Codex Askewianus (*Pistis Sophia*). In that year the publication of Codex Berolinensis 8502 made accessible the Gospel of Mary, the Apocryphon of John, and the Wisdom of Jesus Christ.

In the meantime, the Nag Hammadi Gnostic texts had been discovered in 1945, and their publication (beginning in 1956) a wealth of Gnostic documents afforded the scholar first-hand insight into Gnostic doctrine and cult (*see* Chenoboskion). Today documents such as the Gospel of Truth, the Epistle of Rheginos, the Epistle of James, the Apocryphon of John, the Gospel of Thomas, the Gospel of Philip, and the Hypostasis of the Archons are available in English. Summaries of several other treatises have been published, and English translations of all 51 texts are projected. *See* Agrapha.

Biblical relationships. The Gnostic literature demonstrates the existence in the 2nd cen. of a NT canon almost identical with the formal canons adopted by the councils of Laodicea, Carthage, and Hippo. It also sheds light on textual variations and the history of textual transmission. The supreme importance of the literature is probably in the field of NT interpretation.

Some scholars have attempted to show that certain NT books are indebted to Gnosticism (John's Gospel) or are reactions against it (Colossians, Luke–Acts, Corinthians, Ephesians, Pastoral Epistles [*q.v.*], Johannine epistles). However, some of these scholars seem to be using the word "gnosticism" in the general meaning rather than referring to the central, unbiblical distinctives of the Great Gnostic sects. *See* Heresy.

Bibliography. Francis Crowfoot Burkitt, *Church and Gnosis,* Cambridge: Cambridge Univ. Press, 1932. Robert M. Grant, *Gnosticism, A Sourcebook of Heretical Writings,* New York: Harper, 1961; *Gnosticism and Early Christianity,* 2nd ed., New York: Harper & Row, 1966. Andrew K. Helmbold, *The Nag Hammadi Gnostic Texts and the Bible,* Grand Rapids: Baker, 1967. Hans Jonas, *The Gnostic Religion,* 2nd ed., Boston: Beacon Press, 1963. G. van Groningen, *First Century Gnosticism, Its Origin and Motifs,* Leiden: Brill, 1967. Robert McLachlan Wilson, *The Gnostic Problem,* London: Mowbrays, 1958.

A. K. H.

GOAD. A pointed stick used for driving animals. It could be used in combat (cf. Shamgar, Jud 3:31, who slew 600 Philistines). When a goad was tipped with iron the metal point had to be sharpened (I Sam 13:21). Eccl 12:11 indicates that words may serve figuratively as goads.

GOAT. *See* Animals, I.9.

GOAT'S HAIR, GOATSKIN. *See* Dress; Tabernacle.

GOATSUCKER. A nighthawk. *See* Animals, III.17.

GOAT, WILD. *See* Animals: Ibex, II.22.

GOATH (gō'ăth). A locality near Jerusalem, apparently near the SW corner of the city, listed after the hill of Gareb in Jer 31:39. In this passage the prophet describes the restored Holy City by proceeding around it in a counterclockwise direction. Goath thus may have been at the junction of the Kidron, Tyropoean, and Hinnom valleys.

GOB (gŏb). The exact location is unknown but at this place David's soldiers fought two battles with the Philistines (II Sam 21:18–19). The parallel passage in I Chr 20:4 lists Gezer as the locale of the contests. Gob, which is mentioned in the Amarna letters as Gubbu, may have been near the better-known Gezer. *See* Gezer.

GOBLET. A basin or curved bowl-shaped vessel. In Song 7:2 the beloved's navel or pelvis is compared to a goblet. The same Heb. term, *'aggān*, occurs in Ex 24:6 as "basins" and in Isa 22:24 as "cups."

GOD. The Bible stresses that man as a creature was especially made for knowledge of his Creator, who reveals Himself to man in nature, in conscience, and, moreover, in particular historical events. This divine disclosure, climaxed in Jesus Christ as God's self-revelation in flesh, is authoritatively narrated and interpreted by the Scriptures. The God of biblical theology is therefore decisively known from scriptural data, that is, from the prophetic-apostolic disclosure, centering in Jesus Christ as the incarnate revelation of Deity. By contrast, expositions by speculative philosophers aim to sketch the nature of God from His works alone, whether nature or man, or from the general movements of history.

The self-revealed God introduces Himself by name. Despite the fall of the human race into sin, He does not retire from the scene of history, but challenges speculative interpreters who introduce Deity simply by their own schematic views (e.g., Plato's Idea of the Good, Aristotle's Prime Mover, Hegel's Absolute, Tillich's Ground of Being). The biblical terms and names of God—generic, proper, and personal—supply, in fact, a dramatic introduction to

the Creator, Preserver, Redeemer and Judge of life.

1. *The generic term: Elohim.* Genesis immediately refers the creation of the universe and man to *Elohim* (a generic term for deity, whose equivalent is *theos* in Greek, *Deus* in Latin, God in English). This plural noun (*'ĕlôah, 'ĕlōhîm*) in pagan usage signified plurality of gods, whereas the OT specifically excludes polytheism. (*a*) In prose, the plural form *elohim* commonly was used for deity (monotheistic or polytheistic), the rare singular form *eloah* being specially reserved for poetry (cf. Job, where *eloah* occurs more often than in all the rest of the OT). (*b*) Except when used of pagan gods (e.g., Gen 31:30; Ex 12:12), the plural *elohim* is uniformly used in the OT but with a singular adjective to exclude polytheistic misunderstanding. The intention or content, therefore, is more important than etymology or derivation for determining meaning. (*c*) The Genesis creation narrative refers the origin of the universe, and particularly man, to *Elohim*, whose creative activity distinguishes Him from the pagan myths of multiple competitive deities. (*d*) Although intimations of the doctrine of the Trinity sometimes have been traced to the plural form *Elohim*, the term more likely is a Heb. idiom that suggests plurality of majesty or plenitude of power in view of God's creation and governance of man and the world. When in the OT *elohim* carries the idea of plurality of persons, the reference is to pagan polytheism rather than to personal distinctions within a single deity. Without other hints in the OT, and without the explicit NT teaching, Trinitarianism could hardly be inferred from the term *elohim* itself. (*e*) Through its OT associations *elohim* does not remain simply a generic term for deity, but becomes a proper name also.

The title *Adonai*, from *'ādôn*, "master," "lord," "sovereign," is an attributive designation in view of the divine sovereignty. The word passed finally into use as a generic term for God. The corresponding NT term is *Kurios*, "Lord."

2. *Proper names: El Elyon, El Shaddai, Yahweh.* The remarkable turn in biblical theology is that the living God is progressively known through actual historical events in which He discloses Himself and His purposes. The generic terms for Deity thereby gain more specific content, become proper names, and these successively give way to later designations that reflect more fully the progressively revealed nature of God.

The word *El*, the most common term for Deity in the Semitic languages (but not the usual OT term), is often coupled with a noun or adjective (cf. *'el 'elyôn*, "God Most High," or *'el shaddai*, "God Almighty"). Thus it became a proper name for God.

El Shaddai became the characteristic patriarchal name for Deity in consequence of the divine covenant with Abraham. Whereas *Elohim* especially depicts God in the role of Creator, Maker and Preserver of man and the world, *El Shaddai* looks further to the divine constraint of natural processes for the purposes of His grace. The birth of Isaac the promised son, in the absence of any natural prospect, illuminates God as omnipotently materializing His gracious purpose in a finite and fallen creation. In the LXX and the NT, *El Shaddai* is translated *pantokratōr,* "Almighty," "Omnipotent One" (cf. II Cor 6:18; Rev 1:8; 4:8).

In the progress of the Heb. religious drama, earlier names for God fade into the background in view of the developing self-disclosure of God. Yet the name *El Shaddai* does not wholly replace *Elohim,* since the Hebrews retain all designations of Deity, sometimes interchangeably, often as circumstances may suggest one or another. The literary use of divine names, therefore, supplies no infallible clue to the literary development and authorship of the sacred writings.

The name par excellence for the God of Israel is *Yahweh,* found 6,823 times in the OT. Through Israel's deliverance from bondage in Egypt, adoption as a nation, and guidance to the Promised Land, the Redeemer-God is especially known by this name. The self-revealing God discloses Himself redemptively in a special way (I AM WHO I AM," Ex 3:14). *See* I Am.

The living God, who had earlier manifested Himself to the patriarchs in the capacity of *El Shaddai* (Ex 6:2 f.), was not wholly unknown to them as *Yahweh,* this name being found frequently in Genesis in the mouth of God, and even in Jacob's blessing (which no redactor would have altered!); from Abram onward, the name of *Yahweh* periodically enters the sacred record. But with the rescue of Israel and establishment of the theocracy, *Yahweh* becomes the distinctive OT name for the living God, who not only conforms fallen nature to grace, but shapes a new order of grace in the midst of this natural course of things. Hence the name *Jehovah* (an artificial English reconstruction of the Heb. YHWH, originally pronounced Yahweh or Yahveh) particularly emphasizes God's redemptive activity. Through superstition, the Hebrews came to avoid pronouncing the tetragrammaton (four-letter name) YHWH and substituted *Adonai.* In recent centuries, *Jehovah* has often served as the equivalent of *Yahweh* in English literature, hymnody, and Bible translations (e.g., the ASV). The Jerusalem Bible has adopted *Yahweh.*

Superimposing a framework of naturalistic development upon the Bible, higher critics have contended that the multiple names for God, especially *Elohim* and *Yahweh,* reflect divergent literary sources. This assumption was long a cornerstone of the now discredited JEDP hypothesis which resolved the Pentateuch (*q.v.*) into conflicting original sources. The attempt to explain the compounded name *Yahweh-Elohim* by documentary conflation has proved untenable, and JEDP are more and more acknowl-

edged as artificially projected sources (on the precise content of which the critical scholars themselves have disagreed). *See* God, Names and Titles of; Lord.

3. *Personal terms: Father, Son, Spirit.* In the OT, God was revealed as Creator of all things, Lord of history, Judge of men and nations, and Redeemer of a chosen people. The NT lifts the revelation of God to even higher dimensions. Over against pagan superstition and speculation about the supernatural, the OT declared God to be transcendent to nature and man. Expressly forbidden were graven images which would not only localize Deity in time and space but also materialize Deity by denying the spirituality (invisibility and immateriality) of God. The NT revelation, presupposing that God is Spirit (Jn 4:24), adds the dramatic emphasis that the invisible God has become uniquely incarnate in Jesus Christ (Jn 1:14, 18).

The revelation of God in Christ discloses that God is a social being. In the one God there exists a society of divine persons; furthermore, this God seeks to restore doomed sinners to personal fellowship even at the cost of sacrificial death. The disclosure of "the name of Jesus," of eternal fatherhood and eternal sonship in the very being of God, moves on to the unveiling of God as triune by the revelation of "the name of the Father, and of the Son, and of the Holy Spirit" (Mt 28:19). The distinctive Christian affirmation about God is the doctrine of the Trinity. In a series of mighty redemptive acts the inner secret of God's being is made known. The God of Sinai, the outraged Creator ranged against transgressors of His law, is also the God of Golgotha, is "God with us," attested both by the gift of the incarnate Christ and by the gift of the indwelling Spirit by whom the Father draws near. *See* Godhead; Sonship of Christ; Trinity.

[The NT emphasizes the fatherhood of God. Jesus' most common designation for God was "Father." In Christian theology this term is reserved primarily for the first person of the Trinity. But the designation Father is sometimes used when referring to the one supreme God (I Pet 1:17; Isa 9:6, where "everlasting Father" connotes Messiah's true deity). The conception of God as Father is present in the OT, where it describes both a creative and a redemptive or covenant relationship. Malachi's contemporaries ask, "Have we not all one father? Hath not one God created us?" (Mal 2:10). Isaiah parallels the ideas of father and potter in calling upon God as Creator (64:8). In a unique sense God is the Father of Jesus Christ by eternal generation, expressive of an essential and timeless relationship.

More commonly in the OT the fatherhood of God expressed His covenant relationship with His people Israel. In His love He chose Israel and redeemed her from Egypt so that collectively the nation was considered the child or son of God (Isa 63:16; Ex 4:22; Hos 11:1). In this adoptive relationship Israel was to call God "my Father" (Jer 3:19) and was expected to honor Him as Father (Mal 1:6). Because the majority refused to show filial love expressed in obedience, the Lord was especially like a father to the God-fearing among the nation (Ps 103:13).

In the NT God's redemption reaches the individual first of all at the spiritual level. Salvation is viewed from two aspects, that of one's standing in Christ and that of the regenerating work of the Holy Spirit in him. Through identification with Christ by faith the believer is adopted into the family of God with all the privileges of an heir to call God "Abba! Father!" (Rom 8:15-17). See Abba. Under the other aspect he is regarded as born anew into the kingdom of God, partaker of the divine nature, and loved by the Father (Jn 3:3-7; II Pet 1:4; I Jn 3:1-2). Nowhere does Christ assume that this relationship exists between God and unbelievers. He never teaches that a redeeming fatherhood of God includes all men, but pointedly says to the censorious Jews, "Ye are of your father the devil" (Jn 8:44). See Father, God the.—J.R.]

4. *The attributive names or divine perfections.* While the personal names apply to the respective centers of consciousness in the one God, the attributes or virtues qualify the Godhead as a whole.

Theologians customarily have distinguished between the incommunicable attributes (self-existence, eternity, immutability, infinity, omniscience, omnipresence, omnipotence, unity) that emphasize His transcendence and are ascribable to God alone, and the communicable attributes that express the immanence of God and are shared in some degree by His creatures.

Through the influence of Kant and Schleiermacher, much Protestant theology in the recent past has been anti-metaphysical in temperament. Its preoccupation has been with God-in-relation to man (hence the communicable attributes) to the neglect of God-in-Himself. Protestant orthodoxy has repudiated this modernist "experiential centering" of theology which substitutes a "relational" for a "metaphysical" exposition of the nature of God. Instead of demeaning theology to an inference or induction from religious experience (as Protestant liberalism did), or trying to expound the divine attributes on a speculative rational basis (so medieval scholasticism), Protestant orthodoxy derives the content of its doctrine of God primarily from the Bible as an objectively communicated propositional revelation. The recent modern disbelief in propositional divine revelation has meant the loss also of objective knowledge of God. Karl Barth, in his later writings, sought to escape such neoorthodox subjectivity. But Barth halted short of affirming the objective inspiration of Scripture, and appealed vulnerably to an internal miracle of divine grace whereby the believer knows God truly.

The communicable attributes may be classified as spiritual (spirituality), mental (wisdom, veracity), moral (goodness, love, holiness, righteousness) and volitional (will, power to act). Theologians have had to contend with numerous temptations in expositing these perfections. Some have regarded these qualities as merely verbal distinctions with no objective basis in the nature of God (the pantheistic philosopher Spinoza reduced the attributes of Deity simply to thought and extension). Others have regarded every distinct biblical term as sufficient basis for attributing a different perfection to the divine nature.

By subordinating the righteousness or holiness of God to the love of God, Protestant liberalism nullified divine wrath. When righteousness is reduced to a form of benevolence, the resulting revision of the character of God leads logically to repudiating the doctrines of propitiatory atonement and of hell, and invites eschatological speculations about universal salvation or ultimate reconciliation for the lost. Neoorthodox theology claims to reaffirm the reality of the wrath of God. But it continues, even in a more complex manner, to submerge divine righteousness in divine love. Historic Protestant theology affirms that a basis exists in the nature of God to discriminate between righteousness and love as two distinct divine attributes which complement rather than exclude one another.

See Election; Godhead; Holiness, Holy; Incarnation; Sovereignty of God; Will of God.

C. F. H. H.

Bibliography. Robert Anderson, *The Silence of God,* Grand Rapids: Kregel, 1952. J. Oliver Buswell, Jr., *A Systematic Theology of the Christian Religion,* Grand Rapids: Zondervan, 1962, I, 29-182. Stephen Charnock, *Discourses upon the Existence and Attributes of God,* London: Henry Bohn, 1849. Gordon H. Clark, "God," BDT, pp. 238-248. R. A. Finlayson, "God," NBD, pp. 474-477. Charles Hodge, *Systematic Theology,* New York: Scribner, 1873, I, 191-441. H. Kleinknecht, G. Quell, E. Stauffer and K. G. Kuhn, "*Theos,* etc.," TDNT, III, 65-123. Robert C. Neville, *God, the Creator,* Chicago: Univ. of Chicago Press, 1968 (a philosophic defense of the transcendence and immanence of God). James Orr, *The Christian View of God and the World,* New York: Scribner, 1907, pp. 73-115. J. Barton Payne, *The Theology of the Older Testament,* Grand Rapids: Zondervan, 1962, pp. 120-176, and an annotated bibliography. J. B. Phillips, *Your God Is Too Small,* New York: Macmillan, 1961. Norman H. Snaith, *The Distinctive Ideas of the Old Testament,* London: Epworth Press, 1944. Augustus H. Strong, *Systematic Theology,* 11th ed., Philadelphia: Judson Press, 1947, pp. 52-110, 243-443. Geerhardus Vos, *Biblical Theology,* Grand Rapids: Eerdmans, 1948.

GOD IS DEAD THEOLOGY. This viewpoint was presented in the 1960's by a new school of theology, calling the movement radical theology. It sprang up in the wake of the theologies of Paul Tillich and Rudolf Bultmann. The movement was composed of a number of theologians who vary considerably in their viewpoints but were united by the common theme "God is dead." They are generally known as the "God is Dead" theologians. They vary widely as to the meaning of this slogan, and were held together as much by other common factors as by their main tenet.

Different Views of the "Death of God"

1. *There never was a God* and now the very idea has died. This was the view of such an atheist as Nietzsche as he spoke of the "death of God," and his Madman cried, "Do we not hear anything yet of the noise of the grave diggers who are burying God? Do we not smell anything yet of God's decomposition? Gods too decompose. God is dead" (*The Madman*).

This atheistic view was presented in another form later by Feuerbach in his *Essence of Christianity* in 1841 as he spoke of religion, and the Christian religion in particular, as merely a projection of the human spirit. Albert Camus, in his famous book *The Rebel,* outlined the entire history of atheism as a movement.

2. *God has actually died.* T. J. J. Altizer, associate professor of Bible and Religion at Emory University, Atlanta, Georgia, wrote in *Radical Theology and the Death of God:* "We must realize that the death of God is an historical event, that God has died in our cosmos, in our history, in our *existenz*" (p. 11).

In a subsequent book, *The Gospel of Christian Atheism,* Altizer explained in detail his theory of how God has died over and over again, to appear each time in another "epiphany" or appearance. The incarnation of Jesus Christ and His crucifixion are to be seen as a Hegelian triadic dialectic in which the God of the OT epiphany, a changeless, immobile quiescent God (as the thesis), has negated Himself to become incarnate or flesh as Jesus Christ (as the antithesis), and then Jesus has negated Himself to become spirit, while God the Father has again negated Himself to become flesh. God the Father, now flesh, united with Jesus, now spirit, in the thesis to form "the Great Humanity Divine" or "the final coming together of God and man" (p. 107).

This triadic dialectic is the process of the death of God. And yet the death of God occurs again and again as a continuous process so that "we can say that God dies in some sense wherever he is present or actual in the world, for God actualizes himself by negating his original or given expressions" (p. 105). Altizer says of his position that "it is an atheistic view but with a difference" (*Radical Theology,* p. x).

3. *The old concept of God is dead.* The old biblical concept of a personal God is out of date and must be discarded, say these radical theologians. Modern man with his scientific viewpoint cannot accept the view of a "God out there." Paul Tillich spoke of the need perhaps to forget the name of God for a generation (*The Shaking of the Foundations,* p. 57) so that we may establish a new view of God as "the God above God" (*The Courage to Be,* pp. 182, 186) who is present as the Power of Being in everything while still being absent. Bishop John A. T. Robinson also speaks along the same lines in his *Honest to God* (p. 7). God is not a person or an object out there, but the Power of Being in everything that is.

4. *The very word "God" is logically meaningless.* The linguistic analyst argues that the term "God" corresponds to no reality which can be tested and proved in an empirical manner, and is therefore entirely contentless. Paul Van Buren reasoned in this manner in his book *The Secular Meaning of the Gospel.* We can talk meaningfully of Jesus Christ, because He was an historical person and there is at least empirical evidence for His existence, but not of "this literally nonsensical entity called 'God' " (p. 84). "Today we cannot even understand the Nietzschian cry 'God is dead,' for if it were so, how could we know? No, the problem now is that the *word* 'God' is dead" (p. 103).

5. *Various other views.* For some, God is merely in eclipse (cf. Martin Buber); for others, the God whom we have thought of as a problem solver is now the God who deals with man as no longer a child but mature (cf. Bonhoeffer's idea of the "coming of age" of humanity). Again, for such a man as William Hamilton, God is now silent, hidden, absent, so we must speak of the death of God, but that time will doubtless pass.

Uniting Characteristics

1. *Revolutionary activism.* The radical theologians see revolutionary action as called for in our day.

2. *Optimism versus pessimism.* The movement is a distinctly American reaction to the pessimism and the subjectivism of European existentialism. Its optimism is undoubtedly partly a result of the economic prosperity being experienced in both Europe and the United States today.

3. *Social action.* The great stress is upon social action in general in distinction to either individual or corporate spiritual renewal. The social, economic, and political aspects of life crowd out all the moral and spiritual.

4. *The slogan "God is dead."* While this is explained in all the diverse ways mentioned, still the slogan does indicate for many that the God of the OT has ceased to exist. God can be known only as He becomes united with universal humanity, that is, in Jesus as universal humanity.

5. *Universal humanity.* According to these

theologians, God has been done away with, but Jesus Christ has become united with fallen humanity. He can be touched in every human hand and seen in every human face.

6. *Secularized Christianity*. Man has become entirely secularized. Bonhoeffer spoke of man "coming of age" and reaching maturity. Man is now self-sufficient and has no need for God. Harvey Cox in *The Secular City* stresses the wholly secularized society of our day and proposes a secular gospel to meet man's needs. Bonhoeffer spoke of a "religionless Christianity" and how man must be spoken to in wholly secular terms; Cox spells this out for our day. The Christian is to work alongside the man of the world in his political, economic, and social endeavors. He should not come to his fellowman to help him with revealed principles or rules, but he should come simply as man with man to work out bit by bit the answers which prove successful because they are found to function.

7. *Situation ethics*. Most of the radical theologians are in distinct rebellion against the revealed ethical standards and moral laws presented in the Bible. They claim all ethical decisions can vary according to the particular circumstances in which a man finds himself as he applies the one principle of love. Premarital relations, adultery, lying and stealing, all may be right under certain circumstances (cf. Joseph Fletcher, *Situation Ethics*).

8. *The failure of the church*. According to their view, the church has failed and is failing, particularly today, to reach the masses of mankind. Its view of God is outdated in a modern scientific world. The church must mix with the world and enter into its social, economic, and political problems with a new secular gospel. The secular must replace the soul-winning gospel.

Historical Background

The God is Dead movement can be traced from early humanism through William Blake the poet, on to Nietzsche, and through Feuerbach, and on to the present. The Christian humanism of Erasmus has blossomed forth in the movement's confidence that man is quite well able to do without God because he can find absolute and radical freedom from all moral laws in a Christ who has become united with fallen humanity. Nietzsche could not bear to have a God who saw into his sinful heart, and therefore wrote, "He had to die; he looked with eyes which saw everything. . . .His pity knew no modesty: he crept into my dirtiest corners . . . on such a witness I would have revenge . . . the God that beheld everything and also man had to die!" With his Madman, Nietzsche put God to death in a literary manner. He finally broke down mentally under the strain, never recovered, and died insane. Altizer leans heavily on Nietzsche for his argument that God has died, and others of the movement also quote him.

After Karl Barth failed to find any way to get propositional revelation from God with his Kierkegaardian theory of revelation (*see* Neoorthodoxy), and Bultmann emptied the teachings of Scripture completely with his demythologization, the radical theologians have turned to Nietzsche with his cry, "God is dead," and given the expression their own particular meanings. Bonhoeffer has given them certain inspirations with his suggestion of a "religionless Christianity" and a wholly secular presentation of the gospel, but since he continued to believe in the existence of God the Father and in confessional Christianity until the time of his death, their view that God is dead is not attributable to him.

The most important men in the American movement are Thomas J. J. Altizer, William Hamilton, Paul Van Buren, and Harvey Cox.

Analysis and Evaluation

The God is Dead theologians with their radical theology and revolutionary activism are challenging the true evangelical church to consider the Christian's responsibility toward the secular needs of man in the areas of economics, politics, and man's social needs. God charged man with the task of subduing and ruling the world (Gen 1:28), and this task has never been revoked. This is God's world, and therefore it is the Christian's world, even if Satan has usurped God's place in the hearts of fallen man. Therefore it is the Christian's duty to do all he can to subdue the world economically, socially, and politically. This was the concept of Abraham Kuyper and it has been worked out in detail by the Free University which he was instrumental in founding. The reformed view is that the Christian has as his duty the task of applying the revealed principles of justice, democracy, and morality found in the Bible to the world's needs. In contrast, these radical theologians think that they can change the world while at the same time denying the divinely revealed principles.

The evangelical Christian finds the God is Dead theology wanting for the following reasons:

1. The movement is essentially a rebellion against God-given law and morals. Man has always wanted absolute radical freedom, and these men are ready to destroy God in their own way, even as Nietzsche did in his way in order to gain such freedom.

2. These men maintain that we live in a scientific age and that modern man must base all his life on the scientific method. In science man finds physical laws by experimentation. If he breaks the physical law, then the law destroys him immediately. There are, however, also moral laws. If he breaks them, they in turn can destroy him; however, they do not necessarily react immediately. They may punish him in his old age or in his children's children. This tempts him to think that such laws may not

exist. The difference between the physical laws and the moral laws is that the former can be discovered by fallen man through functionalism, but the latter only through revelation! The reason functionalism fails at this point is that man, as fallen, cannot correctly in moral matters. His total depravity incapacitates him and even prejudices him against revealed moral law.

3. All the arguments presented for the death of God are based finally upon a refusal to accept Jesus Christ at His own self-evaluation. He spoke of God as His Father, as being a person, and as hearing and answering both His prayers and those who are His children. He maintained that He was the Son of God, and indicated that He forgave sins because He was God. Any attempt, therefore, to take Christ only in part is a denial of who and what He is.

4. The God is Dead theologians are not Christians at all. They are merely humanists.

Bibliography. T. J. J. Altizer, *The Gospel of Christian Atheism*, Philadelphia: Westminster, 1966. Altizer and William Hamilton, *Radical Theology and the Death of God*, New York: Bobbs-Merrill, 1966. Harvey Cox, *The Secular City*, New York: Macmillan, 8th ed., 1966. Joseph Fletcher, *Situation Ethics*, Philadelphia: Westminster, 1966. Kenneth Hamilton, *God Is Dead*, Grand Rapids: Eerdmans, 1966. K. Hamilton, *Revolt Against Heaven*, Grand Rapids: Eerdmans, 1965. William Hamilton, *The New Essence of Christianity*, New York: Association Press, 1961. Gabriel Vahanian, *The Death of God*, New York: George Braziller, 1957. Paul M. Van Buren, *The Secular Meaning of the Gospel*, New York: Macmillan, 1963.

R. A. K.

GOD, NAMES AND TITLES OF. Five OT Heb. terms are of basic importance in discussing the various simple and compound names and titles of God. In the OT, just as in Canaanite religious literature, synonymous divine names often occur for the same deity as well as appellations used in parallelism in poetry. No inferences of polytheism can be drawn from such usage. For the significance in biblical times of the concept of "name," *see* Name(s).

1. *El.* The Heb. word *'ēl,* which has cognate forms in other Semitic languages, signifies "the strong one," a mighty being or leader, a god in the widest sense, whether true or false. Like *theos,* Deus and God, it is the generic term for Deity. The plural form *'ēlîm* in most contexts is to be translated "gods." These gods may be mere idols of wood, metal or stone (Isa 44:10, 15, 17; 46:6). *El* was the name of the "high god" or head of the Canaanite pantheon. Among the Israelites, *El* was often used of their God in describing Him and as an element in compound names (e.g., *El Shaddai,* "Immanuel"). *See* El.

2. *Elohim.* This plural form of the similar word *'ĕlōah* (found 42 times in Job) is used of gods and goddesses of the surrounding nations, but chiefly to signify the true God of Israel in the sense of the one supreme Deity (Gen 1:1, etc.; 3.5; Deut 4:35, 39; Jer 10:10). As the ordinary Heb. word for God, it corresponds to the common noun "god" in English, and is therefore applicable to the concept of deity in contrast to man and created beings. The plural form with reference to one particular deity is not unique to the Heb. OT, but the very frequent usage in Heb. was almost certainly encouraged by the Israelites' belief that their God was the only true God, and therefore that the sum and total of deity was inherent in Him. *See* Elohim; God.

3. *Elyon, El Elyon. Elyon,* the "Most High," is found alone as a designation for God in Num 24:16; Deut 32:8; II Sam 22:14; Ps 9:2, plus 11 times; Isa 14:14; Lam 3:35, 38. In the LXX and NT this title appears as Gr. *hupsistos* (e.g., Lk 1:32; Acts 7:48). The term *'Ēl 'Elyôn,* the "most high God," is particularly significant as used by Melchizedek (Gen 14:18–20). The term refers to divine beings in the sacred literature of the Canaanites found at Ras Shamra (*q.v.*). *See* Most High.

4. *Yahweh.* This is the most significant name of God found in the OT in that it is the personal proper name Israel had for their God. For this reason in post-Exilic times it began to be considered so holy that it was never pronounced. Instead, usually the term *Adonai* was substituted. In the 6th–7th cen. A.D. the Jewish Masoretic scholars combined the vowels of *Adonai* with the consonants YHWH to remind the synagogue reader to pronounce the name as *Adonai*. But those consonants and vowels spell the name Jehovah, a form first attested about A.D. 1220. Jehovah is the spelling often used in the ASV, following its few occurrences in the KJV, to translate *Yahweh*. The substitution of the vowels can only be understood when we realize that the original Heb. Scriptures contained no written vowels. The Heb. words consisted of consonants alone, the vowels being provided by the requirement of the context, or by memory.

Yahweh was doubtless the approximate pronunciation of the tetragrammaton, the four-letter word YHWH, since transliterations into Gr. in early Christian literature have been found in the form of *iaoué* (Clement of Alexander) and *iabé* (Theodoret) pronounced "iave." The name is a variant connected with the verb *hāyâ,* "to be," from an earlier form, *hāwâ*.

Strictly speaking, this is the only personal name of God belonging to Him alone. When Moses asked God what was the significance of His name, He replied, "I AM THAT I AM: and he said, Thus shalt thou say unto the children of Israel, I AM hath sent me unto you" (Ex 3:14). Thus God revealed to Moses what was the very inner meaning of His name as *Yahweh*. God followed with the declaration, "Thus shalt thou say unto the children of Israel, Yahweh the God of your fathers, the God of Abraham, the God of Isaac, and the God of Jacob, hath sent me unto you: this is my name for ever" (Ex 3:15). His very name was His promise to His covenant people that "He is" with them (cf. 3:12) to be their God and to supply every need. He had not explained the import of His name Yahweh to the patriarchs (cf. Ex 6:2-3).

There is strong reason to believe that Jesus picked up the thought inherent in the divine name when He said, "Before Abraham was, I am" (Jn 8:58). This identification of Himself with the declaration of God in Ex 3:14 would then have been so startling as to explain why the Jews took up stones immediately to stone Him (Jn 8:58-59). *See* I Am.

5. *Adonai.* An honorific title used both as an intensive plural of rank meaning "Master," "Sovereign," or "Lord," and as an appellative meaning "my Lord." Its alternate form occurs in Ps 110:1 which reads, "The Lord [*Yahweh*] said unto my Lord ['*ădōnî*]." Mt 22:41-45 shows how Christ identified this title with Himself. The Gr. equivalent is *Kyrios*, "Lord," representing both *Yahweh* and *Adonai* in the OT LXX. In the NT it is applied to Christ equally with the Father and the Spirit.

6. *Composite names for God.* There are in the OT special characterizations of God, both expressing and confessing such truths as:

a. God's power—'*Ēl Shaddai,* "Almighty God," probably meaning originally the "god of the mountain(s)" (Gen 17:1). The term Shaddai occurs alone 31 times in Job as an appellation for God.

b. God's eternity—'*Ēl 'Ôlām,* "the everlasting God" (Gen 21:33) and '*Atîiq Yômîn,* "Ancient of Days," the One who judges and rules over the empires of the world (Dan 7:9, 13, 22).

c. God's special relationship to Israel. Accepting Israel as his new name (cf. Gen 32:28), Jacob confessed '*El-'elōhê-Israel,* "El (is) the God of Israel," when he bought a piece of land and erected an altar at Shechem (Gen 33:18-20, JerusB). Likewise Joshua in establishing the covenant at Mount Ebal (Josh 8:30), Deborah after her victory (Jud 5:3), and the prophets and psalmists (Isa 17:6; Ps 59:5; Zeph 2:9) acknowledged Yahweh to be the "God of Israel." "The Holy One of Israel" was a favorite title (*qᵉdôsh Yiśrā'ēl*) with Isaiah, who used it 29 times. He also spoke of God as the "mighty One of Israel" (Isa 1:24) and the "mighty One of Jacob" (Isa 49:26; 60:16), following Gen 49:24. See also the "Strength of Israel" (I Sam 15:29).

d. God's provision for the believer's needs. Abraham named the hill where he was about to offer Isaac *Jehovah-jireh.* He thus confessed that God had provided the needed sacrifice in the ram caught in the thicket which could substitute as a burnt offering instead of his son (Gen 22:13-14). *Yahweh Rōph'ekā,* "I am the Lord, your healer" (Ex 15:26, RSV), was

God's promise to all who would diligently obey Him.

e. God's leadership—*Jehovah-nissi,* "The Lord is my banner," the name Moses gave to an altar he built to commemorate the defeat of the Amalekites (Ex 17:15). *Yahweh Rō'î,* the best loved name or description of all, is the familiar "The Lord is my shepherd" (Ps 23:1), with its many applications to leadership, provision, and protection.

f. God's peace—*Yahweh-shalom,* "The Lord is (my) peace," exclaimed Gideon after being visited by the angel of the Lord as he erected an altar in Ophrah and knew the peace of God in his heart (Jud 6:24).

g. The Messiah's most precious name, *Yahweh-tsidkenu,* "The Lord our righteousness" (Jer 23:6; cf. 33:16); the name and attribute by which the Messiah, Jesus Christ, was especially to be known (I Cor 1:30; II Cor 5:21; Phil 3:9; II Pet 1:1; I Jn 2:1).

h. The name of the New Jerusalem, *Yahweh-shammah,* "Jehovah is there," a prophecy in Ezk 48:35, which will be fulfilled in the New Jerusalem of Rev 21:22; 22:3.

i. God's heavenly title, *Yahweh Sabaoth,* "the Lord of hosts." This divine title, first found in I Sam 1:3, was used by David as he went to meet Goliath: "You come to me with a sword and with a spear and with a javelin; but I come to you in the name of the Lord of hosts, the God of the armies of Israel, whom you have defied" (I Sam 17:45, RSV). As the Lord of hosts He is mighty in battle (Ps 24:8, 10). The prophets often used the term. It is found in Jeremiah 88 times in the KJV either as "the Lord of hosts" or as "the Lord God of hosts," where it implies that the "hosts" are angelic forces of heaven constantly ready to do God's command (cf. Ps 89:5-8; 148:2; Mt 26:53). The expression "the Lord of Sabaoth" occurs untranslated in Rom 9:29 and Jas 5:4. *See* Host of Heaven.

7. *Other appellations.*

a. Rock (Heb. *sûr,* e.g., Deut 32:4, 15, 18, 31; I Sam 2:2; II Sam 22:3, 32, 47; 23:3; Ps 92:15; Heb. *sela',* e.g., Ps 18:2; 31:3; 42:9).

b. Father (e.g., Isa 63:16; 64:8; Mal 1:6; Mt 5:16, 45, 48; 6:9; etc.). *See* Father, God the; Abba.

c. King (Ps 10:16; 24:7-10; 44:4; 47:7; cf. I Sam 12:12). In the ancient Semitic world it was common practice to address one's deity as "King." Isaiah saw the Lord seated upon a throne and exclaimed, "Mine eyes have seen the King, the Lord of hosts" (Isa 6:1, 5).

d. Judge (e.g., Gen 18:25; Jud 11:27; Ps 50; 75:7; Acts 10:42; II Tim 4:8; Heb 12:23). This title referred to one of the functions of a king as ruler (Isa 33:22).

e. Shepherd. This title was frequently assumed by ancient monarchs to signify their benevolent rule of their people (e.g., Hammurabi in the prologue of his code). God is called the Shepherd of Israel (Ps 80:1), and is likened to one in Isa 40:11; Ezk 34:11–16. Thus it became an important title of the Lord Jesus Christ as the great Shepherd of the sheep (Heb 13:20; cf. I Pet 2:25; 5:4).

f. The First and the Last. Isaiah employs this expression to describe the eternal rule of Yahweh over the entire course of history from beginning to end (Isa 44:6; 48:12; cf. 41:4; 43:10; 45:21; 46:9–10). The risen, glorified Christ assumes the title as He speaks to John on the island of Patmos (Rev 1:11, 17; 2:8; 22:13).

g. Gr. *despotēs,* "lord," "master," "owner," denoted absolute ownership and uncontrolled power over slaves. It is used as a title for God in Lk 2:29; Acts 4:24; Rev 6:10, and for Christ in II Pet 2:1 and Jude 4. *See* God.

Bibliography. William F. Albright, *Yahweh and the Gods of Canaan,* Garden City: Doubleday, 1968. B. W. Anderson, "God, Names of," IDB, II, 407–417. Ada R. Habershon, *The New Testament Names and Titles of the Lord of Glory,* London: Nisbet, 1910. Andrew Jukes, *The Names of God in Holy Scripture,* London: Longmans, 1888. C. J. Labuschagne, *The Incomparability of Yahweh in the Old Testament,* Leiden: E. J. Brill, 1966. G. T. Manley, "God, Names of," NBD, pp. 477–480. Herbert F. Stevenson, *Titles of the Triune God,* Westwood, N.J.: Revell, 1956. Nathan J. Stone, *Names of God in the Old Testament,* Chicago, Moody, 1944. H. W. Webb-Peploe, *The Titles of Jehovah,* London: Nisbet, 1901.

R. A. K.

The goddess Demeter at Izmir. HFV

GODDESS.A term used only twice in the Bible: the Heb. *'ĕlōhîm* used of Ashtoreth, goddess of the Sidonians, in I Kgs 11:5, 33; Gr. *thea* of the goddess Diana in Acts 19:27, 35, 37.

Ashtoreth was the Heb. name of the Canaanite goddess Astarte. It is cognate with the Babylonian Ishtar, the goddess of sensuousness, maternity and fertility. The worship of Ashtoreth included most licentious practices. Israel commenced serving Baal and Ashtoreth in the times of the judges (Jud 2:13; 10:6). Solomon succumbed to her voluptuous worship and built high places for her and other heathen gods (I Kgs 11:5, 7–8, 33; II Kgs 23:13), in spite of God's earlier warnings (I Sam 7:3; 12:10).

Diana *(q.v.),* known among the Greeks as Artemis and the Romans as Diana, represented the same power over fruitfulness and birth which was worshiped as Ashtoreth in Palestine. She was regarded as mother goddess of the earth with her chief place of worship at the temple in Ephesus, where she was served by eunuchs and vestal virgins. The ritual of the temple consisted in sacrifices and ceremonial prostitution.

These two, Ashtoreth and Diana, who are essentially the same mother-goddess of Asia, are examples of the female images man has set up of himself—of his self-projections—mentioned in Rom 1:21–23 and worshiped, while the pagan gods are male examples. They personify man's unbridled passions and lusts and are deities made in man's fallen image and after his own likeness.

See Gods, False.

R. A. K.

GODHEAD. The word "godhead," compounded of "god" and "hood," later changed to "head," means that which is qualitatively of the nature of Deity. It refers not to any one person in the Trinity but rather the whole. The Shorter Catechism uses the term as it asks, "How many persons are there in the Godhead?" Three Gr. words are translated by this term in the KJV.

1. *Theion* is used once in Acts 17:29 by Paul as he speaks to the learned Greeks on Mars Hill about the unknown God whom they ignorantly worshiped, and contrasts His "Deity" (RSV) or "Divine Nature" (NASB) to the images of gold, silver and stone formed by the art and imagination of man.

2. *Theiotēs* in Rom 1:20 is a term particularly of quality and stresses the nature of God as divine. As man looks at creation he should come to two conclusions: the existence of a God who is powerful enough to cause it all to exist, and His "Diety" (RSV) or "Divine Nature" (NASB). By the use of *theiotēs* God's invisible qualities or attributes are indicated (see NASB, TEV).

3. *Theotēs* occurs in Col 2:9 and stresses the divine essence rather than attributes. "In him dwelleth all the fulness of the Godhead bodily." In Christ only, since He alone of the

Trinity became incarnate, does absolute and perfect Deity, all the divine essence, dwell in One who has a body.

The term Godhead stresses monotheism and the unity of the three persons of the Trinity, and guards against a polytheistic view of God. The OT categorically states, "The Lord our God is one Lord" (Deut 6:4). In the NT Christ declares, "I and my Father are one" (Jn 10:30). The doctrine of the Godhead develops this monotheistic concept further.

The doctrine of three persons in the one Godhead supplies certain very important philosophical needs. If God were a unitary person rather than a trinity of persons, the world and man would add basic new dimensions to Him. He would know added relationships when they came into being. To this extent a unitarian concept of God fails in that the God proposed by all Unitarians—be they Jewish, Muslim or Christian—needs the world and man to be fully developed. The world adds an "I-It" relationship; man adds an "I-Thou" and a "We-You" or social relationship. The Christian Trinity in contrast possesses all of these. The Son and the Spirit are objects to the Father, and each to the other. The Father and the Son have always enjoyed the "I-Thou" relationship, the personal encounter. Any two of the Trinity can minister to the third, and thus God forever knows the "We-You" or social relationship.

See God; I Am; Trinity.

R. A. K.

GODLINESS. Normally, "godliness" in the KJV is a translation of the Gr. *euseheia*. Godliness broadly means practical Christian piety. It finds its basis in a proper knowledge of God (I Jn 5:18), its outworking in a yielded life to God through Jesus Christ (Rom 12:1), and its final goal as the development of the consciousness of God, and of such similar traits as righteousness, faith, love, patience, and meekness (I Tim 6:11; II Pet 1:6). The concept is developed extensively in the Pastoral Epistles, and is crystallized in the words, "but godliness with contentment is great gain" (I Tim 6:6; cf. I Tim 2:2, 10; 3:16; 4:7-8; 6:3, 5, 11; II Tim 3:5, 12; Tit 1:1; 2:12).

GODS, FALSE

Introduction

The most common Heb. words for "gods" are *'ēlîm* and *'ĕlōhîm*, denoting men of might and rank, angels, gods, and (*'ĕlōhîm* only) the Supreme Being. Whether or not both words are traceable to a single root is debatable. The former is probably from the root *'wl*, "to be in front of, precede." Some think the latter may come from a root *'lh*, "to be in awe of." The Gr. word *theoi*, used in the NT and the LXX to render *'ēlîm*, *'ĕlōhîm*, may be connected with a root "to supplicate, to implore."

The meaning of the term must be determined by its actual usage. The ancient Near Eastern concept of "gods" varied somewhat from mod-

A Syrian deity standing on the back of a lion.
LM

ern ideas of "gods" as supernatural beings who were immortal. This was also true of the concepts of the pagan nations with whom Israel came in contact. For example, some gods, such as Baal and Tammuz, could and did die.

To the Hebrews, the "gods" of the nations about them were simply the powers in whom their neighbors and contemporaries believed. Those powers were the activators of the forces of nature: sun, moon, storm, flood, disease, etc. Each event had its activator. Hence there could be a multitude of gods according to pagan and primitive conceptions. Since there was no concept of an organized cosmos, there was no idea of a solitary Supreme Being, although each religion had its own chief, or father-god. Some gods were assumed to be local (I Kgs 20:28; II Kgs 17:26 f.) and limited in power. Other gods were conceived of as unlimited by geography, so certain prominent gods were worshiped across political and cultural lines (e.g., Ashtoreth, Baal, Hadad).

The biblical viewpoint regarding heathen deities affirms their subjective existence (Jer 2:28) in the mind and life of the devotee, but denies their objective reality (Jer 2:11). Of course, where deity and its image or idol were fused into one, the idol was an objective reality which the biblical writers acknowledge, while denying the objective existence of the deity represented by it.

In studying the gods of the Bible, a distinction must be made between the deities proper, and the idols or cult objects by which they were represented or worshiped. Sometimes the two were fused into one, while at other times the deity was kept distinct from his cult object. Baalim, asherim (sacred trees, groves), calves, the brazen serpent, and the teraphim (household idols) were all objects of worship. It is doubtful that there was a deity behind either of the latter two. The Baalim were representations of the local Baals, possibly in the form of bulls or calves. Sometimes the word is used of the deities without any reference to a cultic representation. The same is true of the asherim.

The golden calves of Jeroboam (I Kgs 12:28–30) have been thought by some to have been pedestals for Yahweh to ride on, replacing the ark as Yahweh's place of meeting His people. However, in keeping with the widespread use of the bull as a cultic symbol, it seems more likely that the calves were intended to be a fusion of deity and image, the deity being perhaps a fusion of Yahweh and the local Baal. Aaron's golden calf (Ex 32) may have been a fusion of Yahweh with the Egyptian god Apis, worshiped under the representation of a bull. Calf worship was denounced by Hosea (8:5–6; 10:5; 13:2).

A distinction must also be made between gods and demons. Frequently, when a nation conquered another nation, it demoted its gods to the status of demons and myths. Traces of this can be seen in the OT in such vague figures as satyrs (Lev 17:7; II Chr 11:15, both RSV, NEB), Lilith (Isa 34:14, JerusB), and Resheph (see below). Eventually the demoted pagan deity survived only in a language in mere hints of his former existence, such as in poetic symbolism (cf. Albright, *Yahweh and the Gods of Canaan*, pp. 183–193). This is evident in English in such expressions as "love-struck," i.e., "smitten by the arrows of Cupid." In this category can be put some of the OT references to Leviathan, the primeval serpent, the dragon, Rahab, and the Sea.

National Pantheons

Frequently the OT speaks of the gods of the various nations surrounding Israel in general terms. Here one encounters practically all the nations with whom Israel had contacts. Commonly the word "pantheon" is used in listing and discussing the gods of any ethnic or political group. However, this is a misleading anachronism. The Semitic idiom is "the assembly of the gods." This conclave is to be envisioned as an assemblage for concerted decision or action (as, e.g., U.S. Senate may meet without all senators being present) rather than a formal, methodical catalog of the deities worshiped by a particular people. With this distinction in mind,

one can note the following pantheons mentioned in the Bible.

1. The gods of the Ammonites (Jud 10:6). The chief god was Moloch/Molech or Milcom.

2. The gods of the Amorites (Josh 24:2, 15; Jud 6:10; I Kgs 21:26; II Kgs 21:11). Since little Amorite literature has come down to us, secondary sources and inferences must be depended on for knowledge of this pantheon. Evidently it was somewhat like the later and succeeding Canaanite pantheon. The temple of Ishtar at Mari and the temple of Dagon at Babylon were probably Amorite shrines. Dagon/Dagan, Hadad, and Anath seem to have been Amorite deities forced upon the Canaanites by the invading Amorites from the middle Euphrates region, as inferred from the discoveries at Ras Shamra (Oldenburg, *The Conflict Between El and Ba'al*, pp. 146–163).

3. The gods of the Assyrians (Nah 1:14) come into purview in the OT in the 9th to the 7th cen. B.C. Chief god of this pantheon was Asshur, replacing the Sumerian Ea. The Assyrian pantheon was somewhat like that of Babylonia. In both localities Semitic deities replaced the older Sumerian gods, in some cases absorbing their functions and titles.

Stone tablet recording the refoundation of the temple of the sun god at Sippar, Babylonia, ninth century B.C. BM

4. The gods of the Babylonians (Isa 21:9; Ezr 1:7) were important to Israel in the closing centuries of the kingdom and during the Exile. There were more than 700 deities listed in Babylonia. The Semitic conquerors of the Sumerians accepted the native gods and added their own. This situation was further complicated by the fact that each city-state had its own pantheon.

At Lagash, in early times, Anu, the god of heaven, was worshiped along with Antu his wife. At Eridu the chief god was Enlil, god of earth, who was later succeeded by Marduk.

The Assyrian god Ashur. ORINST

Enlil's wife was Damkina, and his son was Marduk. These figures (except Marduk) were all Sumerian. Other gods of the Babylonians included Sin (Sumerian Nanna), the moon-god; Shamash, the sun-god and son of Sin; Ningal, the wife of Sin; Ishtar (Sumerian Innina), the fertility goddess, and her husband Tammuz; Allatu (Sumerian Ereshkigal), the goddess of the underworld; Namtar, herald of the god of death; Irra, the plague god; Kingsu, the goddess of Chaos; Apsu, the god of the underworld ocean; Nabu, the patron saint of science and learning; and Nusku, the god of fire. *See* Babylonia.

5. The gods of the Canaanites (*q.v.*) are mentioned along with those of other inhabitants of Canaan in connection with the Heb. conquest of the land. Other tribes mentioned in Ex 23:23; 34:11–17; Jud 3:5 f. and other passages include the Amorites, the Hittites, the Perizzites, the Hivites and the Jebusites. Except for the Hittites, and possibly the Hivites (Horites? i.e., Hurrians; cf. Gr. Gen 34:2; Josh 9:7), the other tribes were closely allied to the Canaanites and probably worshiped the same deities. The same was true of the Syrians mentioned in Jud 10:6, but there probably was some change in that pantheon in later times (see 11 below). The Canaanite pantheon is best known from the mythological texts of Ras Shamra, although other information comes from Philo of Byblos and biblical sources, as well as shorter literary texts in Aramaic and Phoenician.

The chief god and creator was El. His son (sometimes called his grandson) Baal (see below) was the storm and vegetation god. He was called "the one who prevails," "the exalted one, lord of the earth." In mythology, Baal is enthroned on a lofty mountain in the N. During Ahab's reign he became the chief god of Israel. Asherah was the wife of El and mother of 70 gods. In the Ras Shamra texts the goddess Anath is the sister and usually the wife of Baal, but in the OT Ashtoreth (i.e., Asherah) is usually his wife. At Tyre, home of Jezebel, Asherah is Baal's wife (cf. RSV; I Kgs 15:13;

18:19; II Kgs 21:7; 23:4). Other prominent Canaanite gods were Dagon, Moloch, Resheph and Rimmon (see below), and Mot (death).

6. The gods of Egypt are mentioned in the Heb. early premonarchic history and again in the 7th to the 6th cen. B.C. (Ex 12:12; Josh 24:14; Jer 43:12–13; 46:25). Since the gods of Egypt were constantly changing, fusing and syncretizing, depending in part upon the political fortunes of the nome or city at which a particular deity was paramount, it is difficult to give a brief survey of Egypt's "pantheon." However, the chief god was known by different names at different times and places. At Heliopolis he was known as Aten-Re-Khepri; at Elephantine as Khnum-Re; at Thebes as Amon-Re (see below); and at Amarna (*q.v.*) as Aton-Re. Re, the sun-god was thus fused with the local god of the nome. Triads of chief gods are noted at various times: Ptah, Sekhmet, Nefer Tem; Amon-Re, Mut, and Khonsu; Osiris, Isis, and Horus. These are all father-mother-son triads.

According to the Pyramid texts, the Book of the Dead, and other early Egyptian literature, there were over 1,200 deities known to the Egyptians. Chief of these deities were the following: Apis, the bull of Memphis (Ex 32; I Kgs 12:25–33 may refer to his worship); Hapi, the Nile god; Hathor, the goddess of love and beauty; Ma'at, the god of right and order;

The goddess Sekhmet. LM

The temple of Bacchus, god of wine, at Baalbek. HFV

Sothis, the dog star; Sihor, the god of the underworld; Shu, the god of the air; Thoth, the scribal god.

7. The gods of the Edomites are sometimes mentioned as the gods of Seir (II Chr 25:14; cf. v. 20).

8. The gods of the Hittites, although not referred to by name in the OT, are alluded to in Ex 23:23–24; 34:11–15; Jud 3:5–6. The chief Hittite god, Teshub, was a storm-god roughly equivalent to Baal. Possibly, therefore, the Hittites worshiped Canaanite deities as a result of their contact with the Canaanites, although Hittite proper names indicate that Indo-European deities were worshiped at least for a brief time (cf. William F. Albright, *Archaeology of Palestine*, p. 183).

9. The gods of the Moabites are mentioned in Num 25:1–2; Jud 10:6; Ruth 1:15; Jer 48:35. Their chief god was Chemosh, who is also called Athtar. In Babylonia in the 2nd mil. B.C., he was equated with Nergal, the god of the underworld.

10. The gods of the Philistines included Dagon, worshiped at Gaza and Ashdod (Jud 16:23; I Sam 5:1–7; I Macc 10:83); Ashtoreth,

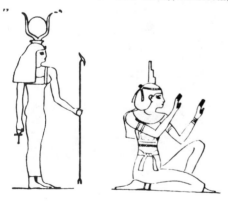

Picture of Hathor and Isis as is.

worshiped at Ashkelon (Herodotus i.105); and Baalzebub, worshiped at Ekron (II Kgs 1:2, 6, 16).

11. The gods of the Syrians (II Kgs 17:31; 18:34; II Chr 28:23; Isa 36:19) are probably variants of the older Canaanite pantheon. Theophoric names such as Ben-hadad and Tabrimmon bear witness to the worship of Baal under the guise of the Amorite Hadad, also known as Rimmon.

12. The Gr. and Rom. pantheons are not mentioned except in a general way (Acts 17:16, 18) in the NT.

The worship of astral deities is mentioned in Deut 4:19; II Kgs 23:5; Jer 19:13; Amos 5:26; Acts 7:43. An indirect reference to such entities may be found in Neh 9:6; Ps 148:1–4. A number of these astral deities are treated separately below.

The OT constantly condemns the worship of foreign deities (Deut 6:14) and pronounces judgment upon idolatry (Ex 20:3–5; 32:35; Num 25:1–9; Deut 5:7–9). Behind the awful judgment of Joel 1:4–20 was Israel's lapse into idolatry (cf. Joel 2:12 f.). The captivity is depicted as being brought on by the worship of other gods (II Kgs 22:17).

Individual Gods

Adrammelech (*á*-drăm′ĕ-lĕk) – A deity worshiped by the people of Sepharvaim who were settled in Samaria by the Assyrians after 722 B.C. (II Kgs 17:31). Since "d" and "r" look alike in ancient Heb. script, the name may be a confusion of a NW Mesopotamian god Adad-Milki ("Adad is my king"). There is no evidence of a god named Adar. Cf. Anammelech below.

Amon (ăm′ŏn) – The chief deity of Thebes (Jer 46:25, RSV, NASB). He was represented by a ram with upward curving horns. When Thebes dominated Egypt following the fall of the Old Kingdom, Amon became the most important god and was called Amon-Re. His great temple at Karnak with its famous hypostyle hall has the highest columns in the world (70 feet). He became the national god par excellence, except for a brief time during the reform of Akhenaton (*q.v.*).

Anammelech (*á*-năm′ĕ-lĕk) – A deity worshiped by the people of Sepharvaim (probably Sabraim, located between Hamath and Damascus, II Kgs 17:31), who were settled in Samaria by the Assyrians after 722 B.C. The name probably means "Anu is king." There was a temple dedicated to Anu and Adad at Assur about this time. The worship of the Sepharvites, presumably including that of Anammelech, involved the sacrifice of children as burnt offerings.

Anath (ā′năth) – The name of a popular but savage Canaanite goddess of fertility who played a key role as the sister and consort of Baal in the important corpus of 15th cen. B.C. Semitic literature from Ras Shamra, known as the Ugaritic tablets. The Bible makes no direct

700

The god Amon. MM

The worship of the Ephesian Artemis extended into Greece, Gaul, Rome, and Syria. The Nabateans of the 1st cen. A.D. worshiped the deity Atargatis, who is equated with Artemis. In NT times there was a temple of Artemis at Gerasa. *See* Diana; Goddess.

Asherah (*à*-shĕr'*à*) – A deity whose name is frequently mistranslated in KJV following the LXX "groves." In a Sumerian inscription to Hammurabi she is called "the bride of Anu (heaven)." She was the chief goddess of Tyre, *c*. 1500 B.C. In the Ugaritic pantheon she is called *"Athiratu-yammi"* ("She who walks on the sea"). She was the consort or wife of El, and the mother of 70 gods, including Baal. Animal sacrifices were offered to her. She also bore the title "Holiness" as attested by an Egyptian nude figure of her bearing that inscription.

In Babylonian records Ashratum was known as a deity. In the Tell el-Amarna tablets her name occurs in the proper name "Abdi-Ashirta." The name is also found in S Arabia, indicating the widespread prevalence of her worship.

This goddess is not to be confused with Astarte, known in the OT in its plural form as Ashtaroth or Ashtoreth (*see* Ashtoreth below). In the OT her worship is associated with that of Baal (RSV: Jud 3:7; I Kgs 18:19; II Kgs 23:4).

The goddess Artemis or Diana in the Ephesus Museum. HFV

reference to her as a goddess, but rather to her sister goddess of fertility Astarte (Ashtoreth, I Kgs 11:5, 33). The two goddesses were at least partly fused in Canaanite thinking since Astarte and Anath were both worshiped as the spouse of Baal (cf. Jud 10:6; I Sam 7:4); this may be the reason for biblical silence on Anath.

Artemis (är'tĕ-mĭs) – In classical mythology, the sister of Apollo, daughter of Leto and Zeus, equated with the Roman Diana, the moon-goddess who was a huntress and protector of womanhood. However, Artemis of Acts 19:23–40 (NASB) has little in common with her classical namesake. She was really a Lydian mother-goddess, worshiped at the mouth of the Cayster River long before the Greeks came to Ephesus. At Ephesus, Artemis was the goddess of fertility. Her temple retinue included eunuch priests, attendants, and hierodules. Her image (Acts 19:35) probably was a meteorite. The silver shrines (Acts 19:24), as well as models of clay and marble, may have been replicas of the primitive sanctuary. The temple of Paul's day was one of the seven wonders of the world.

A column base from the temple of Artemis or Diana at Ephesus sculptured with life-size figures. BM

Gideon had to destroy his father's altar to Baal and the accompanying Asherah in order to qualify as a leader of Israel (Jud 6:25–30, RSV). Her worship during the Heb. kingdom is attested by the image made by Asa's mother (I Kgs 15:13, RSV) and the image set up by Manasseh in the temple (II Kgs 21:7, RSV). Josiah attempted to stamp out her worship (II Kgs 23:4–7, RSV).

Some OT passages indicate a coalescence of the deity with the cult object used in her worship (RSV: Ex 34:13; Jud 6:25–30; II Kgs 18:4), a phenomenon common in many religions. As a cult object, an *'ǎshērâ* (pl. *'ǎshērîm, 'ǎshērôth*) (*see* Plants: Grove) could be made and destroyed by men (II Kgs 17:16; 23:6, 15, RSV); was made of wood (Ex 34:13; II Kgs 23:6–7, RSV); could be burned (Deut 12:3, RSV); stood upright (Isa 27:9, RSV); and was used in the worship of Asherah. Some scholars, on the basis of Deut 16:21 (RSV) and other evidence think it was a living tree. Most scholars, however, think it was an image of Asherah, perhaps a stylized tree of life, otherwise the silence of the prophets concerning it would be strange. But they do denounce idolatry, which would include the *'ǎshērîm*.

Ashima (*á-shī'má*)—A deity worshiped by colonists from Hamath settled in Samaria by the Assyrians after 722 B.C. (II Kgs 17:30; Amos 8:14, RSV). There may be some connection with the deity mentioned in the Elephantine Papyri called Ashembethel.

Astarte—*See* Ashtoreth (following paragraph).

Ashtoreth (ăsh'tŏ-rĕth; pl. ăsh'tá-rŏth)—A deity variously known as Ishtar, Astarte, Venus, sometimes called the "queen of heaven." She was the goddess of the evening star or planet Venus, but may have been androgynous originally and thus also god of the morning star, likewise Venus (cf. S Arabic *'aṭtar*, "god of the morning star"). She was principally the goddess of sex and war. God's people altered her name from Astarte to Ashtoreth, vocalized with the vowels of the Heb. word *bōsheth*, "shame," as was Molech. Her association with Baal in the OT (Jud 2:13; 10:6; I Sam 7:4; 12:10) may indicate that she can be equated with Asherah in Palestine. Astarte grew in importance in Phoenicia and Palestine, while the cruel goddess of war Anath, sister and consort of Baal, occupies the place of prominence in the Ugaritic texts (Albright, *Yahweh and the Gods of Canaan*, pp. 128–135).

In the OT Ashtoreth is mentioned as being worshiped among the Hebrews during the days of the judges (Jud 2:13; 10:6); at Beth-shan where Saul's armor was placed in her temple (I Sam 31:10; I Chr 10:10); by the Zidonians (I Kgs 11:5, 33; II Kgs 23:13). Jezebel's father was an Astarte priest. Philo of Byblos says she was worshiped at Byblos and Tyre. The town name Ashteroth Karnaim (Gen 14:5) suggests a shrine for her worship existed E of the Jordan. Her fame spread to Egypt as evidenced by Astarte figurines and the translation of the poem "Astarte and the Sea Dragon." In Moab (Moabite inscription, ANET, p. 320) the name of her male equivalent Ashtar is compounded with Chemosh.

Baal (bā'ăl, bāl; lit., "master, owner, husband")—The most important god of the Canaanite pantheon (*see* Canaan). From the 3rd mil. to *c*. 1500 B.C. the title is applied to the Amorite god of winter rain and storm, Hadad (see below). Hence, in the Canaanite pantheon he became the god of fertility with the bull as his symbol.

The widespread prevalence of his cult is attested by his name appearing in Babylonian, Aramaic, Phoenician, Punic, Ugaritic and Egyptian sources. During the Ramesside period he was equated with Seth. His titles were Zabûl, "exalted, lord of earth"; Ba'al Shamen, "lord of heaven" (in Phoenician, but not in the earlier Ugaritic); *Rōkēb 'ǎrufôt*, "rider on the clouds." The Egyptian place name Baal Saphon (lit., Baal of the N, Baal of Mount Casius) indicates his cult was known in Egypt. The OT refers to the many local Baal images as the Baalim, the plural form of Baal.

In the Ras Shamra texts he is the son of El (or, once, the son of Dagon). He overcomes the primeval waters. However he is slain by Mot and revived by Anath (fused with Athirat/Astarte). He also may have been identified with the Tyrian Melcarth, "lord of the city."

In the OT his worship became a serious rival to that of Yahweh. He was worshiped in the high places of Moab (Num 22:41). There were altars to him in the days of the judges (Jud 2:13; 6:28–32). Perhaps his worship reached its height in the days of Ahab and Jezebel (I Kgs 16:32; 18:17–40), although there were later revivals (II Kgs 3:2 f.; 10:18–28; 18:4, 22; 21:3; II Chr 21:6; 22:3). His worship was suppressed by **Jehoiada** (II Kgs 11:18) and Josiah (II Kgs 23:4–5).

The worship of Baal was accompanied with lascivious rites (I Kgs 14:24; II Kgs 23:7). Kissing his image is attested (I Kgs 19:18; Hos 13:2). Child sacrifice by fire was part of his cult (Jer 19:5).

The worship of Baal was associated with Ashtoreth (see above; Jud 2:13). He is also associated with the goddess Asherah (see above; I Kgs 18:19; II Kgs 23:4, both RSV), and his altars frequently had asherahs nearby (RSV: Jud 6:30; I Kgs 16:32–33). It seems likely that during the Heb. monarchy Ashtoreth and Asherah had fused into one figure. Ahaz made images for the Baalim (II Chr 28:2); these may have been brazen bulls or calves. The worship of Baal was denounced by the prophets (Jer 19:4–5; Hos 2:17).

In addition to the direct influence of the Baal cult on the Hebrews, much of the Canaanite imagery applied to him is sublimated and applied to Yahweh in the OT. Yahweh is the "rider on the clouds" or heavens (cf. Deut 33:26; Ps 68:4; 104:3). Like Marduk in the conflict with Tiamat, the Canaanite Baal was the conqueror of the upsurging waters. This conflict, sometimes with a monster called Rahab or Leviathan, is re-echoed throughout the OT where Yahweh is depicted as the victor over all His foes. The motif of Yahweh's kingship and annual worship at the new year (Zech 14:16–19) has been traced by some to the idea of Baal's revivification, at the close of the combat, by the coming of the seasonal rains.

Baal of Thunder from Ras Shamra, Syria. LM

Baal-berith (băl-bĕ-rîth′), "lord of the covenant"—An Amorite god with a shrine at Shechem (Jud 9:1-6). He is associated with the local Baals (Jud 8:33), so perhaps may be a local manifestation of the great fertility god of Canaan. Perhaps he was the same deity as El-berith (Jud 9:46, RSV), and is to be equated with the Semitic god of the underworld Hauron/Horon, whose name appears in Canaanite personal and place names.

Baal-peor (băl pē′ôr), "the lord of Mount Peor"—A Moabite and Midianite god (Num 25:1–5; Deut 4:3; Ps 106:28; Hos 9:10).

Baal-zebub (băl zē′bŭb)—The god of the Philistine city of Ekron (II Kgs 1:2, 6, 16). Opinion varies as to the meaning of this name. It was formerly thought to come from the Heb. root zbb, "to fly," hence as in the LXX, "lord of the flies." Most scholars now believe that the name of the god was Baal-zebul, "lord, prince" or "Baal the prince." In the Ugaritic texts Baal is described repeatedly as zbl b'l 'arṣ, "prince, lord of earth." The present form is explained as a mocking distortion, just as bōsheth, "shame," is often substituted for ba'al in personal names. The name of Jezebel, whose father's name was Ethbaal, contains the element zbl as an equivalent for ba'al. It is not surprising that her son Ahaziah preferred Baal-zebul to Yahweh. On the other hand, golden images of flies found in the excavations of Philistine sites may indicate that there truly was a god known as Baal-zebub, worshiped to appease the bothersome flies, or who gave oracles by the flight or buzzing of a fly (T. H. Gaster, "Baalzebub," IDB, I, 332).

Beelzebul (bē-ĕl′zĕ-bŭl)—A NT name applied to Satan (RSV, NASB: Mt 10:25; 12:24, 27; Mk 3:22; Lk 11:15, 18–19). KJV, following the Vulg., renders it Beelzebub (q.v.), probably a throwback, erroneously, to the Philistine god of Ekron, Baal-zebub, as found in the Heb. MT.

Bel (bĕl)—The name of the Babylonian national sun-god. Marduk. As Marduk, the son of Ea, he assumed the role of the Sumerian En-lil as conqueror of the chaotic waters. He was credited with conceiving the idea for the creation of man (ANET, p. 68), contra Canaanite El as the creator. In the OT Bel is associated with Nebo (Isa 46:1) and with Marduk (Jer 50:2). Other references to him are found in Jer 51:44, the apocryphal Bel and the Dragon (3:22), and Herodotus (i. 181).

Berith (Jud 9:46)—See Baal-berith.

Castor and Pollux (kăs-tŏr, pŏl′ŭks)—Astral deities, "the Twin Brothers," were children of Zeus and Leda (wife of the king of Sparta). They were the patron gods of sailors; the ship on which Paul sailed from Malta to Puteoli bore their insignia (Acts 28:11). Poseidon gave them power over winds and waves. Their temple at Rome stood next to the Basilica Julia in the Forum.

Chemosh (kē′mŏsh)—The name or title of the god of the Moabites (Num 21:29; Jer 48:46). According to II Kgs 3:27 and the Mesha inscription (ANET, p. 320) he was worshiped with child sacrifices. A sanctuary was built for him by Solomon (I Kgs 11:7), which was destroyed by Josiah (II Kgs 23:13-14). In the Mesha inscription he was equated with Ashtar (*see* Ashtoreth above). In addressing the king of the Ammonites Jephthah speaks of Chemosh as "thy god" (Jud 11:24), whereas the Ammonite deity was called Milcom/Molech (see below). But Molech may simply be a title of Chemosh, a god worshiped in common by the two related peoples. Jephthah's reference to Chemosh implying he admitted the god's existence was probably an *ad hominem* argument in appealing to the Ammonite king.

Chiun — *See* Kaiwan.

A bronze lion from the temple of Dagon in Mari (Iraq), second millennium B.C. LM

Dagon (dā'gŏn) — A name presumed to be related to Heb. *dāgān*, "grain," hence a vegetation deity. This is supported by a Ugaritic reference to Baal as "son of Dagon," perhaps viewing Baal as the dying and reviving vegetation deity. The idea of Dagon as a fish-god is not traceable earlier than Jerome, but is probably due to false etymology from Heb. *dāg*, "a fish."

Dagon is attested as a Babylonian deity. The name is found in theophoric names *c.* 2200 B.C. among the Amorites of Mesopotamia. There was a temple with two votive stelae commemorating sacrifices to Dagon found beside it, and older than that of Baal, at Ras Shamra, *c.* 2000 B.C. Philo of Byblos says Dagon was associated with El, the senior Phoenician god. First El and then Dagon may have been worshiped at that temple.

A theophoric place name (Josh 15:41; 19:27) indicates his worship in Canaan before the Philistine invasions. However, in the OT he is most famous as the god of the Philistines (Jud 16:23-24), who had an image of him at Ashdod (I Sam 5:2-4). He also was worshiped at Beth-shan (I Chr 10:10). The Ashdod temple was the locale where the Philistines put the Israelite ark. It was still in use in the Hasmo-

nean period and was destroyed by Jonathan, the brother of Judas Maccabaeus, 147 B.C. (I Macc 10:83-84; 11:4).

Day Star (KJV, Lucifer), Heb. *hêlēl,* "bright one" (Isa 14:12) — He was evidently a deity who wanted to rise higher than all stars, but was obliged to come down to earth. This is illuminated by the Ugaritic story of Ashtar (Venus star) who was proposed as the occupant of Baal's throne when it was vacant during the dry season. However, Ashtar was too small to fill the throne so had to descend (ANET, p. 140).

The traditional exegesis of Isa 14:12 has equated Day Star (Lucifer) with Satan. This is based on the belief that Lk 10:18 refers to Isa 14:15. Some modern exegetes see the Day Star merely as a title for the king of Babylon.

Diana (Acts 19:24) — *See* Diana; *also* Artemis above.

El-berith (Jud 9:46, RSV), "god of the covenant" — *See* Baal-berith above.

Gad (găd) — A god of fortune (see Isa 65:11, KJV, RSV, JerusB). This name for a deity is found in Phoenician, Assyrian, and Aramaic. The LXX translates it *daimon.* ASV, RSV, NEB and NASB translate the name instead of transliterating it, but by capitalization show the translators believed it to be a deity or a hypostatization. In an Aramaic-Greek bilingual text from Palmyra, he is identified with *Tyche,* "fortune." Evidently his cult was popular in the Hauran region.

Hadad (hā'dăd), "thunderer" — A Semitic god known variously as Adad, Addu, Haddu, Had. He is equated with Rimmon and Teshub (Hittite storm-god). Haddu/Hadad was originally the proper name of Baal. In Babylonian and Assyrian art he is represented as a bull. His name is found on the Panamua inscription from Zinjirli where there was also a statue dedicated to Hadad. His worship persisted down to Hellenistic times. At Tannur in Transjordan there was a Nabatean temple to Hadad who assumed the role of Zeus (or vice versa).

The name Hadad may lie behind the KJV "Hadar" of Gen 25:15; 36:39. It was the divine element in names given to kings and princes of Edom in Gen 36:35-39; I Kgs 11:14-21; I Chr 1:46-51. He was worshiped at Damascus (II Kgs 5:18). Cf. above under heading "Baal."

Hadadrimmon (hā'dăd-rĭm'ŏn) — A deity worshiped with ritual mourning at Megiddo (Zech 12:11). Perhaps this is to be compared with Anath weeping for Baal her brother in Ugaritic text I AB (Cyrus H. Gordon, *Ugaritic Manual,* text 49; ANET, p. 139). Cf. preceding paragraph and Rimmon below. *See also* Hadadrimmon.

Hermes (hẽr'mēz) — A Gr. deity mentioned in Acts 14:12 (RSV) which reflects his character as the god of eloquence and the divine herald. He was the son of Zeus, and half-brother of Apollo. As a master thief and trickster and god of good luck (whether honestly or dishonestly achieved) he was the patron saint of traders and thieves. In astral religion he was identified with Mercury. In Hellenistic times he was equated with the Egyptian scribal god Thoth. His epithet, "Hermes Trismegistus" ("thrice great"), indicates something of the importance he attained in the Hermetic religion of post-NT times.

Jupiter (joō'pĭ-tĕr) — Sky god of the Latins, identified with Zeus in Hellenistic times. He is mentioned in Acts 14:12–13 and II Macc 6:2. *See* Zeus below.

Head of the god Hadad, from Carchemish, Syria. LM

Kaiwan (kī'wăn); KJV, Chiun (Amos 5:26) — He is probably identical with Remphan (KJV), Rompha (NASB) of Acts 7:43, and was probably an astral deity. In Babylonian the name *kayawânu* is given to Saturn; it is translated by *Raiphan* in the LXX of Amos. *See* Remphan below.

Lilith (lĭl'ĭth) — The "night hag" (RSV) or "screech owl" (KJV) of Isa 34:14. In Akkad, *lilītu* is a night demon who tempts men in their sleep. She was later associated in Semitic thought with the child-stealing witch. In Isaiah her companions are unclean birds and devouring animals.

Marduk (mär'dŭk) — The state god of Babylon and foremost son of Ea. In the time of Hammurabi he was acknowledged as the chief deity with the functions of the Sumerian En-lil. In the new year festival ritual he was victorious over chaotic waters, thus re-enacting creation (cf. ANET, pp. 66 f.). Some recent scholars see

these motifs influencing the OT in such concepts as enthronement and divine kingship. In Neo-Babylonian times Marduk is equated with Bel (cf. parallelism of Jer 50:2). The name is Hebraized as Merodach (II Kgs 25:27; Isa 39:1; Jer 52:31).

Meni (mĕ-nî') — A god of destiny and good luck mentioned in Isa 65:11 (JerusB). The word is translated in KJV as "that number," RSV and NASB as "Destiny," and NEB as "Fate." Perhaps the name is derived from the Egyptian god Menu. He is possibly an astral deity, one of the Pleiades. However, a god Manat is known in pre-Islamic Arabic culture (Koran, Sura 53:20). During the Assyrian Empire he was equated with Asshur, the chief god. There is probably no connection with the Phrygian god Men of Hellenistic times, who had his principal temple at Antioch of Galatia and was a god of healing and prosperous agriculture.

Mercurus (mĕ-kyū'ĭ-ŭs), **Mercury** (mēr'cū-rĭ), Acts 14:12 — *See* Hermes above.

Merodach — *See* Marduk above.

Milcom — *See* Molech, Moloch.

Molech (mō'lĕk), **Moloch** (mō'lŏk) — An Ammonite deity worshiped with human sacrifice (II Kgs 23:10; Jer 32:35). The first vocalization is based on Heb. *bōsheth,* "shame." There is evidence for a god Muluk in Mari *c.* 1700 B.C. Jud 11:24 may indicate the identity of Molech with Chemosh (see above), Molech/Moloch being a title. The name of Chemosh was compounded with Ashtar on the Moabite Stone. Since Ashtar equals the planet Venus, the evening star, and the latter appears as Shalim, "dusk," at Ras Shamra, Moloch could be an old Canaanite deity in another guise (cf. Jer 32:35).

This deity is called Milcom (same Heb. root) in I Kgs 11:7, Heb.; 11:33; II Kgs 23:13; Jer 49:1, 3 (RSV, following LXX; KJV translates "king," from same Heb. consonants). This is reversed in Amos 5:26 where RSV translates "king," while KJV reads "Moloch." Stephen quotes this passage in Acts 7:42–43, where "Molech" is strangely retained in RSV. Solomon built a sanctuary for Molech (I Kgs 11:7, 33) which was desecrated by Josiah (II Kgs 23:13). His worship was reproved by Zephaniah (1:5) in words which indicate he was an astral deity.

The forbidden practice of human sacrifice (Lev 18:21; 20:2–5) seems to have been widespread in Israel (II Kgs 16:3; 17:17; Ps 106:38; Jer 19:4–5, and many other passages). A recent attempt by Eissfeldt (followed by Albright, *Yahweh and the Gods of Canaan,* pp. 235–242) to remove Moloch from the list of deities to whom human sacrifice was offered does not seem to be satisfactory. On the basis of Punic inscriptions where *mlk* means a sacrifice made to confirm a vow, he said the OT "pass through the fire to Moloch" means "as a votive offering." However, while this would help explain the association of Baal and Moloch in Jer 32:35, yet Lev 20:5 (where harlotry certainly refers to idolatrous worship, not to an offering) and II Kgs 17:31 (where "to" Adrammelech and Anammelech certainly cannot mean "as") show that Moloch and other gods with names ending in the compound _____-melech must be understood as deities to whom sacrifices were offered.

Nebo (nē'bō) — Probably a transliteration of Akkad. *nabû*, "to announce." This Babylonian deity was regarded as the son of Marduk. Originally a water deity, he was later associated with writing and speech. His image was carried in the new year's procession. The cult of Nebo was popular in the Neo-Babylonian period (625–539 B.C.) where his name is the theophoric element in three of the six kings' names, e.g., Nebuchadnezzar. He had a special temple at Borsippa.

Nergal (nēr'găl), probably from Sumerian *Ne-uru-gal*, "lord of the great city" — A Mesopotamian deity (II Kgs 17:30) worshiped by the Cuthites settled in Samaria after 722 B.C. by the Assyrians. Originally he was a god of fire and heat of the sun; then of hunting and disaster; finally the lord of the underworld. He was the consort of Ereshkigal, the mistress of hell. He was called "lord of weapons," which may be connected with the Heb. "Reshepho of the bow" (Ps 76:4[3]). As god of the underworld city he may have been equated with Mot of Ras Shamra. The Tyrian deity Melcarth (lit., "king of the city") was also an underworld god.

Nibhaz (nĭb'hăz) — A deity worshiped by Syrian colonists settled in Samaria after 722 B.C. by the Assyrians (II Kgs 17:31). There is to date no archaeological evidence for such a deity; so it has been suggested that the name is a corruption of Heb. *mizbēaḥ*, "altar," as also the temple was deified in the divine name "Bethel" at Elephantine two centuries later. The rabbis thought the name came from Heb. *nbḥ*, "to bark," but this is probably wrong.

Nisroch (nĭz'rŏk) — A deity worshiped by Sennacherib (II Kgs 19:37; Isa 37:38), who was killed in his temple. Several variant spellings of the name in the LXX all begin with *spiritus asper*. Since the name is unknown in Mesopotamian sources, it may be a corruption of the Assyrian Nusku. Nusku was a fire god, the son of the moon-god Sin and Nergal. His cult is attested at this period.

Queen of Heaven — [A pagan goddess to whom Israel, especially the women, offered sacrifice and worship in the last days of Judah (Jer 7:18). After the fall of Jerusalem and the disobedient departure of many of the Jews to Egypt, with a wicked perversion of reason, they insisted that it was while they worshiped the queen of heaven that things went well with them, and that only when Jeremiah had persuaded them to return to Yahweh had their troubles begun (Jer 44:17 ff.).

The false goddess is the Assyrian Ishtar or Astarte, the equivalent of the Ugaritic Ashirat. She was a mother-goddess and a symbol of fertility. Worship of the queen of heaven was to insure the fertility of field, flock and family (cf. Jer 44:17, "then had we plenty of victuals, and were well, and saw no evil"). In the 5th cen. B.C. the Jewish colony in Egypt on the island of Elephantine (Yeb) included in their strange syncretistic worship a goddess called Anath-bethel, who may be that same queen of heaven. — P. C. J.]

Pollux — *See* Castor and Pollux above.

Remphan (KJV, Vulg.), **Rephan** (RSV) (rĕm'făn, rē'făn) — An astral deity worshiped by the Israelites in the wilderness (Acts 7:43). The name is derived from the LXX Raiphan (Amos 5:26) where it is a corruption of Kaiwan (see above).

Resheph (rē'shĕf) — A Canaanite deity noted in offering lists and theophoric names from Ugarit, Egypt (Papyrus Harris, *c.* 13th cen.) and 8th cen. B.C. Syrian Aram. inscriptions. He is reportedly found sculptured in Egypt, holding the *ankh* ("life") sign. Conversely, in the Keret epic he is the god of plague and mass destruction. Many OT passages translate the name as a common noun, "pestilence," "thunderbolt,"

The god Reshef.

"flame," etc., where there is a covert allusion to this god. In the theophany of Hab 3:5, "and plague followed close behind" (RSV), some scholars consider it possible that the proper noun is meant. In Cyprian inscriptions (George A. Cooke, *Northwest Semitic Inscriptions*, pp. 55, 57), Resheph is equated with Apollo, who (*Iliad* i.51, 52) also caused plagues. As an underworld god, perhaps Resheph was identified with Nergal, Hauron and Melcarth.

Rimmon (rĭm'ŏn)—The name was originally thought to come from Heb. *rimmôn,* "a pomegranate," but now is clearly seen to be from Akkad. *ramānu,* "to roar," hence, "the thunderer." The chief god of Damascus, he was worshiped by Naaman and the king of Syria (II Kgs 5:18). He was the god of rain and storm. He was known among the Assyrians as Ramanu, a title of Hadad (see above), and identical with the Syrian Baal (see above). His name occurs in the Syrian name Tabrimmon, father of Ben-hadad (I Kgs 15:18).

Saccuth (săk'ŭth), **Siccuth** (sĭk'ŭth)—The latter spelling (ERV), based on the Heb. MT, is probably a variant (Heb. *paronomasia* using vowels of *shiqquṣ,* "abominable thing") of Mesopotamian Sakkut (Amos 5:26, RSV). The LXX took it to be some form of Heb. *sukkāh,* "tabernacle." The KJV follows the LXX here, as do the KJV and RSV in Stephen's citation of Amos (Acts 7:43). In Mesopotamia, Sakkut has the same ideogram as Ninib, so it was an astral deity.

Succoth-benoth (sŭk'ŏth-bē'nŏth)—A deity worshiped by the colonists from Babylonia settled in Samaria after 722 B.C. by the Assyrians (II Kgs 17:30). The name in Heb. lit. means "booths of girls," but this must be a corruption. Assyriologists Rawlinson and Schroeder supposed the deity to be Ṣarpanitu, the consort of Marduk, who was popularly called *Zir-baṅîtu,* "seed creating." Franz Delitzsch thought the name might be the Heb. equivalent of *sakkut biṅîti,* "supreme judge," i.e., Marduk. The name may have some relation to Sakkuth (properly vocalized) of Amos 5:26 who is the same as Akkad. Ninib.

Tammuz (tăm'ŭz)—[A Mesopotamian deity after whom the fourth Jewish-Babylonian month (June–July) was named. The name occurs when the prophet Ezekiel finds some women in Jerusalem weeping for the god Tammuz (8:14). Tammuz was famous as a husband of Ishtar (*see* Ashtoreth above). His Sumerian prototype Dumuzi was a king of Erech in the early 3rd mil. B.C. who was deified as the consort of the city's protectress Ïnanna or Innin (corresponding to the Akkad. Ishtar). Gilgamesh accused her of betraying Tammuz, her lover, in the famous epic (ANET, p. 84). In Hellenistic times Tammuz was equated with Adonis, and Ishtar with Aphrodite/Venus. Swine, often associated with underworld cults, were his sacrificial animals.

It has long been supposed that the purpose of Inanna's (or Ishtar's) mythical descent to the underworld (ANET, pp. 52–57) was to resurrect her lover. Hence he was identified by Sir James Frazer in 1906, along with Adonis, Attis and Osiris, as an example of the dying and rising god. Although he was a shepherd and not a vegetation deity, Tammuz was represented as a fertility god who, like the vegetation, died in the heat of summer (at which time there was cultic wailing for him) and arose in the spring.

Thanks to the work of the sumerologist Samuel Kramer, we now have clear evidence that Dumuzi (Tammuz) was not thought to rise from the dead at all. In a newly translated poem, "The Death of Dumuzi," Inanna, in fact, has her husband dragged down to the netherworld as her substitute for not having properly mourned her absence. Henceforth all the identifications of Tammuz with Adonis and with other resurrected gods will have to be abandoned (e.g., A. Moortgat, *Tammuz*), and likewise those attempts to interpret the Bible on the basis of such an identification (e.g., Alfred Jeremias on the Joseph story, and Theophile Meek on the Song of Solomon [*q.v.*]). There is evidence of a *hieros gamos* or "sacred marriage" rite to insure the fertility of the land (not to be confused with the New Year *Akitu* rite in Babylon) between King Iddin-Dagan (*c.* 1900 B.C.), who was addressed as Dumuzi, and Inanna, who was probably represented by a hierodule. Sumerian love songs were also used in the Dumuzi-Inanna cult.—E. M. Y.]

Tartak (tär'tăk)—A deity worshiped by Arvites who were settled in Samaria after 722 B.C. by the Assyrians (II Kgs 17:31). The name may be a corruption of Atargatis, a goddess worshiped in Syria by the Aramaeans of Mesopotamia whose worship persisted down into Hellenistic times. Atargatis, in turn, may be a composite figure of Athirat (Ashtoreth of the OT) and Anath of the Ras Shamra pantheon.

Zeus (zūs)—The head of the Gr. Olympian pantheon mentioned in Acts 14:12 (RSV). His statue at Olympia was one of the seven wonders of the ancient world. His temple at Athens was the largest in Greece. His worship was still widespread in NT times, with representations in art found at Tarsus and temples at Gerasa, Tannur, and Salamis. In the Latin pantheon his equivalent was Jupiter. The fused figure of Zeus-Jupiter is in view in the NT reference. Oxen and sheep were sacrificed to him.

Bibliography. William F. Albright, *Archaeology and the Religion of Israel,* 3rd ed., Baltimore: Johns Hopkins Press, 1953; *Yahweh and the Gods of Canaan,* Garden City: Doubleday, 1968. Lloyd R. Bailey, "Israelite Êl Šadday and Amorite Bêl Šadê, JBL, LXXXVII (1968), 434–438. G. Cornfeld (ed.), "Canaan, Gods and Idols, Cult," CornPBE, pp. 179–191. G. R. Driver, *Canaanite Myths and Legends,* Edinburgh: T. & T. Clark, 1956. Henri Frankfort, *Ancient Egyptian Religion,* New York: Columbia Univ. Press, 1948. O. R. Gurney, "Tammuz Reconsidered," JSS, VII (1962),

Head of Zeus, Ephesus Museum. HFV

147-159. Arvid S. Kapelrud, *Baal in the Ras Shamra Texts*, Copenhagen: G. E. C. Gad, 1952; *The Violent Goddess: Anat in the Ras Shamra Texts*, Oslo: Scandinavian Univ. Books, 1969. Samuel N. Kramer (ed.), *Mythologies of the Ancient World*, Garden City: Doubleday Anchor Books, 1961; *Sumerian Mythology*, rev. ed., New York: Harper Torchbooks, 1961; *The Sacred Marriage Rite*, Bloomington: Indiana Univ. Press, 1969. Ulf Oldenburg, *The Conflict Between El and Baal in Canaanite Religion*, Leiden: Brill, 1969. Jean Ouellette, "More on 'Ēl Šadday and Bêl Šadê," *JBL*, LXXXVIII (1969), 470 f. Raphael Patai, "The Goddess Asherah," *JNES*, XXIV (1965), 37-56. Edwin M. Yamauchi, "Tammuz and the Bible," *JBL*, LXXXIV (1965), 283-290; "Additional Notes on Tammuz," *JSS*, XI (1966), 10-15. For bibliography of Gr. religion and deities *see under* Diana.

A. K. H.

GOG (gŏg)

1. A Reubenite, son of Shemaiah (I Chr 5:4).

2. The prince of Meshech and Tubal (the Mushku and Tabali of the Assyrian inscriptions, Ezk 38:3). "Land of Magog" of Ezk 38:2 and "Magog" of Ezk 39:6 are probably incorrect since the former is not paralleled in 38:3 and the latter stands alone among several references to Gog. In Gen 10:2 Magog was the second son of Japheth, here the place being substituted for the personal name Gog. Placed between Gomer (Assyrian: *Gimirrai*; D. D. Luckenbill, *Ancient Records of Assyria and Babylonia*, II, 298, 352) and the Cimmerians,

the land of Gog appears to be located in northern Armenia, W of the Caspian Sea. *See* Gomer.

Gog as a mighty commander of many peoples is to come from the N against Israel "brought forth out of the nations," dwelling "safely all of them" (Ezk 38:8) in unwalled villages, where Gog attacks them (vv. 11-12). He comes with great numbers (v.16), reminiscent of the Scythians (Ashkenaz, Gen 10:3) who invaded Asia Minor *c*. 630 B.C. The Lord will judge Gog with mighty plagues and will destroy him by the elements (Ezk 38:22-23). His forces will be buried in numberless graves (Ezk 39:5-16).

Rev 20:8-15 places the invasion of this people in the future; thus. Gog cannot be fulfilled in Gyges, king of Lydia in Asia Minor (d. 662 B.C.). Since the last recall of Israel from exile is that one just before the Millennium, and since Satan is loosed after that age for one last assault against God, some scholars believe that this invasion out of the N comes after the Millennium. The hordes would be the unconverted millennial descendants of the dwellers of the area N of eastern Turkey. Others hold that there will be one invasion from present-day Russia led by Gog before Christ returns (Ezk 38-39), and another led by Satan, similar to Gog's, after Christ's 1000-year reign (Rev 20:7-9).

See Hamon-Gog; Magog.

H. G. S.

GOLAN (gō'lán). A city in Bashan of the Transjordanian half-tribe of Manasseh. Moses set it aside to be one of the three cities of refuge E of the Jordan (Deut 4:43; Josh 20:8), and it was one of the 48 Levitical cities (Josh 21:27; I Chr 6:71). It is probably to be identified with the modern Saḥem el-Jolan, *c*. 17 miles E of the Sea of Galilee. It later gave its name to the division of Bashan called Gaulanitis (*q.v.*), a flat and fertile tableland that was widely populated in Maccabean and Herodian times (Jos *Ant*. xiii.15. 3-4; xvii.8.1; xviii.4.6; *Wars* iii.3.5). It is called Jolan by the Arabs today.

GOLD. *See* Minerals and Metals: Gold; Ophir.

GOLDEN CITY. Isa 14, the taunt-song against Babylon, speaks (v.4) of the end of the golden city (Heb. *madhēbâ*). The translators, not finding the root in Heb., took it as Aramaic *dhb*, "gold," and therefore the derivation as "golden one," or "exactress of gold" (marg.). But now the Dead Sea Scroll 1Q Is[a] helps us see that the LXX, Syriac and possibly the Targum must have read *marhēbâ*. Heb. *d* and *r*, much alike, are often confused. This root means "storm against," "act arrogantly." The line is therefore better translated with its preceding parallel thought in the poetic couplet, "how the oppressor has ceased, how his arrogance has ceased!"

GOLDSMITH. *See* Occupations: Goldsmith

GOLGOTHA (gŏl'gŏ-thå). This is a Gr. word, derived from the Aramaic *gulgaltā'*, which means "a skull." Three times the place of the crucifixion is called the "place of a skull" (Mt 27:33; Mk 15:22; Jn 19:17). But what does this signify? Jerome said it was a place of public execution, where skulls lay around. In the past century the view has become popular that it means a skull-shaped hill. Gordon's Calvary, with its skull-shaped rock, holds sentimental attachment for many Protestants. The older tradition identifies Golgotha with the Church of the Holy Sepulchre, inside the walls. Both sites are uncertain. *See* Calvary.

GOLIATH (gŏ-lī'ăth). Goliath was either a descendant of the Rephaim (*q.v.*), a tall aboriginal people living in the Transjordan area of Ammon, of whom a scattered remnant took refuge with the Philistines after their dispersion by the Ammonites (Deut 2:20–21), or of the Anakim (*q.v.*; cf. Num 13:33; Josh 11:22), noted for their tall stature. The LXX (I Sam 17:4) and Josephus (*Ant.* vi. 9.1) say he was four cubits and a span, i.e., six feet nine inches tall, while the Heb. text states that he was six cubits and a span, or nine feet nine inches tall. Recovered skeletons of equal height from archaeological excavations at Gezer and other sites bear out the unusually tall stature of individuals in ancient Palestine at roughly the same period. *See* Giant.

Rabbinic literature records many legends about Goliath. According to these, his mother was Orpah (cf. Ruth 1:14), who walked 40 paces with Naomi and Ruth, and then returned to a profligate life in Moab. Goliath was born of her illegitimately. He boasted of having slain Eli's two sons (I Sam 4:11), and that he had stolen the ark of Israel (I Sam 4:17). The 40 days of his challenge to the Israelite army (I Sam 17:4–10) compared to the 40 paces of his mother Orpah, and it was done at the time of the reciting of the Shema!

The Vulgate calls him *vir spurius*, a bastard. The LXX refers to him as "the middleman" (I Sam 17:23); the Heb. text calls him "the man of the intervals" (I Sam 17:4, 23), i.e., the man who goes out as the champion in the space between two opposing armies. The cognate term in a prose text found at Ugarit signifies a middleman or intermediary (BASOR #150, p. 38).

The place where Goliath met his death was in the valley of Elah (I Sam 17:2), between Shochoh and Azekah, in the land of the tribe of Judah. The Israelites under King Saul were encamped on the N slope of the valley of Elah, and the Philistines were entrenched on the opposite slope. A narrow valley through which flowed a brook separated the two armies. Goliath the Philistine champion was attired in a bronze helmet and coat of mail, and carried both a spear and a sword. Bronze scales for

Golgotha. HFV

coats of mail dating to the 15th cen. B.C. were uncovered at Nuzu. Records of such coats of mail and drawings of them were found in the inscriptions of the pharaohs engraved on temple walls of Karnak at Luxor, Egypt. The bronze "target" (KJV) or "javelin" (RSV), Heb. *kîdôn*, may have been a curved scimitar, since the *kîdôn* is so described in the Dead Sea War Scroll. A shield bearer preceded Goliath into the fray. The custom of two warriors engaging in a duel to settle a battle is well represented in the Homeric epics of Greece and in an Egyptian text that dates from the 20th cen. B.C. In the latter, Sinuhe shot his Retenu challenger with an arrow from a distance; then he finished off his fallen foe with the Retenu's own battle-axe and shouted the cry of victory over his back ("The Story of Sinuhe," ANET, p. 20, lines 109–145).

The religious significance of the contest is seen in the powerlessness of the Philistine gods to carry out Goliath's curse on David and in the battle cry of David, "I come against you in the name of Yahweh Sabaoth, the God of the armies of Israel that you have dared to insult" (I Sam 17:43, 45, JerusB). Also there is the fact that David placed the sword of Goliath, perhaps as an offering, in the sanctuary of Yahweh at Nob (I Sam 21:9). Ps 144 and Ps 151 (LXX and DSS) seem to be in tribute of David's victory.

An alleged contradicton seems to occur in II Sam 21:19 (ASV, RSV, etc.) which reports that "Elhanan the son of Jaare-oregim, the Bethlehemite, slew Goliath the Gittite, the shaft of whose spear was like a weaver's beam," while I Sam 17:50–51 (cf. 19:5; 21:9; 22:10, 13) asserts that David did so. Moreover, I Chr 20:5, clearly parallel to II Sam 21:19, states that "Elhanan the son of Jairi slew Lahmi the brother of Goliath the Gittite, the shaft of whose spear was like a weaver's beam" (RSV). It can be demonstrated in the Heb. that in the course of transmission of the text some copyists' errors have evidently been made in II Sam 21:19. While there are possible slight alternatives in seeking to harmonize the Heb. of

II Sam 21:19 and I Chr 20:5, it is clear that (*a*) David slew Goliath, and (*b*) Elhanan slew the brother of Goliath. For full discussion of the problem and possible emendation see S. R. Driver, *Notes on the Hebrew Text of the Books of Samuel*, Oxford, 1913; E. J. Young, *Introduction to the Old Testament*, Eerdmans, 1949, pp. 181f.; Archer, SOTI, p. 274.

F. E. Y. and J. R.

GOMER (gō'mĕr)

1. The eldest son of Japheth, and the father of Ashkenaz, Riphath, and Togarmah (Gen 10:2-3; I Chr 1:5-6). Gomer represents the people termed Gimirra by the Assyrians and Cimmerians by the Greeks. Indo-European nomads, in the 8th cen. B.C. they invaded the Near East from northern Europe via the Caucasus under pressure of the Scythians (*q.v.*). The Cimmerians attacked Urartu (Ararat) and Tabal N of Assyria, but were driven westward into Cappadocia by Sargon II. They went on to destroy the Phrygian kingdom (*see* Meshech) c. 695 B.C. and ransacked Lydia (*see* Sardis) before Esarhaddon and Ashurbanipal of Assyria defeated them. Alyattes of Lydia (605-560 B.C.) finally expelled them from Asia Minor. Their contemporary, Ezekiel, prophesied of a people called Gomer, evidently from the former territory of the Cimmerians, as joining the ranks of Gog (*q.v.*) in the end time (Ezk 38:6).

2. Daughter of Diblaim, the unfaithful wife of Hosea the prophet (Hos 1:3), and mother of Jezreel, Lo-ruhamah, and Lo-ammi (the second and third children may have been illegitimate). Her marital infidelity provided the stage for Hosea's dramatic parable of Israel's unfaithfulness to God. *See* Hosea.

J. R.

GOMORRAH (gŏ-mŏr'ă). Direct information on this city is very scant and can be arrived at mainly through its association with the cities which "were joined together in the vale of Siddim" near the Dead Sea. They are listed as Sodom, Gomorrah, Admah, Zeboiim, and Zoar (Gen 14:2-3). The twin cities of Sodom and Gomorrah were most intimately associated as cities of gross sin (Gen 18:20; Mt 10:15). Condemnation of Sodom is shared by the city of Gomorrah (Gen 18:20; II Pet 2:6; Jude 7).

It is generally assumed that these cities were located on the sloping plains between the hills of Judea and the shore of the Dead Sea, somewhere at the southern end. Archaeological probings have been made in this area, but no conclusive evidence has been found to identify Sodom or Gomorrah positively.

At the present time the southern end of the Dead Sea is very shallow. A broad delta or tongue of sand and stones, known in Arabic as el-Lisan, has been washed into this area from the E shore so that the water between the tip of el-Lisan and the W shore is only about three miles wide and not much deeper than the height of a man.

Jebel Usdum, a mountain of almost pure salt, is located on the SW shore of the Dead Sea. W. F. Albright and Melvin G. Kyle in 1924 made a thorough exploration of the southern shoreline of the Dead Sea S of el-Lisan. Their conclusion was that Sodom and Gomorrah must have been on the western side of the narrow plain, since Zoar (*q.v.;* Gen 19:20-23, 30), in an easterly direction toward the hills of Moab, seems to have been a safe place of refuge. This puts the doomed cities in a small plain, now covered by the Dead Sea, in front of the eastern side of Mount Usdum (see Melvin G. Kyle, *Explorations in Sodom*, 1928, pp. 130-138). *See* Sodom; Dead Sea.

H. A. Han.

GOOD. Good is that which is worthy of approbation because of its inherent moral value and because of its beneficial external effect. The Scriptures use the term in both of these moral and amoral senses. In the amoral sense, gold is spoken of as good (Gen 2:12), as well as cattle (Gen 41:26), trees (Mt 7:17), treasures (Lk 6:45), ground (Lk 8:8), etc. If salt has lost its savor it is "good for nothing" or of no practical value (Mt 5:13; Lk 14:34).

But the Bible speaks particularly of good in the moral sense; its teachings about this can be classified in the following manner.

God is the standard of all that is good. When the Scriptures describe what is good they do not apply some categorical imperative or moral standard to God, but present God Himself as the standard. The psalmist writes, "For the Lord is good; his mercy is everlasting; and his truth endureth to all generations" (Ps 100:5). This is neither an abstract quality in God nor a secular ideal of man, because all He plans, does, creates, commands and approves is good. In fact, no one is good without qualification but God (Mk 10:18). He is the norm, judge and decider of what is good, and man and things are good to the extent that they conform to Him and to His will.

God's works are good. They reveal His attributes of wisdom and power (Ps 104:24-32; Rom 1:19-20) and display His glory (Ps 19). Step by step as He formed creation He examined it to prove that it was good (Gen 1:4, 10, 12, 18, 21, 25), and when He finished it, "God saw everything" including man, "and, behold, it was very good" (v.31). There is no Barthian "*Das Nichtige*" or Manichean dualism, nor are there Roman Catholic degrees of being, in God's creation. Sin was originated by the creature and not the Creator. Sin (*q.v.*) did not come into existence because God could not do good without causing evil, but because the creature in his freedom of will caused it to exist.

God's gifts are good, because they express His beneficence, love, and mercy, and are for the good of the creature. James writes that every good and perfect gift comes from God (Jas 1:17). In His providence He does good to all men, both the just and the unjust (Mt 5:45; Lk 6:35; Acts 14:17), while as a perfect heavenly Father He gives good gifts in particular to His children (Mt 7:11).

In the OT God's goodness to His covenant people is foretold in the many promises of millennial blessings, which include the possession of the entire promised land (Deut 30:1-10; Isa 11:11-12; 66:19-20; Joel 3:1-20), a thousand years of peace (Isa 9:7; Rev 20:1-6); prosperity and plenty (Joel 3:17-20; Amos 9:13-15).

For the Christian, "all things work together for good to them that love God" (Rom 8:28), including chastening (Heb 12:10), temptations (Jas 1:2-12), trials (Ps 119:67, 71) and persecutions (II Cor 4:17). They drive him to God and to seek His blessing and the presence and power of the Holy Spirit.

God's commands are good. As God's law is a reflection of His holy character, so His commands are a revelation of His moral perfection and perfect will. The ideal moral standard of the Bible is to be like God the Father (Mt 5:48), as this has been revealed in the Scriptures and in the life and teachings of Jesus Christ. Christ came not to destroy the law of God but to fulfill it for our justification, and commended it as the guide for the walk of faith and obedience (Mt 5:17-19, 48).

Obedience to God's commands is good. Obedience pleases Him, is the basis of blessing and answered prayer (I Jn 3:22; 5:2-3), and blossoms forth into the performance of those good works for which the Christian has been saved (Mt 5:16; Eph 2:10; Col 1:10; II Cor 9:8).

In what sense can any works be called good? When they are in accordance with God's revealed standard and will (II Tim 3:16-17). When they stem from the right motive, namely, love to others and gratitude to God (II Cor 5:14; I Thess 1:3; Heb 6:10). When they are performed with the right aim, that is, for the extension of a knowledge of God and His glory (Mt 5:16; I Cor 10:31; cf. 6:20; I Pet 2:12).

The law of God is revealed to man in two ways: in positive form—love God and love your neighbor, which is the basis of the law (Rom 13:8-10); and in negative form—(except for the fourth and fifth commandments) as summarized in the Ten Commandments. God is love, and His holiness and love go hand in hand. Man too must combine love with righteousness in a Spirit-filled walk if his acts are to be truly good (Rom 8:3-4; Gal 5:22-23). Thus good works are works of love, such as Mary's anointing of Jesus Christ which is called by Him a good work (Mk 14:3-6; cf. Mt 5:13-16; Rom 12:9-21; 13:8-10).

In our understanding of good works, it is necessary to distinguish the three main uses of the law of God found in Scripture: (1) For justification. All men are born sinners and are therefore lost and need salvation. But they cannot save themselves since they cannot keep the holy law of God. One infraction breaks all the law (Jas 2:10). Christ, in contrast, came into the world sinless, kept the law of God perfectly, and then died under the penalty of the broken law—both for our justification. Therefore the Bible never presents to fallen man the keeping of the law as a means of self-justification, but says, "By the deeds of the law there shall no flesh be justified in his sight: for by the law is the knowledge of sin" (Rom 3:20). (2) For condemnation. The law of God convicts us of our sins and makes us guilty before God (Gal 3:24; cf. Lk 10:25-37; 18:20-22). (3) For sanctification. After we are converted, God's law becomes the standard for the Christian life as seen in the teachings of both Christ and Paul (Mt 5:17-48; Rom 13:8-10). It is only in the third sense that the Christian is spoken of as keeping the law of God, and then only by the indwelling power of the Holy Spirit.

See Example; Goodness; Law; Law of Moses; Sermon on the Mount.

R. A. K.

GOODLY TREES. *See* Plants.

GOODMAN. An archaic English word meaning the head of a family or master of a household. In 1611 the word meant "husband," as it still does in Scotland; hence in Prov 7:19 according to the context it is an accurate rendering of Heb. *hā'îsh,* "the man," RSV "my husband." In the NT Gr. *oikodespotēs* is translated "goodman" in KJV in Mt 20:11; 24:43; Mk 14:14; Lk 12:39; 22:11; and seven other times as "householder" or "master of the house." That he is the owner and not merely the chief steward is clear from a comparison of Mt 21:33 with verses 37-38 where his son is called the heir.

GOODNESS. In both the OT and the NT two elements appear in particular: a goodness which rests upon mercy (*ḥesed, chrēstotēs*) and one that rests upon God's moral goodness (*tôb, agathōsunē*). Thus, in some places God's kindness comes to the fore: "The earth is full of the goodness [loving-kindness, ASV] of the Lord" (Ps 33:5; cf. Ps 52:1; 107:8); "Despisest thou the riches of his goodness [kindness] . . . not knowing that the goodness of God leadeth thee to repentance?" (Rom 2:4). In others, God's perfection and goodness come forth (Num 10:32; Ps 16:2; 23:6; Gal 5:22; II Thess 1:11).

One of the fruits of the Spirit is goodness (*agathōsunē*), in the sense of Christian holiness and righteousness (Gal 5:22). This is in keeping with the goal of the Christian life, which is to be like our heavenly Father, both in character and action, even as Christ taught in the Sermon on the Mount (Mt 5:48).

See Good; Kindness.

R. A. K.

GOOSE. *See* Animals, III.18.

GOPHER WOOD. *See* Plants.

GOSHEN (gō'shĕn)

1. Goshen was the territory in Egypt in which Jacob and his family were granted royal permission to settle. It is called either "the land of Goshen" or simply "Goshen," and is related to "the land of Rameses" (Gen 47:11) and the store cities of Ex 1:11.

Goshen was located in the easternmost section of the Delta, NE of Heliopolis (biblical On, Gen 41:45). It is associated with the Wadi Tumeilat, a very fertile area which joins the Nile at Bubastis (Pibeseth, *q.v.*) with Lake Timsah at modern Isma'iliya, N of the Bitter Lakes. *See* Succoth.

The LXX relates Goshen (Gesem) to the Egyptian nome of "Arabia" (the twentieth nome of Lower Egypt, on the E border of the Delta, according to Ptolemy the geographer), preserving a tradition of the Hellenistic Jews of Egypt (cf. Gen 45:10; 46:34).

Joseph selected Goshen as the residence for his relatives, so that they would be near him and probably because the district was best suited for their pastoral livelihood (Gen 45:10; cf. 47:4; for a later parallel, see Breasted, *Ancient Records of Egypt*, III, §§ 636–638, and ANET, p. 259). When Jacob arrived in Goshen, Joseph went to meet him there (Gen 46:28–29; the LXX adds "at Heroonpolis"). Joseph told Pharaoh of the arrival of his family in Goshen (Gen 47:1) and presented five of his brothers to the king, who suggested that Joseph settle his relatives in "the best of the land" (v. 6), in Goshen, in accordance with their request (v. 4). Here the Israelites prospered and multiplied (v. 27). From here a large funeral procession went to Canaan to bury Jacob (Gen 50:7–9). At the time of the Exodus, Goshen was protected from the plagues of "swarms" (Ex 8:22) and of hail (Ex 9:26), which affected all the rest of Egypt. *See* Exodus, The; Plagues.

2. A district called Goshen was situated in the southern part of Judah, between the hill country and the Negeb (Josh 10:41; 11:16).

Plowing in the land of Goshen. MPS

3. There was a town by this name in the southern hill country of Judah (Josh 15:51); its location is uncertain. Aharoni (*The Land of the Bible,* p. 184) suggests that it is Tell el-Khuweilifeh, a site which others have identified as Ziklag (*q.v.*).

C. E. D.

GOSPEL. A word used only in the NT to denote the message of Christ. The Gr. *euangelion,* meaning "good tidings," became a technical term for the essential message of salvation. It is modified by various descriptive phrases, such as, "the gospel of God" (Mk 1:14, ASV; Rom 15:16), "the gospel of Jesus Christ" (Mk 1:1; I Cor 9:12), "the gospel of his Son" (Rom 1:9), "the gospel of the kingdom" (Mt 4:23; 9:35; 24:14), "the gospel of the grace of God" (Acts 20:24), "the gospel of the glory of Christ" (II Cor 4:4, ASV), "the gospel of peace" (Eph 6:15), "an eternal gospel" (Rev 14:6, RSV). Although distinctive aspects of the message are indicated by the various modifiers, the gospel is essentially one. Paul speaks of "another gospel" which is not an equivalent, for the gospel of God is His revelation, not the result of discovery (Gal 1:6–11).

The content of the gospel is clearly defined in the NT. It is the accepted message of the Christian church, for it was received by all believers, defended by their reason, and was a vital part of their experience. It was historical in its content, biblical in its meaning, and transforming in its effect. "Christ died for our sins according to the scriptures . . . he was buried . . . he hath been raised on the third day according to the scriptures . . . he appeared to Cephas . . ." are Paul's descriptive words (I Cor 15:1–6, ASV).

The gospel was not a loose accretion of early legends about Jesus, but was a well-organized set of teachings about His life and its significance, preached by the leaders of the early church in the first generation after His death. Although it was not reduced to a catechetical formulation, it was sufficiently uniform to be reflected in the writings of Matthew, Mark, and Luke, now called the Synoptic Gospels. A different form of the same preaching appeared in the Gospel of John. Because of the unique quality and content of the message, the writings embodying it were called the "Gospels." It is probable, however, that this technical use of the term does not appear in the narrative passages of the NT. Invariably when it is used it refers to the content rather than to the vehicle; the application of "Gospel" to the written work is later than the 1st cen.

The central truth of the gospel is that God has provided a way of salvation for men through the gift of His Son to the world. He suffered as a sacrifice for sin, overcame death, and now offers a share in His triumph to all who will accept it. The gospel is good news because it is a gift of God, not something that must be earned by penance or by self-improvement (Jn 3:16; Rom 5:8-11; II Cor 5:14-19; Tit 2:11-14). The gospel presents Christ as the mediator between God and men, who has been ordained by God to bring an erring humanity back to Himself.

See Evangelist; Glad Tidings; Law of Moses.

Bibliography. Gerhard Friedrich, *"Euaggelizomai,* etc.," TDNT, II, 707-737.

M. C. T.

GOSPELS, THE FOUR. The first four books of the NT canon, Matthew, Mark, Luke, and John, are called Gospels because they are the written record of the early preaching of the good news concerning Christ. They constitute a distinctive type of literature. They are not wholly biography, for they do not attempt to narrate all the facts of Jesus' career; nor are they only history; nor are they sermons, though they include preaching and discourses; nor are they simply news reports. All of these elements appear in them, combined in a new form of organization which appears only in Christian writings. These writings were intended to express the basic message of the early Christian preachers which was written to instruct believers in the certainties of their faith.

The first three, because of their close resemblance to each other in content and in viewpoint, are called the Synoptic Gospels. Although they differ in many respects, they follow the same general order of events, and deal largely with the ministry of Jesus in Galilee. John, the fourth Gospel, contains a different selection of events, narrates chiefly the work of Jesus in Judea, and interprets His life more from a theological standpoint than do the others.

From the very earliest period of the Christian church the Gospels have been acknowledged as valid records of the life of Jesus. The first writer to mention them by name was Papias of Hierapolis, who lived in the first third of the 2nd cen. According to the record given in the *Historia Ecclesiae* of Eusebius (iii.39), A.D. 350, Papias reported that "Matthew composed his history in the Hebrew dialect . . .," and that "Mark, being the interpreter of Peter, whatsoever he recorded he wrote with great accuracy, but not however in the order in which it was spoken or done by our Lord. . . ." Justin Martyr, *c.* A.D. 150, mentioned "the memoirs of the apostles, which are called Gospels," "composed by the apostles and those that followed them" (I *Apology* 66-67; *Dialogue with Trypho,* 10, 100, 103). Tatian, a Gnostic writer of the middle of the 2nd cen., combined the four Gospels into one harmony. They must, therefore, have been known and accepted as authority not later than the opening of the 2nd cen. Other works of the early 2nd cen., such as the Didache, the Epistles of Ignatius, and the Epistle of Barnabas, contain allusions which can be traced to Gospel sources, chiefly to Matthew's account. The recent discovery of the

Gospel According to Thomas, containing very early specimens of the sayings of Jesus, simply confirms the previous existence of basic Gospel writings.

The Origin of the Gospels

The Christian church did not begin its evangelism by the distribution of literature but by public preaching. The witness of the apostles centered on the death and resurrection of Jesus (Acts 4:10), who, Paul said, "was delivered up for our trespasses, and was raised for our justification" (Rom 4:25, ASV). Wherever the early disciples went, they proclaimed the coming of Jesus as the promised Messiah of the OT, and told the story of His life and works. The climactic events of His passion constituted the initial message preached in any given locality. Paul reminded the Corinthians that "first of all" he had declared to them that "Christ died for our sins according to the scriptures; and that he was buried; and that he hath been raised on the third day according to the scriptures; and that he appeared . . ." (I Cor 15:3-5, ASV). Undoubtedly, however, the apostles did not confine themselves to these few facts, for their hearers would have desired more information about Jesus. The significant events of His life must have been narrated in order, making an account corresponding generally to the content of the existing Gospels.

Because of the numerous witnesses and the wide variety of discourses, parables, and episodes attributed to Jesus, there must have been many versions of the gospel story. The main facts, however, were fairly well fixed, and consequently the gospel tradition, as this oral preaching can be called, tended to become uniform in content.

From the beginning the new disciples were instructed formally in the "teaching of the apostles" (Acts 2:42), which must have contained the history and interpretation of Jesus' life, death, and resurrection. Without such teaching the Christian church would have lost its distinctive message. While the oral preaching may not have become stereotyped, constant repetition and the use of the material in the instruction of believers probably gave it a relatively settled form. Luke alludes to such procedure when writing to his friend Theophilus: ". . . that thou mightest know the certainty concerning the things wherein thou wast *instructed,"* Gr. *catechized* (Lk 1:4, ASV). The Gr. word implies the impartation of knowledge by word of mouth, and may mean formal teaching. Theophilus had already been orally informed of the general content of the gospel; Luke put the material into writing to confirm the facts that he already knew.

Since new believers constantly needed instruction, and since the original witnesses were gradually becoming unavailable either because of dispersion or death, a more permanent record became necessary. The transition from preaching to literature has not been preserved by any single account, and must be derived by inference from the hints that survive in the existing Gospels and in other early writings. Various theories have been propounded to explain the origin of the Gospels, particularly of the Synoptics, which present the peculiar problem of close verbal resemblances in some parts, and of widely differing content in others. The existence of these similarities and differences gave rise to the "Synoptic problem." Why, if these three Gospels were independently composed, do they resemble each other so closely? If they are not independent, why do they differ? See also Gospels, Synoptic.

Oral tradition. The apostles of Jesus who had associated closely with Him during the years of His ministry would have a vast fund of reminiscences from which to draw the outline of His life and the illustrations of His teachings. Since it would be impossible to recount in one message all that He did and said, the facts would have to be sorted so that only the most significant would be used. As they preached, they tended to repeat the essential events and teachings, such as the Sermon on the Mount, or the account of the passion, and to omit the smaller events which seemed of lesser importance. This constant repetition crystallized the message so that it became uniform with occasional variations. In writing, each author repeated the main narrative, endeavoring to reproduce it in accordance with the needs of his audience and with his divinely given purpose. The general facts and their significance would thus be the same for all; the organization and the illustrations would differ. Resemblances in the Gospels thus repeat facts common to all the preaching of the message by the church; differences are the result of varying selection of episodes and discourses fitted to the author's purpose.

The interdependence theories. Explanation of the resemblances and differences in the Synoptics by reproduction of various parts of the oral tradition, some identical and some different, did not satisfy the scholars of the late 18th cen. They and their successors pointed out that the resemblances were too close to be explained by purely verbal transmission. They argued that the Gospels must be dependent on each other. All possible permutations of order were suggested, but none could prove a conclusive case. Interdependence has been generally abandoned as an explanation of the Synoptic problem.

The documentary theories. A more recent theory proposes that the Synoptics were built on two primary sources, the Gospel of Mark and a hypothetical collection of Jesus' sayings and parables called "Q," from the German Quelle meaning "source." The theory owes its origin to the observation that almost the entire content of Mark is embedded in Luke and Matthew, and that while Mark and Matthew may agree against Luke, or Luke and Mark against Matthew, Matthew and Luke never agree against Mark. "Q" has been presumably reconstructed from the common discourse material existing in Matthew and Luke which does not occur in Mark. According to this "two-document" theory, Mark incorporated the main facts of the life of Jesus as they were currently preached and taught in the church. "Q" was composed of sayings and deeds of Jesus which had been noted for proclamation, but it was not an organized narrative. B. H. Streeter (The Four Gospels, 1936) extended the hypothesis to include two other "sources," "M" for Matthew's peculiar material, and "L" for Luke's specific contribution.

A plausible defense for the general documentary hypothesis can be offered on the ground that almost all the Markan narrative is incorporated into Matthew and Luke, and that collections similar to "Q" are known to have existed. Papyrus fragments of the sayings of Jesus have been discovered in the rubbish heaps of Egypt (see B. P. Grenfell and A. S. Hunt, The Logia of Jesus, and R. M. Grant, The Secret Sayings of Jesus, New York: Doubleday, 1960).

Such a theory, however, raises grave doubts concerning the independence and accuracy of Matthew and Luke. If the writers of these documents incorporated Mark wholesale, or with such modifications and additions as they saw fit, have they produced works which can be classed with his for authority and importance? Furthermore, no trace of "Q" has ever been found. Its existence is purely conjectural, founded on the assumption that Matthew and Luke must have had a single source for their common non-Markan material. The construction of the theory is wholly subjective, and there is disagreement among its proponents concerning what portions of the Gospel text may or may not belong to "Q." E. F. Scott, who accepts the documentary hypothesis, admits that "Q" does not represent a single document but a series of collections of Jesus' sayings that may have existed in many copies or editions (E. F. Scott, Literature of the New Testament, p. 41).

While it is possible that the writers of the Gospels may have used written sources, there is no reason why they could not have depended largely on firsthand knowledge or upon direct oral information for the bulk of their material; and there is little convincing evidence for the support of theories that place the time of production of the Gospels late in the 1st cen. or early in the 2nd. The writers themselves could have supplied most of the material credited to "sources." Streeter's theory does not necessitate two additional sources; he has simply assigned letters to the authors themselves.

Formgeschichte. The theory of Formgeschichte, a German word meaning "Form history" (English title, Form Criticism) was proposed by Martin Dibelius in 1919, who attempted to penetrate behind the "sources" to the oral tradition. He suggested that the material from which the Gospels were constructed originally circulated as short independent accounts which could be classified by their literary form for which he proposed a series of labels: the Passion Story concerning the end of Jesus' life; Paradigms, or stories of Jesus' works that were used as illustrations of His message; Tales, miraculous events which were narrated for the pleasure that they afforded the hearer; Legends, or stories of the lives of holy men, cited as examples; Sayings, epigrammatic utterances of Jesus which were used in exhortations. From the miscellaneous array of quotations and anecdotes, according to this theory, the first sermons were composed and later edited into the Gospels.

While it is not impossible that separate sayings and acts of Jesus may have been quoted and recorded in the Gospels, it is dubious whether so complicated a process really took place. Each of the Gospels bears marks of purposeful organization rather than of being the accidental accumulation of floating tradition.

The most definite evidence available concerning the origin of the Synoptic Gospels may be gleaned from the introduction to Luke. The writer acknowledges at the outset that others had attempted to produce narratives of the life of Jesus (1:1), but either he regarded them as unreliable, or else they were not available to his addressee. His statement, "It seemed good to me also . . . to write unto thee in order" (1:3), shows that he assumed an equal right with the others to create a life of Jesus, and that he possessed information which was superior in quality. The substance of his account would not be novel; it concerned "those matters which have been fulfilled [fully established] among us" (1:1, ASV). Luke took for granted that they were accepted by the church as a whole, and affirmed that they had been transmitted to him by men "who from the beginning were eyewitnesses, and ministers of the word" (1:2). The word "minister" is identical with the one used in Acts 13:5 to describe John Mark who was the attendant of Barnabas and Paul in their early ministry. Since Luke was not with them at that time, he may have obtained from Mark part of the information in his Gospel—a fact which might explain to some extent the identity of wording. In any case, Luke was careful to use authoritative informants. Furthermore, he was a contemporary of the general course of events (1:3), alert and conscientious both in the acquisition and in the transmission of information. Although the other two writers of the Synoptic Gospels do not explain their procedure with similar definiteness, the general order and content of their narratives bespeak equal accuracy.

The closing words of the fourth Gospel shed some additional light on this problem of composition. The writer states that "many other signs therefore did Jesus in the presence of the disciples, which are not written in this book: but these are written, that ye may believe . . ."

(Jn 20:30-31, ASV). John was selective, taking from the store of facts about Jesus' life and teaching only such items as would serve his purpose. His Gospel has a specific objective, and he used only the materials that enabled him to attain his goal. Since the Gospels were not intended to be exhaustive, they should not be expected to provide a complete account of all that Jesus said and did, nor should they be regarded as inaccurate because they differ among themselves.

Perhaps the best explanation of the process of writing is that each of the four authors endeavored to present the central message about Jesus to his own constituency, and consequently used and arranged the materials independently. On the other hand, the message had been so often repeated that much of it was already fixed in form, so that it would be expressed in identical phraseology by anybody who used it. Furthermore, it is not impossible that the three authors, Matthew, Mark, and Luke, may have met each other at one time or another in their careers, and exchanged notes. The possibility of personal contact is at least as valid as that of documentary dependence.

The Gospel of Matthew

The Gospel of Matthew is the earliest known and the most widely used of the Gospels. As previously noted, Eusebius, a church historian, of the 4th cen. after Christ, quoted Papias who said that "Matthew composed his history in the Hebrew dialect, and everyone translated it as he was able" (Eusebius, *Historia Ecclesiae*, iii.39). Since Eusebius did not quote all that Papias said, the meaning is uncertain. By "Hebrew" Papias could have meant Aramaic, the then current speech of Jewish Palestine. He does imply that Matthew contributed some definite information concerning Jesus which antedated the Gentile expansion of the church, and which consequently must have been known before A.D. 50. The Gospel quotations or allusions in the Didache (A.D. 125), the Epistle of Barnabas (A.D. 150), Ignatius' Epistle to the Smyrneans (A.D. 118), and Justin Martyr's *Dialogue with Trypho*, xlix (*c*. A.D. 140), accord more closely with Matthew than with any other Synoptic. The Gospel must have been in circulation by the end of the 1st cen., and probably considerably earlier.

Of the traditional author little is known. Matthew (Levi, as the Gospels call him) was a tax collector, stationed near Capernaum (Mt 9:9-10). He entertained Jesus at a dinner in his home, and abandoned his profession to become a disciple. There is no other mention of him except in the general list of the apostles (Mk 2:14; Lk 6:15; Acts 1:13). He must have been literate, for he would be compelled to keep accounts when he served the government. *See* Matthew.

The date of the Gospel is unknown, but its silence concerning the destruction of Jerusalem, its interest in Jewish prophecy, and its awareness of Jewish sentiment (Mt 28:15) point to an origin not much later than A.D. 50. Since the present Gospel exists only in Greek, it may be that its wide use among the Gentile Christians began with the dispersion from Antioch, and that it was first circulated extensively there between A.D. 50 and 65. Irenaeus (c. A.D. 180) stated that "Matthew also issued a written Gospel among the Hebrews in their own dialect" (*Against Heresies* iii, 1.1), confirming Papias' statement. Perhaps Matthew's Gospel was the first to incorporate in one account the teachings of Jesus which Matthew had transcribed, and the acts of Jesus which formed the core of apostolic preaching, as proclaimed by Peter and later digested by Mark. It may have been the earliest written account used in the transition from the Aramaic church of Jerusalem to the Gr. church of the Gentile mission.

The theme of the Gospel is the messiahship of Jesus, a topic prominent in primitive apostolic preaching. The opening genealogy makes Jesus heir of the promises given to Abraham and David. Six times in the first four chapters (Mt 1:22–23; 2:5–6, 15, 17–18; 3:3; 4:14) the events in His life are connected with the fulfillment of prophecy. The Sermon on the Mount emphasizes Jesus' relation to the law (5:17–20). He claimed to be a greater prophet than Jonah, and a greater king than Solomon (12:41–42). He accepted and commended Peter's confession that He was the Messiah (16:13–20), and He confirmed the claim on oath before the high priest (26:63–64).

Matthew's treatment of the gospel is predominantly topical. Rather than chronicling Jesus' activities by short episodes, as Mark does, he prefers to use large blocks of text, each of which is devoted to some one aspect of Christ's life and teaching. The first four chapters are concerned chiefly with the relation of the OT to the advent of the Messiah. The Sermon on the Mount (chaps. 5 – 7) is a sample of Jesus' preaching which states His essential ethical principles, and summarizes the main content of His teaching. Another block of text from 8:1 to 11:1 comprises a list of miracles of various types all illustrative of Jesus' power over nature, disease, and death. Chap. 13 contains eight parables of the kingdom, portraying both its inward and outward aspects. The conflict of Jesus with His opponents occupies chaps. 19–25, including the famous Olivet Discourse (24–25). The rest of the Gospel is devoted to the narrative of the passion.

The structure follows generally the chronological pattern of the other Synoptics. In biographical sequence it does not differ from them greatly, though it contains some material that they lack. The two largest sections of the book are marked by the phrase "from that time" (4:17; 16:21), which introduces first the beginning of Jesus' popular public ministry, and second, the decline which led to the cross. Matthew combines this rise and decline of Jesus' career with His messianic manifestation.

Several features of Matthew's Gospel are not duplicated in the others. The dream of Joseph (1:20–24), the visit of the Magi (2:1–12), the withdrawal into Egypt (2:13–15), the slaughter of the infants at Bethlehem (2:16), the dream of Pilate's wife (27:19), the suicide of Judas (27:3–10), the resuscitation of dead saints at the crucifixion (27:52), the bribing of the guard (28:12–15), and the baptismal commission (28:19–20) appear nowhere else. Ten parables are given only by Matthew: the tares (13:24–30, 36–43), the hidden treasure (13:44), the pearl (13:45–46), the dragnet (13:47–50), the unmerciful servant (18:23–35), the laborers in the vineyard (20:1–16), the two sons (21:28–32), the marriage of the king's son (22:1–13), the ten virgins (25:1–13), and the talents (25:14–30).

This Gospel stresses discourses and teaching. Seven important addresses are recorded: the preaching of John (3:1–12), the Sermon on the Mount (5:1 – 7:29), the commission of the disciples (10:1–42), the parables of the kingdom (13:1–52), the meaning of forgiveness (18:1–35), denunciation and prediction of the end (23:1 – 25:46), and the Great Commission (28:18–20). The emphasis is much more on teaching than on action or character development.

This Gospel is the only one in which the Church is mentioned (16:18; 18:17). The inclusion of Jesus' references to the Church indicates that the author was interested in the rise and growth of the institution. Perhaps he had in mind the development of the church at Antioch.

See Matthew, Gospel of.

The Gospel of Mark

Beginning with Papias, the early writers of the church unanimously ascribe the second Gospel to John Mark, a young companion of the apostolic band. The current tradition of the 2nd cen. was well summarized by Irenaeus (c. A.D. 180): "After their [Peter's and Paul's] departure, Mark, the disciple and interpreter of Peter, did also hand down to us in writing what had been preached by Peter" (*Against Heresies* iii. 1.1). This statement is repeated in substance by Origen of Alexandria (c. A.D. 250), Tertullian of Carthage (c. A.D. 200), and Jerome (c. A.D. 400), the translator of the Latin Vulgate. Neither on external nor on internal grounds is there any good reason for challenging the traditional authorship. The direct and artless narrative of Mark accords well with the known character of Peter, and with the type of preaching that was employed in the Apostolic Age.

According to the records of the NT, John Mark was the son of a woman named Mary who owned a home in Jerusalem, and was sufficiently affluent to have servants (Acts 12:12–13). It is possible that the "upper room" of the last supper was in her house, and that the pre-Pentecostal prayer meeting was held there. John Mark must have been acquainted with all the apostles, and must have been familiar with their preaching. It is probable that he may have seen Jesus during the last week of His life, if not before. He was a cousin of Barnabas, who took him to Antioch to work in the church with himself and Paul (Acts 12:25). He accompanied Barnabas and Paul on their first missionary journey (13:5), but left them at Perga (13:13). Paul refused to take him on the second missionary tour (15:36–39), but Mark continued in service with Barnabas. Evidently he succeeded, for in Paul's later epistles Mark is commended as a Christian worker (Col 4:10; II Tim 4:11). *See* Mark.

Mark was qualified to write a narrative of Jesus' life because he was personally acquainted with the apostolic band, because he had participated in the evangelistic ministry of the church, and because he may himself have been an eyewitness of the last scenes of Jesus' career. Two references in the Gospel seemingly point to Mark. One alludes to a young man who was in the garden of Gethsemane when Jesus was captured, and who narrowly escaped from the clutches of the arresting party (Mk 14:51–52). The episode does not occur in the other accounts, and is irrelevant to the main teaching of the passage. It takes on meaning only if it is an experience of the writer, who speaks from firsthand knowledge. Perhaps Mark, curious about the fate of Jesus, went to the garden to investigate, and was almost involved in the capture. He may have been the only witness to the prayer which the Lord offered on that occasion. The other reference relates to Simon, the Cyrenian, who carried Jesus' cross. Mark informs the reader that Simon was the father of Alexander and Rufus (15:21). There would have been no reason for this statement had the author not expected the two men to be known to his readers. Evidently he was a contemporary of the generation that immediately followed that of Jesus. While this allusion does not definitely identify him as Mark, it places him in the period and circle to which Mark belonged.

The place of writing is uncertain, but the general tradition connects the publication of Mark's Gospel with Rome. Mark's clear, terse, and concrete style would appeal to the practical Roman mind, for it stresses action rather than teaching. There are more Latinisms here in the Gr. text than in the other Gospels, such as the words "census" for "tribute" (12:14); "speculator" for "executioner" (6:27, KJV); *phragelloun* for Latin *flagellare*, "to scourge" (15:15); and *centurio* for "centurion" (15:39), where Matthew and Luke employ a Gr. equivalent. If Mark were not writing for a Roman audience, he may have been influenced by a Roman environment. Possibly he composed the substance of the Gospel in Palestine and finished it in Rome. It may have been written as a summary of the apostolic preaching to the Gentiles, to provide a résumé of Christian truth for the early converts.

The content of the Gospel is brief but inclusive. It contains a minimum of discourse material and a maximum of action, compressed into a series of episodes like candid camera pictures. Each presents Jesus in some one pose or action, and calls for a personal reaction on the part of the reader. In many instances the reaction of the public to Jesus is a part of the narrative.

The last 12 verses of the Gospel are lacking in the oldest MSS of the NT, Codex Vaticanus and Codex Sinaiticus, both of the 4th cen. Numerous other copies either omit them, or mark them with an asterisk to indicate that they are not contained in all the sources known to the scribe, and several of the early Church Fathers never quote them. In the existing MS tradition there are three different endings: the longer ending familiar to most readers, and two shorter ones which are obviously attempts to fill a gap. It is possible that Mark intended to conclude his Gospel at 16:8, as R. H. Lightfoot argues (*Locality and Doctrine in the Gospels*, pp. 1–23), but the ending is so abrupt that early damage to the original manuscript seems more probable. The longer ending, which is printed in most English translations, may date back to the 2nd cen., and represents a very early summary of the postresurrection events, whether it is Markan or not.

Mark's Gospel has certain definite characteristics. It emphasizes action rather than teaching. Very few discourses or parables of Jesus are reported, but Mark narrates more miracles than any of the other Gospel writers in proportion to length. He uses the historic present tense 151 times to make the story vivid. His language is terse but pictorial: "He saw the heavens *rent asunder*" (1:10, ASV); "The herd [of swine] *rushed* down the steep into the sea" (5:13, ASV); "They *laughed him to scorn*" (5:40); "They had a *few small fishes*" (8:7). The italicized words are phrases which illustrate the concise and vigorous quality of the Markan writing. The narrative moves rapidly, and is more concerned with changing the scenes than with continuity of reasoning. Nevertheless, this Gospel conveys a definite picture of Jesus, and from the variety of His acts it composes a unified portrait of a supernatural Person who can forgive sins, legislate human ethics, feed hungry crowds, heal the sick, and debate successfully with the sharpest intellects of His nation.

Mark specializes in portraying Jesus by the popular reactions which He evoked. He notes repeatedly that the crowds or disciples were "amazed" (1:27), resentful of His claims (2:7), querulous about His behavior (2:16), fearful of His power (4:41), "astonished" at His teaching (10:26; 11:18), awed by His wisdom (12:34). There are 23 such expressions of feeling that reflect the impressions that Jesus made on those who met Him. Mark does not attempt a general evaluation of Jesus; he simply records the popular reactions, and lets the reader form his own judgments.

The purpose of this Gospel seems to be evangelistic. It contains less teaching than Matthew and is less apologetic than Luke. The style is that of a street preacher, who attempts to hold the interest of his audience by lively anecdotes, pointed sentences, and pungent applications of truth. Mark makes his reader feel that he has witnessed the scenes described in the Gospel, and evokes from him the response that Jesus Himself would have created.

See Mark, Gospel of.

The Gospel of Luke

More information concerning the composition of the third Gospel is available than concerning the origin of Matthew and Mark, for the author has supplied a brief introduction (Lk 1:1-4) that explains his method and purpose in writing. This preface is a key to the book, which enables the reader to understand the motives which directed the writing of the Gospel and the circumstances under which it was produced. A comparison of this introduction with that of the book of Acts shows that the two documents were written by the same man, for both are addressed to Theophilus, and the introduction to Acts (1:1-5) speaks of a "former treatise" containing the life and works of Jesus. Since the vocabulary and style of the two works resemble each other closely, there can be no reasonable doubt that they had a common author.

This author was undoubtedly Luke, a companion of Paul, who is mentioned in the epistles as "the beloved physician" (Col 4:14). His birthplace is unknown, though it may have been Antioch of Syria, with which he seemed to be familiar. He joined Paul's company at Troas, on the second journey (Acts 16:10), and traveled with him to Philippi, where he probably remained as pastor of the church until Paul returned on the third journey (Acts 20:6 ff.). Throughout the rest of Paul's itinerary Luke was a constant associate, except that he seems to have been at liberty during Paul's imprisonment at Caesarea, for he is not mentioned in the account. He rejoined Paul on the voyage to Rome (Acts 27:1-2 ff.) and stayed with him for the rest of his life (II Tim 4:11).

See Luke.

Early tradition unanimously credits this work to Luke. Justin Martyr (A.D. 140) definitely quoted Luke 23:46, and ascribed his quotation to "the memoirs" (*Dialogue with Trypho* cv). The Muratorian Fragment (A.D. 170) attributed the third Gospel to Luke. Tatian (A.D. 140-150) included it in his *Diatessaron*. Marcion, the Gnostic (A.D. 140), accepted Luke as the only Gospel in his canon, though he altered its text considerably. Irenaeus (A.D. 170) quoted it extensively and acknowledged Luke explicitly as the author (*Against Heresies* iii.1.1).

The traditional view is supported by the internal evidence, for Luke is the only one of Paul's companions who could have written the book of Acts and, consequently, this Gospel.

The language of both books shows a physician's interest in the sick and diseased, and some of his vocabulary is that which a doctor would be more likely to employ than a layman. Mark (1:30), in describing the illness of Peter's mother-in-law, says that she was sick with fever, but Luke (4:38) says that she was afflicted with "a great fever." Mark (1:40) speaks of a leper; Luke (5:12) says that he was "full of leprosy." Mark (3:1), in describing a cripple, says that he had a withered hand; Luke (6:6) observes that his *right* hand was affected. Mark (5:25-26) says that the woman with the issue of blood was not helped by the physicians but rather grew worse; Luke (8:43-44) implies that she was an incurable case.

Cadbury has objected that the language of Luke is not the technical jargon of a physician because there was none in the days of the NT (*The Style and Literary Method of Luke,* in *Harvard Theological Studies,* VI, 39 ff.). Cadbury may be right that the Gr. physicians did not have a separate medical terminology in the 1st cen., but his argument does not change the fact that Luke's vocabulary exhibits a physician's interests and viewpoint.

Furthermore, the writer seems to have had access to some informants that would have been available only to one who moved both in official circles and among the earliest associates of Jesus and the apostles. The first two chapters contain facts that could have been derived only from the family of Jesus. The author knew some of the apostles; among the women he mentions Mary Magdalene, and Joanna, the wife of Chuza, Herod's steward, who would have known Herod's court; and it is possible that he became acquainted with some of the persons mentioned in this Gospel, such as Zacchaeus, the publican of Jericho (19:2), and Cleopas, one of the two who traveled to Emmaus on the resurrection day (24:13, 18). Some of these witnesses, because of their convictions, had become active workers in the church, "ministers of the word" (1:2). Both by their experience and by their position they would be adequate sources for reliable information. Luke claims that he had been a contemporary of these men ("having traced the course of all things . . .,"ASV) for a considerable length of time, and that he was therefore qualified to write authoritatively concerning their testimony.

Luke's introduction implies that numerous accounts of the life of Jesus were already in circulation when he composed his Gospel (1:1). Whether he stated this fact solely to justify his right to produce another, or whether he was dissatisfied with the scope and accuracy of those already written is not perfectly clear. In any case, some attempts to write the facts concerning Jesus had already been made, so that the church was not devoid of literature. This Gospel presupposes a demand for such works, and the use of documents to propagate the faith.

The content of Luke's Gospel, according to

his own testimony, consists of "those matters which have been fulfilled among us" (1:1, ASV). The margin of the ASV reads "fully established," and the expression means "the facts generally accepted as settled." Luke was not attempting to introduce a novel teaching, but was transcribing the general story of Jesus' life as it had been confirmed by his own research or by the testimony of reliable witnesses. These matters were not novelties to his reader, for he had been "instructed" in them. The word instructed means literally, "to be informed by word of mouth," and may connote a regular course of instruction or catechizing. Evidently Luke did not confine himself to repeating church teaching, but he professed to convey the substance of the common oral instruction strengthened by information that he had acquired, and motivated by the consciousness that he possessed the authority of truth.

Luke did not specify whether by "order" he meant chronological sequence, logical continuity, or homiletical procedure. In general, his narrative followed the same order as those of Mark and Matthew, with some insertions. Perhaps he combined the biographical or homiletical sequence of the current preaching with his own didactic purpose, for he organized Luke and Acts around the ministry of the Holy Spirit in the life of Christ and of the early church. The governing purpose of this Gospel was to produce certainty in the thinking of its readers. The author could not have achieved this end had he built his narrative upon fiction or upon legend.

Although the date of production cannot be fixed exactly, it is most probable that the Gospel was written not later than A.D. 62. As the first half of the two-volume work of Luke-Acts, it must have been written before Acts. The latter was probably completed while Paul was still alive, quite likely at the end of his first Roman imprisonment. If the writer knew more concerning Paul's fate than the book of Acts records, it is unlikely that he would have ended his narrative without disclosing the facts. Probably he wrote no more because there was no more to tell. Paul's two years in Rome must have ended about A.D. 62. In that case the collection of material for the Gospel and its composition probably preceded that time. Luke would have had ample opportunity to interview the witnesses of Jesus' life and to visit the scenes of His ministry during Paul's two-year imprisonment in Caesarea. Even so radical a critic as Harnack argued that the Gospel of Luke cannot be much later than A.D. 80 (see Adolf Harnack, *Luke the Physician*, p. 163). It may be that it represents in some measure the gospel which Paul and other members of the Gentile mission preached.

The place of publication is not clear. Although the Gospel may have been composed during the first part of Paul's imprisonment, it may have been sent privately to Theophilus. After the completion of Acts, both may have been given to the Gentile Gr. churches. Both were probably published before the destruction of Jerusalem, for there is no reference to that event within their pages.

The destination is plainly marked in the introduction. The Gospel was dedicated to the "most excellent Theophilus" (Lk 1:3). "Most excellent" was an epithet usually reserved for royalty and nobility (Acts 23:26; 24:3; 26:25). Theophilus was almost certainly a man of high position and culture, probably a government official, who had become a friend of Luke and who was a new Christian. Perhaps the instruction which he had received in the church conflicted with the rumors concerning Jesus that had been familiar to him as a government officer, and he was desirous of ascertaining the truth of the matter. Luke wrote to him as a personal friend that he might dispel his doubts and lead him into an intelligent faith.

Luke's Gospel is the most literary of the four. Its introduction accords closely with the classical literary form for books. The ancestry, birth, youth, and introduction of Jesus to His public ministry are described with more detail than in other Gospels. In the section of the Gospel which is peculiarly Lucan (9:51—18:14), there are numerous parables and anecdotes which are unique, and which disclose the discernment and arrangement of a literary artist. The parables of the lost sheep, the lost coin, and the two sons in Lk 15 are short stories of high quality. Allowing for the fact that they were originally spoken by Jesus, their transcription shows the hand of a facile craftsman who knew how to write effectively.

Luke presents Christ as the Saviour of men, who is interested in the poor and downtrodden, and who has come to bring them deliverance.

Because of his desire to make the message of Christ convincing to Theophilus, Luke stresses the historical aspect of the gospel. He explains fully the environment from which Jesus came, gives His genealogy by natural descent rather than by tracing the royal line as Matthew does, and places the entire narrative in a chronological setting that relates it to the contemporary current of world affairs (Lk 2:1-2; 3:1-2). Though his approach is less didactic than Matthew's, he includes a large amount of Jesus' teaching so that His thought is adequately represented. Luke deals more with personalities than the other Synoptic writers, both in the contacts of Jesus with individuals, and in the literary characters of His parables. The connection of the Gospel with Acts reveals his historical perspective, for he was considering Jesus' life not as a unit by itself, but as the first part of the ministry which was continued through the leaders of the church who finally took the gospel from Jerusalem, the center of the Jewish world, to Rome, the center of the Gentile world. He saw in Christianity the manifestation of God's world plan, not simply the origin of a sect.

Tradition says that Luke was an artist who painted a picture of the Virgin Mary. Assuredly he was an artist in words. He alone of the Gospel writers preserves the four songs: the *Magnificat* (1:46–55), the *Benedictus* of Zacharias (1:68–79), the *Gloria in Excelsis* of the angels at Christ's birth (2:14), and the *Nunc Dimittis* of Simeon (2:29–32). His vocabulary is varied and colorful. His reproduction of the parables of Jesus, particularly those in the section peculiar to him (9:51 – 18:14), reveals literary skill of highest quality.

The Gospel is universal in its appeal. It presents Jesus as the Son of Man, who belongs to all humanity and who sympathizes with everybody. Luke alone relates the parable of the Good Samaritan, which shows that a neighbor is not determined by race or by culture, but by love. Women and children obtain greater recognition in his Gospel than in any other. He magnifies Jesus' ministry among the poor and oppressed. The *Magnificat* (1:53) says:

"The hungry he hath filled with good things;.
And the rich he hath sent empty away."

Jesus' first words in the synagogue at Nazareth were a quotation from Isa 61:1: "The Spirit of the Lord is upon me, because he anointed me to preach good tidings to the poor . . ." (Lk 4:18, ASV). In the parables of the rich fool (12:16–21), the great supper (14:15–24), and the rich man and Lazarus (16:19–31), Luke has reflected Jesus' concern for the plight of the poor.

Luke stresses particularly two theological themes. Prayer is one of his most prominent topics. He notes Jesus' prayer at His baptism (3:21), at His withdrawal into the desert (5:16), before the choice of the twelve disciples (6:12), before the prediction of His death (9:18), before teaching His disciples (11:1), special intercession for Simon Peter (22:32), the prayer in Gethsemane (22:41), and on the cross (23:34, 46). A second theme is the Holy Spirit, who is mentioned more times than in Matthew and Mark combined. Luke indicates that all of Jesus' life was lived by the Spirit. The Spirit created His body (1:35); He was baptized with the Spirit (3:22), tried by the Spirit (4:1), commissioned by the Spirit for His life work (4:14, 18), encouraged by the Spirit in His work (10:21), and He enjoined His disciples to await the Spirit before they undertook their labors (24:49). Both of these themes are carried forward by Acts, which shows that they represent the author's interest as well as being historical facts.

The doctrinal content is not so pronounced as that of Matthew or John, but is sufficient to reveal the undercurrent of Christian theology. Luke presents Christ as the Son of God, whose sonship is attested by angels (1:35), by demons (4:41), and by God Himself (9:35). The concept of salvation is stated in Jesus' own words: "The Son of man came to seek and to save that which was lost" (19:10, ASV). In the concluding chapter Luke stresses the truth that Jesus is the predicted Messiah of the OT Scriptures, who "should suffer, and rise again from the dead the third day; and that repentance and remission of sins should be preached in his name unto all the nations . . ." (24:46–47, ASV). The climax of his teaching fulfills his avowed purpose to impart spiritual certainty to his reader.

See Luke, Gospel of.

The Gospel of John

The fourth Gospel differs strongly from the Synoptics in content and organization. So radical is the difference that some scholars have challenged its authenticity, saying that the Synoptic and Johannine accounts of the life of Christ cannot both be true. The Gospel of John contains no parables, few of the epigrammatic sayings of Jesus which are so common in the Synoptics, only seven miracles, five of which the Synoptics do not record, and a number of long argumentative discourses related to the person of Jesus that the Synoptics do not duplicate. The Gospel of John is organized more like a sermon than a biography, and deals with the life of Jesus as an incentive to faith rather than an attempt to summarize historical occurrences. By the critics of the 19th cen., from Bretschneider (1820) on, to more recent writers like James Moffatt (*Introduction to the Literature of the New Testament*, pp. 566–619) and Pierson Parker ("John the Son of Zebedee and the Fourth Gospel," JBL, LXXXI [1962], 35–43), the Johannine authorship has been widely denied.

The tradition that John the son of Zebedee was the writer is early, and is supported by considerable evidence. The Rylands Fragment, a small scrap of papyrus bearing on its two sides a few words from John, dates from the first quarter of the 2nd cen., and demonstrates that the Gospel was copied probably by A.D. 125. There are allusions in the Epistle to Barnabas (A.D. 125), the Epistles of Ignatius (A.D. 110), and Justin Martyr (A.D. 140) that seem traceable to this Gospel. Heracleon, a Gnostic who belonged to a school of thought flourishing between A.D. 140 and 180, wrote a commentary on the fourth Gospel. Tatian (A.D. 140) used it in his *Diatessaron,* so that there can be no doubt of its existence before the middle of the 2nd cen. From the time of Irenaeus (A.D. 170–180) the patristic testimony is almost unanimous that the fourth Gospel was the authentic product of John the beloved disciple.

The Gospel itself bears marks of its authorship. The writer was familiar with Jewish customs and traditions, and knew the OT. He was familiar with locations in Palestine, and had lived in Jerusalem and its environs. He professed to have seen Jesus, for he remarked that "we beheld his glory . . ." (1:14), and to have been present at the crucifixion (19:35). He noted the hour at which Jesus sat by the well of Sychar (4:6), the number and size of the waterpots at the wedding of Cana (2:6), the grass at the place of the feeding of the 5,000 (6:10), the numerous details concerning the death and burial of Jesus (chaps. 18–19). The final chapter of the book identifies him with the unnamed "beloved disciple" who was Peter's companion on the fishing expedition after the resurrection (21:7) and also in the investigation of the tomb (20:2). He must have been an intimate associate of Jesus, for he reclined next to Him at the last supper. Of Jesus' disciples who are mentioned by name, Peter, Andrew, Philip, or Nathanael cannot fill the requirement since they are mentioned in the third person. James and John, the sons of Zebedee, were present at the occasions mentioned above, but James could not have been the author since he was martyred at an early date, probably about A.D. 44 (Acts 12:2). By the simple process of elimination John the son of Zebedee is the one remaining possibility for authorship.

The objections that he was "unlearned" (Acts 4:13), that he was a Galilean rather than a Judean, and that his known character does not accord with the temperament of the author as deduced from the writing are not valid. Greek was spoken in Galilee, and although John may not have been primarily a literary man, he could have learned to express himself in the simple but good Greek of the fourth Gospel. If the book were written toward the close of his life, he would have had ample opportunity to improve both his language and his theological knowledge. The language of the fourth Gospel shows that its author possessed an ardent temperament which had been disciplined by contact with the world, and that he wrote from a perspective of many years in the ministry of Christ. The explanation of the words of Jesus concerning his longevity (Jn 21:22–23) implies that he must have survived to old age, or the explanation would not have been necessary for the author to include.

The great differences between the content of this Gospel and that of the Synoptics can be largely explained by assuming that the author was acquainted with the Synoptic tradition, the account of Jesus' life currently preached and incorporated in Matthew, Mark, and Luke, and that he was consciously attempting to add a supplement to it, while integrating with it simultaneously a new estimate of Jesus' life. A few chronological difficulties, such as the placing of the cleansing of the temple early in Jesus' ministry (2:13–22) and the sequence of the last hours of Jesus' life, have not yet been perfectly resolved. The Gospel is, however, authentic history, and should not be dismissed as mere theologizing.

Comparatively little is known concerning John, son of Zebedee. His father was a prosperous Galilean fisherman, who owned boats, and had hired servants (Mk 1:19–20). His mother was Salome, who may have been the older sister of Mary, Jesus' mother (Mt 27:56; Mk 15:40; Jn 19:25). John was a partner in the fishing business with his brother James, and

with Peter and Andrew (Lk 5:10). All four men were probably among the early disciples of John the Baptist; perhaps John was the second member of the pair who first followed Jesus (Jn 1:35–37). If he were, he witnessed the wedding at Cana (2:2), and later quit the fishing trade to follow Jesus.

In the later ministry he participated in the general preaching of the Twelve (Mt 10:1–2). Both he and his brother were so aggressive that they were called "sons of thunder" (Mk 3:17), but Jesus' reproof disciplined their hasty tempers (Lk 9:49–55). John took the responsibility for Jesus' mother at the crucifixion (Jn 19:26–27), and was one of the first to realize the meaning of the resurrection (20:8). Both by his intimate knowledge of Christ and by his long spiritual experience he was well qualified to write an interpretative Gospel. See John.

The date of the fourth Gospel has been placed at various intervals from A.D. 40 to 140. Goodenough and Albright both argue, for different reasons, that John may have been written as early as A.D. 40 (Erwin R. Goodenough, "John a Primitive Gospel," JBL, LXIV [1945], 145–182; W. F. Albright, "Recent Discoveries in Palestine and the Gospel of John" in Davies and Daube, ed., *The Background of the New Testament and Its Eschatology,* pp. 153–171). A fair median date would be A.D. 85, at a time when the general gospel tradition had crystallized, and when doctrinal interpretation and controversy called for an authoritative presentation of the meaning of Jesus' career.

The place of production is unknown. Numerous hypotheses have been suggested: Palestine, Alexandria, and others. Irenaeus states (*Against Heresies* iii.1.1) that John published this Gospel during his residence at Ephesus in Asia. It was probably written for a church which had grown to maturity, and which was confronting the opposition of pagan philosophy. The explanation of Jewish phrases and customs (1:38; 2:6, 13; 4:9; 9:22; 18:28; etc.) indicates that it was intended for a Gentile audience. Quite probably the Gospel and the epistles were directed to the Gr. church of Asia.

The fourth Gospel is carefully organized, with definite literary and chronological divisions. Although the writer followed the sequence of Jesus' ministry by the successive Passovers, he paid less attention to biographical detail than to the interpretation of personality. His avowed aim was to create faith in Jesus as the Messiah, and to lead his readers into a new life as they believed. To this end his illustrative material and the progress of his argument are directed. The theme is eternal life, the life of God manifested among men, and it is developed in orderly fashion by presenting selected episodes from the life of Jesus that illustrate its meaning.

The prologue of the Gospel introduces the person of Christ as the Eternal Word, the expression of the Father, who became flesh in order to manifest eternal life to men. The plot of the Gospel is stated at the outset in the words, "The light shineth in the darkness; and the darkness apprehended [overcame, marg.] it not" (1:5, ASV). The manifestation of the life, like light, encountered the darkness, and a conflict immediately ensued. The history of this spiritual conflict is the scheme of interpretation for the life of Jesus. Two alternatives are presented: belief, which means receiving the light (1:11-12), and unbelief, which means rejecting the light (1:10-11). In the episodes that follow through the narrative, belief and unbelief, with their symptoms and consequences, are graphically illustrated.

The basis for belief consists of seven selected miracles or "signs" of Jesus: (1) turning the water into wine (2:1-11); (2) the healing of the nobleman's son (4:46-54); (3) the cure of the impotent man (5:1-9); (4) the feeding of the 5,000 (6:1-14); (5) the walking on the water (6:16-21); (6) the healing of the man born blind (9:1-41); (7) the raising of Lazarus (11:1-44). Each of these signs represents the sovereign power of Christ in some particular area of human need, and cumulatively they show His competence to cope with the forces that depress and degrade human life. Each miracle was a response to the faith of the principals involved, and at least five of them were performed to educate the disciples. John said specifically that these signs were selected for the purpose of promoting belief that Jesus is the Messiah (20:30-31).

The person of Christ is more important in this Gospel than His actions. His claims are stated in seven major uses of the phrase "I am." He said, "I am" the bread of life (6:35), the light of the world (8:12; 9:5), the door of the sheepfold (10:7), the good shepherd (10:11, 14), the resurrection and the life (11:25), the way, the truth, and the life (14:6), the true vine (15:1). Each of these equates Him figuratively with a common object which indicates one of His functions. As the bread, He is the sustenance of men; as the light, He is the guide of men; as the door, He provides access to security; as the shepherd, He assures protection; as the resurrection and the life, He achieves victory over death; as the way, the truth, and the life, He imparts certainty; as the true vine, He provides the vitality for fruitage.

More personal interviews are recounted in John than in any of the other Gospels. Some are short, like the conversation with the nobleman; some are long, like the trial before Pilate. Almost all of them illustrate Jesus' endeavor to evoke belief in Himself from the person with whom He was conversing.

The Johannine vocabulary is so distinctive that excerpts from this Gospel are easily identifiable. "Word," "life," "flesh," "hour," "sign," "lifted up," "works," "love" (two different Gr. verbs), "send," "beginning," "know" (two different Gr. verbs), "glory," "glorify," "abide," "perish," "Comforter," "the Father"

contain concepts that are exclusively Johannine and that create a new representation of truth.

The Gospel emphasizes the deity of Jesus Christ, both in the claims of the Gospel itself, and in the confessions from the mouths of its characters. The prologue calls Him the Word of God (1:1-2); John the Baptist declared Him to be the Son of God (1:34); He descended from heaven (3:13); He was sent by God (3:34); the Samaritans called Him the Saviour of the world (4:42); He claimed equal honor with the Father (5:23), and professed to possess the same kind of life (5:26); the officers sent to arrest Him returned empty-handed, saying, "Never man [in contrast to God] so spake" (7:46, ASV). His statements, "Before Abraham was born, I am" (8:58, ASV) and "I and the Father are one" (10:30, ASV), were understood by His enemies to be claims to deity. At the same time, His humanity is stressed. He "became flesh" (1:14); He was tired (4:6), exasperated (4:48), harsh (8:44), sympathetic (11:33), agitated (12:27), affectionate (13:1), unselfish (18:8), loyal to family ties (19:26). John portrays the perfections of God manifested in the perfect humanity of Christ.

The characters are numerous and diverse. Among the disciples the writer characterizes by a few quick strokes of his pen the impulsive Peter, the quiet Andrew, Philip the materialist, Nathanael the student, Thomas the skeptic, Judas Iscariot the selfish, and "the beloved disciple" the confidant of Jesus. Among those whom Jesus encountered in His ministry were Nicodemus the learned teacher of Israel, the sharp but untaught Samaritan woman, the desperate nobleman of Cana, the supercilious and unbelieving brethren, the devoted Mary of Bethany, the indifferent Pilate, and the loyal Joseph of Arimathea. These and many others of lesser importance constitute the galaxy of men and women whose faith or unbelief reflected Jesus' influence upon them.

The language of John is simple, direct, and at times repetitious because of the constantly recurring technical terms which he uses. The structure of the Greek shows that the author had a good command of vocabulary and grammar, but that he possibly thought in Aramaic. The prologue has the form of Heb. poetry, somewhat resembling the Psalms in structure. The frequent use of "and" as a connective, the occasional use of Aramaic names such as Cephas (1:42), and the reiteration of propositions in slightly different wording (5:26-27) may indicate Semitic origin, though there is no proof that the Gospel was originally written in Aramaic.

The selection concerning the woman taken in adultery (7:53-8:11) is not found in the oldest MSS. Some include it, but indicate that it is not generally regarded as authentic, and one group of MSS locates it after Luke 21:38. Several Old Latin versions, three of the Old Syriac, the Coptic, Gothic, and the oldest Armenian version also omit it; nor is it contained in the recently discovered Bodmer Papyrus of the early 3rd cen. None of the earlier Church Fathers quote it, though it was recognized from the 5th cen. onward. A. T. Robertson said: "It is clear that it is not a genuine part of the Gospel of John" (*An Introduction to the Textual Criticism of the New Testament*, p. 210). It may, nevertheless, be a genuine episode in the life of Jesus, which was included in this text because it fitted the setting of the narrative. Its introduction shows that it was formerly part of a larger narrative, and it seems strange that this short anecdote should survive the loss of its context if it were not accepted as truth.

See John, Gospel of.

Each of the quartet of Gospels is needed for a rounded picture of Christ. Matthew depicts Him as the Messiah who fulfills OT prophecy and completes the redemptive purpose of God. Mark presents Him as the man of authority, who can overcome sickness, sin, and death, and who is Lord of all. Luke portrays Him as the perfect humanitarian, concerned with every aspect of human affairs. John declares that He is Deity, truly man and truly God. However much they may differ in approach and detail, they agree on the identity of the person of Christ, and they bear united testimony to His supernatural character.

Bibliography. F. F. Bruce, *Are the New Testament Documents Reliable?* London: Inter-Varsity, 1943. Austin Marsden Farrer, "On Dispensing with Q," *Studies in the Gospels*, ed. by D. E. Nineham, Oxford: Basil Blackwell, 1955, pp. 55–88. Edgar J. Goodspeed, *Matthew, Apostle and Evangelist*, Philadelphia: Winston, 1959. R. M. Grant and D. N. Friedman, *The Secret Sayings of Jesus, with an English Translation of the Gospel of Thomas* by William R. Schoedel, Garden City, N.Y.: Doubleday, 1960. Adolph Harnack, *The Sayings of Jesus*, trans. by J. R. Wilkinson, London: Williams and Norgate, 1908; contains Harnack's reconstruction of "Q." David Martin McIntyre, *Some Notes on the Gospels*, ed. by F. F. Bruce, London: Inter-Varsity, 1943. Edwin B. Redlich, *Form Criticism: Its Value and Limitations*, New York: Scribner's, 1939. A. T. Robertson, *Studies in Mark's Gospel*, New York: Macmillan, 1919; *Luke the Historian in the Light of Research*, New York: Scribner's, 1923. W. Graham Scroggie, *A Guide to the Gospels*, London: Pickering and Inglis, 1948. Vincent Henry Stanton, *The Gospels as Historical Documents*, Parts I, II, III, Cambridge: Univ. Press, 1923–1930. Burnett Hillman Streeter, *The Four Gospels*, 4th impression rev., London: Macmillan, 1936, pp. xxiv, 624. Theodor Zahn, *Introduction to the New Testament*, ed. by M. W. Jacobus, Grand Rapids: Kregel, 1953; see II, 307–617 and III, 1–354.

M. C. T.

GOSPELS, SYNOPTIC. As the term synoptic suggests (from *syn*, "together with," and *opsis*, "a sight, a view," thus "a seeing together"), Matthew, Mark, and Luke provide a presentation of Jesus and His ministry that has much in common. These features set them apart from the Gospel according to John, in which most of the material is peculiar to itself. In the Synoptics the public ministry of Jesus is prefaced by the preparatory work of John the Baptist and the baptism and temptation of our Lord. The ministry itself is pictured as occurring mainly in Galilee, consisting of Jesus' activities of teaching and healing, usually in terms of great throngs of people, as He moved here and there in the company of His disciples. The climax comes in the journey to Jerusalem and the events of the passion and resurrection.

The Synoptic Problem

When these three Gospels are considered apart from John and in relation to one another, certain agreements and differences come to light which in turn raise questions as to the origin of these writings. Did they emerge independently of one another, or did they make use of one another to some extent? If they made use of one another, this may help to explain the agreements, but by the same token the differences will be the more puzzling.

The measure of agreement between the Synoptics is actually quite surprising in view of the fact that Jesus was engaged for a period of approximately three years in an almost continuous ministry by word and deed. The amount of material available must have been tremendous. However hyperbolic Jn 21:25 may be in its affirmation that the world itself could not contain the books that should be written if all the deeds of Jesus were recorded, the clear intent is to give the impression that the reports in our Gospels are quite fragmentary. All we have is a selection.

The Synoptic problem, so-called, has to do with the mutual relations in the accounts. How can the similarities and also the differences in these three Gospels be explained? Before any kind of answer can be attempted, it is necessary to examine the phenomena of the Synoptics more closely.

The Data

First of all, as to the agreements among the Synoptics, one should consider *content* or subject matter. Westcott's analysis, though only approximate, is sufficiently precise for our purpose. Mark is found to have 93 percent of his material in common with Matthew and/or Luke; only 7 percent is peculiar to this Gospel. Matthew has 58 percent in common with other Synoptics and 42 percent that does not appear in the other two. Luke has 41 percent in common with the other two and 59 percent peculiar to this Gospel. To state the coincidences differently, roughly two-thirds of Mark is found in both Matthew and Luke, and almost one-third more in either Matthew or Luke. Mark has only thirty to forty verses that fail to appear in one or the other of the two remaining Synoptics.

As to *order* or sequence of the material, Mark's arrangement is usually shared both by Matthew and Luke. Where this is not the case, one or the other agrees with Mark. Matthew and Luke do not unite against Mark. When the Markan order is shared by the others, it is generally shared from the beginning to the end of a narrative.

With regard to *language and style,* one who is in position to study a Gr. synopsis where the accounts are placed side by side can better appreciate the situation, but an English harmony will provide considerable information. A good passage to test, one which contains the triple tradition (Matthew, Mark, Luke), is the account of the healing of the paralytic (Mt 9:1–8; Mk 2:1–12; Lk 5:17–26). While there is some variation, especially in the opening and closing statements, the main part of the narrative shows remarkable agreement in the vocabulary employed by all three writers. What is most striking of all is the preservation of a broken construction in the report of the actual performance of the miracle: " 'But that you may know that the Son of man has authority on earth to forgive sins'—he says to the paralytic—'I say to you, rise, take up your pallet and go home' " (Mk 2:10–11, RSV, and parallels).

With respect to *differences,* it should be observed that as far as content is concerned, Mark has little to report of the *didachē* or teaching of Jesus, whereas Matthew and Luke contain many parables and considerable discourse material that is not parabolic. Lk 9:51 – 18:14 has much that appears only in this Gospel. Various details of the crucifixion and resurrection appearances turn up in a single record only. Matthew's account of the Sermon on the Mount is much more extensive than Luke's. The order of events in the temptation of Jesus varies between Matthew and Luke. Jesus' visit to the synagogue at Nazareth is put earlier in the Lucan narrative than in the other two. Many more examples could be given, including the use of synonymous terms rather than identical words in parallel accounts.

Explanation

While various attempts have been made to explain the relationship between them, no solution for the phenomena of the Synoptic Gospels has yet won universal acceptance.

1. *Oral tradition.* B. F. Westcott and Arthur Wright have suggested that oral tradition was the decisive influence, since several decades passed before our Gospels began to be written. During that time presumably the core of the material became somewhat fixed from telling and retelling. This could account for the agreements in the Synoptics, which were written to preserve this oral tradition. The differences could then be attributed to the special interests of the individual writers as well as to the particular needs of the people for whom they wrote.

This view, however, is not without difficulties. It is hard to see how the tradition could have been sufficiently safeguarded from alteration as it spread into the widely separated regions from which the written Gospels arose. Further, it is hard to understand how Mark, depending on this common tradition along with Matthew and Luke, could have utilized so little of our Lord's teaching. Furthermore, one would expect greater uniformity in the reports of what Jesus said in instituting the supper of His new covenant. It should be granted, however, that oral tradition must have played an important role, if not an exclusive one, in the preservation of the Gospel material, and even in the choice of written materials by each writer.

2. *Direct literary dependence.* The many agreements in content, in sequence, and in construction (language and style) are best explained in terms of some sort of literary dependence (recall especially Mk 2:10–11 and parallels). There can be little doubt that Mark is the source for the material in Matthew and Luke that agrees with it. Here the habitual following of the Markan order by the other evangelists is especially impressive. The conclusion of Markan priority is buttressed by the fact that Matthew and Luke contain alterations of Markan material at times in the interest of grammatical smoothness. In other words, Mark's record appears to be the more primitive. It is worth noting, too, that where the three Gospels have the same material, Mark's narratives are usually longer and more graphic. Matthew and Luke may have contracted Mark in such cases in order to allow room for material not derived from Mark. Ancient authors had to exercise care lest their book, which was in the form of a scroll, would become too unwieldy for convenient use.

There were people such as Augustine in the early centuries of the church who thought that Mark abbreviated Matthew. If this were the case, it is difficult to conceive how Mark could have omitted so much of the teaching of Jesus, such as that which is contained in the Sermon on the Mount. So this opinion has not been able to maintain itself.

3. *Two-document hypothesis.* It is clear, however, that Matthew and Luke could not have depended on Mark for everything, since they contain much discourse material that is absent from Mark. There is a strong possibility that they depended on a source, whether oral or written, that specialized in the sayings of Jesus. Modern scholars often refer to such a source by the designation "Q" derived from the first letter of the German word for source (*Quelle*). It is granted that the objective existence of such a source cannot be demonstrated historically, but it is felt that the data of Matthew and Luke

point to the necessity for such a source. Possible support for this theory may be found in the statement of Papias, quoted by Eusebius, that "Matthew collected the oracles (*logia*) in the Hebrew language, and each interpreted them as best he could." There is no clear evidence, however, that Matthew drew on Luke or vice versa. They seem to have written independently of each other.

Conclusion

If Mark and Q were sources for Matthew and Luke, most of the material in the latter two Gospels is accounted for, but not all. Judging from their nativity and passion narratives, as well as some other features, they each must have had access to information that was not a part of the central tradition of the early church. Some of it may have been gained by personal investigation. From Luke's prologue (1:1-4) it is evident that he had available to him the oral testimony of eye-witnesses plus the accounts of those who had written before he undertook his Gospel. The prologue informs us that he did some investigating of his own. So the possible sources for Gospel materials must have been many and varied. Apparently there was no prejudice against the use of sources, and this is quite natural, since much of the historical material in the OT was written up with the aid of earlier records (cf. Kings, Chronicles).

It would be a mistake, however, to look on the human authors of the Gospels as mere editors. Each one had a molding influence, under God, on the materials used, so that it is possible to detect a definite individuality impressed on each Gospel.

The search for the human factors that entered into the composition of the Gospels can go only so far. Beyond the sphere of this kind of investigation lies the mysterious and powerful inspiration or influence of the Holy Spirit upon the writers, leading them to the selection and use of their material. This is what gives their work authority for the church.

See Gospels, The Four.

E. F. Har.

Bibliography. Everett F. Harrison, *Introduction to the New Testament,* Grand Rapids: Eerdmans, 1964, pp. 136-145. Ned B. Stonehouse, *Origins of the Synoptic Gospels,* Grand Rapids: Eerdmans, 1963. B. H. Streeter, *The Four Gospels,* London: Macmillan, 1930. Merrill C. Tenney, *The Genius of the Gospels,* Grand Rapids: Eerdmans, 1951.

GOURD. *See* Plants.

GOUT. *See* Diseases.

GOVERNMENT OF GOD. *See* Theocracy; Israel; Israel, Kingdom of; King.

GOVERNMENT OF ISRAEL. *See* Israel; Israel, Kingdom of.

GOVERNOR. The English term is used broadly by the KJV in the OT for a variety of specialized Heb. words which designate some type of delegated official (e.g., Gen 42:6; 45:26; Jud 5:9; II Chr 1:2; 28:7; Jer 20:1; Zech 9:7). Heb. *peḥâ* (Akkadian *paḥatu*) was a general term that came to be used for governor during the Assyrian through the Persian periods (I Kgs 10:15; Ezr 5:3; 8:36; Neh 2:7; 5:15; Est 3:12). The *peḥâ* often exercised control by military power and is thus called a "captain" (e.g., II Kgs 18:24; Jer 51:23, 28, 57). This word has been found on several stamped jar handles from the post-Exilic level of Ramat Raḥel (IEJ, IX, 273 f.), proving that it was used as the title of the governor of the province of Judah during the Persian administration (Neh 5:14; 12:26; Hag 1:1; Mal 1:8). The Tirshatha (*q.v.*) was the honorific title for the governor of a province (Ezr 2:63; Neh 7:65; etc.).

In the NT, "governor" occurs most frequently for *hēgemōn,* "one who goes before," which denotes the emperor-appointed administrators in the provinces (Mt 10:18; I Pet 2:14) and especially the procurators in Judea (e.g., Pilate, Mt 27:2; cf. Acts 23:24; 26:30). *See* Pilate.

"Governor" is also used in II Cor 11:32 for the Gr. *ethnarchēs* (NASB, "ethnarch") of Damascus; in Gal 4:2 rendering *oikonomos* (RSV, "trustee"); in Jn 2:8-9 for *architriklinos* (RSV, "steward of the feast"); and in Jas 3:4 for the participial form, *euthynontos* (RSV, "pilot"). *See* Deputy; Ethnarch; Steward.

F. G. C. and J. R.

GOZAN (gō'zăn). A region along the Habor River near the Euphrates where the Israelites deported from Samaria were settled (II Kgs 17:6; 18:11). It is frequently mentioned in Assyrian records as Guzani. Assyria had already conquered it in 808 B.C. (cf. II Kgs 19:12). Oppenheim identified it with Tel Halaf on that river. Excavations have revealed documents of the 7th cen. B.C. with such Israelite names as Hoshea and Ishmael.

See Habor.

GRACE. The concept of grace is many-sided and subject to development in the Scriptures. In the OT *ḥēn,* "favor," is the unmerited favor of a superior to an inferior. In the case of God and man, *ḥēn* is demonstrated usually in temporal though occasionally in spiritual blessings, and in deliverance in both physical and spiritual senses (Jer 31:2; Ex 33:19). *Ḥesed,* "loving-kindness," is the firm loving-kindness expressed between related people and particularly in the covenants into which God entered with His people and which His *ḥesed* firmly guaranteed (II Sam 7:15; Ex 20:6).

In Gr. literature *charis* had the following meanings: (1) It was used of that which causes attractiveness, such as grace of appearance or speech. (2) It was used of a favorable regard felt toward a person. (3) It was used of a favor. (4) It was used to mean gratitude. (5) It was used adverbially in phrases such as "for the sake of a thing," *charin tinos*.

But it was not until the coming of Christ that grace took on its fullest meaning. His self-sacrifice is grace itself (II Cor 8:9). This grace is absolutely free (Rom 6:14; 5:15–18; Eph 1:7; 2:8–9). When it is received by the believer, it governs his spiritual life by compounding favor upon favor. It equips, strengthens, and controls all phases of his life (II Cor 8:6–7; Col 4:6; II Thess 2:16; II Tim 2:1). Consequently, the Christian gives thanks (*charis*) to God for the riches of grace in His unspeakable gift (II Cor 9:15).

The apostle Paul was the principal human instrument to convey the full meaning of grace in Christ. The NT offers grace to all, in contrast to the OT which generally restricted the offer of grace to God's elect people Israel. Grace in its fullest definition is God's unmerited favor in the gift of His Son, who offers salvation to all and who gives to those who receive Him as their personal Saviour added grace for this life and hope for the future.

Sovereign grace is not an arbitrary display of God's grace. In order to receive it man must believe. In order to enjoy it the believer must be obedient. Grace provides acceptance (Rom 3:24), enablement (Col 1:29), a new position (I Pet 2:5, 9), and an inheritance (Eph 1:3, 14). At least three motives are indicated in the NT as to why God acts in grace, especially in salvation. He does it to express His love (Eph 2:4; Jn 3:16), to be able to display His grace in the ages to come (Eph 2:7), and that redeemed man will produce good works (Eph 2:10). Sovereign grace is always purposeful, for the life under grace is a life of good works.

Bibliography. Leo G. Cox, "Prevenient Grace—a Wesleyan View," JETS, XII (1969), 143–150. Charles C. Ryrie, *The Grace of God,* Chicago: Moody Press, 1970.

C. C. R.

GRACE AT MEALS. Among the Jews, it was apparently customary at meals to give thanks over the bread, representing all the food, and over the wine, representing all the drink. This, says Edersheim, was because Psalm 24:1 states, "The earth is the Lord's, and the fulness thereof." Christians carried this custom over into their practice. It is suggested in the NT. Jesus gave thanks before distributing food to the 5,000 (Mt 14:19) and the 4,000 (Mt 15:36), before partaking of the Lord's Supper (Lk 22:19), and before eating with the two disciples at Emmaus (Lk 24:30). Cf. Acts 27:33–35; Rom 14:6; I Cor 10:30; I Tim 4:3–5.

GRAFF, GRAFT. This is a horticultural process by which the branches from a cultivated tree may be inserted and grafting take place. In Rom 11:17 ff. the apostle Paul employs this

practice in reverse: the wild branches, the Gentiles, are pictured as grafted in to the good stock of the parent tree, the Israelites. This deliberate inversion heightens the picturesque figure of speech conveying the eternal truth of the rejection of national Israel and composition of true Israel—all believers. However, Paul warns that the new branch could be cut away if it proved faithless.

GRAIN. *See* Plants.

GRANARY. *See* Storehouse.

GRAPES. *See* Plants.

GRASS. *See* Plants.

GRASSHOPPER. *See* Animals: Locust, III.29.

GRATE. A bronze grating (RSV) or lattice for the altar of burnt offering before the tabernacle (Ex 27:4; 35:16; 38:4–5, 30; 39:39). The grating probably surrounded the lower half of the altar as a skirt, fastened to the ledge halfway up the altar and extending down to the ground, perhaps to prevent the priests from stepping in the sacrificial blood poured out at the base of the altar (Lev 4:7). Each corner of the grating had a bronze ring; through these went two bronze-covered poles to carry the entire altar (D. W. Gooding, "Tabernacle," NBD, p. 1233; fig. 176). *See* Altar; Tabernacle.

Herodian family tomb, Jerusalem (illustrates a "rolling stone" that would seal a tomb). HFV

Tombs carved from the mountainside at Petra. MIS

GRAVE. The words translated "grave" in KJV are the Heb. words *'î,* "ruin" (once); *qeber* and *qᵉbûrâ,* "tomb" (about 40 times); *shᵉ'ôl* (31 times); *shahat,* "destruction" (once); and the Gr. words *hadēs* (once); *mnēma* (once) and *mnēmion,* "tomb" (eight times). These words are also translated in other ways. *Qeber* and *qᵉbûrâ* many times are rendered "sepulcher" or "burying place" as are *mnēma* and *mnēmion.* The translation "tomb" also is used. Heb. *shᵉ'ôl* is also translated "hell" (31 times) and "pit" (three times) in the KJV. The RSV usually transliterates both *shᵉ'ôl* and *hadēs.*

The burial customs of the Israelites are fairly clear from archaeology and biblical references. The OT speaks of burials both in house gardens (II Kgs 21:18) and in tomb complexes (Gen 23:20; I Kgs 14:31). Graves of the poor often were undoubtedly only shallow trenches, as in the large cemetery at Qumran. In other cases a cairn of stones was erected over the burial, as for Achan (Josh 7:26), enemy kings (Josh 8:29; 10:27), and Absalom (II Sam 18:17). Doubtless burial customs varied somewhat through the centuries.

The Hebrews apparently did not use coffins—none are found in native tombs—but buried their dead on a bier or low couch (II Sam 3:31; II Chr 16:14; Ezk 32:25; Lk 7:14), following a Canaanite custom as found in Middle Bronze Age tombs at Jericho.

Perhaps the most extensive burial chamber of Heb. times was found by Dr. Joseph P. Free at Dothan (BASOR, Dec. 1960, pp. 10–13; there is later unpublished material). Many bodies were found in the one tomb. The skeletons of those buried earlier were pushed to the sides to make room for the most recent burial. A notable feature was the many lamps found. Was the tomb left with a lamp burning or were the lamps used in funerary rites? Miss K. Kenyon found niches for lamps cut in the walls of tombs of an earlier date at Jericho (Kathleen Kenyon, *Archaeology in the Holy Land,* p. 139). Notice the mention of a burning at a burial in II Chr 16:14; 21:19. This was probably not a cremation, which was exceptional among the Hebrews.

In NT times tomb complexes were dug, as witnessed by the references to the tomb of Joseph of Arimathea. The Herodian family tomb in Jerusalem, Israel, is an undoubted example. The rolling stone that closed the low doorway is still intact. The so-called tombs of the Sanhedrin NW of modern Jerusalem, with their many chambers and niches for bodies, also may be dated prior to A.D. 70.

The poor were doubtless buried more simply.

The tomb of Clytemnestra at Mycenae, Greece, one of the so-called "beehive tombs." Mimosa

From NT times come many ossuaries which perhaps reflect poorer burials. These are small stone boxes containing the bones of the dead which were collected after decomposition. They did not contain ashes; the Roman custom of cremation was apparently rejected. Some of these ossuaries are famous. NT names such as Miriam and Bar Jonah have been noted, but it is difficult to tell if these are Christian burials or Jewish (cf. G. E. Wright, *Biblical Archaeology*, p. 242). The famous Uzziah inscription refers to such a regathering of the bones of King Uzziah (*q.v.*).

The word *qeber* usually means simply "sepulcher." Occasionally it has a figurative use, e.g., Ps 5:9. In Isa 14:19 and Ezk 32:22, 25-26 the word is used in the dramatic scene of the kings of the earth who lie in their graves but stir themselves up to meet the kings of Babylon and Egypt as they also come to the grave. In these contexts *she'ôl* is also used.

The word *she'ôl* brings many problems. It is now usually defined as the place of departed spirits. This does not entirely fit the 31 places translated "grave" in KJV. Neither does it do justice to the statements that *she'ôl* is a place of darkness, silence, and forgetfulness (Job 17:13; Ps 31:17; 88:3, 12). Some have concluded from such verses that the soul sleeps in *she'ôl*. However, the problem is solved if these verses refer to the sleep of the body in the grave (*see* Dead). A. Heidel argues extensively that *she'ôl* sometimes refers to the realm of the dead, sometimes to the grave (A. Heidel, *The Gilgamesh Epic and OT Parallels*, pp. 173 ff.). It may be argued that *she'ôl* is a poetic word for "grave." It is used in poetic parallelism with *māwet*, "death," and *qeber*, "sepulcher" (R. L. Harris, "The Meaning of the Word Sheol," BETS, IV [1961], 129-135).

Of details of actual burial customs of the Hebrews, there is little evidence. Ananias and Sapphira were buried very promptly, as is still done among the Jews. G. E. Wright some time ago expressed doubt that food was left with the dead, though vessels clearly were (BA, VIII [1945], 17). Miss Kenyon found food in Jericho tombs, but this was of pre-Israelite date (*op. cit.*, p. 191). The Bible shows no cult of the dead in orthodox Heb. religion.

See Burial; Dead, The; Embalm; Funeral; Mourning; Sheol; Tomb.

R. L. H.

The false door from the Tomb of Nakht at Amarna, Egypt. Gaddis

GRAVE CLOTHES. The expression translates Gr. *keiriai* in Jn 11:44, the bandages or strips of cloth wrapped around a corpse to bind the arms and legs in a Jewish burial. After the body was washed (Acts 9:37)—but not further embalmed—it was generally wrapped first in a "clean linen shroud" (Mt 27:59, RSV).

GRAVEN IMAGE. An image (Heb. *pesel*) carved or sculpted from stone, wood, or metal, mentioned in the OT along with the molten image cast in a mold (e.g., Deut 27:15; Jud 17:3-4; II Chr 34:3). Since the Canaanites used these as idols—as archaeological discoveries in Palestine and Syria have verified—they were forbidden to the Israelites (Ex 20:4; Lev 26:1; etc.). *See* Idol.

GRAVER, GRAVING. *See* Occupations: Carving. Engraver.

GRAY, GREY. *See* Colors; Hair.

GREAT COMMISSION. *See* Commission, Great.

GREAT OWL. *See* Animals, III.37.

GREAT SEA. The large body of water known to us as the Mediterranean Sea (Num 34:6; Josh 1:4; 9:1; 15:12, 47; Ezk 47:10; etc.). It is also called the "uttermost sea" or the "hinder sea," i.e., the western sea (Deut 11:24; 34:2; Joel 2:20; Zech 14:8), the "sea of the Philistines" (Ex 23:31), the "sea of Joppa" (Ezr 3:7), or simply "the sea" (Num 13:29; Ezk 26:5, 16–18; 27:3; etc.; Jon 1:4; etc.; Acts 10:6, 32; 27:30; etc.). About 2,300 miles long, it was the chief sea known to the Israelites. According to some commentators, the expression may also be used figuratively in Dan 7:26 of the ocean or the masses of humanity. *See* Sea.

Violent winds from the NE made shipping unsafe during the winter months from October through February or March (Acts 27:14–28:11). Sandbars and rocky reefs were constant hazards, because the captains hesitated to leave the sight of land. Modern diving expeditions have found the wrecks of many an ancient ship with its cargo of wine jars or copper ingots or marble columns intended for the cities of Greece and Rome.

The "Great Sea." MIS

From 3000 B.C. onward the Egyptians carried cedar timber in their ships hugging the Mediterranean coast from Byblos (*see* Gebal) in Lebanon to the Nile delta. Minoan traders from Crete and later the Mycenaean Greeks dominated the Mediterranean during the 2nd mil. B.C. Throughout the 1st mil. B.C. the Phoenicians from Tyre and Sidon plied its waters and colonized its shores. With no natural harbors, the Hebrews never became a seafaring people; consequently they depended on Phoenician ships and sailors for maritime commerce and travel. Solomon employed the skills of Hiram's mariners (I Kgs 9:26–28; 10:11, 22). Jonah took passage on a Phoenician ship sailing from Joppa to Tarshish in Spain.

By NT times the Mediterranean had become virtually a Roman lake (*mare nostrum*) to connect Rome with many parts of her vast empire and to transport grain and other products to the capital from the provinces. A harbor was built at Acco in the Hellenistic period and renamed Ptolemais (Acts 21:7), and Herod the Great had constructed artificial harbor installations at Caesarea (*q.v.*). Thus Palestine came into direct communication with the western world, and since then has been at the crossroads of three continents.

J. R.

The Egyptian god Osiris cast in bronze. LM

GREAVES. *See* Armor.

GRECIANS (grē'shánz)

1. Used in the OT once (Joel 3:6, KJV) for "the sons of Javanim," Javan being the Heb. word for Ionia or Greece.

The contacts of Jews with Greeks in OT times were limited but became considerable in the period between the Testaments. By the beginning of the Christian era the three centers of Jewish population outside of Palestine were Babylonia, Syria, and Egypt, the latter two areas being also centers of Hellenism. Large numbers of Jews were also located in Asia Minor and Rome. The contact of Jews with Gr. culture found creative literary expression at Alexandria, where the translation of the OT into Gr. was begun in the 3rd cen. B.C. and where Philo in the 1st Christian cen. expounded the OT in terms of Gr. philosophy. Even Palestinian Jews came under the Hellenizing influence.

2. In the NT "Grecians" (Gr. *Hellēnistai*) are mentioned in Acts 6:1; 9:29; and in some MSS at 11:20, and *Hellēnes* in the rest of Acts (14:1; 16:1, 3; 17:4, 12; etc.). This distinction is maintained by the translation of *Hellēnistai* as "Grecians" and *Hellēnes* as "Greeks."

"Grecians" (Gr. *Hellēnistai*) is a relatively rare word. It has not been found in Gr. or in Hellenistic Jewish literature. The verb form *hellēnizē* is more common. It is used by Christian writers to mean "to speak Greek," "to speak good Greek" (the classical meanings), or "to practice paganism," "to be pagan." Etymologically the verb has no special reference to language, and on the analogy of similar word formations should mean one who practices Gr. ways (whether a Gr. or a foreigner). It is this meaning which lies behind the usage for "pagan."

The following identifications of the "Grecians" in Acts (6:1; 9:29; 11:20) have been proposed.

a. The usual explanation is that they were Gr.-speaking Jews who were contrasted with the Aram.-speaking Palestinian Jews (*Ioudaioi*). This interpretation goes back to Chrysostom's homilies on Acts. There is difficulty in the contrast with "Hebrews" in Acts 6:1. "Hebrews" is not commonly used in a linguistic sense, and Paul, a Gr.-speaking Jew, called himself a Hebrew (Phil 3:5; II Cor 11:22).

b. A variation on the above takes "Grecians" and "Hebrews" in Acts 6:1 as meaning respectively, Jews who spoke *only* Greek, and Jews who *also* knew a Semitic language, without denying that both words in other contexts had wider connotations. This distinction between the two groups may have been reflected in the language used in their worship services and in the form of the Scriptures they read publicly. Such differences could account for the possibility of tensions, and at the same time avoid the problem that many Palestinian Jews would have spoken Gr. by preference so that a language distinction would not have been absolute between Palestinian and Diaspora Jews.

c. "Grecians" were Gr.-speaking Jews of the Diaspora living in Palestine, as opposed to the *Hellēnes* of the fourth gospel who were Gr.-speaking Jews living beyond Palestine. It seems natural to connect the seven deacons whose names are all Gr., with the "Grecians" of Acts 6:1, and then to see a connection with the synagogues of the residents of Cyrene, Alexandria, Cilicia, and Asia (Acts 6:9) with whom Stephen was in dispute (see Acts 21:8, 16 for an association of Philip with Cypriot Jews). The same circle comes to mind as the antagonists of Saul, a native of Cilicia. Converts native to these regions opened up the

Gentile mission at Antioch (Acts 11:19 f.; cf. 13:1).

d. The most radical interpretation is that "Grecians" are no different from "Greeks" (Gentiles). This view destroys the whole structure of Acts.

e. That Jewish proselytes are meant is unlikely, for it is more natural to distinguish Nicolas (Acts 6:5) as the only proselyte in the group than to consider all seven as proselytes and distinguish him only as from Antioch. His presence shows that those of pure Gr. culture were included among the "Grecians."

f. It has been argued that the "Grecians" were a religious party in Judaism opposed to the temple and its sacrificial cultus who were so named by their opponents. "Grecians" does appear only in the first half of Acts, which reflects Palestinian tradition.

g. The word may have its literal meaning of "act like a Greek," and so may describe both Jews (native or Diaspora) who did not conform to Palestinian customs and traditions (but were doctrinally orthodox) as well as Gentile pagans (at Antioch).

h. The word may be left as a general word for "Greek speakers," with the context deciding what kind — Jewish Christians in Acts 6:1, Jews of the synagogues in Acts 9:29, Gentiles in Acts 11:20.

In support of this last and broadest view, namely, "Greek speakers," in Acts 11:20 the MS evidence may slightly favor "Grecians" over the variant "Greeks." It seems unlikely that a scribe would have changed a common word into a rarer word and particularly one which introduces a more difficult reading. At the same time, the context demands that the preaching be done to non-Jews. The demands can be reconciled in "Grecian" as used in the sense of "Greek speakers," these imitating the Greeks in language, customs, or both, and so refer to the general population of Antioch.

Following the same line of thinking, if Stephen and his associates in Acts 6 can be identified with the Grecian party, then the first thrust of missionary activity in the early church came from this group and, as argued above, they were composed of those who spoke Gr. whether Jewish Christians, Jews of the synagogue, or Greeks. Philip began the mission to Samaria, and unnamed Jews from the Dispersion launched the work among the Gentiles at Antioch.

Bibliography. F. F. Bruce, *The Acts of the Apostles,* Grand Rapids: Eerdmans, 1952. Henry J. Cadbury, "The Hellenists," *The Beginnings of Christianity,* London: Macmillan, Vol. V, 1933. CornPBE, "Hellenism," pp. 379–388. C. F. D. Moule, "Once More, Who Were the Hellenists?" *Expository Times,* LXX (Jan., 1959), 100–102. Marcel Simon, *St. Stephen and the Hellenists in the Primitive Church,* New York: Longmans, Green, 1958. B. B. Warfield, "The Readings *Hellenas* and

Hellenistas, Acts xi.20," JBL, III (Dec., 1883), 113–127. Hans Windisch, "*Hellēn,* etc.," TDNT, II, 504–516.

E. F. and R. A. K.

GREECE. The reputation of Greece as a classical land has long been established. Its distinction as a Bible land is not so well fixed. Yet Greece provides the geographical stage for much of the NT drama. Here Paul preached at the prayer meeting site at Philippi and first brought the gospel to Europe, later becoming involved in the midnight scene at the local jail. Here he made his dramatic bid for acceptance before the Areopagus court on Mars Hill in Athens. Here he ministered at Corinth for 18 months. Numerous other Gr. towns figure in the NT account.

While Greece represents a national entity to the contemporary observer, it was never a whole sovereign state until winning its full independence from Turkey in 1829, and did not reach its present territorial limits until 1947. In ancient times Hellas (Greece) was that area inhabited by Gr. peoples, including the Gr. peninsula, islands of the Aegean and for many centuries the Asia Minor coast. Macedonia was not really a part of the Gr. world until the 4th cen. B.C., when Philip II and his son Alexander the Great made a conscious effort to bring Gr. culture to their kingdom. In most ancient times Greece was a collection of kingdoms and city-states; Alexander never really united it. Under the Romans it became two provinces, Macedonia and Achaia. With the decline of Rome in the W, Greece remained within the Byzantine Empire and with the fall of Byzantium passed on into the Ottoman Empire, of which it was a part until the last century.

Geography. If one includes in Greece the Gr. peninsula stretching S from Thessaly and Epirus and the Aegean islands, which is what Greece was in most of classical times, he is dealing with an area of about 30,000 square miles. This approximates the state of Maine. Like Maine, Greece is very mountainous; in fact, mountains cover about 70 percent of the land surface. No other country of the Mediterranean area presents a more tumbled surface than Greece. Although the placement of mountains in Greece is chaotic, there is a degree of symmetry. The Magnesian range extends S from Olympus in E Greece; the Pindus range lies between Thessaly and Epirus in central Greece; and the Epirus range stretches along the W coast. These are crossed by other ridges, dividing the country into a vast checkerboard of tiny valleys, few of which are more than a dozen miles long and more than half as wide. With communications so hampered, a provincialism developed in Greece such as has probably existed in no other historically important area of the world.

The coast of Greece is so deeply indented that she has the longest coastline in proportion to enclosed area of all important historical re-

The Lion Gate at Mycenae. HFV

gions. The many indentations afforded numerous harbors. So the Greeks, unable to wrest a living from their rocky farms, became a seafaring people. It is easy, however, to overemphasize the place of the sea in Gr. economic life. The mountains sometimes cut off access to the sea and often were too barren to provide good ship timber. And during much of the year the sea was too stormy for sailing. Moreover, overseas trade was not vital in the early days when most of the communities of Greece were self-sufficient. It is important to observe that the best ports of Greece and many of her valleys lay on the E coast. Therefore her E areas received civilizing influences from the Orient first.

History. The earliest high development of civilization in the Gr. world occurred not on the mainland but on the island of Crete. There Minoan civilization began *c.* 3000 B.C. A combination of oriental and native elements, Minoan culture was palace-centered and reached its greatest prosperity 1600–1400 B.C. Often called "educators of Hellas," the Minoans left an indelible stamp on mainland developments. There, sometime after *c.* 2000 B.C., a wave of Indo-European peoples moved in from the N and established themselves. Ultimately they gained sufficient power to bring the Minoans of Crete under their control (*c.* 1500 B.C.). The greatest days of these Mycenaen peoples lasted 1400–1200 B.C. During this time they ranged far and wide over the Mediterranean, marketing their wares and in the latter part of the period tangled with Troy.

About 1200 B.C. another wave of Indo-European peoples moved in from the N and destroyed the Mycenaean kingdoms. The years *c.* 1100–800 are often known as the Greek Middle Age; at that time the old order

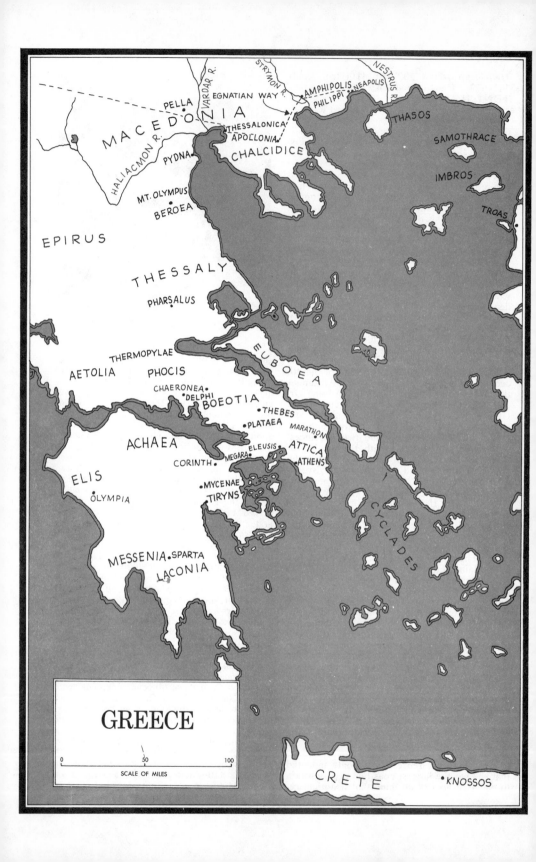

MACEDONIA

PELLA

EGNATIAN WAY

STRYMON R.

VARDAR R.

HALIACMON R.

AMPHIPOLIS

NEAPOLIS

PHILIPPI

NESTRUS R.

THASOS

SAMOTHRACE

THESSALONICA

APOLLONIA

CHALCIDICE

IMBROS

PYDNA

TROAS

MT. OLYMPUS

BEROEA

EPIRUS

THESSALY

PHARSALUS

EUBOEA

THERMOPYLAE

AETOLIA

PHOCIS

CHAERONEA

DELPHI

BOEOTIA

THEBES

PLATAEA

MARATHON

ACHAEA

ATTICA

CORINTH

MEGARA

ELEUSIS

ATHENS

ELIS

MYCENAE

TIRYNS

OLYMPIA

CYCLADES

MESSENIA

SPARTA

LACONIA

GREECE

0   50   100

SCALE OF MILES

CRETE

KNOSSOS

was dying out and a new order of small city-states was rising. Homer wrote his great epics around 850 B.C. The period 800–500 is frequently dubbed the Formative Age because at this time the typical political, economic, religious, and social institutions of the city-states of the Classical Age gradually appeared on the scene. At this time too Gr. peoples migrated all over the Mediterranean area – to Italy, France, Spain, Egypt, and elsewhere. To this deposit of Gr. peoples and culture Alexander and his successors would add. And Romans would imbibe a very large portion of the Gr. cultural heritage. As a result Greek was the language of communication of the entire Mediterranean world by the time of Christ, facilitating the spread of a gospel preached and written in Gr. And by that time the OT had been translated into Gr. (the Septuagint [LXX]) and was being studied in the some 150 synagogues of the Roman world, thus making preparation for the coming of the gospel.

In 512 B.C. Greece faced a new crisis when the Persians crossed the Hellespont and invaded Thrace. During subsequent years dramatic battles were fought at such places as Marathon, Thermopylae, Salamis, and Plataea, with the result that the Persians broke off attempts to subjugate the Greeks. Now the Greeks were free to experiment with their unique institutions in the small city-states of the Classical Age. Such experimentation would have been impossible if the superpower to the E had elected to make further efforts to bring the Hellenes to heel.

During the 5th cen. Athens converted the league formed to turn back the Persians into an Athenian Empire. And she used the resources of empire to make possible her golden age (461–431 B.C.). Under the leadership of Pericles she developed her democracy, empire, drama, architectural achievements of the acropolis, and other aspects of culture. Meanwhile Sparta put together a Peloponnesian league to offset the rising power of Athens. Other city-states arose to be sure, but they could not operate without reference to one or the other of the two chief powers of Hellas.

Perhaps it was inevitable that Athens and Sparta would ultimately go to war. At any rate they did; and the conflict dragged on from 431 to 404 B.C., ending in the destruction of the Athenian Empire. After a few decades of Spartan dominance in Greece, Thebes seized the hegemony temporarily. Meanwhile Macedonian power was building in the N and after 337 B.C. dominated the peninsula. Philip II did most to build the military capability of Macedon and passed on to his son Alexander an excellent army with which to launch the Panhellenic war of revenge against Persia. This had been brewing for some time because of Persian interference in Gr. affairs. For instance, Persians had provided Spartans with naval help necessary to defeat the Athenians during the Peloponnesian war. Parenthetically it should be

The Temple of Hephaestus (Vulcan) overlooking the Agora at Athens. HFV

noted that Philip employed Aristotle as tutor for the young Alexander, and Plato was partially contemporary with Aristotle.

After the assassination of his father, Alexander was left to fight the Persians. He launched the attack in 334 B.C. and within about three years conquered most of the territory of the colossus of the E. Before he could reorganize the empire, he fell victim to a fever in Babylon in 323 B.C. Sparring for power among leading members of Alexander's entourage finally led to a division of the empire into Syrian, Egyptian, and Macedonian kingdoms. Confusion reigned in Macedon after the death of Alexander, as one general after another tried to secure the throne. Finally Antigonus Gonatas, grandson of the great Antigonus of Alexander's staff, secured control over Macedon and established his dynasty there.

Although Macedon was dominant in Greece during the 3rd cen., it did not control the entire country. In central Greece Aetolian and Achaean leagues organized and in the W the kingdom of Epirus arose. King Pyrrhus of Epirus led an army to Italy to help Greeks of the S part of the peninsula take a stand against Roman efforts to unify Italy. He returned to Greece in 275 B.C. to face Macedon. After Pyrrhus was killed in battle in 272, his kingdom rapidly declined. At the end of the 3rd cen. Macedon allied with Hannibal during the second Punic war between Carthage and Rome. Naturally this act brought undying determination on the part of Rome to subjugate this new enemy in Greece.

Roman warfare in Greece lasted a half century and ended with Roman annexation of Greece and creation of the provinces of Macedonia (148 B.C.) and Achaia (146 B.C.). Now Greece was to suffer new woes, for Roman civil wars of the 1st cen. B.C. brought terrible destruction to Gr. soil. Both the decisive battles between Pompey and Julius Caesar, and Antony and Augustus Caesar were fought in Greece, as was the battle of Brutus and Cassius against Augustus at Philippi. More settled conditions under the empire after Augustus brought peace and political reorganization restored a degree of

The Temple of Apollo and Acropolis at Corinth. Mimosa

prosperity to Greece. By the time the apostle Paul came through during the middle of the 1st cen. A.D., many of the scars of war had healed. But Greece was not destined to recover the greatness of earlier centuries.

Greece as a Bible land. The claim of Greece to be a Bible land is mostly connected with Paul's second and third missionary journeys. His itinerary on his second journey is associated with Neapolis, Philippi, Amphipolis, Apollonia, Thessalonica, Berea, Athens, and Corinth (Acts 16:11–18:18). Later he addressed two epistles each to Thessalonica and Corinth and one to Philippi. Separate articles are devoted to each of these towns and epistles. After his first imprisonment in Rome Paul apparently returned to Greece briefly, and even did missionary work on Crete (*q.v.*), where he subsequently sent Titus (*q.v.*) to minister and gave him instructions in the epistle to Titus (*q.v.*).

Bibliography. M. Cary, *The Geographic Background of Greek and Roman History,* Oxford: Clarendon Press, 1949. N. G. L. Hammond, *A History of Greece to 322 B.C.,* Oxford: Clarendon Press, 1959. M. L. W. Laistner, *A History of the Greek World from 479 to 323 B.C.,* 2d ed., London: Methuen & Co., 1947. Carl Roebuck, *The World of Ancient Times,* New York: Scribner's Sons, 1966. Chester Starr, *A History of the Ancient World,* New York: Oxford Univ. Press, 1965.

H. F. V.

GREED. *See* Covetousness.

GREEK LANGUAGE. Gr. is an Indo-European language probably coming through the Sanskrit dialect, which shows a close relation to classical Gr.

The literary period began with Homer (*c.* 850 B.C.), who ushered in the classical period running to Alexander the Great (330 B.C.). This period had many dialects for the many tribes in Greece, but three chief families, Doric, Aeolic, and Ionic, emerged.

The Attic branch of the Ionic became supreme through Athens' political power by the 6th cen. B.C.; Persian wars with victories at Marathon, Salamis, and Thermopylae which prevented Greece and Europe from becoming oriental; and the 5th cen. B.C. literary giants, Sophocles, Euripides, and Aeschylus. Even after the decline of Athens, the Attic dialect continued through the writings of Plato, Aristotle, Xenophon, and Thucydides. Aristotle's pupil Alexander the Great extended the empire and pushed a program of Hellenization, making Attic Gr. a universal language even in Palestine, so that it still flourished there in Christ's time although modified to Hellenistic form since 300 B.C. Although the Hellenistic Gr. was followed by Byzantine (A.D. 550–1453) and modern (since A.D. 1453), today's Athens newspaper could no doubt be read by Plato.

Hellenistic Gr. consisted of a literary and non-literary form. Literary writers, such as Josephus, Philo, and Strabo, imitated the Attic, while the non-literary or Koine Gr. was the

Athena, patron deity of ancient Athens. Mimosa

734

everyday language of the masses. The literary has been found in stone inscriptions and extra-biblical literature and may appear in the NT Luke. The non-literary Koine has been found in papyri remains of letters, wills, and contracts, as well as in the ostraca (pottery fragments), and was used by the LXX and NT writers.

The Koine stressed clarity and emphasis by using the historical present tense, by piling up prepositions and adverbs before and after verbs, by using compound verbs instead of simple, and by using prepositions for simple cases and dropping the dual and optative forms. For some time many NT scholars thought the differences in vocabulary and style between biblical and classical were caused by a "Holy Spirit language" to convey divine truth, but the discovery of the papyri and ostraca in Egypt in the 1890's showed it to be the everyday living Gr. of the people, although some common words assumed new meanings or uses in the religious context of the OT and NT.

E. B. R.

GREEN. *See* Colors.

GREEN HERBS. *See* Plants.

GREETING. *See* Salutation.

GREYHOUND. *See* Animals: Fowl, Domestic, III.14.

GRIEF. Grief can be caused by many things, hence the use of a variety of words, most of which reflect the cause of the particular grief. All told, there are about 20 words in the Bible which have been translated "grief" in the KJV. In the RSV an attempt has been made to translate these in such a manner as to do credit to the root meanings.

The different words used. Such words as those listed below are to be found in both Heb. and Gr., each with its own root meaning bearing on the particular choice of the word to express a certain grief. For easy classification they are listed here alphabetically, according to their English meanings. The nature, the cause, or the motivation for grief comes out in the various words used.

1. Anger – Heb. *ḥārâ,* "to burn," "be wroth" (Gen 4:6, "Why art thou wroth"; Gen 45:5, "Now therefore be not grieved, nor angry with yourselves"; I Sam 18:8, "Samuel was very wroth"). A righteous indignation or grievance at the effects of sin in death is expressed by the Gr. *embrimaomai* ("And Jesus again boiling over within himself [*embrimōmenos*] came to the tomb," Jn 11:38, lit.). Heb. *ka'as,* "provocation," "anger," "sadness" (I Sam 1:16, "out of the abundance of my complaint and grief [my great anxiety and vexation, RSV] have I spoken"; Prov 17:25, "A foolish son is a grief to his father"; Ps 31:9, "mine eye is consumed with grief" [cf. Eccl 1:18; 2:23; Dan 11:30]). Heb. *ka'as,* "provocation," "anger" (Job 6:2,

"Oh that my grief [my vexation, RSV] were throughly weighed").

2. Bitterness – Heb. *mārar,* "to be bitter" (I Sam 30:6, "The soul of all the people was grieved" ["all the people were bitter in soul," RSV]; cf. Ruth 1:13; Lam 1:20). The place where the water was bitter was called Marah (Ex 15:23; Num 33:8-9).

3. Disgust – "weariness at," Heb. *qûṭ* (Ps 139:21, "Am not I grieved with [do I not loathe, RSV] those that rise up against thee"). Gr. *prosochthizō* (Heb 3:10, "I was grieved with [provoked with, RSV] that generation").

4. Evil – Heb. *ra',* "evil," "calamity" (Jon 4:6, "to deliver him from his grief [discomfort, RSV]"). Heb. *yēra',* "to be evil" (Gen 21:11-12, "The thing was very grievous [very displeasing, RSV] in Abraham's sight"; cf. Isa 15:4). Gr. *kakōs,* "evilly" (Mt 15:22, "My daughter is grievously [severely, RSV] vexed with a devil").

5. Exhaustion – Heb. *lā'â,* "to be weary," "faint," "exhausted" (Prov 26:15 [cf. Job 4:2], "The slothful hideth his hand in his bosom; it grieveth him [wears him out, RSV] to bring it again to his mouth"). *diaponeo,* "to labor through," "exert oneself," "get worked up," "grieve self" (Acts 4:2, "Being grieved [annoyed, RSV] that they taught the people"; Acts 16:18, "Paul, being grieved [annoyed, RSV], turned and said . . .").

6. Frustration – Heb. *pûqâ,* "a stumbling block" (I Sam 25:31, "that this shall be no grief unto thee").

7. Pain – Heb. *mak'ôb,* "pain," "sorrow," "suffering" (II Chr 6:29, "When every one shall know . . . his own grief [affliction, RSV]"; Ps 69:26, "they talk to the grief of [afflict still more, RSV] those whom thou hast wounded"; Isa 53:3, "a man of sorrows").

8. Showing of grief – Heb. *yāgôn,* "showing of grief," "sorrow," "affliction" (Ps 31:10, "My life is spent with grief [sorrow, RSV]"; Jer 45:3, "The Lord hath added grief to my sorrow"). Gr. *lupē,* "grief," "grievance" (I Pet 2:19, "for conscience toward God endure grief [endures pain, RSV]"; cf. Heb 12:11). Gr. *lupeō,* "to grieve," "afflict" (Mk 10:22, "He was sad . . . and went away grieved [sorrowful, RSV]"; Jn 21:17, "Peter was grieved"; cf. Rom 14:15; II Cor 2:4; Mk 3:5). Gr. *stenazō,* "to groan," "sigh" (Heb 13:17, "they may do it with joy, and not with grief").

9. Sullenness – Heb. *ḥāmēṣ,* "be sour," "leavened" (Ps 73:21, "for my heart was grieved [embittered, RSV]").

10. Vexation – Heb. *'āṣab,* "to annoy or vex," "to grieve" (Ps 78:40, "How oft did they . . . grieve him"; Gen 45:5, "be not grieved [distressed, RSV]"; cf. I Sam 20:3, 34; II Sam 19:2; Neh 8:11).

11. Weakness – Heb. *ḥālâ,* "to be sick," "be weak" (Isa 57:10, "therefore thou wast not grieved [you were not faint, RSV]"; Amos 6:6, "they are not grieved"; also Jer 10:19; 14:17; 30:12; Nah 3:19). Heb. *ḥŏlî,* "sickness,"

"weakness," "pain" (Isa 53:3, "a man of sorrows"; Isa 53:4, "Surely he hath borne our griefs"; also Jer 6:7; 10:19).

The causes of grief.

1. Grief over man's sin. This is seen in Isa 53 where Jesus is called a man of sorrows (v. 3).

2. Grief over our own sin. Sorrow over the consequences of what we have done when it is not accompanied by true repentance is remorse (Heb 12:15-17), in contrast to godly sorrow over the sinful act itself, that accompanies real repentance (II Cor 7:9-10; II Sam 12:13; Ps 32; 38:18).

3. Grief over loved ones who have died. David grieved over the loss of his first son by Bathsheba (II Sam 12:15-23), but was comforted by the fact that his child was in heaven and therefore said, "I shall go to him, but he shall not return to me." Mary and Martha and Christ grieved at the death of Lazarus (Jn 11:19, 35, 38). The one comfort they had was that Jesus could raise the dead – and did, in the particular case of Lazarus, right at that time, though he must have died again to await the resurrection like other men. The comfort for the Christian is that Jesus will not let him die eternally, that is, experience the second death, but will raise him at the time of the rapture (*q.v.,* Jn 11:25; I Thess 4:14-18; I Cor 15:52-55).

4. Grief over loved ones who are eternally lost. This God will Himself care for, particularly in the eternal era of the kingdom of God, in fulfillment of His promise, "God shall wipe away all tears from their eyes; and there shall be no more death, neither sorrow, nor crying" (Rev 21:4). This is to be accomplished in two ways. First, by the removal of the old heavens and the old earth so completely (Rev 20:11; 21:1, 4) that God can say, "Behold, I create new heavens and a new earth: and the former shall not be remembered, nor come to mind" (Isa 65:17). Second, there will be that direct comfort which God will give to His own. In Isa 65:18 God says, "Be ye glad and rejoice forever in that which I create: for, behold, I create Jerusalem a rejoicing, and her people a joy" (cf. Isa 51:11). He also promised to Israel to do away with death. "He will swallow up death in victory; and the Lord God will wipe away tears from all faces; and the rebuke of his people shall he take away from off all the earth: for the Lord hath spoken it" (Isa 25:8). Paul uses this verse in I Cor 15:54 as a proof of the resurrection and rapture of all believers at Christ's second coming.

See Suffering.

R. A. K.

GRIND. In Isa 3:15 "to grind the faces of the poor" means to oppress the poor still further by extortion. "Let my wife grind for another" (Job 31:10, RSV) means "let her become a slave in grinding grain for another man" (cf. Ex 11:5; Isa 47:2). In Eccl 12:3 the "grinders" that "cease because they are few" portray the teeth largely decayed in old age, whereas in v. 4 ears becoming deaf can hardly hear the noise of millstones grinding grain (cf. Jer 25:10). *See* Mill.

GRISLED, GRIZZLED. *See* Colors.

GROVE. This is a translation of two words:

1. Heb. *'ēshel,* "tamarisk." Abraham planted a grove (KJV), more appropriately "a tamarisk," at Beer-sheba (see Gen 21:33, RSV; cf. "tree" [*'ēshel*] in I Sam 22:6 and 31:13). *See* Plants: Tamarisk.

2. Heb. *'ăshērâ.* In its various forms it is rendered "grove" or sometimes "shrine" in KJV, an erroneous translation going back to the LXX. It is known now, however, that Asherah is Heb. for *athirat (yam)* of the Ugaritic texts of Ras Shamra. Asherah was the mother-goddess, the wife of El, who gave birth to 70 gods and goddesses including Baal. She was the foremost fertility deity of the Canaanites and she became a formidable rival to Yahweh especially during the time of Jezebel. *See* Gods, False: Asherah.

GUARD. A man or group of men who protected an important person or special object.

1. Heb. *mĩshma'at,* "bodyguard," i.e., a group bound to another person by obedience. David was a bodyguard's captain under Saul (I Sam 22:14, RSV); Benaiah, the group's captain under David (II Sam 23:23).

2. Heb. *rāṣîm* (from *rûṣ,* "to run"), "guards," runners or a royal escort for Absalom (II Sam 15:1) and for Adonijah (I Kgs 1:5); the royal bodyguard who not only protected the king but also carried out his wishes (I Sam 22:17, RSV; I Kgs 14:27; II Kgs 10:25; 11:4; etc.).

3. Heb. *mishmār,* "gaol or prison" (Gen 40:3; etc.); in later times the man on watch (Neh 4:22-23) and also a guard or watchman waiting for orders (Ezk 38:7).

4. Heb. *ṭabbāḥ,* "guard" (lit., "slaughterer," "executioner"), exclusively of non-Israelites: of Potiphar the Egyptian over Joseph (Gen 37:36), of Nebuzaradan (II Kgs 25:8).

In the NT the RSV translation is "guard" instead of "watch" (KJV) in Mt 27:65-66; 28:11, and "executioner" in Mk 6:27.

GUARDIAN ANGELS. *See* Angels.

GUDGODAH (gŭd-gō'dä). An Israelite campground in the Negeb after Aaron's death (Deut 10:7), probably the same as Hor-hagidgad (*q.v.*).

GUEST. *See* Hospitality.

GUEST CHAMBER. *See* House.

GUIDANCE, GUIDE. *See* Lead, Leader.

GUILE. Three Heb words and one Gr. word are so translated in KJV. The verbal form "to beguile" represents three words in the OT and four in the NT.

The basic meaning of the word is trickery or deception, and related to attitudes held by people or actions involving people.

In Israel, taking of life "with guile" (*'ormâ,* "trickery" or "subtlety," Ex 21:14) was a crime punishable by death. (See Deissmann, LAE, pp. 214–217, on a Jewish prayer for vengeance on an ancient gravestone now in Athens.) The Lord would bless the man in whose spirit there was no guile (*remîyâ,* "treachery," Ps 32:2). One was to refrain from speaking guile (*mirmâ,* "deceit" or "fraud," Ps 34:13).

The verbal forms convey the idea of deceiving, as in Gen 3:13 (*nāshâ,* "lead astray" or "delude"), Gen 29:25 (*rāmâ',* "delude" or "betray") or Num 25:18 (*nākal,* "defraud"). Emphatic in these examples is wrongful behavior on the part of one or more persons.

In the NT, the single noun form is *dolos* (see, e.g., Jn 1:47; I Pet 2:22). The word referred to a "taint" in material things, as gold or silver (see MM, *Lexicon, s.v.*). By application it meant "deceit," "cunning" or "treachery" in a person's attitudes or dealings. One's motives (Acts 13:10), speech (I Pet 3:10) or actions (Mt 26:4) are so described.

The verb forms translated by "beguile" are varied. In Col 2:4 *paralogizomai* means to delude by false reasoning; in 2:18 *katabrabeuō* means to render an umpire's decision, here to rob one of his true reward. In I Cor 11:3 *exapataō* conveys the idea of being completely deceived (cf. Gen 3:13). II Pet 2:14 has *deleazō,* a fisherman's term meaning to catch by means of a bait.

See Deceit.

W. M. D.

GUILT. *See* Sin.

GULF. A translation of Gr. *chasma,* RSV "chasm," in Lk 16:26; a deep cleft separating two places. The Lord Jesus Christ lends His authority to the concept that a vast chasm has been fixed by an irrevocable decree between paradise ("Abraham's bosom," *q.v.*) and hades, in order that persons in the next life cannot cross it (cf. Heb 9:27). Gr. *chasma* may be found in other descriptions of final judgment in I Enoch 18:11; Diogenes Laertius 8:31; Plato *Republic* X.614.

GULL. *See* Animals: Cuckoo, III.8, 45.

GUM. *See* Plants: Gum.

GUNI (gū'nī), **GUNITES** (gū'nīts)
1. The second son of Naphtali, founder of the family of the Gunites (Gen 46:24; I Chr 7:13; Num 26:48).
2. Father of Abdiel and grandfather of Ahi, who was a chief man of the Gadites (I Chr 5:15).

GUR (gûr). An ascent near Ibleam, between Jezreel and Beth-haggan, where Ahaziah, king of Judah, was mortally wounded by Jehu, king of Israel (II Kgs 9:27). It is equated with Akkad. *Gurra* by Albright (BASOR, 94 [1944], 21). J. Simons, finding no ancient site in this short stretch, adopts the reading of the LXX, "at the ascent of the valley (*Gai*), which is Jeblaam" (*The Geographical and Topographical Texts of the Old Testament,* Leiden: E. J. Brill, 1959, pp. 916–918).

GUR-BAAL (gûr'bāl). A town in the Negeb, whose Arab occupants were defeated by King Uzziah (II Chr 26:7). Possibly the same as Jagur of Josh 15:21 (Khirbet Gharra), ten miles E of Beer-sheba.

GUTTER
1. The rendering of the Heb. *rahat* (Gen 30:38, 41); Assyrian *râtu,* "vessel," "water container"; a depression in the trough, *shōqet* (Gen 24:20; 30:38). In Moses' time (Ex 2:16) *rahat* was used alone for the watering trough. Jacob's placing peeled rods in the troughs simply was his own adherence to local superstition. Common sense dictated putting the rods where the animals would be found in largest numbers at one time. There was no biological value to the practice. God would have multiplied Jacob's herds in any event.
2. The "gutter" (*sinnôr*) of II Sam 5:8 almost certainly is a term for the vertical tunnel, known as Warren's shaft, in the water system of Jebusite Jerusalem. By sneaking into the spring Gihon and clambering up the 40 foot high watershaft, Joab and his men were able to enter the stronghold and take the Jebusites by surprise (see FLAP, p. 178). *See* Gihon.

H

HAAHASHTARI (hā'a-hăsh'tȧ-rī). A son of Naarah and Ashur, the "father" or founder of Tekoa and a descendant of Judah (I Chr 4:6).

HABAIAH (hȧ-bā'yȧ). Father of one of the families of returned exiles claiming priestly descent, but put out of the priesthood since their names were not found in the genealogical register (Ezr 2:61; cf. vv. 62–63; Neh 7:63).

HABAKKUK (hȧ-băk'ŭk). Information about Habakkuk is limited to the book that bears his name. Two references ascribe the oracle which the author saw (1:1) and the prayer he prayed (3:1) to the prophet Habakkuk. The only clear historical reference in this book is to the Chaldeans (1:6), which provides the basis for dating this prophet near the close of the 7th cen. B.C.

Very likely Habakkuk witnessed the decline and fall of the Assyrian Empire. He possibly may have known about the fall of Nineveh in 612 B.C., and very likely was aware of the rising power of the Babylonians when this message was revealed to him. Conditions prevailing in Judah after Josiah's death in 609 B.C. and before the Chaldean invasion of Judah in 605 make this period a favorable time for dating the prophecy of Habakkuk.

HABAKKUK, BOOK OF. The uniqueness of this book is apparent in two distinctive features. First of all, Habakkuk records his dialogue with God in which he raises theological problems and listens to the answers. In addition, chap. 3 is a psalm with musical terms noted in the first and last verses.

In outline form the message of Habakkuk may be summarized as follows:
  I. Why Does God Tolerate Violence? 1:1–4
  II. Chaldeans Will Bring Punishment on Judah, 1:5–11
  III. Why Should Heathen Be Used to Punish God's People? 1:12–2:1
  IV. The Righteous Trust God to Do Right, 2:2–20
  V. Prayer of Confidence and Praise, 3:1–19

Habakkuk (*q.v.*) appeals to God in prayer concerning the violence, injustice, destruction, and indifference to the teaching of the law that prevailed in Judah. He could not understand why a righteous God should tolerate this. When God replied, indicating that the Chaldean invaders would bring judgment on the guilty citizens of Judah, Habakkuk became more concerned. Should the Chaldeans, whose own might was their god, be allowed to punish the Jews who actually were less wicked than these pagan invaders? In response, Habakkuk is bidden to record that ultimately the unrighteous would fail but the righteous would live by his faith or faithfulness. The upright should not draw his conclusion on the basis of a limited temporal perspective, but should wait and look at the ultimate outcome. The unrighteous about him — aggressors, evildoers, murderers, deceivers, and idolators (2:6–19) — would finally perish, while the righteous would live, since the Lord is in His holy temple. Consequently all the earth should keep silence before Him (2:20). In a prayer appealing to God that in His wrath He would remember mercy, the prophet expresses his praise and thanksgiving to God. He is determined to continue this even though everything temporal should fail.

A midrash or commentary on the book of Habakkuk was found among the Dead Sea Scrolls in Qumran Cave # 1. Apparently it was written by a Jewish sectarian of Palestine interpreting the first two chapters in the light of

The Habakkuk Commentary. Y. Yadin and the Shrine of the Book

the history of the Qumran sect. It does not offer much insight on the meaning of the prophecy.

The theory held currently by some OT scholars is that chap. 3 was not part of the original book. The fact that the Qumran commentary does not include this chapter does not prove this theory. Since chap. 3 is a psalm, it does not lend itself to such use as was made of the first two chapters in the midrash. The probability exists that the commentary never was finished. The LXX has all three chapters. There is no evidence that disallows for the prophet to have composed a psalm of praise and thanksgiving. The writings of the prophets frequently were in highly poetic form.

Bibliography. W. F. Albright, "The Psalm of Habakkuk," in *Studies in Old Testament Prophecy,* ed. by H. H. Rowley, Edinburgh: T. & T. Clark, 1950, pp. 1–18. Gleason L. Archer, SOTI, pp. 343–346. Millar Burrows, *The Dead Sea Scrolls,* New York: Viking Press, 1955. Frank E. Gaebelein, *Four Minor Prophets,* Chicago: Moody Press, 1970. David W. Kerr, "Habakkuk," WBC, pp. 871–881. D. Martin Lloyd-Jones, *From Fear to Faith,* London: Inter-Varsity, 1953. Samuel J. Schultz, *The Old Testament Speaks,* New York: Harper and Row, 1960, pp. 406 ff.

S. J. S.

HABAZINIAH (hăb'á-zĭ-nī'á). Grandfather of Jaaziniah and his brothers, Rechabites, who were tested by the prophet Jeremiah in the temple (Jer 35:3).

HABERGEON (hăb'ĕr-jĕn)

1. An obsolete term for coat of mail or breastplate (II Chr 26:14; Neh 4:16) to protect the neck and shoulders, but later reaching the thighs or knees. Goliath's coat of mail (I Sam 17:5) seems to have been a coat of leather covered with bronze scales, weighing *c.* 125 pounds. A fragment of such bronze scale armor from the 15th cen. B.C. was found at Nuzu (Yigael Yadin, *The Art of Warfare in Biblical Lands,* New York: McGraw-Hill, 1963, I, 196 f.). David found Saul's coat of mail too heavy for him (I Sam 17:38). *See* Armor.

2. The term used in Job 41:26 probably denotes a pointed shaft or javelin (cf. RSV).

3. Habergeon in Ex 28:32; 39:23 translates a word of uncertain meaning, some kind of garment (cf. RSV). It may be a loan word from the Egyptian, denoting a garment used in ritual services to deck the image-statue of a god on certain festivals.

HABITATION. The translation of 20 different words in the Bible, including the ideas of temporary dwelling (sojourn), permanent home (dwelling place), fixed abode or place, and resting place.

The temple is called God's habitation (*zebûl,* II Chr 6:2). The heavens also are His dwelling place (*shibtô,* from *yāshab,* Ps 33:13–14). Jus-

tice and judgment are likewise His habitation (*mākôn,* "fixed place," Ps 89:14). In the NT the Church is called the habitation of God (*katoikētērion,* "place of habitation," Eph 2:22).

Canaan was Israel's habitation (*môshāb,* I Chr 4:33, etc.). After the Exile God promised to return Israel to her habitation (*nāweh,* "resting place," Isa 32:18; 33:20; Jer 50:19). God has also determined the limits of men's habitation (*katoikia,* "dwelling place," Acts 17:26). The Christian disciple may look forward to being received into everlasting habitations (*skēnē,* "tent," Lk 16:9).

HABOR (hā'bôr). The modern Khabur River, the eastern of the two main tributaries of the upper Euphrates, entering it from the N near Tirqah. To the Gozan district near its headwaters captives from the ten tribes were deported by Tiglath-pileser III in 732 B.C. and by Sargon II in King Hoshea's ninth year, 722 B.C. (II Kgs 17:6 and 18:11, RSV; I Chr 5:26). *See* Gozan; Halah.

HACHALIAH (hăk'á-lī'á). The father of Nehemiah, governor of Judea after the Captivity (Neh 1:1; 10:1).

HACHILAH (há-kī'lá). A hill in the wilderness of Judah E of Ziph, SE of Hebron, facing the Jeshimon ("desolate") district where David took refuge when fleeing from Saul (I Sam 23:19; 26:1, 3). It is a wild area of cliffs and gorges W of En-gedi.

HACHMONI (hăk'mō-nī). Hachmoni, the "wise one," was the father or ancestor of Jashobeam (*q.v.*), the illustrious first of the mighty men of David (I Chr 11:11, lit., "Jashobeam son of *Hakmônî*"). In II Sam 23:8 this family name is spelled Tachmonite (KJV) or Tah-chemonite (RSV), perhaps a scribal error for "the Hachmonite." In I Chr 27:32 another son of Hachmoni is mentioned, Jehiel, who was with David's sons as their adviser. The actual father of Jashobeam may have been Zabdiel, or Zabdiel may have been the more distant ancestor (I Chr 27:2). Possibly this family belonged to the tribe of Levi, because Jashobeam is called a Korahite (I Chr 12:6, RSV).

HADAD (hā'dăd)

1. The eighth son of Ishmael (Gen 25:15, "Hadar" [*q.v.*] in Heb. and KJV; I Chr 1:30).

2. The fourth early king of Edom (in Avith) who defeated Midian (Gen 36:35 f.; I Chr 1:46 f.).

3. The eighth (and last) king of Edom (Gen 36:39; I Chr 1:50 f.), in Pau or Pai.

4. An Edomite prince whom God raised up to be an adversary against Solomon (I Kgs 11:14–25). As a child, he escaped to Egypt from Joab's slaughter in David's reign. He was sponsored by Pharaoh, giving him the queen's sister as wife and rearing his son. On David's death, he obtained release from Pharaoh and

returned to lead the Edomites in overthrowing Israel's dominance. By divine appointment, he was God's agent of punishment against Solomon by constituting a major threat and continual harassment.

5. Hadad was the name of an ancient Semitic storm-god among the Syrians and Assyrians. This name was adopted by kings, e.g., Ben-hadad (I Kgs 15:18; II Kgs 13) and Hadadezer (II Sam 10:16, 19, RSV). This deity was also called Hadadrimmon (Zech 12:11), following the identification by the Assyrians with Ramman, their god of wind and storm. *See* Gods, False.

HADADEZER (hăd′a-dē′zĕr). Son of Rehob, Hadadezer was king of Zobah (II Sam 8:3), a Syrian region lying to the N of Damascus. In David's time Hadadezer sought with various allies to conquer Israel, but without success. II Sam 8 describes two occasions when David subdued Hadadezer, the second campaign bringing much booty of gold and brass. Solomon used this brass to make the brazen sea, the pillars, and the vessels of brass for the temple (I Chr 18:8). II Sam 10 describes a third successful campaign of David against Hadadezer, who had become allied with the Ammonites and Syrians.

HADADRIMMON (hā′dăd-rĭm′ŏn). A combination of the names of two gods, the Aramean Hadad ("thunderer") and the Akkad. Rimmon, *Ramânu* ("thunderer"; cf. II Kgs 5:18), for whom public mourning was made in the plain of Esdraelon at Megiddo (Zech 12:11). In the Ras Shamra mythology, the Canaanite Baal, same as the Amorite storm-god Hadad, was pictured as a kilted striding warrior with mace and thunderbolt, and a helmet with bull's horns. He was also the vegetation god. Mourning for Hadadrimmon, the dead Baal, and Tammuz (Ezk 18:14) are common motifs in Mesopotamian mythology. *See* Gods, False.

Hadadrimmon formerly was thought to be a place name of a locality near Megiddo where King Josiah's death was lamented after he was mortally wounded at Megiddo; but he died in Jerusalem, where the mourning took place (II Chr 35:22–25).

HADAR (hā′där)

1. Alternate form of Hadad (*q.v.*), son of Ishmael (Gen 25:15). The letters *resh* (*r*) and *daleth* (*d*) are similar in Heb. and were frequently confused. He founded a tribe of the same name, attested in cuneiform records as the *Ḥudadu*.

2. Variant for Hadad, last of the ancient kings of Edom's elective monarchy, whose city was Pau (Gen 36:39).

HADAREZER (hăd′a-rē′zĕr). Alternate spelling of Hadadezer (*q.v.*), king of the Aramean state of Zobah, defeated by King David (II Sam 10:16, 19; I Chr 18:3, 5, 7–10; 19:16, 19; cf. spelling Hadadezer, II Sam 8:3–12).

HADASHAH (hă-dăsh′a). A village of Judah in the Shephelah or foothills district, possibly between Lachish and Gath (Josh 15:37).

HADASSAH (hă-dăs′a). The earlier name of Esther, who became queen and the wife of Ahasuerus or Xerxes I (Est 2:7). In Heb. the name means "myrtle." Possibly it could be a title given to her, derived from Akkad. *ḫaddaš-šatu*, "bride"; it was so used for Ishtar. *See* Esther.

HADATTAH (hă-dăt′a). Part of the name of the town Hazor-Hadattah in Judah (Josh 15:25, RSV), located in the Negeb, perhaps at el-Hudeira, S of Tuwāni, *c.* 20 miles E of Beer-sheba toward the Dead Sea.

HADES (hā′dēz). Hades is another name of Pluto the Gr. god of the underworld. The name was transferred to the realm of the dead itself. The Hades of the Greeks was in two parts. The deeper part, where souls were punished, was sometimes called Tartarus, and the place of blessed souls was called the Elysian Fields (Edith Hamilton, *Mythology,* p. 39). We must beware of importing these pagan Gr. ideas into the Christian vocabulary. Just as the Gr. word *theos,* "god," attained new meaning in Jewish-Christian thought, so Hades is not to be defined from pagan Gr. usage but from the NT.

The word *hadēs* is used some ten times in the NT. These are:

1. Mt 11:23 and Lk 10:15 (ASV, RSV). Here, as remarked in ExpB, heaven and *hadēs* are proverbial expressions for the highest exaltation and the deepest degradation.

2. Mt 16:18. The expression "gates of hell" is wholly figurative (cf. Job 38:17; Isa 38:10). Possibly the figure is of a walled city with gates and bars. The verse could possibly refer to an assault from Satan's kingdom—which will fail.

3. Lk 16:23 (ASV, RSV). This is a clear reference. *Hadēs* is used of the place of torment as distinguished from the place of bliss. Some have called this a parable, although there is no indication of that. But in any case the word is used to designate a place of punishment.

4. Acts 2:27, 31 (ASV, RSV). This passage is complicated by the fact that it is an OT quotation and its exact meaning unsure. A common view is that this refers to Christ's descent into the realm of the dead to preach to sinners or to deliver righteous ones from the upper compartment of Hades into heaven. One problem with this explanation is that Christ had already spoken of Hades as a place of torment. And elsewhere He says that at His death He was not going to such a place, but to paradise (Lk 23:43) and to be with God (Jn 16:28).

An alternative view would interpret the pas-

Dagger of Mes-kalam-dug (*c.* 2500 B.C.) with hilt of lapis lazuli and sheath of gold filigree, 14½ inches long. BM

sage by its OT original, Ps 16:10. There, the statement "thou wilt not leave my soul in hell" surely does not refer to the spiritual nature going to the netherworld. The word *nepesh* often means just the "individual." It seldom means the "spirit nature." The parallel is "neither wilt thou suffer thine holy one to see corruption." It is logical to take the first part as a synonymous parallel meaning "Thou wilt not abandon me to the grave." (See treatment in C. F. H. Henry, ed., *The Biblical Expositor,* II, 59 f.). In this case *hadēs* in this OT quotation would be used in the meaning of its Heb. original *she'ōl,* which many times means simply "grave" (*q.v.*).

5. Rev 1:18; 6:8; 20:13-14 (ASV, RSV). These verses also are figurative. In the first (Rev 1:18) Christ holds the keys of *hadēs* and death. This expression reminds one of "gates of *hadēs*" in Mt 16:18 (ASV). Hades is pictured as a walled city, in this case a prison possibly. In the next passage (Rev 6:8) *hadēs* is also linked with death and they are personified as enemies of God and men. In Rev. 20:13-14 death and *hadēs* are linked again and they deliver up the wicked dead who are in them for final judgment. This usage is reminiscent of the passage in Lk 16:23 and strengthens the idea that in the NT Hades signifies the abode of the wicked dead.

See Dead, The; Gehenna; Hell; Sheol.

R. L. H.

HADID (hā'dĭd). A town of Benjamin at the NW edge of the Shephelah, near the mouth of the Ajalon Valley, probably modern el-Ḥadītheh, about three miles ENE of Lod or Lydda (Ezr 2:33; Neh 7:37; 11:34). An earlier town of this name is included in the Karnak list of Thutmose III.

HADLAI (hăd'lī). Father of Amasa, who was one of the chiefs of the tribe of Ephraim in the reign of Pekah (II Chr 28:12).

HADORAM (ha-dôr'am)
1. The fifth son of Joktan (Gen 10:27; I Chr 1:21), a Shemite sixth from Noah.
2. Son of Tou (Toi), king of Hamath, who was sent with congratulatory gifts for David on

his defeat of Hadarezer (I Chr 18:10; called Joram in II Sam 8:10).
3. A taskmaster to Solomon (I Kgs 4:6, called Adoniram, *q.v.*) and Rehoboam, who was stoned to death when he delivered Rehoboam's message to the ten tribes (II Chr 10:18; called Adoram in I Kgs 12:18).

HAFT. The handle of a knife or dagger, occurring only in Jud 3:22, in the account of Ehud's stabbing of Eglon, king of Moab. Translated "hilt" in RSV.

HAGAB (hā'găb). Head of a family of Nethinim who returned with Zerubbabel to Jerusalem (Ezr 2:46). The name is omitted in Nehemiah's list (Neh 7:48). A man of this name was mentioned in Jeremiah's time on Ostracon I of the Lachish letters.

HAGABA, HAGABAH (hăg'a-ba). Founder of a family of Nethinim or temple servants that returned from Exile with Zerubbabel (Neh 7:48; Ezr 2:45). Evidently different from that of Hagab in Ezr 2:46).

Hagar in the Wilderness by Corot. MM

HAGAR (hā'gär). An Egyptian woman who belonged to Sarai, the wife of Abram. Sarai was prevented from bearing children, so she gave Hagar to Abram as a wife, hoping that she might have a child through her (Gen 16). The Nuzu tablets reveal that this practice was common, and some of the marriage contracts specify that a barren wife must provide a woman for her husband for the purpose of procreation. After Hagar conceived she looked on Sarai with contempt. Sarai, with Abram's assent, treated Hagar harshly. Hagar fled into the wilderness and was found beside a spring of water by the angel of the Lord, who instructed her to return. She was promised that her son would have innumerable descendants. After her return Ishmael was born.

Later God granted to Sarah (whose name God changed from Sarai to Sarah, and also

Abram to Abraham) a child of her own—Isaac. After the weaning of Isaac, Sarah demanded of Abraham that he send Ishmael away. According to the Nuzu tablets, such action was prohibited, and this may be the reason Abraham was so reluctant to expel Ishmael until God Himself gave him permission to do so. Hagar and Ishmael were sent away with only bread and a skin of water. The angel appeared to her again in the wilderness when she had given up hope of survival, and again promised a bright future for her son. Hagar took a wife for Ishmael from the land of Egypt.

The apostle Paul used the story of Hagar (spelled Agar in the NT) as an allegory (Gal 4:21-31). There she symbolizes the old covenant of flesh given on Mount Sinai. In contrast, Sarah the freewoman represents the new covenant of faith instituted by Christ.

R. E. H.

HAGARENES. See Hagarites.

HAGARITES (hăg′ȧ-rīts). Variant form of Hagarenes, Hagerites, and Hagrites (RSV).

A tribe, or confederation of tribes, dwelling in the Syrian and N Arabian desert. They were of Bedouin stock, whether Arabian or Aramean is uncertain, and their wealth consisted in livestock (I Chr 5:20-21). During the reign of Saul, the Reubenites waged war against them (I Chr 5:10). I Chr 5:18-22 indicates that the Reubenites formed a coalition with the Gadites and the half tribe of Manasseh against the Hagarites, Nodab, Jetur, and Nephish. The last two are Arab tribes and are named in Gen 25:15 as sons of Ishmael. The Ituraeans of Roman times took their name from Jetur. From the close association of the Hagarites with these Arab tribes and the similarity to the name Hagar, this people has often been assumed to be descended from Ishmael's mother (see also Ps 83:6). However, the region assigned to her descendants was near Beer-sheba. Also, both Tiglath-pileser III and Sennacherib list the *Hagaranu* (Hagarenes) with other tribes as Arameans. The Gr. geographers Strabo and Ptolemy mention the *Agraioi* as living in N Arabia. An individual Hagerite, Jaziz, was a steward of King David "over the flocks" (I Chr 27:31).

R. E. H.

HAGERITES. See Hagarites.

HAGGAI (hăg′ā-ī). A post-Exilic prophet who was active in Judah during the building of the second temple, 520-515 B.C. References to Haggai outside the book bearing his name are Ezr 5:1 and 6:14. His name means "festal," derived from Heb. *ḥag,* "festival." Possibly he was so named by godly parents because he was born on some major Jewish feast day. Very likely he was born in Babylonia and came to Jerusalem after Cyrus, the king of Persia, issued a decree in 538 B.C. allowing Jews to return to their homeland (II Chr 36:22-23; Ezr 1:1-4).

In his prophetic ministry Haggai was supported by the prophet Zechariah. The four messages recorded in his book are dated within three or four months in the year 520 B.C., the second year of Darius I (Hystaspes), king of Persia (521-485 B.C.). See Darius Hystaspes.

HAGGAI, BOOK OF. With enthusiasm the exiles, who returned after the decree of Cyrus in 538 B.C., began to rebuild the temple (536 B.C.). See Haggai; Zechariah. The opposition by the Samaritans was effective to the point of stopping the building efforts during the reigns of Cyrus and Cambyses until the second year of Darius in 520 B.C. (Ezr 4:4-5, 20). Marauding Persians under Cambyses en route to Egypt during this period (c. 525 B.C.) may have overrun Palestine to such an extent that any hope for a permanent effort to rebuild the temple was halted.

This book in the OT is unusual in being uncontested by practically all critics. There is no evidence for the conjecture that the present book is a fragment of longer writings by the prophet or a compilation of his oracles and narrative writings. Oesterly and Robinson, without recognizing the usual practice of the writing prophets, have conjectured that this collection comes from the hand of a contemporary of Haggai who wrote down the salient points of the prophet's sermons, because the third person is used for the prophet.

The book of Haggai may represent merely outlines of his messages, written under inspiration of the Holy Spirit. The Lord had spoken through him to stir up the people to a successful effort to rebuild the temple (Hag 1:12-15; Ezr 5:1-2; 6:13-15).

The conditions during this period are vividly reflected in his approach to the people. Although they were deeply engaged in private housing projects, Haggai reminded them that the Lord of hosts was the controller of the material blessings which they were lacking through drought and crop failure (1:2-11). Assuring the builders that God through His Spirit was working in their midst so that the latter glory of this temple would be greater than the former glory of the temple in Solomon's time (2:7-9, RSV), Haggai encouraged the leaders as well as the laity. To God and Haggai there was only *one* temple, not three or four (Solomon's, Zerubbabel's, Herod's, millennial); therefore this prophecy was not necessarily fulfilled before A.D. 70.

Better crops were promised (2:15-19). Zerubbabel as a representative of the Davidic throne is designated as a signet (2:23) or seal guaranteeing to God's people the fulfillment of the Davidic covenant (II Sam 7:12-16) and providing the basis for the hope that God, who shakes the heavens and the earth, will destroy the strength of the heathen nations. Consequently God's work through His chosen nation will ultimately be established (2:20–23).

The messages of Haggai may be outlined as follows:

I. Haggai Promotes Involvement, 1:1–15
II. Potential of Greater Glory in the New Temple, 2:1–9
III. Material Blessings Assured, 2:10–19
IV. God's Promise, 2:20–23

Bibliography. Charles L. Feinberg, "Haggai," WBC, pp. 889–896, with bibliography. Hobart E. Freeman, *An Introduction to the Old Testament Prophets,* Chicago: Moody Press, 1968, pp. 326–332. Frank E. Gaebelein, *Four Minor Prophets,* Chicago: Moody Press, 1970. A. Gelston, "The Foundations of the Second Temple," VT, XVI (April, 1966), 232–235, on Hag 2:18.

S. J. S.

HAGGERI (hăg'ĕ-rī). The father or ancestor of Mibhar, one of David's heroes (I Chr 11:38).

HAGGI (hăg'ī), **HAGGITES** (hăg'īts). The second son of Gad, founder of the clan called Haggites (Gen 46:16; Num 26:15). The name occurs in a Phoenician text and has been found in a number of ancient Heb. inscriptions.

HAGGIAH (hă-gī'à). A descendant of Merari, the son of Levi (I Chr 6:30).

HAGGITH (hăg'ĭth). A wife of King David and mother of his fourth son Adonijah, who later claimed the throne (II Sam 3:4; I Kgs 1:5, 11; 2:13; I Chr 3:2).

HAGIOGRAPHA (hăg'ĭ-ŏg'rà-fà; "holy writings"). Adopted from the Gr., this is an alternate name for the last of the traditional three divisions (see Lk 24:44) of the Heb. Scriptures (*Ketûbîm,* the Writings), comprising the books not included under the Law and the Prophets. This division was so manifestly arbitrary that it was never accepted as a proper one by the Church Fathers.

The miscellaneous collection of 11 books (in Heb.) includes the following: (1) three large books of poetry: Psalms, Proverbs, Job; (2) the five scrolls or *Megilloth,* which came to be read in synagogues at five sacred occasions: Song of Solomon at Passover, Ruth at Feast of Weeks (Pentecost), Lamentations at the ninth of Ab (the anniversary of the destruction of the temple), Ecclesiastes at Feast of Tabernacles, and Esther at Feast of Purim; (3) three late narrative books: Daniel, Ezra-Nehemiah, and Chronicles. The order in our English Bibles, following the LXX and Vulgate, differs considerably from the Heb. *See* Canon of Scripture, the OT.

A. T. P.

HAI (hā'ī). Same as Ai *(q.v.),* in the vicinity of Bethel, where Abraham pitched his tent (Gen 12:8; 13:3). Here the KJV expressed the definite article *(hā)* with which Ai is always accompanied in the Heb. text (one exception, Jer 49:3).

HAIL, HAILSTONES. Hailstorms occur in hot as well as cold climates, frequently accompanying violent thunderstorms. Raindrops within the cumulonimbus cloud are carried to great altitudes where the temperature drops below 0°F; turning to ice pellets, they grow in size as they are blown up and down. Hailstones exceeding a pound in weight have been picked up after a storm. In October, 1937, roof tiles were broken by hail near Tel Aviv in Palestine.

Hailstorms affect the area along a narrow line, so that one place might suffer from the storm while an adjoining one might escape (Ex 9:26; Josh 10:11). Driving rain (Isa 28:17), storm winds (Ezk 13:11), and snow (Job 38:22) often accompanied hailstorms. An unparalleled fall of hail, the seventh judgment on Egypt, destroyed crops and trees and injured animals and men (Ex 9:18–34), becoming a prototype for the end-time judgments in the books of Ezekiel (38:22) and Revelation (8:7; 11:19; 16:21). The hailstorm over Beth-horon (Josh 10:10–11) was miraculous both in its intensity and probably in its being unseasonal, since Joshua's campaign against the Amorites seems to have been waged in the dry summer season, within a few months after Passover (Josh 5:10).

A. T. P. and J. R.

HAIR. Hair is frequently mentioned in Scripture, especially with reference to the head. The manner and customs of wearing the hair varied considerably among the nations.

Egyptians. The Egyptian men shaved their hair, except in time of mourning. Even the heads of children were shaved, leaving a few locks as a sign of youth. Slaves, when brought from other countries to serve in the court, had their heads and beards shaved. This was why Joseph, before going in to Pharaoh, shaved himself (Gen 41:14). However, the women wore their natural hair long and plaited, often reaching down in the form of strings to the bottom of the shoulder blades. Wigs sometimes were worn for disguise. The pharaoh wore a false beard as a symbol of deity.

Assyrians. The Assyrian men had the opposite custom in allowing the hair of both head and beard to grow full length. They sometimes curled the beard and added false hair to provide a headdress.

Greeks and Romans. The Greeks admired long hair on both men and women. They believed that the hair was the cheapest of ornaments. Customs varied, however, and they first wore it long, then in a knot, and at a later period short. Romans at first wore the hair long, but the men began to wear it short about three centuries B.C. Shaving was also customary, and a long beard was a mark of slovenliness. Plaiting or braiding women's hair was so elaborately done that Peter and Paul counseled against it (I Pet 3:3; I Tim 2:9).

Hebrews. The Hebrews considered the hair an important part of personal beauty for both young and old (Song 5:11; Prov 16:31). The sexes were distinguished by the long hair of the women (Lk 7:38; Jn 11:2; 12:3; I Cor 11:6) and the frequent clipping to a moderate length by the men. The ordinance for the priests, and thereby probably followed by the rest of the community, was that the hair was to be polled, i.e., neither shaved nor allowed to grow too long (Lev 21:5; Ezk 44:20). Absalom's luxuriant hair was greatly admired (II Sam 14:26). The Nazarites *(q.v.),* for the term of their vow, wore long hair (Num 6:5). The Hebrews dreaded baldness as it was frequently the result of leprosy (Lev 13:40), and hence formed one of the disqualifications for the priesthood (Lev 21:5). Calling Elisha "bald" was therefore meant as an insult (II Kgs 2:23). In times of affliction, the hair was completely cut off (Isa 3:17, 24; Jer 7:29; 48:37; Amos 8:10). Job was bald in the day of his affliction (Job 1:20), probably as a symbol of desolation (cf. Isa 3:24; 15:2; Jer 7:29).

The usual and favorite color of the hair was black (Song 5:11). Josephus indicates that gold dust was occasionally sprinkled on the hair, but

dyeing was not practiced. Pure white hair represented the divine majesty (Dan 7:9; Rev 1:14). Gray hair was considered beautiful on old men (Prov 20:29), in keeping with their age (Job 15:10; I Sam 12:2; Ps 71:18). Curls, whether natural or artificial, were considered beautiful. Jezebel attired or adorned her head (II Kgs 9:30), and Samson's hair was arranged into seven braids (Jud 16:13, 19). Sometimes ornaments were placed in the hair with combs and hairpins as mentioned in the Talmud. The hair was also profusely anointed with fragrant ointments (Ruth 3:3; II Sam 14:2; Ps 23:5; 45:7; Isa 3:24), especially for festive occasions (Mt 6:17; 26:7; Lk 7:46). Barbers *(q.v.)* have existed from ancient times (Ezk 5:1).

The beard was regarded in much the same manner as the head. With the exception of the Egyptians, most Asiatics cherished the beard as the mark of manhood. The Hebrews did not shave the beard, but trimmed it (II Sam 19:24). It was the object of an oath (Mt 5:36), shaved or plucked in mourning (Isa 50:6; Jer 41:5; Ezr 9:3), neglected during affliction (II Sam 19:24), and the object of salutation (II Sam 20:9). The shaving of the beard as well as all the hair was part of the ceremonial cleansing of a leper (Lev 14:9). The Mosaic law forbade one to "round the corners of your heads, neither shalt thou mar the corners of thy beard" (Lev 19:27; 21:5). This probably means that the hair was not to be cut from one temple to the other in a circle, as among the Arabs (cf. Jer 9:26, RSV). Also, the place where the hair and beard met was not to be shaved. Other nations may have had such customs in their idolatrous worship and as a rite of mourning or offering in behalf of the dead (Deut 14:1; Jer 16:6), and thus God prevented Israel from such by these regulations.

Figurative. The hair represented an innumerable group (Ps 40:12; 69:4), and what was of least value of a man (I Sam 14:45; II Sam 14:11; I Kgs 1:52; Mt 10:30; Lk 12:7; 21:18; Acts 27:34). White hair or the hoary head was the symbol of respect due to age (Lev 19:32; Prov 16:31). Thus God, the Ancient of Days, appears as such (Dan 7:9; cf. Rev 1:14). On the other hand, the shaving of the head signified affliction, poverty, and disgrace. "Cutting off the hair" was a figure used to denote the entire destruction of a people by God (Isa 7:20). Gray hairs here and there represent the decline of the kingdom of Israel (Hos 7:9).

The capacity of hair for continual growth made it an evidence or symbol of life; thus, letting the hair grow long was symbolic of the dedication of one's life to the Lord (Num 6:1–21; Jud 13:5; etc.). Such a vow brought God's blessing and strength, as in the case of Samson. Cutting the hair signified that the period of the vow, if temporary, was at an end (Num 6:18; Acts 18:18; 21:23 f.). Warriors anticipating battle often let their hair grow and hang loose, perhaps as a sign of dedication to their deity in a holy war (Deut 32:42, RSV; see

Pharaoh Tutankhamon of Egypt with a false beard. LL

An Assyrian god with curled hair and beard.
LM

comment on Jud 5:2 in *Wycliffe Bible Commentary*).

E. C. J.

HAKKATAN (hăk'á-tăn). The father of Johanan, chief of the family of Azgad, who returned from the Babylonian Exile with Ezra (Ezr 8:12). The name is Katan, "little," with the definite article prefixed. The name occurs in Akkad. as *Qitinu* and *Kuttunu*.

HAKKOZ. *See* Koz.

HAKUPHA (há-kū'fá). The sons of Hakupha were among the post-Exilic temple servants of lower rank who returned from Babylon with Zerubbabel (Ezr 2:51; Neh 7:53).

HALAH (hā 'lá). City or district, unidentified, in Mesopotamia, perhaps near Gozan in the basin of the Habor River to which a portion of the northern tribes of Israel were deported by the Assyrian kings in 732 and 722 B.C. (II Kgs, 17:6; 18:11; I Chr 5:26). Since a city gate of Nineveh facing NE was called "Gate of the land *Halaḫḫu*," Halah may have been considerably E of the other locations to which Israelite captives were taken. *See* Habor.

HALAK (hā'lăk). A mountain, named as the southern limit of Joshua's conquests and rising toward Seir (Josh 11:17; 12:7), probably Jebel Halâq in the Negeb *c.* 30 miles SW of the Dead Sea, halfway to Kadesh-barnea. Apparently Mount Halak faced Avdat and the mountainous terrain of Seir which lay S of Wadi Zin (Wadi Fuqrah), for prior to the 13th cen. B.C. expansion of the Edomites, their territory of Seir lay W of the Arabah, on the way from Horeb to Kadesh-barnea (Deut 1:2).

HALHUL (hăl'hŭl). A village in the hill country of Judah beside Beth-zur and Gedor (Josh 15:58), about three miles N of Hebron.

HALI (hā'lĭ). A village on the boundary of Asher, named between Helkath and Beten (Josh 19:25). Its site is unknown.

HALL. *See* Court; Praetorium.

HALL OF JUDGMENT. *See* Praetorium; Gabbatha.

HALLEL (hăl'lĕl). This term, not found in the English Bible, comes from a Heb. verb meaning "to praise" (e.g., Ezr 3:11; II Chr 7:6). It later became a Jewish liturgical term referring to certain psalms. The "Egyptian" Hallel (Ps 113–118) was sung in the homes at the Passover (Mt 26:30), in the temple, and in the synagogues at the great annual festivals and at the day of the new moon. The "Great" Hallel (Ps 120–136, or 135–136, or just 136) praises God for rain (135:1, 7) and food (136:25). *See also* Alleluia.

HALLELUJAH (hăl'ĕ-lōō'yá). *See* Alleluia.

HALLOHESH, HALOHESH (hă-lō'hĕsh). Father of the Shallum who ruled over part of Jerusalem and helped Nehemiah rebuild the wall (Neh 3:12). He also set his seal to a covenant with Ezra and Nehemiah to worship the Lord (Neh 10:24).

HALLOW, HALLOWED. Both words (also "holy") mean basically "to be clean," ceremonially and morally, and hence "sacred." The words are used of persons and things set apart for God. The sabbath was hallowed (Ex 20:11), as well as the priests (Ex 29:1), the tabernacle and its equipment (Ex 40:9), and Solomon's temple (I Kgs 9:3). God was hallowed, and He hallowed the people (Lev 22:32) and the firstborn (Num 3:13).

See Holiness; Sanctification.

HAM (hăm)

1. A city of the Zuzim, smitten by Chedorlaomer and his allies in the time of Abraham (Gen 14:5).

2. One of the three sons of Noah (Gen 5:32; 10:6–14). His descendants, who spread also to Mesopotamia, included the civilizations of Babylon, Erech (modern Warka), Akkad, Calneh, and Assyria (Gen 10:8–12). Cush was Ham's firstborn, the ancient Cassites, followed by Mizraim, Phut, and Canaan (Gen 10:6). Cush was the father of the peoples of Arabia (Gen 10:7). Mizraim produced the inhabitants of Egypt and adjoining countries, including the Philistines (Gen 10:13–14). Canaan was the father of the peoples spread from Sihon to Gaza and to Sodom and Gomorrah.

The history of the Canaanites is foreshadowed in the dishonoring of Noah by Ham when his father lay in a drunken stupor (Gen 9:20–23). The story of Gen 9:20–25 and the genealogy of Gen 10:6, 15–20 are included to show the origin of the Canaanites and the source of their licentious practices in the days of Joshua. Since Ham was not included in the blessing of Shem and Japheth, some have argued that the curse included Ham. It was applied, however, particularly to Canaan. Historically the curse was fulfilled in the destruction of the Canaanites and their descendants the Phoenicians (*see* Phoenicia). The curse pertained in a secondary way to the religious aspect of the Hamites of the OT period in that the religions of Egypt, Canaan, and Assyria were filled with a gross, sensual polytheism. The genealogy of Gen 10 demonstrates the truth that ancestry influences morality.

H. G. S.

"HAM, THEY OF." Descendants of Ham, the youngest son of Noah, either Egyptians, Ethiopians, or more probably Canaanites (cf. Gen 10:6), who had settled in the rich pastureland of southern Palestine. Their territory was seized by the descendants of Simeon, Jacob's second son (I Chr 4:40).

HAMAN (hā'măn). The "son of Hammedatha the Agagite." *See* Agagite. Haman was an influential official in the court of King Ahasuerus (Est 3:1). One of the least admirable characters of the OT, this prince was the embodiment of ignoble delusions of grandeur. After his promotion his vanity was gratified by the adulation of his associates, with the exception of Mordecai who, as a Jewish monotheist, did not venerate him (Est 3:2). In his childish fury Haman determined to destroy not only Mordecai but all Jews. His plans were thwarted by the heroism of Queen Esther, and, with poetic justice, his life ended on the gallows he had prepared for Mordecai (Est 7).

HAMATH (hā'măth). KJV uses Hemath in I Chr 13:5; Amos 6:14.

A city and a state (Isa 11:11; Jer 39:5; Zech 9:2) in Syria, located just N of the ideal boundary of Israel (Num 13:21; 34:8; Josh 13:5; *see* Lebo-hamath). The present site of the city, Hama on the Nahr el-Asi (the ancient Orontes), was excavated by H. Ingholt (1932–38), who discovered 12 levels of occupation. The city was founded in Neolithic times. Level H corresponds to the age of Hammurabi of Babylon, but Hamath was uninhabited during the Hyksos period (1750–1500 B.C.). Thutmose III of Egypt captured the city (ANET, p. 242); during the Amarna period it was the capital of an Amorite kingdom. Later it flourished as a local Hittite city-state, and eventually became Aramean under an influx of immigrants or by conquest.

Located as it was on the important trade route halfway between Aleppo and Damascus, with the more powerful states of Israel and Aram as its neighbors, Hamath had to defend its independence by alliances of one sort or another. Its king Toi sought the friendship of David after the latter's victories over the Arameans (II Sam 8:9 f.). Solomon built storecities in the land of Hamath (II Chr 8:4).

In 853 B.C. it was the third state in the coalition that faced Shalmaneser III of Assyria in the battle of Qarqar (ANET, p. 279). An inscription of its king Zakir, c. 800 B.C., records a successful war against a group of kings headed by Ben-hadad of Damascus (ANET, pp. 501 f.). It is possible that this Zakir was the unnamed "savior" who helped Israel against the Arameans in the time of Jehoahaz (II Kgs 13:5). Jeroboam II recaptured land from Damascus and Hamath that had once belonged to David (II Kgs 14:28).

The prophet Amos, who was active about 760 B.C., describes Hamath as being in ruins in his time (Amos 6:2), possibly as a result of the Aramean attack. Subsequently Hamath was conquered by Sargon II of Assyria c. 721 B.C. (as alluded to in Isa 10:9), and its inhabitants transported to other countries. Some of them were sent to repeople the cities of Samaria, where for a time they worshiped their god Ashima (II Kgs 17:24, 30).

S. C.

HAMATH, ENTRANCE OF; ENTERING IN OF. *See* Lebo-hamath.

HAMATH-ZOBAH (hā'măth-zō'ba). Perhaps Hamath of Zobah. It is mentioned only in II Chr 8:3 in connection with the conquests of Solomon, who is said to have conquered it. But the reference is uncertain. The site has not been identified. Some believe that Hamath-zobah refers to the neighbor kingdoms of Hamath and Zobah, or that it is identical with Hamath (*q.v.;* Num 34:8), and that Zobah is used here in a broader sense. It is perhaps better to accept it as another Hamath located in the territory of Zobah.

HAMMATH (hăm'ăth)
1. The ancestral head of the Rechabite clan (I Chr 2:55, RSV; KJV has Hemath, *q.v.*).
2. A fortified town in the territory of Naphtali (Josh 19:35). It was probably located at Hammam Tabariyeh, a village with hot springs just S of Tiberias on the W shore of Galilee. Nearly all agree that Hammoth-dor (*q.v.*; Josh 21:32) and the Hammon (*q.v.*) of I Chr 6:76 are identical with Hammath.

HAMMEDATHA (hăm'ĕ-dā'tha). The father of Haman, the Jews' enemy in the book of Esther (Est 3:1, 10; 8:5; 9:10, 24). His name is typically Persian, possibly from *mâh*, "moon," and *data*, "given," "given by the moon."

HAMMELECH (hăm'ĕ-lĕk). A proper name in the KJV, but the word is better rendered as the ordinary Heb. word for "the king." Jerahmeel and Malchiah are each designated as "the son of the king" (Jer 36:26; 38:6, RSV), making them royal princes.

HAMMER. Several Heb. words have been translated "hammer" in the KJV. In OT times the head of a hammer was usually of a hard stone, less often of bronze or iron. Since it was used as a cutting tool, metal tended to be too soft.
1. Heb. *paṭṭîsh* was the hammer of the smith used for smoothing metals (Isa 41:7), and the large hammer used in quarrying (Jer 23:29; 50:23).
2. Heb. *maqqebet* was the smaller hammer of the stonecutter (I Kgs 6:7). It was also used by artisans in the manufacture of idols (Isa 44:12; Jer 10:4), and served as a mallet to drive Jael's tent pin (Jud 4:21). The name Maccabee, "the hammerer," is traditionally derived from this word.
3. In the poetic version, Jael's feat was performed with a *halmût,* a hammer or mallet (Jud 5:26).
4. In Ps 74:6, Heb. *kêlappôt,* a loan word from Akkad. *kalapâti,* would refer to crowbars rather than hammers.

A. T. P.

HAMMOLEKETH (hă-mŏl'ĕ-kĕth). Daughter of Machir and sister of Gilead, the grandson of Manasseh. Gideon the judge was descended from her (I Chr 7:17–18).

HAMMON (hăm'ŏn)
1. A border village of Asher (Josh 19:28), possibly Umm el-'Awamîd, ten miles S of Tyre, where two Phoenician inscriptions mentioning the worship of the god Baal Hammon have been found.
2. A Levitical town in Naphtali (I Chr 6:76), probably the same as Hammath (*q.v.*).

HAMMOTH-DOR (hăm'ŏth-dôr'). A city of Naphtali, allotted to the Gershonites and appointed a city of refuge (Josh 21:32). Called

Hammon in I Chr 6:76, possibly modern Hammam Tabariyeh, the hot springs just S of Tiberias on the W shore of the Sea of Galilee, but seemingly not of sufficient antiquity. Probably the same as Hammath (*q.v.*).

Presumed head of Hammurabi. LM

HAMMURABI (hăm'ŭ-rä'bĭ). A common Amorite name in the early 2nd mil. B.C. At least two kings of Yamhad (Aleppo) and a ruler of Qurda were so named. But its most famous holder was the sixth ruler of the First Dynasty of Babylon who reigned *c.* 1792–1750 B.C. (according to Sidney Smith) or 1728–1686 B.C. (according to W. F. Albright).

Amraphel, king of Shinar, whose allies attacked Sodom (Gen 14:1 f.), formerly thought to be a Heb. rendering of the name Hammurabi, is rather to be compared with such forms as the Amorite Amud-pi-el ("enduring is the word of El") found at Mari *c.* 1750 B.C.

Hammurabi of Babylon, as all rulers of city-states in the ancient Near East, recorded the legal cases he judged. Toward the end of his reign he rendered to his deity Shamash an account of his wisdom shown in the law and order, justice and truth which he had made prevail in the land. Selected cases and new laws were inscribed on stone stelae and erected in the principal temples of Babylonia. One of these, an eight foot tall black diorite pillar taken as loot to Susa, was recovered by French archaeologists in December, 1901, and is now in the Louvre in Paris. It is likely that similar written records of legal decisions were kept by the kings of Israel and Judah (JSS, VII [1962], 161–172).

From the prologue to the laws of Hammurabi as well as from the references in numerous contemporary texts of his reign (*see* Mari), the main events of his day can be retraced. At first the king worked to establish the internal economy; then the power of Babylon was gradually extended over the southern cities of Uruk (Erech) and Isin in a series of military campaigns. The capture of cities in the Diyala region and lower Euphrates brought him into direct contact with the powerful kings of Assyria, Mari and Aleppo. One Mari letter tells how at this time Hammurabi had 10 to 15 vassal rulers under him, about half the number claimed by

Code of Hammurabi. LM

the king of Aleppo. By his thirty-eighth year Hammurabi had beaten his rival Rim-Sin of Larsa, defeated the hill tribes of the Gutians and Eshnunna, and had captured Mari on the middle Euphrates from Zimri-Lim. He had thus won an empire of an area not to be exceeded by a Babylonian king until the time of Nebuchadrezzar II (605–562 B.C.).

Hammurabi's laws (ANET, pp. 163–180), which in a large measure continued the legal tradition of his predecessors Urukagina of Lagash, Lipit-Ishtar of Isin and Bilalama of Eshnunna, were a testimony to his administrative ability. These 282 judgments and stipulations covered a wide range of subjects: marriage, divorce, adoption, apprenticeship, theft, assault, farming, trade, property and wages. The penalties imposed varied according to the status of the offender or injured party whether freeman, palace dependent or slave. Capital punishment, physical penalties *(lex talionis),* property confiscation and money fines were imposed. Women had specific rights. All this shows a definite legal tradition which, at numerous points of form and detail, offers close parallels to the OT legal sections; e.g., the law of the goring ox (Ex 21:28 ff.) or of incest (Lev 20:14). The laws of Hammurabi thus afford an extrabiblical insight into legal traditions common throughout much of the ancient Near East.

Bibliography. G. R. Driver and John C. Miles, *The Babylonian Laws,* 2 vols., Oxford: Clarendon Press, 1952, 1955.

D. J. W.

HAMONAH (hȧ-mō'nȧ; "multitude"). Symbolical name of the place near which the multitudes of Gog are to be buried after the great slaughter (Ezk 39:16).

HAMON-GOG (hā'mŏn-gŏg̕). A glen previously known as the "valley of the passers-by" opposite the sea (Dead Sea?), where the hosts which Gog brings with him will be slain and buried (Ezk 39:11, 15). *See* Gog.

HAMOR (hā'môr). The ruler of Shechem at the time of Jacob's return from Padan-aram. Shechem, Hamor's son, humiliated Dinah, Jacob's daughter; and her brothers, Simeon and Levi, avenged her wrong by killing all the men of Shechem (Gen 34:1–31).

Jacob bought a parcel of land from Hamor on which to pitch his tent (Gen 33:19). Later, Joseph was buried on this parcel of ground (Josh 24:32). As late as the judges, Hamor's name was still attached to Shechem (Jud 9:28). *See* Shechem.

The name Hamor means "ass," a fact that has led some scholars to consider the term as the name of a "totem clan." However, this theory is not necessarily true. Animal personal names were common in the ancient world; for example, Caleb means "dog," and Rachel means "ewe." It is possible that Hamor was an

Amorite or a Hittite, and practiced sacrificing an ass as a part of covenant making. (Cf. Mendenhall, BASOR #133 [1954], p. 26, n. 3.)

HAMUEL (hăm'ū-ĕl). A son of Mishma, a Simeonite, of the family of Shaul (I Chr 4:26).

HAMUL (hā'mŭl), **HAMULITES** (hā'mŭ-līts). The younger son of Pharez, sòn of Judah by Tamar. Hamul was founder of a tribal family (Gen 46:12; Num 26:21; I Chr 2:4–5).

HAMUTAL (ha-mū'tăl). A daughter of Jeremiah of Libnah, one of King Josiah's wives, and mother of King Jehoahaz and King Zedekiah (II Kgs 23:31; 24:18; Jer 52:1).

HANAMEEL (hăn'a-mēl). Son of Shallum and cousin of Jeremiah the prophet, who purchased an ancestral field from him at Anathoth during the siege of Jerusalem (Jer 32:7–9, 12).

HANAN (hā'nàn)
1. The son or descendant of Shashak, one of the chief men of Benjamin (I Chr 8:23).
2. One of the six sons of Azel of Benjamin (I Chr 8:38; 9:44).
3. The son of Maachah. He was one of David's mighty men (I Chr 11:43).
4. The sons or descendants of Hanan were among the Nethinim (KJV) or temple servants (RSV) who returned with Zerubbabel (Ezr 2:46; Neh 7:49).
5. A Levite active in the days of Ezra and Nehemiah. He was one of those who helped the people understand the law as it was read by Ezra (Neh 8:7). He is probably the same Levite who signed the great covenant of Nehemiah and was appointed assistant to the treasurers of the storehouses who distributed the temple revenue among the priests and Levites (Neh 10:10; 13:13).
6. One of the chiefs of the people who signed the covenant of Nehemiah (Neh 10:22).
7. Another chief who signed the covenant (Neh 10:26).
8. The son of Igdaliah; he was an officer of the temple. Jeremiah brought the Rechabites into the chamber of Hanan's sons to test their faithfulness (Jer 35:4).

P. C. J.

HANANEEL, TOWER OF (hăn'a-nēl). A tower in the N wall of Jerusalem between the sheep gate and the fish gate (Neh 3:1; 12:39; Jer 31:38; Zech 14:10). Together with the Tower of Meah (q.v.) it was probably part of the temple fortress. King Herod later replaced these by the Tower of Antonia (q.v.). See Jerusalem: Gates and Towers 3.

HANANI (ha-nā'nĭ)
1. One of the sons of Heman who was set apart for the service of music in the sanctuary. He and his family were chosen as the 18th class in the order of service organized by David (I Chr 25:4, 25).

2. The prophet who rebuked King Asa and proclaimed God's judgment upon him because he had appealed to Syria for aid in his fight against Israel, instead of to the Lord. The angry and impenitent king put the prophet in prison (II Chr 16:7–10). He is probably the same man who was father of the prophet Jehu who condemned Asa's rival Baasha and counseled his own successor, King Jehoshaphat (I Kgs 16:1, 7; II Chr 19:2; 20:34).
3. A priest in the days of Ezra who was convicted of marrying a foreign woman and pledged himself to put her away (Ezr 10:19–20).
4. A brother of Nehemiah. It was he who led the group that informed Nehemiah of the deplorable condition of Jerusalem (Neh 1:2). After the restoration of the city, Hanani, along with Hananiah, the "ruler of the palace," was given charge over Jerusalem (Neh 7:2).
5. A priest in the days of Nehemiah, who with others played "with the musical instruments of David" at the great dedication of the completed wall (Neh 12:36).

P. C. J.

HANANIAH (hăn'a-nī'a)
1. A son of Heman, appointed to blow the horn for temple and royal services (I Chr 25:4–5), and head of the 16th course of Levite musicians (I Chr 25:23). See Heman.
2. A captain of the army under King Uzziah (II Chr 26:11).
3. The father of Zedekiah, a prince of Judah in the reign of Jehoiakim, king of Judah (Jer 36:12).
4. A son of Azur, a false prophet in the fourth year of Zedekiah, king of Judah. He falsely and publicly proclaimed in the temple that within two full years the booty Nebuchadnezzar had taken would be returned and Jeconiah and the captives restored. When Jeremiah denounced him as a false prophet, Hananiah removed the yoke from Jeremiah's neck which he had been wearing as a symbol of his counsel to submit to Babylon. Thereupon, declaring Hananiah's yoke of wood was to become iron, that is, Babylonian control would become stronger, Jeremiah predicted Hananiah's death within the year. Hananiah died two months later (Jer 28).
5. Grandfather of Irijah who arrested Jeremiah in the "gate of Benjamin" as he sought to go to Nebuchadnezzar in obedience tò God's word (Jer 37:13).
6. Son of Shashak, head of a Benjamite house (I Chr 8:24).
7. The Heb. name of Shadrach, one of the three young men taken to Babylon with Daniel (Dan 1:6–7, 11, 19; 2:17).
8. A son of Zerubbabel and ancestor of Jesus (I Chr 3:19, 21).
9. A son of Bebai, a repatriot with Ezra (Ezr 10:28).
10. An apothecary who helped repair the walls (Neh 3:8).

11. Son of Shelemiah, who with Hanun helped repair the walls (Neh 3:30).

12. A ruler of the palace in Nehemiah's time (Neh 7:2).

13. A sealer of the covenant to keep God's commands (Neh 10:23).

14. A priest in the time of Joiakim, the high priest (Neh 12:12, 41).

H. G. S.

HAND. The hand is the principal organ of touch and the member of the body chiefly employed in active service. As such, it is the symbol of human action. Pure hands mean pure actions, while hands full of blood symbolize deeds of iniquity (Ps 90:17; Job 9:30; I Tim 2:8; Isa 1:15). Washing of the hands was a sign of innocence, expiation, and sanctification (Ps 26:6; 24:3-4). *See* Ablution; Hands, Washing of.

The lifting up of the hands was a sign of prayer (I Tim 2:8; Job 11:13-14). Probably with this sense in mind, the term *yad* is used of a monument (II Sam 18:18; Isa 56:5, RSV). Such a stone pillar carved with two hands uplifted to divine symbols was found at Canaanite Hazor in 1955. The raising of the right hand *(cheir)* was evidently the method of voting in assemblies (cf. *cheirotoneō:* "ordained," Acts 14:23; "chosen," II Cor 8:19). A high hand (Ex 14:8) meant a brandished fist and signified defiance (Num 15:30, RSV; Deut 32:27; Isa 10:32; Acts 13:17).

The hand, especially the right one, was the emblem of power and strength. To hold by the right hand meant protection and favor (Ps 28:2, 5). To give the hand, as to a master, was a sign of future obedience (II Chr 30:8, marg.; Ps 68:31). To kiss the hand was an act of homage (I Kgs 19:18; Job 31:27). To pour water on another's hands meant to serve him (II Kgs 3:11). To seal up the hand was to stop man's work because of the ice and snow of winter (Job 37:7). Marks or scars on the hands or wrists signified a servant. Such marks showed a heathen's devotion to false gods (Zech 13:6). To stand at one's right hand was to aid or sustain anyone (Ps 16:8; 109:31). The right hand stretched out signified immediate exertion of power (Ex 15:12) and sometimes mercy (Isa 65:2; Prov 1:24). Being at the right hand of a person was the chief place of honor, dignity, and power (Ps 45:9). Such a place of position is accorded Christ Himself and shows His pre-eminence (Ps 110:1; Rom 8:34; Heb 1:3).

The hand of God as an anthropomorphism is His instrument of power. It is that which belongs to God Himself (Job 27:11; Acts 4:28; I Pet 5:6). The hand of the Lord upon anyone denotes favor (Ezr 7:6, 28; Acts 11:21), and against anyone signifies discipline (Ex 9:3; Amos 1:8; Acts 13:11). The hand of God upon a prophet denoted the enablement of the Holy Spirit (I Kgs 18:46; Ezk 8:1). The finger of God designated His power or Spirit (Lk 11:20; cf. Mt 12:28) and spoke of a work which only God could perform (Ex 8:19).

The laying on of hands marked out an individual and set him apart for service (Num 27:18-19; Acts 8:15-17; I Tim 4:14; II Tim 1:6). A perversion of this doctrine is seen when Simon offered money to obtain such a gift for himself in order to sell it or the powers to others (Acts 8:18), hence, simony. *See* Hands, Laying on of.

E. C. J.

HANDBREADTH. The breadth of the hand at the base of the four fingers, about three inches (Ex 25:25; 37:12; I Kgs 7:26; II Chr 4:5). Six handbreadths were a cubit. Ezekiel's cubit consisted of seven handbreadths (Ezk 40:5; 43:13), as did the royal systems of Egypt and Babylon. *See* Weights, Measures, and Coins.

In Ps 39:5 a handbreadth figuratively expresses the shortness of life.

HANDKERCHIEF. This word occurs only in the NT. A cloth used for wiping away perspiration. Handkerchiefs touched by Paul were carried away to heal the sick (Acts 19:12). The same Gr. word is translated "napkin" in Lk 19:20; Jn 11:44; 20:7. *See* Napkin.

In KJV "kerchiefs" apparently refers to veils of different lengths used by false prophetesses in divination to shroud persons consulting them (Ezk 13:18, 21).

HANDLE. Found only in Song 5:5 as part of a door bolt. The greatest diversity of handles in the ancient Near Eastern world is found on clay jars: e.g., loop handles, ledge handles, pierced lug handles, and high pitcher handles being characteristic of the Early Bronze Age; and wishbone, band, and stirrup handles seen in Late Bronze ware. *See* Pottery.

HANDMAID, HANDMAIDEN. The KJV rendering of *'āmâ* and *shiphâ*, terms denoting female slave, bondmaid, bondwoman, or maidservant. They attended to the personal needs of the mistress of the house (Gen 16:1; 25:12; 29:24), or nursed the children (Gen 24:59; II Sam 4:4; II Kgs 11:2). They had rights under the law (Ex 21:7-11; Lev 25:6), and could even become concubines when the first wife was sterile (Gen 16:1-2; 30:3, 9). The captive slave girl acquired new rights when taken to wife (Deut 21:10-14). Heb. slaves were to be emancipated in the year of jubilee (Lev 25:40) or after serving six years (Deut 15:12-17), but foreign slaves generally were slaves for life (Lev 25:45-46).

The term was sometimes used in expressing humility and submission (I Sam 25:24; II Sam 14:12; Lk 1:38).

A. T. P.

HANDS, LAYING ON OF. This is a religious act which signifies the impartation of a special blessing. *See* Hand. It was used to set aside the Levites for their special office (Num 8:5-20) and to dedicate animals (Lev 1:4). Thus Isaac blessed the sons of Joseph (Gen 48:14–19) and Jesus the little children (Mk 10:16). Jesus healed the sick by laying His hands on them (Lk 4:40; 13:13).

The seven deacons in Jerusalem were thus set aside by the apostles (Acts 6:6), and in Antioch Barnabas and Paul (Acts 13:3) were consecrated by this means. Peter and John laid their hands on certain Samaritans "and they received the Holy Ghost" (Acts 8:14–17). At Ephesus Paul did the same, with the same result (Acts 19:6). Here the believers received the gift of tongues and· prophesied. Timothy (I Tim 4:14; II Tim 1:6) received a special gift by Paul laying his hands on him. Blessing, healing, and consecration are associated with the act.

In churches today it is used in official acts of the public ministry, such as baptism, confirmation, and ordination. In the Roman Catholic church, laying on of hands is regarded as a sacrament by which the fitness for an office is conferred.

Calvin (*Institutes,* IV, 19, 6) disallowed the example of the apostolic laying on of hands, because "those miraculous powers and manifest workings, which were dispensed by the laying on of hands have ceased; and they have rightly lasted only as a time." The Lutheran Apology of the Augsburg Confession allowed it to be called "a sacrament," if it referred to teaching the gospel and administering the sacraments.

C. S. M.

HANDS, WASHING OF. Ceremonial washing of the body is universally recognized as a religious symbol or an effective sacrament for cleansing from the defilement and guilt of sin. In the OT, the brass laver was placed between the altar and the holy place of the tabernacle and temple so that the priests who were ministering unto the Lord might wash hands and feet (Ex 30:17–21). The baptism of John was a symbol of the cleansing from sins that followed repen-

A large ablution basin at the entrance to the Hittite temple of the storm god at Boghazköy.
HFV

Highly decorated ablution basin at the Temple of Jupiter, Baalbek, HFV

tance (Mt 3:6–11). Pilate the governor called for water and washed his hands before the multitude as though this would absolve him from the guilt of the crucifixion of Christ (Mt 27:24).

The Pharisees, in their zeal for the law, had deduced innumerable ways in which a person might contact ceremonial defilement, which, while not sinful, nevertheless made one Levitically unclean and unable to approach God in worship. Correspondingly, they had developed an elaborate program of washings to counteract this defilement. The discussion with Jesus in regard to the unwashed hands of His disciples had to do with this ceremonial act and not with ordinary cleansing. Jesus condemned the Pharisees because by the innumerable, burdensome details of their washings they had obscured the will as well as the Word of God. "Ye reject the commandment of God, that ye may keep your own tradition" (Mk 7:1–9). They had made a moral obligation out of what was only symbolic and ceremonial. (See Edersheim, *Life and Times of Jesus the Messiah,* II, 9 ff., for an extended treatment.)

See Ablution; Hand.

P. C. J.

HANDSTAFF. *See* Armor.

HANDWRITING. In Col 2:14 the KJV expression "handwriting" (Gr. *cheirographon*) is a hand-written document, often found in the Gr. papyri with the specific sense of a certificate of indebtedness (see NASB) ·or bond (RSV). In this passage the term presumably refers to the written Mosaic law. Its decrees or obligations which stood "against us" were fulfilled by Christ, and then it was cancelled and cast aside by "nailing it to His cross." *See* Writing.

HANES (hā'něz). A city in Egypt to which Judah sent envoys (Isa 30:4), almost certainly a site just S of the Fayyum, 55 miles S of Memphis on the W bank of the Nile, still known as Ahnas. The Greeks identified the local deity

Herishef with Hercules and called the city Heracleopolis Magna. Hanes was the home of the Twenty-second Dynasty (935–735 B.C.), and remained a city of great importance. In the reign of Psamtik I (663–609 B.C., Twenty-sixth Dynasty) Hanes was the center of government of Upper Egypt. On the basis of the Aramaic targum of the passage, however, some scholars have identified Hanes with Taphanes, a fortress on the E frontier.

HANGING. *See* Gallows; Crime and Punishment.

HANIEL (hăn′ĭ-ĕl). A son of Ulla and a prince and hero of the tribe of Asher (I Chr 7:39). The name is spelled Hanniel (*q.v.*) in RSV.

HANNAH (hăn′a). Only one woman of this name appears in the Bible, although "Anna" (the Gr. equivalent) is the name of another woman mentioned in Lk 2:36. The name means "grace" or "graciousness."

The story of Hannah, the mother of Samuel, is found in I Sam 1–2. She was one of the two wives of Elkanah, a Levite of the line of Kohath, who lived in Mount Ephraim. Perhaps because Hannah was barren he had married Penninah, his second wife, who bore him children. Hannah was a woman of prayer and faith as well as a woman of strong desires. She begged God for a son, and promised that if God gave her one, she would give him back to the Lord. This she did when Samuel was born, taking him to the tabernacle as a small boy and leaving him in the care of Eli the high priest. She later became the mother of five more children (I Sam 2:21).

Hannah's prophetic prayer (I Sam 2:1–10) reveals much regarding her spiritual maturity and insight. She was filled with joy, she recognized God's holiness and strength, His sovereignty and grace. She spoke of His keeping power and of the fact that He would some day "judge the ends of the earth." Furthermore, she seems, however vaguely, to have foreseen the eventual establishment of God's Anointed to be King, a prophecy that began to be fulfilled in David a century later (I Sam 2:10; cf. Ps 18:50; 89:19–37).

J. A. S.

HANNATHON (hăn′a-thŏn). A town on the N border of Zebulun (Josh 19:14). It is mentioned twice in the Amarna tablets (EA 8:17; 245:32) of the 14th cen. B.C., where it is called Hinnatuni and Hinatuna respectively, and once in the records of Tiglath-pileser III.

Perhaps it was located at Tell el-Bedeiwîyeh, a site approximately six miles N of Nazareth. Some identify it with el-Harbaj at the S end of the plain of Acco.

HANNIEL (hăn′ĭ-ĕl)
1. The son of Ephod and a prince of Manasseh who assisted in dividing Canaan among the tribes. Appointed to superintend the distribution of the W Jordanian territory among ten tribes to be settled in that area (Num 34:23).

2. A man of Asher (I Chr 7:39, RSV). Spelled Haniel (*q.v.*) in KJV.

HANOCH (hā′nŏk)
1. Head of a Midianite clan whose ancestry is traced to Abraham through Keturah (Gen 25:4; I Chr 1:33; KJV, Henoch).

2. The eldest son of Reuben (Gen 46:9; Ex 6:14; Num 26:5; I Chr 5:3).

HANUN (hā′nŭn)
1. The son and heir of Nahash, king of the Ammonites. When David sent a message of consolation to Hanun upon the death of his father, the new king chose to interpret the act as one of espionage. The ambassadors were arrested and disgraced by having half of each man's beard shaved off and his garments cut off at the middle, before being ejected from Ammon. This insult was considered by David an act of war, and he prepared his army to invade Ammon. Hanun, anticipating the invasion, had already sent for help to the Syrians. David's army, led by Joab and Abishai, was trapped between Ammonites and Syrians, but valiantly defeated both forces. This was the beginning of a war with Ammon that went on for some time (II Sam 10; I Chr 19).

2. The sixth son of Zalaph who repaired part of the wall of Jerusalem (Neh 3:30).

3. Another Hanun who with the inhabitants of Zanoah repaired the valley gate of Jerusalem and part of the wall (Neh 3:13).

P. C. J.

HAPHRAIM (hăf-rā′ĭm). A town in Issachar mentioned as between Shunem and Shion (Josh 19:19). Spelled *ḥprm* in Shishak's list of conquered Palestinian towns. Probably located at et-Taiyibeh NW of Bethshan and seven miles NE of Jezreel.

HARA (hâr′a). Named in I Chr 5:26 along with Halah, Habor, and the river Gozan, to which Tiglath-pileser III of Assyria exiled the Heb. tribes of Reuben, Gad, and half of Manasseh.

In II Kgs 17:6; 18:11 where the Heb. has "cities of Media," the LXX has "mountains of Media." Perhaps the Heb. *Hārā* in I Chr 5:26 is a corruption of this. Others have suggested Hara should be read Haran.

HARADAH (ha-rā′da). A stopping place in the journey of the Israelites from Sinai to Kadesh-barnea (Num 33:24–25). The location is unknown.

HARAN (hā′răn). An important crossroads and commercial city of Syria, situated about 20 miles S of Edessa on the Belias (now Belikh) River, on the high road which ran from Nineveh to Carchemish and on to the shores of the

Mediterranean. Its name (Heb. *ḫārān,* Akkad. *ḫarrānu*) means "road, route, caravan." In Hittite it became *ḫarvana,* the basis of our English word caravan.

Haran is first mentioned in the Bible as the place to which Terah journeyed from Ur of the Chaldeans. Here Terah died and Abraham received the call of God to leave his kindred and go to Canaan. Abraham left with his wife and his nephew Lot, while the other members of the clan remained behind (Gen 11:31 – 12:4). Though it is not specifically stated, Haran was apparently the place where the servant of Abraham, seeking a wife for Isaac, met Rebekah at the well; the traditional site of this well is still shown. Later Jacob fled to his uncle Laban, who lived in or near Haran (Gen 28:10), and spent 20 years before returning (Gen 28–30).

The only other biblical reports about Haran are that it was once destroyed by the Assyrians (II Kgs 19:12) and that its merchants exported blue embroidered garments and choice carpets (Ezk 27:23–24).

Haran is frequently mentioned in sources outside the Bible. Its name appears in a letter from Mari written about 2000 B.C., close to the time of Abraham. The city was a center of worship of the moon-god Sin. The other great center of Sin worship was Ur of the Chaldeans; hence it is very probable that Haran was founded by colonists sent out from Ur. Thus it is possible that Terah made the long journey from the fertile, prosperous lands of Babylonia to the less favorable regions of Syria as the leader of such a band of colonists. In the early centuries of the 2nd mil. B.C. Haran was near the center of the Hurrian occupation, so that the patriarchs undoubtedly came in contact with this dominant social element known to us through the Nuzu tablets (*see* Horites: Nuzu). Later records show that the city passed through various vicissitudes; it was at times in the hands of Mitannians, Assyrians, and Arameans.

When the Assyrian Empire was supreme in western Asia after 730 B.C., Haran was a strong fortress and the residence of a *turtan* ("commander," usually of royal blood). According to the *Babylonian Chronicle,* when Nineveh fell to the Medes and Babylonians in 612 B.C., the turtan of Haran, Ashur-uballit II, headed a short-lived Assyrian kingdom. Haran was besieged and taken by the Babylonians, and although the Assyrians had Egyptian aid, they failed to recover it; thus ended the Assyrian Empire.

Haran appears again in the story of Nabonidus, the last king of Babylonia (555–539 B.C.), who restored the famous temple of Sin, called Ehulhul, intending it for the chief religious center of his empire. The Romans kept the town as a fortress (Carrhae); nearby the army of Crassus was annihilated by the Parthians in 53 B.C.

The present-day town marks the site of the old settlement. Ancient inscriptions have been found in Eski-haran (Turkish, "old Haran") six

miles farther N, so that this may be the site of the famous temple of Sin.

Bibliography. William Hallo, "Haran, Harran," BW, pp. 280–283.

S. C.

HARARITE (hăr′à-rīt). The designation of three of David's mighty men known as the "thirty," perhaps signifying each was a "mountaineer": (1) Agee (II Sam 23:11); (2) Shammah (II Sam 23:33; Shage in I Chr 11:34); (3) Sharar (II Sam 23:33; Sacar in I Chr 11:35).

HARBONA(H) (här-bō′nà). The third of the seven eunuchs who served as chamberlains for Ahasuerus (Xerxes) mentioned in Est 1:10. He suggested Haman be hanged upon the gallows prepared for Mordecai (Est 7:9; Harbonah in KJV).

HARDNESS OF HEART. An expression found several times in the NT describing a certain moral attitude and firm set of mind. This stubbornness, impenitence (Rom 2:5) and impenetrability of man's heart as a condition is caused by wickedness and sin (Ex 9:34; Heb 3:13). Jesus Christ was grieved at the hardness *(pōrōsis)* or callousness of the Pharisees' hearts as He was about to perform a miracle on the sabbath (Mk 3:5). This callousness or ossification often resulted in inability to understand (Eph 4:18, "blindness," KJV; "hardness," RSV; cf. the verb *pōroō,* Mk 6:52; 8:17; II Cor 3:14). Another Gr. term *(sklērokardia)* signifies the dryness or stiff, unbending quality of mind in the realms of both faith (Mk 16:14; cf. the verb *sklērunō* used in Acts 19:9; Heb 3:8, 13, 15; 4:7) and practice (Mt 19:8; Mk 10:5).

In the Bible the act of hardening is attributed both to man (Ex 8:15; Heb 3:8) and to God (Ex 9:12; Deut 2:30; Josh 11:20; Isa 63:17; Rom 9:18). Many of the passages referring to hardening the heart relate to the refusal of Pharaoh to let God's people go out from Egypt. The Heb. verbs *qāshâ,* "make sharp, hard, obstinate" (Ex 7:3; Prov 28:14; 29:1); *kābēd,* "be heavy, insensible" (Ex 7:14; 8:15, 32; 9:7, 34; 10:1; I Sam 6:6); and *ḥāzaq,* "make strong, headstrong, stiff, unyielding" (Ex 4:21; 7:13, 22; 8:19; 9:12, 35; etc.) are used interchangeably, both of Pharaoh's own action and of the Lord's causing the hardness. While the Lord told Moses He would harden Pharaoh's heart (Ex 4:21; 7:3), seven times it is said the king of Egypt hardened his heart himself (7:13, properly "was hardened," RSV; 7:14, 22; 8:15, 19, 32; 9:7) before God actually hardened it (9:12): Thus both in the OT (I Sam 6:6, where even the heathen recognized the Egyptians and Pharaoh were responsible for their hardness) and in the NT (Rom 9:17–18) Pharaoh's hardening is mentioned as typical.

The theological problem of who bears the responsibility for hardness of the heart is thus resolved by a close study of Pharaoh's example. Men, by acting in accordance with their own self-will, carry out God's purpose in history. The Lord finally confirmed Pharaoh's attitude, lest out of sheer human weakness the king might give in before God had fully accomplished His will in judging Egypt. Israel in the wilderness was responsible for hardening their necks (Neh 9:16–17, 29) in manifesting a lack of faith and a disobedient, rebellious spirit (Ps 95:8; Heb 3:7–4:11).

Regarding salvation, it is well to remember that God takes no pleasure in the death of the wicked and is not willing that any should perish (Ezk 33:11; II Pet 3:9; cf. I Tim 2:4). Nevertheless, the same manifestation of divine mercy softens the hearts of those who repent and find forgiveness in Christ, but hardens the hearts of those who resist and obstinately refuse to heed God's invitation. Rom 9:14–18 is not specifically speaking of the sovereign grace that leads men to salvation, but rather that chooses certain men through whom God may advance His will on earth. *See* Heart.

Bibliography. K. L. and M. A. Schmidt, *"Pachunō, . . . , Sklēras, . . . ,"* TDNT, V, 1022–1031.

J. R.

HARE. *See* Animals, II.16.

HAREPH (hâr'ĕf). A Judahite chief, descended from Caleb, who founded Beth-gader, located somewhere in the region of Bethlehem and Kirjath-jearim (I Chr 2:51).

HARETH (hâr'ĕth). A forest between Adullam and Giloh in which David hid after his sojourn in Moab (I Sam 22:5; Hereth in RSV). Possibly the scene of the incident narrated in II Sam 23:14–17; I Chr 11:16–19.

HARHAIAH (här-hā'yȧ). Father of Uzziel, who helped repair the walls of Jerusalem under Nehemiah (Neh 3:8).

HARHAS (här'hăs). Grandfather of Shallum, husband of the prophetess Huldah (II Kgs 22:14). In II Chr 34:22 the name is spelled Hasrah *(q.v.);* the transposition of letters is probably a scribal error.

HARHUR (här'hûr). The ancestral head of a family of temple servants listed among the returned exiles (Ezr 2:51; Neh 7:53).

HARIM (hâr'ĭm)
1. The priest who was appointed by lot and thus gave his name to the third of 24 divisions or courses into which the priests were separated for service (I Chr 24:8). The 1,017 "sons of Harim" who came back from Babylon (Ezr 2:39; Neh 7:42) simply belonged to this course of Harim. Five of them took foreign wives (Ezr 10:21). The Harim who signed Nehemiah's covenant (Neh 10:5) and the priest Adna (Neh

12:15) seem to have belonged to this family. If the conjecture is correct that Rehum (Neh 12:3) is a scribal error for Harim, the name is also listed among the priests who returned with Zerubbabel from Babylon.
2. The ancestor of a large family of lay Israelites which bore his name. Accompanying Zerubbabel, 320 male members of this clan returned from Exile (Ezr 2:32; Neh 7:35). One of them was among the leaders who sealed the covenant with Nehemiah (Neh 10:27). Eight of these laymen were guilty of marrying foreign women (Ezr 10:31; cf. 10:44). One of the eight, Malchijah, helped repair the wall of Jerusalem (Neh 3:11).

P. C. J.

HARIPH (hâr'ĭf)
1. Head of a family whose 112 male members returned to Jerusalem after the Exile (Neh 7:24); apparently called Jorah in Ezr 2:18.
2. One of those who sealed Ezra's covenant (Neh 10:19).

HARLOT, WHORE. A woman guilty of illicit sexual relationships for reasons other than sexual pleasure is normally referred to in the English versions of the Bible as a whore, harlot, or prostitute, with the latter two designations being the terms normally used in the more recent versions.

In biblical times, harlotry was practiced for both mercenary and religious purposes. This fact is to be seen in the usage of the various Heb. words that refer to harlot. Heb. *zônâ,* the usual word, normally refers to a woman engaging in the practice for monetary purposes. The religious prostitute was normally called a *qedēshâ,* designating a female who belonged to a special class of religiously consecrated individuals. It was nothing unusual for the heathen religious systems of both OT and NT times to regularly employ prostitutes in their worship rituals at their idol shrines, and the Canaanite religions were no exception in this regard. It was a system which deified the reproductive organs and forces, the assumption being that reproduction and fertility in nature were controlled by sexual relations between gods and goddesses. The worshipers in the shrines of these cults would engage in sexual intercourse with the religious prostitutes (both male and female) of the shrine in the belief that this would prompt the gods and goddesses to do the same, thus bringing fertility and productivity to family, fields, and flocks. *See* Cults.

Inasmuch as the idolatrous practices of the Canaanites made inroads into the worship of the one true God, it is not at all surprising to find some indications in the OT that a syncretism of these fertility rites with the worship of Yahweh had been attempted (Amos 2:7; Hos 4:13 ff.; Jer 3:1–2).

Two other phrases occur in the Heb. of Proverbs which refer to harlots, i.e., *'ishshâ nokrîyâ* (foreign woman) and *'ishshâ zārâ* (strange woman). From the frequency of these terms in Proverbs it may be inferred that during the time of Solomon the foreign influences to which Israel was subjected caused a rise in prostitution, with many of these prostitutes being foreigners.

In the Gr. NT the one word that designates a harlot is *pornē*. Though it does not occur with great frequency in the NT, it was a common word; words related to it etymologically, two nouns and a verb, are of frequent occurrence.

The Bible consistently advocates moral purity and stands against prostitution of whatever type. Various bans are to be found in the Mosaic law (Lev 19:29; 21:7, 14; Deut 22:21). Proverbs is replete with its warnings to those who would go in to prostitutes. The same dangers confronted NT believers, for fertility cults of various types were still existent in the Roman Empire and the general moral tone in the 1st cen. was anything but high. Prohibition of prostitution would be included in those general prohibitions of illicit sexual relationships which pervade the NT. *See* Fornication.

The words for harlot and the concept of harlotry also have a significant figurative usage in Scripture in which those who are supposedly God's people, but who are also guilty of apostasy, are said to be guilty of harlotry. There is a twofold reason for this figurative usage. First, apostasy might actually involve one in the type of religious prostitution that has already been described. But the second aspect is probably the more significant. The relationship between God and His people is compared in Scripture to the marriage relationship involving union with and fidelity to one another. Thus when God's people apostatize they are in a figurative sense guilty of harlotry, for they have violated that relationship with God which is likened to marriage (cf. Num 25:1–2; Jud 2:13–17; 8:27, 33;

Jer 3:1–6; Ezk 6:9; Hos 4:12; I Cor 6:15; Rev 2:21–22).

In Rev 14:8 and 17:1–19:2 the harlot named Babylon designates a future apostate religious system that is both unfaithful to and hostile to God.

Bibliography. William F. Albright, *Archaeology and the Religion of Israel*, Baltimore: Johns Hopkins Press, 1953, pp. 74–78, 93, 114 f., 158 f.; *Yahweh and the Gods of Canaan*, Garden City, N.Y.: Doubleday, 1968, pp. 119–152. Friedrick Hauck and Siegfried Schulz, "*Pornē*, etc.," TDNT, VI, 579–595.

S. N. G.

HARNEPHER (här'nĕ-fĕr). One of the sons of Zophah, a chief of the tribe of Asher (I Chr 7:36); a transliteration of the Egyptian *hr-nfr*, "Horus is merciful."

HARNESS. Found in the KJV translation of Heb. *shiryon* in I Kgs 22:34 and II Chr 18:33 where there is a marginal reading of "breastplate." The RSV translates "breastplate" in both passages. The KJV translates Heb. *nesheq* as "harness" in II Chr 9:24; the RSV translates this as "myrrh," while the Jerusalem Bible has "armour," as in I Kgs 10:25; II Kgs 10:2; Isa 22:8.

In Jer 46:4 the expression "harness the horses" has its modern meaning of fastening animals to a vehicle, from Heb. *'āsar*, "to bind, tie," used also of the two milch cows tied or harnessed to a cart by the Philistines (I Sam 6:7, 10).

The harness of Egyptian war chariots was of leather, richly decorated and studded with gold and silver. Likewise the three horses drawing Ashurnasirpal II's royal hunting chariot were

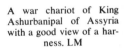

A war chariot of King Ashurbanipal of Assyria with a good view of a harness. LM

bedecked with elaborate harness (ANEP #184).

HAROD (hâr'ŏd). A spring (not a "well," KJV) which was the site of Gideon's encampment while preparing for battle with the Midianites (Jud 7:1). Possibly the fountain where Saul made camp against the Philistines (I Sam 29:1). It has been identified by some with 'Ain Jalud, a spring located on the NW slope of Mount Gilboa, eight miles WNW of Beth-shean. The water flows out of a natural cavern into a large pool, from which Gideon's men likely slaked their thirst. It is one of the most copious springs in Palestine, an important consideration for any military movements in the neighborhood.

HARODITE (hâr'ŏ-dīt). Two of David's men (Shammah and Elika) are called Harodites in II Sam 23:25. "Harorite" (I Chr 11:27) is a common scribal error for Harodite.

HAROEH. *See* Reaiah.

HARORITE (hâr'ŏ-rīt). This term (I Chr 11:27) should probably be read Harodite (cf. II Sam 23:25) since the *r* and *d* are very similar in Hebrew. *See* Harodite.

HAROSHETH OF THE GENTILES (hă-rō'shĕth). The term occurs only in Jud 4:2, 13, 16 in connection with the confrontation between the Israelites under Deborah and Barak, and Sisera, general of the Canaanite army. If Harosheth was a city, the text calls for proximity to the Kishon River at a place near the W end of the Plain of Esdraelon where it could flood to an extent required in Jud 5:21. This would be in the Kishon pass c. ten miles NNW of Megiddo. The site is generally identified with either the village of *el-Hârithîyeh* or *Tell 'Amr* nearby, both of which are doubtful because of soundings which indicate neither are of sufficient antiquity. Some scholars prefer *Tell Harbaj,* three miles N of *el-Hârithîyeh.* That Sisera "dwelt" (*yôshēb,* Jud 4:2) there may mean he was (military) governor of the area, and this may explain why a specific city has been so hard to find (cf. with use of *yôshēb* in Num 33:40; Jud 4:5; 10:1, and *l.*8 of the Moabite Stone which states Omri "dwelt" in or occupied the land of Medeba, ANET, p. 320).

P. W. F.

HARP. *See* Musical Instruments.

HARPOON. Found in Job 41:7, RSV and Jerusalem Bible as the translation of Heb. *śukkâ.* KJV has "barbed irons."

HARROW. The word so translated in II Sam 12:31 and I Chr 20:3 (Heb. *ḥārîṣ*) was a sharp instrument made of iron. It may have been some kind of threshing instrument (cf. *ḥārîṣ,* Isa 28:27; 41:15; Amos 1:3) or it may have been an agricultural implement like a hoe or pick-axe drawn over plowed land to level it and

break the clods before sowing the seed, and then to cover the seed which had been sown. A different word *(śādad)* used in Job 39:10; Isa 28:24; Hos 10:11 expresses the breaking of clods or fallow ground in some manner, but it is doubtful that it was the same as the modern harrow.

HARSHA (här'shá). Eponym of family of temple servants who returned from Babylon with Zerubbabel (Ezr 2:52; Neh 7:54).

HART. *See* Animals: Deer, II.10.

HARUM (hâr'ŭm). The father of Aharhel, listed among the posterity of Coz (I Chr 4:8) of the tribe of Judah.

HARUMAPH (hà-rū'măf). The father of Jedaiah, who helped repair the walls of Jerusalem in the time of Nehemiah (Neh 3:10).

HARUPHITE (hà-rū'fīt). The appellative of Shephatiah, one of the Benjamite warriors who joined David at Ziklag (I Chr 12:5). Possibly there is some relation between this designation and the Calebite Hareph of I Chr 2:51 or the Hariph family of Neh 7:24; 10:19, since no place of this name is known.

HARUZ (hâr'ŭz). Maternal grandfather of Amon, king of Judah (II Kgs 21:19). His place of origin was Jotbah.

HARVEST. The gathering of crops was the most important season on Israel's calendar. The Hebrews were primarily dependent on their harvests for livelihood (Gen 45:6; Prov 10:5; 20:4; Jer 5:17). Events were dated from harvests (Gen 30:14; Josh 3:15; Jud 15:1; Ruth 1:22; 2:23; I Sam 6:13; II Sam 21:9; 23:13). The three principal feasts of the Jews corresponded to their main harvest seasons (Ex 23:14–17; 34:18, 22–23): (1) the Passover, April-May, early in the barley harvest (cf. II Sam 21:9); (2) the Feast of Pentecost, seven weeks later, May-June, after the wheat harvest (Ex 34:22); (3) the Feast of Tabernacles (or Booths) during the fruit harvest, September-October. (Cf. G. E. Wright, BA, pp. 180 ff., for the Gezer Calendar.)

Both in the OT and NT the harvest figure is used to teach spiritual truths. A devastated harvest signified devastation or affliction (Job 5:5; Isa 16:9; 17:11; Jer 5:17; 50:16). The "time of harvest" could mean the day of destruction (Jer 51:33; Hos 6:11; Joel 3:13). "Joy in the harvest" suggested abounding joy (Isa 9:3); "harvest of Nile," an abundant harvest for profitable commerce (Isa 23:3, ASV, RSV). "The harvest is past" meant disappointment (Jer 8:20) or lost opportunity. "A cloud of dew in the heat of harvest" (Isa 18:4–5) spoke of the calm of summer approaching harvest season, to illustrate the Lord's waiting quietly until He would annihilate the wicked. The Master frequently referred to the harvest of souls (Mt

Harvest in the Fields of Boaz at Bethlehem. MPS

9:37-38; 13:30, 39; Mk 4:29; Jn 4:35). Also He employed the term in explaining the parable of the tares, "the harvest is the end of the age" (Mt 13:39, NASB; cf. Rev 14:15).

See Agriculture.

D. W. D.

HASADIAH (hăs'ȧ-dī'ȧ). One of the sons of Zerubbabel (I Chr 3:20).

HASENUAH (hăs'ĕ-noo'ȧ). The name means "the hated one."

1. A Benjamite, the father of Hodaviah (I Chr 9:7).

2. Without the definite article in Heb. the name is Senuah (KJV), a Benjamite whose son Judah was the second in command of Jerusalem (Neh 11:9). Neh 11:9 and I Chr 9:7 may refer to the same person.

See Hassenaah.

HASHABIAH (hăsh'ȧ-bī'ȧ)

1. The father of Malluch and son of Amaziah, a Levite of the family of Merari, a musician in the temple (I Chr 6:45).

2. A returned exile, the father of Azrikam and son of Bunni of the Levite family of Merari (I Chr 9:14; Neh 11:15).

3. One of the six musician sons of Jeduthun, appointed by David to head the 12th course of singers in the temple (I Chr 25:3, 19).

4. Hashabiah of Hebron, appointed by David to have oversight of Israel W of the Jordan; 1,700 men worked under him (I Chr 26:30).

5. The son of Kemuel, chief officer of the tribe of Levi in David's time (I Chr 27:17).

6. A leading man among the Levites in the days of Josiah who gave liberally for the great Passover (II Chr 35:9).

7. One of the chiefs of the Levites who went up with Ezra to Jerusalem (Ezr 8:19) and who was entrusted with the great treasure brought to Jerusalem (Ezr 8:24). He was probably the same Hashabiah who became ruler of half the district of Keilah (Neh 3:17). He was active in the days of Nehemiah, repairing the wall, sealing the covenant (Neh 10:11), and taking part in the dedication of the completed wall (Neh 12:24).

8. A Levite, son of Mattaniah and father of Bani, after the Exile (Neh 11:22).

9. The head of the priestly family of Hilkiah in the days of the high priest Joiakim (Neh 12:21), perhaps the same as 7.

P. C. J.

HASHABNAH (há-shăb'na). One of the chiefs of the people who with Nehemiah set their seal on Ezra's renewal of the covenant (Neh 10:25).

HASHABNIAH (hăsh'ăb-nī'ȧ)

1. Father of a certain Hattush, who helped repair the walls of Jerusalem in the time of Nehemiah (Neh 3:10).

2. One of a group of Levites who participated in a blessing offered to God during the time of Ezra as preparation for the sealing of the covenant (Neh 9:5).

HASHBADANA (hăsh-băd'á-na). One of the men who stood at Ezra's left when the law was read to the people at the great assembly (Neh 8:4).

HASHEM (hā'shĕm). A Gizonite, one of the 30 mighty men of the armies of David (I Chr 11:34), called Jashen (*q.v.*) in II Sam 23:32.

HASHMONAH (hăsh-mo'na) One of the camping places of the Israelites in their journey from

757

Sinai to Canaan (Num 33:29-30), perhaps to be identified with Wadi Hashim in the vicinity of Kadesh-barnea.

HASHUB (hā'shŭb)
1. A Levite, the son of Azrikam of the family of Merari. His son Shemaiah was one of the supervisors of the temple in the days of Nehemiah (I Chr 9:14, spelled Hasshub; Neh 11:15).
2. The son of Pahath-moab, a repairer of part of the wall of Jerusalem (Neh 3:11).
3. Another who worked under Nehemiah on the wall (Neh 3:23).
4. One of the leading Israelites who sealed the covenant of Nehemiah. He could be either 2 or 3 (Neh 10:23).

HASHUBAH (há-shoo'bá). One of the sons of Zerubbabel and a descendant of Jehoiakim, king of Judah (I Chr 3:20).

HASHUM (hā'shŭm)
1. The "children of Hashum" were among the Israelites who returned with Zerubbabel to rebuild the temple (Ezr 2:19; Neh 7:22). They are also listed among those who put away their foreign wives in the time of Ezra (Ezr 10:33).
2. One of the men who stood beside Ezra as he read the law before the people (Neh 8:4).
3. One of the chiefs of the people who signed the covenant made by Nehemiah to obey God's law (Neh 10:18).

HASHUPHA (há-shoo'fá), **HASUPHA** (há-soo'fá). The ancestral head of a family of Nethinim (q.v.) which returned from Exile with Zerubbabel (Ezr 2:43; Neh 7:46).

HASMONEANS. See Maccabees.

HASRAH (hăz'rá). Grandfather of Shallum, the husband of Huldah, the prophetess who was consulted about the book of the law found during Josiah's reign (II Chr 34:22). Called Harhas (q.v.) in II Kgs 22:14.

HASSENAAH (hăs'ĕ-nā'á). Identical with Senaah (Ezr 2:35; Neh 7:38) where it appears without the article. See Senaah. The "sons" or men of Hassenaah rebuilt the fish gate when the wall of Jerusalem was repaired after the exiles returned from Babylon (Neh 3:3). The name is probably identical with Hasenuah (q.v.) in I Chr 9:7 or Senuah in Neh 11:9, seemingly a personal name. But the number of sons of Senaah, nearly 4,000 (Ezr 2:35; Neh 7:38), is extraordinarily large for one family or clan. Thus Senaah may be a term for a category of persons who come from several places or families (GTT, ¶ 1035, pp. 382 f.).

HASSHUB. See Hashub.

HASUPHA. See Hashupha.

HAT. An article of clothing (Aram. *karbᵉlâ*) mentioned only in Dan 3:21. A loan word from Akkad. *karballatu,* it probably signified the high, pointed cap of a style worn sometimes by the Assyrians and Babylonians and more especially by the Cimmerians. See Dress.

HATACH (hăt'ák). A chamberlain (eunuch) of King Ahasuerus who was appointed to attend Queen Esther. Through him she learned from Mordecai of Haman's plot to have the Jews destroyed (Est 4:5-6, 9-10).

HATE, HATRED. Hatred (a strong dislike for) may be a work of the "flesh" (Rom 8:7; Gal 5:19 f.) and a sign of unregeneracy (I Jn 3:15). The unregenerate hate God (Ex 20:5; Ps 83:2; Rom 1:30), the light (Jn 3:20), the righteous (Ps 35:19; 69:4; Jn 15:25), and one another (Tit 3:3). They hate Christians as disciples of Christ (Lk 6:22; 21:17; Jn 15:18-25; 17:14).

But hatred can be a mark of spirituality. God's people must actively hate evil (Ps 97:10; 119:104, 128, 163; Jude 23). They must even hate their own lives for Christ's sake (Lk 14:26; Jn 12:25). However, hatred as a malicious attitude is incompatible with the Christian life (I Jn 2:9, 11; 3:15; 4:20). Christians must not hate others (Mt 5:43 f.; Lk 6:27 f.) except as God hates the workers of iniquity (Ps 26:5; 101:3; 139:21 f.; cf. II Chr 19:2).

Bibliography. Werner Foerster, *"Echthros,* etc.," TDNT, II, 811-815. O. Michel, *"Mis-eō,"* TDNT, IV, 683-694.

HATHATH (hā'thǎth). A son of Othniel, of the family of Caleb (I Chr 4:13).

HATIPHA (há-tī'fá). Ancestral head of a family of Nethinim (temple servants) who returned from captivity with Zerubbabel (Ezr 2:54; Neh 7:56).

HATITA (há-tī'tá). The ancestral head of a family of porters or gatekeepers (Ezr 2:42; Neh 7:45) some of whose members returned from Babylon.

HATTIL (hăt'ĭl). One of Solomon's servants, some of whose descendants returned from captivity with Zerubbabel (Ezr 2:57; Neh 7:59).

HATTUSH (hăt'ŭsh)
1. One of the sons of Shemaiah, a descendant of Zerubbabel (I Chr 3:22).
2. A descendant of David who went with Ezra to Jerusalem (Ezr 8:2). He may be the same as 1 or 3.
3. The son of Hashabniah who helped in building the wall under Nehemiah (Neh 3:10).
4. One of those who sealed the covenant of Nehemiah. He may be the same as 3 (Neh 10:4).
5. A priest who returned to Jerusalem with Zerubbabel (Neh 12:2).

758

HAURAN (hôr'ǎn). A district of Palestine E of the Sea of Galilee, S of Damascus on the edge of the Arabian desert, N of the Yarmuk River. It was at times included in Bashan, the kingdom of Og (Num 21:33-35). In NT times the territory was practically identical with the region of Auranitis in the tetrarchy of Philip. Mainly, it is a fertile basin about 50 miles square and 2,000 feet above sea level. The area is practically treeless and is known for its production of wheat. The soil is rich because of the lava deposits. Some burned out volcanic craters remain to this day. The basin is protected from the desert sands on the E by a volcanic mountain range (Jebel Hawran). The region is still called el-Hauran. In the Bible Hauran is mentioned only by Ezekiel in his delineation of the NE boundaries of ideal Israel (Ezk 47:16, 18).

HAVEN. A port or harbor for ships (Gen 49:13; Acts 27:12). Used metaphorically of the peace and rest which come with salvation and dwell in the heart of the fully consecrated believer as he surrenders his trials and problems to God (Ps 107:30).

HAVILAH (hǎv'ĭ-là)
1. A land associated with the garden of Eden and cited as the source of gold, bdellium gum, and onyx stone, surrounded or drained by the river Pishon (Gen 2:11-12, ASV, RSV). Most authorities locate Havilah in central Arabia N of Yemen. The basis for this location is the association of the term with Hazarmaveth (the area now called Hadramaut) and Sheba (Gen 10:26-29), sections of S Arabia, and also the fact that the products from the area are the same as the products from central Arabia. It is probable that this area extended N for several hundred miles (I Sam 15:7; Gen 25:18). Some authorities believe that there are two places designated by this name because of the difficulty of locating the Pishon River in the Arabian peninsula, and that originally Havilah referred to the area of West Pakistan, the Pishon being the Indus River. *See* Pison.
2. A son of Cush and a descendant of Ham (Gen 10:7; I Chr 1:9).
3. A son of Joktan and a grandson of Eber (Gen 10:29; I Chr 1:23), of the family of Shem.
G. A. T.

HAVOTH-JAIR (hā'vǒth-jā'ĩr). A group of tent villages on the border of Bashan and Gilead, E of the Jordan, taken by Jair the Manassite who renamed them after himself (Num 32:41; Deut 3:14). I Chr 2:21-24 shows that Jair was a descendant of Judah, but that his grandmother was a daughter of Machir of the tribe of Manasseh. Twenty-three towns continued to belong to Jair and his descendants in Gilead. In later times, however, Geshur and Aram took those "villages of Jair" including Kenath, which were in Bashan (I Chr 2:23, RSV). This loss evidently came after the time of Solomon who ruled over the tent villages of Jair and the 60

walled cities in Bashan (I Kgs 4:13); perhaps this occurred during the reign of Hazael (II Kgs 10:32 f.). In Jud 10:3-4 there is reference to Jair the Gileadite, probably a direct descendant of the earlier Jair, as one of the judges who had 30 sons who ruled over 30 cities in the land of Gilead.

There seems to be some confusion as to the number of towns that belonged to Jair. In Deut 3:4 Moses claims that Israel had captured the 60 cities of Og in Bashan; Jair then took over the whole region of Bashan and renamed it Havvoth-Jair (Deut 3:14, Berkeley; see also Josh 13:30); Jud 10:4 says 30, I Chr 2:22 says 23. It has been suggested that the number was liable to fluctuation because the sites lay in contested land (I Chr 2:23), and because the very nature of such tent encampments was mobile and temporary.
F. B. H.

HAWK. *See* Animals, III.19.

HAY. The rendering of the KJV in Prov 27:25 and Isa 15:6 of Heb. term *(ḥāṣîr)* that occurs elsewhere in the OT as "grass." *See* Plants: Grass. The Hebrews probably did not distinguish carefully between the different grasses and grass-like herbs. Grass is not usually cut and dried for hay in the Near East.

Grass, which becomes brown during the summer dry season, is used to symbolize the shortness of man's life on earth (Ps 90:5; 103:15; Isa 51:12). Paul uses "hay" *(chortos)*, i.e., grass, figuratively to denote the inferior and non-enduring quality of the work which some men are building on the foundation of Christ (I Cor 3:12).

HAZAEL (hā'zĭ-ăl). The ruler of Damascus during the years *c.* 843-796 B.C.; a contemporary of Joram, Jehu, and Jehoahaz of Israel. He troubled Israel often during their reigns. He is first met in the OT in I Kgs 19:15 when Elijah was commissioned to anoint him as one of God's agents in the destruction of Baal worship in Israel. At the time Ben-hadad II was ruler in Damascus. Next we hear of him when he visited Elisha, who happened to be in Damascus, to inquire on behalf of the ailing Ben-hadad whether he would recover (II Kgs 8:7-10). On that occasion Elisha wept as he told Hazael that the king would die and that he would be the next ruler and would become an oppressor of Israel (II Kgs 8:11-14). Hazael put the prophecy into effect by murdering Ben-hadad (II Kgs 8:15). Before long he was in conflict with Joram at Ramoth-gilead (II Kgs 8:28-29; 9:14-15). Joram was wounded and as he rested at Jezreel he was slain by Jehu the Israelite army captain who then seized the throne of Israel (II Kgs 9:16-26).

During the reign of Jehu (841-814 B.C.) Hazael continued to attack Israel until he overran the whole of Transjordan as far S as the river Arnon (II Kgs 10:32-33). In the time of Jehoahaz (814–798), Hazael's attacks continued (II Kgs 13:3, 22–25), and he actually penetrated into SW Palestine, capturing Gath and threatening Jerusalem. J(eh)oash, king of Judah, bought him off with the temple treasures (II Kgs 12:17–18). At one stage during Hazael's campaigns against Israel the former large chariot force of Israel was reduced to 50 horsemen and ten chariots in the days of Jehoahaz (II Kgs 13:7). Jehoahaz called upon God for deliverance, which came through a change in the international situation (II Kgs 13:4–5).

The key to Israel's deliverance lies in the activity of the Assyrians during these years. In 843 B.C. at the start of his reign, Hazael had to face renewed attacks from Shalmaneser III of Assyria and withstood a long siege in which he and his lands suffered severely. In the years that followed he was comparatively free from Assyrian attack and campaigned against Israel. But in 805–803 B.C. Adad-nirari III of Assyria attacked Hazael again, and shortly after, in 797 B.C., Shalmaneser IV followed up the assault. These repeated campaigns so weakened Hazael that Israel was able to recover towns on her northern frontier formerly lost to Hazael in the days of J(eh)oash (798–782; II Kgs 13:25). By then, however, Hazael was nearing the end of his life and he must have died shortly after J(eh)oash, perhaps in 797 or 796 B.C.

During his long reign of over 40 years he was the scourge of Israel. Even a century later Amos spoke of the rulers of Damascus as the house of Hazael and prophesied that they would yet experience the fire of God's judgment (Amos 1:4).

Hazael was known to the Assyrians and his name appears in several Assyrian texts as an opponent of Shalmaneser. He was known to be a usurper and is called on one document "a son of a nobody" (ANET, p. 280). Adad-nirari referred to him as *mari'*, lord (ANET, pp. 281 f.). A piece of ivory found at Nimrud bearing the inscription "belonging to our lord Hazael" may have been part of Assyrian spoils from Damascus.

See Syria.

Bibliography. Merrill F. Unger, *Israel and the Arameans of Damascus*, London: James Clark, 1957.

J. A. T.

HAZAIAH (há-zā'yà). An ancestor of Maaseiah, who was a Jewish lay leader living in post-Exilic Jerusalem (Neh 11:5). Son of Adaiah and father of Col-hozeh, he was a descendant of Pharez, Judah's son.

HAZAR (hā'zár). A term meaning unwalled settlements (Lev 25:31; Josh 19:8). Hazar was frequently prefixed to the name of a nearby village. *See* Hazar-addar; Hazar-enan; Hazar-gaddah; Hazar-hatticon; Hazarmaveth; Hazar-shual; Hazar-susah.

HAZAR-ADDAR (hā'zár-ăd'ár). A place in the S part of Palestine near Kadesh-barnea and Azmon (Num 34:4); simply called Adar in Josh 15:3. Possibly it was modern 'Ain Qedeis, five miles SE of 'Ain el-Qudeirat (Kadesh-barnea; Y. Aharoni, *The Land of the Bible*, p. 65). *See* Hazar.

HAZAR-ENAN (hā'zár-ē'nán). According to Num 34:7–10, the site at the end of the N frontier between Palestine and Hamath (cf. Ezk 47:16–17) where the border turned southward. It may be identified with the desert oasis of el-Qaryatein, half way between Damascus and Palmyra. *See* Hazar-hatticon.

HAZAR-GADDAH (hā'zár-găd'à). A city in the southern part of Judah (Josh 15:27), near Moladah and Heshmon.

HAZAR-HATTICON (hā'zár-hăt'à-kŏn). Named by Ezekiel as the ultimate boundary of Israel (Ezk 47:16). Possibly it is an alternate form of Hazar-enan (*q.v.*).

HAZARMAVETH (hā'zar-mā'vĕth). Found in the Table of Nations (Gen 10:26; I Chr 1:20). One of the sons of Joktan and ancestor of a tribe in S Arabia which gave its name to the Wadi Hadhramaut. By the 5th cen. B.C. this area supported a flourishing state with its capital at Shabwa, 220 miles NE of Aden. Hadhramaut was famed for its traffic in frankincense.

HAZAR-SHUAL (hā'zár-shū'ál). A town of Simeon in the extreme S of Judah, always mentioned in close connection with Beer-sheba (Josh 15:28; 19:3; I Chr 4:28). It was reoccupied by Jews after the Exile (Neh 11:27).

HAZAR-SUSAH (hā'zár-sū'sà). A city of Simeon in the SW part of Judah (Josh 19:5). Called Hazar-susim ("village of horses") in I Chr 4:31, it perhaps contained stables where Solomon kept some of the horses he imported from Egypt and sold to Hittites and Syrians (I Kgs 4:26; 9:19; 10:29; cf. cities of horsemen in II Chr 8:6). It is possibly modern Sbalat Abû Sûsein, 20 miles W of Beer-sheba. It may be that the Hyksos or Canaanites had kept horses here. Sir Flinders Petrie discovered Late Bronze Age burial of horses which may have been sacrificed at Tell el-'Ajjul SW of Gaza on the seacoast.

HAZAZON-TAMAR (hăz'á-zŏn-tā'már). Hazazon-tamar is a town identified with Engedi in II Chr 20:2, but this note may only indicate the general direction. After Chedorlaomer and the other four Mesopotamian kings had subdued the cities of the plain for 12 years, the citizens of the plain rebelled and sent the once-conquering but now-defeated kings on their way. It appears that these kings attacked the small nations to the S and in the vicinity of Mount Seir, including the dwellers in Ashteroth Karnaim, in Ham, in Shaveh Kiriathaim, etc. (Gen 14:1–6). Later, they returned to Sodom and Gomorrah and en route they smote the Amorites that dwelt in Hazazon-tamar (Gen 14:7, spelled Hazezon-tamar in KJV). Engedi (q.v.) is an oasis below a beautiful waterfall about 25 miles up the W coast of the Dead Sea from the S end (II Chr 20:2).

Hazazon-tamar may otherwise be the Tamar (q.v.) fortified by Solomon to guard a trade route from the Arabah to the Negeb, located at 'Ain Hasevah near the foot of Scorpion Pass (Akrabbim, q.v.), according to M. Harel ("The Roman Road at Ma'aleh 'Aqrabbim," IEJ, IX, 175–179).

H. A. Han.

HAZEL. *See* Plants.

HAZELELPONI (hāz'ĕ-lĕl-pō'nī). A sister of the sons of Etam, descendants of Judah (I Chr 4:3).

HAZERIM (hȧ-zēr'ĭm). The Avim (q.v.) lived in unwalled villages (Hazerim) as far as Gaza until destroyed by the Caphtorim (Deut 2:23). Heb. ḥāṣēr often denotes a settlement or village dependent on a fortified city nearby for the protection of its inhabitants (Lev 25:31; Josh 15:45–47; 19:8).

HAZEROTH (hȧ-zēr'ŏth). The camping place of the Israelites after leaving Kibroth-hattaavah (Num 11:35; 12:16; 33:17–18; Deut 1:1). It was there that Miriam and Aaron complained against Moses because of his marriage to a Cushite (Ethiopian) woman and because of his unique authority as mediator between God and the people (Num 12). The location has been identified with 'Ain Khadra, c. 35 miles NE of Mount Sinai (GTT, pp. 255 f.).

HAZEZON-TAMAR. *See* Hazazon-tamar.

HAZIEL (hā'zĭ-ĕl). The head of a clan of Gershonite Levites, the son of Shimei (I Chr 23:9).

HAZO (hā'zō). The fifth of the eight sons of Nahor and Milcah (Gen 22:22) and the ancestor of an Aramean tribe. The name has been identified with the mountainous region of Ḥazû in N Arabia or the Syrian desert, mentioned in Esarhaddon's Arabian campaign.

HAZOR (hā'zôr). The name of at least five towns mentioned in the Bible.

1. A Canaanite city ruled in the days of Joshua by Jabin (Josh 11:1). At that time Hazor was considered "the head of all those kingdoms" (v. 10), the petty city-states in N Palestine and S Lebanon. Jabin led them out with their chariots against Joshua, who almost annihilated them after surprising them at the waters of Merom, thought now to be a stream

Excavations at Hazor. Yigael Yadin

flowing S from springs in the highest mountain of Galilee. Joshua turned back and captured Hazor, killed Jabin, and burned the city with fire (vv. 10–11). Later, another Jabin (Jud 4) ruling at Hazor was considered king of Canaan; but using Deborah and Barak, God subdued and destroyed him also. Located strategically on a principal trade route from Damascus to the Mediterranean coast, Hazor was fortified by Solomon (I Kgs 9:15). Its Israelite inhabitants were carried away captive (II Kgs 15:29) to Assyria by Tiglath-pileser III on his campaign of 732 B.C.

The ancient site was located by John Garstang digging in 1926 and 1928 at Tell el-Qedah on the Wadi Waqqas, five miles SW of the now-drained Lake Huleh and ten miles N of the Sea of Galilee. Hazor is mentioned in the early 18th cen. B.C. Execration texts which list potential enemies of Egypt, the 18th cen. Mari letters, records of pharaohs who conquered Palestinian cities (Thutmose III, Amen-hotep II, Sethos I), in four of the Amarna letters (14th cen.), and in the 13th cen. Papyrus Anastasi I from Egypt.

Systematic excavation of the site began with Yigael Yadin's work in 1955, who directed further seasons in '56, '57, '58, and '68–'69. Hazor consisted of two distinct areas, the 30-acre 130 foot high acropolis mound at the SW corner known as the upper city, and the huge rectangular enclosure to the N encompassing 175 acres where it is estimated 40,000 inhabitants once lived. It was by far the largest city in Palestine in OT times. This lower city was first settled before 1750 B.C., presumably by the Hyksos, who then fortified it with mighty earthen ramparts in the Middle Bronze II B and C periods (1750–1550 B.C.).

After destruction in the mid-16th cen. B.C., Hazor reached its zenith in the Late Bronze I period (1550–1400), in which the reign of the earlier Jabin would fall according to the early date of the Exodus (*see* Exodus, Date of). City gates with three pairs of pilasters and a large gate tower on either side gave access to the

Excavating the water system at Hazor. HFV

lower city. In that area the archaeologists uncovered a series of four superimposed Late Bronze Age Canaanite temples lined with basalt orthostats and revealing a floor plan similar to that of Solomon's temple. One of these temples contained a sculptured stone figure of a god seated on a throne in a raised central niche. It was found decapitated, with the head nearby. To the left in a row of stelae, the middle one depicted two hands uplifted in prayer to a sun disk within a crescent. This monument or memorial stela is probably an example of the Heb. *yad* (lit., "hand," Isa 56:5, KJV "place"; 57:8, KJV "remembrance"). The lower city was destroyed *c.* 1230 B.C. (which corresponds with the date of Deborah and Barak) and never rebuilt.

On the acropolis during the Late Bronze I period stood a large structure which most likely was the palace, and adjacent to it a 50-foot-long rectangular temple having an entrance built with orthostats. This building was demolished and abandoned by the end of Late Bronze I. The earliest stratum of the mound or upper city dates back to Early Bronze times, and continued to be occupied after Tiglath-pileser's destruction by a small undefended settlement in the 8th-7th cen., followed by Assyrian, Persian, and Hellenistic forts. Yadin excavated the gate of Solomon's city and proved it to be identical with gateways of his reign at Megiddo and Gezer (cf. I Kgs 9:15). A public building from the time of King Ahab measured 49 by 66 feet and contained two rows of stone columns, nine pillars in each row.

In the fifth season, the elaborate water system of Hazor was discovered. Evidence shows that when Ahab rebuilt the whole upper city of Hazor and refortified it to withstand long siege, his men first dug a shaft 100 feet down with a rock-cut staircase ten feet wide descending its side, and then a tunnel averaging 13 feet both in height and width and sloping down to reach the water table. Larger than comparable water systems at Megiddo, Gezer and Gibeon, this one remained in use until 732 B.C.

Bibliography. John Gray, "Hazor," VT, XVI (1966), 26–52. Yigael Yadin, Hazor articles, BA, XIX. 1 (Feb., 1956), XX. 2 (May, 1957), XXI. 2 (May, 1958), and XXII. 1 (Feb., 1959), edited as one continuous report in *The Biblical Archaeologist Reader,* Garden City: Anchor Books, 1964, pp. 191–224; "The Fifth Season of Excavations at Hazor, 1968–1969," BA, XXXII. 3 (Sept., 1969); "Hazor," TAOTS, pp. 245–263.

2. A town in the extreme S of Judah, mentioned only in Josh 15:23. Perhaps identified with el-Jebariyeh, on the Wadi Umm Ethnan, near Bir Hafir, *c.* nine miles SE of el- 'Auja.

3. Another town in the S of Judah (Josh 15:25). Possibly the same as Kerioth-Hezron. Located in Negeb district of Beer-sheba; possibly identified with Khirbet el-Qaryatein, four and a half miles S of Maon. KJV has "Kerioth and Hezron."

4. A town N of Jerusalem, inhabited by Benjamites during the restoration (Neh 11:33). The name is preserved in Khirbet Hazzur, W of Beit Hanina.

5. A region in N Arabia near Kedar (*q.v.*), inhabited by camel-riding nomads, against which Jeremiah pronounced a "doom" (Jer 49:28-33).

L. L. W.

HAZOR-HADATTAH (hā'zôr-há-dăt'á). A city in the extreme S of the Negeb of Judah (Josh 15:25, RSV). In KJV the words are separated, Hazor Hadattah.

HE (hā). The fifth letter of the Heb. alphabet, used as the heading of the fifth section of Ps 119, where every verse in the section begins with this letter.

HE ASS. *See* Animals: Ass, I.1.

HEAD. There are several uses of the word head.
1. It denotes the most essential part of man and beast. It is used of the serpent's head (Gen 3:15), sacrificial animals (Ex 29:10, 15, 19), and human beings (Gen 40:16–17). The head is considered the seat of the intelligence and sometimes represents the whole man (Prov 10:6). Joy and sorrow, blessing and adversity were said to come on the head of a person. Anointing the head was an emblem of joy (Ps 23:5; Heb 1:9). Hands were placed on the head of a person and blessing invoked (Mt 19:15). Cutting the hair and covering the head were signs of mourning and distress (Josh 7:6; I Sam 4:12; Lam 2:10). Bruising or smiting the head was synonymous with complete destruction (Gen 3:15; Ps 68:21). Bowing the head was a sign of humility and reverence (Isa 58:5).
2. Another meaning is the top or summit of inanimate objects such as mountains, scepters, ladders, and towers (Ex 19:20; Est 5:2; Gen 28:12; Gen 11:4). Christ is called the head-

stone or top stone (Zech 4:7; cf. 10:4, ASV, RSV).

3. Head also denotes the beginning of months, rivers, and streets (Gen 2:10; Ex 12:2; Isa 51:20).

4. It designates one in authority in the sense of foremost or uppermost. It may mean leader, prince, chief, or captain, and is used of cities, nations, men, and God. Damascus is the head or capital of Syria (Isa 7:8), and Israel is to be the head of the nations (Deut 28:13). Men of Israel are called the heads of their fathers' houses (Ex 6:14; Deut 1:15; I Chr 5:24).

5. An important NT use is the headship of Christ. *See* Head of the Church. He is the Head of His Church called His Body (Eph 4:12, 15; 5:23; Col 1:24). Believers are placed into this Body by the Holy Spirit (I Cor 12:13; cf. 12:27). The figure represents the service and manifestation of Christ through believers in union, direction, and control. *See* Body of Christ. Christ is also Head of His Church called His Bride (Eph 5:23–33). This figure shows His love and care for His Church, and looks forward to the marriage to be consummated in heaven (Rev 19:7). *See* Bride of Christ. After this example, the husband is the head of the wife and is to love and care for her (I Cor 11:3; Eph 5:23–33). Christ is also Head of the universe (Eph 1:22) and every cosmic power (Col 2:10). The head of Christ is God (I Cor 11:3).

Bibliography. J. R. Bartlett, "The Use of the Word *Rôsh* as a Title in the Old Testament," VT, XIX (1969), 1–10. Heinrich Schlier, "*Kephalē*," TDNT, III, 673–682.

E. C. J.

HEAD OF THE CHURCH. Paul presents Christ as the Head of the Church (Eph 5:32), and the individual members in the Church as parts of His Body (Eph 4:4–16; I Cor 12:12–27).

In Colossians Christ is seen as Head (Col 1:18; cf. Eph 1:21–22) in contrast to and above all principalities and powers of evil (Col 2:10; cf. Eph 6:12), and to angels (Col 2:18; cf. Heb 1:4 ff.).

In Ephesians He is seen as head of the corner, or chief cornerstone which joins together two walls in one, Jew and Gentile, breaking down the middle wall of partition between them (Eph 2:14–15, 19–20). This union, "that the Gentiles should be fellow heirs" with converted Jews (3:6), which Christ effects as their united head, was so difficult for the OT saints to grasp (Isa 9:2; 11:10; 42:6; 49:6; 60:3; 66:2, 12, 19; Amos 9:12) that it is called "the mystery . . . hid in God" (Eph 3:9).

Three main lessons are drawn. First, that we are to learn to give appropriate submission and honor to those in authority around us, even as we do to Christ (Eph 5:21–6:9). Second, even as Christ loved the Church and each one of us, we are to love our wives and others (Eph 5:25–33). Third, we are to remember we are

like the members of our own body, each being gifted by the Holy Spirit in particular ways (I Cor 12:4–13; Eph 4:7 f.), and yet each needing the other (I Cor 12:14 ff.).

See Head.

R. A. K.

HEADBAND

1. KJV translation for bands or sashes around the waist (Isa 3:20). The same word (*qishshurîm*) is rendered "attire" in Jer 2:32.

2. RSV renders Isa 3:18 as "headband" (KJV "cauls"). It was probably a gold or silver head ornament.

See Dress.

HEADSTONE. This expression is found only in Zech 4:7 (KJV). ASV and RSV translate "top stone"; JerusB has "keystone." The term occurs in Zechariah's vision in which Israel is seen as a lamp of witness, fed with the oil of the Spirit by the Priest-King Messiah.

The immediate occasion was the word of encouragement to Zerubbabel that he would complete the construction of the restored temple (Ezr 5; 6:14–15) begun 14 years before and left unfinished. The urging of Haggai the prophet had initiated and carried forward the work in the second year of Darius, in the sixth, seventh, and ninth months. Zechariah's prophecies began in the eighth month, and the series of eight visions in which the vision of the candelabrum is found came on the twenty-fourth day of the eleventh month. The promised completion came four years later (Ezr 6:15). The messages of the two prophets complement each other. Haggai stirred a sluggish and self-seeking people to work; Zechariah revealed the divine power at work "not by might, nor by power, but by my Spirit, saith the Lord of hosts" (Zech 4:6). Thus the fulfillment of the prediction that Zerubbabel would finish the temple would cause the people to know that God had sent the prophet to them.

The ultimate prophetic significance of this vision is found in Jesus Christ. In almost identical words He is prefigured as "the stone which the builders rejected" who "has become the cornerstone" (Ps 118:22, RSV). Peter twice declared that Christ was the fulfillment of this concept (Acts 4:11; I Pet 2:7). Paul viewed the whole company of believers as a building of God, Christ Himself being the chief cornerstone (Eph 2:19–22). *See* Cornerstone. "In the Millennial Age, toward which the golden candlestick of Zech 4:1–7 points, Christ will be manifested also as the Headstone of the temple of His restored covenant people Israel, the golden candlestick of Zech 4:2 more specifically speaking of converted Israel as the light of the world in the Kingdom Age" (Unger's *Bible Dictionary,* p. 462).

W. B. W.

HEADY. Found in II Tim 3:4 to describe unruly or headstrong men in the last days. RSV translates the word as "reckless." The same Gr. word *propetēs* occurs also in Acts 19:36 as "rashly."

HEALING, HEALTH

Principles of Health

The Bible has much to say about healing and health. Throughout its pages may be found many sound principles for healthful living, both from the medical and the psychological standpoints. The physical strength and well-being of the body is never despised or dismissed, but is aptly summarized by the apostle's prayer: "Beloved, I wish above all things that thou mayest prosper and be in health, even as thy soul prospereth" (III Jn 2).

The law of Moses set forth specific regulations which served to prevent disease and continues to be "a model of sanitary and hygienic insight" (R. K. Harrison, "Healing, Health," IDB, II, 542). The Mosaic sanitary code provided for periodic physical rest through observance of the sabbath; dietary rules which diminished the possibility of tapeworm infestation and such diseases as trichinosis and tularemia; sexual prophylaxis and prohibitions against incestuous relationships common among neighboring peoples; cleanliness through washing the body and clothing; and sanitary procedures for armies in the field that prevented the outbreak of epidemics of infectious diseases (Deut 23:12-13).

Prevention of psychosomatic illnesses is assured by obedience to the Word of God. "Pleasant words are as an honeycomb, sweet to the soul, and health to the bones" (Prov 16:24; cf. 3:8; 4:22; 12:18; 13:17; 15:1, 4). The concept of health includes all areas of the individual's existence—body, mind, and spirit—as the psalmist suggests: "Why art thou cast down, O my soul? and why art thou disquieted within me? Hope thou in God: for I shall yet praise him, who is the health of my countenance, and my God" (Ps 42:11). Forgiveness and cleansing from sin will bring health and healing (Jer 30:12-17; 33:6-8). The redemptive work of Christ is the greatest healing force known to man; for guilt, bitterness, hatred, envy, and other negative attitudes are removed which are in themselves sickness and cause all manner of mental and physical illness. Love is recognized by psychiatrists as "the one and only antidote that can save man from the many diseases produced by the emotions of our evil nature" (S. I. McMillen, *None of These Diseases*, p. 78). Therefore the new commandment of Christ (Jn 13:34) and the various apostolic exhortations (e.g., Eph 4:25-32; Phil 4:4-8; I Pet 3:8-12) lay the foundation for physical and mental healing and health.

Divine Healing

In addition to principles of health the Bible teaches that human beings may look to God for direct healing when other avenues of help have failed. Divine healing is a subject over which differences of opinion have existed from early in the history of the Christian church. Protestants and Roman Catholics have claimed to practice it, as well as Christian Scientists and other so-called Christian cults, along with Muslims and many of the pagan mystery religions.

All Christians agree that the Bible teaches God has healed and can heal men of every kind of disease. The fact that in the OT Miriam was healed of leprosy (Num 12:10-15) and that Christ healed many lepers (Mk 1:40-44; Lk 17:12-19) proves, in view of the fact that disease is still so difficult to handle if not still impossible to cure, that no disease is to be excepted. In proclaiming "I am the Lord, your healer," God promised the Israelites that in consequence of their obedience He would put upon them none of the diseases of the Egyptians (Ex 15:26, RSV; cf. 23:25; Ps 105:37). David could testify regarding the God-fearing man, "The Lord sustains him on his sickbed; in his illness thou healest all his infirmities" (Ps 41:3, RSV). The psalmists repeatedly prayed and thanked God for healing (Ps 6:2; 30:2; 103:3; 107:20; 147:3). Obedience to God's Word and an attitude of mercy are shown to be essential for healing and health (Ps 107:20; Prov 4:20-22; Isa 58:6-8).

Some of the healings recorded in the Bible were with means, as in the case of Hezekiah by means of a poultice of figs (II Kgs 20:2-11; cf. I Tim 5:23; Jas 5:14-15; Ex 15:23-26; Jer 8:22; I Sam 16:16; Mt 9:12). Others were without any means, as in the case of Miriam.

Certainly the Bible is not opposed to the use of means for healing, since Christ Himself considered it normal for people to go to a doctor (Mt 9:12). In the case of Asa, which has been quoted as a proof to the contrary, the "physicians" to whom Asa turned actually were equivalent to pagan magicians (II Chr 16:12). Asa's action revealed a lack of faith in God and a dependence upon men who were much like modern witch doctors. In the parable of the Good Samaritan Jesus states that oil and wine were poured on the wounds of the beaten traveler (Lk 10:34). The woman with the issue of blood suffered from a condition beyond the knowledge of the medicine of her day, and does not justify the Christian refusing proved medical remedies (Mk 5:25-26; Lk 8:43). It is significant that Paul chose Luke, a physician (Col 4:14), as his traveling companion.

There is also a class of healings in which certain additive factors have a part, though they are not of themselves actually therapeutic but rather symbolic. For example, in the healing of Naaman the leper, his stepping into the river Jordan appears to speak of faith on the part of Naaman and cleansing on the part of God (II Kgs 5:14). Also in the healing of the blind man, Jesus spit in his eyes (Mk 8:23), and for the man blind from birth, He made a salve of clay and spittle (Jn 9:6). The laying of hands upon the sick both by Jesus and by the disciples (Lk 13:11–13; Mk 6:13), and anointing the sick person with oil were symbols of the divine presence and healing power (Mk 6:13; Jas 5:14).

Various Theories of Divine Healing

These theories rest upon certain general assumptions.

1. In seeking healing we are choosing between God and the doctor. For example, A. B. Simpson wrote: "If you cannot trust the Lord, then call the doctor . . . if you can't take God's best, take God's second best" (R.V. Bingham, *The Bible and the Body*, p. 20).

The rejection of the use of remedies revealed by God to man as used in modern medicine, in favor of direct divine healing, is in itself not a reasonable act of faith in God's wonderful providence. God may lead certain individuals to glorify Him by such trust and dependence, but Scripture does not seem to indicate this need be a general rule for all believers. Many a Christian is alive today because of the discoveries of modern medicine and surgery.

2. Healing is as much a part of the salvation purchased by Christ on the cross as is the forgiveness of sins. Isa 53:4a and 5c are quoted as proof: "Surely he hath borne our griefs, and carried our sorrows . . . and with his stripes we are healed," in conjunction with Mt 8:16–17: "And he cast out the spirits with his word, and healed all that were sick: that it might be fulfilled which was spoken by Esaias the prophet, saying, Himself took our infirmities, and bare our sicknesses."

It is true that the Heb. word *ḥŏlî* translated "griefs" usually means disease or sickness, and the word *mak'ōbôth* connotes pain whether physical or mental. A. J. Gordon supported the view of healing in the atonement in *The Ministry of Healing* when he wrote: "Something more than sympathetic fellowship with our sufferings is evidently referred to here. The yoke of His cross by which He lifted our iniquities took hold also of our diseases; so that it is in some sense true that as God 'made him to be sin for us who knew no sin,' He also made Him to be sick for us who knew no sickness. . . . The passage seems to teach that Christ endured vicariously our diseases as well as our iniquities" (pp. 16–17).

Most evangelicals disagree, however, with such an exegesis. They feel the passages referred to only prove that Christ bore our sicknesses as a heavy load of sorrow. It is true that the Gr. word *bastazō* used in Mt 8:17 is used of bearing burdens (Gal 6:2; Rom 15:1) and by Galen of removing disease (Arndt, p. 137), but never of Christ's bearing imputed sin. Yet in only one other place in the NT is there any suggestion of healing in the atonement. Peter in I Pet 2:24 connects "by whose stripes ye were healed" with Christ's sacrificial death on the cross, but there is no explicit mention of physical sickness. The argument is also set forth that

Christ has redeemed us from the curse of the law (Gal 3:13), of which sickness is a definite aspect (Deut 28:21–27, 59–61). Furthermore, healing as a first installment of the resurrection is promised for our mortal bodies through the indwelling Holy Spirit (Rom 8:11; cf. 6:12 *re* "mortal body").

3. That sickness is always the result of sin.

While it is true that many sicknesses are a punishment sent by God for sin; e.g., the plagues which struck Israel when they rebelled against God in the wilderness journey (Num 11:33; 14:37; 16:47; 25:8–9, 18), still some sicknesses are used by God for His own glory (Jn 9:3) and others for the good of the sufferer (II Cor 12:7–10; but *see* Thorn in the Flesh).

4. That sickness is to be attributed to the devil. Healing evangelist William Branham, for example, prayed, "Come out of him/her, thou demon of cancer." F. F. Bosworth explained disease as caused by "the oppression of the devil" (*Christ the Healer*, p. 1). He based his argument on what Peter said to the Gentiles concerning Jesus' ministry, He "went about doing good, and healing all that were oppressed of the devil" (Acts 10:38). Oral Roberts agrees with Bosworth (Oral Roberts, *If You Need Healing*, p. 16). Other passages, such as Lk 13:16, which speaks of one "whom Satan hath bound, lo, these eighteen years"; Christ's argument that He did not cast out devils by Beelzebub (Lk 11:14–23); God's permission to Satan to afflict Job with loathsome sores (Job 2:7), as well as certain references to Satan's power (Jn 12:31; Heb 2:14–15; I Jn 3:8; 5:19), are used to support the view.

While it is clear from Scripture that Satan often does inflict sickness upon men, it is equally clear that this occurs only by God's permission. God as sovereign can and does use the suffering originated by Satan and man for His own purposes and glory (Rom 8:18, 22–23, 26, 28). Many illnesses, however, stem from other causes than the direct action of Satan.

Causes of Sickness

Four main reasons for sickness can be found.

1. It is the consequence of the curse that came upon man after the Fall. In this sense, all sickness stems from man's first sin, though it does not follow that an individual's personal sickness is due to his own personal sin. The fact that there is a tree with all manner of fruits for the healing of the nations in Ezk 47:12 and Rev 22:2 does indicate sickness is the result of man's original sin, and is to be removed, even as the curse brought about by that sin will be removed (Rom 8:18–23; cf. Gen 3:18–19).

2. Ignorance and carelessness. There are many cases where sickness is caused by man's ignorance and also by his own carelessness. The high rate of deaths at childbirth until Semmelweis and Lister discovered antiseptics proves the former, and the constant sickness in the homes of some Christians, in contrast to the

wonderful health enjoyed by others, is often due to the latter. As the knowledge of medicine increases, sickness of many kinds decreases and the life span of man lengthens.

3. Individual sin. Sickness may be directly caused by man's sin, as in the spread of venereal disease, or chronic illnesses resulting from alcoholism. Or sickness may be sent by God as a punishment, as in the case of Uzziah's presumptuous sin (II Chr 26:19-20). Christ commanded one of the chronically ill men whom He healed, "Behold, thou art made whole: sin no more, lest a worse thing come unto thee" (Jn 5:14).

4. As a chastisement for the development of character. This particular use of disease and accident, in order to train and develop the child of God, cannot be ignored. It is the one whom the Lord loveth that He chasteneth (Heb 12:6). The believer is to count it all blessing when he enters into various trials and testings (which may include sickness), because if he bears them patiently, they will bring forth the peaceable fruit of righteousness, and he will receive the crown of life as a recompense (Jas 1:2-4, 12). Job was brought to recognize his pride and self-righteous attitude through his afflictions, and repented in dust and ashes (Job 40:4; 42:6). Paul saw his thorn in the flesh as something Satan could use to buffet him (II Cor 12:7), but also as something God used to keep him humble and to cause him to rely upon the Holy Spirit for grace and power (vv. 9-10), and therefore he rejoiced in it. The fact that sickness may be used of God to develop character, faith, and humility in His own children makes it impossible to maintain that it is always the immediate result of sin.

When Jesus not only healed the sick but also forgave them their sins, as with the paralytic borne of four (Mt 9:2-8; Mk 2:3-12; Lk 5:18-26), this in itself did not prove that man's sickness was due to his sin, or that the cures for sin and sickness are both in the cross, but that Christ was exercising His own prerogative as God to forgive sins. And it was in this light the scribes and Pharisees saw it (Mt 9:3; Mk 2:7; Lk 5:21). At the same time, that some are sick because of their sins, is true as seen above.

The fact that though Paul healed so many others (Acts 19:11-12) but he himself was not delivered, even when he prayed for it three times, shows it is God's will for some to suffer for their own good (II Cor 12:10). This further proves that healing does not depend on our faith in God alone; it is dependent on God's will. The "prayer of faith" that heals the sick, in James 5:15, is that prayer which God gives to His own, in which the child of God has the assurance, before or as he asks, that his request is in God's will and is going to be answered. This is made clear in I Jn 5:14-15 where we read: "This is the confidence that we have in him, that, if we ask any thing according to his will, he heareth us: and if we know that he hear us, whatsoever we ask, we know that we have the petitions that we desired of him."

The Healings of Christ and of the Early Church

Because sickness was not part of original creation but an evil thing, Jesus never hesitated to heal the sick. When a leper questioned if it would be His will to cleanse him of the disease, Jesus immediately banished the thought and healed the man (Mk 1:40-42). In His mission to undo the works of the devil (I Jn 3:8), He made every effort to cast out demons and heal the diseased. His ministry was therefore as much to the mind and soul as to the body. His goal was the restoration of the entire personality. Thus biblical healing includes the needs of the whole man.

In one sense Christ's healings must be regarded as in a special category. In them He demonstrated and proved that He was the Son of God. He performed them in His own peculiar power and that of the Holy Spirit which He possessed without measure. They confirmed His person as well as His power (Lk 4:14-21 with Isa 61:1-2; Mt 11:2-5; 15:30-31 with Isa 35:5-6).

The miracles and charismatic gifts of healing (I Cor 12:9, 28) of the disciples and the early church were similar, to the extent that they proved these men were true followers of Christ, and thus corroborated them and their ministry. Philip's miracles at Samaria, the healing of the lame beggar at the temple gate, and of the cripple at Lystra opened up doors of opportunity to testify of Christ (Acts 3-4; 8:6-8; 14:8-18).

On the other hand, neither Jesus' nor the apostles' miracles were simply signs; they were a salutary function of the kingdom of God. In His compassion the Lord brought actual relief to multitudes of sufferers who needed healing. The writings of leaders in the church of the first three centuries testify to the fact that prayer and exorcism as a means to healing continued to be effective, at least in part (see survey by A. Harnack, *The Mission and Expansion of Christianity*, pp. 120-146).

Both Christ, as in the case of the man born blind (Jn 9:1-38), and the apostles, as in the case of the lame man healed by Peter at the temple (Acts 3:1-11), healed some who initially had no faith of their own. Yet Christ and the apostles healed others on the basis of their faith (Mt 9:29; Mk 5:34; 10:52; Lk 7:50; 8:48; 17:19; Acts 14:9). The foregoing proves NT healings were only at times based on the faith of the one healed. The same should be true if there is genuine healing through the ministry of God's servants in our time.

See Aeneas; Demonology; Diseases; Miracles; Spiritual Gifts.

Bibliography. Paul E. Adolph, *Health Shall Spring Forth*, Chicago: Moody Press, 1956. Rowland V. Bingham, *The Bible and the Body*, 3rd ed., London: Marshall, Morgan and Scott, 1939. F. F. Bosworth, *Christ the Healer*, 7th ed. rev., Miami: F. N. Bosworth, 1948. C. B. Eavey, *Principles of Mental Health for Chris-*

tian Living, Chicago: Moody Press, 1956. Arno C. Gaebelein, *The Healing Question,* New York: Our Hope, 1925. A. J. Gordon, *The Ministry of Healing,* New York: Revell, 1882. Adolf Harnack, *The Mission and Expansion of Christianity in the First Three Centuries,* New York: Harper Torchbook, 1961. R. K. Harrison, "Healing, Health," IDB, II, 541–548. D. Martyn Lloyd-Jones, *Spiritual Depression: Its Causes and Cure,* Grand Rapids: Eerdmans, 1965. T. J. McCrossan, *Bodily Healing and the Atonement,* Youngstown, Ohio: C. Humbard, 1930. S. I. McMillen, *None of These Diseases,* Westwood, N.J.: Revell, 1963. Andrew Murray, *Divine Healing,* Fort Washington, Pa.: Christian Literature Crusade, n.d. A. Oepke, "*Iaomai,* etc.," TDNT, III, 194–215. T. C. Osborn, *Healing the Sick,* Tulsa: Osborn Evangelistic Assoc., 1959. A. P. Waterson, "Disease and Healing," NBD, pp. 316 ff.

R. A. K. and J. R.

HEAP

1. Heb. *gal,* designating stones rolled together. A heap or cairn of stones was sometimes placed over a slain person to serve as a reminder of his infamy (Josh 7:26; 8:29; II Sam 18:17); it seems to have been equivalent as a sign of disgrace to death by stoning. A heap or cairn of stones was used as a witness of a covenant between Jacob and Laban (Gen 31:46–52). A city which had become a heap of ruins was a reminder of God's judgment (II Kgs 19:25; Isa 25:2; Jer 9:11; 51:37).

2. Heb. *'î,* a heap of ruins (Ps 79:1; Jer 26:18; Mic 1:6; 3:12) and the cognate word *me'î* (Isa 17:1). The name of the city Ai was derived from this word.

3. Heb. *nēd* denotes a heap or wall of water as if held back by an invisible dike (Ex 15:8; Josh 3:13, 16; Ps 33:7; 78:13).

4. Heb. *'ărēmâ* signified anything piled up, whether grain (Ruth 3:7; Song 7:2; Hag 2:16) or agricultural produce (II Chr 31:5–9), rubbish or debris (Neh 4:2), or city ruins (Jer 50:26).

5. Heb. *tel,* the mound of level upon level of heaped-up ruins of a buried city (Deut 13:16; Josh 8:28; Jer 30:18; 49:2).

F. B. H. and J. R.

HEARING. *See* Ear.

HEART. The heart was considered by the Egyptians to be the central organ of physical life. Since the Hebrews likewise held this opinion instead of taking the liver as the principal internal organ as all Mesopotamian people did, here is undesigned evidence of the long stay of the Israelites in Egypt. Thus the word "heart" in both Heb. and Gr. came to mean that which is central. It is the seat of physical, mental, and spiritual life. It is seldom used of things; when so used, it is in the sense of midst (Ex 15:8). Only rarely is "heart" used of the physical organ (II Sam 18:14; II Kgs 9:24).

As the center of physical life, the "heart" in the sense of the whole body may be strengthened by eating and drinking (Gen 18:5; Jud 19:5; Acts 14:17; Jas 5:5). As the center of

Weighing of the heart of the scribe Ani in the afterlife, a scene from the Egyptian Book of the Dead.
BM

mental and spiritual life, the term is used in a variety of ways:

1. The inner man. In this sense, the heart has secrets and is unsearchable (Ps 44:21; Prov 25:3).

2. The mental center. The heart knows (Deut 29:4; Prov 22:17), understands (Isa 44:18; Acts 16:14), reflects (Lk 2:19), considers (Ex 7:23), and remembers (Isa 42:25).

3. The emotional center. It is the seat of joy (Isa 65:14), courage (Ps 27:14; II Sam 17:10), pain (Prov 25:20), anxiety (Prov 12:25), despair (Eccl 2:20), sorrow (Neh 2:2), and fear (Deut 28:28). Fear is also expressed by being faint or wounded (Lam 5:17; Ps 109:22).

4. The moral center. God tries the heart (Ps 17:3; Jer 12:3), sees the heart (Jer 20:12), refines the heart (Ps 26:2), and searches the heart (Jer 17:10). Man may have an evil heart (Prov 26:23), be godless in heart (Job 36:13), and perverse or deceitful in heart (Prov 11:20; 17:20). However, the work of God gives him a clean heart (Ps 51:10) and a new heart (Ezk 18:31; 36:26). The heart is also the seat of the conscience (Heb 10:22; cf. I Jn 3:19–21) and that which receives the love and peace of God (Rom 5:5; Col 3:15). It is the dwelling place of the Spirit and the Lord (II Cor 1:22; Eph 3:17). *See* Hardness of Heart; Mind.

Bibliography. Johannes Behm, "*Kardia,* etc.," TDNT, III, 605–614.

E. C. J.

HEARTH. The fire pit or depression in the dirt floor of poorer houses, discovered in many archaeological excavations. The pungent smoke from the burning wood, grass, or dried cow dung escaped through the door or a window.

1. A stove (*'āḥ*) in which Jehoiakim burned strips of the scroll of the word of God (Jer 36:22–23). *See* Brazier.

2. A pan (*kiyyôr,* Zech 12:6). The chiefs of Judah will be the pans of coals to set on fire her enemies in days to come.

3. A place of burning (*môqēd,* Ps 102:3). The bones smoulder like the place where the fire is laid.

4. A fireplace (*yāqûd,* Isa 30:14). In breaking the earthenware jar not a sherd will be found large enough to carry coals from the hearth to start another fire.

5. An altar hearth (*'arî'el,* "hearth of God"), a square, horned altar hearth (Ezk 43:15–16). Such will Jerusalem be when she is invaded, drenched with blood, and burning with the fires of God's judgments (Isa 29:1–2, ASV marg.). *See* Ariel.

H. G. S.

HEAT. Heb. *ḥōm* is used of heat in the middle of the day in contrast to other times (Gen 18:1; I Sam 11:11; II Sam 4:5); of summer in contrast to winter (Gen 8:22; Jer 17:8); of harvest time (Isa 18:4).

Heb. *ḥōreb* refers to heat, but particularly of drought (Job 30:30; Isa 4:6; 25:4; Jer 36:30).

Gr. *kauma* means scorching heat of the sun (Rev 7:16; 16:9); *kausōn* means burning heat (Mt 20:12; Lk 12:55; cf. Jas 1:11).

One of the blessings spoken of in salvation is shielding from the heat of the sun which refers to the protection and prosperity which God grants to His own both now in this life (Ps 121:6; Jer 17:8) and in the future kingdom (Isa 4:6; Rev 7:16).

HEATH. *See* Plants.

HEATHEN. *See* Gentiles; Nations; Dispersion of Mankind.

HEAVE OFFERING, HEAVE SHOULDER. *See* Sacrificial Offerings.

HEAVEN. The word heaven, or the heavens, is used in the Scriptures in a number of different senses. In the most general of these it includes all that is distinguished from the earth. When employed this way, the words heaven and earth exclude one another; but when taken together, the two embrace all the universe of God (Gen 1:1). In this sense, the term often is used metaphorically. For example, "From one end of heaven to the other" (Mt 24:31), and "from the one side of heaven unto the other" (Deut 4:32).

In a more limited sense the word is employed to describe the atmosphere which surrounds the earth. Thus we read of the "dew of heaven" (Dan 4:15), the "clouds of heaven" (Dan 7:13), and of heaven giving rain (Jas 5:18). *See* Sky. Again, the word often includes more than just that which is comprehended within the earth's atmosphere. It is used to embrace all that is visible in the expanse of the universe above man. It would be impossible to set specific limits to the visible expanse of space which stretches away to unknown heights; but as such, the term heaven includes the vast realm in which are the sun, the moon, the planets, and the stars (Gen 1:16, 17).

From the theological standpoint, unquestionably the most important use of the term heaven is with reference to the invisible realm of which the visible may be simply the fringe nearest to man. This is the heaven which is best described as God's dwelling place. Before the Christian era, the Jews divided the heavens into seven different strata, a notion which has no basis in the Scriptures, although Paul speaks of having been "caught up to the third heaven" (II Cor 12:2). Unquestionably, the apostle is speaking of the heaven which is the abiding place of God and the blessed dead. The fact that he uses the expression "third heaven" means that he was referring either to heaven in its most exalted character, or to the heaven which is reached by the souls of the blessed when they have passed through the two lower regions of the atmosphere and of outer space containing the celestial bodies. The term "heaven of heavens" (Deut 10:14; I Kgs 8:27; Ps 68:33; 148:4) literally renders the Heb. idiom for the superlative, "the highest heaven." It may express our concept of the uttermost reaches of the universe.

When we speak of heaven as God's dwelling place, or the place where His presence is made manifest, we do not transgress the doctrine of His divine omnipresence. Though the Lord speaks of coming from heaven and going to heaven, He is infinite and therefore manifests Himself where He already was. John 1:18 implies that when the Lord was on earth He was in the bosom of the Father. We simply recognize that the description of infinite divine realities must be given to finite human minds in terms they can understand. Much of the description of heaven in this its strictest sense is given in figurative terms, because it is impossible to express heavenly things except in figurative language which is often symbolical. This language, however, does not at all mean that there is nothing literal about heaven and that it is simply a state or a condition. Jesus said, "I go to prepare *a place* for you" (Jn 14:2). Christ lives forever in His glorified resurrection body. There must be a place where He dwells with His saints. *See* Abraham's Bosom; Father's House.

Certain things are clearly revealed in the Scriptures concerning heaven. Considerable attention is given to the things which are *not* to be found there. For example, there will be no marrying or giving in marriage (Lk 20:34-36). There will be no tears, death, sorrow, crying, or pain, nothing that defiles, and no more curse. There will be no night, nor will there be need for light, because the Son of God will be the light of heaven (Rev 21:4, 27; 22:3, 5).

In addition to the negative description, certain facts are delineated concerning the inhabitants and the activities of heaven. (1) Here, God is present in a special sense, dispensing judgment, grace and glory. We pray to Him as "our Father which art in heaven" (Mt 6:9; cf. also Jon 1:9; Rev 11:13; Ps 2:4; 14:2; 102:19; 103:19; Isa 33:5; 66:1). (2) Jesus Christ descended from heaven (Jn 3:13) and He was taken up into heaven (Acts 1:9-10; 3:21). He is presently at the right hand of God, making intercession for His saints (Heb 7:25; Rom 8:34), and from this place He will come again to judge the quick and the dead (Mt 24:30). (3) Redeemed souls are presently with Christ in heaven (*see* Intermediate State). At least two OT saints, Enoch and Elijah, were translated into heaven (II Kgs 2:1, 11; Heb 11:5). All the redeemed shall ultimately be in heaven in their resurrection bodies when He comes from heaven for them (I Thess 4:16-17; Rev 19:1-4). Furthermore, their treasures and rewards await the saints in heaven (Mt 5:12; I Pet 1:4; II Cor 5:1). (4) Heaven is the dwelling place of angelic beings (Mt 18:10; Eph 1:10; Heb 12:22) and from thence they go to minister to the inhabitants of the earth (Lk 2:13-15; 22:43).

See also Eternal State and Death; Jerusalem, New; New Heavens and New Earth.

Bibliography. Calvin D. Linton, "What's So Great About Heaven?" ChT, XV (Nov. 20, 1970), 163 ff. H. Harold Mare, "The New Testament Concept Regarding the Regions of Heaven with Emphasis on II Cor 12:1-4," *Grace Journal,* XI (1970), 3-12. Wilbur M. Smith, *The Biblical Doctrine of Heaven,* Chicago: Moody Press, 1968, with comprehensive bibliography. Helmut Traub and Gerhard von Rad, "*Ouranos,* etc.," TDNT, V, 497-543.

R. G. R.

HEAVINESS. A term usually signifying grief, used to translate a number of different Heb. and Gr. words. Ezra meant by "heaviness" (Ezr 9:5) his show of humiliation and grief expressed by fasting. In Prov 12:25 the word means anxiety (RSV). The Messiah will give a garment of praise instead of a spirit of fainting or despondency (Isa 61:3, JerusB). Sorrow or grief is the connotation in Ps 119:28 and Prov 10:1 (RSV), as well as in Rom 9:2 and in II Cor 2:1, where the Gr. noun *lupē* is translated "sorrow" and the corresponding verb "make sorry" or "grieve" in the following verses (2:2-7). Trials and temptations may well cause grief and distress to the believer during this present age (I Pet 1:6).

In repenting of his sins one should turn from gaiety to a downcast look or gloomy, dejected expression (Jas 4:9). Epaphroditus was "full of heaviness" (Phil 2:26), i.e., was distressed that the Philippian church had heard that he was ill. This same Gr. verb describes the deep distress of soul that Christ endured in Gethsemane (Mk 14:33).

Our expression "a heavy heart" is found in Prov 25:20, where Heb. *ra'* means "sad," as in Gen 40:7 and Neh 2:1-2.

J. R.

HEAVING AND WAVING. *See* Sacrificial Offerings.

HEBER (hē'bĕr)
1. Son of Beriah, grandson of Asher (Gen 46:17; I Chr 7:31-32). His descendants were called Heberites (Num 26:45).
2. A Kenite of the descendants of Hobab (*q.v.*), brother-in-law of Moses (Jud 4:11). Heber had separated himself from the Kenites and had settled in the plain of Zaanaim near Kedesh when Deborah was judge of Israel. She prophesied to Barak that Sisera, captain of the Canaanitish army, would be delivered into his hand. Sisera attacked Israel, but God intervened and he was defeated by Barak. Sisera attempted to flee on foot and ran to the tent of Jael (*q.v.*), wife of Heber. While he was asleep she drove a tent pin through his temples thus killing him (Jud 4).
3. Son of Mered and Jehudijah, the founder of Socho in Judah (I Chr 4:18).

4. One of the sons of Elpaal and a chief in the tribe of Benjamin (I Chr 8:17).

See also Eber.

R. H. B.

HEBREW LANGUAGE. In the NT the term "Hebrew" is applied to language, but in the OT it is only an ethnic designation. The Hebrews are referred to as speaking "the language of Canaan" (Isa 19:18) or else "the Jews' language" (Neh 13:24). Actually, Heb. was a dialect of the Canaanites, acquired by Abraham after his migration to Canaan, and employed by most of the surrounding nations, such as the Moabites, the Phoenicians, and (probably) the Philistines.

Like other Semitic languages, Heb. is made up of three-consonant roots for the most part (although some of the commonest words were only two-consonant), and variations in meaning were indicated by the vowels inserted between the consonants. Thus *kātab* meant "he wrote"; *kātebû*, "she wrote"; *yiktōb*, "he will write"; *kôtēb*, "writing"; *niktab*, "it was written"; *hiktîb*, "he caused to write"; and so forth. In each case the three root consonants are k-t-b. Pronoun objects were simply tacked on to the end of the verb; thus, "he will write them" is *yiktebēm*. This ability to express so many words in a single word-cluster enabled Heb. to convey much thought in a few words, thereby facilitating a powerful, concentrated mode of expression admirably suited both to poetry and prophetic oratory. The frequency of long vowels gave it an impressive, sonorous character, very pleasing to the ear, and well suited to convey the mood of the poet, the preacher, or the man of prayer.

The Heb. verbal system was not concerned with expressing tenses or time values as such, but rather with the mode of action, whether a complete or single action (perfect tense or state), or an incomplete or prolonged action (imperfect tense or state). The perfect most frequently referred to past actions, and yet it could refer to certain types of present (e.g., "Thus *saith* the Lord"), or even the prophetic future. The imperfect tense usually referred to present or future actions (hence, the RSV often renders as present tense those verb forms which the KJV translated as future—either interpretation is possible, depending on the context); but it could also describe continued action in past time ("he was writing") or potential action ("in order that he may write"). More extended continuous action could be expressed by a participle with a form of the verb "to be" either expressed (in the case of past or future time) or unexpressed (in the case of present time). This lack of precision in regard to time values offers occasional perplexities to one who wishes to translate into modern European languages. It stands in considerable contrast to the Gr. of the NT in this respect. Unlike Gr., Heb. also lacks a neuter gender and treats even inanimate objects or ideas as either masculine or feminine.

The fact that Heb. was originally written in consonants only, and the vowels had to be supplied by the reader in the light of the context, meant that differences of interpretation could easily result where more than one vocalization was possible. Thus the LXX, or OT Gr. translation, vocalized the consonants of h-sh-m-n in Isa 6:10 as *hushmān* ("has been made fat"), whereas the Masoretic Jewish scribes read it as *hashmēn* ("make fat!"). Cf. Mt 13:15 (lit. trans.): "The heart of this people has been made fat," which follows the LXX rendering, in contrast to the Jewish Heb. text (which was supplied with vowel points some time between A.D. 500 and 800), which reads, "Make the heart of this people fat." Usually the Jewish tradition is to be relied upon in regard to these vowel points, but occasionally a better reading is suggested by the ancient translations into Gr., Latin, or Syriac.

All the OT was composed in Heb. except

A Hebrew alphabetic inscription of Shebna, a steward, about 700 B.C., possibly the royal steward rebuked by Isaiah (22:15–16). BM

Dan 2–6 and Ezr 3–6, which were written in Aramaic. Heb. began to fall out of common usage after the 5th cen. B.C., but was still cultivated by the Jewish scholarly class, and was occasionally revived for patriotic reasons during the Jewish revolts against Rome. Much of the Midrash and Talmud, and the rabbinic commentaries on the OT as well, were composed in a later form of Heb. With the establishment of the modern state of Israel, Heb. was reinstated as the language of the Jewish population in the Holy Land, and has been developed into a precise, versatile, linguistic medium suited to modern needs.

"Hebrew" is referred to at least ten times in the NT, but it is not clear how often this term refers to the historic Heb. language and how often the Jewish dialect of Aramaic (then the *lingua franca* of the Semitic Near East) is intended. But it is significant that in every instance where a "Hebrew" word is quoted, or a saying of Jesus is recorded in His native tongue, the quotation or term is Aramaic rather than Heb. (except where the word would be identical in both languages). Cf. Jn 5:2 ("Bethzatha" or "Bethesda"); Jn 19:13 ("Gabbatha"); Jn 19:17 ("Golgotha"); Mk 5:41 ("*talitha koum*," best Gr. text); Mk 7:34 ("*ephphatha*"); and Mt 27:46 ("*lema sabachthani*," best Gr. text). Thus it may be conjectured that Paul's address to the Jerusalem mob in Acts 22 was in Heb. Aramaic rather than in Heb. itself.

G. L. A.

HEBREW OF THE HEBREWS. When Paul asserted he was "a Hebrew out of Hebrews" (Phil 3:5, Gr.), he meant more than "born of" (RSV). Using a standard Semitic idiom (e.g., "holy of holies"), he indicated the superlative degree.

HEBREW PEOPLE. The first person to be referred to as a Hebrew (*'ibrî*) in the Scripture was Abraham (Gen 14:13). His descendants derived from him the ethnic designation of "Hebrews." It would appear that he derived this label from his ancestor Eber (*'ēber*), the son of Salah, son of Arphaxad, son of Shem (Gen 11:10–14). Eber was father of Peleg, grandfather of Reu, great-grandfather of Serug, who begot Nahor, Abraham's grandfather (Gen 11:16–26).

Nevertheless it is difficult to see why no other descendant of Eber was known as an *'ibrî* besides Abraham and his posterity. On the basis of ancestry alone, all the descendants of Joktan (from whom came Arabian tribes like Hadramaut and Sheba, cf. I Chr 1:19–23) could have been called Hebrews, as well as those of Peleg, Abram's forefather (to be sure) but Nahor's as well. Yet not even Terah, Abram's father, is referred to as a "Hebrew," nor his brothers, Nahor the Younger or Haran, the father of Lot. But after Abraham had settled in Canaan, he and his descendants who were of the covenant line became known to the

Canaanites and Egyptians as "Hebrews." Potiphar's wife so referred to Joseph (Gen 39:14, 17), and he so regarded himself (Gen 40:15), referring to the Canaanite area as "the land of the Hebrews." Gen 43:32 affirms that the Egyptians refused to eat with Hebrews (Joseph's brothers who had come to Egypt to buy grain), because that was "an abomination unto the Egyptians" – probably because "every shepherd was an abomination to the Egyptians" (Gen 46:34).

In addition to his being a descendant from Eber, Abraham may have been called an *'ibrî* for another reason. The 2nd mil. B.C. cuneiform records refer to a class of migrant peoples as *Ḥabiru, Ḫabiri, Ḥapiru* or *'Apiru*, and these references occur as early as Warad-Sin and Rim-Sin of the Elamite Dynasty (*c.* 1800 B.C.). The Mari correspondence tells of 2,000 enemy troops of the Ḥapiru led by a certain Ya-pah-Adad (ANET, p. 483). Hittite and Old Babylonian texts mention them as receiving regular rations from the state, manning royal garrisons and worshiping gods invoked in suzerainty treaties (although the names of these "gods" are not given – cf. ANET, p. 206). A Nuzu tablet from about 1500 B.C. refers to a Habiru from Assyria named Mar-Idiglat ("son of the Tigris") as a volunteer slave to a local householder; another mentions a female Ḥabiru named Sin-balti ("the moon-god is my life") as a slave to a woman named Tehip-tilla (ANET, p. 220).

These names are completely pagan or idolatrous. Quite certainly none of these has any relationship to Abraham's family, and therefore could not be considered "Hebrew" in the biblical sense. The same is true of the Ḥabiri at Alalakh in N Syria, who rose to be government officials (*c.* 1450 B.C.) or chariot-owning *maryannu* in that principality.

A different situation arises in connection with the Tell el-Amarna correspondence, a file of letters addressed to Amenhotep III and Akhenaton during the 18th Dynasty (*c.* 1400–1360). *See* Amarna Letters. Invading Ḥabiri are complained of by 'Abdu-Heba king of Jerusalem as plundering all "the lands of the king" (i.e., the territory he held as a vassal of Egypt; see ANET, pp. 487 ff., Nos. 286 and 288). There are numerous other references to these invaders as *SA.GAZ* (the usual cuneiform characters for these Ḥabiri when their name was not phonetically spelled out) in correspondence from other Canaanite rulers as far to N as Syria and Phoenicia (notably Byblos). While the book of Joshua reports no collective military operations by Joshua's troops in these northerly regions, there is nothing in the account in Joshua or Judges to discourage the supposition that after receiving their allotment (Josh 19) the northern Israelite tribes, such as Asher and Naphtali, may have launched tribal expeditions against the Phoenician territories contiguous to their borders.

It is certainly significant that no correspondence has been found at Tell el-Amarna from cities which fell earliest to Israelite power or influence, like Jericho, Ai, Bethel and Gibeon (*see* Exodus, The: Date). Most of the communications come from cities which according to the OT the Israelites were slow in conquering, namely, Megiddo, Ashkelon, Acco, Gezer and Jerusalem. Concerning Shechem, near which the Israelites solemnized their national covenant as they stood between Mount Ebal and Mount Gerizim, 'Abdu-Heba complained that Labayu of Shechem had gone over to the side of the 'Apiru (ANET, p. 489, No. 289).

In the light of the foregoing evidence it seems reasonable to conclude that the term *Ḥabiru* was a general designation originally for migrant peoples who had crossed over national boundaries (from the verb *'ābar,* "pass through, cross over," which may well have been represented by *ḥābiru,* corresponding to the participial form *'ôber)* as nomads or itinerant laborers, whatever their ethnic background may have been. As a migrant from Haran and Ur, then, Abraham would have been considered a *ḥabiru* by the Canaanites, and thus have acquired this label as a sort of surname. Presumably his descendants retained it in later generations, even through the four centuries in Egypt, and were so known at the time of the conquest under Joshua *c.* 1400 B.C.

The wider use of the term remained current as well. In 15th cen. Ugarit in N Syria, the city of Aleppo was still known as Halbu of the *'Apiru,* from which corvee labor was required for the service of the king of Ugarit. The Egyptian references to the *'Apiru* begin with the reign of Thutmose III (1504–1450 B.C.), as witness the tombs of Puyemrē and Antef (who were high officials during his reign); then in the Memphis stela of his son Amenhotep II, who claims to have captured 3,600 'Apiru in battle. Seti I encountered 'Apiru in Jarmuth or Yeroham (*c.* 1310 B.C.); Rameses III dedicated 'Apiru slaves to the temple of Amon in Heliopolis (ANET, p. 261); whereas Rameses IV mentions 800 'Apiru of the bowmen of the Antiu, which implies that they were mercenary soldiers. These Egyptian references can only be understood as immigrants into Canaan, in the more general sense of the term Ḥabiru, rather than as specifically Hebrews or Israelites.

So far as the biblical record goes, the Israelites were commonly referred to as *'ibrîm* by the Egyptians all during the Mosaic period, and the term carries with it covenantal connotations. Moses was quoted as referring to Yahweh as the God of the Hebrews (*'ibrîm*) (Ex 5:3; 7:16; 9:1, 13; 10:3). Under the law a "Hebrew servant" was to be treated with consideration, and to be granted manumission by the seventh year of his servitude (Deut 15:12; cf. Jer 34:9, where there was a move to implement this merciful provision). In the later period of the judges the Philistines are quoted as calling the Israelites by this term quite consistently; in their lips

it appears as a purely ethnic designation, usually tinged with a note of contempt (I Sam 4:6, 9; 14:11; 29:3). After the division of the Solomonic domains into the northern kingdom of Israel and the southern kingdom of Judah (*c.* 930 B.C.), the term Hebrew was occasionally used by Israelites as they identified themselves ethnically in dealings with other nations. Thus Jonah, in explaining to the sailors from Joppa what his religious and national background was, said, "I am a Hebrew, and I worship Yahweh, the God of heaven, who made the sea and the land" (Jon 1:9, JerusB).

In the NT the term *Hebraisti* seems to refer to the Jewish dialect of Aramaic (thus the "Hebrew" name for Calvary is given in Jn 19:17 as Golgothā, a distinctively Aramaic formation with the final emphatic -ā; likewise *gabbathā,* the paved area on which Pilate's judgment throne was set up). Hence the consciousness of nationality was based upon a covenant commitment to Israel's God, rather than upon the language they spoke. In calling himself "a Hebrew of the Hebrews" (*q.v.*; Phil 3:5), Paul claimed to be a full-blooded Israelite, whose parents were both Hebrews (cf. II Cor 11:22).

The distinction between Jew and Gentile was occasionally expressed by this term Hebrew rather than by the usual *Ioudaioi* ("Jews"); e.g., the title of the Epistle to the Hebrews (*pros tous Hebraious*). Or it might even indicate Palestinian Jews in contrast to those of the Dispersion, as in Acts 6:1, which uses the terms *Hebraioi* and *Hellēnistai* for these two groups within the Jerusalem church. Here the term is not only ethnic, but also geographical and cultural. Yet in later times the scope of *Hebraioi* was enlarged, by some writers at least, to include even Jews of the Diaspora. Eusebius of Caesarea in the 4th cen. A.D. referred to Philo, the Alexandrian Jew, as *Hebraiòs (Eccl. Hist.* 2.4, 2), or at least as a descendant of *Hebraioi.* He likewise spoke of Aristobulus (in *Praepar. Evang.* 8.8, 34), who was a Greek-speaking scholar of the Dispersion.

The Heb. language fell into relative disuse during the post-Exilic period, during which a Jewish dialect of Aramaic prevailed among the Jews even in Palestine. Nevertheless the Heb. Scriptures were held in high esteem and were publicly read at every synagogue service – even if they had to be interpreted into Aramaic (the origin of the later written Targums). Moreover, there seems to have been some restricted use of the authentic Heb. language among scholars and students of the Bible, for only continual use as a living speech could account for the development of the Mishnaic type of Heb. found in the Dead Sea Scrolls, especially the Copper Scroll of Cave Three. The letters and legal documents from the second revolt (*c.* A.D. 135) were often couched in Heb., as might be expected in a time of intense nationalistic fervor. Interestingly enough, one such letter in Heb.

seems to have been preserved from Bar Kochba himself, the false Messiah of that unsuccessful uprising. Thus there is a sense in which the Heb. language, especially as enshrined in the sacred Scriptures, was a necessary concomitant for the Heb. people to maintain their consciousness of nationhood, despite the adoption of Aram. or Gr. as the household speech. Always they looked to the Heb. OT as the basis of their status as a covenant people, especially chosen by God to be His own. This linguistic association ultimately proved decisive in modern times, when the Heb. language was deliberately revived and enforced by the founders of modern Israel as the obligatory tongue for all of their citizens.

For history of the Heb. people *see* Nations; Patriarchal Age; Exodus, The; Israel; Israel, Kingdom of; Jew; Judah, Kingdom of; Captivity; Restoration, The. For language *see* Hebrew Language. For religion *see* Covenant; Festivals; Law of Moses; Priest, Priesthood.

Bibliography. G. L. Archer, SOTI, pp. 253–259. John Bright, "Hebrew Religion, History of," IDB, II, 560–570. E. F. Campbell, "The Amarna Letters and the Amarna Period," BA, XXIII (1960), 13–15. Moshe Greenberg, *The Hab|piru,* New Haven: American Oriental Society, 1955. M. G. Kline, "The Ḥa-BI-ru – Kin or Foe of Israel?" WTJ, XIX (1956–7), 1–24, 170–184, XX (1957), 46–70. Julius Lewy, "Origin and Signification of the Biblical Term 'Hebrew,' " HUCA, XXVIII (1957), 1–13. S. Moscati, *Ancient Semitic Civilizations,* New York: Putnam, 1960, pp. 124–166, 242 f. H. H. Rowley, *From Joseph to Joshua,* London: British Academy, 1950, pp. 45–56. Roland de Vaux, "Le Problème des Ḥapiru," JNES, XXVII (1968), 221–228.

G. L. A.

HEBREWS, EPISTLE TO THE. An anonymous epistle of the NT, placed after those identified as Pauline and before the general epistles. It is an exhortation toward a full experience of salvation, presented in a classic Gr. rhetorical style. The epistle is unique, abounding in problems and characteristics peculiar to itself. Nevertheless it contains deep theological insight into the nature of the salvation which God provided in His Son. This is predicated upon rabbinic-type argumentation from OT institutions and statements about the salvation of God. Exhortations and useful principles for the enjoyment of salvation are found throughout. The early church was for a time in a quandary as to what to do with this epistle because of uncertainty about its origin, and contemporary Christians find it an enigma because of uncertainty concerning its meaning.

Authorship and Canonicity

Uncertainty as to author resulted in slow admission to the canon. The concerted efforts of the Church Fathers to attribute it to Paul

were more motivated by zeal for canonicity than nervousness about authorship. Having been admitted, however, its inspiration and authority are clearly attested by the church. Since authorship is not stated by the text, it is a matter of scholarly interest and not theological commitment.

When the Western church first mentioned the epistle, it said nothing about the epistle's authorship. Suggestions that Paul was the author came from the Alexandrian church; however, Origen of Alexandria concluded: "But as to who actually wrote the epistle, God knows the truth of the matter." The subsequent history of the question attests the wisdom of Origen's conclusion, for students of the issue up to the Reformation suggested as author, aside from Paul, Barnabas, Clement of Rome, and Luke.

Luther was the first to suggest Apollos. As biblical scholarship developed from the time of the Reformation, fewer and fewer scholars have held to Pauline authorship so that very few seriously defend it today. However, it continued to be homiletically convenient and is often so asserted uncritically. Also suggested as authors are Philip the deacon, Priscilla and Aquila, Aristion, Silas, Mark, and Jude.

Among the evidence presented for Pauline authorship is Peter's mention of a letter Paul wrote, possibly to Jews (II Pet 3:15–16); association with Timothy (cf. Heb 13:23) and Rome (cf. v. 24); an ending not unlike Paul's; and many points of theological agreement. The most frequently offered evidence, however, is simply tradition. This is, indeed, probably the strongest argument and not to be dismissed without reason. The fact is that Paul was the first widely suggested candidate, and he has been accepted by more people over a longer period of time than any other.

However, a great number of reasons have been posited to dismiss the traditional Pauline authorship. It did take the church a long time to suggest him, and the suggestion came from the part of the church least likely to know and without careful argumentation when the part most likely to know refrained from such. It was held traditional, moreover, during the time of least critical scholarship. Lack of signature and personal greetings and exclusive use of the LXX are unlike Paul's signed epistles. The style is unlike those in that it uses polished rhetoric, Hellenistic spirit, completed thoughts, and balanced sentences. There is also a distinct vocabulary and a peculiar theological viewpoint. Paul pictures Christ indwelling the believer, while Hebrews has Him at "the right hand of the Father"; Paul shows the law to be ethically impossible, while Hebrews argues that it is ceremonially impossible. Moreover, this epistle does not easily fit into the Pauline itinerary (cf. Heb. 13:23). The strongest argument against Pauline authorship is that it would appear impossible for the same man to acknowledge a secondary source of information

(2:3) and elsewhere insist upon primary and direct revelation (Gal 1:11-24).

Apollos is the apostolic character whose biblical description (Acts 18:24-28; I Cor 1:13; 3:4) comes closest to the type of man it took to write an epistle like Hebrews. He was a Jew from Alexandria who was "an eloquent man, well versed in the scriptures" and closely associated with Paul. First suggested by Luther, this has become the position of an increasingly great number of scholars which include T. W. Manson, W. F. Howard, C. Spicq, Alford, F. W. Farrar, and Hugh Montefiore. Yet this still does not account for omission of his name, and it seems strange that the Alexandrian church did not know and eagerly acknowledge Apollos as the author.

Date

Several statements indicate that the epistle was written during the second generation of the apostolic period, e.g., the process of transmission (2:1-4), time for growth (5:12), "former days" past (10:32), leaders dead (13:7), Timothy imprisoned (13:23). Yet the Jewish institutions were still in operation and the temple still standing (13:10-11) although they were soon to be gone (12:37) and persecution was imminent (10:32 ff.; 12:4). These factors seem to put the writing somewhere in the late A.D. 60's, c. 67-69.

Destination and Readers

It is difficult to identify the destination and readers since there are no internal or external statements. The title and OT usage have been taken as indications of a Jewish-Christian readership. But this assumption is increasingly challenged, and it has been suggested that the readers were Gentiles converted from paganism (Moffatt, E. F. Scott). Other recent scholars suggest non-Palestinian Jews (William Manson, F. F. Bruce), Essenes, or former Essenes (C. Spicq, Yadin). It is the wilderness experience of the Hebrews and the tabernacle which are featured and not the restoration state and the temple, and nothing is said of the characteristic Judaistic emphasis upon circumcision. OT quotations and references are not so obscure that they would not be understood by anyone who had studied the OT. Yet the warnings would seem to fit best Christians in danger of falling back into the practices of Judaism. Perhaps it can be assumed that, although the readers were not necessarily Jewish, they were probably Jewish or at least strongly influenced by Judaism. Rome now seems ruled out as the place of writing (see 13:24, RSV) but could be the destination.

Of greater importance than these matters, so far as interpretation of the epistle and its contemporary application, is the spiritual condition of the readers. They were converted to Christianity by those who had known Jesus (2:3 f.) and were, therefore, second generation believers. If this were not from Judaism (most likely some non-Palestinian form), they ac-

quired a strong respect for the ancient Heb. institutions and God's promises to Israel (evidently from a study of the LXX rather than by observance of temple worship in Jerusalem). They early endured significant persecution (10:32 ff.) although not as severe as that which was imminent (12:4). The crisis created in them a practical expression of their faith in ministering to their brothers—especially those most affected by the persecution (6:10; 10:34).

Despite these early experiences, they were no longer growing (5:11-6:20) and, indeed, were beginning to go back (2:1 ff.). It was not that they were consciously rebelling against the gospel of faith or purposely turning to something else, but rather taking salvation for granted and presuming upon God's grace in the sacrifice of His Son (10:26-31). They were lethargic and sluggish in regard to their faith (3:7-4:13) and susceptible to false teachings (13:7-9). They were prone to exaggerate the importance of angels (1:5-14) and the effectiveness of the law, and to depreciate the ultimacy of Christ's sacrifice (9:11-10:31) and His perfection (4:14-5:10; 7:1-8:13), as well as the worth of the ultimate reality promised to them (11:13-16). They possessed salvation but were neglecting to live it. Therefore they were in danger not only of failing to reach the fullness of their salvation but to lose its present

A third century papyrus fragment showing Hebrews 12:1-11. BM

experience. Instead of gaining the better things promised, they might lose the good things already received and be left with only the lesser things of the past.

Purpose and Argument

This epistle makes a significant contribution to NT theology, but its main purpose is not theological. The writer calls it "my word of exhortation" (13:22, RSV), and this is its goal throughout. He writes with the compassion of one who cares about the Christians as a group and has some kind of pastoral responsibility for them. He exhorts them to a determined and active practice of their salvation so that they can achieve all that salvation was meant to give and avoid the disastrous consequences of neglecting it.

What the writer is seeking to accomplish may be seen by a collective study of the warnings and then the hortatory passages. He warns his readers of the inescapable consequence of neglecting salvation (2:1–3), about missing God's rest (3:7–19), about disqualification from the rest (4:1–11), of the impossibility of return from conscious apostasy (6:4–8), and of there being no provision for deliberate and knowledgeable sin (10:26–31). Closely related to these are his exhortations: be alert, lest you drift away (2:1–4); be careful, lest you disbelieve (3:7–4:13); go on, lest you fall back (5:11–6:20); draw near, lest you walk away (10:19–39); build up, lest you fall apart (12:12–29).

Whether his readers were Jewish or Gentile, or whether it was Judaism or paganism to which they were in danger of returning, is not as clear as their current spiritual condition and the danger in which the author found them. This he compares with neither Judaism nor paganism, but with the Hebrews wandering in the wilderness between exodus from sin's bondage and entrance into the Promised Land. That condition was as impoverished and fruitless as the wilderness. Since his readers were guilty of the same kind of unbelief and disobedience as were the Hebrews of Moses' day, they were in as much danger of dying there without ever entering into the promised rest as were the Israelites of old. They were not so much like the Jews of the synagogues overworking their religion, as they were like the Hebrews of the wilderness not exercising their salvation. The purpose of Hebrews is to exhort the Christians to become active in their present experience with God's salvation so that they possess all that God has promised while it is still "today."

Outline

An Exhortation Concerning God's Salvation

Theology

The epistle's theology is so unique that much time has been spent in comparing and contrasting it with the balance of NT theology (especially Pauline). An even greater search has been made to find ideological origins in contemporary religious and philosophic systems. The first associations were made with Philo, then Gr. Gnosticism, and more recently Jewish Essenism. In each case, impressive similarities have been outweighed by more significant divergences.

The writer shows familiarity with a variety of schools of thought, but his theology is distinctly his own. Finding an analogy in the matter-ideal dualism of Platonism, he speaks of present reality as being only a shadow of ultimate reality. Thus to the Gr. dualist Hebrews presents Christ as giving access to ultimate reality in God. Another analogy comes from the Heb. fear of God. The epistle shows that Christ has pioneered the way to God in the ultimate sanctuary of heaven by means of His own atonement "once for all." So to the Jew fearful of God, Hebrews presents Christ as giving bold access into the very presence of God.

The theological concepts of the epistle are all applications of these basic presuppositions: Christ gives access to reality and access to God. No theological concern is developed which does not make a conceptual contribution to the exhortation to live God's salvation.

Christology is important because the concept of perfection grows from soteriology which is based solidly on Christology. Salvation is great because it was provided in the person of God's Son. This epistle has one of the highest concepts of the Sonship of Christ to be found anywhere in the Bible. The Son is superior to patriarchs, prophets, and even the rabbinicly exaggerated angels. And yet the Son of God identifies Himself with man by becoming man. The believer, then, becomes a brother of the Son of God and therefore himself a son of God.

The Son became the ultimate and perfect Priest for all men (rather than exclusively on behalf of the people of the old covenant). He is the ultimate Priest because His atonement need never be repeated year after year and for the same sins, but was done "once for all." He is the perfect Saviour-Priest because He actually accomplished the real removal of sin and the redemption of the sinner rather than covering over what still remains in the consciousness. Maintaining the figure of the Day of Atonement, Jesus is pictured as a High Priest. To show His unique priesthood, the writer calls Him a Melchizedekian Priest by analogy.

The soteriology of Hebrews does not picture salvation as a goal for the lost or a possession of the believer, but exhorts the Christian to make use of his salvation. While the crucifixion and resurrection are effectively assumed and clearly implied, Hebrews focuses upon the sacrifice not as the victim is slain on the altar but as the sacrifice is carried into the holiest (the Father's right hand) and mediated by constant intercession. Salvation is described in ceremonial (ultimate priesthood) and forensic (new covenant) terms rather than ethical (Paul). Hebrews, then, shows the high priest taking the blood of the victim from the altar through the temple veil into the holiest year after year as superseded by Jesus taking His own sacrifice from the cross through the veil between imperfect reality and ultimate reality into heaven once for all.

Sanctification is described in terms highly peculiar to this epistle, and centers around a concept of perfection which is reminiscent of the Platonic dissatisfaction with the incompleteness of the present and anticipation of the ultimateness of the future. The goal of God's salvation is God's rest, which is variously spoken of as arrival at one's destination, as completion of one's task, and as peace with God. The rest of God can, then, be defined as perfect and eternal fellowship with God. But perfection and rest are conceived in dynamic terms so that the believer is always to be in the process of perfection and arriving at his rest. Perfection is not an award to be clutched but an experience to be pursued. Apostasy is to be feared because it is not the loss of a possession but of experience.

Hebrews does not debate eternal security, since the readers were thoroughly convinced of this and indeed were presuming upon it to the point of neglecting the present experience of salvation. Apostasy, he shows, is the failure to be in the process of being saved from sin. When one is not being saved from present sin, he is not experiencing salvation. If one persists in this condition long enough, he will become so hardened that he will never again return to that previous experience of being in the process of being saved.

Rather than faulting the writer with lack of appreciation for the reception of salvation, he should be credited with taking seriously its utilization. He does not teach eternal security, because it is unnecessary to do so. Rather than putting his readers at ease in regard to the end, he puts them in the wholesome tension between security about eternity and loss in the present, and this tension allows possession of the former and avoidance of the latter while assuring a full salvation from inception to culmination.

Bibliography. William Barclay, *The Letter to the Hebrews,* Philadelphia: Westminster Press, 1957. F. F. Bruce, *The Epistle to the Hebrews,* NIC, Grand Rapids: Eerdmans, 1964. Marcus Dods, "The Epistle to the Hebrews," EGT, IV, Grand Rapids: Eerdmans reprint, 1956. William Manson, *The Epistle to the Hebrews,* London: Hodder & Stoughton, 1951. Andrew Murray, *The Holiest of All,* London: Nisbet & Co., n.d. (devotional). Alexander Nairne, *The Epistle to the Hebrews,* Cambridge: Univ. Press, 1921. William R. Newell, *Hebrews Verse by Verse,* Chicago: Moody Press, 1947. John Owen, *Hebrews: The Epistle of Warning,* Grand Rapids: Kregel, 1953 (condensation of Owen's 8 vol. work). Adolph Saphir, *The Epistle to the Hebrews,* 2 vols., New York: Loizeaux Bros., n.d. (warm exposition by a Jewish Christian teacher). B. F. Westcott, *The Epistle to the Hebrews,* Grand Rapids: Eerdmans reprint, 1950. Ronald Williamson, *Philo and the Epistle to the Hebrews,* Leiden: Brill, 1970.

W. A.

HEBRON (hē'brŭn)

1. The third named son of Kohath, the son of Levi (Ex 6:18; Num 3:19, 27; I Chr 6:2, 18; 23:12). His descendants were called Hebronites (Num 3:27; 26:58; I Chr 26:23, 30–31).

2. A descendant of Caleb (I Chr 2:42–43).

3. A very old city 19 miles SSW of Jerusalem on the road to Beer-sheba via Bethlehem. It is 3,040 feet above sea level, the highest town in Palestine. It was originally called Kiriath-arba ("town of Arba" or "town of the four," referring either to a great hero of the Anakim [Josh 14:15] or, taking *'arba'* as a numeral, to the four clans living there, Anak and his three sons [Josh 15:14]). The name Kiriath-arba may have suggested a curious legend that Adam was buried here, and that Abraham, Isaac and Jacob wished to be buried alongside him. Num 13:22 speaks of Hebron as built or rebuilt seven years before Zoan (or Avaris, Ps 78:12) in Egypt. Some scholars believe that this verse implies a connection with

the Hyksos *(q.v.),* who built their capital in the NE delta of Egypt at Avaris *c.* 1700 B.C.

The chief fame of Hebron rests in the fact that Abram dwelt much of the time at Mamre in its environs (Gen 13:18). He was living here when the confederacy of kings overthrew the cities of the plain and captured Lot (Gen 14:1-13). At Hebron his name was changed to Abraham. Here too he entertained the celestial visitors who spoke of the birth of Isaac (Gen 18:1-15). Sarah died at Hebron (Gen 23:2) and Abraham bought the cave of Machpelah nearby as a burial place (Gen 23:9). Ephron the Hittite and "the children of Heth" (Gen 23:5, 10) probably have no racial or political connection with the powerful Indo-European Hittites *(q.v.).* Isaac lived at Hebron (Gen 35:27). Later, Joseph was sent to his brethren by Jacob from that region (Gen 37:14). Abraham, Sarah, Isaac, Rebekah, Jacob and Leah (Gen 49:31; 50:13) were all buried in the cave which Abraham had purchased near Hebron.

The 12 Heb. spies saw Hebron (Num 13:22). Joshua slew the king of the town during the period of conquest (Josh 10:3-27). Caleb claimed it as his inheritance and drove out the Anakim (Josh 14:12-15; 15:13-14). Hebron was assigned to be a city of refuge (Josh 20:7). David was well received by the Hebronites (I Sam 30:31) and reigned as king there for seven and one-half years (II Sam 5:5). Absalom's revolt began in Hebron (II Sam 15:7-12). Rehoboam fortified it as one of the bastion cities to protect his S and W frontier against Egyptian invasion such as that of Shishak (II Chr 11:5, 10; 12:2-4). Royal stamped jar handles of the 8th and 7th cen. B.C., which name Hebron among four cities, suggest that it was the key storage city for army rations in the military defense system initiated by King Uzziah (II Chr 26:10; Y. Yadin, "The Fourfold Division of Judah," BASOR #163, pp. 6-12).

Some of the Jews in the post-Exilic period preferred to live in Hebron (Kiriath-arba) and its surrounding hamlets rather than move to Jerusalem (Neh 11:25). Later the Idumeans occupied Hebron until Judas Maccabaeus captured it (I Macc 5:65). During the first Jewish revolt it was held briefly by Simon bar-Giora, but was attacked and burned by the Romans (Jos *Wars* iv.9. 7, 9).

The present town is known to the Arabs as el-Khalil ("the friend," referring to Abraham as the friend of God; cf. Isa 41:8 and Jas 2:23). It surrounds the sacred Moslem enclosure or Haram, with a large mosque over the traditional site of the cave of Machpelah. The reputation of Hebron is that of great conservatism and almost fanatical dedication to Islam.

A hill to the W of the present city, called Jebel er-Rumeideh, was the site of Hebron up to the time of the Crusades. In 1964 Phillip C. Hammond began excavations which uncovered evidence of occupation from *c.* 3000 B.C., a city wall of the entire Middle Bronze Age (*c.* 2000-1550 B.C.), material from the 15th cen.

B.C., stratified remains of the Israelite period, and evidence from late Roman, Byzantine, and Islamic times (BA, XXVIII [1965], 30-32).

W. C. and J. R.

HEBRONITES (hē'brŏn-īts). A family of Levites, descendants of Hebron, the third son of Kohath (Num 3:27; 26:58; I Chr 26:23, 30-31). *See also* Hebron.

HEDGE. In the NT, a fence of any kind (Mk 12:1; Lk 14:23). The OT uses two Heb. roots, one signifying a stone wall (*gdr,* Ps 80:12; 89:40; Eccl 10:8; Nah 3:17); the other, a thorn hedge (*śûk,* Prov 15:19; Hos 2:6). Hedges were planted to protect vineyards (Isa 5:5). The verb "hedge in," "hedge about" has been used to express God's protection (Job 1:10) or His constraint (Job 3:23). *See* Fence; Plants: Hedge.

HEDGEHOG. *See* Animals, II.18.

HEEL, LIFTED UP HIS. The expression "hath lifted up his heel against me" (Ps 41:9; lit., "made great the heel against me") refers to the treachery of one's closest and most trusted friend. That some such rendering is what the psalmist meant seems clear from the LXX and from the independent translation into Gr. found in Jesus' quotation of the verse in Jn 13:18 as He applied it to Judas Iscariot. Thus Mitchell Dahood's translation of Ps 41:10 (9) in the Anchor Bible, "spun slanderous tales about me," is not a likely one.

HEGAI (hĕg'ī). The officer of King Ahasuerus in charge of the fair virgins from whom the successor to Vashti, the deposed queen, was to be taken (Est 2:8, 15). The name is also spelled Hege (Est 2:3).

HEGE (hĕg'ī). Same as Hegai *(q.v.).*

HEGLAM (hĕg'lăm). An alternate name for Gera *(q.v.),* a son of Ehud (I Chr 8:7, RSV). However, KJV, ASV, JerusB, and Anchor

Hebron. HFV

Bible all treat the name as a verb and translate "he removed them," "he led them into exile," etc.

HEIFER. *See* Animals: Cattle, I.6.

HEIFER, RED. *See* Sacrificial Offerings.

HEIR. *See* Inheritance.

HELAH (hē'lá). A wife of Ashur, a descendant of Hur (I Chr 4:5, 7).

HELAM (hē'lám). A town E of the Jordan River, probably on the southern border of Syria. David's commander Joab defeated the Syrian allies of Ammon here (II Sam 10:16-17). This city seems to appear in the Egyptian Execration texts (BASOR #83, p. 33), and probably is the same as the Alama of I Macc 5:26, which may be modern 'Alma in the plain of Hauran.

HELBAH (hĕl'bá). A town in the tribal territory of Asher (Jud 1:31). Its exact location is unknown. It is possibly Ahlab on the Mediterranean coast N of Tyre.

HELBON (hĕl'bŏn). A town in Syria *c.* 15 miles NNW of Damascus, famous in ancient times for the excellency of its wine (Ezk 27:18). It is modern Ḥalbûn, lying in a steep valley. It is still known for the extensive vineyards on its nearby slopes.

HELDAI (hĕl'dī)
1. A hero under David, Heldai was the captain over the temple services for the 12th month (I Chr 27:15). His name also appears as Heled (*q.v.;* I Chr 11:30) and as Heleb (*q.v.;* II Sam 23:29).
2. One who returned from the Exile in the time of Zerubbabel (*c.* 520 B.C.). His name also appears as Helem (*q.v.;* Zech 6:14) as well as Heldai (Zech 6:10).

HELEB (hē'lĕb). Son of Baanah the Netophathite, one of David's mighty men (II Sam 23:29). Called Heled in I Chr 11:30 (*q.v.*). *See also* Heldai 1.

HELED (hē'lĕd). Found only in I Chr 11:30. *See* Heleb; Heldai 1.

HELEK (hē'lĕk), **HELEKITES** (hē'lĕ-kīts). Second son of Gilead of the tribe of Manasseh and the founder of the family of Helekites (Num 26:30; Josh 17:2).

HELEM (hē'lĕm)
1. A great-grandson of Asher (I Chr 7:35). He is called Hotham (*q.v.*) in I Chr 7:32.
2. The same as Heldai 2 (*q.v.*).

HELEPH (hē'lĕf). A border town of Naphtali near Mount Tabor (Josh 19:33). Its exact site is uncertain.

HELEZ (hē'lĕz)
1. A descendant of Judah of the Jerahmeelite clan (I Chr 2:39).
2. A commander over 24,000 soldiers of David's army in charge of the 7th course. He is identified as being of the tribe of Ephraim (I Chr 27:10). His village may be indicated by the adjectives "Paltite" (II Sam 23:26) and "Pelonite" (I Chr 11:27; 27:10), but neither term refers to a known village; they refer to Beth-pelet near Beer-sheba in southern Judah.

HELI (hē'lī). This is the Gr. form of the Heb. name *'Elî.*

He was the father of Joseph, the husband of Mary, according to the unpunctuated text of the genealogy of Jesus as given by Luke (3:23). The verse, however, may be translated to read: "And when He began His ministry, Jesus Himself was about thirty years of age, being supposedly the son of Joseph, the son of Heli" (NASB). R. C. H. Lenski punctuates the key phrase, "being a son (as was supposed) of Joseph) of Heli." The term *hōs enomizeto,* "as was supposed," may have the sense of "according to custom." As Norval Geldenhuys comments, "Because it was not customary (among the Romans as well as among the Jews) to insert the name of a woman in a lineage list, [Luke] added the words '(as was supposed) the son of Joseph.' He was not afraid that his readers would get the impression that the genealogical tree was that of Joseph and not that of Mary, for in Luke 1 and 2 he had pointed out expressly that Jesus was solely the son of Mary and not of Joseph and Mary" (*Commentary on the Gospel of Luke,* p. 151; see also his further arguments, pp. 150-155). Thus Heli was the father-in-law of Joseph and the maternal grandfather of Jesus.

                                                        J. R.

HELKAI (hĕl'kī). A priest of the family of Meraioth (Neh 12:15), in the high priesthood of Joiakim in the early years of the 5th cen. B.C. This is probably an abbreviation of the name Hilkiah (Neh 8:4).

HELKATH (hĕl'kăth). A city of Asher on the southern border near Mount Carmel (Josh 19:25). It was assigned to the Levitical family of Gershon (Josh 21:31). The exact site is unknown. In I Chr 6:75 it is called Hukok (*q.v.*).

HELKATH-HAZZURIM (hĕl'kăth-hăzh'ŏo-rĭm; "the field of sword edges"). A field at the pool of Gibeon where David's army led by Joab met Ishbosheth's army led by Abner. Twelve men from each army killed each other in individual combat, after which David's army routed the forces of Ishbosheth (II Sam 2:16).

HELL. In common and theological usage, the place of future punishment of the wicked dead. However, since the KJV uses "hell" to signify the grave and the place of disembodied spirits, both good and bad, care must be taken to prevent mistakes and confusion.

Hell, in the sense of a place of future punishment, is certainly distinctly taught in the Bible. Though the doctrine is not nearly so clearly expressed in the OT as in the NT, it is suggested in such passages as Isa 14:9–11 (cf. Ezk 32:21 ff.); Num 16:33; Deut 32:22; Job 24:19; Ps 9:17; Isa 33:14; Dan 12:2. In the NT is Christ, our beloved Saviour, who gives the fullest teaching about hell. Only from the One who loved men enough to die for them can men receive this terrible truth. Paul accepts the doctrine but does not dwell upon it or expound it. The apostle John adds details in the book of Revelation (20:10, 15).

If some object that the teaching of everlasting hell fire cannot be meant to be taken literally, the least that we can conclude is that such words and descriptions as given are metaphors to express the terrible agonies of the soul as it suffers endless remorse in eternity to come, when separated from God and all that is good and confined with all that are bad. Even in this life the agonies of the mind can equal if not exceed those of the body. The biblical teaching of hell cannot be denied without assuming either that Christ knew no better, or knew better but still taught it. If He knew no better, how then does He know enough for us to trust Him to save us? If He knew better but still taught it, He used deception and was not holy enough to die for us.

The four words translated "hell" are:

1. *Sheol.* Two possible derivations of the Heb. word *shĕ'ōl* have been suggested: *shā'al,* "to ask or inquire," and *shō'al,* "hollow" (cf. Isa 40:12, "hollow of his hand," and Num 22:24, "the path [or hollow] of the vineyards"). In postbiblical Heb. the latter word is used for the "deep" of the sea. In the OT *sheol* is used of the grave (Job 17:13; Ps 16:10; Isa 38:10) and of the place of the dead both good (Gen 37:35; Job 14:13; Ps 6:5; Eccl 9:10) and bad (Ps 55:15; Prov 9:18). It was conceived of a world below our world where darkness, decay and forgetfulness prevail and one is remote from God (Ps 6:5; 88:3–12; Isa 38:18).

2. *Hadēs,* the Gr. word which corresponds most closely to *sheol,* and the name of the Gr. god of the underworld. Christ taught that the realm of departed human spirits is divided into two parts: the one described as Abraham's bosom to distinguish it from the other which is called Hades and is the place of the wicked dead (Lk 16:23). The KJV translates the word as "hell" in each of the ten instances of its use (Mt 11:23; 16:18; Lk 10:15; 16:23; Acts 2:27, 31; Rev 1:18; 6:8; 20:13, 14), but the RSV and NASB use the word "Hades." It seems clear that in some instances the translation "hell" in the sense of the place of punishment is satisfactory.

In Acts 2:27, 31, however, Hades is the translation of Sheol in Ps 16:10 and refers simply to the grave or death. In the passages in

Revelation Hades seems to be personified as a synonym of Death in its power over men, probably following the metaphor of Mt 16:18. The consensus of textual critics is that *hadēs* did not appear originally in I Cor 15:55.

3. *Gehenna,* the Grecized form of Heb. *gĕ' hinnōm,* the valley of Hinnom. A ravine on the S side of Jerusalem where rites of the heathen god Moloch were celebrated (I Kgs 11:7; II Chr 28:3; 33:6; Jer 7:32). Converted by Josiah into a place of abomination by the strewing of dead men's bones (II Kgs 23:13), it became the garbage and rubbish heap of Jerusalem, and as a place of continuous fires, a symbol of the place of lost spirits in torment. In every place the word is used it properly means hell (Mt 5:22, 29, 30; 10:28; 18:9; 23:15, 33; Mk 9:43, 45, 47; Lk 12:5; Jas 3:6).

4. *Tartaroō,* a Gr. verb which means "to send into Tartarus," found only in II Pet 2:4. The Greeks thought of Tartarus as a subterranean place lower than Hades where divine punishment was meted out; thus the term came to be so employed in Jewish apocalyptic literature.

Besides these four words, there are several synonyms for hell such as "unquenchable fire" (Mt 3:12); "the blackness of darkness" (Jude 13); "furnace of fire" (Mt 13:42, 50); "tormented with fire and brimstone" (Rev 14:10); "lake which burneth with fire and brimstone" (Rev 21:8); "where their worm dieth not" (Mk 9:48); the place "prepared for the devil and his angels" (Mt 25:41).

See Abyss; Dead, The; Eschatology; Eternal State and Death; Hades; Hinnom; Sheol.

R. A. K.

HELLENISTS. *See* Grecians.

HELMET. *See* Armor.

HELON (hē'lŏn). Father of Eliab, chief of the tribe of Zebulun, who was chosen to serve as an aide to Moses (Num 1:9; 2:7; 7:24, 29; 10:16).

HELP. As a verb this word means "to aid," "to assist," "to succor." Nine Heb. and six Gr. verbs are translated "help" in the KJV.

Besides its usual meaning of "assistance," a technical application is given the noun in two NT passages: (1) "Helps," Gr. plural of *boētheia,* "measures" (RSV), or a method of securing a leaking vessel by means of undergirding with chains, cables, or ropes (Acts 27:17). (2) "Helps," Gr. plural of *antilēmpsis,* "helpful deeds," one of the specific ministries in the church (I Cor 12:28), probably referring to the ministrations of the deacons, and used in the sense of "helpers" (RSV).

HELP MEET, HELPMATE. In Gen 2:18,20 the expression for the spouse for Adam consists of two Heb. words, *'ēzor kĕnegdô,* translated in KJV as "an help meet for him," in RSV as "a helper fit for him," and in JerusB as "a helpmate." The first word is the usual noun for "help" *(q.v.).* The second term means *"according to what is in front of* . . . a help *corresponding to* him, i.e., equal and adequate to himself" (BDB, p. 617). Thus the idea in "meet" is "similarity as well as supplementation" (Gerhard von Rad, *Genesis,* p. 80), the sexual, social, and intellectual counterpart of Adam to complete his being. "She was to be one who could share man's responsibilities, respond to his nature with understanding and love, and wholeheartedly cooperate with him in working out the plan of God" (WBC, p. 5).

HELVE. The wooden handle of an ax. The word is found only in Deut 19:5 ("handle" in RSV).

HEM OF A GARMENT. To remind the Israelites of their obligations to God, the law directed (Num 15:37 ff.; Deut 22:12) them to attach, with blue (i.e., blue-purple or violet) thread, tassels (KJV "hem") of twisted threads to the corners of their outer garments. Pharisees ostentatiously made theirs very large (Mt 23:5). Certain sick persons exercised their faith in reaching out from the crowds to Jesus for help. When they touched even the mere hem or fringe of His garment, they were healed (Mt 9:20–21; 14:36).

HEMAM (hē'măm). Son of Lotan, a descendant of Seir and a member of a group known as Horites (Gen 36:22). In I Chr 1:39 he is called Homam *(q.v.).* He is also called Heman in the LXX in both passages, and this spelling is used in Gen 36:22 in the RSV.

HEMAN (hē'măn)
1. RSV for Hemam (Gen 36:22), a Horite. *See* Hemam.
2. A wise man, one of the sons of Mahol (I Kgs 4:31), i.e., members of the orchestral guild or cantors (Jerusalem Bible). In I Chr 2:6 he is listed as a son of Zerah of the family of Judah. A superscription attributes Ps 88 to him.
3. One of the temple musicians in the reign of David. He was a Kohathite, son of Joel and a descendant of Samuel the prophet (I Chr 6:33; 15:17, 19; 16:41–42). He is called the seer of David (I Chr 25:5). The children of Heman also participated in the temple music services (I Chr 25:1–8; also II Chr 5:12; 29:14; 35:15). Perhaps "children" means the choir members under his direction.

HEMATH (hē'măth). A variant spelling in KJV of Hamath *(q.v.;* I Chr 13:5; Amos 6:14) and Hammath *(q.v.;* I Chr 2:55).

HEMDAN (hĕm'dăn). Son of Dishon (Gen 36:26). In the parallel genealogy of Chronicles (I Chr 1:41) he is called Amram (KJV) or Hamran (RSV) apparently because of a scribal error.

HEMLOCK. *See* Plants.

HEN. *See* Animals: Fowl, Domestic, III.14.

HENA (hĕn'á). A city conquered by Assyria, its exact location unknown. Since the name means "low" and the city is mentioned with two other cities on the Orontes River, Hamath and Arpad, Hena probably was in the same general area (II Kgs 18:34; 19:13; Isa 37:13).

HENADAD (hĕn'á-dăd). The head of a family of Levites in the post-Exilic community of Jerusalem (Ezr 3:9; Neh 3:18, 24; 10:9).

HENNA. *See* Plants.

HENOCH. *See* Hanoch; Enoch.

HEPATOSCOPY (hĕp'á-tŏs'cō-py). From the genitive *hēpatos* of Gr. *hēpar,* "liver," and *skopeō,* "to look at." This was divination based on the examination of the liver of a slain animal. It was a widespread custom among the Babylonians, Greeks, and Romans by which pagan priests ascertained guidance and prognostication. The liver *(q.v.)* was considered by some to be the seat of life; by others, as an organ which reflected the universe and its history. The prognostication was probably based upon the healthiness of the liver as indicated by its depth and uniformity of color, or its unhealthiness as revealed by lack of color and by spots, together with the element of chance in choice of a particular animal for sacrifice.

Hepatoscopy is mentioned in Ezk 21:21 as having been practiced by the king of Babylon, but was never used by the Israelites except when they degenerated to paganism. Numerous clay models of animal livers, usually bearing cuneiform inscriptions to teach temple diviners this art, have been found in Babylonia and a few at Hazor and Megiddo in Late Bronze Age Canaanite levels.

See Divination; Magic.

R. A. K.

HEPHER (hē'fẽr), **HEPHERITES** (hē'fĕ-rīts)
1. The son of Gilead and father of Zelophehad of the tribe of Manasseh. His descendants are called Hepherites. Although Zelophehad had only daughters, the inheritance was continued through them as through sons, thus keeping the family alive in Israel (Num 26:32; 27:1; Josh 17:2–3).
2. A man of the tribe of Judah and a son of Ashur by his wife Naarah (I Chr 4:6).
3. The Mecherathite, one of David's mighty men (I Chr 11:36). He may be the same as Eliphelet the Maacathite who appears in the parallel list (II Sam 23:34).
4. A city in the plain of Sharon NW of Jerusalem. The king of Hepher was conquered by Joshua and the city was used by Solomon as a store city (Josh 12:17; I Kgs 4:10). It may be Tell Ibshar near the coast S of Caesarea.

HEPHZIBAH (hĕf'zĭ-bá)

1. Wife of King Hezekiah of Judah, mother of Manasseh (II Kgs 21:1).

2. Along with the three other feminine names having descriptive meanings in Isa 62:4 (see RSV marg.)—Azubah ("forsaken"), Shemamah ("desolate"), and Beulah ("married")—Hephzibah (KJV) is given symbolically to restored Jerusalem when God will delight in His city. Following LXX, RSV and NASB here translate the term "my delight is in her."

HERALD. One who announces or proclaims a message. The word is found only once in the KJV, referring to the one who announced the king's proclamation (Dan 3:4). The RSV uses the term three times in addition to Dan 3:4. In Isa 40:9 the term is used of Zion-Jerusalem as the "herald of good tidings," while Isa 41:27 mentions a prophet sent from God as the "herald of good tidings." In II Pet 2:5 Noah is called a "herald of righteousness." *See* Ambassador; Evangelist; Messenger; Preacher.

HERB; HERBS, BITTER. *See* Plants.

HERD. Before Joshua's time, Israel was a seminomadic people. Job, a seminomadic chieftain near the Transjordanian trade routes, owned sheep, camels, oxen, and asses (Job 1:3). Even for some time after the conquest of Canaan Israel continued to be largely a pastoral and agricultural people. Usually the herd consisted

A herd of sheep along the Jabbok River. HFV

of larger animals—oxen, cattle, and asses—as contrasted with the flocks of sheep, goats, etc., as demonstrated: "Jacob divided . . . the flocks (*şō'n*), and herds (*bāqār*), and the camels (*gĕmallîm*), into two bands" (Gen 32:7). The word '*ēder* is translated "herd" in Prov 27:23; Joel 1:18. The cognate *miqneh* is translated "herd" in Gen 47:18, "flock" in Num 32:26, and "cattle" in a large number of places. The term "herd" also translates the Gr. *agelē*, used in connection with the drove of swine that charged down the cliff to their destruction near Gadara (Mt 8:30–32). *See* Animals: Cattle, I.6; Sheep, I.15.

HERDMAN. *See* Occupations: Herdman.

HERES (hĭr'ĭz).

1. Mount Heres was a mountain from which the tribe of Dan could not expel the Amorites (Jud 1:35). It was probably on the boundary between Judah and Dan.

2. In Jud 8:13 the RSV mentions Gideon's return from battle "by the ascent of Heres," but the KJV renders the passage as "before the sun was up." It is a mountain pass going up from the Jordan or from the Jabbok River.

HERESH (hĕr'ĕsh). A Levite mentioned among those returning from Exile (I Chr 9:15).

HERESY

1. This term originally meant choice. It is used in this sense only in the LXX.

2. A chosen way of thinking or course of action; hence, an opinion or view held by an individual (I Cor 11:19), or by a party, such as the Pharisees (Acts 15:5; 26:5), the Sadducees (Acts 5:17), or the Christians (Acts 24:5, 14; 28:22).

3. A dissension arising within the church because of a divergent view (I Cor 11:19; Gal 5:20).

4. A doctrinal departure from biblically revealed truth, or an erroneous view (Tit 3:10; II Pet 2:1). Paul says that heresies, in the sense of differing opinions, must needs arise as a necessary step in the development of true doctrine (I Cor 11:19). The great struggles which led to the councils of Nicea and Chalcedon illustrate this well.

The early church fought against certain dangerous doctrinal heresies and rejected those who taught them (cf. Tit 3:10).

The Judaizers. Paul wrote the books of Romans and Galatians to refute those who insisted Christianity must make a synthesis between the legalistic keeping of the law and faith in Christ. He urges the Galatians to stand fast in the liberty wherewith Christ has made them free, for "Christ is become of no effect unto you, whosoever of you are justified by the law; ye are fallen from grace" (Gal 5:4). Physical circumcision has been done away with by spiritual circumcision in Christ (Col 2:11; Phil 3:2–3).

The Gnostics. The books of Colossians and

Mount Hermon. ORINST

I John were written to refute their errors. They taught that Christ was a pantheistic emanation, lower than God, who only seemed to appear in the flesh. John asserts that he preaches a Christ whom he has seen, heard, and touched, and demands that the Christian test orthodoxy on the basis of a confession that Christ became incarnate in human flesh (I Jn 4:2–3). *See* Gnosticism.

The Syncretists. These attempted to make a synthesis between revelation and philosophy. Philo, prior to the time of Christ, tried to combine the Jewish religion with the Stoic concept of a Logos fashioned after Plato's "idea of ideas." Examples of later similar syncretistic endeavors are the union of neoplatonism and Christianity in the medieval church, the influences of which still appear in Roman Catholic views of evil; Hegelianism and Christianity in 19th cen. German liberalism; and Kierkegaardian existentialism and Christianity as seen wedded in modern neoorthodoxy.

R. A. K.

HERETIC. *See* Heresy.

HERITAGE. *See* Inheritance.

HERMAS (hûr'mȧs). A Christian at Rome greeted by Paul (Rom 16:14).

HERMES (hûr'mēz)

1. A Christian at Rome greeted by Paul (Rom 16:14). He is not to be confused with Hermas.

2. The Gr. god of eloquence who was the spokesman for the gods. At Lystra, Barnabas was called Zeus and Paul was called Hermes. The KJV translates the name as Mercurius, but the RSV retains Hermes (Acts 14:12). *See* Gods, False.

HERMOGENES (hĕr-mŏj'ŏ-nēz). One of the "all who are in Asia" who turned away from Paul in his troubles (II Tim 1:15). By being named, it appears that he was one of the leaders.

HERMON (hûr'mŏn). The name means "sacred mountain" or "consecrated place" (from *hā̆ram,* in the *hiph'il,* "to devote," "consecrate"), and probably derived its name from the Baal sanctuaries located there from ancient times, prior to the Exodus (Josh 11:17). It has been called Shenir or Senir by the Amorites, Sirion by the Sidonians (Deut 3:9), Sion (Deut 4:48) and Jebel esh-Sheik by the Arabs.

Hermon formed the northern boundary of the country which Israel took from the Amorites (Deut 3:8) and is the southern terminus of the Anti-Lebanon range. The ridge of Hermon is about 20 miles long, having three peaks that cause it to be referred to on occasion as "the Hermonites" (Ps 42:6, KJV) or "the Hermons" (ASV). Two of these peaks are more than 9,000 feet above sea level, being by far the highest peaks in or near Palestine, and are covered with snow the year around. The melting snows of Hermon constitute the principal source of the Jordan River. The highest peak of Hermon is situated about 30 miles to the SW of Damascus and 40 miles to the NE of the Sea of Galilee.

Many have believed Hermon to be the site of the transfiguration of Jesus (Mt 17:1–9; Mk 9:2, 9; Lk 9:28). About a week before the transfiguration He was in the region of Caesarea Philippi just to the S of Hermon, and it has been held more likely that He went N to the slopes of Hermon rather than SW to Mount Tabor, the traditional site.

H. L. D.

HEROD (hĕr'ŏd)

Herod the Great

The most famous of those who bore the name Herod in biblical times was Herod the Great, the progenitor of a large clan. Although his name occurs in the sacred text only in connection with the historical setting for the birth of John the Baptist (Lk 1:5) and in the account of the coming of the wise men (Mt 2), his influence on Palestine during a long reign as king of Judea was so considerable that a knowledge of his career is essential for a true understanding of NT times. The fact that Josephus devotes so much space to Herod in his *Jewish Antiquities* and in *The Jewish Wars* is proof enough of the importance this historian attached to him.

Family background. Herod was an Idumean. The country of Idumea in the S of Palestine (the Negeb) became occupied by Edomites when their former territory around Petra was taken over by the Arabs or Nabataeans. They in turn were conquered by the Hasmonean rulers of the Jews and compelled to accept Judaism, including circumcision. Herod's father, Antipater, who seems to have been the head of this nation, though his official position is not delineated by Josephus, married an Arab woman. Five children were born of this union, Herod alone bearing a Gr. name. His birth can be put at 73 B.C. or thereabouts.

Before long Antipater, a man of wealth and ambition, became involved in Jewish political affairs. At this time two brothers of the royal line, Aristobulus and Hyrcanus, were struggling for power, with the former having gained the mastery. Antipater intervened to champion the cause of Hyrcanus. It was left to the Romans, however, to settle the dispute and bring to an end the period of Jewish independence.

When Pompey arrived, Herod was about ten years old. As a lad, he gained a lively impression of the Roman military might and also witnessed the sagacity of his father Antipater as he threw his support behind the Roman regime,

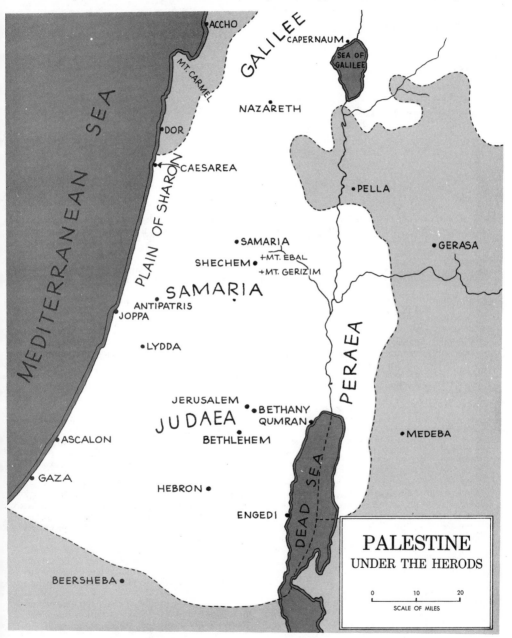

PALESTINE
UNDER THE HERODS

SCALE OF MILES

TABLE OF THE HERODIAN FAMILY

GIVING THE NAMES ONLY OF THOSE MENTIONED IN THE FOREGOING DISCUSSION AND THOSE NAMED IN THE NEW TESTAMENT.

HEROD I[1], or
HEROD THE KING, or
HEROD THE GREAT.

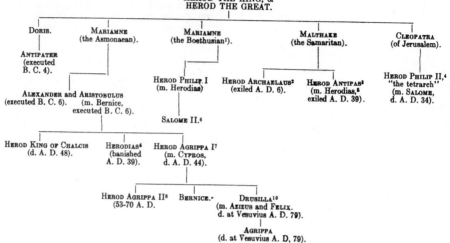

DORIS.	MARIAMNE (the Asmonaean).	MARIAMNE (the Boethusian[1]).	MALTHAKE (the Samaritan).	CLEOPATRA (of Jerusalem).

ANTIPATER (executed B. C. 4).

ALEXANDER and ARISTOBULUS (executed B. C. 6).

HEROD PHILIP I (m. Herodias)

HEROD ARCHAELAUS[2] (exiled A. D. 6).

HEROD ANTIPAS[3] (m. Herodias,[5] exiled A. D. 39).

HEROD PHILIP II,[4] "the tetrarch" (m. SALOME, d. A. D. 34).

Bernice, executed B. C. 6).

SALOME II.[6]

HEROD KING OF CHALCIS (d. A. D. 48).

HERODIAS[6] (banished A. D. 39).

HEROD AGRIPPA I[7] (m. CYPROS, d. A. D. 44).

HEROD AGRIPPA II[8] (53-70 A. D.

BERNICE.[9]

DRUSILLA[10] (m. AZIZUS and FELIX, d. at Vesuvius A. D. 79).

AGRIPPA (d. at Vesuvius A. D, 79).

[1]"Herod the King," Matt. 2; Luke 1:5. [2]Herod "Archaelaus," Luke 19:12-27; Matt. 2:22. [3]"Herod" Antipas "the tetrarch," Matt. 14:1; Luke 3:1, 19; Mark 6:14. [4]Herod "Philip" "the tetrarch," Matt. 14:1, 6; Luke 3:1, 19; 9:7; Mark 6:34. [5]"Herodias," Matt. 14:3, 6; Mark 6:17. [6]Salome, Matt. 14:6; Mark 6:22, 28; Luke 3:19. [7]"Herod" Agrippa [I] "the king," Acts 12:1, 2. [8]Herod "Agrippa" II, Acts 25:13-27; 26. [9]"Bernice," Acts 25:13, 23; 26:30. [10]"Drusilla," Acts 24:24.

and as a result was rewarded with responsibility and influence in Judean affairs. Antipater, who liked to think of himself as a Jew, could point with pride to the generous favors which a later Roman leader, Julius Caesar, bestowed on the Jewish people, since in large part these were due to the help which he gave Caesar in his Egyptian campaign.

Though Hyrcanus continued as the nominal head of the Jewish nation and occupied the office of high priest, the active control of affairs passed to Antipater, who now held the rank of procurator. It was to the great advantage of Rome to have a man like Antipater at the helm, for he knew the Jews far better than the Romans did, and he could be counted on to remain loyal to his overlords. This became the keynote of Herod's own policy in later years. However, no matter how capable and how much interested in the welfare of the Jews an Indumean might be, he could never compete in the affections of the people with one of their own number, and it was bound to be held against him that he was in the service of the hated conqueror from the W (Pompey had besieged Jerusalem, killing thousands of its inhabitants, and had even dared to enter the holy of holies of the temple).

Herod as a young man. At the age of 26 he was appointed by his father as governor or magistrate of Galilee (47 B.C.), and quickly asserted himself by ferreting out nests of brigands and putting them to death. The local people were grateful, but others in the nation, resentful

of Herod's success and popularity, persuaded Hyrcanus to call him to account for the taking of human life contrary to Jewish law. Accordingly Herod was summoned to appear before the Sanhedrin. But when this tall, handsome youth of athletic bearing, ornately clad and surrounded by an escort, appeared before this judicial body, its members were afraid to take action against him, though a majority favored it. Never being one to forget an indignity, Herod got his revenge when he came to power as king by taking the lives of these opponents.

Roman affairs were anything but tranquil during these closing days of the Republic. Caesar, Pompey, and Crassus had formed the first triumvirate in 60 B.C., but Crassus lost his life on the eastern frontier and the other two had a falling out. We have seen how the Jews profited from Caesar's dictatorship. After the assassination of Caesar, a second triumvirate was created by Mark Antony, Octavian (Caesar's nephew), and Lepidus. The first objective was to punish Brutus and Cassius for the murder of Caesar. Herod had loyalties in both directions, since Cassius was his friend and had promised him the kingship of Judea, whereas Antony was an even closer friend, if anything, so Herod could hardly expect less from him if he should emerge victorious. Antipater had been put to death by treachery, so Herod was next in line for promotion.

As long as a prince of the Hasmonean line was available, the spirit of revolution among the Jews could easily be stirred. One such remained, Antigonus the son of Aristobulus. Herod reasoned that if he could somehow overcome the disadvantage of alien blood by marriage with the royal line of the Jews, he might be more acceptable to the Jewish nation. With this in mind he became engaged to Mariamne, a Hasmonean princess, even though he was already married.

About this time Octavian and Antony emerged triumphant in their struggle, which brought Antony to the areas of Syria and Palestine to oversee matters there. Hyrcanus remained in his position as ethnarch (ruler of the nation) and high priest, but Herod and his brother Phasael were appointed tetrarchs and actually controlled the country, being responsible to the Roman authorities.

But Antigonus was active in fomenting rebellion. With Antony a victim of the charms of Cleopatra of Egypt, Herod soon found himself in a precarious position, especially when Antigonus gained the help of the warlike Parthians, who penetrated all the way to Jerusalem. Phasael and Hyrcanus allowed themselves to fall into a trap and were imprisoned. Shortly thereafter Phasael took his own life. Herod resorted to flight, placing his family and some others in the fortress of Masada just W of the Dead Sea, and making his way painfully to Rome in the hope of getting help there. In this hope he was not disappointed. Antony named him king of the Jews. Octavian was favorable also, and introduced this pro-Roman to the senate as one who could well lead their cause against Antigonus and their inveterate enemies, the Parthians. Without a dissenting voice, the senate proclaimed Herod king of Judea (40 B.C.).

Herod as king. At this point Herod was in the position of the man of whom Jesus spoke in the parable, "A nobleman went into a far country to receive kingly power and then return" (Lk 19:12, RSV), although the parable fits Archelaus even better than Herod. He had the title but not the kingdom. Landing at Ptolemais Herod gathered forces, rescued his family at Masada, and began the arduous task of subjugating the country. Galilee had a tendency to defect as soon as his back was turned, and the Roman generals who had been ordered to assist him were bribed into virtual inactivity by Antigonus. But finally he was able to get Roman aid in the form of two legions sent by Antony under the command of Sossius. Antigonus was shut up in Jerusalem. Feeling that the capture of the city was now a matter of course, Herod took time out to marry Mariamne at Samaria. After a siege of five months Jerusalem fell and Antigonus was slain. With him died the hopes of the Jewish nationalists for independence.

Herod's problems were not all solved by this victory. A new threat arose from the ambitions of Cleopatra, the ruler of Egypt. Antony, who had taken Asia as his sphere of influence, had fallen victim, like Caesar before him, to her beauty and blandishments. The wily queen in-

Statuary niches in facade of Herod's palace at New Testament Jericho. HFV

duced Antony to grant her several of Herod's cities and to insist that Herod undertake a war against the Arabs, hoping thereby to weaken both parties that she might the more readily gobble up their territories. After one serious reverse, Herod emerged from this conflict victorious.

Cleopatra's real objective was to erect a sovereign state in the Levant in opposition to the power of Rome in the W. When it became apparent that Antony had thrown in his lot with her, open war with Rome was inevitable. Herod, as the friend of Antony, was desirous of aiding him, and would have gone to battle at his side, but Cleopatra, ever jealous of Herod, would not permit it. In the sea battle at Actium (31 B.C.) Octavian was successful. Antony's army, stationed in Greece, was obliged to capitulate. Cleopatra sailed for Egypt, Antony accompanying her. Both eventually took their own lives.

Herod's loyalty to Antony now placed him in a precarious position with the conqueror. But instead of begging for mercy, he put on a bold front and openly admitted his friendship for Antony, giving the impression that he could be just as loyal and useful to Octavian as he had been to Antony. The tactics were effective. Octavian not only forgave him, but restored the cities Cleopatra had managed to detach from his realm, and eventually increased his territories by the addition of several areas to the E and NE of the Sea of Galilee.

Having cleared this hurdle, Herod seemed to be set for a long and prosperous reign, for the victory of Octavian (who became Augustus Caesar) made possible the *pax Romana*. The internal strife which had marred the latter days of the Republic was now at an end. But tragedy struck the household of the king of the Jews. His wife Mariamne became estranged from him due to the persistent nagging of her mother Alexandra. On top of this, Herod's sister Salome, bitterly jealous of the Hasmonean woman, sowed seeds of distrust in the mind of Herod concerning Mariamne's faithfulness. Although the charges were groundless, Herod

Temple to Augustus built by Herod at Caesarea.

came to believe them and finally had his wife put to death. Afterward he regretted his act and became ill with grief. His physicians thought he would die. Though time and diversionary activity brought healing, he was never the same thereafter, for the sunny side of his nature was gone. He was now a morose and suspicious man, more than ever an easy mark for the shafts of intrigue directed toward him by the women of his household in later days.

Herod found some relief for his spirit by plunging into a vast program of public works which would memorialize his energy and the magnificence of his regime. Foremost among these was the Jewish temple, which he rebuilt and enlarged, employing a thousand priests trained as masons, besides thousands of other workers. Begun in 20 B.C., it was still not wholly completed in the days of Christ. At the NW corner stood the castle of Antonia, named in honor of his old friend Antony. Herod's own palace was laid out on spacious lines and lavishly adorned. Its two wings were named in honor of Augustus Caesar and his minister Agrippa. Samaria was built up into a prominent city and fortress and was given the name Sebaste, the Gr. equivalent of Augustus. At Strato's Tower, on the Mediterranean Sea, the king put in a breakwater and thus provided a port, something the Palestinian coastline had lacked. Renamed as Caesarea, this city included in its construction a large amphitheater where games were held periodically. Some miles to the S Herod established the town of Antipatris in honor of his father, which served as a station on the route up to Jerusalem (Acts 23:31). Far to the N he erected a temple to Rome and the emperor at Paneion, the Caesarea Philippi of the Gospels. As a precaution against uprisings, at several points he built fortresses, one of which, near Jericho, he named Cypros after his mother.

By his munificence the king of the Jews reared temples in communities beyond the border of his realm, for despite the piety which he assumed toward the God of the Hebrews, he was a pagan at heart. To square himself with the Jews he asserted that as a king in the service of Rome he must fall in line with their practices. He also subsidized the Olympian games, which had fallen on evil days and needed help.

His liberality to foreign communities, which included Athens and Sparta, was partly to show his devotion to Hellenic culture and thus receive a measure of gratitude seldom extended to him by his own subjects, and partly to assist the Jews in the Dispersion. Pagan cities were less reluctant to permit the Jews in their midst to send sums of money for the temple in Jerusalem when they were recipients of donations from the king of the Jews.

Herod ruled his subjects with an iron hand. Josephus relates that on occasion he would dress as a private citizen and mingle with the crowds to learn what was being said of him. Any conspiracy was met with speedy retribution. On the other hand, in a year of dearth and threatened famine, the king at great sacrifice to himself brought in grain from Egypt and saved the lives of many of his people. Josephus summarizes the two aspects of his rule by saying, "He kept his subjects submissive in two ways, namely, by fear, since he was inexorable in punishment, and by showing himself greathearted in his care of them when a crisis arose."

The outward glory of Herod's reign was offset by the domestic troubles which continued to plague him. Salome, after having disposed of Mariamne, now schemed against her two sons Aristobulus and Alexander, claiming to Herod that they were plotting against him. To offset their supposed influence, the king brought Antipater, his son by his first wife Doris, into a position of favor and prominence. Malignity thickened on both sides. Herod accused the two sons of Mariamne in the presence of Augustus. Reconciliation was only temporary. Ultimately the two young men were executed. Popular resentment at Herod's treatment of his sons made his life miserable and his position less secure than formerly.

During the final decade of his life Herod became increasingly irritable and correspondingly difficult to deal with. Augustus grew cool toward him, which hurt him in many quarters. Despite all his efforts, he continued unable to gain the support of the Pharisees. Most of all, his domestic situation worsened appreciably. Herod had a total of ten wives. Salome, his sister, was an inveterate plotter who kept the pot boiling, all in Herod's interest, she thought. Antipater was busy at the same game, and in his own interest. Herod's brother Pheroras was involved, along with Antipater, in a plot to poison Herod. This plan of Antipater was foolish, since he was named in Herod's will as his successor, and was simply impatient that the old king lingered so long. One of Herod's last acts was to order the execution of Antipater and to alter his will in favor of another son, Archelaus.

Herod's massacre of the infants of Bethlehem (Mt 2:16) near the end of his reign is strictly in keeping with two evident facts, his bloodthirstiness, which is attested by countless episodes, and his fear of possible aspirants for his throne. His mental and physical condition in these closing days of his life made a virtual madman out of him. Proof of this is forthcoming from another act of the aging king, now nearing 70. Summoning the leading men of the nation, the elders of the various communities, to meet him at Jericho, he then had them shut up in the hippodrome, giving orders to kill them when he himself passed away, that there might be general lamentation when he died. This vicious decree of a bitter and disappointed man fortunately was not carried out.

A Roman procurator attached to Syria, Sabinus by name, went up to Jerusalem and tried to get control of Herod's records and properties, bent on personal gain. He succeeded in inflaming the populace, which was augmented by crowds attending the Feast of Pentecost. The troops of Sabinus, finding themselves in grave danger, set fire to the porticoes of the temple upon which many Jews had taken up positions for combat. Varus, the governor of Syria, answering Sabinus' call for aid, marched into Judea and found the area in dire disorder. After quelling the uprisings and crucifying 2,000 Jews, he departed, leaving behind further grievance against Rome.

Augustus had a difficult decision to make. In addition to the pleas of the claimants, he had to consider the request made by 50 men who had come from Judea, backed by 8,000 more in Rome itself, that Herodian rule be abandoned and that direct Roman rule be substituted for it. Doubtless he wished to honor Herod's desires, but felt that Archelaus was young and lacking in leadership ability. To make him king would only promote dissatisfaction and friction with

the other brothers. The verdict was finally given that Archelaus should have Judea, Samaria, and Idumea, with the title of ethnarch, and might have the title king in due time if he merited it. Antipas was given Galilee and Perea. A third brother, Philip, who had followed the other two to Rome, was given Batanea, Trachonitis, Auranitis, and some additional territory.

Archelaus had the richest area, with an annual tribute equal to twice the combined revenues of the domains of his two brothers. But he proved unequal to his assignment and made some costly mistakes. For one thing, in defiance of Jewish law, he married Glaphyra, who had been the wife of his half-brother Alexander and had borne him several children. This deeply offended the Jews. By A.D. 6 his subjects had had enough, charging him with cruelty and tyranny before Caesar. Since the Samaritans joined the Jews in this, the likelihood is that the charges were well-founded. In anger Caesar sent him into exile in Gaul. Judea was placed under Roman rule, governed by a procurator, and this arrangement obtained thereafter except for a period of three years when Herod Agrippa I (q.v.) was made king of the Jews by a later emperor.

Herod Antipas

This man, who has been rated as the least attractive of the Herods, was the younger son of Herod the Great and Malthace. He is mentioned several times in the Gospels. The ministries of both John the Baptist and of Jesus occurred during his tenure of office as tetrarch of Galilee and Perea (Lk 3:1).

Originally Antipas made Sepphoris, between Nazareth and Cana, his capital, but later built for this purpose Tiberias on the Sea of Galilee,

Roman theater, Caesarea.
IIS

The pillared courtyard of Herod's palace at the Herodian, near Bethlehem HFV

naming it after the emperor Tiberius, who had succeeded Augustus.

On a visit to Rome Antipas became enamored of the wife of his half-brother Herod Philip, and before long married her (Mk 6:17). She insisted that he divorce the wife he had, the daughter of the king of Petra. When the wife learned of Antipas' intentions, she returned to her father's house. *See* Philip 2.

Not only were the Jews in general incensed by the conduct of Antipas, but John the Baptist, in particular, had the courage to charge him with sin. John could have stayed in the territory of Judea and Samaria and attacked Antipas at long range without fear of reprisal, but he dared to press his charges at close quarters, and for this was imprisoned (Mt 14; Mk 6).

Jesus was no more afraid of this Herod than was John, for when the tetrarch let it be known through Pharisaic channels that he was bent on killing Him, our Lord refused to be frightened off and went right on with His work. In calling Antipas a fox (Lk 13:31–32), Jesus was doubtless referring to the sly tactics of the ruler. After having dealt harshly with John the Baptist, he lacked the courage to deal thus with Jesus and hoped to frighten Him by threats.

Antipas was not on good terms with Pilate. Among other things Pilate had killed some of his subjects when they were bent on sacrificing at the temple (Lk 13:1). But the condescension of Pilate in sending Jesus to him as an interlude in the trial pleased him so much that his quarrel with Pilate was mended (Lk 23:12).

Now deaf to the voice of conscience, this ruler was soon to begin paying for his crimes. His troops met resounding defeat at the hand of the Arabs, and his subjects were quick to attrib-
ute this to divine retribution for his marital irregularities and his murder of John. Finally, prodded by his wife Herodias to seek from the emperor the title of king, which had lately been bestowed on Agrippa to the N and E of him, Antipas requested this boon of Caligula, the new emperor, only to be rebuffed and be banished to Gaul, where he ended his days.

Herod Philip

Not to be confused with the Herod Philip whose wife was taken by Antipas, this Herod remained a bachelor through most of his life. His domain, whose territories have already been noted, is partially indicated in Lk 3:1. Little is known of his reign beyond its generally satisfactory character. By moving among the people and providing justice on their behalf, he gained their admiration. Late in life he took as his wife Salome, the daughter of Herodias who danced before Antipas and his court. One of the memorials of his reign is Caesarea Philippi, built and named in honor of Caesar, with which his own name is coupled. *See* Philip 1.

Death was induced by a disease which may well have been cancer of the bowels. His funeral was a state occasion of great magnificence, the casket being carried to the fortress of Herodium for burial. From his large fortune he had arranged for a generous gift to the emperor and another to his wife, with lesser amounts going to his own relatives.

Estimate of Herod. On the whole this ruler must be credited with the achievement of an outwardly prosperous and relatively peaceful reign. As an administrator he possessed insight and initiative and seldom made a mistake in judgment. He sought to maintain the rights of non-Jews throughout his realm, and also to improve the condition of his Jewish subjects.

In personal character he is a fascinating subject for psychological study. He could be generous to a fault and also savagely cruel. He could be calm in a crisis and yet go to pieces when moods of depression or anger swept over him.

Of formal education he had little, but was humble enough to learn at the feet of his court teacher and diplomat, Nicolaus of Damascus, who had a great admiration for Herod and served him well on several occasions.

Herod's story bears testimony to his capacity for friendship. Some of the ablest and finest people of his time were in his circle, and his loyalty to them is one of his best traits.

But his sensuality and his secularism were his undoing. From the former he reaped the nemesis of jealousies, animosities, and killings that haunted his declining days. From the latter came his failure to understand the deeper significance of the religious faith to which he nominally subscribed.

Josephus in one place calls him "the Great," but only, it seems, in a relative sense, as superior in ability and achievement to others of his house who ruled after him.

Herod Archelaus

This son of Herod the Great and Malthace, a Samaritan, is mentioned only once in the biblical text, and that in connection with his accession to the rule over Judea following the death of his father (Mt 2:22). He was named for the king of Cappadocia, to whose daughter Herod and Mariamne's son Alexander had been married.

Herod made four wills altogether, and in the last one, executed shortly before his death, appointed Archelaus, then in his late teens, as his successor. When the will was read to the troops and townspeople of Jericho, the place of Herod's death, they acclaimed Archelaus king, although they were reminded that the will had to be ratified by Caesar before it could become effective. Actually the terms of the will did not award Herod's whole kingdom to Archelaus, but only Judea and Samaria. Galilee and Perea were awarded to Antipas, the full brother of Archelaus, and the rest of the kingdom, involving territories N and E of the Sea of Galilee, was to go to Philip their half-brother.

After seven days of mourning for his father, Archelaus spread a feast for his subjects in Jerusalem, then had a golden throne set on a platform, from which he received the plaudits of his subjects and addressed them graciously, promising to be kinder to them than his father had been. Sensing that the king was young and impressionable, the people began to press him for favors, including the diminution of taxes and the removal of some men honored by Herod, especially the high priest. The people turned to mourning for those lives which had been taken by Herod when they cut down a golden eagle he had set up in the temple area. Messengers

sent by Archelaus were unable to disperse them, the crowds having been augmented by Passover pilgrims from far and near. To forestall any outbreak, the young king sent troops to deal with the situation. Infuriated, the crowd attacked the soldiers. More troops were called out, including the cavalry. Some 3,000 people were killed before the melee ended.

Shortly thereafter, Archelaus departed for Rome to secure the approval of Augustus concerning the arrangements made by Herod. His brother Antipas likewise made the trip to dispute the will on the ground that the previous will, made when Herod was of sound mind, gave him the succession. Caesar deferred making a decision, and in the meantime things were happening in Judea which were destined to influence the final verdict.

Herod Agrippa I

Grandson of Herod the Great and son of Aristobulus, this ruler was named in honor of Agrippa, the able minister of Augustus. His early years were spent in Rome, where he had connections with the royal family. Ambition for political power was checked by lack of appointment and frustrated by financial embarrassment. After occupying minor posts in the E for a time, he returned to Rome, where he cultivated the friendship of Gaius (Caligula). An unguarded remark to his friend to the effect that he hoped Gaius would soon be emperor was reported to Tiberius, who clapped him into prison.

After the death of Tiberius and the accession of Gaius, Agrippa was given the tetrarchy of Philip, who died in A.D. 34, and was allowed to bear the title of king. When Antipas was discredited, Agrippa took over his territory also. In the following year (A.D. 41) Gaius was murdered and was succeeded by Claudius. The new emperor, out of gratitude for help rendered by Agrippa, added Judea and Samaria to his friend's realm, so now he was king of the Jews as was Herod of old.

Posing as one ardently committed to the law and the customs, Agrippa won the favor of the Jews. He risked his position by urging Gaius to give up his plan to put a statue of himself in Jerusalem and claim divine honors. His persecution of the early church and his untimely death shortly thereafter in A.D. 44 in Caesarea are noted in Acts 12.

Herod Agrippa II

At his father's death this young man was too young, in the opinion of Claudius, to be entrusted with the kingship, so direct Roman rule was imposed once again on the Jews.

A few years later Herod succeeded to the throne of the kingdom of Chalcis in Lebanon which had formerly been ruled by a kinsman. About this time Claudius granted him the right of appointing the high priest and the supervision of the temple and its funds, so he became involved in Jewish affairs. His next move took him closer to the Holy Land, as he inherited much of the realm formerly ruled by Philip. Later, Nero added some territory around the Sea of Galilee and in southern Perea. Like his father, he was called king. It was in his presence that Paul made his defense (Acts 26).

As in the case of other Herods, he ingratiated himself with pagan Gr. cities and at the same time maintained the ordinances of Judaism. He is known to have championed the cause of the Alexandrian Jews who were suffering persecution in this period.

In particular he endeavored to stem the rising tide of nationalism among the Palestinian Jews and to dissuade them from acts of violence and insubordination against Rome, even when provoked by unworthy Roman officials. In this he was unsuccessful, and when war broke out, his troops fought with the Romans against the Jews. Josephus states that Agrippa sent him more than 60 letters with information about his part in the conflict, thus assisting Josephus in his account contained in *The Jewish Wars*. Little is known of Agrippa's later years, but he probably lived until the close of the century. With his death the dynasty of Herod came to an end.

Princesses of the House of Herod

Those whose names dot the sacred record are three in number—Herodias, Bernice, and Drusilla—and their reputation is not an enviable one.

Herodias had for her father Aristobulus, who was son of Herod the Great by Mariamne. Her mother was Bernice, the daughter of Herod's sister Salome. After being married to Herod Philip, Herodias left him to be the wife of Antipas. Her hatred of John the Baptist led to the death of the prophet (Mt 14:3–11) and the deterioration in the character of Antipas. *See* Herodias.

Bernice was daughter of Herod Agrippa I. Married first to a Jewish official of Alexandria named Marcus, and then to Herod of Chalcis, she went to live with her brother Herod Agrippa II. Ugly rumors became current of her incestuous relations with him. To allay these, she became married to a certain Polemo, king of Cilicia, but returned to her brother after a short time. In the disorders at Jerusalem which preceded the outbreak of the great war with Rome, she distinguished herself by appealing to Florus, at the risk of her own life, to call off his troops and restore peace to the holy city. In Luke's account of Paul's hearing before Agrippa (Acts 25–26), Bernice appears as accompanying her brother. *See* Bernice.

Drusilla, a full sister of Bernice and Agrippa II *(q.v.)*, was slated to marry Epiphanes of Commagene, but the arrangement was called off when the prince refused to be circumcised. Azizus, king of Emesa, was willing to turn Jew to gain her hand, but the marriage did not last long because Felix, the notorious procurator who hoped to be bribed by Paul, induced her to leave her husband and marry him. Her presence with Felix is noted in Acts 24:24. *See* Drusilla.

Bibliography. Félix Marie Abel, *Histoire de la Palestine depuis la conquête d'Alexandre jusqu' à l'invasion arabe*, Paris: Gabalda, 1952, I, 287–503. F. F. Bruce, "Herod Antipas, Tetrarch of Galilee and Peraea," ALUOS, V (1963–65), 6–23. A. H. M. Jones, *The Herods of Judaea*, Oxford: Clarendon Press, 1938. Flavius Josephus, *Jewish Antiquities; The Jewish War*. Stewart Perowne, *The Life and Times of Herod the Great*, London: Hodder, 1956; *The Later Herods*, London: Hodder, 1958. E. Schürer, *A History of the Jewish People in the Time of Jesus Christ*, trans. by John Macpherson, 2nd and rev. ed., 5 vols., New York: Scribner's, 1891.

E. F. Har.

HERODIANS (hĕ-rō'dĭ-ănz). The Herodians are mentioned in three passages in the Gospels, treating two incidents, the first in Galilee (Mk 3:6) and the second in Jerusalem (Mk 12:13; Mt 22:16), where they are associated with the Pharisees in their opposition to Jesus. Apart from one reference in Josephus (*Wars* i.16.6, *hoi Hērōdeio;* cf. *Ant.* xiv.15.10, "those of Herod's party"), they are not mentioned in any other ancient source, evidence that they were not a religious sect or an organized political party.

The word is of Latin formation (*Herodiani*), indicating adherents or partisans of Herod, and describes a common attitude of allegiance to Herod in a country where large numbers of people chafed under his rule. In Josephus the term clearly denotes those who were sympathizers and supporters of his cause. It is reasonable to understand the term in the Gospels in the same light. The narratives which mention the Herodians presuppose that they were influential men of standing who loyally supported Herod Antipas. From their question concerning the tribute money (Mt 22:17), it seems clear that they were also loyal to the Roman rule upon which the Herodian dynasty depended.

W. L. L.

HERODIAS (hĕ-rō'dĭ-ăs). Daughter of Aristobulus and Bernice. Married first to Herod Philip, a private citizen, who was the son of Herod the Great and Mariamne II (not to be confused with Philip the tetrarch of Iturea in Lk 3:1, who was the son of Herod the Great and Cleopatra of Jerusalem), she left him to marry his half-brother Herod Antipas. It was because of this marriage that John the Baptist reproved Herod Antipas and was put in prison (Mt 14:3; Mk 6:17; Lk 3:19 f.). John was finally beheaded at the request of Salome, Herodias' daughter (Mt 14:8; Mk 6:24) by her first husband.

See Herod.

HERODION (hě-rō′dĭ-ŏn). A Christian to whom Paul sent greetings. Paul called him "my kinsman," which probably meant that he was a Jew in spite of the name (Rom 16:11).

HERON. *See* Animals, III.21.

HESED (hē′sěd). The father of Ben-hesed ("son of Hesed"), who was one of the 12 commissary officers of Solomon in charge of a district of Judah (I Kgs 4:10).

Heshbon. JR

HESHBON (hěsh′bŏn). Built on two small hills on the Transjordan tableland, overlooking the lower Jordan Valley, Heshbon was the capital city of Sihon, king of the Amorites, who had captured it from the Moabites (Num 21:25-30). Taken by the Israelites from Sihon when he would not allow them to pass through his land (Num 21:23-24), Heshbon was among the cities rebuilt and populated by the Reubenites and Gadites (Num 32:37; Josh 13:17, 26). It was one of the cities assigned to the Levites (Josh 21:39).

Heshbon was recaptured by Mesha of Moab and held by the Moabites in the times of Isaiah and Jeremiah (Isa 15:4; 16:8-9; Jer 48:2, 34). Apparently it fell into the hands of the Ammonites during the time of Jeremiah (Jer 49:3). It was part of the Nabatean kingdom during the Hellenistic period, but later was conquered by Alexander Janneus; it was made a garrison city in Transjordan by Herod the Great (Jos *Ant.* xiii.15.4; xv.8.5). It is known today as *Ḥesbân* and is located 17 miles SW of Amman.

Excavations were begun in 1968 at *Ḥesbân*, directed by Dr. Siegfried Horn. Ruins of a Byzantine church were uncovered in addition to much pottery from Roman and Hellenistic times. Other pottery was found representing all the times Heshbon is mentioned in the OT (Late Bronze I to Iron III).

Bibliography. Yohanan Aharoni, *The Land of the Bible,* trans. by A. F. Rainey, Philadelphia: Westminster Press, 1967, pp. 187-191. Siegfried H. Horn, "The 1968 Heshbon Expedition," BA, XXXII (May, 1969), 25-41.

F. B. H.

HESHMON (hěsh′mŏn). A town in the extreme S of Judah near Beer-sheba (Josh 15:27). The exact location is unknown.

HETH (hěth)
1. A son of Canaan (Gen 10:15; I Chr 1:13). His descendants are identified as Hittites by the KJV (Gen 23:10), and by the RSV (Gen 23:3, 5, 7; 27:46; 49:32).
2. The eighth letter of the Heb. alphabet. The eighth section of Ps 119 is headed by this letter in the KJV.

HETHLON (hěth′lŏn). A place mentioned by Ezekiel as situated on the future northern boundary of Israel (Ezk 47:15; 48:1). Its exact location is unknown; possibly it is modern Heitelâ, NE of Tripolis on the coast of Lebanon. The "way of Hethlon" may designate the route through the valley N of the Lebanon Mountain range to Kadesh-on-the-Orontes. Hethlon approximates the Mount Hor of Num 34:7, a northerly summit of the Lebanons (Y. Aharoni, *The Land of the Bible,* p. 67, n. 34).

HEW. Two basically different Heb. verbs are used, one in connection with wood and the other with stone. Heb. *ḥāṭab* means to chop down (a tree) or to cut and gather (firewood). Hewers of wood (Deut 19:5; 29:11; Josh 9:21, 23, 27; II Chr 2:10) were unskilled laborers, often slaves, whose task was menial and dull. On the other hand, Heb. *ḥāṣab* means to quarry and carve stone for building purposes (I Chr 22:2; Prov 9:1), to cut out a sepulcher (Isa 22:16), or to dig a watertight cistern (cf. Jer 2:13). The stonecutter was considered a skilled tradesman and was duly paid for his labor (II Kgs 12:11-12). *See* Occupations: Woodcutter.

HEZEKI (hěz′ě-kī). A Benjamite (I Chr 8:17). The name is transliterated Hizki in RSV.

HEZEKIAH (hěz′ě-kīà)
1. A king of Judah who reigned for 29 years (cf. II Kgs 18-20; II Chr 29-32; Isa 36-39). The chronological references are best harmonized by dating his reign from 716/15 to 687 B.C. He may have been coregent with his father Ahaz beginning *c.* 729 (II Kgs 18:1, 9-10).

The Assyrian domination of the Fertile Crescent posed the major international problem for this period. Ahaz, enthroned in Judah with the support of a pro-Assyrian party, established and maintained a policy of friendship or vassalage to Assyria while Syria and the northern kingdom capitulated. Damascus was conquered by Tiglath-pileser III in 732 B.C. and Samaria by Shalmaneser V in 723/22. Sargon II, the next king of Assyria, 722-706, advanced into Philistia to conquer Ashdod in 711. The crucial time for Judah came during the reign of the Assyrian king Sennacherib, 705-681.

The heathen influence that accompanied the Judeo-Assyrian alliance may have caused a reaction during the decade before Ahaz died.

Hezekiah began his reign with the most extensive reforms in Judah's history. Keenly conscious of the fact that the captivity of the northern kingdom was caused by the breaking of the covenant and disobedience (II Kgs 18:9–12), Hezekiah removed idolatry, repaired and cleansed the temple, restored worship, and extended invitations throughout Judah and the northern tribes for an observance of the Passover that exceeded all celebrations since the time of Solomon. Religiously this reformation was a great success.

Hezekiah also was an outstanding military leader. Anticipating Assyrian attack on Judah, he concentrated on a defense program fortifying Jerusalem. By constructing a 1,777 foot tunnel through solid rock to connect the Siloam pool or cistern—the entrance to which was enclosed within the city by extending the wall—with the spring of Gihon (q.v.) he assured Jerusalem of an adequate water supply. This tunnel was discovered in 1880 and has ever since been an attraction for tourists. With religious and military preparations at its best, Hezekiah assembled his people in the city square and boldly expressed his confidence in God for protection (II Chr 32:1–8).

Crucial were the developments for Hezekiah personally as well as nationally in 701 B.C. That year Sennacherib advanced into the maritime plain W of Jerusalem, conquering numerous cities and exacting excessive sums of tribute from Jerusalem while he besieged Lachish (II Kgs 18:13–16). Emboldened by this submission, Sennacherib sent a large army to encircle Jerusalem and demand its complete surrender, but without success. Both the Bible (II Kgs 18:17–19:8) and Sennacherib's cuneiform records agree in essence concerning this campaign.

About this time Hezekiah became critically ill so that he anticipated death. The prophet Isaiah not only assured the king of Judah that his life would be extended 15 years, but also promised relief for the kingdom from Assyrian pressure (II Kgs 20:1–7). Perhaps the Assyrians left Jerusalem on hearing a rumor of a revolt in Babylon (II Kgs 19:7). At any rate, Assyrian records show that a year later Sennacherib was occupied with suppressing the Babylonians, which ultimately led to his destroying the city of Babylon in 689 B.C.

Probably in 688, although he left no record of such a disastrous campaign, Sennacherib turned toward Egypt, being alarmed by Tirhakah, an Ethiopian king of Egypt and Nubia, from 690 to 664 (II Kgs 19:9). By letter the Assyrian king sent an ultimatum to Hezekiah, who went to the temple to pray, confident that God would deliver him again. Once more Isaiah sent word assuring Hezekiah that the Assyrians would return the way they came (II Kgs 19:9–34). Subsequently by miraculous intervention the Assyrian army—which may have been encamped en route from Babylon across the Arabian desert to Egypt—was de-

pleted by 185,000 troops. Sennacherib returned to Nineveh never to threaten Hezekiah again. In 681 Sennacherib was assassinated by two of his sons. *See* Sennacherib for alternate one campaign theory.

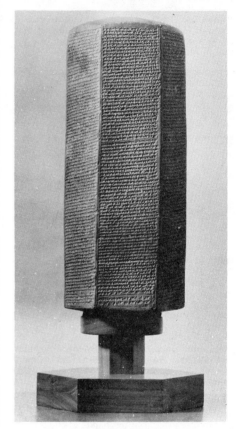

The prism of Sennacherib. ORINST

After the first crisis in 701 B.C. Hezekiah enjoyed a period of peace and prosperity. Acclaimed as the leader who had successfully withstood Assyrian aggression, Hezekiah was very likely supported politically and commercially by the surrounding nations, so that Judah enjoyed a rapid economic recovery. Hezekiah was rebuked, however, for accepting the congratulations of the Babylonians without giving witness to divine deliverance. Isaiah, who had repeatedly assured Judah of protection from Assyrian aggression, subsequently warned that ultimately the Babylonians would conquer Jerusalem, but not during Hezekiah's lifetime (Isa 39).

Hezekiah died in 686. He was succeeded by his son Manasseh, who probably had been made coregent in 696 B.C.

2. A great-great-grandfather of the prophet Zephaniah (Zeph 1:1), very likely King Hezekiah, since other prophets name only their father. (Hizkiah in KJV is spelled Hezekiah in RSV. The names are exactly the same in Heb.)

3. Ancestor of a group of exiles who returned with Zerubbabel; his Babylonian name evidently was Ater (Ezr 2:16; Neh 7:21). He is probably the same as a chief of the people who set his seal to the covenant renewal under Nehemiah (Neh 10:17; KJV, Hizkijah).

4. Son of Neariah, a descendant of the royal family of Judah (I Chr 3:23).

S. J. S.

HEZION (hē'zǐ-ŏn). The grandfather of the Syrian king Ben-hadad (q.v., I Kgs 15:18).

HEZIR (hē'zǐr)
1. The head of the 17th course of priests in the time of David (I Chr 24:15).
2. The head of a family who signed the covenant in the time of Nehemiah (Neh 10:20).

HEZRAI (hěz'rī). One of the mighty men of David. The name is found only in II Sam 23:35, but is probably the same as Hezro (q.v.).

HEZRO (hěz'rō). Found only in I Chr 11:37. It is probably the same as Hezrai (q.v.).

HEZRON (hěz'rŏn), **HEZRONITES** (hěz'-rŏ-nīts)
1. The third named of the sons of Reuben, the firstborn of Jacob (Gen 46:9; Ex 6:14; I Chr 5:3). He is the ancestor of the Hezronites (Num 26:6).
2. A son of Pharez and grandson of Judah. He was the ancestor of David through whom came Jesus (Gen 46:12; Num 26:21; Ruth 4:18–19; I Chr 2:5, 9, 18, 21, 24–25; 4:1). In Mt 1:3 he is called Esrom in KJV but Hezron in RSV.
3. A city on the southern border of Judah, between Kadesh-barnea and Adar. It is also called Hazor (Josh 15:3, 25).

HIDDAI (hǐd'ī). One of David's mighty men from the wilds near Gaash (II Sam 23:30). He is called Hurai in the parallel passage in I Chr 11:32 (q.v.). The alternate spellings probably resulted from a confusion in Heb. of r and d, and of h and ḥ, letters very similar in post-Exilic Heb.

HIDDEKEL (hǐd-dĕk'ĕl). A Heb. rendering of Akkad. Idiqlat, the second major river of Mesopotamia (Gen 2:14; Dan 10:4). The Idiqlat was called Diqlat or Diglat in Aram., Tigrā in Old Persian, and Tigris (q.v.) in Gr.

HIEL (hī'ĕl). A Bethelite (q.v.) who rebuilt Jericho in the days of Ahab (I Kgs 16:34). The curse of Joshua (Josh 6:26) was understood as applying to the sacrifices of his oldest and youngest sons.

Hierapolis, appearing as a frozen waterfall.
James L. Boyer

HIERAPOLIS (hī'ĕ-răp'ŏ-lǐs). A city built on a high terrace overlooking the valley of the Lycus River in the W part of the Roman province of Asia, about six miles N of Laodicea. It was famous for its hot springs, which made it a health resort, and for the Plutonium, a crevasse in the rock which emitted poisonous gases, supposedly the domain of the Phrygian fertility goddess Leto. The church in Hierapolis was probably founded by converts of Paul, and was associated closely with the church in Colosse (Col 4:13). Legend says that Philip the evangelist and John the apostle visited this city.

HIGGAION (hǐ-gā'yŏn). Transliteration of a Heb. term appearing only in Ps 9:16 where it is a musical note or direction. The term is translated "meditation" in Ps 19:14, "solemn sound" in Ps 92:3, and "device" in Lam 3:62.

HIGH PLACE. The original meaning was simply that of a mountain or hill top (Deut 32:13; II Sam 1:19, 25). The overwhelming proportion of uses, however, indicate sanctuaries on an elevated area. These were Canaanite in origin. They may have been used for funeral rites and certainly were often the scenes of fertility rites (Hos 4:11–14; Jer 3:6; 19:5; 48:35).

Ruins of such sanctuaries are scattered throughout Canaan (as at Petra, Bab edh-Dra, Gezer, Megiddo, Hazor, q.v.), and were apparently located near almost every village, sometimes even inside cities (Jer 7:31; 19:13; Ezk 6:3). Every such pagan shrine included in its equipment an altar of stone or earth, stone pillars (masṣēbôth, Deut 12:3; Hos 10:1), wooden poles ('ăshērîm, Ex 34:13), and a basin for ceremonial washings. Some high places possessed an image like Jeroboam's golden calf or Micah's ephod; others, some sacred object such as an ark or ephod. This required a house or temple to shelter it (Jud 17:5; I Kgs 12:31). A place for groups to eat together may also be presumed for the high places (I Sam 9:13, 22; I Kgs 3:4, 15).

Steps leading to the great high place of Petra. MIS

Since the high places were the only local places of worship in early Israel after Shiloh was destroyed, they were the scenes of many religious acts. Here sacrifices were offered (I Sam 9:13; I Kgs 3:3–4; 12:32). This meant at the same time that they were the places for slaughter of all animals to be eaten for meat, for each such slaughter was at the same time a sacrifice. In earliest times this was done by the worshiper himself. Later, priests were attached to each high place to carry out these functions properly.

To the high places tithes and offerings were brought, as men came to "inquire of the Lord" through priestly oracle or prophetic word (I Sam 9:7–12). Here, as "in the gate," justice was administered in the name of the Lord. They were very likely places of asylum supplementing the six Levitical cities. Recent research suggests that they were also mortuary shrines, sometimes achieving their fame and importance as the burial place of a hero or king, or as the place where his monument (*maṣṣēbâ*) or funerary stela (*peger*) was erected (Ezk 43:7; 6:3–6; Lev 26:30).

Undoubtedly the main significance of the high place lay in its use as a local sanctuary. Official Israelitic religion consisted in the great annual pilgrimage festivals. The carryover into every week and every day religion occurred at the high place sanctuaries. They apparently emphasized an area of concern largely ignored in official Israelitic religion: that of death and life after death. By syncretizing the law (Torah) with Canaanite ideology, apostatizing Israelites became concerned with a subject actively opposed by the official religion, that of fertility. Because of these extra-orthodox concerns and the excesses for which their celebration gave occasion, they came under the severe criticism of the prophets. While the religious reform under Hezekiah (II Kgs 18:4, 22) was undone by his son Manasseh (II Kgs 21:1–6), from the time of Josiah on (II Kgs 23:4–20) the high places were summarily condemned. Ceremonial worship was allowed only in Jerusalem.

Bibliography. W. F. Albright, "The High Place in Ancient Palestine," VT, Supplement IV (1957), 242–58; CornPBE, pp. 391–94.

D. W. W.

HIGH PRIEST. *See* Priest, High.

HIGHEST

1. Superlative of the adjective "high." It is used in the KJV in the ordinary sense of elevation (Ezk 41:7; RSV "top"), and as the translation of idioms implying quality rather than elevation; e.g., *rō'sh,* "head," translated "highest" in KJV, and "first" in RSV (Prov 8:26); *prōtoklisia,* "first couch," translated "highest" in KJV, and "place of honor" in RSV (Lk 14:8).

2. Used as a title for God in KJV (Ps 18:13; 87:5; Lk 1:32, 35, 76; 6:35). RSV translates the title as "the Most High."

The great high place or worship center of Petra. MIS

3. Used as a synonym for heaven, God's dwelling place and seat of His throne (Lk 2:14; 19:38; Mt 21:9; Mk 11:10; cf. Job 16:19), equivalent to the "third heaven" (II Cor 12:2) and the "heaven of heavens" (Deut 10:14; I Kgs 8:27; Neh 9:6; Ps 148:4).

HIGHWAY. A travel route for public use. The most frequent Heb. term used is *mᵉsillâ* (Num 20:19; Isa 7:3; 40:3; *et al.*), which means a built-up roadway. In the NT the Gr. term *hodos* is translated "highway" three times by the KJV (Mt 22:10; Mk 10:46; Lk 14:23) and once by the RSV (Lk 14:23). *See* Commerce; King's Highway; Road; Travel and Communication with map showing the principal trade routes in ancient Palestine.

HILEN. *See* Holon.

HILKIAH (hĭl-kī'à)

1. A Levite of the family of Merari, the son of Amzi and father of Amaziah (I Chr 6:45–46).

2. A Levite, the son of Hosah, a Merarite, who was appointed a doorkeeper in the temple by David (I Chr 26:11).

3. The father of Eliakim who was "over the house," that is, prime minister under King Hezekiah (II Kgs 18:18, 26, 37; Isa 22:20; 36:3, 22).

4. The son of Shallum (or Meshullam) and descendant of Zadok who was high priest in the days of Ezra (I Chr 6:13; 9:11; Ezr 7:1). He was also an ancestor of Ezra (I Chr 6:13; 9:11; Ezr 7:1). It was in part under his leadership that the great revival took place in the reign of Josiah. During the repair of the temple, Hilkiah discovered "the book of the law of the Lord given by Moses." This may have been a "foundation" copy, such as we now put in cornerstones, or it may have been in fact the very copy placed in the ark by Moses (Deut 31:9–26). The book was brought to the king who, after reading in it, was convicted of the great sin of his people. He requested Hilkiah and others to "inquire of the Lord" for

him. Hilkiah turned to Huldah the prophetess and through her received of the Lord the pronouncement of judgment upon Judah, but comfort and blessing personally to the devout Josiah. Hilkiah had a leading role in the reformation that followed, marked by a momentous Passover observation (II Kgs 22–23; II Chr 34–35).

5. A priest of Anathoth in Benjamin, the father of Jeremiah the prophet (Jer 1:1).

6. The father of Gemariah, who with Elasah was sent to Babylon by King Zedekiah, bearing the letter of Jeremiah to those already in captivity (Jer 29:3).

7. One of the priests who returned from Babylon with Zerubbabel. The father of Hashabiah who was priest in the days of Joiakim (Neh 12:7, 21).

8. One of the priests who stood with Ezra as he read the law of God to the people (Neh 8:4).

9. The father of Seraiah, one of the chief priests under Nehemiah and "ruler of the house of God" (Neh 11:11).

P. C. J.

HILL, HILL COUNTRY

1. The usual Heb. word for "hill" is *gib'â*, derived from a root that suggests a swelling and yields other words such as "bowl" and "humpbacked." It is peculiarly applicable to the many rounded hills in Palestine. It may refer to the elevated terrain in general of Ephraim (Gen 49:26; Deut 33:15) and the plateau of Moab (Num 23:9), or to specific heights such as the hill of Moreh (Jud 7:1) and the hill of Hachilah (I Sam 23:19; 26:1, 3). As Isa 31:4 indicates, it can be synonymous with the next term.

2. The Heb. word *har* most often refers to a range of mountains or to a particular summit, but is translated as "hill" 61 times in the KJV and once as "hill country" (Josh 13:6). The proper translation of *har* requires a knowledge of the geography of Palestine. Since the mountains of Palestine and Transjordan are seldom more than 3,000 feet in elevation, it is often preferable to refer to them as "hill country." Hence the RSV has rendered the term re-

Holes may be seen in the base and lintel of the Lion Gate at Mycenae for the "pivot" or pole piece (hinge) of the gate. Holes may be seen for inserting bars to lock the gate. HFV

peatedly in this way when the mountainous section of an area is indicated (cf. "hill country of Seir," Gen 36:8, RSV; "hill country of Ephraim," Josh 17:15, 16, 18, RSV). The entire hill country of Judah, Benjamin, and Ephraim, and perhaps of Galilee, once inhabited by Amorites, is referred to as *hāhār*, "the mountain" (Num 13:29). On the other hand, in II Kgs 1:9; 4:27 the use of the word "hill" for *hāhār* obscures the allusion to Mount Carmel, which in other passages concerning Elijah and Elisha (e.g., I Kgs 18:19; II Kgs 4:25) has the translation "mount" correctly attached to it. *See* Palestine II.A.5; B.2.

3. Heb. *ma'ăleh* is once rendered "hill" (I Sam 9:11); better would be "ascent" or "slope" (Jerusalem Bible), the sloping ramp or roadway leading up to the city gate.

4. Gr. *bounos* is used twice in the NT and translated "hill" (Lk 3:5; 23:30).

5. Gr. *oros* is rendered 62 times as "mount" or "mountain" but three times as "hill," twice correctly (Mt 5:14; Lk 4:29). The third passage (Lk 9:37) should have "mountain" to agree with the use of *oros* in Lk 9:28.

6. Gr. *oreinos* properly is translated "hill country" in Lk 1:39, 65.

J. R.

Mount Tabor, a good illustration of one of the rounded hills of Palestine. ORINST

HILLEL (hĭl'ĕl). The father of the judge Abdon (Jud 12:13, 15).

HIN. *See* Weights, Measures, and Coins.

HIND. *See* Animals: Deer, II.10.

HINGE. Two words are translated "hinge" in KJV. The Heb. word *pōt* probably means "socket" (I Kgs 7:50), and *ṣîr* refers to the "pivot" or pole piece of the ancient Palestinian door (Prov 26:14). In contrast with the gold sockets in which the doors of Solomon's temple turned (I Kgs 7:50), the sockets were more often simply a hole in the wood or stone lintel and doorsill. Stone door sockets are commonly found in Palestinian excavated sites. The pivot, to which the door was attached, was an upright beam of wood or metal fitted into the sockets.

In Prov 26:14 a sluggard turning in his bed is compared to a pivot turning in its sockets. *See* Door.

Valley of Hinnom looking north toward the Jaffa Gate. HFV

Using the ancient "pole pieces," a modern gate has been installed at the north gate of Mycenae. HFV

HINNOM (hĭn'ŏm). The valley of Hinnom begins on the W side of Jerusalem at the Joppa (Jaffa) Gate, continuing S until it bends E along the southern limits of the city, joining the valley of the Kidron near the SE corner and the Dung Gate. It is a deep and narrow ravine with steep, rocky sides. *See* Jerusalem.

It is first mentioned in Scripture as a part of the boundary between Judah (to the S) and Benjamin (to the N) in the division of the land among the tribes (Josh 15:8; 18:16). Here was located Topheth, where parents had made their children pass through the fire to the idol Molech (II Chr 28:3; 33:6). Jeremiah warned that God would punish the people so severely because of this wickedness that the place would become known as the valley of slaughter (Jer 7:31–34; 19:3–6; 32:35). King Josiah sought to bring such idolatrous abominations to an end, making the valley the dumping ground for refuse from the city (II Kgs 23:10, 13–14; II Chr 34:4–5).

The Heb. name *Gê ben-Hinnom* (Ge-Hinnom) was transliterated into Gr. as *geenna*. It becomes in the NT the word for "hell," which is found 11 times in the Gospels upon the lips of Jesus (Mt 5:22, 29–30; 10:28; 18:9; 23:15, 33; Mk 9:43, 45, 47; Lk 12:5) and once in Jas 3:6. It became known as a place of putrefaction, decay, and burning, associated with the destruction of waste, a fit symbol for the final destination of the wicked. The references in Rev 14:10; 19:20; 20:10; 21:8 to "the lake of fire" probably have their foundation in the Gehenna concept. *See* Gehenna; Hell.

H. L. D. and F. B. H.

HIP AND THIGH. An idiom used in Jud 15:8 to indicate a slaughter so fierce that the bodies were mutilated.

HIPPOPOTAMUS. *See* Animals, II.20.

HIRAH (hī'rá). An Adullamite, a friend of Judah (Gen 38:1, 12). He was Judah's emissary to the supposed harlot (Gen 38:20 ff.). Both the LXX and the Vulgate read "shepherd" for "friend" in Gen 38:12.

HIRAM (hī'rȧm). A name that is commonly rendered Hiram in I Kings and I Chronicles but Huram in II Chronicles (*q.v.*).

1. King of Tyre. With the reign of Hiram I the great days of Tyre (*q.v.*) began. When he took the reins of government, Tyre consisted of two small islands about a half mile off the Phoenician coast. (Whether or not there was a main-

Ruins of the Roman period at Tyre, a city started on the road to greatness by Hiram.
HFV

land Tyre at the time is uncertain.) These two islands he joined, and then claimed from the sea an area on the E of the larger island. The total circumference of island Tyre was now about two and a half miles. Then he proceeded to rebuild and beautify the temples, and enlarged and improved the harbor and fortifications of the city.

One acceptable chronology based on Josephus' statements (*Ant.* viii.3.1; 5.3; *Against Apion* i.17–18) pegs the 34-year reign of Hiram at 978–944 B.C. His father was Abi-baal and the remaining rulers of his dynasty include Beleazarus, seven years; Abd-Astartus, nine years; Deleastartus, 12 years; Astartus, 12 years; Aserymus, nine years; Pheles, eight months.

After David became king over all Israel, Hiram sent an embassy to David. The result was a supply of cedars of Lebanon (*q.v.*) and Tyrian carpenters and masons to provide a palace for David—on what terms we do not know (II Sam 5:11–12; I Chr 14:1–2). Later, David obtained cedar from Tyre and Sidon for the temple (I Chr 22:4).

When Solomon assumed the task of building the temple in Jerusalem, he sent to Hiram to make specific arrangements for actual construction. The correspondence between the two kings appears in II Chr 2 and I Kgs 5:1–12 (cf. I Kgs 7:13–14). The picture we get is something like this: Solomon needed wood, gold, and artisans in various trades. In exchange for the wood and skilled labor Solomon furnished agricultural products; for the gold, a section of land.

The total amount of what Solomon agreed to furnish annually for the wood and laborers was 20,000 measures (Heb. *kor* = 10–11 bushels each) of wheat, 20,000 measures of barley, 20,000 measures (Heb. *bath* = 4½ gallons each) of wine, and 20,000 measures of oil (thought to be a textual corruption; the amount is seemingly too much) (II Chr 2:10).

The fact that this payment differs from that mentioned in I Kgs 5:11 seems easily explained. The latter reference speaks of a pay-

ment of 20,000 measures of wheat and 20 measures of pure oil and says this was for "his [Hiram's] household." The II Chronicles statistics probably include receipts for public expenditures as well. For gold, Solomon gave Hiram a tract of land in Galilee; this encompassed 20 towns. Upon seeing this district, Hiram was quite unhappy and called it *cabul*. According to Josephus this word is a Phoenician term meaning "that which does not please" (I Kgs 9:10–14; Jos *Ant.* viii.5.3).

Having established an agreement for building purposes, Solomon and Hiram also seem to have drawn up a pact for joint commercial endeavor. Solomon's conquest of the Edomites gave him access to the Red Sea. There he constructed the port of Ezion-geber (*q.v.*) and built a fleet of ships for trade in eastern and southern waters (I Kgs 9:25–28). Up to this point, the Hebrews had never possessed good port facilities and had never engaged extensively in travel by sea. When constructing a port and fleet, the most natural place for the Hebrews to turn for skilled technicians was to the Phoenicians, acknowledged leaders in the field. And the Phoenicians were glad to cooperate in construction of a southern fleet because, on the one hand, such a fleet would not contest their mastery of the Mediterranean, since there was no Suez Canal. On the other hand, the Phoenicians would in this way have access to goods of Arabia and Africa for their Mediterranean trade; these products they previously had had to do without. The land of Ophir (I Kgs 9:28) was either located in SW Arabia (modern Yemen) and perhaps the adjacent coast of Africa, or possibly in western India. The Phoenicians also seem to have helped Solomon develop his copper smelting industry in the area S of the Dead Sea.

Not only did Hiram and Solomon have a public commercial alliance, they seem to have had a private tilt of shrewdness over solving riddles. Josephus relates that the two monarchs exchanged riddles or enigmatical sayings, with the understanding that the one who could not solve those submitted to him was to forfeit a money payment. At first Hiram seems to have been the substantial loser; but later Hiram, with the help of a certain Abdemon of Tyre, managed to solve the riddles. Later, Hiram proposed a number of riddles which even wise Solomon could not figure out, and Solomon paid substantial sums of money to Hiram (Jos *Ant.* viii.5.5; *Against Apion,* i.17). What relation King Ahiram of Byblos (*c.* 1000 B.C.) may have had to Hiram I of Tyre is problematical.

2. A second Hiram of Tyre (not referred to in the OT) is mentioned by Tiglath-pileser III (744–727 B.C.) of Assyria as paying tribute to the Assyrian monarch.

3. An artisan contemporary with King Hiram I, whom the king sent to Solomon to supervise casting of the molten sea (great laver), copper pillars, and other utensils for the temple (I Kgs

7:13–47). While Hiram's father was a Tyrian, his mother was either from the tribe of Naphtali (I Kgs 7:14) or of Dan (II Chr 2:14). Perhaps the discrepancy is a result of a copyist's error, or possibly Hiram's mother was descended from both tribes. Hiram was apparently a very superior craftsman.

H. F. V.

HIRE. *See* Wages.

HIRELING. The word occurs six times in the OT and always means a laborer who receives pay. Job 7:1–2 deals with the hireling's anxiety for the day's end; Isa 16:14; 21:16 refer to the hireling's tenure; Mal 3:5 warns against the mistreatment of the hireling in reference to his wages; Jer 46:21 refers to a mercenary soldier (cf. RSV, NASB; II Sam 10:6; II Kgs 7:6; II Chr 25:6).

The only usage in the NT is in Jn 10:12–13, where the hireling's neglect of the sheep is sharply contrasted with the shepherd's protection and courage. The true owner of the flock leads them to and from pasturage and lays down his life for the sheep. While there is no imputation of unfaithfulness or dishonesty necessarily conveyed by the term, nevertheless, this is usually read into the term because of Jesus' application of the word to the unfaithful shepherd.

HISS. The RSV translates the Heb. verb *shāraq,* "whistle," in the sense of calling or signaling (Isa 5:26; 7:18; Zech 10:8); KJV renders it "hiss." It is also rendered "hiss" in both KJV and RSV in the sense of expressing scorn (I Kgs 9:8; Job 27:23; *et al.*), apparently deriving this sense mimetically from the hissing of air being expelled through clenched teeth. The noun of this same root is frequently employed by Jeremiah in the same sense of derision and scorn (Jer 18:16; 19:8; 25:9, 18; 29:18; 51:37).

HITTITES (hĭt′īts). The term Hittite has a twofold use in the OT. Usually it designates a relatively unimportant ethnic group living in Palestine since the days of the patriarchs (Gen 15:19–21). These people, called the "sons of Heth," were descended from Noah's son Ham through Canaan (Gen 10:15; I Chr 1:13) and were settled in the central hills of Palestine (Num 13:29; Josh 11:3).

In a few cases, however, the term Hittite is used in the OT to designate outsiders, non-Semitic peoples living in the N, who were to be respected and feared as a great power (I Kgs 11:1; II Kgs 7:6–7; II Chr 1:17). These were the Hittites so famous from extrabiblical historical sources. Although it has been suggested that the small enclaves of Hittites in central Palestine were part of the northern Hittites who migrated S early in the 2nd mil. B.C., there need be no connection between the two groups at all, except for a coincidental similarity of name.

The Indo-European Hittites who entered Anatolia and the Near East around 2000 B.C. from the steppes of inner Asia received their name more or less by accident, by virtue of the fact that they settled in territory previously held by an earlier non-Indo-European group called Hatti-people (or Hattians). Henceforth in this article the three groups will be called "sons of Heth," "Hittites," and "Hattians" respectively, to avoid confusion.

[The red and black highly burnished Khirbet Kerah ware in Palestine is virtually identical with pottery in central Anatolia and the Kurgan homeland in Transcaucasia in the 3rd mil. B.C. This may suggest an incursion or migration of Hattians into Palestine in the 23rd cen. B.C.—Ed. See BASOR # 189 (1968), pp. 28f.]

There is no way of knowing how long the Hattians had been living in central Anatolia before the Hittites arrived *c.* 2000 B.C. Although the Hittites acquired territory and political supremacy in central Anatolia around the Halys River partly by force of arms, there was no organized conquest of the land in the manner of Israel's conquest of Palestine. The Hattians ever after formed a minority group within Hittite society, and were very influential in religious matters.

Teshub, the Hittite weather god. LM

Although it is possible that an earlier king, Anitta of Kussar, who subdued five rival cities and moved his capital to Nesa (Kanesh), was related in some way to the later Hittite kings, the Hittite Old Kingdom proper is usually dated (S. Smith's chronology) 1680–1460 B.C. Hattusili I (1650–1620 B.C.) raided and defeated Alalakh, Urshu, and Aleppo in N Syria. Mursili I (1620–1590 B.C.) led the Hittite army down the Euphrates to conquer Aleppo, destroy Mari, and raid and plunder Babylon itself, thus putting an end to the Babylonian dynasty founded by Hammurabi. After Mursili the power of the Hittites declined. It is possible that the first recension of the Hittite laws dates from the reign of Telipinu (1525–1500 B.C.).

Revival of Hittite power began with Tudhaliya II (1460–1440 B.C.), who in cooperation with Thutmose III of Egypt destroyed Aleppo (c. 1457). During the years that followed, however, the Hurrian kingdom of Mittanni established itself in N Syria, restricting the Hittites to their mountainous homeland in central Anatolia. The greatest and most famous of the Hittite kings was Suppiluliuma (1380–1340 B.C.), who reduced the kingdom of Mittanni to a vassal state and controlled Syria S to the Lebanon region. Suppiluliuma laid a solid foundation for the administration of Syrian vassal states, binding each of them to himself in suzerainty treaties, the literary form of which closely resembles that of the covenant which God gave to Israel at Mount Sinai (cf. George Mendenhall, *Law and Covenant in Israel and the Ancient Near East*).

During the reign of Muwatalli (1306–1282 B.C.) Rameses II of Egypt joined battle with the Hittite allied armies at Kadesh on the Orontes. Both sides claimed victory in their annals, but Muwatalli retained Syria and added Abina (Hobah) to his possessions. Rameses later allied himself by treaty with Hattusili III (1275–1250 B.C.) against the mutual threat of the young Assyrian state. The Hittite Empire centered in Asia Minor came to an end when barbarian hordes from Thrace swept over the western lands and c. 1200 B.C. destroyed the capital city of Hattusas (at Boghazköy, 75 miles E of Ankara, Turkey). Sea Peoples from the W and S may have also had a part in the collapse of the Hittites.

The political designation "Hatti" was carried on by a small group of N Syrian city-states, among whom were Carchemish, Aleppo, and Hamath. Hittites from these cities may have served in David's armies (I Sam 26:6; II Sam 11:3), although these may have been the sons of Heth, since Ahimelech is transparently a Semitic name and Uriah may be either Semitic or Hurrian. Semitic names in themselves, however, need not rule out a Syro-Hittite origin, since the Hittites of Syria had long since accommodated themselves to the prevailing Aramean culture.

When Ezekiel accused the profligate Jerusalem of being the offspring of an Amorite father and a Hittite mother (Ezk 16:3), he had in mind the sons of Heth, not the great empire in Asia Minor. Ephron the Hittite of Gen 23 may also have been of the sons of Heth, although some have detected traces of Hittite real estate procedure in the transaction between Ephron and Abraham (Lehmann, BASOR # 129, pp. 15–18; Tucker, JBL, LXXXV, 77–84).

The language of the Hittites was an Indo-European tongue related to early Greek, Latin, and Sanskrit. Other groups in Anatolia related to the Hittites spoke related dialects called Luwian and Palaic. The language of the Hattians was neither Semitic nor Indo-European. The laws of the Hittites, inscribed on clay tablets in cuneiform script, are very similar in form and content to contemporary law codes from Mesopotamia (ANET, pp. 188–197). But unlike Semitic law with its characteristic stress on *lex talionis*, these laws stress compensation for injuries, undoubtedly a residue of the old Indo-European *wergeld* institution.

The Hittites possessed two distinct military advantages over their foes. They were the first to smelt iron on a large scale in the Near East, which gave them superior weapons. Hittites were also in the vanguard of those who developed the breeding and training of chariot horses into a science. Among clay tablets in the Hittite archives were found an extensive series of tablets describing procedures in training chariot horses. The author of these texts was a Hurrian named Kikkuli. Solomon in later times imported fine horses from Cilicia (Kue) for his chariotry (I Kgs 10:28–29).

See Archaeology: Boghazköy.

Bibliography. Kurt Bittel, "Boghazköy: The Excavations of 1967 and 1968," *Archaeology*, XXII (1969), 276–279. O. R. Gurney, "Boghazköy," TAOT, pp. 105–116. Harry A.

Entrance to the great temple of the lower city. Boghazköy. HFV

Lion Gate, Boghazköy, capital of the Hittites. HFV

Hoffner, "Hittites," BW, pp. 290–294, with excellent bibliography; "Some Contributions of Hittitology to Old Testament Study," *Tyndale Bulletin,* XX (1969), 27–55. Manfred R. Lehmann, "Abraham's Purchase of Machpelah and Hittite Law," BASOR #129 (1953), pp. 15–18. Gene M. Tucker, "The Legal Background of Genesis 23," JBL, LXXXV (1966), 77–84.

H. A. Hof.

HIVITES (hī'vīts). Numbered among the descendants of Canaan (Gen 10:17; I Chr 1:15), the Hivites were one of the ethnic groups dwelling in Canaan before the Israelite settlement (Ex 3:8; Deut 7:1; Josh 3:10). Hivite cities and settlements are known to have existed in the vicinity of Sidon and Tyre (II Sam 24:7), in the Lebanon hills (Jud 3:3), in the Hermon range and the valley leading to Hamath (Josh 11:3), and in central Palestine around Shechem (Gen 34:2) and Gibeon N of Jerusalem (Josh 9:7; 11:19). Solomon conscripted Hivites for his building projects (I Kgs 9:20; II Chr 8:7).

Since in the Heb. spelling the words "Hivite" (*ḥiwwî*) and "Horite" (*ḥōrrî*) differ only in one letter (*w* and *r*, which are shaped similarly in Heb.), many scholars assume an early textual error and equate the Hivites with the Horites. Confusion of the two spellings in the course of textual transmission is evident from the Masoretic Heb. text itself, since Zibeon is called a "Hivite" in Gen 36:2 and a "Horite" in Gen 36:20. LXX reads "Horites" for MT "Hivites" in Gen 34:2 and Josh 9:7. Furthermore, Hurrians (biblical "Horites") are known to have settled in Palestine in just the areas where the biblical Hivites were located. Hurrian personal names are attested from central Palestine, Lebanon, and Syria. The prince of Jerusalem around the middle of the 14th cen. B.C., as

known from the Amarna letters, bore the Hurrian personal name Abdi-Hepa.

In David's time a Jebusite prince from the Jerusalem area bore the name (or title) Araunah (II Sam 24:16; variant spelling Ornan, *'rnn,* in I Chr 21:18), which means in Hurrian "the lord." The variant spellings in II Sam 24 in the consonantal text of MT, *'wrnh* (v. 16) and *'rwnh* (vv. 20–24), have been thought to reflect dialectal differences, since "lord" was pronounced *iwri* in some Hurrian dialects and *irwi* in others. But since the term equivalent to Araunah's name is always spelled *'wrn* at Ugarit, and LXX always reads *Orna* (even at II Sam 24:20–24, reflecting *'wrnh* in the Heb. text), it is probable that MT *'rwnh* in II Sam 24:20–24 is a transpositional error for earlier *'wrnh.* The fact that Araunah with his Hurrian name or title is called a Jebusite (II Sam 24:16), along with the fact that in the stereotyped lists Hivites immediately precede Jebusites (Ex 3:8; Deut 7:1; etc.), has been construed as additional evidence that the Hivites were Hurrians (Horites). *See* Horites.

H. A. Hof.

HIZKIAH. *See* Hezekiah.

HIZKIJAH. *See* Hezekiah.

HOARFROST. *See* Frost.

HOBAB (hō'băb). The son of Raguel or Reuel the Midianite (Num 10:29), and thus the brother of Zipporah and brother-in-law of Moses (Ex 2:18, 21; 3:1). The Heb. word *ḥōtēn,* translated "father-in-law" (Num 10:29; Jud 1:16; 4:11; *et al.*), comes from the verb *ḥātan,* "to marry," and simply means a relative by marriage. Since it is no more specific than that, there is no contradiction in the passages in Judges naming Hobab as Moses' "in-law." *See* Jethro.

When Israel set out from Sinai, Moses invited Hobab to accompany them, promising that the blessing of God extended to Israel would be his also. He urged Hobab to come that he might be a guide and help to them since he was experienced in the ways of the wilderness (Num 10:29–32). The record in Numbers does not indicate whether Hobab went with them at the time or not, but people of the same Midianite family, the Kenites, are found among the Israelites from then on. In the time of the judges, Heber, the Kenite, is called a descendant of Hobab. Heber's wife Jael (*q.v.*) was the heroine who slew the oppressor Sisera (Jud 4:11 ff.).

Bibliography. William F. Albright, *Yahweh and the Gods of Canaan,* Garden City: Doubleday, 1968, pp. 38–42.

P. C. J.

HOBAH (hō′bȧ). The place to which Abram pursued the routed army of Chedorlaomer "on the left hand" (i.e., N) of Damascus (Gen 14:15). The exact site is uncertain.

HOD (hŏd). A son of Zophah of the family of Asher (I Chr 7:37).

HODAIAH (hō-dā′yȧ). Variant of Hodaviah (*q.v.*). Hodaiah is found only in I Chr 3:24, referring to a descendant of David. He was one of the seven sons of Elioenai of the descendants of Zerubbabel.

HODAVIAH (hŏd′ȧ-vī′ȧ). Variant of Hodaiah (*q.v.*). The name appears in the Aramaic letters from Elephantine.
1. One of the chief men of Manasseh, a mighty warrior, taken into exile by the Assyrians (I Chr 5:24).
2. The father of Meshullam and son of Hassenuah of the tribe of Benjamin (I Chr 9:7).
3. A Levite, ancestor of 74 who returned to Jerusalem with Zerubbabel (Ezr 2:40). In Ezr 3:9 he is called Judah and in Neh 7:43 the name is spelled Hodevah.

HODESH (hō′dĕsh). A wife of Shaharaim, a Benjamite (I Chr 8:9).

HODEVAH. *See* Hodaviah 3.

HODIAH (hō-dī′ȧ). A man of Judah (I Chr 4:19). *See* Hodijah 1.

HODIJAH (hō-dī′jȧ). The RSV consistently translates Hodiah; the KJV translates Hodiah in I Chr 4:19, but elsewhere uses Hodijah. The Heb. name has been found on an ancient seal in Palestine.
1. A man of Judah (*q.v.*; I Chr 4:19, RSV), whose wife was a sister of Naham. The word order and punctuation of the KJV give the wrong impression that Hodiah was a woman.

2. A Levite active in the days of Nehemiah. He helped the people understand the law as it was read by Ezra and led the people in prayer (Neh 8:7 f.; 9:5). He signed the great covenant of Nehemiah (Neh 10:10).
3. Another Levite who signed Nehemiah's covenant (Neh 10:13).
4. One of the chiefs of the people who signed the covenant (Neh 10:18).

HOGLAH (hŏg′lȧ). One of five daughters of Zelophehad (Num 26:33; 27:1; Josh 17:3). Since there were no sons, the daughters were to receive the inheritance provided they married within their tribe (Num 36:1–12).

HOHAM (hō′hăm). Amorite king of Hebron who joined the coalition against Gibeon. The coalition was defeated by Joshua at Beth-horon. The kings fled but were caught in the cave at Makkedah and killed (Josh 10:3 ff.).

HOLD. This term is used to refer to a stronghold (Jud 9:46, 49); to a cage or jail (Ezk 19:9; Acts 4:3; RSV "in custody"); to a den or lair (Rev 18:2; RSV "haunt"). *See* Fort.

HOLINESS, HOLY. The Heb. words *qādôsh,* "holy"; *qōdesh,* "holiness"; and the Gr. *hagios* and *hagiōsynē* mean basically separation from what is common or unclean, and consecration to God (Lev 20:24–26, RSV; Acts 6:13; 21:28). From the underlying idea of apartness or separation from the profane (Lev 10:10; Ezk 22:26) stem three derived aspects of holiness found in Scripture.
1. *Deity.* Since God is transcendent and independent of His created universe (I Kgs 8:27), He is separate from its inhabitants and feared by them (e.g., Ex 19:10–25; 20:18–21). Thus holiness becomes equivalent to true deity, separating Him from the impotence of the gods of the defeated Egyptians (Ex 15:11): "Who is like unto thee, O Lord, among the gods? who is like thee, glorious in holiness?" "Holy" in many passages is synonymous with "divine": "There is none holy [uniquely divine] as the Lord: for there is none beside thee" (I Sam 2:2; cf. Ps 99:3, 5, 9; Isa 40:25; Hab 3:3). Because He is holy, truly deity and thus infinite, there is no searching of His understanding (Isa 40:28; Ps 145:3). Holiness, then, is what characterizes God, and it includes all His other attributes.
2. *Ceremonial holiness.* While it is true that God as the "wholly other" Being "dwells in the high and holy place," yet He is "with him also that is of a contrite spirit" (Isa 57:15). That is, God shares His holiness with those in covenant relationship with Him. They too are separated from the world around them by being brought near to God (Ex 19:4–6; 33:16; Lev 11:44–45; I Kgs 8:53). Thus divine holiness is not exclusive, but God reaches out to attract others to His state and attitude of separation from the

material world which He created. Israel, therefore, is holy (Ex 19:6), and in the NT believers are called saints (Gr. *hagioi*, lit., "holy ones," Rom 1:7) and a "holy nation" (I Pet 2:9). *See* Saints.

Ceremonial objects are also classed as holy or sacred, set apart entirely for God's use. Thus the tabernacle was sanctified by God's shekinah glory (Ex 29:43-45; 40:34-35; Ps 93:5), especially the holy of holies (*q.v.*). The priests had holy garments (Ex 28:2). The spot where God appeared to Moses in the burning bush was holy ground (Ex 3:5). Such holiness possessed no essentially moral quality. As an extreme example of the root meaning of the Heb. term, the Canaanitish temple prostitute was called a *qᵉdēshâ* (Deut 23:17, RSV) because she was separated for this religious ceremonial. Wars were "sanctified" (Joel 3:9, ASV marg.), declared holy or set apart to punish the enemies of God. *See* War.

Ceremonial holiness could become fearsome, for death might follow contact with God (Ex 33:20; Jud 6:22 f.; 13:22 f.; Isa 6:5). The men of Beth-shemesh, smitten for desecrating the ark by looking into it, cried out, "Who is able to stand before the Lord, this holy God?" (I Sam 6:20, RSV). When David was bringing the ark to Jerusalem, Uzzah was struck down on the spot for merely touching the ark to steady it (II Sam 6:6-7).

As a part of the holy covenant relationship with God, Moses prescribed purifying rites, preparatory to holy ceremonies (Ex 19:14; 29:4; Lev 12-15). Some of the ceremonies and laws included (1) the dedication of the firstborn (Ex 13:2, 12 f.; 22:29 ff.) and the offering of all firstling animals and firstfruits (Deut 26:1-11); (2) the distinction between clean and unclean food (Lev 11; Deut 14); (3) regulations concerning the holiness of the priests (Lev 21:1-22:16), the Levites (Num 8:5-26), and the sacred place of worship (Deut 12); and (4) the regulations regarding the appointed feasts and holy convocations (Lev 23; *see* Festivals). The Nazarite (*q.v.*), by his vow of total separation unto the Lord, epitomized a life of ceremonial holiness (Num 6).

Comparative religionists attribute many of the *qōdesh* passages of Scripture to the primitive concept of taboo: divinely potent objects to be left alone. Superstitions like these are unworthy of the OT, but this much appears true: holy items, permanently set apart for God, were called *ḥērem*, "devoted" things; and what the Canaanites had considered *qōdesh* or taboo, God commanded Israel upon capturing them to make them *ḥērem*, "devoted" either to destruction or, if valuable in the service of the Lord, to sacred uses (Josh 6:17-19). *See* Accursed; Devote; Devoted Thing.

3. *Moral purity.* Since such ceremonial association and covenant fellowship is with the God who is also righteous and sinless, holiness acquires the meaning of separation from sin (Isa

52:11; II Cor 6:17) and conformity to God's moral standards (Lev 20:7-8; Mt 5:48; I Pet 1:15-16). From the beginning God's will has opposed sin and has sought for righteousness in the human race (Gen 6:5-6). It is God's moral wholeness or purity that leads Him to separate Himself from evil (Hab 1:13).

God's holiness, therefore, is entire freedom from moral evil on the one hand and absolute moral perfection on the other. Its greatest revelation is in the sinless character and work of Jesus Christ (*see* arts. on Christ). By the holiness of God it is not implied that He is subject to some law or standard of moral excellence external to Himself, but that all moral law and perfection have their eternal and unchangeable basis in His own nature. In this sense the saints will sing without qualification, "For thou only art holy" (Rev 15:3-4).

The punishment of man's moral infractions stems ultimately from the fact of God's holiness (Ezk 38:16, 23, RSV; Amos 4:2). The greatest loss in such punishment is his separation from the divine favor and presence. In the call of Isaiah, the prophet's natural reaction to God's holiness (Isa 6:3) was to experience conviction about his own sin and the sense of being undone (v. 5, KJV), lost (RSV, NEB), cut off or ruined (Heb. *nidmêtî*). His submission, however, eventuated in his forgiveness and the imputation to him of moral holiness through atonement ("thine iniquity is taken away, and thy sin purged [Heb. *tᵉkuppār*]," v. 7).

The NT teaches that the believer is sanctified positionally before God, with the holiness of Christ imputed to him, at the time of his conversion, by virtue of his being presented "in Christ" (I Cor 1:2, 30). He is being sanctified experientially as he keeps reckoning upon his position in Christ, refusing to yield the members of his body to sin, and presenting himself to God (Rom 6:11-13). He must deliberately "follow peace with all men, and holiness, without which no man shall see the Lord" (Heb 12:14). He will be ultimately sanctified in the sense of full conformity to Christ in glorification (Rom 8:30-31). *See* Sanctification.

Holiness, therefore, is the characteristic mark of a believer in both the OT and the NT. He that would stand in the holy place to worship God must have clean hands and a pure heart and not have sworn to a lie (Ps 24:3-4). To dwell in God's holy mountain—in His presence—one must walk with integrity and do no wrong to his neighbor (Ps 15). God "chose us in Him [Christ] before the foundation of the world, that we should be holy and blameless before Him" (Eph 1:4, NASB). Our sanctification is God's direct and perfect will for us (I Thess 4:3).

Thus every activity of life becomes sacred, for the Christian as well as for Israel. For when a man's aim is that of conformity to the will of God, who executes moral righteousness for all, life cannot be divided between the secular and the sacred. Accordingly, Christ treated the commandments as one: "Thou shalt love the Lord thy God with all thy heart . . . and thy neighbor as thyself. . . . This do . . ." (Lk 10:27-28), and illustrated His teaching with the parable of the Good Samaritan. The all-compelling motivation which determines both our religious and our ethical conduct must be one of response to the grace of God, a motivation not of reward but of gratitude.

See Example; God; Holy Spirit; Sanctification.

Bibliography. R. A. Finlayson, *The Holiness of God,* London: Pickering & Inglis, 1955; "Holiness, Holy, Saints," NBD, pp. 529 ff. Edmond Jacob, *The Theology of the Old Testament,* trans. by A. W. Heathcote and P. J. Allcock, New York: Harper, 1958, pp. 86-93. J. Barton Payne, *The Theology of the Older Testament,* Grand Rapids: Zondervan, 1962. Kenneth F. W. Prior, *The Way of Holiness,* Chicago: Inter-Varsity, 1967. Otto Procksch and Karl G. Kuhn, "*Agios,* etc.," TDNT, I, 88-115. Paul S. Rees, "Holiness, Holy," BDT, pp. 269 f. Norman H. Snaith, *The Distinctive Ideas of the Old Testament,* Philadelphia: Westminster, 1946, pp. 21-50.

J. B. P.

HOLM TREE. *See* Plants.

HOLON (hō'lŏn)
1. A village in the hill country of Judah (Josh 15:51) assigned to the Levites (Josh 21:15). Also called Hilen (I Chr 6:58).
2. A Moabite town included in the judgment upon a group of cities enumerated by Jeremiah (Jer 48:21).

HOLY. *See* Holiness; Saint.

HOLY GHOST. *See* Holy Spirit.

HOLY OF HOLIES. *See* Tabernacle; Temple.

HOLY ONE OF ISRAEL. *See* God, Names and Titles of.

HOLY PLACE. *See* Tabernacle; Temple.

HOLY SPIRIT. In the NT the Holy Spirit clearly reveals Himself as a person and is Deity. He has the attributes of personality: intellect (Rom 8:27; I Cor 2:10-13), emotions (Eph 4:30), and will (I Cor 12:11). He performs the actions of personality: teaches (Jn 14:26), testifies (Jn 15:26), directs (Acts 8:29; 13:2), guides (Rom 8:14), warns (I Tim 4:1). He is Deity because He is the Spirit of God and of Christ (Rom 8:9) and proceeds eternally from the Father (Jn 15:26; Gal 4:6).

Scripture places the Holy Spirit on a par with the Father and the Son (II Cor 13:14; Mt 28:19; I Cor 12:4-6; I Pet 1:2). Accordingly, the works of God always involve all three persons of the Trinity (*q.v.*). It was the triune God who created the world and who reveals Himself in it and by His word to man. It was the triune God who redeemed His people from their sin. Even so, some of these works are specifically the concern of the Holy Spirit. The Holy Spirit brings about the consummation of the works of the triune God.

In Creation
The Spirit hovered over the face of the deep (Gen 1:2), and by His Spirit God garnished the heavens (Job 26:13). The Spirit gives life to men (Job 33:4). He provides them with excellent gifts, both natural abilities and spiritual or charismatic powers (Ex 31:2-3; I Cor 12:8-11). When men sin, He convicts and pleads with them to return unto God (Gen 6:3; Jn 16:8-9; Rom 2:4). It is especially through the Spirit that the triune God bears witness of Himself to men.

In Revelation and Inspiration
The divine Author of God's revelation to mankind is the Holy Spirit. The prophets and apostles, the human instruments, "spake from God, being moved by the Holy Spirit" (II Pet 1:21, ASV). It is clearly stated that OT prophets received the words of the Lord by His Spirit (Zech 7:12; Ezk 2:2; Neh 9:30). A comparison of Acts 28:25 with Isa 6:9-10 teaches that the Holy Spirit is the particular person of the Trinity who delivered God's revelation in words. The Spirit of God is the One who inspired the Scriptures, i.e., taught the very words (I Cor 2:12-13) so that they are accurate, infallible, and authoritative. Jesus promised to send the Holy Spirit to teach His apostles all things and bring to remembrance all that He had said to them (Jn 14:26). *See* Inspiration; Revelation.

In Redemption
It is, however, especially when the triune God comes to redeem His people that the Spirit is clearly evident in His work of consummation.

In the Old Testament. In the period of OT revelation the Spirit prepared the people of God to yearn for their redemption through the coming Messiah. He inspired Moses and the prophets to speak of the Coming One. He broke down the attitude of rebellion in the Israel of God when they refused to obey the word of promise (Isa 63:10-14; Mic 3:8). He taught David, the sweet singer of Israel (II Sam 31:1-2), and through him many others, to say: ". . . thy spirit is good; lead me into the land of uprightness" (Ps 143:10).

Jesus and the Spirit. In the period of NT revelation the Spirit was active before the beginning of the life of Jesus (Lk 1:13-15) to the end (I Pet 3:18). Jesus was conceived by the Holy Spirit (Lk 1:35). The Spirit descended upon Christ at the time of His baptism (Mt 3:16). Then, being "full of the Holy Ghost" Jesus "was led by the Spirit into the wilderness" (Lk 4:1). The Spirit empowered and qualified the Messiah for His official task of destroying the kingdom of Satan and of establishing the kingdom of God.

Soon after His declaration of war against Satan, the Saviour "returned in the power of the Spirit into Galilee" (Lk 4:14) to preach the gospel of the kingdom. He read in the synagogue from the scroll of Isaiah about the coming Messiah: "The Spirit of the Lord is upon me. . . " (Lk 4:18) and said: "This day is this scripture fulfilled in your ears" (Lk 4:21). He told Nicodemus that "except a man be born of water and of the Spirit, he cannot enter into the kingdom of God" (Jn 3:5). By the Spirit He cast out demons (Mt 12:28, RSV). Then when the Pharisees ascribed this cleansing work of the Spirit to Beelzebub, Jesus warned them not to sin against the Spirit lest they become like Satan and their sin could not be forgiven (Mt 12:31-32. *See* Holy Spirit, Sin Against the.

Jesus promised His disciples to pray to the Father that He would give them "another Comforter," "the Spirit of truth" (Jn 14:16-17). By that Spirit the apostles would be enabled to perform their special task as teachers of the church (Jn 14:26). When Jesus would return to glory, then the Spirit would enable the apostles to set forth the full significance of all that He had come to do for His people (Jn 16:13).

Sustained by the Spirit, Jesus had set His face steadfastly to go to Jerusalem. As at the beginning, so at the end, Jesus resisted Satan's ever-present temptation to save His people and establish His kingdom by means other than that of dying in their place for their sins. He knew the prophetic word: "But he was wounded for our transgressions, he was bruised for our iniquities: the chastisement of our peace was upon him; and with his stripes we are healed" (Isa 53:5). He knew that "this day" this Scripture must be fulfilled in Him. Thus was our Saviour sustained by the Spirit in all of His redeeming work (Heb 9:14). Through the Spirit He could say: "It is finished" and could commend His spirit unto the Father.

Pentecost. It was finished indeed. Jesus died but rose again from the dead. He ascended to heaven. Now He is glorified. In accordance with His promise He sent forth His Spirit (Acts 2:3-4). *See* Pentecost.

Peter "wept bitterly" after his denial of Jesus. But from Pentecost on, filled with the Holy Ghost as the Comforter, utter victory came into his heart. Now "filled with the Holy Ghost" as the "Spirit of truth," he saw the vision of "things to come." Filled with the Holy Ghost, he boldly proclaimed that Jesus was not in the final analysis delivered unto death by the people, by the Pharisees, by Pilate, or even by Satan. It was "by the determinate counsel and foreknowledge of God" that all was done (Acts 2:23). What the "wicked hands" of men had done was now defeated. It was impossible that He should be held by the pangs of death (2:24). David the prophet had said that his soul should

not be left in hell and that his flesh should not see corruption (Ps 16:10), and the Spirit taught Peter to interpret this individual as the risen Christ (Acts 2:25-36).

In the church. At Pentecost the church became the universal church. Before leaving for heaven, Jesus said to the Twelve: "But ye shall receive power, after that the Holy Ghost is come upon you: and ye shall be witnesses unto me both in Jerusalem, and in all Judea, and in Samaria, and unto the uttermost part of the earth" (Acts 1:8).

With the coming of Pentecost, the church entered upon "the last days" (Acts 2:17). Slaves ("servants") as well as free, and women ("handmaidens") as well as men, would now "prophesy" (Acts 2:18). Jews from Crete and Arabia heard in their native languages "the wonderful works of God" (Acts 2:11). *See* Tongues, Gift of. When Peter, who spoke at the occasion of Pentecost, explained how the Gentile Cornelius had turned to Christ in an absolutely convincing way, he said, "The Holy Ghost fell on them, as on us at the beginning" (Acts 11:15). The middle wall of partition between Jew and Gentile was now finally removed (Eph 2:14), and the unity of the Spirit was not only possible but should be preserved (Eph 4:3-6).

Henceforth, the "Lord *is* the Spirit" (II Cor 3:17) in the fullness of His redemption for His own. With "open face" believers now constantly behold "the glory of the Lord," the glory of Him who died for their sins and rose again for their justification. In so doing they are "changed into the same image from glory to glory, even as by the Spirit of the Lord" (II Cor 3:18). The "Spirit of life in Christ Jesus" has made them "free from the law of sin and death" (Rom 8:2). In all the days ahead they will know that they have "not received the spirit of bondage again unto fear" but "the Spirit of adoption," whereby they cry, "Abba, Father" (Rom 8:15). In the present age the Holy Spirit indwells believers (I Cor 3:16; 6:19); seals them (II Cor 1:22; Eph 1:13; 4:30); teaches them (Jn 16:12-15); guides them (Rom 8:14); helps them as they pray (Rom 8:26); and seeks to fill them (Eph 5:18).

In the world. Jesus told His disciples: "But you shall receive power when the Holy Spirit has come upon you; and you shall be my witnesses" (Acts 1:8, RSV). And through them He told all His followers the same. How will the world receive them and their witness to them? Jesus told them what their reception would be: "If they have called the master of the house Beelzebub, how much more shall they call them of his household?" (Mt 10:25). "The carnal mind is enmity against God: for it is not subject to the law of God, neither indeed can be" (Rom 8:7; cf. I Cor 2:14; Eph 2:1). But the Holy Spirit was sent to convict the world of sin and righteousness and judgment (Jn 16:7-11).

In spite of persecution nothing can stop the people of God as they "preach the unsearchable riches of Christ" (Eph 3:8). With the early Christians they can pray and be filled with the Holy Spirit and speak the word of God with boldness (Acts 4:31). With Peter they can say to the council, "We are witnesses to these things, and so is the Holy Spirit whom God has given to those who obey him" (Acts 5:32, RSV). With Paul they can exclaim, in the face of all opposition, inspired as it is by Satan: "Now thanks be unto God, which always causeth us to triumph in Christ, and maketh manifest the savour of his knowledge by us in every place" (II Cor 2:14). They know that the Gentiles walk "in the vanity of their mind, having the understanding darkened" (Eph 4:17-18). But by the renewing power of the Holy Spirit (Tit 3:5) human minds are liberated and renewed in their attitudes (Eph 4:23; Rom 12:2). Therefore the work of the Holy Spirit in evangelism is essential for men to be able to hear and receive the gospel.

Finally, the Holy Spirit, the Spirit who rested upon Christ without measure (Jn 1:32-33; 3:34) and made Him to be the faithful witness of God, will sustain those who are the last to make the good confession before men. The "seven Spirits" of God (a Semitic expression for the Spirit in seven aspects, cf. Isa 11:2) are before the throne of Christ, the Victorious One (Rev 1:4). He "who hath sealed us, and given the earnest of the Spirit in our hearts" (II Cor 1:22; cf. Eph 1:14) will seal the final witnesses of His grace when they are confronted with the climactic hatred of Satan as he inspires the Beast. Thus the Holy Spirit will witness to the world through those who are purchased unto God by the blood of the Lamb. When all is finished, the victory over Satan won, then "the Spirit and the bride say, Come" (Rev 22:17).

See Gifts, Spiritual; Holy Spirit, Filling of the; Holy Spirit, Sin Against the; Paraclete; Pentecost; Spirit; Theism; Tongues, Gift of.

Bibliography. Geoffrey W. Bromiley, "The Holy Spirit," Fundamentals of the Faith, ed. by Carl F. H. Henry, Grand Rapids: Zondervan, 1969, pp. 143-165. Frederick D. Bruner, A Theology of the Holy Spirit, Grand Rapids: Eerdmans, 1970. Lewis Sperry Chafer, He That Is Spiritual, Chicago: Moody Press, 1943. James E. Cumming, Through the Eternal Spirit, London: Partridge & Co., 1891; Minneapolis: Bethany Fellowship, reprint, 1965. Hermann Kleinknecht, et al., "Pneuma, etc.," TDNT, VI, 332-455. Abraham Kuyper, The Work of the Holy Spirit, New York: Funk & Wagnalls, 1900; Grand Rapids: Eerdmans, reprint. John Owen, A Discourse Concerning the Holy Spirit, London: 1674; Grand Rapids: Kregel, reprint, 1954. Rene Pache, The Person and Work of the Holy Spirit, Chicago: Moody Press, 1954. Charles C. Ryrie, The Holy Spirit, Chicago: Moody Press, 1965. John F. Walvoord, The Holy Spirit, Grand Rapids: Dunham, 1958; Zondervan, reprint.

C. V. T.

HOLY SPIRIT, FILLING OF THE. The Scriptures teach there is one Father, one Son, one Holy Spirit (I Cor 12:4-6; Eph 4:4-6), and that all Christians are baptized in the Spirit into or in relationship to the Body of Christ (I Cor 12:13). Further, the Holy Spirit distributes particular spiritual gifts to each as He wills (I Cor 12:4-11). At the same time the Bible speaks of the filling of the Holy Spirit which occurs over and over again. Thus, though there is only one baptism in the Holy Spirit (Eph 4:5), there are many fillings (Eph 5:18).

The peerless example of the baptism in the Holy Spirit occurred at Pentecost in fulfillment of Christ's promise to clothe His disciples with supernatural power (Lk 24:49; Acts 1:4-5, 8; 2:1-12). Similar examples of the baptism in the Holy Spirit occurred at Samaria (Acts 8:14-17), for Saul of Tarsus when Ananias laid his hands upon him (Acts 9:17), in Cornelius' home (Acts 10:44-45), and at Ephesus to the disciples of John the Baptist (Acts 19:6). Following these initial baptisms in the Spirit there were many fillings (e.g., Acts 4:8, 31; 13:9, 52). See Baptism in the Spirit.

Several questions arise in regard to the filling of the Holy Spirit.

1. Did the OT believers experience this blessing? To this the answer is yes. To the extent David (II Sam 23:2) and others were inspired in their writing of the OT, they were filled "as they were moved [lit., carried along] by the Holy Ghost" (II Pet 1:21). Such was the testimony of the prophet Micah: "But as for me, I am filled with power, with the Spirit of the Lord ... to declare ... to Israel his sin" (Mic 3:8, RSV).

Joseph (Gen 41:38), Joshua (Num 27:18; Deut 34:9), Bezaleel (Ex 31:3), and Daniel (Dan 4:8, 18; 5:11, 14; 6:3) were recognized as being filled with the Spirit of God by their respective abilities to perform specific tasks. The Spirit of the Lord came upon other men at certain occasions to empower them to deliver God's people (e.g., Othniel, Jud 3:10; Gideon, Jud 6:34; Samson, Jud 14:6, 19; 15:14; Saul, I Sam 11:6) or to prophesy (Num 11:25, 29; I Sam 10:6, 10; II Chr 15:1; 20:14; cf. Lk 1:41, 67). In the Mosaic dispensation, however, charismatically endowed men were the exception; whereas as a result of Pentecost the Spirit has been poured out upon "all flesh," universally upon all believers regardless of race, sex, age, or social status.

2. How can the Holy Spirit dwell in the Christian and fill him when the NT teaches that the believer still has flesh or a fallen nature (Gal 5:17)? The fallen nature in the Christian is a judged thing and stands condemned, because "God sending his own Son in the likeness of sinful flesh, and for sin, condemned sin in the

flesh: that [in order that] the righteousness of the law might be fulfilled in us, who walk not after the flesh, but after the Spirit" (Rom 8:3-4). The blessed Holy Spirit can dwell beside the fallen nature because it is reckoned as crucified or dead, and thus already it stands judged and its days are numbered (Rom 6:6; Gal 2:20; 5:24).

3. If the Holy Spirit is in us, then how does the filling occur? On man's part it depends upon his opening up and surrendering every area of his life, every room in his earthly mansion to the Spirit's presence and control (Acts 5:32; Rom 12:1-2; cf. Rom 6:11-13). He must initially receive the Holy Spirit by a conscious act of faith (Gal 3:2, 5, 14). Some Bible expositors consider this reception to be God's seal or stamp of divine ownership upon the believer (Eph 1:13), even as the Father set His seal upon His Son when the Holy Spirit descended upon Him as a dove (Jn 1:30-34; 6:27). On God's part, it depends upon the Holy Spirit's occupying, enabling, and guiding in all spheres of the believer's life.

4. Is the filling then an option or a matter of indifference? No, because it is a command of the Scriptures that the believer be continuously filled with the Holy Spirit (Eph 5:18), and that he walk by the Spirit (Gal 5:16-25; Rom 8:5-13). At the same time he is warned not to grieve the Spirit (Eph 4:30) or to quench Him (I Thess 5:19).

Results of being filled with the Spirit are many and wonderful. Spirit-filled Christians were men of "good reputation" and filled with wisdom, faith, grace, and power (Acts 6:3, 5, 8, NASB). They are enabled to speak to and thus share with one another on a spiritual level, to sing joyfully praises to the Lord, to thank God for *all* things, and to submit to one another out of reverence to Christ (Eph 5:19-21). They bear the fruit of the Spirit (Gal 5:22-23) and display the manifestations of the Spirit in charismatic knowledge, wisdom, and power (Rom 12:6-8; I Cor 12:7-11; I Pet 4:10-11).

For the view that there is only one filling with the Holy Spirit without need of subsequent refillings, see Howard M. Ervin, *These Are Not Drunken As Ye Suppose* (Plainfield, N.J.: Logos, 1968).

R. A. K. and J. R.

HOLY SPIRIT, SIN AGAINST. The committing of the sin of blasphemy against the Holy Spirit, or the unpardonable sin, grew out of Christ's healing a man who was blind, deaf, and dumb because of demon possession (Mt 12:24-32; Mk 3:22-30; Lk 11:15-20; 12:10). The Pharisees accused Jesus of being in league with Satan and sought to prove it by asserting that Satan was obliging Jesus by withdrawing demons from people. The Lord's answer was twofold: such a divided kingdom could not stand; and how then did the Pharisees explain the success of their own Jewish exorcists? Then

Christ declared that such an accusation as the Pharisees had leveled was an unpardonable sin against the Holy Spirit.

The sin is particularly directed against the Spirit. A similar sin against Christ the Son of Man was forgivable. The reason for this is simply that while the Pharisees might have misunderstood the claims and work of Jesus as Messiah they should have known from their OT Scriptures that the Holy Spirit was powerful enough to cast out demons. Therefore, the sin is a sin against knowledge, or a sin "with a high hand" (lit., "presumptuous," KJV) in contrast to a sin of ignorance (Num 15:30). Such a sin was unforgivable in the OT, for offerings could be brought only for sins of ignorance (Num 15:22-31).

However, in order to commit this unpardonable sin, a special situation is required. It is not simply swearing in the Spirit's name, but it is the charge that the works of Christ originate from Satan, and Christ is therefore Satan's agent. But Jesus was anointed with the Spirit at the river Jordan as God's chosen Servant, and ministered publicly in the power of the Spirit (Lk 4:1, 14). The committing of this sin presupposes the personal presence of Christ in manifestation of divine power. The incident by no means teaches that some sins can be forgiven in the age to come; rather, it emphatically teaches that eternal destiny is determined here and now.

It may be that this specific sin against the Holy Spirit cannot be committed today since the Lord is not personally present on the earth. However, one should beware of attributing the miraculous gifts of the Spirit (I Cor 12:4-11, 28) to demonic or Satanic operations; and the rejection of Christ is of course an unpardonable sin anytime (Jn 3:18). I Jn 5:16 is not speaking of an unpardonable sin, because the reference is to physical death, not spiritual death. *See* Sin unto Death.

C. C. R.

HOLYDAY. Translated "holyday" in the NT only in Col 2:16 (KJV). It was actually a festival or feast day though used for a reverent, holy purpose. In all other cases in the NT it is translated as feast day or festival (e.g., Lk 2:42; Jn 5:1; 7:2; etc.). In the OT, on the other hand, the sabbath is spoken of as a holy day in Ex 35:2, in the sense of being a sacred day.

HOMAM (hō'măm). Variant name for Hemam (*q.v.*), used in I Chr 1:39.

HOME. *See* Family; Household.

HOMEBORN. *See* Service.

HOMER. *See* Weights, Measures, and Coins.

HONESTY. Three words are translated "honest" in KJV.

1. Gr. *kalos,* that which is excellent and in this sense good. We are to provide all things honest in the sight of men (Rom 12:17), and of God and men (II Cor 8:21), and see that our conduct ("conversation," KJV) is excellent before the unsaved (I Pet 2:12).

2. Gr. *semnos,* "venerable or time-proved," "reverent." Paul urges the Christian to fill his mind with what is pure and has the reverence of age ("honest," Phil 4:8), and to live a peaceable life "in all godliness and honesty" ("godly and respectful in every way," I Tim 2:2, RSV).

3. Gr. *euschēmonōs,* "decent," "becoming." The Christian is always to act becomingly, even as he would in clear daylight (Rom 13:13), and what he does is to be decent and becoming in the sight of the unsaved (I Thess 4:12).

HONEY. *See* Food.

HONOR. Honor is the high respect or esteem shown to or received from another person, or a demonstration of such respect. The concept is expressed figuratively in the OT by words which are also translated beauty, majesty, brilliancy, preciousness, weight, and glory. The parallels are significant: glory and honor (I Chr 16:27; Ps 8:5); honor and majesty (Ps 21:5; 96:6; 104:1); honor and dignity (Est 6:3); gifts and rewards and great honor (Dan 2:6); riches and honor (I Kgs 3:13). Thus the concept is involved in worship (*q.v.*), which is *worth-ship,* recognition of worth.

God Himself deserves all honor; recognition of what He is, and ascription of praise is His due. God may also cause men to be recognized by others: "God hath given riches, wealth, and honor" (Eccl 6:2). He has commanded respect to be shown to parents (Ex 20:12) and to the elderly (Lev 19:32). A virtuous wife deserves the esteem of her husband (Prov 31:25; 11:16; I Pet 3:7). Those who honor God will in turn be honored (I Sam 2:30). The man who pursues righteousness and covenant loyalty will find honor (Prov 21:21).

A suggestion of the Lord's reason for redemptively restoring honor to men is given in Ps 8:5: God made man little less than divine. The Representative Man, Jesus, crowned with glory and honor because of His suffering of death, brings redemption and ultimate glory for His redeemed (see Heb 2:5-10). Honor as a by-product of wisdom and godliness is associated with life in a sense which could find fulfillment only in a blessed immortality (Prov 3:16; 8:18; 21:21; 22:4; cf. Rom 2:7, 10).

In the Gr. NT, words meaning weight and glory are translated honor. Ethical values are in view. Honor majestically describes that approbation and mutual esteem between Father and Son (II Pet 1:17; Heb 2:9; Jn 8:49, 54). Honor in redemptive glory is bestowed on men by God (Rom 2:10; I Pet 1:7; Jn 12:26). Men and angels give glory and honor to God (I Tim 1:17; Rev 4:9; 19:1) and to Christ (Jn 5:23; Rev 5:12 f.). Men should seek the honor or approval that comes from God instead of the

approval of men (Jn 12:43). Nevertheless, we are not to deny the honor that is due others (Rom 12:10): to parents (Mt 15:4), to widows (I Tim 5:3), to masters (I Tim 6:1), and to the king (I Pet 2:17). Marriage, also, is to be held in honor by all (Heb 13:4).

W. B. W.

HOOD. The Heb. term *ṣānîp* appears in the KJV as "hoods" (Isa 3:23), and "mitre" (Zech 3:5). The RSV renders the term "turban" in both instances, which is correct as the term means "something wrapped around." *See* Dress.

HOOF. The horny casing of horses' feet (Isa 5:28; Jer 47:3), or other animals (Lev 11:3-7, 26). It is used figuratively to mean "power" or "strength" (Mic 4:13).

HOOK

1. Heb. *wāw,* a hook or ring as the head of a spike driven into wood. These were the gold (Ex 26:32; 36:36) or silver (Ex 27:10; 38:10) fasteners which held the tabernacle curtains and screens in place.

2. Heb. *ḥāḥ,* a hook or ring, such as is placed in the nose of a bull to lead it about (II Kgs 19:28) or in its jaw (Ezk 29:4; 38:4). It was a symbol of divine judgment upon Sennacherib, Pharaoh, and Gog, and upon Judah's princes (Ezk 19:4, 9, RSV). Assyrian sculpture depicts royal captives with ring in lip and attached ropes held by the Assyrian monarch (ANEP # 447), even as happened to King Manasseh of Judah (II Chr 33:11, RSV).

3. Heb. *ḥakkâ,* a hook used in fishing (Isa 19:8; Hab 1:15, RSV), mentioned in the attempts to catch leviathan (Job 41:1).

4. Heb. *ṣinnâ,* a thorn or hook, in parallel with *sîr dûgâ,* "fishhooks," a metaphor for dragging Israel captive (Amos 4:2), according to the practice described in 2.

5. Heb. *shᵉphattayim,* double or forked pegs, upon which the carcasses of beasts were hung for skinning (Ezk 40:43). The word is of doubtful meaning, however; the versions suggest edges or rims, as seen on a dressed stone sacrificial table for Apis bulls at Memphis, Egypt.

6. Gr. *agkistron,* a hook for fishing (Mt 17:27).

See also Fishhook; Flesh Hook; Pruning Hook.

H. E. Fi.

HOOPOE. *See* Animals, III.22.

HOPE. In the OT several Heb. words are translated "hope" which signify "trust," "expectation," or "prospect." In both OT and NT the object of one's hope varies according to human desires (Prov 13:12; e.g., gain, Acts 16:19; physical rescue, Acts 27:20; a husband, Ruth 1:12).

The chief theological use of the term "hope" was of trust in the supernatural, specifically in

Yahweh as the God of Israel (e.g., Ps 130:5; 146:5; Jer 17:7, 13). This trust was sometimes for safety from enemies (Ps 71:4-5; Jer 14:8-9), tending in later usage toward deliverance in the future day of the Lord (Zech 9:12). Chiefly, however, the hope of the godly Israelites was an expectation of and reliance on God's blessing and provision in the present life (Ezr 10:2; Job 11:18, 20; 14:7, 19; Ps 33:18-19, 22; 119:49-50; Lam 3:22-24).

In the NT the believer's hope is Christ (I Tim 1:1). It resides in God (Rom 15:13; I Pet 1:21), who has elected a people (Phil 1:20; Eph 1:18) and given them hope through the gospel (Col 1:23). Properly this is not merely human anticipation of better days (even salvation in one sense is "hoped for," not yet realized, Rom 8:24; 13:11), but of the final consummation of salvation in the resurrection (Acts 23:6; Rom 8:18-25) and at the revelation of Jesus (I Pet 1:13). Christ's indwelling through the Spirit becomes the Christian's "hope of glory" (Col 1:27; cf. I Jn 3:1-3). This hope is variously described: it is "laid up in heaven" (Col 1:5); it is a hope of eternal life (Tit 1:2); it is living (I Pet 1:3); and it is better than former hopes (Heb 7:19).

In the NT hope is associated with affliction and patience. Affliction is sure to come upon the faithful; it produces patience (Rom 5:3-5), and patience, hope. Such hope is an anchor for the soul (Heb 6:18 ff.). Hope in such contexts becomes virtually synonymous with trust in God, a certainty lying beyond earthly doubt (cf. Rom 5:5 with 9:33). In view of their hope Christians are to be pure (I Jn 3:3) and be ready to give their "defense" (reason) for their hope (I Pet 3:15). While living sober, upright, godly lives they are to await the fulfillment of their blessed hope, the glorious appearing of their great God and Saviour Jesus Christ (Tit 2:12-13).

Bibliography. R. Bultmann and Karl H. Rengstorf, "*Elpis,* etc.," TDNT, II, 517-535.

J. W. R.

HOPHNI (hŏf'nī). A son of the high priest Eli. The wickedness of Hophni and his brother Phinehas caused a curse to come on the house of Eli (I Sam 2:34). This curse was fulfilled at the battle of Aphek (I Sam 4:11).

HOPHRA. *See* Pharaoh-Hophra.

HOR, MOUNT (hôr). Num 20:22-29 and 33:38-39 record the death and burial of Aaron at "Hōr hā-hār" (lit., Hor the mountain), but the actual site is quite uncertain. The account in Num 20 might suggest that it lay somewhere on the E side of the Wadi 'Arabah, especially if we are right in identifying the place where Moses made the brazen serpent with the copper mining center of Punon, the modern Feinān (Num 21:6-9; cf. Num 33:42-43).

Deut 10:6, however, places the death of Aaron at Moserah, which must be the same place as Moseroth of Num 33:30. This place is equally unknown, but it was apparently somewhere in the Sinai Desert not far from Kadesh-barnea, which is usually identified with 'Ain Qadeis, close to the 1948-1967 Israeli-Egyptian boundary line. Both Mount Hor and Kadesh-barnea were thought of as being "on the border of Edom" (Num 20:14-21, 23). It seems reasonable, therefore, to look for Mount Hor in the vicinity of Kadesh-barnea. Jebel el-Hamrah has been suggested as a possible site, largely because one of the valleys running near this mountain is called Wādi Hārūniyeh, but it must be admitted that this is very fragile evidence. We are therefore driven to say that we do not know for certain where Aaron was buried.

The problem is further complicated by the difficulty that "Mount Hor" may not be a proper name at all, for *hōr* appears to be a variant of *har* (mountain), and the name may mean merely "mountain of mountains" or "the high mountain." This has some support from the fact that the same name, Hōr hā-hār, is given to a conspicuous mountain on the N frontier of ancient Israel, possibly Mount Hermon (Num 34:7). In any case the traditional identification, which goes back at least to Josephus, of Mount Hor with the towering sandstone mass of Jebel Hārūn at Petra, must with great regret be abandoned. It is too close to Sela, the ancient center of Edomite territory, into which according to the biblical account, the Hebrews were unable to penetrate during their Exodus wanderings.

D.B.

[Ed. note: Yohanan Aharoni, as a result of his explorations in the Sinai during the brief 1956-57 Israeli occupation of that region, has argued strongly for a "sacred mountain" noted first by Nelson Glueck. It is called 'Imaret el-Khureisheh, a flat-topped hill 25 acres in extent, walled about to enclose burials from the various periods of Negeb occupation. It overlooks an important road junction *c.* eight miles N of Kadesh-barnea ("Kadesh-barnea and Mount Sinai," Beno Rothenberg, *God's Wilderness,* London: Thames & Hudson, 1961, pp. 139-141.]

HORAM (hôr'ăm). The king of Gezer (*q.v.*) whom Joshua defeated and killed (Josh 10:33).

HOREB (hôr'ĕb). The name of the mountain at which Moses received the first theophany (Ex 3:1). Here also the covenant was made and the law given (Deut 5:2). The name Horeb is used synonymously with Sinai (*q.v.*). Traditionally the mountain is thought to be in the SW of the Sinai peninsula, but some modern scholars believe the site is in the S of Edom.

HOREM (hôr'ĕm). A fortified city in Naphtali (Josh 19:38). Its exact site is unknown.

HOR-HAGIDGAD (hôr'hȧ-gĭd'găd). A camp-ground during the Israelites' 38 years of wandering through the wilderness after their defeat at Hormah (Num 33:32–33). It is called Gudgodah (*q.v.*) in Deut 10:7. Its location is in the southern Negeb or the Sinai peninsula, but the exact site is unknown.

HORI (hôr'ī)

1. A Horite (*q.v.*), son of Lotan (Gen 36:22; 1 Chr 1:39).

2. The father of Shaphat, the Simeonite spy sent to Canaan by Moses (Num 13:5).

HORIM. *See* Horite.

HORITES (hôr'īts), **HURRIANS** (hŏŏr'ĭ-ȧnz)

1. The Horites (Heb. *hōrî*) were the inhabitants of Mount Seir (Gen 14:6) before the Edomites dispossessed them (Deut 2:12, 22). They were said to be descendants of Seir the Horite (Gen 36:20) and were governed by chieftains or clan leaders (36:21, 29–30). In one passage (Gen 36:2) the MT reading "Hivite" ("Zibeon the Hivite") seems to be a textual error for "Horite" (cf. 36:20, where Zibeon is listed as a son of Seir the Horite). The Heb. term as applied to these people is Semitic in origin, and probably means "cave dwellers" (*hōrîm*, cf. "holes," I Sam 14:11; Isa 42:22; Nah 2:12; "caves," Job 30:6). *See* Hivites; Hori.

According to E. A. Speiser, these Horites cannot be identified with the Hurrians because, (*a*) their personal names (Gen 36:20–30) do not conform to Hurrian patterns, but are instead Semitic (although some scholars believe Dishon and Dishan, *q.v.*, Gen 36:21, are Hurrian names); and (*b*) there is no archaeological evidence for Hurrian settlements in the Negeb (Seir) or in Transjordan ("Horite," IDB, II, 645). Such a distinction seems valid also from the standpoint of chronology, if the events of Gen 14 are to be dated *c.* 2000 B.C., too early for the known spread of Hurrians to Palestine in large numbers.

2. The LXX reads "Horites" *(Gr. chorraios)* for MT "Hivites" in Gen 34:2 and Josh 9:7. Both of these passages deal with inhabitants of central Palestine, as distinct from the Horites (see 1) of Mount Seir. Speiser pointed out in the same article that, conversely, the LXX reads *euaioi*, "Hivites," in Isa 17:9 (RSV), where the MT has *haḥōresh*, which he considers to be an evident corruption of *haḥōrî*, "the Horites."

Thus there seems to be confusion in the various texts of the OT over the matter of the Horites. These Horites in Canaan (at Shechem and Gibeon) may well be connected with the extrabiblical Hurrians, although in local usage they were commonly designated as Hivites (*q.v.*). Thus the dual use of the term "Horite" may be explained by a coincidental similarity in sound between the name of the Horites who were Semitic cave dwellers and a non-Semitic

people pushing in from Mesopotamia via Syria, who are known from ancient texts as the *Ḫurru* (Akkadian), *Ḫry* (Ugaritic), and *Ḫȝrw* (Egyptian). Speiser also explored the possibility of the "children of Heth" (Gen 10:15; 23:3–19) and sometimes "Hittite" (Ezk 16:3, 45) being another biblical term for the Hurrians (E. A. Speiser, *Genesis: The Anchor Bible*, Garden City, N.Y.: Doubleday, 1964, pp. 69, 172 f.).

Various cuneiform tablets from dozens of sites reveal that the Hurrians must have lived in the Armenian or Kurdish mountains in the 3rd mil. B.C., but began to infiltrate the Tigris-Euphrates valley before 2000 B.C. By the 19th cen. B.C. Hurrian names are found in considerable numbers as far W as Alalakh near Antioch-of-Syria, at Chagar Bazar in the Habur valley (E of Haran), at Mari on the Euphrates, and as far E as Dilbat near Babylon. In Asia Minor tablets found at Boghazköy reveal that even before the 18th cen. B.C. Hurrian religious texts were translated into Hittite. It would not be anachronistic, therefore, for Jacob to have met a Hurrian family at Shechem in his day (Gen 34).

It is certain that the Hurrians shared a similar way of life with the patriarchs, who spent many years in the ancestral home region of Haran (*q.v.*). The center of the later Hurrian state, the kingdom of Mitanni, was near Haran in the middle Euphrates valley, an area which was then called Subaru.

A study of tablets found at Nuzu (Yorgan Tepe, *c.* 12 miles SW of Kirkuk in Iraq) reveals the legal customs of the Hurrians during the mid-2nd mil. B.C. Many of the unusual actions of Abraham and Jacob with regard to marriage and children can now be understood as being part of the prevailing social culture and laws that Hurrians and Babylonians alike followed for centuries in the Middle East. *See* Abraham; Archaeology; Jacob; Nuzu; Patriarchal Age.

Under Mitannian leadership the Hurrians rose to a prominent position elsewhere in Syria (as known by tablets found at Alalakh and Ugarit, and Amarna tablets sent from Qatna and Tunip), Hittite territory (Boghazköy tablets), and E Assyria (Nuzu tablets) from *c.* 1550 to *c.* 1150 B.C.

The pressure of the Hurrians on Syria and Palestine probably accounts for the Hyksos invasion of Egypt in the 18th cen. B.C. The first of these invaders were evidently Semites, who perhaps had been pushed out of their own lands. The later waves were Hurrians (*q.v.*), according to a study of the names of the Hyksos kings. Even after the Egyptians expelled the Hyksos from Egypt *c.* 1550 B.C., a strong Hurrian element remained in Canaan, which the Egyptians sometimes called *Ḫuru*. Amenhotep II (1450–1425 B.C.) claims to have brought back 36,300 Kharu or Huru as captives from a military campaign in Palestine (ANET, p. 247).

Hurrian names are found in cuneiform tablets excavated at Taanach and Shechem, dated *c.* 1400 B.C., and in the Amarna letters (*q.v.*), such as 'Abdu-Heba of Jerusalem (ANET, pp. 487 ff.). The long letter from Tushratta, king of Mitanni, to Pharaoh Akhenaton was composed entirely in classical Hurrian. The name of the Jebusite king Araunah (*q.v.*) of Jerusalem (II Sam 24:16) can be explained as a form of Hurrian *ewri-ni,* meaning "the lord." The earliest Hurrian name in the Bible may well be Arioch (*Arĭ-aku* or *Ari-ukku*) in Gen 14:1. The OT documents are correct, therefore, in alluding to the prevalence of Hurrians in Palestine during the 2nd mil. B.C.

Bibliography. I. J. Gelb, *Hurrians and Subarians,* Chicago: Univ. of Chicago Press, 1944. Cyrus H. Gordon, "Biblical Customs and Nuzi Tablets," BA, III (1940), 1–12. Roy Hayden, "Hurrians," BW, pp. 294–298.

J. R.

HORMAH (hôr'má). A city near Ziklag. The tribes of Israel were defeated there when they tried to move into the Promised Land after the death of the ten spies sent out by Moses (Num 14:45; Deut 1:44). The city was taken later by the Israelites (Num 21:3; Josh 12:14); this feat is also attributed to Judah and Simeon (Jud 1:17). The name Hormah, "destruction," is said to come from the fall of the city formerly known as Zephath (Jud 1:17). The city is identified as being in the Negeb and belonging to Judah (Josh 15:30). David divided the spoil of the Amalekites with the city (I Sam 30:30).

HORN. Horns are mentioned in the Bible as having various uses.

1. Trumpets. A ram's horn (*qeren*) perforated at the tip was early used to sound a battle call (Josh 6:5). Similar was the *shôpār,* originally the curved horn of a wild sheep or goat, perhaps later a metal instrument in the shape of a horn which gave a loud, far-reaching note, but always translated "trumpet" (*see* Musical Instruments: Trumpet). It was used to sound an alarm (Jer 4:5, 19; 6:1, 17; Ezk 33:3–6; Joel 2:1; Amos 3:6; Zeph 1:16), to muster troops for war (Jud 3:27; 6:34; I Sam 13:3; Neh 4:18, 20; Zech 9:14) or for return from battle (II Sam 2:28; 18:16; 20:1, 22), to signal for attack (Jud 7:16–22), and to announce the beginning of religious ceremonies (Ex 19:16, 19; 20:18; Lev 25:9; Ps 81:3; Joel 2:15) or the crowning of a king (I Sam 15:10; I Kgs 1:34, 39; II Kgs 9:13). *See* Music.

Heb. *yôbēl,* "ram's horn" (Josh 6:4, 6, 8, 13), loaned its name to the year of jubilee (*q.v.*; Lev 25:8–54; 27:17–24) because the fiftieth year was opened by the blowing of the ram's horn. It is first mentioned, in Ex 19:13, as the "trumpet" blown loud and long at Mount Sinai. The *yôbēl* seems to have a religio-ceremonial significance, announcing the arrival of Yahweh as King, whether to His people to complete His covenant or proclaim release and liberty, or to His enemies to judge and smite them.

2. Containers. Being hollow and easily polished, horns have been used in ancient and modern times for drinking vessels and as flasks to hold oil or cosmetics. Ezk 27:15 describes horns inlaid with ivory and/or ebony; as such they were a much prized possession and symbol of wealth. The name of Job's third daughter reflects this usage, for Keren-happuch (Job 42:14) means "a horn of eye-paint" (jar of mascara or black antimony). The prophets used horns of this type to carry oil for anointing of kings, etc. (I Sam 16:1, 13; I Kgs 1:39).

Military trumpets of copper and silver ornamented with gold. The lowest clear notes are C and D. From tomb of Tutankhamon. LL

3. Horns of the altar. Altars made of stone (the wood and brass altars disintegrated) have been found by archaeologists. The "horn" (*qeren*) on the altar (Ex 38:2) was a hornlike protrusion on each corner. In the sacrificial rites the priest put some of the blood on the horns of the altar (Ex 29:12; Lev 8:15; etc.). Even the golden incense altar had horns on its corners (Ex 30:2–3) which received the blood of the sin offering on the Day of Atonement (Ex 30:10). Since the altar stood for justice, taking hold of the horns of the altar was a sign that one claimed sanctuary from his enemy until his case could be properly adjudicated (I Kgs 1:50–51; 2:28; cf. Ex 21:14).

4. Figurative sense. The tribe of Joseph is described with horns of the wild ox ("unicorn" in KJV) to signify his strength in conquering people (Deut 33:17). Job laments that his horn is thrust into the dust (Job 16:15). Here one's horn (like that of the ram) is the symbol of his dignity, power or strength. This figurative usage of horn is apparently based on the fact that an animal's horns are its weapon of aggressive strength; animals deprived of their horns are notably more docile. Similar usage may be found in Ps 75:4–5; 89:17, 24; 92:10; 112:9; 132:17; 148:14; Jer 48:25. A certain prophet Zedekiah made horns of iron as an object lesson to encourage King Ahab to attack the Syrians (I Kgs 22:11).

In Mary's magnificat in Lk 1:69 (following Hannah's prayer in I Sam 2:1, 10), "the horn of salvation" simply means the Lord has the strength or power to deliver or save.

Prophetic passages in Daniel and Zechariah (1:18–21) use the term specifically of kings or kingdoms that have existed or shall rise up. In Dan 8 the goat with one horn (Greece) rises up against the ram with two horns (Media and Persia). The great beast of Dan 7 which has ten horns plus a little horn that devours three others is similar in appearance to the great red dragon and the beast out of the sea of Rev 12:3; 13:1, both of whom have seven heads and ten horns. Rev 17:9 reveals that the seven heads represent seven mountains and the ten horns (v. 12) are ten kings. Amos has kings in mind when he accuses Israel of boasting that they have taken horns (kings) by their own power (Amos 6:13).

The KJV in Hab 3:4 misunderstands a rarer Heb. word spelled with the same consonants *q-r-n* and translates it "horn" where it should be "ray of light." It was this same misunderstanding of Ex 34:29–30, 35 in the Vulgate which made Michelangelo put horns on his immortal statue of Moses.

E. B. S.

HORNET. *See* Animals: Wasp, III.55.

HORONAIM (hôr′ŏ-nā′ĭm). A city of Moab, site uncertain. It is mentioned in Isa 15:5; Jer 48:3, 5, 34, and on the Moabite Stone (11. 31–32). The references indicate that it was probably between the highlands of Moab and the Arabah.

HORONITE (hôr′ŏ-nīt). A title given to Sanballat, an opponent of Nehemiah (Neh 2:10, 19; 13:28). It probably indicates that he was a native of Beth-horon.

HORSE. *See* Animals, I.11.

HORSE GATE. *See* Jerusalem: Gates and Towers 13.

HORSEMAN. One who rides a horse, almost always for military purposes, i.e., a cavalryman.

Israel was late among the nations to use horses and most references are to foreign armies. OT references are frequently to chariot drivers since chariotry was earlier than cavalry. The Assyrians first developed cavalry tactics, and many references to horsemen in the prophets have in mind the Assyrians, e.g., Isaiah, Jeremiah, Ezekiel, Hosea, Joel and Habakkuk. Elisha cried, "The chariot of Israel, and the horsemen thereof " (II Kgs 2:12; cf. 13:14), referring symbolically to angelic protection or to Elijah's godly influence and power in prayer. King Joram of Israel sent messengers on horseback to meet Jehu in his chariot (II Kgs 9:17–19). In the NT, Paul was escorted from Jerusalem to Caesarea by 70 horsemen (Acts 23:23–32).

Much use is made of horsemen in apocalyptic writing, e.g., in Zechariah and Revelation. Horses of white, red, black and pale have riders (Rev 6:1–8), who have come to be known as "the four horsemen of the Apocalypse." Horsemen are further pictured wearing colorful breastplates (Rev 9:17, 19). The returned Christ and His hosts are pictured as horsemen riding to victory on white horses (Rev 19:11–21).

W. A. A.

A horseman from the early Assyrian site of Halaf. BM

HORSE LEACH. *See* Animals: Leech, V. 6.

HOSAH (hō′zà)

1. A border city of Asher, S or SE of Tyre (Josh 19:29). The exact location is uncertain; possibly to be identified with modern Khirbet el-Hosh. Moore suggests identification with Assyrian *Usu* of Sennacherib's Taylor Cylinder (ICC, *Judges*, p. 51), which in turn may be the mainland settlement of Tyre (ANET, p. 287*b*; cf. p. 300*b*).

2. A Levite who with his family was chosen by David to be a gatekeeper to the ark of the covenant after it was moved to Jerusalem (I Chr 16:38). This family had similar assignments in the later organization of the Levites in preparation for worship in the temple (I Chr 26:10–11, 16).

HOSANNA. An indeclinable exclamation which seems to mean "help (save) now!" It occurs alone (Mk 11:9; Jn 12:13), with "to the son of David" (Mt 21:9*a*, 15), and "in the highest" (Mt 21:9*b*; Mk 11:10). The NT uses it only at the triumphal entry. The Heb. *hôshî*ʿâ nāʾ and Aram. *hôsha nāʾ* occurred in the Hallel (Ps 113–118) and was recited ritually at the Feast of Tabernacles (Ps 118:25, "Save now, we beseech thee, O Jehovah," ASV). It is interesting to note that the Latin versions transliterated the Heb. of this expression in this verse. The Hallel was also sung at the Passover offering, the Passover supper, and the Feasts of Pentecost and Dedication (Edersheim, *Life and Times of Jesus the Messiah,* II, 371 f.). The singing was accompanied by waving palm, myrtle, and willow branches (the *Tulabh*).

Besides liturgical uses, both the Hallel and the branches were used to greet kings and visitors to festivals. The use at the triumphal entry is, therefore, probably to be interpreted as recognition (homage) paid to Jesus by the people as their anticipated promised King. The phrase was adopted by the early church as a part of its ritual (*Didache* 10:6, in the prayer of the Lord's Supper: "Let grace come and let this world pass away. Hosannah to the God of David"). From this it has passed into the modern church ritual.

J. W. R.

HOSEA (hō-zā'à). An OT prophet of the 8th cen., the only writing prophet who lived in the northern kingdom, except possibly Jonah. His name means "salvation" and is identical with the original form of Joshua's name (Num 13:8) and that of Hoshea (*q.v.*), the last king of Israel (II Kgs 15:30).

Hosea, the son of Beeri and a younger contemporary of Amos, began his prophetic ministry before 753 B.C. when Jeroboam II died. Exactly how long his work of proclaiming God's judgment upon the sins of his country continued, is not known. Objections to treaties made with Egypt (Hos 7:11; 12:1) may refer to King Hoshea's sending messengers to the king of Egypt ((II Kgs 17:4), who would be Pharaoh Tefnakhte (726–716 B.C.). If this is the occasion to which the prophet alludes, he ministered to the very closing years of the northern kingdom. His mention of Hezekiah and his three predecessors may indicate he fled to the kingdom of Judah to close out his ministry (Hos 1:1; cf. 1:7, 11; 4:15; 5:5, 10, 12–14; 6:4, 11; 8:14; 10:11; 11:12; 12:2).

Much of what can or cannot be learned of the prophet depends on the interpretation followed in chaps. 1 and 3 of the book. For centuries these chapters have been the subject of much discussion. Basically, the various opinions can be divided into two parts.

1. The allegorical view. This view has been held by many Jewish and Christian interpreters. It maintains that all the passages dealing with Hosea's marriage and family life, such as the command to take "a wife of harlotry" (1:2), are to be understood figuratively. The God of Israel, it is thought, would not require Hosea to marry a corrupt woman, and then use that relationship to teach a lesson on faithfulness.

2. The literal view. According to this view, chaps. 1 and 3 are to be taken together and refer to the same wife. Accordingly, Hosea married a woman named Gomer and she gave birth to three children. In time Gomer proved faithless and left her husband; later, Hosea bought her from her paramour and brought her home again. This view, in spite of obvious difficulties, has commended itself to many exegetes. It is pointed out that certain details of what happened, such as the precise amount of money spent by Hosea in reclaiming his wife (3:2), do not fit an allegorical interpretation. The fact remains, also, that the incidents recorded in these controversial chapters are related as though they were actual historical events. Whatever the correct view, Hosea's personal disappointments in love certainly contributed to his tender prophetic message. In Hosea, human experience became the channel of divine revelation.

See Gomer.

N. R. L.

HOSEA, BOOK OF. The first of the Minor Prophets in the English canon and the Twelve in the Heb. canon. Although it comes from the latter half of the 8th cen. B.C. and Obadiah, Joel, Jonah, and Amos probably belonged to the 9th and early 8th cen. B.C., Hosea seems to have been placed first because it was the longest of the Minor Prophets.

The book bears the name of its author, and is the sole source of information about Hosea's life and ministry. However, more is known of Hosea's home life than of any other prophet, since it was the basis for his message to God's people (*see* Hosea). His prophecy is the only surviving writing from the northern prophet to his own people, although Amos, a southerner who ministered to the northern kingdom, has a book in the sacred canon. Snaith thinks chap. 7 of Hosea shows that the prophet was a baker. The numerous references to agricultural matters may suggest that Hosea had some connection with the soil.

Major Themes

The book of Hosea naturally falls into two parts: the prophet's domestic life (1:1–3:5) and the prophetic discourses (4:1–14:9). In the prophetic discourses there are three dominant themes: the sin of the nation (4:1–8:14; 11:12–13:16); the certainty of divine judgment for this sin (9:1 – 10:15; 11:12 – 13:16); and the ultimate bestowal of God's mercy and love on a repentant people (11:1- 11; 14:1-9).

Theories of Interpretation

The first three chapters of Hosea have constituted an interpretive problem for both Jewish and Christian scholars. It appears that God commanded Hosea to marry Gomer the harlot. An order to do something so morally evil seems to impugn the righteousness and holiness of God. Hence, these various interpretations have arisen with regard to chaps. 1-3. |

1. Jewish interpreters during medieval times (Maimonides, Aben Ezra, Kimchi) held that no such marriage actually took place. The whole affair was the object of a prophetic dream or vision. It was similar to Ezekiel's visit to Jerusalem (Ezk 8- 11).

2. Others have argued that Hosea's marriage was a prophetic allegory. From such an allegory it would be wrong to think that one can deduce what the actual situation was. Against this view is the fact that no clear allegorical meaning can be found for Gomer's name.

3. Luther and Osiander suggested that while Gomer and her children are called adulterous, it was done for parabolic purposes, and was not actually the case.

4. Gomer was already a harlot at the time God ordered Hosea to marry her. Each step in the relationship was taken not at the prophet's impulse but at God's command. That is, the prophet's marriage, the birth of his children, the disruption of his home, and the restoration of Gomer were done deliberately as a medium whereby God could speak to Israel (e.g., Hubbard, *With Bands of Love*, p. 54).

5. Thomas Aquinas and Sebastian Schmidt sought to circumvent the problem by supposing that Gomer was a concubine rather than a wife. It is hard to see how this avoids any of the difficulties.

6. Most likely the correct interpretation was suggested by Gebhard. He held that Hosea married Gomer prior to her harlotry. It was only after the marriage and the birth of Jezreel that Gomer became unfaithful. At the time of her marriage to Hosea she had within her a spirit of harlotry (cf. Hos 4:12; 5:4, NASB), but it had not yet manifested itself. This interpretation has the advantages of preserving the historical character of the account and the holiness of God. *See also* Hosea.

Message

Whatever the difficulties of determining the correct interpretation may be, the basic message of the prophet is clear. Israel is the wife of Yahweh (2:19- 20; cf. 2:2). She has entered into this holy relationship by way of a covenant (6:7; 8:1). However, like Gomer, the nation is guilty of spiritual infidelity, having been corrupted by Baal worship (2:8, 13, 17; 4:13; 11:2).

More fundamental than their idolatry is the

people's lack of personal knowledge of their God (4:1, 6; 5:4; 6:6; 13:4). They have rejected a close, warm contact with His loving heart (4:6). In their return they must press on to know Yahweh (6:1- 3). Coordinate to their infidelity and the spurning of His love is the absence of covenant loyalty and devotion (*ḥesed*) on their part (4:2; 6:4, 6, NASB marg.); a revival of its observance is essential (10:12; 12:6).

Even though Israel has fallen to this despicable level, Yahweh still loves her with yearning compassion (11:8-9; 14:4). If she will but repent (10:12; 12:6; 14:1) He will have mercy and restore her. Whereas Amos *thunders* against the northern kingdom, Hosea *pleads*. In Amos there is portrayed the unapproachable righteousness of God, while in Hosea there is demonstrated the unfailing love (*ḥesed*) of God. Just as Luke writes of the prodigal son, so Hosea tells of the prodigal wife.

Style and Text

The unusual style of the writer of this book poses some difficult problems for the exegete. He uses a great variety of figures of speech in achieving parallel thoughts in the usual pattern of Heb. poetry. The writer merges himself in the message he delivers, so much so that often he appears to be pleading in the capacity of God Himself. This personal vigor accounts for many of the abrupt transitions and makes it unnecessary to relegate parts of the book to later interpolations. Another difficulty is that the Heb. text of Hosea is probably more corrupt than that of any other OT book. The LXX may be used in a number of places to restore the text. Occasionally it may have preserved superior readings as well as additional phrases.

Outline

Title, 1:1

I. The Prologue: The Message in General by Illustration, 1:2 – 3:5
  A. Hosea's first marriage with harlotrous Gomer, 1:2 – 2:23
    1. The children born and named to symbolize Israel's rejection, 1:2- 9
    2. Message of comfort to Hosea concerning Israel, 1:10 – 2:1
    3. Message of chastisement to Israel, 2:2- 13
    4. Message of restoration to Israel, 2:14- 23
  B. Hosea's remarriage to Gomer, 3:1- 5
    1. The buying back and cleansing of his adulterous wife, 3:1- 3
    2. The symbolic meaning: by captivity Israel will be prepared for restoration in the latter days, 3:4-5

II. The Treatise: The Message in Detail by Prophecy, 4:1 – 14:8
  A. God's lawsuit: Israel's sin is intolerable, 4:1 – 6:3

1. The indictment: lack and rejection of experiential knowledge of God, fidelity, and covenant loyalty, 4:1 — 5:7
2. The sentence, 5:8 – 14
3. The prophecy of restoration, 5:15 – 6:3

B. God's judgment: Israel is about to be punished, 6:4 – 10:15
1. The character of their sins demands punishment, 6:4 – 8:14
2. Description of their punishment, 9:1 – 10:15
3. Parenthetical plea for repentance, 10:12

C. God's love: Israel shall be restored, 11:1 – 14:8
1. God's yearning love over Ephraim and future restoration, 11:1-11
2. Yet sinful Ephraim must first be punished, 11:12 – 13:16
3. Final victory of God's love, 14:1-8

Conclusion, 14:9

Bibliography. H. L. Ellison, *The Prophets of Israel,* Grand Rapids: Eerdmans, 1969, pp. 95-167. Charles L. Feinberg, *Hosea: God's Love for Israel,* New York: American Board of Missions to the Jews, 1947. J. B. Hindley, "Hosea," NBC, 3rd ed. rev., pp. 703-715. David A. Hubbard, *With Bands of Love: Studies in Hosea,* Grand Rapids: Eerdmans, 1968. John H. Johansen, "The Prophet Hosea: His Marriage and Message," JETS, XIV (1971), 179-184. G. A. F. Knight, *Hosea: God's Love,* London: SCM Press, 1960. G. Campbell Morgan, *Hosea: The Heart and Holiness of God,* New York: Revell, 1934. Charles F. Pfeiffer, "Hosea," WBC, pp. 801-818 (with good bibliography). Norman H. Snaith, *Mercy and Sacrifice,* London: SCM Press, 1953; *Amos, Hosea, and Micah,* London: Epworth, 1956. Herbert F. Stevenson, *Three Prophetic Voices,* Old Tappan: Revell, 1971, pp. 95-158. James M. Ward, *Hosea: A Theological Commentary,* New York: Harper & Row, 1966; "The Message of the Prophet Hosea," *Interpretation,* XXIII (1969), 387-407.

                                                              P. D. F.

HOSEN. Used only in Dan 3:21, where the context shows it to be wearing apparel. RSV translates the term "tunic." "Hosen" is a 17th cen. English term for a garment such as leggings or trousers covering the hips and legs. The Aramaic word *p^etash* means "undergarment, breeches" (Marcus Jastrow, *A Dictionary of the Targumim, the Talmud Babli and Yerushalmi, and the Midrashic Literature,* ii, 1155). In Daniel its obvious use is to indicate that the men were fully dressed.

HOSHAIAH (hō-shā'yà)
1. The leader of half of the princes of Judah in the procession around the wall of Jerusalem

when it was dedicated by Nehemiah (Neh 12:32).
2. Father of Jezaniah or Azariah, a commander of the forces of Judah after the fall of Jerusalem (Jer 42:1; 43:2).

HOSHAMA (hŏsh'á-má). A son of Jeconiah (Jehoiachin) whom King Nebuchadnezzar carried into captivity with the 10,000 nobles in 597 B.C. (I Chr 3:18).

HOSHEA (hō-shē'á)
1. The original name of Joshua (Deut 32:44), sometimes called Oshea (Num 13:8), but changed by Moses to Joshua (Num 13:16, RSV). *See* Joshua.
2. Son of Azaziah and a prince of the tribe of Ephraim in the time of David (I Chr 27:20).
3. The son of Elah, and the last king of Israel (II Kgs 15:30; 17:1-6; 18:1, 9 – 12). His reign lasted nine years (732-722 B.C.). It seems fairly certain that the anti-Assyrian demonstrations of Pekah, the preceding king, brought down the wrath of Tiglath-pileser III upon the kingdom and reduced Israel to one-third its original size. This produced a pro-Assyrian party led by Hoshea, culminating in the murder of Pekah and the enthronement of the assassin (II Kgs 15:30). But even this reacted unfavorably for Israel, for Tiglath-pileser III brought the pressure of his armed might on Hoshea so that he became a mere viceroy of a foreign power. In the annals of Assyria the monarch boasted, "They overthrew their king Pekah and I placed Hoshea as king over them" (ANET, p. 284).

Apparent chronological inconsistencies within the biblical record and amazing incongruities with contemporary Assyrian history have presented almost insuperable problems to the scholars. This has led some to conclude falsely that there was a period of nine years between the death of Pekah and the accession of Hoshea when there was no king in Israel. But once the principle for unraveling the meaning of the mysterious numbers was discovered, it was evident that the Bible contained a perfect system of chronology. Thus the dates for Hoshea's reign are *c.* 732-722 B.C. (*see* Chronology, OT).

The failure of Hoshea to display full subserviency to the new Assyrian monarch, Shalmaneser V (727-722 B.C.), heralded the end. When Hoshea failed to pay the annual tribute and instead sent envoys for assistance to the king of Egypt at So (Sais) in the western Delta (*see* So), Shalmaneser first imprisoned the king of Israel and then organized the siege of Samaria. After three years of siege the city was captured by Sargon II, the new ruler of Assyria. The northern kingdom came to an end, and thousands were carried into captivity. This was the judgment of God upon Israel (II Kgs 17:7). *See* Hosea.
4. One of the Jewish chiefs who joined in the

renewal of the covenant after the Captivity (Neh 10:23).

H. A. Hoy.

HOSPITALITY. The reception and lodging of travelers was viewed in Bible lands as a binding obligation to be conscientiously fulfilled. The stranger was to be courteously treated as a guest. In fact, the facilities of the household were placed at his disposal. After eating food with his guest, the host considered it his duty to protect him during his stay. This kind of oriental hospitality is seen in Lot's reception of the two angels (Gen 19:1-8; see also Gen 18:2-8; Ex 2:15-20). In NT times, Jesus made the 70 disciples dependent upon the hospitality of the people when He sent them out with no provisions for the journey (Lk 10:1-12). In the judgment scene of Mt 25:31-46, the criterion for judgment is the practice of hospitality toward Christ's brethren. During the Apostolic Age, apostles and itinerant teachers were supported by the hospitality of Christian people while on tour (Acts 16:15; 17:7; 18:7; 21:4-8, 16; 28:7, 14; III Jn 5-8). See II Jn 10-11 for a misuse of this practice by propagators of error. In Rom 12:13 and Heb 13:2, hospitality (*philoxenia*, "love of strangers") is treated as a Christian virtue. The corresponding adjective (*philoxenos*, "loving strangers") expresses a qualification of the bishop (I Tim 3:2; Tit 1:8) as well as a duty of all Christians (I Pet 4:9). Widows being considered for financial aid were to have been known for this quality (I Tim 5:10, "lodged strangers").

Bibliography. W. Ewing, "Hospitality," HDB rev. G. Stählin, *"Xenos . . . Philoxenia . . ."* TDNT, V, 17-25.

D. W. B.

HOST
1. Literally, Gr. *xenos,* as does Latin *hostis,* meant a stranger; then, "guest"; then, one who receives and entertains strangers, or a host such as Gaius in Rom 16:23. *See* Hospitality.
2. An innkeeper who acts as host for his guests (Lk 10:35).
3. Several Heb. words used frequently in a military sense of a large number of fighting men. *See* Army.
4. The meaning, in the plural form, of Sabaoth (*q.v.*) in the title "the Lord of Sabaoth" (Rom 9:29; Jas 5:4). It is transliterated from Heb. *ṣᵉbā'ôth,* "hosts," which occurs hundreds of times in the OT as "the Lord of hosts" and "the Lord God of hosts." God is recognized as the divine Commander of the armies of Israel on earth (Josh 5:14-15) and especially of the heavenly bodies (Isa 51:15; Jer 31:35), and of the angels in heaven (Neh 9:6; Ps 103:20-21; 148:1-6). *See* Host of Heaven.

HOST OF HEAVEN. The Heb. expression *ṣᵉbā' hashshāmayim,* "army of the skies," is found *c.* 18 times in the OT. The Heb. word

ṣābā' occurs nearly 500 times in the OT and usually means "army."

Since the realms of the earth and heaven were closely associated in the thinking of the ancients, the heathen neighbors of Israel imagined the celestial bodies as organized in military array. The sun, moon, and stars were under the symbol of an army. The sun was the king; the moon, the viceregent; and the stars and planets, their attendants (cf. Jud 5:20), i.e., an army, the heavenly host. These creations were thought to be animated by divine spirits constituting a living army which controlled human destiny.

Although the Israelites were warned against such pagan beliefs (Deut 4:19; 17:3), they succumbed to the temptation during the Assyrian and Babylonian periods to worship the heavenly bodies (II Kgs 17:16; 21:3, 5; 23:4-5; II Chr 33:3, 5; Jer 8:2; 19:13; Zeph 1:5; Acts 7:42). Israel's doctrine of the Lord as the Creator of heaven and earth, the one who marshaled the heavenly bodies at His command, was the antidote to this pagan practice (cf. Gen 1:14-19; 2:1; Neh 9:6; Ps 33:6; 103:21; 148:2; Isa 40:26; 45:12)

The concepts of celestial bodies and angelic beings were closely related. Included in the idea of the heavenly host is that of angels (messengers). These heavenly attendants are closely related to the Lord's kingly role. They are His army. As King, He presides over His heavenly council, composed of angelic servants or "sons of God" (cf. Micaiah's vision in I Kgs 22:19; also Gen 1:26; Job 1-2; Ps 82; Isa 6). Divine messengers at intervals were dispatched from the Lord's council to accomplish His purpose (cf. the angelic host, Lk 2:13; Jacob's encounter with a band of angels, Gen 28:12 ff.).

In the OT the LORD (Yahweh) is frequently mentioned as "the LORD (Yahweh), God of hosts," i.e., the LORD God of the armies (cf. Jer 5:14; 38:17; 44:7; Hos 12:5, *et al.*). The apostles Paul (Rom 9:29) and James (Jas 5:4) use the Heb. term *sabaoth,* "hosts," as a title for the Lord. *See* God, Names and Titles of; War.

D. W. D.

HOSTAGE. Literally, the Heb. expression means "son of sureties." It occurs only in II Kgs 14:14 and the parallel passage in II Chr 25:24.

HOTHAM (hō'tham)
1. An Aroerite, father of two of David's mighty men (I Chr 11:44). The name is incorrectly rendered "Hothan" by KJV. *See* Hothan.
2. An Asherite (I Chr 7:32). *See* Helem.

HOTHAN (hō'than). This name is found only in I Chr 11:44, KJV. *See* Hotham 1.

HOTHIR (hō'thir). A son of Heman and head of the 21st course in the temple service in the time of David (I Chr 25:4, 28).

HOUGH. The older form of "hock." In the hind leg of a quadraped it is the joint between the knee and the fetlock. The verb means "to cut the hamstring of an animal," thus permanently crippling it. The word "hough" appears in Josh 11:6, 9; II Sam 8:4; I Chr 18:4. In the RSV all of the above uses are translated "hamstring." In addition, the RSV translates the term in Gen 49:6 "hamstring," while the KJV renders it "they digged down a wall."

HOUR. *See* Time, Divisions of.

HOUSE. This is the translation of some five words in the Bible. The house (Heb. *bayit;* Gr. *oikia*) designates variously the dwelling place of a family, of the king, or the temple of God in Jerusalem. The term may also designate a nation (house of Israel), a tribe, a family (Gen 7:1, etc.).

Historical development. The earliest known dwellings were the natural caves where humans sought shelter from the elements. In the 8th mil. B.C. the cave dwellers were leaving them and moving out into the open after the heavy rains (and the glaciers farther N) of the Ice Age had ceased. Shortly thereafter began the appearance of tents and huts of sticks stuck in the ground in a circular fashion with tops secured together and covered with thatch or leaves. The ingenuity of others developed stone walls across the mouths of caves or in front of them and covered the space with poles or skins.

Reconstruction of a courtyard of a house at Ur in the days of Abraham. Family rooms were located on the second floor; the kitchen, storage, and servants' quarters on the first floor.
University of Pa. Museum

Model of a house and estate at Amarna, Egypt, *c.* 1375–1330 B.C. This is the sort of upper class home Moses would have known there.
ORINST

The evidence of huts grouped together to form houses indicates the need, in the mind of thinking men, to compartmentalize for function, privacy, and — more space. At one stage of development, some groups saw the advantage of protection in building their huts on wooden pilings in lakes, many of two or more rooms. In the European lake dwellings occurred the crossed, overlapping logs at the corners.

At what time men passed in their thinking from the consideration of houses as merely a group of dwellings to view them as a city, is not known. However, Jericho in Palestine, at present considered the oldest known walled city, goes back well before 6000 B.C., thus indicating not too long a period from the cave-dwelling era to the rise of the concept of the city. Early Neolithic agricultural villages, such as Hacilar in Anatolia, Jarmo in Iraq, and Beidha near Petra in Jordan, may slightly antedate the massive defensive wall and moat of Jericho.

In Egypt, Mesopotamia, and the lowlands of Syria and Palestine, bricks of hand-formed, sun-dried mud became the common building material. Frequently in Mesopotamia and Egypt, the seal of the reigning king was stamped upon them, helping to date the structure and to correlate it with the inscriptions of the king describing his building activities. Earlier, however, in the lowlands along the coast of Palestine and around Lake Huleh, the most available building material had been the marsh reed. The technique involved a circular floor plan in which reeds were combined with clay bricks to form beehive-like houses.

In Chalcolithic burials (4000–3200 B.C.) ossuaries, which are modeled after houses, indicate a rectangular plan, with reeds bound together and plastered solid with mud to form the roof. In other places wattle and daub houses were constructed with sticks stuck in the ground and walls formed by basket-weaving reeds (wattles) and surfaces daubed with mud to present a solid face to the weather. During the early Chalcolithic period people in the Beer-sheba plain dug subterranean dwellings in the compacted loess earth.

In the highlands of Palestine, abundance of stone determined the general building material. Frequently two-storied houses are found, along with one-storied kinds, with a flat roof and exterior stairway to it. Stairs were usually of stone or brick, placed against an outer wall or the wall of the courtyard. It is possible that sometimes they passed down inside the dwelling as suggested by Mk 13:15, "not go down *into* the house." Roofs were more often framed with wood beams with smaller cross members on which were placed small branches or straw covered with a packed clay. The OT required a parapet (Heb. *gāg,* "battlement") around the roof to prevent injury by a fall (Deut 22:8).

Ruins of the "House of the Faun" at Pompeii, an example of a Roman villa of St. Paul's day. In the front of the house was a large covered area (atrium) with a pool in the center and surrounded by rooms; in the back was an open pillared courtyard surrounded by rooms. HFV

Evidence of the use of the column reveals considerable imagination. At Neolithic Jericho a building with inner and outer chambers with six columns across the front is an outstanding example. The inner room has two wooden columns supporting the superstructure. The columns in front obviously supported a porch antedating by 3000 years the porch of Solomon's house of the forest. In an Early Bronze Age temple (*c.* 2500 B.C.) at Ai (BA, VII [1944], fig. 3) four limestone bases were found and part of a charred wooden post still *in situ.* The size of the stump and of the neatly trimmed plinths indicate heavy loads above, suggesting a second story. Later, in an Early Iron Age villa (*c.* 1200 B.C.) at the same site four hewn pillars were unearthed which supported the roof or upper story extending over one side of the courtyard. Similar plans appeared in houses dated 900 and 750 B.C. at Hazor (BA, XXI, figs. 7, 10).

As civilization developed in Egypt some of the better houses were built from stone quarried from cliffs. In Palestine from 3000 B.C. onward throughout the Canaanite period (ending *c.* 1200 B.C.), as evidence from Tell Beit

Mirsim (Debir?) indicates during the Hyksos domination, houses were well constructed, and thickness of stone walls suggests a need for protection. The floor plan of the house of a patrician or Hyksos chieftain at Tell Beit Mirsim *c.* 1600 B.C. reveals six rooms on one side of a long courtyard *c.* 20 by 40 feet (Albright, *Archaeology of Palestine,* fig. 16; ANEP # 723).

In the early Israelite period, *c.* 1200–1000 B.C., rudeness of fit shows an unfamiliarity with stone construction. Later, in Solomon's time and afterward, technical advance in understanding and usage is indicated in the fine stone work of house, city wall and palace. When the need arose for monumental buildings, as the temple of Yahweh and Solomon's house of the forest of Lebanon, craftsmen familiar with this type of architecture had to be imported, the source of easiest acquisition being Phoenicia. I Kgs 6 gives some idea of what the house of Yahweh was like as to materials and techniques used. Stones were squared up by marginal drafting and then cut to shape for fitting into the wall. The roof was of timber, with the floors, interior walls and ceilings made of fir and cedar boards with carved and gold-leaf decoration.

Exact technical descriptions pertain to the enclosure wall described as of three courses of stone topped by a row of cedar beams (I Kgs 6:36; 7:12). Some light is shed on this structure by the contemporary Megiddo gate. The substructure of five courses of close-jointed limestone had bond beams four inches thick between the second and third courses. In the case of Solomon's temple, therefore, the reference to the manner of construction might refer only to the substructure.

The temple itself in plan consisted of two rooms,̓ the holy place and the holy of holies where the ark of the covenant was placed. This reflects the familiar plan of temples found elsewhere in Palestine and other countries, indicating only the appropriateness of plan to functions and not an evolution of the worship of Yahweh. *See* Temple.

The House of the Forest of Lebanon (*q.v.*) was named for its many cedar pillars and wall boards. Four rows of pillars divided it lengthwise, and it had three rows of upper chambers of 15 each (I Kgs 7:2–5). This palace was connected to a waiting room (Hall of Pillars?) and the Hall of the Throne, and included private apartments for the king (the palace?) and for Pharaoh's daughter (I Kgs 7:6–8). It housed the golden shields, the ivory throne and precious vessels (I Kgs 10:7, 21; II Chr 9:16, 20; Isa 22:8). The palace adjoined the temple compound on the S, thus combining the house of God and His viceroy. Since no definite archaeological information exists, exact layout cannot be determined.

Plans and construction. In the cities and walled towns of Palestine and elsewhere, houses were built wall to wall. Any open courts lay within the exterior house walls and had rooms opening off them. Houses faced on the narrow streets; where city walls occurred, these commonly formed the rear house wall. When population increased as in later times, houses in Palestine usually became smaller with smaller rooms and thinner walls, and less attention was paid to urban planning. As such, city planning was known in the early history of the Sumerian city-state of Erech, whose king Gilgamesh proposed a threefold division of the town and its environs into houses, temple and fields.

In details the houses had, of course, a doorway and frequently windows. In some of the better homes, the door would be framed with wood lintel and posts. Thick doors of wood during the Bronze Age (3000–1200 B.C.) were evidenced by large threshold stone sockets; these were often absent in houses of David's day, suggestive of an effective police force to protect the inhabitants. In such cases a hanging of cloth or skin would serve as a door. Windows sometimes opened out through the city wall when the house was incorporated into the fortification (cf. Josh 2:15; Acts 9:25; II Cor 11:32–33). Windows on the street would have lattices (q.v.).

Storage pits for grain were dug down into the floor, sometimes lined with plaster, sometimes being large clay jars sunk into the ground. Fire pits were also dug into the floor, or sometimes built up with a low wall around to hold in the fire. Not having a chimney, the smoke found its way out through doors and windows. Such fires also heated the houses, with braziers used to supplement them. Floors were generally of beaten clay, although in the better homes plaster and even stone is found. By NT times the wealthy houses and villas often had mosaic floors, as at Pompeii and Antioch-on-the-Orontes.

Porters or doorkeepers are mentioned (I Chr 15:23–24; Jn 10:3; 18:16–17; Acts 12:13–15); in wealthier homes they determined who should be admitted to the house.

In most cities some attempt at drainage systems to carry off rain water and sometimes

Floor mosaics of wealthy Roman homes were often elaborate and done in many colors. Here the god Dionysus is seated on a panther, from the island of Delos. Hannibal

sewage is found, usually of stone-lined and stone-covered channels, though clay pipe and open half-pipe systems are discovered.

In the Hellenistic period more evidence of city planning is found with more rectangular street plans occurring. The houses assumed a more rectangular or even square shape. Bathrooms with plumbing also occur in the homes of the wealthy. Herodian Jericho had by NT times become a garden paradise with public baths and fine homes (Lk 19:1–10). The homes of the wealthy in Roman Palestine were similar to the well-known Roman houses, with covered atrium or hall and surrounding rooms, behind which was an open court with surrounding rooms, affording utmost privacy.

Furnishings. During most of the biblical period, the house served for both dwelling and storage. Amazement occurs at the charred remains of the variety of implements, goods, animals, etc., stored in them. In very cold or severely inclement weather, the most precious animals shared its shelter (cf. II Sam 12:1–4).

The poorest families had only a few kitchen utensils and their bedding (sometimes only their cloak, Ex 22:26–27), sleeping on only a reed mat (Jn 5:8–12). If a guest room were provided, it would contain only a bed, table, chair and clay lamp (II Kgs 4:10, RSV). If beds were afforded, the rich had high bedsteads (Gen 47:31; 48:2; 49:33; Ezk 23:41); others had a sort of low cot (Ex 8:3; Lk 8:16). Some had chests for storage of clothes and bedding like the ornate boxes found in Tutankhamon's tomb. The wealthy indulged in furniture having inlaid ivory and gold leaf (Amos 6:4).

Cooking was done in good weather in outside fireplaces; in bad weather, inside. Bread ovens occur both inside and out. A pair of millstones

A black-and-white floor mosaic from Delos.
HFV

(Deut 24:6) provided the means for grinding grain for flour. Olive oil was stored in special clay jars. Frequently cisterns are found inside the courtyard for water storage. Cooking pots are found, wide-mouth types for stirring, smaller-mouth types for liquids. Fingers were the most usual eating "utensils." The rich provided themselves with gold and silver tableware. *See* Architecture; City.

Bibliography. W. F. Albright, *Archaeology of Palestine,* Harmondsworth: Penguin, 1960. Emmanuel Anati, *Palestine Before the Hebrews,* New York: Knopf, 1963. H. Keith Beebe, "Ancient Palestinian Dwellings," BA, XXXI (1968), 38–58. A. C. Bouquet, *Everyday Life in New Testament Times,* New York: Scribner, 1954, pp. 27–38. "Cities, Israelite; Building and Houses," CornPBE, pp. 212–217. E. W. Heaton, *Everyday Life in Old Testament Times,* New York: Scribner, 1956, pp. 55–77. Otto Michel, *"Oikos,* etc.," TDNT, V, 119–159. G. Ernest Wright, *Biblical Archaeology,* rev. ed., Philadelphia: Westminster, 1962, pp. 187–190.

H. G. S.

HOUSEHOLD. This is the translation of eight words in the Bible, the most frequent OT word being Heb. *bayit,* "house." Job 1:3 has *'ăbuddâ,* "household," a set of servants for the family. Gr. *therapeia,* of similar meaning, occurs in Lk 12:42. The common Gr. *oikos,* "house(hold)," describes the families of Lydia (Acts 16:15), Stephanas (I Cor 1:16), and Onesiphorus (II Tim 4:19). An attributive form of *oikia* occurs in Mt 10:25, 36, "those of his household" *(oikiakos).*

The household is the object of the care of a virtuous woman (Prov 31:15 ff.). Members are recipients of religious instruction (Gen 18:19), rejoice together at God's mercies (Deut 14:26), and are to be evangelized (Acts 16:15; 16:33–34). Christians were numbered in the household of Caesar (Phil 4:22). Christian believers have become members of a new spiritual family, the "household of the faith" (Gal 6:10, NASB), God's household (Eph 2:19, NASB). *See* Family; Home.

HOUSEHOLDER. *See* Goodman; Household.

HOUSE OF THE FOREST OF LEBANON. A great hall of Solomon's palace in Jerusalem, named from the material imported from Mount Lebanon. It consisted of a rectangular structure 150 by 75 feet, divided by rows of pillars, possibly with an upper story of chambers distributed in rows of 15 each (I Kgs 7:2–5). It served as a royal armory and as an antechamber for audience with the king. It connected with the throne room and other public rooms of the palace, as well as with the private apartments of the king and of the daughter of Pharaoh (I Kgs 7:6–8).

References are made to the golden shields, the ivory throne, and the precious vessels that were kept in the house of the forest (I Kgs 10:17, 21; II Chr 9:16, 20; Isa 22:8).

HOUSETOP. The flat roof of a house where the family could find rest in the cool of evening, or where various activities might take place, as drying of flax (Josh 2:6) and prayer (Acts 10:9). The surface was usually a marly clay. It was kept in water-shedding condition between rains by rolling with stone rollers. Parapets were required around the housetop to prevent accidental falls (Deut 22:8). In NT times roof tiles of the curved type came into use (Lk 5:19).

HUKKOK (hŭk'ŏk). A border village of Naphtali (Josh 19:34). It may be identified with Yāqûq, a site *c.* three miles W of Chinnereth near the spot where the Waters of Merom enter the Sea of Galilee (Herbert G. May, *Oxford Bible Atlas,* p. 62).

HUKOK (hū'kŏk). A Levitical town in Asher (I Chr 6:75), an alternate name for Helkath *(q.v.).*

HUL (hŭl). Son of Aram and grandson of Shem, the son of Noah (Gen 10:23). The parallel in I Chr 1:17 identifies him as a son of Shem.

HULDAH (hŭl'dá). The wife of Shallum, wardrobe keeper in Josiah's court, who lived in the second quarter of Jerusalem as a recognized prophetess. When Josiah felt convicted by the book of the law which had been found during the temple repair, he directed officials to inquire of God for its meaning. Although Jeremiah was contemporary, they went to Huldah, who prophesied judgment upon the nation but peace for Josiah who then began his reforms (II Kgs 22:14–20).

HUMAN SACRIFICE. *See* Sacrifice, Human.

HUMANITY OF CHRIST. *See* Christ, Humanity of.

HUMBLENESS. The term appears only once in the KJV (Col 3:12), not at all in the RSV. The Gr. word *tapeinophrosynē* is used six other times and is translated in the KJV as "lowliness" of mind (Phil 2:3; Eph 4:2), "humility" (Acts 20:19; Col 2:18, 23; I Pet 5:5). The RSV renders it "humility" (Phil 2:3; Acts 20:19; I Pet 5:5), "lowliness" (Eph 4:2), "self-abasement" (Col 2:18, 23). *See* Humility.

HUMILIATION OF CHRIST. *See* Christ, Humiliation of.

HUMILITY. A Christian characteristic, epitomized in Rom 12:3: "For I say . . . to every man that is among you, not to think of himself more highly than he ought to think." Humility (Gr. *tapeinophrosynē,* I Pet 5:5) is a mental attitude of lowliness (Eph 4:2; Phil 2:3), the opposite of pride (*q.v.*). It is that specific grace developed in the Christian by the Spirit of God wherein the believer frankly acknowledges that all he has and is he owes to the Triune God who is dynamically operative in his behalf. He then willingly submits himself under the hand of God (Jas 4:6–10; I Pet 5:5–7). Thus humility should not be equated with a pious inferiority complex. It can be pretended on the part of false teachers (Col 2:18, 23) in acts of self-abasement (NASB).

In the OT this quality is praised (Prov 15:33; 18:12; 22:4). The Heb. term *'ānāwâ* (from *'ānāh*, "be afflicted") implies that humility of spirit often results from affliction. According to this characteristic the lives of many of the kings of Judah and Israel were assessed (I Kgs 21:29; II Chr 32:26; 33:23; 34:27; 36:12). Humbling oneself is the first step in true revival (II Chr 7:14; cf. Mic 6:8), for God Himself, the high and lofty One, delights to dwell with him who has a contrite and humble spirit in order to revive him (Isa 57:15).

Jesus Christ, as the supreme example of humility (Mt 11:29), furnished His disciples with visible demonstration of it in serving them by washing their feet (Jn 13:3–16). A major Christological passage in the NT (Phil 2:5–11) finds its key in the cultivation of this trait of Jesus Christ by the believer. *See* Humbleness; Christ, Humiliation of.

F. R. H.

HUMTAH (hŭm'tȧ). One of nine cities in the hill country of Hebron inherited by Judah (Josh 15:54). Its exact location is not now known.

HUNDREDS. While the term "hundred" appears in both the OT and the NT in the normal use, where the term "hundreds" appears it usually refers to the formal grouping of society (Ex 18:21, *et al.*), soldiers (Num 31:14, *et al.*), a crowd for a specific purpose (Mk 6:40).

HUNGER. This word is used three ways in the Scriptures: (1) with reference to physiological starvation and famine (Ex 16:3; Lk 15:17); (2) with reference to the normal physiological desire for food (Rom 12:20); (3) with reference to desire for spiritual satisfaction and sustenance (Mt 5:6). See L. Goppelt, *"Peinaō,"* TDNT, VI, 12–22.

HUNT, HUNTER, HUNTING. The two most noted hunters of the Bible are Nimrod (Gen 10:9) and Esau (Gen 25:27). In the ancient Near East a hunter had special heroic standing, which reflected the non-urban life of nomadic society where men spent much time providing food by hunting, while a little agriculture was carried on by women. The very word *ṣayid* used for "hunter" and "hunting" in the OT is often translated "victuals" (Neh 13:15), "food" (Job 38:41), and "venison" (Gen 27:3, 5, 7, 19; in v. 30, "hunting").

The oldest paintings known to be done by

The Assyrian king Ashurbanipal hunting lions. BM

human hands (at Lauscaux, France; Altamira, Spain, etc.) depict prehistoric man as primarily a hunter. These amazingly life-like rock carvings and paintings have been explained as a kind of sympathetic magic whereby men sought to have good fortune in their hunting through recreating the hunt scenes with red ochre and carbon deep inside caves.

With the domestication of animals and establishment of settled agricultural communities, hunting as a necessity for livelihood became obsolete. It continued, however, in the Bible world especially as a sport for kings and nobles. This has been depicted on reliefs and murals of Egypt, Mesopotamia, Greece and Rome (ANEP # 182–190). The grand hunting scenes of the Assyrian monarchs are best illustrated by the reliefs in Ashurbanipal's palace at Nineveh.

The free and naturalistic treatment of wounded lions marks a high point in Assyrian art. The reliefs reveal that the lions were first captured and kept in cages, then released for the king to hunt down. The sporting aspect of this kind of hunting must not be interpreted in 20th cen. A.D. terms. The sport was strictly practical not for food but because it led to skill in warfare. The king, whether of Egypt or Assyria, had to be the invincible warrior, and the hunting games were used both to improve and prove his strength and accuracy with the instruments of war.

The art of these various cultures also shows the use of dogs in hunting. The Theban tomb of the Eighteenth Dynasty noble Rekh-mi-Re has a relief showing dogs attacking wild animals of the desert. Paintings from the war-like Myceneans show dogs similar to the modern greyhound assisting in a lion hunt. Palestine in OT times was infested with lions (Jud 14:5), bears (II Kgs 2:24), wild boars (Ps 80:13), etc., all of which are now extinct in that area. The Levitical statutes allowed for the taking of game in the hunt, provided the animals were clean according to the dietary laws and all blood was carefully removed (Lev 17:13). *See* Animals.

There is wide metaphorical treatment of the Heb. verb *ṣûd*, "to hunt." Jeremiah's enemies "chased" (hunted) his steps (Lam 3:52; cf. 4:18). The Lord "hunted" Job as if the latter were a fierce lion (Job 10:16). To Ezekiel, the false prophets and sorceresses hunt and capture souls (Ezk 13:18); but to Jeremiah it is the Lord who hunts out the rebellious "from every mountain, and from every hill, and out of the holes of the rocks" (Jer 16:16).

See Bow and Arrow; Occupations: Hunter.

E. B. S.

HUPHAM (hū'făm), **HUPHAMITES** (hū'fá-mīts). A descendant of Benjamin; eponymous ancestor of the Huphamites (Num 26:39). "Huppim" in Gen 46:21 and I Chr 7:12, 15 is probably a variant.

HUPPAH (hŭp'á). A priest in the time of David in charge of the 13th course in the temple (I Chr 24:13).

HUPPIM. *See* Hupham.

HUR (hûr). Possibly an Egyptian name similar to Horus, the Egyptian god; or perhaps a pet name for a child (cf. Akkad. *ḫuru*, "child"); or a shortened form of Asshur.

1. A descendant of Judah, son of Caleb and Ephrath, and an ancestor of Bezaleel the craftsman (Ex 31:2; 35:30; I Chr 2:19-20). He is listed also as "the firstborn of Ephrathah, the father of Bethlehem" (I Chr 4:4), so the name may have been used to denote a tribe such as Hurrian or Horite (Gen 36:20).

2. Moses' assistant who in the battle against the Amalekites held up one hand of Moses while Aaron held the other until the going down of the sun and Joshua had defeated the enemy (Ex 17:10, 12). He also assisted Aaron in the rule of the Israelites while Moses was on the mount at the giving of the Ten Commandments (Ex 24:14). He may be the same as 1 and may have been the husband of Miriam, the sister of Moses, according to Josephus (*Ant.* iii.2.4). However, the OT says nothing about this.

3. Listed as one of the five kings of Midian, slain by Moses in a battle in which he killed all Midianite males, and took the women captive, while the flocks and herds were added to those of the Hebrews (Num 31:8; Josh 13:21).

4. Father of one of the officers of Solomon in the hill country of Ephraim (I Kgs 4:8).

5. Father of Rephaiah who helped rebuild the walls of Jerusalem (Neh 3:9).

A. W. W.

HURAI (hyŏŏr'ī). A mighty man of David (I Chr 11:32). In the parallel passage of II Sam 23:30 he is called Hiddai (*q.v.*).

HURAM (hyŭr'ám). Variant of the name Hiram (*q.v.*). Huram is used by the Chronicler in every instance except I Chr 14:1.

1. Son of Bela and grandson of Benjamin (I Chr 8:5).

2. The Tyrian craftsman employed by Solomon (II Chr 4:11), called Hiram in I Kgs 7:13.

3. The king of Tyre during the reign of Solomon (II Chr 2:3, 11; cf. I Kgs 5:1 ff.).

HURI (hyŏŏr'ī). A descendant of Gad and the father of Abihail (I Chr 5:14).

HURRIAN. *See* Horite.

HUSBAND. *See* Family; Marriage.

HUSBANDMAN. *See* Occupations: Farmer, Husbandman.

HUSBANDRY. *See* Agriculture.

HUSHAH (hŏŏsh'á). Mentioned in I Chr 4:4 as the son of Ezer of the tribe of Judah. Some accept the name as a designation of a family or a place.

HUSHAI (hŏŏsh'ī). An Archite and friend of David who aided the king during Absalom's rebellion by counteracting the sound advice of Ahithophel to Absalom (II Sam 15:32-37; 16:18-19; 17:5-14). Hushai sent word of Absalom's plans to David by Ahimaaz and Jonathan, sons of the priests Zadok and Abiathar respectively (II Sam 17:15-17), and thus David escaped Absalom's plot. Hushai apparently is to be identified as the father of Baanah, one of the 12 officers appointed to provide food for Solomon's household (I Kgs 4:16).

HUSHAM (hŏŏsh'ám). A Temanite who succeeded Jobab as king of Edom (Gen 36:34-35; I Chr 1:45-46).

HUSHATHITE (hŏŏsh'á-thīt). The family name of Sibbechai, one of David's 30 heroic followers (II Sam 21:18; I Chr 11:29; 20:4; 27:11); also apparently called by the name of Mebunnai (II Sam 23:27).

HUSHIM (hŏŏsh'ĭm)

1. Family name of the children of Dan (Gen 46:23), also called Shuham (Num 26:42).

2. The name given to the sons of Aher, a Benjamite (I Chr 7:12).

3. One of the two wives of Shaharaim, a Benjamite, and the mother of Abitub and Elpaal (I Chr 8:8, 11).

HUSK. *See* Plants.

HUZ (hŭz). The eldest son of Nahor by his wife Milcah (Gen 22:21). He is called Uz in the ASV and RSV. *See* Uz.

HUZZAB (hŭz'áb). A word of doubtful meaning found in Nah 2:7. Older commentators took it as a proper noun referring to the queen of Nineveh or to a female idol such as Ishtar, or perhaps a personification of Nineveh itself; but no such name is known in Assyrian inscriptions. Another view sees it as a verb meaning "it is decreed." Others read it as "country of Zab," or "river country," designating a fertile tract of Assyria E of the Tigris River. RSV conjectures it to mean "its mistress."

HYENA. *See* Animals, II.21.

HYKSOS (hĭk'sŏs). The Hyksos were non-Egyptian rulers of Egypt who formed the 15th and 16th Dynasties in the Egyptian historical outline by the 3rd cen. B.C. priest-historian Manetho. He referred to them as "shepherd kings" and ascribed to them a rule of 511 years. The name "Hyksos" is derived from the Egyptian "rulers of foreign countries"; current chronologies assign them only some 150 years of domination in Egypt (*c.* 1730–1570 B.C.).

The Hyksos established their capital in the Nile Delta at Avaris (later Tanis; biblical Zoan). They were Asiatics who are thought to have dominated most of the Syro-Palestinian area during the Middle Bronze II period (1850–1550 B.C.) and who infiltrated Egypt, eventually gaining control of the country without warfare. The names of some of the Hyksos kings contain Semitic elements. This factor contributes to the view that Joseph, a Semitic slave, rose to power in Egypt during the Hyksos period. Josephus (*Against Apion*, i.14, 16) even confuses the Hyksos and the Israelites (FLAP, p. 95).

The Hyksos became quite Egyptianized but also made certain contributions to Egyptian culture. They left the knowledge of how to use the horse and chariot in warfare, and introduced new types of daggers and swords and especially the strong compound Asiatic bow. The relationships of the Hyksos were widespread, for objects bearing the name of a Hyksos king have been found as far distant as Crete and Mesopotamia. Sites occupied by them usually show a typical rectangular fortification with a sloping rampart (glacis) made of beaten earth (*terre pisée*).

The native Egyptian rulers of the Theban area led by Sekenenre began the war of liberation against the Hyksos. Ahmose, his son, the founder of the 18th Dynasty, besieged Avaris and defeated the Hyksos, who fled to Palestine. Pursuing, Ahmose successfully climaxed three campaigns against them at Sharuhen W of Beer-sheba. A century later the expeditions of Thutmose III (1504–1450 B.C.) were still attributable in part to the desire to crush the Hyksos.

See Egypt; Exodus, The; Joseph.

C. E. D.

HYMENAEUS (hĭ-mĕ-nē'ŭs). A teacher in Ephesus (?), mentioned in I Tim 1:20 and II Tim 2:17, condemned by Paul for false teaching. He appears to have rejected the apostolic teaching and the dictates of conscience. For this Paul delivered him over to Satan (cf. I Cor 5:5) to teach him the error of blaspheming. Whether this punishment was limited to excommunication from the church only, or involved physical suffering as well (cf. Acts 5:1–11; I Cor 11:30), is difficult to ascertain. Seemingly, however, it was remedial and not simply penal in nature. (See further in Deissmann, *Light from the Ancient East*, pp. 301–303, for examples of Execration texts in antiquity.)

The second error of Hymenaeus was the affirmation that the resurrection had already taken place. Like cancer, the error was apparently spreading and doing injury to the faith of certain persons. Possibly this case was parallel to the incident in Corinth where some taught that there is no resurrection of the dead (I Cor 15:12). To the Gr. mind at least, the idea of bodily resurrection was absurd (cf. Acts 17:32).

Again, it may have been a teaching that the resurrection was spiritual in nature, referring to the regeneration of one dead in sins (see Eph 2:6; Col 3:1; Rom 6:3–4). However, both Paul (I Cor 15:4, 20–23, 51–54; Phil 3:11, 21) and our Lord before him (Jn 5:28–29) taught a bodily resurrection. This is the ordinary sense of the Gr. word *anastasis* in the NT. Some continued to spiritualize the idea, and these heretical views are recorded by 2nd cen. writers (Justin Martyr, Irenaeus and Tertullian). *See also* Resurrection.

W. M. D.

HYMN. *See* Music.

HYPOCRISY, HYPOCRITE. In the context of Gr. drama the term hypocrite was applied to an actor on the theater stage. Since an actor pretends to be someone other than himself, *hypokritēs* was applied metaphorically to a person who "acts a part" in real life, pretending to be better than he actually is, one who simulates goodness. In secular Gr. literature, therefore, *hypokritēs* may be either neutral or undesirable. In the NT, however, it is always undesirable, signifying one who works a deception by feigned piety.

This concept of pretended goodness was foreign to OT thought. The Heb. root *ḥ-n-p*, translated "hypocrisy" or "hypocrite" in the KJV, was translated in the LXX by *anomos*, "lawless," "criminal," or "godless," parallel to *ponēros*, "an evil doer" (Isa 9:17); and by *asebēs*, "godless," "irreverent" (Isa 33:14).

In the book of Job it is clear that the *ḥānēp* is one radically opposed to God, one who forgets God (Job 8:13; 15:34–35; 20:5; 27:8). The verb *ḥānap* means to pollute or corrupt (cf. Num 35:33; Ps 106:38; Isa 24:5; Jer 3:1). Theodotion's translation of Job, later incorporated into the LXX, rendered Heb. *ḥānēp* as *hypo-*

Masks used by Greek and Roman actors were made of stiffened linen. These Roman masks were made in marble for decorative purposes.
BM

kritēs in two verses (Job 34:30; 36:13). Thus it seems that Greek-speaking Jews were employing *hypokrisis* in another sense in addition to its metaphorical meaning of feigning to be what one is not.

This background in the OT indicates the broader sense in which the term is used in our Lord's ministry. "Hypocrite" occurs 18 times and "hypocrisy" twice in the words of Jesus. He warned His disciples of "the leaven of the Pharisees, which is hypocrisy" (Lk 12:1). He diagnosed them as appearing righteous to men, but being full of hypocrisy and iniquity within (Mt 23:28). That He accused the Pharisees of more than mere pretending is suggested by the parallels to the reading "their hypocrisy" in Mk 12:15. In Mt 22:18 it is "their wickedness" or malice, and in Lk 20:23 it is "their craftiness." Only in Lk 20:20 does the verb *hypokrinō* retain the original Gr. meaning of pretending: the scribes and chief priests, attempting to arrest Jesus, sent spies "who pretended to be sincere" (RSV).

Outside the Gospels *hypokrisis* occurs three times. Paul rebuked Peter for "dissimulation," his deliberate inconsistency of first eating with Gentile converts at Antioch and then, fearing the circumcision party, refusing to associate with them further (Gal 2:13, verb and noun)—and this following God's vision to Peter prior to his visiting Cornelius (Acts 10). Paul reveals that in the last times there will be those who follow evil spirits and doctrines of demons and speak lies in hypocrisy (I Tim 4:1-2). The Christian himself is warned to get rid of all hypocrisy in his life (I Pet 2:1).

There are six occurrences in the NT of the verbal adjective *anupokritos*, "without hypocrisy" (Jas 3:17; also Rom 12:9, "without dissimulation"; and II Cor 6:6; I Tim 1:5; II Tim 1:5; I Pet 1:22, "unfeigned").

J. H. G. and R. A. K.

HYSSOP. *See* Plants.

I

I AM. The name God gave Himself when He commissioned Moses to deliver the Israelites from Egypt (Ex 3:14). God is the one independent, entirely self-subsistent Being in the universe. All that is, depends upon Him (Gen 1:1; cf. Col 1:17; Heb 1:3, 10). He does not need anyone or anything, since in Himself He possesses all possible relationships – the I-it or the subject-object, the I-Thou or the personal encounter, and the we-you or the social relationship (*see* Godhead; Trinity). All that exists has been created by Him for His own glory.

Christ declared Himself to be the great "I AM." In Jn 8 He maintains that He tells the truth, and supports this by claiming He is saying what He has heard (v. 26), seen (v. 38), and been taught by the Father (v. 28), and can corroborate with Him at any time (v. 29). He concludes His argument by using the expression "I am" (v. 58). The Jews realized when He said "Before Abraham was, I am," that this was a claim to deity, particularly since He was returning to the "I am" of v. 24: "If ye believe not that I am [the word "he" is not in the Gr.], ye shall die in your sins." This is why they took up stones to kill Him. He was identifying Himself, they realized, with the "I AM THAT I AM" of Ex 3:14.

Theodor Zahn found similar "I am" expressions in Jn 4:26; 9:9; 18:5; Mt 14:27; Mk 13:6; 14:62; Lk 22:70; 24:39. Greijdanus objected that in these other places a predicate is either given or implied. However, at least in Mt 14:27, as Christ came to the disciples walking on the storm-tossed waters, He announced Himself as "I am" (Gr. *egō eimi*). And again in Mk 13:6 He uses the term without any predicate saying, "Many shall come in my name, saying, I am [Gr. omits Christ]; and shall deceive many." Lk 22:70, on the other hand, has an implied predicate, and though in Lk 24:39 Christ again says "I am," He makes it clear that He is merely identifying Himself to the disciples as He adds the word *autos,* meaning "the same," "Myself."

R. A. K.

IBEX or WILD GOAT. *See* Animals, II. 22.

IBHAR (ĭb'här). A son of David, born in Jerusalem, by a wife not mentioned by name and otherwise unknown (II Sam 5:15; I Chr 3:6; 14:5).

IBIS. *See* Animals, III. 24.

IBLEAM (ĭb'lē-ȧm). A Canaanite city in northern Manasseh, whose territory extended to Issachar (Josh 17:11), and in I Chr 6:70 called Bileam (*q.v.*). However, the native inhabitants were never expelled and continued to live alongside the Israelites (Jud 1:27). King Ahaziah of Judah was slain by Jehu's men near there (II Kgs 9:27). According to LXX of II Kgs 15:10, King Zachariah of Israel was also killed there (see RSV). It is near modern Jenin, on the road from Jezreel to Dothan, now called Tell Bel'ameh. Its name occurs as *ybr'm* in Thutmose III's list of conquered towns, about 1470 B.C.

IBNEIAH (ĭb-nē'yȧ). A son of Jeroham and a chief of the tribe of Benjamin in the first settlement in Jerusalem (I Chr 9:8).

IBNIJAH (ĭb-nī'jȧ). A member of the tribe of Benjamin and the father of Reuel (I Chr 9:8).

IBRI (ĭb'rī). A Merarite Levite and son of Jaaziah in the time of David (I Chr 24:27).

IBZAN (ĭb'zăn). A judge of Israel for seven years following the death of Jephthah. He was a native of Bethlehem, whether of Judah or Zebulun is not certain. He had 30 sons and 30 daughters, all of whom took marriage partners outside his clan (Jud 12:8–10).

ICE. Frost is somewhat rare in Palestine except on the highest mountains. Three biblical references to ice or frost (Job 37:10; 38:29; Ps 147:17) stress the power of God. In a figurative sense, insincere friends are compared with brooks "which are blackish by reason of the ice" (Job 6:16).

ICHABOD (ĭk'ȧ-bŏd; "no glory"). Son of Phinehas and grandson of Eli (I Sam 4:21). The shocking news of Israel's defeat by the Philistines (I Sam 4:19–22) with the consequent slaughter of Phinehas, the taking of the ark, and the death of Eli, induced labor in the pregnant wife of Phinehas and she gave birth to a son. As death laid hold upon her in this experience she named the child Ichabod, partly on account of her own personal tragedy but mainly for the national catastrophe and the loss of the ark as the visible representation of the presence of God (I Sam 4:22). Her own words of explanation of the name were, "The glory has departed from Israel" (v. 21, RSV).

ICONIUM (ī-kō'nĭ-ŭm). An ancient city of Asia Minor, now called Konya, that was visited several times by Paul on his missionary journeys. The chief city of Lycaonia in the Hellenistic period, Iconium lay on the border of the districts of Phrygia and Lycaonia. It was incorporated into the Roman province of Galatia in 25 B.C. It stood on a level plateau 3,400 feet above sea level, with 5,000–6,000 foot mountains a few miles to the W.

Paul brought the gospel there on his first missionary journey (Acts 13:51; 14:1–6, 21) and returned there on his second journey (Acts 16:2), and probably on his third as well (Acts 18:23). It was possibly to Iconium as well as the other cities in that area that Paul wrote his epistle to the Galatians to combat the inroads of the Judaizers.

IDALAH (ĭd'a-la). A border town of Zebulun (Josh 19:15). The Jerusalem Talmud (*Megillah,* I, 1) calls it Iralah and identifies it with Heireiah. It may be represented by the modern Khirbet el-Ḥuwārah, little more than half a mile S of Beit Lahm, the Bethlehem in Galilee.

IDBASH (ĭd'băsh). A man of Judah and one belonging to the "father" of Etam (I Chr 4:3). "Father" here probably means "founder" of the town of Etam, two miles SW of Bethlehem; Idbash was likely one of his sons.

IDDO (ĭd'ō)
1. A Gershomite Levite whom David set over the service of song (I Chr 6:21).
2. Son of Zechariah and ruler of the half tribe of Manasseh in Gilead, E of the Jordan (I Chr 27:21).
3. Father of Ahinadab, one of Solomon's 12 provisioners (I Kgs 4:14).
4. A seer (II Chr 9:29; 12:15) and prophet (II Chr 13:22) who lived in the days of Solomon, Jeroboam, and Rehoboam and recorded some of their activities. His records concerning Solomon (II Chr 9:29), Rehoboam (II Chr 12:15), and Abijah (II Chr 13:22) are unknown to us, but may form the basis for part of our Chronicles.
5. The chief of the Jews of the Captivity in Casiphia (Ezr 8:17). Ezra sent to him to requisition from the Levites and Nethinim a contingent to join his expedition to Jerusalem.
6. Grandfather of the prophet Zechariah (Zech 1:1, 7) who was contemporary with Haggai (Ezr 6:14) and author of the OT book bearing that name. Iddo was one of those who returned from the Exile with Zerubbabel, and is listed among the chiefs of the priests and heads of households (Neh 12:4, 16).

J. K. M.

IDLE. Laziness or indolence which, according to Heb. wisdom literature, leads to poverty (Prov 19:15; Eccl 10:18). Earlier Pharaoh had accused the complaining Israelites of idleness (Ex 5:8–17). The NT word *argos* (Mt 12:36; 20:3, 6; I Tim 5:13) means "inactive" or "useless."

IDOL. *See* Gods, False; Idolatry; Imagery.

IDOLATRY

Definition

This is a transliteration of the Gr. word *eidōlolatria,* which we understand to mean "the worship of idols; the worship of images as divine or sacred." *See* Imagery. This Gr. term is a compound of two. The first is *eidō* (cf. the Latin *video*), meaning "to see" and "to know"; hence it carries the basic concept "to know by seeing." On this term was formed the word *eidōlon,* "image," which came to mean specifically an image of a god as an object of worship, or a material symbol of the supernatural as such an object. The second term is *latreia,* meaning "service" or, more especially, "the service or worship of the gods."

Idolatry, then, is paying divine honors to any item of human fabrication, or the ascription of divine powers to purely natural agencies.

Description

As a time-space creature, man has been specially inclined to give adoration and worship to some sort of visible symbol of the deity. He seems to crave tangible manifestations of the divine presence. During man's history this has taken varied forms and manifestations. If he departed from the worship of the true God, he did not renounce religion but sought to substitute for the true God a false one after his own liking.

Animism was the worship or reverence of inanimate objects, such as stones, trees, rivers, springs, and other natural objects. There was also the worship of animate things: such animals as the sacred bulls or calves, symbolical of the principle of reproduction and procreation; the serpent, as a symbol of yearly renewal, since it sheds its old skin for a new one; and birds, such as the hawk, the eagle, and the falcon, as symbols of wisdom and insight. These animal forms were sometimes combined with the human as objects of worship—theriomorphism. There were the astral deities, such as the sun, moon and stars. Nature's elements and forces were also reverenced and worshiped: storm, air, fire, water, and earth; hence the vegetation gods and the *genii loci* received status.

The fertility principle was often deified as a mother-goddess (*see* Diana), as images from Ephesus indicate. This involved the worship of sex and the glorification of prostitution.

There was the common tendency toward

hero worship which also included the dead ancestors of the tribe or clan.

Totemism represented not only activity in arts and crafts, but the worship of the patron god or goddess of the clan under whatever image the deity may have been conceived. Usually this was a wild animal or a bird, or a combination of one of the animal forms with the human.

Idealism involved the worship of abstract concepts such as wisdom and justice.

Emperor worship must be included. Kings, because they had the power of life and death over their subjects, came to be deified. "*Ave Caesar*" meant more than "long live the king" or "Heil Hitler"; it was an act of worship.

The Greek goddess Aphrodite, identified with the Assyrian Ishtar. Corinth Museum, Mimosa

Man alone possesses the gift of image making. In doing so he seeks the reproduction of vanished ocular impressions or imagined sacred objects. So idolatry stands closely related to man's advance in arts and crafts. His history is filled with attempts to give material shapes to religious ideals and ideas. Once these became objectivized as concrete objects, then reverence and worship could be expressed toward them by the burning of incense, bowing the knee, kissing the image, coating it over with silver and gold, bedecking it with precious stones and jewels, or clothing it in sumptuous apparel. It was only another step to consulting it as an oracle of divine wisdom and a means of predicting one's future or the outcome of some

military or political project. A cult-statue was therefore a thing of worship and delight because the visible image gave evidence of the presence of the divinity. It was customarily housed in some shrine, and an entire cultus for its worship evolved. *See* Graven Image; Imagery.

In a larger sense idolatry in theoretical forms may include the vain philosophies of men, for these detract from God's glory (Rom 1:23) and give divine honors to another. Thus naturalism, humanism, rationalism are types of idolatry. Likewise, attachment to horoscopes and any occult practices of witchcraft and spiritism must be condemned as idolatrous. *See* Magic; Sorcery.

The Idolatry of Israel's Neighbors

Heathen practices came to Israel chiefly via the Egyptians, the Canaanites and the Assyro-Babylonian nations.

Ancient Egyptian art and writing have left evidence of thousands of deities. The Pharaohs themselves were regarded to be incarnations of deity. In addition to such humans, a bull, a crocodile, a fish, a tree, a hawk, etc., might also be indwelt by a spirit and thus deified. There were many animal- or bird-headed deities with human bodies.

Among the Canaanites the many Baals with their respective fertility cults were the sponsors of orgiastic worship of nature and the productivity principle.

Chief among the deities of the Babylonians and the Assyrians was the Mesopotamian immoral goddess of lust and procreation—Ishtar. The Babylonians seemed willing to import gods from many surrounding neighbors, or from nations they had conquered and placed under tribute. Hence they had a god for almost anything: learning, war, fire, motherhood, virginity, fertility, the sky, the wind, water, earth, and the underworld, along with the usual sun, moon, and stars. The Assyrians were just as idolatrous and in addition gained the unenviable reputation of being the cruelest and most sadistic of all the ancient nations of the Near East.

The History of Idolatry Among the Israelites

Abraham lived in a world of idolatry. His westward trek was to abandon idolatrous Ur of the Chaldees and seek a new home in which to worship the one true God. It is significant that from his descendants have come the three great monotheistic religions of the world: Judaism, Christianity, and Islam.

The prohibition of idolatry is one of the few immutable absolutes in the Jewish system of ethics (along with incest and murder). The imageless worship of Yahweh announced not merely that He was greater than nature but also that He was unbounded by it. In the OT there are many Heb. terms used in derision of idolatry indicating its foulness and obscenity as well as its sheer emptiness.

All strata of Jewish law bear witness to the opposition to a portrayal of God. The first two

Altar in the Temple of Vespasian (Pompeii), sacred to the imperial cult. It portrays a sacrificing priest, a flute player, and administration of sacred oaths. HFV

commandments prohibit image worship as well as the worship of any other god (cf. Ex 20:1 ff.; Deut 5:7-8; Lev 19:4). Idolatry was classed as a state offense and savored of treason, punishable by death (Deut 17:2-7).

Heb. prophecy likewise shows an uncompromising hostility to idolatry. An image is the mere handiwork of man (Amos 5:26; Hos 13:2; Isa 2:8), an imitation of creatures (Deut 4:16 ff.) formed out of dead matter (Hos 4:12, RSV; Isa 44:9-10; Ps 115). Thus its worship is sheer folly. God alone is to be worshiped, since He alone is the living Creator of all things and a Spirit who cannot be pictured in any form. Yet among the Israelites may be noted the worship of Yahweh under the form of some image or symbol; the worship of the gods of the surrounding nations under whatever symbol was appropriate; and the worship of images and symbols themselves (the brazen serpent, II Kgs 18:4).

The story of idolatry among the Hebrews begins with the account of Rachel's stealing Laban's teraphim (Gen 31:19), which were probably statuettes of household gods. These of course were not rated on an equal basis with the God of Abraham and Nahor (Gen 31:53). Rachel may not have been interested in the teraphim for worship purposes, however, because discoveries at Nuzu indicate that with possession of the teraphim went headship of the family. She may have been trying to transfer headship of the patriarchal family from her father to her husband.

Years in Egypt resulted in Israel's infatuation with Egyptian idols (cf. Josh 24:14; Ezk 20:7-8), and thus Moses found it imperative to challenge the gods of Egypt (Num 33:4).

During the absence of Moses from the camp at the foot of Mount Sinai, the Israelites clamored for some visible representation of Yahweh (Ex 32:1). Only a mind thoroughly accustomed to the profound respect paid to the sacred bulls of Egypt could hit upon so strange a representation of Yahweh (Ex 32:4; see JerusB). Nor could any people not familiar with this Egyptian practice have responded so readily as did these Israelites. The feast that Aaron proclaimed to Yahweh (Ex 32:5), which resulted in the people singing and dancing naked before the idol (32:6, 18, 19, 25), was like the feast of Apis; it led if not publicly yet privately to indecency (the word "play," ṣaḥēq, in 32:6 implies sexual gestures or acts; cf. "fondling," Gen 26:8, RSV). Thus the great wrath of both the Lord and Moses is understandable (32:4, 8). Aaron called the calf Yahweh (32:5), but to represent Him thus was idolatry (Ps 106:19-20).

There was temporary apostasy at Shittim when the men of Israel, yielding to the charms of the daughters of Moab, gave way to Baalism (Num 25).

On entering Palestine, Israel came in contact with varied forms of idolatry. And though they were commanded to destroy all these (Deut 12:2-3), the command was not in all instances fully obeyed (Jud 2:12, 14).

Gideon's father had erected or had come into the possession of an altar to Baal which Gideon was obliged to destroy (Jud 6:25-32). The ephod of Gideon may have been a votive offering to Yahweh, but it became a snare to all Israel as well as his own household (Jud 8:27). No sooner was Gideon dead than Israel returned to the idolatrous worship of "Baal of the covenant" (Jud 8:33; 9:4).

The episode of Micah in Jud 17 and 18 gives evidence of secret idolatry on the part of many individuals (Jud 17:1-6). Here a Levite, of all people, becomes a priest of images (cf. Deut 27:15). Samuel, as he took over the judgeship of Israel, found it necessary to rebuke their possession of foreign gods (I Sam 7:3-4).

Solomon had already set the stage for a great apostasy to idolatry by his importation of so many foreign wives, and with them their respective forms of heathen worship, each with its false god. There was Ashteroth of the Zidonians, Chemosh of the Moabites, Milcom of the Ammonites, to mention but a few. Three of the summits of Mount Olivet were crowned with high places to these deities respectively, and the fourth was named "the Mount of Corruption" (I Kgs 11:5-8; II Kgs 23:13-14).

Solomon's son Rehoboam was of an Ammonitish mother, with whose religion was introduced some of the worst features of licentious idolatry (I Kgs 14:21-24). Jeroboam, fresh from his exile in Egypt, erected sacred bulls in honor of Yahweh at Dan and Bethel (I Kgs 12:26-33). In practice, however, the worship seems to have been directed to the animals of gold rather than to the Lord Himself (cf. Amos 4:4-5). This worship of the calves is thought of by Hosea as the "sin of Israel" (Hos 10:5-8, NASB).

One of the greatest promoters of idolatry in Heb. history was King Ahab with his Zidonian princess wife, Jezebel (I Kgs 21:25-26). He not only built a temple and an altar to Baal of the Zidonians — Melkart, but engaged in active persecution of the prophets of Yahweh (I Kgs 16:31-33). With the prophets of Baal and Asherah Elijah staged his famous contest for the vindication of the true God (I Kgs 18).

The story of the northern kingdom now becomes successively, with each of its kings, a reenactment of the sin of Jeroboam. It came to be known as "the way of the kings of Israel." (II Kgs 16:3; cf. 17:7-18). Thus there was a long line of royal apostates in the nation of Israel, which did not cease until the conquest of that kingdom by the Assyrians.

A sponsor of idolatry in the southern kingdom was King Ahaz. He built an altar after a model he had seen in Damascus, right on the site of the brazen altar of the Jewish temple (II Kgs 16:10-15). He also caused his son to pass through the fire (II Kgs 16:3) and offered sacrifices to the gods of Damascus (II Chr 28:23).

One of the longest and most idolatrous reigns in Judah was that of wicked King Manasseh, who, though he returned to the Lord just before his death (II Chr 33:10-17), could not undo the results of a lifetime of patronage of enchantments, divinations, witchcraft, profanation of the temple courts with altars to astral deities, and an image of Asherah in the holy place (II Kgs 21:1-9; Jer 32:34). Consequently, not long after his repentance and death his own son restored the altars of the Baalim and the images of Asherah.

Yet as in the days of Elijah in the northern kingdom (I Kgs 19:18), so during the reigns of the wicked kings of Judah God seems to have had a righteous remnant who refused to bow the knee to Baal.

The most deplorable type of idolatry was that led by the false prophets, who as leaders of the apostasy joined ranks with corrupt priests (II Kgs 23:5) and prophesied by Baal and followed "things that do not profit," i.e., idols with no power in them (Jer 2:8; cf. II Chr 15:3).

There seem to have been some attempts to worship the true God under idolatrous imagery and a contamination of the true worship with idolatrous rites (II Kgs 17:32; 18:22; Jer 41:5). Of course intermarriage with idolatrous nations was invariably a first step toward idolatry (Ex 34:14-16; Deut 7:3-4; Ezr 9:2; 10:18; Neh 13:23-27).

Ezekiel describes a chamber of images at Jerusalem (Ezk 8:7-12), derived no doubt from Egypt. The brazen serpent seems to have become something of an idol, with the people offering incense to it (II Kgs 18:4). Even the worship of Moloch was resorted to at times (II Kgs 17:17), though this practice of tossing their infants into the fire was basically revolting to the Heb. mind.

The Babylonian Exile came as a direct rebuke to their idolatry (Jer 29:8-10), as God had forewarned in Hezekiah's day (Isa 39:6).

In post-Exilic times, especially under Alex-

ander and his successors, the Jews once again faced the issue of idolatry (I Macc 1:41-50, 54-64). Let it be said to the credit of many that they chose death rather than idolatry (I Macc 2:23-26, 45-48).

Later, Herod's golden eagle above one of the doors of the sanctuary aroused a storm of protest (Jos *Ant.* xvii.6.3).

Ashurbanipal, king of Assyria (*c.* 650) beginning ceremonially the work of rebuilding the temple of a god. BM

New Testament Evaluation

The early Christians unavoidably came in contact with Gentile idolatry (Acts 17:16). Thus they often had to face questions concerning the festive meals and meat offered to idols (Acts 15:20; I Pet 4:3; Rev 2:14, 20), especially at Corinth (I Cor 8, 10).

Idolater is the name given to worshipers of heathen gods and personal idols in the NT (I Cor 5:10-11; 6:9; 10:7; Rev 21:8; 22:15). Idolatry is specifically equated with covetousness which makes a god of mammon (i.e., money) and renders a man unfaithful in his stewardship (Mt 6:24; Lk 16:13; Col 3:5; Eph 5:5). The injunctions against evil concupiscence surely have a reference not only to the idolatry in the early Christian environment but also to our sex-obsessed age (Gal 5:19-20; Phil 3:19;

cf. Rom 16:18). The source of idolatry is basically an impure heart and will (Rom 1:21). Paul agrees with Isaiah that man degenerated to heathenism rather than evolved from it (cf. Rom 1; Isa 44). Therefore he commands Christians to flee from idolatry (I Cor 10:14), as does John (I Jn 5:21).

Bibliography. John Calvin, *Institutes of the Christian Religion,* Grand Rapids: Eerdmans, I, Chap. XI, 1957 reprint. E. La B. Cherbonnier, "Idolatry," *Handbook of Christian Theology,* M. Halverson, ed., New York: Meridian Books, 1958, pp. 176–183. CornPBE, "Idol Worship in Israel," pp. 398–401. John Gray, "Idolatry," IDB, II, 675–678. Gerhard Kittel, *"Eikōn,"* TDNT, II, 381–397. Adolphe Lods, "Images and Idols (Hebrew and Canaanite)," Hastings' *Encyclopedia of Religion and Ethics,* VII, 138–142. McClintock and Strong, "Idolatry," *Cyclopedia of Biblical, Theological and Ecclesiastical Literature,* IV, 471–486. H. M. Schulweis, "Jewish Ethics," *Encyclopedia of Morals,* V, Ferm, ed., New York: Philosophical Library, 1956, pp. 253–265.

R. E. Pr.

IDOLS, THINGS OFFERED TO. The idea of flesh that has been offered to idols is expressed by a single Gr. word, *eidōlothyton.* The word is used ten times in the NT. It is translated once "meats offered to idols" (Acts 15:29); and "things sacrificed unto idols" (Rev 2:14, 20; cf. I Cor 10:19, 28). It refers to meat from an animal which has been slain in sacrifice to an idol. Only certain parts of the carcass were used in the sacrificial ceremony, the remainder being sold for food in the markets. Jewish law forbade the eating of this meat. The Jerusalem council (Acts 15:29) agreed that Gentile believers should abstain from meats offered to idols out of deference to their Jewish brethren. Paul urged (I Cor 8; Rom 14) Christians to consider their weaker brethren and refrain from eating such meat. *See* Expediency; Weaker Brother.

IDUMAEA (ĭd'yŏŏ-mē'á). This term was used by the Greeks and Romans (with slightly different spellings) to refer to the region inhabited by the descendants of Esau—the Edomites of the OT. *See* Esau. The word appears once in the Bible, Mk 3:8 (the KJV uses it in Isa 34:5–6; Ezk 35:15; 36:5, but Edom is given by other translations).

The Edomites were closely associated with the Israelites in origin, culture, and language. Their primary importance in the NT is that Herod the Great's father (Antipater) was Idumaean. His mother was Nabataean, an Arab group that lived to the S of the Idumaeans (Jos *Ant.* xiv.1.3; 7.3). The Edomites (*q.v.*) are frequently mentioned in the OT. *See also* Edom; Seir.

The richest part of the land of Edom was on the eastern side of the Arabah (the continuation of the Jordan-Dead Sea cleft), but the Naba-

taeans had driven the Edomites westward by the 4th cen. B.C. There appears to have been an earlier migration westward, for even Hebron was probably an Edomite city by the time of Ezra and Nehemiah. Since Hebron, famous for the burial place of the patriarchs and David's one-time capital, was not mentioned as one of the cities of Judah reoccupied after the Exile, it may be assumed it was occupied by Edomites.

The Idumaean period was the last time of any greatness in the history of the Edomites, from c. 100 B.C. to A.D. 70. Judas Maccabaeus had defeated the Idumaeans and recaptured Hebron in 164 B.C. (I Macc 5:1–5, 65), and John Hyrcanus warred against them successfully, subjected them, and forced them to adopt Judaism and be circumcised c. 120 B.C. Yet it was the rise of the Herodian dynasty that lends a prominence to the Idumaeans that otherwise they never would have earned. In A.D. 66–70 they fanatically helped to defend Jerusalem over whose fall their ancestors had gloated some 600 years earlier. The last of the Idumaeans were slaughtered by Titus in A.D. 72.

D. R. S.

IGAL (ī'găl)

1. The son of Joseph of the tribe of Issachar and one of the 12 men sent out by Moses to spy out the land of Canaan (Num 13:7, 17).

2. One of David's mighty warriors, son of Nathan (II Sam 23:36), referred to in I Chr 11:38 as "Joel the brother of Nathan."

3. One of the sons of Shemaiah of the royal house of David (I Chr 3:22), called Igeal in the KJV. *See* Igeal.

IGDALIAH (ĭg'dá-lī'á). The father of Hanan the prophet (Jer 35:4).

IGEAL (ī'gē-ál). One of the sons of Shemaiah of the royal house of David (I Chr 3:22), called Igal in the ASV and RSV. *See* Igal 3.

IGNORANCE. In the OT God made provision for sins committed in "ignorance" (Heb. *she-gāgâ,* "error," "wandering astray") as seen in Lev 4, 5; Num 15:22–29, in distinction to sins of presumption. Such sins produced guilt. They were not necessarily done unconsciously but unintentionally, out of weakness or waywardness, and had to be atoned for. These sinners had no intent to rebel against the rule of God; but those who despised His word were to be cut off with no remedy (Num 15:30–31).

The Gr. word *agnoia* means a lack of knowledge because one is uninformed. Paul frequently wrote that he did not wish the early Christians to be ignorant in this sense (Rom 1:13; 11:25; I Cor 10:1; 12:1; etc.). Paul declared he received mercy because he acted in the ignorance of unbelief when persecuting Christians (I Tim 1:13). At Athens he preached that God overlooks the times of ignorance of the heathen (Acts 17:30; cf. 3:17). Thus we see there is special allowance both for the sins committed by the believer in ignorance, and for the ignorance of the heathen.

On the other hand, ignorance in the unconverted is linked with blindness of heart (Eph 4:18) and lust (I Pet 1:14). The heathen are without excuse in not worshiping the one true God, for what can be known about God is plain to them. Therefore their rejection of God is at heart willful and deliberate (Rom 1:18–32; II Pet 3:5; cf. Rom 10:3).

The word *idiōtēs,* meaning a private person in ordinary Gr., is used once in Acts 4:13 by the Sanhedrin of the disciples in the sense of an untrained layman: "they were unlearned [unlettered] and ignorant men [common men with no rabbinic training]."

Bibliography. Rudolf Bultmann, *"Agnoeō,* etc.," TDNT, I, 115–121.

R. A. K.

IIM (ī'ĭm)

1. The contracted form of Ije-abarim, one of the encampments of the Israelites during their exodus from Egypt (Num 33:44–45).

2. A town in the territory of Judah near Edom, the exact location of which is uncertain (Josh 15:29).

IJE-ABARIM (ī'jĕ-ăb'a-rĭm). An encampment of the Israelites, said to be near Moab, during their journey from Egypt to the Promised Land (Num 33:44); also called Iim (Num 33:45).

IJON (ī'jŏn). A city of Israel in the territory of Naphtali that was captured by Ben-hadad, king of Syria, at the suggestion of Asa, king of Judah (I Kgs 15:20; II Chr 16:4). Subsequently, during the reign of Pekah, its inhabitants were taken captive into Assyria by Tiglath-pileser. The city is situated about eight miles NW of Banias.

IKKESH (ĭk'ĕsh). A man from Tekoa, the father of Ira, one of David's 30 heroic men (II Sam 23:26; I Chr 11:28; 27:9).

ILAI (ī'lī). An Ahohite, one of David's mighty warriors (I Chr 11:29), also called Zalmon (II Sam 23:28).

ILLNESS. *See* Diseases.

ILLUMINATION. A theological term used to express the manner in which the Holy Spirit makes clear to man the Word of God, whether preached or in written form. Without an illumination of the Holy Scriptures, no man can understand God's divine, infallible revelation because spiritual things are only spiritually — i.e., by the aid of the Holy Spirit — understood or discerned (I Cor 2:11–14; Jn 16:13). Therefore Paul prayed that the "eyes" of our hearts might be enlightened (Eph 1:18). The Bible in its original text is the inspired, infallible Word of God. Inspiration therefore describes the work of the Spirit in the authors of the Scriptures and the Scriptures themselves; illumination, the means by which the Scriptures are made clear to the reader.

Enlightenment or illumination of the darkened mind, whether it be of Jew (Heb 6:4; 10:32) or Gentile (II Cor 4:4–6), is a necessary aspect of the salvation experience. David acknowledged that the Lord lightened his darkness (Ps 18:28). By linking this concept with the term "commandment" he implied that only as the Word of God is obeyed, does further enlightenment come (Ps 19:8).

Karl Barth and the neoorthodox theologians remove inspiration from the writer of Scripture and the Scriptures themselves and place it in the hearer or reader. Barth speaks of men being verbally inspired and means by this that the fallible, contradictory Bible becomes the Word of God as man enjoys a subjective experience of revelation. This view denies both the teaching of Christ concerning the Bible and the view which the Bible presents of itself. *See* Inspiration; Neoorthodoxy.

R. A. K.

ILLYRICUM (ĭ-lĭr'ĭ-cŭm). A Roman province (also called Dalmatia) lying N of Macedonia, W of Moesia and S of Pannonia, and on the E coast of the Adriatic Sea. It is approximately equivalent to the territory of modern Yugoslavia. It is only mentioned in the NT as the western limits of Paul's travels at the end of his third missionary journey (Rom 15:19).

The geographer Strabo (*Geography* VII.317) described the Illyrians as wild and given to piracy, and the land as warm on the coast but cold in the mountainous interior. Both the Greeks and the Romans carried on military campaigns against them, often not too successfully. The land was finally incorporated as a province of the Roman Empire in the first decade of the 1st cen. A.D.

IMAGE. *See* Idolatry; Imagery.

IMAGE, NEBUCHADNEZZAR'S. The only record of the golden image which Nebuchadnezzar made is in Dan 3. Images of gods and the kings themselves were common in Babylonia, and fit in with our knowledge of religious conditions under Nebuchadnezzar. This image on the plain of Dura may have had the form of an obelisk with a nine-foot base and towering 90 feet high, plated with glittering gold. The refusal of Daniel's three friends to worship this image was readily apparent. The method of punishment by fire for those refusing to bow seems to have been common to that period (cf. Jer 29:22). Although Daniel is not mentioned, it is unreasonable to infer, on the basis of Daniel's character as portrayed in the book bearing his name, that he worshiped this image.

Possibly the great image which the king saw in his dream and which Daniel described (Dan 2:31–35) and interpreted for him, was the inspiration for the golden monument which Nebuchadnezzar created (3:1). In so doing he was defying.God's express declaration that his kingdom would fall and be succeeded by other kingdoms (2:38–45).

S. J. S.

IMAGE OF GOD. Man, as created in the image of God, is distinguished from all other creatures. He is unique in that he was made for communion with and to be responsible to his Creator. God made man like Himself, as a personal being, and for Himself in an "I-Thou" relationship (Gen 1:26–27; 5:1–2; 9:6; I Cor 11:7; Eph 4:24; Col 3:10; Jas 3:9). Only in obedient response to God can man truly fulfill the purpose for which he was created. It is in Jesus Christ alone that the image of God may be perfectly seen; He is the true and perfect man (Col 1:15; II Cor 4:4).

Three aspects of this doctrine may be distinguished.

1. *The image as created by God.* The image of God bears a natural or a formal likeness to God, which consists in personality, for this is essentially what God is, a personal Spirit. It also bears a moral or relational likeness, which consisted originally in positive holiness and original righteousness. Man was not created merely in a state of innocence or moral neutrality; but his mind, affections, and will were positively directed toward God as his supreme end. As such, the first man's moral nature was a finite reflection of God's moral nature. However, he was capable of testing, probation, development and progress through the exercise of free choice in the face of temptation. His was a responsibility in freedom. It was possible for Adam to choose good or evil; his moral condition was not immutable or indefectible.

As a gift from God, man in God's image was endowed with immortality (not merely as naturally possessing endless existence in virtue of the simplicity of his soul). He was not subject to the law of death, since there was no principle of death or of sin at work in his original state of created goodness.

While God is not physical in any way, there is a sense in which even man's body is included in the image of God, for man is a unitary being composed of both body and soul. His body is a fit instrument for the self-expression of a soul made for fellowship with the Creator and is suited eschatologically to become a "spiritual body" (I Cor 15:44). There was no antagonism or contrariety between soul and body in the original state (dualism is ruled out). The body was not something to be despised as inferior to the soul or as a hindrance to the higher life of man. It was not something apart from the real self of Adam, but was essentially one with it. As such, there was a subjection of the sensuous impulses to the control of the human spirit.

Included in Adam's creation in the image of God was his dominion over the lower creation, the animals and the world of nature. This is indicative of the glory and honor with which man was crowned as the head and apex of the entire creation. Physical surroundings in the garden of Eden were fitted to bring happiness and to favor the development of the whole of nature. *See* Anthropology; on Christ as the image of God (II Cor 4:4; Phil 2:6;.Col 1:15) *see* Christ, Humiliation of; Kenosis.

2. *The image as marred by the Fall.* Disobedience brought disastrous consequences to the original image of God in the first man. Sin impaired the entire natural likeness (personality), so that man's mind, emotions, and will became corrupt (total depravity). Yet man did not lose this natural likeness, however sullied it became because of sin, for it is this which constitutes him as man in distinction from other creatures. It is intrinsic to human nature and constitutes his receptivity for redemption. Even the unregenerate retain the natural image of God, otherwise they would cease to be men (rational and moral beings).

Whereas the natural likeness is still retained after the Fall, the moral image is entirely lost. Now man is destitute of original righteousness; he is dead in trespasses and sin. His affections and will are not inclined in an upward direction toward God and holiness, but in a downward, carnal direction. He has lost fellowship with God and has become an alien and enemy through the estrangement produced by disobedience (Gen 3:8–10; Rom 5:10a; Col 1:21a). Cut off from the Source of life he became a dying creature (Gen 2:17; Rom 6:23a).

The body is no longer such a fit instrument of the soul; it is often a hindrance to the higher life of man because it easily enters into alliance with his depraved affections and perverted will. The original subjection of the sensuous to the spiritual now seems reversed with the Fall. Adam was driven from the garden of Eden, and dominion over nature became difficult and laborious. *See* Fall of Man.

3. *The image as restored by Christ.* Through the redemption that is in Christ the believer is regenerated: he is renewed in knowledge, his affections are reorientated, his will is transformed, his body is made a temple of the Holy Spirit. The image of God is re-created in righteousness and true holiness and is restored to communion and favor with God; by faith man inherits eternal life. Indeed, through the Lord's saving work the believer has regained far more than was lost through Adam's sin (I Cor 15:44–49). The Christian is to be gradually transformed into the very image of the Son of God, which will ultimately involve not only perfect moral and spiritual likeness to Christ but also a glorified body like that of the resurrected last Adam (Rom 8:29; II Cor 3:18; I Cor 15:42 ff.). *See* New Creation.

Divergent views respecting the image of God. In Roman Catholic theology an unwarranted distinction is made between the synonymous terms "image" and "likeness." The former designates the natural image, they claim, and belongs to the very nature of man as man, including spirituality, freedom, and immortality. The latter designates the moral image, righteousness, and holiness, and is a superadded, supernatural gift given to make obedience easier in view of concupiscence, which is a natural tendency toward the lower appetites (but not itself sin, according to Catholic theology). Sometimes the "likeness" is described as a merited product of obedience, a reward for the proper use of nature, so that by it man is enabled to merit eternal life. In the Fall Adam lost only the likeness; the natural image remained unimpaired. Thus, the natural man is now in a moral condition similar to that of the unfallen Adam but before being endowed with original righteousness. This original righteousness can be regained through the sacraments of the Catholic Church.

Among other modern views is the very influential doctrine that the image of God is not at all substantial, as is personality, but is simply relational. This is the view of S. Kierkegaard, Karl Barth and a host of contemporary theologians. They teach that man stands in the image of God only when he is mirroring God's spiritual nature in his own life. This occurs when man obediently responds to God's confrontation in the point of contact between God and man which is experienced in an act of true worship. In such an experience, man at times resembles God and thus (and then) stands in the divine image.

An evolutionary view distinguishes between the image which man originally possessed and which he lost in the Fall (happiness and responsive obedience), and the image acquired by the Fall (rational powers and moral responsibility). This came about when *Homo*, or man, became *Homo sapiens*, or rational man, through the first act that involved moral accountability. In this act man lost his animal-like innocence and happiness, and gained a rational and moral nature.

Bibliography. J. Behm, "*Morphē*, etc.," TDNT, IV, 742-759. G. C. Berkouwer, *Man—The Image of God*, Grand Rapids: Eerdmans, 1962. David S. Cairns, *The Image of God in Man*, New York: Philosophical Library, 1953. Gordon H. Clark, "The Image of God in Man," JETS, XII (1969), 215-222. Carl F. H. Henry, "Man," BDT, pp. 338-342. James Gresham Machen, *The Christian View of Man*, New York: Macmillan, 1937. James Orr, *God's Image in Man*, Grand Rapids: Eerdmans, 1948. J. Schneider, "*Homoios*, etc.," TDNT, V, 186-199. A. H. Strong, *Systematic Theology*, 11th ed., Philadelphia: Judson Press, 1947, pp. 514-532. Charles L. Feinberg, "The Image of God," BS, CXXIX (1972), 235-246.

R. E. Po.

IMAGERY. Very early in human history there came to be employed various artificial representations of objects, animals, persons or gods designed to be used in worship. Some were similitudes of that which actually exists, others were pictorial representations of the imagination, and others assumed symbolic forms. Often they were employed simply for ornamental purposes, as in the tabernacle and the temple, but commonly they came to be used in idolatrous ways.

The Egyptians used images in their burial ceremonies which were distinct from their idols used in pagan worship, such as miniatures of servants, pets, foods, vehicles, etc. By means of magical formulas painted on the inside of his coffin or written on a papyrus scroll buried with the dead, the deceased was expected to bring to life these images in order to serve him in the next world.

Constantly repeated denunciations and prohibitions of images and likenesses of created things in the OT show how persistent was the tendency to idolatry among the Hebrews (e.g., Deut 5:8; 7:5; 16:22; Ps 97:7; Isa 42:17; 44:9; Jer 10:14; Ezk 7:20; Hos 10:2; Mic 1:7; Hab 2:18). Use of graven (or carved) and molten (or cast) idols and images was forbidden to Israelites by the second commandment (Ex 20:4-5), because the idol inevitably became a rival and substitute for God (not merely a symbol). Idolatry not only misrepresents the spiritual nature of God (every bodily representation is a misrepresentation), but divides or alienates devotion by placing an object between (and before) God and the worshiper. It is a root of evil; it leads to every kind of corruption of religion and morality. *See* Idolatry.

R. E. Po.

IMAGINATION. The formation of mental images by a synthesis of elements experienced separately. It presents new views and applications of ideas, events and truths already experienced. The verb "to imagine" in KJV has the meaning of "purpose, scheme, contrive." The ASV translates it "think," "meditate," "devise."

The Heb. word *sheriruth* (Deut 29:19; Jer 3:17; etc.) is lit., "firmness" and is generally used in the bad sense of stubbornness, as in RSV, NEB. Heb. *yēṣer* (Gen 6:5; I Chr 28:9; 29:18; etc.) means "form, conception," what is framed in the mind. The Gr. words are *dialogismos*, "thought, opinion, reasoning, design" (Rom 1:21); *dianoia*, "understanding, intelligence, mind, purpose, plan" (Lk 1:51); and *logismos*, "calculation, reasoning, reflection, reasoning power" (II Cor 10:5).

IMITATE. *See* Example.

IMLA, IMLAH (ĭm'là). Father of Micaiah, the prophet of God who was consulted by Ahab and Jehoshaphat before they went to battle against the Syrians at Ramoth-gilead (I Kgs 22:8-9; II Chr 18:7-8).

IMMANUEL. *See* Emmanuel.

IMMATERIALITY. Immateriality is the negative term for which spirituality is its positive expression. It denotes the qualities of simplicity (not divisible), having no parts (not composite), indestructibility (cannot be dissolved), and incorporeality (not of the nature of matter). The Bible describes God and the human soul in terms that indicate they are immaterial.

God is pure spirit (Jn 4:24); He stands in absolute contrast to matter. God cannot be separated into parts; He is free from the limitations of time and space. He is "eternal, immortal, invisible" (I Tim 1:17; cf. 6:16). The divine immateriality is sometimes said to be the basis for God's attributes of eternity, omnipresence and unchangeableness. The fact of the immateriality of the human soul is usually used as one of the arguments for immortality.

Immateriality when used in biblical and theological language should not be understood as it is often used in ordinary language, as the quality of being unessential, flimsy or unimportant.

R. E. Po.

IMMER (ĭm'ĕr)

1. A priest, head of the 16th course of priests appointed by David (I Chr 24:14), the father of Meshillemith (I Chr 9:12) and founder of a family which was very active after the return from Exile. A total of 1,052 of his descendants returned (I Chr 9:12; Ezr 2:37; 10:20; Neh 7:40; 11:13).

2. Among those who returned to Jerusalem with Zerubbabel were some who could not prove their Israelitish descent. The record is not clear whether Immer is the name of one of their ancestors (see 1 above) or the village in Babylon from which some of them came (Ezr 2:59; Neh 7:61).

3. Father of Zadok the priest who worked on the wall of Jerusalem (Neh 3:29). If "father" here means ancestor, he may be the same as 1 above.

4. The father of Pashur the priest who had Jeremiah beaten and put in stocks because of his dire warnings (Jer 20:1). If "ancestor" is meant, he may be 1 above.

P. C. J.

IMMORTALITY. *Athanasia* ("deathlessness") and *aphtharsia* ("incorruptibility") are the two Gr. words designating immortality. *Athanasia* is found in I Cor 15:53 f.; I Tim 6:16; *aphtharsia* is found in Rom 2:7; I Cor 15:42, 50, 53 f.; Eph 6:24 (translated "sincerity"); II Tim 1:10; and the adjective *aphthartos* ("incorruptible") is found in Rom 1:23; I Cor 9:25; 15:52; I Tim 1:17; I Pet 1:4, 23; 3:4.

Immortality may be defined as that state of deathlessness and incorruptibility that resides absolutely and eternally in God and relatively and derivatively in man. This article is limited to the various aspects of man's immortality as revealed in the Scriptures.

God's eternal plan. God's plan involved not only the creation of man but also the redemption of some of fallen man's posterity through the grace of God offered to sinful men in the atoning death of Jesus Christ (Gen 1:26–28; 3:15; Isa 53:1–12; Jn 3:14–16; Rom 3:21–30; Eph 2:1–10). This plan considered man as a created being whose life would continue forever. Those of sinful man's posterity who savingly enter into God's kingdom of grace become inheritors of eternal life in Christ Jesus (Jn 17:2–3; Acts 13:48; Rom 8:28–30; Rev 13:8); but those of sinful man's posterity who reject the offer of salvation in Christ become the objects of God's eternal wrath (Mt 25:41, 46; Rom 2:5–9; 9:22; II Thess 1:8–9; II Pet 2:9; 3:7; Rev 14:9–11). It is evident, therefore, that God's decrees from eternity envisioned a creature called man whose destiny, whether in heaven or in hell, would be eternal. Thus man's immortality is an integral part of God's eternal plan.

Man's creation. The immortality of man's nature is implicit in the creation of man in God's "image" (Gen 1:26–27). Although this term is never defined as such, it is quite evident that "image" describes a kinship with God (cf. II Pet 1:4) that puts man in a category by himself among God's creatures. Even death cannot destroy man's soul (Mt 10:28; Heb 12:23; Rev 6:9–11; 20:4). Paul's interpretation of Gen 2:7 in I Cor 15:45–48 in no wise invalidates the doctrine of man's original and innate immortality, for Paul is contrasting "the image of the earthy" which we now bear as a result of our sin in Eden with "the image of the heavenly" which the redeemed will bear as a result of the resurrection of their bodies at Christ's second advent. Thus it is quite evident that the divine "image" planted in man's nature at creation included man's immortality as an integral part.

Man's apostasy. The question arises at this point whether Adam's sin in Eden (Gen 3:1–21; Rom 5:12–14) disrobed man of his essential immortality. Some believe man lost his immortality in Eden. This view finds apparent support in the fact the divine image received some serious damage as a result of Adam's sin. It is evident that man's moral nature (Rom 1:18–32; 3:9–20; Eph 2:1–3, 12; 4:18) and volitional powers (Mt 12:34; Jn 3:19; 8:43–44; II Pet 2:14) were radically affected by man's apostasy from a state of original rectitude.

It cannot be deduced, however, from these devastations upon man's original nature that man likewise lost his immortality. Such a conclusion would run contrary to three important facts: (1) the still resident image of God in man long after his fall in Eden (Gen 9:6), thus justifying the stern punishment inflicted upon the willful murderer (Num 35:33); (2) the "more than" and "much more" teaching of our Lord regarding man's intrinsic value before God (Mt 6:25–26); (3) the provision made by God in the gospel for the salvation of lost mankind (Lk 19:10; Jn 3:14–16; I Tim 1:12–16).

Moreover, the death attached to Adam's disobedience (Gen 2:17) affected primarily the *na*-

ture of his existence rather than the *fact* of his existence. This fact is confirmed by what the Bible describes as the state of spiritual death resulting from the Fall (Eph 2:1, 5; Col 2:13). Actually, Adam did not die physically on the day of his disobedience; thus the death threatened and actualized must have meant spiritual death with its eventual consequence in physical death (Rom 5:12–14). But neither of these involves the non-existence of the soul. Man did not lose his immortality when he became a sinner in the garden of Eden.

Man's redemption. Promises designed to effectuate man's recovery and restoration began to flow from the heart of God as soon as man sinned in Eden (Gen 3:15). But attached to these promises is the warning that the one who disbelieves the Son of God will "perish" (Jn 3:16, 36).

Again the question of immortality crops up, for some insist that only those who savingly believe in Jesus Christ receive immortal or eternal life (i.e., the restoration of the immortality supposedly lost in Eden), while all others perish (i.e., become non-existent at death). It is perfectly true that the Bible applies such terms as "perish" (Lk 13:3, 5; Jn 3:15–16; II Thess 2:10), "destroy" (Mt 10:28; I Cor 3:17; Jude 5; Rev 11:18), "destruction" (Mt 7:13; Rom 9:22; Phil 3:19; II Thess 1:9), "perdition" (Phil 1:28; I Tim 6:9; II Pet 3:7), "lose" (Lk 9:24–25; 17:33), and "lost" (Lk 19:10; Jn 17:12; II Cor 4:3) to those who reject Jesus Christ as their Lord and Saviour. Yet nowhere in these passages is the theory of the annihilation of the unbeliever taught or implied.

"Eternal life" is the spiritual counterpart of "eternal sin" (Mk 3:29, ASV), "eternal punishment" (Mt 25:46), and "eternal destruction" (II Thess 1:9). However, the word "eternal" in these descriptions designates not only length of existence but also the kind or nature of existence. For example, "eternal life" introduces the believer into a new kind of life—a life receiving its energy and motivation from its union with the living Lord (Jn 10:10; 17:23; Gal 2:20; Col 1:27; I Jn 5:11–12). This life continues forever (Mt 25:34; Jn 6:37–51). On the opposite side, "eternal destruction" represents a kind of life, already begun in the present world (Jn 3:36), which issues in eternal separation from the living God (Lk 16:23, 26; Eph 4:18–19; II Thess 1:9).

Thus the gospel offer of mercy in Christ does not restore to the repentant sinner an immortality which he supposedly lost in Eden; nor does this offer when rejected confirm the non-immortality supposedly brought upon man by his transgression in Eden. In other words, man's immortality as such is not affected by the acceptance or rejection of the gospel offer of mercy; but the *kind* of immortality man will experience is tremendously affected by his attitude toward Christ in the present life (cf. Mt 26:24).

The intermediate state. Both the righteous

and the unrighteous die physically as a result of Adam's transgression in Eden (Gen 3:17–19; 5:1–31; Rom 5:12–14). But the Scriptures teach that the soul survives the dissolution of soul and body at physical death. The ancient patriarchs believed in the soul's continuance after death (Gen 25:8, 17; 35:29; 49:29, 33). These men looked for the City of God beyond the present life (Heb 11:10, 13–16). Job's "I know" (19:25–27) is re-echoed by Paul's "I know" (II Cor 5:1–10; II Tim 1:12; 4:18) centuries later. David believed his child (II Sam 12:23) entered a state of blessedness comparable to that state promised to the repentant thief on the cross (Lk 23:43). True, the body dies and returns to the dust (Gen 3:19); but the soul of the righteous returns to God (Eccl 12:7; Acts 7:59).

There are places in the OT revelation where the disembodied or intermediate state of the soul is described somewhat disparagingly (Ps 6:5; 30:9; 88:10–12; 115:17; Eccl 9:10; Isa 38:18). On the other hand, there are other places (Job 19:25–27; Ps 16:8–11) where faith in a life beyond the present is presented in terms prophetic of the fuller light of NT revelation (II Cor 5:1–10; Phil 1:21–23; II Tim 4:8, 18; Rev 6:9–11). This faith in the soul's immortality after death is vividly and dramatically confirmed by the appearance of Moses and Elijah with Christ on the Mount of Transfiguration (Mt 17:1–8). If further confirmation were necessary, Paul surely received it when he was transported from this world to the heavenly scene for a vision of the eternal world (II Cor 12:1–7). And still further confirmation can be found in the fact that Lazarus (Jn 11:1–44) and others (Mt 9:18–25; Lk 7:11–17; Acts 9: 36–43) were temporarily restored to the present life after the soul had left their bodies at death. Our Lord's own resurrection gives, of course, the greatest confirmation to the soul's continuance beyond the present life (I Cor 15:1–23).

The fact that the believer's state after death is sometimes called a "sleep" (Dan 12:2; Mt 27:52; Jn 11:11; Acts 13:36; I Cor 15:6, 18, 20; I Thess 4:13–18) in no wise sustains the idea that the soul enters into a state of unconsciousness after death; in fact, this very disembodied state is described as "very much better" (Phil 1:23, NASB) than the present life. There is very little in the Bible about the soul of the unbeliever after death, but there is enough to warrant the firm conclusion that he is in a state of unrelenting agony (Lk 16:22–31).

The resurrection of the righteous. The intermediate state of the soul is completed and consummated in the resurrection of the body of the redeemed at the time of Christ's return in glory (I Thess 4:13–18; I Jn 3:1–3). The beauty and grandeur of this resurrection are majestically described in the Scriptures (Job 19:25–27; Isa 25:6–8; 26:19, NASB; Mt 22:30; I Cor 15:35–49; Phil 3:20–21). There will be, of course, a generation of believers who will be ushered·immediately into the next life without experiencing death (I Cor 15:51-53; I Thess 4:15, 17; 5:10).

A striking similarity exists between the immortality of the resurrected and glorified body of our Lord and the immortality of the resurrected and glorified body of the believer (Rom 8:29; I Cor 15:43, 49; Phil 3:21; Col 3:4; I Jn 3:2). A striking dissimilarity also exists in the fact that, though Christ's body did not undergo corruption (Ps 16:10; Acts 2:27; 13:35), the believer's body must return to the dust unless he is in that last generation on earth at the time of Christ's second coming (Gen 3:19; Ps 90:3; Heb 9:27-28). "The redemption of the body" is the last stage in the total restoration of the disrupted-by-sin personality of the believer (Rom 8:18-25). This blessed immortality of the redeemed shall never end (Rev 22:1-5). It is the grand and glorious climax of God's eternal plan for the salvation of some of Adam's fallen posterity (Mt 25:34; Rom 9:23-24; Heb 12:22-24; Rev 7:9⊥10).

The resurrection of the wicked. The Bible positively asserts that there will be a resurrection of the wicked (Dan 12:2; Jn 5:28-29; Acts 24:15; Rev 20:11-15). Their resurrection will issue in what is called "the second death" (Rev 20:6, 14; cf. 2:11; 21:8), from which state there is not the slightest hope of relief, release or restoration (Mt 10:15; 11:22-24; 25:41; II Thess 1:8-9; II Pet 2:9; 3:7; Rev 14:10 f.; 20:14; 21:8). Such terms as "perish" (Rom 2:12; II Thess 2:10), "destroy" (I Cor 3:17; Rev 11:18), and the like (see under "Man's Redemption" above) give no support to the theory of annihilationism; nor do such passages as Acts 3:21; I Cor 15:22; Eph 1:10; Col 1:20; I Pet 3:18-20 give the slightest hope, when correctly interpreted, to any theory of restorationism.

Conclusions. The following conclusions regarding man's immortality are justifiable in the light of the discussion given above: (1) Only in the Bible do we find evidence sufficient to sustain the doctrine of man's immortality; all other sources of help on this subject are vain and hopeless. (2) The biblical evidence for the immortality of the soul pervades the Scriptures from the earliest times (Job 19:23-27) and reaches its climax in the resurrection of Christ from the grave (Ps 16:8-11; Acts 2:25-28; I Cor 15:1-23). (3) This evidence is not only casual and indirect (Gen 25:8; 35:29; Ex 3:6; Mt 22:31-32) but also studied and systematic (Mt 22:29-30; Jn 5:28-29; 11:25-26; 14:1-3; Rom 2:1-11; I Cor 15:1-58; II Cor 5:1-10). (4) The Bible presents the immortality of the righteous and the immortality of the wicked with equal cogency; it is thus impossible to deny the one without denying the other (Mt 25:34, 41, 46; Lk 16:19-31).

See Anthropology; Dead, The; Eternal State and Death; Incorruption; Mortality; Resurrection.

Bibliography. Loraine Boettner, *Immortality,* Grand Rapids: Eerdmans, 1956. P. T. Forsyth, *This Life and the Next: The Effect on This Life of Faith in Another,* Boston: Pilgrim Press, 1948, reprint. W. E. Hocking, *The Meaning of Immortality in Human Experience,* New York: Harper, 1957. E. E. Holmes, *Immortality,* London: Longmans, Green, and Co., 1908. A. Kuyper, *The Shadow of Death,* Grand Rapids: Eerdmans, 1929. Carroll E. Simcox, *Is Death the End? The Christian Answer,* Greenwich, Conn.: Seabury Press, 1959.

W. B.

IMMUTABILITY. The term appears in the KJV in Heb 6:17-18: "Wherein God, willing more abundantly to show unto the heirs of promise the immutability of his counsel, confirmed it by an oath: that by two immutable things, in which it was impossible for God to lie. . . ." By the immutability of God is meant that in His essence, attributes, consciousness and will God is unchangeable.

The doctrine of God's immutability is further deduced from biblical passages such as: "They shall be changed, but thou art the same" (Ps 102:26-27); "I am the Lord, I change not" (Mal 3:6); "Jesus Christ the same yesterday, and today, and for ever" (Heb 13:8); and "with whom can be no variation, neither shadow that is cast by turning" (Jas 1:17, ASV). In such verses change is explicitly denied to God. This does not mean God is immobile, however, for He acts in history. His immutability is dynamic, not static.

Immutability is also indicated in other verses where the idea is implicit rather than explicit. For example, all those passages that teach omniscience (*q.v.*) imply immutability; for if the amount of knowledge in the divine mind increased or diminished, there would be a time in which God would not know all things (but cf. Heb 4:13). Omniscience allows no change nor temporal sequence of ideas in God's mind. God can neither forget what He now knows nor think of something additional that He never thought of before. Omniscience therefore involves immutability.

Occasionally the Bible attributes repentance or regret to God. In I Sam 15:11, 35 it is stated that God repented (Heb. *niḥam,* "feel compassion, grief, sorrow") of having made Saul king over Israel. This seems to indicate a change of mind or emotion in God. But between these two verses, in v. 29 we read that "the Strength of Israel will not lie nor repent: for he is not a man, that he should repent." God's seeming change of mind or attitude therefore should be taken as an anthropopathism, the attributing of human emotions to God, just as we understand the arms and eyes of the Lord as anthropomorphisms.

Other passages which speak of God as repenting of judgment (e.g., against Israel, Ex 32:14; Nineveh, Jon 3:10) reveal that His threats are often conditional upon human repentance (cf. Jer 18:7-10; 26:3, 13, 19). Therefore God abides by the same unchanging moral principles in all dispensations of His government. *See* Repentance.

A greater difficulty relates to the act of creating the world. All orthodox Christians admit that God eternally willed to create; but since He actually created at a particular moment, this act seems to be a change in God. Charnock, the Puritan theologian (VI, iv, 1 [p. 213]), tried to resolve the difficulty by saying, "There was no change in God by the act of creation, because ... there was no new act of his will which was not before. The creation began in time, but the will of creating was from eternity.... But though God spake that word which he had not spoke before, whereby the world was brought into act, yet he did not will that will he willed not before. God did not create by a new counsel or new will, but by that which was from eternity (Eph 1:9)."

Bibliography. Thomas Aquinas, *Summa Theologica,* Book I, question IX, answers 1, 2. J. Oliver Buswell, Jr., *A Systematic Theology of the Christian Religion,* Grand Rapids: Zondervan, 1962, I, 40-71. Stephen Charnock, *Discourses upon the Existence and Attributes of God,* London: Henry Bohn, 1849, pp. 195-230. Charles A. Hodge, *Systematic Theology,* New York: Scribner's, 1872, I, v, 7.

G. H. C.

IMNA (ĭm'nà). A son of Helem from the tribe of Asher (I Chr 7:35).

IMNAH (ĭm'nà)
1. Eldest son of Asher (I Chr 7:30), also called Jimna and Jimnah (Gen 46:17; Num 26:44).
2. A Levite, the father of Kore in the time of Hezekiah (II Chr 31:14).

IMPORTUNITY. The Gr. *anaideia,* "shamelessness," "impudence," "importunity," appears only in Lk 11:8, to describe a person who is persistent in his entreaties and exemplifies perseverance in prayer (cf. Lk 18:1-8; I Thess 5:17).

IMPOSITION OF HANDS. *See* Hands, Laying on of.

IMPOTENT. *See* Diseases.

IMPRECATION. *See* Curse.

IMPRECATORY PSALMS. *See* Psalms; Prayer.

IMPRISONMENT. Imprisonment (Gr. *phylakē,* usually "watch" or "prison") was one of the trials suffered by OT believers (Heb 11:36) and by Paul and other early Christians (II Cor 6:5).

Several long imprisonments were those of Joseph (Gen 39:20-41:14), Jeremiah (Jer 32:2 ff.), and Paul at Caesarea (Acts 23:23-26:32) and at Rome (Acts 28:16-31). Imprisonment (Heb. *'esûr,* from *'āsar,* "to bind") was one form of punishment imposed for disobeying the law of the Persian kings (Ezr 7:26). *See* Crime and Punishment; Prison.

Entrance to the Mamertine Prison in Rome, where Paul was presumably held when he wrote 2 Timothy. HFV

IMPURITY. *See* Ablution; Uncleanness.

IMPUTATION, IMPUTE. In the OT this concept is found in the common Heb. verb *ḥāshab,* "to think, count, be accounted" (KJV "impute," Lev 7:18; 17:4; II Sam 19:19; Ps 32:2). In the NT it is represented by the Gr. *ellogeō,* "to impute, lay to one's charge" (used only twice, in Rom 5:13 and Phm 18), and *logizomai,* "to place to the account of, reckon to, to impute" (used 41 times, KJV "impute," Rom 4:6, etc.; II Cor 5:19; Jas 2:23). The concept is beautifully illustrated when Paul writes to Philemon concerning the runaway slave Onesimus: "If he has wronged you in any way, or owes you anything, charge that to my account" (*touto emoi elloga,* Phm 18, NASB).

There are two kinds of imputation: immediate and mediate. The transmission of Adam's fallen nature consecutively to and through each following generation, from parents to their children, is mediate. For it some theologians would not even use the term imputation. They would reserve it for the three separate acts of immediate imputation: (1) the imputation of Adam's sin to his posterity (Rom 5:12; I Cor 15:22); (2) the imputation of our sins to Christ (II Cor 5:21; Gal 3:13); (3) the imputation of Christ's righteousness to us (Rom 4:1–25; I Cor 1:30). These three major imputations are fully explained in Scripture:

1. The imputation of Adam's sin to the race is clearly set forth in Rom 5:12: Death came "upon all men, for that [because] all have sinned." All died in Adam, Paul teaches in I Cor 15:22. Death reigned right from the time of Adam, and not just from the days of Moses when the Jewish law was first given — though sin is not imputed when there is no law — because Adam's sin was every man's sin (Rom 5:13–14). Because of the reconciliation (*q.v.*) which God has effected through Christ, He no longer accounts men's trespasses against them (II Cor 5:19). But this word must be preached so that men may appropriate it.

2. The imputation of the sins of man to Christ entails judicial imputation inasmuch as it is the reckoning to Christ of that which is not antecedently His own. While the theological term impute is not used to express this in Scripture, equivalent expressions are employed, such as "the Lord hath laid upon him the iniquity of us all" (Isa 53:6); "who his own self bare our sins" (I Pet 2:24); "He hath made him to be sin for us, who knew no sin" (II Cor 5:21).

3. The imputation of righteousness (*q.v.*) to the believer. The "righteousness of God" is the theme of Romans (1:17; 3:5, 21–22, 25–26). The term is used in two senses in Romans: (*a*) God's own inherent righteousness (Rom 1:17; 3:5, 25–26); (*b*) the righteousness of Christ which is imputed to the believer (Rom 3:21–22; 10:3; cf. II Cor 5:21).

Christ's righteousness is the basis of the Christian's acceptance and standing before God. God made Him to be "unto us wisdom, and righteousness, and sanctification, and redemption" (I Cor 1:30). God identifies us positionally with all that Christ did in His death, burial and resurrection, and baptizes us into Christ (Rom 6:3–6; I Cor 12:13; *see* Baptism). Thus we become recipients of the very righteousness of God, "For he hath made him to be sin for us, who knew no sin; that we might be made the righteousness of God" (II Cor 5:21). The believer is perfected in Christ (Heb 10:14), entirely complete in Him (Col 2:9–10; cf. Jn 1:16; Col 1:19), and thereby fit to appear in the presence of God (Col 1:12; Phil 3:9). As in the case of Abraham, who believed God and it was counted (Heb. *ḥāshab,* Gen 15:6; Gr. *logi-*

zomai, Rom 4:3) to him as righteousness, so faith, not works, is the basis for receiving this righteousness (Rom 4:9–25). *See* Justification.

R. A. K.

IMRAH (ĭm′rà). A prominent chief of the tribe of Asher and the son of Zophah (I Chr 7:36).

IMRI (ĭm′rī)

1. A descendant of Pharez, the son of Judah (I Chr 9:4).

2. The father of Zaccur who assisted Nehemiah in the rebuilding of the wall of Jerusalem (Neh 3:2).

INABILITY. Scripture describes the unsaved man in such a way as to deny to him the ability of himself without special divine grace to turn to God, to do perfectly the will of God, or wholly to please God (Jn 1:13; 6:44; Rom 7:18; 8:7–8; I Cor 2:14; Eph 2:1). Sin has so weakened man's being and powers that he is by nature morally and spiritually unable to perform an act which is truly and entirely good in God's sight. When seen from God's viewpoint, all the works of the unregenerate are radically defective because they are not motivated by love to God and for the glory of God.

INCANTATION. *See* Magic.

INCARNATION. A term derived from the Latin version of Jn 1:14. Incarnation refers exclusively to that action by which the Son of God, often spoken of as the Second Person of the Godhead, became man. It presupposes the essential deity and eternal sonship of the Person who became incarnate. The doctrine is vitiated if it is conceived of as the beginning of existence of Him who is uniquely the Son of God. When John writes, "And the Word was made flesh" (Jn 1:14), the Word had already been identified as eternally subsistent, as eternally with God, and as Himself God (Jn 1:1–3). When Paul says that He "was made in the likeness of men" (Phil 2:7), he means that this Person was originally in the form of God and therefore on an equality with God (Phil 2:6).

The fact. The incarnation is a stupendous fact; it is the mystery of godliness, the grand miracle of the Christian faith. It means that He who never began to be but eternally existed, and who ever continued to be what He eternally was, began to be what He eternally was not. It is an event that occurred in time with reference to Him who Himself was eternal. There are, therefore, the sustained contrasts: the Eternal entered time and became subject to its conditions; the Infinite became the finite; the Immutable became mutable; the Invisible became visible; the Almighty became the weak and infirm; the Creator became the creature; God became man.

It would have been humiliation for the Son of God to become man under the most ideal earthly conditions, because of the discrepancy between the majesty of God the Creator and the humble status of the most dignified creation. But it was not into an ideal world that He came; it was into this world of sin, of misery, and of death. That He came into such a world indicates the peculiarity of the humiliation undertaken and the redemptive purpose designed. He came, therefore, "in the likeness of sinful flesh" (Rom 8:3), into the closest relation to sinful humanity that it was possible for Him to come without thereby becoming Himself sinful. *See* Christ, Humiliation of.

The mode. The mode is generally spoken of as the virgin birth. Christ was in truth born of the virgin because Mary had not yet known a man. The mode was, therefore, supernatural. Three considerations point up the supernatural character.

1. Jesus was not conceived by the conjunction of man and woman, by spermal communication from the man. He was begotten in the womb of Mary by the power of the Holy Spirit (Mt 1:20; Lk 1:35). The miracle appears first of all in supernatural begetting. In this respect it is not strictly accurate to say that Jesus was conceived by the Holy Spirit. It was Mary who conceived and our attention is expressly drawn to this fact (Lk 1:31). That is said of Mary which is said also of Elisabeth (Lk 1:24, 36). But Mary conceived only because the Holy Spirit had begotten Jesus in her womb and hence the birth was virgin. Paul reflects this doctrine in Gal 4:4 when he writes, "God sent forth his Son, born of woman" (RSV). The prophecy of Isa 7:14 foretold the supernatural manner of Jesus' birth. *See* Virgin.

2. It was not a mere baby who was conceived of Mary. It was the eternal Son of God who was conceived. Only in respect of His human nature was He formed in the womb, but it was He in this unchanged identity. The most stupendous aspect of the supernatural was the begetting and conception of this supernatural, eternal Person. Hence there is no point at which the supernatural is not present, and it is not merely in the fact of supernatural begetting that the miracle appears. It is only when this fact is overlooked that difficulty with the doctrine of the virgin birth is entertained. Natural generation would be incongruous, while supernatural generation is in perfect accord with the supernatural character of the Person.

3. The dogma of Mary's immaculate conception is an imposture; it has no warrant from the data of revelation (*see* Mary). The supernatural is evident in the preservation of the infant Jesus from the defilement that belonged to His human mother. Supernatural generation was necessary to preserve immunity to hereditary depravity, because "that which is born of the flesh is flesh" (Jn 3:6). Yet this does not appear to be of itself an adequate explanation of Jesus' spotless purity. He was made of the seed of David according to the flesh. This seed was corrupt. But Jesus was holy, undefiled, and separate from sinners.

Jesus came by a mode that was supernatural and therefore by a mode consonant with His supernatural person. He came by a mode that guaranteed His sinlessness, and therefore by a mode consonant with His divine perfection and with the redemptive design of His coming. But He came by a mode that preserved fully His genetic connection with sinful humanity. This is the meaning of conception by and birth from a virgin who herself was conceived in sin like all the other offspring of Adam by natural generation. And this belongs to the marvel and grace of the incarnation. *See* Christ, Sinlessness of.

The nature. The proposition "God became man" must not be interpreted to mean that Godhood was exchanged for manhood; it means no subtraction or divestiture. The Son of God did not cease to be what He eternally was when He became human. The incarnation was by addition. In Jn 1:14 there is no suggestion that the Word in becoming flesh surrendered that which He had been defined to be in vv. 1–3. John proceeds immediately to obviate any such conception. It is this Word, he says, who dwelt among us, and the glory beheld was the glory of the only begotten from the Father. To confirm this doctrine John adds that the revelation given by the incarnate Son was given by Him in His identity as God only begotten in the bosom of the Father (v. 18).

The idea of self-emptying, derived from a mistranslation of Phil 2:7, has no basis in Scripture. The rendering of the KJV that He "made himself of no reputation" is shown by the context and by the usage of the NT to be correct. Our Lord made no account of Himself and so He took the form of a servant and humbled Himself, becoming obedient unto death, even the death of the cross (vv. 7–8). *See* Kenosis.

The incarnation means that the Son of God took human nature in its pristine integrity, with all its essential properties and sinless limitations, into union with His divine person. The result is that human nature now belongs to His person and to His personal life and experience. He thinks and wills and acts as God, and He thinks and wills and acts as man. He possesses all divine attributes and prerogatives equally with God the Father and God the Holy Spirit. But also of Him must be predicated all that belongs to human creaturehood.

This great truth of the coexistence of both Godhood and manhood in the one divine Person was set forth in the creed of Chalcedon in A.D. 451 as follows: "We, then . . . all with one consent, teach men to confess one and the same Son, our Lord Jesus Christ . . . to be acknowledged in two natures, inconfusedly, unchangeably, indivisibly, inseparably; the distinction of natures being by no means taken away by the union, but rather the property of each nature being preserved, and concurring in one Person . . . not parted or divided into two persons, but one and the same Son, and only be-gotten, God the Word, the Lord Jesus Christ."

A great deal of more recent discussion has been devoted to the question, Is the man Jesus to be regarded as a human person? Catholic orthodoxy, following the Chalcedonian creed, has maintained that Jesus was one person, and that since He was divine, He was a divine person. This means that His human nature must not be regarded as personal. This is not to deny the reality and integrity of His human nature but to insist that the center of person-ality in His case was the deity. This doctrine reflects the witness of the NT.

In the various situations recorded in the Gospels, Jesus always recognized Himself as sustaining a unique relation to God the Father. This means that He was aware of His divine identity. And even when the limitations belong-ing to Him in virtue of His human nature were most in evidence (cf. Mt 24:36), He identified Himself in terms of His divine relationship. When the NT writers refer to those actions of Jesus which were performed in human nature, such as the death on the cross, they always say that *He Himself* wrought these works (cf. Phil 2:7-8; Heb 1:3; I Pet 2:24); and the personal pronoun as applied to Him has always in view His divine identity and could never be regarded as merely human.

This doctrine of one person in two distinct natures is closely related to the character and efficacy of our Lord's redemptive accom-plishments. It was the God-Man who wrought salvation, and in that same capacity in His ex-alted glory He carries on His heavenly ministry unto the consummation of God's redemptive purpose.

See Christ, Humanity of; Christ, Sinlessness of; Jesus Christ.

Bibliography. E. C. Blackman. "Incarnation," IDB, II, 691-697. A. B. Bruce, *The Humili-ation of Christ,* Grand Rapids: Eerdmans, 1955. J. Gresham Machen, *The Virgin Birth of Christ,* New York: Harper, 1932. James Orr, *The Virgin Birth of Christ,* New York: Scrib-ner's, 1915. R. L. Ottley, "Incarnation, The," HDB, II, 458-467. H. C. Powell, *The Prin-ciple of the Incarnation,* New York: Long-mans, Green & Co., 1896. W. Childs Robinson, "A Restudy of the Virgin Birth of Christ," EQ, XXXVII (1965), 198-211. Thomas A. Thomas, "The Kenosis Question," EQ, XLII (1970), 142-151. B. B. Warfield, *The Person and Work of Christ,* Philadelphia: Presbyterian and Reformed, 1950.

J. M.

INCENSE. A mixture of spices and gums used for burning in Israel's worship; sometimes the sweet odor issuing from the burning. The recipe for the incense to be used in the temple is given in Ex 30:34-38. It includes stacte, onycha, gal-banum, and frankincense (*see* Plants; Spice). The use of this formula was banned for private use, and any who violated this prohibition were to be excommunicated from the congregation of Israel. The use of incense was not peculiar to Israel, and in the land of promise itself incense was offered by priests on profane high places (I Kgs 13:1-2; II Kgs 17:11, and elsewhere).

Incense was to be burned on the altar of incense which stood in the tent of meeting in the holy place directly before the inner sanc-tuary, the holy of holies. The priest would take pieces of coal from the altar of burnt offering on a kind of shovel, sprinkle the incense powder on the burning embers, and place the whole on the altar of incense. This was to be done morn-ing and evening (Ex 30:7-8). Once a year, on the Day of Atonement, the high priest was to take a censer of coals within the veil into the holy of holies and sprinkle incense on the fire preparatory to sprinkling the sacrificial blood before the mercy seat (Lev 16:12-14).

Altar of incense

Once the burning of incense in censers was resorted to by Moses to show that only the family of Aaron was entitled to the priesthood, and the challengers of this prerogative received the extreme penalty (Num 16:17 f.). Nadab and Abihu, Aaron's sons, were slain for guiltily offering incense improperly at the outset of the institution (Lev 10:1-3). King Uzziah was stricken with leprosy for presumptuously in-sisting on offering incense in the temple against the protests of the priests (II Chr 26:16-21). It was while offering the incense in the temple that Zacharias, John the Baptist's father, was told by the angel that he would have a son (Lk 1:8–13). The ascent of the sweet perfumed smoke appropriately signifies the prayers of God's people coming before their God (Ps 141:2; Rev 5:8; 8:3–4).

Bibliography. Gus W. Van Beek, "Frankincense and Myrrh," BA, XXIII (1960), 69–95.

N. B. B.

INCEST. The crime of cohabitation or sexual intercourse with those kin or relatives who are forbidden in the Mosaic law (Lev 18:1–18).

The list given by Moses is preceded with a warning that Israel was not to indulge in the sins of the Egyptians whom they had just left, or the Canaanites to whom God was bringing them. The list of those forbidden includes (1) mother, (2) stepmother, (3) sister or half sister, (4) granddaughter, (5) daughter of a stepmother, (6) an aunt on either side, (7) an uncle's wife on the father's side, (8) daughter-in-law, (9) sister-in-law, (10) a woman and her daughter or her granddaughter, (11) the sister of a living wife.

A daughter and a full sister are not mentioned specifically since covered by "near of kin" (v. 6). A mother-in-law is included in # 10. Those mentioned in # 1, 2, 3, 8, 10 were to be punished by the death penalty (Lev 20:11, 12, 14, 17) as accursed crimes. Those mentioned in # 6, 7, 9 were to bear their iniquity and die childless (Lev 20:19–21).

In the NT a case of incest, a man cohabiting with his father's wife, is mentioned in I Cor 5:1. Paul instructs the Corinthian church to judge this evil and "deliver such an one unto Satan for the destruction of the flesh, that the spirit may be saved in the day of the Lord Jesus" (v. 5).

R. A. K.

INCONTINENCY. Lack of self-control. Used once in I Cor 7:5 where Paul warns those who are married against withdrawing from proper regular sexual intercourse lest Satan tempt either party to extramarital relations. Since the imperative is used in v. 2: "Let every man have his own wife," both marriage and its relations are not discouraged but rather encouraged by Paul, except in certain particular cases and situations.

See Divorce.

INCORRUPTION. A term (Gr. *aphtharsia,* "perpetuity, incorruption") used by Paul in I Cor 15:42, 50, 53–54 of the resurrection body which the Christian will receive at the time of the rapture along with the departed saints, shortly before they return to reign with Christ (I Thess 4:13–18; cf. Rev 20:4–6). The Gr. word is also translated "immortality" in Rom 2:7 and II Tim 1:10, "sincerity" in the sense of incorruptibleness in Eph 6:24, and "uncorruptness" in Tit 2:7. *See* Immortality.

An eleventh century B.C. shrine model from Bethshean used as an incense burner. BM

The adjective *aphthartos* describes the incorruptible or imperishable crown the victorious believer will receive in contrast to the fading crown of laurel leaves won by the Gr. athlete (I Cor 9:25). Our heavenly inheritance is incorruptible (I Pet 1:4); so also is the Word of God viewed as seed (1:23), and the inner spirit of the godly wife (3:4). God is *aphthartos* in the sense of immortal (Rom 1:23; I Tim 1:17).

INDIA. The word is mentioned only twice in the Scriptures, both occurrences being in the book of Esther (1:1; 8:9) and referring to the extent of the realm of Ahasuerus, the Persian king. Scholars are generally agreed that the word "India" (Heb. *hōddû,* from Old Persian *hidauw* and *hinduish,* from Sanskrit *sindhu,* "stream"—i.e., the Indus River) refers not to the peninsula of Hindustan but to the territory adjoining the Indus River, i.e., the Punjab. Some identify it with the land of Havilah of Gen 2:11 and equate the Indus with the Pishon. The seafaring country of *Meluḥḥa,* mentioned often in Sumerian texts, was probably the Gujerat region of W India where the Indus civilization flourished *c.* 2000 B.C. (W. F. Leemans, *Old Babylonian Letters and Economic History,* Leiden: Brill, 1968, pp. 219–226).

INFANT BAPTISM. *See* Baptism.

INFANT SALVATION. *See* Salvation.

INFINITY. Though the Bible does not give any abstract discussion of infinity (or of the infinitesimal), yet the simple literal concept of limitlessness in certain specified aspects of being is consistently assumed. Thus, God is omnipresent in infinite space in all dimensions. Every part of all space is immediately in His presence (Ps 139:1–12). God is eternal in infinite time, both past and future (Ps 90:1–2). God is infinite in power, the Almighty (*pantokratōr,* II Cor 6:18 and frequently in Revelation). He is infinite in wisdom and knowledge, omniscient (Ps 139; Col 2:3).

On the other hand, God is never regarded as "the Infinite" without specification. Spinoza's idea that the "Infinitely Infinite" is "the All," simply means pantheism (just as "the Absolute" without specification means absolutely nothing). If God were infinite in all respects He would be infinitely evil, infinitely cruel, etc.

Modern mathematicians, such as Georg Cantor (*Contributions to the Founding of the Theory of Transfinite Numbers,* trans. by P. E. B. Jourdain, New York: Dover Publications, 1952), have developed supposed paradoxes in the concept of infinity. It is alleged that ". . . the series of odd integers can be put into one-one correlation with the complete series of integers and is therefore of the same number. This capacity to have proper parts which are equal in number to the whole can be taken as definitory of transfinite aggregates" (*Encyclopaedia Britannica,* 1967 ed., XII, 237).

The fallacy of such a paradox is in the treating of an infinite series as a whole which can be equal to another infinite whole. "Infinite whole" is a palpable contradiction.

J. O. B., Jr.

INFIRMITY. *See* Diseases.

INFLAMMATION. *See* Diseases.

INGATHERING, FEAST OF. *See* Festivals: Feast of Tabernacles.

INHERITANCE. While the OT develops the Heb. law of legal inheritance, the theological significance of inheritance is prominent in God's dealings with man in both the OT and NT.

The basic idea is settled possession of land and personal property by a stable and permanent title irrespective of how that possession has been acquired. Frequently included is the concept of the acquisition by succession of property belonging to one's forebears, the allocation or distribution of this property having

been effected by God. Closely related to inheritance are the ideas of covenant (in the OT) and sonship (in the NT).

Inheritance in the Old Testament

Although statistical analysis of the Heb. words for inheritance is difficult (since the term inheritance in the English versions does not always represent the same Heb. word, nor are the pertinent Heb. words always translated inheritance), it is seen that *nāḥal* ("to give inheritance," "to receive possession") and *naḥălâ* ("inheritance") are the more relevant and frequent Heb. words. Note also: *ḥēleq* ("portion," Ps 16:5); *yerushshâ* ("possession," "thing occupied," Jud 21:17; Jer 32:8); *mô-rāshâ* ("possession," "thing occupied," Deut 33:4); *yārash* ("to subdue," "occupy," "possess," "inherit," Josh 1:11).

The Promised Land, the inheritance of Israel. Material inheritance in OT law and custom cannot be understood apart from the theological significance of inheritance as derived from the Abrahamic covenant. The promise to Abraham (Gen 12:1–3; 13:14–17; etc.) had a double object: an heir (Isaac, then the nation, and ultimately Christ) and an inheritance (the land of Canaan). Israel's messianic expectancy and the gradual deepening of the inheritance theme in the OT both grow out of the Abrahamic promise.

While all the earth is God's (Ex 19:5; Deut 10:14) which He as Creator gave to man to hold, cultivate and enjoy (Ps 115:16), yet He selected a specific people for His inheritance and selected a specific portion of land to give this people as their inheritance (I Kgs 8:36). Although Israel did not initially receive Canaan from her fathers, yet, to the degree that God's promises are a reality when uttered, the land which was to be their inheritance for all generations is viewed retrospectively as an inheritance from the time of the original grant by God. Thus, the possession of Canaan, either as a whole or in its various portions, belongs to the nation Israel, or to each tribe or family or individual.

The basis of this possession is the grace of God in fulfillment of promise. God supervised the conquest by entrusting Joshua with the task (Deut 1:38) and by intervening in behalf of Israel (Josh 21:43–45). Thus, the nature of this inheritance of the land is not a simple succession from generation to generation but an inheritance which God has granted to Israel (Deut 12:9–10).

Not only did God fulfill His promise by supervising the conquest of the land which He allotted to Israel, but He also fulfilled it by directing its partitioning among the tribes, effected by lot which was regarded as a divine decision (Num 33:54; Josh 14:2). In this division, each tribe received its lot or portion in the inheritance (Josh 14:2; 15:1; 16:1; 17:1; 18:1–11). The partitioning extended to each family (Josh 15:1, 20) and to individuals (Caleb,

Josh 15:13; Joshua, Josh 19:49-50). However, the tribe of Levi had no inheritance, although assigned 48 cities (Num 35:2-8).

While God's ultimate promise regarding the land is immutable, full possession of the land by any particular generation of Israelites is conditional upon obedience to the divine commands (1 Chr 28:8; cf. Deut 4:1). Punishment for disobedience includes loss of the land (Deut 4:25-26; I Kgs 14:15) as illustrated in the Babylonian captivity. Consequently, repentance is related to restoration to the land (Ezk 36:8-15; 37:21-28). The dispossession of any particular generation of Israelites because of unbelief does not invalidate God's unconditional promise, for the generation living at Christ's second advent will "inherit the land for ever" (Isa 60:21) and enjoy it in perfect happiness, a promise which will begin fulfillment in the future messianic or millennial kingdom (Deut 30:1-6). In this connection, the Davidic King is also promised the nations as His inheritance (Ps 2:8).

Israel, the land and the people, the inheritance of God. Since God gave the land, He is the ultimate Landowner and the land is viewed as His inheritance (Lev 25:23); not that He received it from someone else, but that He has chosen it for His own possession and it is His by right. Therefore, Israel is God's tenant and ought to live on the land not for itself but for God. Likewise, the people whom God has chosen are regarded as His inheritance, which He has allotted to Himself for eternal possession (Deut 4:20; 32:9). Inheritance is once more linked to covenant relationship by the formula of the covenant: "They shall be my people, and I will be their God" (Jer 24:7). *See* Land and Property.

Inheritance in Old Testament law and custom. In general, inherited property included both land and personal possessions, such as cattle, household goods, servants, and even wives. Since the land was given by God and was held in trust for Him, it properly belonged to the family and only to the individual heir as representing the family. Personal possessions, however, could be distributed among all the sons. Since given by God, the land was not to be alienated (Lev 25:23) and, though sold temporarily, the land must be returned to the original owner in the year of jubilee (Lev 25:25-34). One exception was a dwelling house in a walled city which, if not redeemed within one year of sale, did not return to the original owner in the year of jubilee (Lev 25:29-30).

The firstborn son inherited a double portion of all his father's possessions (Deut 21:17), the remainder being divided equally among the other sons. A father sometimes made disposition of his property during his lifetime (Gen 24:35-36; 25:5-6), and the patriarchal blessing seemed to function much like wills and testaments of modern times. While a father was prohibited from arbitrarily depriving his firstborn of the birthright (Deut 21:15-17), it

could be taken from him because of trespass against the father (I Chr 5:1). The cases of transfer of birthright appear as exceptions which exemplify divine election (Ishmael and Isaac, Gen 21:10; cf. 21:12; Esau and Jacob, Gen 27:37; cf. Mal 1:2-3; Rom 9:13; Reuben and Joseph, I Chr 5:1; cf. Gen 49:22-26; Adonijah and Solomon, I Kgs 1:5 ff.; cf. I Chr 22:9-10).

At first a daughter could not receive the inheritance (Job 42:15 is exceptional), but a change was introduced after the death of Zelophehad so that daughters were entitled to inheritance if there were no sons in the family (Num 27:1-11). But even in this case, heiresses had to marry only within their father's tribe. If there were no direct heirs, then brothers, paternal uncles, or the next of kin could inherit. A widow had no immediate place in the succession, but if she were left without children, the nearest kinsman on her husband's side had the right of marrying her to raise up children to the name of his dead brother (Deut 25:5-10; cf. Ruth 3:12-13; 4:1 ff.). *See* Marriage, Levirate.

Other Old Testament uses of inheritance. God Himself came to be viewed as the inheritance of the righteous (Ps 16:5-6; 73:26) as He had been in a particular way the inheritance of the Levites (Deut 10:9). The law itself (Deut 33:4) and even children (Ps 127:3) are spoken of as an inheritance. Inheritance also describes the portion allotted to man in the sense of his personal destiny (Job 20:29; 27:13).

Inheritance in the New Testament

Gr. *klēronomos* (heir) and *klēronomia* (inheritance) and their cognates occur about 45 times in the NT, principally in the Synoptic Gospels, Pauline epistles (especially Galatians) and Hebrews.

While inheritance is used in the ordinary sense (Lk 12:13) and with reference to the OT usage of possession of the Promised Land (Acts 7:5; Heb 11:8), the concept of inheritance is further developed in the NT in two ways: (1) the heir is related to sonship (especially is Christ Son and Heir), and (2) the inheritance is related to the kingdom which Christ inaugurates. Both elements are present side by side in the parable of the vinedressers (Mt 21:33-46; Mk 12:1-12; Lk 20:9-19) where Jesus Christ is seen to be the Heir by virtue of being the Son (Mk 12:6-7; cf. Heb 1:2) and the inheritance is the kingdom (Mt 21:43).

Not only is Christ the Son and Heir, but in Christ believers are also sons and therefore heirs (Rom 8:17; Gal 4:7). This Pauline concept of spiritual heirship is not based on the Heb. concept of inheritance but rather upon Roman law under which all the children inherited equally. As in Roman law where the testator lived on in the group of his co-heirs, so Christ lives in believers who derive their heirship by being co-heirs with Him (Rom 8:17). While the Holy Spirit now indwells the believer as the Guarantor of his inheritance (Eph 1:14), the inheritance itself is a future one (I Cor 6:9–10; Gal 5:21; Eph 5:5; Jas 2:5; I Pet 1:3–4) into which eternal inheritance the believer will enter after resurrection (Heb 9:15).

The inheritance awaited includes the glory (Rom 8:17–18) and incorruption (I Cor 15:50–57; cf. I Pet 1:4) of resurrection life into which the believer will enter, after which he shall reign with Christ in the millennial kingdom. The inheritance of resurrected believers includes also a heavenly city in a new heaven and a new earth (Heb 11:10, 16; 12:22–24; Rev 21:1 ff.).

See also Adoption; Allotment; Family; Patrimony.

Bibliography. Francois Dreyfus and Pierre Grelot, "Inheritance," *Dictionary of Biblical Theology,* Xavier Leon-Dufour, ed., New York: Desclee Co., 1967. Werner Foerster and J. Herrmann, "*Klēronomos,* etc.," TDNT, III, 758–785. J.-Cl. Margot, "Inheritance," *A Companion to the Bible,* J.-J. von Allmen, ed., New York: Oxford Univ. Press, 1958, pp. 181–185. Merrill F. Unger, "Inheritance," UBD, pp. 525 f.

F. D. L.

INIQUITY. Sixteen Heb. and Gr. words are translated "iniquity" in the KJV. The more important are as follows: Heb. *'āwen,* "iniquity, vanity"; *'āwel,* "perversity, perverseness"; *āwôn,* "that which is crooked, perversity (most common), depravity, sin." Gr. *adikia,* "unrighteousness"; *anomia,* "lawlessness."

The Heb. *āwôn* refers primarily to the character of an action, as seen in Isa 64:6 where iniquities are paralleled to self-righteous deeds that are like filthy rags. From this it expands to express the idea of guilt (Gen 15:16; Num 15:31; II Sam 14:32; Ps 32:5; Jer 2:22; 30:14–15, RSV), followed by punishment for guilt in the sense of Gen 4:13, "My punishment is greater than I can bear" (cf. Lev 26:41, 43, KJV, NEB; Lam 4:6, 22; Ezk 14:10).

In the NT *adikia* stresses the idea of a negative righteousness, but in the sense of actual unrighteousness as seen in the reference to the 30 pieces of silver paid to Judas as the "reward of iniquity" (Acts 1:18), and the condemnation of Simon the sorcerer's offer to buy the power of the Holy Spirit (Acts 8:23; cf. I Cor 13:6; II Tim 2:19; Jas 3:6).

The Gr. *anomia* stresses, in contrast, the rejection and breaking of God's holy law. Jesus condemns this lawlessness (Mt 7:23; 13:41; 23:28; 24:12), as well as Paul (Rom 6:19) and the writer of Hebrews (Heb 8:12; 10:17). In II Thess 2:7 we learn that the mystery of iniquity (*anomia*) – the real origin of lawlessness being the revolt of the devil and his angels, followed by the revolt of man against God – is already present and will continue right up until

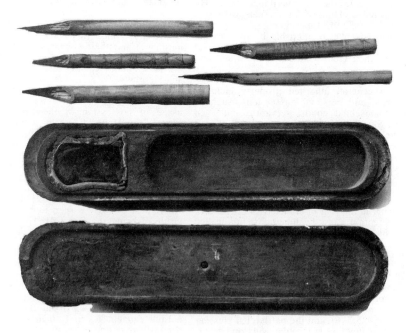

Ancient writing equipment from Egypt. At one end of the pen case was an inkwell. BM

INK

Ruins of the traditional Good Samaritan Inn on the Jericho Road. HFV

the Antichrist is revealed and destroyed by the coming of Christ as the rider on the white horse of Rev 19:11–20.

See Evil; Sin; Wickedness.

Bibliography. W. Gutbrod, *"Anomia,"* TDNT, IV, 1085 ff.

R. A. K.

INK. Ink was used in Egypt as early as 2500 B.C. One OT reference says that Baruch wrote Jeremiah's prophecies "with ink" (Jer 36:18). The word ink occurs in the NT in II Cor 3:3; II Jn 12; III Jn 13 as the translation of Gr. *melan* (black), probably referring to lampblack carbon or soot mixed with gum (three parts to one) and water to make it adhere and have some gloss. The mass was molded into sticks and later cut off as needed and moistened for use.

Carbon's chemical inertness kept such ink black for centuries as shown by ostraca found at Lachish and Samaria from the time of the OT prophets. A rusty-brown ink of powdered nutgalls and ferrous sulfate was used in some MSS such as Codex Vaticanus and Codex Bezae. Several Egyptian papyri used a red ink (rubric) made from pulverized minerals. *See* Writing.

INKHORN. Scribes throughout the centuries have carried in their girdle a long tube or case in which they kept their pens (reeds), with a small cup or container for ink attached to the upper end. It is called in Heb. *qĕsĕth* and translated "inkhorn" (KJV, ASV). It occurs only in Ezk 9:2, 3, 11, and is translated "writing case" in RSV. The Egyptian and Syrian scribes used a palette (Egyp. *gsty*), a narrow rectangular wooden board with a long groove to hold the rush pens and circular hollows for the cakes of red and black ink. For illustrations of these palettes see ANEP, Nos. 232–234, 460. *See* Ink; Writing.

INN. The inn of Bible days was not at all like a modern hotel or motel, but is generally considered to have been similar to the Oriental caravansary or khan, which is said to still exist in rural areas of Asia. The caravansary is a large square edifice built around an open inner courtyard. In the center of the courtyard a well is provided. Often the building is two stories, with the lower one containing stalls for beasts and the upper consisting of small rooms for use of the human travelers.

The KJV terms the place where Joseph's brothers stopped (Gen 42:27; 43:21) an "inn," as well as a similar place where Moses and his family lodged (Ex 4:24). But *mālôn,* camping place for the night, was merely a resting place, not an inn in each of these references, as in Josh 4:3. On the other hand, Jewish archaeologists have discovered scores of small settlements in the Negeb and the desert of north-central Sinai, dating back to the Middle Bronze I Age or patriarchal period. These are considered to be caravan stations on the trade route to Egypt (W. F. Albright, *Yahweh and the Gods of Canaan,* Garden City: Doubleday, 1968, pp. 62–73).

The inn where there was no room for Joseph and Mary (Lk 2:7) has traditionally been thought of as a caravansary, which they found to be completely full of people and beasts, forcing them to lodge in a nearby cave used as a sheepfold. Some authorities, however, hold that the Gr. word here used (*katalyma*) refers not to a caravansary at all but to a guest chamber or lodging place in a private home, *katalyma* obviously referring to something of this kind in its only other NT usages (Mk 14:14; Lk 22:11). According to this view, Joseph and Mary planned to stay at the home of friends or relatives, but the small dwelling and its guest chamber were so full that they had to be housed in the lower portion where the animals were quartered.

The inn of the Good Samaritan parable (Gr. *pandocheion,* Lk 10:34) evidently was a caravansary between Jerusalem and Jericho, the host, or innkeeper, being a man who supplied provisions and other needs to travelers.

G. C. L.

INNER MAN. Inner or inward man is the KJV translation of *ho esō anthrōpos* in Rom 7:22; Eph 3:16; II Cor 4:16 (in last reference only *ho esō* appears, with *anthrōpos* clearly to be supplied from the immediate context). It is a Pauline expression referring to man's rational, moral and spiritual nature, that total sphere in which the Holy Spirit carries on His convicting, renewing and sanctifying work. In short, it is synonymous with man's soul. Thus it is *not* the "new man," that is, the new capacity to serve God and righteousness, which God graciously gives the sinner in regeneration. *See* New Creation.

In Rom 7:22 Paul is describing his attitude toward the divine law as a self-righteous Pharisee. (For a vindication of the view that Rom 7:14-25 describes Paul the legalistic Pharisee, cf. J. Oliver Buswell, Jr., *A Systematic Theology of the Christian Religion,* II, 115-119.) As a Pharisee, trained in and possessing a high respect for the law of God, Paul could say that even prior to his conversion he concurred with and took pleasure in God's law. But being unregenerate at the time in his life described in Rom 7, Paul had to admit that he possessed at that time no gracious enablement whereby he might obey the law in its *intended* sense. This being the case, Paul could nonetheless declare that as a highly trained religious man he respected the divine law in the "inner man."

[For the view that in Rom 7:14-25 Paul is describing his continuing experience as a believer, see Charles C. Ryrie, *Balancing the Christian Life,* Chicago: Moody Press, 1969, pp. 45-48. According to this interpretation all believers have two capacities within their being: to serve sin *and* to delight in the law of God. These two capacities remain with the Christian throughout life on earth, with the constant possibility of conflict. By his freedom of choice the believer activates either the old or the new capacity.—Ed.]

In II Cor 4:16 Paul is simply expressing his confidence that, though his physical body wear away because of the stress and strain of his work, his "inner man," that is, his soul (or spirit) would be renewed daily.

In Eph 3:16 Paul prays that the Ephesian believers might experience a fresh invigorating from the Holy Spirit in the "inner man." Here he is merely expressing his prayerful desire that they grow spiritually.

R. L. R.

INNOCENCY. In addition to this noun and its adjective "innocent" several words are used in the KJV for the idea of innocence, such as "harmless" and "blameless." Together they express the idea of freedom from corruption, taint, evil or guilt. Likewise various Heb. and Gr. terms suggest this concept. The Heb. verb *nāqâ* and its derivatives have the primary meaning of emptied out and clean, hence free from guilt, innocent (e.g., Ps 19:13; Jer 2:35). Its adjective often appears in the idiom "innocent blood" (e.g., Deut 19:10; 21:8). Its noun is translated "innocency" in Gen 20:5; Ps 26:6; 73:13; Hos 8:5. In the RSV, Heb. *ṣādîq* (*see* Righteousness) is eight times translated "innocent" (e.g., Gen 20:4; Deut 25:1; Job 9:15). The Heb. word *tāmîm* signifies wholeness, integrity and perfection (e.g., Noah, Gen 6:9; 7:1; Job, Job 1:1; David, Ps 18:23).

Absolute innocence (incapable of sinning) is an attribute of God and Christ alone (Heb 7:26, NASB) and of the saints when glorified. Adam and Eve were innocent ("very good," Gen 1:31) before the Fall, but not yet confirmed in holiness. In a relative sense those who are not morally accountable (infants and imbeciles) may be considered innocent. Innocency may also express that simplicity, childlikeness, singleness of mind and wholehearted devotion to God which our Lord requires of the citizens of His kingdom (e.g., "innocent as doves," Mt 10:16; "blameless and innocent," Phil 2:15; both RSV and NASB).

R. E. Po.

INNOCENTS, SLAUGHTER OF. This term refers to the slaughter by Herod the Great of all the male children two years old and under in Bethlehem and its environs, in his effort to destroy the Christ Child (Mt 2:16). Description of the children as "innocents" may be traced to Cyprian in the 3rd cen. Since Bethlehem was a small village, the number of children slain probably was fewer than 50 and certainly not so large a number as sometimes imagined. Matthew considered the slaughter to be a fulfillment of Jer 31:15, probably because Rachel died on the way to Bethlehem and her tomb is traditionally considered to be just N of the town. But the connection of the OT verse with Bethlehem is not clear, because Ramah was in the territory of Benjamin and Rachel was not the mother of Judah, ancestor of the inhabitants of Bethlehem. Rachel, however, *died* near Bethlehem. The primary fulfillment of Jer 31:15 is to be found in Jer 40:1.

See Ramah 1.

INSCRIPTION. *See* Writing.

INSECTS. *See* Animals, IV.

INSPIRATION. The theological concept of inspiration has reference to the fact that Holy Scripture is the utterance of the God who cannot lie and is hence the infallible Word of God. The term itself occurs seldom in Scripture (Job 32:8; II Tim 3:16).

Definition

The English word "inspiration" (Lat. *inspiratio*) alters the biblical sense somewhat by implying a merely psychological heightening of a writer's powers, rather than emphasizing the divine "inspiration" of Scripture. The Gr. adjective *theopneustos* (translated in II Tim 3:16, RSV, by "is inspired by God") has only a passive sense, affirming that Scripture was "breathed out" by God so that it is His word and oracle. Thus Scripture is what God the Holy Spirit says (Heb 3:7), as "men moved by the Holy Spirit spoke from God" (II Pet 1:21, RSV).

Inspiration is the miracle of redemptive, divine revelation by which sacred writings were called forth, the product of God's creative breath, possessing absolute divine authority. God's breath or Spirit denotes the outgoing of His dynamic power, whether in creation (Ps 33:6), preservation (Job 34:14–15), revelation (Isa 48:16), regeneration (Ezk 36:26–27), or judgment (Isa 30:28). God's breath created Scripture to be His very word in man's language.

Inspiration and Revelation

1. *Revelation a divine activity.* Inspiration needs to be understood within and not apart from divine special revelation. Inspired Scripture enjoys its dignity as the medium of, record of, and witness to divine revelation. The nature of inspiration is an aspect in the pattern of revelation. Revelation is the divine activity of self-disclosure by which the living God unveils something of His character and purposes for mankind (Deut 29:29; II Cor 4:6). Scripture is a product of that revealing activity, its linguistic residue and written embodiment. God reveals Himself on the plane of history by His saving *acts* (Acts 2:11) and on the plane of truth by His gracious *word* (Isa 55:11).

2. *Biblical balance.* The Neoprotestant understanding of revelation, under the influence of existential philosophical *a prioris,* plays down the cognitive side of revelation and refuses to recognize Scripture as written revelation. There i a shift from the propositional to the personal, and from the literary to the historical. But the two new emphases fail to observe the biblical balance. In Scripture, the personal encounter with God occurs in the context of valid knowledge (Heb 1:1 f.), and God's saving acts in history are accompanied by the prophetic interpretation (Amos 3:7). The divine acting and the divine speaking are correlative concepts of equal dignity. Act and interpretation are perfectly blended together.

3. *Purpose of revelation.* Neoprotestantism to the contrary, the *word* of God is central to the biblical idea of revelation (Jer 23:9, 16, 18, 22, 28). Pagan idols may be dumb, but the Lord is a living and a speaking God (Amos 3:8). Truth is fundamental to trust. Biblical faith means walking in the light of the divine promises. Both acts and words are divine events, forming an inseparable unity. The NT attitude to the OT is that written Scripture is a primary product of divine revelation, the locus in which the revealing activity now takes place. In Scripture God addresses the church (Mt 22:43; Acts 28:25; Heb 10:15). Thus we can say that revelation *generates* Scripture.

4. *Purpose of inspiration.* Inspiration, in other words, is the miracle of conservation whereby the truths of divine revelation have been *preserved* in an authentic and sufficient form. Scripture is nothing other than an extension of the revelation modality of the divine speaking. It exists so that the church might know God's word and distinguish it from her own sinful self-consciousness.

The purpose of Scripture is the same as that

of revelation, to bear witness to the divine plan for redeeming sinners (II Tim 3:15). It is a seamless robe of truth-telling language, designed to lead men to Christ the Saviour (Lk 24:27). Christians love and reverence the Holy Scriptures because they are the locus of their confrontation and fellowship with the living Word. It contains the truths of revelation which conserve and deepen our relationship with God.

The high doctrine of biblical inspiration is not at all the result of an antiquated brand of scholastic thinking. It arises naturally out of the pattern of revelation at the heart of Christian faith. The divine activity of revelation led to the production of inspired Scripture, the written transcript of revealed truth.

The Biblical Concept of Inspiration

1. *Biblical testimony to its inspiration.* The self-attestation of the Bible to its own authority is in reality the teachings of Jesus Christ and of His apostles and prophets. Christians who have been convinced that God has revealed Himself in a historical mode culminating in Christ cannot but regard this evidence with deep seriousness. Any attempt to silence the evidence one text at a time is like trying to stop an avalanche one stone at a time.

There is a strong, pervasive, and complete testimony to the inspiration of Scripture in the biblical record. All Scripture (plenary inspiration) is of divine authorship (verbal inspiration) according to Paul (II Tim 3:16), and may be personified as God Himself speaking (Gal 3:8). Scripture records what God says (Acts 13:32–33). Peter affirms that the OT Scriptures are what the Holy Spirit spoke beforehand (Acts 1:16). Scripture is the written word of God, and cannot err because He cannot lie (Acts 4:25; Jn 10:35). Scripture was not initiated by men (II Pet 1:21). The Spirit of the Lord spoke by their tongues (II Sam 23:2).

2. *The testimony of Christ.* Jesus regarded the Scripture in its entire extent and in every part to be God-given and of indefectible authority (Mt 5:17 f.). It is the word of God (Mk 7:13), the divine commandment (Mt 19:4 f.), and had to be fulfilled in every particular (Mk 14:49).

Christ Himself constituted Christianity a religion of divine authority based on Scripture. Unless His ministry was founded upon a fallacy of no small magnitude and His divine authority an illusion, His followers are bound to His teachings in this respect. It is consistent to accept both Christ and Scripture, or to reject both; but it is neither consistent nor honest to accept one and reject the other. Where Christ is acknowledged as Lord, the matter of biblical authority is settled. What Scripture says, God says. The words of the law and the prophets are regarded as God's own speech (Ps 119; Jer 1:4, 9). The OT is a divine oracle (Rom 3:2); not merely the record of what Moses or David said, but of what God said through them (Acts 28:25). The

NT continually cites the OT as the utterance of God (Rom 9:17). Thus the testimony of the prophets, Christ, and the apostles is uniformly consistent.

3. *The divine authorship of Scripture.* While little is said regarding the mode of divine inspiration, it is clear that the role of the biblical writers was to transmit what they received. God was the primary author of Scripture, and its message is a divine creation. Scripture is a body of literature bearing prophetic witness to Christ (Jn 5:39 f.; II Cor 3:14–18) and designed to instruct believers in divine things (Rom 15:4; I Cor 10:11). The entire Scripture is a deposit of heavenly instruction, the authentic voice of God (Mt 4:4). The OT Scripture was seen as the written complement and product of old covenant revelation, called forth and generated by that divine activity. In the same way, the NT finds its validity as the witness to a new and better covenant.

4. *Attributes of the inspired Word.* On the basis of such evidence it is possible to construct a doctrinal model for biblical inspiration. Holy Scripture is God's written word to man (Mt 4:4). All its high attributes rest on this single fact. Scripture and the word of God *ought* to be identified (Mk 7:9–13). It is a *divine*, and not merely human, witness to revelation. The OT is repeatedly cited in the NT as the univocal word of God (Mt 1:22). As a consequence the Scripture is *infallible* (incapable of wandering from the truth) and *inerrant* (not guilty of mistakes or errors), fully trustworthy and authoritative (Prov 30:5–6). If the Scripture deceived its readers or erred in its teachings, it would not be *God*'s word (Ps 19:7). An erring standard provides no sure measurement of truth and error.

Inerrancy is a necessary concomitant of the doctrine of inspiration. As Wesley put it, "If there be any mistakes in the Bible, there may well be a thousand. If there be one falsehood in that book, it did not come from the God of truth." Hardly a theologian of any note failed to draw this conclusion from the evidence until very recently. Divine inspiration is essentially incompatible with error. Christ's attitude to Scripture was one of *total trust* (Mt 22:29).

5. *Inspiration of the autographs.* Strictly speaking, inspiration has to do with the original text (i.e., the autographs) of Scripture, and not with the corruptions which intruded in the course of textual transmission. For instance, in reading Hamlet, it is of the greatest interest to the student of Shakespeare to know what part of the text is authentic and what is not. Textual criticism of the Bible has shown that the Heb. and Gr. texts we possess are *virtually* identical to the original, and may therefore be said to be virtually inspired as well. Inspiration terminates on *graphē* (written Scripture), not on scribal copies made from it (II Tim 3:16). Faith in the providence of God and evidence from lower criticism warrant an attitude of confidence that the text is sufficiently trustworthy so as not to lead us astray.

6. *Plenary verbal inspiration.* Inspiration is *plenary* and *verbal*, and Scripture a language deposit inspired in the whole, not merely in the parts (Rom 15:4; II Tim 3:16). Without plenary inspiration, the Bible is an equivocal authority. The control of the Spirit over the biblical writers was so complete as to ensure that they were the mouthpieces of infallible revelation.

Although many denounce verbal inspiration as a detestable theory, it is in fact the only biblical and meaningful one. Inspiration has to do with *words* and with language: "which things we also speak, not in words taught by human wisdom, but in those taught by the Spirit, combining spiritual thoughts with spiritual words" (I Cor 2:13, NASB). Scripture is the text through which God speaks to us. "And the Lord said unto me, Behold, I have put my words in thy mouth" (Jer 1:9); "thou shalt speak my words unto them" (Ezk 2:7). This word deposit is veracious, and conveys successfully the freight of divine revelation. Words signify and safeguard meaning. We get at the meaning of the Bible by the words it employs. Inspiration assures us that this verbal text is the trustworthy and sufficient vehicle of divine revelation.

7. *Dual authorship.* The authorship of Scripture is *dual*, the word of God in the words of men (e.g., Mt 2:15). In one sense the human writers contributed much to the making of Scripture (style, research, fervor), and in another sense they contributed nothing. The Spirit worked concurrently alongside the activity of the human authors (not penmen), He Himself being the principle and they the instrumental cause, with the result that their writing was both free and spontaneous on their part and divinely elicited and controlled. It is an axiom of biblical theism that divine providence can reach its ends *without* dehumanizing the agents it employs (cf. Acts 2:23).

Mechanical dictation is not involved here at all. The sacred writers retained their full individuality and made use of the full range of their capacities. They may be likened to the first violinist or concertmaster, playing with his own style, in a symphony orchestra which is directed in person by the composer of the music. Inspiration simply assured that the humanity of Scripture was not corrupted by the errancy of the human race. As Christ was truly human yet free from sin, so Scripture is truly human yet free from error. Because Scripture is the word of God, it is truthful in all that it teaches, and possesses the following properties.

8. *Inherent properties of Scripture.* The *authority* of Scripture means that it enjoys the right to rule and command our obedience. It is the *principium cognoscendi* (the beginning of knowledge) of Christian theology, and the *causa media* (intermediate instrument) of our knowledge of God. Hence, inspiration is perennially at the center of theological discussion.

The *sufficiency* and *clarity* of Scripture point to the fact that Scripture has enough light to save sinners and direct the church. All that believers need to know is contained therein (II Tim 3:17). This is not to say that Scripture contains all possible or even all actual revelation, or that a total theological system may be deduced from it, or that every text is alike clear unto all. It is nonetheless a "light shining in a dark place" (II Pet 1:19) and a lamp unto our path (Ps 119:105). There is enough clear truth in it to lead every sincere seeker to God through Jesus Christ (Jn 14:6; Acts 4:12; I Pet 3:18).

The Word of God is also *efficacious* (Heb 4:12). It possesses the capability in the presence of faith and the Spirit of convicting and converting sinners (Isa 55:11; I Pet 1:23). Therefore, it is called a "hammer" and "fire" (Jer 23:29), "seed" and "wheat" (Isa 55:10; Jer 23:28), and "spiritual milk" (I Pet 2:2). Scripture is a means of grace, a sacramental vehicle, bearing authoritative testimony to Christ who is its focus and center.

Inspiration and Authority

1. *Scripture as the source of theology.* Christian theology is the science of articulating the truth content of divine revelation. The historic church from the beginning has given the Bible a place of preeminence in providing *revelation data* for this task.

2. *The modern departure from this source.* Theologians always found it easier to accept the plenary inspiration of Scripture than to believe that Christ, His disciples, and the entire church from the first erred in their view. The reason why the doctrine was never incorporated in a formal creed may be found in the fact that scarcely anyone dreamed of challenging it. The new, higher critical views of Scripture, therefore, are a deliberate break with historic Christian opinion.

The chaos and ambiguity of so much modern theology result from the crisis in biblical authority. Suddenly, in place of a divine Word, only a human voice is heard (cf. Amos 8:11 f.). As a historical religion, Christianity depends on her historical sources. Once the strong link between divine revelation and the Hebrew-Christian Scriptures is broken, theological methodology is in shambles.

3. *The Protestant basis of authority.* Scripture is the epistemological base of theology, i.e., the foundation or grounds for our knowledge of God. Luther's motto, *Sola Scriptura* ("Scripture alone"), is the Protestant principle. Scripture constitutes, determines, and rules the entire theological endeavor. Our source of authority is the Holy Spirit speaking in the Scripture, the product of His own creative breath. In it the church has an objective check against demonic self-delusion and a resource for her correction. Scripture is the authentic map of the spiritual order. By it we encounter the living God in His gracious self-disclosure. God-talk becomes possible because grounded in ascertainable revelation data couched in human language. It is inspiring to its readers because it is in itself inspired by God.

Bibliography. Theodore Engelder, *Scripture Cannot Be Broken,* St. Louis: Concordia, 1944. Louis Gaussen, *Theopneustia, The Plenary Inspiration of the Holy Scriptures,* Chicago: Moody Press, 1949. Carl F. H. Henry, ed., *Revelation and the Bible,* Grand Rapids: Baker, 1958. James Orr, *Revelation and Inspiration,* Grand Rapids: Eerdmans, 1952. René Pache, *The Inspiration and Authority of Scripture,* trans. by Helen I. Needham, Chicago: Moody Press, 1969. James I. Packer, *'Fundamentalism' and the Word of God,* London: Inter-Varsity, 1958. Clark H. Pinnock, *A Defense of Biblical Infallibility,* Philadelphia: Presbyterian and Reformed, 1967; *Sola Scriptura,* Chicago: Moody Press, 1970. Bernard Ramm, *Special Revelation and the Word of God,* Grand Rapids: Eerdmans, 1961. Ned B. Stonehouse and P. Wooley, ed., *The Infallible Word,* Grand Rapids: Eerdmans, 1946. John F. Walvoord, ed., *Inspiration and Interpretation,* Grand Rapids: Eerdmans, 1957. Benjamin B. Warfield, *The Inspiration and Authority of the Bible,* Philadelphia: Presbyterian and Reformed, 1948.

C. H. P.

INSTANT, INSTANTLY. The KJV uses these words in translating several different Heb. and Gr. words. Although in modern English the words refer only to time, they are used predominantly in the KJV in the sense of urgency (cf. Lk 23:23; II Tim 4:2). In Isa 29:5; 30:13; Jer 18:7, 9 the concept of time is evident.

INSTRUCTION. See Disciple; Education; Family; Schools.

INSTRUMENT. In the OT the word "instrument" has three uses.

1. Utensils used in connection with the sanctuary of the tabernacle (cf. Num 31:6) and later of the temple. See Tabernacle; Temple.

2. Weapons of war (cf. I Chr 12:33). See Armor.

3. Musical instruments (cf. II Chr 7:6). See Music.

Paul refers to the members of the body as instruments to be used in the cause of righteousness whereas formerly they were used in the cause of unrighteousness (Rom 6:13).

INTEGRITY. The state or quality of being ethically sound, morally well-adjusted, from Heb. *tōm, tummâ,* "completeness, integrity." The Heb. term is used in a coordinate sense of simplicity in the phrase "a certain man drew a bow at a venture" (lit., in his simplicity or innocence, I Kgs 22:34; II Chr 18:33; cf. II Sam 15:11). It is translated "integrity" in all places where it signifies sincerity and honesty of heart (e.g., Gen 20:5; I Kgs 9:4; Job 2:3; 27:5; 31:6; Ps 7:8; 25:21; 26:1; 41:12; 78:72; Prov 11:3;

19:1; 20:7; etc.). In the plural it is used in one of the words ("thummim," *see* Urim and Thummim) on the breastplate of the high priest (Ex 28:30; Deut 33:8; Ezr 2:63; Neh 7:65) indicating possibly innocence or integrity. While the word does not occur in the NT, the concept is covered by such terms as "sincerity," "pure in heart," "single eye," and is synonymous with honesty, genuineness, sincerity.

INTENTION. The purpose, design, aim or goal which is intended by the mind or heart (Heb 4:12, NASB; "intents," KJV). It often involves the determination of the will, as in Lk 14:28. The aim or intent behind an action is most important both in ethics and in criminal law. The killing of a man when done with "malice aforethought" is murder, but when done by mistake, simply manslaughter.

Intent or purpose, however, does not of itself make an act good. It is the fault of Paul Tillich's ethics that he maintains anything done in love is thereby justified. Many serious mistakes and much evil can occur when intent and moral law are divorced, as in his theology when he denies that the laws of God and the commands of Christ apply to us today. Christ's teaching is perfectly clear that only those who have both righteous motives in the heart and do the will of God will enter the kingdom of heaven (Mt 5:17-20; 7:21). *See* Sermon on the Mount.

R. A. K.

INTERCESSION
Meaning. The Heb. word for intercede (*pāga'*) originally meant "to strike upon," and thus came to mean "to assail anyone with petitions." When such assailing was done on behalf of others this was intercession.

The Gr. word (*entygchanō*) means "to appeal or petition." The verb is used five times in the NT (Acts 25:24 [RSV "petitioned me"]; Rom 8:27, 34; 11:2; Heb 7:25). The noun occurs twice (I Tim 2:1; 4:5). In I Tim 2:1 intercession is contrasted with supplications, prayers, and giving of thanks. On the difference in meaning of these words Trench says: " 'Intercession,' by which the AV translates it, is not, as we now understand 'intercession,' a satisfactory rendering. For *enteuxis* does not necessarily mean what intercession at present commonly does mean—namely, prayer in relation to others (at I Tim 4:5 such meaning is impossible); a pleading either for them or against them ... but, as its connexion with *entugchanein*, to fall in with a person, to draw close to him so as to enter into familiar speech and communion with him ... implies, it is free familiar prayer, such as boldly draws near to God" (*Synonyms of the New Testament,* pp. 189-90). Intercession, then, highlights naturalness, boldness, and familiarity in prayer.

Illustrations of intercession. Abraham's earnest pleading for Sodom is an outstanding OT illustration of intercession (Gen 18:23-33).

Moses prayed in like vein for Israel after they had made the golden calf (Ex 32:31-32). Elijah's boldness in prayer on Mount Carmel is similar (I Kgs 18:36-37). Likewise, there are many illustrations of intercession in the NT (see below).

The intercession of Christ. As Priest Christ is pictured as drawing near to God interceding for His people (Rom 8:34; Heb 7:25). This ministry has two aspects: that of advocate, pleading when we have sinned (I Jn 2:1-2), and that preventive work of keeping us from evil (Jn 17:15). This work of Christ is illustrated in His conversation with Peter in which He assured him that "I have prayed for thee, that thy faith fail not" (Lk 22:32).

The intercession of the Holy Spirit. The Spirit also intercedes on behalf of the believer (Rom 8:26) with unutterable groanings. "Thus, at the moment when the believer already feels the impulse of hope failing within him, a groan more elevated, holy, and intense than anything which can go forth even from his renewed heart is uttered within him, coming from God and going to God, like a pure breath, and relieves the poor downcast heart" (Godet, *Romans,* II, 102).

The intercession of Christians. The intercessory work of believers is in behalf of all men with a view that they might come to a knowledge of the truth of salvation in Christ (I Tim 2:1-4). In this, all believers are priests.

See Mediation; Prayer.

C. C. R.

INTEREST. *See* Usury.

INTERMEDIATE STATE. The doctrine of the intermediate state is concerned with the condition of men immediately following physical death and prior to the resurrection.

Since all Bible-believing Christians believe in the resurrection of the body and the future judgment, it follows that all believe in an intermediate state between death and the resurrection. Not all Christians, however, agree as to the condition of the dead during this interval. All recognize that it is different from the condition of those living on earth, and some believe that it is, at least in certain details, quite different from what it will be subsequent to the resurrection. The problem in the doctrine of the intermediate state, then, is the nature of the existence of the righteous and the wicked dead prior to the resurrection.

Just as the Scriptures affirm the future resurrection of both the righteous and the wicked, they also teach the continuous personal and conscious existence of both in that period immediately after death and the dissolution of the physical body. Neither the righteous nor the wicked receive bodies before the resurrection. The righteous are to receive theirs "at the last trump" (I Cor 15:52), which is identified with the personal return of the Lord (I Thess

4:16–17; cf. Rev 20:4–5). For the wicked dead there is also a resurrection (Acts 24:15; Jn 5:28–30).

The Nature of Existence in the Intermediate State

The righteous dead. Although their souls are without bodies, the intermediate state is for the righteous one of conscious joy and exaltation because they have been made perfect in holiness, are free from sin and suffering, and have passed into the presence of the Lord in glory. Their bodies, which are the Lord's, rest, or sleep, in their graves until the day of resurrection. The apostle Paul taught that believers were "confident ... and willing rather to be absent from the body, and to be present with the Lord" (II Cor 5:8). The dying thief was told by Christ, "Today shalt thou be with me in paradise" (Lk 23:43). Being present with the Lord certainly implies conscious bliss, since Christ obviously did not sleep in unconsciousness. Although His body was taken from the cross and rested in Joseph's tomb, He had commended His spirit into God's hands (Lk 23:46).

According to the Scriptures the eternal destiny of man has been settled at his death. There is no passing from one state of existence to another after death. The parable of the rich man and Lazarus makes this clear (Lk 16:25–26; cf. Heb 9:27). It is therefore consistent with the Scripture to believe that the righteous, whose salvation has been wrought by Christ through the offering of Himself once for all, are on death immediately changed from imperfect to perfect holiness. It is this state which Paul had in view when he spoke of his "desire to depart, and to be with Christ; which is far better" (Phil 1:23). With his burning zeal for the proclamation of the gospel throughout the earth, Paul would certainly have preferred to live on and continue his labors on earth if death had held for him the prospect of unconsciousness or of inactivity. Certainly, in the presence of Christ there is "fullness of joy" (Ps 16:11) and deliverance from "every evil work" (II Tim 4:18). In the light of II Cor 12:3–4 and Heb 12:23 the "paradise" in which Christ and the righteous dead are together can only be heaven itself.

That the intermediate state for the believer does not include all of the full blessedness of the resurrection, however, is revealed by the fact that Paul hoped to avoid the period of "nakedness" for the soul and live until the rapture at the coming of the Lord (II Cor 5:2–8). The ultimate, glorious anticipation of the Christian is the resurrection. *See* Heaven.

The wicked dead. Concerning those who die in sin and unbelief, the Scriptures teach that they are in a definitely fixed and conscious state of suffering and punishment, although the degree of this punishment is not specifically identified as the same as that of the eternal state following the resurrection of the unrighteous.

Eternal punishment is connected with those who are in their bodies (cf. Mt 10:28). It is spoken of in the NT in relation to a specific place, Gehenna (*q.v.*), which is a metaphorical designation of the lake of fire; and the sufferings of the intermediate state are never mentioned as occurring there. This does not mean, however, that any fundamental distinction should be made between the sufferings of hell as a place of eternal torment and the suffering which the wicked experience in the invisible world before the resurrection. *See* Hell.

Wherever the sphere of punishment in the intermediate state is localized, it is referred to in the Gr. of the NT as Hades (*q.v.*). This is the equivalent of OT Sheol (*q.v.*). It seems clear that the words Sheol and Hades do not always indicate a locality in the Scripture, but often simply denote the state of death, or the separation of the soul and body (I Sam 2:6; Ps 89:48; Acts 2:27, 31). There are also some passages in which Sheol seems merely to designate the grave in a general sense (Gen 37:35; 44:29; Job 14:13; Ps 6:5).

The principal passage in which Hades is given a localized conception is Lk 16:23. Because this is in a parable, it may be argued that the Lord in using the term did not intend to reveal any truth concerning a specific locality as distinct from Gehenna, e.g., but simply used imagery which was well known in His day. Whether this be true or not, this parable does prove that the intermediate state is for the wicked not an abiding place of a neutral character where they await the final judgment, but rather a place of conscious suffering and punishment from which there is no return. The fact that the departed are spoken of as though they were possessed of bodily organs does not mean that they actually have bodies prior to the resurrection, for God and the angels are spoken of in the same manner.

Four Common Errors

It is necessary in considering the doctrine of the intermediate state to point out the fact that the Scriptures enable us to refute four commonly held errors respecting the abode of the soul after death.

1. The doctrine that the souls of both the righteous and the wicked sleep between death and the resurrection. This view has been held by small sects since very early days in the history of the church. While it is true that the Scripture often speaks of death as a sleep (Mt 9:24; Acts 7:60; I Cor 15:51; I Thess 4:13), and there are certain passages which might seem to teach that the departed are unconscious (Ps 6:5; 30:9; Isa 38:18–19), the Scriptures never speak of the soul or the person falling asleep, but only the body. The term sleep is used because there is great similarity between a sleeping body and a dead body; and, furthermore, the sleep in death of the body is to be broken by a quickening at the resurrection.

Those passages which are thought to indicate that the dead are unconscious actually do no more than emphasize the fact that the dead are unable to take part any longer in the activity of the world of living men. The Scriptures nowhere encourage the living to seek or expect any kind of converse with the dead (Deut 18:9–12; I Sam 28:7–10; Isa 8:19–20). It should never be forgotten that the Scriptures clearly portray the righteous as enjoying conscious communion with God and with the Lord Jesus Christ immediately after their death (see section on "The righteous dead" above).

2. The doctrine that the intermediate state is one of further probation. This theory teaches that salvation through Christ is still possible in the intermediate state for certain classes of people, and perhaps for all. Some teach that this is the time when salvation will be offered to all children who die in infancy and to the heathen who never heard the gospel. The scriptures frequently used to support this theory are I Pet 3:19 and 4:6. Even though they are understood as teaching that Christ went into the underworld to preach (which interpretation is not necessary), certainly they do not prove that any offer of salvation was extended to persons there.

The Word of God uniformly represents the state of all men, whether believers or unbelievers, as completely fixed when they have died. The most important passage is Lk 16:19–31, but one should also consider Jn 8:21, 24; II Pet 2:4, 9; Jude 7–13. Furthermore, the Scriptures never represent the eternal destiny of a soul as determined by that which is done in the intermediate state (see Mt 7:22–23; Lk 12:47–48; Gal 6:7–8; II Thess 1:8; Heb 9:27).

3. The doctrine taught by the Church of Rome, that souls at peace with the church but not perfectly pure at death (and almost none are considered to be) must undergo a period of purging before they are permitted to enter into the perfect and unlimited bliss of heaven. This purifying is carried on in a place called purgatory, where all souls endure suffering for the purpose of both expiation and purification. Romanist doctrine places no limit except the final judgment on the time souls may continue in purgatory, since the extent of their suffering is determined by their guilt and impurity. They may be aided by the prayers of living saints and especially by the sacrifice of the Mass offered on their behalf.

The Roman Catholic authority for the doctrine of purgatory is almost exclusively the teaching of the Church of Rome itself. The Pope is supposed to have jurisdiction over purgatory. No proper appeal can be made to the Scripture, for as has been pointed out above, the Scriptures teach that the soul of the believer is immediately transported into the presence of Christ when he dies, just as the wicked pass into eternal torment. More than this, however, the doctrine of purgatory would destroy the clearest and most vital teachings of the gospel in the NT. The sinner's salvation rests not upon his own works or merits, but entirely upon the infinitely meritorious sacrifice of Christ to which sinners can add nothing in making satisfaction for sin (Eph 2:8–9).

There are other unscriptural doctrines which have arisen in the Church of Rome in connection with the doctrine of purgatory. For example, the doctrine of supererogation, the idea that a man may be more than perfect himself and with his superfluous merit aid those suffering in purgatory. Strangely, the Romanist believes that one human's merit can be imputed to another, yet he cannot believe that Christ's perfect righteousness is imputed to sinners. The Roman doctrine of purgatory presupposes two impossibilities: first, that any man can be better than he ought to be; and second, that man can add to the perfect work of salvation which Christ accomplished by His death and resurrection.

4. Finally, there is the error of the doctrine of annihilationism. According to this teaching, there is no conscious existence for the wicked after death. A distinction can be made between those who teach that the soul of the unbeliever is deprived of immortality by an act of God and is thus deprived of consciousness after death, and those who teach that immortality is a gift of God only to those who believe, so the soul that does not receive it simply ceases to exist.

The Scriptures are clear on the fact that the wicked as well as the righteous will live forever, and that their existence will be one of conscious suffering and punishment (Eccl 12:7; Mt 25:46; Rom 2:8–10; Rev 14:11; 20:10, 12–15).

See Dead, The; Death; Eschatology; Immortality.

R. G. R.

INTERPRET, INTERPRETER. The noun "interpreter" (Gr. *diermēneutēs*, one who explains fully or interprets) is used in the NT only in I Cor 14:28. The verb of that root occurs in I Cor 12:30; 14:5, 13, 27. In chap. 14 Paul instructs that speaking in tongues in a church assembly is to occur in an orderly manner but only when there is an "interpreter" present, for only then is it edifying. The one who speaks in a tongue ought to pray that he himself may interpret (v. 13). One purpose of the gift of tongues was that thus an unconverted man should hear a message in his own language, as did those present at Pentecost (Acts 2:8), and then hear it interpreted by another who knew not that tongue. It was thus to be a double miracle, yet one which would corroborate itself in this peculiar manner to the hearer. *See* Tongues, Gift of; Gifts, Spiritual.

The Gr. *hermēneuō* and its compound *methermeneuomai* denote interpreting by translating from one language to another (e.g., Mt 1:23; Jn 1:38, 41–42). In Ezra's time royal decrees were translated (*mᵉturgām*, Ezr 4:7), and the Aramaic translations with expositions of the Heb. Scriptures became known as the Targums or Targumim.

In II Pet 1:20 the word for "interpretation" is *epilusis*, unloosing or unfolding. Interpreting Scripture is not a matter of one's own private opinion.

In the OT Joseph acted as the interpreter (from Heb. *pāthar*) of various dreams (Gen 40–41). Daniel convinced Nebuchadnezzar of his God-given ability to give the interpretation (Aram. *peshar*) or explanation of the king's dream, by first of all telling the king what he saw in the dream (Dan 2:5–45). Later Daniel gave the interpretation of Nebuchadnezzar's dream of the great tree that was cut down (4:8–27) and of the handwriting on the wall of Belshazzar's palace (5:12–28). The word *pesher*, "interpretation" (Eccl 8:1), became the standard term for the sectarian explanations or commentaries of the canonical books of the OT by members of the Qumran community. *See* Dead Sea Scrolls.

R. A. K.

INTERPRETATION OF SCRIPTURE. *See* Bible Interpretation.

IPHEDEIAH (ĭf'ĕ-dē'yȧ). A descendant of Benjamin, son of Shashak (I Chr 8:25).

IPHTAHEL. *See* Jiphthael.

IR (ĭr). A descendant of Benjamin (I Chr 7:12), father of Shuppim and Huppim.

IRA (ī'rȧ)
1. A chief ruler (KJV) or priest (RSV) of David (II Sam 20:26), also designated as a Jairite, perhaps a Jattirite, according to the Syriac text.
2. An Ithrite (perhaps Jattirite), one of David's mighty men and possibly the same as 1 (II Sam 23:38; I Chr 11:40).
3. Another of David's heroic followers, the son of Ikkesh the Tekoite (II Sam 23:26; I Chr 11:28).

IRAD (ī'răd). A grandson of Cain, son of Enoch, and father of Mehujael (Gen 4:18).

IRAM (ī'răm). A "duke" or chief of Edom and descendant of Esau (Gen 36:43; I Chr 1:54).

IRHAHERES (ĭr-hă-hē'rĕs). A term which appears only in the Heb. text of Isa 19:18, where it is stated that one of a certain five Egyptian cities will be called by this name or title. Though various interpretations may be found, the name usually is taken as a play on words relating to the city of Heliopolis (biblical On, Aven; Egpt. *Iwnw*), whose name means "city of the sun" (see RSV), which can be written in Heb. as *'ir haheres*, as the complete Isaiah scroll from Cave 1 at Qumran, *c.* 15 later Heb.

MSS, Symmachus, the Vulgate, and the Talmud attest. *See* On. But the MT states that the one city will be called *'ir haheres*, "city of destruction" (KJV, NASB), possibly because the temples and other physical elements of sun-worship will have been destroyed. For an extended discussion of the textual problem see Carl W. E. Naegelsbach, *Isaiah, Lange's Commentary*, Grand Rapids: Zondervan, n.d., pp. 226 ff.

IRI (ī'rī). A Benjamite, the son of Bela (I Chr 7:7).

IRIJAH (ī-rī'jȧ). A captain of the guard who arrested Jeremiah at the gate of Benjamin during the Chaldean siege, and having falsely accused the prophet of deserting to the enemy he took Jeremiah back to the princes of Judah (Jer 37:13–14).

IR-NAHASH (ĭr-nā'hȧsh). Perhaps a city founded by Tehinnah, since he is called "father" of it (I Chr 4:12). On the other hand, it could refer to a man, the son of Tehinnah.

IRON
1. *See* Minerals and Metals.
2. A fortified city in the territory of Naphtali (Josh 19:38), called Yiron in RSV. It is probably the present village of Yārûn, 10 miles NW of Hazor. Tiglath-pileser III captured Iron and took away 650 captives (ANET, p. 283).

IRPEEL (ĭr'pē-ĕl). A city of Benjamin, the identity of which is not certainly known. Some have taken it to be a site near ancient Gibeon (Josh 18:27).

IRRIGATION. This word is not found in Heb. or Gr., although the practice of irrigation for watering plants and trees is frequently implied in biblical literature (cf. Gen 13:10; Eccl 2:5–6; Isa 58:11). The term refers to artificial means of watering crops throughout biblical times in the form of aqueducts, cisterns, dams, canals, etc.

A Roman aqueduct near Caesarea. HFV

A Roman dam with a sluice gate near Samaria.
HFV

The Heb. *peleg,* translated "rivers" in KJV, often refers to irrigation canals (Ps 1:3; 46:4; Prov 21:1; Isa 30:25; 32:2). Because of inadequate rainfall, Babylonia and Egypt have always had to be supplied with water from their respective rivers. The water was conducted from the river along canals via various mechanical devices and at great cost of labor. There was less need in Palestine and Syria than in Egypt and Babylonia (cf. Deut 11:10). Generally, the winter rains were ample for the cereal crops; however, the vegetable and fruit gardens would be parched by the long summer drought. These gardens were always planted near natural supplies of water. The water was made to flow from its sources (either directly or by aqueduct, or raised from a well by an endless chain of buckets drawn by a horse or donkey, cf. Num 24:7; Isa 40:15) into little channels running through the garden. Artificial water pools for gardens are referred to in Eccl 2:6. A storage pool is an almost universal feature in such gardens. Large numbers of cisterns have been unearthed on every major site in Palestine (cf. II Chr 26:10; Neh 9:25). Before the development of watertight cisterns, the farmer had to depend entirely on springs and perennial streams, such as the Jabbok and the Wadi Qelt near Jericho, for artificial irrigation. *See* Agriculture.

D. W. D.

IR-SHEMESH (ĭr-shĕm′ĭsh). A city of Dan, apparently the same as Beth-shemesh (*q.v.*) and connected with Mount Heres (Josh 19:41).

IRU (ī′rōō). The eldest son of Caleb (I Chr 4:15). The word is perhaps to be read "Ir," the *-u* being the conjunction "and" belonging to the succeeding word.

ISAAC (ī′zĭk). The name, given by God before the birth of the child (Gen 17:19), signifies "he laughs" or "he who laughs." See references to laughter in Gen 17:17; 18:12–15; 21:6.
History. Isaac was born (probably in Gerar)

to Abraham and Sarah when they were 100 and 90 years old respectively. He was the first to be circumcised in the normal course, when eight days old (Gen 21:4), in recognition of the covenant promise (Gen 17:2–17). The presence of Hagar and her son Ishmael was a disturbing factor in the covenant household, and by divine command they were dismissed. If the events are related in chronological order, Ishmael would be at this time about 16 or 17 years old; he is depicted in the story as an immature youth who suffered exhaustion sooner than his mother (Gen 21:15, 18). But he was old enough to be a mocker (v. 9)!

Nothing is known of the early boyhood of Isaac. We next see him big and strong enough to carry the wood for the altar fire up the mountain slope, not knowing that he himself would mount that altar. The experience of being bound as a sacrificial victim and then delivered by divine intervention must have deeply affected his whole life.

Isaac was 37 years old when his mother died in Hebron. Three years later his marriage to Rebekah took place at Lahai-roi. In this he accepted the arrangement made by his father, as evidently the ordering of the Lord.

To safeguard the inheritance, Abraham sent all his other sons away, as he had done Ishmael, making Isaac sole heir (Gen 25:1–6). This would prevent any dispute about the birthright. The death of Abraham at the ripe age of 175 brought Ishmael and Isaac together, probably for the last time.

Isaac was 40 years old when he married, and he waited 20 years for offspring. Then came the twins, Esau and Jacob, bringing new conflict into the covenant home. The favoritism of the parents fostered the struggle for power in the children, culminating in Jacob's deception by which he secured the patriarchal blessing.

In the meantime Isaac's sojourn in Gerar brought out behavior reminiscent of his father (Gen 26:6–11). Isaac passed off Rebekah as his sister, reckoning that a brother would not be in the same danger as a husband in the event of

A *shaduf,* an Egyptian irrigation "machine."
JR

someone else wanting her. His prosperity in Gerar made him unpopular, so that not only did the Philistine chief invite him to leave, but the herdsmen disputed his right to the wells which his servants dug.

The return to Beer-sheba was attended with the Lord's blessing and a renewal of the divine promise (Gen 26:23–24). But Isaac had his sorrows there too. Esau's wives distressed both him and Rebekah, but still more painful was his son Jacob's deceit, instigated by his mother. There Isaac saw his two sons part company. Isaac was already old and dim of sight when Jacob left for Padan-aram. Twenty years later, when Jacob returned, Isaac was still alive, but dwelling in Hebron, where he had buried Rebekah. There he died, at the age of 180, and there his half-reconciled sons buried him.

See Patriarchal Age.

Character. Isaac was neither as great as Abraham nor as colorful as Jacob. Yet he was great, and filled an important place between the father of the nation and the father of the tribes.

The meekness of Isaac is seen in his unresisting submission to his father in becoming the sacrifice on the altar of Moriah, and in his refusal to argue when the herdsmen of Gerar laid claim to the wells.

He was of an affectionate nature, deeply attached to his mother, grieving her passing, and then comforted in his love for Rebekah. His meditative spirit may have contributed to his outgoing affection.

He was a man in touch with God. If he did not have the dramatic visitations granted his father Abraham, he nevertheless had communication with heaven, and obeyed God's commandments. The altar, the tent, and the well symbolize the chief interests of his life.

He is included in the roster of heroes of faith in Heb 11. His benedictions upon Jacob and Esau are there declared to be acts of faith. No doubt his experience on Mount Moriah helped to make him a man of faith.

Another admirable trait in Isaac was his willingness not to hold grudges. He was treated very meanly by Abimelech and his servants, yet when Abimelech, realizing the strength of Isaac, sought a non-aggression pact, he forgave the past and gave every token of goodwill.

Like all men, Isaac had his faults. Two grave ones can be mentioned. He lacked the wisdom to avoid paternal favoritism. Perhaps it was Rebekah's manifest partiality for Jacob that induced Isaac to champion Esau. At the same time he admired the prowess and sportsmanship of Esau – and incidentally enjoyed venison! No doubt this created a feeling of inferiority in Jacob and urged him to compensate with guile.

But Isaac could lie too, like his father before him. A beautiful woman was dangerous company. A would-be suitor would give dowry to a brother in the absence of the father, but might kill a husband to gain the prize. So Isaac used the tactics of Abraham (though with less justifi-

cation, for Sarah was actually half sister to Abraham), and said, "She is my sister." It was neither truthful nor heroic.

Spiritual applications

1. At the burning bush God introduced Himself to Moses as "the God of thy father, the God of Abraham, the God of Isaac, and the God of Jacob" (Ex 3:6), so establishing the covenant relationship. Our Lord took up the triple designation of God to confute the Sadducees and to confirm faith in the resurrection (Mt 22:31–32). Notice how the singular form "father" covers Abraham, Isaac and Jacob. Here is a distinction in unity and a unity in distinction not generally ascribed to men.

2. Isaac is presented in Rom 9:7 as a typical case of sovereign election. So far as the covenant was concerned, Ishmael was ruled out, as were the sons of Keturah. Natural generation does not give one a place in the kingdom of God. That is the privilege of the called, whose calling is made evident by their faith.

3. The birth of Isaac was the fruit of faith – not only Abraham's, but Sarah's (Heb 11:11). Her incredulous laughter gave place to faith, and the senile womb revived. So spiritual birth is always a miraculous operation in response to faith.

4. Abraham's faith also centered in Isaac. He believed the word of God in face of all natural impossibilities. He took a hard look at his own impotence and at Sarah's 90 years, and still believed God. It was this faith that gave Abraham a standing in righteousness before God. Isaac, therefore, was the fruit of justifying faith (see Rom 4:18–22).

The command to offer Isaac on the altar further tested Abraham's faith. How could the death of Isaac fit in with all the divine promises? Abraham had the answer of faith, that "God was able to raise him up, even from the dead." So Isaac became a figure of life from the dead, or, to give it a NT turn, the new life in Christ (see Heb 11:17–19; Rom 6:3–5). He also appears here as a prefiguration of Christ, the obedient Son, who was "obedient unto death, yea, the death of the cross."

5. The most elaborate spiritual application is in Gal 4:21–31. There the contrast is drawn between Hagar and Ishmael on the one hand, and Sarah and Isaac on the other. Historically we see the conflict between the slave girl and the wife, and between their offspring; but it was left to the apostle Paul to indicate that this feud was an allegory, pointing up the antagonisms between the flesh and the Spirit, between the bondage of the law and the freedom of grace. Any attempt at coexistence between these is bound to fail. Isaac speaks to us of "the liberty wherewith Christ hath made us free" (Gal 5:1).

J. C. M.

ISAIAH (ī-zā'á). The Heb. name of Isaiah is Y^{e}sha'-yahu, meaning "Yahweh is (the source of) salvation." It is fitting that his underlying message to God's covenant nation is that salvation will come to them on the basis of divine grace and power and not by their own strength and religious works.

The fact that Isaiah is called "the son of Amoz" 13 times in the OT may mean that his father was a man of prominence. *See* Amoz. Isaiah apparently made his home in Jerusalem, since his small son Shear-jashub walked with him to meet King Ahaz outside the city (Isa 7:3). His wife was known as a prophetess, and they had another son whom the Lord commanded to be named Maher-shalal-hashbaz (8:1-4). These names were significant, constant reminders to king and to people of the prophet's message. The name of his older son means "a remnant shall return," a promise to the godly in the kingdom of Judah; the name of the younger son, meaning "swift is the booty, speedy is the prey" (Isa 8:3, NASB marg.), pointed to judgment near at hand by the king of Assyria.

It is believed that Isaiah ministered by word and pen for 60 years or more. His call to the prophetic ministry of warning and rebuke came in the year of King Uzziah's death (739 B.C.). Whether he had preached before that event is not certain. He states in the opening verse that he received revelations from God during the reigns of Uzziah, Jotham (750-731 B.C.), Ahaz (745-715), and Hezekiah (729-687). Yet he must have lived longer to be able to record the death of Sennacherib in 681 B.C. and to know the name of the succeeding Assyrian monarch, Esarhaddon (37:38). Thus Isaiah lived on into the reign of Manasseh. Whereas he had been actively engaged in the life of the court during the previous reigns (see chaps. 7, 8, 20, 22, 28-31, 36-39 and II Kgs 19:2-7, 20; 20:1-19), by now he had undoubtedly retired from public life and felt under no compulsion to list the name of the ruler whose wickedness he opposed so strongly in his later writings. II Kgs 21 is the terse historical account of the prevailing apostate worship and civil injustice that evoked from the prophet God's warning of vengeance (56:9-12; 44:9-20; 57:1-21; 58:1-4; 59:1-15; 65:2-7, 11-15). II Chr 33 indicates that Manasseh's idolatrous rampage was the worst during his early years before Esarhaddon displayed him as a vassal in chains in Babylon in 679 B.C. (II Chr 33:11; cf. ANET, p. 291). Thus the tradition that Isaiah was sawn in sunder at the order of Manasseh is credible (perhaps alluded to in Heb 11:37).

The prophets Hosea and Micah were Isaiah's contemporaries. Mic 4:1-3 is practically identical with Isa 2:2-4; which prophet quoted the other we cannot say. Perhaps they were familiar with each other's preaching. Numerous other literary resemblances may be seen between Micah and Isa 40-66, a fact which lends credence to the unity of the book of Isaiah.

Isaiah is by general consent the greatest of all the Heb. writers. His words indicate that he was a man of refinement and culture, a truly poetic soul, a lover and a profound observer of creation and of human nature, a statesman who looked upon the world as the scene of God's working, who looked upon it with fiery indignation because of its wickedness, and yet ever with a note of hope and comfort for the repentant and God-fearing remnant. So fully does he describe the person and offices of the coming Messiah, that from the time of Jerome he has been known as the "evangelist" of the OT. His reputation greatly increased after the fulfillment of many of his prophecies by the Babylonian exile, the victories of Cyrus, and the deliverance of a remnant from captivity. According to Josephus, Cyrus was induced to set the Jews at liberty by the prophecies of Isaiah concerning himself (Jos *Ant.* xi.1.2).

O. T. A.

ISAIAH, BOOK OF. In the Heb. Bible Isaiah is the first of the Latter Prophets (Isaiah, Jeremiah, Ezekiel, the Twelve).

Historical Setting

The book of Isaiah is centered in one of the most troublous and tragic periods of Jewish history. In Isaiah's day the kingdom of Judah was under five kings both good and bad — Uzziah, Jotham, Ahaz, Hezekiah, and Manasseh. It was a sinful nation. Although they were God's people, yet they were apostate and richly deserved chastisement. During Isaiah's lifetime several powerful enemies at one time or another were bent on Judah's destruction: the northern kingdom of Israel, ruled by Pekah; Syria, whose king was Rezin; and Assyria, under such warlike kings as Tiglath-pileser III, Sargon II, and Sennacherib. In addition, other neighbors such as the Philistines, the Moabites, and the Edomites harassed the tiny kingdom from time to time. Egypt was only a "broken reed" to lean upon for help against the Assyrian invader. Babylon, with whom Hezekiah made an alliance, was predicted to become the future destroyer. By revelation Isaiah foresaw Cyrus as the distant, and the Messiah as the far distant, deliverers yet to come. All of these the prophet viewed as God's instruments for the chastising and redeeming of His chosen people.

Date and Authorship

The book itself gives only scanty information about Isaiah's literary activity. According to 8:1 (RSV) and 30:8 he made notations on a tablet or writing board, but also he is commanded to inscribe a certain prophecy in a book or scroll (30:8). The divine exhortation to seek and read from the book of the Lord (34:16) implies that the entire prophecy regarding Edom has been recorded so that in the day of its fulfillment the reader may check every detail with the Scripture. Isaiah's name is specifically attached to chaps. 1, 2, and 13. This prophet is known to have been a court historian for the reigns of Kings Uzziah and Hezekiah (II Chr 26:22; 32:32). It is probable, therefore, that Isaiah wrote the words originally of II Kgs

18:13–20:19, which is essentially parallel to Isa 36–39.

Critical theories of the composition of this prophecy abound today, however, which deny that Isaiah of Jerusalem wrote all 66 chapters himself. Under the influence of deism in the late 18th cen. J. C. Doederlein published in 1789 a systematic argument that chaps. 40–66 were composed in the 6th cen. B.C. Since then it has been common for critics to speak of a "second Isaiah" who allegedly wrote in the period immediately before the end of the Babylonian Captivity (c. 550–539 B.C.). H. F. W. Gesenius supported this view in 1819, but Ernst Rosenmuller assigned a number of passages in chaps. 1–39 (such as chaps. 13 and 14 re Babylon) to the later unknown writer. Bernhard Duhm went even further in 1892 by proposing a "third Isaiah" who wrote chaps. 56–66 in Jerusalem in the time of Ezra. In 1928 C. C. Torrey in his book *The Second Isaiah* argued for a single author for chaps. 34–66 (36–39 excluded), composed by a writer who lived in Palestine near the end of the 5th cen. Some recent scholars, such as W. H. Brownlee, hold 'that all 66 chapters come from a circle of disciples who followed or later studied Isaiah and his oral prophecies. These writings were collected and arranged by an able practitioner of this Isaianic school, living perhaps in the 3rd cen.

Numerous evidences in refutation of these critical views may be given, arguing for the unity of the book and for its authorship by the historical Isaiah.

1. Jewish tradition. Later prophets allude to expressions in Isaiah (cf. Nah 1:15 with Isa 52:7; Zeph 2:15 with Isa 47:8, 10). In Ecclesiasticus the son of Sirach c. 180 B.C. speaks of Isaiah as the one who "comforted them that mourned in Zion" (48:22–25), a clear allusion to the subject matter of Isa 40–66 and to 40:1 in particular. This is the first appearance of any tradition concerning the authorship of Isaiah. Not a word is said of any later prophet of the Exile or of the time of Ezra adding to Isaiah's writings. None of the many MS copies of Isaiah found in the caves of Qumran and transcribed before and during the time of Christ give any clue to dual or multiple authorship. Nor does Josephus. The LXX has one heading for the entire book. And rabbinic tradition has remained uniform down to the period of modern rational criticism that Isaiah wrote all 66 chapters.

2. The NT witness. Christ referred to Isaiah the prophet as a distinct individual (Mt 15:7–9). The NT writers clearly regarded the author of both main sections of the prophecy to be one and the same (see Mt 3:3; 8:17; 12:17–21; 13:14–15; Mk 1:2; Lk 3:4; 4:17; Acts 8:28–32; 28:25–27; Rom 9:27–29; 10:16, 20–21). "The most conclusive NT citation is John 12:38–41. Verse 38 quotes Isa 53:1; verse 40 quotes Isa 6:9, 10. Then the inspired apostle comments in verse 41: 'These things said Isaiah, when he saw his glory, and spoke of him.' Obviously it was the same Isaiah who personally beheld the glory of Christ in the temple vision of Isa 6 who also made the statement in Isa 53:1: 'Who hath believed our report? and to whom is the arm of the Lord revealed?' If it was not the same author who composed both chap. 6 and chap. 53 (and advocates of the Deutero-Isaiah theory stoutly affirm that it was not), then the inspired apostle himself must have been in error. It therefore follows that advocates of the two-Isaiah theory must by implication concede the existence of errors in the NT" (Archer, SOTI, p. 336). It is inconceivable that the identity of so great a prophet as the author of Isa 40–66 would have been utterly forgotten by both the Jewish nation and the Christian church, by pious, God-fearing men who believed, taught, copied, and cherished the prophets as well as the law from generation to generation. It was essential among the ancient Hebrews to know the name of the prophet for his writing to be accepted and to be registered in the house of Israel (cf. Ezk 13:9).

3. Palestinian background. Rationalistic critics have asserted that chaps. 40–66 were written in Babylon, which is flat country. But both parts of the book of Isaiah tell of the rocks, mountains, valley streams, flocks and herds of Judah. If the second part had been written in Babylon, allusions to the landscape of that country would have been included. The local coloring in both parts is Judaic, showing that the entire book was written in Judah, thus pointing to the single authorship of Isaiah.

4. Historical and religious background. The fact that Babylon is mentioned in both parts of the book does not in itself necessitate a later date than Isaiah's time for those chapters. The warnings re Babylon were already relevant in his own day (see chap. 39). The events either prophesied or described in 21:9; 43:14; 46:1–2; and in part in 47:1–6, were fulfilled in history more particularly by Sennacherib's destruction of Babylon in 689 B.C. than by Cyrus' capture of the city in 539 B.C. Furthermore, the forms of idolatry condemned in Isa 57:5–9; 59:3–15; 65:3–5; 66:17 were practiced by the Jews in Judah during the reign of Manasseh (II Kgs 21:1–16), but not by the Jewish exiles in Babylon nor by the returned Jews in the post-Exilic period. Still more, the ideal completeness of the restoration of Israel depicted in chaps. 40–58 is more likely to have been written by one contemplating the return of the exiles from a distance, than by one who, as a contemporary, watched the somewhat meager results as recorded by Ezra, Nehemiah, and Haggai.

5. Language and style. All 66 chapters are written in perfectly pure Heb., without Aramaisms and Babylonian terms which characterize the known post-Exilic books. Likewise the stylistic resemblances between chaps. 1–39

One of the most important of the Dead Sea Scrolls is the complete manuscript of Isaiah (IQIs*a*) dating prior to 100 B.C. Courtesy *Biblical Archaeologist*

and 40–66 are striking. For example, the title of God "the Holy One of Israel," used but 31 times in the entire OT, is found 25 times in Isaiah; it occurs 12 times in chaps. 1–39, and 13 times in chaps. 40–66.

Another marked feature of Isaiah's style is his frequent use of the so-called prophetic perfect tense of the verb, i.e., he often speaks of future events as at hand or already come to pass (e.g., 5:13; 8:23; 9:1–7; 10:28–31); of Cyrus as already embarked on his conquering career (41:25; 45:13); or of the Servant of the Lord as having died as an offering for sin (53:1–12). The prophet could speak thus because he viewed these future events as already accomplished in the purpose of God.

This vivid way of speaking which Isaiah shares with the other prophets is especially significant in his case because of its bearing on the question of the unity of the book. Many scholars claim today that chaps. 40–66 cannot be the words of Isaiah but must come from an unknown author who lived at the close of the Babylonian Captivity (Deutero-Isaiah) or even later.

Many who accept this view fail to realize that this argument proves too much. If 41:2–4 must be the words of a contemporary of Cyrus, then chap. 53 must be the words of a witness of the crucifixion. This is of course impossible. Consequently, those who deny that Isaiah could have uttered the prophecies regarding Cyrus must either hold that the same argument does not apply to chap. 53 or they must deny that Isa 53 is a messianic prophecy, despite the clear testimony of the NT that it is fulfilled in Jesus' death (Mk 15:28; Lk 22:37; Acts 8:35; I Pet 2:22).

Back of this argument against the unity of Isaiah is of course the modern doctrine regarding prophecy, which is that the prophet was a man of his own time who spoke only to the people of his own time and not to future generations. This is a dangerous half-truth. The prophets did witness most earnestly to the men of their own day. But they also spoke about things to come, about "that day," "the day of

the Lord." Without saying it in so many words, this modernistic definition of prophecy minimizes or eliminates from it the predictive element. Yet according to the clear teachings of Scripture, nowhere stated more clearly than by Isaiah himself, it is the predictions which when fulfilled are the clearest evidence that the word of the prophet is a message from God.

The denial of prediction in prophecy severs the link between the "and it shall come to pass" of the OT and the "that it might be fulfilled" of the NT (cf. Jn 12:38–41). Anti-supernaturalists deny this connection. But Bible-believers throughout the centuries have seen in predictive prophecy the clear and conclusive evidence that God has spoken. So they have rejoiced in the unity of the entire book, and have recognized Isaiah to be the "evangelist" of the OT pointing forward to a suffering Messiah as the sinbearer for all mankind.

As if to guard against the claim that Cyrus is represented as one with whom the prophet is contemporary, it is to be noted that while the prophet usually alludes to Cyrus as one present or about to appear, he introduces the name of Cyrus in the climax of a remarkable poem (44:24–28). The words "I am the Lord" are followed in the KJV by nine "that clauses," which are arranged in three groups, each group longer than the one preceding it. The first group deals with the past (v. 24*b*), the second with the present (vv. 25–26*a*), the third with the future (vv. 26*b*–28). The structure of the poem is climactic and indicates that the words, "that saith of Cyrus, He is my shepherd, etc.," refer to a future so remote that the definiteness of the prediction is to be regarded as very remarkable. Cyrus is not yet a known figure, for the prophet nowhere states his nationality.

Outline of Contents

I. Introduction, Chaps. 1–6
II. The Book of Immanuel, Chaps. 7–12
III. Oracles Concerning the Nations, Chaps. 13–23
IV. The Little Apocalypse, Chaps. 24–27
V. The Book of Woes, Chaps. 28–35
VI. The Book of Hezekiah, Chaps. 36–39
VII. The Book of Consolation, Chaps. 40–66
   A. Deliverance from sin and captivity, Chaps. 40–48
   B. The Deliverer—the Servant of Yahweh, Chaps. 49–57
   C. The delivered people and their future glory, Chaps. 58–66

Analysis of the Book

Chapters 1–6 are introductory. In the "great arraignment" (chap. 1) God's people are charged with formalism and hypocrisy, with greed and cruelty, with utter disregard of their covenant relation with their God. They deserve the fate of Sodom. But here as everywhere in the book of Isaiah there is a wonderful mingling of exhortation and comfort with denunciation and doom. "Zion shall be redeemed with judgment, and her converts with righteousness" (1:27). The glorious promise of universal peace (2:2–5) and of the Branch (4:2–6) appear amid direful threatenings. The parable of the vineyard (5:1–7) is followed by six "woes" ending with the threat of the sword, punishment at the hand of invading armies (cf. 1:20). Chap. 6 contains the call of the prophet, a vision of the holiness of God, which makes "the Holy One of Israel" Isaiah's favorite title for the God whom he serves. Whether its occurrence already in 1:4; 5:19, 24 justifies the inference that in temporal sequence Isaiah's call belongs before chap. 1 is not clear.

Chaps. 7–12, often called the "book of Immanuel," relate to the first great crisis, the Syro-Ephraimitic war, which because of Ahaz's unbelief led to the first Assyrian invasion. Isaiah's scornful references to Rezin and Pekah might, but for II Chr 28:6, lead us to minimize the greatness of this threat, which accounts for Ahaz's appeal to Assyria for help. The wonderful Immanuel prophecies (7:14; 8:8, 10; 9:6 f.; 11:1–6) end with blessing for the Gentiles (11:10) and with a song of praise to the God of Israel (chap. 12): "For great is the Holy One of Israel in the midst of thee" (v. 6).

Chaps. 13–23 contain "burdens" (weighty and grievous prophecies) against nations which threaten Israel's very existence: Babylon (and Assyria), Philistia, Moab, Damascus, Ethiopia and Egypt, Babylon, Edom, Arabia, Jerusalem (her sin makes her her own worst enemy), and Tyre. Here, as elsewhere, compassion and hope pierce the thunderclouds of ·wrath (14:1–3, 24–27, 32; 17:7 f.; 18:7; etc.). Especially striking is 19:23–25, where Isaiah uses his favorite figure of the "highway" to describe the future safe and friendly intercourse of ancient enemies. Egypt is called "my people" (19:25; cf. Ex 5:1); Assyria, "the work of my hands" (cf. 45:11); Israel, "my inheritance" (Zech 2:12)—a wonderful prophecy developing Isa 2:2–5.

Chap. 24 is a vision of world judgment, an apocalypse, which ends in blessing; the Lord shall reign on Mount Zion. Chap. 25, a hymn of praise, is followed by a song which like that in chap. 12 will be sung by redeemed Israel. Chap. 27 ends with a promise of deliverance.

Chaps. 28–31 contain further judgments on the nations, apparently Assyria, Babylon, and Egypt. The woe on Samaria (chap. 28), uttered probably before Sargon besieged it, is followed by the promise of the "tried cornerstone" which the Lord will lay in Zion (28:16). In chap. 29 the woe on Ariel (the hearth of God, where the altar fires are ever burning, and therefore a figurative name of Jerusalem) ends likewise with promise (vv. 22–24). It is followed by warnings against alliance with Egypt (chaps. 30–31). Yet this warning too is combined with a promise of blessing (30:18–33), and is followed in chap. 32 with the promise of a king (Messiah) who shall "reign in righ-

teousness"; and "the work of righteousness shall be peace." Chap. 33 is directed against Assyria, "the spoiler that was not spoiled." Yet Jerusalem shall be "a quiet habitation, a tabernacle that shall not be taken down" (33:20). The terrible woe on Edom (chap. 34) is followed by a glorious picture of blessedness to come (chap. 35).

Chaps. 36–37 tell of Sennacherib's invasion, one of the most thrilling stories in the Bible. The raging bull who has blasphemed the Holy One of Israel will be led away with a hook in his nose to perish in his own land at the hand of his own sons. Hezekiah's sickness and the embassy of Merodach-baladan (chaps. 38–39) apparently belong chronologically before chaps. 36–37. These accounts are placed after them, however, in order that the ominous prophecy of 39:6 f. may be immediately followed by the great message of consolation for future generations, a deliverance which Hezekiah could only look for in his own day.

The book of consolation (chaps. 40–66) may aptly be called a prophetic sermon with Isaiah's name ("salvation of the Lord") as its theme. It has its counterpart in the words of John the Baptist and of Jesus, "Repent ye: for the kingdom of heaven is at hand" (Mt 3:2; Mk 1:15). The awfulness of human sin and the wonders of divine grace are its recurring and alternating themes. It is apparently divided into three parts by the warning words of 48:22; 57:21, and ends with the terrible words of 66:24 (cf. Mk 9:48). The major themes in these chapters are:

1. The transcendence of Yahweh. He "has made all things" (44:24; cf. 45:12), "all nations before him are as nothing" (40:17). "To whom will ye liken me?" (46:5) is His challenge to mortal men. He will "create new heavens and a new earth" (65:17; 66:22; cf. 55:9).

2. The sinful folly of idolatry, man worshiping the work of his own hands (44:9–20; 46:1–2, 6–8).

3. Israel's God, who alone can foretell future events and bring them to pass (41:22–25; 42:9; 43:9–12; 44:7; 45:21; 46:10; 48:3–5).

4. A prominent figure is Cyrus. God has raised him up "from the east" (41:2–5); he comes in righteousness (45:13); he comes as a ravening bird from a far country (46:11); he will humble Babylon (43:14; 48:14); he will cause Jerusalem to be built and the temple restored (44:28; 45:1–7).

5. A more prominent figure is the Servant of the Lord. He is called Israel (49:3), Jacob (48:20), Jacob-Israel (41:8 f.; 44:1, 21; 45:4). He is described as "deaf and blind" (42:18 f.), sinful and needing redemption (43:25; 44:22), as having a mission to Israel and the Gentiles (42:1–7; 49:1–6), as one in whom the Lord will be glorified (49:3), as one who has suffered though innocent (50:5–9), as one who has suffered vicariously for others (52:13 — 53:12).

The reference cannot be the same in all of these passages. Where sinfulness is attributed to the servant, he must be sinful Israel; where unmerited suffering is described and a mission to Israel and the Gentiles is referred to, the pious remnant which the Lord will use to bring blessing to Israel and the nations may be in part referred to. In chap. 53 the Servant can only be the Messiah, who in 61:1-3 speaks of His mission in words which in the synagogue at Nazareth Jesus appropriated to Himself (Lk 4: 17-21). *See* Servant of the Lord.

6. The world-embracing extent of this promised salvation is especially stressed in the closing chapters. The "every one" of 55:1 has its echo in the "whosoever will" of Jn 3:16, and the promises of 56:7 and 66:1 f. have their fulfillment in Jn 4:24.

Bibliography. Conservative: J. A. Alexander, *Commentary on the Prophecies of Isaiah,* 1846; Grand Rapids: Zondervan, reprinted 1953. O. T. Allis, *The Unity of Isaiah,* Philadelphia: Presbyterian and Reformed, 1950. Charles Boutflower, *The Book of Isaiah (Chapters I–XXXIX) in the Light of the Assyrian Monuments,* New York: Macmillan, 1930. Franz Delitzsch, *Biblical Commentary on the Prophecies of Isaiah,* 2 vols. 1866; Grand Rapids: Eerdmans, reprinted 1949. Seth Erlandsson, *The Burden of Babylon: A Study of Isaiah 13:2–14:23,* Lund: CWK Gleerup, 1970. F. Derek Kidner, "Isaiah," NBC, 2nd ed. H. C. Leupold, *Exposition of Isaiah,* Vol. I, Grand Rapids: Baker, 1968. G. L. Robinson, "Isaiah," ISBE, III, 1495-1508. E. J. Young, *Studies in Isaiah,* Grand Rapids: Eerdmans, 1954; *Who Wrote Isaiah?* Grand Rapids: Eerdmans, 1958; *The Book of Isaiah,* Grand Rapids: Eerdmans, Vol. I, 1965; Vol. II, 1969; Vol. III, 1972.

Critical or radical: B. Duhm, *Das Buch Jesaja,* 1892; 3rd ed., Göttingen, GHK, 1914. G. B. Gray, *A Critical and Exegetical Commentary on the Book of Isaiah* (Chaps. 1-27), ICC, New York: Scribner's, 1912. J. L. McKenzie, *Second Isaiah,* Anchor Bible, Garden City: Doubleday, 1968. C. R. North, "Isaiah," IDB, II, 731-744; *The Second Isaiah: Introduction, Translation and Commentary to Chapters XL–LV,* Oxford: Clarendon Press, 1964. J. Skinner, *The Book of the Prophet Isaiah,* 2 vols., rev. ed., Cambridge Bible, Cambridge: Univ. Press, 1925.

O. T. A.

ISCAH (ĭz'kà). A daughter of Haran, the brother of Abraham, and a sister of Milcah and Lot (Gen 11:29). Jewish tradition, with insufficient reasons, identified her with Sarah.

ISCARIOT. *See* Judas 8.

ISHBAH (ĭsh'bà). A member of the tribe of Judah, father of Eshtemoa (I Chr 4:17).

ISHBAK (ĭsh'băk). The name carried by the descendants of Ishbak, one of the sons of Abraham and Keturah (Gen 25:2). According to the Annals of Shalmaneser III (858-824), they seem to have settled in N Syria (ANET, pp. 277 f.).

ISHBI-BENOB (ĭsh'bī-bē'nŏb). A Philistine giant who attempted to kill David but instead was slain by Abishai, brother of Joab (II Sam 21:16-17). His name in Heb., *Yishbî-benōb,* is the *Qere* reading of the text, the emendation vocalization of the Masoretes. The *Kethib* or unpointed Heb. text can also be read, "And they dwelt in Nob where there was one among the descendants of the giant, the weight of whose spear...." If the latter reading is adopted the name disappears.

ISHBOSHETH (ĭsh-bō'shĕth). A Heb. name meaning "man of shame." Comparison of several OT passages indicates that this man was referred to under several names. In I Sam 14:49 the name is probably Ishvi (ASV) or Ishui (KJV), unless this is another name for Abinadab (I Sam 31:2). In II Sam 2:8 the name is Ishbosheth. In I Chr 8:33 it is Esh-baal, a compound which was probably the original name. Some think it exalts Yahweh as Lord, but was changed to Ishbosheth when the story of his shameful murder was related, in order to make it refer prophetically to the manner of his death.

When Saul and his three eldest sons were slain on the field of battle at Mount Gilboa (I Sam 31:1 ff.), Abner, the captain of Saul's hosts, took Ishbosheth, the remaining son of Saul, across Jordan to Mahanaim and there proclaimed him king over Israel (II Sam 2:8-9). Since the men of Judah acknowledged the sovereignty of David, it was inevitable that the opposing forces must meet. The first encounter was at Gibeon (II Sam 2:12 ff.). A preliminary attempt was made to settle the issue by the outcome of combat between 12 champions representing each side. All 24 fell mortally wounded. This led to full scale battle, and the resulting defeat of Abner and the death of Joab's brother Asahel. Ishbosheth was 40 years old when he was invested with sovereignty over Israel (II Sam 2:10). This was approximately 1011 B.C. Though the biblical account declares that he reigned only two years, it appears that he and his general Abner exercised combined control over Israel for a period of seven years, or until 1004 B.C., when David was crowned king over the entire nation.

Abner was alienated from Ishbosheth when the latter apprehended him in an intrigue with Saul's concubine Rizpah, and virtually charged him with an act of treason (II Sam 3:6-11). This was more than Abner could endure, and deep resentment led him to transfer his allegiance to David.

In reprisal for the death of his brother Asahel, Joab treacherously murdered Abner (II Sam 3:27). Very shortly thereafter Ishbosheth was cruelly murdered by two of his officers. Thinking to gain favor with David by this act, they were overwhelmed with denunciation and condemned to instant death (II Sam 4:5–12). Though David had no part in the misfortunes that befell Ishbosheth and his general Abner, God used these events to establish David as king over all Israel.

H. A. Hoy.

ISHI (ĭsh'ī). A term meaning "my husband," symbolizing the Israelites' relationship with God after they returned to Him from their idolatry (Hos 2:16). Ishi was also the name of four men:

1. A son of Appaim of the tribe of Judah (I Chr 2:31).

2. A man of Judah, father of Zoheth (I Chr 4:20).

3. A descendant of Simeon, father of Pelatiah, Neariah, Rephaiah, and Uzziel who fought against the Amalekites (I Chr 4:42–43).

4. Head of a family of the tribe of Manasseh (I Chr 5:24).

ISHIAH (ĭ-shī'à). The KJV variant of Isshiah 4 (q.v.). A descendant of Issachar who is mentioned among David's valiant men (I Chr 7:3, 5).

ISHIJAH (ĭ-shī'jà). Son of Harim (Ezr 10:31) who along with others put away his foreign wife at the command of Ezra.

ISHMA (ĭsh'mà). A descendant of Hur of Judah through Etam, a brother of Jezreel and Idbash (I Chr 4:3).

ISHMAEL (ĭsh'mā-ĕl). The name means "may God hear" and is related to the experience wherein God heard the anguished prayer of Hagar in her flight from the household of Abraham (Gen 16:11).

1. The firstborn son of Abraham by Hagar, the Egyptian maid of his wife Sarah. Abraham was 86 at the time and had lived in Canaan for 11 years. Sarah, the barren wife, in keeping with the customs of her time as seen in both the Babylonian law code of Hammurabi (q.v.) and the Nuzu tablets, gave her slave Hagar to Abraham to produce an heir for the family.

When Abraham was 99 God renewed His covenant with him and enjoined circumcision as an external sign of membership in the covenant community (Gen 17:1–14). God also announced that He would fulfill the divine promise of a son through his wife Sarah, although Abraham looked on Ishmael with deep affection and prayed that he might be the promised heir (Gen 17:18). When Ishmael was circumcised, Abraham and all his household — those born to the men and women who had grown up in his employ and newcomers to the household through purchase from foreigners — were also circumcised. Ishmael was then 13 years old. Many Arab tribes still circumcise their youths at the age of 13.

Fourteen years after the birth of Ishmael, Isaac was born to Sarah and Abraham. The jealousy that had long separated Sarah from Hagar came to the breaking point at an anniversary celebrating the weaning of Isaac. Sarah insisted, contrary to the customs of the times as evidenced by Abraham's displeasure (Gen 21:11; cf. Nuzu legal tablet HV 67:22), that Hagar and Ishmael be sent away. Although Hagar and Ishmael left the house of Abraham and went to live in the wilderness of Beer-sheba, and later in the wilderness of Paran, there is no record of any animosity developing between Ishmael and Isaac. Both sons tended to the burial of Abraham in the cave of Machpelah (Gen 25:9). While Isaac was his sole heir, Abraham endowed the sons of his concubines (Hagar and Keturah) while he was still living (Gen 25:6). Therefore Ishmael received some of Abraham's material goods. Keturah's sons were sent away eastward, whereas Ishmael went to the SW.

Hagar took for him an Egyptian wife and he became the father of 12 sons and a daughter called Mahalath (Gen 28:9) or Basemath (Gen 36:3). She became one of the wives of Esau. The names of Ishmael's sons were Nebajoth, Kedar, Adbeel, Mibsam, Mishma, Dumah, Massa, Hadad, Tema, Jetur, Naphish, and Kedemah (Gen 25:13–15). Since most of these names occur as tribal entities of considerable influence in other places, some scholars look upon this genealogy list as ethnic rather than personal.

The epithet "a wild ass of a man" ascribed to Ishmael in Gen 16:12 (RSV, NASB) is not to be considered one of opprobrium but one of praise. The wild onager was the choicest animal on the Assyrian king's hunting list and a delicacy on the menus at royal banquets. Here it depicts the Bedouin freedom of the Ishmaelites in the southern wilderness (Gen 25:16–18).

Ishmael died at the age of 137 (Gen 25:17). His burial place is unknown. The Muslims claim that he and his mother Hagar were buried in the Ka'aba at Mecca.

In Gal 4:21–5:1 Paul interprets the narratives of Ishmael and Isaac allegorically. He uses the word "persecute" (v. 29; cf. mocking, Gen 21:9) to indicate the action of those Jews who, though clinging to the ordinances of the Mosaic law which must pass away (as Ishmael was sent away), persecute those who are the free born in Christ, the true heirs of the promise.

2. The third son of Azel, a Benjamite descendant from the family of Saul through Mephibosheth, son of Jonathan (I Chr 8:38; 9:44).

3. The father of Zebadiah, the governor of the house of Judah in the reign of Jehoshaphat (II Chr 19:11).

4. The son of Jehohanan, a captain of a "hundred." He aided Jehoiada in restoring Joash, the crown prince, to the throne of Judah (II Chr 23:1).

5. The third son of Pashur, who relinquished

his Gentile wife in the reforms of Ezra in the post-Exilic period (Ezr 10:22).

6. The son of Nethaniah, a member of the royal house of David. During Nebuchadnezzar's siege of Jerusalem he fled with many others to Transjordan and found refuge at the court of Baalis, then king of Ammon (cf. Jos *Ant.* x. 9.2). He pretended friendship with Gedaliah, the Heb. governor appointed by Nebuchadnezzar to care for the needs of those left in Judah following the sacking of Jerusalem in 586 B.C. Gedaliah's headquarters was in Mizpah, a few miles N of Jerusalem. Although Gedaliah was warned of the treacherous plot of Ishmael to slay him, Johanan volunteering to put Ishmael to death, Gedaliah refused to believe the report and held a banquet in Ishmael's honor. Ten companions of Ishmael, called princes of the king, also attended the banquet. Gedaliah, the governor of Judah, and some of the Babylonian soldiers stationed at Mizpah were murdered at the feast. Ishmael and his men escaped. So secretly was the deed accomplished that several days elapsed before anyone detected the murder. Ishmael was able to abduct King Zedekiah's daughter and several townspeople, and headed for Ammon. Johanan caught up with him at the great waters of Gibeon (Jer 41:1-12). In the ensuing battle, the abducted party was retrieved, but Ishmael and eight of his men escaped to Ammon. Nothing further is recorded of Ishmael or of his activities (II Kgs 25:25; Jer 40:7—41:18).

F. E. Y.

ISHMAELITES (ĭsh'mā-ĕ-līts). The term occurs in Gen 37:25, 27, 28; 39:1; Jud 8:24 and Ps 83:6 as a general designation for a people dwelling in the territory from Egypt to the Euphrates. According to the biblical tradition, the Ishmaelites had Egyptian as well as Semitic blood in their veins, for the mother and the wife of Ishmael were Egyptians. His descendants dwelt in a twelvefold division in settlements and in movable camps in the desert of N Arabia, in the region between Havilah, Egypt, and the Euphrates. These tribes included the Nebajoth, Kedar, Adbeel, Dumah, Massa, and Tema—all mentioned in the 8th and 7th cen. Assyrian texts; Jetur, Naphish, and Kedemah—a more or less homogeneous group; Mibsam, Mishma, and Hadar—so far not identified in any extrabiblical source. The Nabataeans (*q.v.*; the descendants of Nebajoth?) in Greco-Roman times settled permanently in Petra and in Palmyra and developed a flourishing civilization. The Muslim Arabs, following Muhammad's example, claim descent from Ishmael.

The Ishmaelite mode of life was that of itinerant caravan traders, tent dwellers, and cameleers (I Chr 27:30). They were characterized by their spirit of independence and adventurousness. They carried aromatic gum and incense from Gilead to Egyptian markets (Gen 37:25). One such caravan bought Joseph and

sold him into slavery in Egypt. Following the tradition of Ishmael's skill in archery, the sons of Kedar were noted for their deftness with the bow (Isa 21:17).

II Sam 17:25 states that Amasa, commander of Absalom's army, was the son of Ithra an Israelite; according to I Chr 2:17 the father of Amasa was Jether (Ithra) the Ishmaelite. Perhaps Jether was an Israelite living in the land of Ishmael (cf. Obed-edom the Gittite).

F. E. Y.

ISHMAIAH (ĭsh-mā'yȧ). Chief of the army contingent of the Zebulunites during David's reign (I Chr 27:19).

ISHMEELITE. KJV spelling of Ishmaelite (*q.v.*) in the Genesis references and I Chr 2:17.

ISHMERAI (ĭsh'mḗ-rī). A descendant of Benjamin, son of Elpaal, and one of the chief men of the tribe (I Chr 8:18).

ISHOD (ĭsh'ŏd). A member of the tribe of Manasseh, whose mother was Hammoleketh (I Chr 7:18).

ISHPAN (ĭsh'păn). A member of the tribe of Benjamin, the son of Shashak (I Chr 8:22).

ISHTOB (ĭsh'tŏb). Ishtob is the KJV reading for "men of Tob." It was a place in Syria or Palestine, perhaps a small state, that supplied 12,000 men to support the Ammonites in their war against Joab and his forces (II Sam 10:6, 8). Jephthah had fled there from Gilead (Jud 11:3, 5). *See* Tob.

ISHUAH (ĭsh'ū-ȧ), **ISUAH** (ĭs'ū-ȧ). The second son of Asher (Gen 46:17; I Chr 7:30). The name is spelled Ishvah in the RSV.

ISHUAI. *See* Ishui.

ISHUI (ĭsh'ū-ī). Variant in KJV of Isui, Ishuai, and Jesui.

1. The third son of Asher (Gen 46:17; I Chr 7:30), his name being called Jesui and his family Jesuites in Num 26:44, with Ishvi and Ishvites being the reading of the RSV.

2. The second son of Saul by his wife Ahinoam (I Sam 14:49). His name is omitted in Saul's genealogy in I Chr 8:9 (some claim he died young) and in I Sam 31:2 his place is taken by Abinadab (*q.v.*), with whom others identify him.

ISLAND, ISLE. The Heb. word 'î is used in a much broader sense than the English, since it is based upon the idea of a mariner who sees any dry land as a place of peace from the sea and of rest, whether it be simply the seacoast or an island. Therefore the word has to be understood in context to decide whether it is to be translated island or simply coast. There are passages where an island is clearly signified (Isa

40:15), and others where it is simply the land at the coast or the coastline (Isa 20:6). It can also be used to refer to far off places of the earth in the sense of foreign shores (Isa 41:5; 66:19).

In the NT specific islands are designated by *nēsos,* and such islands are mentioned as Chios, Crete, Cyprus, Melita, Rhodes, and Samos. John was exiled to the isle of Patmos where he received "the Revelation of Jesus Christ" (Rev 1:1, 9).

R. A. K.

ISMACHIAH (ĭz′mȧ-kī′ȧ). One of the overseers in connection with the temple during the reign of Hezekiah (II Chr 31:13).

ISMAIAH (ĭs-mā′yȧ). A Gibeonite, chief of David's 30 mighty men, who came to him at Ziklag (I Chr 12:4).

ISPAH (ĭs′pȧ). A descendant of Benjamin and a son of Beriah (I Chr 8:16).

ISRAEL (ĭz′rā-ĕl). The name Israel first appears in Gen 32:28, where the Angel of the Lord bestowed it upon Jacob (*q.v.*) during His encounter with him at Peniel. Jacob had refused to let Him go until He had given him a blessing, and so God granted him the new title of Yis-rā′ēl, stating that he had persistently struggled (*śārîtā* from *śārāh,* "exert oneself, persist") with God (*'elōhîm,* the shorter form of which is *'Ēl*) and had prevailed (i.e., in his earnest prayer). Thus it would appear that the name meant "he persists with God"; the more obvious "God persists" would not fit the circumstances of this episode very well. At any rate, this became the specific covenant name for Jacob, just as Abraham had been for Abram (Gen 17:5).

The national designation of the Heb. people was "the sons of Israel" (*benê Yiśrā'ēl*) rather than "the sons of Jacob" by the time the members of Joseph's family had multiplied (Ex 1:9, 12) and were ready to leave Egypt for the Promised Land under Moses' leadership (Ex 2:23, 25; 3:9; etc.). The expression "sons of Jacob" never appears in the Pentateuch after the book of Genesis (where it occurs only in connection with Jacob's immediate children). For the sake of brevity the "sons of" was occasionally omitted, and "Israel" by itself could refer to the Hebrews as a race. Thus the pursuing Egyptians by the Red Sea were quoted as saying, "Let us flee from the face of Israel," when they found themselves bogged down and threatened with destruction (Ex 14:25).

In surviving Egyptian records the Israelites may have been referred to by the general designation of *'Apiru* (which seems to have included other Canaanite and Semitic groups than the Hebrews alone; *see* Hebrew People). There is one reference, however, to the name of Israel in the well-known "Israel stela" of King Merneptah of the 19th Dynasty. After speaking of his military success in plundering Canaan, Ashkelon, Gezer, and Yanoam, the triumphal

hymn goes on to state, "Israel is laid waste, his seed is not" (ANET, p. 378). The Egyptian spelling of the name is "Y-s-r-'-r" (Egyptian made no distinction between *l* and *r* until after the Gr. conquest), and it is followed by the man-woman-plural-strokes determinative, indicating that Israel was a tribe or nation, rather than a local city-state. The date of this inscription was about 1230 B.C., so it must refer to an Egyptian incursion which took place during the period of the judges.

Correspondingly there is only one reference to the name Israel in the Assyrian cuneiform inscriptions thus far discovered, namely, in the Balawat inscription of Shalmaneser III (ANET, p. 279) which records the battle of Karkar (853 B.C.) as fought against Hadadezer of Damascus and Ahab the Israelite (*A-ḫa-ab-bu Sir-'i-la-ai*). Otherwise the extant Assyrian records refer to Israel (and especially the northern kingdom) as "the land of Omri" (*mat Ḫumri*), apparently because it was during the reign of this dynasty that the Assyrians first came in contact with the Heb. monarchy (cf. ANET, pp. 281, 283–285). But in adjacent Moab the name "Israel" was the usual designation, if we may judge from the four or five references in the inscription of King Mesha (*c.* 840 B.C.; ANET, p. 320). In the comparatively meager collection of Phoenician inscriptions surviving to us, no reference to Israel has been found; the same is true of the Old Aramaic inscriptions.

In biblical usage, as already mentioned, the name Israel has a covenantal or theological connotation, even on the lips of Jacob himself. In Gen 49:2 he gathers his sons about him for a final blessing: "Hearken unto Israel your father." Then follows a specific characterization of each of the 12, accompanied by a prophecy of their role in the life of the future nation. In v. 28 we read: "All these are the twelve tribes of Israel; and this is what their father spoke to them as he blessed them." *See* Tribe; for the individual tribes *see* under their respective names.

In the days of Moses, Yahweh ("Jehovah") declares Himself to be the Father of Israel: "Israel is my son, even my firstborn" (Ex 4:22); in 5:1 (ASV) we read: "Thus saith Jehovah, the God of Israel, Let my people go. . . ." As "Israel" the Heb. nation was to play a special role as a theocracy governed by the specially revealed law of God, and He was to be their only King. The powerful leader Gideon reaffirmed this principle when he rejected the proposal to make him king over Israel, saying, "I will not rule over you, neither shall my son rule over you: Jehovah shall rule over you" (Jud 8:23, ASV). Even when a human king was at last anointed by the prophet Samuel, it was made clear that he was chosen and appointed by Yahweh, and was under obligation to obey His law (I Sam 10:25; 12:13–15, 24–25).

In his subsequent career, however, as the first king of Israel, Saul proved unfaithful to his trust, substituting his own will and judgment for the revealed will of God, first, in offering a sacrifice at Gilgal (I Sam 13:9–10) as if he were an ordained priest; and second, in sparing the king of the Amalekites and their cattle despite Yahweh's command to destroy them utterly (15:17–26). The result was that the Lord revoked his commission as theocratic king (I Sam 13:13–14; 15:23), and sent Samuel to Bethlehem to anoint David, the youngest son of Jesse, although under conditions of secrecy (16:13). Eventually Saul began to suspect that his valiant young harpist, the slayer of Goliath, was God's chosen successor to him and the supplanter of his dynasty (18:29), and he became obsessed with a desire to see him dead (20:31). Much of the remainder of his reign was spent in an unsuccessful attempt to capture and slay David. Finally Saul and his sons became involved in a disastrous campaign with the invading Philistines, who fatally wounded him in the battle of Mount Gilboa. After seven and a half years of intermittent civil war, Saul's youngest son, Ishbosheth, was assassinated, and the ten northern tribes acknowledged David as their king, after he had reigned over Judah and Simeon from the time of Saul's death. This confirmed the principle that Israel's king had to be chosen by God Himself, and was responsible to keep His law as His agent upon earth.

As a godly and dedicated ruler under the divine mandate David reigned over the united monarchy of Israel. He subdued not only the Philistines but also the other neighboring nations (Edomites, Moabites, Ammonites and Syrians of Damascus, and Hamath) in a long series of successful campaigns. David never experienced defeat on the battlefield. Yahweh used him to give Israel "rest" from all their enemies round about, and to take possession of the entire territory originally promised to Abraham's seed (Gen 15:18), all the way from the "river of Egypt" (the Wadi el-'Arish) to the Euphrates at Tiphsah (cf. I Kgs 4:24). In a sense the conquest of Canaan was not completed until Yahweh found in David a man after His own heart (I Sam 13:14). It was he who, as a dutiful theocratic ruler, subdued all of Israel's foes and took the city of Jerusalem from its heathen owners, the Jebusites, and secured a suitable permanent resting place for the Lord's sanctuary (according to the promise of Deut 12:10–11).

Yet because of his involvement in bloody warfare (which he sometimes conducted with cruel severity, cf. II Sam 8:2; 12:31), David was denied the privilege of building the temple itself (I Chr 22:8). Nevertheless, he assembled most of the costly materials necessary for its construction and devised the building plans for his son Solomon to carry out (I Chr 28:11–19). He was promised by the prophet Nathan, speaking in the name of the Lord, that Solomon would live to carry out his design and erect a beautiful structure to house the ark of the covenant and to serve as a focal point for the worship of all Israel (II Sam 7:12–13; I Chr 28:5–6).

Even more important than the temple itself was the divine promise that Solomon would be a type of the Messianic King who would some day come to establish God's kingdom upon earth (II Sam 7:13; I Chr 28:7). This promise was inherent in the angel's announcement to Mary: "The Lord God will give unto him the throne of his father David: and he shall reign over the house of Jacob forever; and of his kingdom there shall be no end" (Lk 1:32–33).

David, then, fulfilled the pattern of a theocratic king responsible to God under the covenant. But even though he received God's approval earlier in his reign, he later fell into grievous personal sin in the matter of Bathsheba (with whom he committed adultery) and in the contrived murder of her husband Uriah (II Sam 11). After the prophet Nathan privately denounced him for these sins, David broke down in grief and repentance, and was therefore forgiven and restored to fellowship with God.

Nevertheless, he had so gravely violated his role as king of Israel that the baneful consequence was pronounced: "Now therefore the sword shall never depart from thine house; because thou hast despised me. . . .Behold, I will raise up evil against thee out of thine own house" (II Sam 12:10–11). This meant that violence, cruelty and treachery would plague the dynasty of David throughout the ensuing generations. In David's own lifetime he suffered the loss of the baby first conceived by Bathsheba out of wedlock; the grief from the sordid episode of his firstborn son, Amnon, who raped his own half sister Tamar; and the subsequent revenge of Absalom, who later assassinated Amnon as a guest at his table (13:28–29). Even more serious was the rebellion raised against David by Absalom, who drove him out of Jerusalem to take refuge in Mahanaim on the other side of the Jordan (17:24). Although David's general Joab managed to defeat the pursuing forces of Absalom and put him to death, David's latter days were lived under the cloud of this sorrow.

David also brought Israel into trouble by undertaking a complete census of the 12 tribes without any divine mandate to do so (such as Moses had received in the days of the Exodus). In the resultant plague that afflicted the nation no remedy could be found until David purchased the threshing floor of Araunah the Jebusite (where the destroying angel had halted his course) and offered up sacrifice to Yahweh on the very spot which was later to be the site of the temple of Solomon (II Sam 24).

David's son by Bathsheba, Solomon the Wise, took over responsibility as Israel's theocratic king under the rule of God. His wealth, wisdom, and prosperity became proverbial, and his prestige was such that he retained control of the enlarged borders of David's empire without having to use his large and formidable chariot forces in warfare with his foes. But his most notable achievement was the erection of a beautiful temple, twice the dimensions of the Mosaic tabernacle (i.e., 60 cubits by 20 cubits, or 90 feet by 30 feet), and possessing ten times as many lampstands and tables of showbread (for the tabernacle had been furnished with only one of each). An enormous bronze altar of sacrifice replaced the smaller Mosaic one, and likewise a huge basin (15 feet in diameter) took the place of the earlier laver before the door of the temple. This structure of unparalleled beauty and costliness was solemnly dedicated to the Lord as the meeting place between Yahweh and His covenant people Israel, and the shekinah glory of God came down upon the inner sanctum once again, as it had in the days of Moses (I Kgs 8:10–11). Under Solomon's rule, then, the united monarchy of Israel enjoyed its highest degree of prosperity and glory.

Unfortunately, however, Solomon's constitutional limitations under the law (Deut 17:14–20) could not be enforced by any human authority, so absolute was his power. Thus he could violate with impunity the commandments against multiplying horses and wives, and it was the policy of permitting Pharaoh's daughter to worship her Egyptian gods in Jerusalem that first led to the introduction of idolatry. This precedent led to religious tolerance for all his other wives of heathen background, and Israel's testimony for Yahweh was greatly impaired. Extravagant building programs and costly palace expenses resulted in excessive taxation and the employment of forced labor which aroused general antagonism throughout the kingdom. Thus the way was paved for the division of Israel into the northern and southern kingdoms once Solomon had passed away, and the succession fell to his arrogant and tactless son Rehoboam, who promised his subjects an even more oppressive rule than that of his father. This marked the end of the united monarchy, and the beginning of the kingdom of the ten tribes, which came to be known as the kingdom of Israel (in contradistinction to the kingdom of Judah). *See* Israel, Kingdom of; Judah, Kingdom of; Hebrew People.

Bibliography. John Bright, *A History of Israel,* Philadelphia: Westminster, 1959. F. F. Bruce, "Israel," NBD, pp. 578–588. "Government, Authority, and Kingship," CornPBE, pp. 354–369. G. von Rad, K. G. Kuhn, and W. Gutbrod, "*Israel, Ioudaios, Hebraios, etc.,*" TDNT, III, 356–391. H. H. Rowley, "Israel, History of (Israelites)," IDB, II, 750–765. Roland de Vaux, *Ancient Israel,* trans. by John McHugh, New York: McGraw-Hill, 1961.

G. L. A.

ISRAEL, KINGDOM OF. In 930 B.C., after the death of Solomon and the accession of his son Rehoboam, the united monarchy of Israel

Tirzah. JR

broke up into two realms. Finding that the young king was determined to maintain an even more tyrannous and oppressive rule than Solomon had done (especially in his latter years), the northern ten tribes resolved to set up a new kingdom of their own, under the leadership of a promising young Ephraimite, Jeroboam the son of Nebat. But the roots of this division went back to the days of Saul and David and to the tribal jealousy that manifested itself when the leadership passed from Benjamin to Judah. For seven years after Saul's death at the battle of Mount Gilboa the northern tribes had remained loyal to Ishbosheth, Saul's youngest son, even after Judah had installed David as king at Hebron. It was only after both Abner, commander of the army under Saul, and Ishbosheth himself had been assassinated that the ten tribes resolved to submit to David's rule and enjoy the benefits of the success that invariably attended him on the battlefield.

Even in David's case their loyalty was somewhat compromised during the rebellion of Absalom against his father. After Absalom's defeat and death contention arose between Judah, whose troops had accompanied David back across the Jordan, and the forces of the northern tribes. The latter had insisted, "We have ten parts in the king, and we have also more right in David than you" (II Sam 19:43). Their resentment paved the way for a brief but abortive revolt under Sheba, a Benjamite, who declared, "We have no part in David, neither have we inheritance in the son of Jesse; every man to his tents, O Israel" (II Sam 20:1). In practically the same words the representatives of the ten tribes cast off their allegiance to the Davidic dynasty in 930 B.C. (I Kgs 12:16), feeling confident that their spokesman, Jeroboam, would be able to lead them in a successful defense of their liberties. He had been an official under Solomon in the department of public works, but after he had been proclaimed by the prophet Ahijah as the Lord's choice as ruler over the ten tribes (I Kgs 11:31–38), he fled to Egypt and there became a protégé of

Pharaoh Shishak. After Solomon's death Jeroboam returned to act as chief spokesman for the northern Israelites, and through Rehoboam's folly he became chosen as king of the revolting tribes. (Only Judah and Simeon and the southern part of Benjamin adjacent to Jerusalem remained loyal to Solomon's son.)

Jeroboam, son of Nebat, had been commissioned by God to serve as a covenant-keeping ruler obedient to the Mosaic law, in contrast to the idolatrous tendencies of Solomon's later reign (I Kgs 11:33). He was promised a long and enduring dynasty if he proved faithful to his trust. When Rehoboam massed an army of 180,000 troops to compel the submission of the ten tribes, God even restrained him through the prophet Shemaiah from attempting this invasion (I Kgs 12:21-24).

But when Jeroboam faced the problem of the yearly pilgrimages of his subjects to the temple at Jerusalem, he felt compelled by the national interest to terminate this practice (which might have eroded their loyalty to himself), and to erect new sanctuaries at Bethel and Dan where they might carry on their worship of Yahweh according to the religious calendar of the Torah. Lacking the prestigious ark of the covenant enshrined in the Jerusalem temple, he decided upon a golden calf as the focal point of worship at these new temples, and declared them to be the "gods who brought up Israel out of the land of Egypt" (I Kgs 12:28). At best this new arrangement had to be regarded as an idolatrous worship of Yahweh. The inauguration of this new cult, therefore, was attended by a divine rebuke, administered by an unnamed prophet from Judah (I Kgs 13:2), who prophesied that this schismatic altar and sanctuary would one day be destroyed by a king named Josiah (fulfilled three centuries later around 630 B.C.). Despite this solemn warning, accompanied by two miraculous signs (13:4-6), Jeroboam persisted in his religious policy, and appointed as priests any of his citizens who applied for ordi-

nation (II Chr 11:13-16), even though they were not of the tribe of Levi (most Levites having migrated to Judah after the schism).

This evil example of the first king of Israel was subsequently followed by all his successors until the final demise of Samaria in 722 B.C. Even so zealous a worshiper of Yahweh as Jehu failed to depart from the "sins of Jeroboam the son of Nebat ... the golden calves that were in Bethel and ... in Dan" (II Kgs 10:29). As for Jeroboam himself, he was sternly warned by Ahijah that his line would be cut off completely, and that all ten tribes would some day be taken off into captivity to the E of the Euphrates (I Kgs 14:10, 15). His oldest son predeceased him by mortal illness, and his younger son, Nadab, did not survive him by more than two years, when he was assassinated by Baasha the son of Ahijah, of the tribe of Issachar (I Kgs 15:25-28).

After exterminating all the descendants of Jeroboam, Baasha continued a policy of hostility against Judah, fortifying Ramah as a staging area for invasion. King Asa of Judah was able to counter this move by bribing Ben-hadad of Damascus to break his treaty of alliance with Israel and attack Baasha from his rear, destroying the wealthiest cities of Naphtali (II Chr 16:2-4). While Baasha marched N to meet this threat, Asa overran Ramah and removed all of its fortifications. Following Baasha's death in 886 B.C., his son Elah lasted barely two years before he was assassinated by his chariot commander, Zimri, during a drinking bout. After destroying all of Baasha's household, Zimri himself came under attack from Omri, the chief commander of the army, who overwhelmed him in Tirzah, the capital. Omri assumed the crown in 885 B.C. and crushed the followers of Tibni, a rival pretender to the throne (I Kgs 16:15-22).

Omri proved to be a strong and successful king, and eventually the northern kingdom came to be known abroad as "the land of Omri" (or "Humri," as the Assyrians spelled it). He transferred the capital to a new site, the easily defended hill of Samaria, and acquired sufficient prestige to secure in marriage a brilliant match for his son Ahab, that is, Jezebel, the daughter of King Ethbaal of the Phoenicians. After 12 years of rule Omri passed on (874 B.C.), leaving his throne to Ahab, who was almost completely dominated by Jezebel.

As a zealous Baal-worshiper the queen persecuted the prophets of Yahweh who still adhered to the revealed faith. Only those hidden in caves were able to survive. But the prophet Elijah called for a total drought upon the entire kingdom (which affected much of Phoenicia as well, judging from the famine at Zarephath), and it lasted for three and a half years. Elijah finally came out of hiding and challenged Ahab and his followers to a contest on Mount Carmel. After Jezebel's prophets of Baal and Asherah (totaling 850) had vainly prayed all day for fire to ignite their offering, Elijah called down fire from heaven upon his sacrifice. He so con-

Samaria. HFV

The Black Obelisk of Shalmaneser III of Assyria, showing Jehu of Israel paying tribute to the Assyrians in the second register. BM

vinced his countrymen of the sovereignty of Yahweh that they followed his leadership in executing all the prophets of Baal. Despite the miraculous termination of the drought by a copious rain, Elijah fled for his life because of Jezebel's grim threats, and he did not stop until he met with God on Mount Sinai.

Ahab was subjected to great pressure by Ben-hadad of Damascus, but by following the directions of some unnamed prophets of Yahweh he managed to defeat and even to capture Ben-hadad at Aphek, despite the latter's overwhelming advantage in manpower and chariotry. Yet Ahab let his captive go in return for a promise of commercial concessions, and Ben-hadad lived on to plague Israel. After the

sordid affair of Naboth's judicial murder (I Kgs 21), Ahab was again confronted by Elijah as he was gloating over the confiscated vineyard, and was warned that he would die a violent death. This was fulfilled later when he died of an arrow wound at the battle of Ramoth-gilead (853 B.C.), despite his alliance with Jehoshaphat of Judah, who had come to help him against the Syrians (I Kgs 22:29–37). His son Ahaziah died two years later as the result of an accidental fall, and the crown passed to his younger son, Jehoram, who carried on the struggle against the Syrians of Damascus.

It was during Jehoram's reign that Moab regained its independence under King Mesha, despite a punitive expedition in alliance with Jehoshaphat and aided by Elisha, Elijah's chosen successor (II Kgs 3). During an interlude of peace with Damascus, General Naaman came to Samaria and was cured by Elisha of his leprosy. Nevertheless the Syrians later resumed their aggression, vainly endeavoring to capture the troublesome Elisha at Dothan (II Kgs 6:8–18), and then besieging Jehoram at Samaria, until they were miraculously chased away by a sudden panic (6:24–7:16). Upon his deathbed King Ben-hadad sent down his trusted general Hazael to seek healing from the Heb. prophet. But in the end he was smothered in bed by Hazael, just as Elisha predicted, and Hazael became an even more dangerous aggressor against Israel than his predecessor had been. It was from the battlefront at Ramoth-gilead that Jehu, Jehoram's army commander, hurried back to assassinate his king (having been anointed by an emissary of Elisha), and likewise King Ahaziah of Judah, who happened to be visiting Jehoram at the time. (As a grandson of Jezebel, Ahaziah was marked for destruction along with all other descendants of the house of Omri.)

A zealous partisan of Yahweh-worship, Jehu (841–814 B.C.) followed up the extermination of Ahab's 70 sons by a massacre of all the worshipers of Baal, whom he had craftily enticed into the great Baal temple in Samaria under guise of being a Baal worshiper himself. Yet he failed to remove the cult of the golden calves at Bethel and Dan, and forfeited divine favor by this compromise with expediency. Not only did he sustain reverses from Hazael, but in the year of his accession he even had to pay tribute to the Assyrian Shalmaneser III (who had battled Ahab and Ben-hadad at Qarqar in 853 B.C.). His son Jehoahaz (814–798) was reduced to ignominious vassalage by the Syrians (II Kgs 13:7), but his grandson Jehoash (798–782), in accordance with Elisha's dying prophecy, gained three notable victories over Hazael and regained Israel's independence. Challenged to battle by Amaziah of Judah (the cordial entente with the southern kingdom had ceased in 841), Jehoash defeated and captured him at Beth-shemesh, destroyed much of the wall of Jerusalem and rifled the treasures of its temple and palace.

Jeroboam II (782–753 B.C.), the son of Jehoash, was even more successful in battle. He succeeded in reconquering all the dominions once subject to Jeroboam I, and even subdued the Syrian kingdoms of Damascus and Hamath (II Kgs 14:28). During this military success, however, the wealthy classes in Israel secured all the booty for themselves and the poor became poorer still. It was during this period of continued moral decline that the prophets Amos and Hosea began their ministry, vainly calling for repentance and reform. Jeroboam's incompetent son Zechariah was murdered by an army officer named Shallum in 752 B.C. Shallum in turn was vanquished and killed by another general, named Menahem, within a month, and thus the achievement of Jeroboam II gave way to civil war and national enfeeblement that presaged early disaster to the whole realm.

Ominously for Israel, Menahem (752–742 B.C.) found it necessary to pay tribute to the resurgent power of Assyria under the aggressive Tiglath-pileser III (744–727 B.C.) and to follow a pro-Assyrian policy until his death. His son Pekahiah was soon cut down (in 740) by an aide-de-camp named Pekah, who had apparently claimed the throne in Gilead back in 752 (cf. II Kgs 15:27). This led to an anti-Assyrian policy which welded Pekah and King Rezin of Damascus into a defensive coalition against Tiglath-pileser. When Ahaz of Judah refused to join with them, they launched devastating invasions which smashed the Judean armed forces (II Chr 28:5–8), although they did not capture Jerusalem itself. Bribed by Ahaz, Tiglath-pileser invaded Syria with overwhelming force, storming the capital of Damascus in 732, and reducing Israel to vassalage.

That same year Pekah's assassin Hoshea was installed as king and was compelled to cede northern Galilee to Assyria. Vainly he sought Egyptian alliance against Shalmaneser V, the new Assyrian ruler. But Hoshea was arrested and imprisoned and his capital beseiged. Samaria held out for nearly three years before it finally succumbed, apparently early in 721 B.C., and was totally destroyed by Sargon II (722/1–705 B.C.). All its surviving population was removed from Israel and settled by the Assyrians in territories E of the Tigris. Only a fraction of the rural population remained behind, and these were eventually submerged by large contingents of settlers from Cuthah, Ava, Hamath, Sepharvaim (II Kgs 17:24), Babylonia, Susa, Elam and elsewhere (Ezr 4:9–10), to form the hybrid people and culture which later came to be known as the Samaritans (q.v.).

See Israel; Judah, Kingdom of; Chronology, O.T.

Bibliography. "Israel and Judah, Monarchies of," CornPBE, pp. 422–444. Edwin R. Thiele, *The Mysterious Numbers of the Hebrew Kings,* 2nd ed., Grand Rapids: Eerdmans, 1965.

G. L. A.

ISSACHAR (ĭs'á-kär). The ninth son of Jacob, the fifth by Leah (Gen 30:17–18; 35:23). The sons of Issachar were "Tola, and Phuvah, and Job, and Shimron" (Gen 46:13), and were among those who moved to Egypt when Joseph sent the wagons from Egypt for his father Jacob and his family.

Before Jacob died he called his sons into his presence to pronounce a benediction and a prophetic utterance over each one. Jacob said, "Issachar is a strong ass couching down between two burdens" (Gen 49:14). The descendants of Issachar developed into five tribal clans, increasing in number from 54,400 at the first numbering (Num 1:29) to 64,300 at the second census (Num 26:25), and to 87,000 during the reign of David (I Chr 7:1–5).

Representatives from the tribe of Issachar stood on Mount Gerizim to bless the people (Deut 27:12). Moses predicted a joyous and quiet life for Issachar (Deut 33:18). Such notables as the judge Tola (Jud 10:1), and King Baasha (I Kgs 15:27) belonged to the tribe of Issachar. The descendants of this tribe "were men that had understanding of the times, to know what Israel ought to do," and changed their political allegiance from Saul to David at the opportune time (I Chr 12:32, 38).

At the division of the land of Canaan, the fourth lot was assigned to Issachar after the ark was taken to Shiloh. The tribe occupied most of the plain of Jezreel or Esdraelon (Josh 19:17–23). This low, fertile plain of the Kishon proved to have advantages as well as disadvantages. Its location was a disadvantage because the Canaanites long dominated that area (Jud 1:27 f.), foreign invaders often pillaged the crops (e.g., Jud 6:3–6, 33), and enemy war chariots more than once engaged in battle here, thus fulfilling Jacob's prophecy in Gen 49:15. Yet the story of Sisera indicates that this tribe possessed qualities of valor (Jud 5:15). On the positive side, the "way of the sea" passed through Issachar's allotment and became a source of lucrative revenue to its occupants (Deut 33:19).

H. A. Han.

ISSHIAH (ĭ-shī'á). Variant of Ishiah and Jesiah (q.v.).

1. A Levite, the eldest son of Rehabiah and great-grandson of Moses (I Chr 24:21; cf. 23:14–17).

2. A Levite, son of Uzziel (I Chr 24:24–25; cf. 23:20, RSV).

3. One of David's mighty men whose name is spelled Jesiah in KJV (see I Chr 12:6, RSV).

4. A man of the tribe of Issachar whose name is spelled Ishiah in KJV (see I Chr 7:3, 5, RSV).

ISSUE. *See* Diseases.

ISUAH. *See* Ishuah.

ISUI. *See* Ishui.

ITALY (ĭt'á-lĭ). Slashing diagonally across the center of the Mediterranean, Italy is strategically located for control of that sea, and Rome is strategically located for controlling the peninsula of Italy. The area of Italy comprises about 90,000 square miles and divides into two regions: the peninsula and the continental region. The boot-shaped peninsula stretches some 700 miles toward Africa and is never more than 125 miles wide.

The Alps extend in an irregular 1,200-mile arc across the N and the Apennines extend the full length of the peninsula in a bow-shaped range about 800 miles long. These 4,000-foot mountains have passes which do not hinder communications and which thrust out spurs to the W to divide the land into such plains as Etruria, Latium, and Campania. The rivers of Italy (except for the Po) are generally not navigable and deposit silt at their mouths to create malarial marshes.

Italy's primary source of wealth was always agricultural and pastoral. There were also notable mine fields in ancient times, especially copper and iron beds in Etruria and Elba. Marble, limestone, timber, and abundance of good clay were also available during the early centuries after Christ.

Italy figures in the NT narrative in connection with Paul's journey to Rome and imprisonment there (Acts 27:1, 6). Aquila and Priscilla had come from Italy to Corinth (Acts 18:2). The writer of the epistle to the Hebrews extended greetings from Christians from Italy (Heb 13:24), a factor in determining the place of writing and the destination of that epistle. The military unit commanded by the centurion was called the Italian cohort (Acts 10:1, NASB).

See Rome; Roman Empire.

H. F. V.

ITCH. *See* Diseases.

ITHAI. *See* Ittai.

ITHAMAR (ĭth'á-mär). Fourth and youngest son of Aaron (Ex 6:23). He was consecrated to the priesthood along with his brothers (Ex 28:1 ff.), and after the death of Nadab and Abihu he and Eleazar were appointed to take their places in the priestly office (Num 3:4; I Chr 24:2). Treasurer of the offerings of the tabernacle (Ex 38:21), Ithamar was also super-

Italy at peace, and rich in crops, flocks and herds, as symbolized on the Altar of Peace of Augustus in Rome. HFV

ITALY

SCALE OF MILES
0 25 50 100 200

intendent of the work of the Gershonites and Merarites (Num 4:27-28, 33). He was founder of the priestly line to which Eli (*q.v.*) belonged (I Chr 24:5-6). A descendant of Ithamar named Daniel was among the exiles who returned from Babylon (Ezr 8:2).

ITHIEL (ĭth′ĭ-ĕl)
1. A Benjamite, the son of Jesaiah, in the time of Nehemiah (Neh 11:7).
2. A man to whom, along with Ucal, the words of Agur were addressed (Prov 30:1).

ITHMAH (ĭth′ma). A Moabite, one of David's valiant men (I Chr 11:46).

ITHNAN (ĭth′năn). A town in the southern extreme of Judah, mentioned along with Kedesh and Hazor (Josh 15:23).

ITHRA (ĭth′ra). The father of Amasa, the commander of Absalom's rebel army (II Sam 17:25). He is called "Ithra an Israelite" in II Sam 17:25, but a better reading is "Jether the Ishmeelite" in I Chr 2:17. *See* Jether. His mother was Abigail, the sister of David.

ITHRAN (ĭth′răn)
1. A son of Dishon, a Horite (Gen 36:26; I Chr 1:41).
2. Son of Zophah, a descendant of Asher (I Chr 7:37).

ITHREAM (ĭth′rē-ăm). The sixth son of David, born in Hebron. His mother's name was Eglah (II Sam 3:5; I Chr 3:3).

ITHRITES (ĭth′rīts). A family in Israel that lived at Kirjath-jearim (I Chr 2:53). Two of David's valiant warriors, Ira and Gareb, belonged to this family (II Sam 23:38; I Chr 11:40).

ITTAH-KAZIN (ĭt′a-kā′zĭn). The same as Eth-kazin (RSV), a place on the border of Zebulun (Josh 19:13).

ITTAI (ĭt′ī)
1. A Benjamite, son of Ribai, one of David's mighty men (II Sam 23:29; I Chr 11:31).
2. A Gittite, native of Gath, thus a Philistine, who became a dear friend of David and commander of one-third of David's forces during the revolt of Absalom, serving in equal capacity with Joab and Abishai (II Sam 15:18-22; 18:2, 5). When David urged him to remain in Jerusalem rather than risk his life, Ittai refused, choosing rather to serve his king.

ITURAEA (ĭt′yŏŏr-ē′a). This term appears only once in the Scriptures (Lk 3:1), where it designates a portion of the territory ruled over by Philip, the son of Herod the Great and brother of Herod Antipas. It was adjacent to Trachonitis in NE Palestine, beyond the Jordan River. It received its name from Jetur, son of Ishmael (Gen 25:15-16), and after the conquest by the Israelites it was occupied by the tribe of Manasseh (I Chr 5:19-20).

IVAH (ī′va). A city conquered by the Assyrians and mentioned along with Hamath, Arpad, Sepharvaim, and Hena, according to the boast of Rabshakeh, a representative of Sennacherib (II Kgs 18:34; 19:13; Isa 37:13). Although its exact location has not been determined, it apparently was in Babylonia and perhaps is to be identified with Ava (II Kgs 17:24) from which the Assyrians took people to occupy Samaria after its fall. *See* Ava.

Small ivory panel with an Egyptian scene from an Assyrian palace at Nimrud. Assyria. BM

IVORY. The Heb. word *shēn*, translated "ivory," means "tooth"; and the compound word *shenhabbîm*, also translated "ivory," means "elephant's tooth." *See* Animals: Elephant, II, 12.

Ivory is mentioned several times in the Bible, first of all with reference to Solomon's reign when he shipped it in through his Red Sea port at Ezion-geber and decorated his throne with ivory veneer or inlays (I Kgs 10:18, 22). Solomon very likely imported his ivory from Punt (Somaliland in E Africa), where the Egyptians sent trading expeditions via the Red Sea to obtain ivory. In his beautiful love song he compares the body of the bridegroom and the neck of the bride to white ivory (Song 5:14; 7:4).

Ahab is said to have built an "ivory house"

(I Kgs 22:39), undoubtedly meaning that the walls and doors of his palace and pieces of furniture were inlaid with ivory panels and carvings (cf. Ps 45:8). Amos condemned ivory houses and beds along with the other luxuries of the royalty and nobility of the northern kingdom (Amos 3:15; 6:4).

A large number of ivory pieces were found in the excavations of Samaria. They apparently date to the reign of Ahab in the 9th cen. B.C. Some are carved panels with frame and tenon on the side for attaching to woodwork. The merchants of Tyre even boasted of inlaying the decks of their ships with ivory (Ezk 27:6, RSV, NASB), which they received in the form of tusks from the Sudan by the traders of Dedan in Arabia (27:15). In Rev 18:12 articles of ivory are listed among the cargoes to be brought to the eschatological Babylon.

Both Egyptian and Assyrian texts frequently list chairs and couches decorated with ivory that were taken as booty (ANET, pp. 237, 282, 288). Archaeological excavations of many Near Eastern sites from Cyprus to Ur in lower Mesopotamia have uncovered exquisite ivory objects. A catalogue published in 1957 listed 1,271 separate pieces, such as figurines of gods and animals, plaques, combs, gaming boards, cosmetic tools, and jewel boxes (R. D. Barnett, *A Catalogue of Nimrud Ivories and Other Examples of Ancient Near Eastern Ivories;* see also ANEP, # 58, 67, 69, 70, 125–132, 203, 213–215, 290, 293, 332, 464, 566, 649, 663).

The most important collections of Palestinian ivory work have come from Samaria and Megiddo. A hoard of 383 pieces dating from 1350–1150 B.C. was discovered at the latter site. Nimrud (biblical Calah) has yielded the finest collection of all. Some of its ivories are so similar in technique to those of Samaria that it may be assumed the same Phoenician craftsmen made pieces in each group. Most of the ivory used in Assyria, Syria, and Palestine came from Asiatic elephants which inhabited the marshes along the upper Euphrates. They

were hunted to extinction sometime after 850 B.C.

J. R.

IVY. *See* Plants: Ivy.

IZEHARITES. *See* Izharites.

IZHAR (ĭz'här), **IZEHAR** (ĭz'ĕ-här)
1. A Levite (Heb. *yiṣhar*), son of Kohath and father of Korah (Num 16:1), head of a tribal family called Izharites and Izeharites (see also Ex 6:18, 21; Num 3:19, 27; I Chr 6:18, 38; etc.); called Amminadab in I Chr 6:22 (*see* Amminadab 2).
2. A descendant of Judah (Heb. *yiṣhar*), whose mother was named Helah (I Chr 4:7, RSV). The KJV renders his name Jezoar.

IZHARITES (ĭz'hȧ-rīts), **IZEHARITES** (ĭz'ĕ-hä-rīts). The descendants of Izhar, son of Kohath and the father of Korah (I Chr 3:27; I Chr 24:22; 26:23, 29). These Levites during the reign of David helped to supervise the treasures of the tabernacle (I Chr 26:23), and some also served as "officers and judges" (I Chr 26:29).

IZLIAH. *See* Jezliah.

IZRAHIAH (ĭz'rȧ-hī'ȧ). A descendant of Issachar and grandson of Tola, a chief of the tribe (I Chr 7:3). *See* Jezrahiah.

IZRAHITE (ĭz'rȧ-hīt). The family name of Shamhuth, one of David's heroic men and designated as "the fifth captain for the fifth month" (I Chr 27:8). The name is possibly a corruption of "Zerahite," a descendant of Zerah of Judah (I Chr 27:11, RSV).

IZRI (ĭz'rī). Apparently one of the sons of Jeduthun and also called Zeri (I Chr 25:3), leader of the fourth group of musicians in the Levitical choir during the reign of David (I Chr 25:11).

J

JAAKAN (jā′á-kản). A descendant of a nomadic clan of the Horites (Hurrians) of Mount Seir who maintained their identity among the Edomites. He was a son of Ezer, called Jakan in I Chr 1:42 and Akan (*q.v.*) in Gen 36:27. The name also is spelled Jaakan in Deut 10:6, where it is disclosed that the Israelites had rested in the area of the wells (Beeroth) of the "children of Jaakan." Num 33:31 –32 records that the Israelites pitched tent in Bene-jaakan ("sons of Jaakan"). It is to be noted that the so-called Horites have been identified with a cultured people known as the Hurrians, who migrated southward into N Mesopotamia around 2000 B.C. Later they spread over Syria and Palestine, so that by the time of Moses the Egyptians frequently called this area Kharu or Hurru.

JAAKOBAH (jā′á-kō′bả). A descendant of Simeon (I Chr 4:36).

JAALA, JAALAH (jā′á-lả). A servant of Solomon whose children returned from the Babylonian Exile under Zerubbabel (Ezr 2:56; Neh 7:58).

JAALAM (jā′á-lảm). A son of Esau by Aholibamah, a Hivite woman (Gen 36:5). He is referred to as a "duke" or chief (Gen 36:18).

JAANAI (jā′á-nī). A chief of the tribe of Gad (I Chr 5:12).

JAARE-OREGIM (jā′á-rĕ-ôr′ĕ-jǐm). The name given to the father of Elhanan, a Bethlehemite who killed the brother of Goliath (II Sam 21:19). The name "Jaare-oregim" may result from a scribe having inserted the word *'ōreḡîm* from the next line of the same verse (an error of dittography), since the same man is also called Jair (*q.v.;* I Chr 20:5).

JAASAU (jā′á-sô). Called Jaasu in the RSV. He was a descendant of Bani and one of the Jews who put away their foreign wives upon the demand of a council headed by Ezra (Ezr 10:37).

JAASIEL (jā-ā′sǐ-ĕl), **JASIEL** (jā′sǐ-ĕl)
1. A son of Abner of the tribe of Benjamin

and one of the princes of the tribe (I Chr 27:21).
2. Jasiel the Mesobaite (I Chr 11:47), one of David's mighty men. Some authorities identify the two.

JAAZANIAH (jā-ăz′á-nī-á). The name occurs on an agate Heb. seal, "Jaazaniah, servant of the king," found at Tell en-Nasbeh, and in one of the Lachish letters.

1. The son of Hoshaiah the Maacathite. He was one of the Jewish army officers remaining after the desolation of Jerusalem by Babylon. With the other leaders, he pledged his support to Gedaliah, and after the murder of Gedaliah, pursued and defeated Ishmael, recovering all the captives. All the commanders appealed to Jeremiah for God's guidance, but disregarded him when he counseled them to remain in the land and trust in God. Jaazaniah last appears with the other "insolent men" rejecting God's will and preparing to go to Egypt and oblivion (II Kgs 25:23; Jer 40:8; 42:1; 43:2 – 5). In Jeremiah the name is spelled Jezaniah, and in Jer 43:2 he is called Azariah.

2. The leader of the Rechabites (*q.v.*) in the days of Jeremiah, when the prophet tempted them with wine that they might afford Judah a symbol of faithfulness (Jer 35:3ff.).

3. The son of Shaphan, seen by Ezekiel in a vision worshiping abominable things with the other elders of Israel (Ezk 8:10 –13).

4. The son of Azur, a prince of Judah, seen in Ezekiel's vision worshiping the sun with his back to the temple (Ezk 11:1 – 4).

P. C. J.

JAAZER (jā-ā′zẽr), **JAZER** (jā′zẽr). Jaazer occurs twice in the KJV (Num 21:32; 32:35); otherwise the name is spelled Jazer. It was a city located E of the Jordan, belonging originally to the Amorite kingdom of Sihon, captured by the Israelites (Num 21:32), and later allotted to the tribe of Gad (Josh 13:25). It furnished warriors for David (I Chr 26:31; II Sam 24:5). In the 8th cen. B.C. it was captured by the Moabites (Isa 16:8 –9; Jer 48:32). In the 2nd cen. B.C. it was captured and destroyed by the Maccabees (I Macc 5:7 –8). The site may be Khirbet Jazzir near es-Salt, 12 miles WNW of Amman.

JAAZIAH (jä'à-zī'à). A Levite, son or descendant of Merari, in the time of David (I Chr 24:26 - 27). However, there is a textual problem concerning this passage, with the LXX reading *Ozeiá*, which may mean Uzziah.

JAAZIEL (jä-ā'zī-ĕl). A Levite musician who was appointed to play an instrument at the return of the ark by David following its capture by the Philistines (I Chr 15:18). He also is called Aziel (*q.v.*; I Chr 15:20), and apparently the same man is referred to as Jeiel (*q.v.;* I Chr 16:5).

JABAL (jä'bàl). The son of Lamech by Adah and the originator of the nomadic way of life, as well as one who raised cattle (Gen 4:20).

The Jabbok River. Richard E. Ward

JABBOK (jăb'ŏk). An E tributary of the Jordan River *c.* 60 miles long. Now called Nahr ez-Zerqa from the blue look of its water, it rises near the ancient Rabbath-Ammon, the Ammonite capital. It flows N for 20 miles or more, gradually swinging to the W, where it descends rapidly through a steep-banked gorge. This gives it a strong current, especially in the rainy season. Reaching the Jordan Valley, it flows SW to enter the Jordan River about 24 miles N of the Dead Sea.

It was a natural boundary between the kingdoms of Sihon of Heshbon and Og of Bashan before the conquest of Canaan under Joshua (Num 21:24); and it was the W boundary of the Ammonites (Deut 3:16). Later it formed the S border of the tribal territory of Manasseh (Deut 3:12 - 17).

Jacob forded the river with his family before wrestling there at night with an angel who gave him the name Israel (Gen 32:22 - 29). In memory of this event the Israelites may have named the stream, for Jabbok in Heb. is *yabbōq*, while "and . . . wrestled" (Gen 32:24) is *way-yē'ābēq*, which contains only one additional consonant, a silent aleph.

N. B. B.

JABESH (jä'bĕsh)
1. The father of Shallum, who killed Zachariah, the king of Israel, and reigned in his stead (II Kgs 15:10, 13 - 14).
2. A shortened form of Jabesh-gilead (*q.v.*; I Sam 11:1, 3, 5, 9- 10; 31:12- 13; I Chr 10:12).

JABESH-GILEAD (jä'bĕsh-gĭl'ē-àd). A town in Gilead, about ten miles SE of the ancient Beth-shan, and about two miles E of the Jordan River. The site has been identified by Glueck with Tell Abu Kharaz on the Wadi Yabis two miles E of the Jordan. Israel early put the town to the sword because its citizens would not share in the war against Benjamin (Jud 21:8 - 15). Later, Saul rescued the town when Nahash the Ammonite threatened to gouge out the right eyes of the men when they surrendered to him in return for sparing their lives (I Sam 11:1 - 11). After Saul's death at the battle of Gilboa, the Philistines beheaded his body and hung it on the fortress of Beth-shan, but the men of Jabesh-gilead nine miles away recovered the body in a daring night-long raid and gave his remains an honorable burial (I Sam 31:8 - 13). David sent them a message praising them for their action (II Sam 2:4 - 7), doubtless hoping that this would help win their support to his kingship.

N. B. B.

JABEZ (jä'bĕz)
1. Jabez was a descendant of Judah, but he can be related to no time or family. His brief record appears like a bright light in the otherwise drab genealogies of Chronicles. He had been named Jabez, "he causes pain or sorrow." In faith he laid hold upon God and sought His blessing, and that faith triumphed, for "God granted what he asked" (I Chr 4:9 - 10).
2. A town, apparently in Judah, where "the families of the scribes" dwelt (I Chr 2:55).

JABIN (jä'bĭn). According to W. F. Albright (*Yahweh and the Gods of Canaan*, Garden City: Doubleday, 1968, p. 49, n. 99), this name is an abbreviation of the longer *Yabni-Hadad*, the name of a king of Hazor in the 17th cen. B.C. It is similar to *Yabni-el*, the name of a 14th cen. prince of Lachish.
1. King of Hazor (*q.v.*) who formed a coalition with several other kings to fight against the Israelites, but who instead was defeated by Joshua and his forces near the waters of Merom (*q.v.*). After the battle Jabin was slain and Hazor burned (Josh 11:1 - 14).
2. A later king of Hazor, possibly a descendant of the former Jabin. He oppressed Israel for 20 years during the time of the judges. His forces, led by Sisera, were defeated by the Israelite forces under Barak and Deborah (Jud 4:1 - 24). The latest level of the great Canaanite city of Hazor may be associated with his reign. The archaeological excavations of Yigael Yadin indicate it was destroyed *c.*1230 B.C.

F. D. H.

Remains of a public building of Ahab's day at the city of Hazor. HFV

JABNEEL (jăb′nē-ĕl)

1. A town on the NW border of Judah (Josh 15:11) four miles inland from the Mediterranean Sea and nine miles NE of Ashdod. It is probably to be identified with Jabneh, a Philistine city which was captured by Uzziah (II Chr 26:6). Jabneh was called Jamnia in the Gr. and Rom. periods, and it was at this city that the Sanhedrin re-formed after the destruction of Jerusalem in A.D. 70 and that the canon of the Jewish Scriptures was confirmed (c. A.D. 100).

2. A town of Naphtali (Josh 19:33), identified by some with modern Kirbet Yamma, about seven miles S of Tiberias.

JABNEH (jăb′nĕ). *See* Jabneel 1.

JACHAN (jā′kăn). A Gadite chief, probably head of a father's house (I Chr 5:13; RSV, "Jacan").

JACHIN (jā′kĭn)

1. The son of Simeon, son of Jacob, who came down to Egypt when Jacob migrated there and became founder of the family of Jachinites (Gen 46:10; Ex 6:15; Num 26:12). Called Jarib (*q.v.*) in I Chr 4:24.

2. Jachin and Boaz (*q.v.*) were the names given to two enormous free-standing bronze columns that stood before the temple of Solomon (I Kgs 7:15–22; II Chr 3:17). Such free-standing twin pillars were a common feature of ancient temples from Assyria throughout the Mediterranean area, as noted in architectural ruins, on clay models, and by representations on coins and seals. Each name may be the first word of a promise of God inscribed on it; e.g., "Yahweh will establish [*yākîn*] thy throne forever," and, "In the strength [*be'āz*] of Yahweh shall the king rejoice" (cf. Ps 21:1; R. B. Y. Scott, JBL, LVIII [1939], 143f.; P. Garber, BA, XIV [1951], 8). The tremendous pillars and their ornamented capitals (chapiter,

q.v.) were about 35 feet high and 18 feet in circumference. The capitals were covered with sculpture in the form of flowering lilies, below which was a band of network with two rows of ornamental pomegranates (I Kgs 7:17–22).

On the basis of recent archaeological studies, Albright suggests that these were gigantic fire altars, like great torches standing before the temple of God, and reminding the people of the pillar(s) of fire and cloud that led them through the wilderness (Ex 13:21f.; Albright, *Archaeology and the Religion of Israel*, pp. 144–148). Yeivin contends that the pommel shape of the capitals prohibited their use as giant lamps, and believes the pillars signified that God was present in His sacred dwelling (S. Yeivin, PEQ, XCI [1959], 6–22). *See* Temple.

3. A priest who dwelt in Jerusalem after the return from Captivity (I Chr 9:10; Neh 11:10).

4. Head of the 21st course of priests appointed by David (I Chr 24:17).

P. C. J.

The pillars Jachin and Boaz stand before this model of Solomon's temple at the Lebanonorama near Beirut. HFV

JACINTH. *See* Jewels.

JACKAL. *See* Animals, II. 23.

JACOB (jā′kŏb). In Heb. the name *ya'ăqōb* means "heel catcher," "trickster," or "supplanter." In S Arabic and Ethiopic the word means "may God protect," from the verb *'aqaba,* "to guard," "watch," or "protect." The root *'āqab* is a general Semitic word which occurs in Arabic personal names, in Akkad. and Aram. inscriptions, as well as Syriac and Palmyrene. The noun meaning "heel" occurs in Heb. (*'āqēb*), Aram., Syriac, Arabic, Ugaritic, and Akkad. Jacob's name was thus an ancient member of the Near Eastern onomastica rather than a uniquely biblical name.

1. The patriarch. The younger twin son of Isaac and Rebekah; later called Israel.

Life in Palestine (Gen 25–27). The birth of Jacob and Esau is recorded in Gen 25:21–28.

Isaac married Rebekah when he was 40 years of age (see Gen 24 for this beautiful picturesque episode). Rebekah, like Sarah (cf. Gen 11:30; 16:1 – 2), was barren. Isaac's prayer for his wife was heard and rewarded. She gave birth to twin boys, who wrestled in the womb as their posterity nations did in real life (*see* Esau for the history of this long and bitter struggle). Esau, the firstborn, was so named because he was hairy. The second was named Jacob because he came forth from the womb grasping his brother's heel. Rebekah's twin sons inherited her chief characteristics: Esau, her open-mindedness; Jacob, her craftiness or guile. Esau grew into a skilled hunter, a man of the field, whom Isaac loved because Esau gave him venison to eat. In contrast, Jacob was a quiet, meditative, settled, and well-integrated man, dwelling in tents, whom Rebekah loved.

God promised Abraham that through his seed Isaac, He would make of him a great nation. This promise was renewed with Isaac. The question was through which seed, Jacob or Esau? This struggle resulted in a domestic conflict and forced Jacob to live under constant tension. Gen 25:23 states that by divine choice Jacob would be the heir of promise; but two interesting events occur to implement the divine purpose.

First, the buying of Esau's birthright (Gen 25:29 – 34). When Esau the hunter came from the field hungry and empty-handed, he desired some of that red stuff (Gen 25:30, lit.), a stew which the shepherd brother Jacob was preparing. In his famished condition Esau bargained away his birthright. Jacob insisted on an oath, considered irretractable (Gen 25:33; cf. Josh 9:19). So by shrewd foresight (as well as taking unfair advantage) Jacob lived up to the reputation of his name and gained the right of precedence which his order of birth did not give. God's intention (Gen 25:23) was working itself out with Jacob's help. However, along with Jacob's good fortune, seeds of hostility were sown that would goad Jacob in years to come (Gen 27:41). The Nuzu tablets discovered SE of Nineveh in 1926 reveal that in the prevailing culture in Mesopotamia in the first half of the 2nd mil. B.C., the birthright could be bought and sold. *See* Firstborn; Nuzu.

Second, the stealing of the covenant blessing (Gen 27:1 – 46). Aged Isaac, fearful of imminent death (137 years of age – but 43 years before his death) instructed Esau to prepare for him his favorite dish, that he might transmit to his firstborn the patriarchal blessing contained in his soul (Gen 27:4). As innocent Esau was out stalking his kill, Jacob cooperated with Rebekah's scheme to wrest the blessing for himself. He executed the deceit as outlined by his mother with boldness, and to his crass lies (Gen 27:19, 24) he added shocking blasphemy (v. 20: "Because the Lord your God granted me success," RSV). The pathos of the occasion is deepened by Isaac's blindness. Torn by suspicion and doubt (Jacob's voice but Esau's

hands, 27:22), the blind father finally conveyed upon Jacob his final, deathbed benediction (Gen 27:27 – 29; cf. 24:1 – 9; 49:1 – 33). On Esau's return and Isaac's awareness of the guile, the blessing could not be recalled nor altered (27:37 – 38). So only ill-fortune remained for Esau (27:39 – 40).

Life in Haran (Gen 28 – 30). When the full import of the plot was uncovered, Jacob was sent away to his relatives in Haran. En route from Beer-sheba Jacob, as a weary, troubled, and sinful fugitive, spent his first night near the ancient Canaanite sanctuary of Luz. In a night vision God revealed Himself to this wanderer as the God of his father. He also renewed the covenant blessing (Gen 12:7; 13:14–17; 26:3–5), promised him the land, appointed him to a universal mission, and assured him of divine guidance and a prosperous life. Jacob responded with a personal vow and renamed the place Bethel (*q.v.*).

Jacob arrived in Aram-naharaim and good fortune came to his rescue again. He met Rachel at the well and it was love at first sight. She in turn brought Jacob to her father's house and introduced him to Laban, Jacob's uncle (Gen 29:10–11, 18, 20). Jacob's love for Rachel issued in permanent employment with Laban. Jacob worked to gain her as wife for seven years. The morning after the marriage ceremony he discovered that instead of soft-voiced Rachel, he had married weak-eyed Leah. The deceitful Laban was equal to Jacob's anger and agreed to give him Rachel after the customary one week's marriage festivities if Jacob would serve him another seven years. Jacob brought his father-in-law great prosperity (Gen 30:30), and shrewd Laban recognized a bargain when he saw one.

Jacob's fortune increased as well as his family. Twelve children were born to Jacob in Mesopotamia. Leah was the mother of Reuben, Simeon, Levi, Judah, Issachar, Zebulun, and a daughter Dinah (Gen 29:31 – 35; 30:17 – 21). From Leah's handmaid Zilpah came Gad and Asher (Gen 30:9 – 13). Rachel's handmaid Bilhah bore Dan and Naphtali (Gen 29:31; 30:1 – 2; cf. 16:2; 25:21; 30:3 – 8). Finally, God opened Rachel's womb and she bore Joseph and later on in Canaan, Benjamin (Gen 30:22 – 24; 35:16 – 18).

Jacob's preparation to return home (Gen 31). Jacob desired to return to Palestine (Gen 30:25). Realizing his prosperity came because of Jacob, Laban urged him to stay (Gen 30:27), and Jacob agreed on one condition (Gen 30:29ff.). But now the Lord instructed Jacob to go back home (Gen 31:3, 11 – 13). Jacob talked with his wives and reminded them that their father Laban had changed his wages "ten times" (Gen 31:4 –7). They assured him that they acquiesced in his plans (vv. 14 – 16).

While Laban was shearing his sheep, Jacob with his wives and children, servants, flocks, herds, and substance departed for his fatherland (Gen 31:17 – 20). They crossed the Euphrates

Jacob Blessing Ephraim and Manasseh. Painting by Benjamin West.
Allen Memorial Art Museum, Oberlin

River and headed toward Gilead. After three days, Laban, hearing of their flight, pursued and overtook them after a seven-day chase in the mountain of Gilead, c. 400 miles from Haran (vv. 21–25). Angrily Laban leveled three charges against Jacob (vv. 26–30): (1) he fled in secret; (2) he kidnapped his daughters; (3) he stole Laban's household gods (teraphim; cf. G. E. Wright, *Biblical Archaeology,* p. 44). Jacob countered with the 20 years of hard service and Laban's attempt to defraud him of wages. After much haranguing, in which each sought to outdo the other in exaggeration of wrongs endured, Laban suggested a truce which was marked by setting up a pillar and a mound of stones and which climaxed in an all-night covenant feast (vv. 31–54). The next morning Laban returned to Haran and Jacob journeyed on southward.

Return to Palestine (Gen 32–33). Twenty years had elapsed since Jacob had deceived Isaac and stolen Esau's blessing. As Jacob drew near to the land of his heart, an angelic band met him (32:1–2), assuring him once again of God's protection as if to welcome and congratulate him on his auspicious return. Fording the brook Jabbok (*q.v.*) to protect his family from Esau, Jacob met "a man" who wrestled with him until daybreak (v. 24). Although wounded in his hip Jacob prevailed and won from his assailant a blessing which changed his name from Jacob ("supplanter") to

Israel ("he persists with God"; *see* Israel). The stranger revealed His true identity both by blessing Jacob and by changing his name—He was the Eternal Himself (cf. Gen 17:5; 35:9–15; Isa 65:15; Hos 2:23; 12:3–4).

Jacob's next hurdle was to appease his wronged brother Esau. Jacob's meeting with Esau is recorded in Gen 33:1–16. Fearful that Esau's anger was still aflame, Jacob had dispatched messengers to spy out Esau's plans, and they reported that Esau was marching with 400 armed men. So Jacob, still the clever one, had sought both to pacify his wronged twin brother and to protect himself and his family from attack (Gen 32:3–8, 13–21; 33:1–3). In addition to this strategy, he had prayed (32:9–12) and petitioned the God of Abraham and Isaac who combines past events (32:9), the present need (32:11), and the promise of the future (32:12). Amid the tangled mess of human actions, Jacob recognized the need of the Lord's hand. He not only won God's favor, but Esau's in spite of his armed men. In a scene of great tenderness, Jacob met Esau, and the breach was healed at least temporarily with magnanimity and affection.

Life in Palestine the second time (Gen 33:17–45:5). Esau went to Seir and there sired a nation (Gen 33:16; cf. the fulfillment of the promise of Gen 25:23; 27:39–40; 36:1–43). Jacob resided in Canaan to assume his inheritance. He was now indeed the patriarch.

After Esau left, Jacob remained E of Jordan and camped near Succoth; then to Shechem where he purchased ground and reconstructed an altar (Gen 33:17 – 20). Under God's order, he went to Bethel and there the Lord renewed the patriarchal promises (35:1 – 15). Jacob and his company drifted southward, and during this journey Jacob's beloved Rachel died in childbirth (during the birth of Benjamin) and was buried on the way to Ephrath (Bethlehem, 35:16 – 20). Jacob joined Esau at Mamre (Hebron) and there laid their father away in the cave of Machpelah, the family sepulchre (35:27 – 29; 49:30 – 31).

Jacob's latter years demonstrated Moses' later warning to Israel: "Be sure your sin will find you out" (Num 32:23). Domestic trials tracked down Jacob in the sunset of his life. First, there was severe conflict between his rash sons Simeon and Levi with the sons of Hamor at Shechem over the matter of Dinah (Gen 34:1 – 31). Then Deborah (Rebekah's nurse), the confidante and counselor of the family, died and the entire family was crushed (35:8). Rachel, the object of Jacob's dearest love, was taken soon afterward (35:16ff.). "Reuben went and lay with Bilhah his father's concubine: and Israel heard it" (35:22). Joseph, his favorite son, was snatched away and gray-headed Jacob was overwhelmed with grief (37:34f.). Last of all the aged patriarch was forced to expatriate himself to Egypt in order to preserve his own life and the life of his family (46:3).

The final years of Jacob. These years in Egypt (Gen 46:6 – 50:13) are intertwined in the Joseph story (Gen 37 – 50). *See*Joseph.

When seven years of famine gripped the land of Canaan, Jacob and his sons went down to Egypt. Along the way, at Beer-sheba he was assured of God's favor (46:1 – 4). Joseph arranged for Jacob and his company to settle in the land of Goshen where he remained until his death. At the age 130 he had an audience with the pharaoh and blessed him (47:7 – 10).

Before he died at the advanced age of 147 (47:28) Jacob bestowed a patriarchal blessing on Joseph's sons, Ephraim and Manasseh (48:8 – 20), and subsequently on his own sons (49:1 – 33). God's promise to Jacob was fulfilled. At his death the Egyptians paid him great homage. His sons, led by Joseph, the prime minister of Egypt, carried his body back to Canaan and buried him at Machpelah with Abraham and Isaac (49:29 – 50:13; cf. 25:9 – 10; 35:28 – 29), fulfilling the desire of the ancients to be buried in their homeland (cf. the Egyptian Sinuhe, ANET, pp. 20ff.). *See* Patriarchal Age.

Jacob is a typical example of God's redeeming grace. In himself he was a coarse, selfish, scheming, and passionate rogue with a capacity for business. But he had time in his heart for God. His nature was sensitive to the touch of the Lord and capable of great development. He dreamed dreams and had visions; angels visited him and he prayed. He coveted the best gifts; he developed fixed religious principles; and he finally became steady in his habits. But Jacob's life was fraught with conflict. The struggle in his soul was a long and fierce one – but grace conquered and Jacob the "overreacher" became Israel the one who "persists with God."

The use of "Jacob" in the Scriptures. The name "Jacob" appears many times in the Bible. "Jacob" occurs as an individual as a marked child of favor (cf. Mal 1:2; Rom 9:10 – 13), an heir of divine promise (cf. Heb 11:9), and a man of blessing (Heb 11:20 – 21). As the third notable patriarch, Jacob is frequently linked with Abraham and Isaac. So the God of the three renowned worthies is El Shaddai (Ex 6:3) and Yahweh (Ex 3:6, 15), faithful to His covenant (Ex 2:24; 32:13; Deut 29:12), compassionate toward Israel (II Kgs 13:23). The Jewish patriarchs dwell with Him (Mk 12:26 – 27), and sit at His table in the kingdom of heaven (Mt 8:11).

As the name-bearer of the nation Israel, Jacob appears frequently in the Scriptures: Israel is the "house of Jacob" (Lk 1:33); its God is the "King of Jacob" (Isa 41:21); and His temple is a habitation of the God of Jacob (Acts 7:46). The figure of Jacob (Israel) is epitomized in the title "servant of Yahweh" (Isa 41:8; 44:1 – 2, 21; 48:20; 49:3), of whom Messiah was the fulfillment (Isa 42:1 – 7; 49:1 – 10; 50:4 – 9; 52:13 – 53:12; Mt 8:17; 12:15 – 21; Mk 10:45; Lk 2:30 – 32; Acts 3:13, 26; 4:27, 30, NASB; 8:30 – 35; I Pet 2:21 – 25).*See* Servant of the Lord.

Bibliography. S. R. Driver, *The Book of Genesis, Westminster Commentaries,* 9th ed., London: Methuen Co., Ltd., 1913, pp. 244 – 401. L. Hicks, "Jacob (Israel)," IDB, II, 782 – 787. William S. Lasor, *Great Personalities of the Old Testament,* New York: Revell, 1959, pp. 31 – 39. A. R. Millard, "Jacob," NBD, pp. 593 – 596. John Muilenberg, "The Birth of Benjamin," JBL, LXXV (1956), 194 – 200. Martin Noth, *The History of Israel,* New York: Harper, 1958, pp. 1 – 7, 53 – 84, 120 – 126. G. E. Wright, *Biblical Archaeology,* Philadelphia: Westminster, 1951, pp. 40 – 68.

2. Joseph's father. The name of the father of Joseph, Mary's husband, according to the genealogy of Christ in Mt 1:15 – 16.

D. W. D.

JACOB'S WELL. The well, mentioned only in Jn 4:5 – 12, where Jesus talked to the Samaritan woman. By unanimous tradition, most probably correct, it is *Bîr Ya'qûb* lying *c.* five-eighths of a mile SW of the Arab village of 'Askar (perhaps NT Sychar, *q. v.*) and over 300 yards SSE of Tell Balatah, the site of OT Shechem. At this spot the road from Jerusalem, 40 miles to the S, forks. The W branch heads toward the Mediterranean and the city of Samaria; the E branch continues N to Tirzah and Beth-shan, which Jesus would have taken to Capernaum. One may look up directly to the W

Jacob's Well

at Mount Gerizim (*q.v.*), where the Samaritans have worshiped for over 2000 years (Jn 4:20).

Evidently the well was dug by Jacob after he purchased a plot of ground near Shechem (Gen 33:18–20) in order to have his own supply of water independent of the city. *Bir Ya'qûb* is seven and a half feet in diameter, its upper part lined with masonry and its lower part cut through layers of limestone. G. Ernest Wright reports that after cleaning out the well in 1935 its depth was *c.* 138 feet, with the water level in summertime standing 75–80 feet below the surface (*Shechem: The Biography of a Biblical City,* New York: McGraw-Hill, 1965, p. 216). It is described both as a well fed by a spring (Gr. *pēgē,* Jn 4:6) and as a cistern (Gr. *phrear,* Jn 4:11–12) because apparently it is also fed by surface water.

The site is now surrounded by an unfinished Greek Orthodox church, built over the crypt of a Crusader church which contains the well. In the 4th cen. A.D. a cruciform church had been erected here with the well in the center of the transept.

See Sychar.

J. R.

JADA (jā'dá). A Jerahmeelite, the son of Onam (I Chr 2:28, 32).

JADAU (jā'dô). A son of Nebo and one of those who was compelled by Ezra to give up his foreign wife (Ezr 10:43). The name appears in the RSV as Jaddai.

JADDUA (jăd'ū-á)

1. One of the chiefs of the people who set their seal to the covenant of Nehemiah to keep the law (Neh 10:21).

2. The son of Jonathan and the last of the high priests named in the OT (Neh 12:11, 22). According to the Elephantine papyri, written in the last decade of the 5th cen. B.C., the high priest in 400 B.C. was Jonathan (Johanan), the

father of Jaddua. Josephus says (*Ant.* xi. 8. 3 – 6) that Jaddua was high priest when Alexander the Great came to Jerusalem in 332 B.C. While this is possible if Jaddua lived to be nearly 100 years old, yet it may be a second priest of the same name.

JADON (jā'dŏn). A Meronothite who worked with Melatiah the Gibeonite and the men of Gibeon and of Mizpah in repairing the wall of Jerusalem during the time of Nehemiah (Neh 3:7).

JAEL (jā'ĕl). The wife of Heber the Kenite in the days of the judges (*see* Heber). The Kenites were Midianites of the family into which Moses had married. Hobab, Moses' brother-in-law, had come to the Promised Land with Israel, and his descendants still lived there.

In the battle between Hazor and the northern tribes, Heber the Kenite was not considered one of his Israelite enemies by Jabin, king of Hazor. Therefore Sisera, Jabin's general, fleeing from his disastrous defeat at the hands of Barak, felt safe in turning aside for rest and refuge at the tent of Heber. Jael, having welcomed and given refreshment to Sisera, stood guard at the door of the tent until the exhausted man fell asleep. Then she took a tent peg and hammer and with a few vigorous strokes killed the sleeping warrior. When the pursuing Israelites arrived, Jael led them to their fallen foe. She was honored, as Deborah had prophesied, as the true heroine of the battle (Jud 4:11 – 5:31).

P. C. J.

JAGUR (jā'gŭr). A town in the SE part of Judah, near the border of Edom (Josh 15:21). The site is unknown; however, it may be the same as Gur-Baal, modern Tell Ghurr, eight miles E of Beer-sheba.

JAH (jä). An abbreviated form of the sacred name Yahweh. It is found in poetry, as in Ps 68:4; 118:4, ASV marg., and in various other places where it is rendered Lord in the KJV. *See* God, Names of; Lord.

JAHATH (jā'hăth)

1. The son of Reaiah of the tribe of Judah and father of Ahumai and Lahad (I Chr 4:2).

2. The son of Libni of the Levitical family of Gershom (I Chr 6:20, 43). In the genealogy of I Chr 23:9–11, Jahath is said to be the son of Shimei, Gershom's second son, but the passage is obscure.

3. The son of Shelomoth of the Levitical family of Izhar, appointed by David for service in the temple (I Chr 24:22).

4. A Levite of the family of Merari who was appointed one of the overseers of repairs to the temple in the reform of Josiah (II Chr 34:12).

JAHAZ (jā'hăz). This name occurs also in several other forms: Jahaza (Josh 13:18); Jahazah

(Josh 21:36; Jer 48:21); Jahzah (I Chr 6:78).

Jahaz was a town in the plains of Moab, where Sihon, the Amorite king, was defeated by Israel (Num 21:23; Deut 2:32; Jud 11:20). It fell in Reuben's portion (Josh 13:18) and was assigned to the Merarite Levites (Josh 21:34, 36). The area in which Jahaz was located was later lost to Israel, but Omri reconquered the land as far as Jahaz. The Moabite Stone (lines 18–20) indicates that the town was finally taken by Mesha, king of Moab, and added to his domains. It was held by Moab in the time of Isaiah and Jeremiah (Isa 15:4; Jer 48:21, 34). Jahaz was probably N of the Arnon and not far S of Heshbron, but its location is uncertain.

JAHAZA. *See* Jahaz.

JAHAZIAH (jā′à-zī′à). A son of Tikvah and one of the four men mentioned in connection with the controversy over "strange" (foreign) wives (Ezr 10:15). The KJV regards Jahaziah and his companions as supporters of Ezra. The RSV regards the four men as opposed to Ezra's action. The Heb. (lit., "stood against this") would seem to support the RSV rendering.

JAHAZIEL (jà-hā′zĭ-ĕl)

1. One of the Benjamites, mighty warriors, who deserted Saul to join David at Ziklag (I Chr 12:4).

2. A priest appointed by David to blow the trumpet before the ark after it was brought to Jerusalem (I Chr 16:6).

3. The third named of the sons of Hebron the Levite, appointed by David to serve in the temple (I Chr 23:19; 24:23).

4. The son of Zechariah of the Levitical family of Asaph. The Spirit of the Lord inspired him to prophesy a great victory by God on behalf of Jehoshaphat (II Chr 20:14–17).

5. The father of Shechaniah, a chieftain who returned with Ezra with 300 men (Ezr 8:5).

JAHDAI (jä′dī). One of Caleb's wives, or (more likely) a descendant of Caleb whose six sons are listed in I Chr 2:47.

JAHDIEL (jä′dĭ-ĕl). A leading man in the half tribe of Manasseh E of Jordan (I Chr 5:24). He is spoken of as one of the "mighty men of valor" and the head of a household.

JAHDO (jä′dō). A member of the tribe of Gad and a son of Buz (I Chr 5:14).

JAHLEEL (jä′lē-ĕl), **JAHLEELITES** (jä′lē-ĕ-līts). The third son of Zebulun and the founder of a tribal family called the Jahleelites (Gen 46:14; Num 26:26).

JAHMAI (jä′mī). Listed as grandson of Issachar and son of Tola (I Chr 7:2).

JAHZAH. *See* Jahaz.

JAHZEEL (jä′zē-ĕl), **JAHZEELITES** (jä′zē-ĕ-līts). The firstborn son of Naphtali and founder of a tribal family (Gen 46:24; Num 26:48). In I Chr 7:13 he is called Jahziel.

JAHZERAH (jä′zĕ-rà). A priest of the family of Immer (I Chr 9:12), and an ancestor of a priest among the returned exiles. The name parallels Ahasai in Neh 11:13.

JAHZIEL. *See* Jahzeel.

Traditional site of the prison in which Paul was kept at Philippi. HFV

JAILOR. A guard of a prison or jail (Gr. *desmophylax*). It is used once in the NT in Acts 16:23 of the keeper of the jail in Philippi. The jailer was impressed by the songs of Paul and Silas as they ached from their beating in the stocks, and by their refusal to escape after an earthquake opened their stocks. Moreover, he was terror stricken at the obvious hand of God in the events of the night. The combined effect of apostolic testimony and divine intervention brought about his conversion and baptism. His baptism involved his whole household and occurred sometime after midnight (Acts 16:25–34).

JAIR (jā′ĭr)

1. The son of Segub who was of the tribe of Manasseh on his mother's side and of Judah on his father's. During the conquest of Palestine Gilead was given to Manasseh, and Jair won for himself a number of villages in the plateau of Argob which came to be known as Havvoth-jair, "villages of Jair" (Num 32:41; Deut 3:14; I Kgs 4:13; I Chr 2:22).

2. The Gileadite who was the eighth judge of Israel and a descendant of 1 above. Although he judged Israel 22 years, nothing is known of him except that he had 30 sons and the 30 cities of Havvoth-jair (Jud 10:3–5).

3. The son of Shimei and father of Mordecai, the guardian of Esther (Est 2:5).

4. The father of Elhanan who slew Lahmi, the brother of Goliath (I Chr 20:5).

JAIRITE. *See* Ira.

JAIRUS (jā-ī′rŭs). The name of a ruler of a synagogue (Mk 5:22; Lk 8:41), probably at Capernaum. His daughter was raised from the dead by Jesus.

JAKAN. *See* Jaakan.

JAKEH (jā′kĕ). The father of Agur, the author of the proverbs recorded in Prov 30:1 (see v. 1).

JAKIM (jā′kĭm)
1. A son of Shimhi, a Benjamite (I Chr 8:19).
2. A priest and a descendant of Aaron. His family was made the 12th of the 24 courses into which David divided the priests (I Chr 24:12).

JALON (jā′lŏn). A descendant of Caleb the spy and son of Ezra (I Chr 4:17). This Ezra is called Ezrah in the RSV.

JAMBRES (jăm′brēz). *See* Jannes and Jambres.

JAMES (jāmz). At least four persons mentioned in the NT bore this name (Gr. *Iakōbos,* from Heb. *ya'ăqōb,* Jacob, *q.v.*). Two were among the 12 apostles, one was a half-brother of Jesus, and one was the father of Judas, one of the Twelve. Probably James the leader of the church in Jerusalem and James the author of the epistle were one and the same and one of the above. James the Less (Mk 15:40) may or may not have been one of the above.
1. One of the sons of Zebedee (Mt 4:21; Mk 1:19; Lk 5:10) and Salome (cf. Mt 20:20; Mk 15:40; 16:1) and the elder brother of John the apostle (James is nearly always named first, e.g., Mk 5:37). *See* John the Apostle. He was a fisherman with his brother John, netting fish in the Sea of Galilee and using the boat of their father Zebedee (Mt 4:18 – 22; Mk 1:16 – 20). Since Zebedee had hired servants (Mk 1:20) and John was acquainted with the high priest in Jerusalem so that he could enter his house unchallenged on the night of Jesus' betrayal (Jn 18:16), many have concluded that Zebedee and his sons were prosperous with some degree of social standing. James became one of the "inner three," the specially favored disciples of Christ, apparently because they understood more fully the person and work of Jesus during His ministry (Mk 5:37; 9:2; 14:33; cf. 13:3; also Peter, James and John are named first among the Twelve, Mk 3:16 – 19). The epithet Boanerges (*q.v.*), meaning "sons of thunder" (Mk 3:17), evidently characterized James and John as impetuous and quick to take offense (Lk 9:54 – 55) and to offend the other disciples by wanting the chief positions in Jesus' kingdom (Mk 10:35 – 41). James was the first of the apostles to suffer martyrdom, executed at the order of Herod Agrippa 1 *c.* A.D. 44 (Acts 12:1 – 2). James thus figuratively drank the cup

Traditional tomb of St. James (center foreground) in the Kidron Valley, Jerusalem

of suffering that he and John had rashly declared they were able to drink (Mk 10:38 – 39).
2. The son of Alphaeus, one of the Twelve (Mt 10:3; Mk 3:18; Lk 6:15; Acts 1:13). Nothing else certain is known of him. Levi (Matthew) was also the son of an Alphaeus (Mk 2:14), so that James and Matthew may have been brothers.
3. The author of the epistle of James identifies himself only as "James, a servant of God and of the Lord Jesus Christ" (Jas 1:1). He could not have been the son of Zebedee and brother of John (Mt 4:21; 10:2) because that James was martyred before the epistle was written (Acts 12:2). This leaves the James who presided over the Jerusalem church as the undoubted author (Acts 15:13).

The fact that he is called "James the Lord's brother" (Gal 1:19) makes untenable the view that he was James the son of Alphaeus (Mt 10:3). Ps 69:8 makes it clear that Jesus' mother had other children, one of whom was named James (Mt 13:55; Mk 6:3).

Biographical items regarding James abound in the NT, although there are none in the epistle itself. It is assumed from I Cor 9:5 that he was a married man. He was not one of the Twelve (Mt 10:2 – 4). Not at first a believer (Jn 7:5), he later was probably included as one of Jesus' brothers with those who awaited Pentecost in the upper room (Acts 1:13 – 14). (This latter passage distinguishes between the brother of Jesus and the two apostles, James and James the son of Alphaeus.) The risen Saviour appeared to him personally after first appearing to the Twelve (I Cor 15:5, 7).

In his capacity as leader of the Jerusalem council of apostles and elders, James announced his authoritative judgment when the discussion had ended (Acts 15:13, 19). There is an undesigned coincidence in the fact that when James' decision was sent by letter from the council, he used a Gr. word rendered "greeting" in the salutation (Acts 15:23) which appears in the address of only one NT epistle, in the salutation of James 1:1.

Peter, after being miraculously released from prison, instructed the household of John Mark to report the event to James (Acts 12:17). Paul recognized "James, Cephas, and John" as pillars of the church at Jerusalem (Gal 2:9). Obviously James was the leader, for representatives who came from that church to Antioch were said to have come from James (Gal 2:12). In Acts 21:18-19 Paul reported to James the things God had wrought among the Gentiles during his third missionary journey.

Tradition describes James as very zealous for the law, combining OT righteousness with evangelical faith. He is said to have abstained from strong drink and to have refrained from cutting his hair, like a Nazarite (*q.v.*). A man of great virtue, he was called "James the Just." Because he spent so much time in prayer, he was described as having knees "hard skinned like a camel's." His epistle reveals that he spoke with an air of patriarchal authority, for its pages glow with stern and severe utterances and the fervency of his spirit. *See* James, Epistle of.

The death of James is mentioned by Josephus (*Ant.* xx. 9.1), and described by Hegesippus (Eusebius II.23), a Jewish Christian who wrote in the middle of the 2nd cen. Some time before the destruction of Jerusalem in A.D. 70, the Pharisees had him thrown down from the temple, stoned, and then beaten with a club for having faithfully witnessed to his Saviour. He is said to have died praying, "Father forgive them, for they know not what they do."

4. The father (not the "brother" as in KJV) of Judas (not Iscariot), one of the Twelve (Lk 6:16, NASB).

5. James the Less (Mk 15:40), less in stature or in age, is said to be the son of a certain Mary (*see* Mary 3) and brother of Joses or Joseph (also Mt 27:56; Lk 24:10). James the brother of our Lord also had a brother named Joses or Joseph (Mk 6:3; Mt 13:55), so that this James may be the same as 3. But it would seem strange for Mary the mother of Jesus to be identified only as the mother of James and Joses when standing near the cross, especially when Christ spoke directly to her and asked the beloved disciple to care for her (Jn 19:25-27). Some have identified James the Less with James the son of Alphaeus 2; however, there is no proof for this.

S. M. C.

JAMES, EPISTLE OF. This oldest of NT epistles is first among the General Epistles, as Eusebius termed James and Jude in the 4th cen., possibly because of their general content or readership.

Author. The writer of this epistle is generally considered to be James the brother of our Lord (*see* James 3). Since James is Jacob in the original, this may be called the Epistle of Jacob to the Twelve Tribes (1:1).

Theme. The book treats of faith demonstrated, tested, and perfected by works. This has been called the epistle of holy living, of practical Christianity, of Christian ethics, Christianity in coveralls.

Style. The style is terse, vivid, abounding in aphorisms, antithetic. Since many thoughts are grouped together in short proverbial expressions, this epistle is regarded as the Proverbs of the NT. James' imagery is drawn from nature, in contrast with Paul's which is drawn from the activities of men. Some of the terms used aptly describe the country where the author lived: near the sea (1:6), with salt springs (3:12); a place of olives, vines, and figs (3:12), burning sun and drought (1:11); early and latter rain (5:7); a place of synagogues (2:2). There is an unusual double use of words (cf. patience, perfect, 1:3-4), and a contrasting of positive and negative statements (cf. "perfect and entire, wanting nothing," 1:4).

Characteristics. James begins and ends abruptly, lacks the autobiographical data of Paul, contains more references to nature than all Paul's epistles, and more parallels to Christ's discourses than any other part of the NT. For striking similarities to the Sermon on the Mount, cf. Mt 5:34-37; 6:19; 7:1 with Jas 5:12; 5:2; 4:11-12. James is closer in style to Peter than to Paul. For similarities to I Peter cf. I Pet 1:7; 1:24; 1:23; 2:11; 5:5-6 with Jas 1:3, 11, 18; 4:1; 4:6-10.

James contains no apostolic benediction, perhaps because it sternly condemns non-Christians among its readers (4:4; 5:1-6). Although it has been criticized because it lacks such NT words as gospel, redemption, incarnation, resurrection, ascension, it does speak of the Lord Jesus Christ (1:1; 2:1), the new birth (1:18), faith (2:14-26), and the return of the Lord (5:7-8). Clearly addressed to the Jews (1:1; 2:1, 21) and reminding the reader of Matthew, the "Jewish" Gospel, James is sometimes called "Jewish," but it reveals a noticeable absence of the Jewish elements which were done away in Christ: sacrifices, circumcision, priesthood, feast days, the sabbath. In contrast, it speaks of teachers and elders in the church (3:1; 5:14).

Outline. An outline is difficult to construct because of an apparent lack of logical order. Nevertheless, a structure is clearly evident.

1. Believers and Outward Circumstances, 1:1-12
2. Believers and Inward Desire, 1:13-16
3. Believers and the Word of God, 1:17-27
4. Believers and Their Neighbors, 2:1-13
5. The Believer's Faith and Works, 2:14-26
6. The Believer's Tongue, 3:1-12
7. Heavenly Wisdom, 3:13-18
8. World, Flesh, and Devil, 4:1-7
9. God and His Law, 4:8-17
10. The Last Days, 5:1-9
11. Patience and Prayer in Trials, 5:10-20

James begins and ends with a discussion of testings, patience, the prayer of faith. Certain words occur at approximately the same distance from each end of the epistle (cf. Scripture, rich, adultery, tongue). The heart of James is the remarkable statement in 3:2 that a perfect man is one who can control his tongue. Just as an old family doctor diagnoses a disease by having his patient stick out his tongue, James diagnoses spiritual disease by examining the tongue and its manifestations. This is the most prominent theme of the epistle.

Prominent teachings. Prayer: for wisdom (1:5 – 7), unanswered (4:2 – 3), of faith (5:13 – 18). The Word: begotten by (1:18), receiving (1:21), obeying (1:25). Three tests of religion: self-control, love, purity (1:26 – 27). Trials bring perfection now (1:1 – 4), the crown of life later (1:12). How to make the devil flee, and bring God near (4:7 – 8). A definition of sin (4:17).

The charge that Jas 2:24 contradicts Rom 3:28 falls before the fact that James refers to justification before men (2:18), while Paul refers to justification before God (Rom 4:2). James deprecates only that faith which a man may *say* he has, while lacking works to demonstrate its genuineness (2:20).

Bibliography. F. J. A. Hort, *The Epistle of St. James 1:1 – 4:7,* London: Macmillan, 1909. Richard J. Knowling, *The Epistle of St. James,* WC, 2nd ed., London: Methuen, 1910. Joseph B. Mayor, *The Epistle of St. James,* 3rd ed., London: Macmillan, 1913. C. L. Mitton, *The Epistle of James,* Grand Rapids: Eerdmans, 1966. James H. Ropes, *The Epistle of James,* ICC, New York: Scribner's, 1916. Alexander Ross, *The Epistles of James and John,* NIC, Grand Rapids: Eerdmans, 1954. M. H. Shepherd, Jr., "The Epistle of James and the Gospel of Matthew," JBL, LXXV (1956), 40 – 51. R. V. G. Tasker, *The General Epistle of James,* TNTC, Grand Rapids: Eerdmans, 1956.

S. M. C.

JAMIN (jā'mĭn)

1. A son of Simeon, the second son of Jacob (Gen 46:10; Ex 6:15; I Chr 4:24). He was the founder of a tribal family called the Jaminites (Num 26:12).

2. A member of the tribe of Judah and of the family of Jerahmeel (I Chr 2:27).

3. One of the Levites who, under the supervision of Ezra, read the law to the people and helped them to understand it (Neh 8:7).

JAMLECH (jăm'lĕk). A descendant of Simeon and a prince among his people (I Chr 4:34, 38).

JANGLING. The word is used in I Tim 1:6 in the expression "vain jangling" (cf. Tit 1:10). The RSV has "vain discussion." A good translation of the word would be "chatter." Evidently it means proud, self-conceited talking against what God has revealed and against God Himself.

JANNA (jăn'à). An ancestor of Jesus (Lk 3:24). Spelled Jannai in RSV and NASB.

JANNES AND JAMBRES (jăn'ēz, jăm'brēz). These are given by Paul as the names of the two Egyptian magicians who withstood Moses (II Tim 3:8). The reference is to the incidents described in Ex 7:11 – 12, 22; 8:7, 18 – 19; 9:11, where, however, the names of the magicians are not given nor their number. These two names appear in various forms in the Talmud, Targums, and rabbinic writings. Since in II Timothy and in the literature of the Qumran community they are referred to as familiarly known, it would seem that some Jewish apocryphon concerned with their story was in circulation in the 1st cen. B.C. This, or a Christian version of it, was known in the early Christian centuries. Certain references in Origen and the Decree of Gelasius point to the existence of a non-canonical writing describing and condemning their activities. Christian tradition is largely dependent on II Timothy, and has used them as figures symbolic of Satanic arts and opposition to truth.

J. A. R.

JANOAH (jà-nō'à). Variant of Janohah (*q.v.*).

A town in the northern part of Naphtali near Kedesh. It was captured by Tiglath-pileser III of Assyria in the days of Pekah, king of Israel (II Kgs 15:29). The site is uncertain.

JANOHAH (jà-nō'hà). A border town in Ephraim (Josh 16:6 – 7). It is to be identified with Khirbet Yanun, about seven miles SE of Shechem.

JANUM (jā'nŭm). A town in the hill country district of Hebron, near Beth-tappuah (Josh 15:53). It is possibly to be identified with modern Beni Na'im.

JAPHETH (jā'fĕth). The third son of Noah (Gen 10:1), father of some 14 nations forming the Indo-Germanic family, originally inhabiting the Caucasus, thence spreading E and W. His descendants erected the civilizations of the Medes and Persians, produced the Ionians of western Asia Minor, Cappadocians (including the Hittites), Cimmerians, Scythians, and the island kingdoms of the Aegean. At the time of the Flood he was married but had no children.

When his father Noah became drunken, Japheth acted to protect him. For this he was blessed by his father, under the figure of "dwelling in the tents of Shem," i.e., to find protection and deliverance (Gen 9:27). The blessing of Noah included the following points: the gospel, revealed and developed in the Jewish world, was written in Gr. and preached to the Gentiles by Paul, the Semite. The gospel went first to Asia Minor and then to Macedonia (cf. Acts 16:9), Greece, and finally Rome, and thence over all the western world, bringing myriads of Japhetic peoples into the "tents of

Shem." As was the curse of Ham, so the blessing of Japheth was essentially religious.

H. G. S.

JAPHIA (jȧ-fī'ȧ)

1. The Amorite king of Lachish who joined with four other kings to oppose Joshua. They were completely routed at the battle of Gibeon and slain after they tried to hide in the cave of Makkedah (Josh 10).

2. A town on the SE border of the territory of Zebulun. It has been located as modern Yafa, a mile and a half SW of Nazareth (Josh 19:12).

3. One of the sons of David born to him in Jerusalem; his mother's name is not given (II Sam 5:15; I Chr 3:7; 14:6).

JAPHLET (jăf'lĕt). A member of the tribe of Asher and of the family of Heber (I Chr 7:32–33).

JAPHLETI (jăf'lē-tī). The descendants of a certain Japhlet, apparently not the same as the Asherite of that name. The area of the Japhleti is mentioned in stating the boundaries of the children of Joseph. The Japhletites lived in an area E of Gezer (Josh 16:3).

JAPHO (jā'fō). The KJV for Joppa in Josh 19:46. Belonging to the Philistines, it was located on the coast of the Mediterranean Sea, and bordered on the territory of the Danites. *See* Joppa.

JARAH (jār'ȧ). A descendant of King Saul through Jonathan (I Chr 9:42). Instead of this name, I Chr 8:36 has Jehoadah (*q.v.*).

JAREB (jār'ĭb). The name or epithet of an Assyrian king who received tribute from Israel (Hos 5:13; 10:6). It is not safe to be dogmatic about the text and meaning. But if we adhere to the current text, we must regard Jareb as a nickname coined by Hosea to indicate the love of conflict which characterized the Assyrian king. Thus "King Jareb" is equivalent to "King Warrior" or "King Striver." The RSV rendering is "great king." Linguistic and present historical evidence is against the idea that Jareb is the proper name of an Assyrian monarch.

JARED (jār'ĭd). An antediluvian patriarch of the line of Seth. He was the son of Mahalaleel and the father of Enoch (Gen 5:15–20; Lk 3:37). In I Chr 1:2 his name appears as Jered.

JARESIAH (jăr'ē-sī'ȧ). A son of Jeroham and a Benjamite chief who dwelt in Jerusalem (I Chr 8:27). The name is spelled Jaareshiah in the RSV.

JARHA (jär'hȧ). An Egyptian slave to whom his master Sheshan of Judah, not having a living son, gave his daughter as a wife (I Chr 2:34–35; cf. v. 31). Sheshan may first have legally adopted Jarha in light of customs revealed in tablets from Nuzu (*q.v.*).

JARIB (jār'ĭb)

1. A son of Simeon and the founder of a tribal family (I Chr 4:24). He is called Jachin (*q.v.*) in Gen 46:10; Ex 6:15; Num 26:12.

2. One of the leading men who helped Ezra in securing temple servants before the return to Palestine (Ezr 8:16).

3. A priest who had married a foreign wife and who was compelled by Ezra to give her up (Ezr 10:18).

JARMUTH (jär'mŭth)

1. A city of the Canaanites in the Shephelah whose king was defeated, captured, and slain by Joshua (Josh 10:3, 5, 23; 12:11). After its capture it was assigned to Judah (Josh 15:35) and was inhabited after the captivity (Neh 11:29). It is identified with modern Khirbet Yarmuk, about eight miles N of Beit Jibrin and about 18 miles SW of Jerusalem.

2. A town in Issachar allotted to the Gershonite Levites (Josh 21:29). It corresponds to Ramoth (I Chr 6:73) and Remeth (Josh 19:21). The site is unknown.

JAROAH (jȧ-rō'ȧ). A descendant of Gad through Buz (I Chr 5:14).

JASHAR, BOOK OF (jā'shȧr), KJV, Jasher. The Book of Jashar (lit., "Book of the Righteous One") belongs to an ancient collection of national songs, now lost, from which the biblical writers draw some of their material (*see also* Wars of the Lord, Book of). There are two acknowledged quotes from Jashar in the Bible: Josh 10:12–13 (the event of the sun and moon standing still at Gibeon) and II Sam 1:17–27 (David's lament over Saul). A third conjectured extract appears in I Kgs 8:12–13. Other passages may be Ex 15:1 ff.; Num 21:17 f.; Num 21:27–30. The material in this book, if the dating is correct, is quite ancient. As a collection, however, it probably dates to the period 1000–800 B.C. Another view relates the Book of Jashar to the E Mediterranean Heroic Age (15th–10th cen. B.C.), its songs being used as a part of military training. II Sam 1:18 should then read, "He instructed them to train the Judeans in bowmanship, the training-poem for which is written in the Book of Jashar" (R. K. Harrison, IOT, Grand Rapids: Eerdmans, 1969, p. 670).

R. A. M.

JASHEN (jā'shĕn). The father of one of David's "mighty men" (II Sam 23:32). In the parallel list in I Chr 11:34 he appears as Hashem the Gizonite. *See* Hashem.

JASHOBEAM (jả-shǒ'bē-ảm)

1. The son of Zabdiel the Hachmonite, chief of the 30 mighty men of David. He was renowned as a great warrior who had fought with his spear against 300 at one time and had slain them (I Chr 11:11). He may also have been one of the three nameless heroes who broke through the enemy lines at Bethlehem in order to bring David a drink of water from the city well (I Chr 11:15 – 19). When as king David organized his army, Jashobeam was chief of the army unit of 24,000 men on duty for the first month (I Chr 27:2 – 3).

The Heb. of the parallel text in II Sam 23:8 is very obscure but it seems to refer to the same man. The RSV translates it "Josheb-basshebeth a Tahchemonite" who slew "eight hundred." Scribal errors in transmission have confused the text. Some MSS of the LXX at I Chr 11:11 give his name as Ishbaal, which possibly was the original form. See also Hachmoni; Josheb-Basshebeth.

2. A warrior who joined David at Ziklag; from the Levitical family of Korah (I Chr 12:6), residing in Benjamite territory (v. 2). Perhaps he is the same as 1 above.

P. C. J.

JASHUB (jā'shǔb)

1. One of the four sons of Issachar and the founder of a tribal family called Jashubites (Num 26:24; I Chr 7:1). He is called Job in Gen 46:13.

2. A son of Bani, who, after his return from Exile, was persuaded by Ezra to divorce his foreign wife (Ezr 10:29).

3. In Isa 7:3 it is part of the name Shear-jashub.

JASHUBI-LEHEM (jả-shoō'bī-lē 'hěm). A member of the family of Shelah and of the tribe of Judah (I Chr 4:22). The RSV rendering is "returned to Lehem."

JASIEL. See Jaasiel.

JASON (jā'sǒn). A resident of Thessalonica who entertained Paul and Silas. As a consequence the citizens mobbed his house and cast him in prison when they did not find his guests. Jason was released on security (Acts 17:5 –9).

The Jason who sent greetings in Rom 16:21 was a kinsman or fellow countryman of Paul, i.e., a Jew. If the same individual as in Acts 17:5 –9, Jason had by then moved to Corinth.

JASPER. See Jewels.

JATHNIEL (jăth'nǐ-ĕl). The fourth son of Meshelemiah of the house of Korah (I Chr 26:2). He was a gatekeeper at the temple.

JATTIR (jăt'ẽr). A Levitical city in the southern mountains of Judah (Josh 15:48; 21:14;

I Chr 6:57). It was one of the cities which shared in David's spoil from Ziklag (I Sam 30:27). The site is identified as Khirbet 'Attir, about 13 miles SSW of Hebron.

JAVAN (jā'vản; Heb. *yāwān*). This name refers to one of Japheth's descendants (Gen 10:2; I Chr 1:5) from whom "the coastland peoples spread" (Gen 10:5, RSV) NW from Upper Mesopotamia and Syria (*see* Nations). Heb. *yāwān* appears as *yamānu* in the cuneiform inscriptions of Sargon II of Assyria and of Darius I of Persia, and is doubtless related to the *Iaonēs* (Ionians) of Homer's *Iliad* (xiii.685). The Ionians are referred to in Egyptian records from the time of Rameses II (*c.* 1300 B.C.). The connection of Javan (approximately Greece) with slave trade (cf. Ezk 27:13; Joel 3:6) is perhaps illustrated by a S Arabic inscription which notes *Ywnm* as one of the countries from which female temple attendants were secured (cf. ANET², p. 508). Javan (KJV, Grecia) was one of the four great empires of Daniel (Dan 8:21; 10:20; 11:2) and would one day receive a declaration of God's glory (Isa 66:19; cf. also Zech 9:13, KJV, Greece).

In Ezk 27:19, LXX reads *yyn* ("wine") for *ywn* ("Greece"; cf. v. 18 and RSV in *loc. cit.*).

R. Y.

JAVELIN. See Armor.

JAW. Three Heb. words are used in connection with the English word "jaw":(1) *lᵉḥî*, meaning "cheek" or "cheekbone" (Jud 15:15– 17, 19; Job 41:2; Isa 30:28; Ezk 29:4; 38:4; Hos 11:4); (2) *malqôaḥ*, meaning "jaw" (Ps 22:15); (3) *mᵉtallᵉ'ôt*, meaning "jaw teeth" (Job 29:17; Prov 30:14).

Jaw is used figuratively: (1) of the power of the wicked with reference to divine constraint and discipline (Job 29:17; Prov 30:14;, Isa 30:28; Ezk 29:4; 38:4); (2) of human labor and trials eased by divine gentleness (Hos 11:4).

JAZER. See Jaazer.

JAZIZ (jā'zĭz). A Hagerite who was a royal steward and in charge of David's flocks (I Chr 27:31).

JEALOUSY. In the OT the Heb. word *qin'â* has the basic idea of deep emotional ardor. It may be the ardor (1) of jealousy (Num 5:14; Song 8:6), (2) of zeal (Num 25:11; Isa 42:13; 63:15), or (3) of anger (Ezk 35:11; 36:6). God's jealousy is that of a lover who demands the exclusive attention, worship and faithfulness of His people (Ex 34:14; Num 25:11; Deut 32:16, 21; Joel 2:18; Zech 1:14; 8:2).

In the NT the basic Gr. word is *zēlos* which may be used in the good sense of zeal (II Cor 7:11; 9:2; 11:2) or a bad sense of jealousy (RSV, Rom 13:13; I Cor 3:3). A synonym *phthonos* is always employed in the evil sense of envy (Mt 27:18; Phil 1:15). See Envy; Zeal.

JEALOUSY, IMAGE OF. An image mentioned in Ezk 8:3, 5. The reference may be to a "figured slab," containing cultic and mythological scenes of the type found in northern Syria, Asia Minor, and northern Mesopotamia. On the other hand, the reference could be to Tammuz (v. 14). Jealousy was not the name of the idol, but it was probably called "image of jealousy" because in a special way this particular image seems to have been drawing the people from the worship of God and therefore provoking Him to jealousy.

JEALOUSY OFFERING. The basis for this offering is to be found in Num 5:11–31. If a man had reason to suspect his wife of unfaithfulness or if a "spirit of jealousy" came upon him, a provision was made for a trial by ordeal. The man was to bring his wife to the priest along with a prescribed offering consisting of a tenth part of an ephah of barley. No oil or frankincense was to be placed upon it, thus symbolizing that the occasion was not a happy one. The object of the offering was to draw God's attention to the alleged crime so that He might render a right decision.

The woman, with hair down and the offering in her hand, was "brought before the Lord," whereupon she took an oath calling for punishment if guilty. She drank the "water of bitterness" consisting of water from an earthen vessel to which had been added dust from the temple floor and ashes from a part of the barley which had been burned. The words of the curse were written down and washed off into the water. The woman then drank the water of bitterness. If no ill effect came upon her, she was judged to be guiltless. No penalty was prescribed for a man who falsely accused his wife.

R. O. C.

JEALOUSY, WATERS OF. See Jealousy Offering.

JEARIM (jē'a-rǐm). A mountain on the northern border of Judah, and identified with Chesalon (Josh 15:10) near Kirjath-jearim. It is modern Kesla.

JEATERAI (jē-ăt'ĕ-rī). A descendant of Gershon, son of Levi (I Chr 6:21). In v. 41 he is called Ethni.

JEBERECHIAH (jē-bĕr'ĕ-kī'à). The father of Zechariah, a trusted friend of Isaiah, who lived in the time of King Ahaz (Isa 8:2).

JEBUS (jē'bŭs), **JEBUSITES** (jĕb'yŭ-sīts). Jebus refers in the OT to a name for pre-Davidic Jerusalem (Josh 15:8; 18:28; Jud 19:10; I Chr 11:4), derived from the clan name of its inhabitants who occupied the site during most of the 2nd mil. B.C. (although "Jebusite" is used also of their descendants in later times; cf. I Kgs 9:20–21; II Chr 8:7–8; Ezr 9:1). The inhabitants of Jebus were classified as

Canaanites (Gen 10:15–16; I Chr 1:13–14), but only in a geographical sense (contrast Jos *Ant.* vii.3.1), for they are elsewhere carefully distinguished from ethnic Canaanites (e.g., Gen 15:21; Ex 3:8, 17). Its ruler Adonizedek is listed as one of the five Amorite kings in league against Joshua (Josh 10:5). Melchizedek in Gen 14:18 was also an Amorite name (*Malki-ṣaduqa*). The only purely Jebusite name or title in the OT is the non-Semitic Araunah (Ornan; cf. II Sam 24:16, 18; I Chr 21:15, 18, 28; II Chr 3:1). Scholars believe Araunah is a Hurrian or Hittite title meaning "lord" or "noble." The prince of Jerusalem mentioned in the Amarna letters (*c.* 1375 B.C.) likewise had a non-Semitic Hittite name ('Abdu-Heba, ANET, pp. 487ff.). These details concur with God's statement to Jerusalem that her aboriginal population had consisted of Amorites and Hittites (Ezk 16:3, 45).

Jebus was located in the hill country (Josh 11:3) between the Kidron and Tyropoeon valleys on a long narrow spur (cf. Josh 15:8; 18:16) that extends S from the later temple area and is naturally fortified by steep descents on all sides but the N. Situated on the border between Judah and Benjamin, Jebus defended itself successfully against both tribes during the conquest period and thereafter (Josh 15:63; Jud 1:21). In spite of its vaunted strength, however, it finally succumbed to David (II Sam 5:6–9; I Chr 11:4–8) and became the capital city of his kingdom. David was lenient with the Jebusites, but Solomon subjected them to bond service (I Kgs 9:20–22). They seem ultimately to have been absorbed into the Israelite population.

R. Y. and J. R.

JECAMIAH (jĕk'à-mī'à). The fifth son of King Jeconiah, a descendant of Solomon (I Chr 3:10–18). See Jekamiah.

JECHOLIAH (jĕk-ŏ-lī'à). Wife of King Amaziah and mother of Azariah (Uzziah), king of Judah (II Kgs 15:1–2). In II Chr 26:3 her name is given as Jecoliah.

JECHONIAS (jĕk'ŏ-nī'às). Jechonias is the Gr. form of Jeconiah (*q.v.*). It is found in Mt 1:11–12.

JECOLIAH. See Jecholiah.

JECONIAH (jĕk'ŏ-nī'à). An altered form of Jehoiachin (*q.v.*). The name is also contracted to Coniah. Jeconiah is found in I Chr 3:16–17; Est 2:6; Jer 24:1; 27:20; 28:4; 29:2.

JEDAIAH (jē-dā'yà).
1. The son of Shimri and father of Allon, he is listed in the genealogy of the Simeonites who settled in the valley of Gedor in Hezekiah's time (I Chr 4:37).
2. The son of Harumaph; one of those who labored with Nehemiah in rebuilding the wall of Jerusalem (Neh 3:10).

3. A priest in the time of David, the head of the second of the 24 priestly courses (I Chr 24:7).

4. The name of a priest who returned from Exile with Zerubbabel and whose descendants are mentioned down to the time of Joiakim. It is difficult to tell whether this is one or several priests with the same name (I Chr 9:10; Ezr 2:36; Neh 7:39; 11:10; 12:6, 19).

5. Another priest after the Exile. He appears in the same list as 4, but as a distinct person (Neh 12:7, 21).

6. One of the exiles taken by Zechariah as witness to the symbolic crowning of Joshua. He may be the same as 4 or 5 (Zech 6:10 – 14).

P. C. J.

JEDIAEL (jē-dī'ĕl)

1. One of the three sons of Benjamin. He was the ancestor of a great family, renowned as warriors and numbering 17,200 men "ready for service in war" in David's time (I Chr 7:6, 10 – 11, RSV).

2. The son of Shimri, he is listed as one of David's mighty men (I Chr 11:45).

3. One of the men of the tribe of Manasseh who deserted Saul and joined David at Ziklag. He may be the same as 2 (I Chr 12:20).

4. The son of Meshelemiah of the Levitical family of Korah who was appointed a door-keeper of the temple by David (I Chr 26:2).

JEDIDAH (jē-dī'dá). The mother of King Josiah of the southern kingdom of Judah. She was the daughter of Adaiah of Bozcath (II Kgs 22:1).

JEDIDIAH (jĕd'ĭ-dī'á). David named his second child by Bathsheba Solomon; but Nathan' the prophet received word from God that the child was to be named Jedidiah, meaning "Jehovah is a friend" or "beloved of Jehovah," perhaps to indicate divine forgiveness (II Sam 12:24 – 25).

JEDUTHUN (jē-dū'thŭn). A Levite who was one of the great musicians of Israel. He was appointed by David along with Asaph and Heman to take charge of the temple music, and he continued to serve in the days of Solomon. Jeduthun's six sons and descendants are mentioned, some as continuing the musical heritage and others as serving the Lord in other capacities (I Chr 16:38, 41 – 42; 25:1, 3, 6; II Chr 5:12). Jeduthun's descendants are mentioned as active in the reformation of Hezekiah (II Chr 29:14). In the days of Josiah the liturgy of the temple arranged by the three great musicians was still being observed (II Chr 35:15). Descendants of Jeduthun ministered once more after the return from Exile (I Chr 9:16; Neh 11:17). The editorial notations to Ps 39, 62, and 77 relate them to Jeduthun.

JEEZER (jē-ē'zer), **JEEZERITES** (jē-ē 'ze-rīts). The name seems to be a contracted form of Abiezer (q.v.; Josh 17:2). It is the name of a clan of Gilead (Num 26:30) and is called Iezer in the RSV.

JEGAR-SAHADUTHA (jē'gár-sā'á-dū'thá). The word means "heap of witness" or "mound of witness," and refers to the stones raised by Laban and Jacob to be a sign of their covenant (Gen 31:47). Laban called it Jegar-sahadutha, while Jacob referred to it as Galeed. Laban's designation is Aramaic and Jacob's Hebrew. Both terms have the same meaning.

JEHALELEEL (jē-há-lē'lē-ĕl). A more correct form of Jehallelel (RSV). The word means "he shall praise God."

1. The name of a Judahite (I Chr 4:16).

2. A Levite, a descendant of Merari (II Chr 29:12; "Jehalelel" in KJV).

JEHALELEL. See Jehaleleel.

JEHDEIAH (jē-dē'yá)

1. A descendant of Moses in the time of David. He was the son of Shubael (I Chr 24:20; cf. 23:16).

2. Jehdeiah the Meronothite who had charge of David's asses (I Chr 27:30).

JEHEZEKEL (jē-hĕz'ĕ-kĕl). A priest in David's time who was made 20th in course of service (I Chr 24:16).

JEHIAH (jē-hī'á). One of the two gatekeepers for the ark when it was brought to Jerusalem by David (I Chr 15:24).

JEHIEL (jē-hī'ĕl)

1. The "father" or founder of Gibeon, husband of Maacah and father of a number of sons (I Chr 9:35), including Kish, the father of King Saul (vv. 36, 39).

2. The son of Hotham the Aroerite. With his brother Shama, Jehiel was one of David's mighty men (I Chr 11:44).

3. A Levite musician who was appointed with others to play music before the ark as it was brought by David to Jerusalem (I Chr 15:18, 20). Afterward he was appointed to the permanent ministry of music in the sanctuary (I Chr 16:5).

4. A Levite, son of the Gershonite Laadan. He was in charge of the treasury of the temple, an office that seems to have continued with the family (I Chr 23:8; 29:8). Also spelled Jehieli (q.v.) in I Chr 26:20 – 22.

5. The son of Hachmoni, who with Jonathan, David's uncle, "a counselor . . . and a scribe," was appointed to "attend" the king's sons, probably as a tutor (I Chr 27:32).

6. The son of Jehoshaphat. He and five brothers were slain by Jehoram when he became king (II Chr 21:2 – 4).

7. A Levite of the family of Heman, he dedicated himself with others for the cleansing of the temple in the time of Hezekiah (II Chr 29:14ff.). He may be the same Levite who was assigned to oversee the reception and distribution of the sacred offerings (II Chr 31:13ff.).

8. One of the chief officers (RSV) or rulers

(KJV) of the temple who contributed many sacrifices for the great Passover service of Josiah (II Chr 35:8).

9. The father of Obadiah, who with 218 of the family of Joab returned from the Exile with Ezra (Ezr 8:9).

10. One of the sons of Elam, the father of Shechaniah, who proposed that the Gentile wives who had drawn the Jews away from God be put away (Ezr 10:2). Jehiel himself was one who put away his wife (Ezr 10:26).

11. A priest of the sons of Harim who put away his Gentile wife (Ezr 10:21).

P. C. J.

JEHIELI (jē-hī'ē̌-lī). A son of Laadan the Gershonite whose two sons were in charge of the treasury (I Chr 26:22). *See* Jehiel 4.

JEHIZKIAH (jē'hĭz-kī'à). An Ephraimite in the days of Ahaz who opposed making slaves of captives from Judah, declaring that God's judgment would be upon the northern kingdom if they proceeded to do so (II Chr 28:12 – 13).

JEHOADAH (jē-hō'à-dà). The son of Ahaz, a descendant of Saul through Jonathan (I Chr 8:36). The same person is referred to in I Chr 9:42 as Jarah (*q.v.*).

JEHOADDAN (je-hō'à-dán). The wife of Joash and the mother of Amaziah, both kings of Judah (II Chr 25:1; II Kgs 14:1 – 2).

JEHOAHAZ (jē-hō'à-hăz)

1. In contracted form, Joahaz, or Ahaziah (*q.v.*), youngest son of Jehoram, king of Judah (II Chr 21:17).

2. King of Israel, son of Jehu, who reigned in Samaria for 17 years (II Kgs 13:1–9). He was subject to Hazael, king of Syria, throughout his rule. He followed the religious practices of Jeroboam I.

3. King of Judah, son of Josiah. Although he was not the eldest, he was chosen by the people (II Kgs 23:30 – 31). He ruled under the tragic circumstances of the death of Josiah, which ended the hope of a great empire under the Davidic line. After only three months he was deposed by Pharaoh-Necho and taken to Egypt in chains (II Kgs 23:32 – 33; Jer 22:10). The people mourned his death, the first king of Judah to die in exile.

JEHOASH (jē-hō'ăsh). Alternate form of Joash.

1. The son of Ahaziah, king of Judah (II Kgs 11 – 12). *See* Joash 3.

2. The son of Jehoahaz and father of Jeroboam II, kings of Israel (II Kgs 13:9 — 14:16). *See* Joash 4.

JEHOHANAN (jē'hō-hā'nán)

1. The sixth son of Meshelemiah, a Levite, in the days of David. He was appointed to the office of porter or doorkeeper in the temple (I Chr 26:3).

2. One of the chief generals of the army of Judah in the days of Jehoshaphat. He commanded a corps of 280,000 (II Chr 17:15). It was probably his son, another soldier, who supported Jehoiada in overthrowing the wicked Athaliah and placing the boy Joash on the throne (II Chr 23:1).

3. An Israelite in the days of Ezra who had married a Gentile wife and put her away in the time of reformation (Ezr 10:28).

4. A priest of the family of Amariah in the days of Jehoiakim. Amariah had returned from Exile with Zerubbabel (Neh 12:13).

5. A priest in the days of Nehemiah, he is listed with those who took part in the dedication of the completed wall of Jerusalem (Neh 12:42; perhaps the same as 4).

P. C. J.

JEHOIACHIN (jě-hoi'à-kĭn). Also called Jeconiah (I Chr 3:16 – 17; Est 2:6; Jer 24:1; 27:20; 28:4; 29:2) and Coniah (Jer 22:24, 28; 37:1). Mt 1:11– 12 uses the Gr. form Jechonias.

Son of Jehoiakim, Jehoiachin became king of Judah in December, 598 B.C. He was 18 years old (the "eight years old" of II Chr 36:9 is considered a scribal error) when he began his reign, which lasted three months and ten days (II Kgs 24:8). He came on the throne when Judah was suffering from raids by neighboring people which had been incited by Nebuchadnezzar because of Jehoiakim's reckless bid for independence (II Kgs 24:1 – 7).

Jehoiachin's short rule gave little chance to tell what sort of king he would have made, but he is charged with doing evil as his father had done (II Kgs 24:9). When Nebuchadnezzar finished his war with Egypt, he mobilized his army to invade Judah, and Jehoiachin was forced to capitulate. A cuneiform tablet in the series of the court chronicles of the Babylonian kings states the exact date that Nebuchadnezzar took him captive, equivalent to March 16, 597 B.C. On April 22 he left Jerusalem to begin his exile in Babylon, along with 10,000 others including his mother, the leading men and women of Judah such as Ezekiel the prophet, and the royal treasures. There was only a poor and feeble remnant left behind, with no leadership or protection (II Kgs 24:10 – 16).

Jehoiachin was kept a captive for most of the rest of his life. At least two Babylonian tablets dated to 592 B.C. list Jehoiachin and his five sons among those who received rations from the king in Babylon (ANET, p. 308). He seems to have enjoyed a certain amount of freedom within the city at this time, but was imprisoned later, perhaps during the final siege of Jerusalem. After about 36 years Evil-merodach set him free from prison and made him eat at his table (II Kgs 25:27 – 30).

Jehoiachin remained a figure of nationalistic hope to his people during his long captivity, for he was the legitimate Davidic king and was even called "king of Judah." As long as he lived he kept the nationalistic spirit of his people on fire. Clay impressions of the stamp seal of his steward Eliakim have been found at Tell Beit Mirsim and Beth-shemesh in Palestine (VBW, II, 297). These suggest that while in exile Jehoiachin's royal estates were not confiscated but continued to be managed in his name by his chief steward. The time of his death is uncertain. He was the last of Solomon's line as predicted by Jeremiah (Jer 22:30), and the succession passed to the line of Nathan.

A. W. W.

JEHOIADA (jē-hoi'á-dá)

1. Father of Benaiah, David's general (II Sam 8:16, 18; 20:23) who succeeded Joab after serving under him (I Kgs 4:4) and under Solomon (I Chr 11:22, 24). He is probably the same one who led many Aaronites to join forces with David at Hebron (I Chr 12:27).

2. A son of Benaiah, one of David's counselors who succeeded Ahithophel (I Chr 27:33–34), and thus a grandson of the above, although some believe these to be the same.

3. The high priest during the time Athaliah usurped the throne of Judah, who overthrew her and placed the boy king Joash (Jehoash) on the throne (II Kgs 11:4–21). He made a covenant between God, the king and Judah (II Kgs 11:17) which led to some religious reforms and enabled Jehoiada to serve as the king's adviser. Jehoiada's wife was the daughter of King Joram and sister of King Ahaziah, so the priest was the uncle of the young king he aided. Jehoiada lived to be 130, and was honored for his service to the nation by burial among the kings of Judah in the old city of David (II Chr 24:15–16). His godly influence gone, Joash quickly lapsed into idolatrous ways and slew Jehoiada's son (II Chr 24:2, 17–22).

4. A priest during the time of Jeremiah who was succeeded by Zephaniah as overseer of the temple (Jer 29:26).

5. One who helped repair the old gate of Jerusalem (Neh 3:6).

A. W. W.

JEHOIAKIM (jē-hoi'á-kĭm). King of Judah, son of Josiah by his wife Zebudah. He was first called Eliakim, but after deposing Jehoiahaz Pharaoh-Necho set him on the throne of Judah and changed his name to Jehoiakim, in the latter half of 609 B.C. (II Kgs 23:34, 36). He was subject to Egypt for four years and required to exact heavy tribute from his people. The battle of Carchemish in May-June 605 B.C. ended the rule of Egypt.

Nebuchadnezzar entered Jerusalem and received the submission of Jehoiakim (II Kgs 24:1; Jer 46:2) and took some captives including Daniel and his three friends and the golden vessels from the temple to Babylon (Dan 1:1–2, 6). Nebuchadnezzar had bound Jehoiakim in chains to take him along with the others to Babylon (II Chr 36:6), but evidently released him after receiving assurance that he

would be a loyal vassal. Judah began a period of moral and religious decay. Baal and Ashtoreth were worshiped in the very gates of the temple and sacrifices may have been resumed in the valley of Hinnom. Cruelty, corruption and oppression were commonplace in the city.

Jeremiah wrote on a scroll in protest, telling how divine judgment would surely come to Judah (Jer 36), but the king, after reading a few leaves, took his knife and cut them in strips and then burned them. After three years Jehoiakim rashly rebelled against Babylonia while Nebuchadnezzar was too busy with battles elsewhere to take any action at that time.

Jehoiakim died on Dec. 10, 598 B.C. according to calculations based on the Babylonian chronicle. The people did not mourn and he was evidently given a shameful burial as Jeremiah had prophesied (Jer 22:18f.; 36:30). His young son Jehoiachin (q.v.) inherited his throne and all the unsolved problems.

A. W. W.

JEHOIARIB (jē-hoi'á-rĭb). Also appears as Joiarib (q.v.) both in Heb. and in English. It is difficult always to tell whether the name refers to an individual or a member of the priestly course.

1. A priest, the head of the first of the 24 courses of the priesthood in the days of David (I Chr 24:7).

2. A priest who returned with the first of the exiles from Babylon (I Chr 9:10).

JEHONADAB (jē-hō'ná-dăb). Alternate form of Jonadab (q.v.). The English in II Sam 13 and Jer 35 consistently calls him Jonadab, but the Heb. varies the longer and shorter forms. Jehonadab is found only in II Kgs 10:15, 23.

JEHONATHAN (jē-hŏn'á-thán). A shorter form of the name is Jonathan (q.v.).

1. The son of Uzziah and an overseer of King David's treasuries or storehouses (I Chr 27:25).

2. One of the Levites sent out by King Jehoshaphat through the cities of Judah to teach the law of the Lord to the people (II Chr 17:8–9).

3. A priest, head of the family of Shemaiah, in the days of Nehemiah (Neh 12:18).

JEHORAM (jē-hôr'ám). Same as Joram (q.v.), an abbreviated form of the name.

1. A son of Ahab (II Kgs 3:1) king of Israel, nearly contemporary with the king of Judah by the same name. He succeeded his elder brother Ahaziah. Jehoram destroyed an image of Baal which his father had made (3:2), but continued to uphold the calf worship instituted by Jeroboam I. Israel and Judah were friendly allies during his reign as a result of the alliance between Ahab and Jehoshaphat. Together they put down a revolt of King Mesha of Moab (II Kgs 3:1–27). Mesha's record of the campaign is recorded on the Moabite Stone (q.v.).

Jehoram must have been the unidentified king of Israel to whom Naaman was sent to be cured of leprosy (II Kgs 5:1-8), to whom Elisha revealed the movements of the Syrian army and who sent the helpless enemy troops back to Damascus after feeding them (II Kgs 6:8-23), and who witnessed the seige of Samaria by the Syrians (II Kgs 6:24—7:20). Wounded in the battle over Ramoth-gilead against Hazael of Syria, Jehoram went to Jezreel to seek a cure (II Kgs 8:28-29), but instead was assassinated by an arrow from the bow of Jehu; thus ending the dynasty of Omri on the very land Jezebel had procured for Ahab by having Naboth slain (I Kgs 21).

2. Jehoshaphat's son, who served as his father's regent for about five years before succeeding him on the throne of Judah in 848 B.C. at the age of 32 (I Kgs 22:50; II Chr 21:1, 3, 5). To strengthen his father's political alliance with Israel (II Chr 18:1) he had been married to the older Athaliah, daughter of Ahab and Jezebel, who evidently influenced him to allow the worship of Baal-Melkart (II Kgs 8:18). He murdered his brothers and some of the princes of Judah (II Chr 21:4). Jehoram fought against the Philistines and Arabians (II Chr 21:16-17), who captured his wives and all his sons except Ahaziah (Jehoahaz). In 841 B.C. he died of a lingering, painful disease, but none mourned (II Chr 21:18-20).

3. A priest appointed by King Jehoshaphat to teach the law (II Chr 17:8).

A. W. W.

JEHOSHABEATH. *See* Jehosheba.

JEHOSHAPHAT (jē-hŏsh'ȧ-făt)
1. A recorder under David and Solomon, the son of Ahilud (II Sam 8:16; 20:24; I Kgs 4:3). He is listed as one of the chief officials of the kingdom.

2. One of the priests during the reign of David, appointed to blow the trumpet in front of the ark as it was brought to the city of David from Obed-edom (I Chr 15:24; Heb. *Yôshpāṭ*).

3. One of the 12 administrative officers of Solomon whose responsibility was to provide food for the king and his household for one month of each year. He was charged with the collection from the district of Issachar (I Kgs 4:17).

4. King of Judah (873-848 B.C.), son of Asa and his successor. At the age of 35 he became coregent with his father Asa until the latter's death in 870, and ruled for 25 years (I Kgs 22:42). His mother was Azubah, daughter of Shilhi. He was contemporary with Ahab, Ahaziah, and Jehoram of Israel. He made an alliance with Israel by marrying his son Jehoram to Athaliah, the daughter of Ahab and Jezebel (II Kgs 8:18). In spite of the fact that this act opened the door to the worship of Baal in the kingdom of Judah, he was considered a good king.

In his third year he carried out some reforms to improve the religious situation, instructing his people himself as well as sending out the Levites with the book of the law to teach in the cities of Judah (II Chr 17:7-9). The Philistines and the Arabians paid tribute (vv. 10-11), and he further fortified the cities of his kingdom (vv. 12-19).

In 853 B.C. Ahab persuaded him to join Israel in an attempt to wrest Ramoth-gilead from Syria. Ahab was mortally wounded but Jehoshaphat survived (I Kgs 22:1-38; II Chr 18:1-34). He was severely reproved by the prophet Jehu for having anything to do with King Ahab (II Chr 19:1-2). Judah clearly occupied a subordinate position but the alliance was temporarily a source of strength for both kingdoms. On his return Jehoshaphat again encouraged Yahweh worship (II Chr 19:4).

He had previously strengthened the defenses of Judah and brought Edom under his control (II Chr 17:1-2; I Kgs 22:47). This gave him command of the caravan routes from Arabia and brought him additional wealth (II Chr 17:5; 18:1). He attempted to build a fleet of ships at Ezion-geber in cooperation with Ahaziah, king of Israel, but the ships were wrecked. Jehoshaphat refused any new ventures, probably fearing encroachment on his territory and because the prophet Eliezer rebuked him for joining Ahaziah (I Kgs 22:48-49). Jehoshaphat introduced important administrative changes (II Chr 19:5-11) by appointing judges in the fortified cities of Judah to replace the local elders, and establishing a final court of appeals in Jerusalem made up of Levites and priests and heads of families, with the chief priest in charge.

Once again the king of Israel, this time Jehoram, persuaded Jehoshaphat into a new venture to make Moab a tributary to Israel, but it was only partly successful (II Kgs 3:5-7). Near the end of his reign the Ammonites, Edomites, and Moabites joined forces to invade Judah by crossing what is now the Dead Sea toward Engedi. Jehoshaphat sought the Lord and heeded the words of the prophet Jahaziel to stand still and see the salvation of the Lord on their behalf. In the confusion caused by Judah's songs of praise the enemies began to ambush one another until they destroyed themselves (II Chr 20:1-30).

During his last five years Jehoshaphat had his son Jehoram reign with him on the throne (II Kgs 8:16 with 1:17). Jehoshaphat died at the age of 60 and was buried in the city of David (I Kgs 22:50).

5. Father of Jehu, king of Israel, he lived in the 9th cen. B.C. (II Kgs 9:2, 14).

A. W. W.

JEHOSHAPHAT, VALLEY OF (jē-hŏs'ȧ-făt). A valley in which the Lord will gather all nations together for judgment (Joel 3:2, 12). The name itself is significant, meaning "Yahweh judges."

It is called the valley of decision (v. 14), meaning judicial decision to determine punishment, not an opportunity to believe unto salvation. The historical event of II Chr 20: 20 – 26 seems to have been used here as a symbol of an eschatological event (see Armageddon). No actual valley bore this name in pre-Christian antiquity. Since the 4th cen. A.D. Christian tradition has commonly identified it with the Kidron Valley (between Jerusalem and the Mount of Olives). Some have identified it with the Valley of Berachah near Bethlehem. Probably neither view is correct.

The exact geographical location of the valley in which Jehoshaphat's enemies came to their destruction cannot be ascertained. It must have been somewhere in the wilderness of Judah below the heights of Tekoa (II Chr 20:20), in the direction of En-gedi (v. 2), and should probably be identified with the valley of the "ascent to Ziz" (see Ziz) in the vicinity of the "wilderness of Jeruel" (see Jeruel; II Chr 20:16).

A. F. R.

JEHOSHEBA (jĕ-hŏsh'ĕ-bà). Also called Jehoshabeath (II Chr 22:11).

Jehosheba was the daughter of King Jehoram of Judah and the sister of King Ahaziah. She was probably not the daughter of Jehoram's infamous wife Athaliah but the offspring of another wife. She was the wife of Jehoiada the high priest at the time when Athaliah attempted to kill all the heirs of the murdered Ahaziah and seize the throne. Jehosheba rescued the infant Joash and protected him for six years until the tyrant queen could be safely defied and the child Joash proclaimed king (II Kgs 11:1 – 3).

JEHOSHUA, JEHOSHUAH (jĕ-hŏsh'u-à). A peculiar spelling sometimes given to Joshua the son of Nun (Num 13:16). Another spelling adds the final "h" (I Chr 7:27). See Joshua.

JEHOVAH. See God; God, Names and Titles of.

JEHOVAH-JIREH (jĕ-hō'và-jī'rĕ). The phrase means "Jehovah (Yahweh) sees," or "Jehovah (Yahweh) will provide." It refers to the place named by Abraham when the ram appeared in the thicket and was sacrificed instead of Isaac (Gen 22:14, KJV). See God, Names and Titles of.

JEHOVAH-NISSI (jĕ-hō'và-nĭs'ĭ). The phrase means "Jehovah (Yahweh) is my banner," and is the name of the altar Moses built after defeating the Amalekites at Rephidim (Ex 17:15, KJV). See God, Names and Titles of.

JEHOVAH-SHALOM (jĕ-hō'và-shā'lŏm). The phrase means "Jehovah (Yahweh) is peace," and is the name of the altar Gideon built at Ophrah to memorialize the words of God's message to him, "Peace be unto thee" (Jud 6:23 – 24, KJV). See God, Names and Titles of.

JEHOZABAD (jĕ-hō'zà-bǎd)

1. The son of Shomer (or Shimrith), a Moabitess. He was one of the two servants of Joash of Judah who assassinated the king at the house of Millo (II Kgs 12:20 – 21; II Chr 24:26).

2. A Levite, the second son of Obed-edom. He was appointed a doorkeeper of the temple by David (I Chr 26:4).

3. A soldier from the tribe of Benjamin. He was one of the generals of Jehoshaphat, commanding 180,000 men (II Chr 17:18).

JEHOZADAK. Alternate form of Jozadak and Josedech. See Josedech.

JEHU (jē'hū)

1. A servant of David born at Anathoth, one of David's chief slingers who met him at Ziklag (I Chr 12:3).

2. A prophet, son of Hanani, who prophesied against King Baasha (I Kgs 16:1, 7, 12) and later recorded events of the reign of Jehoshaphat in the chronicles of Jehu mentioned in II Chr 20:34.

3. A man of the tribe of Judah, son of Obed, descendant of Jerahmeel (I Chr 2:38).

4. A man of the tribe of Simeon, son of Joshibiah (I Chr 4:35).

5. Tenth king of Israel, son of Jehoshaphat, grandson of Nimshi (II Kgs 9:2), first king of the fourth dynasty in Israel (841 – 814 B.C.).

Before becoming king, Jehu played a quiet and subordinate role under Ahab, Ahaziah, and Jehoram. His earliest known military position was as a bodyguard of Ahab. In this capacity he was present at Ahab's encounter with Elijah in the vineyard of Naboth as well as the legalized murder of Naboth and his sons (II Kgs 9:25 – 26; cf. I Kgs 21:15 – 16). Under Jehoram, he was captain of the army of Israel in the defense of Ramoth-gilead (II Kgs 9:1 – 5). During the fighting against the Syrians in Transjordan, Jehoram was forced to return to Jezreel

Jehu doing homage to Shalmaneser III, a panel from the Black Obelisk of Shalmaneser. BM

because of wounds (II Kgs 8:28-29; 9:15), leaving Jehu in charge of the besieged city.

His anointment. The prophet Elisha recognized the strategic nature of the circumstances. He recalled that his predecessor, Elijah, had been commissioned to anoint Jehu as the future king of Israel. The reason for such a long delay is not given in the biblical record. Now conditions were ripe for a successful revolution against the house of Ahab. Elisha sent a messenger to anoint Jehu as the new king. The young messenger of wild appearance (II Kgs 9:11) secretly poured a vial of sacred oil over Jehu's head (vv. 6-10). However, the secret was short-lived as Jehu soon revealed the mission of the young prophet. Enthusiasm swept over the soldiers, causing them to throw down their garments under Jehu's feet, sound their trumpets, and proclaim him king (vv. 12-13).

His coup. Jehu wasted no time in striking against the house of Ahab. Making certain that no one would ride to warn Jehoram, he took a small group of men toward Jezreel. Jehoram, seeing the approaching troops, sent out messengers who did not return. Then he and Ahaziah, king of Judah, rode out to inquire of Jehu's business at Jezreel. Jehoram's question, "Is it peace?" was answered by Jehu's fierce denunciation of Jezebel. With positive and passionless speed, Jehu began the bloody massacre which continued for several days. Jehoram was pierced by Jehu's arrow while Jehu's men mortally wounded Ahaziah. Riding into Jezreel, Jehu ordered two servants to throw down Jezebel from the palace window. He and his men completed her demise with the wheels of their chariots (II Kgs 9:14-37).

Next Jehu challenged the leading citizens to set up one of the princes in opposition to his rulership. Once they had submitted to him, he ordered them to prove their allegiance by appearing the next day with the heads of the 70 heirs of Ahab. The heads were then piled up on either side of the gate leading into Jezreel as a reminder to anyone still inclined to resist (II Kgs 10:1-11).

The ruthless slaughter continued with the death of 42 kinsmen of Ahaziah who unluckily came from Judah for a visit at this time. The bloodbath was finally ended with the wholesale slaughter of all the worshipers of Baal who could be gathered together and the eradication of the foreign cult of Baal. Jehu showed his cunning and calculating side as he pretended to be loyal to Baal. Calling a solemn assembly and leading out in the ritual, he quietly stepped aside while 80 of his trusty guards killed everyone who had accepted his invitation (II Kgs 10:12-28).

His foreign policy. Although Jehu had ruthlessly disposed of his potential enemies, he soon found he had no friends. He had broken completely with Phoenicia by the murder of the Phoenician-bred queen mother and the overthrow of the Phoenician-inspired worship. He had destroyed all hope of close ties with Judah

when he killed Ahaziah and his close kinsmen. Since Ahab had already broken the bonds with Syria and obligated his nation to Assyria, Jehu had little choice in regard to his foreign policy. During the first year of Jehu's reign, 842 B.C., Shalmaneser III directed a triumphant campaign against Hazael of Damascus. It was expedient, if not courageous, for Jehu to follow a policy of vassalage to Assyria. The Black Obelisk of Shalmaneser, found by Layard at Nimrud, describes this submission in word and picture. It tells of tribute paid by Jehu as well as the inhabitants of Tyre and Sidon—gold, silver, vessels of metal and wooden objects (ANET, pp. 280f.). It also gives an actual representation of Israelites offering their tribute to the Assyrian monarch. This is the earliest known artistic representation of an Israelite (ANEP, #351, 355).

In the years which followed, Israel was constantly threatened by Syria, as Assyria failed to keep the Syrians in check. Hazael was able to gain sufficient power to overrun all the territories of Israel E of the Jordan (II Kgs 10:32-33).

His religious zeal. The various motives behind Jehu's acts are difficult to untangle. However, a deep religious motivation is obvious since the revolution was prophet-inspired. Although Elijah was no longer on the scene, his name was associated with the movement through the memory of his words to Ahab in Naboth's vineyard. Jehu became the agent in satisfying the prophecy of Elijah as he left Jehoram's body in the vineyard of Naboth and carried out the prophetic promise concerning Jezebel. Elisha's name was inseparably connected with Jehu's rebellion by his action in ordering the anointing of the young leader.

In the final phase of his plans, Jehu linked himself with another element of Israel's religious heritage. He took Jehonadab the Rechabite with him to Samaria as his associate in eradicating the worshipers of Baal (II Kgs 9:15-16, 23). Even as he had the backing of the best in the prophetic tradition, Elijah and Elisha, he could likewise claim the sanction of the most fanatical group as well in the Rechabites.

Although there was prophetic backing of the revolution, later writers looked back with censure upon the extreme nature of Jehu's actions. The writer of II Kgs 10:29-31 views the events in the light of his toleration of the idolatrous cult instituted by Jeroboam I at Bethel and Dan. Hosea likewise decries the violence and bloodshed (Hos 1:4).

His character. Jehu was a man possessed by dominant traits of personality. In making preparation for carrying out his purposes, he was prudent, calculating, masterful, and ambitious. In executing his plans, he was bold, daring, impetuous, and stern. His zeal approached the point of ruthless fanaticism. He was seemingly lacking in the regal qualities which inspire respect, trust, and appreciation. His extreme policies alienated friend and foe, hastening the demise of Israel. The fact that he continued the identification of the sacred bulls with the Yahweh worship suggests that his prophetic zeal for God was probably leavened by his ambitious zeal for Jehu.

K. M. Y.

JEHUBBAH (jḗ-hŭb'á). An Asherite, the son of Shemer (I Chr 7:34).

JEHUCAL (jḗ-hū'kál). Also spelled Jucal in Jer 38:1. The son of Shelemiah who was sent by Zedekiah, the king of Judah, to entreat Jeremiah to pray for him (Jer 37:3). After hearing Jeremiah, Jehucal, among others, encouraged the king to put Jeremiah to death on the grounds that his message of judgment and destruction was undermining the safety of the city (Jer 38:1–6).

JEHUD (jē'hŭd). A town in the tribal territory of Dan in the time of Joshua. Its location seems to be about seven miles E of Joppa and near the modern city of Tel Aviv (Josh 19:45).

JEHUDI (jḗ-hū'dī). The word refers to a man of Judah, a Jew. He was a messenger of King Jehoiakim (Jer 36:14, 21, 23) sent to Baruch to request him to bring the scroll in the presence of the king, who proceeded to cut and burn it as it was read by Jehudi.

JEHUDIJAH (jē'hŭ-dī'já). The KJV lists Jehudijah as a proper name, but it is an adjective meaning "Jewess." The term is used in reference to the Jewish wife of Mered and distinguishes her from his Egyptian wife (I Chr 4:18).

JEHUSH. See Jeush 3.

JEIEL (jḗ-ī'ĕl)
1. A Reubenite chief at the time when Tiglath-pileser took into captivity the Transjordanic tribes (I Chr 5:7).
2. The founder of Israelite Gibeon, father of Ner who was grandfather of King Saul (I Chr 9:35, ASV, RSV; Jehiel in KJV).
3. The son of Hotham the Aroerite, one of David's mighty men (I Chr 11:44, ASV, RSV; Jehiel in KJV).
4. A Levite, appointed by David as doorkeeper and musician (I Chr 15:18, 21). He took part in the ministry of music before the ark as it was brought to Jerusalem (I Chr 16:5).
5. A Levite, the great-grandfather of Jahaziel who prophesied the victory of Jehoshaphat (II Chr 20:14ff.).
6. A scribe who kept account of the numbers of King Uzziah's army (II Chr 26:11).
7. A Levite, son of Elizaphan, who assisted in the cleansing of the temple under Hezekiah (II Chr 29:13, KJV; Jeuel in ASV, RSV).
8. A chief Levite who took part in the great Passover of Josiah (II Chr 35:9).

9. One of the descendants, "sons," of Adonikam who returned with Ezra (Ezr 8:13, KJV; ASV, RSV have Jeuel).
10. A son or descendant of Nebo, who had taken a foreign wife in the days of Ezra (Ezr 10:43).

P. C. J.

JEKABZEEL (jḗ-kăb'zḗ-ĕl). A city in the southern part of Judah (Neh 11:25), probably identical with Kabzeel (q.v.).

JEKAMEAM (jĕk'á-mē'ám). The son of Hebron, a descendant of Levi (I Chr 23:19; 24:23).

JEKAMIAH (jĕk'á-mī'á). A man of Judah, the son of Shallum (I Chr 2:41). See also Jecamiah.

JEKUTHIEL (jḗ-kū'thĭ-ĕl). The son of Mered by his Jewish wife (I Chr 4:18).

JEMIMA (jḗ-mī'má). Eldest of Job's three daughters, all of exceeding beauty, born to him after his restoration to prosperity (Job 42:14). Her name perhaps means "dove," with reference to the Egyptian turtledove.

JEMUEL (jĕm'ū-ĕl). The eldest son of Simeon (Gen 46:10; Ex 6:15). The same person is mentioned under the name of Nemuel (q.v.)in Num 26:12; I Chr 4:24.

JEPHTHAE. See Jephthah.

JEPHTHAH (jĕf'thá). One of the important leaders from the period of the judges (Jud 11:1–12:7). He was from the area of Gilead and was a son of a man named Gilead. His mother was a harlot, so Gilead's legitimate children drove Jephthah from home. He went to live at Tob, possibly just E of Ramoth-gilead. Here he gathered around him a band of dubious character but great courage, who lived by preying on other groups. Jephthah was himself a mighty warrior, a charismatic leader empowered by the Spirit of the Lord (11:29), but one with pride in his just and honest treatment of others.

When the area of Gilead had trouble with Ammon, its Israelite leaders could not cope with the situation. For 18 long years they smarted under the ruthless subjection of the Ammonites. Finally they begged Jephthah to help them since they had heard of his great prowess. Doubtless his brothers were in the group of elders of Gilead, for after a bitter denunciation of them he agreed to become the leader of their clan. The story suggests that they may have felt him to be especially close to God, for they may have noticed that he had taught his daughter his faith.

When Jephthah became judge he asked the tribe of Ephraim to help defeat the Ammonites, but they ignored him. Before the outcome of the battle was certain, Jephthah made a vow to sacrifice the first thing to come out his door on his return if he were successful. Some believe that this was a rash vow given in a moment of ecstacy or despair and that he little dreamed of what would actually happen. Others feel that he was quite aware of the probable consequences of his act. That he expected to make a human sacrifice is likely when one considers the alternative of an animal sacrifice. There is no reason to believe that a leader such as Jephthah would have kept in his house animals which he deemed worthy of sacrificing to fulfill his vow. The victory was important enough to him to warrant a comparably important payment, even a human life.

At any rate, he did defeat the Ammonites, and when he returned home he was greeted by his lovely young daughter. This tragedy nearly broke the heart of Jephthah, but he was loyal to his vow. His grief and her courageous faith are beautifully told by the Hebrew storyteller (11:34–40). She retired to the mountains for two months of prayer and mourning over her virginity. This may have been a delicate way of leaving the end of the story to the reader's imagination, or it might have been a way of saying she had no husband or child to come to her defense and prohibit this dreadful deed. The story may have been an acknowledgement of the fact that the pagan neighbors made human sacrifices but the Hebrews did not. Since a vow was very sacred, perhaps Jephthah did sacrifice her (II Kgs 3:27). Or he may have redeemed her with money (Lev 27:1–8) and then had her set aside to live the rest of her life in celibacy. This may have started the custom of the women of Israel setting aside four days of the year to mourn her sad fate (Jud 11:40).

Sometimes the idea is presented that Jephthah gave her to the tabernacle where she spent the remainder of her life working as a priest's servant, never marrying, for she would be devoted to the sacred duties of religion as a holy virgin (cf. Ex 38:8; I Sam 2:22). However, there is no specific OT example for the concept of the celibate female temple servant, though there were women performing various religious functions. Historically, this interpretation apparently rose from the allegorical explanation posited by the Rabbis Kimchi in the 11th and 12th cen. This interpretation was subsequently adopted by many Christian expositors but has little biblical basis.

A final campaign of Jephthah's is related, this time against the Ephraimites. They accused him of not inviting them to participate in the battle against the Ammonites (Jud 12:1–6). There seems to have been some resentment in their not being given an important place in the campaign since they claimed leadership of the northern tribes, and they considered his treatment of them a question of their honor. They demanded an immediate explanation and threatened to burn his house. He went into battle against them and won another victory. The Ephraimites were scattered, and when some of

those who had escaped attempted to cross over to go home by way of the Jordan fords, they were asked by Jephthah's men if they were Ephraimites. If they said no, the famous Shibboleth-Sibboleth test was applied. If they could say the word correctly they were allowed to pass on, otherwise they were slain immediately.

Jephthah judged Israel for six years (Jud 12:7). Samuel uses him as an illustration of how God raised up a leader to deliver Israel from trouble (I Sam 12:11). He is included among the heroes of the faith in Heb 11:32.

A. W. W.

JEPHUNNEH (jḗ-fŭn'ĕ)
1. The father of Caleb, one of the two faithful spies of Canaan (Num 13:6). *See* Kenezite.
2. An Asherite, son of Jether (I Chr 7:38).

JERAH (jēr'ȧ). A son of Joktan (Gen 10:26; I Chr 1:20), presumably the origin of an Arabic tribe.

JERAHMEEL (jḗ-rä'mḗ-ĕl)
1. A son of Hezron and a grandson of Judah (I Chr 2:9).
2. A son of Kish, a Levite (I Chr 24:29).
3. One of the officers sent by King Jehoiakim to arrest Baruch (Jer 36:26).

JERAHMEELITE (jḗ-rä'mḗ-ĕ-līt). The name is a collective noun in use before the proper name. It refers to a tribe of people raided by David when he was fleeing from Saul and had taken refuge with Achish, the Philistine (I Sam 27:10).

JERED (jēr'ĕd). The son of Mered by his Jewish wife (I Chr 4:18).

JEREMAI (jĕr'ĕ-mī). One of the Hebrews whom Ezra persuaded to put away his wife (Ezr 10:33).

JEREMIAH (jĕr'ĕ-mī'ȧ)
1. The head of a clan in the tribe of Manasseh (I Chr 5:24).
2, 3, and 4. Three warriors who joined David at Ziklag. The second and third were Gadites (I Chr 12:4, 10, 13).
5. An Israelite resident of Libnah whose daughter Hamutal became the wife of King Josiah and mother of the kings Jehoahaz and Zedekiah (II Kgs 23:31; 24:18; Jer 52:1).
6. A Rechabite and the father of Jaazaniah, a contemporary of Jeremiah the prophet (Jer 35:3).
7. A priest who returned from Babylon with Zerubbabel (Neh 12:1, 12).
8. One of the priests who signed Ezra's covenant to keep the law (Neh 10:2).
9. An official of Judah who joined in the dedication ceremony for the Jerusalem wall under Nehemiah (Neh 12:34).

10. The major prophet during the period of the decline and fall of Judah in the 7th and 6th cen. B.C.

His birth. The latter part of the 7th cen. B.C. produced four prophets in Judah: Jeremiah the humanist, Zephaniah the orator, Nahum the poet, and Habakkuk the philosopher. The greatest of these, and the one enjoying the longest period of prophetic activity was Jeremiah.

His birthplace was Anathoth, a little village perched on a limestone ridge *c.* two miles NE of Jerusalem. Jeremiah was born *c.* 650 B.C. (Jer 1:2, 6), during the closing period of King Manasseh's reign (*c.* 695 – 642 B.C.).

About 70 years previously Samaria, the capital of the northern kingdom, had fallen, and about 65 years later Jerusalem, the capital of the southern kingdom, would fall. Immediately before Jeremiah's birth, Egypt and the small Palestinian states had formed a coalition to throw off the Assyrian yoke; so war clouds were threatening on the world's horizon. This international turmoil could be responsible for the prophet's name. Like Isaiah, there are two Heb. spellings of the English name Jeremiah – the long form *yirmᵉyāhû* and the shorter form *yirmᵉyâ* (Gr. Ieremias and Vulg. Jeremias). There are two probable meanings of the Heb. name, "the Lord [Yahweh] founds" or "establishes"; and, "whom the Lord [Yahweh] hurls" or "casts forth." If the latter interpretation is accepted, no name could be more descriptive of the character or mission of the prophet from Anathoth. Indeed, he was a spiritual missile, hurled forth in a darkened world. Hilkiah was his father's name (Jer 1:1) – a common Heb. name meaning "the Lord [Yahweh] is my portion." Both names (Jeremiah's and Hilkiah's) suggest that the family was loyal to the God of Israel during the tyrannical reign of the ungodly King Manasseh.

His formative years. Probably the family of Jeremiah descended from Eli, for Abiathar, the last of that descent to hold the priestly office, possessed an ancestral estate at Anathoth, to which he retired upon his dismissal by Solomon (I Kgs 2:26). Hence Jeremiah had a background of the finest religious traditions and grew up in the atmosphere of a pious Heb. home. Everything that was good in Heb. life was a part of his intellectual, moral, and spiritual inheritance.

Jeremiah's earliest writings reflect a thorough knowledge and insight of the prophecies of Amos, Hosea, and Isaiah. The prophet Hosea made an indelible imprint upon the young prophet (Jer 2 – 4). Yet when Jeremiah began to prophesy, he demonstrated a firsthand awareness of divine knowledge and the divine call. Like all great prophets (cf. Paul of the NT), Jeremiah shook himself free of all secondary and human sources of inspiration. He knew in his heart that God had called him, for he had heard the voice of the Lord: "Before I fashioned you in the womb I knew you, and before you were born I dedicated you; I designed you for a prophet to the nations" (Jer 1:5, Berkeley).

Anathoth, the birthplace of Jeremiah, since the time of David had been a priestly residence (Jer 1:1; 29:27; 32:7). It is known today as Ras el-Kharrubeh, *c.* two miles NE of Jerusalem, on a hill overlooking the Jordan valley. Its open range and arid landscape were a good cradle for a prophet. Jeremiah reflected his country environment: the hot desert, the village herds, the parched hills, the wild animals, etc. The city was located in the territory of Benjamin, the tribe of mad Saul and cursing Shimei. Its soil was hard and thorny, which demanded deep plowing. Frequently strong men are reared in such soil. "What," asked an English visitor to New England, surveying for the first time its rocky soil, "can you raise here?" "Here," was the proud response, "we raise men!" (G. A. Smith, *Jeremiah,* pp. 67ff.).

Since Jerusalem was less than an hour's walk from Anathoth, Jeremiah was in close touch with the heart of the nation and the pulse of the world. All the political and social news would trickle eventually to the prophet's village and the reverberations of the Assyrian, Scythian, and Babylonian campaigns sounded forth.

Jeremiah was no recluse. He was both a townsman and countryman. He had an eye for events and his sensitive soul felt the impression of the eternal God. Jeremiah possessed a knack for the commonplace. Nature made an indelible imprint on his life. He observed the farmer in the field(Jer 4:3), the children in the street (6:1), the silver refiners and the potters at their work (6:28, 30; 18:3, 6). Also he knew firsthand the strifes of debtors and creditors (15:10), the humiliation of thieves when apprehended (2:26), the lamentations for the dead (16:4), and the joy of festivals of brides and weddings (2:32; 7:34). These changing moods later were reflected in his own soul.

His call. Manasseh died when Jeremiah was about ten years old. Amon, Manasseh's son, ruled two years (642 – 640 B.C.). Then young King Josiah (640 – 609 B.C.) ascended the Judean throne at only eight years of age. Thirteen years later, 627 B.C. (Jer 1:2), during Josiah's reign, Jeremiah was drafted by the Lord to be His prophet to the nations.

The year 627/626 B.C. was an epochal year in world history. Ashurbanipal, the last great Assyrian king, died; and Nabopolassar, the first great neo-Babylonian king, came to the throne of Babylon. Ten years later the Babylonians and Medes, along with the Scythians, launched a combined attack on Nineveh. The death rattle could already be detected in the throat of the mistress of the world.

During this shaking of the nations, God's hand laid hold on Jeremiah on the quiet pathway of life, and overpowered him as recorded in chap. 1. Behind that call were inheritance, tradition, and training; but the experience itself was sudden, abrupt, and fraught with terrific weight and meaning. Also it was accompanied by a stupendous consciousness and inrush of God possessing the whole of his being. From that day, Jeremiah moved upon the stage of history as a God-possessed soul.

His apprenticeship. Jeremiah's prophetic ministry began in Anathoth, and apparently he remained there for several years as more or less an insignificant prophet. In 622 –621 B.C. a religious reformation occurred. Josiah had taken over the reigns of government and decided to restore faith in the God of Israel. In the 18th year of his reign he issued a decree to repair the temple. In the process of cleaning the debris from the temple, the book of the law was found by Hilkiah the priest. He immediately sent it to Josiah, who read it and "rent his clothes." The young king resolved to make the religious life of the nation conform to the laws of the new-found book; so he inaugurated his great reform movement, intended to bring about a national revival of the true religion. All religious worship was to be centered in the temple. All other shrines were to be destroyed.

Jeremiah probably threw himself into this revival movement and went on itinerant preaching tours. But later he broke with the movement because it failed to change the inner life of the nation. He perceived religion as an affair of the heart (see J. Skinner, *Prophecy and Religion,* pp. 89 – 107).

His arrival as a prophet. There is a strange period of silence of *c.* 13 years (621 –609 B.C.) concerning the life of Jeremiah. Evidently during this period he shifted his base of operation from Anathoth to the capital city, Jerusalem. He became the respected prophet of the state.

At the death of Josiah in 609 B.C. at the battle of Megiddo, the Judean people passed over Jehoiakim, the oldest son of Josiah, and placed Jehoahaz (who reigned only three months) on the Judean throne. He was deposed by Pharaoh-necho of Egypt, and Jehoiakim (609 – 598 B.C.) was set on Judah's throne as the puppet of Egypt. Jeremiah immediately clashed with this selfish, covetous, tyrannical, spoiled son of his father's harem, who paneled his roomy palace with cedar (Jer 22:13 – 14). The famous temple sermon (7:1 – 8:3) was preached during the early part of Jehoiakim's reign. As a result, Jeremiah was banned from the temple and nearly lost his life (cf. Jer 7 with 26).

In 612 B.C. Nineveh fell before the Babylonians, and in 605 B.C. at the battle of Carchemish (Jer 46:2) the Babylonians defeated a combined coalition of the remnant army of Assyria and Egypt. Now the Babylonians stepped out upon the world stage as the undisputed master.

Jehoiakim became the vassal of Nebuchadnezzar (605 – 562 B.C.); Judah was reduced to a tributary vassal of Babylon. Jehoiakim remained loyal to Babylon for a few years. Then Pharaoh-necho of Egypt encouraged him to join the westland countries in a revolt. So in 598 B.C., the Judean king revolted and refused to pay annual tribute to his Babylonian overlord. The Babylonian army marched swiftly toward Jerusalem to suppress the revolt. Jehoiakim was probably slain outside the walls of Jerusalem and received an ignominious burial of an ass just as Jeremiah had predicted (Jer 22:18 – 19; 36:30). Jehoiachin, his 17-year-old son, took over the Judean throne. In three months he capitulated unconditionally to Nebuchadnezzar. The Babylonians did not destroy Jerusalem but took away about 3,000 captives, the king, the king's mother, and all the king's court to Babylonia as hostages.

Zedekiah was appointed king of Judah, and Jeremiah continued preaching his theme song that the Babylonians were God's instruments of judgment on Judah for her sins. To resist her would be futile! To submit was wisdom and the only way to survival! In Jeremiah's eyes, the Lord had ordered Babylon to invade Judah; so in the teeth of the king, priests, prophets, and people he opposed any alliance with Egypt and freely predicted the supremacy of Babylon and the destruction of the Jewish state. Also Jeremiah perceived that the hope of future Israel was wrapped up solely in the band of the Jewish captives in Babylon (Jer 31), not in Jerusalem. The leftovers in the capital city were not the true remnant.

His final years. In 588 B.C. Zedekiah, who had long been plotting against Babylon, openly revolted against his Babylonian master. Babylonian vengeance was swift and final. They marched through Judah and Jerusalem in 588 B.C. In July of 586 B.C., after a long and terrible siege of about 18 months, the city was captured. Nebuchadnezzar's patience was exhausted, so he ordered a systematic destruction of the city. The temple was pillaged and demolished. The king was carried to Riblah in chains, his sons and cabinet were slain, his eyes seared, and many Jews taken into captivity—only the poorest people were left behind to be vinedressers and husbandmen.

Jeremiah was released from the prison in Jerusalem by Nebuchadnezzar to stay with the people of the land (Jer 39:11 – 14). His friend Gedaliah was appointed governor of the Judean province. Jeremiah threw his influence behind the governor as he began "to rebuild" and "to replant" the nation (see 1:10).

In 581 B.C., Gedaliah was murdered by a Jewish fanatic, Ishmael, who massacred also all of Gedaliah's adherents. This brought the Babylonian army back to Palestine. In the wake of this return the people, panic-stricken over fear of Babylonian reprisal, fled to Egypt. They kidnapped Jeremiah and carried him with them (43:1 – 7). There on the banks of the Nile he preached against the fanatic worship practiced by the Jewish women to the Queen of Heaven (44:15 – 30). The prophet of Anathoth probably lost his life under an avalanche of stones hurled by the husbands of the female devotees.

His personality. Jeremiah is a personality of complexes—protest and agony. Our knowledge of the personal history of Jeremiah is more extensive than for any other OT prophet. Baruch, his scribe, recorded extensively Jeremiah's spiritual battles.

Also Jeremiah was an honest man, so his utterances laid bare his soul before God. Sprinkled throughout chaps. 1–20 of his book are snatches composing a spiritual diary of his inner life which are commonly termed "the confessions of Jeremiah" (Jer 1; 4:10, 19; 6:11; 11:10–23; 12:1–3, 5–6; 14:17; 15:10–21; 17:9–10; 18:18–23; 20:7–18). These prophecies reveal the conflicts which repeatedly churned within the prophet's soul as he sought to wrestle with the problems of his day.

Even though he was assured of Yahweh's strength (Jer 1:8, 17ff.) for the prophetic ministry, when he encountered persecution and abuse he stormed back with all his soul. He was a laughingstock all day long, an object of derision (20:7–8); his enemies cut him with their tongues (18:18); everyone cursed him (15:10). He was lonely and rejected by his countrymen (15:17; 16:18). Even his home townsmen plotted to assassinate him (18:18, 22; 20:10). His reaction was one of resentment and he rained down imprecations on his enemies (11:20–23; 15:15; 17:18; 20:11–12). He was haunted with apparent failure and he was a man of moods: "See, they say to me, Why tarries the word of the Lord? Let it come!" (17:15, Berkeley; cf. also 15:15; 20:8). At times his fellowship with God was a source of deep spiritual joy (15:16), but at other times he experienced deep spiritual depressions that the Lord had let him down (15:17–18). However he must go on (20:7, 9), for the Lord was stronger than he and had prevailed!

Jeremiah was a man of prayer. He said very little about prayer; he just prayed! He poured out his soul's dregs and all to the One who sees and hears in secret and rewards openly. He prayed for healing (17:14)—spiritual healing of his sick heart (17:9) and the removal of complexes which blocked him and sapped his physical energy. He prayed for relief from his adversaries, for the cause for which he was giving his life, and for vengeance on his persecutors (18:18–23). His prayers were more than petitions. They were communication with God in which his inner life was laid bare, with his frustrations, struggles, temptations, and sins. It was the exercise of his soul in which he unburdened himself of the loads and weights of life (15:15–18).

But Jeremiah was a prophet, the Lord's spokesman. Whereas Isaiah was a volunteer (he accepted his mission and sprang to it with enthusiasm), Jeremiah was a draftee. He shrank, protested, and craved leave to retire. He felt keenly his own sense of inadequacy in view of the order to be a "prophet to the nations." Yet in the midst of pressure of outward events and his own inward tumults, he was the Lord's mouthpiece—a God-possessed, God-controlled, and God-directed man. God's word was a burning fire in his heart (6:11; 20:9); he preached from an inner compulsion. He stood like a flint against the false prophets in Babylon and Jerusalem (23:9–40).

Also Jeremiah was a moral analyst, an assayer of man's thoughts, motives, and actions (5:1–5; especially 6:27: "I have made you an assayer and examiner among my people, so that you may test and analyze their actions"—Berkeley). In examining society he self-analyzed himself (12:3; 15:10, 15–18; 17:16; 18:20).

Again, Jeremiah was a crusader. What Luther was at the Diet of Worms, Jeremiah was to Israel in his famous temple sermon of 609/608 B.C. (chap. 7 for content, chap. 26 for narrative). The word of the Lord came to him, and he had to strike the fatal blow to temple superstition and empty formalism as substitutes for true religion which is an affair of the heart.

Finally, Jeremiah was an optimist. He believed that God would eventually be victorious. When he looked at the generations he was a pessimist. But when he looked at the centuries he was an optimist, and so he spoke of a new king, a good shepherd, and a Davidic righteous branch (Jer 23:5).

According to his conception of the righteousness of God, Jeremiah knew the nation was doomed, the Exile certain, and a new order was inevitable. So in the book of hope (Jer 30–33, especially 31:31ff.) a new day would dawn, a new Israel would return, and God would accomplish His purpose through the Israel of tomorrow. In that day the word of God would be written on the heart of man. Believers would have firsthand experience with the true and living God. This is the OT conception of the new birth.

Because Jeremiah so loved Jerusalem and so aligned himself with the purpose of God, there arose the tradition that Jeremiah would be raised from the dead. The Church Fathers report the belief that he was stoned to death at Tahpanhes by the Jews. He was expected by some to appear and restore the tabernacle, the ark, and the altar of incense which he supposedly had hidden in a cave (II Macc 2:1–8). So when Jesus asked His disciples for the grass roots report, "Who do people say that the Son of Man is?" they replied, "Some say . . . Jeremiah" (Mt 16:13–14, NASB).

D. W. D.

JEREMIAH, BOOK OF. The book of Jeremiah opens with the prophet's call (chap. 1) and closes with the fall of Jerusalem (chap. 52). It spans the historical period *c.* 626–581 B.C.

The Chronological Enigma

The book of Jeremiah consists of prophetic

discourses, biographical materials, and historical narratives not arranged in strict chronological sequence. A vivid illustration is chaps. 21 and 24 which are dated during the reign of King Zedekiah (597 – 586 B.C.), but chap. 25 is dated during Jehoiakim's reign (608 – 597 B.C.). Also chaps. 27 and 28 are from the reign of King Zedekiah, while chaps. 35 and 36 belong to Jehoiakim's reign. Therefore every outline of Jeremiah is somewhat arbitrary.

Since Jeremiah had a faithful secretary, Baruch, one would normally expect better order. Why all the confusion? A plausible explanation of this state of bewilderment is: the materials in the book of Jeremiah originally circulated in the form of separate scrolls, each one illustrating a Jeremianic teaching (cf. F. M. Wood, *Fire in My Bones*, pp. 9 – 11). Later these topically arranged rolls were compressed into the modern book of Jeremiah. Between the various scrolls a number of narratives have been interwoven from the biography of Jeremiah. Seven major scrolls may be detected:

1. Jeremiah's earlier prophecies, chaps. 1 – 6
2. False and true wisdom, 8:4 – 10:25
3. Messages of discouragement, chaps. 11 – 20
4. Condemnations against the kings and prophets, chaps. 22 – 29
5. The book of hope, chaps. 30– 33
6. Historical section, the siege of Jerusalem through the flight into Egypt, chaps. 37 – 44
7. Oracles against the foreign nations, chaps. 46 – 51

The famous temple sermon (7:1 – 8:3) was inserted between scrolls one and two; and between the third and fourth rolls there is a narrative (chap. 21) containing Jeremiah's advice during the siege of the capital city. Three narratives (chaps. 34– 36) concerning Israel's reception of the word of the Lord provide the connecting link for scrolls five and six. Jeremiah's advice to discouraged Baruch (chap. 45) ties the historical section to the foreign prophecies. The oracles to the foreign powers appear in chaps. 46 – 51 (cf. books of Isaiah and Ezekiel for similar sections), and they are followed by a historical appendix (chap. 52), possibly lifted from II Kgs 25. Since Jeremiah spent his life in warning the city of Jerusalem, this is a fitting climax to the romantic ministry of the prophet from Anathoth. Hence this arrangement offers an explanation for the chronological maze (see C. F. Francisco, *Studies in Jeremiah*, p. 13).

The Composition

The beginning point for the writing of the book of Jeremiah is recounted in 36:1 – 8. The date for the nucleus of the roll was 605 B.C. Jeremiah was under a temple interdict from the temple sermon he preached in 609/8 B.C. In the fourth year of the reign of Jehoiakim (605 B.C.) the word of the Lord came to Jeremiah and he dictated the message to Baruch who recorded it in a roll of a book. Then Baruch took it to the temple area and read the sermon during several of the annual religious festivals. The king heard of the message and called for the scroll. After hearing its words of warning, he cut it to bits with his penknife (36:9 – 26). Baruch reported this to Jeremiah and later the Lord ordered Jeremiah to dictate another roll and add many more words to it (Jer 36:27 – 32). This second scroll, apparently the first edition of the extant prophecy, probably contained the heart of chaps. 1 – 25, i.e., the prophecies of Jeremiah which spanned the prophetic period 626 – 605 B.C.

Interspersed throughout this section are the confessions of Jeremiah (Jer 1:4 ff.; 4:10, 19; 6:11; 11:18; 12:6; 15:10– 16; 17:14– 18; 18:23; 20:7 – 18) which lay bare the prophet's soul. The biblical world is indebted to Jeremiah's faithful amanuensis, Baruch, for recording these passing shadows of a great soul. Later this loyal scribe, who accompanied Jeremiah step by step along his prophetic pilgrimage, added the biographies of Jeremiah (25:45) as the prophet's life unfolded during the Judean crisis, 604 – 581 B.C.

Also Baruch could have recorded chaps. 46 – 51 as Jeremiah dictated them. These oracles to the foreign nations perhaps were circulated among the neighboring peoples, in addition to being read by the Jews. This section may have been written during the siege of Jerusalem (588 – 586 B.C.). These foreign prophecies consist of oracles against Egypt (chap. 46), Philistia (chap. 47), Moab (chap. 48), Ammon (49:1 – 6), Edom (49:7 – 22), Syria (49:23 – 27), Arabia (49:28 – 33), Elam (49:34 – 39), and Babylon (chaps. 50 – 51).

It is possible that Jeremiah and his scribe Baruch revised the book more than once, so that it went through successive editions. This conclusion depends in part on the evidence of the LXX.

The Relationship to the Septuagint Text

A comparison of the Gr. and Heb. MSS reveal textual difficulties. The LXX (translated 250 – 100 B.C.) differs considerably from the Heb. Masoretic Text (MT): 2,700 words fewer than the MT, i.e., *c.* 120 verses, or four to five average chapters; the Gr. text has nearly 100 words not found in the MT. Frequently where parallel passages occur, the meaning is different.

Various explanations have been offered to explain these differences: The LXX is not a literal translation of the Heb. text. Also the MSS were often illegible; so many of the errors were unconscious mistakes of the copyists. No doubt some of the changes were intentional (see G. A. Smith, *Jeremiah*, pp. 11 – 14).

These apologies account for many of the different readings, but not the two most glaring discrepancies between the LXX and the MT: the absence of so many passages in the Gr. which appear in the MT, and the rearrangement of oracles to the foreign nations. In the LXX chaps. 46-51 are placed between vv. 13 and 15 of chap. 25. Verse 14 is absent in the Gr. version. Evidently the translators of the Gr. were using a Heb. text which differed from the present day MT.

G. L. Archer suggests that the LXX represents an earlier edition compiled during the prophet's own lifetime and first circulated in Egypt. Then, after Jeremiah's death, Baruch made a more complete collection of his master's sermons which came into the hands of the Jews returning from Babylonian Exile—the MT (SOTI, pp. 349 f.). Others believe there were two streams of compilation which continued until c. 200 B.C., both coming from a parent source. Since the discovery of the Qumran scrolls, the questionable texts can be studied in light of the LXX, the MT, and the Qumran scrolls.

The Literary Analysis

The book of Jeremiah has become since 1901 a kind of happy hunting ground for the literary analysis by scholars. In that year B. Duhm assigned to Jeremiah himself only 60 short poems. He contended that Jeremiah's original words were all written in the *Qinah* poetical form (3:2 rhythm) in c. 280 verses. Also Baruch's biography accounts for c. 200 verses. Roughly speaking, then, Duhm attributed about two-thirds of the book to later editors and supplementers (see A. S. Peake, *The New Century Bible*, I, 48-57). Less radical scholars ascribe all but a few chapters to Jeremiah and his scribe Baruch. Happily, scholars do not destroy the message. For a more complete survey of the various critical positions, see R. K. Harrison, *Introduction to the Old Testament*, pp. 809-817. He concludes that the process of transmission from the lips of the prophet to the present form of the book was considerably less complex than the majority of liberal writers have assumed, and that it was completed by 520 B.C.

The Testimony of Scripture

The Gr. version of the OT ascribes Lamentations to Jeremiah; but the poems themselves do not claim Jeremianic authorship. Jeremiah is quoted in II Chr 36:21-23 and Ezr 1:1-2. Sir 49:6-7 reflects passages from it as well as from Lamentations. Daniel (9:2) refers to "the word of the Lord to Jeremiah the prophet" (Jer 25:12), and II Macc 2:1-8 contains echoes of the book of Jeremiah (cf. the relationship of Jer 33:15 with Isa 4:2; 11:1; 53:2; Zech 3:8; 6:12).

The NT writers show that the book of Jeremiah was held in high regard and considered canonical by often quoting and referring to it (cf. the new covenant in Jer 31:31 ff. with Heb 8:8-13; 10:15-17; Jer 31:15 with Mt 2:17 f.; Jer 23:5 with Lk 1:32 f.; Jer 11:20 and 17:10 with Rev 2:23; Jer 51:7-9 with Rev 14:8; 17:2-4; 18:3-5; Jer 10:7 with Rev 15:4; Jer 51:6, 9, 45 with Rev 18:4; Jer 51:63 f. with Rev 18:21; Jer 25:10 with Rev 18:22 f.; Jer 9:23 f. with I Cor 1:31; Jer 7:11 with Mt 21:13; Jer 22:5 with Mt 23:38).

The Teachings

The nature and character of God. The Lord is one God, righteous and just, pure and holy, merciful and gracious, slow to anger and a punisher of evildoers for their sins.

The message of warning to Israel.

1. Israel sustains a special relation wih the Lord (Jer 2:2-3; 7:23; 11:2-5; 13:11). Hosea and Jeremiah used the metaphors of marriage and filial relation which reflect this relationship (Hos 2:2; Jer 31:9).

2. Israel was faithless and was guilty of base apostasy (Jer 2:5-8, 13, 28; 3:1; 5:12, 23-24; 6:7; 7:30).

3. The nation of Israel was self-complacent and blindly trusted in religious externals (Jer 6:20; 7:4, 9-11; 8:8, 12; 16:10-12).

4. Judgment threatened Israel because of her sin (Jer 4:3-4; 6:8; 7:16-20; 14:12; 15:1-9).

The message of hope. Future restoration was a certainty. The political nation of Judah may perish, but the chosen people of God will survive. The eternal purposes of God would be realized (cf. the book of hope, chaps. 30-33). Elements of the future glory are:

1. The preservation of a remnant (Jer 4:27; 5:10, 18; 29:11; 30:11; 46:28).

2. The return from Exile (3:12, 21-22; 16:14-15; 25:11-14; 30:7-11; 31:23).

3. The new Jerusalem (33:16, to be associated with the name "the Lord our righteousness").

4. The ideal ruler (23:4-6; 30:9, 21).

5. The new and everlasting covenant (31:31-34; 32:40; 33:8).

6. The spirituality of religion (24:7), so that the exiles in Babylon (or anywhere else), separated from the temple worship, may seek the Lord directly in prayer (29:4-14).

7. Individual responsibility as the foundation of moral character and spiritual life (31:29-30).

8. The salvation of the nations (3:17; 4:2; 16:19; 33:9).

The visible nation may fall, but true Israel would live on. In the prophecy of the new covenant of grace and forgiveness of sins (31:31 f.) Jeremiah equals the most evangelical sections of Isaiah and other OT prophets.

Bibliography. Kenneth L. Barker, "Jeremiah's Ministry and Ours," BS, CXXVII (1970), 223-231. S. H. Blank, *Jeremiah, Man and Prophet*, Cincinnati: Hebrew Union College, 1961. John Bright, *Jeremiah*, Anchor Bible, Vol. XXI, Garden City: Doubleday, 1965. F. Cawley, "Jeremiah," NBC, pp. 608-639. Clyde F. Francisco, *Studies in Jeremiah*, Nashville: Convention Press, 1961. J. P. Hyatt, *Jeremiah—Prophet of Courage and Hope*, Nashville, Abingdon, 1958. C. F. Keil, *The Prophecies of Jeremiah*, KD. Irving L. Jensen,

Jeremiah: Prophet of Judgment, Chicago: Moody, 1966. Theodore Laetsch, *Jeremiah,* St. Louis: Concordia, 1952. Elmer A. Leslie, *Jeremiah,* Nashville: Abingdon, 1954. A. S. Peake, ed., *Jeremiah and Lamentations,* The New Century Bible, Edinburgh: T. C. & C. C. Jack, 1910. George A. Smith, *Jeremiah,* 4th ed., New York: Harper, 1940. A. Stewart, *Jeremiah, The Man and His Message,* Edinburgh: Henderson, 1936. C. von Orelli, *The Prophecies of Jeremiah,* Edinburgh: T. & T. Clark, 1889. A. C. Welch, *Jeremiah—His Time and His Work,* Oxford: Blackwell, 1951. Fred M. Wood, *Fire in My Bones,* Nashville: Broadman, 1959.

D. W. D.

JEREMIAS. NT form of Jeremiah (Mt 16:14). *See* Jeremiah.

JEREMOTH (jĕr′á-mŏth)
1. A Benjamite, son of Beriah. He dwelt in Jerusalem, head of a father's house (I Chr 8:14, 28).
2. A Levite, son of Mushi, of the family of Merari (I Chr 23:23; called Jerimoth in 24:30).
3. A Levite, son of Heman, and head of the 15th course of temple musicians (I Chr 25:22; called Jerimoth in 25:4).
4. An Israelite of the family of Elam who put away his Gentile wife in the days of Ezra (Ezr 10:26).
5. One of the family of Zattu, another who put away his foreign wife (Ezr 10:27).
6. One of the sons of Bani who put away his Gentile wife (Ezr 10:29, ASV, RSV; KJV reads "and Ramoth").

JEREMY. NT form of Jeremiah (*q.v.*). See Mt 2:17; 27:9.

JERIAH (jĕ-rī′á). A descendant of Levi through Hebron (I Chr 23:19; 24:23). An alternate spelling of Jerijah is used in I Chr 26:31.

JERIBAI (jĕr′ĭ-bī). One of David's "mighty men," a category used to distinguish them from the "three" and the "thirty" (I Chr 11:46).

JERICHO (jĕr′ĭ-kō). At the present stage of archaeological research OT Jericho is considered by the excavator Kathleen Kenyon to be the most ancient instance of urban civilization known to man. The site, located in the Jordan Valley about eight miles NW of the junction of the Jordan River with the Dead Sea, was supplied by a very excellent spring called 'Ayin es-Sultan and Elisha's Fountain (based on the incident in II Kgs 2:19–22). Even before pottery was used a sophisticated culture came into being near this spring. It was a walled town with solid stone structures showing an excellent architectural technique consisting of large dwellings and public buildings. The most remarkable feature of this pre-pottery neolithic culture was a number of human skulls covered with plaster molded to form the facial features, with inset shell eyes. This probably represented a form of ancestor worship, because the features resemble individual portraits; hence some concept of the spiritual nature of man was undoubtedly present. The strong fortifications and evidences of trade reveal these early people were not an isolated society. *See* Archaeology.

The following culture in Jericho was a retrogression. Sometime a little before 5000 B.C. a people using a red burnished coarse handmade pottery arrived. There was no continuity of occupation between these people and the pre-pottery culture; and though the use of pottery was a distinct advantage, the later culture as a whole was by far inferior. However, ascribed to this group is a kind of plastic art similar to, though in more ways different from, the plastered-skull art of the earlier group. A kind of idol was made with plaster smeared in a base of reeds rather than a skull. The shape is that of a flat disc on which are molded inexact features embellished with painted hair and beard and eyes again made of shell.

These people dug quarry pits into the pre-pottery level to obtain clay for their own building bricks formed in a distinctive bun shape. Little, however, is known of this 5th mil. neolithic culture because no burials have been discovered. There were two phases of this culture, the latter with a better handmade pottery which for the first time can be linked with other neolithic pottery from places like Byblos just N of Beirut and Sha'ar ha-Golan at the junction of the Yarmuk and Jordan rivers. Indeed, these crude villagers at Jericho were part of a great and wide movement of people throughout the Fertile Crescent and were making progress toward the age of metal and the dawn of history.

A well-known Chalcolithic culture called Ghassulian, which flourished throughout Palestine in the 4th mil. B.C., is completely absent at Jericho. After a period of no occupation (part of 4th mil.) Jericho came to life again *c.*3200 B.C. But the people were probably semi-nomadic because the evidence comes mostly from their rock tombs with very little from the city mound. The pottery from these tombs is of several types, each of which can be linked with separate sites in the Palestinian hill country. Hence in the late 4th mil. Palestine was receiving several new peoples. Many of them came in through Jericho from the E, a repetitive experience for this age-old city. This was a period of merging newly arrived cultures in Palestine which laid the foundation for the strong urban civilization of the coming Early Bronze Age.

During the Early Bronze Age (c. 2900–2300 B.C.) Jericho flourished as a fortified city. Its succession of defenses shows the constant struggle with eastern nomads and possibly the contest with other city-states like Jerusalem, Bethshan and Megiddo, which also helped to create this age of urbanization. The Early Bronze walls of Jericho give dramatic evidence of many destructions by fire. Other causes were

Airview of Old Testament Jericho

widespread erosion of the mud brick of which these walls were made and the not infrequent earthquakes to which this area is subjected. Two of these walls were thought by the 1930–36 excavators of Jericho (directed by Garstang) to be a double Late Bronze Age wall destroyed under Joshua. Kenyon's work has proved the two walls were not contemporary but both were of the Early Bronze Age.

Interesting architectural innovations appear at Jericho in this period: the use of a single and sometimes double ditch outside the walls to make them less accessible, and the abundant use of timbers in the walls for more stability but also as roof beams and roof supports in the mud brick houses. Kenyon believes this reflects the process of deforestation of Palestine which coincides with the period of major erosion at the end of the Early Bronze Age.

Perhaps the biggest change of population in Palestine came at the end of the Early Bronze Age. In the Middle Bronze Age there was a considerable technical advance in pottery through use of the fast wheel and the introduction of entirely new forms. In Jericho this change begins with a strong incursion of no-madic people whose distinctive tombs tell the story. The last Early Bronze wall was hastily built and destroyed by fire before it was completed. The newcomers usher in an intermediate period which Kenyon calls Early Bronze-Middle Bronze. At first living as nomads they built nothing, though eventually their meager building efforts were done with a unique greenish brick. Their pottery had some connection with the earlier period and was usually handmade except for the flaring necks and rims which were added on a fast wheel. Rough with no burnishing or paint, the only decoration is wavy and straight lined incisions sometimes having folded ledge handles. One house of this period seemed to be a temple with altar-like structures and an infant foundation sacrifice.

But the numerous single burial tombs make the clearest distinction with the earlier and later times. Dug into the limestone hills nearby these tombs reveal several distinct types of burial customs pointing to the separate tribes which joined to overthrow Early Bronze Age Jericho. There was the dagger tomb, a small neat type with a single dagger accompanying the articulate bones. Then there was the large roughly cut tomb where the individual was interred as a bag of bones with a batch of small pots and a four-spouted lamp set in a niche. A third square-shaft type had pots and a dagger and sometimes a javelin with curled tangs. One such tomb contained a tribal chief still wearing a copper headband. Finally there was a very large type tomb involving the removal of over 150 tons of rock simply to bury one or two individuals, who also may have been prominent personages. Though there is very little of an artistic nature about the roughly incised unburnished pottery and very utilitarian weapons of these people, yet some graffiti from a tomb shaft wall ties in with similar pottery painting of the Near East. Here are outlines of trees and desert animals with long horns like an ibex or goat, also two warriors holding javelins and small square shields.

Kenyon dates the beginning of this incursion *c*. 2300 B.C. and identifies it with that movement of nomads called in various ancient sources the Amorites.

About 1900 B.C. the Middle Bronze Age makes a full appearance at Jericho. This time the new people came from the N, perhaps pushed out of their former homes, for they came with a developed urban culture. The pottery was made completely on a fast wheel with many shapes derived from metalic prototypes. Bronze instead of copper made their tools and weapons more efficient, and building techniques reached a zenith at Jericho.

An entirely new type of defense system appears, similar to others like it in coastal Syria, Palestine and the Nile delta region. This consisted of a huge plastered embankment supported by a stone revetment at the bottom and having the town wall at the top. Such fortification is usually associated with the Asiatic invaders whom the Egyptians called the Hyksos, perhaps as a defense against new methods of warfare.

The E side of the Jericho mound yielded abundant witness to the town life of the latter part of he Middle Bronze Age. Here are ten

Major ruins of New Testament Jericho stand on the mound to the right of the mosque in right center. J. L. Kelso

strata of buildings. This Jericho came to a violent end shortly after the overthrow of the Hyksos in Egypt (*c*. 1570 B.C.). The Egyptians pursued them to Palestine and one by one destroyed many of their fortified cities such as Sharuhen, by 1550 B.C. Excavation of the last strata uncovered many houses and two steep "streets" with cobbled steps built on the E slope. One street had an underground drain; many ground level shops or storage rooms with the carbonized grain still in great jars; many clay loom-weights witnessing to a weaving industry. A single residence with dozens of querns for grinding flour was perhaps the premises of a flour merchant. Proof that this Jericho had strong contacts with Egypt comes from the presence of Hyksos-type scarabs; but also from well-preserved Egyptian-type furniture in the family tombs which were supplied with food and equipment for the after-life. The perishable items such as long, narrow wooden tables, stools, bowls, a bed, boxes, baskets, mats, etc., represent a most unusual departure for Palestinian archaeology where usually dampness puts strict limits on what is to be found. Probably volcanic gases stopped the decomposition in these sealed tombs.

On the important subject of Late Bronze Age Jericho and Joshua's conquest the Kenyon digging has produced little information. Proof of a 15th–14th cen. occupation is shown in the tombs. As to the mound, erosion is again extensive. But on the E slope erosion was stopped for 150 years by the Late Bronze town of *c*. 1400 B.C. According to Kenyon, no trace of the walls of Joshua's time remains. The reason for this seems to be that the walls were mud brick, as were most of Jericho's walls, and subject to erosion as well as to centuries of quarrying of the decayed mud brick by later peoples. The presence of the modern road over the most likely place where the wash from erosion might be found seems to be additional reason for finding sparse evidence of the Late Bronze Age. It must also be remembered that Garstang's excavations (1930–36) provided considerable uncontroverted Late Bronze material with little or no Mycenaean pottery which was entering Palestine by 1400 B.C. Yet quantities of such pottery have been found recently at Deir Allah and Tell es-Sa'idiyeh 30 miles up the Jordan. Thus Garstang dated the conquest of Jericho no later than 1385 B.C. Kenyon put the fall of Jericho to Joshua at *c*. 1350–1325 B.C. (*Digging up Jericho*, pp. 261–63). *See* Exodus, The: The Date.

Joshua's curse (Josh 6:26–27) was fulfilled on Hiel the Bethelite who rebuilt Jericho (I Kgs 16:34) in the days of Ahab (*c*. 880 B.C.). Most of this Iron Age stratum has also eroded, the earliest remains showing a prosperous community in the 7th cen. which was later destroyed by Nebuchadnezzar's army and rebuilt in the time of Ezra and Nehemiah (cf. Ezr 2:34; Neh 3:2; 7:36).

Herodian palace, New Testament Jericho. HFV

The excavations of J. L. Kelso and J. B. Pritchard in 1950 and 1951 uncovered a Roman style winter palace of Herod the Great at a town site about one and three-quarter miles SW of the OT mound. This was the Jericho where Zacchaeus (*q.v.*), the chief tax collector, lived in Jesus' time (Lk 19:1-2). It was dependent on waters brought from springs in the Wadi Qelt, up which the Roman road went to Jerusalem. Other Jews were evidently living in a village also known as Jericho but much nearer to the copious spring, for Matthew and Mark report that blind Bartimaeus (*q.v.*) was healed along the roadside as Jesus was leaving Jericho (Mt 20:29-34; Mk 10:46-52). Luke, however, states that Jesus was approaching Jericho at the time (18:35). The moving of medieval and modern Jericho a mile closer to Jordan should remind us that it was the oasis, not just the OT mound, which received the epithet "Jericho"—in its origin probably a reference to the moon-god worshiped here by the early Canaanite inhabitants.

Bibliography. John and J. B. E. Garstang, *The Story of Jericho,* London: Marshall, Morgan and Scott, 1948. Kathleen M. Kenyon, *Digging up Jericho,* London: Ernest Benn, 1957; "Jericho," TAOTS, pp. 264-275. Leon T. Wood, "Date of the Exodus," NPOT, pp. 69-73.

E. B. S.

JERIEL (jĕr'ĭ-ĕl). A man of the tribe of Issachar, the son of Tola (I Chr 7:2).

JERIJAH (jĕ-rī'ja). An alternate form of Jeriah (*q.v.*).

JERIMOTH (jĕr'ĭ-mŏth)
1. One of the five sons of Bela, son of Benjamin. He was head of his clan and a warrior in David's time (I Chr 7:7).
2. A son or descendant of Becher, son of Benjamin, head of another Benjamite clan (I Chr 7:8).
3. A Benjamite warrior who joined David at Ziklag. He could be 1 or 2 (I Chr 12:5).

4. A Levite, the son of Mushi of the family of Merari (I Chr 24:30; called Jeremoth in 23:23).
5. A Levite, son of Heman, and head of the 15th course of Levitical musicians (I Chr 25:4; called Jeremoth in 25:22).
6. The son of Azriel, chief of the tribe of Naphtali during David's reign (I Chr 27:19).
7. A son of David and father of Mahalath the wife of Rehoboam (II Chr 11:18). He is not listed among the sons of David. Jewish tradition holds that he was the son of a concubine.
8. A Levite appointed an overseer of the temple offerings by Hezekiah (II Chr 31:13).

JERIOTH (jĕr'ĭ-ŏth). One of the wives of Caleb, the son of Hezron (I Chr 2:18).

JEROBOAM (jĕr'ŏ-bō'ăm). Two kings of Israel carried this name. The name appears on a jasper seal found at Megiddo with the inscription "Shema, servant of Jeroboam," probably an official of Jeroboam II.
1. Jeroboam I (931-910 B.C.), of the tribe of Ephraim, son of Nebat and Zeruah. His energy and skill were recognized by Solomon in connection with the building of the tower of Millo, and he was put in charge of the Ephraimite draftees. The prophecy of Ahijah that Jeroboam would become king of the ten northern tribes instead of Rehoboam, the son of Solomon, came to the king's ears, and Jeroboam fled to Egypt for safety (I Kgs 11:26-40). Returning to Palestine after the death of Solomon, he headed up the delegation of the northern tribes seeking from Rehoboam an alleviation of the oppressions practiced by his father. When this was refused, the northern tribes broke away from the house of David and made Jeroboam king (I Kgs 12:2-15, 19-20).
Jeroboam rebuilt Shechem of Ephraim, which Abimelech, son of Gideon, had destroyed, and made it the royal residence. Next he built Penuel in Transjordan (I Kgs 12:25), either as a winter residence or as an alternate

Bethel, where Jeroboam set up one of his centers of calf worship. HFV capital because of Pharaoh Shishak's campaign *c*. 926 B.C. Finally he moved his royal residence to Tirzah (*q.v.*; 1 Kgs 14:17), a city NE of Shechem. His training under Solomon made him a great builder. He is chiefly known as "Jeroboam, the son of Nebat, who made Israel to sin." His sin was the erecting of the calves at Dan and Bethel, establishing in Israel the calf worship which he had doubtless seen in Egypt. His purpose was political, to keep the people away from the temple in Jerusalem, where their hearts might be drawn back to the house of David. The priests and Levites whose homes were in his territory were given no place in the new worship, others being indiscriminately chosen for the priesthood. He was undeterred in his purpose by the warnings of the unnamed prophet from Judah (1 Kgs 12:25 – 13:10, 33 – 34).

While his reign was prosperous, his sin brought on him the stern judgment of God, seen in the death of his young son Abijah, and in the tragic ending of his dynasty in the second generation (1 Kgs 14:1 – 20).

2. Jeroboam II (782 – 753 B.C.), son of Joash, and third in succession to Jehu. The duration of his reign given in II Kgs 14:23 (41 years) includes a coregency with his father of approximately 12 years, 794 – 782 B.C. His reign was one of great prosperity, militarily and economically. He continued the conquests which his father Joash had begun, restoring the borders of Israel which had been overrun by the Syrians and actually subjugating Damascus. As his father had received encouragement in this from Elisha, so Jeroboam was encouraged by the prophet Jonah. It was a period of great wealth. Extravagances and luxuries abounded, as excavations at the capital city of Samaria (*q.v.*) have verified; yet the poor were oppressed, and moral standards were sinking fast. The book of Amos gives a vivid picture of the godless abandonment to pleasure in the days of Jeroboam. Outwardly prosperous, his kingdom was on the verge of disintegration. On the one hand Jeroboam was a savior of Israel (II Kgs 14:27), but on the other hand his long reign brought the nation to the brink of judgment. About 30 years after his death, the kingdom of Israel ceased to exist.

J. C. M.

The Stele of Amrith, Syria, sixth century B.C., illustrates how pagans of the eastern Mediterranean area often viewed their gods as standing on the backs of animals. Some think Jeroboam sought to have Israelites envision Yahweh invisibly standing or seated on his golden calves. LM

JEROHAM (jĕ-rō′hăm)

1. The son of Elihu and father of Elkanah the father of Samuel (I Sam 1:1; I Chr 6:27, 34).

2. A Benjamite, father of several sons who lived in Jerusalem after the Exile (I Chr 8:27).

3. The father of Ibneiah, a chief of Benjamin after the Exile (I Chr 9:8). Possibly the same as 2.

4. A priest whose son Adaiah resided in Jerusalem after the Exile (I Chr 9:12; Neh 11:12).

5. Jeroham of Gedor, a village in Judah. His sons Joelah and Zebadiah joined David at Ziklag (I Chr 12:7).

6. The father of Azarel, chief of the tribe of Dan in the time of David (I Chr 27:22).

7. The father of Azariah, one of the captains who helped Jehoiada restore Joash to the throne of Judah (II Chr 23:1).

JERUBBAAL (jĕr′ŭ-bāl). The name means "let Baal contend," and is the name given to Gideon by his father Joash upon his destruction of the altar of Baal (Jud 6:32; 7:1). *See* Gideon.

JERUBBESHETH (jĕ-rŭb′ĕ-shĕth). A substitute name for Gideon in place of Jerubbaal used to avoid connecting Gideon with Baal worship (II Sam 11:21). *See* Gideon.

JERUEL (jĕ-rū′ĕl). A section of the wilderness of Judah, above and W of the cliffs overlooking the Dead Sea (II Chr 20:16, RSV), between Tekoa and En-gedi.

JERUSALEM (jĕ-rū′sà-lĕm). This city has been aptly called the "spiritual capital of the world," a judgment underscored by the United Nations' resolution of 1947 to designate it an international holy city. To students of the Bible and of history it is perhaps the world's most fascinating community, being one of the world's best preserved medieval walled cities, and sacred to the three leading monotheistic faiths— Judaism, Christianity, and Islam.

Name

The assumption that the name came originally from Heb. *'Ir Shalēm*, meaning "city of peace," appears now to be untenable. The Amarna letters (*q.v.*) written in Akkadian cuneiform have the word *Urusalim;* the Assyrian inscriptions of Sennacherib spell it *Urusalimmu*; and Egyptian hieroglyphics (19th – 18th cen. B.C.) have the equivalent of *Urushamem.* Modern scholars take these to mean "founded by the god Shalem," a god of the Amorites meaning "prosperer" (cf. Ezk 16:2). Its ancient biblical name appears to have been Salem (Gen 14:18; cf. Heb 7:2; Ps 76:2), a form of Heb. *shālôm*, "peace." God's people are to pray for the peace of Jerusalem (Ps 122:6). In the future age God will extend peace to her like a river (Isa 66:12), and here He will give peace (Hag 2:9). The correct Gr. transliteration *Ierousalēm* (Mt 23:37), used regularly in the LXX, follows the Aram. pronunciation *yerùshelēm* (Ezr 4:8, 12, etc.). The alternate form in the Gr. NT, *Hierosolyma*, is deliberately Hellenized to make a Gr.-sounding name.

After the time of the Conquest Jerusalem was known as Jebus (Jud 19:10 – 11), named after its inhabitants the Jebusites (*q.v.*) who were descendants of Hittites and Amorites. Other names include "Ariel" (Isa 29:1), "City of Righteousness" (Isa 1:26), "The Holy City" (Isa 48:2; 52:1; Neh 11:1, 18; 27:53). Today Muslims call it *Al-Quds al-Sharîf* ("the noble sanctuary"), or simply *Al-Quds.*

Location and Topography

Jerusalem is located 33 miles E of the Mediterranean and 14 miles due W of the N end of the Dead Sea, at approximately 31° N latitude and 35° E longitude.

The ancient city was built on top of a hill (Ps 48:1 –2; Zech 8:3) and yet was surrounded by higher hills on all sides except one (Ps 125:1 –2). The oldest portion—the Jebusite city—lay on a rocky spur projecting S to the confluence of the Kidron and Tyropoeon Val-

leys. It could be easily defended, and safeguarded the only adequate spring in the vicinity. North on the same spur was the temple site, Mount Moriah. To the W, across the Tyropoeon Valley lay the "upper city," slightly higher than the eastern ridge. Thus the city was in the shape of a U with the open end facing S toward the wilderness of Judea. To the E across the Kidron lies a saddle-shaped ridge 300 feet higher, dominated by Mount Scopus to the NE and Mount Olivet directly E. The view to the W is obstructed by the watershed of the hill country of Judea *c.* 2,800 feet above sea level. *Jebel Deir abu Tor* ("the hill of evil counsel," cf. Mt 26:14 – 16) cuts off much of the view to the S, so the only distant view is to the SE overlooking the desert, a fact which may account for the city's atmosphere of rugged independence.

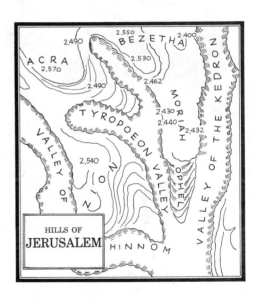

Hills of Jerusalem map

Water

The city's chief natural source of water in OT times was the spring Gihon (*q.v.*) in the Kidron Valley at the foot of the E slope of the Jebusite stronghold. It overflows intermittently three to five times a day. This is caused by underground cavities which fill up and initiate a siphoning process. Water from this source was denied to the Assyrian invaders and was made available to the besieged city by Hezekiah's famous tunnel which still conveys the water to the Pool of Siloam at the SW tip of the ridge (II Chr 32:3 –4, 30; Isa 22:11; Jn 9:7).

The Palestine Archaeological Museum, Jerusalem, where many of the treasures excavated in Palestine have been housed. HFV

A well known as Bir Eyyub, the biblical En-rogel (Josh 15:7; I Kgs 1:9), had early been dug SE of the city where the Kidron and Hinnom Valleys meet. In Roman times water was conveyed by an aqueduct built by Pilate from "Solomon's Pools" S of Bethlehem and by a high level aqueduct (A.D. 165) from Arrub, toward Hebron. In modern times water is pumped from copious springs N of Anathoth and from Ras el-'Ain in the Shephelah to the W.

The Walls of Jerusalem

The walls originally enclosed the tiny elongated "city of David" on the SE hill. Later, they were extended to enclose the enlarged city and temple area. The main sources for present knowledge of the ancient walls are Nehemiah and Josephus. In Jesus' time, the S wall crossed the Tyropoeon Valley and embraced both David's burg and the upper city where the Church of the Dormition now stands. The first N wall in His day ran due W from the temple area. The disputed "second wall" of Josephus ran from the vicinity of the Joppa Gate N and then E to join the fortress Antonia N of the temple. The "third wall," begun, according to Josephus, in A.D. 42, either lies under the existing N wall or it may be the line of massive stones far to the N of the present wall between the American Consulate and the American School of Oriental Re-

search. The present walls are those of Suleiman, built in A.D. 1542, and probably follow the Roman walls of Aelia Capitolina.

The Gates and Towers of Jerusalem

The gates and towers of the city wall at the time of its rebuilding during the governorship of Nehemiah are named in order, beginning with the Sheep Gate near the NE corner of the temple area, and proceeding counterclockwise around the fortifications (Neh 3). Either in connection with Nehemiah's preliminary inspection by night or with the dedication of the wall of Jerusalem most of the gates are mentioned again (Neh 2:12–15; 12:27–39).

1. *Sheep Gate* (Neh 3:1, 32; 12:39). It was on the N side of the city, between the Tower of Meah to the W and the Miphkad Gate to the E which was near the "going up of the corner," probably meaning the roof-chamber at the NE corner of the city (Neh 3:31, NEB). It is probable that the "sheep market" near the Pool of Bethesda (Jn 5:2) is actually the Sheep Gate (so RSV, NASB), the word "market" having been added by the KJV translators. Buying and selling was often done in the gateway area in ancient cities.

2. *Tower of Meah* (Neh 3:1; 12:39). Modern versions translate the name as Tower of the Hundred.

3. *Tower of Hananeel* (Neh 3:1; 12:39 ; Jer 31:38). This tower and the Tower of Meah guarded the temple area on the N, as the massive "castle" or Tower of Antonia built by King Herod did in the NT period (Acts 21:34, etc.; *see* Castle).

4. *Fish Gate* (Neh 3:3; 12:39; II Chr 33:14; Zeph 1:10). First mentioned in connection with the outer wall built by Manasseh, this gate in the N wall must have been near the present Damascus Gate, where the wall crosses the upper Tyropoeon Valley. The name probably came from the fact that fish from the Sea of Galilee were brought through it into the city, or because of a fish market located near it. This would be the Middle Gate of Jer 39:3 where the Babylonian officials sat, while King Zedekiah fled through a gate on the S side of the city (39:4).

5. *Old Gate* (Neh 3:6; 12:39). From this point onward to the Fountain Gate the line which the fortifications followed is very uncertain, for archaeologists have not yet been able to excavate sufficiently on the W hill to determine how much of it and at what periods it was enclosed within the city wall during OT times. NEB transliterates the name of this gate as the Jeshanah Gate and suggests in a footnote it was the gate of the old city. Depending on the extent of the city, it may have opened into the area called Ophel or the temple area on its W side, near the E end of Robinson's Arch. On the other hand, since Nehemiah does not mention the Corner Gate (II Kgs 14:13; II Chr 25:23; 26:9; Zech 14:10), that may be an alternate name for the Old Gate. The Corner Gate

may have been near the present citadel and Jaffa Gate, where Herod's palace stood in NT times.

6. *Ephraim Gate* (II Kgs 14:13; II Chr 25:23; Neh 8:16; 12:39). The location of this gate of pre-Exilic Jerusalem is given in II Kgs 14:13 and II Chr 25:23 as 400 cubits, or approximately 600 feet, from the Corner Gate. Because of its name it must have led out northward to the territory of Ephraim, thus serving the same purpose as the present Damascus Gate. Neh 8:16 refers to the broad place before the gate within the city walls where booths were built for the observance of the Feast of Tabernacles. Apparently this gate had been rebuilt before Nehemiah returned to Jeruslaem, since it is not mentioned in Neh 3 but is spoken of in Neh 12:39. In NT times the gate which Josephus called Gennath ("garden") stood on or near this spot (*Wars* v.4.2). Jesus may have been led out that gate, carrying His cross (Mt 27:31–32), since there was a garden near the crucifixion site (Jn 19:41).

7. *Broad Wall* (Neh 3:8; 12:38). Excavations in 1970 uncovered a 35 meter-long section of a city wall probably built by Hezekiah (*c.* 700 B.C.) on the western hill. Its unusual thickness of seven meters (23 feet) suggests that it may have been the Broad Wall, still standing in part after Nebuchadnezzar's de-

structions in 586 B.C. It is much farther E, however, than the present W wall built by Suleiman in A.D. 1542, the newly discovered section lying *c.* 275 meters W of the temple enclosure and *c.* 400 meters E of the Jaffa Gate (N. Avigad, "Excavations in the Jewish Quarter," IEJ, XX [1970], 129–135).

8. *Tower of the Furnaces* (Neh 3:11; 12:38). This tower may be one of those constructed during Uzziah's reign, perhaps the one to fortify the Valley Gate (II Chr 26:9). The "furnaces" or "ovens" (RSV) may refer to pottery kilns which were probably located near Jeremiah's "Potsherd Gate" (Jer 19:2, RSV, NASB), the Valley Gate.

9. *Valley Gate* (Neh 2:13; 3:13; II Chr 26:9). This is the same as the "East Gate" of Jer 19:2 (KJV), a faulty translation of Heb. *sha'ar haharsit,* "the Potsherd Gate" (RSV), where broken pottery from the potters' shops was thrown out into the Valley of Hinnom on the refuse heaps. The Valley Gate must have stood high on the western hill and faced SW, since it was 1,000 cubits (1,500 feet) W of the Dung Gate (Neh 3:13).

10. *Dung Gate* (Neh 2:13; 3:13–14; 12:31). It was so named because the refuse of the city was taken through it to be burned in the Valley of Hinnom. Josephus called it the Gate of the Essenes (*Wars* v.4.2). It may have been at or

Jerusalem from the Mount of Olives with the Temple area in foreground. HFV

near the S tip of the walled city, somewhat S of the Pool of Siloam, where the wall must have crossed the mouth of the Tyropoeon Valley. Remains of an ancient gate have been found here. In Jeremiah's time the gate in this section was described as "the gate between the two walls" (II Kgs 25:4; Jer 39:4; 52:7), through which King Zedekiah fled toward the Jordan Valley. Near this gate lay the "king's garden" (II Kgs 25:4; Neh 3:15).

11. *Fountain Gate* (Neh 2:14; 3:15; 12:37). This gate can be located quite closely, since it was near the Pool of Siloam or King's Pool within the city and led directly to the "stairs of the city of David" (Neh 12:37). The remains of a staircase cut in the rock, leading up from the Kidron Valley, show that the Fountain Gate was just N of the SE corner of the city. Its name may indicate that it opened to the "dragon well" (Neh 2:13), the well named En-rogel (II Sam 17:17; I Kgs 1:9), a little way down the Kidron Valley.

12. *Water Gate* (Neh 3:26; 8:1, 3, 16; 12:37). Undoubtedly this gate, which was "toward the east," provided a surface route in peaceful times to descend to the spring Gihon at the foot of the hill. When under siege the defenders walled up the mouth of Gihon, and its waters flowed through Hezekiah's tunnel to the Pool of Siloam. The gate may have been considerably N of Gihon, however, much closer to the temple, as Neh 8:1–5 might suggest. The walls between the Fountain and Water Gates must have been in an extremely bad state of disrepair, judging from the number of men who worked on rebuilding it (Neh 3:15–26).

Miss Kenyon found in her excavations that the terraces supporting houses within the pre-Exilic wall had eroded and collapsed after the Babylonian destruction of Jerusalem. She also discovered that the N wall of the Jebusite city curved from the slope not far N of Gihon and up to the top of the ridge in a northwesterly direction. The Israelite wall connecting this part of the city to the temple mount ran along the E crest on a northeasterly course, forming a right angle in the city wall where it began (cf. "the Angle," II Chr 26:9; Neh 3:19, 20, 24, 25, RSV).

Near the Water Gate was built the "great tower that lieth out" (Neh 3:27), a large projecting tower adjacent to the wall guarding the E side of Ophel, the section of the city just S of the temple area.

13. *Horse Gate* (Neh 3:28; II Kgs 11:16; II Chr 23:15; Jer 31:40). Queen Athaliah was killed at the Horse Gate, which at that time led from the temple to the palace (II Chr 23:15). By Jeremiah's time a city gate of that name marked the easternmost part of the city, probably a little N of "the corner" (Jer 31:40) where the city wall became the E wall of the temple enclosure.

14. *East Gate* (Neh 3:29). Since the East Gate is not stated to have been repaired in

Nehemiah's time, it may have been the eastern gate of the temple (cf. Ezk 10:19; 11:1), which had already been rebuilt under Zerubbabel. It would have been opposite the temple building, somewhat S of the present walled-up Golden Gate. For the "east gate" of Jer 19:2 (KJV) *see* Valley Gate, 9 above.

15. *Miphkad Gate* (Neh 3:31, KJV). Other versions translate the name of this gate as "Muster Gate" (RSV), "Mustering Gate" (NEB), or "Inspection Gate" (NASB). This may have been the Benjamin Gate of Jer 20:2; 37:13; 38:7; Zech 14:10, which seems definitely to have been adjacent to the temple and near the NE corner of the city and leading to the territory of Benjamin. The "upper Benjamin Gate" where Jeremiah was imprisoned (Jer 20:2, NASB) was probably a temple gate, perhaps the same as the Gate of the Guards (II Kgs 11:19). The Miphkad Gate must have been at or near the present Golden Gate. Jesus may have come into Jerusalem through this or the East Gate in His triumphal entry. Just N of the Miphkad Gate was the corner of the city defense where the wall turned to the NW, with the Sheep Gate in that section.

16. *Gates of the temple.* In addition to the gates of the city wall certain gates of the temple are named: (1) *Gate Sur* (II Kgs 11:6)—*Gate of the Foundation* (II Chr 23:5); (2) *Gate of the Guards* (II Kgs 11:6, 19; Neh 12:39, KJV, "prison gate"; cf. Jer 20:2); (3) *Gate Shallecheth* (I Chr 26:16), on the W side of the temple area opening on the Tyropoeon Valley; (4) *New Gate* (Jer 36:10); (5) *Beautiful Gate* (*see* Gate, Beautiful; Acts 3:10), perhaps the Nicanor Gate of the Mishnaic tractate Middoth, on the E side of the court of the women (cf. Jos *Wars* v.5.3); (6) the *East Gate* (*see* 14 above).

Excavations

Captain Charles Warren, a British mining engineer, was the first man to conduct any sort of scientific investigation of Jerusalaem. In 1867–70 he excavated around the walls of the temple area, probing the four sides of the *Haram esh-Sherif* with a system of shafts and tunnels. F. J. Bliss and A. C. Dickie explored the S end of the western hill in 1894–97 and found a large wall across the mouth of the Tyropoeon Valley. While the wall has never been accurately dated, it does not seem to go back to OT times. In 1909–11 Montague Parker, with the aid of Père L.H. Vincent, explored and interpreted the maze of tunnels leading from Gihon spring, thus explaining how the Jebusites obtained water during a siege. Raymond Weill excavated parts of the SE hill in 1913–14 and demonstrated once and for all that it was the site of the Jebusite city which David captured and called Zion.

After World War I during the 1920's Weill conducted further excavations at the S tip of the old city. J. Garrow Duncan and R. A. S. Macalister investigated the ridge and along the slope above Gihon. They dated a portion of the wall to the Jebusites, but in 1961 this was proved to belong to the 2nd cen. B.C. Two other British archaeologists, J. W. Crowfoot and G. M. Fitzgerald, dug a trench from the Ophel area on the crest of the Jebusite hill down its W slope and across the Tyropoeon Valley. They uncovered a massive city gate and wall on this side of the SE hill, proving it had been encircled by walls as late as the Maccabean period. Quite far N of the walled old city E. L. Sukenik and L. A. Mayer discovered sections of a wall seemingly built by Herod Agrippa I (A.D. 40 – 44).

In excavations extending between 1934 and 1948 C. N. Johns carried out extensive examinations of the citadel. A city wall curved around here from the crest above the Valley of Hinnom, and then ran E toward the temple. On it were three towers, the latest Herodian and the earliest Hellenistic or early Hasmonean. Some 7th cen. B.C. pottery was found in the citadel area. A portion of a pre-Hasmonean, probably Israelite, wall built of squared but rough blocks of stone was found under the Herodian tower known as Phasael in further diggings since 1967.

After World War II and the birth of the State of Israel in 1948 no large-scale excavation in Jerusalem was undertaken until 1961. In that year and through 1967 Kathleen A. Kenyon and Pere R. de Vaux directed annual campaigns to investigate a number of areas in Jerusalem using the most up-to-date stratigraphical techniques. These excavations established with reasonable certainty the position of the earliest city and its wall. The Jebusite defenses were built well down the slope of the Kidron Valley in order to protect the entrance to the tunnel leading to the shaft above the cave of Gihon spring. From its origin c. 1800 B.C. the city wall was located on this course at least until the 7th cen. B.C., well into the Israelite period.

Since the Six Day War in 1967 Israeli archaeologists led by Benjamin Mazar have excavated S and SW of the temple precinct. A beautifully paved Herodian street was found running along the S and W enclosure walls of Herod's temple. The remains of the great bridge crossing the Tyropoeon Valley from the palace area on the western hill to the Royal Stoa in the temple area (connecting at "Robinson's Arch") were investigated. Instead of a series of arches, the 48-foot-wide viaduct stretched c. 40 feet above the street to a finely constructed pier on the W side of the valley. Four small rooms, which probably served as shops, were built into the pier and faced the Herodian avenue. Beneath the paving slabs ran a great aqueduct hewn into bedrock by Herod's workmen (BA, XXXIII [1970], 47 – 60). Monumental stairs were discovered leading up from the old city of David to one of the Hulda Gates in the S wall of Herod's temple. Beneath one of these gates was found a rock-cut tunnel

New excavations near the Western Wall of the Temple. HFV

which, according to the Mishnah, may have served for priestly access to the sanctuary.

Other excavations have uncovered numerous Jewish tombs, including a 1st cen. A.D. cemetery N of the old city. In one of these tombs were bones of a young Jew who had been crucified (see Cross).

History

Jerusalem's prehistory goes back at least to the Early Bronze Age when nomadic tribes camped on the SE hill and left some of their kitchen pots and flint tools in a cave c. 3000 B.C. It must have been regarded as a holy city from patriarchal times, for Abraham is reported as having paid tithes to Melchizedek (q.v.), its unique priest-king (Gen 14:18 – 20). It was inhabited during the period of the Amorite influx into Palestine, listed as Aushamem in the Egyptian Execration texts (c. 1900 B.C.) now in the Berlin Museum (ANET, p. 329).

At the time of the Israelite invasion (c. 1400 B.C.) Adoni-zedec, king of Jerusalem, led a coalition which unsuccessfully challenged Joshua's advance (Josh 10:1 – 26). During the Amarna period its ruler 'Abdu-Heba wrote a number of letters to pharaoh begging for military assistance (ANET, pp. 487 ff.). Afterward the Israelites captured the city outside the walls and set it on fire (Jud 1:7 – 8); but apparently they did not occupy the citadel, for it was listed as an unconquered city of Jebusites (Jud 1:21; 19:10 – 12). Because of its natural defenses the Jebusites later felt strong enough to challenge David and his men. Joab and his warriors very likely gained access to the citadel through the large water tunnel leading up from the spring Gihon (II Sam 5:6 – 9; I Chr 11:6).

In 1867 Charles Warren discovered a vertical shaft 40 feet high within the hill. It enabled residents to draw water from a reservoir filled by means of a horizontal tunnel leading back from the spring. An erratic passage led from the top of the shaft to the surface. The entrance to the passage lay within the town wall, which was 160 feet down from the crest of the ridge and originally built in Middle Bronze Age II (*c.* 1800 B.C.).

With David's capture of the city, Jerusalem entered the realm of world history. His choice of a capital proved to be a wise one. It was a pagan city, not previously claimed by any of the tribes of Israel, and hence it could not be a source of jealousy. It was on the border line of Judah and Benjamin, adjacent to both David's tribe and that of his predecessor. In addition to these political advantages of the time there were the long-range assets of a site easily defended, a secure water supply, and a healthy climate. With an elevation of 2,600 feet it remains one of the highest national capitals in the world. Even in summer the nights are fairly cool because of the elevation and breeze.

David's first act was to strengthen the fortifications of the city by construction of Millo (*q.v.*), perhaps a fortification on the same ridge and to the N of "David's city" in the area called Ophel (Neh 3:26–27). Miss Kenyon believes the *millo* or "filling" was a series of terraces with massive substructures on the eastern slope, built to enlarge the residential area of the crowded city. With the accession of Solomon, extensive building operations transformed the hill N of Ophel into one of the architectural wonders of the world. On that hill was erected Solomon's temple, over the probable site of Abraham's sacrifice of Isaac (Gen 22) and the site of the threshing floor of Araunah the Jebusite (II Sam 24:16–25). The enormous walls built during Solomon's time are probably buried under the present *Haram esh-Sherîf,* the enclosure around Herod's temple which he had enlarged to nearly twice its former size.

Jerusalem experienced numerous vicissitudes after the "golden age" of Solomon. Shishak, *c.* 926 B.C., invaded Judah and threatened Jerusalem (I Kgs 14:25–26) but was content with exacting a heavy tribute. During the reign of Jehoram the city was attacked by Philistines and Arabs (II Chr 21:16–17). When Amaziah was king, a portion of the city wall was destroyed by Jehoash of the northern kingdom, and much booty was taken (II Kgs 14:8 ff.). During the reign of Uzziah, however, the city was greatly built up and strengthened and its prestige, in a large measure, restored (II Chr 26:7–8). Another crisis in the city's history occurred when Ahaz was on the throne at the time of the Syro-Ephraimitic war (cf. Isa 7:1–9); then the nation was threatened by a coalition of Israel and Syria (II Kgs 16:5–6).

A major crisis came in 701 B.C. The Assyrians under Sennacherib invaded Judah and besieged Jerusalem (Isa 36–37). In spite of extensive precautions taken by Hezekiah—strengthening the walls and safeguarding the water supply—the city escaped destruction only by divine intervention as stated in II Kgs 18:13–19:37 (cf. Isa 22:1–14). Hezekiah's idolatrous son Manasseh further strengthened the defenses (II Chr 33:14), and it was now one of the most impregnable cities in the world.

Nevertheless, the beginning of the end may be seen in Nebuchadnezzar's occupation of the city in 597 B.C. when he carried into captivity its best citizens and its treasure (II Kgs 24:10–16). The final tragedy occurred in 587/6 B.C. with the complete destruction of the city and the transfer of most of the citizens and artifacts to Babylonia. The seriousness of this ruin can scarcely be overestimated, and the deep scar was never to be effaced (Lam 1:1–19; Ps 79:1–9). Archaeology confirms the biblical account of the thoroughness of the destruction of both city and countryside.

Hope did not die with the city, however. After the accession of Cyrus (539 B.C.) the Jewish emigrants were allowed to return and rebuild. One of their first acts was to lay the foundations of the second temple. After a 20-year period of neglect and apathy, the house of the Lord was completed and dedicated in 516 B.C. The city and environs maintained a precarious existence thereafter with only a vestige of its former glory and influence (Ezra, Nehemiah, Haggai; *see* Restoration and Persian Period).

In the 2nd cen. B.C. another major crisis arose when the Seleucids of Syria gained control of Palestine from the Ptolemies and Antiochus IV began a campaign to force Hellenism upon the Jews. In the ensuing struggle, Jerusalem was captured in 168 B.C., its temple desecrated. But it was recaptured in 165 B.C. by Jewish patriots led by the Maccabbean family of five brothers. The temple, cleansed and rededicated at the Feast of Lights, continued to serve as the focus of Jewish religious and political life until NT times.

Pompey the Roman general arrived in Jerusalem in 63 B.C. at the invitation of one of the warring factions of the Pharisees. Roman rule remained in Palestine thereafter until the Byzantine Empire became dominant. During these

The Western Wall of the Temple (Wailing Wall).
HFV

years Jerusalem remained the religious center of the Jews both of Palestine and of the Dispersion. Here on Passover occasions and other festivals throngs of pilgrims converged on the city. At such times it often became the scene of violence, as at the accession of Herod's successor Archelaus (when 3,000 died), at the death of Jesus, and when Paul was rescued from a mob (Acts 21:30). The temple of Herod, in Jewish thinking still the second temple although enlarged and completely remodeled, was begun in 19 B.C. and completed in A.D. 64, six years before the total destruction of the city in A.D. 70 following a four-year rebellion against Rome.

Jerusalem was leveled to the ground after the second Jewish revolt under Bar Kochba in A.D. 134 and rebuilt by Hadrian as a pagan city called Aelia Capitolina. Gradually Christians became more and more numerous in the city; Christian churches were erected there from the 4th cen. until the Muslim conquest in A.D. 637. Muslim influence has been dominant in the city from then until the present with the exception of the Latin Kingdom (A.D. 1099 – 1188) and other short intervals during the Crusades. Palestine was occupied by the Ottoman Empire for four centuries (1517 – 1917).

Since the last quarter of the 19th cen. Jewish immigration from all over the world has greatly increased the size of the city until at the present time there is a population of about 300,000 Jews and 80,000 Arabs.

After the termination of Ottoman rule in Palestine by World War I, Great Britain held a Mandate over Palestine from the League of Nations for 30 years. When this terminated in 1948 Arabs and Jews fought to a standstill along armistice lines which divided the city until 1967. After the Six Day War in 1967, Israel united the Holy City and declares she will not surrender the eastern section regardless of what decision is made on other occupied territories.

While the capitals of mighty empires — Tyre, Thebes, Nineveh, Babylon — have laid in ruins for millennia, Jerusalem survives as a commercial and political center, but most of all as a museum of the past and a symbol of hope for the future.

Bibliography. D. R. Ap-Thomas, "Jerusalem," TAOTS, pp. 276 - 295. M. Avi-Yonah, *Jerusalem,* New York: Orion, 1960. Millar Burrows, "Jerusalem," IDB, II, 843 – 866. Joseph A. Callaway, "Jerusalem," BW, pp. 309 – 323. G. Cornfeld, "Ancient Cities: Jerusalem," CornPBE, pp. 80 – 89. G. Fohrer and E. Lohse, "*Sion, Ierousalēm,* etc.," TDNT, VII, 292 – 338. John Gray, *A History of Jerusalem,* London: Hale, 1969. Joachim Jeremias, *Jerusalem in the Time of Jesus,* Philadelphia: Fortress, 1969. Kathleen M. Kenyon, *Jerusalem,* New York: McGraw-Hill, 1967; "Israelite Jerusalem," *Near Eastern Archaeology in the Twentieth Century,* ed. by J. A. Sanders, Garden City: Doubleday, 1970, pp. 232 – 253.

André Parrot, *Golgotha and the Church of the Holy Sepulchre,* London: SCM Press, 1957. D. F. Payne, "Jerusalem," NBD, pp. 614 – 620. Stewart Perowne, *Jerusalem and Bethlehem,* New York: Barnes, 1965. Charles F. Pfeiffer, *Jerusalem Through the Ages,* Grand Rapids: Baker, 1967. J. Simons, *Jerusalem in the Old Testament,* Leiden: Brill, 1952. George A. Smith, *Jerusalem,* 2 vols., New York: Armstrong, 1907 - 8. Wilbur M. Smith, "Jerusalem," ZPBD, pp. 417 - 427. Hermann Strathmann, "*Polis,* etc.," TDNT, VI, 516 – 536. L. H. Vincent, *Jerusalem de l' Ancien Testament,* Paris: Gabalda, 1954- 6.

G. A. T. and J. R.

JERUSALEM COUNCIL. *See* Apostolic Council.

JERUSALEM, NEW. The New Jerusalem (Rev 3:12; 21:2, 10) was looked for by Abraham (Heb 11:10, 16), promised by Christ (Jn 14:2 - 3), referred to as Zion the mountain and city of the living God (Heb 12:22), alluded to by Paul (Gal 4:26), employed as an incentive (Rev 3:12), and described in Rev 21:1 – 22:5. It is not identical with the earthly Jerusalem of the Millennium, nor is it equivalent to the new heaven. This city comes down out of heaven from God after the Millennium, and is the center of the new order. It is the habitation of Christ and the Church and is accessible to the saved nations.

The city is described first from the standpoint of its population, the Church (Rev 21:1 - 9); then from the viewpoint of its material proportions, a cube 1,500 miles each way, made of gold and precious stones (Rev 21:10 - 23); and finally from the viewpoint of its eternal provisions (Rev 21:24 — 22:5). This divine architectural achievement has material reality — the resurrected saints and Christ will inhabit it with physically real bodies, though its details symbolize great spiritual realities. *See* City of God; City, Holy; Heaven; Zion.

H. A. Hoy.

JERUSHA, JERUSHAH (jĕ-rū′shȧ). The mother of Jotham, the wife of King Uzziah, and the daughter of Zadok (II Kgs 15:33). The alternate spelling of Jerushah is found in II Chr 27:1.

JESAIAH (jĕ-sā′yȧ), **JESHAIAH** (jĕ-shā′yȧ)

1. A son of Hananiah, son of Zerubbabel (I Chr 3:21).

2. A Levite, one of the sons of Jeduthun. He was a harpist and appointed by David to be head of the eighth course of musicians (I Chr 25:3, 15).

3. A Levite, the son of Rehabiah. A descendant, Shelomoth, was over the treasury of things dedicated by David and the other leaders to the Lord (I Chr 24:21, Isshiah; 26:25 - 26).

4. The son of Athaliah, chief of the family of

Elam. He returned to Jerusalem with Ezra (Ezr 8:7).

5. A Levite of the family of Merari. With Hashabiah and 20 sons and brethren he joined Ezra at Ahava on the way to Jerusalem (Ezr 8:19).

6. A Benjamite, father of Ithiel, whose descendants dwelt in Jerusalem after the Exile (Neh 11:7).

JESHANAH (jĕsh'à-nà). One of the cities taken by King Abijah of Judah in a war with Jeroboam II (II Chr 13:19). The RSV has Jeshanah for Shen in I Sam 7:12. The most probable location is Burj el-Isaneh, about three miles N of Jifneh.

JESHARELAH (jĕsh'à-rē'là). A musician among the sons of Asaph during the time of David (I Chr 25:14). He is called Asarelah in v. 2.

JESHEBEAB (jē-shĕb'ē-ăb). The head of the 14th order of priests (I Chr 24:13).

JESHER (jē'shẽr). A son of Caleb (I Chr 2:18).

JESHIMON (jē-shī'mŏn)

1. A barren place at the NE end of the Dead Sea E of Jordan ("Jeshimon," KJV; "desert," ASV, RSV). Mount Pisgah and Mount Peor look down upon it; mentioned in connection with Israel's journey to Canaan (Num 21:20; 23:28).

2. A place N of the hill Hachilah and the wilderness of Maon, and S of Hebron. Rendered "Jeshimon" in the KJV and RSV; ASV, "desert," but marg., "Jeshimon." Apparently part of the general wilderness of Judah in which David was a fugitive when Saul was hunting for him (I Sam 23:19, 24; 26:1, 3).

JESHISHAI (jē-shĭsh'ī). A member of the tribe of Gad, a descendant of Buz (I Chr 5:14).

JESHOHAIAH (jĕsh'ŏ-hā'yà). A Simeonite prince (I Chr 4:36).

JESHUA (jĕsh'ōō-à)

1. A priest in the time of David to whom the ninth course was assigned by lot (I Chr 24:11). Descendants of the house of Jeshua returned after the Exile (Ezr 2:36; Neh 7:39).

2. A Levite appointed by Hezekiah to distribute the offerings among his brethren (II Chr 31:15).

3. A Levite whose descendants, "the children of Jeshua," returned with Zerubbabel (Ezr 2:40; Neh 7:43). Perhaps the same as 2.

4. The son of Jozadak, who returned with Zerubbabel to Jerusalem as high priest. He is of historic importance as the one under whom the temple was rebuilt and the worship restored. From him descended 14 successive high priests. Jeshua is named with the prince Zerubbabel as an equal not only in the work of the

temple but in the relations of the Jews with other peoples (Ezr 2:2; 3:2, 8, 9 f.; 4:3; 5:2; 10:18; Neh 7:7; 12:1, 7, 10, 26). The word of the Lord through the prophet Haggai was addressed to Zerubbabel and Jeshua (called Joshua in Hag 1:1, 12, 14; 2:2, 4). He is used by Zechariah as a symbol of the restored, forgiven remnant, a "brand plucked out of the fire" (Zech 3:1 – 3), and also as a type of Christ, the "Branch" and the "priest upon his throne" (Zech 3:6 ff.; 6:11 – 13).

5. The father of Jozabad the Levite, appointed by Ezra as one of those to receive the treasure delivered to the temple (Ezr 8:33).

6. Of the town of Pahath-moab. His descendants are named along with Joab among those who returned with Zerubbabel (Ezr 2:6; Neh 7:11).

7. Ezer, son of Jeshua, ruler of Mizpah, helped in the repair of the wall of Jerusalem with Nehemiah (Neh 3:19).

8. A prominent Levite during the time of Nehemiah. Jeshua, son of Kadmiel, stood with Ezra as he read the law and helped explain it to the people (Neh 8:7 – 8). He took part in the great prayer of confession at the Feast of Tabernacles (Neh 9:4 – 5). He is listed among the heads of his father's houses among Levites (Neh 12:8, 24).

9. Joshua the son of Nun, called Jeshua in Neh 8:17.

10. A Levite, son of Azaniah, who sealed the covenant of Nehemiah (Neh 10:9). He is difficult to distinguish from 8.

11. A city of Judah inhabited after the Exile (Neh 11:26).

P. C. J.

JESHUAH. See Jeshua.

JESHURUN (jĕsh'ū-rŭn). A poetic term for Israel meaning "upright one." If the ending -un is a diminutive, it means "little upright one" (Deut 32:15; 33:5, 26; Isa 44:2).

JESIAH (jē-sī'à)

1. KJV variant of Isshiah 3 (q.v.). One of David's mighty men when he was at Ziklag (I Chr 12:6).

2. KJV variant of Isshiah 2 (q.v.). A Levite, son of Uzziel (I Chr 23:20).

JESIMIEL (jē-sĭm'ĭ-ĕl). A prince of the tribe of Simeon (I Chr 4:36).

JESSE (jĕs'ĭ). A descendant of Obed, the son of Boaz and Ruth (Ruth 4:17, 22), in the clan of Nahshon, chief of the tribe of Judah in the time of Moses. Jesse had eight sons, of whom David was the youngest, and two daughters (I Sam 17:12). The daughters were by a different wife from David's mother. Jesse lived in Bethlehem and was supported through shepherding and goat herding

The humble status of his family is alluded to by the opprobius epithet "son of Jesse" given to David by those who disliked him (e.g., I Sam 20:27, 30; 22:7; 25:10; II Sam 20:1). Jesse sought asylum in Moab during David's flight from Saul (I Sam 22:3–4). The expression "shoot from the stump of Jesse" and "the root of Jesse" in Isa 11:1, 10 (RSV), which indicate the insignificant and lowly background of the royal line of David, became symbols of messianism.

F. E. Y.

JESTING. In the KJV the term is used only in Eph 5:4, where it means having a coarse, frivolous attitude toward serious matters. In the RSV it is used only in Gen 19:14, where Lot's sons-in-law thought he was joking about the coming destruction.

JESUI (jĕsʹū-ī). A son of Asher (Num 26:44). *See* Ishui.

JESURUN. *See* Jeshurun.

JESUS CHRIST. Jesus Christ is unique in several respects, not the least of which is the fact that in Him alone centers the gospel of the grace of God. He has changed the face of history, for in Him eternity has invaded time, God has become man, and human life has achieved through His redemption a significance that lifts it above the natural order and fits it for God's fellowship and service.

But is such a life possible? The philosopher may be inclined to deny it on the ground that the gulf between God and man is too great to be bridged in a single being and that the elements involved are too discrete to be combined in a unified personality. Yet the Gospel records present just such a personality. One has the choice between supposing a literary miracle based on fancy and accepting a historical miracle based on the sovereign action of Almighty God, adequately attested by competent witnesses. *See* Christ, Deity of; Christ, Humanity of; Christ, Humiliation of; Christ, Sinlessness of.

The historian may feel that he cannot dismiss Jesus Christ as unhistorical, in view of the substantial character of the evidence, but nevertheless acknowledges misgivings as to the factuality of many elements of the story as given in our sources. After all, the earliest of the Gospels emerged some 30 years after the latest of the events it recounts. Granted the interval exists, yet it is not an empty interval. Memories of Jesus of Nazareth lived on in scores, yes hundreds of lives, and these memories were kept vivid by frequent recollection stimulated both by meditation and by proclamation.

Though Jesus wrote nothing for posterity, He gave assurance to His closest followers that the Spirit of God would have as a peculiar part of His ministry the bringing to remembrance in the minds of these men of the things that Jesus had said (Jn 14:26). Even apart from supernatural aid the disciples could never forget the

Traditional site of the manger in which Jesus was born inside the Church of the Nativity, Bethlehem.
Giovanni Trimboli

stirring scenes that they had shared with the Master. Some incidents involved Jesus alone, such as the temptation, but there is no reason to suppose that He would have refrained from informing them of what transpired.

It is not possible to demonstrate that the materials in the Gospels are always arranged in strict chronological order. But it is clear that all the records preserve an order of events that proceeds from those that belong to the commencement of the ministry to those that mark its close, so that there is a sense of progress and also of symmetry. One does not get an impression of erratic or fanciful composition.

The setting for this greatest of all lives is the land of Palestine at a time when Rome had established her sovereignty over much of the Near East. Government officials, military men and tax gatherers were constant and unpleasant reminders that Israel was not free. Restlessness, at least among the Zealots, was gradually building up toward open revolt. In such an atmosphere it would not be easy to carry on a ministry grounded in spiritual considerations. Jesus' teaching and personal claims could be easily misconstrued. Any assertion of kingly right was bound to be distorted by some into a bid for temporal power. Any talk of freedom was all too readily lifted from its context of bondage to sin and made to apply to the current political situation. It was only with the greatest difficulty that even the Twelve were weaned from these notions. By the time this adjustment was made (Acts 1) Jesus was on the point of departure from the world. Thus even if the temporal concept of the kingdom had persisted, it would have lacked any possibility of realization, since the Master was no longer on the scene. Under the control of the Holy Spirit the church could move only along the lines laid down by Jesus—a kingdom free from worldly motives and methods. Rome need have no fears of competition from this quarter.

Although Jesus spent His days on earth under the Roman eagle, His life was far more heavily influenced by His Jewish inheritance. Born of a Jewish mother, nurtured in a home of piety and possibly of near poverty, encouraged to love the Scriptures, trained in the worship and instruction of the synagogue, He steeped His mind in the history and traditions of His people. The readiness with which He could quote Scripture and the appropriateness of His references to it testify to prolonged and thoughtful study. His boyhood development along this line is hidden from us; but this much is clear, that He turned to the Word not only for spiritual nourishment but also to find the indications of His own mission (Lk 4:18 – 19; 22:37; 24:44 – 47). Lacking formal rabbinic training, He was able to assess the spiritual needs of His nation in an independent manner and could point out the various ways in which the religious leaders had led the people astray.

This ability to be in Judaism and yet to stand over against it is reflected in a certain duality that runs through Jesus' ministry, namely, loyalty to Israel (Jn 4:22; Mt 10:6; 15:24) yet admiration for the faith of those who were outside the covenant nation (Mt 8:10); compassion for His own countrymen (Mt 23:37) yet forthright prediction that others would step into Israel's inheritance (Mt 8:11 – 12). Jesus the Jew was in many ways the most unjewish of men. He was, in fact, the universal man. Perhaps that is part of what He sought to convey by calling Himself the Son of man (*see* Son of Man). To be sure, He was the son of David and the son of Abraham (Mt 1:1), but He was also the son of Adam (Lk 3:38). There is nothing surprising in this if He came to fulfill the promises made to the fathers and also to insure that the Gentiles might be able to glorify God for His mercy (Rom 15:8 – 9). *See* Messiah.

Birth and boyhood. Herod the Great was still reigning at the time Jesus was born (Mt 2:1). Herod's jealous apprehension made it unwise

A mosque at Beeroth, a day's journey from Jerusalem, where presumably Joseph and Mary discovered that Jesus was missing from the company returning from the Temple to Nazareth (Lk 2). HFV

for Jews to show any great enthusiasm over the heralded arrival of their promised King. Yet the response of the shepherds (Lk 2:8 –18) presaged a kindly reception from the common people of a godly sort even as the Magi constituted the firstfruits of the Gentiles.

The circumstances surrounding the conception of Jesus were such as to give rise among unbelieving Jews to ugly rumors to the effect that He was an illegitimate child. Medieval Jewish legends made much of this. Matthew's account of the nativity seems designed to answer such misrepresentations, treating the matter particularly from the side of Joseph; whereas Luke's account, probably derived ultimately from Mary herself, presents the Lord's dealings with her in a special way. Occasional insinuations may have been made against Jesus during His lifetime (cf. Jn 8:41). The nativity accounts gave to the church all it needed to know on this subject. Although the doctrine of the virgin birth took its place also in the Apostles' Creed, it was not a part of the apostolic preaching so far as the records reveal. *See* Incarnation.

Little information is given about the boyhood of Jesus, and this very fact underscores the truth that our Gospels were not intended to be biographies in the accepted sense of that word. Although they provide some materials for a life of Christ, they were not written from the biographical standpoint but rather as furnishing information leading to a better understanding of the message of the gospel. The silence concerning this period of Jesus' life is relieved by the account of the visit to the temple at the age of twelve, preceded and followed by summary statements about His development (Lk 2:40– 52). In His discussions on the Scripture Jesus the lad appears as a hearer of the Word, and in His continuing obedience to His parents in the home at NazarethHe is seen as a doer of it.

Preparations for the ministry. In the providence of God Jesus had a herald who prepared the way for Him. John the Baptist, fully aware of the impact he was making on Israel, nevertheless publicly proclaimed that a greater was coming, One who was both Saviour (Jn 1:29) and Judge (Mt 3:12), and that men must repent of their sins in view of the approach of the kingdom (Mt 3:2). Similar announcements were made by Jesus Himself. Although the two were very different in appearance and habits (Mt 11:18 – 19), they were akin in possessing a large following and in creating opposition in leading circles of Judaism, an opposition that did not stop short of taking their lives (Mt 17:12).

Jesus' baptism at the hands of John marked the abandonment of the secluded life in Nazareth and the assumption of His role as the Servant of Yahweh (Mt 3:17; cf. Ps 2:7; Isa 42:1). To equip Him for this mission the Holy Spirit came upon Him and heaven acknowledged Him. The keynote of that mission was sounded in the avowed readiness of the Son to identify

Himself with the sinful nation He had come to redeem (Mt 3:15). The full implications of that identification were to become apparent in His baptism of blood at the cross (Mk 10:38; Lk 12:50).

The Son of God was not yet ready to launch out in His work, even though He had divine approval and equipment to add to His own dedication to the task. He must first be subjected to a grueling temptation at the hands of Satan. Jesus would be dealing with minds blinded by Satan, with people whose bodies were bound by him and reduced to virtual helplessness, with lives darkened and tortured by his emissaries the unclean spirits. By meeting every test of the evil one Jesus earned the right to banish the demons and deliver men from the fearful grip of the devil. He could challenge the sway of Satan's kingdom by having defeated the prince of this world, blunting every dart on the shield of faith and pinning down His opponent by means of the sword of the Spirit, the Word of God. Out of the temptation experience came a pattern of resolute dependence on God that remained a permanent feature of His ministry.

The locale and length of the ministry. A day by day chronicle of Jesus' activity is lacking. Notices of time and place are occasionally given, but they are insufficient to provide more than a sketchy outline. It is clear from the Synoptics that the bulk of the ministry took place in Galilee, with considerable itinerating among the towns and villages. Capernaum proved a suitable headquarters, because of its central location. A journey to Tyre and Sidon on one occasion took Jesus and the disciples outside the bounds of Palestine (Mk 7:24). Another trip took them through a portion of the Decapolis region consisting of a scattered group of Gr. communities to the E of the Sea of Galilee (Mk 7:31). In addition there was a withdrawal N to Caesarea Philippi (Mk 8:27) and some activity in Perea, the territory E of the Jordan (Mk 10:1).

From the Gospel according to John, on the other hand, we learn little about Jesus' work in Galilee, for most of the narrative centers around visits to Jerusalem, especially in connection with the various annual festivals of the Jews. These include Passover (Jn 2:23; 6:4; 13:1), Tabernacles (7:2), Dedication (10:22) and an unnamed feast (5:1). The Synoptics mention only one Passover, the occasion of the passion. From Acts 10:37 it is possible to assume that Jesus had a ministry in other parts of Judea than Jerusalem and vicinity.

With the help of these references to festivals in John, the duration of the ministry can be calculated roughly. It must have exceeded two years and probably approximated three. Some advocate a four year period (E. Stauffer, *Jesus and His Story*, pp. 6 – 7).

Jesus' teaching. The Gospel writers give many pen pictures of our Lord surrounded by large crowds and holding their attention by the fascination of His instruction. People were im-

Traditional site of the baptism of Jesus. HFV

pressed by the manner in which He spoke — with authority (Mk 1:22). He did not quote the sayings of the rabbis. He dared to put His own statements on a par with the teaching of the OT and even to supersede the authoritative declarations of the past (Mk 7:9 – 14; Mt 5:33 – 34, 38 – 39). In contrast to most teachers among His people, He did not become lost in a maze of inconsequential details or resort to hairsplitting, but confined His discourse to essential truths. Great simplicity marked His utterances, aided by His avoidance of technical terms and by the frequent use of illustration, especially in connection with parables. He knew how to lead people from the known to the unknown.

The teaching was carried on in various settings — on the hillside, at the edge of the lake, in homes, in the synagogues, and at the temple in Jerusalem. It was all open and public (Jn 18:20). Teaching as He did for hours at a time, He must have suffered a severe drain on His energy (Mk 4:36 – 38).

In His public teaching Jesus could build on the fact that His hearers were believers in God and fairly familiar with the OT. Probably for this reason He gave less formal instruction on the nature of God than would otherwise have been the case. The truth that God is Spirit was disclosed to a Samaritan rather than a Jew (Jn 4:24). Considerable attention was given to God's goodness (Mt 5:45; 7:11; 19:17), His care over His children (Mt 6:26, 30, 32), and the perfection of His love (Mt 5:46 – 48). Assurance was given of God's forgiveness of the trespasses of His people (Mk 11:25) and of His readiness to hear the prayer of faith (Mk 11:22 – 24). His righteousness is acknowledged (Mt 6:33) and His work as Judge (Mt 10:28). But above all Jesus set forth God as Father. The language of fatherhood had been used in the OT in the sense of Creator (Isa 64:8), but

Jesus conveyed to His hearers a richness of meaning hitherto unknown, especially in the area of personal relationship. Here He could speak out of immediate and intimate knowledge (Mt 11:27). He graciously welcomed His true followers into the heavenly family, which entitled them to call upon God as their Father also (Mt 6:9). *See* God.

Central to the teaching of Christ was His exposition of the kingdom of God. Those who have a part in it are not the mighty of this world or the self-righteous, but rather the poor in spirit and the persecuted (Mt 5:3, 10). In fact, Christ as King exhibits the very traits which are demanded of His subjects (Mt 11:29; 21:5). One could say He *is* the kingdom in its essence. With His coming into the world the kingdom came in an initial sense. In His teaching the principles of the kingdom stood revealed. After His departure the kingdom continued to make its appeal (Acts 28:31), and according to His prediction will be consummated in power and glory at His return (Mt 25:31 – 34). *See* Kingdom of God.

Jesus' evaluation of man is to be gleaned not so much from His spoken word as from His readiness to sacrifice His own life for the sake of bringing about man's redemption. Obviously mankind must in all faithfulness be pronounced evil by Him who best knows the heart (Mt 7:11). The corruption comes from within rather than from environmental influences (Mk 7:18 – 23).

Two blemishes on the society of that time were especially distressing to the Master. One was the result of religious factors centering in the scribes and Pharisees. By their scrupulous attention to the minutiae of the law and the traditions of the elders, to the comparative neglect of the weightier issues of justice and love, these blind leaders were strangling the religious impulses of the covenant nation. The people were like shepherdless sheep. Another distressing feature, influenced by the first, was the drift of the common man toward materialism. He was too often found serving Mammon, imagining that he could give himself to covetousness and still honor God in passable fashion. Jesus had to warn of the danger of losing one's soul in the vain attempt to gain the world (Mk 8:36 – 37).

No one could listen to Jesus without sensing in Him a tremendous earnestness about life and the way it should be lived. It was the vestibule of eternity. Heaven and hell were solemn realities to Him, and He challenged His hearers to consider their destiny in the light of their beliefs and practices.

Jesus' miracles. There can be no doubt that along with His teaching the mighty works of our Lord were highly influential in awakening popular enthusiasm for Him, especially at the height of His Galilean campaign. He could not be hid. Wherever He went the crowds surged about Him. It may not be possible to trace a consistent pattern of relationship between His teaching and the miracles in this matter of attracting a following; but with Mt 4:24 – 5:1 as a guide one may reasonably conclude that frequently the crowds were bent on securing healing for themselves and their loved ones, and when this was granted, large numbers of them remained to hear the Lord teach. Something of the same supernatural power that was unveiled in the works of healing shone forth from the teaching. The one activity complemented the other.

Modern Cana, possibly on the same location as the biblical town where Jesus performed His first miracle.
HFV

Can the miracles be verified? Their very prevalence in the narratives of the Gospels makes it exceedingly difficult to treat them as pious creations of the writers. One has to ponder the fact that the early church, according to the testimony of the book of Acts and of the epistles, enjoyed similar miraculous power, which it attributed to Jesus Christ (Acts 4:10; 9:34; Rom 15:18 – 19; Heb 2:4). Our sources attest the spiritual transformation of a host of people, including the apostles. These are the same sources that claim miraculous power for Jesus and His followers. How is it possible to have truth and fraud jumbled together? The total picture must stand or fall in terms not of one ingredient only but of all. The transformed lives are no less marvelous than the signs and wonders, and without them the church could not have made its way in the world. It is well to remember this also, that the miracles were not doubted in Jesus' time, even by those who were counted His enemies (Mk 3:22; Mt 27:42).

A motivating purpose behind these marvelous deeds is suggested by one of the terms used for them. They were signs. This means they were intended to bear a testimony to the One who performed them or to the truth He proclaimed. They were calculated to assure those who experienced them or witnessed them that God's Anointed was at work in their midst (see Lk 4:16 – 21). They were counted on to add weight to the spoken word that bade men break with their sins and turn to God in penitence and faith. That this result did not always follow when miracles were performed, shows the hardness of the human heart (Mt 11:20 – 21). One of the Gospels openly connects the inclusion in its record of certain signs of Jesus with the expectation that as a result faith will be quickened in the heart toward Him as the Christ, the Son of God (Jn 20:30 – 31). It would be most extraordinary to expect such a result from the reading of this Gospel if in point of fact people had not previously been led to such faith by the witnessing of the signs during Jesus' ministry.

But to insist on this purpose as the sole reason for the miracles would be one-sided. It would hardly explain the healing of all the needy who confronted Jesus time after time. To show His power on a few would have been adequate as a demonstration of His messianic office. The plain intimations of Scripture that another motive was present cannot be ignored. Our Lord was so moved with compassion over the plight of those who flocked to Him that He could not refrain from helping them. As Peter put it, He "went about doing good, and healing all that were oppressed of the devil" (Acts 10:38). So the miracles are rightly regarded as revelations of the love of God in Christ as well as tokens of divine appointment. *See* Miracles.

Response to the ministry. This ran the gamut from bitter opposition to adoring devotion. Leading opponents were the scribes and Pharisees. At first they were content to observe Him in action, but before long they became vocal, challenging Him on a variety of counts. They took offense when He accused them of setting aside the commandments of God in favor of their traditions (Mk 7:9). His rebuke was particularly hard for them to bear because He was not trained as a rabbi, yet took the liberty of sitting in judgment on them. Friction arose also over Jesus' insistence on conducting His healing ministry on the sabbath as well as on other days (Mk 3:1 – 6). Delay in relieving human suffering was senseless in His eyes. But the religious leaders did not look on the matter in the same light. They became so infuriated that they determined to put Him to death. Another cause of offense was Jesus' claim to be able to forgive sins. To the opposition, this was plain blasphemy, for it meant that He was assuming a prerogative of God (Mk 2:7). This charge of blasphemy loomed large in the eyes of the Sanhedrin, especially when it involved an admission on Jesus' part of divine sonship (Mk 14:61 – 64).

Among the people in general the response varied from indifference to genuine faith. Perhaps the most disappointing feature to our Lord was the utterly selfish motivation governing many who followed Him. On one occasion He accused the multitude of seeking Him merely for the sake of what He could provide for them in the form of material good (Jn 6:26).

Yet there were a few in those days who gladly forsook their possessions, their gainful pursuits, their homes and their loved ones in order to become His intimate followers (Mt 19:27). It would be rash to assert that the Twelve were more devoted than any others, especially in view of the ministry of certain women (Lk 8:1 – 3) and the close tie that Jesus enjoyed with His friends at Bethany (Lk 10:38 – 42; Jn 11). Nevertheless the Gospels emphasize the fidelity of the apostles and correspondingly the attention that Jesus bestowed on them to prepare them for their future work as leaders in the church. Here was a ministry within a ministry. Jesus taught them to trust the Father and pray to Him for their needs, to look with compassion on the sufferings and trials of those about them, and to cultivate their discipleship with an ever deepening understanding of its implications. The more clearly they were able to perceive in the ministry of Jesus the outline of their own, the more meaningful became their call.

It was a shock to these men to hear from Jesus' own lips that He must go to Jerusalem and there be rejected and put to death (Mt 16:21 – 22). Even further instruction on this subject left them perplexed and disturbed, but they did not desert the cause. Only with difficulty did Jesus communicate to them the basic nature of His mission—obedience to the Father and self-surrender to the point of giving Himself a ransom for many (Mk 10:45).

Naturally the Twelve had difficulty in the area of humility until they had accepted their Lord's interpretation of His ministry and had adjusted themselves to it. But it was a hard lesson to learn. Even at the beginning of those sacred last hours with Christ in the upper room they were still disputing with one another as to which one of them was to be regarded as the greatest (Lk 22:24). But the sight of His bending down to wash their feet, then softly speaking of His great love for them, hearing Him pray for their unity in Himself, then seeing Him quietly submit to capture by sinners, ready to drink the cup that the Father had given Him—all this made a deep impression. Coupled with their own regrets for their numerous shortcomings, including their desertion in the hour of crisis, was their sadness over the detention, crucifixion and entombment of the Master.

Out of this abyss of penitence and sorrow came the rebirth of joy and a new usefulness to their Lord as they fellowhiped with Him in His risen state. Only the enduement with the Spirit remained to fit them for their apostolic labors. Jesus had been father and friend, teacher and critic to them. Now that He must be recognized as universal Lord as well, His faithfulness and patience in the days of their training loomed larger in their thinking. What a privilege to serve such a one as He! *See* Apostle; Disciple.

The culmination of the ministry. Even as Caesarea Philippi was a milestone in the spiritual progress of the disciples, so was it a turning point in the earthly career of Jesus (Mt 16:13 – 21). Here the passion was divulged, not as something tentative but as something already

Garden of Gethsemane with adjacent Church of All Nations (center) which covers traditional Rock of Agony. Giovanni Trimboli

determined and embraced. From this time on the Lord returned to the subject more than once, showing that it was engrossing His thoughts.

The transfiguration, for all the mystery that invests it on account of the visible glory that broke from the Saviour's person, must be understood in close relation to Caesarea Philippi. The divine voice with its stern admonition to the disciples to hearken to the Son (Mt 17:5), finds its explanation in Peter's audacity in rebuking Jesus for broaching the subject of the cross (Mt 16:22 – 23). Moses and Elijah talked about this very thing on the mount. The glory was there, too, as though to dramatize the truth of the resurrection and the triumphs that would follow. Most significant as binding the transfiguration to the remainder of Jesus' ministry is Luke's observation that shortly thereafter He set His face to go to Jerusalem (Lk 9:51). Jesus was already envisioning the end, no matter how much remained to fill the interim. He would hasten on to His baptism of blood (Lk 12:50).

This period between the transfiguration and the passion presents problems as soon as one tries to trace the movements of Jesus. Suffice it to say that part of this interval was spent along the border of Galilee and Samaria, and part of it in Perea. Much that is peculiar to Luke (9:51 – 19:27) belongs here. Gradually the Lord worked His way toward Jerusalem. Increasingly crowds of people thronged Him (Lk 18:36; 19:3) in a way reminiscent of His busiest days in Galilee.

Two topics seemed to dominate His teaching as the hour of His passion (Jn 12:23 –27) approached. One was His rejection by His own people, and the other His return in glory. He is the nobleman who goes into a far country to get a kingdom and returns, whose citizens hate him and insist they will not have this man to rule over them (Lk 19:14). He is the son and heir whom the tenant farmers kill that they may

seize the inheritance, only to be destroyed themselves (Mt 21:33 – 41). He is the stone rejected by the builders (Mt 21:42). He is the king's son whose wedding guests spurn the invitation and go their way to other pursuits (Mt 22:2 ff.). He is the bridegroom who expects watchfulness in view of his return (Mt 25:1 ff.). He is the lord who will check the faithfulness of his servants when he comes again (Mt 25:14 ff.) and the king who will judge the nations (Mt 25:31ff.).

If the words of the Prophet from Galilee could be judged inflammatory by the Jews, His actions were no less so — the daring ride into the city accompanied by the enthusiastic acclaim of the crowd, the bold move to rid the temple area of those who commercialized its courts and ruined it as a house of prayer, and all this in broad daylight, under the eyes of the priests who were profiting from this traffic.

The questions thrown at our Lord during holy week reflect the anger and frustration of the Jewish leaders. To think that this outsider can come right into their own territory and disturb the status quo in this fashion! How exasperating! Yet they are not able to trip Him up in a verbal encounter and thus discredit Him. Desperately they confer and confess their impotence. The only course apparently open to them is to accept the dictum of Caiaphas the high priest, laid down sometime before, that this one life had better be sacrificed rather than have the whole nation thrown into turmoil and revolution. He spoke beyond his own wisdom in thus prophesying the death of the Saviour (Jn 11:49 – 51). Even so, the rulers of the Jews would have been at a loss to know how to

St. Peter's of the Cock Crowing which covers traditional site of Caiaphas' Palace. Photo courtesy of the Church

implement their decision without incurring the wrath of the people had not Judas come forward with an offer to betray the Master (Mt 26:2 – 5, 14 – 16).

Aware of Judas' intrigue, Jesus kept from him the knowledge of the place where He would meet with the disciples to eat the Passover, and in this way was able to enjoy a period of uninterrupted intercourse with His own in the upper room. The words spoken on that occasion (Jn 13 – 16) and the prayer offered (Jn 17) are among the most precious deposits left to us from His entire ministry. They bear the marks of the stress and pathos of Jesus' approaching "hour," but they also possess the calm assurance of the victory that He would achieve and communicate to His own for their life and service in coming days.

Then came the soul struggle in Gethsemane (*q.v.*). That Jesus should have to agonize as He did in remaining true to the Father's will is our best indication of the severity of the conflict. The cross as an instrument of torture can hardly account for it, but the cross as the focus of the sin of the ages upon the Crucified furnishes the necessary key. Only a soul with complete freedom from sin could feel the horror, as Jesus did, of taking the sins of the world on Himself.

In a matter of hours He was on the cross. The Jewish authorities, after apprehending Him in the garden, used the remainder of the night for deliberation, and in the early morning decreed His condemnation on the charge of blasphemy (Mk 14:60 – 64). Hurrying Him off to Pilate, the Roman governor, before the city was fully alert, the chief priests secured a verdict based ostensibly on the charge that Jesus had declared Himself King of the Jews (Mk 15:26; cf. Jn 19:21). By nine o'clock in the morning He was hanging on the accursed tree. *See* Christ, Passion of; Cross.

From His lips came no execration, but instead a prayer for His tormentors. His accusers remained hardened, but others went home beating their breasts (Lk 23:48). In awe the centurion voiced his feeling that this One could only be God's Son (Mk 15:39). One of the thieves discovered that Jesus held the key to Paradise and that his own death on a cross was no barrier to his entrance upon its joys (Lk 23:39 – 43). So soon did the saving power of the crucified Son of God assert itself. *See* Atonement.

As Jesus had affirmed in advance (Jn 10:18), He died a voluntary death, yielding up His spirit to God (Mt 27:50; Jn 19:30). Would He be able to make good the companion claim that He would take up His life again? The paradox is that the disciples, despite several utterances of this sort promising resurrection, were not looking for it, whereas the enemies of Jesus, with much less to go on, were determined that no basis for such a claim could be provided (Mt 27:62 – 66). The former group did not doubt that God *could* raise Him, but were not expecting that He would; the latter group counted

Roman steps leading to St. Peter's of the Cock Crowing, on which Jesus may have walked. HFV

only on human action, by the removal of the body, as providing a specious basis for the claim of resurrection. The one group, in joyful surprise, welcomed the resurrection because they loved the Saviour. The other group became the prototype of those who deny this great event and remain strangers to its transforming power. *See* Resurrection of Christ.

The resurrection appearances were occasions of renewed fellowship between the Lord and His own, but also gave opportunity for explanation of what had happened in terms of OT prophecy and for commissioning the apostles to preach the gospel everywhere with His universal authority (Lk 24:44 – 49; Mt 28:18 – 20). *See* Commission, Great. These appearances terminated with the ascension (*see* Ascension of Christ), which in turn opened a new era characterized by the Lord's appearance in heaven on behalf of His people (Heb 9:24). As the Head of the Church He continues to make real His presence and power on the earth ere He fulfills His promise to return and consummate all things. *See* Christ, Coming of; Eschatology; Jesus, Offices of.

Bibliography. William Barclay, *The Mind of Jesus*, New York: Harper, 1961. G. C. Berkouwer, *The Person of Christ*, Grand Rapids:

Chapel of the Ascension on top of the Mount of Olives. HFV

Eerdmans, 1955. Alfred Edersheim, *The Life and Times of Jesus the Messiah*, 2 vols., 8th ed. rev., New York: Longmans, Green & Co., 1901. Werner Foerster, "*Iēsous*," TDNT, III, 284–293. Everett F. Harrison, *Short Life of Christ*, Grand Rapids: Eerdmans, 1968. A. M. Hunter, *The Work and Words of Jesus*, Philadelphia: Westminster, 1950. T. W. Manson, *The Servant-Messiah*, Cambridge: Univ. Press, 1953. G. Campbell Morgan, *The Crises of the Christ*, New York: Revell, 1936. A. T. Olmstead, *Jesus in the Light of History*, New York: Scribner's, 1942. A. E. J. Rawlinson, *Christ in the Gospels*, London: Oxford Univ. Press, 1944. Wilbur M. Smith, *The Supernaturalness of Christ*, Boston: Wilde, 1954. Ethelbert Stauffer, *Jesus and His Story*, New York: Knopf, 1960. James S. Stewart, *The Life and Teaching of Jesus Christ*, New York: Abingdon, n.d. Vincent Taylor, *The Names of Jesus*, London: Macmillan, 1953. Howard F. Vos, *The Life of Our Divine Lord*, Grand Rapids: Zondervan, 1958. John F. Walvoord, *Jesus Christ Our Lord*, Chicago: Moody, 1969 (with extensive bibliography).

E. F. Har.

JESUS, OFFICES OF. The offices of Christ, the Anointed of God, are threefold: that of prophet, priest, and king. These were the three offices among the Israelites in OT times whose holders were recognized by anointing with oil (prophet,

I Kgs 19:16; priest, Ex 29:7; 30:25, 30; king, 1 Sam 9:16; 16:1, 13).

Calvin was the first theologian to recognize the importance of distinguishing the three and devoted a chapter to them in his *Institutes*. Lutheran theologians have adopted the threefold offices somewhat reluctantly and slowly. They accepted Christ's prophetical and kingly offices, but tended to reject His priestly office. Liberal theologians on the whole place such stress on Christ as a teacher that His offices lose all value. The Barthians have so reinterpreted Christ's prophetical office, with their view of existential revelation here and now through hearing or reading a "fallible, contradictory Bible" or a sermon, that the offices of Christ are largely absorbed in that of revealer.

Christ as Prophet. The office of prophet required a person to be: (1) God's spokesman, His mouthpiece to man. This ministry of the prophet is seen in Ex 7:1 where God says, "I have made thee a god to Pharaoh: and Aaron thy brother shall be thy prophet." The prophet was to hear the word of God or see a vision and declare it (Deut 18:18). His ministry was both passive, to receive; and active, to proclaim. It was not merely passive, since Abimelech, Pharaoh, and Nebuchadnezzar all received revelations but were not considered prophets. (2) A foreteller of the future. The prophet gave revelation concerning future events. He foretold the future.

Christ exercised both these functions but in such a manner that they are generally fused. His ministry as spokesman and teacher was most clearly described by Himself in John 8 where He says that He speaks what He has heard of the Father (v. 26), has seen (v. 38), been taught (v. 28), and can verify with Him (v. 29). His ministry of foretelling the future is seen in Mt 24:2–31 and 25:31–46 (cf. Lk 21:6–28).

OT Scripture foretells that the Messiah is to be a prophet (Deut 18:15; cf. Acts 3:22–23). Jesus spoke of Himself as a prophet (Mt 13:57; Lk 13:33) and claimed to bring a message from the Father (Jn 8:26–28; 12:49–50; 14:10). The people received Him as a prophet (Mt 21:11, 46; Lk 7:16; 24:19; Jn 3:2; 4:19; 6:14; 7:40; 9:17). *See* Prophecy; Prophet.

Christ as Priest. The OT foretells His priestly ministry (Ps 40:6–8; 110:4). The office of priest entails offering sacrifices (Heb 5:1–3) and making intercession (Deut 5:5; 9:18; I Sam 7:5; etc.). Both of these He does. However, the sacrifice He offered was not that of bulls and goats but of Himself, His own body (Ps 40:6–8; Heb 10:5–14; cf. Heb 9:25–28). The intercession He makes is not in an earthly temple but at the very throne of God (I Jn 2:1–2; Rom 8:34; Heb 7:25; 9:24). The OT priesthood and sacrifices were only types of Christ and His sacrifice on Calvary, and pointed to Him as the Lamb of God (Jn 1:29).

Christ as King. The third office is that of king or ruler. This office Christ already exercises over all the members of His Church, but will exercise it over the whole earth at His second coming (Zech 14:9, 16 – 17; Rev 19:6; 20:4 ff.). The order of events leading to His final rule are: (1) The promise of the Davidic covenant (II Sam 7:16; Ps 89:20 – 27; cf. Isa 11:1 – 16; 55:3 – 4). (2) His announcement and birth as a king (Mt 2:2; Lk 1:32 – 33). (3) His rejection as a king (Mk 15:12 – 13; Lk 19:14). (4) His death as a sacrifice to satisfy divine justice (Isa 53:11), and yet as a king (Mt 27:37). (5) His return in glory to reign as king in Jerusalem (Mt 24:27 – 31; 26:64; Zech 14:8 – 9, 16 – 17). His kingly reign is to last forever (II Sam 7:15 – 16; Ps 89:36 – 37; Isa 9:6 – 7; Dan 7:13 – 14).

R. A. K.

JETHER (jē′thĕr)

1. Same as Jethro, father-in-law of Moses (Ex 4:18, Heb.).

2. The firstborn son of Gideon. Exhorted by his father to kill the captive Midianite princes Zebah and Zalmunna, Jether, who was very young, declined (Jud 8:20). He probably died in the conspiracy of Abimelech in which all the sons of Gideon were murdered (Jud 9:18).

3. The father of Amasa, commander of Absalom's army, who was made captain of David's forces after the rebellion. Jether was the husband of Abigail, David's sister. In II Sam 17:25 he is called Ithra the Israelite. This is probably a scribal corruption from the correct Jether the Ishmaelite in I Chr 2:17; I Kgs 2:5, 32.

4. A son of Jada of the family of Hezron of Judah (I Chr 2:32).

5. A son of Ezrah in the genealogy of Judah (I Chr 4:17).

6. A chief prince and warrior of the tribe of Asher (I Chr 7:38, 40).

JETHETH (jē′thĕth). The chief of an Edomite clan (Gen 36:40; I Chr 1:51).

JETHLAH (jĕth′lȧ). Called Ithlah in RSV. A town of the tribe of Dan (Josh 19:42), probably in the vicinity of Aijalon.

JETHRO (jĕth′rō). Apparently also called Reuel (Ex 2:18) and Raguel (Num 10:29). He was a priest of the nomadic Midianites (*q.v.*) living near Mount Sinai (Ex 2:16; 3:1; 4:18). A descendant of Abraham by Keturah (Gen 25:1 – 2), he consequently possessed remnants of the true knowledge of Yahweh (Ex 18:10 – 12).

Moses married Zipporah, one of Jethro's seven daughters, during his 40-year stay with Jethro (Ex 2:16 – 21). She bore two sons to him (Ex 2:22; 4:20; 18:3 – 4; Acts 7:29). Moses asked for and received from Jethro permission to return to Egypt (Ex 4:18 – 20). Zipporah and her two sons accompanied Moses, but he sent them back to Jethro for some unknown reason (Ex 4:24 – 26; 18:2).

After the exodus from Egypt and while the Israelites were in the vicinity of Mount Sinai (cf. Ex 3:12 with 19:2 – 3), Jethro brought Zipporah and her two sons back to Moses (18:1 – 6). Jethro did two notable things at this reunion: (1) he initiated and observed with Israel's leaders a sacrifice of thanksgiving for the recent deliverance from Egypt (18:10 – 12); (2) he wisely counseled Moses to make certain changes in his burdensome system of judging the people, which changes were apparently instituted immediately (18:13 – 26). *See* Judge. Jethro then returned to his own land (18:27).

Jethro's further contacts with the Israelites are linked with the almost insoluble problem regarding the identity of the Hobab mentioned in Num 10:29. This man was either Jethro or Jethro's son or grandson, at any rate an in-law of Moses. The family descendants dwelt among the Israelites after the conquest of Canaan (Jud 1:16; 4:11; I Sam 15:6). *See* Hobab; Raguel; Reuel. (See also W. F. Albright, *Yahweh and the Gods of Canaan*, Garden City: Doubleday, 1968, pp. 38 – 40; Wick Broomall, "Jethro: Wise Counselor," *The Presbyterian Journal*, September 29, 1965, pp. 16 – 18.)

W. B.

JETUR (jē′tûr). One of the sons of Ishmael, founder of a tribe (Gen 25:15; I Chr 1:31; 5:19). *See* Ituraea.

JEUEL (joo′ĕl). Listed as head of one of the families of Judah which returned to Jerusalem after the Exile (I Chr 9:6). *See also* Jeiel 7 (spelled Jeuel in RSV).

JEUSH (jē′ŭsh)

1. A son of Esau by his Hivite wife Aholibamah, born in the land of Canaan. He was one of the earliest Edomite chiefs or sheiks (Gen 36:5, 14, 18; I Chr 1:35).

2. A Benjamite, the son of Bilhan of the family of Jediael (I Chr 7:10).

3. A Benjamite, son of Eshek, a descendant of Saul (I Chr 8:39; here spelled Jehush).

4. A Levite of the family of Gershom, the son of Shimei. He and his brother Beriah were counted one "father's house" or clan because they did not have many children (I Chr 23:10 – 11).

5. The son of King Rehoboam by his second wife Abihail, daughter of Eliab the brother of David (II Chr 11:18 – 19).

JEUZ (jē′ŭz). The fifth of seven sons of the Benjamite Shaharaim and his wife Hodesh. His sons are called "heads of the fathers" (I Chr 8:10), i.e., heads of families (NEB).

JEW (joo). Heb. *yᵉhûdî* specifically refers to a descendant of Judah; the name is applied to members of the tribe of that name or to those of the country of Judah (II Kgs 16:6; 18:26, 28; 25:25; II Chr 32:18; Est 2:5; 3:6; Jer 32:12; 38:19; 52:28; etc.). I Chr 9:3 indicates that members of other tribes resided in Jerusalem in Judah. Many from the seceded northern kingdom went over to Judah to worship the true God (II Chr 11:13 – 16; 15:9; 30:1 – 18).

The Jews who finished rebuilding the temple in the reign of Darius I probably included members of various tribes, for they sacrificed twelve goats for the twelve tribes (Ezr 6:14 – 17). Therefore after the Babylonian captivity the term was used for all Israelites since Judah then formed the larger part of the returning remnant (II Macc 9:17; Mt 2:2; 27:11; Jn 4:9; Act 2:5, 8 – 10; 10:28; etc.).

As descendants of Abraham the Hebrew (Gen 14:13), the Jews were also called Hebrews; hence Paul appropriately called himself such (Phil 3:5). *See* Hebrew People; Israel.

R. A. K.

JEWELS, JEWELRY. The love of adornment has been expressed in the wearing of precious stones and the making of jewelry since the beginning of history. The practice of burying such treasures with the remains of their owners has been of inestimable help to archaeologists in tracing the history and culture of perished races and civilizations.

Jewelry of Queen Shubad of Ur, *c.* 2500 B.C. BM

Scriptural terms. The following words are rendered "jewel" in the KJV:

1. Heb. *ḥălî,* meaning "ornament" and probably coming from Aram. "to adorn." It is a necklace or trinket, a symbol of grace and beauty (Song 7:1; "ornament," Prov 25:12).

2. Heb. *ḥelyâ,* a piece of jewelry, probably a necklace or female ornament (Hos 2:13).

3. Heb. *kelî,* meaning an article, utensil, or vessel of any kind. When used in the sense of jewelry, it is an article of silverware or other precious metal (Gen 24:53; Ex 3:22; 11:2; 12:35; Num 31:50 – 51; I Sam 6:8, 15; Prov 20:15), money (Job 28:17), or a piece of finery in dress (Isa 61:10; Ezk 16:17, 39; 23:26).

4. Heb. *nezem,* a ring always of gold when the material is mentioned. It is generally rendered "earring" (Gen 35:4; Ex 32:2; Ezk 16:12) but also nose ring (Prov 11:22; Isa 3:21). Thus it is a specific term. However, the part of the body on which it is worn is not specified. *See* Earring.

5. Heb. *segullâ,* a piece of valued property (Mal 3:17) or peculiar treasure, used of the choice relationship between God and His people Israel (Ex 19:5; Ps 135:4).

As indicated, only the word *nezem* is specific while the others are of general character. The KJV usually translates the specific kinds of jewelry by their specific words, such as, bracelet, necklace, earring, nose ring, etc. The term "precious stones" (*'eben ye qārâ*) occurs 13 times in the OT, as well as other expressions such as "pleasant stones" (Isa 54:12) and "stones of a crown" (Zech 9:16).

Materials. The jewels and other materials used in the making of jewelry consisted of the available precious stones and metals. Many of the Heb. and Gr. terms are difficult to identify because some are foreign loan-words, and because the ancients described their gems according to color and hardness and not according to chemical structure. Pliny's *Natural History* (A.D. 77), which describes precious stones according to their Gr. names close to the very time John wrote the book of Revelation, is of inestimable help.

Agate (*shebô,* Ex 28:19; 39:12; *kadkōd,* Isa 54:12; Ezk 27:16, "red jasper," NEB). Among the many varieties of quartz, agate is distinguished as a translucent cryptocrystalline form with certain distinctive markings, usually in the form of layers of variegated colors. The term agate is often used interchangeably with chalcedony. This material has been widely used since Sumerian times both as jewelry and as a talisman because of its supposed magical powers. Pieces of agate could be gathered in certain desert areas of Egypt. The *kadkōd,* cognate to Arabic *kadkadatu,* "bright redness," is to be used in the battlements of the future Zion. This suggests red jasper, used by the Assyrians in their buildings.

Amethyst (*'aḥlāmâ,* Ex 28:19; 39:12; *amethystos,* Rev 21:20). A clear purple variety of quartz crystal, ranging from barely perceptible tinting to an intense purple. Pliny noted its occurrence in Egypt, but the finest amethysts came from India and Ceylon.

Beryl (*tarshîsh*, Ex 28:20; Song 5:14; Ezk 1:16; 28:13; Dan 10:6; *bēryllos*, Rev 21:20). A mineral, beryllium aluminum silicate, hexagonal crystal system, hardness 8. Color distinguishes the gem varieties of this mineral: emerald — green; aquamarine — light blue; golden beryl — yellow. Only the green beryl was used in Egypt in Moses' time, the aquamarine and the yellow and white beryls not being known.

The *tarshîsh* may have been another stone, however. The Heb. name is the same as for the land of Spain, so that it may have signified the "stone of Spain." Of the various suggestions for *tarshîsh* Spain produces only "chrysolith" according to Pliny (*Natural History*, xxxvii. 43), a yellow rock crystal or citrine quartz.

Carbuncle (*bāreqet*, Ex 28:13, 17; *'eben 'eqdāḥ*, Isa 54:12). Any of several precious or semiprecious red gemstones such as red garnet. The KJV translators confused the *bāreqet* with the following *nōphek* in the list of stones in the high priest's breastplate and reversed their meanings. Therefore the *bāreqet* should have been translated "emerald," or more correctly "green beryl," because the true emerald has never been found among the many precious gems of ancient Egypt.

Carnelian (cornelian). A variety of translucent chalcedony without crystal form, usually reddish in color, though sometimes orange-red or reddish-brown. One of the gems found most frequently in Palestinian excavations, it was widely used for seals, beads, and scarabs. A richly furnished tomb of the 13th –12th cen. B.C. discovered in 1964 at Tell es-Sa'idiyeh near Succoth in the Jordan Valley held a woman's skeleton with a necklace of 670 orange carnelian beads and 72 beads of gold. The golden necklace of Queen Shubad of Ur (*c.* 2500 B.C.) was set with alternating triangles of carnelian and lapis lazuli. The NJPS version identifies it with the Heb. *'ōdem*, the sardius of the KJV (Ex 28:17; 39:10; Ezk 28:13). The deserts of Arabia and Egypt were sources of fine carnelians.

Chalcedony (Gr. *chalkēdōn*, Rev 21:19). A cryptocrystalline translucent variety of quartz. By common usage the chalcedony is milky white or light gray or blue. Specimens having special markings are more generally known as agate, while the reddish varieties are called carnelian, sardius, or sardin(e). It was much used for engraved seals and gems, especially by the Greeks in the 5th and 4th cen. B.C., and is one of the foundation stones of the walls in the New Jerusalem. Another interpretation of the Gr. word is that the stone referred to is the green dioptose (silicate of copper) from the copper mines of Chalcedon in Asia Minor.

Chrysolite (Gr. *chrysolithos*, Rev 21:20). The modern meaning of the term is the gem variety of the mineral olivine, a peridot. Its chemical composition is iron magnesium silicate, hard-

ness 7. Peridot is valued for its hardness, transparency, and greenish to yellowish color. According to its Gr. name the ancient gem was a "gold stone," probably our topaz, or some other yellow-hued gem such as beryl or zircon. The NEB and NJPS translate Heb. *piṭᵉdâ*, the second stone of the priestly breastplate (Ex 28:17, KJV "topaz"), as chrysolite. The Heb. name seems to be an Indian loan-word, for it is cognate to Sanskrit *pīta*, "yellow." The RSV renders Heb. *tarshîsh* as chrysolite in Ezk 1:16; 10:9; 28:13.

Chrysoprasus (Gr. *chrysoprasos*, Rev. 21:20). The modern chrysoprase is an apple-green variety of chalcedony colored by nickel oxide. Its Gr. name suggests a gold-tinted, leek-green gemstone. It may be carved into exquisite cameos, and occurs in slabs large enough to make tops for small tables. It is the 10th foundation stone of the New Jerusalem.

Coral (Heb. *rā'môt*, Job 28:18; Ezk 27:16). The solid calcareous skeleton secreted by a class of minute marine coelenterate animals. Colors range from white to red to the rare black coral which comes from the Indian Ocean and has recently been discovered in the Gulf of Aqaba. Black coral is the NEB translation of *rā'môt*. Dark pink to red coral was so highly prized in the ancient Near East that it was considered one of the precious stones. The NEB translates Heb. *pᵉnînîm* (KJV "rubies") as "coral" or "red coral" (e.g., Job 28:18; Prov 3:15). The cognate Arabic word *fananu*, "branch(es)," suggests that the Heb. means something branched, like the coral organism (Lam 4:7, NEB). Superstition held that coral worn as an amulet bestowed magical benefits upon the wearer. *See* Animals.

Crystal (Heb. *zᵉkôkît*, Job 28:17; *qeraḥ*, Ezk 1:22; Gr. *krystallos*, Rev 4:6; 22:1). Transparent colorless quartz (silicon dioxide), hardness 7, acid resisting, does not cleave under impact. Crystal was fashioned for many different uses, such as jewelry for adornment, spheres for crystal gazing and other magical purposes, and costly utensils for table service. The Romans carved blocks of crystal into great bowls and vases as well as smaller goblets and drinking cups. Heb. *zᵉkôkît* may not mean crystal but instead glass (RSV, NASB). The Egyptians were making colored opaque glass vases by 2000 B.C. and glass beads even earlier. The word *qeraḥ* should be translated "ice," as in Job 6:16; 37:10; 38:29; Ps 147:17. However, the sixth stone of the breastplate (Heb. *yāhǎlōm*, KJV "diamond") is probably a rock crystal, because the Heb. word signifies a stone hard enough to withstand the blow of a heavy hammer, yet the true diamond was unknown in the ancient Near East.

Diamond (Heb. *yāhǎlōm*, Ex 28:18; Ezk 28:13; *shāmîr*, Jer 17:1). A mineral composed of pure carbon, it is the hardest natural substance known, 10 on the hardness scale. Before modern times the only sources of diamond were

India and Borneo. Knowledge of them in India predates written history. The famous Kohinoor diamond is reputed to have belonged to an Indian king some 5,000 years ago. The Heb. words translated diamond mean "hard" and may refer to other hard stones (*see* Jewels: Crystal; Minerals: Adamant). The point of Jeremiah's engraving tool was almost certainly corundum (Jer 17:1). In the Mediterranean world the first sufficiently detailed descriptions to positively identify diamonds are from the 1st cen. A.D.

Emerald (Heb. *nōphek*, Ex 28:18; Ezk 27:16; 28:13; Gr. *smaragdos*, Rev. 4:3; 21:19). A transparent brilliant green variety of beryl colored by minute amounts of chromium oxide. Unflawed specimens of good color are extremely rare, which contributes to the establishment of emerald as the most precious of all gems. The most famous come from Colombia where the Incas mined them. The true emerald was probably not known in OT times, for none has ever been found in ancient tombs or ruins. Heb. *nōphek* may be compared with Egyptian *mfk3t*, which is probably turquoise, the blue-green semiprecious stone mined in OT times in the Sinai peninsula; NJPS so translates *nōphek*. Some scholars believe the *bāreqet*, the third stone of the breastplate (Ex 28:17), should be translated "emerald" (NJPS) or "green feldspar" (NEB). Many of the gems called "emerald" in Egyptian jewelry are actually green feldspar, although beads and scarabs were carved from emerald matrix. Cleopatra wore emeralds from mines in Upper Egypt, so that the Gr. *smaragdos* may be a true emerald. On the other hand, the Gr. word probably included all green-hued gems from emerald to green jasper and chrysoprase.

Garnet. The garnet group of minerals contains several mineral species with a hardness of about 7. The best gem mineral in this group is pyrope, a magnesium aluminum silicate, noted for its deep wine-red color. This may be the carbuncle listed in Scripture. The garnet beads discovered by archaeologists in Egypt were fashioned from dark red or reddish-brown translucent native stone. NEB translates Heb. *nōphek*, the fourth gem of the breastplate, as "purple garnet."

Jacinth (Gr. *hyakinthos*, Rev 9:17; 21:20). The modern hyacinth is a transparent colored zircon, usually red or reddish-brown. The gem referred to in the book of Revelation was almost certainly a blue stone, possibly aquamarine, turquoise (NEB, TEV) or amethyst (Pliny, *Natural History*, xxxvii. 41).

Jasper (Heb. *yāshepēh*, Ex 28:20; Ezk 28:13; Gr. *iaspis*, Rev 4:3; 21:11, 18, 19). Chalcedony rendered opaque by the inclusion of brightly colored iron oxides with shades of brown, yellow, red or green. The last in the list of stones of the breastplate is almost certainly a jasper. It was the first hard stone carved by the Babylonians and was usually green and some-

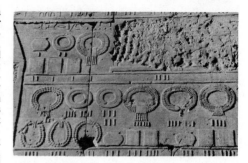

Necklaces of Queen Hatshepsut of Egypt, *c.* 1500 B.C., as portrayed on a wall of the Temple of Karnak, Luxor, Egypt. HFV

times even transparent. The jasper of the NT was "clear as crystal" (Rev 21:11), i.e., translucent at least. Therefore jade (either nephrite or jadeite), which has been suggested, is excluded as a possibility.

Ligure (Heb. *leshem*, Ex 28:19; 39:12). The identity of this stone in Aaron's breastplate is problematical. Amber or jacinth are two strong possibilities. Golden sapphire, orange zircon, turquoise, agate and opal have also been suggested. Yellow jacinth or orange zircon are the two most likely possibilities.

Onyx (Heb. *shōham*, Gen 2:12; Ex 28:9, 20; 1 Chr 29:2; Job 28:16; Ezk 28:13). A non-transparent variety of agate structured with parallel layers of alternating colors, as red and white, brown and white, black and white. Onyx has long been used for cutting "eye" agates, rounded forms having an eye on one or opposite sides. Cameos are carved in a manner which gives a design of one color with a recessed background of another color. As the Vulgate translates it, the eleventh stone in the breastplate was probably a sardonyx, a red and white variegated gem. NEB renders *shōham* as "(red) carnelian," a favorite stone of the ancient world which could be picked up in the deserts, as its presence in the "land of Havilah" (probably N Arabia, Gen 2:12) suggests. Both the onyx and carnelian were much used for seals, stones engraved with an inscription (intaglio carving, the opposite of a cameo). The two shoulder stones of the high priest's ephod were of this material, with the names of six of the tribes engraved on each (Ex 28:9 –12).

Pearl (Heb. *gābîsh*, Job 28:18; Gr. *margarites*, Mt 7:6; 13:45; etc.). A dense lustrous irridescent spherical mass of calcium carbonate formed in the mantle of many species of mollusk. The best pearls have always come from a few species of pearl oyster. They have been prized through all of recorded history for their beauty, rarity, warmth of color and symmetry, and for a variety of superstitious reasons. While the *gābîsh* is more likely to be alabaster (so NEB at Job 28:18), the *penînim* (KJV rubies) were pearls from the Red Sea, where an especially lovely pink pearl is sometimes found. *See* Pearl.

Ruby. A clear, deep red, extremely hard precious gemstone, a variety of aluminum oxide (corundum), colored by traces of chromium. A really fine ruby is so rare that it is worth more than a diamond of the same weight. Ruby in this sense was not known in the biblical world until the 3rd cen. B.C. Therefore the rubies of the OT (Heb. *pᵉnînîm*) are more likely to have been either pink pearls from the Red Sea or red coral from the same body of water (Job 28:18; Prov 3:15; 8:11; 20:15; 31:10; Lam 4:7).

Sapphire (Heb. *sappîr*, Ex 24:10; 28:18; Job 28:16; Ezk 28:13; Gr. *sappheiros*, Rev 21:19). In modern usage a transparent gem variety of corundum of any color. The more common application of the word reserves sapphire for the dark blue gem and gives other names to other colors. The normally colorless aluminum oxide is tinted blue by traces of iron or titanium. The OT references using this word are to an opaque blue speckled stone called lapis lazuli. Job 28:6 gives the clue to the identity of this mineral which was mined out of the mountains: "and out of its rocks comes lapis lazuli, dusted with flecks of gold" (NEB); the azure-blue stone contains golden flecks of iron pyrites. It is a silicate of calcium, aluminum, and sodium.

Objects of lapis lazuli date back to 3500 B.C. in the ancient Middle East. Wooden frames of harps inlaid with lapis lazuli are among the finest treasures recovered by Leonard Woolley from the royal cemetery at Ur, dating to 2500 B.C. A golden ram standing upright by a tree had its mane, beard and horns of lapis, and thousands of beads and the queen's cylinder seal were of the same substance. A relatively soft gem stone (hardness 5.5), lapis can be carved quite easily and therefore was in great demand for inlays in furniture and caskets. The innermost gold mummy case and the gold death mask of Tutankhamen were decorated with lapis, carnelian, and turquoise, and on each the false beard was of solid lapis lazuli. Other pharaohs of Egypt also employed this prized stone on a lavish scale. Its use in highly decorated statuary is suggested in Song 5:14: "His hands are golden rods set in topaz; his belly a plaque of ivory overlaid with lapis lazuli" (NEB).

The amazing fact about this gem rock is that the only known deposit where it was mined in the ancient East is at Badakshan in N Afghanistan. Discoveries of objects made from lapis lazuli at sites in the Middle East and the Sumerian tablets both point to this source, and also testify to the extensive trading of the ancient world (V. I. Sarianidi, "The Lapis Lazuli Route in the Ancient East," *Archaeology*, XXIV [1971], 12–15; G. Hermann, "Lapis Lazuli: The Early Phases of Its Trade," *Iraq*, XXX [1968], 21–57; Joan C. Payne, "Lapis Lazuli in Early Egypt," *Iraq*, XXX [1968], 58–61).

Sardius, Sardine (Heb. *'ōdem*, Ex 28:17; Ezk 28:13; Gr. *sardion*, Rev 4:3; 21:20). The stone today called sard or sardin(e) is a clear or translucent variety of chalcedony quartz, ranging from deep orange-red to brownish-red. The sardius of the Bible probably included the blood-red jasper, the sard, and the carnelian (*see* Jewels: Carnelian). The Heb. name, *'ōdem*, signifies a reddish or ruddy-colored stone, which could vary from rich chestnut brown to blood red. Along with carnelian, the sard has been found frequently in the excavated tombs and cities of Egypt, Palestine, and Babylonia. These gems most likely were cut from pieces of chalcedony lying on the surface of the surrounding deserts. It is believed that the ultraviolet rays of sunlight produce a deeper color by affecting the iron salts included as impurities in that mineral.

Sardonyx (Gr. *sardonyx*, Rev 21:20). Parallel layers of red and white chalcedony. The eleventh stone of the breastplate (Ex 28:20, Heb. *shōham*) was probably a sardonyx (*see* Jewels: Onyx).

Topaz (Heb. *piṭᵉdâ*, Ex 28:17; Job 28:19; Ezk 28:13; Gr. *topazion*, Rev 21:20). The mineral now known as topaz is an aluminum fluorosilicate which forms as brownish-yellow to clear crystals of hardness 8. Topaz of the 1st cen. A.D. and earlier was some other softer material which "yielded to the file" (Pliny), possibly yellow chrysolite (*see* Jewels: Chrysolite). Pliny said the topaz came from islands of the Red Sea.

Turquoise. A greenish-blue hydrous copper aluminum phosphate mineral, hardness 6, long valued for its beauty and for certain magical benefits bestowed upon its wearer. Because turquoise was a favorite stone among the Egyptians and because it was readily obtainable from their Sinai mines, it seems very likely that one of the jewels of Aaron's breastplate would have been a turquoise. The most probable of the twelve stones to identify with turquoise is the fourth, Heb. *nōphek* (KJV "emerald"). Emeralds were unknown in the time of Moses. NEB translates the blue jacinth of Rev 21:20 as "turquoise." The famous turquoise mines at Wady Maghara and Serabit el-Khadem were worked by Egyptians from predynastic times to the 20th Dynasty. At the latter site was a temple to the goddess Hathor, with many inscriptions there and at the entrances to the mines (ANET, pp. 229 f.). Some of these are in the so-called Proto-Sinaitic alphabetic script and dated to the 15th cen. B.C.

Manufacture. The method of making jewelry depended upon the geographical location and the civilization. In Egypt, perfection in the art of manufacturing was reached very early. The elegance of the jeweled treasures of the 12th Dynasty surpasses most ancient gilt or gem-work. The jewelry found in the tomb of Tutankhamen of the 18th Dynasty was incredibly magnificent. Although most of the tombs were robbed in ancient times, large quantities of jewelry were found in this one after it was opened on Nov. 25, 1922. Among the treasures were the three mummiform coffins and death mask; exquisitely carved alabaster jars; inlaid chests containing garments, jewelry, or cosmetics; the gilded throne chair with its jeweled back panel portraying the king and queen; and many gold rings, necklaces, bracelets, etc., set with turquoise, pearls, carnelian, green feldspar, amethyst, lapis lazuli, glass, and colored frit paste. The form of Egyptian jewelry most familiar to us is the scaraboid seal of carved stone or glazed ware. Although this was useful as a signet, it had a religious purpose as well to signify belief in eternal existence.

The Canaanite Phoenician artisans in Palestine were probably itinerants with shops in the main cities (I Kgs 20:34) and selling their wares from place to place. Even today this custom may be observed in the East with the artificer making jewelry from the treasured coins of the townspeople with his portable furnace and crucible. Jewelry from the rich finds at Ugarit and in the royal tombs of Byblos, and other displays in the National Museum of Lebanon, are evidences of the Phoenician skill. A great hoard of gold and electrum jewelry belonging to the 14th – 13th cen. B.C. was found in tombs at Tell el-'Ajjul near Gaza by Petrie (ANEP, #74 – 75).

The Assyrian and Babylonian jewelry was generally not so graceful or delicate as that of Egypt but rather was large, heavy, and showy. The gorgeous musical instruments and crowns or chaplets from Queen Shubad's tomb at Ur (2500 B.C.) are an exception, however, and many of the gold vessels are masterpieces of design and proportion. Necklaces of carnelian and lapis lazuli beads discovered at Mari illustrate the type of jewelry worn by Sarah and Rebekah. The "Chaldean cylinders" or rolling seals were popular throughout the Near East, and have been found in Palestinian excavations. These were worn largely for ornamental purposes. Herodotus mentions that they were part of the dress wardrobe for Babylonian men (cf. Gen 38:18).

The Israelites probably learned to make jewelry from those under whose dominance and influence they came. The first such people were the Egyptians. The workmanship associated with the tabernacle, especially the high priest's breastplate, was probably Egyptian in style and character. At a later period the Israelites came under Phoenician and then finally Chaldean influence.

In ancient times, stones were not cut in facets, but rather en cabochon, i.e., in rounded forms with smooth or polished convex surfaces. Thus, there was not the demand as today for transparent stones to give the brilliant flashing caused by the reflection and refraction of light from the numerous facets.

Uses. The Scriptures mention several different ways that jewelry was used. These include: (1) personal adornment and ornamentation (Ex 11:2; Isa 3:19 – 20); (2) gifts or tokens of friendship (Gen 24:22, 53; Ezk 16:11); (3) adornment of idols (Jer 10:4); (4) in political and religious ceremonies of foreign lands (Gen 41:42; Dan 5:7, 16, 29); and (5) as symbols of those precious to the Lord—the priestly jewels (Ex 28, 39).

Aaron's breastplate. The "breastplate of judgment" (Ex 28:15, 30, NASB) was a highly ornamented pouch to hold the sacred lots known as the Urim and Thummin (*q.v.*), by means of which judgment was given in certain cases. The "breastplate" or pectoral was made of a rectangular piece of richly woven linen. When folded in two, it formed a square of a span (nine inches) on each side. It was attached by golden cords to the two shoulder pieces of the high priest's ephod, and secured at its lower corners by a blue cord to rings on the ephod itself. On the front of the breastpiece were mounted in gold settings four rows of precious stones, three to a row. The gems were cut *en cabochon*, and each was engraved like a seal with the name of one of the 12 tribes of Israel. The KJV name, the Heb. word and its probable true meaning, and the approximate color of each stone follows:

Row 1: Sardius — '*ōdem*, carnelian or sard; orange-red
Topaz — *piṭᵉdā*, chrysolite; yellow
Carbuncle — *bāreqet*, beryl or feldspar; green
Row 2: Emerald — *nōphek*, turquoise; blue-green
Sapphire — *sappîr*, lapis lazuli; azure blue
Diamond — *yahᵃlōm*, rock crystal; clear, colorless
Row 3: Ligure — *leshem*, jacinth or zircon; amber yellow or orange
Agate — *shᵉbô*, agate; variegated black and white
Amethyst — '*aḥlāmâ*, amethyst; purple
Row 4: Beryl — *tarshîsh*, citrine quartz; yellow
Onyx — *shōham*, sardonyx; variegated red and white
Jasper — *yāshᵉpēh*, jasper; green

Ornaments. Besides the jewels employed in ceremonial worship, the Israelites wore a variety of types of jewelry in everyday life. Many men for business reasons wore a signet seal or ring which served as the personal signature of its owner (Gen 38:18; Song 8:6; Lk 15:22). This was generally worn on the right hand or suspended from the neck by a cord. *See* Seal, Signet. However, sometimes the position of the man (princes, etc.) required more of a display of jewelry (II Sam 12:30).

The women decorated themselves more elaborately and wore several types of ornaments (Ezk 16:10 – 13). One such type was earrings, which were universally worn by women (Ex 32:2; Ezk 16:12). They were made of bone, horn, or metal, and some that have been found have been rather large (as much as four fingers breadth in diameter). Some women would puncture the earlobe with as many openings as possible, and would then put a ring through each. *See* Earring. Nose rings were also a favorite and were used from the earliest times (Gen 24:22, 47, RSV). They were made of ivory or metal and often decorated with precious jewels. Nose rings and earrings were sometimes worn by men (Jud 8:24).

The necklace was a favorite ornament among the women. Men of rank and rulers of foreign nations also wore them (Gen 41:42; Prov 1:9; Dan 5:29). They were made of precious metal, often inlaid with gems, stones, or pearls, or of beads strung on a cord. Attached to them sometimes were other articles of finery, such as half-moons or crescents (Isa 3:18, RSV), smelling bottles (Isa 3:20, RSV), and stellated studs (Song 1:11).

Another favorite with the women from the earliest times was the armlet or bracelet (Gen 24:22, 30, 47). They were also worn by princes and nobles of rank (II Sam 1:10). These were made of ivory, precious metals, horn, cords, or chains. They could be worn on both arms, and some covered the forearm to the elbow.

The anklet was worn about the feet (Isa 3:18). These were generally so arranged that in walking a tinkling or clapping sound was made which called attention to the wearer and made her proud (Isa 3:16). Sometimes small chains were fastened from one ankle to the other in order to secure a more elegant step (Isa 3:20, NASB). Isaiah lists these as well as other articles of ornamentation in rebuking the women of Jerusalem (Isa 3:18–26). The Egyptian nobles and commoners had a profusion of such ornaments, which were demanded by the Israelite slaves as they left in the Exodus (Ex 11:2; 12:35–36, NASB). These articles of gold and silver supplied sufficient material for making the sacred utensils for the tabernacle (Ex 35:4–29). *See* Minerals and Metals.

Bibliography. Howard Carter, *The Tomb of Tut-ank-Amen,* 3 vols., London: Cassell, 1923–1933. A. Paul Davis, *Aaron's Breastplate,* St. Louis: A. P. Davis, 1960. G. R. Driver, "Jewels and Precious Stones," HDB rev., pp. 496–500. Paul L. Garber and R. W. Funk, "Jewels and Precious Stones," IDB, II, 898–905. John S. Harris, "An Introduction to the Study of Personal Ornaments of Precious, Semi-Precious and Imitation Stones Used Throughout Biblical History," *Annual of Leeds University Oriental Society,* IV (1962–63), 49–83; "The Stones of the High Priest's Breastplate," ALUOS, V (1963–65), 40–62. Ruth V. Wright and R. L. Chadbourne, *Gems and Minerals of the Bible,* New York: Harper & Row, 1970.

E.C.J., G.H.H. and J.R.

JEWESS. A female Jew by blood or conversion to Judaism. Timothy's mother was a Jewess and his father a Greek (Acts 16:1). Drusilla,

the wife of Felix the Roman governor who trembled at Paul's preaching, was a Jewess (Acts 24:24). She was a descendant of Herod the Great, the offspring of converts to Judaism. *See* Drusilla.

JEWISH, JEWS'. Belonging to a Jew (Heb. y^e-*hûdîth,* adverb meaning "in Jewish," "in the language of Judah"). Used of the language of the Jews or people of Judah dwelling at Jerusalem when Hezekiah's representatives pleaded with the Assyrians not to talk with his people in their own tongue (II Kgs 18:26, 28; II Chr 32:18; Isa 36:11, 13), and again in Nehemiah of the children of the remnant that returned who could not speak their own language (Neh 13:24). Paul employed the term once when he spoke of Jewish fables (Tit 1:14).

JEWRY (jōo'rĭ). A KJV translation of Aram. *yehûd,* the Jewish nation, i.e., the kingdom of Judah (Dan 5:13); and in the NT of Gr. *Ioudaia,* Judea in contrast to Galilee (Lk 23:5; Jn 7:1; see RSV, NASB).

JEZANIAH. *See* Jaazaniah.

JEZEBEL (jĕz'ĕ-bĕl). The wife of Ahab, king of Israel (874–853 B.C.), and daughter of Ethbaal, king of the Zidonians. Jezebel was a devotee of Baal-Melkart, the god of Phoenecia (I Kgs 18:19). She encouraged Ahab to build shrines for worship and brought hundreds of the religion's priests and prophets to Israel. She persecuted the prophets of Yahweh and ordered those slain who spoke against her idolatrous ways (I Kgs 18:4). She seems to have had considerable influence over Ahab, who allowed her to do as she pleased. She raised her two sons to use the same practices, and her daughter Athaliah (II Kgs 8:18) even carried her ideas to Judah when she married the son of Jehoshaphat.

Jezebel's chief opponent in Israel was Elijah (I Kgs 18:21–46), who held a contest on Mount Carmel to prove who was the true God. After his success, he was threatened by Jezebel and fled to Mount Horeb. Her lack of respect for the property of others is demonstrated by the story of Naboth. Ahab at first respected Naboth's desire to keep the land of his inheritance, but Jezebel seized it ruthlessly.

When Jehu came to the throne he purged the kingdom of the house of Ahab. Jezebel was thrown from the palace tower and Jehu's chariot ran over her. Later, he sent his servants to bury her but the dogs had already eaten her, thus fulfilling Elijah's prophecy (II Kgs 9:30–37).

In Rev 2:20 the name Jezebel is given to a prophetess or a group within the church at Thyatira who encouraged idolatry and immorality. Evidently the name already was symbolic of apostasy.

A. W. W.

JEZER (jē′zẽr). The third son of Naphtali, he was head of the clan of Jezerites (Gen 46:24; Num 26:49; I Chr 7:13).

JEZIAH (jē-zī′á). The KJV form of Izziah. An Israelite of the family of Parosh. One of those compelled by Ezra to put away their foreign wives after the Exile (Ezr 10:25).

JEZIEL (jē′zǐ-ĕl). A son of Azmaveth, and one of the skilled Benjamite archers and slingers who defected from Saul to join David's band at Ziklag (I Chr 12:3).

JEZLIAH (jĕz-lī′á). ASV and RSV have Izliah. A son or descendant of Elpaal, a Benjamite who resided at Jerusalem (I Chr 8:18).

JEZOAR (jē-zō′ẽr). ASV and RSV have Izhar.
1. Son of Helah, a wife of Ashur, the father (founder) of Tekoa (I Chr 4:7). A descendant of Judah. *See also* Zohar.
2. Father of Korah (Num 16:1). A Levite, descended from Kohath, whose descendants formed a family in the tribe of Levi (Ex 6:18, 21; Num 3:19, 27; I Chr 6:18, 38); called Amminadab in I Chr 6:22.

JEZRAHIAH (jĕz′rȧ-hī′á). Overseer of the singers performing at the purification of the people on the occasion of Nehemiah's reforms (Neh 12:42). *See* Izrahiah.

JEZREEL (jĕz′rē-ĕl)
1. A town in the Judean hill country (Josh 15:56). It was the home of Ahinoam the Jezreelitess (q.v.), one of David's wives (I Sam 25:43). It is possibly Khirbet Tarrama, about six miles SW of Hebron.
2. A descendant of Judah (I Chr 4:3), who presumably may have been the eponymous ancestor of Jezreel in Judah.
3. A town of Issachar (Josh 19:18) in the southern area along the border of Manasseh's territory. It is identified with modern ꞁZer′în about ten miles E of Megiddo, a village at the

foot of the NW spur of Mount Gilboa with a commanding view of the plain of Jezreel (see 4). In ancient times it was at the intersection of trade routes from the Mediterranean coast to the Jordan Valley and those from S to N Palestine. Solomon selected it as one of his 12 administrative centers, with Baana its first resident governor (I Kgs 4:12). Ahab made it one of his royal residences since it was especially pleasant in winter (I Kgs 18:45–46). It was the place of the horrible murder of Naboth perpetrated by Jezebel (I Kgs 21). Joram fled to it after suffering wounds in a battle with Hazael of Syria (II Kgs 8:29; II Chr 22:6). It witnessed excessive bloodshed during Jehu's revolt (II Kgs 9:1–10:11). The tower of Jezreel (II Kgs 9:17) was a tower or bastion guarding the entrance of Jezreel the city.
4. The fertile plain which separated Galilee from Samaria (see Josh 17:16; Jud 6:33; Hos 1:5). It is a geological fault basin with a fairly deep alluvial covering, well watered, and thus very fertile. In some later sources, Esdraelon is designated as the western portion of this plain and Jezreel its eastern portion. The entire plain was occupied by Canaanites based principally at Megiddo before the Israelite conquest. Thus the western half is sometimes called the Valley of Har Megiddo ("mound of Megiddo") or Armageddon (q.v.). *See* Palestine, II.B.2.b.
5. The name of Hosea's first son. It was given as a symbol of the bloodshed committed by Jehu at Jezreel to grab the throne of the northern kingdom (II Kgs 9:17–10:11), as well as foretelling the divine judgment on the dynasty of Jehu for that slaughter (Hos 1:4–5).
H. E. Fi.

JEZREELITE (jĕz′rē-ĕ-līt). Applied to Naboth, a native resident of the town of Jezreel (I Kgs 21:1, 4, 6, 7, 15, 16; II Kgs 9:21, 25).

JEZREELITESS (jĕz′rē-ĕ-lī-tĭs). Used of Ahinoam, one of David's first two wives, a native

A view across the Valley of Jezreel showing the richness of the soil and its agricultural potential. IIS

Valley of Jezreel with road to Nazareth at right. IIS

of Jezreel in Judah (I Sam 27:3; 30:5; II Sam 2:2; 3:2; I Chr 3:1).

JIBSAM (jĭb'săm). The son of Tola and a grandson of Issachar (I Chr 7:2). Spelled Ibsam in RSV.

JIDLAPH (jĭd'lăf). A son of Nahor and Milcah (Gen 22:22). He became the ancestral head of a Nahorite clan.

JIMMA, JIMNAH. *See* Imnah.

JIMNITE (jĭm'nīt). Used only in Num 26:44. Descendants of Jimna or Imnah (*q.v.*), a son of Asher.

JIPHTAH (jĭf'tȧ). Called Iphtah in RSV. A town of Judah in the Shephelah region, in the same district as Libnah (Josh 15:43).

JIPHTHAH-EL (jĭf'thȧ-ĕl). This form used in KJV, but Iphtah-el used in other versions. A valley on the boundary line between Zebulun and Asher (Josh 19:14, 27). The name is perhaps found in Jotopata, the modern Tell Jefat, nine miles NW of Nazareth.

JOAB (jō'ăb)
1. The son of Zeruiah, half sister of David (II Sam 2:18), and brother of Abishai and Asahel. The only thing known about his father is that his tomb was in Bethlehem (II Sam 2:32).

The first mention of Joab's activities is the battle between David's men led by Joab and Ishbosheth's forces under Abner near the pool of Gibeon. Joab's men bested Abner's. When Abner reluctantly slew Joab's younger brother Asahel (II Sam 2:23), a blood revenge developed between the two leaders that led first to the death of Abner (II Sam 3:26–27), and second to David's pronouncement of death on Joab for killing him (a doubly heinous crime since Hebron was a Levitical city of refuge, II Sam 3:28–39).

Joab's capture of the Jebusite city of Jerusalem led to his appointment as commander-in-chief of the armies of Israel (I Chr 11:6).

Nahari of Beeroth was his chief armor bearer (II Sam 23:37), and ten attendants carried his equipment (II Sam 18:15). Joab also superintended the reconstruction program of David in Jerusalem (I Chr 11:8). He led the armies of David in war against Syria, Ammon (II Sam 10:7–11:1; 12:26), and Edom (II Sam 8:13, 16). His undue cruelty toward the Edomites may be seen in his attempt to exterminate all the Edomite males (I Kgs 11:15–16). He also led the forces of David in putting down the revolts of Absalom (II Sam 18) and of Sheba (II Sam 20). His military prowess and ruthless strategy are evidenced in the manner in which he removed all barriers to the success of his master David, whom he wanted to be first, and in the severe measures he took to see to it that he, Joab, was a close second in command. Abner and Amasa, potential threats to Joab's position, were summarily executed in typical bedouin fashion.

Joab's biggest mistake was to side with Abiathar in championing Adonijah to become the next king (I Kgs 1:7, 19, 41). On his deathbed David named Solomon to succeed him, and Joab fled to the altar at Gibeon for asylum. There he was executed according to royal decree by Benaiah, chief of the royal bodyguard, the man who would succeed to Joab's position (I Kgs 2:28–35). Joab's life ended where his career began—in Gibeon!

2. Son of Seraiah, a descendant of Kenaz (I Chr 4:14; Neh 11:35), a Judahite "father" or founder of Ge-Harashim, that is, the Valley of Craftsmen.

3. The founder of a family, some of whom are listed among those who returned from the Exile with Zerubbabel (Ezr 2:6; Neh 7:11).

F. E. Y.

The pool of Gibeon where Joab's and Abner's men fought. HFV

JOAH (jō'ȧ)
1. The son of Asaph, recorder or court chronicler to Hezekiah. He was a member of the delegation that went outside Jerusalem to bargain with the Rabshakeh, emissary of Sennacherib (II Kgs 18:18, 26; Isa 36:3, 11, 22).

2. A Levite, the son of Zimmah, of the family of Gershom (I Chr 6:21); he is called Ethan in v. 42. He took part in the cleansing of the temple during the reform of Hezekiah (II Chr 29:12 ff.).

3. The third son of Obed-edom, appointed a doorkeeper of the sanctuary in the time of David (I Chr 26:4).

4. The recorder or chronicler of King Josiah, appointed one of the directors of repairs for the temple (II Chr 34:8).

JOAHAZ (jō'ȧ-hăz)

1. Father of Joah, the recorder under King Josiah (II Chr 34:8).

2. Alternate form of Jehoahaz (q.v.).

JOANNA (jō-ăn'ȧ)

1. An ancestor of Jesus (Lk 3:27), properly spelled Joanan in RSV.

2. Wife of Chuza, the steward of Herod Antipas, one of the women who ministered to Jesus (Lk 8:3) and who went with the other women of Galilee to the tomb of Jesus (Lk 23:55 – 24:10).

JOASH (jō'ăsh). Two different Heb. names appear in English as Joash. The first, Heb. yō'ash, means "Yahweh has given." It is a shorter form of Jehoash (q.v.). At least six people bear this Heb. name in the OT. The name occurs as Y'wsh in the Heb. Lachish ostraca. The other Heb. name is yō'ash, which means "Yahweh has helped." The name with this spelling occurs also on the Samaria ostraca. Heb. yō'ash is the actual name of 3 and 5 below; yō'ash is the name of the other men listed.

1. The father of Gideon of the tribe of Manasseh (Jud 6:11). Joash may have been a man of wealth and status since Gideon was in a position to command ten servants to destroy the altar of Baal and Asherah erected by his father (Jud 6:27–34).

2. A son of Shelah, of Judah (I Chr 4:21–22).

3. A Benjamite of the clan of Becher (I Chr 7:8).

4. The second in command of those who joined David at Ziklag (I Chr 12:3).

5. An official of David in charge of the storage of olive oil (I Chr 27:28).

6. A son of Ahab, king of Israel. When Micaiah prophesied before Jehoshaphat and Ahab, the latter was displeased and sent the prophet to Joash, his son, for imprisonment limited to bread and water rations (I Kgs 22:26; II Chr 18:25).

7. A son of Ahaziah, king of Judah, and his wife Zibiah (II Kgs 11:2; 12:1; II Chr 24:1); also called Jehoash. He was born during a period of excessive royal bloodshed in Judah. His grandfather Jehoram had killed six of his own brothers (II Chr 21:2-4), whereas Jehoram's other sons were killed by the Arabs, leaving only Ahaziah, who ruled but one year (II Chr 21:16 f.; 22:1 f.). When Ahaziah was killed by Jehu of the northern kingdom (II Kgs 9:27 f.), the queen mother Athaliah seized the opportunity to usurp the throne by murdering all the children of Ahaziah. The infant heir Joash, however, was saved by his aunt Jehosheba, wife of the high priest Jehoiada. The child was hidden for six years in the temple until resistance to the evil queen was well established. In the seventh year (835 B.C.), Jehoiada plotted with supporters loyal to the family of David, and they successfully proclaimed Joash king and put Athaliah to death (II Kgs 11:1–16; II Chr 22:10 – 23:15).

Under the guidance of Jehoiada the reign of Joash was a good and godly one. Baal worship was destroyed, the temple was repaired, and a return to Yahweh spread among the people.

On the death of the godly Jehoiada, Joash radically changed. Influenced by worldly princes he forsook the Lord and reverted to idolatry and Asherim worship. He even went so far as to have his cousin Zechariah, son of his rescuer Jehoiada, stoned to death in the temple court for rebuking him. God's judgment came upon him quickly. The Syrians under Hazael invaded the land and took Gath, and were only bribed from destroying Jerusalem with an immense temple treasure (II Kgs 12:17-18). Later, Hazael entered Jerusalem, massacring the princes and severely wounding King Joash (II Chr 24:23-24, RSV). His own servants conspired against Joash and assassinated him. In a final gesture of contempt they refused him burial with the kings (II Chr 24:23-25). The names Joash and Jehoash are used interchangeably throughout II Kgs 11-12; II Chr 23-24. He is one of the three kings omitted in the royal genealogy in Mt 1.

8. The son of Jehoahaz and father of Jeroboam II, kings of Israel. As third king in the Jehu dynasty, he ruled 798-782 B.C. Joash succeeded to the throne of Israel at a time when the nation was all but destroyed. Repeated defeats at the hands of Hazael and Ben-hadad II, kings of Syria, during the days of Jehoahaz had reduced the strength of the nation to its lowest point (II Kgs 13:1-7). It was the glory of Joash during his 16 year reign that, capitalizing on the death of the powerful Hazael c. 800 B.C., he restored the position and power of Israel and prepared it for its highest prosperity under Jeroboam II. Although he promoted idolatry, Joash might have done even greater things had his faith matched that of the dying prophet Elisha who exhorted him to smite the ground repeatedly with arrows in symbol of victories over the Syrian enemy (II Kgs 13:14-25).

Somewhat unwillingly, Joash also went to fight against the presumptuous and perhaps jealous king Amaziah of Judah. He thoroughly defeated Amaziah, even destroying part of the wall of Jerusalem and taking many hostages and much treasure (II Kgs 14:8-16; II Chr 25:17-24). Amaziah himself may have been among the captives. Joash died a natural death and was buried in Samaria.

According to a stela excavated in 1967 at Tell al-Rimah in Iraq, the Assyrian king Adad-nirari III (810–783 B.C.) received tribute from Ia'asu (Joash) the Samaritan (*Iraq*, XXX [1968], 139–153; VT, XIX [1969], 483 f.). This text provides the earliest known mention of Samaria by that name.

S. J. S. and P. C. J.

JOATHAM. *See* Jotham.

JOB (jōb). Although the semipoetic character of the Prologue-Epilogue of the book of Job and the poetry of the central discourses suggest that not all features of the Joban history are described with prosaic literalness, nevertheless the narrative of Job and his experiences is history, not fiction. This conclusion is required by the reference to Job elsewhere in the Bible (see Ezk 14:14, 20; Jas 5:11), and it is confirmed by the purpose of the book of Job, which is to magnify the name of God for His sovereign soteric accomplishments in history.

Job's homeland was somewhere to the E of Palestine near the border of the desert. There are several indications that he lived in the patriarchal age: the longevity of Job (he apparently lived some two centuries), the flourishing of true religion supported by special divine revelation outside the community of the Abrahamic covenant, and certain early social and ethnic features such as the still nomadic status of the Chaldeans and the patriarchal form of worship and sacrifice. Furthermore, he had a name that was borne by a number of W Semites in the earlier part of the 2nd mil. B.C., but which is not found in the 1st mil. The name occurs in the Berlin Execration texts from Egypt as Ayyabum (ANET, p. 329) and in the Amarna letters as Ayal (ANET, p. 486), as well as in Akkadian texts from Mari and Alalakh.

Materially prosperous and genuinely pious Job continued for perhaps some 70 years in the manifest favor of God and men. Then the sudden, well-nigh total reversal of all his earthly circumstances introduced the great crisis that gives Job's life special significance for redemptive history (Job 1 and 2).

Out of the agony and enigma of his sufferings arose the complaint of Job (Job 3) and a long formal discussion between him and his three philosophical friends (Job 4–31). The debate served to demonstrate the foolishness of the traditional wisdom of the world, which led the friends to the utterly false judgment that Job's sufferings were the condign consequence of a radical defection from the fear of God.

But it took the revelation of the voice of the Lord Himself out of the whirlwind, a revelation prepared for by the ministry of His young servant Elihu (Job 32–37), to bring the anguished sufferer back to the peace of a humble and trusting devotion to his Lord (Job 38:1 – 42:6). Thus was Job proved, contrary to the allegations of the evil Adversary, to be a trophy of divine grace.

As vindication of Job before the eyes of his human accusers, God crowned the earthly life of his servant with twofold restoration (Job 42:7– 17).

M. G. K.

JOB, BOOK OF

Background

There was a rich ancient literature devoted to probing the mystery of human life and particularly to discovering the relation of cultic fidelity to material prosperity. The literary motif of the problem of the righteous sufferer was treated in Sumerian literature at least as early as 2000 B.C. A Babylonian text going back to Kassite times (1600–1150 B.C.) and entitled "I Will Praise the Lord of Wisdom" is often called the "Babylonian Job."

This theme figures prominently in the book of Job, but it is there subordinated to a grander theocentric interest, and it is treated within the biblical context of the historical realities of the Fall of man and of God's redemptive dispensation which lead to answers altogether different from those suggested in the pagan poems.

Date and Author

It is difficult to determine when the book of Job was written. Dates ranging from the Mosaic to the Persian period continue to find support among current OT scholars. Conservative scholarship has tended to associate the composition of the book with the flourishing of biblical Wisdom Literature in the age of Solomon. For the most part higher critical investigations have favored a date no earlier than the Exile, and yet a significant minority has argued for an origin in the 2nd mil. B.C.

Most scholars do not believe that one author was responsible for the entire book. Often regarded as later additions to an original work are the Elihu section, the poem on wisdom in chap. 28, and parts of the Lord's discourses. Also called in question is the integrity of the Prologue-Epilogue. The evidence for these misgivings, however, is completely subjective. On the other hand, it is compatible with the proper view of Scripture to recognize that the inspired author of the canonical book of Job made use of a (possibly quite extensive) tradition concerning the life of Job, which may have been written as well as oral.

[For the book to have been accepted in Israel as canonical, its author must have been recognized as an Israelite in the prophetic tradition. He was a poet of rare genius with a deeply sensitive soul. In order to write as he did he himself must have suffered intensely. He was well acquainted with Egypt as well as the ways of the desert, and he seems to have been familiar with the wisdom and lore of the ancient Near East. Therefore individual Israelites ranging from Joseph to Moses to Solomon, who knew Egypt well and had wide-ranging contacts and great personal ability, have been suggested as candidates for author of the book of Job. – Ed.]

Outline

I. Desolation: The Trial of Job's Wisdom, 1:1 – 2:10
II. Complaint: The Way of Wisdom Lost, 2:11 – 3:26
III. Judgment: The Way of Wisdom Darkened and Illuminated, 4:1 – 41:34
    A. The verdicts of men, 4:1 – 37:24
        1. First cycle of debate, 4:1 – 14:22
        2. Second cycle of debate, 15:1 – 21:34
        3. Third cycle of debate, 22:1 – 31:40
        4. Ministry of Elihu, 32:1 – 37:24
    B. The voice of God, 38:1 – 41:34
IV. Confession: The Way of Wisdom Regained, 42:1-6
V. Restoration: The Triumph of Job's Wisdom, 42:7- 17

Purpose

Wisdom Literature that it is, the purpose of the book of Job is to extol God the Creator as the Lord of wisdom and, particularly, to praise the divine wisdom revealed in the redemptive might by which God delivers the slaves of Satan from the power of sin and from the hopelessness of the grave, and establishes them as His own in a triumphant service of pure devotion. As the corollary of this, the book inculcates the fear of this God of all wisdom as the true way of wisdom for man. *See* Wisdom Literature.

Content

The Prologue discloses how a demonstration of God's saving power was afforded through Job and his sufferings. God declared that Job was His servant, but Satan contradicted the divine boast. A test of strength was agreed upon to reveal whether God or Satan owned the allegiance of Job's heart. The full meaning of Job's steadfastness in his fierce temptation must be found, therefore, in the legal framework of the trial by ordeal between God and the Accuser (Job 1-2).

The doxology of Job marked the beginning of the end for Satan, but before the final bruising of Satan under foot Job was to be all but overwhelmed by the dark mystery of his experience. The arrival of his three colleagues from the ranks of the Wise precipitated a process of philosophizing which lured Job away from the simplicity of faith. Afraid now that he had lost the favor of God, Job broke into complaint (Job 3).

In their response to the complaint, Eliphaz, Bildad, and Zophar thought to defend the honor of God. But their commitment to the traditional wisdom of the world with its doctrine of proportionate sin and suffering in this life resulted in their condemnation of the sufferer and thus,

in effect, in their advocacy of Satan's cause. Although Job managed to silence the three philosophers and, in the process, to attain to new insights into the ultimate beatitude of those who know God as their Redeemer, complaint continued to accompany his lament, and his longing for an immediate hearing before the great Judge became ever more consuming (Job 4-31).

A quieting of Job's inflamed spirit must precede the desired trial. Such was the service rendered by Elihu, who, anticipating the judgments of God, rebuked the friends and brought Job to silence and a humility appropriate to his imminent confrontations with God (Job 32-37).

The voice of the Almighty summoned Job to his trial, which turned out to be another trial by ordeal. It was by victory in this ordeal with Job that God purposed to perfect his triumph in his ordeal against Satan. The wrestling of God with Job took the form of a wisdom contest, and Job found himself unable to answer even one of his Creator's questions (Job 38:1 – 41:34).

In Job's repentant confession while still without intimation of earthly restoration, there was a final confirmation of the genuineness of his consecration. Thereby Satan was exposed as a liar still, and God's name and word were honored (Job 42:1-6).

The restoration of Job described in the Epilogue vindicated God's servant against the devil's unwitting advocates and served as a sign of the validity of that hope of ultimate justification and peace which Job had laid hold on by faith (Job 42:7- 17).

Bibliography. Franz Delitzsch, *Job*, KD, 1869 (1949 reprint). E. Dhorme, *A Commentary on the Book of Job*, trans. by Harold Knight, London: Nelson & Sons, 1967. H. L. Ellison, *From Tragedy to Triumph: The Message of the Book of Job*, Grand Rapids: Eerdmans, 1958; "Job," "Job, Book of," NBD, pp. 635-637. Robert Gordis, *The Book of God and Man: A Study of Job*, Chicago: Univ. of Chicago, 1965. W. H. Green, *The Argument of the Book of Job Unfolded*, New York: Carter, 1881. A. Guillaume, *Studies in the Book of Job*, Leiden: Brill, 1968. R. K. Harrison, *Introduction to the Old Testament*, Grand Rapids: Eerdmans, 1969, pp. 1022-1046. Meredith G. Kline, "Job," WBC, pp. 459-490. Marvin H. Pope, "Job, Book of," IDB, II, 911-925; *Job*, Anchor Bible, Garden City: Doubleday, 1965. Nathan M. Sarna, "Epic Substratum in the Prose of Job," JBL, LXXVI (1957), 13-25. Elmer B. Smick, "Mythology and the Book of Job," JETS, XIII (1970), 101-108. Norman H. Snaith, *The Book of Job: Its Origin and Purpose*, Naperville: Allenson, 1968.

M. G. K.

JOBAB (jō'băb)

1. The son of Joktan of the family of Sher (Gen 10:29; I Chr 1:23).

2. The son of Zerah, one of the early kings of Edom (Gen 36:33-34; I Chr 1:44-45).

3. King of the N Canaanite city of Madon, he was allied with Jabin of Hazor against Joshua (Josh 11:1; 12:19).

4. The son of a Benjamite, Shaharaim, by his wife Hodesh (I Chr 8:8-9).

5. Another Benjamite, the son or descendant of Elpaal (I Chr 8:18).

JOCHEBED (jŏk′ĕ-bĕd). The wife of Amram (*q.v.*) and the mother of Moses, Aaron, and Miriam (Ex 6:20; Num 26:59). The faith, courage, and resourcefulness of Amram and Jochebed not only preserved the life of Moses, but his mother obtained from Pharaoh's daughter the privilege of nursing and caring for her own son (Ex 2:1-10; Heb 11:23). Jochebed was the aunt of Amram, his father's sister (Ex 6:20). Marriage of such close relations is forbidden by the Mosaic law (Lev 18:12; 20:19); but there seems to have been no law against it at the time, and even closer relatives were married (cf. Gen 20:12).

Jochebed's Heb. name, *yŏkebed*, meaning "Yah is glory," reveals that the name Yahweh was known and revered by the Israelites before Moses' burning bush experience when God revealed the fuller significance of His divine name (Ex 3:1-15).

JOD. The tenth letter of the Heb. alphabet. *See* Alphabet. This letter is used in the KJV as the heading of the tenth section of Ps 119, where each verse begins with this letter.

JOED (jō′ĕd). A Benjamite living in Jerusalem during the time of Nehemiah (Neh 11:7).

JOEL (jō′ĕl). This name, meaning "Yahweh is God," was popular among the Hebrews.

1. The prophet who wrote the book of Joel (1:1; Acts 2:16). There is no reference to him in the OT historical books but his writings indicate he was the son of Pethuel and lived in Judah, probably in Jerusalem. His date depends on the dating of his book (*see* Joel, Book of), but perhaps c. 835 B.C. Some consider him non-historical and the name only indicative of the prophecy's theme (2:26-28). Since this is unnecessary and the NT refers to an historical character, he should be seen as historical.

2. Samuel's elder son (I Sam 8:2), father of Heman the singer (I Chr 6:33; 15:17). The KJV reads "Vashni" in I Chr 6:28, which is a transliteration of the Heb. probably meaning "and the second"; ASV and RSV so render it and correct the text by adding "Joel" on the basis of Lucian's recession of the LXX, the Syriac, v. 33 and I Sam 8:2. He and his younger brother, Abijah, were appointed by Samuel as judges at Beer-sheba. Their perversion of the office precipitated the elders' demand for a king over Israel.

3. A prince of the Simeonites who emigrated to the valley of Geder c. 715 B.C. (I Chr 4:35).

4. A Reubenite (I Chr 5:4, 8).

5. A chief of the Gadites in Bashan (I Chr 5:12).

6. An ancestor of 2 above and Samuel, son of Azariah and father of an Elkanah (I Chr 6:36).

7. Chief in Issachar, son of Izrahiah, in David's time (I Chr 7:3).

8. One of David's mighty men (I Chr 11:38), brother of Nathan. (In II Sam 23:36 he is called Igal and is referred to as "son.")

9. The Gershonite chief from the Levites (son of Laadan, I Chr 23:8) appointed by David to help return the ark from the house of Obed-edom (I Chr 15:7, 11) and a keeper of the temple treasury (I Chr 26:22).

10. The son of Pedaiah and David's chief over western Manasseh (I Chr 27:20).

11. A Kohathite Levite who assisted Hezekiah in the restoration of temple services (II Chr 29:12).

12. A son of Nebo listed as one of those pledging to put away their foreign wives (Ezr 10:43; also mentioned in I Esd 9:35).

13. A son of Zichri and overseer of the post-Exilic Benjamites in Jerusalem c. 456 B.C. (Neh 11:9).

14. The son of Bani (called Uel in Ezr 10:34 but Joel in I Esd 9:34) in the same list as 12 above.

Sometimes 4 and 5 are seen as one man, and 9 as two.

W. A. A.

JOEL, BOOK OF

Authorship

The author cannot be identified with any of the other OT persons bearing this name, and nothing is known of him outside the book. Thus identification hinges on whether the name is historical or symbolic (*see* Joel). However well his name ("Yahweh is God") expresses his message, it is usually taken as historical. He was the son of Pethuel (1:1; LXX, Bethuel), and Peter speaks of him as the author of the book (Acts 2:16).

Date

With only internal evidence, dating is the greatest problem of the book. Suggestions range from the 10th to the 2nd cen. B.C., 830 and 400 B.C. being the most common. While the earlier date is most characteristic of conservatives and the later of liberals, this lack of agreement seems to be more the result of honest uncertainty about historical possibilities rather than theological predisposition. The same data are presented in favor of both dates. Were the priests in favor (1:13 f.; 2:12-17) because they had not yet fallen into disfavor, or were they again in favor? Significantly, no king is mentioned. This implies either the regency under Jehoiada the priest early in the reign of Joash (835-796 B.C.), or the post-monarchial period after the Exile. The priests and elders as leaders could indicate either an early or a late date. A post-Exilic setting for both of these would seem more certain. No mention of Assyria or Babylon could point to a late date, but the silence regarding them can also be accounted for by proposing the early date before these nations began to harass the kingdom of Judah.

Scattered people and divided land (3:2 f.), Greeks (3:6), no mention of the northern kingdom, and alleged post-Exilic language favor the late date. None of these is conclusive, each raises additional problems, and each can be explained. Phoenicians, Philistines, Egyptians, and Edomites (3:4, 19) as early enemies, and Amos seeming to use Joel (e.g., Joel 2:2, 10; 3:16, 18 with Amos 5:18, 20; 8:8; 1:2; 9:13, respectively) are as strongly in favor of the early date. Most conclusive is the ancient position in the canon which almost obliges a cautious scholar to accept it at face value until contrary evidence compels change of opinion. It is suggested here that the evidence for the early date—while not conclusive—is sufficient to accept the ancient understanding, and that the arguments for the late date—while forceful—are not sufficient to require a departure. Joel's message, moreover, seems to make sense as an early statement which was further developed by later prophets (e.g., the day of the Lord concept, cf. Zephaniah; Joel 3:10, cf. Isa 2:4; Mic 4:3). Therefore, a date c. 830 B.C. seems more likely as the time when Joel wrote; thus he is one of the earliest prophets. He may have been one of the prophets mentioned in II Chr 24:19 whom God sent to warn Judah and Jerusalem after a new outburst of idolatry following Jehoiada's death.

Occasion and Purpose

While a recent locust plague and drought were surely involved as illustrations, the occasion for Joel's prophetic message is most properly seen in the spiritual conditions of the day. The people needed revival in light of the coming day of the Lord and God's climactic disposition of the universe and human society. There is none of the bitter condemnation of blatant sin and gross corruption of later prophets because the people of Judah had simply drifted in Joel's day rather than rebelled against God. While continuing to observe the mechanics of the old covenant, they had become thoughtless in their understanding and careless in their practice. They were spiritually fruitless—rather like the land after the recent locust attacks.

This condition cannot long be tolerated, Joel is convinced, because the day of the Lord is coming when God will make a final disposition of Judah. He not only draws attention to the present spiritual need and to the terribleness of the day of the Lord relative to it, but he sees a glorious future for those who will return to the Lord. The purpose of this prophecy, then, is to call Judah back to God before the day of the Lord comes, to assure the return of God's blessings, and to promise future restoration and vindication.

Structure and Style

The Heb. text is composed of four chapters so that the English 2:28–32 is chap. 3 in the Heb. and the third English chapter is chap. 4 in Heb. Moreover, the first two Heb. chapters are thought to pertain mainly to the present, while the latter two deal only with the future. Therefore, the English 2:28 is a turning point at which to divide the text in analysis, and most scholars do so.

Another way of outlining the book makes the major division before 2:18–19 where the Heb. verbs indicate a past tense. But the verb translated "I will remove" in 2:20 is in the imperfect state, indicating a future tense, so that vv. 18–19 may be interpreted as prophetic perfects foretelling a future period, as in KJV and NASB. Then everything from 2:18 to 3:21 is future in the Messianic Age.

Since the second division is markedly different from the first (apocalyptic rather than historical), many years ago the more liberal scholars began to suggest that it was written by another prophet much later. No other factor suggests dual authorship, and this is adequately accounted for by the dual aspect of God's judgment with future blessings promised for repentance after present punishment is threatened. Therefore, the face value unity of the book commends itself.

Classical among the earlier writing prophets (cf. Amos, Hosea and Micah), Joel's style includes purposeful structure, vivid illustrations, and finely polished language. The bulk of the book is metered poetry with a short prose section (3:4–8).

Outline

Superscription, 1:1
I. Decline of Judah's Prosperity, 1:2–2:11
   A. Description of the present crisis, 1:2–20
     Assemble and cry out to the Lord because locusts have left His land without fruit and His house without offerings—and the day of the Lord is coming.
   B. Description of the coming day of the Lord, 2:1–11
     The day of the Lord is coming with a terrible army and unparalleled destruction.
II. Return of the Lord and His Blessings, 2:12–27
   A. The conditions for return, 2:12–17
     Let all the people return to the Lord with repentance—perhaps He will relent and provide blessings.
   B. The Lord's response, 2:18–20
     With jealousy for His land and pity for His people, Yahweh then promised satisfying food and removal of foreign reproach and the northern enemy.

C. The prophet's song of rejoicing, 2:21-24
Be glad, for the land is productive, for the Lord has caused all the rains to fall as before.

D. Establishment of the Lord and His people, 2:25-27
"I will restore the food lost to locusts and My great army, and you will praise Me with conviction as Israel's exclusive God who has wondrously satisfied you. And My people will never again be put to shame."

III. Reconstitution of Society, 2:28-3:21

A. The Lord's Spirit and salvation, 2:28-32
"Before the day of the Lord will be cosmic upheaval, but I will first pour out My Spirit on all mankind. I will provide deliverance to those who call upon Me as I call them to escape."

B. The Lord's judgment of the nations, 3:1-15
"I will judge the nations for their oppression of Judah at the time when they will come to besiege Jerusalem."

C. The Lord's vindication of Judah, 3:16-21
The Lord acts from Zion to drive away alien nations and to guard Judah in prosperity.

The Locusts

Despite their simply instrumental function, the locusts are so dramatically described that their importance is sometimes exaggerated. The 'arbeh, gāzām, yeleq, and ḥāsîl are explained as different insects, varieties or stages; but whatever, they indicate the cumulative effect of unrelenting attacks. See Animals, III.29. While the immediate references are to literal insects in chap. 1, it becomes difficult to be sure whether they or horses are being pictured in 2:1-11 since a locust's head resembles a horse's head in miniature. The narrative can describe equally well swarms of locusts instinctively doing as they were created, or squadrons of cavalry obediently doing as they were trained. The eschatological features of this day of the Lord passage have led many commentators to connect it with the demonic locusts of Rev 9:1-11. See Hobart E. Freeman, An Introduction to the Old Testament Prophets, Chicago: Moody Press, 1968, pp. 150-154 for arguments in favor of apocalyptic symbolism in 2:1-11.

The Day of the Lord

This is a major motif which is announced with alarm and described as great and dark destruction (1:15; 2:1, 11), but this negative aspect is balanced with a bright picture of restoration (3:1, 18). It is that era in which God no longer restrains the full execution of His judgment, but directly intervenes in human society

and even the cosmos according to the analysis of holiness and in terms of the execution of justice. While the negative is emphasized because Judah most needed to be warned, the positive is present as an encouragement to the faithful remnant and a further motivation to those warned. However unclear the theological understanding of the time sequence of this prophecy may be, the practical implication is clear: God's judgment is coming soon; there is just enough time to repent effectively, but not enough to delay safely.

The Outpouring of the Spirit

Both Peter at Pentecost (Acts 2:21) and Paul to the Romans (10:13) quote Joel 2:32. It is Peter, however, who makes the fullest use (Acts 2:17-21) when he quotes Joel 2:28-32. In correcting those who thought the Jerusalem disciples were drunk because of their glossolalia (see Tongues, Gift of), Peter said, "This is that which was spoken by the prophet Joel" (Acts 2:16). The apostle may have been making specific reference only to that portion of the prophecy which speaks of the Spirit's outpouring and the consequent prophesying, for the events of the day of Pentecost do not seem to have exhausted the prophecy. The effect of the reference seems to be that this is one of the things Joel had in mind, but just the beginning of these things. From that day, the public inauguration of the Messianic Age, and onward to the day of the Lord, the promised Holy Spirit is being given to believers of every age, sex and race (Acts 2:38-39). Thus Joel is the first of the prophets to link the outpouring of the Spirit with the coming of Messiah (cf. Isa 11:2; 32:15; 42:1; 44:3; 59:21; 61:1-3; Ezk 36:27; 39:29; Zech 12:10). See Freeman, op. cit., pp. 154-156 for discussion of the various views of the fulfillment of Joel 2:28-32.

The Apocalypse and the Restoration of Israel

Already indicated is that the last two Heb. chapters (2:28-3:21 in English) are clearly apocalyptic. The ultimate restoration of Israel in the land is obvious, but the exact nature and order of events is less clear. Joel's apocalypse is a significant early statement in the progression of eschatological prophecy, and one cannot formulate a doctrine of future events without inclusion of his data. This prophecy offers a needed corrective to those who are naively optimistic about world peace because of presumptions upon the promise that men will one day "beat their swords into plowshares and their spears into pruning hooks" (Isa 2:4; Mic 4:3). Joel calls upon the nations to do just the opposite (3:10) because of the day of the Lord coming upon their evil. God's promise through Isaiah and Micah, then, will only be realized after His threat through Joel has been experienced.

Significance

The contemporary and eschatological significance of Joel's prophecy is very great; the former because the people of Judah in his day were so much like Christians today; the latter because so much of his predictive prophecy remains unfulfilled. Its message should warn Christians who are beginning to drift spiritually that the consequences are already determined, but that God's blessings can be revived in their lives and that they can anticipate even fuller blessings in the days to come.

Bibliography. J. A. Brewer, ICC. J. T. Carson, "Joel," NBC, Grand Rapids: Eerdmans, 1953. S. R. Driver, *Cambridge Bible*, 1934. A. S. Kapelrud, *Joel Studies*, Uppsala: Uppsala Univ., 1948. E. B. Pusey, *The Minor Prophets*, Vol I, New York: Funk & Wagnalls, 1885. G. A. Smith, *The Expositor's Bible*, rev. ed., New York: Harper, 1928.

W. A. A.

JOELAH (jō-ē'lȧ). One of the sons of Jeroham of Gedor who joined David's forces at Ziklag (I Chr 12:7).

JOEZER (jō-ē'zẽr). A Korahite who joined David's army while David was exiled at Ziklag (I Chr 12:6). The name was inscribed on an ancient Heb. seal as *Yhw'zr*.

JOGBEHAH (jŏg'bẽ-hȧ). A fortified town of Gad (Num 32:35). Gideon passed E of the city in attacking the Midianites (Jud 8:11). This is the modern village of Jubeihât, six miles NW of Amman.

JOGLI (jŏg'lī). The father of Bukki, a Danite chief (Num 34:22).

JOHA (jō'hȧ)

1. A son of Beriah listed in the genealogy of the tribe of Benjamin (I Chr 8:16).

2. A Tizite included, with his brother Jediael, among David's 30 mighty men (I Chr 11:45).

JOHANAN (jō-hā'năn)

1. One of the captains of the remnant that remained in Judah after the fall of Jerusalem. He led the others in warning Gedaliah of the danger to his life from Ishmael. After the governor had been slain, Johanan led the force that pursued Ishmael and recovered the captives taken. Fearful of what the Babylonians would do in reprisal for the murder, Johanan and the other captains approached Jeremiah for advice. When he told them it was the Lord's will that they abide in the land and trust God for protection, Johanan "and all the proud men" rejected the prophet and led the remnant of people to Egypt. There Johanan passes from the record (II Kgs 25:23; Jer 40–43).

2. The oldest son of King Josiah. He probably died young as there is no further mention of him (I Chr 3:15).

3. The son of Elioenai, a descendant of Zerubbabel, after the Exile (I Chr 3:24).

4. A priest, the son of Azariah and father of another Azariah (I Chr 6:9–10).

5. A Benjamite warrior who joined David at Ziklag (I Chr 12:4).

6. A mighty Gadite warrior who joined David in the wilderness (I Chr 12:12, 14).

7. The father of Azariah who was one of the Ephraimites who insisted on returning the captives of Judah taken by Pekah (II Chr 28:12).

8. The son of Hakkatan, one of the descendants of Azgad who returned to Jerusalem with Ezra (Ezr 8:12).

9. One of the chief priests in the days of Ezra and Nehemiah. Ezra retired to the chamber of Johanan in the temple to mourn over the mixed marriages (Ezr 10:6; Neh 12:22–23).

10. The son of Tobiah the Ammonite. He married the daughter of Meshullam the priest (Neh 6:18).

P. C. J.

JOHN (jŏn). In its Heb. form *yôḥānān*, this name was once common among the Jews (*see* Johanan). At least four men named John are mentioned in I and II Maccabees. The following appear in the NT:

1. John the father of Simon Peter (Jn 1:42; 21:15–17, RSV, NASB). Jesus called Peter, Simon Bar-jona (Mt 16:17), Aram. for "son of Jonah." It is not clear whether "Jonah" and "John" represent two Gr. forms of the same Heb. name, or are two different names for Peter's father.

2. John the Baptist (*q.v.*).

3. John the apostle (*q.v.*).

4. John Mark (*see* Mark).

5. A Jewish priest who participated in the questioning of Peter and John (Acts 4:6), otherwise unknown.

JOHN, GOSPEL OF. The fourth Gospel of the NT, regarded by many as the most profound book in the NT. Simple in language and structure, it is nevertheless a deeply perceptive exposition of the person of Christ in a historical setting.

Theme

Like the Synoptic Gospels (*see* Gospels, Synoptic), the Gospel of John has as its theme the presentation of the ministry of Jesus Christ to His own nation, including the preparation for it by the work of John the Baptist, the gathering of disciples about Him, the teaching of the people, the performing of miracles, the stirring of opposition on the part of the religious leaders of Israel, and His condemnation to death by the high council, which was implemented by Pilate the Roman governor, leading to His crucifixion and resurrection, with appearances to His chosen disciples.

Purpose

The author's purpose in writing is plainly stated: to induce faith in Jesus as the Christ, the Son of God, so that life may come through His name (20:31). It is not life in the abstract but the divine life communicated to those willing to receive the Messiah. Because the nation as a whole was unwilling to do this (1:11; 18:35), it was left in its sins. Judaism, despite the glamour of its festivals and the enlightenment of its law and the self-confidence of its leaders, shows how pathetic is its blindness. It refused to recognize its Messiah and thereby forfeited all claim to a genuine knowledge of the God who had sent Him (chap. 8).

The appeal of the book is mainly to the Jewish Diaspora, those who because of their residence outside the land lacked the opportunity for immediate contact with Jesus. Let them see clearly the solemnity of the issues involved and choose life in the Son rather than the condemnation that belongs to those who refuse Him. It is a striking fact that despite the "whosoever" of the gospel invitation, the word Gentile does not once occur in the book—although the term "Greeks" in 7:35 apparently means Gentiles, and the Greeks who came to see Jesus (12:20) were undoubtedly Gentile proselytes.

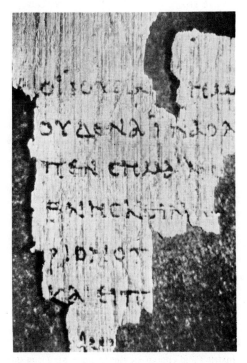

The John Rylands Fragment of John 18: 31–33. John Rylands Library

Author and Date

Who wrote this "spiritual Gospel," as Clement of Alexandria called it? The traditional answer is John, the son of Zebedee. Irenaeus is the leading patristic writer who affirms this, and he was in a favorable position to know because of his contact with Polycarp and Pothinus, who had been associated with John in Asia Minor during the latter days of his life. Other 2nd cen. witnesses were Theophilus of Antioch, the author of the Muratorian Canon, and Clement of Alexandria.

This testimony has been widely challenged in modern times on various grounds, such as the silence of Ignatius about John when writing to the Ephesian church early in the 2nd cen., the claim that an Ephesian by the same name, John the Elder, may have written it, or that reports of the early martyrdom of John rule out the possibility of his authorship. These objections are rather easily answered.

More serious are the allegations that a fisherman could not be expected to display such a grasp of theological thought as the author of this book manifestly had (cf. Acts 4:13). It seems strange also that a Galilean would give such slight attention to Jesus' ministry in Galilee. And if the writer was a member of the apostolic circle, why did he omit a description of the transfiguration and of Jesus' agony in Gethsemane, at which he was a privileged witness?

In the face of problems such as these, many have concluded that while John may have furnished much of the material of the Gospel, another—probably one of his close disciples—actually wrote it. But it is still possible to maintain John's authorship, since no decisive argument against it has been raised, and no satisfactory alternative has been offered. The writer was familiar with Samaria (cf. 3:23; 4:5–12) and with Jerusalem prior to its destruction in A.D. 70, knowing details verified by archaeological discoveries about the pool of Bethesda (5:2) and the Pavement (19:13). He seems to have been an eyewitness of many of the events (e.g., 6:10; 19:31–35), and was conversant with the religious terminology current among pious Jews in Palestine prior to A.D. 68, according to the Qumran literature.

For many years it was popular, following F. C. Baur of the Tübingen School in Germany, to insist that the Gospel of John was a product of the mid-2nd cen. A.D. But the John Rylands fragment (P⁵²) of the text of this Gospel, found in Egypt in modern times and dated by paleographers during the first half of the 2nd cen., helps to fix the writing of the fourth Gospel by the close of the 1st cen. The use of John as an authoritative Gospel along with the other three is attested by the Egerton Papyrus 2, a harmony dated not later than A.D. 150, published in *Fragments of an Unknown Gospel and Other Early Christian Papyri*, by H. I. Bell and T. C. Sheat (1935). Furthermore, the fourth Gospel seems to have been quoted by the Gnostic writer Valentinus in his Gospel of Truth, originally composed c. A.D. 140 (see Gnosticism). Also in catacombs in Rome there are paintings of Christ as the Good Shepherd and of the raising of Lazarus that can be dated c. A.D. 150. Thus the origin of the Gospel of John can be placed during the last decade or so of the 1st cen., although some would make it even earlier, with Ephesus as the probable place of writing.

Outline

I. Prologue, 1:1–18
II. The Son of God Working and Witnessing Among Men, 1:19–12:50
III. The Son of God Teaching His Own, 13:1–17:26
IV. The Son of God Glorifying the Father in Death and Resurrection, 18:1–20:31
V. Epilogue, 21:1–25

Differences from Other Gospels

Though in its general nature this Gospel is similar in broad outline to the Synoptics, it differs from them in various respects. About nine-tenths of its material is not found in the Synoptics at all. Much more emphasis is put on Jesus' ministry in Judea than in Galilee. The Lord is represented as going to Jerusalem on several occasions, especially for the festivals of the Jewish year. On the basis of these, it is possible to hold that His ministry must have lasted about three years, whereas the items included in the Synoptics need not have covered more than one year, with a single Passover being mentioned.

One misses the parables that so abound in Jesus' teaching as it is reported in the Synoptics. The teaching material occurs mainly in discourses which do not center in the kingdom of God, as in the other Gospels, but in the person of Christ. It is here that the "I am" sayings are to be found. Not infrequently dialogues between Jesus and various individuals are introduced, as in the case of Nicodemus and of the Samaritan woman. A cleansing of the temple is included at an early point in the Gospel and none is mentioned at the close, where the Synoptics place it. The resurrection of Lazarus, which fails to appear in the Synoptics, is introduced in connection with the deepening of official opposition to Jesus. Much more sharply than in the Synoptics the issue of His messiahship is the focus of discussion.

In Jesus' self-revelation, as here presented, the most outstanding feature is His relation to the Father as the Son. He is conscious of pre-existence (17:5) and claims equality with the Father (10:30; 5:23). Yet along with this high claim goes an oft-repeated recognition of subordination and dependence on the Father. His words (14:24) and His works (14:10) are traced to the Father. His glorification is not merely reserved for the resurrection and what follows (12:16; 7:39), but actually includes His death (12:23; 13:31), since this fulfilled the Father's will.

That a Gospel of this character could be written in the early church and accepted by it, despite these and other differences from the Synoptics, suggests the variety and richness of the Christian tradition as it was recalled by those who had companied with the Saviour. It is wholly unlikely that this Gospel was written to replace the Synoptics since it is so different from them. While it may have been designed to supplement the other accounts, it seems to stand largely apart from them, as though springing from a source that had independent information. See Gospels, The Four.

Bibliography. C. K. Barrett, *The Gospel According to St. John*, London: SPCK, 1955. T. D. Bernard, *The Central Teaching of Jesus Christ*, New York: Macmillan, 1892. Raymond E. Brown, *The Gospel According to John*, Anchor Bible, 2 vols., Garden City: Doubleday, 1966, 1970. F. Lamar Cribbs, "A Reassessment of the Date of the Origin and the Destination of the Gospel of John," JBL, LXXXIX (1970), 38-55. C. H. Dodd, *The Interpretation of the Fourth Gospel*, Cambridge: Univ. Press, 1953. F. Godet, *Commentary on the Gospel of St. John*, 3 vols., 3rd ed., Edinburgh: T. & T. Clark, 1895. William Hendriksen, *The Gospel of John*, 2 vols., Grand Rapids: Baker, 1953. E. C. Hoskyns, *The Fourth Gospel*, rev. ed., by F. N. Davey, London: Faber & Faber, 1940. W. F. Howard, *Christianity According to St. John,* London: Duckworth, 1943. Leon Morris, *The Gospel of John*, Grand Rapids: Eerdmans, 1971; *Studies in the Fourth Gospel*, Grand Rapids: Eerdmans, 1969. H. P. V. Nunn, *The Authorship of the Fourth Gospel*, Oxford: Blackwell, 1952. R. V. G. Tasker, *The Gospel According to St. John*, TNTC, Grand Rapids: Eerdmans, 1960. William Temple, *Readings in St. John's Gospel*, London: Macmillan, 1945. Merrill C. Tenney, *John: The Gospel of Belief*, Grand Rapids: Eerdmans, 1948. W. H. Griffith Thomas, "The Plan of the Fourth Gospel," BS, CXXV (1968), 313-323. George A. Turner and Julius R. Mantey, *The Gospel According to John*, Grand Rapids: Eerdmans, 1964. B. F. Westcott, *The Gospel According to St. John: The Greek Text with Introduction and Notes*, London: John Murray, 1908.

E. F. Har.

JOHN, I, II AND III EPISTLES OF. These are often described as catholic or general epistles, but the designation is somewhat faulty since the second and third letters are addressed to local situations and the first to believers in a limited area, probably that portion of Asia Minor that looked to Ephesus as its hub city.

I John

Purpose. This letter was written partly to instruct and encourage the readers, majoring on such fundamental terms as light, truth, knowledge (verb), belief (verb), love, and righteousness. These are not developed one after another in systematic fashion, but are intertwined to a degree as the author repeats his themes with variations.

It is not difficult to detect along with this positive purpose a desire to warn against false teaching (e.g., 2:26). The particular error in view is Gnosticism (*q.v.*) of a Jewish type that denied that Jesus is the Christ (2:22) and that He had come in the flesh (4:2-3). The Gnostics tended to be proud and exclusive, boasting of their superior insights, and for this reason drew the fire of the writer as he insisted that genuine believers are not deficient in knowledge (2:20-21, 27). Neither must they be deficient in love, in contrast to the errorists (4:20). It is diabolical to claim superior knowledge and live on a low moral and ethical plane (3:7-8).

Author. From various references in the Church Fathers, it is known that the early church ascribed the epistle to John the apostle (*q.v.*). Agreeable to this identification is the close similarity between the introduction (1:1-4) of I John and the prologue of the Gospel of John. Much the same vocabulary is found in the two works. There are differences, of course, but these are natural in view of the diverse nature of the two writings.

Recipients. The readers of the epistle cannot be identified with certainty. If the word "idols" in 5:21 must be taken literally, then the readers were Gentile Christians. But it is perhaps more logical to understand the word in a broader sense of the fascination with false teaching and the vagaries that belong to it. At any rate, the prominence given to the confession of Jesus as the Christ (2:22) suggests that the readers were Jewish Christians (cf. Jn 20:31).

Date. The exact time of writing cannot be fixed. It was probably sometime in the last decade of the 1st cen.

Characteristics. Simplicity of language and sentence structure characterize the book. Its challenge lies in its sharply enunciated teaching on the nature of the Christian life. One is either walking in the light with God or is in darkness. To profess one thing and be another is the mark of a liar. No man can live rightly unless he is born of God (2:29; 3:9; 4:7; 5:4). The doctrinal emphasis centers mainly in Christology—the oneness of the Son with the Father (1:2-3; 2:23), His incarnation (1:2; 4:2), atonement (1:7; 2:2; 3:5), victory over the evil one (3:8), and future appearing (3:2). The Spirit is given attention also, particularly in the capacity of witness to the truth (5:7-8; cf. 4:2) and to the divine indwelling of the believer (3:24; 4:13). As in the Gospel according to John, the world, ethically considered, is pictured as evil, something to be shunned (2:15-17; 3:13; 4:5; 5:4-5, 19).

Outline

I. Introduction, 1:1-4

II. Fellowship with God (Walking in the Light), 1:5-2:28

Tested by:
1. Righteousness of life, 1:8-2:6
2. Love for the brethren, 2:7-17
3. Belief in Jesus as God incarnate, 2:18-28

III. Divine Sonship, 2:29-4:6
Tested by:
1. Righteousness, 2:29-3:10*a*
2. Love, 3:10*b*-24
3. Belief, 4:1-6

IV. The Commandment of Christian Love, 4:7-21

V. The Necessity of Christian Belief, 5:1-12

VI. The Certainties of the Christian Life, 5:13-20

VII. Concluding Exhortation, 5:21

II John

The writer makes himself known only as "the elder." This was sufficient since the recipient, identified as "the elect lady," was evidently a close friend. The elder was following the spiritual development of her children faithfully, and hoped to come in person for a visit before long. Others believe the "lady" refers to a local church or Christian community, perhaps at Pergamum, the members of which are called "her children." *See* Elect Lady.

If there was a special reason for the writing of this brief letter, it is probably to be found in the counsel not to receive visiting teachers who fail to measure up to the church's confession concerning the incarnation (vv. 7-11). The elder could not resist the urge to underscore also the need for continued love toward the saints (vv. 5-6).

Several features of this brief letter suggest John the apostle as the writer, such as the emphasis on truth and love, and especially the insistence on the incarnation. Other items looking in the same direction are the mention of Antichrist (v. 7; cf I Jn 2:18, 22; 4:3) and the word "abide" (v.9). It would be pedantic to insist that the use of "elder" rules out apostolic status (cf. I Pet 5:1). The early church generally accepted the book as emanating from John. Presumably the recipient lived fairly close to Ephesus (v. 12). The probable date is late in the 1st cen.

Outline

I. Commendation for Fidelity to the Truth, 1-3

II. Commandment of Love in Which to Walk, 4-6

III. Importance of Holding the Doctrine of Christ, 7-9

IV. Refusal of Fellowship with False Teachers, 10-11

V. Conclusion, 12-13

III John

This short missive, likewise from "the elder," is addressed to a certain Gaius who is a faithful believer (v. 3) and a leader in a local church. He had distinguished himself by his hospitality toward traveling Christian workers (vv. 5 – 6), in contrast to Diotrephes, who belonged either in the same church or in one close by. This man not only had refused to receive the brethren whom John had sent (apparently wishing to show his authority in the local situation by rejecting the elder's recommendation contained in his letter), but had gone so far as to put out of the church those who welcomed these visitors (v. 10). Now the elder was writing Gaius, appealing to him to help the missionaries even at the cost of bringing down upon himself the wrath of Diotrephes.

The letter bears marks of similarity to II John, not only in the person of the writer, but in the strong emphasis on the truth and the preference for a personal visit over communication by letter (v. 13).

In all probability the date of the letter is roughly the same as for II John, and the destination some spot not far distant from Ephesus.

Outline

- I. Introduction, 1 – 4
- II. Praise for Kindness to Traveling Brethren, 5 – 8
- III. Condemnation of Diotrephes, 9 – 11
- IV. Recommendation of Demetrius, 12
- V. Conclusion, 13 – 14

Bibliography. Donald W. Burdick, *The Epistles of John,* Chicago: Moody Press, 1970. Robert S. Candlish, *The First Epistle of John,* Grand Rapids: Zondervan, n.d. C. H. Dodd, *The Johannine Epistles,* New York: Harper, 1946. George G. Findlay, *Fellowship in the Life Eternal,* London: Hodder & Stoughton, n.d. Robert Law, *The Tests of Life, A Study of the First Epistle of John,* Edinburgh: T. & T. Clark, 1909. Alexander Ross, *Commentary on the Epistles of James and John,* NIC, Grand Rapids: Eerdmans, 1954. Charles C. Ryrie, "I, II

Ruins of the Church of St. John at Ephesus. HFV

and III John," WBC, pp. 1463 – 1485. John R. W. Stott, *The Epistles of John,* TNTC, Grand Rapids: Eerdmans, 1964. B. F. Westcott, *The Epistles of John,* Cambridge: Macmillan, 1892. Reginald E. O. White, *Open Letter to Evangelicals, A Devotional and Homiletic Commentary on the First Epistle of John,* Grand Rapids: Eerdmans, 1964.

E. F. Har.

JOHN MARK. *See* Mark.

JOHN THE APOSTLE. According to the testimony of the NT and of the ancient church, this John was one of the leading figures in shaping the course of Christianity, whether by his writings (the fourth Gospel, three epistles, and the Apocalypse), his missionary and pastoral labors, or his defense of the faith against the attempted inroads of Gnostic error.

Personal history. The biblical data furnish considerable information about him, at least more than is available on most of the apostles. Zebedee was his father (Mk 1:20) and Salome his mother (Mk 15:40; Mt 27:56). A comparison with Jn 19:25 makes it probable that Salome was the sister of Mary, the mother of Jesus. John was likely younger than his brother James, for, with the exception of a few Lucan passages (Lk 8:51, RSV; 9:28; Acts 1:13, RSV), he is regularly named after James. The family was engaged in the fishing business, with servants assisting the father and his sons (Mk 1:20). A partnership had been formed with another pair of brothers, Simon Peter and Andrew (Lk 5:10). Since the latter lived at Bethsaida on the northern shore of the Sea of Galilee (Jn 1:44), it may be assumed that this was John's residence also.

Whereas John is named rather frequently in the Synoptic Gospels especially in Mark, this is not true of the fourth Gospel, which merely refers to the sons of Zebedee (Jn 21:2). However, there are several references to "the disciple whom Jesus loved" (Jn 13:23; 19:26; 20:2; 21:7, 20) and to "another disciple" (Jn 18:15) who brought Peter into the court of the high priest's house. Since Peter's companion a short time afterward was the beloved disciple (Jn 20:2) and since John was closely associated with Peter both in the Synoptic Gospels and Acts, it is reasonable to infer that John was the beloved disciple. This is supported by the consideration that the absence of John's name from the fourth Gospel, in view of its prominence in the Synoptics, can best be explained on the supposition that John was the writer of the fourth Gospel, who for some reason, probably modesty, preferred to keep his name out of the record (in Jn 21:24 the writer of the Gospel is identified with the beloved disciple).

It is highly probable that John was that unnamed disciple who, in company with Andrew, spent several hours with Jesus after John the Baptist had pointed Him out (Jn 1:35 – 40). If so, this means that he and a number of other disciples of Jesus had been followers of the Baptist before transferring their allegiance to the Nazarene. However, the more definite call to discipleship came somewhat later, in Galilee, when John and his brother James were summoned from their nets to become fishers of men (Mk 1:19). Later still, when 12 men were set apart as apostles, John was included. He appears as a member of the inner circle of three (Peter, James, and John) who were with Jesus at the raising of Jairus' daughter (Mk 5:37), at the transfiguration (Mk 9:2), and at the night vigil in Gethsemane (Mk 14:33). On another occasion Andrew was present with the three (Mk 13:3). With Peter, John was delegated to prepare the Passover feast for Jesus and the Twelve (Lk 22:8).

If the reference in Jn 18:15 to the acquaintanceship between a certain disciple and the high priest really refers to John, as seems most natural, then he is not to be regarded simply as an ordinary fisherman. It is quite possible that John's family possessed means. His mother was likely a member of that group of women who ministered to Jesus of their substance (Lk 8:2–3; cf. Jn 19:25). From Jn 19:26–27 it appears that the family maintained a home in the Jerusalem area. Jesus knew that in committing His mother to John He was insuring her comfort as well as spiritual solace. Although it is only conjecture, one may conclude perhaps that it was during John's days in Judea as a disciple of John the Baptist that he secured quarters in Jerusalem and also became known to the high priest. He wanted to be near in order to keep in the closest possible touch with the new awakening that centered in the ministry of the Baptist.

Characteristics. Something of the character of John may be gleaned from the epithet given to him and his brother James by the Lord. Although "sons of thunder" (Mk 3:17) is not explained in the text, it seems to refer to the disposition or to the zeal of these brothers, or both. Fortunately, a few episodes are recorded that help to fill out the picture. On his own initiative John forbade a man to continue casting out demons in Jesus' name, on the ground that he did not belong to Jesus' chosen band of disciples. Christ would not own this narrowness, but rebuked it (Lk 9:49–50).

On two other occasions John teamed with his brother James in exhibiting undesirable traits of character. Using their mother as a go-between, they asked for the choice places of honor on either side of Jesus when His kingdom glory was achieved (Mk 10:35; Mt 20:20). They had not yet learned to crucify selfish ambition. At another time, on the way up to Jerusalem, the brothers proposed that they call down fire from heaven upon a Samaritan village that refused hospitality to their Master. Apparently it did not dawn on them that a vindictive use of miraculous power was completely alien to Him who had called them into His service (Lk 9:51–55). They were "sons of thunder" indeed.

Traditional tomb of John inside Church of St. John at Ephesus. HFV

Despite his weaknesses, and perhaps even because of them, John was given a specially close relationship to the Lord as "the disciple whom Jesus loved," leaning on His breast at supper. He was the first of the apostolic company to believe in the resurrection on the basis of what he saw in the empty tomb (Jn 20:8). It was his insight that detected the risen Lord as the one responsible for the great catch of fish (Jn 21:7). With reference to him the Lord indicated that quite a different future might unfold than that reserved for Simon Peter (Jn 21:22).

After Pentecost. Information on John for the period after Pentecost centers around his association with Simon Peter. He regularly took a subordinate role, content to let the initiative in speech and action rest with his friend. Because of his participation in the healing of the lame man (Acts 3:1, 4, 11), he was brought before the Sanhedrin, along with Peter, and almost certainly made some statement, because the boldness of both men impressed the council (Acts 4:13; cf. v. 19). These same two were deputed by the other apostles to go to Samaria to oversee the results of Philip's labors there (Acts 8:14).

Some time later, when his brother James was beheaded by order of Herod Agrippa I and his friend Peter imprisoned with a view to the same fate, John was not included in the persecution. Gradually tradition sponsored the idea that he suffered martyrdom, based mainly, one may suppose, on Jesus' prediction (Mk 10:39); but Luke knows nothing of it. This late tradition may safely be rejected. Our last glimpse of John in the Jerusalem area is furnished by Paul, who met with James the Lord's brother and Peter and John to discuss the nature of the gospel and their relation to it as servants of Christ (Gal 2:9). Here John is accounted a pillar of the Jerusalem church. It may be that John remained in the city until the troubled days prior to the siege of Jerusalem by the Roman armies under Titus, although he is not mentioned in connection with Paul's last visit (Acts 21).

Christian writers of the 2nd cen. and later tell of John's work in Asia Minor, centering in the city of Ephesus. According to Rev 1:9, John was exiled to the isle of Patmos for his testimony to the gospel. Irenaeus asserts that this occurred near the end of the reign of Domitian, which terminated in A.D. 96 (Eusebius HE iii.18.3). The same writer alleges that John lived on into the reign of Trajan, which began in the year 98 (*Against Heresies* iii.3.4).

John may well have supervised the work among the various churches in Asia Minor such as are named in Rev 2 – 3. Clement of Alexandria indicates a varied ministry in this area even after John's return from Patmos, when he must have been a very old man, including a moving story of his pastoral concern for a young man who fell into evil ways after his baptism. John allowed himself to be captured by the robbers over whom this young man was now chief, exhorted him, prayed with him, and brought him back to the Lord and to the church (*The Rich Man's Salvation*, p. 42).

In those days Gnosticism (*q.v.*) was gaining ground and seriously challenging the apostolic faith. John showed that he was capable not only of manifesting love for the brethren, but that he was still in measure a son of thunder. Irenaeus relates that on entering a bathhouse in Ephesus and seeing the heretic Cerinthus within, John rushed out crying, "Let us fly, lest even the bathhouse fall down, because Cerinthus, the enemy of the truth, is within" (*Against Heresies* iii.3.4).

For bibliography, *see* John, Gospel of.

E. F. Har.

JOHN THE BAPTIST. Born (*c.* 7 B.C.) of elderly parents, Zacharias and Elisabeth, both of whom were of a priestly family, John grew up in the wilderness of Judea (Lk 1:80), and there (*c.* A.D. 27) he was called to his prophetic ministry (Lk 3:2). Under what influences he lived during his formative years we can only speculate. Even if he had some association in the wilderness with the Essenes (whether those of Qumran or others; *see* Essenes; Dead Sea Scrolls), it was a new spiritual experience that launched him on his distinctive task of making ready "a people prepared for the Lord" (Lk 1:17), and this probably involved a break with his previous association. Now he rapidly gained fame as a preacher of repentance. Great numbers of Jews flocked out to the wilderness to listen to him, from Judea and the neighboring regions. Many of them received at his hands the baptism of repentance in the river Jordan, confessing their sins as they did so.

John's attitude to the Jewish "establishment" of the day was one of radical condemnation. The existing order could not be reformed; the axe was already being swung to cut down the tree at the root (Mt 3:10; Lk 3:9). The Pharisees and other religious leaders of the nation

Ein Kerem, birthplace of John the Baptist, with Church of St. John over his traditional place of birth.

IIS

he denounced as a brood of vipers, trying to escape the flames of divine judgment which were overtaking them. He denied any value in natural descent from Abraham; he called for a new beginning. From the Jewish people at large he called out a loyal and repentant remnant that would make ready for the imminent advent of the greater than John who was to inaugurate the work of judgment. John spoke of himself as the preparer of the way for this Coming One, for whom he declared himself unworthy to perform even the humblest service. His own baptizing with water was to be followed by the more powerful baptism with the Spirit and fire which the Coming One would carry out.

That John's converts formed a distinct group in Israel is implied both by the fourth Gospel, with its references to the disciples of John, and by Josephus, who records that John bade his hearers "come together by means of baptism" (*Ant.* xviii.5.2). Josephus means probably that John called a religious community into being by his baptism of repentance. But when he further represents John as teaching that "baptism was acceptable to God provided that it was undergone not to procure remission of sins but for the purification of the body, when the soul had first been purified by righteousness," his account deviates from that of the Gospel writers, and probably reflects the baptismal doctrine of the Essenes, with which Josephus had some acquaintance.

To those of his disciples who sought his practical guidance, John gave some simple rules of charity and justice which demanded no such abandonment of their normal vocation as the strictest Essene code required.

Among those who received baptism from John was Jesus. After Jesus' baptism (which took place by His own request), John recognized in Him the Coming One of whom he had spoken—although later, during his imprisonment, he began to doubt this, and had to be reassured that the features of Jesus' ministry were precisely those which the prophets had said would mark the new age.

John exercised a baptismal ministry in Samaria, at Aenon near to Salim (Jn 3:23), as well as in the Judean wilderness. This ministry, which was probably of short duration, would explain certain features which emerged subsequently in Samaritan religion, and it also explains Jesus' words to His disciples in Jn 4:35–38, referring to that neighborhood: "Others have labored, and ye are entered into their labor" (ASV).

The last phase of John's career was located in the Perean region of Herod Antipas' tetrarchy. John aroused Herod's suspicion as the leader of a popular movement which might have political implications. He also incurred the personal animosity of Herodias, Herod's wife, by denouncing the illegality of their marriage. He was accordingly arrested and imprisoned in Herod's Transjordanian fortress of Machaerus (q.v.), where some months later he was beheaded (c. A.D. 29). His disciples preserved their identity for some decades after his death.

To the NT writers John's chief significance lies in his being Christ's forerunner. For a time his ministry and Christ's overlapped (Jn 3:22 f.). His imprisonment was the signal for the beginning of Christ's Galilean ministry (Mk 1:14); his baptism provided the starting point for the apostolic preaching (Acts 10:37; 13:24 f.). Jesus declared him to be the promised Elijah of Mal 4:5–6 (Mk 9:13; Mt 11:14; cf. Lk 1:17), and the last and greatest of the prophets (Lk 7:24–28; 16:16). His ministry summed up the burden of divine revelation under the old order: "The law and the prophets were until John: since that time the kingdom of God is preached." But while unsurpassed in personal stature, John was inferior in privilege, said Jesus, to the lowest in the kingdom of God. Like Moses viewing the Promised Land from Pisgah, John stood on the threshold of the new age as its herald, but did not enter it in this life.

Bibliography. W. H. Brownlee, "John the Baptist in the New Light of Ancient Scrolls," *The Scrolls and the New Testament,* ed. by K. Stendahl, London: SCM, 1958, pp. 33 ff. C. H. Kraeling, *John the Baptist,* New York: Scribner's, 1951. J. A. T. Robinson, *Twelve New Testament Studies,* London: SCM, 1962, pp. 11 ff. J. Steinmann, *Saint John the Baptist and the Desert Tradition,* London: Longmans, 1958.

F. F. B.

JOIADA (joi'á-dá). An abbreviation of Jehoiada (q.v.).

1. A son of Paseah who helped Nehemiah rebuild the wall of Jerusalem (Neh 3:6, RSV; KJV, Jehoiada).

2. A high priest and great-grandson of Jeshua (Neh 12:10, 22). One of his sons married a daughter of Sanballat, for which cause Nehemiah expelled him from the priesthood (Neh 13:28; here RSV has Jehoiada).

JOIAKIM (joi'á-kǐm). The son of Jeshua the priest who returned with Zerubbabel (Neh 12:10, 12, 26).

JOIARIB (joi'á-rǐb)

1. A priest in the time of David (I Chr 24:7).

2. One of the "men of understanding" or teachers sent by Ezra to Casiphia to request that ministers for the temple be sent to accompany them to Jerusalem (Ezr 8:16–17).

3. The son of Zechariah of the tribe of Judah whose descendants dwelt in Jerusalem in Nehemiah's day (Neh 11:5).

4. The father of Jedaiah and founder of one of the priestly houses after the Exile (Neh 11:10; 12:19). His name is given as Jehoiarib (q.v.) in I Chr 9:10.

5. One of the chief priests who returned to Jerusalem with Zerubbabel. A son Mattenai was contemporary with Joiakim (Neh 12:6, 19). Probably the same as 4.

JOINING. Two different Heb. words are translated "joining" in KJV.

1. A form of *ḥābar,* meaning "to join together, connect" (I Chr 22:3). It is translated "coupling" in ASV and "clamps" in RSV.

2. An adjective from *dābaq,* meaning "to cleave, adhere, join" (II Chr 3:12).

JOKDEAM (jǒk'dě-ăm). An unidentified town in the hill country of Judah, listed with Maon, Carmel and Ziph in Josh 15:56.

JOKIM (jō'kǐm). A son or descendant of Shelah, Judah's youngest son (I Chr 4:22).

JOKMEAM (jǒk'mē-ăm). A town in Ephraim assigned to the Kohathite Levites (I Chr 6:66, 68); perhaps the same as Kibzaim in Josh 21:22. In KJV of I Kgs 4:12 the name is incorrectly spelled Jokneam (see ASV and RSV for correction); this passage indicates Jokmeam is S of Abel-meholah in the Jordan Valley, perhaps Tell el-Mazar on the S side of the Wadi Far'ah, across from Adam (Tell ed-Damiyeh).

JOKNEAM (jǒk'nē-ăm). A royal Canaanite city (Josh 12:22) assigned to the Merarite Levites (Josh 21:34). Located on the W side of the Kishon stream at the foot of the Carmel ridge on Zebulun's boundary (Josh 19:11), it is now identified as Tell Qeimun, 12 miles SW of Nazareth and seven miles NW of Megiddo. The site guards the E end of the northernmost and lowest pass through the Carmel range, connecting the Plain of Sharon and the Valley of Jezreel. Jokneam is # 113 in the list of towns captured by Thutmose III. Jokneam in KJV of I Kgs 4:12 should read Jokmeam (as in ASV and RSV). *See* Jokmeam.

JOKSHAN (jǒk'shăn). A son of Abraham and Keturah, and the ancestor of the Sheba and Dedan tribes of Arabia (Gen 25:1–3; I Chr

1:32). The supposition that Jokshan is to be identified with Joktan (Gen 10:25; I Chr 1:20) is unsupported historically and philologically.

JOKTAN (jŏk'tăn). A descendant of Shem and the son of Eber and brother of Peleg (Gen 10:25; I Chr 1:19). He was the progenitor of 13 sons or Semitic tribal groups who inhabited the S Arabian peninsula (Gen 10:26–30; I Chr 1:20–23).

JOKTHEEL (jŏk'thē-ĕl)
1. An unidentified town in the Shephelah region of Judah near Lachish (Josh 15:38).
2. A name given to Sela(h) (now Petra) after King Amaziah of Judah captured it from the Edomites (II Kgs 14:7).

JONA (jō'nà). KJV form of John (Jn 1:42, RSV), used in order to harmonize with Bar-jona in Mt 16:17.

JONADAB (jō'nà-dăb). A shorter and alternate form of Jehonadab (q.v.).
1. Son of Shimeah and nephew of David (II Sam 13:3, 5, 32, 35). A crafty man, he suggested how Amnon might rape his half-sister Tamar. Later he reported the details of Amnon's death to King David. He may have been the same as or brother of the man called Jonathan son of Shimeah, who slew one of the Gittite giants (II Sam 21:21).
2. Son of Rechab and titular head of the Rechabites (q.v.), a clan maintaining strict principles of a nomadic life and abstinence from wine in obedience to the teachings of their father Jonadab (Jer 35:6–19). He accompanied Jehu to Samaria and participated with him in the destruction of the worshipers of Baal (II Kgs 10:15, 23). He must have been known for his piety and faithfulness to God, for Jehu invited him to go through the doomed worshipers of Baal gathered in the temple to make sure no followers of the Lord were there. Jonadab's household traced its lineage back to the Kenites (I Chr 2:55).

JONAH (jō'nà). The son of Amittai from Gath-hepher in Zebulun, who prophesied the restoration of Israel's borders, which was accomplished by Jeroboam II (782–753 B.C.) (II Kgs 14:25), and the hero of the book of Jonah (1:1). Since Jonah probably spoke the word concerning Jeroboam c. 790 B.C. during the latter's coregency with his father Jehoash, Jonah almost certainly knew Elisha (d. 797 B.C.) and may have been one of the "sons of the prophets" trained by Elisha (cf. II Kgs 6:1–7).

Most liberal scholars deny both that the events of Jonah happened and that he wrote the book. The claim is that a 4th cen. B.C. anonymous writer fabricated the story, since the early Jonah had the exclusively nationalistic spirit which was common among post-Exilic Jews and, therefore, he was a convenient illustration.

According to the book of Jonah, the Lord directed him to go to Nineveh and to "cry against it." The prophet, however, went to Joppa, where he boarded a ship scheduled to sail to Tarshish, which was either Corsica or part of Spain, as far W from Israel as Nineveh was E. When the Lord sent a great storm which endangered the ship, its captain found Jonah asleep and ordered him to pray to his deity in hope that they might be spared. The casting of lots indicated that it was Jonah whose guilt had caused the calamity. He told them to cast him overboard since he was responsible for the storm. The Lord had "prepared a great fish to swallow up Jonah" and thus to rescue him, and he stayed in it for three days and nights. After Jonah prayed a psalm of thanksgiving, the fish vomited him out on the shore, probably farther along the Syrian coast.

God again directed him to Nineveh. This time he responded and there preached: "Yet forty days, and Nineveh shall be overthrown!" Because the people repented and the king proclaimed a fast, God turned from the threatened calamity; but Jonah became very angry. It is at this point that his motive for fleeing the original order is revealed, i.e., jealousy or antipathy toward a heathen people who were the enemies of his own country. He said that he knew God, being gracious, would turn from His judgment upon Nineveh if they would repent, and asked the Lord to take his life. God caused a plant to grow up and shade the pouting Jonah as he watched the city from a distance. The next day God as quickly destroyed the plant, so that Jonah again became angry and asked once again to die. Using as an illustration Jonah's pity for the plant for which he was not responsible (in contrast to his complete lack of pity on the people to whom he had been appointed), the Lord taught him that it was morally right for Him to have pity on the people of Nineveh.

Jonah's story ends abruptly and there is no further OT record of him. It may be assumed that he learned this lesson since its story was written. Jesus Christ referred both to Jonah's three day stay in the fish and to the repentance of Nineveh (Mt 12:39–41; 16:4; Lk 11:29–32).

W. A. A.

JONAH, BOOK OF. Standing fifth among the writings of the Twelve Minor Prophets, the book of Jonah is perhaps the best known of these. It is at once one of the more appreciated, but also one of the most controversial.

Historicity

The chief critical problem of the book is its historicity. This is almost unanimously acclaimed by conservatives and denied by liberals. Upon the solution to this problem hang most others in the book. The fact is that the style and language used give every evidence of an historical narrative and both Jews (cf. Tobit 14:4 ff.; Jos *Ant.* ix.10.1) and Christians have understood it in this sense until recently. The identification of Jonah with the historical prophet (II Kgs 14:25; *see* Jonah the man) is a further indication, as is the testimony of Jesus Christ (Mt 12:38 –41; 16:4; Lk 11:29 –32). The historicity of Jonah's three days and nights in the fish and the repentance of Nineveh were accepted facts not only by Jesus who referred to them as such, but also by the scribes and Pharisees to whom He commended the event as a sign.

The claim that Jesus was accommodating to the historical ignorance of His audience is unconvincing, since it results from the circular argument of saying that Jesus could not have been certifying to its historicity since it could not have been historical. Moreover, this is to ignore the fact that a "sign" from fiction would hardly have been offered by Jesus as sufficient to answer the scribes and Pharisees who demanded a sign from Him. Liberals challenge the historicity, however, on the basis of miraculous elements, statements about Nineveh, language and form, and political outlook.

While the book has also been cast as mythological, symbolic, or fiction, the allegorical or parabolic character is most often suggested by the non-historicists. According to the allegorical interpretation, every feature has a corresponding element in Israel's experience. Jonah stands for the nation, his flight is Israel's avoidance of its mission to the peoples, the ship in the sea is the ship of diplomatic intrigue in the sea of the world, the sailors are the Gentiles, the storm is the power shift from Assyria to Babylon, the fish is the Exile, and the vomiting out is the return. Many liberals feel that an allegorical interpretation "depends too much upon the imaginative fancies of the interpreter" and have, therefore, claimed it to be a simple parable with more general analogy rather than precise parallelism.

Authorship

Those who recognize the historicity of the book, usually assume that Jonah was the author of his own story. While all the book except the psalm (2:2 –9) is written in the third person, this may only mean, if Jonah himself did not write it, that someone else (even an amanuensis) committed it to writing, but the facts came from Jonah. More likely is the possibility that this was a literary device used by Jonah not uncharacteristic of historical narrative. (Moses always referred to himself in the third person in Exodus to Deuteronomy.) The psalm may well have been a literary unit from the prophet in which the first person was retained because of its uniquely personal nature. Many liberals, however, believe that the psalm came from an entirely different pen than that of the anonymous author of the balance. That supposed author is usually suggested as a 4th cen. B.C. writer who simply used the earlier historical figure as a peg upon which to hang his fabrication.

Date

Acceptance of the historicity of Jonah seemingly requires dating the events in the book during the reign of Jeroboam II (782 –753 B.C.). The book was probably written before 745 B.C. when Assyria rebounded to dominance in the Near East under Tiglath-pileser III. R. Dick Wilson, G. L. Archer (SOTI, pp. 300 f.), and others have shown that certain unusual words and alleged Aramaisms do not prove a post-Exilic date. The non-historicist nevertheless puts most of the writing in the 4th cen. with the psalm as late as the 2nd cen. B.C. Those who deny its historicity never put it before the Exile, while those who accept such have no reason to make it later.

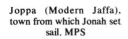

Joppa (Modern Jaffa), town from which Jonah set sail. MPS

Structure and Style

Unlike the rest of the Twelve, this book is entirely an historical narrative and not at all a collection of prophetic oracles. In point of fact, the only prophetic utterance in the book is: "Yet forty days, and Nineveh shall be overthrown!" (3:4*b*). Only the fact that Jonah was recognized as a true prophet can account for its inclusion in the canonical Book of the Twelve. The narrative is vivid but uncomplicated, and the action moves without unnecessary description. The structure is exceedingly simple with four chapters, each containing a distinct unit of thought. The only complication to the four-chapter structure is the fact that 1:17 of the English is 2:1 of the Heb. text.

Occasion and Purpose

During a time of national rebirth, Israel had to know what God's attitude was toward others. Although foreign evangelism was not the principal mission of Israel as the chosen people (see Freeman, *An Introduction to the Old Testament Prophets*, p. 163), they had to learn that the Lord still loves the other nations and wills to bring salvation to them through (or, at least, because of) His chosen people. The book was obviously addressed to the northern kingdom of Israel and takes its place with Hosea and Amos in this regard.

Outline

I. Refusal of God's Command, or Fighting God's Will, 1:1 – 16
  A. Flight by sea, 1:1 – 6
    When the Lord ordered him to cry against wicked Nineveh, Jonah boarded a ship for Tarshish to flee God's presence, only to have God threaten all aboard with a storm.
  B. Disposal into the sea, 1:7 – 16
    Recognizing divine retribution upon Jonah's flight, the sailors sought to escape the storm and then cast Jonah into the sea.
II. Surrendering to God's Will, 1:17 – 2:10
  A. Repentance, 1:17 – 2:1
    When Jonah was swallowed by a divinely prepared fish, he prayed to God.
  B. Prayer, 2:2 – 9
    "The Lord answered my cry from the depths of the sea, and I will sacrifice to Him with thanksgiving because of His deliverance."
  C. Deliverance, 2:10
    The Lord caused the fish to release Jonah.
III. Doing God's Will, 3:1 – 10
  A. Effective prophecy, 3:1 – 5
    Obeying the Lord's second order to go to Nineveh, Jonah prophesied its destruction and the people believed God.
  B. Effective repentance, 3:6 – 10
    The king repented and decreed, "Let every man repent"; thus God relented from the evil planned.
IV. Selfishness about God's Blessings, or Understanding God's Will, 4:1 – 11
  A. Jonah's objection to the Lord's compassion, 4:1 – 5
    Angrily Jonah prayed, "I knew You would relent," but God rebuked him and he waited outside the city.
  B. The Lord's illustration of the need for compassion, 4:6 – 11
    The Lord appointed a plant to shade Jonah and later destroyed it, and then asked Jonah, "How can you pity a plant but deny My pity on the people of Nineveh?"

The Problem of the Miraculous

This is often considered to be the biggest problem. The frequent mistake of theologically conservative scholars is to be too preoccupied with proving the fish-swallowing by historical parallels. While survival of such an experience is well documented relative to sperm whales, it is unnecessary since 1:17 makes clear that "the Lord had *prepared* a great fish."

There are also the miracles of Nineveh's repentance and of the plant. All three of these are involved in a complex of miracles. The reliability of any miracle depends upon the ability of God to perform it and not of man to explain it. Jonah prophesied close to the time of Elijah and Elisha in the northern kingdom, whose contacts with Phoenicia (I Kgs 17:9 –24) and Syria (II Kgs 5) were likewise accompanied by miracles.

The Problem of the Psalm

The psalm (2:2 – 9) stands out from the prose of the book and presents not only a literary problem but also a logical problem. While many commentators cite a variety of individual psalms which may have been quoted, the words fit none well enough to conclude that these are specific quotations. More likely, many psalms were in mind and freely paraphrased to fit the particular situation and in a manner which expressed Jonah's appropriate emotions. The non-historicists, again, assigned this portion to a 2nd cen. B.C. writer who was even later than the anonymous writer of the narrative.

Even when understood as the composition of Jonah and forming a unity with the balance of the book, problems exist. Is Jonah thanking God for having delivered him from the sea by means of a fish? Could a man pray so eloquently in the midst of such a traumatic experience? Perhaps Jonah prayed from the fish thanking God for saving him from the sea and, on the basis of that initial salvation, he anticipated its completion. Moreover, the psalm as found in the text may represent his general thoughts at the moment as polished in poetic style upon reflection later.

The Problems of Nineveh

If this story be the creation of a 4th cen.

writer, he was foolishly careless when constructing his references to Nineveh because he has left himself open to many points of criticism. It is charged that a city never has a "king" (3:6); that Nineveh was never "three days' journey" in breadth (3:3); that Jonah could not have spoken their language in preaching; that it is not reasonable for such a city to have repented so easily and that there is no secular record of such. Moreover, the greatness of the city is spoken of in the past tense (3:3).

The term "the king of Nineveh" (3:6) is a metonymy with adequate precedent in the OT; e.g., there were kings of such cities as Samaria (I Kgs 21:1), Damascus (II Chr 24:23), Salem (Gen 14:18), and Zion (Jer 8:19). Furthermore, since Nineveh was not yet the capital of Assyria, the author may have used the word *melek* ("king") as a transliteration of the Akkad. *malku* meaning "governor."

The size of the city could refer to its circumference as well as diameter; the city as a metropolitan area could include its immediately neighboring cities (e.g., Calah, Rehoboth-Ir, Resen of Gen 10:11 ff.); or the "journey" could well have been a walk, preaching his message throughout the city's precincts. Aramaic was already becoming a widespread trade language (cf. II Kgs 18:26) which Jonah is likely to have known and which would have been known by enough in Nineveh to pass his message on. The question should center around what God can do rather than what the prophet could not do.

The severe plagues of 765 and 759 and the total eclipse of 763 B.C. could have been used by God to alert the people to their need; and certainly when combined with the work of the Spirit of God before and through His prophet there is sufficient cause for the great repentance recorded. The fact that this national repentance is not found in extant Assyrian annals is an argument from silence. Many other events and people known only through the Bible have only recently been confirmed by modern archaeological discoveries. That the repentance obviously did not last is not surprising and gives an added reason why the Assyrians would not have mentioned it in their official records. The past tense relative to Nineveh need mean nothing more than the fact that the events which took place there were past when the record was written.

Significance

Few OT books have more obvious application to the contemporary church. It can well be used to help the Christian overcome the barrier of his foreignness in evangelistic mission as he is assured of God's love for the world and His will to use the saved to reach all lost men. But the book of Jonah does not teach simple willingness to go to a foreign country as a missionary for the reward of being obedient. In point of fact, this is one of the deficiencies the book seeks to correct. It is not enough to be obedient to the command; one must be sympathetic with it. Evangelism is for the sake of the lost and not the evangelist. One must obey God—but for the right reason. The motive for missions is acknowledgment of God's will—but also obedience to it and agreement with it.

Bibliography. G. C. Aalders, *The Problem of the Book of Jonah,* London: Tyndale Press, 1948. J. A. Bewer, ICC. Hobart E. Freeman, *An Introduction to the Old Testament Prophets,* Chicago: Moody Press, 1968, pp. 160–171. Frank E. Gaebelein, *Four Minor Prophets,* Chicago: Moody Press, 1970. Don W. Hillis, *The Book of Jonah,* Grand Rapids: Baker, 1967. James H. Kennedy, *Studies in the Book of Jonah,* Nashville: Broadman Press, 1956. G. Herbert Livingston, "Jonah," WBC, pp. 843–850. E. B. Pusey, *The Minor Prophets,* Grand Rapids: Baker, 1960 (reprint). George L. Robinson, *The Twelve Minor Prophets,* Grand Rapids: Baker, 1962 (reprint).

W. A. A.

JONAN (jō'năn). An ancestor of Christ (Lk 3:30) who lived about 200 years after David. Jonam is the correct spelling (ASV and RSV), based on the Gr. *Iōnam.*

JONAS (jō'nás)
1. KJV form of Jonah (Gr. *Iōna*), the OT prophet (Mt 12:39–41; 16:4; Lk 11:29–32). *See* Jonah.
2. KJV form of John (Jn 21:15–17, RSV), used in order to harmonize with Bar-jona in Mt. 16:17.

JONATHAN (jŏn'á-thán). This name occurs frequently in biblical literature.
1. The son of Gershom, son of Manasseh (Jud 18:30, KJV). The Masoretic scribes inserted an *n* (*nun*) above the line in the name of Moses, so that in the Heb. spelling it would read Manasseh (*m-n-sh-h*) instead of Moses (*m-sh-h*). Thus they thought to spare Moses the disgrace of having a grandson become an idolatrous priest. Jonathan was a Levite from Bethlehem, said to be of the tribe of Judah, probably on his mother's side (Jud 17:7). He acted as house priest in the sanctuary founded by the Ephraimite Micah and later founded the priesthood which served the Danites (Jud 17–18).
2. The eldest son of King Saul of Israel.
His military prowess. After his decisive victory over the Ammonites (I Sam 11), King Saul divided his army into two divisions: about 2,000 men were stationed in Michmash under him and about 1,000 men were garrisoned under his son Jonathan about five miles S at Gibeah. Midway between the two military camps was a Philistine outpost at Geba. Jonathan killed the garrison (or, governor, NEB) there, which the Philistines interpreted as a revolt of the Israelite forces (I Sam 13:3). They decided to attack immediately, and they compelled Saul to abandon Michmash. The king withdrew to Gilgal to recoup his forces, and then returned

The mound of Beth-Shan, where the bodies of Jonathan and the rest of Saul's family were displayed for public ridicule. Remains of a great Roman theater appear at right. HFV

to the hill country to make his base at Geba (I Sam 13:16, NASB). Jonathan made a surprise attack on the Philistines who were guarding the gorge S of Michmash and slew all of them single-handedly (I Sam 14:6 – 14). God matched Jonathan's feat with an earthquake, and the Philistines fled in panic. The Israelites, fighting only with crude agricultural implements (I Sam 13:20), pursued them to complete the rout.

This victory was marred by King Saul who, seized with religious superstition, ordered all his warriors to fast until sundown (I Sam 14:24). When Jonathan unwittingly broke the command, the king ordered the prince executed. But the people remembering Jonathan's military skill and courage intervened and saved his life (I Sam 14:25 – 45).

His friendship with David. Jonathan and David's friendship is a most inspiring epic. After David slew the Philistine giant Goliath and won for himself a permanent place in the royal court, Jonathan loved the shepherd lad with all his soul. He recognized that David was a man chosen for the throne of Israel. He acquiesced to this by making a covenant and presenting to David his own princely robe and armor (I Sam 18:1 – 4).

The meteoric rise of David's military fame and his place in the people's affections were more, however, than the melancholic King Saul could take. He not only planned to slay David but attempted to press Jonathan and his courtiers to wield the javelin against this potential supplanter. Soon Saul drove David from the court. Jonathan was disgusted with his father's behavior and intervened by securing for David a temporary visa for reinstatement in the king's court (I Sam 19:1 – 7). This truce was abruptly ended when Saul suffered a fit of melancholia and threw his javelin at David; so David fled to Naioth in Ramah. During the new moon festival Jonathan discovered that his father's anger toward David was permanent and he relayed the sad news to his beloved friend by way of an

arrow and lad at the appointed rendezvous (I Sam 20).

The final and romantic conference between these friends took place in the wilderness of Ziph, S of Hebron. There they made a pact that when David became the next king, Jonathan would be his prime minister, and they renewed their covenant to protect each other's posterity forever (I Sam 23:16 – 18; cf. I Sam 20:12 – 17, 42; II Sam 9:1).

His final history. During the days when Saul pursued David, Jonathan remained in the background — evidently he refused to be a party to this futile chase. The activity of the Philistines compelled Saul to terminate his hunt for David and to turn his energies to do battle with Israel's perpetual enemy. This battle was short and decisive — Saul lost! Jonathan, Saul, and his other sons, Abinadad and Malchishua, were killed in battle. Their corpses were despoiled the day following the battle and exposed by the Philistines on a wall overlooking the public square of Beth-shan (II Sam 21:12). The Jabesh-gileadites, out of gratitude to King Saul's rescuing their town at the beginning of his reign, crossed the Jordan and stormed Beth-shan, retrieved the bodies and buried them in Jabesh (I Sam 31; I Chr 10:1 – 12; cf. II Sam 2:5 – 7).

When the sad tidings of the disaster on Mount Gilboa reached David, he uttered a moving elegy lamenting the death of Saul and the loss of his true friend Jonathan (II Sam 1). David later reinterred the remains of Saul and his sons in the tomb of Saul's father Kish in Zelah of the territory of Benjamin (II Sam 21:12 – 14).

His character. Jonathan undoubtedly was one of the greatest souls of all time. He had a granite-like character. He was athletic and courageous (I Sam 14:13; II Sam 1:22 – 23). Swift as an eagle and strong as a lion, this Israelite prince inspired and led the renowned Benjamite archers in warfare. When secrecy was mandatory, he could maintain a tight lip! He could always analyze a situation, plan a strategy, and in turn act at the auspicious moment. Also he was a great lover. His unqualified love for David in the midst of adverse pressures in his father's court vindicated David's elegy: "Thy love to me was wonderful, passing the love of women" (II Sam 1:26).

His family tree. Jonathan had one son, whose name was Meribaal (Mephibosheth). He was only five years of age at the slaughter on Gilboa (II Sam 4:4). David's honoring the pledge which he forged with Jonathan assured this survivor of gaining Saul's inheritance, as well as membership in the royal court and the sparing of his head (II Sam 9; 21:7). Jonathan's posterity which passed through this lame prince lived through several generations (I Chr 8:33 – 38; 9:40 – 44; II Sam 9:12).

Jonathan's mother was Ahinoam (daughter of Ahimaaz), characterized by Saul during one of his temper tantrums as "a perverse, rebellious woman" (I Sam 20:30, RSV). Besides Abinadad and Malchishua he had another brother, Ish-baal (Ishbosheth or Ishui, a probable corruption of Ishyahu, I Sam 14:49), and two sisters, Merab and Michal. The former was promised to David but given to Adriel the Meholathite (I Sam 18:17–20); Michal instead of her sister was married to David for a dowry of a hundred Philistine foreskins (I Sam 18:20 ff.).

His family loyalty. The solidarity of the Hebraic family remained intact in Saul's family. Jonathan's independence and capacity to do his own thinking naturally collided with the impetuosity and unreasonableness of his father Saul. But in the midst of these adverse tensions, the prince struggled to conform as nearly as possible to the strong will of the king. Convinced of the high promise of David and conscious of Saul's reaction, Jonathan sought to mediate between the irresistible force and the immovable object and partially succeeded (I Sam 19:6). Filial duty was supremely tested but Jonathan's conduct toward both men is unquestionable. When Saul, under gross provocation impugned the honor of his mother and sought to kill even Jonathan, the prince's loyalty temporarily snapped. However, this estrangement was short-lived. Saul and Jonathan were one in life and one in death (II Sam 1:23)–father and son went down together!

3. A son of Abiathar, a high priest in David's cabinet who was loyal to David during Absalom's rebellion (II Sam 15:27, 36; 17:15–22). Abiathar and Zadok were dispatched to Jerusalem to assist Hushai in counteracting the betrayal of Ahithophel. As they secured valuable information from Hushai, they relayed the secrets to the couriers Jonathan and Ahimaaz, sons of Abiathar and Zadok, respectively, who were stationed at En-rogel. The young men in turn were to relay the information to King David (II Sam 15:24 ff.). When this espionage was uncovered, the couriers fled with a message of warning for David in his camp by the W bank of the Jordan (II Sam 17:15–21).

During David's latter days when his heirs were jockeying for the throne, Jonathan along with his father Abiathar joined in Adonijah's plot to snatch the Israelite throne. It was Jonathan's sad lot to bring the frustrating news to the abortive kingly sacrificial feast at En-rogel, that Solomon had been anointed in Gihon as king of Israel with the blessings and by the strong hand of David (I Kgs 1:42–48). Apparently this involvement marked Jonathan as a dispensable man, and he probably was exiled along with his father when Abiathar was stripped of the high priesthood and banished to Anathoth by Solomon (I Kgs 2:26–27).

4. A son of Shimeah, David's brother, who slew a Philistine giant who jeered the Israelites at Gath (II Sam 21:21; I Chr 20:7).

5. A son of Shage the Hararite, who was one of David's heroes (the mighty men of David, known as the "thirty," II Sam 23:32; I Chr 11:34).

6. A son of Jada and the father of Peleth and Zaza who were members of the family of Jerahmeel of the tribe of Judah (I Chr 2:32–33).

7. An uncle of David who was a wise, trusted counselor as well as a royal scribe (I Chr 27:32).

8. A son of Uzziah who had supervision of King David's storehouses in the cities, hamlets, and towns outside Jerusalem (I Chr 27:25; Jehonathan, KJV).

9. A scribe in whose house Jeremiah was imprisoned during the siege of Jerusalem by the Babylonians (588–586 B.C.), when the prophet's enemies charged Jeremiah with defecting to the enemy (Jer 37:15, 20; 38:26).

10. A son of Kareah, a Judean field captain, who settled with Gedaliah at Mizpah, after the fall of Jerusalem in 586 B.C. (Jer 40:8; KJV, NASB, NEB following Masoretic Text, list both Johanan and Jonathan; but RSV and others have only Johanan. Possibly the name Jonathan is a dittography since it is omitted by LXX and the parallel passage in II Kgs 25:23).

11. The father of Ebed who, along with 50 members of his family, returned with Ezra in 457 B.C. (Ezr 8:6).

12. A priest who descended from Melicu (KJV; others, Malluchi) during Joiakim's high priesthood (Neh 12:14).

13. A son of Joiada and one of the high priests during the post-Exilic period. His son was Jaddua, the last-named priest in the OT (Neh 12:11). The corrupted text probably should read Johanan (Ezr 10:6; Neh 12:22–23; I Esd 9:1).

14. A son of Shemaiah and father of Zechariah who was a priestly trumpeter in the thanksgiving convocation during the rededication of the walls of Jerusalem under the governorship of Nehemiah (Neh 12:35).

15. A son of Asahel, during the period of Ezra, who opposed the appointment of the marital commission in Jerusalem to investigate the Jews who had married foreign wives (Ezr 10:15).

D. W. D.

JONATH-ELEM-RECHOKIM (jō'năth-ē'lĕm-rē-kō'kĭm). This transliterated Heb. phrase in the KJV and ASV heading of Ps 56, perhaps meaning "the dove of the far-off terebinths" (cf. Ps 55:6–7), may be understood in one or all of the following ways: (1) an enigmatical reference to David among the Philistines in Gath (I Sam 21:10–15); (2) a mystical reference to Israel or God's people generally as exiles from their real home (cf. Phil 3:20; Heb 11:8–10, 13–16); (3) a technical phrase indicating the rhythm or melody to which this psalm is set (see ASV).

JOPPA (jŏp'á). The modern Jaffa, it was the only seaport on the coast of Palestine between Haifa and Egypt, and is now the southern section of Tel Aviv. It is mentioned in the Tell el-Amarna letters. It was assigned to the tribe of Dan in the division of the land after the conquest of Joshua (Josh 19:46), though the Israelites may not have actually possessed it. Timber for the building of Solomon's temple was floated from Tyre to Joppa (II Chr 2:16), and also for the building of the second temple in the restoration (Ezr 3:7). In the time of the divided kingdom it was controlled by the Phoenicians. Jonah fled from Israel via Joppa (Jon 1:3).

In NT times Peter there restored Dorcas to life (Acts 9:36–43), and afterward stayed at the home of Simon the tanner, where he received the vision that summoned him to preach at the house of the Gentile Cornelius (Acts 10:1–23).

The city was built on the rocky heights above the harbor, which was formed by a natural breakwater of rocks. In the 1st cen. B.C. it was held successively by the Syrians, the Maccabees, the Romans, and by freebooters who made it a center of piracy. The harbor is too dangerous for modern shipping, and is not used extensively at present.

M. C. T.

JORAH (jôr′á). The head of a family of returnees from Babylon with Zerubbabel (Ezr 2:18). Called Hariph in Neh 7:24.

JORAI (jôr′ī). One of seven Gadite chiefs who were descendants of Abihail (I Chr 5:13–14).

JORAM (jôr′ăm). Abbrev. form of Jehoram (q.v.).

1. Son of Toi, king of Hamath (II Sam 8:9–10). Also called Hadoram (I Chr 18:10).

2. King of Judah, son and successor of Jehoshaphat (II Kgs 8:21–24; I Chr 3:11; Mt 1:8). Also called Jehoram (see Jehoram 2).

3. King of Israel, son of Ahab and successor of his brother Ahaziah (II Kgs 8:16; cf. 1:2, 17). Also called Jehoram (see Jehoram 1).

4. A Levite, descendant of Eliezer, son of Moses (I Chr 26:25; cf. 23:15, 17).

JORDAN (jôr′dăn). In Heb. the name of the most famous river in the Bible is *yardēn.* Most scholars consider the word Semitic and derive it from the root *yārad,* "to descend." The name thus means "the descender," an apt description of the river. Others theorize that the word may have an Indo-Aryan origin, in which case it would mean "perennial river." The oldest form of the name is found in Nineteenth Dynasty Egyptian records as *ya-ar-du-na* (Simon Cohen, "Jordan," IDB, II, 973).

A series of gigantic faults in the crust of the earth brought about the collapse of land which now forms the Jordan Valley. From that deep trough called the Dead Sea (the Salt Sea in the OT) the earth rises both to the N and S. It ascends from 2,598 feet below sea level at the bottom of the Dead Sea to a height of plus 800 feet at one hump in the Arabah (area S of the Dead Sea) and to 9,166 foot high Mount Hermon in the N. The geological fault extends through the Red Sea deep into E Africa.

The distance by air from the sources of the Jordan to the Dead Sea is *c.* 80 miles, but the river itself is over 200 miles long on account of its circuitous course between the Galilee and Dead Seas. The valley may be said to begin in the N with the Huleh Basin, an area of about three by nine miles culminating, until recently drained, in a marsh and a shallow lake created by a dam of natural rock.

The sudden descent from about 1,600 feet in altitude at the Merj 'Ayun to 230 feet above sea level in the Huleh Basin allows two small source streams, Nahr Bareighit and Nahr Hasbani, to pour their water into the basin. The two major Jordan sources flow out of the rock as sizable streams on the slopes of Mount Hermon. The Nahr el-Leddan arises from strong springs out of the ground at Tel el-Qadi, the site of ancient Dan, the northernmost city of the land (formerly Laish, Jud 18:7, 27). The Nahr Banias originates in a large cave farther up the slope at a village called Banias (Paneas), which derives its name from the Roman god Pan. In NT times this town was called Caesarea Philippi in honor of Caesar and because it was in the tetrarchy of Philip. In this region Jesus asked His disciples, "Whom say ye that I am?" (Mk 8:27–29), and was transfigured before three of them on some part of Mount Hermon nearby (Mk 9:2). Three of these headwater streams meet about two miles S of Dan and then divide again to enter the Huleh Basin as two streams, the Tur'ah and the Jordan.

On a plateau overlooking the Huleh Basin stand the ruins of the OT city of Hazor (recently excavated) and the NT city of Chorazin (Khirbet Kerazeh). The Jordan alone flows out of Huleh for two miles to "the Bridge of the Daughters of Jacob" where travelers on the road between Galilee and Damascus forded it. After this the Jordan enters a gorge, flowing with vigor until it finally leaves these walls and gently enters the Sea of Galilee at 696 feet below sea level. The sea is really a lake surrounded almost completely by hills, but here

The Nahr Hasbani, one of the sources of the Jordan.
HFV

and there these hills withdraw creating some plains like the famous plain of Gennesaret on the NW shore near Capernaum. In addition to the still inhabited Tiberias, several biblical lake cities are identifiable, namely Capernaum at Tel Hum on the NW and Magdala at Majdal on the W shore at the foot of "the Valley of the Robbers." In NT times the northern part of the Jordan region was controlled by the league of ten independent cities called Decapolis. Of the cities, those in or near the Jordan Valley were Scythopolis (Beisan or Bethshan), Gadara (Umm Keis) and Pella (Fahil) across the river from Scythopolis.

The first dozen miles from the Sea of Galilee the Jordan Valley never reaches a breadth of more than four miles. Bethany beyond the Jordan where John was baptizing (Jn 1:28, NASB), or Bethabara (KJV; q.v.) is thought to have been in the vicinity, c. 12 miles S of the lake. If Elisha (q.v.) were living at Shunem or Mount Carmel or Dothan at the time of Naaman's visit, the Syrian general was probably sent to this stretch of the Jordan to dip seven times in its muddy waters (II Kgs 5:10, 14). At the plain of Bethshan the valley widens to six or seven miles, rising on the W side by terraces toward the level of the plain of Esdraelon.

The Jordan itself is but a groove cut into the bottom of this valley which is said to be an old seabed. Its current does not look swift but can be treacherous, the water dropping in the N about 40 feet per mile, although the average drop per mile is about nine feet. The formidable barrier created by the river is the result of other factors than the width or swiftness of the stream. Indeed, in the N the river is not so great a barrier because the distinct features of the valley are less pronounced there. The valley itself is the real barrier consisting of three interesting features: the Ghor or lowland, Qattara or sterile chalk hills, and the Zor or thicket.

The Ghor is the valley floor itself bounded by mountains or high plateaus on either side. Here are layers of alluvial deposits which need only irrigation to make rich farmland. The results of such irrigation may be seen today along the E side of the Ghor where water is available. Geological faults meet the Ghor at an angle and help form the river valleys which join the Jordan. On the E side the river has two major tributaries, the Yarmuk and the Jabbok. The Yarmuk just S of the Sea of Galilee provides almost as much water as the Jordan itself. On the N side of the Yarmuk gorge some seven or more miles from the confluence stands the ancient el-Hammeh, a famous hot springs. A high culture flourished here from as early as the 4th mil. B.C., and its warm curative waters have been popular throughout history. Between the Yarmuk and the Jabbok nine other streams flow into the Jordan from the E. This well-watered area explains why many settlements grew up on the E side of the Ghor, towns such as Pella, Jabesh-gilead, Zaphon, Zaretan and Adam.

About 13 miles from the Sea of Galilee the

The Springs of Banias which give rise to another source of the Jordan. HFV

river Jalud joins from the W flowing through the plain of Bethshan. Here the Ghor widens to about seven miles, only to be constricted again farther S by the hills of Samaria. Farther S the Wadi Fari'a joins from the W and the Jabbok on the E near Succoth. Here the patriarchs had entered Canaan, coming from Haran and Padan-aram far to the NE (Gen 12:5-6; 32:22; 33:17-18). Near here the Midianites must have fled across the Jordan with Gideon in pursuit (Jud 7:24; 8:4-5). The floor widens again to eight miles, from whence it continues to widen to a maximum of 14 miles at Jericho. 'Ain Fari'a at the head of its wadi, near OT Tirzah, supplies a rich quantity of water, but little of it ever reaches the Jordan. The same is true of Wadi Qelt which helps create the rich green oasis at Jericho. Such irrigation of the land has to come from the sweet water streams before they reach the Jordan because the Jordan also receives mineral salts which make its water increasingly unfit for irrigation.

Near Gilgal, NE of Jericho, was a well-known ford that David used in his flight from Absalom (II Sam 17:22-24) and in his victorious return (19:15-40). Perhaps this was the very spot where Elijah and Elisha crossed the Jordan prior to the former's translation (II Kgs 2:7-8, 13-14). Also in this region of the lower Jordan the two Israelite spies had swum the flooded river (Josh 2:1, 23), and soon afterward the entire nation crossed miraculously over the dry riverbed (Josh 3-4).

The Bible uses various terms to describe the Ghor. Often it is simply called the *'emeq*, the vale or lowland as in Josh 13:19, 27. But in Deut 34:3 the Ghor is described as "the *kikkār* even the *biq'â* of Jericho." *Kikkār* means a circuit and the *biq'â* means a broad valley. Here at Jericho the Ghor is some 14 miles across. The term *'ărābâ* meaning "a plain" is also used of the Jordan Valley. The E side of the Ghor opposite Jericho was called "the plains of Moab" (Num 22:1), an area well-irrigated and inhabited from Chalcolithic times as at Teleilat Ghassul. The Ghor was sometimes so heavily inhabited that Gen 13:10 tells us Lot beheld the *"kikkār* of the Jordan and lo, all of it was well watered (irrigated)... like the garden of the Lord." When one visits this region especially in summer he may be impressed with its aridity. However, it was not only one of the first settled sections of the country but at one time was one of the richest parts of all ancient Palestine. Nelson Glueck discovered at least 70 sites where people had lived and worked in the Jordan Valley S of Galilee in ancient times.

About 100 – 150 feet below the main valley floor is the depression called in Arabic the Zor through which the Jordan itself flows. The Zor can get nearly a mile wide when the river twists upon itself, though the river is only from 90 to 100 feet wide and normally ranges from 3 to 12 feet in depth. The Zor always contains the river when it floods in the spring (Josh 3:15; I Chr 12:15), but unlike the Nile, the flood is violent, carrying soil away and leaving debris, so that the rank growth of tamarisks, oleanders, willows, bushes and vines which is left is well called. Zor or thicket. The OT describes the Zor as *ge'on hay-yarden*, "the jungle of the Jordan" ("Behold like a lion ... out of the jungle of the Jordan," Jer 49:19; cf. 12:5; 50:44; Zech 11:3). Indeed, the Zor was infested with lions in ancient times and elephants in pre-historic times and was until very recently the haunt of the wild boar. Because of the twistings within the fickle snakelike route of the Jordan, the Zor jungle becomes a formidable barrier and to this barrier is added the sterile marl hills of the "qattara" separating the Ghor and the Zor.

When the OT speaks of Jordan as a barrier it certainly means the whole valley complex, not just the little river itself. Josh 22:25 expresses the fear that Reuben, Gad and half the tribe of Manasseh might become alienated by the natural border formed by the valley: "Your children might speak ... saying, 'What have ye to do with the Lord God of Israel? For the Lord hath made Jordan a border between us- and you ... ye have no part in the Lord.' " It is curiously true that not only in OT times but even today a distinct alienation of spirit exists between those who live on either side of the Jordan Valley.

The Jordan flows into the Dead Sea at about 1,290 feet below sea level. The Dead Sea is about 45 miles long and 10 miles wide. A tongue of land juts out into the E side of the Dead Sea. At one time this formed its S boundary, but the sea having no outlet has risen continuously covering erstwhile cities on its S shore, probably including Sodom (*q.v.*) and Gomorrah. The Dead Sea itself is about one-fourth to one-third mineral salts, coming largely from the many hot and cold springs which line the valley. As may be expected, the entire region is an area of above normal earthquake activity averaging about four per century. The E slopes of the sea like the wilderness of Judea are almost devoid of rain and so supply little water except from a few underground springs (e.g., 'Ain Feshkha near Qumran and Engedi, due E of Hebron).

See Arabah; Dead Sea; Galilee, Sea of; Palestine. II.B.3.*d*; River.

Bibliography. Denis Baly, *The Geography of the Bible*, New York: Harper, 1957, pp. 14 – 26, 193 – 216. Nelson Glueck, *The River Jordan*, 2nd ed., New York: McGraw-Hill, 1968. Karl H. Rengstorf, *'Potamos ... Iordanēs*," TDNT, VI, 608 – 623.

E. B. S.

JORIM (jôr'ĭm). An ancestor of Christ (Lk 3:29) and descendant of David.

JORKOAM (jôr'kō-ăm). The son of Raham, and a descendant of Caleb (I Chr 2:44; Jorkeam in ASV and RSV). Two suppositions are held regarding this name: (1) that it designates a place in the tribe of Judah; (2) that it is to be identified with Jokdeam (*q.v.*) in Josh 15:56:

JOSABAD. *See* Jozabad.

JOSAPHAT. *See* Jehoshaphat.

JOSE (jō'sě). A man in Christ's ancestry not mentioned in the OT (Lk 3:29). KJV incorrectly takes the *Iōsēs* of TR as a genitive of the nominative *Iōsē*. The correct form (genitive of *Iēsous*) found in earlier Gr. MSS reads Jesus as in ASV, i.e., Joshua as-in RSV and NASB.

JOSEDECH (jō'zě-děk). Father of Joshua, the high priest during the post-Captivity era (Hag 1:1, 12, 14; 2:2, 4; Zech 6:11). In all these verses ASV and RSV have Jehozadak. In Ezr 3:2, 8; 5:2; 10:18 and Neh 12:26 the same Heb. name is spelled Jozadak in KJV, ASV and RSV. This man, having been carried captive to Babylon by Nebuchadnezzar (I Chr 6:14 – 15), was presumably high priest during most of the Babylonian Captivity. His father, Seraiah, the last high priest who officiated in the

The Jordan River as it flows out of the Sea of Galilee at its southern end. HFV

temple before its destruction in 586 B.C., was slain by the Babylonians (II Kgs 25:18–21).

JOSEPH (jō'zĕf)

1. The eleventh son of Jacob and the first son of his favorite wife Rachel, after her sister Leah had borne Jacob six sons and a daughter. Long barren and desirous of children, Rachel named her first son Joseph (Heb. *yôsēp, yᵉhô-sēp*), "May He (i.e., the Lord) add," as she explains, "May the Lord add to me another son" (Gen 30:24, RSV).

Joseph sold by his brethren, painted by **Maggiotto**. MM

Joseph was Rachel's only child at the time of the return to Palestine from the Haran area, and consequently was his father's favorite son. When Jacob went to meet Esau he put Rachel and Joseph in the safest position in the caravan. This favoritism receives comment in Gen 37:3, which states that Joseph was favored because he was the son of Jacob's old age. Joseph was a shepherd like his brothers, and incurred their hostility by bringing his father a report of their bad conduct. Jacob's partiality was demonstrated by his giving to Joseph a long robe with sleeves (lit., a robe of soles and palms). Possibly it was also a robe of patterned cloth and many colors (cf. the garments of the Asiatics, shown in the Middle Kingdom tomb of Khnumhotep II at Beni Hasan). This gift indicated that Jacob intended to make Joseph his principal heir, and further incited Joseph's brothers against him (37:4).

Fuel was added to the flames of hatred by Joseph's sharing with his brothers two dreams by which the Lord had shown him that he would rule over them. The jealousy of the brothers led them to take action against him. When Joseph was sent to check on the herding activities of the brothers, he found them at Dothan with the flocks. They planned to kill him (37:18–19), but were deterred by the eldest of them, Reuben, who wished to save him from harm (vv. 22–24). When an Ishmaelite-Midianite caravan appeared (see Kitchen, *Ancient Orient and the Old Testament*, pp. 119 f.), on its way from Gilead to Egypt, the broth-

ers conceived the notion of getting rid of Joseph at a profit. They sold him to the traders and callously deceived Jacob into believing Joseph had been killed by wild animals; they brought to Jacob the robe, which they had dipped in the blood of a goat.

In Egypt the merchants sold Joseph to Potiphar, an officer of the king, the captain of the guard. The Lord blessed Joseph with success in his work, so that he was promoted to the office of overseer of the house, a typical Egyptian title and function. The wife of Potiphar was attracted to the young official and continually sought to seduce him (39:10). Egyptian domestic architecture, as illustrated by the excavations at Amarna, indicates that the duties of Joseph demanded his presence in parts of the estate in which he would of necessity encounter the woman. Though far from home and family, the young Hebrew was true to his ideals and rejected her propositions on the basis that his compliance would be both wickedness and a sin against God (39:9).

This interesting account (39:6–20) gives many details of Egyptian life. Novelists and popular writers have often presented an unsavory view of Egyptian morals, which seem to have been quite commendable, though proper conduct was often based on primarily practical reasons. Egyptian civilization did have its seamy side, however, and the Papyrus D'Orbiney relates a story of seduction which is common to many times and places. The story is titled "The Tale of Two Brothers" and confirms the virtuous attitude of the brothers as opposed to the immoral motives of the wife of the elder brother. Though the parallels to the biblical account are interesting, the differences are even greater (see ANET, pp. 23–25). *See* Egypt.

Potiphar accepted his wife's dramatic testimony, and Joseph was consigned to a prison for political offenders. In prison Joseph again was signally blessed by the Lord and soon rose to a position of responsibility even here. In this particular place of imprisonment he was brought into contact with officials from the royal court. He interpreted dreams which the royal butler and baker had on the same night.

The dreams contain many items of Egyptian background, for viticulture was important in ancient Egypt and a great variety of bake goods was known. Dreams were often regarded as omens in the Near East. A hieratic papyrus relating to the interpretation of dreams dates from the 19th Dynasty and may go back to the Middle Kingdom. It has the punning allusions which are typical of Egyptian literature and which occur in Gen 40 as marks of local color. Since Joseph's ability to interpret dreams was a gift from God, there is no other relationship between this papyrus and Joseph (see ANET, p. 495).

While the butler was pardoned and the baker executed, Joseph remained in prison for at least two more years (41:1). When Pharaoh's strange

Traditional tomb of Joseph at Shechem. HFV

dreams could not be interpreted by the Egyptian experts, the butler remembered Joseph, who then was summoned to the royal court. Before appearing in the presence of the king, Joseph shaved (41:14), in good Egyptian fashion (see ANET, p. 22). In Egyptian reliefs and paintings smooth-shaven Egyptians contrast markedly with bearded Asiatics; many razors have been found in excavations in Egypt. Pharaoh's dreams included the ever-present Nile, the cattle that commonly grazed along the river, and the grain which made Egypt the breadbasket of the Mediterranean world. The interpretation given by Joseph indicated that seven years of plenty would be followed by seven years of scarcity. The Nile was very regular in its annual flooding (*see* Nile). There were exceptions to this rule, however, and ancient texts preserve statements of officials who boast of providing for the needy in such lean years (see ANET, pp. 31 – 32).

Joseph then suggested that provision be made for the bad years by collecting one-fifth of the produce during the years of abundance. This proposal met with the approval of the king and his advisers, with the result that Joseph was given the office second only to that of the king. This office is well-known from the documents of Egypt and usually is designated by the Near Eastern term "vizier." The vizier was the chief administrative officer and his duties were quite varied; he was in charge of the treasury, justice, and the execution of all royal decrees.

Joseph was given an Egyptian name (*see* Zaphnath-paaneah) and was married to Asenath, the daughter of Potiphera, priest of On, the solar religious center better known as Heliopolis (*see* On). During the prosperous years Asenath bore two sons, Manasseh and Ephraim, who later took their place as Joseph's representatives among the sons of Jacob (Israel).

Joseph made adequate preparation for the years of famine, so that not only all Egypt but

also people from neighboring lands came to buy grain from Joseph. Here the progress of the earlier prophecies of Joseph's dreams becomes apparent (42:9), for among those who came to Egypt to purchase grain were Joseph's brothers (42:5). Joseph recognized them but they did not know him (42:7 – 8); consequently he was able to subject them to a series of tests. He interrogated them, accused them of being spies, and finally put them in prison for three days. As proof of their honesty he demanded that they leave one of their number as a hostage and return to Canaan to get their youngest brother, Benjamin, who they said was yet in Canaan. Verses 21 – 23 graphically describe the workings of conscience in the reasonings of the brothers. Simeon remained in Egypt while the others returned to Palestine.

To add to the perplexity of the brothers, Joseph had their grain purchase money returned to them in their grain bags. They discovered this en route to Canaan and brought a report of their adventures to the aged Jacob, who finally was forced by circumstances to accede to the necessity for the brothers to take Benjamin with them when they again went to Egypt for grain. Every effort was made to secure the favor of the vizier, and Israel sent his sons to Egypt with his blessing and with confidence in God (43:14).

Several additional tests lay before the brothers (43:18). They were invited to eat wth Joseph, though he was served by himself, according to Egyptian custom (43:32). The final trial for the brothers lay in a framed accusation of theft, which brought them back to Egypt after they had begun their return to Palestine (chap. 44). Since the supposedly stolen silver cup was found in the grain sack of Benjamin, the most severe anxiety fell upon them.

At last Joseph arranged to disclose his identity to them. This was done with considerable emotion on his part; he wept loudly, so that all the Egyptians heard it (45:2; cf. 42:24; 43:30 – 31). The sensitive and understanding character of Joseph is clear from his immediate assurance to his brothers, showing that he had forgiven them and was concerned for their welfare. Beyond even this, Joseph saw the hand of God in his career, for God had designed to preserve Israel through him (45:7 – 8).

Joseph then made arrangements for informing his father of the good turn of events and for moving the entire family to Egypt. The titles which Joseph ascribes to himself, "a father to Pharaoh, and lord of all his house, and a ruler over all the land of Egypt" (45:8), are quite typical for an Egyptian official of his rank. Pharaoh was pleased at the report of the arrival of Joseph's brothers and personally suggested provision for bringing Joseph's family to the best part of Egypt (45:16 – 20). Transportation was provided in the form of the usual patient donkeys, which carried gifts and supplies, and by wagons, which were for the transport of the people. Wagons are strange to the Egyptian

954

tomb scenes but perhaps they were a concession to the Asiatic origin of Joseph's family. Some regard the references to wagons and to chariots (41:43) as indications that Joseph was vizier during the Hyksos rule. Jacob responded favorably to the invitation and was also directed by God to go to Egypt, where God would make Israel a great nation (46:2–4).

Joseph went to Goshen to meet his father (46:29) and began plans to settle his relatives in that area (*see* Goshen). Because of the antipathy between cattlemen and sheep raisers, Joseph advised his family to emphasize their cattle (see 46:6) when questioned by Pharaoh about their occupation (46:31–34); in spite of this his brothers spoke primarily of their flocks (47:3–4). Pharaoh received them cordially, confirmed their locating in Goshen, and requested that capable men from among them be put in charge of his cattle (47:6). Jacob was presented before the king and in answer to Pharaoh's inquiry stated that he was 130 years old, but contrasted his age with the years of his ancestors, "few and evil have been the days of the years of my life" (47:9).

As the famine continued Joseph traded grain for land, so that the throne became the virtual possessor of Egypt, with the exception of the lands owned by the priests (47:20–22; see Breasted, *History of Egypt*, pp. 229, 238, 244). It is recognized that for some reason during the reign of Sesostris III (1878–1843 B.C.) the provincial nobles were shorn of their traditional rights and privileges and the provinces became administered by appointed officials (William C. Hayes, "The Middle Kingdom in Egypt," CAH, rev. ed., fasc. 3, pp. 44 f.). The benefactions provided for the priests by the king (47:22) are well-known from ancient documents, such as the long Papyrus Harris I, which lists the gifts of Ramses III to the temples (see ANET, pp. 260–62; Breasted, ARE, IV, §§ 151–412).

After 17 years of residence in Egypt Jacob became ill. Previously he had extracted a promise from Joseph that he would be buried in the family burial place in Canaan (47:29–31). He also gave a particular blessing to Joseph's sons (Gen 48) and individualized prophetic blessings to his own sons (Gen 49; for Joseph, see vv. 22–26). Joseph fulfilled his promise to his father, having him mummified in the Egyptian manner (50:2–13; *see* Embalm) and buried in the cave of Machpelah near Hebron. After Jacob's death Joseph's brothers feared that he would yet take vengeance upon them, but again he insisted that God in His providence had intended all of this for good.

Joseph died in Egypt at the ideal Egyptian age of 110 years (see ANET, p. 414, n.33). He too was mummified and placed in a sarcophagus or wooden mummy case (50:26). He had requested that when the Israelites left Egypt they should take his remains with them (50:25). This was faithfully performed by Moses at the time of the exodus (Ex 13:19).

See Exodus, The. Joseph was buried at Shechem in a plot of ground which Jacob had acquired (Josh 24:32).

Joseph is not mentioned in the Egyptian records. It is of interest, however, that the name Joseph-El appears as a Palestinian place name in the lists of cities conquered by Thutmose III (see ANET, p. 242; J. Simons, *Egyptian Topographical Lists*, pp. 112, 118, 127–128). *See* Chronology, OT; Genesis; Patriarchal Age.

Bibliography. K. A. Kitchen, "Joseph," NBD, pp. 656–660. H. H. Rowley, *From Joseph to Joshua*, London: British Academy, 1950. J. Vergote, *Joseph en Egypte*, Louvain: Publications Universitaires, 1959. W. A. Ward, "Egyptian Titles in Genesis 39–50," BS, CXIV (1957), 40–59; "The Egyptian Office of Joseph," JSS, V (1960), 144–150.

2. The descendants of 1 (Gen 49:22; Deut 33:13; Jud 1:22–23; etc.).

3. The father of Igal, one of the spies sent out by Moses, of the tribe of Issachar (Num 13:7).

4. A son of Asaph whose name appears twice in the description of the religious services under David (I Chr 25:2, 9).

5. A man of the family of Bani (Binnui) who married a woman from outside Israel but put her away in response to a religious revival (Ezr 10:42, 44).

6. A priest in the time of Joiakim, from the family of Shebaniah (Neh 12:14).

7-9. Three men listed in the genealogy of Lk 3:24, 26 (here another reading gives "Josech," RSV), and 30.

10. The husband of Mary, the mother of Jesus. His genealogy is given in Mt 1 (cf. Lk 3:23–38). He was a carpenter (Mt 13:55; Mk 6:3), who lived in Nazareth (Lk 2:4), but as a descendant of David his ancestral home was in Bethlehem. He was engaged to Mary at the time Jesus was conceived by the Holy Spirit (Mt 1:18; Lk 1:27; 2:5). When he learned that Mary was pregnant he was unwilling to put her to public shame but considered divorcing or putting her away secretly. He was informed by God in a dream that Mary's conception was divine and was encouraged to marry her (Mt 1:20–25). To register for the imperial tax, he and Mary went to Bethlehem, where Jesus was born. Joseph is mentioned along with Mary and Jesus at the visit of the shepherds (Lk 2:16) and at the presentation of Jesus in the temple (Lk 2:27, 33). In a dream the Lord instructed Joseph to flee Herod's wrath by taking Jesus and Mary to Egypt for a while (Mt 2:13–15). The last mentioned participation of Joseph in the events of the Gospels relates to the annual festival visit to Jerusalem when Jesus was 12 years old (Lk 2:41–52). He is not included with Mary and their children in Mt 12:46–50; Mk 3:31–35; and Lk 8:19–21 (cf. Mk 6:3), though Jn 6:42 may indicate that Joseph was

still living during part of Jesus' ministry. Joseph does not appear at the crucifixion, when Jesus gave His mother into the care of the apostle John (Jn 19:26 – 27); hence it may be concluded that Joseph had died previous to this. The Jews of Jesus' time regarded Jesus as a son of Joseph (see Lk 3:23; 4:22; Jn 1:45; 6:42).

11. Joseph of Arimathea, a wealthy man (Mt 27:57), a member of the council or Sanhedrin (Lk 23:50, RSV), and a secret disciple of Jesus, for fear of the Jews (Jn 19:38). He is characterized as honorable, bold, and awaiting the kingdom of God (Mk 15:43; Lk 23:50 – 51). After Jesus' death Joseph went to Pilate to request the body of Jesus (Mt 27:57 – 58; Mk 15:43; Lk 23:52; Jn 19:38). With Nicodemus, Joseph prepared Jesus' body for burial and placed Him in the tomb which Joseph had prepared for his own use (Mt 27:60).

12. A half-brother of Jesus (Mt 13:55; some MSS read "Joses" or "John").

13. A candidate for the place of Judas among the apostles, identified as "Joseph called Barsabas, who was surnamed Justus" (Acts 1:23).

14. The original name of Barnabas (q.v.), a Levite of Cyprian birth (Acts 4:36, NASB). The KJV, following the Textus Receptus, calls him Joses.

C. E. D.

JOSEPHUS, FLAVIUS (jō-sē′fŭs flā′vĭ-ŭs). The life of Josephus (c. A.D. 37 – 103) is a study in contrasts. Son of a priest and reared in traditional Judaism, Josephus, or Joseph ben Matthias (his Heb. name), could boast of royal blood through his Hasmonean mother. He was so dissatisfied with the three prevailing sects of Judaism that he retired for several years to a monastery near Jerusalem under the hermit Banus. Caught up in the Jewish anti-Roman resistance movement which he had been unable to dispel, he found himself the general in charge of the Jotapata fortress in Galilee (A.D. 66). Though he refused to surrender until guaranteed his life, it was his successful prophecy that Vespasian would become emperor that brought imperial favor. He was permitted to accompany Titus to Jerusalem, but he could not persuade the besieged city to surrender.

Claiming to be a Pharisee and true patriot, he was generally thought by Romans, as well as Jews, to behave as an opportunist. He had the "abstract principles of a Pharisee, but with the principles and temper of an Herodian." Thus he later lived and wrote in despised favor at Rome.

After the destruction of Jerusalem, Josephus was given a chance to retire near Jerusalem, but he chose rather to return to Rome with Titus. Here he received Roman citizenship and was commissioned to write a history of the Jewish people.

As the Apostolic Fathers are virtually the only source for early 2nd cen. Christianity, so were it not for Josephus very little would be known of 1st cen. Judaism or its outlook on Christianity. This is the main reason for the high esteem in which his writings were held by early Church Fathers, such as Jerome.

Josephus' first literary work was his *History of the Jewish War* (against Rome), published in the closing years of the reign of Vespasian: Written first in Aramaic for the benefit of Jews in Mesopotamia and then rewritten in Gr., this is a detailed account of the futile struggle against Rome. The narrative begins in the intertestamental period with Antiochus Epiphanes and the Maccabean revolt, culminating in the insurrection against Rome and the fall of Jerusalem in A.D. 70 and Masada in 73. Josephus writes as a moderate Jew attempting to trace the faults of his compatriots to the extremities of the Zealots. While he describes the siege and fall of Jerusalem in pitiful detail, there is no explicit reference whatever to Christ or Christians in the Gr. text of this volume. The historical accuracy of much of his writing has been confirmed through various discoveries such as at Machaerus (q.v.).

Antiquities of the Jews is the product of Josephus' scholarly leisure under Roman patronage. He wrote it to answer his chief critic, Justus of Tiberius, and to win the favor of his pagan patrons for the Jewish religion. This may account for his naturalistic demythologizing tendency in describing OT miracles. He was also hopeful of regaining the favor of his kinsmen who distrusted him. The account ends as did *The Jewish War* with the fall of Jerusalem, but begins with the creation. Relying on the Heb. Scriptures for the earliest history, Josephus later incorporates other sources, including the Apocrypha and popular traditions but with only slight reference to the NT, except for one statement better known to the world in general than all the rest of the writings combined. The "Testimonium Flavianum" (*Ant.* xviii.3.3) is by far the most significant witness in Josephus to Christianity. Its authenticity has been seriously questioned. In this most celebrated and most debated extra-Christian testimony of antiquity, Christ is described as "a wise man, if indeed one should call him a man." Such a momentous Jewish statement not being attested by Christian writers before Eusebius (*History of the Christian Church*, i.11.7 f.) would make it appear to be non-genuine. In spite of this, however, A. von Harnack, Rendel Harris and others have championed its originality. While most contemporary scholars believe it to be spurious in its present form, some are persuaded it has a pristine Josephan ingredient.

Bibliography. Norman Bentwich, *Josephus,* Philadelphia: Jewish Pub. Society, 1914. William R. Farmer, *Maccabees, Zealots and Josephus,* New York: Columbia Univ. Press, 1956. Frederick J. Foakes-Jackson, *Josephus and the Jews,* New York: R. R. Smith, 1930. J. Rendel Harris, *Josephus and His Testimony,* Cambridge, 1931. Hugh W. Montefiore, *Josephus and the New Testament,* London: A. R.

Mowbray & Co., 1962. Henry St. John Thackeray, *Josephus, the Man and the Historian,* New York: Ktav Pub. House, 1968. Solomon Zeitlin, *Josephus on Jesus,* Philadelphia: Dropsie College, 1931.

J. H. G.

JOSES (jō'sēz). Possibly a Gr. form of Joseph, although the name *Iōsēs* is attested in Gr. inscriptions.

1. A brother of Jesus (Mk 6:3). Called "Joseph" in Mt 13:55, ASV, RSV, and NASB according to best MSS evidence.

2. A son of Mary and Cleophas (Clopas in best Gr. MSS, Jn 19:25) and brother of James the Less (Mt 27:56, KJV according to TR; called "Joseph" in RSV and NASB following a different Gr. text; Mk 15:40, 47 has the genitive of *Iōsēs* in nearly all MSS).

3. The natal name of Barnabas, a prominent missionary and early companion of Paul (Acts 4:36, KJV according to TR; called "Joseph" in ASV, RSV, NASB according to earlier Gr. MSS). *See* Barnabas.

JOSHAH (jŏsh'ȧ). A Simeonite chief who with others invaded the valley of Gedor in the time of King Hezekiah and destroyed the native Hamites there (I Chr 4:34–41).

JOSHAPHAT (jŏsh'ȧ-făt)
1. A Mithnite among David's mighty men (I Chr 11:43).

2. One of seven priests who blew the trumpet before the ark in David's time (I Chr 15:24) in accordance with the law of Moses (Num 10:8). He is called Jehoshaphat in KJV, but the Heb. text supports Joshaphat as in ASV and RSV.

JOSHAVIAH (jŏsh'ȧ-vī'ȧ). A son of Elnaam listed among David's mighty men (I Chr 11:46).

JOSHBEKASHAH (jŏsh'bĕ-kā'shȧ). A member of the house of Heman who headed the 17th course of musicians appointed by David for the sanctuary service (I Chr 25:4, 24).

JOSHEB-BASSHEBETH (jō'shĕb-bȧ-sē'bĕt). The name of David's most eminent warrior among his mighty men as given in ASV and RSV as a probable substitute for the meaningless "that sat in the seat" in II Sam 23:8 of KJV. In the parallel passage in I Chr 11:11 this man is identified as "Jashobeam, an Hachmonite." *See* Jashobeam.

JOSHUA (jŏsh'ū-ȧ). The leader of the Israelites in their conquest of the Promised Land. His full name Jehoshua (Num 13:16) means "Yahweh is salvation," and is the same as the Hellenized form of the name Jesus (Acts 7:45; Heb 4:8). His name is spelled "Jeshua" in Neh 8:17. His original name was Oshea (RSV, Hoshea, Num 13:8).

House remains of the Israelite period at Et Tell, commonly identfied as Ai. HFV

Joshua was the son of Nun, of the tribe of Ephraim (Num 13:8). After directing the allotment of tribal territories he settled in the highlands of Ephraim at Timnath-serah, where he was buried (Josh 19:50; 24:30).

Since he was over 40 when he left Egypt and seemed well-qualified to command the Israelite forces who fought off the Amalekites at Rephidim (Ex 17:8–16), it is possible that he had been trained in Pharaoh's army. During the year at Mount Sinai Joshua served as personal attendant to Moses when the latter was receiving the law and whenever he went to the tent of meeting to hear the Lord (Ex 24:13; 32:17; 33:11). Even after leaving Sinai, Moses considered Joshua to be "young" and found it necessary to rebuke him for trying to forbid two elders in the camp from prophesying (Num 11:27–29).

In addition to whatever contacts he may have had before the Exodus with Canaan and its inhabitants as they came to trade in Egypt or as he may have traveled there on an Egyptian military campaign, Joshua gained experience of that land as one of the 12 spies. He was selected as the representative from the tribe of Ephraim (Num 13:8). They scouted Canaan thoroughly from the Negeb to Rehob, near Lebo-hamath (Lebweh, 14 miles NE of Baalbek between the Lebanon ranges). As Joshua and Caleb opposed the defaming majority report and urged the Israelites to enter the "exceedingly good land" (Num 14:7) instead of rebelling against the Lord, they grew in spiritual stature. The other ten who disparaged the land died by plague (Num 14:36–38). Only Joshua and Caleb of those over 20 at the beginning of the wilderness journey remained alive at the end of the 40 years and were permitted to enter Canaan (Num 26:65; 32:12; Deut 1:34–40).

The Lord ordered Moses to give Joshua a commission as the new shepherd of His people when the lawgiver realized he would soon die

The mound of Gibeon, with whose ancient Canaanite inhabitants Joshua made a treaty. HFV

instead of crossing into Canaan (Num 27:12–23; Deut 3:21–29). Moses invested Joshua solemnly with honor or authority before Eleazar the high priest and the entire congregation, and imparted to him a spirit of wisdom as he laid his hands upon him (Num 27:18, 23; Deut 34:9). As part of Moses' final arrangements for covenant continuity he charged Joshua publicly to be strong and courageous in order to bring Israel to the land of its promised inheritance (Deut 31:3, 7–8). When Moses and his successor went and stood at the door of the tent of meeting, God directly commissioned Joshua (Deut 31:14–15, 23). After Moses' death the Lord graciously repeated this charge to Joshua privately, enlarging His promises to encourage him on the eve of the invasion of Canaan (Josh 1:1–9).

Encamped E of the Jordan, Joshua faced two stupendous problems, how to cross the flooded river and how to overcome the defending Canaanites. Would they be waiting with drawn swords on the opposite bank? He sent two spies to reconnoiter the bastion of Jericho and commanded them to keep their mission secret lest their report discourage the people as the ten spies had done (Josh 2; cf. Num 13; 14). God undertook for both obstacles by filling the inhabitants of the land with terror (Josh 2:9–11), and by stopping the Jordan when the people marched to the river in faith and at the moment the priests carrying the ark stepped in the waters (3:14–17).

In obedience to the Lord, Joshua had the men born in the wilderness circumcised (5:2–9). The nation was willing once again to walk by faith with Yahweh their God in the promises of the Abrahamic covenant and to submit to circumcision, the covenant sign. Thus God removed the reproach or disgrace of their idolatrous and sensual ways in Egypt (5:9).

Joshua exhibited great faith and discipline in obeying God's unusual tactics for reducing Jericho. He commanded the priests and people to march round the city each day and to refrain from shouts and retorts to the undoubted mockery of the defending Canaanites (6:6–10). Except for Achan, the Israelite troops followed his orders in not looting the ruins for their own benefit. Feeling a personal responsibility, Joshua agonized over the defeat and loss of 36 of his men at Ai, and fell on his face in desperation before the Lord (7:6–9).

The details of the second attack on Ai illustrate the thorough planning and strategy that went into Joshua's campaigns. He was swift and decisive in his movements, as the all-night forced march up from Gilgal to relieve the siege of Gibeon would indicate (10:9). When the Amorite ranks broke, he urged his army to follow up the victory (10:19–20). He had prayed for God to help him destroy in the open field the enemy's fighting potential, and after the divinely sent hailstorm he pressed his advantage as the Amorite armies fled to fortresses 20 miles away (10:10–14).

With blitzkrieg speed he assaulted the key southern strongholds one after another, aiming at killing their troops rather than occupying and holding the cities (10:28–43). He counted on divine direction and support (10:25, 30, 32, 42; 11:6–9, 15), on surprise and ruse, on discipline and incentive among his own troops, and on collapse of enemy morale rather than on superior weapons and numbers. Since his desert army was untrained in siege operations, he could not afford to get bogged down outside a walled city. Many Canaanites probably fled to the hills and caves, later to return and reoccupy their towns. Other cities, such as Gibeon and her allies, capitulated outright. Thus, except at Jericho, Ai, and Hazor, which Joshua burned (11:13), archaeologists can expect to find little clear-cut evidence of city destruction as a result of Joshua's incursions. He subdued the country as a whole and secured it sufficiently to enable each tribe to enter and claim its allotted inheritance. Israelite settlement and city building followed gradually during the time from the judges to David. See Exodus, The.

Joshua possessed the qualities of a true leader. He displayed great courage from his first battle with the Amalekites at Rephidim, grimly holding fast whenever they began to prevail, to his attack on the combined Canaanite kings at the waters of Merom. He was quick to receive and obey orders from his divine Commander-in-Chief (e.g., 5:13–6:5), humble enough to recognize his constant need to depend on the Lord—although he failed to seek God as to the identity of the envoys from Gibeon (9:14–15). He was a man of honor. He carried out the agreement made by the two spies with the household of Rahab and spared her family when Jericho fell (6:22–25). Nor did he abrogate the treaty made by the Israelite princes with the Gibeonites (9:18–26).

His finest quality was his utter devotion to the law of God. He saturated his mind and heart with the Word of the Lord. Thus the nation had confidence in his decisions (see 1:13 – 18; 11:12, 15; 14:1 – 5). In the midst of his early campaigns Joshua took time to establish Israel's covenant as the new law of the land at its very center, at Gerizim and Ebal (8:30 – 35). In his farewell addresses he appealed to the people to renew their covenant commitment with the Lord and exhorted them "to keep and to do all that is written in the book of the law of Moses" (23:6).

His godly example continued to influence the nation even after his death, during the lifetime of the elders who outlived Joshua (24:31).

For bibliography *see* Joshua, Book of.

J. R.

JOSHUA, BOOK OF. The sixth book of the OT, and the first of the historical books, named after its principal character, Joshua. Under God he led the nation of Israel across the Jordan, in their conquest of Canaan, in occupying their tribal territories, and in renewing their covenant allegiance to the Lord. In Jewish tradition Joshua is the first book of The Prophets, the second major division of the Heb. Bible, heading the subdivision known as the Former Prophets (Joshua, Judges, I and II Samuel, I and II Kings).

Position in the Canon

In 1792 Alexander Geddes proposed a theory that Joshua was the sixth book of a late Jewish collection which modern critics have called the Hexateuch. Developing this view along with the documentary (JEDP) theory of the Pentateuch, such scholars as Bleek, Knobel, and Nöldeke argued that there must have been a suitable conclusion to the story of Israel's beginnings described in the first five books of the OT. Since the land which God swore to give to the patriarchs is mentioned from Gen 12 to Deut 34, the fulfillment of the divine promise would not be provided without Joshua. Source analysts thought they could detect the styles of the supposed Pentateuchal sources in the sixth book.

There is no ancient Jewish tradition or MS evidence, however, that Joshua ever formed a unit with the five books of the law to constitute a so-called Hexateuch. The law was always distinguished from the other books. Josephus clearly states that the Jews of his day had five books belonging to Moses, 13 by prophets who wrote down what was done in their times from the death of Moses until the reign of Artaxerxes, and four others containing hymns to God and precepts for daily living (Jos *Apion* 1.8). Nor were any portions of Joshua ever included in the annual and triennial systems of the public reading of the law.

The strongest argument against a Hexateuch is that the Samaritans considered only the five books of Moses to be canonical, but never the book of Joshua. Yet Joshua contains various features which would aid the cause of the Samaritan sectarians. Both Mount Gerizim (Josh

8:33), where the Samaritans later worshiped, and Shechem (Josh 20:7; 24:1, 32), their home (Jos *Ant.* xi.8.6), are mentioned, with no intimation of Jerusalem becoming Israel's center of worship. Thus, since there was no reason to reject the book of Joshua and every reason to keep it, Joshua could not have been part of the Torah at the time of the Samaritan schism (see G. L. Archer, SOTI, p. 253).

More recently, Martin Noth (*Das Buch Joshua*, 1938) and others have claimed that there existed in Israel a theological history that began with Deuteronomy and continued through II Kings. While there are some similarities of style in Deuteronomy and Joshua, it must be recognized that in Jewish history Deuteronomy was always considered as part of the Torah, as one of the five books of the law. Deut 24:16 is quoted in II Kgs 14:6, indicating it was "written in the book of the law of Moses." Both Jesus and the apostles quoted or referred to portions of Deuteronomy as belonging to the law (cf. Mt 22:36 – 38 with Deut 6:5; Mt 19:8 with Deut 24:1 – 4; Acts 3:22 with Deut 18:15; I Cor 9:9 with Deut 25:4; Heb 10:28 with Deut 17:6; 19:15; Heb 10:30 with Deut 32:35 – 36).

Certainly no one in the early church doubted the inspiration of the book of Joshua. In Heb 13:5, Josh 1:5 is quoted as the Word of God. Numerous other references may be found in the NT to persons and events in Joshua, stamping the record of its events as authentic.

Authorship and Date

The book appears to be a literary unit, composed by a single author. Critical scholars, however, have held varying views leading to the general conclusion that it is a composite work of several late source documents, still later compiled and edited by the Deuteronomic school. Some think they find clues of the Elohist (E) and Yahwist (J) writers and claim there was a major Deuteronomic (D) revision during Josiah's reign, with Priestly (P) writers adding most of the contents of chaps. 13 – 22 in Ezra's time. Other liberal scholars, such as Martin Noth and John Bright (IB, II, 541 – 548), reject this analysis and recognize only the Deuteronomic style in the book.

Unquestionably sources were used in writing Joshua. The author specifically refers to the book of Jasher (Josh 10:13) and mentions that Joshua had ordered a description of the land to be written in a book (18:8 – 9). Joshua himself wrote "in the book of the law of God" the stipulations of the renewed covenant as part of the ceremony at Shechem (24:25 – 26).

Yet Joshua could not have been the final author of the book bearing his name since it records his death (24:29 – 30). Furthermore, several events are recorded which apparently did not happen until after Joshua's death: Caleb's conquest of Hebron (Josh 15:13*b* – 14; cf. Jud 1:1, 10, 20), Othniel's capture of Debir

(Josh 15:15 – 19; cf. Jud 1:1, 11 –15), and the migration of the Danites to Leshem (Josh 15:17; 19:47; 24:31; cf. Jud 1:1, 17– 18). The name Hormah is used for the town of Zephath (Josh 12:14; 15:30; 19:4), which was not changed until the following era (Jud 1:1, 17). But the author was a contemporary of Joshua, having participated in the Jordan crossing ("we," Josh 5:1). Also, Rahab was still alive at the time of writing (6:25).

The book gives other evidence of having been written prior to 1200 B.C. because the Philistines are barely mentioned (only in Josh 13:2 – 3) and certainly were not yet considered to be a threat. The author knew them only as occupying a part of the "south," the Negeb, along with the Geshurites and the Avvim; and the territory as a whole was counted as Canaanite. Rameses III (1198 – 1166 B.C.) boasted of crushing an attempted invasion of Egypt by land and sea by the Philistines and their Aegean allies in his eighth year (ANET, pp. 262 f.). The remnants settled the Palestinian coastal plain in force from that time on. On the other hand, the phrase "all the land of the Hittites" (Josh 1:4; *not* in Deut 11:24!) in referring to Syria-Lebanon would not have been historically accurate until the Hittite king Suppiluliumas (1380 – 1346 B.C.) crushed the Mitanni in Syria *c.* 1370 B.C. Furthermore, the term may have been less significant after the treaty between Rameses II and Hattusilis III *c.* 1284 B.C. Widespread Hittite control had disappeared altogether in S Syria before 1200 B.C.

If Joshua himself did not write the major portion of the book to which a short appendix about his death was added, then a possible author might be the high priest Phinehas, the last-named person in the book (24:33). He, rather than Joshua, is the prominent person in settling the dispute over the altar built by the two and one-half tribes at the Jordan frontier (Josh 22:10 – 34). Another possibility is a nameless priest closely associated with Phinehas but who resided in Judah. The lengthy list of the borders and towns of Judah (15:1 – 63) may indicate that he settled in that territory. In comparison, the borders of Ephraim and Manasseh are traced rather briefly, even though within them lay the important religious centers of Shiloh and Shechem (Josh 16 – 17). A special interest in the city of Hebron may be detected (14:6 – 15; 15:13 – 14; 21:11 – 13), suggesting perhaps the author's home.

Biblical data and archaeological discoveries provide evidence by which one may arrive at a date for the Exodus and thus the Conquest (*see* Exodus, The: Date). If Moses led the Israelites through the Red Sea *c.* 1445 B.C., 480 years before Solomon began to build the temple (I Kgs 6:1), then Joshua's invasion of Canaan took place *c.* 1405 B.C., at the close of the Late Bronze I Age (1550 – 1400). The division of the land began 45 years after Moses at Kadesh-barnea had promised Caleb an inheritance

(Josh 14:1 – 10), thus *c.* 1400 B.C. After making the tribal allotments Joshua lived on until 1390 – 1380, or even later. Thus the book was probably written early in the period of the judges, *c.* 1370 – 1350 B.C. According to the late date theory of the Exodus and Conquest the Israelites would have crossed the Jordan *c.* 1250 – 1230 B.C. or even later. It would be difficult, however, to reconcile this view with a date before 1200 B.C. for the time of the writing of Joshua which seems preferable as discussed above: *c.* 1200 B.C. the Philistines came in strength to Palestine and the Hittite Empire collapsed.

Purpose

The book of Joshua seems to have been written as the official record of God's providential leading in Israel's triumph and settlement in the land He had promised their forefathers. Hence the record was undoubtedly added to the existing scrolls of the law kept beside the ark in the tabernacle (Deut 31:9, 24 – 27). Samuel, for instance, wrote additional material "in the book" (I Sam 10:25, ASV marg.) and laid it up before the Lord. As part of the recognized and accepted sacred Scriptures, Joshua would be read periodically at the annual feasts and on special occasions of covenant renewal (e.g., Neh 8 – 9). The book of Joshua declares the faithfulness of the Lord to His covenants with the patriarchs and with the nation as mediated to it by Moses. God is demonstrated as keeping His promises in full (Josh 21:43 – 45). On their part, the future generations are inspired to renew their own covenant commitment and to imitate the faith and unity and high morale of Joshua's era.

Outline

I. Entrance into the Promised Land, 1:1 – 5:12
    A. God's commission to Joshua, 1:1 – 9
    B. Joshua's mobilization for crossing the Jordan, 1:10 – 18
    C. Mission of the spies, 2:1 – 24
    D. Crossing of the Jordan, 3:1 – 5:1
    E. Renewal of circumcision and Passover observance, 5:2– 12
II. Conquest of the Promised Land, 5:13 – 12:24
    A. Appearance of the divine Commander-in-Chief, 5:13 – 6:5
    B. The central campaign, 6:6 – 8:29
      1. Capture of Jericho, 6:6 – 27
      2. Repulse at Ai because of Achan's sin, 7:1 – 26
      3. Second attack and the burning of Ai, 8:1 – 29
    C. Establishment of Israel's covenant as the law of the land, 8:30 – 35
    D. The southern campaign, 9:1 – 10:43
      1. Treaty with the Gibeonite tetrapolis, 9:1 – 27
      2. Defeat and hanging of the five Amorite kings, 10:1 – 27

Teaching and Value

Joshua is the first of the books of prophetic history that describe God's dealings with His chosen people after the death of Moses, the mediator of the Sinaitic covenant. There is a strong sense of historical continuity as God in faithfulness to His covenants with the patriarchs and the theocratic nation brings Israel into the land of blessing and settles the tribes in their promised homeland. By real and mighty acts of redemption He displays His presence and power. These acts are both actual and prophetic of the second Joshua, even Jesus our Saviour.

The era of Joshua is the high water mark of corporate faith and faithfulness in the OT. As such it is also prophetic of the faith of Israel's remnant in the end-time as they will triumph over their enemies in the day of the Lord. Likewise the book of Joshua illustrates the present-day conflict of the people of God with evil powers—with the evil kings and princes of the unseen world, the cosmic rulers of this dark age, the spirit hosts of wickedness in the supernatural sphere—and with Satan himself (Eph 6:10 – 18). Such spiritual warfare is encountered as the believer earnestly strives to possess all that God has promised to him in Christ (Eph 1:3). As in Josh 10, all strongholds must be destroyed and every thought brought captive to the obedience of Christ (II Cor 10:4 – 5). Such warfare is won by faith in the finished redemptive work of Christ and His present authority (Eph 1:19 – 22), which believers share as they are enthroned together with Him in the supernatural realm (Eph 2:6). The book of Joshua thus is filled with spiritual lessons on how the believer may live the victorious life, how he may enter the land of rest of Heb 3 – 4. In this NT passage the rest in Canaan from vain wilderness strivings is set forth as typical of the present spiritual rest as believers abide in Christ. It is He who made complete atonement and is continually interceding for the believer to enable him to conquer self and Satan.

Not only are God's faithfulness and His miraculous saving power portrayed in the book of Joshua, but also His holiness is seen in His judgment upon the iniquitous Canaanites and in His insistence that in fighting the holy war against them Israel must put away everything evil from their own use. The teaching concerning *ḥērem*, the "accursed thing" (Josh 6:17 – 21; Deut 7:2, 26), meant that every person and thing hostile to theocracy by its having been associated with another deity must be devoted to the Lord, either to be utterly destroyed or to be taken out of common use and dedicated only to sacred use.

Contents and Problems

For specific discussion of Joshua's career *see* Joshua; and of various theological, archaeological, and exegetical problems in the book *see* War on the extermination of Canaanites and holy war; Jericho; Ai; Shechem; Hazor; *see* Sun on Josh 10:12 – 14.

Bibliography. Carl Armerding, *The Fight for Palestine in the Days of Joshua*, Wheaton: Van Kampen Press, 1949. William G. Blaikie, "Joshua," ExpB. Hugh J. Blair, "Joshua," NBC. John Bright, "Joshua," IB. "Conquest," CornPBE, pp. 230 – 236. John J. Davis, *Conquest and Crisis*, Grand Rapids: Baker, 1970. John Garstang, *Joshua-Judges: the Foundation of Bible History*, New York: Richard Smith, Inc., 1931. Irving Jensen, *Joshua: Rest-Land Won*, Chicago: Moody Press, 1966. Yehezkel Kaufmann, *The Biblical Account of the Conquest of Palestine*, Jerusalem: Magnes Press, 1953. Carl F. Keil, "Joshua," KD. William S. LaSor, *Great Personalities of the OT*, Westwood, N.J.: Revell, 1959, pp. 69 – 77. George E. Mendenhall, *Law and Covenant in Israel and the Ancient Near East*, Pittsburgh: The Biblical Colloquium, 1955. F. B. Meyer, *Joshua and the Land of Promise*, London: Morgan & Scott, n.d. John Rea, "Joshua," WBC. Alan Redpath, *Victorious Christian Living: Studies in the Book of Joshua*, Revell, 1955.

J. R.

JOSIAH (jō-sī'ȧ)

1. Grandson of Manasseh and son and successor of Amon as king of Judah. The primary biblical information concerning him comes from II Kgs 22–23; II Chr 34–35; Jeremiah (many references); and Zephaniah. His birth was supernaturally predicted by name in the time of Jeroboam I (I Kgs 13:2). He was one of the good kings of Judah who led a reform. The "people of the land" placed him on the throne at the age of eight, and he reigned c. 639–609 B.C. In the eighth year of his reign (at 16 years of age) he "began to seek after the God of David, his father" (II Chr 34:3). In his twelfth year he began his reforms in Judah and Jerusalem, and evidently in northern Israel as well. (Jeremiah received his call to the prophetic ministry in Josiah's thirteenth year, c. 626 B.C.)

In his eighteenth year (621 B.C.) Josiah arranged for the temple repairs. It was at this time that a most important event in his reign occurred. Hilkiah the high priest found the "book of the law" in the temple. If this work is not to be identified solely as the book of Deuteronomy, it is quite certain that it at least included that book, or parts of it. This lawbook was responsible for the renewal of the covenant and further reforms, which by now certainly extended even to Bethel and Naphtali. Apparently, Assyrian control had weakened enough to allow such a widespread cleansing of the land from idolatry. In doing this, Josiah centralized public worship in Jerusalem. He also observed the Passover on the grandest scale since the days of the judges. But in spite of all this, Jeremiah (e.g., Jer 2–6, 11) makes it clear that Josiah's reform was only superficial, external, and temporary. No genuine repentance or lasting inner change of the people resulted from it.

Josiah adopted an anti-Assyrian policy and thereby met an untimely death in 609 B.C. by injudiciously leading a little army against Neco II, king of Egypt. The latter was actually on a march with his army to aid the Assyrians in making their last ditch stand against the Babylonians at Haran. At the very beginning of this encounter with the Egyptian army at Megiddo, Josiah was killed. His religious reformation was soon forgotten, and three months later the kingdom of Judah lost its political independence to Egypt.

Yet Josiah was the last good and godly king of Judah before the destruction of Jerusalem and the Babylonian captivity. The finest tribute is paid to him in II Kgs 23:25: "And like unto him was there no king before him [i.e., in the area of obedience to the law, as the following explains], that turned to the Lord with all his heart, and with all his soul, and with all his might, according to all the law of Moses; neither after him arose there any like him."

2. A son of Zephaniah who returned with other Jews from Exile (Zech 6:10).

K. L. B.

JOSIAS. *See* Josiah.

JOSIBIAH (jŏs'ĭ-bī'ȧ). A Simeonite (I Chr 4:35).

JOSIPHIAH (jŏs'ĭ-fī'ȧ). The father of a returnee to Palestine with Ezra (Ezr 8:10).

JOT. A word used in Mt 5:18 to represent the Gr. *iōta*, a letter equivalent to *i* in English. However, *iōta* was used here to designate *yōd*, the smallest letter in the Heb. alphabet, and thereby to set forth the indestructibility of the law in its smallest details. The inviolability of all of God's revelation in the Scriptures is, by implication, likewise upheld. The importance of such a minute detail as a *yōd* can be accounted for only by recognizing that Christ regarded the individual words of Scripture as inspired and authoritative, for the change of a letter might well change the whole word and its meaning.

Modern versions offer a large variety of translations of *iōta* in Mt 5:18: "jot" (ASV), "iota" (Montgomery, Moffatt, Berkeley, RSV), "smallest letter" (Weymouth, NASB), "dotting an *i*" (Goodspeed, Williams), "single dot" (Phillips), "letter" (NEB), "least point" (Today's English Version), etc.

JOTBAH (jŏt'bȧ). A town where Meshullemeth, the mother of King Amon of Judah, lived (II Kgs 21:19). Its exact site is unknown, although some identify it with Khirbet Jefat, known as Jotapata in Roman times, a town near Cana of Galilee. Josephus tried unsuccessfully to defend this city against Vespasian's army (Jos *Wars* iii.7).

JOTBATH. *See* Jotbathah.

JOTBATHAH (jŏt'bȧ-thȧ). A place or district where Israel encamped twice during the wilderness wanderings (Num 33:33–34; Deut 10:7, Jotbath). The two references represent the beginning and the close of the period of wilderness wandering. The place is usually identified with some wady or valley (Deut 10:7, ASV, "a land of brooks of water") N of the Gulf of Aqabah, perhaps Ain el-Ghadian, 25 miles N of Ezion-geber in the Arabah. Another possible location is the luxurious oasis at Taba, six miles SW of Eilat on the western shore of the gulf (Beno Rothenberg, *God's Wilderness*, London: Thames & Hudson, 1961, pp. 163 f.).

JOTHAM (jō'thȧm)

1. A king of Judah who was a son of Azariah (or Uzziah) and father of Ahaz (II Kgs 15:5, 7, 30–38; II Chr 27:1–9). He was coregent with his father c. 750–742 B.C. because his father had leprosy and was unable to administer efficiently the affairs of the kingdom. He was sole king c. 742–735 B.C., continuing the anti-Assyrian policy of his father (*see* Uzziah). He abdicated the actual rulership in favor of his pro-Assyrian son Ahaz, and died in 731 B.C.

Jotham won a military victory over the Ammonites (II Chr 27:5). He was also responsible for several building projects. For example, he built the high gate of the temple (i.e., the northern gate of the inner court), fortified the wall of Ophel in Jerusalem, built cities in the hill country of Judah, and established forts and towers on the hills (II Kgs 15:35; II Chr 27:3). It may be correctly surmised from such activity that this was a period of prosperity, and this is confirmed by archaeology.

A signet ring has been found at Ezion-geber (Elath) with a seal inscribed "belonging to Jotham." This Jotham has been identified as the son of Uzziah. The fact that it was discovered at Ezion-geber evidently indicates that at that time Judah's control extended to that seaport on the Gulf of Aqabah.

2. Gideon's youngest son who escaped the massacre of Gideon's 70 sons ordered by Abimelech (Jud 9:5). After his escape, and after Abimelech was made king by the people of Shechem, he appeared on Mount Gerizim to protest their action by relating the parable of the trees selecting the bramble to be their king (which "honor" had already been declined by the cedar, the olive, and the vine). Thus he warned the Shechemites against Abimelech and pronounced a curse on them, which was fulfilled three years later (Jud 9:57).

3. A son of Jahdai and a descendant of Caleb (I Chr 2:47).

K. L. B.

JOURNEY, SABBATH DAY'S. *See* Sabbath Day's Journey.

JOY, REJOICE. Joy is inseparably connected with the life of God's people in the OT and NT (Deut 12:7, 12; Phil 4:4). It characterizes the heavenly hosts before the throne of God (Rev 19:6 – 7), and the consecrated life of the Christian on earth with his hope for future glory (I Pet 4:13).

In the OT joy is expressed by a number of synonyms, signifying an overflowing adoration before God, particularly in worship. This exuberant delight is often quite demonstrative in loud shouting, clapping, and dancing. God is its source and object (Ps 35:9 – 10). Especially in the Psalms this exultant gladness is emphasized in God's nearness (Ps 16:11), His pardon (Ps 51:8, 15), His steadfast love (Ps 31:7), His Word (Ps 119:14), and His promises (Ps 106:5). Joy is to be the characteristic of the Messianic Age and the fulfillment of Israel's hopes (Isa 35; 55:12; 65:18 – 19).

The chief NT words (Gr. *chara* and *chairō*) come from the same root as "grace" (*charis*). The ministry of Jesus is described as the joy of the bridegroom with his friends (Jn 3:29; cf. Mk 2:19). He Himself supplies His deep inner joy to the believer (Jn 15:11; 16:24; 17:13). His joy was a constant satisfying delight in doing the will of God (Ps 40:8), the absolute self-sacrifice of Himself to His Father. Luke particularly stresses joy in the ministry of Jesus (Lk 10:17; 13:17; 15:5, 7, 10; 19:37) and also in the preaching of the gospel ("joyous news") with

its conversions (Acts 8:8; 13:48, 52; 15:3). Paul lists joy among the fruit of the Spirit (Gal 5:22), and the result of God's nearness to those whom He has graciously justified in Christ (Rom 5:20). It constantly expresses itself toward others (Phil 1:26; 2:2) in glad obedience arising from love in the fellowship of the church.

Thus joy, which comes from the indwelling of the Holy Spirit in the Christian community, is a basic characteristic of the kingdom of God (Rom 14:17; cf. 15:13; I Thess 1:6). Christian joy is lasting because it is based on a right relationship to God through Christ. Its most remarkable expression, however, is in times of suffering for Christ's sake (Mt 5:12; Acts 5:41; Rom 12:12; Col 1:24; I Pet 4:13). He went to His cross for joy (Heb 12:2). The NT opens with the angelic choruses of joy at Christ's birth and closes with the hallelujahs of His reign.

In the KJV the Gr. verb *kauchaomai*, "to boast, exult," is several times rendered "to joy" (Rom 5:11) or "rejoice" (Rom 5:2; Phil 3:3; Jas 1:9; 4:16) and the nouns *kauchēma* and *kauchēsis* as "rejoicing." This root suggests joy in the sense of proud confidence (II Cor 1:12, NASB) or glorying and boasting (II Cor 7:4; 8:24; etc.). *See* Glory.

F. P.

JOZABAD (jŏ′zȧ-băd)
1. A volunteer from Gederah in David's army at Ziklag (I Chr 12:4; KJV, Josabad).
2, 3. Two Manassite captains in David's army at Ziklag (I Chr 12:20).
4. A Levite overseer under King Hezekiah (II Chr 31:13).
5. A chief Levite under King Josiah (II Chr 35:9).
6. A priest who divorced his non-Jewish wife (Ezr 10:22).
7. A Levite, son of Jeshua (Ezr 8:33).
8. A priest who divorced his non-Jewish wife (Ezr 10:23).
9. A Levite expounder of the law (Neh 8:7).
10. A chief of the Levites (Neh 11:16). The same person may be represented in 7 – 10.

JOZACHAR (jŏ′zȧ-kär). A son of Shimeath and one of two murderers of King Joash of Judah (II Kgs 12:21), identified as Zabad in II Chr 24:26).

JOZADAK. *See* Josedech.

JUBAL (jōō′bȧl). The younger son of Lamech by Adah who first played the lyre and flute, and thus probably invented these musical instruments (Gen 4:21).

JUBILEE. *See* Festivals.

JUCAL (jōō′kȧl). An abbreviated form of Jehucal (*q.v.*), found in Jer 38:1.

JUDA. *See* Judah.

JUDAEA. *See* Judea.

JUDAH (jōō'dȧ)

1. The fourth son of Jacob whose mother was Leah (Gen 29:35). He married a Canaanite, a daughter of Shuah of Adullam, and they had three sons, Er, Onan, and Shelah. Because of their wickedness and contempt of God the two older sons were slain by the Lord (Gen 38:1 – 10). Through guile, Judah also became the father of twins (Gen 38:11 – 30), Pharez and Zarah, by Tamar, widow of Er. It is to be noted that Judah through Pharez became the ancestor of both David (Ruth 4:18 – 22) and the Lord Jesus Christ (Mt 1:3, 16).

Judah was the leader of the sons of Jacob. He proposed that Joseph be spared instead of murdering him and that he be sold as a slave to the Midianite traders who took him to Egypt (Gen 37:12 – 13, 18 – 28). Judah pleaded with the vizier of Egypt, whom he did not suspect to be Joseph, that he be kept a prisoner instead of Benjamin. This resulted in Joseph's making himself known to his brothers (Gen 44:33 – 34; 45:1). Jacob chose Judah to be the leader to show the way to Goshen (Gen 46:28), and bestowed the privilege of the birthright (including the ancestry of Messiah) on Judah whom he chose over his three older brothers (Gen 49:8 – 12).

2. The name of the tribe descended from Judah (Num 26:19 – 21). The men of Judah played no very important part in the Exodus from Egypt and in the wilderness wanderings except that they led in vanguard (Num 2:9). They numbered 74,600 (Num 1:26 – 27) in the first census at Sinai, and in the second census taken at Shittim before entering Canaan they had increased in 40 years only to 76,500 (Num 26:22). When the tribes would meet at Mount Gerizim, Judah was to stand there to bless the people (Deut 27:12).

Judah was the first tribe authorized to take possession of its assigned territory after the initial conquest of Canaan (Josh 14:6 – 15:63). They continued to drive out the Canaanites from their towns and from the hill country (Jud 1:1 – 20). Caleb, one of the 12 spies, was of the tribe of Judah, and with the help of Othniel, his nephew, he made sure his allotment. The territory that Judah occupied was one of the largest, measuring from the Dead Sea W toward the Mediterranean Sea about 30 miles. From the N border which extended from the N end of the Dead Sea W through all the mountains and hilly wilderness to include the Negeb, its length was about 80 miles. Included with that of Judah was the territory of Simeon. During the period of the judges Judah was often cut off from the other tribes by the remaining pagan peoples, such as the Gibeonites, Jebusites, etc., dwelling along the N part of their allotment.

During the latter period of the judges they were in constant conflict with the Philistines who lived along the coast and in the Shephelah (Jud 3:31; 10:7; 13:1). The men of Judah joined

in the formation of the kingdom of the combined tribes of Israel. After King Saul died they turned to David and crowned him king with the capital at Hebron. *See* Judah, Kingdom of.

3. A Levite who was one of the overseers of the temple repair workmen (Ezr 3:9).

4. A Levite who put away his foreign wife (Ezr 10:23).

5. A Benjamite, second ruler of Jerusalem in the time of Nehemiah (Neh 11:9).

6. A Levite, one of the choir directors who returned with Zerubbabel (Neh 12:8).

7. One who marched in the parade at the dedication of the restored walls of Jerusalem (Neh 12:34). He may also have been a musician (v. 36).

8. An ancestor of Jesus in the line of Mary, several generations after David (Lk 3:30; KJV, Juda).

C. L. F. and E. L. C.

JUDAH, KINGDOM OF. Not until the time of

David did Jacob's prophesied preeminence of Judah (Gen 49:10) begin to reach its fulfillment. After seven years and six months in Hebron (II Sam 5:5), David took Jerusalem from the Jebusites by stealth and made it his capital and center of worship. But Jerusalem and the house of David were to experience the bitterness of schism. King Solomon, in spite of all his administrative genius, only deepened the distrust between the N and S, and his son foolishly consummated the division about 931 B.C. (I Kgs 12).

The kingdoms of Judah and Israel fought for the first 60 years after the division (I Kgs 14:30) until Jehoshaphat helped Ahab with his wars against Damascus. Sadly, this resulted in the toleration of Baal worship in Judah. Under Jehoshaphat, Judah was strong enough to control Edom, but Jehoram, his son, lost both the copper mines and Elath, the seaport on the Gulf of Aqabah, to the rebellious Edomites.

This same Jehoram married Athaliah, the daughter of Ahab and Jezebel, whose treachery almost brought an end to the house of David. The son of this unholy union, Ahaziah, was caught in Jehu's purge of the house of Ahab and mercilessly slain with his cousin Jehoram, king of Israel. Athaliah used this incident to seize the throne and kill all the Davidic seed, missing only the babe Joash, who was saved by his aunt and hidden for six years. A coup lead by Jehoiada the priest brought about the demise of Athaliah, and young Joash ruled under a regency. Joash on the one hand repaired the temple but on the other gave as tribute to Hazael of Syria many of its hallowed treasures.

Amaziah who came to the throne about 800 B.C. had limited success in reviving the fortunes of Judah. With the help of mercenaries he recovered the city of Selah from the Edomites (II Kgs 14:7), but his rule was marred by a foolish challenge to Jehoash of Israel who sacked Jerusalem. Azariah (Uzziah) restored the seaport Elath to Judah and rebuilt it.

Jotham's undistinguished reign was followed by the proud Ahaz. Ahaz reacted faithlessly to a bad political situation. Rezin of Syria and Pekah of Israel were in league against him. Despite pleadings and warnings of Isaiah, Ahaz secured a treaty with the Assyrian king, Tiglath-pileser III, designed to protect him against his northern neighbors. Tiglath-pileser soon laid seige to the city of Damascus and put Samaria under heavy tribute, but then came on to Jerusalem and demanded a large ransom (II Chr 28:16 – 21).

Judah's good king Hezekiah brought about a spiritual revival. He eventually showed his contempt for Assyrian power when Sennacherib first came into Judah c. 705 B.C. Hezekiah probably paid tribute at this time, but the Assyrian king Sennacherib had troubles in many parts of his realm and left Judah. Shabako, the Ethiopian who united Egypt, and Merodach-baladan the Chaldean in Babylon, encouraged Hezekiah to slough off the Assyrian yoke. So once again in 701 Sennacherib brought his hordes into the Judean countryside. He took Lachish and many other cities and used psychological warfare against Hezekiah (II Kgs 18; Isa 36); but by divine intervention, as predicted by Isaiah (Isa 37:21 – 38), Sennacherib's army was so weakened that he had to give up the seige and leave again. Hezekiah engaged in missionary activities in the northern half of the land. The chronicler tells us that these met with some success in Galilee but not in Ephraim (II Chr 30:1 – 11).

Assyrian power was so complete it was hard for Judah to escape its influence. Consequently Manasseh, the son of Hezekiah, capitulated to the heathen forces and built altars for Baal worship. He even set up the practice of idolatry in the house of the Lord. He made his sons pass through the fire, used enchantments and dealt with familiar spirits, and tradition tells that he martyred the prophet Isaiah. Following the death of Ashurbanipal (c. 630 B.C.), Assyrian power began to wane.

Josiah, the new king of Judah, came to the throne with a strong instinct to bring about reform. He too extended his revival into the N, especially Galilee. In keeping with the instructions of the book of the law which Hilkiah the priest found, Josiah kept the Passover and destroyed the cult at Bethel which was in active competition with the temple. Josiah also had visions of restoring the political sovereignty of Judah over all the land. So when Pharaoh Necho marched through the land to help the dying embers of the Assyrian Empire, Josiah challenged him at Meggido, but lost his life in the battle.

Josiah's son Jehoahaz was deposed by Pharaoh Necho, who set up Jehoiakim as a puppet king. Jehoiakim became the vassal of the new Babylonian monarch Nebuchadnezzar. In due course he rebelled against the Chaldeans, but soon died, and his 18-year-old son Jehoiachin was taken into captivity by Nebuchadnezzar

The Babylonians carried away 10,000 captives, all the mighty men of valor, the craftsmen and smiths, and left only the poorest of the land (II Kgs 24:14).

Nebuchadnezzar now set up Zedekiah, Jehoiachin's uncle, as king. He was destined to be the last king of the house of David. Provoked by another rebellion Nebuchadnezzar laid seige to the city of Jerusalem, and in Zedekiah's eleventh year famine prevailed so severely that Zedekiah made an attempt to escape. He was captured and witnessed the slaying of his sons before his own eyes were gouged out. The house of the Lord and all the city were burned. Not a single important city of Judah was left unburned.

At Lachish pieces of broken pottery have been found inscribed with messages from various army officials, which indicate something of the restriction of movement experienced by the Judean army during the years preceding the fall of Jerusalem (ANET, p. 321). Administrative documents found at the Ishtar gate at Babylon reveal how Jehoiachin and his five sons and other captives with him were provided for by the Babylonians (ANET, p. 308). Indeed, the post-Exilic Jewish community in Babylon fared well for many years and became a much more important Jewish community than that in Judea.

With the fall of Jerusalem in 586 B.C. Judah ceased to be a kingdom and became a small province of the Arabaya satrapy of the Persian Empire. Later, Zerubbabel, a descendant of David, became the civil ruler of this province, but never again did a Judean king of the house of David rule in Jerusalem. By NT times the messianic hope for restoration of the monarchy under the house of David ran high, but the NT teaches that this aspect of God's promise to David still awaits fulfillment (Lk 1:32 – 33; Acts 2:30 – 31; 15:15 – 16; Rom 11:26).

See Chronology, OT; Judah; Israel, Kingdom of.

E. B. S.

JUDAIZERS (jōo′dĭ-īz′ẽrs). An extrabiblical term for those who acted like Jews and/or sought so to influence others, based on Paul's charge that Peter's attitude would force Gentiles "to Judaize" (Gr. *'ioudaizein*, "to live like Jews," Gal 2:14, RSV).

Commentaries refer to men as Judaizers who sought to enforce Jewish circumcision and other legalisms upon Gentiles, e.g., the "false brethren" who wanted to bring the whole church into the bondage of the law (Gal 2:4), and those who taught "unless you are circumcised . . . you cannot be saved" (Acts 15:1 ff., RSV). Paul attacked Judaizers in Galatia who "would compel you to be circumcised" (Gal 6:12, RSV). In a few places (Acts 11:2; Gal 2:12; Tit 1:10) "they of the circumcision" seems to refer not to Jews generally but Judaizers specifically (cf. RSV's "circumcision party").

They may have taught that one had to become Jewishly legalistic to receive grace, and did teach that one had to live legalistically despite grace. The Jerusalem council (Acts 15; perhaps Gal 2:1 – 10?) supported Paul as over against those who carried their scruples to the extreme of Judaizing.

W. A. A.

JUDAS (jōō'dăs). The name is so spelled in the NT after Gr. *Ioudas*, for the Heb. name Judah (*q.v.*). The latter comes from the Heb. root *yādā* meaning "to give thanks, laud, praise."

1. Judah the son of Jacob and father of the tribe that was known by that name (Gen 35:23), called Judas in NT (Mt 1:2 – 3).

2. Judas (Jude), one of four brothers of Jesus, named along with James, Joses, and Simon as sons of Mary (Mk 6:3; Mt 13:55). Probably author of Epistle of Jude (*q.v.*).

3. Judas Lebbaeus (Mt 10:3) surnamed Thaddaeus (Mt 3:18), one of the 12 apostles, "not Iscariot" (Jn 14:22). *See* Lebbaeus. He is called "Judas of James" (Lk 6:16; Acts 1:13) which is translated "the son of James" in both the RSV and NASB.

4. A Galilean zealot who stirred up rebellion among the Jews *c.* A.D. 6 over the right of the Romans to impose a direct tax upon the Jews. He was destroyed and his followers dispersed by Cyrenius (*q.v.*), proconsul of Syria (cf. Acts 5:37; also Jos *Ant.* xviii.1.6; xx.5.2; *War* ii.8.1; 18:8; vii.8.1). Although his movement failed, there grew out of it the party of the Zealots (*q.v.*).

5. A man with whom Paul lodged in Damascus on "the street called straight" (Acts 9:11).

6. A man surnamed Barsabas and a member of the delegation sent from the Jerusalem church to the church at Antioch in Syria (Acts 15:22, 27, 32). He and Silas had the gift of prophecy with which they encouraged the brethren.

7. There are at least five men who bear this name in the Apocryphal literature.

8. Judas Iscariot. Gr. *Iskariōtēs*, meaning "inhabitant of Kerioth," derived from the Heb. *'ish,* "man," plus *qᵉriyôt,* hence "man of Kerioth." Kerioth is probably to be identified with the modern Khirbet el-Qaryatein, located *c.* 18 miles NE of Beer-sheba, halfway between Maon and Arad, *c.* four and a half miles S of Tell-Ma'in.

He is designated by the stigma "who also betrayed him" (Mt 10:4; Mk 3:19) and "which was the traitor" (Lk 6:16; cf. Jn 18:2, 5) in the list of the 12 apostles chosen by Christ. At the same time he is also called "one of the twelve" (Mk 14:10, 20; Jn 6:71; 12:4). There is no mention of him prior to his choice by Christ.

His position. Judas was appointed treasurer for Christ and the apostolic band (Jn 12:4 – 6; 13:29). He embezzled the funds under his care and became a thief (Jn 12:6). His true character, with its avarice and covetousness, revealed itself at the anointing of Jesus by Mary with the expensive alabaster box of ointment. He pretended, along with that of the other disciples, that his concern had to do with such wastage and protested that it could have been sold for 300 pence and given to the poor (Jn 12:1 – 8; cf. Mt 26:6 – 13; Mk 14:3 – 9).

His career. Though he became a disciple and follower of Jesus, Judas did not accept Him as his Lord and Saviour. He never called Him more than Rabbi (Mt 26:25, NASB). Judas expected Christ to establish an earthly kingdom in which he would have an important position. Till that happened he was happy to enrich himself from the common funds. It undoubtedly troubled him to hear the Lord declare that His was a spiritual kingdom which none could enter except by the Father's enabling (Jn 6:44, 63 – 65). The refusal of Christ to accept an earthly kingdom angered Judas as did Christ's periodic reference to His death. The final incident which drove Judas to betray Jesus was the expensive anointing at Bethany coupled with Christ's clear declarations: "She did it for my burial" (Mt 26:12); "She is come aforehand to anoint my body to the burying" (Mk 14:8); and His admonition, "Let her alone: against the day of my burying hath she kept this" (Jn 12:7). Seeing the end of his hopes and plans, Judas determined to sell his Master for what he could get.

His responsibility. How can we reconcile Christ's knowledge of Judas' character and perfidy, together with the OT prophecies concerning Judas (Ps 41:9; 69:25; 109:8), with any true responsibility on Judas' part for his own action? Two things can be said.

First, Christ's concern. Though Christ chose Judas knowing he would betray Him, still He showed him constant compassion, gave him a complete revelation of Himself and many warnings. He humbly washed Judas' feet along with the other disciples and then said: "Ye are clean, but not all" (Jn 13:10). He sadly told His disciples at the last supper that one of them would betray Him. When they were all bewildered and asked, "Is it I?" Jesus whispered to John that it was the one to whom He should give the sop – that morsel given as an honor by the host at a feast (Jn 13:21 – 26). But this sign of love was of no avail. From none of His great messages and not even from the work of evangelism, when He sent out the Twelve (Mt 10:1 – 11:1; Lk 9:1 – 6), did Christ exclude Judas.

From time to time, even from the first, Jesus had warned Judas. For example, when many had deserted and this brought forth Peter's confession, Jesus openly said, "Have not I chosen you twelve, and one of you is a devil?" (Jn 6:67 – 70). He spoke of the dangers of avarice, covetousness and hypocrisy (Mt 6:20; Lk 12:1 – 3, 15 ff., 22 f.; Mk 7:17, 21 – 22). But it all fell upon a seared conscience. It was surely not Christ's fault that Judas refused to turn from his wicked way. Judas is an example of what sin does in the life of the unsaved unless God exercises sovereign saving grace.

966

Second, the true nature of prophecy and foreordination. How can Judas be condemned for what he did if it had already been foreordained and foretold (Ps 41:9; 69:25; 109:8)? Judas acted in entire freedom. He chose to steal from the common funds; he chose to betray his Master for the 30 pieces of silver paid for a slave (Ex 21:32). He should have known the prophecy of Zechariah (Zech 11:12). If he did, he ignored it. God foresaw this action on Judas' part and chose to let him act according to his fallen freedom—He foreordained it be so. There was, therefore, no curtailment of Judas' freedom or his responsibility, any more than there is of any other man's.

Judas' end. Before the supper the devil had already put it in Judas' heart to betray Jesus (Jn 13:2) and as soon as Judas took the sop "Satan entered into him" (Jn 13:27).Hurrying to the chief priests, he said that he would lead them to Christ and identify Him with a kiss. Since he knew the secret of the garden he was able to lead a great multitude with swords and staves from the chief priests, and coming up to Jesus "kissed him" (Mt 26:49; Mk 14:45). Jesus reached out in a last word of love and said, "Friend, why art thou come?" (Mt 26:50).

After Judas saw Christ condemned to be crucified, he was filled with remorse (Mt 27:3 f.), and coming to the chief priests and elders he confessed his crime, saying, "I have betrayed innocent blood" (v.4). Then he went out and committed suicide by hanging himself. When Peter says, "This man purchased a field with the reward of iniquity; and falling headlong, he burst asunder in the midst" (Acts 1:18), we can accept Edersheim's reconciliation of the two accounts in Matthew and Acts: In a figurative sense Judas bought the field, the Jews considering him the buyer in that he provided the money they used for it (*Life and Times of Jesus the Messiah,* II, 575 f.).

Many reasons have been given for Judas' actions, such as the following: (1) He was a victim of circumstances. (2) He was predestined to this course and chosen for this deed and, therefore, powerless. (3) He was a deluded soul who thought that by betrayal he could force Jesus to exert His power miraculously and take control. (4) He was a true friend of Jesus trying merely to disillusion Him of His messianic claims. (5) He was a Jewish patriot and thought it better one die than the nation perish. (6) He was a real hero who as Christ's friend tried to save Him from misguided allegiance to the God of the OT (cf. E. S. Bates, *The Friend of Jesus,* New York: Simon & Schuster, 1928). All such explanations are inadequate or in error and leave us unsatisfied.

Judas made his decisions freely, as any other man. Money is "a root of all evil," of evil of every kind (I Tim 6:10), and covetousness as his besetting sin led from thievery to hypocrisy, and finally to betrayal of the Lord of glory for a handful of money.

One thing more must be said. Karl Barth

The traditional Aceldama or field of blood bought with Judas' betrayal money (Ac 1:19). It is located just east of Jerusalem along the Kidron. HFV

pleads for Judas' final salvation, arguing that though he sinned, he sinned no more grievously than Peter when he denied Christ thrice. After all, Barth continues, he did repent according to Scripture and this is all that is required of the sinner (*Church Dogmatics,* Edinburgh: T. & T. Clark, 1957, Vol. II, 2, 458–506). Why does Barth reason in this manner when Scripture says he went to his own place (Acts 1:25), and the psalmist pronounces upon him the most awful curse issued against the wicked recorded in the Bible (Ps 109:6–20)? According to Barth, predestination is not an individual matter. It is centered entirely in Christ. He is the rejected and the elected one, and all are both rejected and elected in Him! If Judas is lost, particularly when he "repented," then Christocentric election fails.

The evangelical Christian must reject such a basis for a case for Judas' salvation since it conflicts with the prophetic curse upon Judas in the psalm, removes all necessity for believing in Christ to be saved, and leads to the false doctrine of the salvation of all men, called universal salvation or ultimate reconciliation. Moreover, repentance involves a "turning" and may in Judas' case simply describe a revulsion over a reprehensible deed and need not also comprehend a personal commitment to Christ.

For the term "son of perdition" as applied to Judas Iscariot, *see* Perdition, Son of.

Bibliography. A. B. Bruce, *The Training of the Twelve,* New York: Armstrong, 1902, Chap. XXIII. Alfred Edersheim, *The Life and Times of Jesus the Messiah,* 2 vols., New York: Longmans, Green & Co., 1901.

R. A. K.

JUDE (jo͞od). Called Judas in the Gr. It is a striking fact that the writer of the last NT letter, the epistle of the apostasy, should have borne the same name as the traitor and greatest apostate, last named of the Twelve (Mt 10:4).

As "brother of James," the Lord's brother (Jude 1; Gal 1:19), Jude was also a brother of the Lord, one of His "mother's children" (Ps 69:8) who are named in Mt 13:55; Mk 6:3. He is therefore not to be confused with the Judas of Jn 14:22 (cf. Lk 6:16), who is called Thaddaeus and Lebbaeus in Mt 10:3. In cherishing the words spoken by the apostles (Jude 17), he clearly implied that he was not one of them.

Jude was characterized by humility, claiming only to be James' brother and a bondslave (lit.) of Jesus Christ; by diligence (v.3), which may have been one reason why the Holy Spirit selected him; by a knowledge of revealed truth (vv. 5 – 7, 11, 17), and by being chosen as the recipient of truth not previously recorded by the pen of inspiration (vv.9, 14 – 15).

S. M. C.

JUDE, EPISTLE OF. The last epistle of the NT was written by Judas (Gr.), the brother of James. They probably were the brothers of our Lord (Mt 13:55; Mk 6:3; *see* Judas; Jude; James). It is coincidental that the author's name, like a title, stands as the first word of the only book devoted entirely to the theme of apostasy, since Judas was also the name of the greatest apostate.

Date and Destination

[The similarity of the epistle of Jude to II Pet 2 raises the question of literary dependence. If we accept II Peter as a genuine writing of Peter (*see* Peter, Second Epistle of), then Jude is probably later, after the fall of Jerusalem (v. 17 refers to the apostles in the past). But it is not likely that Jude is directly dependent on II Peter 2. Most likely both epistles derive from a common tradition of preaching against false teachers. Two grandsons of a certain Judas (probably this Jude) were summoned by the emperor Domitian (A.D. 81 –96) when he was informed that they belonged to the dynastic house of David. He dismissed them when he found they were merely poor farmers and no threat to Rome (Eusebius, Hist. Eccl. iii. 19:1 – 20:6). This event suggests the importance of Jude before the reign of Domitian, since he himself was not involved in the emperor's inquiry.

[It seems clear that this book was written with more regard for Jewish Christian readers than was II Peter. The Exodus (v.5) and OT figures such as Michael, Cain, and Korah's sons (vv. 9, 11) are mentioned in Jude but not in II Peter. Also, the Jewish apocalypse of First Enoch is quoted as prophecy (vv. 14 – 15). Thus, as Reicke (p. 191) argues, the audience Jude had in mind probably consisted of Jewish Christians. – Ed.]

Purpose

As the Acts of the Apostles begins the history of the church on earth, so Jude, in Acts of

the Apostates, brings it to a close, and prepares the reader for the judgments of the book of Revelation.

The inspiration of the epistle is declared in v. 3. While the author was preparing to write about our common salvation, a divine compulsion came upon him to· write instead about contending for the apostolic faith against an early antinomian form of Gnosticism (*q.v.*). The word "needful" (v. 3) is rendered "necessity" in I Cor 9:16.

Content

An astonishing sweep of revelation moves the reader from sin in the dawn of human history (v. 11) to its future judgment at Christ's return (v. 15). It speaks of the sea and the stars (v. 13), of eternal fire and everlasting darkness (vv. 7, 13), of the unseen world of angelic activity (vv. 6, 9).

New truths revealed through Jude include details about the sin of fallen angels (v. 6), Michael's dispute with the devil (v. 9), and the antediluvian prophecy of Enoch (vv. 14 – 15). In citing the book of Enoch and referring to Michael's contest known only from the Assumption of Moses, Jude was not endorsing pseudepigraphical literature. Rather he was employing literature used by the false teachers in question in order to silence them with their own material. Jude merely held that the passages he quoted contain remnants of truth (cf. Paul in Acts 17:28; Gal 3:19; II Tim 3:8; Tit 1:12 f.). *See* Michael.

Subject matter is clustered in orderly fashion about a common center. The salutation matches the benediction. Lest believers fear that they too may fall away from the truth, words of tender love and assurance appear in the opening and closing sentences. Salvation is the theme of vv. 3 and 23. Contending for the faith (v. 3) stands in contrast with building upon the faith (v. 20). "Remember the OT" describes the section beginning with v. 5; "remember the NT"describes the section beginning with v. 17. Apostasy in the supernatural realm (v. 9) is matched by apostasy in the natural realm (vv. 12 – 13).

In the heart of Jude (v. 11) appears an ancient trio of men who perfectly illustrate the three outstanding characteristics of apostasy described in vv. 4, 16, 19, which are further illustrated by three corporate examples in vv. 5 – 7. Verse 11 is typical of the progress of thought found throughout the epistle. Apostates enter upon a wrong way, rush headlong down that way, and perish at its end. The wrong way starts with wandering, ends with open rebellion (v.11, RSV). The *way* of Cain contrasts with Christ the way, the *error* of Balaam with Christ the truth, the *perishing* of Core (Korah, *q.v.*) with Christ the life (Jn 14:6).

The fourfold rule for Christian living given in vv. 20 – 21 ties Jude into other NT books. The Christian is to be building, praying, keeping, and looking. Help for soul winners is found in a threefold classification of unsaved persons (vv. 22 – 23, RSV). Some need compassionate tenderness because they have sincere doubts, some demand urgent boldness because they are close to the fire, some require cautious ministration lest their form of sin contaminate the believer.

In a glorious benediction, Jude suggests the rapture of the Church by suddenly passing from the possibility of present stumbling on a pilgrim pathway to the presentation of the people of God, by their Saviour and Lord, before the presence of His glory in heaven (v. 24).

Outline

I. Salutation, 1 – 2
II. Occasion and Purpose: Exhortation to Defend the Faith, 3 – 4
III. Illustrations of the Necessity of Defending the Faith, 5 – 16
    A. Three historic examples of judgment on corporate apostasy, 5 – 7
    B. Historic examplesand descriptions of false teachers, 8 – 16
IV. Charge to True Christians: How to Defend the Faith, 17 – 23
V. Conclusion: A Doxology, 24 – 25

Bibliography. Charles Bigg, *The Epistles of St. Peter and St. Jude,* ICC, New York: Scribner's, 1901. F. F. Bruce, "Jude, Epistle of," NBD, pp. 675 f. J. B. Mayor, *Epistle of St. Jude and the Second Epistle of St. Peter,* London: Macmillan, 1907. James Moffatt, *The General Epistles,* MNT, Garden City: Doubleday, Doran & Co., 1928. Bo Reicke, *The Epistles of James, Peter, and Jude,* Anchor Bible, Garden City: Doubleday, 1964, pp. 189 – 219. Robert Robertson, "The General Epistle of Jude," NBC, pp. 1161 – 1167.

S. M. C.

JUDEA (jōō-dē′á). In Persian times Judea was a tiny province of the Arabaya Satrapy lying S of Samaria and corresponding approximately to the earlier kingdom of Judah except that the coastal cities were excluded. The term Judea (*Ioudaia*) represents the Hellenizing process which took place following the conquests of Alexander the Great. A network of Hellenistic cities surrounded the province of Judea, and little by little as the country was Hellenized cities took Greek names; many of the upper class and educated Jews encouraged this. II Macc 6:8 speaks of Hellenistic cities within the boundaries of Judea. It is not surprising, then, to find the territory itself called Judea, a Gr. equivalent of the Aram. word for Judah, *yᵉhûd.*

Geographically the territory has natural boundaries on all sides except the N. On the E is the steep ascent from the Jordan and the Dead Sea with dry chalky soil forming the barren wilderness of Judea or Jeshimon. On the W the Shephelah foothills meet the slopes of the

central mountains at a moat-like depression which continues around the S end of Judea to join the chalk wilderness on the E. In the S there is a sudden drop of *c.* 650 feet about halfway between Hebron and Beer-sheba. In the days of Judas Maccabeus (165– 161 B.C.) the garrison at Beth-Zur was the S frontier until he took Hebron and generally overthrew the Idumeans (I Macc 5:3, 65). The N frontier was even less defined, for here there was no protective valley. From early OT times the small tribe of Benjamin marked the N boundary of Judea (Judah).

The Maccabeans under Jonathan extended these boundaries in all directions so that when Pompey, the Roman conqueror, entered Jewish territory the northernmost town in Jewish hands was at Koraea in the Wadi Fari'a. The Romans appointed various Asmonean rulers over Judea until Herod the Great, who *c.* 40 B.C. was declared by the senate to be king of Judea. Following Herod's death Judea, until A.D. 64, was under Roman procurators (imperial governors) except for the brief reign of Herod Agrippa (Acts 26) who was proclaimed king by Claudius Caesar in A.D. 41.

The term Judea may occasionally be used to mean all the region occupied by the Jewish nation. Several of Luke's references seem to be the most conclusive, e.g., "throughout all Judea, beginning from Galilee to this place" (Lk 23:5, RSV; cf. Acts 10:37). Acts 26:20 could better be translated "the whole Jewish country," while Mt 19:1 (cf. Mk 10:1) should not be taken to imply that there was any land E of Jordan that was considered a part of Judea. This passage should be translated, "unto the territory of Judea adjacent to Jordan." The wider sense for Judea, i.e., including Samaria and Galilee, seems to be employed by secular writers of NT times, among them being Strabo, Tacitus and Philo.

See Judah, Kingdom of.

E. B. S.

The Wilderness of Judea. HFV

JUDGE, JUDGING

God As Judge

God is the supreme and absolute Judge of all the earth (Gen 18:25; Ps 94:2; Rom 3:6). God's right to be Judge is based primarily on three divine attributes: (1) God's absolute righteousness (Ps 9:8; 96:13; 98:2, 9); (2) God's infinite knowledge of the secrets of man's life (Job 34:21 – 28; Isa 28:17; Rom 2:16); (3) God's irresistible power to bestow rewards or inflict punishment (Ps 11:5 – 7; Rom 2:1 – 16).

God's throne is eternally set for judging mankind "righteously" (Ps 9:4, 7 – 8; 89:14; 97:2). His unimpeachable character makes any kind of error in His judgments utterly impossible (Gen 18:25; Deut 32:4; Job 8:3; 34:10, 12; Rom 3:5). God always judges "according to truth" (Rom 2:2). He "will render to every man according to his deeds" (Rom 2:6; Rev 20:12). His judgments are not vitiated by such human faults as favoritism (Rom 2:11; I Pet 1:17), superficial appearance (I Sam 16:7; Jn 7:24), fleshly standards (Jn 8:15), or bribe-taking (II Chr 19:7). Thus God's will, not man's, becomes the standard of all judgment. *See* Will of God.

Though the wicked may seem to escape for a while the righteous judgment of God (Ps 10; 73) as they ignore God's present goodness toward them (Rom 2:3 – 4; Acts 14:16 – 17), yet a day is inexorably set in the divine plan (Rom 2:1 – 16) for the judgment of all men (Mt 11:22 – 24; 25:31 – 46; Acts 17:31; II Pet 2:9; 3:7; Rev 20:11 – 15).

Examples of God's judgments may be seen in the following instances: (1) the judgment pronounced upon Adam and Eve and upon all mankind in Eden (Gen 3; Rom 5:12); (2) the destruction of the ancient world by flood (Gen 6 – 8; Lk 17:26 – 27; II Pet 2:5; 3:5 – 6); (3) the destruction of Sodom and Gomorrah (Gen 19; Lk 17:28 – 30; II Pet 2:6); (4) the destruction of Egypt's army (Ex 14); (5) the punishments visited upon Israel at Sinai (Ex 32), in the wilderness (Num 14; 16; 25), and at many subsequent times in her history; (6) the definitive judgment upon Israel for her rejection of her Messiah (Lk 21:20 – 24; I Thess 2:14 – 16); (7) the final punishment upon all those who reject the Lord Jesus Christ (Jn 3:36; 5:24; II Thess 1:8 – 9; Heb 10:26 – 31; 12:25; II Pet 2:1 – 10; 3:7).

The Judge in Israel's Judiciary System

The following stages of development may be clearly seen in Israel's history:

The patriarchal period. Judicial functions were largely in the hands of the family head during this period (Gen 21 – 22; 38:24). God's law, although not officially promulgated as at Sinai, was nevertheless known to the patriarchs. This knowledge was derived from the general knowledge of God's will given to all mankind (Rom 1:18 – 23), from God's law written upon man's heart (Rom 2:14 – 15), and from specific legislation given to man (e.g., Gen 9:5 – 6). Thus the family head became the principal agent in God's plan for transmission of concepts regarding righteousness and justice from one generation to another (Gen 18:19). Back of all this was the resident conviction that the Judge of all the earth shall do right (Gen 18:25).

The early Mosaic period. Moses, fully prepared by his extensive knowledge of worldly matters (Acts 7:21 – 22), was ready for the office of judge that soon was to fall upon him as leader of the people of God redeemed from Egypt. Even while in Egypt, however, he was accused of assuming this office presumptuously as he sought to render justice with his own hands (Ex 2:11 – 15; Acts 7:23 – 28, 35). Nevertheless, the exodus of the people of Israel from Egypt thrust upon them the imperative need for an authoritative judge to adjudicate lawsuits and disputes. This need was fully met by Moses, who was universally recognized by the Israelites as the mouthpiece of God, i.e., as the agent through whom the will of God was made known to the people (Ex 18:15; Num 9:8; 27:5). Thus, after the pattern of Moses, the judgeship in Israel was invested with divine rights that constituted the human judge as God's representative of justice on earth (cf. Ex 21:6, ASV; II Chr 19:6; Ps 82:1, 6; Jn 10:34).

The Jethro episode at Sinai. Jethro, Moses' father-in-law, instinctively sensing the burden that human nature could not long endure with-

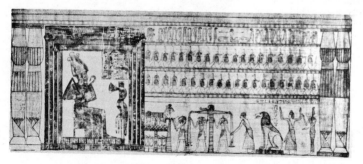

A judgment scene, "weighing of the heart" after death, from the Egyptian *Book of the Dead*, as pictured on an ancient papyrus. ORINST

out help, made some very judicious suggestions to Moses for the betterment of the legal system among the Israelites (Ex 18:17 – 26). The basic elements in Jethro's proposed revision were these: (1) a series of ascending courts; (2) an implicit "supreme court" (in Moses himself); (3) the accessibility of the courts to all the people in "all seasons"; (4) an instructional program regarding the nature and content of the laws; (5) qualifications for those entrusted with the office of judge.

Moses saw immediately the wisdom of Jethro's suggestions; they were all adopted as integral parts of Israel's system of jurisprudence. Subsequent history and legislation, even while at Sinai, simply supplied the details of Jethro's epoch-making wise counsel.

The Sinaitic legislation. The law of Sinai strengthened the revisions suggested by Jethro in the following ways: (1) by outlining more specifically the qualifications of judges (Deut 1:13 – 18; 16:18 – 20); (2) by giving preeminence to the tribe of Levi as custodians and interpreters of the law (Deut 17:8 – 13, 18 – 20); (3) by giving specific principles for the guidance of the court in rendering a verdict (Deut 19:15 – 21; 21:1 – 9; 25:1 – 3).

However, it must be admitted that there were allowable fluctuations in Israel's system of jurisprudence. There were cases, for example, when the congregation of all Israel became the absolute judge (Num 35:12, 22 – 28). At a later date, even the people could veto the unwise oath of their king (I Sam 14:24 – 46). It seems quite certain, in periods of Israel's history after Sinai, that historical and political factors influenced materially the kind of justice prevalent in any particular era.

The period of the judges. This period, graphically described in the book of Judges (*q.v.*), constitutes a transition from the rule of Moses and Joshua to the rule of kings in Israel. God raised up during this period persons especially endowed to judge a part or all of Israel (Jud 2:16 – 23; 3:9 – 10; I Sam 12:9 – 11; II Sam 7:11). The following statements may be made concerning these judges: (1) They were raised up by God in times of crisis (Jud 2:16 – 23; cf. Ps 106:43 – 45; Acts 13:20). (2) They were especially empowered by the Holy Spirit (Jud 3:10; 13:25; 14:19; cf. Num 11:25 – 29; 24:2). (3) They continued in office until the time of their death (Jud 2:19; I Sam 4:18; 7:15). (4) They rejected the temptation to establish hereditary rulership over Israel (Jud 8:22 – 23). (5) They considered their judicial functions as involving them in spiritual leadership over the people (I Chr 17:6; cf. II Sam 7:7).

The periods of the united and divided kingdoms. It is indeed difficult to trace any consistent system of jurisprudence during the long period from Samuel, the last judge, to the end of the OT dispensation. Many of the safeguards in the Sinaitic legislation against the perversion of justice were undoubtedly neglected under wicked kings or in times of religious declension.

The columned entrance to the basilica at the forum of Pompeii, where civil and commercial court cases were heard. HFV

The prophets often complain against such perversion (Isa 1:23; 5:23; 10:1 – 2; Amos 5:12; 6:12; Mic 3:9 – 11; 7:3).

Although Samuel had performed his duties as judge impeccably, and had even established a system of circuit courts (I Sam 7:15 – 16), nevertheless, his sons corrupted justice (8:1 – 3) and thus gave added weight to the people's desire to change from judgeship to kingship (8:4 – 22; 12:1 – 25).

However, even after the kings became the absolute judges, local or subordinate courts, after the precedent set by Samuel, were established by David and Solomon (I Chr 23:3 – 4; 26:29 – 32). It is to Solomon's credit that he sensed the need of divine wisdom in judging Israel (I Kgs 3:9). This wisdom was soon manifested in a most difficult case brought before him for adjudication (I Kgs 3:16 – 28). Nevertheless, some kings were notoriously wicked in the execution of justice (I Kgs 21:1 – 16; II Kgs 21:16). Lawlessness arose spontaneously in such times (Hab 1:2 – 4).

Both David (II Sam 1:15 – 16; 4:9 – 12) and Solomon (I Kgs 2:5 – 9, 13 – 46) pronounced sentences and executed offenders in a very decisive manner. The precedent set by these two notable kings probably became the standard of justice throughout most of OT history (e.g., II Kgs 11:12 – 20), even in the case of unjust judgments (e.g., I Kgs 21:7 – 16).

Jehoshaphat, it appears, was a most efficient king in the system of jurisprudence which he established throughout his kingdom (II Chr 19:4 – 11). It is even probable that the courts he placed in "the fortified cities of Judah, city by city" (v.5, ASV) were what we would call today superior courts. Jerusalem itself became, in this system, a kind of supreme court, with Amariah, the high priest, as chief justice (vv. 8 – 11). Thus Jehoshaphat finalized to a large extent the OT judicial system, a system which found its ultimate fulfillment in the Jewish Sanhedrin of NT times (e.g., Acts 5:27 – 41; 6:10 – 15; 23:1 – 10).

Christ As Judge

The various aspects of Christ's judgeship may be set forth in the following manner:

As messianically endowed. The prophets depict the coming Messiah as possessing all the attributes of a true judge (Ps 89:14; 97:2; Isa 11:1 – 5). This One was destined to bring in "everlasting righteousness" (Dan 9:24) in a world where justice could hardly be found (Isa 59:1 – 21).

As legislator of true judgment. One of the first acts performed by Christ after His mission on earth had been inaugurated was to set forth the true meaning of the law of God. This was done in His Sermon on the Mount (Mt 5 – 7), in which He categorically corrected the false dogmas of the Jews imposed upon the law of God. Christ's whole ministry was one of judgment upon the Jews for their perversion of God's law (e.g., Mt 15:1 – 20).

As non-participant in man's litigations. Christ refused to become a judge in matters affecting man's material possessions (Lk 12: 13 – 14). Even while before Pilate, He refrained from any involvement in the case against Him on the ground that His kingdom was "not of this world" (Jn 18:33 – 39).

As refiner of false judges. This implication of Christ's judgeship had prophetic antecedents (Mal 3:1 – 6). With all the passion of a true judge, Christ pronounced devastating judgments against the Pharisees and other leaders of the Jews as false judges "sitting in Moses' seat" (Mt 23; Lk 12:57 – 59; Jn 7:24).

As sent to save rather than to judge. Christ's advent to earth was designed to bring salvation to men, not to judge men (Jn 3:16 – 21; 12:46 – 47). This does not mean, however, that Christ refused to judge evil now (Jn 8:15 – 16). But the present time is definitely "the day of salvation" (II Cor 6:2).

As custodian of the Father's judgment. Christ plainly taught that all judgment had been committed unto Him by His heavenly Father (Jn 5:22, 30). Even now, before the future judgments, there is a decisive exercise of Christ's definitive judgment against those who refuse to accept Him as Messiah and Lord (Lk 19:41 – 44; 21:20 – 24; Jn 9:39). Such men are "judged already" (Jn 3:18; 5:24).

As final judge. Christ will be the judge of all mankind (Mt 7:21 – 23; 25:36 – 46). Christ Himself will be the righteous judge (II Tim 4:8) in that last day when His word will be the basis of man's judgment (Jn 12:48). He is the One "ordained of God to be the Judge of the living and the dead" (Acts 10:42, ASV; cf. 17:31; II Tim 4:1; I Pet 4:5).

The Christian As Judge and As Judged

The various aspects of this subject may be summed up thus:

Censorious judgment. This kind of criticism comes under the prohibition expressed by Christ in Mt 7:1 – 4 and Lk 6:37 – 42. "Judge not" (the aorist negative imperative in the Gr.)

The Basilica Julia at Corinth, where Christians probably launched lawsuits against other Christians. HFV

states a definitive prohibition against the pernicious habit of criticizing others while passing over our own faults (cf. Jas 4:11 – 12).

Civil litigations. Two sides of this subject are presented in the NT. On the one side, Paul was certainly justified in demanding as a civil right before Roman authorities his complete vindication against the false charges of the Jews (Acts 25:9 – 12). This was at least a minimum benefit of his Roman citizenship (Acts 16:37 – 39; 22:27 – 29; cf. Rom 13:1 – 7). On the other side, Christians are urged to undergo injustice rather than to engage in lawsuits against other Christians before unbelievers (I Cor 6:1, 5 – 8). Paul's case before the Roman authorities was entirely different from the situation existing among believers in the Corinthian church. Paul's appeal to Caesar was thrust upon him as the only alternative to almost certain death at Jerusalem. The Christians at Corinth were in no such exigency.

Questions of conscience. The following principles may clarify this somewhat difficult area of Christian conduct: (1) The freedom of the new man in Christ must be maintained (Jn 8:32, 36; Rom 8:15; Gal 2:4; 5:1, 13; Col 2:16 – 23). (2) This freedom, however, must not degenerate into license or licentiousness (Gal 5:13; I Pet 2:16; II Pet 2:7, 10, 14; Jude 4). (3) The sometimes dubious or debatable area between freedom and licentiousness may be traversed by Christian love for "the weaker brother" (Rom 14:1 – 23; I Cor 8:9 – 13; 10:23 – 33; Gal 5:13 – 15), by a proper concern for one's own weakness (Gal 6:1) and proneness toward superiority (Jas 2:8 – 13), and by a proper application of Christ's "judge not" (Mt 7:1 – 5; cf. Jas 4:11 – 12).

Self-judgment. The Christian is called upon not only to judge or examine himself (II Cor 13:5) but also to realize that God Himself is the Examiner (I Thess 2:4; cf. Ps 139:1 – 6, 23). This self-judgment should be a part of the spiritual preparation for the Lord's Supper (I Cor 11:27 – 34). When properly conducted by the assistance of the Holy Spirit (Rom 8:26 – 27), this self-examination puts the Lord's Supper in its true perspective and thus obviates the divine judgment visited upon those who fail to discriminate between the ordinary meal and the Lord's Supper.

Judgments concerning faith and practice. Christians are required to "examine everything carefully" and to "hold fast to that which is good" (I Thess 5:21, NASB). They are also obligated to "test the spirits to see whether they are from God" (I Jn 4:1, NASB). Even in Christian gatherings they must "pass judgment" on what they hear (I Cor 14:29, NASB). The Corinthian Christians were commanded to pass immediate judgment on the immorality existing in their membership (I Cor 5:1 – 8). Even the passing stranger is not to be entertained if it is ascertained that he is not true in the faith (II Jn 10 – 11). And an anathema must be pronounced against those who would introduce a different kind of gospel (Gal 1:9). The principle back of all this required spiritual discrimination is that the Christian should never bring the Lord's judgment upon himself because of the things in doctrine or in practice which he approves (Rom 14:22).

The spiritual man of I Cor 2:14-15. This man is above the judgment of the unregenerate man for the simple reason that the two men are on different levels of spiritual insight and ability. The unregenerate man is a child of the devil (Jn 8:44; I Jn 3:10 – 12), devoid of the Holy Spirit (Jude 19), spiritually dead (Eph 2:1, 5; Col 2:13) and spiritually blind (Mt 23:16, 24; Jn 9:39 – 41), and a willing captive of sin (Rom 6:6, 16 – 23; II Pet 2:14). Thus such a person is morally unable to pass judgment on the spiritual man who has been resurrected into a new life in Christ (Col 3:1 – 3), indwelt by the Holy Spirit (Rom 8:11) and by Christ (II Cor 13:5), and completely transformed as a new creature (II Cor 5:17).

Judgment in abeyance. In I Cor 4:3 – 5 Paul speaks of three judgments: (1) by "man's judgment," i.e., by a day in any human court (NASB) or by the world's public opinion; (2) by his own conscience, which while not condemning him is still inadequate to justify (i.e., definitively approve) his stewardship; and (3) by the Lord Jesus, who at His second coming will render full judgment. Thus the believer is urged to judge nothing, i.e., to pass judgment on no one else's ministry, until that future event. All the unknown factors that now motivate man's actions will then be revealed by the Lord; and then each man, beholding the justice of the verdict rendered, will have his praise from God (cf. Jas 5:9).

The Christian and future judgments. The Scriptures reveal a threefold relationship of the believer to future judgments: (1) as one who will be judged to determine his rewards (I Cor 3:11 – 15; II Cor 5:10; II Tim 4:1, 8), but not concerning his salvation (Jn 3:18; 5:24); (2) as one who will participate in the judgment of the world and of angels (I Cor 6:2 – 3; cf. Dan 7:18, 22, 27; Mt 19:28; Rev 2:26 – 27; 3:21); (3) as one who will not be judged with the wicked before the Great White Throne of God, because his name is found written in the book of life (Rev 20:11 – 15). *See* Life, Book of; Judgments.

Bibliography. William A. Beardslee, "Judging," HDB rev., pp. 541 f. A. Marzal, "The Provincial Governor at Mari," JNES, XXX (1971), 186 – 217. Donald A. McKenzie, "The Judge of Israel," VT, XVII (1967), 118 – 121.

W. B.

JUDGE, THE. A civil judge or magistrate is first mentioned in Israel under Moses when Jethro suggested that judges be appointed to relieve Moses in his administrative responsibilities (Ex 18:13 – 26). Subsequently, Israel organized into units within each tribe with a qualified man as judge. These men were to judge righteously, fearlessly, and impartially (Deut 1:16 f.). Only the most important cases were brought before Moses (Deut 1:12 – 18; 21:2). Note also the organization of Israel in Num 1 – 10. Under Joshua a similar plan was followed (Deut 16:18 – 20; 17:2 – 13; 19: 15 – 20; Josh 8:33; 23:2; 24:1; I Sam 8:1).

The era following Joshua's death portrays a modified situation as described in the book of Judges. Here the principal leaders, or judges, of the people were those who had primarily the mission of delivering the Israelites from oppressing nations (Jud 2:16). Charismatically endowed by the Spirit of God they were "saviors" (Jud 3:9, ASV), empowered to save and preserve Israel (Jud 6:34 – 36).

The Heb. word *shōpēṭ* translated "judge" seems to have been a term borrowed from the Canaanites. It appears in the Ugaritic literature as *spt* with the sense of "ruler" or "judge" and a synonym for "king." Later, the chief magistrates of Carthage, descendants of the Phoenicians or Canaanites, bore this title for centuries, and were known to the Romans as *suffetes*. Thus the Heb. term properly includes the concept of leader as well as arbitrator.

The oppressing invaders during the era between the Conquest and the monarchy in Israel were primarily Mesopotamians, Moabites, Canaanites, Midianites, Ammonites, and Philistines. The outstanding judges who were used to counter them were Othniel, Ehud, Deborah and Barak, Gideon, and Samson as narrated in the book of Judges. Additional judges concerning whom very little information is available were Shamgar, Abimelech, Tola, Jair, Ibzan, Elon, and Abdon. *See* individual names. Some of the judges of this era are listed in the book of Hebrews (chap. 11) as heroes of faith. The opening chapters of I Samuel (cf. 4:18) indicate that Eli served as judge of Israel for 40 years. Samuel not only led the Israelites in a successful resistance to Philistine oppression, but also established an organized circuit court. Although he appointed his sons as judges, the changing conditions marked a transition to an organized kingdom requiring the anointing of a king (I Sam 7:15 – 8:5).

During the monarchy the king became the supreme judge in civil matters (II Sam 15:2; I Kgs 3:9, 28). Cases were tried by the king in the palace gate (I Kgs 7:7), but local courts were likewise functioning. David assigned Levites to judicial office and appointed 6,000 men as officers and judges (I Chr 23:4; 26:29). Jehoshaphat enlarged the judicial system in Judah, appointing priests and judges in fortified cities with a supreme court in Jerusalem where religious matters were under the high priest and civil matters under the prince of Judah (II Chr 19:5 – 8).

Prophets frequently asserted that justice was corrupted by bribery and false witness (Isa 1:23; 5:23; 10:1; Amos 5:12; 6:12; Mic 3:11; 7:3). Kings were often unjust in their treatment of the prophet who spoke for God (I Kgs 22:26 – 27; II Kgs 21:16; Jer 36:26). Cf. also I Kgs 21:1 – 13, where the law was disregarded by Ahab and Jezebel and false witnesses were used to the advantage of the king.

See also Judge, Judging; Judges, Book of.

S. J. S.

JUDGES, BOOK OF. The title is derived from the word "judges" (*shōpₑṭîm*, Jud 2:16), since the activities of the judges are recorded in this book. In historical sequence it covers the period of Israel's history between Joshua and Samuel.

The era of the judges was a period in which the Israelites as God's covenant people were frequently in need of divine deliverance. Through Moses the Israelites had experienced release from Egyptian bondage and received the divine revelation as recorded in the Pentateuch. Under Joshua the next generation partially conquered and occupied the land of Canaan. As subsequent generations succumbed to apostasy and idolatry which resulted in oppression, they appealed to God for deliverance. Once more the mighty acts of God were displayed as a number of judges (*see* Judge, The) responded to the call of God to lead the Israelites in military exploits to rout the oppressing nations. These religious-political cycles of sin, sorrow, supplication, and salvation occurred repeatedly, and may have been limited geographically and may have overlapped chronologically.

Purpose

Thus the purpose of the book in presenting this history is definitely didactic, to teach divine retribution upon a sinning people, God's mercy upon repentance, and the futility of man-centered and idolatrous governments.

The ministry of Eli and Samuel, recorded in the opening chapters of I Samuel, concludes this era of the judges. Religion had reached a low ebb and Israel was threatened by the Phil-

istines in spite of Samson's exploits. Through the leadership of Samuel, who served as the law judge, came a revival so that Israel was sufficiently unified to stem the tide of Philistine aggression and occupation.

Outline

Chronology

The chronology of the book of Judges is not so simple as it might appear to the casual reader. A simple addition of the years allotted to each judge totals about 410 years. Even with an early date (*c.* 1400 B.C.) for Joshua, it is impossible to include all these years before David (*c.* 1000 B.C.) and allow time for Eli, Samuel, and Saul. Consequently the careers of these judges overlapped or may even have been contemporaneous. Among numerous studies of this chronology is that of J. B. Payne (*An Outline of Hebrew History,* 1954, p. 79), which accounts for this era beginning with Othniel in 1381 B.C. and ends with the career of Samuel in 1050 B.C. Samson and Jephthah may have been contemporaneous. Scholars who advocate a date of 1300 B.C. or later for Joshua, of necessity compress the time for the judges to two centuries or less. The references in I Kgs 6:1 and Jud 11:26 seem to favor the early date for Joshua, allowing for a longer period of time between the entrance of Israel into Canaan and establishment of the kingdom.

Archaeology

Archaeology has offered significant information to provide further insights on the historical developments in Palestine during the period surveyed in the book of Judges. The initial success of Joshua in the conquest of Canaan may be reflected in the Tell el-Amarna letters written a few decades afterward. Numerous

The Valley of the Dancers, where the events of Judges 21:21 are supposed to have taken place. HFV

city-states had been defeated and they had appealed to Egypt for help. This could account for Joshua's capture of such cities as Lachish and Debir (c. 1400 B.C.), their reoccupation by Canaanites, and their subsequent destruction by fire (c. 1230 – 1200 B.C.), as indicated by archaeology. Deborah and Barak must have judged in the 13th cen., because they fought against Hazor; the occupation of the huge lower city and of Level XIII of the *tell* came to an end in the second half of that century. Abimelech, the son of Gideon, burned Shechem, and this destruction has been dated to the 12th cen. B.C. Very likely Egypt continued to control the main trade routes along the coast of Palestine and through Galilee into the 12th cen. Witness to this are the inscriptions of the name of Rameses III (1198 – 1167 B.C.) in such cities as Beth-shean and Megiddo. Garstang in his study (*Joshua-Judges,* 1931) suggests a synchronism between Egyptian control and the periods of rest as indicated in the book of Judges.

Author

The author of this book is unknown. Internal evidence points to the years after the death of Samson and after the coronation of King Saul (Jud 17:6; 18:1; 19:1; 21:25) but before the conquest of Jerusalem by David as the time of composition (c. 1100 – 1000 B.C.; cf. Jud 1:21; 18:1; 19:1). The assertion in Jud 1:29 that the Canaanites were still in control of Gezer dates the writing prior to the time when the king of Egypt conquered this city (c. 970 B.C.) and gave it to Solomon. Some of the content, such as the song of Deborah, reflects the date of composition as having been at the time of the event. It is possible that Samuel or one of his disciples may have compiled the history of this period as given in the book of Judges. *See also* Ruth.

Bibliography. Gleason L. Archer, Jr., SOTI, pp. 262 – 267. C. F. Burney, *The Book of Judges,* 2nd ed., London: Rivington, 1930. Arthur E. Cundall, *Judges,* and Leon Morris, *Ruth,* Tyndale OT Commentaries, London: IVCF, 1968. John J. Davis, *Conquest and Crisis,* Grand Rapids: Baker, 1970. John Garstang, *Joshua-Judges,* London: Constable & Co., 1931. *Joshua, Judges, Ruth,* KD. C. F. Kraft, "Judges, Book of," IDB, II, 1013 – 1023. J. Barton Payne, "Judges, Book of," NBD, pp. 676 – 679. Charles F. Pfeiffer, "Judges," WBC, pp. 233 – 265. M. B. Rowton, "Chronology: Ancient Western Asia," CAH, 2nd ed., fascicle # 4, pp. 67 ff. G. Ernest Wright, *Shechem: The Biography of a Biblical City,* New York: McGraw-Hill, 1964, pp. 123 – 128. Y. Yadin, "Hazor," TAOTS, pp. 244 – 263.

S. J. S.

JUDGMENT HALL. Judgment hall (Gr. *praitō-rion*) related to the Latin word *praetorium* which originally referred to the praetor's (military officer's) tent in camp with its surroundings. The Gr. word is translated "praetorium" almost exclusively in the ASV and RSV. In the KJV it is translated "common hall" in Mt 27:27; "praetorium" in Mk 15:16; "judgment hall" in Jn 18:28, 33; 19:9; Acts 23:35; and "palace" in Phil 1:13.

The term judgment hall, or praetorium, came eventually to be applied to the residence of the civil governor in provinces and cities of the Roman Empire. More particularly, this was the part of the residence where justice was administered, or the court at the entrance to the praetorian residence. The judgment hall (praetorium) in the capital of a province was usually a large palace or palatial residence.

In Jerusalem, Pilate's judgment hall, where

Jesus was brought to trial, was either the fortified palace of Herod the Great or the Tower of Antonia. According to Josephus it was Herod's palace at the W side of the walled city, but according to some church traditions and a number of modern scholars, it was the Tower of Antonia NW of the temple. The discovery of large paving stones at the site of the latter corresponding to the Pavement of Jn 19:13 now seems to be conclusive (*see* Gabbatha; Pavement). Acts 23:35 indicates that Herod's palace in Caesarea was used as a praetorium by the Roman governor Felix.

In Phil 1:13, the Gr. word *praitōrion* is translated "palace" in the KJV but the ASV, RSV and NASB paraphrase slightly to clarify Paul's statement that the cause of his imprisonment had become well-known "throughout the whole praetorian guard and to everyone else" (NASB). Here it refers either to the guard assigned to Paul during his house arrest in Rome (Acts 28:16, 30) or, as F. F. Bruce (*The Letters of Paul: An Expanded Paraphrase,* Grand Rapids: Eerdmans, 1965, pp. 160, 165) and other scholars have suggested, to the governor's headquarters in Ephesus for the Roman province of Asia.

B. M. W.

The presumed pavement of Pilate's judgment hall (Jn 19:13). Giovanni Trimboli

JUDGMENTS. The principal words translated "judgment" are Heb. *mishpāṭ* and Gr. *krima* and *krisis.* Derived from *shāphaṭ,* "to judge," the Heb. word denotes a dynamic "right-doing" as the result of distinguishing between the right and the wrong (I Kgs 3:9).

Among God's covenant people judgment is based upon His revelation and instruction (*tôrâ*) to them. It is to be a religious activity (Mic 6:8), to punish the wrongdoer, vindicate the righteous, and deliver the weak from unjust condemnation, in order to perform real justice (Isa 1:17; Zech 8:16 – 17). *Mishpāṭ* is fundamental right, frequently occurring in the sense of a law, being usually translated then as "ordi-

nance" (II Kgs 17:34, 37; Isa 58:2). God's judgment is perfectly just, not arbitrary. It is "a blend of reliability and clemency, of law and love" (Morris, *The Biblical Doctrine of Judgment,* p. 21). The judgment of the Lord is the outworking of His mercy and of His wrath, bringing deliverance to the meek (Ps 25:9; Deut 10:18; Isa 30:18 f.) as well as doom to the wicked (Deut 32:41). The OT "concept of judgment has a legal basis, arising as it does from that judicial activity of discrimination in accordance with right which separates the righteous from the wicked and takes action as a result" (*ibid.,* p. 29).

In the NT, when the two Gr. words can be distinguished in meaning, *krisis* suggests more the process of judgment, how it works (Jn 3:19), whereas *krima* denotes condemnation, the sentence pronounced by the judge (Rom 2:2 – 3; Jas 3:1; Jude 4).

Judgments of Men

The Scriptures teach that, under proper limitations, men should be free to form and express private judgments relative to the Word of God, to the state, and to their fellowmen. Men are to govern one another as well as to judge themselves.

1. Protestants generally hold that the Bible is a book for the people, to be read and understood by the people themselves. The OT prophets spoke to the entire nation, and the Gospels and epistles were for popular use and instruction. The Holy Spirit is the ultimate Teacher for every man (I Jn 2:20 – 21, 27). Roman Catholics have maintained that the church is the divinely authorized and infallible interpreter of Scripture revelation, and that the individual must submit unreservedly to the judgment of the church. Protestants claim that not tradition and formal papal decisions but the Bible alone is the only and sufficient rule of faith and practice.

2. Civil or human government is clearly recognized by the Scriptures as resting upon divine authority (Gen 9:5 – 6; Ex 18:13 – 26). Obedience to the state in general, therefore, is a commandment of God (Rom 13:1 – 5; I Pet 2:13 – 15). But it is equally clear that in order to demand obedience from citizens or subjects, the state must confine its action within its proper sphere. The function of human government is to protect life and property, and to preserve social order. All rulers and judges are to remember that they are subject to the judgment of God, and should exercise their office equitably and with due moderation. When the state, however, attempts to enforce assent to religious doctrines, or to enact laws which require disobedience to the commandments of God, then the right of private judgment must be asserted. As Peter declared, "We ought to obey God rather than men" (Acts 5:29).

3. Private, unofficial judgment of others is necessary in order to protect one's own life and character. We must constantly form estimates

of the conduct and character of others for our own guidance and safety and usefulness. For example, we are to beware of false prophets whom we shall be able to recognize by their fruits (Mt 7:15 – 20). We are to prove or examine all things, holding fast to what is good and avoiding the evil (I Thess 5:21 – 22). We need to be able to discriminate, abounding in knowledge and discernment (Phil 1:9 – 10, NEB, NASB marg.). The prohibition of judging (Mt 7:1) is not opposed to this (cf. 7:6), but refers to criticizing and condemning. We are forbidden to usurp God's place as judge, or to pass rash, unjust, uncharitable judgments on others (see "Judgment," *Unger's Bible Dictionary*, pp. 620 f.).

4. The Christian is told to examine himself (II Cor 13:5), to judge his own walk. This self-judgment refers to the believer's criticism of his own ways (I Cor 11:31 – 32), and it results in his seeing and confessing his sin (I Jn 1:7 – 9). Restoration to full fellowship through the advocacy of Jesus Christ ensues (I Jn 2:1 – 2).

Judgments of God

1. The basis of divine judgment. This depends for the unsaved entirely on their works. They are not without a knowledge of the truth for they are: (*a*) the recipients of general revelation and therefore without excuse (Rom 1:18 – 20); (*b*) they once knew God but changed what they knew into a lie (vv. 21 – 24); (*c*) they have the work of the law written in their hearts (Rom 2:15). God will judge them according to the truth (Rom 2:2); according to their deeds (v. 6); by the law if they have it, and by the work of the law written in their hearts if they do not (vv. 12 – 15).

Some will be punished with few stripes and some many, according to the degree of their responsibility and the seriousness of their sins (Lk 12:48), but none of them will be saved (Rom 2:19 – 20; Eph 2:9).

For the believers there remains only a judgment of valuation and rewards, since Christ has kept the law in their stead and suffered and died in their place (Isa 53:5, 10 – 11) under the penalty of the broken law (II Cor 5:21).

2. The description of the divine judgments. Theologians have often maintained that there is one general judgment. This is a tenet strongly entrenched in Christian theology, more the result of rationalization than of thorough biblical exegesis. But a careful inductive study of all the Scriptures involved demonstrates that there are at least seven distinct divine judgments described in the Bible.

a. The judgment of the cross. Christ as our substitutionary atonement bore the punishment for our sins on the cross (Isa 53; Heb 10:10 – 12; I Pet 2:24). He bore the curse of sin (Gal 3:13) and became our sinbearer (Jn 1:29; II Cor 5:21; Heb 9:26 – 28), and before He commended His spirit finally to God He could say, "It is finished" (Jn 19:30). When we acknowledge our sin and accept Christ as our Saviour, God identifies us with His Son and sees us as having both died in our Representative and risen in Him in newness of life (Rom 5:12 ff.; 6:3 – 5; I Cor 15:22). Because of this we read in Rom 8:1, "There is therefore now no condemnation [judgment to damnation] to them which are in Christ Jesus." As a result, the believer will never again be judged for his sins. God has put them behind His back and they shall be remembered no more (Isa 38:17; 43:25; Ps 103:12; Jer 31:34; Heb 10:17).

b. The judgment of the believer's walk. This comes in the form of divine correction and chastisement (I Cor 11:30 – 32; Jn 15:1 – 8; Heb 12:3 – 15). God inflicts it on the Christian so that he may not be judged with the world (I Cor 11:32). It may take the form of severe afflictions at the hand of Satan in order to subjugate his fleshly nature (I Cor 5:5). It may end in the removal of the Christian by death if he does not repent (I Cor 11:30). The "sin unto death" spoken of in I Jn 5:16, however, is punished by eternal death in the case of the one who deliberately continues in sin (Heb 10:26) and persistently denies the incarnation of God's Son (I Jn 2:22; 4:3; II Jn 7) or His deity. *See* Sin unto Death.

c. The judgment of the believer's works. Since his sins have already been judged in the person of his substitute, the Lord Jesus Christ (Rom 8:3; II Cor 5:21; I Pet 2:24), the Christian is not judged again for his sins along with the world (I Cor 5:5). He must, however, appear or be made manifest (ASV) before what is called the judgment seat (Gr. *bēma*) of Christ (II Cor 5:10; Rom 14:10), "that each one may receive the things done in the body, according to what he hath done, whether it be good or bad" (ASV). His works must be openly displayed at the *bēma* or judge's tribunal (cf. Acts 25:6, 10, 17, NASB), also the stand or platform in an amphitheater where awards were given, as at Caesarea (Acts 12:21). It is quite necessary that the service of every child of God be scrutinized and evaluated (Mt 12:36; II Cor 9:6; Gal 6:7, 9; Eph 6:8; Col 3:24 – 25). As a result of this judgment of the believer's works there will be reward or loss of reward. Even in the latter case, if his work is burned up, the truly born-again believer will be saved, "yet so as through fire" (I Cor 3:12 – 15).

Since we are to reign with Christ and some will be appointed rulers of five and some of ten cities in His millennial kingdom, this judgment must occur prior to the return of the saints to rule with Christ (Zech 14:5; Jude 14; Rev 20:4). It may be a continuous process, each saint being judged for his works immediately on going to be with the Lord (I Cor 3:12 – 15). Or the judgment seat may be set up in heaven after the rapture of the Church and before Christ's glorious return to earth to establish His reign at Jerusalem. *See* Judgment Seat.

d. The judgment of Israel. The Lord will judge His chosen nation Israel when He returns with all His saints, before setting up His kingdom (Ezk 20:33 – 44; Mal 3:2 – 6). This action is the final stage of His continuing judgment of national Israel, foretold so often (e.g., Deut 28:15 – 68; Isa 1; 3; 5; etc.; Jer 2 – 9) and carried out so severely in history.

e. The judgment of the nations. This is the most difficult judgment to place and define. It is spoken of in two parts. First, that poured out by Christ as He comes to punish those nations that have united under the Antichrist to destroy Israel (Joel 3:12 – 16; cf. Zech 12:2, 9; 14:2 f.). Such destruction is the climax of God's judgments against specific nations that harmed His chosen people Israel, as announced by the OT prophets (e.g., Isa 13 – 23; Jer 46 – 51; Ezk 25 – 32). Second, a judgment of all the nations after Christ's second coming (Mt 25:31 – 46).

The Lord cannot take up His millennial rulership over the earth without first judging the nations for what they have been doing. In Mt 25:32 the word "nations" is a translation of Gr. *ethnē,* the equivalent of Heb. *gôyim,* meaning also "peoples," "Gentiles." Here they seem to be all the civilian peoples not killed in the battle of Armageddon when their armies were destroyed (Rev 16:14, 16; 19:19 – 21). The basis of this judgment is to be how these peoples as individuals have treated "one of the least of these my brethren" (Mt 25:40), and refers to their treatment of both the Christian (Heb 2:11 – 14) and God's people Israel (Ps 22:22; 69:8).

The crux of the difficulty in deciding the nature of this judgment lies in the fact that it speaks of previously unsaved people receiving either eternal blessing or eternal condemnation on the basis of their works. Since no man can be justified by his works (Rom 3:19 – 20; Gal 2:16), it cannot form a part of any general judgment of the righteous and the wicked. However, for this very reason, it does fit the situation existent at Christ's second coming and describes the judgment due the "nations" for their actions toward believers and Israelites during the Great Tribulation.

The one difficulty which remains with any interpretation is the statement that while the goats "shall go away into everlasting punishment . . . the righteous [the sheep] shall go into life eternal" (Mt 25:46). If this be taken to refer merely to entry into the millennial kingdom without implying salvation, then we can understand the verdict. Or it may mean into a life which leads on to eternal life since it is one and the same with the Lord. The most likely explanation is that because the Scripture speaks of a national repentance by all Israel at that time (Zech 12:10 – 13:1; Deut 30:1 – 10; Hos 5:15 – 6:3; Rev 1:7), and the salvation of that nation in a day (Isa 66:8; Zech 3:9; Rom 11:26), the same will occur in those nations which did treat the Christian and the Jew well. Being permitted to enter the kingdom, they will immediately repent, acknowledge Christ and be saved, and therefore can be spoken of by Christ as going into life eternal.

f. The judgment of angels. In this the Christian is to have a part (I Cor 6:3). It would appear to occur at the time of the judgment of Satan and in connection with that of the Great White Throne (Rev 20:11 ff.; cf. II Pet 2:4; Jude 6).

g. The judgment of the wicked. There is no indication of any judgment of the wicked before Rev 20:11, except for the wicked nations in Mt 25. Only the righteous dead are to be resurrected at the beginning of Christ's millennial reign (Rev 20:4), and the second death has no power over them. All the wicked, in contrast, called "the rest of the dead," will not live again until the thousand years are finished (v. 5). They are the participants in the final judgment. Their judgment rests upon two things: their works, which alone cannot save them; and the presence or absence of their names in the book of life. All not found in the book of life are to be cast into the lake of fire (v. 15).

See Crime and Punishment; Eternal State and Death; Judge, Judging; Justice (of God).

Bibliography. F. Büchsel and V. Herntrich, "*Krinō,* etc.," TDNT, III, 921 – 954. Leon Morris, *The Biblical Doctrine of Judgment,* London: Tyndale Press, 1960. Norman H. Snaith, *The Distinctive Ideas of the Old Testament,* London: Epworth Press, 1944, pp. 74 – 77.

R. A. K. and J. R.

JUDGMENT SEAT. A step or raised place; hence a rostrum or stage for speakers. It was used of the official seat or chair of a judge in the Gr. and Rom. courts of law. The Gr. word *bēma* appears 12 times in the NT, and is translated in the KJV and ASV as "judgment seat" in ten of them (Mt 27:19; Jn 19:13; Acts 18:12, 16 – 17; 25:6, 10, 17; Rom 14:10; II Cor 5:10).

The judgment seat or bema where Paul stood before Gallio at Corinth (Acts 18). HFV

Generally the word designates the official seat (tribunal, judicial bench) of a judge, usually the Rom. governor or procurator (although in Acts 25:10, "of Caesar"; Rom 14:10, "of God," ASV, RSV; II Cor 5:10, "of Christ"). However, in Acts 12:21 it refers to the throne-like speaker's platform of Herod Agrippa in Caesarea. For judgment seat of Christ, *see* Judgments: Judgments of God 2, *c*.

JUDICIAL BLINDNESS. The paralysis of spiritual perception which comes on the mind and heart of one who trifles with or rejects God's gracious offer of salvation. This is a subject which occupies an important place in both OT and NT.

A judgment of God. In Ps 69:23 ("Let their eyes be darkened, that they see not"), Messiah is heard through the voice of the psalmist calling for this judgment on the people because of their sin and rebellion against the Lord's Anointed. Even more striking is God's commission to the prophet Isaiah which he is given to pronounce to the people: "Go, and tell this people, Hear ye indeed, but understand not; and see ye indeed, but perceive not. Make the heart of this people fat . . . and shut their eyes; lest they see with their eyes . . . and convert, and be healed" (Isa 6:9 – 10). While the strange-sounding "lest they turn again and be healed" must not be made to mean that God does not want Israel to truly repent, it does mean that He wants no more of the external profession in which (Isa 29:10 – 13) they "draw near with their mouth . . . but have removed their heart far from me."

Not an arbitrary judgment. In every OT passage referring to this judgment the cause is shown to be man's unbelief, rebellion, and apostasy in heart from God. Thus the judgment, far from being arbitrary, is actually a sealing of their own decision in spiritual hardness, just as Paul in Rom 1 declares that God gave men over in awful judgment to the very sins they had deliberately chosen. A further comment on the depth of this spiritual blindness and deception of heart is given by Isaiah when he describes a man worshiping a part of a piece of wood, the rest of which he burns to bake a bit of bread (Isa 44:9 – 20).

Its relation to the parables. In a parable there is a certain concealment of the truth. Jesus explained to His disciples that it was for this reason that He used this method of teaching. He was carrying out the declared judgment of God in Isaiah's prophecy by hiding God's revelation from the superficial, self-righteous rejecters of God's grace, while at the same time making it abidingly vivid to the penitent, responsive heart (Mt 13:10 – 17).

A reason for the Jewish rejection of Christ. The apostle John (Jn 12:39 –40) cites this judicial blindness as the cause of Jewish unbelief and presents the situation as a fulfillment of Isa

53:1. Paul likewise gives it as the reason for the rejection of the gospel by the Jewish leadership in Rome (Acts 28:26).

Its presentation in the Pauline epistles. In Rom 11:7 – 10 Paul shows that Israel, except for an elect remnant, has failed to obtain the promise of God, and states the cause is this blindness. God is using His rejection of Israel as a foil to win the Gentiles (11:11 – 22). In the end, after this present period of blindness or hardening on the part of Israel, the Jew himself will be saved (11:25 – 26).

In II Cor 3:14 – 16 the apostle compares this blindness on the hearts of the Jews to a veil, like the one on Moses' face. It keeps them from seeing the glory of Christ in the OT. When their hearts turn to the Lord, the veil is removed. In II Cor 4:4 Paul shows Satan's part in this blindness. He is the promoter of the superficiality, self-righteousness, and self-seeking that lead to unbelief and spiritual blindness. In this aspect the blindness is not restricted to the Jew but comes on everyone who rejects the offer of God's grace (Eph 4:18). The very darkness in which he walks in his hatred of others blinds his eyes (I Jn 2:11).

This judgment of blindness stands as a strong warning in this life against disregarding the revelation which God has given to us. In eternity the lost will be eternally conscious of the inestimable worth of that which they have rejected (Lk 16:27 – 28).

See Blindness; Hardness of Heart.

M. A. K.

JUDITH (jōō′dĭth). The Heb. name *y*ᵉ*hŭdĭth* means "Jewess," and is a feminine form of *ye-hŭdî* "Jew."

1. One of Esau's wives and daughter of Beeri the Hittite (Gen 26:34); perhaps also called Aholibamah (Oholibamah in ASV and RSV) in Gen 36:2.

2. The heroine of the apocryphal book of Judith (Jth 8:1; 9:2). Since her name means "Jewess," it suggests the personification of piety to the Mosaic law and devotion to the cause of her nation.

JULIA (jōōl′yȧ). A Christian woman at Rome to whom Paul sent greetings; probably the wife or sister of Philologus (Rom 16:15).

JULIUS (jōōl′yŭs). This centurion, mentioned half a dozen times in Acts 27, and once in Acts 28:16 according to some MSS but not in the best texts, was the man put in charge of Paul the prisoner when he was sent to Rome after his appeal to Caesar. Julius was presumably his family name. There is no certainty that he was a Roman citizen. Soldiers in Palestine were not members of the legionary forces but rather auxiliary troops recruited from the *peregrini* or provincial subjects. Julius treated Paul kindly (Acts 27:3) and spared his life when his soldiers counseled killing him prior to the shipwreck (Acts 27:42 –43).

JUNIA (joo'ni-å), **JUNIAS** (joo'nĭ-ăs). A Christian at Rome (most probably a man, although the accusative form [Ioynian] in Rom 16:7 is ambiguous as to gender). He, with Andronicus, is greeted by Paul as a fellow Jew (cf. Rom 9:3), a fellow prisoner (during some otherwise unknown imprisonment; II Cor 11:23), a man "of note among the apostles" (using "apostles" of Christian teachers and evangelists in general; cf. Acts 14:4, 14; Gal 1:19; 2:9), and a Christian before Paul's conversion.

JUNIPER. *See* Plants.

JUPITER. *See* Gods, False.

JUSHAB-HESED (joo'shăb-hē'sĕd). A son or grandson of Zerubbabel (I Chr 3:20).

JUSTICE (ETHICS). In two of Plato's dialogues, *The Republic* and the *Gorgias,* the subject of justice is disputed at such a fundamental level that the divergent opinions recur throughout all subsequent ages. The conflict is between those who say that might makes right and those who say that power can be either justly or unjustly used, that justice is of a higher order than utility.

In the 17th cen. Hobbes and Spinoza took a position similar to the "might makes right" view. In essence they held that the stronger party can do no injustice in serving his own interests and the weaker suffers no injustice if he is inexpedient enough to suffer when resisting the will of those who have the rule over him. For Hobbes (*Leviathan*), the word justice has no meaning until men voluntarily form a state invested with sufficient power to coerce men to submit to it who do not obey civil laws. In a natural state, according to Spinoza, nothing can be called just or unjust, but only in a civil society. Hence justice for the individual consists of keeping the laws of the state, and for the state, in enforcing whatever laws it has the power to promulgate in the interest of its own self-preservation. This is the view taken by humanists and naturalists in our own day, and graphically put into practice by the modern dictators.

The opposite view, to which all Christians together with many others subscribe, is that justice transcends and judges the will of the state. This does not deny that the preservation of justice is the task of the state. Paul stated that the governing authorities have been instituted by God (Rom 13:1 –7; cf. I Pet 2:13 –17). Justice is the organizing principle of the state, the bond which holds men together in civil societies, without which, as Augustine said, the state is no better than a band of robbers. The principle of justice is higher than the constitution of the state; therefore justice can-

not be understood as merely right based upon might.

This second view believes that there is a natural justice which transcends the relativities of history and holds for all men everywhere. For the founding fathers of our country, this natural justice consisted in certain rights granted to all men by the Creator. These rights were inalienable in the sense that the state could guarantee them, but never deny them. The philosopher Locke (*On Civil Government*) regarded it as a self-evident axiom of reason that all men should enjoy that measure of equality and liberty which forbids injury to one's neighbor in his life, health or property. Thomas Aquinas seems to regard this natural justice as a part of the concept of natural law.

Analyzing the concept a bit more closely, thinkers who speak of justice as a natural law of human life consider it as involving the obligation to render to one's neighbor that which is due to him as his own. The idea of justice as the rendering to others what is their due lies close to the idea of fairness. This is a term employed to describe justice in economics, the exchange of goods according to an equivalent value, and the distribution of goods according to need and merit.

Aristotle in this regard employs the notion of equality, distinguishing between arithmetic (or simple) and geometric (or proportional) equality. Since arithmetic or simple justice includes remedial or corrective justice, it may involve either remuneration in kind for the loss or damage of goods, or punishment which is graded in severity to the seriousness of the crime. This is analogous to *lex talionis,* a limitation upon measureless vengeance which is expressed in the OT concept of an eye for an eye and a tooth for a tooth (Ex 21:22 –25; Lev 24:17 –20).

Ever since Marx wrote *Das Kapital,* much attention has been given to the special problems of economic justice. For Marx it is a self-evident principle of justice that the wealth acquired by the sale of goods should reward only the labor of the one who produced the goods. Marx also assumes that originally men possessed all things in common, and that therefore distributive justice requires a revamping of the whole order of private property in terms of public ownership of the materials and means of production to insure the laboring man the full fruits of his work. The Scriptures also say that the laborer is worthy of his hire (Lk 10:7; I Tim 5:18); but even in the early Christian community where they voluntarily had all things in common, it is clear that the right of private property was never questioned (Ananias and Sapphira did not have to sell their property and share it, Acts 5:1 –4). *See* Community of Goods. Furthermore, the Marxist views of economic justice, framed in the name of equality, have proved a threat to individual liberty, and liberty has ever been, from the days of Greek Idealism, a basic co-ordinate of the concept of justice.

For the Christian, justice involves conformity to the law of God as the final and unchanging norm of right action, in contrast to the Marxist that it is determined by communistic state ownership and control, and the evolutionary view that justice is determined by social progress.

See Example; Justice of God; Law.

Bibliography. Aristotle, *Politics,* I, 6; III, 13; VI, 3; VII, 2. Augustine, *City of God,* XIX, 21. Plato, *Gorgias; The Republic,* I -11; *Laws,* IV, X.   P. K. J.

JUSTICE OF GOD. Justice is an attribute of God that manifests His holiness. Several biblical words translated "justice," Heb. *sᵉdāqâ* *ṣedeq,* Gr. *dikaiosunē,* are more often rendered "righteousness." The Heb. words sometimes appear in conjunction after *mishpāṭ,* which the KJV renders as "judgment and justice" (e.g., II Sam 8:15) but which RSV gives as "justice and equity" or "justice and righteousness" (I Kgs 10:9; Jer 22:15; 23:5).

Assuming the uniform doctrine of the church that God is a personal Being, the statement means, "God is just," that He always acts in a way consistent with the requirements of His character as revealed in His law. He rules His creation with rectitude, He keeps His word, He renders to all His creatures their due. "Righteous art thou, O Lord, and upright in thy judgments. Thy testimonies that thou hast commanded are righteous and very faithful" (Ps 119:137 - 138). The justice of God is a necessary correlate of His holiness, or moral excellence. Since God is infinitely perfect, He must be impartial in His judgments and always treat His creatures with equity. "That be far from thee," says Abraham to the Lord, "to do after this manner, to slay the righteous with the wicked: and that the righteous should be as the wicked, that be far from thee. Shall not the Judge of all the earth do right?" (Gen 18:25).

The doctrine of God's justice has many ramifications but it is most often discussed in connection with man's sin, and in this connection it is close in meaning to the severity of God. Severity is the way the sinner feels the justice of God.

With the rise of German liberalism, this aspect of God's moral being was softened to the point of being emptied of all meaning. The doctrines of vicarious satisfaction and especially eternal hell were repudiated as vestigial remains of the angry God of the OT and unworthy of the heavenly Father whom Jesus revealed, who loves all His creatures and is worshiped by Christians. The Scripture, however, will sustain no such bifurcation. The God of Jesus and the apostles is the God of the OT. Jesus Himself had more to say about hell specifically, than can be found in the whole OT put together; probably more than can be found in the remainder of the NT.

As for vicarious satisfaction, this is at the heart of Paul's interpretation of the meaning of the death of Christ. As the leading theological thinker of the apostolic church, he wrote a treatise on the righteousness of God (1:16 - 17) to the Romans, the epistle which is justly viewed as the major exposition of the gospel from his pen. Regarding God's justice or righteousness he stated that "all have sinned, and come short of the glory of God; being justified freely by his grace through the redemption that is in Christ Jesus: whom God hath set forth to be a propitiation through faith in his blood, to declare his righteousness for the remission of sins that are past, through the forbearance of God; to declare, I say, at this time his righteousness: that he might be just, and the justifier of him which believeth in Jesus" (Rom 3:23 - 26). This passage has been happily called the "acropolis of the gospel," the good news that through Christ the requirements of divine justice have been met.

Scripture does not teach that God's justice is purely remedial. It is not an expression of God's benevolence. It is that quality in God which guarantees to all His creatures that sin must be punished because of its inherent ill-desert, and that rectitude must be acknowledged and rewarded because of its intrinsic merit and worthiness.

See God; Judgments; Justification; Righteousness; Sin.

Bibliography. J. Barton Payne, "Justice," NBD, pp. 680 - 683.
                                    P. K. J.

JUSTIFICATION. Justification (Gr. *dikaiōsis*) is a term that has reference to judicial judgment. It does not mean to make upright or holy, but to announce a favorable verdict, to declare to be righteous. This meaning is patent in both Testaments (Heb. *hiphil* stem of *ṣādaq,* "to declare righteous"; Gr. *dikaioō,* "to vindicate, acquit, pronounce and treat as just"). "To justify" is contrasted with "to condemn" (cf. Deut 25:1; I Kgs 8:32; Prov 17:15; Rom 8:33) and no more means to make upright than condemn means to make wicked.

It is this declarative force of the term that raises the question: how can God justify the ungodly? In God's justification of sinners there is a unique ingredient that holds in no other case of justification. This unique feature is that He causes to be the new relation which He has declared to be. This operation is expressly stated in Scripture to be the act of constituting many righteous (Rom 5:19), the bestowal of the free gift of righteousness (Rom 5:17), and making us the righteousness of God in Christ (II Cor 5:21). It is by this action that the sentence of condemnation (*q.v.*) under which we rest as sinners is changed to one of justification; there is, therefore, no condemnation to them who are in Christ Jesus (Rom 8:1). This constitutive act is properly spoken of as the imputation to us of the righteousness of Christ. It is thereby shown to have no affinity with what is inwardly wrought in us either by regeneration (*q.v.*) or sanctification (*q.v.*). Imputation is the reckoning to our account of a righteousness not our own but based on the obedience of Christ (Phil 3:9; Rom 5:17, 19). It is therefore distinguished from the forgiveness of sins, although forgiveness is necessarily included in it (Acts 13:38 – 39).

As the *nature* of justification is thus shown to be declarative, constitutive, and imputative, so the *ground* resides in nothing else but the accomplished work of Christ, and its *source* in the free grace of God. We are justified freely by God's grace "through the redemption that is in Christ Jesus" (Rom 3:24). This truth comes to focal expression in the designation "the righteousness of God" (Rom 1:17; 3:21 – 22; 10:3; II Cor 5:21; Phil 3:9). Christ's work was obedience (Rom 5:19; Phil 2:8; Heb 5:8 – 9). As such it was righteousness (Mt 3:15; Rom 5:17 – 18, 21). It was wrought by Him as the God-man and is, therefore, a righteousness with divine property, a God-righteousness contrasted not only with human unrighteousness but with all human righteousness. This righteousness alone meets the desperateness of our sinful situation and measures up to all the demands of God's holiness. It not only warrants God's justification but wherever reckoned to our account demands our justification. Grace reigns "through righteousness unto eternal life" (Rom 5:21).

As justification is of grace, it is through faith (Rom 1:17; 5:1). Faith is congruous with all the other features. This is true not because faith is the gift of God, for all grace exercised by us is the gift of God, but because the distinctive character of faith is to receive and rest upon Christ for salvation. It is the self-abandoning and self-entrusting quality of faith that makes it the fitting instrument of all else that justification involves. It is by faith we are justified and by faith alone, though never by a faith that is alone.

Justification is the basic religious question. It is not now simply the question: how can man be just with God? It is the more pressing question: how can man as a sinner *become* just with God? Justification by grace through faith is the answer.

See Faith; Forgiveness; Impartation; Righteousness; Salvation.

Bibliography. See commentaries on Romans. John A. Faulkner, "Justification," ISBE, III, 1782 – 1788. Leon Morris, *The Apostolic Preaching of the Cross,* Grand Rapids: Eerdmans, 1956, pp. 224 – 274. James I. Packer, "Just, Justify, Justification," BDT, pp. 303 – 308; "Justification," NBD, pp. 683 – 686. Gottlob Schrenk, "*Dikaios,* etc.," TDNT, II, 182 – 225.

J. M.

JUSTUS (jŭs'tŭs). The surname for three men of the apostolic period.

1. Joseph called Barsabas who was eliminated when Matthias was chosen to complete the Twelve (Acts 1:23).

2. Titus (or Titius), a Roman and converted God-fearer, who opened his home next to the Corinth synagogue to Paul as a meeting place when the apostle turned from the Jews (Acts 18:7). Most later Gr. MSS have only "Justus" (so KJV), but earlier MSS and versions have either "Titius Justus" or "Titus Justus."

3. Jesus (or Joshua) Justus, a Jew possibly from Colosse, who was with Paul during his first Rome imprisonment and, along with John Mark and Aristarchus, sent greetings to the Colosse church (Col 4:11).

JUTTAH (jŭt'å). A town in Judah (now identified with Yatta), about five miles S of Hebron (Josh 15:55), assigned to the sons of Aaron as a refuge city (Josh 21:16). A parallel listing in I Chr 6:59 omits this town. The conjecture which equates this city with "Juda" (KJV) in Lk 1:39 is now generally rejected as linguistically indefensible.